THE OFFICIAL®
1991 PRICE GUIDE TO
BASEBALL CARDS

BY DR. JAMES BECKETT

TENTH EDITION
HOUSE OF COLLECTIBLES • NEW YORK

Errata

There are thousands of names, more than 100,000 prices, and untold other words in this book. There are going to be a few typographical errors, a few misspellings, and possibly, a number or two out of place. If you catch a blooper, drop me a note directly or in care of the publisher, and we will fix it up in the next year's edition.

Published by: The House of Collectibles
201 East 50th Street
New York, New York 10022

Distributed by Ballantine Books, a division of Random House, Inc., New York, and simultaneously in Canada by Random House of Canada Limited, Toronto.

Manufactured in the United States of America

Library of Congress Catalog Card Number: 84-645496

ISBN: 0-876-37807-6

Tenth Edition: April 1990

10 9 8 7 6 5 4 3 2 1

Table of Contents

About the Author

Jim Beckett, the leading authority on sports card values in the United States, maintains a wide range of activities in the world of sports. He possesses one of the finest collections of sports cards and autographs in the world, has made numerous appearances on radio and television, and has been frequently cited in many national publications. He was awarded the first "Special Achievement Award" for Contributions to the Hobby by the National Sports Collectors Convention in 1980 and the "Jock-Jasperson Award" for Hobby Dedication in 1983.

Dr. Beckett is the author of *The Sport Americana Baseball Card Price Guide, The Official Price Guide to Baseball Cards, The Sport Americana Football, Hockey, Basketball and Boxing Price Guide, The Official Price Guide to Football Cards, The Official Price Guide to Hockey and Basketball Cards, The Sport Americana Price Guide to Baseball Collectibles, The Sport Americana Baseball Memorabilia and Autograph Price Guide,* and *The Sport Americana Alphabetical Baseball Card Checklist*. In addition, he is the founder, author, and editor of *Beckett Baseball Card Monthly, Beckett Basketball Card Magazine,* and *Beckett Football Card Magazine,* magazines dedicated to advancing the card collecting hobby.

Jim Beckett received his Ph.D. in Statistics from Southern Methodist University in 1975. He resides in Dallas with his wife Patti and their daughters, Christina, Rebecca, and Melissa.

Preface

Isn't it great? Every year this book gets bigger and bigger with all the new sets coming out. But even more exciting is that every year there are more collectors, more shows, more stores, and . . . more interest in the cards we love so much. This edition has been enhanced and expanded from the previous edition. The cards you collect—who they are, what they look like, where they are from, and (most important to many of you) what their current values are—are enumerated within. Many of the features contained in the other *Beckett Price Guides* have been incorporated into this volume since condition grading, nomenclature, and many other aspects of collecting are common to the card hobby in general. We hope you find the book both interesting and useful in your collecting pursuits.

The *Beckett Guide* has been successful where other attempts have failed because it is complete, current, and valid. This price guide contains not just one, but three, prices by condition for the baseball cards in the issues listed. These account for almost all the baseball cards in existence. The prices were added to the card lists just prior to printing and reflect not the author's opinions or desires but the going retail prices for each card, based on the marketplace (sports memorabilia conventions and shows, hobby papers, current mail order catalogs, local club meetings, auction results, and other firsthand reportings of actually realized prices).

What is the BEST price guide available (on the market) today? Of course, card sellers will prefer the price guide with the highest prices as the best—while card buyers will naturally prefer the one with the lowest prices. Accuracy, however, is the true test. Use the price guide used by more collectors and dealers than all the others combined. Look for the Beckett name. I won't put my name on anything I won't stake my reputation on. Not the lowest and not the highest—but the most accurate, with integrity. To facilitate your use of this book, read the complete introductory section in the pages following before going to the pricing pages. Every collectible field has its own terminology; we've tried to capture most of these terms and definitions in our glossary. Please read carefully the section on grading and the condition of your cards, as you will not be able to determine which price column is appropriate for a given card without first knowing its condition.

Welcome to the world of baseball cards.

Sincerely, Dr. James Beckett

Acknowledgments

A great deal of hard work went into this volume, and it could not have been done without help from many people. Our thanks are extended to each and every one of you.

Those who have worked closely with us on this, and many other books, have again proven themselves invaluable—Frank and Vivian Barning (*Baseball Hobby News*), Chris Benjamin, Sy Berger (Topps), Card Collectors Co., Cartophilium (Andrew Pywowarczuk), Ira Cetron, Mike Cramer (Pacific Trading Cards), Bill and Diane Dodge, Richard Duglin (Baseball Cards-n-More), Steve Freedman, Gervise Ford, Larry and Jeff Fritsch, Tony Galovich (American Card Exchange), Georgia Music and Sports (Dick DeCourcy and Floyd Parr), Bill Goodwin (St. Louis Baseball Cards), Mike and Howard Gordon, John Greenwald, Wayne Grove, Bill Haber, Bill Henderson, Danny Hitt, Tom Imboden, Allan Kaye (*Baseball Card News*), Rick Keplinger, David Kohler (SportsCards Plus), Don Lepore, Paul Lewicki, Neil Lewis (Leaf), Lew Lipset, Norman and Ken Liss (Topps), Major League Marketing (Dan Shedrick, Tom Day, George Martin), Mid-Atlantic Coin Exchange (Bill Bossert), David "Otis" Miller, Dick Millerd, Brian Morris, Paul Mullen and Vincent Murray (Fleer), Ralph Nozaki, Optigraphics (Anne Flavin and Ed Fick), Jack Pollard, Gavin Riley, Alan Rosen ("Mr. Mint"), John Rumierz, San Diego Sport Collectibles (Bill Goepner and Nacho Arredondo), Kevin Savage (Sports Gallery), Mike Schechter, Barry Sloate, John Spalding, Phil Spector (Scoreboard, Inc.), Sports Collectors Store, Frank Steele, Murvin Sterling, Lee Temanson, Ed Twombly (New England Bullpen), Gary Walter, Kit Young, and Ted Zanidakis. Finally we owe a special acknowledgment to Dennis W. Eckes, "Mr. Sport Americana." The success of the *Beckett Price Guides* has always been the result of a team effort.

This price guide is our best one yet and you can thank all of the contributors (listed above and below) as well as our staff here for that. But two people on our staff here have made direct and important specific contributions to this work. Theo Chen has done many things to help, e.g., he's done a great job on Readers Write, freeing me up for more attention to pricing, and has, in fact, provided most of the R/W answers which I then only need to review. He's also primarily responsible for the paragraph descriptions for the new sets this year. B.A. Murry's contribution has been significant with respect to virtually all aspects of pricing cards. It is very difficult to be "accurate"—one can only do one's best, but this job is especially difficult since we're shooting at a moving target as prices are fluctuating all the time. Having two full-time pricing experts has definitely proven to be better than one, and I thank B.A. for coming on board and making a difference, resulting in more accurate prices for you, our readers.

Many people have provided price input, illustrative material, checklist verifications, errata, and/or background information. We should like to individually thank AbD Cards (Dale Wesolewski), Carl Abrams, Jerry Adamic, Ron Adelson, Tony Adkins, A.J.'s Sport Stop, Ercu Aktay, Bob Alexander, Jay Alicea, All Star Sports Collectibles, Jason Allen, Paul Allen, Kent W. Alverson, Pat Alvey, Doug Amerman, Jon Andell, Read Andersen, Dennis Anderson, Roberto Ansourian, Ric Apter, Mark Argo (Olde South Cards), Neil Armstrong (World Series Cards), Troy Arnold, Hury Askotzky, Sammy Ayres, B&F Sports Cards, Joel Bachman, Josh Bakk, Ball Four Cards, Brad Bane, Joe Barney, Fernando Barriga, Ed Barry (Ed's Collectibles), Bob Bartosz (Baseball Card Shop), Bay State Cards (Lenny DeAngelico), Tom Beckley, Karen Bell, Jason Beloro, Chris Berbermeyer, Carl Berg, Frank Bernatt, Bernie's Bullpen, Curtis Bethea, Beulah Sports, BH Baseball Cards, Darin Blang, Eddy Blaw, Levi Bleam, Bob Boffa, Moni Boling, Tim Bond (Tim's Cards & Comics), Bobby Bono, Charlie Botello, Travis Boyer, Randy Bradford, Peter T. Brennan, David Brewer, John Brigandi, Chuck Brooks, Casey Brough, Richard Brown, Derek Brusko, William Bryfia, Hans Buchsteiner, Eric Bush, Patrick Buss, California Card Co., David Call (9th Inning Baseball Card Shop), Joe Callahan, Jim Carballido, Paul C. Carpenter, Michael Cary, Sandy Chan, David Chang, Dwight Chapin, Erick Chapman, Chris Charles, Jared Chasteen, Ray Cherry, Wayne Christian, Dick Cianciotto, Cincinnati Baseball Cards, Terry Circle, Ron Citrenbaum, James Clark, Alexander Clarke, Daniel Cleaveland, Ronald Cochran, Barry Colla, Collectibles Unlimited (John Alward and Deb Ingram), Collection de Sport AZ (Ronald Villaneuve), Ryan Collins, Nathan Cooper, Curt Cooter, Steve Corbin, S. Alan Corlew, Douglas Covelli, Matt Craig, Taylor Crane, Chad Cripe, James Critzer, John Curtis, and Allen Custer.

Paul Dainesi, Eugene Dalager, Dave Dame, Don Daniel III, Cameron Davis, Kevin Davis, Paul R. Davis, Ben Deaton, Jason Decena, Jeff Dickenson, Howard J. Didier Jr., Ken Diemer, Andrew Dilg, Ken Dinerman (California Cruizers), Jeff Ding, D.L. Ditto, George Doherty, George Dolence, Richard Dolloff (Dolloff Coin Center), George Dougherty, Jonathon Drye, Irving Eichenthal, Karen Ellison, Doak Ewing, Matthew Falewicz, Josh Feinkind, Tom Feldman, Eric Fellows, Chuck Ferrero, David Festberg, Jay Finglass, Danny Fitzgerald, Doug Flatau, Roger Flood, Kirk Fogg, Fremont Fong, Perry Fong, Tim Fong, Tommy Fox, Andrew France, Walter Franklin, Steve Freeburne, Mark Friedman, Robert Garren, David Garrett, Mike Garrett, Willie George Jr., Stanley Gilbert, Bob Gill, Timothy Gilman, Deric Glissmeyer, Dick Goddard, Steve Gold (AU Sports), Greg Goldstein (Dragon's Den), Jeff Goldstein, Jerry Goodman, Jim Goodreid, Robert Gottberg, Keith Gradwohl, Grauer's Collectibles, Stephen Grave, Justin Greenwald, Gabe Greer, Alex Gregg, Al Gritter, Bob Gullic, and Steve Gungormez.

Chris Hackman, Hall's Nostalgia, Hershell Hanks, A.R. Hanson, Mike Harrigan, Chris Hathaway, Aaron Hecht, Billy Heffner, Joel Hellman, Mark Hellman, Stacy Henderson, Dennis Henry, John Higley, James Hilgert, Zack Hill, Scott Hill, Curtis Hoggatt, Home Plate of Utah (Ken Edick), Joan Hoole, David Horie, Rich Hovoroka,

Jimmy Howell, David A. Hunt, Keith Huskamp, Matt and Marc Hutcheson, Heath Ingersoll, Richard Iozia, Ryan Jansen, Paul Jastrzembski, Nancy Jennings, JJ's Budget Baseball Cards, Bryan D. Johnson, Jay Johnson, Kevin M. Johnson, Jack L. Johnstone, Stewart W. Jones, Steve Juon, Dave Jurgensmeier, Aaron Kalina, Eric Karabagli, Jay and Mary Kasper, Frank Katen, Neil Katz, Tim Kelley, Mike Kelly, Paul M. Kelly, Justin Kerstetter, Phil Kidel, Leroy King, Chad Kisner, Richard Klein, Rob H. Klein, Eric Knodel, David Kohler, Jim Kohlmeyer, Ernie Kohlstruk, Koinz and Kards, David Koslik, David Kreskai, William and Curt Kruschwitz, Michael Kullkewski, Thomas Kunnecke, Jared Kvapil, Andy Kwang, John Kyranos, Tim Langan, Shawn Larson, Jason Lassic, Dan Lavin, Sylvia Leasure, Phil Lee, Morley Leeking, Michael Lenart, Glenn Lerch, Irv Lerner, Dale E. Loebs, Mike London, Damian Lopez, Ray Luangsuwan, and Jeff Lupke.

David Macaray, Robert Macasinag, Jim Macie, Mark Macrae, Adam Magary, Paul Manning, Andy Mar, Paul Marchant, Dick Marshall, Bill Mastro, P.M. Mathis, Jeffrey Maxey, Dr. William McAvoy, Alex McCollum, Mike McConnell, Scott McCoy, Michael McDonald (The Sports Page), Dan McIlhargey, Ryan McKee, Reed McKenney, Scott McKevitt, Tony McLaughlin, Michael McLean, Scott McNutt, W. Terry McPherson, Mendal Mearkle, Raj Mehta, Ken Melanson, Randy Messel, Blake Meyer (Lone Star Sportscards), Joe Michalowicz, Eric Miller, Cary Miller, Linda Miller, Wayne Miller, Dick Millerd, Patrick Montagu, Leland Morris, Bill Morton, Brian Munger, Zachary Myles, Edward Nazzaro (The Collector), Lloyd Neider, Robby Nelson, James W. Niels, Rusty Nighbert, Will Norris, Neal Obermeyer, Mike O'Brien, Keith Olbermann, Oldies and Goodies, Scott Orgera, Ron Oser, Jeff Osner, Jamie O'Sullivan, Tom Overson, Nelson Paine, Jason Parker, Gary Parnell, John Pash, Clay Pasternack, Mark Patzschke, Bernie Paul, Mark A. Paulson, Daniel Payne, Michael Pensabene, Michael Perrotta, Trevor Perry, Jeff Pfeil, Tom Pfirrmann, John Phillips, Mark L. Phillips, Dan Piepenbrock, Curtis Pires, Bob Poet, Edward Pope, Seth Poppel, Mark Porath, Chip Porter, Michael Poynter, Don Prestia, Kelby Joe Price, Jeff Prillaman (Southern Cards), Donald Prindle, and James Quintong.

David Rae, Sam Ramirez, Victor Ramos, Rick Rapa and Barry Sanders (Atlanta Sports Cards), R.W. Ray, Dylan Reach, Steve Reardon, Matt Reghitto, Tom Reid, Paula Ann Reinke, Frank J. Retcho, Jeff Reynolds, Stephen Ricci, Dave Ring, Al Rocca, Jeff Rockholt, Doug Rodman, Carlyle Rood, Avi Rosenfeld, Rick Ross, Clifton Rouse, Deedrick Rowe III, George Rusnak, Gregory Russell, Terry Sack, Todd Sackmann, Harry Sacks, Joe Sak, Jennifer Salems, John San Martino Jr., Gary Sawatzki, Evan Schenkman, Bruce Schwartz, David Seaverns, Tom Shanyfelt, Gerry Shebib, Farr N. Shepherd, Wayne Sherman, Tom Sherry, Rey Silva, Rick Sinchak, Bob Singer, Robert Smathers, Art Smith, Brian W. Smith, Chad Smith, Michael Snowden, Fred Mo Snyder, Brian E. South, Martin Spitzer, Linda Spitzer, Howard Staples, John Stephens, Kim A. Stigall, Tim Strandberg, Edward Strauss, Richard Strobino, Jon Strohl, Alan Sugahara, Superior Sport Card, Matt Swarner, J. and A. Swenson, Ian Taylor, Jason Terry, Jim Thompson, Carl Thrower, Joshua Tjiong, Karrie Tompkins, Dan Trimble, Dr. Ralph Triplette, Howard Tung, Ralph

Turkenkopf, Jim Turner, Matthew Turner, Matt Tyson, Andrew Uzarowski, Todd Van
Der Kruik, Mark Vanden Busch, Jeff Varnado, Michael Vrooman, Tom R. Walton,
Greg Watanabe, Joe Webb, Mark Weber, R.R. Webster, Douglas Weddleton, Tony
Weiand, Josh Weis, Andy Wemmer, Melvin D. Werling, Bill Wesslund, Richard
West, Mark Whiteside, Timothy Wiley, Matt Wilgenbush, Jeff Williams, Mark Willis,
Andy Wilson, David Wilson, Eric Wilson, Jesse Wilson, Opry Winston, John Witmer,
Dylan Wolfe, Kyle Wolfe, Jay Wolt (Cavalcade of Sports), Lawrence Wong, Leon
Wong, Pete Wooten, Vida Yancy, Chris Yang, Mike Yanke, Dan Yaw, Sandy Yelnick,
Yesterday's Heroes, V.P. Young Jr., Eddy Yuan, Robert Zanze, and Chris Ziemba.

Every year we make active solicitations for input to that year's edition and we
are particularly appreciative of help (large and small) provided for this volume. While
we receive many inquiries, comments, and questions regarding material within this
book—and, in fact, each and every one is read and digested—time constraints
prevent us from personally replying. We hope that the letters will continue, and that
even though no reply is received, you will feel that you are making significant contributions to the hobby through your interest and comments.

Special thanks go the staff of *Beckett Publications* for their help. Editorial Director
Fred Reed was very helpful with the editing of the introductory section, the produc-
tion of the advertising pages, and the supervision of the extensive production
support team. He was ably assisted by Jeff Amano, Therese Bellar, Michael Bolduc,
Lou Cather, Theo Chen, Susan Elliott, Julie Fulton, Pepper Hastings, Sara Jenks,
Jay Johnson, Tricia Jones, Rudy Klancnik, Frances Knight, Omar Mediano, and
Reed Poole. The rest of the overall operations of *Beckett Monthly* were skillfully
directed by Claire Backus and Joe Galindo. Working with them were Nancy Barton,
Lisa Borden, Chris Calandro, Mary Campana, Paige Crosby, Jan Dickerson, Louise
Ebaugh, Mary Gregory, Julie Grove, Beth Hartke, Laura Kelley, Monte King, Debbie
Kingsbury, Amy Kirk, Renee MacElvaine, Glen Morante, Ruth Price, Cindy Struble,
Mark Whitesell, and Jay Yarid. James and Sandi Beane performed several major
system programming jobs for us this year in order to help us accomplish our work
faster and more accurately. The whole *Beckett Publications* team has my thanks
for jobs well done. Thank you, everyone.

I also thank my family, especially my wife, Patti, and daughters, Christina,
Rebecca, and Melissa, for putting up with me again.

Introduction

Welcome to the exciting world of baseball card collecting, America's fastest-growing avocation. You have made a good choice in buying this book, since it will open up to you the entire panorama of this field in the simplest, most concise way.

It is estimated that nearly a third of a million different baseball cards have been issued during the past century. The number of total cards put out by all manufacturers last year has been estimated at several billion, with an initial retail value of more than $300 million. Sales of older cards by dealers may account for a like amount. With all that cardboard available in the marketplace, it should be no surprise that several million sports fans like you collect baseball cards today, and that number is growing by hundreds of thousands each year.

The growth of *Beckett Baseball Card Monthly* is another indication of this rising crescendo of popularity for baseball cards. Founded less than five years ago by Dr. James Beckett, the author of this price guide, *Beckett Monthly* has grown to the pinnacle of the baseball card hobby, with more than a half million readers anxiously awaiting each enjoyable issue.

So collecting baseball cards—while still pursued as a hobby with youthful exuberance by kids in the neighborhood—has also taken on the trappings of an industry, with thousands of full- and part-time card dealers, as well as vendors of supplies, clubs, and conventions. In fact, each year since 1980 thousands of hobbyists have assembled for a National Sports Collectors Convention, at which hundreds of dealers have displayed their wares, seminars have been conducted, autographs penned by sports notables, and millions of cards have changed hands. These colossal affairs have been staged in Los Angeles, Detroit, St. Louis, Chicago, New York, Anaheim, Arlington (TX), San Francisco, Atlantic City, Chicago, and, this year, back in Arlington, Texas, at the Convention Center. So baseball card collecting really is national in scope!

This increasing interest has been reflected in card values. As more collectors compete for available supplies, card prices (especially for premium-grade cards) rise. A national publication indicated a "very strong advance" in baseball card prices during the past decade, and a quick perusal of prices in this book compared to the figures in earlier editions of this price guide will quickly confirm this. Which brings us back around again to the book you have in your hands. Many prices have literally doubled! It is the best annual guide available to this exciting world of baseball cards. Read it and use it. May your enjoyment and your card collection increase in the coming months and years.

How to Collect

Each collection is personal and reflects the individuality of its owner. There are no set rules on how to collect cards. Since card collecting is a hobby or leisure pastime, what you collect, how much you collect, and how much time and money you spend collecting are entirely up to you. The funds you have available for collecting and your own personal taste should determine how you collect. Information and ideas presented here are intended to help you get the most enjoyment from this hobby.

It is impossible to collect every card ever produced. Therefore, beginners as well as intermediate and advanced collectors usually specialize in some way. One of the reasons this hobby is popular is that individual collectors can define and tailor their collecting methods to match their own tastes. To give you some ideas of the various approaches to collecting, we will list some of the more popular areas of specialization.

Many collectors select complete sets from particular years. For example, they may concentrate on assembling complete sets from all the years since their birth or since they became avid sports fans. They may try to collect a card for every player during that specified period of time. Many others wish to acquire only certain players. Usually such players are the superstars of the sport, but occasionally collectors will specialize in all the cards of players who attended certain colleges or came from certain towns. Some collectors are only interested in the first cards or rookie cards of certain players. A handy guide for collectors interested in pursuing the hobby this way is the just-released *Sport Americana Alphabetical Checklist No. 4*. Another fun way to collect cards is by team. Most fans have a favorite team, and it is natural for that loyalty to be translated into a desire for cards of the players on that favorite team. For most of the recent years, team sets (all the cards from a given team for that year) are readily available at a reasonable price. *The Sport Americana Team Baseball Card Checklist* will open up this field to the collector.

Obtaining Cards

Several avenues are open to card collectors. Cards can be purchased in the traditional way at the local candy, grocery, or drug stores, with the bubble gum or other products included. In recent years, it has also become possible to purchase complete sets of baseball cards through mail order advertisers found in traditional sports media publications, such as *The Sporting News*, *Baseball Digest*, *Street & Smith* yearbooks, and others. These sets are also advertised in the card collecting periodicals. Many collectors will begin by subscribing to at least one of the hobby periodicals, all with good up-to-date information. In fact, subscription offers can be found in the advertising section of this book.

Most serious card collectors obtain old (and new) cards from one or more of several main sources: (1) trading or buying from other collectors or dealers; (2) responding to sale or auction ads in the hobby publications; and/or (3) attending sports collectibles shows or conventions. We advise that you try all three methods since each has its own distinct advantages: (1) trading is a great way to make new friends; (2) hobby periodicals help you keep up with what's going on in the hobby (including when and where the conventions are happening); and (3) shows provide enjoyment and the opportunity to view millions of collectibles under one roof, in addition to meeting some of the hundreds or even thousands of other collectors with similar interests who also attend the shows.

Preserving Your Cards

Cards are fragile. They must be handled properly in order to retain their value. Careless handling can easily result in creased or bent cards. It is, however, not recommended that tweezers or tongs be used to pick up your cards since such utensils might mar or indent card surfaces and thus reduce those cards' conditions and values. In general, your cards should be handled directly as little as possible. This is sometimes easier to say than to do. Although there are still many who use custom boxes, storage trays, or even shoe boxes, plastic sheets are the preferred method of storing cards. A collection stored in plastic pages in a three-ring album allows you to view your collection at any time without the need to touch the card itself. For a large collection, some collectors may use a combination of the above methods. When purchasing plastic sheets for your cards, be sure that you find the pocket size that fits the cards snugly. Don't put your 1951 Bowmans in a sheet designed to fit 1981 Topps. Most hobby and collectibles shops and virtually all collectors' conventions will have these plastic pages available in quantity for the various sizes offered or you can purchase them directly from the advertisers in this book. Also remember that pocket size isn't the only factor to consider when looking for plastic sheets. Some collectors concerned with long-term storage of their cards in plastic sheets are cautious to avoid sheets containing PVC and request non-PVC sheets from their dealer.

Damp, sunny, and/or hot conditions—no, this is not a weather forecast—are three elements to avoid in extremes if you are interested in preserving your collection. Too much (or too little) humidity can cause gradual deterioration of a card. Direct, bright sun (or fluorescent light) over time will bleach out the color of a card. Extreme heat accelerates the decomposition of the card. On the other hand, many cards have lasted more than 50 years without much scientific intervention. So be cautious, even if the above factors typically present a problem only when present in the extreme. It never hurts to be prudent.

Collecting/Investing

Collecting individual players and collecting complete sets are both popular vehicles for investment and speculation. Most investors and speculators stock up on complete sets or on quantities of players they think have good investment potential. There is obviously no guarantee in this book, or anywhere else for that matter, that cards will outperform the stock market or other investment alternatives in the future. After all, baseball cards do not pay quarterly dividends, and cards cannot be sold at their "current values" as easily as stocks or bonds. Nevertheless, investors have noticed a favorable trend in the past performance of baseball and other sports collectibles, and certain cards and sets have outperformed just about any other investment in some years.

Some of the obvious questions are: Which cards? When to buy? When to sell? The best investment you can make is in your own education. The more you know about your collection and the hobby, the more informed the decisions you will be able to make. We're not selling investment tips. We're selling information about the current value of baseball cards. It's up to you to use that information to your best advantage.

Nomenclature

Each hobby has its own language to describe its area of interest. The nomenclature traditionally used for trading cards is derived from the *American Card Catalog*, published in 1960 by Nostalgia Press. That catalog, written by Jefferson Burdick (who is called the "Father of Card Collecting" for his pioneering work), uses letter and number designations for each separate set of cards.

The letter used in the *ACC* designation refers to the generic type of card. While both sport and non-sport issues are classified in the *ACC*, we shall confine ourselves to the sport issues. The following list defines the letters and their meanings as used by the *American Card Catalog*.

(none) or   N —19th Century U.S.
                 Tobacco
            B — Blankets
            D — Bakery Inserts Including Bread
            E — Early Candy and Gum
            F — Food Inserts
            H — Advertising
            M — Periodicals
           PC — Postcards
            R — Candy and Gum Cards, 1930 to
                 Present
            T — 20th Century U.S. Tobacco
           UO — Gas and Oil Inserts
            V — Canadian Candy
            W — Exhibits, Strip Cards, Team Issues

Following the letter prefix and an optional hyphen are one-, two-, or three-digit numbers, 1-999. These typically represent the company or entity issuing the cards. In several cases, the *ACC* number is extended by an additional hyphen and another one- or two-digit numerical suffix. For example, the 1957 Topps regular series base-ball card issue carries an *ACC* designation of R414-11. The "R" indicates a Candy or Gum Card produced since 1930. The "414" is the *ACC* designation for Topps Chewing Gum baseball card issues, and the "11" is the *ACC* designation for the 1957 regular issue (Topps' eleventh baseball set).

Like other traditional methods of identification, this system provides order to the process of cataloging cards; however, most serious collectors learn the *ACC* designation of the popular sets by repetition and familiarity, rather than by attempting to "figure out" what they might or should be.

From 1948 forward, collectors and dealers commonly refer to all sets by their year, maker, type of issue, and any other distinguishing characteristic. For example, such a characteristic could be an unusual issue or one of several regular issues put out by a specific maker in a single year. Regional issues are usually referred to by year, maker, and sometimes by title or theme of the set.

Glossary/Legend

Our glossary defines terms frequently used in the card collecting hobby. Many of these terms are also common to other types of sports memorabilia collecting. Some terms may have several meanings depending on use.

AAS. Action All Stars, a postcard-size set issued by the Donruss Company.

ACC. Acronym for American Card Catalog.

ALL STAR CARD. A card portraying an All Star Player of the previous year that says "All Star" on its face.

ALPH. Alphabetical.

AS. Abbreviation for All Star (card).

ATG. All Time Great card.

BLANKET. A felt square (normally 5" to 6") portraying a baseball player.

BOX. Card issued on a box or a card depicting a Boxer.

BRICK. A group of 50 or more cards having common characteristics that is intended to be bought, sold, or traded as a unit.

CABINETS. Popular and highly valuable photographs on thick card stock produced in the 19th and early 20th century.

CHECKLIST. A list of the cards contained in a particular set. The list is always in numerical order if the cards are numbered. Some unnumbered sets are artificially numbered in alphabetical order, by team and alphabetically within the team, or by uniform number for convenience.

CHECKLIST CARD. A card that lists in order the cards and players in the set or series. Older checklist cards in mint condition that have not been checked off or marked off are very desirable.

CL. Abbreviation for Checklist.

COA. Abbreviation for Coach.

COIN. A small disc of metal or plastic portraying a player in its center.

COLLECTOR. A person who engages in the hobby of collecting cards primarily for his own enjoyment, with any profit motive being secondary.

COLLECTOR ISSUE. A set produced for the sake of the card itself with no product or service sponsor. It derives its name from the fact that most of these sets are produced for sale directly to the hobby market.

COMBINATION CARD. A single card depicting two or more players (but not a team card).

COMMON CARD. The typical card of any set; it has no premium value accruing from subject matter, numerical scarcity, popular demand, or anomaly.

COM. Card issued by the Post Cereal Company through their mail-in offer.

CONVENTION. A large weekend gathering of dealers and collectors at a single location for the purpose of buying, selling, and sometimes trading sports memorabilia items. Conventions are open to the public and sometimes feature celebrities, door prizes, films, contests, etc. They are frequently referred to simply as "shows."

CONVENTION ISSUE. A set produced in conjunction with a sports collectibles convention to commemorate or promote the show.

COR. Correct or corrected card.

COUPON. See Tab.

CREASE. A wrinkle on the card, usually caused by bending the card. Creases are a common (and serious) defect from careless handling.

CY. Cy Young Award.

DEALER. A person who engages in buying, selling, and trading sports collectibles or supplies. A dealer may also be a collector, but as a dealer, he anticipates a profit.

DIE-CUT. A card with part of its stock partially cut, allowing one or more parts to be folded or removed. After removal or appropriate folding, the remaining part of the card can frequently be made to stand up.

DISC. A circular-shaped card.

DISPLAY CARD. A sheet, usually containing three to nine cards, that is printed and used by the manufacturer to advertise and/or display the packages containing his products and cards. The backs of display cards are blank or contain advertisements.

DK. Diamond King (artwork produced by Perez-Steele for Donruss).

DP. Double Print (a card that was printed in double the quantity compared to the other cards in the same series).

ERA. Earned Run Average.

ERR. Error card (see also COR).

ERROR CARD. A card with erroneous information, spelling, or depiction on either side of the card. Most errors are not corrected by the producing card company.

EXHIBIT. The generic name given to thick-stock, postcard-size cards with single-color obverse pictures. The name is derived from the Exhibit Supply Co. of Chicago, the principal manufacturer of this type of card. These are also known as Arcade cards since they were found in many arcades.

FDP. First Draft Pick.

FULL SHEET. A complete sheet of cards that has not been cut up into individual cards by the manufacturer. Also called an uncut sheet.

HALL OF FAMER (HOF'er). A card that portrays a player who has been inducted into the Hall of Fame.

HIGH NUMBER. The cards in the last series of numbers in a year in which such higher-numbered cards were printed or distributed in significantly lesser amounts than the lower-numbered cards. The high-number designation refers to a scarcity of the high-numbered cards. Not all years have high numbers in terms of this definition.

HOC. House of Collectibles.

HOF. Hall of Fame.

HOR. Horizontal pose on card as opposed to the standard vertical orientation found on most cards.

HR. Home Run.

IA. In Action (type of card).

INSERT. A card of a different type, e.g., a poster, or any other sports collectible contained and sold in the same package along with a card or cards of a major set.

ISSUE. Synonymous with set, but usually used in conjunction with a manufacturer, e.g., a Topps issue.

K. Strikeout.

KP. Kid Picture (a sub-series issued in the Topps baseball sets of 1972 and 1973).

LAYERING. The separation or peeling of one or more layers of the card stock, usually at the corner of the card.

LEGITIMATE ISSUE. A set produced to promote or boost sales of a product or service, e.g., bubble gum, cereal, cigarettes, etc. Most collector issues are not legitimate issues in this sense.

LHP. Left-Handed Pitcher.

LID. A circular-shaped card (possibly with tab) that forms the top of the container for the product being promoted.

LL. Living Legends (Donruss 1984) or large letters.

MAJOR SET. A set produced by a national manufacturer of cards containing a large number of cards. Usually 100 or more different cards comprise the set.

MG. Abbreviation for Manager.

MINI. A small card; specifically, a Topps baseball card of identical design but smaller dimensions than the regular Topps issue of 1975.

ML. Major League.

MVP. Most Valuable Player.

NNOF. No Name on Front (see 1949 Bowman).

NOF. Name on Front (see 1949 Bowman).

NON-SPORT CARD. A card from a set whose major theme is a subject other than a sports subject. A card of a sports figure or event that is part of a non-sport set is still a non-sport card, e.g., while the "Look 'N' See" non-sport card set contains a card of Babe Ruth, a sports figure, that card is a non-sport card.

NOTCHING. The grooving of the card, usually caused by fingernails, rubber bands, or bumping card edges against other objects.

NY. New York.

OBVERSE. The front, face, or pictured side of the card.

OLY. Olympics (see 1985 Topps baseball and 1988 Topps Traded sets; the members of the U.S. Olympic baseball teams were featured subsets in both of these sets).

OPT. Option.

P. Pitcher or Pitching pose.

P1. First Printing.

P2. Second Printing.

P3. Third Printing.

PANEL. An extended card that is composed of two or more individual cards. Often the panel forms the back part of the container for the product being promoted, e.g., a Hostess panel, a Bazooka panel, an Esskay Meat panel.

PCL. Pacific Coast League.

PG. Price Guide.

PLASTIC SHEET. A clear, plastic page that is punched for insertion into a binder (with standard three-ring spacing) containing pockets for displaying cards. Many different styles of sheets exist with pockets of varying sizes to hold the many differing card formats.

PREMIUM. A card, sometimes on photographic stock, that is purchased or obtained in conjunction with, or redemption for, another card or product. The premium is not packaged in the same unit as the primary item.

PUZZLE CARD. A card whose back contains a part of a picture which, when joined correctly with other puzzle cards, forms the completed picture.

PUZZLE PIECE. A die-cut piece designed to interlock with similar pieces.

PVC. Polyvinyl Chloride, a substance used to make many of the popular card display protective sheets. Non-PVC sheets are considered preferable for long-term storage of cards.

RARE. A card or series of cards of very limited availability. Unfortunately, "rare" is a subjective term sometimes used indiscriminately. "Rare" cards are harder to obtain than "scarce" cards.

RB. Record Breaker card.

REGIONAL. A card or set of cards issued and distributed only in a limited geographical area of the country.

REVERSE. The back or narrative side of the card.

RHP. Right-Handed Pitcher.

ROY. Rookie of the Year.

RP. Relief Pitcher.

RR. Rated Rookies (a subset featured in the Donruss Baseball sets).

SA. Super Action or Sport Americana.

SASE. Self-Addressed, Stamped Envelope.

SB. Stolen Bases.

SCARCE. A card or series of cards of limited availability. This subjective term is sometimes used indiscriminately to promote or hype value. "Scarce" cards are not as difficult to obtain as "rare" cards.

SCR. Script name on back (see 1949 Bowman baseball).

SEMI-HIGH. A card from the next to last series of a sequentially issued set. It has more value than an average card and generally less value than a high number. A card is not called a semi-high unless the next to last series in which it exists has an additional premium attached to it.

SERIES. The entire set of cards issued by a particular producer in a particular year, e.g., the 1971 Topps series. Also, within a particular set, series can refer to a group of (consecutively numbered) cards printed at the same time, e.g., the first series of the 1957 Topps issue (numbers 1 through 88).

SET. One each of the entire run of cards of the same type produced by a particular manufacturer during a single year. In other words, if you have a (complete) set of 1976 Topps, then you have every card from number 1 up through and including number 660, i.e., all the different cards that were produced.

SKIP-NUMBERED. A set that has many unissued card numbers between the lowest number in the set and the highest number in the set, e.g., the 1948 Leaf baseball set contains 98 cards skip-numbered from number 1 to number 168. A major set in which a few numbers were not printed is not considered to be skip-numbered.

SO. Strikeouts.

SP. Single or Short Print (a card which was printed in lesser quantity compared to the other cards in the same series; see also DP and TP).

SPECIAL CARD. A card that portrays something other than a single player or team, for example, a card that portrays the previous year's statistical leaders or the results from the previous year's post-season action.

SS. Shortstop.

STAMP. Adhesive-backed papers depicting a player. The stamp may be individual or in a sheet of many stamps. Moisture must be applied to the adhesive in order for the stamp to be attached to another surface.

STAR CARD. A card that portrays a player of some repute, usually determined by his ability; however, sometimes referring to sheer popularity.

STICKER. A card with a removable layer that can be affixed to (stuck onto) another surface.

STOCK. The cardboard or paper on which the card is printed.

STRIP CARDS. A sheet or strip of cards, particularly popular in the 1920s and 1930s, with the individual cards usually separated by broken or dotted lines.

SUPERSTAR CARD. A card that portrays a superstar, e.g., a Hall of Fame member or one with strong Hall of Fame potential.

SV. Super Veteran (see 1982 Topps).

TAB. A card portion set off from the rest of the card, usually with perforations, that may be removed without damaging the central character or event depicted by the card.

TBC. Turn Back the Clock cards.

TC. Team Checklist cards (see 1989 and 1990 Upper Deck).

TEAM CARD. A card that depicts an entire team.

TEST SET. A set, usually containing a small number of cards, issued by a national card producer and distributed in a limited section or sections of the country. Presumably, the purpose of a test set is to test market appeal for a particular type of card.

TL. Team Leader card.

TP. Triple Print (a card that was printed in triple the quantity compared to the other cards in the same series).

TR. Trade or Traded.

TRIMMED. A card cut down from its original size. Trimmed cards are undesirable to most collectors.

VARIATION. One of two or more cards from the same series with the same number (or player with identical pose if the series is unnumbered) differing from one another by some aspect, the different feature stemming from the printing or stock of the card. This can be caused when the manufacturer of the cards notices an error in one (or more) of the cards, makes the changes, and then resumes the print run. In this case there will be two versions or variations of the same card. Sometimes one of the variations is relatively scarce.

VERT. Vertical pose on card.

WAS. Washington.

WS. World Series card.

History of Baseball Cards

Today's version of the baseball card, with its colorful front and statistical back, is a far cry from its earliest predecessors. The issue remains cloudy as to which was the very first baseball card ever produced, but the institution of baseball cards dates from the latter half of the 19th century, more than 100 years ago. Early issues, generally printed on heavy cardboard, were of poor quality, with photographs, drawings, and printing far short of today's standards.

Goodwin & Co., of New York, makers of Gypsy Queen, Old Judge, and other cigarette brands, is considered by many to be the first issuer of baseball and other sports cards. Their issues, predominantly in the 1½ by 2½ size, generally consisted of photographs of baseball players, boxers, wrestlers, and other subjects mounted on stiff cardboard. More than 2,000 different photos of baseball players alone have been identified. These "Old Judges," a collective name commonly used for the Goodwin & Co. cards, were issued from 1886 to 1890 and are treasured parts of many collections today.

Among the other cigarette companies which issued baseball cards that still attract attention today are Allen & Ginter, D. Buchner & Co. (Gold Coin Chewing Tobacco), and P.H. Mayo & Brother. Cards from the first two companies bore colored line drawings, while the Mayos are sepia photographs on black cardboard.

In addition to the small-size cards from this era, several tobacco companies issued cabinet-size baseball cards. These "cabinets" were considerably larger than the small cards, usually about 4¼" by 6½", and were printed on heavy stock. Goodwin & Co.'s Old Judge cabinets and the National Tobacco Works' "Newsboy" baseball photos are two that remain popular today.

By 1895 the American Tobacco Company began to dominate its competition. They discontinued baseball card inserts in their cigarette packages (actually slide boxes in those days). The lack of competition in the cigarette market had made these inserts unnecessary. This marked the end of the first era of the baseball card.

At the dawn of the 20th century, few baseball cards were being issued. But once again it was the cigarette companies—particularly, the American Tobacco Company—followed to a lesser extent by the candy and gum makers that revived the practice of including baseball cards with their products. The bulk of these cards, identified in the *American Card Catalog* (designated hereafter as *ACC*) as T or E cards for 20th-century "Tobacco" or "Early Candy and Gum" issues respectively, were released from 1909 to 1915.

This romantic and popular era of baseball card collecting produced many desirable items. The most outstanding is the fabled T-206 Honus Wagner card. Other perennial favorites among collectors are the T-206 Eddie Plank card and the T-206 Magee error card. The former was once the second most valuable card and only recently relinquished that position to a more distinctive and aesthetically pleasing Napoleon Lajoie card from the 1933/34 Goudey Gum series. The latter misspells the player's name as "Magie," the most famous and valuable blooper card.

The ingenuity and distinctiveness of this era has yet to be surpassed. Highlights include the T-202 Hassan triple-folders, one of the best looking and the most distinctive cards ever issued; the durable T-201 Mecca double-folders, one of the first sets with players' records on the reverse; the T-3 Turkey Reds, the hobby's most popular cabinet card; the E-145 Cracker Jacks, the only major set containing Federal League player cards; and the T-204 Ramlys, with their distinctive black and white oval photos and ornate gold borders. These are but a few of the varieties issued during this period.

While the American Tobacco Company dominated the field, several other tobacco companies, as well as clothing manufacturers, newspapers and periodicals, game makers, and companies whose identities remain anonymous, also issued cards during this period. In fact, the Collins-McCarthy Candy Company, makers of Zeenuts Pacific Coast League baseball cards, issued cards yearly from 1911 to 1938. Their record for continuous annual card production has been exceeded only by the Topps Chewing Gum Company. The era of the tobacco card issues closed with the onset of World War I, with the exception of the Red Man chewing tobacco sets produced from 1952 to 1955.

The next flurry of card issues broke out in the roaring and prosperous 1920s, the era of the E card. The caramel companies (National Caramel, American Caramel, York Caramel) were the leading distributors of these E cards. In addition, the strip card, a continous strip with several cards divided by dotted lines or other sectioning features, flourished during this time. While the E cards and the strip cards are generally considered less imaginative than the T cards or the recent candy and gum issues, they are still sought after by many advanced collectors.

Another significant event of the 1920s was the introduction of the Arcade card. Taking its designation from its issuer, the Exhibit Supply Company of Chicago, it is usually known as the "Exhibit" card. Once a trademark of the penny arcades, amusement parks, and county fairs across the country, Exhibit machines dispensed nearly postcard-size photos on thick stock for one penny. These picture cards bore likenesses of a favorite cowboy, actor, actress, or baseball player. Exhibit Supply and its associated companies produced baseball cards during a longer time span, although discontinuous, than any other manufacturer. Its first cards appeared in 1921, while its last issue was in 1966. In 1979, the Exhibit Supply Company was bought and somewhat revived by a collector/dealer who has since reprinted Exhibit photos of the past.

If the T card period, from 1909 to 1915, can be said to be the "Golden Age" of baseball card collecting, then perhaps the "Silver Age" commenced with the introduction of the Big League Gum series of 239 cards in 1933 (a 240th card was added in 1934). These are the forerunners of today's baseball gum cards, and the Goudey Gum Company of Boston is responsible for their success. This era spanned the period from the Depression days of 1933 to America's formal involvement in World War II in 1941.

Goudey's attractive designs, with full-color line drawings on thick card stock, influenced greatly other cards being issued at that time. As a result, the most attractive and popular cards in collecting history were produced in this "Silver Age." The 1933 Goudey Big League Gum series also owes its popularity to the more than 40 Hall of Fame players in the set. These include four cards of Babe Ruth and two of Lou Gehrig. Goudey's reign continued in 1934 when it issued a 96-card set in color, together with the single remaining card from the 1933 series, #106, the Napoleon Lajoie card.

In addition to Goudey, several other bubble gum manufacturers issued baseball cards during this era. DeLong Gum Company issued an extremely attractive set in 1933. National Chicle Company's 192-card "Batter-Up" series of 1934–1936 became the largest die-cut set in card history. In addition, that company offered the popular "Diamond Stars" series during the same period. Other popular sets included the "Tattoo Orbit" set of 60 color cards issued in 1933 and Gum Products' 75-card "Double Play" set, featuring sepia depictions of two players per card.

In 1939 Gum Inc., which later became Bowman Gum, replaced Goudey Gum as the leading baseball card producer. In 1939 and the following year, it issued two important sets of black and white cards. In 1939 its "Play Ball America" set consisted of 162 cards. The larger, 240-card "Play Ball" set of 1940 is still considered by many to be the most attractive black and white cards ever produced. That firm introduced its only color set in 1941, consisting of 72 cards entitled "Play Ball Sports Hall of Fame." Many of these were colored repeats of poses from the black and white 1940 series.

In addition to regular gum cards, many manufacturers distributed premium issues during the 1930s. These premiums were printed on paper or photographic stock, rather than card stock. They were much larger than the regular cards and were sold for a penny across the counter with gum (which was packaged separately from the premium). They were often redeemed at the store or through the mail in exchange for the wrappers of previously purchased gum cards, à la proof-of-purchase box-top premiums today. The gum premiums are scarcer than the card issues of the 1930s, and in most cases no manufacturer's name is present.

World War II brought an end to this popular era of card collecting when paper and rubber shortages curtailed the production of bubble gum baseball cards. They were resurrected again in 1948 by the Bowman Gum Company (the direct descendant of Gum, Inc.). This marked the beginning of the modern era of card collecting.

In 1948, Bowman Gum issued a 48-card set in black and white consisting of one card and one slab of gum in every one-cent pack. That same year, the Leaf Gum Company also issued a set of cards. Although rather poor in quality, these cards were issued in color. A squabble over the rights to use players' pictures developed between Bowman and Leaf. Eventually Leaf dropped out of the card market, but not before it had left a lasting heritage to the hobby by issuing some of the rarest cards now in existence. Leaf's baseball card series of 1948-49 contained 98 cards, skip numbered to #168 (not all numbers were printed). Of these 98 cards, 49 are relatively plentiful; however, the other 49 are rare and quite valuable.

Bowman continued its production of cards in 1949 with a color series of 240 cards. Because there are many scarce "high numbers," this series remains the most difficult Bowman regular issue to complete. Although the set was printed in color and commands great interest due to its scarcity, it is considered aesthetically inferior to the Goudey and National Chicle issues of the 1930s. In addition to the regular issue of 1949, Bowman also produced a set of 36 Pacific Coast League players. While this was not a regular issue, it is still prized by collectors. In fact, it has become the most valuable Bowman series.

In 1950 (Bowman's one-year monopoly of the baseball card market), the company began a string of top quality cards which continued until its demise in 1955. The 1950 series was itself something of an oddity because the "low" numbers, rather than the traditional high numbers, were the more difficult cards to obtain.

The year 1951 marked the beginning of the most competitive and perhaps the highest quality period of baseball card production. In that year Topps Chewing Gum Company of Brooklyn entered the market. Topps' 1951 series consisted of two sets of 52 cards each, one set with red backs and the other with blue backs. In addition, Topps also issued 31 insert cards, three of which remain the rarest Topps cards ("Current All-Stars" Konstanty, Roberts, and Stanky). The 1951 Topps cards were unattractive and paled in comparison to the 1951 Bowman issues. However, they were successful, and Topps has continued to produce cards ever since.

Topps issued a larger and much more attractive card in 1952. This larger size became standard for the next five years. (Bowman followed with larger-size baseball cards in 1953.) This 1952 Topps set has become, like the 1933 Goudey series and the T-206 white border series, the classic set of its era. The 407-card set is a collector's dream of scarcities, rarities, errors, and variations. It also contains the first Topps issues of Mickey Mantle and Willie Mays.

As with Bowman and Leaf in the late 1940s, competition over player rights arose. Ensuing court battles occurred between Topps and Bowman. The market split due to stiff competition, and in January 1956, Topps bought out Bowman. Topps remained relatively unchallenged as the primary producer of baseball cards through 1980. So, the story of major baseball card sets from 1956 through 1980 is by and large the story of Topps' issues with few exceptions. Fleer Gum produced small sets in 1959, 1960, 1961, and 1963, and several cartoon sets in the 1970s, and more recently Kellogg's Cereal and Hostess Cakes issued baseball cards to promote their products.

A court decision in 1980 paved the way for two other large gum companies to enter, or reenter, the baseball card arena. The Fleer Corporation, which had last made photo cards in 1963, and the Donruss Company (then a division of General Mills) secured rights to produce baseball cards of current players, breaking Topps' monopoly. Each company issued major card sets in 1981 with bubble gum products.

Then a higher court decision in that year overturned the lower court ruling against Topps. It appeared that Topps had regained its sole position as a producer of baseball cards. Undaunted by the revocation ruling, Fleer and Donruss continued to issue cards in 1982 but without bubble gum or any other edible product. Fleer issued its current player baseball cards with "team logo stickers," while Donruss issued its cards with a piece of a baseball jigsaw puzzle.

Since 1981, these three major baseball card producers have all thrived, sharing relatively equal recognition. Each has steadily increased its involvement in terms of numbers of issues per year. To the delight of collectors, their competition has generated novel, and in some cases exceptional, issues of current major league baseball players. Collectors have also been impressed with the efforts of Score (1988) and Upper Deck (1989), the newest companies to enter the baseball card-producing derby. All these major producers have become increasingly aware of the organized collecting market. While the corner candy store remains the major marketplace for card sales, an increasing number of issues have been directed to this organized hobby marketplace. In fact, many of these issues have been distributed exclusively through hobby channels. Although no one can ever say what the future will bring, one can only surmise that the hobby market will play a significant role in future plans of all the major baseball card producers.

The above has been a thumbnail sketch of card collecting from its inception in the 1880s to the present. It is difficult to tell the whole story in just a few pages—there are several other good sources of information. Serious collectors should subscribe to at least one of the excellent hobby periodicals. We also suggest that collectors attend a sports collectibles convention in their area. Card collecting is still a young and informal hobby. Chances are good that you will run into one or more of the "experts" at such a show. They are usually more than happy to share their knowledge with you.

Business of Baseball Card Collecting

Determining Value

Why are some cards more valuable than others? Obviously, the economic laws of supply and demand are applicable to card collecting just as they are to any other field where a commodity is bought, sold, or traded in a free, unregulated market.

Supply (the number of cards available on the market) is less than the total number of cards originally produced since attrition diminishes that original quantity. Each year a percentage of cards is typically thrown away, destroyed, or otherwise lost to collectors. This percentage is much smaller today than it was in the past because more and more people have become increasingly aware of the value of their cards. For those who collect only "mint" condition cards, the supply of older cards can be quite small indeed. Until recently, collectors were not so conscious of the need to preserve the condition of their cards. For this reason, it is difficult to know exactly how many 1953 Topps are currently available, mint or otherwise. It is generally accepted that there are fewer 1953 Topps available than 1963, 1973, or 1983 Topps cards. If demand were equal for each of these sets, the law of supply and demand would increase the price for the least available sets. Demand, however, is not equal for all sets, so price correlations can be complicated.

The demand for a card is influenced by many factors. These include: (1) the age of the card; (2) the number of cards printed; (3) the player(s) portrayed on the card; (4) the attractiveness and popularity of the set; and perhaps most important, (5) the physical condition of the card.

In general, (1) the older the card, (2) the fewer the number of the cards printed, (3) the more famous the player, (4) the more attractive and popular the set, or (5) the better the condition of the card, the higher the value of the card will be. There are exceptions to all but one of these factors: the condition of the card. Given two cards similar in all respects except condition, the one in the best condition will ALWAYS be valued higher.

While there are certain guidelines that help to establish the value of a card, the exceptions and peculiarities make any simple, direct mathematical formula to determine card values impossible.

Regional Variation

Two types of price variations exist among the sections of the country where a card is bought or sold. The first is the general price variation on all cards bought and sold in one geographical area as compared to another. Card prices are slightly higher on the East and West coasts, and slightly lower in the middle of the country. Although prices may vary from the East to the West, or from the Southwest to the Midwest, the prices listed in this guide are nonetheless presented as a consensus of all sections of this large and diverse country.

Still, prices for a particular player's cards may well be higher in his home team's area than in other regions. This exhibits the second type of regional price variation in which local players are favored over those from distant areas. For example, an Al Kaline card would be valued higher in Detroit than in Cincinnati because Kaline played in Detroit; therefore, the demand there for Al Kaline cards is higher than it is in Cincinnati. On the other hand, a Johnny Bench card would be priced higher in Cincinnati, where he played, than in Detroit for similar reasons. Sometimes even common player cards command such a premium from hometown collectors.

Set Prices

A somewhat paradoxical situation exists in the price of a complete set versus the combined cost of the individual cards in the set. In nearly every case, the sum of the prices for the individual cards is higher than the cost for the complete set. This is especially prevalent in the cards of the past few years. The reasons for this apparent anomaly stem from the habits of collectors and from the carrying costs to dealers. Today each card in a set is normally produced in the same quantity as all others in its set. However, many collectors pick up only stars, superstars, and particular teams. As a result, the dealer is left with a shortage of certain player cards and an abundance of others. He therefore incurs an expense in simply "carrying" these less desirable cards in stock. On the other hand, if he sells a complete set, he gets rid of large numbers of cards at one time. For this reason, he is often willing to receive less money for a complete set. By doing this, he recovers all of his costs and also receives some profit.

The disparity between the price of the complete set and that for the sum of the individual cards has also been influenced by the fact that the major manufacturers are now pre-collating card sets. Since "pulling" individual cards from the sets of all three manufacturers involves a specific type of labor (and cost), the singles or star card market is not affected significantly by pre-collation.

Set prices also do not include rare card varieties, unless specifically stated. Of course, the prices for sets do include one example of each type for the given set, but this is the least expensive variety.

Scarce Series

Scarce series occur because cards issued before 1974 were made available to the public each year in several series of finite numbers of cards, rather than all cards of the set being available for purchase at one time. At some point during the year, usually toward the end of the baseball season, interest in current year baseball cards waned. Consequently, the manufacturers produced smaller numbers of these later series of cards. Nearly all nationwide issues from post-World War II manufacturers (1948 to 1973) exhibit these series variations. In the past Topps, for example, may have issued series consisting of many different numbers of cards, including 55, 66, 80, 88, and others. Recently Topps has settled on what is now their standard sheet size of 132 cards, six of which comprise its 792-card set.

While the number of cards within a given series is usually the same as the number of cards on one printed sheet, this is not always the case. For example, Bowman used 36 cards on its standard printed sheets, but in 1948 substituted 12 cards during later print runs of that year's baseball cards. Twelve of the cards from the initial sheet of 36 cards were removed and replaced by 12 different cards giving, in effect, a first series of 36 cards and a second series of 12 new cards. This replacement produced a scarcity of 24 cards—the 12 cards removed from the original sheet and the 12 new cards added to the sheet. A full sheet of 1948 Bowman cards (second printing) shows that card numbers 37 through 48 have replaced 12 of the cards on the first printing sheet.

The Topps Gum Company has also created scarcities and/or excesses of certain cards in many of their sets. Topps, however, has most frequently gone the other direction by double printing some of the cards. Double printing causes an abundance of cards of the players who are on the same sheet more than one time. During the years from 1978 to 1981, Topps double printed 66 cards out of their large 726-card set. The Topps' practice of double printing cards in earlier years is the most logical explanation for the known scarcities of particular cards in some of these Topps sets. Recently Donruss has always been short printing or double printing certain cards in its major sets. Ostensibly this is due to their addition of Bonus MVP cards in their regular issue wax packs.

We are always looking for information or photographs of printing sheets of cards for research. Each year we try to update the hobby's knowledge of distribution anomalies. Please let us know at the address in this book if you have first-hand knowledge that would be helpful in this pursuit.

Grading Your Cards

Each hobby has its own grading terminology—stamps, coins, comic books, beer cans, right down the line. Collectors of sports cards are no exception. The one invariable criterion for determining the value of a card is its condition: the better the condition of the card, the more valuable it is. However, condition grading is very subjective. Individual card dealers and collectors differ in the strictness of their grading, but the stated condition of a card should be determined without regard to whether it is being bought or sold.

The physical defects which lower the condition of a card are usually quite apparent, but each individual places his own estimation (negative value in this case) on these defects. We present the condition guide for use in determining values listed in this price guide in the hopes that excess subjectivity can be minimized.

The defects listed in the condition guide below are those either placed in the card at the time of printing—uneven borders, focus—or those defects that can occur to a card under normal handling—corner sharpness, gloss, edge wear, light creases —and finally, environmental conditions—browning. Other defects to cards are caused by human carelessness and in all cases should be noted separately and in addition to the condition grade. Among the more common alterations are heavy creases, tape, tape stains, rubber band marks, water damage, smoke damage, trimming, paste, tears, writing, pin or tack holes, any back damage, and missing parts (tabs, tops, coupons, backgrounds).

Centering

It is important to define in words and pictures what is meant by certain frequently used hobby terms relating to grading cards. The following pictures portray various stages of centering. Centering can range from well-centered to slightly off-centered to off-centered to badly off-centered to miscut.

Slightly Off-Centered: A slightly off-center card is one which upon close inspection is found to have one border bigger than the opposite border. This degree is only offensive to a purist.

Off-Centered: An off-center card has one border which is noticeably more than twice as wide as the opposite border.

Badly Off-Centered: A badly off-center card has virtually no border on one side of the card.

Miscut: A miscut card actually shows part of the adjacent card in its larger border and consequently a corresponding amount of its card is cut off.

Centering

SLIGHTLY OFF-CENTERED

OFF-CENTERED

BADLY OFF-CENTERED

MISCUT

Corner Wear

Degrees of corner wear generate several common terms used and useful to accurate grading. The wear on card corners can be expressed as fuzzy corners, corner wear or slightly rounded corners, rounded corners, badly rounded corners.

Fuzzy Corners: Fuzzy corners still come to a right angle (to a point) but the point has begun to fray slightly.

Corner Wear or Slightly Rounded Corners: The slight fraying of the corners has increased to where there is no longer a point to the corner. Nevertheless the corner is still reasonably sharp. There may be evidence of some slight loss of color in the corner also.

Rounded Corners: The corner is definitely no longer sharp but is not badly rounded.

Badly Rounded Corners: The corner is rounded to an objectionable degree. Excessive wear and rough handling are evident.

Creases

The third, and perhaps most frequent, common defect is the crease; the degree of creasing in a card is very difficult to show in a drawing or picture. On giving the specific condition of an expensive card for sale, the seller should note any creases additionally. Creases can be categorized as to severity according to the following scale.

Light Crease: A light crease is a crease which is barely noticeable on close inspection. In fact when cards are in plastic sheets or holders, a light crease may not be seen (until the card is taken out of the holder). A light crease on the front is much more serious than a light crease on the card back only.

Medium Crease: A medium crease is noticeable when held and studied at arm's length by the naked eye, but does not overly detract from the appearance of the card. It is an obvious crease, but not one that breaks the picture surface of the card.

Heavy Crease: A heavy crease is one which has torn or broken through the card's picture surface, e.g., puts a tear in the photo surface.

Alterations

Deceptive Trimming: Deceptive trimming occurs when someone alters the card in order (1) to shave off edge wear; (2) to improve the sharpness of the corners; or (3) to improve centering—obviously their objective is to falsely increase the perceived value of the card to an unsuspecting buyer. The shrinkage is usually only evident if the trimmed card is compared to an adjacent full-sized card or if the trimmed card is itself measured.

Obvious Trimming: Obvious trimming is noticeable and unfortunate. It is usually performed by non-collectors who give no thought to the present or future value of their cards.

Deceptively Retouched Borders: This occurs when the borders (especially on those cards with dark borders) are touched up on the edges and corners with magic marker of appropriate color in order to make the card appear to be mint.

Categorization of Defects

A "Micro Defect" would be fuzzy corners, slight off-centering, printers' lines, printers' spots, slightly out of focus, or slight loss of original gloss. An NrMT card may have one micro defect. An EX-MT card may have two or more micro defects.

A "Minor Defect" would be corner wear or slight rounding, off-centering, light crease on back, wax or gum stains on reverse, loss of original gloss, writing or tape marks on back, or rubber band marks. An Excellent card may have minor defects.

A "Major Defect" would be rounded corner(s), badly off-centering, crease(s), deceptive trimming, deceptively retouched borders, pin hole, staple hole, incidental writing or tape marks on front, warping, water stains, or sun fading. A VG card may have one major defect. A Good card may have two or more major defects.

A "Catastrophic Defect" is the worst kind of defect and would include such defects as badly rounded corner(s), miscutting, heavy crease(s), obvious trimming, punch hole, tack hole, tear(s), corner missing or clipped, destructive writing on front. A Fair card may have one catastrophic defect. A Poor card has two or more catastrophic defects.

Condition Guide

MINT (M OR MT): A card with no defects. The card has sharp corners, even borders, original gloss or shine on the surface, sharp focus of the picture, smooth edges, no signs of wear, and white borders. A Mint card (that is, a card that is worth a "Mint" price) does NOT have printers' lines or other printing defects or other serious quality control problems that should have been discovered by the producing card company before distribution. Note also that there is no allowance made for the age of the card.

NEAR MINT (NrMT): A card with a micro defect. Any of the following would be sufficient to lower the grade of a card from Mint to the Near Mint category: layering at some of the corners (fuzzy corners), a very small amount of the original gloss lost, very minor wear on the edges, slightly off-center borders, slight wear visible only on close inspection, slight off-whiteness of the borders.

EXCELLENT-MINT (EX-MT): A card with micro defects, but no minor defects. Two or three of the following would be sufficient to lower the grade of a card from Mint to the Excellent-Mint category: layering at some of the corners (fuzzy corners), a very small amount of the original gloss lost, minor wear on the edges, slightly off-center borders, slight wear visible only on close inspection, slight off-whiteness of the borders.

EXCELLENT (EX OR E): A card with minor defects. Any of the following would be sufficient to lower the grade of a card from Mint to the Excellent category: slight rounding at some of the corners, a small amount of the original gloss lost, minor wear on the edges, off-center borders, wear visible only on close inspection; off-whiteness of the borders.

VERY GOOD (VG): A card that has been handled but not abused. Some rounding at all corners, slight layering or scuffing at one or two corners, slight notching on edges, gloss lost from the surface but not scuffed, borders might be somewhat uneven but some white is visible on all borders, noticeable yellowing or browning of borders, pictures may be slightly off focus.

GOOD (G): A well-handled card, rounding and some layering at the corners, scuffing at the corners and minor scuffing on the face, borders noticeably uneven and browning, loss of gloss on the face, notching on the edges.

FAIR (F): Round and layering corners, brown and dirty borders, frayed edges, noticeable scuffing on the face, white not visible on one or more borders, cloudy focus.

POOR (P): An abused card. The lowest grade of card, frequently some major physical alteration has been performed on the card, collectible only as a filler until a better-condition replacement can be obtained.

Categories between these major condition grades are frequently used, such as Very Good to Excellent (VG-E), Fair to Good (F-G), etc. Such grades indicate a card with all qualities at least in the lower of the two categories, but with several qualities in the higher of the two categories. In the case of EX-MT, it essentially refers to a card which is halfway between Excellent and Mint.

Unopened "Mint" cards and factory-collated sets are considered Mint in their unknown (and presumed perfect) state. However, once opened or broken out, each of these cards is graded (and valued) in its own right by taking into account any quality control defects (such as off-centering, printers' lines, machine creases, or gum stains) that may be present in spite of the fact that the card has never been handled.

Cards before 1980 that are priced in the price guide in a top condition of NrMT are obviously worth an additional premium when offered in strict Mint condition. This additional premium increases relative to the age and scarcity of the card. For example, Mint cards from the late '70s may bring only a 10% premium for Mint (above NrMT), whereas high demand (or condition rarity) cards from early vintage sets can be sold for as much as double (and occasionally even more) the NrMT price when offered in strict Mint condition.

Cards before 1946 that are priced in the price guide in a top condition of EX-MT, are obviously worth an additional premium when offered in strict Near Mint or better condition. This additional premium increases relative to the age and scarcity of the card.

Selling Your Cards

Just about every collector sells cards or will sell cards eventually. Someday you may be interested in selling your duplicates or maybe even your whole collection. You may sell to other collectors, friends, or dealers. You may even sell cards you purchased from a certain dealer back to that same dealer. In any event, it helps to know some of the mechanics of the typical transaction between buyer and seller.

Dealers will buy cards in order to resell them to other collectors who are interested in the cards. Dealers will always pay a higher percentage for items which (in their opinion) can be resold quickly, and a much lower percentage for those items which are perceived as having low demand and hence are slow moving. In either case, dealers must buy at a price that allows for the expense of doing business and a fair margin for profit.

If you have cards for sale, the best advice we can give is that you get three offers for your cards and take the best offer, all things considered. Note, the "best" offer may not be the one for the highest amount. And remember, if a dealer really wants your cards, he won't let you get away without making his best competitive offer. Another alternative is to take your cards to a nearby convention and either auction them off in the show auction or offer them for sale to some of the dealers present.

Many people think nothing of going into a department store and paying $15 for an item of clothing for which the store paid $5. But, if you were selling your $15 card to a dealer and he offered you only $5 for it, you might think his mark-up unreasonable. To complete the analogy: most department stores (and card dealers) that pay $10 for $15 items eventually go out of business. An exception to this is when the dealer knows that a willing buyer for the merchandise you are attempting to sell is only a phone call away. Then an offer of two-thirds or maybe 70% of the book value will still allow him to make a reasonable profit due to the short time he will need to hold the merchandise. Nevertheless, most cards and collections will bring offers in the range of 25% to 50% of retail price. Material from the past five to ten years or so is very plentiful. Don't be surprised if your best offer is only 20% of the book value for these recent years.

Interesting Notes

The numerically first card of an issue is the single card most likely to obtain excessive wear. Consequently, you will typically find the price on the number one card (in mint condition) somewhat higher than might otherwise be the case. Similarly, but to a lesser extent (because normally the less important, reverse side of the card is the one exposed), the numerically last card in an issue is also prone to abnormal wear. This extra wear and tear occurs because the first and last cards are exposed to the elements (human element included) more than any other cards. They are generally end cards in any brick formations, rubber bandings, stackings on wet surfaces, and like activities.

Sports cards have no intrinsic value. The value of a card, like the value of other collectibles, can only be determined by you and your enjoyment in viewing and possessing these cardboard swatches.

Remember, the buyer ultimately determines the price of each baseball card. You are the determining price factor because you have the ability to say "No" to the price of any card by not exchanging your hard-earned money for a given card. When the cost of a trading card exceeds the enjoyment you will receive from it, your answer should be "No." We assess and report the prices. You set them!

We are always interested in receiving the price input of collectors and dealers from around the country. We happily credit major contributors. We welcome your opinions, since your contributions assist us in ensuring a better guide each year. If you would like to join our survey list for the next editions of this book and others authored by Dr. Beckett, please send your name and address to Dr. James Beckett, 4887 Alpha Road, Suite 200, Dallas, Texas 75244.

Advertising

Within this price guide you will find advertisements for sports memorabilia material, mail order, and retail sports collectibles establishments. All advertisements were accepted in good faith based on the reputation of the advertiser; however, neither the author, the publisher, the distributors, nor the other advertisers in the price guide accept any responsibility for any particular advertiser not complying with the terms of his or her ad.

Readers should also be aware that prices in advertisements are subject to change over the annual period before a new edition of this volume is issued each spring. When replying to an advertisement late in the baseball year, the reader should take this into account, and contact the dealer by phone or in writing for up-to-date price information. Should you come into contact with any of the advertisers in this guide as a result of their advertisement herein, please mention to them this source as your contact.

Additional Reading

With the increase in popularity of the hobby in recent years, there has been a corresponding increase in available literature. Below is a list of the books and periodicals which receive our highest recommendation and which we hope will further advance your knowledge and enjoyment of our great hobby.

The Sport Americana Price Guide to Baseball Collectibles by Dr. James Beckett (Second Edition, $12.95, released 1988, published by Edgewater Book Company)—the complete guide/checklist with up-to-date values for box cards, coins, labels, Canadian cards, stamps, stickers, pins, etc.

The Sport Americana Football, Hockey, Basketball and Boxing Card Price Guide by Dr. James Beckett (Sixth Edition, $14.95, released 1989, published by Edgewater Book Company)—the most comprehensive price guide/checklist ever issued on football and other non-baseball sports cards. No serious hobbyist should be without it.

The Official Price Guide to Football Cards by Dr. James Beckett (Ninth Edition, $5.95, released 1989, published by the House of Collectibles)—an abridgement of the *Sport Americana Price Guide* listed above in a convenient and economical pocket-size format providing Dr. Beckett's pricing of the major football sets since 1948.

The Official Price Guide to Hockey and Basketball Cards by Dr. James Beckett (First Edition, $5.95, released 1989, published by the House of Collectibles)—an abridgement of the *Sport Americana Price Guide* listed above in a convenient and economical pocket-size format providing Dr. Beckett's pricing of the major hockey and basketball sets since 1948.

The Sport Americana Baseball Memorabilia and Autograph Price Guide by Dr. James Beckett and Dennis W. Eckes (First Edition, $8.95, released 1982, co-published by Den's Collectors Den and Edgewater Book Company)—the most complete book ever produced on baseball memorabilia other than baseball cards. This book presents in an illustrated, logical fashion information on baseball memorabilia and autographs that had been heretofore unavailable to the collector.

The Sport Americana Alphabetical Baseball Card Checklist by Dr. James Beckett (Fourth Edition, $12.95, released 1990, published by Edgewater Book Company)—an alphabetical listing, by the last name of the player portrayed on the card, of virtually all baseball cards (Major League and Minor League) produced up through the 1990 major sets.

The Sport Americana Price Guide to the Non-Sports Cards by Christopher Benjamin and Dennis W. Eckes (Third Edition [Part Two], $12.95, released 1988, published by Edgewater Book Company)—the definitive guide to all popular non-sports American tobacco and bubble gum cards. In addition to cards, illustrations and prices for wrappers are also included. Part Two covers non-sports cards from 1961 through 1987.

The Sport Americana Baseball Address List by Jack Smalling and Dennis W. Eckes (Fifth Edition, $10.95, released 1988, published by Edgewater Book Company)—the definitive guide for autograph hunters, giving addresses and deceased information for virtually all major league baseball players past and present.

The Sport Americana Baseball Card Team Checklist by Jeff Fritsch and Dennis W. Eckes (Fifth Edition, $12.95, released 1990, published by Edgewater Book Company)—includes all Topps, Bowman, Donruss, Fleer, Score, Play Ball, Goudey, and Upper Deck cards, with the players portrayed on the cards listed with the teams for whom they played. The book is invaluable to the collector who specializes in an individual team because it is the most complete baseball card team checklist available.

The Encyclopedia of Baseball Cards, Volume I: 19th Century Cards by Lew Lipset ($11.95, released 1983, published by the author)—everything you ever wanted to know about 19th-century cards.

The Encyclopedia of Baseball Cards, Volume II: Early Gum and Candy Cards by Lew Lipset ($10.95, released 1984, published by the author)—everything you ever wanted to know about Early Candy and Gum cards.

The Encyclopedia of Baseball Cards, Volume III: 20th Century Tobacco Cards, 1909–1932 by Lew Lipset ($12.95, released 1986, published by the author) — everything you ever wanted to know about old tobacco cards.

Beckett Baseball Card Monthly authored and edited by Dr. James Beckett—contains the most extensive and accepted monthly price guide, feature articles, "who's hot and who's not" section, convention calendar, and numerous letters to and responses from the editor. Published 12 times annually, it is the hobby's largest paid circulation periodical.

Beckett Football Card Magazine (eight times a year) and *Beckett Basketball Card Magazine* (six times a year) are both very similar to *Beckett Baseball Card Monthly* in style and content.

Prices in This Guide

Prices found in this guide reflect current retail rates just prior to the printing of this book. They do not reflect the FOR SALE prices of the author, the publisher, the distributors, the advertisers, or any card dealers associated with this guide. No one is obligated in any way to buy, sell, or trade his or her cards based on these prices. The price listings were compiled by the author from actual buy/sell transactions at sports conventions, buy/sell advertisements in the hobby papers, for sale prices from dealer catalogs and price lists, and discussions with leading hobbyists in the United States and Canada. All prices are in U.S. dollars.

1952 Topps

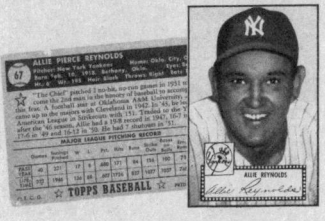

*The cards in this 407-card set measure 2 ⅝"
by 3 ¾". The 1952 Topps set is Topps' first
truly major set. Card numbers 1 to 80 were
issued with red or black backs, both of which
are less plentiful than card numbers 81 to 250.
In fact, the first series is considered the most
difficult with respect to finding mint condition
cards. Card number 48 (Joe Page) and number 49 (Johnny Sain) can be found with each
other's write-up on their back. Card numbers
251 to 310 are somewhat scarce and numbers
311 to 407 are quite scarce. Cards 281-300
were single printed compared to the other
cards in the next to last series. Cards 311-313
were double printed on the last high number
printing sheet. The key card in the set is obviously Mickey Mantle #311, Mickey's first of
many Topps cards. Although rarely seen, there
exists a salesman's sample panel of three
cards containing the fronts of Bob Mahoney,
Robin Roberts, and Sid Hudson with ad information on the back.*

	NRMT	VG-E	GOOD
COMPLETE SET (407) ...	42000.00	18000.00	6000.00
COMMON PLAYER (1-80) ...	50.00	25.00	5.00
COMMON PLAYER (81-250) ...	25.00	12.50	2.50
COMMON PLAYER (251-280) ...	40.00	20.00	4.00
COMMON PLAYER (281-300) ...	50.00	25.00	5.00
COMMON PLAYER (301-310) ..	40.00	20.00	4.00
COMMON PLAYER (311-407) ..	150.00	75.00	15.00

			NRMT	VG-E	GOOD
☐	1	Andy Pafko	1200.00	75.00	10.00
☐	2	Pete Runnels	55.00	27.50	5.50
☐	3	Hank Thompson	55.00	27.50	5.50
☐	4	Don Lenhardt	50.00	25.00	5.00
☐	5	Larry Jansen	50.00	25.00	5.00
☐	6	Grady Hatton	50.00	25.00	5.00
☐	7	Wayne Terwilliger ...	50.00	25.00	5.00
☐	8	Fred Marsh	50.00	25.00	5.00
☐	9	Robert Hogue	50.00	25.00	5.00
☐	10	Al Rosen	70.00	35.00	7.00
☐	11	Phil Rizzuto	150.00	75.00	15.00
☐	12	Romanus Basgall	50.00	25.00	5.00
☐	13	Johnny Wyrostek	50.00	25.00	5.00
☐	14	Bob Elliott	55.00	27.50	5.50
☐	15	Johnny Pesky	55.00	27.50	5.50
☐	16	Gene Hermanski	50.00	25.00	5.00
☐	17	Jim Hegan	55.00	27.50	5.50
☐	18	Merrill Combs	50.00	25.00	5.00
☐	19	Johnny Bucha	50.00	25.00	5.00
☐	20	Billy Loes	90.00	45.00	9.00
☐	21	Ferris Fain	55.00	27.50	5.50
☐	22	Dom DiMaggio	75.00	37.50	7.50
☐	23	Billy Goodman	55.00	27.50	5.50
☐	24	Luke Easter	55.00	27.50	5.50
☐	25	Johnny Groth	50.00	25.00	5.00
☐	26	Monte Irvin	100.00	50.00	10.00
☐	27	Sam Jethroe	55.00	27.50	5.50
☐	28	Jerry Priddy	50.00	25.00	5.00
☐	29	Ted Kluszewski	70.00	35.00	7.00
☐	30	Mel Parnell	55.00	27.50	5.50
☐	31	Gus Zernial	60.00	30.00	6.00
☐	32	Eddie Robinson	50.00	25.00	5.00
☐	33	Warren Spahn	175.00	85.00	18.00
☐	34	Elmer Valo	50.00	25.00	5.00
☐	35	Hank Sauer	65.00	32.50	6.50
☐	36	Gil Hodges	125.00	60.00	12.50
☐	37	Duke Snider	250.00	125.00	25.00
☐	38	Wally Westlake	50.00	25.00	5.00
☐	39	Dizzy Trout	55.00	27.50	5.50
☐	40	Irv Noren	50.00	25.00	5.00
☐	41	Bob Wellman	50.00	25.00	5.00
☐	42	Lou Kretlow	50.00	25.00	5.00
☐	43	Ray Scarborough	50.00	25.00	5.00
☐	44	Con Dempsey	50.00	25.00	5.00
☐	45	Eddie Joost	50.00	25.00	5.00
☐	46	Gordon Goldsberry ..	50.00	25.00	5.00
☐	47	Willie Jones	50.00	25.00	5.00
☐	48A	Joe Page COR	65.00	32.50	6.50
☐	48B	Joe Page ERR	300.00	150.00	30.00

			NRMT	VG-E	GOOD
		(bio for Sain)			
☐	49A	Johnny Sain COR	80.00	40.00	8.00
☐	49B	Johnny Sain ERR	300.00	150.00	30.00
		(bio for Page)			
☐	50	Marv Rickert	50.00	25.00	5.00
☐	51	Jim Russell	50.00	25.00	5.00
☐	52	Don Mueller	60.00	30.00	6.00
☐	53	Chris Van Cuyk	50.00	25.00	5.00
☐	54	Leo Kiely	50.00	25.00	5.00
☐	55	Ray Boone	55.00	27.50	5.50
☐	56	Tommy Glaviano	50.00	25.00	5.00
☐	57	Ed Lopat	90.00	45.00	9.00
☐	58	Bob Mahoney	50.00	25.00	5.00
☐	59	Robin Roberts	125.00	60.00	12.50
☐	60	Sid Hudson	50.00	25.00	5.00
☐	61	Tookie Gilbert	50.00	25.00	5.00
☐	62	Chuck Stobbs	50.00	25.00	5.00
☐	63	Howie Pollet	50.00	25.00	5.00
☐	64	Roy Sievers	55.00	27.50	5.50
☐	65	Enos Slaughter	125.00	60.00	12.50
☐	66	Preacher Roe	90.00	45.00	9.00
☐	67	Allie Reynolds	90.00	45.00	9.00
☐	68	Cliff Chambers	50.00	25.00	5.00
☐	69	Virgil Stallcup	50.00	25.00	5.00
☐	70	Al Zarilla	50.00	25.00	5.00
☐	71	Tom Upton	50.00	25.00	5.00
☐	72	Karl Olson	50.00	25.00	5.00
☐	73	Bill Werle	50.00	25.00	5.00
☐	74	Andy Hansen	50.00	25.00	5.00
☐	75	Wes Westrum	50.00	25.00	5.00
☐	76	Eddie Stanky	60.00	30.00	6.00
☐	77	Bob Kennedy	55.00	27.50	5.50
☐	78	Ellis Kinder	50.00	25.00	5.00
☐	79	Jerald Staley	50.00	25.00	5.00
☐	80	Herman Wehmeier	50.00	25.00	5.00
☐	81	Vernon Law	30.00	15.00	3.00
☐	82	Duane Pillette	25.00	12.50	2.50
☐	83	Billy Johnson	25.00	12.50	2.50
☐	84	Vern Stephens	30.00	15.00	3.00
☐	85	Bob Kuzava	25.00	12.50	2.50
☐	86	Ted Gray	25.00	12.50	2.50
☐	87	Dale Coogan	25.00	12.50	2.50
☐	88	Bob Feller	125.00	60.00	12.50
☐	89	Johnny Lipon	25.00	12.50	2.50
☐	90	Mickey Grasso	25.00	12.50	2.50
☐	91	Red Schoendienst	65.00	32.50	6.50
☐	92	Dale Mitchell	30.00	15.00	3.00
☐	93	Al Sima	25.00	12.50	2.50
☐	94	Sam Mele	25.00	12.50	2.50
☐	95	Ken Holcombe	25.00	12.50	2.50
☐	96	Willard Marshall	25.00	12.50	2.50
☐	97	Earl Torgeson	25.00	12.50	2.50
☐	98	Billy Pierce	30.00	15.00	3.00
☐	99	Gene Woodling	45.00	22.50	4.50
☐	100	Del Rice	25.00	12.50	2.50
☐	101	Max Lanier	25.00	12.50	2.50
☐	102	Bill Kennedy	25.00	12.50	2.50
☐	103	Cliff Mapes	25.00	12.50	2.50
☐	104	Don Kolloway	25.00	12.50	2.50
☐	105	Johnny Pramesa	25.00	12.50	2.50
☐	106	Mickey Vernon	30.00	15.00	3.00
☐	107	Connie Ryan	25.00	12.50	2.50
☐	108	Jim Konstanty	30.00	15.00	3.00
☐	109	Ted Wilks	25.00	12.50	2.50
☐	110	Dutch Leonard	25.00	12.50	2.50
☐	111	Peanuts Lowrey	25.00	12.50	2.50
☐	112	Hank Majeski	25.00	12.50	2.50
☐	113	Dick Sisler	25.00	12.50	2.50
☐	114	Willard Ramsdell	25.00	12.50	2.50
☐	115	Red Munger	25.00	12.50	2.50
☐	116	Carl Scheib	25.00	12.50	2.50
☐	117	Sherm Lollar	30.00	15.00	3.00
☐	118	Ken Raffensberger	25.00	12.50	2.50
☐	119	Mickey McDermott	25.00	12.50	2.50
☐	120	Bob Chakales	25.00	12.50	2.50
☐	121	Gus Niarhos	25.00	12.50	2.50
☐	122	Jackie Jensen	65.00	32.50	6.50
☐	123	Eddie Yost	25.00	12.50	2.50
☐	124	Monte Kennedy	25.00	12.50	2.50
☐	125	Bill Rigney	25.00	12.50	2.50
☐	126	Fred Hutchinson	30.00	15.00	3.00
☐	127	Paul Minner	25.00	12.50	2.50
☐	128	Don Bollweg	25.00	12.50	2.50
☐	129	Johnny Mize	75.00	37.50	7.50
☐	130	Sheldon Jones	25.00	12.50	2.50
☐	131	Morrie Martin	25.00	12.50	2.50
☐	132	Clyde Klutz	25.00	12.50	2.50
☐	133	Al Widmar	25.00	12.50	2.50
☐	134	Joe Tipton	25.00	12.50	2.50
☐	135	Dixie Howell	25.00	12.50	2.50
☐	136	Johnny Schmitz	25.00	12.50	2.50
☐	137	Roy McMillan	25.00	12.50	2.50
☐	138	Bill MacDonald	25.00	12.50	2.50
☐	139	Ken Wood	25.00	12.50	2.50
☐	140	Johnny Antonelli	30.00	15.00	3.00
☐	141	Clint Hartung	25.00	12.50	2.50
☐	142	Harry Perkowski	25.00	12.50	2.50
☐	143	Les Moss	25.00	12.50	2.50

		NRMT	VG-E	GOOD			NRMT	VG-E	GOOD
☐ 144	Ed Blake	25.00	12.50	2.50	☐ 193	Harry Simpson	25.00	12.50	2.50
☐ 145	Joe Haynes	25.00	12.50	2.50	☐ 194	Joe Hatton	25.00	12.50	2.50
☐ 146	Frank House	25.00	12.50	2.50	☐ 195	Minnie Minoso	60.00	30.00	6.00
☐ 147	Bob Young	25.00	12.50	2.50	☐ 196	Solly Hemus	25.00	12.50	2.50
☐ 148	Johnny Klippstein	25.00	12.50	2.50	☐ 197	George Strickland	25.00	12.50	2.50
☐ 149	Dick Kryhoski	25.00	12.50	2.50	☐ 198	Phil Haugstad	25.00	12.50	2.50
☐ 150	Ted Beard	25.00	12.50	2.50	☐ 199	George Zuverink	25.00	12.50	2.50
☐ 151	Wally Post	30.00	15.00	3.00	☐ 200	Ralph Houk	60.00	30.00	6.00
☐ 152	Al Evans	25.00	12.50	2.50	☐ 201	Alex Kellner	25.00	12.50	2.50
☐ 153	Bob Rush	25.00	12.50	2.50	☐ 202	Joe Collins	35.00	17.50	3.50
☐ 154	Joe Muir	25.00	12.50	2.50	☐ 203	Curt Simmons	30.00	15.00	3.00
☐ 155	Frank Overmire	25.00	12.50	2.50	☐ 204	Ron Northey	25.00	12.50	2.50
☐ 156	Frank Hiller	25.00	12.50	2.50	☐ 205	Clyde King	25.00	12.50	2.50
☐ 157	Bob Usher	25.00	12.50	2.50	☐ 206	Joe Ostrowski	25.00	12.50	2.50
☐ 158	Eddie Waitkus	25.00	12.50	2.50	☐ 207	Mickey Harris	25.00	12.50	2.50
☐ 159	Saul Rogovin	25.00	12.50	2.50	☐ 208	Marlin Stuart	25.00	12.50	2.50
☐ 160	Owen Friend	25.00	12.50	2.50	☐ 209	Howie Fox	25.00	12.50	2.50
☐ 161	Bud Byerly	25.00	12.50	2.50	☐ 210	Dick Fowler	25.00	12.50	2.50
☐ 162	Del Crandall	30.00	15.00	3.00	☐ 211	Ray Coleman	25.00	12.50	2.50
☐ 163	Stan Rojek	25.00	12.50	2.50	☐ 212	Ned Garver	25.00	12.50	2.50
☐ 164	Walt Dubiel	25.00	12.50	2.50	☐ 213	Nippy Jones	25.00	12.50	2.50
☐ 165	Eddie Kazak	25.00	12.50	2.50	☐ 214	Johnny Hopp	30.00	15.00	3.00
☐ 166	Paul LaPalme	25.00	12.50	2.50	☐ 215	Hank Bauer	40.00	20.00	4.00
☐ 167	Bill Howerton	25.00	12.50	2.50	☐ 216	Richie Ashburn	80.00	40.00	8.00
☐ 168	Charlie Silvera	30.00	15.00	3.00	☐ 217	Snuffy Stirnweiss	30.00	15.00	3.00
☐ 169	Howie Judson	25.00	12.50	2.50	☐ 218	Clyde McCullough	25.00	12.50	2.50
☐ 170	Gus Bell	30.00	15.00	3.00	☐ 219	Bobby Shantz	35.00	17.50	3.50
☐ 171	Ed Erautt	25.00	12.50	2.50	☐ 220	Joe Presko	25.00	12.50	2.50
☐ 172	Eddie Miksis	25.00	12.50	2.50	☐ 221	Granny Hamner	25.00	12.50	2.50
☐ 173	Roy Smalley	25.00	12.50	2.50	☐ 222	Hoot Evers	25.00	12.50	2.50
☐ 174	Clarence Marshall	25.00	12.50	2.50	☐ 223	Del Ennis	30.00	15.00	3.00
☐ 175	Billy Martin	300.00	150.00	30.00	☐ 224	Bruce Edwards	25.00	12.50	2.50
☐ 176	Hank Edwards	25.00	12.50	2.50	☐ 225	Frank Baumholtz	25.00	12.50	2.50
☐ 177	Bill Wight	25.00	12.50	2.50	☐ 226	Dave Philley	25.00	12.50	2.50
☐ 178	Cass Michaels	25.00	12.50	2.50	☐ 227	Joe Garagiola	80.00	40.00	8.00
☐ 179	Frank Smith	25.00	12.50	2.50	☐ 228	Al Brazle	25.00	12.50	2.50
☐ 180	Charley Maxwell	30.00	15.00	3.00	☐ 229	Gene Bearden	25.00	12.50	2.50
☐ 181	Bob Swift	25.00	12.50	2.50	☐ 230	Matt Batts	25.00	12.50	2.50
☐ 182	Billy Hitchcock	25.00	12.50	2.50	☐ 231	Sam Zoldak	25.00	12.50	2.50
☐ 183	Erv Dusak	25.00	12.50	2.50	☐ 232	Billy Cox	30.00	15.00	3.00
☐ 184	Bob Ramazotti	25.00	12.50	2.50	☐ 233	Bob Friend	30.00	15.00	3.00
☐ 185	Bill Nicholson	25.00	12.50	2.50	☐ 234	Steve Souchock	25.00	12.50	2.50
☐ 186	Walt Masterson	25.00	12.50	2.50	☐ 235	Walt Dropo	30.00	15.00	3.00
☐ 187	Bob Miller	25.00	12.50	2.50	☐ 236	Ed Fitzgerald	25.00	12.50	2.50
☐ 188	Clarence Podbielan	25.00	12.50	2.50	☐ 237	Jerry Coleman	30.00	15.00	3.00
☐ 189	Pete Reiser	35.00	17.50	3.50	☐ 238	Art Houtteman	25.00	12.50	2.50
☐ 190	Don Johnson	25.00	12.50	2.50	☐ 239	Rocky Bridges	25.00	12.50	2.50
☐ 191	Yogi Berra	350.00	175.00	35.00	☐ 240	Jack Phillips	25.00	12.50	2.50
☐ 192	Myron Ginsberg	25.00	12.50	2.50	☐ 241	Tommy Byrne	25.00	12.50	2.50

		NRMT	VG-E	GOOD			NRMT	VG-E	GOOD
☐ 242	Tom Poholsky	25.00	12.50	2.50	☐ 291	Gil Coan SP	50.00	25.00	5.00
☐ 243	Larry Doby	40.00	20.00	4.00	☐ 292	Floyd Baker SP	50.00	25.00	5.00
☐ 244	Vic Wertz	30.00	15.00	3.00	☐ 293	Sibby Sisti SP	50.00	25.00	5.00
☐ 245	Sherry Robertson	25.00	12.50	2.50	☐ 294	Walker Cooper SP	50.00	25.00	5.00
☐ 246	George Kell	65.00	32.50	6.50	☐ 295	Phil Cavarretta SP	60.00	30.00	6.00
☐ 247	Randy Gumpert	25.00	12.50	2.50	☐ 296	Red Rolfe SP	60.00	30.00	6.00
☐ 248	Frank Shea	25.00	12.50	2.50	☐ 297	Andy Seminick SP	50.00	25.00	5.00
☐ 249	Bobby Adams	25.00	12.50	2.50	☐ 298	Bob Ross SP	50.00	25.00	5.00
☐ 250	Carl Erskine	50.00	25.00	5.00	☐ 299	Ray Murray SP	50.00	25.00	5.00
☐ 251	Chico Carrasquel	40.00	20.00	4.00	☐ 300	Barney McCosky SP	55.00	27.50	5.50
☐ 252	Vern Bickford	40.00	20.00	4.00	☐ 301	Bob Porterfield	40.00	20.00	4.00
☐ 253	Johnny Berardino	45.00	22.50	4.50	☐ 302	Max Surkont	40.00	20.00	4.00
☐ 254	Joe Dobson	40.00	20.00	4.00	☐ 303	Harry Dorish	40.00	20.00	4.00
☐ 255	Clyde Vollmer	40.00	20.00	4.00	☐ 304	Sam Dente	40.00	20.00	4.00
☐ 256	Pete Suder	40.00	20.00	4.00	☐ 305	Paul Richards	50.00	25.00	5.00
☐ 257	Bobby Avila	45.00	22.50	4.50	☐ 306	Lou Sleater	40.00	20.00	4.00
☐ 258	Steve Gromek	40.00	20.00	4.00	☐ 307	Frank Campos	40.00	20.00	4.00
☐ 259	Bob Addis	40.00	20.00	4.00	☐ 308	Luis Aloma	40.00	20.00	4.00
☐ 260	Pete Castiglione	40.00	20.00	4.00	☐ 309	Jim Busby	40.00	20.00	4.00
☐ 261	Willie Mays	1100.00	450.00	100.00	☐ 310	George Metkovich	60.00	30.00	6.00
☐ 262	Virgil Trucks	45.00	22.50	4.50	☐ 311	Mickey Mantle DP	6600	2500	600
☐ 263	Harry Brecheen	45.00	22.50	4.50	☐ 312	Jackie Robinson DP	850.00	425.00	85.00
☐ 264	Roy Hartsfield	40.00	20.00	4.00	☐ 313	Bobby Thomson DP	175.00	85.00	18.00
☐ 265	Chuck Diering	40.00	20.00	4.00	☐ 314	Roy Campanella	1250.00	500.00	150.00
☐ 266	Murry Dickson	40.00	20.00	4.00	☐ 315	Leo Durocher	275.00	135.00	27.00
☐ 267	Sid Gordon	40.00	20.00	4.00	☐ 316	Dave Williams	175.00	85.00	18.00
☐ 268	Bob Lemon	150.00	75.00	15.00	☐ 317	Conrado Marrero	150.00	75.00	15.00
☐ 269	Willard Nixon	40.00	20.00	4.00	☐ 318	Harold Gregg	150.00	75.00	15.00
☐ 270	Lou Brissie	40.00	20.00	4.00	☐ 319	Al Walker	150.00	75.00	15.00
☐ 271	Jim Delsing	40.00	20.00	4.00	☐ 320	John Rutherford	150.00	75.00	15.00
☐ 272	Mike Garcia	50.00	25.00	5.00	☐ 321	Joe Black	225.00	110.00	22.00
☐ 273	Erv Palica	40.00	20.00	4.00	☐ 322	Randy Jackson	150.00	75.00	15.00
☐ 274	Ralph Branca	75.00	37.50	7.50	☐ 323	Bubba Church	150.00	75.00	15.00
☐ 275	Pat Mullin	40.00	20.00	4.00	☐ 324	Warren Hacker	150.00	75.00	15.00
☐ 276	Jim Wilson	40.00	20.00	4.00	☐ 325	Bill Serena	150.00	75.00	15.00
☐ 277	Early Wynn	150.00	75.00	15.00	☐ 326	George Shuba	175.00	85.00	18.00
☐ 278	Allie Clark	40.00	20.00	4.00	☐ 327	Al Wilson	150.00	75.00	15.00
☐ 279	Eddie Stewart	40.00	20.00	4.00	☐ 328	Bob Borkowski	150.00	75.00	15.00
☐ 280	Cloyd Boyer	45.00	22.50	4.50	☐ 329	Ike Delock	150.00	75.00	15.00
☐ 281	Tommy Brown SP	50.00	25.00	5.00	☐ 330	Turk Lown	150.00	75.00	15.00
☐ 282	Birdie Tebbetts SP	55.00	27.50	5.50	☐ 331	Tom Morgan	150.00	75.00	15.00
☐ 283	Phil Masi SP	50.00	25.00	5.00	☐ 332	Anthony Bartirome	150.00	75.00	15.00
☐ 284	Hank Arft SP	50.00	25.00	5.00	☐ 333	Pee Wee Reese	650.00	325.00	65.00
☐ 285	Cliff Fannin SP	50.00	25.00	5.00	☐ 334	Wilmer Mizell	150.00	75.00	15.00
☐ 286	Joe DeMaestri SP	50.00	25.00	5.00	☐ 335	Ted Lepcio	150.00	75.00	15.00
☐ 287	Steve Bilko SP	50.00	25.00	5.00	☐ 336	Dave Koslo	150.00	75.00	15.00
☐ 288	Chet Nichols SP	50.00	25.00	5.00	☐ 337	Jim Hearn	150.00	75.00	15.00
☐ 289	Tommy Holmes SP	60.00	30.00	6.00	☐ 338	Sal Yvars	150.00	75.00	15.00
☐ 290	Joe Astroth SP	50.00	25.00	5.00	☐ 339	Russ Meyer	150.00	75.00	15.00

		NRMT	VG-E	GOOD
☐ 340	Bob Hooper	150.00	75.00	15.00
☐ 341	Hal Jeffcoat	150.00	75.00	15.00
☐ 342	Clem Labine	175.00	85.00	18.00
☐ 343	Dick Gernert	150.00	75.00	15.00
☐ 344	Ewell Blackwell	175.00	85.00	18.00
☐ 345	Sammy White	150.00	75.00	15.00
☐ 346	George Spencer	150.00	75.00	15.00
☐ 347	Joe Adcock	200.00	100.00	20.00
☐ 348	Robert Kelly	150.00	75.00	15.00
☐ 349	Bob Cain	150.00	75.00	15.00
☐ 350	Cal Abrams	150.00	75.00	15.00
☐ 351	Alvin Dark	200.00	100.00	20.00
☐ 352	Karl Drews	150.00	75.00	15.00
☐ 353	Bobby Del Greco	150.00	75.00	15.00
☐ 354	Fred Hatfield	150.00	75.00	15.00
☐ 355	Bobby Morgan	150.00	75.00	15.00
☐ 356	Toby Atwell	150.00	75.00	15.00
☐ 357	Smoky Burgess	175.00	85.00	18.00
☐ 358	John Kucab	150.00	75.00	15.00
☐ 359	Dee Fondy	150.00	75.00	15.00
☐ 360	George Crowe	150.00	75.00	15.00
☐ 361	William Posedel	150.00	75.00	15.00
☐ 362	Ken Heintzelman	150.00	75.00	15.00
☐ 363	Dick Rozek	150.00	75.00	15.00
☐ 364	Clyde Sukeforth	150.00	75.00	15.00
☐ 365	Cookie Lavagetto	150.00	75.00	15.00
☐ 366	Dave Madison	150.00	75.00	15.00
☐ 367	Ben Thorpe	150.00	75.00	15.00
☐ 368	Ed Wright	150.00	75.00	15.00
☐ 369	Dick Groat	250.00	125.00	25.00
☐ 370	Billy Hoeft	150.00	75.00	15.00
☐ 371	Bobby Hofman	150.00	75.00	15.00
☐ 372	Gil McDougald	275.00	135.00	27.00
☐ 373	Jim Turner CO	175.00	85.00	18.00
☐ 374	John Benton	150.00	75.00	15.00
☐ 375	John Merson	150.00	75.00	15.00
☐ 376	Faye Throneberry	150.00	75.00	15.00
☐ 377	Chuck Dressen MG	175.00	85.00	18.00
☐ 378	Leroy Fusselman	150.00	75.00	15.00
☐ 379	Joe Rossi	150.00	75.00	15.00
☐ 380	Clem Koshorek	150.00	75.00	15.00
☐ 381	Milton Stock	150.00	75.00	15.00
☐ 382	Sam Jones	175.00	85.00	18.00
☐ 383	Del Wilber	150.00	75.00	15.00
☐ 384	Frank Crosetti CO	250.00	125.00	25.00
☐ 385	Herman Franks	175.00	85.00	18.00
☐ 386	John Yuhas	150.00	75.00	15.00
☐ 387	Billy Meyer	150.00	75.00	15.00
☐ 388	Bob Chipman	150.00	75.00	15.00

		NRMT	VG-E	GOOD
☐ 389	Ben Wade	150.00	75.00	15.00
☐ 390	Glenn Nelson	150.00	75.00	15.00
☐ 391	Ben Chapman (photo actually Sam Chapman)	150.00	75.00	15.00
☐ 392	Hoyt Wilhelm	500.00	250.00	50.00
☐ 393	Ebba St.Claire	150.00	75.00	15.00
☐ 394	Billy Herman CO	250.00	125.00	25.00
☐ 395	Jake Pitler CO	150.00	75.00	15.00
☐ 396	Dick Williams	250.00	125.00	25.00
☐ 397	Forrest Main	150.00	75.00	15.00
☐ 398	Hal Rice	150.00	75.00	15.00
☐ 399	Jim Fridley	150.00	75.00	15.00
☐ 400	Bill Dickey CO	500.00	250.00	50.00
☐ 401	Bob Schultz	150.00	75.00	15.00
☐ 402	Earl Harrist	150.00	75.00	15.00
☐ 403	Bill Miller	150.00	75.00	15.00
☐ 404	Dick Brodowski	150.00	75.00	15.00
☐ 405	Eddie Pellagrini	150.00	75.00	15.00
☐ 406	Joe Nuxhall	200.00	100.00	20.00
☐ 407	Eddie Mathews	1600.00	500.00	100.00

1953 Topps

The cards in this 274-card set measure 2 ⅝" by 3 ¾". Although the last card is numbered 280, there are only 274 cards in the set since numbers 253, 261, 267, 268, 271, and 275 were never issued. The 1953 Topps series contains line drawings of players in full color. The name and team panel at the card base is easily damaged, making it very difficult to complete a mint set. The high number series, 221 to 280, was produced in shorter supply late in the year and hence is more difficult to complete than the lower numbers. The key cards in the set are Mickey Mantle #82 and Willie Mays #244. There are a number of double-printed cards (actually not double but 50% more of each of these numbers were printed compared to the other cards in the series) indicated by DP in the checklist below. In addition, there are five numbers which were printed in with the more plentiful series 166-220; these cards (94, 107, 131, 145, and 156) are also indicated by DP in the checklist below. There were some three-card advertising panels produced by Topps; the players include Johnny Mize, Clem Koshorek, and Toby Atwell and Mickey Mantle, Johnny Wyrostek, and Sal Yvars. When cut apart, these advertising cards are distinguished by the non-standard card back, i.e., part of an advertisement for the 1953 Topps set instead of the typical statistics and biographical information about the player pictured.

		NRMT	VG-E	GOOD
COMPLETE SET (274)		12500.00	6000.00	1750.00
COMMON PLAYER (1-165)		22.00	11.00	2.20
COMMON DP (1-165)		16.00	8.00	1.60
COMMON PLAYER (166-220)		16.00	8.00	1.60
COMMON PLAYER (221-280)		80.00	40.00	8.00
COMMON DP (221-280)		40.00	20.00	4.00

			NRMT	VG-E	GOOD
☐	1	Jackie Robinson DP	550.00	150.00	30.00
☐	2	Luke Easter DP	16.00	8.00	1.60
☐	3	George Crowe	22.00	11.00	2.20
☐	4	Ben Wade	22.00	11.00	2.20
☐	5	Joe Dobson	22.00	11.00	2.20
☐	6	Sam Jones	22.00	11.00	2.20
☐	7	Bob Borkowski DP	16.00	8.00	1.60
☐	8	Clem Koshorek DP	16.00	8.00	1.60
☐	9	Joe Collins	30.00	15.00	3.00
☐	10	Smoky Burgess	25.00	12.50	2.50
☐	11	Sal Yvars	22.00	11.00	2.20
☐	12	Howie Judson DP	16.00	8.00	1.60
☐	13	Conrado Marrero DP	16.00	8.00	1.60
☐	14	Clem Labine DP	22.00	11.00	2.20
☐	15	Bobo Newsom DP	20.00	10.00	2.00
☐	16	Peanuts Lowrey DP	16.00	8.00	1.60
☐	17	Billy Hitchcock	22.00	11.00	2.20
☐	18	Ted Lepcio DP	16.00	8.00	1.60
☐	19	Mel Parnell DP	22.00	11.00	2.20
☐	20	Hank Thompson	25.00	12.50	2.50
☐	21	Billy Johnson	22.00	11.00	2.20
☐	22	Howie Fox	22.00	11.00	2.20
☐	23	Toby Atwell DP	16.00	8.00	1.60
☐	24	Ferris Fain	25.00	12.50	2.50
☐	25	Ray Boone	25.00	12.50	2.50
☐	26	Dale Mitchell DP	18.00	9.00	1.80
☐	27	Roy Campanella DP	200.00	100.00	20.00
☐	28	Eddie Pellagrini	22.00	11.00	2.20
☐	29	Hal Jeffcoat	22.00	11.00	2.20
☐	30	Willard Nixon	22.00	11.00	2.20
☐	31	Ewell Blackwell	35.00	17.50	3.50
☐	32	Clyde Vollmer	22.00	11.00	2.20
☐	33	Bob Kennedy DP	16.00	8.00	1.60
☐	34	George Shuba	25.00	12.50	2.50
☐	35	Irv Noren DP	16.00	8.00	1.60
☐	36	Johnny Groth DP	16.00	8.00	1.60
☐	37	Eddie Mathews DP	80.00	40.00	8.00
☐	38	Jim Hearn DP	16.00	8.00	1.60
☐	39	Eddie Miksis	22.00	11.00	2.20
☐	40	John Lipon	22.00	11.00	2.20
☐	41	Enos Slaughter	65.00	32.50	6.50
☐	42	Gus Zernial DP	16.00	8.00	1.60
☐	43	Gil McDougald	35.00	17.50	3.50
☐	44	Ellis Kinder	22.00	11.00	2.20
☐	45	Grady Hatton DP	16.00	8.00	1.60
☐	46	Johnny Klippstein DP	16.00	8.00	1.60
☐	47	Bubba Church DP	16.00	8.00	1.60
☐	48	Bob Del Greco DP	16.00	8.00	1.60
☐	49	Faye Throneberry DP	16.00	8.00	1.60
☐	50	Chuck Dressen MG DP	20.00	10.00	2.00
☐	51	Frank Campos DP	16.00	8.00	1.60
☐	52	Ted Gray DP	16.00	8.00	1.60
☐	53	Sherm Lollar DP	18.00	9.00	1.80
☐	54	Bob Feller DP	90.00	45.00	9.00
☐	55	Maurice McDermott DP	16.00	8.00	1.60
☐	56	Jerry Staley DP	16.00	8.00	1.60
☐	57	Carl Scheib	22.00	11.00	2.20
☐	58	George Metkovich	22.00	11.00	2.20
☐	59	Karl Drews DP	16.00	8.00	1.60
☐	60	Cloyd Boyer DP	16.00	8.00	1.60
☐	61	Early Wynn	65.00	32.50	6.50
☐	62	Monte Irvin DP	40.00	20.00	4.00
☐	63	Gus Niarhos DP	16.00	8.00	1.60
☐	64	Dave Philley	22.00	11.00	2.20
☐	65	Earl Harrist	22.00	11.00	2.20
☐	66	Minnie Minoso	35.00	17.50	3.50
☐	67	Roy Sievers DP	18.00	9.00	1.80

		NRMT	VG-E	GOOD
☐ 68	Del Rice	22.00	11.00	2.20
☐ 69	Dick Brodowski	22.00	11.00	2.20
☐ 70	Ed Yuhas	22.00	11.00	2.20
☐ 71	Tony Bartirome	22.00	11.00	2.20
☐ 72	Fred Hutchinson	25.00	12.50	2.50
☐ 73	Eddie Robinson	22.00	11.00	2.20
☐ 74	Joe Rossi	22.00	11.00	2.20
☐ 75	Mike Garcia	25.00	12.50	2.50
☐ 76	Pee Wee Reese	90.00	45.00	9.00
☐ 77	Johnny Mize DP	55.00	27.50	5.50
☐ 78	Al (Red) Schoendienst	50.00	25.00	5.00
☐ 79	Johnny Wyrostek	22.00	11.00	2.20
☐ 80	Jim Hegan	25.00	12.50	2.50
☐ 81	Joe Black	45.00	22.50	4.50
☐ 82	Mickey Mantle	1750.00	600.00	150.00
☐ 83	Howie Pollet	22.00	11.00	2.20
☐ 84	Bob Hooper DP	16.00	8.00	1.60
☐ 85	Bobby Morgan DP	16.00	8.00	1.60
☐ 86	Billy Martin	90.00	45.00	9.00
☐ 87	Ed Lopat	35.00	17.50	3.50
☐ 88	Willie Jones DP	16.00	8.00	1.60
☐ 89	Chuck Stobbs DP	16.00	8.00	1.60
☐ 90	Hank Edwards DP	16.00	8.00	1.60
☐ 91	Ebba St.Claire DP	16.00	8.00	1.60
☐ 92	Paul Minner DP	16.00	8.00	1.60
☐ 93	Hal Rice DP	16.00	8.00	1.60
☐ 94	Bill Kennedy DP	16.00	8.00	1.60
☐ 95	Willard Marshall DP	16.00	8.00	1.60
☐ 96	Virgil Trucks	25.00	12.50	2.50
☐ 97	Don Kolloway DP	16.00	8.00	1.60
☐ 98	Cal Abrams DP	16.00	8.00	1.60
☐ 99	Dave Madison	22.00	11.00	2.20
☐ 100	Bill Miller	22.00	11.00	2.20
☐ 101	Ted Wilks	22.00	11.00	2.20
☐ 102	Connie Ryan DP	16.00	8.00	1.60
☐ 103	Joe Astroth DP	16.00	8.00	1.60
☐ 104	Yogi Berra	180.00	90.00	18.00
☐ 105	Joe Nuxhall DP	18.00	9.00	1.80
☐ 106	Johnny Antonelli	25.00	12.50	2.50
☐ 107	Danny O'Connell DP	16.00	8.00	1.60
☐ 108	Bob Porterfield DP	16.00	8.00	1.60
☐ 109	Alvin Dark	27.00	13.50	2.70
☐ 110	Herman Wehmeier DP	16.00	8.00	1.60
☐ 111	Hank Sauer DP	18.00	9.00	1.80
☐ 112	Ned Garver DP	16.00	8.00	1.60
☐ 113	Jerry Priddy	22.00	11.00	2.20
☐ 114	Phil Rizzuto	75.00	37.50	7.50
☐ 115	George Spencer	22.00	11.00	2.20
☐ 116	Frank Smith DP	16.00	8.00	1.60
☐ 117	Sid Gordon DP	16.00	8.00	1.60
☐ 118	Gus Bell DP	18.00	9.00	1.80
☐ 119	Johnny Sain	35.00	17.50	3.50
☐ 120	Davey Williams	30.00	15.00	3.00
☐ 121	Walt Dropo	25.00	12.50	2.50
☐ 122	Elmer Valo	22.00	11.00	2.20
☐ 123	Tommy Byrne DP	18.00	9.00	1.80
☐ 124	Sibby Sisti DP	16.00	8.00	1.60
☐ 125	Dick Williams DP	20.00	10.00	2.00
☐ 126	Bill Connelly DP	16.00	8.00	1.60
☐ 127	Clint Courtney DP	16.00	8.00	1.60
☐ 128	Wilmer Mizell DP	16.00	8.00	1.60
☐ 129	Keith Thomas	22.00	11.00	2.20
☐ 130	Turk Lown DP	16.00	8.00	1.60
☐ 131	Harry Byrd DP	16.00	8.00	1.60
☐ 132	Tom Morgan	22.00	11.00	2.20
☐ 133	Gil Coan	22.00	11.00	2.20
☐ 134	Rube Walker	25.00	12.50	2.50
☐ 135	Al Rosen DP	30.00	15.00	3.00
☐ 136	Ken Heintzelman DP	16.00	8.00	1.60
☐ 137	John Rutherford DP	16.00	8.00	1.60
☐ 138	George Kell	45.00	22.50	4.50
☐ 139	Sammy White	22.00	11.00	2.20
☐ 140	Tommy Glaviano	22.00	11.00	2.20
☐ 141	Allie Reynolds DP	30.00	15.00	3.00
☐ 142	Vic Wertz	25.00	12.50	2.50
☐ 143	Billy Pierce	30.00	15.00	3.00
☐ 144	Bob Schultz DP	16.00	8.00	1.60
☐ 145	Harry Dorish DP	16.00	8.00	1.60
☐ 146	Granny Hamner	22.00	11.00	2.20
☐ 147	Warren Spahn	90.00	45.00	9.00
☐ 148	Mickey Grasso	22.00	11.00	2.20
☐ 149	Dom DiMaggio DP	30.00	15.00	3.00
☐ 150	Harry Simpson DP	16.00	8.00	1.60
☐ 151	Hoyt Wilhelm	55.00	27.50	5.50
☐ 152	Bob Adams DP	16.00	8.00	1.60
☐ 153	Andy Seminick DP	16.00	8.00	1.60
☐ 154	Dick Groat	30.00	15.00	3.00
☐ 155	Dutch Leonard	22.00	11.00	2.20
☐ 156	Jim Rivera DP	16.00	8.00	1.60
☐ 157	Bob Addis DP	16.00	8.00	1.60
☐ 158	Johnny Logan	25.00	12.50	2.50
☐ 159	Wayne Terwilliger DP	16.00	8.00	1.60
☐ 160	Bob Young	22.00	11.00	2.20
☐ 161	Vern Bickford DP	16.00	8.00	1.60
☐ 162	Ted Kluszewski	35.00	17.50	3.50
☐ 163	Fred Hatfield DP	16.00	8.00	1.60
☐ 164	Frank Shea DP	16.00	8.00	1.60

	NRMT	VG-E	GOOD			NRMT	VG-E	GOOD
☐ 165 Billy Hoeft	22.00	11.00	2.20	☐ 214 Bill Bruton		18.00	9.00	1.80
☐ 166 Billy Hunter	16.00	8.00	1.60	☐ 215 Gene Conley		18.00	9.00	1.80
☐ 167 Art Schult	16.00	8.00	1.60	☐ 216 Jim Hughes		16.00	8.00	1.60
☐ 168 Willard Schmidt	16.00	8.00	1.60	☐ 217 Murray Wall		16.00	8.00	1.60
☐ 169 Dizzy Trout	16.00	8.00	1.60	☐ 218 Les Fusselman		16.00	8.00	1.60
☐ 170 Bill Werle	16.00	8.00	1.60	☐ 219 Pete Runnels		18.00	9.00	1.80
☐ 171 Bill Glynn	16.00	8.00	1.60	(photo actually Don				
☐ 172 Rip Repulski	16.00	8.00	1.60	Johnson)				
☐ 173 Preston Ward	16.00	8.00	1.60	☐ 220 Satchel Paige UER		350.00	175.00	35.00
☐ 174 Billy Loes	18.00	9.00	1.80	(misspelled Satchell				
☐ 175 Ron Kline	16.00	8.00	1.60	on card front)				
☐ 176 Don Hoak	20.00	10.00	2.00	☐ 221 Bob Milliken		80.00	40.00	8.00
☐ 177 Jim Dyck	16.00	8.00	1.60	☐ 222 Vic Janowicz DP		45.00	22.50	4.50
☐ 178 Jim Waugh	16.00	8.00	1.60	☐ 223 Johnny O'Brien DP		45.00	22.50	4.50
☐ 179 Gene Hermanski	16.00	8.00	1.60	☐ 224 Lou Sleater DP		40.00	20.00	4.00
☐ 180 Virgil Stallcup	16.00	8.00	1.60	☐ 225 Bobby Shantz		90.00	45.00	9.00
☐ 181 Al Zarilla	16.00	8.00	1.60	☐ 226 Ed Erautt		80.00	40.00	8.00
☐ 182 Bobby Hofman	16.00	8.00	1.60	☐ 227 Morrie Martin		80.00	40.00	8.00
☐ 183 Stu Miller	16.00	8.00	1.60	☐ 228 Hal Newhouser		100.00	50.00	10.00
☐ 184 Hal Brown	16.00	8.00	1.60	☐ 229 Rockey Krsnich		80.00	40.00	8.00
☐ 185 Jim Pendleton	16.00	8.00	1.60	☐ 230 Johnny Lindell DP		40.00	20.00	4.00
☐ 186 Charlie Bishop	16.00	8.00	1.60	☐ 231 Solly Hemus DP		40.00	20.00	4.00
☐ 187 Jim Fridley	16.00	8.00	1.60	☐ 232 Dick Kokos		80.00	40.00	8.00
☐ 188 Andy Carey	20.00	10.00	2.00	☐ 233 Al Aber		80.00	40.00	8.00
☐ 189 Ray Jablonski	16.00	8.00	1.60	☐ 234 Ray Murray DP		40.00	20.00	4.00
☐ 190 Dixie Walker	16.00	8.00	1.60	☐ 235 John Hetki DP		40.00	20.00	4.00
☐ 191 Ralph Kiner	45.00	22.50	4.50	☐ 236 Harry Perkowski DP		40.00	20.00	4.00
☐ 192 Wally Westlake	16.00	8.00	1.60	☐ 237 Bud Podbielan DP		40.00	20.00	4.00
☐ 193 Mike Clark	16.00	8.00	1.60	☐ 238 Cal Hogue DP		40.00	20.00	4.00
☐ 194 Eddie Kazak	16.00	8.00	1.60	☐ 239 Jim Delsing		80.00	40.00	8.00
☐ 195 Ed McGhee	16.00	8.00	1.60	☐ 240 Fred Marsh		80.00	40.00	8.00
☐ 196 Bob Keegan	16.00	8.00	1.60	☐ 241 Al Sima DP		40.00	20.00	4.00
☐ 197 Del Crandall	18.00	9.00	1.80	☐ 242 Charlie Silvera		80.00	40.00	8.00
☐ 198 Forrest Main	16.00	8.00	1.60	☐ 243 Carlos Bernier DP		40.00	20.00	4.00
☐ 199 Marion Fricano	16.00	8.00	1.60	☐ 244 Willie Mays		1400.00	500.00	125.00
☐ 200 Gordon Goldsberry	16.00	8.00	1.60	☐ 245 Bill Norman		80.00	40.00	8.00
☐ 201 Paul LaPalme	16.00	8.00	1.60	☐ 246 Roy Face DP		40.00	20.00	4.00
☐ 202 Carl Sawatski	16.00	8.00	1.60	☐ 247 Mike Sandlock DP		40.00	20.00	4.00
☐ 203 Cliff Fannin	16.00	8.00	1.60	☐ 248 Gene Stephens DP		40.00	20.00	4.00
☐ 204 Dick Bokelman	16.00	8.00	1.60	☐ 249 Eddie O'Brien		80.00	40.00	8.00
☐ 205 Vern Benson	16.00	8.00	1.60	☐ 250 Bob Wilson		80.00	40.00	8.00
☐ 206 Ed Bailey	18.00	9.00	1.80	☐ 251 Sid Hudson		80.00	40.00	8.00
☐ 207 Whitey Ford	110.00	55.00	11.00	☐ 252 Hank Foiles		80.00	40.00	8.00
☐ 208 Jim Wilson	16.00	8.00	1.60	☐ 253 Does not exist		00.00	00.00	0.00
☐ 209 Jim Greengrass	16.00	8.00	1.60	☐ 254 Preacher Roe DP		80.00	40.00	8.00
☐ 210 Bob Cerv	20.00	10.00	2.00	☐ 255 Dixie Howell		80.00	40.00	8.00
☐ 211 J.W. Porter	16.00	8.00	1.60	☐ 256 Les Peden		80.00	40.00	8.00
☐ 212 Jack Dittmer	16.00	8.00	1.60	☐ 257 Bob Boyd		80.00	40.00	8.00
☐ 213 Ray Scarborough	16.00	8.00	1.60	☐ 258 Jim Gilliam		275.00	135.00	27.00

		NRMT	VG-E	GOOD
☐ 259	Roy McMillan DP ...	40.00	20.00	4.00
☐ 260	Sam Calderone	80.00	40.00	8.00
☐ 261	Does not exist	00.00	00.00	0.00
☐ 262	Bob Oldis	80.00	40.00	8.00
☐ 263	Johnny Podres	250.00	125.00	25.00
☐ 264	Gene Woodling DP .	60.00	30.00	6.00
☐ 265	Jackie Jensen	100.00	50.00	10.00
☐ 266	Bob Cain	80.00	40.00	8.00
☐ 267	Does not exist	00.00	00.00	0.00
☐ 268	Does not exist	00.00	00.00	0.00
☐ 269	Duane Pillette	80.00	40.00	8.00
☐ 270	Vern Stephens	90.00	45.00	9.00
☐ 271	Does not exist	00.00	00.00	0.00
☐ 272	Bill Antonello	80.00	40.00	8.00
☐ 273	Harvey Haddix	100.00	50.00	10.00
☐ 274	John Riddle	80.00	40.00	8.00
☐ 275	Does not exist	00.00	00.00	0.00
☐ 276	Ken Raffensberger .	80.00	40.00	8.00
☐ 277	Don Lund	80.00	40.00	8.00
☐ 278	Willie Miranda	80.00	40.00	8.00
☐ 279	Joe Coleman DP	40.00	20.00	4.00
☐ 280	Milt Bolling	300.00	50.00	10.00

1954 Topps

pitcher NEW YORK YANKEES

*The cards in this 250-card set measure 2 ⅝"
by 3 ¾". Each of the cards in the 1954 Topps
set contains a large "head" shot of the player
in color plus a smaller full-length photo in black
and white set against a color background. This
series contains the rookie cards of Hank Aaron,*

*Ernie Banks, and Al Kaline and two separate
cards of Ted Williams (number 1 and number
250). Conspicuous by his absence is Mickey
Mantle who apparently was the exclusive pro-
perty of Bowman during 1954 (and 1955).*

		NRMT	VG-E	GOOD
COMPLETE SET (250)		7000.00	3500.00	900.00
COMMON PLAYER (1-50)		8.00	4.00	.80
COMMON PLAYER (51-75)		22.00	10.00	2.00
COMMON PLAYER (76-125) ..		9.00	4.50	.90
COMMON PLAYER (126-250) ..		10.00	5.00	1.00
☐	1	Ted Williams	500.00	150.00	30.00
☐	2	Gus Zernial	8.00	4.00	.80
☐	3	Monte Irvin	25.00	12.50	2.50
☐	4	Hank Sauer	9.00	4.50	.90
☐	5	Ed Lopat	16.00	8.00	1.60
☐	6	Pete Runnels	9.00	4.50	.90
☐	7	Ted Kluszewski ...	16.00	8.00	1.60
☐	8	Bob Young	8.00	4.00	.80
☐	9	Harvey Haddix	10.00	5.00	1.00
☐	10	Jackie Robinson ..	200.00	100.00	20.00
☐	11	Paul Leslie Smith ..	8.00	4.00	.80
☐	12	Del Crandall	9.00	4.50	.90
☐	13	Billy Martin	60.00	30.00	6.00
☐	14	Preacher Roe	16.00	8.00	1.60
☐	15	Al Rosen	14.00	7.00	1.40
☐	16	Vic Janowicz	9.00	4.50	.90
☐	17	Phil Rizzuto	55.00	27.50	5.50
☐	18	Walt Dropo	9.00	4.50	.90
☐	19	Johnny Lipon	8.00	4.00	.80
☐	20	Warren Spahn	70.00	35.00	7.00
☐	21	Bobby Shantz	10.00	5.00	1.00
☐	22	Jim Greengrass ...	8.00	4.00	.80
☐	23	Luke Easter	9.00	4.50	.90
☐	24	Granny Hamner ...	8.00	4.00	.80
☐	25	Harvey Kuenn	25.00	12.50	2.50
☐	26	Ray Jablonski	8.00	4.00	.80
☐	27	Ferris Fain	9.00	4.50	.90
☐	28	Paul Minner	8.00	4.00	.80
☐	29	Jim Hegan	9.00	4.50	.90
☐	30	Eddie Mathews	65.00	32.50	6.50
☐	31	Johnny Klippstein ..	8.00	4.00	.80
☐	32	Duke Snider	100.00	50.00	10.00
☐	33	Johnny Schmitz ...	8.00	4.00	.80
☐	34	Jim Rivera	8.00	4.00	.80
☐	35	Jim Gilliam	15.00	7.50	1.50
☐	36	Hoyt Wilhelm	30.00	15.00	3.00
☐	37	Whitey Ford	70.00	35.00	7.00

			NRMT	VG-E	GOOD				NRMT	VG-E	GOOD
☐	38	Eddie Stanky	9.00	4.50	.90	☐	87	Roy Face	12.00	6.00	1.20
☐	39	Sherm Lollar	9.00	4.50	.90	☐	88	Matt Batts	9.00	4.50	.90
☐	40	Mel Parnell	9.00	4.50	.90	☐	89	Howie Pollet	9.00	4.50	.90
☐	41	Willie Jones	8.00	4.00	.80	☐	90	Willie Mays	325.00	160.00	32.00
☐	42	Don Mueller	9.00	4.50	.90	☐	91	Bob Oldis	9.00	4.50	.90
☐	43	Dick Groat	10.00	5.00	1.00	☐	92	Wally Westlake	9.00	4.50	.90
☐	44	Ned Garver	8.00	4.00	.80	☐	93	Sid Hudson	9.00	4.50	.90
☐	45	Richie Ashburn	27.00	13.50	2.70	☐	94	Ernie Banks	600.00	300.00	60.00
☐	46	Ken Raffensberger	8.00	4.00	.80	☐	95	Hal Rice	9.00	4.50	.90
☐	47	Ellis Kinder	8.00	4.00	.80	☐	96	Charlie Silvera	9.00	4.50	.90
☐	48	Billy Hunter	8.00	4.00	.80	☐	97	Jerald Hal Lane	9.00	4.50	.90
☐	49	Ray Murray	8.00	4.00	.80	☐	98	Joe Black	12.00	6.00	1.20
☐	50	Yogi Berra	180.00	90.00	18.00	☐	99	Bobby Hofman	9.00	4.50	.90
☐	51	Johnny Lindell	22.00	10.00	2.00	☐	100	Bob Keegan	9.00	4.50	.90
☐	52	Vic Power	22.00	10.00	2.00	☐	101	Gene Woodling	12.00	6.00	1.20
☐	53	Jack Dittmer	22.00	10.00	2.00	☐	102	Gil Hodges	65.00	32.50	6.50
☐	54	Vern Stephens	27.00	12.50	2.50	☐	103	Jim Lemon	10.00	5.00	1.00
☐	55	Phil Cavarretta	27.00	12.50	2.50	☐	104	Mike Sandlock	9.00	4.50	.90
☐	56	Willie Miranda	22.00	10.00	2.00	☐	105	Andy Carey	12.00	6.00	1.20
☐	57	Luis Aloma	22.00	10.00	2.00	☐	106	Dick Kokos	9.00	4.50	.90
☐	58	Bob Wilson	22.00	10.00	2.00	☐	107	Duane Pillette	9.00	4.50	.90
☐	59	Gene Conley	27.00	12.50	2.50	☐	108	Thornton Kipper	9.00	4.50	.90
☐	60	Frank Baumholtz	22.00	10.00	2.00	☐	109	Bill Bruton	10.00	5.00	1.00
☐	61	Bob Cain	22.00	10.00	2.00	☐	110	Harry Dorish	9.00	4.50	.90
☐	62	Eddie Robinson	27.00	12.50	2.50	☐	111	Jim Delsing	9.00	4.50	.90
☐	63	Johnny Pesky	27.00	12.50	2.50	☐	112	Bill Renna	9.00	4.50	.90
☐	64	Hank Thompson	27.00	12.50	2.50	☐	113	Bob Boyd	9.00	4.50	.90
☐	65	Bob Swift	22.00	10.00	2.00	☐	114	Dean Stone	9.00	4.50	.90
☐	66	Ted Lepcio	22.00	10.00	2.00	☐	115	Rip Repulski	9.00	4.50	.90
☐	67	Jim Willis	22.00	10.00	2.00	☐	116	Steve Bilko	9.00	4.50	.90
☐	68	Sam Calderone	22.00	10.00	2.00	☐	117	Solly Hemus	9.00	4.50	.90
☐	69	Bud Podbielan	22.00	10.00	2.00	☐	118	Carl Scheib	9.00	4.50	.90
☐	70	Larry Doby	40.00	20.00	4.00	☐	119	Johnny Antonelli	12.00	6.00	1.20
☐	71	Frank Smith	22.00	10.00	2.00	☐	120	Roy McMillan	9.00	4.50	.90
☐	72	Preston Ward	22.00	10.00	2.00	☐	121	Clem Labine	12.00	6.00	1.20
☐	73	Wayne Terwilliger	22.00	10.00	2.00	☐	122	Johnny Logan	10.00	5.00	1.00
☐	74	Bill Taylor	22.00	10.00	2.00	☐	123	Bobby Adams	9.00	4.50	.90
☐	75	Fred Haney	22.00	10.00	2.00	☐	124	Marion Fricano	9.00	4.50	.90
☐	76	Bob Scheffing	9.00	4.50	.90	☐	125	Harry Perkowski	9.00	4.50	.90
☐	77	Ray Boone	10.00	5.00	1.00	☐	126	Ben Wade	10.00	5.00	1.00
☐	78	Ted Kazanski	9.00	4.50	.90	☐	127	Steve O'Neill	10.00	5.00	1.00
☐	79	Andy Pafko	10.00	5.00	1.00	☐	128	Hank Aaron	1100.00	450.00	125.00
☐	80	Jackie Jensen	14.00	7.00	1.40	☐	129	Forrest Jacobs	10.00	5.00	1.00
☐	81	Dave Hoskins	9.00	4.50	.90	☐	130	Hank Bauer	20.00	10.00	2.00
☐	82	Milt Bolling	9.00	4.50	.90	☐	131	Reno Bertoia	10.00	5.00	1.00
☐	83	Joe Collins	12.00	6.00	1.20	☐	132	Tom Lasorda	150.00	75.00	15.00
☐	84	Dick Cole	9.00	4.50	.90	☐	133	Dave Baker	10.00	5.00	1.00
☐	85	Bob Turley	20.00	10.00	2.00	☐	134	Cal Hogue	10.00	5.00	1.00
☐	86	Billy Herman	18.00	9.00	1.80	☐	135	Joe Presko	10.00	5.00	1.00

		NRMT	VG-E	GOOD			NRMT	VG-E	GOOD
☐ 136	Connie Ryan	10.00	5.00	1.00	☐ 182	Chuck Harmon	10.00	5.00	1.00
☐ 137	Wally Moon	18.00	9.00	1.80	☐ 183	Earle Combs CO	18.00	9.00	1.80
☐ 138	Bob Borkowski	10.00	5.00	1.00	☐ 184	Ed Bailey	10.00	5.00	1.00
☐ 139	The O'Briens	21.00	10.50	2.10	☐ 185	Chuck Stobbs	10.00	5.00	1.00
	Johnny O'Brien				☐ 186	Karl Olson	10.00	5.00	1.00
	Eddie O'Brien				☐ 187	Henry Manush CO	18.00	9.00	1.80
☐ 140	Tom Wright	10.00	5.00	1.00	☐ 188	Dave Jolly	10.00	5.00	1.00
☐ 141	Joey Jay	12.00	6.00	1.20	☐ 189	Floyd Ross	10.00	5.00	1.00
☐ 142	Tom Poholsky	10.00	5.00	1.00	☐ 190	Ray Herbert	10.00	5.00	1.00
☐ 143	Ralston Hemsley	10.00	5.00	1.00	☐ 191	John (Dick) Schofield	12.00	6.00	1.20
☐ 144	Bill Werle	10.00	5.00	1.00	☐ 192	Ellis Deal	10.00	5.00	1.00
☐ 145	Elmer Valo	10.00	5.00	1.00	☐ 193	Johnny Hopp	12.00	6.00	1.20
☐ 146	Don Johnson	10.00	5.00	1.00	☐ 194	Bill Sarni	10.00	5.00	1.00
☐ 147	Johnny Riddle	10.00	5.00	1.00	☐ 195	Billy Consolo	10.00	5.00	1.00
☐ 148	Bob Trice	10.00	5.00	1.00	☐ 196	Stan Jok	10.00	5.00	1.00
☐ 149	Al Robertson	10.00	5.00	1.00	☐ 197	Lynwood Rowe	12.00	6.00	1.20
☐ 150	Dick Kryhoski	10.00	5.00	1.00	☐ 198	Carl Sawatski	10.00	5.00	1.00
☐ 151	Alex Grammas	10.00	5.00	1.00	☐ 199	Glenn (Rocky)			
☐ 152	Michael Blyzka	10.00	5.00	1.00		Nelson	10.00	5.00	1.00
☐ 153	Al Walker	12.00	6.00	1.20	☐ 200	Larry Jansen	12.00	6.00	1.20
☐ 154	Mike Fornieles	10.00	5.00	1.00	☐ 201	Al Kaline	600.00	300.00	60.00
☐ 155	Bob Kennedy	12.00	6.00	1.20	☐ 202	Bob Purkey	10.00	5.00	1.00
☐ 156	Joe Coleman	10.00	5.00	1.00	☐ 203	Harry Brecheen	12.00	6.00	1.20
☐ 157	Don Lenhardt	10.00	5.00	1.00	☐ 204	Angel Scull	10.00	5.00	1.00
☐ 158	Peanuts Lowrey	10.00	5.00	1.00	☐ 205	Johnny Sain	21.00	10.50	2.10
☐ 159	Dave Philley	10.00	5.00	1.00	☐ 206	Ray Crone	10.00	5.00	1.00
☐ 160	Ralph Kress	10.00	5.00	1.00	☐ 207	Tom Oliver	10.00	5.00	1.00
☐ 161	John Hetki	10.00	5.00	1.00	☐ 208	Grady Hatton	10.00	5.00	1.00
☐ 162	Herman Wehmeier	10.00	5.00	1.00	☐ 209	Chuck Thompson	10.00	5.00	1.00
☐ 163	Frank House	10.00	5.00	1.00	☐ 210	Bob Buhl	12.00	6.00	1.20
☐ 164	Stu Miller	12.00	6.00	1.20	☐ 211	Don Hoak	12.00	6.00	1.20
☐ 165	Jim Pendleton	10.00	5.00	1.00	☐ 212	Bob Micelotta	10.00	5.00	1.00
☐ 166	Johnny Podres	21.00	10.50	2.10	☐ 213	Johnny Fitzpatrick	10.00	5.00	1.00
☐ 167	Don Lund	10.00	5.00	1.00	☐ 214	Arnie Portocarrero	10.00	5.00	1.00
☐ 168	Morrie Martin	10.00	5.00	1.00	☐ 215	Warren McGhee	10.00	5.00	1.00
☐ 169	Jim Hughes	10.00	5.00	1.00	☐ 216	Al Sima	10.00	5.00	1.00
☐ 170	James (Dusty)				☐ 217	Paul Schreiber	10.00	5.00	1.00
	Rhodes	14.00	7.00	1.40	☐ 218	Fred Marsh	10.00	5.00	1.00
☐ 171	Leo Kiely	10.00	5.00	1.00	☐ 219	Chuck Kress	10.00	5.00	1.00
☐ 172	Harold Brown	10.00	5.00	1.00	☐ 220	Ruben Gomez	10.00	5.00	1.00
☐ 173	Jack Harshman	10.00	5.00	1.00	☐ 221	Dick Brodowski	10.00	5.00	1.00
☐ 174	Tom Qualters	10.00	5.00	1.00	☐ 222	Bill Wilson	10.00	5.00	1.00
☐ 175	Frank Leja	12.00	6.00	1.20	☐ 223	Joe Haynes	10.00	5.00	1.00
☐ 176	Robert Keeley	10.00	5.00	1.00	☐ 224	Dick Weik	10.00	5.00	1.00
☐ 177	Bob Milliken	10.00	5.00	1.00	☐ 225	Don Liddle	10.00	5.00	1.00
☐ 178	Bill Glynn	10.00	5.00	1.00	☐ 226	Jehosie Heard	10.00	5.00	1.00
☐ 179	Gair Allie	10.00	5.00	1.00	☐ 227	Colonel Mills	10.00	5.00	1.00
☐ 180	Wes Westrum	12.00	6.00	1.20	☐ 228	Gene Hermanski	10.00	5.00	1.00
☐ 181	Mel Roach	10.00	5.00	1.00	☐ 229	Bob Talbot	10.00	5.00	1.00

			NRMT	VG-E	GOOD
☐ 230	Bob Kuzava		12.00	6.00	1.20
☐ 231	Roy Smalley		10.00	5.00	1.00
☐ 232	Lou Limmer		10.00	5.00	1.00
☐ 233	Augie Galan		10.00	5.00	1.00
☐ 234	Jerry Lynch		12.00	6.00	1.20
☐ 235	Vernon Law		12.00	6.00	1.20
☐ 236	Paul Penson		10.00	5.00	1.00
☐ 237	Dominic Ryba		10.00	5.00	1.00
☐ 238	Al Aber		10.00	5.00	1.00
☐ 239	Bill Skowron		45.00	22.50	4.50
☐ 240	Sam Mele		10.00	5.00	1.00
☐ 241	Robert Miller		10.00	5.00	1.00
☐ 242	Curt Roberts		10.00	5.00	1.00
☐ 243	Ray Blades		10.00	5.00	1.00
☐ 244	Leroy Wheat		10.00	5.00	1.00
☐ 245	Roy Sievers		12.00	6.00	1.20
☐ 246	Howie Fox		10.00	5.00	1.00
☐ 247	Ed Mayo		10.00	5.00	1.00
☐ 248	Al Smith		12.00	6.00	1.20
☐ 249	Wilmer Mizell		12.00	6.00	1.20
☐ 250	Ted Williams		550.00	150.00	30.00

1955 Topps

ED STANKY manager ST. LOUIS CARDINALS

The cards in this 206-card set measure 2 ⅝" by 3 ¾". Both the large "head" shot and the smaller full-length photos used on each card of the 1955 Topps set are in color. The card fronts were designed horizontally for the first time in Topps' history. The first card features Dusty Rhodes, hitting star for the Giants' 1954 World Series sweep over the Indians. A "high"

series, 161 to 210, is more difficult to find than cards 1 to 160. Numbers 175, 186, 203, and 209 were never issued. To fill in for the four cards not issued in the high number series, Topps double printed four players, those appearing on cards 170, 172, 184, and 188.

			NRMT	VG-E	GOOD
COMPLETE SET (206)			5600.00	2700.00	700.00
COMMON PLAYER (1-150)			6.00	3.00	.60
COMMON PLAYER (151-160)			12.00	6.00	1.20
COMMON PLAYER (161-210)			15.00	7.50	1.50

			NRMT	VG-E	GOOD
☐ 1	Dusty Rhodes		30.00	5.00	1.00
☐ 2	Ted Williams		300.00	150.00	30.00
☐ 3	Art Fowler		6.00	3.00	.60
☐ 4	Al Kaline		125.00	60.00	12.50
☐ 5	Jim Gilliam		11.00	5.50	1.10
☐ 6	Stan Hack		6.00	3.00	.60
☐ 7	Jim Hegan		6.00	3.00	.60
☐ 8	Harold Smith		6.00	3.00	.60
☐ 9	Robert Miller		6.00	3.00	.60
☐ 10	Bob Keegan		6.00	3.00	.60
☐ 11	Ferris Fain		6.00	3.00	.60
☐ 12	Vernon Thies		6.00	3.00	.60
☐ 13	Fred Marsh		6.00	3.00	.60
☐ 14	Jim Finigan		6.00	3.00	.60
☐ 15	Jim Pendleton		6.00	3.00	.60
☐ 16	Roy Sievers		7.00	3.50	.70
☐ 17	Bobby Hofman		6.00	3.00	.60
☐ 18	Russ Kemmerer		6.00	3.00	.60
☐ 19	Billy Herman		10.00	5.00	1.00
☐ 20	Andy Carey		8.00	4.00	.80
☐ 21	Alex Grammas		6.00	3.00	.60
☐ 22	Bill Skowron		12.00	6.00	1.20
☐ 23	Jack Parks		6.00	3.00	.60
☐ 24	Hal Newhouser		10.00	5.00	1.00
☐ 25	Johnny Podres		12.00	6.00	1.20
☐ 26	Dick Groat		8.00	4.00	.80
☐ 27	Billy Gardner		7.00	3.50	.70
☐ 28	Ernie Banks		110.00	55.00	11.00
☐ 29	Herman Wehmeier		6.00	3.00	.60
☐ 30	Vic Power		6.00	3.00	.60
☐ 31	Warren Spahn		60.00	30.00	6.00
☐ 32	Warren McGhee		6.00	3.00	.60
☐ 33	Tom Qualters		6.00	3.00	.60
☐ 34	Wayne Terwilliger		6.00	3.00	.60
☐ 35	Dave Jolly		6.00	3.00	.60
☐ 36	Leo Kiely		6.00	3.00	.60
☐ 37	Joe Cunningham		7.00	3.50	.70

			NRMT	VG-E	GOOD				NRMT	VG-E	GOOD
☐	38	Bob Turley	10.00	5.00	1.00	☐	87	Frank House	6.00	3.00	.60
☐	39	Bill Glynn	6.00	3.00	.60	☐	88	Bob Skinner	7.00	3.50	.70
☐	40	Don Hoak	6.00	3.00	.60	☐	89	Joe Frazier	6.00	3.00	.60
☐	41	Chuck Stobbs	6.00	3.00	.60	☐	90	Karl Spooner	7.00	3.50	.70
☐	42	John (Windy) McCall	6.00	3.00	.60	☐	91	Milt Bolling	6.00	3.00	.60
☐	43	Harvey Haddix	7.00	3.50	.70	☐	92	Don Zimmer	21.00	10.50	2.10
☐	44	Harold Valentine	6.00	3.00	.60	☐	93	Steve Bilko	6.00	3.00	.60
☐	45	Hank Sauer	7.00	3.50	.70	☐	94	Reno Bertoia	6.00	3.00	.60
☐	46	Ted Kazanski	6.00	3.00	.60	☐	95	Preston Ward	6.00	3.00	.60
☐	47	Hank Aaron	250.00	125.00	25.00	☐	96	Chuck Bishop	6.00	3.00	.60
☐	48	Bob Kennedy	6.00	3.00	.60	☐	97	Carlos Paula	6.00	3.00	.60
☐	49	J.W. Porter	6.00	3.00	.60	☐	98	John Riddle	6.00	3.00	.60
☐	50	Jackie Robinson	175.00	85.00	18.00	☐	99	Frank Leja	6.00	3.00	.60
☐	51	Jim Hughes	6.00	3.00	.60	☐	100	Monte Irvin	21.00	10.50	2.10
☐	52	Bill Tremel	6.00	3.00	.60	☐	101	Johnny Gray	6.00	3.00	.60
☐	53	Bill Taylor	6.00	3.00	.60	☐	102	Wally Westlake	6.00	3.00	.60
☐	54	Lou Limmer	6.00	3.00	.60	☐	103	Chuck White	6.00	3.00	.60
☐	55	Rip Repulski	6.00	3.00	.60	☐	104	Jack Harshman	6.00	3.00	.60
☐	56	Ray Jablonski	6.00	3.00	.60	☐	105	Chuck Diering	6.00	3.00	.60
☐	57	Billy O'Dell	6.00	3.00	.60	☐	106	Frank Sullivan	6.00	3.00	.60
☐	58	Jim Rivera	6.00	3.00	.60	☐	107	Curt Roberts	6.00	3.00	.60
☐	59	Gair Allie	6.00	3.00	.60	☐	108	Al Walker	6.00	3.00	.60
☐	60	Dean Stone	6.00	3.00	.60	☐	109	Ed Lopat	11.00	5.50	1.10
☐	61	Forrest Jacobs	6.00	3.00	.60	☐	110	Gus Zernial	7.00	3.50	.70
☐	62	Thornton Kipper	6.00	3.00	.60	☐	111	Bob Milliken	6.00	3.00	.60
☐	63	Joe Collins	8.00	4.00	.80	☐	112	Nelson King	6.00	3.00	.60
☐	64	Gus Triandos	7.00	3.50	.70	☐	113	Harry Brecheen	6.00	3.00	.60
☐	65	Ray Boone	6.00	3.00	.60	☐	114	Louis Ortiz	6.00	3.00	.60
☐	66	Ron Jackson	6.00	3.00	.60	☐	115	Ellis Kinder	6.00	3.00	.60
☐	67	Wally Moon	7.00	3.50	.70	☐	116	Tom Hurd	6.00	3.00	.60
☐	68	Jim Davis	6.00	3.00	.60	☐	117	Mel Roach	6.00	3.00	.60
☐	69	Ed Bailey	6.00	3.00	.60	☐	118	Bob Purkey	6.00	3.00	.60
☐	70	Al Rosen	9.00	4.50	.90	☐	119	Bob Lennon	6.00	3.00	.60
☐	71	Ruben Gomez	6.00	3.00	.60	☐	120	Ted Kluszewski	11.00	5.50	1.10
☐	72	Karl Olson	6.00	3.00	.60	☐	121	Bill Renna	6.00	3.00	.60
☐	73	Jack Shepard	6.00	3.00	.60	☐	122	Carl Sawatski	6.00	3.00	.60
☐	74	Bob Borkowski	6.00	3.00	.60	☐	123	Sandy Koufax	650.00	325.00	65.00
☐	75	Sandy Amoros	9.00	4.50	.90	☐	124	Harmon Killebrew	250.00	125.00	25.00
☐	76	Howie Pollet	6.00	3.00	.60	☐	125	Ken Boyer	40.00	20.00	4.00
☐	77	Arnie Portocarrero	6.00	3.00	.60	☐	126	Dick Hall	6.00	3.00	.60
☐	78	Gordon Jones	6.00	3.00	.60	☐	127	Dale Long	7.00	3.50	.70
☐	79	Clyde Schell	6.00	3.00	.60	☐	128	Ted Lepcio	6.00	3.00	.60
☐	80	Bob Grim	9.00	4.50	.90	☐	129	Elvin Tappe	6.00	3.00	.60
☐	81	Gene Conley	6.00	3.00	.60	☐	130	Mayo Smith MG	6.00	3.00	.60
☐	82	Chuck Harmon	6.00	3.00	.60	☐	131	Grady Hatton	6.00	3.00	.60
☐	83	Tom Brewer	6.00	3.00	.60	☐	132	Bob Trice	6.00	3.00	.60
☐	84	Camilo Pascual	8.00	4.00	.80	☐	133	Dave Hoskins	6.00	3.00	.60
☐	85	Don Mossi	8.00	4.00	.80	☐	134	Joey Jay	6.00	3.00	.60
☐	86	Bill Wilson	6.00	3.00	.60	☐	135	Johnny O'Brien	6.00	3.00	.60

		NRMT	VG-E	GOOD
☐ 136	Vernon Stewart	6.00	3.00	.60
☐ 137	Harry Elliott	6.00	3.00	.60
☐ 138	Ray Herbert	6.00	3.00	.60
☐ 139	Steve Kraly	6.00	3.00	.60
☐ 140	Mel Parnell	8.00	4.00	.80
☐ 141	Tom Wright	6.00	3.00	.60
☐ 142	Jerry Lynch	6.00	3.00	.60
☐ 143	John (Dick) Schofield	6.00	3.00	.60
☐ 144	John (Joe) Amalfitano	6.00	3.00	.60
☐ 145	Elmer Valo	6.00	3.00	.60
☐ 146	Dick Donovan	6.00	3.00	.60
☐ 147	Hugh Pepper	6.00	3.00	.60
☐ 148	Hector Brown	6.00	3.00	.60
☐ 149	Ray Crone	6.00	3.00	.60
☐ 150	Mike Higgins	6.00	3.00	.60
☐ 151	Ralph Kress	12.00	6.00	1.20
☐ 152	Harry Agganis	60.00	30.00	6.00
☐ 153	Bud Podbielan	12.00	6.00	1.20
☐ 154	Willie Miranda	12.00	6.00	1.20
☐ 155	Eddie Mathews	80.00	40.00	8.00
☐ 156	Joe Black	16.00	8.00	1.60
☐ 157	Robert Miller	12.00	6.00	1.20
☐ 158	Tommy Carroll	14.00	7.00	1.40
☐ 159	Johnny Schmitz	12.00	6.00	1.20
☐ 160	Ray Narleski	14.00	7.00	1.40
☐ 161	Chuck Tanner	27.00	13.50	2.70
☐ 162	Joe Coleman	15.00	7.50	1.50
☐ 163	Faye Throneberry	15.00	7.50	1.50
☐ 164	Roberto Clemente	950.00	475.00	95.00
☐ 165	Don Johnson	15.00	7.50	1.50
☐ 166	Hank Bauer	30.00	15.00	3.00
☐ 167	Thomas Casagrande	15.00	7.50	1.50
☐ 168	Duane Pillette	15.00	7.50	1.50
☐ 169	Bob Oldis	15.00	7.50	1.50
☐ 170	Jim Pearce DP	9.00	4.50	.90
☐ 171	Dick Brodowski	15.00	7.50	1.50
☐ 172	Frank Baumholtz DP	9.00	4.50	.90
☐ 173	Johnny Kline	15.00	7.50	1.50
☐ 174	Rudy Minarcin	15.00	7.50	1.50
☐ 175	Does not exist	0.00	0.00	0.00
☐ 176	Norm Zauchin	15.00	7.50	1.50
☐ 177	Al Robertson	15.00	7.50	1.50
☐ 178	Bobby Adams	15.00	7.50	1.50
☐ 179	Jim Bolger	15.00	7.50	1.50
☐ 180	Clem Labine	20.00	10.00	2.00
☐ 181	Roy McMillan	15.00	7.50	1.50
☐ 182	Humberto Robinson	15.00	7.50	1.50
☐ 183	Anthony Jacobs	15.00	7.50	1.50
☐ 184	Harry Perkowski DP	9.00	4.50	.90

		NRMT	VG-E	GOOD
☐ 185	Don Ferrarese	15.00	7.50	1.50
☐ 186	Does not exist	0.00	0.00	0.00
☐ 187	Gil Hodges	120.00	60.00	12.00
☐ 188	Charlie Silvera DP	9.00	4.50	.90
☐ 189	Phil Rizzuto	120.00	60.00	12.00
☐ 190	Gene Woodling	20.00	10.00	2.00
☐ 191	Eddie Stanky	20.00	10.00	2.00
☐ 192	Jim Delsing	15.00	7.50	1.50
☐ 193	Johnny Sain	27.00	13.50	2.70
☐ 194	Willie Mays	400.00	200.00	40.00
☐ 195	Ed Roebuck	20.00	10.00	2.00
☐ 196	Gale Wade	15.00	7.50	1.50
☐ 197	Al Smith	18.00	9.00	1.80
☐ 198	Yogi Berra	200.00	100.00	20.00
☐ 199	Odbert Hamric	15.00	7.50	1.50
☐ 200	Jackie Jensen	45.00	22.50	4.50
☐ 201	Sherm Lollar	18.00	9.00	1.80
☐ 202	Jim Owens	15.00	7.50	1.50
☐ 203	Does not exist	0.00	0.00	0.00
☐ 204	Frank Smith	15.00	7.50	1.50
☐ 205	Gene Freese	15.00	7.50	1.50
☐ 206	Pete Daley	15.00	7.50	1.50
☐ 207	Billy Consolo	15.00	7.50	1.50
☐ 208	Ray Moore	15.00	7.50	1.50
☐ 209	Does not exist	0.00	0.00	0.00
☐ 210	Duke Snider	400.00	100.00	25.00

1956 Topps

The cards in this 340-card set measure 2 5/8"
by 3 3/4". Following up with another horizontally
oriented card in 1956, Topps improved the

format by layering the color "head" shot onto an actual action sequence involving the player. Cards 1 to 180 come with either white or gray backs: in the 1 to 100 sequence, gray backs are less common (worth about 10% more) and in the 101 to 180 sequence, white backs are less common (worth 30% more). The team cards, used for the first time in a regular set by Topps, are found dated 1955, or undated, with the team name appearing on either side. The dated team cards in the first series were not printed on the gray stock. The two un-numbered checklist cards are highly prized (must be unmarked to qualify as excellent or mint). The complete set price below does not include the unnumbered checklist cards or any of the variations.

			NRMT	VG-E	GOOD
	COMPLETE SET (340)		6000.00	3000.00	700.00
	COMMON PLAYER (1-100)		5.00	2.50	.50
	COMMON PLAYER (101-180)		6.00	3.00	.60
	COMMON PLAYER (181-260)		11.00	5.00	1.00
	COMMON PLAYER (261-340)		7.00	3.50	.70
☐	1	William Harridge (AL President)	100.00	10.00	2.00
☐	2	Warren Giles DP (NL President)	12.00	6.00	1.20
☐	3	Elmer Valo	5.00	2.50	.50
☐	4	Carlos Paula	5.00	2.50	.50
☐	5	Ted Williams	200.00	100.00	20.00
☐	6	Ray Boone	5.00	2.50	.50
☐	7	Ron Negray	5.00	2.50	.50
☐	8	Walter Alston MG	25.00	11.00	2.25
☐	9	Ruben Gomez	5.00	2.50	.50
☐	10	Warren Spahn DP	45.00	22.50	4.50
☐	11A	Chicago Cubs (centered)	15.00	7.50	1.50
☐	11B	Cubs Team (dated 1955)	40.00	20.00	4.00
☐	11C	Cubs Team (name at far left)	15.00	7.50	1.50
☐	12	Andy Carey	6.00	3.00	.60
☐	13	Roy Face	7.00	3.50	.70
☐	14	Ken Boyer	10.00	5.00	1.00
☐	15	Ernie Banks DP	55.00	27.50	5.50
☐	16	Hector Lopez	5.00	2.50	.50
☐	17	Gene Conley	5.00	2.50	.50
☐	18	Dick Donovan	5.00	2.50	.50

			NRMT	VG-E	GOOD
☐	19	Chuck Diering	5.00	2.50	.50
☐	20	Al Kaline	65.00	32.50	6.50
☐	21	Joe Collins	6.00	3.00	.60
☐	22	Jim Finigan	5.00	2.50	.50
☐	23	Fred Marsh	5.00	2.50	.50
☐	24	Dick Groat	7.00	3.50	.70
☐	25	Ted Kluszewski	12.00	6.00	1.20
☐	26	Grady Hatton	5.00	2.50	.50
☐	27	Nelson Burbrink	5.00	2.50	.50
☐	28	Bobby Hofman	5.00	2.50	.50
☐	29	Jack Harshman	5.00	2.50	.50
☐	30	Jackie Robinson DP	125.00	60.00	12.50
☐	31	Hank Aaron DP (small photo actually W. Mays)	160.00	80.00	16.00
☐	32	Frank House	5.00	2.50	.50
☐	33	Roberto Clemente	250.00	125.00	25.00
☐	34	Tom Brewer	5.00	2.50	.50
☐	35	Al Rosen DP	8.00	4.00	.80
☐	36	Rudy Minarcin	5.00	2.50	.50
☐	37	Alex Grammas	5.00	2.50	.50
☐	38	Bob Kennedy	5.00	2.50	.50
☐	39	Don Mossi	6.00	3.00	.60
☐	40	Bob Turley	8.00	4.00	.80
☐	41	Hank Sauer	6.00	3.00	.60
☐	42	Sandy Amoros	7.00	3.50	.70
☐	43	Ray Moore	5.00	2.50	.50
☐	44	Windy McCall	5.00	2.50	.50
☐	45	Gus Zernial	5.00	2.50	.50
☐	46	Gene Freese	5.00	2.50	.50
☐	47	Art Fowler	5.00	2.50	.50
☐	48	Jim Hegan	5.00	2.50	.50
☐	49	Pedro Ramos	5.00	2.50	.50
☐	50	Dusty Rhodes	6.00	3.00	.60
☐	51	Ernie Oravetz	5.00	2.50	.50
☐	52	Bob Grim	6.00	3.00	.60
☐	53	Arnie Portocarrero	5.00	2.50	.50
☐	54	Bob Keegan	5.00	2.50	.50
☐	55	Wally Moon	7.00	3.50	.70
☐	56	Dale Long	6.00	3.00	.60
☐	57	Duke Maas	5.00	2.50	.50
☐	58	Ed Roebuck	6.00	3.00	.60
☐	59	Jose Santiago	5.00	2.50	.50
☐	60	Mayo Smith MG	5.00	2.50	.50
☐	61	Bill Skowron	10.00	5.00	1.00
☐	62	Hal Smith	5.00	2.50	.50
☐	63	Roger Craig	18.00	9.00	1.80
☐	64	Luis Arroyo	6.00	3.00	.60
☐	65	Johnny O'Brien	5.00	2.50	.50

		NRMT	VG-E	GOOD
☐ 66	Bob Speake	5.00	2.50	.50
☐ 67	Vic Power	5.00	2.50	.50
☐ 68	Chuck Stobbs	5.00	2.50	.50
☐ 69	Chuck Tanner	7.00	3.50	.70
☐ 70	Jim Rivera	5.00	2.50	.50
☐ 71	Frank Sullivan	5.00	2.50	.50
☐ 72A	Phillies Team DP (centered)	15.00	7.50	1.50
☐ 72B	Phillies Team (dated 1955)	40.00	20.00	4.00
☐ 72C	Phillies Team (name at far left)	15.00	7.50	1.50
☐ 73	Wayne Terwilliger	5.00	2.50	.50
☐ 74	Jim King	5.00	2.50	.50
☐ 75	Roy Sievers	6.00	3.00	.60
☐ 76	Ray Crone	5.00	2.50	.50
☐ 77	Harvey Haddix	6.00	3.00	.60
☐ 78	Herman Wehmeier	5.00	2.50	.50
☐ 79	Sandy Koufax	225.00	110.00	22.00
☐ 80	Gus Triandos	6.00	3.00	.60
☐ 81	Wally Westlake	5.00	2.50	.50
☐ 82	Bill Renna	5.00	2.50	.50
☐ 83	Karl Spooner	6.00	3.00	.60
☐ 84	Babe Birrer	5.00	2.50	.50
☐ 85A	Cleveland Indians (centered)	15.00	7.50	1.50
☐ 85B	Indians Team (dated 1955)	40.00	20.00	4.00
☐ 85C	Indians Team (name at far left)	15.00	7.50	1.50
☐ 86	Ray Jablonski	5.00	2.50	.50
☐ 87	Dean Stone	5.00	2.50	.50
☐ 88	Johnny Kucks	6.00	3.00	.60
☐ 89	Norm Zauchin	5.00	2.50	.50
☐ 90A	Cincinnati Redlegs Team (centered)	15.00	7.50	1.50
☐ 90B	Reds Team (dated 1955)	40.00	20.00	4.00
☐ 90C	Reds Team (name at far left)	15.00	7.50	1.50
☐ 91	Gail Harris	5.00	2.50	.50
☐ 92	Bob (Red) Wilson	5.00	2.50	.50
☐ 93	George Susce	5.00	2.50	.50
☐ 94	Ron Kline	5.00	2.50	.50
☐ 95A	Milwaukee Braves Team (centered)	15.00	7.50	1.50
☐ 95B	Braves Team (dated 1955)	40.00	20.00	4.00
☐ 95C	Braves Team	15.00	7.50	1.50
	(name at far left)			
☐ 96	Bill Tremel	5.00	2.50	.50
☐ 97	Jerry Lynch	5.00	2.50	.50
☐ 98	Camilo Pascual	6.00	3.00	.60
☐ 99	Don Zimmer	12.00	6.00	1.20
☐ 100A	Baltimore Orioles Team (centered)	15.00	7.50	1.50
☐ 100B	Orioles Team (dated 1955)	40.00	20.00	4.00
☐ 100C	Orioles Team (name at far left)	15.00	7.50	1.50
☐ 101	Roy Campanella	110.00	55.00	11.00
☐ 102	Jim Davis	6.00	3.00	.60
☐ 103	Willie Miranda	6.00	3.00	.60
☐ 104	Bob Lennon	6.00	3.00	.60
☐ 105	Al Smith	6.00	3.00	.60
☐ 106	Joe Astroth	6.00	3.00	.60
☐ 107	Eddie Mathews	45.00	22.50	4.50
☐ 108	Laurin Pepper	6.00	3.00	.60
☐ 109	Enos Slaughter	22.00	11.00	2.20
☐ 110	Yogi Berra	110.00	55.00	11.00
☐ 111	Boston Red Sox Team Card	15.00	7.50	1.50
☐ 112	Dee Fondy	6.00	3.00	.60
☐ 113	Phil Rizzuto	35.00	17.50	3.50
☐ 114	Jim Owens	6.00	3.00	.60
☐ 115	Jackie Jensen	10.00	5.00	1.00
☐ 116	Eddie O'Brien	6.00	3.00	.60
☐ 117	Virgil Trucks	7.00	3.50	.70
☐ 118	Nellie Fox	18.00	9.00	1.80
☐ 119	Larry Jackson	6.00	3.00	.60
☐ 120	Richie Ashburn	20.00	10.00	2.00
☐ 121	Pittsburgh Pirates Team Card	15.00	7.50	1.50
☐ 122	Willard Nixon	6.00	3.00	.60
☐ 123	Roy McMillan	6.00	3.00	.60
☐ 124	Don Kaiser	6.00	3.00	.60
☐ 125	Minnie Minoso	12.00	6.00	1.20
☐ 126	Jim Brady	6.00	3.00	.60
☐ 127	Willie Jones	6.00	3.00	.60
☐ 128	Eddie Yost	6.00	3.00	.60
☐ 129	Jake Martin	6.00	3.00	.60
☐ 130	Willie Mays	225.00	110.00	22.00
☐ 131	Bob Roselli	6.00	3.00	.60
☐ 132	Bobby Avila	7.00	3.50	.70
☐ 133	Ray Narleski	6.00	3.00	.60
☐ 134	St. Louis Cardinals Team Card	15.00	7.50	1.50
☐ 135	Mickey Mantle	750.00	375.00	75.00

		NRMT	VG-E	GOOD
☐ 136	Johnny Logan	7.00	3.50	.70
☐ 137	Al Silvera	6.00	3.00	.60
☐ 138	Johnny Antonelli	8.00	4.00	.80
☐ 139	Tommy Carroll	7.00	3.50	.70
☐ 140	Herb Score	16.00	8.00	1.60
☐ 141	Joe Frazier	6.00	3.00	.60
☐ 142	Gene Baker	6.00	3.00	.60
☐ 143	Jim Piersall	9.00	4.50	.90
☐ 144	Leroy Powell	6.00	3.00	.60
☐ 145	Gil Hodges	32.00	16.00	3.20
☐ 146	Washington Nationals	15.00	7.50	1.50
	Team Card			
☐ 147	Earl Torgeson	6.00	3.00	.60
☐ 148	Alvin Dark	8.00	4.00	.80
☐ 149	Dixie Howell	6.00	3.00	.60
☐ 150	Duke Snider	100.00	50.00	10.00
☐ 151	Spook Jacobs	6.00	3.00	.60
☐ 152	Billy Hoeft	6.00	3.00	.60
☐ 153	Frank Thomas	7.00	3.50	.70
☐ 154	Dave Pope	6.00	3.00	.60
☐ 155	Harvey Kuenn	8.00	4.00	.80
☐ 156	Wes Westrum	6.00	3.00	.60
☐ 157	Dick Brodowski	6.00	3.00	.60
☐ 158	Wally Post	7.00	3.50	.70
☐ 159	Clint Courtney	6.00	3.00	.60
☐ 160	Billy Pierce	8.00	4.00	.80
☐ 161	Joe DeMaestri	6.00	3.00	.60
☐ 162	Dave (Gus) Bell	7.00	3.50	.70
☐ 163	Gene Woodling	8.00	4.00	.80
☐ 164	Harmon Killebrew	75.00	37.50	7.50
☐ 165	Red Schoendienst	24.00	12.00	2.40
☐ 166	Brooklyn Dodgers	150.00	75.00	15.00
	Team Card			
☐ 167	Harry Dorish	6.00	3.00	.60
☐ 168	Sammy White	6.00	3.00	.60
☐ 169	Bob Nelson	6.00	3.00	.60
☐ 170	Bill Virdon	10.00	5.00	1.00
☐ 171	Jim Wilson	6.00	3.00	.60
☐ 172	Frank Torre	7.50	3.50	.70
☐ 173	Johnny Podres	12.00	6.00	1.20
☐ 174	Glen Gorbous	6.00	3.00	.60
☐ 175	Del Crandall	7.00	3.50	.70
☐ 176	Alex Kellner	6.00	3.00	.60
☐ 177	Hank Bauer	12.00	6.00	1.20
☐ 178	Joe Black	8.00	4.00	.80
☐ 179	Harry Chiti	6.00	3.00	.60
☐ 180	Robin Roberts	24.00	12.00	2.40
☐ 181	Billy Martin	60.00	30.00	6.00
☐ 182	Paul Minner	11.00	5.00	1.00
☐ 183	Stan Lopata	11.00	5.00	1.00
☐ 184	Don Bessent	11.00	5.00	1.00
☐ 185	Bill Burton	11.00	5.00	1.00
☐ 186	Ron Jackson	11.00	5.00	1.00
☐ 187	Early Wynn	30.00	15.00	3.00
☐ 188	Chicago White Sox	24.00	12.00	2.40
	Team Card			
☐ 189	Ned Garver	11.00	5.00	1.00
☐ 190	Carl Furillo	18.00	9.00	1.80
☐ 191	Frank Lary	12.50	6.00	1.20
☐ 192	Smoky Burgess	12.50	6.00	1.20
☐ 193	Wilmer Mizell	11.00	5.00	1.00
☐ 194	Monte Irvin	25.00	12.50	2.50
☐ 195	George Kell	25.00	12.50	2.50
☐ 196	Tom Poholsky	11.00	5.00	1.00
☐ 197	Granny Hamner	11.00	5.00	1.00
☐ 198	Ed Fitzgerald	11.00	5.00	1.00
☐ 199	Hank Thompson	12.50	6.00	1.20
☐ 200	Bob Feller	80.00	40.00	8.00
☐ 201	Rip Repulski	11.00	5.00	1.00
☐ 202	Jim Hearn	11.00	5.00	1.00
☐ 203	Bill Tuttle	11.00	5.00	1.00
☐ 204	Art Swanson	11.00	5.00	1.00
☐ 205	Whitey Lockman	12.50	6.00	1.20
☐ 206	Erv Palica	11.00	5.00	1.00
☐ 207	Jim Small	11.00	5.00	1.00
☐ 208	Elston Howard	30.00	15.00	3.00
☐ 209	Max Surkont	11.00	5.00	1.00
☐ 210	Mike Garcia	12.50	6.00	1.20
☐ 211	Murry Dickson	11.00	5.00	1.00
☐ 212	Johnny Temple	12.50	6.00	1.20
☐ 213	Detroit Tigers	30.00	15.00	3.00
	Team Card			
☐ 214	Bob Rush	11.00	5.00	1.00
☐ 215	Tommy Byrne	12.50	6.00	1.20
☐ 216	Jerry Schoonmaker	11.00	5.00	1.00
☐ 217	Billy Klaus	11.00	5.00	1.00
☐ 218	Joe Nuxall	12.50	6.00	1.20
	(sic, Nuxhall)			
☐ 219	Lew Burdette	16.00	8.00	1.60
☐ 220	Del Ennis	12.50	6.00	1.20
☐ 221	Bob Friend	12.50	6.00	1.20
☐ 222	Dave Philley	11.00	5.00	1.00
☐ 223	Randy Jackson	11.00	5.00	1.00
☐ 224	Bud Podbielan	11.00	5.00	1.00
☐ 225	Gil McDougald	18.00	9.00	1.80
☐ 226	New York Giants	50.00	25.00	5.00
	Team Card			
☐ 227	Russ Meyer	11.00	5.00	1.00

		NRMT	VG-E	GOOD			NRMT	VG-E	GOOD
☐ 228	Mickey Vernon	14.00	7.00	1.40	☐ 274	Frank Baumholtz	7.00	3.50	.70
☐ 229	Harry Brecheen	12.50	6.00	1.20	☐ 275	Jim Greengrass	7.00	3.50	.70
☐ 230	Chico Carrasquel	11.00	5.00	1.00	☐ 276	George Zuverink	7.00	3.50	.70
☐ 231	Bob Hale	11.00	5.00	1.00	☐ 277	Daryl Spencer	7.00	3.50	.70
☐ 232	Toby Atwell	11.00	5.00	1.00	☐ 278	Chet Nichols	7.00	3.50	.70
☐ 233	Carl Erskine	16.00	8.00	1.60	☐ 279	Johnny Groth	7.00	3.50	.70
☐ 234	Pete Runnels	12.50	6.00	1.20	☐ 280	Jim Gilliam	12.00	6.00	1.20
☐ 235	Don Newcombe	30.00	15.00	3.00	☐ 281	Art Houtteman	7.00	3.50	.70
☐ 236	Kansas City Athletics	20.00	10.00	2.00	☐ 282	Warren Hacker	7.00	3.50	.70
	Team Card				☐ 283	Hal Smith	7.00	3.50	.70
☐ 237	Jose Valdivielso	11.00	5.00	1.00	☐ 284	Ike Delock	7.00	3.50	.70
☐ 238	Walt Dropo	12.50	6.00	1.20	☐ 285	Eddie Miksis	7.00	3.50	.70
☐ 239	Harry Simpson	11.00	5.00	1.00	☐ 286	Bill Wight	7.00	3.50	.70
☐ 240	Whitey Ford	85.00	42.50	8.50	☐ 287	Bobby Adams	7.00	3.50	.70
☐ 241	Don Mueller UER	14.00	7.00	1.40	☐ 288	Bob Cerv	11.00	5.50	1.10
	(6" tall)				☐ 289	Hal Jeffcoat	7.00	3.50	.70
☐ 242	Hershell Freeman	11.00	5.00	1.00	☐ 290	Curt Simmons	9.00	4.50	.90
☐ 243	Sherm Lollar	12.50	6.00	1.20	☐ 291	Frank Kellert	7.00	3.50	.70
☐ 244	Bob Buhl	11.00	5.00	1.00	☐ 292	Luis Aparicio	100.00	50.00	10.00
☐ 245	Billy Goodman	12.50	6.00	1.20	☐ 293	Stu Miller	8.00	4.00	.80
☐ 246	Tom Gorman	11.00	5.00	1.00	☐ 294	Ernie Johnson	8.00	4.00	.80
☐ 247	Bill Sarni	11.00	5.00	1.00	☐ 295	Clem Labine	9.00	4.50	.90
☐ 248	Bob Porterfield	11.00	5.00	1.00	☐ 296	Andy Seminick	7.00	3.50	.70
☐ 249	Johnny Klippstein	11.00	5.00	1.00	☐ 297	Bob Skinner	8.00	4.00	.80
☐ 250	Larry Doby	15.00	7.50	1.50	☐ 298	Johnny Schmitz	7.00	3.50	.70
☐ 251	New York Yankees	150.00	75.00	15.00	☐ 299	Charlie Neal	14.00	7.00	1.40
	Team Card				☐ 300	Vic Wertz	8.00	4.00	.80
☐ 252	Vern Law	12.50	6.00	1.20	☐ 301	Marv Grissom	7.00	3.50	.70
☐ 253	Irv Noren	12.50	6.00	1.20	☐ 302	Eddie Robinson	7.00	3.50	.70
☐ 254	George Crowe	11.00	5.00	1.00	☐ 303	Jim Dyck	7.00	3.50	.70
☐ 255	Bob Lemon	30.00	15.00	3.00	☐ 304	Frank Malzone	14.00	7.00	1.40
☐ 256	Tom Hurd	11.00	5.00	1.00	☐ 305	Brooks Lawrence	7.00	3.50	.70
☐ 257	Bobby Thomson	14.00	7.00	1.40	☐ 306	Curt Roberts	7.00	3.50	.70
☐ 258	Art Ditmar	12.50	6.00	1.20	☐ 307	Hoyt Wilhelm	25.00	12.50	2.50
☐ 259	Sam Jones	12.50	6.00	1.20	☐ 308	Chuck Harmon	7.00	3.50	.70
☐ 260	Pee Wee Reese	100.00	50.00	10.00	☐ 309	Don Blasingame	7.00	3.50	.70
☐ 261	Bobby Shantz	10.00	5.00	1.00	☐ 310	Steve Gromek	7.00	3.50	.70
☐ 262	Howie Pollet	7.00	3.50	.70	☐ 311	Hal Naragon	7.00	3.50	.70
☐ 263	Bob Miller	7.00	3.50	.70	☐ 312	Andy Pafko	8.00	4.00	.80
☐ 264	Ray Monzant	7.00	3.50	.70	☐ 313	Gene Stephens	7.00	3.50	.70
☐ 265	Sandy Consuegra	7.00	3.50	.70	☐ 314	Hobie Landrith	7.00	3.50	.70
☐ 266	Don Ferrarese	7.00	3.50	.70	☐ 315	Milt Bolling	7.00	3.50	.70
☐ 267	Bob Nieman	7.00	3.50	.70	☐ 316	Jerry Coleman	9.00	4.50	.90
☐ 268	Dale Mitchell	8.00	4.00	.80	☐ 317	Al Aber	7.00	3.50	.70
☐ 269	Jack Meyer	7.00	3.50	.70	☐ 318	Fred Hatfield	7.00	3.50	.70
☐ 270	Billy Loes	8.00	4.00	.80	☐ 319	Jack Crimian	7.00	3.50	.70
☐ 271	Foster Castleman	7.00	3.50	.70	☐ 320	Joe Adcock	9.00	4.50	.90
☐ 272	Danny O'Connell	7.00	3.50	.70	☐ 321	Jim Konstanty	8.00	4.00	.80
☐ 273	Walker Cooper	7.00	3.50	.70	☐ 322	Karl Olson	7.00	3.50	.70

			NRMT	VG-E	GOOD
☐ 323	Willard Schmidt	....	7.00	3.50	.70
☐ 324	Rocky Bridges	.....	7.00	3.50	.70
☐ 325	Don Liddle	.....	7.00	3.50	.70
☐ 326	Connie Johnson	.....	7.00	3.50	.70
☐ 327	Bob Wiesler	.....	7.00	3.50	.70
☐ 328	Preston Ward	.....	7.00	3.50	.70
☐ 329	Lou Berberet	.....	7.00	3.50	.70
☐ 330	Jim Busby	....	7.00	3.50	.70
☐ 331	Dick Hall	....	7.00	3.50	.70
☐ 332	Don Larsen	.....	21.00	10.50	2.10
☐ 333	Rube Walker	.....	8.00	4.00	.80
☐ 334	Bob Miller	.....	7.00	3.50	.70
☐ 335	Don Hoak	.....	8.00	4.00	.80
☐ 336	Ellis Kinder	.....	7.00	3.50	.70
☐ 337	Bobby Morgan	.....	7.00	3.50	.70
☐ 338	Jim Delsing	.....	7.00	3.50	.70
☐ 339	Rance Pless	.....	7.00	3.50	.70
☐ 340	Mickey McDermott	..	20.00	4.00	.70
☐ 341	Checklist 1/3 (unnumbered)		225.00	25.00	5.00
☐ 342	Checklist 2/4 (unnumbered)		225.00	25.00	5.00

1957 Topps

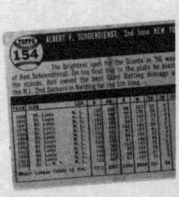

The cards in this 407-card set measure 2 ½" by 3 ½". In 1957, Topps returned to the vertical obverse, adopted what we now call the standard card size, and used a large, un- cluttered color photo for the first time since 1952. Cards in the series 265 to 352 and the unnumbered checklist cards are scarcer than

other cards in the set. However within this scarce series (265-352) there are 22 cards which were printed in double the quantity of the other cards in the series; these 22 double prints are indicated by DP in the checklist below. The first star combination cards, #400 and #407, are quite popular with collectors. They feature the big stars of the previous season's World Series teams, the Dodgers (Furillo, Hodges, Campanella, and Snider) and Yankees (Berra and Mantle). The complete set price below does not include the unnumbered checklist cards.

	NRMT	VG-E	GOOD
COMPLETE SET (407)	6900.00	3300.00	850.00
COMMON PLAYER (1-88)	5.00	2.50	.50
COMMON PLAYER (89-176)	4.00	2.00	.40
COMMON PLAYER (177-264) ..	3.00	1.50	.30
COMMON PLAYER (265-352) ..	15.00	7.50	1.50
COMMON DP (265-352)	10.00	5.00	1.00
COMMON PLAYER (353-407) ..	4.00	2.00	.40

			NRMT	VG-E	GOOD
☐	1	Ted Williams	....	400.00	100.00	20.00
☐	2	Yogi Berra	....	125.00	60.00	12.50
☐	3	Dale Long	.....	6.00	3.00	.60
☐	4	Johnny Logan	.....	6.00	3.00	.60
☐	5	Sal Maglie	.....	8.00	4.00	.80
☐	6	Hector Lopez	.....	5.00	2.50	.50
☐	7	Luis Aparicio	.....	25.00	12.50	2.50
☐	8	Don Mossi	.....	6.00	3.00	.60
☐	9	Johnny Temple	.....	6.00	3.00	.60
☐	10	Willie Mays	.....	180.00	90.00	18.00
☐	11	George Zuverink	.....	5.00	2.50	.50
☐	12	Dick Groat	.....	8.00	4.00	.80
☐	13	Wally Burnette	.....	5.00	2.50	.50
☐	14	Bob Nieman	.....	5.00	2.50	.50
☐	15	Robin Roberts	.....	20.00	10.00	2.00
☐	16	Walt Moryn	.....	5.00	2.50	.50
☐	17	Billy Gardner	.....	6.00	3.00	.60
☐	18	Don Drysdale	.....	175.00	85.00	18.00
☐	19	Bob Wilson	.....	5.00	2.50	.50
☐	20	Hank Aaron (reverse negative photo on front)		200.00	100.00	20.00
☐	21	Frank Sullivan	.....	5.00	2.50	.50
☐	22	Jerry Snyder (photo actually Ed Fitzgerald)		5.00	2.50	.50
☐	23	Sherm Lollar	....	6.00	3.00	.60

		NRMT	VG-E	GOOD				NRMT	VG-E	GOOD
☐	24 Bill Mazeroski	25.00	12.50	2.50	☐	72 Bill Tuttle		5.00	2.50	.50
☐	25 Whitey Ford	50.00	25.00	5.00	☐	73 George Crowe		5.00	2.50	.50
☐	26 Bob Boyd	5.00	2.50	.50	☐	74 Vito Valentinetti		5.00	2.50	.50
☐	27 Ted Kazanski	5.00	2.50	.50	☐	75 Jim Piersall		8.00	4.00	.80
☐	28 Gene Conley	5.00	2.50	.50	☐	76 Roberto Clemente		160.00	80.00	16.00
☐	29 Whitey Herzog	20.00	10.00	2.00	☐	77 Paul Foytack		5.00	2.50	.50
☐	30 Pee Wee Reese	45.00	22.50	4.50	☐	78 Vic Wertz		6.00	3.00	.60
☐	31 Ron Northey	5.00	2.50	.50	☐	79 Lindy McDaniel		6.00	3.00	.60
☐	32 Hershell Freeman	5.00	2.50	.50	☐	80 Gil Hodges		32.00	16.00	3.20
☐	33 Jim Small	5.00	2.50	.50	☐	81 Herman Wehmeier		5.00	2.50	.50
☐	34 Tom Sturdivant	5.00	2.50	.50	☐	82 Elston Howard		10.00	5.00	1.00
☐	35 Frank Robinson	200.00	100.00	20.00	☐	83 Lou Skizas		5.00	2.50	.50
☐	36 Bob Grim	6.00	3.00	.60	☐	84 Moe Drabowsky		5.00	2.50	.50
☐	37 Frank Torre	5.00	2.50	.50	☐	85 Larry Doby		8.00	4.00	.80
☐	38 Nellie Fox	13.00	6.50	1.30	☐	86 Bill Sarni		5.00	2.50	.50
☐	39 Al Worthington	5.00	2.50	.50	☐	87 Tom Gorman		5.00	2.50	.50
☐	40 Early Wynn	18.00	9.00	1.80	☐	88 Harvey Kuenn		8.00	4.00	.80
☐	41 Hal W. Smith	5.00	2.50	.50	☐	89 Roy Sievers		5.00	2.50	.50
☐	42 Dee Fondy	5.00	2.50	.50	☐	90 Warren Spahn		45.00	22.50	4.50
☐	43 Connie Johnson	5.00	2.50	.50	☐	91 Mack Burk		4.00	2.00	.40
☐	44 Joe DeMaestri	5.00	2.50	.50	☐	92 Mickey Vernon		5.00	2.50	.50
☐	45 Carl Furillo	9.00	4.50	.90	☐	93 Hal Jeffcoat		4.00	2.00	.40
☐	46 Robert J. Miller	5.00	2.50	.50	☐	94 Bobby Del Greco		4.00	2.00	.40
☐	47 Don Blasingame	5.00	2.50	.50	☐	95 Mickey Mantle		750.00	375.00	75.00
☐	48 Bill Bruton	6.00	3.00	.60	☐	96 Hank Aguirre		4.00	2.00	.40
☐	49 Daryl Spencer	5.00	2.50	.50	☐	97 New York Yankees		33.00	15.00	3.00
☐	50 Herb Score	8.00	4.00	.80		Team Card				
☐	51 Clint Courtney	5.00	2.50	.50	☐	98 Alvin Dark		6.00	3.00	.60
☐	52 Lee Walls	5.00	2.50	.50	☐	99 Bob Keegan		4.00	2.00	.40
☐	53 Clem Labine	6.00	3.00	.60	☐	100 Giles and Harridge		6.00	3.00	.60
☐	54 Elmer Valo	5.00	2.50	.50		League Presidents				
☐	55 Ernie Banks	65.00	32.50	6.50	☐	101 Chuck Stobbs		4.00	2.00	.40
☐	56 Dave Sisler	5.00	2.50	.50	☐	102 Ray Boone		5.00	2.50	.50
☐	57 Jim Lemon	6.00	3.00	.60	☐	103 Joe Nuxhall		5.00	2.50	.50
☐	58 Ruben Gomez	5.00	2.50	.50	☐	104 Hank Foiles		4.00	2.00	.40
☐	59 Dick Williams	6.00	3.00	.60	☐	105 Johnny Antonelli		5.00	2.50	.50
☐	60 Billy Hoeft	5.00	2.50	.50	☐	106 Ray Moore		4.00	2.00	.40
☐	61 James "Dusty"				☐	107 Jim Rivera		4.00	2.00	.40
	Rhodes	6.00	3.00	.60	☐	108 Tommy Byrne		5.00	2.50	.50
☐	62 Billy Martin	40.00	20.00	4.00	☐	109 Hank Thompson		5.00	2.50	.50
☐	63 Ike Delock	5.00	2.50	.50	☐	110 Bill Virdon		6.00	3.00	.60
☐	64 Pete Runnels	6.00	3.00	.60	☐	111 Hal R. Smith		4.00	2.00	.40
☐	65 Wally Moon	6.00	3.00	.60	☐	112 Tom Brewer		4.00	2.00	.40
☐	66 Brooks Lawrence	5.00	2.50	.50	☐	113 Wilmer Mizell		4.00	2.00	.40
☐	67 Chico Carrasquel	5.00	2.50	.50	☐	114 Milwaukee Braves		9.00	4.50	.90
☐	68 Ray Crone	5.00	2.50	.50		Team Card				
☐	69 Roy McMillan	5.00	2.50	.50	☐	115 Jim Gilliam		8.00	4.00	.80
☐	70 Richie Ashburn	15.00	7.50	1.50	☐	116 Mike Fornieles		4.00	2.00	.40
☐	71 Murry Dickson	5.00	2.50	.50	☐	117 Joe Adcock		6.00	3.00	.60

			NRMT	VG-E	GOOD
☐	118	Bob Porterfield	4.00	2.00	.40
☐	119	Stan Lopata	4.00	2.00	.40
☐	120	Bob Lemon	16.00	8.00	1.60
☐	121	Clete Boyer	12.00	6.00	1.20
☐	122	Ken Boyer	8.00	4.00	.80
☐	123	Steve Ridzik	4.00	2.00	.40
☐	124	Dave Philley	4.00	2.00	.40
☐	125	Al Kaline	65.00	32.50	6.50
☐	126	Bob Wiesler	4.00	2.00	.40
☐	127	Bob Buhl	4.00	2.00	.40
☐	128	Ed Bailey	5.00	2.50	.50
☐	129	Saul Rogovin	4.00	2.00	.40
☐	130	Don Newcombe	8.00	4.00	.80
☐	131	Milt Bolling	4.00	2.00	.40
☐	132	Art Ditmar	5.00	2.50	.50
☐	133	Del Crandall	5.00	2.50	.50
☐	134	Don Kaiser	4.00	2.00	.40
☐	135	Bill Skowron	10.00	5.00	1.00
☐	136	Jim Hegan	5.00	2.50	.50
☐	137	Bob Rush	4.00	2.00	.40
☐	138	Minnie Minoso	8.00	4.00	.80
☐	139	Lou Kretlow	4.00	2.00	.40
☐	140	Frank Thomas	5.00	2.50	.50
☐	141	Al Aber	4.00	2.00	.40
☐	142	Charley Thompson	4.00	2.00	.40
☐	143	Andy Pafko	5.00	2.50	.50
☐	144	Ray Narleski	4.00	2.00	.40
☐	145	Al Smith	4.00	2.00	.40
☐	146	Don Ferrarese	4.00	2.00	.40
☐	147	Al Walker	4.00	2.00	.40
☐	148	Don Mueller	5.00	2.50	.50
☐	149	Bob Kennedy	4.00	2.00	.40
☐	150	Bob Friend	5.00	2.50	.50
☐	151	Willie Miranda	4.00	2.00	.40
☐	152	Jack Harshman	4.00	2.00	.40
☐	153	Karl Olson	4.00	2.00	.40
☐	154	Red Schoendienst	18.50	9.00	2.00
☐	155	Jim Brosnan	5.00	2.50	.50
☐	156	Gus Triandos	5.00	2.50	.50
☐	157	Wally Post	5.00	2.50	.50
☐	158	Curt Simmons	5.00	2.50	.50
☐	159	Solly Drake	4.00	2.00	.40
☐	160	Billy Pierce	6.00	3.00	.60
☐	161	Pittsburgh Pirates Team Card	8.00	4.00	.80
☐	162	Jack Meyer	4.00	2.00	.40
☐	163	Sammy White	4.00	2.00	.40
☐	164	Tommy Carroll	4.00	2.00	.40
☐	165	Ted Kluszewski	12.00	6.00	1.20
☐	166	Roy Face	6.00	3.00	.60
☐	167	Vic Power	5.00	2.50	.50
☐	168	Frank Lary	5.00	2.50	.50
☐	169	Herb Plews	4.00	2.00	.40
☐	170	Duke Snider	80.00	40.00	8.00
☐	171	Boston Red Sox Team Card	9.00	4.50	.90
☐	172	Gene Woodling	6.00	3.00	.60
☐	173	Roger Craig	9.00	4.50	.90
☐	174	Willie Jones	4.00	2.00	.40
☐	175	Don Larsen	10.00	5.00	1.00
☐	176	Gene Baker	4.00	2.00	.40
☐	177	Eddie Yost	3.00	1.50	.30
☐	178	Don Bessent	3.00	1.50	.30
☐	179	Ernie Oravetz	3.00	1.50	.30
☐	180	Dave (Gus) Bell	4.00	2.00	.40
☐	181	Dick Donovan	3.00	1.50	.30
☐	182	Hobie Landrith	3.00	1.50	.30
☐	183	Chicago Cubs Team Card	7.00	3.50	.70
☐	184	Tito Francona	4.00	2.00	.40
☐	185	Johnny Kucks	4.00	2.00	.40
☐	186	Jim King	3.00	1.50	.30
☐	187	Virgil Trucks	4.00	2.00	.40
☐	188	Felix Mantilla	3.00	1.50	.30
☐	189	Willard Nixon	3.00	1.50	.30
☐	190	Randy Jackson	3.00	1.50	.30
☐	191	Joe Margoneri	3.00	1.50	.30
☐	192	Jerry Coleman	4.00	2.00	.40
☐	193	Del Rice	3.00	1.50	.30
☐	194	Hal Brown	3.00	1.50	.30
☐	195	Bobby Avila	3.00	1.50	.30
☐	196	Larry Jackson	3.00	1.50	.30
☐	197	Hank Sauer	4.00	2.00	.40
☐	198	Detroit Tigers Team Card	9.00	4.50	.90
☐	199	Vern Law	4.00	2.00	.40
☐	200	Gil McDougald	8.00	4.00	.80
☐	201	Sandy Amoros	4.00	2.00	.40
☐	202	Dick Gernert	3.00	1.50	.30
☐	203	Hoyt Wilhelm	16.00	8.00	1.60
☐	204	Kansas City Athletics Team Card	7.00	3.50	.70
☐	205	Charlie Maxwell	3.00	1.50	.30
☐	206	Willard Schmidt	3.00	1.50	.30
☐	207	Gordon (Billy) Hunter	3.00	1.50	.30
☐	208	Lou Burdette	5.00	2.50	.50

		NRMT	VG-E	GOOD
☐ 209	Bob Skinner	4.00	2.00	.40
☐ 210	Roy Campanella	80.00	40.00	8.00
☐ 211	Camilo Pascual	4.00	2.00	.40
☐ 212	Rocco Colavito	40.00	20.00	4.00
☐ 213	Les Moss	3.00	1.50	.30
☐ 214	Philadelphia Phillies Team Card	7.00	3.50	.70
☐ 215	Enos Slaughter	18.00	9.00	1.80
☐ 216	Marv Grissom	3.00	1.50	.30
☐ 217	Gene Stephens	3.00	1.50	.30
☐ 218	Ray Jablonski	3.00	1.50	.30
☐ 219	Tom Acker	3.00	1.50	.30
☐ 220	Jackie Jensen	7.00	3.50	.70
☐ 221	Dixie Howell	3.00	1.50	.30
☐ 222	Alex Grammas	3.00	1.50	.30
☐ 223	Frank House	3.00	1.50	.30
☐ 224	Marv Blaylock	3.00	1.50	.30
☐ 225	Harry Simpson	3.00	1.50	.30
☐ 226	Preston Ward	3.00	1.50	.30
☐ 227	Jerry Staley	3.00	1.50	.30
☐ 228	Smoky Burgess	4.00	2.00	.40
☐ 229	George Susce	3.00	1.50	.30
☐ 230	George Kell	15.00	7.50	1.50
☐ 231	Solly Hemus	3.00	1.50	.30
☐ 232	Whitey Lockman	4.00	2.00	.40
☐ 233	Art Fowler	3.00	1.50	.30
☐ 234	Dick Cole	3.00	1.50	.30
☐ 235	Tom Poholsky	3.00	1.50	.30
☐ 236	Joe Ginsberg	3.00	1.50	.30
☐ 237	Foster Castleman	3.00	1.50	.30
☐ 238	Eddie Robinson	3.00	1.50	.30
☐ 239	Tom Morgan	3.00	1.50	.30
☐ 240	Hank Bauer	8.00	4.00	.80
☐ 241	Joe Lonnett	3.00	1.50	.30
☐ 242	Charlie Neal	4.00	2.00	.40
☐ 243	St. Louis Cardinals Team Card	9.00	4.50	.90
☐ 244	Billy Loes	4.00	2.00	.40
☐ 245	Rip Repulski	3.00	1.50	.30
☐ 246	Jose Valdivielso	3.00	1.50	.30
☐ 247	Turk Lown	3.00	1.50	.30
☐ 248	Jim Finigan	3.00	1.50	.30
☐ 249	Dave Pope	3.00	1.50	.30
☐ 250	Eddie Mathews	25.00	12.50	2.50
☐ 251	Baltimore Orioles Team Card	8.00	4.00	.80
☐ 252	Carl Erskine	7.00	3.50	.70
☐ 253	Gus Zernial	4.00	2.00	.40
☐ 254	Ron Negray	3.00	1.50	.30
☐ 255	Charlie Silvera	3.00	1.50	.30
☐ 256	Ron Kline	3.00	1.50	.30
☐ 257	Walt Dropo	3.00	1.50	.30
☐ 258	Steve Gromek	3.00	1.50	.30
☐ 259	Eddie O'Brien	3.00	1.50	.30
☐ 260	Del Ennis	4.00	2.00	.40
☐ 261	Bob Chakales	3.00	1.50	.30
☐ 262	Bobby Thomson	7.00	3.50	.70
☐ 263	George Strickland	3.00	1.50	.30
☐ 264	Bob Turley	8.00	4.00	.80
☐ 265	Harvey Haddix DP	15.00	7.50	1.50
☐ 266	Ken Kuhn DP	10.00	5.00	1.00
☐ 267	Danny Kravitz	15.00	7.50	1.50
☐ 268	Jack Collum	15.00	7.50	1.50
☐ 269	Bob Cerv	18.00	9.00	1.80
☐ 270	Washington Senators Team Card	30.00	15.00	3.00
☐ 271	Danny O'Connell DP	10.00	5.00	1.00
☐ 272	Bobby Shantz	22.00	11.00	2.20
☐ 273	Jim Davis	15.00	7.50	1.50
☐ 274	Don Hoak	18.00	9.00	1.80
☐ 275	Cleveland Indians Team Card	30.00	15.00	3.00
☐ 276	Jim Pyburn	15.00	7.50	1.50
☐ 277	Johnny Podres DP	45.00	20.00	4.00
☐ 278	Fred Hatfield DP	10.00	5.00	1.00
☐ 279	Bob Thurman	15.00	7.50	1.50
☐ 280	Alex Kellner	15.00	7.50	1.50
☐ 281	Gail Harris	15.00	7.50	1.50
☐ 282	Jack Dittmer DP	10.00	5.00	1.00
☐ 283	Wes Covington DP	12.00	6.00	1.20
☐ 284	Don Zimmer	22.00	11.00	2.20
☐ 285	Ned Garver	15.00	7.50	1.50
☐ 286	Bobby Richardson	90.00	45.00	9.00
☐ 287	Sam Jones	18.00	9.00	1.80
☐ 288	Ted Lepcio	15.00	7.50	1.50
☐ 289	Jim Bolger DP	10.00	5.00	1.00
☐ 290	Andy Carey DP	15.00	7.50	1.50
☐ 291	Windy McCall	15.00	7.50	1.50
☐ 292	Billy Klaus	15.00	7.50	1.50
☐ 293	Ted Abernathy DP	15.00	7.50	1.50
☐ 294	Rocky Bridges DP	10.00	5.00	1.00
☐ 295	Joe Collins DP	15.00	7.50	1.50
☐ 296	Johnny Klippstein	15.00	7.50	1.50
☐ 297	Jack Crimian	15.00	7.50	1.50
☐ 298	Irv Noren DP	10.00	5.00	1.00
☐ 299	Chuck Harmon	15.00	7.50	1.50
☐ 300	Mike Garcia	18.00	9.00	1.80
☐ 301	Sammy Esposito DP	10.00	5.00	1.00

		NRMT	VG-E	GOOD
☐ 302	Sandy Koufax DP	300.00	125.00	30.00
☐ 303	Billy Goodman	18.00	9.00	1.80
☐ 304	Joe Cunningham	18.00	9.00	1.80
☐ 305	Chico Fernandez	15.00	7.50	1.50
☐ 306	Darrell Johnson DP	15.00	7.50	1.50
☐ 307	Jack D. Phillips DP	10.00	5.00	1.00
☐ 308	Dick Hall	15.00	7.50	1.50
☐ 309	Jim Busby DP	10.00	5.00	1.00
☐ 310	Max Surkont DP	10.00	5.00	1.00
☐ 311	Al Pilarcik DP	10.00	5.00	1.00
☐ 312	Tony Kubek DP	100.00	45.00	9.00
☐ 313	Mel Parnell	18.00	9.00	1.80
☐ 314	Ed Bouchee DP	10.00	5.00	1.00
☐ 315	Lou Berberet DP	10.00	5.00	1.00
☐ 316	Billy O'Dell	15.00	7.50	1.50
☐ 317	New York Giants Team Card	50.00	25.00	5.00
☐ 318	Mickey McDermott	15.00	7.50	1.50
☐ 319	Gino Cimoli	18.00	9.00	1.80
☐ 320	Neil Chrisley	15.00	7.50	1.50
☐ 321	John (Red) Murff	15.00	7.50	1.50
☐ 322	Cincinnati Reds Team Card	50.00	25.00	5.00
☐ 323	Wes Westrum	18.00	9.00	1.80
☐ 324	Brooklyn Dodgers Team Card	100.00	50.00	10.00
☐ 325	Frank Bolling	15.00	7.50	1.50
☐ 326	Pedro Ramos	15.00	7.50	1.50
☐ 327	Jim Pendleton	15.00	7.50	1.50
☐ 328	Brooks Robinson	350.00	175.00	35.00
☐ 329	Chicago White Sox Team Card	30.00	15.00	3.00
☐ 330	Jim Wilson	15.00	7.50	1.50
☐ 331	Ray Katt	15.00	7.50	1.50
☐ 332	Bob Bowman	15.00	7.50	1.50
☐ 333	Ernie Johnson	18.00	9.00	1.80
☐ 334	Jerry Schoonmaker	15.00	7.50	1.50
☐ 335	Granny Hamner	15.00	7.50	1.50
☐ 336	Haywood Sullivan	18.00	9.00	1.80
☐ 337	Rene Valdes	15.00	7.50	1.50
☐ 338	Jim Bunning	100.00	50.00	10.00
☐ 339	Bob Speake	15.00	7.50	1.50
☐ 340	Bill Wight	15.00	7.50	1.50
☐ 341	Don Gross	15.00	7.50	1.50
☐ 342	Gene Mauch	18.00	9.00	1.80
☐ 343	Taylor Phillips	15.00	7.50	1.50
☐ 344	Paul LaPalme	15.00	7.50	1.50
☐ 345	Paul Smith	15.00	7.50	1.50
☐ 346	Dick Littlefield	15.00	7.50	1.50
☐ 347	Hal Naragon	15.00	7.50	1.50
☐ 348	Jim Hearn	15.00	7.50	1.50
☐ 349	Nellie King	15.00	7.50	1.50
☐ 350	Eddie Miksis	15.00	7.50	1.50
☐ 351	Dave Hillman	15.00	7.50	1.50
☐ 352	Ellis Kinder	15.00	7.50	1.50
☐ 353	Cal Neeman	4.00	2.00	.40
☐ 354	W. (Rip) Coleman	4.00	2.00	.40
☐ 355	Frank Malzone	5.00	2.50	.50
☐ 356	Faye Throneberry	4.00	2.00	.40
☐ 357	Earl Torgeson	4.00	2.00	.40
☐ 358	Jerry Lynch	4.00	2.00	.40
☐ 359	Tom Cheney	4.00	2.00	.40
☐ 360	Johnny Groth	4.00	2.00	.40
☐ 361	Curt Barclay	4.00	2.00	.40
☐ 362	Roman Mejias	4.00	2.00	.40
☐ 363	Eddie Kasko	4.00	2.00	.40
☐ 364	Cal McLish	4.00	2.00	.40
☐ 365	Ozzie Virgil	4.00	2.00	.40
☐ 366	Ken Lehman	4.00	2.00	.40
☐ 367	Ed Fitzgerald	4.00	2.00	.40
☐ 368	Bob Purkey	4.00	2.00	.40
☐ 369	Milt Graff	4.00	2.00	.40
☐ 370	Warren Hacker	4.00	2.00	.40
☐ 371	Bob Lennon	4.00	2.00	.40
☐ 372	Norm Zauchin	4.00	2.00	.40
☐ 373	Pete Whisenant	4.00	2.00	.40
☐ 374	Don Cardwell	4.00	2.00	.40
☐ 375	Jim Landis	4.00	2.00	.40
☐ 376	Don Elston	4.00	2.00	.40
☐ 377	Andre Rodgers	4.00	2.00	.40
☐ 378	Elmer Singleton	4.00	2.00	.40
☐ 379	Don Lee	4.00	2.00	.40
☐ 380	Walker Cooper	4.00	2.00	.40
☐ 381	Dean Stone	4.00	2.00	.40
☐ 382	Jim Brideweser	4.00	2.00	.40
☐ 383	Juan Pizarro	4.00	2.00	.40
☐ 384	Bobby G. Smith	4.00	2.00	.40
☐ 385	Art Houtteman	4.00	2.00	.40
☐ 386	Lyle Luttrell	4.00	2.00	.40
☐ 387	Jack Sanford	7.00	3.50	.70
☐ 388	Pete Daley	4.00	2.00	.40
☐ 389	Dave Jolly	4.00	2.00	.40
☐ 390	Reno Bertoia	4.00	2.00	.40
☐ 391	Ralph Terry	8.00	4.00	.80
☐ 392	Chuck Tanner	6.00	3.00	.60
☐ 393	Raul Sanchez	4.00	2.00	.40
☐ 394	Luis Arroyo	5.00	2.50	.50
☐ 395	J.M. (Bubba) Phillips	4.00	2.00	.40

		NRMT	VG-E	GOOD
☐ 396	K. (Casey) Wise	4.00	2.00	.40
☐ 397	Roy Smalley	4.00	2.00	.40
☐ 398	Al Cicotte	5.00	2.50	.50
☐ 399	Billy Consolo	4.00	2.00	.40
☐ 400	Dodgers' Sluggers ..	150.00	75.00	15.00
	Carl Furillo			
	Gil Hodges			
	Roy Campanella			
	Duke Snider			
☐ 401	Earl Battey	5.00	2.50	.50
☐ 402	Jim Pisoni	4.00	2.00	.40
☐ 403	Dick Hyde	4.00	2.00	.40
☐ 404	Harry Anderson	4.00	2.00	.40
☐ 405	Duke Maas	4.00	2.00	.40
☐ 406	Bob Hale	4.00	2.00	.40
☐ 407	Yankee Power Hitters	300.00	100.00	20.00
	Mickey Mantle			
	Yogi Berra			
☐ 408	Checklist 1/2	100.00	10.00	2.00
	(unnumbered)			
☐ 409	Checklist 2/3	250.00	25.00	5.00
	(unnumbered)			
☐ 410	Checklist 3/4	300.00	30.00	6.00
	(unnumbered)			
☐ 411	Checklist 4/5	500.00	50.00	10.00
	(unnumbered)			

1958 Topps

Harmon Killebrew

*The cards in this 494-card set measure 2 ½"
by 3 ½". Although the last card is numbered*
495, number 145 was not issued, bringing the
set total to 494 cards. The 1958 Topps set contains the first Sport Magazine All-Star Selection
series (475-495) and expanded use of combination cards. The team cards carried series
checklists on back (Milwaukee, Detroit, Baltimore, and Cincinnati are also found with players listed alphabetically). Cards with the scarce
yellow name (YL) or team (YT) lettering, as opposed to the common white lettering, are noted
in the checklist. In the last series, cards of Stan
Musial and Mickey Mantle were triple printed;
the cards they replaced (443, 446, 450, and
462) on the printing sheet were hence printed
in shorter supply than other cards in the last
series and are marked with an SP in the list
below.

	NRMT	VG-E	GOOD
COMPLETE SET (494)	4000.00	2000.00	500.00
COMMON PLAYER (1-110)	4.00	2.00	.40
COMMON PLAYER (111-198) ..	3.00	1.50	.30
COMMON PLAYER (199-352) ..	2.50	1.25	.25
COMMON PLAYER (353-440) ..	2.25	1.10	.22
COMMON PLAYER (441-474) .	2.00	1.00	.20
COMMON PLAYER (475-495) ..	2.50	1.25	.25

			NRMT	VG-E	GOOD
☐	1	Ted Williams	325.00	100.00	20.00
☐	2A	Bob Lemon	15.00	7.50	1.50
☐	2B	Bob Lemon YT	35.00	17.50	3.50
☐	3	Alex Kellner	4.00	2.00	.40
☐	4	Hank Foiles	4.00	2.00	.40
☐	5	Willie Mays	135.00	65.00	13.50
☐	6	George Zuverink ...	4.00	2.00	.40
☐	7	Dale Long	5.00	2.50	.50
☐	8A	Eddie Kasko	4.00	2.00	.40
☐	8B	Eddie Kasko YL	21.00	10.50	2.10
☐	9	Hank Bauer	7.00	3.50	.70
☐	10	Lou Burdette	6.00	3.00	.60
☐	11A	Jim Rivera	4.00	2.00	.40
☐	11B	Jim Rivera YT	16.00	8.00	1.60
☐	12	George Crowe	4.00	2.00	.40
☐	13A	Billy Hoeft	4.00	2.00	.40
☐	13B	Billy Hoeft YL	21.00	10.50	2.10
☐	14	Rip Repulski	4.00	2.00	.40
☐	15	Jim Lemon	5.00	2.50	.50
☐	16	Charlie Neal	5.00	2.50	.50
☐	17	Felix Mantilla	4.00	2.00	.40
☐	18	Frank Sullivan	4.00	2.00	.40
☐	19	New York Giants	15.00	8.00	.80

		NRMT	VG-E	GOOD
	Team Card (checklist on back)			
☐ 20A	Gil McDougald	8.00	4.00	.80
☐ 20B	Gil McDougald YL	25.00	12.50	2.50
☐ 21	Curt Barclay	4.00	2.00	.40
☐ 22	Hal Naragon	4.00	2.00	.40
☐ 23A	Bill Tuttle	4.00	2.00	.40
☐ 23B	Bill Tuttle YL	21.00	10.50	2.10
☐ 24A	Hobie Landrith	4.00	2.00	.40
☐ 24B	Hobie Landrith YL	21.00	10.50	2.10
☐ 25	Don Drysdale	40.00	20.00	4.00
☐ 26	Ron Jackson	4.00	2.00	.40
☐ 27	Bud Freeman	4.00	2.00	.40
☐ 28	Jim Busby	4.00	2.00	.40
☐ 29	Ted Lepcio	4.00	2.00	.40
☐ 30A	Hank Aaron	135.00	65.00	13.50
☐ 30B	Hank Aaron YL	275.00	125.00	25.00
☐ 31	Tex Clevenger	4.00	2.00	.40
☐ 32A	J.W. Porter	4.00	2.00	.40
☐ 32B	J.W. Porter YL	21.00	10.50	2.10
☐ 33A	Cal Neeman	4.00	2.00	.40
☐ 33B	Cal Neeman YT	16.00	8.00	1.60
☐ 34	Bob Thurman	4.00	2.00	.40
☐ 35A	Don Mossi	5.00	2.50	.50
☐ 35B	Don Mossi YT	16.00	8.00	1.60
☐ 36	Ted Kazanski	4.00	2.00	.40
☐ 37	Mike McCormick (photo actually Ray Monzant)	6.00	3.00	.60
☐ 38	Dick Gernert	4.00	2.00	.40
☐ 39	Bob Martyn	4.00	2.00	.40
☐ 40	George Kell	12.50	6.25	1.25
☐ 41	Dave Hillman	4.00	2.00	.40
☐ 42	John Roseboro	7.00	3.50	.70
☐ 43	Sal Maglie	7.00	3.50	.70
☐ 44	Washington Senators Team Card (checklist on back)	7.50	2.50	.50
☐ 45	Dick Groat	6.00	3.00	.60
☐ 46A	Lou Sleater	4.00	2.00	.40
☐ 46B	Lou Sleater YL	21.00	10.50	2.10
☐ 47	Roger Maris	300.00	150.00	30.00
☐ 48	Chuck Harmon	4.00	2.00	.40
☐ 49	Smoky Burgess	5.00	2.50	.50
☐ 50A	Billy Pierce	6.00	3.00	.60
☐ 50B	Billy Pierce YT	21.00	10.50	2.10
☐ 51	Del Rice	4.00	2.00	.40
☐ 52A	Bob Clemente	90.00	45.00	9.00
☐ 52B	Bob Clemente YT	160.00	80.00	16.00
☐ 53A	Morrie Martin	4.00	2.00	.40
☐ 53B	Morrie Martin YL	21.00	10.50	2.10
☐ 54	Norm Siebern	4.00	2.00	.40
☐ 55	Chico Carrasquel	4.00	2.00	.40
☐ 56	Bill Fischer	4.00	2.00	.40
☐ 57A	Tim Thompson	4.00	2.00	.40
☐ 57B	Tim Thompson YL	21.00	10.50	2.10
☐ 58A	Art Schult	4.00	2.00	.40
☐ 58B	Art Schult YT	16.00	8.00	1.60
☐ 59	Dave Sisler	4.00	2.00	.40
☐ 60A	Del Ennis	5.00	2.50	.50
☐ 60B	Del Ennis YL	21.00	10.50	2.10
☐ 61A	Darrell Johnson	5.00	2.50	.50
☐ 61B	Darrell Johnson YL	21.00	10.50	2.10
☐ 62	Joe DeMaestri	4.00	2.00	.40
☐ 63	Joe Nuxhall	5.00	2.50	.50
☐ 64	Joe Lonnett	4.00	2.00	.40
☐ 65A	Von McDaniel	4.00	2.00	.40
☐ 65B	Von McDaniel YL	21.00	10.50	2.10
☐ 66	Lee Walls	4.00	2.00	.40
☐ 67	Joe Ginsberg	4.00	2.00	.40
☐ 68	Daryl Spencer	4.00	2.00	.40
☐ 69	Wally Burnette	4.00	2.00	.40
☐ 70A	Al Kaline	55.00	27.50	5.50
☐ 70B	Al Kaline YL	110.00	55.00	11.00
☐ 71	Dodgers Team (checklist on back)	20.00	6.00	1.25
☐ 72	Bud Byerly	4.00	2.00	.40
☐ 73	Pete Daley	4.00	2.00	.40
☐ 74	Roy Face	6.00	3.00	.60
☐ 75	Gus Bell	5.00	2.50	.50
☐ 76A	Dick Farrell	5.00	2.50	.50
☐ 76B	Dick Farrell YT	21.00	10.50	2.10
☐ 77A	Don Zimmer	7.00	3.50	.70
☐ 77B	Don Zimmer YT	21.00	10.50	2.10
☐ 78A	Ernie Johnson	5.00	2.50	.50
☐ 78B	Ernie Johnson YL	21.00	10.50	2.10
☐ 79A	Dick Williams	5.00	2.50	.50
☐ 79B	Dick Williams YT	21.00	10.50	2.10
☐ 80	Dick Drott	4.00	2.00	.40
☐ 81A	Steve Boros	5.00	2.50	.50
☐ 81B	Steve Boros YT	21.00	10.50	2.10
☐ 82	Ron Kline	4.00	2.00	.40
☐ 83	Bob Hazle	5.00	2.50	.50
☐ 84	Billy O'Dell	4.00	2.00	.40
☐ 85A	Luis Aparicio	16.00	8.00	1.60
☐ 85B	Luis Aparicio YT	32.00	16.00	3.20
☐ 86	Valmy Thomas	4.00	2.00	.40
☐ 87	Johnny Kucks	4.00	2.00	.40

			NRMT	VG-E	GOOD
☐	88	Duke Snider	50.00	25.00	5.00
☐	89	Billy Klaus	4.00	2.00	.40
☐	90	Robin Roberts	13.00	6.50	1.30
☐	91	Chuck Tanner	5.00	2.50	.50
☐	92A	Clint Courtney	4.00	2.00	.40
☐	92B	Clint Courtney YL	20.00	10.00	2.00
☐	93	Sandy Amoros	5.00	2.50	.50
☐	94	Bob Skinner	4.00	2.00	.40
☐	95	Frank Bolling	4.00	2.00	.40
☐	96	Joe Durham	4.00	2.00	.40
☐	97A	Larry Jackson	4.00	2.00	.40
☐	97B	Larry Jackson YL	21.00	10.50	2.10
☐	98A	Billy Hunter	4.00	2.00	.40
☐	98B	Billy Hunter YL	21.00	10.50	2.10
☐	99	Bobby Adams	4.00	2.00	.40
☐	100A	Early Wynn	13.00	6.50	1.30
☐	100B	Early Wynn YT	30.00	15.00	3.00
☐	101A	Bobby Richardson	10.00	5.00	1.00
☐	101B	Bobby Richardson YL	30.00	15.00	3.00
☐	102	George Strickland	4.00	2.00	.40
☐	103	Jerry Lynch	4.00	2.00	.40
☐	104	Jim Pendleton	4.00	2.00	.40
☐	105	Billy Gardner	5.00	2.50	.50
☐	106	Dick Schofield	4.00	2.00	.40
☐	107	Ossie Virgil	4.00	2.00	.40
☐	108A	Jim Landis	4.00	2.00	.40
☐	108B	Jim Landis YT	16.00	8.00	1.60
☐	109	Herb Plews	4.00	2.00	.40
☐	110	Johnny Logan	5.00	2.50	.50
☐	111	Stu Miller	3.00	1.50	.30
☐	112	Gus Zernial	4.00	2.00	.40
☐	113	Jerry Walker	3.00	1.50	.30
☐	114	Irv Noren	3.00	1.50	.30
☐	115	Jim Bunning	12.00	6.00	1.20
☐	116	Dave Philley	3.00	1.50	.30
☐	117	Frank Torre	3.00	1.50	.30
☐	118	Harvey Haddix	4.00	2.00	.40
☐	119	Harry Chiti	3.00	1.50	.30
☐	120	Johnny Podres	7.00	3.50	.70
☐	121	Eddie Miksis	3.00	1.50	.30
☐	122	Walt Moryn	3.00	1.50	.30
☐	123	Dick Tomanek	3.00	1.50	.30
☐	124	Bobby Usher	3.00	1.50	.30
☐	125	Alvin Dark	4.00	2.00	.40
☐	126	Stan Palys	3.00	1.50	.30
☐	127	Tom Sturdivant	4.00	2.00	.40
☐	128	Willie Kirkland	4.00	2.00	.40
☐	129	Jim Derrington	3.00	1.50	.30
☐	130	Jackie Jensen	7.00	3.50	.70

			NRMT	VG-E	GOOD
☐	131	Bob Henrich	3.00	1.50	.30
☐	132	Vern Law	4.00	2.00	.40
☐	133	Russ Nixon	5.00	2.50	.50
☐	134	Philadelphia Phillies Team Card (checklist on back)	7.50	2.50	.50
☐	135	Mike (Moe) Drabowsky	4.00	2.00	.40
☐	136	Jim Finigan	3.00	1.50	.30
☐	137	Russ Kemmerer	3.00	1.50	.30
☐	138	Earl Torgeson	3.00	1.50	.30
☐	139	George Brunet	3.00	1.50	.30
☐	140	Wes Covington	4.00	2.00	.40
☐	141	Ken Lehman	3.00	1.50	.30
☐	142	Enos Slaughter	16.00	8.00	1.60
☐	143	Billy Muffett	3.00	1.50	.30
☐	144	Bobby Morgan	3.00	1.50	.30
☐	145	Never issued	0.00	.00	.00
☐	146	Dick Gray	3.00	1.50	.30
☐	147	Don McMahon	4.00	2.00	.40
☐	148	Billy Consolo	3.00	1.50	.30
☐	149	Tom Acker	3.00	1.50	.30
☐	150	Mickey Mantle	500.00	250.00	50.00
☐	151	Buddy Pritchard	3.00	1.50	.30
☐	152	Johnny Antonelli	4.00	2.00	.40
☐	153	Les Moss	3.00	1.50	.30
☐	154	Harry Byrd	3.00	1.50	.30
☐	155	Hector Lopez	3.00	1.50	.30
☐	156	Dick Hyde	3.00	1.50	.30
☐	157	Dee Fondy	3.00	1.50	.30
☐	158	Cleveland Indians Team Card (checklist on back)	7.50	2.50	.50
☐	159	Taylor Phillips	3.00	1.50	.30
☐	160	Don Hoak	4.00	2.00	.40
☐	161	Don Larsen	7.00	3.50	.70
☐	162	Gil Hodges	18.00	9.00	1.80
☐	163	Jim Wilson	3.00	1.50	.30
☐	164	Bob Taylor	3.00	1.50	.30
☐	165	Bob Nieman	3.00	1.50	.30
☐	166	Danny O'Connell	3.00	1.50	.30
☐	167	Frank Baumann	3.00	1.50	.30
☐	168	Joe Cunningham	4.00	2.00	.40
☐	169	Ralph Terry	5.00	2.50	.50
☐	170	Vic Wertz	4.00	2.00	.40
☐	171	Harry Anderson	3.00	1.50	.30
☐	172	Don Gross	3.00	1.50	.30
☐	173	Eddie Yost	3.00	1.50	.30
☐	174	Athletics Team	7.50	2.50	.50

		NRMT	VG-E	GOOD			NRMT	VG-E	GOOD
	(checklist on back)				☐ 219	Camilo Pascual	3.00	1.50	.30
☐ 175	Marv Throneberry	7.00	3.50	.70	☐ 220	Tom Brewer	2.50	1.25	.25
☐ 176	Bob Buhl	3.00	1.50	.30	☐ 221	Jerry Kindall	3.00	1.50	.30
☐ 177	Al Smith	3.00	1.50	.30	☐ 222	Bud Daley	2.50	1.25	.25
☐ 178	Ted Kluszewski	7.00	3.50	.70	☐ 223	Andy Pafko	3.00	1.50	.30
☐ 179	Willie Miranda	3.00	1.50	.30	☐ 224	Bob Grim	3.00	1.50	.30
☐ 180	Lindy McDaniel	4.00	2.00	.40	☐ 225	Billy Goodman	3.00	1.50	.30
☐ 181	Willie Jones	3.00	1.50	.30	☐ 226	Bob Smith	2.50	1.25	.25
☐ 182	Joe Caffie	3.00	1.50	.30	☐ 227	Gene Stephens	2.50	1.25	.25
☐ 183	Dave Jolly	3.00	1.50	.30	☐ 228	Duke Maas	2.50	1.25	.25
☐ 184	Elvin Tappe	3.00	1.50	.30	☐ 229	Frank Zupo	2.50	1.25	.25
☐ 185	Ray Boone	4.00	2.00	.40	☐ 230	Richie Ashburn	10.00	5.00	1.00
☐ 186	Jack Meyer	3.00	1.50	.30	☐ 231	Lloyd Merritt	2.50	1.25	.25
☐ 187	Sandy Koufax	100.00	50.00	10.00	☐ 232	Reno Bertoia	2.50	1.25	.25
☐ 188	Milt Bolling	3.00	1.50	.30	☐ 233	Mickey Vernon	3.50	1.75	.35
	(photo actually Lou				☐ 234	Carl Sawatski	2.50	1.25	.25
	Berberet)				☐ 235	Tom Gorman	2.50	1.25	.25
☐ 189	George Susce	3.00	1.50	.30	☐ 236	Ed Fitzgerald	2.50	1.25	.25
☐ 190	Red Schoendienst	14.00	7.00	1.40	☐ 237	Bill Wight	2.50	1.25	.25
☐ 191	Art Ceccarelli	3.00	1.50	.30	☐ 238	Bill Mazeroski	8.00	4.00	.80
☐ 192	Milt Graff	3.00	1.50	.30	☐ 239	Chuck Stobbs	2.50	1.25	.25
☐ 193	Jerry Lumpe	3.00	1.50	.30	☐ 240	Bill Skowron	8.00	4.00	.80
☐ 194	Roger Craig	7.00	3.50	.70	☐ 241	Dick Littlefield	2.50	1.25	.25
☐ 195	Whitey Lockman	4.00	2.00	.40	☐ 242	Johnny Klippstein	2.50	1.25	.25
☐ 196	Mike Garcia	4.00	2.00	.40	☐ 243	Larry Raines	2.50	1.25	.25
☐ 197	Haywood Sullivan	4.00	2.00	.40	☐ 244	Don Demeter	2.50	1.25	.25
☐ 198	Bill Virdon	4.00	2.00	.40	☐ 245	Frank Lary	3.50	1.75	.35
☐ 199	Don Blasingame	2.50	1.25	.25	☐ 246	New York Yankees	33.00	8.00	2.00
☐ 200	Bob Keegan	2.50	1.25	.25		Team Card (checklist			
☐ 201	Jim Bolger	2.50	1.25	.25		on back)			
☐ 202	Woody Held	2.50	1.25	.25	☐ 247	Casey Wise	2.50	1.25	.25
☐ 203	Al Walker	2.50	1.25	.25	☐ 248	Herman Wehmeier	2.50	1.25	.25
☐ 204	Leo Kiely	2.50	1.25	.25	☐ 249	Ray Moore	2.50	1.25	.25
☐ 205	Johnny Temple	3.00	1.50	.30	☐ 250	Roy Sievers	3.50	1.75	.35
☐ 206	Bob Shaw	3.00	1.50	.30	☐ 251	Warren Hacker	2.50	1.25	.25
☐ 207	Solly Hemus	2.50	1.25	.25	☐ 252	Bob Trowbridge	2.50	1.25	.25
☐ 208	Cal McLish	2.50	1.25	.25	☐ 253	Don Mueller	3.00	1.50	.30
☐ 209	Bob Anderson	2.50	1.25	.25	☐ 254	Alex Grammas	2.50	1.25	.25
☐ 210	Wally Moon	3.50	1.75	.35	☐ 255	Bob Turley	7.00	3.50	.70
☐ 211	Pete Burnside	2.50	1.25	.25	☐ 256	Chicago White Sox	7.50	2.50	.50
☐ 212	Bubba Phillips	2.50	1.25	.25		Team Card (checklist			
☐ 213	Red Wilson	2.50	1.25	.25		on back)			
☐ 214	Willard Schmidt	2.50	1.25	.25	☐ 257	Hal Smith	2.50	1.25	.25
☐ 215	Jim Gilliam	7.00	3.50	.70	☐ 258	Carl Erskine	5.50	2.75	.55
☐ 216	St. Louis Cardinals	9.00	2.50	.50	☐ 259	Al Pilarcik	2.50	1.25	.25
	Team Card (checklist				☐ 260	Frank Malzone	3.50	1.75	.35
	on back)				☐ 261	Turk Lown	2.50	1.25	.25
☐ 217	Jack Harshman	2.50	1.25	.25	☐ 262	Johnny Groth	2.50	1.25	.25
☐ 218	Dick Rand	2.50	1.25	.25	☐ 263	Eddie Bressoud	2.50	1.25	.25

		NRMT	VG-E	GOOD
☐ 264	Jack Sanford	3.00	1.50	.30
☐ 265	Pete Runnels	3.00	1.50	.30
☐ 266	Connie Johnson	2.50	1.25	.25
☐ 267	Sherm Lollar	3.00	1.50	.30
☐ 268	Granny Hamner	2.50	1.25	.25
☐ 269	Paul Smith	2.50	1.25	.25
☐ 270	Warren Spahn	32.00	16.00	3.20
☐ 271	Billy Martin	14.00	7.00	1.40
☐ 272	Ray Crone	2.50	1.25	.25
☐ 273	Hal Smith	2.50	1.25	.25
☐ 274	Rocky Bridges	2.50	1.25	.25
☐ 275	Elston Howard	8.00	4.00	.80
☐ 276	Bobby Avila	3.00	1.50	.30
☐ 277	Virgil Trucks	3.00	1.50	.30
☐ 278	Mack Burk	2.50	1.25	.25
☐ 279	Bob Boyd	2.50	1.25	.25
☐ 280	Jim Piersall	6.00	3.00	.60
☐ 281	Sammy Taylor	2.50	1.25	.25
☐ 282	Paul Foytack	2.50	1.25	.25
☐ 283	Ray Shearer	2.50	1.25	.25
☐ 284	Ray Katt	2.50	1.25	.25
☐ 285	Frank Robinson	55.00	27.50	5.50
☐ 286	Gino Cimoli	3.00	1.50	.30
☐ 287	Sam Jones	3.00	1.50	.30
☐ 288	Harmon Killebrew	45.00	22.50	4.50
☐ 289	Series Hurling Rivals Lou Burdette Bobby Shantz	4.00	2.00	.40
☐ 290	Dick Donovan	2.50	1.25	.25
☐ 291	Don Landrum	2.50	1.25	.25
☐ 292	Ned Garver	2.50	1.25	.25
☐ 293	Gene Freese	2.50	1.25	.25
☐ 294	Hal Jeffcoat	2.50	1.25	.25
☐ 295	Minnie Minoso	7.00	3.50	.70
☐ 296	Ryne Duren	7.00	3.50	.70
☐ 297	Don Buddin	2.50	1.25	.25
☐ 298	Jim Hearn	2.50	1.25	.25
☐ 299	Harry Simpson	2.50	1.25	.25
☐ 300	Harridge and Giles League Presidents	6.00	3.00	.60
☐ 301	Randy Jackson	2.50	1.25	.25
☐ 302	Mike Baxes	2.50	1.25	.25
☐ 303	Neil Chrisley	2.50	1.25	.25
☐ 304	Tigers' Big Bats Harvey Kuenn Al Kaline	9.00	4.50	.90
☐ 305	Clem Labine	3.50	1.75	.35
☐ 306	Whammy Douglas	2.50	1.25	.25
☐ 307	Brooks Robinson	60.00	30.00	6.00
☐ 308	Paul Giel	2.50	1.25	.25
☐ 309	Gail Harris	2.50	1.25	.25
☐ 310	Ernie Banks	50.00	25.00	5.00
☐ 311	Bob Purkey	2.50	1.25	.25
☐ 312	Boston Red Sox Team Card (checklist on back)	9.00	2.50	.50
☐ 313	Bob Rush	2.50	1.25	.25
☐ 314	Dodgers' Boss and Power: Duke Snider Walt Alston	15.00	7.50	1.50
☐ 315	Bob Friend	3.50	1.75	.35
☐ 316	Tito Francona	2.50	1.25	.25
☐ 317	Albie Pearson	3.50	1.75	.35
☐ 318	Frank House	2.50	1.25	.25
☐ 319	Lou Skizas	2.50	1.25	.25
☐ 320	Whitey Ford	35.00	17.50	3.50
☐ 321	Sluggers Supreme Ted Kluszewski Ted Williams	25.00	12.50	2.50
☐ 322	Harding Peterson	3.00	1.50	.30
☐ 323	Elmer Valo	2.50	1.25	.25
☐ 324	Hoyt Wilhelm	13.00	6.50	1.30
☐ 325	Joe Adcock	3.50	1.75	.35
☐ 326	Bob Miller	2.50	1.25	.25
☐ 327	Chicago Cubs Team Card (checklist on back)	9.00	2.50	.50
☐ 328	Ike Delock	2.50	1.25	.25
☐ 329	Bob Cerv	3.00	1.50	.30
☐ 330	Ed Bailey	3.00	1.50	.30
☐ 331	Pedro Ramos	2.50	1.25	.25
☐ 332	Jim King	2.50	1.25	.25
☐ 333	Andy Carey	3.50	1.75	.35
☐ 334	Mound Aces Bob Friend Billy Pierce	4.00	2.00	.40
☐ 335	Ruben Gomez	2.50	1.25	.25
☐ 336	Bert Hamric	2.50	1.25	.25
☐ 337	Hank Aguirre	2.50	1.25	.25
☐ 338	Walt Dropo	2.50	1.25	.25
☐ 339	Fred Hatfield	2.50	1.25	.25
☐ 340	Don Newcombe	6.00	3.00	.60
☐ 341	Pittsburgh Pirates Team Card (checklist on back)	7.50	2.50	.50
☐ 342	Jim Brosnan	3.00	1.50	.30
☐ 343	Orlando Cepeda	45.00	22.50	4.50
☐ 344	Bob Porterfield	2.50	1.25	.25

		NRMT	VG-E	GOOD
☐ 345	Jim Hegan	3.00	1.50	.30
☐ 346	Steve Bilko	2.50	1.25	.25
☐ 347	Don Rudolph	2.50	1.25	.25
☐ 348	Chico Fernandez	2.50	1.25	.25
☐ 349	Murry Dickson	2.50	1.25	.25
☐ 350	Ken Boyer	6.00	3.00	.60
☐ 351	Braves Fence Busters	18.00	9.00	1.80
	Del Crandall			
	Eddie Mathews			
	Hank Aaron			
	Joe Adcock			
☐ 352	Herb Score	5.00	2.50	.50
☐ 353	Stan Lopata	2.50	1.25	.25
☐ 354	Art Ditmar	3.00	1.50	.30
☐ 355	Bill Bruton	3.00	1.50	.30
☐ 356	Bob Malkmus	2.50	1.25	.25
☐ 357	Danny McDevitt	2.50	1.25	.25
☐ 358	Gene Baker	2.50	1.25	.25
☐ 359	Billy Loes	2.50	1.25	.25
☐ 360	Roy McMillan	2.50	1.25	.25
☐ 361	Mike Fornieles	2.50	1.25	.25
☐ 362	Ray Jablonski	2.50	1.25	.25
☐ 363	Don Elston	2.50	1.25	.25
☐ 364	Earl Battey	3.00	1.50	.30
☐ 365	Tom Morgan	2.50	1.25	.25
☐ 366	Gene Green	2.50	1.25	.25
☐ 367	Jack Urban	2.50	1.25	.25
☐ 368	Rocky Colavito	10.00	5.00	1.00
☐ 369	Ralph Lumenti	2.50	1.25	.25
☐ 370	Yogi Berra	65.00	32.50	6.50
☐ 371	Marty Keough	2.50	1.25	.25
☐ 372	Don Cardwell	2.50	1.25	.25
☐ 373	Joe Pignatano	2.50	1.25	.25
☐ 374	Brooks Lawrence	2.50	1.25	.25
☐ 375	Pee Wee Reese	35.00	17.50	3.50
☐ 376	Charley Rabe	2.50	1.25	.25
☐ 377A	Milwaukee Braves	7.50	3.50	.70
	Team Card			
	(alphabetical)			
☐ 377B	Milwaukee Team	60.00	10.00	2.00
	numerical checklist			
☐ 378	Hank Sauer	3.50	1.75	.35
☐ 379	Ray Herbert	2.50	1.25	.25
☐ 380	Charley Maxwell	3.00	1.50	.30
☐ 381	Hal Brown	2.50	1.25	.25
☐ 382	Al Cicotte	3.00	1.50	.30
☐ 383	Lou Berberet	2.50	1.25	.25
☐ 384	John Goryl	2.50	1.25	.25
☐ 385	Wilmer Mizell	2.50	1.25	.25

		NRMT	VG-E	GOOD
☐ 386	Birdie's Sluggers	6.00	3.00	.60
	Ed Bailey			
	Birdie Tebbetts			
	Frank Robinson			
☐ 387	Wally Post	3.00	1.50	.30
☐ 388	Billy Moran	2.50	1.25	.25
☐ 389	Bill Taylor	2.50	1.25	.25
☐ 390	Del Crandall	3.00	1.50	.30
☐ 391	Dave Melton	2.50	1.25	.25
☐ 392	Bennie Daniels	2.50	1.25	.25
☐ 393	Tony Kubek	12.50	6.25	1.25
☐ 394	Jim Grant	3.00	1.50	.30
☐ 395	Willard Nixon	2.50	1.25	.25
☐ 396	Dutch Dotterer	2.50	1.25	.25
☐ 397A	Detroit Tigers	7.50	3.50	.70
	Team Card			
	(alphabetical)			
☐ 397B	Detroit Team	60.00	10.00	2.00
	numerical checklist			
☐ 398	Gene Woodling	3.50	1.75	.35
☐ 399	Marv Grissom	2.50	1.25	.25
☐ 400	Nellie Fox	9.00	4.50	.90
☐ 401	Don Bessent	3.00	1.50	.30
☐ 402	Bobby Gene Smith	2.50	1.25	.25
☐ 403	Steve Korcheck	2.50	1.25	.25
☐ 404	Curt Simmons	3.50	1.75	.35
☐ 405	Ken Aspromonte	2.50	1.25	.25
☐ 406	Vic Power	3.00	1.50	.30
☐ 407	Carlton Willey	2.50	1.25	.25
☐ 408A	Baltimore Orioles	7.50	3.50	.70
	Team Card			
	(alphabetical)			
☐ 408B	Baltimore Team	60.00	10.00	2.00
	numerical checklist			
☐ 409	Frank Thomas	3.00	1.50	.30
☐ 410	Murray Wall	2.50	1.25	.25
☐ 411	Tony Taylor	2.50	1.25	.25
☐ 412	Jerry Staley	2.50	1.25	.25
☐ 413	Jim Davenport	3.00	1.50	.30
☐ 414	Sammy White	2.50	1.25	.25
☐ 415	Bob Bowman	2.50	1.25	.25
☐ 416	Foster Castleman	2.50	1.25	.25
☐ 417	Carl Furillo	6.00	3.00	.60
☐ 418	World Series Batting	125.00	60.00	12.50
	Foes: Mickey Mantle			
	Hank Aaron			
☐ 419	Bobby Shantz	5.00	2.50	.50
☐ 420	Vada Pinson	16.00	8.00	1.60
☐ 421	Dixie Howell	2.50	1.25	.25

		NRMT	VG-E	GOOD
☐ 422	Norm Zauchin	2.50	1.25	.25
☐ 423	Phil Clark	2.50	1.25	.25
☐ 424	Larry Doby	5.00	2.50	.50
☐ 425	Sammy Esposito	2.50	1.25	.25
☐ 426	Johnny O'Brien	2.50	1.25	.25
☐ 427	Al Worthington	2.50	1.25	.25
☐ 428A	Cincinnati Reds Team Card (alphabetical)	7.50	3.50	.70
☐ 428B	Cincinnati Team numerical checklist	60.00	10.00	2.00
☐ 429	Gus Triandos	3.00	1.50	.30
☐ 430	Bobby Thomson	4.00	2.00	.40
☐ 431	Gene Conley	3.00	1.50	.30
☐ 432	John Powers	2.50	1.25	.25
☐ 433A	Pancho Herrer ERR	500.00	250.00	50.00
☐ 433B	Pancho Herrera COR	2.50	1.25	.25
☐ 434	Harvey Kuenn	5.00	2.50	.50
☐ 435	Ed Roebuck	3.00	1.50	.30
☐ 436	Rival Fence Busters Willie Mays Duke Snider	45.00	22.50	4.50
☐ 437	Bob Speake	2.50	1.25	.25
☐ 438	Whitey Herzog	5.00	2.50	.50
☐ 439	Ray Narleski	2.50	1.25	.25
☐ 440	Eddie Mathews	27.00	13.50	2.70
☐ 441	Jim Marshall	2.00	1.00	.20
☐ 442	Phil Paine	2.00	1.00	.20
☐ 443	Billy Harrell SP	8.00	4.00	.80
☐ 444	Danny Kravitz	2.00	1.00	.20
☐ 445	Bob Smith	2.00	1.00	.20
☐ 446	Carroll Hardy SP	8.00	4.00	.80
☐ 447	Ray Monzant	2.00	1.00	.20
☐ 448	Charlie Lau	5.00	2.50	.50
☐ 449	Gene Fodge	2.00	1.00	.20
☐ 450	Preston Ward SP	8.00	4.00	.80
☐ 451	Joe Taylor	2.00	1.00	.20
☐ 452	Roman Mejias	2.00	1.00	.20
☐ 453	Tom Qualters	2.00	1.00	.20
☐ 454	Harry Hanebrink	2.00	1.00	.20
☐ 455	Hal Griggs	2.00	1.00	.20
☐ 456	Dick Brown	2.00	1.00	.20
☐ 457	Milt Pappas	5.00	2.50	.50
☐ 458	Julio Becquer	2.00	1.00	.20
☐ 459	Ron Blackburn	2.00	1.00	.20
☐ 460	Chuck Essegian	2.00	1.00	.20
☐ 461	Ed Mayer	2.00	1.00	.20
☐ 462	Gary Geiger SP	8.00	4.00	.80
☐ 463	Vito Valentinetti	2.00	1.00	.20
☐ 464	Curt Flood	11.00	5.50	1.10
☐ 465	Arnie Portocarrero	2.00	1.00	.20
☐ 466	Pete Whisenant	2.00	1.00	.20
☐ 467	Glen Hobbie	2.00	1.00	.20
☐ 468	Bob Schmidt	2.00	1.00	.20
☐ 469	Don Ferrarese	2.00	1.00	.20
☐ 470	R.C. Stevens	2.00	1.00	.20
☐ 471	Lenny Green	2.00	1.00	.20
☐ 472	Joey Jay	2.50	1.25	.25
☐ 473	Bill Renna	2.00	1.00	.20
☐ 474	Roman Semproch	2.00	1.00	.20
☐ 475	Haney/Stengel AS (checklist back)	13.50	5.00	1.00
☐ 476	Stan Musial AS TP	25.00	12.50	2.50
☐ 477	Bill Skowron AS	4.00	2.00	.40
☐ 478	Johnny Temple AS	2.50	1.25	.25
☐ 479	Nellie Fox AS	6.00	3.00	.60
☐ 480	Eddie Mathews AS	11.00	5.50	1.10
☐ 481	Frank Malzone AS	2.50	1.25	.25
☐ 482	Ernie Banks AS	12.50	6.25	1.25
☐ 483	Luis Aparicio AS	8.00	4.00	.80
☐ 484	Frank Robinson AS	12.50	6.25	1.25
☐ 485	Ted Williams AS	45.00	22.50	4.50
☐ 486	Willie Mays AS	32.00	16.00	3.20
☐ 487	Mickey Mantle AS TP	65.00	32.50	6.50
☐ 488	Hank Aaron AS	32.00	16.00	3.20
☐ 489	Jackie Jensen AS	3.50	1.75	.35
☐ 490	Ed Bailey AS	2.50	1.25	.25
☐ 491	Sherm Lollar AS	2.50	1.25	.25
☐ 492	Bob Friend AS	2.50	1.25	.25
☐ 493	Bob Turley AS	3.00	1.50	.30
☐ 494	Warren Spahn AS	12.50	6.25	1.25
☐ 495	Herb Score AS	5.00	1.50	.30

1959 Topps

al kaline

DETROIT TIGERS
OUTFIELD

*The cards in this 572-card set measure 2 ½"
by 3 ½". The 1959 Topps set contains bust
pictures of the players in a colored circle. Card
numbers 551 to 572 are Sporting News All-Star
Selections. High numbers 507 to 572 have the
card number in a black background on the
reverse rather than a green background as in
the lower numbers. The high numbers are
more difficult to obtain. Several cards in the
300s exist with or without an extra traded or
option line on the back of the card. Cards 199
to 286 exist with either white or gray backs.
Cards 461 to 470 contain "Highlights" while
cards 116 to 146 give an alphabetically ordered
listing of "Rookie Prospects." These Rookie
Prospects (RP) were Topps' first organized inclusion of untested "Rookie" cards. Card 440
features Lew Burdette erroneously posing as
a left-handed pitcher. There were some three-
card advertising panels produced by Topps;
the players included are from the first series—
one panel shows Don McMahon, Red Wilson,
and Bob Boyd on the front with Ted
Kluszewski's reverse on one of the backs.
When cut apart, these advertising cards are
distinguished by the non-standard card back,
i.e., part of an advertisement for the 1959
Topps set instead of the typical statistics and
biographical information about the player pictured.*

			NRMT	VG-E	GOOD
	COMPLETE SET (572)		4000.00	2000.00	500.00
	COMMON PLAYER (1-110)		3.00	1.50	.30
	COMMON PLAYER (111-506) ..		2.00	1.00	.20
	COMMON PLAYER (507-550) ..		8.50	4.25	.85
	COMMON PLAYER (551-572) ..		10.00	5.00	1.00
☐	1	Ford Frick	40.00	6.00	1.25
☐	2	Eddie Yost	3.00	1.50	.30
☐	3	Don McMahon	3.00	1.50	.30
☐	4	Albie Pearson	3.00	1.50	.30
☐	5	Dick Donovan	3.00	1.50	.30
☐	6	Alex Grammas	3.00	1.50	.30
☐	7	Al Pilarcik	3.00	1.50	.30
☐	8	Phillies Team	7.50	2.50	.50
		(checklist on back)			
☐	9	Paul Giel	3.00	1.50	.30
☐	10	Mickey Mantle	300.00	150.00	30.00
☐	11	Billy Hunter	3.00	1.50	.30
☐	12	Vern Law	4.00	2.00	.40
☐	13	Dick Gernert	3.00	1.50	.30
☐	14	Pete Whisenant	3.00	1.50	.30
☐	15	Dick Drott	3.00	1.50	.30
☐	16	Joe Pignatano	3.00	1.50	.30
☐	17	Danny's Stars	4.00	2.00	.40
		Frank Thomas			
		Ted Kluszewski			
☐	18	Jack Urban	3.00	1.50	.30
☐	19	Eddie Bressoud	3.00	1.50	.30
☐	20	Duke Snider	42.00	20.00	4.00
☐	21	Connie Johnson	3.00	1.50	.30
☐	22	Al Smith	3.00	1.50	.30
☐	23	Murry Dickson	3.00	1.50	.30
☐	24	Red Wilson	3.00	1.50	.30
☐	25	Don Hoak	3.00	1.50	.30
☐	26	Chuck Stobbs	3.00	1.50	.30
☐	27	Andy Pafko	3.00	1.50	.30
☐	28	Al Worthington	3.00	1.50	.30
☐	29	Jim Bolger	3.00	1.50	.30
☐	30	Nellie Fox	8.00	4.00	.80
☐	31	Ken Lehman	3.00	1.50	.30
☐	32	Don Buddin	3.00	1.50	.30
☐	33	Ed Fitzgerald	3.00	1.50	.30
☐	34	Pitchers Beware ...	7.00	3.50	.70
		Al Kaline			
		Charley Maxwell			
☐	35	Ted Kluszewski	6.00	3.00	.60
☐	36	Hank Aguirre	3.00	1.50	.30
☐	37	Gene Green	3.00	1.50	.30
☐	38	Billy Hunter	3.00	1.50	.30

			NRMT	VG-E	GOOD
☐	39	Ed Bouchee	3.00	1.50	.30
☐	40	Warren Spahn	32.00	16.00	3.20
☐	41	Bob Martyn	3.00	1.50	.30
☐	42	Murray Wall	3.00	1.50	.30
☐	43	Steve Bilko	3.00	1.50	.30
☐	44	Vito Valentinetti	3.00	1.50	.30
☐	45	Andy Carey	4.00	2.00	.40
☐	46	Bill R. Henry	3.00	1.50	.30
☐	47	Jim Finigan	3.00	1.50	.30
☐	48	Orioles Team (checklist on back)	7.50	2.50	.50
☐	49	Bill Hall	3.00	1.50	.30
☐	50	Willie Mays	110.00	55.00	11.00
☐	51	Rip Coleman	3.00	1.50	.30
☐	52	Coot Veal	3.00	1.50	.30
☐	53	Stan Williams	3.00	1.50	.30
☐	54	Mel Roach	3.00	1.50	.30
☐	55	Tom Brewer	3.00	1.50	.30
☐	56	Carl Sawatski	3.00	1.50	.30
☐	57	Al Cicotte	3.00	1.50	.30
☐	58	Eddie Miksis	3.00	1.50	.30
☐	59	Irv Noren	3.00	1.50	.30
☐	60	Bob Turley	6.00	3.00	.60
☐	61	Dick Brown	3.00	1.50	.30
☐	62	Tony Taylor	3.00	1.50	.30
☐	63	Jim Hearn	3.00	1.50	.30
☐	64	Joe DeMaestri	3.00	1.50	.30
☐	65	Frank Torre	3.00	1.50	.30
☐	66	Joe Ginsberg	3.00	1.50	.30
☐	67	Brooks Lawrence	3.00	1.50	.30
☐	68	Dick Schofield	3.00	1.50	.30
☐	69	Giants Team (checklist on back)	7.50	2.50	.50
☐	70	Harvey Kuenn	5.00	2.50	.50
☐	71	Don Bessent	3.00	1.50	.30
☐	72	Bill Renna	3.00	1.50	.30
☐	73	Ron Jackson Jim Lemon Roy Sievers	3.00	1.50	.30
☐	74	Directing Power Jim Lemon Cookie Lavagetto Roy Sievers	4.00	2.00	.40
☐	75	Sam Jones	4.00	2.00	.40
☐	76	Bobby Richardson	8.00	4.00	.80
☐	77	John Goryl	3.00	1.50	.30
☐	78	Pedro Ramos	3.00	1.50	.30
☐	79	Harry Chiti	3.00	1.50	.30
☐	80	Minnie Minoso	6.00	3.00	.60

			NRMT	VG-E	GOOD
☐	81	Hal Jeffcoat	3.00	1.50	.30
☐	82	Bob Boyd	3.00	1.50	.30
☐	83	Bob Smith	3.00	1.50	.30
☐	84	Reno Bertoia	3.00	1.50	.30
☐	85	Harry Anderson	3.00	1.50	.30
☐	86	Bob Keegan	3.00	1.50	.30
☐	87	Danny O'Connell	3.00	1.50	.30
☐	88	Herb Score	5.00	2.50	.50
☐	89	Billy Gardner	4.00	2.00	.40
☐	90	Bill Skowron	7.00	3.50	.70
☐	91	Billy Hunter	3.00	1.50	.30
☐	92	Dave Philley	3.00	1.50	.30
☐	93	Julio Becquer	3.00	1.50	.30
☐	94	White Sox Team (checklist on back)	7.50	2.50	.50
☐	95	Carl Willey	3.00	1.50	.30
☐	96	Lou Berberet	3.00	1.50	.30
☐	97	Jerry Lynch	3.00	1.50	.30
☐	98	Arnie Portocarrero	3.00	1.50	.30
☐	99	Ted Kazanski	3.00	1.50	.30
☐	100	Bob Cerv	4.00	2.00	.40
☐	101	Alex Kellner	3.00	1.50	.30
☐	102	Felipe Alou	7.00	3.50	.70
☐	103	Billy Goodman	4.00	2.00	.40
☐	104	Del Rice	3.00	1.50	.30
☐	105	Lee Walls	3.00	1.50	.30
☐	106	Hal Woodeschick	3.00	1.50	.30
☐	107	Norm Larker	4.00	2.00	.40
☐	108	Zack Monroe	3.00	1.50	.30
☐	109	Bob Schmidt	3.00	1.50	.30
☐	110	George Witt	3.00	1.50	.30
☐	111	Redlegs Team (checklist on back)	7.50	2.50	.50
☐	112	Billy Consolo	2.00	1.00	.20
☐	113	Taylor Phillips	2.00	1.00	.20
☐	114	Earl Battey	2.00	1.00	.20
☐	115	Mickey Vernon	3.00	1.50	.30
☐	116	Bob Allison RP	5.00	2.50	.50
☐	117	Bob Blanchard RP	3.00	1.50	.30
☐	118	John Buzhardt RP	2.00	1.00	.20
☐	119	John Callison RP	4.00	2.00	.40
☐	120	Chuck Coles RP	2.00	1.00	.20
☐	121	Bob Conley RP	2.00	1.00	.20
☐	122	Bennie Daniels RP	2.00	1.00	.20
☐	123	Don Dillard RP	2.00	1.00	.20
☐	124	Dan Dobbek RP	2.00	1.00	.20
☐	125	Ron Fairly RP	4.00	2.00	.40
☐	126	Ed Haas RP	2.50	1.25	.25
☐	127	Kent Hadley RP	2.00	1.00	.20

		NRMT	VG-E	GOOD
☐ 128	Bob Hartman RP	2.00	1.00	.20
☐ 129	Frank Herrera RP ...	2.00	1.00	.20
☐ 130	Lou Jackson RP	2.00	1.00	.20
☐ 131	Deron Johnson RP ..	3.00	1.50	.30
☐ 132	Don Lee RP	2.00	1.00	.20
☐ 133	Bob Lillis	3.00	1.50	.30
☐ 134	Jim McDaniel RP	2.00	1.00	.20
☐ 135	Gene Oliver RP	2.00	1.00	.20
☐ 136	Jim O'Toole RP	3.00	1.50	.30
☐ 137	Dick Ricketts RP	2.00	1.00	.20
☐ 138	John Romano RP	2.50	1.25	.25
☐ 139	Ed Sadowski RP	2.00	1.00	.20
☐ 140	Charlie Secrest RP .	2.00	1.00	.20
☐ 141	Joe Shipley RP	2.00	1.00	.20
☐ 142	Dick Stigman RP	2.00	1.00	.20
☐ 143	Willie Tasby RP	2.00	1.00	.20
☐ 144	Jerry Walker RP	2.00	1.00	.20
☐ 145	Dom Zanni RP	2.00	1.00	.20
☐ 146	Jerry Zimmerman RP	2.00	1.00	.20
☐ 147	Cubs Clubbers	7.00	3.50	.70
	Dale Long			
	Ernie Banks			
	Walt Moryn			
☐ 148	Mike McCormick	3.00	1.50	.30
☐ 149	Jim Bunning	8.00	4.00	.80
☐ 150	Stan Musial	110.00	55.00	11.00
☐ 151	Bob Malkmus	2.00	1.00	.20
☐ 152	Johnny Klippstein ...	2.00	1.00	.20
☐ 153	Jim Marshall	2.00	1.00	.20
☐ 154	Ray Herbert	2.00	1.00	.20
☐ 155	Enos Slaughter	12.50	6.25	1.25
☐ 156	Ace Hurlers	4.00	2.00	.40
	Billy Pierce			
	Robin Roberts			
☐ 157	Felix Mantilla	2.00	1.00	.20
☐ 158	Walt Dropo	2.00	1.00	.20
☐ 159	Bob Shaw	2.00	1.00	.20
☐ 160	Dick Groat	4.00	2.00	.40
☐ 161	Frank Baumann	2.00	1.00	.20
☐ 162	Bobby G. Smith	2.00	1.00	.20
☐ 163	Sandy Koufax	100.00	50.00	10.00
☐ 164	Johnny Groth	2.00	1.00	.20
☐ 165	Bill Bruton	2.50	1.25	.25
☐ 166	Destruction Crew	5.00	2.50	.50
	Minnie Minoso			
	Rocky Colavito			
	(misspelled Colovito			
	on card back)			
	Larry Doby			
☐ 167	Duke Maas	2.00	1.00	.20
☐ 168	Carroll Hardy	2.00	1.00	.20
☐ 169	Ted Abernathy	2.00	1.00	.20
☐ 170	Gene Woodling	3.00	1.50	.30
☐ 171	Willard Schmidt	2.00	1.00	.20
☐ 172	Athletics Team	7.50	2.50	.50
	(checklist on back)			
☐ 173	Bill Monbouquette ...	2.00	1.00	.20
☐ 174	Jim Pendleton	2.00	1.00	.20
☐ 175	Dick Farrell	2.00	1.00	.20
☐ 176	Preston Ward	2.00	1.00	.20
☐ 177	John Briggs	2.00	1.00	.20
☐ 178	Ruben Amaro	2.00	1.00	.20
☐ 179	Don Rudolph	2.00	1.00	.20
☐ 180	Yogi Berra	50.00	25.00	5.00
☐ 181	Bob Porterfield	2.00	1.00	.20
☐ 182	Milt Graff	2.00	1.00	.20
☐ 183	Stu Miller	2.50	1.25	.25
☐ 184	Harvey Haddix	3.00	1.50	.30
☐ 185	Jim Busby	2.00	1.00	.20
☐ 186	Mudcat Grant	2.00	1.00	.20
☐ 187	Bubba Phillips	2.00	1.00	.20
☐ 188	Juan Pizzaro	2.00	1.00	.20
☐ 189	Neil Chrisley	2.00	1.00	.20
☐ 190	Bill Virdon	3.50	1.75	.35
☐ 191	Russ Kemmerer	2.00	1.00	.20
☐ 192	Charlie Beamon	2.00	1.00	.20
☐ 193	Sammy Taylor	2.00	1.00	.20
☐ 194	Jim Brosnan	2.50	1.25	.25
☐ 195	Rip Repulski	2.00	1.00	.20
☐ 196	Billy Moran	2.00	1.00	.20
☐ 197	Ray Semproch	2.00	1.00	.20
☐ 198	Jim Davenport	2.50	1.25	.25
☐ 199	Leo Kiely	2.00	1.00	.20
☐ 200	Warren Giles	4.00	2.00	.40
	(NL President)			
☐ 201	Tom Acker	2.00	1.00	.20
☐ 202	Roger Maris	100.00	50.00	10.00
☐ 203	Ossie Virgil	2.00	1.00	.20
☐ 204	Casey Wise	2.00	1.00	.20
☐ 205	Don Larsen	4.00	2.00	.40
☐ 206	Carl Furillo	5.00	2.50	.50
☐ 207	George Strickland ...	2.00	1.00	.20
☐ 208	Willie Jones	2.00	1.00	.20
☐ 209	Lenny Green	2.00	1.00	.20
☐ 210	Ed Bailey	2.50	1.25	.25
☐ 211	Bob Blaylock	2.00	1.00	.20
☐ 212	Fence Busters	25.00	11.00	2.20
☐ 213	Jim Rivera	2.00	1.00	.20

		NRMT	VG-E	GOOD			NRMT	VG-E	GOOD
	Hank Aaron								
	Eddie Mathews				☐ 256	Jerry Davie	2.00	1.00	.20
☐ 214	Marcelino Solis	2.00	1.00	.20	☐ 257	Leon Wagner	2.00	1.00	.20
☐ 215	Jim Lemon	2.50	1.25	.25	☐ 258	Fred Kipp	2.00	1.00	.20
☐ 216	Andre Rodgers	2.00	1.00	.20	☐ 259	Jim Pisoni	2.00	1.00	.20
☐ 217	Carl Erskine	3.50	1.75	.35	☐ 260	Early Wynn	12.00	6.00	1.20
☐ 218	Roman Mejias	2.00	1.00	.20	☐ 261	Gene Stephens	2.00	1.00	.20
☐ 219	George Zuverink	2.00	1.00	.20	☐ 262	Hitters' Foes	4.50	2.25	.45
☐ 220	Frank Malzone	2.50	1.25	.25		Johnny Podres			
☐ 221	Bob Bowman	2.00	1.00	.20		Clem Labine			
☐ 222	Bobby Shantz	3.00	1.50	.30		Don Drysdale			
☐ 223	Cardinals Team	7.50	2.50	.50	☐ 263	Bud Daley	2.00	1.00	.20
	(checklist on back)				☐ 264	Chico Carrasquel	2.00	1.00	.20
☐ 224	Claude Osteen	3.50	1.75	.35	☐ 265	Ron Kline	2.00	1.00	.20
☐ 225	Johnny Logan	2.50	1.25	.25	☐ 266	Woody Held	2.00	1.00	.20
☐ 226	Art Ceccarelli	2.00	1.00	.20	☐ 267	John Romonosky	2.00	1.00	.20
☐ 227	Hal W. Smith	2.00	1.00	.20	☐ 268	Tito Francona	2.50	1.25	.25
☐ 228	Don Gross	2.00	1.00	.20	☐ 269	Jack Meyer	2.00	1.00	.20
☐ 229	Vic Power	2.50	1.25	.25	☐ 270	Gil Hodges	12.50	6.25	1.25
☐ 230	Bill Fischer	2.00	1.00	.20	☐ 271	Orlando Pena	2.00	1.00	.20
☐ 231	Ellis Burton	2.00	1.00	.20	☐ 272	Jerry Lumpe	2.00	1.00	.20
☐ 232	Eddie Kasko	2.00	1.00	.20	☐ 273	Joey Jay	2.00	1.00	.20
☐ 233	Paul Foytack	2.00	1.00	.20	☐ 274	Jerry Kindall	2.50	1.25	.25
☐ 234	Chuck Tanner	3.00	1.50	.30	☐ 275	Jack Sanford	2.50	1.25	.25
☐ 235	Valmy Thomas	2.00	1.00	.20	☐ 276	Pete Daley	2.00	1.00	.20
☐ 236	Ted Bowsfield	2.00	1.00	.20	☐ 277	Turk Lown	2.00	1.00	.20
☐ 237	Run Preventers	5.00	2.50	.50	☐ 278	Chuck Essegian	2.50	1.25	.25
	Gil McDougald				☐ 279	Ernie Johnson	2.50	1.25	.25
	Bob Turley				☐ 280	Frank Bolling	2.00	1.00	.20
	Bob Richardson				☐ 281	Walt Craddock	2.00	1.00	.20
☐ 238	Gene Baker	2.00	1.00	.20	☐ 282	R.C. Stevens	2.00	1.00	.20
☐ 239	Bob Trowbridge	2.00	1.00	.20	☐ 283	Russ Heman	2.00	1.00	.20
☐ 240	Hank Bauer	4.50	2.25	.45	☐ 284	Steve Korcheck	2.00	1.00	.20
☐ 241	Billy Muffett	2.00	1.00	.20	☐ 285	Joe Cunningham	2.50	1.25	.25
☐ 242	Ron Samford	2.00	1.00	.20	☐ 286	Dean Stone	2.00	1.00	.20
☐ 243	Marv Grissom	2.00	1.00	.20	☐ 287	Don Zimmer	4.00	2.00	.40
☐ 244	Ted Gray	2.00	1.00	.20	☐ 288	Dutch Dotterer	2.00	1.00	.20
☐ 245	Ned Garver	2.00	1.00	.20	☐ 289	Johnny Kucks	2.50	1.25	.25
☐ 246	J.W. Porter	2.00	1.00	.20	☐ 290	Wes Covington	2.50	1.25	.25
☐ 247	Don Ferrarese	2.00	1.00	.20	☐ 291	Pitching Partners	2.50	1.25	.25
☐ 248	Red Sox Team	9.00	2.50	.50		Pedro Ramos			
	checklist on back					Camilo Pascual			
☐ 249	Bobby Adams	2.00	1.00	.20	☐ 292	Dick Williams	3.00	1.50	.30
☐ 250	Billy O'Dell	2.00	1.00	.20	☐ 293	Ray Moore	2.00	1.00	.20
☐ 251	Clete Boyer	3.50	1.75	.35	☐ 294	Hank Foiles	2.00	1.00	.20
☐ 252	Roy Boone	2.50	1.25	.25	☐ 295	Billy Martin	9.00	4.50	.90
☐ 253	Seth Morehead	2.00	1.00	.20	☐ 296	Ernie Broglio	3.00	1.50	.30
☐ 254	Zeke Bella	2.00	1.00	.20	☐ 297	Jackie Brandt	2.00	1.00	.20
☐ 255	Del Ennis	2.50	1.25	.25	☐ 298	Tex Clevenger	2.00	1.00	.20
					☐ 299	Billy Klaus	2.00	1.00	.20

		NRMT	VG-E	GOOD			NRMT	VG-E	GOOD
☐ 300	Richie Ashburn	9.00	4.50	.90	☐ 332	Ray Monzant	2.00	1.00	.20
☐ 301	Earl Averill	2.00	1.00	.20	☐ 333	Harry Simpson	2.00	1.00	.20
☐ 302	Don Mossi	2.50	1.25	.25	☐ 334	Glen Hobbie	2.00	1.00	.20
☐ 303	Marty Keough	2.00	1.00	.20	☐ 335	Johnny Temple	2.50	1.25	.25
☐ 304	Cubs Team	8.00	2.50	.50	☐ 336A	Billy Loes	2.00	1.00	.20
	(checklist on back)					(with traded line)			
☐ 305	Curt Raydon	2.00	1.00	.20	☐ 336B	Billy Loes	80.00	40.00	8.00
☐ 306	Jim Gilliam	2.00	1.00	.20		(no trade)			
☐ 307	Curt Barclay	2.00	1.00	.20	☐ 337	George Crowe	2.00	1.00	.20
☐ 308	Norm Sieburn	2.00	1.00	.20	☐ 338	Sparky Anderson	16.00	8.00	1.60
☐ 309	Sal Maglie	4.00	2.00	.40	☐ 339	Roy Face	4.00	2.00	.40
☐ 310	Luis Aparicio	12.00	6.00	1.20	☐ 340	Roy Sievers	2.50	1.25	.25
☐ 311	Norm Zauchin	2.00	1.00	.20	☐ 341	Tom Qualters	2.00	1.00	.20
☐ 312	Don Newcombe	3.50	1.75	.35	☐ 342	Ray Jablonski	2.00	1.00	.20
☐ 313	Frank House	2.00	1.00	.20	☐ 343	Billy Hoeft	2.00	1.00	.20
☐ 314	Don Cardwell	2.00	1.00	.20	☐ 344	Russ Nixon	2.50	1.25	.25
☐ 315	Joe Adcock	3.00	1.50	.30	☐ 345	Gil McDougald	5.00	2.50	.50
☐ 316A	Ralph Lumenti	2.00	1.00	.20	☐ 346	Batter Bafflers	2.50	1.25	.25
	(option)					David Sisler			
	(photo actually					Tom Brewer			
	Camilo Pascual)				☐ 347	Bob Buhl	2.00	1.00	.20
☐ 316B	Ralph Lumenti	80.00	40.00	8.00	☐ 348	Ted Lepcio	2.00	1.00	.20
	(no option)				☐ 349	Hoyt Wilhelm	12.00	6.00	1.20
	(photo actually				☐ 350	Ernie Banks	45.00	22.50	4.50
	Camilo Pascual)				☐ 351	Earl Torgeson	2.00	1.00	.20
☐ 317	Hitting Kings	15.00	7.50	1.50	☐ 352	Robin Roberts	12.50	6.25	1.25
	Willie Mays				☐ 353	Curt Flood	4.00	2.00	.40
	Richie Ashburn				☐ 354	Pete Burnside	2.00	1.00	.20
☐ 318	Rocky Bridges	2.00	1.00	.20	☐ 355	Jim Piersall	3.50	1.75	.35
☐ 319	David Hillman	2.00	1.00	.20	☐ 356	Bob Mabe	2.00	1.00	.20
☐ 320	Bob Skinner	2.50	1.25	.25	☐ 357	Dick Stuart	3.00	1.50	.30
☐ 321A	Bob Giallombardo	2.00	1.00	.20	☐ 358	Ralph Terry	3.00	1.50	.30
	(option)				☐ 359	Bill White	15.00	7.50	1.50
☐ 321B	Bob Giallombardo	80.00	40.00	8.00	☐ 360	Al Kaline	45.00	22.50	4.50
	(no option)				☐ 361	Willard Nixon	2.00	1.00	.20
☐ 322A	Harry Hanebrink	2.00	1.00	.20	☐ 362A	Dolan Nichols	2.00	1.00	.20
	(traded)					(with option line)			
☐ 322B	Harry Hanebrink	80.00	40.00	8.00	☐ 362B	Dolan Nichols	80.00	40.00	8.00
	(no trade)					(no option)			
☐ 323	Frank Sullivan	2.00	1.00	.20	☐ 363	Bobby Avila	2.50	1.25	.25
☐ 324	Don Demeter	2.00	1.00	.20	☐ 364	Danny McDevitt	2.00	1.00	.20
☐ 325	Ken Boyer	4.50	2.25	.45	☐ 365	Gus Bell	2.50	1.25	.25
☐ 326	Marv Throneberry	3.00	1.50	.30	☐ 366	Humberto Robinson	2.00	1.00	.20
☐ 327	Gary Bell	2.00	1.00	.20	☐ 367	Cal Neeman	2.00	1.00	.20
☐ 328	Lou Skizas	2.00	1.00	.20	☐ 368	Don Mueller	2.50	1.25	.25
☐ 329	Tigers Team	9.00	2.50	.50	☐ 369	Dick Tomanek	2.00	1.00	.20
	(checklist on back)				☐ 370	Pete Runnels	2.50	1.25	.25
☐ 330	Gus Triandos	2.50	1.25	.25	☐ 371	Dick Brodowski	2.00	1.00	.20
☐ 331	Steve Boros	2.50	1.25	.25	☐ 372	Jim Hegan	2.50	1.25	.25

		NRMT	VG-E	GOOD
☐ 373	Herb Plews	2.00	1.00	.20
☐ 374	Art Ditmar	2.50	1.25	.25
☐ 375	Bob Nieman	2.00	1.00	.20
☐ 376	Hal Naragon	2.00	1.00	.20
☐ 377	John Antonelli	2.50	1.25	.25
☐ 378	Gail Harris	2.00	1.00	.20
☐ 379	Bob Miller	2.00	1.00	.20
☐ 380	Hank Aaron	90.00	45.00	9.00
☐ 381	Mike Baxes	2.00	1.00	.20
☐ 382	Curt Simmons	2.50	1.25	.25
☐ 383	Words of Wisdom Don Larsen Casey Stengel	6.00	3.00	.60
☐ 384	David Sisler	2.00	1.00	.20
☐ 385	Sherm Lollar	2.50	1.25	.25
☐ 386	Jim Delsing	2.00	1.00	.20
☐ 387	Don Drysdale	25.00	12.50	2.50
☐ 388	Bob Will	2.00	1.00	.20
☐ 389	Joe Nuxhall	2.50	1.25	.25
☐ 390	Orlando Cepeda	8.00	4.00	.40
☐ 391	Milt Pappas	3.00	1.50	.30
☐ 392	Whitey Herzog	4.00	2.00	.40
☐ 393	Frank Lary	2.50	1.25	.25
☐ 394	Randy Jackson	2.00	1.00	.20
☐ 395	Elston Howard	5.00	2.50	.50
☐ 396	Bob Rush	2.00	1.00	.20
☐ 397	Senators Team (checklist on back)	7.50	2.50	.50
☐ 398	Wally Post	2.50	1.25	.25
☐ 399	Larry Jackson	2.00	1.00	.20
☐ 400	Jackie Jensen	4.00	2.00	.40
☐ 401	Ron Blackburn	2.00	1.00	.20
☐ 402	Hector Lopez	2.00	1.00	.20
☐ 403	Clem Labine	2.50	1.25	.25
☐ 404	Hank Sauer	2.50	1.25	.25
☐ 405	Roy McMillan	2.00	1.00	.20
☐ 406	Solly Drake	2.00	1.00	.20
☐ 407	Moe Drabowsky	2.00	1.00	.20
☐ 408	Keystone Combo Nellie Fox Luis Aparicio	6.00	3.00	.60
☐ 409	Gus Zernial	2.50	1.25	.25
☐ 410	Billy Pierce	3.00	1.50	.30
☐ 411	Whitey Lockman	2.50	1.25	.25
☐ 412	Stan Lopata	2.00	1.00	.20
☐ 413	Camilo Pascual (listed as Camillo on front and Pasqual on back)	2.50	1.25	.25

		NRMT	VG-E	GOOD
☐ 414	Dale Long	2.50	1.25	.25
☐ 415	Bill Mazeroski	4.50	2.25	.45
☐ 416	Haywood Sullivan	2.50	1.25	.25
☐ 417	Virgil Trucks	2.50	1.25	.25
☐ 418	Gino Cimoli	2.00	1.00	.20
☐ 419	Braves Team (checklist on back)	7.50	2.50	.50
☐ 420	Rocky Colavito	5.00	2.50	.50
☐ 421	Herman Wehmeier	2.00	1.00	.20
☐ 422	Hobie Landrith	2.00	1.00	.20
☐ 423	Bob Grim	2.50	1.25	.25
☐ 424	Ken Aspromonte	2.00	1.00	.20
☐ 425	Del Crandall	2.50	1.25	.25
☐ 426	Jerry Staley	2.00	1.00	.20
☐ 427	Charlie Neal	2.50	1.25	.25
☐ 428	Buc Hill Aces Ron Kline Bob Friend Vernon Law Roy Face	3.00	1.50	.30
☐ 429	Bobby Thomson	3.00	1.50	.30
☐ 430	Whitey Ford	30.00	15.00	3.00
☐ 431	Whammy Douglas	2.00	1.00	.20
☐ 432	Smoky Burgess	2.50	1.25	.25
☐ 433	Billy Harrell	2.00	1.00	.20
☐ 434	Hal Griggs	2.00	1.00	.20
☐ 435	Frank Robinson	35.00	17.50	3.50
☐ 436	Granny Hamner	2.00	1.00	.20
☐ 437	Ike Delock	2.00	1.00	.20
☐ 438	Sammy Esposito	2.00	1.00	.20
☐ 439	Brooks Robinson	35.00	17.50	3.50
☐ 440	Lou Burdette (posing as if lefthanded	6.00	3.00	.60
☐ 441	John Roseboro	3.00	1.50	.30
☐ 442	Ray Narleski	2.00	1.00	.20
☐ 443	Daryl Spencer	2.00	1.00	.20
☐ 444	Ron Hansen	2.50	1.25	.25
☐ 445	Cal McLish	2.00	1.00	.20
☐ 446	Rocky Nelson	2.00	1.00	.20
☐ 447	Bob Anderson	2.00	1.00	.20
☐ 448	Vada Pinson	4.00	2.00	.40
☐ 449	Tom Gorman	2.00	1.00	.20
☐ 450	Eddie Mathews	22.00	11.00	2.20
☐ 451	Jimmy Constable	2.00	1.00	.20
☐ 452	Chico Fernandez	2.00	1.00	.20
☐ 453	Les Moss	2.00	1.00	.20
☐ 454	Phil Clark	2.00	1.00	.20
☐ 455	Larry Doby	4.00	2.00	.40

		NRMT	VG-E	GOOD
☐ 456	Jerry Casale	2.00	1.00	.20
☐ 457	Dodgers Team (checklist on back)	12.50	3.50	.75
☐ 458	Gordon Jones	2.00	1.00	.20
☐ 459	Bill Tuttle	2.00	1.00	.20
☐ 460	Bob Friend	2.50	1.25	.25
☐ 461	Mantle Hits Homer	30.00	15.00	3.00
☐ 462	Colavito's Catch	3.50	1.75	.35
☐ 463	Kaline Batting Champ	8.00	4.00	.80
☐ 464	Mays' Series Catch	15.00	7.50	1.50
☐ 465	Sievers Sets Mark	3.00	1.50	.30
☐ 466	Pierce All-Star	3.00	1.50	.30
☐ 467	Aaron Clubs Homer	15.00	7.50	1.50
☐ 468	Snider's Play	8.00	4.00	.80
☐ 469	Hustler Banks	8.00	4.00	.80
☐ 470	Musial's 3000 Hit	12.00	6.00	1.20
☐ 471	Tom Sturdivant	2.00	1.00	.20
☐ 472	Gene Freese	2.00	1.00	.20
☐ 473	Mike Fornieles	2.00	1.00	.20
☐ 474	Moe Thacker	2.00	1.00	.20
☐ 475	Jack Harshman	2.00	1.00	.20
☐ 476	Indians Team checklist on back	7.50	2.50	.50
☐ 477	Barry Latman	2.00	1.00	.20
☐ 478	Bob Clemente	70.00	35.00	7.00
☐ 479	Lindy McDaniel	2.50	1.25	.25
☐ 480	Red Schoendienst	11.00	5.50	1.10
☐ 481	Charlie Maxwell	2.00	1.00	.20
☐ 482	Russ Meyer	2.00	1.00	.20
☐ 483	Clint Courtney	2.00	1.00	.20
☐ 484	Willie Kirkland	2.00	1.00	.20
☐ 485	Ryne Duren	3.00	1.50	.30
☐ 486	Sammy White	2.00	1.00	.20
☐ 487	Hal Brown	2.00	1.00	.20
☐ 488	Walt Moryn	2.00	1.00	.20
☐ 489	John Powers	2.00	1.00	.20
☐ 490	Frank Thomas	2.50	1.25	.25
☐ 491	Don Blasingame	2.00	1.00	.20
☐ 492	Gene Conley	2.00	1.00	.20
☐ 493	Jim Landis	2.00	1.00	.20
☐ 494	Don Paveletich	2.00	1.00	.20
☐ 495	Johnny Podres	4.00	2.00	.40
☐ 496	Wayne Terwilliger	2.00	1.00	.20
☐ 497	Hal R. Smith	2.00	1.00	.20
☐ 498	Dick Hyde	2.00	1.00	.20
☐ 499	Johnny O'Brien	2.00	1.00	.20
☐ 500	Vic Wertz	3.00	1.00	.20
☐ 501	Bob Tiefenauer	2.00	1.00	.20
☐ 502	Alvin Dark	3.00	1.50	.30

		NRMT	VG-E	GOOD
☐ 503	Jim Owens	2.00	1.00	.20
☐ 504	Ossie Alvarez	2.00	1.00	.20
☐ 505	Tony Kubek	8.00	4.00	.80
☐ 506	Bob Purkey	2.00	1.00	.20
☐ 507	Bob Hale	8.50	4.25	.85
☐ 508	Art Fowler	2.00	1.00	.20
☐ 509	Norm Cash	25.00	12.50	2.50
☐ 510	Yankees Team (checklist on back)	40.00	10.00	2.00
☐ 511	George Susce	8.50	4.25	.85
☐ 512	George Altman	8.50	4.25	.85
☐ 513	Tommy Carroll	8.50	4.25	.85
☐ 514	Bob Gibson	300.00	150.00	30.00
☐ 515	Harmon Killebrew	85.00	42.50	8.50
☐ 516	Mike Garcia	10.00	5.00	1.00
☐ 517	Joe Koppe	8.50	4.25	.85
☐ 518	Mike Cueller	15.00	7.50	1.50
☐ 519	Infield Power Pete Runnels Dick Gernert Frank Malzone	12.00	6.00	1.20
☐ 520	Don Elston	8.50	4.25	.85
☐ 521	Gary Geiger	8.50	4.25	.85
☐ 522	Gene Snyder	8.50	4.25	.85
☐ 523	Harry Bright	8.50	4.25	.85
☐ 524	Larry Osborne	8.50	4.25	.85
☐ 525	Jim Coates	8.50	4.25	.85
☐ 526	Bob Speake	8.50	4.25	.85
☐ 527	Solly Hemus	8.50	4.25	.85
☐ 528	Pirates Team (checklist on back)	22.00	7.00	1.50
☐ 529	George Bamberger	12.00	6.00	1.20
☐ 530	Wally Moon	10.00	5.00	1.00
☐ 531	Ray Webster	8.50	4.25	.85
☐ 532	Mark Freeman	8.50	4.25	.85
☐ 533	Darrell Johnson	10.00	5.00	1.00
☐ 534	Faye Thornberry	8.50	4.25	.85
☐ 535	Ruben Gomez	8.50	4.25	.85
☐ 536	Danny Kravitz	8.50	4.25	.85
☐ 537	Rudolph Arias	8.50	4.25	.85
☐ 538	Chick King	8.50	4.25	.85
☐ 539	Gary Blaylock	8.50	4.25	.85
☐ 540	Willie Miranda	8.50	4.25	.85
☐ 541	Bob Thurman	8.50	4.25	.85
☐ 542	Jim Perry	15.00	7.50	1.50
☐ 543	Corsair Trio Bob Skinner Bill Virdon Roberto Clemente	50.00	25.00	5.00

1960 Topps

			NRMT	VG-E	GOOD
☐	544	Lee Tate	8.50	4.25	.85
☐	545	Tom Morgan	8.50	4.25	.85
☐	546	Al Schroll	8.50	4.25	.85
☐	547	Jim Baxes	8.50	4.25	.85
☐	548	Elmer Singleton	8.50	4.25	.85
☐	549	Howie Nunn	8.50	4.25	.85
☐	550	Roy Campanella	100.00	50.00	10.00
		(Symbol of Courage)			
☐	551	Fred Haney MG AS	10.00	5.00	1.00
☐	552	Casey Stengel MG AS	25.00	12.50	2.50
☐	553	Orlando Cepeda AS	12.50	6.25	1.25
☐	554	Bill Skowron AS	11.00	5.50	1.10
☐	555	Bill Mazeroski AS	11.00	5.50	1.10
☐	556	Nellie Fox AS	14.00	7.00	1.40
☐	557	Ken Boyer AS	12.50	6.25	1.25
☐	558	Frank Malzone AS	10.00	5.00	1.00
☐	559	Ernie Banks AS	30.00	15.00	3.00
☐	560	Luis Aparicio AS	17.00	8.50	1.70
☐	561	Hank Aaron AS	80.00	40.00	8.00
☐	562	Al Kaline AS	30.00	15.00	3.00
☐	563	Willie Mays AS	80.00	40.00	8.00
☐	564	Mickey Mantle AS	175.00	85.00	18.00
☐	565	Wes Covington AS	10.00	5.00	1.00
☐	566	Roy Sievers AS	10.00	5.00	1.00
☐	567	Del Crandall AS	10.00	5.00	1.00
☐	568	Gus Triandos AS	10.00	5.00	1.00
☐	569	Bob Friend AS	10.00	5.00	1.00
☐	570	Bob Turley AS	11.00	5.50	1.10
☐	571	Warren Spahn AS	30.00	15.00	3.00
☐	572	Billy Pierce AS	14.00	5.00	1.00

*The cards in this 572-card set measure 2 ½"
by 3 ½". The 1960 Topps set is the only Topps
standard size issue to use a horizontally oriented design. World Series cards appeared for
the first time (385 to 391), and there is a
Rookie Prospect (RP) series (117-148), the
most famous of which is Carl Yastrzemski, and
a Sport Magazine All-Star Selection (AS) series (553-572). There are 16 manager cards
listed alphabetically from 212 through 227. The
coaching staff of each team was also afforded
their own card in a 16-card subset (455-470).
Cards 375 to 440 come with either gray or
white backs, and the high series (507-572)
were printed on a more limited basis than the
rest of the set. The team cards have series
checklists on the reverse.*

	NRMT	VG-E	GOOD
COMPLETE SET (572)	3500.00	1600.00	400.00
COMMON PLAYER (1-110)	1.25	.60	.12
COMMON PLAYER (111-198)	1.25	.60	.12
COMMON PLAYER (199-286)	1.50	.75	.15
COMMON PLAYER (287-440)	1.75	.85	.17
COMMON PLAYER (441-506)	3.00	1.50	.30
COMMON PLAYER (507-552)	8.00	4.00	.80
COMMON PLAYER (553-572)	10.00	5.00	1.00

☐	1	Early Wynn	30.00	15.00	3.00
☐	2	Roman Mejias	1.25	.60	.12
☐	3	Joe Adcock	1.75	.85	.17
☐	4	Bob Purkey	1.25	.60	.12

			NRMT	VG-E	GOOD
☐	5	Wally Moon	1.75	.85	.17
☐	6	Lou Berberet	1.25	.60	.12
☐	7	Master and Mentor	10.00	5.00	1.00
		Willie Mays			
		Bill Rigney			
☐	8	Bud Daley	1.25	.60	.12
☐	9	Faye Throneberry	1.25	.60	.12
☐	10	Ernie Banks	30.00	13.50	2.70
☐	11	Norm Siebern	1.25	.60	.12
☐	12	Milt Pappas	1.75	.85	.17
☐	13	Wally Post	1.25	.60	.12
☐	14	Jim Grant	1.25	.60	.12
☐	15	Pete Runnels	1.75	.85	.17
☐	16	Ernie Broglio	1.75	.85	.17
☐	17	Johnny Callison	1.75	.85	.17
☐	18	Dodgers Team	10.00	3.00	.50
		(checklist on back)			
☐	19	Felix Mantilla	1.25	.60	.12
☐	20	Roy Face	2.50	1.25	.25
☐	21	Dutch Dotterer	1.25	.60	.12
☐	22	Rocky Bridges	1.25	.60	.12
☐	23	Eddie Fisher	1.25	.60	.12
☐	24	Dick Gray	1.25	.60	.12
☐	25	Roy Sievers	1.75	.85	.17
☐	26	Wayne Terwilliger	1.25	.60	.12
☐	27	Dick Drott	1.25	.60	.12
☐	28	Brooks Robinson	32.00	16.00	3.20
☐	29	Clem Labine	1.75	.85	.17
☐	30	Tito Francona	1.75	.85	.17
☐	31	Sammy Esposito	1.25	.60	.12
☐	32	Sophomore Stalwarts	1.75	.85	.17
		Jim O'Toole			
		Vada Pinson			
☐	33	Tom Morgan	1.25	.60	.12
☐	34	George Anderson	3.50	1.75	.35
☐	35	Whitey Ford	27.00	13.50	2.70
☐	36	Russ Nixon	1.75	.85	.17
☐	37	Bill Bruton	1.25	.60	.12
☐	38	Jerry Casale	1.25	.60	.12
☐	39	Earl Averill	1.25	.60	.12
☐	40	Joe Cunningham	1.75	.85	.17
☐	41	Barry Latman	1.25	.60	.12
☐	42	Hobie Landrith	1.25	.60	.12
☐	43	Senators Team	5.00	2.00	.40
		(checklist on back)			
☐	44	Bobby Locke	1.25	.60	.12
☐	45	Roy McMillan	1.25	.60	.12
☐	46	Jerry Fisher	1.25	.60	.12
☐	47	Don Zimmer	3.00	1.50	.30

			NRMT	VG-E	GOOD
☐	48	Hal W. Smith	1.25	.60	.12
☐	49	Curt Raydon	1.25	.60	.12
☐	50	Al Kaline	27.00	13.50	2.70
☐	51	Jim Coates	1.25	.60	.12
☐	52	Dave Philley	1.25	.60	.12
☐	53	Jackie Brandt	1.25	.60	.12
☐	54	Mike Fornieles	1.25	.60	.12
☐	55	Bill Mazeroski	3.00	1.50	.30
☐	56	Steve Korcheck	1.25	.60	.12
☐	57	Win Savers	1.75	.85	.17
		Turk Lown			
		Jerry Staley			
☐	58	Gino Cimoli	1.25	.60	.12
☐	59	Juan Pizarro	1.25	.60	.12
☐	60	Gus Triandos	1.75	.85	.17
☐	61	Eddie Kasko	1.25	.60	.12
☐	62	Roger Craig	3.50	1.75	.35
☐	63	George Strickland	1.25	.60	.12
☐	64	Jack Meyer	1.25	.60	.12
☐	65	Elston Howard	4.00	2.00	.40
☐	66	Bob Trowbridge	1.25	.60	.12
☐	67	Jose Pagan	1.25	.60	.12
☐	68	Dave Hillman	1.25	.60	.12
☐	69	Billy Goodman	1.75	.85	.17
☐	70	Lew Burdette	2.50	1.25	.25
☐	71	Marty Keough	1.25	.60	.12
☐	72	Tigers Team	7.50	2.50	.50
		(checklist on back)			
☐	73	Bob Gibson	32.00	16.00	3.20
☐	74	Walt Moryn	1.25	.60	.12
☐	75	Vic Power	1.25	.60	.12
☐	76	Bill Fischer	1.25	.60	.12
☐	77	Hank Foiles	1.25	.60	.12
☐	78	Bob Grim	1.25	.60	.12
☐	79	Walt Dropo	1.25	.60	.12
☐	80	Johnny Antonelli	1.75	.85	.17
☐	81	Russ Snyder	1.25	.60	.12
☐	82	Ruben Gomez	1.25	.60	.12
☐	83	Tony Kubek	4.50	2.25	.45
☐	84	Hal R. Smith	1.25	.60	.12
☐	85	Frank Lary	1.75	.85	.17
☐	86	Dick Gernert	1.25	.60	.12
☐	87	John Romonosky	1.25	.60	.12
☐	88	John Roseboro	1.75	.85	.17
☐	89	Hal Brown	1.25	.60	.12
☐	90	Bobby Avila	1.25	.60	.12
☐	91	Bennie Daniels	1.25	.60	.12
☐	92	Whitey Herzog	3.50	1.75	.35
☐	93	Art Schult	1.25	.60	.12

			NRMT	VG-E	GOOD
☐	94	Leo Kiely	1.25	.60	.12
☐	95	Frank Thomas	1.75	.85	.17
☐	96	Ralph Terry	2.50	1.25	.25
☐	97	Ted Lepcio	1.25	.60	.12
☐	98	Gordon Jones	1.25	.60	.12
☐	99	Lenny Green	1.25	.60	.12
☐	100	Nellie Fox	5.00	2.50	.50
☐	101	Bob Miller	1.25	.60	.12
☐	102	Kent Hadley	1.25	.60	.12
☐	103	Dick Farrell	1.25	.60	.12
☐	104	Dick Schofield	1.25	.60	.12
☐	105	Larry Sherry	2.50	1.25	.25
☐	106	Billy Gardner	1.75	.85	.17
☐	107	Carlton Willey	1.25	.60	.12
☐	108	Pete Daley	1.25	.60	.12
☐	109	Clete Boyer	2.50	1.25	.25
☐	110	Cal McLish	1.25	.60	.12
☐	111	Vic Wertz	1.75	.85	.17
☐	112	Jack Harshman	1.25	.60	.12
☐	113	Bob Skinner	1.75	.85	.17
☐	114	Ken Aspromonte	1.25	.60	.12
☐	115	Fork and Knuckler	4.00	2.00	.40
		Roy Face			
		Hoyt Wilhelm			
☐	116	Jim Rivera	1.25	.60	.12
☐	117	Tom Borland RP	1.25	.60	.12
☐	118	Bob Bruce RP	1.25	.60	.12
☐	119	Chico Cardenas RP	1.75	.85	.17
☐	120	Duke Carmel RP	1.25	.60	.12
☐	121	Camilo Carreon RP	1.75	.85	.17
☐	122	Don Dillard RP	1.25	.60	.12
☐	123	Dan Dobbek RP	1.25	.60	.12
☐	124	Jim Donohue RP	1.25	.60	.12
☐	125	Dick Ellsworth RP	2.50	1.25	.25
☐	126	Chuck Estrada RP	2.50	1.25	.25
☐	127	Ron Hansen RP	1.75	.85	.17
☐	128	Bill Harris RP	1.25	.60	.12
☐	129	Bob Hartman RP	1.25	.60	.12
☐	130	Frank Herrera RP	1.25	.60	.12
☐	131	Ed Hobaugh RP	1.25	.60	.12
☐	132	Frank Howard RP	10.00	5.00	1.00
☐	133	Manuel Javier RP	2.50	1.25	.25
		(sic, Julian)			
☐	134	Deron Johnson RP	1.75	.85	.17
☐	135	Ken Johnson RP	1.25	.60	.12
☐	136	Jim Kaat RP	21.00	10.50	2.10
☐	137	Lou Klimchock RP	1.25	.60	.12
☐	138	Art Mahaffey RP	1.75	.85	.17
☐	139	Carl Mathias RP	1.25	.60	.12
☐	140	Julio Navarro RP	1.75	.85	.17
☐	141	Jim Proctor RP	1.25	.60	.12
☐	142	Bill Short RP	1.75	.85	.17
☐	143	Al Spangler RP	1.25	.60	.12
☐	144	Al Stieglitz RP	1.25	.60	.12
☐	145	Jim Umbricht RP	1.25	.60	.12
☐	146	Ted Wieand RP	1.25	.60	.12
☐	147	Bob Will RP	1.25	.60	.12
☐	148	Carl Yastrzemski RP	350.00	175.00	35.00
☐	149	Bob Nieman	1.25	.60	.12
☐	150	Billy Pierce	2.50	1.25	.25
☐	151	Giants Team	6.00	2.00	.40
		(checklist on back)			
☐	152	Gail Harris	1.25	.60	.12
☐	153	Bobby Thomson	2.50	1.25	.25
☐	154	Jim Davenport	1.75	.85	.17
☐	155	Charlie Neal	1.75	.85	.17
☐	156	Art Ceccarelli	1.25	.60	.12
☐	157	Rocky Nelson	1.25	.60	.12
☐	158	Wes Covington	1.75	.85	.17
☐	159	Jim Piersall	2.50	1.25	.25
☐	160	Rival All-Stars	30.00	15.00	3.00
		Mickey Mantle			
		Ken Boyer			
		Ray Narleski			
☐	161		1.25	.60	.12
☐	162	Sammy Taylor	1.25	.60	.12
☐	163	Hector Lopez	1.25	.60	.12
☐	164	Reds Team	6.00	2.00	.40
		(checklist on back)			
☐	165	Jack Sanford	1.75	.85	.17
☐	166	Chuck Essegian	1.25	.60	.12
☐	167	Valmy Thomas	1.25	.60	.12
☐	168	Alex Grammas	1.25	.60	.12
☐	169	Jake Striker	1.25	.60	.12
☐	170	Del Crandall	1.75	.85	.17
☐	171	Johnny Groth	1.25	.60	.12
☐	172	Willie Kirkland	1.25	.60	.12
☐	173	Billy Martin	7.00	3.50	.70
☐	174	Indians Team	5.00	2.00	.40
		(checklist on back)			
☐	175	Pedro Ramos	1.25	.60	.12
☐	176	Vada Pinson	3.00	1.50	.30
☐	177	Johnny Kucks	1.25	.60	.12
☐	178	Woody Held	1.25	.60	.12
☐	179	Rip Coleman	1.25	.60	.12
☐	180	Harry Simpson	1.25	.60	.12
☐	181	Billy Loes	1.25	.60	.12
☐	182	Glen Hobbie	1.25	.60	.12
☐	183	Eli Grba	1.25	.60	.12

		NRMT	VG-E	GOOD
☐ 184	Gary Geiger	1.25	.60	.12
☐ 185	Jim Owens	1.25	.60	.12
☐ 186	Dave Sisler	1.25	.60	.12
☐ 187	Jay Hook	1.25	.60	.12
☐ 188	Dick Williams	2.50	1.25	.25
☐ 189	Don McMahon	1.25	.60	.12
☐ 190	Gene Woodling	1.75	.85	.17
☐ 191	Johnny Klippstein	1.25	.60	.12
☐ 192	Danny O'Connell	1.25	.60	.12
☐ 193	Dick Hyde	1.25	.60	.12
☐ 194	Bobby Gene Smith	1.25	.60	.12
☐ 195	Lindy McDaniel	1.75	.85	.17
☐ 196	Andy Carey	1.75	.85	.17
☐ 197	Ron Kline	1.25	.60	.12
☐ 198	Jerry Lynch	1.25	.60	.12
☐ 199	Dick Donovan	1.50	.75	.15
☐ 200	Willie Mays	80.00	40.00	8.00
☐ 201	Larry Osborne	1.50	.75	.15
☐ 202	Fred Kipp	1.50	.75	.15
☐ 203	Sammy White	1.50	.75	.15
☐ 204	Ryne Duren	2.50	1.25	.25
☐ 205	Johnny Logan	2.00	1.00	.20
☐ 206	Claude Osteen	2.00	1.00	.20
☐ 207	Bob Boyd	1.50	.75	.15
☐ 208	White Sox Team (checklist on back)	5.00	2.00	.40
☐ 209	Ron Blackburn	1.50	.75	.15
☐ 210	Harmon Killebrew	21.00	10.50	2.10
☐ 211	Taylor Phillips	1.50	.75	.15
☐ 212	Walt Alston MG	8.00	4.00	.80
☐ 213	Chuck Dressen MG	2.00	1.00	.20
☐ 214	Jimmy Dykes MG	2.00	1.00	.20
☐ 215	Bob Elliott MG	2.00	1.00	.20
☐ 216	Joe Gordon MG	2.00	1.00	.20
☐ 217	Charlie Grimm MG	2.00	1.00	.20
☐ 218	Solly Hemus MG	2.00	1.00	.20
☐ 219	Fred Hutchinson MG	2.00	1.00	.20
☐ 220	Billy Jurges MG	2.00	1.00	.20
☐ 221	Cookie Lavagetto MG	2.00	1.00	.20
☐ 222	Al Lopez MG	6.00	3.00	.60
☐ 223	Danny Murtaugh MG	2.00	1.00	.20
☐ 224	Paul Richards MG	2.00	1.00	.20
☐ 225	Bill Rigney MG	2.00	1.00	.20
☐ 226	Eddie Sawyer MG	2.00	1.00	.20
☐ 227	Casey Stengel MG	15.00	7.50	1.50
☐ 228	Ernie Johnson	2.00	1.00	.20
☐ 229	Joe M. Morgan	5.00	2.50	.50
☐ 230	Mound Magicians Lou Burdette Warren Spahn Bob Buhl	5.00	2.50	.50
☐ 231	Hal Naragon	1.50	.75	.15
☐ 232	Jim Busby	1.50	.75	.15
☐ 233	Don Elston	1.50	.75	.15
☐ 234	Don Demeter	1.50	.75	.15
☐ 235	Gus Bell	2.00	1.00	.20
☐ 236	Dick Ricketts	1.50	.75	.15
☐ 237	Elmer Valo	1.50	.75	.15
☐ 238	Danny Kravitz	1.50	.75	.15
☐ 239	Joe Shipley	1.50	.75	.15
☐ 240	Luis Aparicio	10.00	5.00	1.00
☐ 241	Albie Pearson	1.50	.75	.15
☐ 242	Cardinals Team (checklist on back)	6.00	2.00	.40
☐ 243	Bubba Phillips	1.50	.75	.15
☐ 244	Hal Griggs	1.50	.75	.15
☐ 245	Eddie Yost	1.50	.75	.15
☐ 246	Lee Maye	1.50	.75	.15
☐ 247	Gil McDougald	3.50	1.75	.35
☐ 248	Del Rice	1.50	.75	.15
☐ 249	Earl Wilson	2.00	1.00	.20
☐ 250	Stan Musial	80.00	40.00	8.00
☐ 251	Bob Malkmus	1.50	.75	.15
☐ 252	Ray Herbert	1.50	.75	.15
☐ 253	Eddie Bressoud	1.50	.75	.15
☐ 254	Arnie Portocarrero	1.50	.75	.15
☐ 255	Jim Gilliam	3.50	1.75	.35
☐ 256	Dick Brown	1.50	.75	.15
☐ 257	Gordy Coleman	2.00	1.00	.20
☐ 258	Dick Groat	3.50	1.75	.35
☐ 259	George Altman	1.50	.75	.15
☐ 260	Power Plus Rocky Colavito Tito Francona	2.00	1.00	.20
☐ 261	Pete Burnside	1.50	.75	.15
☐ 262	Hank Bauer	2.50	1.25	.25
☐ 263	Darrell Johnson	2.00	1.00	.20
☐ 264	Robin Roberts	11.00	5.50	1.10
☐ 265	Rip Repulski	1.50	.75	.15
☐ 266	Joey Jay	1.50	.75	.15
☐ 267	Jim Marshall	1.50	.75	.15
☐ 268	Al Worthington	1.50	.75	.15
☐ 269	Gene Green	1.50	.75	.15
☐ 270	Bob Turley	2.50	1.25	.25
☐ 271	Julio Becquer	1.50	.75	.15
☐ 272	Fred Green	1.50	.75	.15
☐ 273	Neil Chrisley	1.50	.75	.15
☐ 274	Tom Acker	1.50	.75	.15

		NRMT	VG-E	GOOD			NRMT	VG-E	GOOD
☐ 275	Curt Flood	2.50	1.25	.25	☐ 321	Ron Fairly	2.50	1.25	.25
☐ 276	Ken McBride	1.50	.75	.15	☐ 322	Willie Tasby	1.75	.85	.17
☐ 277	Harry Bright	1.50	.75	.15	☐ 323	John Romano	1.75	.85	.17
☐ 278	Stan Williams	1.50	.75	.15	☐ 324	Jim Perry	3.00	1.50	.30
☐ 279	Chuck Tanner	2.00	1.00	.20	☐ 325	Jim O'Toole	2.50	1.25	.25
☐ 280	Frank Sullivan	1.50	.75	.15	☐ 326	Bob Clemente	75.00	37.50	7.50
☐ 281	Ray Boone	2.00	1.00	.20	☐ 327	Ray Sadecki	1.75	.85	.17
☐ 282	Joe Nuxhall	2.00	1.00	.20	☐ 328	Earl Battey	1.75	.85	.17
☐ 283	John Blanchard	2.00	1.00	.20	☐ 329	Zack Monroe	1.75	.85	.17
☐ 284	Don Gross	1.50	.75	.15	☐ 330	Harvey Kuenn	3.50	1.75	.35
☐ 285	Harry Anderson	1.50	.75	.15	☐ 331	Henry Mason	1.75	.85	.17
☐ 286	Ray Semproch	1.50	.75	.15	☐ 332	Yankees Team	20.00	5.00	1.00
☐ 287	Felipe Alou	2.50	1.25	.25		(checklist on back)			
☐ 288	Bob Mabe	1.75	.85	.17	☐ 333	Danny McDevitt	1.75	.85	.17
☐ 289	Willie Jones	1.75	.85	.17	☐ 334	Ted Abernathy	1.75	.85	.17
☐ 290	Jerry Lumpe	1.75	.85	.17	☐ 335	Red Schoendienst	10.00	5.00	1.00
☐ 291	Bob Keegan	1.75	.85	.17	☐ 336	Ike Delock	1.75	.85	.17
☐ 292	Dodger Backstops	2.50	1.25	.25	☐ 337	Cal Neeman	1.75	.85	.17
	Joe Pignatano				☐ 338	Ray Monzant	1.75	.85	.17
	John Roseboro				☐ 339	Harry Chiti	1.75	.85	.17
☐ 293	Gene Conley	1.75	.85	.17	☐ 340	Harvey Haddix	2.50	1.25	.25
☐ 294	Tony Taylor	1.75	.85	.17	☐ 341	Carroll Hardy	1.75	.85	.17
☐ 295	Gil Hodges	11.00	5.50	1.10	☐ 342	Casey Wise	1.75	.85	.17
☐ 296	Nelson Chittum	1.75	.85	.17	☐ 343	Sandy Koufax	80.00	40.00	8.00
☐ 297	Reno Bertoia	1.75	.85	.17	☐ 344	Clint Courtney	1.75	.85	.17
☐ 298	George Witt	1.75	.85	.17	☐ 345	Don Newcombe	3.00	1.50	.30
☐ 299	Earl Torgeson	1.75	.85	.17	☐ 346	J.C. Martin	1.75	.85	.17
☐ 300	Hank Aaron	80.00	40.00	8.00		(face actually Gary			
☐ 301	Jerry Davie	1.75	.85	.17		Peters)			
☐ 302	Phillies Team	5.00	2.00	.40	☐ 347	Ed Bouchee	1.75	.85	.17
	(checklist on back)				☐ 348	Barry Shetrone	1.75	.85	.17
☐ 303	Billy O'Dell	1.75	.85	.17	☐ 349	Moe Drabowsky	1.75	.85	.17
☐ 304	Joe Ginsberg	1.75	.85	.17	☐ 350	Mickey Mantle	300.00	150.00	30.00
☐ 305	Richie Ashburn	7.00	3.50	.70	☐ 351	Don Nottebart	1.75	.85	.17
☐ 306	Frank Baumann	1.75	.85	.17	☐ 352	Cincy Clouters	4.00	2.00	.40
☐ 307	Gene Oliver	1.75	.85	.17		Gus Bell			
☐ 308	Dick Hall	1.75	.85	.17		Frank Robinson			
☐ 309	Bob Hale	1.75	.85	.17		Jerry Lynch			
☐ 310	Frank Malzone	2.50	1.25	.25	☐ 353	Don Larsen	3.00	1.50	.30
☐ 311	Raul Sanchez	1.75	.85	.17	☐ 354	Bob Lillis	2.50	1.25	.25
☐ 312	Charley Lau	2.50	1.25	.25	☐ 355	Bill White	4.00	2.00	.40
☐ 313	Turk Lown	1.75	.85	.17	☐ 356	Joe Amalfitano	1.75	.85	.17
☐ 314	Chico Fernandez	1.75	.85	.17	☐ 357	Al Schroll	1.75	.85	.17
☐ 315	Bobby Shantz	3.00	1.50	.30	☐ 358	Joe DeMaestri	1.75	.85	.17
☐ 316	Willie McCovey	135.00	65.00	13.50	☐ 359	Buddy Gilbert	1.75	.85	.17
☐ 317	Pumpsie Green	1.75	.85	.17	☐ 360	Herb Score	2.50	1.25	.25
☐ 318	Jim Baxes	1.75	.85	.17	☐ 361	Bob Oldis	1.75	.85	.17
☐ 319	Joe Koppe	1.75	.85	.17	☐ 362	Russ Kemmerer	1.75	.85	.17
☐ 320	Bob Allison	3.00	1.50	.30	☐ 363	Gene Stephens	1.75	.85	.17

		NRMT	VG-E	GOOD
☐ 364	Paul Foytack	1.75	.85	.17
☐ 365	Minnie Minoso	3.50	1.75	.35
☐ 366	Dallas Green	7.50	3.75	.75
☐ 367	Bill Tuttle	1.75	.85	.17
☐ 368	Daryl Spencer	1.75	.85	.17
☐ 369	Billy Hoeft	1.75	.85	.17
☐ 370	Bill Skowron	5.00	2.50	.50
☐ 371	Bud Byerly	1.75	.85	.17
☐ 372	Frank House	1.75	.85	.17
☐ 373	Don Hoak	1.75	.85	.17
☐ 374	Bob Buhl	1.75	.85	.17
☐ 375	Dale Long	2.50	1.25	.25
☐ 376	John Briggs	1.75	.85	.17
☐ 377	Roger Maris	85.00	42.50	8.50
☐ 378	Stu Miller	1.75	.85	.17
☐ 379	Red Wilson	1.75	.85	.17
☐ 380	Bob Shaw	1.75	.85	.17
☐ 381	Braves Team (checklist on back)	5.00	2.00	.40
☐ 382	Ted Bowsfield	1.75	.85	.17
☐ 383	Leon Wagner	1.75	.85	.17
☐ 384	Don Cardwell	1.75	.85	.17
☐ 385	World Series Game 1 Neal Steals Second	3.50	1.75	.35
☐ 386	World Series Game 2 Neal Belts 2nd Homer	3.50	1.75	.35
☐ 387	World Series Game 3 Furillo Breaks Game	4.00	2.00	.40
☐ 388	World Series Game 4 Hodges' Homer	5.00	2.50	.50
☐ 389	World Series Game 5 Luis Swipes Base	5.00	2.50	.50
☐ 390	World Series Game 6 Scrambling After Ball	3.50	1.75	.35
☐ 391	World Series Summary The Champs Celebrate	3.50	1.75	.35
☐ 392	Tex Clevenger	1.75	.85	.17
☐ 393	Smoky Burgess	2.50	1.25	.25
☐ 394	Norm Larker	1.75	.85	.17
☐ 395	Hoyt Wilhelm	11.00	5.50	1.10
☐ 396	Steve Bilko	1.75	.85	.17
☐ 397	Don Blasingame	1.75	.85	.17
☐ 398	Mike Cuellar	2.50	1.25	.25
☐ 399	Young Hill Stars Milt Pappas Jack Fisher Jerry Walker	2.50	1.25	.25
☐ 400	Rocky Colavito	4.50	2.25	.45
☐ 401	Bob Duliba	1.75	.85	.17
☐ 402	Dick Stuart	2.50	1.25	.25
☐ 403	Ed Sadowski	1.75	.85	.17
☐ 404	Bob Rush	1.75	.85	.17
☐ 405	Bobby Richardson	4.50	2.25	.45
☐ 406	Billy Klaus	1.75	.85	.17
☐ 407	Gary Peters (face actually J.C. Martin)	2.50	1.25	.25
☐ 408	Carl Furillo	4.00	2.00	.40
☐ 409	Ron Samford	1.75	.85	.17
☐ 410	Sam Jones	1.75	.85	.17
☐ 411	Ed Bailey	1.75	.85	.17
☐ 412	Bob Anderson	1.75	.85	.17
☐ 413	Athletics Team (checklist on back)	5.00	2.00	.40
☐ 414	Don Williams	1.75	.85	.17
☐ 415	Bob Cerv	2.50	1.25	.25
☐ 416	Humberto Robinson	1.75	.85	.17
☐ 417	Chuck Cottier	2.50	1.25	.25
☐ 418	Don Mossi	2.50	1.25	.25
☐ 419	George Crowe	1.75	.85	.17
☐ 420	Eddie Mathews	21.00	10.50	2.10
☐ 421	Duke Maas	1.75	.85	.17
☐ 422	John Powers	1.75	.85	.17
☐ 423	Ed Fitzgerald	1.75	.85	.17
☐ 424	Pete Whisenant	1.75	.85	.17
☐ 425	Johnny Podres	3.50	1.75	.35
☐ 426	Ron Jackson	1.75	.85	.17
☐ 427	Al Grunwald	1.75	.85	.17
☐ 428	Al Smith	1.75	.85	.17
☐ 429	AL Kings Nellie Fox Harvey Kuenn	3.50	1.75	.35
☐ 430	Art Ditmar	1.75	.85	.17
☐ 431	Andre Rodgers	1.75	.85	.17
☐ 432	Chuck Stobbs	1.75	.85	.17
☐ 433	Irv Noren	1.75	.85	.17
☐ 434	Brooks Lawrence	1.75	.85	.17
☐ 435	Gene Freese	1.75	.85	.17
☐ 436	Marv Throneberry	2.50	1.25	.25
☐ 437	Bob Friend	2.50	1.25	.25
☐ 438	Jim Coker	1.75	.85	.17
☐ 439	Tom Brewer	1.75	.85	.17
☐ 440	Jim Lemon	2.50	1.25	.25
☐ 441	Gary Bell	3.00	1.50	.30
☐ 442	Joe Pignatano	3.00	1.50	.30
☐ 443	Charley Maxwell	3.00	1.50	.30
☐ 444	Jerry Kindall	3.00	1.50	.30
☐ 445	Warren Spahn	27.00	13.50	2.70

		NRMT	VG-E	GOOD
☐ 446	Ellis Burton	3.00	1.50	.30
☐ 447	Ray Moore	3.00	1.50	.30
☐ 448	Jim Gentile	4.50	2.25	.45
☐ 449	Jim Brosnan	3.50	1.75	.35
☐ 450	Orlando Cepeda	7.50	3.75	.75
☐ 451	Curt Simmons	4.00	2.00	.40
☐ 452	Ray Webster	3.00	1.50	.30
☐ 453	Vern Law	4.00	2.00	.40
☐ 454	Hal Woodeshick	3.00	1.50	.30
☐ 455	Baltimore Coaches	4.00	2.00	.40
	Eddie Robinson			
	Harry Brecheen			
	Luman Harris			
☐ 456	Red Sox Coaches	5.00	2.50	.50
	Rudy York			
	Billy Herman			
	Sal Maglie			
	Del Baker			
☐ 457	Cubs Coaches	4.00	2.00	.40
	Charlie Root			
	Lou Klein			
	Elvin Tappe			
☐ 458	White Sox Coaches	4.00	2.00	.40
	Johnny Cooney			
	Don Gutteridge			
	Tony Cuccinello			
	Ray Berres			
☐ 459	Reds Coaches	4.00	2.00	.40
	Reggie Otero			
	Cot Deal			
	Wally Moses			
☐ 460	Indians Coaches	5.00	2.50	.50
	Mel Harder			
	Jo-Jo White			
	Bob Lemon			
	Ralph (Red) Kress			
☐ 461	Tigers Coaches	5.00	2.50	.50
	Tom Ferrick			
	Luke Appling			
	Billy Hitchcock			
☐ 462	Athletics Coaches	4.00	2.00	.40
	Fred Fitzsimmons			
	Don Heffner			
	Walker Cooper			
☐ 463	Dodgers Coaches	5.00	2.50	.50
	Bobby Bragan			
	Pete Reiser			
	Joe Becker			
	Greg Mulleavy			
☐ 464	Braves Coaches	4.00	2.00	.40
	Bob Scheffing			
	Whitlow Wyatt			
	Andy Pafko			
	George Myatt			
☐ 465	Yankees Coaches	9.00	4.50	.90
	Bill Dickey			
	Ralph Houk			
	Frank Crosetti			
	Ed Lopat			
☐ 466	Phillies Coaches	4.00	2.00	.40
	Ken Silvestri			
	Dick Carter			
	Andy Cohen			
☐ 467	Pirates Coaches	4.00	2.00	.40
	Mickey Vernon			
	Frank Oceak			
	Sam Narron			
	Bill Burwell			
☐ 468	Cardinals Coaches	4.00	2.00	.40
	Johnny Keane			
	Howie Pollet			
	Ray Katt			
	Harry Walker			
☐ 469	Giants Coaches	4.00	2.00	.40
	Wes Westrum			
	Salty Parker			
	Bill Posedel			
☐ 470	Senators Coaches	4.00	2.00	.40
	Bob Swift			
	Ellis Clary			
	Sam Mele			
☐ 471	Ned Garver	3.00	1.50	.30
☐ 472	Alvin Dark	4.00	2.00	.40
☐ 473	Al Cicotte	3.00	1.50	.30
☐ 474	Haywood Sullivan	3.50	1.75	.35
☐ 475	Don Drysdale	27.00	13.50	2.70
☐ 476	Lou Johnson	3.50	1.75	.35
☐ 477	Don Ferrarese	3.00	1.50	.30
☐ 478	Frank Torre	3.00	1.50	.30
☐ 479	Georges Maranda	3.00	1.50	.30
☐ 480	Yogi Berra	50.00	25.00	5.00
☐ 481	Wes Stock	3.00	1.50	.30
☐ 482	Frank Bolling	3.00	1.50	.30
☐ 483	Camilo Pascual	3.50	1.75	.35
☐ 484	Pirates Team	12.50	4.00	.80
	(checklist on back)			
☐ 485	Ken Boyer	5.00	2.50	.50
☐ 486	Bobby Del Greco	3.00	1.50	.30

		NRMT	VG-E	GOOD
☐ 487	Tom Sturdivant	3.00	1.50	.30
☐ 488	Norm Cash	4.50	2.25	.45
☐ 489	Steve Ridzik	3.00	1.50	.30
☐ 490	Frank Robinson	35.00	17.50	3.50
☐ 491	Mel Roach	3.00	1.50	.30
☐ 492	Larry Jackson	3.00	1.50	.30
☐ 493	Duke Snider	40.00	20.00	4.00
☐ 494	Orioles Team (checklist on back)	7.50	2.50	.50
☐ 495	Sherm Lollar	3.50	1.75	.35
☐ 496	Bill Virdon	4.50	2.25	.45
☐ 497	John Tsitouris	3.00	1.50	.30
☐ 498	Al Pilarcik	3.00	1.50	.30
☐ 499	Johnny James	3.00	1.50	.30
☐ 500	Johnny Temple	3.50	1.75	.35
☐ 501	Bob Schmidt	3.00	1.50	.30
☐ 502	Jim Bunning	7.50	3.75	.75
☐ 503	Don Lee	3.00	1.50	.30
☐ 504	Seth Morehead	3.00	1.50	.30
☐ 505	Ted Kluszewski	4.50	2.25	.45
☐ 506	Lee Walls	3.00	1.50	.30
☐ 507	Dick Stigman	8.00	4.00	.80
☐ 508	Billy Consolo	8.00	4.00	.80
☐ 509	Tommy Davis	15.00	7.50	1.50
☐ 510	Jerry Staley	8.00	4.00	.80
☐ 511	Ken Walters	8.00	4.00	.80
☐ 512	Joe Gibbon	8.00	4.00	.80
☐ 513	Chicago Cubs Team Card (checklist on back)	24.00	7.00	1.50
☐ 514	Steve Barber	8.00	4.00	.80
☐ 515	Stan Lopata	8.00	4.00	.80
☐ 516	Marty Kutyna	8.00	4.00	.80
☐ 517	Charlie James	8.00	4.00	.80
☐ 518	Tony Gonzalez	8.00	4.00	.80
☐ 519	Ed Roebuck	8.00	4.00	.80
☐ 520	Don Buddin	8.00	4.00	.80
☐ 521	Mike Lee	8.00	4.00	.80
☐ 522	Ken Hunt	8.00	4.00	.80
☐ 523	Clay Dalrymple	8.00	4.00	.80
☐ 524	Bill Henry	8.00	4.00	.80
☐ 525	Marv Breeding	8.00	4.00	.80
☐ 526	Paul Giel	8.00	4.00	.80
☐ 527	Jose Valdivielso	8.00	4.00	.80
☐ 528	Ben Johnson	8.00	4.00	.80
☐ 529	Norm Sherry	9.00	4.50	.90
☐ 530	Mike McCormick	9.00	4.50	.90
☐ 531	Sandy Amoros	9.00	4.50	.90
☐ 532	Mike Garcia	10.00	5.00	1.00
☐ 533	Lu Clinton	8.00	4.00	.80
☐ 534	Ken MacKenzie	8.00	4.00	.80
☐ 535	Whitey Lockman	9.00	4.50	.90
☐ 536	Wynn Hawkins	8.00	4.00	.80
☐ 537	Boston Red Sox Team Card (checklist on back)	24.00	11.00	2.20
☐ 538	Frank Barnes	8.00	4.00	.80
☐ 539	Gene Baker	8.00	4.00	.80
☐ 540	Jerry Walker	8.00	4.00	.80
☐ 541	Tony Curry	8.00	4.00	.80
☐ 542	Ken Hamlin	8.00	4.00	.80
☐ 543	Elio Chacon	8.00	4.00	.80
☐ 544	Bill Monbouquette	9.00	4.50	.90
☐ 545	Carl Sawatski	8.00	4.00	.80
☐ 546	Hank Aguirre	8.00	4.00	.80
☐ 547	Bob Aspromonte	8.00	4.00	.80
☐ 548	Don Mincher	9.00	4.50	.90
☐ 549	John Buzhardt	8.00	4.00	.80
☐ 550	Jim Landis	8.00	4.00	.80
☐ 551	Ed Rakow	8.00	4.00	.80
☐ 552	Walt Bond	8.00	4.00	.80
☐ 553	Bill Skowron AS	11.00	5.50	1.10
☐ 554	Willie McCovey AS	33.00	15.00	3.00
☐ 555	Nellie Fox AS	12.50	6.25	1.25
☐ 556	Charlie Neal AS	10.00	5.00	1.00
☐ 557	Frank Malzone AS	10.00	5.00	1.00
☐ 558	Eddie Mathews AS	22.00	11.00	2.20
☐ 559	Luis Aparicio AS	17.00	8.50	1.70
☐ 560	Ernie Banks AS	30.00	15.00	3.00
☐ 561	Al Kaline AS	30.00	15.00	3.00
☐ 562	Joe Cunningham AS	10.00	5.00	1.00
☐ 563	Mickey Mantle AS	175.00	85.00	18.00
☐ 564	Willie Mays AS	80.00	40.00	8.00
☐ 565	Roger Maris AS	60.00	30.00	6.00
☐ 566	Hank Aaron AS	80.00	40.00	8.00
☐ 567	Sherm Lollar AS	10.00	5.00	1.00
☐ 568	Del Crandall AS	10.00	5.00	1.00
☐ 569	Camilo Pascual AS	10.00	5.00	1.00
☐ 570	Don Drysdale AS	20.00	10.00	2.00
☐ 571	Billy Pierce AS	11.00	5.50	1.10
☐ 572	Johnny Antonelli AS	12.00	6.00	1.20

1961 Topps

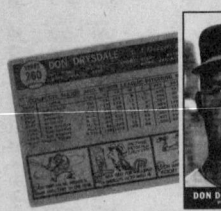

The cards in this 587-card set measure 2 ½" by 3 ½". In 1961, Topps returned to the vertical obverse format. Introduced for the first time were "League Leaders" (41 to 50) and separate, numbered checklist cards. Two number 463s exist: the Braves team card carrying that number was meant to be number 426. There are three versions of the second series checklist card #98; the variations are distinguished by the color of the "CHECKLIST" headline on the front of the card, the color of the printing of the card number on the bottom of the reverse, and the presence of the copyright notice running vertically on the card back. There are two groups of managers (131-139 and 219-226) as well as separate series of World Series cards (306-313), Baseball Thrills (401 to 410), previous MVP's (AL 471-478 and NL 479-486) and Sporting News All-Stars (566 to 589). The usual last series scarcity (523 to 589) exists. The set actually totals 587 cards since numbers 587 and 588 were never issued.

	NRMT	VG-E	GOOD
COMPLETE SET (587)	4800.00	2400.00	600.00
COMMON PLAYER (1-110) ..	1.00	.50	.10
COMMON PLAYER (111-370) ..	1.25	.60	.12
COMMON PLAYER (371-446) ..	1.75	.85	.17
COMMON PLAYER (447-522) ..	2.25	1.10	.22
COMMON PLAYER (523-565) ..	20.00	10.00	2.00
COMMON PLAYER (566-589) ..	21.00	10.50	2.10

			NRMT	VG-E	GOOD
☐	1	Dick Groat	12.00	6.00	1.20
☐	2	Roger Maris	100.00	50.00	10.00
☐	3	John Buzhardt	1.00	.50	.10
☐	4	Lenny Green	1.00	.50	.10
☐	5	John Romano	1.00	.50	.10
☐	6	Ed Roebuck	1.00	.50	.10
☐	7	White Sox Team	3.00	1.50	.30
☐	8	Dick Williams	1.50	.75	.15
☐	9	Bob Purkey	1.00	.50	.10
☐	10	Brooks Robinson ...	25.00	12.50	2.50
☐	11	Curt Simmons	1.50	.75	.15
☐	12	Moe Thacker	1.00	.50	.10
☐	13	Chuck Cottier	1.00	.50	.10
☐	14	Don Mossi	1.50	.75	.15
☐	15	Willie Kirkland	1.00	.50	.10
☐	16	Billy Muffett	1.00	.50	.10
☐	17	Checklist 1	6.00	1.00	.20
☐	18	Jim Grant	1.00	.50	.10
☐	19	Clete Boyer	1.50	.75	.15
☐	20	Robin Roberts	10.00	5.00	1.00
☐	21	Zorro Versalles	1.00	.50	.10
☐	22	Clem Labine	1.50	.75	.15
☐	23	Don Demeter	1.00	.50	.10
☐	24	Ken Johnson	1.00	.50	.10
☐	25	Reds' Heavy Artillery .	4.00	2.00	.40
		Vada Pinson			
		Gus Bell			
		Frank Robinson			
☐	26	Wes Stock	1.00	.50	.10
☐	27	Jerry Kindall	1.00	.50	.10
☐	28	Hector Lopez	1.00	.50	.10
☐	29	Don Nottebart	1.00	.50	.10
☐	30	Nellie Fox	5.00	2.50	.50
☐	31	Bob Schmidt	1.00	.50	.10
☐	32	Ray Sadecki	1.00	.50	.10
☐	33	Gary Geiger	1.00	.50	.10
☐	34	Wynn Hawkins	1.00	.50	.10
☐	35	Ron Santo	12.00	6.00	1.20
☐	36	Jack Kralick	1.00	.50	.10
☐	37	Charley Maxwell	1.00	.50	.10
☐	38	Bob Lillis	1.00	.50	.10
☐	39	Leo Posada	1.00	.50	.10
☐	40	Bob Turley	2.50	1.25	.25
☐	41	NL Batting Leaders ..	5.00	2.50	.50
		Dick Groat			
		Norm Larker			
		Willie Mays			
		Roberto Clemente			

			NRMT	VG-E	GOOD
☐	42	AL Batting Leaders .	2.00	1.00	.20
		Pete Runnels			
		Al Smith			
		Minnie Minoso			
		Bill Skowron			
☐	43	NL Home Run Leaders	7.00	3.50	.70
		Ernie Banks			
		Hank Aaron			
		Ed Mathews			
		Ken Boyer			
☐	44	AL Home Run Leaders	15.00	7.50	1.50
		Mickey Mantle			
		Roger Maris			
		Jim Lemon			
		Rocky Colavito			
☐	45	NL ERA Leaders ...	2.00	1.00	.20
		Mike McCormick			
		Ernie Broglio			
		Don Drysdale			
		Bob Friend			
		Stan Williams			
☐	46	AL ERA Leaders ...	2.00	1.00	.20
		Frank Baumann			
		Jim Bunning			
		Art Ditmar			
		H. Brown			
☐	47	NL Pitching Leaders .	2.00	1.00	.20
		Ernie Broglio			
		Warren Spahn			
		Vern Law			
		Lou Burdette			
☐	48	AL Pitching Leaders .	2.00	1.00	.20
		Chuck Estrada			
		Jim Perry			
		Bud Daley			
		Art Ditmar			
		Frank Lary			
		Milt Pappas			
☐	49	NL Strikeout Leaders .	4.00	2.00	.40
		Don Drysdale			
		Sandy Koufax			
		Sam Jones			
		Ernie Broglio			
☐	50	AL Strikeout Leaders .	2.00	1.00	.20
		Jim Bunning			
		Pedro Ramos			
		Early Wynn			

			NRMT	VG-E	GOOD
		Frank Lary			
☐	51	Detroit Tigers	3.00	1.50	.30
		Team Card			
☐	52	George Crowe	1.00	.50	.10
☐	53	Russ Nixon	1.50	.75	.15
☐	54	Earl Francis	1.00	.50	.10
☐	55	Jim Davenport	1.50	.75	.15
☐	56	Russ Kemmerer	1.00	.50	.10
☐	57	Marv Throneberry ...	1.50	.75	.15
☐	58	Joe Schaffernoth ...	1.00	.50	.10
☐	59	Jim Woods	1.00	.50	.10
☐	60	Woody Held	1.00	.50	.10
☐	61	Ron Piche	1.00	.50	.10
☐	62	Al Pilarcik	1.00	.50	.10
☐	63	Jim Kaat	6.50	3.25	.65
☐	64	Alex Grammas	1.00	.50	.10
☐	65	Ted Kluszewski	3.50	1.75	.35
☐	66	Billy Henry	1.00	.50	.10
☐	67	Ossie Virgil	1.00	.50	.10
☐	68	Deron Johnson	1.50	.75	.15
☐	69	Earl Wilson	1.00	.50	.10
☐	70	Bill Virdon	2.00	1.00	.20
☐	71	Jerry Adair	1.00	.50	.10
☐	72	Stu Miller	1.00	.50	.10
☐	73	Al Spangler	1.00	.50	.10
☐	74	Joe Pignatano	1.00	.50	.10
☐	75	Lindy Shows Larry ..	1.50	.75	.15
		Lindy McDaniel			
		Larry Jackson			
☐	76	Harry Anderson	1.00	.50	.10
☐	77	Dick Stigman	1.00	.50	.10
☐	78	Lee Walls	1.00	.50	.10
☐	79	Joe Ginsberg	1.00	.50	.10
☐	80	Harmon Killebrew ...	18.00	9.00	1.80
☐	81	Tracy Stallard	1.00	.50	.10
☐	82	Joe Christopher	1.00	.50	.10
☐	83	Bob Bruce	1.00	.50	.10
☐	84	Lee Maye	1.00	.50	.10
☐	85	Jerry Walker	1.00	.50	.10
☐	86	Los Angeles Dodgers	4.00	2.00	.40
		Team Card			
☐	87	Joe Amalfitano	1.00	.50	.10
☐	88	Richie Ashburn	6.00	3.00	.60
☐	89	Billy Martin	6.00	3.00	.60
☐	90	Jerry Staley	1.00	.50	.10
☐	91	Walt Moryn	1.00	.50	.10
☐	92	Hal Naragon	1.00	.50	.10
☐	93	Tony Gonzalez	1.00	.50	.10
☐	94	Johnny Kucks	1.00	.50	.10

			NRMT	VG-E	GOOD
☐	95	Norm Cash	2.50	1.25	.25
☐	96	Billy O'Dell	1.00	.50	.10
☐	97	Jerry Lynch	1.00	.50	.10
☐	98A	Checklist 2 (red "Checklist," 98 black on white)	6.00	1.00	.20
☐	98B	Checklist 2 (yellow "Checklist," 98 black on white)	6.00	1.00	.20
☐	98C	Checklist 2 (yellow "Checklist," 98 white on black, no copyright)	6.00	1.00	.20
☐	99	Don Buddin UER (66 HR's)	1.00	.50	.10
☐	100	Harvey Haddix	2.00	1.00	.20
☐	101	Bubba Phillips	1.00	.50	.10
☐	102	Gene Stephens	1.00	.50	.10
☐	103	Ruben Amaro	1.00	.50	.10
☐	104	John Blanchard	1.50	.75	.15
☐	105	Carl Willey	1.00	.50	.10
☐	106	Whitey Herzog	3.00	1.50	.30
☐	107	Seth Morehead	1.00	.50	.10
☐	108	Dan Dobbek	1.00	.50	.10
☐	109	Johnny Podres	2.50	1.25	.25
☐	110	Vada Pinson	2.50	1.25	.25
☐	111	Jack Meyer	1.25	.60	.12
☐	112	Chico Fernandez	1.25	.60	.12
☐	113	Mike Fornieles	1.25	.60	.12
☐	114	Hobie Landrith	1.25	.60	.12
☐	115	Johnny Antonelli	1.75	.85	.17
☐	116	Joe DeMaestri	1.25	.60	.12
☐	117	Dale Long	1.75	.85	.17
☐	118	Chris Cannizzaro	1.25	.60	.12
☐	119	A's Big Armor Norm Siebern Hank Bauer Jerry Lumpe	1.75	.85	.17
☐	120	Eddie Mathews	18.00	9.00	1.80
☐	121	Eli Grba	1.25	.60	.12
☐	122	Chicago Cubs Team Card	3.00	1.50	.30
☐	123	Billy Gardner	1.75	.85	.17
☐	124	J.C. Martin	1.25	.60	.12
☐	125	Steve Barber	1.25	.60	.12
☐	126	Dick Stuart	1.75	.85	.17
☐	127	Ron Kline	1.25	.60	.12
☐	128	Rip Repulski	1.25	.60	.12
☐	129	Ed Hobaugh	1.25	.60	.12

			NRMT	VG-E	GOOD
☐	130	Norm Larker	1.25	.60	.12
☐	131	Paul Richards MG	1.75	.85	.17
☐	132	Al Lopez MG	4.00	2.00	.40
☐	133	Ralph Houk MG	3.00	1.50	.30
☐	134	Mickey Vernon MG	1.75	.85	.17
☐	135	Fred Hutchinson MG	1.75	.85	.17
☐	136	Walt Alston MG	5.00	2.50	.50
☐	137	Chuck Dressen MG	1.75	.85	.17
☐	138	Danny Murtaugh MG	1.75	.85	.17
☐	139	Solly Hemus MG	1.75	.85	.17
☐	140	Gus Triandos	1.75	.85	.17
☐	141	Billy Williams	75.00	37.50	7.50
☐	142	Luis Arroyo	1.75	.85	.17
☐	143	Russ Snyder	1.25	.60	.12
☐	144	Jim Coker	1.25	.60	.12
☐	145	Bob Buhl	1.25	.60	.12
☐	146	Marty Keough	1.25	.60	.12
☐	147	Ed Rakow	1.25	.60	.12
☐	148	Julian Javier	1.25	.60	.12
☐	149	Bob Oldis	1.25	.60	.12
☐	150	Willie Mays	80.00	40.00	8.00
☐	151	Jim Donohue	1.25	.60	.12
☐	152	Earl Torgeson	1.25	.60	.12
☐	153	Don Lee	1.25	.60	.12
☐	154	Bobby Del Greco	1.25	.60	.12
☐	155	Johnny Temple	1.25	.60	.12
☐	156	Ken Hunt	1.25	.60	.12
☐	157	Cal McLish	1.25	.60	.12
☐	158	Pete Daley	1.25	.60	.12
☐	159	Orioles Team	3.00	1.50	.30
☐	160	Whitey Ford	25.00	12.50	2.50
☐	161	Sherman Jones (photo actually Eddie Fisher)	1.25	.60	.12
☐	162	Jay Hook	1.25	.60	.12
☐	163	Ed Sadowski	1.25	.60	.12
☐	164	Felix Mantilla	1.25	.60	.12
☐	165	Gino Cimoli	1.25	.60	.12
☐	166	Danny Kravitz	1.25	.60	.12
☐	167	San Francisco Giants Team Card	3.00	1.50	.30
☐	168	Tommy Davis	2.50	1.25	.25
☐	169	Don Elston	1.25	.60	.12
☐	170	Al Smith	1.25	.60	.12
☐	171	Paul Foytack	1.25	.60	.12
☐	172	Don Dillard	1.25	.60	.12
☐	173	Beantown Bombers Frank Malzone Vic Wertz	1.75	.85	.17

		NRMT	VG-E	GOOD
	Jackie Jensen			
☐ 174	Ray Semproch	1.25	.60	.12
☐ 175	Gene Freese	1.25	.60	.12
☐ 176	Ken Aspromonte	1.25	.60	.12
☐ 177	Don Larsen	2.50	1.25	.25
☐ 178	Bob Nieman	1.25	.60	.12
☐ 179	Joe Koppe	1.25	.60	.12
☐ 180	Bobby Richardson	4.00	2.00	.40
☐ 181	Fred Green	1.25	.60	.12
☐ 182	Dave Nicholson	1.25	.60	.12
☐ 183	Andre Rodgers	1.25	.60	.12
☐ 184	Steve Bilko	1.25	.60	.12
☐ 185	Herb Score	1.75	.85	.17
☐ 186	Elmer Valo	1.25	.60	.12
☐ 187	Billy Klaus	1.25	.60	.12
☐ 188	Jim Marshall	1.25	.60	.12
☐ 189A	Checklist 3	7.50	1.25	.20
	(copyright symbol al-most adjacent to 263 Ken Hamlin)			
☐ 189B	Checklist 3	7.50	1.25	.20
	(copyright symbol ad-jacent to 264 Glen Hobbie)			
☐ 190	Stan Williams	1.25	.60	.12
☐ 191	Mike De La Hoz	1.25	.60	.12
☐ 192	Dick Brown	1.25	.60	.12
☐ 193	Gene Conley	1.25	.60	.12
☐ 194	Gordy Coleman	1.25	.60	.12
☐ 195	Jerry Casale	1.25	.60	.12
☐ 196	Ed Bouchee	1.25	.60	.12
☐ 197	Dick Hall	1.25	.60	.12
☐ 198	Carl Sawatski	1.25	.60	.12
☐ 199	Bob Boyd	1.25	.60	.12
☐ 200	Warren Spahn	22.00	11.00	2.20
☐ 201	Pete Whisenant	1.25	.60	.12
☐ 202	Al Neiger	1.25	.60	.12
☐ 203	Eddie Bressoud	1.25	.60	.12
☐ 204	Bob Skinner	1.25	.60	.12
☐ 205	Billy Pierce	1.75	.85	.17
☐ 206	Gene Green	1.25	.60	.12
☐ 207	Dodger Southpaws	15.00	7.50	1.50
	Sandy Koufax			
	Johnny Podres			
☐ 208	Larry Osborne	1.25	.60	.12
☐ 209	Ken McBride	1.25	.60	.12
☐ 210	Pete Runnels	1.75	.85	.17
☐ 211	Bob Gibson	22.00	11.00	2.20
☐ 212	Haywood Sullivan	1.75	.85	.17

		NRMT	VG-E	GOOD
☐ 213	Bill Stafford	1.25	.60	.12
☐ 214	Danny Murphy	1.25	.60	.12
☐ 215	Gus Bell	1.75	.85	.17
☐ 216	Ted Bowsfield	1.25	.60	.12
☐ 217	Mel Roach	1.25	.60	.12
☐ 218	Hal Brown	1.25	.60	.12
☐ 219	Gene Mauch MG	1.75	.85	.17
☐ 220	Alvin Dark MG	1.75	.85	.17
☐ 221	Mike Higgins MG	1.75	.85	.17
☐ 222	Jimmy Dykes MG	1.75	.85	.17
☐ 223	Bob Scheffing MG	1.75	.85	.17
☐ 224	Joe Gordon MG	1.75	.85	.17
☐ 225	Bill Rigney MG	1.75	.85	.17
☐ 226	Harry Lavagetto MG	1.75	.85	.17
☐ 227	Juan Pizarro	1.25	.60	.12
☐ 228	New York Yankees	15.00	7.50	1.50
	Team Card			
☐ 229	Rudy Hernandez	1.25	.60	.12
☐ 230	Don Hoak	1.25	.60	.12
☐ 231	Dick Drott	1.25	.60	.12
☐ 232	Bill White	3.50	1.75	.35
☐ 233	Joey Jay	1.25	.60	.12
☐ 234	Ted Lepcio	1.25	.60	.12
☐ 235	Camilo Pascual	1.25	.60	.12
☐ 236	Don Gile	1.25	.60	.12
☐ 237	Billy Loes	1.25	.60	.12
☐ 238	Jim Gilliam	2.50	1.25	.25
☐ 239	Dave Sisler	1.25	.60	.12
☐ 240	Ron Hansen	1.25	.60	.12
☐ 241	Al Cicotte	1.25	.60	.12
☐ 242	Hal Smith	1.25	.60	.12
☐ 243	Frank Lary	1.75	.85	.17
☐ 244	Chico Cardenas	1.25	.60	.12
☐ 245	Joe Adcock	1.75	.85	.17
☐ 246	Bob Davis	1.25	.60	.12
☐ 247	Billy Goodman	1.75	.85	.17
☐ 248	Ed Keegan	1.25	.60	.12
☐ 249	Cincinnati Reds	3.50	1.75	.35
	Team Card			
☐ 250	Buc Hill Aces	1.75	.85	.17
	Vern Law			
	Roy Face			
☐ 251	Bill Bruton	1.25	.60	.12
☐ 252	Bill Short	1.25	.60	.12
☐ 253	Sammy Taylor	1.25	.60	.12
☐ 254	Ted Sadowski	1.25	.60	.12
☐ 255	Vic Power	1.25	.60	.12
☐ 256	Billy Hoeft	1.25	.60	.12
☐ 257	Carroll Hardy	1.25	.60	.12

		NRMT	VG-E	GOOD				NRMT	VG-E	GOOD
☐ 258	Jack Sanford	1.75	.85	.17	☐ 300	Mickey Mantle		300.00	150.00	30.00
☐ 259	John Schaive	1.25	.60	.12	☐ 301	Chet Nichols		1.25	.60	.12
☐ 260	Don Drysdale	18.00	9.00	1.80	☐ 302	Al Heist		1.25	.60	.12
☐ 261	Charlie Lau	1.75	.85	.17	☐ 303	Gary Peters		1.25	.60	.12
☐ 262	Tony Curry	1.25	.60	.12	☐ 304	Rocky Nelson		1.25	.60	.12
☐ 263	Ken Hamlin	1.25	.60	.12	☐ 305	Mike McCormick		1.25	.60	.12
☐ 264	Glen Hobbie	1.25	.60	.12	☐ 306	World Series Game 1		3.50	1.75	.35
☐ 265	Tony Kubek	5.00	2.50	.50		Virdon Saves Game				
☐ 266	Lindy McDaniel	1.25	.60	.12	☐ 307	World Series Game 2		25.00	12.50	2.50
☐ 267	Norm Siebern	1.25	.60	.12		Mantle 2 Homers				
☐ 268	Ike Delock	1.25	.60	.12	☐ 308	World Series Game 3		5.00	2.50	.50
☐ 269	Harry Chiti	1.25	.60	.12		Richardson is Hero				
☐ 270	Bob Friend	1.75	.85	.17	☐ 309	World Series Game 4		3.50	1.75	.35
☐ 271	Jim Landis	1.25	.60	.12		Cimoli Safe				
☐ 272	Tom Morgan	1.25	.60	.12	☐ 310	World Series Game 5		3.50	1.75	.35
☐ 273A	Checklist 4	12.00	1.50	.30		Face Saves the Game				
	(copyright symbol adjacent to 336 Don Mincher)				☐ 311	World Series Game 6 Ford Second Shutout		6.00	3.00	.60
☐ 273B	Checklist 4	6.00	1.00	.20	☐ 312	World Series Game 7 Mazeroski's Homer		5.00	2.50	.50
	(copyright symbol adjacent to 339 Gene Baker)				☐ 313	World Series Summary Pirates Celebrate		3.50	1.75	.35
☐ 274	Gary Bell	1.25	.60	.12	☐ 314	Bob Miller		1.25	.60	.12
☐ 275	Gene Woodling	1.75	.85	.17	☐ 315	Earl Battey		1.25	.60	.12
☐ 276	Ray Rippelmeyer	1.25	.60	.12	☐ 316	Bobby Gene Smith		1.25	.60	.12
☐ 277	Hank Foiles	1.25	.60	.12	☐ 317	Jim Brewer		1.25	.60	.12
☐ 278	Don McMahon	1.25	.60	.12	☐ 318	Danny O'Connell		1.25	.60	.12
☐ 279	Jose Pagan	1.25	.60	.12	☐ 319	Valmy Thomas		1.25	.60	.12
☐ 280	Frank Howard	3.00	1.50	.30	☐ 320	Lou Burdette		2.50	1.25	.25
☐ 281	Frank Sullivan	1.25	.60	.12	☐ 321	Marv Breeding		1.25	.60	.12
☐ 282	Faye Throneberry	1.25	.60	.12	☐ 322	Bill Kunkel		1.75	.85	.17
☐ 283	Bob Anderson	1.25	.60	.12	☐ 323	Sammy Esposito		1.25	.60	.12
☐ 284	Dick Gernert	1.25	.60	.12	☐ 324	Hank Aguirre		1.25	.60	.12
☐ 285	Sherm Lollar	1.75	.85	.17	☐ 325	Wally Moon		1.75	.85	.17
☐ 286	George Witt	1.25	.60	.12	☐ 326	Dave Hillman		1.25	.60	.12
☐ 287	Carl Yastrzemski	150.00	75.00	15.00	☐ 327	Matty Alou		4.00	2.00	.40
☐ 288	Albie Pearson	1.25	.60	.12	☐ 328	Jim O'Toole		1.25	.60	.12
☐ 289	Ray Moore	1.25	.60	.12	☐ 329	Julio Becquer		1.25	.60	.12
☐ 290	Stan Musial	75.00	37.50	7.50	☐ 330	Rocky Colavito		4.00	2.00	.40
☐ 291	Tex Clevenger	1.25	.60	.12	☐ 331	Ned Garver		1.25	.60	.12
☐ 292	Jim Baumer	1.25	.60	.12	☐ 332	Dutch Dotterer		1.25	.60	.12
☐ 293	Tom Sturdivant	1.25	.60	.12		(photo actually Tommy Dotterer, Dutch's brother)				
☐ 294	Don Blasingame	1.25	.60	.12						
☐ 295	Milt Pappas	1.75	.85	.17	☐ 333	Fritz Brickell		1.25	.60	.12
☐ 296	Wes Covington	1.25	.60	.12	☐ 334	Walt Bond		1.25	.60	.12
☐ 297	Athletics Team	2.50	1.25	.25	☐ 335	Frank Bolling		1.25	.60	.12
☐ 298	Jim Golden	1.25	.60	.12	☐ 336	Don Mincher		1.25	.60	.12
☐ 299	Clay Dalrymple	1.25	.60	.12	☐ 337	Al's Aces		4.00	2.00	.40

		NRMT	VG-E	GOOD
	Early Wynn			
	Al Lopez			
	Herb Score			
☐ 338	Don Landrum	1.25	.60	.12
☐ 339	Gene Baker	1.25	.60	.12
☐ 340	Vic Wertz	1.75	.85	.17
☐ 341	Jim Owens	1.25	.60	.12
☐ 342	Clint Courtney	1.25	.60	.12
☐ 343	Earl Robinson	1.25	.60	.12
☐ 344	Sandy Koufax	80.00	40.00	8.00
☐ 345	Jim Piersall	2.50	1.25	.25
☐ 346	Howie Nunn	1.25	.60	.12
☐ 347	St. Louis Cardinals Team Card	3.00	1.50	.30
☐ 348	Steve Boros	1.75	.85	.17
☐ 349	Danny McDevitt	1.25	.60	.12
☐ 350	Ernie Banks	27.00	13.50	2.70
☐ 351	Jim King	1.25	.60	.12
☐ 352	Bob Shaw	1.25	.60	.12
☐ 353	Howie Bedell	1.25	.60	.12
☐ 354	Billy Harrell	1.25	.60	.12
☐ 355	Bob Allison	1.75	.85	.17
☐ 356	Ryne Duren	1.75	.85	.17
☐ 357	Daryl Spencer	1.25	.60	.12
☐ 358	Earl Averill	1.25	.60	.12
☐ 359	Dallas Green	3.50	1.75	.35
☐ 360	Frank Robinson	30.00	15.00	3.00
☐ 361A	Checklist 5 (no ad on back)	6.00	1.00	.20
☐ 361B	Checklist 5 (Special Feature ad on back)	12.00	2.00	.40
☐ 362	Frank Funk	1.25	.60	.12
☐ 363	John Roseboro	1.75	.85	.17
☐ 364	Moe Drabowsky	1.25	.60	.12
☐ 365	Jerry Lumpe	1.25	.60	.12
☐ 366	Eddie Fisher	1.25	.60	.12
☐ 367	Jim Rivera	1.25	.60	.12
☐ 368	Bennie Daniels	1.25	.60	.12
☐ 369	Dave Philley	1.25	.60	.12
☐ 370	Roy Face	2.50	1.25	.25
☐ 371	Bill Skowron SP	14.00	7.00	1.40
☐ 372	Bob Hendley	1.75	.85	.17
☐ 373	Boston Red Sox Team Card	3.50	1.75	.35
☐ 374	Paul Giel	1.75	.85	.17
☐ 375	Ken Boyer	4.00	2.00	.40
☐ 376	Mike Roarke	1.75	.85	.17
☐ 377	Ruben Gomez	1.75	.85	.17

		NRMT	VG-E	GOOD
☐ 378	Wally Post	1.75	.85	.17
☐ 379	Bobby Shantz	3.00	1.50	.30
☐ 380	Minnie Minoso	3.00	1.50	.30
☐ 381	Dave Wickersham	1.75	.85	.17
☐ 382	Frank Thomas	2.25	1.10	.22
☐ 383	Frisco First Liners Mike McCormick Jack Sanford Billy O'Dell	2.25	1.10	.22
☐ 384	Chuck Essegian	2.25	1.10	.22
☐ 385	Jim Perry	3.00	1.50	.30
☐ 386	Joe Hicks	1.75	.85	.17
☐ 387	Duke Maas	1.75	.85	.17
☐ 388	Bob Clemente	70.00	35.00	7.00
☐ 389	Ralph Terry	3.00	1.50	.30
☐ 390	Del Crandall	2.25	1.10	.22
☐ 391	Winston Brown	1.75	.85	.17
☐ 392	Reno Bertoia	1.75	.85	.17
☐ 393	Batter Bafflers Don Cardwell Glen Hobbie	2.25	1.10	.22
☐ 394	Ken Walters	1.75	.85	.17
☐ 395	Chuck Estrada	2.25	1.10	.22
☐ 396	Bob Aspromonte	1.75	.85	.17
☐ 397	Hal Woodeshick	1.75	.85	.17
☐ 398	Hank Bauer	2.25	1.10	.22
☐ 399	Cliff Cook	1.75	.85	.17
☐ 400	Vern Law	2.25	1.10	.22
☐ 401	Ruth 60th Homer	15.00	7.50	1.50
☐ 402	Perfect Game (Don Larsen)	7.50	3.75	.75
☐ 403	26 Inning Tie	3.50	1.75	.35
☐ 404	Hornsby .424 Average	4.00	2.00	.40
☐ 405	Gehrig's Streak	10.00	5.00	1.00
☐ 406	Mantle 565 Ft. Homer	35.00	17.50	3.50
☐ 407	Chesbro Wins 41	3.50	1.75	.35
☐ 408	Mathewson Fans 267	4.00	2.00	.40
☐ 409	Johnson Shutouts	4.00	2.00	.40
☐ 410	Haddix 12 Perfect Innings	3.50	1.75	.35
☐ 411	Tony Taylor	1.75	.85	.17
☐ 412	Larry Sherry	2.25	1.10	.22
☐ 413	Eddie Yost	1.75	.85	.17
☐ 414	Dick Donovan	1.75	.85	.17
☐ 415	Hank Aaron	85.00	42.50	8.50
☐ 416	Dick Howser	7.00	3.50	.70
☐ 417	Juan Marichal	80.00	40.00	8.00
☐ 418	Ed Bailey	1.75	.85	.17
☐ 419	Tom Borland	1.75	.85	.17

		NRMT	VG-E	GOOD			NRMT	VG-E	GOOD
☐ 420	Ernie Broglio	2.25	1.10	.22	☐ 461	Smoky Burgess	3.00	1.50	.30
☐ 421	Ty Cline	1.75	.85	.17	☐ 462	Lou Klimchock	2.25	1.10	.22
☐ 422	Bud Daley	1.75	.85	.17	☐ 463	Jack Fisher	3.00	1.50	.30
☐ 423	Charlie Neal SP	4.00	2.00	.40		(See also 426)			
☐ 424	Turk Lown	1.75	.85	.17	☐ 464	Lee Thomas	4.50	2.25	.45
☐ 425	Yogi Berra	55.00	27.50	5.50	☐ 465	Roy McMillan	2.25	1.10	.22
☐ 426	Milwaukee Braves	6.50	3.25	.65	☐ 466	Ron Moeller	2.25	1.10	.22
	Team Card				☐ 467	Cleveland Indians	4.50	2.25	.45
	(back numbered 463)					Team Card			
☐ 427	Dick Ellsworth	2.25	1.10	.22	☐ 468	John Callison	3.00	1.50	.30
☐ 428	Ray Barker SP	3.50	1.75	.35	☐ 469	Ralph Lumenti	2.25	1.10	.22
☐ 429	Al Kaline	33.00	15.00	3.00	☐ 470	Roy Sievers	3.00	1.50	.30
☐ 430	Bill Mazeroski SP	9.00	4.50	.90	☐ 471	Phil Rizzuto MVP	10.00	5.00	1.00
☐ 431	Chuck Stobbs	1.75	.85	.17	☐ 472	Yogi Berra MVP	30.00	15.00	3.00
☐ 432	Coot Veal	1.75	.85	.17	☐ 473	Bob Shantz MVP	3.00	1.50	.30
☐ 433	Art Mahaffey	1.75	.85	.17	☐ 474	Al Rosen MVP	3.50	1.75	.35
☐ 434	Tom Brewer	1.75	.85	.17	☐ 475	Mickey Mantle MVP	80.00	40.00	8.00
☐ 435	Orlando Cepeda	6.00	3.00	.60	☐ 476	Jackie Jensen MVP	3.50	1.75	.35
☐ 436	Jim Maloney	6.00	3.00	.60	☐ 477	Nellie Fox MVP	4.00	2.00	.40
☐ 437A	Checklist 6	9.00	1.50	.30	☐ 478	Roger Maris MVP	30.00	15.00	3.00
	440 Louis Aparicio				☐ 479	Jim Konstanty MVP	3.00	1.50	.30
☐ 437B	Checklist 6	9.00	1.50	.30	☐ 480	Roy Campanella			
	440 Luis Aparicio					MVP	22.00	11.00	2.20
☐ 438	Curt Flood	3.00	1.50	.30	☐ 481	Hank Sauer MVP	3.00	1.50	.30
☐ 439	Phil Regan	2.25	1.10	.22	☐ 482	Willie Mays MVP	32.00	16.00	3.20
☐ 440	Luis Aparicio	11.00	5.50	1.10	☐ 483	Don Newcombe MVP	3.00	1.50	.30
☐ 441	Dick Bertell	1.75	.85	.17	☐ 484	Hank Aaron MVP	32.00	16.00	3.20
☐ 442	Gordon Jones	1.75	.85	.17	☐ 485	Ernie Banks MVP	15.00	7.50	1.50
☐ 443	Duke Snider	35.00	17.50	3.50	☐ 486	Dick Groat MVP	3.00	1.50	.30
☐ 444	Joe Nuxhall	2.25	1.10	.22	☐ 487	Gene Oliver	2.25	1.10	.22
☐ 445	Frank Malzone	2.25	1.10	.22	☐ 488	Joe McClain	2.25	1.10	.22
☐ 446	Bob Taylor	1.75	.85	.17	☐ 489	Walt Dropo	2.25	1.10	.22
☐ 447	Harry Bright	2.25	1.10	.22	☐ 490	Jim Bunning	7.50	3.75	.75
☐ 448	Del Rice	2.25	1.10	.22	☐ 491	Philadelphia Phillies	4.50	2.25	.45
☐ 449	Bob Bolin	2.25	1.10	.22		Team Card			
☐ 450	Jim Lemon	3.00	1.50	.30	☐ 492	Ron Fairly	3.00	1.50	.30
☐ 451	Power for Ernie	3.00	1.50	.30	☐ 493	Don Zimmer UER	4.00	2.00	.40
	Daryl Spencer					(Brooklyn A.L.)			
	Bill White				☐ 494	Tom Cheney	2.25	1.10	.22
	Ernie Broglio				☐ 495	Elston Howard	4.50	2.25	.45
☐ 452	Bob Allen	2.25	1.10	.22	☐ 496	Ken MacKenzie	2.25	1.10	.22
☐ 453	Dick Schofield	2.25	1.10	.22	☐ 497	Willie Jones	2.25	1.10	.22
☐ 454	Pumpsie Green	2.25	1.10	.22	☐ 498	Ray Herbert	2.25	1.10	.22
☐ 455	Early Wynn	10.00	5.00	1.00	☐ 499	Chuck Schilling	2.25	1.10	.22
☐ 456	Hal Bevan	2.25	1.10	.22	☐ 500	Harvey Kuenn	4.00	2.00	.40
☐ 457	John James	2.25	1.10	.22	☐ 501	John DeMerit	2.25	1.10	.22
☐ 458	Willie Tasby	2.25	1.10	.22	☐ 502	Clarence Coleman	2.25	1.10	.22
☐ 459	Terry Fox	2.25	1.10	.22	☐ 503	Tito Francona	3.00	1.50	.30
☐ 460	Gil Hodges	11.00	5.50	1.10	☐ 504	Billy Consolo	2.25	1.10	.22

		NRMT	VG-E	GOOD
☐ 505	Red Schoendienst ..	12.00	6.00	1.20
☐ 506	Willie Davis	7.00	3.50	.70
☐ 507	Pete Burnside	2.25	1.10	.22
☐ 508	Rocky Bridges	2.25	1.10	.22
☐ 509	Camilo Carreon	2.25	1.10	.22
☐ 510	Art Ditmar	2.25	1.10	.22
☐ 511	Joe M. Morgan	3.50	1.75	.35
☐ 512	Bob Will	2.25	1.10	.22
☐ 513	Jim Brosnan	3.00	1.50	.30
☐ 514	Jake Wood	2.25	1.10	.22
☐ 515	Jackie Brandt	2.25	1.10	.22
☐ 516	Checklist 7	9.00	1.50	.30
☐ 517	Willie McCovey	45.00	22.50	4.50
☐ 518	Andy Carey	3.00	1.50	.30
☐ 519	Jim Pagliaroni	2.25	1.10	.22
☐ 520	Joe Cunningham	3.00	1.50	.30
☐ 521	Brother Battery	3.00	1.50	.30
	Norm Sherry			
	Larry Sherry			
☐ 522	Dick Farrell	3.00	1.50	.30
☐ 523	Joe Gibbon	20.00	10.00	2.00
☐ 524	Johnny Logan	22.00	11.00	2.20
☐ 525	Ron Perranoski	22.00	11.00	2.20
☐ 526	R.C. Stevens	20.00	10.00	2.00
☐ 527	Gene Leek	20.00	10.00	2.00
☐ 528	Pedro Ramos	20.00	10.00	2.00
☐ 529	Bob Roselli	20.00	10.00	2.00
☐ 530	Bob Malkmus	20.00	10.00	2.00
☐ 531	Jim Coates	20.00	10.00	2.00
☐ 532	Bob Hale	20.00	10.00	2.00
☐ 533	Jack Curtis	20.00	10.00	2.00
☐ 534	Eddie Kasko	20.00	10.00	2.00
☐ 535	Larry Jackson	20.00	10.00	2.00
☐ 536	Bill Tuttle	20.00	10.00	2.00
☐ 537	Bobby Locke	20.00	10.00	2.00
☐ 538	Chuck Hiller	20.00	10.00	2.00
☐ 539	Johnny Klippstein ...	20.00	10.00	2.00
☐ 540	Jackie Jensen	30.00	15.00	3.00
☐ 541	Roland Sheldon	20.00	10.00	2.00
☐ 542	Minnesota Twins ...	42.00	18.00	4.00
	Team Card			
☐ 543	Roger Craig	30.00	15.00	3.00
☐ 544	George Thomas	20.00	10.00	2.00
☐ 545	Hoyt Wilhelm	55.00	27.50	5.50
☐ 546	Marty Kutyna	20.00	10.00	2.00
☐ 547	Leon Wagner	20.00	10.00	2.00
☐ 548	Ted Wills	20.00	10.00	2.00
☐ 549	Hal R. Smith	20.00	10.00	2.00
☐ 550	Frank Baumann	20.00	10.00	2.00

		NRMT	VG-E	GOOD
☐ 551	George Altman	20.00	10.00	2.00
☐ 552	Jim Archer	20.00	10.00	2.00
☐ 553	Bill Fischer	20.00	10.00	2.00
☐ 554	Pittsburgh Pirates ...	38.00	18.00	3.50
	Team Card			
☐ 555	Sam Jones	22.00	11.00	2.20
☐ 556	Ken R. Hunt	20.00	10.00	2.00
☐ 557	Jose Valdivielso	20.00	10.00	2.00
☐ 558	Don Ferrarese	20.00	10.00	2.00
☐ 559	Jim Gentile	22.00	11.00	2.20
☐ 560	Barry Latman	20.00	10.00	2.00
☐ 561	Charley James	20.00	10.00	2.00
☐ 562	Bill Monbouquette ..	22.00	11.00	2.20
☐ 563	Bob Cerv	22.00	11.00	2.20
☐ 564	Don Cardwell	20.00	10.00	2.00
☐ 565	Felipe Alou	22.00	11.00	2.20
☐ 566	Paul Richards MG AS	21.00	10.50	2.10
☐ 567	Danny Murtaugh MG			
	AS	21.00	10.50	2.10
☐ 568	Bill Skowron AS	22.00	11.00	2.20
☐ 569	Frank Herrera AS ...	21.00	10.50	2.10
☐ 570	Nellie Fox AS	30.00	15.00	3.00
☐ 571	Bill Mazeroski AS ...	22.00	11.00	2.20
☐ 572	Brooks Robinson AS .	75.00	37.50	7.50
☐ 573	Ken Boyer AS	24.00	12.00	2.40
☐ 574	Luis Aparicio AS	40.00	20.00	4.00
☐ 575	Ernie Banks AS	75.00	37.50	7.50
☐ 576	Roger Maris AS	100.00	50.00	10.00
☐ 577	Hank Aaron AS	135.00	65.00	13.50
☐ 578	Mickey Mantle AS ..	300.00	150.00	30.00
☐ 579	Willie Mays AS	135.00	65.00	13.50
☐ 580	Al Kaline AS	75.00	37.50	7.50
☐ 581	Frank Robinson AS ..	75.00	37.50	7.50
☐ 582	Earl Battey AS	21.00	10.50	2.10
☐ 583	Del Crandall AS	21.00	10.50	2.10
☐ 584	Jim Perry AS	21.00	10.50	2.10
☐ 585	Bob Friend AS	21.00	10.50	2.10
☐ 586	Whitey Ford AS	75.00	37.50	7.50
☐ 587	Does not exist	00.00	00.00	0.00
☐ 588	Does not exist	00.00	00.00	0.00
☐ 589	Warren Spahn AS ..	125.00	40.00	8.00

1962 Topps

The cards in this 598-card set measure 2 ½"
by 3 ½". The 1962 Topps set contains a mini-
series spotlighting Babe Ruth (135 to 144).
Other subsets in the set include League
Leaders (51-60), World Series cards (232-
237), In Action cards (311-319), NL All Stars
(390-399), AL All Stars (466-475), and Rookie
Prospects (591-598). The All-Star selections
were again provided by Sport Magazine, as in
1958 and 1960. The second series had two
distinct printings which are distinguishable by
numerous color and pose variations. Card
number 139 exists as A: Babe Ruth Special
card, B: Hal Reniff with arms over head, or C:
Hal Reniff in the same pose as card number
159. In addition, two poses exist for players depicted on card numbers 129, 132, 134, 147,
174, 176, and 190. The high number series,
523 to 598, is somewhat more difficult to obtain
than other cards in the set. Within the last series (523-598) there are 43 cards which were
printed in lesser quantities; these are marked
SP in the checklist below. The set price listed
does not include the pose variations (see
checklist below for individual values).

	NRMT	VG-E	GOOD
COMPLETE SET	4000.00	2000.00	500.00
COMMON PLAYER (1-109)	1.00	.50	.10
COMMON PLAYER (110-196)	1.00	.50	.10
COMMON PLAYER (197-283)	1.25	.60	.12
COMMON PLAYER (284-370)	1.25	.60	.12

	NRMT	VG-E	GOOD
COMMON PLAYER (371-446)	2.00	1.00	.20
COMMON PLAYER (447-522)	3.00	1.50	.30
COMMON PLAYER (523-590)	9.00	4.50	.90
COMMON SP (523-590)	18.00	9.00	1.80
COMMON PLAYER (591-598)	18.00	9.00	1.80

			NRMT	VG-E	GOOD
☐	1	Roger Maris	150.00	40.00	8.00
☐	2	Jim Brosnan	1.00	.50	.10
☐	3	Pete Runnels	1.00	.50	.10
☐	4	John DeMerit	1.00	.50	.10
☐	5	Sandy Koufax	80.00	40.00	8.00
☐	6	Marv Breeding	1.00	.50	.10
☐	7	Frank Thomas	1.00	.50	.10
☐	8	Ray Herbert	1.00	.50	.10
☐	9	Jim Davenport	1.00	.50	.10
☐	10	Bob Clemente	70.00	35.00	7.00
☐	11	Tom Morgan	1.00	.50	.10
☐	12	Harry Craft MG	1.00	.50	.10
☐	13	Dick Howser	2.00	1.00	.20
☐	14	Bill White	2.50	1.25	.25
☐	15	Dick Donovan	1.00	.50	.10
☐	16	Darrell Johnson	1.00	.50	.10
☐	17	John Callison	1.50	.75	.15
☐	18	Managers' Dream	100.00	50.00	10.00
		Mickey Mantle			
		Willie Mays			
☐	19	Ray Washburn	1.00	.50	.10
☐	20	Rocky Colavito	3.00	1.50	.30
☐	21	Jim Kaat	4.00	2.00	.40
☐	22A	Checklist 1 COR	5.00	1.00	
☐	22B	Checklist 1 ERR	6.00	1.00	
		(121-176 on back)			
☐	23	Norm Larker	1.00	.50	.10
☐	24	Tigers Team	3.00	1.50	.30
☐	25	Ernie Banks	25.00	12.50	2.50
☐	26	Chris Cannizzaro	1.00	.50	.10
☐	27	Chuck Cottier	1.00	.50	.10
☐	28	Minnie Minoso	2.00	1.00	.20
☐	29	Casey Stengel MG	12.50	6.25	1.25
☐	30	Eddie Mathews	18.00	9.00	1.80
☐	31	Tom Tresh	8.00	4.00	.80
☐	32	John Roseboro	1.50	.75	.15
☐	33	Don Larsen	2.00	1.00	.20
☐	34	Johnny Temple	1.00	.50	.10
☐	35	Don Schwall	1.00	.50	.10
☐	36	Don Leppert	1.00	.50	.10
☐	37	Tribe Hill Trio	1.50	.75	.15
		Barry Latman			
		Dick Stigman			

			NRMT	VG-E	GOOD
		Jim Perry			
☐	38	Gene Stephens	1.00	.50	.10
☐	39	Joe Koppe	1.00	.50	.10
☐	40	Orlando Cepeda	4.00	2.00	.40
☐	41	Cliff Cook	1.00	.50	.10
☐	42	Jim King	1.00	.50	.10
☐	43	Los Angeles Dodgers	3.50	1.75	.35
		Team Card			
☐	44	Don Taussig	1.00	.50	.10
☐	45	Brooks Robinson ...	25.00	12.50	2.50
☐	46	Jack Baldschun	1.00	.50	.10
☐	47	Bob Will	1.00	.50	.10
☐	48	Ralph Terry	1.50	.75	.15
☐	49	Hal Jones	1.00	.50	.10
☐	50	Stan Musial	70.00	35.00	7.00
☐	51	AL Batting Leaders .	2.00	1.00	.20
		Norm Cash			
		Jim Piersall			
		Al Kaline			
		Elston Howard			
☐	52	NL Batting Leaders .	4.00	2.00	.40
		Bob Clemente			
		Vada Pinson			
		Ken Boyer			
		Wally Moon			
☐	53	AL Home Run Leaders	25.00	12.50	2.50
		Roger Maris			
		Mickey Mantle			
		Jim Gentile			
		Harmon Killebrew			
☐	54	NL Home Run Leaders	4.00	2.00	.40
		Orlando Cepeda			
		Willie Mays			
		Frank Robinson			
☐	55	AL ERA Leaders ...	2.00	1.00	.20
		Dick Donovan			
		Bill Stafford			
		Don Mossi			
		Milt Pappas			
☐	56	NL ERA Leaders ...	3.00	1.50	.30
		Warren Spahn			
		Jim O'Toole			
		Curt Simmons			
		Mike McCormick			
☐	57	AL Wins Leaders ...	3.00	1.50	.30
		Whitey Ford			
		Frank Lary			

			NRMT	VG-E	GOOD
		Steve Barber			
		Jim Bunning			
☐	58	NL Wins Leaders ...	3.00	1.50	.30
		Warren Spahn			
		Joe Jay			
		Jim O'Toole			
☐	59	AL Strikeout Leaders	2.00	1.00	.20
		Camilo Pascual			
		Whitey Ford			
		Jim Bunning			
		Juan Pizzaro			
☐	60	NL Strikeout Leaders	4.00	2.00	.40
		Sandy Koufax			
		Stan Williams			
		Don Drysdale			
		Jim O'Toole			
☐	61	Cardinals Team	3.00	1.50	.30
☐	62	Steve Boros	1.50	.75	.15
☐	63	Tony Cloninger	1.00	.50	.10
☐	64	Russ Snyder	1.00	.50	.10
☐	65	Bobby Richardson ..	4.50	2.25	.45
☐	66	Cuno Barragon	1.00	.50	.10
☐	67	Harvey Haddix	1.50	.75	.15
☐	68	Ken Hunt	1.00	.50	.10
☐	69	Phil Ortega	1.00	.50	.10
☐	70	Harmon Killebrew ..	18.00	9.00	1.80
☐	71	Dick LeMay	1.00	.50	.10
☐	72	Bob's Pupils	1.00	.50	.10
		Steve Boros			
		Bob Scheffing			
		Jake Wood			
☐	73	Nellie Fox	4.50	2.25	.45
☐	74	Bob Lillis	1.00	.50	.10
☐	75	Milt Pappas	1.50	.75	.15
☐	76	Howie Bedell	1.00	.50	.10
☐	77	Tony Taylor	1.00	.50	.10
☐	78	Gene Green	1.00	.50	.10
☐	79	Ed Hobaugh	1.00	.50	.10
☐	80	Vada Pinson	2.50	1.25	.25
☐	81	Jim Pagliaroni	1.00	.50	.10
☐	82	Deron Johnson	1.00	.50	.10
☐	83	Larry Jackson	1.00	.50	.10
☐	84	Lenny Green	1.00	.50	.10
☐	85	Gil Hodges	10.00	5.00	1.00
☐	86	Donn Clendenon ...	1.50	.75	.15
☐	87	Mike Roarke	1.00	.50	.10
☐	88	Ralph Houk MG	2.50	1.25	.25
		(Berra in background)			
☐	89	Barney Schultz	1.00	.50	.10

		NRMT	VG-E	GOOD
☐ 90	Jim Piersall	2.00	1.00	.20
☐ 91	J.C. Martin	1.00	.50	.10
☐ 92	Sam Jones	1.00	.50	.10
☐ 93	John Blanchard	1.50	.75	.15
☐ 94	Jay Hook	1.00	.50	.10
☐ 95	Don Hoak	1.00	.50	.10
☐ 96	Eli Grba	1.00	.50	.10
☐ 97	Tito Francona	1.00	.50	.10
☐ 98	Checklist 2	5.00	1.00	.20
☐ 99	John (Boog) Powell	10.00	5.00	1.00
☐ 100	Warren Spahn	25.00	12.50	2.50
☐ 101	Carroll Hardy	1.00	.50	.10
☐ 102	Al Schroll	1.00	.50	.10
☐ 103	Don Blasingame	1.00	.50	.10
☐ 104	Ted Savage	1.00	.50	.10
☐ 105	Don Mossi	1.50	.75	.15
☐ 106	Carl Sawatski	1.00	.50	.10
☐ 107	Mike McCormick	1.50	.75	.15
☐ 108	Willie Davis	2.00	1.00	.20
☐ 109	Bob Shaw	1.00	.50	.10
☐ 110	Bill Skowron	3.50	1.75	.35
☐ 111	Dallas Green	3.50	1.75	.35
☐ 112	Hank Foiles	1.00	.50	.10
☐ 113	Chicago White Sox Team Card	3.00	1.50	.30
☐ 114	Howie Koplitz	1.00	.50	.10
☐ 115	Bob Skinner	1.00	.50	.10
☐ 116	Herb Score	1.50	.75	.15
☐ 117	Gary Geiger	1.00	.50	.10
☐ 118	Julian Javier	1.00	.50	.10
☐ 119	Danny Murphy	1.00	.50	.10
☐ 120	Bob Purkey	1.00	.50	.10
☐ 121	Billy Hitchcock MG	1.00	.50	.10
☐ 122	Norm Bass	1.00	.50	.10
☐ 123	Mike De La Hoz	1.00	.50	.10
☐ 124	Bill Pleis	1.00	.50	.10
☐ 125	Gene Woodling	1.50	.75	.15
☐ 126	Al Cicotte	1.00	.50	.10
☐ 127	Pride of A's Norm Siebern Hank Bauer Jerry Lumpe	1.50	.75	.15
☐ 128	Art Fowler	1.00	.50	.10
☐ 129A	Lee Walls (facing right)	1.00	.50	.10
☐ 129B	Lee Walls (facing left)	12.50	6.25	1.25
☐ 130	Frank Bolling	1.00	.50	.10
☐ 131	Pete Richert	1.00	.50	.10
☐ 132A	Angels Team (without photo)	3.00	1.50	.30
☐ 132B	Angels Team (with photo)	12.50	6.25	1.25
☐ 133	Felipe Alou	2.00	1.00	.20
☐ 134A	Billy Hoeft (facing right)	1.00	.50	.10
☐ 134B	Billy Hoeft (facing straight)	12.50	6.25	1.25
☐ 135	Babe Ruth Special 1 Babe as a Boy	6.50	3.25	.65
☐ 136	Babe Ruth Special 2 Babe Joins Yanks	6.50	3.25	.65
☐ 137	Babe Ruth Special 3 Babe with Huggins	6.50	3.25	.65
☐ 138	Babe Ruth Special 4 Famous Slugger	6.50	3.25	.65
☐ 139A	Babe Ruth Special 5	10.00	5.00	1.00
☐ 139B	Hal Reniff PORT	10.00	5.00	1.00
☐ 139C	Hal Reniff (pitching)	45.00	22.50	4.50
☐ 140	Babe Ruth Special 6 Gehrig and Ruth	10.00	5.00	1.00
☐ 141	Babe Ruth Special 7 Twilight Years	6.50	3.25	.65
☐ 142	Babe Ruth Special 8 Coaching Dodgers	6.50	3.25	.65
☐ 143	Babe Ruth Special 9 Greatest Sports Hero	6.50	3.25	.65
☐ 144	Babe Ruth Special 10 Farewell Speech	6.50	3.25	.65
☐ 145	Barry Latman	1.00	.50	.10
☐ 146	Don Demeter	1.00	.50	.10
☐ 147A	Bill Kunkel PORT	1.00	.50	.10
☐ 147B	Bill Kunkel (pitching pose)	12.50	6.25	1.25
☐ 148	Wally Post	1.00	.50	.10
☐ 149	Bob Duliba	1.00	.50	.10
☐ 150	Al Kaline	24.00	12.00	2.40
☐ 151	Johnny Klippstein	1.00	.50	.10
☐ 152	Mickey Vernon	1.50	.75	.15
☐ 153	Pumpsie Green	1.00	.50	.10
☐ 154	Lee Thomas	2.00	1.00	.20
☐ 155	Stu Miller	1.00	.50	.10
☐ 156	Merritt Ranew	1.00	.50	.10
☐ 157	Wes Covington	1.00	.50	.10
☐ 158	Braves Team	3.00	1.50	.30
☐ 159	Hal Reniff	1.50	.75	.15
☐ 160	Dick Stuart	1.50	.75	.15

		NRMT	VG-E	GOOD			NRMT	VG-E	GOOD
☐ 161	Frank Baumann	1.00	.50	.10	☐ 199	Gaylord Perry	100.00	45.00	9.00
☐ 162	Sammy Drake	1.00	.50	.10	☐ 200	Mickey Mantle	350.00	175.00	35.00
☐ 163	Hot Corner Guard ..	1.50	.75	.15	☐ 201	Ike Delock	1.25	.60	.12
	Billy Gardner				☐ 202	Carl Warwick	1.25	.60	.12
	Cletis Boyer				☐ 203	Jack Fisher	1.25	.60	.12
☐ 164	Hal Naragon	1.00	.50	.10	☐ 204	Johnny Weekly	1.25	.60	.12
☐ 165	Jackie Brandt	1.00	.50	.10	☐ 205	Gene Freese	1.25	.60	.12
☐ 166	Don Lee	1.00	.50	.10	☐ 206	Senators Team	3.00	1.50	.30
☐ 167	Tim McCarver	15.00	7.50	1.50	☐ 207	Pete Burnside	1.25	.60	.12
☐ 168	Leo Posada	1.00	.50	.10	☐ 208	Billy Martin	6.00	3.00	.60
☐ 169	Bob Cerv	1.50	.75	.15	☐ 209	Jim Fregosi	5.00	2.50	.50
☐ 170	Ron Santo	3.50	1.75	.35	☐ 210	Roy Face	2.00	1.00	.20
☐ 171	Dave Sisler	1.00	.50	.10	☐ 211	Midway Masters	1.25	.60	.12
☐ 172	Fred Hutchinson MG	1.50	.75	.15		Frank Bolling			
☐ 173	Chico Fernandez ...	1.00	.50	.10		Roy McMillan			
☐ 174A	Carl Willey	1.00	.50	.10	☐ 212	Jim Owens	1.25	.60	.12
	(capless)				☐ 213	Richie Ashburn	5.00	2.50	.50
☐ 174B	Carl Willey	12.50	6.25	1.25	☐ 214	Dom Zanni	1.25	.60	.12
	(with cap)				☐ 215	Woody Held	1.25	.60	.12
☐ 175	Frank Howard	2.00	1.00	.20	☐ 216	Ron Kline	1.25	.60	.12
☐ 176A	Eddie Yost PORT ..	1.00	.50	.10	☐ 217	Walt Alston MG	4.50	2.25	.45
☐ 176B	Eddie Yost BATTING	12.50	6.25	1.25	☐ 218	Joe Torre	10.00	5.00	1.00
☐ 177	Bobby Shantz	2.00	1.00	.20	☐ 219	Al Downing	3.00	1.50	.30
☐ 178	Camilo Carreon	1.00	.50	.10	☐ 220	Roy Sievers	1.75	.85	.17
☐ 179	Tom Sturdivant	1.00	.50	.10	☐ 221	Bill Short	1.25	.60	.12
☐ 180	Bob Allison	1.50	.75	.15	☐ 222	Jerry Zimmerman ...	1.25	.60	.12
☐ 181	Paul Brown	1.00	.50	.10	☐ 223	Alex Grammas	1.25	.60	.12
☐ 182	Bob Nieman	1.00	.50	.10	☐ 224	Don Rudolph	1.25	.60	.12
☐ 183	Roger Craig	2.50	1.25	.25	☐ 225	Frank Malzone	1.75	.85	.17
☐ 184	Haywood Sullivan ..	1.50	.75	.15	☐ 226	San Francisco Giants	3.00	1.50	.30
☐ 185	Roland Sheldon ...	1.00	.50	.10		Team Card			
☐ 186	Mack Jones	1.00	.50	.10	☐ 227	Bob Tiefenauer	1.25	.60	.12
☐ 187	Gene Conley	1.00	.50	.10	☐ 228	Dale Long	1.75	.85	.17
☐ 188	Chuck Hiller	1.00	.50	.10	☐ 229	Jesus McFarlane ...	1.25	.60	.12
☐ 189	Dick Hall	1.00	.50	.10	☐ 230	Camilo Pascual	1.75	.85	.17
☐ 190A	Wally Moon PORT ..	1.50	.75	.15	☐ 231	Ernie Bowman	1.25	.60	.12
☐ 190B	Wally Moon BATTING	12.50	6.25	1.25	☐ 232	World Series Game 1	3.00	1.50	.30
☐ 191	Jim Brewer	1.00	.50	.10		Yanks win opener			
☐ 192A	Checklist 3	5.00	1.00	.20	☐ 233	World Series Game 2	3.00	1.50	.30
	(without comma)					Jay ties it up			
☐ 192B	Checklist 3	7.50	1.25	.30	☐ 234	World Series Game 3	9.00	4.50	.90
	(comma after					Maris wins in 9th			
	Checklist)				☐ 235	World Series Game 4	5.00	2.50	.50
☐ 193	Eddie Kasko	1.00	.50	.10		Ford sets new mark			
☐ 194	Dean Chance	2.00	1.00	.20	☐ 236	World Series Game 5	3.00	1.50	.30
☐ 195	Joe Cunningham ...	1.50	.75	.15		Yanks crush Reds			
☐ 196	Terry Fox	1.00	.50	.10	☐ 237	World Series Summary	3.00	1.50	.30
☐ 197	Daryl Spencer	1.25	.60	.12		Yanks celebrate			
☐ 198	Johnny Keane MG ..	1.75	.85	.17	☐ 238	Norm Sherry	1.25	.60	.12

		NRMT	VG-E	GOOD
☐ 239	Cecil Butler	1.25	.60	.12
☐ 240	George Altman	1.25	.60	.12
☐ 241	Johnny Kucks	1.25	.60	.12
☐ 242	Mel McGaha	1.25	.60	.12
☐ 243	Robin Roberts	10.00	5.00	1.00
☐ 244	Don Gile	1.25	.60	.12
☐ 245	Ron Hansen	1.25	.60	.12
☐ 246	Art Ditmar	1.25	.60	.12
☐ 247	Joe Pignatano	1.25	.60	.12
☐ 248	Bob Aspromonte	1.25	.60	.12
☐ 249	Ed Keegan	1.25	.60	.12
☐ 250	Norm Cash	2.50	1.25	.25
☐ 251	New York Yankees Team Card	12.50	6.25	1.25
☐ 252	Earl Francis	1.25	.60	.12
☐ 253	Harry Chiti	1.25	.60	.12
☐ 254	Gordon Windhorn	1.25	.60	.12
☐ 255	Juan Pizarro	1.25	.60	.12
☐ 256	Elio Chacon	1.25	.60	.12
☐ 257	Jack Spring	1.25	.60	.12
☐ 258	Marty Keough	1.25	.60	.12
☐ 259	Lou Klimchock	1.25	.60	.12
☐ 260	Billy Pierce	1.75	.85	.17
☐ 261	George Alusik	1.25	.60	.12
☐ 262	Bob Schmidt	1.25	.60	.12
☐ 263	The Right.Pitch Bob Purkey Jim Turner Joe Jay	1.25	.60	.12
☐ 264	Dick Ellsworth	1.25	.60	.12
☐ 265	Joe Adcock	1.75	.85	.17
☐ 266	John Anderson	1.25	.60	.12
☐ 267	Dan Dobbek	1.25	.60	.12
☐ 268	Ken McBride	1.25	.60	.12
☐ 269	Bob Oldis	1.25	.60	.12
☐ 270	Dick Groat	2.50	1.25	.25
☐ 271	Ray Rippelmeyer	1.25	.60	.12
☐ 272	Earl Robinson	1.25	.60	.12
☐ 273	Gary Bell	1.25	.60	.12
☐ 274	Sammy Taylor	1.25	.60	.12
☐ 275	Norm Siebern	1.25	.60	.12
☐ 276	Hal Kolstad	1.25	.60	.12
☐ 277	Checklist 4	5.00	1.00	.20
☐ 278	Ken Johnson	1.25	.60	.12
☐ 279	Hobie Landrith UER (wrong birthdate)	1.25	.60	.12
☐ 280	Johnny Podres	2.50	1.25	.25
☐ 281	Jake Gibbs	1.25	.60	.12
☐ 282	Dave Hillman	1.25	.60	.12

		NRMT	VG-E	GOOD
☐ 283	Charlie Smith	1.25	.60	.12
☐ 284	Ruben Amaro	1.25	.60	.12
☐ 285	Curt Simmons	1.75	.85	.17
☐ 286	Al Lopez MG	3.00	1.50	.30
☐ 287	George Witt	1.25	.60	.12
☐ 288	Billy Williams	25.00	10.00	2.00
☐ 289	Mike Krsnich	1.25	.60	.12
☐ 290	Jim Gentile	1.75	.85	.17
☐ 291	Hal Stowe	1.25	.60	.12
☐ 292	Jerry Kindall	1.25	.60	.12
☐ 293	Bob Miller	1.25	.60	.12
☐ 294	Phillies Team	3.00	1.50	.30
☐ 295	Vern Law	1.75	.85	.17
☐ 296	Ken Hamlin	1.25	.60	.12
☐ 297	Ron Perranoski	1.75	.85	.17
☐ 298	Bill Tuttle	1.25	.60	.12
☐ 299	Don Wert	1.25	.60	.12
☐ 300	Willie Mays	100.00	50.00	10.00
☐ 301	Galen Cisco	1.25	.60	.12
☐ 302	Johnny Edwards	1.25	.60	.12
☐ 303	Frank Torre	1.25	.60	.12
☐ 304	Dick Farrell	1.25	.60	.12
☐ 305	Jerry Lumpe	1.25	.60	.12
☐ 306	Redbird Rippers Lindy McDaniel Larry Jackson	1.75	.85	.17
☐ 307	Jim Grant	1.25	.60	.12
☐ 308	Neil Chrisley	1.25	.60	.12
☐ 309	Moe Morhardt	1.25	.60	.12
☐ 310	Whitey Ford	25.00	12.50	2.50
☐ 311	Tony Kubek IA	2.50	1.25	.25
☐ 312	Warren Spahn IA	6.00	3.00	.60
☐ 313	Roger Maris IA	12.50	6.25	1.25
☐ 314	Rocky Colavito IA	2.50	1.25	.25
☐ 315	Whitey Ford IA	6.00	3.00	.60
☐ 316	Harmon Killebrew IA	5.00	2.50	.50
☐ 317	Stan Musial IA	10.00	5.00	1.00
☐ 318	Mickey Mantle IA	40.00	20.00	4.00
☐ 319	Mike McCormick IA	1.75	.85	.17
☐ 320	Hank Aaron	100.00	50.00	10.00
☐ 321	Lee Stange	1.25	.60	.12
☐ 322	Alvin Dark	1.75	.85	.17
☐ 323	Don Landrum	1.25	.60	.12
☐ 324	Joe McClain	1.25	.60	.12
☐ 325	Luis Aparicio	10.00	5.00	1.00
☐ 326	Tom Parsons	1.25	.60	.12
☐ 327	Ozzie Virgil	1.25	.60	.12
☐ 328	Ken Walters	1.25	.60	.12
☐ 329	Bob Bolin	1.25	.60	.12

		NRMT	VG-E	GOOD			NRMT	VG-E	GOOD
☐ 330	John Romano	1.25	.60	.12	☐ 376	Bud Daley	2.00	1.00	.20
☐ 331	Moe Drabowsky	1.25	.60	.12	☐ 377	John Orsino	2.00	1.00	.20
☐ 332	Don Buddin	1.25	.60	.12	☐ 378	Bennie Daniels	2.00	1.00	.20
☐ 333	Frank Cipriani	1.25	.60	.12	☐ 379	Chuck Essegian	2.00	1.00	.20
☐ 334	Boston Red Sox	3.00	1.50	.30	☐ 380	Lou Burdette	3.00	1.50	.30
	Team Card				☐ 381	Chico Cardenas	2.00	1.00	.20
☐ 335	Bill Bruton	1.75	.85	.17	☐ 382	Dick Williams	2.50	1.25	.25
☐ 336	Billy Muffett	1.25	.60	.12	☐ 383	Ray Sadecki	2.00	1.00	.20
☐ 337	Jim Marshall	1.25	.60	.12	☐ 384	K.C. Athletics	4.00	2.00	.40
☐ 338	Billy Gardner	1.75	.85	.17		Team Card			
☐ 339	Jose Valdivielso	1.25	.60	.12	☐ 385	Early Wynn	10.00	5.00	1.00
☐ 340	Don Drysdale	24.00	12.00	2.40	☐ 386	Don Mincher	2.50	1.25	.25
☐ 341	Mike Hershberger	1.25	.60	.12	☐ 387	Lou Brock	100.00	50.00	10.00
☐ 342	Ed Rakow	1.25	.60	.12	☐ 388	Ryne Duren	2.50	1.25	.25
☐ 343	Albie Pearson	1.25	.60	.12	☐ 389	Smoky Burgess	2.50	1.25	.25
☐ 344	Ed Bauta	1.25	.60	.12	☐ 390	Orlando Cepeda AS	3.50	1.75	.35
☐ 345	Chuck Schilling	1.25	.60	.12	☐ 391	Bill Mazeroski AS	3.00	1.50	.30
☐ 346	Jack Kralick	1.25	.60	.12	☐ 392	Ken Boyer AS	3.00	1.50	.30
☐ 347	Chuck Hinton	1.25	.60	.12	☐ 393	Roy McMillan AS	2.50	1.25	.25
☐ 348	Larry Burright	1.25	.60	.12	☐ 394	Hank Aaron AS	25.00	12.50	2.50
☐ 349	Paul Foytack	1.25	.60	.12	☐ 395	Willie Mays AS	25.00	12.50	2.50
☐ 350	Frank Robinson	25.00	12.50	2.50	☐ 396	Frank Robinson AS	9.00	4.50	.90
☐ 351	Braves' Backstops	1.75	.85	.17	☐ 397	John Roseboro AS	2.50	1.25	.25
	Joe Torre				☐ 398	Don Drysdale AS	7.50	3.75	.75
	Del Crandall				☐ 399	Warren Spahn AS	8.50	4.25	.85
☐ 352	Frank Sullivan	1.25	.60	.12	☐ 400	Elston Howard	5.00	2.50	.50
☐ 353	Bill Mazeroski	3.00	1.50	.30	☐ 401	AL/NL Homer Kings	25.00	12.00	2.40
☐ 354	Roman Mejias	1.25	.60	.12		Roger Maris			
☐ 355	Steve Barber	1.25	.60	.12		Orlando Cepeda			
☐ 356	Tom Haller	1.75	.85	.17	☐ 402	Gino Cimoli	2.00	1.00	.20
☐ 357	Jerry Walker	1.25	.60	.12	☐ 403	Chet Nichols	2.00	1.00	.20
☐ 358	Tommy Davis	2.50	1.25	.25	☐ 404	Tim Harkness	2.00	1.00	.20
☐ 359	Bobby Locke	1.25	.60	.12	☐ 405	Jim Perry	2.50	1.25	.25
☐ 360	Yogi Berra	45.00	22.50	4.50	☐ 406	Bob Taylor	2.00	1.00	.20
☐ 361	Bob Hendley	1.25	.60	.12	☐ 407	Hank Aguirre	2.00	1.00	.20
☐ 362	Ty Cline	1.25	.60	.12	☐ 408	Gus Bell	2.50	1.25	.25
☐ 363	Bob Roselli	1.25	.60	.12	☐ 409	Pittsburgh Pirates	4.00	2.00	.40
☐ 364	Ken Hunt	1.25	.60	.12		Team Card			
☐ 365	Charlie Neal	1.75	.85	.17	☐ 410	Al Smith	2.00	1.00	.20
☐ 366	Phil Regan	1.75	.85	.17	☐ 411	Danny O'Connell	2.00	1.00	.20
☐ 367	Checklist 5	5.00	1.00	.20	☐ 412	Charlie James	2.00	1.00	.20
☐ 368	Bob Tillman	1.25	.60	.12	☐ 413	Matty Alou	3.00	1.50	.30
☐ 369	Ted Bowsfield	1.25	.60	.12	☐ 414	Joe Gaines	2.00	1.00	.20
☐ 370	Ken Boyer	3.50	1.75	.35	☐ 415	Bill Virdon	3.00	1.50	.30
☐ 371	Earl Battey	2.00	1.00	.20	☐ 416	Bob Scheffing MG	2.00	1.00	.20
☐ 372	Jack Curtis	2.00	1.00	.20	☐ 417	Joe Azcue	2.00	1.00	.20
☐ 373	Al Heist	2.00	1.00	.20	☐ 418	Andy Carey	2.00	1.00	.20
☐ 374	Gene Mauch	2.50	1.25	.25	☐ 419	Bob Bruce	2.00	1.00	.20
☐ 375	Ron Fairly	2.50	1.25	.25	☐ 420	Gus Triandos	2.50	1.25	.25

			NRMT	VG-E	GOOD
☐	421	Ken MacKenzie	2.00	1.00	.20
☐	422	Steve Bilko	2.00	1.00	.20
☐	423	Rival League	4.00	2.00	.40
		Relief Aces:			
		Roy Face			
		Hoyt Wilhelm			
☐	424	Al McBean	2.00	1.00	.20
☐	425	Carl Yastrzemski	150.00	75.00	15.00
☐	426	Bob Farley	2.00	1.00	.20
☐	427	Jake Wood	2.00	1.00	.20
☐	428	Joe Hicks	2.00	1.00	.20
☐	429	Billy O'Dell	2.00	1.00	.20
☐	430	Tony Kubek	7.00	3.50	.70
☐	431	Bob Rodgers	4.00	2.00	.40
☐	432	Jim Pendleton	2.00	1.00	.20
☐	433	Jim Archer	2.00	1.00	.20
☐	434	Clay Dalrymple	2.00	1.00	.20
☐	435	Larry Sherry	2.50	1.25	.25
☐	436	Felix Mantilla	2.00	1.00	.20
☐	437	Ray Moore	2.00	1.00	.20
☐	438	Dick Brown	2.00	1.00	.20
☐	439	Jerry Buchek	2.00	1.00	.20
☐	440	Joey Jay	2.00	1.00	.20
☐	441	Checklist 6	6.00	1.00	.20
☐	442	Wes Stock	2.50	1.25	.25
☐	443	Del Crandall	2.50	1.25	.25
☐	444	Ted Wills	2.00	1.00	.20
☐	445	Vic Power	2.00	1.00	.20
☐	446	Don Elston	2.00	1.00	.20
☐	447	Willie Kirkland	3.00	1.50	.30
☐	448	Joe Gibbon	3.00	1.50	.30
☐	449	Jerry Adair	3.00	1.50	.30
☐	450	Jim O'Toole	3.00	1.50	.30
☐	451	Jose Tartabull	3.00	1.50	.30
☐	452	Earl Averill	3.00	1.50	.30
☐	453	Cal McLish	3.00	1.50	.30
☐	454	Floyd Robinson	3.00	1.50	.30
☐	455	Luis Arroyo	3.00	1.50	.30
☐	456	Joe Amalfitano	3.00	1.50	.30
☐	457	Lou Clinton	3.00	1.50	.30
☐	458A	Bob Buhl	3.00	1.50	.30
		(Braves' cap emblem)			
☐	458B	Bob Buhl	40.00	20.00	4.00
		(no emblem on cap)			
☐	459	Ed Bailey	3.00	1.50	.30
☐	460	Jim Bunning	7.50	3.75	.75
☐	461	Ken Hubbs	7.50	3.75	.75
☐	462A	Willie Tasby	3.00	1.50	.30

			NRMT	VG-E	GOOD
		(Senators' cap emblem)			
☐	462B	Willie Tasby	40.00	20.00	4.00
		(no emblem on cap)			
☐	463	Hank Bauer	4.00	2.00	.40
☐	464	Al Jackson	3.00	1.50	.30
☐	465	Reds Team	6.00	3.00	.60
☐	466	Norm Cash AS	3.50	1.75	.35
☐	467	Chuck Schilling AS	3.00	1.50	.30
☐	468	Brooks Robinson AS	11.00	5.50	1.10
☐	469	Luis Aparicio AS	6.50	3.25	.65
☐	470	Al Kaline AS	11.00	5.50	1.10
☐	471	Mickey Mantle AS	80.00	40.00	8.00
☐	472	Rocky Colavito AS	3.50	1.75	.35
☐	473	Elston Howard AS	3.50	1.75	.35
☐	474	Frank Lary AS	3.00	1.50	.30
☐	475	Whitey Ford AS	10.00	5.00	1.00
☐	476	Orioles Team	6.00	3.00	.60
☐	477	Andre Rodgers	3.00	1.50	.30
☐	478	Don Zimmer	4.50	2.25	.45
☐	479	Joel Horlen	3.00	1.50	.30
☐	480	Harvey Kuenn	4.50	2.25	.45
☐	481	Vic Wertz	3.50	1.75	.35
☐	482	Sam Mele MG	3.00	1.50	.30
☐	483	Don McMahon	3.00	1.50	.30
☐	484	Dick Schofield	3.00	1.50	.30
☐	485	Pedro Ramos	3.00	1.50	.30
☐	486	Jim Gilliam	5.00	2.50	.50
☐	487	Jerry Lynch	3.00	1.50	.30
☐	488	Hal Brown	3.00	1.50	.30
☐	489	Julio Gotay	3.00	1.50	.30
☐	490	Clete Boyer	3.50	1.75	.35
☐	491	Leon Wagner	3.00	1.50	.30
☐	492	Hal W. Smith	3.00	1.50	.30
☐	493	Danny McDevitt	3.00	1.50	.30
☐	494	Sammy White	3.00	1.50	.30
☐	495	Don Cardwell	3.00	1.50	.30
☐	496	Wayne Causey	3.00	1.50	.30
☐	497	Ed Bouchee	3.00	1.50	.30
☐	498	Jim Donohue	3.00	1.50	.30
☐	499	Zoilo Versalles	3.00	1.50	.30
☐	500	Duke Snider	35.00	17.50	3.50
☐	501	Claude Osteen	3.50	1.75	.35
☐	502	Hector Lopez	3.00	1.50	.30
☐	503	Danny Murtaugh MG	3.00	1.50	.30
☐	504	Eddie Bressoud	3.00	1.50	.30
☐	505	Juan Marichal	30.00	15.00	3.00
☐	506	Charlie Maxwell	3.00	1.50	.30
☐	507	Ernie Broglio	3.00	1.50	.30

		NRMT	VG-E	GOOD
☐ 508	Gordy Coleman	3.50	1.75	.35
☐ 509	Dave Giusti	3.50	1.75	.35
☐ 510	Jim Lemon	3.50	1.75	.35
☐ 511	Bubba Phillips	3.00	1.50	.30
☐ 512	Mike Fornieles	3.00	1.50	.30
☐ 513	Whitey Herzog	4.50	2.25	.45
☐ 514	Sherm Lollar	3.50	1.75	.35
☐ 515	Stan Williams	3.00	1.50	.30
☐ 516	Checklist 7	9.00	1.25	.30
☐ 517	Dave Wickersham	3.00	1.50	.30
☐ 518	Lee Maye	3.00	1.50	.30
☐ 519	Bob Johnson	3.00	1.50	.30
☐ 520	Bob Friend	3.50	1.75	.35
☐ 521	Jacke Davis	3.00	1.50	.30
☐ 522	Lindy McDaniel	3.50	1.75	.35
☐ 523	Russ Nixon SP	18.00	9.00	1.80
☐ 524	Howie Nunn SP	18.00	9.00	1.80
☐ 525	George Thomas	9.00	4.50	.90
☐ 526	Hal Woodeshick SP	18.00	9.00	1.80
☐ 527	Dick McAuliffe	12.00	6.00	1.20
☐ 528	Turk Lown	9.00	4.50	.90
☐ 529	John Schaive SP	18.00	9.00	1.80
☐ 530	Bob Gibson SP	100.00	50.00	10.00
☐ 531	Bobby G. Smith	9.00	4.50	.90
☐ 532	Dick Stigman	9.00	4.50	.90
☐ 533	Charley Lau SP	18.00	9.00	1.80
☐ 534	Tony Gonzalez SP	18.00	9.00	1.80
☐ 535	Ed Roebuck	9.00	4.50	.90
☐ 536	Dick Gernert	9.00	4.50	.90
☐ 537	Cleveland Indians Team Card	18.00	9.00	1.80
☐ 538	Jack Sanford SP	18.00	9.00	1.80
☐ 539	Billy Moran	9.00	4.50	.90
☐ 540	Jim Landis SP	18.00	9.00	1.80
☐ 541	Don Nottebart SP	18.00	9.00	1.80
☐ 542	Dave Philley	9.00	4.50	.90
☐ 543	Bob Allen SP	18.00	9.00	1.80
☐ 544	Willie McCovey SP	100.00	50.00	10.00
☐ 545	Hoyt Wilhelm SP	50.00	25.00	5.00
☐ 546	Moe Thacker SP	18.00	9.00	1.80
☐ 547	Don Ferrarese	9.00	4.50	.90
☐ 548	Bobby Del Greco	9.00	4.50	.90
☐ 549	Bill Rigney MG SP	18.00	9.00	1.80
☐ 550	Art Mahaffey SP	18.00	9.00	1.80
☐ 551	Harry Bright	9.00	4.50	.90
☐ 552	Chicago Cubs SP Team Card	30.00	15.00	3.00
☐ 553	Jim Coates SP	18.00	9.00	1.80
☐ 554	Bubba Morton SP	18.00	9.00	1.80

		NRMT	VG-E	GOOD
☐ 555	John Buzhardt SP	18.00	9.00	1.80
☐ 556	Al Spangler	9.00	4.50	.90
☐ 557	Bob Anderson	9.00	4.50	.90
☐ 558	John Goryl	9.00	4.50	.90
☐ 559	Mike Higgins MG	9.00	4.50	.90
☐ 560	Chuck Estrada SP	18.00	9.00	1.80
☐ 561	Gene Oliver SP	18.00	9.00	1.80
☐ 562	Bill Henry	9.00	4.50	.90
☐ 563	Ken Aspromonte	9.00	4.50	.90
☐ 564	Bob Grim	9.00	4.50	.90
☐ 565	Jose Pagan	9.00	4.50	.90
☐ 566	Marty Kutyna SP	18.00	9.00	1.80
☐ 567	Tracy Stallard SP	18.00	9.00	1.80
☐ 568	Jim Golden	9.00	4.50	.90
☐ 569	Ed Sadowski SP	18.00	9.00	1.80
☐ 570	Bill Stafford SP	18.00	9.00	1.80
☐ 571	Billy Klaus SP	18.00	9.00	1.80
☐ 572	Bob G. Miller SP	18.00	9.00	1.80
☐ 573	Johnny Logan	12.00	6.00	1.20
☐ 574	Dean Stone	9.00	4.50	.90
☐ 575	Red Schoendienst	40.00	20.00	4.00
☐ 576	Russ Kemmerer SP	18.00	9.00	1.80
☐ 577	Dave Nicholson SP	18.00	9.00	1.80
☐ 578	Jim Duffalo	9.00	4.50	.90
☐ 579	Jim Schaffer SP	18.00	9.00	1.80
☐ 580	Bill Monbouquette	9.00	4.50	.90
☐ 581	Mel Roach	9.00	4.50	.90
☐ 582	Ron Piche	9.00	4.50	.90
☐ 583	Larry Osborne	9.00	4.50	.90
☐ 584	Minnesota Twins SP Team Card	30.00	15.00	3.00
☐ 585	Glen Hobbie	9.00	4.50	.90
☐ 586	Sammy Esposito SP	18.00	9.00	1.80
☐ 587	Frank Funk SP	18.00	9.00	1.80
☐ 588	Birdie Tebbetts MG	9.00	4.50	.90
☐ 589	Bob Turley	15.00	6.00	1.20
☐ 590	Curt Flood	15.00	6.00	1.20
☐ 591	Rookie Pitchers SP	30.00	15.00	3.00
	Sam McDowell			
	Ron Taylor			
	Ron Nischwitz			
	Art Quirk			
	Dick Radatz			
☐ 592	Rookie Pitchers SP	40.00	20.00	4.00
	Dan Pfister			
	Bo Belinsky			
	Dave Stenhouse			
	Jim Bouton			
	Joe Bonikowski			

1963 Topps

		NRMT	VG-E	GOOD
☐ 593	Rookie Pitchers SP	20.00	10.00	2.00
	Jack Lamabe			
	Craig Anderson			
	Jack Hamilton			
	Bob Moorhead			
	Bob Veale			
☐ 594	Rookie Catchers SP	125.00	50.00	10.00
	Doc Edwards			
	Ken Retzer			
	Bob Uecker			
	Doug Camilli			
	Don Pavletich			
☐ 595	Rookie Infielders SP	18.00	9.00	1.80
	Bob Sadowski			
	Felix Torres			
	Marlan Coughtry			
	Ed Charles			
☐ 596	Rookie Infielders SP	30.00	15.00	3.00
	Bernie Allen			
	Joe Pepitone			
	Phil Linz			
	Rich Rollins			
☐ 597	Rookie Infielders SP	18.00	9.00	1.80
	Jim McKnight			
	Rod Kanehl			
	Amado Samuel			
	Denis Menke			
☐ 598	Rookie Outfielders SP	40.00	15.00	3.00
	Al Luplow			
	Manny Jimenez			
	Howie Goss			
	Jim Hickman			
	Ed Olivares			

*The cards in this 576-card set measure 2 ½"
by 3 ½". The sharp color photographs of the
1963 set are a vivid contrast to the drab pictures of 1962. In addition to the "League
Leaders" series (1-10) and World Series
cards (142-148), the seventh and last series of cards
(523-576) contains seven rookie cards (each
depicting four players). This set has gained
special prominence in recent years since it
contains the rookie card of Pete Rose, #537.*

		NRMT	VG-E	GOOD
COMPLETE SET (576)		4000.00	2000.00	500.00
COMMON PLAYER (1-109)		.75	.35	.07
COMMON PLAYER (110-196)		.85	.40	.08
COMMON PLAYER (197-283)		1.00	.50	.10
COMMON PLAYER (284-446)		1.50	.75	.15
COMMON PLAYER (447-522)		7.00	3.50	.70
COMMON PLAYER (523-576)		5.00	2.50	.50
☐ 1	NL Batting Leaders	20.00	5.00	1.00
	Tommy Davis			
	Frank Robinson			
	Stan Musial			
	Hank Aaron			
	Bill White			
☐ 2	AL Batting Leaders	10.00	5.00	1.00
	Pete Runnels			
	Mickey Mantle			
	Floyd Robinson			
	Norm Siebern			
	Chuck Hinton			

			NRMT	VG-E	GOOD
☐	3	NL Home Run Leaders .... Willie Mays Hank Aaron Frank Robinson Orlando Cepeda Ernie Banks	10.00	5.00	1.00
☐	4	AL Home Run Leaders .... Harmon Killebrew Norm Cash Rocky Colavito Roger Maris Jim Gentile Leon Wagner	3.00	1.50	.30
☐	5	NL ERA Leaders ... Sandy Koufax Bob Shaw Bob Purkey Bob Gibson Don Drysdale	3.00	1.50	.30
☐	6	AL ERA Leaders ... Hank Aguirre Robin Roberts Whitey Ford Eddie Fisher Dean Chance	2.50	1.25	.25
☐	7	AL Pitching Leaders . Don Drysdale Jack Sanford Bob Purkey Billy O'Dell Art Mahaffey Joe Jay	2.00	1.00	.20
☐	8	AL Pitching Leaders . Ralph Terry Dick Donovan Ray Herbert Jim Bunning Camilo Pascual	1.50	.75	.15
☐	9	NL Strikeout Leaders Don Drysdale Sandy Koufax Bob Gibson Billy O'Dell Dick Farrell	3.50	1.75	.35
☐	10	AL Strikeout Leaders Camilo Pascual Jim Bunning	1.50	.75	.15

			NRMT	VG-E	GOOD
		Ralph Terry Juan Pizarro Jim Kaat			
☐	11	Lee Walls	.75	.35	.07
☐	12	Steve Barber	.75	.35	.07
☐	13	Philadelphia Phillies . Team Card	1.75	.85	.17
☐	14	Pedro Ramos	.75	.35	.07
☐	15	Ken Hubbs	1.75	.85	.17
☐	16	Al Smith	.75	.35	.07
☐	17	Ryne Duren	1.00	.50	.10
☐	18	Buc Blasters ...... Smoky Burgess Dick Stuart Bob Clemente Bob Skinner	7.50	3.75	.75
☐	19	Pete Burnside	.75	.35	.07
☐	20	Tony Kubek	3.00	1.50	.30
☐	21	Marty Keough	.75	.35	.07
☐	22	Curt Simmons	1.00	.50	.10
☐	23	Ed Lopat MG	1.50	.75	.15
☐	24	Bob Bruce	.75	.35	.07
☐	25	Al Kaline	24.00	12.00	2.40
☐	26	Ray Moore	.75	.35	.07
☐	27	Choo Choo Coleman	.75	.35	.07
☐	28	Mike Fornieles	.75	.35	.07
☐	29 A	1962 Rookie Stars ... Sammy Ellis Ray Culp John Boozer Jesse Gonder	4.00	2.00	.40
☐	29 B	1963 Rookie Stars .. Sammy Ellis Ray Culp John Boozer Jesse Gonder	1.50	.75	.15
☐	30	Harvey Kuenn	1.50	.75	.15
☐	31	Cal Koonce	.75	.35	.07
☐	32	Tony Gonzalez	.75	.35	.07
☐	33	Bo Belinsky	1.00	.50	.10
☐	34	Dick Schofield	.75	.35	.07
☐	35	John Buzhardt	.75	.35	.07
☐	36	Jerry Kindall	.75	.35	.07
☐	37	Jerry Lynch	.75	.35	.07
☐	38	Bud Daley	.75	.35	.07
☐	39	Angels Team	1.75	.85	.17
☐	40	Vic Power	.75	.35	.07
☐	41	Charley Lau	1.00	.50	.10
☐	42	Stan Williams	.75	.35	.07

			NRMT	VG-E	GOOD
☐	43	Veteran Masters	3.50	1.75	.35
		Casey Stengel			
		Gene Woodling			
☐	44	Terry Fox	.75	.35	.07
☐	45	Bob Aspromonte	.75	.35	.07
☐	46	Tommy Aaron	1.00	.50	.10
☐	47	Don Lock	.75	.35	.07
☐	48	Birdie Tebbetts MG ..	.75	.35	.07
☐	49	Dal Maxvill	.75	.35	.07
☐	50	Billy Pierce	1.00	.50	.10
☐	51	George Alusik	.75	.35	.07
☐	52	Chuck Schilling	.75	.35	.07
☐	53	Joe Moeller	.75	.35	.07
☐	54A	1962 Rookie Stars ..	7.50	3.75	.75
		Nelson Mathews			
		Harry Fanok			
		Jack Cullen			
		Dave DeBusschere			
☐	54B	1963 Rookie Stars ..	3.50	1.75	.35
		Nelson Mathews			
		Harry Fanok			
		Jack Cullen			
		Dave DeBusschere			
☐	55	Bill Virdon	1.50	.75	.15
☐	56	Dennis Bennett	.75	.35	.07
☐	57	Billy Moran	.75	.35	.07
☐	58	Bob Will	.75	.35	.07
☐	59	Craig Anderson	.75	.35	.07
☐	60	Elston Howard	4.00	2.00	.40
☐	61	Ernie Bowman	.75	.35	.07
☐	62	Bob Hendley	.75	.35	.07
☐	63	Reds Team	1.75	.85	.17
☐	64	Dick McAuliffe	.75	.35	.07
☐	65	Jackie Brandt	.75	.35	.07
☐	66	Mike Joyce	.75	.35	.07
☐	67	Ed Charles	.75	.35	.07
☐	68	Friendly Foes	7.50	3.75	.75
		Duke Snider			
		Gil Hodges			
☐	69	Bud Zipfel	.75	.35	.07
☐	70	Jim O'Toole	.75	.35	.07
☐	71	Bobby Wine	.75	.35	.07
☐	72	Johnny Romano	.75	.35	.07
☐	73	Bobby Bragan MG ..	.75	.35	.07
☐	74	Denny Lemaster	.75	.35	.07
☐	75	Bob Allison	1.00	.50	.10
☐	76	Earl Wilson	.75	.35	.07
☐	77	Al Spangler	.75	.35	.07
☐	78	Marv Throneberry ...	1.00	.50	.10

			NRMT	VG-E	GOOD
☐	79	Checklist 1	4.00	.75	.15
☐	80	Jim Gilliam	2.00	1.00	.20
☐	81	Jim Schaffer	.75	.35	.07
☐	82	Ed Rakow	.75	.35	.07
☐	83	Charley James	.75	.35	.07
☐	84	Ron Kline	.75	.35	.07
☐	85	Tom Haller	.75	.35	.07
☐	86	Charley Maxwell	.75	.35	.07
☐	87	Bob Veale	.75	.35	.07
☐	88	Ron Hansen	.75	.35	.07
☐	89	Dick Stigman	.75	.35	.07
☐	90	Gordy Coleman	.75	.35	.07
☐	91	Dallas Green	2.00	1.00	.20
☐	92	Hector Lopez	.75	.35	.07
☐	93	Galen Cisco	.75	.35	.07
☐	94	Bob Schmidt	.75	.35	.07
☐	95	Larry Jackson	.75	.35	.07
☐	96	Lou Clinton	.75	.35	.07
☐	97	Bob Duliba	.75	.35	.07
☐	98	George Thomas	.75	.35	.07
☐	99	Jim Umbricht	.75	.35	.07
☐	100	Joe Cunningham	1.00	.50	.10
☐	101	Joe Gibbon	.75	.35	.07
☐	102A	Checklist 2	5.00	1.00	.20
		(red on yellow)			
☐	102B	Checklist 2	7.00	1.25	.25
		(white on red)			
☐	103	Chuck Essegian	.75	.35	.07
☐	104	Lew Krausse	.75	.35	.07
☐	105	Ron Fairly	1.00	.50	.10
☐	106	Bobby Bolin	.75	.35	.07
☐	107	Jim Hickman	.75	.35	.07
☐	108	Hoyt Wilhelm	7.50	3.75	.75
☐	109	Lee Maye	.75	.35	.07
☐	110	Rich Rollins	.85	.40	.08
☐	111	Al Jackson	.85	.40	.08
☐	112	Dick Brown	.85	.40	.08
☐	113	Don Landrum UER ..	1.25	.60	.12
		(photo actually Ron			
		Santo)			
☐	114	Dan Osinski	.85	.40	.08
☐	115	Carl Yastrzemski ...	75.00	37.50	7.50
☐	116	Jim Brosnan	.85	.40	.08
☐	117	Jacke Davis	.85	.40	.08
☐	118	Sherm Lollar	.85	.40	.08
☐	119	Bob Lillis	.85	.40	.08
☐	120	Roger Maris	45.00	22.50	4.50
☐	121	Jim Hannan	.85	.40	.08
☐	122	Julio Gotay	.85	.40	.08

		NRMT	VG-E	GOOD
☐ 123	Frank Howard	2.00	1.00	.20
☐ 124	Dick Howser	1.50	.75	.15
☐ 125	Robin Roberts	9.00	4.50	.90
☐ 126	Bob Uecker	25.00	12.50	2.50
☐ 127	Bill Tuttle	.85	.40	.08
☐ 128	Matty Alou	1.25	.60	.12
☐ 129	Gary Bell	.85	.40	.08
☐ 130	Dick Groat	1.50	.75	.15
☐ 131	Washington Senators Team Card	1.75	.85	.17
☐ 132	Jack Hamilton	.85	.40	.08
☐ 133	Gene Freese	.85	.40	.08
☐ 134	Bob Scheffing MG	.85	.40	.08
☐ 135	Richie Ashburn	4.50	2.25	.45
☐ 136	Ike Delock	.85	.40	.08
☐ 137	Mack Jones	.85	.40	.08
☐ 138	Pride of NL Willie Mays Stan Musial	25.00	12.50	2.50
☐ 139	Earl Averill	.85	.40	.08
☐ 140	Frank Lary	1.25	.60	.12
☐ 141	Manny Mota	5.00	2.50	.50
☐ 142	World Series Game 1 Ford wins series opener	4.50	2.25	.45
☐ 143	World Series Game 2 Sanford flashes shutout magic	3.00	1.50	.30
☐ 144	World Series Game 3 Maris sparks Yankee rally	7.50	3.75	.75
☐ 145	World Series Game 4 Hiller blasts grand slammer	3.00	1.50	.30
☐ 146	World Series Game 5 Tresh's homer defeats Giants	3.00	1.50	.30
☐ 147	World Series Game 6 Pierce stars in 3 hit victory	3.00	1.50	.30
☐ 148	World Series Game 7 Yanks celebrate as Terry wins	3.00	1.50	.30
☐ 149	Marv Breeding	.85	.40	.08
☐ 150	Johnny Podres	2.00	1.00	.20
☐ 151	Pirates Team	1.75	.85	.17
☐ 152	Ron Nischwitz	.85	.40	.08
☐ 153	Hal Smith	.85	.40	.08
☐ 154	Walt Alston MG	3.50	1.75	.35
☐ 155	Bill Stafford	.85	.40	.08
☐ 156	Roy McMillan	.85	.40	.08
☐ 157	Diego Segui	.85	.40	.08
☐ 158	Rookie Stars Rogelio Alvares Dave Roberts Tommy Harper Bob Saverine	1.25	.60	.12
☐ 159	Jim Pagliaroni	.85	.40	.08
☐ 160	Juan Pizarro	.85	.40	.08
☐ 161	Frank Torre	.85	.40	.08
☐ 162	Twins Team	1.75	.85	.17
☐ 163	Don Larsen	1.75	.85	.17
☐ 164	Bubba Morton	.85	.40	.08
☐ 165	Jim Kaat	3.50	1.75	.35
☐ 166	Johnny Keane MG	1.25	.60	.12
☐ 167	Jim Fregosi	1.75	.85	.17
☐ 168	Russ Nixon	1.25	.60	.12
☐ 169	Rookie Stars Dick Egan Julio Navarro Tommie Sisk Gaylord Perry	18.00	9.00	1.80
☐ 170	Joe Adcock	1.25	.60	.12
☐ 171	Steve Hamilton	.85	.40	.08
☐ 172	Gene Oliver	.85	.40	.08
☐ 173	Bombers' Best Tom Tresh Mickey Mantle Bobby Richardson	40.00	20.00	4.00
☐ 174	Larry Burright	.85	.40	.08
☐ 175	Bob Buhl	.85	.40	.08
☐ 176	Jim King	.85	.40	.08
☐ 177	Bubba Phillips	.85	.40	.08
☐ 178	Johnny Edwards	.85	.40	.08
☐ 179	Ron Piche	.85	.40	.08
☐ 180	Bill Skowron	1.75	.85	.17
☐ 181	Sammy Esposito	.85	.40	.08
☐ 182	Albie Pearson	.85	.40	.08
☐ 183	Joe Pepitone	2.50	1.25	.25
☐ 184	Vern Law	1.25	.60	.12
☐ 185	Chuck Hiller	.85	.40	.08
☐ 186	Jerry Zimmerman	.85	.40	.08
☐ 187	Willie Kirkland	.85	.40	.08
☐ 188	Eddie Bressoud	.85	.40	.08
☐ 189	Dave Giusti	1.25	.60	.12
☐ 190	Minnie Minoso	2.00	1.00	.20
☐ 191	Checklist 3	4.50	.75	.15
☐ 192	Clay Dalrymple	.85	.40	.08

		NRMT	VG-E	GOOD
☐ 193	Andre Rodgers	.85	.40	.08
☐ 194	Joe Nuxhall	1.25	.60	.12
☐ 195	Manny Jimenez	.85	.40	.08
☐ 196	Doug Camilli	.85	.40	.08
☐ 197	Roger Craig	2.50	1.25	.25
☐ 198	Lenny Green	1.00	.50	.10
☐ 199	Joe Amalfitano	1.00	.50	.10
☐ 200	Mickey Mantle	300.00	150.00	30.00
☐ 201	Cecil Butler	1.00	.50	.10
☐ 202	Boston Red Sox Team Card	2.50	1.25	.25
☐ 203	Chico Cardenas	1.00	.50	.10
☐ 204	Don Nottebart	1.00	.50	.10
☐ 205	Luis Aparicio	11.00	5.50	1.10
☐ 206	Ray Washburn	1.00	.50	.10
☐ 207	Ken Hunt	1.00	.50	.10
☐ 208	Rookie Stars	1.00	.50	.10
	Ron Herbel			
	John Miller			
	Wally Wolf			
	Ron Taylor			
☐ 209	Hobie Landrith	1.00	.50	.10
☐ 210	Sandy Koufax	110.00	55.00	11.00
☐ 211	Fred Whitfield	1.00	.50	.10
☐ 212	Glen Hobbie	1.00	.50	.10
☐ 213	Billy Hitchcock MG	1.00	.50	.10
☐ 214	Orlando Pena	1.00	.50	.10
☐ 215	Bob Skinner	1.00	.50	.10
☐ 216	Gene Conley	1.00	.50	.10
☐ 217	Joe Christopher	1.00	.50	.10
☐ 218	Tiger Twirlers	1.50	.75	.15
	Frank Lary			
	Don Mossi			
	Jim Bunning			
☐ 219	Chuck Cottier	1.00	.50	.10
☐ 220	Camilo Pascual	1.00	.50	.10
☐ 221	Cookie Rojas	2.00	1.00	.20
☐ 222	Cubs Team	2.50	1.25	.25
☐ 223	Eddie Fisher	1.00	.50	.10
☐ 224	Mike Roarke	1.00	.50	.10
☐ 225	Joey Jay	1.00	.50	.10
☐ 226	Julian Javier	1.00	.50	.10
☐ 227	Jim Grant	1.00	.50	.10
☐ 228	Rookie Stars	30.00	15.00	3.00
	Max Alvis			
	Bob Bailey			
	Pedro Oliva			
	Ed Kranepool			
☐ 229	Willie Davis	1.50	.75	.15

		NRMT	VG-E	GOOD
☐ 230	Pete Runnels	1.00	.50	.10
☐ 231	Eli Grba (large photo is Ryne Duren)	1.00	.50	.10
☐ 232	Frank Malzone	1.00	.50	.10
☐ 233	Casey Stengel MG	12.00	6.00	1.20
☐ 234	Dave Nicholson	1.00	.50	.10
☐ 235	Billy O'Dell	1.00	.50	.10
☐ 236	Bill Bryan	1.00	.50	.10
☐ 237	Jim Coates	1.00	.50	.10
☐ 238	Lou Johnson	1.00	.50	.10
☐ 239	Harvey Haddix	1.50	.75	.15
☐ 240	Rocky Colavito	3.00	1.50	.30
☐ 241	Bob Smith	1.00	.50	.10
☐ 242	Power Plus	18.00	9.00	1.80
	Ernie Banks			
	Hank Aaron			
☐ 243	Don Leppert	1.00	.50	.10
☐ 244	John Tsitouris	1.00	.50	.10
☐ 245	Gil Hodges	11.00	5.50	1.10
☐ 246	Lee Stange	1.00	.50	.10
☐ 247	Yankees Team	10.00	5.00	1.00
☐ 248	Tito Francona	1.00	.50	.10
☐ 249	Leo Burke	1.00	.50	.10
☐ 250	Stan Musial	80.00	40.00	8.00
☐ 251	Jack Lamabe	1.00	.50	.10
☐ 252	Ron Santo	2.50	1.25	.25
☐ 253	Rookie Stars	1.00	.50	.10
	Len Gabrielson			
	Pete Jernigan			
	John Wojcik			
	Deacon Jones			
☐ 254	Mike Hershberger	1.00	.50	.10
☐ 255	Bob Shaw	1.00	.50	.10
☐ 256	Jerry Lumpe	1.00	.50	.10
☐ 257	Hank Aguirre	1.00	.50	.10
☐ 258	Alvin Dark MG	1.50	.75	.15
☐ 259	Johnny Logan	1.50	.75	.15
☐ 260	Jim Gentile	1.50	.75	.15
☐ 261	Bob Miller	1.00	.50	.10
☐ 262	Ellis Burton	1.00	.50	.10
☐ 263	Dave Stenhouse	1.00	.50	.10
☐ 264	Phil Linz	1.50	.75	.15
☐ 265	Vada Pinson	2.50	1.25	.25
☐ 266	Bob Allen	1.00	.50	.10
☐ 267	Carl Sawatski	1.00	.50	.10
☐ 268	Don Demeter	1.00	.50	.10
☐ 269	Don Mincher	1.00	.50	.10
☐ 270	Felipe Alou	1.50	.75	.15

		NRMT	VG-E	GOOD			NRMT	VG-E	GOOD
☐ 271	Dean Stone	1.00	.50	.10		Team Card			
☐ 272	Danny Murphy	1.00	.50	.10	☐ 313	Ernie Broglio	1.50	.75	.15
☐ 273	Sammy Taylor	1.00	.50	.10	☐ 314	John Goryl	1.50	.75	.15
☐ 274	Checklist 4	4.50	.75	.15	☐ 315	Ralph Terry	2.00	1.00	.20
☐ 275	Eddie Mathews	16.00	8.00	1.60	☐ 316	Norm Sherry	1.50	.75	.15
☐ 276	Barry Shetrone	1.00	.50	.10	☐ 317	Sam McDowell	2.50	1.25	.25
☐ 277	Dick Farrell	1.00	.50	.10	☐ 318	Gene Mauch MG	2.00	1.00	.20
☐ 278	Chico Fernandez	1.00	.50	.10	☐ 319	Joe Gaines	1.50	.75	.15
☐ 279	Wally Moon	1.50	.75	.15	☐ 320	Warren Spahn	24.00	12.00	2.40
☐ 280	Bob Rodgers	1.50	.75	.15	☐ 321	Gino Cimoli	1.50	.75	.15
☐ 281	Tom Sturdivant	1.00	.50	.10	☐ 322	Bob Turley	2.50	1.25	.25
☐ 282	Bobby Del Greco	1.00	.50	.10	☐ 323	Bill Mazeroski	2.50	1.25	.25
☐ 283	Roy Sievers	1.50	.75	.15	☐ 324	Rookie Stars	2.50	1.25	.25
☐ 284	Dave Sisler	1.50	.75	.15		George Williams			
☐ 285	Dick Stuart	2.00	1.00	.20		Pete Ward			
☐ 286	Stu Miller	1.50	.75	.15		Vic Davalillo			
☐ 287	Dick Bertell	1.50	.75	.15	☐ 325	Jack Sanford	2.00	1.00	.20
☐ 288	Chicago White Sox	3.00	1.50	.30	☐ 326	Hank Foiles	1.50	.75	.15
	Team Card				☐ 327	Paul Foytack	1.50	.75	.15
☐ 289	Hal Brown	1.50	.75	.15	☐ 328	Dick Williams	2.00	1.00	.20
☐ 290	Bill White	2.50	1.25	.25	☐ 329	Lindy McDaniel	2.00	1.00	.20
☐ 291	Don Rudolph	1.50	.75	.15	☐ 330	Chuck Hinton	1.50	.75	.15
☐ 292	Pumpsie Green	1.50	.75	.15	☐ 331	Series Foes	2.00	1.00	.20
☐ 293	Bill Pleis	1.50	.75	.15		Bill Stafford			
☐ 294	Bill Rigney MG	1.50	.75	.15		Bill Pierce			
☐ 295	Ed Roebuck	1.50	.75	.15	☐ 332	Joel Horlen	1.50	.75	.15
☐ 296	Doc Edwards	2.00	1.00	.20	☐ 333	Carl Warwick	1.50	.75	.15
☐ 297	Jim Golden	1.50	.75	.15	☐ 334	Wynn Hawkins	1.50	.75	.15
☐ 298	Don Dillard	1.50	.75	.15	☐ 335	Leon Wagner	1.50	.75	.15
☐ 299	Rookie Stars	1.50	.75	.15	☐ 336	Ed Bauta	1.50	.75	.15
	Dave Morehead				☐ 337	Dodgers Team	8.00	4.00	.80
	Bob Dustal				☐ 338	Russ Kemmerer	1.50	.75	.15
	Tom Butters				☐ 339	Ted Bowsfield	1.50	.75	.15
	Dan Schneider				☐ 340	Yogi Berra	60.00	27.50	5.50
☐ 300	Willie Mays	100.00	50.00	10.00	☐ 341	Jack Baldschun	1.50	.75	.15
☐ 301	Bill Fischer	1.50	.75	.15	☐ 342	Gene Woodling	2.00	1.00	.20
☐ 302	Whitey Herzog	2.50	1.25	.25	☐ 343	Johnny Pesky MG	2.00	1.00	.20
☐ 303	Earl Francis	1.50	.75	.15	☐ 344	Don Schwall	2.00	1.00	.20
☐ 304	Harry Bright	1.50	.75	.15	☐ 345	Brooks Robinson	35.00	17.50	3.50
☐ 305	Don Hoak	1.50	.75	.15	☐ 346	Billy Hoeft	1.50	.75	.15
☐ 306	Star Receivers	2.50	1.25	.25	☐ 347	Joe Torre	3.50	1.75	.35
	Earl Battey				☐ 348	Vic Wertz	1.50	.75	.15
	Elston Howard				☐ 349	Zoilo Versalles	1.50	.75	.15
☐ 307	Chet Nichols	1.50	.75	.15	☐ 350	Bob Purkey	1.50	.75	.15
☐ 308	Camilo Carreon	1.50	.75	.15	☐ 351	Al Luplow	1.50	.75	.15
☐ 309	Jim Brewer	1.50	.75	.15	☐ 352	Ken Johnson	1.50	.75	.15
☐ 310	Tommy Davis	2.50	1.25	.25	☐ 353	Billy Williams	18.00	9.00	1.80
☐ 311	Joe McClain	1.50	.75	.15	☐ 354	Dom Zanni	1.50	.75	.15
☐ 312	Houston Colts	8.00	4.00	.80					

			NRMT	VG-E	GOOD
☐	355	Dean Chance	2.00	1.00	.20
☐	356	John Schaive	1.50	.75	.15
☐	357	George Altman	1.50	.75	.15
☐	358	Milt Pappas	2.00	1.00	.20
☐	359	Haywood Sullivan	2.00	1.00	.20
☐	360	Don Drysdale	18.00	9.00	1.80
☐	361	Clete Boyer	2.50	1.25	.25
☐	362	Checklist 5	5.00	1.00	.20
☐	363	Dick Radatz	2.50	1.25	.25
☐	364	Howie Goss	1.50	.75	.15
☐	365	Jim Bunning	6.00	3.00	.60
☐	366	Tony Taylor	1.50	.75	.15
☐	367	Tony Cloninger	1.50	.75	.15
☐	368	Ed Bailey	1.50	.75	.15
☐	369	Jim Lemon MG	2.00	1.00	.20
☐	370	Dick Donovan	1.50	.75	.15
☐	371	Rod Kanehl	1.50	.75	.15
☐	372	Don Lee	1.50	.75	.15
☐	373	Jim Campbell	1.50	.75	.15
☐	374	Claude Osteen	2.00	1.00	.20
☐	375	Ken Boyer	3.50	1.75	.35
☐	376	John Wyatt	1.50	.75	.15
☐	377	Baltimore Orioles Team Card	3.00	1.50	.30
☐	378	Bill Henry	1.50	.75	.15
☐	379	Bob Anderson	1.50	.75	.15
☐	380	Ernie Banks	36.00	18.00	3.60
☐	381	Frank Baumann	1.50	.75	.15
☐	382	Ralph Houk MG	2.50	1.25	.25
☐	383	Pete Richert	1.50	.75	.15
☐	384	Bob Tillman	1.50	.75	.15
☐	385	Art Mahaffey	1.50	.75	.15
☐	386	Rookie Stars	2.00	1.00	.20
		Ed Kirkpatrick			
		John Bateman			
		Larry Bearnarth			
		Garry Roggenburk			
☐	387	Al McBean	1.50	.75	.15
☐	388	Jim Davenport	2.00	1.00	.20
☐	389	Frank Sullivan	1.50	.75	.15
☐	390	Hank Aaron	100.00	50.00	10.00
☐	391	Bill Dailey	1.50	.75	.15
☐	392	Tribe Thumpers	2.00	1.00	.20
		Johnny Romano			
		Tito Francona			
☐	393	Ken MacKenzie	1.50	.75	.15
☐	394	Tim McCarver	6.00	3.00	.60
☐	395	Don McMahon	1.50	.75	.15
☐	396	Joe Koppe	1.50	.75	.15
☐	397	Kansas City Athletics Team Card	3.00	1.50	.30
☐	398	Boog Powell	7.50	3.75	.75
☐	399	Dick Ellsworth	2.00	1.00	.20
☐	400	Frank Robinson	32.00	16.00	3.20
☐	401	Jim Bouton	3.50	1.75	.35
☐	402	Mickey Vernon	2.00	1.00	.20
☐	403	Ron Perranoski	2.00	1.00	.20
☐	404	Bob Oldis	1.50	.75	.15
☐	405	Floyd Robinson	1.50	.75	.15
☐	406	Howie Koplitz	1.50	.75	.15
☐	407	Rookie Stars	1.50	.75	.15
		Frank Kostro			
		Chico Ruiz			
		Larry Elliot			
		Dick Simpson			
☐	408	Billy Gardner	1.50	.75	.15
☐	409	Roy Face	2.50	1.25	.25
☐	410	Earl Battey	1.50	.75	.15
☐	411	Jim Constable	1.50	.75	.15
☐	412	Dodger Big Three	25.00	12.50	2.50
		Johnny Podres			
		Don Drysdale			
		Sandy Koufax			
☐	413	Jerry Walker	1.50	.75	.15
☐	414	Ty Cline	1.50	.75	.15
☐	415	Bob Gibson	27.00	13.50	2.70
☐	416	Alex Grammas	1.50	.75	.15
☐	417	Giants Team	3.00	1.50	.30
☐	418	John Orsino	1.50	.75	.15
☐	419	Tracy Stallard	1.50	.75	.15
☐	420	Bobby Richardson	5.00	2.50	.50
☐	421	Tom Morgan	1.50	.75	.15
☐	422	Fred Hutchinson MG	2.00	1.00	.20
☐	423	Ed Hobaugh	1.50	.75	.15
☐	424	Charlie Smith	1.50	.75	.15
☐	425	Smoky Burgess	2.00	1.00	.20
☐	426	Barry Latman	1.50	.75	.15
☐	427	Bernie Allen	1.50	.75	.15
☐	428	Carl Boles	1.50	.75	.15
☐	429	Lou Burdette	2.50	1.25	.25
☐	430	Norm Siebern	1.50	.75	.15
☐	431A	Checklist 6 (white on red)	5.00	1.00	.20
☐	431B	Checklist 6 (black on orange)	10.00	2.00	.40
☐	432	Roman Mejias	1.50	.75	.15
☐	433	Denis Menke	1.50	.75	.15
☐	434	John Callison	2.00	1.00	.20

		NRMT	VG-E	GOOD
☐ 435	Woody Held	1.50	.75	.15
☐ 436	Tim Harkness	1.50	.75	.15
☐ 437	Bill Bruton	1.50	.75	.15
☐ 438	Wes Stock	1.50	.75	.15
☐ 439	Don Zimmer	2.50	1.25	.25
☐ 440	Juan Marichal	18.00	9.00	1.80
☐ 441	Lee Thomas	2.50	1.25	.25
☐ 442	J.C. Hartman	1.50	.75	.15
☐ 443	Jim Piersall	2.50	1.25	.25
☐ 444	Jim Maloney	2.50	1.25	.25
☐ 445	Norm Cash	3.00	1.50	.30
☐ 446	Whitey Ford	32.00	16.00	3.20
☐ 447	Felix Mantilla	7.00	3.50	.70
☐ 448	Jack Kralick	7.00	3.50	.70
☐ 449	Jose Tartabull	7.00	3.50	.70
☐ 450	Bob Friend	8.00	4.00	.80
☐ 451	Indians Team	12.50	6.25	1.25
☐ 452	Buddy Schultz	7.00	3.50	.70
☐ 453	Jake Wood	7.00	3.50	.70
☐ 454A	Art Fowler	7.00	3.50	.70
	(card number on			
	white background)			
☐ 454B	Art Fowler	15.00	7.50	1.50
	(card number on or-			
	ange background)			
☐ 455	Ruben Amaro	7.00	3.50	.70
☐ 456	Jim Coker	7.00	3.50	.70
☐ 457	Tex Clevenger	7.00	3.50	.70
☐ 458	Al Lopez MG	12.00	6.00	1.20
☐ 459	Dick LeMay	7.00	3.50	.70
☐ 460	Del Crandall	8.00	4.00	.80
☐ 461	Norm Bass	7.00	3.50	.70
☐ 462	Wally Post	7.00	3.50	.70
☐ 463	Joe Schaffernoth	7.00	3.50	.70
☐ 464	Ken Aspromonte	7.00	3.50	.70
☐ 465	Chuck Estrada	8.00	4.00	.80
☐ 466	Rookie Stars SP	24.00	12.00	2.40
	Nate Oliver			
	Tony Martinez			
	Bill Freehan			
	Jerry Robinson			
☐ 467	Phil Ortega	7.00	3.50	.70
☐ 468	Carroll Hardy	7.00	3.50	.70
☐ 469	Jay Hook	7.00	3.50	.70
☐ 470	Tom Tresh SP	24.00	12.00	2.40
☐ 471	Ken Retzer	7.00	3.50	.70
☐ 472	Lou Brock	100.00	45.00	9.00
☐ 473	New York Mets	40.00	17.50	3.50
	Team Card			

		NRMT	VG-E	GOOD
☐ 474	Jack Fisher	7.00	3.50	.70
☐ 475	Gus Triandos	8.00	4.00	.80
☐ 476	Frank Funk	7.00	3.50	.70
☐ 477	Donn Clendenon	8.00	4.00	.80
☐ 478	Paul Brown	7.00	3.50	.70
☐ 479	Ed Brinkman	7.00	3.50	.70
☐ 480	Bill Monbouquette	7.00	3.50	.70
☐ 481	Bill Taylor	7.00	3.50	.70
☐ 482	Felix Torres	7.00	3.50	.70
☐ 483	Jim Owens	7.00	3.50	.70
☐ 484	Dale Long	8.00	4.00	.80
☐ 485	Jim Landis	7.00	3.50	.70
☐ 486	Ray Sadecki	7.00	3.50	.70
☐ 487	John Roseboro	8.00	4.00	.80
☐ 488	Jerry Adair	7.00	3.50	.70
☐ 489	Paul Toth	7.00	3.50	.70
☐ 490	Willie McCovey	80.00	40.00	8.00
☐ 491	Harry Craft MG	7.00	3.50	.70
☐ 492	Dave Wickersham	7.00	3.50	.70
☐ 493	Walt Bond	7.00	3.50	.70
☐ 494	Phil Regan	8.00	4.00	.80
☐ 495	Frank Thomas	8.00	4.00	.80
☐ 496	Rookie Stars	8.00	4.00	.80
	Steve Dalkowski			
	Fred Newman			
	Jack Smith			
	Carl Bouldin			
☐ 497	Bennie Daniels	7.00	3.50	.70
☐ 498	Eddie Kasko	7.00	3.50	.70
☐ 499	J.C. Martin	7.00	3.50	.70
☐ 500	Harmon Killebrew	60.00	30.00	6.00
☐ 501	Joe Azcue	7.00	3.50	.70
☐ 502	Daryl Spencer	7.00	3.50	.70
☐ 503	Braves Team	12.50	6.25	1.25
☐ 504	Bob Johnson	7.00	3.50	.70
☐ 505	Curt Flood	14.00	7.00	1.40
☐ 506	Gene Green	7.00	3.50	.70
☐ 507	Roland Sheldon	7.00	3.50	.70
☐ 508	Ted Savage	7.00	3.50	.70
☐ 509A	Checklist 7	15.00	3.00	.40
	(copyright centered)			
☐ 509B	Checklist 7	15.00	3.00	.40
	(copyright to right)			
☐ 510	Ken McBride	7.00	3.50	.70
☐ 511	Charlie Neal	7.00	3.50	.70
☐ 512	Cal McLish	7.00	3.50	.70
☐ 513	Gary Geiger	7.00	3.50	.70
☐ 514	Larry Osborne	7.00	3.50	.70
☐ 515	Don Elston	7.00	3.50	.70

		NRMT	VG-E	GOOD			NRMT	VG-E	GOOD
☐ 516	Purnell Goldy	7.00	3.50	.70		Elmo Plaskett			
☐ 517	Hal Woodeshick	7.00	3.50	.70	☐ 550	Duke Snider	65.00	32.50	6.50
☐ 518	Don Blasingame	7.00	3.50	.70	☐ 551	Billy Klaus	5.00	2.50	.50
☐ 519	Claude Raymond	7.00	3.50	.70	☐ 552	Detroit Tigers	20.00	10.00	2.00
☐ 520	Orlando Cepeda	15.00	7.00	1.40		Team Card			
☐ 521	Dan Pfister	7.00	3.50	.70	☐ 553	Rookie Stars	200.00	100.00	20.00
☐ 522	Rookie Stars	7.00	3.50	.70		Brock Davis			
	Mel Nelson					Jim Gosger			
	Gary Peters					Willie Stargell			
	Jim Roland					John Herrnstein			
	Art Quirk				☐ 554	Hank Fischer	5.00	2.50	.50
☐ 523	Bill Kunkel	5.00	2.50	.50	☐ 555	John Blanchard	6.00	3.00	.60
☐ 524	Cardinals Team	12.00	6.00	1.20	☐ 556	Al Worthington	5.00	2.50	.50
☐ 525	Nellie Fox	12.00	6.00	1.20	☐ 557	Cuno Barragan	5.00	2.50	.50
☐ 526	Dick Hall	5.00	2.50	.50	☐ 558	Rookie Stars	5.00	2.50	.50
☐ 527	Ed Sadowski	5.00	2.50	.50		Bill Faul			
☐ 528	Carl Willey	5.00	2.50	.50		Ron Hunt			
☐ 529	Wes Covington	6.00	3.00	.60		Al Moran			
☐ 530	Don Mossi	6.00	3.00	.60		Bob Lipski			
☐ 531	Sam Mele MG	5.00	2.50	.50	☐ 559	Danny Murtaugh MG	5.00	2.50	.50
☐ 532	Steve Boros	6.00	3.00	.60	☐ 560	Ray Herbert	5.00	2.50	.50
☐ 533	Bobby Shantz	7.00	3.50	.70	☐ 561	Mike De La Hoz	5.00	2.50	.50
☐ 534	Ken Walters	5.00	2.50	.50	☐ 562	Rookie Stars	9.00	4.50	.90
☐ 535	Jim Perry	7.00	3.50	.70		Randy Cardinal			
☐ 536	Norm Larker	5.00	2.50	.50		Dave McNally			
☐ 537	Rookie Stars	650.00	325.00	65.00		Ken Rowe			
	Pedro Gonzales					Don Rowe			
	Ken McMullen				☐ 563	Mike McCormick	6.00	3.00	.60
	Al Weis				☐ 564	George Banks	5.00	2.50	.50
	Pete Rose				☐ 565	Larry Sherry	6.00	3.00	.60
☐ 538	George Brunet	5.00	2.50	.50	☐ 566	Cliff Cook	5.00	2.50	.50
☐ 539	Wayne Causey	5.00	2.50	.50	☐ 567	Jim Duffalo	5.00	2.50	.50
☐ 540	Bob Clemente	150.00	75.00	15.00	☐ 568	Bob Sadowski	5.00	2.50	.50
☐ 541	Ron Moeller	5.00	2.50	.50	☐ 569	Luis Arroyo	6.00	3.00	.60
☐ 542	Lou Klimchock	5.00	2.50	.50	☐ 570	Frank Bolling	5.00	2.50	.50
☐ 543	Russ Snyder	5.00	2.50	.50	☐ 571	Johnny Klippstein	5.00	2.50	.50
☐ 544	Rookie Stars	27.00	13.50	2.70	☐ 572	Jack Spring	5.00	2.50	.50
	Duke Carmel				☐ 573	Coot Veal	5.00	2.50	.50
	Bill Haas				☐ 574	Hal Kolstad	5.00	2.50	.50
	Rusty Staub				☐ 575	Don Cardwell	5.00	2.50	.50
	Dick Phillips				☐ 576	Johnny Temple	7.50	2.50	.50
☐ 545	Jose Pagan	5.00	2.50	.50					
☐ 546	Hal Reniff	5.00	2.50	.50					
☐ 547	Gus Bell	6.00	3.00	.60					
☐ 548	Tom Satriano	5.00	2.50	.50					
☐ 549	Rookie Stars	5.00	2.50	.50					
	Marcelino Lopez								
	Pete Lovrich								
	Paul Ratliff								

1964 Topps

The cards in this 587-card set measure 2 ½"
by 3 ½". Players in the 1964 Topps baseball
series were easy to sort by team due to the
giant block lettering found at the top of each
card. The name and position of the player are
found underneath the picture, and the card is
numbered in a ball design on the orange-col-
ored back. The usual last series scarcity holds
for this set (523 to 587). Subsets within this
set include League Leaders (1-12) and World Series cards (136-140).

		NRMT	VG-E	GOOD
COMPLETE SET (587)	.....	2500.00	1200.00	300.00
COMMON PLAYER (1-196)	...	.75	.35	.07
COMMON PLAYER (197-370)	..	.85	.40	.08
COMMON PLAYER (371-522)	..	1.50	.75	.15
COMMON PLAYER (523-587)	..	5.00	2.50	.50

			NRMT	VG-E	GOOD
☐	1	NL ERA Leaders ... Sandy Koufax Dick Ellsworth Bob Friend	10.00	2.50	.50
☐	2	AL ERA Leaders ... Gary Peters Juan Pizarro Camilo Pascual	1.50	.75	.15
☐	3	NL Pitching Leaders . Sandy Koufax Juan Marichal Warren Spahn Jim Maloney	6.00	3.00	.60
☐	4	AL Pitching Leaders . Whitey Ford Camilo Pascual Jim Bouton	2.00	1.00	.20
☐	5	NL Strikeout Leaders Sandy Koufax Jim Maloney Don Drysdale	5.00	2.50	.50
☐	6	AL Strikeout Leaders Camilo Pascual Jim Bunning Dick Stigman	1.50	.75	.15
☐	7	NL Batting Leaders .. Tommy Davis Bob Clemente Dick Groat Hank Aaron	3.50	1.75	.35
☐	8	AL Batting Leaders .. Carl Yastrzemski Al Kaline Rich Rollins	5.00	2.50	.50
☐	9	NL Home Run Leaders .... Hank Aaron Willie McCovey Willie Mays Orlando Cepeda	9.00	4.50	.90
☐	10	AL Home Run Leaders .... Harmon Killebrew Dick Stuart Bob Allison	1.50	.75	.15
☐	11	NL RBI Leaders .... Hank Aaron Ken Boyer Bill White	3.00	1.50	.30
☐	12	AL RBI Leaders .... Dick Stuart Al Kaline Harmon Killebrew	2.00	1.00	.20
☐	13	Hoyt Wilhelm	7.50	3.75	.75
☐	14	Dodgers Rookies ... Dick Nen Nick Willhite	.75	.35	.07
☐	15	Zoilo Versalles	.75	.35	.07
☐	16	John Boozer	.75	.35	.07
☐	17	Willie Kirkland	.75	.35	.07
☐	18	Billy O'Dell	.75	.35	.07
☐	19	Don Wert	.75	.35	.07

		NRMT	VG-E	GOOD
☐ 20	Bob Friend	1.00	.50	.10
☐ 21	Yogi Berra	30.00	15.00	3.00
☐ 22	Jerry Adair	.75	.35	.07
☐ 23	Chris Zachary	.75	.35	.07
☐ 24	Carl Sawatski	.75	.35	.07
☐ 25	Bill Monbouquette	.75	.35	.07
☐ 26	Gino Cimoli	.75	.35	.07
☐ 27	New York Mets	3.00	1.50	.30
	Team Card			
☐ 28	Claude Osteen	1.00	.50	.10
☐ 29	Lou Brock	25.00	12.50	2.50
☐ 30	Ron Perranoski	1.00	.50	.10
☐ 31	Dave Nicholson	.75	.35	.07
☐ 32	Dean Chance	1.25	.60	.12
☐ 33	Reds Rookies	1.00	.50	.10
	Sammy Ellis			
	Mel Queen			
☐ 34	Jim Perry	1.25	.60	.12
☐ 35	Eddie Mathews	12.00	6.00	1.20
☐ 36	Hal Reniff	.75	.35	.07
☐ 37	Smoky Burgess	1.00	.50	.10
☐ 38	Jim Wynn	2.00	1.00	.20
☐ 39	Hank Aguirre	.75	.35	.07
☐ 40	Dick Groat	1.25	.60	.12
☐ 41	Friendly Foes	3.00	1.50	.30
	Willie McCovey			
	Leon Wagner			
☐ 42	Moe Drabowsky	.75	.35	.07
☐ 43	Roy Sievers	1.00	.50	.10
☐ 44	Duke Carmel	.75	.35	.07
☐ 45	Milt Pappas	1.00	.50	.10
☐ 46	Ed Brinkman	.75	.35	.07
☐ 47	Giants Rookies	1.00	.50	.10
	Jesus Alou			
	Ron Herbel			
☐ 48	Bob Perry	.75	.35	.07
☐ 49	Bill Henry	.75	.35	.07
☐ 50	Mickey Mantle	200.00	100.00	20.00
☐ 51	Pete Richert	.75	.35	.07
☐ 52	Chuck Hinton	.75	.35	.07
☐ 53	Denis Menke	.75	.35	.07
☐ 54	Sam Mele MG	.75	.35	.07
☐ 55	Ernie Banks	22.00	11.00	2.20
☐ 56	Hal Brown	.75	.35	.07
☐ 57	Tim Harkness	.75	.35	.07
☐ 58	Don Demeter	.75	.35	.07
☐ 59	Ernie Broglio	.75	.35	.07
☐ 60	Frank Malzone	1.00	.50	.10
☐ 61	Angel Backstops	1.00	.50	.10

		NRMT	VG-E	GOOD
	Bob Rodgers			
	Ed Sadowski			
☐ 62	Ted Savage	.75	.35	.07
☐ 63	John Orsino	.75	.35	.07
☐ 64	Ted Abernathy	.75	.35	.07
☐ 65	Felipe Alou	1.25	.60	.12
☐ 66	Eddie Fisher	.75	.35	.07
☐ 67	Tigers Team	2.00	1.00	.20
☐ 68	Willie Davis	1.25	.60	.12
☐ 69	Clete Boyer	1.00	.50	.10
☐ 70	Joe Torre	2.00	1.00	.20
☐ 71	Jack Spring	.75	.35	.07
☐ 72	Chico Cardenas	.75	.35	.07
☐ 73	Jimmie Hall	1.00	.50	.10
☐ 74	Pirates Rookies	.75	.35	.07
	Bob Priddy			
	Tom Butters			
☐ 75	Wayne Causey	.75	.35	.07
☐ 76	Checklist 1	4.00	.75	.15
☐ 77	Jerry Walker	.75	.35	.07
☐ 78	Merritt Ranew	.75	.35	.07
☐ 79	Bob Heffner	.75	.35	.07
☐ 80	Vada Pinson	2.00	1.00	.20
☐ 81	All-Star Vets	5.00	2.50	.50
	Nellie Fox			
	Harmon Killebrew			
☐ 82	Jim Davenport	1.00	.50	.10
☐ 83	Gus Triandos	1.00	.50	.10
☐ 84	Carl Willey	.75	.35	.07
☐ 85	Pete Ward	.75	.35	.07
☐ 86	Al Downing	.75	.35	.07
☐ 87	St. Louis Cardinals	2.00	1.00	.20
	Team Card			
☐ 88	John Roseboro	.50		.10
☐ 89	Boog Powell	2.50	1.25	.25
☐ 90	Earl Battey	.75	.35	.07
☐ 91	Bob Bailey	.75	.35	.07
☐ 92	Steve Ridzik	.75	.35	.07
☐ 93	Gary Geiger	.75	.35	.07
☐ 94	Braves Rookies	.75	.35	.07
	Jim Britton			
	Larry Maxie			
☐ 95	George Altman	.75	.35	.07
☐ 96	Bob Buhl	.75	.35	.07
☐ 97	Jim Fregosi	1.25	.60	.12
☐ 98	Bill Bruton	.75	.35	.07
☐ 99	Al Stanek	.75	.35	.07
☐ 100	Elston Howard	2.50	1.25	.25
☐ 101	Walt Alston MG	3.00	1.50	.30

		NRMT	VG-E	GOOD				NRMT	VG-E	GOOD
☐ 102	Checklist 2	4.00	.75	.15			Dodgers celebrate			
☐ 103	Curt Flood	1.75	.85	.17	☐ 141	Danny Murtaugh MG	.75	.35	.07
☐ 104	Art Mahaffey	.75	.35	.07	☐ 142	John Bateman	.75	.35	.07
☐ 105	Woody Held	.75	.35	.07	☐ 143	Bubba Phillips	.75	.35	.07
☐ 106	Joe Nuxhall	1.00	.50	.10	☐ 144	Al Worthington	.75	.35	.07
☐ 107	White Sox Rookies .	.75	.35	.07	☐ 145	Norm Siebern	.75	.35	.07
	Bruce Howard				☐ 146	Indians Rookies ...	45.00	22.50	4.50
	Frank Kreutzer					Tommy John			
☐ 108	John Wyatt	.75	.35	.07		Bob Chance			
☐ 109	Rusty Staub	5.00	2.50	.50	☐ 147	Ray Sadecki	.75	.35	.07
☐ 110	Albie Pearson	.75	.35	.07	☐ 148	J.C. Martin	.75	.35	.07
☐ 111	Don Elston	.75	.35	.07	☐ 149	Paul Foytack	.75	.35	.07
☐ 112	Bob Tillman	.75	.35	.07	☐ 150	Willie Mays	65.00	32.50	6.50
☐ 113	Grover Powell	.75	.35	.07	☐ 151	Athletics Team	1.75	.85	.17
☐ 114	Don Lock	.75	.35	.07	☐ 152	Denny Lemaster ...	.75	.35	.07
☐ 115	Frank Bolling	.75	.35	.07	☐ 153	Dick Williams	1.00	.50	.10
☐ 116	Twins Rookies	8.00	3.75	.75	☐ 154	Dick Tracewski ...	.75	.35	.07
	Jay Ward				☐ 155	Duke Snider	20.00	10.00	2.00
	Tony Oliva				☐ 156	Bill Dailey	.75	.35	.07
☐ 117	Earl Francis	.75	.35	.07	☐ 157	Gene Mauch MG ...	1.00	.50	.10
☐ 118	John Blanchard	.75	.35	.07	☐ 158	Ken Johnson	.75	.35	.07
☐ 119	Gary Kolb	.75	.35	.07	☐ 159	Charlie Dees	.75	.35	.07
☐ 120	Don Drysdale	12.50	6.25	1.25	☐ 160	Ken Boyer	4.00	2.00	.40
☐ 121	Pete Runnels	.75	.35	.07	☐ 161	Dave McNally	1.50	.75	.15
☐ 122	Don McMahon	.75	.35	.07	☐ 162	Hitting Area	1.00	.50	.10
☐ 123	Jose Pagan	.75	.35	.07		Dick Sisler			
☐ 124	Orlando Pena	.75	.35	.07		Vada Pinson			
☐ 125	Pete Rose	175.00	85.00	18.00	☐ 163	Donn Clendenon ...	1.00	.50	.10
☐ 126	Russ Snyder	.75	.35	.07	☐ 164	Bud Daley	.75	.35	.07
☐ 127	Angels Rookies	.75	.35	.07	☐ 165	Jerry Lumpe	.75	.35	.07
	Aubrey Gatewood				☐ 166	Marty Keough	.75	.35	.07
	Dick Simpson				☐ 167	Senators Rookies ..	20.00	10.00	2.00
☐ 128	Mickey Lolich	10.00	5.00	1.00		Mike Brumley			
☐ 129	Amado Samuel	.75	.35	.07		Lou Piniella			
☐ 130	Gary Peters	.75	.35	.07	☐ 168	Al Weis	.75	.35	.07
☐ 131	Steve Boros	.75	.35	.07	☐ 169	Del Crandall	1.00	.50	.10
☐ 132	Braves Team	2.00	1.00	.20	☐ 170	Dick Radatz	1.25	.60	.12
☐ 133	Jim Grant	.75	.35	.07	☐ 171	Ty Cline	.75	.35	.07
☐ 134	Don Zimmer	1.50	.75	.15	☐ 172	Indians Team	1.75	.85	.17
☐ 135	Johnny Callison	1.00	.50	.10	☐ 173	Ryne Duren	1.00	.50	.10
☐ 136	World Series Game 1	8.00	4.00	.80	☐ 174	Doc Edwards	1.50	.75	.15
	Koufax strikes out 15				☐ 175	Billy Williams	11.00	5.50	1.10
☐ 137	World Series Game 2	2.50	1.25	.25	☐ 176	Tracy Stallard	.75	.35	.07
	Davis sparks rally				☐ 177	Harmon Killebrew ..	12.50	6.25	1.25
☐ 138	World Series Game 3	2.50	1.25	.25	☐ 178	Hank Bauer MG ...	1.25	.60	.12
	LA 3 straight				☐ 179	Carl Warwick	.75	.35	.07
☐ 139	World Series Game 4	2.50	1.25	.25	☐ 180	Tommy Davis	1.50	.75	.15
	Sealing Yanks doom				☐ 181	Dave Wickersham ..	.75	.35	.07
☐ 140	World Series Summary	2.50	1.25	.25	☐ 182	Sox Sockers	8.00	4.00	.80

		NRMT	VG-E	GOOD
	Carl Yastrzemski			
	Chuck Schilling			
☐ 183	Ron Taylor	.75	.35	.07
☐ 184	Al Luplow	.75	.35	.07
☐ 185	Jim O'Toole	.75	.35	.07
☐ 186	Roman Mejias	.75	.35	.07
☐ 187	Ed Roebuck	.75	.35	.07
☐ 188	Checklist 3	4.00	.75	.15
☐ 189	Bob Hendley	.75	.35	.07
☐ 190	Bobby Richardson	3.50	1.75	.35
☐ 191	Clay Dalrymple	.75	.35	.07
☐ 192	Cubs Rookies	.75	.35	.07
	John Boccabella			
	Billy Cowan			
☐ 193	Jerry Lynch	.75	.35	.07
☐ 194	John Goryl	.75	.35	.07
☐ 195	Floyd Robinson	.75	.35	.07
☐ 196	Jim Gentile	1.00	.50	.10
☐ 197	Frank Lary	1.25	.60	.12
☐ 198	Len Gabrielson	.85	.40	.08
☐ 199	Joe Azcue	.85	.40	.08
☐ 200	Sandy Koufax	65.00	32.50	6.50
☐ 201	Orioles Rookies	1.25	.60	.12
	Sam Bowens			
	Wally Bunker			
☐ 202	Galen Cisco	.85	.40	.08
☐ 203	John Kennedy	.85	.40	.08
☐ 204	Matty Alou	1.25	.60	.12
☐ 205	Nellie Fox	3.50	1.75	.35
☐ 206	Steve Hamilton	.85	.40	.08
☐ 207	Fred Hutchinson MG	1.25	.60	.12
☐ 208	Wes Covington	.85	.40	.08
☐ 209	Bob Allen	.85	.40	.08
☐ 210	Carl Yastrzemski	70.00	35.00	7.00
☐ 211	Jim Coker	.85	.40	.08
☐ 212	Pete Lovrich	.85	.40	.08
☐ 213	Angels Team	1.75	.85	.17
☐ 214	Ken McMullen	.85	.40	.08
☐ 215	Ray Herbert	.85	.40	.08
☐ 216	Mike De La Hoz	.85	.40	.08
☐ 217	Jim King	.85	.40	.08
☐ 218	Hank Fischer	.85	.40	.08
☐ 219	Young Aces	2.00	1.00	.20
	Al Downing			
	Jim Bouton			
☐ 220	Dick Ellsworth	1.25	.60	.12
☐ 221	Bob Saverine	.85	.40	.08
☐ 222	Billy Pierce	1.25	.60	.12
☐ 223	George Banks	.85	.40	.08

		NRMT	VG-E	GOOD
☐ 224	Tommie Sisk	.85	.40	.08
☐ 225	Roger Maris	40.00	20.00	4.00
☐ 226	Colts Rookies	1.25	.60	.12
	Gerald Grote			
	Larry Yellen			
☐ 227	Barry Latman	.85	.40	.08
☐ 228	Felix Mantilla	.85	.40	.08
☐ 229	Charley Lau	1.25	.60	.12
☐ 230	Brooks Robinson	24.00	12.00	2.40
☐ 231	Dick Calmus	.85	.40	.08
☐ 232	Al Lopez MG	2.50	1.25	.25
☐ 233	Hal Smith	.85	.40	.08
☐ 234	Gary Bell	.85	.40	.08
☐ 235	Ron Hunt	.85	.40	.08
☐ 236	Bill Faul	.85	.40	.08
☐ 237	Cubs Team	2.00	1.00	.20
☐ 238	Roy McMillan	.85	.40	.08
☐ 239	Herm Starrette	.85	.40	.08
☐ 240	Bill White	2.00	1.00	.20
☐ 241	Jim Owens	.85	.40	.08
☐ 242	Harvey Kuenn	1.50	.75	.15
☐ 243	Phillies Rookies	10.00	5.00	1.00
	Richie Allen			
	John Herrnstein			
☐ 244	Tony LaRussa	8.00	4.00	.80
☐ 245	Dick Stigman	.85	.40	.08
☐ 246	Manny Mota	1.25	.60	.12
☐ 247	Dave DeBusschere	2.50	1.25	.25
☐ 248	Johnny Pesky MG	1.25	.60	.12
☐ 249	Doug Camilli	.85	.40	.08
☐ 250	Al Kaline	21.00	10.50	2.10
☐ 251	Choo Choo Coleman	.85	.40	.08
☐ 252	Ken Aspromonte	.85	.40	.08
☐ 253	Wally Post	.85	.40	.08
☐ 254	Don Hoak	.85	.40	.08
☐ 255	Lee Thomas	1.25	.60	.12
☐ 256	Johnny Weekly	.85	.40	.08
☐ 257	San Francisco Giants	2.00	1.00	.20
	Team Card			
☐ 258	Garry Roggenburk	.85	.40	.08
☐ 259	Harry Bright	.85	.40	.08
☐ 260	Frank Robinson	15.00	7.50	1.50
☐ 261	Jim Hannan	.85	.40	.08
☐ 262	Cards Rookies	4.00	2.00	.40
	Mike Shannon			
	Harry Fanok			
☐ 263	Chuck Estrada	1.25	.60	.12
☐ 264	Jim Landis	.85	.40	.08
☐ 265	Jim Bunning	4.00	2.00	.40

		NRMT	VG-E	GOOD
☐ 266	Gene Freese	.85	.40	.08
☐ 267	Wilbur Wood	1.25	.60	.12
☐ 268	Bill's Got It	1.25	.60	.12
	Danny Murtaugh			
	Bill Virdon			
☐ 269	Ellis Burton	.85	.40	.08
☐ 270	Rich Rollins	1.25	.60	.12
☐ 271	Bob Sadowski	.85	.40	.08
☐ 272	Jake Wood	.85	.40	.08
☐ 273	Mel Nelson	.85	.40	.08
☐ 274	Checklist 4	4.00	.75	.15
☐ 275	John Tsitouris	.85	.40	.08
☐ 276	Jose Tartabull	.85	.40	.08
☐ 277	Ken Retzer	.85	.40	.08
☐ 278	Bobby Shantz	1.50	.75	.15
☐ 279	Joe Koppe	1.25	.60	.12
	(glove on wrong hand)			
☐ 280	Juan Marichal	9.00	4.50	.90
☐ 281	Yankees Rookies	1.25	.60	.12
	Jake Gibbs			
	Tom Metcalf			
☐ 282	Bob Bruce	.85	.40	.08
☐ 283	Tom McCraw	.85	.40	.08
☐ 284	Dick Schofield	.85	.40	.08
☐ 285	Robin Roberts	8.00	4.00	.80
☐ 286	Don Landrum	.85	.40	.08
☐ 287	Red Sox Rookies	10.00	5.00	1.00
	Tony Conigliaro			
	Bill Spanswick			
☐ 288	Al Moran	.85	.40	.08
☐ 289	Frank Funk	.85	.40	.08
☐ 290	Bob Allison	1.25	.60	.12
☐ 291	Phil Ortega	.85	.40	.08
☐ 292	Mike Roarke	.85	.40	.08
☐ 293	Phillies Team	2.00	1.00	.20
☐ 294	Ken L. Hunt	.85	.40	.08
☐ 295	Roger Craig	1.75	.85	.17
☐ 296	Ed Kirkpatrick	.85	.40	.08
☐ 297	Ken MacKenzie	.85	.40	.08
☐ 298	Harry Craft MG	.85	.40	.08
☐ 299	Bill Stafford	.85	.40	.08
☐ 300	Hank Aaron	70.00	35.00	7.00
☐ 301	Larry Brown	.85	.40	.08
☐ 302	Dan Pfister	.85	.40	.08
☐ 303	Jim Campbell	.85	.40	.08
☐ 304	Bob Johnson	.85	.40	.08
☐ 305	Jack Lamabe	.85	.40	.08
☐ 306	Giant Gunners	15.00	7.50	1.50
	Willie Mays			

		NRMT	VG-E	GOOD
	Orlando Cepeda			
☐ 307	Joe Gibbon	.85	.40	.08
☐ 308	Gene Stephens	.85	.40	.08
☐ 309	Paul Toth	.85	.40	.08
☐ 310	Jim Gilliam	2.25	1.10	.22
☐ 311	Tom Brown	.85	.40	.08
☐ 312	Tigers Rookies	.85	.40	.08
	Fritz Fisher			
	Fred Gladding			
☐ 313	Chuck Hiller	.85	.40	.08
☐ 314	Jerry Buchek	.85	.40	.08
☐ 315	Bo Belinsky	1.25	.60	.12
☐ 316	Gene Oliver	.85	.40	.08
☐ 317	Al Smith	.85	.40	.08
☐ 318	Minnesota Twins	2.00	1.00	.20
	Team Card			
☐ 319	Paul Brown	.85	.40	.08
☐ 320	Rocky Colavito	2.50	1.10	.22
☐ 321	Bob Lillis	.85	.40	.08
☐ 322	George Brunet	.85	.40	.08
☐ 323	John Buzhardt	.85	.40	.08
☐ 324	Casey Stengel MG	10.00	5.00	1.00
☐ 325	Hector Lopez	.85	.40	.08
☐ 326	Ron Brand	.85	.40	.08
☐ 327	Don Blasingame	.85	.40	.08
☐ 328	Bob Shaw	.85	.40	.08
☐ 329	Russ Nixon	1.25	.60	.12
☐ 330	Tommy Harper	1.25	.60	.12
☐ 331	AL Bombers	60.00	30.00	6.00
	Roger Maris			
	Norm Cash			
	Mickey Mantle			
	Al Kaline			
☐ 332	Ray Washburn	.85	.40	.08
☐ 333	Billy Moran	.85	.40	.08
☐ 334	Lew Krausse	.85	.40	.08
☐ 335	Don Mossi	.85	.40	.08
☐ 336	Andre Rodgers	.85	.40	.08
☐ 337	Dodgers Rookies	2.50	1.25	.25
	Al Ferrara			
	Jeff Torborg			
☐ 338	Jack Kralick	.85	.40	.08
☐ 339	Walt Bond	.85	.40	.08
☐ 340	Joe Cunningham	1.25	.60	.12
☐ 341	Jim Roland	.85	.40	.08
☐ 342	Willie Stargell	36.00	18.00	3.60
☐ 343	Senators Team	1.75	.85	.17
☐ 344	Phil Linz	1.25	.60	.12
☐ 345	Frank Thomas	1.25	.60	.12

		NRMT	VG-E	GOOD
☐ 346	Joey Jay	.85	.40	.08
☐ 347	Bobby Wine	.85	.40	.08
☐ 348	Ed Lopat MG	1.50	.75	.15
☐ 349	Art Fowler	.85	.40	.08
☐ 350	Willie McCovey	17.00	8.50	1.70
☐ 351	Dan Schneider	.85	.40	.08
☐ 352	Eddie Bressoud	.85	.40	.08
☐ 353	Wally Moon	1.25	.60	.12
☐ 354	Dave Giusti	1.25	.60	.12
☐ 355	Vic Power	.85	.40	.08
☐ 356	Reds Rookies	1.25	.60	.12
	Bill McCool			
	Chico Ruiz			
☐ 357	Charley James	.85	.40	.08
☐ 358	Ron Kline	.85	.40	.08
☐ 359	Jim Schaffer	.85	.40	.08
☐ 360	Joe Pepitone	1.75	.85	.17
☐ 361	Jay Hook	.85	.40	.08
☐ 362	Checklist 5	4.00	1.00	.20
☐ 363	Dick McAuliffe	1.25	.60	.12
☐ 364	Joe Gaines	.85	.40	.08
☐ 365	Cal McLish	.85	.40	.08
☐ 366	Nelson Mathews	.85	.40	.08
☐ 367	Fred Whitfield	.85	.40	.08
☐ 368	White Sox Rookies	1.50	.75	.15
	Fritz Ackley			
	Don Buford			
☐ 369	Jerry Zimmerman	.85	.40	.08
☐ 370	Hal Woodeshick	.85	.40	.08
☐ 371	Frank Howard	2.00	1.00	.20
☐ 372	Howie Koplitz	1.50	.75	.15
☐ 373	Pirates Team	3.00	1.50	.30
☐ 374	Bobby Bolin	1.50	.75	.15
☐ 375	Ron Santo	2.50	1.25	.25
☐ 376	Dave Morehead	1.50	.75	.15
☐ 377	Bob Skinner	1.50	.75	.15
☐ 378	Braves Rookies	2.50	1.25	.25
	Woody Woodward			
	Jack Smith			
☐ 379	Tony Gonzalez	1.50	.75	.15
☐ 380	Whitey Ford	20.00	10.00	2.00
☐ 381	Bob Taylor	1.50	.75	.15
☐ 382	Wes Stock	1.50	.75	.15
☐ 383	Bill Rigney MG	1.50	.75	.15
☐ 384	Ron Hansen	1.50	.75	.15
☐ 385	Curt Simmons	2.00	1.00	.20
☐ 386	Lenny Green	1.50	.75	.15
☐ 387	Terry Fox	1.50	.75	.15
☐ 388	A's Rookies	1.50	.75	.15

		NRMT	VG-E	GOOD
	John O'Donoghue			
	George Williams			
☐ 389	Jim Umbricht	1.50	.75	.15
☐ 390	Orlando Cepeda	5.50	2.75	.55
☐ 391	Sam McDowell	2.50	1.25	.25
☐ 392	Jim Pagliaroni	1.50	.75	.15
☐ 393	Casey Teaches	4.00	2.00	.40
	Casey Stengel			
	Ed Kranepool			
☐ 394	Bob Miller	1.50	.75	.15
☐ 395	Tom Tresh	2.50	1.25	.25
☐ 396	Dennis Bennett	1.50	.75	.15
☐ 397	Chuck Cottier	1.50	.75	.15
☐ 398	Mets Rookies	1.50	.75	.15
	Bill Haas			
	Dick Smith			
☐ 399	Jackie Brandt	1.50	.75	.15
☐ 400	Warren Spahn	21.00	10.50	2.10
☐ 401	Charlie Maxwell	1.50	.75	.15
☐ 402	Tom Sturdivant	1.50	.75	.15
☐ 403	Reds Team	3.00	1.50	.30
☐ 404	Tony Martinez	1.50	.75	.15
☐ 405	Ken McBride	1.50	.75	.15
☐ 406	Al Spangler	1.50	.75	.15
☐ 407	Bill Freehan	3.00	1.50	.30
☐ 408	Cubs Rookies	1.50	.75	.15
	Jim Stewart			
	Fred Burdette			
☐ 409	Bill Fischer	1.50	.75	.15
☐ 410	Dick Stuart	2.00	1.00	.20
☐ 411	Lee Walls	1.50	.75	.15
☐ 412	Ray Culp	1.50	.75	.15
☐ 413	Johnny Keane MG	2.00	1.00	.20
☐ 414	Jack Sanford	2.00	1.00	.20
☐ 415	Tony Kubek	5.00	2.50	.50
☐ 416	Lee Maye	1.50	.75	.15
☐ 417	Don Cardwell	1.50	.75	.15
☐ 418	Orioles Rookies	2.00	1.00	.20
	Darold Knowles			
	Les Narum			
☐ 419	Ken Harrelson	4.50	2.25	.45
☐ 420	Jim Maloney	2.50	1.25	.25
☐ 421	Camilo Carreon	1.50	.75	.15
☐ 422	Jack Fisher	1.50	.75	.15
☐ 423	Tops in NL	60.00	27.50	5.50
	Hank Aaron			
	Willie Mays			
☐ 424	Dick Bertell	1.50	.75	.15
☐ 425	Norm Cash	2.50	1.25	.25

		NRMT	VG-E	GOOD
☐ 426	Bob Rodgers	2.00	1.00	.20
☐ 427	Don Rudolph	1.50	.75	.15
☐ 428	Red Sox Rookies	1.50	.75	.15
	Archie Skeen			
	Pete Smith			
☐ 429	Tim McCarver	5.00	2.50	.50
☐ 430	Juan Pizarro	1.50	.75	.15
☐ 431	George Alusik	1.50	.75	.15
☐ 432	Ruben Amaro	1.50	.75	.15
☐ 433	Yankees Team	10.00	5.00	1.00
☐ 434	Don Nottebart	1.50	.75	.15
☐ 435	Vic Davalillo	1.50	.75	.15
☐ 436	Charlie Neal	1.50	.75	.15
☐ 437	Ed Bailey	1.50	.75	.15
☐ 438	Checklist 6	5.00	1.00	.20
☐ 439	Harvey Haddix	2.00	1.00	.20
☐ 440	Bob Clemente	65.00	32.50	6.50
☐ 441	Bob Duliba	1.50	.75	.15
☐ 442	Pumpsie Green	1.50	.75	.15
☐ 443	Chuck Dressen MG	2.00	1.00	.20
☐ 444	Larry Jackson	1.50	.75	.15
☐ 445	Bill Skowron	2.50	1.25	.25
☐ 446	Julian Javier	1.50	.75	.15
☐ 447	Ted Bowsfield	1.50	.75	.15
☐ 448	Cookie Rojas	2.00	1.00	.20
☐ 449	Deron Johnson	2.00	1.00	.20
☐ 450	Steve Barber	1.50	.75	.15
☐ 451	Joe Amalfitano	1.50	.75	.15
☐ 452	Giants Rookies	2.50	1.25	.25
	Gil Garrido			
	Jim Ray Hart			
☐ 453	Frank Baumann	1.50	.75	.15
☐ 454	Tommie Aaron	2.00	1.00	.20
☐ 455	Bernie Allen	1.50	.75	.15
☐ 456	Dodgers Rookies	2.50	1.25	.25
	Wes Parker			
	John Werhas			
☐ 457	Jesse Gonder	1.50	.75	.15
☐ 458	Ralph Terry	2.00	1.00	.20
☐ 459	Red Sox Rookies	1.50	.75	.15
	Pete Charton			
	Dalton Jones			
☐ 460	Bob Gibson	22.00	11.00	2.20
☐ 461	George Thomas	1.50	.75	.15
☐ 462	Birdie Tebbetts MG	1.50	.75	.15
☐ 463	Don Leppert	1.50	.75	.15
☐ 464	Dallas Green	2.50	1.25	.25
☐ 465	Mike Hershberger	1.50	.75	.15
☐ 466	A's Rookies	1.50	.75	.15
	Dick Green			
	Aurelio Monteagudo			
☐ 467	Bob Aspromonte	1.50	.75	.15
☐ 468	Gaylord Perry	22.00	11.00	2.20
☐ 469	Cubs Rookies	1.50	.75	.15
	Fred Norman			
	Sterling Slaughter			
☐ 470	Jim Bouton	3.00	1.50	.30
☐ 471	Gates Brown	2.50	1.25	.25
☐ 472	Vern Law	2.00	1.00	.20
☐ 473	Baltimore Orioles	3.00	1.50	.30
	Team Card			
☐ 474	Larry Sherry	2.00	1.00	.20
☐ 475	Ed Charles	1.50	.75	.15
☐ 476	Braves Rookies	5.00	2.50	.50
	Rico Carty			
	Dick Kelley			
☐ 477	Mike Joyce	1.50	.75	.15
☐ 478	Dick Howser	2.50	1.25	.25
☐ 479	Cardinals Rookies	1.50	.75	.15
	Dave Bakenhaster			
	Johnny Lewis			
☐ 480	Bob Purkey	1.50	.75	.15
☐ 481	Chuck Schilling	1.50	.75	.15
☐ 482	Phillies Rookies	2.00	1.00	.20
	John Briggs			
	Danny Cater			
☐ 483	Fred Valentine	1.50	.75	.15
☐ 484	Bill Pleis	1.50	.75	.15
☐ 485	Tom Haller	1.50	.75	.15
☐ 486	Bob Kennedy MG	1.50	.75	.15
☐ 487	Mike McCormick	2.00	1.00	.20
☐ 488	Yankees Rookies	1.50	.75	.15
	Pete Mikkelsen			
	Bob Meyer			
☐ 489	Julio Navarro	1.50	.75	.15
☐ 490	Ron Fairly	2.00	1.00	.20
☐ 491	Ed Rakow	1.50	.75	.15
☐ 492	Colts Rookies	1.50	.75	.15
	Jim Beauchamp			
	Mike White			
☐ 493	Don Lee	1.50	.75	.15
☐ 494	Al Jackson	1.50	.75	.15
☐ 495	Bill Virdon	2.50	1.25	.25
☐ 496	White Sox Team	3.00	1.50	.30
☐ 497	Jeoff Long	1.50	.75	.15
☐ 498	Dave Stenhouse	1.50	.75	.15
☐ 499	Indians Rookies	1.50	.75	.15
	Chico Salmon			

		NRMT	VG-E	GOOD
	Gordon Seyfried			
☐ 500	Camilo Pascual	2.00	1.00	.20
☐ 501	Bob Veale	1.50	.75	.15
☐ 502	Angels Rookies	2.00	1.00	.20
	Bobby Knoop			
	Bob Lee			
☐ 503	Earl Wilson	1.50	.75	.15
☐ 504	Claude Raymond	1.50	.75	.15
☐ 505	Stan Williams	1.50	.75	.15
☐ 506	Bobby Bragan MG	1.50	.75	.15
☐ 507	Johnny Edwards	1.50	.75	.15
☐ 508	Diego Segui	1.50	.75	.15
☐ 509	Pirates Rookies	2.50	1.25	.25
	Gene Alley			
	Orlando McFarlane			
☐ 510	Lindy McDaniel	2.00	1.00	.20
☐ 511	Lou Jackson	1.50	.75	.15
☐ 512	Tigers Rookies	5.00	2.50	.50
	Willie Horton			
	Joe Sparma			
☐ 513	Don Larsen	2.50	1.25	.25
☐ 514	Jim Hickman	1.50	.75	.15
☐ 515	Johnny Romano	1.50	.75	.15
☐ 516	Twins Rookies	1.50	.75	.15
	Jerry Arrigo			
	Dwight Siebler			
☐ 517A	Checklist 7 ERR	10.00	2.00	.40
	(incorrect numbering			
	sequence on back)			
☐ 517B	Checklist 7 COR	6.00	1.00	.20
	(correct numbering			
	on back)			
☐ 518	Carl Bouldin	1.50	.75	.15
☐ 519	Charlie Smith	1.50	.75	.15
☐ 520	Jack Baldschun	1.50	.75	.15
☐ 521	Tom Satriano	1.50	.75	.15
☐ 522	Bob Tiefenauer	1.50	.75	.15
☐ 523	Lou Burdette UER	7.00	3.50	.70
	(pitching lefty)			
☐ 524	Reds Rookies	5.00	2.50	.50
	Jim Dickson			
	Bobby Klaus			
☐ 525	Al McBean	5.00	2.50	.50
☐ 526	Lou Clinton	5.00	2.50	.50
☐ 527	Larry Bearnarth	5.00	2.50	.50
☐ 528	A's Rookies	6.00	3.00	.60
	Dave Duncan			
	Tommie Reynolds			
☐ 529	Alvin Dark MG	6.00	3.00	.60

		NRMT	VG-E	GOOD
☐ 530	Leon Wagner	5.00	2.50	.50
☐ 531	Los Angeles Dodgers	10.00	5.00	1.00
	Team Card			
☐ 532	Twins Rookies	5.00	2.50	.50
	Bud Bloomfield			
	(Bloomfield photo			
	actually Jay Ward)			
	Joe Nossek			
☐ 533	Johnny Klippstein	5.00	2.50	.50
☐ 534	Gus Bell	6.00	3.00	.60
☐ 535	Phil Regan	6.00	3.00	.60
☐ 536	Mets Rookies	5.00	2.50	.50
	Larry Elliot			
	John Stephenson			
☐ 537	Dan Osinski	5.00	2.50	.50
☐ 538	Minnie Minoso	7.00	3.50	.70
☐ 539	Roy Face	6.00	3.00	.60
☐ 540	Luis Aparicio	12.50	6.25	1.25
☐ 541	Braves Rookies	125.00	60.00	12.50
	Phil Roof			
	Phil Niekro			
☐ 542	Don Mincher	6.00	3.00	.60
☐ 543	Bob Uecker	45.00	22.50	4.50
☐ 544	Colts Rookies	5.00	2.50	.50
	Steve Hertz			
	Joe Hoerner			
☐ 545	Max Alvis	5.00	2.50	.50
☐ 546	Joe Christopher	5.00	2.50	.50
☐ 547	Gil Hodges	11.00	5.50	1.10
☐ 548	NL Rookies	5.00	2.50	.50
	Wayne Schurr			
	Paul Speckenback			
☐ 549	Joe Moeller	5.00	2.50	.50
☐ 550	Ken Hubbs	10.00	5.00	1.00
	(in memoriam)			
☐ 551	Billy Hoeft	5.00	2.50	.50
☐ 552	Indians Rookies	6.00	3.00	.60
	Tom Kelley			
	Sonny Siebert			
☐ 553	Jim Brewer	5.00	2.50	.50
☐ 554	Hank Foiles	5.00	2.50	.50
☐ 555	Lee Stange	5.00	2.50	.50
☐ 556	Mets Rookies	5.00	2.50	.50
	Steve Dillon			
	Ron Locke			
☐ 557	Leo Burke	5.00	2.50	.50
☐ 558	Don Schwall	5.00	2.50	.50
☐ 559	Dick Phillips	5.00	2.50	.50
☐ 560	Dick Farrell	5.00	2.50	.50

1965 Topps

		NRMT	VG-E	GOOD
☐ 561	Phillies Rookies	6.00	3.00	.60
	Dave Bennett			
	(19 ... is 18)			
	Rick Wise			
☐ 562	Pedro Ramos	5.00	2.50	.50
☐ 563	Dal Maxvill	5.00	2.50	.50
☐ 564	AL Rookies	5.00	2.50	.50
	Joe McCabe			
	Jerry McNertney			
☐ 565	Stu Miller	5.00	2.50	.50
☐ 566	Ed Kranepool	6.00	3.00	.60
☐ 567	Jim Kaat	9.00	4.50	.90
☐ 568	NL Rookies	5.00	2.50	.50
	Phil Gagliano			
	Cap Peterson			
☐ 569	Fred Newman	5.00	2.50	.50
☐ 570	Bill Mazeroski	7.00	3.50	.70
☐ 571	Gene Conley	5.00	2.50	.50
☐ 572	Al Rookies	5.00	2.50	.50
	Dave Gray			
	Dick Egan			
☐ 573	Jim Duffalo	5.00	2.50	.50
☐ 574	Manny Jimenez	5.00	2.50	.50
☐ 575	Tony Cloninger	5.00	2.50	.50
☐ 576	Mets Rookies	5.00	2.50	.50
	Jerry Hinsley			
	Bill Wakefield			
☐ 577	Gordy Coleman	5.00	2.50	.50
☐ 578	Glen Hobbie	5.00	2.50	.50
☐ 579	Red Sox Team	10.00	5.00	1.00
☐ 580	Johnny Podres	7.00	3.50	.70
☐ 581	Yankees Rookies	5.00	2.50	.50
	Pedro Gonzalez			
	Archie Moore			
☐ 582	Rod Kanehl	5.00	2.50	.50
☐ 583	Tito Francona	5.00	2.50	.50
☐ 584	Joel Horlen	5.00	2.50	.50
☐ 585	Tony Taylor	5.00	2.50	.50
☐ 586	Jim Piersall	6.00	3.00	.60
☐ 587	Bennie Daniels	5.00	2.50	.50

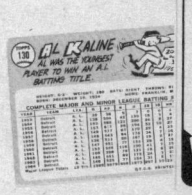

The cards in this 598-card set measure 2 ½" by 3 ½". The cards comprising the 1965 Topps set have team names located within a distinctive pennant design below the picture. The cards have blue borders on the reverse and were issued by series. Cards 523 to 598 are more difficult to obtain than all other series. Within this last series there are 44 cards that were printed in lesser quantities than the other cards in that series; these shorter-printed cards are marked by SP in the checklist below. In addition, the sixth series (447-522) is more difficult to obtain than series one through five. Featured subsets within this set include League Leaders (1-12) and World Series cards (132-139). Key cards in this set include Steve Carlton's rookie, Mickey Mantle, and Pete Rose.

	NRMT	VG-E	GOOD
COMPLETE SET (598)	2700.00	1300.00	350.00
COMMON PLAYER (1-196)	.75	.35	.07
COMMON PLAYER (197-283)	.85	.40	.08
COMMON PLAYER (284-370)	1.00	.50	.10
COMMON PLAYER (371-446)	1.25	.60	.12
COMMON PLAYER (447-522)	3.00	1.50	.30
COMMON PLAYER (523-598)	3.50	1.75	.35
COMMON SP (523-598)	7.00	3.50	.70

		NRMT	VG-E	GOOD
☐ 1	AL Batting Leaders	9.00	1.50	.30
	Tony Oliva			
	Elston Howard			

			NRMT	VG-E	GOOD
		Brooks Robinson			
☐	2	NL Batting Leaders ..	5.00	2.50	.50
		Bob Clemente			
		Hank Aaron			
		Rico Carty			
☐	3	AL Home Run			
		Leaders	8.00	4.00	.80
		Harmon Killebrew			
		Mickey Mantle			
		Boog Powell			
☐	4	NL Home Run			
		Leaders	5.00	2.50	.50
		Willie Mays			
		Billy Williams			
		Jim Ray Hart			
		Orlando Cepeda			
		Johnny Callison			
☐	5	AL RBI Leaders	8.00	4.00	.80
		Brooks Robinson			
		Harmon Killebrew			
		Mickey Mantle			
		Dick Stuart			
☐	6	NL RBI Leaders	2.50	1.25	.25
		Ken Boyer			
		Willie Mays			
		Ron Santo			
☐	7	AL ERA Leaders	1.50	.75	.15
		Dean Chance			
		Joel Horlen			
☐	8	NL ERA Leaders	6.00	3.00	.60
		Sandy Koufax			
		Don Drysdale			
☐	9	AL Pitching Leaders	1.50	.75	.15
		Dean Chance			
		Gary Peters			
		Dave Wickersham			
		Juan Pizarro			
		Wally Bunker			
☐	10	NL Pitching Leaders	1.50	.75	.15
		Larry Jackson			
		Ray Sadecki			
		Juan Marichal			
☐	11	AL Strikeout Leaders	1.50	.75	.15
		Al Downing			
		Dean Chance			
		Camilo Pascual			
☐	12	NL Strikeout Leaders	2.50	1.25	.25
		Bob Veale			
		Don Drysdale			

			NRMT	VG-E	GOOD
		Bob Gibson			
☐	13	Pedro Ramos	.75	.35	.07
☐	14	Len Gabrielson	.75	.35	.07
☐	15	Robin Roberts	7.00	3.50	.70
☐	16	Houston Rookies ...	110.00	55.00	11.00
		Joe Morgan			
		Sonny Jackson			
☐	17	Johnny Romano	.75	.35	.07
☐	18	Bill McCool	.75	.35	.07
☐	19	Gates Brown	1.00	.50	.10
☐	20	Jim Bunning	3.50	1.75	.35
☐	21	Don Blasingame	.75	.35	.07
☐	22	Charlie Smith	.75	.35	.07
☐	23	Bob Tiefenauer	.75	.35	.07
☐	24	Minnesota Twins ...	2.50	1.25	.25
		Team Card			
☐	25	Al McBean	.75	.35	.07
☐	26	Bobby Knoop	.75	.35	.07
☐	27	Dick Bertell	.75	.35	.07
☐	28	Barney Schultz	.75	.35	.07
☐	29	Felix Mantilla	.75	.35	.07
☐	30	Jim Bouton	1.50	.75	.15
☐	31	Mike White	.75	.35	.07
☐	32	Herman Franks MG .	.75	.35	.07
☐	33	Jackie Brandt	.75	.35	.07
☐	34	Cal Koonce	.75	.35	.07
☐	35	Ed Charles	.75	.35	.07
☐	36	Bobby Wine	.75	.35	.07
☐	37	Fred Gladding	.75	.35	.07
☐	38	Jim King	.75	.35	.07
☐	39	Gerry Arrigo	.75	.35	.07
☐	40	Frank Howard	1.50	.75	.15
☐	41	White Sox Rookies ..	.75	.35	.07
		Bruce Howard			
		Marv Staehle			
☐	42	Earl Wilson	.75	.35	.07
☐	43	Mike Shannon	1.25	.60	.12
☐	44	Wade Blasingame ...	.75	.35	.07
☐	45	Roy McMillan	.75	.35	.07
☐	46	Bob Lee	.75	.35	.07
☐	47	Tommy Harper	1.00	.50	.10
☐	48	Claude Raymond	.75	.35	.07
☐	49	Orioles Rookies	1.25	.60	.12
		Curt Blefary			
		John Miller			
☐	50	Juan Marichal	7.50	3.75	.75
☐	51	Bill Bryan	.75	.35	.07
☐	52	Ed Roebuck	.75	.35	.07
☐	53	Dick McAuliffe	1.00	.50	.10

			NRMT	VG-E	GOOD				NRMT	VG-E	GOOD
☐	54	Joe Gibbon	.75	.35	.07	☐	99	Gil Hodges MG	5.50	2.75	.55
☐	55	Tony Conigliaro	3.50	1.75	.35	☐	100	Ken Boyer	2.50	1.25	.25
☐	56	Ron Kline	.75	.35	.07	☐	101	Fred Newman	.75	.35	.07
☐	57	Cardinals Team	1.75	.85	.17	☐	102	Steve Boros	1.00	.50	.10
☐	58	Fred Talbot	.75	.35	.07	☐	103	Harvey Kuenn	1.50	.75	.15
☐	59	Nate Oliver	.75	.35	.07	☐	104	Checklist 2	4.00	.75	.15
☐	60	Jim O'Toole	.75	.35	.07	☐	105	Chico Salmon	.75	.35	.07
☐	61	Chris Cannizzaro	.75	.35	.07	☐	106	Gene Oliver	.75	.35	.07
☐	62	Jim Katt (sic, Kaat)	4.00	2.00	.40	☐	107	Phillies Rookies	1.50	.75	.15
☐	63	Ty Cline	.75	.35	.07			Pat Corrales			
☐	64	Lou Burdette	1.50	.75	.15			Costen Shockley			
☐	65	Tony Kubek	3.00	1.50	.30	☐	108	Don Mincher	.75	.35	.07
☐	66	Bill Rigney MG	.75	.35	.07	☐	109	Walt Bond	.75	.35	.07
☐	67	Harvey Haddix	1.00	.50	.10	☐	110	Ron Santo	1.75	.85	.17
☐	68	Del Crandall	1.00	.50	.10	☐	111	Lee Thomas	1.25	.60	.12
☐	69	Bill Virdon	1.25	.60	.12	☐	112	Derrell Griffith	.75	.35	.07
☐	70	Bill Skowron	1.50	.75	.15	☐	113	Steve Barber	.75	.35	.07
☐	71	John O'Donoghue	.75	.35	.07	☐	114	Jim Hickman	.75	.35	.07
☐	72	Tony Gonzalez	.75	.35	.07	☐	115	Bobby Richardson	2.50	1.25	.25
☐	73	Dennis Ribant	.75	.35	.07	☐	116	Cardinals Rookies	1.25	.60	.12
☐	74	Red Sox Rookies	3.50	1.75	.35			Dave Dowling			
		Rico Petrocelli						Bob Tolan			
		Jerry Stephenson				☐	117	Wes Stock	.75	.35	.07
☐	75	Deron Johnson	1.00	.50	.10	☐	118	Hal Lanier	1.50	.75	.15
☐	76	Sam McDowell	1.00	.50	.10	☐	119	John Kennedy	.75	.35	.07
☐	77	Doug Camilli	.75	.35	.07	☐	120	Frank Robinson	15.00	7.50	1.50
☐	78	Dal Maxvill	.75	.35	.07	☐	121	Gene Alley	1.00	.50	.10
☐	79	Checklist 1	4.00	.75	.15	☐	122	Bill Pleis	.75	.35	.07
☐	80	Turk Farrell	.75	.35	.07	☐	123	Frank Thomas	1.00	.50	.10
☐	81	Don Buford	.75	.35	.07	☐	124	Tom Satriano	.75	.35	.07
☐	82	Braves Rookies	1.25	.60	.12	☐	125	Juan Pizarro	.75	.35	.07
		Santos Alomar				☐	126	Dodgers Team	3.50	1.75	.35
		John Braun				☐	127	Frank Lary	1.00	.50	.10
☐	83	George Thomas	.75	.35	.07	☐	128	Vic Davalillo	.75	.35	.07
☐	84	Ron Herbel	.75	.35	.07	☐	129	Bennie Daniels	.75	.35	.07
☐	85	Willie Smith	.75	.35	.07	☐	130	Al Kaline	18.00	9.00	1.80
☐	86	Les Narum	.75	.35	.07	☐	131	Johnny Keane MG	1.00	.50	.10
☐	87	Nelson Mathews	.75	.35	.07	☐	132	World Series Game 1	2.25	1.10	.22
☐	88	Jack Lamabe	.75	.35	.07			Cards take opener			
☐	89	Mike Hershberger	.75	.35	.07	☐	133	World Series Game 2	2.25	1.10	.22
☐	90	Rich Rollins	1.00	.50	.10			Stottlemyre wins			
☐	91	Cubs Team	1.75	.85	.17	☐	134	World Series Game 3	25.00	12.50	2.50
☐	92	Dick Howser	1.50	.75	.15			Mantle's homer			
☐	93	Jack Fisher	.75	.35	.07	☐	135	World Series Game 4	3.00	1.50	.30
☐	94	Charlie Lau	1.00	.50	.10			Boyer's grand-slam			
☐	95	Bill Mazeroski	1.50	.75	.15	☐	136	World Series Game 5	2.25	1.10	.22
☐	96	Sonny Siebert	1.00	.50	.10			10th inning triumph			
☐	97	Pedro Gonzalez	.75	.35	.07	☐	137	World Series Game 6	3.00	1.50	.30
☐	98	Bob Miller	.75	.35	.07			Bouton wins again			

			NRMT	VG-E	GOOD
☐	138	World Series Game 7	5.00	2.50	.50
		Gibson wins finale			
☐	139	World Series Summary	2.25	1.10	.22
		Cards celebrate			
☐	140	Dean Chance	1.00	.50	.10
☐	141	Charlie James	.75	.35	.07
☐	142	Bill Monbouquette	.75	.35	.07
☐	143	Pirates Rookies	.75	.35	.07
		John Gelnar			
		Jerry May			
☐	144	Ed Kranepool	1.25	.60	.12
☐	145	Luis Tiant	7.50	3.75	.75
☐	146	Ron Hansen	.75	.35	.07
☐	147	Dennis Bennett	.75	.35	.07
☐	148	Willie Kirkland	.75	.35	.07
☐	149	Wayne Schurr	.75	.35	.07
☐	150	Brooks Robinson	18.00	9.00	1.80
☐	151	Athletics Team	1.75	.85	.17
☐	152	Phil Ortega	.75	.35	.07
☐	153	Norm Cash	1.50	.75	.15
☐	154	Bob Humphreys	.75	.35	.07
☐	155	Roger Maris	40.00	20.00	4.00
☐	156	Bob Sadowski	.75	.35	.07
☐	157	Zoilo Versalles	.75	.35	.07
☐	158	Dick Sisler	.75	.35	.07
☐	159	Jim Duffalo	.75	.35	.07
☐	160	Bob Clemente	55.00	27.50	5.50
☐	161	Frank Baumann	.75	.35	.07
☐	162	Russ Nixon	1.00	.50	.10
☐	163	Johnny Briggs	.75	.35	.07
☐	164	Al Spangler	.75	.35	.07
☐	165	Dick Ellsworth	1.00	.50	.10
☐	166	Indians Rookies	1.25	.60	.12
		George Culver			
		Tommie Agee			
☐	167	Bill Wakefield	.75	.35	.07
☐	168	Dick Green	.75	.35	.07
☐	169	Dave Vineyard	.75	.35	.07
☐	170	Hank Aaron	60.00	30.00	6.00
☐	171	Jim Roland	.75	.35	.07
☐	172	Jim Piersall	1.25	.60	.12
☐	173	Detroit Tigers	1.75	.85	.17
		Team Card			
☐	174	Joey Jay	.75	.35	.07
☐	175	Bob Aspromonte	.75	.35	.07
☐	176	Willie McCovey	12.00	6.00	1.20
☐	177	Pete Mikkelsen	.75	.35	.07
☐	178	Dalton Jones	.75	.35	.07
☐	179	Hal Woodeshick	.75	.35	.07

			NRMT	VG-E	GOOD
☐	180	Bob Allison	1.00	.50	.10
☐	181	Senators Rookies	.75	.35	.07
		Don Loun			
		Joe McCabe			
☐	182	Mike De La Hoz	.75	.35	.07
☐	183	Dave Nicholson	.75	.35	.07
☐	184	John Boozer	.75	.35	.07
☐	185	Max Alvis	.75	.35	.07
☐	186	Billy Cowan	.75	.35	.07
☐	187	Casey Stengel MG	10.00	5.00	1.00
☐	188	Sam Bowens	.75	.35	.07
☐	189	Checklist 3	4.00	.75	.15
☐	190	Bill White	1.50	.75	.15
☐	191	Phil Regan	1.00	.50	.10
☐	192	Jim Coker	.75	.35	.07
☐	193	Gaylord Perry	10.00	5.00	1.00
☐	194	Rookie Stars	1.00	.50	.10
		Bill Kelso			
		Rick Reichardt			
☐	195	Bob Veale	.75	.35	.07
☐	196	Ron Fairly	1.00	.50	.10
☐	197	Diego Segui	.85	.40	.08
☐	198	Smoky Burgess	1.00	.50	.10
☐	199	Bob Heffner	.85	.40	.08
☐	200	Joe Torre	1.75	.85	.17
☐	201	Twins Rookies	1.25	.60	.12
		Sandy Valdespino			
		Cesar Tovar			
☐	202	Leo Burke	.85	.40	.08
☐	203	Dallas Green	2.00	1.00	.20
☐	204	Russ Snyder	.85	.40	.08
☐	205	Warren Spahn	15.00	7.50	1.50
☐	206	Willie Horton	1.50	.75	.15
☐	207	Pete Rose	150.00	75.00	15.00
☐	208	Tommy John	10.00	5.00	1.00
☐	209	Pirates Team	1.75	.85	.17
☐	210	Jim Fregosi	1.50	.75	.15
☐	211	Steve Ridzik	.85	.40	.08
☐	212	Ron Brand	.85	.40	.08
☐	213	Jim Davenport	1.25	.60	.12
☐	214	Bob Purkey	.85	.40	.08
☐	215	Pete Ward	.85	.40	.08
☐	216	Al Worthington	.85	.40	.08
☐	217	Walt Alston MG	3.50	1.75	.35
☐	218	Dick Schofield	.85	.40	.08
☐	219	Bob Meyer	.85	.40	.08
☐	220	Billy Williams	8.00	4.00	.80
☐	221	John Tsitouris	.85	.40	.08
☐	222	Bob Tillman	.85	.40	.08

			NRMT	VG-E	GOOD
☐	223	Dan Osinski	.85	.40	.08
☐	224	Bob Chance	.85	.40	.08
☐	225	Bo Belinsky	1.25	.60	.12
☐	226	Yankees Rookies	1.25	.60	.12
		Elvio Jimenez			
		Jake Gibbs			
☐	227	Bobby Klaus	.85	.40	.08
☐	228	Jack Sanford	1.25	.60	.12
☐	229	Lou Clinton	.85	.40	.08
☐	230	Ray Sadecki	.85	.40	.08
☐	231	Jerry Adair	.85	.40	.08
☐	232	Steve Blass	1.50	.75	.15
☐	233	Don Zimmer	1.50	.75	.15
☐	234	White Sox Team	1.75	.85	.17
☐	235	Chuck Hinton	.85	.40	.08
☐	236	Denny McLain	12.00	6.00	1.20
☐	237	Bernie Allen	.85	.40	.08
☐	238	Joe Moeller	.85	.40	.08
☐	239	Doc Edwards	1.50	.75	.15
☐	240	Bob Bruce	.85	.40	.08
☐	241	Mack Jones	.85	.40	.08
☐	242	George Brunet	.85	.40	.08
☐	243	Reds Rookies	2.00	1.00	.20
		Ted Davidson			
		Tommy Helms			
☐	244	Lindy McDaniel	1.25	.60	.12
☐	245	Joe Pepitone	1.75	.85	.17
☐	246	Tom Butters	.85	.40	.08
☐	247	Wally Moon	1.25	.60	.12
☐	248	Gus Triandos	1.25	.60	.12
☐	249	Dave McNally	1.50	.75	.15
☐	250	Willie Mays	75.00	37.50	7.50
☐	251	Billy Herman MG	2.00	1.00	.20
☐	252	Pete Richert	.85	.40	.08
☐	253	Danny Cater	1.25	.60	.12
☐	254	Roland Sheldon	.85	.40	.08
☐	255	Camilo Pascual	1.25	.60	.12
☐	256	Tito Francona	1.25	.60	.12
☐	257	Jim Wynn	1.75	.85	.17
☐	258	Larry Bearnarth	.85	.40	.08
☐	259	Tigers Rookies	2.00	1.00	.20
		Jim Northrup			
		Ray Oyler			
☐	260	Don Drysdale	12.50	6.25	1.25
☐	261	Duke Carmel	.85	.40	.08
☐	262	Bud Daley	.85	.40	.08
☐	263	Marty Keough	.85	.40	.08
☐	264	Bob Buhl	.85	.40	.08
☐	265	Jim Pagliaroni	.85	.40	.08

			NRMT	VG-E	GOOD
☐	266	Bert Campaneris	3.50	1.75	.35
☐	267	Senators Team	1.75	.85	.17
☐	268	Ken McBride	.85	.40	.08
☐	269	Frank Bolling	.85	.40	.08
☐	270	Milt Pappas	1.25	.60	.12
☐	271	Don Wert	.85	.40	.08
☐	272	Chuck Schilling	.85	.40	.08
☐	273	Checklist 4	4.00	.75	.15
☐	274	Lum Harris MG	.85	.40	.08
☐	275	Dick Groat	1.50	.75	.15
☐	276	Hoyt Wilhelm	7.50	3.75	.75
☐	277	Johnny Lewis	.85	.40	.08
☐	278	Ken Retzer	.85	.40	.08
☐	279	Dick Tracewski	.85	.40	.08
☐	280	Dick Stuart	1.25	.60	.12
☐	281	Bill Stafford	.85	.40	.08
☐	282	Giants Rookies	1.25	.60	.12
		Dick Estelle			
		Masanori Murakami			
☐	283	Fred Whitfield	.85	.40	.08
☐	284	Nick Willhite	1.00	.50	.10
☐	285	Ron Hunt	1.00	.50	.10
☐	286	Athletics Rookies	1.00	.50	.10
		Jim Dickson			
		Aurelio Monteagudo			
☐	287	Gary Kolb	1.00	.50	.10
☐	288	Jack Hamilton	1.00	.50	.10
☐	289	Gordy Coleman	1.25	.60	.12
☐	290	Wally Bunker	1.25	.60	.12
☐	291	Jerry Lynch	1.00	.50	.10
☐	292	Larry Yellen	1.00	.50	.10
☐	293	Angels Team	2.00	1.00	.20
☐	294	Tim McCarver	2.50	1.25	.25
☐	295	Dick Radatz	1.50	.75	.15
☐	296	Tony Taylor	1.00	.50	.10
☐	297	Dave Debusschere	2.50	1.25	.25
☐	298	Jim Stewart	1.00	.50	.10
☐	299	Jerry Zimmerman	1.00	.50	.10
☐	300	Sandy Koufax	75.00	37.50	7.50
☐	301	Birdie Tebbetts MG	1.00	.50	.10
☐	302	Al Stanek	1.00	.50	.10
☐	303	John Orsino	1.00	.50	.10
☐	304	Dave Stenhouse	1.00	.50	.10
☐	305	Rico Carty	1.50	.75	.15
☐	306	Bubba Phillips	1.00	.50	.10
☐	307	Barry Latman	1.00	.50	.10
☐	308	Mets Rookies	1.50	.75	.15
		Cleon Jones			
		Tom Parsons			

		NRMT	VG-E	GOOD
☐ 309	Steve Hamilton	1.00	.50	.10
☐ 310	Johnny Callison	1.50	.75	.15
☐ 311	Orlando Pena	1.00	.50	.10
☐ 312	Joe Nuxhall	1.50	.75	.15
☐ 313	Jim Schaffer	1.00	.50	.10
☐ 314	Sterling Slaughter	1.00	.50	.10
☐ 315	Frank Malzone	1.50	.75	.15
☐ 316	Reds Team	2.50	1.25	.25
☐ 317	Don McMahon	1.00	.50	.10
☐ 318	Matty Alou	1.50	.75	.15
☐ 319	Ken McMullen	1.00	.50	.10
☐ 320	Bob Gibson	18.00	9.00	1.80
☐ 321	Rusty Staub	3.00	1.50	.30
☐ 322	Rick Wise	1.50	.75	.15
☐ 323	Hank Bauer MG	1.50	.75	.15
☐ 324	Bobby Locke	1.00	.50	.10
☐ 325	Donn Clendenon	1.50	.75	.15
☐ 326	Dwight Siebler	1.00	.50	.10
☐ 327	Denis Menke	1.00	.50	.10
☐ 328	Eddie Fisher	1.00	.50	.10
☐ 329	Hawk Taylor	1.00	.50	.10
☐ 330	Whitey Ford	18.00	9.00	1.80
☐ 331	Dodgers Rookies	1.00	.50	.10
	Al Ferrara			
	John Purdin			
☐ 332	Ted Abernathy	1.00	.50	.10
☐ 333	Tom Reynolds	1.00	.50	.10
☐ 334	Vic Roznovsky	1.00	.50	.10
☐ 335	Mickey Lolich	3.00	1.50	.30
☐ 336	Woody Held	1.00	.50	.10
☐ 337	Mike Cuellar	1.50	.75	.15
☐ 338	Philadelphia Phillies	2.00	1.00	.20
	Team Card			
☐ 339	Ryne Duren	1.50	.75	.15
☐ 340	Tony Oliva	4.50	2.00	.40
☐ 341	Bob Bolin	1.00	.50	.10
☐ 342	Bob Rodgers	1.50	.75	.15
☐ 343	Mike McCormick	1.50	.75	.15
☐ 344	Wes Parker	1.50	.75	.15
☐ 345	Floyd Robinson	1.00	.50	.10
☐ 346	Bobby Bragan MG	1.00	.50	.10
☐ 347	Roy Face	2.00	1.00	.20
☐ 348	George Banks	1.00	.50	.10
☐ 349	Larry Miller	1.00	.50	.10
☐ 350	Mickey Mantle	375.00	175.00	37.00
☐ 351	Jim Perry	1.50	.75	.15
☐ 352	Alex Johnson	1.50	.75	.15
☐ 353	Jerry Lumpe	1.00	.50	.10
☐ 354	Cubs Rookies	1.00	.50	.10

		NRMT	VG-E	GOOD
	Billy Ott			
	Jack Warner			
☐ 355	Vada Pinson	1.50	.75	.15
☐ 356	Bill Spanswick	1.00	.50	.10
☐ 357	Carl Warwick	1.00	.50	.10
☐ 358	Albie Pearson	1.00	.50	.10
☐ 359	Ken Johnson	1.00	.50	.10
☐ 360	Orlando Cepeda	4.00	2.00	.40
☐ 361	Checklist 5	4.00	.75	.15
☐ 362	Don Schwall	1.00	.50	.10
☐ 363	Bob Johnson	1.00	.50	.10
☐ 364	Galen Cisco	1.00	.50	.10
☐ 365	Jim Gentile	1.50	.75	.15
☐ 366	Dan Schneider	1.00	.50	.10
☐ 367	Leon Wagner	1.00	.50	.10
☐ 368	White Sox Rookies	1.50	.75	.15
	Ken Berry			
	Joel Gibson			
☐ 369	Phil Linz	1.50	.75	.15
☐ 370	Tommy Davis	1.50	.75	.15
☐ 371	Frank Kreutzer	1.25	.60	.12
☐ 372	Clay Dalrymple	1.25	.60	.12
☐ 373	Curt Simmons	1.50	.75	.15
☐ 374	Angels Rookies	1.50	.75	.15
	Jose Cardenal			
	Dick Simpson			
☐ 375	Dave Wickersham	1.25	.60	.12
☐ 376	Jim Landis	1.25	.60	.12
☐ 377	Willie Stargell	21.00	10.50	2.10
☐ 378	Chuck Estrada	1.25	.60	.12
☐ 379	Giants Team	2.50	1.25	.25
☐ 380	Rocky Colavito	2.25	1.10	.22
☐ 381	Al Jackson	1.25	.60	.12
☐ 382	J.C. Martin	1.25	.60	.12
☐ 383	Felipe Alou	1.50	.75	.15
☐ 384	Johnny Klippstein	1.25	.60	.12
☐ 385	Carl Yastrzemski	80.00	40.00	8.00
☐ 386	Cubs Rookies	1.50	.75	.15
	Paul Jaeckel			
	Fred Norman			
☐ 387	Johnny Podres	1.75	.85	.17
☐ 388	John Blanchard	1.50	.75	.15
☐ 389	Don Larsen	1.75	.85	.17
☐ 390	Bill Freehan	2.50	1.25	.25
☐ 391	Mel McGaha MG	1.25	.60	.12
☐ 392	Bob Friend	1.50	.75	.15
☐ 393	Ed Kirkpatrick	1.25	.60	.12
☐ 394	Jim Hannan	1.25	.60	.12
☐ 395	Jim Ray Hart	1.50	.75	.15

		NRMT	VG-E	GOOD
☐ 396	Frank Bertaina	1.25	.60	.12
☐ 397	Jerry Buchek	1.25	.60	.12
☐ 398	Reds Rookies	1.50	.75	.15
	Dan Neville			
	Art Shamsky			
☐ 399	Ray Herbert	1.25	.60	.12
☐ 400	Harmon Killebrew	15.00	7.50	1.50
☐ 401	Carl Willey	1.25	.60	.12
☐ 402	Joe Amalfitano	1.25	.60	.12
☐ 403	Boston Red Sox	2.50	1.25	.25
	Team Card			
☐ 404	Stan Williams	1.50	.75	.15
☐ 405	John Roseboro	1.50	.75	.15
☐ 406	Ralph Terry	1.50	.75	.15
☐ 407	Lee Maye	1.25	.60	.12
☐ 408	Larry Sherry	1.50	.75	.15
☐ 409	Astros Rookies	1.75	.85	.17
	Jim Beauchamp			
	Larry Dierker			
☐ 410	Luis Aparicio	7.50	3.75	.75
☐ 411	Roger Craig	2.50	1.25	.25
☐ 412	Bob Bailey	1.25	.60	.12
☐ 413	Hal Reniff	1.25	.60	.12
☐ 414	Al Lopez MG	2.50	1.25	.25
☐ 415	Curt Flood	2.50	1.25	.25
☐ 416	Jim Brewer	1.25	.60	.12
☐ 417	Ed Brinkman	1.25	.60	.12
☐ 418	Johnny Edwards	1.25	.60	.12
☐ 419	Ruben Amaro	1.25	.60	.12
☐ 420	Larry Jackson	1.25	.60	.12
☐ 421	Twins Rookies	1.25	.60	.12
	Gary Dotter			
	Jay Ward			
☐ 422	Aubrey Gatewood	1.25	.60	.12
☐ 423	Jesse Gonder	1.25	.60	.12
☐ 424	Gary Bell	1.25	.60	.12
☐ 425	Wayne Causey	1.25	.60	.12
☐ 426	Braves Team	2.50	1.25	.25
☐ 427	Bob Saverine	1.25	.60	.12
☐ 428	Bob Shaw	1.25	.60	.12
☐ 429	Don Demeter	1.25	.60	.12
☐ 430	Gary Peters	1.50	.75	.15
☐ 431	Cards Rookies	2.00	1.00	.20
	Nelson Briles			
	Wayne Spiezio			
☐ 432	Jim Grant	1.25	.60	.12
☐ 433	John Bateman	1.25	.60	.12
☐ 434	Dave Morehead	1.25	.60	.12
☐ 435	Willie Davis	1.75	.85	.17

		NRMT	VG-E	GOOD
☐ 436	Don Elston	1.25	.60	.12
☐ 437	Chico Cardenas	1.25	.60	.12
☐ 438	Harry Walker MG	1.25	.60	.12
☐ 439	Moe Drabowsky	1.25	.60	.12
☐ 440	Tom Tresh	1.75	.85	.17
☐ 441	Denny Lemaster	1.25	.60	.12
☐ 442	Vic Power	1.25	.60	.12
☐ 443	Checklist 6	4.50	.75	.15
☐ 444	Bob Hendley	1.25	.60	.12
☐ 445	Don Lock	1.25	.60	.12
☐ 446	Art Mahaffey	1.25	.60	.12
☐ 447	Julian Javier	3.00	1.50	.30
☐ 448	Lee Stange	3.00	1.50	.30
☐ 449	Mets Rookies	3.00	1.50	.30
	Jerry Hinsley			
	Gary Kroll			
☐ 450	Elston Howard	4.50	2.25	.45
☐ 451	Jim Owens	3.00	1.50	.30
☐ 452	Gary Geiger	3.00	1.50	.30
☐ 453	Dodgers Rookies	3.50	1.75	.35
	Willie Crawford			
	John Werhas			
☐ 454	Ed Rakow	3.00	1.50	.30
☐ 455	Norm Siebern	3.00	1.50	.30
☐ 456	Bill Henry	3.00	1.50	.30
☐ 457	Bob Kennedy MG	3.00	1.50	.30
☐ 458	John Buzhardt	3.00	1.50	.30
☐ 459	Frank Kostro	3.00	1.50	.30
☐ 460	Richie Allen	5.00	2.50	.50
☐ 461	Braves Rookies	35.00	17.50	3.50
	Clay Carroll			
	Phil Niekro			
☐ 462	Lew Krausse	3.00	1.50	.30
	(photo actually			
	Pete Lovrich)			
☐ 463	Manny Mota	3.50	1.75	.35
☐ 464	Ron Piche	3.00	1.50	.30
☐ 465	Tom Haller	3.00	1.50	.30
☐ 466	Senators Rookies	3.00	1.50	.30
	Pete Craig			
	Dick Nen			
☐ 467	Ray Washburn	3.00	1.50	.30
☐ 468	Larry Brown	3.00	1.50	.30
☐ 469	Don Nottebart	3.00	1.50	.30
☐ 470	Yogi Berra MG	45.00	22.50	4.50
☐ 471	Billy Hoeft	3.00	1.50	.30
☐ 472	Don Pavletich	3.00	1.50	.30
☐ 473	Orioles Rookies	10.00	5.00	1.00
	Paul Blair			

		NRMT	VG-E	GOOD
	Dave Johnson			
☐ 474	Cookie Rojas	3.50	1.75	.35
☐ 475	Clete Boyer	3.50	1.75	.35
☐ 476	Billy O'Dell	3.00	1.50	.30
☐ 477	Cards Rookies	250.00	110.00	22.00
	Fritz Ackley			
	Steve Carlton			
☐ 478	Wilbur Wood	3.50	1.75	.35
☐ 479	Ken Harrelson	4.00	2.00	.40
☐ 480	Joel Horlen	3.00	1.50	.30
☐ 481	Cleveland Indians	6.00	3.00	.60
	Team Card			
☐ 482	Bob Priddy	3.00	1.50	.30
☐ 483	George Smith	3.00	1.50	.30
☐ 484	Ron Perranoski	3.50	1.75	.35
☐ 485	Nellie Fox	6.00	3.00	.60
☐ 486	Angels Rookies	3.00	1.50	.30
	Tom Egan			
	Pat Rogan			
☐ 487	Woody Woodward	3.50	1.75	.35
☐ 488	Ted Wills	3.00	1.50	.30
☐ 489	Gene Mauch MG	3.50	1.75	.35
☐ 490	Earl Battey	3.00	1.50	.30
☐ 491	Tracy Stallard	3.00	1.50	.30
☐ 492	Gene Freese	3.00	1.50	.30
☐ 493	Tigers Rookies	3.00	1.50	.30
	Bill Roman			
	Bruce Brubaker			
☐ 494	Jay Ritchie	3.00	1.50	.30
☐ 495	Joe Christopher	3.00	1.50	.30
☐ 496	Joe Cunningham	3.50	1.75	.35
☐ 497	Giants Rookies	3.50	1.75	.35
	Ken Henderson			
	Jack Hiatt			
☐ 498	Gene Stephens	3.00	1.50	.30
☐ 499	Stu Miller	3.00	1.50	.30
☐ 500	Eddie Mathews	22.00	11.00	2.20
☐ 501	Indians Rookies	3.00	1.50	.30
	Ralph Gagliano			
	Jim Rittwage			
☐ 502	Don Cardwell	3.00	1.50	.30
☐ 503	Phil Gagliano	3.00	1.50	.30
☐ 504	Jerry Grote	3.00	1.50	.30
☐ 505	Ray Culp	3.00	1.50	.30
☐ 506	Sam Mele MG	3.00	1.50	.30
☐ 507	Sammy Ellis	3.00	1.50	.30
☐ 508	Checklist 7	7.00	1.00	.20
☐ 509	Red Sox Rookies	3.00	1.50	.30
	Bob Guindon			

		NRMT	VG-E	GOOD
	Gerry Vezendy			
☐ 510	Ernie Banks	45.00	22.50	4.50
☐ 511	Ron Locke	3.00	1.50	.30
☐ 512	Cap Peterson	3.00	1.50	.30
☐ 513	New York Yankees	10.00	5.00	1.00
	Team Card			
☐ 514	Joe Azcue	3.00	1.50	.30
☐ 515	Vern Law	3.50	1.75	.35
☐ 516	Al Weis	3.00	1.50	.30
☐ 517	Angels Rookies	3.00	1.50	.30
	Paul Schaal			
	Jack Warner			
☐ 518	Ken Rowe	3.00	1.50	.30
☐ 519	Bob Uecker	40.00	20.00	4.00
☐ 520	Tony Cloninger	3.00	1.50	.30
☐ 521	Phillies Rookies	3.00	1.50	.30
	Dave Bennett			
	Morrie Stevens			
☐ 522	Hank Aguirre	3.00	1.50	.30
☐ 523	Mike Brumley SP	7.00	3.50	.70
☐ 524	Dave Giusti SP	7.00	3.50	.70
☐ 525	Eddie Bressoud	3.50	1.75	.35
☐ 526	Athletics Rookies SP	100.00	45.00	9.00
	Rene Lachemann			
	Johnny Odom			
	Jim Hunter ERR			
	("Tim" on back)			
	Skip Lockwood			
☐ 527	Jeff Torborg SP	9.00	4.50	.70
☐ 528	George Altman	3.50	1.75	.35
☐ 529	Jerry Fosnow SP	7.00	3.50	.70
☐ 530	Jim Maloney	5.00	2.25	.45
☐ 531	Chuck Hiller	3.50	1.75	.35
☐ 532	Hector Lopez	4.00	1.75	.35
☐ 533	Mets Rookies SP	20.00	9.00	1.75
	Dan Napoleon			
	Ron Swoboda			
	Tug McGraw			
	Jim Bethke			
☐ 534	John Herrnstein	3.50	1.75	.35
☐ 535	Jack Kralick SP	7.00	3.50	.70
☐ 536	Andre Rodgers SP	7.00	3.50	.70
☐ 537	Angels Rookies	4.00	1.75	.35
	Marcelino Lopes			
	Phil Roof			
	Rudy May			
☐ 538	Chuck Dressen MG SP	7.00	3.50	.70
☐ 539	Herm Starrette	3.50	1.75	.35
☐ 540	Lou Brock SP	45.00	20.00	4.00

		NRMT	VG-E	GOOD
☐ 541	White Sox Rookies	3.50	1.75	.35
	Greg Bollo			
	Bob Locker			
☐ 542	Lou Klimchock	3.50	1.75	.35
☐ 543	Ed Connolly SP	7.00	3.50	.70
☐ 544	Howie Reed	3.50	1.75	.35
☐ 545	Jesus Alou SP	7.00	3.50	.70
☐ 546	Indians Rookies	3.50	1.75	.35
	Bill Davis			
	Mike Hedlund			
	Ray Barker			
	Floyd Weaver			
☐ 547	Jake Wood SP	7.00	3.50	.70
☐ 548	Dick Stigman	3.50	1.75	.35
☐ 549	Cubs Rookies SP	10.00	4.50	.90
	Roberto Pena			
	Glenn Beckert			
☐ 550	Mel Stottlemyre SP	20.00	9.00	1.70
☐ 551	New York Mets SP	15.00	6.50	1.20
	Team Card			
☐ 552	Julio Gotay	3.50	1.75	.35
☐ 553	Astros Rookies	3.50	1.75	.35
	Dan Coombs			
	Gene Ratliff			
	Jack McClure			
☐ 554	Chico Ruiz SP	7.00	3.50	.70
☐ 555	Jack Baldschun SP	7.00	3.50	.70
☐ 556	Red Schoendienst	15.00	6.50	1.20
	MG SP			
☐ 557	Jose Santiago	3.50	1.75	.35
☐ 558	Tommie Sisk	3.50	1.75	.35
☐ 559	Ed Bailey SP	7.00	3.50	.70
☐ 560	Boog Powell SP	10.00	4.50	.90
☐ 561	Dodgers Rookies	10.00	4.50	.90
	Dennis Daboll			
	Mike Kekich			
	Hector Valle			
	Jim Lefebvre			
☐ 562	Billy Moran	3.50	1.75	.35
☐ 563	Julio Navarro	3.50	1.75	.35
☐ 564	Mel Nelson	3.50	1.75	.35
☐ 565	Ernie Broglio SP	7.00	3.50	.70
☐ 566	Yankees Rookies SP	7.00	3.50	.70
	Gil Blanco			
	Ross Moschitto			
	Art Lopez			
☐ 567	Tommie Aaron	4.00	1.75	.35
☐ 568	Ron Taylor SP	7.00	3.50	.70
☐ 569	Gino Cimoli SP	7.00	3.50	.70
☐ 570	Claude Osteen SP	7.00	3.50	.70
☐ 571	Ossie Virgil SP	7.00	3.50	.70
☐ 572	Baltimore Orioles SP	10.00	4.50	.90
	Team Card			
☐ 573	Red Sox Rookies SP	15.00	6.50	1.20
	Jim Lonborg			
	Gerry Moses			
	Bill Schlesinger			
	Mike Ryan			
☐ 574	Roy Sievers	4.00	1.75	.35
☐ 575	Jose Pagan	3.50	1.75	.35
☐ 576	Terry Fox SP	7.00	3.50	.70
☐ 577	AL Rookie Stars SP	8.00	3.50	.70
	Darold Knowles			
	Don Buschhorn			
	Richie Scheinblum			
☐ 578	Camilo Carreon SP	7.00	3.50	.70
☐ 579	Dick Smith SP	7.00	3.50	.70
☐ 580	Jimmie Hall SP	8.00	3.50	.70
☐ 581	NL Rookie Stars SP	80.00	35.00	6.50
	Tony Perez			
	Dave Ricketts			
	Kevin Collins			
☐ 582	Bob Schmidt SP	7.00	3.50	.70
☐ 583	Wes Covington SP	7.00	3.50	.70
☐ 584	Harry Bright	3.50	1.75	.35
☐ 585	Hank Fischer	3.50	1.75	.35
☐ 586	Tom McCraw SP	7.00	3.50	.70
☐ 587	Joe Sparma	3.50	1.75	.35
☐ 588	Lenny Green	3.50	1.75	.35
☐ 589	Giants Rookies SP	7.00	3.50	.70
	Frank Linzy			
	Bob Schroder			
☐ 590	John Wyatt	3.50	1.75	.35
☐ 591	Bob Skinner SP	7.00	3.50	.70
☐ 592	Frank Bork SP	7.00	3.50	.70
☐ 593	Tigers Rookies SP	7.00	3.50	.70
	Jackie Moore			
	John Sullivan			
☐ 594	Joe Gaines	3.50	1.75	.35
☐ 595	Don Lee	3.50	1.75	.35
☐ 596	Don Landrum SP	7.00	3.50	.70
☐ 597	Twins Rookies	3.50	1.75	.35
	Joe Nossek			
	John Sevcik			
	Dick Reese			
☐ 598	Al Downing SP	10.00	3.50	.70

1966 Topps

WHITEY FORD pitcher

The cards in this 598-card set measure 2 ½"
by 3 ½". There are the same number of cards
as in the 1965 set. Once again, the seventh
series cards (523 to 598) are considered more
difficult to obtain than the cards of any other
series in the set. Within this last series
there are 43 cards that were printed in lesser
quantities than the other cards in that series;
these shorter-printed cards are marked by SP
in the checklist below. The only featured subset
within this set is League Leaders (215-226).
Noteworthy rookie cards in the set include Jim
Palmer (126) and Don Sutton (288). Palmer is
described in the bio (on his card back) as a
left-hander.

		NRMT	VG-E	GOOD
COMPLETE SET (598)		3600.00	1800.00	450.00
COMMON PLAYER (1-109)		.75	.35	.07
COMMON PLAYER (110-283)		.85	.40	.08
COMMON PLAYER (284-370)		1.00	.50	.10
COMMON PLAYER (371-446)		1.50	.75	.15
COMMON PLAYER (447-522)		3.50	1.75	.35
COMMON PLAYER (523-598)		12.00	6.00	1.20
COMMON SP (523-598)		25.00	12.50	2.50

		NRMT	VG-E	GOOD
☐ 1	Willie Mays	125.00	30.00	6.00
☐ 2	Ted Abernathy	.75	.35	.07
☐ 3	Sam Mele MG	.75	.35	.07
☐ 4	Ray Culp	.75	.35	.07
☐ 5	Jim Fregosi	1.00	.50	.10
☐ 6	Chuck Schilling	.75	.35	.07

		NRMT	VG-E	GOOD
☐ 7	Tracy Stallard	.75	.35	.07
☐ 8	Floyd Robinson	.75	.35	.07
☐ 9	Clete Boyer	1.00	.50	.10
☐ 10	Tony Cloninger	.75	.35	.07
☐ 11	Senators Rookies	.75	.35	.07
	Brant Alyea			
	Pete Craig			
☐ 12	John Tsitouris	.75	.35	.07
☐ 13	Lou Johnson	.75	.35	.07
☐ 14	Norm Siebern	.75	.35	.07
☐ 15	Vern Law	1.00	.50	.10
☐ 16	Larry Brown	.75	.35	.07
☐ 17	John Stephenson	.75	.35	.07
☐ 18	Roland Sheldon	.75	.35	.07
☐ 19	San Francisco Giants	1.75	.85	.17
	Team Card			
☐ 20	Willie Horton	1.00	.50	.10
☐ 21	Don Nottebart	.75	.35	.07
☐ 22	Joe Nossek	.75	.35	.07
☐ 23	Jack Sanford	.75	.35	.07
☐ 24	Don Kessinger	2.00	1.00	.20
☐ 25	Pete Ward	.75	.35	.07
☐ 26	Ray Sadecki	.75	.35	.07
☐ 27	Orioles Rookies	1.00	.50	.10
	Darold Knowles			
	Andy Etchebarren			
☐ 28	Phil Niekro	12.00	6.00	1.20
☐ 29	Mike Brumley	.75	.35	.07
☐ 30	Pete Rose	65.00	32.50	6.50
☐ 31	Jack Cullen	.75	.35	.07
☐ 32	Adolfo Phillips	.75	.35	.07
☐ 33	Jim Pagliaroni	.75	.35	.07
☐ 34	Checklist 1	3.50	.50	.10
☐ 35	Ron Swoboda	1.00	.50	.10
☐ 36	Jim Hunter	25.00	12.50	2.50
☐ 37	Billy Herman MG	1.50	.75	.15
☐ 38	Ron Nischwitz	.75	.35	.07
☐ 39	Ken Henderson	.75	.35	.07
☐ 40	Jim Grant	.75	.35	.07
☐ 41	Don LeJohn	.75	.35	.07
☐ 42	Aubrey Gatewood	.75	.35	.07
☐ 43	Don Landrum	.75	.35	.07
☐ 44	Indians Rookies	.75	.35	.07
	Bill Davis			
	Tom Kelley			
☐ 45	Jim Gentile	1.00	.50	.10
☐ 46	Howie Koplitz	.75	.35	.07
☐ 47	J.C. Martin	.75	.35	.07
☐ 48	Paul Blair	1.00	.50	.10

			NRMT	VG-E	GOOD
☐	49	Woody Woodward ..	1.00	.50	.10
☐	50	Mickey Mantle	175.00	85.00	18.00
☐	51	Gordon Richardson .	.75	.35	.07
☐	52	Power Plus	1.00	.50	.10
		Wes Covington			
		Johnny Callison			
☐	53	Bob Duliba	.75	.35	.07
☐	54	Jose Pagan	.75	.35	.07
☐	55	Ken Harrelson	1.25	.60	.12
☐	56	Sandy Valdespino ..	.75	.35	.07
☐	57	Jim Lefebvre	1.25	.60	.12
☐	58	Dave Wickersham ...	.75	.35	.07
☐	59	Reds Team	1.75	.85	.17
☐	60	Curt Flood	1.25	.60	.12
☐	61	Bob Bolin	.75	.35	.07
☐	62A	Merritt Ranew	.75	.35	.07
		(with sold line)			
☐	62B	Merritt Ranew	30.00	12.50	2.50
		(without sold line)			
☐	63	Jim Stewart	.75	.35	.07
☐	64	Bob Bruce	.75	.35	.07
☐	65	Leon Wagner	.75	.35	.07
☐	66	Al Weis	.75	.35	.07
☐	67	Mets Rookies	1.00	.50	.10
		Cleon Jones			
		Dick Selma			
☐	68	Hal Reniff	.75	.35	.07
☐	69	Ken Hamlin	.75	.35	.07
☐	70	Carl Yastrzemski ...	50.00	25.00	5.00
☐	71	Frank Carpin	.75	.35	.07
☐	72	Tony Perez	12.00	6.00	1.20
☐	73	Jerry Zimmerman ...	.75	.35	.07
☐	74	Don Mossi	1.00	.50	.10
☐	75	Tommy Davis	1.25	.60	.12
☐	76	Red Schoendienst MG	4.00	2.00	.40
☐	77	John Orsino	.75	.35	.07
☐	78	Frank Linzy	.75	.35	.07
☐	79	Joe Pepitone	1.50	.75	.15
☐	80	Richie Allen	2.00	1.00	.20
☐	81	Ray Oyler	.75	.35	.07
☐	82	Bob Hendley	.75	.35	.07
☐	83	Albie Pearson	.75	.35	.07
☐	84	Braves Rookies	.75	.35	.07
		Jim Beauchamp			
		Dick Kelley			
☐	85	Eddie Fisher	.75	.35	.07
☐	86	John Bateman	.75	.35	.07
☐	87	Dan Napoleon	.75	.35	.07
☐	88	Fred Whitfield	.75	.35	.07

			NRMT	VG-E	GOOD
☐	89	Ted Davidson	.75	.35	.07
☐	90	Luis Aparicio	6.50	3.25	.65
☐	91A	Bob Uecker	15.00	7.50	1.50
		(with traded line)			
☐	91B	Bob Uecker	60.00	30.00	6.00
		(no traded line)			
☐	92	Yankees Team	3.50	1.75	.35
☐	93	Jim Lonborg	1.50	.75	.15
☐	94	Matty Alou	1.00	.50	.10
☐	95	Pete Richert	.75	.35	.07
☐	96	Felipe Alou	1.00	.50	.10
☐	97	Jim Merritt	.75	.35	.07
☐	98	Don Demeter	.75	.35	.07
☐	99	Buc Belters	3.50	1.75	.35
		Willie Stargell			
		Donn Clendenon			
☐	100	Sandy Koufax	65.00	32.50	6.50
☐	101A	Checklist 2	5.00	1.00	.20
		(115 Bill Henry)			
☐	101B	Checklist 2	10.00	2.00	.40
		(115 W. Spahn)			
☐	102	Ed Kirkpatrick	.75	.35	.07
☐	103A	Dick Groat	1.25	.60	.12
		(with traded line)			
☐	103B	Dick Groat	30.00	12.50	2.50
		(no traded line)			
☐	104A	Alex Johnson	1.00	.50	.10
		(with traded line)			
☐	104B	Alex Johnson	30.00	12.50	2.50
		(no traded line)			
☐	105	Milt Pappas	1.00	.50	.10
☐	106	Rusty Staub	1.75	.85	.17
☐	107	A's Rookies	.75	.35	.07
		Larry Stahl			
		Ron Tompkins			
☐	108	Bobby Klaus	.75	.35	.07
☐	109	Ralph Terry	1.00	.50	.10
☐	110	Ernie Banks	15.00	7.50	1.50
☐	111	Gary Peters	.85	.40	.08
☐	112	Manny Mota	1.25	.60	.12
☐	113	Hank Aguirre	.85	.40	.08
☐	114	Jim Gosger	.85	.40	.08
☐	115	Bill Henry	.85	.40	.08
☐	116	Walt Alston MG ...	3.00	1.50	.30
☐	117	Jake Gibbs	.85	.40	.08
☐	118	Mike McCormick ...	.85	.40	.08
☐	119	Art Shamsky	.85	.40	.08
☐	120	Harmon Killebrew ...	12.50	6.25	1.25
☐	121	Ray Herbert	.85	.40	.08

		NRMT	VG-E	GOOD
☐ 122	Joe Gaines	.85	.40	.08
☐ 123	Pirates Rookies	.85	.40	.08
	Frank Bork			
	Jerry May			
☐ 124	Tug McGraw	2.50	1.25	.25
☐ 125	Lou Brock	12.00	6.00	1.20
☐ 126	Jim Palmer	150.00	75.00	15.00
☐ 127	Ken Berry	.85	.40	.08
☐ 128	Jim Landis	.85	.40	.08
☐ 129	Jack Kralick	.85	.40	.08
☐ 130	Joe Torre	1.50	.75	.15
☐ 131	Angels Team	1.75	.85	.17
☐ 132	Orlando Cepeda	3.50	1.75	.35
☐ 133	Don McMahon	.85	.40	.08
☐ 134	Wes Parker	1.25	.60	.12
☐ 135	Dave Morehead	.85	.40	.08
☐ 136	Woody Held	.85	.40	.08
☐ 137	Pat Corrales	1.25	.60	.12
☐ 138	Roger Repoz	.85	.40	.08
☐ 139	Cubs Rookies	.85	.40	.08
	Byron Browne			
	Don Young			
☐ 140	Jim Maloney	1.25	.60	.12
☐ 141	Tom McCraw	.85	.40	.08
☐ 142	Don Dennis	.85	.40	.08
☐ 143	Jose Tartabull	.85	.40	.08
☐ 144	Don Schwall	.85	.40	.08
☐ 145	Bill Freehan	1.50	.75	.15
☐ 146	George Altman	.85	.40	.08
☐ 147	Lum Harris MG	.85	.40	.08
☐ 148	Bob Johnson	.85	.40	.08
☐ 149	Dick Nen	.85	.40	.08
☐ 150	Rocky Colavito	1.50	.75	.15
☐ 151	Gary Wagner	.85	.40	.08
☐ 152	Frank Malzone	1.25	.60	.12
☐ 153	Rico Carty	1.50	.75	.15
☐ 154	Chuck Hiller	.85	.40	.08
☐ 155	Marcelino Lopez	.85	.40	.08
☐ 156	Double Play Combo	1.25	.60	.12
	Dick Schofield			
	Hal Lanier			
☐ 157	Rene Lachemann	1.50	.75	.15
☐ 158	Jim Brewer	.85	.40	.08
☐ 159	Chico Ruiz	.85	.40	.08
☐ 160	Whitey Ford	13.00	6.50	1.30
☐ 161	Jerry Lumpe	.85	.40	.08
☐ 162	Lee Maye	.85	.40	.08
☐ 163	Tito Francona	.85	.40	.08
☐ 164	White Sox Rookies	1.25	.60	.12

		NRMT	VG-E	GOOD
	Tommie Agee			
	Marv Staehle			
☐ 165	Don Lock	.85	.40	.08
☐ 166	Chris Krug	.85	.40	.08
☐ 167	Boog Powell	2.00	1.00	.20
☐ 168	Dan Osinski	.85	.40	.08
☐ 169	Duke Sims	.85	.40	.08
☐ 170	Cookie Rojas	.85	.40	.08
☐ 171	Nick Willhite	.85	.40	.08
☐ 172	Mets Team	2.00	1.00	.20
☐ 173	Al Spangler	.85	.40	.08
☐ 174	Ron Taylor	.85	.40	.08
☐ 175	Bert Campaneris	1.25	.60	.12
☐ 176	Jim Davenport	1.25	.60	.12
☐ 177	Hector Lopez	.85	.40	.08
☐ 178	Bob Tillman	.85	.40	.08
☐ 179	Cards Rookies	1.25	.60	.12
	Dennis Aust			
	Bob Tolan			
☐ 180	Vada Pinson	1.50	.75	.15
☐ 181	Al Worthington	.85	.40	.08
☐ 182	Jerry Lynch	.85	.40	.08
☐ 183	Checklist 3	3.50	.50	.10
☐ 184	Denis Menke	.85	.40	.08
☐ 185	Bob Buhl	.85	.40	.08
☐ 186	Ruben Amaro	.85	.40	.08
☐ 187	Chuck Dressen MG	.85	.40	.08
☐ 188	Al Luplow	.85	.40	.08
☐ 189	John Roseboro	.85	.40	.08
☐ 190	Jimmie Hall	.85	.40	.08
☐ 191	Darrell Sutherland	.85	.40	.08
☐ 192	Vic Power	.85	.40	.08
☐ 193	Dave McNally	1.25	.60	.12
☐ 194	Senators Team	1.75	.85	.17
☐ 195	Joe Morgan	32.00	16.00	3.20
☐ 196	Don Pavletich	.85	.40	.08
☐ 197	Sonny Siebert	.85	.40	.08
☐ 198	Mickey Stanley	1.25	.60	.12
☐ 199	Chisox Clubbers	1.25	.60	.12
	Bill Skowron			
	Johnny Romano			
	Floyd Robinson			
☐ 200	Eddie Mathews	9.00	4.50	.90
☐ 201	Jim Dickson	.85	.40	.08
☐ 202	Clay Dalrymple	.85	.40	.08
☐ 203	Jose Santiago	.85	.40	.08
☐ 204	Cubs Team	1.75	.85	.17
☐ 205	Tom Tresh	1.50	.75	.15
☐ 206	Al Jackson	.85	.40	.08

		NRMT	VG-E	GOOD
☐ 207	Frank Quilici	.85	.40	.08
☐ 208	Bob Miller	.85	.40	.08
☐ 209	Tigers Rookies	1.50	.75	.15
	Fritz Fisher			
	John Hiller			
☐ 210	Bill Mazeroski	1.50	.75	.15
☐ 211	Frank Kreutzer	.85	.40	.08
☐ 212	Ed Kranepool	1.25	.60	.12
☐ 213	Fred Newman	.85	.40	.08
☐ 214	Tommy Harper	1.25	.60	.12
☐ 215	NL Batting Leaders	12.00	6.00	1.20
	Bob Clemente			
	Hank Aaron			
	Willie Mays			
☐ 216	AL Batting Leaders	3.00	1.50	.30
	Tony Oliva			
	Carl Yastrzemski			
	Vic Davalillo			
☐ 217	NL Home Run Leaders	9.00	4.50	.90
	Willie Mays			
	Willie McCovey			
	Billy Williams			
☐ 218	AL Home Run Leaders	2.00	1.00	.20
	Tony Conigliaro			
	Norm Cash			
	Willie Horton			
☐ 219	NL RBI Leaders	3.00	1.50	.30
	Deron Johnson			
	Frank Robinson			
	Willie Mays			
☐ 220	AL RBI Leaders	1.50	.75	.15
	Rocky Colavito			
	Willie Horton			
	Tony Oliva			
☐ 221	NL ERA Leaders	3.00	1.50	.30
	Sandy Koufax			
	Juan Marichal			
	Vern Law			
☐ 222	AL ERA Leaders	1.50	.75	.15
	Sam McDowell			
	Eddie Fisher			
	Sonny Siebert			
☐ 223	NL Pitching Leaders	3.00	1.50	.30
	Sandy Koufax			
	Tony Cloninger			
	Don Drysdale			
☐ 224	AL Pitching Leaders	1.50	.75	.15

		NRMT	VG-E	GOOD
	Jim Grant			
	Mel Stottlemyre			
	Jim Kaat			
☐ 225	NL Strikeout Leaders	3.00	1.50	.30
	Sandy Koufax			
	Bob Veale			
	Bob Gibson			
☐ 226	AL Strikeout Leaders	1.50	.75	.15
	Sam McDowell			
	Mickey Lolich			
	Dennis McLain			
	Sonny Siebert			
☐ 227	Russ Nixon	1.25	.60	.12
☐ 228	Larry Dierker	1.25	.60	.12
☐ 229	Hank Bauer MG	1.25	.60	.12
☐ 230	Johnny Callison	1.25	.60	.12
☐ 231	Floyd Weaver	.85	.40	.08
☐ 232	Glenn Beckert	1.25	.60	.12
☐ 233	Dom Zanni	.85	.40	.08
☐ 234	Yankees Rookies	3.50	1.75	.35
	Rich Beck			
	Roy White			
☐ 235	Don Cardwell	.85	.40	.08
☐ 236	Mike Hershberger	.85	.40	.08
☐ 237	Billy O'Dell	.85	.40	.08
☐ 238	Dodgers Team	2.25	1.10	.22
☐ 239	Orlando Pena	.85	.40	.08
☐ 240	Earl Battey	.85	.40	.08
☐ 241	Dennis Ribant	.85	.40	.08
☐ 242	Jesus Alou	.85	.40	.08
☐ 243	Nelson Briles	1.25	.60	.12
☐ 244	Astros Rookies	.85	.40	.08
	Chuck Harrison			
	Sonny Jackson			
☐ 245	John Buzhardt	.85	.40	.08
☐ 246	Ed Bailey	.85	.40	.08
☐ 247	Carl Warwick	.85	.40	.08
☐ 248	Pete Mikkelsen	.85	.40	.08
☐ 249	Bill Rigney MG	.85	.40	.08
☐ 250	Sammy Ellis	.85	.40	.08
☐ 251	Ed Brinkman	.85	.40	.08
☐ 252	Denny Lemaster	.85	.40	.08
☐ 253	Don Wert	.85	.40	.08
☐ 254	Phillies Rookies	33.00	15.00	3.00
	Ferguson Jenkins			
	Bill Sorrell			
☐ 255	Willie Stargell	15.00	7.50	1.50
☐ 256	Lew Krausse	.85	.40	.08
☐ 257	Jeff Torborg	1.50	.75	.15

		NRMT	VG-E	GOOD
☐ 258	Dave Giusti	1.25	.60	.12
☐ 259	Boston Red Sox Team Card	2.00	1.00	.20
☐ 260	Bob Shaw	.85	.40	.08
☐ 261	Ron Hansen	.85	.40	.08
☐ 262	Jack Hamilton	.85	.40	.08
☐ 263	Tom Egan	.85	.40	.08
☐ 264	Twins Rookies Andy Kosco Ted Uhlaender	.85	.40	.08
☐ 265	Stu Miller	.85	.40	.08
☐ 266	Pedro Gonzalez (misspelled Gonzales on card back)	.85	.40	.08
☐ 267	Joe Sparma	.85	.40	.08
☐ 268	John Blanchard	.85	.40	.08
☐ 269	Don Heffner MG	.85	.40	.08
☐ 270	Claude Osteen	1.25	.60	.12
☐ 271	Hal Lanier	1.25	.60	.12
☐ 272	Jack Baldschun	.85	.40	.08
☐ 273	Astro Aces Bob Aspromonte Rusty Staub	1.25	.60	.12
☐ 274	Buster Narum	.85	.40	.08
☐ 275	Tim McCarver	2.00	1.00	.20
☐ 276	Jim Bouton	1.50	.75	.15
☐ 277	George Thomas	.85	.40	.08
☐ 278	Cal Koonce	.85	.40	.08
☐ 279	Checklist 4	3.50	.50	.10
☐ 280	Bobby Knoop	.85	.40	.08
☐ 281	Bruce Howard	.85	.40	.08
☐ 282	Johnny Lewis	.85	.40	.08
☐ 283	Jim Perry	1.25	.60	.12
☐ 284	Bobby Wine	1.00	.50	.10
☐ 285	Luis Tiant	2.00	1.00	.20
☐ 286	Gary Geiger	1.00	.50	.10
☐ 287	Jack Aker	1.00	.50	.10
☐ 288	Dodgers Rookies Bill Singer Don Sutton	90.00	45.00	9.00
☐ 289	Larry Sherry	1.25	.60	.12
☐ 290	Ron Santo	1.75	.85	.17
☐ 291	Moe Drabowsky	1.00	.50	.10
☐ 292	Jim Coker	1.00	.50	.10
☐ 293	Mike Shannon	1.50	.75	.15
☐ 294	Steve Ridzik	1.00	.50	.10
☐ 295	Jim Ray Hart	1.25	.60	.12
☐ 296	Johnny Keane MG	1.25	.60	.12
☐ 297	Jim Owens	1.00	.50	.10

		NRMT	VG-E	GOOD
☐ 298	Rico Petrocelli	1.50	.75	.15
☐ 299	Lou Burdette	1.75	.85	.17
☐ 300	Bob Clemente	65.00	32.50	6.50
☐ 301	Greg Bollo	1.00	.50	.10
☐ 302	Ernie Bowman	1.00	.50	.10
☐ 303	Cleveland Indians Team Card	2.00	1.00	.20
☐ 304	John Herrnstein	1.00	.50	.10
☐ 305	Camilo Pascual	1.25	.60	.12
☐ 306	Ty Cline	1.00	.50	.10
☐ 307	Clay Carroll	1.00	.50	.10
☐ 308	Tom Haller	1.25	.60	.12
☐ 309	Diego Segui	1.00	.50	.10
☐ 310	Frank Robinson	24.00	12.00	2.40
☐ 311	Reds Rookies Tommy Helms Dick Simpson	1.25	.60	.12
☐ 312	Bob Saverine	1.00	.50	.10
☐ 313	Chris Zachary	1.00	.50	.10
☐ 314	Hector Valle	1.00	.50	.10
☐ 315	Norm Cash	1.75	.85	.17
☐ 316	Jack Fisher	1.00	.50	.10
☐ 317	Dalton Jones	1.00	.50	.10
☐ 318	Harry Walker MG	1.00	.50	.10
☐ 319	Gene Freese	1.00	.50	.10
☐ 320	Bob Gibson	14.00	7.00	1.40
☐ 321	Rick Reichardt	1.00	.50	.10
☐ 322	Bill Faul	1.00	.50	.10
☐ 323	Ray Barker	1.00	.50	.10
☐ 324	John Boozer	1.00	.50	.10
☐ 325	Vic Davalillo	1.00	.50	.10
☐ 326	Braves Team	2.00	1.00	.20
☐ 327	Bernie Allen	1.00	.50	.10
☐ 328	Jerry Grote	1.00	.50	.10
☐ 329	Pete Charton	1.00	.50	.10
☐ 330	Ron Fairly	1.25	.60	.12
☐ 331	Ron Herbel	1.00	.50	.10
☐ 332	Bill Bryan	1.00	.50	.10
☐ 333	Senators Rookies Joe Coleman Jim French	1.00	.50	.10
☐ 334	Marty Keough	1.00	.50	.10
☐ 335	Juan Pizarro	1.00	.50	.10
☐ 336	Gene Alley	1.25	.60	.12
☐ 337	Fred Gladding	1.00	.50	.10
☐ 338	Dal Maxvill	1.00	.50	.10
☐ 339	Del Crandall	1.25	.60	.12
☐ 340	Dean Chance	1.25	.60	.12
☐ 341	Wes Westrum MG	1.00	.50	.10

		NRMT	VG-E	GOOD
☐ 342	Bob Humphreys	1.00	.50	.10
☐ 343	Joe Christopher	1.00	.50	.10
☐ 344	Steve Blass	1.25	.60	.12
☐ 345	Bob Allison	1.25	.60	.12
☐ 346	Mike De La Hoz	1.00	.50	.10
☐ 347	Phil Regan	1.25	.60	.12
☐ 348	Orioles Team	2.00	1.00	.20
☐ 349	Cap Peterson	1.00	.50	.10
☐ 350	Mel Stottlemyre	2.50	1.25	.25
☐ 351	Fred Valentine	1.00	.50	.10
☐ 352	Bob Aspromonte	1.00	.50	.10
☐ 353	Al McBean	1.00	.50	.10
☐ 354	Smoky Burgess	1.25	.60	.12
☐ 355	Wade Blasingame	1.00	.50	.10
☐ 356	Red Sox Rookies	1.00	.50	.10
	Owen Johnson			
	Ken Sanders			
☐ 357	Gerry Arrigo	1.00	.50	.10
☐ 358	Charlie Smith	1.00	.50	.10
☐ 359	Johnny Briggs	1.00	.50	.10
☐ 360	Ron Hunt	1.00	.50	.10
☐ 361	Tom Satriano	1.00	.50	.10
☐ 362	Gates Brown	1.25	.60	.12
☐ 363	Checklist 5	3.50	.50	.10
☐ 364	Nate Oliver	1.00	.50	.10
☐ 365	Roger Maris	40.00	20.00	4.00
☐ 366	Wayne Causey	1.00	.50	.10
☐ 367	Mel Nelson	1.00	.50	.10
☐ 368	Charlie Lau	1.25	.60	.12
☐ 369	Jim King	1.00	.50	.10
☐ 370	Chico Cardenas	1.00	.50	.10
☐ 371	Lee Stange	1.50	.75	.15
☐ 372	Harvey Kuenn	2.50	1.25	.25
☐ 373	Giants Rookies	1.50	.75	.15
	Jack Hiatt			
	Dick Estelle			
☐ 374	Bob Locker	1.50	.75	.15
☐ 375	Donn Clendenon	2.00	1.00	.20
☐ 376	Paul Schaal	1.50	.75	.15
☐ 377	Turk Farrell	1.50	.75	.15
☐ 378	Dick Tracewski	1.50	.75	.15
☐ 379	Cardinal Team	3.00	1.50	.30
☐ 380	Tony Conigliaro	3.50	1.75	.35
☐ 381	Hank Fischer	1.50	.75	.15
☐ 382	Phil Roof	1.50	.75	.15
☐ 383	Jackie Brandt	1.50	.75	.15
☐ 384	Al Downing	2.00	1.00	.20
☐ 385	Ken Boyer	2.50	1.25	.25
☐ 386	Gil Hodges MG	4.50	2.25	.45

		NRMT	VG-E	GOOD
☐ 387	Howie Reed	1.50	.75	.15
☐ 388	Don Mincher	1.50	.75	.15
☐ 389	Jim O'Toole	1.50	.75	.15
☐ 390	Brooks Robinson	17.00	8.50	1.70
☐ 391	Chuck Hinton	1.50	.75	.15
☐ 392	Cubs Rookies	1.75	.85	.17
	Bill Hands			
	Randy Hundley			
☐ 393	George Brunet	1.50	.75	.15
☐ 394	Ron Brand	1.50	.75	.15
☐ 395	Len Gabrielson	1.50	.75	.15
☐ 396	Jerry Stephenson	1.50	.75	.15
☐ 397	Bill White	2.00	1.00	.20
☐ 398	Danny Cater	1.50	.75	.15
☐ 399	Ray Washburn	1.50	.75	.15
☐ 400	Zoilo Versalles	1.50	.75	.15
☐ 401	Ken McMullen	1.50	.75	.15
☐ 402	Jim Hickman	1.50	.75	.15
☐ 403	Fred Talbot	1.50	.75	.15
☐ 404	Pittsburgh Pirates	3.00	1.50	.30
	Team Card			
☐ 405	Elston Howard	3.00	1.50	.30
☐ 406	Joey Jay	1.50	.75	.15
☐ 407	John Kennedy	1.50	.75	.15
☐ 408	Lee Maye	2.00	1.00	.20
☐ 409	Billy Hoeft	1.50	.75	.15
☐ 410	Al Kaline	18.00	9.00	1.80
☐ 411	Gene Mauch MG	2.00	1.00	.20
☐ 412	Sam Bowens	1.50	.75	.15
☐ 413	Johnny Romano	1.50	.75	.15
☐ 414	Dan Coombs	1.50	.75	.15
☐ 415	Max Alvis	1.50	.75	.15
☐ 416	Phil Ortega	1.50	.75	.15
☐ 417	Angels Rookies	1.50	.75	.15
	Jim McGlothlin			
	Ed Sukla			
☐ 418	Phil Gagliano	1.50	.75	.15
☐ 419	Mike Ryan	1.50	.75	.15
☐ 420	Juan Marichal	7.50	3.75	.75
☐ 421	Roy McMillan	1.50	.75	.15
☐ 422	Ed Charles	1.50	.75	.15
☐ 423	Ernie Broglio	1.50	.75	.15
☐ 424	Reds Rookies	3.50	1.75	.35
	Lee May			
	Darrell Osteen			
☐ 425	Bob Veale	1.50	.75	.15
☐ 426	White Sox Team	3.00	1.50	.30
☐ 427	John Miller	1.50	.75	.15
☐ 428	Sandy Alomar	2.00	1.00	.20

		NRMT	VG-E	GOOD			NRMT	VG-E	GOOD
☐ 429	Bill Monbouquette ...	1.50	.75	.15		Dooley Womack			
☐ 430	Don Drysdale	12.00	6.00	1.20	☐ 470	Sam McDowell	4.50	2.25	.45
☐ 431	Walt Bond	1.50	.75	.15	☐ 471	Bob Skinner	3.50	1.75	.35
☐ 432	Bob Heffner	1.50	.75	.15	☐ 472	Terry Fox	3.50	1.75	.35
☐ 433	Alvin Dark MG	2.00	1.00	.20	☐ 473	Rich Rollins	3.50	1.75	.35
☐ 434	Willie Kirkland	1.50	.75	.15	☐ 474	Dick Schofield	3.50	1.75	.35
☐ 435	Jim Bunning	4.50	2.25	.45	☐ 475	Dick Radatz	4.50	2.25	.45
☐ 436	Julian Javier	1.50	.75	.15	☐ 476	Bobby Bragan MG ...	3.50	1.75	.35
☐ 437	Al Stanek	1.50	.75	.15	☐ 477	Steve Barber	3.50	1.75	.35
☐ 438	Willie Smith	1.50	.75	.15	☐ 478	Tony Gonzalez	3.50	1.75	.35
☐ 439	Pedro Ramos	1.50	.75	.15	☐ 479	Jim Hannan	3.50	1.75	.35
☐ 440	Deron Johnson	1.50	.75	.15	☐ 480	Dick Stuart	4.50	2.25	.45
☐ 441	Tommie Sisk	1.50	.75	.15	☐ 481	Bob Lee	3.50	1.75	.35
☐ 442	Orioles Rookies	1.50	.75	.15	☐ 482	Cubs Rookies	3.50	1.75	.35
	Ed Barnowski					John Boccabella			
	Eddie Watt					Dave Dowling			
☐ 443	Bill Wakefield	1.50	.75	.15	☐ 483	Joe Nuxhall	4.50	2.25	.45
☐ 444	Checklist 6	5.00	1.00	.20	☐ 484	Wes Covington	3.50	1.75	.35
☐ 445	Jim Kaat	5.00	2.50	.50	☐ 485	Bob Bailey	3.50	1.75	.35
☐ 446	Mack Jones	1.50	.75	.15	☐ 486	Tommy John	8.00	4.00	.80
☐ 447	Dick Ellsworth	4.50	2.25	.45	☐ 487	Al Ferrara	3.50	1.75	.35
	(photo actually				☐ 488	George Banks	3.50	1.75	.35
	Ken Hubbs)				☐ 489	Curt Simmons	4.50	2.25	.45
☐ 448	Eddie Stanky MG ...	4.50	2.25	.45	☐ 490	Bobby Richardson ...	8.00	4.00	.80
☐ 449	Joe Moeller	3.50	1.75	.35	☐ 491	Dennis Bennett	3.50	1.75	.35
☐ 450	Tony Oliva	6.50	3.00	.60	☐ 492	Athletics Team	7.00	3.50	.70
☐ 451	Barry Latman	3.50	1.75	.35	☐ 493	Johnny Klippstein ...	3.50	1.75	.35
☐ 452	Joe Azcue	3.50	1.75	.35	☐ 494	Gordy Coleman	3.50	1.75	.35
☐ 453	Ron Kline	3.50	1.75	.35	☐ 495	Dick McAuliffe	3.50	1.75	.35
☐ 454	Jerry Buchek	3.50	1.75	.35	☐ 496	Lindy McDaniel	3.50	1.75	.35
☐ 455	Mickey Lolich	5.00	2.50	.50	☐ 497	Chris Cannizzaro ...	3.50	1.75	.35
☐ 456	Red Sox Rookies ...	3.50	1.75	.35	☐ 498	Pirates Rookies	4.50	2.25	.45
	Darrell Brandon					Luke Walker			
	Joe Foy					Woody Fryman			
☐ 457	Joe Gibbon	3.50	1.75	.35	☐ 499	Wally Bunker	3.50	1.75	.35
☐ 458	Manny Jimenez	3.50	1.75	.35	☐ 500	Hank Aaron	75.00	37.50	7.50
☐ 459	Bill McCool	3.50	1.75	.35	☐ 501	John O'Donoghue ...	3.50	1.75	.35
☐ 460	Curt Blefary	3.50	1.75	.35	☐ 502	Lenny Green	3.50	1.75	.35
☐ 461	Roy Face	4.50	2.25	.45	☐ 503	Steve Hamilton	3.50	1.75	.35
☐ 462	Bob Rodgers	4.50	2.25	.45	☐ 504	Grady Hatton MG ...	3.50	1.75	.35
☐ 463	Philadelphia Phillies .	7.00	3.50	.70	☐ 505	Jose Cardenal	3.50	1.75	.35
	Team Card				☐ 506	Bo Belinsky	3.50	1.75	.35
☐ 464	Larry Bearnarth	3.50	1.75	.35	☐ 507	Johnny Edwards	3.50	1.75	.35
☐ 465	Don Buford	4.50	2.25	.45	☐ 508	Steve Hargan	3.50	1.75	.35
☐ 466	Ken Johnson	3.50	1.75	.35	☐ 509	Jake Wood	3.50	1.75	.35
☐ 467	Vic Roznovsky	3.50	1.75	.35	☐ 510	Hoyt Wilhelm	11.00	5.50	1.10
☐ 468	Johnny Podres	5.00	2.50	.50	☐ 511	Giants Rookies	3.50	1.75	.35
☐ 469	Yankees Rookies ...	9.00	4.50	.90		Bob Barton			
	Bobby Murcer					Tito Fuentes			

		NRMT	VG-E	GOOD
☐ 512	Dick Stigman	3.50	1.75	.35
☐ 513	Camilo Carreon	3.50	1.75	.35
☐ 514	Hal Woodeshick	3.50	1.75	.35
☐ 515	Frank Howard	4.50	2.25	.45
☐ 516	Eddie Bressoud	3.50	1.75	.35
☐ 517A	Checklist 7	10.00	1.50	.30
	529 White Sox Rookies			
	544 Cardinals Rookies			
☐ 517B	Checklist 7	10.00	1.50	.30
	529 W. Sox Rookies			
	544 Cards Rookies			
☐ 518	Braves Rookies	3.50	1.75	.35
	Herb Hippauf			
	Arnie Umbach			
☐ 519	Bob Friend	4.50	2.25	.45
☐ 520	Jim Wynn	4.50	2.25	.45
☐ 521	John Wyatt	3.50	1.75	.35
☐ 522	Phil Linz	4.50	2.25	.45
☐ 523	Bob Sadowski	12.00	6.00	1.20
☐ 524	Giants Rookies SP	25.00	12.50	2.50
	Ollie Brown			
	Don Mason			
☐ 525	Gary Bell SP	25.00	12.50	2.50
☐ 526	Twins Team SP	50.00	22.50	4.50
☐ 527	Julio Navarro	12.00	6.00	1.20
☐ 528	Jesse Gonder SP	25.00	12.50	2.50
☐ 529	White Sox Rookies	16.00	8.00	1.60
	Lee Elia			
	Dennis Higgins			
	Bill Voss			
☐ 530	Robin Roberts	35.00	17.50	3.50
☐ 531	Joe Cunningham	12.00	6.00	1.20
☐ 532	Aurelio Monteagudo	25.00	12.50	2.50
☐ 533	Jerry Adair SP	25.00	12.50	2.50
☐ 534	Mets Rookies	12.00	6.00	1.20
	Dave Eilers			
	Rob Gardner			
☐ 535	Willie Davis SP	30.00	15.00	3.00
☐ 536	Dick Egan	12.00	6.00	1.20
☐ 537	Herman Franks MG	12.00	6.00	1.20
☐ 538	Bob Allen SP	25.00	12.50	2.50
☐ 539	Astros Rookies	12.00	6.00	1.20
	Bill Heath			
	Carroll Sembera			
☐ 540	Denny McLain SP	50.00	22.50	4.50
☐ 541	Gene Oliver SP	25.00	12.50	2.50
☐ 542	George Smith	12.00	6.00	1.20
☐ 543	Roger Craig SP	30.00	15.00	3.00
☐ 544	Cardinals Rookies SP	25.00	12.50	2.50

		NRMT	VG-E	GOOD
	Joe Hoerner			
	George Kernek			
	Jimmy Williams			
☐ 545	Dick Green SP	25.00	12.50	2.50
☐ 546	Dwight Siebler	12.00	6.00	1.20
☐ 547	Horace Clarke SP	35.00	15.00	3.00
☐ 548	Gary Kroll SP	25.00	12.50	2.50
☐ 549	Senators Rookies	12.00	6.00	1.20
	Al Closter			
	Casey Cox			
☐ 550	Willie McCovey SP	100.00	45.00	9.00
☐ 551	Bob Purkey SP	25.00	12.50	2.50
☐ 552	Birdie Tebbetts	25.00	12.50	2.50
	MG SP			
☐ 553	Rookie Stars	12.00	6.00	1.20
	Pat Garrett			
	Jackie Warner			
☐ 554	Jim Northrup SP	30.00	15.00	3.00
☐ 555	Ron Perranoski SP	30.00	15.00	3.00
☐ 556	Mel Queen SP	25.00	12.50	2.50
☐ 557	Felix Mantilla SP	25.00	12.50	2.50
☐ 558	Red Sox Rookies	18.00	9.00	1.80
	Guido Grilli			
	Pete Magrini			
	George Scott			
☐ 559	Roberto Pena SP	25.00	12.50	2.50
☐ 560	Joel Horlen	12.00	6.00	1.20
☐ 561	ChooChoo Coleman			
	SP	30.00	15.00	3.00
☐ 562	Russ Snyder	12.00	6.00	1.20
☐ 563	Twins Rookies	12.00	6.00	1.20
	Pete Cimino			
	Cesar Tovar			
☐ 564	Bob Chance SP	25.00	12.50	2.50
☐ 565	Jim Piersall SP	30.00	15.00	3.00
☐ 566	Mike Cuellar SP	30.00	15.00	3.00
☐ 567	Dick Howser SP	30.00	15.00	3.00
☐ 568	Athletics Rookies	12.00	6.00	1.20
	Paul Lindblad			
	Rod Stone			
☐ 569	Orlando McFarlane			
	SP	25.00	12.50	2.50
☐ 570	Art Mahaffey SP	25.00	12.50	2.50
☐ 571	Dave Roberts SP	25.00	12.50	2.50
☐ 572	Bob Priddy	12.00	6.00	1.20
☐ 573	Derrell Griffith	12.00	6.00	1.20
☐ 574	Mets Rookies	12.00	6.00	1.20
	Bill Hepler			
	Bill Murphy			

		NRMT	VG-E	GOOD
☐ 575	Earl Wilson	12.00	6.00	1.20
☐ 576	Dave Nicholson SP	25.00	12.50	2.50
☐ 577	Jack Lamabe SP	25.00	12.50	2.50
☐ 578	Chi Chi Olivo SP	25.00	12.50	2.50
☐ 579	Orioles Rookies ..... Frank Bertaina Gene Brabender Dave Johnson	18.00	9.00	1.80
☐ 580	Billy Williams SP	75.00	35.00	6.00
☐ 581	Tony Martinez	12.00	6.00	1.20
☐ 582	Garry Roggenburk ...	12.00	6.00	1.20
☐ 583	Tigers Team SP	90.00	42.50	8.50
☐ 584	Yankees Rookies .... Frank Fernandez Fritz Peterson	12.00	6.00	1.20
☐ 585	Tony Taylor	12.00	6.00	1.20
☐ 586	Claude Raymond SP	25.00	12.50	2.50
☐ 587	Dick Bertell	12.00	6.00	1.20
☐ 588	Athletics Rookies ... Chuck Dobson Ken Suarez	12.00	6.00	1.20
☐ 589	Lou Klimchock SP ..	25.00	12.50	2.50
☐ 590	Bill Skowron SP	35.00	17.50	3.50
☐ 591	NL Rookies SP ..... Bart Shirley Grant Jackson	30.00	15.00	3.00
☐ 592	Andre Rodgers	12.00	6.00	1.20
☐ 593	Doug Camilli SP	25.00	12.50	2.50
☐ 594	Chico Salmon	12.00	6.00	1.20
☐ 595	Larry Jackson	12.00	6.00	1.20
☐ 596	Astros Rookies SP .. Nate Colbert Greg Sims	25.00	12.50	2.50
☐ 597	John Sullivan	12.00	6.00	1.20
☐ 598	Gaylord Perry SP ...	200.00	50.00	10.00

1967 Topps

The cards in this 609-card set measure 2 ½"
by 3 ½". The 1967 Topps series is considered
by some collectors to be one of the company's
finest accomplishments in baseball card production. Excellent color photographs are combined with easy-to-read backs. Cards 458 to
533 are slightly harder to find than numbers 1
to 457, and the inevitable (difficult to find) high
series (534 to 609) exists. Each checklist card
features a small circular picture of a popular
player included in that series. Printing discrep-
ancies resulted in some high series cards
being in shorter supply. The checklist below
identifies (by DP) 22 double-printed high
numbers; of the 76 cards in the last series, 54
cards were short printed and the other 22 are
much more plentiful. Featured subsets
within this set include World Series cards (151-
155) and League Leaders (233-244). Although
there are several relatively expensive cards in
this popular set, the key cards in the set are
undoubtedly the Tom Seaver rookie card (581)
and the Rod Carew rookie card (569). Although
rarely seen, there exists a salesman's sample
panel of three cards, which pictures Earl
Battey, Manny Mota, and Gene Brabender with
ad information on the back about the "new"
Topps cards.

	NRMT	VG-E	GOOD
COMPLETE SET (609)	4000.00	2000.00	500.00
COMMON PLAYER (1-109)	.75	.35	.07

			NRMT	VG-E	GOOD				NRMT	VG-E	GOOD
	COMMON PLAYER (110-370) ..		.85	.40	.08		Sal Bando				
	COMMON PLAYER (371-457) ..		1.50	.75	.15		Randy Schwartz				
	COMMON PLAYER (458-533) ..		4.00	2.00	.40	☐ 34	Pete Cimino		.75	.35	.07
	COMMON PLAYER (534-609) ..		15.00	7.50	1.50	☐ 35	Rico Carty		1.00	.50	.10
	COMMON DP (534-609)		6.00	3.00	.60	☐ 36	Bob Tillman		.75	.35	.07
						☐ 37	Rick Wise		1.00	.50	.10
☐ 1	The Champs		10.00	1.25	.25	☐ 38	Bob Johnson		.75	.35	.07
	Frank Robinson					☐ 39	Curt Simmons		1.00	.50	.10
	Hank Bauer					☐ 40	Rick Reichardt		.75	.35	.07
	Brooks Robinson					☐ 41	Joe Hoerner		.75	.35	.07
☐ 2	Jack Hamilton		.75	.35	.07	☐ 42	Mets Team		2.00	1.00	.20
☐ 3	Duke Sims		.75	.35	.07	☐ 43	Chico Salmon		.75	.35	.07
☐ 4	Hal Lanier		1.00	.50	.10	☐ 44	Joe Nuxhall		1.00	.50	.10
☐ 5	Whitey Ford UER ...		13.00	6.00	1.20	☐ 45	Roger Maris		30.00	15.00	3.00
	(1953 listed as 1933					☐ 46	Lindy McDaniel		1.00	.50	.10
	in stats on back)					☐ 47	Ken McMullen		.75	.35	.07
☐ 6	Dick Simpson		.75	.35	.07	☐ 48	Bill Freehan		1.50	.75	.15
☐ 7	Don McMahon		.75	.35	.07	☐ 49	Roy Face		1.25	.60	.12
☐ 8	Chuck Harrison		.75	.35	.07	☐ 50	Tony Oliva		3.50	1.50	.30
☐ 9	Ron Hansen		.75	.35	.07	☐ 51	Astros Rookies		.75	.35	.07
☐ 10	Matty Alou		1.00	.50	.10		Dave Adlesh				
☐ 11	Barry Moore		.75	.35	.07		Wes Bales				
☐ 12	Dodgers Rookies ...		1.00	.50	.10	☐ 52	Dennis Higgins		.75	.35	.07
	Jim Campanis					☐ 53	Clay Dalrymple		.75	.35	.07
	Bill Singer					☐ 54	Dick Green		.75	.35	.07
☐ 13	Joe Sparma		.75	.35	.07	☐ 55	Don Drysdale		9.00	4.50	.90
☐ 14	Phil Linz		1.00	.50	.10	☐ 56	Jose Tartabull		.75	.35	.07
☐ 15	Earl Battey		.75	.35	.07	☐ 57	Pat Jarvis		.75	.35	.07
☐ 16	Bill Hands		.75	.35	.07	☐ 58	Paul Schaal		.75	.35	.07
☐ 17	Jim Gosger		.75	.35	.07	☐ 59	Ralph Terry		1.00	.50	.10
☐ 18	Gene Oliver		.75	.35	.07	☐ 60	Luis Aparicio		6.00	3.00	.60
☐ 19	Jim McGlothlin		.75	.35	.07	☐ 61	Gordy Coleman		.75	.35	.07
☐ 20	Orlando Cepeda		5.00	2.50	.50	☐ 62	Checklist 1		3.00	.40	.10
☐ 21	Dave Bristol MG ...		.75	.35	.07		Frank Robinson				
☐ 22	Gene Brabender ...		.75	.35	.07	☐ 63	Cards' Clubbers ...		5.00	2.50	.50
☐ 23	Larry Elliot		.75	.35	.07		Lou Brock				
☐ 24	Bob Allen		.75	.35	.07		Curt Flood				
☐ 25	Elston Howard		2.50	1.25	.25	☐ 64	Fred Valentine		.75	.35	.07
☐ 26A	Bob Priddy		.75	.35	.07	☐ 65	Tom Haller		.75	.35	.07
	(with traded line)					☐ 66	Manny Mota		1.00	.50	.10
☐ 26B	Bob Priddy		25.00	12.50	2.50	☐ 67	Ken Berry		.75	.35	.07
	(no traded line)					☐ 68	Bob Buhl		.75	.35	.07
☐ 27	Bob Saverine		.75	.35	.07	☐ 69	Vic Davalillo		.75	.35	.07
☐ 28	Barry Latman		.75	.35	.07	☐ 70	Ron Santo		1.50	.75	.15
☐ 29	Tom McCraw		.75	.35	.07	☐ 71	Camilo Pascual		1.00	.50	.10
☐ 30	Al Kaline		14.00	6.00	1.20	☐ 72	Tigers Rookies		.75	.35	.07
☐ 31	Jim Brewer		.75	.35	.07		George Korince				
☐ 32	Bob Bailey		.75	.35	.07		(Photo actually				
☐ 33	Athletic Rookies		2.00	1.00	.20		James Murray Brown)				

			NRMT	VG-E	GOOD
		John (Tom) Matchick			
☐ 73	Rusty Staub		1.50	.75	.15
☐ 74	Wes Stock		.75	.35	.07
☐ 75	George Scott		1.25	.60	.12
☐ 76	Jim Barbieri		.75	.35	.07
☐ 77	Dooley Womack		.75	.35	.07
☐ 78	Pat Corrales		1.00	.50	.10
☐ 79	Bubba Morton		.75	.35	.07
☐ 80	Jim Maloney		1.00	.50	.10
☐ 81	Eddie Stanky MG		1.00	.50	.10
☐ 82	Steve Barber		.75	.35	.07
☐ 83	Ollie Brown		.75	.35	.07
☐ 84	Tommie Sisk		.75	.35	.07
☐ 85	Johnny Callison		1.00	.50	.10
☐ 86A	Mike McCormick		1.00	.50	.10
	(with traded line)				
☐ 86B	Mike McCormick		25.00	12.50	2.50
	(no traded line)				
☐ 87	George Altman		.75	.35	.07
☐ 88	Mickey Lolich		2.00	1.00	.20
☐ 89	Felix Millan		.75	.35	.07
☐ 90	Jim Nash		.75	.35	.07
☐ 91	Johnny Lewis		.75	.35	.07
☐ 92	Ray Washburn		.75	.35	.07
☐ 93	Yankees Rookies		2.50	1.25	.25
	Stan Bahnsen				
	Bobby Murcer				
☐ 94	Ron Fairly		1.00	.50	.10
☐ 95	Sonny Siebert		.75	.35	.07
☐ 96	Art Shamsky		.75	.35	.07
☐ 97	Mike Cuellar		1.00	.50	.10
☐ 98	Rich Rollins		1.00	.50	.10
☐ 99	Lee Stange		.75	.35	.07
☐ 100	Frank Robinson		13.00	6.00	1.20
☐ 101	Ken Johnson		.75	.35	.07
☐ 102	Philadelphia Phillies		1.75	.85	.17
	Team Card				
☐ 103	Checklist 2		6.00	1.00	.20
	Mickey Mantle				
☐ 104	Minnie Rojas		.75	.35	.07
☐ 105	Ken Boyer		1.50	.75	.15
☐ 106	Randy Hundley		.75	.35	.07
☐ 107	Joel Horlen		.75	.35	.07
☐ 108	Alex Johnson		.75	.35	.07
☐ 109	Tribe Thumpers		1.00	.50	.10
	Rocky Colavito				
	Leon Wagner				
☐ 110	Jack Aker		.85	.40	.08
☐ 111	John Kennedy		.85	.40	.08

			NRMT	VG-E	GOOD
☐ 112	Dave Wickersham		.85	.40	.08
☐ 113	Dave Nicholson		.85	.40	.08
☐ 114	Jack Baldschun		.85	.40	.08
☐ 115	Paul Casanova		.85	.40	.08
☐ 116	Herman Franks MG		.85	.40	.08
☐ 117	Darrell Brandon		.85	.40	.08
☐ 118	Bernie Allen		.85	.40	.08
☐ 119	Wade Blasingame		.85	.40	.08
☐ 120	Floyd Robinson		.85	.40	.08
☐ 121	Eddie Bressoud		.85	.40	.08
☐ 122	George Brunet		.85	.40	.08
☐ 123	Pirates Rookies		.85	.40	.08
	Jim Price				
	Luke Walker				
☐ 124	Jim Stewart		.85	.40	.08
☐ 125	Moe Drabowsky		.85	.40	.08
☐ 126	Tony Taylor		.85	.40	.08
☐ 127	John O'Donoghue		.85	.40	.08
☐ 128	Ed Spiezio		.85	.40	.08
☐ 129	Phil Roof		.85	.40	.08
☐ 130	Phil Regan		1.25	.60	.12
☐ 131	Yankees Team		3.00	1.50	.30
☐ 132	Ozzie Virgil		.85	.40	.08
☐ 133	Ron Kline		.85	.40	.08
☐ 134	Gates Brown		1.25	.60	.12
☐ 135	Deron Johnson		1.25	.60	.12
☐ 136	Carroll Sembera		.85	.40	.08
☐ 137	Twins Rookies		.85	.40	.08
	Ron Clark				
	Jim Ollum				
☐ 138	Dick Kelley		.85	.40	.08
☐ 139	Dalton Jones		.85	.40	.08
☐ 140	Willie Stargell		14.00	7.00	1.40
☐ 141	John Miller		.85	.40	.08
☐ 142	Jackie Brandt		.85	.40	.08
☐ 143	Sox Sockers		.85	.40	.08
	Pete Ward				
	Don Buford				
☐ 144	Bill Hepler		.85	.40	.08
☐ 145	Larry Brown		.85	.40	.08
☐ 146	Steve Carlton		60.00	30.00	6.00
☐ 147	Tom Egan		.85	.40	.08
☐ 148	Adolfo Phillips		.85	.40	.08
☐ 149	Joe Moeller		.85	.40	.08
☐ 150	Mickey Mantle		200.00	100.00	20.00
☐ 151	World Series Game 1		2.00	1.00	.20
	Moe mows down 11				
☐ 152	World Series Game 2		4.00	2.00	.40
	Palmer blanks Dodgers				

		NRMT	VG-E	GOOD
☐ 153	World Series Game 3 Blair's homer defeats L.A.	2.00	1.00	.20
☐ 154	World Series Game 4 Orioles 4 straight	2.00	1.00	.20
☐ 155	World Series Summary Winners celebrate	2.00	1.00	.20
☐ 156	Ron Herbel	.85	.40	.08
☐ 157	Danny Cater	.85	.40	.08
☐ 158	Jimmie Coker	.85	.40	.08
☐ 159	Bruce Howard	.85	.40	.08
☐ 160	Willie Davis	1.25	.60	.12
☐ 161	Dick Williams MG	1.25	.60	.12
☐ 162	Billy O'Dell	.85	.40	.08
☐ 163	Vic Roznovsky	.85	.40	.08
☐ 164	Dwight Siebler	.85	.40	.08
☐ 165	Cleon Jones	.85	.40	.08
☐ 166	Eddie Mathews	9.00	4.50	.90
☐ 167	Senators Rookies Joe Coleman Tim Cullen	.85	.40	.08
☐ 168	Ray Culp	.85	.40	.08
☐ 169	Horace Clarke	.85	.40	.08
☐ 170	Dick McAuliffe	.85	.40	.08
☐ 171	Cal Koonce	.85	.40	.08
☐ 172	Bill Heath	.85	.40	.08
☐ 173	St. Louis Cardinals Team Card	1.75	.85	.17
☐ 174	Dick Radatz	1.25	.60	.12
☐ 175	Bobby Knoop	.85	.40	.08
☐ 176	Sammy Ellis	.85	.40	.08
☐ 177	Tito Fuentes	.85	.40	.08
☐ 178	John Buzhardt	.85	.40	.08
☐ 179	Braves Rookies Charles Vaughan Cecil Upshaw	.85	.40	.08
☐ 180	Curt Blefary	.85	.40	.08
☐ 181	Terry Fox	.85	.40	.08
☐ 182	Ed Charles	.85	.40	.08
☐ 183	Jim Pagliaroni	.85	.40	.08
☐ 184	George Thomas	.85	.40	.08
☐ 185	Ken Holtzman	1.50	.75	.15
☐ 186	Mets Maulers Ed Kranepool Ron Swoboda	1.25	.60	.12
☐ 187	Pedro Ramos	.85	.40	.08
☐ 188	Ken Harrelson	1.50	.75	.15
☐ 189	Chuck Hinton	.85	.40	.08
☐ 190	Turk Farrell	.85	.40	.08

		NRMT	VG-E	GOOD
☐ 191A	Checklist 3 (214 Tom Kelley) (Willie Mays)	4.00	.40	.10
☐ 191B	Checklist 3 (214 Dick Kelley) (Willie Mays)	8.00	.80	.15
☐ 192	Fred Gladding	.85	.40	.08
☐ 193	Jose Cardenal	.85	.40	.08
☐ 194	Bob Allison	1.25	.60	.12
☐ 195	Al Jackson	.85	.40	.08
☐ 196	Johnny Romano	.85	.40	.08
☐ 197	Ron Perranoski	1.25	.60	.12
☐ 198	Chuck Hiller	.85	.40	.08
☐ 199	Billy Hitchcock MG	.85	.40	.08
☐ 200	Willie Mays	60.00	27.50	5.50
☐ 201	Hal Reniff	.85	.40	.08
☐ 202	Johnny Edwards	.85	.40	.08
☐ 203	Al McBean	.85	.40	.08
☐ 204	Orioles Rookies Mike Epstein Tom Phoebus	1.25	.60	.12
☐ 205	Dick Groat	1.50	.75	.15
☐ 206	Dennis Bennett	.85	.40	.08
☐ 207	John Orsino	.85	.40	.08
☐ 208	Jack Lamabe	.85	.40	.08
☐ 209	Joe Nossek	.85	.40	.08
☐ 210	Bob Gibson	14.00	6.50	1.30
☐ 211	Twins Team	1.75	.85	.17
☐ 212	Chris Zachary	.85	.40	.08
☐ 213	Jay Johnstone	1.50	.75	.15
☐ 214	Dick Kelley	.85	.40	.08
☐ 215	Ernie Banks	14.00	6.50	1.30
☐ 216	Bengal Belters Norm Cash Al Kaline	4.00	2.00	.40
☐ 217	Rob Gardner	.85	.40	.08
☐ 218	Wes Parker	1.25	.60	.12
☐ 219	Clay Carroll	.85	.40	.08
☐ 220	Jim Ray Hart	1.25	.60	.12
☐ 221	Woodie Fryman	.85	.40	.08
☐ 222	Reds Rookies Darrell Osteen Lee May	1.50	.75	.15
☐ 223	Mike Ryan	.85	.40	.08
☐ 224	Walt Bond	.85	.40	.08
☐ 225	Mel Stottlemyre	1.75	.85	.17
☐ 226	Julian Javier	.85	.40	.08
☐ 227	Paul Lindblad	.85	.40	.08
☐ 228	Gil Hodges MG	4.00	2.00	.40

		NRMT	VG-E	GOOD
☐ 229	Larry Jackson	.85	.40	.08
☐ 230	Boog Powell	2.00	1.00	.20
☐ 231	John Bateman	.85	.40	.08
☐ 232	Don Buford	.85	.40	.08
☐ 233	AL ERA Leaders	1.50	.75	.15
	Gary Peters			
	Joel Horlen			
	Steve Hargan			
☐ 234	NL ERA Leaders	4.50	2.25	.45
	Sandy Koufax			
	Mike Cuellar			
	Juan Marichal			
☐ 235	AL Pitching Leaders	1.50	.75	.15
	Jim Kaat			
	Denny McLain			
	Earl Wilson			
☐ 236	NL Pitching Leaders	9.00	4.50	.90
	Sandy Koufax			
	Juan Marichal			
	Bob Gibson			
	Gaylord Perry			
☐ 237	AL Strikeout Leaders	1.50	.75	.15
	Sam McDowell			
	Jim Kaat			
	Earl Wilson			
☐ 238	NL Strikeout Leaders	3.00	1.50	.30
	Sandy Koufax			
	Jim Bunning			
	Bob Veale			
☐ 239	AL Batting Leaders	4.00	2.00	.40
	Frank Robinson			
	Tony Oliva			
	Al Kaline			
☐ 240	NL Batting Leaders	1.50	.75	.15
	Matty Alou			
	Felipe Alou			
	Rico Carty			
☐ 241	AL RBI Leaders	3.00	1.50	.30
	Frank Robinson			
	Harmon Killebrew			
	Boog Powell			
☐ 242	NL RBI Leaders	5.00	2.50	.50
	Hank Aaron			
	Bob Clemente			
	Richie Allen			
☐ 243	AL Home Run Leaders	3.00	1.50	.30
	Frank Robinson			
	Harmon Killebrew			

		NRMT	VG-E	GOOD
	Boog Powell			
☐ 244	NL Home Run Leaders	5.00	2.50	.50
	Hank Aaron			
	Richie Allen			
	Willie Mays			
☐ 245	Curt Flood	1.25	.60	.12
☐ 246	Jim Perry	1.25	.60	.12
☐ 247	Jerry Lumpe	.85	.40	.08
☐ 248	Gene Mauch MG	1.25	.60	.12
☐ 249	Nick Willhite	.85	.40	.08
☐ 250	Hank Aaron	60.00	30.00	6.00
☐ 251	Woody Held	.85	.40	.08
☐ 252	Bob Bolin	.85	.40	.08
☐ 253	Indians Rookies	.85	.40	.08
	Bill Davis			
	Gus Gil			
☐ 254	Milt Pappas	1.25	.60	.12
☐ 255	Frank Howard	1.50	.75	.15
☐ 256	Bob Hendley	.85	.40	.08
☐ 257	Charlie Smith	.85	.40	.08
☐ 258	Lee Maye	.85	.40	.08
☐ 259	Don Dennis	.85	.40	.08
☐ 260	Jim Lefebvre	1.50	.75	.15
☐ 261	John Wyatt	.85	.40	.08
☐ 262	Athletics Team	1.75	.85	.17
☐ 263	Hank Aguirre	.85	.40	.08
☐ 264	Ron Swoboda	1.25	.60	.12
☐ 265	Lou Burdette	1.75	.85	.17
☐ 266	Pitt Power	3.50	1.75	.35
	Willie Stargell			
	Donn Clendenon			
☐ 267	Don Schwall	.85	.40	.08
☐ 268	Johnny Briggs	.85	.40	.08
☐ 269	Don Nottebart	.85	.40	.08
☐ 270	Zoilo Versalles	.85	.40	.08
☐ 271	Eddie Watt	.85	.40	.08
☐ 272	Cubs Rookies	.85	.40	.08
	Bill Connors			
	Dave Dowling			
☐ 273	Dick Lines	.85	.40	.08
☐ 274	Bob Aspromonte	.85	.40	.08
☐ 275	Fred Whitfield	.85	.40	.08
☐ 276	Bruce Brubaker	.85	.40	.08
☐ 277	Steve Whitaker	.85	.40	.08
☐ 278	Checklist 4	3.00	.40	.10
	Jim Kaat			
☐ 279	Frank Linzy	.85	.40	.08
☐ 280	Tony Conigliaro	2.50	1.25	.25

		NRMT	VG-E	GOOD
☐ 281	Bob Rodgers	1.25	.60	.12
☐ 282	John Odom	.85	.40	.08
☐ 283	Gene Alley	1.25	.60	.12
☐ 284	Johnny Podres	1.75	.85	.17
☐ 285	Lou Brock	13.00	6.50	1.30
☐ 286	Wayne Causey	.85	.40	.08
☐ 287	Mets Rookies	.85	.40	.08
	Greg Goossen			
	Bart Shirley			
☐ 288	Denny Lemaster	.85	.40	.08
☐ 289	Tom Tresh	1.50	.75	.15
☐ 290	Bill White	1.50	.75	.15
☐ 291	Jim Hannan	.85	.40	.08
☐ 292	Don Pavletich	.85	.40	.08
☐ 293	Ed Kirkpatrick	.85	.40	.08
☐ 294	Walt Alston MG	2.50	1.25	.25
☐ 295	Sam McDowell	1.25	.60	.12
☐ 296	Glenn Beckert	1.25	.60	.12
☐ 297	Dave Morehead	.85	.40	.08
☐ 298	Ron Davis	.85	.40	.08
☐ 299	Norm Siebern	.85	.40	.08
☐ 300	Jim Kaat	3.50	1.75	.35
☐ 301	Jesse Gonder	.85	.40	.08
☐ 302	Orioles Team	1.75	.85	.17
☐ 303	Gil Blanco	.85	.40	.08
☐ 304	Phil Gagliano	.85	.40	.08
☐ 305	Earl Wilson	.85	.40	.08
☐ 306	Bud Harrelson	1.25	.60	.12
☐ 307	Jim Beauchamp	.85	.40	.08
☐ 308	Al Downing	1.25	.60	.12
☐ 309	Hurlers Beware	1.25	.60	.12
	Johnny Callison			
	Richie Allen			
☐ 310	Gary Peters	.85	.40	.08
☐ 311	Ed Brinkman	.85	.40	.08
☐ 312	Don Mincher	.85	.40	.08
☐ 313	Bob Lee	.85	.40	.08
☐ 314	Red Sox Rookies	3.00	1.50	.30
	Mike Andrews			
	Reggie Smith			
☐ 315	Billy Williams	7.50	3.75	.75
☐ 316	Jack Kralick	.85	.40	.08
☐ 317	Cesar Tovar	.85	.40	.08
☐ 318	Dave Giusti	.85	.40	.08
☐ 319	Paul Blair	.85	.40	.08
☐ 320	Gaylord Perry	7.00	3.50	.70
☐ 321	Mayo Smith MG	.85	.40	.08
☐ 322	Jose Pagan	.85	.40	.08
☐ 323	Mike Hershberger	.85	.40	.08

		NRMT	VG-E	GOOD
☐ 324	Hal Woodeshick	.85	.40	.08
☐ 325	Chico Cardenas	.85	.40	.08
☐ 326	Bob Uecker	15.00	7.50	1.50
☐ 327	California Angels	1.75	.85	.17
	Team Card			
☐ 328	Clete Boyer	1.25	.60	.12
☐ 329	Charlie Lau	1.25	.60	.12
☐ 330	Claude Osteen	1.25	.60	.12
☐ 331	Joe Foy	.85	.40	.08
☐ 332	Jesus Alou	.85	.40	.08
☐ 333	Fergie Jenkins	6.50	3.25	.65
☐ 334	Twin Terrors	3.50	1.75	.35
	Bob Allison			
	Harmon Killebrew			
☐ 335	Bob Veale	.85	.40	.08
☐ 336	Joe Azcue	.85	.40	.08
☐ 337	Joe Morgan	14.00	7.00	1.40
☐ 338	Bob Locker	.85	.40	.08
☐ 339	Chico Ruiz	.85	.40	.08
☐ 340	Joe Pepitone	1.50	.75	.15
☐ 341	Giants Rookies	.85	.40	.08
	Dick Dietz			
	Bill Sorrell			
☐ 342	Hank Fischer	.85	.40	.08
☐ 343	Tom Satriano	.85	.40	.08
☐ 344	Ossie Chavarria	.85	.40	.08
☐ 345	Stu Miller	.85	.40	.08
☐ 346	Jim Hickman	.85	.40	.08
☐ 347	Grady Hatton MG	.85	.40	.08
☐ 348	Tug McGraw	1.50	.75	.15
☐ 349	Bob Chance	.85	.40	.08
☐ 350	Joe Torre	1.50	.75	.15
☐ 351	Vern Law	1.25	.60	.12
☐ 352	Ray Oyler	.85	.40	.08
☐ 353	Bill McCool	.85	.40	.08
☐ 354	Cubs Team	1.75	.85	.17
☐ 355	Carl Yastrzemski	90.00	45.00	9.00
☐ 356	Larry Jaster	.85	.40	.08
☐ 357	Bill Skowron	1.50	.75	.15
☐ 358	Ruben Amaro	.85	.40	.08
☐ 359	Dick Ellsworth	1.25	.60	.12
☐ 360	Leon Wagner	.85	.40	.08
☐ 361	Checklist 5	4.00	.40	.10
	Roberto Clemente			
☐ 362	Darold Knowles	.85	.40	.08
☐ 363	Dave Johnson	2.00	1.00	.20
☐ 364	Claude Raymond	.85	.40	.08
☐ 365	John Roseboro	1.25	.60	.12
☐ 366	Andy Kosco	.85	.40	.08

		NRMT	VG-E	GOOD
☐ 367	Angels Rookies	.85	.40	.08
	Bill Kelso			
	Don Wallace			
☐ 368	Jack Hiatt	.85	.40	.08
☐ 369	Jim Hunter	12.00	6.00	1.20
☐ 370	Tommy Davis	1.25	.60	.12
☐ 371	Jim Lonborg	2.50	1.25	.25
☐ 372	Mike De La Hoz	1.50	.75	.15
☐ 373	White Sox Rookies ..	1.50	.75	.15
	Duane Josephson			
	Fred Klages			
☐ 374	Mel Queen	1.50	.75	.15
☐ 375	Jake Gibbs	1.50	.75	.15
☐ 376	Don Lock	1.50	.75	.15
☐ 377	Luis Tiant	2.50	1.25	.25
☐ 378	Detroit Tigers	3.50	1.75	.35
	Team Card			
☐ 379	Jerry May	1.50	.75	.15
☐ 380	Dean Chance	2.00	1.00	.20
☐ 381	Dick Schofield	1.50	.75	.15
☐ 382	Dave McNally	2.00	1.00	.20
☐ 383	Ken Henderson	1.50	.75	.15
☐ 384	Cardinals Rookies ..	1.50	.75	.15
	Jim Cosman			
	Dick Hughes			
☐ 385	Jim Fregosi	2.00	1.00	.20
	(batting wrong)			
☐ 386	Dick Selma	1.50	.75	.15
☐ 387	Cap Peterson	1.50	.75	.15
☐ 388	Arnold Earley	1.50	.75	.15
☐ 389	Alvin Dark MG	2.00	1.00	.20
☐ 390	Jim Wynn	2.00	1.00	.20
☐ 391	Wilbur Wood	2.00	1.00	.20
☐ 392	Tommy Harper	2.00	1.00	.20
☐ 393	Jim Bouton	2.50	1.25	.25
☐ 394	Jake Wood	1.50	.75	.15
☐ 395	Chris Short	1.50	.75	.15
☐ 396	Atlanta Aces	1.50	.75	.15
	Denis Menke			
	Tony Cloninger			
☐ 397	Willie Smith	1.50	.75	.15
☐ 398	Jeff Torborg	2.00	1.00	.20
☐ 399	Al Worthington	1.50	.75	.15
☐ 400	Bob Clemente	55.00	27.50	5.50
☐ 401	Jim Coates	1.50	.75	.15
☐ 402	Phillies Rookies	1.50	.75	.15
	Grant Jackson			
	Billy Wilson			
☐ 403	Dick Nen	1.50	.75	.15
☐ 404	Nelson Briles	1.50	.75	.15
☐ 405	Russ Snyder	1.50	.75	.15
☐ 406	Lee Elia	2.00	1.00	.20
☐ 407	Reds Team	3.00	1.50	.30
☐ 408	Jim Northrup	2.00	1.00	.20
☐ 409	Ray Sadecki	1.50	.75	.15
☐ 410	Lou Johnson	1.50	.75	.15
☐ 411	Dick Howser	2.50	1.25	.25
☐ 412	Astros Rookies	2.50	1.25	.25
	Norm Miller			
	Doug Rader			
☐ 413	Jerry Grote	1.50	.75	.15
☐ 414	Casey Cox	1.50	.75	.15
☐ 415	Sonny Jackson	1.50	.75	.15
☐ 416	Roger Repoz	1.50	.75	.15
☐ 417A	Bob Bruce ERR	25.00	10.00	2.00
	(RBAVES on back)			
☐ 417B	Bob Bruce COR	2.00	1.00	.20
☐ 418	Sam Mele MG	1.50	.75	.15
☐ 419	Don Kessinger	2.00	1.00	.20
☐ 420	Denny McLain	3.50	1.75	.35
☐ 421	Dal Maxvill	1.50	.75	.15
☐ 422	Hoyt Wilhelm	7.50	3.75	.75
☐ 423	Fence Busters	12.50	6.25	1.25
	Willie Mays			
	Willie McCovey			
☐ 424	Pedro Gonzalez	1.50	.75	.15
☐ 425	Pete Mikkelsen	1.50	.75	.15
☐ 426	Lou Clinton	1.50	.75	.15
☐ 427	Ruben Gomez	1.50	.75	.15
☐ 428	Dodgers Rookies ...	2.00	1.00	.20
	Tom Hutton			
	Gene Michael			
☐ 429	Garry Roggenburk ..	1.50	.75	.15
☐ 430	Pete Rose	75.00	37.50	7.50
☐ 431	Ted Uhlaender	1.50	.75	.15
☐ 432	Jimmie Hall	1.50	.75	.15
☐ 433	Al Luplow	1.50	.75	.15
☐ 434	Eddie Fisher	1.50	.75	.15
☐ 435	Mack Jones	1.50	.75	.15
☐ 436	Pete Ward	1.50	.75	.15
☐ 437	Senators Team	3.00	1.50	.30
☐ 438	Chuck Dobson	1.50	.75	.15
☐ 439	Byron Browne	1.50	.75	.15
☐ 440	Steve Hargan	1.50	.75	.15
☐ 441	Jim Davenport	2.00	1.00	.20
☐ 442	Yankees Rookies ...	2.00	1.00	.20
	Bill Robinson			
	Joe Verbanic			

	NRMT	VG-E	GOOD		NRMT	VG-E	GOOD
☐ 443 Tito Francona	1.50	.75	.15	☐ 481 Leo Durocher MG	6.00	3.00	.60
☐ 444 George Smith	1.50	.75	.15	☐ 482 Bill Monbouquette	4.00	2.00	.40
☐ 445 Don Sutton	18.00	9.00	1.80	☐ 483 Jim Landis	4.00	2.00	.40
☐ 446 Russ Nixon	2.00	1.00	.20	☐ 484 Jerry Adair	4.00	2.00	.40
☐ 447 Bo Belinsky	2.00	1.00	.20	☐ 485 Tim McCarver	8.00	4.00	.80
☐ 448 Harry Walker MG	1.50	.75	.15	☐ 486 Twins Rookies	4.00	2.00	.40
☐ 449 Orlando Pena	1.50	.75	.15	Rich Reese			
☐ 450 Richie Allen	3.00	1.50	.30	Bill Whitby			
☐ 451 Fred Newman	1.50	.75	.15	☐ 487 Tommie Reynolds	4.00	2.00	.40
☐ 452 Ed Kranepool	2.00	1.00	.20	☐ 488 Gerry Arrigo	4.00	2.00	.40
☐ 453 Aurelio Monteagudo	1.50	.75	.15	☐ 489 Doug Clemens	4.00	2.00	.40
☐ 454A Checklist 6	4.00	.40	.10	☐ 490 Tony Cloninger	4.00	2.00	.40
Juan Marichal (missing left ear)				☐ 491 Sam Bowens	4.00	2.00	.40
☐ 454B Checklist 6	8.00	.75	.15	☐ 492 Pittsburgh Pirates Team Card	8.00	4.00	.80
Juan Marichal (left ear showing)				☐ 493 Phil Ortega	4.00	2.00	.40
☐ 455 Tommy Agee	2.00	1.00	.20	☐ 494 Bill Rigney MG	4.00	2.00	.40
☐ 456 Phil Niekro	9.00	4.50	.90	☐ 495 Fritz Peterson	4.00	2.00	.40
☐ 457 Andy Etchebarren	1.50	.75	.15	☐ 496 Orlando McFarlane	4.00	2.00	.40
☐ 458 Lee Thomas	5.00	2.50	.50	☐ 497 Ron Campbell	4.00	2.00	.40
☐ 459 Senators Rookies	4.00	2.00	.40	☐ 498 Larry Dierker	4.00	2.00	.40
Dick Bosman				☐ 499 Indians Rookies	4.00	2.00	.40
Pete Craig				George Culver			
☐ 460 Harmon Killebrew	35.00	15.00	3.00	Jose Vidal			
☐ 461 Bob Miller	4.00	2.00	.40	☐ 500 Juan Marichal	14.00	7.00	1.40
☐ 462 Bob Barton	4.00	2.00	.40	☐ 501 Jerry Zimmerman	4.00	2.00	.40
☐ 463 Hill Aces	5.00	2.50	.50	☐ 502 Derrell Griffith	4.00	2.00	.40
Sam McDowell				☐ 503 Los Angeles Dodgers Team Card	8.00	4.00	.80
Sonny Siebert				☐ 504 Orlando Martinez	4.00	2.00	.40
☐ 464 Dan Coombs	4.00	2.00	.40	☐ 505 Tommy Helms	5.00	2.50	.50
☐ 465 Willie Horton	5.00	2.50	.50	☐ 506 Smoky Burgess	5.00	2.50	.50
☐ 466 Bobby Wine	4.00	2.00	.40	☐ 507 Orioles Rookies	4.00	2.00	.40
☐ 467 Jim O'Toole	4.00	2.00	.40	Ed Barnowski			
☐ 468 Ralph Houk MG	5.00	2.50	.50	Larry Haney			
☐ 469 Len Gabrielson	4.00	2.00	.40	☐ 508 Dick Hall	4.00	2.00	.40
☐ 470 Bob Shaw	4.00	2.00	.40	☐ 509 Jim King	4.00	2.00	.40
☐ 471 Rene Lachemann	5.00	2.50	.50	☐ 510 Bill Mazeroski	6.00	3.00	.60
☐ 472 Rookies Pirates	4.00	2.00	.40	☐ 511 Don Wert	4.00	2.00	.40
John Gelnar				☐ 512 Red Schoendienst MG	8.00	4.00	.80
George Spriggs				☐ 513 Marcelino Lopez	4.00	2.00	.40
☐ 473 Jose Santiago	4.00	2.00	.40	☐ 514 John Werhas	4.00	2.00	.40
☐ 474 Bob Tolan	5.00	2.50	.50	☐ 515 Bert Campaneris	5.00	2.50	.50
☐ 475 Jim Palmer	65.00	30.00	6.00	☐ 516 Giants Team	8.00	4.00	.80
☐ 476 Tony Perez SP	50.00	25.00	5.00	☐ 517 Fred Talbot	4.00	2.00	.40
☐ 477 Braves Team	8.00	4.00	.80	☐ 518 Denis Menke	4.00	2.00	.40
☐ 478 Bob Humphreys	4.00	2.00	.40	☐ 519 Ted Davidson	4.00	2.00	.40
☐ 479 Gary Bell	4.00	2.00	.40	☐ 520 Max Alvis	4.00	2.00	.40
☐ 480 Willie McCovey	20.00	10.00	2.00				

		NRMT	VG-E	GOOD
□ 521	Bird Bombers	5.00	2.50	.50
	Boog Powell			
	Curt Blefary			
□ 522	John Stephenson ...	4.00	2.00	.40
□ 523	Jim Merritt	4.00	2.00	.40
□ 524	Felix Mantilla	4.00	2.00	.40
□ 525	Ron Hunt	4.00	2.00	.40
□ 526	Tigers Rookies	5.50	2.75	.55
	Pat Dobson			
	George Korince			
	(See 67T-72)			
□ 527	Dennis Ribant	4.00	2.00	.40
□ 528	Rico Petrocelli	5.00	2.50	.50
□ 529	Gary Wagner	4.00	2.00	.40
□ 530	Felipe Alou	5.00	2.50	.50
□ 531	Checklist 7	8.00	.75	.15
	Brooks Robinson			
□ 532	Jim Hicks	4.00	2.00	.40
□ 533	Jack Fisher	4.00	2.00	.40
□ 534	Hank Bauer MG DP .	7.50	3.50	.75
□ 535	Donn Clendenon	20.00	10.00	2.00
□ 536	Cubs Rookies	30.00	12.50	2.50
	Joe Niekro			
	Paul Popovich			
□ 537	Chuck Estrada DP ..	6.00	3.00	.60
□ 538	J.C. Martin	15.00	7.50	1.50
□ 539	Dick Egan DP	6.00	3.00	.60
□ 540	Norm Cash	30.00	15.00	3.00
□ 541	Joe Gibbon	15.00	7.50	1.50
□ 542	Athletics Rookies DP	10.00	5.00	1.00
	Rick Monday			
	Tony Pierce			
□ 543	Dan Schneider	15.00	7.50	1.50
□ 544	Cleveland Indians ...	30.00	10.00	2.00
	Team Card			
□ 545	Jim Grant	15.00	7.50	1.50
□ 546	Woody Woodward ...	15.00	7.50	1.50
□ 547	Red Sox Rookies DP	6.00	3.00	.60
	Russ Gibson			
	Bill Rohr			
□ 548	Tony Gonzalez DP ...	6.00	3.00	.60
□ 549	Jack Sanford	15.00	7.50	1.50
□ 550	Vada Pinson DP	9.00	4.50	.90
□ 551	Doug Camilli DP	6.00	3.00	.60
□ 552	Ted Savage	15.00	7.50	1.50
□ 553	Yankees Rookies	25.00	12.50	2.50
	Mike Hegan			
	Thad Tillotson			
□ 554	Andre Rodgers DP ..	6.00	3.00	.60

		NRMT	VG-E	GOOD
□ 555	Don Cardwell	15.00	7.50	1.50
□ 556	Al Weis DP	6.00	3.00	.60
□ 557	Al Ferrara	15.00	7.50	1.50
□ 558	Orioles Rookies	35.00	17.50	3.50
	Mark Belanger			
	Bill Dillman			
□ 559	Dick Tracewski DP ..	6.00	3.00	.60
□ 560	Jim Bunning	40.00	18.00	3.60
□ 561	Sandy Alomar	15.00	7.50	1.50
□ 562	Steve Blass DP	6.00	3.00	.60
□ 563	Joe Adcock	20.00	10.00	2.00
□ 564	Astros Rookies DP ..	6.00	3.00	.60
	Alonzo Harris			
	Aaron Pointer			
□ 565	Lew Krausse	15.00	7.50	1.50
□ 566	Gary Geiger DP	6.00	3.00	.60
□ 567	Steve Hamilton	15.00	7.50	1.50
□ 568	John Sullivan	15.00	7.50	1.50
□ 569	AL Rookies DP	300.00	135.00	27.00
	Rod Carew			
	Hank Allen			
□ 570	Maury Wills	80.00	37.50	7.50
□ 571	Larry Sherry	15.00	7.50	1.50
□ 572	Don Demeter	15.00	7.50	1.50
□ 573	Chicago White Sox .	30.00	15.00	3.00
	Team Card UER			
	(Indians team stats			
	on back)			
□ 574	Jerry Buchek	15.00	7.50	1.50
□ 575	Dave Boswell	15.00	7.50	1.50
□ 576	NL Rookies	20.00	10.00	2.00
	Ramon Hernandez			
	Norm Gigon			
□ 577	Bill Short	15.00	7.50	1.50
□ 578	John Boccabella	15.00	7.50	1.50
□ 579	Bill Henry	15.00	7.50	1.50
□ 580	Rocky Colavito	35.00	15.00	3.00
□ 581	Mets Rookies	950.00	400.00	75.00
	Bill Denehy			
	Tom Seaver			
□ 582	Jim Owens DP	6.00	3.00	.60
□ 583	Ray Barker	15.00	7.50	1.50
□ 584	Jim Piersall	22.00	10.00	2.00
□ 585	Wally Bunker	15.00	7.50	1.50
□ 586	Manny Jimenez	15.00	7.50	1.50
□ 587	NL Rookies	20.00	10.00	2.00
	Don Shaw			
	Gary Sutherland			
□ 588	Johnny Klippstein DP	6.00	3.00	.60

1968 Topps

		NRMT	VG-E	GOOD
☐ 589	Dave Ricketts DP ...	6.00	3.00	.60
☐ 590	Pete Richert	15.00	7.50	1.50
☐ 591	Ty Cline	15.00	7.50	1.50
☐ 592	NL Rookies	20.00	10.00	2.00
	Jim Shellenback			
	Ron Willis			
☐ 593	Wes Westrum MG	20.00	10.00	2.00
☐ 594	Dan Osinski	15.00	7.50	1.50
☐ 595	Cookie Rojas	20.00	10.00	2.00
☐ 596	Galen Cisco DP	6.00	3.00	.60
☐ 597	Ted Abernathy	15.00	7.50	1.50
☐ 598	White Sox Rookies ..	20.00	10.00	2.00
	Walt Williams			
	Ed Stroud			
☐ 599	Bob Duliba DP	6.00	3.00	.60
☐ 600	Brooks Robinson	200.00	100.00	20.00
☐ 601	Bill Bryan DP	6.00	3.00	.60
☐ 602	Juan Pizarro	15.00	7.50	1.50
☐ 603	Athletics Rookies ...	15.00	7.50	1.50
	Tim Talton			
	Ramon Webster			
☐ 604	Red Sox Team	100.00	50.00	10.00
☐ 605	Mike Shannon	40.00	20.00	4.00
☐ 606	Ron Taylor	15.00	7.50	1.50
☐ 607	Mickey Stanley	30.00	15.00	3.00
☐ 608	Cubs Rookies DP ...	6.00	3.00	.60
	Rich Nye			
	John Upham			
☐ 609	Tommy John	100.00	25.00	5.00

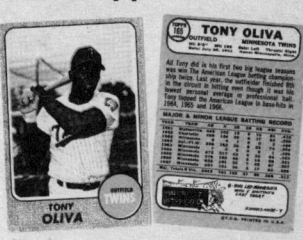

*The cards in this 598-card set measure 2 ½"
by 3 ½". The 1968 Topps set includes Sporting
News All-Star Selections as card numbers 361
to 380. Other subsets in the set include League
Leaders (1-12) and World Series cards (151-
158). The front of each checklist card features
a picture of a popular player inside a circle.
High numbers 534 to 598 are slightly more difficult to obtain. The first series looks different
from the other series, as it has a lighter, wider
mesh background on the card front. The later
series all had a much darker, finer mesh
pattern. Key cards in the set are the rookie
cards of Johnny Bench (247) and Nolan Ryan
(177).*

		NRMT	VG-E	GOOD
COMPLETE SET (598)	......	2500.00	1200.00	300.00
COMMON PLAYER (1-109)	....	.65	.30	.06
COMMON PLAYER (110-196)	..	.65	.30	.06
COMMON PLAYER (197-457)	..	.65	.30	.06
COMMON PLAYER (458-533)	..	.80	.40	.08
COMMON PLAYER (534-598)	..	.80	.40	.08
☐ 1	NL Batting Leaders .	7.00	1.50	.30
	Bob Clemente			
	Tony Gonzales			
	Matty Alou			
☐ 2	AL Batting Leaders ..	6.00	3.00	.60
	Carl Yastrzemski			
	Frank Robinson			
	Al Kaline			

			NRMT	VG-E	GOOD
☐	3	NL RBI Leaders .... Orlando Cepeda Bob Clemente Hank Aaron	4.00	2.00	.40
☐	4	AL RBI Leaders .... Carl Yastrzemski Harmon Killebrew Frank Robinson	6.00	3.00	.60
☐	5	NL Home Run Leaders .... Hank Aaron Jim Wynn Ron Santo Willie McCovey	3.00	1.50	.30
☐	6	NL Home Run Leaders .... Carl Yastrzemski Harmon Killebrew Frank Howard	4.00	2.00	.40
☐	7	NL ERA Leaders .... Phil Niekro Jim Bunning Chris Short	1.50	.75	.15
☐	8	AL ERA Leaders .... Joel Horlen Gary Peters Sonny Siebert	1.25	.60	.12
☐	9	NL Pitching Leaders . Mike McCormick Ferguson Jenkins Jim Bunning Claude Osteen	1.25	.60	.12
☐	10	AL Pitching Leaders . Jim Lonborg Earl Wilson Dean Chance	1.25	.60	.12
☐	11	NL Strikeout Leaders . Jim Bunning Ferguson Jenkins Gaylord Perry	1.50	.75	.15
☐	12	AL Strikeout Leaders . Jim Lonborg UER (misspelled Longberg on card back) Sam McDowell Dean Chance	1.25	.60	.12
☐	13	Chuck Hartenstein ..	.65	.30	.06
☐	14	Jerry McNertney	.65	.30	.06
☐	15	Ron Hunt	.65	.30	.06

			NRMT	VG-E	GOOD
☐	16	Indians Rookies .... Lou Piniella Richie Scheinblum	2.00	1.00	.20
☐	17	Dick Hall	.65	.30	.06
☐	18	Mike Hershberger ...	.65	.30	.06
☐	19	Juan Pizarro	.65	.30	.06
☐	20	Brooks Robinson ...	13.00	6.00	1.20
☐	21	Ron Davis	.65	.30	.06
☐	22	Pat Dobson	.65	.30	.06
☐	23	Chico Cardenas	.65	.30	.06
☐	24	Bobby Locke	.65	.30	.06
☐	25	Julian Javier	.65	.30	.06
☐	26	Darrell Brandon	.65	.30	.06
☐	27	Gil Hodges MG	3.50	1.75	.35
☐	28	Ted Uhlaender	.65	.30	.06
☐	29	Joe Verbanic	.65	.30	.06
☐	30	Joe Torre	1.25	.60	.12
☐	31	Ed Stroud	.65	.30	.06
☐	32	Joe Gibbon	.65	.30	.06
☐	33	Pete Ward	.65	.30	.06
☐	34	Al Ferrara	.65	.30	.06
☐	35	Steve Hargan	.65	.30	.06
☐	36	Pirates Rookies .... Bob Moose Bob Robertson	1.00	.50	.10
☐	37	Billy Williams	6.50	3.25	.65
☐	38	Tony Pierce	.65	.30	.06
☐	39	Cookie Rojas	.65	.30	.06
☐	40	Denny McLain	4.00	2.00	.40
☐	41	Julio Gotay	.65	.30	.06
☐	42	Larry Haney	.65	.30	.06
☐	43	Gary Bell	.65	.30	.06
☐	44	Frank Kostro	.65	.30	.06
☐	45	Tom Seaver	125.00	60.00	12.50
☐	46	Dave Ricketts	.65	.30	.06
☐	47	Ralph Houk MG	1.00	.50	.10
☐	48	Ted Davidson	.65	.30	.06
☐	49A	Eddie Brinkman .... (white team name)	.65	.30	.06
☐	49B	Eddie Brinkman .... (yellow team name)	40.00	20.00	4.00
☐	50	Willie Mays	50.00	22.50	4.50
☐	51	Bob Locker	.65	.30	.06
☐	52	Hawk Taylor	.65	.30	.06
☐	53	Gene Alley	.65	.30	.06
☐	54	Stan Williams	.65	.30	.06
☐	55	Felipe Alou	1.00	.50	.10
☐	56	Orioles Rookies ..... Dave Leonhard	.65	.30	.06

			NRMT	VG-E	GOOD				NRMT	VG-E	GOOD
		Dave May				☐	97	Tom Phoebus	.65	.30	.06
☐	57	Dan Schneider	.65	.30	.06	☐	98	Gary Sutherland	.65	.30	.06
☐	58	Eddie Mathews	7.00	3.50	.70	☐	99	Rocky Colavito	1.50	.75	.15
☐	59	Don Lock	.65	.30	.06	☐	100	Bob Gibson	13.50	6.00	1.25
☐	60	Ken Holtzman	1.00	.50	.10	☐	101	Glenn Beckert	.65	.30	.06
☐	61	Reggie Smith	1.25	.60	.12	☐	102	Jose Cardenal	.65	.30	.06
☐	62	Chuck Dobson	.65	.30	.06	☐	103	Don Sutton	6.50	3.25	.65
☐	63	Dick Kenworthy	.65	.30	.06	☐	104	Dick Dietz	.65	.30	.06
☐	64	Jim Merritt	.65	.30	.06	☐	105	Al Downing	.65	.30	.06
☐	65	John Roseboro	.65	.30	.06	☐	106	Dalton Jones	.65	.30	.06
☐	66A	Casey Cox	.65	.30	.06	☐	107A	Checklist 2	3.00	.35	.10
		(white team name)						Juan Marichal			
☐	66B	Casey Cox	40.00	20.00	4.00			(tan wide mesh)			
		(yellow team name)				☐	107B	Checklist 2	3.00	.35	.10
☐	67	Checklist 1	3.00	.40	.10			Juan Marichal			
		Jim Kaat						(brown fine mesh)			
☐	68	Ron Willis	.65	.30	.06	☐	108	Don Pavletich	.65	.30	.06
☐	69	Tom Tresh	1.00	.50	.10	☐	109	Bert Campaneris	1.00	.50	.10
☐	70	Bob Veale	.65	.30	.06	☐	110	Hank Aaron	50.00	22.50	4.50
☐	71	Vern Fuller	.65	.30	.06	☐	111	Rich Reese	.65	.30	.06
☐	72	Tommy John	4.00	2.00	.40	☐	112	Woodie Fryman	.65	.30	.06
☐	73	Jim Ray Hart	.65	.30	.06	☐	113	Tigers Rookies	.65	.30	.06
☐	74	Milt Pappas	.65	.30	.06			Tom Matchick			
☐	75	Don Mincher	.65	.30	.06			Daryl Patterson			
☐	76	Braves Rookies	.65	.30	.06	☐	114	Ron Swoboda	1.00	.50	.10
		Jim Britton				☐	115	Sam McDowell	1.00	.50	.10
		Ron Reed				☐	116	Ken McMullen	.65	.30	.06
☐	77	Don Wilson	.65	.30	.06	☐	117	Larry Jaster	.65	.30	.06
☐	78	Jim Northrup	1.00	.50	.10	☐	118	Mark Belanger	1.00	.50	.10
☐	79	Ted Kubiak	.65	.30	.06	☐	119	Ted Savage	.65	.30	.06
☐	80	Rod Carew	80.00	37.50	7.50	☐	120	Mel Stottlemyre	1.25	.60	.12
☐	81	Larry Jackson	.65	.30	.06	☐	121	Jimmie Hall	.65	.30	.06
☐	82	Sam Bowens	.65	.30	.06	☐	122	Gene Mauch MG	1.00	.50	.10
☐	83	John Stephenson	.65	.30	.06	☐	123	Jose Santiago	.65	.30	.06
☐	84	Bob Tolan	.65	.30	.06	☐	124	Nate Oliver	.65	.30	.06
☐	85	Gaylord Perry	6.00	3.00	.60	☐	125	Joel Horlen	.65	.30	.06
☐	86	Willie Stargell	8.00	4.00	.80	☐	126	Bobby Etheridge	.65	.30	.06
☐	87	Dick Williams MG	1.00	.50	.10	☐	127	Paul Lindblad	.65	.30	.06
☐	88	Phil Regan	.65	.30	.06	☐	128	Astros Rookies	.65	.30	.06
☐	89	Jake Gibbs	.65	.30	.06			Tom Dukes			
☐	90	Vada Pinson	1.00	.50	.10			Alonzo Harris			
☐	91	Jim Ollom	.65	.30	.06	☐	129	Mickey Stanley	1.00	.50	.10
☐	92	Ed Kranepool	1.00	.50	.10	☐	130	Tony Perez	6.00	3.00	.60
☐	93	Tony Cloninger	.65	.30	.06	☐	131	Frank Bertaina	.65	.30	.06
☐	94	Lee Maye	.65	.30	.06	☐	132	Bud Harrelson	.65	.30	.06
☐	95	Bob Aspromonte	.65	.30	.06	☐	133	Fred Whitfield	.65	.30	.06
☐	96	Senator Rookies	.65	.30	.06	☐	134	Pat Jarvis	.65	.30	.06
		Frank Coggins				☐	135	Paul Blair	.65	.30	.06
		Dick Nold				☐	136	Randy Hundley	.65	.30	.06

		NRMT	VG-E	GOOD
☐ 137	Twins Team	1.50	.75	.15
☐ 138	Ruben Amaro	.65	.30	.06
☐ 139	Chris Short	.65	.30	.06
☐ 140	Tony Conigliaro	1.50	.75	.15
☐ 141	Dal Maxvill	.65	.30	.06
☐ 142	White Sox Rookies	.65	.30	.06
	Buddy Bradford			
	Bill Voss			
☐ 143	Pete Cimino	.65	.30	.06
☐ 144	Joe Morgan	10.00	5.00	1.00
☐ 145	Don Drysdale	7.50	3.75	.75
☐ 146	Sal Bando	1.00	.50	.10
☐ 147	Frank Linzy	.65	.30	.06
☐ 148	Dave Bristol MG	.65	.30	.06
☐ 149	Bob Saverine	.65	.30	.06
☐ 150	Bob Clemente	40.00	17.50	3.50
☐ 151	World Series Game 1	4.00	2.00	.40
	Brock socks 4 hits in			
	opener			
☐ 152	World Series Game 2	6.00	3.00	.60
	Yaz smashes 2			
	homers			
☐ 153	World Series Game 3	2.00	1.00	.20
	Briles cools Boston			
☐ 154	World Series Game 4	4.00	2.00	.40
	Gibson hurls shutout			
☐ 155	World Series Game 5	2.00	1.00	.20
	Lonborg wins again			
☐ 156	World Series Game 6	2.00	1.00	.20
	Petrocelli 2 homers			
☐ 157	World Series Game 7	2.00	1.00	.20
	St. Louis wins it			
☐ 158	World Series Summary	2.00	1.00	.20
	Cardinals celebrate			
☐ 159	Don Kessinger	.65	.30	.06
☐ 160	Earl Wilson	.65	.30	.06
☐ 161	Norm Miller	.65	.30	.06
☐ 162	Cards Rookies	1.00	.50	.10
	Hal Gilson			
	Mike Torrez			
☐ 163	Gene Brabender	.65	.30	.06
☐ 164	Ramon Webster	.65	.30	.06
☐ 165	Tony Oliva	3.00	1.50	.30
☐ 166	Claude Raymond	.65	.30	.06
☐ 167	Elston Howard	2.25	1.10	.22
☐ 168	Dodgers Team	1.50	.75	.15
☐ 169	Bob Bolin	.65	.30	.06
☐ 170	Jim Fregosi	1.00	.50	.10
☐ 171	Don Nottebart	.65	.30	.06

		NRMT	VG-E	GOOD
☐ 172	Walt Williams	.65	.30	.06
☐ 173	John Boozer	.65	.30	.06
☐ 174	Bob Tillman	.65	.30	.06
☐ 175	Maury Wills	3.50	1.75	.35
☐ 176	Bob Allen	.65	.30	.06
☐ 177	Mets Rookies	950.00	475.00	95.00
	Jerry Koosman			
	Nolan Ryan			
☐ 178	Don Wert	.65	.30	.06
☐ 179	Bill Stoneman	.65	.30	.06
☐ 180	Curt Flood	1.00	.50	.10
☐ 181	Jerry Zimmerman	.65	.30	.06
☐ 182	Dave Giusti	.65	.30	.06
☐ 183	Bob Kennedy MG	.65	.30	.06
☐ 184	Lou Johnson	.65	.30	.06
☐ 185	Tom Haller	.65	.30	.06
☐ 186	Eddie Watt	.65	.30	.06
☐ 187	Sonny Jackson	.65	.30	.06
☐ 188	Cap Peterson	.65	.30	.06
☐ 189	Bill Landis	.65	.30	.06
☐ 190	Bill White	1.25	.60	.12
☐ 191	Dan Frisella	.65	.30	.06
☐ 192	Checklist 3	3.50	.40	.10
	Carl Yastrzemski			
☐ 193	Jack Hamilton	.65	.30	.06
☐ 194	Don Buford	.65	.30	.06
☐ 195	Joe Pepitone	1.25	.60	.12
☐ 196	Gary Nolan	.65	.30	.06
☐ 197	Larry Brown	.65	.30	.06
☐ 198	Roy Face	1.25	.60	.12
☐ 199	A's Rookies	.65	.30	.06
	Roberto Rodriquez			
	Darrell Osteen			
☐ 200	Orlando Cepeda	3.00	1.50	.30
☐ 201	Mike Marshall	1.25	.60	.12
☐ 202	Adolfo Phillips	.65	.30	.06
☐ 203	Dick Kelley	.65	.30	.06
☐ 204	Andy Etchebarren	.65	.30	.06
☐ 205	Juan Marichal	5.50	2.75	.55
☐ 206	Cal Ermer MG	.65	.30	.06
☐ 207	Carroll Sembera	.65	.30	.06
☐ 208	Willie Davis	1.00	.50	.10
☐ 209	Tim Cullen	.65	.30	.06
☐ 210	Gary Peters	.65	.30	.06
☐ 211	J.C. Martin	.65	.30	.06
☐ 212	Dave Morehead	.65	.30	.06
☐ 213	Chico Ruiz	.65	.30	.06
☐ 214	Yankees Rookies	1.00	.50	.10
	Stan Bahnsen			

		NRMT	VG-E	GOOD
	Frank Fernandez			
☐ 215	Jim Bunning	3.00	1.50	.30
☐ 216	Bubba Morton	.65	.30	.06
☐ 217	Turk Farrell	.65	.30	.06
☐ 218	Ken Suarez	.65	.30	.06
☐ 219	Rob Gardner	.65	.30	.06
☐ 220	Harmon Killebrew	11.00	5.00	1.00
☐ 221	Braves Team	1.50	.75	.15
☐ 222	Jim Hardin	.65	.30	.06
☐ 223	Ollie Brown	.65	.30	.06
☐ 224	Jack Aker	.65	.30	.06
☐ 225	Richie Allen	1.50	.75	.15
☐ 226	Jimmie Price	.65	.30	.06
☐ 227	Joe Hoerner	.65	.30	.06
☐ 228	Dodgers Rookies	.65	.30	.06
	Jack Billingham			
	Jim Fairey			
☐ 229	Fred Klages	.65	.30	.06
☐ 230	Pete Rose	50.00	25.00	5.00
☐ 231	Dave Baldwin	.65	.30	.06
☐ 232	Denis Menke	.65	.30	.06
☐ 233	George Scott	1.00	.50	.10
☐ 234	Bill Monbouquette	.65	.30	.06
☐ 235	Ron Santo	1.25	.60	.12
☐ 236	Tug McGraw	1.25	.60	.12
☐ 237	Alvin Dark MG	1.00	.50	.10
☐ 238	Tom Satriano	.65	.30	.06
☐ 239	Bill Henry	.65	.30	.06
☐ 240	Al Kaline	14.00	7.00	1.40
☐ 241	Felix Millan	.65	.30	.06
☐ 242	Moe Drabowsky	.65	.30	.06
☐ 243	Rich Rollins	.65	.30	.06
☐ 244	John Donaldson	.65	.30	.06
☐ 245	Tony Gonzalez	.65	.30	.06
☐ 246	Fritz Peterson	.65	.30	.06
☐ 247	Reds Rookies	375.00	175.00	37.00
	Johnny Bench			
	Ron Tompkins			
☐ 248	Fred Valentine	.65	.30	.06
☐ 249	Bill Singer	.65	.30	.06
☐ 250	Carl Yastrzemski	33.00	15.00	3.00
☐ 251	Manny Sanguillen	2.00	1.00	.20
☐ 252	Angels Team	1.50	.75	.15
☐ 253	Dick Hughes	.65	.30	.06
☐ 254	Cleon Jones	.65	.30	.06
☐ 255	Dean Chance	1.00	.50	.10
☐ 256	Norm Cash	2.00	1.00	.20
☐ 257	Phil Niekro	5.00	2.50	.50
☐ 258	Cubs Rookies	.65	.30	.06

		NRMT	VG-E	GOOD
	Jose Arcia			
	Bill Schlesinger			
☐ 259	Ken Boyer	1.25	.60	.12
☐ 260	Jim Wynn	1.00	.50	.10
☐ 261	Dave Duncan	.65	.30	.06
☐ 262	Rick Wise	.65	.30	.06
☐ 263	Horace Clarke	.65	.30	.06
☐ 264	Ted Abernathy	.65	.30	.06
☐ 265	Tommy Davis	1.00	.50	.10
☐ 266	Paul Popovich	.65	.30	.06
☐ 267	Herman Franks MG	.65	.30	.06
☐ 268	Bob Humphreys	.65	.30	.06
☐ 269	Bob Tiefenauer	.65	.30	.06
☐ 270	Matty Alou	1.00	.50	.10
☐ 271	Bobby Knoop	.65	.30	.06
☐ 272	Ray Culp	.65	.30	.06
☐ 273	Dave Johnson	1.25	.60	.12
☐ 274	Mike Cuellar	1.00	.50	.10
☐ 275	Tim McCarver	1.50	.75	.15
☐ 276	Jim Roland	.65	.30	.06
☐ 277	Jerry Buchek	.65	.30	.06
☐ 278	Checklist 4	3.00	.30	.10
	Orlando Cepeda			
☐ 279	Bill Hands	.65	.30	.06
☐ 280	Mickey Mantle	175.00	85.00	18.00
☐ 281	Jim Campanis	.65	.30	.06
☐ 282	Rick Monday	1.00	.50	.10
☐ 283	Mel Queen	.65	.30	.06
☐ 284	Johnny Briggs	.65	.30	.06
☐ 285	Dick McAuliffe	.65	.30	.06
☐ 286	Cecil Upshaw	.65	.30	.06
☐ 287	White Sox Rookies	.65	.30	.06
	Mickey Abarbanel			
	Cisco Carlos			
☐ 288	Dave Wickersham	.65	.30	.06
☐ 289	Woody Held	.65	.30	.06
☐ 290	Willie McCovey	7.50	3.75	.75
☐ 291	Dick Lines	.65	.30	.06
☐ 292	Art Shamsky	.65	.30	.06
☐ 293	Bruce Howard	.65	.30	.06
☐ 294	Red Schoendienst MG	3.00	1.50	.30
☐ 295	Sonny Siebert	.65	.30	.06
☐ 296	Byron Browne	.65	.30	.06
☐ 297	Russ Gibson	.65	.30	.06
☐ 298	Jim Brewer	.65	.30	.06
☐ 299	Gene Michael	1.00	.50	.10
☐ 300	Rusty Staub	1.25	.60	.12
☐ 301	Twins Rookies	.65	.30	.06
	George Mitterwald			

		NRMT	VG-E	GOOD
	Rick Renick			
☐ 302	Gerry Arrigo	.65	.30	.06
☐ 303	Dick Green	.65	.30	.06
☐ 304	Sandy Valdespino	.65	.30	.06
☐ 305	Minnie Rojas	.65	.30	.06
☐ 306	Mike Ryan	.65	.30	.06
☐ 307	John Hiller	1.00	.50	.10
☐ 308	Pirates Team	1.50	.75	.15
☐ 309	Ken Henderson	.65	.30	.06
☐ 310	Luis Aparicio	5.00	2.50	.50
☐ 311	Jack Lamabe	.65	.30	.06
☐ 312	Curt Blefary	.65	.30	.06
☐ 313	Al Weis	.65	.30	.06
☐ 314	Red Sox Rookies	.65	.30	.06
	Bill Rohr			
	George Spriggs			
☐ 315	Zoilo Versalles	.65	.30	.06
☐ 316	Steve Barber	.65	.30	.06
☐ 317	Ron Brand	.65	.30	.06
☐ 318	Chico Salmon	.65	.30	.06
☐ 319	George Culver	.65	.30	.06
☐ 320	Frank Howard	1.25	.60	.12
☐ 321	Leo Durocher MG	1.50	.75	.15
☐ 322	Dave Boswell	.65	.30	.06
☐ 323	Deron Johnson	.65	.30	.06
☐ 324	Jim Nash	.65	.30	.06
☐ 325	Manny Mota	1.00	.50	.10
☐ 326	Dennis Ribant	.65	.30	.06
☐ 327	Tony Taylor	.65	.30	.06
☐ 328	Angels Rookies	.65	.30	.06
	Chuck Vinson			
	Jim Weaver			
☐ 329	Duane Josephson	.65	.30	.06
☐ 330	Roger Maris	24.00	12.00	2.40
☐ 331	Dan Osinski	.65	.30	.06
☐ 332	Doug Rader	1.00	.50	.10
☐ 333	Ron Herbel	.65	.30	.06
☐ 334	Orioles Team	1.50	.75	.15
☐ 335	Bob Allison	1.00	.50	.10
☐ 336	John Purdin	.65	.30	.06
☐ 337	Bill Robinson	1.00	.50	.10
☐ 338	Bob Johnson	.65	.30	.06
☐ 339	Rich Nye	.65	.30	.06
☐ 340	Max Alvis	.65	.30	.06
☐ 341	Jim Lemon MG	.65	.30	
☐ 342	Ken Johnson	.65	.30	.06
☐ 343	Jim Gosger	.65	.30	.06
☐ 344	Donn Clendenon	1.00	.50	.10
☐ 345	Bob Hendley	.65	.30	.06

		NRMT	VG-E	GOOD
☐ 346	Jerry Adair	.65	.30	.06
☐ 347	George Brunet	.65	.30	.06
☐ 348	Phillies Rookies	.65	.30	.06
	Larry Colton			
	Dick Thoenen			
☐ 349	Ed Spiezio	.65	.30	.06
☐ 350	Hoyt Wilhelm	5.50	2.75	.55
☐ 351	Bob Barton	.65	.30	.06
☐ 352	Jackie Hernandez	.65	.30	.06
☐ 353	Mack Jones	.65	.30	.06
☐ 354	Pete Richert	.65	.30	.06
☐ 355	Ernie Banks	11.00	5.50	1.10
☐ 356A	Checklist 5	3.00	.30	.10
	Ken Holtzman			
	(head centered within			
	circle)			
☐ 356B	Checklist 5	3.00	.30	.10
	Ken Holtzman			
	(head shifted right			
	within circle)			
☐ 357	Len Gabrielson	.65	.30	.06
☐ 358	Mike Epstein	.65	.30	.06
☐ 359	Joe Moeller	.65	.30	.06
☐ 360	Willie Horton	1.00	.50	.10
☐ 361	Harmon Killebrew AS	4.50	2.25	.45
☐ 362	Orlando Cepeda AS	1.50	.75	.15
☐ 363	Rod Carew AS	9.00	4.50	.90
☐ 364	Joe Morgan AS	5.00	2.25	.45
☐ 365	Brooks Robinson AS	5.00	2.50	.50
☐ 366	Ron Santo AS	1.00	.50	.10
☐ 367	Jim Fregosi AS	1.00	.50	.10
☐ 368	Gene Alley AS	.65	.30	.06
☐ 369	Carl Yastrzemski AS	10.00	5.00	1.00
☐ 370	Hank Aaron AS	10.00	5.00	1.00
☐ 371	Tony Oliva AS	1.25	.60	.12
☐ 372	Lou Brock AS	5.00	2.50	.50
☐ 373	Frank Robinson AS	5.00	2.50	.50
☐ 374	Bob Clemente AS	9.00	4.50	.90
☐ 375	Bill Freehan AS	1.00	.50	.10
☐ 376	Tim McCarver AS	1.00	.50	.10
☐ 377	Joel Horlen AS	.65	.30	.06
☐ 378	Bob Gibson AS	4.50	2.25	.45
☐ 379	Gary Peters AS	.65	.30	.06
☐ 380	Ken Holtzman AS	.65	.30	.06
☐ 381	Boog Powell	1.50	.75	.15
☐ 382	Ramon Hernandez	.65	.30	.06
☐ 383	Steve Whitaker	.65	.30	.06
☐ 384	Reds Rookies	4.50	2.25	.45
	Bill Henry			

		NRMT	VG-E	GOOD
	Hal McRae			
☐ 385	Jim Hunter	8.50	4.25	.85
☐ 386	Greg Goossen	.65	.30	.06
☐ 387	Joe Foy	.65	.30	.06
☐ 388	Ray Washburn	.65	.30	.06
☐ 389	Jay Johnstone	1.00	.50	.10
☐ 390	Bill Mazeroski	1.25	.60	.12
☐ 391	Bob Priddy	.65	.30	.06
☐ 392	Grady Hatton MG	.65	.30	.06
☐ 393	Jim Perry	1.00	.50	.10
☐ 394	Tommie Aaron	1.00	.50	.10
☐ 395	Camilo Pascual	.65	.30	.06
☐ 396	Bobby Wine	.65	.30	.06
☐ 397	Vic Davalillo	.65	.30	.06
☐ 398	Jim Grant	.65	.30	.06
☐ 399	Ray Oyler	.65	.30	.06
☐ 400A	Mike McCormick	.65	.30	.06
	(yellow letters)			
☐ 400B	Mike McCormick	40.00	20.00	4.00
	(team name in white			
	letters)			
☐ 401	Mets Team	1.75	.85	.17
☐ 402	Mike Hegan	.65	.30	.06
☐ 403	John Buzhardt	.65	.30	.06
☐ 404	Floyd Robinson	.65	.30	.06
☐ 405	Tommy Helms	.65	.30	.06
☐ 406	Dick Ellsworth	.65	.30	.06
☐ 407	Gary Kolb	.65	.30	.06
☐ 408	Steve Carlton	33.00	15.00	3.00
☐ 409	Orioles Rookies	.65	.30	.06
	Frank Peters			
	Don Stone			
☐ 410	Fergie Jenkins	4.00	2.00	.40
☐ 411	Ron Hansen	.65	.30	.06
☐ 412	Clay Carroll	.65	.30	.06
☐ 413	Tom McCraw	.65	.30	.06
☐ 414	Mickey Lolich	2.25	1.10	.22
☐ 415	Johnny Callison	1.00	.50	.10
☐ 416	Bill Rigney MG	.65	.30	.06
☐ 417	Willie Crawford	.65	.30	.06
☐ 418	Eddie Fisher	.65	.30	.06
☐ 419	Jack Hiatt	.65	.30	.06
☐ 420	Cesar Tovar	.65	.30	.06
☐ 421	Ron Taylor	.65	.30	.06
☐ 422	Rene Lachemann	1.00	.50	.10
☐ 423	Fred Gladding	.65	.30	.06
☐ 424	Chicago White Sox	1.50	.75	.15
	Team Card			
☐ 425	Jim Maloney	1.00	.50	.10

		NRMT	VG-E	GOOD
☐ 426	Hank Allen	.65	.30	.06
☐ 427	Dick Calmus	.65	.30	.06
☐ 428	Vic Roznovsky	.65	.30	.06
☐ 429	Tommie Sisk	.65	.30	.06
☐ 430	Rico Petrocelli	1.00	.50	.10
☐ 431	Dooley Womack	.65	.30	.06
☐ 432	Indians Rookies	.65	.30	.06
	Bill Davis			
	Jose Vidal			
☐ 433	Bob Rodgers	1.00	.50	.10
☐ 434	Ricardo Joseph	.65	.30	.06
☐ 435	Ron Perranoski	1.00	.50	.10
☐ 436	Hal Lanier	1.00	.50	.10
☐ 437	Don Cardwell	.65	.30	.06
☐ 438	Lee Thomas	1.00	.50	.10
☐ 439	Lum Harris MG	.65	.30	.06
☐ 440	Claude Osteen	.65	.30	.06
☐ 441	Alex Johnson	.65	.30	.06
☐ 442	Dick Bosman	.65	.30	.06
☐ 443	Joe Azcue	.65	.30	.06
☐ 444	Jack Fisher	.65	.30	.06
☐ 445	Mike Shannon	1.00	.50	.10
☐ 446	Ron Kline	.65	.30	.06
☐ 447	Tigers Rookies	.65	.30	.06
	George Korince			
	Fred Lasher			
☐ 448	Gary Wagner	.65	.30	.06
☐ 449	Gene Oliver	.65	.30	.06
☐ 450	Jim Kaat	3.00	1.50	.30
☐ 451	Al Spangler	.65	.30	.06
☐ 452	Jesus Alou	.65	.30	.06
☐ 453	Sammy Ellis	.65	.30	.06
☐ 454A	Checklist 6	3.00	.30	.10
	Frank Robinson			
	(cap complete within			
	circle)			
☐ 454B	Checklist 6	3.00	.30	.10
	Frank Robinson			
	(cap partially within			
	circle)			
☐ 455	Rico Carty	1.00	.50	.10
☐ 456	John O'Donoghue	.65	.30	.06
☐ 457	Jim Lefebvre	1.25	.60	.12
☐ 458	Lew Krausse	.80	.40	.08
☐ 459	Dick Simpson	.80	.40	.08
☐ 460	Jim Lonborg	1.50	.75	.15
☐ 461	Chuck Hiller	.80	.40	.08
☐ 462	Barry Moore	.80	.40	.08
☐ 463	Jim Schaffer	.80	.40	.08

		NRMT	VG-E	GOOD
☐ 464	Don McMahon	.80	.40	.08
☐ 465	Tommie Agee	1.00	.50	.10
☐ 466	Bill Dillman	.80	.40	.08
☐ 467	Dick Howser	1.25	.60	.12
☐ 468	Larry Sherry	1.00	.50	.10
☐ 469	Ty Cline	.80	.40	.08
☐ 470	Bill Freehan	1.50	.75	.15
☐ 471	Orlando Pena	.80	.40	.08
☐ 472	Walt Alston MG	2.00	1.00	.20
☐ 473	Al Worthington	.80	.40	.08
☐ 474	Paul Schaal	.80	.40	.08
☐ 475	Joe Niekro	1.50	.75	.15
☐ 476	Woody Woodward	1.00	.50	.10
☐ 477	Philadelphia Phillies Team Card	1.75	.85	.17
☐ 478	Dave McNally	1.25	.60	.12
☐ 479	Phil Gagliano	.80	.40	.08
☐ 480	Manager's Dream Tony Oliva Chico Cardenas Bob Clemente	15.00	7.50	1.50
☐ 481	John Wyatt	.80	.40	.08
☐ 482	Jose Pagan	.80	.40	.08
☐ 483	Darold Knowles	.80	.40	.08
☐ 484	Phil Roof	.80	.40	.08
☐ 485	Ken Berry	.80	.40	.08
☐ 486	Cal Koonce	.80	.40	.08
☐ 487	Lee May	1.25	.60	.12
☐ 488	Dick Tracewski	.80	.40	.08
☐ 489	Wally Bunker	.80	.40	.08
☐ 490	Super Stars Harmon Killebrew Willie Mays Mickey Mantle	45.00	22.50	4.50
☐ 491	Denny Lemaster	.80	.40	.08
☐ 492	Jeff Torborg	1.25	.60	.12
☐ 493	Jim McGlothlin	.80	.40	.08
☐ 494	Ray Sadecki	.80	.40	.08
☐ 495	Leon Wagner	.80	.40	.08
☐ 496	Steve Hamilton	.80	.40	.08
☐ 497	Cards Team	1.75	.85	.17
☐ 498	Bill Bryan	.80	.40	.08
☐ 499	Steve Blass	1.00	.50	.10
☐ 500	Frank Robinson	12.00	6.00	1.20
☐ 501	John Odom	.80	.40	.08
☐ 502	Mike Andrews	.80	.40	.08
☐ 503	Al Jackson	.80	.40	.08
☐ 504	Russ Snyder	.80	.40	.08
☐ 505	Joe Sparma	.80	.40	.08
☐ 506	Clarence Jones	.80	.40	.08
☐ 507	Wade Blasingame	.80	.40	.08
☐ 508	Duke Sims	.80	.40	.08
☐ 509	Dennis Higgins	.80	.40	.08
☐ 510	Ron Fairly	1.00	.50	.10
☐ 511	Bill Kelso	.80	.40	.08
☐ 512	Grant Jackson	.80	.40	.08
☐ 513	Hank Bauer MG	1.25	.60	.12
☐ 514	Al McBean	.80	.40	.08
☐ 515	Russ Nixon	1.00	.50	.10
☐ 516	Pete Mikkelsen	.80	.40	.08
☐ 517	Diego Segui	.80	.40	.08
☐ 518A	Checklist 7 (539 ML Rookies) (Clete Boyer)	4.00	.40	.10
☐ 518B	Checklist 7 (539 AL Rookies) (Clete Boyer)	8.00	.60	.15
☐ 519	Jerry Stephenson	.80	.40	.08
☐ 520	Lou Brock	13.00	6.00	1.20
☐ 521	Don Shaw	.80	.40	.08
☐ 522	Wayne Causey	.80	.40	.08
☐ 523	John Tsitouris	.80	.40	.08
☐ 524	Andy Kosco	.80	.40	.08
☐ 525	Jim Davenport	1.00	.50	.10
☐ 526	Bill Denehy	.80	.40	.08
☐ 527	Tito Francona	.80	.40	.08
☐ 528	Tigers Team	15.00	6.00	1.20
☐ 529	Bruce Von Hoff	.80	.40	.08
☐ 530	Bird Belters Brooks Robinson Frank Robinson	6.00	3.00	.60
☐ 531	Chuck Hinton	.80	.40	.08
☐ 532	Luis Tiant	1.50	.75	.15
☐ 533	Wes Parker	1.00	.50	.10
☐ 534	Bob Miller	.80	.40	.08
☐ 535	Danny Cater	.80	.40	.08
☐ 536	Bill Short	.80	.40	.08
☐ 537	Norm Siebern	.80	.40	.08
☐ 538	Manny Jimenez	.80	.40	.08
☐ 539	Major League Rookies Jim Ray Mike Ferraro	1.25	.60	.12
☐ 540	Nelson Briles	1.00	.50	.10
☐ 541	Sandy Alomar	1.00	.50	.10
☐ 542	John Boccabella	.80	.40	.08
☐ 543	Bob Lee	.80	.40	.08
☐ 544	Mayo Smith MG	.80	.40	.08
☐ 545	Lindy McDaniel	1.00	.50	.10

		NRMT	VG-E	GOOD
☐ 546	Roy White	1.25	.60	.12
☐ 547	Dan Coombs	.80	.40	.08
☐ 548	Bernie Allen	.80	.40	.08
☐ 549	Orioles Rookies	.80	.40	.08
	Curt Motton			
	Roger Nelson			
☐ 550	Clete Boyer	1.25	.60	.12
☐ 551	Darrell Sutherland	.80	.40	.08
☐ 552	Ed Kirkpatrick	.80	.40	.08
☐ 553	Hank Aguirre	.80	.40	.08
☐ 554	A's Team	2.00	1.00	.20
☐ 555	Jose Tartabull	.80	.40	.08
☐ 556	Dick Selma	.80	.40	.08
☐ 557	Frank Quilici	.80	.40	.08
☐ 558	Johnny Edwards	.80	.40	.08
☐ 559	Pirates Rookies	1.00	.50	.10
	Carl Taylor			
	Luke Walker			
☐ 560	Paul Casanova	.80	.40	.08
☐ 561	Lee Elia	1.25	.60	.12
☐ 562	Jim Bouton	1.50	.75	.15
☐ 563	Ed Charles	.80	.40	.08
☐ 564	Eddie Stanky MG	1.00	.50	.10
☐ 565	Larry Dierker	1.00	.50	.10
☐ 566	Ken Harrelson	1.50	.75	.15
☐ 567	Clay Dalrymple	.80	.40	.08
☐ 568	Willie Smith	.80	.40	.08
☐ 569	NL Rookies	.80	.40	.09
	Ivan Murrell			
	Les Rohr			
☐ 570	Rick Reichardt	.80	.40	.08
☐ 571	Tony LaRussa	2.00	1.00	.20
☐ 572	Don Bosch	.80	.40	.08
☐ 573	Joe Coleman	.80	.40	.08
☐ 574	Cincinnati Reds	2.00	1.00	.20
	Team Card			
☐ 575	Jim Palmer	25.00	12.50	2.50
☐ 576	Dave Adlesh	.80	.40	.08
☐ 577	Fred Talbot	.80	.40	.08
☐ 578	Orlando Martinez	.80	.40	.08
☐ 579	NL Rookies	1.00	.50	.10
	Larry Hisle			
	Mike Lum			
☐ 580	Bob Bailey	.80	.40	.08
☐ 581	Garry Roggenburk	.80	.40	.08
☐ 582	Jerry Grote	.80	.40	.08
☐ 583	Gates Brown	1.00	.50	.10
☐ 584	Larry Shepard MG	.80	.40	.08
☐ 585	Wilbur Wood	1.00	.50	.10

		NRMT	VG-E	GOOD
☐ 586	Jim Pagliaroni	.80	.40	.08
☐ 587	Roger Repoz	.80	.40	.08
☐ 588	Dick Schofield	.80	.40	.08
☐ 589	Twins Rookies	.80	.40	.08
	Ron Clark			
	Moe Ogier			
☐ 590	Tommy Harper	1.00	.50	.10
☐ 591	Dick Nen	.80	.40	.08
☐ 592	John Bateman	.80	.40	.08
☐ 593	Lee Stange	.80	.40	.08
☐ 594	Phil Linz	1.00	.50	.10
☐ 595	Phil Ortega	.80	.40	.08
☐ 596	Charlie Smith	.80	.40	.08
☐ 597	Bill McCool	.80	.40	.08
☐ 598	Jerry May	1.50	.50	.10

1969 Topps

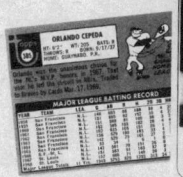

*The cards in this 664-card set measure 2 ½"
by 3 ½". The 1969 Topps set includes Sporting
News All-Star Selections as card numbers 416
to 435. Other popular subsets within this set
include League Leaders (1-12) and World Series cards (162-169). The fifth series contains
several variations; the more difficult variety
consists of cards with the player's first name,
last name, and/or position in white letters instead of lettering in some other color. These
are designated in the checklist below by WL
(white letters). Each checklist card features a
different popular player's picture inside a circle
on the front of the checklist card. Two different*

poses of Clay Dalrymple and Donn Clendenon exist, as indicated in the checklist.

			NRMT	VG-E	GOOD
COMPLETE SET (664)			2000.00	1000.00	250.00
COMMON PLAYER (1-218)			.50	.25	.05
COMMON PLAYER (219-327)			.80	.40	.08
COMMON PLAYER (328-512)			.50	.25	.05
COMMON PLAYER (513-588)			.60	.30	.06
COMMON PLAYER (589-664)			.80	.40	.08

			NRMT	VG-E	GOOD
☐	1	AL Batting Leaders	7.50	1.50	.30
		Carl Yastrzemski			
		Danny Cater			
		Tony Oliva			
☐	2	NL Batting Leaders	3.50	1.75	.35
		Pete Rose			
		Matty Alou			
		Felipe Alou			
☐	3	AL RBI Leaders	1.50	.75	.15
		Ken Harrelson			
		Frank Howard			
		Jim Northrup			
☐	4	NL RBI Leaders	2.50	1.25	.25
		Willie McCovey			
		Ron Santo			
		Billy Williams			
☐	5	AL Home Run Leaders	1.50	.75	.15
		Frank Howard			
		Willie Horton			
		Ken Harrelson			
☐	6	NL Home Run Leaders	2.50	1.25	.25
		Willie McCovey			
		Richie Allen			
		Ernie Banks			
☐	7	AL ERA Leaders	1.50	.75	.15
		Luis Tiant			
		Sam McDowell			
		Dave McNally			
☐	8	NL ERA Leaders	1.50	.75	.15
		Bob Gibson			
		Bobby Bolin			
		Bob Veale			
☐	9	AL Pitching Leaders	1.50	.75	.15
		Denny McLain			
		Dave McNally			
		Luis Tiant			
		Mel Stottlemyre			

			NRMT	VG-E	GOOD
☐	10	NL Pitching Leaders	2.50	1.25	.25
		Juan Marichal			
		Bob Gibson			
		Fergie Jenkins			
☐	11	AL Strikeout Leaders	1.50	.75	.15
		Sam McDowell			
		Denny McLain			
		Luis Tiant			
☐	12	NL Strikeout Leaders	1.50	.75	.15
		Bob Gibson			
		Fergie Jenkins			
		Bill Singer			
☐	13	Mickey Stanley	.75	.35	.07
☐	14	Al McBean	.50	.25	.05
☐	15	Boog Powell	1.50	.75	.15
☐	16	Giants Rookies	.50	.25	.05
		Cesar Gutierrez			
		Rich Robertson			
☐	17	Mike Marshall	.75	.35	.07
☐	18	Dick Schofield	.50	.25	.05
☐	19	Ken Suarez	.50	.25	.05
☐	20	Ernie Banks	10.00	5.00	1.00
☐	21	Jose Santiago	.50	.25	.05
☐	22	Jesus Alou	.50	.25	.05
☐	23	Lew Krausse	.50	.25	.05
☐	24	Walt Alston MG	1.75	.85	.17
☐	25	Roy White	.75	.35	.07
☐	26	Clay Carroll	.50	.25	.05
☐	27	Bernie Allen	.50	.25	.05
☐	28	Mike Ryan	.50	.25	.05
☐	29	Dave Morehead	.50	.25	.05
☐	30	Bob Allison	.75	.35	.07
☐	31	Mets Rookies	1.50	.75	.15
		Gary Gentry			
		Amos Otis			
☐	32	Sammy Ellis	.50	.25	.05
☐	33	Wayne Causey	.50	.25	.05
☐	34	Gary Peters	.75	.35	.07
☐	35	Joe Morgan	8.00	4.00	.80
☐	36	Luke Walker	.50	.25	.05
☐	37	Curt Motton	.50	.25	.05
☐	38	Zoilo Versalles	.50	.25	.05
☐	39	Dick Hughes	.50	.25	.05
☐	40	Mayo Smith MG	.50	.25	.05
☐	41	Bob Barton	.50	.25	.05
☐	42	Tommy Harper	.75	.35	.07
☐	43	Joe Niekro	1.00	.50	.10
☐	44	Danny Cater	.50	.25	.05
☐	45	Maury Wills	2.00	1.00	.20

		NRMT	VG-E	GOOD
☐ 46	Fritz Peterson	.50	.25	.05
☐ 47A	Paul Popovich (no helmet emblem)	.50	.25	.05
☐ 47B	Paul Popovich (C emblem on helmet)	15.00	7.50	1.50
☐ 48	Brant Alyea	.50	.25	.05
☐ 49A	Royals Rookies Steve Jones E. Rodriguez "g"	.50	.25	.05
☐ 49B	Royals Rookies Steve Jones E. Rodriguez "q"	15.00	7.50	1.50
☐ 50	Bob Clemente UER (Bats Right listed twice)	35.00	15.00	3.00
☐ 51	Woodie Fryman	.50	.25	.05
☐ 52	Mike Andrews	.50	.25	.05
☐ 53	Sonny Jackson	.50	.25	.05
☐ 54	Cisco Carlos	.50	.25	.05
☐ 55	Jerry Grote	.50	.25	.05
☐ 56	Rich Reese	.50	.25	.05
☐ 57	Checklist 1 Denny McLain	2.50	.30	.10
☐ 58	Fred Gladding	.50	.25	.05
☐ 59	Jay Johnstone	.75	.35	.07
☐ 60	Nelson Briles	.50	.25	.05
☐ 61	Jimmie Hall	.50	.25	.05
☐ 62	Chico Salmon	.50	.25	.05
☐ 63	Jim Hickman	.50	.25	.05
☐ 64	Bill Monbouquette	.50	.25	.05
☐ 65	Willie Davis	.75	.35	.07
☐ 66	Orioles Rookies Mike Adamson Merv Rettenmund	.75	.35	.07
☐ 67	Bill Stoneman	.50	.25	.05
☐ 68	Dave Duncan	.50	.25	.05
☐ 69	Steve Hamilton	.50	.25	.05
☐ 70	Tommy Helms	.75	.35	.07
☐ 71	Steve Whitaker	.50	.25	.05
☐ 72	Ron Taylor	.50	.25	.05
☐ 73	Johnny Briggs	.50	.25	.05
☐ 74	Preston Gomez MG	.50	.25	.05
☐ 75	Luis Aparicio	5.00	2.50	.50
☐ 76	Norm Miller	.50	.25	.05
☐ 77A	Ron Perranoski (no emblem on cap)	.75	.35	.07
☐ 77B	Ron Perranoski (LA on cap)	15.00	7.50	1.50
☐ 78	Tom Satriano	.50	.25	.05
☐ 79	Milt Pappas	.75	.35	.07
☐ 80	Norm Cash	1.25	.60	.12
☐ 81	Mel Queen	.50	.25	.05
☐ 82	Pirates Rookies Rich Hebner Al Oliver	8.00	4.00	.80
☐ 83	Mike Ferraro	.75	.35	.07
☐ 84	Bob Humphreys	.50	.25	.05
☐ 85	Lou Brock	10.00	5.00	1.00
☐ 86	Pete Richert	.50	.25	.05
☐ 87	Horace Clarke	.50	.25	.05
☐ 88	Rich Nye	.50	.25	.05
☐ 89	Russ Gibson	.50	.25	.05
☐ 90	Jerry Koosman	2.00	1.00	.20
☐ 91	Alvin Dark MG	.75	.35	.07
☐ 92	Jack Billingham	.50	.25	.05
☐ 93	Joe Foy	.50	.25	.05
☐ 94	Hank Aguirre	.50	.25	.05
☐ 95	Johnny Bench	125.00	60.00	12.50
☐ 96	Denny Lemaster	.50	.25	.05
☐ 97	Buddy Bradford	.50	.25	.05
☐ 98	Dave Giusti	.75	.35	.07
☐ 99A	Twins Rookies Danny Morris Graig Nettles (no loop)	15.00	7.50	1.50
☐ 99B	Twins Rookies (errant loop in upper left corner of obverse)	30.00	15.00	3.00
☐ 100	Hank Aaron	40.00	17.50	3.50
☐ 101	Daryl Patterson	.50	.25	.05
☐ 102	Jim Davenport	.75	.35	.07
☐ 103	Roger Repoz	.50	.25	.05
☐ 104	Steve Blass	.75	.35	.07
☐ 105	Rick Monday	.75	.35	.07
☐ 106	Jim Hannan	.50	.25	.05
☐ 107A	Checklist 2 (161 Jim Purdin) (Bob Gibson)	2.50	.30	.10
☐ 107B	Checklist 2 (161 John Purdin) (Bob Gibson)	6.00	.75	.15
☐ 108	Tony Taylor	.50	.25	.05
☐ 109	Jim Lonborg	1.00	.50	.10
☐ 110	Mike Shannon	.75	.35	.07
☐ 111	Johnny Morris	.50	.25	.05
☐ 112	J.C. Martin	.50	.25	.05
☐ 113	Dave May	.50	.25	.05
☐ 114	Yankees Rookies	.50	.25	.05

		NRMT	VG-E	GOOD
	Alan Closter			
	John Cumberland			
☐ 115	Bill Hands	.50	.25	.05
☐ 116	Chuck Harrison	.50	.25	.05
☐ 117	Jim Fairey	.50	.25	.05
☐ 118	Stan Williams	.50	.25	.05
☐ 119	Doug Rader	.75	.35	.07
☐ 120	Pete Rose	35.00	17.50	3.50
☐ 121	Joe Grzenda	.50	.25	.05
☐ 122	Ron Fairly	.75	.35	.07
☐ 123	Wilbur Wood	.75	.35	.07
☐ 124	Hank Bauer MG	.75	.35	.07
☐ 125	Ray Sadecki	.50	.25	.05
☐ 126	Dick Tracewski	.50	.25	.05
☐ 127	Kevin Collins	.50	.25	.05
☐ 128	Tommie Aaron	.75	.35	.07
☐ 129	Bill McCool	.50	.25	.05
☐ 130	Carl Yastrzemski	28.00	13.50	2.70
☐ 131	Chris Cannizzaro	.50	.25	.05
☐ 132	Dave Baldwin	.50	.25	.05
☐ 133	Johnny Callison	.75	.35	.07
☐ 134	Jim Weaver	.50	.25	.05
☐ 135	Tommy Davis	1.00	.50	.10
☐ 136	Cards Rookies	.75	.35	.07
	Steve Huntz			
	Mike Torrez			
☐ 137	Wally Bunker	.50	.25	.05
☐ 138	John Bateman	.50	.25	.05
☐ 139	Andy Kosco	.50	.25	.05
☐ 140	Jim Lefebvre	1.00	.50	.10
☐ 141	Bill Dillman	.50	.25	.05
☐ 142	Woody Woodward	.75	.35	.07
☐ 143	Joe Nossek	.50	.25	.05
☐ 144	Bob Hendley	.50	.25	.05
☐ 145	Max Alvis	.50	.25	.05
☐ 146	Jim Perry	.75	.35	.07
☐ 147	Leo Durocher MG	1.25	.60	.12
☐ 148	Lee Stange	.50	.25	.05
☐ 149	Ollie Brown	.50	.25	.05
☐ 150	Denny McLain	2.50	1.25	.25
☐ 151A	Clay Dalrymple	.50	.25	.05
	(Portrait, Orioles)			
☐ 151B	Clay Dalrymple	15.00	7.50	1.50
	(Catching, Phillies)			
☐ 152	Tommie Sisk	.50	.25	.05
☐ 153	Ed Brinkman	.50	.25	.05
☐ 154	Jim Britton	.50	.25	.05
☐ 155	Pete Ward	.50	.25	.05
☐ 156	Houston Rookies	.50	.25	.05

		NRMT	VG-E	GOOD
	Hal Gilson			
	Leon McFadden			
☐ 157	Bob Rodgers	.75	.35	.07
☐ 158	Joe Gibbon	.50	.25	.05
☐ 159	Jerry Adair	.50	.25	.05
☐ 160	Vada Pinson	1.00	.50	.10
☐ 161	John Purdin	.50	.25	.05
☐ 162	World Series Game 1	3.50	1.75	.35
	Gibson fans 17			
☐ 163	World Series Game 2	2.00	1.00	.20
	Tiger homers			
	deck the Cards			
☐ 164	World Series Game 3	2.50	1.25	.25
	McCarver's homer			
☐ 165	World Series Game 4	3.50	1.75	.35
	Brock lead-off homer			
☐ 166	World Series Game 5	4.50	2.25	.45
	Kaline's key hit			
☐ 167	World Series Game 6	2.00	1.00	.20
	Northrup grandslam			
☐ 168	World Series Game 7	3.50	1.75	.35
	Lolich outduels			
	Bob Gibson			
☐ 169	World Series Summary	2.00	1.00	.20
	Tigers celebrate			
☐ 170	Frank Howard	1.00	.50	.10
☐ 171	Glenn Beckert	.75	.35	.07
☐ 172	Jerry Stephenson	.50	.25	.05
☐ 173	White Sox Rookies	.50	.25	.05
	Bob Christian			
	Gerry Nyman			
☐ 174	Grant Jackson	.50	.25	.05
☐ 175	Jim Bunning	2.50	1.25	.25
☐ 176	Joe Azcue	.50	.25	.05
☐ 177	Ron Reed	.50	.25	.05
☐ 178	Ray Oyler	.50	.25	.05
☐ 179	Don Pavletich	.50	.25	.05
☐ 180	Willie Horton	.75	.35	.07
☐ 181	Mel Nelson	.50	.25	.05
☐ 182	Bill Rigney MG	.50	.25	.05
☐ 183	Don Shaw	.50	.25	.05
☐ 184	Roberto Pena	.50	.25	.05
☐ 185	Tom Phoebus	.50	.25	.05
☐ 186	Johnny Edwards	.50	.25	.05
☐ 187	Leon Wagner	.50	.25	.05
☐ 188	Rick Wise	.75	.35	.07
☐ 189	Red Sox Rookies	.50	.25	.05
	Joe Lahoud			
	John Thibodeau			

		NRMT	VG-E	GOOD
☐ 190	Willie Mays	40.00	17.50	3.50
☐ 191	Lindy McDaniel	.75	.35	.07
☐ 192	Jose Pagan	.50	.25	.05
☐ 193	Don Cardwell	.50	.25	.05
☐ 194	Ted Uhlaender	.50	.25	.05
☐ 195	John Odom	.50	.25	.05
☐ 196	Lum Harris MG	.50	.25	.05
☐ 197	Dick Selma	.50	.25	.05
☐ 198	Willie Smith	.50	.25	.05
☐ 199	Jim French	.50	.25	.05
☐ 200	Bob Gibson	9.00	4.50	.90
☐ 201	Russ Snyder	.50	.25	.05
☐ 202	Don Wilson	.50	.25	.05
☐ 203	Dave Johnson	1.00	.50	.10
☐ 204	Jack Hiatt	.50	.25	.05
☐ 205	Rick Reichardt	.50	.25	.05
☐ 206	Phillies Rookies	.75	.35	.07
	Larry Hisle			
	Barry Lersch			
☐ 207	Roy Face	.75	.35	.07
☐ 208A	Donn Clendenon	.75	.35	.07
	(Houston)			
☐ 208B	Donn Clendenon	15.00	7.50	1.50
	(Expos)			
☐ 209	Larry Haney	.50	.25	.05
	(reverse-negative)			
☐ 210	Felix Millan	.50	.25	.05
☐ 211	Galen Cisco	.50	.25	.05
☐ 212	Tom Tresh	.75	.35	.07
☐ 213	Gerry Arrigo	.50	.25	.05
☐ 214	Checklist 3	2.50	.30	.10
	With 69T deckle CL			
	on back (no player)			
☐ 215	Rico Petrocelli	.75	.35	.07
☐ 216	Don Sutton	5.00	2.50	.50
☐ 217	John Donaldson	.50	.25	.05
☐ 218	John Roseboro	.75	.35	.07
☐ 219	Freddie Patek	1.25	.60	.12
☐ 220	Sam McDowell	1.25	.60	.12
☐ 221	Art Shamsky	.85	.40	.08
☐ 222	Duane Josephson	.85	.40	.08
☐ 223	Tom Dukes	.85	.40	.08
☐ 224	Angels Rookies	.85	.40	.08
	Bill Harrelson			
	Steve Kealey			
☐ 225	Don Kessinger	1.25	.60	.12
☐ 226	Bruce Howard	.85	.40	.08
☐ 227	Frank Johnson	.85	.40	.08
☐ 228	Dave Leonhard	.85	.40	.08
☐ 229	Don Lock	.85	.40	.08
☐ 230	Rusty Staub	1.75	.85	.17
☐ 231	Pat Dobson	1.25	.60	.12
☐ 232	Dave Ricketts	.85	.40	.08
☐ 233	Steve Barber	.85	.40	.08
☐ 234	Dave Bristol MG	.85	.40	.08
☐ 235	Jim Hunter	9.00	4.50	.90
☐ 236	Manny Mota	1.25	.60	.12
☐ 237	Bobby Cox	1.25	.60	.12
☐ 238	Ken Johnson	.85	.40	.08
☐ 239	Bob Taylor	.85	.40	.08
☐ 240	Ken Harrelson	1.50	.75	.15
☐ 241	Jim Brewer	.85	.40	.08
☐ 242	Frank Kostro	.85	.40	.08
☐ 243	Ron Kline	.85	.40	.08
☐ 244	Indians Rookies	1.25	.60	.12
	Ray Fosse			
	George Woodson			
☐ 245	Ed Charles	.85	.40	.08
☐ 246	Joe Coleman	.85	.40	.08
☐ 247	Gene Oliver	.85	.40	.08
☐ 248	Bob Priddy	.85	.40	.08
☐ 249	Ed Spiezio	.85	.40	.08
☐ 250	Frank Robinson	15.00	7.50	1.50
☐ 251	Ron Herbel	.85	.40	.08
☐ 252	Chuck Cottier	.85	.40	.08
☐ 253	Jerry Johnson	.85	.40	.08
☐ 254	Joe Schultz	.85	.40	.08
☐ 255	Steve Carlton	30.00	15.00	3.00
☐ 256	Gates Brown	1.25	.60	.12
☐ 257	Jim Ray	.85	.40	.08
☐ 258	Jackie Hernandez	.85	.40	.08
☐ 259	Bill Short	.85	.40	.08
☐ 260	Reggie Jackson	350.00	175.00	35.00
☐ 261	Bob Johnson	.85	.40	.08
☐ 262	Mike Kekich	.85	.40	.08
☐ 263	Jerry May	.85	.40	.08
☐ 264	Bill Landis	.85	.40	.08
☐ 265	Chico Cardenas	.85	.40	.08
☐ 266	Dodger Rookies	.85	.40	.08
	Tom Hutton			
	Alan Foster			
☐ 267	Vicente Romo	.85	.40	.08
☐ 268	Al Spangler	.85	.40	.08
☐ 269	Al Weis	.85	.40	.08
☐ 270	Mickey Lolich	1.75	.85	.17
☐ 271	Larry Stahl	.85	.40	.08
☐ 272	Ed Stroud	.85	.40	.08
☐ 273	Ron Willis	.85	.40	.08

		NRMT	VG-E	GOOD
☐ 274	Clyde King MG	.85	.40	.08
☐ 275	Vic Davalillo	.85	.40	.08
☐ 276	Gary Wagner	.85	.40	.08
☐ 277	Elrod Hendricks	.85	.40	.08
☐ 278	Gary Geiger	1.25	.60	.12
	(Batting wrong)			
☐ 279	Roger Nelson	.85	.40	.08
☐ 280	Alex Johnson	1.25	.60	.12
☐ 281	Ted Kubiak	.85	.40	.08
☐ 282	Pat Jarvis	.85	.40	.08
☐ 283	Sandy Alomar	.85	.40	.08
☐ 284	Expos Rookies	.85	.40	.08
	Jerry Robertson			
	Mike Wegener			
☐ 285	Don Mincher	.85	.40	.08
☐ 286	Dock Ellis	1.25	.60	.12
☐ 287	Jose Tartabull	.85	.40	.08
☐ 288	Ken Holtzman	1.25	.60	.12
☐ 289	Bart Shirley	.85	.40	.08
☐ 290	Jim Kaat	3.50	1.75	.35
☐ 291	Vern Fuller	.85	.40	.08
☐ 292	Al Downing	1.25	.60	.12
☐ 293	Dick Dietz	.85	.40	.08
☐ 294	Jim Lemon MG	1.25	.60	.12
☐ 295	Tony Perez	6.00	3.00	.60
☐ 296	Andy Messersmith	1.50	.75	.15
☐ 297	Deron Johnson	1.25	.60	.12
☐ 298	Dave Nicholson	.85	.40	.08
☐ 299	Mark Belanger	1.25	.60	.12
☐ 300	Felipe Alou	1.25	.60	.12
☐ 301	Darrell Brandon	.85	.40	.08
☐ 302	Jim Pagliaroni	.85	.40	.08
☐ 303	Cal Koonce	.85	.40	.08
☐ 304	Padres Rookies	2.00	1.00	.20
	Bill Davis			
	Clarence Gaston			
☐ 305	Dick McAuliffe	1.25	.60	.12
☐ 306	Jim Grant	.85	.40	.08
☐ 307	Gary Kolb	.85	.40	.08
☐ 308	Wade Blasingame	.85	.40	.08
☐ 309	Walt Williams	.85	.40	.08
☐ 310	Tom Haller	.85	.40	.08
☐ 311	Sparky Lyle	6.00	3.00	.60
☐ 312	Lee Elia	1.25	.60	.12
☐ 313	Bill Robinson	1.25	.60	.12
☐ 314	Checklist 4	3.00	.30	.10
	Don Drysdale			
☐ 315	Eddie Fisher	.85	.40	.08
☐ 316	Hal Lanier	1.25	.60	.12

		NRMT	VG-E	GOOD
☐ 317	Bruce Look	.85	.40	.08
☐ 318	Jack Fisher	.85	.40	.08
☐ 319	Ken McMullen	.85	.40	.08
☐ 320	Dal Maxvill	.85	.40	.08
☐ 321	Jim McAndrew	.85	.40	.08
☐ 322	Jose Vidal	.85	.40	.08
☐ 323	Larry Miller	.85	.40	.08
☐ 324	Tiger Rookies	.85	.40	.08
	Les Cain			
	Dave Campbell			
☐ 325	Jose Cardenal	.85	.40	.08
☐ 326	Gary Sutherland	.85	.40	.08
☐ 327	Willie Crawford	.85	.40	.08
☐ 328	Joel Horlen	.50	.25	.05
☐ 329	Rick Joseph	.50	.25	.05
☐ 330	Tony Conigliaro	1.50	.75	.15
☐ 331	Braves Rookies	.75	.35	.07
	Gil Garrido			
	Tom House			
☐ 332	Fred Talbot	.50	.25	.05
☐ 333	Ivan Murrell	.50	.25	.05
☐ 334	Phil Roof	.50	.25	.05
☐ 335	Bill Mazeroski	1.00	.50	.10
☐ 336	Jim Roland	.50	.25	.05
☐ 337	Marty Martinez	.50	.25	.05
☐ 338	Del Unser	.50	.25	.05
☐ 339	Reds Rookies	.50	.25	.05
	Steve Mingori			
	Jose Pena			
☐ 340	Dave McNally	.75	.35	.07
☐ 341	Dave Adlesh	.50	.25	.05
☐ 342	Bubba Morton	.50	.25	.05
☐ 343	Dan Frisella	.50	.25	.05
☐ 344	Tom Matchick	.50	.25	.05
☐ 345	Frank Linzy	.50	.25	.05
☐ 346	Wayne Comer	.50	.25	.05
☐ 347	Randy Hundley	.75	.35	.07
☐ 348	Steve Hargan	.50	.25	.05
☐ 349	Dick Williams MG	.75	.35	.07
☐ 350	Richie Allen	1.25	.60	.12
☐ 351	Carroll Sembera	.50	.25	.05
☐ 352	Paul Schaal	.50	.25	.05
☐ 353	Jeff Torborg	.75	.35	.07
☐ 354	Nate Oliver	.50	.25	.05
☐ 355	Phil Niekro	4.00	2.00	.40
☐ 356	Frank Quilici MG	.50	.25	.05
☐ 357	Carl Taylor	.50	.25	.05
☐ 358	Athletics Rookies	.50	.25	.05
	George Lauzerique			

		NRMT	VG-E	GOOD			NRMT	VG-E	GOOD
	Roberto Rodriquez				☐ 403	Bob Miller	.50	.25	.05
☐ 359	Dick Kelley	.50	.25	.05	☐ 404	Cubs Rookies	.50	.25	.05
☐ 360	Jim Wynn	.75	.35	.07		Vic LaRose			
☐ 361	Gary Holman	.50	.25	.05		Gary Ross			
☐ 362	Jim Maloney	.75	.35	.07	☐ 405	Lee May	.75	.35	.07
☐ 363	Russ Nixon	.75	.35	.07	☐ 406	Phil Ortega	.50	.25	.05
☐ 364	Tommie Agee	.75	.35	.07	☐ 407	Tom Egan	.50	.25	.05
☐ 365	Jim Fregosi	.75	.35	.07	☐ 408	Nate Colbert	.50	.25	.05
☐ 366	Bo Belinsky	.75	.35	.07	☐ 409	Bob Moose	.50	.25	.05
☐ 367	Lou Johnson	.50	.25	.05	☐ 410	Al Kaline	10.00	5.00	1.00
☐ 368	Vic Roznovsky	.50	.25	.05	☐ 411	Larry Dierker	.75	.35	.07
☐ 369	Bob Skinner	.50	.25	.05	☐ 412	Checklist 5	6.00	1.00	.20
☐ 370	Juan Marichal	4.50	2.25	.45		Mickey Mantle			
☐ 371	Sal Bando	.75	.35	.07	☐ 413	Roland Sheldon	.50	.25	.05
☐ 372	Adolfo Phillips	.50	.25	.05	☐ 414	Duke Sims	.50	.25	.05
☐ 373	Fred Lasher	.50	.25	.05	☐ 415	Ray Washburn	.50	.25	.05
☐ 374	Bob Tillman	.50	.25	.05	☐ 416	Willie McCovey AS	4.50	2.25	.45
☐ 375	Harmon Killebrew	12.00	5.50	1.10	☐ 417	Ken Harrelson AS	.75	.35	.07
☐ 376	Royals Rookies	.75	.35	.07	☐ 418	Tommy Helms AS	.75	.35	.07
	Mike Fiore				☐ 419	Rod Carew AS	6.00	3.00	.60
	Jim Rooker				☐ 420	Ron Santo AS	.75	.35	.07
☐ 377	Gary Bell	.50	.25	.05	☐ 421	Brooks Robinson AS	4.50	2.25	.45
☐ 378	Jose Herrera	.50	.25	.05	☐ 422	Don Kessinger AS	.75	.35	.07
☐ 379	Ken Boyer	1.00	.50	.10	☐ 423	Bert Campaneris AS	.75	.35	.07
☐ 380	Stan Bahnsen	.50	.25	.05	☐ 424	Pete Rose AS	10.00	5.00	1.00
☐ 381	Ed Kranepool	.75	.35	.07	☐ 425	Carl Yastrzemski AS	9.00	4.50	.90
☐ 382	Pat Corrales	.75	.35	.07	☐ 426	Curt Flood AS	.75	.35	.07
☐ 383	Casey Cox	.50	.25	.05	☐ 427	Tony Oliva AS	1.00	.50	.10
☐ 384	Larry Shepard MG	.50	.25	.05	☐ 428	Lou Brock AS	4.50	2.25	.45
☐ 385	Orlando Cepeda	2.50	1.25	.25	☐ 429	Willie Horton AS	.75	.35	.07
☐ 386	Jim McGlothlin	.50	.25	.05	☐ 430	Johnny Bench AS	12.00	6.00	1.20
☐ 387	Bobby Klaus	.50	.25	.05	☐ 431	Bill Freehan AS	.75	.35	.07
☐ 388	Tom McCraw	.50	.25	.05	☐ 432	Bob Gibson AS	4.00	2.00	.40
☐ 389	Dan Coombs	.50	.25	.05	☐ 433	Denny McLain AS	.75	.35	.07
☐ 390	Bill Freehan	1.00	.50	.10	☐ 434	Jerry Koosman AS	.75	.35	.07
☐ 391	Ray Culp	.50	.25	.05	☐ 435	Sam McDowell AS	.75	.35	.07
☐ 392	Bob Burda	.50	.25	.05	☐ 436	Gene Alley	.75	.35	.07
☐ 393	Gene Brabender	.50	.25	.05	☐ 437	Luis Alcaraz	.50	.25	.05
☐ 394	Pilots Rookies	3.00	1.50	.30	☐ 438	Gary Waslewski	.50	.25	.05
	Lou Piniella				☐ 439	White Sox Rookies	.50	.25	.05
	Marv Staehle					Ed Herrmann			
☐ 395	Chris Short	.50	.25	.05		Dan Lazar			
☐ 396	Jim Campanis	.50	.25	.05	☐ 440A	Willie McCovey	15.00	7.50	1.50
☐ 397	Chuck Dobson	.50	.25	.05	☐ 440B	Willie McCovey WL	80.00	40.00	8.00
☐ 398	Tito Francona	.75	.35	.07		(McCovey white)			
☐ 399	Bob Bailey	.50	.25	.05	☐ 441A	Dennis Higgins	.50	.25	.05
☐ 400	Don Drysdale	7.00	3.50	.70	☐ 441B	Dennis Higgins WL	15.00	7.50	1.50
☐ 401	Jake Gibbs	.50	.25	.05		(Higgins white)			
☐ 402	Ken Boswell	.50	.25	.05	☐ 442	Ty Cline	.50	.25	.05

		NRMT	VG-E	GOOD
☐ 443	Don Wert	.50	.25	.05
☐ 444A	Joe Moeller	.50	.25	.05
☐ 444B	Joe Moeller WL (Moeller white)	15.00	7.50	1.50
☐ 445	Bobby Knoop	.50	.25	.05
☐ 446	Claude Raymond	.50	.25	.05
☐ 447A	Ralph Houk MG	.75	.35	.07
☐ 447B	Ralph Houk WL MG (Houk white)	15.00	7.50	1.50
☐ 448	Bob Tolan	.75	.35	.07
☐ 449	Paul Lindblad	.50	.25	.05
☐ 450	Billy Williams	6.00	3.00	.60
☐ 451A	Rich Rollins	.75	.35	.07
☐ 451B	Rich Rollins WL (Rich and 3B white)	15.00	7.50	1.50
☐ 452A	Al Ferrara	.50	.25	.05
☐ 452B	Al Ferrara WL (Al and OF white)	15.00	7.50	1.50
☐ 453	Mike Cuellar	1.00	.50	.10
☐ 454A	Phillies Rookies Larry Colton Don Money	.75	.35	.07
☐ 454B	Phillies Rookies WL Larry Colton Don Money (names in white)	15.00	7.50	1.50
☐ 455	Sonny Siebert	.75	.35	.07
☐ 456	Bud Harrelson	.75	.35	.07
☐ 457	Dalton Jones	.50	.25	.05
☐ 458	Curt Blefary	.50	.25	.05
☐ 459	Dave Boswell	.50	.25	.05
☐ 460	Joe Torre	1.00	.50	.10
☐ 461A	Mike Epstein	.50	.25	.05
☐ 461B	Mike Epstein WL (Epstein white)	15.00	7.50	1.50
☐ 462	Red Schoendienst MG	2.50	1.25	.25
☐ 463	Dennis Ribant	.50	.25	.05
☐ 464A	Dave Marshall	.50	.25	.05
☐ 464B	Dave Marshall WL (Marshall white)	15.00	7.50	1.50
☐ 465	Tommy John	3.50	1.75	.35
☐ 466	John Boccabella	.50	.25	.05
☐ 467	Tommie Reynolds	.50	.25	.05
☐ 468A	Pirates Rookies Bruce Dal Canton Bob Robertson	.50	.25	.05
☐ 468B	Pirates Rookies WL Bruce Dal Canton Bob Robertson	15.00	7.50	1.50

		NRMT	VG-E	GOOD
	(names in white)			
☐ 469	Chico Ruiz	.50	.25	.05
☐ 470A	Mel Stottlemyre	1.25	.60	.12
☐ 470B	Mel Stottlemyre WL (Stottlemyre white)	18.00	9.00	1.80
☐ 471A	Ted Savage	.50	.25	.05
☐ 471B	Ted Savage WL (Savage white)	15.00	7.50	1.50
☐ 472	Jim Price	.50	.25	.05
☐ 473A	Jose Arcia	.50	.25	.05
☐ 473B	Jose Arcia WL (Jose and 2B white)	15.00	7.50	1.50
☐ 474	Tom Murphy	.50	.25	.05
☐ 475	Tim McCarver	1.50	.75	.15
☐ 476A	Boston Rookies Ken Brett Gerry Moses	.75	.35	.07
☐ 476B	Boston Rookies WL Ken Brett Gerry Moses (names in white)	15.00	7.50	1.50
☐ 477	Jeff James	.50	.25	.05
☐ 478	Don Buford	.75	.35	.07
☐ 479	Richie Scheinblum	.50	.25	.05
☐ 480	Tom Seaver	80.00	40.00	8.00
☐ 481	Bill Melton	.50	.25	.05
☐ 482A	Jim Gosger	.50	.25	.05
☐ 482B	Jim Gosger WL (Jim and OF white)	15.00	7.50	1.50
☐ 483	Ted Abernathy	.50	.25	.05
☐ 484	Joe Gordon MG	.75	.35	.07
☐ 485A	Gaylord Perry	6.00	3.00	.60
☐ 485B	Gaylord Perry WL (Perry white)	60.00	30.00	6.00
☐ 486A	Paul Casanova	.50	.25	.05
☐ 486B	Paul Casanova WL (Casanova white)	15.00	7.50	1.50
☐ 487	Denis Menke	.50	.25	.05
☐ 488	Joe Sparma	.50	.25	.05
☐ 489	Clete Boyer	.75	.35	.07
☐ 490	Matty Alou	.75	.35	.07
☐ 491A	Twins Rookies Jerry Crider George Mitterwald	.50	.25	.05
☐ 491B	Twins Rookies WL Jerry Crider George Mitterwald (names in white)	15.00	7.50	1.50
☐ 492	Tony Cloninger	.50	.25	.05

	NRMT	VG-E	GOOD
☐ 493A Wes Parker	.75	.35	.07
☐ 493B Wes Parker WL	15.00	7.50	1.50
(Parker white)			
☐ 494 Ken Berry	.50	.25	.05
☐ 495 Bert Campaneris	.75	.35	.07
☐ 496 Larry Jaster	.50	.25	.05
☐ 497 Julian Javier	.50	.25	.05
☐ 498 Juan Pizarro	.50	.25	.05
☐ 499 Astro Rookies	.50	.25	.05
Don Bryant			
Steve Shea			
☐ 500A Mickey Mantle	175.00	85.00	18.00
☐ 500B Mickey Mantle WL	500.00	250.00	50.00
(Mantle white)			
☐ 501A Tony Gonzalez	.50	.25	.05
☐ 501B Tony Gonzalez WL	15.00	7.50	1.50
(Tony and OF white)			
☐ 502 Minnie Rojas	.50	.25	.05
☐ 503 Larry Brown	.50	.25	.05
☐ 504 Checklist 6	3.00	.30	.10
Brooks Robinson			
☐ 505A Bobby Bolin	.50	.25	.05
☐ 505B Bobby Bolin WL	15.00	7.50	1.50
(Bolin white)			
☐ 506 Paul Blair	.75	.35	.07
☐ 507 Cookie Rojas	.75	.35	.07
☐ 508 Moe Drabowsky	.50	.25	.05
☐ 509 Manny Sanguillen	1.00	.50	.10
☐ 510 Rod Carew	45.00	20.00	4.00
☐ 511A Diego Segui	.50	.25	.05
☐ 511B Diego Segui WL	15.00	7.50	1.50
(Diego and P white)			
☐ 512 Cleon Jones	.50	.25	.05
☐ 513 Camilo Pascual	.85	.40	.08
☐ 514 Mike Lum	.60	.30	.06
☐ 515 Dick Green	.60	.30	.06
☐ 516 Earl Weaver MG	5.00	2.50	.50
☐ 517 Mike McCormick	.85	.40	.08
☐ 518 Fred Whitfield	.60	.30	.06
☐ 519 Yankees Rookies	.60	.30	.06
Gerry Kenney			
Len Boehmer			
☐ 520 Bob Veale	.85	.40	.08
☐ 521 George Thomas	.60	.30	.06
☐ 522 Joe Hoerner	.60	.30	.06
☐ 523 Bob Chance	.60	.30	.06
☐ 524 Expos Rookies	.60	.30	.06
Jose Laboy			
Floyd Wicker			

	NRMT	VG-E	GOOD
☐ 525 Earl Wilson	.60	.30	.06
☐ 526 Hector Torres	.60	.30	.06
☐ 527 Al Lopez MG	2.50	1.25	.25
☐ 528 Claude Osteen	.85	.40	.08
☐ 529 Ed Kirkpatrick	.60	.30	.06
☐ 530 Cesar Tovar	.60	.30	.06
☐ 531 Dick Farrell	.60	.30	.06
☐ 532 Bird Hill Aces	.85	.40	.08
Tom Phoebus			
Jim Hardin			
Dave McNally			
Mike Cuellar			
☐ 533 Nolan Ryan	225.00	110.00	22.00
☐ 534 Jerry McNertney	.60	.30	.06
☐ 535 Phil Regan	.85	.40	.08
☐ 536 Padres Rookies	.60	.30	.06
Danny Breeden			
Dave Roberts			
☐ 537 Mike Paul	.60	.30	.06
☐ 538 Charlie Smith	.60	.30	.06
☐ 539 Ted Shows How	4.00	2.00	.40
Mike Epstein			
Ted Williams			
☐ 540 Curt Flood	1.00	.50	.10
☐ 541 Joe Verbanic	.60	.30	.06
☐ 542 Bob Aspromonte	.60	.30	.06
☐ 543 Fred Newman	.60	.30	.06
☐ 544 Tigers Rookies	.60	.30	.06
Mike Kilkenny			
Ron Woods			
☐ 545 Willie Stargell	10.00	5.00	1.00
☐ 546 Jim Nash	.60	.30	.06
☐ 547 Billy Martin MG	3.00	1.50	.30
☐ 548 Bob Locker	.60	.30	.06
☐ 549 Ron Brand	.60	.30	.06
☐ 550 Brooks Robinson	12.00	5.50	1.10
☐ 551 Wayne Granger	.60	.30	.06
☐ 552 Dodgers Rookies	.85	.40	.08
Ted Sizemore			
Bill Sudakis			
☐ 553 Ron Davis	.60	.30	.06
☐ 554 Frank Bertaina	.60	.30	.06
☐ 555 Jim Ray Hart	.85	.40	.08
☐ 556 A's Stars	.85	.40	.08
Sal Bando			
Bert Campaneris			
Danny Cater			
☐ 557 Frank Fernandez	.60	.30	.06
☐ 558 Tom Burgmeier	.85	.40	.08

		NRMT	VG-E	GOOD
☐ 559	Cardinals Rookies ..	.60	.30	.06
	Joe Hague			
	Jim Hicks			
☐ 560	Luis Tiant	1.25	.60	.12
☐ 561	Ron Clark	.60	.30	.06
☐ 562	Bob Watson	2.50	1.25	.25
☐ 563	Marty Pattin	.60	.30	.06
☐ 564	Gil Hodges MG ...	6.00	3.00	.60
☐ 565	Hoyt Wilhelm	5.50	2.75	.55
☐ 566	Ron Hansen	.60	.30	.06
☐ 567	Pirates Rookies	.60	.30	.06
	Elvio Jimenez			
	Jim Shellenback			
☐ 568	Cecil Upshaw	.60	.30	.06
☐ 569	Billy Harris	.60	.30	.06
☐ 570	Ron Santo	1.50	.75	.15
☐ 571	Cap Peterson	.60	.30	.06
☐ 572	Giants Heroes	7.00	3.50	.70
	Willie McCovey			
	Juan Marichal			
☐ 573	Jim Palmer	20.00	10.00	2.00
☐ 574	George Scott	.85	.40	.08
☐ 575	Bill Singer	.85	.40	.08
☐ 576	Phillies Rookies	.60	.30	.06
	Ron Stone			
	Bill Wilson			
☐ 577	Mike Hegan	.60	.30	.06
☐ 578	Don Bosch	.60	.30	.06
☐ 579	Dave Nelson	.85	.40	.08
☐ 580	Jim Northrup	.85	.40	.08
☐ 581	Gary Nolan	.60	.30	.06
☐ 582A	Checklist 7	3.00	.30	.10
	(white circle on back)			
	(Tony Oliva)			
☐ 582B	Checklist 7	5.00	.50	.10
	(red circle on back)			
	(Tony Oliva)			
☐ 583	Clyde Wright	.60	.30	.06
☐ 584	Don Mason	.60	.30	.06
☐ 585	Ron Swoboda	.85	.40	.08
☐ 586	Tim Cullen	.60	.30	.06
☐ 587	Joe Rudi	2.00	1.00	.20
☐ 588	Bill White	1.50	.75	.15
☐ 589	Joe Pepitone	1.25	.60	.12
☐ 590	Rico Carty	1.25	.60	.12
☐ 591	Mike Hedlund	.80	.40	.08
☐ 592	Padres Rookies	.80	.40	.08
	Rafael Robles			
	Al Santorini			

		NRMT	VG-E	GOOD
☐ 593	Don Nottebart	.80	.40	.08
☐ 594	Dooley Womack	.80	.40	.08
☐ 595	Lee Maye	.80	.40	.08
☐ 596	Chuck Hartenstein ..	.80	.40	.08
☐ 597	A.L. Rookies	40.00	20.00	4.00
	Bob Floyd			
	Larry Burchart			
	Rollie Fingers			
☐ 598	Ruben Amaro	.80	.40	.08
☐ 599	John Boozer	.80	.40	.08
☐ 600	Tony Oliva	3.00	1.50	.30
☐ 601	Tug McGraw	1.50	.75	.15
☐ 602	Cubs Rookies	.80	.40	.08
	Alec Distaso			
	Don Young			
	Jim Qualls			
☐ 603	Joe Keough	.80	.40	.08
☐ 604	Bobby Etheridge ...	.80	.40	.08
☐ 605	Dick Ellsworth	1.25	.60	.12
☐ 606	Gene Mauch MG ...	1.25	.60	.12
☐ 607	Dick Bosman	.80	.40	.08
☐ 608	Dick Simpson	.80	.40	.08
☐ 609	Phil Gagliano	.80	.40	.08
☐ 610	Jim Hardin	.80	.40	.08
☐ 611	Braves Rookies	1.25	.60	.12
	Bob Didier			
	Walt Hriniak			
	Gary Neibauer			
☐ 612	Jack Aker	.80	.40	.08
☐ 613	Jim Beauchamp	.80	.40	.08
☐ 614	Houston Rookies ...	.80	.40	.08
	Tom Griffin			
	Skip Guinn			
☐ 615	Len Gabrielson	.80	.40	.08
☐ 616	Don McMahon	.80	.40	.08
☐ 617	Jesse Gonder	.80	.40	.08
☐ 618	Ramon Webster	.80	.40	.08
☐ 619	Royals Rookies	1.25	.60	.12
	Bill Butler			
	Pat Kelly			
	Juan Rios			
☐ 620	Dean Chance	1.25	.60	.12
☐ 621	Bill Voss	.80	.40	.08
☐ 622	Dan Osinski	.80	.40	.08
☐ 623	Hank Allen	.80	.40	.08
☐ 624	NL Rookies	.80	.40	.08
	Darrel Chaney			
	Duffy Dyer			
	Terry Harmon			

		NRMT	VG-E	GOOD
☐ 625	Mack Jones	.80	.40	.08
	(Batting wrong)			
☐ 626	Gene Michael	1.25	.60	.12
☐ 627	George Stone	.80	.40	.08
☐ 628	Red Sox Rookies ...	1.25	.60	.12
	Bill Conigliaro			
	Syd O'Brien			
	Fred Wenz			
☐ 629	Jack Hamilton	.80	.40	.08
☐ 630	Bobby Bonds	10.00	5.00	1.00
☐ 631	John Kennedy	.80	.40	.08
☐ 632	Jon Warden	.80	.40	.08
☐ 633	Harry Walker MG	.80	.40	.08
☐ 634	Andy Etchebarren ...	.80	.40	.08
☐ 635	George Culver	.80	.40	.08
☐ 636	Woody Held	.80	.40	.08
☐ 637	Padres Rookies	.80	.40	.08
	Jerry DaVanon			
	Frank Reberger			
	Clay Kirby			
☐ 638	Ed Sprague	.80	.40	.08
☐ 639	Barry Moore	.80	.40	.08
☐ 640	Fergie Jenkins	4.00	2.00	.40
☐ 641	NL Rookies	.80	.40	.08
	Bobby Darwin			
	John Miller			
	Tommy Dean			
☐ 642	John Hiller	1.25	.60	.12
☐ 643	Billy Cowan	.80	.40	.08
☐ 644	Chuck Hinton	.80	.40	.08
☐ 645	George Brunet	.80	.40	.08
☐ 646	Expos Rookies	.80	.40	.08
	Dan McGinn			
	Carl Morton			
☐ 647	Dave Wickersham ..	.80	.40	.08
☐ 648	Bobby Wine	.80	.40	.08
☐ 649	Al Jackson	.80	.40	.08
☐ 650	Ted Williams MG	8.00	4.00	.80
☐ 651	Gus Gil	.80	.40	.08
☐ 652	Eddie Watt	.80	.40	.08
☐ 653	Aurelio Rodriguez ...	1.50	.75	.15
	(photo actually			
	Angels' batboy)			
☐ 654	White Sox Rookies .	1.25	.60	.12
	Carlos May			
	Don Secrist			
	Rich Morales			
☐ 655	Mike Hershberger ..	.80	.40	.08
☐ 656	Dan Schneider	.80	.40	.08

		NRMT	VG-E	GOOD
☐ 657	Bobby Murcer	1.50	.75	.15
☐ 658	AL Rookies	.80	.40	.08
	Tom Hall			
	Bill Burbach			
	Jim Miles			
☐ 659	Johnny Podres	1.50	.75	.15
☐ 660	Reggie Smith	1.50	.75	.15
☐ 661	Jim Merritt	.80	.40	.08
☐ 662	Royals Rookies	1.25	.60	.12
	Dick Drago			
	George Spriggs			
	Bob Oliver			
☐ 663	Dick Radatz	1.25	.60	.12
☐ 664	Ron Hunt	1.25	.60	.12

1970 Topps

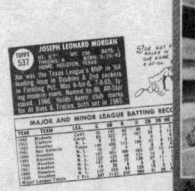 

*The cards in this 720-card set measure 2 ½"
by 3 ½". The Topps set for 1970 has color photos surrounded by white frame lines and gray
borders. The backs have a blue biographical
section and a yellow record section. All-Star
selections are featured on cards 450 to 469.
Other topical subsets within this set include
League Leaders (61-72), Playoffs cards (195-
202), and World Series cards (305-310). There
are graduations of scarcity, terminating in the
high series (634-720), which are outlined in the
value summary.*

			NRMT	VG-E	GOOD
		COMPLETE SET (720)	1650.00	800.00	200.00
		COMMON PLAYER (1-132)	.30	.15	.03
		COMMON PLAYER (133-263)	.35	.17	.03
		COMMON PLAYER (264-459)	.40	.20	.04
		COMMON PLAYER (460-546)	.55	.27	.05
		COMMON PLAYER (547-633)	1.00	.50	.10
		COMMON PLAYER (634-720)	2.25	1.10	.22
☐	1	New York Mets Team Card	6.00	1.00	.20
☐	2	Diego Segui	.30	.15	.03
☐	3	Darrel Chaney	.30	.15	.03
☐	4	Tom Egan	.30	.15	.03
☐	5	Wes Parker	.50	.25	.05
☐	6	Grant Jackson	.30	.15	.03
☐	7	Indians Rookies Gary Boyd Russ Nagelson	.30	.15	.03
☐	8	Jose Martinez	.30	.15	.03
☐	9	Checklist 1	2.00	.20	.04
☐	10	Carl Yastrzemski	27.00	12.50	2.50
☐	11	Nate Colbert	.30	.15	.03
☐	12	John Hiller	.50	.25	.05
☐	13	Jack Hiatt	.30	.15	.03
☐	14	Hank Allen	.30	.15	.03
☐	15	Larry Dierker	.50	.25	.05
☐	16	Charlie Metro MG	.30	.15	.03
☐	17	Hoyt Wilhelm	3.50	1.75	.35
☐	18	Carlos May	.30	.15	.03
☐	19	John Boccabella	.30	.15	.03
☐	20	Dave McNally	.50	.25	.05
☐	21	A's Rookies Vida Blue Gene Tenace	2.50	1.25	.25
☐	22	Ray Washburn	.30	.15	.03
☐	23	Bill Robinson	.50	.25	.05
☐	24	Dick Selma	.30	.15	.03
☐	25	Cesar Tovar	.30	.15	.03
☐	26	Tug McGraw	1.00	.50	.10
☐	27	Chuck Hinton	.30	.15	.03
☐	28	Billy Wilson	.30	.15	.03
☐	29	Sandy Alomar	.30	.15	.03
☐	30	Matty Alou	.50	.25	.05
☐	31	Marty Pattin	.30	.15	.03
☐	32	Harry Walker MG	.30	.15	.03
☐	33	Don Wert	.30	.15	.03
☐	34	Willie Crawford	.30	.15	.03
☐	35	Joel Horlen	.30	.15	.03
☐	36	Red Rookies	.50	.25	.05
		Danny Breeden			
		Bernie Carbo			
☐	37	Dick Drago	.30	.15	.03
☐	38	Mack Jones	.30	.15	.03
☐	39	Mike Nagy	.30	.15	.03
☐	40	Rich Allen	1.00	.50	.10
☐	41	George Lauzerique	.30	.15	.03
☐	42	Tito Fuentes	.30	.15	.03
☐	43	Jack Aker	.30	.15	.03
☐	44	Roberto Pena	.30	.15	.03
☐	45	Dave Johnson	.75	.35	.07
☐	46	Ken Rudolph	.30	.15	.03
☐	47	Bob Miller	.30	.15	.03
☐	48	Gil Garrido	.30	.15	.03
☐	49	Tim Cullen	.30	.15	.03
☐	50	Tommie Agee	.50	.25	.05
☐	51	Bob Christian	.30	.15	.03
☐	52	Bruce Dal Canton	.30	.15	.03
☐	53	John Kennedy	.30	.15	.03
☐	54	Jeff Torborg	.50	.25	.05
☐	55	John Odom	.30	.15	.03
☐	56	Phillies Rookies Joe Lis Scott Reid	.30	.15	.03
☐	57	Pat Kelly	.30	.15	.03
☐	58	Dave Marshall	.30	.15	.03
☐	59	Dick Ellsworth	.50	.25	.05
☐	60	Jim Wynn	.50	.25	.05
☐	61	NL Batting Leaders Pete Rose Bob Clemente Cleon Jones	3.50	1.75	.35
☐	62	AL Batting Leaders Rod Carew Reggie Smith Tony Oliva	1.50	.75	.15
☐	63	NL RBI Leaders Willie McCovey Ron Santo Tony Perez	1.50	.75	.15
☐	64	AL RBI Leaders Harmon Killebrew Boog Powell Reggie Jackson	2.50	1.25	.25
☐	65	NL Home Run Leaders Willie McCovey Hank Aaron Lee May	2.50	1.25	.25

			NRMT	VG-E	GOOD
☐	66	AL Home Run Leaders .... Harmon Killebrew Frank Howard Reggie Jackson	2.50	1.25	.25
☐	67	NL ERA Leaders ... Juan Marichal Steve Carlton Bob Gibson	3.50	1.75	.35
☐	68	AL ERA Leaders ... Dick Bosman Jim Palmer Mike Cuellar	1.50	.75	.15
☐	69	NL Pitching Leaders . Tom Seaver Phil Niekro Fergie Jenkins Juan Marichal	2.50	1.25	.25
☐	70	AL Pitching Leaders . Dennis McLain Mike Cuellar Dave Boswell Dave McNally Jim Perry Mel Stottlemyre	1.50	.75	.15
☐	71	NL Strikeout Leaders Fergie Jenkins Bob Gibson Bill Singer	1.50	.75	.15
☐	72	AL Strikeout Leaders Sam McDowell Mickey Lolich Andy Messersmith	1.50	.75	.15
☐	73	Wayne Granger	.30	.15	.03
☐	74	Angels Rookies .... Greg Washburn Wally Wolf	.30	.15	.03
☐	75	Jim Kaat	2.00	1.00	.20
☐	76	Carl Taylor	.30	.15	.03
☐	77	Frank Linzy	.30	.15	.03
☐	78	Joe Lahoud	.30	.15	.03
☐	79	Clay Kirby	.30	.15	.03
☐	80	Don Kessinger	.50	.25	.05
☐	81	Dave May	.30	.15	.03
☐	82	Frank Fernandez ...	.30	.15	.03
☐	83	Don Cardwell	.30	.15	.03
☐	84	Paul Casanova	.30	.15	.03
☐	85	Max Alvis	.30	.15	.03
☐	86	Lum Harris MG	.30	.15	.03

			NRMT	VG-E	GOOD
☐	87	Steve Renko	.30	.15	.03
☐	88	Pilots Rookies ...... Miguel Fuentes Dick Baney	.30	.15	.03
☐	89	Juan Rios	.30	.15	.03
☐	90	Tim McCarver	1.00	.50	.10
☐	91	Rich Morales	.30	.15	.03
☐	92	George Culver	.30	.15	.03
☐	93	Rick Renick	.30	.15	.03
☐	94	Freddie Patek	.50	.25	.05
☐	95	Earl Wilson	.30	.15	.03
☐	96	Cardinals Rookies .. Leron Lee Jerry Reuss	2.00	1.00	.20
☐	97	Joe Moeller	.30	.15	.03
☐	98	Gates Brown	.50	.25	.05
☐	99	Bobby Pfeil	.30	.15	.03
☐	100	Mel Stottlemyre	1.00	.50	.10
☐	101	Bobby Floyd	.30	.15	.03
☐	102	Joe Rudi	.75	.35	.07
☐	103	Frank Reberger	.30	.15	.03
☐	104	Gerry Moses	.30	.15	.03
☐	105	Tony Gonzalez	.30	.15	.03
☐	106	Darold Knowles	.30	.15	.03
☐	107	Bobby Etheridge ...	.30	.15	.03
☐	108	Tom Burgmeier	.30	.15	.03
☐	109	Expos Rookies ..... Garry Jestadt Carl Morton	.50	.25	.05
☐	110	Bob Moose	.30	.15	.03
☐	111	Mike Hegan	.30	.15	.03
☐	112	Dave Nelson	.30	.15	.03
☐	113	Jim Ray	.30	.15	.03
☐	114	Gene Michael	.50	.25	.05
☐	115	Alex Johnson	.50	.25	.05
☐	116	Sparky Lyle	1.00	.50	.10
☐	117	Don Young	.30	.15	.03
☐	118	George Mitterwald ..	.30	.15	.03
☐	119	Chuck Taylor	.30	.15	.03
☐	120	Sal Bando	.75	.35	.07
☐	121	Orioles Rookies .... Fred Beene Terry Crowley	.50	.25	.05
☐	122	George Stone	.30	.15	.03
☐	123	Don Gutteridge	.30	.15	.03
☐	124	Larry Jaster	.30	.15	.03
☐	125	Deron Johnson	.30	.15	.03
☐	126	Marty Martinez	.30	.15	.03
☐	127	Joe Coleman	.30	.15	.03

		NRMT	VG-E	GOOD				NRMT	VG-E	GOOD
☐ 128	Checklist 2	2.00	.20	.04	☐ 171	Jim Nash		.35	.17	.03
☐ 129	Jimmie Price	.30	.15	.03	☐ 172	Braves Rookies		1.00	.50	.10
☐ 130	Ollie Brown	.30	.15	.03		Garry Hill				
☐ 131	Dodgers Rookies	.30	.15	.03		Ralph Garr				
	Ray Lamb				☐ 173	Jim Hicks		.35	.17	.03
	Bob Stinson				☐ 174	Ted Sizemore		.50	.25	.05
☐ 132	Jim McGlothlin	.30	.15	.03	☐ 175	Dick Bosman		.35	.17	.03
☐ 133	Clay Carroll	.35	.17	.03	☐ 176	Jim Ray Hart		.50	.25	.05
☐ 134	Danny Walton	.35	.17	.03	☐ 177	Jim Northrup		.50	.25	.05
☐ 135	Dick Dietz	.35	.17	.03	☐ 178	Denny Lemaster		.35	.17	.03
☐ 136	Steve Hargan	.35	.17	.03	☐ 179	Ivan Murrell		.35	.17	.03
☐ 137	Art Shamsky	.35	.17	.03	☐ 180	Tommy John		2.50	1.25	.25
☐ 138	Joe Foy	.35	.17	.03	☐ 181	Sparky Anderson MG		1.00	.50	.10
☐ 139	Rich Nye	.35	.17	.03	☐ 182	Dick Hall		.35	.17	.03
☐ 140	Reggie Jackson	75.00	37.50	7.50	☐ 183	Jerry Grote		.35	.17	.03
☐ 141	Pirates Rookies	.50	.25	.05	☐ 184	Ray Fosse		.35	.17	.03
	Dave Cash				☐ 185	Don Mincher		.50	.25	.05
	Johnny Jeter				☐ 186	Rick Joseph		.35	.17	.03
☐ 142	Fritz Peterson	.35	.17	.03	☐ 187	Mike Hedlund		.35	.17	.03
☐ 143	Phil Gagliano	.35	.17	.03	☐ 188	Manny Sanguillen		.75	.35	.07
☐ 144	Ray Culp	.35	.17	.03	☐ 189	Yankees Rookies		60.00	30.00	6.00
☐ 145	Rico Carty	.75	.35	.07		Thurman Munson				
☐ 146	Danny Murphy	.35	.17	.03		Dave McDonald				
☐ 147	Angel Hermoso	.35	.17	.03	☐ 190	Joe Torre		1.00	.50	.10
☐ 148	Earl Weaver MG	1.00	.50	.10	☐ 191	Vicente Romo		.35	.17	.03
☐ 149	Billy Champion	.35	.17	.03	☐ 192	Jim Qualls		.35	.17	.03
☐ 150	Harmon Killebrew	5.00	2.50	.50	☐ 193	Mike Wegener		.35	.17	.03
☐ 151	Dave Roberts	.35	.17	.03	☐ 194	Chuck Manuel		.35	.17	.03
☐ 152	Ike Brown	.35	.17	.03	☐ 195	NL Playoff Game 1		3.50	1.75	.35
☐ 153	Gary Gentry	.35	.17	.03		Seaver wins opener				
☐ 154	Senators Rookies	.35	.17	.03	☐ 196	NL Playoff Game 2		1.50	.75	.15
	Jim Miles					Mets show muscle				
	Jan Dukes				☐ 197	NL Playoff Game 3		4.00	2.00	.40
☐ 155	Denis Menke	.35	.17	.03		Ryan saves the day				
☐ 156	Eddie Fisher	.35	.17	.03	☐ 198	NL Playoff Summary		1.50	.75	.15
☐ 157	Manny Mota	.50	.25	.05		Mets celebrate				
☐ 158	Jerry McNertney	.35	.17	.03	☐ 199	AL Playoff Game 1		1.50	.75	.15
☐ 159	Tommy Helms	.50	.25	.05		Orioles win squeaker				
☐ 160	Phil Niekro	3.50	1.75	.35		(Cuellar)				
☐ 161	Richie Scheinblum	.35	.17	.03	☐ 200	AL Playoff Game 2		1.50	.75	.15
☐ 162	Jerry Johnson	.35	.17	.03		Powell scores winn-				
☐ 163	Syd O'Brien	.35	.17	.03		ing run				
☐ 164	Ty Cline	.35	.17	.03	☐ 201	AL Playoff Game 3		1.50	.75	.15
☐ 165	Ed Kirkpatrick	.35	.17	.03		Birds wrap it up				
☐ 166	Al Oliver	2.00	1.00	.20	☐ 202	AL Playoff Summary		1.50	.75	.15
☐ 167	Bill Burbach	.35	.17	.03		Orioles celebrate				
☐ 168	Dave Watkins	.35	.17	.03	☐ 203	Rudy May		.35	.17	.03
☐ 169	Tom Hall	.35	.17	.03	☐ 204	Len Gabrielson		.35	.17	.03
☐ 170	Billy Williams	4.00	2.00	.40	☐ 205	Bert Campaneris		.50	.25	.05

		NRMT	VG-E	GOOD
☐ 206	Clete Boyer	.50	.25	.05
☐ 207	Tigers Rookies	.35	.17	.03
	Norman McRae			
	Bob Reed			
☐ 208	Fred Gladding	.35	.17	.03
☐ 209	Ken Suarez	.35	.17	.03
☐ 210	Juan Marichal	4.50	2.25	.45
☐ 211	Ted Williams MG	6.00	3.00	.60
☐ 212	Al Santorini	.35	.17	.03
☐ 213	Andy Etchebarren	.35	.17	.03
☐ 214	Ken Boswell	.35	.17	.03
☐ 215	Reggie Smith	1.00	.50	.10
☐ 216	Chuck Hartenstein	.35	.17	.03
☐ 217	Ron Hansen	.35	.17	.03
☐ 218	Ron Stone	.35	.17	.03
☐ 219	Jerry Kenney	.35	.17	.03
☐ 220	Steve Carlton	14.00	6.00	1.25
☐ 221	Ron Brand	.35	.17	.03
☐ 222	Jim Rooker	.35	.17	.03
☐ 223	Nate Oliver	.35	.17	.03
☐ 224	Steve Barber	.35	.17	.03
☐ 225	Lee May	.50	.25	.05
☐ 226	Ron Perranoski	.50	.25	.05
☐ 227	Astros Rookies	1.00	.50	.10
	John Mayberry			
	Bob Watkins			
☐ 228	Aurelio Rodriguez	.35	.17	.03
☐ 229	Rich Robertson	.35	.17	.03
☐ 230	Brooks Robinson	8.00	4.00	.80
☐ 231	Luis Tiant	1.00	.50	.10
☐ 232	Bob Didier	.35	.17	.03
☐ 233	Lew Krausse	.35	.17	.03
☐ 234	Tommy Dean	.35	.17	.03
☐ 235	Mike Epstein	.35	.17	.03
☐ 236	Bob Veale	.50	.25	.05
☐ 237	Russ Gibson	.35	.17	.03
☐ 238	Jose Laboy	.35	.17	.03
☐ 239	Ken Berry	.35	.17	.03
☐ 240	Fergie Jenkins	3.00	1.50	.30
☐ 241	Royals Rookies	.35	.17	.03
	Al Fitzmorris			
	Scott Northey			
☐ 242	Walter Alston MG	1.50	.75	.15
☐ 243	Joe Sparma	.35	.17	.03
☐ 244A	Checklist 3	2.50	.25	.05
	(red bat on front)			
☐ 244B	Checklist 3	3.00	.25	.05
	(brown bat on front)			
☐ 245	Leo Cardenas	.35	.17	.03

		NRMT	VG-E	GOOD
☐ 246	Jim McAndrew	.35	.17	.03
☐ 247	Lou Klimchock	.35	.17	.03
☐ 248	Jesus Alou	.35	.17	.03
☐ 249	Bob Locker	.35	.17	.03
☐ 250	Willie McCovey	6.50	3.25	.65
☐ 251	Dick Schofield	.35	.17	.03
☐ 252	Lowell Palmer	.35	.17	.03
☐ 253	Ron Woods	.35	.17	.03
☐ 254	Camilo Pascual	.50	.25	.05
☐ 255	Jim Spencer	.35	.17	.03
☐ 256	Vic Davalillo	.35	.17	.03
☐ 257	Dennis Higgins	.35	.17	.03
☐ 258	Paul Popovich	.35	.17	.03
☐ 259	Tommie Reynolds	.35	.17	.03
☐ 260	Claude Osteen	.50	.25	.05
☐ 261	Curt Motton	.35	.17	.03
☐ 262	Padres Rookies	.50	.25	.05
	Jerry Morales			
	Jim Williams			
☐ 263	Duane Josephson	.35	.17	.03
☐ 264	Rich Hebner	.75	.35	.07
☐ 265	Randy Hundley	.50	.25	.05
☐ 266	Wally Bunker	.40	.20	.04
☐ 267	Twins Rookies	.40	.20	.04
	Herman Hill			
	Paul Ratliff			
☐ 268	Claude Raymond	.40	.20	.04
☐ 269	Cesar Gutierrez	.40	.20	.04
☐ 270	Chris Short	.40	.20	.04
☐ 271	Greg Goossen	.40	.20	.04
☐ 272	Hector Torres	.40	.20	.04
☐ 273	Ralph Houk MG	.50	.25	.05
☐ 274	Gerry Arrigo	.40	.20	.04
☐ 275	Duke Sims	.40	.20	.04
☐ 276	Ron Hunt	.40	.20	.04
☐ 277	Paul Doyle	.40	.20	.04
☐ 278	Tommie Aaron	.50	.25	.05
☐ 279	Bill Lee	.75	.35	.07
☐ 280	Donn Clendenon	.50	.25	.05
☐ 281	Casey Cox	.40	.20	.04
☐ 282	Steve Huntz	.40	.20	.04
☐ 283	Angel Bravo	.40	.20	.04
☐ 284	Jack Baldschun	.40	.20	.04
☐ 285	Paul Blair	.50	.25	.05
☐ 286	Dodgers Rookies	6.00	3.00	.60
	Jack Jenkins			
	Bill Buckner			
☐ 287	Fred Talbot	.40	.20	.04
☐ 288	Larry Hisle	.50	.25	.05

		NRMT	VG-E	GOOD
☐ 289	Gene Brabender	.40	.20	.04
☐ 290	Rod Carew	18.00	8.50	1.70
☐ 291	Leo Durocher MG	1.25	.60	.12
☐ 292	Eddie Leon	.40	.20	.04
☐ 293	Bob Bailey	.40	.20	.04
☐ 294	Jose Azcue	.40	.20	.04
☐ 295	Cecil Upshaw	.40	.20	.04
☐ 296	Woody Woodward	.50	.25	.05
☐ 297	Curt Blefary	.40	.20	.04
☐ 298	Ken Henderson	.40	.20	.04
☐ 299	Buddy Bradford	.40	.20	.04
☐ 300	Tom Seaver	45.00	22.50	4.50
☐ 301	Chico Salmon	.40	.20	.04
☐ 302	Jeff James	.40	.20	.04
☐ 303	Brant Alyea	.40	.20	.04
☐ 304	Bill Russell	1.50	.75	.15
☐ 305	World Series Game 1	1.50	.75	.15
	Buford leadoff homer			
☐ 306	World Series Game 2	1.50	.75	.15
	Clendenon's homer			
	breaks ice			
☐ 307	World Series Game 3	1.50	.75	.15
	Agee's catch saves			
	the day			
☐ 308	World Series Game 4	1.50	.75	.15
	Martin's bunt ends			
	deadlock			
☐ 309	World Series Game 5	1.50	.75	.15
	Koosman shuts door			
☐ 310	World Series Summary	1.50	.75	.15
	Mets whoop it up			
☐ 311	Dick Green	.40	.20	.04
☐ 312	Mike Torrez	.50	.25	.05
☐ 313	Mayo Smith MG	.40	.20	.04
☐ 314	Bill McCool	.40	.20	.04
☐ 315	Luis Aparicio	3.50	1.75	.35
☐ 316	Skip Guinn	.40	.20	.04
☐ 317	Red Sox Rookies	.50	.25	.05
	Billy Conigliaro			
	Luis Alvarado			
☐ 318	Willie Smith	.40	.20	.04
☐ 319	Clay Dalrymple	.40	.20	.04
☐ 320	Jim Maloney	.50	.25	.05
☐ 321	Lou Piniella	1.25	.60	.12
☐ 322	Luke Walker	.40	.20	.04
☐ 323	Wayne Comer	.40	.20	.04
☐ 324	Tony Taylor	.40	.20	.04
☐ 325	Dave Boswell	.40	.20	.04
☐ 326	Bill Voss	.40	.20	.04

		NRMT	VG-E	GOOD
☐ 327	Hal King	.40	.20	.04
☐ 328	George Brunet	.40	.20	.04
☐ 329	Chris Cannizzaro	.40	.20	.04
☐ 330	Lou Brock	6.00	3.00	.60
☐ 331	Chuck Dobson	.40	.20	.04
☐ 332	Bobby Wine	.40	.20	.04
☐ 333	Bobby Murcer	1.00	.50	.10
☐ 334	Phil Regan	.50	.25	.05
☐ 335	Bill Freehan	.75	.35	.07
☐ 336	Del Unser	.40	.20	.04
☐ 337	Mike McCormick	.50	.25	.05
☐ 338	Paul Schaal	.40	.20	.04
☐ 339	Johnny Edwards	.40	.20	.04
☐ 340	Tony Conigliaro	1.00	.50	.10
☐ 341	Bill Sudakis	.40	.20	.04
☐ 342	Wilbur Wood	.50	.25	.05
☐ 343A	Checklist 4	2.50	.25	.05
	(red bat on front)			
☐ 343B	Checklist 4	3.00	.25	.05
	(brown bat on front)			
☐ 344	Marcelino Lopez	.40	.20	.04
☐ 345	Al Ferrara	.40	.20	.04
☐ 346	Red Schoendienst MG	1.75	.85	.17
☐ 347	Russ Snyder	.40	.20	.04
☐ 348	Mets Rookies	.50	.25	.05
	Mike Jorgensen			
	Jesse Hudson			
☐ 349	Steve Hamilton	.40	.20	.04
☐ 350	Roberto Clemente	35.00	16.00	3.20
☐ 351	Tom Murphy	.40	.20	.04
☐ 352	Bob Barton	.40	.20	.04
☐ 353	Stan Williams	.50	.25	.05
☐ 354	Amos Otis	1.00	.50	.10
☐ 355	Doug Rader	.75	.35	.07
☐ 356	Fred Lasher	.40	.20	.04
☐ 357	Bob Burda	.40	.20	.04
☐ 358	Pedro Borbon	.40	.20	.04
☐ 359	Phil Roof	.40	.20	.04
☐ 360	Curt Flood	1.00	.50	.10
☐ 361	Ray Jarvis	.40	.20	.04
☐ 362	Joe Hague	.40	.20	.04
☐ 363	Tom Shopay	.40	.20	.04
☐ 364	Dan McGinn	.40	.20	.04
☐ 365	Zoilo Versalles	.40	.20	.04
☐ 366	Barry Moore	.40	.20	.04
☐ 367	Mike Lum	.40	.20	.04
☐ 368	Ed Herrmann	.40	.20	.04
☐ 369	Alan Foster	.40	.20	.04
☐ 370	Tommy Harper	.50	.25	.05

		NRMT	VG-E	GOOD
☐ 371	Rod Gaspar	.40	.20	.04
☐ 372	Dave Giusti	.50	.25	.05
☐ 373	Roy White	.75	.35	.07
☐ 374	Tommie Sisk	.40	.20	.04
☐ 375	Johnny Callison	.50	.25	.05
☐ 376	Lefty Phillips MG	.40	.20	.04
☐ 377	Bill Butler	.40	.20	.04
☐ 378	Jim Davenport	.50	.25	.05
☐ 379	Tom Tischinski	.40	.20	.04
☐ 380	Tony Perez	3.50	1.75	.35
☐ 381	Athletics Rookies	.40	.20	.04
	Bobby Brooks			
	Mike Olivo			
☐ 382	Jack DiLauro	.40	.20	.04
☐ 383	Mickey Stanley	.75	.35	.07
☐ 384	Gary Neibauer	.40	.20	.04
☐ 385	George Scott	.75	.35	.07
☐ 386	Bill Dillman	.40	.20	.04
☐ 387	Baltimore Orioles	1.25	.60	.12
	Team Card			
☐ 388	Byron Browne	.40	.20	.04
☐ 389	Jim Shellenback	.40	.20	.04
☐ 390	Willie Davis	.75	.35	.07
☐ 391	Larry Brown	.40	.20	.04
☐ 392	Walt Hriniak	.50	.25	.05
☐ 393	John Gelnar	.40	.20	.04
☐ 394	Gil Hodges MG	3.50	1.75	.35
☐ 395	Walt Williams	.40	.20	.04
☐ 396	Steve Blass	.50	.25	.05
☐ 397	Roger Repoz	.40	.20	.04
☐ 398	Bill Stoneman	.40	.20	.04
☐ 399	New York Yankees	1.50	.75	.15
	Team Card			
☐ 400	Denny McLain	1.00	.50	.10
☐ 401	Giants Rookies	.40	.20	.04
	John Harrell			
	Bernie Williams			
☐ 402	Ellie Rodriguez	.40	.20	.04
☐ 403	Jim Bunning	2.50	1.25	.25
☐ 404	Rich Reese	.50	.25	.05
☐ 405	Bill Hands	.40	.20	.04
☐ 406	Mike Andrews	.40	.20	.04
☐ 407	Bob Watson	.75	.35	.07
☐ 408	Paul Lindblad	.40	.20	.04
☐ 409	Bob Tolan	.50	.25	.05
☐ 410	Boog Powell	2.50	1.25	.25
☐ 411	Los Angeles Dodgers	1.50	.75	.15
	Team Card			
☐ 412	Larry Burchart	.40	.20	.04

		NRMT	VG-E	GOOD
☐ 413	Sonny Jackson	.40	.20	.04
☐ 414	Paul Edmondson	.40	.20	.04
☐ 415	Julian Javier	.50	.25	.05
☐ 416	Joe Verbanic	.40	.20	.04
☐ 417	John Bateman	.40	.20	.04
☐ 418	John Donaldson	.40	.20	.04
☐ 419	Ron Taylor	.40	.20	.04
☐ 420	Ken McMullen	.40	.20	.04
☐ 421	Pat Dobson	.50	.25	.05
☐ 422	Royals Team	1.00	.50	.10
☐ 423	Jerry May	.40	.20	.04
☐ 424	Mike Kilkenny	.40	.20	.04
	(inconsistent design,			
	card # in white circle)			
☐ 425	Bobby Bonds	2.25	1.10	.22
☐ 426	Bill Rigney MG	.40	.20	.04
☐ 427	Fred Norman	.40	.20	.04
☐ 428	Don Buford	.50	.25	.05
☐ 429	Cubs Rookies	.40	.20	.04
	Randy Bobb			
	Jim Cosman			
☐ 430	Andy Messersmith	.50	.25	.05
☐ 431	Ron Swoboda	.50	.25	.05
☐ 432A	Checklist 5	2.50	.25	.05
	("Baseball" in yellow			
	letters)			
☐ 432B	Checklist 5	3.00	.25	.05
	("Baseball" in white			
	letters)			
☐ 433	Ron Bryant	.40	.20	.04
☐ 434	Felipe Alou	.50	.25	.05
☐ 435	Nelson Briles	.50	.25	.05
☐ 436	Philadelphia Phillies	1.00	.50	.10
	Team Card			
☐ 437	Danny Cater	.40	.20	.04
☐ 438	Pat Jarvis	.40	.20	.04
☐ 439	Lee Maye	.40	.20	.04
☐ 440	Bill Mazeroski	1.00	.50	.10
☐ 441	John O'Donoghue	.40	.20	.04
☐ 442	Gene Mauch MG	.50	.25	.05
☐ 443	Al Jackson	.40	.20	.04
☐ 444	White Sox Rookies	.40	.20	.04
	Billy Farmer			
	John Matias			
☐ 445	Vada Pinson	1.00	.50	.10
☐ 446	Billy Grabarkewitz	.40	.20	.04
☐ 447	Lee Stange	.40	.20	.04
☐ 448	Houston Astros	1.00	.50	.10
	Team Card			

		NRMT	VG-E	GOOD
☐ 449	Jim Palmer	12.00	6.00	1.20
☐ 450	Willie McCovey AS	3.50	1.75	.35
☐ 451	Boog Powell AS	.75	.35	.07
☐ 452	Felix Millan AS	.50	.25	.05
☐ 453	Rod Carew AS	4.50	2.25	.45
☐ 454	Ron Santo AS	.50	.25	.05
☐ 455	Brooks Robinson AS	4.00	2.00	.40
☐ 456	Don Kessinger AS	.50	.25	.05
☐ 457	Rico Petrocelli AS	.50	.25	.05
☐ 458	Pete Rose AS	10.00	5.00	1.00
☐ 459	Reggie Jackson AS	10.00	5.00	1.00
☐ 460	Matty Alou AS	.75	.35	.07
☐ 461	Carl Yastrzemski AS	8.00	4.00	.80
☐ 462	Hank Aaron AS	8.00	4.00	.80
☐ 463	Frank Robinson AS	4.00	2.00	.40
☐ 464	Johnny Bench AS	8.00	4.00	.80
☐ 465	Bill Freehan AS	.75	.35	.07
☐ 466	Juan Marichal AS	3.00	1.50	.30
☐ 467	Denny McLain AS	.75	.35	.07
☐ 468	Jerry Koosman AS	.75	.35	.07
☐ 469	Sam McDowell AS	.75	.35	.07
☐ 470	Willie Stargell	6.50	3.25	.65
☐ 471	Chris Zachary	.60	.30	.06
☐ 472	Braves Team	1.25	.60	.12
☐ 473	Don Bryant	.60	.30	.06
☐ 474	Dick Kelley	.60	.30	.06
☐ 475	Dick McAuliffe	.75	.35	.07
☐ 476	Don Shaw	.60	.30	.06
☐ 477	Orioles Rookies	.60	.30	.06
	Al Severinsen			
	Roger Freed			
☐ 478	Bobby Heise	.60	.30	.06
☐ 479	Dick Woodson	.60	.30	.06
☐ 480	Glenn Beckert	.75	.35	.07
☐ 481	Jose Tartabull	.60	.30	.06
☐ 482	Tom Hilgendorf	.60	.30	.06
☐ 483	Gail Hopkins	.60	.30	.06
☐ 484	Gary Nolan	.60	.30	.06
☐ 485	Jay Johnstone	.75	.35	.07
☐ 486	Terry Harmon	.60	.30	.06
☐ 487	Cisco Carlos	.60	.30	.06
☐ 488	J.C. Martin	.60	.30	.06
☐ 489	Eddie Kasko MG	.60	.30	.06
☐ 490	Bill Singer	.75	.35	.07
☐ 491	Graig Nettles	4.00	2.00	.40
☐ 492	Astros Rookies	.60	.30	.06
	Keith Lampard			
	Scipio Spinks			
☐ 493	Lindy McDaniel	.75	.35	.07
☐ 494	Larry Stahl	.60	.30	.06
☐ 495	Dave Morehead	.60	.30	.06
☐ 496	Steve Whitaker	.60	.30	.06
☐ 497	Eddie Watt	.60	.30	.06
☐ 498	Al Weis	.60	.30	.06
☐ 499	Skip Lockwood	.60	.30	.06
☐ 500	Hank Aaron	30.00	13.50	2.70
☐ 501	Chicago White Sox	1.25	.60	.12
	Team Card			
☐ 502	Rollie Fingers	7.00	3.50	.70
☐ 503	Dal Maxvill	.60	.30	.06
☐ 504	Don Pavletich	.60	.30	.06
☐ 505	Ken Holtzman	.75	.35	.07
☐ 506	Ed Stroud	.60	.30	.06
☐ 507	Pat Corrales	.75	.35	.07
☐ 508	Joe Niekro	1.00	.50	.10
☐ 509	Montreal Expos	1.50	.75	.15
	Team Card			
☐ 510	Tony Oliva	1.50	.75	.15
☐ 511	Joe Hoerner	.60	.30	.06
☐ 512	Billy Harris	.60	.30	.06
☐ 513	Preston Gomez MG	.60	.30	.06
☐ 514	Steve Hovley	.60	.30	.06
☐ 515	Don Wilson	.60	.30	.06
☐ 516	Yankees Rookies	.60	.30	.06
	John Ellis			
	Jim Lyttle			
☐ 517	Joe Gibbon	.60	.30	.06
☐ 518	Bill Melton	.60	.30	.06
☐ 519	Don McMahon	.60	.30	.06
☐ 520	Willie Horton	.75	.35	.07
☐ 521	Cal Koonce	.60	.30	.06
☐ 522	Angels Team	1.25	.60	.12
☐ 523	Jose Pena	.60	.30	.06
☐ 524	Alvin Dark MG	.75	.35	.07
☐ 525	Jerry Adair	.60	.30	.06
☐ 526	Ron Herbel	.60	.30	.06
☐ 527	Don Bosch	.60	.30	.06
☐ 528	Elrod Hendricks	.60	.30	.06
☐ 529	Bob Aspromonte	.60	.30	.06
☐ 530	Bob Gibson	8.00	4.00	.80
☐ 531	Ron Clark	.60	.30	.06
☐ 532	Danny Murtaugh MG	.60	.30	.06
☐ 533	Buzz Stephen	.60	.30	.06
☐ 534	Twins Team	1.25	.60	.12
☐ 535	Andy Kosco	.60	.30	.06
☐ 536	Mike Kekich	.60	.30	.06
☐ 537	Joe Morgan	6.50	3.25	.65
☐ 538	Bob Humphreys	.60	.30	.06

		NRMT	VG-E	GOOD
☐ 539	Phillies Rookies .... Dennis Doyle Larry Bowa	4.00	2.00	.40
☐ 540	Gary Peters	.60	.30	.06
☐ 541	Bill Heath	.60	.30	.06
☐ 542	Checklist 6	3.00	.25	.05
☐ 543	Clyde Wright	.60	.30	.06
☐ 544	Cincinnati Reds Team Card	1.50	.75	.15
☐ 545	Ken Harrelson	1.25	.60	.12
☐ 546	Ron Reed	.60	.30	.06
☐ 547	Rick Monday	1.50	.75	.15
☐ 548	Howie Reed	1.00	.50	.10
☐ 549	Cardinals Team	2.00	1.00	.20
☐ 550	Frank Howard	1.50	.75	.15
☐ 551	Dock Ellis	1.00	.50	.10
☐ 552	Royals Rookies .... Don O'Riley Dennis Paepke Fred Rico	1.00	.50	.10
☐ 553	Jim Lefebvre	1.50	.75	.15
☐ 554	Tom Timmermann ..	1.00	.50	.10
☐ 555	Orlando Cepeda	3.00	1.50	.30
☐ 556	Dave Bristol MG	1.00	.50	.10
☐ 557	Ed Kranepool	1.50	.75	.15
☐ 558	Vern Fuller	1.00	.50	.10
☐ 559	Tommy Davis	1.50	.75	.15
☐ 560	Gaylord Perry	6.00	3.00	.60
☐ 561	Tom McCraw	1.00	.50	.10
☐ 562	Ted Abernathy	1.00	.50	.10
☐ 563	Boston Red Sox .... Team Card	2.00	1.00	.20
☐ 564	Johnny Briggs	1.00	.50	.10
☐ 565	Jim Hunter	7.00	3.50	.70
☐ 566	Gene Alley	1.00	.50	.10
☐ 567	Bob Oliver	1.00	.50	.10
☐ 568	Stan Bahnsen	1.00	.50	.10
☐ 569	Cookie Rojas	1.00	.50	.10
☐ 570	Jim Fregosi	1.50	.75	.15
☐ 571	Jim Brewer	1.00	.50	.10
☐ 572	Frank Quilici MG ...	1.00	.50	.10
☐ 573	Padres Rookies .... Mike Corkins Rafael Robles Ron Slocum	1.00	.50	.10
☐ 574	Bobby Bolin	1.00	.50	.10
☐ 575	Cleon Jones	1.00	.50	.10
☐ 576	Milt Pappas	1.50	.75	.15
☐ 577	Bernie Allen	1.00	.50	.10
☐ 578	Tom Griffin	1.00	.50	.10
☐ 579	Detroit Tigers ...... Team Card	2.50	1.25	.25
☐ 580	Pete Rose	75.00	37.50	7.50
☐ 581	Tom Satriano	1.00	.50	.10
☐ 582	Mike Paul	1.00	.50	.10
☐ 583	Hal Lanier	1.50	.75	.15
☐ 584	Al Downing	1.50	.75	.15
☐ 585	Rusty Staub	1.75	.85	.17
☐ 586	Rickey Clark	1.00	.50	.10
☐ 587	Jose Arcia	1.00	.50	.10
☐ 588A	Checklist 7 .... (666 Adolfo)	6.50	.50	.10
☐ 588B	Checklist 7 .... (666 Adolpho)	3.50	.25	.05
☐ 589	Joe Keough	1.00	.50	.10
☐ 590	Mike Cuellar	1.50	.75	.15
☐ 591	Mike Ryan	1.00	.50	.10
☐ 592	Daryl Patterson	1.00	.50	.10
☐ 593	Chicago Cubs ...... Team Card	2.00	1.00	.20
☐ 594	Jake Gibbs	1.00	.50	.10
☐ 595	Maury Wills	2.50	1.25	.25
☐ 596	Mike Hershberger ..	1.00	.50	.10
☐ 597	Sonny Siebert	1.00	.50	.10
☐ 598	Joe Pepitone	1.50	.75	.15
☐ 599	Senators Rookies ... Dick Stelmaszek Gene Martin Dick Such	1.00	.50	.10
☐ 600	Willie Mays	45.00	20.00	4.00
☐ 601	Pete Richert	1.00	.50	.10
☐ 602	Ted Savage	1.00	.50	.10
☐ 603	Ray Oyler	1.00	.50	.10
☐ 604	Clarence Gaston	1.50	.75	.15
☐ 605	Rick Wise	1.50	.75	.15
☐ 606	Chico Ruiz	1.00	.50	.10
☐ 607	Gary Waslewski	1.00	.50	.10
☐ 608	Pittsburgh Pirates ... Team Card	2.00	1.00	.20
☐ 609	Buck Martinez ..... (inconsistent design, card in white circle)	1.00	.50	.10
☐ 610	Jerry Koosman	1.50	.75	.15
☐ 611	Norm Cash	1.50	.75	.15
☐ 612	Jim Hickman	1.00	.50	.10
☐ 613	Dave Baldwin	1.00	.50	.10
☐ 614	Mike Shannon	1.50	.75	.15
☐ 615	Mark Belanger	1.50	.75	.15

		NRMT	VG-E	GOOD
☐ 616	Jim Merritt	1.00	.50	.10
☐ 617	Jim French	1.00	.50	.10
☐ 618	Billy Wynne	1.00	.50	.10
☐ 619	Norm Miller	1.00	.50	.10
☐ 620	Jim Perry	1.50	.75	.15
☐ 621	Braves Rookies	14.00	6.25	1.25
	Mike McQueen			
	Darrell Evans			
	Rick Kester			
☐ 622	Don Sutton	6.50	3.25	.65
☐ 623	Horace Clarke	1.00	.50	.10
☐ 624	Clyde King MG	1.00	.50	.10
☐ 625	Dean Chance	1.50	.75	.15
☐ 626	Dave Ricketts	1.00	.50	.10
☐ 627	Gary Wagner	1.00	.50	.10
☐ 628	Wayne Garrett	1.00	.50	.10
☐ 629	Merv Rettenmund	1.00	.50	.10
☐ 630	Ernie Banks	17.00	8.00	1.60
☐ 631	Oakland Athletics	2.50	1.25	.25
	Team Card			
☐ 632	Gary Sutherland	1.00	.50	.10
☐ 633	Roger Nelson	1.00	.50	.10
☐ 634	Bud Harrelson	3.00	1.50	.30
☐ 635	Bob Allison	3.00	1.50	.30
☐ 636	Jim Stewart	2.25	1.10	.22
☐ 637	Cleveland Indians	4.50	2.25	.45
	Team Card			
☐ 638	Frank Bertaina	2.25	1.10	.22
☐ 639	Dave Campbell	2.25	1.10	.22
☐ 640	Al Kaline	33.00	15.00	3.00
☐ 641	Al McBean	2.25	1.10	.22
☐ 642	Angels Rookies	2.25	1.10	.22
	Greg Garrett			
	Gordon Lund			
	Jarvis Tatum			
☐ 643	Jose Pagan	2.25	1.10	.22
☐ 644	Gerry Nyman	2.25	1.10	.22
☐ 645	Don Money	2.25	1.10	.22
☐ 646	Jim Britton	2.25	1.10	.22
☐ 647	Tom Matchick	2.25	1.10	.22
☐ 648	Larry Haney	2.25	1.10	.22
☐ 649	Jimmie Hall	2.25	1.10	.22
☐ 650	Sam McDowell	3.00	1.50	.30
☐ 651	Jim Gosger	2.25	1.10	.22
☐ 652	Rich Rollins	2.25	1.10	.22
☐ 653	Moe Drabowsky	2.25	1.10	.22
☐ 654	NL Rookies	3.50	1.75	.35
	Oscar Gamble			
	Boots Day			

		NRMT	VG-E	GOOD
	Angel Mangual			
☐ 655	John Roseboro	2.25	1.10	.22
☐ 656	Jim Hardin	2.25	1.10	.22
☐ 657	San Diego Padres	4.50	2.25	.45
	Team Card			
☐ 658	Ken Tatum	2.25	1.10	.22
☐ 659	Pete Ward	2.25	1.10	.22
☐ 660	Johnny Bench	135.00	65.00	13.50
☐ 661	Jerry Robertson	2.25	1.10	.22
☐ 662	Frank Lucchesi MG	2.25	1.10	.22
☐ 663	Tito Francona	2.25	1.10	.22
☐ 664	Bob Robertson	2.25	1.10	.22
☐ 665	Jim Lonborg	3.00	1.50	.30
☐ 666	Adolpho Phillips	2.25	1.10	.22
☐ 667	Bob Meyer	2.25	1.10	.22
☐ 668	Bob Tillman	2.25	1.10	.22
☐ 669	White Sox Rookies	2.25	1.10	.22
	Bart Johnson			
	Dan Lazar			
	Mickey Scott			
☐ 670	Ron Santo	4.00	2.00	.40
☐ 671	Jim Campanis	2.25	1.10	.22
☐ 672	Leon McFadden	2.25	1.10	.22
☐ 673	Ted Uhlaender	2.25	1.10	.22
☐ 674	Dave Leonhard	2.25	1.10	.22
☐ 675	Jose Cardenal	2.25	1.10	.22
☐ 676	Senators Team	4.50	2.25	.45
☐ 677	Woodie Fryman	2.25	1.10	.22
☐ 678	Dave Duncan	2.25	1.10	.22
☐ 679	Ray Sadecki	2.25	1.10	.22
☐ 680	Rico Petrocelli	3.00	1.50	.30
☐ 681	Bob Garibaldi	2.25	1.10	.22
☐ 682	Dalton Jones	2.25	1.10	.22
☐ 683	Reds Rookies	4.00	2.00	.40
	Vern Geishert			
	Hal McRae			
	Wayne Simpson			
☐ 684	Jack Fisher	2.25	1.10	.22
☐ 685	Tom Haller	2.25	1.10	.22
☐ 686	Jackie Hernandez	2.25	1.10	.22
☐ 687	Bob Priddy	2.25	1.10	.22
☐ 688	Ted Kubiak	2.25	1.10	.22
☐ 689	Frank Tepedino	2.25	1.10	.22
☐ 690	Ron Fairly	2.25	1.10	.22
☐ 691	Joe Grzenda	2.25	1.10	.22
☐ 692	Duffy Dyer	2.25	1.10	.22
☐ 693	Bob Johnson	2.25	1.10	.22
☐ 694	Gary Ross	2.25	1.10	.22
☐ 695	Bobby Knoop	2.25	1.10	.22

1971 Topps

			NRMT	VG-E	GOOD
☐	696	San Francisco Giants Team Card	4.50	2.25	.45
☐	697	Jim Hannan	2.25	1.10	.22
☐	698	Tom Tresh	4.00	2.00	.40
☐	699	Hank Aguirre	2.25	1.10	.22
☐	700	Frank Robinson	33.00	15.00	3.00
☐	701	Jack Billingham	2.25	1.10	.22
☐	702	AL Rookies	2.25	1.10	.22
		Bob Johnson			
		Ron Klimkowski			
		Bill Zepp			
☐	703	Lou Marone	2.25	1.10	.22
☐	704	Frank Baker	2.25	1.10	.22
☐	705	Tony Cloninger	2.25	1.10	.22
☐	706	John McNamara MG	6.00	3.00	.60
☐	707	Kevin Collins	2.25	1.10	.22
☐	708	Jose Santiago	2.25	1.10	.22
☐	709	Mike Fiore	2.25	1.10	.22
☐	710	Felix Millan	2.25	1.10	.22
☐	711	Ed Brinkman	2.25	1.10	.22
☐	712	Nolan Ryan	225.00	110.00	22.00
☐	713	Pilots Team	12.00	6.00	1.20
☐	714	Al Spangler	2.25	1.10	.22
☐	715	Mickey Lolich	4.50	2.25	.45
☐	716	Cardinals Rookies	2.25	1.10	.22
		Sal Campisi			
		Reggie Cleveland			
		Santiago Guzman			
☐	717	Tom Phoebus	2.25	1.10	.22
☐	718	Ed Spiezio	2.25	1.10	.22
☐	719	Jim Roland	2.25	1.10	.22
☐	720	Rick Reichardt	3.00	1.50	.30

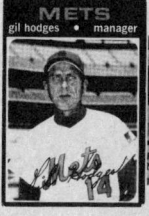 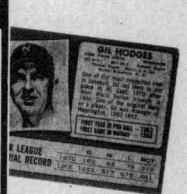

*The cards in this 752-card set measure 2 ½"
by 3 ½". The 1971 Topps set is a challenge to
complete in strict mint condition because the
black obverse border is easily scratched and
damaged. An unusual feature of this set is that
the player is also pictured in black and white
on the back of the card. Featured subsets
within this set include League Leaders (61-72),
Playoffs cards (195-202), and World Series
cards (327-332). Cards 524-643 and the last
series (644-752) are somewhat scarce. The
last series was printed in two sheets of 132.
On the printing sheets 44 cards were printed
in 50% greater quantity than the other 66
cards. These 66 (slightly) shorter-printed
numbers are identified in the checklist below
by SP.*

	NRMT	VG-E	GOOD
COMPLETE SET (752)	1600.00	750.00	200.00
COMMON PLAYER (1-263)	.35	.17	.03
COMMON PLAYER (264-393)	.40	.20	.04
COMMON PLAYER (394-523)	.60	.30	.06
COMMON PLAYER (524-643)	1.00	.50	.10
COMMON PLAYER (644-752)	2.50	1.10	.22
COMMON SP (644-752)	3.50	1.50	.30

☐	1	Baltimore Orioles Team Card	6.00	1.00	.20
☐	2	Dock Ellis	.35	.17	.03
☐	3	Dick McAuliffe	.35	.17	.03
☐	4	Vic Davalillo	.35	.17	.03

			NRMT	VG-E	GOOD
☐	5	Thurman Munson ...	21.00	10.50	2.10
☐	6	Ed Spiezio	.35	.17	.03
☐	7	Jim Holt	.35	.17	.03
☐	8	Mike McQueen	.35	.17	.03
☐	9	George Scott	.50	.25	.05
☐	10	Claude Osteen	.50	.25	.05
☐	11	Elliott Maddox	.35	.17	.03
☐	12	Johnny Callison	.50	.25	.05
☐	13	White Sox Rookies	.35	.17	.03
		Charlie Brinkman			
		Dick Moloney			
☐	14	Dave Concepcion	6.00	3.00	.60
☐	15	Andy Messersmith	.50	.25	.05
☐	16	Ken Singleton	2.00	1.00	.20
☐	17	Billy Sorrell	.35	.17	.03
☐	18	Norm Miller	.35	.17	.03
☐	19	Skip Pitlock	.35	.17	.03
☐	20	Reggie Jackson	36.00	16.00	3.50
☐	21	Dan McGinn	.35	.17	.03
☐	22	Phil Roof	.35	.17	.03
☐	23	Oscar Gamble	.50	.25	.05
☐	24	Rich Hand	.35	.17	.03
☐	25	Clarence Gaston	.75	.35	.07
☐	26	Bert Blyleven	30.00	15.00	3.00
☐	27	Pirates Rookies	.35	.17	.03
		Fred Cambria			
		Gene Clines			
☐	28	Ron Klimkowski	.35	.17	.03
☐	29	Don Buford	.50	.25	.05
☐	30	Phil Niekro	3.50	1.75	.35
☐	31	Eddie Kasko MG	.35	.17	.03
☐	32	Jerry DaVanon	.35	.17	.03
☐	33	Del Unser	.35	.17	.03
☐	34	Sandy Vance	.35	.17	.03
☐	35	Lou Piniella	1.00	.50	.10
☐	36	Dean Chance	.50	.25	.05
☐	37	Rich McKinney	.35	.17	.03
☐	38	Jim Colborn	.35	.17	.03
☐	39	Tiger Rookies	.35	.17	.03
		Lerrin LaGrow			
		Gene Lamont			
☐	40	Lee May	.50	.25	.05
☐	41	Rick Austin	.35	.17	.03
☐	42	Boots Day	.35	.17	.03
☐	43	Steve Kealey	.35	.17	.03
☐	44	Johnny Edwards	.35	.17	.03
☐	45	Jim Hunter	4.50	2.25	.45
☐	46	Dave Campbell	.35	.17	.03
☐	47	Johnny Jeter	.35	.17	.03

			NRMT	VG-E	GOOD
☐	48	Dave Baldwin	.35	.17	.03
☐	49	Don Money	.35	.17	.03
☐	50	Willie McCovey	6.00	3.00	.60
☐	51	Steve Kline	.35	.17	.03
☐	52	Braves Rookies	.50	.25	.05
		Oscar Brown			
		Earl Williams			
☐	53	Paul Blair	.50	.25	.05
☐	54	Checklist 1	2.00	.20	.04
☐	55	Steve Carlton	14.00	6.50	1.25
☐	56	Duane Josephson	.35	.17	.03
☐	57	Von Joshua	.35	.17	.03
☐	58	Bill Lee	.50	.25	.05
☐	59	Gene Mauch MG	.50	.25	.05
☐	60	Dick Bosman	.35	.17	.03
☐	61	AL Batting Leaders	2.00	1.00	.20
		Alex Johnson			
		Carl Yastrzemski			
		Tony Oliva			
☐	62	NL Batting Leaders	1.25	.60	.12
		Rico Carty			
		Joe Torre			
		Manny Sanguillen			
☐	63	AL RBI Leaders	1.25	.60	.12
		Frank Howard			
		Tony Conigliaro			
		Boog Powell			
☐	64	NL RBI Leaders	2.00	1.00	.20
		Johnny Bench			
		Tony Perez			
		Billy Williams			
☐	65	AL HR Leaders	2.00	1.00	.20
		Frank Howard			
		Harmon Killebrew			
		Carl Yastrzemski			
☐	66	NL HR Leaders	2.00	1.00	.20
		Johnny Bench			
		Billy Williams			
		Tony Perez			
☐	67	AL ERA Leaders	1.25	.60	.12
		Diego Segui			
		Jim Palmer			
		Clyde Wright			
☐	68	NL ERA Leaders	1.25	.60	.12
		Tom Seaver			
		Wayne Simpson			
		Luke Walker			
☐	69	AL Pitching Leaders	1.25	.60	.12
		Mike Cuellar			

		NRMT	VG-E	GOOD
	Dave McNally			
	Jim Perry			
☐ 70	NL Pitching Leaders .	2.00	1.00	.20
	Bob Gibson			
	Gaylord Perry			
	Fergie Jenkins			
☐ 71	AL Strikeout Leaders	1.25	.60	.12
	Sam McDowell			
	Mickey Lolich			
	Bob Johnson			
☐ 72	NL Strikeout Leaders	2.00	1.00	.20
	Tom Seaver			
	Bob Gibson			
	Fergie Jenkins			
☐ 73	George Brunet	.35	.17	.03
☐ 74	Twins Rookies	.35	.17	.03
	Pete Hamm			
	Jim Nettles			
☐ 75	Gary Nolan	.35	.17	.03
☐ 76	Ted Savage	.35	.17	.03
☐ 77	Mike Compton	.35	.17	.03
☐ 78	Jim Spencer	.35	.17	.03
☐ 79	Wade Blasingame	.35	.17	.03
☐ 80	Bill Melton	.35	.17	.03
☐ 81	Felix Millan	.35	.17	.03
☐ 82	Casey Cox	.35	.17	.03
☐ 83	Met Rookies	.50	.25	
	Tim Foli			
	Randy Bobb			
☐ 84	Marcel Lachemann	.50	.25	.05
☐ 85	Billy Grabarkewitz	.35	.17	.03
☐ 86	Mike Kilkenny	.35	.17	.03
☐ 87	Jack Heidemann	.35	.17	.03
☐ 88	Hal King	.35	.17	.03
☐ 89	Ken Brett	.50	.25	.05
☐ 90	Joe Pepitone	.75	.35	.07
☐ 91	Bob Lemon MG	1.50	.75	.15
☐ 92	Fred Wenz	.35	.17	.03
☐ 93	Senators Rookies	.35	.17	.03
	Norm McRae			
	Denny Riddleberger			
☐ 94	Don Hahn	.35	.17	.03
☐ 95	Luis Tiant	.75	.35	.07
☐ 96	Joe Hague	.35	.17	.03
☐ 97	Floyd Wicker	.35	.17	.03
☐ 98	Joe Decker	.35	.17	.03
☐ 99	Mark Belanger	.50	.25	.05
☐ 100	Pete Rose	45.00	22.50	4.50
☐ 101	Les Cain	.35	.17	.03

		NRMT	VG-E	GOOD
☐ 102	Astros Rookies	1.00	.50	.10
	Ken Forsch			
	Larry Howard			
☐ 103	Rich Severson	.35	.17	.03
☐ 104	Dan Frisella	.35	.17	.03
☐ 105	Tony Conigliaro	1.00	.50	.10
☐ 106	Tom Dukes	.35	.17	.03
☐ 107	Roy Foster	.35	.17	.03
☐ 108	John Cumberland	.35	.17	.03
☐ 109	Steve Hovley	.35	.17	.03
☐ 110	Bill Mazeroski	.75	.35	.07
☐ 111	Yankee Rookies	.35	.17	.03
	Loyd Colson			
	Bobby Mitchell			
☐ 112	Manny Mota	.50	.25	.05
☐ 113	Jerry Crider	.35	.17	.03
☐ 114	Billy Conigliaro	.50	.25	.05
☐ 115	Donn Clendenon	.50	.25	.05
☐ 116	Ken Sanders	.35	.17	.03
☐ 117	Ted Simmons	8.00	4.00	.80
☐ 118	Cookie Rojas	.50	.25	.05
☐ 119	Frank Lucchesi MG	.35	.17	.03
☐ 120	Willie Horton	.50	.25	.05
☐ 121	Cubs Rookies	.35	.17	.03
	Jim Dunegan			
	Roe Skidmore			
☐ 122	Eddie Watt	.35	.17	.03
☐ 123A	Checklist 2	2.50	.25	
	(card number at bottom right)			
☐ 123B	Checklist 2	3.00	.25	.05
	(card number centered)			
☐ 124	Don Gullett	.75	.35	.07
☐ 125	Ray Fosse	.35	.17	.03
☐ 126	Danny Coombs	.35	.17	.03
☐ 127	Danny Thompson	.35	.17	.03
☐ 128	Frank Johnson	.35	.17	.03
☐ 129	Aurelio Monteagudo	.35	.17	.03
☐ 130	Denis Menke	.35	.17	.03
☐ 131	Curt Blefary	.35	.17	.03
☐ 132	Jose Laboy	.35	.17	.03
☐ 133	Mickey Lolich	1.00	.50	.10
☐ 134	Jose Arcia	.35	.17	.03
☐ 135	Rick Monday	.50	.25	.05
☐ 136	Duffy Dyer	.35	.17	.03
☐ 137	Marcelino Lopez	.35	.17	.03
☐ 138	Phillies Rookies	.50	.25	.05
	Joe Lis			
	Willie Montanez			

		NRMT	VG-E	GOOD			NRMT	VG-E	GOOD
☐ 139	Paul Casanova	.35	.17	.03	☐ 181	Hal Lanier	.50	.25	.05
☐ 140	Gaylord Perry	3.50	1.75	.35	☐ 182	Al Downing	.50	.25	.05
☐ 141	Frank Quilici	.35	.17	.03	☐ 183	Gil Hodges MG	3.00	1.50	.30
☐ 142	Mack Jones	.35	.17	.03	☐ 184	Stan Bahnsen	.35	.17	.03
☐ 143	Steve Blass	.50	.25	.05	☐ 185	Julian Javier	.35	.17	.03
☐ 144	Jackie Hernandez	.35	.17	.03	☐ 186	Bob Spence	.35	.17	.03
☐ 145	Bill Singer	.50	.25	.05	☐ 187	Ted Abernathy	.35	.17	.03
☐ 146	Ralph Houk MG	.50	.25	.05	☐ 188	Dodgers Rookies	2.00	1.00	.20
☐ 147	Bob Priddy	.35	.17	.03		Bob Valentine			
☐ 148	John Mayberry	.50	.25	.05		Mike Strahler			
☐ 149	Mike Hershberger	.35	.17	.03	☐ 189	George Mitterwald	.35	.17	.03
☐ 150	Sam McDowell	.50	.25	.05	☐ 190	Bob Tolan	.50	.25	.05
☐ 151	Tommy Davis	.50	.25	.05	☐ 191	Mike Andrews	.35	.17	.03
☐ 152	Angels Rookies	.35	.17	.03	☐ 192	Billy Wilson	.35	.17	.03
	Lloyd Allen				☐ 193	Bob Grich	2.25	1.10	.22
	Winston Llenas				☐ 194	Mike Lum	.35	.17	.03
☐ 153	Gary Ross	.35	.17	.03	☐ 195	AL Playoff Game 1	1.50	.75	.15
☐ 154	Cesar Gutierrez	.35	.17	.03		Powell muscles Twins			
☐ 155	Ken Henderson	.35	.17	.03	☐ 196	AL Playoff Game 2	1.50	.75	.15
☐ 156	Bart Johnson	.35	.17	.03		McNally makes it two			
☐ 157	Bob Bailey	.35	.17	.03		straight			
☐ 158	Jerry Reuss	.75	.35	.07	☐ 197	AL Playoff Game 3	2.50	1.25	.25
☐ 159	Jarvis Tatum	.35	.17	.03		Palmer mows 'em			
☐ 160	Tom Seaver	30.00	15.00	3.00		down			
☐ 161	Coin Checklist	2.00	.20	.04	☐ 198	AL Playoff Summary	1.50	.75	.15
☐ 162	Jack Billingham	.35	.17	.03		Orioles celebrate			
☐ 163	Buck Martinez	.35	.17	.03	☐ 199	NL Playoff Game 1	1.50	.75	.15
☐ 164	Reds Rookies	.50	.25	.05		Cline pinch-triple de-			
	Frank Duffy					cides it			
	Milt Wilcox				☐ 200	NL Playoff Game 2	1.50	.75	.15
☐ 165	Cesar Tovar	.35	.17	.03		Tolan scores for third			
☐ 166	Joe Hoerner	.35	.17	.03		time			
☐ 167	Tom Grieve	1.00	.50	.10	☐ 201	NL Playoff Game 3	1.50	.75	.15
☐ 168	Bruce Dal Canton	.35	.17	.03		Cline scores winning			
☐ 169	Ed Herrmann	.35	.17	.03		run			
☐ 170	Mike Cuellar	.50	.25	.05	☐ 202	NL Playoff Summary	1.50	.75	.15
☐ 171	Bobby Wine	.35	.17	.03		Reds celebrate			
☐ 172	Duke Sims	.35	.17	.03	☐ 203	Larry Gura	.75	.35	.07
☐ 173	Gil Garrido	.35	.17	.03	☐ 204	Brewers Rookies	.35	.17	.03
☐ 174	Dave LaRoche	.35	.17	.03		Bernie Smith			
☐ 175	Jim Hickman	.35	.17	.03		George Kopacz			
☐ 176	Red Sox Rookies	.35	.17	.03	☐ 205	Gerry Moses	.35	.17	.03
	Bob Montgomery				☐ 206	Checklist 3	2.00	.20	.04
	Doug Griffin				☐ 207	Alan Foster	.35	.17	.03
☐ 177	Hal McRae	.75	.35	.07	☐ 208	Billy Martin MG	2.50	1.25	.25
☐ 178	Dave Duncan	.35	.17	.03	☐ 209	Steve Renko	.35	.17	.03
☐ 179	Mike Corkins	.35	.17	.03	☐ 210	Rod Carew	18.00	8.50	1.70
☐ 180	Al Kaline UER	12.00	5.00	1.00	☐ 211	Phil Hennigan	.35	.17	.03
	(Home instead of Birth)				☐ 212	Rich Hebner	.50	.25	.05

		NRMT	VG-E	GOOD
☐ 213	Frank Baker	.35	.17	.03
☐ 214	Al Ferrara	.35	.17	.03
☐ 215	Diego Segui	.35	.17	.03
☐ 216	Cards Rookies	.35	.17	.03
	Reggie Cleveland			
	Luis Melendez			
☐ 217	Ed Stroud	.35	.17	.03
☐ 218	Tony Cloninger	.35	.17	.03
☐ 219	Elrod Hendricks	.35	.17	.03
☐ 220	Ron Santo	1.00	.50	.10
☐ 221	Dave Morehead	.35	.17	.03
☐ 222	Bob Watson	.50	.25	.05
☐ 223	Cecil Upshaw	.35	.17	.03
☐ 224	Alan Gallagher	.35	.17	.03
☐ 225	Gary Peters	.35	.17	.03
☐ 226	Bill Russell	.75	.35	.07
☐ 227	Floyd Weaver	.35	.17	.03
☐ 228	Wayne Garrett	.35	.17	.03
☐ 229	Jim Hannan	.35	.17	.03
☐ 230	Willie Stargell	6.50	3.25	.65
☐ 231	Indians Rookies	.50	.25	.05
	Vince Colbert			
	John Lowenstein			
☐ 232	John Strohmayer	.35	.17	.03
☐ 233	Larry Bowa	1.75	.85	.17
☐ 234	Jim Lyttle	.35	.17	.03
☐ 235	Nate Colbert	.35	.17	.03
☐ 236	Bob Humphreys	.35	.17	.03
☐ 237	Cesar Cedeno	1.50	.75	.15
☐ 238	Chuck Dobson	.35	.17	.03
☐ 239	Red Schoendienst MG	1.25	.60	.12
☐ 240	Clyde Wright	.35	.17	.03
☐ 241	Dave Nelson	.35	.17	.03
☐ 242	Jim Ray	.35	.17	.03
☐ 243	Carlos May	.35	.17	.03
☐ 244	Bob Tillman	.35	.17	.03
☐ 245	Jim Kaat	2.00	1.00	.20
☐ 246	Tony Taylor	.35	.17	.03
☐ 247	Royals Rookies	.75	.35	.07
	Jerry Cram			
	Paul Splittorff			
☐ 248	Hoyt Wilhelm	3.50	1.75	.35
☐ 249	Chico Salmon	.35	.17	.03
☐ 250	Johnny Bench	36.00	16.00	3.50
☐ 251	Frank Reberger	.35	.17	.03
☐ 252	Eddie Leon	.35	.17	.03
☐ 253	Bill Sudakis	.35	.17	.03
☐ 254	Cal Koonce	.35	.17	.03
☐ 255	Bob Robertson	.35	.17	.03

		NRMT	VG-E	GOOD
☐ 256	Tony Gonzalez	.35	.17	.03
☐ 257	Nelson Briles	.35	.17	.03
☐ 258	Dick Green	.35	.17	.03
☐ 259	Dave Marshall	.35	.17	.03
☐ 260	Tommy Harper	.50	.25	.05
☐ 261	Darold Knowles	.35	.17	.03
☐ 262	Padres Rookies	.35	.17	.03
	Jim Williams			
	Dave Robinson			
☐ 263	John Ellis	.35	.17	.03
☐ 264	Joe Morgan	6.00	3.00	.60
☐ 265	Jim Northrup	.50	.25	.05
☐ 266	Bill Stoneman	.40	.20	.04
☐ 267	Rich Morales	.40	.20	.04
☐ 268	Phillies Team	1.00	.50	.10
☐ 269	Gail Hopkins	.40	.20	.04
☐ 270	Rico Carty	.75	.35	.07
☐ 271	Bill Zepp	.40	.20	.04
☐ 272	Tommy Helms	.50	.25	.05
☐ 273	Pete Richert	.40	.20	.04
☐ 274	Ron Slocum	.40	.20	.04
☐ 275	Vada Pinson	1.00	.50	.10
☐ 276	Giants Rookies	5.00	2.50	.50
	Mike Davison			
	George Foster			
☐ 277	Gary Waslewski	.40	.20	.04
☐ 278	Jerry Grote	.40	.20	.04
☐ 279	Lefty Phillips MG	.40	.20	.04
☐ 280	Fergie Jenkins	3.00	1.50	.30
☐ 281	Danny Walton	.40	.20	.04
☐ 282	Jose Pagan	.40	.20	.04
☐ 283	Dick Such	.40	.20	.04
☐ 284	Jim Gosger	.40	.20	.04
☐ 285	Sal Bando	.75	.35	.07
☐ 286	Jerry McNertney	.40	.20	.04
☐ 287	Mike Fiore	.40	.20	.04
☐ 288	Joe Moeller	.40	.20	.04
☐ 289	White Sox Team	1.00	.50	.10
☐ 290	Tony Oliva	2.00	1.00	.20
☐ 291	George Culver	.40	.20	.04
☐ 292	Jay Johnstone	.75	.35	.07
☐ 293	Pat Corrales	.50	.25	.05
☐ 294	Steve Dunning	.40	.20	.04
☐ 295	Bobby Bonds	1.50	.75	.15
☐ 296	Tom Timmermann	.40	.20	.04
☐ 297	Johnny Briggs	.40	.20	.04
☐ 298	Jim Nelson	.40	.20	.04
☐ 299	Ed Kirkpatrick	.40	.20	.04
☐ 300	Brooks Robinson	9.00	4.50	.90

		NRMT	VG-E	GOOD			NRMT	VG-E	GOOD
☐ 301	Earl Wilson	.40	.20	.04	☐ 337	Jesus Alou	.40	.20	.04
☐ 302	Phil Gagliano	.40	.20	.04	☐ 338	Gene Tenace	.75	.35	.07
☐ 303	Lindy McDaniel	.50	.25	.05	☐ 339	Wayne Simpson	.40	.20	.04
☐ 304	Ron Brand	.40	.20	.04	☐ 340	Rico Petrocelli	.50	.25	.05
☐ 305	Reggie Smith	.75	.35	.07	☐ 341	Steve Garvey	75.00	37.50	7.50
☐ 306	Jim Nash	.40	.20	.04	☐ 342	Frank Tepedino	.40	.20	.04
☐ 307	Don Wert	.40	.20	.04	☐ 343	Pirates Rookies	.40	.20	.04
☐ 308	St. Louis Cardinals	1.00	.50	.10		Ed Acosta			
	Team Card					Milt May			
☐ 309	Dick Ellsworth	.50	.25	.05	☐ 344	Ellie Rodriguez	.40	.20	.04
☐ 310	Tommie Agee	.50	.25	.05	☐ 345	Joel Horlen	.40	.20	.04
☐ 311	Lee Stange	.40	.20	.04	☐ 346	Lum Harris MG	.40	.20	.04
☐ 312	Harry Walker MG	.40	.20	.04	☐ 347	Ted Uhlaender	.40	.20	.04
☐ 313	Tom Hall	.40	.20	.04	☐ 348	Fred Norman	.40	.20	.04
☐ 314	Jeff Torborg	.50	.25	.05	☐ 349	Rich Reese	.40	.20	.04
☐ 315	Ron Fairly	.50	.25	.05	☐ 350	Billy Williams	4.00	2.00	.40
☐ 316	Fred Scherman	.40	.20	.04	☐ 351	Jim Shellenback	.40	.20	.04
☐ 317	Athletic Rookies	.40	.20	.04	☐ 352	Denny Doyle	.40	.20	.04
	Jim Driscoll				☐ 353	Carl Taylor	.40	.20	.04
	Angel Mangual				☐ 354	Don McMahon	.40	.20	.04
☐ 318	Rudy May	.40	.20	.04	☐ 355	Bud Harrelson	.50	.25	.05
☐ 319	Ty Cline	.40	.20	.04	☐ 356	Bob Locker	.40	.20	.04
☐ 320	Dave McNally	.50	.25	.05	☐ 357	Reds Team	1.00	.50	.10
☐ 321	Tom Matchick	.40	.20	.04	☐ 358	Danny Cater	.40	.20	.04
☐ 322	Jim Beauchamp	.40	.20	.04	☐ 359	Ron Reed	.40	.20	.04
☐ 323	Billy Champion	.40	.20	.04	☐ 360	Jim Fregosi	.75	.35	.07
☐ 324	Graig Nettles	2.25	1.10	.22	☐ 361	Don Sutton	3.50	1.75	.35
☐ 325	Juan Marichal	4.50	2.25	.45	☐ 362	Orioles Rookies	.40	.20	.04
☐ 326	Richie Scheinblum	.40	.20	.04		Mike Adamson			
☐ 327	World Series Game 1	1.50	.75	.15		Roger Freed			
	Powell homers to op-				☐ 363	Mike Nagy	.40	.20	.04
	posite field				☐ 364	Tommy Dean	.40	.20	.04
☐ 328	World Series Game 2	1.50	.75	.15	☐ 365	Bob Johnson	.40	.20	.04
	Don Buford				☐ 366	Ron Stone	.40	.20	.04
☐ 329	World Series Game 3	2.00	1.00	.20	☐ 367	Dalton Jones	.40	.20	.04
	Frank Robinson				☐ 368	Bob Veale	.50	.25	.05
	shows muscle				☐ 369	Checklist 4	2.00	.20	.04
☐ 330	World Series Game 4	1.50	.75	.15	☐ 370	Joe Torre	2.00	1.00	.20
	Reds stay alive				☐ 371	Jack Hiatt	.40	.20	.04
☐ 331	World Series Game 5	2.00	1.00	.20	☐ 372	Lew Krausse	.40	.20	.04
	Brooks Robinson com-				☐ 373	Tom McCraw	.40	.20	.04
	mits robbery				☐ 374	Clete Boyer	.50	.25	.05
☐ 332	World Series Summary	1.50	.75	.15	☐ 375	Steve Hargan	.40	.20	.04
	Orioles celebrate				☐ 376	Expos Rookies	.40	.20	.04
☐ 333	Clay Kirby	.40	.20	.04		Clyde Mashore			
☐ 334	Roberto Pena	.40	.20	.04		Ernie McAnally			
☐ 335	Jerry Koosman	.75	.35	.07	☐ 377	Greg Garrett	.40	.20	.04
☐ 336	Detroit Tigers	1.00	.50	.10	☐ 378	Tito Fuentes	.40	.20	.04
	Team Card				☐ 379	Wayne Granger	.40	.20	.04

		NRMT	VG-E	GOOD
☐ 380	Ted Williams MG	5.00	2.50	.50
☐ 381	Fred Gladding	.40	.20	.04
☐ 382	Jake Gibbs	.40	.20	.04
☐ 383	Rod Gaspar	.40	.20	.04
☐ 384	Rollie Fingers	4.00	2.00	.40
☐ 385	Maury Wills	1.50	.75	.15
☐ 386	Red Sox Team	1.00	.50	.10
☐ 387	Ron Herbel	.40	.20	.04
☐ 388	Al Oliver	1.75	.85	.17
☐ 389	Ed Brinkman	.40	.20	.04
☐ 390	Glenn Beckert	.50	.25	.05
☐ 391	Twins Rookies	.50	.25	.05
	Steve Brye			
	Cotton Nash			
☐ 392	Grant Jackson	.40	.20	.04
☐ 393	Merv Rettenmund	.40	.20	.04
☐ 394	Clay Carroll	.60	.30	.06
☐ 395	Roy White	.75	.35	.07
☐ 396	Dick Schofield	.60	.30	.06
☐ 397	Alvin Dark MG	.75	.35	.07
☐ 398	Howie Reed	.60	.30	.06
☐ 399	Jim French	.60	.30	.06
☐ 400	Hank Aaron	30.00	14.00	2.80
☐ 401	Tom Murphy	.60	.30	.06
☐ 402	Dodgers Team	1.25	.60	.12
☐ 403	Joe Coleman	.60	.30	.06
☐ 404	Astros Rookies	.60	.30	.06
	Buddy Harris			
	Roger Metzger			
☐ 405	Leo Cardenas	.60	.30	.06
☐ 406	Ray Sadecki	.60	.30	.06
☐ 407	Joe Rudi	.75	.35	.07
☐ 408	Rafael Robles	.60	.30	.06
☐ 409	Don Pavletich	.60	.30	.06
☐ 410	Ken Holtzman	.75	.35	.07
☐ 411	George Spriggs	.60	.30	.06
☐ 412	Jerry Johnson	.60	.30	.06
☐ 413	Pat Kelly	.60	.30	.06
☐ 414	Woodie Fryman	.60	.30	.06
☐ 415	Mike Hegan	.60	.30	.06
☐ 416	Gene Alley	.75	.35	.07
☐ 417	Dick Hall	.60	.30	.06
☐ 418	Adolfo Phillips	.60	.30	.06
☐ 419	Ron Hansen	.60	.30	.06
☐ 420	Jim Merritt	.60	.30	.06
☐ 421	John Stephenson	.60	.30	.06
☐ 422	Frank Bertaina	.60	.30	.06
☐ 423	Tigers Rookies	.60	.30	.06
	Dennis Saunders			

		NRMT	VG-E	GOOD
	Tim Marting			
☐ 424	R. Rodriquez	.60	.30	.06
☐ 425	Doug Rader	1.00	.50	.10
☐ 426	Chris Cannizzaro	.60	.30	.06
☐ 427	Bernie Allen	.60	.30	.06
☐ 428	Jim McAndrew	.60	.30	.06
☐ 429	Chuck Hinton	.60	.30	.06
☐ 430	Wes Parker	.75	.35	.07
☐ 431	Tom Burgmeier	.60	.30	.06
☐ 432	Bob Didier	.60	.30	.06
☐ 433	Skip Lockwood	.60	.30	.06
☐ 434	Gary Sutherland	.60	.30	.06
☐ 435	Jose Cardenal	.60	.30	.06
☐ 436	Wilbur Wood	.75	.35	.07
☐ 437	Danny Murtaugh MG	.60	.30	.06
☐ 438	Mike McCormick	.75	.35	.07
☐ 439	Phillies Rookies	2.25	1.10	.22
	Greg Luzinski			
	Scott Reid			
☐ 440	Bert Campaneris	.75	.35	.07
☐ 441	Milt Pappas	.75	.35	.07
☐ 442	California Angels	1.25	.60	.12
	Team Card			
☐ 443	Rich Robertson	.60	.30	.06
☐ 444	Jimmie Price	.60	.30	.06
☐ 445	Art Shamsky	.60	.30	.06
☐ 446	Bobby Bolin	.60	.30	.06
☐ 447	Cesar Geronimo	.60	.30	.06
☐ 448	Dave Roberts	.60	.30	.06
☐ 449	Brant Alyea	.60	.30	.06
☐ 450	Bob Gibson	7.50	3.75	.75
☐ 451	Joe Keough	.60	.30	.06
☐ 452	John Boccabella	.60	.30	.06
☐ 453	Terry Crowley	.60	.30	.06
☐ 454	Mike Paul	.60	.30	.06
☐ 455	Don Kessinger	.75	.35	.07
☐ 456	Bob Meyer	.60	.30	.06
☐ 457	Willie Smith	.60	.30	.06
☐ 458	White Sox Rookies	.60	.30	.06
	Ron Lolich			
	Dave Lemonds			
☐ 459	Jim Lefebvre	1.00	.50	.10
☐ 460	Fritz Peterson	.60	.30	.06
☐ 461	Jim Ray Hart	.75	.35	.07
☐ 462	Senators Team	1.25	.60	.12
☐ 463	Tom Kelley	.60	.30	.06
☐ 464	Aurelio Rodriguez	.60	.30	.06
☐ 465	Tim McCarver	1.25	.60	.12
☐ 466	Ken Berry	.60	.30	.06

		NRMT	VG-E	GOOD
☐ 467	Al Santorini	.60	.30	.06
☐ 468	Frank Fernandez	.60	.30	.06
☐ 469	Bob Aspromonte	.60	.30	.06
☐ 470	Bob Oliver	.60	.30	.06
☐ 471	Tom Griffin	.60	.30	.06
☐ 472	Ken Rudolph	.60	.30	.06
☐ 473	Gary Wagner	.60	.30	.06
☐ 474	Jim Fairey	.60	.30	.06
☐ 475	Ron Perranoski	.75	.35	.07
☐ 476	Dal Maxvill	.60	.30	.06
☐ 477	Earl Weaver MG	1.00	.50	.10
☐ 478	Bernie Carbo	.60	.30	.06
☐ 479	Dennis Higgins	.60	.30	.06
☐ 480	Manny Sanguillen	1.00	.50	.10
☐ 481	Daryl Patterson	.60	.30	.06
☐ 482	Padres Team	1.25	.60	.12
☐ 483	Gene Michael	.75	.35	.07
☐ 484	Don Wilson	.60	.30	.06
☐ 485	Ken McMullen	.60	.30	.06
☐ 486	Steve Huntz	.60	.30	.06
☐ 487	Paul Schaal	.60	.30	.06
☐ 488	Jerry Stephenson	.60	.30	.06
☐ 489	Luis Alvarado	.60	.30	.06
☐ 490	Deron Johnson	.75	.35	.07
☐ 491	Jim Hardin	.60	.30	.06
☐ 492	Ken Boswell	.60	.30	.06
☐ 493	Dave May	.60	.30	.06
☐ 494	Braves Rookies	.75	.35	.07
	Ralph Garr			
	Rick Kester			
☐ 495	Felipe Alou	.75	.35	.07
☐ 496	Woody Woodward	.75	.35	.07
☐ 497	Horacio Pina	.60	.30	.06
☐ 498	John Kennedy	.60	.30	.06
☐ 499	Checklist 5	2.00	.20	.04
☐ 500	Jim Perry	1.00	.50	.10
☐ 501	Andy Etchebarren	.60	.30	.06
☐ 502	Cubs Team	1.25	.60	.12
☐ 503	Gates Brown	.75	.35	.07
☐ 504	Ken Wright	.60	.30	.06
☐ 505	Ollie Brown	.60	.30	.06
☐ 506	Bobby Knoop	.60	.30	.06
☐ 507	George Stone	.60	.30	.06
☐ 508	Roger Repoz	.60	.30	.06
☐ 509	Jim Grant	.60	.30	.06
☐ 510	Ken Harrelson	1.00	.50	.10
☐ 511	Chris Short	.60	.30	.06
☐ 512	Red Sox Rookies	.60	.30	.06
	Dick Mills			

		NRMT	VG-E	GOOD
	Mike Garman			
☐ 513	Nolan Ryan	90.00	37.50	7.50
☐ 514	Ron Woods	.60	.30	.06
☐ 515	Carl Morton	.60	.30	.06
☐ 516	Ted Kubiak	.60	.30	.06
☐ 517	Charlie Fox MG	.60	.30	.06
☐ 518	Joe Grzenda	.60	.30	.06
☐ 519	Willie Crawford	.60	.30	.06
☐ 520	Tommy John	2.50	1.25	.25
☐ 521	Leron Lee	.60	.30	.06
☐ 522	Twins Team	1.25	.60	.12
☐ 523	John Odom	.60	.30	.06
☐ 524	Mickey Stanley	1.50	.75	.15
☐ 525	Ernie Banks	17.00	7.50	1.50
☐ 526	Ray Jarvis	1.00	.50	.10
☐ 527	Cleon Jones	1.00	.50	.10
☐ 528	Wally Bunker	1.00	.50	.10
☐ 529	NL Rookie Infielders	3.50	1.75	.35
	Enzo Hernandez			
	Bill Buckner			
	Marty Perez			
☐ 530	Carl Yastrzemski	35.00	17.50	3.50
☐ 531	Mike Torrez	1.00	.50	.10
☐ 532	Bill Rigney MG	1.00	.50	.10
☐ 533	Mike Ryan	1.00	.50	.10
☐ 534	Luke Walker	1.00	.50	.10
☐ 535	Curt Flood	1.50	.75	.15
☐ 536	Claude Raymond	1.00	.50	.10
☐ 537	Tom Egan	1.00	.50	.10
☐ 538	Angel Bravo	1.00	.50	.10
☐ 539	Larry Brown	1.00	.50	.10
☐ 540	Larry Dierker	1.00	.50	.10
☐ 541	Bob Burda	1.00	.50	.10
☐ 542	Bob Miller	1.00	.50	.10
☐ 543	New York Yankees	2.50	1.25	.25
	Team Card			
☐ 544	Vida Blue	3.00	1.50	.30
☐ 545	Dick Dietz	1.00	.50	.10
☐ 546	John Matias	1.00	.50	.10
☐ 547	Pat Dobson	1.00	.50	.10
☐ 548	Don Mason	1.00	.50	.10
☐ 549	Jim Brewer	1.00	.50	.10
☐ 550	Harmon Killebrew	12.00	6.00	1.20
☐ 551	Frank Linzy	1.00	.50	.10
☐ 552	Buddy Bradford	1.00	.50	.10
☐ 553	Kevin Collins	1.00	.50	.10
☐ 554	Lowell Palmer	1.00	.50	.10
☐ 555	Walt Williams	1.00	.50	.10
☐ 556	Jim McGlothlin	1.00	.50	.10

	NRMT	VG-E	GOOD			NRMT	VG-E	GOOD
☐ 557 Tom Satriano	1.00	.50	.10	☐ 597 Ken Suarez	1.00	.50	.10
☐ 558 Hector Torres	1.00	.50	.10	☐ 598 Rick Wise	1.50	.75	.15
☐ 559 AL Rookie Pitchers	1.00	.50	.10	☐ 599 Norm Cash	2.00	1.00	.20
Terry Cox				☐ 600 Willie Mays	50.00	20.00	4.00
Bill Gogolewski				☐ 601 Ken Tatum	1.00	.50	.10
Gary Jones				☐ 602 Marty Martinez	1.00	.50	.10
☐ 560 Rusty Staub	2.00	1.00	.20	☐ 603 Pirates Team	2.00	1.00	.20
☐ 561 Syd O'Brien	1.00	.50	.10	☐ 604 John Gelnar	1.00	.50	.10
☐ 562 Dave Giusti	1.00	.50	.10	☐ 605 Orlando Cepeda	3.50	1.75	.35
☐ 563 Giants Team	2.00	1.00	.20	☐ 606 Chuck Taylor	1.00	.50	.10
☐ 564 Al Fitzmorris	1.00	.50	.10	☐ 607 Paul Ratliff	1.00	.50	.10
☐ 565 Jim Wynn	1.50	.75	.15	☐ 608 Mike Wegener	1.00	.50	.10
☐ 566 Tim Cullen	1.00	.50	.10	☐ 609 Leo Durocher MG	2.00	1.00	.20
☐ 567 Walt Alston MG	2.50	1.25	.25	☐ 610 Amos Otis	1.50	.75	.15
☐ 568 Sal Campisi	1.00	.50	.10	☐ 611 Tom Phoebus	1.00	.50	.10
☐ 569 Ivan Murrell	1.00	.50	.10	☐ 612 Indians Rookies	1.00	.50	.10
☐ 570 Jim Palmer	14.00	6.00	1.20	Lou Camilli			
☐ 571 Ted Sizemore	1.00	.50	.10	Ted Ford			
☐ 572 Jerry Kenney	1.00	.50	.10	Steve Mingori			
☐ 573 Ed Kranepool	1.50	.75	.15	☐ 613 Pedro Borbon	1.00	.50	.10
☐ 574 Jim Bunning	2.50	1.25	.25	☐ 614 Billy Cowan	1.00	.50	.10
☐ 575 Bill Freehan	1.50	.75	.15	☐ 615 Mel Stottlemyre	2.00	1.00	.20
☐ 576 Cubs Rookies	1.00	.50	.10	☐ 616 Larry Hisle	1.00	.50	.10
Adrian Garrett				☐ 617 Clay Dalrymple	1.00	.50	.10
Brock Davis				☐ 618 Tug McGraw	2.00	1.00	.20
Garry Jestadt				☐ 619A Checklist 6	3.00	.25	.05
☐ 578 Jim Lonborg	1.50	.75	.15	(copyright on back)			
☐ 578 Ron Hunt	1.00	.50	.10	☐ 619B Checklist 6	4.00	.25	.05
☐ 579 Marty Pattin	1.00	.50	.10	(no copyright)			
☐ 580 Tony Perez	4.00	2.00	.40	☐ 620 Frank Howard	2.00	1.00	.20
☐ 581 Roger Nelson	1.00	.50	.10	☐ 621 Ron Bryant	1.00	.50	.10
☐ 582 Dave Cash	1.00	.50	.10	☐ 622 Joe Lahoud	1.00	.50	.10
☐ 583 Ron Cook	1.00	.50	.10	☐ 623 Pat Jarvis	1.00	.50	.10
☐ 584 Indians Team	2.00	1.00	.20	☐ 624 Athletics Team	2.00	1.00	.20
☐ 585 Willie Davis	1.50	.75	.15	☐ 625 Lou Brock	12.00	6.00	1.20
☐ 586 Dick Woodson	1.00	.50	.10	☐ 626 Freddie Patek	1.50	.75	.15
☐ 587 Sonny Jackson	1.00	.50	.10	☐ 627 Steve Hamilton	1.00	.50	.10
☐ 588 Tom Bradley	1.00	.50	.10	☐ 628 John Bateman	1.00	.50	.10
☐ 589 Bob Barton	1.00	.50	.10	☐ 629 John Hiller	1.50	.75	.15
☐ 590 Alex Johnson	1.00	.50	.10	☐ 630 Roberto Clemente	35.00	15.00	3.00
☐ 591 Jackie Brown	1.00	.50	.10	☐ 631 Eddie Fisher	1.00	.50	.10
☐ 592 Randy Hundley	1.00	.50	.10	☐ 632 Darrel Chaney	1.00	.50	.10
☐ 593 Jack Aker	1.00	.50	.10	☐ 633 AL Rookie Outfielders	1.00	.50	.10
☐ 594 Cards Rookies	2.00	1.00	.20	Bobby Brooks			
Bob Chlupsa				Pete Koegel			
Bob Stinson				Scott Northey			
Al Hrabosky				☐ 634 Phil Regan	1.50	.75	.15
☐ 595 Dave Johnson	2.00	1.00	.20	☐ 635 Bobby Murcer	2.00	1.00	.20
☐ 596 Mike Jorgensen	1.00	.50	.10	☐ 636 Denny Lemaster	1.00	.50	.10

		NRMT	VG-E	GOOD
☐ 637	Dave Bristol MG	1.00	.50	.10
☐ 638	Stan Williams	1.00	.50	.10
☐ 639	Tom Haller	1.00	.50	.10
☐ 640	Frank Robinson	18.00	8.00	1.60
☐ 641	New York Mets	3.00	1.50	.30
	Team Card			
☐ 642	Jim Roland	1.00	.50	.10
☐ 643	Rick Reichardt	1.00	.50	.10
☐ 644	Jim Stewart SP	3.50	1.50	.30
☐ 645	Jim Maloney SP ...	3.50	1.50	.30
☐ 646	Bobby Floyd SP ...	3.50	1.50	.30
☐ 647	Juan Pizarro	2.50	1.10	.22
☐ 648	Mets Rookies SP ...	4.50	2.00	.40
	Rich Folkers			
	Ted Martinez			
	John Matlack			
☐ 649	Sparky Lyle SP	4.50	2.00	.40
☐ 650	Rich Allen SP	8.00	3.75	.75
☐ 651	Jerry Robertson SP .	3.50	1.50	.30
☐ 652	Braves Team	5.00	2.25	.45
☐ 653	Russ Snyder SP ...	3.50	1.50	.30
☐ 654	Don Shaw SP	3.50	1.50	.30
☐ 655	Mike Epstein SP ...	3.50	1.50	.30
☐ 656	Gerry Nyman SP ...	3.50	1.50	.30
☐ 657	Jose Azcue	2.50	1.10	.22
☐ 658	Paul Lindblad SP ...	3.50	1.50	.30
☐ 659	Byron Browne SP ...	3.50	1.50	.30
☐ 660	Ray Culp	2.50	1.10	.22
☐ 661	Chuck Tanner MG SP	4.00	1.75	.35
☐ 662	Mike Hedlund SP ...	3.50	1.50	.30
☐ 663	Marv Staehle	2.50	1.10	.22
☐ 664	Rookie Pitchers SP .	3.50	1.50	.30
	Archie Reynolds			
	Bob Reynolds			
	Ken Reynolds			
☐ 665	Ron Swoboda SP ...	3.50	1.50	.30
☐ 666	Gene Brabender SP .	3.50	1.50	.30
☐ 667	Pete Ward	2.50	1.10	.22
☐ 668	Gary Neibauer	2.50	1.10	.22
☐ 669	Ike Brown SP	3.50	1.50	.30
☐ 670	Bill Hands	2.50	1.10	.22
☐ 671	Bill Voss SP	3.50	1.50	.30
☐ 672	Ed Crosby SP	3.50	1.50	.30
☐ 673	Gerry Janeski SP ...	3.50	1.50	.30
☐ 674	Montreal Expos	5.00	2.25	.45
	Team Card			
☐ 675	Dave Boswell	2.50	1.10	.22
☐ 676	Tommie Reynolds ...	2.50	1.10	.22
☐ 677	Jack DiLauro	3.50	1.50	.30

		NRMT	VG-E	GOOD
☐ 678	George Thomas	2.50	1.10	.22
☐ 679	Don O'Riley	2.50	1.10	.22
☐ 680	Don Mincher SP	3.50	1.50	.30
☐ 681	Bill Butler	2.50	1.10	.22
☐ 682	Terry Harmon	2.50	1.10	.22
☐ 683	Bill Burbach SP	3.50	1.50	.30
☐ 684	Curt Motton	2.50	1.10	.22
☐ 685	Moe Drabowsky	2.50	1.10	.22
☐ 686	Chico Ruiz SP	3.50	1.50	.30
☐ 687	Ron Taylor SP	3.50	1.50	.30
☐ 688	Sparky Anderson MG			
	SP	6.50	3.00	.60
☐ 689	Frank Baker	2.50	1.10	.22
☐ 690	Bob Moose	2.50	1.10	.22
☐ 691	Bobby Heise	2.50	1.10	.22
☐ 692	AL Rookie Pitchers SP	3.50	1.50	.30
	Hal Haydel			
	Rogelio Moret			
	Wayne Twitchell			
☐ 693	Jose Pena SP	3.50	1.50	.30
☐ 694	Rick Renick SP	3.50	1.50	.30
☐ 695	Joe Niekro	4.00	2.00	.40
☐ 696	Jerry Morales	2.50	1.10	.22
☐ 697	Rickey Clark SP	3.50	1.50	.30
☐ 698	Milwaukee Brewers			
	SP Team Card ...	7.00	3.00	.60
☐ 699	Jim Britton	2.50	1.10	.22
☐ 700	Boog Powell SP	6.50	3.00	.60
☐ 701	Bob Garibaldi	2.50	1.10	.22
☐ 702	Milt Ramirez	2.50	1.10	.22
☐ 703	Mike Kekich	2.50	1.10	.22
☐ 704	J.C. Martin SP	3.50	1.50	.30
☐ 705	Dick Selma SP	3.50	1.50	.30
☐ 706	Joe Foy SP	3.50	1.50	.30
☐ 707	Fred Lasher	2.50	1.10	.22
☐ 708	Russ Nagelson SP ..	3.50	1.50	.30
☐ 709	Rookie Outfielders SP	25.00	12.50	2.50
	Dusty Baker			
	Don Baylor			
	Tom Paciorek			
☐ 710	Sonny Siebert	2.50	1.10	.22
☐ 711	Larry Stahl SP	3.50	1.50	.30
☐ 712	Jose Martinez	2.50	1.10	.22
☐ 713	Mike Marshall SP ..	4.00	1.75	.35
☐ 714	Dick Williams MG SP	4.00	1.75	.35
☐ 715	Horace Clarke SP ..	4.00	1.50	.30
☐ 716	Dave Leonhard	2.50	1.10	.22
☐ 717	Tommie Aaron SP ..	4.00	1.75	.35
☐ 718	Billy Wynne	2.50	1.10	.22

1972 Topps

			NRMT	VG-E	GOOD
☐ 719	Jerry May SP	....	3.50	1.50	.30
☐ 720	Matty Alou	....	3.50	1.50	.30
☐ 721	John Morris	....	2.50	1.10	.22
☐ 722	Houston Astros SP Team Card	..	7.00	3.00	.60
☐ 723	Vicente Romo SP	...	3.50	1.50	.30
☐ 724	Tom Tischinski SP	...	3.50	1.50	.30
☐ 725	Gary Gentry SP	...	3.50	1.50	.30
☐ 726	Paul Popovich	....	2.50	1.10	.22
☐ 727	Ray Lamb SP	....	3.50	1.50	.30
☐ 728	NL Rookie Outfielders Wayne Redmond Keith Lampard Bernie Williams		2.50	1.10	.22
☐ 729	Dick Billings	....	2.50	1.10	.22
☐ 730	Jim Rooker	....	2.50	1.10	.22
☐ 731	Jim Qualls SP	...	3.50	1.50	.30
☐ 732	Bob Reed	....	2.50	1.10	.22
☐ 733	Lee Maye SP	......	3.50	1.50	.30
☐ 734	Rob Gardner SP	....	3.50	1.50	.30
☐ 735	Mike Shannon SP	...	4.50	2.00	.40
☐ 736	Mel Queen SP	.....	3.50	1.50	.30
☐ 737	Preston Gomez MG SP		3.50	1.50	.30
☐ 738	Russ Gibson SP	....	3.50	1.50	.30
☐ 739	Barry Lersch SP	....	3.50	1.50	.30
☐ 740	Luis Aparicio SP	...	12.50	6.00	1.20
☐ 741	Skip Guinn	....	2.50	1.10	.22
☐ 742	Kansas City Royals Team Card	..	5.00	2.25	.45
☐ 743	John O'Donoghue SP	..	3.50	1.50	.30
☐ 744	Chuck Manuel SP	..	3.50	1.50	.30
☐ 745	Sandy Alomar SP	...	3.50	1.50	.30
☐ 746	Andy Kosco	....	2.50	1.10	.22
☐ 747	NL Rookie Pitchers Al Severinsen Scipio Spinks Balor Moore		2.50	1.10	.22
☐ 748	John Purdin SP	....	3.50	1.50	.30
☐ 749	Ken Szotkiewicz	....	2.50	1.10	.22
☐ 750	Denny McLain SP	...	6.00	3.00	.50
☐ 751	Al Weis SP	....	4.00	1.50	.30
☐ 752	Dick Drago	....	3.50	1.50	.30

*The cards in this 787-card set measure 2 ½"
by 3 ½". The 1972 Topps set contained the
most cards ever for a Topps set to that point
in time. Features appearing for the first time
were "Boyhood Photos" (KP: 341-348 and 491-
498), Awards and Trophy cards (621-626), "In
Action" (distributed throughout the set), and
"Traded Cards" (TR: 751-757). Other subsets
included League Leaders (85-96), Playoffs
cards (221-222), and World Series cards (223-
230). The curved lines of the color picture are
a departure from the rectangular designs of
other years. There is a series of intermediate
scarcity (526-656) and the usual high numbers
(657-787).*

		NRMT	VG-E	GOOD
COMPLETE SET (787)	....	1500.00	750.00	200.00
COMMON PLAYER (1-132)	....	.30	.15	.03
COMMON PLAYER (133-263)	...	.35	.17	.03
COMMON PLAYER (264-394)	...	.40	.20	.04
COMMON PLAYER (395-525)	...	.60	.30	.06
COMMON PLAYER (526-656)	...	1.00	.50	.10
COMMON PLAYER (657-787)	...	2.25	1.10	.22
☐ 1	Pittsburgh Pirates Team Card	4.00	.75	.15
☐ 2	Ray Culp	....	.30	.15	.03
☐ 3	Bob Tolan	....	.30	.15	.03
☐ 4	Checklist 1	....	1.50	.20	.04
☐ 5	John Bateman	......	.30	.15	.03
☐ 6	Fred Scherman	......	.30	.15	.03

			NRMT	VG-E	GOOD
☐	7	Enzo Hernandez	.30	.15	.03
☐	8	Ron Swoboda	.30	.15	.03
☐	9	Stan Williams	.30	.15	.03
☐	10	Amos Otis	.50	.25	.05
☐	11	Bobby Valentine	.75	.35	.07
☐	12	Jose Cardenal	.30	.15	.03
☐	13	Joe Grzenda	.30	.15	.03
☐	14	Phillies Rookies	.30	.15	.03
		Pete Koegel			
		Mike Anderson			
		Wayne Twitchell			
☐	15	Walt Williams	.30	.15	.03
☐	16	Mike Jorgensen	.30	.15	.03
☐	17	Dave Duncan	.30	.15	.03
☐	18A	Juan Pizarro	.30	.15	.03
		(yellow underline C			
		and S of Cubs)			
☐	18B	Juan Pizarro	5.00	2.50	.50
		(green underline C			
		and S of Cubs)			
☐	19	Billy Cowan	.30	.15	.03
☐	20	Don Wilson	.30	.15	.03
☐	21	Braves Team	.75	.35	.07
☐	22	Rob Gardner	.30	.15	.03
☐	23	Ted Kubiak	.30	.15	.03
☐	24	Ted Ford	.30	.15	.03
☐	25	Bill Singer	.50	.25	.05
☐	26	Andy Etchebarren	.30	.15	.03
☐	27	Bob Johnson	.30	.15	.03
☐	28	Twins Rookies	.30	.15	.03
		Bob Gebhard			
		Steve Brye			
		Hal Haydel			
☐	29A	Bill Bonham	.30	.15	.03
		(yellow underline C			
		and S of Cubs)			
☐	29B	Bill Bonham	5.00	2.50	.50
		(green underline C			
		and S of Cubs)			
☐	30	Rico Petrocelli	.50	.25	.05
☐	31	Cleon Jones	.30	.15	.03
☐	32	Jones In Action	.30	.15	.03
☐	33	Billy Martin MG	2.50	1.25	.25
☐	34	Martin In Action	1.00	.50	.10
☐	35	Jerry Johnson	.30	.15	.03
☐	36	Johnson In Action	.30	.15	.03
☐	37	Carl Yastrzemski	16.00	8.00	1.60
☐	38	Yastrzemski In Action	6.50	3.25	.65
☐	39	Bob Barton	.30	.15	.03

			NRMT	VG-E	GOOD
☐	40	Barton In Action	.30	.15	.03
☐	41	Tommy Davis	.50	.25	.05
☐	42	Davis In Action	.30	.15	.03
☐	43	Rick Wise	.30	.15	.03
☐	44	Wise In Action	.30	.15	.03
☐	45A	Glenn Beckert	.50	.25	.05
		(yellow underline C			
		and S of Cubs)			
☐	45B	Glenn Beckert	5.00	2.50	.50
		(green underline C			
		and S of Cubs)			
☐	46	Beckert In Action	.30	.15	.03
☐	47	John Ellis	.30	.15	.03
☐	48	Ellis In Action	.30	.15	.03
☐	49	Willie Mays	20.00	9.00	1.80
☐	50	Mays In Action	7.50	3.50	.70
☐	51	Harmon Killebrew	4.00	2.00	.40
☐	52	Killebrew In Action	1.50	.75	.15
☐	53	Bud Harrelson	.50	.25	.05
☐	54	Harrelson In Action	.30	.15	.03
☐	55	Clyde Wright	.30	.15	.03
☐	56	Rich Chiles	.30	.15	.03
☐	57	Bob Oliver	.30	.15	.03
☐	58	Ernie McAnally	.30	.15	.03
☐	59	Fred Stanley	.30	.15	.03
☐	60	Manny Sanguillen	.50	.25	.05
☐	61	Cubs Rookies	.75	.35	.07
		Burt Hooton			
		Gene Hiser			
		Earl Stephenson			
☐	62	Angel Mangual	.30	.15	.03
☐	63	Duke Sims	.30	.15	.03
☐	64	Pete Broberg	.30	.15	.03
☐	65	Cesar Cedeno	.75	.35	.07
☐	66	Ray Corbin	.30	.15	.03
☐	67	Red Schoendienst MG	1.25	.60	.12
☐	68	Jim York	.30	.15	.03
☐	69	Roger Freed	.30	.15	.03
☐	70	Mike Cuellar	.50	.25	.05
☐	71	Angels Team	.75	.35	.07
☐	72	Bruce Kison	.75	.35	.07
☐	73	Steve Huntz	.30	.15	.03
☐	74	Cecil Upshaw	.30	.15	.03
☐	75	Bert Campaneris	.50	.25	.05
☐	76	Don Carrithers	.30	.15	.03
☐	77	Ron Theobald	.30	.15	.03
☐	78	Steve Arlin	.30	.15	.03
☐	79	Red Sox Rookies	60.00	30.00	6.00
		Mike Garman			

			NRMT	VG-E	GOOD
		Cecil Cooper			
		Carlton Fisk			
☐	80	Tony Perez	2.50	1.25	.25
☐	81	Mike Hedlund	.30	.15	.03
☐	82	Ron Woods	.30	.15	.03
☐	83	Dalton Jones	.30	.15	.03
☐	84	Vince Colbert	.30	.15	.03
☐	85	NL Batting Leaders	1.00	.50	.10
		Joe Torre			
		Ralph Garr			
		Glenn Beckert			
☐	86	AL Batting Leaders	1.00	.50	.10
		Tony Oliva			
		Bobby Murcer			
		Merv Rettenmund			
☐	87	NL RBI Leaders	2.00	1.00	.20
		Joe Torre			
		Willie Stargell			
		Hank Aaron			
☐	88	AL RBI Leaders	1.50	.75	.15
		Harmon Killebrew			
		Frank Robinson			
		Reggie Smith			
☐	89	NL Home Run Leaders	2.00	1.00	.20
		Willie Stargell			
		Hank Aaron			
		Lee May			
☐	90	AL Home Run Leaders	1.50	.75	.15
		Bill Melton			
		Norm Cash			
		Reggie Jackson			
☐	91	NL ERA Leaders	1.50	.75	.15
		Tom Seaver			
		Dave Roberts			
		(photo actually			
		Danny Coombs)			
		Don Wilson			
☐	92	AL ERA Leaders	1.00	.50	.10
		Vida Blue			
		Wilbur Wood			
		Jim Palmer			
☐	93	NL Pitching Leaders	1.50	.75	.15
		Fergie Jenkins			
		Steve Carlton			
		Al Downing			
		Tom Seaver			
☐	94	AL Pitching Leaders	1.00	.50	.10

			NRMT	VG-E	GOOD
		Mickey Lolich			
		Vida Blue			
		Wilbur Wood			
☐	95	NL Strikeout Leaders	1.50	.75	.15
		Tom Seaver			
		Fergie Jenkins			
		Bill Stoneman			
☐	96	AL Strikeout Leaders	1.00	.50	.10
		Mickey Lolich			
		Vida Blue			
		Joe Coleman			
☐	97	Tom Kelley	.30	.15	.03
☐	98	Chuck Tanner MG	.50	.25	.05
☐	99	Ross Grimsley	.30	.15	.03
☑	100	Frank Robinson	4.50	2.25	.45
☐	101	Astros Rookies	1.50	.75	.15
		Bill Greif			
		J.R. Richard			
		Ray Busse			
☐	102	Lloyd Allen	.30	.15	.03
☐	103	Checklist 2	1.50	.20	.04
☐	104	Toby Harrah	1.25	.60	.12
☐	105	Gary Gentry	.30	.15	.03
☐	106	Brewers Team	.75	.35	.07
☐	107	Jose Cruz	1.50	.75	.15
☐	108	Gary Waslewski	.30	.15	.03
☐	109	Jerry May	.30	.15	.03
☐	110	Ron Hunt	.30	.15	.03
☐	111	Jim Grant	.30	.15	.03
☐	112	Greg Luzinski	1.00	.50	.10
☐	113	Rogelio Moret	.30	.15	.03
☐	114	Bill Buckner	1.50	.75	.15
☐	115	Jim Fregosi	.50	.25	.05
☐	116	Ed Farmer	.30	.15	.03
☐	117A	Cleo James	.30	.15	.03
		(yellow underline C			
		and S of Cubs)			
☐	117B	Cleo James	5.00	2.50	.50
		(green underline C			
		and S of Cubs)			
☐	118	Skip Lockwood	.30	.15	.03
☐	119	Marty Perez	.30	.15	.03
☐	120	Bill Freehan	.75	.35	.07
☐	121	Ed Sprague	.30	.15	.03
☐	122	Larry Biittner	.30	.15	.03
☐	123	Ed Acosta	.30	.15	.03
☐	124	Yankees Rookies	.30	.15	.03
		Alan Closter			
		Rusty Torres			

		NRMT	VG-E	GOOD
	Roger Hambright			
☐ 125	Dave Cash	.30	.15	.03
☐ 126	Bart Johnson	.30	.15	.03
☐ 127	Duffy Dyer	.30	.15	.03
☐ 128	Eddie Watt	.30	.15	.03
☐ 129	Charlie Fox MG	.30	.15	.03
☐ 130	Bob Gibson	4.50	2.25	.45
☐ 131	Jim Nettles	.30	.15	.03
☐ 132	Joe Morgan	4.50	2.25	.45
☐ 133	Joe Keough	.35	.17	.03
☐ 134	Carl Morton	.35	.17	.03
☐ 135	Vada Pinson	.75	.35	.07
☐ 136	Darrell Chaney	.35	.17	.03
☐ 137	Dick Williams MG	.50	.25	.05
☐ 138	Mike Kekich	.35	.17	.03
☐ 139	Tim McCarver	.75	.35	.07
☐ 140	Pat Dobson	.50	.25	.05
☐ 141	Mets Rookies	.50	.25	.05
	Buzz Capra			
	Leroy Stanton			
	Jon Matlack			
☐ 142	Chris Chambliss	1.50	.75	.15
☐ 143	Garry Jestadt	.35	.17	.03
☐ 144	Marty Pattin	.35	.17	.03
☐ 145	Don Kessinger	.50	.25	.05
☐ 146	Steve Kealey	.35	.17	.03
☐ 147	Dave Kingman	5.00	2.50	.50
☐ 148	Dick Billings	.35	.17	.03
☐ 149	Gary Neibauer	.35	.17	.03
☐ 150	Norm Cash	1.00	.50	.10
☐ 151	Jim Brewer	.35	.17	.03
☐ 152	Gene Clines	.35	.17	.03
☐ 153	Rick Auerbach	.35	.17	.03
☐ 154	Ted Simmons	1.50	.75	.15
☐ 155	Larry Dierker	.50	.25	.05
☐ 156	Minnesota Twins	.75	.35	.07
	Team Card			
☐ 157	Don Gullett	.50	.25	.05
☐ 158	Jerry Kenney	.35	.17	.03
☐ 159	John Boccabella	.35	.17	.03
☐ 160	Andy Messersmith	.50	.25	.05
☐ 161	Brock Davis	.35	.17	.03
☐ 162	Brewers Rookies			
	UER	.75	.35	.07
	Jerry Bell			
	Darrell Porter			
	Bob Reynolds			
	(Porter and Bell			
	photos switched)			

		NRMT	VG-E	GOOD
☐ 163	Tug McGraw	.75	.35	.07
☐ 164	McGraw In Action	.50	.25	.05
☐ 165	Chris Speier	.50	.25	.05
☐ 166	Speier In Action	.35	.17	.03
☐ 167	Deron Johnson	.35	.17	.03
☐ 168	Johnson In Action	.35	.17	.03
☐ 169	Vida Blue	.75	.35	.07
☐ 170	Blue In Action	.50	.25	.05
☐ 171	Darrell Evans	1.50	.75	.15
☐ 172	Evans In Action	.50	.25	.05
☐ 173	Clay Kirby	.35	.17	.03
☐ 174	Kirby In Action	.35	.17	.03
☐ 175	Tom Haller	.35	.17	.03
☐ 176	Haller In Action	.35	.17	.03
☐ 177	Paul Schaal	.35	.17	.03
☐ 178	Schaal In Action	.35	.17	.03
☐ 179	Dock Ellis	.35	.17	.03
☐ 180	Ellis In Action	.35	.17	.03
☐ 181	Ed Kranepool	.50	.25	.05
☐ 182	Kranepool In Action	.35	.17	.03
☐ 183	Bill Melton	.35	.17	.03
☐ 184	Melton In Action	.35	.17	.03
☐ 185	Ron Bryant	.35	.17	.03
☐ 186	Bryant In Action	.35	.17	.03
☐ 187	Gates Brown	.50	.25	.05
☐ 188	Frank Lucchesi MG	.35	.17	.03
☐ 189	Gene Tenace	.50	.25	.05
☐ 190	Dave Giusti	.50	.25	.05
☐ 191	Jeff Burroughs	.75	.35	.07
☐ 192	Cubs Team	.75	.35	.07
☐ 193	Kurt Bevacqua	.35	.17	.03
☐ 194	Fred Norman	.35	.17	.03
☐ 195	Orlando Cepeda	1.75	.85	.17
☐ 196	Mel Queen	.35	.17	.03
☐ 197	Johnny Briggs	.35	.17	.03
☐ 198	Dodgers Rookies	1.75	.85	.17
	Charlie Hough			
	Bob O'Brien			
	Mike Strahler			
☐ 199	Mike Fiore	.35	.17	.03
☐ 200	Lou Brock	4.50	2.25	.45
☐ 201	Phil Roof	.35	.17	.03
☐ 202	Scipio Spinks	.35	.17	.03
☐ 203	Ron Blomberg	.35	.17	.03
☐ 204	Tommy Helms	.50	.25	.05
☐ 205	Dick Drago	.35	.17	.03
☐ 206	Dal Maxvill	.35	.17	.03
☐ 207	Tom Egan	.35	.17	.03
☐ 208	Milt Pappas	.50	.25	.05

		NRMT	VG-E	GOOD
☐ 209	Joe Rudi	.50	.25	.05
☐ 210	Denny McLain	1.00	.50	.10
☐ 211	Gary Sutherland	.35	.17	.03
☐ 212	Grant Jackson	.35	.17	.03
☐ 213	Angels Rookies	.35	.17	.03
	Billy Parker			
	Art Kusnyer			
	Tom Silverio			
☐ 214	Mike McQueen	.35	.17	.03
☐ 215	Alex Johnson	.50	.25	.05
☐ 216	Joe Niekro	.75	.35	.07
☐ 217	Roger Metzger	.35	.17	.03
☐ 218	Eddie Kasko MG	.35	.17	.03
☐ 219	Rennie Stennett	.50	.25	.05
☐ 220	Jim Perry	.75	.35	.07
☐ 221	NL Playoffs	1.00	.50	.10
	Bucs champs			
☐ 222	AL Playoffs	1.50	.75	.15
	Orioles champs			
	(Brooks Robinson)			
☐ 223	World Series Game 1	1.00	.50	.10
	(McNally pitching)			
☐ 224	World Series Game 2	1.00	.50	.10
	(Dave Johnson and			
	Mark Belanger)			
☐ 225	World Series Game 3	1.00	.50	.10
	(Sanguillen scoring)			
☐ 226	World Series Game 4	2.25	1.10	.22
	(Clemente on 2nd)			
☐ 227	World Series Game 5	1.00	.50	.10
	(Briles pitching)			
☐ 228	World Series Game 6	1.25	.60	.12
	(Frank Robinson and			
	Manny Sanguillen)			
☐ 229	World Series Game 7	1.00	.50	.10
	(Blass pitching)			
☐ 230	World Series Summary	1.00	.50	.10
	Pirates celebrate			
☐ 231	Casey Cox	.35	.17	.03
☐ 232	Giants Rookies	.35	.17	.03
	Chris Arnold			
	Jim Barr			
	Dave Rader			
☐ 233	Jay Johnstone	.50	.25	.05
☐ 234	Ron Taylor	.35	.17	.03
☐ 235	Merv Rettenmund	.35	.17	.03
☐ 236	Jim McGlothlin	.35	.17	.03
☐ 237	Yankees Team	1.00	.50	.10
☐ 238	Leron Lee	.35	.17	.03

		NRMT	VG-E	GOOD
☐ 239	Tom Timmermann	.35	.17	.03
☐ 240	Rich Allen	1.75	.85	.17
☐ 241	Rollie Fingers	3.00	1.50	.30
☐ 242	Don Mincher	.35	.17	.03
☐ 243	Frank Linzy	.35	.17	.03
☐ 244	Steve Braun	.35	.17	.03
☐ 245	Tommie Agee	.50	.25	.05
☐ 246	Tom Burgmeier	.35	.17	.03
☐ 247	Milt May	.35	.17	.03
☐ 248	Tom Bradley	.35	.17	.03
☐ 249	Harry Walker MG	.35	.17	.03
☐ 250	Boog Powell	1.00	.50	.10
☐ 251	Checklist 3	1.50	.20	.04
☐ 252	Ken Reynolds	.35	.17	.03
☐ 253	Sandy Alomar	.50	.25	.05
☐ 254	Boots Day	.35	.17	.03
☐ 255	Jim Lonborg	.75	.35	.07
☐ 256	George Foster	1.50	.75	.15
☐ 257	Tigers Rookies	.35	.17	.03
	Jim Foor			
	Tim Hosley			
	Paul Jata			
☐ 258	Randy Hundley	.50	.25	.05
☐ 259	Sparky Lyle	.75	.35	.07
☐ 260	Ralph Garr	.50	.25	.05
☐ 261	Steve Mingori	.35	.17	.03
☐ 262	San Diego Padres	1.00	.50	.10
	Team Card			
☐ 263	Felipe Alou	.50	.25	.05
☐ 264	Tommy John	2.00	1.00	.20
☐ 265	Wes Parker	.50	.25	.05
☐ 266	Bobby Bolin	.40	.20	.04
☐ 267	Dave Concepcion	1.50	.75	.15
☐ 268	A's Rookies	.40	.20	.04
	Dwain Anderson			
	Chris Floethe			
☐ 269	Don Hahn	.40	.20	.04
☐ 270	Jim Palmer	7.00	3.50	.70
☐ 271	Ken Rudolph	.40	.20	.04
☐ 272	Mickey Rivers	1.00	.50	.10
☐ 273	Bobby Floyd	.40	.20	.04
☐ 274	Al Severinsen	.40	.20	.04
☐ 275	Cesar Tovar	.40	.20	.04
☐ 276	Gene Mauch MG	.50	.25	.05
☐ 277	Elliott Maddox	.40	.20	.04
☐ 278	Dennis Higgins	.40	.20	.04
☐ 279	Larry Brown	.40	.20	.04
☐ 280	Willie McCovey	4.50	2.25	.45
☐ 281	Bill Parsons	.40	.20	.04

		NRMT	VG-E	GOOD
☐ 282	Astros Team	1.00	.50	.10
☐ 283	Darrell Brandon	.40	.20	.04
☐ 284	Ike Brown	.40	.20	.04
☐ 285	Gaylord Perry	4.50	2.25	.45
☐ 286	Gene Alley	.50	.25	.05
☐ 287	Jim Hardin	.40	.20	.04
☐ 288	Johnny Jeter	.40	.20	.04
☐ 289	Syd O'Brien	.40	.20	.04
☐ 290	Sonny Siebert	.50	.25	.05
☐ 291	Hal McRae	.75	.35	.07
☐ 292	McRae in Action	.50	.25	.05
☐ 293	Dan Frisella	.40	.20	.04
☐ 294	Frisella in Action	.40	.20	.04
☐ 295	Dick Dietz	.40	.20	.04
☐ 296	Dietz In Action	.40	.20	.04
☐ 297	Claude Osteen	.50	.25	.05
☐ 298	Osteen In Action	.40	.20	.04
☐ 299	Hank Aaron	20.00	9.00	1.80
☐ 300	Aaron in Action	7.50	3.50	.70
☐ 301	George Mitterwald	.40	.20	.04
☐ 302	Mitterwald In Action	.40	.20	.04
☐ 303	Joe Pepitone	.75	.35	.07
☐ 304	Pepitone In Action	.50	.25	.05
☐ 305	Ken Boswell	.40	.20	.04
☐ 306	Boswell In Action	.40	.20	.04
☐ 307	Steve Renko	.40	.20	.04
☐ 308	Renko In Action	.40	.20	.04
☐ 309	Roberto Clemente	17.00	8.00	1.60
☐ 310	Clemente In Action	6.00	3.00	.60
☐ 311	Clay Carroll	.40	.20	.04
☐ 312	Carroll In Action	.40	.20	.04
☐ 313	Luis Aparicio	3.00	1.50	.30
☐ 314	Aparicio In Action	1.25	.60	.12
☐ 315	Paul Splittorff	.50	.25	.05
☐ 316	Cardinals Rookies	.50	.25	.05
	Jim Bibby			
	Jorge Roque			
	Santiago Guzman			
☐ 317	Rich Hand	.40	.20	.04
☐ 318	Sonny Jackson	.40	.20	.04
☐ 319	Aurelio Rodriguez	.40	.20	.04
☐ 320	Steve Blass	.50	.25	.05
☐ 321	Joe Lahoud	.40	.20	.04
☐ 322	Jose Pena	.40	.20	.04
☐ 323	Earl Weaver MG	.75	.35	.07
☐ 324	Mike Ryan	.40	.20	.04
☐ 325	Mel Stottlemyre	.75	.35	.07
☐ 326	Pat Kelly	.40	.20	.04
☐ 327	Steve Stone	.75	.35	.07

		NRMT	VG-E	GOOD
☐ 328	Red Sox Team	1.00	.50	.10
☐ 329	Roy Foster	.40	.20	.04
☐ 330	Jim Hunter	3.00	1.50	.30
☐ 331	Stan Swanson	.40	.20	.04
☐ 332	Buck Martinez	.40	.20	.04
☐ 333	Steve Barber	.40	.20	.04
☐ 334	Rangers Rookies	.40	.20	.04
	Bill Fahey			
	Jim Mason			
	Tom Ragland			
☐ 335	Bill Hands	.40	.20	.04
☐ 336	Marty Martinez	.40	.20	.04
☐ 337	Mike Kilkenny	.40	.20	.04
☐ 338	Bob Grich	.75	.35	.07
☐ 339	Ron Cook	.40	.20	.04
☐ 340	Roy White	.50	.25	.05
☐ 341	KP: Joe Torre	.50	.25	.05
☐ 342	KP: Wilbur Wood	.40	.20	.04
☐ 343	KP: Willie Stargell	1.00	.50	.10
☐ 344	KP: Dave McNally	.40	.20	.04
☐ 345	KP: Rick Wise	.40	.20	.04
☐ 346	KP: Jim Fregosi	.50	.25	.05
☐ 347	KP: Tom Seaver	1.50	.75	.15
☐ 348	KP: Sal Bando	.40	.20	.04
☐ 349	Al Fitzmorris	.40	.20	.04
☐ 350	Frank Howard	.75	.35	.07
☐ 351	Braves Rookies	.50	.25	.05
	Tom House			
	Rick Kester			
	Jimmy Britton			
☐ 352	Dave LaRoche	.40	.20	.04
☐ 353	Art Shamsky	.40	.20	.04
☐ 354	Tom Murphy	.40	.20	.04
☐ 355	Bob Watson	.50	.25	.05
☐ 356	Gerry Moses	.40	.20	.04
☐ 357	Woodie Fryman	.40	.20	.04
☐ 358	Sparky Anderson MG	1.00	.50	.10
☐ 359	Don Pavletich	.40	.20	.04
☐ 360	Dave Roberts	.40	.20	.04
☐ 361	Mike Andrews	.40	.20	.04
☐ 362	New York Mets	1.00	.50	.10
	Team Card			
☐ 363	Ron Klimkowski	.40	.20	.04
☐ 364	Johnny Callison	.50	.25	.05
☐ 365	Dick Bosman	.40	.20	.04
☐ 366	Jimmy Rosario	.40	.20	.04
☐ 367	Ron Perranoski	.50	.25	.05
☐ 368	Danny Thompson	.40	.20	.04
☐ 369	Jim Lefebvre	.75	.35	.07

		NRMT	VG-E	GOOD
☐ 370	Don Buford	.50	.25	.05
☐ 371	Denny Lemaster	.40	.20	.04
☐ 372	Royals Rookies	.40	.20	.04
	Lance Clemons			
	Monty Montgomery			
☐ 373	John Mayberry	.50	.25	.05
☐ 374	Jack Heidemann	.40	.20	.04
☐ 375	Reggie Cleveland	.40	.20	.04
☐ 376	Andy Kosco	.40	.20	.04
☐ 377	Terry Harmon	.40	.20	.04
☐ 378	Checklist 4	1.50	.20	.04
☐ 379	Ken Berry	.40	.20	.04
☐ 380	Earl Williams	.40	.20	.04
☐ 381	Chicago White Sox	1.00	.50	.10
	Team Card			
☐ 382	Joe Gibbon	.40	.20	.04
☐ 383	Brant Alyea	.40	.20	.04
☐ 384	Dave Campbell	.40	.20	.04
☐ 385	Mickey Stanley	.50	.25	.05
☐ 386	Jim Colborn	.40	.20	.04
☐ 387	Horace Clarke	.40	.20	.04
☐ 388	Charlie Williams	.40	.20	.04
☐ 389	Bill Rigney MG	.40	.20	.04
☐ 390	Willie Davis	.50	.25	.05
☐ 391	Ken Sanders	.40	.20	.04
☐ 392	Pirates Rookies	.75	.35	.07
	Fred Cambria			
	Richie Zisk			
☐ 393	Curt Motton	.40	.20	.04
☐ 394	Ken Forsch	.50	.25	.05
☐ 395	Matty Alou	.75	.35	.07
☐ 396	Paul Lindblad	.60	.30	.06
☐ 397	Philadelphia Phillies	1.25	.60	.12
	Team Card			
☐ 398	Larry Hisle	.75	.35	.07
☐ 399	Milt Wilcox	.60	.30	.06
☐ 400	Tony Oliva	1.50	.75	.15
☐ 401	Jim Nash	.60	.30	.06
☐ 402	Bobby Heise	.60	.30	.06
☐ 403	John Cumberland	.60	.30	.06
☐ 404	Jeff Torborg	.75	.35	.07
☐ 405	Ron Fairly	.75	.35	.07
☐ 406	George Hendrick	1.00	.50	.10
☐ 407	Chuck Taylor	.60	.30	.06
☐ 408	Jim Northrup	.75	.35	.07
☐ 409	Frank Baker	.60	.30	.06
☐ 410	Fergie Jenkins	2.00	1.00	.20
☐ 411	Bob Montgomery	.60	.30	.06
☐ 412	Dick Kelley	.60	.30	.06

		NRMT	VG-E	GOOD
☐ 413	White Sox Rookies	.60	.30	.06
	Don Eddy			
	Dave Lemonds			
☐ 414	Bob Miller	.60	.30	.06
☐ 415	Cookie Rojas	.60	.30	.06
☐ 416	Johnny Edwards	.60	.30	.06
☐ 417	Tom Hall	.60	.30	.06
☐ 418	Tom Shopay	.60	.30	.06
☐ 419	Jim Spencer	.60	.30	.06
☐ 420	Steve Carlton	15.00	7.00	1.40
☐ 421	Ellie Rodriguez	.60	.30	.06
☐ 422	Ray Lamb	.60	.30	.06
☐ 423	Oscar Gamble	.75	.35	.07
☐ 424	Bill Gogolewski	.60	.30	.06
☐ 425	Ken Singleton	1.00	.50	.10
☐ 426	Singleton In Action	.75	.35	.07
☐ 427	Tito Fuentes	.60	.30	.06
☐ 428	Fuentes In Action	.60	.30	.06
☐ 429	Bob Robertson	.60	.30	.06
☐ 430	Robertson In Action	.60	.30	.06
☐ 431	Clarence Gaston	1.00	.50	.10
☐ 432	Gaston In Action	.75	.35	.07
☐ 433	Johnny Bench	30.00	14.00	2.80
☐ 434	Bench In Action	10.00	5.00	1.00
☐ 435	Reggie Jackson	27.00	12.50	2.50
☐ 436	Jackson In Action	9.00	4.50	.90
☐ 437	Maury Wills	1.25	.60	.12
☐ 438	Wills In Action	.75	.35	.07
☐ 439	Billy Williams	3.00	1.50	.30
☐ 440	Williams In Action	1.25	.60	.12
☐ 441	Thurman Munson	13.00	6.50	1.30
☐ 442	Munson In Action	5.00	2.50	.50
☐ 443	Ken Henderson	.60	.30	.06
☐ 444	Henderson In Action	.60	.30	.06
☐ 445	Tom Seaver	18.00	9.00	1.80
☐ 446	Seaver In Action	7.00	3.50	.70
☐ 447	Willie Stargell	5.00	2.50	.50
☐ 448	Stargell In Action	2.00	1.00	.20
☐ 449	Bob Lemon MG	1.00	.50	.10
☐ 450	Mickey Lolich	1.00	.50	.10
☐ 451	Tony LaRussa	1.00	.50	.10
☐ 452	Ed Herrmann	.60	.30	.06
☐ 453	Barry Lersch	.60	.30	.06
☐ 454	Oakland A's	1.25	.60	.12
	Team Card			
☐ 455	Tommy Harper	.75	.35	.07
☐ 456	Mark Belanger	.75	.35	.07
☐ 457	Padres Rookies	.60	.30	.06
	Darcy Fast			

		NRMT	VG-E	GOOD
	Derrel Thomas			
	Mike Ivie			
☐ 458	Aurelio Monteagudo	.60	.30	.06
☐ 459	Rick Renick	.60	.30	.06
☐ 460	Al Downing	.75	.35	.07
☐ 461	Tim Cullen	.60	.30	.06
☐ 462	Rickey Clark	.60	.30	.06
☐ 463	Bernie Carbo	.60	.30	.06
☐ 464	Jim Roland	.60	.30	.06
☐ 465	Gil Hodges MG	2.50	1.25	.25
☐ 466	Norm Miller	.60	.30	.06
☐ 467	Steve Kline	.60	.30	.06
☐ 468	Richie Scheinblum	.60	.30	.06
☐ 469	Ron Herbel	.60	.30	.06
☐ 470	Ray Fosse	.75	.35	.07
☐ 471	Luke Walker	.60	.30	.06
☐ 472	Phil Gagliano	.60	.30	.06
☐ 473	Dan McGinn	.60	.30	.06
☐ 474	Orioles Rookies	2.00	1.00	.20
	Don Baylor			
	Roric Harrison			
	Johnny Oates			
☐ 475	Gary Nolan	.60	.30	.06
☐ 476	Lee Richard	.60	.30	.06
☐ 477	Tom Phoebus	.60	.30	.06
☐ 478	Checklist 5	1.50	.20	.04
☐ 479	Don Shaw	.60	.30	.06
☐ 480	Lee May	.75	.35	.07
☐ 481	Billy Conigliaro	.60	.30	.06
☐ 482	Joe Hoerner	.60	.30	.06
☐ 483	Ken Suarez	.60	.30	.06
☐ 484	Lum Harris MG	.60	.30	.06
☐ 485	Phil Regan	.75	.35	.07
☐ 486	John Lowenstein	.60	.30	.06
☐ 487	Tigers Team	1.25	.60	.12
☐ 488	Mike Nagy	.60	.30	.06
☐ 489	Expos Rookies	.60	.30	.06
	Terry Humphrey			
	Keith Lampard			
☐ 490	Dave McNally	.75	.35	.07
☐ 491	KP: Lou Piniella	.75	.35	.07
☐ 492	KP: Mel Stottlemyre	.75	.35	.07
☐ 493	KP: Bob Bailey	.60	.30	.06
☐ 494	KP: Willie Horton	.60	.30	.06
☐ 495	KP: Bill Melton	.60	.30	.06
☐ 496	KP: Bud Harrelson	.60	.30	.06
☐ 497	KP: Jim Perry	.60	.30	.06
☐ 498	KP: Brooks Robinson	1.50	.75	.15
☐ 499	Vicente Romo	.60	.30	.06
☐ 500	Joe Torre	1.00	.50	.10
☐ 501	Pete Hamm	.60	.30	.06
☐ 502	Jackie Hernandez	.60	.30	.06
☐ 503	Gary Peters	.60	.30	.06
☐ 504	Ed Spiezio	.60	.30	.06
☐ 505	Mike Marshall	.75	.35	.07
☐ 506	Indians Rookies	.75	.35	.07
	Terry Ley			
	Jim Moyer			
	Dick Tidrow			
☐ 507	Fred Gladding	.60	.30	.06
☐ 508	Elrod Hendricks	.60	.30	.06
☐ 509	Don McMahon	.60	.30	.06
☐ 510	Ted Williams MG	6.00	3.00	.60
☐ 511	Tony Taylor	.60	.30	.06
☐ 512	Paul Popovich	.60	.30	.06
☐ 513	Lindy McDaniel	.75	.35	.07
☐ 514	Ted Sizemore	.75	.35	.07
☐ 515	Bert Blyleven	7.00	3.50	.70
☐ 516	Oscar Brown	.60	.30	.06
☐ 517	Ken Brett	.60	.30	.06
☐ 518	Wayne Garrett	.60	.30	.06
☐ 519	Ted Abernathy	.60	.30	.06
☐ 520	Larry Bowa	1.50	.75	.15
☐ 521	Alan Foster	.60	.30	.06
☐ 522	Dodgers Team	1.25	.60	.12
☐ 523	Chuck Dobson	.60	.30	.06
☐ 524	Reds Rookies	.60	.30	.06
	Ed Armbrister			
	Mel Behney			
☐ 525	Carlos May	1.00	.30	.06
☐ 526	Bob Bailey	1.00	.50	.10
☐ 527	Dave Leonhard	1.00	.50	.10
☐ 528	Ron Stone	1.00	.50	.10
☐ 529	Dave Nelson	1.00	.50	.10
☐ 530	Don Sutton	4.00	2.00	.40
☐ 531	Freddie Patek	1.50	.75	.15
☐ 532	Fred Kendall	1.00	.50	.10
☐ 533	Ralph Houk MG	1.50	.75	.15
☐ 534	Jim Hickman	1.00	.50	.10
☐ 535	Ed Brinkman	1.00	.50	.10
☐ 536	Doug Rader	1.50	.75	.15
☐ 537	Bob Locker	1.00	.50	.10
☐ 538	Charlie Sands	1.00	.50	.10
☐ 539	Terry Forster	1.50	.75	.15
☐ 540	Felix Millan	1.00	.50	.10
☐ 541	Roger Repoz	1.00	.50	.10
☐ 542	Jack Billingham	1.00	.50	.10
☐ 543	Duane Josephson	1.00	.50	.10

		NRMT	VG-E	GOOD			NRMT	VG-E	GOOD
☐ 544	Ted Martinez	1.00	.50	.10	☐ 592	Lew Krausse	1.00	.50	.10
☐ 545	Wayne Granger	1.00	.50	.10	☐ 593	Rich Morales	1.00	.50	.10
☐ 546	Joe Hague	1.00	.50	.10	☐ 594	Jim Beauchamp	1.00	.50	.10
☐ 547	Indians Team	2.00	1.00	.20	☐ 595	Nolan Ryan	65.00	30.00	6.00
☐ 548	Frank Reberger	1.00	.50	.10	☐ 596	Manny Mota	1.50	.75	.15
☐ 549	Dave May	1.00	.50	.10	☐ 597	Jim Magnuson	1.00	.50	.10
☐ 550	Brooks Robinson	14.00	6.00	1.25	☐ 598	Hal King	1.00	.50	.10
☐ 551	Ollie Brown	1.00	.50	.10	☐ 599	Billy Champion	1.00	.50	.10
☐ 552	Brown In Action	1.00	.50	.10	☐ 600	Al Kaline	15.00	6.00	1.25
☐ 553	Wilbur Wood	1.00	.50	.10	☐ 601	George Stone	1.00	.50	.10
☐ 554	Wood In Action	1.00	.50	.10	☐ 602	Dave Bristol MG	1.00	.50	.10
☐ 555	Ron Santo	2.00	1.00	.20	☐ 603	Jim Ray	1.00	.50	.10
☐ 556	Santo In Action	1.50	.75	.15	☐ 604A	Checklist 6	4.00	.40	.10
☐ 557	John Odom	1.00	.50	.10		(copyright on back			
☐ 558	Odom In Action	1.00	.50	.10		bottom right)			
☐ 559	Pete Rose	60.00	30.00	6.00	☐ 604B	Checklist 6	6.00	.50	.10
☐ 560	Rose In Action	20.00	10.00	2.00		(copyright on back			
☐ 561	Leo Cardenas	1.00	.50	.10		bottom left)			
☐ 562	Cardenas In Action	1.00	.50	.10	☐ 605	Nelson Briles	1.00	.50	.10
☐ 563	Ray Sadecki	1.00	.50	.10	☐ 606	Luis Melendez	1.00	.50	.10
☐ 564	Sadecki In Action	1.00	.50	.10	☐ 607	Frank Duffy	1.00	.50	.10
☐ 565	Reggie Smith	1.50	.75	.15	☐ 608	Mike Corkins	1.00	.50	.10
☐ 566	Smith In Action	1.00	.50	.10	☐ 609	Tom Grieve	1.50	.75	.15
☐ 567	Juan Marichal	5.00	2.50	.50	☐ 610	Bill Stoneman	1.00	.50	.10
☐ 568	Marichal In Action	2.00	1.00	.20	☐ 611	Rich Reese	1.00	.50	.10
☐ 569	Ed Kirkpatrick	1.00	.50	.10	☐ 612	Joe Decker	1.00	.50	.10
☐ 570	Kirkpatrick In Action	1.00	.50	.10	☐ 613	Mike Ferraro	1.00	.50	.10
☐ 571	Nate Colbert	1.00	.50	.10	☐ 614	Ted Uhlaender	1.00	.50	.10
☐ 572	Colbert In Action	1.00	.50	.10	☐ 615	Steve Hargan	1.00	.50	.10
☐ 573	Fritz Peterson	1.00	.50	.10	☐ 616	Joe Ferguson	1.00	.50	.10
☐ 574	Peterson In Action	1.00	.50	.10	☐ 617	Kansas City Royals	2.00	1.00	.20
☐ 575	Al Oliver	1.75	.85	.17		Team Card			
☐ 576	Leo Durocher MG	1.50	.75	.15	☐ 618	Rich Robertson	1.00	.50	.10
☐ 577	Mike Paul	1.00	.50	.10	☐ 619	Rich McKinney	1.00	.50	.10
☐ 578	Billy Grabarkewitz	1.00	.50	.10	☐ 620	Phil Niekro	4.00	2.00	.40
☐ 579	Doyle Alexander	3.00	1.50	.30	☐ 621	Commissioners			
☐ 580	Lou Piniella	2.50	1.25	.25		Award	1.00	.50	.10
☐ 581	Wade Blasingame	1.00	.50	.10	☐ 622	MVP Award	1.00	.50	.10
☐ 582	Montreal Expos	2.00	1.00	.20	☐ 623	Cy Young Award	1.00	.50	.10
	Team Card				☐ 624	Minor League Player	1.00	.50	.10
☐ 583	Darold Knowles	1.00	.50	.10	☐ 625	Rookie of the Year	1.00	.50	.10
☐ 584	Jerry McNertney	1.00	.50	.10	☐ 626	Babe Ruth Award	1.50	.75	.15
☐ 585	George Scott	1.50	.75	.15	☐ 627	Moe Drabowsky	1.00	.50	.10
☐ 586	Denis Menke	1.00	.50	.10	☐ 628	Terry Crowley	1.00	.50	.10
☐ 587	Billy Wilson	1.00	.50	.10	☐ 629	Paul Doyle	1.00	.50	.10
☐ 588	Jim Holt	1.00	.50	.10	☐ 630	Rich Hebner	1.00	.50	.10
☐ 589	Hal Lanier	1.50	.75	.15	☐ 631	John Strohmayer	1.00	.50	.10
☐ 590	Graig Nettles	2.50	1.25	.25	☐ 632	Mike Hegan	1.00	.50	.10
☐ 591	Paul Casanova	1.00	.50	.10	☐ 633	Jack Hiatt	1.00	.50	.10

		NRMT	VG-E	GOOD
☐ 634	Dick Woodson	1.00	.50	.10
☐ 635	Don Money	1.00	.50	.10
☐ 636	Bill Lee	1.50	.75	.15
☐ 637	Preston Gomez MG	1.00	.50	.10
☐ 638	Ken Wright	1.00	.50	.10
☐ 639	J.C. Martin	1.00	.50	.10
☐ 640	Joe Coleman	1.00	.50	.10
☐ 641	Mike Lum	1.00	.50	.10
☐ 642	Dennis Riddleberger	1.00	.50	.10
☐ 643	Russ Gibson	1.00	.50	.10
☐ 644	Bernie Allen	1.00	.50	.10
☐ 645	Jim Maloney	1.50	.75	.15
☐ 646	Chico Salmon	1.00	.50	.10
☐ 647	Bob Moose	1.00	.50	.10
☐ 648	Jim Lyttle	1.00	.50	.10
☐ 649	Pete Richert	1.00	.50	.10
☐ 650	Sal Bando	1.50	.75	.15
☐ 651	Cincinnati Reds Team Card	2.00	1.00	.20
☐ 652	Marcelino Lopez	1.00	.50	.10
☐ 653	Jim Fairey	1.00	.50	.10
☐ 654	Horacio Pina	1.00	.50	.10
☐ 655	Jerry Grote	1.00	.50	.10
☐ 656	Rudy May	1.00	.50	.10
☐ 657	Bobby Wine	2.25	1.10	.22
☐ 658	Steve Dunning	2.25	1.10	.22
☐ 659	Bob Aspromonte	2.25	1.10	.22
☐ 660	Paul Blair	3.00	1.50	.30
☐ 661	Bill Virdon	3.50	1.75	.35
☐ 662	Stan Bahnsen	2.25	1.10	.22
☐ 663	Fran Healy	2.25	1.10	.22
☐ 664	Bobby Knoop	2.25	1.10	.22
☐ 665	Chris Short	2.25	1.10	.22
☐ 666	Hector Torres	2.25	1.10	.22
☐ 667	Ray Newman	2.25	1.10	.22
☐ 668	Texas Rangers Team Card	5.00	2.50	.50
☐ 669	Willie Crawford	2.25	1.10	.22
☐ 670	Ken Holtzman	3.00	1.50	.30
☐ 671	Donn Clendenon	3.00	1.50	.30
☐ 672	Archie Reynolds	2.25	1.10	.22
☐ 673	Dave Marshall	2.25	1.10	.22
☐ 674	John Kennedy	2.25	1.10	.22
☐ 675	Pat Jarvis	2.25	1.10	.22
☐ 676	Danny Cater	2.25	1.10	.22
☐ 677	Ivan Murrell	2.25	1.10	.22
☐ 678	Steve Luebber	2.25	1.10	.22
☐ 679	Astros Rookies Bob Fenwick Bob Stinson	2.25	1.10	.22
☐ 680	Dave Johnson	4.00	2.00	.40
☐ 681	Bobby Pfeil	2.25	1.10	.22
☐ 682	Mike McCormick	3.00	1.50	.30
☐ 683	Steve Hovley	2.25	1.10	.22
☐ 684	Hal Breeden	2.25	1.10	.22
☐ 685	Joel Horlen	2.25	1.10	.22
☐ 686	Steve Garvey	75.00	37.50	7.50
☐ 687	Del Unser	2.25	1.10	.22
☐ 688	St. Louis Cardinals Team Card	4.50	2.25	.45
☐ 689	Eddie Fisher	2.25	1.10	.22
☐ 690	Willie Montanez	2.25	1.10	.22
☐ 691	Curt Blefary	2.25	1.10	.22
☐ 692	Blefary In Action	2.25	1.10	.22
☐ 693	Alan Gallagher	2.25	1.10	.22
☐ 694	Gallagher In Action	2.25	1.10	.22
☐ 695	Rod Carew	70.00	35.00	7.00
☐ 696	Carew In Action	25.00	12.50	2.50
☐ 697	Jerry Koosman	5.00	2.50	.50
☐ 698	Koosman In Action	3.00	1.50	.30
☐ 699	Bobby Murcer	5.00	2.50	.50
☐ 700	Murcer In Action	3.00	1.50	.30
☐ 701	Jose Pagan	2.25	1.10	.22
☐ 702	Pagan In Action	2.25	1.10	.22
☐ 703	Doug Griffin	2.25	1.10	.22
☐ 704	Griffin In Action	2.25	1.10	.22
☐ 705	Pat Corrales	3.00	1.50	.30
☐ 706	Corrales In Action	2.25	1.10	.22
☐ 707	Tim Foli	2.25	1.10	.22
☐ 708	Foli In Action	2.25	1.10	.22
☐ 709	Jim Kaat	7.50	3.75	.75
☐ 710	Kaat In Action	3.50	1.75	.35
☐ 711	Bobby Bonds	6.00	3.00	.60
☐ 712	Bonds In Action	3.50	1.75	.35
☐ 713	Gene Michael	3.00	1.50	.30
☐ 714	Michael In Action	2.25	1.10	.22
☐ 715	Mike Epstein	2.25	1.10	.22
☐ 716	Jesus Alou	2.25	1.10	.22
☐ 717	Bruce Dal Canton	2.25	1.10	.22
☐ 718	Del Rice MG	2.25	1.10	.22
☐ 719	Cesar Geronimo	2.25	1.10	.22
☐ 720	Sam McDowell	3.00	1.50	.30
☐ 721	Eddie Leon	2.25	1.10	.22
☐ 722	Bill Sudakis	2.25	1.10	.22
☐ 723	Al Santorini	2.25	1.10	.22
☐ 724	AL Rookie Pitchers John Curtis Rich Hinton	3.00	1.50	.30

		NRMT	VG-E	GOOD
	Mickey Scott			
☐ 725	Dick McAuliffe	2.25	1.10	.22
☐ 726	Dick Selma	2.25	1.10	.22
☐ 727	Jose LaBoy	2.25	1.10	.22
☐ 728	Gail Hopkins	2.25	1.10	.22
☐ 729	Bob Veale	2.25	1.10	.22
☐ 730	Rick Monday	3.00	1.50	.30
☐ 731	Baltimore Orioles	4.50	2.25	.45
	Team Card			
☐ 732	George Culver	2.25	1.10	.22
☐ 733	Jim Ray Hart	2.25	1.10	.22
☐ 734	Bob Burda	2.25	1.10	.22
☐ 735	Diego Segui	2.25	1.10	.22
☐ 736	Bill Russell	3.50	1.75	.35
☐ 737	Len Randle	2.25	1.10	.22
☐ 738	Jim Merritt	2.25	1.10	.22
☐ 739	Don Mason	2.25	1.10	.22
☐ 740	Rico Carty	3.00	1.50	.30
☐ 741	Rookie First Basemen	3.00	1.50	.30
	Tom Hutton			
	John Milner			
	Rick Miller			
☐ 742	Jim Rooker	2.25	1.10	.22
☐ 743	Cesar Gutierrez	2.25	1.10	.22
☐ 744	Jim Slaton	2.25	1.10	.22
☐ 745	Julian Javier	2.25	1.10	.22
☐ 746	Lowell Palmer	2.25	1.10	.22
☐ 747	Jim Stewart	2.25	1.10	.22
☐ 748	Phil Hennigan	2.25	1.10	.22
☐ 749	Walter Alston MG	5.00	2.50	.50
☐ 750	Willie Horton	3.00	1.50	.30
☐ 751	Steve Carlton TR	36.00	18.00	3.60
☐ 752	Joe Morgan TR	28.00	14.00	2.80
☐ 753	Denny McLain TR	5.00	2.50	.50
☐ 754	Frank Robinson TR	22.00	11.00	2.20
☐ 755	Jim Fregosi TR	3.50	1.75	.35
☐ 756	Rick Wise TR	3.00	1.50	.30
☐ 757	Jose Cardenal TR	3.00	1.50	.30
☐ 758	Gil Garrido	2.25	1.10	.22
☐ 759	Chris Cannizzaro	2.25	1.10	.22
☐ 760	Bill Mazeroski	4.00	2.00	.40
☐ 761	Rookie Outfielders	11.00	5.50	1.10
	Ben Oglivie			
	Ron Cey			
	Bernie Williams			
☐ 762	Wayne Simpson	2.25	1.10	.22
☐ 763	Ron Hansen	2.25	1.10	.22
☐ 764	Dusty Baker	4.00	2.00	.40
☐ 765	Ken McMullen	2.25	1.10	.22

		NRMT	VG-E	GOOD
☐ 766	Steve Hamilton	2.25	1.10	.22
☐ 767	Tom McCraw	2.25	1.10	.22
☐ 768	Denny Doyle	2.25	1.10	.22
☐ 769	Jack Aker	2.25	1.10	.22
☐ 770	Jim Wynn	3.00	1.50	.30
☐ 771	San Francisco Giants	4.50	2.25	.45
	Team Card			
☐ 772	Ken Tatum	2.25	1.10	.22
☐ 773	Ron Brand	2.25	1.10	.22
☐ 774	Luis Alvarado	2.25	1.10	.22
☐ 775	Jerry Reuss	3.00	1.50	.30
☐ 776	Bill Voss	2.25	1.10	.22
☐ 777	Hoyt Wilhelm	10.00	5.00	1.00
☐ 778	Twins Rookies	4.00	2.00	.40
	Vic Albury			
	Rick Dempsey			
	Jim Strickland			
☐ 779	Tony Cloninger	2.25	1.10	.22
☐ 780	Dick Green	2.25	1.10	.22
☐ 781	Jim McAndrew	2.25	1.10	.22
☐ 782	Larry Stahl	2.25	1.10	.22
☐ 783	Les Cain	2.25	1.10	.22
☐ 784	Ken Aspromonte	2.25	1.10	.22
☐ 785	Vic Davalillo	2.25	1.10	.22
☐ 786	Chuck Brinkman	2.25	1.10	.22
☐ 787	Ron Reed	3.00	1.50	.30

1973 Topps

CARL
YASTRZEMSKI 1st BASE

*The cards in this 660-card set measure 2 ½"
by 3 ½". The 1973 Topps set marked the last
year in which Topps marketed baseball cards*

in consecutive series. The last series (529-660) is more difficult to obtain. Beginning in 1974, all Topps cards were printed at the same time, thus eliminating the "high number" factor. The set features team leader cards with small individual pictures of the coaching staff members and a larger picture of the manager. The "background" variations below with respect to these leader cards are subtle and are best understood after a side-by-side comparison of the two varieties. An "All-Time Leaders" series (471-478) appeared for the first time in this set. Kid Pictures appeared again for the second year in a row (341-346). Other topical subsets within the set included League Leaders (61-68), Playoffs cards (201-202), World Series cards (203-210), and Rookie Prospects (601-616).

		NRMT	VG-E	GOOD
	COMPLETE SET (660)	900.00	350.00	90.00
	COMMON PLAYER (1-264)	.25	.12	.02
	COMMON PLAYER (265-396) ..	.30	.15	.03
	COMMON PLAYER (397-528) ..	.50	.25	.05
	COMMON PLAYER (529-660) ..	1.50	.75	.15
☐ 1	All-Time HR Leaders	15.00	4.00	.75
	Babe Ruth 714			
	Hank Aaron 673			
	Willie Mays 654			
☐ 2	Rich Hebner	.25	.12	.02
☐ 3	Jim Lonborg	.50	.25	.05
☐ 4	John Milner	.25	.12	.02
☐ 5	Ed Brinkman	.25	.12	.02
☐ 6	Mac Scarce	.25	.12	.02
☐ 7	Texas Rangers Team	.60	.30	.06
☐ 8	Tom Hall	.25	.12	.02
☐ 9	Johnny Oates	.25	.12	.02
☐ 10	Don Sutton	2.25	1.10	.22
☐ 11	Chris Chambliss	.50	.25	.05
☐ 12A	Padres Leaders	.50	.25	.05
	Don Zimmer MG			
	Dave Garcia CO			
	Johnny Podres CO			
	Bob Skinner CO			
	Whitey Wietelmann CO			
	(Podres no right ear)			
☐ 12B	Padres Leaders	1.00	.50	.10
	(Podres has right ear)			
☐ 13	George Hendrick ...	.50	.25	.05

		NRMT	VG-E	GOOD
☐ 14	Sonny Siebert	.25	.12	.02
☐ 15	Ralph Garr	.25	.12	.02
☐ 16	Steve Braun	.25	.12	.02
☐ 17	Fred Gladding	.25	.12	.02
☐ 18	Leroy Stanton	.25	.12	.02
☐ 19	Tim Foli	.25	.12	.02
☐ 20	Stan Bahnsen	.25	.12	.02
☐ 21	Randy Hundley	.25	.12	.02
☐ 22	Ted Abernathy	.25	.12	.02
☐ 23	Dave Kingman	1.50	.75	.15
☐ 24	Al Santorini	.25	.12	.02
☐ 25	Roy White	.50	.25	.05
☐ 26	Pittsburgh Pirates ...	.60	.30	.06
	Team Card			
☐ 27	Bill Gogolewski	.25	.12	.02
☐ 28	Hal McRae	.50	.25	.05
☐ 29	Tony Taylor	.25	.12	.02
☐ 30	Tug McGraw	.75	.35	.07
☐ 31	Buddy Bell	4.00	2.00	.40
☐ 32	Fred Norman	.25	.12	.02
☐ 33	Jim Breazeale	.25	.12	.02
☐ 34	Pat Dobson	.25	.12	.02
☐ 35	Willie Davis	.50	.25	.05
☐ 36	Steve Barber	.25	.12	.02
☐ 37	Bill Robinson	.50	.25	.05
☐ 38	Mike Epstein	.25	.12	.02
☐ 39	Dave Roberts	.25	.12	.02
☐ 40	Reggie Smith	.60	.30	.06
☐ 41	Tom Walker	.25	.12	.02
☐ 42	Mike Andrews	.25	.12	.02
☐ 43	Randy Moffitt	.25	.12	.02
☐ 44	Rick Monday	.50	.25	.05
☐ 45	Ellie Rodriguez	.25	.12	.02
	(photo actually John			
	Felske)			
☐ 46	Lindy McDaniel	.25	.12	.02
☐ 47	Luis Melendez	.25	.12	.02
☐ 48	Paul Splittorff	.25	.12	.02
☐ 49A	Twins Leaders	.50	.25	.05
	Frank Quilici MG			
	Vern Morgan CO			
	Bob Rodgers CO			
	Ralph Rowe CO			
	Al Worthington CO			
	(solid backgrounds)			
☐ 49B	Twins Leaders	1.00	.50	.10
	(natural backgrounds)			
☐ 50	Roberto Clemente ...	20.00	10.00	2.00
☐ 51	Chuck Seelbach	.25	.12	.02

		NRMT	VG-E	GOOD
☐ 52	Denis Menke	.25	.12	.02
☐ 53	Steve Dunning	.25	.12	.02
☐ 54	Checklist 1	1.50	.20	.04
☐ 55	Jon Matlack	.25	.12	.02
☐ 56	Merv Rettenmund	.25	.12	.02
☐ 57	Derrel Thomas	.25	.12	.02
☐ 58	Mike Paul	.25	.12	.02
☐ 59	Steve Yeager	.60	.30	.06
☐ 60	Ken Holtzman	.50	.25	.05
☐ 61	Batting Leaders	1.50	.75	.15
	Billy Williams			
	Rod Carew			
☐ 62	Home Run Leaders	1.50	.75	.15
	Johnny Bench			
	Dick Allen			
☐ 63	RBI Leaders	1.50	.75	.15
	Johnny Bench			
	Dick Allen			
☐ 64	Stolen Base Leaders	1.00	.50	.10
	Lou Brock			
	Bert Campaneris			
☐ 65	ERA Leaders	1.00	.50	.10
	Steve Carlton			
	Luis Tiant			
☐ 66	Victory Leaders	1.00	.50	.10
	Steve Carlton			
	Gaylord Perry			
	Wilbur Wood			
☐ 67	Strikeout Leaders	4.00	2.00	.40
	Steve Carlton			
	Nolan Ryan			
☐ 68	Leading Firemen	.75	.35	.07
	Clay Carroll			
	Sparky Lyle			
☐ 69	Phil Gagliano	.25	.12	.02
☐ 70	Milt Pappas	.50	.25	.05
☐ 71	Johnny Briggs	.25	.12	.02
☐ 72	Ron Reed	.25	.12	.02
☐ 73	Ed Herrmann	.25	.12	.02
☐ 74	Billy Champion	.25	.12	.02
☐ 75	Vada Pinson	.60	.30	.06
☐ 76	Doug Rader	.50	.25	.05
☐ 77	Mike Torrez	.25	.12	.02
☐ 78	Richie Scheinblum	.25	.12	.02
☐ 79	Jim Willoughby	.25	.12	.02
☐ 80	Tony Oliva UER	1.00	.50	.10
	(Minnseota on front)			
☐ 81A	Cubs Leaders	.50	.25	.05
	Whitey Lockman MG			
	Hank Aguirre CO			
	Ernie Banks CO			
	Larry Jansen CO			
	Pete Reiser CO			
	(solid backgrounds)			
☐ 81B	Cubs Leaders	1.00	.50	.10
	(natural backgrounds)			
☐ 82	Fritz Peterson	.25	.12	.02
☐ 83	Leron Lee	.25	.12	.02
☐ 84	Rollie Fingers	2.25	1.10	.22
☐ 85	Ted Simmons	1.00	.50	.10
☐ 86	Tom McCraw	.25	.12	.02
☐ 87	Ken Boswell	.25	.12	.02
☐ 88	Mickey Stanley	.50	.25	.05
☐ 89	Jack Billingham	.25	.12	.02
☐ 90	Brooks Robinson	4.00	2.00	.40
☐ 91	Dodgers Team	.75	.35	.07
☐ 92	Jerry Bell	.25	.12	.02
☐ 93	Jesus Alou	.25	.12	.02
☐ 94	Dick Billings	.25	.12	.02
☐ 95	Steve Blass	.50	.25	.05
☐ 96	Doug Griffin	.25	.12	.02
☐ 97	Willie Montanez	.25	.12	.02
☐ 98	Dick Woodson	.25	.12	.02
☐ 99	Carl Taylor	.25	.12	.02
☐ 100	Hank Aaron	16.00	8.00	1.60
☐ 101	Ken Henderson	.25	.12	.02
☐ 102	Rudy May	.25	.12	.02
☐ 103	Celerino Sanchez	.25	.12	.02
☐ 104	Reggie Cleveland	.25	.12	.02
☐ 105	Carlos May	.25	.12	.02
☐ 106	Terry Humphrey	.25	.12	.02
☐ 107	Phil Hennigan	.25	.12	.02
☐ 108	Bill Russell	.50	.25	.05
☐ 109	Doyle Alexander	.75	.35	.07
☐ 110	Bob Watson	.50	.25	.05
☐ 111	Dave Nelson	.25	.12	.02
☐ 112	Gary Ross	.25	.12	.02
☐ 113	Jerry Grote	.25	.12	.02
☐ 114	Lynn McGlothen	.25	.12	.02
☐ 115	Ron Santo	.75	.35	.07
☐ 116A	Yankees Leaders	.60	.30	.06
	Ralph Houk MG			
	Jim Hegan CO			
	Elston Howard CO			
	Dick Howser CO			
	Jim Turner CO			
	(solid backgrounds)			
☐ 116B	Yankees Leaders	1.00	.50	.10

		NRMT	VG-E	GOOD
	(natural backgrounds)			
☐ 117	Ramon Hernandez	.25	.12	.02
☐ 118	John Mayberry	.50	.25	.05
☐ 119	Larry Bowa	.75	.35	.07
☐ 120	Joe Coleman	.25	.12	.02
☐ 121	Dave Rader	.25	.12	.02
☐ 122	Jim Strickland	.25	.12	.02
☐ 123	Sandy Alomar	.25	.12	.02
☐ 124	Jim Hardin	.25	.12	.02
☐ 125	Ron Fairly	.25	.12	.02
☐ 126	Jim Brewer	.25	.12	.02
☐ 127	Brewers Team	.60	.30	.06
☐ 128	Ted Sizemore	.25	.12	.02
☐ 129	Terry Forster	.50	.25	.05
☐ 130	Pete Rose	20.00	10.00	2.00
☐ 131A	Red Sox Leaders	.50	.25	.05
	Eddie Kasko MG			
	Doug Camilli CO			
	Don Lenhardt CO			
	Eddie Popowski CO			
	(no right ear)			
	Lee Stange CO			
☐ 131B	Red Sox Leaders	1.00	.50	.10
	(Popowski has right			
	ear showing)			
☐ 132	Matty Alou	.50	.25	.05
☐ 133	Dave Roberts	.25	.12	.02
☐ 134	Milt Wilcox	.25	.12	.02
☐ 135	Lee May UER	.50	.25	.05
	(career average .000)			
☐ 136A	Orioles Leaders	.75	.35	.07
	Earl Weaver MG			
	George Bamberger CO			
	Jim Frey CO			
	Billy Hunter CO			
	George Staller CO			
	(orange backgrounds)			
☐ 136B	Orioles Leaders	1.00	.50	.10
	(dark pale			
	backgrounds)			
☐ 137	Jim Beauchamp	.25	.12	.02
☐ 138	Horacio Pina	.25	.12	.02
☐ 139	Carmen Fanzone	.25	.12	.02
☐ 140	Lou Piniella	.75	.35	.07
☐ 141	Bruce Kison	.25	.12	.02
☐ 142	Thurman Munson	7.50	3.75	.75
☐ 143	John Curtis	.25	.12	.02
☐ 144	Marty Perez	.25	.12	.02
☐ 145	Bobby Bonds	.75	.35	.07

		NRMT	VG-E	GOOD
☐ 146	Woodie Fryman	.25	.12	.02
☐ 147	Mike Anderson	.25	.12	.02
☐ 148	Dave Goltz	.25	.12	.02
☐ 149	Ron Hunt	.25	.12	.02
☐ 150	Wilbur Wood	.25	.12	.02
☐ 151	Wes Parker	.50	.25	.05
☐ 152	Dave May	.25	.12	.02
☐ 153	Al Hrabosky	.50	.25	.05
☐ 154	Jeff Torborg	.50	.25	.05
☐ 155	Sal Bando	.50	.25	.05
☐ 156	Cesar Geronimo	.25	.12	.02
☐ 157	Denny Riddleberger	.25	.12	.02
☐ 158	Astros Team	.60	.30	.06
☐ 159	Clarence Gaston	.60	.30	.06
☐ 160	Jim Palmer	5.50	2.75	.55
☐ 161	Ted Martinez	.25	.12	.02
☐ 162	Pete Broberg	.25	.12	.02
☐ 163	Vic Davalillo	.25	.12	.02
☐ 164	Monty Montgomery	.25	.12	.02
☐ 165	Luis Aparicio	2.50	1.25	.25
☐ 166	Terry Harmon	.25	.12	.02
☐ 167	Steve Stone	.50	.25	.05
☐ 168	Jim Northrup	.50	.25	.05
☐ 169	Ron Schueler	.25	.12	.02
☐ 170	Harmon Killebrew	3.50	1.75	.35
☐ 171	Bernie Carbo	.25	.12	.02
☐ 172	Steve Kline	.25	.12	.02
☐ 173	Hal Breeden	.25	.12	.02
☐ 174	Rich Gossage	7.50	3.75	.75
☐ 175	Frank Robinson	3.50	1.75	.35
☐ 176	Chuck Taylor	.25	.12	.02
☐ 177	Bill Plummer	.25	.12	.02
☐ 178	Don Rose	.25	.12	.02
☐ 179A	A's Leaders	.50	.25	.05
	Dick Williams MG			
	Jerry Adair CO			
	Vern Hoscheit CO			
	Irv Noren CO			
	Wes Stock CO			
	(orange backgrounds)			
☐ 179B	A's Leaders	1.00	.50	.10
	(dark pale			
	backgrounds)			
☐ 180	Fergie Jenkins	1.50	.75	.15
☐ 181	Jack Brohamer	.25	.12	.02
☐ 182	Mike Caldwell	.50	.25	.05
☐ 183	Don Buford	.25	.12	.02
☐ 184	Jerry Koosman	.75	.35	.07
☐ 185	Jim Wynn	.50	.25	.05

		NRMT	VG-E	GOOD
☐ 186	Bill Fahey	.25	.12	.02
☐ 187	Luke Walker	.25	.12	.02
☐ 188	Cookie Rojas	.25	.12	.02
☐ 189	Greg Luzinski	.75	.35	.07
☐ 190	Bob Gibson	3.50	1.75	.35
☐ 191	Tigers Team	.75	.35	.07
☐ 192	Pat Jarvis	.25	.12	.02
☐ 193	Carlton Fisk	12.00	5.00	1.00
☐ 194	Jorge Orta	.25	.12	.02
☐ 195	Clay Carroll	.25	.12	.02
☐ 196	Ken McMullen	.25	.12	.02
☐ 197	Ed Goodson	.25	.12	.02
☐ 198	Horace Clarke	.25	.12	.02
☐ 199	Bert Blyleven	3.50	1.75	.35
☐ 200	Billy Williams	3.00	1.50	.30
☐ 201	A.L. Playoffs	.75	.35	.07
	A's over Tigers; Hendrick scores winning run			
☐ 202	N.L. Playoffs	.75	.35	.07
	Reds over Pirates Foster's run decides			
☐ 203	World Series Game 1	.75	.35	.07
	Tenace the Menace			
☐ 204	World Series Game 2	.75	.35	.07
	A's two straight			
☐ 205	World Series Game 3	.75	.35	.07
	Reds win squeeker			
☐ 206	World Series Game 4	.75	.35	.07
	Tenace singles in ninth			
☐ 207	World Series Game 5	.75	.35	.07
	Odom out at plate			
☐ 208	World Series Game 6	.75	.35	.07
	Red's slugging ties series			
☐ 209	World Series Game 7	.75	.35	.07
	Campy stars winning rally			
☐ 210	World Series Summary	.75	.35	.07
	World champions: A's Win			
☐ 211	Balor Moore	.25	.12	.02
☐ 212	Joe Lahoud	.25	.12	.02
☐ 213	Steve Garvey	13.00	6.50	1.30
☐ 214	Steve Hamilton	.25	.12	.02
☐ 215	Dusty Baker	.60	.30	.06
☐ 216	Toby Harrah	.50	.25	.05
☐ 217	Don Wilson	.25	.12	.02

		NRMT	VG-E	GOOD
☐ 218	Aurelio Rodriguez	.25	.12	.02
☐ 219	Cardinals Team	.60	.30	.06
☐ 220	Nolan Ryan	30.00	15.00	3.00
☐ 221	Fred Kendall	.25	.12	.02
☐ 222	Rob Gardner	.25	.12	.02
☐ 223	Bud Harrelson	.25	.12	.02
☐ 224	Bill Lee	.25	.12	.02
☐ 225	Al Oliver	1.00	.50	.10
☐ 226	Ray Fosse	.25	.12	.02
☐ 227	Wayne Twitchell	.25	.12	.02
☐ 228	Bobby Darwin	.25	.12	.02
☐ 229	Roric Harrison	.25	.12	.02
☐ 230	Joe Morgan	4.50	2.25	.45
☐ 231	Bill Parsons	.25	.12	.02
☐ 232	Ken Singleton	.50	.25	.05
☐ 233	Ed Kirkpatrick	.25	.12	.02
☐ 234	Bill North	.25	.12	.02
☐ 235	Jim Hunter	3.00	1.50	.30
☐ 236	Tito Fuentes	.25	.12	.02
☐ 237A	Braves Leaders	1.00	.50	.10
	Eddie Mathews MG Lew Burdette CO Jim Busby CO Roy Hartsfield CO Ken Silvestri CO (orange backgrounds)			
☐ 237B	Braves Leaders	1.50	.75	.15
	(dark pale backgrounds)			
☐ 238	Tony Muser	.25	.12	.02
☐ 239	Pete Richert	.25	.12	.02
☐ 240	Bobby Murcer	.60	.30	.06
☐ 241	Dwain Anderson	.25	.12	.02
☐ 242	George Culver	.25	.12	.02
☐ 243	Angels Team	.60	.30	.06
☐ 244	Ed Acosta	.25	.12	.02
☐ 245	Carl Yastrzemski	13.00	6.50	1.30
☐ 246	Ken Sanders	.25	.12	.02
☐ 247	Del Unser	.25	.12	.02
☐ 248	Jerry Johnson	.25	.12	.02
☐ 249	Larry Biittner	.25	.12	.02
☐ 250	Manny Sanguillen	.50	.25	.05
☐ 251	Roger Nelson	.25	.12	.02
☐ 252A	Giants Leaders	.50	.25	.05
	Charlie Fox MG Joe Amalfitano CO Andy Gilbert CO Don McMahon CO John McNamara CO			

			NRMT	VG-E	GOOD
	(orange backgrounds)				
☐ 252B	Giants Leaders		1.00	.50	.10
	(dark pale				
	backgrounds)				
☐ 253	Mark Belanger		.50	.25	.05
☐ 254	Bill Stoneman		.25	.12	.02
☐ 255	Reggie Jackson		17.00	8.50	1.70
☐ 256	Chris Zachary		.25	.12	.02
☐ 257A	Mets Leaders		1.50	.75	.15
	Yogi Berra MG				
	Roy McMillan CO				
	Joe Pignatano CO				
	Rube Walker CO				
	Eddie Yost CO				
	(orange backgrounds)				
☐ 257B	Mets Leaders		2.00	1.00	.20
	(dark pale				
	backgrounds)				
☐ 258	Tommy John		1.50	.75	.15
☐ 259	Jim Holt		.25	.12	.02
☐ 260	Gary Nolan		.25	.12	.02
☐ 261	Pat Kelly		.25	.12	.02
☐ 262	Jack Aker		.25	.12	.02
☐ 263	George Scott		.50	.25	.05
☐ 264	Checklist 2		1.50	.20	.04
☐ 265	Gene Michael		.50	.25	.05
☐ 266	Mike Lum		.30	.15	.03
☐ 267	Lloyd Allen		.30	.15	.03
☐ 268	Jerry Morales		.30	.15	.03
☐ 269	Tim McCarver		.75	.35	.07
☐ 270	Luis Tiant		.75	.35	.07
☐ 271	Tom Hutton		.30	.15	.03
☐ 272	Ed Farmer		.30	.15	.03
☐ 273	Chris Speier		.30	.15	.03
☐ 274	Darold Knowles		.30	.15	.03
☐ 275	Tony Perez		1.50	.75	.15
☐ 276	Joe Lovitto		.30	.15	.03
☐ 277	Bob Miller		.30	.15	.03
☐ 278	Baltimore Orioles		.75	.35	.07
	Team Card				
☐ 279	Mike Strahler		.30	.15	.03
☐ 280	Al Kaline		5.00	2.50	.50
☐ 281	Mike Jorgensen		.30	.15	.03
☐ 282	Steve Hovley		.30	.15	.03
☐ 283	Ray Sadecki		.30	.15	.03
☐ 284	Glenn Borgmann		.30	.15	.03
☐ 285	Don Kessinger		.50	.25	.05
☐ 286	Frank Linzy		.30	.15	.03
☐ 287	Eddie Leon		.30	.15	.03

			NRMT	VG-E	GOOD
☐ 288	Gary Gentry		.30	.15	.03
☐ 289	Bob Oliver		.30	.15	.03
☐ 290	Cesar Cedeno		.60	.30	.06
☐ 291	Rogelio Moret		.30	.15	.03
☐ 292	Jose Cruz		.60	.30	.06
☐ 293	Bernie Allen		.30	.15	.03
☐ 294	Steve Arlin		.30	.15	.03
☐ 295	Bert Campaneris		.50	.25	.05
☐ 296	Reds Leaders		.75	.35	.07
	Sparky Anderson MG				
	Alex Grammas CO				
	Ted Kluszewski CO				
	George Scherger CO				
	Larry Shepard CO				
☐ 297	Walt Williams		.30	.15	.03
☐ 298	Ron Bryant		.30	.15	.03
☐ 299	Ted Ford		.30	.15	.03
☐ 300	Steve Carlton		8.00	4.00	.80
☐ 301	Billy Grabarkewitz		.30	.15	.03
☐ 302	Terry Crowley		.30	.15	.03
☐ 303	Nelson Briles		.30	.15	.03
☐ 304	Duke Sims		.30	.15	.03
☐ 305	Willie Mays		20.00	10.00	2.00
☐ 306	Tom Burgmeier		.30	.15	.03
☐ 307	Boots Day		.30	.15	.03
☐ 308	Skip Lockwood		.30	.15	.03
☐ 309	Paul Popovich		.30	.15	.03
☐ 310	Dick Allen		.60	.30	.06
☐ 311	Joe Decker		.30	.15	.03
☐ 312	Oscar Brown		.30	.15	.03
☐ 313	Jim Ray		.30	.15	.03
☐ 314	Ron Swoboda		.30	.15	.03
☐ 315	John Odom		.30	.15	.03
☐ 316	San Diego Padres		.75	.35	.07
	Team Card				
☐ 317	Danny Cater		.30	.15	.03
☐ 318	Jim McGlothlin		.30	.15	.03
☐ 319	Jim Spencer		.30	.15	.03
☐ 320	Lou Brock		4.00	2.00	.40
☐ 321	Rich Hinton		.30	.15	.03
☐ 322	Garry Maddox		.60	.30	.06
☐ 323	Tigers Leaders		1.00	.50	.10
	Billy Martin MG				
	Art Fowler CO				
	Charlie Silvera CO				
	Dick Tracewski CO				
☐ 324	Al Downing		.30	.15	.03
☐ 325	Boog Powell		.75	.35	.07
☐ 326	Darrell Brandon		.30	.15	.03

		NRMT	VG-E	GOOD			NRMT	VG-E	GOOD
☐ 327	John Lowenstein	.30	.15	.03	☐ 368	Bill Buckner	.75	.35	.07
☐ 328	Bill Bonham	.30	.15	.03	☐ 369	Lerrin LaGrow	.30	.15	.03
☐ 329	Ed Kranepool	.50	.25	.05	☐ 370	Willie Stargell	3.50	1.75	.35
☐ 330	Rod Carew	9.00	4.00	.80	☐ 371	Mike Kekich	.30	.15	.03
☐ 331	Carl Morton	.30	.15	.03	☐ 372	Oscar Gamble	.50	.25	.05
☐ 332	John Felske	.30	.15	.03	☐ 373	Clyde Wright	.30	.15	.03
☐ 333	Gene Clines	.30	.15	.03	☐ 374	Darrell Evans	.75	.35	.07
☐ 334	Freddie Patek	.30	.15	.03	☐ 375	Larry Dierker	.50	.25	.05
☐ 335	Bob Tolan	.30	.15	.03	☐ 376	Frank Duffy	.30	.15	.03
☐ 336	Tom Bradley	.30	.15	.03	☐ 377	Expos Leaders	.50	.25	.05
☐ 337	Dave Duncan	.30	.15	.03		Gene Mauch MG			
☐ 338	Checklist 3	1.50	.20	.04		Dave Bristol CO			
☐ 339	Dick Tidrow	.30	.15	.03		Larry Doby CO			
☐ 340	Nate Colbert	.30	.15	.03		Cal McLish CO			
☐ 341	KP: Jim Palmer	1.25	.60	.12		Jerry Zimmerman CO			
☐ 342	KP: Sam McDowell	.30	.15	.03	☐ 378	Len Randle	.30	.15	.03
☐ 343	KP: Bobby Murcer	.40	.20	.04	☐ 379	Cy Acosta	.30	.15	.03
☐ 344	KP: Jim Hunter	.75	.35	.07	☐ 380	Johnny Bench	16.00	7.50	1.50
☐ 345	KP: Chris Speier	.30	.15	.03	☐ 381	Vicente Romo	.30	.15	.03
☐ 346	KP: Gaylord Perry	.75	.35	.07	☐ 382	Mike Hegan	.30	.15	.03
☐ 347	Kansas City Royals	.75	.35	.07	☐ 383	Diego Segui	.30	.15	.03
	Team Card				☐ 384	Don Baylor	1.00	.50	.10
☐ 348	Rennie Stennett	.30	.15	.03	☐ 385	Jim Perry	.50	.25	.05
☐ 349	Dick McAuliffe	.30	.15	.03	☐ 386	Don Money	.30	.15	.03
☐ 350	Tom Seaver	14.00	6.50	1.30	☐ 387	Jim Barr	.30	.15	.03
☐ 351	Jimmy Stewart	.30	.15	.03	☐ 388	Ben Oglivie	.50	.25	.05
☐ 352	Don Stanhouse	.30	.15	.03	☐ 389	New York Mets	1.50	.75	.15
☐ 353	Steve Brye	.30	.15	.03		Team Card			
☐ 354	Billy Parker	.30	.15	.03	☐ 390	Mickey Lolich	.75	.35	.07
☐ 355	Mike Marshall	.50	.25	.05	☐ 391	Lee Lacy	.50	.25	.05
☐ 356	White Sox Leaders	.50	.25	.05	☐ 392	Dick Drago	.30	.15	.03
	Chuck Tanner MG				☐ 393	Jose Cardenal	.30	.15	.03
	Joe Lonnett CO				☐ 394	Sparky Lyle	.60	.30	.06
	Jim Mahoney CO				☐ 395	Roger Metzger	.30	.15	.03
	Al Monchak CO				☐ 396	Grant Jackson	.30	.15	.03
	Johnny Sain CO				☐ 397	Dave Cash	.50	.25	.05
☐ 357	Ross Grimsley	.30	.15	.03	☐ 398	Rich Hand	.50	.25	.05
☐ 358	Jim Nettles	.30	.15	.03	☐ 399	George Foster	1.50	.75	.15
☐ 359	Cecil Upshaw	.30	.15	.03	☐ 400	Gaylord Perry	2.50	1.25	.25
☐ 360	Joe Rudi	.50	.25	.05	☐ 401	Clyde Mashore	.50	.25	.05
	(photo actually Gene				☐ 402	Jack Hiatt	.50	.25	.05
	Tenace)				☐ 403	Sonny Jackson	.50	.25	.05
☐ 361	Fran Healy	.30	.15	.03	☐ 404	Chuck Brinkman	.50	.25	.05
☐ 362	Eddie Watt	.30	.15	.03	☐ 405	Cesar Tovar	.50	.25	.05
☐ 363	Jackie Hernandez	.30	.15	.03	☐ 406	Paul Lindblad	.50	.25	.05
☐ 364	Rick Wise	.50	.25	.05	☐ 407	Felix Millan	.50	.25	.05
☐ 365	Rico Petrocelli	.50	.25	.05	☐ 408	Jim Colborn	.50	.25	.05
☐ 366	Brock Davis	.30	.15	.03	☐ 409	Ivan Murrell	.50	.25	.05
☐ 367	Burt Hooton	.50	.25	.05	☐ 410	Willie McCovey	3.50	1.75	.35

		NRMT	VG-E	GOOD
	(Bench behind plate)			
☐ 411	Ray Corbin	.50	.25	.05
☐ 412	Manny Mota	.75	.35	.07
☐ 413	Tom Timmermann	.50	.25	.05
☐ 414	Ken Rudolph	.50	.25	.05
☐ 415	Marty Pattin	.50	.25	.05
☐ 416	Paul Schaal	.50	.25	.05
☐ 417	Scipio Spinks	.50	.25	.05
☐ 418	Bob Grich	.75	.35	.07
☐ 419	Casey Cox	.50	.25	.05
☐ 420	Tommie Agee	.50	.25	.05
☐ 421A	Angels Leaders	.75	.35	.07
	Bobby Winkles MG			
	Tom Morgan CO			
	Salty Parker CO			
	Jimmie Reese CO			
	John Roseboro CO			
	(orange backgrounds)			
☐ 421B	Angels Leaders	1.00	.50	.10
	(dark pale			
	backgrounds)			
☐ 422	Bob Robertson	.50	.25	.05
☐ 423	Johnny Jeter	.50	.25	.05
☐ 424	Denny Doyle	.50	.25	.05
☐ 425	Alex Johnson	.50	.25	.05
☐ 426	Dave LaRoche	.50	.25	.05
☐ 427	Rick Auerbach	.50	.25	.05
☐ 428	Wayne Simpson	.50	.25	.05
☐ 429	Jim Fairey	.50	.25	.05
☐ 430	Vida Blue	.75	.35	.07
☐ 431	Gerry Moses	.50	.25	.05
☐ 432	Dan Frisella	.50	.25	.05
☐ 433	Willie Horton	.75	.35	.07
☐ 434	San Francisco Giants Team Card	1.25	.60	.12
☐ 435	Rico Carty	.75	.35	.07
☐ 436	Jim McAndrew	.50	.25	.05
☐ 437	John Kennedy	.50	.25	.05
☐ 438	Enzo Hernandez	.50	.25	.05
☐ 439	Eddie Fisher	.50	.25	.05
☐ 440	Glenn Beckert	.75	.35	.07
☐ 441	Gail Hopkins	.50	.25	.05
☐ 442	Dick Dietz	.50	.25	.05
☐ 443	Danny Thompson	.50	.25	.05
☐ 444	Ken Brett	.50	.25	.05
☐ 445	Ken Berry	.50	.25	.05
☐ 446	Jerry Reuss	.75	.35	.07
☐ 447	Joe Hague	.50	.25	.05
☐ 448	John Hiller	.75	.35	.07

		NRMT	VG-E	GOOD
☐ 449A	Indians Leaders	.75	.35	.07
	Ken Aspromonte MG			
	Rocky Colavito CO			
	Joe Lutz CO			
	Warren Spahn CO			
	(Spahn's right ear pointed)			
☐ 449B	Indians Leaders	1.00	.50	.10
	(Spahn's right ear round)			
☐ 450	Joe Torre	1.00	.50	.10
☐ 451	John Vukovich	.50	.25	.05
☐ 452	Paul Casanova	.50	.25	.05
☐ 453	Checklist 4	1.50	.20	.04
☐ 454	Tom Haller	.50	.25	.05
☐ 455	Bill Melton	.50	.25	.05
☐ 456	Dick Green	.50	.25	.05
☐ 457	John Strohmayer	.50	.25	.05
☐ 458	Jim Mason	.50	.25	.05
☐ 459	Jimmy Howarth	.50	.25	.05
☐ 460	Bill Freehan	1.00	.50	.10
☐ 461	Mike Corkins	.50	.25	.05
☐ 462	Ron Blomberg	.50	.25	.05
☐ 463	Ken Tatum	.50	.25	.05
☐ 464	Chicago Cubs Team Card	1.25	.60	.12
☐ 465	Dave Giusti	.75	.35	.07
☐ 466	Jose Arcia	.50	.25	.05
☐ 467	Mike Ryan	.50	.25	.05
☐ 468	Tom Griffin	.50	.25	.05
☐ 469	Dan Monzon	.50	.25	.05
☐ 470	Mike Cuellar	.75	.35	.07
☐ 471	Hits Leaders Ty Cobb 4191	3.00	1.50	.30
☐ 472	Grand Slam Leaders Lou Gehrig 23	3.00	1.50	.30
☐ 473	Total Bases Leaders Hank Aaron 6172	3.00	1.50	.30
☐ 474	RBI Leaders Babe Ruth 2209	5.00	2.50	.50
☐ 475	Batting Leaders Ty Cobb .367	3.00	1.50	.30
☐ 476	Shutout Leaders Walter Johnson 113	1.50	.75	.15
☐ 477	Victory Leaders Cy Young 511	1.50	.75	.15
☐ 478	Strikeout Leaders Walter Johnson 3508	1.50	.75	.15
☐ 479	Hal Lanier	.75	.35	.07

		NRMT	VG-E	GOOD
☐ 480	Juan Marichal	3.50	1.75	.35
☐ 481	Chicago White Sox Team Card	1.25	.60	.12
☐ 482	Rick Reuschel	6.00	3.00	.60
☐ 483	Dal Maxvill	.50	.25	.05
☐ 484	Ernie McAnally	.50	.25	.05
☐ 485	Norm Cash	1.00	.50	.10
☐ 486A	Phillies Leaders Danny Ozark MG Carroll Beringer CO Billy DeMars CO Ray Rippelmeyer CO Bobby Wine CO (orange backgrounds)	.75	.35	.07
☐ 486B	Phillies Leaders (dark pale backgrounds)	1.00	.50	.10
☐ 487	Bruce Dal Canton	.50	.25	.05
☐ 488	Dave Campbell	.50	.25	.05
☐ 489	Jeff Burroughs	.75	.35	.07
☐ 490	Claude Osteen	.75	.35	.07
☐ 491	Bob Montgomery	.50	.25	.05
☐ 492	Pedro Borbon	.50	.25	.05
☐ 493	Duffy Dyer	.50	.25	.05
☐ 494	Rich Morales	.50	.25	.05
☐ 495	Tommy Helms	.75	.35	.07
☐ 496	Ray Lamb	.50	.25	.05
☐ 497A	Cardinals Leaders Red Schoendienst MG Vern Benson CO George Kissell CO Barney Schultz CO (orange backgrounds)	1.00	.50	.10
☐ 497B	Cardinals Leaders (dark pale backgrounds)	1.50	.75	.15
☐ 498	Graig Nettles	2.25	1.10	.22
☐ 499	Bob Moose	.50	.25	.05
☐ 500	Oakland A's Team	1.25	.60	.12
☐ 501	Larry Gura	.75	.35	.07
☐ 502	Bobby Valentine	1.00	.50	.10
☐ 503	Phil Niekro	3.50	1.75	.35
☐ 504	Earl Williams	.50	.25	.05
☐ 505	Bob Bailey	.50	.25	.05
☐ 506	Bart Johnson	.50	.25	.05
☐ 507	Darrel Chaney	.50	.25	.05
☐ 508	Gates Brown	.75	.35	.07
☐ 509	Jim Nash	.50	.25	.05
☐ 510	Amos Otis	1.00	.50	.10

		NRMT	VG-E	GOOD
☐ 511	Sam McDowell	.75	.35	.07
☐ 512	Dalton Jones	.50	.25	.05
☐ 513	Dave Marshall	.50	.25	.05
☐ 514	Jerry Kenney	.50	.25	.05
☐ 515	Andy Messersmith	.75	.35	.07
☐ 516	Danny Walton	.50	.25	.05
☐ 517A	Pirates Leaders Bill Virdon MG Don Leppert CO Bill Mazeroski CO Dave Ricketts CO Mel Wright CO (Mazeroski has no right ear)	.75	.35	.07
☐ 517B	Pirates Leaders (Mazeroski has right ear)	1.00	.50	.10
☐ 518	Bob Veale	.75	.35	.07
☐ 519	Johnny Edwards	.50	.25	.05
☐ 520	Mel Stottlemyre	1.00	.50	.10
☐ 521	Atlanta Braves Team Card	1.25	.60	.12
☐ 522	Leo Cardenas	.50	.25	.05
☐ 523	Wayne Granger	.50	.25	.05
☐ 524	Gene Tenace	.75	.35	.07
☐ 525	Jim Fregosi	.75	.35	.07
☐ 526	Ollie Brown	.50	.25	.05
☐ 527	Dan McGinn	.50	.25	.05
☐ 528	Paul Blair	.75	.35	.07
☐ 529	Milt May	1.50	.75	.15
☐ 530	Jim Kaat	3.50	1.75	.35
☐ 531	Ron Woods	1.50	.75	.15
☐ 532	Steve Mingori	1.50	.75	.15
☐ 533	Larry Stahl	1.50	.75	.15
☐ 534	Dave Lemonds	1.50	.75	.15
☐ 535	Johnny Callison	2.00	1.00	.20
☐ 536	Philadelphia Phillies Team Card	3.00	1.50	.30
☐ 537	Bill Slayback	1.50	.75	.15
☐ 538	Jim Ray Hart	2.00	1.00	.20
☐ 539	Tom Murphy	1.50	.75	.15
☐ 540	Cleon Jones	2.00	1.00	.20
☐ 541	Bob Bolin	1.50	.75	.15
☐ 542	Pat Corrales	2.00	1.00	.20
☐ 543	Alan Foster	1.50	.75	.15
☐ 544	Von Joshua	1.50	.75	.15
☐ 545	Orlando Cepeda	3.00	1.50	.30
☐ 546	Jim York	1.50	.75	.15
☐ 547	Bobby Heise	1.50	.75	.15

		NRMT	VG-E	GOOD
☐ 548	Don Durham	1.50	.75	.15
☐ 549	Rangers Leaders	2.50	1.25	.25
	Whitey Herzog MG			
	Chuck Estrada CO			
	Chuck Hiller CO			
	Jackie Moore CO			
☐ 550	Dave Johnson	2.50	1.25	.25
☐ 551	Mike Kilkenny	1.50	.75	.15
☐ 552	J.C. Martin	1.50	.75	.15
☐ 553	Mickey Scott	1.50	.75	.15
☐ 554	Dave Concepcion	3.00	1.50	.30
☐ 555	Bill Hands	1.50	.75	.15
☐ 556	New York Yankees	3.50	1.75	.35
	Team Card			
☐ 557	Bernie Williams	1.50	.75	.15
☐ 558	Jerry May	1.50	.75	.15
☐ 559	Barry Lersch	1.50	.75	.15
☐ 560	Frank Howard	2.50	1.25	.25
☐ 561	Jim Geddes	1.50	.75	.15
☐ 562	Wayne Garrett	1.50	.75	.15
☐ 563	Larry Haney	1.50	.75	.15
☐ 564	Mike Thompson	1.50	.75	.15
☐ 565	Jim Hickman	1.50	.75	.15
☐ 566	Lew Krausse	1.50	.75	.15
☐ 567	Bob Fenwick	1.50	.75	.15
☐ 568	Ray Newman	1.50	.75	.15
☐ 569	Dodgers Leaders	3.00	1.50	.30
	Walt Alston MG			
	Red Adams CO			
	Monty Basgall CO			
	Jim Gilliam CO			
	Tom Lasorda CO			
☐ 570	Bill Singer	2.00	1.00	.20
☐ 571	Rusty Torres	1.50	.75	.15
☐ 572	Gary Sutherland	1.50	.75	.15
☐ 573	Fred Beene	1.50	.75	.15
☐ 574	Bob Didier	1.50	.75	.15
☐ 575	Dock Ellis	1.50	.75	.15
☐ 576	Montreal Expos	3.00	1.50	.30
	Team Card			
☐ 577	Eric Soderholm	1.50	.75	.15
☐ 578	Ken Wright	1.50	.75	.15
☐ 579	Tom Grieve	2.00	1.00	.20
☐ 580	Joe Pepitone	2.00	1.00	.20
☐ 581	Steve Kealey	1.50	.75	.15
☐ 582	Darrell Porter	1.50	.75	.15
☐ 583	Bill Grief	1.50	.75	.15
☐ 584	Chris Arnold	1.50	.75	.15
☐ 585	Joe Niekro	2.50	1.25	.25

		NRMT	VG-E	GOOD
☐ 586	Bill Sudakis	1.50	.75	.15
☐ 587	Rich McKinney	1.50	.75	.15
☐ 588	Checklist 5	12.00	1.50	.30
☐ 589	Ken Forsch	2.00	1.00	.20
☐ 590	Deron Johnson	1.50	.75	.15
☐ 591	Mike Hedlund	1.50	.75	.15
☐ 592	John Boccabella	1.50	.75	.15
☐ 593	Royals Leaders	2.50	1.25	.25
	Jack McKeon MG			
	Galen Cisco CO			
	Harry Dunlop CO			
	Charlie Lau CO			
☐ 594	Vic Harris	1.50	.75	.15
☐ 595	Don Gullett	2.00	1.00	.20
☐ 596	Red Sox Team	3.00	1.50	.30
☐ 597	Mickey Rivers	2.00	1.00	.20
☐ 598	Phil Roof	1.50	.75	.15
☐ 599	Ed Crosby	1.50	.75	.15
☐ 600	Dave McNally	2.00	1.00	.20
☐ 601	Rookie Catchers	1.50	.75	.15
	Sergio Robles			
	George Pena			
	Rick Stelmaszek			
☐ 602	Rookie Pitchers	1.50	.75	.15
	Mel Behney			
	Ralph Garcia			
	Doug Rau			
☐ 603	Rookie 3rd Basemen	1.50	.75	.15
	Terry Hughes			
	Bill McNulty			
	Ken Reitz			
☐ 604	Rookie Pitchers	1.50	.75	.15
	Jesse Jefferson			
	Dennis O'Toole			
	Bob Strampe			
☐ 605	Rookie 1st Basemen	1.50	.75	.15
	Enos Cabell			
	Pat Bourque			
	Gonzalo Marquez			
☐ 606	Rookie Outfielders	2.50	1.25	.25
	Gary Matthews			
	Tom Paciorek			
	Jorge Roque			
☐ 607	Rookie Shortstops	1.50	.75	.15
	Pepe Frias			
	Ray Busse			
	Mario Guerrero			
☐ 608	Rookie Pitchers	1.50	.75	.15
	Steve Busby			

		NRMT	VG-E	GOOD
	Dick Colpaert			
	George Medich			
☐ 609	Rookie 2nd Basemen	3.00	1.50	.30
	Larvell Blanks			
	Pedro Garcia			
	Dave Lopes			
☐ 610	Rookie Pitchers	2.00	1.00	.20
	Jimmy Freeman			
	Charlie Hough			
	Hank Webb			
☐ 611	Rookie Outfielders ..	1.50	.75	.15
	Rich Coggins			
	Jim Wohlford			
	Richie Zisk			
☐ 612	Rookie Pitchers	1.50	.75	.15
	Steve Lawson			
	Bob Reynolds			
	Brent Strom			
☐ 613	Rookie Catchers	20.00	10.00	2.00
	Bob Boone			
	Skip Jutze			
	Mike Ivie			
☐ 614	Rookie Outfielders ..	50.00	25.00	5.00
	Alonza Bumbry			
	Dwight Evans			
	Charlie Spikes			
☐ 615	Rookie 3rd Basemen	325.00	160.00	32.00
	Ron Cey			
	John Hilton			
	Mike Schmidt			
☐ 616	Rookie Pitchers	1.50	.75	.15
	Norm Angelini			
	Steve Blateric			
	Mike Garman			
☐ 617	Rich Chiles	1.50	.75	.15
☐ 618	Andy Etchebarren ..	1.50	.75	.15
☐ 619	Billy Wilson	1.50	.75	.15
☐ 620	Tommy Harper	2.00	1.00	.20
☐ 621	Joe Ferguson	1.50	.75	.15
☐ 622	Larry Hisle	1.50	.75	.15
☐ 623	Steve Renko	1.50	.75	.15
☐ 624	Astros Leaders	2.50	1.25	.25
	Leo Durocher MG			
	Preston Gomez CO			
	Grady Hatton CO			
	Hub Kittle CO			
	Jim Owens CO			
☐ 625	Angel Mangual	1.50	.75	.15
☐ 626	Bob Barton	1.50	.75	.15

		NRMT	VG-E	GOOD
☐ 627	Luis Alvarado	1.50	.75	.15
☐ 628	Jim Slaton	1.50	.75	.15
☐ 629	Indians Team	3.00	1.50	.30
☐ 630	Denny McLain	3.00	1.50	.30
☐ 631	Tom Matchick	1.50	.75	.15
☐ 632	Dick Selma	1.50	.75	.15
☐ 633	Ike Brown	1.50	.75	.15
☐ 634	Alan Closter	1.50	.75	.15
☐ 635	Gene Alley	1.50	.75	.15
☐ 636	Rickey Clark	1.50	.75	.15
☐ 637	Norm Miller	1.50	.75	.15
☐ 638	Ken Reynolds	1.50	.75	.15
☐ 639	Willie Crawford	1.50	.75	.15
☐ 640	Dick Bosman	1.50	.75	.15
☐ 641	Cincinnati Reds	3.00	1.50	.30
	Team Card			
☐ 642	Jose LaBoy	1.50	.75	.15
☐ 643	Al Fitzmorris	1.50	.75	.15
☐ 644	Jack Heidemann	1.50	.75	.15
☐ 645	Bob Locker	1.50	.75	.15
☐ 646	Brewers Leaders ...	2.00	1.00	.20
	Del Crandall MG			
	Harvey Kuenn CO			
	Joe Nossek CO			
	Bob Shaw CO			
	Jim Walton CO			
☐ 647	George Stone	1.50	.75	.15
☐ 648	Tom Egan	1.50	.75	.15
☐ 649	Rich Folkers	1.50	.75	.15
☐ 650	Felipe Alou	2.00	1.00	.20
☐ 651	Don Carrithers	1.50	.75	.15
☐ 652	Ted Kubiak	1.50	.75	.15
☐ 653	Joe Hoerner	1.50	.75	.15
☐ 654	Twins Team	3.00	1.50	.30
☐ 655	Clay Kirby	1.50	.75	.15
☐ 656	John Ellis	1.50	.75	.15
☐ 657	Bob Johnson	1.50	.75	.15
☐ 658	Elliott Maddox	1.50	.75	.15
☐ 659	Jose Pagan	1.50	.75	.15
☐ 660	Fred Scherman	2.50	1.25	.25

1974 Topps

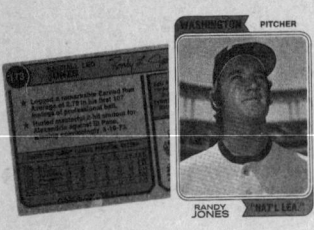

The cards in this 660-card set measure 2 ½"
by 3 ½". This year marked the first time Topps
issued all the cards of its baseball set at the
same time rather than in series. Some interesting variations were created by the rumored
move of the San Diego Padres to Washington.
Fifteen cards (13 players, the team card, and
the rookie card #599) of the Padres were
printed either as "San Diego" (SD) or "Washington." The latter are the scarcer variety and
are denoted in the checklist below by WAS.
Each team's manager and his coaches again
have a combined card with small pictures of
each coach below the larger photo of the
team's manager. The first six cards in the set
(1-6) feature Hank Aaron and his illustrious career. Other topical subsets included in the set
are League Leaders (201-208), All-Star
selections (331-339), Playoffs cards (470-471),
World Series cards (472-479), and Rookie Prospects (596-608).

		NRMT	VG-E	GOOD
COMPLETE SET (660)		450.00	200.00	40.00
COMMON PLAYER (1-660)		.25	.12	.02
☐ 1	Hank Aaron	20.00	5.00	1.00
	Complete ML record			
☐ 2	Aaron Special 54-57	3.50	1.75	.35
	Records on back			
☐ 3	Aaron Special 58-61	3.50	1.75	.35
	Memorable homers			

		NRMT	VG-E	GOOD
☐ 4	Aaron Special 62-65	3.50	1.75	.35
	Life in ML's 1954-63			
☐ 5	Aaron Special 66-69	3.50	1.75	.35
	Life in ML's 1964-73			
☐ 6	Aaron Special 70-73	3.50	1.75	.35
	Milestone homers			
☐ 7	Jim Hunter	3.00	1.50	.30
☐ 8	George Theodore	.25	.12	.02
☐ 9	Mickey Lolich	.60	.30	.06
☐ 10	Johnny Bench	11.00	5.50	1.10
☐ 11	Jim Bibby	.25	.12	.02
☐ 12	Dave May	.25	.12	.02
☐ 13	Tom Hilgendorf	.25	.12	.02
☐ 14	Paul Popovich	.25	.12	.02
☐ 15	Joe Torre	.60	.30	.06
☐ 16	Baltimore Orioles	.60	.30	.06
	Team Card			
☐ 17	Doug Bird	.25	.12	.02
☐ 18	Gary Thomasson	.25	.12	.02
☐ 19	Gerry Moses	.25	.12	.02
☐ 20	Nolan Ryan	24.00	12.00	2.40
☐ 21	Bob Gallagher	.25	.12	.02
☐ 22	Cy Acosta	.25	.12	.02
☐ 23	Craig Robinson	.25	.12	.02
☐ 24	John Hiller	.40	.20	.04
☐ 25	Ken Singleton	.50	.25	.05
☐ 26	Bill Campbell	.25	.12	.02
☐ 27	George Scott	.40	.20	.04
☐ 28	Manny Sanguillen	.40	.20	.04
☐ 29	Phil Niekro	2.00	1.00	.20
☐ 30	Bobby Bonds	.60	.30	.06
☐ 31	Astros Leaders	.40	.20	.04
	Preston Gomez MG			
	Roger Craig CO			
	Hub Kittle CO			
	Grady Hatton CO			
	Bob Lillis CO			
☐ 32A	Johnny Grubb SD	.25	.12	.02
☐ 32B	Johnny Grubb WAS	4.00	2.00	.40
☐ 33	Don Newhauser	.25	.12	.02
☐ 34	Andy Kosco	.25	.12	.02
☐ 35	Gaylord Perry	2.25	1.10	.22
☐ 36	St. Louis Cardinals	.60	.30	.06
	Team Card			
☐ 37	Dave Sells	.25	.12	.02
☐ 38	Don Kessinger	.40	.20	.04
☐ 39	Ken Suarez	.25	.12	.02
☐ 40	Jim Palmer	5.00	2.50	.50
☐ 41	Bobby Floyd	.25	.12	.02

		NRMT	VG-E	GOOD
☐ 42	Claude Osteen	.25	.12	.02
☐ 43	Jim Wynn	.50	.25	.05
☐ 44	Mel Stottlemyre	.60	.30	.06
☐ 45	Dave Johnson	.60	.30	.06
☐ 46	Pat Kelly	.25	.12	.02
☐ 47	Dick Ruthven	.25	.12	.02
☐ 48	Dick Sharon	.25	.12	.02
☐ 49	Steve Renko	.25	.12	.02
☐ 50	Rod Carew	6.50	3.25	.65
☐ 51	Bobby Heise	.25	.12	.02
☐ 52	Al Oliver	.75	.35	.07
☐ 53A	Fred Kendall SD	.25	.12	.02
☐ 53B	Fred Kendall WAS	4.00	2.00	.40
☐ 54	Elias Sosa	.25	.12	.02
☐ 55	Frank Robinson	3.50	1.75	.35
☐ 56	New York Mets Team	.75	.35	.07
☐ 57	Darold Knowles	.25	.12	.02
☐ 58	Charlie Spikes	.25	.12	.02
☐ 59	Ross Grimsley	.25	.12	.02
☐ 60	Lou Brock	3.50	1.75	.35
☐ 61	Luis Aparicio	2.00	1.00	.20
☐ 62	Bob Locker	.25	.12	.02
☐ 63	Bill Sudakis	.25	.12	.02
☐ 64	Doug Rau	.25	.12	.02
☐ 65	Amos Otis	.50	.25	.05
☐ 66	Sparky Lyle	.50	.25	.05
☐ 67	Tommy Helms	.40	.20	.04
☐ 68	Grant Jackson	.25	.12	.02
☐ 69	Del Unser	.25	.12	.02
☐ 70	Dick Allen	.60	.30	.06
☐ 71	Dan Frisella	.25	.12	.02
☐ 72	Aurelio Rodriguez	.25	.12	.02
☐ 73	Mike Marshall	.40	.20	.04
☐ 74	Twins Team	.60	.30	.06
☐ 75	Jim Colborn	.25	.12	.02
☐ 76	Mickey Rivers	.40	.20	.04
☐ 77A	Rich Troedson SD	.25	.12	.02
☐ 77B	Rich Troedson WAS	4.00	2.00	.40
☐ 78	Giants Leaders	.40	.20	.04
	Charlie Fox MG			
	John McNamara CO			
	Joe Amalfitano CO			
	Andy Gilbert CO			
	Don McMahon CO			
☐ 79	Gene Tenace	.40	.20	.04
☐ 80	Tom Seaver	8.00	4.00	.80
☐ 81	Frank Duffy	.25	.12	.02
☐ 82	Dave Giusti	.25	.12	.02
☐ 83	Orlando Cepeda	1.00	.50	.10
☐ 84	Rick Wise	.25	.12	.02
☐ 85	Joe Morgan	3.50	1.75	.35
☐ 86	Joe Ferguson	.25	.12	.02
☐ 87	Fergie Jenkins	1.25	.60	.12
☐ 88	Freddie Patek	.25	.12	.02
☐ 89	Jackie Brown	.25	.12	.02
☐ 90	Bobby Murcer	.60	.30	.06
☐ 91	Ken Forsch	.25	.12	.02
☐ 92	Paul Blair	.25	.12	.02
☐ 93	Rod Gilbreath	.25	.12	.02
☐ 94	Tigers Team	.60	.30	.06
☐ 95	Steve Carlton	6.00	3.00	.60
☐ 96	Jerry Hairston	.25	.12	.02
☐ 97	Bob Bailey	.25	.12	.02
☐ 98	Bert Blyleven	2.00	1.00	.20
☐ 99	Brewers Leaders	.40	.20	.04
	Del Crandall MG			
	Harvey Kuenn CO			
	Joe Nossek CO			
	Jim Walton CO			
	Al Widmar CO			
☐ 100	Willie Stargell	3.00	1.50	.30
☐ 101	Bobby Valentine	.50	.25	.05
☐ 102A	Bill Greif SD	.25	.12	.02
☐ 102B	Bill Greif WAS	4.00	2.00	.40
☐ 103	Sal Bando	.50	.25	.05
☐ 104	Ron Bryant	.25	.12	.02
☐ 105	Carlton Fisk	6.00	3.00	.60
☐ 106	Harry Parker	.25	.12	.02
☐ 107	Alex Johnson	.25	.12	.02
☐ 108	Al Hrabosky	.25	.12	.02
☐ 109	Bob Grich	.50	.25	.05
☐ 110	Billy Williams	2.75	1.35	.27
☐ 111	Clay Carroll	.25	.12	.02
☐ 112	Dave Lopes	.50	.25	.05
☐ 113	Dick Drago	.25	.12	.02
☐ 114	Angels Team	.60	.30	.06
☐ 115	Willie Horton	.40	.20	.04
☐ 116	Jerry Reuss	.40	.20	.04
☐ 117	Ron Blomberg	.25	.12	.02
☐ 118	Bill Lee	.25	.12	.02
☐ 119	Phillies Leaders	.40	.20	.04
	Danny Ozark MG			
	Ray Ripplemeyer CO			
	Bobby Wine CO			
	Carroll Beringer CO			
	Billy DeMars CO			
☐ 120	Wilbur Wood	.25	.12	.02
☐ 121	Larry Lintz	.25	.12	.02

	NRMT	VG-E	GOOD
☐ 122 Jim Holt	.25	.12	.02
☐ 123 Nelson Briles	.25	.12	.02
☐ 124 Bobby Coluccio	.25	.12	.02
☐ 125A Nate Colbert SD	.25	.12	.02
☐ 125B Nate Colbert WAS	4.00	2.00	.40
☐ 126 Checklist 1	1.25	.15	.03
☐ 127 Tom Paciorek	.25	.12	.02
☐ 128 John Ellis	.25	.12	.02
☐ 129 Chris Speier	.25	.12	.02
☐ 130 Reggie Jackson	11.00	5.50	1.10
☐ 131 Bob Boone	2.25	1.10	.22
☐ 132 Felix Millan	.25	.12	.02
☐ 133 David Clyde	.25	.12	.02
☐ 134 Denis Menke	.25	.12	.02
☐ 135 Roy White	.40	.20	.04
☐ 136 Rick Reuschel	1.75	.85	.17
☐ 137 Al Bumbry	.25	.12	.02
☐ 138 Eddie Brinkman	.25	.12	.02
☐ 139 Aurelio Monteagudo	.25	.12	.02
☐ 140 Darrell Evans	.60	.30	.06
☐ 141 Pat Bourque	.25	.12	.02
☐ 142 Pedro Garcia	.25	.12	.02
☐ 143 Dick Woodson	.25	.12	.02
☐ 144 Dodgers Leaders	1.00	.50	.10
Walter Alston MG			
Tom Lasorda CO			
Jim Gilliam CO			
Red Adams CO			
Monty Basgall CO			
☐ 145 Dock Ellis	.25	.12	.02
☐ 146 Ron Fairly	.25	.12	.02
☐ 147 Bart Johnson	.25	.12	.02
☐ 148A Dave Hilton SD	.25	.12	.02
☐ 148B Dave Hilton WAS	4.00	2.00	.40
☐ 149 Mac Scarce	.25	.12	.02
☐ 150 John Mayberry	.40	.20	.04
☐ 151 Diego Segui	.25	.12	.02
☐ 152 Oscar Gamble	.40	.20	.04
☐ 153 Jon Matlack	.25	.12	.02
☐ 154 Astros Team	.60	.30	.06
☐ 155 Bert Campaneris	.40	.20	.04
☐ 156 Randy Moffitt	.25	.12	.02
☐ 157 Vic Harris	.25	.12	.02
☐ 158 Jack Billingham	.25	.12	.02
☐ 159 Jim Ray Hart	.25	.12	.02
☐ 160 Brooks Robinson	4.00	2.00	.40
☐ 161 Ray Burris	.50	.25	.05
☐ 162 Bill Freehan	.50	.25	.05
☐ 163 Ken Berry	.25	.12	.02
☐ 164 Tom House	.25	.12	.02
☐ 165 Willie Davis	.40	.20	.04
☐ 166 Royals Leaders	.40	.20	.04
Jack McKeon MG			
Charlie Lau CO			
Harry Dunlop CO			
Galen Cisco CO			
☐ 167 Luis Tiant	.60	.30	.06
☐ 168 Danny Thompson	.25	.12	.02
☐ 169 Steve Rogers	.50	.25	.05
☐ 170 Bill Melton	.25	.12	.02
☐ 171 Eduardo Rodriguez	.25	.12	.02
☐ 172 Gene Clines	.25	.12	.02
☐ 173A Randy Jones SD	.60	.30	.06
☐ 173B Randy Jones WAS	4.00	2.00	.40
☐ 174 Bill Robinson	.40	.20	.04
☐ 175 Reggie Cleveland	.25	.12	.02
☐ 176 John Lowenstein	.25	.12	.02
☐ 177 Dave Roberts	.25	.12	.02
☐ 178 Garry Maddox	.40	.20	.04
☐ 179 Mets Leaders	1.25	.60	.12
Yogi Berra MG			
Rube Walker CO			
Eddie Yost CO			
Roy McMillan CO			
Joe Pignatano CO			
☐ 180 Ken Holtzman	.40	.20	.04
☐ 181 Cesar Geronimo	.25	.12	.02
☐ 182 Lindy McDaniel	.25	.12	.02
☐ 183 Johnny Oates	.25	.12	.02
☐ 184 Texas Rangers	.60	.30	.06
Team Card			
☐ 185 Jose Cardenal	.25	.12	.02
☐ 186 Fred Scherman	.25	.12	.02
☐ 187 Don Baylor	1.00	.50	.10
☐ 188 Rudy Meoli	.25	.12	.02
☐ 189 Jim Brewer	.25	.12	.02
☐ 190 Tony Oliva	1.00	.50	.10
☐ 191 Al Fitzmorris	.25	.12	.02
☐ 192 Mario Guerrero	.25	.12	.02
☐ 193 Tom Walker	.25	.12	.02
☐ 194 Darrell Porter	.25	.12	.02
☐ 195 Carlos May	.25	.12	.02
☐ 196 Jim Fregosi	.40	.20	.04
☐ 197A Vicente Romo SD	.25	.12	.02
☐ 197B Vicente Romo WAS	4.00	2.00	.40
☐ 198 Dave Cash	.25	.12	.02
☐ 199 Mike Kekich	.25	.12	.02
☐ 200 Cesar Cedeno	.40	.20	.04

		NRMT	VG-E	GOOD
☐ 201	Batting Leaders	3.50	1.75	.35
	Rod Carew			
	Pete Rose			
☐ 202	Home Run Leaders .	2.00	1.00	.20
	Reggie Jackson			
	Willie Stargell			
☐ 203	RBI Leaders	2.00	1.00	.20
	Reggie Jackson			
	Willie Stargell			
☐ 204	Stolen Base Leaders	.75	.35	.07
	Tommy Harper			
	Lou Brock			
☐ 205	Victory Leaders	.60	.30	.06
	Wilbur Wood			
	Ron Bryant			
☐ 206	ERA Leaders	2.50	1.25	.25
	Jim Palmer			
	Tom Seaver			
☐ 207	Strikeout Leaders ...	3.00	1.50	.30
	Nolan Ryan			
	Tom Seaver			
☐ 208	Leading Firemen ...	.60	.30	.06
	John Hiller			
	Mike Marshall			
☐ 209	Ted Sizemore	.25	.12	.02
☐ 210	Bill Singer	.25	.12	.02
☐ 211	Chicago Cubs Team	.60	.30	.06
☐ 212	Rollie Fingers	2.25	1.10	.22
☐ 213	Dave Rader	.25	.12	.02
☐ 214	Billy Grabarkewitz ..	.25	.12	.02
☐ 215	Al Kaline	4.50	2.25	.45
☐ 216	Ray Sadecki	.25	.12	.02
☐ 217	Tim Foli	.25	.12	.02
☐ 218	Johnny Briggs	.25	.12	.02
☐ 219	Doug Griffin	.25	.12	.02
☐ 220	Don Sutton	2.00	1.00	.20
☐ 221	White Sox Leaders .	.40	.20	.04
	Chuck Tanner MG			
	Jim Mahoney CO			
	Alex Monchak CO			
	Johnny Sain CO			
	Joe Lonnett CO			
☐ 222	Ramon Hernandez ..	.25	.12	.02
☐ 223	Jeff Burroughs	.50	.25	.05
☐ 224	Roger Metzger	.25	.12	.02
☐ 225	Paul Splittorff	.25	.12	.02
☐ 226A	Padres Team SD ...	1.00	.50	.10
☐ 226B	Padres Team WAS ..	5.00	2.50	.50
☐ 227	Mike Lum	.25	.12	.02
☐ 228	Ted Kubiak	.25	.12	.02
☐ 229	Fritz Peterson	.25	.12	.02
☐ 230	Tony Perez	1.50	.75	.15
☐ 231	Dick Tidrow	.25	.12	.02
☐ 232	Steve Brye	.25	.12	.02
☐ 233	Jim Barr	.25	.12	.02
☐ 234	John Milner	.25	.12	.02
☐ 235	Dave McNally	.40	.20	.04
☐ 236	Cardinals Leaders ..	.60	.30	.06
	Red Schoendienst MG			
	Barney Schultz CO			
	George Kissell CO			
	Johnny Lewis CO			
	Vern Benson CO			
☐ 237	Ken Brett	.25	.12	.02
☐ 238	Fran Healy HOR ...	.40	.20	.04
	(Munson sliding in			
	background)			
☐ 239	Bill Russell	.40	.20	.04
☐ 240	Joe Coleman	.25	.12	.02
☐ 241A	Glenn Beckert SD ..	.40	.20	.04
☐ 241B	Glenn Beckert WAS	4.00	2.00	.40
☐ 242	Bill Gogolewski	.25	.12	.02
☐ 243	Bob Oliver	.25	.12	.02
☐ 244	Carl Morton	.25	.12	.02
☐ 245	Cleon Jones	.25	.12	.02
☐ 246	Athletics Team	.60	.30	.06
☐ 247	Rick Miller	.25	.12	.02
☐ 248	Tom Hall	.25	.12	.02
☐ 249	George Mitterwald ..	.25	.12	.02
☐ 250A	Willie McCovey SD ..	4.00	2.00	.40
☐ 250B	Willie McCovey WAS	25.00	12.50	2.50
☐ 251	Graig Nettles	1.50	.75	.15
☐ 252	Dave Parker	25.00	12.50	2.50
☐ 253	John Boccabella ...	.25	.12	.02
☐ 254	Stan Bahnsen	.25	.12	.02
☐ 255	Larry Bowa	.60	.30	.06
☐ 256	Tom Griffin	.25	.12	.02
☐ 257	Buddy Bell	1.00	.50	.10
☐ 258	Jerry Morales	.25	.12	.02
☐ 259	Bob Reynolds	.25	.12	.02
☐ 260	Ted Simmons	1.00	.50	.10
☐ 261	Jerry Bell	.25	.12	.02
☐ 262	Ed Kirkpatrick	.25	.12	.02
☐ 263	Checklist 2	1.25	.15	.03
☐ 264	Joe Rudi	.40	.20	.04
☐ 265	Tug McGraw	.60	.30	.06
☐ 266	Jim Northrup	.40	.20	.04
☐ 267	Andy Messersmith ..	.40	.20	.04

		NRMT	VG-E	GOOD
☐ 268	Tom Grieve	.40	.20	.04
☐ 269	Bob Johnson	.25	.12	.02
☐ 270	Ron Santo	.60	.30	.06
☐ 271	Bill Hands	.25	.12	.02
☐ 272	Paul Casanova	.25	.12	.02
☐ 273	Checklist 3	1.25	.15	.03
☐ 274	Fred Beene	.25	.12	.02
☐ 275	Ron Hunt	.25	.12	.02
☐ 276	Angels Leaders	.40	.20	.04
	Bobby Winkles MG			
	John Roseboro CO			
	Tom Morgan CO			
	Jimmie Reese CO			
	Salty Parker CO			
☐ 277	Gary Nolan	.25	.12	.02
☐ 278	Cookie Rojas	.25	.12	.02
☐ 279	Jim Crawford	.25	.12	.02
☐ 280	Carl Yastrzemski	11.00	5.50	1.10
☐ 281	Giants Team	.60	.30	.06
☐ 282	Doyle Alexander	.50	.25	.05
☐ 283	Mike Schmidt	65.00	32.50	6.50
☐ 284	Dave Duncan	.25	.12	.02
☐ 285	Reggie Smith	.50	.25	.05
☐ 286	Tony Muser	.25	.12	.02
☐ 287	Clay Kirby	.25	.12	.02
☐ 288	Gorman Thomas	1.75	.85	.17
☐ 289	Rick Auerbach	.25	.12	.02
☐ 290	Vida Blue	.50	.25	.05
☐ 291	Don Hahn	.25	.12	.02
☐ 292	Chuck Seelbach	.25	.12	.02
☐ 293	Milt May	.25	.12	.02
☐ 294	Steve Foucault	.25	.12	.02
☐ 295	Rick Monday	.40	.20	.04
☐ 296	Ray Corbin	.25	.12	.02
☐ 297	Hal Breeden	.25	.12	.02
☐ 298	Roric Harrison	.25	.12	.02
☐ 299	Gene Michael	.40	.20	.04
☐ 300	Pete Rose	16.00	8.00	1.60
☐ 301	Bob Montgomery	.25	.12	.02
☐ 302	Rudy May	.25	.12	.02
☐ 303	George Hendrick	.40	.20	.04
☐ 304	Don Wilson	.25	.12	.02
☐ 305	Tito Fuentes	.25	.12	.02
☐ 306	Orioles Leaders	.75	.35	.07
	Earl Weaver MG			
	Jim Frey CO			
	George Bamberger CO			
	Billy Hunter CO			

		NRMT	VG-E	GOOD
	George Staller CO			
☐ 307	Luis Melendez	.25	.12	.02
☐ 308	Bruce Dal Canton	.25	.12	.02
☐ 309A	Dave Roberts SD	.25	.12	.02
☐ 309B	Dave Roberts WAS	5.00	2.50	.50
☐ 310	Terry Forster	.40	.20	.04
☐ 311	Jerry Grote	.25	.12	.02
☐ 312	Deron Johnson	.25	.12	.02
☐ 313	Barry Lersch	.25	.12	.02
☐ 314	Milwaukee Brewers Team Card	.60	.30	.06
☐ 315	Ron Cey	1.00	.50	.10
☐ 316	Jim Perry	.40	.20	.04
☐ 317	Richie Zisk	.25	.12	.02
☐ 318	Jim Merritt	.25	.12	.02
☐ 319	Randy Hundley	.25	.12	.02
☐ 320	Dusty Baker	.50	.25	.05
☐ 321	Steve Braun	.25	.12	.02
☐ 322	Ernie McAnally	.25	.12	.02
☐ 323	Richie Scheinblum	.25	.12	.02
☐ 324	Steve Kline	.25	.12	.02
☐ 325	Tommy Harper	.40	.20	.04
☐ 326	Reds Leaders	.75	.35	.07
	Sparky Anderson MG			
	Larry Shephard CO			
	George Scherger CO			
	Alex Grammas CO			
	Ted Kluszewski CO			
☐ 327	Tom Timmermann	.25	.12	.02
☐ 328	Skip Jutze	.25	.12	.02
☐ 329	Mark Belanger	.40	.20	.04
☐ 330	Juan Marichal	2.50	1.25	.25
☐ 331	All-Star Catchers	2.00	1.00	.20
	Carlton Fisk			
	Johnny Bench			
☐ 332	All-Star 1B	1.75	.85	.17
	Dick Allen			
	Hank Aaron			
☐ 333	All-Star 2B	2.00	1.00	.20
	Rod Carew			
	Joe Morgan			
☐ 334	All-Star 3B	1.00	.50	.10
	Brooks Robinson			
	Ron Santo			
☐ 335	All-Star SS	.40	.20	.04
	Bert Campaneris			
	Chris Speier			
☐ 336	All-Star LF	2.50	1.25	.25
	Bobby Murcer			

		NRMT	VG-E	GOOD				NRMT	VG-E	GOOD
	Pete Rose				☐ 373	John Curtis		.25	.12	.02
☐ 337	All-Star CF	.40	.20	.04	☐ 374	Marty Perez		.25	.12	.02
	Amos Otis				☐ 375	Earl Williams		.25	.12	.02
	Cesar Cedeno				☐ 376	Jorge Orta		.25	.12	.02
☐ 338	All-Star RF	2.50	1.25	.25	☐ 377	Ron Woods		.25	.12	.02
	Reggie Jackson				☐ 378	Burt Hooton		.40	.20	.04
	Billy Williams				☐ 379	Rangers Leaders		1.00	.50	.10
☐ 339	All-Star Pitchers	.50	.25	.05		Billy Martin MG				
	Jim Hunter					Frank Lucchesi CO				
	Rick Wise					Art Fowler CO				
☐ 340	Thurman Munson	5.00	2.50	.50		Charlie Silvera CO				
☐ 341	Dan Driessen	.75	.35	.07		Jackie Moore CO				
☐ 342	Jim Lonborg	.40	.20	.04	☐ 380	Bud Harrelson		.40	.20	.04
☐ 343	Royals Team	.60	.30	.06	☐ 381	Charlie Sands		.25	.12	.02
☐ 344	Mike Caldwell	.40	.20	.04	☐ 382	Bob Moose		.25	.12	.02
☐ 345	Bill North	.25	.12	.02	☐ 383	Phillies Team		.60	.30	.06
☐ 346	Ron Reed	.25	.12	.02	☐ 384	Chris Chambliss		.50	.25	.05
☐ 347	Sandy Alomar	.25	.12	.02	☐ 385	Don Gullett		.40	.20	.04
☐ 348	Pete Richert	.25	.12	.02	☐ 386	Gary Matthews		.50	.25	.05
☐ 349	John Vukovich	.25	.12	.02	☐ 387A	Rich Morales SD		.25	.12	.02
☐ 350	Bob Gibson	3.00	1.50	.30	☐ 387B	Rich Morales WAS		5.00	2.50	.50
☐ 351	Dwight Evans	7.50	3.75	.75	☐ 388	Phil Roof		.25	.12	.02
☐ 352	Bill Stoneman	.25	.12	.02	☐ 389	Gates Brown		.40	.20	.04
☐ 353	Rich Coggins	.25	.12	.02	☐ 390	Lou Piniella		.60	.30	.06
☐ 354	Cubs Leaders	.40	.20	.04	☐ 391	Billy Champion		.25	.12	.02
	Whitey Lockman MG				☐ 392	Dick Green		.25	.12	.02
	J.C. Martin CO				☐ 393	Orlando Pena		.25	.12	.02
	Hank Aguirre CO				☐ 394	Ken Henderson		.25	.12	.02
	Al Spangler CO				☐ 395	Doug Rader		.40	.20	.04
	Jim Marshall CO				☐ 396	Tommy Davis		.40	.20	.04
☐ 355	Dave Nelson	.25	.12	.02	☐ 397	George Stone		.25	.12	.02
☐ 356	Jerry Koosman	.60	.30	.06	☐ 398	Duke Sims		.25	.12	.02
☐ 357	Buddy Bradford	.25	.12	.02	☐ 399	Mike Paul		.25	.12	.02
☐ 358	Dal Maxvill	.25	.12	.02	☐ 400	Harmon Killebrew		3.00	1.50	.30
☐ 359	Brent Strom	.25	.12	.02	☐ 401	Elliott Maddox		.25	.12	.02
☐ 360	Greg Luzinski	.75	.35	.07	☐ 402	Jim Rooker		.25	.12	.02
☐ 361	Don Carrithers	.25	.12	.02	☐ 403	Red Sox Leaders		.40	.20	.04
☐ 362	Hal King	.25	.12	.02		Darrell Johnson MG				
☐ 363	Yankees Team	.60	.30	.06		Eddie Popowski CO				
☐ 364A	Cito Gaston SD	.50	.25	.05		Lee Stange CO				
☐ 364B	Cito Gaston WAS	5.00	2.50	.50		Don Zimmer CO				
☐ 365	Steve Busby	.40	.20	.04		Don Bryant CO				
☐ 366	Larry Hisle	.40	.20	.04	☐ 404	Jim Howarth		.25	.12	.02
☐ 367	Norm Cash	.75	.35	.07	☐ 405	Ellie Rodriguez		.25	.12	.02
☐ 368	Manny Mota	.40	.20	.04	☐ 406	Steve Arlin		.25	.12	.02
☐ 369	Paul Lindblad	.25	.12	.02	☐ 407	Jim Wohlford		.25	.12	.02
☐ 370	Bob Watson	.40	.20	.04	☐ 408	Charlie Hough		.50	.25	.05
☐ 371	Jim Slaton	.25	.12	.02	☐ 409	Ike Brown		.25	.12	.02
☐ 372	Ken Reitz	.25	.12	.02	☐ 410	Pedro Borbon		.25	.12	.02

		NRMT	VG-E	GOOD
☐ 411	Frank Baker	.25	.12	.02
☐ 412	Chuck Taylor	.25	.12	.02
☐ 413	Don Money	.25	.12	.02
☐ 414	Checklist 4	1.25	.15	.03
☐ 415	Gary Gentry	.25	.12	.02
☐ 416	White Sox Team	.60	.30	.06
☐ 417	Rich Folkers	.25	.12	.02
☐ 418	Walt Williams	.25	.12	.02
☐ 419	Wayne Twitchell	.25	.12	.02
☐ 420	Ray Fosse	.25	.12	.02
☐ 421	Dan Fife	.25	.12	.02
☐ 422	Gonzalo Marquez	.25	.12	.02
☐ 423	Fred Stanley	.25	.12	.02
☐ 424	Jim Beauchamp	.25	.12	.02
☐ 425	Pete Broberg	.25	.12	.02
☐ 426	Rennie Stennett	.25	.12	.02
☐ 427	Bobby Bolin	.25	.12	.02
☐ 428	Gary Sutherland	.25	.12	.02
☐ 429	Dick Lange	.25	.12	.02
☐ 430	Matty Alou	.40	.20	.04
☐ 431	Gene Garber	.40	.20	.04
☐ 432	Chris Arnold	.25	.12	.02
☐ 433	Lerrin LaGrow	.25	.12	.02
☐ 434	Ken McMullen	.25	.12	.02
☐ 435	Dave Concepcion	.75	.35	.07
☐ 436	Don Hood	.25	.12	.02
☐ 437	Jim Lyttle	.25	.12	.02
☐ 438	Ed Herrmann	.25	.12	.02
☐ 439	Norm Miller	.25	.12	.02
☐ 440	Jim Kaat	1.00	.50	.10
☐ 441	Tom Ragland	.25	.12	.02
☐ 442	Alan Foster	.25	.12	.02
☐ 443	Tom Hutton	.25	.12	.02
☐ 444	Vic Davalillo	.25	.12	.02
☐ 445	George Medich	.25	.12	.02
☐ 446	Len Randle	.25	.12	.02
☐ 447	Twins Leaders	.40	.20	.04
	Frank Quilici MG			
	Ralph Rowe CO			
	Bob Rodgers CO			
	Vern Morgan CO			
☐ 448	Ron Hodges	.25	.12	.02
☐ 449	Tom McCraw	.25	.12	.02
☐ 450	Rich Hebner	.25	.12	.02
☐ 451	Tommy John	1.50	.75	.15
☐ 452	Gene Hiser	.25	.12	.02
☐ 453	Balor Moore	.25	.12	.02
☐ 454	Kurt Bevacqua	.25	.12	.02
☐ 455	Tom Bradley	.25	.12	.02
☐ 456	Dave Winfield	40.00	20.00	4.00
☐ 457	Chuck Goggin	.25	.12	.02
☐ 458	Jim Ray	.25	.12	.02
☐ 459	Cincinnati Reds Team Card	.60	.30	.06
☐ 460	Boog Powell	.60	.30	.06
☐ 461	John Odom	.25	.12	.02
☐ 462	Luis Alvarado	.25	.12	.02
☐ 463	Pat Dobson	.25	.12	.02
☐ 464	Jose Cruz	.50	.25	.05
☐ 465	Dick Bosman	.25	.12	.02
☐ 466	Dick Billings	.25	.12	.02
☐ 467	Winston Llenas	.25	.12	.02
☐ 468	Pepe Frias	.25	.12	.02
☐ 469	Joe Decker	.25	.12	.02
☐ 470	AL Playoffs (Reggie Jackson)	2.50	1.25	.25
☐ 471	NL Playoffs (Matlack pitching)	.75	.35	.07
☐ 472	World Series Game 1 (Knowles pitching)	.75	.35	.07
☐ 473	World Series Game 2 (Willie Mays batting)	2.50	1.25	.25
☐ 474	World Series Game 3 (Campaneris stealing)	.75	.35	.07
☐ 475	World Series Game 4 (Staub batting)	.75	.35	.07
☐ 476	World Series Game 5 Cleon Jones scoring)	.75	.35	.07
☐ 477	World Series Game 6 (Reggie Jackson)	2.50	1.25	.25
☐ 478	World Series Game 7 (Campaneris batting)	.75	.35	.07
☐ 479	World Series Summary A's celebrate; win 2nd consecutive championship	.75	.35	.07
☐ 480	Willie Crawford	.25	.12	.02
☐ 481	Jerry Terrell	.25	.12	.02
☐ 482	Bob Didier	.25	.12	.02
☐ 483	Atlanta Braves Team Card	.60	.30	.06
☐ 484	Carmen Fanzone	.25	.12	.02
☐ 485	Felipe Alou	.40	.20	.04
☐ 486	Steve Stone	.40	.20	.04
☐ 487	Ted Martinez	.25	.12	.02
☐ 488	Andy Etchebarren	.25	.12	.02

		NRMT	VG-E	GOOD			NRMT	VG-E	GOOD
☐ 489	Pirates Leaders	.40	.20	.04	☐ 530	Mickey Stanley	.40	.20	.04
	Danny Murtaugh MG				☐ 531	Expos Leaders	.40	.20	.04
	Don Osborn CO					Gene Mauch MG			
	Don Leppert CO					Dave Bristol CO			
	Bill Mazeroski CO					Cal McLish CO			
	Bob Skinner CO					Larry Doby CO			
☐ 490	Vada Pinson	.60	.30	.06		Jerry Zimmerman CO			
☐ 491	Roger Nelson	.25	.12	.02	☐ 532	Skip Lockwood	.25	.12	.02
☐ 492	Mike Rogodzinski ...	.25	.12	.02	☐ 533	Mike Phillips	.25	.12	.02
☐ 493	Joe Hoerner	.25	.12	.02	☐ 534	Eddie Watt	.25	.12	.02
☐ 494	Ed Goodson	.25	.12	.02	☐ 535	Bob Tolan	.25	.12	.02
☐ 495	Dick McAuliffe	.25	.12	.02	☐ 536	Duffy Dyer	.25	.12	.02
☐ 496	Tom Murphy	.25	.12	.02	☐ 537	Steve Mingori	.25	.12	.02
☐ 497	Bobby Mitchell	.25	.12	.02	☐ 538	Cesar Tovar	.25	.12	.02
☐ 498	Pat Corrales	.40	.20	.04	☐ 539	Lloyd Allen	.25	.12	.02
☐ 499	Rusty Torres	.25	.12	.02	☐ 540	Bob Robertson	.25	.12	.02
☐ 500	Lee May	.40	.20	.04	☐ 541	Cleveland Indians	.60	.30	.06
☐ 501	Eddie Leon	.25	.12	.02		Team Card			
☐ 502	Dave LaRoche	.25	.12	.02	☐ 542	Rich Gossage	1.75	.85	.17
☐ 503	Eric Soderholm	.25	.12	.02	☐ 543	Danny Cater	.25	.12	.02
☐ 504	Joe Niekro	.50	.25	.05	☐ 544	Ron Schueler	.25	.12	.02
☐ 505	Bill Buckner	.60	.30	.06	☐ 545	Billy Conigliaro	.25	.12	.02
☐ 506	Ed Farmer	.25	.12	.02	☐ 546	Mike Corkins	.25	.12	.02
☐ 507	Larry Stahl	.25	.12	.02	☐ 547	Glenn Borgmann	.25	.12	.02
☐ 508	Expos Team	.60	.30	.06	☐ 548	Sonny Siebert	.25	.12	.02
☐ 509	Jesse Jefferson	.25	.12	.02	☐ 549	Mike Jorgensen	.25	.12	.02
☐ 510	Wayne Garrett	.25	.12	.02	☐ 550	Sam McDowell	.40	.20	.04
☐ 511	Toby Harrah	.40	.20	.04	☐ 551	Von Joshua	.25	.12	.02
☐ 512	Joe Lahoud	.25	.12	.02	☐ 552	Denny Doyle	.25	.12	.02
☐ 513	Jim Campanis	.25	.12	.02	☐ 553	Jim Willoughby	.25	.12	.02
☐ 514	Paul Schaal	.25	.12	.02	☐ 554	Tim Johnson	.25	.12	.02
☐ 515	Willie Montanez	.25	.12	.02	☐ 555	Woodie Fryman	.25	.12	.02
☐ 516	Horacio Pina	.25	.12	.02	☐ 556	Dave Campbell	.25	.12	.02
☐ 517	Mike Hegan	.25	.12	.02	☐ 557	Jim McGlothlin	.25	.12	.02
☐ 518	Derrel Thomas	.25	.12	.02	☐ 558	Bill Fahey	.25	.12	.02
☐ 519	Bill Sharp	.25	.12	.02	☐ 559	Darrell Chaney	.25	.12	.02
☐ 520	Tim McCarver	.60	.30	.06	☐ 560	Mike Cuellar	.40	.20	.04
☐ 521	Indians Leaders	.40	.20	.04	☐ 561	Ed Kranepool	.40	.20	.04
	Ken Aspromonte MG				☐ 562	Jack Aker	.25	.12	.02
	Clay Bryant CO				☐ 563	Hal McRae	.40	.20	.04
	Tony Pacheco CO				☐ 564	Mike Ryan	.25	.12	.02
☐ 522	J.R. Richard	.50	.25	.05	☐ 565	Milt Wilcox	.25	.12	.02
☐ 523	Cecil Cooper	1.75	.85	.17	☐ 566	Jackie Hernandez ...	.25	.12	.02
☐ 524	Bill Plummer	.25	.12	.02	☐ 567	Red Sox Team	.60	.30	.06
☐ 525	Clyde Wright	.25	.12	.02	☐ 568	Mike Torrez	.40	.20	.04
☐ 526	Frank Tepedino	.25	.12	.02	☐ 569	Rick Dempsey	.40	.20	.04
☐ 527	Bobby Darwin	.25	.12	.02	☐ 570	Ralph Garr	.40	.20	.04
☐ 528	Bill Bonham	.25	.12	.02	☐ 571	Rich Hand	.25	.12	.02
☐ 529	Horace Clarke	.25	.12	.02	☐ 572	Enzo Hernandez ...	.25	.12	.02

		NRMT	VG-E	GOOD
☐ 573	Mike Adams	.25	.12	.02
☐ 574	Bill Parsons	.25	.12	.02
☐ 575	Steve Garvey	11.00	5.50	1.10
☐ 576	Scipio Spinks	.25	.12	.02
☐ 577	Mike Sadek	.25	.12	.02
☐ 578	Ralph Houk MG	.40	.20	.04
☐ 579	Cecil Upshaw	.25	.12	.02
☐ 580	Jim Spencer	.25	.12	.02
☐ 581	Fred Norman	.25	.12	.02
☐ 582	Bucky Dent	1.50	.75	.15
☐ 583	Marty Pattin	.25	.12	.02
☐ 584	Ken Rudolph	.25	.12	.02
☐ 585	Merv Rettenmund	.25	.12	.02
☐ 586	Jack Brohamer	.25	.12	.02
☐ 587	Larry Christenson	.25	.12	.02
☐ 588	Hal Lanier	.40	.20	.04
☐ 589	Boots Day	.25	.12	.02
☐ 590	Roger Moret	.25	.12	.02
☐ 591	Sonny Jackson	.25	.12	.02
☐ 592	Ed Bane	.25	.12	.02
☐ 593	Steve Yeager	.40	.20	.04
☐ 594	Leroy Stanton	.25	.12	.02
☐ 595	Steve Blass	.40	.20	.04
☐ 596	Rookie Pitchers	.40	.20	.04
	Wayne Garland			
	Fred Holdsworth			
	Mark Littell			
	Dick Pole			
☐ 597	Rookie Shortstops	.60	.30	.06
	Dave Chalk			
	John Gamble			
	Pete MacKanin			
	Manny Trillo			
☐ 598	Rookie Outfielders	4.50	2.25	.45
	Dave Augustine			
	Ken Griffey			
	Steve Ontiveros			
	Jim Tyrone			
☐ 599A	Rookie Pitchers WAS	.60	.30	.06
	Ron Diorio			
	Dave Freisleben			
	Frank Riccelli			
	Greg Shanahan			
☐ 599B	Rookie Pitchers SD	3.00	1.50	.30
	(SD in large print)			
☐ 599C	Rookie Pitchers SD	4.50	2.25	.45
	(SD in small print)			
☐ 600	Rookie Infielders	5.00	2.50	.50
	Ron Cash			

		NRMT	VG-E	GOOD
	Jim Cox			
	Bill Madlock			
	Reggie Sanders			
☐ 601	Rookie Outfielders	2.50	1.25	.25
	Ed Armbrister			
	Rich Bladt			
	Brian Downing			
	Bake McBride			
☐ 602	Rookie Pitchers	.50	.25	.05
	Glen Abbott			
	Rick Henninger			
	Craig Swan			
	Dan Vossler			
☐ 603	Rookie Catchers	.50	.25	.05
	Barry Foote			
	Tom Lundstedt			
	Charlie Moore			
	Sergio Robles			
☐ 604	Rookie Infielders	3.50	1.75	.35
	Terry Hughes			
	John Knox			
	Andy Thornton			
	Frank White			
☐ 605	Rookie Pitchers	2.00	1.00	.20
	Vic Albury			
	Ken Frailing			
	Kevin Kobel			
	Frank Tanana			
☐ 606	Rookie Outfielders	.40	.20	.04
	Jim Fuller			
	Wilbur Howard			
	Tommy Smith			
	Otto Velez			
☐ 607	Rookie Shortstops	.40	.20	.04
	Leo Foster			
	Tom Heintzelman			
	Dave Rosello			
	Frank Taveras			
☐ 608A	Rookie Pitchers: ERR	2.00	1.00	.20
	Bob Apodaca (sic)			
	Dick Baney			
	John D'Acquisto			
	Mike Wallace			
☐ 608B	Rookie Pitchers: COR	.40	.20	.04
	Bob Apodaca			
	Dick Baney			
	John D'Acquisto			
	Mike Wallace			

		NRMT	VG-E	GOOD
☐ 609	Rico Petrocelli	.40	.20	.04
☐ 610	Dave Kingman	1.00	.50	.10
☐ 611	Rich Stelmaszek	.25	.12	.02
☐ 612	Luke Walker	.25	.12	.02
☐ 613	Dan Monzon	.25	.12	.02
☐ 614	Adrian Devine	.25	.12	.02
☐ 615	Johnny Jeter	.25	.12	.02
☐ 616	Larry Gura	.40	.20	.04
☐ 617	Ted Ford	.25	.12	.02
☐ 618	Jim Mason	.25	.12	.02
☐ 619	Mike Anderson	.25	.12	.02
☐ 620	Al Downing	.40	.20	.04
☐ 621	Bernie Carbo	.25	.12	.02
☐ 622	Phil Gagliano	.25	.12	.02
☐ 623	Celerino Sanchez	.25	.12	.02
☐ 624	Bob Miller	.25	.12	.02
☐ 625	Ollie Brown	.25	.12	.02
☐ 626	Pittsburgh Pirates Team Card	.60	.30	.06
☐ 627	Carl Taylor	.25	.12	.02
☐ 628	Ivan Murrell	.25	.12	.02
☐ 629	Rusty Staub	.60	.30	.06
☐ 630	Tommy Agee	.40	.20	.04
☐ 631	Steve Barber	.25	.12	.02
☐ 632	George Culver	.25	.12	.02
☐ 633	Dave Hamilton	.25	.12	.02
☐ 634	Braves Leaders Eddie Mathews MG Herm Starrette CO Connie Ryan CO Jim Busby CO Ken Silvestri CO	1.00	.50	.10
☐ 635	Johnny Edwards	.25	.12	.02
☐ 636	Dave Goltz	.25	.12	.02
☐ 637	Checklist 5	1.25	.15	.03
☐ 638	Ken Sanders	.25	.12	.02
☐ 639	Joe Lovitto	.25	.12	.02
☐ 640	Milt Pappas	.40	.20	.04
☐ 641	Chuck Brinkman	.25	.12	.02
☐ 642	Terry Harmon	.25	.12	.02
☐ 643	Dodgers Team	.75	.35	.07
☐ 644	Wayne Granger	.25	.12	.02
☐ 645	Ken Boswell	.25	.12	.02
☐ 646	George Foster	1.25	.60	.12
☐ 647	Juan Beniquez	.60	.30	.06
☐ 648	Terry Crowley	.25	.12	.02
☐ 649	Fernando Gonzalez	.25	.12	.02
☐ 650	Mike Epstein	.25	.12	.02
☐ 651	Leron Lee	.25	.12	.02

		NRMT	VG-E	GOOD
☐ 652	Gail Hopkins	.25	.12	.02
☐ 653	Bob Stinson	.25	.12	.02
☐ 654A	Jesus Alou ERR (no position)	6.00	3.00	.60
☐ 654B	Jesus Alou COR (outfield)	.40	.20	.04
☐ 655	Mike Tyson	.25	.12	.02
☐ 656	Adrian Garrett	.25	.12	.02
☐ 657	Jim Shellenback	.25	.12	.02
☐ 658	Lee Lacy	.25	.12	.02
☐ 659	Joe Lis	.25	.12	.02
☐ 660	Larry Dierker	.50	.25	.05

1974 Topps Traded

The cards in this 44-card set measure 2 ½" by 3 ½". The 1974 Topps Traded set contains 43 player cards and one unnumbered checklist card. The obverses have the word "traded" in block letters and the backs are designed in newspaper style. Card numbers are the same as in the regular set except they are followed by a "T." No known scarcities exist for this set.

		NRMT	VG-E	GOOD
COMPLETE SET (44)		7.00	3.25	.65
COMMON PLAYER		.12	.06	.01
☐ 23T	Craig Robinson	.12	.06	.01
☐ 42T	Claude Osteen	.20	.10	.02
☐ 43T	Jim Wynn	.20	.10	.02

1975 Topps

		NRMT	VG-E	GOOD
☐	51T Bobby Heise	.12	.06	.01
☐	59T Ross Grimsley	.12	.06	.01
☐	62T Bob Locker	.12	.06	.01
☐	63T Bill Sudakis	.12	.06	.01
☐	73T Mike Marshall	.30	.15	.03
☐	123T Nelson Briles	.20	.10	.02
☐	139T Aurelio Monteagudo	.12	.06	.01
☐	151T Diego Segui	.12	.06	.01
☐	165T Willie Davis	.25	.12	.02
☐	175T Reggie Cleveland	.12	.06	.01
☐	182T Lindy McDaniel	.20	.10	.02
☐	186T Fred Scherman	.12	.06	.01
☐	249T George Mitterwald	.12	.06	.01
☐	262T Ed Kirkpatrick	.12	.06	.01
☐	269T Bob Johnson	.12	.06	.01
☐	270T Ron Santo	.40	.20	.04
☐	313T Barry Lersch	.12	.06	.01
☐	319T Randy Hundley	.20	.10	.02
☐	330T Juan Marichal	1.50	.75	.15
☐	348T Pete Richert	.12	.06	.01
☐	373T John Curtis	.12	.06	.01
☐	390T Lou Piniella	.35	.17	.03
☐	428T Gary Sutherland	.12	.06	.01
☐	454T Kurt Bevacqua	.12	.06	.01
☐	458T Jim Ray	.12	.06	.01
☐	485T Felipe Alou	.20	.10	.02
☐	486T Steve Stone	.20	.10	.02
☐	496T Tom Murphy	.12	.06	.01
☐	516T Horacio Pina	.12	.06	.01
☐	534T Eddie Watt	.12	.06	.01
☐	538T Cesar Tovar	.12	.06	.01
☐	544T Ron Schueler	.12	.06	.01
☐	579T Cecil Upshaw	.12	.06	.01
☐	585T Merv Rettenmund	.12	.06	.01
☐	612T Luke Walker	.12	.06	.01
☐	616T Larry Gura	.20	.10	.02
☐	618T Jim Mason	.12	.06	.01
☐	630T Tommie Agee	.15	.07	.01
☐	648T Terry Crowley	.12	.06	.01
☐	649T Fernando Gonzalez	.12	.06	.01
☐	xxxT Traded Checklist	.50	.25	.05
	(unnumbered)			

DAVE PARKER

The cards in the 1975 Topps set were issued in two different sizes: a regular standard size (2 ½" by 3 ½") and a mini size (2 ½" by 3 ⅛") which was issued as a test in certain areas of the country. The 660-card Topps baseball set for 1975 was radically different in appearance from sets of the preceding years. The most prominent change was the use of a two-color frame surrounding the picture area rather than a single, subdued color. A facsimile autograph appears on the picture, and the backs are printed in red and green on gray. Cards 189-212 depict the MVP's of both leagues from 1951 through 1974. The first seven cards (1-7) feature players breaking records or achieving milestones during the previous season. Cards 306-313 picture league leaders in various statistical categories. Cards 459-466 depict the results of post-season action. Team cards feature a checklist back for players on that team and show a small inset photo of the manager on the front. The Phillies Team card #46 erroneously lists Terry Harmon as #339 instead of #399. This set is quite popular with collectors, at least in part due to the fact that the rookie cards of Robin Yount, George Brett, Jim Rice, Gary Carter, Fred Lynn, and Keith Hernandez are all in the set. Topps minis have the same checklist and are worth approximately double the prices listed below.

		NRMT	VG-E	GOOD
	COMPLETE SET (660)	650.00	300.00	65.00
	COMMON PLAYER (1-132)	.25	.12	.02
	COMMON PLAYER (133-660)	.25	.12	.02
☐ 1	RB: Hank Aaron Sets Homer Mark	15.00	4.00	.75
☐ 2	RB: Lou Brock 118 Stolen Bases	2.25	1.10	.22
☐ 3	RB: Bob Gibson 3000th Strikeout	2.25	1.10	.22
☐ 4	RB: Al Kaline 3000 Hit Club	2.25	1.10	.22
☐ 5	RB: Nolan Ryan Fans 300 for 3rd Year in a Row	4.50	2.25	.45
☐ 6	RB: Mike Marshall Hurls 106 Games	.50	.25	.05
☐ 7	No Hitters Steve Busby Dick Bosman Nolan Ryan	1.00	.50	.10
☐ 8	Rogelio Moret	.25	.12	.02
☐ 9	Frank Tepedino	.25	.12	.02
☐ 10	Willie Davis	.40	.20	.04
☐ 11	Bill Melton	.25	.12	.02
☐ 12	David Clyde	.25	.12	.02
☐ 13	Gene Locklear	.25	.12	.02
☐ 14	Milt Wilcox	.25	.12	.02
☐ 15	Jose Cardenal	.25	.12	.02
☐ 16	Frank Tanana	.60	.30	.06
☐ 17	Dave Concepcion	.60	.30	.06
☐ 18	Tigers: Team/Mgr. Ralph Houk (checklist back)	.75	.35	.07
☐ 19	Jerry Koosman	.60	.30	.06
☐ 20	Thurman Munson	4.00	2.00	.40
☐ 21	Rollie Fingers	1.75	.85	.17
☐ 22	Dave Cash	.25	.12	.02
☐ 23	Bill Russell	.40	.20	.04
☐ 24	Al Fitzmorris	.25	.12	.02
☐ 25	Lee May	.40	.20	.04
☐ 26	Dave McNally	.40	.20	.04
☐ 27	Ken Reitz	.25	.12	.02
☐ 28	Tom Murphy	.25	.12	.02
☐ 29	Dave Parker	8.00	4.00	.80
☐ 30	Bert Blyleven	1.75	.85	.17
☐ 31	Dave Rader	.25	.12	.02
☐ 32	Reggie Cleveland	.25	.12	.02
☐ 33	Dusty Baker	.40	.20	.04
☐ 34	Steve Renko	.25	.12	.02
☐ 35	Ron Santo	.50	.25	.05
☐ 36	Joe Lovitto	.25	.12	.02
☐ 37	Dave Freisleben	.25	.12	.02
☐ 38	Buddy Bell	.75	.35	.07
☐ 39	Andre Thornton	.50	.25	.05
☐ 40	Bill Singer	.25	.12	.02
☐ 41	Cesar Geronimo	.25	.12	.02
☐ 42	Joe Coleman	.25	.12	.02
☐ 43	Cleon Jones	.25	.12	.02
☐ 44	Pat Dobson	.25	.12	.02
☐ 45	Joe Rudi	.40	.20	.04
☐ 46	Phillies: Team/Mgr. Danny Ozark (checklist back)	.75	.35	.07
☐ 47	Tommy John	1.25	.60	.12
☐ 48	Freddie Patek	.25	.12	.02
☐ 49	Larry Dierker	.25	.12	.02
☐ 50	Brooks Robinson	3.50	1.75	.35
☐ 51	Bob Forsch	1.00	.50	.10
☐ 52	Darrell Porter	.25	.12	.02
☐ 53	Dave Giusti	.25	.12	.02
☐ 54	Eric Soderholm	.25	.12	.02
☐ 55	Bobby Bonds	.50	.25	.05
☐ 56	Rick Wise	.25	.12	.02
☐ 57	Dave Johnson	.50	.25	.05
☐ 58	Chuck Taylor	.25	.12	.02
☐ 59	Ken Henderson	.25	.12	.02
☐ 60	Fergie Jenkins	1.25	.60	.12
☐ 61	Dave Winfield	12.00	6.00	1.20
☐ 62	Fritz Peterson	.25	.12	.02
☐ 63	Steve Swisher	.25	.12	.02
☐ 64	Dave Chalk	.25	.12	.02
☐ 65	Don Gullett	.40	.20	.04
☐ 66	Willie Horton	.40	.20	.04
☐ 67	Tug McGraw	.50	.25	.05
☐ 68	Ron Blomberg	.25	.12	.02
☐ 69	John Odom	.25	.12	.02
☐ 70	Mike Schmidt	36.00	18.00	3.60
☐ 71	Charlie Hough	.50	.25	.05
☐ 72	Royals: Team/Mgr. Jack McKeon (checklist back)	.75	.35	.07
☐ 73	J.R. Richard	.40	.20	.04
☐ 74	Mark Belanger	.40	.20	.04
☐ 75	Ted Simmons	.75	.35	.07
☐ 76	Ed Sprague	.25	.12	.02
☐ 77	Richie Zisk	.25	.12	.02
☐ 78	Ray Corbin	.25	.12	.02

		NRMT	VG-E	GOOD			NRMT	VG-E	GOOD
☐ 79	Gary Matthews	.40	.20	.04	☐ 122	Al Hrabosky	.25	.12	.02
☐ 80	Carlton Fisk	4.00	2.00	.40	☐ 123	Johnny Briggs	.25	.12	.02
☐ 81	Ron Reed	.25	.12	.02	☐ 124	Jerry Reuss	.40	.20	.04
☐ 82	Pat Kelly	.25	.12	.02	☐ 125	Ken Singleton	.40	.20	.04
☐ 83	Jim Merritt	.25	.12	.02	☐ 126	Checklist 1-132	1.00	.10	.02
☐ 84	Enzo Hernandez	.25	.12	.02	☐ 127	Glenn Borgmann	.25	.12	.02
☐ 85	Bill Bonham	.25	.12	.02	☐ 128	Bill Lee	.40	.20	.04
☐ 86	Joe Lis	.25	.12	.02	☐ 129	Rick Monday	.40	.20	.04
☐ 87	George Foster	1.25	.60	.12	☐ 130	Phil Niekro	2.25	1.10	.22
☐ 88	Tom Egan	.25	.12	.02	☐ 131	Toby Harrah	.40	.20	.04
☐ 89	Jim Ray	.25	.12	.02	☐ 132	Randy Moffitt	.25	.12	.02
☐ 90	Rusty Staub	.50	.25	.05	☐ 133	Dan Driessen	.40	.20	.04
☐ 91	Dick Green	.25	.12	.02	☐ 134	Ron Hodges	.25	.12	.02
☐ 92	Cecil Upshaw	.25	.12	.02	☐ 135	Charlie Spikes	.25	.12	.02
☐ 93	Dave Lopes	.50	.25	.05	☐ 136	Jim Mason	.25	.12	.02
☐ 94	Jim Lonborg	.40	.20	.04	☐ 137	Terry Forster	.40	.20	.04
☐ 95	John Mayberry	.40	.20	.04	☐ 138	Del Unser	.25	.12	.02
☐ 96	Mike Cosgrove	.25	.12	.02	☐ 139	Horacio Pina	.25	.12	.02
☐ 97	Earl Williams	.25	.12	.02	☐ 140	Steve Garvey	6.50	3.25	.65
☐ 98	Rich Folkers	.25	.12	.02	☐ 141	Mickey Stanley	.40	.20	.04
☐ 99	Mike Hegan	.25	.12	.02	☐ 142	Bob Reynolds	.25	.12	.02
☐ 100	Willie Stargell	3.00	1.50	.30	☐ 143	Cliff Johnson	.25	.12	.02
☐ 101	Expos: Team/Mgr.	.75	.35	.07	☐ 144	Jim Wohlford	.25	.12	.02
	Gene Mauch (check-				☐ 145	Ken Holtzman	.40	.20	.04
	list back)				☐ 146	Padres: Team/Mgr.	.75	.35	.07
☐ 102	Joe Decker	.25	.12	.02		John McNamara			
☐ 103	Rick Miller	.25	.12	.02		(checklist back)			
☐ 104	Bill Madlock	1.25	.60	.12	☐ 147	Pedro Garcia	.25	.12	.02
☐ 105	Buzz Capra	.25	.12	.02	☐ 148	Jim Rooker	.25	.12	.02
☐ 106	Mike Hargrove	.75	.35	.07	☐ 149	Tim Foli	.25	.12	.02
☐ 107	Jim Barr	.25	.12	.02	☐ 150	Bob Gibson	3.00	1.50	.30
☐ 108	Tom Hall	.25	.12	.02	☐ 151	Steve Brye	.25	.12	.02
☐ 109	George Hendrick	.40	.20	.04	☐ 152	Mario Guerrero	.25	.12	.02
☐ 110	Wilbur Wood	.25	.12	.02	☐ 153	Rick Reuschel	.75	.35	.07
☐ 111	Wayne Garrett	.25	.12	.02	☐ 154	Mike Lum	.25	.12	.02
☐ 112	Larry Hardy	.25	.12	.02	☐ 155	Jim Bibby	.40	.20	.04
☐ 113	Elliott Maddox	.25	.12	.02	☐ 156	Dave Kingman	1.00	.50	.10
☐ 114	Dick Lange	.25	.12	.02	☐ 157	Pedro Borbon	.25	.12	.02
☐ 115	Joe Ferguson	.25	.12	.02	☐ 158	Jerry Grote	.25	.12	.02
☐ 116	Lerrin LaGrow	.25	.12	.02	☐ 159	Steve Arlin	.25	.12	.02
☐ 117	Orioles: Team/Mgr.	.75	.35	.07	☐ 160	Graig Nettles	1.25	.60	.12
	Earl Weaver (check-				☐ 161	Stan Bahnsen	.25	.12	.02
	list back)				☐ 162	Willie Montanez	.25	.12	.02
☐ 118	Mike Anderson	.25	.12	.02	☐ 163	Jim Brewer	.25	.12	.02
☐ 119	Tommy Helms	.40	.20	.04	☐ 164	Mickey Rivers	.40	.20	.04
☐ 120	Steve Busby	.25	.12	.02	☐ 165	Doug Rader	.40	.20	.04
	(photo actually Fran				☐ 166	Woodie Fryman	.25	.12	.02
	Healy)				☐ 167	Rich Coggins	.25	.12	.02
☐ 121	Bill North	.25	.12	.02	☐ 168	Bill Greif	.25	.12	.02

		NRMT	VG-E	GOOD
☐ 169	Cookie Rojas	.25	.12	.02
☐ 170	Bert Campaneris	.40	.20	.04
☐ 171	Ed Kirkpatrick	.25	.12	.02
☐ 172	Red Sox: Team/Mgr.	.75	.35	.07
	Darrell Johnson			
	(checklist back)			
☐ 173	Steve Rogers	.40	.20	.04
☐ 174	Bake McBride	.40	.20	.04
☐ 175	Don Money	.25	.12	.02
☐ 176	Burt Hooton	.25	.12	.02
☐ 177	Vic Correll	.25	.12	.02
☐ 178	Cesar Tovar	.25	.12	.02
☐ 179	Tom Bradley	.25	.12	.02
☐ 180	Joe Morgan	5.00	2.50	.50
☐ 181	Fred Beene	.25	.12	.02
☐ 182	Don Hahn	.25	.12	.02
☐ 183	Mel Stottlemyre	.50	.25	.05
☐ 184	Jorge Orta	.25	.12	.02
☐ 185	Steve Carlton	5.50	2.75	.55
☐ 186	Willie Crawford	.25	.12	.02
☐ 187	Denny Doyle	.25	.12	.02
☐ 188	Tom Griffin	.25	.12	.02
☐ 189	1951 MVP's	1.50	.75	.15
	Larry (Yogi) Berra			
	Roy Campanella			
	(Campy never issued)			
☐ 190	1952 MVP's	.50	.25	.05
	Bobby Shantz			
	Hank Sauer			
☐ 191	1953 MVP's	.75	.35	.07
	Al Rosen			
	Roy Campanella			
☐ 192	1954 MVP's	1.50	.75	.15
	Yogi Berra			
	Willie Mays			
☐ 193	1955 MVP's	1.50	.75	.15
	Yogi Berra			
	Roy Campanella			
	(Campy never issued)			
☐ 194	1956 MVP's	4.00	2.00	.40
	Mickey Mantle			
	Don Newcombe			
☐ 195	1957 MVP's	5.00	2.50	.50
	Mickey Mantle			
	Hank Aaron			
☐ 196	1958 MVP's	.60	.30	.06
	Jackie Jensen			
	Ernie Banks			
☐ 197	1959 MVP's	.60	.30	.06

		NRMT	VG-E	GOOD
	Nellie Fox			
	Ernie Banks			
☐ 198	1960 MVP's	.75	.35	.07
	Roger Maris			
	Dick Groat			
☐ 199	1961 MVP's	1.00	.50	.10
	Roger Maris			
	Frank Robinson			
☐ 200	1962 MVP's	4.00	2.00	.40
	Mickey Mantle			
	Maury Wills			
	(Wills never issued)			
☐ 201	1963 MVP's	.75	.35	.07
	Elston Howard			
	Sandy Koufax			
☐ 202	1964 MVP's	.60	.30	.06
	Brooks Robinson			
	Ken Boyer			
☐ 203	1965 MVP's	.75	.35	.07
	Zoilo Versalles			
	Willie Mays			
☐ 204	1966 MVP's	1.00	.50	.10
	Frank Robinson			
	Bob Clemente			
☐ 205	1967 MVP's	1.00	.50	.10
	Carl Yastrzemski			
	Orlando Cepeda			
☐ 206	1968 MVP's	.60	.30	.06
	Denny McLain			
	Bob Gibson			
☐ 207	1969 MVP's	.75	.35	.07
	Harmon Killebrew			
	Willie McCovey			
☐ 208	1970 MVP's	.75	.35	.07
	Boog Powell			
	Johnny Bench			
☐ 209	1971 MVP's	.50	.25	.05
	Vida Blue			
	Joe Torre			
☐ 210	1972 MVP's	.75	.35	.07
	Rich Allen			
	Johnny Bench			
☐ 211	1973 MVP's	3.00	1.50	.30
	Reggie Jackson			
	Pete Rose			
☐ 212	1974 MVP's	.60	.30	.06
	Jeff Burroughs			
	Steve Garvey			
☐ 213	Oscar Gamble	.40	.20	.04

		NRMT	VG-E	GOOD			NRMT	VG-E	GOOD
☐ 214	Harry Parker	.25	.12	.02	☐ 257	Checklist: 133-264	1.00	.10	.02
☐ 215	Bobby Valentine	.50	.25	.05	☐ 258	Dave LaRoche	.25	.12	.02
☐ 216	Giants: Team/Mgr.	.75	.35	.07	☐ 259	Len Randle	.25	.12	.02
	Wes Westrum (check-list back)				☐ 260	Johnny Bench	8.50	4.25	.85
					☐ 261	Andy Hassler	.25	.12	.02
☐ 217	Lou Piniella	.60	.30	.06	☐ 262	Rowland Office	.25	.12	.02
☐ 218	Jerry Johnson	.25	.12	.02	☐ 263	Jim Perry	.40	.20	.04
☐ 219	Ed Herrmann	.25	.12	.02	☐ 264	John Milner	.25	.12	.02
☐ 220	Don Sutton	2.00	1.00	.20	☐ 265	Ron Bryant	.25	.12	.02
☐ 221	Aurelio Rodriguez	.25	.12	.02	☐ 266	Sandy Alomar	.25	.12	.02
☐ 222	Dan Spillner	.25	.12	.02	☐ 267	Dick Ruthven	.25	.12	.02
☐ 223	Robin Yount	110.00	55.00	11.00	☐ 268	Hal McRae	.40	.20	.04
☐ 224	Ramon Hernandez	.25	.12	.02	☐ 269	Doug Rau	.25	.12	.02
☐ 225	Bob Grich	.40	.20	.04	☐ 270	Ron Fairly	.25	.12	.02
☐ 226	Bill Campbell	.25	.12	.02	☐ 271	Gerry Moses	.25	.12	.02
☐ 227	Bob Watson	.40	.20	.04	☐ 272	Lynn McGlothen	.25	.12	.02
☐ 228	George Brett	90.00	45.00	9.00	☐ 273	Steve Braun	.25	.12	.02
☐ 229	Barry Foote	.25	.12	.02	☐ 274	Vicente Romo	.25	.12	.02
☐ 230	Jim Hunter	2.25	1.10	.22	☐ 275	Paul Blair	.25	.12	.02
☐ 231	Mike Tyson	.25	.12	.02	☐ 276	White Sox Team/Mgr.	.75	.35	.07
☐ 232	Diego Segui	.25	.12	.02		Chuck Tanner (check-list back)			
☐ 233	Billy Grabarkewitz	.25	.12	.02					
☐ 234	Tom Grieve	.40	.20	.04	☐ 277	Frank Taveras	.25	.12	.02
☐ 235	Jack Billingham	.25	.12	.02	☐ 278	Paul Lindblad	.25	.12	.02
☐ 236	Angels: Team/Mgr.	.75	.35	.07	☐ 279	Milt May	.25	.12	.02
	Dick Williams (check-list back)				☐ 280	Carl Yastrzemski	8.50	4.25	.85
☐ 237	Carl Morton	.25	.12	.02	☐ 281	Jim Slaton	.25	.12	.02
☐ 238	Dave Duncan	.25	.12	.02	☐ 282	Jerry Morales	.25	.12	.02
☐ 239	George Stone	.25	.12	.02	☐ 283	Steve Foucault	.25	.12	.02
☐ 240	Garry Maddox	.40	.20	.04	☐ 284	Ken Griffey	.75	.35	.07
☐ 241	Dick Tidrow	.25	.12	.02	☐ 285	Ellie Rodriguez	.25	.12	.02
☐ 242	Jay Johnstone	.40	.20	.04	☐ 286	Mike Jorgensen	.25	.12	.02
☐ 243	Jim Kaat	1.00	.50	.10	☐ 287	Roric Harrison	.25	.12	.02
☐ 244	Bill Buckner	.50	.25	.05	☐ 288	Bruce Ellingsen	.25	.12	.02
☐ 245	Mickey Lolich	.50	.25	.05	☐ 289	Ken Rudolph	.25	.12	.02
☐ 246	Cardinals: Team/Mgr.	.75	.35	.07	☐ 290	Jon Matlack	.40	.20	.04
	Red Schoendienst (checklist back)				☐ 291	Bill Sudakis	.25	.12	.02
					☐ 292	Ron Schueler	.25	.12	.02
☐ 247	Enos Cabell	.25	.12	.02	☐ 293	Dick Sharon	.25	.12	.02
☐ 248	Randy Jones	.40	.20	.04	☐ 294	Geoff Zahn	.25	.12	.02
☐ 249	Danny Thompson	.25	.12	.02	☐ 295	Vada Pinson	.50	.25	.05
☐ 250	Ken Brett	.25	.12	.02	☐ 296	Alan Foster	.25	.12	.02
☐ 251	Fran Healy	.25	.12	.02	☐ 297	Craig Kusick	.25	.12	.02
☐ 252	Fred Scherman	.25	.12	.02	☐ 298	Johnny Grubb	.25	.12	.02
☐ 253	Jesus Alou	.25	.12	.02	☐ 299	Bucky Dent	.75	.35	.07
☐ 254	Mike Torrez	.25	.12	.02	☐ 300	Reggie Jackson	10.00	5.00	1.00
☐ 255	Dwight Evans	3.00	1.50	.30	☐ 301	Dave Roberts	.25	.12	.02
☐ 256	Billy Champion	.25	.12	.02	☐ 302	Rick Burleson	.50	.25	.05
					☐ 303	Grant Jackson	.25	.12	.02

		NRMT	VG-E	GOOD
☐ 304	Pirates: Team/Mgr.	.75	.35	.07
	Danny Murtaugh			
	(checklist back)			
☐ 305	Jim Colborn	.25	.12	.02
☐ 306	Batting Leaders	.75	.35	.07
	Rod Carew			
	Ralph Garr			
☐ 307	Home Run Leaders	1.00	.50	.10
	Dick Allen			
	Mike Schmidt			
☐ 308	RBI Leaders	.75	.35	.07
	Jeff Burroughs			
	Johnny Bench			
☐ 309	Stolen-Base Leaders	.75	.35	.07
	Bill North			
	Lou Brock			
☐ 310	Victory Leaders	.75	.35	.07
	Jim Hunter			
	Fergie Jenkins			
	Andy Messersmith			
	Phil Niekro			
☐ 311	ERA Leaders	.75	.35	.07
	Jim Hunter			
	Buzz Capra			
☐ 312	Strikeout Leaders	3.00	1.50	.30
	Nolan Ryan			
	Steve Carlton			
☐ 313	Leading Firemen	.60	.30	.06
	Terry Forster			
	Mike Marshall			
☐ 314	Buck Martinez	.25	.12	.02
☐ 315	Don Kessinger	.40	.20	.04
☐ 316	Jackie Brown	.25	.12	.02
☐ 317	Joe Lahoud	.25	.12	.02
☐ 318	Ernie McAnally	.25	.12	.02
☐ 319	Johnny Oates	.25	.12	.02
☐ 320	Pete Rose	15.00	7.50	1.50
☐ 321	Rudy May	.25	.12	.02
☐ 322	Ed Goodson	.25	.12	.02
☐ 323	Fred Holdsworth	.25	.12	.02
☐ 324	Ed Kranepool	.40	.20	.04
☐ 325	Tony Oliva	.75	.35	.07
☐ 326	Wayne Twitchell	.25	.12	.02
☐ 327	Jerry Hairston	.25	.12	.02
☐ 328	Sonny Siebert	.25	.12	.02
☐ 329	Ted Kubiak	.25	.12	.02
☐ 330	Mike Marshall	.40	.20	.04
☐ 331	Indians: Team/Mgr.	.75	.35	.07

		NRMT	VG-E	GOOD
	Frank Robinson			
	(checklist back)			
☐ 332	Fred Kendall	.25	.12	.02
☐ 333	Dick Drago	.25	.12	.02
☐ 334	Greg Gross	.25	.12	.02
☐ 335	Jim Palmer	4.50	2.25	.45
☐ 336	Rennie Stennett	.25	.12	.02
☐ 337	Kevin Kobel	.25	.12	.02
☐ 338	Rich Stelmaszek	.25	.12	.02
☐ 339	Jim Fregosi	.40	.20	.04
☐ 340	Paul Splittorff	.25	.12	.02
☐ 341	Hal Breeden	.25	.12	.02
☐ 342	Leroy Stanton	.25	.12	.02
☐ 343	Danny Frisella	.25	.12	.02
☐ 344	Ben Oglivie	.40	.20	.04
☐ 345	Clay Carroll	.25	.12	.02
☐ 346	Bobby Darwin	.25	.12	.02
☐ 347	Mike Caldwell	.25	.12	.02
☐ 348	Tony Muser	.25	.12	.02
☐ 349	Ray Sadecki	.25	.12	.02
☐ 350	Bobby Murcer	.50	.25	.05
☐ 351	Bob Boone	1.00	.50	.10
☐ 352	Darold Knowles	.25	.12	.02
☐ 353	Luis Melendez	.25	.12	.02
☐ 354	Dick Bosman	.25	.12	.02
☐ 355	Chris Cannizzaro	.25	.12	.02
☐ 356	Rico Petrocelli	.40	.20	.04
☐ 357	Ken Forsch	.25	.12	.02
☐ 358	Al Bumbry	.25	.12	.02
☐ 359	Paul Popovich	.25	.12	.02
☐ 360	George Scott	.40	.20	.04
☐ 361	Dodgers: Team/Mgr.	1.00	.50	.10
	Walter Alston (check-			
	list back)			
☐ 362	Steve Hargan	.25	.12	.02
☐ 363	Carmen Fanzone	.25	.12	.02
☐ 364	Doug Bird	.25	.12	.02
☐ 365	Bob Bailey	.25	.12	.02
☐ 366	Ken Sanders	.25	.12	.02
☐ 367	Craig Robinson	.25	.12	.02
☐ 368	Vic Albury	.25	.12	.02
☐ 369	Merv Rettenmund	.25	.12	.02
☐ 370	Tom Seaver	7.00	3.50	.70
☐ 371	Gates Brown	.40	.20	.04
☐ 372	John D'Acquisto	.25	.12	.02
☐ 373	Bill Sharp	.25	.12	.02
☐ 374	Eddie Watt	.25	.12	.02
☐ 375	Roy White	.40	.20	.04
☐ 376	Steve Yeager	.40	.20	.04

		NRMT	VG-E	GOOD
☐ 377	Tom Hilgendorf	.25	.12	.02
☐ 378	Derrel Thomas	.25	.12	.02
☐ 379	Bernie Carbo	.25	.12	.02
☐ 380	Sal Bando	.40	.20	.04
☐ 381	John Curtis	.25	.12	.02
☐ 382	Don Baylor	.75	.35	.07
☐ 383	Jim York	.25	.12	.02
☐ 384	Brewers: Team/Mgr. Del Crandall (checklist back)	.75	.35	.07
☐ 385	Dock Ellis	.25	.12	.02
☐ 386	Checklist: 265-396	1.00	.10	.02
☐ 387	Jim Spencer	.25	.12	.02
☐ 388	Steve Stone	.40	.20	.04
☐ 389	Tony Solaita	.25	.12	.02
☐ 390	Ron Cey	.60	.30	.06
☐ 391	Don DeMola	.25	.12	.02
☐ 392	Bruce Bochte	.40	.20	.04
☐ 393	Gary Gentry	.25	.12	.02
☐ 394	Larvell Blanks	.25	.12	.02
☐ 395	Bud Harrelson	.40	.20	.04
☐ 396	Fred Norman	.25	.12	.02
☐ 397	Bill Freehan	.50	.25	.05
☐ 398	Elias Sosa	.25	.12	.02
☐ 399	Terry Harmon	.25	.12	.02
☐ 400	Dick Allen	.50	.25	.05
☐ 401	Mike Wallace	.25	.12	.02
☐ 402	Bob Tolan	.25	.12	.02
☐ 403	Tom Buskey	.25	.12	.02
☐ 404	Ted Sizemore	.25	.12	.02
☐ 405	John Montague	.25	.12	.02
☐ 406	Bob Gallagher	.25	.12	.02
☐ 407	Herb Washington	.25	.12	.02
☐ 408	Clyde Wright	.25	.12	.02
☐ 409	Bob Robertson	.25	.12	.02
☐ 410	Mike Cueller (sic, Cuellar)	.40	.20	.04
☐ 411	George Mitterwald	.25	.12	.02
☐ 412	Bill Hands	.25	.12	.02
☐ 413	Marty Pattin	.25	.12	.02
☐ 414	Manny Mota	.40	.20	.04
☐ 415	John Hiller	.40	.20	.04
☐ 416	Larry Lintz	.25	.12	.02
☐ 417	Skip Lockwood	.25	.12	.02
☐ 418	Leo Foster	.25	.12	.02
☐ 419	Dave Goltz	.25	.12	.02
☐ 420	Larry Bowa	.50	.25	.05
☐ 421	Mets: Team/Mgr.	1.00	.50	.10
	Yogi Berra (checklist back)			
☐ 422	Brian Downing	.50	.25	.05
☐ 423	Clay Kirby	.25	.12	.02
☐ 424	John Lowenstein	.25	.12	.02
☐ 425	Tito Fuentes	.25	.12	.02
☐ 426	George Medich	.25	.12	.02
☐ 427	Clarence Gaston	.50	.25	.05
☐ 428	Dave Hamilton	.25	.12	.02
☐ 429	Jim Dwyer	.25	.12	.02
☐ 430	Luis Tiant	.50	.25	.05
☐ 431	Rod Gilbreath	.25	.12	.02
☐ 432	Ken Berry	.25	.12	.02
☐ 433	Larry Demery	.25	.12	.02
☐ 434	Bob Locker	.25	.12	.02
☐ 435	Dave Nelson	.25	.12	.02
☐ 436	Ken Frailing	.25	.12	.02
☐ 437	Al Cowens	.40	.20	.04
☐ 438	Don Carrithers	.25	.12	.02
☐ 439	Ed Brinkman	.25	.12	.02
☐ 440	Andy Messersmith	.40	.20	.04
☐ 441	Bobby Heise	.25	.12	.02
☐ 442	Maximino Leon	.25	.12	.02
☐ 443	Twins: Team/Mgr. Frank Quilici (checklist back)	.75	.35	.07
☐ 444	Gene Garber	.25	.12	.02
☐ 445	Felix Millan	.25	.12	.02
☐ 446	Bart Johnson	.25	.12	.02
☐ 447	Terry Crowley	.25	.12	.02
☐ 448	Frank Duffy	.25	.12	.02
☐ 449	Charlie Williams	.25	.12	.02
☐ 450	Willie McCovey	3.00	1.50	.30
☐ 451	Rick Dempsey	.40	.20	.04
☐ 452	Angel Mangual	.25	.12	.02
☐ 453	Claude Osteen	.40	.20	.04
☐ 454	Doug Griffin	.25	.12	.02
☐ 455	Don Wilson	.25	.12	.02
☐ 456	Bob Coluccio	.25	.12	.02
☐ 457	Mario Mendoza	.25	.12	.02
☐ 458	Ross Grimsley	.25	.12	.02
☐ 459	1974 AL Champs A's over Orioles (2B action pictured)	.60	.30	.06
☐ 460	1974 NL Champs Dodgers over Pirates (Taveras/Garvey at 2B)	.75	.35	.07
☐ 461	World Series Game 1 (Reggie Jackson)	2.00	1.00	.20

		NRMT	VG-E	GOOD
☐ 462	World Series Game 2 (Dodger dugout)	.60	.30	.06
☐ 463	World Series Game 3 (Fingers pitching)	.75	.35	.07
☐ 464	World Series Game 4 (A's batter)	.60	.30	.06
☐ 465	World Series Game 5 (Rudi rounding third)	.60	.30	.06
☐ 466	World Series Summary A's do it again; win third straight (A's group picture)	.60	.30	.06
☐ 467	Ed Halicki	.25	.12	.02
☐ 468	Bobby Mitchell	.25	.12	.02
☐ 469	Tom Dettore	.25	.12	.02
☐ 470	Jeff Burroughs	.40	.20	.04
☐ 471	Bob Stinson	.25	.12	.02
☐ 472	Bruce Dal Canton	.25	.12	.02
☐ 473	Ken McMullen	.25	.12	.02
☐ 474	Luke Walker	.25	.12	.02
☐ 475	Darrell Evans	.60	.30	.06
☐ 476	Ed Figueroa	.25	.12	.02
☐ 477	Tom Hutton	.25	.12	.02
☐ 478	Tom Burgmeier	.25	.12	.02
☐ 479	Ken Boswell	.25	.12	.02
☐ 480	Carlos May	.25	.12	.02
☐ 481	Will McEnaney	.25	.12	.02
☐ 482	Tom McCraw	.25	.12	.02
☐ 483	Steve Ontiveros	.25	.12	.02
☐ 484	Glenn Beckert	.40	.20	.04
☐ 485	Sparky Lyle	.50	.25	.05
☐ 486	Ray Fosse	.25	.12	.02
☐ 487	Astros: Team/Mgr. Preston Gomez (checklist back)	.75	.35	.07
☐ 488	Bill Travers	.25	.12	.02
☐ 489	Cecil Cooper	1.00	.50	.10
☐ 490	Reggie Smith	.50	.25	.05
☐ 491	Doyle Alexander	.50	.25	.05
☐ 492	Rich Hebner	.25	.12	.02
☐ 493	Don Stanhouse	.25	.12	.02
☐ 494	Pete LaCock	.25	.12	.02
☐ 495	Nelson Briles	.25	.12	.02
☐ 496	Pepe Frias	.25	.12	.02
☐ 497	Jim Nettles	.25	.12	.02
☐ 498	Al Downing	.25	.12	.02
☐ 499	Marty Perez	.25	.12	.02
☐ 500	Nolan Ryan	22.00	11.00	2.20
☐ 501	Bill Robinson	.40	.20	.04
☐ 502	Pat Bourque	.25	.12	.02
☐ 503	Fred Stanley	.25	.12	.02
☐ 504	Buddy Bradford	.25	.12	.02
☐ 505	Chris Speier	.25	.12	.02
☐ 506	Leron Lee	.25	.12	.02
☐ 507	Tom Carroll	.25	.12	.02
☐ 508	Bob Hansen	.25	.12	.02
☐ 509	Dave Hilton	.25	.12	.02
☐ 510	Vida Blue	.50	.25	.05
☐ 511	Rangers: Team/Mgr. Billy Martin (checklist back)	1.00	.50	.10
☐ 512	Larry Milbourne	.25	.12	.02
☐ 513	Dick Pole	.25	.12	.02
☐ 514	Jose Cruz	.40	.20	.04
☐ 515	Manny Sanguillen	.40	.20	.04
☐ 516	Don Hood	.25	.12	.02
☐ 517	Checklist: 397-528	1.00	.10	.02
☐ 518	Leo Cardenas	.25	.12	.02
☐ 519	Jim Todd	.25	.12	.02
☐ 520	Amos Otis	.40	.20	.04
☐ 521	Dennis Blair	.25	.12	.02
☐ 522	Gary Sutherland	.25	.12	.02
☐ 523	Tom Paciorek	.25	.12	.02
☐ 524	John Doherty	.25	.12	.02
☐ 525	Tom House	.25	.12	.02
☐ 526	Larry Hisle	.25	.12	.02
☐ 527	Mac Scarce	.25	.12	.02
☐ 528	Eddie Leon	.25	.12	.02
☐ 529	Gary Thomasson	.25	.12	.02
☐ 530	Gaylord Perry	2.25	1.10	.22
☐ 531	Reds: Team/Mgr. Sparky Anderson (checklist back)	1.00	.50	.10
☐ 532	Gorman Thomas	.60	.30	.06
☐ 533	Rudy Meoli	.25	.12	.02
☐ 534	Alex Johnson	.25	.12	.02
☐ 535	Gene Tenace	.40	.20	.04
☐ 536	Bob Moose	.25	.12	.02
☐ 537	Tommy Harper	.40	.20	.04
☐ 538	Duffy Dyer	.25	.12	.02
☐ 539	Jesse Jefferson	.25	.12	.02
☐ 540	Lou Brock	3.00	1.50	.30
☐ 541	Roger Metzger	.25	.12	.02
☐ 542	Pete Broberg	.25	.12	.02
☐ 543	Larry Biittner	.25	.12	.02
☐ 544	Steve Mingori	.25	.12	.02
☐ 545	Billy Williams	2.50	1.25	.25
☐ 546	John Knox	.25	.12	.02

		NRMT	VG-E	GOOD
☐ 547	Von Joshua	.25	.12	.02
☐ 548	Charlie Sands	.25	.12	.02
☐ 549	Bill Butler	.25	.12	.02
☐ 550	Ralph Garr	.25	.12	.02
☐ 551	Larry Christenson	.25	.12	.02
☐ 552	Jack Brohamer	.25	.12	.02
☐ 553	John Boccabella	.25	.12	.02
☐ 554	Rich Gossage	1.25	.60	.12
☐ 555	Al Oliver	.75	.35	.07
☐ 556	Tim Johnson	.25	.12	.02
☐ 557	Larry Gura	.40	.20	.04
☐ 558	Dave Roberts	.25	.12	.02
☐ 559	Bob Montgomery	.25	.12	.02
☐ 560	Tony Perez	1.25	.60	.12
☐ 561	A's: Team/Mgr.	.75	.35	.07
	Alvin Dark (checklist back)			
☐ 562	Gary Nolan	.25	.12	.02
☐ 563	Wilbur Howard	.25	.12	.02
☐ 564	Tommy Davis	.40	.20	.04
☐ 565	Joe Torre	.60	.30	.06
☐ 566	Ray Burris	.25	.12	.02
☐ 567	Jim Sundberg	.60	.30	.06
☐ 568	Dale Murray	.25	.12	.02
☐ 569	Frank White	.75	.35	.07
☐ 570	Jim Wynn	.40	.20	.04
☐ 571	Dave Lemanczyk	.25	.12	.02
☐ 572	Roger Nelson	.25	.12	.02
☐ 573	Orlando Pena	.25	.12	.02
☐ 574	Tony Taylor	.25	.12	.02
☐ 575	Gene Clines	.25	.12	.02
☐ 576	Phil Roof	.25	.12	.02
☐ 577	John Morris	.25	.12	.02
☐ 578	Dave Tomlin	.25	.12	.02
☐ 579	Skip Pitlock	.25	.12	.02
☐ 580	Frank Robinson	3.00	1.50	.30
☐ 581	Darrel Chaney	.25	.12	.02
☐ 582	Eduardo Rodriguez	.25	.12	.02
☐ 583	Andy Etchebarren	.25	.12	.02
☐ 584	Mike Garman	.25	.12	.02
☐ 585	Chris Chambliss	.50	.25	.05
☐ 586	Tim McCarver	.50	.25	.05
☐ 587	Chris Ward	.25	.12	.02
☐ 588	Rick Auerbach	.25	.12	.02
☐ 589	Braves: Team/Mgr.	.75	.35	.07
	Clyde King (checklist back)			
☐ 590	Cesar Cedeno	.40	.20	.04
☐ 591	Glenn Abbott	.25	.12	.02

		NRMT	VG-E	GOOD
☐ 592	Balor Moore	.25	.12	.02
☐ 593	Gene Lamont	.25	.12	.02
☐ 594	Jim Fuller	.25	.12	.02
☐ 595	Joe Niekro	.50	.25	.05
☐ 596	Ollie Brown	.25	.12	.02
☐ 597	Winston Llenas	.25	.12	.02
☐ 598	Bruce Kison	.25	.12	.02
☐ 599	Nate Colbert	.25	.12	.02
☐ 600	Rod Carew	5.00	2.50	.50
☐ 601	Juan Beniquez	.40	.20	.04
☐ 602	John Vukovich	.25	.12	.02
☐ 603	Lew Krausse	.25	.12	.02
☐ 604	Oscar Zamora	.25	.12	.02
☐ 605	John Ellis	.25	.12	.02
☐ 606	Bruce Miller	.25	.12	.02
☐ 607	Jim Holt	.25	.12	.02
☐ 608	Gene Michael	.40	.20	.04
☐ 609	Elrod Hendricks	.25	.12	.02
☐ 610	Ron Hunt	.25	.12	.02
☐ 611	Yankees: Team/Mgr.	1.00	.50	.10
	Bill Virdon (checklist back)			
☐ 612	Terry Hughes	.25	.12	.02
☐ 613	Bill Parsons	.25	.12	.02
☐ 614	Rookie Pitchers	.40	.20	.04
	Jack Kucek			
	Dyar Miller			
	Vern Ruhle			
	Paul Siebert			
☐ 615	Rookie Pitchers	1.00	.50	.10
	Pat Darcy			
	Dennis Leonard			
	Tom Underwood			
	Hank Webb			
☐ 616	Rookie Outfielders	30.00	15.00	3.00
	Dave Augustine			
	Pepe Mangual			
	Jim Rice			
	John Scott			
☐ 617	Rookie Infielders	1.75	.85	.17
	Mike Cubbage			
	Doug DeCinces			
	Reggie Sanders			
	Manny Trillo			
☐ 618	Rookie Pitchers	2.50	1.25	.25
	Jamie Easterly			
	Tom Johnson			
	Scott McGregor			
	Rick Rhoden			

		NRMT	VG-E	GOOD
☐ 619	Rookie Outfielders ..	.40	.20	.04
	Benny Ayala			
	Nyls Nyman			
	Tommy Smith			
	Jerry Turner			
☐ 620	Rookie Catcher/OF .	35.00	17.50	3.50
	Gary Carter			
	Marc Hill			
	Danny Meyer			
	Leon Roberts			
☐ 621	Rookie Pitchers	.75	.35	.07
	John Denny			
	Rawly Eastwick			
	Jim Kern			
	Juan Veintidos			
☐ 622	Rookie Outfielders ..	12.00	6.00	1.20
	Ed Armbrister			
	Fred Lynn			
	Tom Poquette			
	Terry Whitfield			
☐ 623	Rookie Infielders ...	24.00	12.00	2.40
	Phil Garner			
	Keith Hernandez			
	(sic, bats right)			
	Bob Sheldon			
	Tom Veryzer			
☐ 624	Rookie Pitchers	.40	.20	.04
	Doug Konieczny			
	Gary Lavelle			
	Jim Otten			
	Eddie Solomon			
☐ 625	Boog Powell	.50	.25	.05
☐ 626	Larry Haney	.25	.12	.02
	(photo actually			
	Dave Duncan)			
☐ 627	Tom Walker	.25	.12	.02
☐ 628	Ron LeFlore	.50	.25	.05
☐ 629	Joe Hoerner	.25	.12	.02
☐ 630	Greg Luzinski	.60	.30	.06
☐ 631	Lee Lacy	.25	.12	.02
☐ 632	Morris Nettles	.25	.12	.02
☐ 633	Paul Casanova	.25	.12	.02
☐ 634	Cy Acosta	.25	.12	.02
☐ 635	Chuck Dobson	.25	.12	.02
☐ 636	Charlie Moore	.25	.12	.02
☐ 637	Ted Martinez	.25	.12	.02
☐ 638	Cubs: Team/Mgr. ..	.75	.35	.07
	Jim Marshall (check-			
	list back)			

		NRMT	VG-E	GOOD
☐ 639	Steve Kline	.25	.12	.02
☐ 640	Harmon Killebrew ..	3.00	1.50	.30
☐ 641	Jim Northrup	.40	.20	.04
☐ 642	Mike Phillips	.25	.12	.02
☐ 643	Brent Strom	.25	.12	.02
☐ 644	Bill Fahey	.25	.12	.02
☐ 645	Danny Cater	.25	.12	.02
☐ 646	Checklist: 529-660 .	1.00	.10	.02
☐ 647	Claudell Washington .	2.50	1.25	.25
☐ 648	Dave Pagan	.25	.12	.02
☐ 649	Jack Heidemann	.25	.12	.02
☐ 650	Dave May	.25	.12	.02
☐ 651	John Morlan	.25	.12	.02
☐ 652	Lindy McDaniel	.25	.12	.02
☐ 653	Lee Richard	.25	.12	.02
☐ 654	Jerry Terrell	.25	.12	.02
☐ 655	Rico Carty	.40	.20	.02
☐ 656	Bill Plummer	.25	.12	.02
☐ 657	Dob Olivor	.25	.12	.02
☐ 658	Vic Harris	.25	.12	.02
☐ 659	Bob Apodaca	.25	.12	.02
☐ 660	Hank Aaron	16.00	4.00	.75

1976 Topps

The 1976 Topps set of 660 cards (measuring 2 ½" by 3 ½") is known for its sharp color photographs and interesting presentation of subjects. Team cards feature a checklist back for players on that team and show a small inset photo of the manager on the front. A "Father and Son" series (66-70) spotlights five Major

Leaguers whose fathers also made the "Big Show." Other subseries include "All Time All Stars" (341-350), "Record Breakers" from the previous season (1-6), League Leaders (191-205), Post-season cards (461-462), and Rookie Prospects (589-599).

		NRMT	VG-E	GOOD
	COMPLETE SET (660)	325.00	150.00	30.00
	COMMON PLAYER (1-660)	.20	.10	.02
☐ 1	RB: Hank Aaron Most RBI's, 2262	10.00	2.50	.50
☐ 2	RB: Bobby Bonds Most leadoff HR's 32; plus three seasons 30 homers/30 steals	.40	.20	.04
☐ 3	RB: Mickey Lolich Lefthander, Most Strikeouts, 2679	.40	.20	.04
☐ 4	RB: Dave Lopes Most Consecutive SB attempts, 38	.30	.15	.03
☐ 5	RB: Tom Seaver Most Cons. seasons with 200 SO's, 8	1.75	.85	.17
☐ 6	RB: Rennie Stennett Most Hits in a 9 inning game, 7	.30	.15	.03
☐ 7	Jim Umbarger	.20	.10	.02
☐ 8	Tito Fuentes	.20	.10	.02
☐ 9	Paul Lindblad	.20	.10	.02
☐ 10	Lou Brock	2.50	1.25	.25
☐ 11	Jim Hughes	.20	.10	.02
☐ 12	Richie Zisk	.30	.15	.03
☐ 13	John Wockenfuss	.20	.10	.02
☐ 14	Gene Garber	.20	.10	.02
☐ 15	George Scott	.30	.15	.03
☐ 16	Bob Apodaca	.20	.10	.02
☐ 17	New York Yankees Team Card (checklist back)	1.00	.50	.10
☐ 18	Dale Murray	.20	.10	.02
☐ 19	George Brett	22.00	11.00	2.20
☐ 20	Bob Watson	.30	.15	.03
☐ 21	Dave LaRoche	.20	.10	.02
☐ 22	Bill Russell	.30	.15	.03
☐ 23	Brian Downing	.40	.20	.04
☐ 24	Cesar Geronimo	.20	.10	.02
☐ 25	Mike Torrez	.20	.10	.02
☐ 26	Andre Thornton	.30	.15	.03
☐ 27	Ed Figueroa	.20	.10	.02
☐ 28	Dusty Baker	.40	.20	.04
☐ 29	Rick Burleson	.30	.15	.03
☐ 30	John Montefusco	.30	.15	.03
☐ 31	Len Randle	.20	.10	.02
☐ 32	Danny Frisella	.20	.10	.02
☐ 33	Bill North	.20	.10	.02
☐ 34	Mike Garman	.20	.10	.02
☐ 35	Tony Oliva	.75	.35	.07
☐ 36	Frank Taveras	.20	.10	.02
☐ 37	John Hiller	.30	.15	.03
☐ 38	Garry Maddox	.30	.15	.03
☐ 39	Pete Broberg	.20	.10	.02
☐ 40	Dave Kingman	.75	.35	.07
☐ 41	Tippy Martinez	.30	.15	.03
☐ 42	Barry Foote	.20	.10	.02
☐ 43	Paul Splittorff	.20	.10	.02
☐ 44	Doug Rader	.30	.15	.03
☐ 45	Boog Powell	.50	.25	.05
☐ 46	Dodgers Team (checklist back)	.75	.35	.07
☐ 47	Jesse Jefferson	.20	.10	.02
☐ 48	Dave Concepcion	.50	.25	.05
☐ 49	Dave Duncan	.20	.10	.02
☐ 50	Fred Lynn	2.25	1.10	.22
☐ 51	Ray Burris	.20	.10	.02
☐ 52	Dave Chalk	.20	.10	.02
☐ 53	Mike Beard	.20	.10	.02
☐ 54	Dave Rader	.20	.10	.02
☐ 55	Gaylord Perry	1.75	.85	.17
☐ 56	Bob Tolan	.20	.10	.02
☐ 57	Phil Garner	.30	.15	.03
☐ 58	Ron Reed	.20	.10	.02
☐ 59	Larry Hisle	.30	.15	.03
☐ 60	Jerry Reuss	.30	.15	.03
☐ 61	Ron LeFlore	.30	.15	.03
☐ 62	Johnny Oates	.20	.10	.02
☐ 63	Bobby Darwin	.20	.10	.02
☐ 64	Jerry Koosman	.50	.25	.05
☐ 65	Chris Chambliss	.40	.20	.04
☐ 66	Father and Son Gus Bell Buddy Bell	.40	.20	.04
☐ 67	Father and Son Ray Boone Bob Boone	.40	.20	.04
☐ 68	Father and Son Joe Coleman	.25	.12	.02

			NRMT	VG-E	GOOD
		Joe Coleman Jr.			
☐	69	Father and Son	.25	.12	.02
		Jim Hegan			
		Mike Hegan			
☐	70	Father and Son	.25	.12	.02
		Roy Smalley			
		Roy Smalley Jr.			
☐	71	Steve Rogers	.30	.15	.03
☐	72	Hal McRae	.40	.20	.04
☐	73	Baltimore Orioles	.75	.35	.07
		Team Card			
		(checklist back)			
☐	74	Oscar Gamble	.30	.15	.03
☐	75	Larry Dierker	.30	.15	.03
☐	76	Willie Crawford	.20	.10	.02
☐	77	Pedro Borbon	.20	.10	.02
☐	78	Cecil Cooper	.90	.45	.09
☐	79	Jerry Morales	.20	.10	.02
☐	80	Jim Kaat	.75	.35	.07
☐	81	Darrell Evans	.60	.30	.06
☐	82	Von Joshua	.20	.10	.02
☐	83	Jim Spencer	.20	.10	.02
☐	84	Brent Strom	.20	.10	.02
☐	85	Mickey Rivers	.30	.15	.03
☐	86	Mike Tyson	.20	.10	.02
☐	87	Tom Burgmeier	.20	.10	.02
☐	88	Duffy Dyer	.20	.10	.02
☐	89	Vern Ruhle	.20	.10	.02
☐	90	Sal Bando	.40	.20	.04
☐	91	Tom Hutton	.20	.10	.02
☐	92	Eduardo Rodriguez	.20	.10	.02
☐	93	Mike Phillips	.20	.10	.02
☐	94	Jim Dwyer	.20	.10	.02
☐	95	Brooks Robinson	2.50	1.25	.25
☐	96	Doug Bird	.20	.10	.02
☐	97	Wilbur Howard	.20	.10	.02
☐	98	Dennis Eckersley	5.00	2.50	.50
☐	99	Lee Lacy	.20	.10	.02
☐	100	Jim Hunter	2.25	1.10	.22
☐	101	Pete LaCock	.20	.10	.02
☐	102	Jim Willoughby	.20	.10	.02
☐	103	Biff Pocoroba	.20	.10	.02
☐	104	Reds Team	.75	.35	.07
		(checklist back)			
☐	105	Gary Lavelle	.20	.10	.02
☐	106	Tom Grieve	.30	.15	.03
☐	107	Dave Roberts	.20	.10	.02
☐	108	Don Kirkwood	.20	.10	.02
☐	109	Larry Lintz	.20	.10	.02
☐	110	Carlos May	.20	.10	.02
☐	111	Danny Thompson	.20	.10	.02
☐	112	Kent Tekulve	1.00	.50	.10
☐	113	Gary Sutherland	.20	.10	.02
☐	114	Jay Johnstone	.30	.15	.03
☐	115	Ken Holtzman	.30	.15	.03
☐	116	Charlie Moore	.20	.10	.02
☐	117	Mike Jorgensen	.20	.10	.02
☐	118	Red Sox Team	.75	.35	.07
		(checklist back)			
☐	119	Checklist 1-132	.90	.10	.02
☐	120	Rusty Staub	.50	.25	.05
☐	121	Tony Solaita	.20	.10	.02
☐	122	Mike Cosgrove	.20	.10	.02
☐	123	Walt Williams	.20	.10	.02
☐	124	Doug Rau	.20	.10	.02
☐	125	Don Baylor	.60	.30	.06
☐	126	Tom Dettore	.20	.10	.02
☐	127	Larvell Blanks	.20	.10	.02
☐	128	Ken Griffey	.50	.25	.05
☐	129	Andy Etchebarren	.20	.10	.02
☐	130	Luis Tiant	.50	.25	.05
☐	131	Bill Stein	.20	.10	.02
☐	132	Don Hood	.20	.10	.02
☐	133	Gary Matthews	.30	.15	.03
☐	134	Mike Ivie	.20	.10	.02
☐	135	Bake McBride	.30	.15	.03
☐	136	Dave Goltz	.20	.10	.02
☐	137	Bill Robinson	.30	.15	.03
☐	138	Lerrin LaGrow	.20	.10	.02
☐	139	Gorman Thomas	.50	.25	.05
☐	140	Vida Blue	.40	.20	.04
☐	141	Larry Parrish	.90	.45	.09
☐	142	Dick Drago	.20	.10	.02
☐	143	Jerry Grote	.20	.10	.02
☐	144	Al Fitzmorris	.20	.10	.02
☐	145	Larry Bowa	.50	.25	.05
☐	146	George Medich	.20	.10	.02
☐	147	Astros Team	.75	.35	.07
		(checklist back)			
☐	148	Stan Thomas	.20	.10	.02
☐	149	Tommy Davis	.30	.15	.03
☐	150	Steve Garvey	5.00	2.50	.50
☐	151	Bill Bonham	.20	.10	.02
☐	152	Leroy Stanton	.20	.10	.02
☐	153	Buzz Capra	.20	.10	.02
☐	154	Bucky Dent	.50	.25	.05
☐	155	Jack Billingham	.20	.10	.02
☐	156	Rico Carty	.30	.15	.03

		NRMT	VG-E	GOOD
☐ 157	Mike Caldwell	.30	.15	.03
☐ 158	Ken Reitz	.20	.10	.02
☐ 159	Jerry Terrell	.20	.10	.02
☐ 160	Dave Winfield	6.00	3.00	.60
☐ 161	Bruce Kison	.20	.10	.02
☐ 162	Jack Pierce	.20	.10	.02
☐ 163	Jim Slaton	.20	.10	.02
☐ 164	Pepe Mangual	.20	.10	.02
☐ 165	Gene Tenace	.30	.15	.03
☐ 166	Skip Lockwood	.20	.10	.02
☐ 167	Freddie Patek	.20	.10	.02
☐ 168	Tom Hilgendorf	.20	.10	.02
☐ 169	Graig Nettles	1.00	.50	.10
☐ 170	Rick Wise	.30	.15	.03
☐ 171	Greg Gross	.20	.10	.02
☐ 172	Rangers Team	.75	.35	.07
	(checklist back)			
☐ 173	Steve Swisher	.20	.10	.02
☐ 174	Charlie Hough	.40	.20	.04
☐ 175	Ken Singleton	.40	.20	.04
☐ 176	Dick Lange	.20	.10	.02
☐ 177	Marty Perez	.20	.10	.02
☐ 178	Tom Buskey	.20	.10	.02
☐ 179	George Foster	1.00	.50	.10
☐ 180	Rich Gossage	1.25	.60	.12
☐ 181	Willie Montanez	.20	.10	.02
☐ 182	Harry Rasmussen	.20	.10	.02
☐ 183	Steve Braun	.20	.10	.02
☐ 184	Bill Greif	.20	.10	.02
☐ 185	Dave Parker	4.00	2.00	.40
☐ 186	Tom Walker	.20	.10	.02
☐ 187	Pedro Garcia	.20	.10	.02
☐ 188	Fred Scherman	.20	.10	.02
☐ 189	Claudell Washington	.50	.25	.05
☐ 190	Jon Matlock	.30	.15	.03
☐ 191	NL Batting Leaders	.40	.20	.04
	Bill Madlock			
	Ted Simmons			
	Manny Sanguillen			
☐ 192	AL Batting Leaders	1.50	.75	.15
	Rod Carew			
	Fred Lynn			
	Thurman Munson			
☐ 193	NL Home Run Leaders	.75	.35	.07
	Mike Schmidt			
	Dave Kingman			
	Greg Luzinski			

		NRMT	VG-E	GOOD
☐ 194	AL Home Run Leaders	.75	.35	.07
	Reggie Jackson			
	George Scott			
	John Mayberry			
☐ 195	AL RBI Leaders	.60	.30	.06
	Greg Luzinski			
	Johnny Bench			
	Tony Perez			
☐ 196	AL RBI Leaders	.40	.20	.04
	George Scott			
	John Mayberry			
	Fred Lynn			
☐ 197	NL Steals Leaders	.75	.35	.07
	Dave Lopes			
	Joe Morgan			
	Lou Brock			
☐ 198	AL Steals Leaders	.40	.20	.04
	Mickey Rivers			
	Claudell Washington			
	Amos Otis			
☐ 199	NL Victory Leaders	.60	.30	.06
	Tom Seaver			
	Randy Jones			
	Andy Messersmith			
☐ 200	AL Victory Leaders	1.00	.50	.10
	Jim Hunter			
	Jim Palmer			
	Vida Blue			
☐ 201	NL ERA Leaders	.50	.25	.05
	Randy Jones			
	Andy Messersmith			
	Tom Seaver			
☐ 202	AL ERA Leaders	1.50	.75	.15
	Jim Palmer			
	Jim Hunter			
	Dennis Eckersley			
☐ 203	NL Strikeout Leaders	.60	.30	.06
	Tom Seaver			
	John Montefusco			
	Andy Messersmith			
☐ 204	AL Strikeout Leaders	.50	.25	.05
	Frank Tanana			
	Bert Blyleven			
	Gaylord Perry			
☐ 205	Leading Firemen	.40	.20	.04
	Al Hrabosky			
	Rich Gossage			
☐ 206	Manny Trillo	.20	.10	.02

		NRMT	VG-E	GOOD			NRMT	VG-E	GOOD
☐ 207	Andy Hassler	.20	.10	.02	☐ 253	Bill Buckner	.40	.20	.04
☐ 208	Mike Lum	.20	.10	.02	☐ 254	Rudy Meoli	.20	.10	.02
☐ 209	Alan Ashby	.30	.15	.03	☐ 255	Fritz Peterson	.20	.10	.02
☐ 210	Lee May	.30	.15	.03	☐ 256	Rowland Office	.20	.10	.02
☐ 211	Clay Carroll	.20	.10	.02	☐ 257	Ross Grimsley	.20	.10	.02
☐ 212	Pat Kelly	.20	.10	.02	☐ 258	Nyls Nyman	.20	.10	.02
☐ 213	Dave Heaverlo	.20	.10	.02	☐ 259	Darrel Chaney	.20	.10	.02
☐ 214	Eric Soderholm	.20	.10	.02	☐ 260	Steve Busby	.30	.15	.03
☐ 215	Reggie Smith	.40	.20	.04	☐ 261	Gary Thomasson	.20	.10	.02
☐ 216	Expos Team	.65	.30	.06	☐ 262	Checklist 133-264	.90	.10	.02
	(checklist back)				☐ 263	Lyman Bostock	.50	.25	.05
☐ 217	Dave Freisleben	.20	.10	.02	☐ 264	Steve Renko	.20	.10	.02
☐ 218	John Knox	.20	.10	.02	☐ 265	Willie Davis	.30	.15	.03
☐ 219	Tom Murphy	.20	.10	.02	☐ 266	Alan Foster	.20	.10	.02
☐ 220	Manny Sanguillen	.30	.15	.03	☐ 267	Aurelio Rodriguez	.20	.10	.02
☐ 221	Jim Todd	.20	.10	.02	☐ 268	Del Unser	.20	.10	.02
☐ 222	Wayne Garrett	.20	.10	.02	☐ 269	Rick Austin	.20	.10	.02
☐ 223	Ollie Brown	.20	.10	.02	☐ 270	Willie Stargell	3.00	1.50	.30
☐ 224	Jim York	.20	.10	.02	☐ 271	Jim Lonborg	.30	.15	.03
☐ 225	Roy White	.30	.15	.03	☐ 272	Rick Dempsey	.30	.15	.03
☐ 226	Jim Sundberg	.30	.15	.03	☐ 273	Joe Niekro	.40	.20	.04
☐ 227	Oscar Zamora	.20	.10	.02	☐ 274	Tommy Harper	.30	.15	.03
☐ 228	John Hale	.20	.10	.02	☐ 275	Rick Manning	.20	.10	.02
☐ 229	Jerry Remy	.30	.15	.03	☐ 276	Mickey Scott	.20	.10	.02
☐ 230	Carl Yastrzemski	7.50	3.75	.75	☐ 277	Cubs Team	.75	.35	.07
☐ 231	Tom House	.30	.15	.03		(checklist back)			
☐ 232	Frank Duffy	.20	.10	.02	☐ 278	Bernie Carbo	.20	.10	.02
☐ 233	Grant Jackson	.20	.10	.02	☐ 279	Roy Howell	.20	.10	.02
☐ 234	Mike Sadek	.20	.10	.02	☐ 280	Burt Hooton	.30	.15	.03
☐ 235	Bert Blyleven	1.50	.75	.15	☐ 281	Dave May	.20	.10	.02
☐ 236	Kansas City Royals	.75	.35	.07	☐ 282	Dan Osborn	.20	.10	.02
	Team Card				☐ 283	Merv Rettenmund	.20	.10	.02
	(checklist back)				☐ 284	Steve Ontiveros	.20	.10	.02
☐ 237	Dave Hamilton	.20	.10	.02	☐ 285	Mike Cuellar	.30	.15	.03
☐ 238	Larry Biittner	.20	.10	.02	☐ 286	Jim Wohlford	.20	.10	.02
☐ 239	John Curtis	.20	.10	.02	☐ 287	Pete Mackanin	.20	.10	.02
☐ 240	Pete Rose	15.00	7.50	1.50	☐ 288	Bill Campbell	.20	.10	.02
☐ 241	Hector Torres	.20	.10	.02	☐ 289	Enzo Hernandez	.20	.10	.02
☐ 242	Dan Meyer	.20	.10	.02	☐ 290	Ted Simmons	.75	.35	.07
☐ 243	Jim Rooker	.20	.10	.02	☐ 291	Ken Sanders	.20	.10	.02
☐ 244	Bill Sharp	.20	.10	.02	☐ 292	Leon Roberts	.20	.10	.02
☐ 245	Felix Millan	.20	.10	.02	☐ 293	Bill Castro	.20	.10	.02
☐ 246	Cesar Tovar	.20	.10	.02	☐ 294	Ed Kirkpatrick	.20	.10	.02
☐ 247	Terry Harmon	.20	.10	.02	☐ 295	Dave Cash	.20	.10	.02
☐ 248	Dick Tidrow	.20	.10	.02	☐ 296	Pat Dobson	.30	.15	.03
☐ 249	Cliff Johnson	.20	.10	.02	☐ 297	Roger Metzger	.20	.10	.02
☐ 250	Fergie Jenkins	.75	.35	.07	☐ 298	Dick Bosman	.20	.10	.02
☐ 251	Rick Monday	.30	.15	.03	☐ 299	Champ Summers	.20	.10	.02
☐ 252	Tim Nordbrook	.20	.10	.02	☐ 300	Johnny Bench	6.50	3.25	.65

		NRMT	VG-E	GOOD
☐ 301	Jackie Brown	.20	.10	.02
☐ 302	Rick Miller	.20	.10	.02
☐ 303	Steve Foucault	.20	.10	.02
☐ 304	Angels Team (checklist back)	.75	.35	.07
☐ 305	Andy Messersmith	.30	.15	.03
☐ 306	Rod Gilbreath	.20	.10	.02
☐ 307	Al Bumbry	.20	.10	.02
☐ 308	Jim Barr	.20	.10	.02
☐ 309	Bill Melton	.20	.10	.02
☐ 310	Randy Jones	.30	.15	.03
☐ 311	Cookie Rojas	.20	.10	.02
☐ 312	Don Carrithers	.20	.10	.02
☐ 313	Dan Ford	.20	.10	.02
☐ 314	Ed Kranepool	.30	.15	.03
☐ 315	Al Hrabosky	.30	.15	.03
☐ 316	Robin Yount	28.00	14.00	2.80
☐ 317	John Candelaria	2.00	1.00	.20
☐ 318	Bob Boone	.75	.35	.07
☐ 319	Larry Gura	.30	.15	.03
☐ 320	Willie Horton	.30	.15	.03
☐ 321	Jose Cruz	.40	.20	.04
☐ 322	Glenn Abbott	.20	.10	.02
☐ 323	Rob Sperring	.20	.10	.02
☐ 324	Jim Bibby	.20	.10	.02
☐ 325	Tony Perez	.90	.45	.09
☐ 326	Dick Pole	.20	.10	.02
☐ 327	Dave Moates	.20	.10	.02
☐ 328	Carl Morton	.20	.10	.02
☐ 329	Joe Ferguson	.20	.10	.02
☐ 330	Nolan Ryan	16.00	8.00	1.60
☐ 331	San Diego Padres Team Card (checklist back)	.75	.35	.07
☐ 332	Charlie Williams	.20	.10	.02
☐ 333	Bob Coluccio	.20	.10	.02
☐ 334	Dennis Leonard	.30	.15	.03
☐ 335	Bob Grich	.40	.20	.04
☐ 336	Vic Albury	.20	.10	.02
☐ 337	Bud Harrelson	.30	.15	.03
☐ 338	Bob Bailey	.20	.10	.02
☐ 339	John Denny	.30	.15	.03
☐ 340	Jim Rice	7.50	3.75	.75
☐ 341	All-Time 1B Lou Gehrig	3.00	1.50	.30
☐ 342	All-Time 2B Rogers Hornsby	1.50	.75	.15
☐ 343	All-Time 3B Pie Traynor	.75	.35	.07

		NRMT	VG-E	GOOD
☐ 344	All-Time SS Honus Wagner	1.50	.75	.15
☐ 345	All-Time OF Babe Ruth	5.00	2.50	.50
☐ 346	All-Time OF Ty Cobb	3.00	1.50	.30
☐ 347	All-Time OF Ted Williams	3.00	1.50	.30
☐ 348	All-Time C Mickey Cochrane	.75	.35	.07
☐ 349	All-Time RHP Walter Johnson	1.50	.75	.15
☐ 350	All-Time LHP Lefty Grove	1.25	.60	.12
☐ 351	Randy Hundley	.20	.10	.02
☐ 352	Dave Giusti	.20	.10	.02
☐ 353	Sixto Lezcano	.20	.10	.02
☐ 354	Ron Blomberg	.20	.10	.02
☐ 355	Steve Carlton	4.50	2.25	.45
☐ 356	Ted Martinez	.20	.10	.02
☐ 357	Ken Forsch	.20	.10	.02
☐ 358	Buddy Bell	.50	.25	.05
☐ 359	Rick Reuschel	.60	.30	.06
☐ 360	Jeff Burroughs	.30	.15	.03
☐ 361	Detroit Tigers Team Card (checklist back)	.75	.35	.07
☐ 362	Will McEnaney	.20	.10	.02
☐ 363	Dave Collins	.60	.30	.06
☐ 364	Elias Sosa	.20	.10	.02
☐ 365	Carlton Fisk	2.50	1.25	.25
☐ 366	Bobby Valentine	.40	.20	.04
☐ 367	Bruce Miller	.20	.10	.02
☐ 368	Wilbur Wood	.20	.10	.02
☐ 369	Frank White	.40	.20	.04
☐ 370	Ron Cey	.50	.25	.05
☐ 371	Elrod Hendricks	.20	.10	.02
☐ 372	Rick Baldwin	.20	.10	.02
☐ 373	Johnny Briggs	.20	.10	.02
☐ 374	Dan Warthen	.20	.10	.02
☐ 375	Ron Fairly	.30	.15	.03
☐ 376	Rich Hebner	.20	.10	.02
☐ 377	Mike Hegan	.20	.10	.02
☐ 378	Steve Stone	.30	.15	.03
☐ 379	Ken Boswell	.20	.10	.02
☐ 380	Bobby Bonds	.40	.20	.04
☐ 381	Denny Doyle	.20	.10	.02
☐ 382	Matt Alexander	.20	.10	.02
☐ 383	John Ellis	.20	.10	.02

		NRMT	VG-E	GOOD
☐ 384	Phillies Team (checklist back)	.75	.35	.07
☐ 385	Mickey Lolich	.40	.20	.04
☐ 386	Ed Goodson	.20	.10	.02
☐ 387	Mike Miley	.20	.10	.02
☐ 388	Stan Perzanowski	.20	.10	.02
☐ 389	Glenn Adams	.20	.10	.02
☐ 390	Don Gullett	.30	.15	.03
☐ 391	Jerry Hairston	.20	.10	.02
☐ 392	Checklist 265-396	.90	.10	.02
☐ 393	Paul Mitchell	.20	.10	.02
☐ 394	Fran Healy	.20	.10	.02
☐ 395	Jim Wynn	.30	.15	.03
☐ 396	Bill Lee	.30	.15	.03
☐ 397	Tim Foli	.20	.10	.02
☐ 398	Dave Tomlin	.20	.10	.02
☐ 399	Luis Melendez	.20	.10	.02
☐ 400	Rod Carew	4.50	2.00	.40
☐ 401	Ken Brett	.20	.10	.02
☐ 402	Don Money	.20	.10	.02
☐ 403	Geoff Zahn	.20	.10	.02
☐ 404	Enos Cabell	.20	.10	.02
☐ 405	Rollie Fingers	1.25	.60	.12
☐ 406	Ed Herrmann	.20	.10	.02
☐ 407	Tom Underwood	.20	.10	.02
☐ 408	Charlie Spikes	.20	.10	.02
☐ 409	Dave Lemanczyk	.20	.10	.02
☐ 410	Ralph Garr	.30	.15	.03
☐ 411	Bill Singer	.20	.10	.02
☐ 412	Toby Harrah	.30	.15	.03
☐ 413	Pete Varney	.20	.10	.02
☐ 414	Wayne Garland	.20	.10	.02
☐ 415	Vada Pinson	.40	.20	.04
☐ 416	Tommy John	1.00	.50	.10
☐ 417	Gene Clines	.20	.10	.02
☐ 418	Jose Morales	.20	.10	.02
☐ 419	Reggie Cleveland	.20	.10	.02
☐ 420	Joe Morgan	4.50	2.25	.45
☐ 421	A's Team (checklist back)	.75	.35	.07
☐ 422	Johnny Grubb	.20	.10	.02
☐ 423	Ed Halicki	.20	.10	.02
☐ 424	Phil Roof	.20	.10	.02
☐ 425	Rennie Stennett	.20	.10	.02
☐ 426	Bob Forsch	.20	.10	.02
☐ 427	Kurt Bevacqua	.20	.10	.02
☐ 428	Jim Crawford	.20	.10	.02
☐ 429	Fred Stanley	.20	.10	.02
☐ 430	Jose Cardenal	.20	.10	.02

		NRMT	VG-E	GOOD
☐ 431	Dick Ruthven	.20	.10	.02
☐ 432	Tom Veryzer	.20	.10	.02
☐ 433	Rick Waits	.20	.10	.02
☐ 434	Morris Nettles	.20	.10	.02
☐ 435	Phil Niekro	1.75	.85	.17
☐ 436	Bill Fahey	.20	.10	.02
☐ 437	Terry Forster	.30	.15	.03
☐ 438	Doug DeCinces	.60	.30	.06
☐ 439	Rick Rhoden	.60	.30	.06
☐ 440	John Mayberry	.30	.15	.03
☐ 441	Gary Carter	9.00	4.50	.90
☐ 442	Hank Webb	.20	.10	.02
☐ 443	Giants Team (checklist back)	.75	.35	.07
☐ 444	Gary Nolan	.20	.10	.02
☐ 445	Rico Petrocelli	.30	.15	.03
☐ 446	Larry Haney	.20	.10	.02
☐ 447	Gene Locklear	.20	.10	.02
☐ 448	Tom Johnson	.20	.10	.02
☐ 449	Bob Robertson	.20	.10	.02
☐ 450	Jim Palmer	4.50	2.25	.45
☐ 451	Buddy Bradford	.20	.10	.02
☐ 452	Tom Hausman	.20	.10	.02
☐ 453	Lou Piniella	.40	.20	.04
☐ 454	Tom Griffin	.20	.10	.02
☐ 455	Dick Allen	.40	.20	.04
☐ 456	Joe Coleman	.20	.10	.02
☐ 457	Ed Crosby	.20	.10	.02
☐ 458	Earl Williams	.20	.10	.02
☐ 459	Jim Brewer	.20	.10	.02
☐ 460	Cesar Cedeno	.30	.15	.03
☐ 461	NL and AL Champs Reds sweep Bucs, Bosox surprise A's	.40	.20	.04
☐ 462	'75 World Series Reds Champs	.40	.20	.04
☐ 463	Steve Hargan	.20	.10	.02
☐ 464	Ken Henderson	.20	.10	.02
☐ 465	Mike Marshall	.30	.15	.03
☐ 466	Bob Stinson	.20	.10	.02
☐ 467	Woodie Fryman	.20	.10	.02
☐ 468	Jesus Alou	.20	.10	.02
☐ 469	Rawly Eastwick	.20	.10	.02
☐ 470	Bobby Murcer	.40	.20	.04
☐ 471	Jim Burton	.20	.10	.02
☐ 472	Bob Davis	.20	.10	.02
☐ 473	Paul Blair	.30	.15	.03
☐ 474	Ray Corbin	.20	.10	.02
☐ 475	Joe Rudi	.30	.15	.03

		NRMT	VG-E	GOOD
☐ 476	Bob Moose	.20	.10	.02
☐ 477	Indians Team (checklist back)	.75	.35	.07
☐ 478	Lynn McGlothen	.20	.10	.02
☐ 479	Bobby Mitchell	.20	.10	.02
☐ 480	Mike Schmidt	20.00	10.00	2.00
☐ 481	Rudy May	.20	.10	.02
☐ 482	Tim Hosley	.20	.10	.02
☐ 483	Mickey Stanley	.30	.15	.03
☐ 484	Eric Raich	.20	.10	.02
☐ 485	Mike Hargrove	.30	.15	.03
☐ 486	Bruce Dal Canton	.20	.10	.02
☐ 487	Leron Lee	.20	.10	.02
☐ 488	Claude Osteen	.30	.15	.03
☐ 489	Skip Jutze	.20	.10	.02
☐ 490	Frank Tanana	.40	.20	.04
☐ 491	Terry Crowley	.20	.10	.02
☐ 492	Marty Pattin	.20	.10	.02
☐ 493	Derrel Thomas	.20	.10	.02
☐ 494	Craig Swan	.30	.15	.03
☐ 495	Nate Colbert	.20	.10	.02
☐ 496	Juan Beniquez	.20	.10	.02
☐ 497	Joe McIntosh	.20	.10	.02
☐ 498	Glenn Borgmann	.20	.10	.02
☐ 499	Mario Guerrero	.20	.10	.02
☐ 500	Reggie Jackson	8.00	4.00	.80
☐ 501	Billy Champion	.20	.10	.02
☐ 502	Tim McCarver	.40	.20	.04
☐ 503	Elliott Maddox	.20	.10	.02
☐ 504	Pirates Team (checklist back)	.75	.35	.07
☐ 505	Mark Belanger	.30	.15	.03
☐ 506	George Mitterwald	.20	.10	.02
☐ 507	Ray Bare	.20	.10	.02
☐ 508	Duane Kuiper	.20	.10	.02
☐ 509	Bill Hands	.20	.10	.02
☐ 510	Amos Otis	.40	.20	.04
☐ 511	Jamie Easterley	.20	.10	.02
☐ 512	Ellie Rodriguez	.20	.10	.02
☐ 513	Bart Johnson	.20	.10	.02
☐ 514	Dan Driessen	.30	.15	.03
☐ 515	Steve Yeager	.20	.10	.02
☐ 516	Wayne Granger	.20	.10	.02
☐ 517	John Milner	.20	.10	.02
☐ 518	Doug Flynn	.20	.10	.02
☐ 519	Steve Brye	.20	.10	.02
☐ 520	Willie McCovey	2.50	1.25	.25
☐ 521	Jim Colborn	.20	.10	.02
☐ 522	Ted Sizemore	.20	.10	.02
☐ 523	Bob Montgomery	.20	.10	.02
☐ 524	Pete Falcone	.20	.10	.02
☐ 525	Billy Williams	1.75	.85	.17
☐ 526	Checklist 397-528	.90	.10	.02
☐ 527	Mike Anderson	.20	.10	.02
☐ 528	Dock Ellis	.20	.10	.02
☐ 529	Deron Johnson	.20	.10	.02
☐ 530	Don Sutton	1.50	.75	.15
☐ 531	New York Mets Team Card (checklist back)	.90	.45	.09
☐ 532	Milt May	.20	.10	.02
☐ 533	Lee Richard	.20	.10	.02
☐ 534	Stan Bahnsen	.20	.10	.02
☐ 535	Dave Nelson	.20	.10	.02
☐ 536	Mike Thompson	.20	.10	.02
☐ 537	Tony Muser	.20	.10	.02
☐ 538	Pat Darcy	.20	.10	.02
☐ 539	John Balaz	.20	.10	.02
☐ 540	Bill Freehan	.40	.20	.04
☐ 541	Steve Mingori	.20	.10	.02
☐ 542	Keith Hernandez	6.00	3.00	.60
☐ 543	Wayne Twitchell	.20	.10	.02
☐ 544	Pepe Frias	.20	.10	.02
☐ 545	Sparky Lyle	.40	.20	.04
☐ 546	Dave Rosello	.20	.10	.02
☐ 547	Roric Harrison	.20	.10	.02
☐ 548	Manny Mota	.30	.15	.03
☐ 549	Randy Tate	.20	.10	.02
☐ 550	Hank Aaron	11.00	5.50	1.10
☐ 551	Jerry DaVanon	.20	.10	.02
☐ 552	Terry Humphrey	.20	.10	.02
☐ 553	Randy Moffitt	.20	.10	.02
☐ 554	Ray Fosse	.20	.10	.02
☐ 555	Dyar Miller	.20	.10	.02
☐ 556	Twins Team (checklist back)	.75	.35	.07
☐ 557	Dan Spillner	.20	.10	.02
☐ 558	Clarence Gaston	.40	.20	.04
☐ 559	Clyde Wright	.20	.10	.02
☐ 560	Jorge Orta	.20	.10	.02
☐ 561	Tom Carroll	.20	.10	.02
☐ 562	Adrian Garrett	.20	.10	.02
☐ 563	Larry Demery	.20	.10	.02
☐ 564	Bubble Gum Champ Kurt Bevacqua	.20	.10	.02
☐ 565	Tug McGraw	.40	.20	.04
☐ 566	Ken McMullen	.20	.10	.02
☐ 567	George Stone	.20	.10	.02

		NRMT	VG-E	GOOD
☐ 568	Rob Andrews	.20	.10	.02
☐ 569	Nelson Briles	.20	.10	.02
☐ 570	George Hendrick	.30	.15	.03
☐ 571	Don DeMola	.20	.10	.02
☐ 572	Rich Coggins	.20	.10	.02
☐ 573	Bill Travers	.20	.10	.02
☐ 574	Don Kessinger	.30	.15	.03
☐ 575	Dwight Evans	2.00	1.00	.20
☐ 576	Maximino Leon	.20	.10	.02
☐ 577	Marc Hill	.20	.10	.02
☐ 578	Ted Kubiak	.20	.10	.02
☐ 579	Clay Kirby	.20	.10	.02
☐ 580	Bert Campaneris	.30	.15	.03
☐ 581	Cardinals Team (checklist back)	.75	.35	.07
☐ 582	Mike Kekich	.20	.10	.02
☐ 583	Tommy Helms	.30	.15	.03
☐ 584	Stan Wall	.20	.10	.02
☐ 585	Joe Torre	.50	.25	.05
☐ 586	Ron Schueler	.20	.10	.02
☐ 587	Leo Cardenas	.20	.10	.02
☐ 588	Kevin Kobel	.20	.10	.02
☐ 589	Rookie Pitchers	2.00	1.00	.20
	Santo Alcala			
	Mike Flanagan			
	Joe Pactwa			
	Pablo Torrealba			
☐ 590	Rookie Outfielders	1.00	.50	.10
	Henry Cruz			
	Chet Lemon			
	Ellis Valentine			
	Terry Whitfield			
☐ 591	Rookie Pitchers	.30	.15	.03
	Steve Grilli			
	Craig Mitchell			
	Jose Sosa			
	George Throop			
☐ 592	Rookie Infielders	5.00	2.50	.50
	Willie Randolph			
	Dave McKay			
	Jerry Royster			
	Roy Staiger			
☐ 593	Rookie Pitchers	.40	.20	.04
	Larry Anderson			
	Ken Crosby			
	Mark Littell			
	Butch Metzger			
☐ 594	Rookie Catchers/OF	.40	.20	.04
	Andy Merchant			

		NRMT	VG-E	GOOD
	Ed Ott			
	Royle Stillman			
	Jerry White			
☐ 595	Rookie Pitchers	.40	.20	.04
	Art DeFillipis			
	Randy Lerch			
	Sid Monge			
	Steve Barr			
☐ 596	Rookie Infielders	.50	.25	.05
	Craig Reynolds			
	Lamar Johnson			
	Johnnie LeMaster			
	Jerry Manuel			
☐ 597	Rookie Pitchers	.60	.30	.06
	Don Aase			
	Jack Kucek			
	Frank LaCorte			
	Mike Pazik			
☐ 598	Rookie Outfielders	.30	.15	.03
	Hector Cruz			
	Jamie Quirk			
	Jerry Turner			
	Joe Wallis			
☐ 599	Rookie Pitchers	10.00	5.00	1.00
	Rob Dressler			
	Ron Guidry			
	Bob McClure			
	Pat Zachry			
☐ 600	Tom Seaver	6.00	2.75	.55
☐ 601	Ken Rudolph	.20	.10	.02
☐ 602	Doug Konieczny	.20	.10	.02
☐ 603	Jim Holt	.20	.10	.02
☐ 604	Joe Lovitto	.20	.10	.02
☐ 605	Al Downing	.30	.15	.03
☐ 606	Milwaukee Brewers Team Card (checklist back)	.75	.35	.07
☐ 607	Rich Hinton	.20	.10	.02
☐ 608	Vic Correll	.20	.10	.02
☐ 609	Fred Norman	.20	.10	.02
☐ 610	Greg Luzinski	.50	.25	.05
☐ 611	Rich Folkers	.20	.10	.02
☐ 612	Joe Lahoud	.20	.10	.02
☐ 613	Tim Johnson	.20	.10	.02
☐ 614	Fernando Arroyo	.20	.10	.02
☐ 615	Mike Cubbage	.20	.10	.02
☐ 616	Buck Martinez	.20	.10	.02
☐ 617	Darold Knowles	.20	.10	.02
☐ 618	Jack Brohamer	.20	.10	.02

1976 Topps Traded

			NRMT	VG-E	GOOD
☐	619	Bill Butler	.20	.10	.02
☐	620	Al Oliver	.50	.25	.05
☐	621	Tom Hall	.20	.10	.02
☐	622	Rick Auerbach	.20	.10	.02
☐	623	Bob Allietta	.20	.10	.02
☐	624	Tony Taylor	.20	.10	.02
☐	625	J.R. Richard	.30	.15	.03
☐	626	Bob Sheldon	.20	.10	.02
☐	627	Bill Plummer	.20	.10	.02
☐	628	John D'Acquisto	.20	.10	.02
☐	629	Sandy Alomar	.20	.10	.02
☐	630	Chris Speier	.20	.10	.02
☐	631	Braves Team (checklist back)	.75	.35	.07
☐	632	Rogelio Moret	.20	.10	.02
☐	633	John Stearns	.30	.15	.03
☐	634	Larry Christenson	.20	.10	.02
☐	635	Jim Fregosi	.30	.15	.03
☐	636	Joe Decker	.20	.10	.02
☐	637	Bruce Bochte	.20	.10	.02
☐	638	Doyle Alexander	.30	.15	.03
☐	639	Fred Kendall	.20	.10	.02
☐	640	Bill Madlock	.75	.35	.07
☐	641	Tom Paciorek	.20	.10	.02
☐	642	Dennis Blair	.20	.10	.02
☐	643	Checklist 529-660	.90	.10	.02
☐	644	Tom Bradley	.20	.10	.02
☐	645	Darrell Porter	.20	.10	.02
☐	646	John Lowenstein	.20	.10	.02
☐	647	Ramon Hernandez	.20	.10	.02
☐	648	Al Cowens	.30	.15	.03
☐	649	Dave Roberts	.20	.10	.02
☐	650	Thurman Munson	5.50	2.75	.55
☐	651	John Odom	.20	.10	.02
☐	652	Ed Armbrister	.20	.10	.02
☐	653	Mike Norris	.30	.15	.03
☐	654	Doug Griffin	.20	.10	.02
☐	655	Mike Vail	.20	.10	.02
☐	656	Chicago White Sox Team Card (checklist back)	.75	.35	.07
☐	657	Roy Smalley	.50	.25	.05
☐	658	Jerry Johnson	.20	.10	.02
☐	659	Ben Oglivie	.40	.20	.04
☐	660	Dave Lopes	.65	.15	.03

The cards in this 44-card set measure 2 ½" by 3 ½". The 1976 Topps Traded set contains 43 players and one unnumbered checklist card. The individuals pictured were traded after the Topps regular set was printed. A "Sports Extra" heading design is found on each picture and is also used to introduce the biographical section of the reverse. Each card is numbered according to the player's regular 1976 card with the addition of "T" to indicate his new status.

			NRMT	VG-E	GOOD
		COMPLETE SET (44)	7.00	3.25	.65
		COMMON PLAYER	.12	.06	.01
☐	27T	Ed Figueroa	.12	.06	.01
☐	28T	Dusty Baker	.30	.15	.03
☐	44T	Doug Rader	.20	.10	.02
☐	58T	Ron Reed	.15	.07	.01
☐	74T	Oscar Gamble	.20	.10	.02
☐	80T	Jim Katt	.75	.35	.07
☐	83T	Jim Spencer	.12	.06	.01
☐	85T	Mickey Rivers	.15	.07	.01
☐	99T	Lee Lacy	.15	.07	.01
☐	120T	Rusty Staub	.40	.20	.04
☐	127T	Larvell Blanks	.12	.06	.01
☐	146T	George Medich	.12	.06	.01
☐	158T	Ken Reitz	.12	.06	.01
☐	208T	Mike Lum	.12	.06	.01
☐	211T	Clay Carroll	.12	.06	.01
☐	231T	Tom House	.15	.07	.01
☐	250T	Fergie Jenkins	.75	.35	.07

	NRMT	VG-E	GOOD
☐ 259T Darrel Chaney	.12	.06	.01
☐ 292T Leon Roberts	.12	.06	.01
☐ 296T Pat Dobson	.15	.07	.01
☐ 309T Bill Melton	.12	.06	.01
☐ 338T Bob Bailey	.12	.06	.01
☐ 380T Bobby Bonds	.30	.15	.03
☐ 383T John Ellis	.12	.06	.01
☐ 385T Mickey Lolich	.30	.15	.03
☐ 401T Ken Brett	.12	.06	.01
☐ 410T Ralph Garr	.15	.07	.01
☐ 411T Bill Singer	.12	.06	.01
☐ 428T Jim Crawford	.12	.06	.01
☐ 434T Morris Nettles	.12	.06	.01
☐ 464T Ken Henderson	.12	.06	.01
☐ 497T Joe McIntosh	.12	.06	.01
☐ 524T Pete Falcone	.12	.06	.01
☐ 527T Mike Anderson	.12	.06	.01
☐ 528T Dock Ellis	.12	.06	.01
☐ 532T Milt May	.12	.06	.01
☐ 554T Ray Fosse	.12	.06	.01
☐ 579T Clay Kirby	.12	.06	.01
☐ 583T Tommy Helms	.15	.07	.01
☐ 592T Willie Randolph	.90	.45	.09
☐ 618T Jack Brohamer	.12	.06	.01
☐ 632T Rogelio Moret	.12	.06	.01
☐ 649T Dave Roberts	.12	.06	.01
☐ xxxT Traded Checklist ... (unnumbered)	.50	.25	.05

1977 Topps

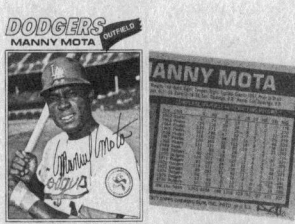

The cards in this 660-card set measure 2 ½" by 3 ½". In 1977 for the fifth consecutive year,

Topps produced a 660-card baseball set. The player's name, team affiliation, and his position are compactly arranged over the picture area and a facsimile autograph appears on the photo. Team cards feature a checklist of that team's players in the set and a small picture of the manager on the front of the card. Appearing for the first time are the series "Brothers" (631-634) and "Turn Back the Clock" (433-437). Other subseries in the set are League Leaders (1-8), Record Breakers (231-234), Playoffs cards (276-277), World Series cards (411-413), and Rookie Prospects (472-479 and 487-494). The key card in the set is the rookie card of Dale Murphy (476). Cards numbered 23 or lower, which feature Yankees and do not follow the numbering checklisted below, are not necessarily error cards. They are probably Burger King cards, a separate set with its own pricing and mass distribution. Burger King cards are indistinguishable from the corresponding Topps cards except for the card numbering difference and the fact that Burger King cards do not have a printing sheet designation (such as A through F like the regular Topps) anywhere on the card back in very small print. There was an aluminum version of the Dale Murphy rookie card #476 produced (legally) in the early '80s; proceeds from the sales (originally priced at $10) of this "card" went to the Huntington's Disease Foundation.

			NRMT	VG-E	GOOD
		COMPLETE SET (660)	325.00	150.00	30.00
		COMMON PLAYER (1-660)	.16	.08	.01
☐	1	Batting Leaders .... George Brett Bill Madlock	2.00	.30	.06
☐	2	Home Run Leaders Graig Nettles Mike Schmidt	.75	.35	.07
☐	3	RBI Leaders .... Lee May George Foster	.30	.15	.03
☐	4	Stolen Base Leaders Bill North Dave Lopes	.30	.15	.03
☐	5	Victory Leaders ...... Jim Palmer	.40	.20	.04

		NRMT	VG-E	GOOD
	Randy Jones			
☐ 6	Strikeout Leaders	2.50	1.25	.25
	Nolan Ryan			
	Tom Seaver			
☐ 7	ERA Leaders	.30	.15	.03
	Mark Fidrych			
	John Denny			
☐ 8	Leading Firemen	.30	.15	.03
	Bill Campbell			
	Rawly Eastwick			
☐ 9	Doug Rader	.25	.12	.02
☐ 10	Reggie Jackson	7.00	3.50	.70
☐ 11	Rob Dressler	.16	.08	.01
☐ 12	Larry Haney	.16	.08	.01
☐ 13	Luis Gomez	.16	.08	.01
☐ 14	Tommy Smith	.16	.08	.01
☐ 15	Don Gullett	.25	.12	.02
☐ 16	Bob Jones	.16	.08	.01
☐ 17	Steve Stone	.25	.12	.02
☐ 18	Indians Team/Mgr.	.65	.30	.06
	Frank Robinson			
	(checklist back)			
☐ 19	John D'Acquisto	.16	.08	.01
☐ 20	Graig Nettles	.75	.35	.07
☐ 21	Ken Forsch	.16	.08	.01
☐ 22	Bill Freehan	.25	.12	.02
☐ 23	Dan Driessen	.25	.12	.02
☐ 24	Carl Morton	.16	.08	.01
☐ 25	Dwight Evans	1.75	.85	.17
☐ 26	Ray Sadecki	.16	.08	.01
☐ 27	Bill Buckner	.35	.17	.03
☐ 28	Woodie Fryman	.16	.08	.01
☐ 29	Bucky Dent	.35	.17	.03
☐ 30	Greg Luzinski	.35	.17	.03
☐ 31	Jim Todd	.16	.08	.01
☐ 32	Checklist 1	.80	.10	.02
☐ 33	Wayne Garland	.16	.08	.01
☐ 34	Angels Team/Mgr.	.65	.30	.06
	Norm Sherry (checklist back)			
☐ 35	Rennie Stennett	.16	.08	.01
☐ 36	John Ellis	.16	.08	.01
☐ 37	Steve Hargan	.16	.08	.01
☐ 38	Craig Kusick	.16	.08	.01
☐ 39	Tom Griffin	.16	.08	.01
☐ 40	Bobby Murcer	.35	.17	.03
☐ 41	Jim Kern	.16	.08	.01
☐ 42	Jose Cruz	.25	.12	.02
☐ 43	Ray Bare	.16	.08	.01

		NRMT	VG-E	GOOD
☐ 44	Bud Harrelson	.25	.12	.02
☐ 45	Rawly Eastwick	.16	.08	.01
☐ 46	Buck Martinez	.16	.08	.01
☐ 47	Lynn McGlothen	.16	.08	.01
☐ 48	Tom Paciorek	.16	.08	.01
☐ 49	Grant Jackson	.16	.08	.01
☐ 50	Ron Cey	.35	.17	.03
☐ 51	Brewers Team/Mgr.	.65	.30	.06
	Alex Grammas (checklist back)			
☐ 52	Ellis Valentine	.16	.08	.01
☐ 53	Paul Mitchell	.16	.08	.01
☐ 54	Sandy Alomar	.16	.08	.01
☐ 55	Jeff Burroughs	.25	.12	.02
☐ 56	Rudy May	.16	.08	.01
☐ 57	Marc Hill	.16	.08	.01
☐ 58	Chet Lemon	.25	.12	.02
☐ 59	Larry Christenson	.16	.08	.01
☐ 60	Jim Rice	4.00	2.00	.40
☐ 61	Manny Sanguillen	.25	.12	.02
☐ 62	Eric Raich	.16	.08	.01
☐ 63	Tito Fuentes	.16	.08	.01
☐ 64	Larry Biittner	.16	.08	.01
☐ 65	Skip Lockwood	.16	.08	.01
☐ 66	Roy Smalley	.25	.12	.02
☐ 67	Joaquin Andujar	.75	.35	.07
☐ 68	Bruce Bochte	.16	.08	.01
☐ 69	Jim Crawford	.16	.08	.01
☐ 70	Johnny Bench	5.50	2.75	.55
☐ 71	Dock Ellis	.16	.08	.01
☐ 72	Mike Anderson	.16	.08	.01
☐ 73	Charlie Williams	.16	.08	.01
☐ 74	A's Team/Mgr.	.65	.30	.06
	Jack McKeon (checklist back)			
☐ 75	Dennis Leonard	.25	.12	.02
☐ 76	Tim Foli	.16	.08	.01
☐ 77	Dyar Miller	.16	.08	.01
☐ 78	Bob Davis	.16	.08	.01
☐ 79	Don Money	.16	.08	.01
☐ 80	Andy Messersmith	.25	.12	.02
☐ 81	Juan Beniquez	.16	.08	.01
☐ 82	Jim Rooker	.16	.08	.01
☐ 83	Kevin Bell	.16	.08	.01
☐ 84	Ollie Brown	.16	.08	.01
☐ 85	Duane Kuiper	.16	.08	.01
☐ 86	Pat Zachry	.16	.08	.01
☐ 87	Glenn Borgmann	.16	.08	.01
☐ 88	Stan Wall	.16	.08	.01

		NRMT	VG-E	GOOD
☐ 89	Butch Hobson	.16	.08	.01
☐ 90	Cesar Cedeno	.25	.12	.02
☐ 91	John Verhoeven	.16	.08	.01
☐ 92	Dave Rosello	.16	.08	.01
☐ 93	Tom Poquette	.16	.08	.01
☐ 94	Craig Swan	.16	.08	.01
☐ 95	Keith Hernandez	3.00	1.50	.30
☐ 96	Lou Piniella	.35	.17	.03
☐ 97	Dave Heaverlo	.16	.08	.01
☐ 98	Milt May	.16	.08	.01
☐ 99	Tom Hausman	.16	.08	.01
☐ 100	Joe Morgan	2.00	1.00	.20
☐ 101	Dick Bosman	.16	.08	.01
☐ 102	Jose Morales	.16	.08	.01
☐ 103	Mike Bacsik	.16	.08	.01
☐ 104	Omar Moreno	.25	.12	.02
☐ 105	Steve Yeager	.25	.12	.02
☐ 106	Mike Flanagan	.35	.17	.03
☐ 107	Bill Melton	.16	.08	.01
☐ 108	Alan Foster	.16	.08	.01
☐ 109	Jorge Orta	.16	.08	.01
☐ 110	Steve Carlton	4.50	2.00	.40
☐ 111	Rico Petrocelli	.25	.12	.02
☐ 112	Bill Greif	.16	.08	.01
☐ 113	Blue Jays Leaders	.50	.25	.05
	Roy Hartsfield MG			
	Don Leppert CO			
	Bob Miller CO			
	Jackie Moore CO			
	Harry Warner CO			
	(checklist back)			
☐ 114	Bruce Dal Canton	.16	.08	.01
☐ 115	Rick Manning	.16	.08	.01
☐ 116	Joe Niekro	.35	.17	.03
☐ 117	Frank White	.35	.17	.03
☐ 118	Rick Jones	.16	.08	.01
☐ 119	John Stearns	.16	.08	.01
☐ 120	Rod Carew	4.50	2.00	.40
☐ 121	Gary Nolan	.16	.08	.01
☐ 122	Ben Oglivie	.25	.12	.02
☐ 123	Fred Stanley	.16	.08	.01
☐ 124	George Mitterwald	.16	.08	.01
☐ 125	Bill Travers	.16	.08	.01
☐ 126	Rod Gilbreath	.16	.08	.01
☐ 127	Ron Fairly	.16	.08	.01
☐ 128	Tommy John	1.00	.50	.10
☐ 129	Mike Sadek	.16	.08	.01
☐ 130	Al Oliver	.40	.20	.04
☐ 131	Orlando Ramirez	.16	.08	.01

		NRMT	VG-E	GOOD
☐ 132	Chip Lang	.16	.08	.01
☐ 133	Ralph Garr	.25	.12	.02
☐ 134	Padres Team/Mgr.	.65	.30	.06
	John McNamara			
	(checklist back)			
☐ 135	Mark Belanger	.25	.12	.02
☐ 136	Jerry Mumphrey	.35	.17	.03
☐ 137	Jeff Terpko	.16	.08	.01
☐ 138	Bob Stinson	.16	.08	.01
☐ 139	Fred Norman	.16	.08	.01
☐ 140	Mike Schmidt	14.00	7.00	1.40
☐ 141	Mark Littell	.16	.08	.01
☐ 142	Steve Dillard	.16	.08	.01
☐ 143	Ed Herrmann	.16	.08	.01
☐ 144	Bruce Sutter	2.50	1.25	.25
☐ 145	Tom Veryzer	.16	.08	.01
☐ 146	Dusty Baker	.25	.12	.02
☐ 147	Jackie Brown	.16	.08	.01
☐ 148	Fran Healy	.16	.08	.01
☐ 149	Mike Cubbage	.16	.08	.01
☐ 150	Tom Seaver	5.00	2.25	.45
☐ 151	Johnny LeMaster	.16	.08	.01
☐ 152	Gaylord Perry	1.75	.85	.17
☐ 153	Ron Jackson	.16	.08	.01
☐ 154	Dave Giusti	.16	.08	.01
☐ 155	Joe Rudi	.25	.12	.02
☐ 156	Pete Mackanin	.16	.08	.01
☐ 157	Ken Brett	.16	.08	.01
☐ 158	Ted Kubiak	.16	.08	.01
☐ 159	Bernie Carbo	.16	.08	.01
☐ 160	Will McEnaney	.16	.08	.01
☐ 161	Garry Templeton	1.00	.50	.10
☐ 162	Mike Cuellar	.25	.12	.02
☐ 163	Dave Hilton	.16	.08	.01
☐ 164	Tug McGraw	.35	.17	.03
☐ 165	Jim Wynn	.25	.12	.02
☐ 166	Bill Campbell	.16	.08	.01
☐ 167	Rich Hebner	.16	.08	.01
☐ 168	Charlie Spikes	.16	.08	.01
☐ 169	Darold Knowles	.16	.08	.01
☐ 170	Thurman Munson	4.00	2.00	.40
☐ 171	Ken Sanders	.16	.08	.01
☐ 172	John Milner	.16	.08	.01
☐ 173	Chuck Scrivener	.16	.08	.01
☐ 174	Nelson Briles	.16	.08	.01
☐ 175	Butch Wynegar	.50	.25	.05
☐ 176	Bob Robertson	.16	.08	.01
☐ 177	Bart Johnson	.16	.08	.01
☐ 178	Bombo Rivera	.16	.08	.01

		NRMT	VG-E	GOOD
☐ 179	Paul Hartzell	.16	.08	.01
☐ 180	Dave Lopes	.25	.12	.02
☐ 181	Ken McMullen	.16	.08	.01
☐ 182	Dan Spillner	.16	.08	.01
☐ 183	Cardinals Team/Mgr. Vern Rapp (checklist back)	.65	.30	.06
☐ 184	Bo McLaughlin	.16	.08	.01
☐ 185	Sixto Lezcano	.16	.08	.01
☐ 186	Doug Flynn	.16	.08	.01
☐ 187	Dick Pole	.16	.08	.01
☐ 188	Bob Tolan	.16	.08	.01
☐ 189	Rick Dempsey	.25	.12	.02
☐ 190	Ray Burris	.16	.08	.01
☐ 191	Doug Griffin	.16	.08	.01
☐ 192	Clarence Gaston	.35	.17	.03
☐ 193	Larry Gura	.25	.12	.02
☐ 194	Gary Matthews	.25	.12	.02
☐ 195	Ed Figueroa	.16	.08	.01
☐ 196	Len Randle	.16	.08	.01
☐ 197	Ed Ott	.16	.08	.01
☐ 198	Wilbur Wood	.25	.12	.02
☐ 199	Pepe Frias	.16	.08	.01
☐ 200	Frank Tanana	.35	.17	.03
☐ 201	Ed Kranepool	.25	.12	.02
☐ 202	Tom Johnson	.16	.08	.01
☐ 203	Ed Armbrister	.16	.08	.01
☐ 204	Jeff Newman	.16	.08	.01
☐ 205	Pete Falcone	.16	.08	.01
☐ 206	Boog Powell	.40	.20	.04
☐ 207	Glenn Abbott	.16	.08	.01
☐ 208	Checklist 2	.80	.10	.02
☐ 209	Rob Andrews	.16	.08	.01
☐ 210	Fred Lynn	1.50	.75	.15
☐ 211	Giants Team/Mgr. Joe Altobelli (checklist back)	.65	.30	.06
☐ 212	Jim Mason	.16	.08	.01
☐ 213	Maximino Leon	.16	.08	.01
☐ 214	Darrell Porter	.16	.08	.01
☐ 215	Butch Metzger	.16	.08	.01
☐ 216	Doug DeCinces	.25	.12	.02
☐ 217	Tom Underwood	.16	.08	.01
☐ 218	John Wathan	1.50	.75	.15
☐ 219	Joe Coleman	.16	.08	.01
☐ 220	Chris Chambliss	.35	.17	.03
☐ 221	Bob Bailey	.16	.08	.01
☐ 222	Francisco Barrios	.16	.08	.01
☐ 223	Earl Williams	.16	.08	.01

		NRMT	VG-E	GOOD
☐ 224	Rusty Torres	.16	.08	.01
☐ 225	Bob Apodaca	.16	.08	.01
☐ 226	Leroy Stanton	.16	.08	.01
☐ 227	Joe Sambito	.25	.12	.02
☐ 228	Twins Team/Mgr. Gene Mauch (checklist back)	.65	.30	.06
☐ 229	Don Kessinger	.25	.12	.02
☐ 230	Vida Blue	.35	.17	.03
☐ 231	RB: George Brett Most cons. games with 3 or more hits	2.00	1.00	.20
☐ 232	RB: Minnie Minoso Oldest to hit safely	.25	.12	.02
☐ 233	RB: Jose Morales, Most pinch-hits, season	.25	.12	.05
☐ 234	RB: Nolan Ryan Most seasons, 300 or more strikeouts	3.00	1.50	.30
☐ 235	Cecil Cooper	.50	.25	.05
☐ 236	Tom Buskey	.16	.08	.01
☐ 237	Gene Clines	.16	.08	.01
☐ 238	Tippy Martinez	.25	.12	.02
☐ 239	Bill Plummer	.16	.08	.01
☐ 240	Ron LeFlore	.25	.12	.02
☐ 241	Dave Tomlin	.16	.08	.01
☐ 242	Ken Henderson	.16	.08	.01
☐ 243	Ron Reed	.16	.08	.01
☐ 244	John Mayberry (cartoon mentions T206 Wagner)	.35	.17	.03
☐ 245	Rick Rhoden	.25	.12	.02
☐ 246	Mike Vail	.16	.08	.01
☐ 247	Chris Knapp	.16	.08	.01
☐ 248	Wilbur Howard	.16	.08	.01
☐ 249	Pete Redfern	.16	.08	.01
☐ 250	Bill Madlock	.50	.25	.05
☐ 251	Tony Muser	.16	.08	.01
☐ 252	Dale Murray	.16	.08	.01
☐ 253	John Hale	.16	.08	.01
☐ 254	Doyle Alexander	.25	.12	.02
☐ 255	George Scott	.25	.12	.02
☐ 256	Joe Hoerner	.16	.08	.01
☐ 257	Mike Miley	.16	.08	.01
☐ 258	Luis Tiant	.35	.17	.03
☐ 259	Mets Team/Mgr. Joe Frazier (checklist back)	.75	.35	.07
☐ 260	J.R. Richard	.25	.12	.02

		NRMT	VG-E	GOOD			NRMT	VG-E	GOOD
☐ 261	Phil Garner	.25	.12	.02	☐ 305	Mickey Rivers	.25	.12	.02
☐ 262	Al Cowens	.25	.12	.02	☐ 306	Rick Waits	.16	.08	.01
☐ 263	Mike Marshall	.25	.12	.02	☐ 307	Gary Sutherland	.16	.08	.01
☐ 264	Tom Hutton	.16	.08	.01	☐ 308	Gene Pentz	.16	.08	.01
☐ 265	Mark Fidrych	.50	.25	.05	☐ 309	Red Sox Team/Mgr.	.65	.30	.06
☐ 266	Derrel Thomas	.16	.08	.01		Don Zimmer (check-			
☐ 267	Ray Fosse	.16	.08	.01		list back)			
☐ 268	Rick Sawyer	.16	.08	.01	☐ 310	Larry Bowa	.40	.20	.04
☐ 269	Joe Lis	.16	.08	.01	☐ 311	Vern Ruhle	.16	.08	.01
☐ 270	Dave Parker	2.75	1.35	.27	☐ 312	Rob Belloir	.16	.08	.01
☐ 271	Terry Forster	.25	.12	.02	☐ 313	Paul Blair	.25	.12	.02
☐ 272	Lee Lacy	.16	.08	.01	☐ 314	Steve Mingori	.16	.08	.01
☐ 273	Eric Soderholm	.16	.08	.01	☐ 315	Dave Chalk	.16	.08	.01
☐ 274	Don Stanhouse	.16	.08	.01	☐ 316	Steve Rogers	.25	.12	.02
☐ 275	Mike Hargrove	.25	.12	.02	☐ 317	Kurt Bevacqua	.16	.08	.01
☐ 276	AL Champs	.35	.17	.03	☐ 318	Duffy Dyer	.16	.08	.01
	Chambliss' homer de-				☐ 319	Rich Gossage	.75	.35	.07
	cides it				☐ 320	Ken Griffey	.35	.17	.03
☐ 277	NL Champs	.35	.17	.03	☐ 321	Dave Goltz	.16	.08	.01
	Reds sweep Phillies				☐ 322	Bill Russell	.25	.12	.02
☐ 278	Danny Frisella	.16	.08	.01	☐ 323	Larry Lintz	.16	.08	.01
☐ 279	Joe Wallis	.16	.08	.01	☐ 324	John Curtis	.16	.08	.01
☐ 280	Jim Hunter	2.00	1.00	.20	☐ 325	Mike Ivie	.16	.08	.01
☐ 281	Roy Staiger	.16	.08	.01	☐ 326	Jesse Jefferson	.16	.08	.01
☐ 282	Sid Monge	.16	.08	.01	☐ 327	Astros Team/Mgr.	.65	.30	.06
☐ 283	Jerry DaVanon	.16	.08	.01		Bill Virdon (checklist			
☐ 284	Mike Norris	.16	.08	.01		back)			
☐ 285	Brooks Robinson	2.50	1.25	.25	☐ 328	Tommy Boggs	.16	.08	.01
☐ 286	Johnny Grubb	.16	.08	.01	☐ 329	Ron Hodges	.16	.08	.01
☐ 287	Reds Team/Mgr.	.75	.35	.07	☐ 330	George Hendrick	.25	.12	.02
	Sparky Anderson				☐ 331	Jim Colborn	.16	.08	.01
	(checklist back)				☐ 332	Elliott Maddox	.16	.08	.01
☐ 288	Bob Montgomery	.16	.08	.01	☐ 333	Paul Reuschel	.16	.08	.01
☐ 289	Gene Garber	.16	.08	.01	☐ 334	Bill Stein	.16	.08	.01
☐ 290	Amos Otis	.35	.17	.03	☐ 335	Bill Robinson	.25	.12	.02
☐ 291	Jason Thompson	.25	.12	.02	☐ 336	Denny Doyle	.16	.08	.01
☐ 292	Rogelio Moret	.16	.08	.01	☐ 337	Ron Schueler	.16	.08	.01
☐ 293	Jack Brohamer	.16	.08	.01	☐ 338	Dave Duncan	.16	.08	.01
☐ 294	George Medich	.16	.08	.01	☐ 339	Adrian Devine	.16	.08	.01
☐ 295	Gary Carter	5.00	2.50	.50	☐ 340	Hal McRae	.25	.12	.02
☐ 296	Don Hood	.16	.08	.01	☐ 341	Joe Kerrigan	.16	.08	.01
☐ 297	Ken Reitz	.16	.08	.01	☐ 342	Jerry Remy	.16	.08	.01
☐ 298	Charlie Hough	.25	.12	.02	☐ 343	Ed Halicki	.16	.08	.01
☐ 299	Otto Velez	.16	.08	.01	☐ 344	Brian Downing	.25	.12	.02
☐ 300	Jerry Koosman	.35	.17	.03	☐ 345	Reggie Smith	.35	.17	.03
☐ 301	Toby Harrah	.25	.12	.02	☐ 346	Bill Singer	.16	.08	.01
☐ 302	Mike Garman	.16	.08	.01	☐ 347	George Foster	1.25	.60	.12
☐ 303	Gene Tenace	.25	.12	.02	☐ 348	Brent Strom	.16	.08	.01
☐ 304	Jim Hughes	.16	.08	.01	☐ 349	Jim Holt	.16	.08	.01

		NRMT	VG-E	GOOD
☐ 350	Larry Dierker	.16	.08	.01
☐ 351	Jim Sundberg	.25	.12	.02
☐ 352	Mike Phillips	.16	.08	.01
☐ 353	Stan Thomas	.16	.08	.01
☐ 354	Pirates Team/Mgr. Chuck Tanner (checklist back)	.65	.30	.06
☐ 355	Lou Brock	2.50	1.25	.25
☐ 356	Checklist 3	.80	.10	.02
☐ 357	Tim McCarver	.35	.17	.03
☐ 358	Tom House	.25	.12	.02
☐ 359	Willie Randolph	.90	.45	.09
☐ 360	Rick Monday	.25	.12	.02
☐ 361	Eduardo Rodriguez	.16	.08	.01
☐ 362	Tommy Davis	.35	.17	.03
☐ 363	Dave Roberts	.16	.08	.01
☐ 364	Vic Correll	.16	.08	.01
☐ 365	Mike Torrez	.25	.12	.02
☐ 366	Ted Sizemore	.16	.08	.01
☐ 367	Dave Hamilton	.16	.08	.01
☐ 368	Mike Jorgensen	.16	.08	.01
☐ 369	Terry Humphrey	.16	.08	.01
☐ 370	John Montefusco	.25	.12	.02
☐ 371	Royals Team/Mgr. Whitey Herzog (checklist back)	.65	.30	.06
☐ 372	Rich Folkers	.16	.08	.01
☐ 373	Bert Campaneris	.25	.12	.02
☐ 374	Kent Tekulve	.25	.12	.02
☐ 375	Larry Hisle	.25	.12	.02
☐ 376	Nino Espinosa	.16	.08	.01
☐ 377	Dave McKay	.16	.08	.01
☐ 378	Jim Umbarger	.16	.08	.01
☐ 379	Larry Cox	.16	.08	.01
☐ 380	Lee May	.25	.12	.02
☐ 381	Bob Forsch	.25	.12	.02
☐ 382	Charlie Moore	.16	.08	.01
☐ 383	Stan Bahnsen	.16	.08	.01
☐ 384	Darrel Chaney	.16	.08	.01
☐ 385	Dave LaRoche	.16	.08	.01
☐ 386	Manny Mota	.25	.12	.02
☐ 387	Yankees Team (checklist back)	.75	.35	.07
☐ 388	Terry Harmon	.16	.08	.01
☐ 389	Ken Kravec	.16	.08	.01
☐ 390	Dave Winfield	4.00	2.00	.40
☐ 391	Dan Warthen	.16	.08	.01
☐ 392	Phil Roof	.16	.08	.01
☐ 393	John Lowenstein	.16	.08	.01
☐ 394	Bill Laxton	.16	.08	.01
☐ 395	Manny Trillo	.16	.08	.01
☐ 396	Tom Murphy	.16	.08	.01
☐ 397	Larry Herndon	.25	.12	.02
☐ 398	Tom Burgmeier	.16	.08	.01
☐ 399	Bruce Boisclair	.16	.08	.01
☐ 400	Steve Garvey	3.50	1.75	.35
☐ 401	Mickey Scott	.16	.08	.01
☐ 402	Tommy Helms	.25	.12	.02
☐ 403	Tom Grieve	.25	.12	.02
☐ 404	Eric Rasmussen	.16	.08	.01
☐ 405	Claudell Washington	.35	.17	.03
☐ 406	Tim Johnson	.16	.08	.01
☐ 407	Dave Freisleben	.16	.08	.01
☐ 408	Cesar Tovar	.16	.08	.01
☐ 409	Pete Broberg	.16	.08	.01
☐ 410	Willie Montanez	.16	.08	.01
☐ 411	W.S. Games 1 and 2 Morgan homers opener; Bench stars as Reds take 2nd game	.60	.30	.06
☐ 412	W.S. Games 3 and 4 Reds stop Yankees; Bench's two homers wrap it up	.60	.30	.06
☐ 413	World Series Summary Cincy wins 2nd straight series	.50	.25	.05
☐ 414	Tommy Harper	.25	.12	.02
☐ 415	Jay Johnstone	.25	.12	.02
☐ 416	Chuck Hartenstein	.16	.08	.01
☐ 417	Wayne Garrett	.16	.08	.01
☐ 418	White Sox Team/Mgr. Bob Lemon (checklist back)	.65	.30	.06
☐ 419	Steve Swisher	.16	.08	.01
☐ 420	Rusty Staub	.35	.17	.03
☐ 421	Doug Rau	.16	.08	.01
☐ 422	Freddie Patek	.16	.08	.01
☐ 423	Gary Lavelle	.16	.08	.01
☐ 424	Steve Brye	.16	.08	.01
☐ 425	Joe Torre	.35	.17	.03
☐ 426	Dick Drago	.16	.08	.01
☐ 427	Dave Rader	.16	.08	.01
☐ 428	Rangers Team/Mgr. Frank Lucchesi (checklist back)	.65	.30	.06
☐ 429	Ken Boswell	.16	.08	.01

		NRMT	VG-E	GOOD
☐ 430	Fergie Jenkins	.75	.35	.07
☐ 431	Dave Collins	.25	.12	.02
	(photo actually Bobby Jones)			
☐ 432	Buzz Capra	.16	.08	.01
☐ 433	Turn back clock 1972 Nate Colbert	.25	.12	.02
☐ 434	Turn back clock 1967 Yaz Triple Crown	2.00	1.00	.20
☐ 435	Turn back clock 1962 Wills 104 steals	.35	.17	.03
☐ 436	Turn back clock 1957 Keegan hurls Majors' only no-hitter	.25	.12	.02
☐ 437	Turn back clock 1952 Kiner leads NL HR's 7th straight year	.40	.20	.04
☐ 438	Marty Perez	.16	.08	.01
☐ 439	Gorman Thomas	.35	.17	.03
☐ 440	Jon Matlack	.25	.12	.02
☐ 441	Larvell Blanks	.16	.08	.01
☐ 442	Braves Team/Mgr. Dave Bristol (checklist back)	.65	.30	.06
☐ 443	Lamar Johnson	.16	.08	.01
☐ 444	Wayne Twitchell	.16	.08	.01
☐ 445	Ken Singleton	.25	.12	.02
☐ 446	Bill Bonham	.16	.08	.01
☐ 447	Jerry Turner	.16	.08	.01
☐ 448	Ellie Rodriguez	.16	.08	.01
☐ 449	Al Fitzmorris	.16	.08	.01
☐ 450	Pete Rose	9.00	4.50	.90
☐ 451	Checklist 4	.80	.10	.02
☐ 452	Mike Caldwell	.16	.08	.01
☐ 453	Pedro Garcia	.16	.08	.01
☐ 454	Andy Etchebarren	.16	.08	.01
☐ 455	Rick Wise	.16	.08	.01
☐ 456	Leon Roberts	.16	.08	.01
☐ 457	Steve Luebber	.16	.08	.01
☐ 458	Leo Foster	.16	.08	.01
☐ 459	Steve Foucault	.16	.08	.01
☐ 460	Willie Stargell	2.50	1.25	.25
☐ 461	Dick Tidrow	.16	.08	.01
☐ 462	Don Baylor	.60	.30	.06
☐ 463	Jamie Quirk	.16	.08	.01
☐ 464	Randy Moffitt	.16	.08	.01
☐ 465	Rico Carty	.25	.12	.02
☐ 466	Fred Holdsworth	.16	.08	.01
☐ 467	Phillies Team/Mgr.	.65	.30	.06

		NRMT	VG-E	GOOD
	Danny Ozark (checklist back)			
☐ 468	Ramon Hernandez	.16	.08	.01
☐ 469	Pat Kelly	.16	.08	.01
☐ 470	Ted Simmons	.50	.25	.05
☐ 471	Del Unser	.16	.08	.01
☐ 472	Rookie Pitchers Don Aase Bob McClure Gil Patterson Dave Wehrmeister	.35	.17	.03
☐ 473	Rookie Outfielders Andre Dawson Gene Richards John Scott Denny Walling	32.00	16.00	3.20
☐ 474	Rookie Shortstops Bob Bailor Kiko Garcia Craig Reynolds Alex Taveras	.25	.12	.02
☐ 475	Rookie Pitchers Chris Batton Rick Camp Scott McGregor Manny Sarmiento	.40	.20	.04
☐ 476	Rookie Catchers Gary Alexander Rick Cerone Dale Murphy Kevin Pasley	50.00	25.00	5.00
☐ 477	Rookie Infielders Doug Ault Rich Dauer Orlando Gonzalez Phil Mankowski	.25	.12	.02
☐ 478	Rookie Pitchers Jim Gideon Leon Hooten Dave Johnson Mark Lemongello	.25	.12	.02
☐ 479	Rookie Outfielders Brian Asselstine Wayne Gross Sam Mejias Alvis Woods	.25	.12	.02
☐ 480	Carl Yastrzemski	5.50	2.75	.55
☐ 481	Roger Metzger	.16	.08	.01
☐ 482	Tony Solaita	.16	.08	.01

		NRMT	VG-E	GOOD
☐ 483	Richie Zisk	.16	.08	.01
☐ 484	Burt Hooton	.16	.08	.01
☐ 485	Roy White	.25	.12	.02
☐ 486	Ed Bane	.16	.08	.01
☐ 487	Rookie Pitchers	.25	.12	.02
	Larry Anderson			
	Ed Glynn			
	Joe Henderson			
	Greg Terlecky			
☐ 488	Rookie Outfielders	18.00	9.00	1.80
	Jack Clark			
	Ruppert Jones			
	Lee Mazzilli			
	Dan Thomas			
☐ 489	Rookie Pitchers	.35	.17	.03
	Len Barker			
	Randy Lerch			
	Greg Minton			
	Mike Overy			
☐ 490	Rookie Shortstops	.25	.12	.02
	Billy Almon			
	Mickey Klutts			
	Tommy McMillan			
	Mark Wagner			
☐ 491	Rookie Pitchers	2.00	1.00	.20
	Mike Dupree			
	Denny Martinez			
	Craig Mitchell			
	Bob Sykes			
☐ 492	Rookie Outfielders	1.00	.50	.10
	Tony Armas			
	Steve Kemp			
	Carlos Lopez			
	Gary Woods			
☐ 493	Rookie Pitchers	.75	.35	.07
	Mike Krukow			
	Jim Otten			
	Gary Wheelock			
	Mike Willis			
☐ 494	Rookie Infielders	.50	.25	.05
	Juan Bernhardt			
	Mike Champion			
	Jim Gantner			
	Bump Wills			
☐ 495	Al Hrabosky	.25	.12	.02
☐ 496	Gary Thomasson	.16	.08	.01
☐ 497	Clay Carroll	.16	.08	.01
☐ 498	Sal Bando	.25	.12	.02
☐ 499	Pablo Torrealba	.16	.08	.01

		NRMT	VG-E	GOOD
☐ 500	Dave Kingman	.50	.25	.05
☐ 501	Jim Bibby	.16	.08	.01
☐ 502	Randy Hundley	.16	.08	.01
☐ 503	Bill Lee	.25	.12	.02
☐ 504	Dodgers Team/Mgr.	.75	.35	.07
	Tom Lasorda (check-list back)			
☐ 505	Oscar Gamble	.25	.12	.02
☐ 506	Steve Grilli	.16	.08	.01
☐ 507	Mike Hegan	.16	.08	.01
☐ 508	Dave Pagan	.16	.08	.01
☐ 509	Cookie Rojas	.25	.12	.02
☐ 510	John Candelaria	.60	.30	.06
☐ 511	Bill Fahey	.16	.08	.01
☐ 512	Jack Billingham	.16	.08	.01
☐ 513	Jerry Terrell	.16	.08	.01
☐ 514	Cliff Johnson	.16	.08	.01
☐ 515	Chris Speier	.16	.08	.01
☐ 516	Bake McBride	.16	.08	.01
☐ 517	Pete Vuckovich	.50	.25	.05
☐ 518	Cubs Team/Mgr.	.65	.30	.06
	Herman Franks (checklist back)			
☐ 519	Don Kirkwood	.16	.08	.01
☐ 520	Garry Maddox	.25	.12	.02
☐ 521	Bob Grich	.25	.12	.02
☐ 522	Enzo Hernandez	.16	.08	.01
☐ 523	Rollie Fingers	1.00	.50	.10
☐ 524	Rowland Office	.16	.08	.01
☐ 525	Dennis Eckersley	1.50	.75	.15
☐ 526	Larry Parrish	.25	.12	.02
☐ 527	Dan Meyer	.16	.08	.01
☐ 528	Bill Castro	.16	.08	.01
☐ 529	Jim Essian	.16	.08	.01
☐ 530	Rick Reuschel	.50	.25	.05
☐ 531	Lyman Bostock	.25	.12	.02
☐ 532	Jim Willoughby	.16	.08	.01
☐ 533	Mickey Stanley	.25	.12	.02
☐ 534	Paul Splittorff	.16	.08	.01
☐ 535	Cesar Geronimo	.16	.08	.01
☐ 536	Vic Albury	.16	.08	.01
☐ 537	Dave Roberts	.16	.08	.01
☐ 538	Frank Taveras	.16	.08	.01
☐ 539	Mike Wallace	.16	.08	.01
☐ 540	Bob Watson	.25	.12	.02
☐ 541	John Denny	.25	.12	.02
☐ 542	Frank Duffy	.16	.08	.01
☐ 543	Ron Blomberg	.16	.08	.01
☐ 544	Gary Ross	.16	.08	.01

		NRMT	VG-E	GOOD			NRMT	VG-E	GOOD
☐ 545	Bob Boone	.50	.25	.05	☐ 592	Dan Briggs	.16	.08	.01
☐ 546	Orioles Team/Mgr.	.75	.35	.07	☐ 593	Dennis Blair	.16	.08	.01
	Earl Weaver (check-				☐ 594	Biff Pocoroba	.16	.08	.01
	list back)				☐ 595	John Hiller	.25	.12	.02
☐ 547	Willie McCovey	2.25	1.10	.22	☐ 596	Jerry Martin	.16	.08	.01
☐ 548	Joel Youngblood	.16	.08	.01	☐ 597	Mariners Leaders	.50	.25	.05
☐ 549	Jerry Royster	.16	.08	.01		Darrell Johnson MG			
☐ 550	Randy Jones	.16	.08	.01		Don Bryant CO			
☐ 551	Bill North	.16	.08	.01		Jim Busby CO			
☐ 552	Pepe Mangual	.16	.08	.01		Vada Pinson CO			
☐ 553	Jack Heidemann	.16	.08	.01		Wes Stock CO			
☐ 554	Bruce Kimm	.16	.08	.01		(checklist back)			
☐ 555	Dan Ford	.16	.08	.01	☐ 598	Sparky Lyle	.50	.25	.05
☐ 556	Doug Bird	.16	.08	.01	☐ 599	Mike Tyson	.16	.08	.01
☐ 557	Jerry White	.16	.08	.01	☐ 600	Jim Palmer	2.50	1.25	.25
☐ 558	Elias Sosa	.16	.08	.01	☐ 601	Mike Lum	.16	.08	.01
☐ 559	Alan Bannister	.16	.08	.01	☐ 602	Andy Hassler	.16	.08	.01
☐ 560	Dave Concepcion	.35	.17	.03	☐ 603	Willie Davis	.25	.12	.02
☐ 561	Pete LaCock	.16	.08	.01	☐ 604	Jim Slaton	.16	.08	.01
☐ 562	Checklist 5	.80	.10	.02	☐ 605	Felix Millan	.16	.08	.01
☐ 563	Bruce Kison	.16	.08	.01	☐ 606	Steve Braun	.16	.08	.01
☐ 564	Alan Ashby	.25	.12	.02	☐ 607	Larry Demery	.16	.08	.01
☐ 565	Mickey Lolich	.35	.17	.03	☐ 608	Roy Howell	.16	.08	.01
☐ 566	Rick Miller	.16	.08	.01	☐ 609	Jim Barr	.16	.08	.01
☐ 567	Enos Cabell	.16	.08	.01	☐ 610	Jose Cardenal	.16	.08	.01
☐ 568	Carlos May	.16	.08	.01	☐ 611	Dave Lemanczyk	.16	.08	.01
☐ 569	Jim Lonborg	.25	.12	.02	☐ 612	Barry Foote	.16	.08	.01
☐ 570	Bobby Bonds	.35	.17	.03	☐ 613	Reggie Cleveland	.16	.08	.01
☐ 571	Darrell Evans	.50	.25	.05	☐ 614	Greg Gross	.16	.08	.01
☐ 572	Ross Grimsley	.16	.08	.01	☐ 615	Phil Niekro	1.50	.75	.15
☐ 573	Joe Ferguson	.16	.08	.01	☐ 616	Tommy Sandt	.16	.08	.01
☐ 574	Aurelio Rodriguez	.16	.08	.01	☐ 617	Bobby Darwin	.16	.08	.01
☐ 575	Dick Ruthven	.16	.08	.01	☐ 618	Pat Dobson	.25	.12	.02
☐ 576	Fred Kendall	.16	.08	.01	☐ 619	Johnny Oates	.16	.08	.01
☐ 577	Jerry Augustine	.16	.08	.01	☐ 620	Don Sutton	1.50	.75	.15
☐ 578	Bob Randall	.16	.08	.01	☐ 621	Tigers Team/Mgr.	.75	.35	.07
☐ 579	Don Carrithers	.16	.08	.01		Ralph Houk (checklist			
☐ 580	George Brett	11.00	5.50	1.10		back)			
☐ 581	Pedro Borbon	.16	.08	.01	☐ 622	Jim Wohlford	.16	.08	.01
☐ 582	Ed Kirkpatrick	.16	.08	.01	☐ 623	Jack Kucek	.16	.08	.01
☐ 583	Paul Lindblad	.16	.08	.01	☐ 624	Hector Cruz	.16	.08	.01
☐ 584	Ed Goodson	.16	.08	.01	☐ 625	Ken Holtzman	.25	.12	.02
☐ 585	Rick Burleson	.25	.12	.02	☐ 626	Al Bumbry	.16	.08	.01
☐ 586	Steve Renko	.16	.08	.01	☐ 627	Bob Myrick	.16	.08	.01
☐ 587	Rick Baldwin	.16	.08	.01	☐ 628	Mario Guerrero	.16	.08	.01
☐ 588	Dave Moates	.16	.08	.01	☐ 629	Bobby Valentine	.35	.17	.03
☐ 589	Mike Cosgrove	.16	.08	.01	☐ 630	Bert Blyleven	.90	.45	.09
☐ 590	Buddy Bell	.40	.20	.04	☐ 631	Big League Brothers	1.50	.75	.15
☐ 591	Chris Arnold	.16	.08	.01		George Brett			

1978 Topps

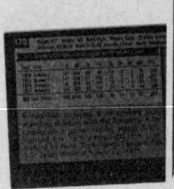

		NRMT	VG-E	GOOD
☐ 632	Ken Brett Big League Brothers . Bob Forsch	.25	.12	.02
☐ 633	Ken Forsch Big League Brothers . Lee May	.25	.12	.02
☐ 634	Carlos May Big League Brothers . Paul Reuschel Rick Reuschel) (photos switched)	.25	.12	.02
☐ 635	Robin Yount	14.00	7.00	1.40
☐ 636	Santo Alcala	.16	.08	.01
☐ 637	Alex Johnson	.16	.08	.01
☐ 638	Jim Kaat	.60	.30	.06
☐ 639	Jerry Morales	.16	.08	.01
☐ 640	Carlton Fisk	2.00	1.00	.20
☐ 641	Dan Larson	.16	.08	.01
☐ 642	Willie Crawford	.16	.08	.01
☐ 643	Mike Pazik	.16	.08	.01
☐ 644	Matt Alexander	.16	.08	.01
☐ 645	Jerry Reuss	.25	.12	.02
☐ 646	Andres Mora	.16	.08	.01
☐ 647	Expos Team/Mgr. Dick Williams (check-list back)	.65	.30	.06
☐ 648	Jim Spencer	.16	.08	.01
☐ 649	Dave Cash	.16	.08	.01
☐ 650	Nolan Ryan	13.00	6.50	1.30
☐ 651	Von Joshua	.16	.08	.01
☐ 652	Tom Walker	.16	.08	.01
☐ 653	Diego Segui	.16	.08	.01
☐ 654	Ron Pruitt	.16	.08	.01
☐ 655	Tony Perez	.75	.35	.07
☐ 656	Ron Guidry	2.75	1.35	.27
☐ 657	Mick Kelleher	.16	.08	.01
☐ 658	Marty Pattin	.16	.08	.01
☐ 659	Merv Rettenmund ...	.16	.08	.01
☐ 660	Willie Horton	.25	.12	.02

*The cards in this 726-card set measure 2 ½"
by 3 ½". The 1978 Topps set experienced an
increase in number of cards from the previous
five regular issue sets of 660. Cards 1 through
7 feature Record Breakers (RB) of the 1977
season. Other subsets within this set include
League Leaders (201-208), Post-season cards
(411-413), and Rookie Prospects (701-711).
While no scarcities exist, 66 of the cards are
more abundant in supply, as they were "double
printed." These 66 double-printed cards are
noted in the checklist by DP. Team cards again
feature a checklist of that team's players in the
set on the back. Cards numbered 23 or lower,
which feature Astros, Rangers, Tigers, or
Yankees and do not follow the numbering
checklisted below, are not necessarily error
cards. They are probably Burger King cards, a
separate set with its own pricing and mass distribution. Burger King cards are indistinguishable from the corresponding Topps cards
except for the card numbering difference and
the fact that Burger King cards do not have a
printing sheet designation (such as A through
F like the regular Topps) anywhere on the card
back in very small print.*

	NRMT	VG-E	GOOD
COMPLETE SET (726)	225.00	90.00	25.00
COMMON PLAYER (1-726)	.12	.06	.01
COMMON DP's (1-726)	.06	.03	.00

			NRMT	VG-E	GOOD
☐	1	RB: Lou Brock ..... Most steals, lifetime	2.00	.50	.10
☐	2	RB: Sparky Lyle .... Most games, pure relief, lifetime	.20	.10	.02
☐	3	RB: Willie McCovey . Most times, 2 HR's in inning, lifetime	1.00	.50	.10
☐	4	RB: Brooks Robinson Most consecutive seasons with one club	1.00	.50	.10
☐	5	RB: Pete Rose ..... Most hits, switch hit- ter, lifetime	2.25	1.10	.22
☐	6	RB: Nolan Ryan ..... Most games with 10 or more strikeouts, lifetime	2.50	1.25	.25
☐	7	RB: Reggie Jackson Most homers, one World Series	2.25	1.10	.22
☐	8	Mike Sadek	.12	.06	.01
☐	9	Doug DeCinces ...	.20	.10	.02
☐	10	Phil Niekro	1.25	.60	.12
☐	11	Rick Manning	.12	.06	.01
☐	12	Don Aase	.20	.10	.02
☐	13	Art Howe	.40	.20	.04
☐	14	Lerrin LaGrow	.12	.06	.01
☐	15	Tony Perez DP	.30	.15	.03
☐	16	Roy White	.20	.10	.02
☐	17	Mike Krukow	.20	.10	.02
☐	18	Bob Grich	.20	.10	.02
☐	19	Darrell Porter	.12	.06	.01
☐	20	Pete Rose DP	4.00	2.00	.40
☐	21	Steve Kemp	.20	.10	.02
☐	22	Charlie Hough	.20	.10	.02
☐	23	Bump Wills	.12	.06	.01
☐	24	Don Money DP	.06	.03	.00
☐	25	Jon Matlack	.20	.10	.02
☐	26	Rich Hebner	.12	.06	.01
☐	27	Geoff Zahn	.12	.06	.01
☐	28	Ed Ott	.12	.06	.01
☐	29	Bob Lacey	.12	.06	.01
☐	30	George Hendrick ...	.20	.10	.02
☐	31	Glenn Abbott	.12	.06	.01
☐	32	Garry Templeton ...	.20	.10	.02
☐	33	Dave Lemanczyk ...	.12	.06	.01
☐	34	Willie McCovey	2.00	1.00	.20
☐	35	Sparky Lyle	.30	.15	.03

			NRMT	VG-E	GOOD
☐	36	Eddie Murray	35.00	17.50	3.50
☐	37	Rick Waits	.12	.06	.01
☐	38	Willie Montanez	.12	.06	.01
☐	39	Floyd Bannister	.90	.45	.09
☐	40	Carl Yastrzemski ...	3.75	1.85	.37
☐	41	Burt Hooton	.12	.06	.01
☐	42	Jorge Orta	.12	.06	.01
☐	43	Bill Atkinson	.12	.06	.01
☐	44	Toby Harrah	.20	.10	.02
☐	45	Mark Fidrych	.30	.15	.03
☐	46	Al Cowens	.12	.06	.01
☐	47	Jack Billingham	.12	.06	.01
☐	48	Don Baylor	.50	.25	.05
☐	49	Ed Kranepool	.20	.10	.02
☐	50	Rick Reuschel	.45	.20	.04
☐	51	Charlie Moore DP ..	.06	.03	.00
☐	52	Jim Lonborg	.20	.10	.02
☐	53	Phil Garner DP	.06	.03	.00
☐	54	Tom Johnson	.12	.06	.01
☐	55	Mitchell Page	.12	.06	.01
☐	56	Randy Jones	.12	.06	.01
☐	57	Dan Meyer	.12	.06	.01
☐	58	Bob Forsch	.20	.10	.02
☐	59	Otto Velez	.12	.06	.01
☐	60	Thurman Munson ...	2.75	1.35	.27
☐	61	Larvell Blanks	.12	.06	.01
☐	62	Jim Barr	.12	.06	.01
☐	63	Don Zimmer	.20	.10	.02
☐	64	Gene Pentz	.12	.06	.01
☐	65	Ken Singleton	.20	.10	.02
☐	66	White Sox Team ...	.50	.25	.05
☐		(checklist back)			
☐	67	Claudell Washington	.20	.10	.02
☐	68	Steve Foucault DP ..	.06	.03	.00
☐	69	Mike Vail	.12	.06	.01
☐	70	Rich Gossage	.75	.35	.07
☐	71	Terry Humphrey ...	.12	.06	.01
☐	72	Andre Dawson	6.50	3.25	.65
☐	73	Andy Hassler	.12	.06	.01
☐	74	Checklist 1	.50	.05	.01
☐	75	Dick Ruthven	.12	.06	.01
☐	76	Steve Ontiveros ...	.12	.06	.01
☐	77	Ed Kirkpatrick	.12	.06	.01
☐	78	Pablo Torrealba ...	.12	.06	.01
☐	79	Darrell Johnson DP .	.06	.03	.00
☐	80	Ken Griffey	.30	.15	.03
☐	81	Pete Redfern	.12	.06	.01
☐	82	Giants Team	.50	.25	.05
☐		(checklist back)			

		NRMT	VG-E	GOOD
☐ 83	Bob Montgomery	.12	.06	.01
☐ 84	Kent Tekulve	.20	.10	.02
☐ 85	Ron Fairly	.12	.06	.01
☐ 86	Dave Tomlin	.12	.06	.01
☐ 87	John Lowenstein	.12	.06	.01
☐ 88	Mike Phillips	.12	.06	.01
☐ 89	Ken Clay	.12	.06	.01
☐ 90	Larry Bowa	.30	.15	.03
☐ 91	Oscar Zamora	.12	.06	.01
☐ 92	Adrian Devine	.12	.06	.01
☐ 93	Bobby Cox DP	.06	.03	.00
☐ 94	Chuck Scrivener	.12	.06	.01
☐ 95	Jamie Quirk	.12	.06	.01
☐ 96	Orioles Team	.50	.25	.05
	(checklist back)			
☐ 97	Stan Bahnsen	.12	.06	.01
☐ 98	Jim Essian	.12	.06	.01
☐ 99	Willie Hernandez	.90	.45	.09
☐ 100	George Brett	5.00	2.50	.50
☐ 101	Sid Monge	.12	.06	.01
☐ 102	Matt Alexander	.12	.06	.01
☐ 103	Tom Murphy	.12	.06	.01
☐ 104	Lee Lacy	.12	.06	.01
☐ 105	Reggie Cleveland	.12	.06	.01
☐ 106	Bill Plummer	.12	.06	.01
☐ 107	Ed Halicki	.12	.06	.01
☐ 108	Von Joshua	.12	.06	.01
☐ 109	Joe Torre	.30	.15	.03
☐ 110	Richie Zisk	.12	.06	.01
☐ 111	Mike Tyson	.12	.06	.01
☐ 112	Astros Team	.50	.25	.05
	(checklist back)			
☐ 113	Don Carrithers	.12	.06	.01
☐ 114	Paul Blair	.12	.06	.01
☐ 115	Gary Nolan	.12	.06	.01
☐ 116	Tucker Ashford	.12	.06	.01
☐ 117	John Montague	.12	.06	.01
☐ 118	Terry Harmon	.12	.06	.01
☐ 119	Denny Martinez	.30	.15	.03
☐ 120	Gary Carter	3.00	1.50	.30
☐ 121	Alvis Woods	.12	.06	.01
☐ 122	Dennis Eckersley	1.00	.50	.10
☐ 123	Manny Trillo	.12	.06	.01
☐ 124	Dave Rozema	.12	.06	.01
☐ 125	George Scott	.20	.10	.02
☐ 126	Paul Moskau	.12	.06	.01
☐ 127	Chet Lemon	.20	.10	.02
☐ 128	Bill Russell	.20	.10	.02
☐ 129	Jim Colborn	.12	.06	.01
☐ 130	Jeff Burroughs	.20	.10	.02
☐ 131	Bert Blyleven	.75	.35	.07
☐ 132	Enos Cabell	.12	.06	.01
☐ 133	Jerry Augustine	.12	.06	.01
☐ 134	Steve Henderson	.12	.06	.01
☐ 135	Ron Guidry DP	.60	.30	.06
☐ 136	Ted Sizemore	.12	.06	.01
☐ 137	Craig Kusick	.12	.06	.01
☐ 138	Larry Demery	.12	.06	.01
☐ 139	Wayne Gross	.12	.06	.01
☐ 140	Rollie Fingers	.75	.35	.07
☐ 141	Ruppert Jones	.12	.06	.01
☐ 142	John Montefusco	.20	.10	.02
☐ 143	Keith Hernandez	2.50	1.25	.25
☐ 144	Jesse Jefferson	.12	.06	.01
☐ 145	Rick Monday	.20	.10	.02
☐ 146	Doyle Alexander	.20	.10	.02
☐ 147	Lee Mazzilli	.12	.06	.01
☐ 148	Andre Thornton	.20	.10	.02
☐ 149	Dale Murray	.12	.06	.01
☐ 150	Bobby Bonds	.30	.15	.03
☐ 151	Milt Wilcox	.12	.06	.01
☐ 152	Ivan DeJesus	.12	.06	.01
☐ 153	Steve Stone	.20	.10	.02
☐ 154	Cecil Cooper DP	.20	.10	.02
☐ 155	Butch Hobson	.12	.06	.01
☐ 156	Andy Messersmith	.20	.10	.02
☐ 157	Pete LaCock DP	.06	.03	.00
☐ 158	Joaquin Andujar	.30	.15	.03
☐ 159	Lou Piniella	.30	.15	.03
☐ 160	Jim Palmer	2.50	1.25	.25
☐ 161	Bob Boone	.45	.20	.04
☐ 162	Paul Thormodsgard	.12	.06	.01
☐ 163	Bill North	.12	.06	.01
☐ 164	Bob Owchinko	.12	.06	.01
☐ 165	Rennie Stennett	.12	.06	.01
☐ 166	Carlos Lopez	.12	.06	.01
☐ 167	Tim Foli	.12	.06	.01
☐ 168	Reggie Smith	.30	.15	.03
☐ 169	Jerry Johnson	.12	.06	.01
☐ 170	Lou Brock	2.00	1.00	.20
☐ 171	Pat Zachry	.12	.06	.01
☐ 172	Mike Hargrove	.20	.10	.02
☐ 173	Robin Yount	7.50	3.75	.75
☐ 174	Wayne Garland	.12	.06	.01
☐ 175	Jerry Morales	.12	.06	.01
☐ 176	Milt May	.12	.06	.01
☐ 177	Gene Garber DP	.06	.03	.00
☐ 178	Dave Chalk	.12	.06	.01

		NRMT	VG-E	GOOD
☐ 179	Dick Tidrow	.12	.06	.01
☐ 180	Dave Concepcion	.30	.15	.03
☐ 181	Ken Forsch	.12	.06	.01
☐ 182	Jim Spencer	.12	.06	.01
☐ 183	Doug Bird	.12	.06	.01
☐ 184	Checklist 2	.50	.05	.01
☐ 185	Ellis Valentine	.12	.06	.01
☐ 186	Bob Stanley DP	.30	.15	.03
☐ 187	Jerry Royster DP	.06	.03	.00
☐ 188	Al Bumbry	.12	.06	.01
☐ 189	Tom Lasorda MG	.30	.15	.03
☐ 190	John Candelaria	.30	.15	.03
☐ 191	Rodney Scott	.12	.06	.01
☐ 192	Padres Team (checklist back)	.50	.25	.05
☐ 193	Rich Chiles	.12	.06	.01
☐ 194	Derrel Thomas	.12	.06	.01
☐ 195	Larry Dierker	.12	.06	.01
☐ 196	Bob Bailor	.12	.06	.01
☐ 197	Nino Espinosa	.12	.06	.01
☐ 198	Ron Pruitt	.12	.06	.01
☐ 199	Craig Reynolds	.12	.06	.01
☐ 200	Reggie Jackson	4.00	2.00	.40
☐ 201	Batting Leaders Dave Parker Rod Carew	.60	.30	.06
☐ 202	Home Run Leaders DP George Foster Jim Rice	.12	.06	.01
☐ 203	RBI Leaders George Foster Larry Hisle	.20	.10	.02
☐ 204	Steals Leaders DP Frank Taveras Freddie Patek	.12	.06	.01
☐ 205	Victory Leaders Steve Carlton Dave Goltz Dennis Leonard Jim Palmer	.50	.25	.05
☐ 206	Strikeout Leaders DP Phil Niekro Nolan Ryan	.30	.15	.03
☐ 207	ERA Leaders DP John Candelaria Frank Tanana	.12	.06	.01
☐ 208	Top Firemen Rollie Fingers Bill Campbell	.20	.10	.02

		NRMT	VG-E	GOOD
☐ 209	Dock Ellis	.12	.06	.01
☐ 210	Jose Cardenal	.12	.06	.01
☐ 211	Earl Weaver MG DP	.12	.06	.01
☐ 212	Mike Caldwell	.12	.06	.01
☐ 213	Alan Bannister	.12	.06	.01
☐ 214	Angels Team (checklist back)	.50	.25	.05
☐ 215	Darrell Evans	.40	.20	.04
☐ 216	Mike Paxton	.12	.06	.01
☐ 217	Rod Gilbreath	.12	.06	.01
☐ 218	Marty Pattin	.12	.06	.01
☐ 219	Mike Cubbage	.12	.06	.01
☐ 220	Pedro Borbon	.12	.06	.01
☐ 221	Chris Speier	.12	.06	.01
☐ 222	Jerry Martin	.12	.06	.01
☐ 223	Bruce Kison	.12	.06	.01
☐ 224	Jerry Tabb	.12	.06	.01
☐ 225	Don Gullett DP	.12	.06	.01
☐ 226	Joe Ferguson	.12	.06	.01
☐ 227	Al Fitzmorris	.12	.06	.01
☐ 228	Manny Mota DP	.12	.06	.01
☐ 229	Leo Foster	.12	.06	.01
☐ 230	Al Hrabosky	.12	.06	.01
☐ 231	Wayne Nordhagen	.12	.06	.01
☐ 232	Mickey Stanley	.20	.10	.02
☐ 233	Dick Pole	.12	.06	.01
☐ 234	Herman Franks MG	.12	.06	.01
☐ 235	Tim McCarver	.30	.15	.03
☐ 236	Terry Whitfield	.12	.06	.01
☐ 237	Rich Dauer	.12	.06	.01
☐ 238	Juan Beniquez	.12	.06	.01
☐ 239	Dyar Miller	.12	.06	.01
☐ 240	Gene Tenace	.20	.10	.02
☐ 241	Pete Vuckovich	.20	.10	.02
☐ 242	Barry Bonnell DP	.12	.06	.01
☐ 243	Bob McClure	.12	.06	.01
☐ 244	Expos Team DP (checklist back)	.20	.10	.02
☐ 245	Rick Burleson	.20	.10	.02
☐ 246	Dan Driessen	.12	.06	.01
☐ 247	Larry Christenson	.12	.06	.01
☐ 248	Frank White DP	.12	.06	.01
☐ 249	Dave Goltz DP	.06	.03	.00
☐ 250	Graig Nettles DP	.20	.10	.02
☐ 251	Don Kirkwood	.12	.06	.01
☐ 252	Steve Swisher DP	.06	.03	.00
☐ 253	Jim Kern	.12	.06	.01
☐ 254	Dave Collins	.12	.06	.01
☐ 255	Jerry Reuss	.20	.10	.02

		NRMT	VG-E	GOOD

		NRMT	VG-E	GOOD
☐ 256	Joe Altobelli MG	.12	.06	.01
☐ 257	Hector Cruz	.12	.06	.01
☐ 258	John Hiller	.20	.10	.02
☐ 259	Dodgers Team (checklist back)	.50	.25	.05
☐ 260	Bert Campaneris	.20	.10	.02
☐ 261	Tim Hosley	.12	.06	.01
☐ 262	Rudy May	.12	.06	.01
☐ 263	Danny Walton	.12	.06	.01
☐ 264	Jamie Easterly	.12	.06	.01
☐ 265	Sal Bando DP	.12	.06	.01
☐ 266	Bob Shirley	.12	.06	.01
☐ 267	Doug Ault	.12	.06	.01
☐ 268	Gil Flores	.12	.06	.01
☐ 269	Wayne Twitchell	.12	.06	.01
☐ 270	Carlton Fisk	1.50	.75	.15
☐ 271	Randy Lerch DP	.06	.03	.00
☐ 272	Royle Stillman	.12	.06	.01
☐ 273	Fred Norman	.12	.06	.01
☐ 274	Freddie Patek	.12	.06	.01
☐ 275	Dan Ford	.12	.06	.01
☐ 276	Bill Bonham DP	.06	.03	.00
☐ 277	Bruce Boisclair	.12	.06	.01
☐ 278	Enrique Romo	.12	.06	.01
☐ 279	Bill Virdon MG	.20	.10	.02
☐ 280	Buddy Bell	.30	.15	.03
☐ 281	Eric Rasmussen DP	.06	.03	.00
☐ 282	Yankees Team (checklist back)	.60	.30	.06
☐ 283	Omar Moreno	.12	.06	.01
☐ 284	Randy Moffitt	.12	.06	.01
☐ 285	Steve Yeager DP	.12	.06	.01
☐ 286	Ben Oglivie	.20	.10	.02
☐ 287	Kiko Garcia	.12	.06	.01
☐ 288	Dave Hamilton	.12	.06	.01
☐ 289	Checklist 3	.50	.05	.01
☐ 290	Willie Horton	.20	.10	.02
☐ 291	Gary Ross	.12	.06	.01
☐ 292	Gene Richards	.12	.06	.01
☐ 293	Mike Willis	.12	.06	.01
☐ 294	Larry Parrish	.20	.10	.02
☐ 295	Bill Lee	.20	.10	.02
☐ 296	Biff Pocoroba	.12	.06	.01
☐ 297	Warren Brusstar DP	.06	.03	.00
☐ 298	Tony Armas	.20	.10	.02
☐ 299	Whitey Herzog MG	.20	.10	.02
☐ 300	Joe Morgan	1.75	.85	.17
☐ 301	Buddy Schultz	.12	.06	.01
☐ 302	Cubs Team	.50	.25	.05
	(checklist back)			
☐ 303	Sam Hinds	.12	.06	.01
☐ 304	John Milner	.12	.06	.01
☐ 305	Rico Carty	.20	.10	.02
☐ 306	Joe Niekro	.30	.15	.03
☐ 307	Glenn Borgmann	.12	.06	.01
☐ 308	Jim Rooker	.12	.06	.01
☐ 309	Cliff Johnson	.12	.06	.01
☐ 310	Don Sutton	1.25	.60	.12
☐ 311	Jose Baez DP	.06	.03	.00
☐ 312	Greg Minton	.12	.06	.01
☐ 313	Andy Etchebarren	.12	.06	.01
☐ 314	Paul Lindblad	.12	.06	.01
☐ 315	Mark Belanger	.20	.10	.02
☐ 316	Henry Cruz DP	.06	.03	.00
☐ 317	Dave Johnson	.30	.15	.03
☐ 318	Tom Griffin	.12	.06	.01
☐ 319	Alan Ashby	.12	.06	.01
☐ 320	Fred Lynn	.75	.35	.07
☐ 321	Santo Alcala	.12	.06	.01
☐ 322	Tom Paciorek	.12	.06	.01
☐ 323	Jim Fregosi DP	.12	.06	.01
☐ 324	Vern Rapp MG	.12	.06	.01
☐ 325	Bruce Sutter	.60	.30	.06
☐ 326	Mike Lum DP	.06	.03	.00
☐ 327	Rick Langford DP	.06	.03	.00
☐ 328	Milwaukee Brewers Team Card (checklist back)	.50	.25	.05
☐ 329	John Verhoeven	.12	.06	.01
☐ 330	Bob Watson	.20	.10	.02
☐ 331	Mark Littell	.12	.06	.01
☐ 332	Duane Kuiper	.12	.06	.01
☐ 333	Jim Todd	.12	.06	.01
☐ 334	John Stearns	.12	.06	.01
☐ 335	Bucky Dent	.30	.15	.03
☐ 336	Steve Busby	.12	.06	.01
☐ 337	Tom Grieve	.20	.10	.02
☐ 338	Dave Heaverlo	.12	.06	.01
☐ 339	Mario Guerrero	.12	.06	.01
☐ 340	Bake McBride	.12	.06	.01
☐ 341	Mike Flanagan	.30	.15	.03
☐ 342	Aurelio Rodriguez	.12	.06	.01
☐ 343	John Wathan DP	.12	.06	.01
☐ 344	Sam Ewing	.12	.06	.01
☐ 345	Luis Tiant	.30	.15	.03
☐ 346	Larry Biittner	.12	.06	.01
☐ 347	Terry Forster	.20	.10	.02
☐ 348	Del Unser	.12	.06	.01

		NRMT	VG-E	GOOD
☐ 349	Rick Camp DP	.06	.03	.00
☐ 350	Steve Garvey	3.00	1.50	.30
☐ 351	Jeff Torborg	.20	.10	.02
☐ 352	Tony Scott	.12	.06	.01
☐ 353	Doug Bair	.12	.06	.01
☐ 354	Cesar Geronimo	.12	.06	.01
☐ 355	Bill Travers	.12	.06	.01
☐ 356	New York Mets	.50	.25	.05
	Team Card (checklist back)			
☐ 357	Tom Poquette	.12	.06	.01
☐ 358	Mark Lemongello	.12	.06	.01
☐ 359	Marc Hill	.12	.06	.01
☐ 360	Mike Schmidt	7.50	3.75	.75
☐ 361	Chris Knapp	.12	.06	.01
☐ 362	Dave May	.12	.06	.01
☐ 363	Bob Randall	.12	.06	.01
☐ 364	Jerry Turner	.12	.06	.01
☐ 365	Ed Figueroa	.12	.06	.01
☐ 366	Larry Milbourne DP	.06	.03	.00
☐ 367	Rick Dempsey	.12	.06	.01
☐ 368	Balor Moore	.12	.06	.01
☐ 369	Tim Nordbrook	.12	.06	.01
☐ 370	Rusty Staub	.30	.15	.03
☐ 371	Ray Burris	.12	.06	.01
☐ 372	Brian Asselstine	.12	.06	.01
☐ 373	Jim Willoughby	.12	.06	.01
☐ 374	Jose Morales	.12	.06	.01
☐ 375	Tommy John	.75	.35	.07
☐ 376	Jim Wohlford	.12	.06	.01
☐ 377	Manny Sarmiento	.12	.06	.01
☐ 378	Bobby Winkles MG	.12	.06	.01
☐ 379	Skip Lockwood	.12	.06	.01
☐ 380	Ted Simmons	.40	.20	.04
☐ 381	Phillies Team	.50	.25	.05
	(checklist back)			
☐ 382	Joe Lahoud	.12	.06	.01
☐ 383	Mario Mendoza	.12	.06	.01
☐ 384	Jack Clark	4.00	2.00	.40
☐ 385	Tito Fuentes	.12	.06	.01
☐ 386	Bob Gorinski	.12	.06	.01
☐ 387	Ken Holtzman	.20	.10	.02
☐ 388	Bill Fahey DP	.06	.03	.00
☐ 389	Julio Gonzalez	.12	.06	.01
☐ 390	Oscar Gamble	.12	.06	.01
☐ 391	Larry Haney	.12	.06	.01
☐ 392	Billy Almon	.12	.06	.01
☐ 393	Tippy Martinez	.12	.06	.01
☐ 394	Roy Howell DP	.06	.03	.00

		NRMT	VG-E	GOOD
☐ 395	Jim Hughes	.12	.06	.01
☐ 396	Bob Stinson DP	.06	.03	.00
☐ 397	Greg Gross	.12	.06	.01
☐ 398	Don Hood	.12	.06	.01
☐ 399	Pete Mackanin	.12	.06	.01
☐ 400	Nolan Ryan	9.00	4.50	.90
☐ 401	Sparky Anderson MG	.20	.10	.02
☐ 402	Dave Campbell	.12	.06	.01
☐ 403	Bud Harrelson	.12	.06	.01
☐ 404	Tigers Team	.50	.25	.05
	(checklist back)			
☐ 405	Rawly Eastwick	.12	.06	.01
☐ 406	Mike Jorgensen	.12	.06	.01
☐ 407	Odell Jones	.12	.06	.01
☐ 408	Joe Zdeb	.12	.06	.01
☐ 409	Ron Schueler	.12	.06	.01
☐ 410	Bill Madlock	.50	.25	.05
☐ 411	AL Champs	.50	.25	.05
	Yankees rally to defeat Royals			
☐ 412	NL Champs	.50	.25	.05
	Dodgers overpower Phillies in four			
☐ 413	World Series	1.50	.75	.15
	Reggie and Yankees reign supreme			
☐ 414	Darold Knowles DP	.06	.03	.00
☐ 415	Ray Fosse	.12	.06	.01
☐ 416	Jack Brohamer	.12	.06	.01
☐ 417	Mike Garman DP	.06	.03	.00
☐ 418	Tony Muser	.12	.06	.01
☐ 419	Jerry Garvin	.12	.06	.01
☐ 420	Greg Luzinski	.30	.15	.03
☐ 421	Junior Moore	.12	.06	.01
☐ 422	Steve Braun	.12	.06	.01
☐ 423	Dave Rosello	.12	.06	.01
☐ 424	Boston Red Sox	.50	.25	.05
	Team Card (checklist back)			
☐ 425	Steve Rogers DP	.12	.06	.01
☐ 426	Fred Kendall	.12	.06	.01
☐ 427	Mario Soto	.60	.30	.06
☐ 428	Joel Youngblood	.12	.06	.01
☐ 429	Mike Barlow	.12	.06	.01
☐ 430	Al Oliver	.30	.15	.03
☐ 431	Butch Metzger	.12	.06	.01
☐ 432	Terry Bulling	.12	.06	.01
☐ 433	Fernando Gonzalez	.12	.06	.01
☐ 434	Mike Norris	.12	.06	.01

		NRMT	VG-E	GOOD
☐ 435	Checklist 4	.50	.05	.01
☐ 436	Vic Harris DP	.06	.03	.00
☐ 437	Bo McLaughlin	.12	.06	.01
☐ 438	John Ellis	.12	.06	.01
☐ 439	Ken Kravec	.12	.06	.01
☐ 440	Dave Lopes	.20	.10	.02
☐ 441	Larry Gura	.12	.06	.01
☐ 442	Elliott Maddox	.12	.06	.01
☐ 443	Darrel Chaney	.12	.06	.01
☐ 444	Roy Hartsfield MG	.12	.06	.01
☐ 445	Mike Ivie	.12	.06	.01
☐ 446	Tug McGraw	.30	.15	.03
☐ 447	Leroy Stanton	.12	.06	.01
☐ 448	Bill Castro	.12	.06	.01
☐ 449	Tim Blackwell DP	.06	.03	.00
☐ 450	Tom Seaver	3.50	1.60	.32
☐ 451	Minnesota Twins Team Card (checklist back)	.50	.25	.05
☐ 452	Jerry Mumphrey	.12	.06	.01
☐ 453	Doug Flynn	.12	.06	.01
☐ 454	Dave LaRoche	.12	.06	.01
☐ 455	Bill Robinson	.20	.10	.02
☐ 456	Vern Ruhle	.12	.06	.01
☐ 457	Bob Bailey	.12	.06	.01
☐ 458	Jeff Newman	.12	.06	.01
☐ 459	Charlie Spikes	.12	.06	.01
☐ 460	Jim Hunter	1.50	.75	.15
☐ 461	Rob Andrews DP	.06	.03	.00
☐ 462	Rogelio Moret	.12	.06	.01
☐ 463	Kevin Bell	.12	.06	.01
☐ 464	Jerry Grote	.12	.06	.01
☐ 465	Hal McRae	.20	.10	.02
☐ 466	Dennis Blair	.12	.06	.01
☐ 467	Alvin Dark MG	.12	.06	.01
☐ 468	Warren Cromartie	.30	.15	.03
☐ 469	Rick Cerone	.20	.10	.02
☐ 470	J.R. Richard	.20	.10	.02
☐ 471	Roy Smalley	.12	.06	.01
☐ 472	Ron Reed	.12	.06	.01
☐ 473	Bill Buckner	.30	.15	.03
☐ 474	Jim Slaton	.12	.06	.01
☐ 475	Gary Matthews	.20	.10	.02
☐ 476	Bill Stein	.12	.06	.01
☐ 477	Doug Capilla	.12	.06	.01
☐ 478	Jerry Remy	.12	.06	.01
☐ 479	Cardinals Team (checklist back)	.50	.25	.05
☐ 480	Ron LeFlore	.12	.06	.01

		NRMT	VG-E	GOOD
☐ 481	Jackson Todd	.12	.06	.01
☐ 482	Rick Miller	.12	.06	.01
☐ 483	Ken Macha	.12	.06	.01
☐ 484	Jim Norris	.12	.06	.01
☐ 485	Chris Chambliss	.20	.10	.02
☐ 486	John Curtis	.12	.06	.01
☐ 487	Jim Tyrone	.12	.06	.01
☐ 488	Dan Spillner	.12	.06	.01
☐ 489	Rudy Meoli	.12	.06	.01
☐ 490	Amos Otis	.20	.10	.02
☐ 491	Scott McGregor	.20	.10	.02
☐ 492	Jim Sundberg	.12	.06	.01
☐ 493	Steve Renko	.12	.06	.01
☐ 494	Chuck Tanner MG	.12	.06	.01
☐ 495	Dave Cash	.12	.06	.01
☐ 496	Jim Clancy DP	.20	.10	.02
☐ 497	Glenn Adams	.12	.06	.01
☐ 498	Joe Sambito	.12	.06	.01
☐ 499	Seattle Mariners Team Card (checklist back)	.50	.25	.05
☐ 500	George Foster	.60	.30	.06
☐ 501	Dave Roberts	.12	.06	.01
☐ 502	Pat Rockett	.12	.06	.01
☐ 503	Ike Hampton	.12	.06	.01
☐ 504	Roger Freed	.12	.06	.01
☐ 505	Felix Millan	.12	.06	.01
☐ 506	Ron Blomberg	.12	.06	.01
☐ 507	Willie Crawford	.12	.06	.01
☐ 508	Johnny Oates	.12	.06	.01
☐ 509	Brent Strom	.12	.06	.01
☐ 510	Willie Stargell	2.00	1.00	.20
☐ 511	Frank Duffy	.12	.06	.01
☐ 512	Larry Herndon	.12	.06	.01
☐ 513	Barry Foote	.12	.06	.01
☐ 514	Rob Sperring	.12	.06	.01
☐ 515	Tim Corcoran	.12	.06	.01
☐ 516	Gary Beare	.12	.06	.01
☐ 517	Andres Mora	.12	.06	.01
☐ 518	Tommy Boggs DP	.06	.03	.00
☐ 519	Brian Downing	.20	.10	.02
☐ 520	Larry Hisle	.12	.06	.01
☐ 521	Steve Staggs	.12	.06	.01
☐ 522	Dick Williams MG	.12	.06	.01
☐ 523	Donnie Moore	.20	.10	.02
☐ 524	Bernie Carbo	.12	.06	.01
☐ 525	Jerry Terrell	.12	.06	.01
☐ 526	Reds Team (checklist back)	.50	.25	.05

		NRMT	VG-E	GOOD
☐ 527	Vic Correll	.12	.06	.01
☐ 528	Rob Picciolo	.12	.06	.01
☐ 529	Paul Hartzell	.12	.06	.01
☐ 530	Dave Winfield	2.50	1.25	.25
☐ 531	Tom Underwood	.12	.06	.01
☐ 532	Skip Jutze	.12	.06	.01
☐ 533	Sandy Alomar	.12	.06	.01
☐ 534	Wilbur Howard	.12	.06	.01
☐ 535	Checklist 5	.50	.05	.01
☐ 536	Roric Harrison	.12	.06	.01
☐ 537	Bruce Bochte	.12	.06	.01
☐ 538	Johnny LeMaster	.12	.06	.01
☐ 539	Vic Davalillo DP	.06	.03	.00
☐ 540	Steve Carlton	2.75	1.35	.27
☐ 541	Larry Cox	.12	.06	.01
☐ 542	Tim Johnson	.12	.06	.01
☐ 543	Larry Harlow DP	.06	.03	.00
☐ 544	Len Randle DP	.06	.03	.00
☐ 545	Bill Campbell	.12	.06	.01
☐ 546	Ted Martinez	.12	.06	.01
☐ 547	John Scott	.12	.06	.01
☐ 548	Billy Hunter MG DP	.06	.03	.00
☐ 549	Joe Kerrigan	.12	.06	.01
☐ 550	John Mayberry	.20	.10	.02
☐ 551	Atlanta Braves	.50	.25	.05
	Team Card (checklist back)			
☐ 552	Francisco Barrios	.12	.06	.01
☐ 553	Terry Puhl	.40	.20	.04
☐ 554	Joe Coleman	.12	.06	.01
☐ 555	Butch Wynegar	.12	.06	.01
☐ 556	Ed Armbrister	.12	.06	.01
☐ 557	Tony Solaita	.12	.06	.01
☐ 558	Paul Mitchell	.12	.06	.01
☐ 559	Phil Mankowski	.12	.06	.01
☐ 560	Dave Parker	2.25	1.10	.22
☐ 561	Charlie Williams	.12	.06	.01
☐ 562	Glenn Burke	.12	.06	.01
☐ 563	Dave Rader	.12	.06	.01
☐ 564	Mick Kelleher	.12	.06	.01
☐ 565	Jerry Koosman	.30	.15	.03
☐ 566	Merv Rettenmund	.12	.06	.01
☐ 567	Dick Drago	.12	.06	.01
☐ 568	Tom Hutton	.12	.06	.01
☐ 569	Lary Sorensen	.12	.06	.01
☐ 570	Dave Kingman	.50	.25	.05
☐ 571	Buck Martinez	.12	.06	.01
☐ 572	Rick Wise	.12	.06	.01
☐ 573	Luis Gomez	.12	.06	.01
☐ 574	Bob Lemon MG	.30	.15	.03
☐ 575	Pat Dobson	.20	.10	.02
☐ 576	Sam Mejias	.12	.06	.01
☐ 577	Oakland A's	.50	.25	.05
	Team Card (checklist back)			
☐ 578	Buzz Capra	.12	.06	.01
☐ 579	Rance Mulliniks	.30	.15	.03
☐ 580	Rod Carew	2.50	1.25	.25
☐ 581	Lynn McGlothen	.12	.06	.01
☐ 582	Fran Healy	.12	.06	.01
☐ 583	George Medich	.12	.06	.01
☐ 584	John Hale	.12	.06	.01
☐ 585	Woodie Fryman DP	.06	.03	.00
☐ 586	Ed Goodson	.12	.06	.01
☐ 587	John Urrea	.12	.06	.01
☐ 588	Jim Mason	.12	.06	.01
☐ 589	Bob Knepper	1.25	.60	.12
☐ 590	Bobby Murcer	.30	.15	.03
☐ 591	George Zeber	.12	.06	.01
☐ 592	Bob Apodaca	.12	.06	.01
☐ 593	Dave Skaggs	.12	.06	.01
☐ 594	Dave Freisleben	.12	.06	.01
☐ 595	Sixto Lezcano	.12	.06	.01
☐ 596	Gary Wheelock	.12	.06	.01
☐ 597	Steve Dillard	.12	.06	.01
☐ 598	Eddie Solomon	.12	.06	.01
☐ 599	Gary Woods	.12	.06	.01
☐ 600	Frank Tanana	.20	.10	.02
☐ 601	Gene Mauch MG	.12	.06	.01
☐ 602	Eric Soderholm	.12	.06	.01
☐ 603	Will McEnaney	.12	.06	.01
☐ 604	Earl Williams	.12	.06	.01
☐ 605	Rick Rhoden	.20	.10	.02
☐ 606	Pirates Team	.50	.25	.05
	(checklist back)			
☐ 607	Fernando Arroyo	.12	.06	.01
☐ 608	Johnny Grubb	.12	.06	.01
☐ 609	John Denny	.20	.10	.02
☐ 610	Garry Maddox	.20	.10	.02
☐ 611	Pat Scanlon	.12	.06	.01
☐ 612	Ken Henderson	.12	.06	.01
☐ 613	Marty Perez	.12	.06	.01
☐ 614	Joe Wallis	.12	.06	.01
☐ 615	Clay Carroll	.12	.06	.01
☐ 616	Pat Kelly	.12	.06	.01
☐ 617	Joe Nolan	.12	.06	.01
☐ 618	Tommy Helms	.20	.10	.02
☐ 619	Thad Bosley DP	.12	.06	.01

		NRMT	VG-E	GOOD			NRMT	VG-E	GOOD
☐ 620	Willie Randolph	.40	.20	.04	☐ 667	Jeff Byrd	.12	.06	.01
☐ 621	Craig Swan DP	.12	.06	.01	☐ 668	Dusty Baker	.20	.10	.02
☐ 622	Champ Summers	.12	.06	.01	☐ 669	Pete Falcone	.12	.06	.01
☐ 623	Eduardo Rodriguez	.12	.06	.01	☐ 670	Jim Rice	3.50	1.75	.35
☐ 624	Gary Alexander DP	.06	.03	.00	☐ 671	Gary Lavelle	.12	.06	.01
☐ 625	Jose Cruz	.20	.10	.02	☐ 672	Don Kessinger	.20	.10	.02
☐ 626	Blue Jays Team DP	.20	.10	.02	☐ 673	Steve Brye	.12	.06	.01
	(checklist back)				☐ 674	Ray Knight	1.25	.60	.12
☐ 627	David Johnson	.12	.06	.01	☐ 675	Jay Johnstone	.20	.10	.02
☐ 628	Ralph Garr	.12	.06	.01	☐ 676	Bob Myrick	.12	.06	.01
☐ 629	Don Stanhouse	.12	.06	.01	☐ 677	Ed Herrmann	.12	.06	.01
☐ 630	Ron Cey	.30	.15	.03	☐ 678	Tom Burgmeier	.12	.06	.01
☐ 631	Danny Ozark MG	.12	.06	.01	☐ 679	Wayne Garrett	.12	.06	.01
☐ 632	Rowland Office	.12	.06	.01	☐ 680	Vida Blue	.20	.10	.02
☐ 633	Tom Veryzer	.12	.06	.01	☐ 681	Rob Belloir	.12	.06	.01
☐ 634	Len Barker	.12	.06	.01	☐ 682	Ken Brett	.12	.06	.01
☐ 635	Joe Rudi	.20	.10	.02	☐ 683	Mike Champion	.12	.06	.01
☐ 636	Jim Bibby	.12	.06	.01	☐ 684	Ralph Houk MG	.20	.10	.02
☐ 637	Duffy Dyer	.12	.06	.01	☐ 685	Frank Taveras	.12	.06	.01
☐ 638	Paul Splittorff	.12	.06	.01	☐ 686	Gaylord Perry	1.75	.85	.17
☐ 639	Gene Clines	.12	.06	.01	☐ 687	Julio Cruz	.20	.10	.02
☐ 640	Lee May DP	.12	.06	.01	☐ 688	George Mitterwald	.12	.06	.01
☐ 641	Doug Rau	.12	.06	.01	☐ 689	Indians Team	.50	.25	.05
☐ 642	Denny Doyle	.12	.06	.01		(checklist back)			
☐ 643	Tom House	.12	.06	.01	☐ 690	Mickey Rivers	.20	.10	.02
☐ 644	Jim Dwyer	.12	.06	.01	☐ 691	Ross Grimsley	.12	.06	.01
☐ 645	Mike Torrez	.12	.06	.01	☐ 692	Ken Reitz	.12	.06	.01
☐ 646	Rick Auerbach DP	.06	.03	.00	☐ 693	Lamar Johnson	.12	.06	.01
☐ 647	Steve Dunning	.12	.06	.01	☐ 694	Elias Sosa	.12	.06	.01
☐ 648	Gary Thomasson	.12	.06	.01	☐ 695	Dwight Evans	1.25	.60	.12
☐ 649	Moose Haas	.20	.10	.02	☐ 696	Steve Mingori	.12	.06	.01
☐ 650	Cesar Cedeno	.20	.10	.02	☐ 697	Roger Metzger	.12	.06	.01
☐ 651	Doug Rader	.20	.10	.02	☐ 698	Juan Bernhardt	.12	.06	.01
☐ 652	Checklist 6	.50	.05	.01	☐ 699	Jackie Brown	.12	.06	.01
☐ 653	Ron Hodges DP	.06	.03	.00	☐ 700	Johnny Bench	3.75	1.85	.37
☐ 654	Pepe Frias	.12	.06	.01	☐ 701	Rookie Pitchers	.30	.15	.03
☐ 655	Lyman Bostock	.20	.10	.02		Tom Hume			
☐ 656	Dave Garcia MG	.12	.06	.01		Larry Landreth			
☐ 657	Bombo Rivera	.12	.06	.01		Steve McCatty			
☐ 658	Manny Sanguillen	.20	.10	.02		Bruce Taylor			
☐ 659	Rangers Team	.50	.25	.05	☐ 702	Rookie Catchers	.20	.10	.02
	(checklist back)					Bill Nahorodny			
☐ 660	Jason Thompson	.20	.10	.02		Kevin Pasley			
☐ 661	Grant Jackson	.12	.06	.01		Rick Sweet			
☐ 662	Paul Dade	.12	.06	.01		Don Werner			
☐ 663	Paul Reuschel	.12	.06	.01	☐ 703	Rookie Pitchers DP	6.00	3.00	.60
☐ 664	Fred Stanley	.12	.06	.01		Larry Andersen			
☐ 665	Dennis Leonard	.20	.10	.02		Tim Jones			
☐ 666	Billy Smith	.12	.06	.01		Mickey Mahler			

		NRMT	VG-E	GOOD
	Jack Morris			
☐ 704	Rookie 2nd Basemen	12.00	6.00	1.20
	Garth Iorg			
	Dave Oliver			
	Sam Perlozzo			
	Lou Whitaker			
☐ 705	Rookie Outfielders	.40	.20	.04
	Dave Bergman			
	Miguel Dilone			
	Clint Hurdle			
	Willie Norwood			
☐ 706	Rookie 1st Basemen	.20	.10	.02
	Wayne Cage			
	Ted Cox			
	Pat Putnam			
	Dave Revering			
☐ 707	Rookie Shortstops	42.00	20.00	4.00
	Mickey Klutts			
	Paul Molitor			
	Alan Trammell			
	U.L. Washington			
☐ 708	Rookie Catchers	24.00	12.00	2.40
	Bo Diaz			
	Dale Murphy			
	Lance Parrish			
	Ernie Whitt			
☐ 709	Rookie Pitchers	.40	.20	.04
	Steve Burke			
	Matt Keough			
	Lance Rautzhan			
	Dan Schatzeder			
☐ 710	Rookie Outfielders	.60	.30	.06
	Dell Alston			
	Rick Bosetti			
	Mike Easler			
	Keith Smith			
☐ 711	Rookie Pitchers DP	.12	.06	.01
	Cardell Camper			
	Dennis Lamp			
	Craig Mitchell			
	Roy Thomas			
☐ 712	Bobby Valentine	.30	.15	.03
☐ 713	Bob Davis	.12	.06	.01
☐ 714	Mike Anderson	.12	.06	.01
☐ 715	Jim Kaat	.50	.25	.05
☐ 716	Clarence Gaston	.30	.15	.03
☐ 717	Nelson Briles	.12	.06	.01
☐ 718	Ron Jackson	.12	.06	.01
☐ 719	Randy Elliott	.12	.06	.01

		NRMT	VG-E	GOOD
☐ 720	Fergie Jenkins	.60	.30	.06
☐ 721	Billy Martin MG	.60	.30	.06
☐ 722	Pete Broberg	.12	.06	.01
☐ 723	John Wockenfuss	.12	.06	.01
☐ 724	Kansas City Royals	.50	.25	.05
	Team Card (checklist back)			
☐ 725	Kurt Bevacqua	.12	.06	.01
☐ 726	Wilbur Wood	.20	.10	.02

1979 Topps

The cards in this 726-card set measure 2 ½" by 3 ½". Topps continued with the same number of cards as in 1978. Various series spotlight "League Leaders" (1-8), "Season and Career Record Holders" (411-418), "Record Breakers of 1978" (201-206), and one "Prospects" card for each team (701-726). Team cards feature a checklist on back of that team's players in the set and a small picture of the manager on the front of the card. There are 66 cards that were double printed and these are noted in the checklist by the abbreviation DP. Bump Wills was initially depicted in a Ranger uniform but with a Blue Jays affiliation; later printings correctly labeled him with Texas. The set price listed does not include the scarcer Wills (Rangers) card. Cards numbered 23 or lower, which feature Phillies or Yankees and do not follow the numbering checklisted below, are not necessarily error cards. They are probably Burger King cards, a separate set with *its own pricing and mass distribution. Burger King cards are indistinguishable from the corresponding Topps cards except for the card numbering difference and the fact that Burger King cards do not have a printing sheet designation (such as A through F like the regular Topps) anywhere on the card back in very small print.*

			NRMT	VG-E	GOOD
		COMPLETE SET (726)	175.00	75.00	15.00
		COMMON PLAYER (1-726)	.10	.05	.01
		COMMON DP's (1-726)	.05	.02	.00
☐	1	Batting Leaders	1.50	.30	.06
		Rod Carew			
		Dave Parker			
☐	2	Home Run Leaders	.30	.15	.03
		Jim Rice			
		George Foster			
☐	3	RBI Leaders	.30	.15	.03
		Jim Rice			
		George Foster			
☐	4	Stolen Base Leaders	.20	.10	.02
		Ron LeFlore			
		Omar Moreno			
☐	5	Victory Leaders	.30	.15	.03
		Ron Guidry			
		Gaylord Perry			
☐	6	Strikeout Leaders	1.00	.50	.10
		Nolan Ryan			
		J.R. Richard			
☐	7	ERA Leaders	.20	.10	.02
		Ron Guidry			
		Craig Swan			
☐	8	Leading Firemen	.30	.15	.03
		Rich Gossage			
		Rollie Fingers			
☐	9	Dave Campbell	.10	.05	.01
☐	10	Lee May	.20	.10	.02
☐	11	Marc Hill	.10	.05	.01
☐	12	Dick Drago	.10	.05	.01
☐	13	Paul Dade	.10	.05	.01
☐	14	Rafael Landestoy	.10	.05	.01
☐	15	Ross Grimsley	.10	.05	.01
☐	16	Fred Stanley	.10	.05	.01
☐	17	Donnie Moore	.10	.05	.01
☐	18	Tony Solaita	.10	.05	.01
☐	19	Larry Gura DP	.10	.05	.01
☐	20	Joe Morgan DP	.60	.30	.06

			NRMT	VG-E	GOOD
☐	21	Kevin Kobel	.10	.05	.01
☐	22	Mike Jorgensen	.10	.05	.01
☐	23	Terry Forster	.20	.10	.02
☐	24	Paul Molitor	4.00	2.00	.40
☐	25	Steve Carlton	2.25	1.10	.22
☐	26	Jamie Quirk	.10	.05	.01
☐	27	Dave Goltz	.10	.05	.01
☐	28	Steve Brye	.10	.05	.01
☐	29	Rick Langford	.10	.05	.01
☐	30	Dave Winfield	2.50	1.25	.25
☐	31	Tom House DP	.05	.02	.00
☐	32	Jerry Mumphrey	.10	.05	.01
☐	33	Dave Rozema	.10	.05	.01
☐	34	Rob Andrews	.10	.05	.01
☐	35	Ed Figueroa	.10	.05	.01
☐	36	Alan Ashby	.10	.05	.01
☐	37	Joe Kerrigan DP	.05	.02	.00
☐	38	Bernie Carbo	.10	.05	.01
☐	39	Dale Murphy	7.50	3.75	.75
☐	40	Dennis Eckersley	.75	.35	.07
☐	41	Twins Team/Mgr.	.40	.20	.04
		Gene Mauch (checklist back)			
☐	42	Ron Blomberg	.10	.05	.01
☐	43	Wayne Twitchell	.10	.05	.01
☐	44	Kurt Bevacqua	.10	.05	.01
☐	45	Al Hrabosky	.10	.05	.01
☐	46	Ron Hodges	.10	.05	.01
☐	47	Fred Norman	.10	.05	.01
☐	48	Merv Rettenmund	.10	.05	.01
☐	49	Vern Ruhle	.10	.05	.01
☐	50	Steve Garvey DP	1.25	.60	.12
☐	51	Ray Fosse DP	.05	.02	.00
☐	52	Randy Lerch	.10	.05	.01
☐	53	Mick Kelleher	.10	.05	.01
☐	54	Dell Alston DP	.05	.02	.00
☐	55	Willie Stargell	2.00	1.00	.20
☐	56	John Hale	.10	.05	.01
☐	57	Eric Rasmussen	.10	.05	.01
☐	58	Bob Randall DP	.05	.02	.00
☐	59	John Denny DP	.10	.05	.01
☐	60	Mickey Rivers	.20	.10	.02
☐	61	Bo Diaz	.20	.10	.02
☐	62	Randy Moffitt	.10	.05	.01
☐	63	Jack Brohamer	.10	.05	.01
☐	64	Tom Underwood	.10	.05	.01
☐	65	Mark Belanger	.20	.10	.02
☐	66	Tigers Team/Mgr.	.40	.20	.04

		NRMT	VG-E	GOOD
	Les Moss (checklist back)			
☐ 67	Jim Mason DP	.05	.02	.00
☐ 68	Joe Niekro DP	.10	.05	.01
☐ 69	Elliott Maddox	.10	.05	.01
☐ 70	John Candelaria	.30	.15	.03
☐ 71	Brian Downing	.20	.10	.02
☐ 72	Steve Mingori	.10	.05	.01
☐ 73	Ken Henderson	.10	.05	.01
☐ 74	Shane Rawley	.90	.45	.09
☐ 75	Steve Yeager	.10	.05	.01
☐ 76	Warren Cromartie	.10	.05	.01
☐ 77	Dan Briggs DP	.05	.02	.00
☐ 78	Elias Sosa	.10	.05	.01
☐ 79	Ted Cox	.10	.05	.01
☐ 80	Jason Thompson	.10	.05	.01
☐ 81	Roger Erickson	.10	.05	.01
☐ 82	Mets Team/Mgr.	.40	.20	.04
	Joe Torre (checklist back)			
☐ 83	Fred Kendall	.10	.05	.01
☐ 84	Greg Minton	.10	.05	.01
☐ 85	Gary Matthews	.20	.10	.02
☐ 86	Rodney Scott	.10	.05	.01
☐ 87	Pete Falcone	.10	.05	.01
☐ 88	Bob Molinaro	.10	.05	.01
☐ 89	Dick Tidrow	.10	.05	.01
☐ 90	Bob Boone	.40	.20	.04
☐ 91	Terry Crowley	.10	.05	.01
☐ 92	Jim Bibby	.10	.05	.01
☐ 93	Phil Mankowski	.10	.05	.01
☐ 94	Len Barker	.10	.05	.01
☐ 95	Robin Yount	6.00	3.00	.60
☐ 96	Indians Team/Mgr.	.40	.20	.04
	Jeff Torborg (checklist back)			
☐ 97	Sam Mejias	.10	.05	.01
☐ 98	Ray Burris	.10	.05	.01
☐ 99	John Wathan	.30	.15	.03
☐ 100	Tom Seaver DP	1.50	.75	.15
☐ 101	Roy Howell	.10	.05	.01
☐ 102	Mike Anderson	.10	.05	.01
☐ 103	Jim Todd	.10	.05	.01
☐ 104	Johnny Oates DP	.05	.02	.00
☐ 105	Rick Camp DP	.05	.02	.00
☐ 106	Frank Duffy	.10	.05	.01
☐ 107	Jesus Alou DP	.05	.02	.00
☐ 108	Eduardo Rodriguez	.10	.05	.01
☐ 109	Joel Youngblood	.10	.05	.01
☐ 110	Vida Blue	.20	.10	.02
☐ 111	Roger Freed	.10	.05	.01
☐ 112	Phillies Team/Mgr.	.40	.20	.04
	Danny Ozark (checklist back)			
☐ 113	Pete Redfern	.10	.05	.01
☐ 114	Cliff Johnson	.10	.05	.01
☐ 115	Nolan Ryan	7.00	3.50	.70
☐ 116	Ozzie Smith	30.00	14.00	2.80
☐ 117	Grant Jackson	.10	.05	.01
☐ 118	Bud Harrelson	.10	.05	.01
☐ 119	Don Stanhouse	.10	.05	.01
☐ 120	Jim Sundberg	.10	.05	.01
☐ 121	Checklist 1 DP	.10	.02	.00
☐ 122	Mike Paxton	.10	.05	.01
☐ 123	Lou Whitaker	3.00	1.50	.30
☐ 124	Dan Schatzeder	.10	.05	.01
☐ 125	Rick Burleson	.20	.10	.02
☐ 126	Doug Bair	.10	.05	.01
☐ 127	Thad Bosley	.10	.05	.01
☐ 128	Ted Martinez	.10	.05	.01
☐ 129	Marty Pattin DP	.05	.02	.00
☐ 130	Bob Watson DP	.10	.05	.01
☐ 131	Jim Clancy	.10	.05	.01
☐ 132	Rowland Office	.10	.05	.01
☐ 133	Bill Castro	.10	.05	.01
☐ 134	Alan Bannister	.10	.05	.01
☐ 135	Bobby Murcer	.30	.15	.03
☐ 136	Jim Kaat	.40	.20	.04
☐ 137	Larry Wolfe DP	.05	.02	.00
☐ 138	Mark Lee	.10	.05	.01
☐ 139	Luis Pujols	.10	.05	.01
☐ 140	Don Gullett	.20	.10	.02
☐ 141	Tom Paciorek	.10	.05	.01
☐ 142	Charlie Williams	.10	.05	.01
☐ 143	Tony Scott	.10	.05	.01
☐ 144	Sandy Alomar	.10	.05	.01
☐ 145	Rick Rhoden	.20	.10	.02
☐ 146	Duane Kuiper	.10	.05	.01
☐ 147	Dave Hamilton	.10	.05	.01
☐ 148	Bruce Boisclair	.10	.05	.01
☐ 149	Manny Sarmiento	.10	.05	.01
☐ 150	Wayne Cage	.10	.05	.01
☐ 151	John Hiller	.20	.10	.02
☐ 152	Rick Cerone	.20	.10	.02
☐ 153	Dennis Lamp	.10	.05	.01
☐ 154	Jim Gantner DP	.10	.05	.01
☐ 155	Dwight Evans	1.00	.50	.10
☐ 156	Buddy Solomon	.10	.05	.01

		NRMT	VG-E	GOOD
☐ 157	U.L. Washington UER (sic, bats left, should be right)	.10	.05	.01
☐ 158	Joe Sambito	.10	.05	.01
☐ 159	Roy White	.20	.10	.02
☐ 160	Mike Flanagan	.30	.15	.03
☐ 161	Barry Foote	.10	.05	.01
☐ 162	Tom Johnson	.10	.05	.01
☐ 163	Glenn Burke	.10	.05	.01
☐ 164	Mickey Lolich	.30	.15	.03
☐ 165	Frank Taveras	.10	.05	.01
☐ 166	Leon Roberts	.10	.05	.01
☐ 167	Roger Metzger DP	.05	.02	.00
☐ 168	Dave Freisleben	.10	.05	.01
☐ 169	Bill Nahorodny	.10	.05	.01
☐ 170	Don Sutton	1.25	.60	.12
☐ 171	Gene Clines	.10	.05	.01
☐ 172	Mike Bruhert	.10	.05	.01
☐ 173	John Lowenstein	.10	.05	.01
☐ 174	Rick Auerbach	.10	.05	.01
☐ 175	George Hendrick	.20	.10	.02
☐ 176	Aurelio Rodriguez	.10	.05	.01
☐ 177	Ron Reed	.10	.05	.01
☐ 178	Alvis Woods	.10	.05	.01
☐ 179	Jim Beattie DP	.10	.05	.01
☐ 180	Larry Hisle	.10	.05	.01
☐ 181	Mike Garman	.10	.05	.01
☐ 182	Tim Johnson	.10	.05	.01
☐ 183	Paul Splittorff	.10	.05	.01
☐ 184	Darrel Chaney	.10	.05	.01
☐ 185	Mike Torrez	.10	.05	.01
☐ 186	Eric Soderholm	.10	.05	.01
☐ 187	Mark Lemongello	.10	.05	.01
☐ 188	Pat Kelly	.10	.05	.01
☐ 189	Eddie Whitson	.90	.45	.09
☐ 190	Ron Cey	.30	.15	.03
☐ 191	Mike Norris	.10	.05	.01
☐ 192	Cardinals Team/Mgr. Ken Boyer (checklist back)	.40	.20	.04
☐ 193	Glenn Adams	.10	.05	.01
☐ 194	Randy Jones	.10	.05	.01
☐ 195	Bill Madlock	.40	.20	.04
☐ 196	Steve Kemp DP	.10	.05	.01
☐ 197	Bob Apodaca	.10	.05	.01
☐ 198	Johnny Grubb	.10	.05	.01
☐ 199	Larry Milbourne	.10	.05	.01
☐ 200	Johnny Bench DP	1.50	.75	.15
☐ 201	RB: Mike Edwards	.10	.05	.01

		NRMT	VG-E	GOOD
	Most unassisted DP's, second basemen			
☐ 202	RB: Ron Guidry, Most strikeouts, lefthander, nine inning game	.30	.15	.03
☐ 203	RB: J.R. Richard, Most strikeouts, season, righthander	.20	.10	.02
☐ 204	RB: Pete Rose, Most consecutive games batting safely	1.50	.75	.15
☐ 205	RB: John Stearns, Most SB's by catcher, season	.10	.05	.01
☐ 206	RB: Sammy Stewart, 7 straight SO's, first ML game	.10	.05	.01
☐ 207	Dave Lemanczyk	.10	.05	.01
☐ 208	Clarence Gaston	.20	.10	.02
☐ 209	Reggie Cleveland	.10	.05	.01
☐ 210	Larry Bowa	.30	.15	.03
☐ 211	Denny Martinez	.30	.15	.03
☐ 212	Carney Lansford	5.00	2.50	.50
☐ 213	Bill Travers	.10	.05	.01
☐ 214	Red Sox Team/Mgr. Don Zimmer (checklist back)	.40	.20	.04
☐ 215	Willie McCovey	1.50	.75	.15
☐ 216	Wilbur Wood	.20	.10	.02
☐ 217	Steve Dillard	.10	.05	.01
☐ 218	Dennis Leonard	.20	.10	.02
☐ 219	Roy Smalley	.10	.05	.01
☐ 220	Cesar Geronimo	.10	.05	.01
☐ 221	Jesse Jefferson	.10	.05	.01
☐ 222	Bob Beall	.10	.05	.01
☐ 223	Kent Tekulve	.20	.10	.02
☐ 224	Dave Revering	.10	.05	.01
☐ 225	Rich Gossage	.50	.25	.05
☐ 226	Ron Pruitt	.10	.05	.01
☐ 227	Steve Stone	.20	.10	.02
☐ 228	Vic Davalillo	.10	.05	.01
☐ 229	Doug Flynn	.10	.05	.01
☐ 230	Bob Forsch	.10	.05	.01
☐ 231	John Wockenfuss	.10	.05	.01
☐ 232	Jimmy Sexton	.10	.05	.01
☐ 233	Paul Mitchell	.10	.05	.01
☐ 234	Toby Harrah	.20	.10	.02
☐ 235	Steve Rogers	.10	.05	.01

		NRMT	VG-E	GOOD
☐ 236	Jim Dwyer	.10	.05	.01
☐ 237	Billy Smith	.10	.05	.01
☐ 238	Balor Moore	.10	.05	.01
☐ 239	Willie Horton	.20	.10	.02
☐ 240	Rick Reuschel	.40	.20	.04
☐ 241	Checklist 2 DP	.10	.02	.00
☐ 242	Pablo Torrealba	.10	.05	.01
☐ 243	Buck Martinez DP	.05	.02	.00
☐ 244	Pirates Team/Mgr.	.40	.20	.04
	Chuck Tanner (checklist back)			
☐ 245	Jeff Burroughs	.20	.10	.02
☐ 246	Darrell Jackson	.10	.05	.01
☐ 247	Tucker Ashford DP	.05	.02	.00
☐ 248	Pete LaCock	.10	.05	.01
☐ 249	Paul Thormodsgard	.10	.05	.01
☐ 250	Willie Randolph	.30	.15	.03
☐ 251	Jack Morris	2.50	1.25	.25
☐ 252	Bob Stinson	.10	.05	.01
☐ 253	Rick Wise	.20	.10	.02
☐ 254	Luis Gomez	.10	.05	.01
☐ 255	Tommy John	.60	.30	.06
☐ 256	Mike Sadek	.10	.05	.01
☐ 257	Adrian Devine	.10	.05	.01
☐ 258	Mike Phillips	.10	.05	.01
☐ 259	Reds Team/Mgr.	.40	.20	.04
	Sparky Anderson (checklist back)			
☐ 260	Richie Zisk	.10	.05	.01
☐ 261	Mario Guerrero	.10	.05	.01
☐ 262	Nelson Briles	.10	.05	.01
☐ 263	Oscar Gamble	.10	.05	.01
☐ 264	Don Robinson	.75	.35	.07
☐ 265	Don Money	.10	.05	.01
☐ 266	Jim Willoughby	.10	.05	.01
☐ 267	Joe Rudi	.20	.10	.02
☐ 268	Julio Gonzalez	.10	.05	.01
☐ 269	Woodie Fryman	.10	.05	.01
☐ 270	Butch Hobson	.10	.05	.01
☐ 271	Rawly Eastwick	.10	.05	.01
☐ 272	Tim Corcoran	.10	.05	.01
☐ 273	Jerry Terrell	.10	.05	.01
☐ 274	Willie Norwood	.10	.05	.01
☐ 275	Junior Moore	.10	.05	.01
☐ 276	Jim Colborn	.10	.05	.01
☐ 277	Tom Grieve	.20	.10	.02
☐ 278	Andy Messersmith	.20	.10	.02
☐ 279	Jerry Grote DP	.05	.02	.00
☐ 280	Andre Thornton	.20	.10	.02
☐ 281	Vic Correll DP	.05	.02	.00
☐ 282	Blue Jays Team/Mgr.	.30	.15	.03
	Roy Hartsfield (checklist back)			
☐ 283	Ken Kravec	.10	.05	.01
☐ 284	Johnnie LeMaster	.10	.05	.01
☐ 285	Bobby Bonds	.30	.15	.03
☐ 286	Duffy Dyer	.10	.05	.01
☐ 287	Andres Mora	.10	.05	.01
☐ 288	Milt Wilcox	.10	.05	.01
☐ 289	Jose Cruz	.20	.10	.02
☐ 290	Dave Lopes	.20	.10	.02
☐ 291	Tom Griffin	.10	.05	.01
☐ 292	Don Reynolds	.10	.05	.01
☐ 293	Jerry Garvin	.10	.05	.01
☐ 294	Pepe Frias	.10	.05	.01
☐ 295	Mitchell Page	.10	.05	.01
☐ 296	Preston Hanna	.10	.05	.01
☐ 297	Ted Sizemore	.10	.05	.01
☐ 298	Rich Gale	.10	.05	.01
☐ 299	Steve Ontiveros	.10	.05	.01
☐ 300	Rod Carew	2.25	1.10	.22
☐ 301	Tom Hume	.10	.05	.01
☐ 302	Braves Team/Mgr.	.40	.20	.04
	Bobby Cox (checklist back)			
☐ 303	Lary Sorensen	.10	.05	.01
☐ 304	Steve Swisher	.10	.05	.01
☐ 305	Willie Montanez	.10	.05	.01
☐ 306	Floyd Bannister	.20	.10	.02
☐ 307	Larvell Blanks	.10	.05	.01
☐ 308	Bert Blyleven	.60	.30	.06
☐ 309	Ralph Garr	.20	.10	.02
☐ 310	Thurman Munson	2.00	1.00	.20
☐ 311	Gary Lavelle	.10	.05	.01
☐ 312	Bob Robertson	.10	.05	.01
☐ 313	Dyar Miller	.10	.05	.01
☐ 314	Larry Harlow	.10	.05	.01
☐ 315	Jon Matlack	.10	.05	.01
☐ 316	Milt May	.10	.05	.01
☐ 317	Jose Cardenal	.10	.05	.01
☐ 318	Bob Welch	3.00	1.50	.30
☐ 319	Wayne Garrett	.10	.05	.01
☐ 320	Carl Yastrzemski	3.00	1.50	.30
☐ 321	Gaylord Perry	1.50	.75	.15
☐ 322	Danny Goodwin	.10	.05	.01
☐ 323	Lynn McGlothen	.10	.05	.01
☐ 324	Mike Tyson	.10	.05	.01
☐ 325	Cecil Cooper	.40	.20	.04

		NRMT	VG-E	GOOD
☐ 326	Pedro Borbon	.10	.05	.01
☐ 327	Art Howe	.20	.10	.02
☐ 328	Oakland A's Team/Mgr.	.40	.20	.04
	Jack McKeon (checklist back)			
☐ 329	Joe Coleman	.10	.05	.01
☐ 330	George Brett	4.00	2.00	.40
☐ 331	Mickey Mahler	.10	.05	.01
☐ 332	Gary Alexander	.10	.05	.01
☐ 333	Chet Lemon	.20	.10	.02
☐ 334	Craig Swan	.10	.05	.01
☐ 335	Chris Chambliss	.20	.10	.02
☐ 336	Bobby Thompson	.10	.05	.01
☐ 337	John Montague	.10	.05	.01
☐ 338	Vic Harris	.10	.05	.01
☐ 339	Ron Jackson	.10	.05	.01
☐ 340	Jim Palmer	2.00	1.00	.20
☐ 341	Willie Upshaw	.50	.25	.05
☐ 342	Dave Roberts	.10	.05	.01
☐ 343	Ed Glynn	.10	.05	.01
☐ 344	Jerry Royster	.10	.05	.01
☐ 345	Tug McGraw	.30	.15	.03
☐ 346	Bill Buckner	.30	.15	.03
☐ 347	Doug Rau	.10	.05	.01
☐ 348	Andre Dawson	5.00	2.50	.50
☐ 349	Jim Wright	.10	.05	.01
☐ 350	Garry Templeton	.20	.10	.02
☐ 351	Wayne Nordhagen	.10	.05	.01
☐ 352	Steve Renko	.10	.05	.01
☐ 353	Checklist 3	.40	.05	.01
☐ 354	Bill Bonham	.10	.05	.01
☐ 355	Lee Mazzilli	.10	.05	.01
☐ 356	Giants Team/Mgr.	.40	.20	.04
	Joe Altobelli (checklist back)			
☐ 357	Jerry Augustine	.10	.05	.01
☐ 358	Alan Trammell	6.00	3.00	.60
☐ 359	Dan Spillner DP	.05	.02	.00
☐ 360	Amos Otis	.20	.10	.02
☐ 361	Tom Dixon	.10	.05	.01
☐ 362	Mike Cubbage	.10	.05	.01
☐ 363	Craig Skok	.10	.05	.01
☐ 364	Gene Richards	.10	.05	.01
☐ 365	Sparky Lyle	.30	.15	.03
☐ 366	Juan Bernhardt	.10	.05	.01
☐ 367	Dave Skaggs	.10	.05	.01
☐ 368	Don Aase	.10	.05	.01
☐ 369A	Bump Wills ERR	3.00	1.50	.30

		NRMT	VG-E	GOOD
	(Blue Jays)			
☐ 369B	Bump Wills COR	3.50	1.75	.35
	(Rangers)			
☐ 370	Dave Kingman	.40	.20	.04
☐ 371	Jeff Holly	.10	.05	.01
☐ 372	Lamar Johnson	.10	.05	.01
☐ 373	Lance Rautzhan	.10	.05	.01
☐ 374	Ed Herrmann	.10	.05	.01
☐ 375	Bill Campbell	.10	.05	.01
☐ 376	Gorman Thomas	.30	.15	.03
☐ 377	Paul Moskau	.10	.05	.01
☐ 378	Rob Picciolo DP	.05	.02	.00
☐ 379	Dale Murray	.10	.05	.01
☐ 380	John Mayberry	.20	.10	.02
☐ 381	Astros Team/Mgr.	.40	.20	.04
	Bill Virdon (checklist back)			
☐ 382	Jerry Martin	.10	.05	.01
☐ 383	Phil Garner	.10	.05	.01
☐ 384	Tommy Boggs	.10	.05	.01
☐ 385	Dan Ford	.10	.05	.01
☐ 386	Francisco Barrios	.10	.05	.01
☐ 387	Gary Thomasson	.10	.05	.01
☐ 388	Jack Billingham	.10	.05	.01
☐ 389	Joe Zdeb	.10	.05	.01
☐ 390	Rollie Fingers	.75	.35	.07
☐ 391	Al Oliver	.30	.15	.03
☐ 392	Doug Ault	.10	.05	.01
☐ 393	Scott McGregor	.20	.10	.02
☐ 394	Randy Stein	.10	.05	.01
☐ 395	Dave Cash	.10	.05	.01
☐ 396	Bill Plummer	.10	.05	.01
☐ 397	Sergio Ferrer	.10	.05	.01
☐ 398	Ivan DeJesus	.10	.05	.01
☐ 399	David Clyde	.10	.05	.01
☐ 400	Jim Rice	2.50	1.25	.25
☐ 401	Ray Knight	.30	.15	.03
☐ 402	Paul Hartzell	.10	.05	.01
☐ 403	Tim Foli	.10	.05	.01
☐ 404	White Sox Team/Mgr	.40	.20	.04
	Don Kessinger (checklist back)			
☐ 405	Butch Wynegar DP	.05	.02	.00
☐ 406	Joe Wallis DP	.05	.02	.00
☐ 407	Pete Vuckovich	.10	.05	.01
☐ 408	Charlie Moore DP	.05	.02	.00
☐ 409	Willie Wilson	1.50	.75	.15
☐ 410	Darrell Evans	.30	.15	.03
☐ 411	Hits Record	.40	.20	.04

		NRMT	VG-E	GOOD
	Season: G. Sisler			
	Career: Ty Cobb			
☐ 412	RBI Record	.40	.20	.04
	Season: Hack Wilson			
	Career: Hank Aaron			
☐ 413	Home Run Record ..	.60	.30	.06
	Season: Roger Maris			
	Career: Hank Aaron			
☐ 414	Batting Record	.40	.20	.04
	Season: R. Hornsby			
	Career: Ty Cobb			
☐ 415	Steals Record	.40	.20	.04
	Season: Lou Brock			
	Career: Lou Brock			
☐ 416	Wins Record	.20	.10	.02
	Season: Jack Chesbro			
	Career: Cy Young			
☐ 417	Strikeout Record DP	.20	.10	.02
	Season: Nolan Ryan			
	Career: W. Johnson			
☐ 418	ERA Record DP	.10	.05	.01
	Season: Dutch			
	Leonard			
	Career: W. Johnson			
☐ 419	Dick Ruthven	.10	.05	.01
☐ 420	Ken Griffey	.30	.15	.03
☐ 421	Doug DeCinces	.20	.10	.02
☐ 422	Ruppert Jones	.10	.05	.01
☐ 423	Bob Montgomery ...	.10	.05	.01
☐ 424	Angels Team/Mgr. ..	.40	.20	.04
	Jim Fregosi (checklist back)			
☐ 425	Rick Manning	.10	.05	.01
☐ 426	Chris Speier	.10	.05	.01
☐ 427	Andy Replogle	.10	.05	.01
☐ 428	Bobby Valentine	.20	.10	.02
☐ 429	John Urrea DP	.05	.02	.00
☐ 430	Dave Parker	1.25	.60	.12
☐ 431	Glenn Borgmann ...	.10	.05	.01
☐ 432	Dave Heaverlo	.10	.05	.01
☐ 433	Larry Biittner	.10	.05	.01
☐ 434	Ken Clay	.10	.05	.01
☐ 435	Gene Tenace	.10	.05	.01
☐ 436	Hector Cruz	.10	.05	.01
☐ 437	Rick Williams	.10	.05	.01
☐ 438	Horace Speed	.10	.05	.01
☐ 439	Frank White	.20	.10	.02
☐ 440	Rusty Staub	.30	.15	.03
☐ 441	Lee Lacy	.10	.05	.01

		NRMT	VG-E	GOOD
☐ 442	Doyle Alexander	.20	.10	.02
☐ 443	Bruce Bochte	.10	.05	.01
☐ 444	Aurelio Lopez	.20	.10	.02
☐ 445	Steve Henderson ...	.10	.05	.01
☐ 446	Jim Lonborg	.20	.10	.02
☐ 447	Manny Sanguillen ...	.20	.10	.02
☐ 448	Moose Haas	.10	.05	.01
☐ 449	Bombo Rivera	.10	.05	.01
☐ 450	Dave Concepcion ...	.20	.10	.02
☐ 451	Royals Team/Mgr. ..	.40	.20	.04
	Whitey Herzog (checklist back)			
☐ 452	Jerry Morales	.10	.05	.01
☐ 453	Chris Knapp	.10	.05	.01
☐ 454	Len Randle	.10	.05	.01
☐ 455	Bill Lee DP	.10	.05	.01
☐ 456	Chuck Baker	.10	.05	.01
☐ 457	Bruce Sutter	.60	.30	.06
☐ 458	Jim Essian	.10	.05	.01
☐ 459	Sid Monge	.10	.05	.01
☐ 460	Graig Nettles	.40	.20	.04
☐ 461	Jim Barr DP	.05	.02	.00
☐ 462	Otto Velez	.10	.05	.01
☐ 463	Steve Comer	.10	.05	.01
☐ 464	Joe Nolan	.10	.05	.01
☐ 465	Reggie Smith	.20	.10	.02
☐ 466	Mark Littell	.10	.05	.01
☐ 467	Don Kessinger DP ..	.10	.05	.01
☐ 468	Stan Bahnsen DP ..	.05	.02	.00
☐ 469	Lance Parrish	3.00	1.50	.30
☐ 470	Garry Maddox DP ..	.10	.05	.01
☐ 471	Joaquin Andujar ...	.20	.10	.02
☐ 472	Craig Kusick	.10	.05	.01
☐ 473	Dave Roberts	.10	.05	.01
☐ 474	Dick Davis	.10	.05	.01
☐ 475	Dan Driessen	.10	.05	.01
☐ 476	Tom Poquette	.10	.05	.01
☐ 477	Bob Grich	.20	.10	.02
☐ 478	Juan Beniquez	.10	.05	.01
☐ 479	Padres Team/Mgr. ..	.40	.20	.04
	Roger Craig (checklist back)			
☐ 480	Fred Lynn	.75	.35	.07
☐ 481	Skip Lockwood	.10	.05	.01
☐ 482	Craig Reynolds	.10	.05	.01
☐ 483	Checklist 4 DP	.10	.02	.00
☐ 484	Rick Waits	.10	.05	.01
☐ 485	Bucky Dent	.30	.15	.03
☐ 486	Bob Knepper	.20	.10	.02

		NRMT	VG-E	GOOD
☐ 487	Miguel Dilone	.10	.05	.01
☐ 488	Bob Owchinko	.10	.05	.01
☐ 489	Larry Cox UER (photo actually Dave Rader)	.10	.05	.01
☐ 490	Al Cowens	.10	.05	.01
☐ 491	Tippy Martinez	.10	.05	.01
☐ 492	Bob Bailor	.10	.05	.01
☐ 493	Larry Christenson	.10	.05	.01
☐ 494	Jerry White	.10	.05	.01
☐ 495	Tony Perez	.50	.25	.05
☐ 496	Barry Bonnell DP	.05	.02	.00
☐ 497	Glenn Abbott	.10	.05	.01
☐ 498	Rich Chiles	.10	.05	.01
☐ 499	Rangers Team/Mgr. Pat Corrales (checklist back)	.40	.20	.04
☐ 500	Ron Guidry	1.00	.50	.10
☐ 501	Junior Kennedy	.10	.05	.01
☐ 502	Steve Braun	.10	.05	.01
☐ 503	Terry Humphrey	.10	.05	.01
☐ 504	Larry McWilliams	.30	.15	.03
☐ 505	Ed Kranepool	.10	.05	.01
☐ 506	John D'Acquisto	.10	.05	.01
☐ 507	Tony Armas	.20	.10	.02
☐ 508	Charlie Hough	.20	.10	.02
☐ 509	Mario Mendoza	.10	.05	.01
☐ 510	Ted Simmons	.40	.20	.04
☐ 511	Paul Reuschel DP	.05	.02	.00
☐ 512	Jack Clark	2.25	1.10	.22
☐ 513	Dave Johnson	.20	.10	.02
☐ 514	Mike Proly	.10	.05	.01
☐ 515	Enos Cabell	.10	.05	.01
☐ 516	Champ Summers DP	.05	.02	.00
☐ 517	Al Bumbry	.10	.05	.01
☐ 518	Jim Umbarger	.10	.05	.01
☐ 519	Ben Oglivie	.20	.10	.02
☐ 520	Gary Carter	2.50	1.25	.25
☐ 521	Sam Ewing	.10	.05	.01
☐ 522	Ken Holtzman	.20	.10	.02
☐ 523	John Milner	.10	.05	.01
☐ 524	Tom Burgmeier	.10	.05	.01
☐ 525	Freddie Patek	.10	.05	.01
☐ 526	Dodgers Team/Mgr. Tom Lasorda (checklist back)	.50	.25	.05
☐ 527	Lerrin LaGrow	.10	.05	.01
☐ 528	Wayne Gross DP	.05	.02	.00
☐ 529	Brian Asselstine	.10	.05	.01
☐ 530	Frank Tanana	.20	.10	.02
☐ 531	Fernando Gonzalez	.10	.05	.01
☐ 532	Buddy Schultz	.10	.05	.01
☐ 533	Leroy Stanton	.10	.05	.01
☐ 534	Ken Forsch	.10	.05	.01
☐ 535	Ellis Valentine	.10	.05	.01
☐ 536	Jerry Reuss	.20	.10	.02
☐ 537	Tom Veryzer	.10	.05	.01
☐ 538	Mike Ivie DP	.05	.02	.00
☐ 539	John Ellis	.10	.05	.01
☐ 540	Greg Luzinski	.30	.15	.03
☐ 541	Jim Slaton	.10	.05	.01
☐ 542	Rick Bosetti	.10	.05	.01
☐ 543	Kiko Garcia	.10	.05	.01
☐ 544	Fergie Jenkins	.60	.30	.06
☐ 545	John Stearns	.10	.05	.01
☐ 546	Bill Russell	.20	.10	.02
☐ 547	Clint Hurdle	.10	.05	.01
☐ 548	Enrique Romo	.10	.05	.01
☐ 549	Bob Bailey	.10	.05	.01
☐ 550	Sal Bando	.20	.10	.02
☐ 551	Cubs Team/Mgr. Herman Franks (checklist back)	.40	.20	.04
☐ 552	Jose Morales	.10	.05	.01
☐ 553	Denny Walling	.10	.05	.01
☐ 554	Matt Keough	.10	.05	.01
☐ 555	Biff Pocoroba	.10	.05	.01
☐ 556	Mike Lum	.10	.05	.01
☐ 557	Ken Brett	.10	.05	.01
☐ 558	Jay Johnstone	.20	.10	.02
☐ 559	Greg Pryor	.10	.05	.01
☐ 560	John Montefusco	.20	.10	.02
☐ 561	Ed Ott	.10	.05	.01
☐ 562	Dusty Baker	.30	.15	.03
☐ 563	Roy Thomas	.10	.05	.01
☐ 564	Jerry Turner	.10	.05	.01
☐ 565	Rico Carty	.20	.10	.02
☐ 566	Nino Espinosa	.10	.05	.01
☐ 567	Richie Hebner	.10	.05	.01
☐ 568	Carlos Lopez	.10	.05	.01
☐ 569	Bob Sykes	.10	.05	.01
☐ 570	Cesar Cedeno	.20	.10	.02
☐ 571	Darrell Porter	.10	.05	.01
☐ 572	Rod Gilbreath	.10	.05	.01
☐ 573	Jim Kern	.10	.05	.01
☐ 574	Claudell Washington	.20	.10	.02
☐ 575	Luis Tiant	.30	.15	.03
☐ 576	Mike Parrott	.10	.05	.01

		NRMT	VG-E	GOOD
☐ 577	Brewers Team/Mgr.	.40	.20	.04
	George Bamberger			
	(checklist back)			
☐ 578	Pete Broberg	.10	.05	.01
☐ 579	Greg Gross	.10	.05	.01
☐ 580	Ron Fairly	.10	.05	.01
☐ 581	Darold Knowles	.10	.05	.01
☐ 582	Paul Blair	.10	.05	.01
☐ 583	Julio Cruz	.10	.05	.01
☐ 584	Jim Rooker	.10	.05	.01
☐ 585	Hal McRae	.20	.10	.02
☐ 586	Bob Horner	1.50	.75	.15
☐ 587	Ken Reitz	.10	.05	.01
☐ 588	Tom Murphy	.10	.05	.01
☐ 589	Terry Whitfield	.10	.05	.01
☐ 590	J.R. Richard	.20	.10	.02
☐ 591	Mike Hargrove	.20	.10	.02
☐ 592	Mike Krukow	.20	.10	.02
☐ 593	Rick Dempsey	.20	.10	.02
☐ 594	Bob Shirley	.10	.05	.01
☐ 595	Phil Niekro	1.25	.60	.12
☐ 596	Jim Wohlford	.10	.05	.01
☐ 597	Bob Stanley	.10	.05	.01
☐ 598	Mark Wagner	.10	.05	.01
☐ 599	Jim Spencer	.10	.05	.01
☐ 600	George Foster	.60	.30	.06
☐ 601	Dave LaRoche	.10	.05	.01
☐ 602	Checklist 5	.40	.05	.01
☐ 603	Rudy May	.10	.05	.01
☐ 604	Jeff Newman	.10	.05	.01
☐ 605	Rick Monday DP	.10	.05	.01
☐ 606	Expos Team/Mgr.	.40	.20	.04
	Dick Williams (check-			
	list back)			
☐ 607	Omar Moreno	.10	.05	.01
☐ 608	Dave McKay	.10	.05	.01
☐ 609	Silvio Martinez	.10	.05	.01
☐ 610	Mike Schmidt	5.00	2.50	.50
☐ 611	Jim Norris	.10	.05	.01
☐ 612	Rick Honeycutt	.50	.25	.05
☐ 613	Mike Edwards	.10	.05	.01
☐ 614	Willie Hernandez	.40	.20	.04
☐ 615	Ken Singleton	.20	.10	.02
☐ 616	Billy Almon	.10	.05	.01
☐ 617	Terry Puhl	.10	.05	.01
☐ 618	Jerry Remy	.10	.05	.01
☐ 619	Ken Landreaux	.30	.15	.03
☐ 620	Bert Campaneris	.20	.10	.02
☐ 621	Pat Zachry	.10	.05	.01

		NRMT	VG-E	GOOD
☐ 622	Dave Collins	.10	.05	.01
☐ 623	Bob McClure	.10	.05	.01
☐ 624	Larry Herndon	.10	.05	.01
☐ 625	Mark Fidrych	.20	.10	.02
☐ 626	Yankees Team/Mgr.	.50	.25	.05
	Bob Lemon (checklist			
	back)			
☐ 627	Gary Serum	.10	.05	.01
☐ 628	Del Unser	.10	.05	.01
☐ 629	Gene Garber	.10	.05	.01
☐ 630	Bake McBride	.10	.05	.01
☐ 631	Jorge Orta	.10	.05	.01
☐ 632	Don Kirkwood	.10	.05	.01
☐ 633	Rob Wilfong DP	.05	.02	.00
☐ 634	Paul Lindblad	.10	.05	.01
☐ 635	Don Baylor	.75	.35	.07
☐ 636	Wayne Garland	.10	.05	.01
☐ 637	Bill Robinson	.20	.10	.02
☐ 638	Al Fitzmorris	.10	.05	.01
☐ 639	Manny Trillo	.10	.05	.01
☐ 640	Eddie Murray	5.00	2.50	.50
☐ 641	Bobby Castillo	.10	.05	.01
☐ 642	Wilbur Howard DP	.05	.02	.00
☐ 643	Tom Hausman	.10	.05	.01
☐ 644	Manny Mota	.20	.10	.02
☐ 645	George Scott DP	.10	.05	.01
☐ 646	Rick Sweet	.10	.05	.01
☐ 647	Bob Lacey	.10	.05	.01
☐ 648	Lou Piniella	.30	.15	.03
☐ 649	John Curtis	.10	.05	.01
☐ 650	Pete Rose	4.50	2.25	.45
☐ 651	Mike Caldwell	.10	.05	.01
☐ 652	Stan Papi	.10	.05	.01
☐ 653	Warren Brusstar DP	.05	.02	.00
☐ 654	Rick Miller	.10	.05	.01
☐ 655	Jerry Koosman	.30	.15	.03
☐ 656	Hosken Powell	.10	.05	.01
☐ 657	George Medich	.10	.05	.01
☐ 658	Taylor Duncan	.10	.05	.01
☐ 659	Mariners Team/Mgr.	.40	.20	.04
	Darrell Johnson			
	(checklist back)			
☐ 660	Ron LeFlore DP	.10	.05	.01
☐ 661	Bruce Kison	.10	.05	.01
☐ 662	Kevin Bell	.10	.05	.01
☐ 663	Mike Vail	.10	.05	.01
☐ 664	Doug Bird	.10	.05	.01
☐ 665	Lou Brock	1.50	.75	.15
☐ 666	Rich Dauer	.10	.05	.01

		NRMT	VG-E	GOOD
☐ 667	Don Hood	.10	.05	.01
☐ 668	Bill North	.10	.05	.01
☐ 669	Checklist 6	.40	.05	.01
☐ 670	Jim Hunter DP	.60	.30	.06
☐ 671	Joe Ferguson DP	.05	.02	.00
☐ 672	Ed Halicki	.10	.05	.01
☐ 673	Tom Hutton	.10	.05	.01
☐ 674	Dave Tomlin	.10	.05	.01
☐ 675	Tim McCarver	.30	.15	.03
☐ 676	Johnny Sutton	.10	.05	.01
☐ 677	Larry Parrish	.20	.10	.02
☐ 678	Geoff Zahn	.10	.05	.01
☐ 679	Derrel Thomas	.10	.05	.01
☐ 680	Carlton Fisk	1.25	.60	.12
☐ 681	John Henry Johnson	.10	.05	.01
☐ 682	Dave Chalk	.10	.05	.01
☐ 683	Dan Meyer DP	.05	.02	.00
☐ 684	Jamie Easterly DP	.05	.02	.00
☐ 685	Sixto Lezcano	.10	.05	.01
☐ 686	Ron Schueler DP	.05	.02	.00
☐ 687	Rennie Stennett	.10	.05	.01
☐ 688	Mike Willis	.10	.05	.01
☐ 689	Orioles Team/Mgr. (checklist back) Earl Weaver	.50	.25	.05
☐ 690	Buddy Bell DP	.10	.05	.01
☐ 691	Dock Ellis DP	.05	.02	.00
☐ 692	Mickey Stanley	.10	.05	.01
☐ 693	Dave Rader	.10	.05	.01
☐ 694	Burt Hooton	.10	.05	.01
☐ 695	Keith Hernandez	2.25	1.10	.22
☐ 696	Andy Hassler	.10	.05	.01
☐ 697	Dave Bergman	.10	.05	.01
☐ 698	Bill Stein	.10	.05	.01
☐ 699	Hal Dues	.10	.05	.01
☐ 700	Reggie Jackson DP	1.75	.85	.17
☐ 701	Orioles Prospects Mark Corey John Flinn Sammy Stewart	.20	.10	.02
☐ 702	Red Sox Prospects Joel Finch Garry Hancock Allen Ripley	.20	.10	.02
☐ 703	Angels Prospects Jim Anderson Dave Frost Bob Slater	.10	.05	.01
☐ 704	White Sox Prospects Ross Baumgarten Mike Colbern Mike Squires	.10	.05	.01
☐ 705	Indians Prospects Alfredo Griffin Tim Norrid Dave Oliver	1.00	.50	.10
☐ 706	Tigers Prospects Dave Stegman Dave Tobik Kip Young	.10	.05	.01
☐ 707	Royals Prospects Randy Bass Jim Gaudet Randy McGilberry	.30	.15	.03
☐ 708	Brewers Prospects Kevin Bass Eddie Romero Ned Yost	1.25	.60	.12
☐ 709	Twins Prospects Sam Perlozzo Rick Sofield Kevin Stanfield	.10	.05	.01
☐ 710	Yankees Prospects Brian Doyle Mike Heath Dave Rajsich	.30	.15	.03
☐ 711	A's Prospects Dwayne Murphy Bruce Robinson Alan Wirth	.30	.15	.03
☐ 712	Mariners Prospects Bud Anderson Greg Biercevicz Byron McLaughlin	.10	.05	.01
☐ 713	Rangers Prospects Danny Darwin Pat Putnam Billy Sample	.40	.20	.04
☐ 714	Blue Jays Prospects Victor Cruz Pat Kelly Ernie Whitt	.40	.20	.04
☐ 715	Braves Prospects Bruce Benedict Glenn Hubbard Larry Whisenton	.30	.15	.03
☐ 716	Cubs Prospects Dave Geisel	.10	.05	.01

1980 Topps

		NRMT	VG-E	GOOD
	Karl Pagel			
	Scot Thompson			
☐ 717	Reds Prospects	.40	.20	.04
	Mike LaCoss			
	Ron Oester			
	Harry Spilman			
☐ 718	Astros Prospects ...	.10	.05	.01
	Bruce Bochy			
	Mike Fischlin			
	Don Pisker			
☐ 719	Dodgers Prospects ..	10.00	5.00	1.00
	Pedro Guerrero			
	Rudy Law			
	Joe Simpson			
☐ 720	Expos Prospects ...	.30	.15	.03
	Jerry Fry			
	Jerry Pirtle			
	Scott Sanderson			
☐ 721	Mets Prospects	.30	.15	.03
	Juan Berenguer			
	Dwight Bernard			
	Dan Norman			
☐ 722	Phillies Prospects ...	2.50	1.10	.22
	Jim Morrison			
	Lonnie Smith			
	Jim Wright			
☐ 723	Pirates Prospects ...	.30	.15	.03
	Dale Berra			
	Eugenio Cotes			
	Ben Wiltbank			
☐ 724	Cardinals Prospects .	.40	.20	.04
	Tom Bruno			
	George Frazier			
	Terry Kennedy			
☐ 725	Padres Prospects ...	.10	.05	.01
	Jim Beswick			
	Steve Mura			
	Broderick Perkins			
☐ 726	Giants Prospects ...	.20	.10	.02
	Greg Johnston			
	Joe Strain			
	John Tamargo			

*The cards in this 726-card set measure 2 ½"
by 3 ½". In 1980 Topps released another set
of the same size and number of cards as the
previous two years. As with those sets, Topps
again has produced 66 double-printed cards in
the set; they are noted by DP in the checklist
below. The player's name appears over the
picture and his position and team are found in
pennant design. Every card carries a facsimile
autograph. Team cards feature a team checklist of players in the set on the back and the
manager's name on the front. Cards 1-6 show
Highlights (HL) of the 1979 season, cards 201-
207 are League Leaders, and cards 661-686
feature American and National League rookie
"Future Stars," one card for each team showing
three young prospects.*

		MINT	EXC	G-VG
COMPLETE SET (726)		165.00	75.00	15.00
COMMON PLAYER (1-726) ..		.10	.05	.01
COMMON DP's (1-726)		.05	.02	.00
☐ 1	HL: Brock and Yaz, . Enter 3000 hit circle	1.50	.35	.07
☐ 2	HL: Willie McCovey, . 512th homer sets new mark for NL lefties	.75	.35	.07
☐ 3	HL: Manny Mota, All- time pinch-hits, 145	.20	.10	.02

			MINT	EXC	G-VG
☐	4	HL: Pete Rose, Career Record 10th season with 200 or more hits	2.00	1.00	.20
☐	5	HL: Garry Templeton, First with 100 hits from each side of plate	.20	.10	.02
☐	6	HL: Del Unser, 3rd cons. pinch homer sets new ML standard	.10	.05	.01
☐	7	Mike Lum	.10	.05	.01
☐	8	Craig Swan	.10	.05	.01
☐	9	Steve Braun	.10	.05	.01
☐	10	Denny Martinez	.20	.10	.02
☐	11	Jimmy Sexton	.10	.05	.01
☐	12	John Curtis DP	.05	.02	.00
☐	13	Ron Pruitt	.10	.05	.01
☐	14	Dave Cash	.10	.05	.01
☐	15	Bill Campbell	.10	.05	.01
☐	16	Jerry Narron	.10	.05	.01
☐	17	Bruce Sutter	.40	.20	.04
☐	18	Ron Jackson	.10	.05	.01
☐	19	Balor Moore	.10	.05	.01
☐	20	Dan Ford	.10	.05	.01
☐	21	Manny Sarmiento	.10	.05	.01
☐	22	Pat Putnam	.10	.05	.01
☐	23	Derrel Thomas	.10	.05	.01
☐	24	Jim Slaton	.10	.05	.01
☐	25	Lee Mazzilli	.10	.05	.01
☐	26	Marty Pattin	.10	.05	.01
☐	27	Del Unser	.10	.05	.01
☐	28	Bruce Kison	.10	.05	.01
☐	29	Mark Wagner	.10	.05	.01
☐	30	Vida Blue	.20	.10	.02
☐	31	Jay Johnstone	.20	.10	.02
☐	32	Julio Cruz DP	.10	.05	.01
☐	33	Tony Scott	.10	.05	.01
☐	34	Jeff Newman DP	.05	.02	.00
☐	35	Luis Tiant	.20	.10	.02
☐	36	Rusty Torres	.10	.05	.01
☐	37	Kiko Garcia	.10	.05	.01
☐	38	Dan Spillner DP	.05	.02	.00
☐	39	Rowland Office	.10	.05	.01
☐	40	Carlton Fisk	1.25	.60	.12
☐	41	Rangers Team/Mgr. Pat Corrales (checklist back)	.35	.17	.03
☐	42	David Palmer	.35	.17	.03

			MINT	EXC	G-VG
☐	43	Bombo Rivera	.10	.05	.01
☐	44	Bill Fahey	.10	.05	.01
☐	45	Frank White	.30	.15	.03
☐	46	Rico Carty	.20	.10	.02
☐	47	Bill Bonham DP	.05	.02	.00
☐	48	Rick Miller	.10	.05	.01
☐	49	Mario Guerrero	.10	.05	.01
☐	50	J.R. Richard	.20	.10	.02
☐	51	Joe Ferguson DP	.05	.02	.00
☐	52	Warren Brusstar	.10	.05	.01
☐	53	Ben Oglivie	.20	.10	.02
☐	54	Dennis Lamp	.10	.05	.01
☐	55	Bill Madlock	.30	.15	.03
☐	56	Bobby Valentine	.20	.10	.02
☐	57	Pete Vuckovich	.10	.05	.01
☐	58	Doug Flynn	.10	.05	.01
☐	59	Eddy Putman	.10	.05	.01
☐	60	Bucky Dent	.30	.15	.03
☐	61	Gary Serum	.10	.05	.01
☐	62	Mike Ivie	.10	.05	.01
☐	63	Bob Stanley	.10	.05	.01
☐	64	Joe Nolan	.10	.05	.01
☐	65	Al Bumbry	.10	.05	.01
☐	66	Royals Team/Mgr. Jim Frey (checklist back)	.35	.17	.03
☐	67	Doyle Alexander	.20	.10	.02
☐	68	Larry Harlow	.10	.05	.01
☐	69	Rick Williams	.10	.05	.01
☐	70	Gary Carter	2.00	1.00	.20
☐	71	John Milner DP	.05	.02	.00
☐	72	Fred Howard DP	.05	.02	.00
☐	73	Dave Collins	.10	.05	.01
☐	74	Sid Monge	.10	.05	.01
☐	75	Bill Russell	.20	.10	.02
☐	76	John Stearns	.10	.05	.01
☐	77	Dave Stieb	4.00	2.00	.40
☐	78	Ruppert Jones	.10	.05	.01
☐	79	Bob Owchinko	.10	.05	.01
☐	80	Ron LeFlore	.10	.05	.01
☐	81	Ted Sizemore	.10	.05	.01
☐	82	Astros Team/Mgr. Bill Virdon (checklist back)	.35	.17	.03
☐	83	Steve Trout	.30	.15	.03
☐	84	Gary Lavelle	.10	.05	.01
☐	85	Ted Simmons	.40	.20	.04
☐	86	Dave Hamilton	.10	.05	.01
☐	87	Pepe Frias	.10	.05	.01

		MINT	EXC	G-VG
☐ 88	Ken Landreaux	.10	.05	.01
☐ 89	Don Hood	.10	.05	.01
☐ 90	Manny Trillo	.10	.05	.01
☐ 91	Rick Dempsey	.10	.05	.01
☐ 92	Rick Rhoden	.20	.10	.02
☐ 93	Dave Roberts DP	.05	.02	.00
☐ 94	Neil Allen	.40	.20	.04
☐ 95	Cecil Cooper	.30	.15	.03
☐ 96	A's Team/Mgr.	.35	.17	.03
	Jim Marshall (checklist back)			
☐ 97	Bill Lee	.10	.05	.01
☐ 98	Jerry Terrell	.10	.05	.01
☐ 99	Victor Cruz	.10	.05	.01
☐ 100	Johnny Bench	2.75	1.35	.27
☐ 101	Aurelio Lopez	.10	.05	.01
☐ 102	Rich Dauer	.10	.05	.01
☐ 103	Bill Caudill	.30	.15	.03
☐ 104	Manny Mota	.20	.10	.02
☐ 105	Frank Tanana	.20	.10	.02
☐ 106	Jeff Leonard	1.50	.75	.15
☐ 107	Francisco Barrios	.10	.05	.01
☐ 108	Bob Horner	.75	.35	.07
☐ 109	Bill Travers	.10	.05	.01
☐ 110	Fred Lynn DP	.35	.17	.03
☐ 111	Bob Knepper	.20	.10	.02
☐ 112	White Sox Team/Mgr.	.35	.17	.03
	Tony LaRussa (checklist back)			
☐ 113	Geoff Zahn	.10	.05	.01
☐ 114	Juan Beniquez	.10	.05	.01
☐ 115	Sparky Lyle	.20	.10	.02
☐ 116	Larry Cox	.10	.05	.01
☐ 117	Dock Ellis	.10	.05	.01
☐ 118	Phil Garner	.10	.05	.01
☐ 119	Sammy Stewart	.10	.05	.01
☐ 120	Greg Luzinski	.20	.10	.02
☐ 121	Checklist 1	.30	.04	.01
☐ 122	Dave Rosello DP	.05	.02	.00
☐ 123	Lynn Jones	.10	.05	.01
☐ 124	Dave Lemanczyk	.10	.05	.01
☐ 125	Tony Perez	.50	.25	.05
☐ 126	Dave Tomlin	.10	.05	.01
☐ 127	Gary Thomasson	.10	.05	.01
☐ 128	Tom Burgmeier	.10	.05	.01
☐ 129	Craig Reynolds	.10	.05	.01
☐ 130	Amos Otis	.20	.10	.02
☐ 131	Paul Mitchell	.10	.05	.01
☐ 132	Biff Pocoroba	.10	.05	.01

		MINT	EXC	G-VG
☐ 133	Jerry Turner	.10	.05	.01
☐ 134	Matt Keough	.10	.05	.01
☐ 135	Bill Buckner	.30	.15	.03
☐ 136	Dick Ruthven	.10	.05	.01
☐ 137	John Castino	.10	.05	.01
☐ 138	Ross Baumgarten	.10	.05	.01
☐ 139	Dane Iorg	.20	.10	.02
☐ 140	Rich Gossage	.50	.25	.05
☐ 141	Gary Alexander	.10	.05	.01
☐ 142	Phil Huffman	.10	.05	.01
☐ 143	Bruce Bochte DP	.10	.05	.01
☐ 144	Steve Comer	.10	.05	.01
☐ 145	Darrell Evans	.30	.15	.03
☐ 146	Bob Welch	.60	.30	.06
☐ 147	Terry Puhl	.10	.05	.01
☐ 148	Manny Sanguillen	.20	.10	.02
☐ 149	Tom Hume	.10	.05	.01
☐ 150	Jason Thompson	.10	.05	.01
☐ 151	Tom Hausman DP	.05	.02	.00
☐ 152	John Fulgham	.10	.05	.01
☐ 153	Tim Blackwell	.10	.05	.01
☐ 154	Lary Sorensen	.10	.05	.01
☐ 155	Jerry Remy	.10	.05	.01
☐ 156	Tony Brizzolara	.10	.05	.01
☐ 157	Willie Wilson DP	.20	.10	.02
☐ 158	Rob Picciolo DP	.05	.02	.00
☐ 159	Ken Clay	.10	.05	.01
☐ 160	Eddie Murray	3.50	1.75	.35
☐ 161	Larry Christenson	.10	.05	.01
☐ 162	Bob Randall	.10	.05	.01
☐ 163	Steve Swisher	.10	.05	.01
☐ 164	Greg Pryor	.10	.05	.01
☐ 165	Omar Moreno	.10	.05	.01
☐ 166	Glenn Abbott	.10	.05	.01
☐ 167	Jack Clark	2.00	1.00	.20
☐ 168	Rick Waits	.10	.05	.01
☐ 169	Luis Gomez	.10	.05	.01
☐ 170	Burt Hooton	.10	.05	.01
☐ 171	Fernando Gonzalez	.10	.05	.01
☐ 172	Ron Hodges	.10	.05	.01
☐ 173	John Henry Johnson	.10	.05	.01
☐ 174	Ray Knight	.20	.10	.02
☐ 175	Rick Reuschel	.35	.15	.03
☐ 176	Champ Summers	.10	.05	.01
☐ 177	Dave Heaverlo	.10	.05	.01
☐ 178	Tim McCarver	.30	.15	.03
☐ 179	Ron Davis	.20	.10	.02
☐ 180	Warren Cromartie	.10	.05	.01
☐ 181	Moose Haas	.10	.05	.01

		MINT	EXC	G-VG
☐ 182	Ken Reitz	.10	.05	.01
☐ 183	Jim Anderson DP	.05	.02	.00
☐ 184	Steve Renko DP	.05	.02	.00
☐ 185	Hal McRae	.20	.10	.02
☐ 186	Junior Moore	.10	.05	.01
☐ 187	Alan Ashby	.10	.05	.01
☐ 188	Terry Crowley	.10	.05	.01
☐ 189	Kevin Kobel	.10	.05	.01
☐ 190	Buddy Bell	.30	.15	.03
☐ 191	Ted Martinez	.10	.05	.01
☐ 192	Braves Team/Mgr.	.35	.17	.03
	Bobby Cox (checklist back)			
☐ 193	Dave Goltz	.10	.05	.01
☐ 194	Mike Easler	.20	.10	.02
☐ 195	John Montefusco	.20	.10	.02
☐ 196	Lance Parrish	1.50	.75	.15
☐ 197	Byron McLaughlin	.10	.05	.01
☐ 198	Dell Alston DP	.05	.02	.00
☐ 199	Mike LaCoss	.20	.10	.02
☐ 200	Jim Rice	1.50	.75	.15
☐ 201	Batting Leaders	.30	.15	.03
	Keith Hernandez			
	Fred Lynn			
☐ 202	Home Run Leaders	.20	.10	.02
	Dave Kingman			
	Gorman Thomas			
☐ 203	RBI Leaders	.30	.15	.03
	Dave Winfield			
	Don Baylor			
☐ 204	Stolen Base Leaders	.20	.10	.02
	Omar Moreno			
	Willie Wilson			
☐ 205	Victory Leaders	.20	.10	.02
	Joe Niekro			
	Phil Niekro			
	Mike Flanagan			
☐ 206	Strikeout Leaders	1.00	.50	.10
	J.R. Richard			
	Nolan Ryan			
☐ 207	ERA Leaders	.20	.10	.02
	J.R. Richard			
	Ron Guidry			
☐ 208	Wayne Cage	.10	.05	.01
☐ 209	Von Joshua	.10	.05	.01
☐ 210	Steve Carlton	2.25	1.10	.22
☐ 211	Dave Skaggs DP	.05	.02	.00
☐ 212	Dave Roberts	.10	.05	.01
☐ 213	Mike Jorgensen DP	.05	.02	.00

		MINT	EXC	G-VG
☐ 214	Angels Team/Mgr.	.35	.17	.03
	Jim Fregosi (checklist back)			
☐ 215	Sixto Lezcano	.10	.05	.01
☐ 216	Phil Mankowski	.10	.05	.01
☐ 217	Ed Halicki	.10	.05	.01
☐ 218	Jose Morales	.10	.05	.01
☐ 219	Steve Mingori	.10	.05	.01
☐ 220	Dave Concepcion	.30	.15	.03
☐ 221	Joe Cannon	.10	.05	.01
☐ 222	Ron Hassey	.30	.15	.03
☐ 223	Bob Sykes	.10	.05	.01
☐ 224	Willie Montanez	.10	.05	.01
☐ 225	Lou Piniella	.30	.15	.03
☐ 226	Bill Stein	.10	.05	.01
☐ 227	Len Barker	.10	.05	.01
☐ 228	Johnny Oates	.10	.05	.01
☐ 229	Jim Bibby	.10	.05	.01
☐ 230	Dave Winfield	2.00	1.00	.20
☐ 231	Steve McCatty	.10	.05	.01
☐ 232	Alan Trammell	2.50	1.25	.25
☐ 233	LaRue Washington	.10	.05	.01
☐ 234	Vern Ruhle	.10	.05	.01
☐ 235	Andre Dawson	2.50	1.25	.25
☐ 236	Marc Hill	.10	.05	.01
☐ 237	Scott McGregor	.20	.10	.02
☐ 238	Rob Wilfong	.10	.05	.01
☐ 239	Don Aase	.10	.05	.01
☐ 240	Dave Kingman	.30	.15	.03
☐ 241	Checklist 2	.30	.04	.01
☐ 242	Lamar Johnson	.10	.05	.01
☐ 243	Jerry Augustine	.10	.05	.01
☐ 244	Cardinals Team/Mgr.	.35	.17	.03
	Ken Boyer (checklist back)			
☐ 245	Phil Niekro	.90	.45	.09
☐ 246	Tim Foli DP	.05	.02	.00
☐ 247	Frank Riccelli	.10	.05	.01
☐ 248	Jamie Quirk	.10	.05	.01
☐ 249	Jim Clancy	.10	.05	.01
☐ 250	Jim Kaat	.40	.20	.04
☐ 251	Kip Young	.10	.05	.01
☐ 252	Ted Cox	.10	.05	.01
☐ 253	John Montague	.10	.05	.01
☐ 254	Paul Dade DP	.05	.02	.00
☐ 255	Dusty Baker DP	.10	.05	.01
☐ 256	Roger Erickson	.10	.05	.01
☐ 257	Larry Herndon	.10	.05	.01
☐ 258	Paul Moskau	.10	.05	.01

		MINT	EXC	G-VG
☐ 259	Mets Team/Mgr. Joe Torre (checklist back)	.40	.20	.04
☐ 260	Al Oliver	.30	.15	.03
☐ 261	Dave Chalk	.10	.05	.01
☐ 262	Benny Ayala	.10	.05	.01
☐ 263	Dave LaRoche DP	.05	.02	.00
☐ 264	Bill Robinson	.20	.10	.02
☐ 265	Robin Yount	4.00	2.00	.40
☐ 266	Bernie Carbo	.10	.05	.01
☐ 267	Dan Schatzeder	.10	.05	.01
☐ 268	Rafael Landestoy	.10	.05	.01
☐ 269	Dave Tobik	.10	.05	.01
☐ 270	Mike Schmidt DP	2.00	1.00	.20
☐ 271	Dick Drago DP	.05	.02	.00
☐ 272	Ralph Garr	.10	.05	.01
☐ 273	Eduardo Rodriguez	.10	.05	.01
☐ 274	Dale Murphy	6.00	3.00	.60
☐ 275	Jerry Koosman	.30	.15	.03
☐ 276	Tom Veryzer	.10	.05	.01
☐ 277	Rick Bosetti	.10	.05	.01
☐ 278	Jim Spencer	.10	.05	.01
☐ 279	Rob Andrews	.10	.05	.01
☐ 280	Gaylord Perry	1.00	.50	.10
☐ 281	Paul Blair	.10	.05	.01
☐ 282	Mariners Team/Mgr. Darrell Johnson (checklist back)	.35	.17	.03
☐ 283	John Ellis	.10	.05	.01
☐ 284	Larry Murray DP	.05	.02	.00
☐ 285	Don Baylor	.40	.20	.04
☐ 286	Darold Knowles DP	.05	.02	.00
☐ 287	John Lowenstein	.10	.05	.01
☐ 288	Dave Rozema	.10	.05	.01
☐ 289	Bruce Bochy	.10	.05	.01
☐ 290	Steve Garvey	2.00	1.00	.20
☐ 291	Randy Scarberry	.10	.05	.01
☐ 292	Dale Berra	.10	.05	.01
☐ 293	Elias Sosa	.10	.05	.01
☐ 294	Charlie Spikes	.10	.05	.01
☐ 295	Larry Gura	.10	.05	.01
☐ 296	Dave Rader	.10	.05	.01
☐ 297	Tim Johnson	.10	.05	.01
☐ 298	Ken Holtzman	.20	.10	.02
☐ 299	Steve Henderson	.10	.05	.01
☐ 300	Ron Guidry	.75	.35	.07
☐ 301	Mike Edwards	.10	.05	.01
☐ 302	Dodgers Team/Mgr.	.45	.22	.04

		MINT	EXC	G-VG
	Tom Lasorda (checklist back)			
☐ 303	Bill Castro	.10	.05	.01
☐ 304	Butch Wynegar	.10	.05	.01
☐ 305	Randy Jones	.10	.05	.01
☐ 306	Denny Walling	.10	.05	.01
☐ 307	Rick Honeycutt	.10	.05	.01
☐ 308	Mike Hargrove	.20	.10	.02
☐ 309	Larry McWilliams	.10	.05	.01
☐ 310	Dave Parker	1.25	.60	.12
☐ 311	Roger Metzger	.10	.05	.01
☐ 312	Mike Barlow	.10	.05	.01
☐ 313	Johnny Grubb	.10	.05	.01
☐ 314	Tim Stoddard	.20	.10	.02
☐ 315	Steve Kemp	.20	.10	.02
☐ 316	Bob Lacey	.10	.05	.01
☐ 317	Mike Anderson DP	.05	.02	.00
☐ 318	Jerry Reuss	.20	.10	.02
☐ 319	Chris Speier	.10	.05	.01
☐ 320	Dennis Eckersley	.50	.25	.05
☐ 321	Keith Hernandez	1.50	.75	.15
☐ 322	Claudell Washington	.20	.10	.02
☐ 323	Mick Kelleher	.10	.05	.01
☐ 324	Tom Underwood	.10	.05	.01
☐ 325	Dan Driessen	.10	.05	.01
☐ 326	Bo McLaughlin	.10	.05	.01
☐ 327	Ray Fosse DP	.05	.02	.00
☐ 328	Twins Team/Mgr. Gene Mauch (checklist back)	.35	.17	.03
☐ 329	Bert Roberge	.10	.05	.01
☐ 330	Al Cowens	.10	.05	.01
☐ 331	Richie Hebner	.10	.05	.01
☐ 332	Enrique Romo	.10	.05	.01
☐ 333	Jim Norris DP	.05	.02	.00
☐ 334	Jim Beattie	.10	.05	.01
☐ 335	Willie McCovey	1.50	.75	.15
☐ 336	George Medich	.10	.05	.01
☐ 337	Carney Lansford	1.50	.75	.15
☐ 338	John Wockenfuss	.10	.05	.01
☐ 339	John D'Acquisto	.10	.05	.01
☐ 340	Ken Singleton	.20	.10	.02
☐ 341	Jim Essian	.10	.05	.01
☐ 342	Odell Jones	.10	.05	.01
☐ 343	Mike Vail	.10	.05	.01
☐ 344	Randy Lerch	.10	.05	.01
☐ 345	Larry Parrish	.20	.10	.02
☐ 346	Buddy Solomon	.10	.05	.01
☐ 347	Harry Chappas	.10	.05	.01

		MINT	EXC	G-VG
☐ 348	Checklist 3	.30	.04	.01
☐ 349	Jack Brohamer	.10	.05	.01
☐ 350	George Hendrick	.20	.10	.02
☐ 351	Bob Davis	.10	.05	.01
☐ 352	Dan Briggs	.10	.05	.01
☐ 353	Andy Hassler	.10	.05	.01
☐ 354	Rick Auerbach	.10	.05	.01
☐ 355	Gary Matthews	.20	.10	.02
☐ 356	Padres Team/Mgr. Jerry Coleman (checklist back)	.35	.17	.03
☐ 357	Bob McClure	.10	.05	.01
☐ 358	Lou Whitaker	1.50	.75	.15
☐ 359	Randy Moffitt	.10	.05	.01
☐ 360	Darrell Porter DP	.10	.05	.01
☐ 361	Wayne Garland	.10	.05	.01
☐ 362	Danny Goodwin	.10	.05	.01
☐ 363	Wayne Gross	.10	.05	.01
☐ 364	Ray Burris	.10	.05	.01
☐ 365	Bobby Murcer	.30	.15	.03
☐ 366	Rob Dressler	.10	.05	.01
☐ 367	Billy Smith	.10	.05	.01
☐ 368	Willie Aikens	.25	.12	.02
☐ 369	Jim Kern	.10	.05	.01
☐ 370	Cesar Cedeno	.20	.10	.02
☐ 371	Jack Morris	1.25	.60	.12
☐ 372	Joel Youngblood	.10	.05	.01
☐ 373	Dan Petry DP	.40	.20	.04
☐ 374	Jim Gantner	.20	.10	.02
☐ 375	Ross Grimsley	.10	.05	.01
☐ 376	Gary Allenson	.10	.05	.01
☐ 377	Junior Kennedy	.10	.05	.01
☐ 378	Jerry Mumphrey	.10	.05	.01
☐ 379	Kevin Bell	.10	.05	.01
☐ 380	Garry Maddox	.20	.10	.02
☐ 381	Cubs Team/Mgr. Preston Gomez (checklist back)	.35	.17	.03
☐ 382	Dave Freisleben	.10	.05	.01
☐ 383	Ed Ott	.10	.05	.01
☐ 384	Joey McLaughlin	.10	.05	.01
☐ 385	Enos Cabell	.10	.05	.01
☐ 386	Darrell Jackson	.10	.05	.01
☐ 387A	Fred Stanley (yellow name on front)	1.00	.50	.10
☐ 387B	Fred Stanley (red name on front)	.10	.05	.01
☐ 388	Mike Paxton	.10	.05	.01
☐ 389	Pete LaCock	.10	.05	.01

		MINT	EXC	G-VG
☐ 390	Fergie Jenkins	.40	.20	.04
☐ 391	Tony Armas DP	.10	.05	.01
☐ 392	Milt Wilcox	.10	.05	.01
☐ 393	Ozzie Smith	4.50	2.25	.45
☐ 394	Reggie Cleveland	.10	.05	.01
☐ 395	Ellis Valentine	.10	.05	.01
☐ 396	Dan Meyer	.10	.05	.01
☐ 397	Roy Thomas DP	.05	.02	.00
☐ 398	Barry Foote	.10	.05	.01
☐ 399	Mike Proly DP	.05	.02	.00
☐ 400	George Foster	.50	.25	.05
☐ 401	Pete Falcone	.10	.05	.01
☐ 402	Merv Rettenmund	.10	.05	.01
☐ 403	Pete Redfern DP	.05	.02	.00
☐ 404	Orioles Team/Mgr. Earl Weaver (checklist back)	.40	.20	.04
☐ 405	Dwight Evans	.80	.40	.08
☐ 406	Paul Molitor	1.50	.75	.15
☐ 407	Tony Solaita	.10	.05	.01
☐ 408	Bill North	.10	.05	.01
☐ 409	Paul Splittorff	.10	.05	.01
☐ 410	Bobby Bonds	.30	.15	.03
☐ 411	Frank LaCorte	.10	.05	.01
☐ 412	Thad Bosley	.10	.05	.01
☐ 413	Allen Ripley	.10	.05	.01
☐ 414	George Scott	.10	.05	.01
☐ 415	Bill Atkinson	.10	.05	.01
☐ 416	Tom Brookens	.10	.05	.01
☐ 417	Craig Chamberlain DP	.05	.02	.00
☐ 418	Roger Freed DP	.05	.02	.00
☐ 419	Vic Correll	.10	.05	.01
☐ 420	Butch Hobson	.10	.05	.01
☐ 421	Doug Bird	.10	.05	.01
☐ 422	Larry Milbourne	.10	.05	.01
☐ 423	Dave Frost	.10	.05	.01
☐ 424	Yankees Team/Mgr. Dick Howser (checklist back)	.40	.20	.04
☐ 425	Mark Belanger	.20	.10	.02
☐ 426	Grant Jackson	.10	.05	.01
☐ 427	Tom Hutton DP	.05	.02	.00
☐ 428	Pat Zachry	.10	.05	.01
☐ 429	Duane Kuiper	.10	.05	.01
☐ 430	Larry Hisle DP	.10	.05	.01
☐ 431	Mike Krukow	.20	.10	.02
☐ 432	Willie Norwood	.10	.05	.01
☐ 433	Rich Gale	.10	.05	.01
☐ 434	Johnnie LeMaster	.10	.05	.01

		MINT	EXC	G-VG
☐ 435	Don Gullett	.20	.10	.02
☐ 436	Billy Almon	.10	.05	.01
☐ 437	Joe Niekro	.30	.15	.03
☐ 438	Dave Revering	.10	.05	.01
☐ 439	Mike Phillips	.10	.05	.01
☐ 440	Don Sutton	1.00	.50	.10
☐ 441	Eric Soderholm	.10	.05	.01
☐ 442	Jorge Orta	.10	.05	.01
☐ 443	Mike Parrott	.10	.05	.01
☐ 444	Alvis Woods	.10	.05	.01
☐ 445	Mark Fidrych	.20	.10	.02
☐ 446	Duffy Dyer	.10	.05	.01
☐ 447	Nino Espinosa	.10	.05	.01
☐ 448	Jim Wohlford	.10	.05	.01
☐ 449	Doug Bair	.10	.05	.01
☐ 450	George Brett	4.00	2.00	.40
☐ 451	Indians Team/Mgr.	.35	.17	.03
	Dave Garcia (checklist back)			
☐ 452	Steve Dillard	.10	.05	.01
☐ 453	Mike Bacsik	.10	.05	.01
☐ 454	Tom Donohue	.10	.05	.01
☐ 455	Mike Torrez	.10	.05	.01
☐ 456	Frank Taveras	.10	.05	.01
☐ 457	Bert Blyleven	.50	.25	.05
☐ 458	Billy Sample	.10	.05	.01
☐ 459	Mickey Lolich DP	.10	.05	.01
☐ 460	Willie Randolph	.30	.15	.03
☐ 461	Dwayne Murphy	.10	.05	.01
☐ 462	Mike Sadek DP	.05	.02	.00
☐ 463	Jerry Royster	.10	.05	.01
☐ 464	John Denny	.20	.10	.02
☐ 465	Rick Monday	.20	.10	.02
☐ 466	Mike Squires	.10	.05	.01
☐ 467	Jesse Jefferson	.10	.05	.01
☐ 468	Aurelio Rodriguez	.10	.05	.01
☐ 469	Randy Niemann DP	.05	.02	.00
☐ 470	Bob Boone	.40	.20	.04
☐ 471	Hosken Powell DP	.05	.02	.00
☐ 472	Willie Hernandez	.30	.15	.03
☐ 473	Bump Wills	.10	.05	.01
☐ 474	Steve Busby	.10	.05	.01
☐ 475	Cesar Geronimo	.10	.05	.01
☐ 476	Bob Shirley	.10	.05	.01
☐ 477	Buck Martinez	.10	.05	.01
☐ 478	Gil Flores	.10	.05	.01
☐ 479	Expos Team/Mgr.	.30	.15	.03
	Dick Williams (checklist back)			
☐ 480	Bob Watson	.20	.10	.02
☐ 481	Tom Paciorek	.10	.05	.01
☐ 482	Rickey Henderson	60.00	22.00	4.00
☐ 483	Bo Diaz	.10	.05	.01
☐ 484	Checklist 4	.30	.04	.01
☐ 485	Mickey Rivers	.20	.10	.02
☐ 486	Mike Tyson DP	.05	.02	.00
☐ 487	Wayne Nordhagen	.10	.05	.01
☐ 488	Roy Howell	.10	.05	.01
☐ 489	Preston Hanna DP	.05	.02	.00
☐ 490	Lee May	.10	.05	.01
☐ 491	Steve Mura DP	.05	.02	.00
☐ 492	Todd Cruz	.10	.05	.01
☐ 493	Jerry Martin	.10	.05	.01
☐ 494	Craig Minetto	.10	.05	.01
☐ 495	Bake McBride	.10	.05	.01
☐ 496	Silvio Martinez	.10	.05	.01
☐ 497	Jim Mason	.10	.05	.01
☐ 498	Danny Darwin	.10	.05	.01
☐ 499	Giants Team/Mgr.	.35	.17	.03
	Dave Bristol (checklist back)			
☐ 500	Tom Seaver	2.00	1.00	.20
☐ 501	Rennie Stennett	.10	.05	.01
☐ 502	Rich Wortham DP	.05	.02	.00
☐ 503	Mike Cubbage	.10	.05	.01
☐ 504	Gene Garber	.10	.05	.01
☐ 505	Bert Campaneris	.20	.10	.02
☐ 506	Tom Buskey	.10	.05	.01
☐ 507	Leon Roberts	.10	.05	.01
☐ 508	U.L. Washington	.10	.05	.01
☐ 509	Ed Glynn	.10	.05	.01
☐ 510	Ron Cey	.30	.15	.03
☐ 511	Eric Wilkins	.10	.05	.01
☐ 512	Jose Cardenal	.10	.05	.01
☐ 513	Tom Dixon DP	.05	.02	.00
☐ 514	Steve Ontiveros	.10	.05	.01
☐ 515	Mike Caldwell	.10	.05	.01
☐ 516	Hector Cruz	.10	.05	.01
☐ 517	Don Stanhouse	.10	.05	.01
☐ 518	Nelson Norman	.10	.05	.01
☐ 519	Steve Nicosia	.10	.05	.01
☐ 520	Steve Rogers	.10	.05	.01
☐ 521	Ken Brett	.10	.05	.01
☐ 522	Jim Morrison	.10	.05	.01
☐ 523	Ken Henderson	.10	.05	.01
☐ 524	Jim Wright DP	.05	.02	.00
☐ 525	Clint Hurdle	.10	.05	.01
☐ 526	Phillies Team/Mgr.	.40	.20	.04

		MINT	EXC	G-VG
	Dallas Green (checklist back)			
☐ 527	Doug Rau DP	.05	.02	.00
☐ 528	Adrian Devine	.10	.05	.01
☐ 529	Jim Barr	.10	.05	.01
☐ 530	Jim Sundberg DP	.10	.05	.01
☐ 531	Eric Rasmussen	.10	.05	.01
☐ 532	Willie Horton	.20	.10	.02
☐ 533	Checklist 5	.30	.04	.01
☐ 534	Andre Thornton	.20	.10	.02
☐ 535	Bob Forsch	.10	.05	.01
☐ 536	Lee Lacy	.10	.05	.01
☐ 537	Alex Trevino	.20	.10	.02
☐ 538	Joe Strain	.10	.05	.01
☐ 539	Rudy May	.10	.05	.01
☐ 540	Pete Rose	4.00	2.00	.40
☐ 541	Miguel Dilone	.10	.05	.01
☐ 542	Joe Coleman	.10	.05	.01
☐ 543	Pat Kelly	.10	.05	.01
☐ 544	Rick Sutcliffe	3.50	1.75	.35
☐ 545	Jeff Burroughs	.10	.05	.01
☐ 546	Rick Langford	.10	.05	.01
☐ 547	John Wathan	.20	.10	.02
☐ 548	Dave Rajsich	.10	.05	.01
☐ 549	Larry Wolfe	.10	.05	.01
☐ 550	Ken Griffey	.30	.15	.03
☐ 551	Pirates Team/Mgr.	.35	.17	.03
	Chuck Tanner (checklist back)			
☐ 552	Bill Nahorodny	.10	.05	.01
☐ 553	Dick Davis	.10	.05	.01
☐ 554	Art Howe	.20	.10	.02
☐ 555	Ed Figueroa	.10	.05	.01
☐ 556	Joe Rudi	.20	.10	.02
☐ 557	Mark Lee	.10	.05	.01
☐ 558	Alfredo Griffin	.20	.10	.02
☐ 559	Dale Murray	.10	.05	.01
☐ 560	Dave Lopes	.20	.10	.02
☐ 561	Eddie Whitson	.20	.10	.02
☐ 562	Joe Wallis	.10	.05	.01
☐ 563	Will McEnaney	.10	.05	.01
☐ 564	Rick Manning	.10	.05	.01
☐ 565	Dennis Leonard	.20	.10	.02
☐ 566	Bud Harrelson	.10	.05	.01
☐ 567	Skip Lockwood	.10	.05	.01
☐ 568	Gary Roenicke	.20	.10	.02
☐ 569	Terry Kennedy	.20	.10	.02
☐ 570	Roy Smalley	.10	.05	.01
☐ 571	Joe Sambito	.10	.05	.01
☐ 572	Jerry Morales DP	.05	.02	.00
☐ 573	Kent Tekulve	.20	.10	.02
☐ 574	Scot Thompson	.10	.05	.01
☐ 575	Ken Kravec	.10	.05	.01
☐ 576	Jim Dwyer	.10	.05	.01
☐ 577	Blue Jays Team/Mgr.	.30	.15	.03
	Bobby Mattick (checklist back)			
☐ 578	Scott Sanderson	.20	.10	.02
☐ 579	Charlie Moore	.10	.05	.01
☐ 580	Nolan Ryan	5.00	2.50	.50
☐ 581	Bob Bailor	.10	.05	.01
☐ 582	Brian Doyle	.10	.05	.01
☐ 583	Bob Stinson	.10	.05	.01
☐ 584	Kurt Bevacqua	.10	.05	.01
☐ 585	Al Hrabosky	.20	.10	.02
☐ 586	Mitchell Page	.10	.05	.01
☐ 587	Garry Templeton	.20	.10	.02
☐ 588	Greg Minton	.10	.05	.01
☐ 589	Chet Lemon	.10	.05	.01
☐ 590	Jim Palmer	1.75	.85	.17
☐ 591	Rick Cerone	.10	.05	.01
☐ 592	Jon Matlack	.10	.05	.01
☐ 593	Jesus Alou	.10	.05	.01
☐ 594	Dick Tidrow	.10	.05	.01
☐ 595	Don Money	.10	.05	.01
☐ 596	Rick Matula	.10	.05	.01
☐ 597	Tom Poquette	.10	.05	.01
☐ 598	Fred Kendall DP	.05	.02	.00
☐ 599	Mike Norris	.10	.05	.01
☐ 600	Reggie Jackson	2.50	1.25	.25
☐ 601	Buddy Schultz	.10	.05	.01
☐ 602	Brian Downing	.20	.10	.02
☐ 603	Jack Billingham DP	.05	.02	.00
☐ 604	Glenn Adams	.10	.05	.01
☐ 605	Terry Forster	.20	.10	.02
☐ 606	Reds Team/Mgr.	.35	.17	.03
	John McNamara (checklist back)			
☐ 607	Woodie Fryman	.10	.05	.01
☐ 608	Alan Bannister	.10	.05	.01
☐ 609	Ron Reed	.10	.05	.01
☐ 610	Willie Stargell	1.50	.75	.15
☐ 611	Jerry Garvin DP	.05	.02	.00
☐ 612	Cliff Johnson	.10	.05	.01
☐ 613	Randy Stein	.10	.05	.01
☐ 614	John Hiller	.20	.10	.02
☐ 615	Doug DeCinces	.20	.10	.02
☐ 616	Gene Richards	.10	.05	.01

		MINT	EXC	G-VG
☐ 617	Joaquin Andujar	.20	.10	.02
☐ 618	Bob Montgomery DP	.05	.02	.00
☐ 619	Sergio Ferrer	.10	.05	.01
☐ 620	Richie Zisk	.10	.05	.01
☐ 621	Bob Grich	.20	.10	.02
☐ 622	Mario Soto	.20	.10	.02
☐ 623	Gorman Thomas	.20	.10	.02
☐ 624	Lerrin LaGrow	.10	.05	.01
☐ 625	Chris Chambliss	.20	.10	.02
☐ 626	Tigers Team/Mgr.	.40	.20	.04
	Sparky Anderson			
	(checklist back)			
☐ 627	Pedro Borbon	.10	.05	.01
☐ 628	Doug Capilla	.10	.05	.01
☐ 629	Jim Todd	.10	.05	.01
☐ 630	Larry Bowa	.30	.15	.03
☐ 631	Mark Littell	.10	.05	.01
☐ 632	Barry Bonnell	.10	.05	.01
☐ 633	Bob Apodaca	.10	.05	.01
☐ 634	Glenn Borgmann DP	.05	.02	.00
☐ 635	John Candelaria	.30	.15	.03
☐ 636	Toby Harrah	.20	.10	.02
☐ 637	Joe Simpson	.10	.05	.01
☐ 638	Mark Clear	.20	.10	.02
☐ 639	Larry Biittner	.10	.05	.01
☐ 640	Mike Flanagan	.20	.10	.02
☐ 641	Ed Kranepool	.10	.05	.01
☐ 642	Ken Forsch DP	.10	.05	.01
☐ 643	John Mayberry	.20	.10	.02
☐ 644	Charlie Hough	.20	.10	.02
☐ 645	Rick Burleson	.20	.10	.02
☐ 646	Checklist 6	.30	.04	.01
☐ 647	Milt May	.10	.05	.01
☐ 648	Roy White	.20	.10	.02
☐ 649	Tom Griffin	.10	.05	.01
☐ 650	Joe Morgan	1.50	.75	.15
☐ 651	Rollie Fingers	.60	.30	.06
☐ 652	Mario Mendoza	.10	.05	.01
☐ 653	Stan Bahnsen	.10	.05	.01
☐ 654	Bruce Boisclair DP ..	.05	.02	.00
☐ 655	Tug McGraw	.30	.15	.03
☐ 656	Larvell Blanks	.10	.05	.01
☐ 657	Dave Edwards	.10	.05	.01
☐ 658	Chris Knapp	.10	.05	.01
☐ 659	Brewers Team/Mgr.	.35	.17	.03
	George Bamberger			
	(checklist back)			
☐ 660	Rusty Staub	.30	.15	.03
☐ 661	Orioles Rookies	.20	.10	.02

		MINT	EXC	G-VG
	Mark Corey			
	Dave Ford			
	Wayne Krenchicki			
☐ 662	Red Sox Rookies ...	.20	.10	.02
	Joel Finch			
	Mike O'Berry			
	Chuck Rainey			
☐ 663	Angels Rookies	.60	.30	.06
	Ralph Botting			
	Bob Clark			
	Dickie Thon			
☐ 664	White Sox Rookies ..	.20	.10	.02
	Mike Colbern			
	Guy Hoffman			
	Dewey Robinson			
☐ 665	Indians Rookies	.30	.15	.03
	Larry Andersen			
	Bobby Cuellar			
	Sandy Wihtol			
☐ 666	Tigers Rookies	.20	.10	.02
	Mike Chris			
	Al Greene			
	Bruce Robbins			
☐ 667	Royals Rookies	1.50	.75	.15
	Renie Martin			
	Bill Paschall			
	Dan Quisenberry			
☐ 668	Brewers Rookies ...	.20	.10	.02
	Danny Boitano			
	Willie Mueller			
	Lenn Sakata			
☐ 669	Twins Rookies	.40	.20	.04
	Dan Graham			
	Rick Sofield			
	Gary Ward			
☐ 670	Yankees Rookies ...	.20	.10	.02
	Bobby Brown			
	Brad Gulden			
	Darryl Jones			
☐ 671	A's Rookies	1.00	.50	.10
	Derek Bryant			
	Brian Kingman			
	Mike Morgan			
☐ 672	Mariners Rookies ...	.20	.10	.02
	Charlie Beamon			
	Rodney Craig			
	Rafael Vasquez			
☐ 673	Rangers Rookies ...	.20	.10	.02
	Brian Allard			

		MINT	EXC	G-VG
	Jerry Don Gleaton			
	Greg Mahlberg			
☐ 674	Blue Jays Rookies ..	.20	.10	.02
	Butch Edge			
	Pat Kelly			
	Ted Wilborn			
☐ 675	Braves Rookies	.20	.10	.02
	Bruce Benedict			
	Larry Bradford			
	Eddie Miller			
☐ 676	Cubs Rookies	.20	.10	.02
	Dave Geisel			
	Steve Macko			
	Karl Pagel			
☐ 677	Reds Rookies	.20	.10	.02
	Art DeFreites			
	Frank Pastore			
	Harry Spilman			
☐ 678	Astros Rookies	.20	.10	.02
	Reggie Baldwin			
	Alan Knicely			
	Pete Ladd			
☐ 679	Dodgers Rookies ...	.50	.25	.05
	Joe Beckwith			
	Mickey Hatcher			
	Dave Patterson			
☐ 680	Expos Rookies	.35	.17	.03
	Tony Bernazard			
	Randy Miller			
	John Tamargo			
☐ 681	Mets Rookies	10.00	5.00	1.00
	Dan Norman			
	Jesse Orosco			
	Mike Scott			
☐ 682	Phillies Rookies	.30	.15	.03
	Ramon Aviles			
	Dickie Noles			
	Kevin Saucier			
☐ 683	Pirates Rookies	.20	.10	.02
	Dorian Boyland			
	Alberto Lois			
	Harry Saferight			
☐ 684	Cardinals Rookies ..	.75	.35	.07
	George Frazier			
	Tom Herr			
	Dan O'Brien			
☐ 685	Padres Rookies	.30	.15	.03
	Tim Flannery			
	Brian Greer			

		MINT	EXC	G-VG
	Jim Wilhelm			
☐ 686	Giants Rookies	.20	.10	.02
	Greg Johnston			
	Dennis Littlejohn			
	Phil Nastu			
☐ 687	Mike Heath DP	.05	.02	.00
☐ 688	Steve Stone	.20	.10	.02
☐ 689	Red Sox Team/Mgr. .	.35	.17	.03
	Don Zimmer (check-			
	list back)			
☐ 690	Tommy John	.50	.25	.05
☐ 691	Ivan DeJesus	.10	.05	.01
☐ 692	Rawly Eastwick DP ..	.05	.02	.00
☐ 693	Craig Kusick	.10	.05	.01
☐ 694	Jim Rooker	.10	.05	.01
☐ 695	Reggie Smith	.20	.10	.02
☐ 696	Julio Gonzalez	.10	.05	.01
☐ 697	David Clyde	.10	.05	.01
☐ 698	Oscar Gamble	.10	.05	.01
☐ 699	Floyd Bannister	.10	.05	.01
☐ 700	Rod Carew DP	1.25	.60	.12
☐ 701	Ken Oberkfell	.30	.15	.03
☐ 702	Ed Farmer	.10	.05	.01
☐ 703	Otto Velez	.10	.05	.01
☐ 704	Gene Tenace	.20	.10	.02
☐ 705	Freddie Patek	.10	.05	.01
☐ 706	Tippy Martinez	.10	.05	.01
☐ 707	Elliott Maddox	.10	.05	.01
☐ 708	Bob Tolan	.10	.05	.01
☐ 709	Pat Underwood	.10	.05	.01
☐ 710	Graig Nettles	.30	.15	.03
☐ 711	Bob Galasso	.10	.05	.01
☐ 712	Rodney Scott	.10	.05	.01
☐ 713	Terry Whitfield	.10	.05	.01
☐ 714	Fred Norman	.10	.05	.01
☐ 715	Sal Bando	.20	.10	.02
☐ 716	Lynn McGlothen	.10	.05	.01
☐ 717	Mickey Klutts DP ...	.05	.02	.00
☐ 718	Greg Gross	.10	.05	.01
☐ 719	Don Robinson	.20	.10	.02
☐ 720	Carl Yastrzemski DP .	1.75	.85	.17
☐ 721	Paul Hartzell	.10	.05	.01
☐ 722	Jose Cruz	.20	.10	.02
☐ 723	Shane Rawley	.20	.10	.02
☐ 724	Jerry White	.10	.05	.01
☐ 725	Rick Wise	.10	.05	.01
☐ 726	Steve Yeager	.20	.10	.02

1981 Topps

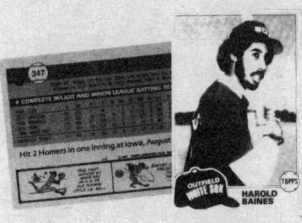

The cards in this 726-card set measure 2 ½"
by 3 ½". League Leaders (1-8), Record Breakers (201-208), and Post-season cards (401-
404) are topical subsets found in this set
marketed by Topps in 1981. The team cards
are all grouped together (661-686) and feature
team checklist backs and a very small photo
of the team's manager in the upper right corner
of the obverse. The obverses carry the player's
position and team in a baseball cap design,
and the company name is printed in a small
baseball. The backs are red and gray. The 66
double-printed cards are noted in the checklist
by DP. The set is quite popular with collectors
partly due to the presence of rookie cards of
Fernando Valenzuela, Tim Raines, Kirk Gib-
son, Harold Baines, John Tudor, Lloyd Mose-
by, Hubie Brooks, Mike Boddicker, and Tony Pena.

	MINT	EXC	G-VG
COMPLETE SET (726)	90.00	45.00	9.00
COMMON PLAYER (1-726)	.08	.04	.01
COMMON DP's (1-726)	.04	.02	.00

			MINT	EXC	G-VG
☐	1	Batting Leaders .... George Brett Bill Buckner	.65	.15	.03
☐	2	Home Run Leaders . Reggie Jackson Ben Oglivie Mike Schmidt	.35	.17	.03
☐	3	RBI Leaders .... Cecil Cooper Mike Schmidt	.20	.10	.02
☐	4	Stolen Base Leaders Rickey Henderson Ron LeFlore	.18	.09	.01
☐	5	Victory Leaders ...... Steve Stone Steve Carlton	.15	.07	.01
☐	6	Strikeout Leaders ... Len Barker Steve Carlton	.15	.07	.01
☐	7	ERA Leaders .... Rudy May Don Sutton	.12	.06	.01
☐	8	Leading Firemen .... Dan Quisenberry Rollie Fingers Tom Hume	.12	.06	.01
☐	9	Pete LaCock DP	.04	.02	.00
☐	10	Mike Flanagan	.12	.06	.01
☐	11	Jim Wohlford DP ..	.04	.02	.00
☐	12	Mark Clear	.08	.04	.01
☐	13	Joe Charboneau	.12	.06	.01
☐	14	John Tudor	1.50	.75	.15
☐	15	Larry Parrish	.12	.06	.01
☐	16	Ron Davis	.08	.04	.01
☐	17	Cliff Johnson	.08	.04	.01
☐	18	Glenn Adams	.08	.04	.01
☐	19	Jim Clancy	.08	.04	.01
☐	20	Jeff Burroughs	.12	.06	.01
☐	21	Ron Oester	.12	.06	.01
☐	22	Danny Darwin	.08	.04	.01
☐	23	Alex Trevino	.08	.04	.01
☐	24	Don Stanhouse	.08	.04	.01
☐	25	Sixto Lezcano	.08	.04	.01
☐	26	U.L. Washington	.08	.04	.01
☐	27	Champ Summers DP ..	.04	.02	.00
☐	28	Enrique Romo	.08	.04	.01
☐	29	Gene Tenace	.12	.06	.01
☐	30	Jack Clark	.65	.30	.06
☐	31	Checklist 1-121 DP ..	.08	.01	.00
☐	32	Ken Oberkfell	.08	.04	.01
☐	33	Rick Honeycutt	.08	.04	.01
☐	34	Aurelio Rodriguez ..	.08	.04	.01
☐	35	Mitchell Page	.08	.04	.01
☐	36	Ed Farmer	.08	.04	.01
☐	37	Gary Roenicke	.08	.04	.01
☐	38	Win Remmerswaal ..	.08	.04	.01
☐	39	Tom Veryzer	.08	.04	.01

			MINT	EXC	G-VG
☐	40	Tug McGraw	.15	.07	.01
☐	41	Ranger Rookies	.12	.06	.01
		Bob Babcock			
		John Butcher			
		Jerry Don Gleaton			
☐	42	Jerry White DP	.04	.02	.00
☐	43	Jose Morales	.08	.04	.01
☐	44	Larry McWilliams	.08	.04	.01
☐	45	Enos Cabell	.08	.04	.01
☐	46	Rick Bosetti	.08	.04	.01
☐	47	Ken Brett	.08	.04	.01
☐	48	Dave Skaggs	.08	.04	.01
☐	49	Bob Shirley	.08	.04	.01
☐	50	Dave Lopes	.15	.07	.01
☐	51	Bill Robinson DP	.04	.02	.00
☐	52	Hector Cruz	.08	.04	.01
☐	53	Kevin Saucier	.08	.04	.01
☐	54	Ivan DeJesus	.08	.04	.01
☐	55	Mike Norris	.08	.04	.01
☐	56	Buck Martinez	.08	.04	.01
☐	57	Dave Roberts	.08	.04	.01
☐	58	Joel Youngblood	.08	.04	.01
☐	59	Dan Petry	.12	.06	.01
☐	60	Willie Randolph	.15	.07	.01
☐	61	Butch Wynegar	.08	.04	.01
☐	62	Joe Pettini	.08	.04	.01
☐	63	Steve Renko DP	.04	.02	.00
☐	64	Brian Asselstine	.08	.04	.01
☐	65	Scott McGregor	.12	.06	.01
☐	66	Royals Rookies	.12	.06	.01
		Manny Castillo			
		Tim Ireland			
		Mike Jones			
☐	67	Ken Kravec	.08	.04	.01
☐	68	Matt Alexander DP	.04	.02	.00
☐	69	Ed Halicki	.08	.04	.01
☐	70	Al Oliver DP	.12	.06	.01
☐	71	Hal Dues	.08	.04	.01
☐	72	Barry Evans DP	.04	.02	.00
☐	73	Doug Bair	.08	.04	.01
☐	74	Mike Hargrove	.12	.06	.01
☐	75	Reggie Smith	.15	.07	.01
☐	76	Mario Mendoza	.08	.04	.01
☐	77	Mike Barlow	.08	.04	.01
☐	78	Steve Dillard	.08	.04	.01
☐	79	Bruce Robbins	.08	.04	.01
☐	80	Rusty Staub	.20	.10	.02
☐	81	Dave Stapleton	.12	.06	.01
☐	82	Astros Rookies DP	.12	.06	.01

			MINT	EXC	G-VG
		Danny Heep			
		Alan Knicely			
		Bobby Sprowl			
☐	83	Mike Proly	.08	.04	.01
☐	84	Johnnie LeMaster	.08	.04	.01
☐	85	Mike Caldwell	.08	.04	.01
☐	86	Wayne Gross	.08	.04	.01
☐	87	Rick Camp	.08	.04	.01
☐	88	Joe Lefebvre	.12	.06	.01
☐	89	Darrell Jackson	.08	.04	.01
☐	90	Bake McBride	.08	.04	.01
☐	91	Tim Stoddard DP	.08	.04	.01
☐	92	Mike Easler	.12	.06	.01
☐	93	Ed Glynn DP	.04	.02	.00
☐	94	Harry Spilman DP	.04	.02	.00
☐	95	Jim Sundberg	.12	.06	.01
☐	96	A's Rookies	.15	.07	.01
		Dave Beard			
		Ernie Camacho			
		Pat Dempsey			
☐	97	Chris Speier	.08	.04	.01
☐	98	Clint Hurdle	.08	.04	.01
☐	99	Eric Wilkins	.08	.04	.01
☐	100	Rod Carew	1.25	.60	.12
☐	101	Benny Ayala	.08	.04	.01
☐	102	Dave Tobik	.08	.04	.01
☐	103	Jerry Martin	.08	.04	.01
☐	104	Terry Forster	.12	.06	.01
☐	105	Jose Cruz	.15	.07	.01
☐	106	Don Money	.08	.04	.01
☐	107	Rich Wortham	.08	.04	.01
☐	108	Bruce Benedict	.08	.04	.01
☐	109	Mike Scott	1.75	.85	.17
☐	110	Carl Yastrzemski	1.75	.85	.17
☐	111	Greg Minton	.08	.04	.01
☐	112	White Sox Rookies	.12	.06	.01
		Rusty Kuntz			
		Fran Mullin			
		Leo Sutherland			
☐	113	Mike Phillips	.08	.04	.01
☐	114	Tom Underwood	.08	.04	.01
☐	115	Roy Smalley	.08	.04	.01
☐	116	Joe Simpson	.08	.04	.01
☐	117	Pete Falcone	.08	.04	.01
☐	118	Kurt Bevacqua	.08	.04	.01
☐	119	Tippy Martinez	.08	.04	.01
☐	120	Larry Bowa	.15	.07	.01
☐	121	Larry Harlow	.08	.04	.01
☐	122	John Denny	.12	.06	.01

		MINT	EXC	G-VG
☐ 123	Al Cowens	.08	.04	.01
☐ 124	Jerry Garvin	.08	.04	.01
☐ 125	Andre Dawson	1.00	.50	.10
☐ 126	Charlie Leibrandt	.40	.20	.04
☐ 127	Rudy Law	.08	.04	.01
☐ 128	Gary Allenson DP	.04	.02	.00
☐ 129	Art Howe	.15	.07	.01
☐ 130	Larry Gura	.12	.06	.01
☐ 131	Keith Moreland	.40	.20	.04
☐ 132	Tommy Boggs	.08	.04	.01
☐ 133	Jeff Cox	.08	.04	.01
☐ 134	Steve Mura	.08	.04	.01
☐ 135	Gorman Thomas	.20	.10	.02
☐ 136	Doug Capilla	.08	.04	.01
☐ 137	Hosken Powell	.08	.04	.01
☐ 138	Rich Dotson DP	.25	.12	.02
☐ 139	Oscar Gamble	.12	.06	.01
☐ 140	Bob Forsch	.08	.04	.01
☐ 141	Miguel Dilone	.08	.04	.01
☐ 142	Jackson Todd	.08	.04	.01
☐ 143	Dan Meyer	.08	.04	.01
☐ 144	Allen Ripley	.08	.04	.01
☐ 145	Mickey Rivers	.12	.06	.01
☐ 146	Bobby Castillo	.08	.04	.01
☐ 147	Dale Berra	.08	.04	.01
☐ 148	Randy Niemann	.08	.04	.01
☐ 149	Joe Nolan	.08	.04	.01
☐ 150	Mark Fidrych	.15	.07	.01
☐ 151	Claudell Washington	.15	.07	.01
☐ 152	John Urrea	.08	.04	.01
☐ 153	Tom Poquette	.08	.04	.01
☐ 154	Rick Langford	.08	.04	.01
☐ 155	Chris Chambliss	.15	.07	.01
☐ 156	Bob McClure	.08	.04	.01
☐ 157	John Wathan	.15	.07	.01
☐ 158	Fergie Jenkins	.30	.15	.03
☐ 159	Brian Doyle	.08	.04	.01
☐ 160	Garry Maddox	.12	.06	.01
☐ 161	Dan Graham	.08	.04	.01
☐ 162	Doug Corbett	.12	.06	.01
☐ 163	Bill Almon	.08	.04	.01
☐ 164	LaMarr Hoyt	.25	.12	.02
☐ 165	Tony Scott	.08	.04	.01
☐ 166	Floyd Bannister	.12	.06	.01
☐ 167	Terry Whitfield	.08	.04	.01
☐ 168	Don Robinson DP	.04	.02	.00
☐ 169	John Mayberry	.12	.06	.01
☐ 170	Ross Grimsley	.08	.04	.01
☐ 171	Gene Richards	.08	.04	.01

		MINT	EXC	G-VG
☐ 172	Gary Woods	.08	.04	.01
☐ 173	Bump Wills	.08	.04	.01
☐ 174	Doug Rau	.08	.04	.01
☐ 175	Dave Collins	.08	.04	.01
☐ 176	Mike Krukow	.12	.06	.01
☐ 177	Rick Peters	.08	.04	.01
☐ 178	Jim Essian DP	.04	.02	.00
☐ 179	Rudy May	.08	.04	.01
☐ 180	Pete Rose	3.50	1.75	.35
☐ 181	Elias Sosa	.08	.04	.01
☐ 182	Bob Grich	.15	.07	.01
☐ 183	Dick Davis DP	.04	.02	.00
☐ 184	Jim Dwyer	.08	.04	.01
☐ 185	Dennis Leonard	.12	.06	.01
☐ 186	Wayne Nordhagen	.08	.04	.01
☐ 187	Mike Parrott	.08	.04	.01
☐ 188	Doug DeCinces	.15	.07	.01
☐ 189	Craig Swan	.12	.06	.01
☐ 190	Cesar Cedeno	.15	.07	.01
☐ 191	Rick Sutcliffe	.60	.30	.06
☐ 192	Braves Rookies	.30	.15	.03
	Terry Harper			
	Ed Miller			
	Rafael Ramirez			
☐ 193	Pete Vuckovich	.12	.06	.01
☐ 194	Rod Scurry	.08	.04	.01
☐ 195	Rich Murray	.08	.04	.01
☐ 196	Duffy Dyer	.08	.04	.01
☐ 197	Jim Kern	.08	.04	.01
☐ 198	Jerry Dybzinski	.08	.04	.01
☐ 199	Chuck Rainey	.08	.04	.01
☐ 200	George Foster	.25	.12	.02
☐ 201	RB: Johnny Bench	.40	.20	.04
	Most homers, lifetime, catcher			
☐ 202	RB: Steve Carlton	.35	.17	.03
	Most strikeouts, lefthander, lifetime			
☐ 203	RB: Bill Gullickson	.12	.06	.01
	Most strikeouts, game, rookie			
☐ 204	RB: Ron LeFlore and Rodney Scott	.12	.06	.01
	Most stolen bases, teammates, season			
☐ 205	RB: Pete Rose	.75	.35	.07
	Most cons. seasons 600 or more at-bats			
☐ 206	RB: Mike Schmidt	.50	.25	.05

		MINT	EXC	G-VG
	Most homers, third baseman, season			
☐ 207	RB: Ozzie Smith	.15	.07	.01
	Most assists season, shortstop			
☐ 208	RB: Willie Wilson ...	.12	.06	.01
	Most at-bats, season			
☐ 209	Dickie Thon DP	.12	.06	.01
☐ 210	Jim Palmer	1.25	.60	.12
☐ 211	Derrel Thomas	.08	.04	.01
☐ 212	Steve Nicosia	.08	.04	.01
☐ 213	Al Holland	.12	.06	.01
☐ 214	Angels Rookies	.12	.06	.01
	Ralph Botting			
	Jim Dorsey			
	John Harris			
☐ 215	Larry Hisle	.12	.06	.01
☐ 216	John Henry Johnson	.08	.04	.01
☐ 217	Rich Hebner	.08	.04	.01
☐ 218	Paul Splittorff	.08	.04	.01
☐ 219	Ken Landreaux	.08	.04	.01
☐ 220	Tom Seaver	1.25	.60	.12
☐ 221	Bob Davis	.08	.04	.01
☐ 222	Jorge Orta	.08	.04	.01
☐ 223	Roy Lee Jackson ...	.08	.04	.01
☐ 224	Pat Zachry	.08	.04	.01
☐ 225	Ruppert Jones	.08	.04	.01
☐ 226	Manny Sanguillen DP	.08	.04	.01
☐ 227	Fred Martinez	.08	.04	.01
☐ 228	Tom Paciorek	.08	.04	.01
☐ 229	Rollie Fingers	.60	.30	.06
☐ 230	George Hendrick ...	.12	.06	.01
☐ 231	Joe Beckwith	.08	.04	.01
☐ 232	Mickey Klutts	.08	.04	.01
☐ 233	Skip Lockwood	.08	.04	.01
☐ 234	Lou Whitaker	.50	.25	.05
☐ 235	Scott Sanderson ...	.12	.06	.01
☐ 236	Mike Ivie	.08	.04	.01
☐ 237	Charlie Moore	.08	.04	.01
☐ 238	Willie Hernandez ...	.25	.12	.02
☐ 239	Rick Miller DP	.04	.02	.00
☐ 240	Nolan Ryan	2.75	1.35	.27
☐ 241	Checklist 122-242 DP	.08	.01	.00
☐ 242	Chet Lemon	.12	.06	.01
☐ 243	Sal Butera	.08	.04	.01
☐ 244	Cardinals Rookies ..	.15	.07	.01
	Tito Landrum			
	Al Olmsted			
	Andy Rincon			

		MINT	EXC	G-VG
☐ 245	Ed Figueroa	.08	.04	.01
☐ 246	Ed Ott DP	.04	.02	.00
☐ 247	Glenn Hubbard DP ..	.04	.02	.00
☐ 248	Joey McLaughlin ...	.08	.04	.01
☐ 249	Larry Cox	.08	.04	.01
☐ 250	Ron Guidry	.50	.25	.05
☐ 251	Tom Brookens	.08	.04	.01
☐ 252	Victor Cruz	.08	.04	.01
☐ 253	Dave Bergman	.08	.04	.01
☐ 254	Ozzie Smith	2.00	1.00	.20
☐ 255	Mark Littell	.08	.04	.01
☐ 256	Bombo Rivera	.08	.04	.01
☐ 257	Rennie Stennett ...	.08	.04	.01
☐ 258	Joe Price	.12	.06	.01
☐ 259	Mets Rookies	2.00	1.00	.20
	Juan Berenguer			
	Hubie Brooks			
	Mookie Wilson			
☐ 260	Ron Cey	.25	.12	.02
☐ 261	Rickey Henderson ..	6.50	3.25	.65
☐ 262	Sammy Stewart	.08	.04	.01
☐ 263	Brian Downing	.12	.06	.01
☐ 264	Jim Norris	.08	.04	.01
☐ 265	John Candelaria ...	.15	.07	.01
☐ 266	Tom Herr	.20	.10	.02
☐ 267	Stan Bahnsen	.08	.04	.01
☐ 268	Jerry Royster	.08	.04	.01
☐ 269	Ken Forsch	.08	.04	.01
☐ 270	Greg Luzinski	.20	.10	.02
☐ 271	Bill Castro	.08	.04	.01
☐ 272	Bruce Kimm	.08	.04	.01
☐ 273	Stan Papi	.08	.04	.01
☐ 274	Craig Chamberlain ..	.08	.04	.01
☐ 275	Dwight Evans	.40	.20	.04
☐ 276	Dan Spillner	.08	.04	.01
☐ 277	Alfredo Griffin	.15	.07	.01
☐ 278	Rick Sofield	.08	.04	.01
☐ 279	Bob Knepper	.15	.07	.01
☐ 280	Ken Griffey	.20	.10	.02
☐ 281	Fred Stanley	.08	.04	.01
☐ 282	Mariners Rookies ..	.12	.06	.01
	Rick Anderson			
	Greg Biercevicz			
	Rodney Craig			
☐ 283	Billy Sample	.08	.04	.01
☐ 284	Brian Kingman	.08	.04	.01
☐ 285	Jerry Turner	.08	.04	.01
☐ 286	Dave Frost	.08	.04	.01
☐ 287	Lenn Sakata	.08	.04	.01

		MINT	EXC	G-VG
☐ 288	Bob Clark	.08	.04	.01
☐ 289	Mickey Hatcher	.12	.06	.01
☐ 290	Bob Boone DP	.12	.06	.01
☐ 291	Aurelio Lopez	.08	.04	.01
☐ 292	Mike Squires	.08	.04	.01
☐ 293	Charlie Lea	.20	.10	.02
☐ 294	Mike Tyson DP	.04	.02	.00
☐ 295	Hal McRae	.12	.06	.01
☐ 296	Bill Nahorodny DP	.04	.02	.00
☐ 297	Bob Bailor	.08	.04	.01
☐ 298	Buddy Solomon	.08	.04	.01
☐ 299	Elliott Maddox	.08	.04	.01
☐ 300	Paul Molitor	.50	.25	.05
☐ 301	Matt Keough	.08	.04	.01
☐ 302	Dodgers Rookies	6.00	3.00	.60
	Jack Perconte			
	Mike Scioscia			
	Fernando Valenzuela			
☐ 303	Johnny Oates	.08	.04	.01
☐ 304	John Castino	.08	.04	.01
☐ 305	Ken Clay	.08	.04	.01
☐ 306	Juan Beniquez DP	.04	.02	.00
☐ 307	Gene Garber	.08	.04	.01
☐ 308	Rick Manning	.08	.04	.01
☐ 309	Luis Salazar	.20	.10	.02
☐ 310	Vida Blue DP	.12	.06	.01
☐ 311	Freddie Patek	.08	.04	.01
☐ 312	Rick Rhoden	.12	.06	.01
☐ 313	Luis Pujols	.08	.04	.01
☐ 314	Rich Dauer	.08	.04	.01
☐ 315	Kirk Gibson	7.00	3.50	.70
☐ 316	Craig Minetto	.08	.04	.01
☐ 317	Lonnie Smith	.20	.10	.02
☐ 318	Steve Yeager	.08	.04	.01
☐ 319	Rowland Office	.08	.04	.01
☐ 320	Tom Burgmeier	.08	.04	.01
☐ 321	Leon Durham	.40	.20	.04
☐ 322	Neil Allen	.12	.06	.01
☐ 323	Jim Morrison DP	.08	.04	.01
☐ 324	Mike Willis	.08	.04	.01
☐ 325	Ray Knight	.20	.10	.02
☐ 326	Biff Pocoroba	.08	.04	.01
☐ 327	Moose Haas	.12	.06	.01
☐ 328	Twins Rookies	.20	.10	.02
	Dave Engle			
	Greg Johnston			
	Gary Ward			
☐ 329	Joaquin Andujar	.15	.07	.01
☐ 330	Frank White	.15	.07	.01
☐ 331	Dennis Lamp	.08	.04	.01
☐ 332	Lee Lacy DP	.08	.04	.01
☐ 333	Sid Monge	.08	.04	.01
☐ 334	Dane Iorg	.08	.04	.01
☐ 335	Rick Cerone	.12	.06	.01
☐ 336	Eddie Whitson	.12	.06	.01
☐ 337	Lynn Jones	.08	.04	.01
☐ 338	Checklist 243-363	.20	.03	.01
☐ 339	John Ellis	.08	.04	.01
☐ 340	Bruce Kison	.08	.04	.01
☐ 341	Dwayne Murphy	.08	.04	.01
☐ 342	Eric Rasmussen DP	.04	.02	.00
☐ 343	Frank Taveras	.08	.04	.01
☐ 344	Byron McLaughlin	.08	.04	.01
☐ 345	Warren Cromartie	.08	.04	.01
☐ 346	Larry Christenson DP	.04	.02	.00
☐ 347	Harold Baines	3.75	1.85	.37
☐ 348	Bob Sykes	.08	.04	.01
☐ 349	Glenn Hoffman	.08	.04	.01
☐ 350	J.R. Richard	.15	.07	.01
☐ 351	Otto Velez	.08	.04	.01
☐ 352	Dick Tidrow DP	.04	.02	.00
☐ 353	Terry Kennedy	.12	.06	.01
☐ 354	Mario Soto	.15	.07	.01
☐ 355	Bob Horner	.25	.12	.02
☐ 356	Padres Rookies	.12	.06	.01
	George Stablein			
	Craig Stimac			
	Tom Tellmann			
☐ 357	Jim Slaton	.08	.04	.01
☐ 358	Mark Wagner	.08	.04	.01
☐ 359	Tom Hausman	.08	.04	.01
☐ 360	Willie Wilson	.25	.12	.02
☐ 361	Joe Strain	.08	.04	.01
☐ 362	Bo Diaz	.12	.06	.01
☐ 363	Geoff Zahn	.08	.04	.01
☐ 364	Mike Davis	.35	.17	.03
☐ 365	Graig Nettles DP	.12	.06	.01
☐ 366	Mike Ramsey	.08	.04	.01
☐ 367	Dennis Martinez	.15	.07	.01
☐ 368	Leon Roberts	.08	.04	.01
☐ 369	Frank Tanana	.15	.07	.01
☐ 370	Dave Winfield	1.25	.60	.12
☐ 371	Charlie Hough	.15	.07	.01
☐ 372	Jay Johnstone	.15	.07	.01
☐ 373	Pat Underwood	.08	.04	.01
☐ 374	Tommy Hutton	.08	.04	.01
☐ 375	Dave Concepcion	.15	.07	.01
☐ 376	Ron Reed	.08	.04	.01

		MINT	EXC	G-VG
☐ 377	Jerry Morales	.08	.04	.01
☐ 378	Dave Rader	.08	.04	.01
☐ 379	Lary Sorensen	.08	.04	.01
☐ 380	Willie Stargell	1.00	.50	.10
☐ 381	Cubs Rookies	.12	.06	.01
	Carlos Lezcano			
	Steve Macko			
	Randy Martz			
☐ 382	Paul Mirabella	.08	.04	.01
☐ 383	Eric Soderholm DP	.04	.02	.00
☐ 384	Mike Sadek	.08	.04	.01
☐ 385	Joe Sambito	.08	.04	.01
☐ 386	Dave Edwards	.08	.04	.01
☐ 387	Phil Niekro	.70	.35	.07
☐ 388	Andre Thornton	.12	.06	.01
☐ 389	Marty Pattin	.08	.04	.01
☐ 390	Cesar Geronimo	.08	.04	.01
☐ 391	Dave Lemanczyk DP	.04	.02	.00
☐ 392	Lance Parrish	.60	.30	.06
☐ 393	Broderick Perkins	.08	.04	.01
☐ 394	Woodie Fryman	.08	.04	.01
☐ 395	Scot Thompson	.08	.04	.01
☐ 396	Bill Campbell	.08	.04	.01
☐ 397	Julio Cruz	.08	.04	.01
☐ 398	Ross Baumgarten	.08	.04	.01
☐ 399	Orioles Rookies	1.50	.75	.15
	Mike Boddicker			
	Mark Corey			
	Floyd Rayford			
☐ 400	Reggie Jackson	1.75	.85	.17
☐ 401	AL Champs	.50	.25	.05
	Royals sweep Yanks			
	(Brett swinging)			
☐ 402	NL Champs	.20	.10	.02
	Phillies squeak			
	past Astros			
☐ 403	1980 World Series	.20	.10	.02
	Phillies beat			
	Royals in six			
☐ 404	1980 World Series	.20	.10	.02
	Phillies win first			
	World Series			
☐ 405	Nino Espinosa	.08	.04	.01
☐ 406	Dickie Noles	.08	.04	.01
☐ 407	Ernie Whitt	.15	.07	.01
☐ 408	Fernando Arroyo	.08	.04	.01
☐ 409	Larry Herndon	.08	.04	.01
☐ 410	Bert Campaneris	.12	.06	.01
☐ 411	Terry Puhl	.12	.06	.01

		MINT	EXC	G-VG
☐ 412	Britt Burns	.25	.12	.02
☐ 413	Tony Bernazard	.12	.06	.01
☐ 414	John Pacella DP	.04	.02	.00
☐ 415	Ben Oglivie	.12	.06	.01
☐ 416	Gary Alexander	.08	.04	.01
☐ 417	Dan Schatzeder	.08	.04	.01
☐ 418	Bobby Brown	.08	.04	.01
☐ 419	Tom Hume	.08	.04	.01
☐ 420	Keith Hernandez	.75	.35	.07
☐ 421	Bob Stanley	.08	.04	.01
☐ 422	Dan Ford	.08	.04	.01
☐ 423	Shane Rawley	.12	.06	.01
☐ 424	Yankees Rookies	.12	.06	.01
	Tim Lollar			
	Bruce Robinson			
	Dennis Werth			
☐ 425	Al Bumbry	.08	.04	.01
☐ 426	Warren Brusstar	.08	.04	.01
☐ 427	John D'Acquisto	.08	.04	.01
☐ 428	John Stearns	.08	.04	.01
☐ 429	Mick Kelleher	.08	.04	.01
☐ 430	Jim Bibby	.08	.04	.01
☐ 431	Dave Roberts	.08	.04	.01
☐ 432	Len Barker	.08	.04	.01
☐ 433	Rance Mulliniks	.08	.04	.01
☐ 434	Roger Erickson	.08	.04	.01
☐ 435	Jim Spencer	.08	.04	.01
☐ 436	Gary Lucas	.12	.06	.01
☐ 437	Mike Heath DP	.04	.02	.00
☐ 438	John Montefusco	.12	.06	.01
☐ 439	Denny Walling	.08	.04	.01
☐ 440	Jerry Reuss	.15	.07	.01
☐ 441	Ken Reitz	.08	.04	.01
☐ 442	Ron Pruitt	.08	.04	.01
☐ 443	Jim Beattie DP	.04	.02	.00
☐ 444	Garth Iorg	.08	.04	.01
☐ 445	Ellis Valentine	.08	.04	.01
☐ 446	Checklist 364-484	.20	.03	.01
☐ 447	Junior Kennedy DP	.04	.02	.00
☐ 448	Tim Corcoran	.08	.04	.01
☐ 449	Paul Mitchell	.08	.04	.01
☐ 450	Dave Kingman DP	.12	.06	.01
☐ 451	Indians Rookies	.12	.06	.01
	Chris Bando			
	Tom Brennan			
	Sandy Wihtol			
☐ 452	Renie Martin	.08	.04	.01
☐ 453	Rob Wilfong DP	.04	.02	.00
☐ 454	Andy Hassler	.08	.04	.01

		MINT	EXC	G-VG
☐ 455	Rick Burleson	.12	.06	.01
☐ 456	Jeff Reardon	1.25	.60	.12
☐ 457	Mike Lum	.08	.04	.01
☐ 458	Randy Jones	.08	.04	.01
☐ 459	Greg Gross	.08	.04	.01
☐ 460	Rich Gossage	.35	.17	.03
☐ 461	Dave McKay	.08	.04	.01
☐ 462	Jack Brohamer	.08	.04	.01
☐ 463	Milt May	.08	.04	.01
☐ 464	Adrian Devine	.08	.04	.01
☐ 465	Bill Russell	.12	.06	.01
☐ 466	Bob Molinaro	.08	.04	.01
☐ 467	Dave Stieb	.60	.30	.06
☐ 468	John Wockenfuss	.08	.04	.01
☐ 469	Jeff Leonard	.25	.12	.02
☐ 470	Manny Trillo	.08	.04	.01
☐ 471	Mike Vail	.08	.04	.01
☐ 472	Dyar Miller DP	.04	.02	.00
☐ 473	Jose Cardenal	.08	.04	.01
☐ 474	Mike LaCoss	.08	.04	.01
☐ 475	Buddy Bell	.20	.10	.02
☐ 476	Jerry Koosman	.15	.07	.01
☐ 477	Luis Gomez	.08	.04	.01
☐ 478	Juan Eichelberger	.08	.04	.01
☐ 479	Expos Rookies	8.50	4.25	.85
	Tim Raines			
	Roberto Ramos			
	Bobby Pate			
☐ 480	Carlton Fisk	.65	.30	.06
☐ 481	Bob Lacey DP	.04	.02	.00
☐ 482	Jim Gantner	.08	.04	.01
☐ 483	Mike Griffin	.08	.04	.01
☐ 484	Max Venable DP	.04	.02	.00
☐ 485	Garry Templeton	.15	.07	.01
☐ 486	Marc Hill	.08	.04	.01
☐ 487	Dewey Robinson	.08	.04	.01
☐ 488	Damaso Garcia	.15	.07	.01
☐ 489	John Littlefield	.08	.04	.01
☐ 490	Eddie Murray	1.50	.75	.15
☐ 491	Gordy Pladson	.08	.04	.01
☐ 492	Barry Foote	.08	.04	.01
☐ 493	Dan Quisenberry	.25	.12	.02
☐ 494	Bob Walk	.35	.17	.03
☐ 495	Dusty Baker	.12	.06	.01
☐ 496	Paul Dade	.08	.04	.01
☐ 497	Fred Norman	.08	.04	.01
☐ 498	Pat Putnam	.08	.04	.01
☐ 499	Frank Pastore	.08	.04	.01
☐ 500	Jim Rice	.75	.35	.07

		MINT	EXC	G-VG
☐ 501	Tim Foli DP	.04	.02	.00
☐ 502	Giants Rookies	.12	.06	.01
	Chris Bourjos			
	Al Hargesheimer			
	Mike Rowland			
☐ 503	Steve McCatty	.08	.04	.01
☐ 504	Dale Murphy	2.25	1.10	.22
☐ 505	Jason Thompson	.08	.04	.01
☐ 506	Phil Huffman	.08	.04	.01
☐ 507	Jamie Quirk	.08	.04	.01
☐ 508	Rob Dressler	.08	.04	.01
☐ 509	Pete Mackanin	.08	.04	.01
☐ 510	Lee Mazzilli	.08	.04	.01
☐ 511	Wayne Garland	.08	.04	.01
☐ 512	Gary Thomasson	.08	.04	.01
☐ 513	Frank LaCorte	.08	.04	.01
☐ 514	George Riley	.08	.04	.01
☐ 515	Robin Yount	2.25	1.10	.22
☐ 516	Doug Bird	.08	.04	.01
☐ 517	Richie Zisk	.12	.06	.01
☐ 518	Grant Jackson	.08	.04	.01
☐ 519	John Tamargo DP	.04	.02	.00
☐ 520	Steve Stone	.12	.06	.01
☐ 521	Sam Mejias	.08	.04	.01
☐ 522	Mike Colbern	.08	.04	.01
☐ 523	John Fulgham	.08	.04	.01
☐ 524	Willie Aikens	.12	.06	.01
☐ 525	Mike Torrez	.08	.04	.01
☐ 526	Phillies Rookies	.15	.07	.01
	Marty Bystrom			
	Jay Loviglio			
	Jim Wright			
☐ 527	Danny Goodwin	.08	.04	.01
☐ 528	Gary Matthews	.12	.06	.01
☐ 529	Dave LaRoche	.08	.04	.01
☐ 530	Steve Garvey	1.25	.60	.12
☐ 531	John Curtis	.08	.04	.01
☐ 532	Bill Stein	.08	.04	.01
☐ 533	Jesus Figueroa	.08	.04	.01
☐ 534	Dave Smith	.45	.22	.04
☐ 535	Omar Moreno	.08	.04	.01
☐ 536	Bob Owchinko DP	.04	.02	.00
☐ 537	Ron Hodges	.08	.04	.01
☐ 538	Tom Griffin	.08	.04	.01
☐ 539	Rodney Scott	.08	.04	.01
☐ 540	Mike Schmidt DP	1.50	.75	.15
☐ 541	Steve Swisher	.08	.04	.01
☐ 542	Larry Bradford DP	.04	.02	.00
☐ 543	Terry Crowley	.08	.04	.01

		MINT	EXC	G-VG
☐ 544	Rich Gale	.08	.04	.01
☐ 545	Johnny Grubb	.08	.04	.01
☐ 546	Paul Moskau	.08	.04	.01
☐ 547	Mario Guerrero	.08	.04	.01
☐ 548	Dave Goltz	.08	.04	.01
☐ 549	Jerry Remy	.08	.04	.01
☐ 550	Tommy John	.35	.17	.03
☐ 551	Pirates Rookies	2.00	1.00	.20
	Vance Law			
	Tony Pena			
	Pascual Perez			
☐ 552	Steve Trout	.12	.06	.01
☐ 553	Tim Blackwell	.08	.04	.01
☐ 554	Bert Blyleven	.35	.17	.03
☐ 555	Cecil Cooper	.25	.12	.02
☐ 556	Jerry Mumphrey	.08	.04	.01
☐ 557	Chris Knapp	.08	.04	.01
☐ 558	Barry Bonnell	.08	.04	.01
☐ 559	Willie Montanez	.08	.04	.01
☐ 560	Joe Morgan	.65	.30	.06
☐ 561	Dennis Littlejohn	.08	.04	.01
☐ 562	Checklist 485-605	.20	.03	.01
☐ 563	Jim Kaat	.25	.12	.02
☐ 564	Ron Hassey DP	.08	.04	.01
☐ 565	Burt Hooton	.08	.04	.01
☐ 566	Del Unser	.08	.04	.01
☐ 567	Mark Bomback	.08	.04	.01
☐ 568	Dave Revering	.08	.04	.01
☐ 569	Al Williams DP	.04	.02	.00
☐ 570	Ken Singleton	.15	.07	.01
☐ 571	Todd Cruz	.08	.04	.01
☐ 572	Jack Morris	.50	.25	.05
☐ 573	Phil Garner	.08	.04	.01
☐ 574	Bill Caudill	.08	.04	.01
☐ 575	Tony Perez	.30	.15	.03
☐ 576	Reggie Cleveland	.08	.04	.01
☐ 577	Blue Jays Rookies	.15	.07	.01
	Luis Leal			
	Brian Milner			
	Ken Schrom			
☐ 578	Bill Gullickson	.30	.15	.03
☐ 579	Tim Flannery	.08	.04	.01
☐ 580	Don Baylor	.25	.12	.02
☐ 581	Roy Howell	.08	.04	.01
☐ 582	Gaylord Perry	.50	.25	.05
☐ 583	Larry Milbourne	.08	.04	.01
☐ 584	Randy Lerch	.08	.04	.01
☐ 585	Amos Otis	.15	.07	.01
☐ 586	Silvio Martinez	.08	.04	.01

		MINT	EXC	G-VG
☐ 587	Jeff Newman	.08	.04	.01
☐ 588	Gary Lavelle	.08	.04	.01
☐ 589	Lamar Johnson	.08	.04	.01
☐ 590	Bruce Sutter	.25	.12	.02
☐ 591	John Lowenstein	.08	.04	.01
☐ 592	Steve Comer	.08	.04	.01
☐ 593	Steve Kemp	.12	.06	.01
☐ 594	Preston Hanna DP	.04	.02	.00
☐ 595	Butch Hobson	.08	.04	.01
☐ 596	Jerry Augustine	.08	.04	.01
☐ 597	Rafael Landestoy	.08	.04	.01
☐ 598	George Vukovich DP	.04	.02	.00
☐ 599	Dennis Kinney	.08	.04	.01
☐ 600	Johnny Bench	1.50	.75	.15
☐ 601	Don Aase	.08	.04	.01
☐ 602	Bobby Murcer	.15	.07	.01
☐ 603	John Verhoeven	.08	.04	.01
☐ 604	Rob Picciolo	.08	.04	.01
☐ 605	Don Sutton	.60	.30	.06
☐ 606	Reds Rookies DP	.04	.02	.01
	Bruce Berenyi			
	Geoff Combe			
	Paul Householder			
☐ 607	David Palmer	.12	.06	.01
☐ 608	Greg Pryor	.08	.04	.01
☐ 609	Lynn McGlothen	.08	.04	.01
☐ 610	Darrell Porter	.08	.04	.01
☐ 611	Rick Matula DP	.04	.02	.00
☐ 612	Duane Kuiper	.08	.04	.01
☐ 613	Jim Anderson	.08	.04	.01
☐ 614	Dave Rozema	.08	.04	.01
☐ 615	Rick Dempsey	.08	.04	.01
☐ 616	Rick Wise	.08	.04	.01
☐ 617	Craig Reynolds	.08	.04	.01
☐ 618	John Milner	.08	.04	.01
☐ 619	Steve Henderson	.08	.04	.01
☐ 620	Dennis Eckersley	.35	.17	.03
☐ 621	Tom Donohue	.08	.04	.01
☐ 622	Randy Moffitt	.08	.04	.01
☐ 623	Sal Bando	.12	.06	.01
☐ 624	Bob Welch	.20	.10	.02
☐ 625	Bill Buckner	.20	.10	.02
☐ 626	Tigers Rookies	.12	.06	.01
	Dave Steffen			
	Jerry Ujdur			
	Roger Weaver			
☐ 627	Luis Tiant	.15	.07	.01
☐ 628	Vic Correll	.08	.04	.01
☐ 629	Tony Armas	.15	.07	.01

		MINT	EXC	G-VG
☐ 630	Steve Carlton	1.25	.50	.10
☐ 631	Ron Jackson	.08	.04	.01
☐ 632	Alan Bannister	.08	.04	.01
☐ 633	Bill Lee	.12	.06	.01
☐ 634	Doug Flynn	.08	.04	.01
☐ 635	Bobby Bonds	.15	.07	.01
☐ 636	Al Hrabosky	.12	.06	.01
☐ 637	Jerry Narron	.08	.04	.01
☐ 638	Checklist 606-726 ..	.20	.03	.01
☐ 639	Carney Lansford	.45	.22	.04
☐ 640	Dave Parker	.50	.25	.05
☐ 641	Mark Belanger	.12	.06	.01
☐ 642	Vern Ruhle	.08	.04	.01
☐ 643	Lloyd Moseby	1.00	.50	.10
☐ 644	Ramon Aviles DP ...	.04	.02	.00
☐ 645	Rick Reuschel	.25	.12	.02
☐ 646	Marvis Foley	.08	.04	.01
☐ 647	Dick Drago	.08	.04	.01
☐ 648	Darrell Evans	.25	.12	.02
☐ 649	Manny Sarmiento ...	.08	.04	.01
☐ 650	Bucky Dent	.20	.10	.02
☐ 651	Pedro Guerrero	2.25	1.10	.22
☐ 652	John Montague	.08	.04	.01
☐ 653	Bill Fahey	.08	.04	.01
☐ 654	Ray Burris	.08	.04	.01
☐ 655	Dan Driessen	.08	.04	.01
☐ 656	Jon Matlack	.08	.04	.01
☐ 657	Mike Cubbage DP ..	.04	.02	.00
☐ 658	Milt Wilcox	.08	.04	.01
☐ 659	Brewers Rookies ...	.12	.06	.01
	John Flinn			
	Ed Romero			
	Ned Yost			
☐ 660	Gary Carter	1.50	.75	.15
☐ 661	Orioles Team/Mgr. ..	.25	.12	.02
	Earl Weaver (checklist back)			
☐ 662	Red Sox Team/Mgr. .	.20	.10	.02
	Ralph Houk (checklist back)			
☐ 663	Angels Team/Mgr. ..	.20	.10	.02
	Jim Fregosi (checklist back)			
☐ 664	White Sox Team/Mgr.	.20	.10	.02
	Tony LaRussa (checklist back)			
☐ 665	Indians Team/Mgr. ..	.20	.10	.02
	Dave Garcia (checklist back)			

		MINT	EXC	G-VG
☐ 666	Tigers Team/Mgr. ...	.25	.12	.02
	Sparky Anderson (checklist back)			
☐ 667	Royals Team/Mgr. ..	.20	.10	.02
	Jim Frey (checklist back)			
☐ 668	Brewers Team/Mgr. ..	.20	.10	.02
	Bob Rodgers (checklist back)			
☐ 669	Twins Team/Mgr.	.20	.10	.02
	John Goryl (checklist back)			
☐ 670	Yankees Team/Mgr. ..	.25	.12	.02
	Gene Michael (checklist back)			
☐ 671	A's Team/Mgr.	.25	.12	.02
	Billy Martin (checklist back)			
☐ 672	Mariners Team/Mgr. ..	.20	.10	.02
	Maury Wills (checklist back)			
☐ 673	Rangers Team/Mgr. ..	.20	.10	.02
	Don Zimmer (checklist back)			
☐ 674	Blue Jays Team/Mgr. .	.20	.10	.02
	Bobby Mattick (checklist back)			
☐ 675	Braves Team/Mgr. ..	.20	.10	.02
	Bobby Cox (checklist back)			
☐ 676	Cubs Team/Mgr.	.20	.10	.02
	Joe Amalfitano (checklist back)			
☐ 677	Reds Team/Mgr.	.20	.10	.02
	John McNamara (checklist back)			
☐ 678	Astros Team/Mgr. ...	.20	.10	.02
	Bill Virdon (checklist back)			
☐ 679	Dodgers Team/Mgr. ..	.25	.12	.02
	Tom Lasorda (checklist back)			
☐ 680	Expos Team/Mgr. ...	.20	.10	.02
	Dick Williams (checklist back)			
☐ 681	Mets Team/Mgr.	.25	.12	.02
	Joe Torre (checklist back)			
☐ 682	Phillies Team/Mgr. ..	.20	.10	.02

		MINT	EXC	G-VG
	Dallas Green (checklist back)			
☐ 683	Pirates Team/Mgr. ...	.20	.10	.02
	Chuck Tanner (checklist back)			
☐ 684	Cardinals Team/Mgr.	.20	.10	.02
	Whitey Herzog (checklist back)			
☐ 685	Padres Team/Mgr.	.20	.10	.02
	Frank Howard (checklist back)			
☐ 686	Giants Team/Mgr. ...	.20	.10	.02
	Dave Bristol (checklist back)			
☐ 687	Jeff Jones	.08	.04	.01
☐ 688	Kiko Garcia	.08	.04	.01
☐ 689	Red Sox Rookies ...	2.50	1.25	.25
	Bruce Hurst			
	Keith MacWhorter			
	Reid Nichols			
☐ 690	Bob Watson	.12	.06	.01
☐ 691	Dick Ruthven	.08	.04	.01
☐ 692	Lenny Randle	.08	.04	.01
☐ 693	Steve Howe	.12	.06	.01
☐ 694	Bud Harrelson DP ..	.04	.02	.00
☐ 695	Kent Tekulve	.12	.06	.01
☐ 696	Alan Ashby	.08	.04	.01
☐ 697	Rick Waits	.08	.04	.01
☐ 698	Mike Jorgensen	.08	.04	.01
☐ 699	Glenn Abbott	.08	.04	.01
☐ 700	George Brett	2.25	1.10	.22
☐ 701	Joe Rudi	.12	.06	.01
☐ 702	George Medich	.08	.04	.01
☐ 703	Alvis Woods	.08	.04	.01
☐ 704	Bill Travers DP	.04	.02	.00
☐ 705	Ted Simmons	.25	.12	.02
☐ 706	Dave Ford	.08	.04	.01
☐ 707	Dave Cash	.08	.04	.01
☐ 708	Doyle Alexander ...	.12	.06	.01
☐ 709	Alan Trammell DP ..	.30	.15	.03
☐ 710	Ron LeFlore DP	.08	.04	.01
☐ 711	Joe Ferguson	.08	.04	.01
☐ 712	Bill Bonham	.08	.04	.01
☐ 713	Bill North	.08	.04	.01
☐ 714	Pete Redfern	.08	.04	.01
☐ 715	Bill Madlock	.15	.07	.01
☐ 716	Glenn Borgmann ...	.08	.04	.01
☐ 717	Jim Barr DP	.04	.02	.00
☐ 718	Larry Biittner	.08	.04	.01

		MINT	EXC	G-VG
☐ 719	Sparky Lyle	.15	.07	.01
☐ 720	Fred Lynn	.30	.15	.03
☐ 721	Toby Harrah	.12	.06	.01
☐ 722	Joe Niekro	.15	.07	.01
☐ 723	Bruce Bochte	.08	.04	.01
☐ 724	Lou Piniella	.15	.07	.01
☐ 725	Steve Rogers	.12	.06	.01
☐ 726	Rick Monday	.20	.10	.02

1981 Topps Traded

*The cards in this 132-card set measure 2 ½"
by 3 ½". For the first time since 1976, Topps
issued a "traded" set in 1981. Unlike the small
traded sets of 1974 and 1976, this set contains
a larger number of cards and was sequentially
numbered, alphabetically, from 727 to 858.
Thus, this set gives the impression it is a continuation of their regular issue of this year. The
sets were issued only through hobby card dealers and were boxed in complete sets of 132
cards.*

		MINT	EXC	G-VG
COMPLETE SET (132)		25.00	12.50	2.50
COMMON PLAYER (727-858) ..		.08	.04	.01
☐ 727	Danny Ainge	.75	.35	.07
☐ 728	Doyle Alexander	.20	.10	.02

		MINT	EXC	G-VG
☐ 729	Gary Alexander	.08	.04	.01
☐ 730	Bill Almon	.08	.04	.01
☐ 731	Joaquin Andujar	.15	.07	.01
☐ 732	Bob Bailor	.08	.04	.01
☐ 733	Juan Beniquez	.08	.04	.01
☐ 734	Dave Bergman	.08	.04	.01
☐ 735	Tony Bernazard	.08	.04	.01
☐ 736	Larry Biittner	.08	.04	.01
☐ 737	Doug Bird	.08	.04	.01
☐ 738	Bert Blyleven	.75	.35	.07
☐ 739	Mark Bomback	.08	.04	.01
☐ 740	Bobby Bonds	.25	.12	.02
☐ 741	Rick Bosetti	.08	.04	.01
☐ 742	Hubie Brooks	1.50	.75	.15
☐ 743	Rick Burleson	.15	.07	.01
☐ 744	Ray Burris	.08	.04	.01
☐ 745	Jeff Burroughs	.15	.07	.01
☐ 746	Enos Cabell	.08	.04	.01
☐ 747	Ken Clay	.08	.04	.01
☐ 748	Mark Clear	.08	.04	.01
☐ 749	Larry Cox	.08	.04	.01
☐ 750	Hector Cruz	.08	.04	.01
☐ 751	Victor Cruz	.08	.04	.01
☐ 752	Mike Cubbage	.08	.04	.01
☐ 753	Dick Davis	.08	.04	.01
☐ 754	Brian Doyle	.08	.04	.01
☐ 755	Dick Drago	.08	.04	.01
☐ 756	Leon Durham	.40	.20	.04
☐ 757	Jim Dwyer	.08	.04	.01
☐ 758	Dave Edwards	.08	.04	.01
☐ 759	Jim Essian	.08	.04	.01
☐ 760	Bill Fahey	.08	.04	.01
☐ 761	Rollie Fingers	1.00	.50	.10
☐ 762	Carlton Fisk	1.50	.75	.15
☐ 763	Barry Foote	.08	.04	.01
☐ 764	Ken Forsch	.08	.04	.01
☐ 765	Kiko Garcia	.08	.04	.01
☐ 766	Cesar Geronimo	.08	.04	.01
☐ 767	Gary Gray	.08	.04	.01
☐ 768	Mickey Hatcher	.20	.10	.02
☐ 769	Steve Henderson	.08	.04	.01
☐ 770	Marc Hill	.08	.04	.01
☐ 771	Butch Hobson	.08	.04	.01
☐ 772	Rick Honeycutt	.08	.04	.01
☐ 773	Roy Howell	.08	.04	.01
☐ 774	Mike Ivie	.08	.04	.01
☐ 775	Roy Lee Jackson	.08	.04	.01
☐ 776	Cliff Johnson	.08	.04	.01
☐ 777	Randy Jones	.15	.07	.01
☐ 778	Ruppert Jones	.08	.04	.01
☐ 779	Mick Kelleher	.08	.04	.01
☐ 780	Terry Kennedy	.15	.07	.01
☐ 781	Dave Kingman	.35	.17	.03
☐ 782	Bob Knepper	.15	.07	.01
☐ 783	Ken Kravec	.08	.04	.01
☐ 784	Bob Lacey	.08	.04	.01
☐ 785	Dennis Lamp	.08	.04	.01
☐ 786	Rafael Landestoy	.08	.04	.01
☐ 787	Ken Landreaux	.15	.07	.01
☐ 788	Carney Lansford	1.00	.50	.10
☐ 789	Dave LaRoche	.08	.04	.01
☐ 790	Joe Lefebvre	.08	.04	.01
☐ 791	Ron LeFlore	.15	.07	.01
☐ 792	Randy Lerch	.08	.04	.01
☐ 793	Sixto Lezcano	.08	.04	.01
☐ 794	John Littlefield	.08	.04	.01
☐ 795	Mike Lum	.08	.04	.01
☐ 796	Greg Luzinski	.25	.12	.02
☐ 797	Fred Lynn	.50	.25	.05
☐ 798	Jerry Martin	.08	.04	.01
☐ 799	Buck Martinez	.08	.04	.01
☐ 800	Gary Matthews	.15	.07	.01
☐ 801	Mario Mendoza	.08	.04	.01
☐ 802	Larry Milbourne	.08	.04	.01
☐ 803	Rick Miller	.08	.04	.01
☐ 804	John Montefusco	.15	.07	.01
☐ 805	Jerry Morales	.08	.04	.01
☐ 806	Jose Morales	.08	.04	.01
☐ 807	Joe Morgan	1.50	.75	.15
☐ 808	Jerry Mumphrey	.08	.04	.01
☐ 809	Gene Nelson	.40	.20	.04
☐ 810	Ed Ott	.08	.04	.01
☐ 811	Bob Owchinko	.08	.04	.01
☐ 812	Gaylord Perry	1.25	.60	.12
☐ 813	Mike Phillips	.08	.04	.01
☐ 814	Darrell Porter	.15	.07	.01
☐ 815	Mike Proly	.08	.04	.01
☐ 816	Tim Raines	8.00	3.75	.75
☐ 817	Lenny Randle	.08	.04	.01
☐ 818	Doug Rau	.08	.04	.01
☐ 819	Jeff Reardon	.75	.35	.07
☐ 820	Ken Reitz	.08	.04	.01
☐ 821	Steve Renko	.08	.04	.01
☐ 822	Rick Reuschel	.40	.20	.04
☐ 823	Dave Revering	.08	.04	.01
☐ 824	Dave Roberts	.08	.04	.01
☐ 825	Leon Roberts	.08	.04	.01
☐ 826	Joe Rudi	.15	.07	.01

		MINT	EXC	G-VG
☐ 827	Kevin Saucier	.08	.04	.01
☐ 828	Tony Scott	.08	.04	.01
☐ 829	Bob Shirley	.08	.04	.01
☐ 830	Ted Simmons	.50	.25	.05
☐ 831	Lary Sorensen	.08	.04	.01
☐ 832	Jim Spencer	.08	.04	.01
☐ 833	Harry Spilman	.08	.04	.01
☐ 834	Fred Stanley	.08	.04	.01
☐ 835	Rusty Staub	.25	.12	.02
☐ 836	Bill Stein	.08	.04	.01
☐ 837	Joe Strain	.08	.04	.01
☐ 838	Bruce Sutter	.40	.20	.04
☐ 839	Don Sutton	1.25	.60	.12
☐ 840	Steve Swisher	.08	.04	.01
☐ 841	Frank Tanana	.20	.10	.02
☐ 842	Gene Tenace	.15	.07	.01
☐ 843	Jason Thompson	.08	.04	.01
☐ 844	Dickie Thon	.35	.17	.03
☐ 845	Bill Travers	.08	.04	.01
☐ 846	Tom Underwood	.08	.04	.01
☐ 847	John Urrea	.08	.04	.01
☐ 848	Mike Vail	.08	.04	.01
☐ 849	Ellis Valentine	.08	.04	.01
☐ 850	Fernando Valenzuela	4.50	2.25	.45
☐ 851	Pete Vuckovich	.15	.07	.01
☐ 852	Mark Wagner	.08	.04	.01
☐ 853	Bob Walk	.25	.12	.02
☐ 854	Claudell Washington	.20	.10	.02
☐ 855	Dave Winfield	2.50	1.25	.25
☐ 856	Geoff Zahn	.08	.04	.01
☐ 857	Richie Zisk	.15	.07	.01
☐ 858	Checklist 727-858	.08	.01	.00

1982 Topps

*The cards in this 792-card set measure 2 ½"
by 3 ½". The 1982 baseball series is the largest set Topps has ever issued at one printing.
The 66-card increase from the previous year's
total eliminated the "double print" practice,
which had occurred in every regular issue
since 1978. Cards 1-6 depict Highlights (HL)
of the 1981 season, cards 161-168 picture
League Leaders, and there are mini-series of
AL (547-557) and NL (337-347) All-Stars (AS).
The abbreviation "SA" in the checklist is given
for the 40 "Super Action" cards introduced in
this set. The team cards are actually Team
Leader (TL) cards picturing the batting and
pitching leader for that team with a checklist
back.*

		MINT	EXC	G-VG
COMPLETE SET (792)		90.00	45.00	9.00
COMMON PLAYER (1-792)		.06	.03	.00
☐ 1	HL: Steve Carlton Sets new NL strikeout record	.45	.10	.02
☐ 2	HL: Ron Davis Fans 8 straight in relief	.10	.05	.01
☐ 3	HL: Tim Raines Swipes 71 bases as rookie	.25	.12	.02
☐ 4	HL: Pete Rose Sets NL career	.75	.35	.07

		MINT	EXC	G-VG
	hits mark			
☐ 5	HL: Nolan Ryan	.75	.35	.07
	Pitches fifth			
	career no-hitter			
☐ 6	HL: Fern. Valenzuela	.20	.10	.02
	8 shutouts as rookie			
☐ 7	Scott Sanderson ...	.06	.03	.00
☐ 8	Rich Dauer	.06	.03	.00
☐ 9	Ron Guidry	.30	.15	.03
☐ 10	SA: Ron Guidry	.15	.07	.01
☐ 11	Gary Alexander	.06	.03	.00
☐ 12	Moose Haas	.06	.03	.00
☐ 13	Lamar Johnson	.06	.03	.00
☐ 14	Steve Howe	.06	.03	.00
☐ 15	Ellis Valentine	.06	.03	.00
☐ 16	Steve Comer	.06	.03	.00
☐ 17	Darrell Evans	.15	.07	.01
☐ 18	Fernando Arroyo ...	.06	.03	.00
☐ 19	Ernie Whitt	.10	.05	.01
☐ 20	Garry Maddox	.10	.05	.01
☐ 21	Orioles Rookies	12.50	6.25	1.25
	Bob Bonner			
	Cal Ripken			
	Jeff Schneider			
☐ 22	Jim Beattie	.06	.03	.00
☐ 23	Willie Hernandez ...	.20	.10	.02
☐ 24	Dave Frost	.06	.03	.00
☐ 25	Jerry Remy	.06	.03	.00
☐ 26	Jorge Orta	.06	.03	.00
☐ 27	Tom Herr	.15	.07	.01
☐ 28	John Urrea	.06	.03	.00
☐ 29	Dwayne Murphy	.06	.03	.00
☐ 30	Tom Seaver	.75	.35	.07
☐ 31	SA: Tom Seaver	.35	.17	.03
☐ 32	Gene Garber	.06	.03	.00
☐ 33	Jerry Morales	.06	.03	.00
☐ 34	Joe Sambito	.06	.03	.00
☐ 35	Willie Aikens	.06	.03	.00
☐ 36	Rangers TL	.15	.07	.01
	Mgr. Don Zimmer			
	Batting: Al Oliver			
	Pitching: Doc Medich			
☐ 37	Dan Graham	.06	.03	.00
☐ 38	Charlie Lea	.06	.03	.00
☐ 39	Lou Whitaker	.35	.17	.03
☐ 40	Dave Parker	.30	.15	.03
☐ 41	SA: Dave Parker ...	.15	.07	.01
☐ 42	Rick Sofield	.06	.03	.00
☐ 43	Mike Cubbage	.06	.03	.00

		MINT	EXC	G-VG
☐ 44	Britt Burns	.06	.03	.00
☐ 45	Rick Cerone	.06	.03	.00
☐ 46	Jerry Augustine	.06	.03	.00
☐ 47	Jeff Leonard	.10	.05	.01
☐ 48	Bobby Castillo	.06	.03	.00
☐ 49	Alvis Woods	.06	.03	.00
☐ 50	Buddy Bell	.15	.07	.01
☐ 51	Cubs Rookies	.45	.22	.04
	Jay Howell			
	Carlos Lezcano			
	Ty Waller			
☐ 52	Larry Andersen	.06	.03	.00
☐ 53	Greg Gross	.06	.03	.00
☐ 54	Ron Hassey	.06	.03	.00
☐ 55	Rick Burleson	.10	.05	.01
☐ 56	Mark Littell	.06	.03	.00
☐ 57	Craig Reynolds	.06	.03	.00
☐ 58	John D'Acquisto ...	.06	.03	.00
☐ 59	Rich Gedman	.50	.25	.05
☐ 60	Tony Armas	.10	.05	.01
☐ 61	Tommy Boggs	.06	.03	.00
☐ 62	Mike Tyson	.06	.03	.00
☐ 63	Mario Soto	.10	.05	.01
☐ 64	Lynn Jones	.06	.03	.00
☐ 65	Terry Kennedy	.06	.03	.00
☐ 66	Astros TL	.20	.10	.02
	Mgr. Bill Virdon			
	Batting: Art Howe			
	Pitching: Nolan Ryan			
☐ 67	Rich Gale	.06	.03	.00
☐ 68	Roy Howell	.06	.03	.00
☐ 69	Al Williams	.06	.03	.00
☐ 70	Tim Raines	2.00	1.00	.20
☐ 71	Roy Lee Jackson ...	.06	.03	.00
☐ 72	Rick Auerbach	.06	.03	.00
☐ 73	Buddy Solomon	.06	.03	.00
☐ 74	Bob Clark	.06	.03	.00
☐ 75	Tommy John	.25	.12	.02
☐ 76	Greg Pryor	.06	.03	.00
☐ 77	Miguel Dilone	.06	.03	.00
☐ 78	George Medich	.06	.03	.00
☐ 79	Bob Bailor	.06	.03	.00
☐ 80	Jim Palmer	.75	.35	.07
☐ 81	SA: Jim Palmer	.35	.17	.03
☐ 82	Bob Welch	.15	.07	.01
☐ 83	Yankees Rookies ...	.35	.17	.03
	Steve Balboni			
	Andy McGaffigan			
	Andre Robertson			

		MINT	EXC	G-VG
□ 84	Rennie Stennett	.06	.03	.00
□ 85	Lynn McGlothen	.06	.03	.00
□ 86	Dane Iorg	.06	.03	.00
□ 87	Matt Keough	.06	.03	.00
□ 88	Biff Pocoroba	.06	.03	.00
□ 89	Steve Henderson	.06	.03	.00
□ 90	Nolan Ryan	2.00	1.00	.20
□ 91	Carney Lansford	.30	.12	.02
□ 92	Brad Havens	.06	.03	.00
□ 93	Larry Hisle	.06	.03	.00
□ 94	Andy Hassler	.06	.03	.00
□ 95	Ozzie Smith	.75	.35	.07
□ 96	Royals TL	.20	.10	.02
	Mgr. Jim Frey			
	Batting: George Brett			
	Pitching: Larry Gura			
□ 97	Paul Moskau	.06	.03	.00
□ 98	Terry Bulling	.06	.03	.00
□ 99	Barry Bonnell	.06	.03	.00
□ 100	Mike Schmidt	1.75	.85	.17
□ 101	SA: Mike Schmidt	.75	.35	.07
□ 102	Dan Briggs	.06	.03	.00
□ 103	Bob Lacey	.06	.03	.00
□ 104	Rance Mulliniks	.06	.03	.00
□ 105	Kirk Gibson	1.25	.60	.12
□ 106	Enrique Romo	.06	.03	.00
□ 107	Wayne Krenchicki	.06	.03	.00
□ 108	Bob Sykes	.06	.03	.00
□ 109	Dave Revering	.06	.03	.00
□ 110	Carlton Fisk	.45	.22	.04
□ 111	SA: Carlton Fisk	.35	.17	.03
□ 112	Billy Sample	.06	.03	.00
□ 113	Steve McCatty	.06	.03	.00
□ 114	Ken Landreaux	.06	.03	.00
□ 115	Gaylord Perry	.35	.17	.03
□ 116	Jim Wohlford	.06	.03	.00
□ 117	Rawly Eastwick	.06	.03	.00
□ 118	Expos Rookies	.65	.30	.06
	Terry Francona			
	Brad Mills			
	Bryn Smith			
□ 119	Joe Pittman	.06	.03	.00
□ 120	Gary Lucas	.06	.03	.00
□ 121	Ed Lynch	.10	.05	.01
□ 122	Jamie Easterly UER	.06	.03	.00
	(photo actually			
	Reggie Cleveland)			
□ 123	Danny Goodwin	.06	.03	.00
□ 124	Reid Nichols	.06	.03	.00

		MINT	EXC	G-VG
□ 125	Danny Ainge	.25	.12	.02
□ 126	Braves TL	.15	.07	.01
	Mgr. Bobby Cox			
	Batting: C.Washington			
	Pitching: Rick Mahler			
□ 127	Lonnie Smith	.15	.07	.01
□ 128	Frank Pastore	.06	.03	.00
□ 129	Checklist 1-132	.10	.01	.00
□ 130	Julio Cruz	.06	.03	.00
□ 131	Stan Bahnsen	.06	.03	.00
□ 132	Lee May	.10	.05	.01
□ 133	Pat Underwood	.06	.03	.00
□ 134	Dan Ford	.06	.03	.00
□ 135	Andy Rincon	.06	.03	.00
□ 136	Lenn Sakata	.06	.03	.00
□ 137	George Cappuzzello	.06	.03	.00
□ 138	Tony Pena	.25	.12	.02
□ 139	Jeff Jones	.06	.03	.00
□ 140	Ron LeFlore	.10	.05	.01
□ 141	Indians Rookies	1.50	.75	.15
	Chris Bando			
	Tom Brennan			
	Von Hayes			
□ 142	Dave LaRoche	.06	.03	.00
□ 143	Mookie Wilson	.20	.10	.02
□ 144	Fred Breining	.06	.03	.00
□ 145	Bob Horner	.20	.10	.02
□ 146	Mike Griffin	.06	.03	.00
□ 147	Denny Walling	.06	.03	.00
□ 148	Mickey Klutts	.06	.03	.00
□ 149	Pat Putnam	.06	.03	.00
□ 150	Ted Simmons	.20	.10	.02
□ 151	Dave Edwards	.06	.03	.00
□ 152	Ramon Aviles	.06	.03	.00
□ 153	Roger Erickson	.06	.03	.00
□ 154	Dennis Werth	.06	.03	.00
□ 155	Otto Velez	.06	.03	.00
□ 156	Oakland A's TL	.25	.12	.02
	Mgr. Billy Martin			
	Batting: R. Henderson			
	Pitching: S. McCatty			
□ 157	Steve Crawford	.06	.03	.00
□ 158	Brian Downing	.10	.05	.01
□ 159	Larry Biittner	.06	.03	.00
□ 160	Luis Tiant	.15	.07	.01
□ 161	Batting Leaders	.15	.07	.01
	Bill Madlock			
	Carney Lansford			
□ 162	Home Run Leaders	.20	.10	.02

		MINT	EXC	G-VG
	Mike Schmidt			
	Tony Armas			
	Dwight Evans			
	Bobby Grich			
	Eddie Murray			
☐ 163	RBI Leaders	.35	.17	.03
	Mike Schmidt			
	Eddie Murray			
☐ 164	Stolen Base Leaders	.35	.17	.03
	Tim Raines			
	Rickey Henderson			
☐ 165	Victory Leaders	.15	.07	.01
	Tom Seaver			
	Denny Martinez			
	Steve McCatty			
	Jack Morris			
	Pete Vuckovich			
☐ 166	Strikeout Leaders	.15	.07	.01
	Fernando Valenzuela			
	Len Barker			
☐ 167	ERA Leaders	.35	.17	.03
	Nolan Ryan			
	Steve McCatty			
☐ 168	Leading Firemen	.15	.07	.01
	Bruce Sutter			
	Rollie Fingers			
☐ 169	Charlie Leibrandt	.06	.03	.00
☐ 170	Jim Bibby	.06	.03	.00
☐ 171	Giants Rookies	1.00	.50	.10
	Bob Brenly			
	Chili Davis			
	Bob Tufts			
☐ 172	Bill Gullickson	.06	.03	.00
☐ 173	Jamie Quirk	.06	.03	.00
☐ 174	Dave Ford	.06	.03	.00
☐ 175	Jerry Mumphrey	.06	.03	.00
☐ 176	Dewey Robinson	.06	.03	.00
☐ 177	John Ellis	.06	.03	.00
☐ 178	Dyar Miller	.06	.03	.00
☐ 179	Steve Garvey	.85	.40	.08
☐ 180	SA: Steve Garvey	.35	.17	.03
☐ 181	Silvio Martinez	.06	.03	.00
☐ 182	Larry Herndon	.06	.03	.00
☐ 183	Mike Proly	.06	.03	.00
☐ 184	Mick Kelleher	.06	.03	.00
☐ 185	Phil Niekro	.45	.22	.04
☐ 186	Cardinals TL	.15	.07	.01
	Mgr. Whitey Herzog			
	Batting K. Hernandez			

		MINT	EXC	G-VG
	Pitching Bob Forsch			
☐ 187	Jeff Newman	.06	.03	.00
☐ 188	Randy Martz	.06	.03	.00
☐ 189	Glenn Hoffman	.06	.03	.00
☐ 190	J.R. Richard	.10	.05	.01
☐ 191	Tim Wallach	1.50	.75	.15
☐ 192	Broderick Perkins	.06	.03	.00
☐ 193	Darrell Jackson	.06	.03	.00
☐ 194	Mike Vail	.06	.03	.00
☐ 195	Paul Molitor	.35	.17	.03
☐ 196	Willie Upshaw	.06	.03	.00
☐ 197	Shane Rawley	.06	.03	.00
☐ 198	Chris Speier	.06	.03	.00
☐ 199	Don Aase	.06	.03	.00
☐ 200	George Brett	1.50	.75	.15
☐ 201	SA: George Brett	.60	.30	.06
☐ 202	Rick Manning	.06	.03	.00
☐ 203	Blue Jays Rookies	3.50	1.75	.35
	Jesse Barfield			
	Brian Milner			
	Boomer Wells			
☐ 204	Gary Roenicke	.06	.03	.00
☐ 205	Neil Allen	.10	.05	.01
☐ 206	Tony Bernazard	.06	.03	.00
☐ 207	Rod Scurry	.06	.03	.00
☐ 208	Bobby Murcer	.15	.07	.01
☐ 209	Gary Lavelle	.06	.03	.00
☐ 210	Keith Hernandez	.50	.25	.05
☐ 211	Dan Petry	.06	.03	.00
☐ 212	Mario Mendoza	.06	.03	.00
☐ 213	Dave Stewart	5.00	2.50	.50
☐ 214	Brian Asselstine	.06	.03	.00
☐ 215	Mike Krukow	.10	.05	.01
☐ 216	White Sox TL	.15	.07	.01
	Mgr. Tony LaRussa			
	Batting: Chet Lemon			
	Pitching: Dennis Lamp			
☐ 217	Bo McLaughlin	.06	.03	.00
☐ 218	Dave Roberts	.06	.03	.00
☐ 219	John Curtis	.06	.03	.00
☐ 220	Manny Trillo	.06	.03	.00
☐ 221	Jim Slaton	.06	.03	.00
☐ 222	Butch Wynegar	.06	.03	.00
☐ 223	Lloyd Moseby	.20	.10	.02
☐ 224	Bruce Bochte	.06	.03	.00
☐ 225	Mike Torrez	.06	.03	.00
☐ 226	Checklist 133-264	.10	.01	.00
☐ 227	Ray Burris	.06	.03	.00
☐ 228	Sam Mejias	.06	.03	.00

		MINT	EXC	G-VG
☐ 229	Geoff Zahn	.06	.03	.00
☐ 230	Willie Wilson	.20	.10	.02
☐ 231	Phillies Rookies	1.50	.75	.15
	Mark Davis			
	Bob Dernier			
	Ozzie Virgil			
☐ 232	Terry Crowley	.06	.03	.00
☐ 233	Duane Kuiper	.06	.03	.00
☐ 234	Ron Hodges	.06	.03	.00
☐ 235	Mike Easler	.10	.05	.01
☐ 236	John Martin	.06	.03	.00
☐ 237	Rusty Kuntz	.06	.03	.00
☐ 238	Kevin Saucier	.06	.03	.00
☐ 239	Jon Matlack	.06	.03	.00
☐ 240	Bucky Dent	.15	.07	.01
☐ 241	SA: Bucky Dent	.10	.05	.01
☐ 242	Milt May	.06	.03	.00
☐ 243	Bob Owchinko	.06	.03	.00
☐ 244	Rufino Linares	.06	.03	.00
☐ 245	Ken Reitz	.06	.03	.00
☐ 246	New York Mets TL	.20	.10	.02
	Mgr. Joe Torre			
	Batting: Hubie Brooks			
	Pitching: Mike Scott			
☐ 247	Pedro Guerrero	1.00	.50	.10
☐ 248	Frank LaCorte	.06	.03	.00
☐ 249	Tim Flannery	.06	.03	.00
☐ 250	Tug McGraw	.15	.07	.01
☐ 251	Fred Lynn	.30	.15	.03
☐ 252	SA: Fred Lynn	.15	.07	.01
☐ 253	Chuck Baker	.06	.03	.00
☐ 254	Jorge Bell	8.00	4.00	.80
☐ 255	Tony Perez	.25	.12	.02
☐ 256	SA: Tony Perez	.10	.05	.01
☐ 257	Larry Harlow	.06	.03	.00
☐ 258	Bo Diaz	.06	.03	.00
☐ 259	Rodney Scott	.06	.03	.00
☐ 260	Bruce Sutter	.20	.10	.02
☐ 261	Tigers Rookies	.10	.05	.01
	Howard Bailey			
	Marty Castillo			
	Dave Rucker			
☐ 262	Doug Bair	.06	.03	.00
☐ 263	Victor Cruz	.06	.03	.00
☐ 264	Dan Quisenberry	.20	.10	.02
☐ 265	Al Bumbry	.06	.03	.00
☐ 266	Rick Leach	.06	.03	.00
☐ 267	Kurt Bevacqua	.06	.03	.00
☐ 268	Rickey Keeton	.06	.03	.00

		MINT	EXC	G-VG
☐ 269	Jim Essian	.06	.03	.00
☐ 270	Rusty Staub	.15	.07	.01
☐ 271	Larry Bradford	.06	.03	.00
☐ 272	Bump Wills	.06	.03	.00
☐ 273	Doug Bird	.06	.03	.00
☐ 274	Bob Ojeda	.75	.35	.07
☐ 275	Bob Watson	.10	.05	.01
☐ 276	Angels TL	.20	.10	.02
	Mgr. Gene Mauch			
	Batting: Rod Carew			
	Pitching: Ken Forsch			
☐ 277	Terry Puhl	.06	.03	.00
☐ 278	John Littlefield	.06	.03	.00
☐ 279	Bill Russell	.10	.05	.01
☐ 280	Ben Oglivie	.10	.05	.01
☐ 281	John Verhoeven	.06	.03	.00
☐ 282	Ken Macha	.06	.03	.00
☐ 283	Brian Allard	.06	.03	.00
☐ 284	Bob Grich	.10	.05	.01
☐ 285	Sparky Lyle	.15	.07	.01
☐ 286	Bill Fahey	.06	.03	.00
☐ 287	Alan Bannister	.06	.03	.00
☐ 288	Garry Templeton	.10	.05	.01
☐ 289	Bob Stanley	.06	.03	.00
☐ 290	Ken Singleton	.10	.05	.01
☐ 291	Pirates Rookies	1.25	.60	.12
	Vance Law			
	Bob Long			
	Johnny Ray			
☐ 292	David Palmer	.06	.03	.00
☐ 293	Rob Picciolo	.06	.03	.00
☐ 294	Mike LaCoss	.06	.03	.00
☐ 295	Jason Thompson	.06	.03	.00
☐ 296	Bob Walk	.10	.05	.01
☐ 297	Clint Hurdle	.06	.03	.00
☐ 298	Danny Darwin	.06	.03	.00
☐ 299	Steve Trout	.06	.03	.00
☐ 300	Reggie Jackson	1.25	.60	.12
☐ 301	SA: Reggie Jackson	.60	.30	.06
☐ 302	Doug Flynn	.06	.03	.00
☐ 303	Bill Caudill	.06	.03	.00
☐ 304	Johnnie LeMaster	.06	.03	.00
☐ 305	Don Sutton	.50	.25	.05
☐ 306	SA: Don Sutton	.20	.10	.02
☐ 307	Randy Bass	.10	.05	.01
☐ 308	Charlie Moore	.06	.03	.00
☐ 309	Pete Redfern	.06	.03	.00
☐ 310	Mike Hargrove	.10	.05	.01
☐ 311	Dodgers TL	.15	.07	.01

		MINT	EXC	G-VG
	Mgr. Tom Lasorda			
	Batting: Dusty Baker			
	Pitching: Burt Hooton			
☐ 312	Lenny Randle	.06	.03	.00
☐ 313	John Harris	.06	.03	.00
☐ 314	Buck Martinez	.06	.03	.00
☐ 315	Burt Hooton	.06	.03	.00
☐ 316	Steve Braun	.06	.03	.00
☐ 317	Dick Ruthven	.06	.03	.00
☐ 318	Mike Heath	.06	.03	.00
☐ 319	Dave Rozema	.06	.03	.00
☐ 320	Chris Chambliss	.10	.05	.01
☐ 321	SA: Chris Chambliss	.06	.03	.00
☐ 322	Garry Hancock	.06	.03	.00
☐ 323	Bill Lee	.10	.05	.01
☐ 324	Steve Dillard	.06	.03	.00
☐ 325	Jose Cruz	.10	.05	.01
☐ 326	Pete Falcone	.06	.03	.00
☐ 327	Joe Nolan	.06	.03	.00
☐ 328	Ed Farmer	.06	.03	.00
☐ 329	U.L. Washington	.06	.03	.00
☐ 330	Rick Wise	.06	.03	.00
☐ 331	Benny Ayala	.06	.03	.00
☐ 332	Don Robinson	.06	.03	.00
☐ 333	Brewers Rookies	.10	.05	.01
	Frank DiPino			
	Marshall Edwards			
	Chuck Porter			
☐ 334	Aurelio Rodriguez	.06	.03	.00
☐ 335	Jim Sundberg	.10	.05	.01
☐ 336	Mariners TL	.10	.05	.01
	Mgr. Rene Lachemann			
	Batting: Tom Paciorek			
	Pitching: Glenn Abbott			
☐ 337	Pete Rose AS	.75	.35	.07
☐ 338	Dave Lopes AS	.10	.05	.01
☐ 339	Mike Schmidt AS	.40	.20	.04
☐ 340	Dave Concepcion AS	.10	.05	.01
☐ 341	Andre Dawson AS	.20	.10	.02
☐ 342A	George Foster AS	.25	.12	.02
	(with autograph)			
☐ 342B	George Foster AS	1.75	.85	.17
	(w/o autograph)			
☐ 343	Dave Parker AS	.15	.07	.01
☐ 344	Gary Carter AS	.25	.12	.02
☐ 345	Fern. Valenzuela AS	.15	.07	.01
☐ 346A	Tom Seaver AS ERR	1.00	.50	.10
	("t ed")			
☐ 346B	Tom Seaver AS COR	.30	.15	.03

		MINT	EXC	G-VG
	(tied)			
☐ 347	Bruce Sutter AS	.10	.05	.01
☐ 348	Derrel Thomas	.06	.03	.00
☐ 349	George Frazier	.06	.03	.00
☐ 350	Thad Bosley	.06	.03	.00
☐ 351	Reds Rookies	.10	.05	.01
	Scott Brown			
	Geoff Coumbe			
	Paul Householder			
☐ 352	Dick Davis	.06	.03	.00
☐ 353	Jack O'Connor	.06	.03	.00
☐ 354	Roberto Ramos	.06	.03	.00
☐ 355	Dwight Evans	.25	.12	.02
☐ 356	Denny Lewallyn	.06	.03	.00
☐ 357	Butch Hobson	.06	.03	.00
☐ 358	Mike Parrott	.06	.03	.00
☐ 359	Jim Dwyer	.06	.03	.00
☐ 360	Len Barker	.06	.03	.00
☐ 361	Rafael Landestoy	.06	.03	.00
☐ 362	Jim Wright	.06	.03	.00
☐ 363	Bob Molinaro	.06	.03	.00
☐ 364	Doyle Alexander	.10	.05	.01
☐ 365	Bill Madlock	.15	.07	.01
☐ 366	Padres TL	.10	.05	.01
	Mgr. Frank Howard			
	Batting: Luis Salazar			
	Pitching: Eichelberger			
☐ 367	Jim Kaat	.15	.07	.01
☐ 368	Alex Trevino	.06	.03	.00
☐ 369	Champ Summers	.06	.03	.00
☐ 370	Mike Norris	.06	.03	.00
☐ 371	Jerry Don Gleaton	.06	.03	.00
☐ 372	Luis Gomez	.06	.03	.00
☐ 373	Gene Nelson	.15	.07	.01
☐ 374	Tim Blackwell	.06	.03	.00
☐ 375	Dusty Baker	.10	.05	.01
☐ 376	Chris Welsh	.06	.03	.00
☐ 377	Kiko Garcia	.06	.03	.00
☐ 378	Mike Caldwell	.06	.03	.00
☐ 379	Rob Wilfong	.06	.03	.00
☐ 380	Dave Stieb	.20	.10	.02
☐ 381	Red Sox Rookies	.75	.35	.07
	Bruce Hurst			
	Dave Schmidt			
	Julio Valdez			
☐ 382	Joe Simpson	.06	.03	.00
☐ 383A	Pascual Perez ERR	30.00	15.00	3.00
	(no position on front)			
☐ 383B	Pascual Perez COR	.25	.12	.02

		MINT	EXC	G-VG
☐ 384	Keith Moreland	.06	.03	.00
☐ 385	Ken Forsch	.06	.03	.00
☐ 386	Jerry White	.06	.03	.00
☐ 387	Tom Veryzer	.06	.03	.00
☐ 388	Joe Rudi	.10	.05	.01
☐ 389	George Vukovich	.06	.03	.00
☐ 390	Eddie Murray	1.25	.60	.12
☐ 391	Dave Tobik	.06	.03	.00
☐ 392	Rick Bosetti	.06	.03	.00
☐ 393	Al Hrabosky	.10	.05	.01
☐ 394	Checklist 265-396	.10	.01	.00
☐ 395	Omar Moreno	.06	.03	.00
☐ 396	Twins TL	.10	.05	.01
	Mgr. Billy Gardner			
	Batting: John Castino			
	Pitching: F. Arroyo			
☐ 397	Ken Brett	.06	.03	.00
☐ 398	Mike Squires	.06	.03	.00
☐ 399	Pat Zachry	.06	.03	.00
☐ 400	Johnny Bench	1.00	.50	.10
☐ 401	SA: Johnny Bench	.40	.20	.04
☐ 402	Bill Stein	.06	.03	.00
☐ 403	Jim Tracy	.06	.03	.00
☐ 404	Dickie Thon	.10	.05	.01
☐ 405	Rick Reuschel	.20	.10	.02
☐ 406	Al Holland	.06	.03	.00
☐ 407	Danny Boone	.06	.03	.00
☐ 408	Ed Romero	.06	.03	.00
☐ 409	Don Cooper	.06	.03	.00
☐ 410	Ron Cey	.15	.07	.01
☐ 411	SA: Ron Cey	.10	.05	.01
☐ 412	Luis Leal	.06	.03	.00
☐ 413	Dan Meyer	.06	.03	.00
☐ 414	Elias Sosa	.06	.03	.00
☐ 415	Don Baylor	.15	.07	.01
☐ 416	Marty Bystrom	.06	.03	.00
☐ 417	Pat Kelly	.06	.03	.00
☐ 418	Rangers Rookies	.30	.15	.03
	John Butcher			
	Bobby Johnson			
	Dave Schmidt			
☐ 419	Steve Stone	.10	.05	.01
☐ 420	George Hendrick	.10	.05	.01
☐ 421	Mark Clear	.06	.03	.00
☐ 422	Cliff Johnson	.06	.03	.00
☐ 423	Stan Papi	.06	.03	.00
☐ 424	Bruce Benedict	.06	.03	.00
☐ 425	John Candelaria	.10	.05	.01
☐ 426	Orioles TL	.20	.10	.02

		MINT	EXC	G-VG
	Mgr. Earl Weaver			
	Batting: Eddie Murray			
	Pitching: Sam Stewart			
☐ 427	Ron Oester	.06	.03	.00
☐ 428	LaMarr Hoyt	.10	.05	.01
☐ 429	John Wathan	.10	.05	.01
☐ 430	Vida Blue	.10	.05	.01
☐ 431	SA: Vida Blue	.06	.03	.00
☐ 432	Mike Scott	.75	.35	.07
☐ 433	Alan Ashby	.06	.03	.00
☐ 434	Joe Lefebvre	.06	.03	.00
☐ 435	Robin Yount	1.75	.85	.17
☐ 436	Joe Strain	.06	.03	.00
☐ 437	Juan Berenguer	.06	.03	.00
☐ 438	Pete Mackanin	.06	.03	.00
☐ 439	Dave Righetti	2.00	1.00	.20
☐ 440	Jeff Burroughs	.10	.05	.01
☐ 441	Astros Rookies	.10	.05	.01
	Danny Heep			
	Billy Smith			
	Bobby Sprowl			
☐ 442	Bruce Kison	.06	.03	.00
☐ 443	Mark Wagner	.06	.03	.00
☐ 444	Terry Forster	.10	.05	.01
☐ 445	Larry Parrish	.10	.05	.01
☐ 446	Wayne Garland	.06	.03	.00
☐ 447	Darrell Porter	.06	.03	.00
☐ 448	SA: Darrell Porter	.06	.03	.00
☐ 449	Luis Aguayo	.06	.03	.00
☐ 450	Jack Morris	.45	.22	.04
☐ 451	Ed Miller	.06	.03	.00
☐ 452	Lee Smith	.80	.40	.08
☐ 453	Art Howe	.10	.05	.01
☐ 454	Rick Langford	.06	.03	.00
☐ 455	Tom Burgmeier	.06	.03	.00
☐ 456	Chicago Cubs TL	.10	.05	.01
	Mgr. Joe Amalfitano			
	Batting: Bill Buckner			
	Pitching: Randy Martz			
☐ 457	Tim Stoddard	.06	.03	.00
☐ 458	Willie Montanez	.06	.03	.00
☐ 459	Bruce Berenyi	.06	.03	.00
☐ 460	Jack Clark	.40	.20	.04
☐ 461	Rich Dotson	.10	.05	.01
☐ 462	Dave Chalk	.06	.03	.00
☐ 463	Jim Kern	.06	.03	.00
☐ 464	Juan Bonilla	.06	.03	.00
☐ 465	Lee Mazzilli	.06	.03	.00
☐ 466	Randy Lerch	.06	.03	.00

		MINT	EXC	G-VG
☐ 467	Mickey Hatcher	.10	.05	.01
☐ 468	Floyd Bannister	.06	.03	.00
☐ 469	Ed Ott	.06	.03	.00
☐ 470	John Mayberry	.10	.05	.01
☐ 471	Royals Rookies	.20	.10	.02
	Atlee Hammaker			
	Mike Jones			
	Darryl Motley			
☐ 472	Oscar Gamble	.06	.03	.00
☐ 473	Mike Stanton	.06	.03	.00
☐ 474	Ken Oberkfell	.06	.03	.00
☐ 475	Alan Trammell	.50	.25	.05
☐ 476	Brian Kingman	.06	.03	.00
☐ 477	Steve Yeager	.06	.03	.00
☐ 478	Ray Searage	.06	.03	.00
☐ 479	Rowland Office	.06	.03	.00
☐ 480	Steve Carlton	.90	.45	.09
☐ 481	SA: Steve Carlton	.40	.20	.04
☐ 482	Glenn Hubbard	.06	.03	.00
☐ 483	Gary Woods	.06	.03	.00
☐ 484	Ivan DeJesus	.06	.03	.00
☐ 485	Kent Tekulve	.10	.05	.01
☐ 486	Yankees TL	.15	.07	.01
	Mgr. Bob Lemon			
	Batting: J. Mumphrey			
	Pitching: Tommy John			
☐ 487	Bob McClure	.06	.03	.00
☐ 488	Ron Jackson	.06	.03	.00
☐ 489	Rick Dempsey	.06	.03	.00
☐ 490	Dennis Eckersley	.25	.12	.02
☐ 491	Checklist 397-528	.10	.01	.00
☐ 492	Joe Price	.06	.03	.00
☐ 493	Chet Lemon	.10	.05	.01
☐ 494	Hubie Brooks	.25	.12	.02
☐ 495	Dennis Leonard	.10	.05	.01
☐ 496	Johnny Grubb	.06	.03	.00
☐ 497	Jim Anderson	.06	.03	.00
☐ 498	Dave Bergman	.06	.03	.00
☐ 499	Paul Mirabella	.06	.03	.00
☐ 500	Rod Carew	.85	.40	.08
☐ 501	SA: Rod Carew	.40	.20	.04
☐ 502	Braves Rookies	2.00	1.00	.20
	Steve Bedrosian			
	Brett Butler			
	Larry Owen			
☐ 503	Julio Gonzalez	.06	.03	.00
☐ 504	Rick Peters	.06	.03	.00
☐ 505	Graig Nettles	.20	.10	.02
☐ 506	SA: Graig Nettles	.10	.05	.01

		MINT	EXC	G-VG
☐ 507	Terry Harper	.06	.03	.00
☐ 508	Jody Davis	.50	.25	.05
☐ 509	Harry Spilman	.06	.03	.00
☐ 510	Fernando Valenzuela	1.25	.60	.12
☐ 511	Ruppert Jones	.06	.03	.00
☐ 512	Jerry Dybzinski	.06	.03	.00
☐ 513	Rick Rhoden	.10	.05	.01
☐ 514	Joe Ferguson	.06	.03	.00
☐ 515	Larry Bowa	.15	.07	.01
☐ 516	SA: Larry Bowa	.06	.03	.00
☐ 517	Mark Brouhard	.06	.03	.00
☐ 518	Garth Iorg	.06	.03	.00
☐ 519	Glenn Adams	.06	.03	.00
☐ 520	Mike Flanagan	.10	.05	.01
☐ 521	Bill Almon	.06	.03	.00
☐ 522	Chuck Rainey	.06	.03	.00
☐ 523	Gary Gray	.06	.03	.00
☐ 524	Tom Hausman	.06	.03	.00
☐ 525	Ray Knight	.10	.05	.01
☐ 526	Expos TL	.10	.05	.01
	Mgr. Jim Fanning			
	Batting: W. Cromartie			
	Pitching: B. Gullickson			
☐ 527	John Henry Johnson	.06	.03	.00
☐ 528	Matt Alexander	.06	.03	.00
☐ 529	Allen Ripley	.06	.03	.00
☐ 530	Dickie Noles	.06	.03	.00
☐ 531	A's Rookies	.10	.05	.01
	Rich Bordi			
	Mark Budaska			
	Kelvin Moore			
☐ 532	Toby Harrah	.10	.05	.01
☐ 533	Joaquin Andujar	.10	.05	.01
☐ 534	Dave McKay	.06	.03	.00
☐ 535	Lance Parrish	.30	.15	.03
☐ 536	Rafael Ramirez	.06	.03	.00
☐ 537	Doug Capilla	.06	.03	.00
☐ 538	Lou Piniella	.15	.07	.01
☐ 539	Vern Ruhle	.06	.03	.00
☐ 540	Andre Dawson	.50	.25	.05
☐ 541	Barry Evans	.06	.03	.00
☐ 542	Ned Yost	.06	.03	.00
☐ 543	Bill Robinson	.10	.05	.01
☐ 544	Larry Christenson	.06	.03	.00
☐ 545	Reggie Smith	.10	.05	.01
☐ 546	SA: Reggie Smith	.06	.03	.00
☐ 547	Rod Carew AS	.25	.12	.02
☐ 548	Willie Randolph AS	.10	.05	.01
☐ 549	George Brett AS	.45	.22	.04

		MINT	EXC	G-VG
☐ 550	Bucky Dent AS	.10	.05	.01
☐ 551	Reggie Jackson AS	.40	.20	.04
☐ 552	Ken Singleton AS	.06	.03	.00
☐ 553	Dave Winfield AS	.30	.15	.03
☐ 554	Carlton Fisk AS	.15	.07	.01
☐ 555	Scott McGregor AS	.06	.03	.00
☐ 556	Jack Morris AS	.10	.05	.01
☐ 557	Rich Gossage AS	.10	.05	.01
☐ 558	John Tudor	.30	.15	.03
☐ 559	Indians TL	.10	.05	.01
	Mgr. Dave Garcia			
	Batting: Mike			
	Hargrove			
	Pitching: Bert Blyleven			
☐ 560	Doug Corbett	.06	.03	.00
☐ 561	Cardinals Rookies	.10	.05	.01
	Glenn Brummer			
	Luis DeLeon			
	Gene Roof			
☐ 562	Mike O'Berry	.06	.03	.00
☐ 563	Ross Baumgarten	.06	.03	.00
☐ 564	Doug DeCinces	.10	.05	.01
☐ 565	Jackson Todd	.06	.03	.00
☐ 566	Mike Jorgensen	.06	.03	.00
☐ 567	Bob Babcock	.06	.03	.00
☐ 568	Joe Pettini	.06	.03	.00
☐ 569	Willie Randolph	.10	.05	.01
☐ 570	SA: Willie Randolph	.06	.03	.00
☐ 571	Glenn Abbott	.06	.03	.00
☐ 572	Juan Beniquez	.06	.03	.00
☐ 573	Rick Waits	.06	.03	.00
☐ 574	Mike Ramsey	.06	.03	.00
☐ 575	Al Cowens	.06	.03	.00
☐ 576	Giants TL	.10	.05	.01
	Mgr. Frank Robinson			
	Batting: Milt May			
	Pitching: Vida Blue			
☐ 577	Rick Monday	.10	.05	.01
☐ 578	Shooty Babitt	.06	.03	.00
☐ 579	Rick Mahler	.30	.15	.03
☐ 580	Bobby Bonds	.15	.07	.01
☐ 581	Ron Reed	.06	.03	.00
☐ 582	Luis Pujols	.06	.03	.00
☐ 583	Tippy Martinez	.06	.03	.00
☐ 584	Hosken Powell	.06	.03	.00
☐ 585	Rollie Fingers	.25	.12	.02
☐ 586	SA: Rollie Fingers	.15	.07	.01
☐ 587	Tim Lollar	.06	.03	.00
☐ 588	Dale Berra	.06	.03	.00

		MINT	EXC	G-VG
☐ 589	Dave Stapleton	.06	.03	.00
☐ 590	Al Oliver	.15	.07	.01
☐ 591	SA: Al Oliver	.06	.03	.00
☐ 592	Craig Swan	.06	.03	.00
☐ 593	Billy Smith	.06	.03	.00
☐ 594	Renie Martin	.06	.03	.00
☐ 595	Dave Collins	.06	.03	.00
☐ 596	Damaso Garcia	.10	.05	.01
☐ 597	Wayne Nordhagen	.06	.03	.00
☐ 598	Bob Galasso	.06	.03	.00
☐ 599	White Sox Rookies	.10	.05	.01
	Jay Loviglio			
	Reggie Patterson			
	Leo Sutherland			
☐ 600	Dave Winfield	.75	.35	.07
☐ 601	Sid Monge	.06	.03	.00
☐ 602	Freddie Patek	.06	.03	.00
☐ 603	Rich Hebner	.06	.03	.00
☐ 604	Orlando Sanchez	.06	.03	.00
☐ 605	Steve Rogers	.06	.03	.00
☐ 606	Blue Jays TL	.10	.05	.01
	Mgr. Bobby Mattick			
	Batting: J. Mayberry			
	Pitching: Dave Stieb			
☐ 607	Leon Durham	.10	.05	.01
☐ 608	Jerry Royster	.06	.03	.00
☐ 609	Rick Sutcliffe	.25	.12	.02
☐ 610	Rickey Henderson	3.25	1.60	.32
☐ 611	Joe Niekro	.15	.07	.01
☐ 612	Gary Ward	.10	.05	.01
☐ 613	Jim Gantner	.06	.03	.00
☐ 614	Juan Eichelberger	.06	.03	.00
☐ 615	Bob Boone	.15	.07	.01
☐ 616	SA: Bob Boone	.10	.05	.01
☐ 617	Scott McGregor	.10	.05	.01
☐ 618	Tim Foli	.06	.03	.00
☐ 619	Bill Campbell	.06	.03	.00
☐ 620	Ken Griffey	.15	.07	.01
☐ 621	SA: Ken Griffey	.10	.05	.01
☐ 622	Dennis Lamp	.06	.03	.00
☐ 623	Mets Rookies	1.00	.50	.10
	Ron Gardenhire			
	Terry Leach			
	Tim Leary			
☐ 624	Fergie Jenkins	.20	.10	.02
☐ 625	Hal McRae	.10	.05	.01
☐ 626	Randy Jones	.06	.03	.00
☐ 627	Enos Cabell	.06	.03	.00
☐ 628	Bill Travers	.06	.03	.00

		MINT	EXC	G-VG
☐ 629	John Wockenfuss ...	.06	.03	.00
☐ 630	Joe Charboneau	.10	.05	.01
☐ 631	Gene Tenace	.06	.03	.00
☐ 632	Bryan Clark	.06	.03	.00
☐ 633	Mitchell Page	.06	.03	.00
☐ 634	Checklist 529-660 ...	.10	.01	.00
☐ 635	Ron Davis	.06	.03	.00
☐ 636	Phillies TL	.35	.17	.03
	Mgr. Dallas Green			
	Batting: Pete Rose			
	Pitching: S. Carlton			
☐ 637	Rick Camp	.06	.03	.00
☐ 638	John Milner	.06	.03	.00
☐ 639	Ken Kravec	.06	.03	.00
☐ 640	Cesar Cedeno	.10	.05	.01
☐ 641	Steve Mura	.06	.03	.00
☐ 642	Mike Scioscia	.10	.05	.01
☐ 643	Pete Vuckovich	.10	.05	.01
☐ 644	John Castino	.06	.03	.00
☐ 645	Frank White	.10	.05	.01
☐ 646	SA: Frank White ...	.06	.03	.00
☐ 647	Warren Brusstar ...	.06	.03	.00
☐ 648	Jose Morales	.06	.03	.00
☐ 649	Ken Clay	.06	.03	.00
☐ 650	Carl Yastrzemski ...	1.50	.75	.15
☐ 651	SA: Carl Yastrzemski	.60	.30	.06
☐ 652	Steve Nicosia	.06	.03	.00
☐ 653	Angels Rookies	2.00	1.00	.20
	Tom Brunansky			
	Luis Sanchez			
	Daryl Sconiers			
☐ 654	Jim Morrison	.06	.03	.00
☐ 655	Joel Youngblood	.06	.03	.00
☐ 656	Eddie Whitson	.10	.05	.01
☐ 657	Tom Poquette	.06	.03	.00
☐ 658	Tito Landrum	.06	.03	.00
☐ 659	Fred Martinez	.06	.03	.00
☐ 660	Dave Concepcion ...	.15	.07	.01
☐ 661	SA: Dave Concep-			
	cion	.10	.05	.01
☐ 662	Luis Salazar	.10	.05	.01
☐ 663	Hector Cruz	.06	.03	.00
☐ 664	Dan Spillner	.06	.03	.00
☐ 665	Jim Clancy	.06	.03	.00
☐ 666	Tigers TL	.10	.05	.01
	Mgr. Sparky Anderson			
	Batting: Steve Kemp			
	Pitching: Dan Petry			
☐ 667	Jeff Reardon	.25	.10	.02

		MINT	EXC	G-VG
☐ 668	Dale Murphy	2.00	1.00	.20
☐ 669	Larry Milbourne	.06	.03	.00
☐ 670	Steve Kemp	.10	.05	.01
☐ 671	Mike Davis	.10	.05	.01
☐ 672	Bob Knepper	.10	.05	.01
☐ 673	Keith Drumwright ...	.06	.03	.00
☐ 674	Dave Goltz	.06	.03	.00
☐ 675	Cecil Cooper	.20	.10	.02
☐ 676	Sal Butera	.06	.03	.00
☐ 677	Alfredo Griffin	.10	.05	.01
☐ 678	Tom Paciorek	.06	.03	.00
☐ 679	Sammy Stewart	.06	.03	.00
☐ 680	Gary Matthews	.10	.05	.01
☐ 681	Dodgers Rookies ...	4.00	2.00	.40
	Mike Marshall			
	Ron Roenicke			
	Steve Sax			
☐ 682	Jesse Jefferson	.06	.03	.00
☐ 683	Phil Garner	.06	.03	.00
☐ 684	Harold Baines	.75	.35	.07
☐ 685	Bert Blyleven	.25	.12	.02
☐ 586	Gary Allenson	.06	.03	.00
☐ 687	Greg Minton	.06	.03	.00
☐ 688	Leon Roberts	.06	.03	.00
☐ 689	Lary Sorensen	.06	.03	.00
☐ 690	Dave Kingman	.20	.10	.02
☐ 691	Dan Schatzeder	.06	.03	.00
☐ 692	Wayne Gross	.06	.03	.00
☐ 693	Cesar Geronimo	.06	.03	.00
☐ 694	Dave Wehrmeister ...	.06	.03	.00
☐ 695	Warren Cromartie ...	.06	.03	.00
☐ 696	Pirates TL	.10	.05	.01
	Mgr. Chuck Tanner			
	Batting: Bill Madlock			
	Pitching: Eddie			
	Solomon			
☐ 697	John Montefusco ...	.10	.05	.01
☐ 698	Tony Scott	.06	.03	.00
☐ 699	Dick Tidrow	.06	.03	.00
☐ 700	George Foster	.25	.12	.02
☐ 701	SA: George Foster ..	.10	.05	.01
☐ 702	Steve Renko	.06	.03	.00
☐ 703	Brewers TL	.10	.05	.01
	Mgr. Bob Rodgers			
	Batting: Cecil Cooper			
	Pitching: P. Vuckovich			
☐ 704	Mickey Rivers	.10	.05	.01
☐ 705	SA: Mickey Rivers ..	.06	.03	.00
☐ 706	Barry Foote	.06	.03	.00

		MINT	EXC	G-VG
☐ 707	Mark Bomback	.06	.03	.00
☐ 708	Gene Richards	.06	.03	.00
☐ 709	Don Money	.06	.03	.00
☐ 710	Jerry Reuss	.10	.05	.01
☐ 711	Mariners Rookies	1.00	.50	.10
	Dave Edler			
	Dave Henderson			
	Reggie Walton			
☐ 712	Dennis Martinez	.10	.05	.01
☐ 713	Del Unser	.06	.03	.00
☐ 714	Jerry Koosman	.15	.07	.01
☐ 715	Willie Stargell	.60	.30	.06
☐ 716	SA: Willie Stargell	.25	.12	.02
☐ 717	Rick Miller	.06	.03	.00
☐ 718	Charlie Hough	.10	.05	.01
☐ 719	Jerry Narron	.06	.03	.00
☐ 720	Greg Luzinski	.15	.07	.01
☐ 721	SA: Greg Luzinski	.10	.05	.01
☐ 722	Jerry Martin	.06	.03	.00
☐ 723	Junior Kennedy	.06	.03	.00
☐ 724	Dave Rosello	.06	.03	.00
☐ 725	Amos Otis	.10	.05	.01
☐ 726	SA: Amos Otis	.06	.03	.00
☐ 727	Sixto Lezcano	.06	.03	.00
☐ 728	Aurelio Lopez	.06	.03	.00
☐ 729	Jim Spencer	.06	.03	.00
☐ 730	Gary Carter	.75	.35	.07
☐ 731	Padres Rookies	.10	.05	.01
	Mike Armstrong			
	Doug Gwosdz			
	Fred Kuhaulua			
☐ 732	Mike Lum	.06	.03	.00
☐ 733	Larry McWilliams	.06	.03	.00
☐ 734	Mike Ivie	.06	.03	.00
☐ 735	Rudy May	.06	.03	.00
☐ 736	Jerry Turner	.06	.03	.00
☐ 737	Reggie Cleveland	.06	.03	.00
☐ 738	Dave Engle	.06	.03	.00
☐ 739	Joey McLaughlin	.06	.03	.00
☐ 740	Dave Lopes	.10	.05	.01
☐ 741	SA: Dave Lopes	.06	.03	.00
☐ 742	Dick Drago	.06	.03	.00
☐ 743	John Stearns	.06	.03	.00
☐ 744	Mike Witt	.90	.45	.09
☐ 745	Bake McBride	.06	.03	.00
☐ 746	Andre Thornton	.10	.05	.01
☐ 747	John Lowenstein	.06	.03	.00
☐ 748	Marc Hill	.06	.03	.00
☐ 749	Bob Shirley	.06	.03	.00

		MINT	EXC	G-VG
☐ 750	Jim Rice	.60	.30	.06
☐ 751	Rick Honeycutt	.06	.03	.00
☐ 752	Lee Lacy	.06	.03	.00
☐ 753	Tom Brookens	.06	.03	.00
☐ 754	Joe Morgan	.50	.25	.05
☐ 755	SA: Joe Morgan	.20	.10	.02
☐ 756	Reds TL	.20	.10	.02
	Mgr. John McNamara			
	Batting: Ken Griffey			
	Pitching: Tom Seaver			
☐ 757	Tom Underwood	.06	.03	.00
☐ 758	Claudell Washington	.10	.05	.01
☐ 759	Paul Splittorff	.06	.03	.00
☐ 760	Bill Buckner	.15	.07	.01
☐ 761	Dave Smith	.10	.05	.01
☐ 762	Mike Phillips	.06	.03	.00
☐ 763	Tom Hume	.06	.03	.00
☐ 764	Steve Swisher	.06	.03	.00
☐ 765	Gorman Thomas	.15	.07	.01
☐ 766	Twins Rookies	4.50	2.25	.45
	Lenny Faedo			
	Kent Hrbek			
	Tim Laudner			
☐ 767	Roy Smalley	.06	.03	.00
☐ 768	Jerry Garvin	.06	.03	.00
☐ 769	Richie Zisk	.10	.05	.01
☐ 770	Rich Gossage	.25	.12	.02
☐ 771	SA: Rich Gossage	.10	.05	.01
☐ 772	Bert Campaneris	.10	.05	.01
☐ 773	John Denny	.10	.05	.01
☐ 774	Jay Johnstone	.10	.05	.01
☐ 775	Bob Forsch	.06	.03	.00
☐ 776	Mark Belanger	.10	.05	.01
☐ 777	Tom Griffin	.06	.03	.00
☐ 778	Kevin Hickey	.06	.03	.00
☐ 779	Grant Jackson	.06	.03	.00
☐ 780	Pete Rose	2.25	1.10	.22
☐ 781	SA: Pete Rose	.75	.35	.07
☐ 782	Frank Taveras	.06	.03	.00
☐ 783	Greg Harris	.20	.10	.02
☐ 784	Milt Wilcox	.06	.03	.00
☐ 785	Dan Driessen	.06	.03	.00
☐ 786	Red Sox TL	.10	.05	.01
	Mgr. Ralph Houk			
	Batting: C.Lansford			
	Pitching: Mike Torrez			
☐ 787	Fred Stanley	.06	.03	.00
☐ 788	Woodie Fryman	.06	.03	.00
☐ 789	Checklist 661-792	.10	.01	.00

		MINT	EXC	G-VG
☐	790 Larry Gura	.06	.03	.00
☐	791 Bobby Brown	.06	.03	.00
☐	792 Frank Tanana	.15	.07	.01

1982 Topps Traded

The cards in this 132-card set measure 2 ½" by 3 ½". The 1982 Topps Traded or extended series is distinguished by a "T" printed after the number (located on the reverse). Of the total cards, 70 players represent the American League and 61 represent the National League, with the remaining card a numbered checklist (132T). The Cubs lead the pack with 12 changes, while the Red Sox are the only team in either league to have no new additions. All 131 player photos used in the set are completely new. Of this total, 112 individuals are seen in the uniform of their new team, 11 others have been elevated to single card status from "Future Stars" cards, and eight more are entirely new to the 1982 Topps lineup. The backs are almost completely red in color with black print.

	MINT	EXC	G-VG
COMPLETE SET (132)	30.00	15.00	3.00
COMMON PLAYER (1-132)	.08	.04	.01

		MINT	EXC	G-VG
☐	1T Doyle Alexander	.15	.07	.01
☐	2T Jesse Barfield	2.00	1.00	.20

		MINT	EXC	G-VG
☐	3T Ross Baumgarten	.08	.04	.01
☐	4T Steve Bedrosian	.75	.35	.07
☐	5T Mark Belanger	.15	.07	.01
☐	6T Kurt Bevacqua	.08	.04	.01
☐	7T Tim Blackwell	.08	.04	.01
☐	8T Vida Blue	.15	.07	.01
☐	9T Bob Boone	.35	.17	.03
☐	10T Larry Bowa	.20	.10	.02
☐	11T Dan Briggs	.08	.04	.01
☐	12T Bobby Brown	.08	.04	.01
☐	13T Tom Brunansky	1.50	.75	.15
☐	14T Jeff Burroughs	.15	.07	.01
☐	15T Enos Cabell	.08	.04	.01
☐	16T Bill Campbell	.08	.04	.01
☐	17T Bobby Castillo	.08	.04	.01
☐	18T Bill Caudill	.08	.04	.01
☐	19T Cesar Cedeno	.20	.10	.02
☐	20T Dave Collins	.08	.04	.01
☐	21T Doug Corbett	.08	.04	.01
☐	22T Al Cowens	.08	.04	.01
☐	23T Chili Davis	1.25	.60	.12
☐	24T Dick Davis	.08	.04	.01
☐	25T Ron Davis	.08	.04	.01
☐	26T Doug DeCinces	.20	.10	.02
☐	27T Ivan DeJesus	.08	.04	.01
☐	28T Bob Dernier	.15	.07	.01
☐	29T Bo Diaz	.15	.07	.01
☐	30T Roger Erickson	.08	.04	.01
☐	31T Jim Essian	.08	.04	.01
☐	32T Ed Farmer	.08	.04	.01
☐	33T Doug Flynn	.08	.04	.01
☐	34T Tim Foli	.08	.04	.01
☐	35T Dan Ford	.08	.04	.01
☐	36T George Foster	.40	.20	.04
☐	37T Dave Frost	.08	.04	.01
☐	38T Rich Gale	.08	.04	.01
☐	39T Ron Gardenhire	.15	.07	.01
☐	40T Ken Griffey	.25	.12	.02
☐	41T Greg Harris	.15	.07	.01
☐	42T Von Hayes	1.25	.60	.12
☐	43T Larry Herndon	.08	.04	.01
☐	44T Kent Hrbek	5.00	2.50	.50
☐	45T Mike Ivie	.08	.04	.01
☐	46T Grant Jackson	.08	.04	.01
☐	47T Reggie Jackson	3.00	1.50	.30
☐	48T Ron Jackson	.08	.04	.01
☐	49T Fergie Jenkins	.40	.20	.04
☐	50T Lamar Johnson	.08	.04	.01
☐	51T Randy Johnson	.08	.04	.01

		MINT	EXC	G-VG
☐ 52T	Jay Johnstone	.20	.10	.02
☐ 53T	Mick Kelleher	.08	.04	.01
☐ 54T	Steve Kemp	.15	.07	.01
☐ 55T	Junior Kennedy	.08	.04	.01
☐ 56T	Jim Kern	.08	.04	.01
☐ 57T	Ray Knight	.25	.12	.02
☐ 58T	Wayne Krenchicki	.08	.04	.01
☐ 59T	Mike Krukow	.15	.07	.01
☐ 60T	Duane Kuiper	.08	.04	.01
☐ 61T	Mike LaCoss	.08	.04	.01
☐ 62T	Chet Lemon	.15	.07	.01
☐ 63T	Sixto Lezcano	.08	.04	.01
☐ 64T	Dave Lopes	.20	.10	.02
☐ 65T	Jerry Martin	.08	.04	.01
☐ 66T	Renie Martin	.08	.04	.01
☐ 67T	John Mayberry	.15	.07	.01
☐ 68T	Lee Mazzilli	.08	.04	.01
☐ 69T	Bake McBride	.08	.04	.01
☐ 70T	Dan Meyer	.08	.04	.01
☐ 71T	Larry Milbourne	.08	.04	.01
☐ 72T	Eddie Milner	.15	.07	.01
☐ 73T	Sid Monge	.08	.04	.01
☐ 74T	John Montefusco	.15	.07	.01
☐ 75T	Jose Morales	.08	.04	.01
☐ 76T	Keith Moreland	.15	.07	.01
☐ 77T	Jim Morrison	.08	.04	.01
☐ 78T	Rance Mulliniks	.08	.04	.01
☐ 79T	Steve Mura	.08	.04	.01
☐ 80T	Gene Nelson	.15	.07	.01
☐ 81T	Joe Nolan	.08	.04	.01
☐ 82T	Dickie Noles	.08	.04	.01
☐ 83T	Al Oliver	.20	.10	.02
☐ 84T	Jorge Orta	.08	.04	.01
☐ 85T	Tom Paciorek	.08	.04	.01
☐ 86T	Larry Parrish	.15	.07	.01
☐ 87T	Jack Perconte	.08	.04	.01
☐ 88T	Gaylord Perry	1.00	.50	.10
☐ 89T	Rob Picciolo	.08	.04	.01
☐ 90T	Joe Pittman	.08	.04	.01
☐ 91T	Hosken Powell	.08	.04	.01
☐ 92T	Mike Proly	.08	.04	.01
☐ 93T	Greg Pryor	.08	.04	.01
☐ 94T	Charlie Puleo	.15	.07	.01
☐ 95T	Shane Rawley	.15	.07	.01
☐ 96T	Johnny Ray	1.00	.50	.10
☐ 97T	Dave Revering	.08	.04	.01
☐ 98T	Cal Ripken	11.00	5.50	1.10
☐ 99T	Allen Ripley	.08	.04	.01
☐ 100T	Bill Robinson	.15	.07	.01
☐ 101T	Aurelio Rodriguez	.08	.04	.01
☐ 102T	Joe Rudi	.15	.07	.01
☐ 103T	Steve Sax	4.00	2.00	.40
☐ 104T	Dan Schatzeder	.08	.04	.01
☐ 105T	Bob Shirley	.08	.04	.01
☐ 106T	Eric Show	1.00	.50	.10
☐ 107T	Roy Smalley	.15	.07	.01
☐ 108T	Lonnie Smith	.25	.12	.02
☐ 109T	Ozzie Smith	4.50	2.25	.45
☐ 110T	Reggie Smith	.20	.10	.02
☐ 111T	Lary Sorensen	.08	.04	.01
☐ 112T	Elias Sosa	.08	.04	.01
☐ 113T	Mike Stanton	.08	.04	.01
☐ 114T	Steve Stroughter	.08	.04	.01
☐ 115T	Champ Summers	.08	.04	.01
☐ 116T	Rick Sutcliffe	.45	.22	.04
☐ 117T	Frank Tanana	.15	.07	.01
☐ 118T	Frank Taveras	.08	.04	.01
☐ 119T	Garry Templeton	.15	.07	.01
☐ 120T	Alex Trevino	.08	.04	.01
☐ 121T	Jerry Turner	.08	.04	.01
☐ 122T	Ed VandeBerg	.15	.07	.01
☐ 123T	Tom Veryzer	.08	.04	.01
☐ 124T	Ron Washington	.15	.07	.01
☐ 125T	Bob Watson	.15	.07	.01
☐ 126T	Dennis Werth	.08	.04	.01
☐ 127T	Eddie Whitson	.15	.07	.01
☐ 128T	Rob Wilfong	.08	.04	.01
☐ 129T	Bump Wills	.08	.04	.01
☐ 130T	Gary Woods	.08	.04	.01
☐ 131T	Butch Wynegar	.15	.07	.01
☐ 132T	Checklist: 1-132	.08	.01	.00

1983 Topps

The cards in this 792-card set measure 2 ½"
by 3 ½". Each regular card of the Topps set
for 1983 features a large action shot of a player
with a small cameo portrait at bottom right.
There are special series for AL and NL All Stars
(386-407), League Leaders (701-708), and
Record Breakers (1-6). In addition, there are
34 "Super Veteran" (SV) cards and six
numbered checklist cards. The Super Veteran
cards are oriented horizontally and show two
pictures of the featured player, a recent picture
and a picture showing the player as a rookie
when he broke in. The cards are numbered on
the reverse at the upper left corner. The team
cards are actually Team Leader (TL) cards picturing the batting and pitching leader for that
team with a checklist back.

		MINT	EXC	G-VG
COMPLETE SET (792)		100.00	50.00	10.00
COMMON PLAYER (1-792)		.06	.03	.00
☐ 1	RB: Tony Armas 11 putouts by rightfielder	.12	.03	.01
☐ 2	RB: Rickey Henderson Sets modern record for steals, season	.35	.17	.03
☐ 3	RB: Greg Minton 269 ⅓ homerless innings streak	.10	.05	.01

		MINT	EXC	G-VG
☐ 4	RB: Lance Parrish Threw out three baserunners in All-Star game	.15	.07	.01
☐ 5	RB: Manny Trillo 479 consecutive errorless chances, second baseman	.10	.05	.01
☐ 6	RB: John Wathan ML steals record for catchers, 31	.10	.05	.01
☐ 7	Gene Richards	.06	.03	.00
☐ 8	Steve Balboni	.10	.05	.01
☐ 9	Joey McLaughlin	.06	.03	.00
☐ 10	Gorman Thomas	.15	.07	.01
☐ 11	Billy Gardner MG	.06	.03	.00
☐ 12	Paul Mirabella	.06	.03	.00
☐ 13	Larry Herndon	.06	.03	.00
☐ 14	Frank LaCorte	.06	.03	.00
☐ 15	Ron Cey	.15	.07	.01
☐ 16	George Vukovich	.06	.03	.00
☐ 17	Kent Tekulve	.10	.05	.01
☐ 18	SV: Kent Tekulve	.06	.03	.00
☐ 19	Oscar Gamble	.06	.03	.00
☐ 20	Carlton Fisk	.35	.17	.03
☐ 21	Baltimore Orioles TL BA: Eddie Murray ERA: Jim Palmer	.30	.15	.03
☐ 22	Randy Martz	.06	.03	.00
☐ 23	Mike Heath	.06	.03	.00
☐ 24	Steve Mura	.06	.03	.00
☐ 25	Hal McRae	.10	.05	.01
☐ 26	Jerry Royster	.06	.03	.00
☐ 27	Doug Corbett	.06	.03	.00
☐ 28	Bruce Bochte	.06	.03	.00
☐ 29	Randy Jones	.06	.03	.00
☐ 30	Jim Rice	.35	.17	.03
☐ 31	Bill Gullickson	.10	.05	.01
☐ 32	Dave Bergman	.06	.03	.00
☐ 33	Jack O'Connor	.06	.03	.00
☐ 34	Paul Householder	.06	.03	.00
☐ 35	Rollie Fingers	.30	.15	.03
☐ 36	SV: Rollie Fingers	.15	.07	.01
☐ 37	Darrell Johnson MG	.06	.03	.00
☐ 38	Tim Flannery	.06	.03	.00
☐ 39	Terry Puhl	.06	.03	.00
☐ 40	Fernando Valenzuela	.45	.22	.04
☐ 41	Jerry Turner	.06	.03	.00
☐ 42	Dale Murray	.06	.03	.00

			MINT	EXC	G-VG
☐	43	Bob Dernier	.06	.03	.00
☐	44	Don Robinson	.06	.03	.00
☐	45	John Mayberry	.10	.05	.01
☐	46	Richard Dotson	.10	.05	.01
☐	47	Dave McKay	.06	.03	.00
☐	48	Lary Sorensen	.06	.03	.00
☐	49	Willie McGee	1.75	.85	.17
☐	50	Bob Horner	.20	.10	.02
		('82 RBI total 7)			
☐	51	Chicago Cubs TL	.15	.07	.01
		BA: Leon Durham			
		ERA: Fergie Jenkins			
☐	52	Onix Concepcion	.06	.03	.00
☐	53	Mike Witt	.20	.10	.02
☐	54	Jim Maler	.06	.03	.00
☐	55	Mookie Wilson	.15	.07	.01
☐	56	Chuck Rainey	.06	.03	.00
☐	57	Tim Blackwell	.06	.03	.00
☐	58	Al Holland	.06	.03	.00
☐	59	Benny Ayala	.06	.03	.00
☐	60	Johnny Bench	.75	.35	.07
☐	61	SV: Johnny Bench	.35	.17	.03
☐	62	Bob McClure	.06	.03	.00
☐	63	Rick Monday	.10	.05	.01
☐	64	Bill Stein	.06	.03	.00
☐	65	Jack Morris	.30	.15	.03
☐	66	Bob Lillis MG	.06	.03	.00
☐	67	Sal Butera	.06	.03	.00
☐	68	Eric Show	.40	.20	.04
☐	69	Lee Lacy	.06	.03	.00
☐	70	Steve Carlton	.55	.27	.05
☐	71	SV: Steve Carlton	.25	.12	.02
☐	72	Tom Paciorek	.06	.03	.00
☐	73	Allen Ripley	.06	.03	.00
☐	74	Julio Gonzalez	.06	.03	.00
☐	75	Amos Otis	.10	.05	.01
☐	76	Rick Mahler	.06	.03	.00
☐	77	Hosken Powell	.06	.03	.00
☐	78	Bill Caudill	.06	.03	.00
☐	79	Mick Kelleher	.06	.03	.00
☐	80	George Foster	.20	.10	.02
☐	81	Yankees TL	.15	.07	.01
		BA: Jerry Mumphrey			
		ERA: Dave Righetti			
☐	82	Bruce Hurst	.35	.17	.03
☐	83	Ryne Sandberg	11.00	5.00	1.00
☐	84	Milt May	.06	.03	.00
☐	85	Ken Singleton	.10	.05	.01
☐	86	Tom Hume	.06	.03	.00
☐	87	Joe Rudi	.10	.05	.01
☐	88	Jim Gantner	.06	.03	.00
☐	89	Leon Roberts	.06	.03	.00
☐	90	Jerry Reuss	.10	.05	.01
☐	91	Larry Milbourne	.06	.03	.00
☐	92	Mike LaCoss	.06	.03	.00
☐	93	John Castino	.06	.03	.00
☐	94	Dave Edwards	.06	.03	.00
☐	95	Alan Trammell	.40	.20	.04
☐	96	Dick Howser MG	.10	.05	.01
☐	97	Ross Baumgarten	.06	.03	.00
☐	98	Vance Law	.15	.07	.01
☐	99	Dickie Noles	.06	.03	.00
☐	100	Pete Rose	2.00	1.00	.20
☐	101	SV: Pete Rose	.75	.35	.07
☐	102	Dave Beard	.06	.03	.00
☐	103	Darrell Porter	.06	.03	.00
☐	104	Bob Walk	.10	.05	.01
☐	105	Don Baylor	.15	.07	.01
☐	106	Gene Nelson	.06	.03	.00
☐	107	Mike Jorgensen	.06	.03	.00
☐	108	Glenn Hoffman	.06	.03	.00
☐	109	Luis Leal	.06	.03	.00
☐	110	Ken Griffey	.15	.07	.01
☐	111	Montreal Expos TL	.10	.05	.01
		BA: Al Oliver			
		ERA: Steve Rogers			
☐	112	Bob Shirley	.06	.03	.00
☐	113	Ron Roenicke	.06	.03	.00
☐	114	Jim Slaton	.06	.03	.00
☐	115	Chili Davis	.15	.07	.01
☐	116	Dave Schmidt	.10	.05	.01
☐	117	Alan Knicely	.06	.03	.00
☐	118	Chris Welsh	.06	.03	.00
☐	119	Tom Brookens	.06	.03	.00
☐	120	Len Barker	.06	.03	.00
☐	121	Mickey Hatcher	.10	.05	.01
☐	122	Jimmy Smith	.06	.03	.00
☐	123	George Frazier	.06	.03	.00
☐	124	Marc Hill	.06	.03	.00
☐	125	Leon Durham	.10	.05	.01
☐	126	Joe Torre MG	.10	.05	.01
☐	127	Preston Hanna	.06	.03	.00
☐	128	Mike Ramsey	.06	.03	.00
☐	129	Checklist: 1-132	.10	.01	.00
☐	130	Dave Stieb	.20	.10	.02
☐	131	Ed Ott	.06	.03	.00
☐	132	Todd Cruz	.06	.03	.00
☐	133	Jim Barr	.06	.03	.00

		MINT	EXC	G-VG
☐ 134	Hubie Brooks	.15	.07	.01
☐ 135	Dwight Evans	.20	.10	.02
☐ 136	Willie Aikens	.06	.03	.00
☐ 137	Woodie Fryman	.06	.03	.00
☐ 138	Rick Dempsey	.06	.03	.00
☐ 139	Bruce Berenyi	.06	.03	.00
☐ 140	Willie Randolph	.10	.05	.01
☐ 141	Indians TL	.10	.05	.01
	BA: Toby Harrah			
	ERA: Rick Sutcliffe			
☐ 142	Mike Caldwell	.06	.03	.00
☐ 143	Joe Pettini	.06	.03	.00
☐ 144	Mark Wagner	.06	.03	.00
☐ 145	Don Sutton	.40	.20	.04
☐ 146	SV: Don Sutton	.20	.10	.02
☐ 147	Rick Leach	.06	.03	.00
☐ 148	Dave Roberts	.06	.03	.00
☐ 149	Johnny Ray	.15	.07	.01
☐ 150	Bruce Sutter	.15	.07	.01
☐ 151	SV: Bruce Sutter	.10	.05	.01
☐ 152	Jay Johnstone	.10	.05	.01
☐ 153	Jerry Koosman	.10	.05	.01
☐ 154	Johnnie LeMaster	.06	.03	.00
☐ 155	Dan Quisenberry	.15	.07	.01
☐ 156	Billy Martin MG	.15	.07	.01
☐ 157	Steve Bedrosian	.25	.12	.02
☐ 158	Rob Wilfong	.06	.03	.00
☐ 159	Mike Stanton	.06	.03	.00
☐ 160	Dave Kingman	.15	.07	.01
☐ 161	SV: Dave Kingman	.10	.05	.01
☐ 162	Mark Clear	.06	.03	.00
☐ 163	Cal Ripken	2.50	1.25	.25
☐ 164	David Palmer	.06	.03	.00
☐ 165	Dan Driessen	.06	.03	.00
☐ 166	John Pacella	.06	.03	.00
☐ 167	Mark Brouhard	.06	.03	.00
☐ 168	Juan Eichelberger	.06	.03	.00
☐ 169	Doug Flynn	.06	.03	.00
☐ 170	Steve Howe	.06	.03	.00
☐ 171	Giants TL	.15	.07	.01
	BA: Joe Morgan			
	ERA: Bill Laskey			
☐ 172	Vern Ruhle	.06	.03	.00
☐ 173	Jim Morrison	.06	.03	.00
☐ 174	Jerry Ujdur	.06	.03	.00
☐ 175	Bo Diaz	.06	.03	.00
☐ 176	Dave Righetti	.35	.17	.03
☐ 177	Harold Baines	.35	.17	.03
☐ 178	Luis Tiant	.10	.05	.01

		MINT	EXC	G-VG
☐ 179	SV: Luis Tiant	.06	.03	.00
☐ 180	Rickey Henderson	1.75	.85	.17
☐ 181	Terry Felton	.06	.03	.00
☐ 182	Mike Fischlin	.06	.03	.00
☐ 183	Ed VandeBerg	.10	.05	.01
☐ 184	Bob Clark	.06	.03	.00
☐ 185	Tim Lollar	.06	.03	.00
☐ 186	Whitey Herzog MG	.06	.03	.00
☐ 187	Terry Leach	.15	.07	.01
☐ 188	Rick Miller	.06	.03	.00
☐ 189	Dan Schatzeder	.06	.03	.00
☐ 190	Cecil Cooper	.15	.07	.01
☐ 191	Joe Price	.06	.03	.00
☐ 192	Floyd Rayford	.06	.03	.00
☐ 193	Harry Spilman	.06	.03	.00
☐ 194	Cesar Geronimo	.06	.03	.00
☐ 195	Bob Stoddard	.06	.03	.00
☐ 196	Bill Fahey	.06	.03	.00
☐ 197	Jim Eisenreich	.75	.35	.07
☐ 198	Kiko Garcia	.06	.03	.00
☐ 199	Marty Bystrom	.06	.03	.00
☐ 200	Rod Carew	.75	.30	.06
☐ 201	SV: Rod Carew	.25	.12	.02
☐ 202	Blue Jays TL	.10	.05	.01
	BA: Damaso Garcia			
	ERA: Dave Stieb			
☐ 203	Mike Morgan	.10	.05	.01
☐ 204	Junior Kennedy	.06	.03	.00
☐ 205	Dave Parker	.25	.12	.02
☐ 206	Ken Oberkfell	.06	.03	.00
☐ 207	Rick Camp	.06	.03	.00
☐ 208	Dan Meyer	.06	.03	.00
☐ 209	Mike Moore	2.00	1.00	.20
☐ 210	Jack Clark	.35	.17	.03
☐ 211	John Denny	.10	.05	.01
☐ 212	John Stearns	.06	.03	.00
☐ 213	Tom Burgmeier	.06	.03	.00
☐ 214	Jerry White	.06	.03	.00
☐ 215	Mario Soto	.10	.05	.01
☐ 216	Tony LaRussa MG	.10	.05	.01
☐ 217	Tim Stoddard	.06	.03	.00
☐ 218	Roy Howell	.06	.03	.00
☐ 219	Mike Armstrong	.06	.03	.00
☐ 220	Dusty Baker	.10	.05	.01
☐ 221	Joe Niekro	.10	.05	.01
☐ 222	Damaso Garcia	.06	.03	.00
☐ 223	John Montefusco	.06	.03	.00
☐ 224	Mickey Rivers	.10	.05	.01
☐ 225	Enos Cabell	.06	.03	.00

		MINT	EXC	G-VG			MINT	EXC	G-VG
☐ 226	Enrique Romo	.06	.03	.00	☐ 270	Dennis Eckersley	.25	.12	.02
☐ 227	Chris Bando	.06	.03	.00	☐ 271	Ed Romero	.06	.03	.00
☐ 228	Joaquin Andujar	.10	.05	.01	☐ 272	Frank Tanana	.10	.05	.01
☐ 229	Phillies TL	.15	.07	.01	☐ 273	Mark Belanger	.10	.05	.01
	BA: Bo Diaz				☐ 274	Terry Kennedy	.06	.03	.00
	ERA: Steve Carlton				☐ 275	Ray Knight	.10	.05	.01
☐ 230	Fergie Jenkins	.15	.07	.01	☐ 276	Gene Mauch MG	.06	.03	.00
☐ 231	SV: Fergie Jenkins	.10	.05	.01	☐ 277	Rance Mulliniks	.06	.03	.00
☐ 232	Tom Brunansky	.40	.20	.04	☐ 278	Kevin Hickey	.06	.03	.00
☐ 233	Wayne Gross	.06	.03	.00	☐ 279	Greg Gross	.06	.03	.00
☐ 234	Larry Andersen	.06	.03	.00	☐ 280	Bert Blyleven	.20	.10	.02
☐ 235	Claudell Washington	.10	.05	.01	☐ 281	Andre Robertson	.06	.03	.00
☐ 236	Steve Renko	.06	.03	.00	☐ 282	Reggie Smith	.15	.07	.01
☐ 237	Dan Norman	.06	.03	.00		(Ryne Sandberg			
☐ 238	Bud Black	.25	.12	.02		ducking back)			
☐ 239	Dave Stapleton	.06	.03	.00	☐ 283	SV: Reggie Smith	.06	.03	.00
☐ 240	Rich Gossage	.25	.12	.02	☐ 284	Jeff Lahti	.06	.03	.00
☐ 241	SV: Rich Gossage	.10	.05	.01	☐ 285	Lance Parrish	.30	.15	.03
☐ 242	Joe Nolan	.06	.03	.00	☐ 286	Rick Langford	.06	.03	.00
☐ 243	Duane Walker	.06	.03	.00	☐ 287	Bobby Brown	.06	.03	.00
☐ 244	Dwight Bernard	.06	.03	.00	☐ 288	Joe Cowley	.10	.05	.01
☐ 245	Steve Sax	.65	.30	.06	☐ 289	Jerry Dybzinski	.06	.03	.00
☐ 246	George Bamberger				☐ 290	Jeff Reardon	.20	.10	.02
	MG	.06	.03	.00	☐ 291	Pirates TL	.10	.05	.01
☐ 247	Dave Smith	.10	.05	.01		BA: Bill Madlock			
☐ 248	Bake McBride	.06	.03	.00		ERA: John Candelaria			
☐ 249	Checklist: 133-264	.10	.01	.00	☐ 292	Craig Swan	.06	.03	.00
☐ 250	Bill Buckner	.15	.07	.01	☐ 293	Glenn Gulliver	.06	.03	.00
☐ 251	Alan Wiggins	.15	.07	.01	☐ 294	Dave Engle	.06	.03	.00
☐ 252	Luis Aguayo	.06	.03	.00	☐ 295	Jerry Remy	.06	.03	.00
☐ 253	Larry McWilliams	.06	.03	.00	☐ 296	Greg Harris	.06	.03	.00
☐ 254	Rick Cerone	.06	.03	.00	☐ 297	Ned Yost	.06	.03	.00
☐ 255	Gene Garber	.06	.03	.00	☐ 298	Floyd Chiffer	.06	.03	.00
☐ 256	SV: Gene Garber	.06	.03	.00	☐ 299	George Wright	.06	.03	.00
☐ 257	Jesse Barfield	.60	.30	.06	☐ 300	Mike Schmidt	1.50	.75	.15
☐ 258	Manny Castillo	.06	.03	.00	☐ 301	SV: Mike Schmidt	.60	.30	.06
☐ 259	Jeff Jones	.06	.03	.00	☐ 302	Ernie Whitt	.10	.05	.01
☐ 260	Steve Kemp	.10	.05	.01	☐ 303	Miguel Dilone	.06	.03	.00
☐ 261	Tigers TL	.10	.05	.01	☐ 304	Dave Rucker	.06	.03	.00
	BA: Larry Herndon				☐ 305	Larry Bowa	.10	.05	.01
	ERA: Dan Petry				☐ 306	Tom Lasorda MG	.10	.05	.01
☐ 262	Ron Jackson	.06	.03	.00	☐ 307	Lou Piniella	.10	.05	.01
☐ 263	Renie Martin	.06	.03	.00	☐ 308	Jesus Vega	.06	.03	.00
☐ 264	Jamie Quirk	.06	.03	.00	☐ 309	Jeff Leonard	.10	.05	.01
☐ 265	Joel Youngblood	.06	.03	.00	☐ 310	Greg Luzinski	.10	.05	.01
☐ 266	Paul Boris	.06	.03	.00	☐ 311	Glenn Brummer	.06	.03	.00
☐ 267	Terry Francona	.06	.03	.00	☐ 312	Brian Kingman	.06	.03	.00
☐ 268	Storm Davis	1.00	.50	.10	☐ 313	Gary Gray	.06	.03	.00
☐ 269	Ron Oester	.06	.03	.00	☐ 314	Ken Dayley	.10	.05	.01

		MINT	EXC	G-VG
☐ 315	Rick Burleson	.10	.05	.01
☐ 316	Paul Splittorff	.06	.03	.00
☐ 317	Gary Rajsich	.06	.03	.00
☐ 318	John Tudor	.30	.15	.03
☐ 319	Lenn Sakata	.06	.03	.00
☐ 320	Steve Rogers	.06	.03	.00
☐ 321	Brewers TL	.15	.07	.01
	BA: Robin Yount			
	ERA: Pete Vuckovich			
☐ 322	Dave Van Gorder	.06	.03	.00
☐ 323	Luis DeLeon	.06	.03	.00
☐ 324	Mike Marshall	.30	.15	.03
☐ 325	Von Hayes	.30	.15	.03
☐ 326	Garth Iorg	.06	.03	.00
☐ 327	Bobby Castillo	.06	.03	.00
☐ 328	Craig Reynolds	.06	.03	.00
☐ 329	Randy Niemann	.06	.03	.00
☐ 330	Buddy Bell	.15	.07	.01
☐ 331	Mike Krukow	.10	.05	.01
☐ 332	Glenn Wilson	.45	.22	.04
☐ 333	Dave LaRoche	.06	.03	.00
☐ 334	SV: Dave LaRoche	.06	.03	.00
☐ 335	Steve Henderson	.06	.03	.00
☐ 336	Rene Lachemann MG	.06	.03	.00
☐ 337	Tito Landrum	.06	.03	.00
☐ 338	Bob Owchinko	.06	.03	.00
☐ 339	Terry Harper	.06	.03	.00
☐ 340	Larry Gura	.06	.03	.00
☐ 341	Doug DeCinces	.10	.05	.01
☐ 342	Atlee Hammaker	.10	.05	.01
☐ 343	Bob Bailor	.06	.03	.00
☐ 344	Roger LaFrancois	.06	.03	.00
☐ 345	Jim Clancy	.06	.03	.00
☐ 346	Joe Pittman	.06	.03	.00
☐ 347	Sammy Stewart	.06	.03	.00
☐ 348	Alan Bannister	.06	.03	.00
☐ 349	Checklist: 265-396	.10	.01	.00
☐ 350	Robin Yount	1.00	.50	.10
☐ 351	Reds TL	.10	.05	.01
	BA: Cesar Cedeno			
	ERA: Mario Soto			
☐ 352	Mike Scioscia	.10	.05	.01
☐ 353	Steve Comer	.06	.03	.00
☐ 354	Randy Johnson	.06	.03	.00
☐ 355	Jim Bibby	.06	.03	.00
☐ 356	Gary Woods	.06	.03	.00
☐ 357	Len Matuszek	.06	.03	.00
☐ 358	Jerry Garvin	.06	.03	.00
☐ 359	Dave Collins	.06	.03	.00
☐ 360	Nolan Ryan	2.00	1.00	.20
☐ 361	SV: Nolan Ryan	.75	.35	.07
☐ 362	Bill Almon	.06	.03	.00
☐ 363	John Stuper	.06	.03	.00
☐ 364	Brett Butler	.10	.05	.01
☐ 365	Dave Lopes	.10	.05	.01
☐ 366	Dick Williams MG	.06	.03	.00
☐ 367	Bud Anderson	.06	.03	.00
☐ 368	Richie Zisk	.06	.03	.00
☐ 369	Jesse Orosco	.06	.03	.00
☐ 370	Gary Carter	.50	.25	.05
☐ 371	Mike Richardt	.06	.03	.00
☐ 372	Terry Crowley	.06	.03	.00
☐ 373	Kevin Saucier	.06	.03	.00
☐ 374	Wayne Krenchicki	.06	.03	.00
☐ 375	Pete Vuckovich	.10	.05	.01
☐ 376	Ken Landreaux	.06	.03	.00
☐ 377	Lee May	.10	.05	.01
☐ 378	SV: Lee May	.06	.03	.00
☐ 379	Guy Sularz	.06	.03	.00
☐ 380	Ron Davis	.06	.03	.00
☐ 381	Red Sox TL	.15	.07	.01
	BA: Jim Rice			
	ERA: Bob Stanley			
☐ 382	Bob Knepper	.10	.05	.01
☐ 383	Ozzie Virgil	.06	.03	.00
☐ 384	Dave Dravecky	1.00	.50	.10
☐ 385	Mike Easler	.10	.05	.01
☐ 386	Rod Carew AS	.20	.10	.02
☐ 387	Bob Grich AS	.10	.05	.01
☐ 388	George Brett AS	.30	.15	.03
☐ 389	Robin Yount AS	.30	.15	.03
☐ 390	Reggie Jackson AS	.30	.15	.03
☐ 391	Rickey Henderson AS	.40	.20	.04
☐ 392	Fred Lynn AS	.10	.05	.01
☐ 393	Carlton Fisk AS	.15	.07	.01
☐ 394	Pete Vuckovich AS	.06	.03	.00
☐ 395	Larry Gura AS	.06	.03	.00
☐ 396	Dan Quisenberry AS	.10	.05	.01
☐ 397	Pete Rose AS	.50	.25	.05
☐ 398	Manny Trillo AS	.06	.03	.00
☐ 399	Mike Schmidt AS	.40	.20	.04
☐ 400	Dave Concepcion AS	.06	.03	.00
☐ 401	Dale Murphy AS	.35	.17	.03
☐ 402	Andre Dawson AS	.20	.10	.02
☐ 403	Tim Raines AS	.20	.10	.02
☐ 404	Gary Carter AS	.20	.10	.02
☐ 405	Steve Rogers AS	.06	.03	.00

		MINT	EXC	G-VG
☐ 406	Steve Carlton AS	.20	.10	.02
☐ 407	Bruce Sutter AS	.10	.05	.01
☐ 408	Rudy May	.06	.03	.00
☐ 409	Marvis Foley	.06	.03	.00
☐ 410	Phil Niekro	.35	.17	.03
☐ 411	SV: Phil Niekro	.15	.07	.01
☐ 412	Rangers TL	.10	.05	.01
	BA: Buddy Bell			
	ERA: Charlie Hough			
☐ 413	Matt Keough	.06	.03	.00
☐ 414	Julio Cruz	.06	.03	.00
☐ 415	Bob Forsch	.06	.03	.00
☐ 416	Joe Ferguson	.06	.03	.00
☐ 417	Tom Hausman	.06	.03	.00
☐ 418	Greg Pryor	.06	.03	.00
☐ 419	Steve Crawford	.06	.03	.00
☐ 420	Al Oliver	.10	.05	.01
☐ 421	SV: Al Oliver	.06	.03	.00
☐ 422	George Cappuzzello	.06	.03	.00
☐ 423	Tom Lawless	.10	.05	.01
☐ 424	Jerry Augustine	.06	.03	.00
☐ 425	Pedro Guerrero	.50	.25	.05
☐ 426	Earl Weaver MG	.10	.05	.01
☐ 427	Roy Lee Jackson	.06	.03	.00
☐ 428	Champ Summers	.06	.03	.00
☐ 429	Eddie Whitson	.06	.03	.00
☐ 430	Kirk Gibson	.50	.25	.05
☐ 431	Gary Gaetti	4.50	2.25	.45
☐ 432	Porfirio Altamirano	.06	.03	.00
☐ 433	Dale Berra	.06	.03	.00
☐ 434	Dennis Lamp	.06	.03	.00
☐ 435	Tony Armas	.10	.05	.01
☐ 436	Bill Campbell	.06	.03	.00
☐ 437	Rick Sweet	.06	.03	.00
☐ 438	Dave LaPoint	.45	.22	.04
☐ 439	Rafael Ramirez	.06	.03	.00
☐ 440	Ron Guidry	.20	.10	.02
☐ 441	Astros TL	.10	.05	.01
	BA: Ray Knight			
	ERA: Joe Niekro			
☐ 442	Brian Downing	.10	.05	.01
☐ 443	Don Hood	.06	.03	.00
☐ 444	Wally Backman	.20	.10	.02
☐ 445	Mike Flanagan	.10	.05	.01
☐ 446	Reid Nichols	.06	.03	.00
☐ 447	Bryn Smith	.15	.07	.01
☐ 448	Darrell Evans	.15	.07	.01
☐ 449	Eddie Milner	.10	.05	.01
☐ 450	Ted Simmons	.15	.07	.01

		MINT	EXC	G-VG
☐ 451	SV: Ted Simmons	.10	.05	.01
☐ 452	Lloyd Moseby	.10	.05	.01
☐ 453	Lamar Johnson	.06	.03	.00
☐ 454	Bob Welch	.10	.05	.01
☐ 455	Sixto Lezcano	.06	.03	.00
☐ 456	Lee Elia MG	.06	.03	.00
☐ 457	Milt Wilcox	.06	.03	.00
☐ 458	Ron Washington	.06	.03	.00
☐ 459	Ed Farmer	.06	.03	.00
☐ 460	Roy Smalley	.06	.03	.00
☐ 461	Steve Trout	.06	.03	.00
☐ 462	Steve Nicosia	.06	.03	.00
☐ 463	Gaylord Perry	.30	.15	.03
☐ 464	SV: Gaylord Perry	.15	.07	.01
☐ 465	Lonnie Smith	.15	.07	.01
☐ 466	Tom Underwood	.06	.03	.00
☐ 467	Rufino Linares	.06	.03	.00
☐ 468	Dave Goltz	.06	.03	.00
☐ 469	Ron Gardenhire	.06	.03	.00
☐ 470	Greg Minton	.06	.03	.00
☐ 471	K.C. Royals TL	.10	.05	.01
	BA: Willie Wilson			
	ERA: Vida Blue			
☐ 472	Gary Allenson	.06	.03	.00
☐ 473	John Lowenstein	.06	.03	.00
☐ 474	Ray Burris	.06	.03	.00
☐ 475	Cesar Cedeno	.10	.05	.01
☐ 476	Rob Picciolo	.06	.03	.00
☐ 477	Tom Niedenfuer	.10	.05	.01
☐ 478	Phil Garner	.06	.03	.00
☐ 479	Charlie Hough	.10	.05	.01
☐ 480	Toby Harrah	.10	.05	.01
☐ 481	Scot Thompson	.06	.03	.00
☐ 482	Tony Gwynn	20.00	10.00	2.00
☐ 483	Lynn Jones	.06	.03	.00
☐ 484	Dick Ruthven	.06	.03	.00
☐ 485	Omar Moreno	.06	.03	.00
☐ 486	Clyde King MG	.06	.03	.00
☐ 487	Jerry Hairston	.06	.03	.00
☐ 488	Alfredo Griffin	.10	.05	.01
☐ 489	Tom Herr	.10	.05	.01
☐ 490	Jim Palmer	.50	.25	.05
☐ 491	SV: Jim Palmer	.20	.10	.02
☐ 492	Paul Serna	.06	.03	.00
☐ 493	Steve McCatty	.06	.03	.00
☐ 494	Bob Brenly	.06	.03	.00
☐ 495	Warren Cromartie	.06	.03	.00
☐ 496	Tom Veryzer	.06	.03	.00
☐ 497	Rick Sutcliffe	.20	.10	.02

		MINT	EXC	G-VG			MINT	EXC	G-VG
☐ 498	Wade Boggs	35.00	17.50	3.50	☐ 543	Alan Fowlkes	.06	.03	.00
☐ 499	Jeff Little	.06	.03	.00	☐ 544	Larry Whisenton	.06	.03	.00
☐ 500	Reggie Jackson	1.00	.50	.10	☐ 545	Floyd Bannister	.06	.03	.00
☐ 501	SV: Reggie Jackson	.40	.20	.04	☐ 546	Dave Garcia MG	.06	.03	.00
☐ 502	Atlanta Braves TL	.25	.12	.02	☐ 547	Geoff Zahn	.06	.03	.00
	BA: Dale Murphy				☐ 548	Brian Giles	.06	.03	.00
	ERA: Phil Niekro				☐ 549	Charlie Puleo	.06	.03	.00
☐ 503	Moose Haas	.06	.03	.00	☐ 550	Carl Yastrzemski	1.00	.50	.10
☐ 504	Don Werner	.06	.03	.00	☐ 551	SV: Carl Yastrzemski	.40	.20	.04
☐ 505	Garry Templeton	.10	.05	.01	☐ 552	Tim Wallach	.25	.12	.02
☐ 506	Jim Gott	.35	.17	.03	☐ 553	Dennis Martinez	.10	.05	.01
☐ 507	Tony Scott	.06	.03	.00	☐ 554	Mike Vail	.06	.03	.00
☐ 508	Tom Filer	.15	.07	.01	☐ 555	Steve Yeager	.06	.03	.00
☐ 509	Lou Whitaker	.30	.15	.03	☐ 556	Willie Upshaw	.06	.03	.00
☐ 510	Tug McGraw	.15	.07	.01	☐ 557	Rick Honeycutt	.06	.03	.00
☐ 511	SV: Tug McGraw	.10	.05	.01	☐ 558	Dickie Thon	.10	.05	.01
☐ 512	Doyle Alexander	.10	.05	.01	☐ 559	Pete Redfern	.06	.03	.00
☐ 513	Fred Stanley	.06	.03	.00	☐ 560	Ron LeFlore	.10	.05	.01
☐ 514	Rudy Law	.06	.03	.00	☐ 561	Cardinals TL	.10	.05	.01
☐ 515	Gene Tenace	.06	.03	.00		BA: Lonnie Smith			
☐ 516	Bill Virdon MG	.06	.03	.00		ERA: Joaquin Andujar			
☐ 517	Gary Ward	.10	.05	.01	☐ 562	Dave Rozema	.06	.03	.00
☐ 518	Bill Laskey	.06	.03	.00	☐ 563	Juan Bonilla	.06	.03	.00
☐ 519	Terry Bulling	.06	.03	.00	☐ 564	Sid Monge	.06	.03	.00
☐ 520	Fred Lynn	.25	.12	.02	☐ 565	Bucky Dent	.15	.07	.01
☐ 521	Bruce Benedict	.06	.03	.00	☐ 566	Manny Sarmiento	.06	.03	.00
☐ 522	Pat Zachry	.06	.03	.00	☐ 567	Joe Simpson	.06	.03	.00
☐ 523	Carney Lansford	.25	.10	.02	☐ 568	Willie Hernandez	.10	.05	.01
☐ 524	Tom Brennan	.06	.03	.00	☐ 569	Jack Perconte	.06	.03	.00
☐ 525	Frank White	.10	.05	.01	☐ 570	Vida Blue	.10	.05	.01
☐ 526	Checklist: 397-528	.10	.01	.00	☐ 571	Mickey Klutts	.06	.03	.00
☐ 527	Larry Biittner	.06	.03	.00	☐ 572	Bob Watson	.10	.05	.01
☐ 528	Jamie Easterly	.06	.03	.00	☐ 573	Andy Hassler	.06	.03	.00
☐ 529	Tim Laudner	.06	.03	.00	☐ 574	Glenn Adams	.06	.03	.00
☐ 530	Eddie Murray	.75	.35	.07	☐ 575	Neil Allen	.06	.03	.00
☐ 531	Oakland A's TL	.20	.10	.02	☐ 576	Frank Robinson MG	.15	.07	.01
	BA: Rickey Henderson				☐ 577	Luis Aponte	.06	.03	.00
	ERA: Rick Langford				☐ 578	David Green	.06	.03	.00
☐ 532	Dave Stewart	.75	.35	.07	☐ 579	Rich Dauer	.06	.03	.00
☐ 533	Luis Salazar	.10	.05	.01	☐ 580	Tom Seaver	.75	.35	.07
☐ 534	John Butcher	.06	.03	.00	☐ 581	SV: Tom Seaver	.35	.17	.03
☐ 535	Manny Trillo	.06	.03	.00	☐ 582	Marshall Edwards	.06	.03	.00
☐ 536	John Wockenfuss	.06	.03	.00	☐ 583	Terry Forster	.10	.05	.01
☐ 537	Rod Scurry	.06	.03	.00	☐ 584	Dave Hostetler	.06	.03	.00
☐ 538	Danny Heep	.06	.03	.00	☐ 585	Jose Cruz	.10	.05	.01
☐ 539	Roger Erickson	.06	.03	.00	☐ 586	Frank Viola	6.00	3.00	.60
☐ 540	Ozzie Smith	.60	.30	.06	☐ 587	Ivan DeJesus	.06	.03	.00
☐ 541	Britt Burns	.06	.03	.00	☐ 588	Pat Underwood	.06	.03	.00
☐ 542	Jody Davis	.10	.05	.01	☐ 589	Alvis Woods	.06	.03	.00

		MINT	EXC	G-VG
☐ 590	Tony Pena	.20	.10	.02
☐ 591	White Sox TL	.10	.05	.01
	BA: Greg Luzinski			
	ERA: LaMarr Hoyt			
☐ 592	Shane Rawley	.10	.05	.01
☐ 593	Broderick Perkins	.06	.03	.00
☐ 594	Eric Rasmussen	.06	.03	.00
☐ 595	Tim Raines	.80	.40	.08
☐ 596	Randy Johnson	.06	.03	.00
☐ 597	Mike Proly	.06	.03	.00
☐ 598	Dwayne Murphy	.06	.03	.00
☐ 599	Don Aase	.06	.03	.00
☐ 600	George Brett	1.00	.50	.10
☐ 601	Ed Lynch	.06	.03	.00
☐ 602	Rich Gedman	.10	.05	.01
☐ 603	Joe Morgan	.40	.20	.04
☐ 604	SV: Joe Morgan	.15	.07	.01
☐ 605	Gary Roenicke	.06	.03	.00
☐ 606	Bobby Cox MG	.06	.03	.00
☐ 607	Charlie Leibrandt	.06	.03	.00
☐ 608	Don Money	.06	.03	.00
☐ 609	Danny Darwin	.06	.03	.00
☐ 610	Steve Garvey	.70	.35	.07
☐ 611	Bert Roberge	.06	.03	.00
☐ 612	Steve Swisher	.06	.03	.00
☐ 613	Mike Ivie	.06	.03	.00
☐ 614	Ed Glynn	.06	.03	.00
☐ 615	Garry Maddox	.06	.03	.00
☐ 616	Bill Nahorodny	.06	.03	.00
☐ 617	Butch Wynegar	.06	.03	.00
☐ 618	LaMarr Hoyt	.10	.05	.01
☐ 619	Keith Moreland	.06	.03	.00
☐ 620	Mike Norris	.06	.03	.00
☐ 621	New York Mets TL	.10	.05	.01
	BA: Mookie Wilson			
	ERA: Craig Swan			
☐ 622	Dave Edler	.06	.03	.00
☐ 623	Luis Sanchez	.06	.03	.00
☐ 624	Glenn Hubbard	.06	.03	.00
☐ 625	Ken Forsch	.06	.03	.00
☐ 626	Jerry Martin	.06	.03	.00
☐ 627	Doug Bair	.06	.03	.00
☐ 628	Julio Valdez	.06	.03	.00
☐ 629	Charlie Lea	.06	.03	.00
☐ 630	Paul Molitor	.25	.12	.02
☐ 631	Tippy Martinez	.06	.03	.00
☐ 632	Alex Trevino	.06	.03	.00
☐ 633	Vicente Romo	.06	.03	.00
☐ 634	Max Venable	.06	.03	.00
☐ 635	Graig Nettles	.15	.07	.01
☐ 636	SV: Graig Nettles	.10	.05	.01
☐ 637	Pat Corrales MG	.06	.03	.00
☐ 638	Dan Petry	.06	.03	.00
☐ 639	Art Howe	.10	.05	.01
☐ 640	Andre Thornton	.10	.05	.01
☐ 641	Billy Sample	.06	.03	.00
☐ 642	Checklist: 529-660	.10	.01	.00
☐ 643	Bump Wills	.06	.03	.00
☐ 644	Joe Lefebvre	.06	.03	.00
☐ 645	Bill Madlock	.10	.05	.01
☐ 646	Jim Essian	.06	.03	.00
☐ 647	Bobby Mitchell	.06	.03	.00
☐ 648	Jeff Burroughs	.10	.05	.01
☐ 649	Tommy Boggs	.06	.03	.00
☐ 650	George Hendrick	.10	.05	.01
☐ 651	Angels TL	.20	.10	.02
	BA: Rod Carew			
	ERA: Mike Witt			
☐ 652	Butch Hobson	.06	.03	.00
☐ 653	Ellis Valentine	.06	.03	.00
☐ 654	Bob Ojeda	.15	.07	.01
☐ 655	Al Bumbry	.06	.03	.00
☐ 656	Dave Frost	.06	.03	.00
☐ 657	Mike Gates	.06	.03	.00
☐ 658	Frank Pastore	.06	.03	.00
☐ 659	Charlie Moore	.06	.03	.00
☐ 660	Mike Hargrove	.10	.05	.01
☐ 661	Bill Russell	.10	.05	.01
☐ 662	Joe Sambito	.06	.03	.00
☐ 663	Tom O'Malley	.06	.03	.00
☐ 664	Bob Molinaro	.06	.03	.00
☐ 665	Jim Sundberg	.06	.03	.00
☐ 666	Sparky Anderson MG	.10	.05	.01
☐ 667	Dick Davis	.06	.03	.00
☐ 668	Larry Christenson	.06	.03	.00
☐ 669	Mike Squires	.06	.03	.00
☐ 670	Jerry Mumphrey	.06	.03	.00
☐ 671	Lenny Faedo	.06	.03	.00
☐ 672	Jim Kaat	.15	.07	.01
☐ 673	SV: Jim Kaat	.10	.05	.01
☐ 674	Kurt Bevacqua	.06	.03	.00
☐ 675	Jim Beattie	.06	.03	.00
☐ 676	Biff Pocoroba	.06	.03	.00
☐ 677	Dave Revering	.06	.03	.00
☐ 678	Juan Beniquez	.06	.03	.00
☐ 679	Mike Scott	.45	.22	.04
☐ 680	Andre Dawson	.45	.22	.04
☐ 681	Dodgers Leaders	.25	.12	.02

		MINT	EXC	G-VG
	BA: Pedro Guerrero			
	ERA: Fern.Valenzuela			
☐ 682	Bob Stanley	.06	.03	.00
☐ 683	Dan Ford	.06	.03	.00
☐ 684	Rafael Landestoy	.06	.03	.00
☐ 685	Lee Mazzilli	.06	.03	.00
☐ 686	Randy Lerch	.06	.03	.00
☐ 687	U.L. Washington	.06	.03	.00
☐ 688	Jim Wohlford	.06	.03	.00
☐ 689	Ron Hassey	.06	.03	.00
☐ 690	Kent Hrbek	.75	.35	.07
☐ 691	Dave Tobik	.06	.03	.00
☐ 692	Denny Walling	.06	.03	.00
☐ 693	Sparky Lyle	.10	.05	.01
☐ 694	SV: Sparky Lyle	.06	.03	.00
☐ 695	Ruppert Jones	.06	.03	.00
☐ 696	Chuck Tanner MG	.06	.03	.00
☐ 697	Barry Foote	.06	.03	.00
☐ 698	Tony Bernazard	.06	.03	.00
☐ 699	Lee Smith	.15	.07	.01
☐ 700	Keith Hernandez	.45	.22	.04
☐ 701	Batting Leaders	.10	.05	.01
	AL: Willie Wilson			
	NL: Al Oliver			
☐ 702	Home Run Leaders	.15	.07	.01
	AL: Reggie Jackson			
	AL: Gorman Thomas			
	NL: Dave Kingman			
☐ 703	RBI Leaders	.15	.07	.01
	AL: Hal McRae			
	NL: Dale Murphy			
	NL: Al Oliver			
☐ 704	SB Leaders	.25	.12	.02
	AL: Rickey Henderson			
	NL: Tim Raines			
☐ 705	Victory Leaders	.12	.06	.01
	AL: LaMarr Hoyt			
	NL: Steve Carlton			
☐ 706	Strikeout Leaders	.12	.06	.01
	AL: Floyd Bannister			
	NL: Steve Carlton			
☐ 707	ERA Leaders	.10	.05	.01
	AL: Rick Sutcliffe			
	NL: Steve Rogers			
☐ 708	Leading Firemen	.10	.05	.01
	AL: Dan Quisenberry			
	NL: Bruce Sutter			
☐ 709	Jimmy Sexton	.06	.03	.00
☐ 710	Willie Wilson	.15	.07	.01
☐ 711	Mariners TL	.10	.05	.01
	BA: Bruce Bochte			
	ERA: Jim Beattie			
☐ 712	Bruce Kison	.06	.03	.00
☐ 713	Ron Hodges	.06	.03	.00
☐ 714	Wayne Nordhagen	.06	.03	.00
☐ 715	Tony Perez	.20	.10	.02
☐ 716	SV: Tony Perez	.10	.05	.01
☐ 717	Scott Sanderson	.06	.03	.00
☐ 718	Jim Dwyer	.06	.03	.00
☐ 719	Rich Gale	.06	.03	.00
☐ 720	Dave Concepcion	.15	.07	.01
☐ 721	John Martin	.06	.03	.00
☐ 722	Jorge Orta	.06	.03	.00
☐ 723	Randy Moffitt	.06	.03	.00
☐ 724	Johnny Grubb	.06	.03	.00
☐ 725	Dan Spillner	.06	.03	.00
☐ 726	Harvey Kuenn MG	.06	.03	.00
☐ 727	Chet Lemon	.10	.05	.01
☐ 728	Ron Reed	.06	.03	.00
☐ 729	Jerry Morales	.06	.03	.00
☐ 730	Jason Thompson	.06	.03	.00
☐ 731	Al Williams	.06	.03	.00
☐ 732	Dave Henderson	.15	.07	.01
☐ 733	Buck Martinez	.06	.03	.00
☐ 734	Steve Braun	.06	.03	.00
☐ 735	Tommy John	.20	.10	.02
☐ 736	SV: Tommy John	.10	.05	.01
☐ 737	Mitchell Page	.06	.03	.00
☐ 738	Tim Foli	.06	.03	.00
☐ 739	Rick Ownbey	.06	.03	.00
☐ 740	Rusty Staub	.15	.07	.01
☐ 741	SV: Rusty Staub	.10	.05	.01
☐ 742	Padres TL	.10	.05	.01
	BA: Terry Kennedy			
	ERA: Tim Lollar			
☐ 743	Mike Torrez	.06	.03	.00
☐ 744	Brad Mills	.06	.03	.00
☐ 745	Scott McGregor	.10	.05	.01
☐ 746	John Wathan	.10	.05	.01
☐ 747	Fred Breining	.06	.03	.00
☐ 748	Derrel Thomas	.06	.03	.00
☐ 749	Jon Matlack	.06	.03	.00
☐ 750	Ben Oglivie	.10	.05	.01
☐ 751	Brad Havens	.06	.03	.00
☐ 752	Luis Pujols	.06	.03	.00
☐ 753	Elias Sosa	.06	.03	.00
☐ 754	Bill Robinson	.10	.05	.01
☐ 755	John Candelaria	.10	.05	.01

		MINT	EXC	G-VG
☐ 756	Russ Nixon MG	.06	.03	.00
☐ 757	Rick Manning	.06	.03	.00
☐ 758	Aurelio Rodriguez ..	.06	.03	.00
☐ 759	Doug Bird	.06	.03	.00
☐ 760	Dale Murphy	1.50	.75	.15
☐ 761	Gary Lucas	.06	.03	.00
☐ 762	Cliff Johnson	.06	.03	.00
☐ 763	Al Cowens	.06	.03	.00
☐ 764	Pete Falcone	.06	.03	.00
☐ 765	Bob Boone	.20	.10	.02
☐ 766	Barry Bonnell	.06	.03	.00
☐ 767	Duane Kuiper	.06	.03	.00
☐ 768	Chris Speier	.06	.03	.00
☐ 769	Checklist: 661-792	.10	.01	.00
☐ 770	Dave Winfield	.60	.30	.06
☐ 771	Twins TL	.10	.05	.01
	BA: Kent Hrbek			
	ERA: Bobby Castillo			
☐ 772	Jim Kern	.06	.03	.00
☐ 773	Larry Hisle	.06	.03	.00
☐ 774	Alan Ashby	.06	.03	.00
☐ 775	Burt Hooton	.06	.03	.00
☐ 776	Larry Parrish	.10	.05	.01
☐ 777	John Curtis	.06	.03	.00
☐ 778	Rich Hebner	.06	.03	.00
☐ 779	Rick Waits	.06	.03	.00
☐ 780	Gary Matthews	.10	.05	.01
☐ 781	Rick Rhoden	.10	.05	.01
☐ 782	Bobby Murcer	.10	.05	.01
☐ 783	SV: Bobby Murcer ..	.06	.03	.00
☐ 784	Jeff Newman	.06	.03	.00
☐ 785	Dennis Leonard	.10	.05	.01
☐ 786	Ralph Houk MG	.06	.03	.00
☐ 787	Dick Tidrow	.06	.03	.00
☐ 788	Dane Iorg	.06	.03	.00
☐ 789	Bryan Clark	.06	.03	.00
☐ 790	Bob Grich	.10	.05	.01
☐ 791	Gary Lavelle	.06	.03	.00
☐ 792	Chris Chambliss ...	.15	.07	.01

1983 Topps Traded

The cards in this 132-card set measure 2 ½"
by 3 ½". For the third year in a row, Topps
issued a 132-card Traded (or extended) set
featuring some of the year's top rookies and
players who had changed teams during the
year, but were featured with their old team in
the Topps regular issue of 1983. The cards
were available through hobby dealers only and
were printed in Ireland by the Topps affiliate in
that country. The set is numbered alphabetically by the last name of the player of the card.
The Darryl Strawberry card #108 can be found
with either one or two asterisks (in the lower
left corner of the reverse).

		MINT	EXC	G-VG
COMPLETE SET (132)		90.00	45.00	9.00
COMMON PLAYER (1-132)		.08	.04	.01
☐	1T Neil Allen	.15	.07	.01
☐	2T Bill Almon	.08	.04	.01
☐	3T Joe Altobelli MG ...	.08	.04	.01
☐	4T Tony Armas	.15	.07	.01
☐	5T Doug Bair	.08	.04	.01
☐	6T Steve Baker	.08	.04	.01
☐	7T Floyd Bannister ...	.15	.07	.01
☐	8T Don Baylor	.25	.12	.02
☐	9T Tony Bernazard ...	.08	.04	.01
☐	10T Larry Biittner	.08	.04	.01
☐	11T Dann Bilardello ...	.08	.04	.01
☐	12T Doug Bird	.08	.04	.01
☐	13T Steve Boros MG	.08	.04	.01

		MINT	EXC	G-VG
☐	14T Greg Brock	.35	.17	.03
☐	15T Mike Brown	.15	.07	.01
	(Red Sox pitcher)			
☐	16T Tom Burgmeier	.08	.04	.01
☐	17T Randy Bush	.35	.17	.03
☐	18T Bert Campaneris	.15	.07	.01
☐	19T Ron Cey	.20	.10	.02
☐	20T Chris Codiroli	.15	.07	.01
☐	21T Dave Collins	.08	.04	.01
☐	22T Terry Crowley	.08	.04	.01
☐	23T Julio Cruz	.08	.04	.01
☐	24T Mike Davis	.15	.07	.01
☐	25T Frank DiPino	.08	.04	.01
☐	26T Bill Doran	1.25	.60	.12
☐	27T Jerry Dybzinski	.08	.04	.01
☐	28T Jamie Easterly	.08	.04	.01
☐	29T Juan Eichelberger	.08	.04	.01
☐	30T Jim Essian	.08	.04	.01
☐	31T Pete Falcone	.08	.04	.01
☐	32T Mike Ferraro MG	.08	.04	.01
☐	33T Terry Forster	.15	.07	.01
☐	34T Julio Franco	3.50	1.75	.35
☐	35T Rich Gale	.08	.04	.01
☐	36T Kiko Garcia	.08	.04	.01
☐	37T Steve Garvey	1.50	.75	.15
☐	38T Johnny Grubb	.08	.04	.01
☐	39T Mel Hall	1.25	.60	.12
☐	40T Von Hayes	1.00	.50	.10
☐	41T Danny Heep	.15	.07	.01
☐	42T Steve Henderson	.08	.04	.01
☐	43T Keith Hernandez	1.00	.50	.10
☐	44T Leo Hernandez	.15	.07	.01
☐	45T Willie Hernandez	.25	.12	.02
☐	46T Al Holland	.08	.04	.01
☐	47T Frank Howard MG	.15	.07	.01
☐	48T Bobby Johnson	.08	.04	.01
☐	49T Cliff Johnson	.08	.04	.01
☐	50T Odell Jones	.08	.04	.01
☐	51T Mike Jorgensen	.08	.04	.01
☐	52T Bob Kearney	.08	.04	.01
☐	53T Steve Kemp	.15	.07	.01
☐	54T Matt Keough	.08	.04	.01
☐	55T Ron Kittle	.75	.35	.07
☐	56T Mickey Klutts	.08	.04	.01
☐	57T Alan Knicely	.08	.04	.01
☐	58T Mike Krukow	.15	.07	.01
☐	59T Rafael Landestoy	.08	.04	.01
☐	60T Carney Lansford	.40	.17	.03
☐	61T Joe Lefebvre	.08	.04	.01
☐	62T Bryan Little	.08	.04	.01
☐	63T Aurelio Lopez	.08	.04	.01
☐	64T Mike Madden	.08	.04	.01
☐	65T Rick Manning	.08	.04	.01
☐	66T Billy Martin MG	.30	.15	.03
☐	67T Lee Mazzilli	.08	.04	.01
☐	68T Andy McGaffigan	.08	.04	.01
☐	69T Craig McMurtry	.15	.07	.01
☐	70T John McNamara MG	.15	.07	.01
☐	71T Orlando Mercado	.15	.07	.01
☐	72T Larry Milbourne	.08	.04	.01
☐	73T Randy Moffitt	.08	.04	.01
☐	74T Sid Monge	.08	.04	.01
☐	75T Jose Morales	.08	.04	.01
☐	76T Omar Moreno	.08	.04	.01
☐	77T Joe Morgan	1.50	.75	.15
☐	78T Mike Morgan	.20	.10	.02
☐	79T Dale Murray	.08	.04	.01
☐	80T Jeff Newman	.08	.04	.01
☐	81T Pete O'Brien	1.75	.85	.17
☐	82T Jorge Orta	.08	.04	.01
☐	83T Alejandro Pena	.60	.30	.06
☐	84T Pascual Perez	.30	.15	.03
☐	85T Tony Perez	.60	.30	.06
☐	86T Broderick Perkins	.08	.04	.01
☐	87T Tony Phillips	.40	.20	.04
☐	88T Charlie Puleo	.08	.04	.01
☐	89T Pat Putnam	.08	.04	.01
☐	90T Jamie Quirk	.08	.04	.01
☐	91T Doug Rader MG	.15	.07	.01
☐	92T Chuck Rainey	.08	.04	.01
☐	93T Bobby Ramos	.08	.04	.01
☐	94T Gary Redus	.45	.22	.04
☐	95T Steve Renko	.08	.04	.01
☐	96T Leon Roberts	.08	.04	.01
☐	97T Aurelio Rodriguez	.08	.04	.01
☐	98T Dick Ruthven	.08	.04	.01
☐	99T Daryl Sconiers	.08	.04	.01
☐	100T Mike Scott	1.50	.75	.15
☐	101T Tom Seaver	2.00	1.00	.20
☐	102T John Shelby	.45	.22	.04
☐	103T Bob Shirley	.08	.04	.01
☐	104T Joe Simpson	.08	.04	.01
☐	105T Doug Sisk	.15	.07	.01
☐	106T Mike Smithson	.15	.07	.01
☐	107T Elias Sosa	.08	.04	.01
☐	108T Darryl Strawberry	65.00	32.50	6.50
☐	109T Tom Tellmann	.08	.04	.01
☐	110T Gene Tenace	.15	.07	.01

		MINT	EXC	G-VG
☐ 111T	Gorman Thomas	.20	.10	.02
☐ 112T	Dick Tidrow	.08	.04	.01
☐ 113T	Dave Tobik	.08	.04	.01
☐ 114T	Wayne Tolleson	.15	.07	.01
☐ 115T	Mike Torrez	.08	.04	.01
☐ 116T	Manny Trillo	.08	.04	.01
☐ 117T	Steve Trout	.08	.04	.01
☐ 118T	Lee Tunnell	.15	.07	.01
☐ 119T	Mike Vail	.08	.04	.01
☐ 120T	Ellis Valentine	.08	.04	.01
☐ 121T	Tom Veryzer	.08	.04	.01
☐ 122T	George Vukovich ...	.08	.04	.01
☐ 123T	Rick Waits	.08	.04	.01
☐ 124T	Greg Walker	.60	.30	.06
☐ 125T	Chris Welsh	.08	.04	.01
☐ 126T	Len Whitehouse	.08	.04	.01
☐ 127T	Eddie Whitson	.08	.04	.01
☐ 128T	Jim Wohlford	.08	.04	.01
☐ 129T	Matt Young	.15	.07	.01
☐ 130T	Joel Youngblood	.08	.04	.01
☐ 131T	Pat Zachry	.08	.04	.01
☐ 132T	Checklist 1T-132T ..	.08	.01	.00

1984 Topps

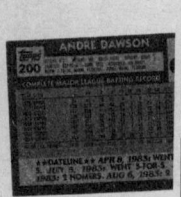

The cards in this 792-card set measure 2 ½" by 3 ½". For the second year in a row, Topps utilized a dual picture on the front of the card. A portrait is shown in a square insert and an action shot is featured in the main photo. Card numbers 1-6 feature 1983 Highlights (HL), cards 131-138 depict League Leaders, card numbers 386-407 feature All-Stars, and card numbers 701-718 feature active Major League career leaders in various statistical categories. Each team leader (TL) card features the team's leading hitter and pitcher pictured on the front with a team checklist back. There are six numerical checklist cards in the set. The player cards feature team logos in the upper right corner of the reverse. Topps also produced a specially boxed "glossy" edition frequently referred to as the Topps Tiffany set. There were supposedly only 10,000 sets of the Tiffany cards produced; they were marketed to hobby dealers. The checklist of cards (792 regular and 132 Traded) is identical to that of the normal non-glossy cards. There are two primary distinguishing features of the Tiffany cards, white card stock reverses and high gloss obverses. These Tiffany cards are valued at approximately five times the values listed below.

		MINT	EXC	G-VG
COMPLETE SET (792)		100.00	50.00	10.00
COMMON PLAYER (1-792)		.05	.02	.00
☐ 1	HL: Steve Carlton ... 300th win and all-time SO king	.30	.07	.01
☐ 2	HL: Rickey Henderson 100 stolen bases, three times	.30	.15	.03
☐ 3	HL: Dan Quisenberry Sets save record	.10	.05	.01
☐ 4	HL: Nolan Ryan, ... Steve Carlton, and Gaylord Perry (All surpass Johnson)	.30	.15	.03
☐ 5	HL: Dave Righetti, .. Bob Forsch, and Mike Warren (All pitch no-hitters)	.10	.05	.01
☐ 6	HL: Johnny Bench, .. Gaylord Perry, and Carl Yastrzemski (Superstars retire)	.30	.15	.03
☐ 7	Gary Lucas	.05	.02	.00
☐ 8	Don Mattingly	27.00	10.00	2.00
☐ 9	Jim Gott	.10	.05	.01

			MINT	EXC	G-VG
☐	10	Robin Yount	.75	.35	.07
☐	11	Minnesota Twins TL	.10	.05	.01
		Kent Hrbek			
		Ken Schrom			
☐	12	Billy Sample	.05	.02	.00
☐	13	Scott Holman	.05	.02	.00
☐	14	Tom Brookens	.05	.02	.00
☐	15	Burt Hooton	.05	.02	.00
☐	16	Omar Moreno	.05	.02	.00
☐	17	John Denny	.08	.04	.01
☐	18	Dale Berra	.05	.02	.00
☐	19	Ray Fontenot	.08	.04	.01
☐	20	Greg Luzinski	.10	.05	.01
☐	21	Joe Altobelli MG	.05	.02	.00
☐	22	Bryan Clark	.05	.02	.00
☐	23	Keith Moreland	.05	.02	.00
☐	24	John Martin	.05	.02	.00
☐	25	Glenn Hubbard	.05	.02	.00
☐	26	Bud Black	.05	.02	.00
☐	27	Daryl Sconiers	.05	.02	.00
☐	28	Frank Viola	.80	.40	.08
☐	29	Danny Heep	.05	.02	.00
☐	30	Wade Boggs	7.00	3.50	.70
☐	31	Andy McGaffigan	.05	.02	.00
☐	32	Bobby Ramos	.05	.02	.00
☐	33	Tom Burgmeier	.05	.02	.00
☐	34	Eddie Milner	.05	.02	.00
☐	35	Don Sutton	.30	.15	.03
☐	36	Denny Walling	.05	.02	.00
☐	37	Texas Rangers TL	.10	.05	.01
		Buddy Bell			
		Rick Honeycutt			
☐	38	Luis DeLeon	.05	.02	.00
☐	39	Garth Iorg	.05	.02	.00
☐	40	Dusty Baker	.08	.04	.01
☐	41	Tony Bernazard	.05	.02	.00
☐	42	Johnny Grubb	.05	.02	.00
☐	43	Ron Reed	.05	.02	.00
☐	44	Jim Morrison	.05	.02	.00
☐	45	Jerry Mumphrey	.05	.02	.00
☐	46	Ray Smith	.05	.02	.00
☐	47	Rudy Law	.05	.02	.00
☐	48	Julio Franco	1.50	.75	.15
☐	49	John Stuper	.05	.02	.00
☐	50	Chris Chambliss	.10	.05	.01
☐	51	Jim Frey MG	.05	.02	.00
☐	52	Paul Splittorff	.05	.02	.00
☐	53	Juan Beniquez	.05	.02	.00
☐	54	Jesse Orosco	.05	.02	.00

			MINT	EXC	G-VG
☐	55	Dave Concepcion	.10	.05	.01
☐	56	Gary Allenson	.05	.02	.00
☐	57	Dan Schatzeder	.05	.02	.00
☐	58	Max Venable	.05	.02	.00
☐	59	Sammy Stewart	.05	.02	.00
☐	60	Paul Molitor	.20	.10	.02
☐	61	Chris Codiroli	.08	.04	.01
☐	62	Dave Hostetler	.05	.02	.00
☐	63	Ed VandeBerg	.05	.02	.00
☐	64	Mike Scioscia	.08	.04	.01
☐	65	Kirk Gibson	.35	.17	.03
☐	66	Houston Astros TL	.20	.10	.02
		Jose Cruz			
		Nolan Ryan			
☐	67	Gary Ward	.08	.04	.01
☐	68	Luis Salazar	.05	.02	.00
☐	69	Rod Scurry	.05	.02	.00
☐	70	Gary Matthews	.08	.04	.01
☐	71	Leo Hernandez	.05	.02	.00
☐	72	Mike Squires	.05	.02	.00
☐	73	Jody Davis	.08	.04	.01
☐	74	Jerry Martin	.05	.02	.00
☐	75	Bob Forsch	.05	.02	.00
☐	76	Alfredo Griffin	.08	.04	.01
☐	77	Brett Butler	.10	.05	.01
☐	78	Mike Torrez	.05	.02	.00
☐	79	Rob Wilfong	.05	.02	.00
☐	80	Steve Rogers	.05	.02	.00
☐	81	Billy Martin MG	.15	.07	.01
☐	82	Doug Bird	.05	.02	.00
☐	83	Richie Zisk	.05	.02	.00
☐	84	Lenny Faedo	.05	.02	.00
☐	85	Atlee Hammaker	.05	.02	.00
☐	86	John Shelby	.25	.12	.02
☐	87	Frank Pastore	.05	.02	.00
☐	88	Rob Picciolo	.05	.02	.00
☐	89	Mike Smithson	.08	.04	.01
☐	90	Pedro Guerrero	.35	.17	.03
☐	91	Dan Spillner	.05	.02	.00
☐	92	Lloyd Moseby	.12	.06	.01
☐	93	Bob Knepper	.08	.04	.01
☐	94	Mario Ramirez	.05	.02	.00
☐	95	Aurelio Lopez	.05	.02	.00
☐	96	K.C. Royals TL	.10	.05	.01
		Hal McRae			
		Larry Gura			
☐	97	LaMarr Hoyt	.08	.04	.01
☐	98	Steve Nicosia	.05	.02	.00
☐	99	Craig Lefferts	.25	.12	.02

		MINT	EXC	G-VG			MINT	EXC	G-VG
☐ 100	Reggie Jackson	.75	.35	.07	☐ 136	Strikeout Leaders	.15	.07	.01
☐ 101	Porfirio Altamirano ..	.05	.02	.00		Steve Carlton			
☐ 102	Ken Oberkfell	.05	.02	.00		Jack Morris			
☐ 103	Dwayne Murphy	.05	.02	.00	☐ 137	ERA Leaders	.08	.04	.01
☐ 104	Ken Dayley	.05	.02	.00		Atlee Hammaker			
☐ 105	Tony Armas	.08	.04	.01		Rick Honeycutt			
☐ 106	Tim Stoddard	.05	.02	.00	☐ 138	Leading Firemen	.08	.04	.01
☐ 107	Ned Yost	.05	.02	.00		Al Holland			
☐ 108	Randy Moffitt	.05	.02	.00		Dan Quisenberry			
☐ 109	Brad Wellman	.05	.02	.00	☐ 139	Bert Campaneris	.08	.04	.01
☐ 110	Ron Guidry	.25	.12	.02	☐ 140	Storm Davis	.12	.06	.01
☐ 111	Bill Virdon MG	.05	.02	.00	☐ 141	Pat Corrales MG	.05	.02	.00
☐ 112	Tom Niedenfuer	.08	.04	.01	☐ 142	Rich Gale	.05	.02	.00
☐ 113	Kelly Paris	.08	.04	.01	☐ 143	Jose Morales	.05	.02	.00
☐ 114	Checklist 1-132	.08	.01	.00	☐ 144	Brian Harper	.25	.12	.02
☐ 115	Andre Thornton	.08	.04	.01	☐ 145	Gary Lavelle	.05	.02	.00
☐ 116	George Bjorkman	.05	.02	.00	☐ 146	Ed Romero	.05	.02	.00
☐ 117	Tom Veryzer	.05	.02	.00	☐ 147	Dan Petry	.05	.02	.00
☐ 118	Charlie Hough	.08	.04	.01	☐ 148	Joe Lefebvre	.05	.02	.00
☐ 119	John Wockenfuss	.05	.02	.00	☐ 149	Jon Matlack	.05	.02	.00
☐ 120	Keith Hernandez	.35	.17	.03	☐ 150	Dale Murphy	1.00	.50	.10
☐ 121	Pat Sheridan	.20	.10	.02	☐ 151	Steve Trout	.05	.02	.00
☐ 122	Cecilio Guante	.08	.04	.01	☐ 152	Glenn Brummer	.05	.02	.00
☐ 123	Butch Wynegar	.05	.02	.00	☐ 153	Dick Tidrow	.05	.02	.00
☐ 124	Damaso Garcia	.05	.02	.00	☐ 154	Dave Henderson	.15	.07	.01
☐ 125	Britt Burns	.05	.02	.00	☐ 155	Frank White	.10	.05	.01
☐ 126	Atlanta Braves TL ...	.15	.07	.01	☐ 156	Oakland A's TL	.15	.07	.01
	Dale Murphy					Rickey Henderson			
	Craig McMurtry					Tim Conroy			
☐ 127	Mike Madden	.05	.02	.00	☐ 157	Gary Gaetti	.75	.35	.07
☐ 128	Rick Manning	.05	.02	.00	☐ 158	John Curtis	.05	.02	.00
☐ 129	Bill Laskey	.05	.02	.00	☐ 159	Darryl Cias	.05	.02	.00
☐ 130	Ozzie Smith	.40	.20	.04	☐ 160	Mario Soto	.05	.02	.00
☐ 131	Batting Leaders	.25	.12	.02	☐ 161	Junior Ortiz	.05	.02	.00
	Bill Madlock				☐ 162	Bob Ojeda	.10	.05	.01
	Wade Boggs				☐ 163	Lorenzo Gray	.05	.02	.00
☐ 132	Home Run Leaders .	.25	.12	.02	☐ 164	Scott Sanderson ...	.05	.02	.00
	Mike Schmidt				☐ 165	Ken Singleton	.10	.05	.01
	Jim Rice				☐ 166	Jamie Nelson	.05	.02	.00
☐ 133	RBI Leaders	.20	.10	.02	☐ 167	Marshall Edwards ...	.05	.02	.00
	Dale Murphy				☐ 168	Juan Bonilla	.05	.02	.00
	Cecil Cooper				☐ 169	Larry Parrish	.08	.04	.01
	Jim Rice				☐ 170	Jerry Reuss	.08	.04	.01
☐ 134	Stolen Base Leaders .	.25	.12	.02	☐ 171	Frank Robinson MG ..	.12	.06	.01
	Tim Raines				☐ 172	Frank DiPino	.05	.02	.00
	Rickey Henderson				☐ 173	Marvell Wynne	.10	.05	.01
☐ 135	Victory Leaders	.08	.04	.01	☐ 174	Juan Berenguer	.05	.02	.00
	John Denny				☐ 175	Graig Nettles	.15	.07	.01
	LaMarr Hoyt				☐ 176	Lee Smith	.10	.05	.01

		MINT	EXC	G-VG
☐ 177	Jerry Hairston	.05	.02	.00
☐ 178	Bill Krueger	.05	.02	.00
☐ 179	Buck Martinez	.05	.02	.00
☐ 180	Manny Trillo	.05	.02	.00
☐ 181	Roy Thomas	.05	.02	.00
☐ 182	Darryl Strawberry	15.00	7.50	1.50
☐ 183	Al Williams	.05	.02	.00
☐ 184	Mike O'Berry	.05	.02	.00
☐ 185	Sixto Lezcano	.05	.02	.00
☐ 186	Cardinal TL	.10	.05	.01
	Lonnie Smith			
	John Stuper			
☐ 187	Luis Aponte	.05	.02	.00
☐ 188	Bryan Little	.05	.02	.00
☐ 189	Tim Conroy	.08	.04	.01
☐ 190	Ben Oglivie	.08	.04	.01
☐ 191	Mike Boddicker	.10	.05	.01
☐ 192	Nick Esasky	2.25	1.10	.22
☐ 193	Darrell Brown	.05	.02	.00
☐ 194	Domingo Ramos	.05	.02	.00
☐ 195	Jack Morris	.20	.10	.02
☐ 196	Don Slaught	.15	.07	.01
☐ 197	Garry Hancock	.05	.02	.00
☐ 198	Bill Doran	.75	.35	.07
☐ 199	Willie Hernandez	.20	.10	.02
☐ 200	Andre Dawson	.40	.20	.04
☐ 201	Bruce Kison	.05	.02	.00
☐ 202	Bobby Cox MG	.05	.02	.00
☐ 203	Matt Keough	.05	.02	.00
☐ 204	Bobby Meacham	.10	.05	.01
☐ 205	Greg Minton	.05	.02	.00
☐ 206	Andy Van Slyke	2.50	1.25	.25
☐ 207	Donnie Moore	.05	.02	.00
☐ 208	Jose Oquendo	.50	.25	.05
☐ 209	Manny Sarmiento	.05	.02	.00
☐ 210	Joe Morgan	.35	.17	.03
☐ 211	Rick Sweet	.05	.02	.00
☐ 212	Broderick Perkins	.05	.02	.00
☐ 213	Bruce Hurst	.20	.10	.02
☐ 214	Paul Householder	.05	.02	.00
☐ 215	Tippy Martinez	.05	.02	.00
☐ 216	White Sox TL	.12	.06	.01
	Carlton Fisk			
	Richard Dotson			
☐ 217	Alan Ashby	.05	.02	.00
☐ 218	Rick Waits	.05	.02	.00
☐ 219	Joe Simpson	.05	.02	.00
☐ 220	Fernando Valenzuela	.30	.15	.03
☐ 221	Cliff Johnson	.05	.02	.00

		MINT	EXC	G-VG
☐ 222	Rick Honeycutt	.05	.02	.00
☐ 223	Wayne Krenchicki	.05	.02	.00
☐ 224	Sid Monge	.05	.02	.00
☐ 225	Lee Mazzilli	.05	.02	.00
☐ 226	Juan Eichelberger	.05	.02	.00
☐ 227	Steve Braun	.05	.02	.00
☐ 228	John Rabb	.05	.02	.00
☐ 229	Paul Owens MG	.05	.02	.00
☐ 230	Rickey Henderson	1.25	.60	.12
☐ 231	Gary Woods	.05	.02	.00
☐ 232	Tim Wallach	.15	.07	.01
☐ 233	Checklist 133-264	.08	.01	.00
☐ 234	Rafael Ramirez	.05	.02	.00
☐ 235	Matt Young	.08	.04	.01
☐ 236	Ellis Valentine	.05	.02	.00
☐ 237	John Castino	.05	.02	.00
☐ 238	Reid Nichols	.05	.02	.00
☐ 239	Jay Howell	.10	.05	.01
☐ 240	Eddie Murray	.55	.27	.05
☐ 241	Bill Almon	.05	.02	.00
☐ 242	Alex Trevino	.05	.02	.00
☐ 243	Pete Ladd	.05	.02	.00
☐ 244	Candy Maldonado	.25	.12	.02
☐ 245	Rick Sutcliffe	.25	.12	.02
☐ 246	New York Mets TL	.15	.07	.01
	Mookie Wilson			
	Tom Seaver			
☐ 247	Onix Concepcion	.05	.02	.00
☐ 248	Bill Dawley	.10	.05	.01
☐ 249	Jay Johnstone	.08	.04	.01
☐ 250	Bill Madlock	.10	.05	.01
☐ 251	Tony Gwynn	3.00	1.50	.30
☐ 252	Larry Christenson	.05	.02	.00
☐ 253	Jim Wohlford	.05	.02	.00
☐ 254	Shane Rawley	.08	.04	.01
☐ 255	Bruce Benedict	.05	.02	.00
☐ 256	Dave Geisel	.05	.02	.00
☐ 257	Julio Cruz	.05	.02	.00
☐ 258	Luis Sanchez	.05	.02	.00
☐ 259	Sparky Anderson MG	.08	.04	.01
☐ 260	Scott McGregor	.08	.04	.01
☐ 261	Bobby Brown	.05	.02	.00
☐ 262	Tom Candiotti	.30	.15	.03
☐ 263	Jack Fimple	.05	.02	.00
☐ 264	Doug Frobel	.05	.02	.00
☐ 265	Donnie Hill	.08	.04	.01
☐ 266	Steve Lubratich	.05	.02	.00
☐ 267	Carmelo Martinez	.25	.12	.02
☐ 268	Jack O'Connor	.05	.02	.00

		MINT	EXC	G-VG
☐ 269	Aurelio Rodriguez ...	.05	.02	.00
☐ 270	Jeff Russell	.50	.25	.05
☐ 271	Moose Haas	.05	.02	.00
☐ 272	Rick Dempsey	.05	.02	.00
☐ 273	Charlie Puleo	.05	.02	.00
☐ 274	Rick Monday	.08	.04	.01
☐ 275	Len Matuszek	.05	.02	.00
☐ 276	Angels TL	.15	.07	.01
	Rod Carew			
	Geoff Zahn			
☐ 277	Eddie Whitson	.08	.04	.01
☐ 278	Jorge Bell	1.25	.60	.12
☐ 279	Ivan DeJesus	.05	.02	.00
☐ 280	Floyd Bannister	.05	.02	.00
☐ 281	Larry Milbourne	.05	.02	.00
☐ 282	Jim Barr	.05	.02	.00
☐ 283	Larry Biittner	.05	.02	.00
☐ 284	Howard Bailey	.05	.02	.00
☐ 285	Darrell Porter	.05	.02	.00
☐ 286	Lary Sorensen	.05	.02	.00
☐ 287	Warren Cromartie ...	.05	.02	.00
☐ 288	Jim Beattie	.05	.02	.00
☐ 289	Randy Johnson	.05	.02	.00
☐ 290	Dave Dravecky	.20	.10	.02
☐ 291	Chuck Tanner MG ..	.05	.02	.00
☐ 292	Tony Scott	.05	.02	.00
☐ 293	Ed Lynch	.05	.02	.00
☐ 294	U.L. Washington	.05	.02	.00
☐ 295	Mike Flanagan	.08	.04	.01
☐ 296	Jeff Newman	.05	.02	.00
☐ 297	Bruce Berenyi	.05	.02	.00
☐ 298	Jim Gantner	.05	.02	.00
☐ 299	John Butcher	.05	.02	.00
☐ 300	Pete Rose	1.25	.60	.12
☐ 301	Frank LaCorte	.05	.02	.00
☐ 302	Barry Bonnell	.05	.02	.00
☐ 303	Marty Castillo	.05	.02	.00
☐ 304	Warren Brusstar ...	.05	.02	.00
☐ 305	Roy Smalley	.05	.02	.00
☐ 306	Dodgers TL	.10	.05	.01
	Pedro Guerrero			
	Bob Welch			
☐ 307	Bobby Mitchell	.05	.02	.00
☐ 308	Ron Hassey	.08	.04	.01
☐ 309	Tony Phillips	.25	.12	.02
☐ 310	Willie McGee	.30	.15	.03
☐ 311	Jerry Koosman	.10	.05	.01
☐ 312	Jorge Orta	.05	.02	.00
☐ 313	Mike Jorgensen	.05	.02	.00

		MINT	EXC	G-VG
☐ 314	Orlando Mercado	.05	.02	.00
☐ 315	Bob Grich	.08	.04	.01
☐ 316	Mark Bradley	.05	.02	.00
☐ 317	Greg Pryor	.05	.02	.00
☐ 318	Bill Gullickson	.05	.02	.00
☐ 319	Al Bumbry	.05	.02	.00
☐ 320	Bob Stanley	.05	.02	.00
☐ 321	Harvey Kuenn MG ..	.05	.02	.00
☐ 322	Ken Schrom	.05	.02	.00
☐ 323	Alan Knicely	.05	.02	.00
☐ 324	Alejandro Pena	.25	.12	.02
☐ 325	Darrell Evans	.15	.07	.01
☐ 326	Bob Kearney	.05	.02	.00
☐ 327	Ruppert Jones	.05	.02	.00
☐ 328	Vern Ruhle	.05	.02	.00
☐ 329	Pat Tabler	.20	.10	.02
☐ 330	John Candelaria	.10	.05	.01
☐ 331	Bucky Dent	.12	.06	.01
☐ 332	Kevin Gross	.35	.17	.03
☐ 333	Larry Herndon	.05	.02	.00
☐ 334	Chuck Rainey	.05	.02	.00
☐ 335	Don Baylor	.12	.06	.01
☐ 336	Seattle Mariners TL ..	.10	.05	.01
	Pat Putnam			
	Matt Young			
☐ 337	Kevin Hagen	.05	.02	.00
☐ 338	Mike Warren	.08	.04	.01
☐ 339	Roy Lee Jackson ...	.05	.02	.00
☐ 340	Hal McRae	.08	.04	.01
☐ 341	Dave Tobik	.05	.02	.00
☐ 342	Tim Foli	.05	.02	.00
☐ 343	Mark Davis	.25	.12	.02
☐ 344	Rick Miller	.05	.02	.00
☐ 345	Kent Hrbek	.45	.22	.04
☐ 346	Kurt Bevacqua	.05	.02	.00
☐ 347	Allan Ramirez	.05	.02	.00
☐ 348	Toby Harrah	.05	.02	.00
☐ 349	Bob L. Gibson	.08	.04	.01
	(Brewers Pitcher)			
☐ 350	George Foster	.20	.10	.02
☐ 351	Russ Nixon MG	.05	.02	.00
☐ 352	Dave Stewart	.60	.30	.06
☐ 353	Jim Anderson	.05	.02	.00
☐ 354	Jeff Burroughs	.05	.02	.00
☐ 355	Jason Thompson ...	.05	.02	.00
☐ 356	Glenn Abbott	.05	.02	.00
☐ 357	Ron Cey	.10	.05	.01
☐ 358	Bob Dernier	.05	.02	.00
☐ 359	Jim Acker	.08	.04	.01

		MINT	EXC	G-VG			MINT	EXC	G-VG
☐ 360	Willie Randolph	.10	.05	.01	☐ 407	Dan Quisenberry AS	.08	.04	.01
☐ 361	Dave Smith	.08	.04	.01	☐ 408	Lou Piniella	.10	.05	.01
☐ 362	David Green	.05	.02	.00	☐ 409	Juan Agosto	.15	.07	.01
☐ 363	Tim Laudner	.05	.02	.00	☐ 410	Claudell Washington	.08	.04	.01
☐ 364	Scott Fletcher	.20	.10	.02	☐ 411	Houston Jimenez	.08	.04	.01
☐ 365	Steve Bedrosian	.15	.07	.01	☐ 412	Doug Rader MG	.05	.02	.00
☐ 366	Padres TL	.10	.05	.01	☐ 413	Spike Owen	.20	.10	.02
	Terry Kennedy,				☐ 414	Mitchell Page	.05	.02	.00
	Dave Dravecky				☐ 415	Tommy John	.20	.10	.02
☐ 367	Jamie Easterly	.05	.02	.00	☐ 416	Dane Iorg	.05	.02	.00
☐ 368	Hubie Brooks	.10	.05	.01	☐ 417	Mike Armstrong	.05	.02	.00
☐ 369	Steve McCatty	.05	.02	.00	☐ 418	Ron Hodges	.05	.02	.00
☐ 370	Tim Raines	.50	.25	.05	☐ 419	John Henry Johnson	.05	.02	.00
☐ 371	Dave Gumpert	.05	.02	.00	☐ 420	Cecil Cooper	.12	.06	.01
☐ 372	Gary Roenicke	.05	.02	.00	☐ 421	Charlie Lea	.05	.02	.00
☐ 373	Bill Scherrer	.05	.02	.00	☐ 422	Jose Cruz	.10	.05	.01
☐ 374	Don Money	.05	.02	.00	☐ 423	Mike Morgan	.10	.05	.01
☐ 375	Dennis Leonard	.08	.04	.01	☐ 424	Dann Bilardello	.05	.02	.00
☐ 376	Dave Anderson	.15	.07	.01	☐ 425	Steve Howe	.05	.02	.00
☐ 377	Danny Darwin	.05	.02	.00	☐ 426	Orioles TL	.15	.07	.01
☐ 378	Bob Brenly	.05	.02	.00		Cal Ripken			
☐ 379	Checklist 265-396	.08	.01	.00		Mike Boddicker			
☐ 380	Steve Garvey	.50	.25	.05	☐ 427	Rick Leach	.05	.02	.00
☐ 381	Ralph Houk MG	.05	.02	.00	☐ 428	Fred Breining	.05	.02	.00
☐ 382	Chris Nyman	.05	.02	.00	☐ 429	Randy Bush	.25	.12	.02
☐ 383	Terry Puhl	.05	.02	.00	☐ 430	Rusty Staub	.10	.05	.01
☐ 384	Lee Tunnell	.10	.05	.01	☐ 431	Chris Bando	.05	.02	.00
☐ 385	Tony Perez	.20	.10	.02	☐ 432	Charles Hudson	.20	.10	.02
☐ 386	George Hendrick AS	.08	.04	.01	☐ 433	Rich Hebner	.05	.02	.00
☐ 387	Johnny Ray AS	.08	.04	.01	☐ 434	Harold Baines	.30	.15	.03
☐ 388	Mike Schmidt AS	.35	.17	.03	☐ 435	Neil Allen	.05	.02	.00
☐ 389	Ozzie Smith AS	.15	.07	.01	☐ 436	Rick Peters	.05	.02	.00
☐ 390	Tim Raines AS	.15	.07	.01	☐ 437	Mike Proly	.05	.02	.00
☐ 391	Dale Murphy AS	.30	.15	.03	☐ 438	Biff Pocoroba	.05	.02	.00
☐ 392	Andre Dawson AS	.15	.07	.01	☐ 439	Bob Stoddard	.05	.02	.00
☐ 393	Gary Carter AS	.15	.07	.01	☐ 440	Steve Kemp	.08	.04	.01
☐ 394	Steve Rogers AS	.08	.04	.01	☐ 441	Bob Lillis MG	.05	.02	.00
☐ 395	Steve Carlton AS	.20	.10	.02	☐ 442	Byron McLaughlin	.05	.02	.00
☐ 396	Jesse Orosco AS	.08	.04	.01	☐ 443	Benny Ayala	.05	.02	.00
☐ 397	Eddie Murray AS	.15	.07	.01	☐ 444	Steve Renko	.05	.02	.00
☐ 398	Lou Whitaker AS	.10	.05	.01	☐ 445	Jerry Remy	.05	.02	.00
☐ 399	George Brett AS	.25	.12	.02	☐ 446	Luis Pujols	.05	.02	.00
☐ 400	Cal Ripken AS	.20	.10	.02	☐ 447	Tom Brunansky	.30	.15	.03
☐ 401	Jim Rice AS	.15	.07	.01	☐ 448	Ben Hayes	.05	.02	.00
☐ 402	Dave Winfield AS	.15	.07	.01	☐ 449	Joe Pettini	.05	.02	.00
☐ 403	Lloyd Moseby AS	.08	.04	.01	☐ 450	Gary Carter	.40	.20	.04
☐ 404	Ted Simmons AS	.08	.04	.01	☐ 451	Bob Jones	.05	.02	.00
☐ 405	LaMarr Hoyt AS	.08	.04	.01	☐ 452	Chuck Porter	.05	.02	.00
☐ 406	Ron Guidry AS	.10	.05	.01	☐ 453	Willie Upshaw	.05	.02	.00

		MINT	EXC	G-VG
☐ 454	Joe Beckwith	.05	.02	.00
☐ 455	Terry Kennedy	.05	.02	.00
☐ 456	Chicago Cubs TL	.10	.05	.01
	Keith Moreland			
	Fergie Jenkins			
☐ 457	Dave Rozema	.05	.02	.00
☐ 458	Kiko Garcia	.05	.02	.00
☐ 459	Kevin Hickey	.05	.02	.00
☐ 460	Dave Winfield	.45	.22	.04
☐ 461	Jim Maler	.05	.02	.00
☐ 462	Lee Lacy	.05	.02	.00
☐ 463	Dave Engle	.05	.02	.00
☐ 464	Jeff A. Jones	.05	.02	.00
	(A's Pitcher)			
☐ 465	Mookie Wilson	.10	.05	.01
☐ 466	Gene Garber	.05	.02	.00
☐ 467	Mike Ramsey	.05	.02	.00
☐ 468	Geoff Zahn	.05	.02	.00
☐ 469	Tom O'Malley	.05	.02	.00
☐ 470	Nolan Ryan	1.75	.85	.17
☐ 471	Dick Howser MG	.08	.04	.01
☐ 472	Mike Brown	.08	.04	.01
	(Red Sox Pitcher)			
☐ 473	Jim Dwyer	.05	.02	.00
☐ 474	Greg Bargar	.05	.02	.00
☐ 475	Gary Redus	.25	.12	.02
☐ 476	Tom Tellmann	.05	.02	.00
☐ 477	Rafael Landestoy	.05	.02	.00
☐ 478	Alan Bannister	.05	.02	.00
☐ 479	Frank Tanana	.08	.04	.01
☐ 480	Ron Kittle	.25	.12	.02
☐ 481	Mark Thurmond	.10	.05	.01
☐ 482	Enos Cabell	.05	.02	.00
☐ 483	Fergie Jenkins	.20	.10	.02
☐ 484	Ozzie Virgil	.05	.02	.00
☐ 485	Rick Rhoden	.08	.04	.01
☐ 486	N.Y. Yankees TL	.10	.05	.01
	Don Baylor			
	Ron Guidry			
☐ 487	Ricky Adams	.05	.02	.00
☐ 488	Jesse Barfield	.30	.15	.03
☐ 489	Dave Von Ohlen	.05	.02	.00
☐ 490	Cal Ripken	.90	.45	.09
☐ 491	Bobby Castillo	.05	.02	.00
☐ 492	Tucker Ashford	.05	.02	.00
☐ 493	Mike Norris	.05	.02	.00
☐ 494	Chili Davis	.15	.07	.01
☐ 495	Rollie Fingers	.20	.10	.02
☐ 496	Terry Francona	.05	.02	.00
☐ 497	Bud Anderson	.05	.02	.00
☐ 498	Rich Gedman	.08	.04	.01
☐ 499	Mike Witt	.10	.05	.01
☐ 500	George Brett	.75	.35	.07
☐ 501	Steve Henderson	.05	.02	.00
☐ 502	Joe Torre MG	.08	.04	.01
☐ 503	Elias Sosa	.05	.02	.00
☐ 504	Mickey Rivers	.08	.04	.01
☐ 505	Pete Vuckovich	.08	.04	.01
☐ 506	Ernie Whitt	.08	.04	.01
☐ 507	Mike LaCoss	.05	.02	.00
☐ 508	Mel Hall	.45	.22	.04
☐ 509	Brad Havens	.05	.02	.00
☐ 510	Alan Trammell	.35	.17	.03
☐ 511	Marty Bystrom	.05	.02	.00
☐ 512	Oscar Gamble	.05	.02	.00
☐ 513	Dave Beard	.05	.02	.00
☐ 514	Floyd Rayford	.05	.02	.00
☐ 515	Gorman Thomas	.10	.05	.01
☐ 516	Montreal Expos TL	.10	.05	.01
	Al Oliver			
	Charlie Lea			
☐ 517	John Moses	.08	.04	.01
☐ 518	Greg Walker	.40	.20	.04
☐ 519	Ron Davis	.05	.02	.00
☐ 520	Bob Boone	.15	.07	.01
☐ 521	Pete Falcone	.05	.02	.00
☐ 522	Dave Bergman	.05	.02	.00
☐ 523	Glenn Hoffman	.05	.02	.00
☐ 524	Carlos Diaz	.05	.02	.00
☐ 525	Willie Wilson	.12	.06	.01
☐ 526	Ron Oester	.05	.02	.00
☐ 527	Checklist 397-528	.08	.01	.00
☐ 528	Mark Brouhard	.05	.02	.00
☐ 529	Keith Atherton	.05	.02	.00
☐ 530	Dan Ford	.05	.02	.00
☐ 531	Steve Boros MG	.05	.02	.00
☐ 532	Eric Show	.08	.04	.01
☐ 533	Ken Landreaux	.05	.02	.00
☐ 534	Pete O'Brien	.90	.45	.09
☐ 535	Bo Diaz	.05	.02	.00
☐ 536	Doug Bair	.05	.02	.00
☐ 537	Johnny Ray	.12	.06	.01
☐ 538	Kevin Bass	.10	.05	.01
☐ 539	George Frazier	.05	.02	.00
☐ 540	George Hendrick	.08	.04	.01
☐ 541	Dennis Lamp	.05	.02	.00
☐ 542	Duane Kuiper	.05	.02	.00
☐ 543	Craig McMurtry	.08	.04	.01

		MINT	EXC	G-VG			MINT	EXC	G-VG
☐ 544	Cesar Geronimo	.05	.02	.00	☐ 589	Mike Easler	.08	.04	.01
☐ 545	Bill Buckner	.10	.05	.01	☐ 590	Dave Stieb	.18	.09	.01
☐ 546	Indians TL	.10	.05	.01	☐ 591	Tony LaRussa MG	.05	.02	.00
	Mike Hargrove				☐ 592	Andre Robertson	.05	.02	.00
	Lary Sorensen				☐ 593	Jeff Lahti	.05	.02	.00
☐ 547	Mike Moore	.25	.12	.02	☐ 594	Gene Richards	.05	.02	.00
☐ 548	Ron Jackson	.05	.02	.00	☐ 595	Jeff Reardon	.15	.07	.01
☐ 549	Walt Terrell	.45	.22	.04	☐ 596	Ryne Sandberg TL	1.50	.75	.15
☐ 550	Jim Rice	.30	.15	.03	☐ 597	Rick Camp	.05	.02	.00
☐ 551	Scott Ullger	.05	.02	.00	☐ 598	Rusty Kuntz	.05	.02	.00
☐ 552	Ray Burris	.05	.02	.00	☐ 599	Doug Sisk	.08	.04	.01
☐ 553	Joe Nolan	.05	.02	.00	☐ 600	Rod Carew	.50	.22	.04
☐ 554	Ted Power	.05	.02	.00	☐ 601	John Tudor	.15	.07	.01
☐ 555	Greg Brock	.15	.07	.01	☐ 602	John Wathan	.08	.04	.01
☐ 556	Joey McLaughlin	.05	.02	.00	☐ 603	Renie Martin	.05	.02	.00
☐ 557	Wayne Tolleson	.08	.04	.01	☐ 604	John Lowenstein	.05	.02	.00
☐ 558	Mike Davis	.08	.04	.01	☐ 605	Mike Caldwell	.05	.02	.00
☐ 559	Mike Scott	.35	.17	.03	☐ 606	Blue Jays TL	.10	.05	.01
☐ 560	Carlton Fisk	.35	.17	.03		Lloyd Moseby			
☐ 561	Whitey Herzog MG	.05	.02	.00		Dave Stieb			
☐ 562	Manny Castillo	.05	.02	.00	☐ 607	Tom Hume	.05	.02	.00
☐ 563	Glenn Wilson	.08	.04	.01	☐ 608	Bobby Johnson	.05	.02	.00
☐ 564	Al Holland	.05	.02	.00	☐ 609	Dan Meyer	.05	.02	.00
☐ 565	Leon Durham	.08	.04	.01	☐ 610	Steve Sax	.30	.15	.03
☐ 566	Jim Bibby	.05	.02	.00	☐ 611	Chet Lemon	.08	.04	.01
☐ 567	Mike Heath	.05	.02	.00	☐ 612	Harry Spilman	.05	.02	.00
☐ 568	Pete Filson	.05	.02	.00	☐ 613	Greg Gross	.05	.02	.00
☐ 569	Bake McBride	.05	.02	.00	☐ 614	Len Barker	.05	.02	.00
☐ 570	Dan Quisenberry	.12	.06	.01	☐ 615	Garry Templeton	.08	.04	.01
☐ 571	Bruce Bochy	.05	.02	.00	☐ 616	Don Robinson	.05	.02	.00
☐ 572	Jerry Royster	.05	.02	.00	☐ 617	Rick Cerone	.05	.02	.00
☐ 573	Dave Kingman	.15	.07	.01	☐ 618	Dickie Noles	.05	.02	.00
☐ 574	Brian Downing	.08	.04	.01	☐ 619	Jerry Dybzinski	.05	.02	.00
☐ 575	Jim Clancy	.05	.02	.00	☐ 620	Al Oliver	.10	.05	.01
☐ 576	Giants TL	.10	.05	.01	☐ 621	Frank Howard MG	.05	.02	.00
	Jeff Leonard				☐ 622	Al Cowens	.05	.02	.00
	Atlee Hammaker				☐ 623	Ron Washington	.05	.02	.00
☐ 577	Mark Clear	.05	.02	.00	☐ 624	Terry Harper	.05	.02	.00
☐ 578	Lenn Sakata	.05	.02	.00	☐ 625	Larry Gura	.05	.02	.00
☐ 579	Bob James	.20	.10	.02	☐ 626	Bob Clark	.05	.02	.00
☐ 580	Lonnie Smith	.12	.06	.01	☐ 627	Dave LaPoint	.08	.04	.01
☐ 581	Jose DeLeon	.45	.22	.04	☐ 628	Ed Jurak	.05	.02	.00
☐ 582	Bob McClure	.05	.02	.00	☐ 629	Rick Langford	.05	.02	.00
☐ 583	Derrel Thomas	.05	.02	.00	☐ 630	Ted Simmons	.12	.06	.01
☐ 584	Dave Schmidt	.08	.04	.01	☐ 631	Dennis Martinez	.08	.04	.01
☐ 585	Dan Driessen	.05	.02	.00	☐ 632	Tom Foley	.05	.02	.00
☐ 586	Joe Niekro	.10	.05	.01	☐ 633	Mike Krukow	.08	.04	.01
☐ 587	Von Hayes	.18	.09	.01	☐ 634	Mike Marshall	.18	.09	.01
☐ 588	Milt Wilcox	.05	.02	.00	☐ 635	Dave Righetti	.18	.09	.01

			MINT	EXC	G-VG
☐	636	Pat Putnam	.05	.02	.00
☐	637	Phillies TL	.10	.05	.01
		Gary Matthews			
		John Denny			
☐	638	George Vukovich	.05	.02	.00
☐	639	Rick Lysander	.05	.02	.00
☐	640	Lance Parrish	.25	.12	.02
☐	641	Mike Richardt	.05	.02	.00
☐	642	Tom Underwood	.05	.02	.00
☐	643	Mike Brown	.08	.04	.01
		(Angels OF)			
☐	644	Tim Lollar	.05	.02	.00
☐	645	Tony Pena	.15	.07	.01
☐	646	Checklist 529-660	.08	.01	.00
☐	647	Ron Roenicke	.05	.02	.00
☐	648	Len Whitehouse	.05	.02	.00
☐	649	Tom Herr	.10	.05	.01
☐	650	Phil Niekro	.20	.10	.02
☐	651	John McNamara MG	.05	.02	.00
☐	652	Rudy May	.05	.02	.00
☐	653	Dave Stapleton	.05	.02	.00
☐	654	Bob Bailor	.05	.02	.00
☐	655	Amos Otis	.10	.05	.01
☐	656	Bryn Smith	.12	.06	.01
☐	657	Thad Bosley	.05	.02	.00
☐	658	Jerry Augustine	.05	.02	.00
☐	659	Duane Walker	.05	.02	.00
☐	660	Ray Knight	.10	.05	.01
☐	661	Steve Yeager	.05	.02	.00
☐	662	Tom Brennan	.05	.02	.00
☐	663	Johnnie LeMaster	.05	.02	.00
☐	664	Dave Stegman	.05	.02	.00
☐	665	Buddy Bell	.12	.06	.01
☐	666	Detroit Tigers TL	.15	.07	.01
		Lou Whitaker			
		Jack Morris			
☐	667	Vance Law	.08	.04	.01
☐	668	Larry McWilliams	.05	.02	.00
☐	669	Dave Lopes	.08	.04	.01
☐	670	Rich Gossage	.18	.09	.01
☐	671	Jamie Quirk	.05	.02	.00
☐	672	Ricky Nelson	.05	.02	.00
☐	673	Mike Walters	.05	.02	.00
☐	674	Tim Flannery	.05	.02	.00
☐	675	Pascual Perez	.15	.07	.01
☐	676	Brian Giles	.05	.02	.00
☐	677	Doyle Alexander	.08	.04	.01
☐	678	Chris Speier	.05	.02	.00
☐	679	Art Howe	.08	.04	.01

			MINT	EXC	G-VG
☐	680	Fred Lynn	.20	.10	.02
☐	681	Tom Lasorda MG	.08	.04	.01
☐	682	Dan Morogiello	.05	.02	.00
☐	683	Marty Barrett	1.50	.75	.15
☐	684	Bob Shirley	.05	.02	.00
☐	685	Willie Aikens	.05	.02	.00
☐	686	Joe Price	.05	.02	.00
☐	687	Roy Howell	.05	.02	.00
☐	688	George Wright	.05	.02	.00
☐	689	Mike Fischlin	.05	.02	.00
☐	690	Jack Clark	.25	.12	.02
☐	691	Steve Lake	.05	.02	.00
☐	692	Dickie Thon	.08	.04	.01
☐	693	Alan Wiggins	.05	.02	.00
☐	694	Mike Stanton	.05	.02	.00
☐	695	Lou Whitaker	.25	.12	.02
☐	696	Pirates TL	.10	.05	.01
		Bill Madlock			
		Rick Rhoden			
☐	697	Dale Murray	.05	.02	.00
☐	698	Marc Hill	.05	.02	.00
☐	699	Dave Rucker	.05	.02	.00
☐	700	Mike Schmidt	1.00	.50	.10
☐	701	NL Active Batting	.20	.10	.02
		Bill Madlock			
		Pete Rose			
		Dave Parker			
☐	702	NL Active Hits	.20	.10	.02
		Pete Rose			
		Rusty Staub			
		Tony Perez			
☐	703	NL Active Home Run	.15	.07	.01
		Mike Schmidt			
		Tony Perez			
		Dave Kingman			
☐	704	NL Active RBI	.10	.05	.01
		Tony Perez			
		Rusty Staub			
		Al Oliver			
☐	705	NL Active Steals	.10	.05	.01
		Joe Morgan			
		Cesar Cedeno			
		Larry Bowa			
☐	706	NL Active Victory	.20	.10	.02
		Steve Carlton			
		Fergie Jenkins			
		Tom Seaver			
☐	707	NL Active Strikeout	.25	.12	.02
		Steve Carlton			

		MINT	EXC	G-VG
	Nolan Ryan			
	Tom Seaver			
☐ 708	NL Active ERA	.18	.09	.01
	Tom Seaver			
	Steve Carlton			
	Steve Rogers			
☐ 709	NL Active Save	.10	.05	.01
	Bruce Sutter			
	Tug McGraw			
	Gene Garber			
☐ 710	AL Active Batting	.20	.10	.02
	Rod Carew			
	George Brett			
	Cecil Cooper			
☐ 711	AL Active Hits	.18	.09	.01
	Rod Carew			
	Bert Campaneris			
	Reggie Jackson			
☐ 712	AL Active Home Run	.15	.07	.01
	Reggie Jackson			
	Graig Nettles			
	Greg Luzinski			
☐ 713	AL Active RBI	.15	.07	.01
	Reggie Jackson			
	Ted Simmons			
	Graig Nettles			
☐ 714	AL Active Steals	.08	.04	.01
	Bert Campaneris			
	Dave Lopes			
	Omar Moreno			
☐ 715	AL Active Victory	.18	.09	.01
	Jim Palmer			
	Don Sutton			
	Tommy John			
☐ 716	AL Active Strikeout	.08	.04	.01
	Don Sutton			
	Bert Blyleven			
	Jerry Koosman			
☐ 717	AL Active ERA	.15	.07	.01
	Jim Palmer			
	Rollie Fingers			
	Ron Guidry			
☐ 718	AL Active Save	.12	.06	.01
	Rollie Fingers			
	Rich Gossage			
	Dan Quisenberry			
☐ 719	Andy Hassler	.05	.02	.00
☐ 720	Dwight Evans	.18	.09	.01
☐ 721	Del Crandall MG	.05	.02	.00

		MINT	EXC	G-VG
☐ 722	Bob Welch	.08	.04	.01
☐ 723	Rich Dauer	.05	.02	.00
☐ 724	Eric Rasmussen	.05	.02	.00
☐ 725	Cesar Cedeno	.08	.04	.01
☐ 726	Brewers TL	.10	.05	.01
	Ted Simmons			
	Moose Haas			
☐ 727	Joel Youngblood	.05	.02	.00
☐ 728	Tug McGraw	.10	.05	.01
☐ 729	Gene Tenace	.05	.02	.00
☐ 730	Bruce Sutter	.12	.06	.01
☐ 731	Lynn Jones	.05	.02	.00
☐ 732	Terry Crowley	.05	.02	.00
☐ 733	Dave Collins	.05	.02	.00
☐ 734	Odell Jones	.05	.02	.00
☐ 735	Rick Burleson	.08	.04	.01
☐ 736	Dick Ruthven	.05	.02	.00
☐ 737	Jim Essian	.05	.02	.00
☐ 738	Bill Schroeder	.10	.05	.01
☐ 739	Bob Watson	.08	.04	.01
☐ 740	Tom Seaver	.50	.25	.05
☐ 741	Wayne Gross	.05	.02	.00
☐ 742	Dick Williams MG	.05	.02	.00
☐ 743	Don Hood	.05	.02	.00
☐ 744	Jamie Allen	.05	.02	.00
☐ 745	Dennis Eckersley	.25	.10	.02
☐ 746	Mickey Hatcher	.08	.04	.01
☐ 747	Pat Zachry	.05	.02	.00
☐ 748	Jeff Leonard	.10	.05	.01
☐ 749	Doug Flynn	.05	.02	.00
☐ 750	Jim Palmer	.45	.22	.04
☐ 751	Charlie Moore	.05	.02	.00
☐ 752	Phil Garner	.05	.02	.00
☐ 753	Doug Gwosdz	.05	.02	.00
☐ 754	Kent Tekulve	.08	.04	.01
☐ 755	Garry Maddox	.08	.04	.01
☐ 756	Reds TL	.10	.05	.01
	Ron Oester			
	Mario Soto			
☐ 757	Larry Bowa	.10	.05	.01
☐ 758	Bill Stein	.05	.02	.00
☐ 759	Richard Dotson	.08	.04	.01
☐ 760	Bob Horner	.15	.07	.01
☐ 761	John Montefusco	.05	.02	.00
☐ 762	Rance Mulliniks	.05	.02	.00
☐ 763	Craig Swan	.05	.02	.00
☐ 764	Mike Hargrove	.08	.04	.01
☐ 765	Ken Forsch	.05	.02	.00
☐ 766	Mike Vail	.05	.02	.00

1984 Topps Traded

			MINT	EXC	G-VG
☐	767	Carney Lansford	.15	.07	.01
☐	768	Champ Summers	.05	.02	.00
☐	769	Bill Caudill	.05	.02	.00
☐	770	Ken Griffey	.12	.06	.01
☐	771	Billy Gardner MG ..	.05	.02	.00
☐	772	Jim Slaton	.05	.02	.00
☐	773	Todd Cruz	.05	.02	.00
☐	774	Tom Gorman	.08	.04	.01
☐	775	Dave Parker	.20	.10	.02
☐	776	Craig Reynolds	.05	.02	.00
☐	777	Tom Paciorek	.05	.02	.00
☐	778	Andy Hawkins	.60	.30	.06
☐	779	Jim Sundberg	.05	.02	.00
☐	780	Steve Carlton	.35	.17	.03
☐	781	Checklist 661-792 ...	.08	.01	.00
☐	782	Steve Balboni	.08	.04	.01
☐	783	Luis Leal	.05	.02	.00
☐	784	Leon Roberts	.05	.02	.00
☐	785	Joaquin Andujar	.10	.05	.01
☐	786	Red Sox TL	.25	.12	.02
		Wade Boggs			
		Bob Ojeda			
☐	787	Bill Campbell	.05	.02	.00
☐	788	Milt May	.05	.02	.00
☐	789	Bert Blyleven	.20	.07	.01
☐	790	Doug DeCinces	.08	.04	.01
☐	791	Terry Forster	.08	.04	.01
☐	792	Bill Russell	.15	.07	.01

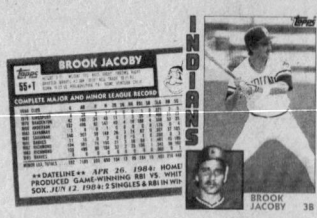

*The cards in this 132-card set measure 2 ½"
by 3 ½". In its now standard procedure, Topps
issued its Traded (or extended) set for the
fourth year in a row. Because all photos and
statistics of its regular set for the year were
developed during the fall and winter months of
the preceding year, players who changed
teams during the fall, winter, and spring months
are portrayed with the teams they were with in
1983. The Traded set amends the shortcomings
of the regular set by presenting the players with
their proper teams for the current year. Rookies
not contained in the regular set are also picked
up in the Traded set. Again this year, the Topps
affiliate in Ireland printed the cards, and the
cards were available through hobby dealers
only. Topps also produced a specially boxed
"glossy" edition, frequently referred to as the
Topps Traded Tiffany set. There were
supposedly only 10,000 sets of the Tiffany
cards produced; they were marketed to hobby
dealers. The checklist of cards is identical to
that of the normal non-glossy cards. There are
two primary distinguishing features of the
Tiffany cards—white card stock reverses and
high gloss obverses. These Tiffany cards are
valued at approximately five times the values
listed below.*

	MINT	EXC	G-VG
COMPLETE SET (132)	100.00	50.00	10.00
COMMON PLAYER (1-132)	.10	.05	.01

		MINT	EXC	G-VG
☐	1T Willie Aikens	.20	.10	.02
☐	2T Luis Aponte	.10	.05	.01
☐	3T Mike Armstrong	.10	.05	.01
☐	4T Bob Bailor	.10	.05	.01
☐	5T Dusty Baker	.20	.10	.02
☐	6T Steve Balboni	.20	.10	.02
☐	7T Alan Bannister	.10	.05	.01
☐	8T Dave Beard	.10	.05	.01
☐	9T Joe Beckwith	.10	.05	.01
☐	10T Bruce Berenyi	.10	.05	.01
☐	11T Dave Bergman	.10	.05	.01
☐	12T Tony Bernazard	.10	.05	.01
☐	13T Yogi Berra MG	.40	.20	.04
☐	14T Barry Bonnell	.10	.05	.01
☐	15T Phil Bradley	2.00	1.00	.20
☐	16T Fred Breining	.10	.05	.01
☐	17T Bill Buckner	.30	.15	.03
☐	18T Ray Burris	.10	.05	.01
☐	19T John Butcher	.10	.05	.01
☐	20T Brett Butler	.30	.15	.03
☐	21T Enos Cabell	.10	.05	.01
☐	22T Bill Campbell	.10	.05	.01
☐	23T Bill Caudill	.10	.05	.01
☐	24T Bob Clark	.10	.05	.01
☐	25T Bryan Clark	.10	.05	.01
☐	26T Jaime Cocanower	.20	.10	.02
☐	27T Ron Darling	5.00	2.50	.50
☐	28T Alvin Davis	7.00	3.50	.70
☐	29T Ken Dayley	.20	.10	.02
☐	30T Jeff Dedmon	.20	.10	.02
☐	31T Bob Dernier	.20	.10	.02
☐	32T Carlos Diaz	.10	.05	.01
☐	33T Mike Easler	.10	.05	.01
☐	34T Dennis Eckersley	.60	.30	.06
☐	35T Jim Essian	.10	.05	.01
☐	36T Darrell Evans	.30	.15	.03
☐	37T Mike Fitzgerald	.20	.10	.02
☐	38T Tim Foli	.10	.05	.01
☐	39T George Frazier	.10	.05	.01
☐	40T Rich Gale	.10	.05	.01
☐	41T Barbaro Garbey	.20	.10	.02
☐	42T Dwight Gooden	42.00	18.00	4.00
☐	43T Rich Gossage	.35	.17	.03
☐	44T Wayne Gross	.10	.05	.01
☐	45T Mark Gubicza	5.00	2.50	.50
☐	46T Jackie Gutierrez	.20	.10	.02
☐	47T Mel Hall	.40	.20	.04
☐	48T Toby Harrah	.20	.10	.02
☐	49T Ron Hassey	.20	.10	.02
☐	50T Rich Hebner	.10	.05	.01
☐	51T Willie Hernandez	.30	.15	.03
☐	52T Ricky Horton	.35	.17	.03
☐	53T Art Howe	.20	.10	.02
☐	54T Dane Iorg	.10	.05	.01
☐	55T Brook Jacoby	1.25	.60	.12
☐	56T Mike Jeffcoat	.20	.10	.02
☐	57T Dave Johnson MG	.30	.15	.03
☐	58T Lynn Jones	.10	.05	.01
☐	59T Ruppert Jones	.10	.05	.01
☐	60T Mike Jorgensen	.10	.05	.01
☐	61T Bob Kearney	.10	.05	.01
☐	62T Jimmy Key	3.00	1.50	.30
☐	63T Dave Kingman	.30	.15	.03
☐	64T Jerry Koosman	.30	.15	.03
☐	65T Wayne Krenchicki	.10	.05	.01
☐	66T Rusty Kuntz	.10	.05	.01
☐	67T Rene Lachemann MG	.10	.05	.01
☐	68T Frank LaCorte	.10	.05	.01
☐	69T Dennis Lamp	.10	.05	.01
☐	70T Mark Langston	18.00	9.00	1.80
☐	71T Rick Leach	.10	.05	.01
☐	72T Craig Lefferts	.30	.15	.03
☐	73T Gary Lucas	.10	.05	.01
☐	74T Jerry Martin	.10	.05	.01
☐	75T Carmelo Martinez	.20	.10	.02
☐	76T Mike Mason	.20	.10	.02
☐	77T Gary Matthews	.20	.10	.02
☐	78T Andy McGaffigan	.10	.05	.01
☐	79T Larry Milbourne	.10	.05	.01
☐	80T Sid Monge	.10	.05	.01
☐	81T Jackie Moore MG	.10	.05	.01
☐	82T Joe Morgan	2.00	1.00	.20
☐	83T Graig Nettles	.40	.20	.04
☐	84T Phil Niekro	1.00	.50	.10
☐	85T Ken Oberkfell	.10	.05	.01
☐	86T Mike O'Berry	.10	.05	.01
☐	87T Al Oliver	.30	.15	.03
☐	88T Jorge Orta	.10	.05	.01
☐	89T Amos Otis	.20	.10	.02
☐	90T Dave Parker	1.00	.50	.10
☐	91T Tony Perez	.60	.30	.06
☐	92T Gerald Perry	1.00	.50	.10
☐	93T Gary Pettis	.40	.20	.04
☐	94T Rob Picciolo	.10	.05	.01
☐	95T Vern Rapp MG	.10	.05	.01
☐	96T Floyd Rayford	.10	.05	.01
☐	97T Randy Ready	.35	.17	.03

1985 Topps

		MINT	EXC	G-VG
☐ 98T	Ron Reed	.10	.05	.01
☐ 99T	Gene Richards	.10	.05	.01
☐ 100T	Jose Rijo	1.50	.75	.15
☐ 101T	Jeff Robinson	.75	.35	.07
	(Giants pitcher)			
☐ 102T	Ron Romanick	.20	.10	.02
☐ 103T	Pete Rose	7.50	3.75	.75
☐ 104T	Bret Saberhagen	21.00	10.50	2.10
☐ 105T	Juan Samuel	3.00	1.50	.30
☐ 106T	Scott Sanderson	.20	.10	.02
☐ 107T	Dick Schofield	.45	.22	.04
☐ 108T	Tom Seaver	3.00	1.50	.30
☐ 109T	Jim Slaton	.10	.05	.01
☐ 110T	Mike Smithson	.10	.05	.01
☐ 111T	Lary Sorensen	.10	.05	.01
☐ 112T	Tim Stoddard	.10	.05	.01
☐ 113T	Champ Summers	.10	.05	.01
☐ 114T	Jim Sundberg	.10	.05	.01
☐ 115T	Rick Sutcliffe	.50	.25	.05
☐ 116T	Craig Swan	.10	.05	.01
☐ 117T	Tim Teufel	.35	.17	.03
☐ 118T	Derrel Thomas	.10	.05	.01
☐ 119T	Gorman Thomas	.30	.15	.03
☐ 120T	Alex Trevino	.10	.05	.01
☐ 121T	Manny Trillo	.10	.05	.01
☐ 122T	John Tudor	.30	.15	.03
☐ 123T	Tom Underwood	.10	.05	.01
☐ 124T	Mike Vail	.10	.05	.01
☐ 125T	Tom Waddell	.20	.10	.02
☐ 126T	Gary Ward	.20	.10	.02
☐ 127T	Curt Wilkerson	.20	.10	.02
☐ 128T	Frank Williams	.30	.15	.03
☐ 129T	Glenn Wilson	.20	.10	.02
☐ 130T	John Wockenfuss	.10	.05	.01
☐ 131T	Ned Yost	.10	.05	.01
☐ 132T	Checklist 1-132	.10	.01	.00

*The cards in this 792-card set measure 2 ½"
by 3 ½". The 1985 Topps set contains full color
cards. The fronts feature both the Topps and
team logos along with the team name, player's
name, and his position. The backs feature
player statistics with ink colors of light green
and maroon on a gray stock. A trivia quiz is
included on the lower portion of the backs. The
first ten cards (1-10) are Record Breakers
(RB), cards 131-143 are Father and Son (FS)
cards, and cards 701 to 722 portray All-Star
selections (AS). Cards 271 to 282 represent
"First Draft Picks" still active in the Major
Leagues and cards 389-404 feature the coach
and players on the 1984 U.S. Olympic Baseball
Team. The manager cards in the set are important in that they contain the checklist of that
team's players on the back. Topps also produced a specially boxed "glossy" edition,
frequently referred to as the Topps Tiffany set.
There were supposedly only 5,000 sets of the
Tiffany cards produced; they were marketed to
hobby dealers. The checklist of cards (792
regular and 132 Traded) is identical to that of
the normal non-glossy sets. There are two
primary distinguishing features of the Tiffany
cards—white card stock reverses and high
gloss obverses. These Tiffany cards are
valued at approximately five times the values
listed below.*

		MINT	EXC	G-VG
	COMPLETE SET (792)	100.00	50.00	10.00
	COMMON PLAYER (1-792)	.04	.02	.00
☐ 1	Carlton Fisk RB .... Longest game by catcher	.20	.04	.01
☐ 2	Steve Garvey RB ... Consecutive errorless games, 1B	.20	.10	.02
☐ 3	Dwight Gooden RB . Most strikeouts, rookie, season	.75	.35	.07
☐ 4	Cliff Johnson RB .... Most pinch homers, lifetime	.04	.02	.00
☐ 5	Joe Morgan RB .... Most homers, 2 CB, lifetime	.12	.06	.01
☐ 6	Pete Rose RB ..... Most singles, lifetime	.50	.25	.05
☐ 7	Nolan Ryan RB .... Most strikeouts, lifetime	.50	.25	.05
☐ 8	Juan Samuel RB ... Most stolen bases, rookie, season	.12	.06	.01
☐ 9	Bruce Sutter RB .... Most saves, season, NL	.07	.03	.01
☐ 10	Don Sutton RB ..... Most seasons, 100 or more K's	.10	.05	.01
☐ 11	Ralph Houk MG .... (checklist back)	.07	.03	.01
☐ 12	Dave Lopes	.07	.03	.01
☐ 13	Tim Lollar	.04	.02	.00
☐ 14	Chris Bando	.04	.02	.00
☐ 15	Jerry Koosman	.07	.03	.01
☐ 16	Bobby Meacham	.04	.02	.00
☐ 17	Mike Scott	.30	.15	.03
☐ 18	Mickey Hatcher	.04	.02	.00
☐ 19	George Frazier	.04	.02	.00
☐ 20	Chet Lemon	.07	.03	.01
☐ 21	Lee Tunnell	.04	.02	.00
☐ 22	Duane Kuiper	.04	.02	.00
☐ 23	Bret Saberhagen ...	5.50	2.75	.55
☐ 24	Jesse Barfield	.25	.12	.02
☐ 25	Steve Bedrosian	.15	.07	.01
☐ 26	Roy Smalley	.04	.02	.00
☐ 27	Bruce Berenyi	.04	.02	.00
☐ 28	Dann Bilardello	.04	.02	.00
☐ 29	Odell Jones	.04	.02	.00
☐ 30	Cal Ripken	.50	.25	.05
☐ 31	Terry Whitfield	.04	.02	.00
☐ 32	Chuck Porter	.04	.02	.00
☐ 33	Tito Landrum	.04	.02	.00
☐ 34	Ed Nunez	.07	.03	.01
☐ 35	Graig Nettles	.10	.05	.01
☐ 36	Fred Breining	.04	.02	.00
☐ 37	Reid Nichols	.04	.02	.00
☐ 38	Jackie Moore MG ... (checklist back)	.07	.03	.01
☐ 39	John Wockenfuss ...	.04	.02	.00
☐ 40	Phil Niekro	.18	.09	.01
☐ 41	Mike Fischlin	.04	.02	.00
☐ 42	Luis Sanchez	.04	.02	.00
☐ 43	Andre David	.04	.02	.00
☐ 44	Dickie Thon	.04	.02	.00
☐ 45	Greg Minton	.04	.02	.00
☐ 46	Gary Woods	.04	.02	.00
☐ 47	Dave Rozema	.04	.02	.00
☐ 48	Tony Fernandez	1.50	.75	.15
☐ 49	Butch Davis	.04	.02	.00
☐ 50	John Candelaria	.07	.03	.01
☐ 51	Bob Watson	.07	.03	.01
☐ 52	Jerry Dybzinski	.04	.02	.00
☐ 53	Tom Gorman	.04	.02	.00
☐ 54	Cesar Cedeno	.07	.03	.01
☐ 55	Frank Tanana	.07	.03	.01
☐ 56	Jim Dwyer	.04	.02	.00
☐ 57	Pat Zachry	.04	.02	.00
☐ 58	Orlando Mercado ...	.04	.02	.00
☐ 59	Rick Waits	.04	.02	.00
☐ 60	George Hendrick	.07	.03	.01
☐ 61	Curt Kaufman	.04	.02	.00
☐ 62	Mike Ramsey	.04	.02	.00
☐ 63	Steve McCatty	.04	.02	.00
☐ 64	Mark Bailey	.04	.02	.00
☐ 65	Bill Buckner	.10	.05	.01
☐ 66	Dick Williams MG ... (checklist back)	.07	.03	.01
☐ 67	Rafael Santana	.25	.12	.02
☐ 68	Von Hayes	.15	.07	.01
☐ 69	Jim Winn	.04	.02	.00
☐ 70	Don Baylor	.10	.05	.01
☐ 71	Tim Laudner	.04	.02	.00
☐ 72	Rick Sutcliffe	.12	.06	.01
☐ 73	Rusty Kuntz	.04	.02	.00

			MINT	EXC	G-VG				MINT	EXC	G-VG
☐	74	Mike Krukow	.04	.02	.00	☐	121	Checklist: 1-132	.07	.01	.00
☐	75	Willie Upshaw	.04	.02	.00	☐	122	Tom Brunansky	.18	.09	.01
☐	76	Alan Bannister	.04	.02	.00	☐	123	Dave Smith	.07	.03	.01
☐	77	Joe Beckwith	.04	.02	.00	☐	124	Rich Hebner	.04	.02	.00
☐	78	Scott Fletcher	.07	.03	.01	☐	125	Kent Tekulve	.07	.03	.01
☐	79	Rick Mahler	.04	.02	.00	☐	126	Ruppert Jones	.04	.02	.00
☐	80	Keith Hernandez	.30	.15	.03	☐	127	Mark Gubicza	1.25	.60	.12
☐	81	Lenn Sakata	.04	.02	.00	☐	128	Ernie Whitt	.07	.03	.01
☐	82	Joe Price	.04	.02	.00	☐	129	Gene Garber	.04	.02	.00
☐	83	Charlie Moore	.04	.02	.00	☐	130	Al Oliver	.10	.05	.01
☐	84	Spike Owen	.04	.02	.00	☐	131	Buddy/Gus Bell FS	.07	.03	.01
☐	85	Mike Marshall	.12	.06	.01	☐	132	Dale/Yogi Berra FS	.15	.07	.01
☐	86	Don Aase	.04	.02	.00	☐	133	Bob/Ray Boone FS	.07	.03	.01
☐	87	David Green	.04	.02	.00	☐	134	Terry/Tito Francona FS	.07	.03	.01
☐	88	Bryn Smith	.07	.03	.01	☐	135	Terry/Bob Kennedy FS	.07	.03	.01
☐	89	Jackie Gutierrez	.07	.03	.01	☐	136	Jeff/Jim Kunkel FS	.07	.03	.01
☐	90	Rich Gossage	.12	.06	.01	☐	137	Vance/Vern Law FS	.07	.03	.01
☐	91	Jeff Burroughs	.04	.02	.00	☐	138	Dick/Dick Schofield FS	.07	.03	.01
☐	92	Paul Owens MG	.07	.03	.01	☐	139	Joel/Bob Skinner FS	.07	.03	.01
		(checklist back)				☐	140	Roy/Roy Smalley FS	.07	.03	.01
☐	93	Don Schulze	.04	.02	.00	☐	141	Mike/D. Stenhouse FS	.07	.03	.01
☐	94	Toby Harrah	.04	.02	.00	☐	142	Steve/Dizzy Trout FS	.07	.03	.01
☐	95	Jose Cruz	.10	.05	.01	☐	143	Ozzie/Ozzie Virgil FS	.07	.03	.01
☐	96	Johnny Ray	.10	.05	.01	☐	144	Ron Gardenhire	.04	.02	.00
☐	97	Pete Filson	.04	.02	.00	☐	145	Alvin Davis	2.00	1.00	.20
☐	98	Steve Lake	.04	.02	.00	☐	146	Gary Redus	.04	.02	.00
☐	99	Milt Wilcox	.04	.02	.00	☐	147	Bill Swaggerty	.04	.02	.00
☐	100	George Brett	.50	.25	.05	☐	148	Steve Yeager	.04	.02	.00
☐	101	Jim Acker	.04	.02	.00	☐	149	Dickie Noles	.04	.02	.00
☐	102	Tommy Dunbar	.04	.02	.00	☐	150	Jim Rice	.25	.12	.02
☐	103	Randy Lerch	.04	.02	.00	☐	151	Moose Haas	.04	.02	.00
☐	104	Mike Fitzgerald	.04	.02	.00	☐	152	Steve Braun	.04	.02	.00
☐	105	Ron Kittle	.12	.06	.01	☐	153	Frank LaCorte	.04	.02	.00
☐	106	Pascual Perez	.10	.05	.01	☐	154	Argenis Salazar	.04	.02	.00
☐	107	Tom Foley	.04	.02	.00	☐	155	Yogi Berra MG	.15	.07	.01
☐	108	Darnell Coles	.10	.05	.01			(checklist back)			
☐	109	Gary Roenicke	.04	.02	.00	☐	156	Craig Reynolds	.04	.02	.00
☐	110	Alejandro Pena	.07	.03	.01	☐	157	Tug McGraw	.10	.05	.01
☐	111	Doug DeCinces	.07	.03	.01	☐	158	Pat Tabler	.07	.03	.01
☐	112	Tom Tellmann	.04	.02	.00	☐	159	Carlos Diaz	.04	.02	.00
☐	113	Tom Herr	.07	.03	.01	☐	160	Lance Parrish	.18	.09	.01
☐	114	Bob James	.04	.02	.00	☐	161	Ken Schrom	.04	.02	.00
☐	115	Rickey Henderson	.60	.30	.06	☐	162	Benny Distefano	.10	.05	.01
☐	116	Dennis Boyd	.20	.10	.02	☐	163	Dennis Eckersley	.15	.07	.01
☐	117	Greg Gross	.04	.02	.00	☐	164	Jorge Orta	.04	.02	.00
☐	118	Eric Show	.07	.03	.01	☐	165	Dusty Baker	.07	.03	.01
☐	119	Pat Corrales MG	.07	.03	.01	☐	166	Keith Atherton	.04	.02	.00
		(checklist back)				☐	167	Rufino Linares	.04	.02	.00
☐	120	Steve Kemp	.07	.03	.01	☐	168	Garth Iorg	.04	.02	.00

		MINT	EXC	G-VG			MINT	EXC	G-VG
☐ 169	Dan Spillner	.04	.02	.00	☐ 216	Jerry Don Gleaton	.04	.02	.00
☐ 170	George Foster	.10	.05	.01	☐ 217	Leon Roberts	.04	.02	.00
☐ 171	Bill Stein	.04	.02	.00	☐ 218	Doyle Alexander	.07	.03	.01
☐ 172	Jack Perconte	.04	.02	.00	☐ 219	Gerald Perry	.30	.15	.03
☐ 173	Mike Young	.10	.05	.01	☐ 220	Fred Lynn	.15	.07	.01
☐ 174	Rick Honeycutt	.04	.02	.00	☐ 221	Ron Reed	.04	.02	.00
☐ 175	Dave Parker	.18	.09	.01	☐ 222	Hubie Brooks	.12	.06	.01
☐ 176	Bill Schroeder	.04	.02	.00	☐ 223	Tom Hume	.04	.02	.00
☐ 177	Dave Von Ohlen	.04	.02	.00	☐ 224	Al Cowens	.04	.02	.00
☐ 178	Miguel Dilone	.04	.02	.00	☐ 225	Mike Boddicker	.10	.05	.01
☐ 179	Tommy John	.15	.07	.01	☐ 226	Juan Beniquez	.04	.02	.00
☐ 180	Dave Winfield	.35	.17	.03	☐ 227	Danny Darwin	.04	.02	.00
☐ 181	Roger Clemens	10.00	5.00	1.00	☐ 228	Dion James	.15	.07	.01
☐ 182	Tim Flannery	.04	.02	.00	☐ 229	Dave LaPoint	.07	.03	.01
☐ 183	Larry McWilliams	.04	.02	.00	☐ 230	Gary Carter	.30	.15	.03
☐ 184	Carmen Castillo	.04	.02	.00	☐ 231	Dwayne Murphy	.04	.02	.00
☐ 185	Al Holland	.04	.02	.00	☐ 232	Dave Beard	.04	.02	.00
☐ 186	Bob Lillis MG	.07	.03	.01	☐ 233	Ed Jurak	.04	.02	.00
	(checklist back)				☐ 234	Jerry Narron	.04	.02	.00
☐ 187	Mike Walters	.04	.02	.00	☐ 235	Garry Maddox	.04	.02	.00
☐ 188	Greg Pryor	.04	.02	.00	☐ 236	Mark Thurmond	.04	.02	.00
☐ 189	Warren Brusstar	.04	.02	.00	☐ 237	Julio Franco	.40	.20	.04
☐ 190	Rusty Staub	.10	.05	.01	☐ 238	Jose Rijo	.45	.22	.04
☐ 191	Steve Nicosia	.04	.02	.00	☐ 239	Tim Teufel	.12	.06	.01
☐ 192	Howard Johnson	4.00	2.00	.40	☐ 240	Dave Stieb	.12	.06	.01
☐ 193	Jimmy Key	1.00	.50	.10	☐ 241	Jim Frey MG	.07	.03	.01
☐ 194	Dave Stegman	.04	.02	.00		(checklist back)			
☐ 195	Glenn Hubbard	.04	.02	.00	☐ 242	Greg Harris	.04	.02	.00
☐ 196	Pete O'Brien	.10	.05	.01	☐ 243	Barbaro Garbey	.04	.02	.00
☐ 197	Mike Warren	.04	.02	.00	☐ 244	Mike Jones	.04	.02	.00
☐ 198	Eddie Milner	.04	.02	.00	☐ 245	Chili Davis	.10	.05	.01
☐ 199	Dennis Martinez	.07	.03	.01	☐ 246	Mike Norris	.04	.02	.00
☐ 200	Reggie Jackson	.45	.22	.04	☐ 247	Wayne Tolleson	.04	.02	.00
☐ 201	Burt Hooton	.04	.02	.00	☐ 248	Terry Forster	.07	.03	.01
☐ 202	Gorman Thomas	.10	.05	.01	☐ 249	Harold Baines	.15	.07	.01
☐ 203	Bob McClure	.04	.02	.00	☐ 250	Jesse Orosco	.04	.02	.00
☐ 204	Art Howe	.07	.03	.01	☐ 251	Brad Gulden	.04	.02	.00
☐ 205	Steve Rogers	.04	.02	.00	☐ 252	Dan Ford	.04	.02	.00
☐ 206	Phil Garner	.04	.02	.00	☐ 253	Sid Bream	.30	.15	.03
☐ 207	Mark Clear	.04	.02	.00	☐ 254	Pete Vuckovich	.04	.02	.00
☐ 208	Champ Summers	.04	.02	.00	☐ 255	Lonnie Smith	.07	.03	.01
☐ 209	Bill Campbell	.04	.02	.00	☐ 256	Mike Stanton	.04	.02	.00
☐ 210	Gary Matthews	.07	.03	.01	☐ 257	Bryan Little	.04	.02	.00
☐ 211	Clay Christiansen	.04	.02	.00	☐ 258	Mike Brown	.04	.02	.00
☐ 212	George Vukovich	.04	.02	.00		(Angels OF)			
☐ 213	Billy Gardner MG	.07	.03	.01	☐ 259	Gary Allenson	.04	.02	.00
	(checklist back)				☐ 260	Dave Righetti	.12	.06	.01
☐ 214	John Tudor	.15	.07	.01	☐ 261	Checklist: 133-264	.07	.01	.00
☐ 215	Bob Brenly	.04	.02	.00	☐ 262	Greg Booker	.04	.02	.00

		MINT	EXC	G-VG
☐ 263	Mel Hall	.10	.05	.01
☐ 264	Joe Sambito	.04	.02	.00
☐ 265	Juan Samuel	.60	.30	.06
☐ 266	Frank Viola	.30	.15	.03
☐ 267	Henry Cotto	.15	.07	.01
☐ 268	Chuck Tanner MG	.07	.03	.01
	(checklist back)			
☐ 269	Doug Baker	.04	.02	.00
☐ 270	Dan Quisenberry	.12	.06	.01
☐ 271	Tim Foli FDP68	.04	.02	.00
☐ 272	Jeff Burroughs FDP69	.04	.02	.00
☐ 273	Bill Almon FDP74	.04	.02	.00
☐ 274	Floyd Bannister FDP76	.04	.02	.00
☐ 275	Harold Baines FDP77	.12	.06	.01
☐ 276	Bob Horner FDP78	.12	.06	.01
☐ 277	Al Chambers FDP79	.04	.02	.00
☐ 278	D.Strawberry FDP80	1.00	.50	.10
☐ 279	Mike Moore FDP81	.10	.05	.01
☐ 280	Sh.Dunston FDP82	1.50	.75	.15
☐ 281	Tim Belcher FDP83	1.50	.75	.15
☐ 282	Shawn Abner FDP84	.35	.17	.03
☐ 283	Fran Mullins	.04	.02	.00
☐ 284	Marty Bystrom	.04	.02	.00
☐ 285	Dan Driessen	.04	.02	.00
☐ 286	Rudy Law	.04	.02	.00
☐ 287	Walt Terrell	.04	.02	.00
☐ 288	Jeff Kunkel	.07	.03	.01
☐ 289	Tom Underwood	.04	.02	.00
☐ 290	Cecil Cooper	.10	.05	.01
☐ 291	Bob Welch	.07	.03	.01
☐ 292	Brad Komminsk	.04	.02	.00
☐ 293	Curt Young	.25	.12	.02
☐ 294	Tom Nieto	.04	.02	.00
☐ 295	Joe Niekro	.07	.03	.01
☐ 296	Ricky Nelson	.04	.02	.00
☐ 297	Gary Lucas	.04	.02	.00
☐ 298	Marty Barrett	.12	.06	.01
☐ 299	Andy Hawkins	.10	.05	.01
☐ 300	Rod Carew	.35	.17	.03
☐ 301	John Montefusco	.04	.02	.00
☐ 302	Tim Corcoran	.04	.02	.00
☐ 303	Mike Jeffcoat	.04	.02	.00
☐ 304	Gary Gaetti	.30	.15	.03
☐ 305	Dale Berra	.04	.02	.00
☐ 306	Rick Reuschel	.12	.06	.01
☐ 307	Sparky Anderson MG	.07	.03	.01
	(checklist back)			

		MINT	EXC	G-VG
☐ 308	John Wathan	.04	.02	.00
☐ 309	Mike Witt	.10	.05	.01
☐ 310	Manny Trillo	.04	.02	.00
☐ 311	Jim Gott	.04	.02	.00
☐ 312	Marc Hill	.04	.02	.00
☐ 313	Dave Schmidt	.07	.03	.01
☐ 314	Ron Oester	.04	.02	.00
☐ 315	Doug Sisk	.04	.02	.00
☐ 316	John Lowenstein	.04	.02	.00
☐ 317	Jack Lazorko	.04	.02	.00
☐ 318	Ted Simmons	.10	.05	.01
☐ 319	Jeff Jones	.04	.02	.00
☐ 320	Dale Murphy	.60	.30	.06
☐ 321	Ricky Horton	.20	.10	.02
☐ 322	Dave Stapleton	.04	.02	.00
☐ 323	Andy McGaffigan	.04	.02	.00
☐ 324	Bruce Bochy	.04	.02	.00
☐ 325	John Denny	.07	.03	.01
☐ 326	Kevin Bass	.10	.05	.01
☐ 327	Brook Jacoby	.25	.12	.02
☐ 328	Bob Shirley	.04	.02	.00
☐ 329	Ron Washington	.04	.02	.00
☐ 330	Leon Durham	.07	.03	.01
☐ 331	Bill Laskey	.04	.02	.00
☐ 332	Brian Harper	.04	.02	.00
☐ 333	Willie Hernandez	.10	.05	.01
☐ 334	Dick Howser MG	.07	.03	.01
	(checklist back)			
☐ 335	Bruce Benedict	.04	.02	.00
☐ 336	Rance Mulliniks	.04	.02	.00
☐ 337	Billy Sample	.04	.02	.00
☐ 338	Britt Burns	.04	.02	.00
☐ 339	Danny Heep	.04	.02	.00
☐ 340	Robin Yount	.50	.25	.05
☐ 341	Floyd Rayford	.04	.02	.00
☐ 342	Ted Power	.04	.02	.00
☐ 343	Bill Russell	.07	.03	.01
☐ 344	Dave Henderson	.10	.05	.01
☐ 345	Charlie Lea	.04	.02	.00
☐ 346	Terry Pendleton	.45	.22	.04
☐ 347	Rick Langford	.04	.02	.00
☐ 348	Bob Boone	.12	.06	.01
☐ 349	Domingo Ramos	.04	.02	.00
☐ 350	Wade Boggs	3.50	1.75	.35
☐ 351	Juan Agosto	.04	.02	.00
☐ 352	Joe Morgan	.20	.10	.02
☐ 353	Julio Solano	.04	.02	.00
☐ 354	Andre Robertson	.04	.02	.00
☐ 355	Bert Blyleven	.15	.07	.01

		MINT	EXC	G-VG
☐ 356	Dave Meier	.04	.02	.00
☐ 357	Rich Bordi	.04	.02	.00
☐ 358	Tony Pena	.10	.05	.01
☐ 359	Pat Sheridan	.04	.02	.00
☐ 360	Steve Carlton	.30	.15	.03
☐ 361	Alfredo Griffin	.07	.03	.01
☐ 362	Craig McMurtry	.04	.02	.00
☐ 363	Ron Hodges	.04	.02	.00
☐ 364	Richard Dotson	.07	.03	.01
☐ 365	Danny Ozark MG	.07	.03	.01
	(checklist back)			
☐ 366	Todd Cruz	.04	.02	.00
☐ 367	Keefe Cato	.04	.02	.00
☐ 368	Dave Bergman	.04	.02	.00
☐ 369	R.J. Reynolds	.20	.10	.02
☐ 370	Bruce Sutter	.10	.05	.01
☐ 371	Mickey Rivers	.07	.03	.01
☐ 372	Roy Howell	.04	.02	.00
☐ 373	Mike Moore	.10	.05	.01
☐ 374	Brian Downing	.07	.03	.01
☐ 375	Jeff Reardon	.10	.05	.01
☐ 376	Jeff Newman	.04	.02	.00
☐ 377	Checklist: 265-396	.07	.01	.00
☐ 378	Alan Wiggins	.04	.02	.00
☐ 379	Charles Hudson	.04	.02	.00
☐ 380	Ken Griffey	.10	.05	.01
☐ 381	Roy Smith	.04	.02	.00
☐ 382	Denny Walling	.04	.02	.00
☐ 383	Rick Lysander	.04	.02	.00
☐ 384	Jody Davis	.07	.03	.01
☐ 385	Jose DeLeon	.07	.03	.01
☐ 386	Dan Gladden	.35	.17	.03
☐ 387	Buddy Biancalana	.07	.03	.01
☐ 388	Bert Roberge	.04	.02	.00
☐ 389	Rod Dedeaux OLY CO	.04	.02	.00
☐ 390	Sid Akins OLY	.07	.03	.01
☐ 391	Flavio Alfaro OLY	.04	.02	.00
☐ 392	Don August OLY	.35	.17	.03
☐ 393	Scott Bankhead OLY	.75	.35	.07
☐ 394	Bob Caffrey OLY	.07	.03	.01
☐ 395	Mike Dunne OLY	.35	.17	.03
☐ 396	Gary Green OLY	.12	.06	.01
☐ 397	John Hoover OLY	.12	.06	.01
☐ 398	Shane Mack OLY	.35	.17	.03
☐ 399	John Marzano OLY	.25	.12	.02
☐ 400	Oddibe McDowell OLY	.65	.30	.06
☐ 401	Mark McGwire OLY	18.00	9.00	1.80
☐ 402	Pat Pacillo OLY	.15	.07	.01
☐ 403	Cory Snyder OLY	4.00	2.00	.40
☐ 404	Billy Swift OLY	.20	.10	.02
☐ 405	Tom Veryzer	.04	.02	.00
☐ 406	Len Whitehouse	.04	.02	.00
☐ 407	Bobby Ramos	.04	.02	.00
☐ 408	Sid Monge	.04	.02	.00
☐ 409	Brad Wellman	.04	.02	.00
☐ 410	Bob Horner	.12	.06	.01
☐ 411	Bobby Cox MG	.07	.03	.01
	(checklist back)			
☐ 412	Bud Black	.04	.02	.00
☐ 413	Vance Law	.07	.03	.01
☐ 414	Gary Ward	.07	.03	.01
☐ 415	Ron Darling UER	1.00	.50	.10
	(no trivia answer)			
☐ 416	Wayne Gross	.04	.02	.00
☐ 417	John Franco	1.25	.60	.12
☐ 418	Ken Landreaux	.04	.02	.00
☐ 419	Mike Caldwell	.04	.02	.00
☐ 420	Andre Dawson	.30	.15	.03
☐ 421	Dave Rucker	.04	.02	.00
☐ 422	Carney Lansford	.12	.06	.01
☐ 423	Barry Bonnell	.04	.02	.00
☐ 424	Al Nipper	.10	.05	.01
☐ 425	Mike Hargrove	.04	.02	.00
☐ 426	Vern Ruhle	.04	.02	.00
☐ 427	Mario Ramirez	.04	.02	.00
☐ 428	Larry Andersen	.04	.02	.00
☐ 429	Rick Cerone	.04	.02	.00
☐ 430	Ron Davis	.04	.02	.00
☐ 431	U.L. Washington	.04	.02	.00
☐ 432	Thad Bosley	.04	.02	.00
☐ 433	Jim Morrison	.04	.02	.00
☐ 434	Gene Richards	.04	.02	.00
☐ 435	Dan Petry	.04	.02	.00
☐ 436	Willie Aikens	.04	.02	.00
☐ 437	Al Jones	.04	.02	.00
☐ 438	Joe Torre MG	.07	.03	.01
	(checklist back)			
☐ 439	Junior Ortiz	.04	.02	.00
☐ 440	Fernando Valenzuela	.25	.12	.02
☐ 441	Duane Walker	.04	.02	.00
☐ 442	Ken Forsch	.04	.02	.00
☐ 443	George Wright	.04	.02	.00
☐ 444	Tony Phillips	.04	.02	.00
☐ 445	Tippy Martinez	.04	.02	.00
☐ 446	Jim Sundberg	.04	.02	.00
☐ 447	Jeff Lahti	.04	.02	.00
☐ 448	Derrel Thomas	.04	.02	.00
☐ 449	Phil Bradley	.65	.30	.06

		MINT	EXC	G-VG
☐ 450	Steve Garvey	.40	.20	.04
☐ 451	Bruce Hurst	.15	.07	.01
☐ 452	John Castino	.04	.02	.00
☐ 453	Tom Waddell	.07	.03	.01
☐ 454	Glenn Wilson	.07	.03	.01
☐ 455	Bob Knepper	.07	.03	.01
☐ 456	Tim Foli	.04	.02	.00
☐ 457	Cecilio Guante	.04	.02	.00
☐ 458	Randy Johnson	.04	.02	.00
☐ 459	Charlie Leibrandt	.04	.02	.00
☐ 460	Ryne Sandberg	.45	.22	.04
☐ 461	Marty Castillo	.04	.02	.00
☐ 462	Gary Lavelle	.04	.02	.00
☐ 463	Dave Collins	.04	.02	.00
☐ 464	Mike Mason	.07	.03	.01
☐ 465	Bob Grich	.07	.03	.01
☐ 466	Tony LaRussa MG (checklist back)	.07	.03	.01
☐ 467	Ed Lynch	.04	.02	.00
☐ 468	Wayne Krenchicki	.04	.02	.00
☐ 469	Sammy Stewart	.04	.02	.00
☐ 470	Steve Sax	.25	.12	.02
☐ 471	Pete Ladd	.04	.02	.00
☐ 472	Jim Essian	.04	.02	.00
☐ 473	Tim Wallach	.10	.05	.01
☐ 474	Kurt Kepshire	.07	.03	.01
☐ 475	Andre Thornton	.07	.03	.01
☐ 476	Jeff Stone	.10	.05	.01
☐ 477	Bob Ojeda	.10	.05	.01
☐ 478	Kurt Bevacqua	.04	.02	.00
☐ 479	Mike Madden	.04	.02	.00
☐ 480	Lou Whitaker	.18	.09	.01
☐ 481	Dale Murray	.04	.02	.00
☐ 482	Harry Spilman	.04	.02	.00
☐ 483	Mike Smithson	.04	.02	.00
☐ 484	Larry Bowa	.10	.05	.01
☐ 485	Matt Young	.04	.02	.00
☐ 486	Steve Balboni	.04	.02	.00
☐ 487	Frank Williams	.12	.06	.01
☐ 488	Joel Skinner	.07	.03	.01
☐ 489	Bryan Clark	.04	.02	.00
☐ 490	Jason Thompson	.04	.02	.00
☐ 491	Rick Camp	.04	.02	.00
☐ 492	Dave Johnson MG (checklist back)	.07	.03	.01
☐ 493	Orel Hershiser	7.00	3.50	.70
☐ 494	Rich Dauer	.04	.02	.00
☐ 495	Mario Soto	.04	.02	.00
☐ 496	Donnie Scott	.04	.02	.00
☐ 497	Gary Pettis UER (photo actually Gary's little brother, Lynn)	.25	.12	.02
☐ 498	Ed Romero	.04	.02	.00
☐ 499	Danny Cox	.20	.10	.02
☐ 500	Mike Schmidt	.60	.30	.06
☐ 501	Dan Schatzeder	.04	.02	.00
☐ 502	Rick Miller	.04	.02	.00
☐ 503	Tim Conroy	.04	.02	.00
☐ 504	Jerry Willard	.04	.02	.00
☐ 505	Jim Beattie	.04	.02	.00
☐ 506	Franklin Stubbs	.25	.12	.02
☐ 507	Ray Fontenot	.04	.02	.00
☐ 508	John Shelby	.04	.02	.00
☐ 509	Milt May	.04	.02	.00
☐ 510	Kent Hrbek	.30	.15	.03
☐ 511	Lee Smith	.07	.03	.01
☐ 512	Tom Brookens	.04	.02	.00
☐ 513	Lynn Jones	.04	.02	.00
☐ 514	Jeff Cornell	.04	.02	.00
☐ 515	Dave Concepcion	.07	.03	.01
☐ 516	Roy Lee Jackson	.04	.02	.00
☐ 517	Jerry Martin	.04	.02	.00
☐ 518	Chris Chambliss	.07	.03	.01
☐ 519	Doug Rader MG (checklist back)	.07	.03	.01
☐ 520	LaMarr Hoyt	.07	.03	.01
☐ 521	Rick Dempsey	.04	.02	.00
☐ 522	Paul Molitor	.15	.07	.01
☐ 523	Candy Maldonado	.10	.05	.01
☐ 524	Rob Wilfong	.04	.02	.00
☐ 525	Darrell Porter	.04	.02	.00
☐ 526	David Palmer	.04	.02	.00
☐ 527	Checklist: 397-528	.07	.01	.00
☐ 528	Bill Krueger	.04	.02	.00
☐ 529	Rich Gedman	.07	.03	.01
☐ 530	Dave Dravecky	.12	.06	.01
☐ 531	Joe Lefebvre	.04	.02	.00
☐ 532	Frank DiPino	.04	.02	.00
☐ 533	Tony Bernazard	.04	.02	.00
☐ 534	Brian Dayett	.04	.02	.00
☐ 535	Pat Putnam	.04	.02	.00
☐ 536	Kirby Puckett	12.00	6.00	1.20
☐ 537	Don Robinson	.04	.02	.00
☐ 538	Keith Moreland	.04	.02	.00
☐ 539	Aurelio Lopez	.04	.02	.00
☐ 540	Claudell Washington	.07	.03	.01
☐ 541	Mark Davis	.15	.07	.01
☐ 542	Don Slaught	.04	.02	.00

		MINT	EXC	G-VG
☐ 543	Mike Squires	.04	.02	.00
☐ 544	Bruce Kison	.04	.02	.00
☐ 545	Lloyd Moseby	.10	.05	.01
☐ 546	Brent Gaff	.04	.02	.00
☐ 547	Pete Rose MG (checklist back)	.45	.22	.04
☐ 548	Larry Parrish	.04	.02	.00
☐ 549	Mike Scioscia	.07	.03	.01
☐ 550	Scott McGregor	.07	.03	.01
☐ 551	Andy Van Slyke	.35	.17	.03
☐ 552	Chris Codiroli	.04	.02	.00
☐ 553	Bob Clark	.04	.02	.00
☐ 554	Doug Flynn	.04	.02	.00
☐ 555	Bob Stanley	.04	.02	.00
☐ 556	Sixto Lezcano	.04	.02	.00
☐ 557	Len Barker	.04	.02	.00
☐ 558	Carmelo Martinez	.04	.02	.00
☐ 559	Jay Howell	.07	.03	.01
☐ 560	Bill Madlock	.07	.03	.01
☐ 561	Darryl Motley	.04	.02	.00
☐ 562	Houston Jimenez	.04	.02	.00
☐ 563	Dick Ruthven	.04	.02	.00
☐ 564	Alan Ashby	.04	.02	.00
☐ 565	Kirk Gibson	.30	.15	.03
☐ 566	Ed VandeBerg	.04	.02	.00
☐ 567	Joel Youngblood	.04	.02	.00
☐ 568	Cliff Johnson	.04	.02	.00
☐ 569	Ken Oberkfell	.04	.02	.00
☐ 570	Darryl Strawberry	3.00	1.50	.30
☐ 571	Charlie Hough	.07	.03	.01
☐ 572	Tom Paciorek	.04	.02	.00
☐ 573	Jay Tibbs	.10	.05	.01
☐ 574	Joe Altobelli MG (checklist back)	.07	.03	.01
☐ 575	Pedro Guerrero	.25	.12	.02
☐ 576	Jaime Cocanower	.04	.02	.00
☐ 577	Chris Speier	.04	.02	.00
☐ 578	Terry Francona	.04	.02	.00
☐ 579	Ron Romanick	.04	.02	.00
☐ 580	Dwight Evans	.12	.06	.01
☐ 581	Mark Wagner	.04	.02	.00
☐ 582	Ken Phelps	.25	.12	.02
☐ 583	Bobby Brown	.04	.02	.00
☐ 584	Kevin Gross	.04	.02	.00
☐ 585	Butch Wynegar	.04	.02	.00
☐ 586	Bill Scherrer	.04	.02	.00
☐ 587	Doug Frobel	.04	.02	.00
☐ 588	Bobby Castillo	.04	.02	.00
☐ 589	Bob Dernier	.04	.02	.00
☐ 590	Ray Knight	.07	.03	.01
☐ 591	Larry Herndon	.04	.02	.00
☐ 592	Jeff Robinson (Giants pitcher)	.30	.15	.03
☐ 593	Rick Leach	.04	.02	.00
☐ 594	Curt Wilkerson	.04	.02	.00
☐ 595	Larry Gura	.04	.02	.00
☐ 596	Jerry Hairston	.04	.02	.00
☐ 597	Brad Lesley	.04	.02	.00
☐ 598	Jose Oquendo	.07	.03	.01
☐ 599	Storm Davis	.10	.05	.01
☐ 600	Pete Rose	1.00	.50	.10
☐ 601	Tom Lasorda MG (checklist back)	.07	.03	.01
☐ 602	Jeff Dedmon	.04	.02	.00
☐ 603	Rick Manning	.04	.02	.00
☐ 604	Daryl Sconiers	.04	.02	.00
☐ 605	Ozzie Smith	.25	.12	.02
☐ 606	Rich Gale	.04	.02	.00
☐ 607	Bill Almon	.04	.02	.00
☐ 608	Craig Lefferts	.07	.03	.01
☐ 609	Broderick Perkins	.04	.02	.00
☐ 610	Jack Morris	.15	.07	.01
☐ 611	Ozzie Virgil	.04	.02	.00
☐ 612	Mike Armstrong	.04	.02	.00
☐ 613	Terry Puhl	.04	.02	.00
☐ 614	Al Williams	.04	.02	.00
☐ 615	Marvell Wynne	.04	.02	.00
☐ 616	Scott Sanderson	.04	.02	.00
☐ 617	Willie Wilson	.10	.05	.01
☐ 618	Pete Falcone	.04	.02	.00
☐ 619	Jeff Leonard	.07	.03	.01
☐ 620	Dwight Gooden	9.00	4.50	.90
☐ 621	Marvis Foley	.04	.02	.00
☐ 622	Luis Leal	.04	.02	.00
☐ 623	Greg Walker	.07	.03	.01
☐ 624	Benny Ayala	.04	.02	.00
☐ 625	Mark Langston	3.25	1.60	.32
☐ 626	German Rivera	.07	.03	.01
☐ 627	Eric Davis	13.50	6.00	1.25
☐ 628	Rene Lachemann MG (checklist back)	.07	.03	.01
☐ 629	Dick Schofield	.12	.06	.01
☐ 630	Tim Raines	.35	.17	.03
☐ 631	Bob Forsch	.04	.02	.00
☐ 632	Bruce Bochte	.04	.02	.00
☐ 633	Glenn Hoffman	.04	.02	.00
☐ 634	Bill Dawley	.04	.02	.00
☐ 635	Terry Kennedy	.04	.02	.00

		MINT	EXC	G-VG
☐ 636	Shane Rawley	.04	.02	.00
☐ 637	Brett Butler	.07	.03	.01
☐ 638	Mike Pagliarulo	.65	.30	.06
☐ 639	Ed Hodge	.04	.02	.00
☐ 640	Steve Henderson	.10	.05	.01
☐ 641	Rod Scurry	.04	.02	.00
☐ 642	Dave Owen	.04	.02	.00
☐ 643	Johnny Grubb	.04	.02	.00
☐ 644	Mark Huismann	.04	.02	.00
☐ 645	Damaso Garcia	.04	.02	.00
☐ 646	Scot Thompson	.04	.02	.00
☐ 647	Rafael Ramirez	.04	.02	.00
☐ 648	Bob Jones	.04	.02	.00
☐ 649	Sid Fernandez	.85	.40	.08
☐ 650	Greg Luzinski	.10	.05	.01
☐ 651	Jeff Russell	.12	.06	.01
☐ 652	Joe Nolan	.04	.02	.00
☐ 653	Mark Brouhard	.04	.02	.00
☐ 654	Dave Anderson	.04	.02	.00
☐ 655	Joaquin Andujar	.10	.05	.01
☐ 656	Chuck Cottier MG	.07	.03	.01
	(checklist back)			
☐ 657	Jim Slaton	.04	.02	.00
☐ 658	Mike Stenhouse	.07	.03	.01
☐ 659	Checklist: 529-660	.07	.01	.00
☐ 660	Tony Gwynn	1.25	.60	.12
☐ 661	Steve Crawford	.04	.02	.00
☐ 662	Mike Heath	.04	.02	.00
☐ 663	Luis Aguayo	.04	.02	.00
☐ 664	Steve Farr	.25	.12	.02
☐ 665	Don Mattingly	9.00	4.50	.90
☐ 666	Mike LaCoss	.04	.02	.00
☐ 667	Dave Engle	.04	.02	.00
☐ 668	Steve Trout	.04	.02	.00
☐ 669	Lee Lacy	.04	.02	.00
☐ 670	Tom Seaver	.30	.15	.03
☐ 671	Dane Iorg	.04	.02	.00
☐ 672	Juan Berenguer	.04	.02	.00
☐ 673	Buck Martinez	.04	.02	.00
☐ 674	Atlee Hammaker	.04	.02	.00
☐ 675	Tony Perez	.15	.07	.01
☐ 676	Albert Hall	.10	.05	.01
☐ 677	Wally Backman	.04	.02	.00
☐ 678	Joey McLaughlin	.04	.02	.00
☐ 679	Bob Kearney	.04	.02	.00
☐ 680	Jerry Reuss	.07	.03	.01
☐ 681	Ben Oglivie	.07	.03	.01
☐ 682	Doug Corbett	.04	.02	.00
☐ 683	Whitey Herzog MG	.07	.03	.01

		MINT	EXC	G-VG
	(checklist back)			
☐ 684	Bill Doran	.10	.05	.01
☐ 685	Bill Caudill	.04	.02	.00
☐ 686	Mike Easler	.04	.02	.00
☐ 687	Bill Gullickson	.04	.02	.00
☐ 688	Len Matuszek	.04	.02	.00
☐ 689	Luis DeLeon	.04	.02	.00
☐ 690	Alan Trammell	.30	.15	.03
☐ 691	Dennis Rasmussen	.25	.12	.02
☐ 692	Randy Bush	.04	.02	.00
☐ 693	Tim Stoddard	.04	.02	.00
☐ 694	Joe Carter	2.50	1.25	.25
☐ 695	Rick Rhoden	.07	.03	.01
☐ 696	John Rabb	.04	.02	.00
☐ 697	Onix Concepcion	.04	.02	.00
☐ 698	Jorge Bell	.50	.25	.05
☐ 699	Donnie Moore	.04	.02	.00
☐ 700	Eddie Murray	.45	.22	.04
☐ 701	Eddie Murray AS	.15	.07	.01
☐ 702	Damaso Garcia AS	.04	.02	.00
☐ 703	George Brett AS	.25	.12	.02
☐ 704	Cal Ripken AS	.20	.10	.02
☐ 705	Dave Winfield AS	.15	.07	.01
☐ 706	Rickey Henderson AS	.30	.15	.03
☐ 707	Tony Armas AS	.07	.03	.01
☐ 708	Lance Parrish AS	.10	.05	.01
☐ 709	Mike Boddicker AS	.07	.03	.01
☐ 710	Frank Viola AS	.10	.05	.01
☐ 711	Dan Quisenberry AS	.07	.03	.01
☐ 712	Keith Hernandez AS	.15	.07	.01
☐ 713	Ryne Sandberg AS	.20	.10	.02
☐ 714	Mike Schmidt AS	.35	.17	.03
☐ 715	Ozzie Smith AS	.15	.07	.01
☐ 716	Dale Murphy AS	.25	.12	.02
☐ 717	Tony Gwynn AS	.30	.15	.03
☐ 718	Jeff Leonard AS	.07	.03	.01
☐ 719	Gary Carter AS	.15	.07	.01
☐ 720	Rick Sutcliffe AS	.07	.03	.01
☐ 721	Bob Knepper AS	.07	.03	.01
☐ 722	Bruce Sutter AS	.07	.03	.01
☐ 723	Dave Stewart	.25	.12	.02
☐ 724	Oscar Gamble	.04	.02	.00
☐ 725	Floyd Bannister	.04	.02	.00
☐ 726	Al Bumbry	.04	.02	.00
☐ 727	Frank Pastore	.04	.02	.00
☐ 728	Bob Bailor	.04	.02	.00
☐ 729	Don Sutton	.25	.12	.02
☐ 730	Dave Kingman	.10	.05	.01
☐ 731	Neil Allen	.04	.02	.00

		MINT	EXC	G-VG
☐ 732	John McNamara MG (checklist back)	.07	.03	.01
☐ 733	Tony Scott	.04	.02	.00
☐ 734	John Henry Johnson	.04	.02	.00
☐ 735	Garry Templeton	.07	.03	.01
☐ 736	Jerry Mumphrey	.04	.02	.00
☐ 737	Bo Diaz	.04	.02	.00
☐ 738	Omar Moreno	.04	.02	.00
☐ 739	Ernie Camacho	.04	.02	.00
☐ 740	Jack Clark	.25	.12	.02
☐ 741	John Butcher	.04	.02	.00
☐ 742	Ron Hassey	.04	.02	.00
☐ 743	Frank White	.07	.03	.01
☐ 744	Doug Bair	.04	.02	.00
☐ 745	Buddy Bell	.10	.05	.01
☐ 746	Jim Clancy	.04	.02	.00
☐ 747	Alex Trevino	.04	.02	.00
☐ 748	Lee Mazzilli	.04	.02	.00
☐ 749	Julio Cruz	.04	.02	.00
☐ 750	Rollie Fingers	.15	.07	.01
☐ 751	Kelvin Chapman	.04	.02	.00
☐ 752	Bob Owchinko	.04	.02	.00
☐ 753	Greg Brock	.04	.02	.00
☐ 754	Larry Milbourne	.04	.02	.00
☐ 755	Ken Singleton	.07	.03	.01
☐ 756	Rob Picciolo	.04	.02	.00
☐ 757	Willie McGee	.25	.12	.02
☐ 758	Ray Burris	.04	.02	.00
☐ 759	Jim Fanning MG (checklist back)	.07	.03	.01
☐ 760	Nolan Ryan	1.00	.50	.10
☐ 761	Jerry Remy	.04	.02	.00
☐ 762	Eddie Whitson	.04	.02	.00
☐ 763	Kiko Garcia	.04	.02	.00
☐ 764	Jamie Easterly	.04	.02	.00
☐ 765	Willie Randolph	.07	.03	.01
☐ 766	Paul Mirabella	.04	.02	.00
☐ 767	Darrell Brown	.04	.02	.00
☐ 768	Ron Cey	.10	.05	.01
☐ 769	Joe Cowley	.04	.02	.00
☐ 770	Carlton Fisk	.25	.12	.02
☐ 771	Geoff Zahn	.04	.02	.00
☐ 772	Johnnie LeMaster	.04	.02	.00
☐ 773	Hal McRae	.07	.03	.01
☐ 774	Dennis Lamp	.04	.02	.00
☐ 775	Mookie Wilson	.10	.05	.01
☐ 776	Jerry Royster	.04	.02	.00
☐ 777	Ned Yost	.04	.02	.00
☐ 778	Mike Davis	.07	.03	.01

		MINT	EXC	G-VG
☐ 779	Nick Esasky	.25	.10	.02
☐ 780	Mike Flanagan	.07	.03	.01
☐ 781	Jim Gantner	.04	.02	.00
☐ 782	Tom Niedenfuer	.04	.02	.00
☐ 783	Mike Jorgensen	.04	.02	.00
☐ 784	Checklist: 661-792	.07	.01	.00
☐ 785	Tony Armas	.07	.03	.01
☐ 786	Enos Cabell	.04	.02	.00
☐ 787	Jim Wohlford	.04	.02	.00
☐ 788	Steve Comer	.04	.02	.00
☐ 789	Luis Salazar	.07	.03	.01
☐ 790	Ron Guidry	.15	.07	.01
☐ 791	Ivan DeJesus	.04	.02	.00
☐ 792	Darrell Evans	.15	.07	.01

1985 Topps Traded

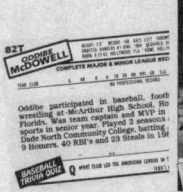

The cards in this 132-card set measure 2 ½" by 3 ½". In its now standard procedure, Topps issued its Traded (or extended) set for the fifth year in a row. Because all photos and statistics of its regular set for the year were developed during the fall and winter months of the preceding year, players who changed teams during the fall, winter, and spring months are portrayed in the 1985 regular issue set with the teams they were with in 1984. The Traded set amends the shortcomings of the regular set by presenting the players with their proper teams for the current year. Rookies not contained in the regular set are also picked up in the Traded set. Again this year, the Topps affiliate in Ire-

land printed the cards, and the cards were available through hobby dealers only. Topps also produced a specially boxed "glossy" edition, frequently referred to as the Topps Traded Tiffany set. There were supposedly only 5,000 sets of the Tiffany cards produced; they were marketed to hobby dealers. The checklist of cards is identical to that of the normal nonglossy cards. There are two primary distinguishing features of the Tiffany cards—white card stock reverses and high gloss obverses. These Tiffany cards are valued at approximately five times the values listed below.

	MINT	EXC	G-VG
COMPLETE SET (132)	15.00	7.50	1.50
COMMON PLAYER (1-132)	.06	.03	.00
☐ 1T Don Aase	.10	.05	.01
☐ 2T Bill Almon	.06	.03	.00
☐ 3T Benny Ayala	.06	.03	.00
☐ 4T Dusty Baker	.10	.05	.01
☐ 5T G. Bamberger MG	.10	.05	.01
☐ 6T Dale Berra	.06	.03	.00
☐ 7T Rich Bordi	.06	.03	.00
☐ 8T Daryl Boston	.10	.05	.01
☐ 9T Hubie Brooks	.25	.12	.02
☐ 10T Chris Brown	.20	.10	.02
☐ 11T Tom Browning	1.25	.60	.12
☐ 12T Al Bumbry	.06	.03	.00
☐ 13T Ray Burris	.06	.03	.00
☐ 14T Jeff Burroughs	.10	.05	.01
☐ 15T Bill Campbell	.06	.03	.00
☐ 16T Don Carman	.25	.12	.02
☐ 17T Gary Carter	.70	.35	.07
☐ 18T Bobby Castillo	.06	.03	.00
☐ 19T Bill Caudill	.06	.03	.00
☐ 20T Rick Cerone	.10	.05	.01
☐ 21T Bryan Clark	.06	.03	.00
☐ 22T Jack Clark	.35	.17	.03
☐ 23T Pat Clements	.10	.05	.01
☐ 24T Vince Coleman	4.50	2.25	.45
☐ 25T Dave Collins	.06	.03	.00
☐ 26T Danny Darwin	.06	.03	.00
☐ 27T Jim Davenport MG	.06	.03	.00
☐ 28T Jerry Davis	.10	.05	.01
☐ 29T Brian Dayett	.06	.03	.00
☐ 30T Ivan DeJesus	.06	.03	.00
☐ 31T Ken Dixon	.12	.06	.01
☐ 32T Mariano Duncan	.20	.10	.02
☐ 33T John Felske MG	.06	.03	.00
☐ 34T Mike Fitzgerald	.06	.03	.00
☐ 35T Ray Fontenot	.06	.03	.00
☐ 36T Greg Gagne	.30	.15	.03
☐ 37T Oscar Gamble	.06	.03	.00
☐ 38T Scott Garrelts	.50	.25	.05
☐ 39T Bob L. Gibson	.06	.03	.00
☐ 40T Jim Gott	.10	.05	.01
☐ 41T David Green	.06	.03	.00
☐ 42T Alfredo Griffin	.10	.05	.01
☐ 43T Ozzie Guillen	1.25	.60	.12
☐ 44T Eddie Haas MG	.06	.03	.00
☐ 45T Terry Harper	.06	.03	.00
☐ 46T Toby Harrah	.10	.05	.01
☐ 47T Greg Harris	.06	.03	.00
☐ 48T Ron Hassey	.06	.03	.00
☐ 49T Rickey Henderson	1.75	.85	.17
☐ 50T Steve Henderson	.06	.03	.00
☐ 51T George Hendrick	.10	.05	.01
☐ 52T Joe Hesketh	.15	.07	.01
☐ 53T Teddy Higuera	2.00	1.00	.20
☐ 54T Donnie Hill	.10	.05	.01
☐ 55T Al Holland	.06	.03	.00
☐ 56T Burt Hooton	.06	.03	.00
☐ 57T Jay Howell	.15	.07	.01
☐ 58T Ken Howell	.20	.10	.02
☐ 59T LaMarr Hoyt	.10	.05	.01
☐ 60T Tim Hulett	.10	.05	.01
☐ 61T Bob James	.10	.05	.01
☐ 62T Steve Jeltz	.10	.05	.01
☐ 63T Cliff Johnson	.06	.03	.00
☐ 64T Howard Johnson	2.25	1.10	.22
☐ 65T Ruppert Jones	.06	.03	.00
☐ 66T Steve Kemp	.10	.05	.01
☐ 67T Bruce Kison	.06	.03	.00
☐ 68T Alan Knicely	.06	.03	.00
☐ 69T Mike LaCoss	.06	.03	.00
☐ 70T Lee Lacy	.06	.03	.00
☐ 71T Dave LaPoint	.10	.05	.01
☐ 72T Gary Lavelle	.06	.03	.00
☐ 73T Vance Law	.10	.05	.01
☐ 74T Johnnie LeMaster	.06	.03	.00
☐ 75T Sixto Lezcano	.06	.03	.00
☐ 76T Tim Lollar	.06	.03	.00
☐ 77T Fred Lynn	.25	.12	.02
☐ 78T Billy Martin MG	.20	.10	.02
☐ 79T Ron Mathis	.10	.05	.01
☐ 80T Len Matuszek	.06	.03	.00
☐ 81T Gene Mauch MG	.06	.03	.00

		MINT	EXC	G-VG
☐	82T Oddibe McDowell ...	.50	.25	.05
☐	83T Roger McDowell	.80	.40	.08
☐	84T John McNamara MG	.10	.05	.01
☐	85T Donnie Moore	.06	.03	.00
☐	86T Gene Nelson	.06	.03	.00
☐	87T Steve Nicosia	.06	.03	.00
☐	88T Al Oliver	.15	.07	.01
☐	89T Joe Orsulak	.20	.10	.02
☐	90T Rob Picciolo	.06	.03	.00
☐	91T Chris Pittaro	.10	.05	.01
☐	92T Jim Presley	.70	.35	.07
☐	93T Rick Reuschel	.20	.10	.02
☐	94T Bert Roberge	.06	.03	.00
☐	95T Bob Rodgers MG ...	.06	.03	.00
☐	96T Jerry Royster	.06	.03	.00
☐	97T Dave Rozema	.06	.03	.00
☐	98T Dave Rucker	.06	.03	.00
☐	99T Vern Ruhle	.06	.03	.00
☐	100T Paul Runge	.10	.05	.01
☐	101T Mark Salas	.12	.06	.01
☐	102T Luis Salazar	.06	.03	.00
☐	103T Joe Sambito	.06	.03	.00
☐	104T Rick Schu	.12	.06	.01
☐	105T Donnie Scott	.06	.03	.00
☐	106T Larry Sheets	.25	.12	.02
☐	107T Don Slaught	.06	.03	.00
☐	108T Roy Smalley	.06	.03	.00
☐	109T Lonnie Smith	.15	.07	.01
☐	110T Nate Snell UER ...	.12	.06	.01
	(headings on back for			
	a batter)			
☐	111T Chris Speier	.06	.03	.00
☐	112T Mike Stenhouse ...	.10	.05	.01
☐	113T Tim Stoddard	.06	.03	.00
☐	114T Jim Sundberg	.06	.03	.00
☐	115T Bruce Sutter	.20	.10	.02
☐	116T Don Sutton	.50	.25	.05
☐	117T Kent Tekulve	.10	.05	.01
☐	118T Tom Tellmann	.06	.03	.00
☐	119T Walt Terrell	.10	.05	.01
☐	120T Mickey Tettleton ..	1.00	.50	.10
☐	121T Derrel Thomas	.06	.03	.00
☐	122T Rich Thompson	.10	.05	.01
☐	123T Alex Trevino	.06	.03	.00
☐	124T John Tudor	.25	.12	.02
☐	125T Jose Uribe	.30	.15	.03
☐	126T Bobby Valentine MG	.10	.05	.01
☐	127T Dave Von Ohlen ...	.06	.03	.00
☐	128T U.L. Washington ...	.06	.03	.00

		MINT	EXC	G-VG
☐	129T Earl Weaver MG	.10	.05	.01
☐	130T Eddie Whitson	.10	.05	.01
☐	131T Herm Winningham ..	.15	.07	.01
☐	132T Checklist 1-132	.06	.01	.00

1986 Topps

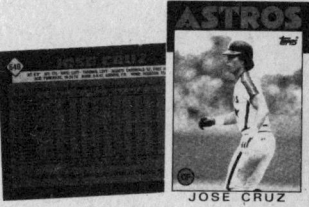

JOSE CRUZ

The cards in this 792-card set are standard size (2 ½" by 3 ½"). The first seven cards are a tribute to Pete Rose and his career. Cards 2-7 show small photos of the given years on the front with biographical information pertaining to those years on the back. The team leader cards were done differently with a simple player action shot on a white background; the player pictured is dubbed the "Dean" of that team, i.e., the player with the longest continuous service with that team. Topps again features a "Turn Back the Clock" series (401-405). Record breakers of the previous year are acknowledged on cards 201 to 207. Cards 701-722 feature All-Star selections from each league. Manager cards feature the team checklist on the reverse. Ryne Sandberg (#690) is the only player card in the set without a Topps logo on the front of the card; this omission was never corrected by Topps. There are two other uncorrected errors involving misnumbered cards; see card numbers 51, 57, 141, and 171 in the checklist below. The backs of all the cards have a distinctive red background. Topps also produced a specially boxed "glossy" edition, frequently referred to as the Topps Tiffany set. There were supposedly only 5,000 sets of the Tiffany cards produced; they were marketed to hobby dealers. The checklist of cards (792 regular and 132 Traded) is identical to that of the normal non-glossy cards. There are two primary distinguishing features of the Tiffany cards—white card stock reverses and high gloss obverses. These Tiffany cards are valued at approximately five times the values listed below.

		MINT	EXC	G-VG
	COMPLETE SET (792)	35.00	17.50	3.50
	COMMON PLAYER (1-792)	.03	.01	.00
☐ 1	Pete Rose	1.00	.20	.04
☐ 2	Rose Special: '63-'66	.30	.15	.03
☐ 3	Rose Special: '67-'70	.30	.15	.03
☐ 4	Rose Special: '71-'74	.30	.15	.03
☐ 5	Rose Special: '75-'78	.30	.15	.03
☐ 6	Rose Special: '79-'82	.30	.15	.03
☐ 7	Rose Special: '83-'85	.30	.15	.03
☐ 8	Dwayne Murphy	.03	.01	.00
☐ 9	Roy Smith	.03	.01	.00
☐ 10	Tony Gwynn	.60	.30	.06
☐ 11	Bob Ojeda	.06	.03	.00
☐ 12	Jose Uribe	.25	.12	.02
☐ 13	Bob Kearney	.03	.01	.00
☐ 14	Julio Cruz	.03	.01	.00
☐ 15	Eddie Whitson	.03	.01	.00
☐ 16	Rick Schu	.06	.03	.00
☐ 17	Mike Stenhouse	.03	.01	.00
☐ 18	Brent Gaff	.03	.01	.00
☐ 19	Rich Hebner	.03	.01	.00
☐ 20	Lou Whitaker	.12	.06	.01
☐ 21	G. Bamberger MG (checklist back)	.06	.03	.00
☐ 22	Duane Walker	.03	.01	.00
☐ 23	Manny Lee	.10	.05	.01
☐ 24	Len Barker	.03	.01	.00
☐ 25	Willie Wilson	.10	.05	.01
☐ 26	Frank DiPino	.03	.01	.00
☐ 27	Ray Knight	.06	.03	.00
☐ 28	Eric Davis	2.50	1.25	.25
☐ 29	Tony Phillips	.03	.01	.00
☐ 30	Eddie Murray	.30	.15	.03
☐ 31	Jamie Easterly	.03	.01	.00
☐ 32	Steve Yeager	.03	.01	.00
☐ 33	Jeff Lahti	.03	.01	.00
☐ 34	Ken Phelps	.06	.03	.00
☐ 35	Jeff Reardon	.08	.04	.01
☐ 36	Tigers Leaders Lance Parrish	.08	.04	.01
☐ 37	Mark Thurmond	.03	.01	.00
☐ 38	Glenn Hoffman	.03	.01	.00
☐ 39	Dave Rucker	.03	.01	.00
☐ 40	Ken Griffey	.08	.04	.01
☐ 41	Brad Wellman	.03	.01	.00
☐ 42	Geoff Zahn	.03	.01	.00
☐ 43	Dave Engle	.03	.01	.00
☐ 44	Lance McCullers	.25	.12	.02
☐ 45	Damaso Garcia	.03	.01	.00
☐ 46	Billy Hatcher	.08	.04	.01
☐ 47	Juan Berenguer	.03	.01	.00
☐ 48	Bill Almon	.03	.01	.00
☐ 49	Rick Manning	.03	.01	.00
☐ 50	Dan Quisenberry	.10	.05	.01
☐ 51	Bobby Wine MG ERR (checklist back) (number of card on back is actually 57)	.08	.04	.01
☐ 52	Chris Welsh	.03	.01	.00
☐ 53	Len Dykstra	.60	.30	.06
☐ 54	John Franco	.12	.06	.01
☐ 55	Fred Lynn	.12	.06	.01
☐ 56	Tom Niedenfuer	.03	.01	.00
☐ 57	Bill Doran (see also 51)	.08	.04	.01
☐ 58	Bill Krueger	.03	.01	.00
☐ 59	Andre Thornton	.06	.03	.00
☐ 60	Dwight Evans	.12	.06	.01
☐ 61	Karl Best	.10	.05	.01
☐ 62	Bob Boone	.08	.04	.01
☐ 63	Ron Roenicke	.03	.01	.00
☐ 64	Floyd Bannister	.03	.01	.00
☐ 65	Dan Driessen	.03	.01	.00
☐ 66	Cardinals Leaders Bob Forsch	.03	.01	.00
☐ 67	Carmelo Martinez	.03	.01	.00
☐ 68	Ed Lynch	.03	.01	.00
☐ 69	Luis Aguayo	.03	.01	.00
☐ 70	Dave Winfield	.25	.12	.02
☐ 71	Ken Schrom	.03	.01	.00
☐ 72	Shawon Dunston	.20	.10	.02

			MINT	EXC	G-VG				MINT	EXC	G-VG
☐	73	Randy O'Neal	.03	.01	.00	☐	116	Brook Jacoby	.06	.03	.00
☐	74	Rance Mulliniks	.03	.01	.00	☐	117	Bruce Kison	.03	.01	.00
☐	75	Jose DeLeon	.06	.03	.00	☐	118	Jerry Royster	.03	.01	.00
☐	76	Dion James	.03	.01	.00	☐	119	Barry Bonnell	.03	.01	.00
☐	77	Charlie Leibrandt	.03	.01	.00	☐	120	Steve Carlton	.20	.10	.02
☐	78	Bruce Benedict	.03	.01	.00	☐	121	Nelson Simmons	.06	.03	.00
☐	79	Dave Schmidt	.03	.01	.00	☐	122	Pete Filson	.03	.01	.00
☐	80	Darryl Strawberry	1.00	.50	.10	☐	123	Greg Walker	.06	.03	.00
☐	81	Gene Mauch MG	.06	.03	.00	☐	124	Luis Sanchez	.03	.01	.00
		(checklist back)				☐	125	Dave Lopes	.06	.03	.00
☐	82	Tippy Martinez	.03	.01	.00	☐	126	Mets Leaders	.06	.03	.00
☐	83	Phil Garner	.03	.01	.00			Mookie Wilson			
☐	84	Curt Young	.03	.01	.00	☐	127	Jack Howell	.30	.15	.03
☐	85	Tony Perez	.20	.10	.02	☐	128	John Wathan	.03	.01	.00
		(Eric Davis also				☐	129	Jeff Dedmon	.03	.01	.00
		shown on card)				☐	130	Alan Trammell	.20	.10	.02
☐	86	Tom Waddell	.03	.01	.00	☐	131	Checklist: 1-132	.06	.01	.00
☐	87	Candy Maldonado	.06	.03	.00	☐	132	Razor Shines	.06	.03	.00
☐	88	Tom Nieto	.03	.01	.00	☐	133	Andy McGaffigan	.03	.01	.00
☐	89	Randy St.Claire	.03	.01	.00	☐	134	Carney Lansford	.08	.04	.01
☐	90	Garry Templeton	.06	.03	.00	☐	135	Joe Niekro	.08	.04	.01
☐	91	Steve Crawford	.03	.01	.00	☐	136	Mike Hargrove	.06	.03	.00
☐	92	Al Cowens	.03	.01	.00	☐	137	Charlie Moore	.03	.01	.00
☐	93	Scot Thompson	.03	.01	.00	☐	138	Mark Davis	.15	.07	.01
☐	94	Rich Bordi	.03	.01	.00	☐	139	Daryl Boston	.06	.03	.00
☐	95	Ozzie Virgil	.03	.01	.00	☐	140	John Candelaria	.06	.03	.00
☐	96	Blue Jays Leaders	.03	.01	.00	☐	141	Chuck Cottier MG	.08	.04	.01
		Jim Clancy						(checklist back)			
☐	97	Gary Gaetti	.10	.05	.01			(see also 171)			
☐	98	Dick Ruthven	.03	.01	.00	☐	142	Bob Jones	.03	.01	.00
☐	99	Buddy Biancalana	.03	.01	.00	☐	143	Dave Van Gorder	.03	.01	.00
☐	100	Nolan Ryan	.60	.30	.06	☐	144	Doug Sisk	.03	.01	.00
☐	101	Dave Bergman	.03	.01	.00	☐	145	Pedro Guerrero	.15	.07	.01
☐	102	Joe Orsulak	.10	.05	.01	☐	146	Jack Perconte	.03	.01	.00
☐	103	Luis Salazar	.03	.01	.00	☐	147	Larry Sheets	.08	.04	.01
☐	104	Sid Fernandez	.12	.06	.01	☐	148	Mike Heath	.03	.01	.00
☐	105	Gary Ward	.03	.01	.00	☐	149	Brett Butler	.06	.03	.00
☐	106	Ray Burris	.03	.01	.00	☐	150	Joaquin Andujar	.06	.03	.00
☐	107	Rafael Ramirez	.03	.01	.00	☐	151	Dave Stapleton	.03	.01	.00
☐	108	Ted Power	.03	.01	.00	☐	152	Mike Morgan	.06	.03	.00
☐	109	Len Matuszek	.03	.01	.00	☐	153	Ricky Adams	.03	.01	.00
☐	110	Scott McGregor	.06	.03	.00	☐	154	Bert Roberge	.03	.01	.00
☐	111	Roger Craig MG	.06	.03	.00	☐	155	Bob Grich	.06	.03	.00
		(checklist back)				☐	156	White Sox Leaders	.03	.01	.00
☐	112	Bill Campbell	.03	.01	.00			Richard Dotson			
☐	113	U.L. Washington	.03	.01	.00	☐	157	Ron Hassey	.03	.01	.00
☐	114	Mike Brown	.03	.01	.00	☐	158	Derrel Thomas	.03	.01	.00
		(Pirates OF)				☐	159	Orel Hershiser UER	1.25	.60	.12
☐	115	Jay Howell	.06	.03	.00			(82 Albuquerque)			

		MINT	EXC	G-VG			MINT	EXC	G-VG
☐ 160	Chet Lemon	.06	.03	.00		Most stolen bases, season, rookie			
☐ 161	Lee Tunnell	.03	.01	.00					
☐ 162	Greg Gagne	.08	.04	.01	☐ 202	RB: Dwight Gooden	.30	.15	.03
☐ 163	Pete Ladd	.03	.01	.00		Youngest 20 game winner			
☐ 164	Steve Balboni	.03	.01	.00					
☐ 165	Mike Davis	.03	.01	.00	☐ 203	RB: Keith Hernandez	.12	.06	.01
☐ 166	Dickie Thon	.03	.01	.00		Most game-winning RBI's			
☐ 167	Zane Smith	.10	.05	.01					
☐ 168	Jeff Burroughs	.03	.01	.00	☐ 204	RB: Phil Niekro	.10	.05	.01
☐ 169	George Wright	.03	.01	.00		Oldest shutout pitcher			
☐ 170	Gary Carter	.25	.12	.02	☐ 205	RB: Tony Perez	.10	.05	.01
☐ 171	Bob Rodgers MG ERR	.08	.04	.01		Oldest grand slammer			
	(checklist back)				☐ 206	RB: Pete Rose	.35	.17	.03
	(number of card on back actually 141)					Most hits, lifetime			
					☐ 207	RB: Fern. Valenzuela	.12	.06	.01
☐ 172	Jerry Reed	.03	.01	.00		Most cons. innings, start of season, no earned runs			
☐ 173	Wayne Gross	.03	.01	.00					
☐ 174	Brian Snyder	.03	.01	.00	☐ 208	Ramon Romero	.03	.01	.00
☐ 175	Steve Sax	.15	.07	.01	☐ 209	Randy Ready	.08	.04	.01
☐ 176	Jay Tibbs	.03	.01	.00	☐ 210	Calvin Schiraldi	.06	.03	.00
☐ 177	Joel Youngblood	.03	.01	.00	☐ 211	Ed Wojna	.06	.03	.00
☐ 178	Ivan DeJesus	.03	.01	.00	☐ 212	Chris Speier	.03	.01	.00
☐ 179	Stu Cliburn	.08	.04	.01	☐ 213	Bob Shirley	.03	.01	.00
☐ 180	Don Mattingly	3.00	1.50	.30	☐ 214	Randy Bush	.03	.01	.00
☐ 181	Al Nipper	.03	.01	.00	☐ 215	Frank White	.06	.03	.00
☐ 182	Bobby Brown	.03	.01	.00	☐ 216	A's Leaders	.03	.01	.00
☐ 183	Larry Andersen	.03	.01	.00		Dwayne Murphy			
☐ 184	Tim Laudner	.03	.01	.00	☐ 217	Bill Scherrer	.03	.01	.00
☐ 185	Rollie Fingers	.12	.06	.01	☐ 218	Randy Hunt	.03	.01	.00
☐ 186	Astros Leaders	.03	.01	.00	☐ 219	Dennis Lamp	.03	.01	.00
	Jose Cruz				☐ 220	Bob Horner	.10	.05	.01
☐ 187	Scott Fletcher	.03	.01	.00	☐ 221	Dave Henderson	.06	.03	.00
☐ 188	Bob Dernier	.03	.01	.00	☐ 222	Craig Gerber	.03	.01	.00
☐ 189	Mike Mason	.03	.01	.00	☐ 223	Atlee Hammaker	.03	.01	.00
☐ 190	George Hendrick	.06	.03	.00	☐ 224	Cesar Cedeno	.06	.03	.00
☐ 191	Wally Backman	.03	.01	.00	☐ 225	Ron Darling	.15	.07	.01
☐ 192	Milt Wilcox	.03	.01	.00	☐ 226	Lee Lacy	.03	.01	.00
☐ 193	Daryl Sconiers	.03	.01	.00	☐ 227	Al Jones	.03	.01	.00
☐ 194	Craig McMurtry	.03	.01	.00	☐ 228	Tom Lawless	.03	.01	.00
☐ 195	Dave Concepcion	.06	.03	.00	☐ 229	Bill Gullickson	.03	.01	.00
☐ 196	Doyle Alexander	.06	.03	.00	☐ 230	Terry Kennedy	.03	.01	.00
☐ 197	Enos Cabell	.03	.01	.00	☐ 231	Jim Frey MG	.06	.03	.00
☐ 198	Ken Dixon	.03	.01	.00		(checklist back)			
☐ 199	Dick Howser MG	.06	.03	.00	☐ 232	Rick Rhoden	.06	.03	.00
	(checklist back)				☐ 233	Steve Lyons	.06	.03	.00
☐ 200	Mike Schmidt	.50	.25	.05	☐ 234	Doug Corbett	.03	.01	.00
☐ 201	RB: Vince Coleman	.20	.10	.02	☐ 235	Butch Wynegar	.03	.01	.00
					☐ 236	Frank Eufemia	.03	.01	.00

		MINT	EXC	G-VG			MINT	EXC	G-VG
☐ 237	Ted Simmons	.08	.04	.01	☐ 283	Mike Fischlin	.03	.01	.00
☐ 238	Larry Parrish	.03	.01	.00	☐ 284	Brian Dayett	.03	.01	.00
☐ 239	Joel Skinner	.03	.01	.00	☐ 285	Buddy Bell	.06	.03	.00
☐ 240	Tommy John	.12	.06	.01	☐ 286	Luis DeLeon	.03	.01	.00
☐ 241	Tony Fernandez	.20	.10	.02	☐ 287	John Christensen	.03	.01	.00
☐ 242	Rich Thompson	.03	.01	.00	☐ 288	Don Aase	.03	.01	.00
☐ 243	Johnny Grubb	.03	.01	.00	☐ 289	Johnnie LeMaster	.03	.01	.00
☐ 244	Craig Lefferts	.06	.03	.00	☐ 290	Carlton Fisk	.20	.10	.02
☐ 245	Jim Sundberg	.03	.01	.00	☐ 291	Tom Lasorda MG	.10	.05	.01
☐ 246	Phillies Leaders	.12	.06	.01		(checklist back)			
	Steve Carlton				☐ 292	Chuck Porter	.03	.01	.00
☐ 247	Terry Harper	.03	.01	.00	☐ 293	Chris Chambliss	.06	.03	.00
☐ 248	Spike Owen	.03	.01	.00	☐ 294	Danny Cox	.06	.03	.00
☐ 249	Rob Deer	.40	.20	.04	☐ 295	Kirk Gibson	.25	.12	.02
☐ 250	Dwight Gooden	1.75	.85	.17	☐ 296	Geno Petralli	.03	.01	.00
☐ 251	Rich Dauer	.03	.01	.00	☐ 297	Tim Lollar	.03	.01	.00
☐ 252	Bobby Castillo	.03	.01	.00	☐ 298	Craig Reynolds	.03	.01	.00
☐ 253	Dann Bilardello	.03	.01	.00	☐ 299	Bryn Smith	.06	.03	.00
☐ 254	Ozzie Guillen	.40	.20	.04	☐ 300	George Brett	.40	.20	.04
☐ 255	Tony Armas	.06	.03	.00	☐ 301	Dennis Rasmussen	.06	.03	.00
☐ 256	Kurt Kepshire	.03	.01	.00	☐ 302	Greg Gross	.03	.01	.00
☐ 257	Doug DeCinces	.06	.03	.00	☐ 303	Curt Wardle	.03	.01	.00
☐ 258	Tim Burke	.25	.12	.02	☐ 304	Mike Gallego	.03	.01	.00
☐ 259	Dan Pasqua	.12	.06	.01	☐ 305	Phil Bradley	.06	.03	.00
☐ 260	Tony Pena	.08	.04	.01	☐ 306	Padres Leaders	.03	.01	.00
☐ 261	Bobby Valentine MG	.06	.03	.00		Terry Kennedy			
	(checklist back)				☐ 307	Dave Sax	.03	.01	.00
☐ 262	Mario Ramirez	.03	.01	.00	☐ 308	Ray Fontenot	.03	.01	.00
☐ 263	Checklist: 133-264	.06	.01	.00	☐ 309	John Shelby	.03	.01	.00
☐ 264	Darren Daulton	.12	.06	.01	☐ 310	Greg Minton	.03	.01	.00
☐ 265	Ron Davis	.03	.01	.00	☐ 311	Dick Schofield	.03	.01	.00
☐ 266	Keith Moreland	.03	.01	.00	☐ 312	Tom Filer	.03	.01	.00
☐ 267	Paul Molitor	.12	.06	.01	☐ 313	Joe DeSa	.03	.01	.00
☐ 268	Mike Scott	.30	.15	.03	☐ 314	Frank Pastore	.03	.01	.00
☐ 269	Dane Iorg	.03	.01	.00	☐ 315	Mookie Wilson	.08	.04	.01
☐ 270	Jack Morris	.12	.06	.01	☐ 316	Sammy Khalifa	.08	.04	.01
☐ 271	Dave Collins	.03	.01	.00	☐ 317	Ed Romero	.03	.01	.00
☐ 272	Tim Tolman	.03	.01	.00	☐ 318	Terry Whitfield	.03	.01	.00
☐ 273	Jerry Willard	.03	.01	.00	☐ 319	Rick Camp	.03	.01	.00
☐ 274	Ron Gardenhire	.03	.01	.00	☐ 320	Jim Rice	.18	.09	.01
☐ 275	Charlie Hough	.06	.03	.00	☐ 321	Earl Weaver MG	.06	.03	.00
☐ 276	Yankees Leaders	.03	.01	.00		(checklist back)			
	Willie Randolph				☐ 322	Bob Forsch	.03	.01	.00
☐ 277	Jaime Cocanower	.03	.01	.00	☐ 323	Jerry Davis	.03	.01	.00
☐ 278	Sixto Lezcano	.03	.01	.00	☐ 324	Dan Schatzeder	.03	.01	.00
☐ 279	Al Pardo	.03	.01	.00	☐ 325	Juan Beniquez	.03	.01	.00
☐ 280	Tim Raines	.25	.12	.02	☐ 326	Kent Tekulve	.03	.01	.00
☐ 281	Steve Mura	.03	.01	.00	☐ 327	Mike Pagliarulo	.08	.04	.01
☐ 282	Jerry Mumphrey	.03	.01	.00	☐ 328	Pete O'Brien	.08	.04	.01

		MINT	EXC	G-VG			MINT	EXC	G-VG
☐ 329	Kirby Puckett	2.50	1.25	.25	☐ 375	Rich Gedman	.03	.01	.00
☐ 330	Rick Sutcliffe	.10	.05	.01	☐ 376	Bill Dawley	.03	.01	.00
☐ 331	Alan Ashby	.03	.01	.00	☐ 377	Joe Carter	.35	.17	.03
☐ 332	Darryl Motley	.03	.01	.00	☐ 378	Bruce Bochte	.03	.01	.00
☐ 333	Tom Henke	.15	.07	.01	☐ 379	Bobby Meacham	.03	.01	.00
☐ 334	Ken Oberkfell	.03	.01	.00	☐ 380	LaMarr Hoyt	.06	.03	.00
☐ 335	Don Sutton	.15	.07	.01	☐ 381	Ray Miller MG	.06	.03	.00
☐ 336	Indians Leaders	.03	.01	.00		(checklist back)			
	Andre Thornton				☐ 382	Ivan Calderon	.50	.25	.05
☐ 337	Darnell Coles	.03	.01	.00	☐ 383	Chris Brown	.15	.07	.01
☐ 338	Jorge Bell	.20	.10	.02	☐ 384	Steve Trout	.03	.01	.00
☐ 339	Bruce Berenyi	.03	.01	.00	☐ 385	Cecil Cooper	.08	.04	.01
☐ 340	Cal Ripken	.30	.15	.03	☐ 386	Cecil Fielder	.15	.07	.01
☐ 341	Frank Williams	.03	.01	.00	☐ 387	Steve Kemp	.03	.01	.00
☐ 342	Gary Redus	.03	.01	.00	☐ 388	Dickie Noles	.03	.01	.00
☐ 343	Carlos Diaz	.03	.01	.00	☐ 389	Glenn Davis	2.25	1.10	.22
☐ 344	Jim Wohlford	.03	.01	.00	☐ 390	Tom Seaver	.30	.15	.03
☐ 345	Donnie Moore	.03	.01	.00	☐ 391	Julio Franco	.20	.10	.02
☐ 346	Bryan Little	.03	.01	.00	☐ 392	John Russell	.03	.01	.00
☐ 347	Teddy Higuera	1.00	.50	.10	☐ 393	Chris Pittaro	.03	.01	.00
☐ 348	Cliff Johnson	.03	.01	.00	☐ 394	Checklist: 265-396	.06	.01	.00
☐ 349	Mark Clear	.03	.01	.00	☐ 395	Scott Garrelts	.25	.12	.02
☐ 350	Jack Clark	.20	.10	.02	☐ 396	Red Sox Leaders	.08	.04	.01
☐ 351	Chuck Tanner MG	.06	.03	.00		Dwight Evans			
	(checklist back)				☐ 397	Steve Buechele	.20	.10	.02
☐ 352	Harry Spilman	.03	.01	.00	☐ 398	Earnie Riles	.20	.10	.02
☐ 353	Keith Atherton	.03	.01	.00	☐ 399	Bill Swift	.06	.03	.00
☐ 354	Tony Bernazard	.03	.01	.00	☐ 400	Rod Carew	.30	.15	.03
☐ 355	Lee Smith	.06	.03	.00	☐ 401	Turn Back 5 Years	.10	.05	.01
☐ 356	Mickey Hatcher	.03	.01	.00		Fern. Valenzuela '81			
☐ 357	Ed VandeBerg	.03	.01	.00	☐ 402	Turn Back 10 Years	.15	.07	.01
☐ 358	Rick Dempsey	.03	.01	.00		Tom Seaver '76			
☐ 359	Mike LaCoss	.03	.01	.00	☐ 403	Turn Back 15 Years	.15	.07	.01
☐ 360	Lloyd Moseby	.08	.04	.01		Willie Mays '71			
☐ 361	Shane Rawley	.03	.01	.00	☐ 404	Turn Back 20 Years	.10	.05	.01
☐ 362	Tom Paciorek	.03	.01	.00		Frank Robinson '66			
☐ 363	Terry Forster	.06	.03	.00	☐ 405	Turn Back 25 Years	.15	.07	.01
☐ 364	Reid Nichols	.03	.01	.00		Roger Maris '61			
☐ 365	Mike Flanagan	.06	.03	.00	☐ 406	Scott Sanderson	.03	.01	.00
☐ 366	Reds Leaders	.03	.01	.00	☐ 407	Sal Butera	.03	.01	.00
	Dave Concepcion				☐ 408	Dave Smith	.06	.03	.00
☐ 367	Aurelio Lopez	.03	.01	.00	☐ 409	Paul Runge	.03	.01	.00
☐ 368	Greg Brock	.03	.01	.00	☐ 410	Dave Kingman	.08	.04	.01
☐ 369	Al Holland	.03	.01	.00	☐ 411	Sparky Anderson MG	.06	.03	.00
☐ 370	Vince Coleman	1.50	.75	.15		(checklist back)			
☐ 371	Bill Stein	.03	.01	.00	☐ 412	Jim Clancy	.03	.01	.00
☐ 372	Ben Oglivie	.06	.03	.00	☐ 413	Tim Flannery	.03	.01	.00
☐ 373	Urbano Lugo	.03	.01	.00	☐ 414	Tom Gorman	.03	.01	.00
☐ 374	Terry Francona	.03	.01	.00	☐ 415	Hal McRae	.06	.03	.00

		MINT	EXC	G-VG			MINT	EXC	G-VG
☐ 416	Dennis Martinez	.06	.03	.00	☐ 462	Domingo Ramos	.03	.01	.00
☐ 417	R.J. Reynolds	.03	.01	.00	☐ 463	Jim Gott	.06	.03	.00
☐ 418	Alan Knicely	.03	.01	.00	☐ 464	Ruppert Jones	.03	.01	.00
☐ 419	Frank Wills	.03	.01	.00	☐ 465	Jesse Orosco	.03	.01	.00
☐ 420	Von Hayes	.08	.04	.01	☐ 466	Tom Foley	.03	.01	.00
☐ 421	David Palmer	.03	.01	.00	☐ 467	Bob James	.03	.01	.00
☐ 422	Mike Jorgensen	.03	.01	.00	☐ 468	Mike Scioscia	.06	.03	.00
☐ 423	Dan Spillner	.03	.01	.00	☐ 469	Storm Davis	.08	.04	.01
☐ 424	Rick Miller	.03	.01	.00	☐ 470	Bill Madlock	.08	.04	.01
☐ 425	Larry McWilliams	.03	.01	.00	☐ 471	Bobby Cox MG	.06	.03	.00
☐ 426	Brewers Leaders	.03	.01	.00		(checklist back)			
	Charlie Moore				☐ 472	Joe Hesketh	.06	.03	.00
☐ 427	Joe Cowley	.03	.01	.00	☐ 473	Mark Brouhard	.03	.01	.00
☐ 428	Max Venable	.03	.01	.00	☐ 474	John Tudor	.10	.05	.01
☐ 429	Greg Booker	.03	.01	.00	☐ 475	Juan Samuel	.12	.06	.01
☐ 430	Kent Hrbek	.15	.07	.01	☐ 476	Ron Mathis	.06	.03	.00
☐ 431	George Frazier	.03	.01	.00	☐ 477	Mike Easler	.03	.01	.00
☐ 432	Mark Bailey	.03	.01	.00	☐ 478	Andy Hawkins	.08	.04	.00
☐ 433	Chris Codiroli	.03	.01	.00	☐ 479	Bob Melvin	.10	.05	.01
☐ 434	Curt Wilkerson	.03	.01	.00	☐ 480	Oddibe McDowell	.12	.06	.01
☐ 435	Bill Caudill	.03	.01	.00	☐ 481	Scott Bradley	.08	.04	.01
☐ 436	Doug Flynn	.03	.01	.00	☐ 482	Rick Lysander	.03	.01	.00
☐ 437	Rick Mahler	.03	.01	.00	☐ 483	George Vukovich	.03	.01	.00
☐ 438	Clint Hurdle	.03	.01	.00	☐ 484	Donnie Hill	.03	.01	.00
☐ 439	Rick Honeycutt	.03	.01	.00	☐ 485	Gary Matthews	.06	.03	.00
☐ 440	Alvin Davis	.18	.09	.01	☐ 486	Angels Leaders	.03	.01	.00
☐ 441	Whitey Herzog MG	.06	.03	.00		Bobby Grich			
	(checklist back)				☐ 487	Bret Saberhagen	.75	.35	.07
☐ 442	Ron Robinson	.08	.04	.01	☐ 488	Lou Thornton	.08	.04	.01
☐ 443	Bill Buckner	.06	.03	.00	☐ 489	Jim Winn	.03	.01	.00
☐ 444	Alex Trevino	.03	.01	.00	☐ 490	Jeff Leonard	.08	.04	.01
☐ 445	Bert Blyleven	.10	.05	.01	☐ 491	Pascual Perez	.08	.04	.01
☐ 446	Lenn Sakata	.03	.01	.00	☐ 492	Kelvin Chapman	.03	.01	.00
☐ 447	Jerry Don Gleaton	.03	.01	.00	☐ 493	Gene Nelson	.03	.01	.00
☐ 448	Herm Winningham	.10	.05	.01	☐ 494	Gary Roenicke	.03	.01	.00
☐ 449	Rod Scurry	.03	.01	.00	☐ 495	Mark Langston	.50	.25	.05
☐ 450	Graig Nettles	.10	.05	.01	☐ 496	Jay Johnstone	.06	.03	.00
☐ 451	Mark Brown	.06	.03	.00	☐ 497	John Stuper	.03	.01	.00
☐ 452	Bob Clark	.03	.01	.00	☐ 498	Tito Landrum	.03	.01	.00
☐ 453	Steve Jeltz	.03	.01	.00	☐ 499	Bob L. Gibson	.03	.01	.00
☐ 454	Burt Hooton	.03	.01	.00	☐ 500	Rickey Henderson	.45	.22	.04
☐ 455	Willie Randolph	.08	.04	.01	☐ 501	Dave Johnson MG	.06	.03	.00
☐ 456	Braves Leaders	.12	.06	.01		(checklist back)			
	Dale Murphy				☐ 502	Glen Cook	.06	.03	.00
☐ 457	Mickey Tettleton	.45	.22	.04	☐ 503	Mike Fitzgerald	.03	.01	.00
☐ 458	Kevin Bass	.08	.04	.01	☐ 504	Denny Walling	.03	.01	.00
☐ 459	Luis Leal	.03	.01	.00	☐ 505	Jerry Koosman	.08	.04	.01
☐ 460	Leon Durham	.06	.03	.00	☐ 506	Bill Russell	.06	.03	.00
☐ 461	Walt Terrell	.03	.01	.00	☐ 507	Steve Ontiveros	.08	.04	.01

		MINT	EXC	G-VG
☐ 508	Alan Wiggins	.03	.01	.00
☐ 509	Ernie Camacho	.03	.01	.00
☐ 510	Wade Boggs	2.00	1.00	.20
☐ 511	Ed Nunez	.03	.01	.00
☐ 512	Thad Bosley	.03	.01	.00
☐ 513	Ron Washington	.03	.01	.00
☐ 514	Mike Jones	.03	.01	.00
☐ 515	Darrell Evans	.08	.04	.01
☐ 516	Giants Leaders	.03	.01	.00
	Greg Minton			
☐ 517	Milt Thompson	.25	.12	.02
☐ 518	Buck Martinez	.03	.01	.00
☐ 519	Danny Darwin	.03	.01	.00
☐ 520	Keith Hernandez	.25	.12	.02
☐ 521	Nate Snell	.06	.03	.00
☐ 522	Bob Bailor	.03	.01	.00
☐ 523	Joe Price	.03	.01	.00
☐ 524	Darrell Miller	.06	.03	.00
☐ 525	Marvell Wynne	.03	.01	.00
☐ 526	Charlie Lea	.03	.01	.00
☐ 527	Checklist: 397-528	.06	.01	.00
☐ 528	Terry Pendleton	.06	.03	.00
☐ 529	Marc Sullivan	.03	.01	.00
☐ 530	Rich Gossage	.10	.05	.01
☐ 531	Tony LaRussa MG	.06	.03	.00
	(checklist back)			
☐ 532	Don Carman	.20	.10	.02
☐ 533	Billy Sample	.03	.01	.00
☐ 534	Jeff Calhoun	.03	.01	.00
☐ 535	Toby Harrah	.03	.01	.00
☐ 536	Jose Rijo	.08	.04	.01
☐ 537	Mark Salas	.03	.01	.00
☐ 538	Dennis Eckersley	.12	.06	.01
☐ 539	Glenn Hubbard	.03	.01	.00
☐ 540	Dan Petry	.03	.01	.00
☐ 541	Jorge Orta	.03	.01	.00
☐ 542	Don Schulze	.03	.01	.00
☐ 543	Jerry Narron	.03	.01	.00
☐ 544	Eddie Milner	.03	.01	.00
☐ 545	Jimmy Key	.10	.05	.01
☐ 546	Mariners Leaders	.03	.01	.00
	Dave Henderson			
☐ 547	Roger McDowell	.35	.17	.03
☐ 548	Mike Young	.06	.03	.00
☐ 549	Bob Welch	.06	.03	.00
☐ 550	Tom Herr	.06	.03	.00
☐ 551	Dave LaPoint	.06	.03	.00
☐ 552	Marc Hill	.03	.01	.00
☐ 553	Jim Morrison	.03	.01	.00

		MINT	EXC	G-VG
☐ 554	Paul Householder	.03	.01	.00
☐ 555	Hubie Brooks	.08	.04	.01
☐ 556	John Denny	.06	.03	.00
☐ 557	Gerald Perry	.10	.05	.01
☐ 558	Tim Stoddard	.03	.01	.00
☐ 559	Tommy Dunbar	.03	.01	.00
☐ 560	Dave Righetti	.10	.05	.01
☐ 561	Bob Lillis MG	.06	.03	.00
	(checklist back)			
☐ 562	Joe Beckwith	.03	.01	.00
☐ 563	Alejandro Sanchez	.03	.01	.00
☐ 564	Warren Brusstar	.03	.01	.00
☐ 565	Tom Brunansky	.12	.06	.01
☐ 566	Alfredo Griffin	.06	.03	.00
☐ 567	Jeff Barkley	.03	.01	.00
☐ 568	Donnie Scott	.03	.01	.00
☐ 569	Jim Acker	.03	.01	.00
☐ 570	Rusty Staub	.08	.04	.01
☐ 571	Mike Jeffcoat	.03	.01	.00
☐ 572	Paul Zuvella	.03	.01	.00
☐ 573	Tom Hume	.03	.01	.00
☐ 574	Ron Kittle	.10	.05	.01
☐ 575	Mike Boddicker	.08	.04	.01
☐ 576	Expos Leaders	.10	.05	.01
	Andre Dawson			
☐ 577	Jerry Reuss	.06	.03	.00
☐ 578	Lee Mazzilli	.03	.01	.00
☐ 579	Jim Slaton	.03	.01	.00
☐ 580	Willie McGee	.12	.06	.01
☐ 581	Bruce Hurst	.12	.06	.01
☐ 582	Jim Gantner	.03	.01	.00
☐ 583	Al Bumbry	.03	.01	.00
☐ 584	Brian Fisher	.18	.09	.01
☐ 585	Garry Maddox	.03	.01	.00
☐ 586	Greg Harris	.03	.01	.00
☐ 587	Rafael Santana	.03	.01	.00
☐ 588	Steve Lake	.03	.01	.00
☐ 589	Sid Bream	.03	.01	.00
☐ 590	Bob Knepper	.06	.03	.00
☐ 591	Jackie Moore MG	.06	.03	.00
	(checklist back)			
☐ 592	Frank Tanana	.06	.03	.00
☐ 593	Jesse Barfield	.18	.09	.01
☐ 594	Chris Bando	.03	.01	.00
☐ 595	Dave Parker	.15	.07	.01
☐ 596	Onix Concepcion	.03	.01	.00
☐ 597	Sammy Stewart	.03	.01	.00
☐ 598	Jim Presley	.15	.07	.01
☐ 599	Rick Aguilera	.25	.12	.02

		MINT	EXC	G-VG
☐ 600	Dale Murphy	.35	.17	.03
☐ 601	Gary Lucas	.03	.01	.00
☐ 602	Mariano Duncan	.15	.07	.01
☐ 603	Bill Laskey	.03	.01	.00
☐ 604	Gary Pettis	.06	.03	.00
☐ 605	Dennis Boyd	.08	.04	.01
☐ 606	Royals Leaders	.03	.01	.00
	Hal McRae			
☐ 607	Ken Dayley	.03	.01	.00
☐ 608	Bruce Bochy	.03	.01	.00
☐ 609	Barbaro Garbey	.03	.01	.00
☐ 610	Ron Guidry	.10	.05	.01
☐ 611	Gary Woods	.03	.01	.00
☐ 612	Richard Dotson	.06	.03	.00
☐ 613	Roy Smalley	.03	.01	.00
☐ 614	Rick Waits	.03	.01	.00
☐ 615	Johnny Ray	.08	.04	.01
☐ 616	Glenn Brummer	.03	.01	.00
☐ 617	Lonnie Smith	.08	.04	.01
☐ 618	Jim Pankovits	.03	.01	.00
☐ 619	Danny Heep	.03	.01	.00
☐ 620	Bruce Sutter	.10	.05	.01
☐ 621	John Felske MG	.06	.03	.00
	(checklist back)			
☐ 622	Gary Lavelle	.03	.01	.00
☐ 623	Floyd Rayford	.03	.01	.00
☐ 624	Steve McCatty	.03	.01	.00
☐ 625	Bob Brenly	.03	.01	.00
☐ 626	Roy Thomas	.03	.01	.00
☐ 627	Ron Oester	.03	.01	.00
☐ 628	Kirk McCaskill	.45	.22	.04
☐ 629	Mitch Webster	.25	.12	.02
☐ 630	Fernando Valenzuela	.20	.10	.02
☐ 631	Steve Braun	.03	.01	.00
☐ 632	Dave Von Ohlen	.03	.01	.00
☐ 633	Jackie Gutierrez	.03	.01	.00
☐ 634	Roy Lee Jackson	.03	.01	.00
☐ 635	Jason Thompson	.03	.01	.00
☐ 636	Cubs Leaders	.03	.01	.00
	Lee Smith			
☐ 637	Rudy Law	.03	.01	.00
☐ 638	John Butcher	.03	.01	.00
☐ 639	Bo Diaz	.03	.01	.00
☐ 640	Jose Cruz	.08	.04	.01
☐ 641	Wayne Tolleson	.03	.01	.00
☐ 642	Ray Searage	.03	.01	.00
☐ 643	Tom Brookens	.03	.01	.00
☐ 644	Mark Gubicza	.20	.07	.01
☐ 645	Dusty Baker	.06	.03	.00

		MINT	EXC	G-VG
☐ 646	Mike Moore	.08	.04	.01
☐ 647	Mel Hall	.08	.04	.01
☐ 648	Steve Bedrosian	.10	.05	.01
☐ 649	Ronn Reynolds	.03	.01	.00
☐ 650	Dave Stieb	.10	.05	.01
☐ 651	Billy Martin MG	.12	.06	.01
	(checklist back)			
☐ 652	Tom Browning	.25	.12	.02
☐ 653	Jim Dwyer	.03	.01	.00
☐ 654	Ken Howell	.08	.04	.01
☐ 655	Manny Trillo	.03	.01	.00
☐ 656	Brian Harper	.03	.01	.00
☐ 657	Juan Agosto	.03	.01	.00
☐ 658	Rob Wilfong	.03	.01	.00
☐ 659	Checklist: 529-660	.06	.01	.00
☐ 660	Steve Garvey	.35	.17	.03
☐ 661	Roger Clemens	2.00	1.00	.20
☐ 662	Bill Schroeder	.03	.01	.00
☐ 663	Neil Allen	.03	.01	.00
☐ 664	Tim Corcoran	.03	.01	.00
☐ 665	Alejandro Pena	.06	.03	.00
☐ 666	Rangers Leaders	.03	.01	.00
	Charlie Hough			
☐ 667	Tim Teufel	.03	.01	.00
☐ 668	Cecilio Guante	.03	.01	.00
☐ 669	Ron Cey	.06	.03	.00
☐ 670	Willie Hernandez	.08	.04	.01
☐ 671	Lynn Jones	.03	.01	.00
☐ 672	Rob Picciolo	.03	.01	.00
☐ 673	Ernie Whitt	.03	.01	.00
☐ 674	Pat Tabler	.08	.04	.01
☐ 675	Claudell Washington	.06	.03	.00
☐ 676	Matt Young	.03	.01	.00
☐ 677	Nick Esasky	.12	.06	.01
☐ 678	Dan Gladden	.06	.03	.00
☐ 679	Britt Burns	.03	.01	.00
☐ 680	George Foster	.10	.05	.01
☐ 681	Dick Williams MG	.06	.03	.00
	(checklist back)			
☐ 682	Junior Ortiz	.03	.01	.00
☐ 683	Andy Van Slyke	.20	.10	.02
☐ 684	Bob McClure	.03	.01	.00
☐ 685	Tim Wallach	.08	.04	.01
☐ 686	Jeff Stone	.03	.01	.00
☐ 687	Mike Trujillo	.03	.01	.00
☐ 688	Larry Herndon	.03	.01	.00
☐ 689	Dave Stewart	.25	.12	.02
☐ 690	Ryne Sandberg	.35	.17	.03
	(no Topps logo			

		MINT	EXC	G-VG
	on front)			
☐ 691	Mike Madden	.03	.01	.00
☐ 692	Dale Berra	.03	.01	.00
☐ 693	Tom Tellmann	.03	.01	.00
☐ 694	Garth Iorg	.03	.01	.00
☐ 695	Mike Smithson	.03	.01	.00
☐ 696	Dodgers Leaders	.03	.01	.00
	Bill Russell			
☐ 697	Bud Black	.03	.01	.00
☐ 698	Brad Komminsk	.03	.01	.00
☐ 699	Pat Corrales MG	.06	.03	.00
	(checklist back)			
☐ 700	Reggie Jackson	.35	.17	.03
☐ 701	Keith Hernandez AS	.12	.06	.01
☐ 702	Tom Herr AS	.06	.03	.00
☐ 703	Tim Wallach AS	.06	.03	.00
☐ 704	Ozzie Smith AS	.10	.05	.01
☐ 705	Dale Murphy AS	.20	.10	.02
☐ 706	Pedro Guerrero AS	.10	.05	.01
☐ 707	Willie McGee AS	.08	.04	.01
☐ 708	Gary Carter AS	.15	.07	.01
☐ 709	Dwight Gooden AS	.30	.15	.03
☐ 710	John Tudor AS	.06	.03	.00
☐ 711	Jeff Reardon AS	.06	.03	.00
☐ 712	Don Mattingly AS	.75	.35	.07
☐ 713	Damaso Garcia AS	.06	.03	.00
☐ 714	George Brett AS	.25	.12	.02
☐ 715	Cal Ripken AS	.20	.10	.02
☐ 716	Rickey Henderson AS	.25	.12	.02
☐ 717	Dave Winfield AS	.15	.07	.01
☐ 718	George Bell AS	.10	.05	.01
☐ 719	Carlton Fisk AS	.12	.06	.01
☐ 720	Bret Saberhagen AS	.12	.06	.01
☐ 721	Ron Guidry AS	.06	.03	.00
☐ 722	Dan Quisenberry AS	.06	.03	.00
☐ 723	Marty Bystrom	.03	.01	.00
☐ 724	Tim Hulett	.03	.01	.00
☐ 725	Mario Soto	.03	.01	.00
☐ 726	Orioles Leaders	.03	.01	.00
	Rick Dempsey			
☐ 727	David Green	.03	.01	.00
☐ 728	Mike Marshall	.10	.05	.01
☐ 729	Jim Beattie	.03	.01	.00
☐ 730	Ozzie Smith	.18	.09	.01
☐ 731	Don Robinson	.03	.01	.00
☐ 732	Floyd Youmans	.25	.12	.02
☐ 733	Ron Romanick	.03	.01	.00
☐ 734	Marty Barrett	.08	.04	.01
☐ 735	Dave Dravecky	.08	.04	.01

		MINT	EXC	G-VG
☐ 736	Glenn Wilson	.03	.01	.00
☐ 737	Pete Vuckovich	.06	.03	.00
☐ 738	Andre Robertson	.03	.01	.00
☐ 739	Dave Rozema	.03	.01	.00
☐ 740	Lance Parrish	.12	.06	.01
☐ 741	Pete Rose MG	.35	.17	.03
	(checklist back)			
☐ 742	Frank Viola	.25	.12	.02
☐ 743	Pat Sheridan	.03	.01	.00
☐ 744	Lary Sorensen	.03	.01	.00
☐ 745	Willie Upshaw	.03	.01	.00
☐ 746	Denny Gonzalez	.03	.01	.00
☐ 747	Rick Cerone	.03	.01	.00
☐ 748	Steve Henderson	.03	.01	.00
☐ 749	Ed Jurak	.03	.01	.00
☐ 750	Gorman Thomas	.06	.03	.00
☐ 751	Howard Johnson	.30	.15	.03
☐ 752	Mike Krukow	.03	.01	.00
☐ 753	Dan Ford	.03	.01	.00
☐ 754	Pat Clements	.08	.04	.01
☐ 755	Harold Baines	.10	.05	.01
☐ 756	Pirates Leaders	.03	.01	.00
	Rick Rhoden			
☐ 757	Darrell Porter	.03	.01	.00
☐ 758	Dave Anderson	.03	.01	.00
☐ 759	Moose Haas	.03	.01	.00
☐ 760	Andre Dawson	.25	.12	.02
☐ 761	Don Slaught	.03	.01	.00
☐ 762	Eric Show	.06	.03	.00
☐ 763	Terry Puhl	.03	.01	.00
☐ 764	Kevin Gross	.03	.01	.00
☐ 765	Don Baylor	.10	.05	.01
☐ 766	Rick Langford	.03	.01	.00
☐ 767	Jody Davis	.06	.03	.00
☐ 768	Vern Ruhle	.03	.01	.00
☐ 769	Harold Reynolds	.60	.30	.06
☐ 770	Vida Blue	.06	.03	.00
☐ 771	John McNamara MG	.06	.03	.00
	(checklist back)			
☐ 772	Brian Downing	.06	.03	.00
☐ 773	Greg Pryor	.03	.01	.00
☐ 774	Terry Leach	.08	.04	.01
☐ 775	Al Oliver	.08	.04	.01
☐ 776	Gene Garber	.03	.01	.00
☐ 777	Wayne Krenchicki	.03	.01	.00
☐ 778	Jerry Hairston	.03	.01	.00
☐ 779	Rick Reuschel	.10	.05	.01
☐ 780	Robin Yount	.35	.17	.03
☐ 781	Joe Nolan	.03	.01	.00

		MINT	EXC	G-VG
☐ 782	Ken Landreaux	.03	.01	.00
☐ 783	Ricky Horton	.03	.01	.00
☐ 784	Alan Bannister	.03	.01	.00
☐ 785	Bob Stanley	.03	.01	.00
☐ 786	Twins Leaders	.03	.01	.00
	Mickey Hatcher			
☐ 787	Vance Law	.03	.01	.00
☐ 788	Marty Castillo	.03	.01	.00
☐ 789	Kurt Bevacqua	.03	.01	.00
☐ 790	Phil Niekro	.15	.07	.01
☐ 791	Checklist: 661-792	.06	.01	.00
☐ 792	Charles Hudson	.06	.03	.00

1986 Topps Traded

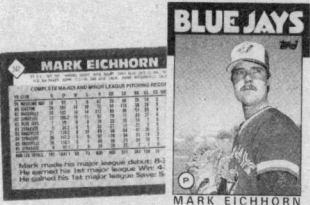

MARK EICHHORN

This 132-card Traded or extended set was distributed by Topps to dealers in a special red and white box as a complete set. The card fronts are identical in style to the Topps regular issue and are also 2 ½" by 3 ½". The backs are printed in red and black on white card stock. Cards are numbered (with a T suffix) alphabetically according to the name of the player. Topps also produced a specially boxed "glossy" edition, frequently referred to as the Topps Traded Tiffany set. There were supposedly only 5,000 sets of the Tiffany cards produced; they were marketed to hobby dealers. The checklist of cards is identical to that of the normal non-glossy cards. There are two primary distinguishing features of the Tiffany cards—white card stock reverses and high gloss obverses. These Tiffany cards are valued at approximately five times the values listed below.

		MINT	EXC	G-VG
COMPLETE SET (132)		30.00	15.00	3.00
COMMON PLAYER (1-132)		.05	.02	.00
☐ 1T	Andy Allanson	.15	.04	.01
☐ 2T	Neil Allen	.05	.02	.00
☐ 3T	Joaquin Andujar	.10	.05	.01
☐ 4T	Paul Assenmacher	.15	.07	.01
☐ 5T	Scott Bailes	.15	.07	.01
☐ 6T	Don Baylor	.10	.05	.01
☐ 7T	Steve Bedrosian	.15	.07	.01
☐ 8T	Juan Beniquez	.05	.02	.00
☐ 9T	Juan Berenguer	.05	.02	.00
☐ 10T	Mike Bielecki	.35	.17	.03
☐ 11T	Barry Bonds	1.00	.50	.10
☐ 12T	Bobby Bonilla	1.00	.50	.10
☐ 13T	Juan Bonilla	.05	.02	.00
☐ 14T	Rich Bordi	.05	.02	.00
☐ 15T	Steve Boros MG	.05	.02	.00
☐ 16T	Rick Burleson	.10	.05	.01
☐ 17T	Bill Campbell	.05	.02	.00
☐ 18T	Tom Candiotti	.10	.05	.01
☐ 19T	John Cangelosi	.15	.07	.01
☐ 20T	Jose Canseco	8.50	4.25	.85
☐ 21T	Carmen Castillo	.05	.02	.00
☐ 22T	Rick Cerone	.05	.02	.00
☐ 23T	John Cerutti	.25	.12	.02
☐ 24T	Will Clark	10.00	5.00	1.00
☐ 25T	Mark Clear	.05	.02	.00
☐ 26T	Darnell Coles	.10	.05	.01
☐ 27T	Dave Collins	.05	.02	.00
☐ 28T	Tim Conroy	.05	.02	.00
☐ 29T	Joe Cowley	.05	.02	.00
☐ 30T	Joel Davis	.15	.07	.01
☐ 31T	Rob Deer	.15	.07	.01
☐ 32T	John Denny	.10	.05	.01
☐ 33T	Mike Easler	.05	.02	.00
☐ 34T	Mark Eichhorn	.10	.05	.01
☐ 35T	Steve Farr	.05	.02	.00
☐ 36T	Scott Fletcher	.10	.05	.01
☐ 37T	Terry Forster	.10	.05	.01
☐ 38T	Terry Francona	.05	.02	.00
☐ 39T	Jim Fregosi MG	.05	.02	.00
☐ 40T	Andres Galarraga	1.50	.75	.15
☐ 41T	Ken Griffey	.15	.07	.01
☐ 42T	Bill Gullickson	.05	.02	.00

		MINT	EXC	G-VG
☐ 43T	Jose Guzman	.20	.10	.02
☐ 44T	Moose Haas	.05	.02	.00
☐ 45T	Billy Hatcher	.10	.05	.01
☐ 46T	Mike Heath	.05	.02	.00
☐ 47T	Tom Hume	.05	.02	.00
☐ 48T	Pete Incaviglia	.70	.35	.07
☐ 49T	Dane Iorg	.05	.02	.00
☐ 50T	Bo Jackson	9.00	4.50	.90
☐ 51T	Wally Joyner	2.00	1.00	.20
☐ 52T	Charlie Kerfeld	.10	.05	.01
☐ 53T	Eric King	.15	.07	.01
☐ 54T	Bob Kipper	.05	.02	.00
☐ 55T	Wayne Krenchicki	.05	.02	.00
☐ 56T	John Kruk	.35	.17	.03
☐ 57T	Mike LaCoss	.05	.02	.00
☐ 58T	Pete Ladd	.05	.02	.00
☐ 59T	Mike Laga	.10	.05	.01
☐ 60T	Hal Lanier MG	.05	.02	.00
☐ 61T	Dave LaPoint	.10	.05	.01
☐ 62T	Rudy Law	.05	.02	.00
☐ 63T	Rick Leach	.05	.02	.00
☐ 64T	Tim Leary	.20	.10	.02
☐ 65T	Dennis Leonard	.10	.05	.01
☐ 66T	Jim Leyland MG	.05	.02	.00
☐ 67T	Steve Lyons	.05	.02	.00
☐ 68T	Mickey Mahler	.05	.02	.00
☐ 69T	Candy Maldonado	.10	.05	.01
☐ 70T	Roger Mason	.10	.05	.01
☐ 71T	Bob McClure	.05	.02	.00
☐ 72T	Andy McGaffigan	.05	.02	.00
☐ 73T	Gene Michael MG	.05	.02	.00
☐ 74T	Kevin Mitchell	5.00	2.50	.50
☐ 75T	Omar Moreno	.05	.02	.00
☐ 76T	Jerry Mumphrey	.05	.02	.00
☐ 77T	Phil Niekro	.30	.15	.03
☐ 78T	Randy Niemann	.05	.02	.00
☐ 79T	Juan Nieves	.15	.07	.01
☐ 80T	Otis Nixon	.15	.07	.01
☐ 81T	Bob Ojeda	.10	.05	.01
☐ 82T	Jose Oquendo	.10	.05	.01
☐ 83T	Tom Paciorek	.05	.02	.00
☐ 84T	David Palmer	.05	.02	.00
☐ 85T	Frank Pastore	.05	.02	.00
☐ 86T	Lou Piniella MG	.10	.05	.01
☐ 87T	Dan Plesac	.30	.15	.03
☐ 88T	Darrell Porter	.05	.02	.00
☐ 89T	Rey Quinones	.20	.10	.02
☐ 90T	Gary Redus	.05	.02	.00
☐ 91T	Bip Roberts	.20	.10	.02
☐ 92T	Billy Jo Robidoux	.10	.05	.01
☐ 93T	Jeff Robinson (Giants pitcher)	.20	.10	.02
☐ 94T	Gary Roenicke	.05	.02	.00
☐ 95T	Ed Romero	.05	.02	.00
☐ 96T	Argenis Salazar	.05	.02	.00
☐ 97T	Joe Sambito	.05	.02	.00
☐ 98T	Billy Sample	.05	.02	.00
☐ 99T	Dave Schmidt	.10	.05	.01
☐ 100T	Ken Schrom	.05	.02	.00
☐ 101T	Tom Seaver	.50	.25	.05
☐ 102T	Ted Simmons	.15	.07	.01
☐ 103T	Sammy Stewart	.05	.02	.00
☐ 104T	Kurt Stillwell	.25	.12	.02
☐ 105T	Franklin Stubbs	.05	.02	.00
☐ 106T	Dale Sveum	.20	.10	.02
☐ 107T	Chuck Tanner MG	.05	.02	.00
☐ 108T	Danny Tartabull	.75	.35	.07
☐ 109T	Tim Teufel	.05	.02	.00
☐ 110T	Bob Tewksbury	.15	.07	.01
☐ 111T	Andres Thomas	.20	.10	.02
☐ 112T	Milt Thompson	.10	.05	.01
☐ 113T	Robby Thompson	.35	.17	.03
☐ 114T	Jay Tibbs	.05	.02	.00
☐ 115T	Wayne Tolleson	.05	.02	.00
☐ 116T	Alex Trevino	.05	.02	.00
☐ 117T	Manny Trillo	.05	.02	.00
☐ 118T	Ed VandeBerg	.05	.02	.00
☐ 119T	Ozzie Virgil	.05	.02	.00
☐ 120T	Bob Walk	.05	.02	.00
☐ 121T	Gene Walter	.10	.05	.01
☐ 122T	Claudell Washington	.10	.05	.01
☐ 123T	Bill Wegman	.10	.05	.01
☐ 124T	Dick Williams MG	.05	.02	.00
☐ 125T	Mitch Williams	.40	.20	.04
☐ 126T	Bobby Witt	.35	.17	.03
☐ 127T	Todd Worrell	.50	.25	.05
☐ 128T	George Wright	.05	.02	.00
☐ 129T	Ricky Wright	.05	.02	.00
☐ 130T	Steve Yeager	.05	.02	.00
☐ 131T	Paul Zuvella	.05	.02	.00
☐ 132T	Checklist 1-132	.05	.01	.00

1987 Topps

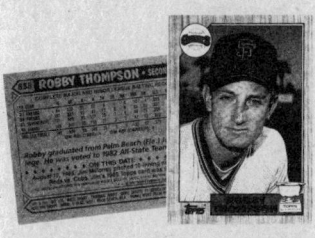

This 792-card set is reminiscent of the 1962 Topps baseball cards with their simulated wood grain borders. The backs are printed in yellow and blue on gray card stock. The manager cards contain a checklist of the respective team's players on the back. Subsets in the set include Record Breakers (1-7), Turn Back the Clock (311-315), and All-Star selections (595-616). The Team Leader cards typically show players conferring on the mound inside a white cloud. The wax pack wrapper gives details of "Spring Fever Baseball" where a lucky collector can win a trip for four to Spring Training. Topps also produced a specially boxed "glossy" edition, frequently referred to as the Topps Tiffany set. This year Topps did not disclose the number of sets they produced or sold. It is apparent from the availability that there were many more sets produced this year compared to the 1984-86 Tiffany sets, perhaps more than three times as many. The checklist of cards (792 regular and 132 Traded) is identical to that of the normal non-glossy cards. There are two primary distinguishing features of the Tiffany cards—white card stock reverses and high gloss obverses. These Tiffany cards are valued at approximately four times the values listed below.

	MINT	EXC	G-VG
COMPLETE SET (792)	35.00	17.50	3.50
COMMON PLAYER (1-792)	.03	.01	.00

			MINT	EXC	G-VG
☐	1	RB: Roger Clemens . Most strikeouts, nine inning game	.40	.10	.02
☐	2	RB: Jim Deshaies ... Most cons. K's, start of game	.06	.03	.00
☐	3	RB: Dwight Evans ... Earliest home run, season	.08	.04	.01
☐	4	RB: Davey Lopes ... Most steals, season, 40-year-old	.06	.03	.00
☐	5	RB: Dave Righetti ... Most saves, season	.08	.04	.01
☐	6	RB: Ruben Sierra ... Youngest player to switch hit homers in game	.25	.12	.02
☐	7	RB: Todd Worrell ... Most saves, season, rookie	.08	.04	.01
☐	8	Terry Pendleton	.03	.01	.00
☐	9	Jay Tibbs	.03	.01	.00
☐	10	Cecil Cooper	.08	.04	.01
☐	11	Indians Team ...... (mound conference)	.03	.01	.00
☐	12	Jeff Sellers	.10	.05	.01
☐	13	Nick Esasky	.10	.05	.01
☐	14	Dave Stewart	.15	.07	.01
☐	15	Claudell Washington ..	.06	.03	.00
☐	16	Pat Clements	.03	.01	.00
☐	17	Pete O'Brien	.08	.04	.01
☐	18	Dick Howser MG .... (checklist back)	.06	.03	.00
☐	19	Matt Young	.03	.01	.00
☐	20	Gary Carter	.18	.09	.01
☐	21	Mark Davis	.12	.06	.01
☐	22	Doug DeCinces	.06	.03	.00
☐	23	Lee Smith	.06	.03	.00
☐	24	Tony Walker	.08	.04	.01
☐	25	Bert Blyleven	.10	.05	.01
☐	26	Greg Brock	.03	.01	.00
☐	27	Joe Cowley	.03	.01	.00
☐	28	Rick Dempsey	.03	.01	.00
☐	29	Jimmy Key	.08	.04	.01
☐	30	Tim Raines	.15	.07	.01
☐	31	Braves Team ...... (Hubbard/Ramirez)	.03	.01	.00

		MINT	EXC	G-VG
☐ 32	Tim Leary	.06	.03	.00
☐ 33	Andy Van Slyke	.15	.07	.01
☐ 34	Jose Rijo	.06	.03	.00
☐ 35	Sid Bream	.03	.01	.00
☐ 36	Eric King	.12	.06	.01
☐ 37	Marvell Wynne	.03	.01	.00
☐ 38	Dennis Leonard	.03	.01	.00
☐ 39	Marty Barrett	.06	.03	.00
☐ 40	Dave Righetti	.10	.05	.01
☐ 41	Bo Diaz	.03	.01	.00
☐ 42	Gary Redus	.03	.01	.00
☐ 43	Gene Michael MG (checklist back)	.06	.03	.00
☐ 44	Greg Harris	.03	.01	.00
☐ 45	Jim Presley	.06	.03	.00
☐ 46	Dan Gladden	.06	.03	.00
☐ 47	Dennis Powell	.03	.01	.00
☐ 48	Wally Backman	.03	.01	.00
☐ 49	Terry Harper	.03	.01	.00
☐ 50	Dave Smith	.03	.01	.00
☐ 51	Mel Hall	.06	.03	.00
☐ 52	Keith Atherton	.03	.01	.00
☐ 53	Ruppert Jones	.03	.01	.00
☐ 54	Bill Dawley	.03	.01	.00
☐ 55	Tim Wallach	.08	.04	.01
☐ 56	Brewers Team (mound conference)	.03	.01	.00
☐ 57	Scott Nielsen	.12	.06	.01
☐ 58	Thad Bosley	.03	.01	.00
☐ 59	Ken Dayley	.03	.01	.00
☐ 60	Tony Pena	.08	.04	.01
☐ 61	Bobby Thigpen	.25	.12	.02
☐ 62	Bobby Meacham	.03	.01	.00
☐ 63	Fred Toliver	.03	.01	.00
☐ 64	Harry Spilman	.03	.01	.00
☐ 65	Tom Browning	.10	.05	.01
☐ 66	Marc Sullivan	.03	.01	.00
☐ 67	Bill Swift	.03	.01	.00
☐ 68	Tony LaRussa MG (checklist back)	.06	.03	.00
☐ 69	Lonnie Smith	.08	.04	.01
☐ 70	Charlie Hough	.06	.03	.00
☐ 71	Mike Aldrete	.15	.07	.01
☐ 72	Walt Terrell	.03	.01	.00
☐ 73	Dave Anderson	.03	.01	.00
☐ 74	Dan Pasqua	.06	.03	.00
☐ 75	Ron Darling	.15	.07	.01
☐ 76	Rafael Ramirez	.03	.01	.00
☐ 77	Bryan Oelkers	.03	.01	.00
☐ 78	Tom Foley	.03	.01	.00
☐ 79	Juan Nieves	.08	.04	.01
☐ 80	Wally Joyner	1.25	.60	.12
☐ 81	Padres Team (Hawkins/Kennedy)	.03	.01	.00
☐ 82	Rob Murphy	.20	.10	.02
☐ 83	Mike Davis	.03	.01	.00
☐ 84	Steve Lake	.03	.01	.00
☐ 85	Kevin Bass	.06	.03	.00
☐ 86	Nate Snell	.03	.01	.00
☐ 87	Mark Salas	.03	.01	.00
☐ 88	Ed Wojna	.03	.01	.00
☐ 89	Ozzie Guillen	.08	.04	.01
☐ 90	Dave Stieb	.10	.05	.01
☐ 91	Harold Reynolds	.06	.03	.00
☐ 92A	Urbano Lugo ERR (no trademark)	.25	.12	.02
☐ 92B	Urbano Lugo COR	.06	.03	.00
☐ 93	Jim Leyland MG (checklist back)	.06	.03	.00
☐ 94	Calvin Schiraldi	.06	.03	.00
☐ 95	Oddibe McDowell	.08	.04	.01
☐ 96	Frank Williams	.03	.01	.00
☐ 97	Glenn Wilson	.03	.01	.00
☐ 98	Bill Scherrer	.03	.01	.00
☐ 99	Darryl Motley	.03	.01	.00
☐ 100	Steve Garvey	.20	.10	.02
☐ 101	Carl Willis	.06	.03	.00
☐ 102	Paul Zuvella	.03	.01	.00
☐ 103	Rick Aguilera	.03	.01	.00
☐ 104	Billy Sample	.03	.01	.00
☐ 105	Floyd Youmans	.06	.03	.00
☐ 106	Blue Jays Team (Bell/Barfield)	.12	.06	.01
☐ 107	John Butcher	.03	.01	.00
☐ 108	Jim Gantner UER (Brewers logo reversed)	.06	.03	.00
☐ 109	R.J. Reynolds	.03	.01	.00
☐ 110	John Tudor	.10	.05	.01
☐ 111	Alfredo Griffin	.06	.03	.00
☐ 112	Alan Ashby	.03	.01	.00
☐ 113	Neil Allen	.03	.01	.00
☐ 114	Billy Beane	.06	.03	.00
☐ 115	Donnie Moore	.03	.01	.00
☐ 116	Bill Russell	.06	.03	.00
☐ 117	Jim Beattie	.03	.01	.00
☐ 118	Bobby Valentine MG (checklist back)	.06	.03	.00

		MINT	EXC	G-VG			MINT	EXC	G-VG
☐ 119	Ron Robinson	.03	.01	.00	☐ 165	Jeff Reardon	.08	.04	.01
☐ 120	Eddie Murray	.18	.09	.01	☐ 166	Bob Boone	.08	.04	.01
☐ 121	Kevin Romine	.10	.05	.01	☐ 167	Jim Deshaies	.20	.10	.02
☐ 122	Jim Clancy	.03	.01	.00	☐ 168	Lou Piniella MG	.08	.04	.01
☐ 123	John Kruk	.30	.15	.03		(checklist back)			
☐ 124	Ray Fontenot	.03	.01	.00	☐ 169	Ron Washington	.03	.01	.00
☐ 125	Bob Brenly	.03	.01	.00	☐ 170	Bo Jackson	3.50	1.75	.35
☐ 126	Mike Loynd	.06	.03	.00	☐ 171	Chuck Cary	.20	.10	.02
☐ 127	Vance Law	.03	.01	.00	☐ 172	Ron Oester	.03	.01	.00
☐ 128	Checklist 1-132	.06	.01	.00	☐ 173	Alex Trevino	.03	.01	.00
☐ 129	Rick Cerone	.03	.01	.00	☐ 174	Henry Cotto	.03	.01	.00
☐ 130	Dwight Gooden	.65	.30	.06	☐ 175	Bob Stanley	.03	.01	.00
☐ 131	Pirates Team	.03	.01	.00	☐ 176	Steve Buechele	.03	.01	.00
	(Bream/Pena)				☐ 177	Keith Moreland	.03	.01	.00
☐ 132	Paul Assenmacher	.06	.03	.00	☐ 178	Cecil Fielder	.06	.03	.00
☐ 133	Jose Oquendo	.03	.01	.00	☐ 179	Bill Wegman	.06	.03	.00
☐ 134	Rich Yett	.03	.01	.00	☐ 180	Chris Brown	.03	.01	.00
☐ 135	Mike Easler	.03	.01	.00	☐ 181	Cardinals Team	.03	.01	.00
☐ 136	Ron Romanick	.03	.01	.00		(mound conference)			
☐ 137	Jerry Willard	.03	.01	.00	☐ 182	Lee Lacy	.03	.01	.00
☐ 138	Roy Lee Jackson	.03	.01	.00	☐ 183	Andy Hawkins	.06	.03	.00
☐ 139	Devon White	1.00	.50	.10	☐ 184	Bobby Bonilla	.75	.35	.07
☐ 140	Bret Saberhagen	.25	.12	.02	☐ 185	Roger McDowell	.06	.03	.00
☐ 141	Herm Winningham	.03	.01	.00	☐ 186	Bruce Benedict	.03	.01	.00
☐ 142	Rick Sutcliffe	.10	.05	.01	☐ 187	Mark Huismann	.03	.01	.00
☐ 143	Steve Boros MG	.06	.03	.00	☐ 188	Tony Phillips	.03	.01	.00
	(checklist back)				☐ 189	Joe Hesketh	.03	.01	.00
☐ 144	Mike Scioscia	.03	.01	.00	☐ 190	Jim Sundberg	.03	.01	.00
☐ 145	Charlie Kerfeld	.03	.01	.00	☐ 191	Charles Hudson	.03	.01	.00
☐ 146	Tracy Jones	.15	.07	.01	☐ 192	Cory Snyder	.40	.20	.04
☐ 147	Randy Niemann	.03	.01	.00	☐ 193	Roger Craig MG	.06	.03	.00
☐ 148	Dave Collins	.03	.01	.00		(checklist back)			
☐ 149	Ray Searage	.03	.01	.00	☐ 194	Kirk McCaskill	.03	.01	.00
☐ 150	Wade Boggs	1.25	.60	.12	☐ 195	Mike Pagliarulo	.06	.03	.00
☐ 151	Mike LaCoss	.03	.01	.00	☐ 196	Randy O'Neal UER	.03	.01	.00
☐ 152	Toby Harrah	.03	.01	.00		(wrong ML career			
☐ 153	Duane Ward	.15	.07	.01		W-L totals)			
☐ 154	Tom O'Malley	.03	.01	.00	☐ 197	Mark Bailey		.01	.00
☐ 155	Eddie Whitson	.03	.01	.00	☐ 198	Lee Mazzilli	.03	.01	.00
☐ 156	Mariners Team	.03	.01	.00	☐ 199	Mariano Duncan	.03	.01	.00
	(mound conference)				☐ 200	Pete Rose	.45	.22	.04
☐ 157	Danny Darwin	.03	.01	.00	☐ 201	John Cangelosi	.08	.04	.01
☐ 158	Tim Teufel	.03	.01	.00	☐ 202	Ricky Wright	.03	.01	.00
☐ 159	Ed Olwine	.06	.03	.00	☐ 203	Mike Kingery	.08	.04	.01
☐ 160	Julio Franco	.12	.06	.01	☐ 204	Sammy Stewart	.03	.01	.00
☐ 161	Steve Ontiveros	.03	.01	.00	☐ 205	Graig Nettles	.08	.04	.01
☐ 162	Mike LaValliere	.15	.07	.01	☐ 206	Twins Team	.06	.03	.00
☐ 163	Kevin Gross	.03	.01	.00		(Frank Viola and			
☐ 164	Sammy Khalifa	.03	.01	.00		Tim Laudner)			

		MINT	EXC	G-VG
☐ 207	George Frazier	.03	.01	.00
☐ 208	John Shelby	.03	.01	.00
☐ 209	Rick Schu	.03	.01	.00
☐ 210	Lloyd Moseby	.06	.03	.00
☐ 211	John Morris	.03	.01	.00
☐ 212	Mike Fitzgerald	.03	.01	.00
☐ 213	Randy Myers	.45	.22	.04
☐ 214	Omar Moreno	.03	.01	.00
☐ 215	Mark Langston	.25	.12	.02
☐ 216	B.J. Surhoff	.35	.17	.03
☐ 217	Chris Codiroli	.03	.01	.00
☐ 218	Sparky Anderson MG	.06	.03	.00
	(checklist back)			
☐ 219	Cecilio Guante	.03	.01	.00
☐ 220	Joe Carter	.25	.12	.02
☐ 221	Vern Ruhle	.03	.01	.00
☐ 222	Denny Walling	.03	.01	.00
☐ 223	Charlie Leibrandt	.03	.01	.00
☐ 224	Wayne Tolleson	.03	.01	.00
☐ 225	Mike Smithson	.03	.01	.00
☐ 226	Max Venable	.03	.01	.00
☐ 227	Jamie Moyer	.15	.07	.01
☐ 228	Curt Wilkerson	.03	.01	.00
☐ 229	Mike Birkbeck	.10	.05	.01
☐ 230	Don Baylor	.08	.04	.01
☐ 231	Giants Team	.03	.01	.00
	(Bob Brenly and			
	Jim Gott)			
☐ 232	Reggie Williams	.06	.03	.00
☐ 233	Russ Morman	.10	.05	.01
☐ 234	Pat Sheridan	.03	.01	.00
☐ 235	Alvin Davis	.10	.05	.01
☐ 236	Tommy John	.10	.05	.01
☐ 237	Jim Morrison	.03	.01	.00
☐ 238	Bill Krueger	.03	.01	.00
☐ 239	Juan Espino	.03	.01	.00
☐ 240	Steve Balboni	.03	.01	.00
☐ 241	Danny Heep	.03	.01	.00
☐ 242	Rick Mahler	.03	.01	.00
☐ 243	Whitey Herzog MG	.06	.03	.00
	(checklist back)			
☐ 244	Dickie Noles	.03	.01	.00
☐ 245	Willie Upshaw	.03	.01	.00
☐ 246	Jim Dwyer	.03	.01	.00
☐ 247	Jeff Reed	.03	.01	.00
☐ 248	Gene Walter	.03	.01	.00
☐ 249	Jim Pankovits	.03	.01	.00
☐ 250	Teddy Higuera	.15	.07	.01
☐ 251	Rob Wilfong	.03	.01	.00

		MINT	EXC	G-VG
☐ 252	Dennis Martinez	.06	.03	.00
☐ 253	Eddie Milner	.03	.01	.00
☐ 254	Bob Tewksbury	.10	.05	.01
☐ 255	Juan Samuel	.10	.05	.01
☐ 256	Royals Team	.10	.05	.01
	(Brett/F. White)			
☐ 257	Bob Forsch	.03	.01	.00
☐ 258	Steve Yeager	.03	.01	.00
☐ 259	Mike Greenwell	4.00	2.00	.40
☐ 260	Vida Blue	.06	.03	.00
☐ 261	Ruben Sierra	2.50	1.25	.25
☐ 262	Jim Winn	.03	.01	.00
☐ 263	Stan Javier	.06	.03	.00
☐ 264	Checklist 133-264	.06	.01	.00
☐ 265	Darrell Evans	.08	.04	.01
☐ 266	Jeff Hamilton	.15	.07	.01
☐ 267	Howard Johnson	.20	.10	.02
☐ 268	Pat Corrales MG	.06	.03	.00
	(checklist back)			
☐ 269	Cliff Speck	.06	.03	.00
☐ 270	Jody Davis	.03	.01	.00
☐ 271	Mike Brown	.03	.01	.00
	(Mariners pitcher)			
☐ 272	Andres Galarraga	.90	.45	.09
☐ 273	Gene Nelson	.03	.01	.00
☐ 274	Jeff Hearron	.10	.05	.01
	(duplicate 1986			
	stat line on back)			
☐ 275	LaMarr Hoyt	.06	.03	.00
☐ 276	Jackie Gutierrez	.03	.01	.00
☐ 277	Juan Agosto	.03	.01	.00
☐ 278	Gary Pettis	.03	.01	.00
☐ 279	Dan Plesac	.25	.12	.02
☐ 280	Jeff Leonard	.06	.03	.00
☐ 281	Reds Team	.10	.05	.01
	(Pete Rose, Bo Diaz,			
	and Bill Gullickson)			
☐ 282	Jeff Calhoun	.03	.01	.00
☐ 283	Doug Drabek	.30	.15	.03
☐ 284	John Moses	.03	.01	.00
☐ 285	Dennis Boyd	.06	.03	.00
☐ 286	Mike Woodard	.03	.01	.00
☐ 287	Dave Von Ohlen	.03	.01	.00
☐ 288	Tito Landrum	.03	.01	.00
☐ 289	Bob Kipper	.03	.01	.00
☐ 290	Leon Durham	.06	.03	.00
☐ 291	Mitch Williams	.30	.15	.03
☐ 292	Franklin Stubbs	.03	.01	.00
☐ 293	Bob Rodgers MG	.06	.03	.00

		MINT	EXC	G-VG			MINT	EXC	G-VG
	(checklist back)				☐ 329	Ron Roenicke	.03	.01	.00
☐ 294	Steve Jeltz	.03	.01	.00	☐ 330	Mike Scott	.20	.10	.02
☐ 295	Len Dykstra	.08	.04	.01	☐ 331	Mets Team	.15	.07	.01
☐ 296	Andres Thomas	.12	.06	.01		(Gary Carter and			
☐ 297	Don Schulze	.03	.01	.00		Darryl Strawberry)			
☐ 298	Larry Herndon	.03	.01	.00	☐ 332	Joe Price	.03	.01	.00
☐ 299	Joel Davis	.03	.01	.00	☐ 333	Ken Phelps	.06	.03	.00
☐ 300	Reggie Jackson	.30	.15	.03	☐ 334	Ed Correa	.10	.05	.01
☐ 301	Luis Aquino	.06	.03	.00	☐ 335	Candy Maldonado	.06	.03	.00
	UER (no trademark,				☐ 336	Allan Anderson	.25	.12	.02
	never corrected)				☐ 337	Darrell Miller	.03	.01	.00
☐ 302	Bill Schroeder	.03	.01	.00	☐ 338	Tim Conroy	.03	.01	.00
☐ 303	Juan Berenguer	.03	.01	.00	☐ 339	Donnie Hill	.03	.01	.00
☐ 304	Phil Garner	.03	.01	.00	☐ 340	Roger Clemens	1.00	.50	.10
☐ 305	John Franco	.08	.04	.01	☐ 341	Mike Brown	.03	.01	.00
☐ 306	Red Sox Team	.08	.04	.01		(Pirates OF)			
	(Tom Seaver,				☐ 342	Bob James	.03	.01	.00
	John McNamara,				☐ 343	Hal Lanier MG	.06	.03	.00
	and Rich Gedman)					(checklist back)			
☐ 307	Lee Guetterman	.12	.06	.01	☐ 344A	Joe Niekro	.10	.05	.01
☐ 308	Don Slaught	.03	.01	.00		(copyright inside			
☐ 309	Mike Young	.03	.01	.00		righthand border)			
☐ 310	Frank Viola	.15	.07	.01	☐ 344B	Joe Niekro	.50	.25	.05
☐ 311	Turn Back 1982	.12	.06	.01		(copyright outside			
	Rickey Henderson					righthand border)			
☐ 312	Turn Back 1977	.12	.06	.01	☐ 345	Andre Dawson	.25	.12	.02
	Reggie Jackson				☐ 346	Shawon Dunston	.12	.06	.01
☐ 313	Turn Back 1972	.12	.06	.01	☐ 347	Mickey Brantley	.12	.06	.01
	Roberto Clemente				☐ 348	Carmelo Martinez	.03	.01	.00
☐ 314	Turn Back 1967 UER	.12	.06	.01	☐ 349	Storm Davis	.08	.04	.01
	Carl Yastrzemski				☐ 350	Keith Hernandez	.18	.09	.01
	(sic, 112 RBI's on				☐ 351	Gene Garber	.03	.01	.00
	back)				☐ 352	Mike Felder	.06	.03	.00
☐ 315	Turn Back 1962	.06	.03	.00	☐ 353	Ernie Camacho	.03	.01	.00
	Maury Wills				☐ 354	Jamie Quirk	.03	.01	.00
☐ 316	Brian Fisher	.03	.01	.00	☐ 355	Don Carman	.03	.01	.00
☐ 317	Clint Hurdle	.03	.01	.00	☐ 356	White Sox Team	.03	.01	.00
☐ 318	Jim Fregosi MG	.06	.03	.00		(mound conference)			
	(checklist back)				☐ 357	Steve Fireovid	.06	.03	.00
☐ 319	Greg Swindell	1.00	.50	.10	☐ 358	Sal Butera	.03	.01	.00
☐ 320	Barry Bonds	.75	.35	.07	☐ 359	Doug Corbett	.03	.01	.00
☐ 321	Mike Laga	.03	.01	.00	☐ 360	Pedro Guerrero	.12	.06	.01
☐ 322	Chris Bando	.03	.01	.00	☐ 361	Mark Thurmond	.03	.01	.00
☐ 323	Al Newman	.06	.03	.00	☐ 362	Luis Quinones	.08	.04	.01
☐ 324	David Palmer	.03	.01	.00	☐ 363	Jose Guzman	.08	.04	.01
☐ 325	Garry Templeton	.06	.03	.00	☐ 364	Randy Bush	.03	.01	.00
☐ 326	Mark Gubicza	.12	.06	.01	☐ 365	Rick Rhoden	.06	.03	.00
☐ 327	Dale Sveum	.15	.07	.01	☐ 366	Mark McGwire	3.00	1.50	.30
☐ 328	Bob Welch	.06	.03	.00	☐ 367	Jeff Lahti	.03	.01	.00

		MINT	EXC	G-VG				MINT	EXC	G-VG
☐ 368	John McNamara MG (checklist back)	.06	.03	.00		☐ 412	Eric Davis	.90	.45	.09
						☐ 413	Moose Haas	.03	.01	.00
☐ 369	Brian Dayett	.03	.01	.00		☐ 414	Joe Orsulak	.03	.01	.00
☐ 370	Fred Lynn	.10	.05	.01		☐ 415	Bobby Witt	.25	.12	.02
☐ 371	Mark Eichhorn	.08	.04	.01		☐ 416	Tom Nieto	.03	.01	.00
☐ 372	Jerry Mumphrey	.03	.01	.00		☐ 417	Pat Perry	.03	.01	.00
☐ 373	Jeff Dedmon	.03	.01	.00		☐ 418	Dick Williams MG (checklist back)	.06	.03	.00
☐ 374	Glenn Hoffman	.03	.01	.00						
☐ 375	Ron Guidry	.10	.05	.01		☐ 419	Mark Portugal	.15	.07	.01
☐ 376	Scott Bradley	.03	.01	.00		☐ 420	Will Clark	5.00	2.50	.50
☐ 377	John Henry Johnson	.03	.01	.00		☐ 421	Jose DeLeon	.06	.03	.00
☐ 378	Rafael Santana	.03	.01	.00		☐ 422	Jack Howell	.03	.01	.00
☐ 379	John Russell	.03	.01	.00		☐ 423	Jaime Cocanower	.03	.01	.00
☐ 380	Rich Gossage	.08	.04	.01		☐ 424	Chris Speier	.03	.01	.00
☐ 381	Expos Team (mound conference)	.03	.01	.00		☐ 425	Tom Seaver	.25	.12	.02
						☐ 426	Floyd Rayford	.03	.01	.00
☐ 382	Rudy Law	.03	.01	.00		☐ 427	Edwin Nunez	.03	.01	.00
☐ 383	Ron Davis	.03	.01	.00		☐ 428	Bruce Bochy	.03	.01	.00
☐ 384	Johnny Grubb	.03	.01	.00		☐ 429	Tim Pyznarski	.08	.04	.01
☐ 385	Orel Hershiser	.30	.15	.03		☐ 430	Mike Schmidt	.35	.17	.03
☐ 386	Dickie Thon	.03	.01	.00		☐ 431	Dodgers Team (mound conference)	.06	.03	.00
☐ 387	T.R. Bryden	.06	.03	.00						
☐ 388	Geno Petralli	.03	.01	.00		☐ 432	Jim Slaton	.03	.01	.00
☐ 389	Jeff Robinson (Giants pitcher)	.08	.04	.01		☐ 433	Ed Hearn	.06	.03	.00
						☐ 434	Mike Fischlin	.03	.01	.00
☐ 390	Gary Matthews	.03	.01	.00		☐ 435	Bruce Sutter	.08	.04	.01
☐ 391	Jay Howell	.06	.03	.00		☐ 436	Andy Allanson	.06	.03	.00
☐ 392	Checklist 265-396	.06	.01	.00		☐ 437	Ted Power	.03	.01	.00
☐ 393	Pete Rose MG (checklist back)	.35	.17	.03		☐ 438	Kelly Downs	.25	.12	.02
						☐ 439	Karl Best	.03	.01	.00
☐ 394	Mike Bielecki	.15	.07	.01		☐ 440	Willie McGee	.10	.05	.01
☐ 395	Damaso Garcia	.03	.01	.00		☐ 441	Dave Leiper	.06	.03	.00
☐ 396	Tim Lollar	.03	.01	.00		☐ 442	Mitch Webster	.03	.01	.00
☐ 397	Greg Walker	.06	.03	.00		☐ 443	John Felske MG (checklist back)	.06	.03	.00
☐ 398	Brad Havens	.03	.01	.00						
☐ 399	Curt Ford	.06	.03	.00		☐ 444	Jeff Russell	.06	.03	.00
☐ 400	George Brett	.30	.15	.03		☐ 445	Dave Lopes	.06	.03	.00
☐ 401	Billy Jo Robidoux	.06	.03	.00		☐ 446	Chuck Finley	.35	.17	.03
☐ 402	Mike Trujillo	.03	.01	.00		☐ 447	Bill Almon	.03	.01	.00
☐ 403	Jerry Royster	.03	.01	.00		☐ 448	Chris Bosio	.30	.15	.03
☐ 404	Doug Sisk	.03	.01	.00		☐ 449	Pat Dodson	.10	.05	.01
☐ 405	Brook Jacoby	.06	.03	.00		☐ 450	Kirby Puckett	.60	.30	.06
☐ 406	Yankees Team (Henderson/Mattingly)	.25	.12	.02		☐ 451	Joe Sambito	.03	.01	.00
						☐ 452	Dave Henderson	.06	.03	.00
☐ 407	Jim Acker	.03	.01	.00		☐ 453	Scott Terry	.25	.12	.02
☐ 408	John Mizerock	.03	.01	.00		☐ 454	Luis Salazar	.03	.01	.00
☐ 409	Milt Thompson	.06	.03	.00		☐ 455	Mike Boddicker	.06	.03	.00
☐ 410	Fernando Valenzuela	.15	.07	.01		☐ 456	A's Team (mound conference)	.03	.01	.00
☐ 411	Darnell Coles	.03	.01	.00						

		MINT	EXC	G-VG
☐ 457	Len Matuszek	.03	.01	.00
☐ 458	Kelly Gruber	.08	.04	.01
☐ 459	Dennis Eckersley	.12	.06	.01
☐ 460	Darryl Strawberry	.50	.25	.05
☐ 461	Craig McMurtry	.03	.01	.00
☐ 462	Scott Fletcher	.03	.01	.00
☐ 463	Tom Candiotti	.03	.01	.00
☐ 464	Butch Wynegar	.03	.01	.00
☐ 465	Todd Worrell	.20	.10	.02
☐ 466	Kal Daniels	.60	.30	.06
☐ 467	Randy St. Claire	.03	.01	.00
☐ 468	George Bamberger MG (checklist back)	.06	.03	.00
☐ 469	Mike Diaz	.10	.05	.01
☐ 470	Dave Dravecky	.08	.04	.01
☐ 471	Ronn Reynolds	.03	.01	.00
☐ 472	Bill Doran	.08	.04	.01
☐ 473	Steve Farr	.03	.01	.00
☐ 474	Jerry Narron	.03	.01	.00
☐ 475	Scott Garrelts	.06	.03	.00
☐ 476	Danny Tartabull	.75	.35	.07
☐ 477	Ken Howell	.03	.01	.00
☐ 478	Tim Laudner	.03	.01	.00
☐ 479	Bob Sebra	.08	.04	.01
☐ 480	Jim Rice	.15	.07	.01
☐ 481	Phillies Team (Glenn Wilson, Juan Samuel, and Von Hayes)	.06	.03	.00
☐ 482	Daryl Boston	.03	.01	.00
☐ 483	Dwight Lowry	.08	.04	.01
☐ 484	Jim Traber	.03	.01	.00
☐ 485	Tony Fernandez	.12	.06	.01
☐ 486	Otis Nixon	.08	.04	.01
☐ 487	Dave Gumpert	.03	.01	.00
☐ 488	Ray Knight	.06	.03	.00
☐ 489	Bill Gullickson	.03	.01	.00
☐ 490	Dale Murphy	.30	.15	.03
☐ 491	Ron Karkovice	.06	.03	.00
☐ 492	Mike Heath	.03	.01	.00
☐ 493	Tom Lasorda MG (checklist back)	.08	.04	.01
☐ 494	Barry Jones	.10	.05	.01
☐ 495	Gorman Thomas	.08	.04	.01
☐ 496	Bruce Bochte	.03	.01	.00
☐ 497	Dale Mohorcic	.12	.06	.01
☐ 498	Bob Kearney	.03	.01	.00
☐ 499	Bruce Ruffin	.12	.06	.01

		MINT	EXC	G-VG
☐ 500	Don Mattingly	1.25	.60	.12
☐ 501	Craig Lefferts	.06	.03	.00
☐ 502	Dick Schofield	.03	.01	.00
☐ 503	Larry Andersen	.03	.01	.00
☐ 504	Mickey Hatcher	.03	.01	.00
☐ 505	Bryn Smith	.06	.03	.00
☐ 506	Orioles Team (mound conference)	.03	.01	.00
☐ 507	Dave Stapleton (infielder)	.03	.01	.00
☐ 508	Scott Bankhead	.08	.04	.01
☐ 509	Enos Cabell	.03	.01	.00
☐ 510	Tom Henke	.08	.04	.01
☐ 511	Steve Lyons	.03	.01	.00
☐ 512	Dave Magadan	.40	.20	.04
☐ 513	Carmen Castillo	.03	.01	.00
☐ 514	Orlando Mercado	.03	.01	.00
☐ 515	Willie Hernandez	.08	.04	.01
☐ 516	Ted Simmons	.08	.04	.01
☐ 517	Mario Soto	.03	.01	.00
☐ 518	Gene Mauch MG (checklist back)	.06	.03	.00
☐ 519	Curt Young	.03	.01	.00
☐ 520	Jack Clark	.18	.09	.01
☐ 521	Rick Reuschel	.08	.04	.01
☐ 522	Checklist 397-528	.06	.01	.00
☐ 523	Earnie Riles	.03	.01	.00
☐ 524	Bob Shirley	.03	.01	.00
☐ 525	Phil Bradley	.08	.04	.01
☐ 526	Roger Mason	.03	.01	.00
☐ 527	Jim Wohlford	.03	.01	.00
☐ 528	Ken Dixon	.03	.01	.00
☐ 529	Alvaro Espinoza	.03	.01	.00
☐ 530	Tony Gwynn	.40	.20	.04
☐ 531	Astros Team (Y. Berra conference)	.10	.05	.01
☐ 532	Jeff Stone	.03	.01	.00
☐ 533	Argenis Salazar	.03	.01	.00
☐ 534	Scott Sanderson	.03	.01	.00
☐ 535	Tony Armas	.06	.03	.00
☐ 536	Terry Mulholland	.08	.04	.01
☐ 537	Rance Mulliniks	.03	.01	.00
☐ 538	Tom Niedenfuer	.03	.01	.00
☐ 539	Reid Nichols	.03	.01	.00
☐ 540	Terry Kennedy	.03	.01	.00
☐ 541	Rafael Belliard	.06	.03	.00
☐ 542	Ricky Horton	.03	.01	.00
☐ 543	Dave Johnson MG (checklist back)	.08	.04	.01

		MINT	EXC	G-VG
☐ 544	Zane Smith	.06	.03	.00
☐ 545	Buddy Bell	.08	.04	.01
☐ 546	Mike Morgan	.06	.03	.00
☐ 547	Rob Deer	.15	.07	.01
☐ 548	Bill Mooneyham	.06	.03	.00
☐ 549	Bob Melvin	.03	.01	.00
☐ 550	Pete Incaviglia	.60	.30	.06
☐ 551	Frank Wills	.03	.01	.00
☐ 552	Larry Sheets	.06	.03	.00
☐ 553	Mike Maddux	.12	.06	.01
☐ 554	Buddy Biancalana	.03	.01	.00
☐ 555	Dennis Rasmussen	.06	.03	.00
☐ 556	Angels Team	.06	.03	.00
	(Lachemann, Witt,			
	and Boone)			
☐ 557	John Cerutti	.15	.07	.01
☐ 558	Greg Gagne	.03	.01	.00
☐ 559	Lance McCullers	.06	.03	.00
☐ 560	Glenn Davis	.25	.12	.02
☐ 561	Rey Quinones	.15	.07	.01
☐ 562	Bryan Clutterbuck	.06	.03	.00
☐ 563	John Stefero	.03	.01	.00
☐ 564	Larry McWilliams	.03	.01	.00
☐ 565	Dusty Baker	.06	.03	.00
☐ 566	Tim Hulett	.03	.01	.00
☐ 567	Greg Mathews	.20	.10	.02
☐ 568	Earl Weaver MG	.08	.04	.01
	(checklist back)			
☐ 569	Wade Rowdon	.06	.03	.00
☐ 570	Sid Fernandez	.12	.06	.01
☐ 571	Ozzie Virgil	.03	.01	.00
☐ 572	Pete Ladd	.03	.01	.00
☐ 573	Hal McRae	.06	.03	.00
☐ 574	Manny Lee	.03	.01	.00
☐ 575	Pat Tabler	.06	.03	.00
☐ 576	Frank Pastore	.03	.01	.00
☐ 577	Dann Bilardello	.03	.01	.00
☐ 578	Billy Hatcher	.06	.03	.00
☐ 579	Rick Burleson	.06	.03	.00
☐ 580	Mike Krukow	.03	.01	.00
☐ 581	Cubs Team	.03	.01	.00
	(Cey/Trout)			
☐ 582	Bruce Berenyi	.03	.01	.00
☐ 583	Junior Ortiz	.03	.01	.00
☐ 584	Ron Kittle	.08	.04	.01
☐ 585	Scott Bailes	.10	.05	.01
☐ 586	Ben Oglivie	.06	.03	.00
☐ 587	Eric Plunk	.06	.03	.00
☐ 588	Wallace Johnson	.06	.03	.00

		MINT	EXC	G-VG
☐ 589	Steve Crawford	.03	.01	.00
☐ 590	Vince Coleman	.20	.10	.02
☐ 591	Spike Owen	.03	.01	.00
☐ 592	Chris Welsh	.03	.01	.00
☐ 593	Chuck Tanner MG	.06	.03	.00
	(checklist back)			
☐ 594	Rick Anderson	.08	.04	.01
☐ 595	Keith Hernandez AS	.10	.05	.01
☐ 596	Steve Sax AS	.08	.04	.01
☐ 597	Mike Schmidt AS	.25	.12	.02
☐ 598	Ozzie Smith AS	.10	.05	.01
☐ 599	Tony Gwynn AS	.20	.10	.02
☐ 600	Dave Parker AS	.08	.04	.01
☐ 601	Darryl Strawberry AS	.20	.10	.02
☐ 602	Gary Carter AS	.12	.06	.01
☐ 603A	Dwight Gooden AS	1.00	.50	.10
	ERR (no trademark)			
☐ 603B	Dwight Gooden AS			
	COR	.30	.15	.03
☐ 604	Fern. Valenzuela AS	.10	.05	.01
☐ 605	Todd Worrell AS	.08	.04	.01
☐ 606A	Don Mattingly AS	2.00	1.00	.20
	ERR (no trademark)			
☐ 606B	Don Mattingly AS			
	COR	.65	.30	.06
☐ 607	Tony Bernazard AS	.06	.03	.00
☐ 608	Wade Boggs AS	.35	.17	.03
☐ 609	Cal Ripken AS	.15	.07	.01
☐ 610	Jim Rice AS	.10	.05	.01
☐ 611	Kirby Puckett AS	.25	.12	.02
☐ 612	George Bell AS	.10	.05	.01
☐ 613	Lance Parrish AS			
	UER	.08	.04	.01
	(Pitcher heading			
	on back)			
☐ 614	Roger Clemens AS	.20	.10	.02
☐ 615	Teddy Higuera AS	.06	.03	.00
☐ 616	Dave Righetti AS	.08	.04	.01
☐ 617	Al Nipper AS	.03	.01	.00
☐ 618	Tom Kelly MG	.08	.04	.01
	(checklist back)			
☐ 619	Jerry Reed	.03	.01	.00
☐ 620	Jose Canseco	4.00	2.00	.40
☐ 621	Danny Cox	.06	.03	.00
☐ 622	Glenn Braggs	.45	.22	.04
☐ 623	Kurt Stillwell	.20	.10	.02
☐ 624	Tim Burke	.06	.03	.00
☐ 625	Mookie Wilson	.06	.03	.00
☐ 626	Joel Skinner	.03	.01	.00

		MINT	EXC	G-VG
☐ 627	Ken Oberkfell	.03	.01	.00
☐ 628	Bob Walk	.03	.01	.00
☐ 629	Larry Parrish	.03	.01	.00
☐ 630	John Candelaria	.06	.03	.00
☐ 631	Tigers Team (mound conference)	.03	.01	.00
☐ 632	Rob Woodward	.06	.03	.00
☐ 633	Jose Uribe	.03	.01	.00
☐ 634	Rafael Palmeiro	.75	.35	.07
☐ 635	Ken Schrom	.03	.01	.00
☐ 636	Darren Daulton	.03	.01	.00
☐ 637	Bip Roberts	.12	.06	.01
☐ 638	Rich Bordi	.03	.01	.00
☐ 639	Gerald Perry	.08	.04	.01
☐ 640	Mark Clear	.03	.01	.00
☐ 641	Domingo Ramos	.03	.01	.00
☐ 642	Al Pulido	.06	.03	.00
☐ 643	Ron Shepherd	.06	.03	.00
☐ 644	John Denny	.06	.03	.00
☐ 645	Dwight Evans	.10	.05	.01
☐ 646	Mike Mason	.03	.01	.00
☐ 647	Tom Lawless	.03	.01	.00
☐ 648	Barry Larkin	1.25	.60	.12
☐ 649	Mickey Tettleton	.10	.05	.01
☐ 650	Hubie Brooks	.08	.04	.01
☐ 651	Benny Distefano	.06	.03	.00
☐ 652	Terry Forster	.06	.03	.00
☐ 653	Kevin Mitchell	3.00	1.50	.30
☐ 654	Checklist 529-660	.06	.01	.00
☐ 655	Jesse Barfield	.15	.07	.01
☐ 656	Rangers Team (Valentine/R. Wright)	.03	.01	.00
☐ 657	Tom Waddell	.03	.01	.00
☐ 658	Robby Thompson	.20	.10	.02
☐ 659	Aurelio Lopez	.03	.01	.00
☐ 660	Bob Horner	.10	.05	.01
☐ 661	Lou Whitaker	.12	.06	.01
☐ 662	Frank DiPino	.03	.01	.00
☐ 663	Cliff Johnson	.03	.01	.00
☐ 664	Mike Marshall	.10	.05	.01
☐ 665	Rod Scurry	.03	.01	.00
☐ 666	Von Hayes	.08	.04	.01
☐ 667	Ron Hassey	.03	.01	.00
☐ 668	Juan Bonilla	.03	.01	.00
☐ 669	Bud Black	.03	.01	.00
☐ 670	Jose Cruz	.06	.03	.00
☐ 671A	Ray Soff ERR (no D* before copyright line)	.08	.04	.01
☐ 671B	Ray Soff COR (D* before copyright line)	.08	.04	.01
☐ 672	Chili Davis	.08	.04	.01
☐ 673	Don Sutton	.12	.06	.01
☐ 674	Bill Campbell	.03	.01	.00
☐ 675	Ed Romero	.03	.01	.00
☐ 676	Charlie Moore	.03	.01	.00
☐ 677	Bob Grich	.06	.03	.00
☐ 678	Carney Lansford	.10	.05	.01
☐ 679	Kent Hrbek	.15	.07	.01
☐ 680	Ryne Sandberg	.20	.10	.02
☐ 681	George Bell	.20	.10	.02
☐ 682	Jerry Reuss	.03	.01	.00
☐ 683	Gary Roenicke	.03	.01	.00
☐ 684	Kent Tekulve	.03	.01	.00
☐ 685	Jerry Hairston	.03	.01	.00
☐ 686	Doyle Alexander	.03	.01	.00
☐ 687	Alan Trammell	.15	.07	.01
☐ 688	Juan Beniquez	.03	.01	.00
☐ 689	Darrell Porter	.03	.01	.00
☐ 690	Dane Iorg	.03	.01	.00
☐ 691	Dave Parker	.12	.06	.01
☐ 692	Frank White	.06	.03	.00
☐ 693	Terry Puhl	.03	.01	.00
☐ 694	Phil Niekro	.12	.06	.01
☐ 695	Chico Walker	.08	.04	.01
☐ 696	Gary Lucas	.03	.01	.00
☐ 697	Ed Lynch	.03	.01	.00
☐ 698	Ernie Whitt	.03	.01	.00
☐ 699	Ken Landreaux	.03	.01	.00
☐ 700	Dave Bergman	.03	.01	.00
☐ 701	Willie Randolph	.06	.03	.00
☐ 702	Greg Gross	.03	.01	.00
☐ 703	Dave Schmidt	.06	.03	.00
☐ 704	Jesse Orosco	.03	.01	.00
☐ 705	Bruce Hurst	.10	.05	.01
☐ 706	Rick Manning	.03	.01	.00
☐ 707	Bob McClure	.03	.01	.00
☐ 708	Scott McGregor	.06	.03	.00
☐ 709	Dave Kingman	.08	.04	.01
☐ 710	Gary Gaetti	.10	.05	.01
☐ 711	Ken Griffey	.08	.04	.01
☐ 712	Don Robinson	.03	.01	.00
☐ 713	Tom Brookens	.03	.01	.00
☐ 714	Dan Quisenberry	.08	.04	.01
☐ 715	Bob Dernier	.03	.01	.00
☐ 716	Rick Leach	.03	.01	.00
☐ 717	Ed VandeBerg	.03	.01	.00

		MINT	EXC	G-VG
☐ 718	Steve Carlton	.20	.10	.02
☐ 719	Tom Hume	.03	.01	.00
☐ 720	Richard Dotson	.06	.03	.00
☐ 721	Tom Herr	.06	.03	.00
☐ 722	Bob Knepper	.06	.03	.00
☐ 723	Brett Butler	.06	.03	.00
☐ 724	Greg Minton	.03	.01	.00
☐ 725	George Hendrick	.03	.01	.00
☐ 726	Frank Tanana	.06	.03	.00
☐ 727	Mike Moore	.08	.04	.01
☐ 728	Tippy Martinez	.03	.01	.00
☐ 729	Tom Paciorek	.03	.01	.00
☐ 730	Eric Show	.06	.03	.00
☐ 731	Dave Concepcion	.06	.03	.00
☐ 732	Manny Trillo	.03	.01	.00
☐ 733	Bill Caudill	.03	.01	.00
☐ 734	Bill Madlock	.08	.04	.01
☐ 735	Rickey Henderson	.30	.15	.03
☐ 736	Steve Bedrosian	.10	.05	.01
☐ 737	Floyd Bannister	.03	.01	.00
☐ 738	Jorge Orta	.03	.01	.00
☐ 739	Chet Lemon	.03	.01	.00
☐ 740	Rich Gedman	.03	.01	.00
☐ 741	Paul Molitor	.10	.05	.01
☐ 742	Andy McGaffigan	.03	.01	.00
☐ 743	Dwayne Murphy	.03	.01	.00
☐ 744	Roy Smalley	.03	.01	.00
☐ 745	Glenn Hubbard	.03	.01	.00
☐ 746	Bob Ojeda	.06	.03	.00
☐ 747	Johnny Ray	.06	.03	.00
☐ 748	Mike Flanagan	.06	.03	.00
☐ 749	Ozzie Smith	.15	.07	.01
☐ 750	Steve Trout	.03	.01	.00
☐ 751	Garth Iorg	.03	.01	.00
☐ 752	Dan Petry	.03	.01	.00
☐ 753	Rick Honeycutt	.03	.01	.00
☐ 754	Dave LaPoint	.06	.03	.00
☐ 755	Luis Aguayo	.03	.01	.00
☐ 756	Carlton Fisk	.15	.07	.01
☐ 757	Nolan Ryan	.35	.17	.03
☐ 758	Tony Bernazard	.03	.01	.00
☐ 759	Joel Youngblood	.03	.01	.00
☐ 760	Mike Witt	.06	.03	.00
☐ 761	Greg Pryor	.03	.01	.00
☐ 762	Gary Ward	.03	.01	.00
☐ 763	Tim Flannery	.03	.01	.00
☐ 764	Bill Buckner	.06	.03	.00
☐ 765	Kirk Gibson	.15	.07	.01
☐ 766	Don Aase	.03	.01	.00

		MINT	EXC	G-VG
☐ 767	Ron Cey	.06	.03	.00
☐ 768	Dennis Lamp	.03	.01	.00
☐ 769	Steve Sax	.12	.06	.01
☐ 770	Dave Winfield	.20	.10	.02
☐ 771	Shane Rawley	.06	.03	.00
☐ 772	Harold Baines	.10	.05	.01
☐ 773	Robin Yount	.25	.12	.02
☐ 774	Wayne Krenchicki	.03	.01	.00
☐ 775	Joaquin Andujar	.06	.03	.00
☐ 776	Tom Brunansky	.10	.05	.01
☐ 777	Chris Chambliss	.06	.03	.00
☐ 778	Jack Morris	.10	.05	.01
☐ 779	Craig Reynolds	.03	.01	.00
☐ 780	Andre Thornton	.06	.03	.00
☐ 781	Atlee Hammaker	.03	.01	.00
☐ 782	Brian Downing	.06	.03	.00
☐ 783	Willie Wilson	.08	.04	.01
☐ 784	Cal Ripken	.20	.10	.02
☐ 785	Terry Francona	.03	.01	.00
☐ 786	Jimy Williams MG (checklist back)	.06	.03	.00
☐ 787	Alejandro Pena	.03	.01	.00
☐ 788	Tim Stoddard	.03	.01	.00
☐ 789	Dan Schatzeder	.03	.01	.00
☐ 790	Julio Cruz	.03	.01	.00
☐ 791	Lance Parrish UER (no trademark, never corrected)	.15	.07	.01
☐ 792	Checklist 661-792	.06	.01	.00

1987 Topps Traded

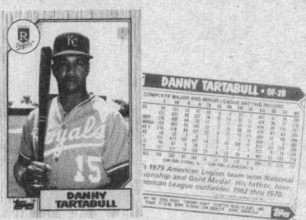

This 132-card Traded or extended set was distributed by Topps to dealers in a special green and white box as a complete set. The card fronts are identical in style to the Topps regular issue and are also 2 ½" by 3 ½". The backs are printed in yellow and blue on white card stock. Cards are numbered (with a T suffix) alphabetically according to the name of the player. Topps also produced a specially boxed "glossy" edition, frequently referred to as the Topps Traded Tiffany set. This year Topps did not disclose the number of sets they produced or sold. It is apparent from the availability that there were many more sets produced this year compared to the 1984-86 Tiffany sets, perhaps more than three times as many. The checklist of cards is identical to that of the normal non-glossy cards. There are two primary distinguishing features of the Tiffany cards—white card stock reverses and high gloss obverses. These Tiffany cards are valued at approximately four times the values listed below.

		MINT	EXC	G-VG
	COMPLETE SET (132)	15.00	7.00	1.40
	COMMON PLAYER (1-132)	.05	.02	.00
☐	1T Bill Almon	.05	.02	.00
☐	2T Scott Bankhead	.10	.05	.01
☐	3T Eric Bell	.10	.05	.01
☐	4T Juan Beniquez	.05	.02	.00
☐	5T Juan Berenguer	.05	.02	.00

		MINT	EXC	G-VG
☐	6T Greg Booker	.05	.02	.00
☐	7T Thad Bosley	.05	.02	.00
☐	8T Larry Bowa MG	.10	.05	.01
☐	9T Greg Brock	.10	.05	.01
☐	10T Bob Brower	.12	.06	.01
☐	11T Jerry Browne	.25	.12	.02
☐	12T Ralph Bryant	.10	.05	.01
☐	13T DeWayne Buice	.10	.05	.01
☐	14T Ellis Burks	2.00	1.00	.20
☐	15T Ivan Calderon	.20	.10	.02
☐	16T Jeff Calhoun	.05	.02	.00
☐	17T Casey Candaele	.10	.05	.01
☐	18T John Cangelosi	.10	.05	.01
☐	19T Steve Carlton	.25	.12	.02
☐	20T Juan Castillo	.10	.05	.01
☐	21T Rick Cerone	.05	.02	.00
☐	22T Ron Cey	.10	.05	.01
☐	23T John Christensen	.05	.02	.00
☐	24T David Cone	1.75	.85	.17
☐	25T Chuck Crim	.10	.05	.01
☐	26T Storm Davis	.15	.07	.01
☐	27T Andre Dawson	.35	.17	.03
☐	28T Rick Dempsey	.10	.05	.01
☐	29T Doug Drabek	.15	.07	.01
☐	30T Mike Dunne	.05	.02	.00
☐	31T Dennis Eckersley	.25	.12	.02
☐	32T Lee Elia MG	.05	.02	.00
☐	33T Brian Fisher	.10	.05	.01
☐	34T Terry Francona	.05	.02	.00
☐	35T Willie Fraser	.10	.05	.01
☐	36T Billy Gardner MG	.05	.02	.00
☐	37T Ken Gerhart	.10	.05	.01
☐	38T Dan Gladden	.10	.05	.01
☐	39T Jim Gott	.05	.02	.00
☐	40T Cecilio Guante	.05	.02	.00
☐	41T Albert Hall	.10	.05	.01
☐	42T Terry Harper	.05	.02	.00
☐	43T Mickey Hatcher	.05	.02	.00
☐	44T Brad Havens	.05	.02	.00
☐	45T Neal Heaton	.05	.02	.00
☐	46T Mike Henneman	.30	.15	.03
☐	47T Donnie Hill	.05	.02	.00
☐	48T Guy Hoffman	.05	.02	.00
☐	49T Brian Holton	.15	.07	.01
☐	50T Charles Hudson	.05	.02	.00
☐	51T Danny Jackson	.15	.07	.01
☐	52T Reggie Jackson	.50	.25	.05
☐	53T Chris James	.45	.22	.04
☐	54T Dion James	.10	.05	.01

		MINT	EXC	G-VG
☐ 55T	Stan Jefferson	.20	.10	.02
☐ 56T	Joe Johnson	.10	.05	.01
☐ 57T	Terry Kennedy	.05	.02	.00
☐ 58T	Mike Kingery	.10	.05	.01
☐ 59T	Ray Knight	.10	.05	.01
☐ 60T	Gene Larkin	.30	.15	.03
☐ 61T	Mike LaValliere	.10	.05	.01
☐ 62T	Jack Lazorko	.05	.02	.00
☐ 63T	Terry Leach	.12	.06	.01
☐ 64T	Tim Leary	.20	.10	.02
☐ 65T	Jim Lindeman	.10	.05	.01
☐ 66T	Steve Lombardozzi	.10	.05	.01
☐ 67T	Bill Long	.12	.06	.01
☐ 68T	Barry Lyons	.35	.17	.03
☐ 69T	Shane Mack	.12	.06	.01
☐ 70T	Greg Maddux	.75	.35	.07
☐ 71T	Bill Madlock	.10	.05	.01
☐ 72T	Joe Magrane	1.25	.60	.12
☐ 73T	Dave Martinez	.20	.10	.02
☐ 74T	Fred McGriff	2.00	1.00	.20
☐ 75T	Mark McLemore	.05	.02	.00
☐ 76T	Kevin McReynolds	.20	.10	.02
☐ 77T	Dave Meads	.10	.05	.01
☐ 78T	Eddie Milner	.05	.02	.00
☐ 79T	Greg Minton	.05	.02	.00
☐ 80T	John Mitchell	.15	.07	.01
☐ 81T	Kevin Mitchell	1.25	.60	.12
☐ 82T	Charlie Moore	.05	.02	.00
☐ 83T	Jeff Musselman	.15	.07	.01
☐ 84T	Gene Nelson	.05	.02	.00
☐ 85T	Graig Nettles	.15	.07	.01
☐ 86T	Al Newman	.05	.02	.00
☐ 87T	Reid Nichols	.05	.02	.00
☐ 88T	Tom Niedenfuer	.05	.02	.00
☐ 89T	Joe Niekro	.10	.05	.01
☐ 90T	Tom Nieto	.05	.02	.00
☐ 91T	Matt Nokes	.45	.22	.04
☐ 92T	Dickie Noles	.05	.02	.00
☐ 93T	Pat Pacillo	.10	.05	.01
☐ 94T	Lance Parrish	.15	.07	.01
☐ 95T	Tony Pena	.15	.07	.01
☐ 96T	Luis Polonia	.25	.12	.02
☐ 97T	Randy Ready	.10	.05	.01
☐ 98T	Jeff Reardon	.15	.07	.01
☐ 99T	Gary Redus	.05	.02	.00
☐ 100T	Jeff Reed	.05	.02	.00
☐ 101T	Rick Rhoden	.10	.05	.01
☐ 102T	Cal Ripken Sr. MG	.05	.02	.00
☐ 103T	Wally Ritchie	.10	.05	.01
☐ 104T	Jeff Robinson (Tigers pitcher)	.35	.17	.03
☐ 105T	Gary Roenicke	.05	.02	.00
☐ 106T	Jerry Royster	.05	.02	.00
☐ 107T	Mark Salas	.05	.02	.00
☐ 108T	Luis Salazar	.05	.02	.00
☐ 109T	Benny Santiago	1.00	.50	.10
☐ 110T	Dave Schmidt	.10	.05	.01
☐ 111T	Kevin Seitzer	1.00	.50	.10
☐ 112T	John Shelby	.05	.02	.00
☐ 113T	Steve Shields	.05	.02	.00
☐ 114T	John Smiley	.35	.17	.03
☐ 115T	Chris Speier	.05	.02	.00
☐ 116T	Mike Stanley	.15	.07	.01
☐ 117T	Terry Steinbach	.50	.25	.05
☐ 118T	Les Straker	.12	.06	.01
☐ 119T	Jim Sundberg	.05	.02	.00
☐ 120T	Danny Tartabull	.30	.15	.03
☐ 121T	Tom Trebelhorn MG	.05	.02	.00
☐ 122T	Dave Valle	.05	.02	.00
☐ 123T	Ed VandeBerg	.05	.02	.00
☐ 124T	Andy Van Slyke	.20	.10	.02
☐ 125T	Gary Ward	.05	.02	.00
☐ 126T	Alan Wiggins	.05	.02	.00
☐ 127T	Bill Wilkinson	.12	.06	.01
☐ 128T	Frank Williams	.05	.02	.00
☐ 129T	Matt Williams	2.00	1.00	.20
☐ 130T	Jim Winn	.05	.02	.00
☐ 131T	Matt Young	.05	.02	.00
☐ 132T	Checklist	.05	.01	.00

1988 Topps

This 792-card set features backs that are printed in orange and black on white card stock. The manager cards contain a checklist of the respective team's players on the back. Subsets in the set include Record Breakers (1-7), Turn Back the Clock (661-665), and All-Star selections (386-407). The Team Leader cards typically show two players together inside a white cloud. Topps also produced a specially boxed "glossy" edition, frequently referred to as the Topps Tiffany set. This year, again, Topps did not disclose the number of Tiffany sets they produced or sold. It is apparent from the availability that there were many more sets produced this year compared to the 1984-86 Tiffany sets, perhaps more than three times as many (similar to the 1987 Tiffany cards). The checklist of cards (792 regular and 132 Traded) is identical to that of the normal non-glossy cards. There are two primary distinguishing features of the Tiffany cards—white card stock reverses and high gloss obverses. These Tiffany cards are valued at approximately four times the values listed below.

	MINT	EXC	G-VG
COMPLETE SET (792)	25.00	12.50	2.50
COMMON PLAYER (1-792)	.03	.01	.00

			MINT	EXC	G-VG
☐	1	Vince Coleman RB .. 100 Steals for Third Cons. Season	.20	.04	.01

			MINT	EXC	G-VG
☐	2	Don Mattingly RB ... Six Grand Slams	.30	.15	.03
☐	3A	Mark McGwire RB .. Rookie Homer Record (white spot behind left foot)	1.00	.50	.10
☐	3B	Mark McGwire RB ... Rookie Homer Record (no white spot)	.30	.15	.03
☐	4A	Eddie Murray RB ... Switch Home Runs, Two Straight Games (caption in box on card front)	1.00	.50	.10
☐	4B	Eddie Murray RB ... Switch Home Runs, Two Straight Games (no caption on front)	.20	.10	.02
☐	5	Phil/Joe Niekro RB .. Brothers Win Record	.06	.03	.00
☐	6	Nolan Ryan RB ..... 11th Season with 200 Strikeouts	.20	.10	.02
☐	7	Benito Santiago RB . 34-Game Hitting Streak, Rookie Record	.10	.05	.01
☐	8	Kevin Elster	.15	.07	.01
☐	9	Andy Hawkins	.03	.01	.00
☐	10	Ryne Sandberg	.15	.07	.01
☐	11	Mike Young	.03	.01	.00
☐	12	Bill Schroeder	.03	.01	.00
☐	13	Andres Thomas	.03	.01	.00
☐	14	Sparky Anderson MG (checklist back)	.06	.03	.00
☐	15	Chili Davis	.06	.03	.00
☐	16	Kirk McCaskill	.03	.01	.00
☐	17	Ron Oester	.03	.01	.00
☐	18A	Al Leiter ERR (photo actually Steve George, right ear visible)	.90	.45	.09
☐	18B	Al Leiter COR (left ear visible)	.60	.30	.06
☐	19	Mark Davidson	.10	.05	.01
☐	20	Kevin Gross	.03	.01	.00
☐	21	Red Sox TL Wade Boggs and Spike Owen	.12	.06	.01

			MINT	EXC	G-VG				MINT	EXC	G-VG
☐	22	Greg Swindell	.12	.06	.01	☐	68	Dave Dravecky	.08	.04	.01
☐	23	Ken Landreaux	.03	.01	.00	☐	69	Mike Hart	.06	.03	.00
☐	24	Jim Deshaies	.03	.01	.00	☐	70	Roger Clemens	.50	.25	.05
☐	25	Andres Galarraga	.15	.07	.01	☐	71	Gary Pettis	.03	.01	.00
☐	26	Mitch Williams	.06	.03	.00	☐	72	Dennis Eckersley	.10	.05	.01
☐	27	R.J. Reynolds	.03	.01	.00	☐	73	Randy Bush	.03	.01	.00
☐	28	Jose Nunez	.10	.05	.01	☐	74	Tom Lasorda MG	.08	.04	.01
☐	29	Argenis Salazar	.03	.01	.00			(checklist back)			
☐	30	Sid Fernandez	.08	.04	.01	☐	75	Joe Carter	.12	.06	.01
☐	31	Bruce Bochy	.03	.01	.00	☐	76	Dennis Martinez	.03	.01	.00
☐	32	Mike Morgan	.06	.03	.00	☐	77	Tom O'Malley	.03	.01	.00
☐	33	Rob Deer	.06	.03	.00	☐	78	Dan Petry	.03	.01	.00
☐	34	Ricky Horton	.03	.01	.00	☐	79	Ernie Whitt	.03	.01	.00
☐	35	Harold Baines	.08	.04	.01	☐	80	Mark Langston	.12	.06	.01
☐	36	Jamie Moyer	.03	.01	.00	☐	81	Reds TL	.03	.01	.00
☐	37	Ed Romero	.03	.01	.00			Ron Robinson			
☐	38	Jeff Calhoun	.03	.01	.00			and John Franco			
☐	39	Gerald Perry	.06	.03	.00	☐	82	Darrel Akerfelds	.08	.04	.01
☐	40	Orel Hershiser	.20	.10	.02	☐	83	Jose Oquendo	.03	.01	.00
☐	41	Bob Melvin	.03	.01	.00	☐	84	Cecilio Guante	.03	.01	.00
☐	42	Bill Landrum	.20	.10	.02	☐	85	Howard Johnson	.12	.06	.01
☐	43	Dick Schofield	.03	.01	.00	☐	86	Ron Karkovice	.03	.01	.00
☐	44	Lou Piniella MG	.06	.03	.00	☐	87	Mike Mason	.03	.01	.00
		(checklist back)				☐	88	Earnie Riles	.03	.01	.00
☐	45	Kent Hrbek	.12	.06	.01	☐	89	Gary Thurman	.18	.09	.01
☐	46	Darnell Coles	.03	.01	.00	☐	90	Dale Murphy	.20	.10	.02
☐	47	Joaquin Andujar	.06	.03	.00	☐	91	Joey Cora	.12	.06	.01
☐	48	Alan Ashby	.03	.01	.00	☐	92	Len Matuszek	.03	.01	.00
☐	49	Dave Clark	.10	.05	.01	☐	93	Bob Sebra	.03	.01	.00
☐	50	Hubie Brooks	.08	.04	.01	☐	94	Chuck Jackson	.08	.04	.01
☐	51	Orioles TL	.15	.07	.01	☐	95	Lance Parrish	.08	.04	.01
		Eddie Murray and				☐	96	Todd Benzinger	.20	.10	.02
		Cal Ripken				☐	97	Scott Garrelts	.06	.03	.00
☐	52	Don Robinson	.03	.01	.00	☐	98	Rene Gonzales	.10	.05	.01
☐	53	Curt Wilkerson	.03	.01	.00	☐	99	Chuck Finley	.06	.03	.00
☐	54	Jim Clancy	.03	.01	.00	☐	100	Jack Clark	.12	.06	.01
☐	55	Phil Bradley	.06	.03	.00	☐	101	Allan Anderson	.06	.03	.00
☐	56	Ed Hearn	.03	.01	.00	☐	102	Barry Larkin	.18	.09	.01
☐	57	Tim Crews	.08	.04	.01	☐	103	Curt Young	.03	.01	.00
☐	58	Dave Magadan	.10	.05	.01	☐	104	Dick Williams MG	.06	.03	.00
☐	59	Danny Cox	.06	.03	.00			(checklist back)			
☐	60	Rickey Henderson	.25	.12	.02	☐	105	Jesse Orosco	.03	.01	.00
☐	61	Mark Knudson	.10	.05	.01	☐	106	Jim Walewander	.10	.05	.01
☐	62	Jeff Hamilton	.06	.03	.00	☐	107	Scott Bailes	.03	.01	.00
☐	63	Jimmy Jones	.10	.05	.01	☐	108	Steve Lyons	.03	.01	.00
☐	64	Ken Caminiti	.18	.09	.01	☐	109	Joel Skinner	.03	.01	.00
☐	65	Leon Durham	.03	.01	.00	☐	110	Teddy Higuera	.08	.04	.01
☐	66	Shane Rawley	.03	.01	.00	☐	111	Expos TL	.03	.01	.00
☐	67	Ken Oberkfell	.03	.01	.00			Hubie Brooks and			

		MINT	EXC	G-VG				MINT	EXC	G-VG
	Vance Law				☐ 157	Atlee Hammaker	...	.03	.01	.00
☐ 112	Les Lancaster	.12	.06	.01	☐ 158	Tim Hulett		.03	.01	.00
☐ 113	Kelly Gruber	.06	.03	.00	☐ 159	Brad Arnsberg		.10	.05	.01
☐ 114	Jeff Russell	.06	.03	.00	☐ 160	Willie McGee		.08	.04	.01
☐ 115	Johnny Ray	.06	.03	.00	☐ 161	Bryn Smith		.06	.03	.00
☐ 116	Jerry Don Gleaton	.03	.01	.00	☐ 162	Mark McLemore		.03	.01	.00
☐ 117	James Steels	.06	.03	.00	☐ 163	Dale Mohorcic		.03	.01	.00
☐ 118	Bob Welch	.06	.03	.00	☐ 164	Dave Johnson MG		.06	.03	.00
☐ 119	Robbie Wine	.08	.04	.01		(checklist back)				
☐ 120	Kirby Puckett	.40	.20	.04	☐ 165	Robin Yount		.20	.10	.02
☐ 121	Checklist 1-132	.06	.01	.00	☐ 166	Rick Rodriquez		.10	.05	.01
☐ 122	Tony Bernazard	.03	.01	.00	☐ 167	Rance Mulliniks		.03	.01	.00
☐ 123	Tom Candiotti	.03	.01	.00	☐ 168	Barry Jones		.03	.01	.00
☐ 124	Ray Knight	.06	.03	.00	☐ 169	Ross Jones		.08	.04	.01
☐ 125	Bruce Hurst	.10	.05	.01	☐ 170	Rich Gossage		.08	.04	.01
☐ 126	Steve Jeltz	.03	.01	.00	☐ 171	Cubs TL		.03	.01	.00
☐ 127	Jim Gott	.03	.01	.00		Shawon Dunston				
☐ 128	Johnny Grubb	.03	.01	.00		and Manny Trillo				
☐ 129	Greg Minton	.03	.01	.00	☐ 172	Lloyd McClendon		.15	.07	.01
☐ 130	Buddy Bell	.06	.03	.00	☐ 173	Eric Plunk		.03	.01	.00
☐ 131	Don Schulze	.03	.01	.00	☐ 174	Phil Garner		.03	.01	.00
☐ 132	Donnie Hill	.03	.01	.00	☐ 175	Kevin Bass		.06	.03	.00
☐ 133	Greg Mathews	.03	.01	.00	☐ 176	Jeff Reed		.03	.01	.00
☐ 134	Chuck Tanner MG	.06	.03	.00	☐ 177	Frank Tanana		.03	.01	.00
	(checklist back)				☐ 178	Dwayne Henry		.06	.03	.00
☐ 135	Dennis Rasmussen	.06	.03	.00	☐ 179	Charlie Puleo		.03	.01	.00
☐ 136	Brian Dayett	.03	.01	.00	☐ 180	Terry Kennedy		.03	.01	.00
☐ 137	Chris Bosio	.06	.03	.00	☐ 181	David Cone		.80	.40	.08
☐ 138	Mitch Webster	.03	.01	.00	☐ 182	Ken Phelps		.06	.03	.00
☐ 139	Jerry Browne	.10	.05	.01	☐ 183	Tom Lawless		.03	.01	.00
☐ 140	Jesse Barfield	.10	.05	.01	☐ 184	Ivan Calderon		.06	.03	.00
☐ 141	Royals TL	.15	.07	.01	☐ 185	Rick Rhoden		.03	.01	.00
	George Brett and				☐ 186	Rafael Palmeiro		.20	.10	.02
	Bret Saberhagen				☐ 187	Steve Kiefer		.03	.01	.00
☐ 142	Andy Van Slyke	.12	.06	.01	☐ 188	John Russell		.03	.01	.00
☐ 143	Mickey Tettleton	.08	.04	.01	☐ 189	Wes Gardner		.15	.07	.01
☐ 144	Don Gordon	.08	.04	.01	☐ 190	Candy Maldonado		.03	.01	.00
☐ 145	Bill Madlock	.06	.03	.00	☐ 191	John Cerutti		.03	.01	.00
☐ 146	Donnell Nixon	.10	.05	.01	☐ 192	Devon White		.12	.06	.01
☐ 147	Bill Buckner	.06	.03	.00	☐ 193	Brian Fisher		.03	.01	.00
☐ 148	Carmelo Martinez	.03	.01	.00	☐ 194	Tom Kelly MG		.06	.03	.00
☐ 149	Ken Howell	.03	.01	.00		(checklist back)				
☐ 150	Eric Davis	.40	.20	.04	☐ 195	Dan Quisenberry		.08	.04	.01
☐ 151	Bob Knepper	.03	.01	.00	☐ 196	Dave Engle		.03	.01	.00
☐ 152	Jody Reed	.30	.15	.03	☐ 197	Lance McCullers		.06	.03	.00
☐ 153	John Habyan	.03	.01	.00	☐ 198	Franklin Stubbs		.03	.01	.00
☐ 154	Jeff Stone	.03	.01	.00	☐ 199	Dave Meads		.08	.04	.01
☐ 155	Bruce Sutter	.08	.04	.01	☐ 200	Wade Boggs		.65	.30	.06
☐ 156	Gary Matthews	.03	.01	.00	☐ 201	Rangers TL		.06	.03	.00

		MINT	EXC	G-VG
	Bobby Valentine, Pete O'Brien, Pete Incaviglia, and Steve Buechele			
☐ 202	Glenn Hoffman	.03	.01	.00
☐ 203	Fred Toliver	.03	.01	.00
☐ 204	Paul O'Neill	.15	.07	.01
☐ 205	Nelson Liriano	.15	.07	.01
☐ 206	Domingo Ramos	.03	.01	.00
☐ 207	John Mitchell	.12	.06	.01
☐ 208	Steve Lake	.03	.01	.00
☐ 209	Richard Dotson	.03	.01	.00
☐ 210	Willie Randolph	.06	.03	.00
☐ 211	Frank DiPino	.03	.01	.00
☐ 212	Greg Brock	.03	.01	.00
☐ 213	Albert Hall	.03	.01	.00
☐ 214	Dave Schmidt	.03	.01	.00
☐ 215	Von Hayes	.08	.04	.01
☐ 216	Jerry Reuss	.03	.01	.00
☐ 217	Harry Spilman	.03	.01	.00
☐ 218	Dan Schatzeder	.03	.01	.00
☐ 219	Mike Stanley	.06	.03	.00
☐ 220	Tom Henke	.06	.03	.00
☐ 221	Rafael Belliard	.03	.01	.00
☐ 222	Steve Farr	.03	.01	.00
☐ 223	Stan Jefferson	.08	.04	.01
☐ 224	Tom Trebelhorn MG (checklist back)	.06	.03	.00
☐ 225	Mike Scioscia	.03	.01	.00
☐ 226	Dave Lopes	.06	.03	.00
☐ 227	Ed Correa	.03	.01	.00
☐ 228	Wallace Johnson	.03	.01	.00
☐ 229	Jeff Musselman	.08	.04	.01
☐ 230	Pat Tabler	.06	.03	.00
☐ 231	Pirates TL Barry Bonds and Bobby Bonilla	.10	.05	.01
☐ 232	Bob James	.03	.01	.00
☐ 233	Rafael Santana	.03	.01	.00
☐ 234	Ken Dayley	.03	.01	.00
☐ 235	Gary Ward	.03	.01	.00
☐ 236	Ted Power	.03	.01	.00
☐ 237	Mike Heath	.03	.01	.00
☐ 238	Luis Polonia	.20	.10	.02
☐ 239	Roy Smalley	.03	.01	.00
☐ 240	Lee Smith	.06	.03	.00
☐ 241	Damaso Garcia	.03	.01	.00
☐ 242	Tom Niedenfuer	.03	.01	.00
☐ 243	Mark Ryal	.08	.04	.01
☐ 244	Jeff D. Robinson (Pirates pitcher)	.06	.03	.00
☐ 245	Rich Gedman	.03	.01	.00
☐ 246	Mike Campbell	.15	.07	.01
☐ 247	Thad Bosley	.03	.01	.00
☐ 248	Storm Davis	.06	.03	.00
☐ 249	Mike Marshall	.08	.04	.01
☐ 250	Nolan Ryan	.30	.15	.03
☐ 251	Tom Foley	.03	.01	.00
☐ 252	Bob Brower	.08	.04	.01
☐ 253	Checklist 133-264	.06	.01	.00
☐ 254	Lee Elia MG (checklist back)	.06	.03	.00
☐ 255	Mookie Wilson	.06	.03	.00
☐ 256	Ken Schrom	.03	.01	.00
☐ 257	Jerry Royster	.03	.01	.00
☐ 258	Ed Nunez	.03	.01	.00
☐ 259	Ron Kittle	.08	.04	.01
☐ 260	Vince Coleman	.12	.06	.01
☐ 261	Giants TL (five players)	.03	.01	.00
☐ 262	Drew Hall	.10	.05	.01
☐ 263	Glenn Braggs	.06	.03	.00
☐ 264	Les Straker	.08	.04	.01
☐ 265	Bo Diaz	.03	.01	.00
☐ 266	Paul Assenmacher	.03	.01	.00
☐ 267	Billy Bean	.15	.07	.01
☐ 268	Bruce Ruffin	.03	.01	.00
☐ 269	Ellis Burks	1.00	.50	.10
☐ 270	Mike Witt	.06	.03	.00
☐ 271	Ken Gerhart	.06	.03	.00
☐ 272	Steve Ontiveros	.03	.01	.00
☐ 273	Garth Iorg	.03	.01	.00
☐ 274	Junior Ortiz	.03	.01	.00
☐ 275	Kevin Seitzer	.65	.30	.06
☐ 276	Luis Salazar	.03	.01	.00
☐ 277	Alejandro Pena	.06	.03	.00
☐ 278	Jose Cruz	.06	.03	.00
☐ 279	Randy St.Claire	.03	.01	.00
☐ 280	Pete Incaviglia	.12	.06	.01
☐ 281	Jerry Hairston	.03	.01	.00
☐ 282	Pat Perry	.03	.01	.00
☐ 283	Phil Lombardi	.08	.04	.01
☐ 284	Larry Bowa MG (checklist back)	.06	.03	.00
☐ 285	Jim Presley	.06	.03	.00
☐ 286	Chuck Crim	.08	.04	.01
☐ 287	Manny Trillo	.03	.01	.00
☐ 288	Pat Pacillo	.06	.03	.00

		MINT	EXC	G-VG
	(Chris Sabo in background of photo)			
☐ 289	Dave Bergman	.03	.01	.00
☐ 290	Tony Fernandez	.10	.05	.01
☐ 291	Astros TL	.06	.03	.00
	Billy Hatcher and Kevin Bass			
☐ 292	Carney Lansford	.08	.04	.01
☐ 293	Doug Jones	.25	.12	.02
☐ 294	Al Pedrique	.08	.04	.01
☐ 295	Bert Blyleven	.08	.04	.01
☐ 296	Floyd Rayford	.03	.01	.00
☐ 297	Zane Smith	.03	.01	.00
☐ 298	Milt Thompson	.03	.01	.00
☐ 299	Steve Crawford	.03	.01	.00
☐ 300	Don Mattingly	1.25	.60	.12
☐ 301	Bud Black	.03	.01	.00
☐ 302	Jose Uribe	.03	.01	.00
☐ 303	Eric Show	.03	.01	.00
☐ 304	George Hendrick	.03	.01	.00
☐ 305	Steve Sax	.10	.05	.01
☐ 306	Billy Hatcher	.03	.01	.00
☐ 307	Mike Trujillo	.03	.01	.00
☐ 308	Lee Mazzilli	.03	.01	.00
☐ 309	Bill Long	.08	.04	.01
☐ 310	Tom Herr	.03	.01	.00
☐ 311	Scott Sanderson	.03	.01	.00
☐ 312	Joey Meyer	.10	.05	.01
☐ 313	Bob McClure	.03	.01	.00
☐ 314	Jimy Williams MG	.06	.03	.00
	(checklist back)			
☐ 315	Dave Parker	.10	.05	.01
☐ 316	Jose Rijo	.03	.01	.00
☐ 317	Tom Nieto	.03	.01	.00
☐ 318	Mel Hall	.06	.03	.00
☐ 319	Mike Loynd	.03	.01	.00
☐ 320	Alan Trammell	.12	.06	.01
☐ 321	White Sox TL	.10	.05	.01
	Harold Baines and Carlton Fisk			
☐ 322	Vicente Palacios	.10	.05	.01
☐ 323	Rick Leach	.03	.01	.00
☐ 324	Danny Jackson	.08	.04	.01
☐ 325	Glenn Hubbard	.03	.01	.00
☐ 326	Al Nipper	.03	.01	.00
☐ 327	Larry Sheets	.06	.03	.00
☐ 328	Greg Cadaret	.15	.07	.01
☐ 329	Chris Speier	.03	.01	.00
☐ 330	Eddie Whitson	.03	.01	.00

		MINT	EXC	G-VG
☐ 331	Brian Downing	.03	.01	.00
☐ 332	Jerry Reed	.03	.01	.00
☐ 333	Wally Backman	.03	.01	.00
☐ 334	Dave LaPoint	.03	.01	.00
☐ 335	Claudell Washington	.06	.03	.00
☐ 336	Ed Lynch	.03	.01	.00
☐ 337	Jim Gantner	.03	.01	.00
☐ 338	Brian Holton	.08	.04	.01
☐ 339	Kurt Stillwell	.03	.01	.00
☐ 340	Jack Morris	.10	.05	.01
☐ 341	Carmen Castillo	.03	.01	.00
☐ 342	Larry Andersen	.03	.01	.00
☐ 343	Greg Gagne	.03	.01	.00
☐ 344	Tony LaRussa MG	.06	.03	.00
	(checklist back)			
☐ 345	Scott Fletcher	.03	.01	.00
☐ 346	Vance Law	.03	.01	.00
☐ 347	Joe Johnson	.03	.01	.00
☐ 348	Jim Eisenreich	.03	.01	.00
☐ 349	Bob Walk	.03	.01	.00
☐ 350	Will Clark	1.00	.50	.10
☐ 351	Cardinals TL	.06	.03	.00
	Red Schoendienst and Tony Pena			
☐ 352	Billy Ripken	.15	.07	.01
☐ 353	Ed Olwine	.03	.01	.00
☐ 354	Marc Sullivan	.03	.01	.00
☐ 355	Roger McDowell	.06	.03	.00
☐ 356	Luis Aguayo	.03	.01	.00
☐ 357	Floyd Bannister	.03	.01	.00
☐ 358	Rey Quinones	.03	.01	.00
☐ 359	Tim Stoddard	.03	.01	.00
☐ 360	Tony Gwynn	.30	.15	.03
☐ 361	Greg Maddux	.35	.17	.03
☐ 362	Juan Castillo	.08	.04	.01
☐ 363	Willie Fraser	.03	.01	.00
☐ 364	Nick Esasky	.08	.04	.01
☐ 365	Floyd Youmans	.03	.01	.00
☐ 366	Chet Lemon	.03	.01	.00
☐ 367	Tim Leary	.06	.03	.00
☐ 368	Gerald Young	.25	.12	.02
☐ 369	Greg Harris	.03	.01	.00
☐ 370	Jose Canseco	1.25	.60	.12
☐ 371	Joe Hesketh	.03	.01	.00
☐ 372	Matt Williams	1.00	.50	.10
☐ 373	Checklist 265-396	.06	.01	.00
☐ 374	Doc Edwards MG	.06	.03	.00
	(checklist back)			
☐ 375	Tom Brunansky	.08	.04	.01

		MINT	EXC	G-VG			MINT	EXC	G-VG
☐ 376	Bill Wilkinson	.10	.05	.01	☐ 421	Ed VandeBerg	.03	.01	.00
☐ 377	Sam Horn	.12	.06	.01	☐ 422	Dave Concepcion	.06	.03	.00
☐ 378	Todd Frohwirth	.08	.04	.01	☐ 423	John Smiley	.25	.12	.02
☐ 379	Rafael Ramirez	.03	.01	.00	☐ 424	Dwayne Murphy	.03	.01	.00
☐ 380	Joe Magrane	.45	.22	.04	☐ 425	Jeff Reardon	.06	.03	.00
☐ 381	Angels TL	.10	.05	.01	☐ 426	Randy Ready	.03	.01	.00
	Wally Joyner and				☐ 427	Paul Kilgus	.10	.05	.01
	Jack Howell				☐ 428	John Shelby	.03	.01	.00
☐ 382	Keith Miller	.20	.10	.02	☐ 429	Tigers TL	.15	.07	.01
	(New York Mets)					Alan Trammell and			
☐ 383	Eric Bell	.03	.01	.00		Kirk Gibson			
☐ 384	Neil Allen	.03	.01	.00	☐ 430	Glenn Davis	.12	.06	.01
☐ 385	Carlton Fisk	.10	.05	.01	☐ 431	Casey Candaele	.03	.01	.00
☐ 386	Don Mattingly AS	.40	.20	.04	☐ 432	Mike Moore	.06	.03	.00
☐ 387	Willie Randolph AS	.06	.03	.00	☐ 433	Bill Pecota	.10	.05	.01
☐ 388	Wade Boggs AS	.25	.12	.02	☐ 434	Rick Aguilera	.03	.01	.00
☐ 389	Alan Trammell AS	.08	.04	.01	☐ 435	Mike Pagliarulo	.06	.03	.00
☐ 390	George Bell AS	.10	.05	.01	☐ 436	Mike Bielecki	.06	.03	.00
☐ 391	Kirby Puckett AS	.15	.07	.01	☐ 437	Fred Manrique	.10	.05	.01
☐ 392	Dave Winfield AS	.10	.05	.01	☐ 438	Rob Ducey	.15	.07	.01
☐ 393	Matt Nokes AS	.10	.05	.01	☐ 439	Dave Martinez	.08	.04	.01
☐ 394	Roger Clemens AS	.20	.10	.02	☐ 440	Steve Bedrosian	.08	.04	.01
☐ 395	Jimmy Key AS	.06	.03	.00	☐ 441	Rick Manning	.03	.01	.00
☐ 396	Tom Henke AS	.06	.03	.00	☐ 442	Tom Bolton	.10	.05	.01
☐ 397	Jack Clark AS	.08	.04	.01	☐ 443	Ken Griffey	.08	.04	.01
☐ 398	Juan Samuel AS	.06	.03	.00	☐ 444	Cal Ripken, Sr. MG	.06	.03	.00
☐ 399	Tim Wallach AS	.06	.03	.00		(checklist back)			
☐ 400	Ozzie Smith AS	.10	.05	.01		UER (two copyrights)			
☐ 401	Andre Dawson AS	.12	.06	.01	☐ 445	Mike Krukow	.03	.01	.00
☐ 402	Tony Gwynn AS	.20	.10	.02	☐ 446	Doug DeCinces	.03	.01	.00
☐ 403	Tim Raines AS	.10	.05	.01	☐ 447	Jeff Montgomery	.25	.12	.02
☐ 404	Benny Santiago AS	.12	.06	.01	☐ 448	Mike Davis	.03	.01	.00
☐ 405	Dwight Gooden AS	.20	.10	.02	☐ 449	Jeff M. Robinson	.25	.12	.02
☐ 406	Shane Rawley AS	.06	.03	.00		(Tigers pitcher)			
☐ 407	Steve Bedrosian AS	.06	.03	.00	☐ 450	Barry Bonds	.15	.07	.01
☐ 408	Dion James	.03	.01	.00	☐ 451	Keith Atherton	.03	.01	.00
☐ 409	Joel McKeon	.03	.01	.00	☐ 452	Willie Wilson	.06	.03	.00
☐ 410	Tony Pena	.06	.03	.00	☐ 453	Dennis Powell	.03	.01	.00
☐ 411	Wayne Tolleson	.03	.01	.00	☐ 454	Marvell Wynne	.03	.01	.00
☐ 412	Randy Myers	.08	.04	.01	☐ 455	Shawn Hillegas	.15	.07	.01
☐ 413	John Christensen	.03	.01	.00	☐ 456	Dave Anderson	.03	.01	.00
☐ 414	John McNamara MG	.06	.03	.00	☐ 457	Terry Leach	.06	.03	.00
	(checklist back)				☐ 458	Ron Hassey	.03	.01	.00
☐ 415	Don Carman	.03	.01	.00	☐ 459	Yankees TL	.10	.05	.01
☐ 416	Keith Moreland	.03	.01	.00		Dave Winfield and			
☐ 417	Mark Ciardi	.08	.04	.01		Willie Randolph			
☐ 418	Joel Youngblood	.03	.01	.00	☐ 460	Ozzie Smith	.12	.06	.01
☐ 419	Scott McGregor	.03	.01	.00	☐ 461	Danny Darwin	.03	.01	.00
☐ 420	Wally Joyner	.30	.15	.03	☐ 462	Don Slaught	.03	.01	.00

		MINT	EXC	G-VG			MINT	EXC	G-VG
☐ 463	Fred McGriff	1.00	.50	.10	☐ 508	Tim Teufel	.03	.01	.00
☐ 464	Jay Tibbs	.03	.01	.00	☐ 509	Bill Dawley	.03	.01	.00
☐ 465	Paul Molitor	.10	.05	.01	☐ 510	Dave Winfield	.15	.07	.01
☐ 466	Jerry Mumphrey	.03	.01	.00	☐ 511	Joel Davis	.03	.01	.00
☐ 467	Don Aase	.03	.01	.00	☐ 512	Alex Trevino	.03	.01	.00
☐ 468	Darren Daulton	.03	.01	.00	☐ 513	Tim Flannery	.03	.01	.00
☐ 469	Jeff Dedmon	.03	.01	.00	☐ 514	Pat Sheridan	.03	.01	.00
☐ 470	Dwight Evans	.10	.05	.01	☐ 515	Juan Nieves	.03	.01	.00
☐ 471	Donnie Moore	.03	.01	.00	☐ 516	Jim Sundberg	.03	.01	.00
☐ 472	Robby Thompson	.03	.01	.00	☐ 517	Ron Robinson	.03	.01	.00
☐ 473	Joe Niekro	.06	.03	.00	☐ 518	Greg Gross	.03	.01	.00
☐ 474	Tom Brookens	.03	.01	.00	☐ 519	Mariners TL	.06	.03	.00
☐ 475	Pete Rose MG	.30	.15	.03		Harold Reynolds and			
	(checklist back)					Phil Bradley			
☐ 476	Dave Stewart	.12	.06	.01	☐ 520	Dave Smith	.03	.01	.00
☐ 477	Jamie Quirk	.03	.01	.00	☐ 521	Jim Dwyer	.03	.01	.00
☐ 478	Sid Bream	.03	.01	.00	☐ 522	Bob Patterson	.08	.04	.01
☐ 479	Brett Butler	.06	.03	.00	☐ 523	Gary Roenicke	.03	.01	.00
☐ 480	Dwight Gooden	.40	.20	.04	☐ 524	Gary Lucas	.03	.01	.00
☐ 481	Mariano Duncan	.03	.01	.00	☐ 525	Marty Barrett	.06	.03	.00
☐ 482	Mark Davis	.12	.06	.01	☐ 526	Juan Berenguer	.03	.01	.00
☐ 483	Rod Booker	.10	.05	.01	☐ 527	Steve Henderson	.03	.01	.00
☐ 484	Pat Clements	.03	.01	.00	☐ 528A	Checklist 397-528	.75	.05	.01
☐ 485	Harold Reynolds	.06	.03	.00		ERR (455 S. Carlton)			
☐ 486	Pat Keedy	.08	.04	.01	☐ 528B	Checklist 397-528	.08	.01	.00
☐ 487	Jim Pankovits	.03	.01	.00		COR (455 S. Hillegas)			
☐ 488	Andy McGaffigan	.03	.01	.00	☐ 529	Tim Burke	.03	.01	.00
☐ 489	Dodgers TL	.12	.06	.01	☐ 530	Gary Carter	.15	.07	.01
	Pedro Guerrero and				☐ 531	Rich Yett	.03	.01	.00
	Fernando Valenzuela				☐ 532	Mike Kingery	.03	.01	.00
☐ 490	Larry Parrish	.03	.01	.00	☐ 533	John Farrell	.20	.10	.02
☐ 491	B.J. Surhoff	.08	.04	.01	☐ 534	John Wathan MG	.06	.03	.00
☐ 492	Doyle Alexander	.03	.01	.00		(checklist back)			
☐ 493	Mike Greenwell	1.25	.60	.12	☐ 535	Ron Guidry	.08	.04	.01
☐ 494	Wally Ritchie	.08	.04	.01	☐ 536	John Morris	.03	.01	.00
☐ 495	Eddie Murray	.15	.07	.01	☐ 537	Steve Buechele	.03	.01	.00
☐ 496	Guy Hoffman	.03	.01	.00	☐ 538	Bill Wegman	.03	.01	.00
☐ 497	Kevin Mitchell	.35	.17	.03	☐ 539	Mike LaValliere	.03	.01	.00
☐ 498	Bob Boone	.08	.04	.01	☐ 540	Bret Saberhagen	.15	.07	.01
☐ 499	Eric King	.03	.01	.00	☐ 541	Juan Beniquez	.03	.01	.00
☐ 500	Andre Dawson	.15	.07	.01	☐ 542	Paul Noce	.08	.04	.01
☐ 501	Tim Birtsas	.03	.01	.00	☐ 543	Kent Tekulve	.03	.01	.00
☐ 502	Dan Gladden	.06	.03	.00	☐ 544	Jim Traber	.03	.01	.00
☐ 503	Junior Noboa	.08	.04	.01	☐ 545	Don Baylor	.08	.04	.01
☐ 504	Bob Rodgers MG	.06	.03	.00	☐ 546	John Candelaria	.06	.03	.00
	(checklist back)				☐ 547	Felix Fermin	.08	.04	.01
☐ 505	Willie Upshaw	.03	.01	.00	☐ 548	Shane Mack	.08	.04	.01
☐ 506	John Cangelosi	.03	.01	.00	☐ 549	Braves TL	.06	.03	.00
☐ 507	Mark Gubicza	.10	.05	.01		Albert Hall,			

		MINT	EXC	G-VG
	Dale Murphy, Ken Griffey, and Dion James			
☐ 550	Pedro Guerrero	.10	.05	.01
☐ 551	Terry Steinbach	.20	.10	.02
☐ 552	Mark Thurmond	.03	.01	.00
☐ 553	Tracy Jones	.03	.01	.00
☐ 554	Mike Smithson	.03	.01	.00
☐ 555	Brook Jacoby	.06	.03	.00
☐ 556	Stan Clarke	.06	.03	.00
☐ 557	Craig Reynolds	.03	.01	.00
☐ 558	Bob Ojeda	.06	.03	.00
☐ 559	Ken Williams	.15	.07	.01
☐ 560	Tim Wallach	.06	.03	.00
☐ 561	Rick Cerone	.03	.01	.00
☐ 562	Jim Lindeman	.06	.03	.00
☐ 563	Jose Guzman	.03	.01	.00
☐ 564	Frank Lucchesi MG (checklist back)	.06	.03	.00
☐ 565	Lloyd Moseby	.06	.03	.00
☐ 566	Charlie O'Brien	.08	.04	.01
☐ 567	Mike Diaz	.03	.01	.00
☐ 568	Chris Brown	.03	.01	.00
☐ 569	Charlie Leibrandt	.03	.01	.00
☐ 570	Jeffrey Leonard	.06	.03	.00
☐ 571	Mark Williamson	.08	.04	.01
☐ 572	Chris James	.15	.07	.01
☐ 573	Bob Stanley	.03	.01	.00
☐ 574	Graig Nettles	.08	.04	.01
☐ 575	Don Sutton	.10	.05	.01
☐ 576	Tommy Hinzo	.08	.04	.01
☐ 577	Tom Browning	.08	.04	.01
☐ 578	Gary Gaetti	.10	.05	.01
☐ 579	Mets TL Gary Carter and Kevin McReynolds	.15	.07	.01
☐ 580	Mark McGwire	1.00	.50	.10
☐ 581	Tito Landrum	.03	.01	.00
☐ 582	Mike Henneman	.20	.10	.02
☐ 583	Dave Valle	.06	.03	.00
☐ 584	Steve Trout	.03	.01	.00
☐ 585	Ozzie Guillen	.06	.03	.00
☐ 586	Bob Forsch	.03	.01	.00
☐ 587	Terry Puhl	.03	.01	.00
☐ 588	Jeff Parrett	.15	.07	.01
☐ 589	Geno Petralli	.03	.01	.00
☐ 590	George Bell	.15	.07	.01
☐ 591	Doug Drabek	.06	.03	.00
☐ 592	Dale Sveum	.03	.01	.00

		MINT	EXC	G-VG
☐ 593	Bob Tewksbury	.03	.01	.00
☐ 594	Bobby Valentine MG (checklist back)	.06	.03	.00
☐ 595	Frank White	.06	.03	.00
☐ 596	John Kruk	.08	.04	.01
☐ 597	Gene Garber	.03	.01	.00
☐ 598	Lee Lacy	.03	.01	.00
☐ 599	Calvin Schiraldi	.03	.01	.00
☐ 600	Mike Schmidt	.30	.15	.03
☐ 601	Jack Lazorko	.03	.01	.00
☐ 602	Mike Aldrete	.03	.01	.00
☐ 603	Rob Murphy	.03	.01	.00
☐ 604	Chris Bando	.03	.01	.00
☐ 605	Kirk Gibson	.15	.07	.01
☐ 606	Moose Haas	.03	.01	.00
☐ 607	Mickey Hatcher	.03	.01	.00
☐ 608	Charlie Kerfeld	.03	.01	.00
☐ 609	Twins TL Gary Gaetti and Kent Hrbek	.10	.05	.01
☐ 610	Keith Hernandez	.12	.06	.01
☐ 611	Tommy John	.08	.04	.01
☐ 612	Curt Ford	.03	.01	.00
☐ 613	Bobby Thigpen	.08	.04	.01
☐ 614	Herm Winningham	.03	.01	.00
☐ 615	Jody Davis	.03	.01	.00
☐ 616	Jay Aldrich	.08	.04	.01
☐ 617	Oddibe McDowell	.06	.03	.00
☐ 618	Cecil Fielder	.03	.01	.00
☐ 619	Mike Dunne (inconsistent design, black name on front)	.08	.04	.01
☐ 620	Cory Snyder	.12	.06	.01
☐ 621	Gene Nelson	.03	.01	.00
☐ 622	Kal Daniels	.12	.06	.01
☐ 623	Mike Flanagan	.06	.03	.00
☐ 624	Jim Leyland MG (checklist back)	.06	.03	.00
☐ 625	Frank Viola	.15	.07	.01
☐ 626	Glenn Wilson	.03	.01	.00
☐ 627	Joe Boever	.10	.05	.01
☐ 628	Dave Henderson	.06	.03	.00
☐ 629	Kelly Downs	.06	.03	.00
☐ 630	Darrell Evans	.06	.03	.00
☐ 631	Jack Howell	.03	.01	.00
☐ 632	Steve Shields	.03	.01	.00
☐ 633	Barry Lyons	.15	.07	.01
☐ 634	Jose DeLeon	.06	.03	.00
☐ 635	Terry Pendleton	.03	.01	.00

		MINT	EXC	G-VG			MINT	EXC	G-VG
☐ 636	Charles Hudson	.03	.01	.00	☐ 671	Tim Laudner	.03	.01	.00
☐ 637	Jay Bell	.15	.07	.01	☐ 672	John Davis	.12	.06	.01
☐ 638	Steve Balboni	.03	.01	.00	☐ 673	Tony Phillips	.03	.01	.00
☐ 639	Brewers TL	.03	.01	.00	☐ 674	Mike Fitzgerald	.03	.01	.00
	Glenn Braggs				☐ 675	Jim Rice	.12	.06	.01
	and Tony Muser CO				☐ 676	Ken Dixon	.03	.01	.00
☐ 640	Garry Templeton	.06	.03	.00	☐ 677	Eddie Milner	.03	.01	.00
	(inconsistent design,				☐ 678	Jim Acker	.03	.01	.00
	green border)				☐ 679	Darrell Miller	.03	.01	.00
☐ 641	Rick Honeycutt	.03	.01	.00	☐ 680	Charlie Hough	.03	.01	.00
☐ 642	Bob Dernier	.03	.01	.00	☐ 681	Bobby Bonilla	.12	.06	.01
☐ 643	Rocky Childress	.08	.04	.01	☐ 682	Jimmy Key	.06	.03	.00
☐ 644	Terry McGriff	.08	.04	.01	☐ 683	Julio Franco	.10	.05	.01
☐ 645	Matt Nokes	.35	.17	.03	☐ 684	Hal Lanier MG	.06	.03	.00
☐ 646	Checklist 529-660	.06	.01	.00		(checklist back)			
☐ 647	Pascual Perez	.08	.04	.01	☐ 685	Ron Darling	.08	.04	.01
☐ 648	Al Newman	.03	.01	.00	☐ 686	Terry Francona	.03	.01	.00
☐ 649	DeWayne Buice	.08	.04	.01	☐ 687	Mickey Brantley	.06	.03	.00
☐ 650	Cal Ripken	.18	.09	.01	☐ 688	Jim Winn	.03	.01	.00
☐ 651	Mike Jackson	.15	.07	.01	☐ 689	Tom Pagnozzi	.08	.04	.01
☐ 652	Bruce Benedict	.03	.01	.00	☐ 690	Jay Howell	.03	.01	.00
☐ 653	Jeff Sellers	.03	.01	.00	☐ 691	Dan Pasqua	.03	.01	.00
☐ 654	Roger Craig MG	.06	.03	.00	☐ 692	Mike Birkbeck	.03	.01	.00
	(checklist back)				☐ 693	Benny Santiago	.45	.22	.04
☐ 655	Len Dykstra	.08	.04	.01	☐ 694	Eric Nolte	.10	.05	.01
☐ 656	Lee Guetterman	.03	.01	.00	☐ 695	Shawon Dunston	.08	.04	.01
☐ 657	Gary Redus	.03	.01	.00	☐ 696	Duane Ward	.03	.01	.00
☐ 658	Tim Conroy	.03	.01	.00	☐ 697	Steve Lombardozzi	.03	.01	.00
	(inconsistent design,				☐ 698	Brad Havens	.03	.01	.00
	name in white)				☐ 699	Padres TL	.20	.10	.02
☐ 659	Bobby Meacham	.03	.01	.00		Benito Santiago			
☐ 660	Rick Reuschel	.06	.04	.01		and Tony Gwynn			
☐ 661	Turn Back Clock 1983	.20	.10	.02	☐ 700	George Brett	.25	.12	.02
	Nolan Ryan				☐ 701	Sammy Stewart	.03	.01	.00
☐ 662	Turn Back Clock 1978	.08	.04	.01	☐ 702	Mike Gallego	.03	.01	.00
	Jim Rice				☐ 703	Bob Brenly	.03	.01	.00
☐ 663	Turn Back Clock 1973	.03	.01	.00	☐ 704	Dennis Boyd	.06	.03	.00
	Ron Blomberg				☐ 705	Juan Samuel	.08	.04	.01
☐ 664	Turn Back Clock 1968	.10	.05	.01	☐ 706	Rick Mahler	.03	.01	.00
	Bob Gibson				☐ 707	Fred Lynn	.10	.05	.01
☐ 665	Turn Back Clock 1963	.15	.07	.01	☐ 708	Gus Polidor	.06	.03	.00
	Stan Musial				☐ 709	George Frazier	.03	.01	.00
☐ 666	Mario Soto	.03	.01	.00	☐ 710	Darryl Strawberry	.35	.17	.03
☐ 667	Luis Quinones	.03	.01	.00	☐ 711	Bill Gullickson	.03	.01	.00
☐ 668	Walt Terrell	.03	.01	.00	☐ 712	John Moses	.03	.01	.00
☐ 669	Phillies TL	.06	.03	.00	☐ 713	Willie Hernandez	.06	.03	.00
	Lance Parrish				☐ 714	Jim Fregosi MG	.06	.03	.00
	and Mike Ryan CO					(checklist back)			
☐ 670	Dan Plesac	.06	.03	.00	☐ 715	Todd Worrell	.10	.05	.01

		MINT	EXC	G-VG
☐ 716	Lenn Sakata	.03	.01	.00
☐ 717	Jay Baller	.03	.01	.00
☐ 718	Mike Felder	.03	.01	.00
☐ 719	Denny Walling	.03	.01	.00
☐ 720	Tim Raines	.15	.07	.01
☐ 721	Pete O'Brien	.06	.03	.00
☐ 722	Manny Lee	.03	.01	.00
☐ 723	Bob Kipper	.03	.01	.00
☐ 724	Danny Tartabull	.15	.07	.01
☐ 725	Mike Boddicker	.03	.01	.00
☐ 726	Alfredo Griffin	.03	.01	.00
☐ 727	Greg Booker	.03	.01	.00
☐ 728	Andy Allanson	.03	.01	.00
☐ 729	Blue Jays TL	.12	.06	.01
	George Bell and			
	Fred McGriff			
☐ 730	John Franco	.08	.04	.01
☐ 731	Rick Schu	.03	.01	.00
☐ 732	David Palmer	.03	.01	.00
☐ 733	Spike Owen	.03	.01	.00
☐ 734	Craig Lefferts	.06	.03	.00
☐ 735	Kevin McReynolds	.15	.07	.01
☐ 736	Matt Young	.03	.01	.00
☐ 737	Butch Wynegar	.03	.01	.00
☐ 738	Scott Bankhead	.06	.03	.00
☐ 739	Daryl Boston	.03	.01	.00
☐ 740	Rick Sutcliffe	.08	.04	.01
☐ 741	Mike Easler	.03	.01	.00
☐ 742	Mark Clear	.03	.01	.00
☐ 743	Larry Herndon	.03	.01	.00
☐ 744	Whitey Herzog MG	.06	.03	.00
	(checklist back)			
☐ 745	Bill Doran	.06	.03	.00
☐ 746	Gene Larkin	.20	.10	.02
☐ 747	Bobby Witt	.06	.03	.00
☐ 748	Reid Nichols	.03	.01	.00
☐ 749	Mark Eichhorn	.03	.01	.00
☐ 750	Bo Jackson	.90	.45	.09
☐ 751	Jim Morrison	.03	.01	.00
☐ 752	Mark Grant	.03	.01	.00
☐ 753	Danny Heep	.03	.01	.00
☐ 754	Mike LaCoss	.03	.01	.00
☐ 755	Ozzie Virgil	.03	.01	.00
☐ 756	Mike Maddux	.03	.01	.00
☐ 757	John Marzano	.08	.04	.01
☐ 758	Eddie Williams	.15	.07	.01
☐ 759	A's TL	.35	.17	.03
	Mark McGwire			
	and Jose Canseco			

		MINT	EXC	G-VG
☐ 760	Mike Scott	.12	.06	.01
☐ 761	Tony Armas	.06	.03	.00
☐ 762	Scott Bradley	.03	.01	.00
☐ 763	Doug Sisk	.03	.01	.00
☐ 764	Greg Walker	.06	.03	.00
☐ 765	Neal Heaton	.03	.01	.00
☐ 766	Henry Cotto	.03	.01	.00
☐ 767	Jose Lind	.18	.09	.01
☐ 768	Dickie Noles	.03	.01	.00
☐ 769	Cecil Cooper	.08	.04	.01
☐ 770	Lou Whitaker	.08	.04	.01
☐ 771	Ruben Sierra	.35	.17	.03
☐ 772	Sal Butera	.03	.01	.00
☐ 773	Frank Williams	.03	.01	.00
☐ 774	Gene Mauch MG	.06	.03	.00
	(checklist back)			
☐ 775	Dave Stieb	.08	.04	.01
☐ 776	Checklist 661-792	.06	.01	.00
☐ 777	Lonnie Smith	.03	.01	.00
☐ 778A	Keith Comstock ERR	7.50	3.75	.75
	(white "Padres")			
☐ 778B	Keith Comstock COR	.15	.07	.01
	(blue "Padres")			
☐ 779	Tom Glavine	.30	.15	.03
☐ 780	Fernando Valenzuela	.12	.06	.01
☐ 781	Keith Hughes	.15	.07	.01
☐ 782	Jeff Ballard	.35	.17	.03
☐ 783	Ron Roenicke	.03	.01	.00
☐ 784	Joe Sambito	.03	.01	.00
☐ 785	Alvin Davis	.08	.04	.01
☐ 786	Joe Price	.03	.01	.00
	(inconsistent design,,			
	orange team name)			
☐ 787	Bill Almon	.03	.01	.00
☐ 788	Ray Searage	.03	.01	.00
☐ 789	Indians' TL	.10	.05	.01
	Joe Carter and			
	Cory Snyder			
☐ 790	Dave Righetti	.08	.04	.01
☐ 791	Ted Simmons	.08	.04	.01
☐ 792	John Tudor	.10	.05	.01

1988 Topps Big Cards

This set of 264 cards was issued as three separately distributed series of 88 cards each. Cards were distributed in wax packs with seven cards for a suggested retail of 40 cents. These cards are very reminiscent in style of the 1956 Topps card set and are popular with collectors perhaps for that reason. The cards measure approximately 2 5/8" by 3 3/4" and are oriented horizontally.

	MINT	EXC	G-VG
COMPLETE SET (264)	27.00	13.50	2.70
COMMON PLAYER (1-88)	.05	.02	.00
COMMON PLAYER (89-176)	.05	.02	.00
COMMON PLAYER (177-264)	.05	.02	.00

			MINT	EXC	G-VG
☐	1	Paul Molitor	.12	.06	.01
☐	2	Milt Thompson	.05	.02	.00
☐	3	Billy Hatcher	.05	.02	.00
☐	4	Mike Witt	.05	.02	.00
☐	5	Vince Coleman	.12	.06	.01
☐	6	Dwight Evans	.12	.06	.01
☐	7	Tim Wallach	.08	.04	.01
☐	8	Alan Trammell	.15	.07	.01
☐	9	Will Clark	1.25	.60	.12
☐	10	Jeff Reardon	.08	.04	.01
☐	11	Dwight Gooden	.50	.25	.05
☐	12	Benny Santiago	.15	.07	.01
☐	13	Jose Canseco	1.25	.60	.12
☐	14	Dale Murphy	.35	.17	.03
☐	15	George Bell	.20	.10	.02
☐	16	Ryne Sandberg	.20	.10	.02
☐	17	Brook Jacoby	.08	.04	.01
☐	18	Fernando Valenzuela	.12	.06	.01
☐	19	Scott Fletcher	.05	.02	.00
☐	20	Eric Davis	.75	.35	.07
☐	21	Willie Wilson	.10	.05	.01
☐	22	B.J. Surhoff	.10	.05	.01
☐	23	Steve Bedrosian	.10	.05	.01
☐	24	Dave Winfield	.30	.15	.03
☐	25	Bobby Bonilla	.15	.07	.01
☐	26	Larry Sheets	.05	.02	.00
☐	27	Ozzie Guillen	.08	.04	.01
☐	28	Checklist 1-88	.05	.02	.00
☐	29	Nolan Ryan	1.00	.50	.10
☐	30	Bob Boone	.12	.06	.01
☐	31	Tom Herr	.08	.04	.01
☐	32	Wade Boggs	1.00	.50	.10
☐	33	Neal Heaton	.05	.02	.00
☐	34	Doyle Alexander	.05	.02	.00
☐	35	Candy Maldonado	.05	.02	.00
☐	36	Kirby Puckett	.50	.25	.05
☐	37	Gary Carter	.20	.10	.02
☐	38	Lance McCullers	.08	.04	.01
☐	39A	Terry Steinbach (Topps logo in black)	.15	.07	.01
☐	39B	Terry Steinbach (Topps logo in white)	.15	.07	.01
☐	40	Gerald Perry	.08	.04	.01
☐	41	Tom Henke	.05	.02	.00
☐	42	Leon Durham	.05	.02	.00
☐	43	Cory Snyder	.15	.07	.01
☐	44	Dale Sveum	.05	.02	.00
☐	45	Lance Parrish	.12	.06	.01
☐	46	Steve Sax	.15	.07	.01
☐	47	Charlie Hough	.05	.02	.00
☐	48	Kal Daniels	.15	.07	.01
☐	49	Bo Jackson	1.25	.60	.12
☐	50	Ron Guidry	.12	.06	.01
☐	51	Bill Doran	.08	.04	.01
☐	52	Wally Joyner	.35	.17	.03
☐	53	Terry Pendleton	.05	.02	.00
☐	54	Marty Barrett	.05	.02	.00
☐	55	Andres Galarraga	.15	.07	.01
☐	56	Larry Herndon	.05	.02	.00
☐	57	Kevin Mitchell	.50	.25	.05
☐	58	Greg Gagne	.05	.02	.00
☐	59	Keith Hernandez	.20	.10	.02
☐	60	John Kruk	.10	.05	.01

	MINT	EXC	G-VG		MINT	EXC	G-VG
☐ 61 Mike LaValliere	.05	.02	.01	☐ 110 Ken Griffey Sr.	.10	.05	.01
☐ 62 Cal Ripken	.30	.15	.03	☐ 111 Danny Cox	.08	.04	.01
☐ 63 Ivan Calderon	.10	.05	.01	☐ 112 Franklin Stubbs	.05	.02	.00
☐ 64 Alvin Davis	.10	.05	.01	☐ 113 Lloyd Moseby	.08	.04	.01
☐ 65 Luis Polonia	.08	.04	.01	☐ 114 Mel Hall	.08	.04	.01
☐ 66 Robin Yount	.50	.25	.05	☐ 115 Kevin Seitzer	.30	.15	.03
☐ 67 Juan Samuel	.10	.05	.01	☐ 116 Tim Raines	.25	.12	.02
☐ 68 Andres Thomas	.08	.04	.01	☐ 117 Juan Castillo	.05	.02	.00
☐ 69 Jeff Musselman	.05	.02	.00	☐ 118 Roger Clemens	.75	.35	.07
☐ 70 Jerry Mumphrey	.05	.02	.00	☐ 119 Mike Aldrete	.05	.02	.00
☐ 71 Joe Carter	.15	.07	.01	☐ 120 Mario Soto	.05	.02	.00
☐ 72 Mike Scioscia	.05	.02	.00	☐ 121 Jack Howell	.05	.02	.00
☐ 73 Pete Incaviglia	.20	.10	.02	☐ 122 Rick Schu	.05	.02	.00
☐ 74 Barry Larkin	.25	.12	.02	☐ 123 Jeff Robinson	.08	.04	.01
☐ 75 Frank White	.08	.04	.01	☐ 124 Doug Drabek	.05	.02	.01
☐ 76 Willie Randolph	.08	.04	.01	☐ 125 Henry Cotto	.05	.02	.00
☐ 77 Kevin Bass	.08	.04	.01	☐ 126 Checklist 89-176	.05	.02	.00
☐ 78 Brian Downing	.05	.02	.00	☐ 127 Gary Gaetti	.12	.06	.01
☐ 79 Willie McGee	.12	.06	.01	☐ 128 Rick Sutcliffe	.10	.05	.01
☐ 80 Ellis Burks	.50	.25	.05	☐ 129 Howard Johnson	.15	.07	.01
☐ 81 Hubie Brooks	.08	.04	.01	☐ 130 Chris Brown	.05	.02	.00
☐ 82 Darrell Evans	.08	.04	.01	☐ 131 Dave Henderson	.05	.02	.00
☐ 83 Robby Thompson	.05	.02	.00	☐ 132 Curt Wilkerson	.05	.02	.00
☐ 84 Kent Hrbek	.15	.07	.01	☐ 133 Mike Marshall	.10	.05	.01
☐ 85 Ron Darling	.10	.05	.01	☐ 134 Kelly Gruber	.08	.04	.01
☐ 86 Stan Jefferson	.08	.04	.01	☐ 135 Julio Franco	.12	.06	.01
☐ 87 Teddy Higuera	.08	.04	.01	☐ 136 Kurt Stillwell	.08	.04	.01
☐ 88 Mike Schmidt	.75	.35	.07	☐ 137 Donnie Hill	.05	.02	.00
☐ 89 Barry Bonds	.15	.07	.01	☐ 138 Mike Pagliarulo	.08	.04	.01
☐ 90 Jim Presley	.08	.04	.01	☐ 139 Von Hayes	.10	.05	.01
☐ 91 Orel Hershiser	.60	.30	.06	☐ 140 Mike Scott	.15	.07	.01
☐ 92 Jesse Barfield	.15	.07	.01	☐ 141 Bob Kipper	.05	.02	.00
☐ 93 Tom Candiotti	.05	.02	.00	☐ 142 Harold Reynolds	.08	.04	.01
☐ 94 Bret Saberhagen	.25	.12	.02	☐ 143 Bob Brenley	.05	.02	.00
☐ 95 Jose Uribe	.05	.02	.00	☐ 144 Dave Concepcion	.10	.05	.01
☐ 96 Tom Browning	.12	.06	.01	☐ 145 Devon White	.10	.05	.01
☐ 97 Johnny Ray	.08	.04	.01	☐ 146 Jeff Stone	.05	.02	.00
☐ 98 Mike Morgan	.08	.04	.01	☐ 147 Chet Lemon	.05	.02	.00
☐ 99 Lou Whitaker	.12	.06	.01	☐ 148 Ozzie Virgil	.05	.02	.00
☐ 100 Jim Sundberg	.05	.02	.00	☐ 149 Todd Worrell	.12	.06	.01
☐ 101 Roger McDowell	.05	.02	.00	☐ 150 Mitch Webster	.05	.02	.00
☐ 102 Randy Ready	.05	.02	.00	☐ 151 Rob Deer	.08	.04	.01
☐ 103 Mike Gallego	.05	.02	.00	☐ 152 Rich Gedman	.05	.02	.00
☐ 104 Steve Buechele	.05	.02	.00	☐ 153 Andre Dawson	.20	.10	.02
☐ 105 Greg Walker	.05	.02	.00	☐ 154 Mike Davis	.05	.02	.00
☐ 106 Jose Lind	.08	.04	.01	☐ 155 Nelson Liriano	.05	.02	.00
☐ 107 Steve Trout	.05	.02	.00	☐ 156 Greg Swindell	.12	.06	.01
☐ 108 Rick Rhoden	.05	.02	.00	☐ 157 George Brett	.35	.17	.03
☐ 109 Jim Pankovits	.05	.02	.00	☐ 158 Kevin McReynolds	.20	.10	.02

		MINT	EXC	G-VG			MINT	EXC	G-VG
☐ 159	Brian Fisher	.05	.02	.00	☐ 208	Mark Eichhorn	.05	.02	.00
☐ 160	Mike Kingery	.05	.02	.00	☐ 209	Rene Gonzalez	.08	.04	.01
☐ 161	Tony Gwynn	.35	.17	.03	☐ 210	Dave Valle	.05	.02	.00
☐ 162	Don Baylor	.10	.05	.01	☐ 211	Tom Brunansky	.10	.05	.01
☐ 163	Jerry Browne	.08	.04	.01	☐ 212	Charles Hudson	.05	.02	.00
☐ 164	Dan Pasqua	.05	.02	.00	☐ 213	John Farrell	.08	.04	.01
☐ 165	Rickey Henderson	.45	.22	.04	☐ 214	Jeff Treadway	.08	.04	.01
☐ 166	Brett Butler	.10	.05	.01	☐ 215	Eddie Murray	.25	.12	.02
☐ 167	Nick Esasky	.12	.06	.01	☐ 216	Checklist 177-264	.05	.02	.00
☐ 168	Kirk McCaskill	.08	.04	.01	☐ 217	Greg Brock	.05	.02	.00
☐ 169	Fred Lynn	.12	.06	.01	☐ 218	John Shelby	.05	.02	.00
☐ 170	Jack Morris	.12	.06	.01	☐ 219	Craig Reynolds	.05	.02	.00
☐ 171	Pedro Guerrero	.15	.07	.01	☐ 220	Dion James	.05	.02	.00
☐ 172	Dave Stieb	.10	.05	.01	☐ 221	Carney Lansford	.12	.06	.01
☐ 173	Pat Tabler	.05	.02	.00	☐ 222	Juan Berenguer	.05	.02	.00
☐ 174	Floyd Bannister	.05	.02	.00	☐ 223	Luis Rivera	.05	.02	.00
☐ 175	Rafael Belliard	.05	.02	.00	☐ 224	Harold Baines	.12	.06	.01
☐ 176	Mark Langston	.15	.07	.01	☐ 225	Shawon Dunston	.12	.06	.01
☐ 177	Greg Mathews	.08	.04	.01	☐ 226	Luis Aguayo	.05	.02	.00
☐ 178	Claudell Washington	.08	.04	.01	☐ 227	Pete O'Brien	.08	.04	.01
☐ 179	Mark McGwire	1.00	.50	.10	☐ 228	Ozzie Smith	.15	.07	.01
☐ 180	Bert Blyleven	.12	.06	.01	☐ 229	Don Mattingly	1.25	.60	.12
☐ 181	Jim Rice	.15	.07	.01	☐ 230	Danny Tartabull	.25	.12	.02
☐ 182	Mookie Wilson	.08	.04	.01	☐ 231	Andy Allanson	.05	.02	.00
☐ 183	Willie Fraser	.05	.02	.00	☐ 232	John Franco	.08	.04	.01
☐ 184	Andy Van Slyke	.12	.06	.01	☐ 233	Mike Greenwell	1.00	.50	.10
☐ 185	Matt Nokes	.15	.07	.01	☐ 234	Bob Ojeda	.08	.04	.01
☐ 186	Eddie Whitson	.05	.02	.00	☐ 235	Chili Davis	.08	.04	.01
☐ 187	Tony Fernandez	.10	.05	.01	☐ 236	Mike Dunne	.05	.02	.00
☐ 188	Rick Reuschel	.10	.05	.01	☐ 237	Jim Morrison	.05	.02	.00
☐ 189	Ken Phelps	.08	.04	.01	☐ 238	Carmelo Martinez	.05	.02	.00
☐ 190	Juan Nieves	.05	.02	.00	☐ 239	Ernie Whitt	.05	.02	.00
☐ 191	Kirk Gibson	.25	.12	.02	☐ 240	Scott Garrelts	.08	.04	.01
☐ 192	Glenn Davis	.25	.12	.02	☐ 241	Mike Moore	.10	.05	.01
☐ 193	Zane Smith	.05	.02	.00	☐ 242	Dave Parker	.12	.06	.01
☐ 194	Jose DeLeon	.08	.04	.01	☐ 243	Tim Laudner	.05	.02	.00
☐ 195	Gary Ward	.05	.02	.00	☐ 244	Bill Wegman	.05	.02	.00
☐ 196	Pascual Perez	.10	.05	.01	☐ 245	Bob Horner	.10	.05	.01
☐ 197	Carlton Fisk	.20	.10	.02	☐ 246	Rafael Santana	.05	.02	.00
☐ 198	Oddibe McDowell	.08	.04	.01	☐ 247	Alfredo Griffin	.05	.02	.00
☐ 199	Mark Gubicza	.12	.06	.01	☐ 248	Mark Bailey	.05	.02	.00
☐ 200	Glenn Hubbard	.05	.02	.00	☐ 249	Ron Gant	.15	.07	.01
☐ 201	Frank Viola	.15	.07	.01	☐ 250	Bryn Smith	.08	.04	.01
☐ 202	Jody Reed	.08	.04	.01	☐ 251	Lance Johnson	.08	.04	.01
☐ 203	Len Dykstra	.08	.04	.01	☐ 252	Sam Horn	.08	.04	.01
☐ 204	Dick Schofield	.05	.02	.00	☐ 253	Darryl Strawberry	.75	.35	.07
☐ 205	Sid Bream	.05	.02	.00	☐ 254	Chuck Finley	.08	.04	.01
☐ 206	Guillermo Hernandez	.08	.04	.01	☐ 255	Darnell Coles	.05	.02	.00
☐ 207	Keith Moreland	.05	.02	.00	☐ 256	Mike Henneman	.08	.04	.01

		MINT	EXC	G-VG
☐ 257	Andy Hawkins	.05	.02	.00
☐ 258	Jim Clancy	.05	.02	.00
☐ 259	Atlee Hammaker	.05	.02	.00
☐ 260	Glenn Wilson	.05	.02	.00
☐ 261	Larry McWilliams ...	.05	.02	.00
☐ 262	Jack Clark	.15	.07	.01
☐ 263	Walt Weiss	.30	.15	.03
☐ 264	Gene Larkin	.10	.05	.01

1988 Topps Traded

This 132-card Traded or extended set was distributed by Topps to dealers in a special blue and white box as a complete set. The card fronts are identical in style to the Topps regular issue and are also 2 ½" by 3 ½". The backs are printed in orange and black on white card stock. Cards are numbered (with a T suffix) alphabetically according to the name of the player. This set has generated additional interest due to the inclusion of the 1988 U.S. Olympic baseball team members. These Olympians are indicated in the checklist below by OLY. Topps also produced a specially boxed "glossy" edition, frequently referred to as the Topps Traded Tiffany set. This year, again, Topps did not disclose the number of Tiffany sets they produced or sold. It is apparent from the availability that there were many more sets produced this year compared to the 1984-86 Tiffany sets, perhaps more than three times as many (similar to the 1987 Tiffany cards). The checklist of cards is identical to that of the nor-

mal non-glossy cards. There are two primary distinguishing features of the Tiffany cards—white card stock reverses and high gloss obverses. These Tiffany cards are valued at approximately four times the values listed below.

		MINT	EXC	G-VG
COMPLETE SET (132)		27.00	13.50	2.70
COMMON PLAYER (1-132)		.06	.03	.00
☐ 1 T	Jim Abbott OLY	10.00	5.00	1.00
☐ 2 T	Juan Agosto	.06	.03	.00
☐ 3 T	Luis Alicea	.10	.05	.01
☐ 4 T	Roberto Alomar	.60	.30	.06
☐ 5 T	Brady Anderson	.35	.17	.03
☐ 6 T	Jack Armstrong	.25	.12	.02
☐ 7 T	Don Aquust	.10	.05	.01
☐ 8 T	Floyd Bannister	.06	.03	.00
☐ 9 T	Bret Barberie OLY ..	.25	.12	.02
☐ 10 T	Jose Bautista	.12	.06	.01
☐ 11 T	Don Baylor	.10	.05	.01
☐ 12 T	Tim Belcher	.20	.10	.02
☐ 13 T	Buddy Bell	.10	.05	.01
☐ 14 T	Andy Benes OLY	3.00	1.50	.30
☐ 15 T	Damon Berryhill	.35	.17	.03
☐ 16 T	Bud Black	.06	.03	.00
☐ 17 T	Pat Borders	.15	.07	.01
☐ 18 T	Phil Bradley	.10	.05	.01
☐ 19 T	Jeff Branson OLY ...	.25	.12	.02
☐ 20 T	Tom Brunansky	.15	.07	.01
☐ 21 T	Jay Buhner	.35	.17	.03
☐ 22 T	Brett Butler	.10	.05	.01
☐ 23 T	Jim Campanis OLY ..	.25	.12	.02
☐ 24 T	Sil Campusano	.20	.10	.02
☐ 25 T	John Candelaria	.10	.05	.01
☐ 26 T	Jose Cecena	.10	.05	.01
☐ 27 T	Rick Cerone	.06	.03	.00
☐ 28 T	Jack Clark	.15	.07	.01
☐ 29 T	Kevin Coffman	.10	.05	.01
☐ 30 T	Pat Combs OLY	1.50	.75	.15
☐ 31 T	Henry Cotto	.06	.03	.00
☐ 32 T	Chili Davis	.10	.05	.01
☐ 33 T	Mike Davis	.06	.03	.00
☐ 34 T	Jose DeLeon	.10	.05	.01
☐ 35 T	Richard Dotson	.06	.03	.00
☐ 36 T	Cecil Espy	.15	.07	.01
☐ 37 T	Tom Filer	.06	.03	.00
☐ 38 T	Mike Fiore OLY	.30	.15	.03
☐ 39 T	Ron Gant	.45	.22	.04

		MINT	EXC	G-VG
☐ 40	T Kirk Gibson	.15	.07	.01
☐ 41	T Rich Gossage	.15	.07	.01
☐ 42	T Mark Grace	3.50	1.75	.35
☐ 43	T Alfredo Griffin	.10	.05	.01
☐ 44	T Ty Griffin OLY	1.25	.60	.12
☐ 45	T Bryan Harvey	.30	.15	.03
☐ 46	T Ron Hassey	.06	.03	.00
☐ 47	T Ray Hayward	.10	.05	.01
☐ 48	T Dave Henderson	.10	.05	.01
☐ 49	T Tom Herr	.10	.05	.01
☐ 50	T Bob Horner	.10	.05	.01
☐ 51	T Ricky Horton	.06	.03	.00
☐ 52	T Jay Howell	.10	.05	.01
☐ 53	T Glenn Hubbard	.06	.03	.00
☐ 54	T Jeff Innis	.20	.10	.02
☐ 55	T Danny Jackson	.15	.07	.01
☐ 56	T Darrin Jackson	.15	.07	.01
☐ 57	T Roberto Kelly	.65	.30	.06
☐ 58	T Ron Kittle	.15	.07	.01
☐ 59	T Ray Knight	.10	.05	.01
☐ 60	T Vance Law	.06	.03	.00
☐ 61	T Jeffrey Leonard	.10	.05	.01
☐ 62	T Mike Macfarlane	.20	.10	.02
☐ 63	T Scotti Madison	.15	.07	.01
☐ 64	T Kirt Manwaring	.15	.07	.01
☐ 65	T Mark Marquess OLY	.06	.03	.00
☐ 66	T Tino Martinez OLY	1.25	.60	.12
☐ 67	T Billy Masse OLY	.25	.12	.02
☐ 68	T Jack McDowell	.15	.07	.01
☐ 69	T Jack McKeon MG	.06	.03	.00
☐ 70	T Larry McWilliams	.06	.03	.00
☐ 71	T Mickey Morandini OLY	.35	.17	.03
☐ 72	T Keith Moreland	.06	.03	.00
☐ 73	T Mike Morgan	.10	.05	.01
☐ 74	T Charles Nagy OLY	.25	.12	.02
☐ 75	T Al Nipper	.06	.03	.00
☐ 76	T Russ Nixon MG	.06	.03	.00
☐ 77	T Jesse Orosco	.06	.03	.00
☐ 78	T Joe Orsulak	.06	.03	.00
☐ 79	T Dave Palmer	.06	.03	.00
☐ 80	T Mark Parent	.20	.10	.02
☐ 81	T Dave Parker	.15	.07	.01
☐ 82	T Dan Pasqua	.10	.05	.01
☐ 83	T Melido Perez	.25	.12	.02
☐ 84	T Steve Peters	.15	.07	.01
☐ 85	T Dan Petry	.06	.03	.00
☐ 86	T Gary Pettis	.06	.03	.00
☐ 87	T Jeff Pico	.15	.07	.01
☐ 88	T Jim Poole OLY	.25	.12	.02
☐ 89	T Ted Power	.06	.03	.00
☐ 90	T Rafael Ramirez	.06	.03	.00
☐ 91	T Dennis Rasmussen	.10	.05	.01
☐ 92	T Jose Rijo	.10	.05	.01
☐ 93	T Ernie Riles	.06	.03	.00
☐ 94	T Luis Rivera	.10	.05	.01
☐ 95	T Doug Robbins OLY	.25	.12	.02
☐ 96	T Frank Robinson MG	.15	.07	.01
☐ 97	T Cookie Rojas MG	.06	.03	.00
☐ 98	T Chris Sabo	1.00	.50	.10
☐ 99	T Mark Salas	.06	.03	.00
☐ 100	T Luis Salazar	.06	.03	.00
☐ 101	T Rafael Santana	.06	.03	.00
☐ 102	T Nelson Santovenia	.25	.12	.02
☐ 103	T Mackey Sasser	.15	.07	.01
☐ 104	T Calvin Schiraldi	.06	.03	.00
☐ 105	T Mike Schooler	.30	.15	.03
☐ 106	T Scott Servais OLY	.25	.12	.02
☐ 107	T Dave Silvestri OLY	.25	.12	.02
☐ 108	T Don Slaught	.06	.03	.00
☐ 109	T Joe Slusarski OLY	.25	.12	.02
☐ 110	T Lee Smith	.10	.05	.01
☐ 111	T Pete Smith	.15	.07	.01
☐ 112	T Jim Snyder MG	.06	.03	.00
☐ 113	T Ed Sprague OLY	.35	.17	.03
☐ 114	T Pete Stanicek	.15	.07	.01
☐ 115	T Kurt Stillwell	.10	.05	.01
☐ 116	T Todd Stottlemyre	.25	.12	.02
☐ 117	T Bill Swift	.15	.07	.01
☐ 118	T Pat Tabler	.10	.05	.01
☐ 119	T Scott Terry	.06	.03	.00
☐ 120	T Mickey Tettleton	.15	.07	.01
☐ 121	T Dickie Thon	.06	.03	.00
☐ 122	T Jeff Treadway	.25	.12	.02
☐ 123	T Willie Upshaw	.06	.03	.00
☐ 124	T Robin Ventura OLY	2.00	1.00	.20
☐ 125	T Ron Washington	.06	.03	.00
☐ 126	T Walt Weiss	.90	.45	.09
☐ 127	T Bob Welch	.15	.07	.01
☐ 128	T David Wells	.15	.07	.01
☐ 129	T Glenn Wilson	.06	.03	.00
☐ 130	T Ted Wood OLY	.35	.17	.03
☐ 131	T Don Zimmer MG	.10	.05	.01
☐ 132	T Checklist 1T-132T	.06	.01	.00

1989 Topps

This 792-card set features backs that are printed in pink and black on gray card stock. The manager cards contain a checklist of the respective team's players on the back. Subsets in the set include Record Breakers (1-7), Turn Back the Clock (661-665), and All-Star selections (386-407). The bonus cards distributed throughout the set, which are indicated on the Topps checklist cards, are actually Team Leader (TL) cards. Also sprinkled throughout the set are Future Stars (FS) and First Draft Picks (FDP). There are subtle variations found in the Future Stars cards with respect to the placement of photo and type on the card; in fact, each card has at least two varieties but they are difficult to detect (requiring precise measurement) as well as difficult to explain. Topps also produced a specially boxed "glossy" edition, frequently referred to as the Topps Tiffany set. This year, again, Topps did not disclose the number of Tiffany sets they produced or sold but it seems that production quantities were roughly similar (or slightly smaller) to the previous two years. The checklist of cards (792 regular and 132 Traded) is identical to that of the normal non-glossy cards. There are two primary distinguishing features of the Tiffany cards—white card stock reverses and high gloss obverses. These Tiffany cards are valued at approximately four times the values listed below.

			MINT	EXC	G-VG
	COMPLETE SET (792)		25.00	12.50	2.50
	COMMON PLAYER (1-792)		.03	.01	.00
☐	1	George Bell RB Slams 3 HR on Opening Day	.12	.02	.01
☐	2	Wade Boggs RB Gets 200 Hits 6th Straight Season	.15	.07	.01
☐	3	Gary Carter RB Sets Record for Career Putouts	.08	.04	.01
☐	4	Andre Dawson RB Logs Double Figures in HR and SB	.08	.04	.01
☐	5	Orel Hershiser RB Pitches 59 Scoreless Innings	.12	.06	.01
☐	6	Doug Jones RB Earns His 15th Straight Save (photo actually Chris Codiroli)	.06	.03	.00
☐	7	Kevin McReynolds RB Steals 21 Without Being Caught	.08	.04	.01
☐	8	Dave Eiland	.12	.06	.01
☐	9	Tim Teufel	.03	.01	.00
☐	10	Andre Dawson	.10	.05	.01
☐	11	Bruce Sutter	.08	.04	.01
☐	12	Dale Sveum	.03	.01	.00
☐	13	Doug Sisk	.03	.01	.00
☐	14	Tom Kelly MG (team checklist back)	.06	.03	.00
☐	15	Robby Thompson	.03	.01	.00
☐	16	Ron Robinson	.03	.01	.00
☐	17	Brian Downing	.03	.01	.00
☐	18	Rick Rhoden	.03	.01	.00
☐	19	Greg Gagne	.03	.01	.00
☐	20	Steve Bedrosian	.08	.04	.01
☐	21	Chicago White Sox TL Greg Walker	.03	.01	.00
☐	22	Tim Crews	.03	.01	.00
☐	23	Mike Fitzgerald Montreal Expos	.03	.01	.00
☐	24	Larry Andersen	.03	.01	.00
☐	25	Frank White	.06	.03	.00

		MINT	EXC	G-VG
☐	26 Dale Mohorcic	.03	.01	.00
☐	27A Orestes Destrade	.20	.10	.02
	(F* next to copyright)			
☐	27B Orestes Destrade	.20	.10	.02
	(E*F* next to copyright)			
☐	28 Mike Moore	.06	.03	.00
☐	29 Kelly Gruber	.06	.03	.00
☐	30 Dwight Gooden	.25	.12	.02
☐	31 Terry Francona	.03	.01	.00
☐	32 Dennis Rasmussen	.06	.03	.00
☐	33 B.J. Surhoff	.06	.03	.00
☐	34 Ken Williams	.03	.01	.00
☐	35 John Tudor UER	.08	.04	.01
	('84 Pirates record, should be Red Sox)			
☐	36 Mitch Webster	.03	.01	.00
☐	37 Bob Stanley	.03	.01	.00
☐	38 Paul Runge	.03	.01	.00
☐	39 Mike Maddux	.03	.01	.00
☐	40 Steve Sax	.10	.05	.01
☐	41 Terry Mulholland	.03	.01	.00
☐	42 Jim Eppard	.08	.04	.01
☐	43 Guillermo Hernandez	.06	.03	.00
☐	44 Jim Snyder MG	.06	.03	.00
	(team checklist back)			
☐	45 Kal Daniels	.08	.04	.01
☐	46 Mark Portugal	.03	.01	.00
☐	47 Carney Lansford	.08	.04	.01
☐	48 Tim Burke	.06	.03	.00
☐	49 Craig Biggio	.35	.17	.03
☐	50 George Bell	.10	.05	.01
☐	51 California Angels TL	.03	.01	.00
	Mark McLemore			
☐	52 Bob Brenly	.03	.01	.00
☐	53 Ruben Sierra	.18	.09	.01
☐	54 Steve Trout	.03	.01	.00
☐	55 Julio Franco	.08	.04	.01
☐	56 Pat Tabler	.06	.03	.00
☐	57 Alejandro Pena	.03	.01	.00
☐	58 Lee Mazzilli	.03	.01	.00
☐	59 Mark Davis	.12	.06	.01
☐	60 Tom Brunansky	.08	.04	.01
☐	61 Neil Allen	.03	.01	.00
☐	62 Alfredo Griffin	.03	.01	.00
☐	63 Mark Clear	.03	.01	.00
☐	64 Alex Trevino	.03	.01	.00
☐	65 Rick Reuschel	.06	.03	.00
☐	66 Manny Trillo	.03	.01	.00

		MINT	EXC	G-VG
☐	67 Dave Palmer	.03	.01	.00
☐	68 Darrell Miller	.03	.01	.00
☐	69 Jeff Ballard	.08	.04	.01
☐	70 Mark McGwire	.50	.25	.05
☐	71 Mike Boddicker	.03	.01	.00
☐	72 John Moses	.03	.01	.00
☐	73 Pascual Perez	.08	.04	.01
☐	74 Nick Leyva MG	.06	.03	.00
	(team checklist back)			
☐	75 Tom Henke	.06	.03	.00
☐	76 Terry Blocker	.12	.06	.01
☐	77 Doyle Alexander	.03	.01	.00
☐	78 Jim Sundberg	.03	.01	.00
☐	79 Scott Bankhead	.03	.01	.00
☐	80 Cory Snyder	.08	.04	.01
☐	81 Montreal Expos TL	.08	.04	.01
	Tim Raines			
☐	82 Dave Leiper	.03	.01	.00
☐	83 Jeff Blauser	.12	.06	.01
☐	84 Bill Bene FDP	.12	.06	.01
☐	85 Kevin McReynolds	.10	.05	.01
☐	86 Al Nipper	.03	.01	.00
☐	87 Larry Owen	.03	.01	.00
☐	88 Darryl Hamilton	.15	.07	.01
☐	89 Dave LaPoint	.03	.01	.00
☐	90 Vince Coleman UER	.10	.05	.01
	(wrong birth year)			
☐	91 Floyd Youmans	.03	.01	.00
☐	92 Jeff Kunkel	.03	.01	.00
☐	93 Ken Howell	.03	.01	.00
☐	94 Chris Speier	.03	.01	.00
☐	95 Gerald Young	.06	.03	.00
☐	96 Rick Cerone	.06	.03	.00
	(Ellis Burks in background of photo)			
☐	97 Greg Mathews	.03	.01	.00
☐	98 Larry Sheets	.03	.01	.00
☐	99 Sherman Corbett	.08	.04	.01
☐	100 Mike Schmidt	.20	.10	.02
☐	101 Les Straker	.03	.01	.00
☐	102 Mike Gallego	.03	.01	.00
☐	103 Tim Birtsas	.03	.01	.00
☐	104 Dallas Green MG	.06	.03	.00
	(team checklist back)			
☐	105 Ron Darling	.08	.04	.01
☐	106 Willie Upshaw	.03	.01	.00
☐	107 Jose DeLeon	.06	.03	.00
☐	108 Fred Manrique	.03	.01	.00
☐	109 Hipolito Pena	.08	.04	.01

		MINT	EXC	G-VG
☐ 110	Paul Molitor	.10	.05	.01
☐ 111	Cincinnati Reds TL .. Eric Davis (swinging bat)	.10	.05	.01
☐ 112	Jim Presley	.03	.01	.00
☐ 113	Lloyd Moseby	.06	.03	.00
☐ 114	Bob Kipper	.03	.01	.00
☐ 115	Jody Davis	.03	.01	.00
☐ 116	Jeff Montgomery	.06	.03	.00
☐ 117	Dave Anderson	.03	.01	.00
☐ 118	Checklist 1-132	.06	.01	.00
☐ 119	Terry Puhl	.03	.01	.00
☐ 120	Frank Viola	.12	.06	.01
☐ 121	Garry Templeton	.06	.03	.00
☐ 122	Lance Johnson	.08	.04	.01
☐ 123	Spike Owen	.03	.01	.00
☐ 124	Jim Traber	.03	.01	.00
☐ 125	Mike Krukow	.03	.01	.00
☐ 126	Sid Bream	.03	.01	.00
☐ 127	Walt Terrell	.03	.01	.00
☐ 128	Milt Thompson	.03	.01	.00
☐ 129	Terry Clark	.10	.05	.01
☐ 130	Gerald Perry	.06	.03	.00
☐ 131	Dave Otto	.08	.04	.01
☐ 132	Curt Ford	.03	.01	.00
☐ 133	Bill Long	.03	.01	.00
☐ 134	Don Zimmer MG (team checklist back)	.06	.03	.00
☐ 135	Jose Rijo	.03	.01	.00
☐ 136	Joey Meyer	.06	.03	.00
☐ 137	Geno Petralli	.03	.01	.00
☐ 138	Wallace Johnson	.03	.01	.00
☐ 139	Mike Flanagan	.03	.01	.00
☐ 140	Shawon Dunston	.06	.03	.00
☐ 141	Cleveland Indians TL Brook Jacoby	.06	.03	.00
☐ 142	Mike Diaz	.03	.01	.00
☐ 143	Mike Campbell	.03	.01	.00
☐ 144	Jay Bell	.03	.01	.00
☐ 145	Dave Stewart	.10	.05	.01
☐ 146	Gary Pettis	.03	.01	.00
☐ 147	DeWayne Buice	.03	.01	.00
☐ 148	Bill Pecota	.03	.01	.00
☐ 149	Doug Dascenzo	.15	.07	.01
☐ 150	Fernando Valenzuela	.10	.05	.01
☐ 151	Terry McGriff	.03	.01	.00
☐ 152	Mark Thurmond	.03	.01	.00
☐ 153	Jim Pankovits	.03	.01	.00
☐ 154	Don Carman	.03	.01	.00
☐ 155	Marty Barrett	.03	.01	.00
☐ 156	Dave Gallagher	.15	.07	.01
☐ 157	Tom Glavine	.06	.03	.00
☐ 158	Mike Aldrete	.03	.01	.00
☐ 159	Pat Clements	.03	.01	.00
☐ 160	Jeffrey Leonard	.06	.03	.00
☐ 161	Gregg Olson FDP .. (born Scribner, NE, should be Omaha, NE)	.65	.30	.06
☐ 162	John Davis	.03	.01	.00
☐ 163	Bob Forsch	.03	.01	.00
☐ 164	Hal Lanier MG (team checklist back)	.06	.03	.00
☐ 165	Mike Dunne	.03	.01	.00
☐ 166	Doug Jennings	.15	.07	.01
☐ 167	Steve Searcy FS	.18	.09	.01
☐ 168	Willie Wilson	.06	.03	.00
☐ 169	Mike Jackson	.03	.01	.00
☐ 170	Tony Fernandez	.08	.04	.01
☐ 171	Atlanta Braves TL Andres Thomas	.03	.01	.00
☐ 172	Frank Williams	.03	.01	.00
☐ 173	Mel Hall	.06	.03	.00
☐ 174	Todd Burns	.20	.10	.02
☐ 175	John Shelby	.03	.01	.00
☐ 176	Jeff Parrett	.03	.01	.00
☐ 177	Monty Fariss FDP	.25	.12	.02
☐ 178	Mark Grant	.03	.01	.00
☐ 179	Ozzie Virgil	.03	.01	.00
☐ 180	Mike Scott	.10	.05	.01
☐ 181	Craig Worthington	.35	.17	.03
☐ 182	Bob McClure	.03	.01	.00
☐ 183	Oddibe McDowell	.06	.03	.00
☐ 184	John Costello	.10	.05	.01
☐ 185	Claudell Washington	.06	.03	.00
☐ 186	Pat Perry	.03	.01	.00
☐ 187	Darren Daulton	.03	.01	.00
☐ 188	Dennis Lamp	.03	.01	.00
☐ 189	Kevin Mitchell	.30	.15	.03
☐ 190	Mike Witt	.06	.03	.00
☐ 191	Sil Campusano	.20	.10	.02
☐ 192	Paul Mirabella	.03	.01	.00
☐ 193	Sparky Anderson MG (team checklist back) UER (553 Salazer)	.06	.03	.00
☐ 194	Greg W. Harris San Diego Padres	.20	.10	.02
☐ 195	Ozzie Guillen	.06	.03	.00

		MINT	EXC	G-VG
☐ 196	Denny Walling	.03	.01	.00
☐ 197	Neal Heaton	.03	.01	.00
☐ 198	Danny Heep	.03	.01	.00
☐ 199	Mike Schooler	.25	.12	.02
☐ 200	George Brett	.20	.10	.02
☐ 201	Blue Jays TL	.06	.03	.00
	Kelly Gruber			
☐ 202	Brad Moore	.12	.06	.01
☐ 203	Rob Ducey	.06	.03	.00
☐ 204	Brad Havens	.03	.01	.00
☐ 205	Dwight Evans	.08	.04	.01
☐ 206	Roberto Alomar	.25	.12	.02
☐ 207	Terry Leach	.06	.03	.00
☐ 208	Tom Pagnozzi	.03	.01	.00
☐ 209	Jeff Bittiger	.10	.05	.01
☐ 210	Dale Murphy	.15	.07	.01
☐ 211	Mike Pagliarulo	.06	.03	.00
☐ 212	Scott Sanderson	.03	.01	.00
☐ 213	Rene Gonzales	.03	.01	.00
☐ 214	Charlie O'Brien	.03	.01	.00
☐ 215	Kevin Gross	.03	.01	.00
☐ 216	Jack Howell	.03	.01	.00
☐ 217	Joe Price	.03	.01	.00
☐ 218	Mike LaValliere	.03	.01	.00
☐ 219	Jim Clancy	.03	.01	.00
☐ 220	Gary Gaetti	.08	.04	.01
☐ 221	Cecil Espy	.08	.04	.01
☐ 222	Mark Lewis FDP	.30	.15	.03
☐ 223	Jay Buhner	.12	.06	.01
☐ 224	Tony LaRussa MG	.06	.03	.00
	(team checklist back)			
☐ 225	Ramon Martinez	.30	.15	.03
☐ 226	Bill Doran	.06	.03	.00
☐ 227	John Farrell	.03	.01	.00
☐ 228	Nelson Santovenia	.12	.06	.01
☐ 229	Jimmy Key	.06	.03	.00
☐ 230	Ozzie Smith	.10	.05	.01
☐ 231	San Diego Padres TL	.10	.05	.01
	Roberto Alomar			
	(G. Carter at plate)			
☐ 232	Ricky Horton	.03	.01	.00
☐ 233	Gregg Jefferies FS	1.75	.85	.17
☐ 234	Tom Browning	.08	.04	.01
☐ 235	John Kruk	.06	.03	.00
☐ 236	Charles Hudson	.03	.01	.00
☐ 237	Glenn Hubbard	.03	.01	.00
☐ 238	Eric King	.03	.01	.00
☐ 239	Tim Laudner	.03	.01	.00
☐ 240	Greg Maddux	.08	.04	.01

		MINT	EXC	G-VG
☐ 241	Brett Butler	.06	.03	.00
☐ 242	Ed Vandeberg	.03	.01	.00
☐ 243	Bob Boone	.08	.04	.01
☐ 244	Jim Acker	.03	.01	.00
☐ 245	Jim Rice	.10	.05	.01
☐ 246	Rey Quinones	.03	.01	.00
☐ 247	Shawn Hillegas	.03	.01	.00
☐ 248	Tony Phillips	.03	.01	.00
☐ 249	Tim Leary	.06	.03	.00
☐ 250	Cal Ripken	.15	.07	.01
☐ 251	John Dopson	.15	.07	.01
☐ 252	Billy Hatcher	.03	.01	.00
☐ 253	Jose Alvarez	.08	.04	.01
☐ 254	Tom Lasorda MG	.06	.03	.00
	(team checklist back)			
☐ 255	Ron Guidry	.08	.04	.01
☐ 256	Benny Santiago	.10	.05	.01
☐ 257	Rick Aguilera	.03	.01	.00
☐ 258	Checklist 133-264	.06	.01	.00
☐ 259	Larry McWilliams	.03	.01	.00
☐ 260	Dave Winfield	.12	.06	.01
☐ 261	St. Louis Cardinals			
	TL	.06	.03	.00
	Tom Brunansky			
	(with Luis Alicea)			
☐ 262	Jeff Pico	.10	.05	.01
☐ 263	Mike Felder	.03	.01	.00
☐ 264	Rob Dibble	.20	.10	.02
☐ 265	Kent Hrbek	.10	.05	.01
☐ 266	Luis Aquino	.03	.01	.00
☐ 267	Jeff Robinson	.06	.03	.00
	Detroit Tigers			
☐ 268	Keith Miller	.15	.07	.01
	Philadelphia Phillies			
☐ 269	Tom Bolton	.03	.01	.00
☐ 270	Wally Joyner	.12	.06	.01
☐ 271	Jay Tibbs	.03	.01	.00
☐ 272	Ron Hassey	.03	.01	.00
☐ 273	Jose Lind	.03	.01	.00
☐ 274	Mark Eichhorn	.03	.01	.00
☐ 275	Danny Tartabull UER	.08	.04	.01
	(Born San Juan, PR			
	should be Miami, FL)			
☐ 276	Paul Kilgus	.03	.01	.00
☐ 277	Mike Davis	.03	.01	.00
☐ 278	Andy McGaffigan	.03	.01	.00
☐ 279	Scott Bradley	.03	.01	.00
☐ 280	Bob Knepper	.03	.01	.00
☐ 281	Gary Redus	.03	.01	.00

		MINT	EXC	G-VG
☐ 282	Cris Carpenter	.15	.07	.01
☐ 283	Andy Allanson	.03	.01	.00
☐ 284	Jim Leyland MG	.06	.03	.00
	(team checklist back)			
☐ 285	John Candelaria	.06	.03	.00
☐ 286	Darrin Jackson	.10	.05	.01
☐ 287	Juan Nieves	.03	.01	.00
☐ 288	Pat Sheridan	.03	.01	.00
☐ 289	Ernie Whitt	.03	.01	.00
☐ 290	John Franco	.06	.03	.00
☐ 291	New York Mets TL	.12	.06	.01
	Darryl Strawberry			
	(with K. Hernandez			
	and K. McReynolds)			
☐ 292	Jim Corsi	.12	.06	.01
☐ 293	Glenn Wilson	.03	.01	.00
☐ 294	Juan Berenguer	.03	.01	.00
☐ 295	Scott Fletcher	.03	.01	.00
☐ 296	Ron Gant	.15	.07	.01
☐ 297	Oswald Peraza	.08	.04	.01
☐ 298	Chris James	.06	.03	.00
☐ 299	Steve Ellsworth	.12	.06	.01
☐ 300	Darryl Strawberry	.30	.15	.03
☐ 301	Charlie Leibrandt	.03	.01	.00
☐ 302	Gary Ward	.03	.01	.00
☐ 303	Felix Fermin	.03	.01	.00
☐ 304	Joel Youngblood	.03	.01	.00
☐ 305	Dave Smith	.03	.01	.00
☐ 306	Tracy Woodson	.10	.05	.01
☐ 307	Lance McCullers	.03	.01	.00
☐ 308	Ron Karkovice	.03	.01	.00
☐ 309	Mario Diaz	.08	.04	.01
☐ 310	Rafael Palmeiro	.10	.05	.01
☐ 311	Chris Bosio	.06	.03	.00
☐ 312	Tom Lawless	.03	.01	.00
☐ 313	Dennis Martinez	.06	.03	.00
☐ 314	Bobby Valentine MG	.06	.03	.00
	(team checklist back)			
☐ 315	Greg Swindell	.08	.04	.01
☐ 316	Walt Weiss	.30	.15	.03
☐ 317	Jack Armstrong	.20	.10	.02
☐ 318	Gene Larkin	.03	.01	.00
☐ 319	Greg Booker	.03	.01	.00
☐ 320	Lou Whitaker	.08	.04	.01
☐ 321	Boston Red Sox TL	.08	.04	.01
	Jody Reed			
☐ 322	John Smiley	.06	.03	.00
☐ 323	Gary Thurman	.03	.01	.00
☐ 324	Bob Milacki	.20	.10	.02

		MINT	EXC	G-VG
☐ 325	Jesse Barfield	.08	.04	.01
☐ 326	Dennis Boyd	.06	.03	.00
☐ 327	Mark Lemke	.10	.05	.01
☐ 328	Rick Honeycutt	.03	.01	.00
☐ 329	Bob Melvin	.03	.01	.00
☐ 330	Eric Davis	.25	.12	.02
☐ 331	Curt Wilkerson	.03	.01	.00
☐ 332	Tony Armas	.06	.03	.00
☐ 333	Bob Ojeda	.06	.03	.00
☐ 334	Steve Lyons	.03	.01	.00
☐ 335	Dave Righetti	.08	.04	.01
☐ 336	Steve Balboni	.03	.01	.00
☐ 337	Calvin Schiraldi	.03	.01	.00
☐ 338	Jim Adduci	.03	.01	.00
☐ 339	Scott Bailes	.03	.01	.00
☐ 340	Kirk Gibson	.12	.06	.01
☐ 341	Jim Deshaies	.03	.01	.00
☐ 342	Tom Brookens	.03	.01	.00
☐ 343	Gary Sheffield FS	1.25	.60	.12
☐ 344	Tom Trebelhorn MG	.06	.03	.00
	(team checklist back)			
☐ 345	Charlie Hough	.03	.01	.00
☐ 346	Rex Hudler	.03	.01	.00
☐ 347	John Cerutti	.03	.01	.00
☐ 348	Ed Hearn	.03	.01	.00
☐ 349	Ron Jones	.25	.12	.02
☐ 350	Andy Van Slyke	.08	.04	.01
☐ 351	San Fran. Giants TL	.03	.01	.00
	Bob Melvin			
	(with Bill Fahey CO)			
☐ 352	Rick Schu	.03	.01	.00
☐ 353	Marvell Wynne	.03	.01	.00
☐ 354	Larry Parrish	.03	.01	.00
☐ 355	Mark Langston	.12	.06	.01
☐ 356	Kevin Elster	.06	.03	.00
☐ 357	Jerry Reuss	.03	.01	.00
☐ 358	Ricky Jordan	1.25	.60	.12
☐ 359	Tommy John	.08	.04	.01
☐ 360	Ryne Sandberg	.15	.07	.01
☐ 361	Kelly Downs	.03	.01	.00
☐ 362	Jack Lazorko	.03	.01	.00
☐ 363	Rich Yett	.03	.01	.00
☐ 364	Rob Deer	.06	.03	.00
☐ 365	Mike Henneman	.03	.01	.00
☐ 366	Herm Winningham	.03	.01	.00
☐ 367	Johnny Paredes	.10	.05	.01
☐ 368	Brian Holton	.03	.01	.00
☐ 369	Ken Caminiti	.03	.01	.00
☐ 370	Dennis Eckersley	.08	.04	.01

		MINT	EXC	G-VG
☐ 371	Manny Lee	.03	.01	.00
☐ 372	Craig Lefferts	.06	.03	.00
☐ 373	Tracy Jones	.03	.01	.00
☐ 374	John Wathan MG	.06	.03	.00
	(team checklist back)			
☐ 375	Terry Pendleton	.03	.01	.00
☐ 376	Steve Lombardozzi	.03	.01	.00
☐ 377	Mike Smithson	.03	.01	.00
☐ 378	Checklist 265-396	.06	.01	.00
☐ 379	Tim Flannery	.03	.01	.00
☐ 380	Rickey Henderson	.25	.12	.02
☐ 381	Baltimore Orioles TL	.03	.01	.00
	Larry Sheets			
☐ 382	John Smoltz	.35	.17	.03
☐ 383	Howard Johnson	.12	.06	.01
☐ 384	Mark Salas	.03	.01	.00
☐ 385	Von Hayes	.08	.04	.01
☐ 386	Andres Galarraga AS	.08	.04	.01
☐ 387	Ryne Sandberg AS	.10	.05	.01
☐ 388	Bobby Bonilla AS	.08	.04	.01
☐ 389	Ozzie Smith AS	.08	.04	.01
☐ 390	Darryl Strawberry AS	.15	.07	.01
☐ 391	Andre Dawson AS	.10	.05	.01
☐ 392	Andy Van Slyke AS	.08	.04	.01
☐ 393	Gary Carter AS	.10	.05	.01
☐ 394	Orel Hershiser AS	.10	.05	.01
☐ 395	Danny Jackson AS	.06	.03	.00
☐ 396	Kirk Gibson AS	.10	.05	.01
☐ 397	Don Mattingly AS	.30	.15	.03
☐ 398	Julio Franco AS	.08	.04	.01
☐ 399	Wade Boggs AS	.25	.12	.02
☐ 400	Alan Trammell AS	.08	.04	.01
☐ 401	Jose Canseco AS	.30	.15	.03
☐ 402	Mike Greenwell AS	.20	.10	.02
☐ 403	Kirby Puckett AS	.15	.07	.01
☐ 404	Bob Boone AS	.08	.04	.01
☐ 405	Roger Clemens AS	.15	.07	.01
☐ 406	Frank Viola AS	.08	.04	.01
☐ 407	Dave Winfield AS	.10	.05	.01
☐ 408	Greg Walker	.03	.01	.00
☐ 409	Ken Dayley	.03	.01	.00
☐ 410	Jack Clark	.08	.04	.01
☐ 411	Mitch Williams	.08	.04	.01
☐ 412	Barry Lyons	.03	.01	.00
☐ 413	Mike Kingery	.03	.01	.00
☐ 414	Jim Fregosi MG	.06	.03	.00
	(team checklist back)			
☐ 415	Rich Gossage	.08	.04	.01
☐ 416	Fred Lynn	.08	.04	.01
☐ 417	Mike LaCoss	.03	.01	.00
☐ 418	Bob Dernier	.03	.01	.00
☐ 419	Tom Filer	.03	.01	.00
☐ 420	Joe Carter	.10	.05	.01
☐ 421	Kirk McCaskill	.03	.01	.00
☐ 422	Bo Diaz	.03	.01	.00
☐ 423	Brian Fisher	.03	.01	.00
☐ 424	Luis Polonia UER	.03	.01	.00
	(wrong birthdate)			
☐ 425	Jay Howell	.06	.03	.00
☐ 426	Dan Gladden	.03	.01	.00
☐ 427	Eric Show	.03	.01	.00
☐ 428	Craig Reynolds	.03	.01	.00
☐ 429	Minnesota Twins TL	.03	.01	.00
	Greg Gagne			
	(taking throw at 2nd)			
☐ 430	Mark Gubicza	.08	.04	.01
☐ 431	Luis Rivera	.03	.01	.00
☐ 432	Chad Kreuter	.10	.05	.01
☐ 433	Albert Hall	.03	.01	.00
☐ 434	Ken Patterson	.08	.04	.01
☐ 435	Len Dykstra	.06	.03	.00
☐ 436	Bobby Meacham	.03	.01	.00
☐ 437	Andy Benes FDP	.75	.35	.07
☐ 438	Greg Gross	.03	.01	.00
☐ 439	Frank DiPino	.03	.01	.00
☐ 440	Bobby Bonilla	.08	.04	.01
☐ 441	Jerry Reed	.03	.01	.00
☐ 442	Jose Oquendo	.03	.01	.00
☐ 443	Rod Nichols	.10	.05	.01
☐ 444	Moose Stubing MG	.06	.03	.00
	(team checklist back)			
☐ 445	Matt Nokes	.08	.04	.01
☐ 446	Rob Murphy	.03	.01	.00
☐ 447	Donell Nixon	.03	.01	.00
☐ 448	Eric Plunk	.03	.01	.00
☐ 449	Carmelo Martinez	.03	.01	.00
☐ 450	Roger Clemens	.25	.12	.02
☐ 451	Mark Davidson	.03	.01	.00
☐ 452	Israel Sanchez	.10	.05	.01
☐ 453	Tom Prince	.08	.04	.01
☐ 454	Paul Assenmacher	.03	.01	.00
☐ 455	Johnny Ray	.06	.03	.00
☐ 456	Tim Belcher	.08	.04	.01
☐ 457	Mackey Sasser	.03	.01	.00
☐ 458	Donn Pall	.08	.04	.01
☐ 459	Seattle Mariners TL	.03	.01	.00
	Dave Valle			
☐ 460	Dave Stieb	.08	.04	.01

		MINT	EXC	G-VG
☐ 461	Buddy Bell	.06	.03	.00
☐ 462	Jose Guzman	.03	.01	.00
☐ 463	Steve Lake	.03	.01	.00
☐ 464	Bryn Smith	.06	.03	.00
☐ 465	Mark Grace	2.50	1.25	.25
☐ 466	Chuck Crim	.03	.01	.00
☐ 467	Jim Walewander	.03	.01	.00
☐ 468	Henry Cotto	.03	.01	.00
☐ 469	Jose Bautista	.10	.05	.01
☐ 470	Lance Parrish	.08	.04	.01
☐ 471	Steve Curry	.10	.05	.01
☐ 472	Brian Harper	.03	.01	.00
☐ 473	Don Robinson	.03	.01	.00
☐ 474	Bob Rodgers MG (team checklist back)	.06	.03	.00
☐ 475	Dave Parker	.08	.04	.01
☐ 476	Jon Perlman	.08	.04	.01
☐ 477	Dick Schofield	.03	.01	.00
☐ 478	Doug Drabek	.06	.03	.00
☐ 479	Mike Macfarlane	.12	.06	.01
☐ 480	Keith Hernandez	.10	.05	.01
☐ 481	Chris Brown	.03	.01	.00
☐ 482	Steve Peters	.10	.05	.01
☐ 483	Mickey Hatcher	.03	.01	.00
☐ 484	Steve Shields	.03	.01	.00
☐ 485	Hubie Brooks	.06	.03	.00
☐ 486	Jack McDowell	.10	.05	.01
☐ 487	Scott Lusader	.08	.04	.01
☐ 488	Kevin Coffman ("Now with Cubs")	.08	.04	.01
☐ 489	Phila. Phillies TL Mike Schmidt	.12	.06	.01
☐ 490	Chris Sabo	.40	.20	.04
☐ 491	Mike Birkbeck	.03	.01	.00
☐ 492	Alan Ashby	.03	.01	.00
☐ 493	Todd Benzinger	.03	.01	.00
☐ 494	Shane Rawley	.03	.01	.00
☐ 495	Candy Maldonado	.03	.01	.00
☐ 496	Dwayne Henry	.03	.01	.00
☐ 497	Pete Stanicek	.08	.04	.01
☐ 498	Dave Valle	.03	.01	.00
☐ 499	Don Heinkel	.08	.04	.01
☐ 500	Jose Canseco	.80	.40	.08
☐ 501	Vance Law	.03	.01	.00
☐ 502	Duane Ward	.03	.01	.00
☐ 503	Al Newman	.03	.01	.00
☐ 504	Bob Walk	.03	.01	.00
☐ 505	Pete Rose MG (team checklist back)	.25	.12	.02

		MINT	EXC	G-VG
☐ 506	Kirt Manwaring	.08	.04	.01
☐ 507	Steve Farr	.03	.01	.00
☐ 508	Wally Backman	.03	.01	.00
☐ 509	Bud Black	.03	.01	.00
☐ 510	Bob Horner	.08	.04	.01
☐ 511	Richard Dotson	.03	.01	.00
☐ 512	Donnie Hill	.03	.01	.00
☐ 513	Jesse Orosco	.03	.01	.00
☐ 514	Chet Lemon	.03	.01	.00
☐ 515	Barry Larkin	.10	.05	.01
☐ 516	Eddie Whitson	.03	.01	.00
☐ 517	Greg Brock	.03	.01	.00
☐ 518	Bruce Ruffin	.03	.01	.00
☐ 519	New York Yankees TL Willie Randolph	.06	.03	.00
☐ 520	Rick Sutcliffe	.08	.04	.01
☐ 521	Mickey Tettleton	.08	.04	.01
☐ 522	Randy Kramer	.10	.05	.01
☐ 523	Andres Thomas	.03	.01	.00
☐ 524	Checklist 397-528	.06	.01	.00
☐ 525	Chili Davis	.06	.03	.00
☐ 526	Wes Gardner	.03	.01	.00
☐ 527	Dave Henderson	.06	.03	.00
☐ 528	Luis Medina (lower left front has white triangle)	.25	.12	.02
☐ 529	Tom Foley	.03	.01	.00
☐ 530	Nolan Ryan	.25	.12	.02
☐ 531	Dave Hengel	.10	.05	.01
☐ 532	Jerry Browne	.03	.01	.00
☐ 533	Andy Hawkins	.03	.01	.00
☐ 534	Doc Edwards MG (team checklist back)	.06	.03	.00
☐ 535	Todd Worrell UER (4 wins in '88, should be 5)	.08	.04	.01
☐ 536	Joel Skinner	.03	.01	.00
☐ 537	Pete Smith	.10	.05	.01
☐ 538	Juan Castillo	.03	.01	.00
☐ 539	Barry Jones	.03	.01	.00
☐ 540	Bo Jackson	.50	.25	.05
☐ 541	Cecil Fielder	.03	.01	.00
☐ 542	Todd Frohwirth	.03	.01	.00
☐ 543	Damon Berryhill	.30	.15	.03
☐ 544	Jeff Sellers	.03	.01	.00
☐ 545	Mookie Wilson	.06	.03	.00
☐ 546	Mark Williamson	.03	.01	.00
☐ 547	Mark McLemore	.03	.01	.00

		MINT	EXC	G-VG
☐ 548	Bobby Witt	.06	.03	.00
☐ 549	Chicago Cubs TL	.03	.01	.00
	Jamie Moyer			
	(pitching)			
☐ 550	Orel Hershiser	.20	.10	.02
☐ 551	Randy Ready	.03	.01	.00
☐ 552	Greg Cadaret	.03	.01	.00
☐ 553	Luis Salazar	.03	.01	.00
☐ 554	Nick Esasky	.06	.03	.00
☐ 555	Bert Blyleven	.08	.04	.01
☐ 556	Bruce Fields	.03	.01	.00
☐ 557	Keith Miller	.03	.01	.00
	New York Mets			
☐ 558	Dan Pasqua	.03	.01	.00
☐ 559	Juan Agosto	.03	.01	.00
☐ 560	Tim Raines	.12	.06	.01
☐ 561	Luis Aguayo	.03	.01	.00
☐ 562	Danny Cox	.03	.01	.00
☐ 563	Bill Schroeder	.03	.01	.00
☐ 564	Russ Nixon MG	.06	.03	.00
	(team checklist back)			
☐ 565	Jeff Russell	.06	.03	.00
☐ 566	Al Pedrique	.03	.01	.00
☐ 567	David Wells UER	.08	.04	.01
	(Complete Pitching			
	Recor)			
☐ 568	Mickey Brantley	.06	.03	.00
☐ 569	German Jimenez	.08	.04	.01
☐ 570	Tony Gwynn UER	.15	.07	.01
	('88 average should			
	be italicized as			
	league leader)			
☐ 571	Billy Ripken	.03	.01	.00
☐ 572	Atlee Hammaker	.03	.01	.00
☐ 573	Jim Abbott FDP	2.00	1.00	.20
☐ 574	Dave Clark	.06	.03	.00
☐ 575	Juan Samuel	.08	.04	.01
☐ 576	Greg Minton	.03	.01	.00
☐ 577	Randy Bush	.03	.01	.00
☐ 578	John Morris	.03	.01	.00
☐ 579	Houston Astros TL	.06	.03	.00
	Glenn Davis			
	(batting stance)			
☐ 580	Harold Reynolds	.06	.03	.00
☐ 581	Gene Nelson	.03	.01	.00
☐ 582	Mike Marshall	.08	.04	.01
☐ 583	Paul Gibson	.10	.05	.01
☐ 584	Randy Velarde UER	.08	.04	.01
	(signed 1935,			

		MINT	EXC	G-VG
	should be 1985)			
☐ 585	Harold Baines	.08	.04	.01
☐ 586	Joe Boever	.03	.01	.00
☐ 587	Mike Stanley	.03	.01	.00
☐ 588	Luis Alicea	.10	.05	.01
☐ 589	Dave Meads	.03	.01	.00
☐ 590	Andres Galarraga	.10	.05	.01
☐ 591	Jeff Musselman	.03	.01	.00
☐ 592	John Cangelosi	.03	.01	.00
☐ 593	Drew Hall	.03	.01	.00
☐ 594	Jimy Williams MG	.06	.03	.00
	(team checklist back)			
☐ 595	Teddy Higuera	.06	.03	.00
☐ 596	Kurt Stillwell	.03	.01	.00
☐ 597	Terry Taylor	.12	.06	.01
☐ 598	Ken Gerhart	.03	.01	.00
☐ 599	Tom Candiotti	.03	.01	.00
☐ 600	Wade Boggs	.50	.25	.05
☐ 601	Dave Dravecky	.08	.04	.01
☐ 602	Devon White	.08	.04	.01
☐ 603	Frank Tanana	.03	.01	.00
☐ 604	Paul O'Neill	.03	.01	.00
☐ 605A	Bob Welch ERR	4.00	2.00	.40
	(missing line on back,			
	"Complete M.L.			
	Pitching Record")			
☐ 605B	Bob Welch COR	.15	.07	.01
☐ 606	Rick Dempsey	.03	.01	.00
☐ 607	Willie Ansley FDP	.35	.17	.03
☐ 608	Phil Bradley	.06	.03	.00
☐ 609	Detroit Tigers TL	.06	.03	.00
	Frank Tanana			
	(with Alan Trammell			
	and Mike Heath)			
☐ 610	Randy Myers	.06	.03	.00
☐ 611	Don Slaught	.03	.01	.00
☐ 612	Dan Quisenberry	.08	.04	.01
☐ 613	Gary Varsho	.10	.05	.01
☐ 614	Joe Hesketh	.03	.01	.00
☐ 615	Robin Yount	.15	.07	.01
☐ 616	Steve Rosenberg	.10	.05	.01
☐ 617	Mark Parent	.10	.05	.01
☐ 618	Rance Mulliniks	.03	.01	.00
☐ 619	Checklist 529-660	.06	.01	.00
☐ 620	Barry Bonds	.08	.04	.01
☐ 621	Rick Mahler	.03	.01	.00
☐ 622	Stan Javier	.03	.01	.00
☐ 623	Fred Toliver	.03	.01	.00
☐ 624	Jack McKeon MG	.06	.03	.00

		MINT	EXC	G-VG
	(team checklist back)			
☐ 625	Eddie Murray	.12	.06	.01
☐ 626	Jeff Reed	.03	.01	.00
☐ 627	Greg Harris	.03	.01	.00
	Philadelphia Phillies			
☐ 628	Matt Williams	.15	.07	.01
☐ 629	Pete O'Brien	.06	.03	.00
☐ 630	Mike Greenwell	.45	.22	.04
☐ 631	Dave Bergman	.03	.01	.00
☐ 632	Bryan Harvey	.18	.09	.01
☐ 633	Daryl Boston	.03	.01	.00
☐ 634	Marvin Freeman	.03	.01	.00
☐ 635	Willie Randolph	.06	.03	.00
☐ 636	Bill Wilkinson	.03	.01	.00
☐ 637	Carmen Castillo	.03	.01	.00
☐ 638	Floyd Bannister	.03	.01	.00
☐ 639	Oakland A's TL	.10	.05	.01
	Walt Weiss			
☐ 640	Willie McGee	.08	.04	.01
☐ 641	Curt Young	.03	.01	.00
☐ 642	Argenis Salazar	.03	.01	.00
☐ 643	Louie Meadows	.08	.04	.01
☐ 644	Lloyd McClendon	.03	.01	.00
☐ 645	Jack Morris	.08	.04	.01
☐ 646	Kevin Bass	.06	.03	.00
☐ 647	Randy Johnson	.18	.09	.01
☐ 648	Sandy Alomar FS ...	.90	.45	.09
☐ 649	Stewart Cliburn	.03	.01	.00
☐ 650	Kirby Puckett	.25	.12	.02
☐ 651	Tom Niedenfuer	.03	.01	.00
☐ 652	Rich Gedman	.03	.01	.00
☐ 653	Tommy Barrett	.10	.05	.01
☐ 654	Whitey Herzog MG ..	.06	.03	.00
	(team checklist back)			
☐ 655	Dave Magadan	.08	.04	.01
☐ 656	Ivan Calderon	.06	.03	.00
☐ 657	Joe Magrane	.08	.04	.00
☐ 658	R.J. Reynolds	.03	.01	.00
☐ 659	Al Leiter	.08	.04	.01
☐ 660	Will Clark	.50	.25	.05
☐ 661	Dwight Gooden			
	TBC84	.12	.06	.01
☐ 662	Lou Brock TBC79 ...	.08	.04	.01
☐ 663	Hank Aaron TBC74 ..	.10	.05	.01
☐ 664	Gil Hodges TBC69 ..	.08	.04	.01
☐ 665A	Tony Oliva TBC64			
	ERR	2.00	1.00	.20
	(fabricated card)			

		MINT	EXC	G-VG
	(Topps copyright miss-			
	ing)			
☐ 665B	Tony Oliva TBC64			
	COR	.10	.05	.01
	(fabricated card)			
☐ 666	Randy St. Claire	.03	.01	.00
☐ 667	Dwayne Murphy	.03	.01	.00
☐ 668	Mike Bielecki	.06	.03	.00
☐ 669	L.A. Dodgers TL	.15	.07	.01
	Orel Hershiser			
	(mound conference			
	with Mike Scioscia)			
☐ 670	Kevin Seitzer	.12	.06	.01
☐ 671	Jim Gantner	.03	.01	.00
☐ 672	Allan Anderson	.06	.03	.00
☐ 673	Don Baylor	.06	.03	.00
☐ 674	Otis Nixon	.03	.01	.00
☐ 675	Bruce Hurst	.08	.04	.01
☐ 676	Ernie Riles	.03	.01	.00
☐ 677	Dave Schmidt	.03	.01	.00
☐ 678	Dion James	.03	.01	.00
☐ 679	Willie Fraser	.03	.01	.00
☐ 680	Gary Carter	.12	.06	.01
☐ 681	Jeff Robinson	.06	.03	.00
	Pittsburgh Pirates			
☐ 682	Rick Leach	.03	.01	.00
☐ 683	Jose Cecena	.08	.04	.01
☐ 684	Dave Johnson MG ..	.06	.03	.00
	(team checklist back)			
☐ 685	Jeff Treadway	.10	.05	.01
☐ 686	Scott Terry	.03	.01	.00
☐ 687	Alvin Davis	.08	.04	.01
☐ 688	Zane Smith	.03	.01	.00
☐ 689A	Stan Jefferson	.10	.05	.01
	(pink triangle on			
	front bottom left)			
☐ 689B	Stan Jefferson	.10	.05	.01
	(violet triangle on			
	front bottom left)			
☐ 690	Doug Jones	.06	.03	.00
☐ 691	Roberto Kelly UER ..	.25	.12	.02
	(83 Oneonita)			
☐ 692	Steve Ontiveros	.03	.01	.00
☐ 693	Pat Borders	.15	.07	.01
☐ 694	Les Lancaster	.03	.01	.00
☐ 695	Carlton Fisk	.10	.05	.01
☐ 696	Don August	.06	.03	.00
☐ 697A	Franklin Stubbs	.10	.05	.01
	(team name on front			

		MINT	EXC	G-VG
	in white)			
☐ 697B	Franklin Stubbs	.10	.05	.01
	(team name on front in gray)			
☐ 698	Keith Atherton	.03	.01	.00
☐ 699	Pittsburgh Pirates TL	.08	.04	.01
	Al Pedrique			
	(Tony Gwynn sliding)			
☐ 700	Don Mattingly	.75	.35	.07
☐ 701	Storm Davis	.06	.03	.00
☐ 702	Jamie Quirk	.03	.01	.00
☐ 703	Scott Garrelts	.06	.03	.00
☐ 704	Carlos Quintana	.25	.12	.02
☐ 705	Terry Kennedy	.03	.01	.00
☐ 706	Pete Incaviglia	.08	.04	.01
☐ 707	Steve Jeltz	.03	.01	.00
☐ 708	Chuck Finley	.06	.03	.00
☐ 709	Tom Herr	.03	.01	.00
☐ 710	David Cone	.15	.07	.01
☐ 711	Candy Sierra	.10	.05	.01
☐ 712	Bill Swift	.03	.01	.00
☐ 713	Ty Griffin FDP	.75	.35	.07
☐ 714	Joe Morgan MG	.06	.03	.00
	(team checklist back)			
☐ 715	Tony Pena	.06	.03	.00
☐ 716	Wayne Tolleson	.03	.01	.00
☐ 717	Jamie Moyer	.03	.01	.00
☐ 718	Glenn Braggs	.06	.03	.00
☐ 719	Danny Darwin	.03	.01	.00
☐ 720	Tim Wallach	.06	.03	.00
☐ 721	Ron Tingley	.08	.04	.01
☐ 722	Todd Stottlemyre	.12	.06	.01
☐ 723	Rafael Belliard	.03	.01	.00
☐ 724	Jerry Don Gleaton ...	.03	.01	.00
☐ 725	Terry Steinbach	.08	.04	.01
☐ 726	Dickie Thon	.03	.01	.00
☐ 727	Joe Orsulak	.03	.01	.00
☐ 728	Charlie Puleo	.03	.01	.00
☐ 729	Texas Rangers TL	.03	.01	.00
	Steve Buechele (inconsistent design, team name on front surrounded by black, should be white)			
☐ 730	Danny Jackson	.08	.04	.01
☐ 731	Mike Young	.03	.01	.00
☐ 732	Steve Buechele	.03	.01	.00
☐ 733	Randy Bockus	.08	.04	.01
☐ 734	Jody Reed	.06	.03	.00

		MINT	EXC	G-VG
☐ 735	Roger McDowell	.06	.03	.00
☐ 736	Jeff Hamilton	.03	.01	.00
☐ 737	Norm Charlton	.12	.06	.01
☐ 738	Darnell Coles	.03	.01	.00
☐ 739	Brook Jacoby	.06	.03	.00
☐ 740	Dan Plesac	.06	.03	.00
☐ 741	Ken Phelps	.06	.03	.00
☐ 742	Mike Harkey FS	.25	.12	.02
☐ 743	Mike Heath	.03	.01	.00
☐ 744	Roger Craig MG	.06	.03	.00
	(team checklist back)			
☐ 745	Fred McGriff	.15	.07	.01
☐ 746	German Gonzalez UER	.10	.05	.01
	(wrong birthdate)			
☐ 747	Will Tejada	.03	.01	.00
☐ 748	Jimmy Jones	.06	.03	.00
☐ 749	Rafael Ramirez	.03	.01	.00
☐ 750	Bret Saberhagen	.12	.06	.01
☐ 751	Ken Oberkfell	.03	.01	.00
☐ 752	Jim Gott	.03	.01	.00
☐ 753	Jose Uribe	.03	.01	.00
☐ 754	Bob Brower	.03	.01	.00
☐ 755	Mike Scioscia	.03	.01	.00
☐ 756	Scott Medvin	.10	.05	.01
☐ 757	Brady Anderson	.20	.10	.02
☐ 758	Gene Walter	.03	.01	.00
☐ 759	Milwaukee Brewers TL	.06	.03	.00
	Rob Deer			
☐ 760	Lee Smith	.06	.03	.00
☐ 761	Dante Bichette	.18	.09	.01
☐ 762	Bobby Thigpen	.06	.03	.00
☐ 763	Dave Martinez	.03	.01	.00
☐ 764	Robin Ventura FDP ...	1.00	.50	.10
☐ 765	Glenn Davis	.10	.05	.01
☐ 766	Cecilio Guante	.03	.01	.00
☐ 767	Mike Capel	.12	.06	.01
☐ 768	Bill Wegman	.03	.01	.00
☐ 769	Junior Ortiz	.03	.01	.00
☐ 770	Alan Trammell	.12	.06	.01
☐ 771	Ron Kittle	.06	.03	.00
☐ 772	Ron Oester	.03	.01	.00
☐ 773	Keith Moreland	.03	.01	.00
☐ 774	Frank Robinson MG .	.10	.05	.01
	(team checklist back)			
☐ 775	Jeff Reardon	.06	.03	.00
☐ 776	Nelson Liriano	.03	.01	.00
☐ 777	Ted Power	.03	.01	.00

		MINT	EXC	G-VG
☐ 778	Bruce Benedict	.03	.01	.00
☐ 779	Craig McMurtry	.03	.01	.00
☐ 780	Pedro Guerrero	.10	.05	.01
☐ 781	Greg Briley	.60	.30	.06
☐ 782	Checklist 661-792	.06	.01	.00
☐ 783	Trevor Wilson	.12	.06	.01
☐ 784	Steve Avery FDP	.50	.25	.05
☐ 785	Ellis Burks	.25	.12	.02
☐ 786	Melido Perez	.12	.06	.01
☐ 787	Dave West	.35	.17	.03
☐ 788	Mike Morgan	.06	.03	.00
☐ 789	Kansas City Royals TL	.15	.07	.01
	Bo Jackson (throwing)			
☐ 790	Sid Fernandez	.08	.04	.01
☐ 791	Jim Lindeman	.03	.01	.00
☐ 792	Rafael Santana	.06	.03	.00

1989 Topps Big Baseball

The 1989 Topps Big Baseball set contains 330 glossy cards measuring 2 ½" by 3 ¾". The fronts feature mug shots superimposed on action photos. The horizontally oriented backs have color cartoons, 1988 and career stats. The set was released in three series of 110 cards. The cards were distributed in seven-card cello packs marked with the series number.

		MINT	EXC	G-VG
	COMPLETE SET (330)	30.00	15.00	3.00
	COMMON PLAYER (1-110)	.05	.02	.00
	COMMON PLAYER (111-220)	.05	.02	.00
	COMMON PLAYER (221-330)	.06	.02	.00
☐ 1	Orel Hershiser	.35	.17	.03
☐ 2	Harold Reynolds	.10	.05	.01
☐ 3	Jody Davis	.05	.02	.00
☐ 4	Greg Walker	.05	.02	.00
☐ 5	Barry Bonds	.12	.06	.01
☐ 6	Bret Saberhagen	.20	.10	.02
☐ 7	Johnny Ray	.08	.04	.01
☐ 8	Mike Fiore	.12	.06	.01
☐ 9	Juan Castillo	.05	.02	.00
☐ 10	Todd Burns	.08	.04	.01
☐ 11	Carmelo Martinez	.05	.02	.00
☐ 12	Geno Petralli	.05	.02	.00
☐ 13	Mel Hall	.08	.04	.01
☐ 14	Tom Browning	.08	.04	.01
☐ 15	Fred McGriff	.20	.10	.02
☐ 16	Kevin Elster	.12	.06	.01
☐ 17	Tim Leary	.08	.04	.01
☐ 18	Jim Rice	.20	.10	.02
☐ 19	Bret Barberie	.20	.10	.02
☐ 20	Jay Buhner	.10	.05	.01
☐ 21	Atlee Hammaker	.05	.02	.00
☐ 22	Lou Whitaker	.12	.06	.01
☐ 23	Paul Runge	.08	.04	.01
☐ 24	Carlton Fisk	.20	.10	.02
☐ 25	Jose Lind	.05	.02	.00
☐ 26	Mark Gubicza	.10	.05	.01
☐ 27	Billy Ripken	.08	.04	.01
☐ 28	Mike Pagliarulo	.05	.02	.00
☐ 29	Jim Deshaies	.05	.02	.00
☐ 30	Mark McLemore	.05	.02	.00
☐ 31	Scott Terry	.05	.02	.00
☐ 32	Franklin Stubbs	.05	.02	.00
☐ 33	Don August	.05	.02	.00
☐ 34	Mark McGwire	.60	.30	.06
☐ 35	Eric Show	.05	.02	.00
☐ 36	Cecil Espy	.08	.04	.01
☐ 37	Ron Tingley	.05	.02	.00
☐ 38	Mickey Brantley	.08	.04	.01
☐ 39	Paul O'Neill	.10	.05	.01
☐ 40	Ed Sprague	.15	.07	.01
☐ 41	Len Dykstra	.08	.04	.01
☐ 42	Roger Clemens	.40	.20	.04
☐ 43	Ron Gant	.10	.05	.01
☐ 44	Dan Pasqua	.05	.02	.00

			MINT	EXC	G-VG				MINT	EXC	G-VG
☐	45	Jeff Robinson	.08	.04	.01	☐	94	Herm Winningham	.05	.02	.00
☐	46	George Brett	.35	.17	.03	☐	95	Kelly Gruber	.08	.04	.01
☐	47	Bryn Smith	.08	.04	.01	☐	96	Terry Leach	.05	.02	.00
☐	48	Mike Marshall	.10	.05	.01	☐	97	Jody Reed	.08	.04	.01
☐	49	Doug Robbins	.10	.05	.01	☐	98	Nelson Santovenia	.08	.04	.01
☐	50	Don Mattingly	.75	.35	.07	☐	99	Tony Armas	.05	.02	.00
☐	51	Mike Scott	.15	.07	.01	☐	100	Greg Brock	.05	.02	.00
☐	52	Steve Jeltz	.05	.02	.00	☐	101	Dave Stewart	.12	.06	.01
☐	53	Dick Schofield	.05	.02	.00	☐	102	Roberto Alomar	.20	.10	.02
☐	54	Tom Brunansky	.10	.05	.01	☐	103	Jim Sundberg	.05	.02	.00
☐	55	Gary Sheffield	.50	.25	.05	☐	104	Albert Hall	.05	.02	.00
☐	56	Dave Valle	.05	.02	.00	☐	105	Steve Lyons	.05	.02	.00
☐	57	Carney Lansford	.12	.06	.01	☐	106	Sid Bream	.05	.02	.00
☐	58	Tony Gwynn	.30	.15	.03	☐	107	Danny Tartabull	.12	.06	.01
☐	59	Checklist 1-110	.05	.02	.00	☐	108	Rick Dempsey	.05	.02	.00
☐	60	Damon Berryhill	.12	.06	.01	☐	109	Rich Renteria	.05	.02	.00
☐	61	Jack Morris	.12	.06	.01	☐	110	Ozzie Smith	.20	.10	.02
☐	62	Brett Butler	.08	.04	.01	☐	111	Steve Sax	.15	.07	.01
☐	63	Mickey Hatcher	.05	.02	.00	☐	112	Kelly Downs	.08	.04	.01
☐	64	Bruce Sutter	.08	.04	.01	☐	113	Larry Sheets	.05	.02	.00
☐	65	Robin Ventura	.40	.20	.04	☐	114	Andy Benes	.50	.25	.05
☐	66	Junior Ortiz	.05	.02	.00	☐	115	Pete O'Brien	.08	.04	.01
☐	67	Pat Tabler	.05	.02	.00	☐	116	Kevin McReynolds	.12	.06	.01
☐	68	Greg Swindell	.10	.05	.01	☐	117	Juan Berenguer	.05	.02	.00
☐	69	Jeff Branson	.10	.05	.01	☐	118	Billy Hatcher	.05	.02	.00
☐	70	Manny Lee	.05	.02	.00	☐	119	Rick Cerone	.05	.02	.00
☐	71	Dave Magadan	.10	.05	.01	☐	120	Andre Dawson	.20	.10	.02
☐	72	Rich Gedman	.05	.02	.00	☐	121	Storm Davis	.08	.04	.01
☐	73	Tim Raines	.15	.07	.01	☐	122	Devon White	.10	.05	.01
☐	74	Mike Maddux	.05	.02	.00	☐	123	Alan Trammell	.15	.07	.01
☐	75	Jim Presley	.05	.02	.00	☐	124	Vince Coleman	.15	.07	.01
☐	76	Chuck Finley	.08	.04	.01	☐	125	Al Leiter	.08	.04	.01
☐	77	Jose Oquendo	.08	.04	.01	☐	126	Dale Sveum	.05	.02	.00
☐	78	Rob Deer	.08	.04	.01	☐	127	Pete Incaviglia	.12	.06	.01
☐	79	Jay Howell	.08	.04	.01	☐	128	Dave Stieb	.12	.06	.01
☐	80	Terry Steinbach	.10	.05	.01	☐	129	Kevin Mitchell	.40	.20	.04
☐	81	Ed Whitson	.05	.02	.00	☐	130	Dave Schmidt	.05	.02	.00
☐	82	Ruben Sierra	.40	.20	.04	☐	131	Gary Redus	.05	.02	.00
☐	83	Bruce Benedict	.05	.02	.00	☐	132	Ron Robinson	.05	.02	.00
☐	84	Fred Manrique	.05	.02	.00	☐	133	Darnell Coles	.05	.02	.00
☐	85	John Smiley	.08	.04	.01	☐	134	Benito Santiago	.20	.10	.02
☐	86	Mike Macfarlane	.08	.04	.01	☐	135	John Farrell	.08	.04	.01
☐	87	Rene Gonzales	.05	.02	.00	☐	136	Willie Wilson	.10	.05	.01
☐	88	Charles Hudson	.05	.02	.00	☐	137	Steve Bedrosian	.10	.05	.01
☐	89	Glenn Davis	.15	.07	.01	☐	138	Don Slaught	.05	.02	.00
☐	90	Les Straker	.05	.02	.00	☐	139	Darryl Strawberry	.50	.25	.05
☐	91	Carmen Castillo	.05	.02	.00	☐	140	Frank Viola	.15	.07	.01
☐	92	Tracy Woodson	.05	.02	.00	☐	141	Dave Silvestri	.12	.06	.01
☐	93	Tino Martinez	.50	.25	.05	☐	142	Carlos Quintana	.12	.06	.01

		MINT	EXC	G-VG
☐ 143	Vance Law	.05	.02	.00
☐ 144	Dave Parker	*.15	.07	.01
☐ 145	Tim Belcher	.15	.07	.01
☐ 146	Will Clark	1.00	.50	.10
☐ 147	Mark Williamson	.05	.02	.00
☐ 148	Ozzie Guillen	.08	.04	.01
☐ 149	Kirk McCaskill	.08	.04	.01
☐ 150	Pat Sheridan	.05	.02	.00
☐ 151	Terry Pendleton	.05	.02	.00
☐ 152	Roberto Kelly	.20	.10	.02
☐ 153	Joey Meyer	.08	.04	.01
☐ 154	Mark Grant	.05	.02	.00
☐ 155	Joe Carter	.15	.07	.01
☐ 156	Steve Buechele	.05	.02	.00
☐ 157	Tony Fernandez	.10	.05	.01
☐ 158	Jeff Reed	.05	.02	.00
☐ 159	Bobby Bonilla	.12	.06	.01
☐ 160	Henry Cotto	.05	.02	.00
☐ 161	Kurt Stillwell	.08	.04	.01
☐ 162	Mickey Morandini	.20	.10	.02
☐ 163	Robby Thompson	.05	.02	.00
☐ 164	Rick Schu	.05	.02	.00
☐ 165	Stan Jefferson	.05	.02	.00
☐ 166	Ron Darling	.10	.05	.01
☐ 167	Kirby Puckett	.40	.20	.04
☐ 168	Bill Doran	.08	.04	.01
☐ 169	Dennis Lamp	.05	.02	.00
☐ 170	Ty Griffin	.60	.30	.06
☐ 171	Ron Hassey	.05	.02	.00
☐ 172	Dale Murphy	.30	.15	.03
☐ 173	Andres Galarraga	.15	.07	.01
☐ 174	Tim Flannery	.05	.02	.00
☐ 175	Cory Snyder	.15	.07	.01
☐ 176	Checklist 111-220	.05	.02	.00
☐ 177	Tommy Barrett	.08	.04	.01
☐ 178	Dan Petry	.05	.02	.00
☐ 179	Billy Masse	.12	.06	.01
☐ 180	Terry Kennedy	.05	.02	.00
☐ 181	Joe Orsulak	.05	.02	.00
☐ 182	Doyle Alexander	.05	.02	.00
☐ 183	Willie McGee	.10	.05	.01
☐ 184	Jim Gantner	.05	.02	.00
☐ 185	Keith Hernandez	.15	.07	.01
☐ 186	Greg Gagne	.05	.02	.00
☐ 187	Kevin Bass	.08	.04	.01
☐ 188	Mark Eichhorn	.05	.02	.00
☐ 189	Mark Grace	.75	.35	.07
☐ 190	Jose Canseco	.75	.35	.07
☐ 191	Bobby Witt	.08	.04	.01

		MINT	EXC	G-VG
☐ 192	Rafael Santana	.05	.02	.00
☐ 193	Dwight Evans	.10	.05	.01
☐ 194	Greg Booker	.05	.02	.00
☐ 195	Brook Jacoby	.08	.04	.01
☐ 196	Rafael Belliard	.05	.02	.00
☐ 197	Candy Maldonado	.05	.02	.00
☐ 198	Mickey Tettleton	.10	.05	.01
☐ 199	Barry Larkin	.15	.07	.01
☐ 200	Frank White	.08	.04	.01
☐ 201	Wally Joyner	.15	.07	.01
☐ 202	Chet Lemon	.05	.02	.00
☐ 203	Joe Magrane	.10	.05	.01
☐ 204	Glenn Braggs	.10	.05	.01
☐ 205	Scott Fletcher	.05	.02	.00
☐ 206	Gary Ward	.05	.02	.00
☐ 207	Nelson Liriano	.05	.02	.00
☐ 208	Howard Johnson	.15	.07	.01
☐ 209	Kent Hrbek	.15	.07	.01
☐ 210	Ken Caminiti	.08	.04	.01
☐ 211	Mike Greenwell	.60	.30	.06
☐ 212	Ryne Sandberg	.25	.12	.02
☐ 213	Joe Slusarski	.15	.07	.01
☐ 214	Donell Nixon	.05	.02	.00
☐ 215	Tim Wallach	.08	.04	.01
☐ 216	John Kruk	.10	.05	.01
☐ 217	Charles Nagy	.20	.10	.02
☐ 218	Alvin Davis	.10	.05	.01
☐ 219	Oswald Peraza	.08	.04	.01
☐ 220	Mike Schmidt	.75	.35	.07
☐ 221	Spike Owen	.06	.02	.00
☐ 222	Mike Smithson	.06	.02	.00
☐ 223	Dion James	.06	.02	.00
☐ 224	Ernie Whitt	.06	.02	.00
☐ 225	Mike Davis	.06	.02	.00
☐ 226	Gene Larkin	.06	.02	.00
☐ 227	Pat Combs	.75	.35	.07
☐ 228	Jack Howell	.06	.02	.00
☐ 229	Ron Oester	.06	.02	.00
☐ 230	Paul Gibson	.06	.02	.00
☐ 231	Mookie Wilson	.08	.04	.01
☐ 232	Glenn Hubbard	.06	.02	.00
☐ 233	Shawon Dunston	.10	.05	.01
☐ 234	Otis Nixon	.06	.02	.00
☐ 235	Melido Perez	.08	.04	.01
☐ 236	Jerry Browne	.08	.04	.01
☐ 237	Rick Rhoden	.06	.02	.00
☐ 238	Bo Jackson	1.00	.50	.10
☐ 239	Randy Velarde	.06	.02	.00
☐ 240	Jack Clark	.12	.06	.01

		MINT	EXC	G-VG			MINT	EXC	G-VG
☐ 241	Wade Boggs	.60	.30	.06	☐ 290	Rich Yett	.06	.02	.00
☐ 242	Lonnie Smith	.10	.05	.01	☐ 291	Scott Servais	.15	.07	.01
☐ 243	Mike Flanagan	.08	.04	.01	☐ 292	Bill Pecota	.06	.02	.00
☐ 244	Willie Randolph	.08	.04	.01	☐ 293	Ken Phelps	.06	.02	.00
☐ 245	Oddibe McDowell	.08	.04	.01	☐ 294	Chili Davis	.08	.04	.01
☐ 246	Ricky Jordan	.50	.25	.05	☐ 295	Manny Trillo	.06	.02	.00
☐ 247	Greg Briley	.25	.12	.02	☐ 296	Mike Boddicker	.06	.02	.00
☐ 248	Rex Hudler	.08	.04	.01	☐ 297	Geronimo Berroa	.06	.02	.00
☐ 249	Robin Yount	.40	.20	.04	☐ 298	Todd Stottlemyre	.08	.04	.01
☐ 250	Lance Parrish	.12	.06	.01	☐ 299	Kirk Gibson	.15	.07	.01
☐ 251	Chris Sabo	.20	.10	.02	☐ 300	Wally Backman	.06	.02	.00
☐ 252	Mike Henneman	.08	.04	.01	☐ 301	Hubie Brooks	.08	.04	.01
☐ 253	Gregg Jefferies	.75	.35	.07	☐ 302	Von Hayes	.10	.05	.01
☐ 254	Curt Young	.06	.02	.00	☐ 303	Matt Nokes	.12	.06	.01
☐ 255	Andy Van Slyke	.12	.06	.01	☐ 304	Dwight Gooden	.30	.15	.03
☐ 256	Rod Booker	.06	.02	.00	☐ 305	Walt Weiss	.20	.10	.02
☐ 257	Rafael Palmeiro	.15	.07	.01	☐ 306	Mike LaValliere	.06	.02	.00
☐ 258	Jose Uribe	.06	.02	.00	☐ 307	Cris Carpenter	.08	.04	.01
☐ 259	Ellis Burks	.35	.17	.03	☐ 308	Ted Wood	.25	.12	.02
☐ 260	John Smoltz	.25	.12	.02	☐ 309	Jeff Russell	.08	.04	.01
☐ 261	Tom Foley	.06	.02	.00	☐ 310	Dave Gallagher	.08	.04	.01
☐ 262	Lloyd Moseby	.08	.04	.01	☐ 311	Andy Allanson	.06	.02	.00
☐ 263	Jim Poole	.12	.06	.01	☐ 312	Craig Reynolds	.06	.02	.00
☐ 264	Gary Gaetti	.10	.05	.01	☐ 313	Kevin Seitzer	.20	.10	.02
☐ 265	Bob Dernier	.06	.02	.00	☐ 314	Dave Winfield	.20	.10	.02
☐ 266	Harold Baines	.12	.06	.01	☐ 315	Andy McGaffigan	.06	.02	.00
☐ 267	Tom Candiotti	.08	.04	.01	☐ 316	Nick Esasky	.10	.05	.01
☐ 268	Rafael Ramirez	.06	.02	.00	☐ 317	Jeff Blauser	.08	.04	.01
☐ 269	Bob Boone	.10	.05	.01	☐ 318	George Bell	.15	.07	.01
☐ 270	Buddy Bell	.08	.04	.01	☐ 319	Eddie Murray	.20	.10	.02
☐ 271	Rickey Henderson	.40	.20	.04	☐ 320	Mark Davidson	.06	.02	.00
☐ 272	Willie Fraser	.06	.02	.00	☐ 321	Juan Samuel	.10	.05	.01
☐ 273	Eric Davis	.50	.25	.05	☐ 322	Jim Abbott	1.00	.50	.10
☐ 274	Jeff Robinson	.08	.04	.01	☐ 323	Kal Daniels	.10	.05	.01
☐ 275	Damaso Garcia	.06	.02	.00	☐ 324	Mike Brumley	.08	.04	.01
☐ 276	Sid Fernandez	.10	.05	.01	☐ 325	Gary Carter	.15	.07	.01
☐ 277	Stan Javier	.08	.04	.01	☐ 326	Dave Henderson	.08	.04	.01
☐ 278	Marty Barrett	.06	.02	.00	☐ 327	Checklist 221-330	.06	.02	.00
☐ 279	Gerald Perry	.08	.04	.01	☐ 328	Garry Templeton	.08	.04	.01
☐ 280	Rob Ducey	.08	.04	.01	☐ 329	Pat Perry	.06	.02	.00
☐ 281	Mike Scioscia	.06	.02	.00	☐ 330	Paul Molitor	.12	.06	.01
☐ 282	Randy Bush	.06	.02	.00					
☐ 283	Tom Herr	.06	.02	.00					
☐ 284	Glenn Wilson	.06	.02	.00					
☐ 285	Pedro Guerrero	.15	.07	.01					
☐ 286	Cal Ripken	.25	.12	.02					
☐ 287	Randy Johnson	.10	.05	.01					
☐ 288	Julio Franco	.12	.06	.01					
☐ 289	Ivan Calderon	.10	.05	.01					

1989 Topps Traded

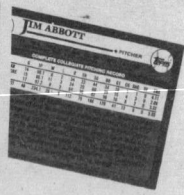

The 1989 Topps Traded set contains 132 standard-size (2 ½" by 3 ½") cards. The fronts have white borders; the horizontally oriented backs are red and pink. From the front the cards' style is indistinguishable from the 1989 Topps regular issue. The cards were distributed as a boxed set. Topps also produced a specially boxed "glossy" edition, frequently referred to as the Topps Traded Tiffany set. This year, again, Topps did not disclose the number of Tiffany sets they produced or sold but it seems that production quantities were roughly similar (or slightly smaller) to the previous two years. The checklist of cards is identical to that of the normal non-glossy cards. There are two primary distinguishing features of the Tiffany cards—white card stock reverses and high gloss obverses. These Tiffany cards are valued at approximately four times the values listed below.

	MINT	EXC	G-VG
COMPLETE SET (132)	12.50	6.25	1.25
COMMON PLAYER (1-132) ...	.05	.02	.00
☐ 1 T Don Aase	.10	.02	.01
☐ 2 T Jim Abbott	1.50	.75	.15
☐ 3 T Kent Anderson	.20	.10	.02
☐ 4 T Keith Atherton	.05	.02	.00
☐ 5 T Wally Backman	.05	.02	.00
☐ 6 T Steve Balboni	.05	.02	.00
☐ 7 T Jesse Barfield	.10	.05	.01

	MINT	EXC	G-VG
☐ 8 T Steve Bedrosian ...	.10	.05	.01
☐ 9 T Todd Benzinger ...	.10	.05	.01
☐ 10 T Geronimo Berroa ...	.10	.05	.01
☐ 11 T Bert Blyleven	.15	.07	.01
☐ 12 T Bob Boone	.15	.07	.01
☐ 13 T Phil Bradley	.10	.05	.01
☐ 14 T Jeff Brantley	.20	.10	.02
☐ 15 T Kevin Brown	.20	.10	.02
☐ 16 T Jerry Browne	.10	.05	.01
☐ 17 T Chuck Cary	.10	.05	.01
☐ 18 T Carmen Castillo ...	.05	.02	.00
☐ 19 T Jim Clancy	.05	.02	.00
☐ 20 T Jack Clark	.12	.06	.01
☐ 21 T Bryan Clutterbuck ...	.05	.02	.00
☐ 22 T Jody Davis	.05	.02	.00
☐ 23 T Mike Devereaux ...	.15	.07	.01
☐ 24 T Frank DiPino	.05	.02	.00
☐ 25 T Benny Distefano ...	.05	.02	.00
☐ 26 T John Dopson	.10	.05	.01
☐ 27 T Len Dykstra	.15	.07	.01
☐ 28 T Jim Eisenreich	.10	.05	.01
☐ 29 T Nick Esasky	.15	.07	.01
☐ 30 T Alvaro Espinoza ...	.10	.05	.01
☐ 31 T Darrell Evans	.10	.05	.01
☐ 32 T Junior Felix	1.00	.50	.10
☐ 33 T Felix Fermin	.05	.02	.00
☐ 34 T Julio Franco	.15	.07	.01
☐ 35 T Terry Francona	.05	.02	.00
☐ 36 T Cito Gaston MG	.10	.05	.01
☐ 37 T Bob Geren UER	.60	.30	.06
(photo actually			
Mike Fennell)			
☐ 38 T Tom Gordon	1.00	.50	.10
☐ 39 T Tommy Gregg	.10	.05	.01
☐ 40 T Ken Griffey Sr.	.15	.07	.01
☐ 41 T Ken Griffey Jr.	3.00	1.50	.30
☐ 42 T Kevin Gross	.05	.02	.00
☐ 43 T Lee Guetterman ...	.05	.02	.00
☐ 44 T Mel Hall	.10	.05	.01
☐ 45 T Erik Hanson	.20	.10	.02
☐ 46 T Gene Harris	.30	.15	.03
☐ 47 T Andy Hawkins	.10	.05	.01
☐ 48 T Rickey Henderson ..	.35	.17	.03
☐ 49 T Tom Herr	.10	.05	.01
☐ 50 T Ken Hill	.20	.10	.02
☐ 51 T Brian Holman	.20	.10	.02
☐ 52 T Brian Holton	.10	.05	.01
☐ 53 T Art Howe MG	.05	.02	.00
☐ 54 T Ken Howell	.05	.02	.00

	MINT	EXC	G-VG		MINT	EXC	G-VG
☐ 55 T Bruce Hurst	.10	.05	.01	☐ 104 T Kenny Rogers	.20	.10	.02
☐ 56 T Chris James	.10	.05	.01	☐ 105 T Ed Romero	.05	.02	.00
☐ 57 T Randy Johnson	.15	.07	.01	☐ 106 T Nolan Ryan	1.25	.60	.12
☐ 58 T Jimmy Jones	.05	.02	.00	☐ 107 T Luis Salazar	.05	.02	.00
☐ 59 T Terry Kennedy	.05	.02	.00	☐ 108 T Juan Samuel	.15	.07	.01
☐ 60 T Paul Kilgus	.05	.02	.00	☐ 109 T Alex Sanchez	.25	.12	.02
☐ 61 T Eric King	.05	.02	.00	☐ 110 T Deion Sanders	1.00	.50	.10
☐ 62 T Ron Kittle	.10	.05	.01	☐ 111 T Steve Sax	.12	.06	.01
☐ 63 T John Kruk	.10	.05	.01	☐ 112 T Rick Schu	.05	.02	.00
☐ 64 T Randy Kutcher	.05	.02	.00	☐ 113 T Dwight Smith	1.50	.75	.15
☐ 65 T Steve Lake	.05	.02	.00	☐ 114 T Lonnie Smith	.15	.07	.01
☐ 66 T Mark Langston	.25	.12	.02	☐ 115 T Billy Spiers	.35	.17	.03
☐ 67 T Dave LaPoint	.05	.02	.00	☐ 116 T Kent Tekulve	.05	.02	.00
☐ 68 T Rick Leach	.05	.02	.00	☐ 117 T Walt Terrell	.05	.02	.00
☐ 69 T Terry Leach	.10	.05	.01	☐ 118 T Milt Thompson	.05	.02	.00
☐ 70 T Jim Lefebvre MG	.05	.02	.00	☐ 119 T Dickie Thon	.05	.02	.00
☐ 71 T Al Leiter	.10	.05	.01	☐ 120 T Jeff Torborg MG	.05	.02	.00
☐ 72 T Jeffrey Leonard	.10	.05	.01	☐ 121 T Jeff Treadway	.05	.02	.00
☐ 73 T Derek Lilliquist	.20	.10	.02	☐ 122 T Omar Vizquel	.25	.12	.02
☐ 74 T Rick Mahler	.05	.02	.00	☐ 123 T Jerome Walton	3.50	1.75	.35
☐ 75 T Tom McCarthy	.15	.07	.01	☐ 124 T Gary Ward	.05	.02	.00
☐ 76 T Lloyd McClendon	.10	.05	.01	☐ 125 T Claudell Washington	.10	.05	.01
☐ 77 T Lance McCullers	.10	.05	.01	☐ 126 T Curt Wilkerson	.05	.02	.00
☐ 78 T Oddibe McDowell	.10	.05	.01	☐ 127 T Eddie Williams	.05	.02	.00
☐ 79 T Roger McDowell	.10	.05	.01	☐ 128 T Frank Williams	.05	.02	.00
☐ 80 T Larry McWilliams	.05	.02	.00	☐ 129 T Ken Williams	.10	.05	.01
☐ 81 T Randy Milligan	.10	.05	.01	☐ 130 T Mitch Williams	.20	.10	.02
☐ 82 T Mike Moore	.10	.05	.01	☐ 131 T Steve Wilson	.15	.07	.01
☐ 83 T Keith Moreland	.05	.02	.00	☐ 132 T Checklist 1T-132T	.05	.01	.00
☐ 84 T Mike Morgan	.10	.05	.01				
☐ 85 T Jamie Moyer	.05	.02	.00				
☐ 86 T Rob Murphy	.05	.02	.00				
☐ 87 T Eddie Murray	.12	.06	.01				
☐ 88 T Pete O'Brien	.10	.05	.01				
☐ 89 T Gregg Olson	.75	.35	.07				
☐ 90 T Steve Ontiveros	.05	.02	.00				
☐ 91 T Jesse Orosco	.05	.02	.00				
☐ 92 T Spike Owen	.05	.02	.00				
☐ 93 T Rafael Palmeiro	.12	.06	.01				
☐ 94 T Clay Parker	.25	.12	.02				
☐ 95 T Jeff Parrett	.10	.05	.01				
☐ 96 T Lance Parrish	.10	.05	.01				
☐ 97 T Dennis Powell	.05	.02	.00				
☐ 98 T Rey Quinones	.05	.02	.00				
☐ 99 T Doug Rader MG	.05	.02	.00				
☐ 100 T Willie Randolph	.10	.05	.01				
☐ 101 T Shane Rawley	.05	.02	.00				
☐ 102 T Randy Ready	.05	.02	.00				
☐ 103 T Bip Roberts	.10	.05	.01				

1990 Topps

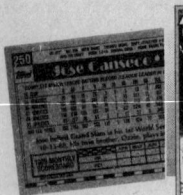

JOSE CANSECO

The 1990 Topps set contains 792 standard-size (2 ½" by 3 ½") cards. The front borders are various colors. The horizontally oriented backs are yellowish green. Cards 385-407 contain the All-Stars. Cards 61-665 contain the Turn Back the Clock cards. The manager cards this year contain information that had been on the backs of the Team Leader cards in the past few years; the Team Leader cards were discontinued, apparently in order to allow better individual player card selection. Topps really concentrated on individual player cards in this set with 725, the most ever in a baseball card set. The checklist cards are oriented alphabetically by team name and player name.

			MINT	EXC	G-VG
		COMPLETE SET (792)	24.00	12.00	2.40
		COMMON PLAYER (1-792)	.03	.01	.00
☐	1	Nolan Ryan	.30	.10	.02
☐	2	Nolan Ryan Salute New York Mets	.12	.06	.01
☐	3	Nolan Ryan Salute California Angels	.12	.06	.01
☐	4	Nolan Ryan Salute Houston Astros	.12	.06	.01
☐	5	Nolan Ryan Salute Texas Rangers	.12	.06	.01
☐	6	Vince Coleman RB (50 consecutive stolen bases)	.08	.04	.01

			MINT	EXC	G-VG
☐	7	Rickey Henderson RB (40 career leadoff home runs)	.10	.05	.01
☐	8	Cal Ripken RB (20 or more homers for 8 consecutive years, record for shortstops)	.08	.04	.01
☐	9	Eric Plunk	.03	.01	.00
☐	10	Barry Larkin	.08	.04	.01
☐	11	Paul Gibson	.03	.01	.00
☐	12	Joe Girardi	.10	.05	.01
☐	13	Mark Williamson	.03	.01	.00
☐	14	Mike Fetters	.15	.07	.01
☐	15	Teddy Higuera	.06	.03	.00
☐	16	Kent Anderson	.10	.05	.01
☐	17	Kelly Downs	.03	.01	.00
☐	18	Carlos Quintana	.06	.03	.00
☐	19	Al Newman	.03	.01	.00
☐	20	Mark Gubicza	.06	.03	.00
☐	21	Jeff Torborg MG	.03	.01	.00
☐	22	Bruce Ruffin	.03	.01	.00
☐	23	Randy Velarde	.03	.01	.00
☐	24	Joe Hesketh	.03	.01	.00
☐	25	Willie Randolph	.06	.03	.00
☐	26	Don Slaught	.03	.01	.00
☐	27	Rick Leach	.03	.01	.00
☐	28	Duane Ward	.03	.01	.00
☐	29	John Cangelosi	.03	.01	.00
☐	30	David Cone	.10	.05	.01
☐	31	Henry Cotto	.03	.01	.00
☐	32	John Farrell	.03	.01	.00
☐	33	Greg Walker	.03	.01	.00
☐	34	Tony Fossas	.10	.05	.01
☐	35	Benito Santiago	.10	.05	.01
☐	36	John Costello	.03	.01	.00
☐	37	Domingo Ramos	.03	.01	.00
☐	38	Wes Gardner	.03	.01	.00
☐	39	Curt Ford	.03	.01	.00
☐	40	Jay Howell	.03	.01	.00
☐	41	Matt Williams	.10	.05	.01
☐	42	Jeff Robinson	.06	.03	.00
☐	43	Dante Bichette	.03	.01	.00
☐	44	Roger Salkeld FDP	.20	.10	.02
☐	45	Dave Parker	.08	.04	.01
☐	46	Rob Dibble	.06	.03	.00
☐	47	Brian Harper	.03	.01	.00
☐	48	Zane Smith	.03	.01	.00

		MINT	EXC	G-VG
☐ 49	Tom Lawless	.03	.01	.00
☐ 50	Glenn Davis	.08	.04	.01
☐ 51	Doug Rader MG	.03	.01	.00
☐ 52	Jack Daugherty	.12	.06	.01
☐ 53	Mike LaCoss	.03	.01	.00
☐ 54	Joel Skinner	.03	.01	.00
☐ 55	Darrell Evans	.06	.03	.00
☐ 56	Franklin Stubbs	.03	.01	.00
☐ 57	Greg Vaughn	1.25	.60	.12
☐ 58	Keith Miller	.03	.01	.00
☐ 59	Ted Power	.03	.01	.00
☐ 60	George Brett	.12	.06	.01
☐ 61	Deion Sanders	.40	.20	.04
☐ 62	Ramon Martinez	.08	.04	.01
☐ 63	Mike Pagliarulo	.06	.03	.00
☐ 64	Danny Darwin	.03	.01	.00
☐ 65	Devon White	.08	.04	.01
☐ 66	Greg Litton	.20	.10	.02
☐ 67	Scott Sanderson	.03	.01	.00
☐ 68	Dave Henderson	.03	.01	.00
☐ 69	Todd Frohwirth	.03	.01	.00
☐ 70	Mike Greenwell	.20	.10	.02
☐ 71	Allan Anderson	.06	.03	.00
☐ 72	Jeff Huson	.12	.06	.01
☐ 73	Bob Milacki	.06	.03	.00
☐ 74	Jeff Jackson FDP	.25	.12	.02
☐ 75	Doug Jones	.06	.03	.00
☐ 76	Dave Valle	.03	.01	.00
☐ 77	Dave Bergman	.03	.01	.00
☐ 78	Mike Flanagan	.03	.01	.00
☐ 79	Ron Kittle	.06	.03	.00
☐ 80	Jeff Russell	.06	.03	.00
☐ 81	Bob Rodgers MG	.03	.01	.00
☐ 82	Scott Terry	.03	.01	.00
☐ 83	Hensley Meulens	.20	.10	.02
☐ 84	Ray Searage	.03	.01	.00
☐ 85	Juan Samuel	.06	.03	.00
☐ 86	Paul Kilgus	.03	.01	.00
☐ 87	Rick Luecken	.12	.06	.01
☐ 88	Glenn Braggs	.06	.03	.00
☐ 89	Clint Zavaras	.12	.06	.01
☐ 90	Jack Clark	.08	.04	.01
☐ 91	Steve Frey	.12	.06	.01
☐ 92	Mike Stanley	.03	.01	.00
☐ 93	Shawn Hillegas	.03	.01	.00
☐ 94	Herm Winningham	.03	.01	.00
☐ 95	Todd Worrell	.08	.04	.01
☐ 96	Jody Reed	.03	.01	.00
☐ 97	Curt Schilling	.08	.04	.01
☐ 98	Jose Gonzalez	.06	.03	.00
☐ 99	Rich Monteleone	.10	.05	.01
☐ 100	Will Clark	.50	.25	.05
☐ 101	Shane Rawley	.03	.01	.00
☐ 102	Stan Javier	.03	.01	.00
☐ 103	Marvin Freeman	.03	.01	.00
☐ 104	Bob Knepper	.03	.01	.00
☐ 105	Randy Myers	.06	.03	.00
☐ 106	Charlie O'Brien	.03	.01	.00
☐ 107	Fred Lynn	.06	.03	.00
☐ 108	Rod Nichols	.03	.01	.00
☐ 109	Roberto Kelly	.08	.04	.01
☐ 110	Tommy Helms MG	.03	.01	.00
☐ 111	Ed Whited	.15	.07	.01
☐ 112	Glenn Wilson	.03	.01	.00
☐ 113	Manny Lee	.03	.01	.00
☐ 114	Mike Bielecki	.06	.03	.00
☐ 115	Tony Pena	.06	.03	.00
☐ 116	Floyd Bannister	.03	.01	.00
☐ 117	Mike Sharperson	.03	.01	.00
☐ 118	Erik Hanson	.10	.05	.01
☐ 119	Billy Hatcher	.03	.01	.00
☐ 120	John Franco	.06	.03	.00
☐ 121	Robin Ventura	.25	.12	.02
☐ 122	Shawn Abner	.03	.01	.00
☐ 123	Rich Gedman	.03	.01	.00
☐ 124	Dave Dravecky	.06	.03	.00
☐ 125	Kent Hrbek	.08	.04	.01
☐ 126	Randy Kramer	.03	.01	.00
☐ 127	Mike Devereaux	.06	.03	.00
☐ 128	Checklist 1	.06	.01	.00
☐ 129	Ron Jones	.06	.03	.00
☐ 130	Bert Blyleven	.08	.04	.01
☐ 131	Matt Nokes	.06	.03	.00
☐ 132	Lance Blankenship	.08	.04	.01
☐ 133	Ricky Horton	.03	.01	.00
☐ 134	Earl Cunningham FDP	.35	.17	.03
☐ 135	Dave Magadan	.06	.03	.00
☐ 136	Kevin Brown	.10	.05	.01
☐ 137	Marty Pevey	.10	.05	.01
☐ 138	Al Leiter	.06	.03	.00
☐ 139	Greg Brock	.03	.01	.00
☐ 140	Andre Dawson	.08	.04	.01
☐ 141	John Hart MG	.03	.01	.00
☐ 142	Jeff Wetherby	.12	.06	.01
☐ 143	Rafael Belliard	.03	.01	.00
☐ 144	Bud Black	.03	.01	.00
☐ 145	Terry Steinbach	.06	.03	.00

		MINT	EXC	G-VG			MINT	EXC	G-VG
☐ 146	Rob Richie	.15	.07	.01	☐ 195	Tim Burke	.06	.03	.00
☐ 147	Chuck Finley	.06	.03	.00	☐ 196	Gerald Young	.03	.01	.00
☐ 148	Edgar Martinez	.03	.01	.00	☐ 197	Doug Drabek	.03	.01	.00
☐ 149	Steve Farr	.03	.01	.00	☐ 198	Mike Marshall	.08	.04	.01
☐ 150	Kirk Gibson	.08	.04	.01	☐ 199	Sergio Valdez	.12	.06	.01
☐ 151	Rick Mahler	.03	.01	.00	☐ 200	Don Mattingly	.50	.25	.05
☐ 152	Lonnie Smith	.06	.03	.00	☐ 201	Cito Gaston MG	.06	.03	.00
☐ 153	Randy Milligan	.06	.03	.00	☐ 202	Mike Macfarlane	.03	.01	.00
☐ 154	Mike Maddux	.03	.01	.00	☐ 203	Mike Roesler	.10	.05	.01
☐ 155	Ellis Burks	.15	.07	.01	☐ 204	Bob Dernier	.03	.01	.00
☐ 156	Ken Patterson	.03	.01	.00	☐ 205	Mark Davis	.08	.04	.01
☐ 157	Craig Biggio	.08	.04	.01	☐ 206	Nick Esasky	.06	.03	.00
☐ 158	Craig Lefferts	.03	.01	.00	☐ 207	Bob Ojeda	.06	.03	.00
☐ 159	Mike Felder	.03	.01	.00	☐ 208	Brook Jacoby	.06	.03	.00
☐ 160	Dave Righetti	.08	.04	.01	☐ 209	Greg Mathews	.03	.01	.00
☐ 161	Harold Reynolds	.06	.03	.00	☐ 210	Ryne Sandberg	.10	.05	.01
☐ 162	Todd Zeile	1.25	.60	.12	☐ 211	John Cerutti	.03	.01	.00
☐ 163	Phil Bradley	.06	.03	.00	☐ 212	Joe Orsulak	.03	.01	.00
☐ 164	Jeff Juden FDP	.25	.12	.02	☐ 213	Scott Bankhead	.06	.03	.00
☐ 165	Walt Weiss	.08	.04	.01	☐ 214	Terry Francona	.03	.01	.00
☐ 166	Bobby Witt	.06	.03	.00	☐ 215	Kirk McCaskill	.03	.01	.00
☐ 167	Kevin Appier	.12	.06	.01	☐ 216	Ricky Jordan	.20	.10	.02
☐ 168	Jose Lind	.03	.01	.00	☐ 217	Don Robinson	.03	.01	.00
☐ 169	Richard Dotson	.03	.01	.00	☐ 218	Wally Backman	.03	.01	.00
☐ 170	George Bell	.08	.04	.01	☐ 219	Donn Pall	.03	.01	.00
☐ 171	Russ Nixon MG	.03	.01	.00	☐ 220	Barry Bonds	.08	.04	.01
☐ 172	Tom Lampkin	.06	.03	.00	☐ 221	Gary Mielke	.10	.05	.01
☐ 173	Tim Belcher	.06	.03	.00	☐ 222	Kurt Stillwell	.03	.01	.00
☐ 174	Jeff Kunkel	.03	.01	.00	☐ 223	Tommy Gregg	.08	.04	.01
☐ 175	Mike Moore	.06	.03	.00	☐ 224	Delino DeShields	.30	.15	.03
☐ 176	Luis Quinones	.03	.01	.00	☐ 225	Jim Deshaies	.03	.01	.00
☐ 177	Mike Henneman	.03	.01	.00	☐ 226	Mickey Hatcher	.03	.01	.00
☐ 178	Chris James	.06	.03	.00	☐ 227	Kevin Tapani	.15	.07	.01
☐ 179	Brian Holton	.03	.01	.00	☐ 228	Dave Martinez	.03	.01	.00
☐ 180	Tim Raines	.10	.05	.01	☐ 229	David Wells	.03	.01	.00
☐ 181	Juan Agosto	.03	.01	.00	☐ 230	Keith Hernandez	.08	.04	.01
☐ 182	Mookie Wilson	.06	.03	.00	☐ 231	Jack McKeon MG	.03	.01	.00
☐ 183	Steve Lake	.03	.01	.00	☐ 232	Darnell Coles	.03	.01	.00
☐ 184	Danny Cox	.03	.01	.00	☐ 233	Ken Hill	.06	.03	.00
☐ 185	Ruben Sierra	.20	.10	.02	☐ 234	Mariano Duncan	.03	.01	.00
☐ 186	Dave LaPoint	.03	.01	.00	☐ 235	Jeff Reardon	.06	.03	.00
☐ 187	Rick Wrona	.15	.07	.01	☐ 236	Hal Morris	.08	.04	.01
☐ 188	Mike Smithson	.03	.01	.00	☐ 237	Kevin Ritz	.15	.07	.01
☐ 189	Dick Schofield	.03	.01	.00	☐ 238	Felix Jose	.08	.04	.01
☐ 190	Rick Reuschel	.06	.03	.00	☐ 239	Eric Show	.03	.01	.00
☐ 191	Pat Borders	.03	.01	.00	☐ 240	Mark Grace	.30	.15	.03
☐ 192	Don August	.03	.01	.00	☐ 241	Mike Krukow	.03	.01	.00
☐ 193	Andy Benes	.30	.15	.03	☐ 242	Fred Manrique	.03	.01	.00
☐ 194	Glenallen Hill	.20	.10	.02	☐ 243	Barry Jones	.03	.01	.00

		MINT	EXC	G-VG			MINT	EXC	G-VG
☐ 244	Bill Schroeder	.03	.01	.00	☐ 293	Mike Gallego	.03	.01	.00
☐ 245	Roger Clemens	.20	.10	.02	☐ 294	Craig McMurtry	.03	.01	.00
☐ 246	Jim Eisenreich	.03	.01	.00	☐ 295	Fred McGriff	.10	.05	.01
☐ 247	Jerry Reed	.03	.01	.00	☐ 296	Jeff Ballard	.06	.03	.00
☐ 248	Dave Anderson	.03	.01	.00	☐ 297	Tommy Herr	.03	.01	.00
☐ 249	Mike Smith	.12	.06	.01	☐ 298	Dan Gladden	.03	.01	.00
☐ 250	Jose Canseco	.50	.25	.05	☐ 299	Adam Peterson	.06	.03	.00
☐ 251	Jeff Blauser	.03	.01	.00	☐ 300	Bo Jackson	.40	.20	.04
☐ 252	Otis Nixon	.03	.01	.00	☐ 301	Don Aase	.03	.01	.00
☐ 253	Mark Portugal	.03	.01	.00	☐ 302	Marcus Lawton	.20	.10	.02
☐ 254	Francisco Cabrera	.15	.07	.01	☐ 303	Rick Cerone	.03	.01	.00
☐ 255	Bobby Thigpen	.06	.03	.00	☐ 304	Marty Clary	.03	.01	.00
☐ 256	Marvell Wynne	.03	.01	.00	☐ 305	Eddie Murray	.10	.05	.01
☐ 257	Jose DeLeon	.06	.03	.00	☐ 306	Tom Niedenfuer	.03	.01	.00
☐ 258	Barry Lyons	.03	.01	.00	☐ 307	Bip Roberts	.03	.01	.00
☐ 259	Lance McCullers	.03	.01	.00	☐ 308	Jose Guzman	.03	.01	.00
☐ 260	Eric Davis	.20	.10	.02	☐ 309	Eric Yelding	.10	.05	.01
☐ 261	Whitey Herzog MG	.03	.01	.00	☐ 310	Steve Bedrosian	.06	.03	.00
☐ 262	Checklist 2	.06	.01	.00	☐ 311	Dwight Smith	.50	.25	.05
☐ 263	Mel Stottlemyre Jr.	.10	.05	.01	☐ 312	Dan Quisenberry	.06	.03	.00
☐ 264	Bryan Clutterbuck	.03	.01	.00	☐ 313	Gus Polidor	.03	.01	.00
☐ 265	Pete O'Brien	.06	.03	.00	☐ 314	Donald Harris FDP	.30	.15	.03
☐ 266	German Gonzalez	.03	.01	.00	☐ 315	Bruce Hurst	.06	.03	.00
☐ 267	Mark Davidson	.03	.01	.00	☐ 316	Carney Lansford	.08	.04	.01
☐ 268	Rob Murphy	.03	.01	.00	☐ 317	Mark Guthrie	.15	.07	.01
☐ 269	Dickie Thon	.03	.01	.00	☐ 318	Wallace Johnson	.03	.01	.00
☐ 270	Dave Stewart	.08	.04	.01	☐ 319	Dion James	.03	.01	.00
☐ 271	Chet Lemon	.03	.01	.00	☐ 320	Dave Stieb	.08	.04	.01
☐ 272	Bryan Harvey	.03	.01	.00	☐ 321	Joe Morgan MG	.03	.01	.00
☐ 273	Bobby Bonilla	.08	.04	.01	☐ 322	Junior Ortiz	.03	.01	.00
☐ 274	Mauro Gozzo	.15	.07	.01	☐ 323	Willie Wilson	.06	.03	.00
☐ 275	Mickey Tettleton	.06	.03	.00	☐ 324	Pete Harnisch	.06	.03	.00
☐ 276	Gary Thurman	.03	.01	.00	☐ 325	Robby Thompson	.03	.01	.00
☐ 277	Lenny Harris	.08	.04	.01	☐ 326	Tom McCarthy	.10	.05	.01
☐ 278	Pascual Perez	.06	.03	.00	☐ 327	Ken Williams	.03	.01	.00
☐ 279	Steve Buechele	.03	.01	.00	☐ 328	Curt Young	.03	.01	.00
☐ 280	Lou Whitaker	.08	.04	.01	☐ 329	Oddibe McDowell	.06	.03	.00
☐ 281	Kevin Bass	.06	.03	.00	☐ 330	Ron Darling	.08	.04	.01
☐ 282	Derek Lilliquist	.08	.04	.01	☐ 331	Juan Gonzalez	.50	.25	.05
☐ 283	Joey Belle	.50	.25	.05	☐ 332	Paul O'Neill	.08	.04	.01
☐ 284	Mark Gardner	.12	.06	.01	☐ 333	Bill Wegman	.03	.01	.00
☐ 285	Willie McGee	.08	.04	.01	☐ 334	Johnny Ray	.06	.03	.00
☐ 286	Lee Guetterman	.03	.01	.00	☐ 335	Andy Hawkins	.03	.01	.00
☐ 287	Vance Law	.03	.01	.00	☐ 336	Ken Griffey Jr.	1.25	.60	.12
☐ 288	Greg Briley	.15	.07	.01	☐ 337	Lloyd McClendon	.03	.01	.00
☐ 289	Norm Charlton	.03	.01	.00	☐ 338	Dennis Lamp	.03	.01	.00
☐ 290	Robin Yount	.25	.12	.02	☐ 339	Dave Clark	.03	.01	.00
☐ 291	Dave Johnson MG	.03	.01	.00	☐ 340	Fernando Valenzuela	.10	.05	.01
☐ 292	Jim Gott	.03	.01	.00	☐ 341	Tom Foley	.03	.01	.00

		MINT	EXC	G-VG			MINT	EXC	G-VG
☐ 342	Alex Trevino	.03	.01	.00	☐ 391	Kirby Puckett AS	.15	.07	.01
☐ 343	Frank Tanana	.03	.01	.00	☐ 392	Carlton Fisk AS	.08	.04	.01
☐ 344	George Canale	.15	.07	.01	☐ 393	Bret Saberhagen AS	.08	.04	.01
☐ 345	Harold Baines	.08	.04	.01	☐ 394	Jeff Ballard AS	.06	.03	.00
☐ 346	Jim Presley	.03	.01	.00	☐ 395	Jeff Russell AS	.06	.03	.00
☐ 347	Junior Felix	.30	.15	.03	☐ 396	A. Bartlett Giamatti	.50	.25	.05
☐ 348	Gary Wayne	.10	.05	.01		(commemorative)			
☐ 349	Steve Finley	.10	.05	.01	☐ 397	Will Clark AS	.20	.10	.02
☐ 350	Bret Saberhagen	.10	.05	.01	☐ 398	Ryne Sandberg AS	.10	.05	.01
☐ 351	Roger Craig MG	.03	.01	.00	☐ 399	Howard Johnson AS	.08	.04	.01
☐ 352	Bryn Smith	.06	.03	.00	☐ 400	Ozzie Smith AS	.08	.04	.01
☐ 353	Sandy Alomar Jr.	.25	.12	.02	☐ 401	Kevin Mitchell AS	.10	.05	.01
☐ 354	Stan Belinda	.10	.05	.01	☐ 402	Eric Davis AS	.12	.06	.01
☐ 355	Marty Barrett	.03	.01	.00	☐ 403	Tony Gwynn AS	.12	.06	.01
☐ 356	Randy Ready	.03	.01	.00	☐ 404	Craig Biggio AS	.08	.04	.01
☐ 357	Dave West	.06	.03	.00	☐ 405	Mike Scott AS	.08	.04	.01
☐ 358	Andres Thomas	.03	.01	.00	☐ 406	Joe Magrane AS	.06	.03	.00
☐ 359	Jimmy Jones	.03	.01	.00	☐ 407	Mark Davis AS	.06	.03	.00
☐ 360	Paul Molitor	.08	.04	.01	☐ 408	Trevor Wilson	.03	.01	.00
☐ 361	Randy McCament	.10	.05	.01	☐ 409	Tom Brunansky	.08	.04	.01
☐ 362	Damon Berryhill	.08	.04	.01	☐ 410	Joe Boever	.03	.01	.00
☐ 363	Dan Petry	.03	.01	.00	☐ 411	Ken Phelps	.03	.01	.00
☐ 364	Rolando Roomes	.08	.04	.01	☐ 412	Jamie Moyer	.03	.01	.00
☐ 365	Ozzie Guillen	.06	.03	.00	☐ 413	Brian Dubois	.12	.06	.01
☐ 366	Mike Heath	.03	.01	.00	☐ 414	Frank Thomas FDP	.30	.15	.03
☐ 367	Mike Morgan	.03	.01	.00	☐ 415	Shawon Dunston	.06	.03	.00
☐ 368	Bill Doran	.06	.03	.00	☐ 416	Dave Johnson (P)	.12	.06	.01
☐ 369	Todd Burns	.03	.01	.00	☐ 417	Jim Gantner	.03	.01	.00
☐ 370	Tim Wallach	.06	.03	.00	☐ 418	Tom Browning	.06	.03	.00
☐ 371	Jimmy Key	.06	.03	.00	☐ 419	Beau Allred	.15	.07	.01
☐ 372	Terry Kennedy	.03	.01	.00	☐ 420	Carlton Fisk	.08	.04	.01
☐ 373	Alvin Davis	.08	.04	.01	☐ 421	Greg Minton	.03	.01	.00
☐ 374	Steve Cummings	.10	.05	.01	☐ 422	Pat Sheridan	.03	.01	.00
☐ 375	Dwight Evans	.08	.04	.01	☐ 423	Fred Toliver	.03	.01	.00
☐ 376	Checklist 3	.06	.01	.00	☐ 424	Jerry Reuss	.03	.01	.00
☐ 377	Mickey Weston	.10	.05	.01	☐ 425	Bill Landrum	.03	.01	.00
☐ 378	Luis Salazar	.03	.01	.00	☐ 426	Jeff Hamilton	.03	.01	.00
☐ 379	Steve Rosenberg	.03	.01	.00	☐ 427	Carmen Castillo	.03	.01	.00
☐ 380	Dave Winfield	.10	.05	.01	☐ 428	Steve Davis	.10	.05	.01
☐ 381	Frank Robinson MG	.08	.04	.01	☐ 429	Tom Kelly MG	.03	.01	.00
☐ 382	Jeff Musselman	.03	.01	.00	☐ 430	Pete Incaviglia	.06	.03	.00
☐ 383	John Morris	.03	.01	.00	☐ 431	Randy Johnson	.03	.01	.00
☐ 384	Pat Combs	.30	.15	.03	☐ 432	Damaso Garcia	.03	.01	.00
☐ 385	Fred McGriff AS	.10	.05	.01	☐ 433	Steve Olin	.10	.05	.01
☐ 386	Julio Franco AS	.06	.03	.00	☐ 434	Mark Carreon	.06	.03	.00
☐ 387	Wade Boggs AS	.15	.07	.01	☐ 435	Kevin Seitzer	.08	.04	.01
☐ 388	Cal Ripken AS	.10	.05	.01	☐ 436	Mel Hall	.06	.03	.00
☐ 389	Robin Yount AS	.15	.07	.01	☐ 437	Les Lancaster	.03	.01	.00
☐ 390	Ruben Sierra AS	.15	.07	.01	☐ 438	Greg Myers	.06	.03	.00

		MINT	EXC	G-VG
☐ 439	Jeff Parrett	.03	.01	.00
☐ 440	Alan Trammell	.08	.04	.01
☐ 441	Bob Kipper	.03	.01	.00
☐ 442	Jerry Browne	.03	.01	.00
☐ 443	Cris Carpenter	.03	.01	.00
☐ 444	Kyle Abbott FDP	.25	.12	.02
☐ 445	Danny Jackson	.06	.03	.00
☐ 446	Dan Pasqua	.03	.01	.00
☐ 447	Atlee Hammaker	.03	.01	.00
☐ 448	Greg Gagne	.03	.01	.00
☐ 449	Dennis Rasmussen	.03	.01	.00
☐ 450	Rickey Henderson	.20	.10	.02
☐ 451	Mark Lemke	.03	.01	.00
☐ 452	Luis De Los Santos	.08	.04	.01
☐ 453	Jody Davis	.03	.01	.00
☐ 454	Jeff King	.10	.05	.01
☐ 455	Jeffrey Leonard	.06	.03	.00
☐ 456	Chris Gwynn	.06	.03	.00
☐ 457	Gregg Jefferies	.30	.15	.03
☐ 458	Bob McClure	.03	.01	.00
☐ 459	Jim Lefebvre MG	.03	.01	.00
☐ 460	Mike Scott	.08	.04	.01
☐ 461	Carlos Martinez	.20	.10	.02
☐ 462	Denny Walling	.03	.01	.00
☐ 463	Drew Hall	.03	.01	.00
☐ 464	Jerome Walton	1.25	.60	.12
☐ 465	Kevin Gross	.03	.01	.00
☐ 466	Rance Mulliniks	.03	.01	.00
☐ 467	Juan Nieves	.03	.01	.00
☐ 468	Bill Ripken	.03	.01	.00
☐ 469	John Kruk	.06	.03	.00
☐ 470	Frank Viola	.08	.04	.01
☐ 471	Mike Brumley	.06	.03	.00
☐ 472	Jose Uribe	.03	.01	.00
☐ 473	Joe Price	.03	.01	.00
☐ 474	Rich Thompson	.03	.01	.00
☐ 475	Bob Welch	.06	.03	.00
☐ 476	Brad Komminsk	.03	.01	.00
☐ 477	Willie Fraser	.03	.01	.00
☐ 478	Mike LaValliere	.03	.01	.00
☐ 479	Frank White	.06	.03	.00
☐ 480	Sid Fernandez	.08	.04	.01
☐ 481	Garry Templeton	.06	.03	.00
☐ 482	Steve Carter	.12	.06	.01
☐ 483	Alejandro Pena	.03	.01	.00
☐ 484	Mike Fitzgerald	.03	.01	.00
☐ 485	John Candelaria	.06	.03	.00
☐ 486	Jeff Treadway	.03	.01	.00
☐ 487	Steve Searcy	.03	.01	.00
☐ 488	Ken Oberkfell	.03	.01	.00
☐ 489	Nick Leyva MG	.03	.01	.00
☐ 490	Dan Plesac	.06	.03	.00
☐ 491	Dave Cochrane	.12	.06	.01
☐ 492	Ron Oester	.03	.01	.00
☐ 493	Jason Grimsley	.12	.06	.01
☐ 494	Terry Puhl	.03	.01	.00
☐ 495	Lee Smith	.06	.03	.00
☐ 496	Cecil Espy	.03	.01	.00
☐ 497	Dave Schmidt	.03	.01	.00
☐ 498	Rick Schu	.03	.01	.00
☐ 499	Bill Long	.03	.01	.00
☐ 500	Kevin Mitchell	.20	.10	.02
☐ 501	Matt Young	.03	.01	.00
☐ 502	Mitch Webster	.03	.01	.00
☐ 503	Randy St.Claire	.03	.01	.00
☐ 504	Tom O'Malley	.03	.01	.00
☐ 505	Kelly Gruber	.06	.03	.00
☐ 506	Tom Glavine	.06	.03	.00
☐ 507	Gary Redus	.03	.01	.00
☐ 508	Terry Leach	.03	.01	.00
☐ 509	Tom Pagnozzi	.03	.01	.00
☐ 510	Dwight Gooden	.20	.10	.02
☐ 511	Clay Parker	.08	.04	.01
☐ 512	Gary Pettis	.03	.01	.00
☐ 513	Mark Eichhorn	.03	.01	.00
☐ 514	Andy Allanson	.03	.01	.00
☐ 515	Len Dykstra	.06	.03	.00
☐ 516	Tim Leary	.06	.03	.00
☐ 517	Roberto Alomar	.08	.04	.01
☐ 518	Bill Krueger	.03	.01	.00
☐ 519	Bucky Dent MG	.06	.03	.00
☐ 520	Mitch Williams	.06	.03	.00
☐ 521	Craig Worthington	.08	.04	.01
☐ 522	Mike Dunne	.03	.01	.00
☐ 523	Jay Bell	.03	.01	.00
☐ 524	Daryl Boston	.03	.01	.00
☐ 525	Wally Joyner	.08	.04	.01
☐ 526	Checklist 4	.06	.01	.00
☐ 527	Ron Hassey	.03	.01	.00
☐ 528	Kevin Wickander	.08	.04	.01
☐ 529	Greg Harris	.03	.01	.00
☐ 530	Mark Langston	.08	.04	.01
☐ 531	Ken Caminiti	.03	.01	.00
☐ 532	Cecilio Guante	.03	.01	.00
☐ 533	Tim Jones	.06	.03	.00
☐ 534	Louie Meadows	.03	.01	.00
☐ 535	John Smoltz	.08	.04	.01
☐ 536	Bob Geren	.15	.07	.01

	MINT	EXC	G-VG		MINT	EXC	G-VG
☐ 537 Mark Grant	.03	.01	.00	☐ 586 Edwin Nunez	.03	.01	.00
☐ 538 Bill Spiers	.20	.10	.02	☐ 587 Lance Johnson	.03	.01	.00
☐ 539 Neal Heaton	.03	.01	.00	☐ 588 Rick Rhoden	.03	.01	.00
☐ 540 Danny Tartabull	.08	.04	.01	☐ 589 Mike Aldrete	.03	.01	.00
☐ 541 Pat Perry	.03	.01	.00	☐ 590 Ozzie Smith	.08	.04	.01
☐ 542 Darren Daulton	.03	.01	.00	☐ 591 Todd Stottlemyre	.06	.03	.00
☐ 543 Nelson Liriano	.03	.01	.00	☐ 592 R.J. Reynolds	.03	.01	.00
☐ 544 Dennis Boyd	.03	.01	.00	☐ 593 Scott Bradley	.03	.01	.00
☐ 545 Kevin McReynolds	.08	.04	.01	☐ 594 Luis Sojo	.12	.06	.01
☐ 546 Kevin Hickey	.03	.01	.00	☐ 595 Greg Swindell	.08	.04	.01
☐ 547 Jack Howell	.03	.01	.00	☐ 596 Jose DeJesus	.03	.01	.00
☐ 548 Pat Clements	.03	.01	.00	☐ 597 Chris Bosio	.06	.03	.00
☐ 549 Don Zimmer MG	.03	.01	.00	☐ 598 Brady Anderson	.03	.01	.00
☐ 550 Julio Franco	.06	.03	.00	☐ 599 Frank Williams	.03	.01	.00
☐ 551 Tim Crews	.03	.01	.00	☐ 600 Darryl Strawberry	.25	.12	.02
☐ 552 Mike Smith	.12	.06	.01	☐ 601 Luis Rivera	.03	.01	.00
☐ 553 Scott Scudder	.15	.07	.01	☐ 602 Scott Garrelts	.06	.03	.00
☐ 554 Jay Buhner	.06	.03	.00	☐ 603 Tony Armas	.06	.03	.00
☐ 555 Jack Morris	.08	.04	.01	☐ 604 Ron Robinson	.03	.01	.00
☐ 556 Gene Larkin	.03	.01	.00	☐ 605 Mike Scioscia	.03	.01	.00
☐ 557 Jeff Innis	.10	.05	.01	☐ 606 Storm Davis	.06	.03	.00
☐ 558 Rafael Ramirez	.03	.01	.00	☐ 607 Steve Jeltz	.03	.01	.00
☐ 559 Andy McGaffigan	.03	.01	.00	☐ 608 Eric Anthony	1.50	.75	.15
☐ 560 Steve Sax	.08	.04	.01	☐ 609 Sparky Anderson MG	.06	.03	.00
☐ 561 Ken Dayley	.03	.01	.00	☐ 610 Pedro Guerrero	.08	.04	.01
☐ 562 Chad Kreuter	.03	.01	.00	☐ 611 Walt Terrell	.03	.01	.00
☐ 563 Alex Sanchez	.08	.04	.01	☐ 612 Dave Gallagher	.03	.01	.00
☐ 564 Tyler Houston FDP	.40	.20	.04	☐ 613 Jeff Pico	.03	.01	.00
☐ 565 Scott Fletcher	.03	.01	.00	☐ 614 Nelson Santovenia	.03	.01	.00
☐ 566 Mark Knudson	.03	.01	.00	☐ 615 Rob Deer	.06	.03	.00
☐ 567 Ron Gant	.06	.03	.00	☐ 616 Brian Holman	.08	.04	.01
☐ 568 John Smiley	.06	.03	.00	☐ 617 Geronimo Berroa	.06	.03	.00
☐ 569 Ivan Calderon	.06	.03	.00	☐ 618 Ed Whitson	.03	.01	.00
☐ 570 Cal Ripken	.12	.06	.01	☐ 619 Rob Ducey	.03	.01	.00
☐ 571 Brett Butler	.06	.03	.00	☐ 620 Tony Castillo	.06	.03	.00
☐ 572 Greg Harris	.03	.01	.00	☐ 621 Melido Perez	.06	.03	.00
☐ 573 Danny Heep	.03	.01	.00	☐ 622 Sid Bream	.03	.01	.00
☐ 574 Bill Swift	.03	.01	.00	☐ 623 Jim Corsi	.03	.01	.00
☐ 575 Lance Parrish	.08	.04	.01	☐ 624 Darrin Jackson	.03	.01	.00
☐ 576 Mike Dyer	.12	.06	.01	☐ 625 Roger McDowell	.06	.03	.00
☐ 577 Charlie Hayes	.08	.04	.01	☐ 626 Bob Melvin	.03	.01	.00
☐ 578 Joe Magrane	.08	.04	.01	☐ 627 Jose Rijo	.03	.01	.00
☐ 579 Art Howe MG	.03	.01	.00	☐ 628 Candy Maldonado	.03	.01	.00
☐ 580 Joe Carter	.10	.05	.01	☐ 629 Eric Hetzel	.06	.03	.00
☐ 581 Ken Griffey Sr.	.06	.03	.00	☐ 630 Gary Gaetti	.08	.04	.01
☐ 582 Rick Honeycutt	.03	.01	.00	☐ 631 John Wetteland	.20	.10	.02
☐ 583 Bruce Benedict	.03	.01	.00	☐ 632 Scott Lusader	.03	.01	.00
☐ 584 Phil Stephenson	.10	.05	.01	☐ 633 Dennis Cook	.10	.05	.01
☐ 585 Kal Daniels	.08	.04	.01	☐ 634 Luis Polonia	.03	.01	.00

		MINT	EXC	G-VG			MINT	EXC	G-VG
☐ 635	Brian Downing	.03	.01	.00	☐ 681	Mike Schooler	.06	.03	.00
☐ 636	Jesse Orosco	.03	.01	.00	☐ 682	Dann Bilardello	.03	.01	.00
☐ 637	Craig Reynolds	.03	.01	.00	☐ 683	Kenny Rogers	.10	.05	.01
☐ 638	Jeff Montgomery	.06	.03	.00	☐ 684	Julio Machado	.12	.06	.01
☐ 639	Tony LaRussa MG	.03	.01	.00	☐ 685	Tony Fernandez	.08	.04	.01
☐ 640	Rick Sutcliffe	.06	.03	.00	☐ 686	Carmelo Martinez	.03	.01	.00
☐ 641	Doug Strange	.12	.06	.01	☐ 687	Tim Birtsas	.03	.01	.00
☐ 642	Jack Armstrong	.06	.03	.00	☐ 688	Milt Thompson	.03	.01	.00
☐ 643	Alfredo Griffin	.03	.01	.00	☐ 689	Rich Yett	.03	.01	.00
☐ 644	Paul Assenmacher	.03	.01	.00	☐ 690	Mark McGwire	.25	.12	.02
☐ 645	Jose Oquendo	.03	.01	.00	☐ 691	Chuck Cary	.03	.01	.00
☐ 646	Checklist 5	.06	.01	.00	☐ 692	Sammy Sosa	.35	.17	.03
☐ 647	Rex Hudler	.03	.01	.00	☐ 693	Calvin Schiraldi	.03	.01	.00
☐ 648	Jim Clancy	.03	.01	.00	☐ 694	Mike Stanton	.20	.10	.02
☐ 649	Dan Murphy	.12	.06	.01	☐ 695	Tom Henke	.06	.03	.00
☐ 650	Mike Witt	.06	.03	.00	☐ 696	B.J. Surhoff	.06	.03	.00
☐ 651	Rafael Santana	.03	.01	.00	☐ 697	Mike Davis	.03	.01	.00
☐ 652	Mike Boddicker	.03	.01	.00	☐ 698	Omar Vizquel	.12	.06	.01
☐ 653	John Moses	.03	.01	.00	☐ 699	Jim Leyland MG	.03	.01	.00
☐ 654	Paul Coleman FDP	.30	.15	.03	☐ 700	Kirby Puckett	.20	.10	.02
☐ 655	Gregg Olson	.25	.12	.02	☐ 701	Bernie Williams	.40	.20	.04
☐ 656	Mackey Sasser	.06	.03	.00	☐ 702	Tony Phillips	.03	.01	.00
☐ 657	Terry Mulholland	.03	.01	.00	☐ 703	Jeff Brantley	.12	.06	.01
☐ 658	Donell Nixon	.03	.01	.00	☐ 704	Chip Hale	.12	.06	.01
☐ 659	Greg Cadaret	.03	.01	.00	☐ 705	Claudell Washington	.06	.03	.00
☐ 660	Vince Coleman	.08	.04	.01	☐ 706	Geno Petralli	.03	.01	.00
☐ 661	Dick Howser TBC '85	.03	.01	.00	☐ 707	Luis Aquino	.03	.01	.00
☐ 662	Mike Schmidt TBC				☐ 708	Larry Sheets	.03	.01	.00
	'80	.12	.06	.01	☐ 709	Juan Berenguer	.03	.01	.00
☐ 663	Fred Lynn TBC '75	.06	.03	.00	☐ 710	Von Hayes	.08	.04	.01
☐ 664	Johnny Bench TBC				☐ 711	Rick Aguilera	.03	.01	.00
	'70	.10	.05	.01	☐ 712	Todd Benzinger	.03	.01	.00
☐ 665	Sandy Koufax TBC				☐ 713	Tim Drummond	.12	.06	.01
	'65	.10	.05	.01	☐ 714	Marquis Grissom	.50	.25	.05
☐ 666	Brian Fisher	.03	.01	.00	☐ 715	Greg Maddux	.06	.03	.00
☐ 667	Curt Wilkerson	.03	.01	.00	☐ 716	Steve Balboni	.03	.01	.00
☐ 668	Joe Oliver	.15	.07	.01	☐ 717	Ron Karkovice	.03	.01	.00
☐ 669	Tom Lasorda MG	.06	.03	.00	☐ 718	Gary Sheffield	.30	.15	.03
☐ 670	Dennis Eckersley	.08	.04	.01	☐ 719	Wally Whitehurst	.10	.05	.01
☐ 671	Bob Boone	.06	.03	.00	☐ 720	Andres Galarraga	.08	.04	.01
☐ 672	Roy Smith	.03	.01	.00	☐ 721	Lee Mazzilli	.03	.01	.00
☐ 673	Joey Meyer	.03	.01	.00	☐ 722	Felix Fermin	.03	.01	.00
☐ 674	Spike Owen	.03	.01	.00	☐ 723	Jeff Robinson	.06	.03	.00
☐ 675	Jim Abbott	.50	.25	.05	☐ 724	Juan Bell	.15	.07	.01
☐ 676	Randy Kutcher	.03	.01	.00	☐ 725	Terry Pendleton	.03	.01	.00
☐ 677	Jay Tibbs	.03	.01	.00	☐ 726	Gene Nelson	.03	.01	.00
☐ 678	Kirt Manwaring	.03	.01	.00	☐ 727	Pat Tabler	.03	.01	.00
☐ 679	Gary Ward	.03	.01	.00	☐ 728	Jim Acker	.03	.01	.00
☐ 680	Howard Johnson	.10	.05	.01	☑ 729	Bobby Valentine MG	.03	.01	.00

		MINT	EXC	G-VG
☐ 730	Tony Gwynn	.15	.07	.01
☐ 731	Don Carman	.03	.01	.00
☐ 732	Ernest Riles	.03	.01	.00
☐ 733	John Dopson	.03	.01	.00
☐ 734	Kevin Elster	.06	.03	.00
☐ 735	Charlie Hough	.03	.01	.00
☐ 736	Rick Dempsey	.03	.01	.00
☐ 737	Chris Sabo	.08	.04	.01
☐ 738	Gene Harris	.15	.07	.01
☐ 739	Dale Sveum	.03	.01	.00
☐ 740	Jesse Barfield	.08	.04	.01
☐ 741	Steve Wilson	.08	.04	.01
☐ 742	Ernie Whitt	.03	.01	.00
☐ 743	Tom Candiotti	.03	.01	.00
☐ 744	Kelly Mann	.15	.07	.01
☐ 745	Hubie Brooks	.06	.03	.00
☐ 746	Dave Smith	.03	.01	.00
☐ 747	Randy Bush	.03	.01	.00
☐ 748	Doyle Alexander	.03	.01	.00
☐ 749	Mark Parent	.03	.01	.00
☐ 750	Dale Murphy	.12	.06	.01
☐ 751	Steve Lyons	.03	.01	.00
☐ 752	Tom Gordon	.45	.22	.04
☐ 753	Chris Speier	.03	.01	.00
☐ 754	Bob Walk	.03	.01	.00
☐ 755	Rafael Palmeiro	.06	.03	.00
☐ 756	Ken Howell	.03	.01	.00
☐ 757	Larry Walker	.20	.10	.02
☐ 758	Mark Thurmond	.03	.01	.00
☐ 759	Tom Trebelhorn MG	.03	.01	.00
☐ 760	Wade Boggs	.25	.12	.02
☐ 761	Mike Jackson	.03	.01	.00
☐ 762	Doug Dascenzo	.03	.01	.00
☐ 763	Dennis Martinez	.03	.01	.00
☐ 764	Tim Teufel	.03	.01	.00
☐ 765	Chili Davis	.06	.03	.00
☐ 766	Brian Meyer	.08	.04	.01
☐ 767	Tracy Jones	.03	.01	.00
☐ 768	Chuck Crim	.03	.01	.00
☐ 769	Greg Hibbard	.12	.06	.01
☐ 770	Cory Snyder	.08	.04	.01
☐ 771	Pete Smith	.03	.01	.00
☐ 772	Jeff Reed	.03	.01	.00
☐ 773	Dave Leiper	.03	.01	.00
☐ 774	Ben McDonald	1.75	.85	.17
☐ 775	Andy Van Slyke	.08	.04	.01
☐ 776	Charlie Leibrandt	.03	.01	.00
☐ 777	Tim Laudner	.03	.01	.00
☐ 778	Mike Jeffcoat	.03	.01	.00
☐ 779	Lloyd Moseby	.06	.03	.00
☐ 780	Orel Hershiser	.10	.05	.01
☐ 781	Mario Diaz	.03	.01	.00
☐ 782	Jose Alvarez	.03	.01	.00
☐ 783	Checklist 6	.06	.01	.00
☐ 784	Scott Bailes	.03	.01	.00
☐ 785	Jim Rice	.08	.04	.01
☐ 786	Eric King	.03	.01	.00
☐ 787	Rene Gonzales	.03	.01	.00
☐ 788	Frank DiPino	.03	.01	.00
☐ 789	John Wathan MG	.03	.01	.00
☐ 790	Gary Carter	.08	.04	.01
☐ 791	Alvaro Espinoza	.03	.01	.00
☐ 792	Gerald Perry	.06	.03	.00

1948 Bowman

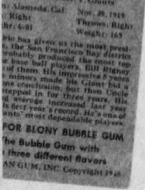

The 48-card Bowman set of 1948 was the first major set of the post-war period. Each 2 1/16" by 2 1/2" card had a black and white photo of a current player, with his biographical information printed in black ink on a gray back. Due to the printing process and the 36-card sheet size upon which Bowman was then printing, the 12 cards marked with an SP in the checklist are scarcer numerically, as they were removed from the printing sheet in order to make room for the 12 high numbers (37-48). Many cards are found with over-printing, transposed, or blank backs. The set features the Rookie Cards of Hall of Famers Yogi Berra, Ralph

Kiner, Stan Musial, Red Schoendienst, and
Warren Spahn.

		NRMT	VG-E	GOOD
COMPLETE SET		2700.00	1300.00	450.00
COMMON PLAYER (1-36)		14.00	7.00	1.40
COMMON PLAYER (37-48)		21.00	10.50	2.10
COMMON PLAYER SP		30.00	15.00	3.00

			NRMT	VG-E	GOOD
☐	1	Bob Elliott	75.00	10.00	2.00
☐	2	Ewell Blackwell	27.00	13.50	2.70
☐	3	Ralph Kiner	125.00	50.00	10.00
☐	4	Johnny Mize	70.00	35.00	7.00
☐	5	Bob Feller	135.00	65.00	13.50
☐	6	Yogi Berra	400.00	200.00	40.00
☐	7	Pete Reiser SP	40.00	20.00	4.00
☐	8	Phil Rizzuto SP	175.00	85.00	18.00
☐	9	Walker Cooper	14.00	7.00	1.40
☐	10	Buddy Rosar	14.00	7.00	1.40
☐	11	Johnny Lindell	14.00	7.00	1.40
☐	12	Johnny Sain	35.00	17.50	3.50
☐	13	Willard Marshall SP	30.00	15.00	3.00
☐	14	Allie Reynolds	35.00	17.50	3.50
☐	15	Eddie Joost	14.00	7.00	1.40
☐	16	Jack Lohrke SP	30.00	15.00	3.00
☐	17	Enos Slaughter	70.00	35.00	7.00
☐	18	Warren Spahn	200.00	100.00	20.00
☐	19	Tommy Henrich	22.00	11.00	2.20
☐	20	Buddy Kerr SP	30.00	15.00	3.00
☐	21	Ferris Fain	18.00	9.00	1.80
☐	22	Floyd Bevens SP	30.00	15.00	3.00
☐	23	Larry Jansen	16.00	8.00	1.60
☐	24	Dutch Leonard SP	30.00	15.00	3.00
☐	25	Barney McCosky	14.00	7.00	1.40
☐	26	Frank Shea SP	30.00	15.00	3.00
☐	27	Sid Gordon	14.00	7.00	1.40
☐	28	Emil Verban SP	30.00	15.00	3.00
☐	29	Joe Page SP	33.00	16.00	3.50
☐	30	Whitey Lockman SP	33.00	16.00	3.50
☐	31	Bill McCahan	14.00	7.00	1.40
☐	32	Bill Rigney	16.00	8.00	1.60
☐	33	Bill Johnson	14.00	7.00	1.40
☐	34	Sheldon Jones SP	30.00	15.00	3.00
☐	35	Snuffy Stirnweiss	18.00	9.00	1.80
☐	36	Stan Musial	600.00	300.00	60.00
☐	37	Clint Hartung	21.00	10.50	2.10
☐	38	Red Schoendienst	100.00	50.00	10.00
☐	39	Augie Galan	21.00	10.50	2.10
☐	40	Marty Marion	50.00	25.00	5.00
☐	41	Rex Barney	21.00	10.50	2.10

			NRMT	VG-E	GOOD
☐	42	Ray Poat	21.00	10.50	2.10
☐	43	Bruce Edwards	21.00	10.50	2.10
☐	44	Johnny Wyrostek	21.00	10.50	2.10
☐	45	Hank Sauer	33.00	16.00	3.50
☐	46	Herman Wehmeier	21.00	10.50	2.10
☐	47	Bobby Thomson	50.00	25.00	5.00
☐	48	Dave Koslo	50.00	12.00	2.50

1949 Bowman

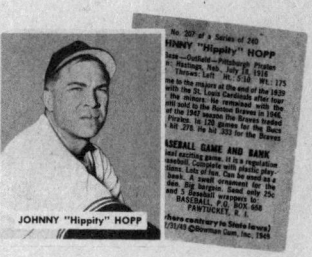

The cards in this 240-card set measure 2 1/16"
by 2 1/2". In 1949 Bowman took an intermediate
step between black and white and full color
with this set of tinted photos on colored backgrounds. Collectors should note the series
price variations, which reflect some in-
consistencies in the printing process. There are
four major varieties in name printing, which are
noted in the checklist below: NOF: name on
front; NNOF: no name on front; PR: printed
name on back; and SCR: script name on back.
These variations resulted when Bowman used
twelve of the lower numbers to fill out the last
press sheet of 36 cards, adding to numbers
217-240. Cards 1-3 and 5-73 can be found with
either gray or white backs. The set features the
Rookie Cards of Hall of Famers Roy
Campanella, Bob Lemon, Robin Roberts, Duke
Snider, and Early Wynn.

	NRMT	VG-E	GOOD
COMPLETE SET	15000.00	7000.00	1800.00
COMMON CARD (1-3/5-36/73)..	14.00	7.00	1.40
COMMON CARD (37-72)	15.00	7.50	1.50
COMMON CARD (4/74-108)	13.00	6.50	1.30
COMMON CARD (109-144)	12.00	6.00	1.20
COMMON CARD (145-180)	80.00	40.00	8.00
COMMON CARD (181-216)	75.00	37.50	7.50
COMMON CARD (217-240)	75.00	37.50	7.50

		NRMT	VG-E	GOOD
☐ 1	Vern Bickford	70.00	8.00	1.50
☐ 2	Whitey Lockman	16.00	8.00	1.60
☐ 3	Bob Porterfield	14.00	7.00	1.40
☐ 4A	Jerry Priddy NNOF	13.00	6.50	1.30
☐ 4B	Jerry Priddy NOF	40.00	20.00	4.00
☐ 5	Hank Sauer	18.00	9.00	1.80
☐ 6	Phil Cavarretta	18.00	9.00	1.80
☐ 7	Joe Dobson	14.00	7.00	1.40
☐ 8	Murry Dickson	14.00	7.00	1.40
☐ 9	Ferris Fain	18.00	9.00	1.80
☐ 10	Ted Gray	14.00	7.00	1.40
☐ 11	Lou Boudreau	50.00	22.50	4.50
☐ 12	Cass Michaels	14.00	7.00	1.40
☐ 13	Bob Chesnes	14.00	7.00	1.40
☐ 14	Curt Simmons	25.00	12.50	2.50
☐ 15	Ned Garver	14.00	7.00	1.40
☐ 16	Al Kozar	14.00	7.00	1.40
☐ 17	Earl Torgeson	14.00	7.00	1.40
☐ 18	Bobby Thomson	21.00	10.50	2.10
☐ 19	Bobby Brown	30.00	15.00	3.00
☐ 20	Gene Hermanski	14.00	7.00	1.40
☐ 21	Frank Baumholtz	14.00	7.00	1.40
☐ 22	Peanuts Lowrey	14.00	7.00	1.40
☐ 23	Bobby Doerr	60.00	30.00	6.00
☐ 24	Stan Musial	450.00	225.00	45.00
☐ 25	Carl Scheib	14.00	7.00	1.40
☐ 26	George Kell	50.00	22.50	4.50
☐ 27	Bob Feller	110.00	55.00	11.00
☐ 28	Don Kolloway	14.00	7.00	1.40
☐ 29	Ralph Kiner	60.00	30.00	6.00
☐ 30	Andy Seminick	14.00	7.00	1.40
☐ 31	Dick Kokos	14.00	7.00	1.40
☐ 32	Eddie Yost	14.00	7.00	1.40
☐ 33	Warren Spahn	110.00	55.00	11.00
☐ 34	Dave Koslo	14.00	7.00	1.40
☐ 35	Vic Raschi	35.00	17.50	3.50
☐ 36	Pee Wee Reese	110.00	50.00	10.00
☐ 37	Johnny Wyrostek	15.00	7.50	1.50
☐ 38	Emil Verban	15.00	7.50	1.50
☐ 39	Billy Goodman	18.00	9.00	1.80
☐ 40	Red Munger	15.00	7.50	1.50
☐ 41	Lou Brissie	15.00	7.50	1.50
☐ 42	Hoot Evers	15.00	7.50	1.50
☐ 43	Dale Mitchell	18.00	9.00	1.80
☐ 44	Dave Philley	15.00	7.50	1.50
☐ 45	Wally Westlake	15.00	7.50	1.50
☐ 46	Robin Roberts	165.00	75.00	15.00
☐ 47	Johnny Sain	25.00	12.50	2.50
☐ 48	Willard Marshall	15.00	7.50	1.50
☐ 49	Frank Shea	15.00	7.50	1.50
☐ 50	Jackie Robinson	600.00	300.00	60.00
☐ 51	Herman Wehmeier	15.00	7.50	1.50
☐ 52	Johnny Schmitz	15.00	7.50	1.50
☐ 53	Jack Kramer	15.00	7.50	1.50
☐ 54	Marty Marion	22.00	11.00	2.20
☐ 55	Eddie Joost	15.00	7.50	1.50
☐ 56	Pat Mullin	15.00	7.50	1.50
☐ 57	Gene Bearden	15.00	7.50	1.50
☐ 58	Bob Elliott	18.00	9.00	1.80
☐ 59	Jack Lohrke	15.00	7.50	1.50
☐ 60	Yogi Berra	250.00	125.00	25.00
☐ 61	Rex Barney	15.00	7.50	1.50
☐ 62	Grady Hatton	15.00	7.50	1.50
☐ 63	Andy Pafko	18.00	9.00	1.80
☐ 64	Dom DiMaggio	22.00	11.00	2.20
☐ 65	Enos Slaughter	60.00	30.00	6.00
☐ 66	Elmer Valo	15.00	7.50	1.50
☐ 67	Alvin Dark	22.00	11.00	2.20
☐ 68	Sheldon Jones	15.00	7.50	1.50
☐ 69	Tommy Henrich	22.00	11.00	2.20
☐ 70	Carl Furillo	45.00	22.50	4.50
☐ 71	Vern Stephens	18.00	9.00	1.80
☐ 72	Tommy Holmes	18.00	9.00	1.80
☐ 73	Billy Cox	22.00	11.00	2.20
☐ 74	Tom McBride	13.00	6.50	1.30
☐ 75	Eddie Mayo	13.00	6.50	1.30
☐ 76	Bill Nicholson	13.00	6.50	1.30
☐ 77	Ernie Bonham	13.00	6.50	1.30
☐ 78A	Sam Zoldak NNOF	13.00	6.50	1.30
☐ 78B	Sam Zoldak NOF	40.00	20.00	4.00
☐ 79	Ron Northey	13.00	6.50	1.30
☐ 80	Bill McCahan	13.00	6.50	1.30
☐ 81	Virgil Stallcup	13.00	6.50	1.30
☐ 82	Joe Page	20.00	10.00	2.00
☐ 83A	Bob Scheffing NNOF	13.00	6.50	1.30
☐ 83B	Bob Scheffing NOF	40.00	20.00	4.00
☐ 84	Roy Campanella	500.00	250.00	50.00
☐ 85A	Johnny Mize NNOF	60.00	30.00	6.00
☐ 85B	Johnny Mize NOF	120.00	60.00	12.00

		NRMT	VG-E	GOOD
☐	86 Johnny Pesky	15.00	7.50	1.50
☐	87 Randy Gumpert	13.00	6.50	1.30
☐	88A Bill Salkeld NNOF	13.00	6.50	1.30
☐	88B Bill Salkeld NOF	40.00	20.00	4.00
☐	89 Mizell Platt	13.00	6.50	1.30
☐	90 Gil Coan	13.00	6.50	1.30
☐	91 Dick Wakefield	13.00	6.50	1.30
☐	92 Willie Jones	13.00	6.50	1.30
☐	93 Ed Stevens	13.00	6.50	1.30
☐	94 Mickey Vernon	22.00	11.00	2.20
☐	95 Howie Pollet	13.00	6.50	1.30
☐	96 Taft Wright	13.00	6.50	1.30
☐	97 Danny Litwhiler	13.00	6.50	1.30
☐	98A Phil Rizzuto NNOF	80.00	40.00	8.00
☐	98B Phil Rizzuto NOF	160.00	80.00	16.00
☐	99 Frank Gustine	13.00	6.50	1.30
☐	100 Gil Hodges	165.00	80.00	16.00
☐	101 Sid Gordon	13.00	6.50	1.30
☐	102 Stan Spence	13.00	6.50	1.30
☐	103 Joe Tipton	13.00	6.50	1.30
☐	104 Eddie Stanky	20.00	10.00	2.00
☐	105 Bill Kennedy	13.00	6.50	1.30
☐	106 Jake Early	13.00	6.50	1.30
☐	107 Eddie Lake	13.00	6.50	1.30
☐	108 Ken Heintzelman	13.00	6.50	1.30
☐	109A Ed Fitzgerald SCR	12.00	6.00	1.20
☐	109B Ed Fitzgerald PR	35.00	17.50	3.50
☐	110 Early Wynn	100.00	50.00	10.00
☐	111 Red Schoendienst	60.00	30.00	6.00
☐	112 Sam Chapman	12.00	6.00	1.20
☐	113 Ray LaManno	12.00	6.00	1.20
☐	114 Allie Reynolds	25.00	12.50	2.50
☐	115 Dutch Leonard	12.00	6.00	1.20
☐	116 Joe Hatton	12.00	6.00	1.20
☐	117 Walker Cooper	12.00	6.00	1.20
☐	118 Sam Mele	12.00	6.00	1.20
☐	119 Floyd Baker	12.00	6.00	1.20
☐	120 Cliff Fannin	12.00	6.00	1.20
☐	121 Mark Christman	12.00	6.00	1.20
☐	122 George Vico	12.00	6.00	1.20
☐	123 Johnny Blatnick	12.00	6.00	1.20
☐	124A Danny Murtaugh SCR	12.00	6.00	1.20
☐	124B Danny Murtaugh PR	35.00	17.50	3.50
☐	125 Ken Keltner	14.00	7.00	1.40
☐	126A Al Brazle SCR	12.00	6.00	1.20
☐	126B Al Brazle PR	35.00	17.50	3.50
☐	127A Hank Majeski SCR	12.00	6.00	1.20
☐	127B Hank Majeski PR	35.00	17.50	3.50
☐	128 Johnny VanderMeer	20.00	10.00	2.00
☐	129 Bill Johnson	12.00	6.00	1.20
☐	130 Harry Walker	12.00	6.00	1.20
☐	131 Paul Lehner	12.00	6.00	1.20
☐	132A Al Evans SCR	12.00	6.00	1.20
☐	132B Al Evans PR	35.00	17.50	3.50
☐	133 Aaron Robinson	12.00	6.00	1.20
☐	134 Hank Borowy	12.00	6.00	1.20
☐	135 Stan Rojek	12.00	6.00	1.20
☐	136 Hank Edwards	12.00	6.00	1.20
☐	137 Ted Wilks	12.00	6.00	1.203
☐	138 Buddy Rosar	12.00	6.00	1.20
☐	139 Hank Arft	12.00	6.00	1.20
☐	140 Ray Scarborough	12.00	6.00	1.20
☐	141 Ulysses Lupien	12.00	6.00	1.20
☐	142 Eddie Waitkus	14.00	7.00	1.40
☐	143A Bob Dillinger SCR	12.00	6.00	1.20
☐	143B Bob Dillinger PR	35.00	17.50	3.50
☐	144 Mickey Haefner	12.00	6.00	1.20
☐	145 Sylvester Donnelly	80.00	40.00	8.00
☐	146 Mike McCormick	80.00	40.00	8.00
☐	147 Bert Singleton	80.00	40.00	8.00
☐	148 Bob Swift	80.00	40.00	8.00
☐	149 Roy Partee	80.00	40.00	8.00
☐	150 Allie Clark	80.00	40.00	8.00
☐	151 Mickey Harris	80.00	40.00	8.00
☐	152 Clarence Maddern	80.00	40.00	8.00
☐	153 Phil Masi	80.00	40.00	8.00
☐	154 Clint Hartung	80.00	40.00	8.00
☐	155 Mickey Guerra	80.00	40.00	8.00
☐	156 Al Zarilla	80.00	40.00	8.00
☐	157 Walt Masterson	80.00	40.00	8.00
☐	158 Harry Brecheen	90.00	45.00	9.00
☐	159 Glen Moulder	80.00	40.00	8.00
☐	160 Jim Blackburn	80.00	40.00	8.00
☐	161 Jocko Thompson	80.00	40.00	8.00
☐	162 Preacher Roe	125.00	60.00	12.50
☐	163 Clyde McCullough	80.00	40.00	8.00
☐	164 Vic Wertz	90.00	45.00	9.00
☐	165 Snuffy Stirnweiss	90.00	45.00	9.00
☐	166 Mike Tresh	80.00	40.00	8.00
☐	167 Babe Martin	80.00	40.00	8.00
☐	168 Doyle Lade	80.00	40.00	8.00
☐	169 Jeff Heath	80.00	40.00	8.00
☐	170 Bill Rigney	90.00	45.00	9.00
☐	171 Dick Fowler	80.00	40.00	8.00
☐	172 Eddie Pellagrini	80.00	40.00	8.00
☐	173 Eddie Stewart	80.00	40.00	8.00
☐	174 Terry Moore	100.00	50.00	10.00
☐	175 Luke Appling	125.00	60.00	12.50

		NRMT	VG-E	GOOD
☐ 176	Ken Raffensberger ..	80.00	40.00	8.00
☐ 177	Stan Lopata	80.00	40.00	8.00
☐ 178	Tom Brown	80.00	40.00	8.00
☐ 179	Hugh Casey	90.00	45.00	9.00
☐ 180	Connie Berry	80.00	40.00	8.00
☐ 181	Gus Niarhos	75.00	37.50	7.50
☐ 182	Hal Peck	75.00	37.50	7.50
☐ 183	Lou Stringer	75.00	37.50	7.50
☐ 184	Bob Chipman	75.00	37.50	7.50
☐ 185	Pete Reiser	90.00	45.00	9.00
☐ 186	Buddy Kerr	75.00	37.50	7.50
☐ 187	Phil Marchildon	75.00	37.50	7.50
☐ 188	Karl Drews	75.00	37.50	7.50
☐ 189	Earl Wooten	75.00	37.50	7.50
☐ 190	Jim Hearn	75.00	37.50	7.50
☐ 191	Joe Haynes	75.00	37.50	7.50
☐ 192	Harry Gumbert	75.00	37.50	7.50
☐ 193	Ken Trinkle	75.00	37.50	7.50
☐ 194	Ralph Branca	100.00	50.00	10.00
☐ 195	Eddie Bockman	75.00	37.50	7.50
☐ 196	Fred Hutchinson	90.00	45.00	9.00
☐ 197	Johnny Lindell	75.00	37.50	7.50
☐ 198	Steve Gromek	75.00	37.50	7.50
☐ 199	Tex Hughson	75.00	37.50	7.50
☐ 200	Jess Dobernic	75.00	37.50	7.50
☐ 201	Sibby Sisti	75.00	37.50	7.50
☐ 202	Larry Jansen	90.00	45.00	9.00
☐ 203	Barney McCosky	75.00	37.50	7.50
☐ 204	Bob Savage	75.00	37.50	7.50
☐ 205	Dick Sisler	75.00	37.50	7.50
☐ 206	Bruce Edwards	75.00	37.50	7.50
☐ 207	Johnny Hopp	90.00	45.00	9.00
☐ 208	Dizzy Trout	90.00	45.00	9.00
☐ 209	Charlie Keller	100.00	50.00	10.00
☐ 210	Joe Gordon	100.00	50.00	10.00
☐ 211	Boo Ferriss	75.00	37.50	7.50
☐ 212	Ralph Hamner	75.00	37.50	7.50
☐ 213	Red Barrett	75.00	37.50	7.50
☐ 214	Richie Ashburn	500.00	250.00	50.00
☐ 215	Kirby Higbe	75.00	37.50	7.50
☐ 216	Schoolboy Rowe	90.00	45.00	9.00
☐ 217	Marino Pieretti	75.00	37.50	7.50
☐ 218	Dick Kryhoski	75.00	37.50	7.50
☐ 219	Virgil "Fire" Trucks .	90.00	45.00	9.00
☐ 220	Johnny McCarthy ...	75.00	37.50	7.50
☐ 221	Bob Muncrief	75.00	37.50	7.50
☐ 222	Alex Kellner	75.00	37.50	7.50
☐ 223	Bobby Hofman	75.00	37.50	7.50
☐ 224	Satchell Paige	1200.00	100.00	20.00

		NRMT	VG-E	GOOD
☐ 225	Gerry Coleman	90.00	45.00	9.00
☐ 226	Duke Snider	1000.00	500.00	100.00
☐ 227	Fritz Ostermueller ..	75.00	37.50	7.50
☐ 228	Jackie Mayo	75.00	37.50	7.50
☐ 229	Ed Lopat	125.00	60.00	12.50
☐ 230	Augie Galan	75.00	37.50	7.50
☐ 231	Earl Johnson	75.00	37.50	7.50
☐ 232	George McQuinn	75.00	37.50	7.50
☐ 233	Larry Doby	125.00	60.00	12.50
☐ 234	Rip Sewell	75.00	37.50	7.50
☐ 235	Jim Russell	75.00	37.50	7.50
☐ 236	Fred Sanford	75.00	37.50	7.50
☐ 237	Monte Kennedy	75.00	37.50	7.50
☐ 238	Bob Lemon	225.00	110.00	22.00
☐ 239	Frank McCormick ...	90.00	45.00	9.00
☐ 240	Babe Young	125.00	60.00	12.50
	(photo actually Bobby Young)			

1950 Bowman

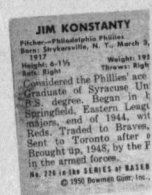

The cards in this 252-card set measure 2 1/16" by 2 1/2". This set, marketed in 1950 by Bowman, represented a major improvement in terms of quality over their previous efforts. Each card was a beautifully colored line drawing developed from a simple photograph. The first 72 cards are the scarcest in the set, while the final 72 cards may be found with or without the copyright line. This was the only Bowman sports set to carry the famous "5-Star" logo.

		NRMT	VG-E	GOOD
	COMPLETE SET	8000	4000	900
	COMMON PLAYER (1-72)	36.00	18.00	3.60
	COMMON PLAYER (73-252)	13.00	6.50	1.30
☐ 1	Mel Parnell	200.00	20.00	4.00
☐ 2	Vern Stephens	40.00	20.00	4.00
☐ 3	Dom DiMaggio	45.00	22.50	4.50
☐ 4	Gus Zernial	45.00	22.50	4.50
☐ 5	Bob Kuzava	36.00	18.00	3.60
☐ 6	Bob Feller	135.00	65.00	13.50
☐ 7	Jim Hegan	40.00	20.00	4.00
☐ 8	George Kell	70.00	35.00	7.00
☐ 9	Vic Wertz	40.00	20.00	4.00
☐ 10	Tommy Henrich	45.00	22.50	4.50
☐ 11	Phil Rizzuto	110.00	55.00	11.00
☐ 12	Joe Page	45.00	22.50	4.50
☐ 13	Ferris Fain	40.00	20.00	4.00
☐ 14	Alex Kellner	36.00	18.00	3.60
☐ 15	Al Kozar	36.00	18.00	3.60
☐ 16	Roy Sievers	45.00	22.50	4.50
☐ 17	Sid Hudson	36.00	18.00	3.60
☐ 18	Eddie Robinson	36.00	18.00	3.60
☐ 19	Warren Spahn	135.00	65.00	13.50
☐ 20	Bob Elliott	40.00	20.00	4.00
☐ 21	Pee Wee Reese	125.00	60.00	12.50
☐ 22	Jackie Robinson	500.00	250.00	50.00
☐ 23	Don Newcombe	80.00	40.00	8.00
☐ 24	Johnny Schmitz	36.00	18.00	3.60
☐ 25	Hank Sauer	40.00	20.00	4.00
☐ 26	Grady Hatton	36.00	18.00	3.60
☐ 27	Herman Wehmeier	36.00	18.00	3.60
☐ 28	Bobby Thomson	45.00	22.50	4.50
☐ 29	Eddie Stanky	40.00	20.00	4.00
☐ 30	Eddie Waitkus	36.00	18.00	3.60
☐ 31	Del Ennis	40.00	20.00	4.00
☐ 32	Robin Roberts	100.00	50.00	10.00
☐ 33	Ralph Kiner	80.00	40.00	8.00
☐ 34	Murry Dickson	36.00	18.00	3.60
☐ 35	Enos Slaughter	80.00	40.00	8.00
☐ 36	Eddie Kazak	36.00	18.00	3.60
☐ 37	Luke Appling	60.00	30.00	6.00
☐ 38	Bill Wight	36.00	18.00	3.60
☐ 39	Larry Doby	50.00	25.00	5.00
☐ 40	Bob Lemon	80.00	40.00	8.00
☐ 41	Hoot Evers	36.00	18.00	3.60
☐ 42	Art Houtteman	36.00	18.00	3.60
☐ 43	Bobby Doerr	70.00	35.00	7.00
☐ 44	Joe Dobson	36.00	18.00	3.60
☐ 45	Al Zarilla	36.00	18.00	3.60
☐ 46	Yogi Berra	350.00	175.00	35.00
☐ 47	Jerry Coleman	45.00	22.50	4.50
☐ 48	Lou Brissie	36.00	18.00	3.60
☐ 49	Elmer Valo	36.00	18.00	3.60
☐ 50	Dick Kokos	36.00	18.00	3.60
☐ 51	Ned Garver	36.00	18.00	3.60
☐ 52	Sam Mele	36.00	18.00	3.60
☐ 53	Clyde Vollmer	36.00	18.00	3.60
☐ 54	Gil Coan	36.00	18.00	3.60
☐ 55	Buddy Kerr	36.00	18.00	3.60
☐ 56	Del Crandall	45.00	22.50	4.50
☐ 57	Vern Bickford	36.00	18.00	3.60
☐ 58	Carl Furillo	50.00	25.00	5.00
☐ 59	Ralph Branca	45.00	22.50	4.50
☐ 60	Andy Pafko	40.00	20.00	4.00
☐ 61	Bob Rush	36.00	18.00	3.60
☐ 62	Ted Kluszewski	50.00	25.00	5.00
☐ 63	Ewell Blackwell	40.00	20.00	4.00
☐ 64	Alvin Dark	45.00	22.50	4.50
☐ 65	Dave Koslo	36.00	18.00	3.60
☐ 66	Larry Jansen	40.00	20.00	4.00
☐ 67	Willie Jones	36.00	18.00	3.60
☐ 68	Curt Simmons	40.00	20.00	4.00
☐ 69	Wally Westlake	36.00	18.00	3.60
☐ 70	Bob Chesnes	36.00	18.00	3.60
☐ 71	Red Schoendienst	75.00	37.50	7.50
☐ 72	Howie Pollet	36.00	18.00	3.60
☐ 73	Willard Marshall	13.00	6.50	1.30
☐ 74	Johnny Antonelli	20.00	10.00	2.00
☐ 75	Roy Campanella	250.00	125.00	25.00
☐ 76	Rex Barney	13.00	6.50	1.30
☐ 77	Duke Snider	250.00	125.00	25.00
☐ 78	Mickey Owen	15.00	7.50	1.50
☐ 79	Johnny VanderMeer	20.00	10.00	2.00
☐ 80	Howard Fox	13.00	6.50	1.30
☐ 81	Ron Northey	13.00	6.50	1.30
☐ 82	Whitey Lockman	15.00	7.50	1.50
☐ 83	Sheldon Jones	13.00	6.50	1.30
☐ 84	Richie Ashburn	50.00	25.00	5.00
☐ 85	Ken Heintzelman	13.00	6.50	1.30
☐ 86	Stan Rojek	13.00	6.50	1.30
☐ 87	Bill Werle	13.00	6.50	1.30
☐ 88	Marty Marion	20.00	10.00	2.00
☐ 89	Red Munger	13.00	6.50	1.30
☐ 90	Harry Brecheen	15.00	7.50	1.50
☐ 91	Cass Michaels	13.00	6.50	1.30
☐ 92	Hank Majeski	13.00	6.50	1.30

		NRMT	VG-E	GOOD			NRMT	VG-E	GOOD
☐ 93	Gene Bearden	13.00	6.50	1.30	☐ 140	Pete Suder	13.00	6.50	1.30
☐ 94	Lou Boudreau	40.00	20.00	4.00	☐ 141	Joe Coleman	13.00	6.50	1.30
☐ 95	Aaron Robinson	13.00	6.50	1.30	☐ 142	Sherm Lollar	15.00	7.50	1.50
☐ 96	Virgil Trucks	15.00	7.50	1.50	☐ 143	Eddie Stewart	13.00	6.50	1.30
☐ 97	Maurice McDermott	13.00	6.50	1.30	☐ 144	Al Evans	13.00	6.50	1.30
☐ 98	Ted Williams	600.00	275.00	55.00	☐ 145	Jack Graham	13.00	6.50	1.30
☐ 99	Billy Goodman	15.00	7.50	1.50	☐ 146	Floyd Baker	13.00	6.50	1.30
☐ 100	Vic Raschi	22.00	11.00	2.20	☐ 147	Mike Garcia	15.00	7.50	1.50
☐ 101	Bobby Brown	25.00	12.50	2.50	☐ 148	Early Wynn	50.00	25.00	5.00
☐ 102	Billy Johnson	13.00	6.50	1.30	☐ 149	Bob Swift	13.00	6.50	1.30
☐ 103	Eddie Joost	13.00	6.50	1.30	☐ 150	George Vico	13.00	6.50	1.30
☐ 104	Sam Chapman	13.00	6.50	1.30	☐ 151	Fred Hutchinson	15.00	7.50	1.50
☐ 105	Bob Dillinger	13.00	6.50	1.30	☐ 152	Ellis Kinder	13.00	6.50	1.30
☐ 106	Cliff Fannin	13.00	6.50	1.30	☐ 153	Walt Masterson	13.00	6.50	1.30
☐ 107	Sam Dente	13.00	6.50	1.30	☐ 154	Gus Niarhos	13.00	6.50	1.30
☐ 108	Ray Scarborough	13.00	6.50	1.30	☐ 155	Frank Shea	13.00	6.50	1.30
☐ 109	Sid Gordon	13.00	6.50	1.30	☐ 156	Fred Sanford	13.00	6.50	1.30
☐ 110	Tommy Holmes	15.00	7.50	1.50	☐ 157	Mike Guerra	13.00	6.50	1.30
☐ 111	Walker Cooper	13.00	6.50	1.30	☐ 158	Paul Lehner	13.00	6.50	1.30
☐ 112	Gil Hodges	70.00	35.00	7.00	☐ 159	Joe Tipton	13.00	6.50	1.30
☐ 113	Gene Hermanski	13.00	6.50	1.30	☐ 160	Mickey Harris	13.00	6.50	1.30
☐ 114	Wayne Terwilliger	13.00	6.50	1.30	☐ 161	Sherry Robertson	13.00	6.50	1.30
☐ 115	Roy Smalley	13.00	6.50	1.30	☐ 162	Eddie Yost	13.00	6.50	1.30
☐ 116	Virgil Stallcup	13.00	6.50	1.30	☐ 163	Earl Torgeson	13.00	6.50	1.30
☐ 117	Bill Rigney	13.00	6.50	1.30	☐ 164	Sibby Sisti	13.00	6.50	1.30
☐ 118	Clint Hartung	13.00	6.50	1.30	☐ 165	Bruce Edwards	13.00	6.50	1.30
☐ 119	Dick Sisler	13.00	6.50	1.30	☐ 166	Joe Hatton	13.00	6.50	1.30
☐ 120	John Thompson	13.00	6.50	1.30	☐ 167	Preacher Roe	25.00	12.50	2.50
☐ 121	Andy Seminick	13.00	6.50	1.30	☐ 168	Bob Scheffing	13.00	6.50	1.30
☐ 122	Johnny Hopp	15.00	7.50	1.50	☐ 169	Hank Edwards	13.00	6.50	1.30
☐ 123	Dino Restelli	13.00	6.50	1.30	☐ 170	Dutch Leonard	13.00	6.50	1.30
☐ 124	Clyde McCullough	13.00	6.50	1.30	☐ 171	Harry Gumbert	13.00	6.50	1.30
☐ 125	Del Rice	13.00	6.50	1.30	☐ 172	Peanuts Lowrey	13.00	6.50	1.30
☐ 126	Al Brazle	13.00	6.50	1.30	☐ 173	Lloyd Merriman	13.00	6.50	1.30
☐ 127	Dave Philley	13.00	6.50	1.30	☐ 174	Hank Thompson	15.00	7.50	1.50
☐ 128	Phil Masi	13.00	6.50	1.30	☐ 175	Monte Kennedy	13.00	6.50	1.30
☐ 129	Joe Gordon	18.00	9.00	1.80	☐ 176	Sylvester Donnelly	13.00	6.50	1.30
☐ 130	Dale Mitchell	15.00	7.50	1.50	☐ 177	Hank Borowy	13.00	6.50	1.30
☐ 131	Steve Gromek	13.00	6.50	1.30	☐ 178	Ed Fitzgerald	13.00	6.50	1.30
☐ 132	James "Mickey" Vernon	15.00	7.50	1.50	☐ 179	Chuck Diering	13.00	6.50	1.30
☐ 133	Don Kolloway	13.00	6.50	1.30	☐ 180	Harry Walker	13.00	6.50	1.30
☐ 134	Paul Trout	13.00	6.50	1.30	☐ 181	Marino Pieretti	13.00	6.50	1.30
☐ 135	Pat Mullin	13.00	6.50	1.30	☐ 182	Sam Zoldak	13.00	6.50	1.30
☐ 136	Warren Rosar	13.00	6.50	1.30	☐ 183	Mickey Haefner	13.00	6.50	1.30
☐ 137	Johnny Pesky	15.00	7.50	1.50	☐ 184	Randy Gumpert	13.00	6.50	1.30
☐ 138	Allie Reynolds	25.00	12.50	2.50	☐ 185	Howie Judson	13.00	6.50	1.30
☐ 139	Johnny Mize	60.00	30.00	6.00	☐ 186	Ken Keltner	15.00	7.50	1.50
					☐ 187	Lou Stringer	13.00	6.50	1.30

		NRMT	VG-E	GOOD
☐ 188	Earl Johnson	13.00	6.50	1.30
☐ 189	Owen Friend	13.00	6.50	1.30
☐ 190	Ken Wood	13.00	6.50	1.30
☐ 191	Dick Starr	13.00	6.50	1.30
☐ 192	Bob Chipman	13.00	6.50	1.30
☐ 193	Pete Reiser	15.00	7.50	1.50
☐ 194	Billy Cox	15.00	7.50	1.50
☐ 195	Phil Cavarretta	15.00	7.50	1.50
☐ 196	Doyle Lade	13.00	6.50	1.30
☐ 197	Johnny Wyrostek	13.00	6.50	1.30
☐ 198	Danny Litwhiler	13.00	6.50	1.30
☐ 199	Jack Kramer	13.00	6.50	1.30
☐ 200	Kirby Higbe	13.00	6.50	1.30
☐ 201	Pete Castiglione	13.00	6.50	1.30
☐ 202	Cliff Chambers	13.00	6.50	1.30
☐ 203	Danny Murtaugh	13.00	6.50	1.30
☐ 204	Granny Hamner	13.00	6.50	1.30
☐ 205	Mike Goliat	13.00	6.50	1.30
☐ 206	Stan Lopata	13.00	6.50	1.30
☐ 207	Max Lanier	13.00	6.50	1.30
☐ 208	Jim Hearn	13.00	6.50	1.30
☐ 209	Johnny Lindell	13.00	6.50	1.30
☐ 210	Ted Gray	13.00	6.50	1.30
☐ 211	Charley Keller	15.00	7.50	1.50
☐ 212	Jerry Priddy	13.00	6.50	1.30
☐ 213	Carl Scheib	13.00	6.50	1.30
☐ 214	Dick Fowler	13.00	6.50	1.30
☐ 215	Ed Lopat	25.00	12.50	2.50
☐ 216	Bob Porterfield	13.00	6.50	1.30
☐ 217	Casey Stengel MG	100.00	50.00	10.00
☐ 218	Cliff Mapes	15.00	7.50	1.50
☐ 219	Hank Bauer	45.00	22.50	4.50
☐ 220	Leo Durocher MG	40.00	20.00	4.00
☐ 221	Don Mueller	24.00	12.00	2.40
☐ 222	Bobby Morgan	13.00	6.50	1.30
☐ 223	Jim Russell	13.00	6.50	1.30
☐ 224	Jack Banta	13.00	6.50	1.30
☐ 225	Eddie Sawyer MG	15.00	7.50	1.50
☐ 226	Jim Konstanty	24.00	12.00	2.40
☐ 227	Bob Miller	13.00	6.50	1.30
☐ 228	Bill Nicholson	13.00	6.50	1.30
☐ 229	Frank Frisch	40.00	20.00	4.00
☐ 230	Bill Serena	13.00	6.50	1.30
☐ 231	Preston Ward	13.00	6.50	1.30
☐ 232	Al Rosen	45.00	22.50	4.50
☐ 233	Allie Clark	13.00	6.50	1.30
☐ 234	Bobby Shantz	21.00	10.50	2.10
☐ 235	Harold Gilbert	13.00	6.50	1.30

		NRMT	VG-E	GOOD
☐ 236	Bob Cain	13.00	6.50	1.30
☐ 237	Bill Salkeld	13.00	6.50	1.30
☐ 238	Vernal Jones	13.00	6.50	1.30
☐ 239	Bill Howerton	13.00	6.50	1.30
☐ 240	Eddie Lake	13.00	6.50	1.30
☐ 241	Neil Berry	13.00	6.50	1.30
☐ 242	Dick Kryhoski	13.00	6.50	1.30
☐ 243	Johnny Groth	13.00	6.50	1.30
☐ 244	Dale Coogan	13.00	6.50	1.30
☐ 245	Al Papai	13.00	6.50	1.30
☐ 246	Walt Dropo	21.00	10.50	2.10
☐ 247	Irv Noren	15.00	7.50	1.50
☐ 248	Sam Jethroe	15.00	7.50	1.50
☐ 249	Snuffy Stirnweiss	15.00	7.50	1.50
☐ 250	Ray Coleman	13.00	6.50	1.30
☐ 251	John Moss	13.00	6.50	1.30
☐ 252	Billy DeMars	70.00	8.00	1.50

1951 Bowman

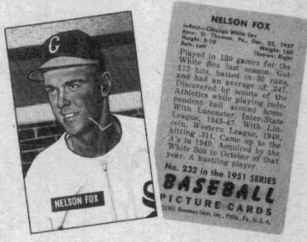

The cards in this 324-card set measure 2 1/16"
by 3 1/8". Many of the obverses of the cards
appearing in the 1951 Bowman set are en-
largements of those appearing in the previous
year. The high number series (253-324) is
highly valued and contains the true "Rookie"
cards of Mickey Mantle and Willie Mays. Card
number 195 depicts Paul Richards in carica-
ture. George Kell's card (#46) incorrectly lists
him as being in the "1941" Bowman series.
Player names are found printed in a panel on

the front of the card. These cards were
supposedly also sold in sheets in variety stores
in the Philadelphia area.

		NRMT	VG-E	GOOD
	COMPLETE SET (324)	16000.00	8000.00	2000.00
	COMMON PLAYER (1-36)	16.00	8.00	1.60
	COMMON PLAYER (37-72)	13.00	6.50	1.30
	COMMON PLAYER (73-252)	12.00	6.00	1.20
	COMMON PLAYER (253-324)	45.00	22.50	4.50
☐ 1	Whitey Ford	1200.00	150.00	30.00
☐ 2	Yogi Berra	350.00	175.00	35.00
☐ 3	Robin Roberts	60.00	30.00	6.00
☐ 4	Del Ennis	18.00	9.00	1.80
☐ 5	Dale Mitchell	18.00	9.00	1.80
☐ 6	Don Newcombe	30.00	15.00	3.00
☐ 7	Gil Hodges	60.00	30.00	6.00
☐ 8	Paul Lehner	16.00	8.00	1.60
☐ 9	Sam Chapman	16.00	8.00	1.60
☐ 10	Red Schoendienst	60.00	30.00	6.00
☐ 11	Red Munger	16.00	8.00	1.60
☐ 12	Hank Majeski	16.00	8.00	1.60
☐ 13	Eddie Stanky	20.00	10.00	2.00
☐ 14	Alvin Dark	22.00	11.00	2.20
☐ 15	Johnny Pesky	18.00	9.00	1.80
☐ 16	Maurice McDermott	16.00	8.00	1.60
☐ 17	Pete Castiglione	16.00	8.00	1.60
☐ 18	Gil Coan	16.00	8.00	1.60
☐ 19	Sid Gordon	16.00	8.00	1.60
☐ 20	Del Crandell (sic, Crandall)	20.00	10.00	2.00
☐ 21	Snuffy Stirnweiss	18.00	9.00	1.80
☐ 22	Hank Sauer	18.00	9.00	1.80
☐ 23	Hoot Evers	16.00	8.00	1.60
☐ 24	Ewell Blackwell	20.00	10.00	2.00
☐ 25	Vic Raschi	22.00	11.00	2.20
☐ 26	Phil Rizzuto	65.00	32.50	6.50
☐ 27	Jim Konstanty	18.00	9.00	1.80
☐ 28	Eddie Waitkus	16.00	8.00	1.60
☐ 29	Allie Clark	16.00	8.00	1.60
☐ 30	Bob Feller	100.00	50.00	10.00
☐ 31	Roy Campanella	225.00	110.00	22.00
☐ 32	Duke Snider	180.00	90.00	18.00
☐ 33	Bob Hooper	16.00	8.00	1.60
☐ 34	Marty Marion	20.00	10.00	2.00
☐ 35	Al Zarilla	16.00	8.00	1.60
☐ 36	Joe Dobson	16.00	8.00	1.60
☐ 37	Whitey Lockman	16.00	8.00	1.60

		NRMT	VG-E	GOOD
☐ 38	Al Evans	13.00	6.50	1.30
☐ 39	Ray Scarborough	13.00	6.50	1.30
☐ 40	Gus Bell	20.00	10.00	2.00
☐ 41	Eddie Yost	13.00	6.50	1.30
☐ 42	Vern Bickford	13.00	6.50	1.30
☐ 43	Billy DeMars	13.00	6.50	1.30
☐ 44	Roy Smalley	13.00	6.50	1.30
☐ 45	Art Houtteman	13.00	6.50	1.30
☐ 46	George Kell 1941	50.00	25.00	5.00
☐ 47	Grady Hatton	13.00	6.50	1.30
☐ 48	Ken Raffensberger	13.00	6.50	1.30
☐ 49	Jerry Coleman	16.00	8.00	1.60
☐ 50	Johnny Mize	50.00	25.00	5.00
☐ 51	Andy Seminick	13.00	6.50	1.30
☐ 52	Dick Sisler	13.00	6.50	1.30
☐ 53	Bob Lemon	45.00	22.50	4.50
☐ 54	Ray Boone	16.00	8.00	1.60
☐ 55	Gene Hermanski	13.00	6.50	1.30
☐ 56	Ralph Branca	20.00	10.00	2.00
☐ 57	Alex Kellner	13.00	6.50	1.30
☐ 58	Enos Slaughter	50.00	25.00	5.00
☐ 59	Randy Gumpert	13.00	6.50	1.30
☐ 60	Chico Carrasquel	13.00	6.50	1.30
☐ 61	Jim Hearn	13.00	6.50	1.30
☐ 62	Lou Boudreau	40.00	20.00	4.00
☐ 63	Bob Dillinger	13.00	6.50	1.30
☐ 64	Bill Werle	13.00	6.50	1.30
☐ 65	Mickey Vernon	18.00	9.00	1.80
☐ 66	Bob Elliott	16.00	8.00	1.60
☐ 67	Roy Sievers	16.00	8.00	1.60
☐ 68	Dick Kokos	13.00	6.50	1.30
☐ 69	Johnny Schmitz	13.00	6.50	1.30
☐ 70	Ron Northey	13.00	6.50	1.30
☐ 71	Jerry Priddy	13.00	6.50	1.30
☐ 72	Lloyd Merriman	13.00	6.50	1.30
☐ 73	Tommy Byrne	15.00	7.50	1.50
☐ 74	Billy Johnson	15.00	7.50	1.50
☐ 75	Russ Meyer	12.00	6.00	1.20
☐ 76	Stan Lopata	12.00	6.00	1.20
☐ 77	Mike Goliat	12.00	6.00	1.20
☐ 78	Early Wynn	45.00	22.50	4.50
☐ 79	Jim Hegan	15.00	7.50	1.50
☐ 80	Pee Wee Reese	90.00	45.00	9.00
☐ 81	Carl Furillo	27.00	13.50	2.70
☐ 82	Joe Tipton	12.00	6.00	1.20
☐ 83	Carl Scheib	12.00	6.00	1.20
☐ 84	Barney McCosky	12.00	6.00	1.20
☐ 85	Eddie Kazak	12.00	6.00	1.20

		NRMT	VG-E	GOOD			NRMT	VG-E	GOOD
☐ 86	Harry Brecheen	15.00	7.50	1.50	☐ 134	Warren Spahn	90.00	45.00	9.00
☐ 87	Floyd Baker	12.00	6.00	1.20	☐ 135	Walker Cooper	12.00	6.00	1.20
☐ 88	Eddie Robinson	12.00	6.00	1.20	☐ 136	Ray Coleman	12.00	6.00	1.20
☐ 89	Hank Thompson	15.00	7.50	1.50	☐ 137	Dick Starr	12.00	6.00	1.20
☐ 90	Dave Koslo	12.00	6.00	1.20	☐ 138	Phil Cavarretta	15.00	7.50	1.50
☐ 91	Clyde Vollmer	12.00	6.00	1.20	☐ 139	Doyle Lade	12.00	6.00	1.20
☐ 92	Vern Stephens	15.00	7.50	1.50	☐ 140	Eddie Lake	12.00	6.00	1.20
☐ 93	Danny O'Connell	12.00	6.00	1.20	☐ 141	Fred Hutchinson	15.00	7.50	1.50
☐ 94	Clyde McCullough	12.00	6.00	1.20	☐ 142	Aaron Robinson	12.00	6.00	1.20
☐ 95	Sherry Robertson	12.00	6.00	1.20	☐ 143	Ted Kluszewski	25.00	12.50	2.50
☐ 96	Sandy Consuegra	12.00	6.00	1.20	☐ 144	Herman Wehmeier	12.00	6.00	1.20
☐ 97	Bob Kuzava	12.00	6.00	1.20	☐ 145	Fred Sanford	12.00	6.00	1.20
☐ 98	Willard Marshall	12.00	6.00	1.20	☐ 146	Johnny Hopp	15.00	7.50	1.50
☐ 99	Earl Torgeson	12.00	6.00	1.20	☐ 147	Ken Heintzelman	12.00	6.00	1.20
☐ 100	Sherm Lollar	15.00	7.50	1.50	☐ 148	Granny Hamner	12.00	6.00	1.20
☐ 101	Owen Friend	12.00	6.00	1.20	☐ 149	Bubba Church	12.00	6.00	1.20
☐ 102	Dutch Leonard	12.00	6.00	1.20	☐ 150	Mike Garcia	15.00	7.50	1.50
☐ 103	Andy Pafko	15.00	7.50	1.50	☐ 151	Larry Doby	21.00	10.50	2.10
☐ 104	Virgil Trucks	15.00	7.50	1.50	☐ 152	Cal Abrams	12.00	6.00	1.20
☐ 105	Don Kolloway	12.00	6.00	1.20	☐ 153	Rex Barney	12.00	6.00	1.20
☐ 106	Pat Mullin	12.00	6.00	1.20	☐ 154	Pete Suder	12.00	6.00	1.20
☐ 107	Johnny Wyrostek	12.00	6.00	1.20	☐ 155	Lou Brissie	12.00	6.00	1.20
☐ 108	Virgil Stallcup	12.00	6.00	1.20	☐ 156	Del Rice	12.00	6.00	1.20
☐ 109	Allie Reynolds	25.00	12.50	2.50	☐ 157	Al Brazle	12.00	6.00	1.20
☐ 110	Bobby Brown	25.00	12.50	2.50	☐ 158	Chuck Diering	12.00	6.00	1.20
☐ 111	Curt Simmons	15.00	7.50	1.50	☐ 159	Eddie Stewart	12.00	6.00	1.20
☐ 112	Willie Jones	12.00	6.00	1.20	☐ 160	Phil Masi	12.00	6.00	1.20
☐ 113	Bill Nicholson	12.00	6.00	1.20	☐ 161	Wes Westrum	12.00	6.00	1.20
☐ 114	Sam Zoldak	12.00	6.00	1.20	☐ 162	Larry Jansen	12.00	6.00	1.20
☐ 115	Steve Gromek	12.00	6.00	1.20	☐ 163	Monte Kennedy	12.00	6.00	1.20
☐ 116	Bruce Edwards	12.00	6.00	1.20	☐ 164	Bill Wight	12.00	6.00	1.20
☐ 117	Eddie Miksis	12.00	6.00	1.20	☐ 165	Ted Williams	450.00	225.00	45.00
☐ 118	Preacher Roe	25.00	12.50	2.50	☐ 166	Stan Rojek	12.00	6.00	1.20
☐ 119	Eddie Joost	12.00	6.00	1.20	☐ 167	Murry Dickson	12.00	6.00	1.20
☐ 120	Joe Coleman	12.00	6.00	1.20	☐ 168	Sam Mele	12.00	6.00	1.20
☐ 121	Jerry Staley	12.00	6.00	1.20	☐ 169	Sid Hudson	12.00	6.00	1.20
☐ 122	Joe Garagiola	100.00	50.00	10.00	☐ 170	Sibby Sisti	12.00	6.00	1.20
☐ 123	Howie Judson	12.00	6.00	1.20	☐ 171	Buddy Kerr	12.00	6.00	1.20
☐ 124	Gus Niarhos	12.00	6.00	1.20	☐ 172	Ned Garver	12.00	6.00	1.20
☐ 125	Bill Rigney	12.00	6.00	1.20	☐ 173	ank Arft	12.00	6.00	1.20
☐ 126	Bobby Thomson	25.00	12.50	2.50	☐ 174	Mickey Owen	15.00	7.50	1.50
☐ 127	Sal Maglie	35.00	17.50	3.50	☐ 175	Wayne Terwilliger	12.00	6.00	1.20
☐ 128	Ellis Kinder	12.00	6.00	1.20	☐ 176	Vic Wertz	15.00	7.50	1.50
☐ 129	Matt Batts	12.00	6.00	1.20	☐ 177	Charlie Keller	15.00	7.50	1.50
☐ 130	Tom Saffell	12.00	6.00	1.20	☐ 178	Ted Gray	12.00	6.00	1.20
☐ 131	Cliff Chambers	12.00	6.00	1.20	☐ 179	Danny Litwhiler	12.00	6.00	1.20
☐ 132	Cass Michaels	12.00	6.00	1.20	☐ 180	Howie Fox	12.00	6.00	1.20
☐ 133	Sam Dente	12.00	6.00	1.20	☐ 181	Casey Stengel MG	80.00	40.00	8.00

		NRMT	VG-E	GOOD				NRMT	VG-E	GOOD
☐ 182	Tom Ferrick	12.00	6.00	1.20		☐ 228	Cloyd Boyer	15.00	7.50	1.50
☐ 183	Hank Bauer	25.00	12.50	2.50		☐ 229	Bill Howerton	12.00	6.00	1.20
☐ 184	Eddie Sawyer MG	15.00	7.50	1.50		☐ 230	Max Lanier	12.00	6.00	1.20
☐ 185	Jimmy Bloodworth	12.00	6.00	1.20		☐ 231	Luis Aloma	12.00	6.00	1.20
☐ 186	Richie Ashburn	45.00	22.50	4.50		☐ 232	Nelson Fox	75.00	30.00	6.00
☐ 187	Al Rosen	22.00	11.00	2.20		☐ 233	Leo Durocher MG	40.00	20.00	4.00
☐ 188	Bobby Avila	15.00	7.50	1.50		☐ 234	Clint Hartung	12.00	6.00	1.20
☐ 189	Erv Palica	12.00	6.00	1.20		☐ 235	Jack Lohrke	12.00	6.00	1.20
☐ 190	Joe Hatton	12.00	6.00	1.20		☐ 236	Warren Rosar	12.00	6.00	1.20
☐ 191	Billy Hitchcock	12.00	6.00	1.20		☐ 237	Billy Goodman	15.00	7.50	1.50
☐ 192	Hank Wyse	12.00	6.00	1.20		☐ 238	Pete Reiser	18.00	9.00	1.80
☐ 193	Ted Wilks	12.00	6.00	1.20		☐ 239	Bill MacDonald	12.00	6.00	1.20
☐ 194	Peanuts Lowrey	12.00	6.00	1.20		☐ 240	Joe Haynes	12.00	6.00	1.20
☐ 195	Paul Richards	15.00	7.50	1.50		☐ 241	Irv Noren	12.00	6.00	1.20
	(caricature)					☐ 242	Sam Jethroe	12.00	6.00	1.20
☐ 196	Billy Pierce	22.00	11.00	2.20		☐ 243	Johnny Antonelli	15.00	7.50	1.50
☐ 197	Bob Cain	12.00	6.00	1.20		☐ 244	Cliff Fannin	12.00	6.00	1.20
☐ 198	Monte Irvin	75.00	37.50	7.50		☐ 245	John Berardino	15.00	7.50	1.50
☐ 199	Sheldon Jones	12.00	6.00	1.20		☐ 246	Bill Serena	12.00	6.00	1.20
☐ 200	Jack Kramer	12.00	6.00	1.20		☐ 247	Bob Ramazotti	12.00	6.00	1.20
☐ 201	Steve O'Neill	12.00	6.00	1.20		☐ 248	Johnny Klippstein	12.00	6.00	1.20
☐ 202	Mike Guerra	12.00	6.00	1.20		☐ 249	Johnny Groth	12.00	6.00	1.20
☐ 203	Vernon Law	20.00	10.00	2.00		☐ 250	Hank Borowy	12.00	6.00	1.20
☐ 204	Vic Lombardi	12.00	6.00	1.20		☐ 251	Willard Ramsdell	12.00	6.00	1.20
☐ 205	Mickey Grasso	12.00	6.00	1.20		☐ 252	Dixie Howell	12.00	6.00	1.20
☐ 206	Conrado Marrero	12.00	6.00	1.20		☐ 253	Mickey Mantle	5000.00	2000.00	500.00
☐ 207	Billy Southworth	12.00	6.00	1.20		☐ 254	Jackie Jensen	100.00	50.00	10.00
☐ 208	Blix Donnelly	12.00	6.00	1.20		☐ 255	Milo Candini	45.00	22.50	4.50
☐ 209	Ken Wood	12.00	6.00	1.20		☐ 256	Ken Sylvestri	45.00	22.50	4.50
☐ 210	Les Moss	12.00	6.00	1.20		☐ 257	Birdie Tebbetts	55.00	27.50	5.50
☐ 211	Hal Jeffcoat	12.00	6.00	1.20		☐ 258	Luke Easter	55.00	27.50	5.50
☐ 212	Bob Rush	12.00	6.00	1.20		☐ 259	Chuck Dressen MG	55.00	27.50	5.50
☐ 213	Neil Berry	12.00	6.00	1.20		☐ 260	Carl Erskine	85.00	42.50	8.50
☐ 214	Bob Swift	12.00	6.00	1.20		☐ 261	Wally Moses	55.00	27.50	5.50
☐ 215	Ken Peterson	12.00	6.00	1.20		☐ 262	Gus Zernial	55.00	27.50	5.50
☐ 216	Connie Ryan	12.00	6.00	1.20		☐ 263	Howie Pollet	45.00	22.50	4.50
☐ 217	Joe Page	18.00	9.00	1.80		☐ 264	Don Richmond	45.00	22.50	4.50
☐ 218	Ed Lopat	25.00	12.50	2.50		☐ 265	Steve Bilko	45.00	22.50	4.50
☐ 219	Gene Woodling	27.00	13.50	2.70		☐ 266	Harry Dorish	45.00	22.50	4.50
☐ 220	Bob Miller	12.00	6.00	1.20		☐ 267	Ken Holcombe	45.00	22.50	4.50
☐ 221	Dick Whitman	12.00	6.00	1.20		☐ 268	Don Mueller	55.00	27.50	5.50
☐ 222	Thurman Tucker	12.00	6.00	1.20		☐ 269	Ray Noble	45.00	22.50	4.50
☐ 223	Johnny VanderMeer	20.00	10.00	2.00		☐ 270	Willard Nixon	45.00	22.50	4.50
☐ 224	Billy Cox	15.00	7.50	1.50		☐ 271	Tommy Wright	45.00	22.50	4.50
☐ 225	Dan Bankhead	15.00	7.50	1.50		☐ 272	Billy Meyer MG	45.00	22.50	4.50
☐ 226	Jimmy Dykes	15.00	7.50	1.50		☐ 273	Danny Murtaugh	45.00	22.50	4.50
☐ 227	Bobby Schantz	18.00	9.00	1.80		☐ 274	George Metkovich	45.00	22.50	4.50
	(sic, Shantz)					☐ 275	Bucky Harris MG	65.00	32.50	6.50

		NRMT	VG-E	GOOD
☐ 276	Frank Quinn	45.00	22.50	4.50
☐ 277	Roy Hartsfield	45.00	22.50	4.50
☐ 278	Norman Roy	45.00	22.50	4.50
☐ 279	Jim Delsing	45.00	22.50	4.50
☐ 280	Frank Overmire	45.00	22.50	4.50
☐ 281	Al Widmar	45.00	22.50	4.50
☐ 282	Frank Frisch	75.00	37.50	7.50
☐ 283	Walt Dubiel	45.00	22.50	4.50
☐ 284	Gene Bearden	45.00	22.50	4.50
☐ 285	Johnny Lipon	45.00	22.50	4.50
☐ 286	Bob Usher	45.00	22.50	4.50
☐ 287	Jim Blackburn	45.00	22.50	4.50
☐ 288	Bobby Adams	45.00	22.50	4.50
☐ 289	Cliff Mapes	55.00	27.50	5.50
☐ 290	Bill Dickey	150.00	75.00	15.00
☐ 291	Tommy Henrich	65.00	32.50	6.50
☐ 292	Eddie Pellegrini	45.00	22.50	4.50
☐ 293	Ken Johnson	45.00	22.50	4.50
☐ 294	Jocko Thompson	45.00	22.50	4.50
☐ 295	Al Lopez MG	75.00	37.50	7.50
☐ 296	Bob Kennedy	55.00	27.50	5.50
☐ 297	Dave Philley	45.00	22.50	4.50
☐ 298	Joe Astroth	45.00	22.50	4.50
☐ 299	Clyde King	55.00	27.50	5.50
☐ 300	Hal Rice	45.00	22.50	4.50
☐ 301	Tommy Glaviano	45.00	22.50	4.50
☐ 302	Jim Busby	45.00	22.50	4.50
☐ 303	Marv Rotblatt	45.00	22.50	4.50
☐ 304	Al Gettell	45.00	22.50	4.50
☐ 305	Willie Mays	1700.00	600.00	150.00
☐ 306	Jim Piersall	90.00	45.00	9.00
☐ 307	Walt Masterson	45.00	22.50	4.50
☐ 308	Ted Beard	45.00	22.50	4.50
☐ 309	Mel Queen	45.00	22.50	4.50
☐ 310	Erv Dusak	45.00	22.50	4.50
☐ 311	Mickey Harris	45.00	22.50	4.50
☐ 312	Gene Mauch	55.00	27.50	5.50
☐ 313	Ray Mueller	45.00	22.50	4.50
☐ 314	Johnny Sain	55.00	27.50	5.50
☐ 315	Zack Taylor	45.00	22.50	4.50
☐ 316	Duane Pillette	45.00	22.50	4.50
☐ 317	Smokey Burgess	55.00	27.50	5.50
☐ 318	Warren Hacker	45.00	22.50	4.50
☐ 319	Red Rolfe	55.00	27.50	5.50
☐ 320	Hal White	45.00	22.50	4.50
☐ 321	Earl Johnson	45.00	22.50	4.50
☐ 322	Luke Sewell	55.00	27.50	5.50
☐ 323	Joe Adcock	65.00	32.50	6.50

		NRMT	VG-E	GOOD
☐ 324	Johnny Pramesa	85.00	25.00	5.00

1952 Bowman

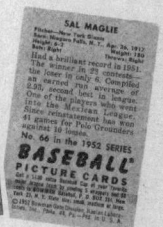

The cards in this 252-card set measure 2 1/16"
by 3 1/8". While the Bowman set of 1952
retained the card size introduced in 1951, it
employed a modification of color tones from the
two preceding years. The cards also appeared
with a facsimile autograph on the front and, for
the first time since 1949, premium advertising
on the back. The 1952 set was sold in sheets
as well as in gum packs. Artwork for 15 cards
that were never issued was recently discovered.

	NRMT	VG-E	GOOD
COMPLETE SET (252)	8200.00	4100.00	900.00
COMMON PLAYER (1-36)	16.00	8.00	1.60
COMMON PLAYER (37-144)	14.00	7.00	1.40
COMMON PLAYER (145-180)	13.00	6.50	1.30
COMMON PLAYER (181-216)	12.00	6.00	1.20
COMMON PLAYER (217-252)	27.00	13.50	2.70

		NRMT	VG-E	GOOD
☐ 1	Yogi Berra	600.00	150.00	30.00
☐ 2	Bobby Thomson	25.00	12.50	2.50
☐ 3	Fred Hutchinson	20.00	10.00	2.00
☐ 4	Robin Roberts	50.00	25.00	5.00
☐ 5	Minnie Minoso	40.00	20.00	4.00

		NRMT	VG-E	GOOD			NRMT	VG-E	GOOD
☐	6 Virgil Stallcup	16.00	8.00	1.60	☐	54 Billy Pierce	18.00	9.00	1.80
☐	7 Mike Garcia	18.00	9.00	1.80	☐	55 Ken Raffensberger	14.00	7.00	1.40
☐	8 Pee Wee Reese	90.00	45.00	9.00	☐	56 Clyde King	16.00	8.00	1.60
☐	9 Vern Stephens	18.00	9.00	1.80	☐	57 Clyde Vollmer	14.00	7.00	1.40
☐	10 Bob Hooper	16.00	8.00	1.60	☐	58 Hank Majeski	14.00	7.00	1.40
☐	11 Ralph Kiner	45.00	22.50	4.50	☐	59 Murry Dickson	14.00	7.00	1.40
☐	12 Max Surkont	16.00	8.00	1.60	☐	60 Sid Gordon	14.00	7.00	1.40
☐	13 Cliff Mapes	16.00	8.00	1.60	☐	61 Tommy Byrne	14.00	7.00	1.40
☐	14 Cliff Chambers	16.00	8.00	1.60	☐	62 Joe Presko	14.00	7.00	1.40
☐	15 Sam Mele	16.00	8.00	1.60	☐	63 Irv Noren	14.00	7.00	1.40
☐	16 Turk Lown	16.00	8.00	1.60	☐	64 Roy Smalley	14.00	7.00	1.40
☐	17 Ed Lopat	25.00	12.50	2.50	☐	65 Hank Bauer	21.00	10.50	2.10
☐	18 Don Mueller	18.00	9.00	1.80	☐	66 Sal Maglie	20.00	10.00	2.00
☐	19 Bob Cain	16.00	8.00	1.60	☐	67 Johnny Groth	14.00	7.00	1.40
☐	20 Willie Jones	16.00	8.00	1.60	☐	68 Jim Busby	14.00	7.00	1.40
☐	21 Nellie Fox	35.00	17.50	3.50	☐	69 Joe Adcock	18.00	9.00	1.80
☐	22 Willard Ramsdell	16.00	8.00	1.60	☐	70 Carl Erskine	21.00	10.50	2.10
☐	23 Bob Lemon	45.00	22.50	4.50	☐	71 Vernon Law	16.00	8.00	1.60
☐	24 Carl Furillo	27.00	13.50	2.70	☐	72 Earl Torgeson	14.00	7.00	1.40
☐	25 Mickey McDermott	16.00	8.00	1.60	☐	73 Gerry Coleman	16.00	8.00	1.60
☐	26 Eddie Joost	16.00	8.00	1.60	☐	74 Wes Westrum	14.00	7.00	1.40
☐	27 Joe Garagiola	60.00	30.00	6.00	☐	75 George Kell	40.00	20.00	4.00
☐	28 Roy Hartsfield	16.00	8.00	1.60	☐	76 Del Ennis	16.00	8.00	1.60
☐	29 Ned Garver	16.00	8.00	1.60	☐	77 Eddie Robinson	14.00	7.00	1.40
☐	30 Red Schoendienst	50.00	25.00	5.00	☐	78 Lloyd Merriman	14.00	7.00	1.40
☐	31 Eddie Yost	16.00	8.00	1.60	☐	79 Lou Brissie	14.00	7.00	1.40
☐	32 Eddie Miksis	16.00	8.00	1.60	☐	80 Gil Hodges	50.00	25.00	5.00
☐	33 Gil McDougald	40.00	20.00	4.00	☐	81 Billy Goodman	16.00	8.00	1.60
☐	34 Alvin Dark	20.00	10.00	2.00	☐	82 Gus Zernial	16.00	8.00	1.60
☐	35 Granny Hamner	14.00	7.00	1.40	☐	83 Howie Pollet	14.00	7.00	1.40
☐	36 Cass Michaels	14.00	7.00	1.40	☐	84 Sam Jethroe	14.00	7.00	1.40
☐	37 Vic Raschi	18.00	9.00	1.80	☐	85 Marty Marion	20.00	10.00	2.00
☐	38 Whitey Lockman	16.00	8.00	1.60	☐	86 Cal Abrams	14.00	7.00	1.40
☐	39 Vic Wertz	16.00	8.00	1.60	☐	87 Mickey Vernon	18.00	9.00	1.80
☐	40 Bubba Church	14.00	7.00	1.40	☐	88 Bruce Edwards	14.00	7.00	1.40
☐	41 Chico Carrasquel	14.00	7.00	1.40	☐	89 Billy Hitchcock	14.00	7.00	1.40
☐	42 Johnny Wyrostek	14.00	7.00	1.40	☐	90 Larry Jansen	14.00	7.00	1.40
☐	43 Bob Feller	80.00	40.00	8.00	☐	91 Don Kolloway	14.00	7.00	1.40
☐	44 Roy Campanella	175.00	85.00	18.00	☐	92 Eddie Waitkus	14.00	7.00	1.40
☐	45 Johnny Pesky	16.00	8.00	1.60	☐	93 Paul Richards	16.00	8.00	1.60
☐	46 Carl Scheib	14.00	7.00	1.40	☐	94 Luke Sewell	16.00	8.00	1.60
☐	47 Pete Castiglione	14.00	7.00	1.40	☐	95 Luke Easter	16.00	8.00	1.60
☐	48 Vern Bickford	14.00	7.00	1.40	☐	96 Ralph Branca	20.00	10.00	2.00
☐	49 Jim Hearn	14.00	7.00	1.40	☐	97 Willard Marshall	14.00	7.00	1.40
☐	50 Jerry Staley	14.00	7.00	1.40	☐	98 Jimmy Dykes	16.00	8.00	1.60
☐	51 Gil Coan	14.00	7.00	1.40	☐	99 Clyde McCullough	14.00	7.00	1.40
☐	52 Phil Rizzuto	55.00	27.50	5.50	☐	100 Sibby Sisti	14.00	7.00	1.40
☐	53 Richie Ashburn	40.00	20.00	4.00	☐	101 Mickey Mantle	1500.00	600.00	150.00

		NRMT	VG-E	GOOD			NRMT	VG-E	GOOD
☐ 102	Peanuts Lowrey	14.00	7.00	1.40	☐ 150	Herman Wehmeier	13.00	6.50	1.30
☐ 103	Joe Haynes	14.00	7.00	1.40	☐ 151	Al Rosen	20.00	10.00	2.00
☐ 104	Hal Jeffcoat	14.00	7.00	1.40	☐ 152	Billy Cox	16.00	8.00	1.60
☐ 105	Bobby Brown	22.00	11.00	2.20	☐ 153	Fred Hatfield	13.00	6.50	1.30
☐ 106	Randy Gumpert	14.00	7.00	1.40	☐ 154	Ferris Fain	15.00	7.50	1.50
☐ 107	Del Rice	14.00	7.00	1.40	☐ 155	Billy Meyer	13.00	6.50	1.30
☐ 108	George Metkovich	14.00	7.00	1.40	☐ 156	Warren Spahn	75.00	37.50	7.50
☐ 109	Tom Morgan	14.00	7.00	1.40	☐ 157	Jim Delsing	13.00	6.50	1.30
☐ 110	Max Lanier	14.00	7.00	1.40	☐ 158	Bucky Harris MG	27.00	13.50	2.70
☐ 111	Hoot Evers	14.00	7.00	1.40	☐ 159	Dutch Leonard	13.00	6.50	1.30
☐ 112	Smokey Burgess	16.00	8.00	1.60	☐ 160	Eddie Stanky	16.00	8.00	1.60
☐ 113	Al Zarilla	14.00	7.00	1.40	☐ 161	Jackie Jensen	25.00	12.50	2.50
☐ 114	Frank Hiller	14.00	7.00	1.40	☐ 162	Monte Irvin	40.00	20.00	4.00
☐ 115	Larry Doby	20.00	10.00	2.00	☐ 163	Johnny Lipon	13.00	6.50	1.30
☐ 116	Duke Snider	150.00	75.00	15.00	☐ 164	Connie Ryan	13.00	6.50	1.30
☐ 117	Bill Wight	14.00	7.00	1.40	☐ 165	Saul Rogovin	13.00	6.50	1.30
☐ 118	Ray Murray	14.00	7.00	1.40	☐ 166	Bobby Adams	13.00	6.50	1.30
☐ 119	Bill Howerton	14.00	7.00	1.40	☐ 167	Bobby Avila	15.00	7.50	1.50
☐ 120	Chet Nichols	14.00	7.00	1.40	☐ 168	Preacher Roe	22.00	11.00	2.20
☐ 121	Al Corwin	14.00	7.00	1.40	☐ 169	Walt Dropo	15.00	7.50	1.50
☐ 122	Billy Johnson	14.00	7.00	1.40	☐ 170	Joe Astroth	13.00	6.50	1.30
☐ 123	Sid Hudson	14.00	7.00	1.40	☐ 171	Mel Queen	13.00	6.50	1.30
☐ 124	Birdie Tebbetts	16.00	8.00	1.60	☐ 172	Ebba St.Claire	13.00	6.50	1.30
☐ 125	Howie Fox	14.00	7.00	1.40	☐ 173	Gene Bearden	13.00	6.50	1.30
☐ 126	Phil Cavarretta	16.00	8.00	1.60	☐ 174	Mickey Grasso	13.00	6.50	1.30
☐ 127	Dick Sisler	14.00	7.00	1.40	☐ 175	Randy Jackson	13.00	6.50	1.30
☐ 128	Don Newcombe	21.00	10.50	2.10	☐ 176	Harry Brecheen	15.00	6.50	1.30
☐ 129	Gus Niarhos	14.00	7.00	1.40	☐ 177	Gene Woodling	18.00	9.00	1.80
☐ 130	Allie Clark	14.00	7.00	1.40	☐ 178	Dave Williams	16.00	8.00	1.60
☐ 131	Bob Swift	14.00	7.00	1.40	☐ 179	Pete Suder	13.00	6.50	1.30
☐ 132	Dave Cole	14.00	7.00	1.40	☐ 180	Ed Fitzgerald	13.00	6.50	1.30
☐ 133	Dick Kryhoski	14.00	7.00	1.40	☐ 181	Joe Collins	15.00	7.50	1.50
☐ 134	Al Brazle	14.00	7.00	1.40	☐ 182	Dave Koslo	12.00	6.00	1.20
☐ 135	Mickey Harris	14.00	7.00	1.40	☐ 183	Pat Mullin	12.00	6.00	1.20
☐ 136	Gene Hermanski	14.00	7.00	1.40	☐ 184	Curt Simmons	15.00	7.50	1.50
☐ 137	Stan Rojek	14.00	7.00	1.40	☐ 185	Eddie Stewart	12.00	6.00	1.20
☐ 138	Ted Wilks	14.00	7.00	1.40	☐ 186	Frank Smith	12.00	6.00	1.20
☐ 139	Jerry Priddy	14.00	7.00	1.40	☐ 187	Jim Hegan	14.00	7.00	1.40
☐ 140	Ray Scarborough	14.00	7.00	1.40	☐ 188	Charlie Dressen MG	15.00	7.50	1.50
☐ 141	Hank Edwards	14.00	7.00	1.40	☐ 189	Jim Piersall	18.00	9.00	1.80
☐ 142	Early Wynn	40.00	20.00	4.00	☐ 190	Dick Fowler	12.00	6.00	1.20
☐ 143	Sandy Consuegra	14.00	7.00	1.40	☐ 191	Bob Friend	18.00	9.00	1.80
☐ 144	Joe Hatton	14.00	7.00	1.40	☐ 192	John Cusick	12.00	6.00	1.20
☐ 145	Johnny Mize	50.00	25.00	5.00	☐ 193	Bobby Young	12.00	6.00	1.20
☐ 146	Leo Durocher MG	36.00	18.00	3.60	☐ 194	Bob Porterfield	12.00	6.00	1.20
☐ 147	Marlin Stuart	13.00	6.50	1.30	☐ 195	Frank Baumholtz	12.00	6.00	1.20
☐ 148	Ken Heintzelman	13.00	6.50	1.30	☐ 196	Stan Musial	400.00	200.00	40.00
☐ 149	Howie Judson	13.00	6.50	1.30	☐ 197	Charlie Silvera	12.00	6.00	1.20

		NRMT	VG-E	GOOD
☐ 198	Chuck Diering	12.00	6.00	1.20
☐ 199	Ted Gray	12.00	6.00	1.20
☐ 200	Ken Silvestri	12.00	6.00	1.20
☐ 201	Ray Coleman	12.00	6.00	1.20
☐ 202	Harry Perkowski	12.00	6.00	1.20
☐ 203	Steve Gromek	12.00	6.00	1.20
☐ 204	Andy Pafko	14.00	7.00	1.40
☐ 205	Walt Masterson	12.00	6.00	1.20
☐ 206	Elmer Valo	12.00	6.00	1.20
☐ 207	George Strickland	12.00	6.00	1.20
☐ 208	Walker Cooper	12.00	6.00	1.20
☐ 209	Dick Littlefield	12.00	6.00	1.20
☐ 210	Archie Wilson	12.00	6.00	1.20
☐ 211	Paul Minner	12.00	6.00	1.20
☐ 212	Solly Hemus	12.00	6.00	1.20
☐ 213	Monte Kennedy	12.00	6.00	1.20
☐ 214	Ray Boone	12.00	6.00	1.20
☐ 215	Sheldon Jones	12.00	6.00	1.20
☐ 216	Matt Batts	12.00	6.00	1.20
☐ 217	Casey Stengel MG	125.00	60.00	12.50
☐ 218	Willie Mays	800.00	400.00	80.00
☐ 219	Neil Berry	27.00	13.50	2.70
☐ 220	Russ Meyer	27.00	13.50	2.70
☐ 221	Lou Kretlow	27.00	13.50	2.70
☐ 222	Dixie Howell	27.00	13.50	2.70
☐ 223	Harry Simpson	27.00	13.50	2.70
☐ 224	Johnny Schmitz	27.00	13.50	2.70
☐ 225	Del Wilber	27.00	13.50	2.70
☐ 226	Alex Kellner	27.00	13.50	2.70
☐ 227	Clyde Sukeforth	27.00	13.50	2.70
☐ 228	Bob Chipman	27.00	13.50	2.70
☐ 229	Hank Arft	27.00	13.50	2.70
☐ 230	Frank Shea	27.00	13.50	2.70
☐ 231	Dee Fondy	27.00	13.50	2.70
☐ 232	Enos Slaughter	65.00	32.50	6.50
☐ 233	Bob Kuzava	27.00	13.50	2.70
☐ 234	Fred Fitzsimmons	27.00	13.50	2.70
☐ 235	Steve Souchock	27.00	13.50	2.70
☐ 236	Tommy Brown	27.00	13.50	2.70
☐ 237	Sherm Lollar	32.00	16.00	3.20
☐ 238	Roy McMillan	32.00	16.00	3.20
☐ 239	Dale Mitchell	32.00	16.00	3.20
☐ 240	Billy Loes	32.00	16.00	3.20
☐ 241	Mel Parnell	32.00	16.00	3.20
☐ 242	Everett Kell	27.00	13.50	2.70
☐ 243	Red Munger	27.00	13.50	2.70
☐ 244	Lew Burdette	50.00	25.00	5.00
☐ 245	George Schmees	27.00	13.50	2.70

		NRMT	VG-E	GOOD
☐ 246	Jerry Snyder	27.00	13.50	2.70
☐ 247	Johnny Pramesa	27.00	13.50	2.70
☐ 248	Bill Werle	27.00	13.50	2.70
☐ 249	Hank Thompson	32.00	16.00	3.20
☐ 250	Ike Delock	27.00	13.50	2.70
☐ 251	Jack Lohrke	27.00	13.50	2.70
☐ 252	Frank Crosetti CO	125.00	25.00	5.00

1953 Bowman Color

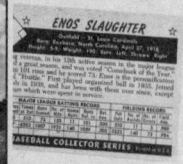

The cards in this 160-card set measure 2 ½"
by 3 ¾". The 1953 Bowman Color set, considered by many to be the best looking set of the
modern era, contains Kodachrome photographs with no names or facsimile autographs on the face. Numbers 113 to 160 are
somewhat more difficult to obtain. There are
two cards of Al Corwin (126 and 149).

		NRMT	VG-E	GOOD
COMPLETE SET (160)		10000.00	5000.00	1250.00
COMMON PLAYER (1-96)		25.00	12.50	2.50
COMMON PLAYER (97-112)		28.00	14.00	2.80
COMMON PLAYER (113-128)		45.00	22.50	4.50
COMMON PLAYER (129-160)		33.00	16.00	3.50
☐ 1	Dave Williams	100.00	15.00	3.00
☐ 2	Vic Wertz	28.00	14.00	2.80
☐ 3	Sam Jethroe	25.00	12.50	2.50
☐ 4	Art Houtteman	25.00	12.50	2.50

#	Player	NRMT	VG-E	GOOD
5	Sid Gordon	25.00	12.50	2.50
6	Joe Ginsberg	25.00	12.50	2.50
7	Harry Chiti	25.00	12.50	2.50
8	Al Rosen	35.00	17.50	3.50
9	Phil Rizzuto	75.00	37.50	7.50
10	Richie Ashburn	50.00	25.00	5.00
11	Bobby Shantz	30.00	15.00	3.00
12	Carl Erskine	35.00	17.50	3.50
13	Gus Zernial	28.00	14.00	2.80
14	Billy Loes	28.00	14.00	2.80
15	Jim Busby	25.00	12.50	2.50
16	Bob Friend	28.00	14.00	2.80
17	Jerry Staley	25.00	12.50	2.50
18	Nellie Fox	48.00	24.00	5.00
19	Alvin Dark	30.00	15.00	3.00
20	Don Lenhardt	25.00	12.50	2.50
21	Joe Garagiola	50.00	25.00	5.00
22	Bob Porterfield	25.00	12.50	2.50
23	Herman Wehmeier	25.00	12.50	2.50
24	Jackie Jensen	32.00	16.00	3.20
25	Hoot Evers	25.00	12.50	2.50
26	Roy McMillan	25.00	12.50	2.50
27	Vic Raschi	32.00	16.00	3.20
28	Smokey Burgess	28.00	14.00	2.80
29	Bobby Avila	28.00	14.00	2.80
30	Phil Cavarretta	28.00	14.00	2.80
31	Jimmy Dykes	28.00	14.00	2.80
32	Stan Musial	425.00	200.00	42.00
33	Pee Wee Reese HOR	225.00	110.00	22.00
34	Gil Coan	25.00	12.50	2.50
35	Maurice McDermott	25.00	12.50	2.50
36	Minnie Minoso	35.00	17.50	3.50
37	Jim Wilson	25.00	12.50	2.50
38	Harry Byrd	25.00	12.50	2.50
39	Paul Richards MG	28.00	14.00	2.80
40	Larry Doby	35.00	17.50	3.50
41	Sammy White	25.00	12.50	2.50
42	Tommy Brown	25.00	12.50	2.50
43	Mike Garcia	28.00	14.00	2.80
44	Berra/Bauer/Mantle	350.00	175.00	35.00
45	Walt Dropo	28.00	14.00	2.80
46	Roy Campanella	225.00	110.00	22.00
47	Ned Garver	25.00	12.50	2.50
48	Hank Sauer	28.00	14.00	2.80
49	Eddie Stanky	30.00	15.00	3.00
50	Lou Kretlow	25.00	12.50	2.50
51	Monte Irvin	50.00	25.00	5.00
52	Marty Marion	32.00	16.00	3.20
53	Del Rice	25.00	12.50	2.50
54	Chico Carrasquel	25.00	12.50	2.50
55	Leo Durocher MG	45.00	22.50	4.50
56	Bob Cain	25.00	12.50	2.50
57	Lou Boudreau MG	50.00	25.00	5.00
58	Willard Marshall	25.00	12.50	2.50
59	Mickey Mantle	1400.00	500.00	150.00
60	Granny Hamner	25.00	12.50	2.50
61	George Kell	50.00	25.00	5.00
62	Ted Kluszewski	35.00	17.50	3.50
63	Gil McDougald	35.00	17.50	3.50
64	Curt Simmons	30.00	15.00	3.00
65	Robin Roberts	55.00	27.50	5.50
66	Mel Parnell	28.00	14.00	2.80
67	Mel Clark	25.00	12.50	2.50
68	Allie Reynolds	35.00	17.50	3.50
69	Charlie Grimm MG	28.00	14.00	2.80
70	Clint Courtney	25.00	12.50	2.50
71	Paul Minner	25.00	12.50	2.50
72	Ted Gray	25.00	12.50	2.50
73	Billy Pierce	28.00	14.00	2.80
74	Don Mueller	28.00	14.00	2.80
75	Saul Rogovin	25.00	12.50	2.50
76	Jim Hearn	25.00	12.50	2.50
77	Mickey Grasso	25.00	12.50	2.50
78	Carl Furillo	35.00	17.50	3.50
79	Ray Boone	28.00	14.00	2.80
80	Ralph Kiner	60.00	30.00	6.00
81	Enos Slaughter	60.00	30.00	6.00
82	Joe Astroth	25.00	12.50	2.50
83	Jack Daniels	25.00	12.50	2.50
84	Hank Bauer	35.00	17.50	3.50
85	Solly Hemus	25.00	12.50	2.50
86	Harry Simpson	25.00	12.50	2.50
87	Harry Perkowski	25.00	12.50	2.50
88	Joe Dobson	25.00	12.50	2.50
89	Sandy Consuegra	25.00	12.50	2.50
90	Joe Nuxhall	28.00	14.00	2.80
91	Steve Souchock	25.00	12.50	2.50
92	Gil Hodges	100.00	50.00	10.00
93	Phil Rizzuto and Billy Martin	200.00	100.00	20.00
94	Bob Addis	25.00	12.50	2.50
95	Wally Moses	28.00	14.00	2.80
96	Sal Maglie	32.00	16.00	3.20
97	Eddie Mathews	150.00	75.00	15.00
98	Hector Rodriguez	28.00	14.00	2.80
99	Warren Spahn	110.00	55.00	11.00
100	Bill Wight	28.00	14.00	2.80
101	Red Schoendienst	75.00	37.50	7.50

		NRMT	VG-E	GOOD
☐ 102	Jim Hegan	30.00	15.00	3.00
☐ 103	Del Ennis	30.00	15.00	3.00
☐ 104	Luke Easter	30.00	15.00	3.00
☐ 105	Eddie Joost	28.00	14.00	2.80
☐ 106	Ken Raffensberger	28.00	14.00	2.80
☐ 107	Alex Kellner	28.00	14.00	2.80
☐ 108	Bobby Adams	28.00	14.00	2.80
☐ 109	Ken Wood	28.00	14.00	2.80
☐ 110	Bob Rush	28.00	14.00	2.80
☐ 111	Jim Dyck	28.00	14.00	2.80
☐ 112	Toby Atwell	28.00	14.00	2.80
☐ 113	Karl Drews	45.00	22.50	4.50
☐ 114	Bob Feller	250.00	125.00	25.00
☐ 115	Cloyd Boyer	45.00	22.50	4.50
☐ 116	Eddie Yost	45.00	22.50	4.50
☐ 117	Duke Snider	500.00	250.00	50.00
☐ 118	Billy Martin	250.00	125.00	25.00
☐ 119	Dale Mitchell	45.00	22.50	4.50
☐ 120	Marlin Stuart	45.00	22.50	4.50
☐ 121	Yogi Berra	500.00	250.00	50.00
☐ 122	Bill Serena	45.00	22.50	4.50
☐ 123	Johnny Lipon	45.00	22.50	4.50
☐ 124	Charlie Dressen MG	55.00	27.50	5.50
☐ 125	Fred Hatfield	45.00	22.50	4.50
☐ 126	Al Corwin	45.00	22.50	4.50
☐ 127	Dick Kryhoski	45.00	22.50	4.50
☐ 128	Whitey Lockman	45.00	22.50	4.50
☐ 129	Russ Meyer	33.00	16.00	3.50
☐ 130	Cass Michaels	33.00	16.00	3.50
☐ 131	Connie Ryan	33.00	16.00	3.50
☐ 132	Fred Hutchinson	40.00	20.00	4.00
☐ 133	Willie Jones	33.00	16.00	3.50
☐ 134	Johnny Pesky	36.00	18.00	3.60
☐ 135	Bobby Morgan	33.00	16.00	3.50
☐ 136	Jim Brideweser	33.00	16.00	3.50
☐ 137	Sam Dente	33.00	16.00	3.50
☐ 138	Bubba Church	33.00	16.00	3.50
☐ 139	Pete Runnels	36.00	18.00	3.60
☐ 140	Al Brazle	33.00	16.00	3.50
☐ 141	Frank Shea	33.00	16.00	3.50
☐ 142	Larry Miggins	33.00	16.00	3.50
☐ 143	Al Lopez MG	65.00	32.50	6.50
☐ 144	Warren Hacker	33.00	16.00	3.50
☐ 145	George Shuba	36.00	18.00	3.60
☐ 146	Early Wynn	110.00	55.00	11.00
☐ 147	Clem Koshorek	33.00	16.00	3.50
☐ 148	Billy Goodman	36.00	18.00	3.60
☐ 149	Al Corwin	33.00	16.00	3.50
☐ 150	Carl Scheib	33.00	16.00	3.50

		NRMT	VG-E	GOOD
☐ 151	Joe Adcock	40.00	20.00	4.00
☐ 152	Clyde Vollmer	33.00	16.00	3.50
☐ 153	Whitey Ford	375.00	175.00	37.00
☐ 154	Turk Lown	33.00	16.00	3.50
☐ 155	Allie Clark	33.00	16.00	3.50
☐ 156	Max Surkont	33.00	16.00	3.50
☐ 157	Sherm Lollar	36.00	18.00	3.60
☐ 158	Howard Fox	33.00	16.00	3.50
☐ 159	Mickey Vernon	40.00	20.00	4.00
	(photo actually Floyd Baker)			
☐ 160	Cal Abrams	60.00	20.00	4.00

1953 Bowman BW

 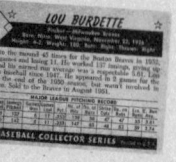

The cards in this 64-card set measure 2 ½" by 3 ¾". Some collectors believe that the high cost of producing the 1953 color series forced Bowman to issue this set in black and white, since the two sets are identical in design except for the element of color. This set was also produced in fewer numbers than its color counterpart, and is popular among collectors for the challenge involved in completing it.

		NRMT	VG-E	GOOD
COMPLETE SET (64)		2250.00	1100.00	300.00
COMMON PLAYER (1-64)		28.00	14.00	2.80
☐ 1	Gus Bell	100.00	15.00	3.00

			NRMT	VG-E	GOOD
☐	2	Willard Nixon	28.00	14.00	2.80
☐	3	Bill Rigney	28.00	14.00	2.80
☐	4	Pat Mullin	28.00	14.00	2.80
☐	5	Dee Fondy	28.00	14.00	2.80
☐	6	Ray Murray	28.00	14.00	2.80
☐	7	Andy Seminick	28.00	14.00	2.80
☐	8	Pete Suder	28.00	14.00	2.80
☐	9	Walt Masterson	28.00	14.00	2.80
☐	10	Dick Sisler	28.00	14.00	2.80
☐	11	Dick Gernert	28.00	14.00	2.80
☐	12	Randy Jackson	28.00	14.00	2.80
☐	13	Joe Tipton	28.00	14.00	2.80
☐	14	Bill Nicholson	28.00	14.00	2.80
☐	15	Johnny Mize	100.00	50.00	10.00
☐	16	Stu Miller	33.00	16.00	3.50
☐	17	Virgil Trucks	33.00	16.00	3.50
☐	18	Billy Hoeft	33.00	16.00	3.50
☐	19	Paul LaPalme	28.00	14.00	2.80
☐	20	Eddie Robinson	28.00	14.00	2.80
☐	21	Clarence Podbielan.	28.00	14.00	2.80
☐	22	Matt Batts	28.00	14.00	2.80
☐	23	Wilmer Mizell	33.00	16.00	3.50
☐	24	Del Wilber	28.00	14.00	2.80
☐	25	Johnny Sain	50.00	25.00	5.00
☐	26	Preacher Roe	50.00	25.00	5.00
☐	27	Bob Lemon	90.00	45.00	9.00
☐	28	Hoyt Wilhelm	100.00	50.00	10.00
☐	29	Sid Hudson	28.00	14.00	2.80
☐	30	Walker Cooper	28.00	14.00	2.80
☐	31	Gene Woodling	40.00	20.00	4.00
☐	32	Rocky Bridges	28.00	14.00	2.80
☐	33	Bob Kuzava	28.00	14.00	2.80
☐	34	Ebba St. Claire	28.00	14.00	2.80
☐	35	Johnny Wyrostek	28.00	14.00	2.80
☐	36	Jim Piersall	40.00	20.00	4.00
☐	37	Hal Jeffcoat	28.00	14.00	2.80
☐	38	Dave Cole	28.00	14.00	2.80
☐	39	Casey Stengel MG	275.00	135.00	27.00
☐	40	Larry Jansen	33.00	16.00	3.50
☐	41	Bob Ramazotti	28.00	14.00	2.80
☐	42	Howie Judson	28.00	14.00	2.80
☐	43	Hal Bevan	28.00	14.00	2.80
☐	44	Jim Delsing	28.00	14.00	2.80
☐	45	Irv Noren	33.00	16.00	3.50
☐	46	Bucky Harris	50.00	25.00	5.00
☐	47	Jack Lohrke	28.00	14.00	2.80
☐	48	Steve Ridzik	28.00	14.00	2.80
☐	49	Floyd Baker	28.00	14.00	2.80

			NRMT	VG-E	GOOD
☐	50	Dutch Leonard	28.00	14.00	2.80
☐	51	Lou Burdette	40.00	20.00	4.00
☐	52	Ralph Branca	36.00	18.00	3.60
☐	53	Morrie Martin	28.00	14.00	2.80
☐	54	Bill Miller	28.00	14.00	2.80
☐	55	Don Johnson	28.00	14.00	2.80
☐	56	Roy Smalley	28.00	14.00	2.80
☐	57	Andy Pafko	33.00	16.00	3.50
☐	58	Jim Konstanty	33.00	16.00	3.50
☐	59	Duane Pillette	28.00	14.00	2.80
☐	60	Billy Cox	33.00	16.00	3.50
☐	61	Tom Gorman	28.00	14.00	2.80
☐	62	Keith Thomas	28.00	14.00	2.80
☐	63	Steve Gromek	28.00	14.00	2.80
☐	64	Andy Hansen	45.00	15.00	3.00

1954 Bowman

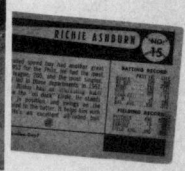

*The cards in this 224-card set measure 2 ½"
by 3 ¾". A contractual problem apparently
resulted in the deletion of the number 66 Ted
Williams card from this Bowman set, thereby
creating a scarcity that is highly valued among
collectors. The set price below does NOT include number 66 Williams. Many errors in
players' statistics exist (and some were corrected) while a few players' names were
printed on the front, instead of appearing as a
facsimile autograph.*

		NRMT	VG-E	GOOD
	COMPLETE SET (224)	3600.00	1800.00	425.00
	COMMON PLAYER (1-128) ..	6.00	3.00	.60
	COMMON PLAYER (129-224) ..	7.00	3.50	.70
☐ 1	Phil Rizzuto	160.00	25.00	5.00
☐ 2	Jackie Jensen	10.00	5.00	1.00
☐ 3	Marion Fricano	6.00	3.00	.60
☐ 4	Bob Hooper	6.00	3.00	.60
☐ 5	Billy Hunter	6.00	3.00	.60
☐ 6	Nellie Fox	16.00	8.00	1.60
☐ 7	Walt Dropo	7.00	3.50	.70
☐ 8	Jim Busby	6.00	3.00	.60
☐ 9	Davey Williams	7.00	3.50	.70
☐ 10	Carl Erskine	10.00	5.00	1.00
☐ 11	Sid Gordon	6.00	3.00	.60
☐ 12	Roy McMillan	6.00	3.00	.60
☐ 13	Paul Minner	6.00	3.00	.60
☐ 14	Jerry Staley	6.00	3.00	.60
☐ 15	Richie Ashburn	22.00	11.00	2.20
☐ 16	Jim Wilson	6.00	3.00	.60
☐ 17	Tom Gorman	6.00	3.00	.60
☐ 18	Hoot Evers	6.00	3.00	.60
☐ 19	Bobby Shantz	8.00	4.00	.80
☐ 20	Art Houtteman	6.00	3.00	.60
☐ 21	Vic Wertz	7.00	3.50	.70
☐ 22	Sam Mele	6.00	3.00	.60
☐ 23	Harvey Kuenn	22.00	11.00	2.20
☐ 24	Bob Porterfield	6.00	3.00	.60
☐ 25	Wes Westrum	6.00	3.00	.60
☐ 26	Billy Cox	7.00	3.50	.70
☐ 27	Dick Cole	6.00	3.00	.60
☐ 28	Jim Greengrass	6.00	3.00	.60
☐ 29	Johnny Klippstein	6.00	3.00	.60
☐ 30	Del Rice	6.00	3.00	.60
☐ 31	Smoky Burgess	7.00	3.50	.70
☐ 32	Del Crandall	7.00	3.50	.70
☐ 33 A	Vic Raschi	10.00	5.00	1.00
	(no mention of trade on back)			
☐ 33 B	Vic Raschi	20.00	10.00	2.00
	(traded to St. Louis)			
☐ 34	Sammy White	6.00	3.00	.60
☐ 35	Eddie Joost	6.00	3.00	.60
☐ 36	George Strickland	6.00	3.00	.60
☐ 37	Dick Kokos	6.00	3.00	.60
☐ 38	Minnie Minoso	10.00	5.00	1.00
☐ 39	Ned Garver	6.00	3.00	.60
☐ 40	Gil Coan	6.00	3.00	.60
☐ 41	Alvin Dark	8.00	4.00	.80
☐ 42	Billy Loes	6.00	3.00	.60
☐ 43	Bob Friend	7.00	3.50	.70
☐ 44	Harry Perkowski	6.00	3.00	.60
☐ 45	Ralph Kiner	30.00	15.00	3.00
☐ 46	Rip Repulski	6.00	3.00	.60
☐ 47	Granny Hamner	6.00	3.00	.60
☐ 48	Jack Dittmer	6.00	3.00	.60
☐ 49	Harry Byrd	6.00	3.00	.60
☐ 50	George Kell	25.00	12.50	2.50
☐ 51	Alex Kellner	6.00	3.00	.60
☐ 52	Joe Ginsberg	6.00	3.00	.60
☐ 53	Don Lenhardt	6.00	3.00	.60
☐ 54	Chico Carrasquel	6.00	3.00	.60
☐ 55	Jim Delsing	6.00	3.00	.60
☐ 56	Maurice McDermott	6.00	3.00	.60
☐ 57	Hoyt Wilhelm	25.00	12.50	2.50
☐ 58	Pee Wee Reese	45.00	22.50	4.50
☐ 59	Bob Schultz	6.00	3.00	.60
☐ 60	Fred Baczewski	6.00	3.00	.60
☐ 61	Eddie Miksis	6.00	3.00	.60
☐ 62	Enos Slaughter	28.00	14.00	2.80
☐ 63	Earl Torgeson	6.00	3.00	.60
☐ 64	Eddie Mathews	40.00	20.00	4.00
☐ 65	Mickey Mantle	750.00	375.00	75.00
☐ 66 A	Ted Williams	2700.00	1200.00	300.00
☐ 66 B	Jim Piersall	100.00	50.00	10.00
☐ 67	Carl Scheib	6.00	3.00	.60
☐ 68	Bobby Avila	7.00	3.50	.70
☐ 69	Clint Courtney	6.00	3.00	.60
☐ 70	Willard Marshall	6.00	3.00	.60
☐ 71	Ted Gray	6.00	3.00	.60
☐ 72	Eddie Yost	6.00	3.00	.60
☐ 73	Don Mueller	7.00	3.50	.70
☐ 74	Jim Gilliam	10.00	5.00	1.00
☐ 75	Max Surkont	6.00	3.00	.60
☐ 76	Joe Nuxhall	7.00	3.50	.70
☐ 77	Bob Rush	6.00	3.00	.60
☐ 78	Sal Yvars	6.00	3.00	.60
☐ 79	Curt Simmons	7.00	3.50	.70
☐ 80	Johnny Logan	7.00	3.50	.70
☐ 81	Jerry Coleman	7.00	3.50	.70
☐ 82	Billy Goodman	7.00	3.50	.70
☐ 83	Ray Murray	6.00	3.00	.60
☐ 84	Larry Doby	10.00	5.00	1.00
☐ 85	Jim Dyck	6.00	3.00	.60
☐ 86	Harry Dorish	6.00	3.00	.60
☐ 87	Don Lund	6.00	3.00	.60

			NRMT	VG-E	GOOD
☐	88	Tom Umphlett	6.00	3.00	.60
☐	89	Willie Mays	275.00	135.00	27.00
☐	90	Roy Campanella	110.00	55.00	11.00
☐	91	Cal Abrams	6.00	3.00	.60
☐	92	Ken Raffensberger	6.00	3.00	.60
☐	93	Bill Serena	6.00	3.00	.60
☐	94	Solly Hemus	6.00	3.00	.60
☐	95	Robin Roberts	27.00	13.50	2.70
☐	96	Joe Adcock	7.00	3.50	.70
☐	97	Gil McDougald	10.00	5.00	1.00
☐	98	Ellis Kinder	6.00	3.00	.60
☐	99	Pete Suder	6.00	3.00	.60
☐	100	Mike Garcia	7.00	3.50	.70
☐	101	Don Larsen	22.00	11.00	2.20
☐	102	Billy Pierce	8.00	4.00	.80
☐	103	Steve Souchock	6.00	3.00	.60
☐	104	Frank Shea	6.00	3.00	.60
☐	105	Sal Maglie	9.00	4.50	.90
☐	106	Clem Labine	7.00	3.50	.70
☐	107	Paul LaPalme	6.00	3.00	.60
☐	108	Bobby Adams	6.00	3.00	.60
☐	109	Roy Smalley	6.00	3.00	.60
☐	110	Red Schoendienst	27.00	13.50	2.70
☐	111	Murry Dickson	6.00	3.00	.60
☐	112	Andy Pafko	7.00	3.50	.70
☐	113	Allie Reynolds	13.00	6.50	1.30
☐	114	Willard Nixon	6.00	3.00	.60
☐	115	Don Bollweg	6.00	3.00	.60
☐	116	Luke Easter	7.00	3.50	.70
☐	117	Dick Kryhoski	6.00	3.00	.60
☐	118	Bob Boyd	6.00	3.00	.60
☐	119	Fred Hatfield	6.00	3.00	.60
☐	120	Mel Hoderlein	6.00	3.00	.60
☐	121	Ray Katt	6.00	3.00	.60
☐	122	Carl Furillo	13.00	6.50	1.30
☐	123	Toby Atwell	6.00	3.00	.60
☐	124	Gus Bell	7.00	3.50	.70
☐	125	Warren Hacker	6.00	3.00	.60
☐	126	Cliff Chambers	6.00	3.00	.60
☐	127	Del Ennis	7.00	3.50	.70
☐	128	Ebba St.Claire	6.00	3.00	.60
☐	129	Hank Bauer	14.00	7.00	1.40
☐	130	Milt Bolling	7.00	3.50	.70
☐	131	Joe Astroth	7.00	3.50	.70
☐	132	Bob Feller	65.00	32.50	6.50
☐	133	Duane Pillette	7.00	3.50	.70
☐	134	Luis Aloma	7.00	3.50	.70
☐	135	Johnny Pesky	8.00	4.00	.80
☐	136	Clyde Vollmer	7.00	3.50	.70
☐	137	Al Corwin	7.00	3.50	.70
☐	138	Gil Hodges	40.00	20.00	4.00
☐	139	Preston Ward	7.00	3.50	.70
☐	140	Saul Rogovin	7.00	3.50	.70
☐	141	Joe Garagiola	33.00	16.00	3.50
☐	142	Al Brazle	7.00	3.50	.70
☐	143	Willie Jones	7.00	3.50	.70
☐	144	Ernie Johnson	7.00	3.50	.70
☐	145	Billy Martin	50.00	25.00	5.00
☐	146	Dick Gernert	7.00	3.50	.70
☐	147	Joe DeMaestri	7.00	3.50	.70
☐	148	Dale Mitchell	8.00	4.00	.80
☐	149	Bob Young	7.00	3.50	.70
☐	150	Cass Michaels	7.00	3.50	.70
☐	151	Pat Mullin	7.00	3.50	.70
☐	152	Mickey Vernon	9.00	4.50	.90
☐	153	Whitey Lockman	8.00	4.00	.80
☐	154	Don Newcombe	13.00	6.50	1.30
☐	155	Frank Thomas	8.00	4.00	.80
☐	156	Rocky Bridges	7.00	3.50	.70
☐	157	Turk Lown	7.00	3.50	.70
☐	158	Stu Miller	8.00	4.00	.80
☐	159	Johnny Lindell	7.00	3.50	.70
☐	160	Danny O'Connell	7.00	3.50	.70
☐	161	Yogi Berra	120.00	60.00	12.00
☐	162	Ted Lepcio	7.00	3.50	.70
☐	163A	Dave Philley (no mention of trade on back)	8.00	4.00	.80
☐	163B	Dave Philley (traded to Cleveland)	18.00	9.00	1.80
☐	164	Early Wynn	25.00	12.50	2.50
☐	165	Johnny Groth	7.00	3.50	.70
☐	166	Sandy Consuegra	7.00	3.50	.70
☐	167	Billy Hoeft	7.00	3.50	.70
☐	168	Ed Fitzgerald	7.00	3.50	.70
☐	169	Larry Jansen	8.00	4.00	.80
☐	170	Duke Snider	110.00	55.00	11.00
☐	171	Carlos Bernier	7.00	3.50	.70
☐	172	Andy Seminick	7.00	3.50	.70
☐	173	Dee Fondy	7.00	3.50	.70
☐	174	Pete Castiglione	7.00	3.50	.70
☐	175	Mel Clark	7.00	3.50	.70
☐	176	Vern Bickford	7.00	3.50	.70
☐	177	Whitey Ford	70.00	35.00	7.00
☐	178	Del Wilber	7.00	3.50	.70
☐	179	Morrie Martin	7.00	3.50	.70

1955 Bowman

		NRMT	VG-E	GOOD
☐ 180	Joe Tipton	7.00	3.50	.70
☐ 181	Les Moss	7.00	3.50	.70
☐ 182	Sherm Lollar	8.00	4.00	.80
☐ 183	Matt Batts	7.00	3.50	.70
☐ 184	Mickey Grasso	7.00	3.50	.70
☐ 185	Daryl Spencer	7.00	3.50	.70
☐ 186	Russ Meyer	7.00	3.50	.70
☐ 187	Vernon Law	8.00	4.00	.80
☐ 188	Frank Smith	7.00	3.50	.70
☐ 189	Randy Jackson	7.00	3.50	.70
☐ 190	Joe Presko	7.00	3.50	.70
☐ 191	Karl Drews	7.00	3.50	.70
☐ 192	Lou Burdette	9.00	4.50	.90
☐ 193	Eddie Robinson	7.00	3.50	.70
☐ 194	Sid Hudson	7.00	3.50	.70
☐ 195	Bob Cain	7.00	3.50	.70
☐ 196	Bob Lemon	25.00	12.50	2.50
☐ 197	Lou Kretlow	7.00	3.50	.70
☐ 198	Virgil Trucks	8.00	4.00	.80
☐ 199	Steve Gromek	7.00	3.50	.70
☐ 200	Conrado Marrero	7.00	3.50	.70
☐ 201	Bobby Thomson	9.00	4.50	.90
☐ 202	George Shuba	8.00	4.00	.80
☐ 203	Vic Janowicz	8.00	4.00	.80
☐ 204	Jack Collum	7.00	3.50	.70
☐ 205	Hal Jeffcoat	7.00	3.50	.70
☐ 206	Steve Bilko	7.00	3.50	.70
☐ 207	Stan Lopata	7.00	3.50	.70
☐ 208	Johnny Antonelli	8.00	4.00	.80
☐ 209	Gene Woodling	9.00	4.50	.90
☐ 210	Jim Piersall	10.00	5.00	1.00
☐ 211	Al Robertson	7.00	3.50	.70
☐ 212	Owen Friend	7.00	3.50	.70
☐ 213	Dick Littlefield	7.00	3.50	.70
☐ 214	Ferris Fain	8.00	4.00	.80
☐ 215	Johnny Bucha	7.00	3.50	.70
☐ 216	Jerry Snyder	7.00	3.50	.70
☐ 217	Hank Thompson	8.00	4.00	.80
☐ 218	Preacher Roe	11.00	5.50	1.10
☐ 219	Hal Rice	7.00	3.50	.70
☐ 220	Hobie Landrith	7.00	3.50	.70
☐ 221	Frank Baumholtz	7.00	3.50	.70
☐ 222	Memo Luna	7.00	3.50	.70
☐ 223	Steve Ridzik	7.00	3.50	.70
☐ 224	Bill Bruton	20.00	5.00	1.00

*The cards in this 320-card set measure 2 ½"
by 3 ¾". The Bowman set of 1955 is known
as the "TV set" because each player photograph is cleverly shown within a television set
design. The set contains umpire cards, some
transposed pictures (e.g., Johnsons and
Bollings), an incorrect spelling for Harvey
Kuenn, and a traded line for Palica (all of which
are noted in the checklist below). Some three-
card advertising strips exist.*

		NRMT	VG-E	GOOD
COMPLETE SET (320)		4400.00	2200.00	525.00
COMMON PLAYER (1-96)		6.00	3.00	.60
COMMON PLAYER (97-224)		4.00	2.00	.40
COMMON PLAYER (225-320)		12.00	6.00	1.20
COMMON UMPIRES (225-320)		16.00	8.00	1.60
☐ 1	Hoyt Wilhelm	100.00	10.00	2.00
☐ 2	Alvin Dark	8.00	4.00	.80
☐ 3	Joe Coleman	6.00	3.00	.60
☐ 4	Eddie Waitkus	6.00	3.00	.60
☐ 5	Jim Robertson	6.00	3.00	.60
☐ 6	Pete Suder	6.00	3.00	.60
☐ 7	Gene Baker	6.00	3.00	.60
☐ 8	Warren Hacker	6.00	3.00	.60
☐ 9	Gil McDougald	10.00	5.00	1.00
☐ 10	Phil Rizzuto	40.00	20.00	4.00
☐ 11	Bill Bruton	7.00	3.50	.70
☐ 12	Andy Pafko	7.00	3.50	.70
☐ 13	Clyde Vollmer	6.00	3.00	.60

		NRMT	VG-E	GOOD
☐ 14	Gus Keriazakos	6.00	3.00	.60
☐ 15	Frank Sullivan	6.00	3.00	.60
☐ 16	Jim Piersall	9.00	4.50	.90
☐ 17	Del Ennis	7.00	3.50	.70
☐ 18	Stan Lopata	6.00	3.00	.60
☐ 19	Bobby Avila	7.00	3.50	.70
☐ 20	Al Smith	6.00	3.00	.60
☐ 21	Don Hoak	7.00	3.50	.70
☐ 22	Roy Campanella	90.00	45.00	9.00
☐ 23	Al Kaline	100.00	50.00	10.00
☐ 24	Al Aber	6.00	3.00	.60
☐ 25	Minnie Minoso	10.00	5.00	1.00
☐ 26	Virgil Trucks	7.00	3.50	.70
☐ 27	Preston Ward	6.00	3.00	.60
☐ 28	Dick Cole	6.00	3.00	.60
☐ 29	Red Schoendienst	22.00	11.00	2.20
☐ 30	Bill Sarni	6.00	3.00	.60
☐ 31	Johnny Temple	7.00	3.50	.70
☐ 32	Wally Post	7.00	3.50	.70
☐ 33	Nellie Fox	16.00	8.00	1.60
☐ 34	Clint Courtney	6.00	3.00	.60
☐ 35	Bill Tuttle	6.00	3.00	.60
☐ 36	Wayne Belardi	6.00	3.00	.60
☐ 37	Pee Wee Reese	45.00	22.50	4.50
☐ 38	Early Wynn	20.00	10.00	2.00
☐ 39	Bob Darnell	6.00	3.00	.60
☐ 40	Vic Wertz	7.00	3.50	.70
☐ 41	Mel Clark	6.00	3.00	.60
☐ 42	Bob Greenwood	6.00	3.00	.60
☐ 43	Bob Buhl	6.00	3.00	.60
☐ 44	Danny O'Connell	6.00	3.00	.60
☐ 45	Tom Umphlett	6.00	3.00	.60
☐ 46	Mickey Vernon	8.00	4.00	.80
☐ 47	Sammy White	6.00	3.00	.60
☐ 48A	Milt Bolling ERR	8.00	4.00	.80
	(name on back is Frank Bolling)			
☐ 48B	Milt Bolling COR	25.00	10.00	2.00
☐ 49	Jim Greengrass	6.00	3.00	.60
☐ 50	Hobie Landrith	6.00	3.00	.60
☐ 51	Elvin Tappe	6.00	3.00	.60
☐ 52	Hal Rice	6.00	3.00	.60
☐ 53	Alex Kellner	6.00	3.00	.60
☐ 54	Don Bollweg	6.00	3.00	.60
☐ 55	Cal Abrams	6.00	3.00	.60
☐ 56	Billy Cox	7.00	3.50	.70
☐ 57	Bob Friend	8.00	4.00	.80
☐ 58	Frank Thomas	7.00	3.50	.70
☐ 59	Whitey Ford	60.00	30.00	6.00
☐ 60	Enos Slaughter	22.00	11.00	2.20
☐ 61	Paul LaPalme	6.00	3.00	.60
☐ 62	Royce Lint	6.00	3.00	.60
☐ 63	Irv Noren	7.00	3.50	.70
☐ 64	Curt Simmons	7.00	3.50	.70
☐ 65	Don Zimmer	16.00	8.00	1.60
☐ 66	George Shuba	7.00	3.50	.70
☐ 67	Don Larsen	13.00	6.50	1.30
☐ 68	Elston Howard	22.00	11.00	2.20
☐ 69	Billy Hunter	6.00	3.00	.60
☐ 70	Lou Burdette	9.00	4.50	.90
☐ 71	Dave Jolly	6.00	3.00	.60
☐ 72	Chet Nichols	6.00	3.00	.60
☐ 73	Eddie Yost	6.00	3.00	.60
☐ 74	Jerry Snyder	6.00	3.00	.60
☐ 75	Brooks Lawrence	6.00	3.00	.60
☐ 76	Tom Poholsky	6.00	3.00	.60
☐ 77	Jim McDonald	6.00	3.00	.60
☐ 78	Gil Coan	6.00	3.00	.60
☐ 79	Willie Miranda	6.00	3.00	.60
☐ 80	Lou Limmer	6.00	3.00	.60
☐ 81	Bobby Morgan	6.00	3.00	.60
☐ 82	Lee Walls	6.00	3.00	.60
☐ 83	Max Surkont	6.00	3.00	.60
☐ 84	George Freese	6.00	3.00	.60
☐ 85	Cass Michaels	6.00	3.00	.60
☐ 86	Ted Gray	6.00	3.00	.60
☐ 87	Randy Jackson	6.00	3.00	.60
☐ 88	Steve Bilko	6.00	3.00	.60
☐ 89	Lou Boudreau MG	20.00	10.00	2.00
☐ 90	Art Ditmar	6.00	3.00	.60
☐ 91	Dick Marlowe	6.00	3.00	.60
☐ 92	George Zuverink	6.00	3.00	.60
☐ 93	Andy Seminick	6.00	3.00	.60
☐ 94	Hank Thompson	7.00	3.50	.70
☐ 95	Sal Maglie	9.00	4.50	.90
☐ 96	Ray Narleski	6.00	3.00	.60
☐ 97	Johnny Podres	10.00	5.00	1.00
☐ 98	Jim Gilliam	10.00	5.00	1.00
☐ 99	Jerry Coleman	7.00	3.50	.70
☐ 100	Tom Morgan	6.00	3.00	.60
☐ 101A	Don Johnson ERR (photo actually Ernie Johnson)	7.00	3.50	.70
☐ 101B	Don Johnson COR	20.00	8.00	1.60
☐ 102	Bobby Thomson	8.00	4.00	.80
☐ 103	Eddie Mathews	33.00	16.00	3.50

		NRMT	VG-E	GOOD
☐ 104	Bob Porterfield	4.00	2.00	.40
☐ 105	Johnny Schmitz	4.00	2.00	.40
☐ 106	Del Rice	4.00	2.00	.40
☐ 107	Solly Hemus	4.00	2.00	.40
☐ 108	Lou Kretlow	4.00	2.00	.40
☐ 109	Vern Stephens	5.00	2.50	.50
☐ 110	Bob Miller	4.00	2.00	.40
☐ 111	Steve Ridzik	4.00	2.00	.40
☐ 112	Granny Hamner	4.00	2.00	.40
☐ 113	Bob Hall	4.00	2.00	.40
☐ 114	Vic Janowicz	5.00	2.50	.50
☐ 115	Roger Bowman	4.00	2.00	.40
☐ 116	Sandy Consuegra	4.00	2.00	.40
☐ 117	Johnny Groth	4.00	2.00	.40
☐ 118	Bobby Adams	4.00	2.00	.40
☐ 119	Joe Astroth	4.00	2.00	.40
☐ 120	Ed Burtschy	4.00	2.00	.40
☐ 121	Rufus Crawford	4.00	2.00	.40
☐ 122	Al Corwin	4.00	2.00	.40
☐ 123	Marv Grissom	4.00	2.00	.40
☐ 124	Johnny Antonelli	6.00	3.00	.60
☐ 125	Paul Giel	4.00	2.00	.40
☐ 126	Billy Goodman	5.00	2.50	.50
☐ 127	Hank Majeski	4.00	2.00	.40
☐ 128	Mike Garcia	6.00	3.00	.60
☐ 129	Hal Naragon	4.00	2.00	.40
☐ 130	Richie Ashburn	16.00	8.00	1.60
☐ 131	Willard Marshall	4.00	2.00	.40
☐ 132A	Harvey Kueen ERR (sic, Kuenn)	8.00	4.00	.80
☐ 132B	Harvey Kuenn COR	20.00	10.00	2.00
☐ 133	Charles King	4.00	2.00	.40
☐ 134	Bob Feller	55.00	27.50	5.50
☐ 135	Lloyd Merriman	4.00	2.00	.40
☐ 136	Rocky Bridges	4.00	2.00	.40
☐ 137	Bob Talbot	4.00	2.00	.40
☐ 138	Davey Williams	5.00	2.50	.50
☐ 139	Shantz Brothers Wilmer and Bobby	6.00	3.00	.60
☐ 140	Bobby Shantz	6.00	3.00	.60
☐ 141	Wes Westrum	5.00	2.50	.50
☐ 142	Rudy Regalado	4.00	2.00	.40
☐ 143	Don Newcombe	9.00	4.50	.90
☐ 144	Art Houtteman	4.00	2.00	.40
☐ 145	Bob Nieman	4.00	2.00	.40
☐ 146	Don Liddle	4.00	2.00	.40
☐ 147	Sam Mele	4.00	2.00	.40
☐ 148	Bob Chakales	4.00	2.00	.40
☐ 149	Cloyd Boyer	4.00	2.00	.40
☐ 150	Billy Klaus	4.00	2.00	.40
☐ 151	Jim Brideweser	4.00	2.00	.40
☐ 152	Johnny Klippstein	4.00	2.00	.40
☐ 153	Eddie Robinson	4.00	2.00	.40
☐ 154	Frank Lary	6.00	3.00	.60
☐ 155	Jerry Staley	4.00	2.00	.40
☐ 156	Jim Hughes	4.00	2.00	.40
☐ 157A	Ernie Johnson ERR (photo actually Don Johnson)	5.00	2.50	.50
☐ 157B	Ernie Johnson COR	20.00	8.00	1.60
☐ 158	Gil Hodges	30.00	15.00	3.00
☐ 159	Harry Byrd	5.00	2.50	.50
☐ 160	Bill Skowron	12.00	6.00	1.20
☐ 161	Matt Batts	4.00	2.00	.40
☐ 162	Charlie Maxwell	4.00	2.00	.40
☐ 163	Sid Gordon	4.00	2.00	.40
☐ 164	Toby Atwell	4.00	2.00	.40
☐ 165	Maurice McDermott	4.00	2.00	.40
☐ 166	Jim Busby	4.00	2.00	.40
☐ 167	Bob Grim	6.00	3.00	.60
☐ 168	Yogi Berra	90.00	45.00	9.00
☐ 169	Carl Furillo	10.00	5.00	1.00
☐ 170	Carl Erskine	9.00	4.50	.90
☐ 171	Robin Roberts	22.00	11.00	2.20
☐ 172	Willie Jones	4.00	2.00	.40
☐ 173	Chico Carrasquel	4.00	2.00	.40
☐ 174	Sherm Lollar	5.00	2.50	.50
☐ 175	Wilmer Shantz	4.00	2.00	.40
☐ 176	Joe DeMaestri	4.00	2.00	.40
☐ 177	Willard Nixon	4.00	2.00	.40
☐ 178	Tom Brewer	4.00	2.00	.40
☐ 179	Hank Aaron	180.00	90.00	18.00
☐ 180	Johnny Logan	5.00	2.50	.50
☐ 181	Eddie Miksis	4.00	2.00	.40
☐ 182	Bob Rush	4.00	2.00	.40
☐ 183	Ray Katt	4.00	2.00	.40
☐ 184	Willie Mays	180.00	90.00	18.00
☐ 185	Vic Raschi	7.00	3.50	.70
☐ 186	Alex Grammas	4.00	2.00	.40
☐ 187	Fred Hatfield	4.00	2.00	.40
☐ 188	Ned Garver	4.00	2.00	.40
☐ 189	Jack Collum	4.00	2.00	.40
☐ 190	Fred Baczewski	4.00	2.00	.40
☐ 191	Bob Lemon	20.00	10.00	2.00
☐ 192	George Strickland	4.00	2.00	.40
☐ 193	Howie Judson	4.00	2.00	.40
☐ 194	Joe Nuxhall	5.00	2.50	.50
☐ 195A	Erv Palica	5.00	2.50	.50

		NRMT	VG-E	GOOD
	(without trade)			
☐ 195B	Erv Palica	20.00	8.00	1.60
	(with trade)			
☐ 196	Russ Meyer	4.00	2.00	.40
☐ 197	Ralph Kiner	24.00	12.00	2.40
☐ 198	Dave Pope	4.00	2.00	.40
☐ 199	Vernon Law	6.00	3.00	.60
☐ 200	Dick Littlefield	4.00	2.00	.40
☐ 201	Allie Reynolds	11.00	5.50	1.10
☐ 202	Mickey Mantle	400.00	200.00	40.00
☐ 203	Steve Gromek	4.00	2.00	.40
☐ 204A	Frank Bolling ERR ..	5.00	2.50	.50
	(name on back is Milt			
	Bolling)			
☐ 204B	Frank Bolling COR ..	20.00	8.00	1.60
☐ 205	Rip Repulski	4.00	2.00	.40
☐ 206	Ralph Beard	4.00	2.00	.40
☐ 207	Frank Shea	4.00	2.00	.40
☐ 208	Ed Fitzgerald	4.00	2.00	.40
☐ 209	Smokey Burgess ...	5.00	2.50	.50
☐ 210	Earl Torgeson	4.00	2.00	.40
☐ 211	Sonny Dixon	4.00	2.00	.40
☐ 212	Jack Dittmer	4.00	2.00	.40
☐ 213	George Kell	20.00	10.00	2.00
☐ 214	Billy Pierce	6.00	3.00	.60
☐ 215	Bob Kuzava	4.00	2.00	.40
☐ 216	Preacher Roe	8.00	4.00	.80
☐ 217	Del Crandall	5.00	2.50	.50
☐ 218	Joe Adcock	6.00	3.00	.60
☐ 219	Whitey Lockman	5.00	2.50	.50
☐ 220	Jim Hearn	4.00	2.00	.40
☐ 221	Hector Brown	4.00	2.00	.40
☐ 222	Russ Kemmerer	4.00	2.00	.40
☐ 223	Hal Jeffcoat	4.00	2.00	.40
☐ 224	Dee Fondy	4.00	2.00	.40
☐ 225	Paul Richards	14.00	7.00	1.40
☐ 226	W. McKinley UMP ...	16.00	8.00	1.60
☐ 227	Frank Baumholtz	12.00	6.00	1.20
☐ 228	John Phillips	12.00	6.00	1.20
☐ 229	Jim Brosnan	14.00	7.00	1.40
☐ 230	Al Brazle	12.00	6.00	1.20
☐ 231	Jim Konstanty	14.00	7.00	1.40
☐ 232	Birdie Tebbetts	14.00	7.00	1.40
☐ 233	Bill Serena ....!	12.00	6.00	1.20
☐ 234	Dick Bartell	12.00	6.00	1.20
☐ 235	J. Paparella UMP ...	16.00	8.00	1.60
☐ 236	Murry Dickson	12.00	6.00	1.20
☐ 237	Johnny Wyrostek	12.00	6.00	1.20
☐ 238	Eddie Stanky	16.00	8.00	1.60
☐ 239	Edwin Rommel UMP	16.00	8.00	1.60

		NRMT	VG-E	GOOD
☐ 240	Billy Loes	14.00	7.00	1.40
☐ 241	Johnny Pesky	14.00	7.00	1.40
☐ 242	Ernie Banks	300.00	150.00	30.00
☐ 243	Gus Bell	14.00	7.00	1.40
☐ 244	Duane Pillette	12.00	6.00	1.20
☐ 245	Bill Miller	12.00	6.00	1.20
☐ 246	Hank Bauer	24.00	12.00	2.40
☐ 247	Dutch Leonard	12.00	6.00	1.20
☐ 248	Harry Dorish	12.00	6.00	1.20
☐ 249	Billy Gardner	14.00	7.00	1.40
☐ 250	Larry Napp UMP	16.00	8.00	1.60
☐ 251	Stan Jok	12.00	6.00	1.20
☐ 252	Roy Smalley	12.00	6.00	1.20
☐ 253	Jim Wilson	12.00	6.00	1.20
☐ 254	Bennett Flowers	12.00	6.00	1.20
☐ 255	Pete Runnels	14.00	7.00	1.40
☐ 256	Owen Friend	12.00	6.00	1.20
☐ 257	Tom Alston	12.00	6.00	1.20
☐ 258	John Stevens UMP ..	16.00	8.00	1.60
☐ 259	Don Mossi	16.00	8.00	1.60
☐ 260	Edwin Hurley UMP ..	16.00	8.00	1.60
☐ 261	Walt Moryn	12.00	6.00	1.20
☐ 262	Jim Lemon	14.00	7.00	1.40
☐ 263	Eddie Joost	12.00	6.00	1.20
☐ 264	Bill Henry	12.00	6.00	1.20
☐ 265	Albert Barlick UMP ..	50.00	25.00	5.00
☐ 266	Mike Fornieles	12.00	6.00	1.20
☐ 267	Jim Honochick UMP .	50.00	25.00	5.00
☐ 268	Roy Lee Hawes	12.00	6.00	1.20
☐ 269	Joe Amalfitano	12.00	6.00	1.20
☐ 270	Chico Fernandez	12.00	6.00	1.20
☐ 271	Bob Hooper	12.00	6.00	1.20
☐ 272	John Flaherty UMP ..	16.00	8.00	1.60
☐ 273	Bubba Church	12.00	6.00	1.20
☐ 274	Jim Delsing	12.00	6.00	1.20
☐ 275	William Grieve UMP .	16.00	8.00	1.60
☐ 276	Ike Delock	12.00	6.00	1.20
☐ 277	Ed Runge UMP	20.00	10.00	2.00
☐ 278	Charlie Neal	18.00	9.00	1.80
☐ 279	Hank Soar UMP	16.00	8.00	1.60
☐ 280	Clyde McCullough ..	12.00	6.00	1.20
☐ 281	Charles Berry UMP .	16.00	8.00	1.60
☐ 282	Phil Cavarretta	16.00	8.00	1.60
☐ 283	Nestor Chylak UMP .	16.00	8.00	1.60
☐ 284	Bill Jackowski UMP .	16.00	8.00	1.60
☐ 285	Walt Dropo	14.00	7.00	1.40
☐ 286	Frank Secory UMP ..	16.00	8.00	1.60
☐ 287	Ron Mrozinski	12.00	6.00	1.20
☐ 288	Dick Smith	12.00	6.00	1.20
☐ 289	Arthur Gore UMP ...	16.00	8.00	1.60

1989 Bowman

		NRMT	VG-E	GOOD
☐ 290	Hershell Freeman ...	12.00	6.00	1.20
☐ 291	Frank Dascoli UMP	16.00	8.00	1.60
☐ 292	Marv Blaylock	12.00	6.00	1.20
☐ 293	Thomas Gorman UMP	16.00	8.00	1.60
☐ 294	Wally Moses	14.00	7.00	1.40
☐ 295	Lee Ballanfant UMP	16.00	8.00	1.60
☐ 296	Bill Virdon	30.00	15.00	3.00
☐ 297	Dusty Boggess UMP	16.00	8.00	1.60
☐ 298	Charlie Grimm	14.00	7.00	1.40
☐ 299	Lon Warneke UMP ..	16.00	8.00	1.60
☐ 300	Tommy Byrne	14.00	7.00	1.40
☐ 301	William Engeln UMP	16.00	8.00	1.60
☐ 302	Frank Malzone	20.00	10.00	2.00
☐ 303	Jocko Conlan UMP ..	65.00	32.50	6.50
☐ 304	Harry Chiti	12.00	6.00	1.20
☐ 305	Frank Umont UMP ...	16.00	8.00	1.60
☐ 306	Bob Cerv	20.00	10.00	2.00
☐ 307	Babe Pinelli UMP ...	20.00	10.00	2.00
☐ 308	Al Lopez MG	40.00	20.00	4.00
☐ 309	Hal Dixon UMP	16.00	8.00	1.60
☐ 310	Ken Lehman	12.00	6.00	1.20
☐ 311	Lawrence Goetz UMP	16.00	8.00	1.60
☐ 312	Bill Wight	12.00	6.00	1.20
☐ 313	Augie Donatelli UMP	25.00	12.50	2.50
☐ 314	Dale Mitchell	14.00	7.00	1.40
☐ 315	Cal Hubbard UMP ..	55.00	27.50	5.50
☐ 316	Marion Fricano	12.00	6.00	1.20
☐ 317	William Summers UMP	16.00	8.00	1.60
☐ 318	Sid Hudson	12.00	6.00	1.20
☐ 319	Al Schroll	12.00	6.00	1.20
☐ 320	George Susce, Jr. ...	25.00	7.00	1.50

The 1989 Bowman set, which was actually produced by Topps, contains 484 cards measuring 2 ½" by 3 ¾". The fronts have white-bordered color photos with facsimile autographs and small Bowman logos. The backs are scarlet and feature charts detailing 1988 player performances vs. each team. The set is arranged in alphabetical team order. The player selection is concentrated on prospects and "name" players. The cards were released in midseason 1989 in wax, rack, and cello pack formats.

		MINT	EXC	G-VG
COMPLETE SET (484)		25.00	12.50	2.50
COMMON PLAYER (1-484)		.03	.01	.00
☐ 1	Oswald Peraza	.10	.02	.01
☐ 2	Brian Holton	.08	.04	.01
☐ 3	Jose Bautista	.08	.04	.01
☐ 4	Pete Harnisch	.10	.05	.01
☐ 5	Dave Schmidt	.03	.01	.00
☐ 6	Gregg Olson	.75	.35	.09
☐ 7	Jeff Ballard	.15	.07	.01
☐ 8	Bob Melvin	.03	.01	.00
☐ 9	Cal Ripken	.15	.07	.01
☐ 10	Randy Milligan	.10	.05	.01
☐ 11	Juan Bell	.20	.10	.02
☐ 12	Billy Ripken	.03	.01	.00
☐ 13	Jim Traber	.03	.01	.00
☐ 14	Pete Stanicek	.08	.04	.01
☐ 15	Steve Finley	.30	.15	.03
☐ 16	Larry Sheets	.03	.01	.00
☐ 17	Phil Bradley	.06	.03	.00

		MINT	EXC	G-VG
☐ 18	Brady Anderson	.20	.10	.02
☐ 19	Lee Smith	.03	.01	.00
☐ 20	Tom Fischer	.08	.04	.01
☐ 21	Mike Boddicker	.03	.01	.00
☐ 22	Rob Murphy	.03	.01	.00
☐ 23	Wes Gardner	.03	.01	.00
☐ 24	John Dopson	.18	.09	.01
☐ 25	Bob Stanley	.03	.01	.00
☐ 26	Roger Clemens	.30	.15	.03
☐ 27	Rich Gedman	.03	.01	.00
☐ 28	Marty Barrett	.03	.01	.00
☐ 29	Luis Rivera	.03	.01	.00
☐ 30	Jody Reed	.03	.01	.00
☐ 31	Nick Esasky	.08	.04	.01
☐ 32	Wade Boggs	.50	.25	.05
☐ 33	Jim Rice	.12	.06	.01
☐ 34	Mike Greenwell	.60	.30	.06
☐ 35	Dwight Evans	.10	.05	.01
☐ 36	Ellis Burks	.25	.12	.02
☐ 37	Mark Clear	.03	.01	.00
☐ 38	Kirk McCaskill	.03	.01	.00
☐ 39	Jim Abbott	2.00	1.00	.20
☐ 40	Bryan Harvey	.20	.10	.02
☐ 41	Bert Blyleven	.08	.04	.01
☐ 42	Mike Witt	.06	.03	.00
☐ 43	Bob McClure	.03	.01	.00
☐ 44	Bill Schroeder	.03	.01	.00
☐ 45	Lance Parrish	.08	.04	.01
☐ 46	Dick Schofield	.03	.01	.00
☐ 47	Wally Joyner	.15	.07	.01
☐ 48	Jack Howell	.03	.01	.00
☐ 49	Johnny Ray	.06	.03	.00
☐ 50	Chili Davis	.06	.03	.00
☐ 51	Tony Armas	.06	.03	.00
☐ 52	Claudell Washington	.06	.03	.00
☐ 53	Brian Downing	.03	.01	.00
☐ 54	Devon White	.12	.06	.01
☐ 55	Bobby Thigpen	.06	.03	.00
☐ 56	Bill Long	.03	.01	.00
☐ 57	Jerry Reuss	.03	.01	.00
☐ 58	Shawn Hillegas	.03	.01	.00
☐ 59	Melido Perez	.08	.04	.01
☐ 60	Jeff Bittiger	.10	.05	.01
☐ 61	Jack McDowell	.10	.05	.01
☐ 62	Carlton Fisk	.10	.05	.01
☐ 63	Steve Lyons	.03	.01	.00
☐ 64	Ozzie Guillen	.06	.03	.00
☐ 65	Robin Ventura	1.00	.50	.10
☐ 66	Fred Manrique	.03	.01	.00
☐ 67	Dan Pasqua	.03	.01	.00

		MINT	EXC	G-VG
☐ 68	Ivan Calderon	.06	.03	.00
☐ 69	Ron Kittle	.08	.04	.01
☐ 70	Daryl Boston	.03	.01	.00
☐ 71	Dave Gallagher	.20	.10	.02
☐ 72	Harold Baines	.08	.04	.01
☐ 73	Charles Nagy	.20	.10	.02
☐ 74	John Farrell	.03	.01	.00
☐ 75	Kevin Wickander	.10	.05	.01
☐ 76	Greg Swindell	.08	.04	.01
☐ 77	Mike Walker	.10	.05	.01
☐ 78	Doug Jones	.06	.03	.00
☐ 79	Rich Yett	.03	.01	.00
☐ 80	Tom Candiotti	.03	.01	.00
☐ 81	Jesse Orosco	.03	.01	.00
☐ 82	Bud Black	.03	.01	.00
☐ 83	Andy Allanson	.03	.01	.00
☐ 84	Pete O'Brien	.06	.03	.00
☐ 85	Jerry Browne	.06	.03	.00
☐ 86	Brook Jacoby	.06	.03	.00
☐ 87	Mark Lewis	.20	.10	.02
☐ 88	Luis Aguayo	.03	.01	.00
☐ 89	Cory Snyder	.08	.04	.01
☐ 90	Oddibe McDowell	.06	.03	.00
☐ 91	Joe Carter	.12	.06	.01
☐ 92	Frank Tanana	.03	.01	.00
☐ 93	Jack Morris	.08	.04	.01
☐ 94	Doyle Alexander	.03	.01	.00
☐ 95	Steve Searcy	.20	.10	.02
☐ 96	Randy Bockus	.08	.04	.01
☐ 97	Jeff Robinson	.06	.03	.00
☐ 98	Mike Henneman	.06	.03	.00
☐ 99	Paul Gibson	.08	.04	.01
☐ 100	Frank Williams	.03	.01	.00
☐ 101	Matt Nokes	.08	.04	.01
☐ 102	Ricco Brogna	.10	.05	.01
☐ 103	Lou Whitaker	.08	.04	.01
☐ 104	Al Pedrique	.03	.01	.00
☐ 105	Alan Trammell	.12	.06	.01
☐ 106	Chris Brown	.03	.01	.00
☐ 107	Pat Sheridan	.03	.01	.00
☐ 108	Gary Pettis	.03	.01	.00
☐ 109	Keith Moreland	.03	.01	.00
☐ 110	Mel Stottlemyre, Jr.	.20	.10	.02
☐ 111	Bret Saberhagen	.15	.07	.01
☐ 112	Floyd Bannister	.03	.01	.00
☐ 113	Jeff Montgomery	.12	.06	.01
☐ 114	Steve Farr	.03	.01	.00
☐ 115	Tom Gordon UER	1.00	.50	.10
	(front shows auto-			
	graph of Don Gordon)			

		MINT	EXC	G-VG			MINT	EXC	G-VG
☐ 116	Charlie Leibrandt	.03	.01	.00	☐ 166	Andy Hawkins	.03	.01	.00
☐ 117	Mark Gubicza	.08	.04	.01	☐ 167	Dave Righetti	.08	.04	.01
☐ 118	Mike Macfarlane	.10	.05	.01	☐ 168	Lance McCullers	.03	.01	.00
☐ 119	Bob Boone	.08	.04	.01	☐ 169	Jimmy Jones	.03	.01	.00
☐ 120	Kurt Stillwell	.03	.01	.00	☐ 170	Al Leiter	.10	.05	.01
☐ 121	George Brett	.20	.10	.02	☐ 171	John Candelaria	.06	.03	.00
☐ 122	Frank White	.06	.03	.00	☐ 172	Don Slaught	.03	.01	.00
☐ 123	Kevin Seitzer	.18	.09	.01	☐ 173	Jamie Quirk	.03	.01	.00
☐ 124	Willie Wilson	.06	.03	.00	☐ 174	Rafael Santana	.03	.01	.00
☐ 125	Pat Tabler	.03	.01	.00	☐ 175	Mike Pagliarulo	.06	.03	.00
☐ 126	Bo Jackson	.85	.40	.08	☐ 176	Don Mattingly	.85	.40	.08
☐ 127	Hugh Walker	.12	.06	.01	☐ 177	Ken Phelps	.06	.03	.00
☐ 128	Danny Tartabull	.08	.04	.01	☐ 178	Steve Sax	.08	.04	.01
☐ 129	Teddy Higuera	.06	.03	.00	☐ 179	Dave Winfield	.12	.06	.01
☐ 130	Don August	.06	.03	.00	☐ 180	Stan Jefferson	.03	.01	.00
☐ 131	Juan Nieves	.03	.01	.00	☐ 181	Rickey Henderson	.25	.12	.02
☐ 132	Mike Birkbeck	.03	.01	.00	☐ 182	Bob Brower	.03	.01	.00
☐ 133	Dan Plesac	.06	.03	.00	☐ 183	Roberto Kelly	.25	.12	.02
☐ 134	Chris Bosio	.06	.03	.00	☐ 184	Curt Young	.03	.01	.00
☐ 135	Bill Wegman	.03	.01	.00	☐ 185	Gene Nelson	.03	.01	.00
☐ 136	Chuck Crim	.03	.01	.00	☐ 186	Bob Welch	.06	.03	.00
☐ 137	B.J. Surhoff	.08	.04	.01	☐ 187	Rick Honeycutt	.03	.01	.00
☐ 138	Joey Meyer	.06	.03	.00	☐ 188	Dave Stewart	.10	.05	.01
☐ 139	Dale Sveum	.03	.01	.00	☐ 189	Mike Moore	.06	.03	.00
☐ 140	Paul Molitor	.10	.05	.01	☐ 190	Dennis Eckersley	.08	.04	.01
☐ 141	Jim Gantner	.03	.01	.00	☐ 191	Eric Plunk	.03	.01	.00
☐ 142	Gary Sheffield	1.00	.50	.10	☐ 192	Storm Davis	.06	.03	.00
☐ 143	Greg Brock	.03	.01	.00	☐ 193	Terry Steinbach	.10	.05	.01
☐ 144	Robin Yount	.20	.10	.02	☐ 194	Ron Hassey	.03	.01	.00
☐ 145	Glenn Braggs	.06	.03	.00	☐ 195	Stan Royer	.12	.06	.01
☐ 146	Rob Deer	.06	.03	.00	☐ 196	Walt Weiss	.20	.10	.02
☐ 147	Fred Toliver	.03	.01	.00	☐ 197	Mark McGwire	.60	.30	.06
☐ 148	Jeff Reardon	.08	.04	.01	☐ 198	Carney Lansford	.08	.04	.01
☐ 149	Allan Anderson	.06	.03	.00	☐ 199	Glenn Hubbard	.03	.01	.00
☐ 150	Frank Viola	.10	.05	.01	☐ 200	Dave Henderson	.03	.01	.00
☐ 151	Shane Rawley	.03	.01	.00	☐ 201	Jose Canseco	.85	.40	.08
☐ 152	Juan Berenguer	.03	.01	.00	☐ 202	Dave Parker	.08	.04	.01
☐ 153	Johnny Ard	.15	.07	.01	☐ 203	Scott Bankhead	.06	.03	.00
☐ 154	Tim Laudner	.03	.01	.00	☐ 204	Tom Niedenfuer	.03	.01	.00
☐ 155	Brian Harper	.03	.01	.00	☐ 205	Mark Langston	.12	.06	.01
☐ 156	Al Newman	.03	.01	.00	☐ 206	Erik Hanson	.20	.10	.02
☐ 157	Kent Hrbek	.10	.05	.01	☐ 207	Mike Jackson	.03	.01	.00
☐ 158	Gary Gaetti	.08	.04	.01	☐ 208	Dave Valle	.03	.01	.00
☐ 159	Wally Backman	.03	.01	.00	☐ 209	Scott Bradley	.03	.01	.00
☐ 160	Gene Larkin	.03	.01	.00	☐ 210	Harold Reynolds	.06	.03	.00
☐ 161	Greg Gagne	.03	.01	.00	☐ 211	Tino Martinez	.75	.35	.07
☐ 162	Kirby Puckett	.40	.20	.04	☐ 212	Rich Renteria	.10	.05	.01
☐ 163	Dan Gladden	.03	.01	.00	☐ 213	Rey Quinones	.03	.01	.00
☐ 164	Randy Bush	.03	.01	.00	☐ 214	Jim Presley	.03	.01	.00
☐ 165	Dave LaPoint	.03	.01	.00	☐ 215	Alvin Davis	.08	.04	.01

		MINT	EXC	G-VG
☐ 216	Edgar Martinez	.10	.05	.01
☐ 217	Darnell Coles	.03	.01	.00
☐ 218	Jeffrey Leonard	.06	.03	.00
☐ 219	Jay Buhner	.15	.07	.01
☐ 220	Ken Griffey, Jr.	3.00	1.50	.30
☐ 221	Drew Hall	.03	.01	.00
☐ 222	Bobby Witt	.06	.03	.00
☐ 223	Jamie Moyer	.03	.01	.00
☐ 224	Charlie Hough	.03	.01	.00
☐ 225	Nolan Ryan	.60	.30	.06
☐ 226	Jeff Russell	.06	.03	.00
☐ 227	Jim Sundberg	.03	.01	.00
☐ 228	Julio Franco	.08	.04	.01
☐ 229	Buddy Bell	.06	.03	.00
☐ 230	Scott Fletcher	.03	.01	.00
☐ 231	Jeff Kunkel	.03	.01	.00
☐ 232	Steve Buechele	.03	.01	.00
☐ 233	Monty Fariss	.15	.07	.01
☐ 234	Rick Leach	.03	.01	.00
☐ 235	Ruben Sierra	.30	.15	.03
☐ 236	Cecil Espy	.08	.04	.01
☐ 237	Rafael Palmeiro	.10	.05	.01
☐ 238	Pete Incaviglia	.08	.04	.01
☐ 239	Dave Stieb	.08	.04	.01
☐ 240	Jeff Musselman	.03	.01	.00
☐ 241	Mike Flanagan	.03	.01	.00
☐ 242	Todd Stottlemyre	.12	.06	.01
☐ 243	Jimmy Key	.06	.03	.00
☐ 244	Tony Castillo	.10	.05	.01
☐ 245	Alex Sanchez	.20	.10	.02
☐ 246	Tom Henke	.06	.03	.00
☐ 247	John Cerutti	.03	.01	.00
☐ 248	Ernie Whitt	.03	.01	.00
☐ 249	Bob Brenly	.03	.01	.00
☐ 250	Rance Mulliniks	.03	.01	.00
☐ 251	Kelly Gruber	.06	.03	.00
☐ 252	Ed Sprague	.20	.10	.02
☐ 253	Fred McGriff	.20	.10	.02
☐ 254	Tony Fernandez	.10	.05	.01
☐ 255	Tom Lawless	.03	.01	.00
☐ 256	George Bell	.12	.06	.01
☐ 257	Jesse Barfield	.08	.04	.01
☐ 258	Roberto Alomar w/Dad	.20	.10	.02
☐ 259	Ken Griffey, Jr./Sr.	.65	.30	.06
☐ 260	Cal Ripken, Jr./Sr.	.08	.04	.01
☐ 261	M. Stottlemyre, Jr./Sr.	.08	.04	.01
☐ 262	Zane Smith	.03	.01	.00
☐ 263	Charlie Puleo	.03	.01	.00
☐ 264	Derek Lilliquist	.20	.10	.02
☐ 265	Paul Assenmacher	.03	.01	.00
☐ 266	John Smoltz	.40	.20	.04
☐ 267	Tom Glavine	.06	.03	.00
☐ 268	Steve Avery	.40	.20	.04
☐ 269	Pete Smith	.08	.04	.01
☐ 270	Jody Davis	.03	.01	.00
☐ 271	Bruce Benedict	.03	.01	.00
☐ 272	Andres Thomas	.03	.01	.00
☐ 273	Gerald Perry	.06	.03	.00
☐ 274	Ron Gant	.15	.07	.01
☐ 275	Darrell Evans	.06	.03	.00
☐ 276	Dale Murphy	.15	.07	.01
☐ 277	Dion James	.03	.01	.00
☐ 278	Lonnie Smith	.06	.03	.00
☐ 279	Geronimo Berroa	.03	.01	.00
☐ 280	Steve Wilson	.15	.07	.01
☐ 281	Rick Sutcliffe	.08	.04	.01
☐ 282	Kevin Coffman	.08	.04	.01
☐ 283	Mitch Williams	.08	.04	.01
☐ 284	Greg Maddux	.10	.05	.01
☐ 285	Paul Kilgus	.03	.01	.00
☐ 286	Mike Harkey	.20	.10	.02
☐ 287	Lloyd McClendon	.08	.04	.01
☐ 288	Damon Berryhill	.25	.12	.02
☐ 289	Ty Griffin	.85	.40	.08
☐ 290	Ryne Sandberg	.15	.07	.01
☐ 291	Mark Grace	2.25	1.10	.22
☐ 292	Curt Wilkerson	.03	.01	.00
☐ 293	Vance Law	.03	.01	.00
☐ 294	Shawon Dunston	.06	.03	.00
☐ 295	Jerome Walton	3.50	1.75	.35
☐ 296	Mitch Webster	.03	.01	.00
☐ 297	Dwight Smith	1.50	.75	.15
☐ 298	Andre Dawson	.12	.06	.01
☐ 299	Jeff Sellers	.03	.01	.00
☐ 300	Jose Rijo	.03	.01	.00
☐ 301	John Franco	.06	.03	.00
☐ 302	Rick Mahler	.03	.01	.00
☐ 303	Ron Robinson	.03	.01	.00
☐ 304	Danny Jackson	.06	.03	.00
☐ 305	Rob Dibble	.20	.10	.02
☐ 306	Tom Browning	.08	.04	.01
☐ 307	Bo Diaz	.03	.01	.00
☐ 308	Manny Trillo	.03	.01	.00
☐ 309	Chris Sabo	.45	.22	.04
☐ 310	Ron Oester	.03	.01	.00
☐ 311	Barry Larkin	.12	.06	.01
☐ 312	Todd Benzinger	.03	.01	.00
☐ 313	Paul O'Neill	.08	.04	.01
☐ 314	Kal Daniels	.10	.05	.01

		MINT	EXC	G-VG			MINT	EXC	G-VG
☐ 315	Joel Youngblood	.03	.01	.00	☐ 365	Andres Galarraga	.10	.05	.01
☐ 316	Eric Davis	.30	.15	.03	☐ 366	Otis Nixon	.03	.01	.00
☐ 317	Dave Smith	.03	.01	.00	☐ 367	Hubie Brooks	.06	.03	.00
☐ 318	Mark Portugal	.03	.01	.00	☐ 368	Mike Aldrete	.03	.01	.00
☐ 319	Brian Meyer	.10	.05	.01	☐ 369	Tim Raines	.10	.05	.01
☐ 320	Jim Deshaies	.03	.01	.00	☐ 370	Dave Martinez	.03	.01	.00
☐ 321	Juan Agosto	.03	.01	.00	☐ 371	Bob Ojeda	.06	.03	.00
☐ 322	Mike Scott	.12	.06	.01	☐ 372	Ron Darling	.08	.04	.01
☐ 323	Rick Rhoden	.03	.01	.00	☐ 373	Wally Whitehurst	.20	.10	.02
☐ 324	Jim Clancy	.03	.01	.00	☐ 374	Randy Myers	.06	.03	.00
☐ 325	Larry Andersen	.03	.01	.00	☐ 375	David Cone	.15	.07	.01
☐ 326	Alex Trevino	.03	.01	.00	☐ 376	Dwight Gooden	.25	.12	.02
☐ 327	Alan Ashby	.03	.01	.00	☐ 377	Sid Fernandez	.08	.04	.01
☐ 328	Craig Reynolds	.03	.01	.00	☐ 378	Dave Proctor	.12	.06	.01
☐ 329	Bill Doran	.06	.03	.00	☐ 379	Gary Carter	.12	.06	.01
☐ 330	Rafael Ramirez	.03	.01	.00	☐ 380	Keith Miller	.03	.01	.00
☐ 331	Glenn Davis	.10	.05	.01	☐ 381	Gregg Jefferies	1.00	.50	.10
☐ 332	Willie Ansley	.25	.12	.02	☐ 382	Tim Teufel	.03	.01	.00
☐ 333	Gerald Young	.03	.01	.00	☐ 383	Kevin Elster	.06	.03	.00
☐ 334	Cameron Drew	.18	.09	.01	☐ 384	Dave Magadan	.08	.04	.01
☐ 335	Jay Howell	.06	.03	.00	☐ 385	Keith Hernandez	.10	.05	.01
☐ 336	Tim Belcher	.20	.10	.02	☐ 386	Mookie Wilson	.06	.03	.00
☐ 337	Fernando Valenzuela	.10	.05	.01	☐ 387	Darryl Strawberry	.40	.20	.04
☐ 338	Ricky Horton	.03	.01	.00	☐ 388	Kevin McReynolds	.10	.05	.01
☐ 339	Tim Leary	.06	.03	.00	☐ 389	Mark Carreon	.10	.05	.01
☐ 340	Bill Bene	.12	.06	.01	☐ 390	Jeff Parrett	.10	.05	.01
☐ 341	Orel Hershiser	.20	.10	.02	☐ 391	Mike Maddux	.03	.01	.00
☐ 342	Mike Scioscia	.03	.01	.00	☐ 392	Don Carman	.03	.01	.00
☐ 343	Rick Dempsey	.03	.01	.00	☐ 393	Bruce Ruffin	.03	.01	.00
☐ 344	Willie Randolph	.06	.03	.00	☐ 394	Ken Howell	.03	.01	.00
☐ 345	Alfredo Griffin	.03	.01	.00	☐ 395	Steve Bedrosian	.08	.04	.01
☐ 346	Eddie Murray	.10	.05	.01	☐ 396	Floyd Youmans	.03	.01	.00
☐ 347	Mickey Hatcher	.03	.01	.00	☐ 397	Larry McWilliams	.03	.01	.00
☐ 348	Mike Sharperson	.03	.01	.00	☐ 398	Pat Combs	.60	.30	.06
☐ 349	John Shelby	.03	.01	.00	☐ 399	Steve Lake	.03	.01	.00
☐ 350	Mike Marshall	.08	.04	.01	☐ 400	Dickie Thon	.06	.03	.00
☐ 351	Kirk Gibson	.10	.05	.01	☐ 401	Ricky Jordan	1.00	.50	.10
☐ 352	Mike Davis	.00	.00	.00	☐ 402	Mike Schmidt	.30	.15	.03
☐ 353	Bryn Smith	.06	.03	.00	☐ 403	Tom Herr	.03	.01	.00
☐ 354	Pascual Perez	.08	.04	.01	☐ 404	Chris James	.06	.03	.00
☐ 355	Kevin Gross	.03	.01	.00	☐ 405	Juan Samuel	.08	.04	.01
☐ 356	Andy McGaffigan	.03	.01	.00	☐ 406	Von Hayes	.08	.04	.01
☐ 357	Brian Holman	.08	.04	.01	☐ 407	Ron Jones	.25	.12	.02
☐ 358	Dave Wainhouse	.10	.05	.01	☐ 408	Curt Ford	.03	.01	.00
☐ 359	Dennis Martinez	.06	.03	.00	☐ 409	Bob Walk	.03	.01	.00
☐ 360	Tim Burke	.06	.03	.00	☐ 410	Jeff Robinson	.06	.03	.00
☐ 361	Nelson Santovenia	.15	.07	.01	☐ 411	Jim Gott	.03	.01	.00
☐ 362	Tim Wallach	.08	.04	.01	☐ 412	Mike Dunne	.06	.03	.00
☐ 363	Spike Owen	.03	.01	.00	☐ 413	John Smiley	.06	.03	.00
☐ 364	Rex Hudler	.03	.01	.00	☐ 414	Bob Kipper	.03	.01	.00

		MINT	EXC	G-VG			MINT	EXC	G-VG
☐ 415	Brian Fisher	.03	.01	.00	☐ 465	Kelly Downs	.06	.03	.00
☐ 416	Doug Drabek	.06	.03	.00	☐ 466	Rick Reuschel	.06	.03	.00
☐ 417	Mike LaValliere	.03	.01	.00	☐ 467	Scott Garrelts	.06	.03	.00
☐ 418	Ken Oberkfell	.03	.01	.00	☐ 468	Wil Tejada	.03	.01	.00
☐ 419	Sid Bream	.03	.01	.00	☐ 469	Kirt Manwaring	.08	.04	.01
☐ 420	Austin Manahan	.10	.05	.01	☐ 470	Terry Kennedy	.03	.01	.00
☐ 421	Jose Lind	.03	.01	.00	☐ 471	Jose Uribe	.03	.01	.00
☐ 422	Bobby Bonilla	.08	.04	.01	☐ 472	Royce Clayton	.10	.05	.01
☐ 423	Glenn Wilson	.03	.01	.00	☐ 473	Robby Thompson	.03	.01	.00
☐ 424	Andy Van Slyke	.10	.05	.01	☐ 474	Kevin Mitchell	.30	.15	.03
☐ 425	Gary Redus	.03	.01	.00	☐ 475	Ernie Riles	.03	.01	.00
☐ 426	Barry Bonds	.08	.04	.01	☐ 476	Will Clark	.85	.40	.08
☐ 427	Don Heinkel	.03	.01	.00	☐ 477	Donell Nixon	.03	.01	.00
☐ 428	Ken Dayley	.03	.01	.00	☐ 478	Candy Maldonado	.03	.01	.00
☐ 429	Todd Worrell	.08	.04	.01	☐ 479	Tracy Jones	.03	.01	.00
☐ 430	Brad DuVall	.10	.05	.01	☐ 480	Brett Butler	.06	.03	.00
☐ 431	Jose DeLeon	.06	.03	.00	☐ 481	Checklist	.06	.01	.00
☐ 432	Joe Magrane	.08	.04	.01	☐ 482	Checklist	.06	.01	.00
☐ 433	John Ericks	.20	.10	.02	☐ 483	Checklist	.06	.01	.00
☐ 434	Frank DiPino	.03	.01	.00	☐ 484	Checklist	.06	.01	.00
☐ 435	Tony Pena	.06	.03	.00					
☐ 436	Ozzie Smith	.10	.05	.01					
☐ 437	Terry Pendleton	.03	.01	.00					
☐ 438	Jose Oquendo	.03	.01	.00					
☐ 439	Tim Jones	.08	.04	.01					
☐ 440	Pedro Guerrero	.10	.05	.01					
☐ 441	Milt Thompson	.03	.01	.00					
☐ 442	Willie McGee	.08	.04	.01					
☐ 443	Vince Coleman	.10	.05	.01					
☐ 444	Tom Brunansky	.08	.04	.01					
☐ 445	Walt Terrell	.03	.01	.00					
☐ 446	Eric Show	.03	.01	.00					
☐ 447	Mark Davis	.12	.06	.01					
☐ 448	Andy Benes	.85	.40	.08					
☐ 449	Ed Whitson	.03	.01	.00					
☐ 450	Dennis Rasmussen	.03	.01	.00					
☐ 451	Bruce Hurst	.08	.04	.01					
☐ 452	Pat Clements	.03	.01	.00					
☐ 453	Benito Santiago	.12	.06	.01					
☐ 454	Sandy Alomar, Jr.	.75	.35	.07					
☐ 455	Garry Templeton	.06	.03	.00					
☐ 456	Jack Clark	.10	.05	.01					
☐ 457	Tim Flannery	.03	.01	.00					
☐ 458	Roberto Alomar	.25	.12	.02					
☐ 459	Carmelo Martinez	.03	.01	.00					
☐ 460	John Kruk	.06	.03	.00					
☐ 461	Tony Gwynn	.20	.10	.02					
☐ 462	Jerald Clark	.20	.10	.02					
☐ 463	Don Robinson	.03	.01	.00					
☐ 464	Craig Lefferts	.06	.03	.00					

1981 Donruss

DAVE PARKER OUTFIELD

*The cards in this 605-card set measure 2 1/2"
by 3 1/2". In 1981 Donruss launched itself into
the baseball card market with a set containing
600 numbered cards and five unnumbered
checklists. Even though the five checklist cards
are unnumbered, they are numbered below
(601-605) for convenience in reference. The
cards are printed on thin stock and more than
one pose exists for several popular players.
The numerous errors of the first print run were*

later corrected by the company. These are
marked P1 and P2 in the checklist below.

		MINT	EXC	G-VG
	COMPLETE SET (P1)	33.00	15.00	3.00
	COMPLETE SET (P2)	27.00	13.50	2.70
	COMMON PLAYER (1-605)	.03	.01	.00
☐ 1	Ozzie Smith	.75	.15	.03
☐ 2	Rollie Fingers	.35	.17	.03
☐ 3	Rick Wise	.03	.01	.00
☐ 4	Gene Richards	.03	.01	.00
☐ 5	Alan Trammell	.45	.22	.04
☐ 6	Tom Brookens	.03	.01	.00
☐ 7A	Duffy Dyer P1	.10	.05	.01
	1980 batting average has decimal point			
☐ 7B	Duffy Dyer P2	.06	.03	.00
	1980 batting average has no decimal point			
☐ 8	Mark Fidrych	.10	.05	.01
☐ 9	Dave Rozema	.03	.01	.00
☐ 10	Ricky Peters	.03	.01	.00
☐ 11	Mike Schmidt	1.50	.75	.15
☐ 12	Willie Stargell	.40	.20	.04
☐ 13	Tim Foli	.03	.01	.00
☐ 14	Manny Sanguillen	.06	.03	.00
☐ 15	Grant Jackson	.03	.01	.00
☐ 16	Eddie Solomon	.03	.01	.00
☐ 17	Omar Moreno	.03	.01	.00
☐ 18	Joe Morgan	.45	.22	.04
☐ 19	Rafael Landestoy	.03	.01	.00
☐ 20	Bruce Bochy	.03	.01	.00
☐ 21	Joe Sambito	.03	.01	.00
☐ 22	Manny Trillo	.03	.01	.00
☐ 23A	Dave Smith P1	.35	.17	.03
	Line box around stats is not complete			
☐ 23B	Dave Smith P2	.35	.17	.03
	Box totally encloses stats at top			
☐ 24	Terry Puhl	.06	.03	.00
☐ 25	Bump Wills	.03	.01	.00
☐ 26A	John Ellis P1 ERR	.60	.30	.06
	Photo on front shows Danny Walton			
☐ 26B	John Ellis P2 COR	.10	.05	.01
☐ 27	Jim Kern	.03	.01	.00
☐ 28	Richie Zisk	.06	.03	.00
☐ 29	John Mayberry	.06	.03	.00
☐ 30	Bob Davis	.03	.01	.00

		MINT	EXC	G-VG
☐ 31	Jackson Todd	.03	.01	.00
☐ 32	Alvis Woods	.03	.01	.00
☐ 33	Steve Carlton	.65	.30	.06
☐ 34	Lee Mazzilli	.03	.01	.00
☐ 35	John Stearns	.03	.01	.00
☐ 36	Roy Lee Jackson	.03	.01	.00
☐ 37	Mike Scott	1.00	.50	.10
☐ 38	Lamar Johnson	.03	.01	.00
☐ 39	Kevin Bell	.03	.01	.00
☐ 40	Ed Farmer	.03	.01	.00
☐ 41	Ross Baumgarten	.03	.01	.00
☐ 42	Leo Sutherland	.03	.01	.00
☐ 43	Dan Meyer	.03	.01	.00
☐ 44	Ron Reed	.03	.01	.00
☐ 45	Mario Mendoza	.03	.01	.00
☐ 46	Rick Honeycutt	.03	.01	.00
☐ 47	Glenn Abbott	.03	.01	.00
☐ 48	Leon Roberts	.03	.01	.00
☐ 49	Rod Carew	.65	.30	.06
☐ 50	Bert Campaneris	.06	.03	.00
☐ 51A	Tom Donahue P1 ERR	.15	.07	.01
	Name on front misspelled Donahue			
☐ 51B	Tom Donohue P2 COR	.10	.05	.01
☐ 52	Dave Frost	.03	.01	.00
☐ 53	Ed Halicki	.03	.01	.00
☐ 54	Dan Ford	.03	.01	.00
☐ 55	Garry Maddox	.06	.03	.00
☐ 56A	Steve Garvey P1 "Surpassed 25 HR"	1.25	.60	.12
☐ 56B	Steve Garvey P2 "Surpassed 21 HR"	.65	.30	.06
☐ 57	Bill Russell	.06	.03	.00
☐ 58	Don Sutton	.30	.15	.03
☐ 59	Reggie Smith	.10	.05	.01
☐ 60	Rick Monday	.06	.03	.00
☐ 61	Ray Knight	.10	.05	.01
☐ 62	Johnny Bench	.75	.35	.07
☐ 63	Mario Soto	.10	.05	.01
☐ 64	Doug Bair	.03	.01	.00
☐ 65	George Foster	.20	.10	.02
☐ 66	Jeff Burroughs	.06	.03	.00
☐ 67	Keith Hernandez	.35	.17	.03
☐ 68	Tom Herr	.15	.07	.01
☐ 69	Bob Forsch	.06	.03	.00
☐ 70	John Fulgham	.03	.01	.00
☐ 71A	Bobby Bonds P1 ERR 986 lifetime HR	.40	.20	.04

		MINT	EXC	G-VG
☐ 71B	Bobby Bonds P2 COR .... 326 lifetime HR	.15	.07	.01
☐ 72A	Rennie Stennett P1 "breaking broke leg"	.10	.05	.01
☐ 72B	Rennie Stennett P2 Word "broke" deleted	.06	.03	.00
☐ 73	Joe Strain	.03	.01	.00
☐ 74	Ed Whitson	.06	.03	.00
☐ 75	Tom Griffin	.03	.01	.00
☐ 76	Billy North	.03	.01	.00
☐ 77	Gene Garber	.03	.01	.00
☐ 78	Mike Hargrove	.06	.03	.00
☐ 79	Dave Rosello	.03	.01	.00
☐ 80	Ron Hassey	.06	.03	.00
☐ 81	Sid Monge	.03	.01	.00
☐ 82A	Joe Charboneau P1 '78 highlights, "For some reason"	.15	.07	.01
☐ 82B	Joe Charboneau P2 phrase "For some reason" deleted	.10	.05	.01
☐ 83	Cecil Cooper	.15	.07	.01
☐ 84	Sal Bando	.06	.03	.00
☐ 85	Moose Haas	.06	.03	.00
☐ 86	Mike Caldwell	.03	.01	.00
☐ 87A	Larry Hisle P1 '77 highlights, line ends with "28 RBI"	.15	.07	.01
☐ 87B	Larry Hisle P2 correct line "28 HR"	.10	.05	.01
☐ 88	Luis Gomez	.03	.01	.00
☐ 89	Larry Parrish	.06	.03	.00
☐ 90	Gary Carter	.50	.25	.05
☐ 91	Bill Gullickson	.25	.12	.02
☐ 92	Fred Norman	.03	.01	.00
☐ 93	Tommy Hutton	.03	.01	.00
☐ 94	Carl Yastrzemski ...	1.00	.50	.10
☐ 95	Glenn Hoffman	.03	.01	.00
☐ 96	Dennis Eckersley ...	.25	.12	.02
☐ 97A	Tom Burgmeier P1 ERR Throws: Right	.10	.05	.01
☐ 97B	Tom Burgmeier P2 COR Throws: Left	.06	.03	.00
☐ 98	Win Remmerswaal ...	.03	.01	.00
☐ 99	Bob Horner	.15	.07	.01
☐ 100	George Brett	.90	.45	.09
☐ 101	Dave Chalk	.03	.01	.00
☐ 102	Dennis Leonard	.06	.03	.00
☐ 103	Renie Martin	.03	.01	.00

		MINT	EXC	G-VG
☐ 104	Amos Otis	.10	.05	.01
☐ 105	Graig Nettles	.15	.07	.01
☐ 106	Eric Soderholm	.03	.01	.00
☐ 107	Tommy John	.20	.10	.02
☐ 108	Tom Underwood	.03	.01	.00
☐ 109	Lou Piniella	.10	.05	.01
☐ 110	Mickey Klutts	.03	.01	.00
☐ 111	Bobby Murcer	.10	.05	.01
☐ 112	Eddie Murray	.80	.40	.08
☐ 113	Rick Dempsey	.06	.03	.00
☐ 114	Scott McGregor	.06	.03	.00
☐ 115	Ken Singleton	.10	.05	.01
☐ 116	Gary Roenicke	.03	.01	.00
☐ 117	Dave Revering	.03	.01	.00
☐ 118	Mike Norris	.03	.01	.00
☐ 119	Rickey Henderson ...	3.00	1.50	.30
☐ 120	Mike Heath	.03	.01	.00
☐ 121	Dave Cash	.03	.01	.00
☐ 122	Randy Jones	.03	.01	.00
☐ 123	Eric Rasmussen	.03	.01	.00
☐ 124	Jerry Mumphrey	.03	.01	.00
☐ 125	Richie Hebner	.03	.01	.00
☐ 126	Mark Wagner	.03	.01	.00
☐ 127	Jack Morris	.30	.15	.03
☐ 128	Dan Petry	.10	.05	.01
☐ 129	Bruce Robbins	.03	.01	.00
☐ 130	Champ Summers	.03	.01	.00
☐ 131A	Pete Rose P1 ...... last line ends with "see card 251"	2.00	1.00	.20
☐ 131B	Pete Rose P2 ...... last line corrected "see card 371"	1.25	.60	.12
☐ 132	Willie Stargell	.40	.20	.04
☐ 133	Ed Ott	.03	.01	.00
☐ 134	Jim Bibby	.03	.01	.00
☐ 135	Bert Blyleven	.20	.10	.02
☐ 136	Dave Parker	.30	.15	.03
☐ 137	Bill Robinson	.06	.03	.00
☐ 138	Enos Cabell	.03	.01	.00
☐ 139	Dave Bergman	.03	.01	.00
☐ 140	J.R. Richard	.10	.05	.01
☐ 141	Ken Forsch	.03	.01	.00
☐ 142	Larry Bowa UER (shortshop on front)	.15	.07	.01
☐ 143	Frank LaCorte UER (photo acutally Randy Niemann)	.03	.01	.00
☐ 144	Denny Walling	.03	.01	.00
☐ 145	Buddy Bell	.15	.07	.01

		MINT	EXC	G-VG
☐ 146	Ferguson Jenkins	.20	.10	.02
☐ 147	Dannny Darwin	.03	.01	.00
☐ 148	John Grubb	.03	.01	.00
☐ 149	Alfredo Griffin	.10	.05	.01
☐ 150	Jerry Garvin	.03	.01	.00
☐ 151	Paul Mirabella	.03	.01	.00
☐ 152	Rick Bosetti	.03	.01	.00
☐ 153	Dick Ruthven	.03	.01	.00
☐ 154	Frank Taveras	.03	.01	.00
☐ 155	Craig Swan	.03	.01	.00
☐ 156	Jeff Reardon	.75	.35	.07
☐ 157	Steve Henderson	.03	.01	.00
☐ 158	Jim Morrison	.03	.01	.00
☐ 159	Glenn Borgmann	.03	.01	.00
☐ 160	LaMarr Hoyt	.25	.12	.02
☐ 161	Rich Wortham	.03	.01	.00
☐ 162	Thad Bosley	.03	.01	.00
☐ 163	Julio Cruz	.03	.01	.00
☐ 164A	Del Unser P1	.10	.05	.01
	no "3B" heading			
☐ 164B	Del Unser P2	.06	.03	.00
	Batting record on back			
	corrected ("3B")			
☐ 165	Jim Anderson	.03	.01	.00
☐ 166	Jim Beattie	.03	.01	.00
☐ 167	Shane Rawley	.06	.03	.00
☐ 168	Joe Simpson	.03	.01	.00
☐ 169	Rod Carew	.65	.30	.06
☐ 170	Fred Patek	.06	.03	.00
☐ 171	Frank Tanana	.10	.05	.01
☐ 172	Alfredo Martinez	.03	.01	.00
☐ 173	Chris Knapp	.03	.01	.00
☐ 174	Joe Rudi	.06	.03	.00
☐ 175	Greg Luzinski	.15	.07	.01
☐ 176	Steve Garvey	.65	.30	.06
☐ 177	Joe Ferguson	.03	.01	.00
☐ 178	Bob Welch	.15	.07	.01
☐ 179	Dusty Baker	.10	.05	.01
☐ 180	Rudy Law	.03	.01	.00
☐ 181	Dave Concepcion	.15	.07	.01
☐ 182	Johnny Bench	.75	.35	.07
☐ 183	Mike LaCoss	.03	.01	.00
☐ 184	Ken Griffey	.12	.06	.01
☐ 185	Dave Collins	.03	.01	.00
☐ 186	Brian Asselstine	.03	.01	.00
☐ 187	Garry Templeton	.10	.05	.01
☐ 188	Mike Phillips	.03	.01	.00
☐ 189	Pete Vuckovich	.06	.03	.00
☐ 190	John Urrea	.03	.01	.00
☐ 191	Tony Scott	.03	.01	.00
☐ 192	Darrell Evans	.15	.07	.01
☐ 193	Milt May	.03	.01	.00
☐ 194	Bob Knepper	.06	.03	.00
☐ 195	Randy Moffitt	.03	.01	.00
☐ 196	Larry Herndon	.03	.01	.00
☐ 197	Rick Camp	.03	.01	.00
☐ 198	Andre Thornton	.06	.03	.00
☐ 199	Tom Veryzer	.03	.01	.00
☐ 200	Gary Alexander	.03	.01	.00
☐ 201	Rick Waits	.03	.01	.00
☐ 202	Rick Manning	.03	.01	.00
☐ 203	Paul Molitor	.35	.17	.03
☐ 204	Jim Gantner	.06	.03	.00
☐ 205	Paul Mitchell	.03	.01	.00
☐ 206	Reggie Cleveland	.03	.01	.00
☐ 207	Sixto Lezcano	.03	.01	.00
☐ 208	Bruce Benedict	.03	.01	.00
☐ 209	Rodney Scott	.03	.01	.00
☐ 210	John Tamargo	.03	.01	.00
☐ 211	Bill Lee	.06	.03	.00
☐ 212	Andre Dawson	.40	.20	.04
☐ 213	Rowland Office	.03	.01	.00
☐ 214	Carl Yastrzemski	1.00	.50	.10
☐ 215	Jerry Remy	.03	.01	.00
☐ 216	Mike Torrez	.03	.01	.00
☐ 217	Skip Lockwood	.03	.01	.00
☐ 218	Fred Lynn	.20	.10	.02
☐ 219	Chris Chambliss	.10	.05	.01
☐ 220	Willie Aikens	.03	.01	.00
☐ 221	John Wathan	.10	.05	.01
☐ 222	Dan Quisenberry	.15	.07	.01
☐ 223	Willie Wilson	.15	.07	.01
☐ 224	Clint Hurdle	.03	.01	.00
☐ 225	Bob Watson	.06	.03	.00
☐ 226	Jim Spencer	.03	.01	.00
☐ 227	Ron Guidry	.20	.10	.02
☐ 228	Reggie Jackson	1.00	.50	.10
☐ 229	Oscar Gamble	.06	.03	.00
☐ 230	Jeff Cox	.03	.01	.00
☐ 231	Luis Tiant	.10	.05	.01
☐ 232	Rich Dauer	.03	.01	.00
☐ 233	Dan Graham	.03	.01	.00
☐ 234	Mike Flanagan	.10	.05	.01
☐ 235	John Lowenstein	.03	.01	.00
☐ 236	Benny Ayala	.03	.01	.00
☐ 237	Wayne Gross	.03	.01	.00
☐ 238	Rick Langford	.03	.01	.00
☐ 239	Tony Armas	.10	.05	.01
☐ 240A	Bob Lacy P1 ERR	.30	.15	.03
	Name misspelled			

		MINT	EXC	G-VG
	Bob "Lacy"			
☐ 240B	Bob Lacey P2 COR	.10	.05	.01
☐ 241	Gene Tenace	.06	.03	.00
☐ 242	Bob Shirley	.03	.01	.00
☐ 243	Gary Lucas	.06	.03	.00
☐ 244	Jerry Turner	.03	.01	.00
☐ 245	John Wockenfuss	.03	.01	.00
☐ 246	Stan Papi	.03	.01	.00
☐ 247	Milt Wilcox	.03	.01	.00
☐ 248	Dan Schatzeder	.03	.01	.00
☐ 249	Steve Kemp	.10	.05	.01
☐ 250	Jim Lentine	.03	.01	.00
☐ 251	Pete Rose	1.25	.60	.12
☐ 252	Bill Madlock	.15	.07	.01
☐ 253	Dale Berra	.03	.01	.00
☐ 254	Kent Tekulve	.06	.03	.00
☐ 255	Enrique Romo	.03	.01	.00
☐ 256	Mike Easler	.06	.03	.00
☐ 257	Chuck Tanner MG	.06	.03	.00
☐ 258	Art Howe	.10	.05	.01
☐ 259	Alan Ashby	.03	.01	.00
☐ 260	Nolan Ryan	1.75	.85	.17
☐ 261A	Vern Ruhle P1 ERR	.60	.30	.06
	Photo on front			
	actually Ken Forsch			
☐ 261B	Vern Ruhle P2 COR	.10	.05	.01
☐ 262	Bob Boone	.20	.10	.02
☐ 263	Cesar Cedeno	.10	.05	.01
☐ 264	Jeff Leonard	.15	.07	.01
☐ 265	Pat Putnam	.03	.01	.00
☐ 266	Jon Matlack	.06	.03	.00
☐ 267	Dave Rajsich	.03	.01	.00
☐ 268	Billy Sample	.03	.01	.00
☐ 269	Damaso Garcia	.10	.05	.01
☐ 270	Tom Buskey	.03	.01	.00
☐ 271	Joey McLaughlin	.03	.01	.00
☐ 272	Barry Bonnell	.03	.01	.00
☐ 273	Tug McGraw	.10	.05	.01
☐ 274	Mike Jorgensen	.03	.01	.00
☐ 275	Pat Zachry	.03	.01	.00
☐ 276	Neil Allen	.06	.03	.00
☐ 277	Joel Youngblood	.03	.01	.00
☐ 278	Greg Pryor	.03	.01	.00
☐ 279	Britt Burns	.15	.07	.01
☐ 280	Rich Dotson	.35	.17	.03
☐ 281	Chet Lemon	.06	.03	.00
☐ 282	Rusty Kuntz	.03	.01	.00
☐ 283	Ted Cox	.03	.01	.00
☐ 284	Sparky Lyle	.10	.05	.01
☐ 285	Larry Cox	.03	.01	.00

		MINT	EXC	G-VG
☐ 286	Floyd Bannister	.06	.03	.00
☐ 287	Byron McLaughlin	.03	.01	.00
☐ 288	Rodney Craig	.03	.01	.00
☐ 289	Bobby Grich	.10	.05	.01
☐ 290	Dickie Thon	.10	.05	.01
☐ 291	Mark Clear	.06	.03	.00
☐ 292	Dave Lemanczyk	.03	.01	.00
☐ 293	Jason Thompson	.03	.01	.00
☐ 294	Rick Miller	.03	.01	.00
☐ 295	Lonnie Smith	.15	.07	.01
☐ 296	Ron Cey	.10	.05	.01
☐ 297	Steve Yeager	.03	.01	.00
☐ 298	Bobby Castillo	.03	.01	.00
☐ 299	Manny Mota	.06	.03	.00
☐ 300	Jay Johnstone	.06	.03	.00
☐ 301	Dan Driessen	.03	.01	.00
☐ 302	Joe Nolan	.03	.01	.00
☐ 303	Paul Householder	.03	.01	.00
☐ 304	Harry Spilman	.03	.01	.00
☐ 305	Cesar Geronimo	.03	.01	.00
☐ 306A	Gary Mathews P1			
	ERR	.30	.15	.03
	Name misspelled			
☐ 306B	Gary Matthews P2	.10	.05	.01
	COR			
☐ 307	Ken Reitz	.03	.01	.00
☐ 308	Ted Simmons	.15	.07	.01
☐ 309	John Littlefield	.03	.01	.00
☐ 310	George Frazier	.03	.01	.00
☐ 311	Dane Iorg	.03	.01	.00
☐ 312	Mike Ivie	.03	.01	.00
☐ 313	Dennis Littlejohn	.03	.01	.00
☐ 314	Gary Lavelle	.03	.01	.00
☐ 315	Jack Clark	.30	.15	.03
☐ 316	Jim Wohlford	.03	.01	.00
☐ 317	Rick Matula	.03	.01	.00
☐ 318	Toby Harrah	.06	.03	.00
☐ 319A	Dwane Kuiper P1			
	ERR	.15	.07	.01
	Name misspelled			
☐ 319B	Duane Kuiper P2			
	COR	.10	.05	.01
☐ 320	Len Barker	.03	.01	.00
☐ 321	Victor Cruz	.03	.01	.00
☐ 322	Dell Alston	.03	.01	.00
☐ 323	Robin Yount	1.00	.50	.10
☐ 324	Charlie Moore	.03	.01	.00
☐ 325	Lary Sorensen	.03	.01	.00
☐ 326A	Gorman Thomas P1	.30	.15	.03
	2nd line on back:			

		MINT	EXC	G-VG
☐ 326B	Gorman Thomas P2 "30 HR mark 4th"	.10	.05	.01
☐ 327	Bob Rodgers MG "30 HR mark 3rd"	.06	.03	.00
☐ 328	Phil Niekro	.30	.15	.03
☐ 329	Chris Speier	.03	.01	.00
☐ 330A	Steve Rodgers P1 ERR Name misspelled	.30	.15	.03
☐ 330B	Steve Rogers P2 COR	.10	.05	.01
☐ 331	Woodie Fryman	.03	.01	.00
☐ 332	Warren Cromartie	.03	.01	.00
☐ 333	Jerry White	.03	.01	.00
☐ 334	Tony Perez	.20	.10	.02
☐ 335	Carlton Fisk	.40	.20	.04
☐ 336	Dick Drago	.03	.01	.00
☐ 337	Steve Renko	.03	.01	.00
☐ 338	Jim Rice	.30	.15	.03
☐ 339	Jerry Royster	.03	.01	.00
☐ 340	Frank White	.10	.05	.01
☐ 341	Jamie Quirk	.03	.01	.00
☐ 342A	Paul Spittorff P1 ERR Name misspelled	.15	.07	.01
☐ 342B	Paul Splittorff P2 COR	.10	.05	.01
☐ 343	Marty Pattin	.03	.01	.00
☐ 344	Pete LaCock	.03	.01	.00
☐ 345	Willie Randolph	.10	.05	.01
☐ 346	Rick Cerone	.06	.03	.00
☐ 347	Rich Gossage	.20	.10	.02
☐ 348	Reggie Jackson	1.00	.50	.10
☐ 349	Ruppert Jones	.03	.01	.00
☐ 350	Dave McKay	.03	.01	.00
☐ 351	Yogi Berra CO	.20	.10	.02
☐ 352	Doug DeCinces	.06	.03	.00
☐ 353	Jim Palmer	.60	.30	.06
☐ 354	Tippy Martinez	.03	.01	.00
☐ 355	Al Bumbry	.03	.01	.00
☐ 356	Earl Weaver MG	.10	.05	.01
☐ 357A	Bob Picciolo P1 ERR Name misspelled	.15	.07	.01
☐ 357B	Rob Picciolo P2 COR	.06	.03	.00
☐ 358	Matt Keough	.03	.01	.00
☐ 359	Dwayne Murphy	.03	.01	.00
☐ 360	Brian Kingman	.03	.01	.00
☐ 361	Bill Fahey	.03	.01	.00
☐ 362	Steve Mura	.03	.01	.00
☐ 363	Dennis Kinney	.03	.01	.00
☐ 364	Dave Winfield	.50	.25	.05
☐ 365	Lou Whitaker	.30	.15	.03

		MINT	EXC	G-VG
☐ 366	Lance Parrish	.25	.12	.02
☐ 367	Tim Corcoran	.03	.01	.00
☐ 368	Pat Underwood	.03	.01	.00
☐ 369	Al Cowens	.06	.03	.00
☐ 370	Sparky Anderson MG	.10	.05	.01
☐ 371	Pete Rose	1.25	.60	.12
☐ 372	Phil Garner	.03	.01	.00
☐ 373	Steve Nicosia	.03	.01	.00
☐ 374	John Candelaria	.10	.05	.01
☐ 375	Don Robinson	.06	.03	.00
☐ 376	Lee Lacy	.03	.01	.00
☐ 377	John Milner	.03	.01	.00
☐ 378	Craig Reynolds	.03	.01	.00
☐ 379A	Luis Pujois P1 ERR Name misspelled	.15	.07	.01
☐ 379B	Luis Pujols P2 COR	.06	.03	.00
☐ 380	Joe Niekro	.10	.05	.01
☐ 381	Joaquin Andujar	.10	.05	.01
☐ 382	Keith Moreland	.30	.15	.03
☐ 383	Jose Cruz	.10	.05	.01
☐ 384	Bill Virdon MG	.06	.03	.00
☐ 385	Jim Sundberg	.06	.03	.00
☐ 386	Doc Medich	.03	.01	.00
☐ 387	Al Oliver	.12	.06	.01
☐ 388	Jim Norris	.03	.01	.00
☐ 389	Bob Bailor	.03	.01	.00
☐ 390	Ernie Whitt	.10	.05	.01
☐ 391	Otto Velez	.03	.01	.00
☐ 392	Roy Howell	.03	.01	.00
☐ 393	Bob Walk	.30	.15	.03
☐ 394	Doug Flynn	.03	.01	.00
☐ 395	Pete Falcone	.03	.01	.00
☐ 396	Tom Hausman	.03	.01	.00
☐ 397	Elliott Maddox	.03	.01	.00
☐ 398	Mike Squires	.03	.01	.00
☐ 399	Marvis Foley	.03	.01	.00
☐ 400	Steve Trout	.06	.03	.00
☐ 401	Wayne Nordhagen	.03	.01	.00
☐ 402	Tony LaRussa MG	.06	.03	.00
☐ 403	Bruce Bochte	.03	.01	.00
☐ 404	Bake McBride	.03	.01	.00
☐ 405	Jerry Narron	.03	.01	.00
☐ 406	Rob Dressler	.03	.01	.00
☐ 407	Dave Heaverlo	.03	.01	.00
☐ 408	Tom Paciorek	.03	.01	.00
☐ 409	Carney Lansford	.25	.10	.02
☐ 410	Brian Downing	.06	.03	.00
☐ 411	Don Aase	.03	.01	.00
☐ 412	Jim Barr	.03	.01	.00
☐ 413	Don Baylor	.15	.07	.01

		MINT	EXC	G-VG
☐ 414	Jim Fregosi	.06	.03	.00
☐ 415	Dallas Green MG	.10	.05	.01
☐ 416	Dave Lopes	.10	.05	.01
☐ 417	Jerry Reuss	.06	.03	.00
☐ 418	Rick Sutcliffe	.30	.15	.03
☐ 419	Derrel Thomas	.03	.01	.00
☐ 420	Tom Lasorda MG	.10	.05	.01
☐ 421	Charles Leibrandt	.30	.15	.03
☐ 422	Tom Seaver	.60	.30	.06
☐ 423	Ron Oester	.06	.03	.00
☐ 424	Junior Kennedy	.03	.01	.00
☐ 425	Tom Seaver	.60	.30	.06
☐ 426	Bobby Cox MG	.03	.01	.00
☐ 427	Leon Durham	.30	.15	.03
☐ 428	Terry Kennedy	.06	.03	.00
☐ 429	Silvio Martinez	.03	.01	.00
☐ 430	George Hendrick	.06	.03	.00
☐ 431	Red Schoendienst MG	.15	.07	.01
☐ 432	Johnnie LeMaster	.03	.01	.00
☐ 433	Vida Blue	.10	.05	.01
☐ 434	John Montefusco	.06	.03	.00
☐ 435	Terry Whitfield	.03	.01	.00
☐ 436	Dave Bristol MG	.03	.01	.00
☐ 437	Dale Murphy	1.25	.60	.12
☐ 438	Jerry Dybzinski	.03	.01	.00
☐ 439	Jorge Orta	.03	.01	.00
☐ 440	Wayne Garland	.03	.01	.00
☐ 441	Miguel Dilone	.03	.01	.00
☐ 442	Dave Garcia MG	.03	.01	.00
☐ 443	Don Money	.03	.01	.00
☐ 444A	Buck Martinez P1 ERR (reverse negative)	.15	.07	.01
☐ 444B	Buck Martinez P2 COR	.06	.03	.00
☐ 445	Jerry Augustine	.03	.01	.00
☐ 446	Ben Oglivie	.06	.03	.00
☐ 447	Jim Slaton	.03	.01	.00
☐ 448	Doyle Alexander	.10	.05	.01
☐ 449	Tony Bernazard	.06	.03	.00
☐ 450	Scott Sanderson	.06	.03	.00
☐ 451	David Palmer	.06	.03	.00
☐ 452	Stan Bahnsen	.03	.01	.00
☐ 453	Dick Williams MG	.06	.03	.00
☐ 454	Rick Burleson	.06	.03	.00
☐ 455	Gary Allenson	.03	.01	.00
☐ 456	Bob Stanley	.03	.01	.00
☐ 457A	John Tudor P1 ERR lifetime W-L "9.7"	1.25	.60	.12
☐ 457B	John Tudor P2 COR corrected "9-7"	1.00	.50	.10
☐ 458	Dwight Evans	.25	.12	.02
☐ 459	Glenn Hubbard	.03	.01	.00
☐ 460	U.L. Washington	.03	.01	.00
☐ 461	Larry Gura	.06	.03	.00
☐ 462	Rich Gale	.03	.01	.00
☐ 463	Hal McRae	.06	.03	.00
☐ 464	Jim Frey MG	.03	.01	.00
☐ 465	Bucky Dent	.12	.06	.01
☐ 466	Dennis Werth	.03	.01	.00
☐ 467	Ron Davis	.03	.01	.00
☐ 468	Reggie Jackson	1.00	.50	.10
☐ 469	Bobby Brown	.03	.01	.00
☐ 470	Mike Davis	.25	.12	.02
☐ 471	Gaylord Perry	.30	.15	.03
☐ 472	Mark Belanger	.06	.03	.00
☐ 473	Jim Palmer	.65	.30	.06
☐ 474	Sammy Stewart	.03	.01	.00
☐ 475	Tim Stoddard	.03	.01	.00
☐ 476	Steve Stone	.06	.03	.00
☐ 477	Jeff Newman	.03	.01	.00
☐ 478	Steve McCatty	.03	.01	.00
☐ 479	Billy Martin MG	.20	.10	.02
☐ 480	Mitchell Page	.03	.01	.00
☐ 481	Cy Young Winner 1980 Steve Carlton	.30	.15	.03
☐ 482	Bill Buckner	.15	.07	.01
☐ 483A	Ivan DeJesus P1 ERR lifetime hits "702"	.10	.05	.01
☐ 483B	Ivan DeJesus P2 COR lifetime hits "642"	.06	.03	.00
☐ 484	Cliff Johnson	.03	.01	.00
☐ 485	Lenny Randle	.03	.01	.00
☐ 486	Larry Milbourne	.03	.01	.00
☐ 487	Roy Smalley	.03	.01	.00
☐ 488	John Castino	.03	.01	.00
☐ 489	Ron Jackson	.03	.01	.00
☐ 490A	Dave Roberts P1 Career Highlights: "Showed pop in"	.10	.05	.01
☐ 490B	Dave Roberts P2 "Declared himself"	.06	.03	.00
☐ 491	MVP: George Brett	.60	.30	.06
☐ 492	Mike Cubbage	.03	.01	.00
☐ 493	Rob Wilfong	.03	.01	.00
☐ 494	Danny Goodwin	.03	.01	.00

		MINT	EXC	G-VG
☐ 495	Jose Morales	.03	.01	.00
☐ 496	Mickey Rivers	.06	.03	.00
☐ 497	Mike Edwards	.03	.01	.00
☐ 498	Mike Sadek	.03	.01	.00
☐ 499	Lenn Sakata	.03	.01	.00
☐ 500	Gene Michael MG	.03	.01	.00
☐ 501	Dave Roberts	.03	.01	.00
☐ 502	Steve Dillard	.03	.01	.00
☐ 503	Jim Essian	.03	.01	.00
☐ 504	Rance Mulliniks	.03	.01	.00
☐ 505	Darrell Porter	.03	.01	.00
☐ 506	Joe Torre MG	.10	.05	.01
☐ 507	Terry Crowley	.03	.01	.00
☐ 508	Bill Travers	.03	.01	.00
☐ 509	Nelson Norman	.03	.01	.00
☐ 510	Bob McClure	.03	.01	.00
☐ 511	Steve Howe	.10	.05	.01
☐ 512	Dave Rader	.03	.01	.00
☐ 513	Mick Kelleher	.03	.01	.00
☐ 514	Kiko Garcia	.03	.01	.00
☐ 515	Larry Biittner	.03	.01	.00
☐ 516A	Willie Norwood P1	.10	.05	.01
	Career Highlights:			
	"Spent most of"			
☐ 516B	Willie Norwood P2	.06	.03	.00
	"Traded to Seattle"			
☐ 517	Bo Diaz	.06	.03	.00
☐ 518	Juan Beniquez	.03	.01	.00
☐ 519	Scot Thompson	.03	.01	.00
☐ 520	Jim Tracy	.03	.01	.00
☐ 521	Carlos Lezcano	.03	.01	.00
☐ 522	Joe Amalfitano MG	.03	.01	.00
☐ 523	Preston Hanna	.03	.01	.00
☐ 524A	Ray Burris P1	.10	.05	.01
	Career Highlights:			
	"Went on ..."			
☐ 524B	Ray Burris P2	.06	.03	.00
	"Drafted by ..."			
☐ 525	Broderick Perkins	.03	.01	.00
☐ 526	Mickey Hatcher	.10	.05	.01
☐ 527	John Goryl MG	.03	.01	.00
☐ 528	Dick Davis	.03	.01	.00
☐ 529	Butch Wynegar	.03	.01	.00
☐ 530	Sal Butera	.03	.01	.00
☐ 531	Jerry Koosman	.10	.05	.01
☐ 532A	Geoff Zahn P1	.10	.05	.01
	Career Highlights:			
	"Was 2nd in"			
☐ 532B	Geoff Zahn P2	.06	.03	.00
	"Signed a 3 year"			

		MINT	EXC	G-VG
☐ 533	Dennis Martinez	.10	.05	.01
☐ 534	Gary Thomasson	.03	.01	.00
☐ 535	Steve Macko	.03	.01	.00
☐ 536	Jim Kaat	.20	.10	.02
☐ 537	Best Hitters	1.25	.60	.12
	George Brett			
	Rod Carew			
☐ 538	Tim Raines	5.00	2.50	.50
☐ 539	Keith Smith	.03	.01	.00
☐ 540	Ken Macha	.03	.01	.00
☐ 541	Burt Hooton	.03	.01	.00
☐ 542	Butch Hobson	.03	.01	.00
☐ 543	Bill Stein	.03	.01	.00
☐ 544	Dave Stapleton	.03	.01	.00
☐ 545	Bob Pate	.03	.01	.00
☐ 546	Doug Corbett	.06	.03	.00
☐ 547	Darrell Jackson	.03	.01	.00
☐ 548	Pete Redfern	.03	.01	.00
☐ 549	Roger Erickson	.03	.01	.00
☐ 550	Al Hrabosky	.06	.03	.00
☐ 551	Dick Tidrow	.03	.01	.00
☐ 552	Dave Ford	.03	.01	.00
☐ 553	Dave Kingman	.15	.07	.01
☐ 554A	Mike Vail P1	.10	.05	.01
	Career Highlights:			
	"After two ..."			
☐ 554B	Mike Vail P2	.06	.03	.00
	"Traded to ..."			
☐ 555A	Jerry Martin P1	.10	.05	.01
	Career Highlights:			
	"Overcame a ..."			
☐ 555B	Jerry Martin P2	.06	.03	.00
	"Traded to ..."			
☐ 556A	Jesus Figueroa P1	.10	.05	.01
	Career Highlights:			
	"Had an ..."			
☐ 556B	Jesus Figueroa P2	.06	.03	.00
	"Traded to ..."			
☐ 557	Don Stanhouse	.03	.01	.00
☐ 558	Barry Foote	.03	.01	.00
☐ 559	Tim Blackwell	.03	.01	.00
☐ 560	Bruce Sutter	.20	.10	.02
☐ 561	Rick Reuschel	.20	.10	.02
☐ 562	Lynn McGlothen	.03	.01	.00
☐ 563A	Bob Owchinko P1	.10	.05	.01
	Career Highlights:			
	"Traded to ..."			
☐ 563B	Bob Owchinko P2	.06	.03	.00
	"Involved in a ..."			
☐ 564	John Verhoeven	.03	.01	.00

		MINT	EXC	G-VG
☐ 565	Ken Landreaux	.03	.01	.00
☐ 566A	Glen Adams P1 ERR	.15	.07	.01
	Name misspelled			
☐ 566B	Glenn Adams P2			
	COR	.06	.03	.00
☐ 567	Hosken Powell	.03	.01	.00
☐ 568	Dick Noles	.03	.01	.00
☐ 569	Danny Ainge	.40	.20	.04
☐ 570	Bobby Mattick MG ..	.03	.01	.00
☐ 571	Joe Lefebvre	.06	.03	.00
☐ 572	Bobby Clark	.03	.01	.00
☐ 573	Dennis Lamp	.03	.01	.00
☐ 574	Randy Lerch	.03	.01	.00
☐ 575	Mookie Wilson	.50	.25	.05
☐ 576	Ron LeFlore	.06	.03	.00
☐ 577	Jim Dwyer	.03	.01	.00
☐ 578	Bill Castro	.03	.01	.00
☐ 579	Greg Minton	.03	.01	.00
☐ 580	Mark Littell	.03	.01	.00
☐ 581	Andy Hassler	.03	.01	.00
☐ 582	Dave Stieb	.35	.17	.03
☐ 583	Ken Oberkfell	.03	.01	.00
☐ 584	Larry Bradford	.03	.01	.00
☐ 585	Fred Stanley	.03	.01	.00
☐ 586	Bill Caudill	.03	.01	.00
☐ 587	Doug Capilla	.03	.01	.00
☐ 588	George Riley	.03	.01	.00
☐ 589	Willie Hernandez ...	.15	.07	.01
☐ 590	MVP: Mike Schmidt	.75	.35	.07
☐ 591	Cy Young Winner			
	1980:	.06	.03	.00
	Steve Stone			
☐ 592	Rick Sofield	.03	.01	.00
☐ 593	Bombo Rivera	.03	.01	.00
☐ 594	Gary Ward	.06	.03	.00
☐ 595A	Dave Edwards P1 ..	.10	.05	.01
	Career Highlights:			
	"Sidelined the"			
☐ 595B	Dave Edwards P2 ..	.06	.03	.00
	"Traded to ..."			
☐ 596	Mike Proly	.03	.01	.00
☐ 597	Tommy Boggs	.03	.01	.00
☐ 598	Greg Gross	.03	.01	.00
☐ 599	Elias Sosa	.03	.01	.00
☐ 600	Pat Kelly	.03	.01	.00
☐ 601A	Checklist 1 P1 ERR	.10	.05	.01
	unnumbered			
	(51 Donahue)			
☐ 601B	Checklist 1 P2 COR .	.75	.35	.07
	unnumbered			

		MINT	EXC	G-VG
	(51 Donohue)			
☐ 602	Checklist 2	.10	.05	.01
☐ 603A	Checklist 3 P1 ERR .	.10	.05	.01
	unnumbered			
	(306 Mathews)			
☐ 603B	Checklist 3 P2 COR .	.10	.05	.01
	unnumbered			
	(306 Matthews)			
☐ 604A	Checklist 4 P1 ERR .	.10	.05	.01
	unnumbered			
	(379 Pujois)			
☐ 604B	Checklist 4 P2 COR .	.10	.05	.01
	unnumbered			
	(379 Pujols)			
☐ 605A	Checklist 5 P1 ERR .	.10	.05	.01
	unnumbered			
	(566 Glen Adams)			
☐ 605B	Checklist 5 P2 COR .	.10	.05	.01
	unnumbered			
	(566 Glenn Adams)			

1982 Donruss

The 1982 Donruss set contains 653 numbered cards and the seven unnumbered checklists; each card measures 2 ½" by 3 ½". The first 26 cards of this set are entitled Donruss Diamond Kings (DK) and feature the artwork of Dick Perez of Perez-Steele Galleries. The set was marketed with puzzle pieces rather than with bubble gum. There are 63 pieces to the puzzle, which, when put together, make a col-

lage of Babe Ruth entitled "Hall of Fame Diamond King." The card stock in this year's Donruss cards is considerably thicker than that of the 1981 cards. The seven unnumbered checklist cards are arbitrarily assigned numbers 654 through 660 and are listed at the end of the list below.

			MINT	EXC	G-VG
	COMPLETE SET (660)		35.00	17.50	3.50
	COMMON PLAYER (1-660)		.03	.01	.00
☐	1	Pete Rose DK	1.75	.50	.10
☐	2	Gary Carter DK	.45	.22	.04
☐	3	Steve Garvey DK	.50	.25	.05
☐	4	Vida Blue DK	.08	.04	.01
☐	5A	Alan Trammel DK ERR	1.50	.75	.15
		(name misspelled)			
☐	5B	Alan Trammell DK COR	.40	.20	.04
☐	6	Len Barker DK	.06	.03	.00
☐	7	Dwight Evans DK	.20	.10	.02
☐	8	Rod Carew DK	.50	.25	.05
☐	9	George Hendrick DK	.06	.03	.00
☐	10	Phil Niekro DK	.25	.12	.02
☐	11	Richie Zisk DK	.06	.03	.00
☐	12	Dave Parker DK	.20	.10	.02
☐	13	Nolan Ryan DK	1.00	.50	.10
☐	14	Ivan DeJesus DK	.06	.03	.00
☐	15	George Brett DK	.75	.35	.07
☐	16	Tom Seaver DK	.50	.25	.05
☐	17	Dave Kingman DK	.10	.05	.01
☐	18	Dave Winfield DK	.45	.22	.04
☐	19	Mike Norris DK	.06	.03	.00
☐	20	Carlton Fisk DK	.20	.10	.02
☐	21	Ozzie Smith DK	.25	.12	.02
☐	22	Roy Smalley DK	.06	.03	.00
☐	23	Buddy Bell DK	.08	.04	.01
☐	24	Ken Singleton DK	.08	.04	.01
☐	25	John Mayberry DK	.06	.03	.00
☐	26	Gorman Thomas DK	.08	.04	.01
☐	27	Earl Weaver MG	.06	.03	.00
☐	28	Rollie Fingers	.20	.10	.02
☐	29	Sparky Anderson MG	.06	.03	.00
☐	30	Dennis Eckersley	.20	.09	.02
☐	31	Dave Winfield	.50	.25	.05
☐	32	Burt Hooton	.03	.01	.00
☐	33	Rick Waits	.03	.01	.00
☐	34	George Brett	.80	.40	.08
☐	35	Steve McCatty	.03	.01	.00

			MINT	EXC	G-VG
☐	36	Steve Rogers	.03	.01	.00
☐	37	Bill Stein	.03	.01	.00
☐	38	Steve Renko	.03	.01	.00
☐	39	Mike Squires	.03	.01	.00
☐	40	George Hendrick	.06	.03	.00
☐	41	Bob Knepper	.08	.04	.01
☐	42	Steve Carlton	.60	.30	.06
☐	43	Larry Biittner	.03	.01	.00
☐	44	Chris Welsh	.03	.01	.00
☐	45	Steve Nicosia	.03	.01	.00
☐	46	Jack Clark	.25	.12	.02
☐	47	Chris Chambliss	.06	.03	.00
☐	48	Ivan DeJesus	.03	.01	.00
☐	49	Lee Mazzilli	.03	.01	.00
☐	50	Julio Cruz	.03	.01	.00
☐	51	Pete Redfern	.03	.01	.00
☐	52	Dave Stieb	.20	.10	.02
☐	53	Doug Corbett	.03	.01	.00
☐	54	Jorge Bell	6.50	3.25	.65
☐	55	Joe Simpson	.03	.01	.00
☐	56	Rusty Staub	.12	.06	.01
☐	57	Hector Cruz	.03	.01	.00
☐	58	Claudell Washington	.08	.04	.01
☐	59	Enrique Romo	.03	.01	.00
☐	60	Gary Lavelle	.03	.01	.00
☐	61	Tim Flannery	.03	.01	.00
☐	62	Joe Nolan	.03	.01	.00
☐	63	Larry Bowa	.15	.07	.01
☐	64	Sixto Lezcano	.03	.01	.00
☐	65	Joe Sambito	.03	.01	.00
☐	66	Bruce Kison	.03	.01	.00
☐	67	Wayne Nordhagen	.03	.01	.00
☐	68	Woodie Fryman	.03	.01	.00
☐	69	Billy Sample	.03	.01	.00
☐	70	Amos Otis	.08	.04	.01
☐	71	Matt Keough	.03	.01	.00
☐	72	Toby Harrah	.06	.03	.00
☐	73	Dave Righetti	1.50	.75	.15
☐	74	Carl Yastrzemski	1.00	.50	.10
☐	75	Bob Welch	.10	.05	.01
☐	76A	Alan Trammell ERR	1.50	.75	.15
		(name misspelled)			
☐	76B	Alan Trammell CORR	.40	.20	.04
☐	77	Rick Dempsey	.03	.01	.00
☐	78	Paul Molitor	.25	.12	.02
☐	79	Dennis Martinez	.08	.04	.01
☐	80	Jim Slaton	.03	.01	.00
☐	81	Champ Summers	.03	.01	.00
☐	82	Carney Lansford	.20	.07	.01
☐	83	Barry Foote	.03	.01	.00

		MINT	EXC	G-VG
☐ 84	Steve Garvey	.50	.25	.05
☐ 85	Rick Manning	.03	.01	.00
☐ 86	John Wathan	.06	.03	.00
☐ 87	Brian Kingman	.03	.01	.00
☐ 88	Andre Dawson	.35	.17	.03
☐ 89	Jim Kern	.03	.01	.00
☐ 90	Bobby Grich	.08	.04	.01
☐ 91	Bob Forsch	.03	.01	.00
☐ 92	Art Howe	.08	.04	.01
☐ 93	Marty Bystrom	.03	.01	.00
☐ 94	Ozzie Smith	.40	.20	.04
☐ 95	Dave Parker	.25	.12	.02
☐ 96	Doyle Alexander	.06	.03	.00
☐ 97	Al Hrabosky	.06	.03	.00
☐ 98	Frank Taveras	.03	.01	.00
☐ 99	Tim Blackwell	.03	.01	.00
☐ 100	Floyd Bannister	.06	.03	.00
☐ 101	Alfredo Griffin	.08	.04	.01
☐ 102	Dave Engle	.03	.01	.00
☐ 103	Mario Soto	.06	.03	.00
☐ 104	Ross Baumgarten	.03	.01	.00
☐ 105	Ken Singleton	.08	.04	.01
☐ 106	Ted Simmons	.15	.07	.01
☐ 107	Jack Morris	.20	.10	.02
☐ 108	Bob Watson	.06	.03	.00
☐ 109	Dwight Evans	.20	.10	.02
☐ 110	Tom Lasorda MG	.08	.04	.01
☐ 111	Bert Blyleven	.20	.10	.02
☐ 112	Dan Quisenberry	.12	.06	.01
☐ 113	Rickey Henderson	1.50	.75	.15
☐ 114	Gary Carter	.45	.22	.04
☐ 115	Brian Downing	.06	.03	.00
☐ 116	Al Oliver	.10	.05	.01
☐ 117	LaMarr Hoyt	.06	.03	.00
☐ 118	Cesar Cedeno	.08	.04	.01
☐ 119	Keith Moreland	.03	.01	.00
☐ 120	Bob Shirley	.03	.01	.00
☐ 121	Terry Kennedy	.03	.01	.00
☐ 122	Frank Pastore	.03	.01	.00
☐ 123	Gene Garber	.03	.01	.00
☐ 124	Tony Pena	.35	.17	.03
☐ 125	Allen Ripley	.03	.01	.00
☐ 126	Randy Martz	.03	.01	.00
☐ 127	Richie Zisk	.03	.01	.00
☐ 128	Mike Scott	.40	.20	.04
☐ 129	Lloyd Moseby	.25	.12	.02
☐ 130	Rob Wilfong	.03	.01	.00
☐ 131	Tim Stoddard	.03	.01	.00
☐ 132	Gorman Thomas	.10	.05	.01
☐ 133	Dan Petry	.06	.03	.00
☐ 134	Bob Stanley	.03	.01	.00
☐ 135	Lou Piniella	.12	.06	.01
☐ 136	Pedro Guerrero	.60	.30	.06
☐ 137	Len Barker	.03	.01	.00
☐ 138	Rich Gale	.03	.01	.00
☐ 139	Wayne Gross	.03	.01	.00
☐ 140	Tim Wallach	1.00	.50	.10
☐ 141	Gene Mauch MG	.03	.01	.00
☐ 142	Doc Medich	.03	.01	.00
☐ 143	Tony Bernazard	.03	.01	.00
☐ 144	Bill Virdon MG	.03	.01	.00
☐ 145	John Littlefield	.03	.01	.00
☐ 146	Dave Bergman	.03	.01	.00
☐ 147	Dick Davis	.03	.01	.00
☐ 148	Tom Seaver	.50	.25	.05
☐ 149	Matt Sinatro	.03	.01	.00
☐ 150	Chuck Tanner MG	.03	.01	.00
☐ 151	Leon Durham	.06	.03	.00
☐ 152	Gene Tenace	.03	.01	.00
☐ 153	Al Bumbry	.03	.01	.00
☐ 154	Mark Brouhard	.03	.01	.00
☐ 155	Rick Peters	.03	.01	.00
☐ 156	Jerry Remy	.03	.01	.00
☐ 157	Rick Reuschel	.15	.07	.01
☐ 158	Steve Howe	.03	.01	.00
☐ 159	Alan Bannister	.03	.01	.00
☐ 160	U.L. Washington	.03	.01	.00
☐ 161	Rick Langford	.03	.01	.00
☐ 162	Bill Gullickson	.06	.03	.00
☐ 163	Mark Wagner	.03	.01	.00
☐ 164	Geoff Zahn	.03	.01	.00
☐ 165	Ron LeFlore	.06	.03	.00
☐ 166	Dane Iorg	.03	.01	.00
☐ 167	Joe Niekro	.10	.05	.01
☐ 168	Pete Rose	1.25	.60	.12
☐ 169	Dave Collins	.03	.01	.00
☐ 170	Rick Wise	.03	.01	.00
☐ 171	Jim Bibby	.03	.01	.00
☐ 172	Larry Herndon	.03	.01	.00
☐ 173	Bob Horner	.15	.07	.01
☐ 174	Steve Dillard	.03	.01	.00
☐ 175	Mookie Wilson	.12	.06	.01
☐ 176	Dan Meyer	.03	.01	.00
☐ 177	Fernando Arroyo	.03	.01	.00
☐ 178	Jackson Todd	.03	.01	.00
☐ 179	Darrell Jackson	.03	.01	.00
☐ 180	Alvis Woods	.03	.01	.00
☐ 181	Jim Anderson	.03	.01	.00
☐ 182	Dave Kingman	.15	.07	.01
☐ 183	Steve Henderson	.03	.01	.00

		MINT	EXC	G-VG
☐ 184	Brian Asselstine	.03	.01	.00
☐ 185	Rod Scurry	.03	.01	.00
☐ 186	Fred Breining	.03	.01	.00
☐ 187	Danny Boone	.03	.01	.00
☐ 188	Junior Kennedy	.03	.01	.00
☐ 189	Sparky Lyle	.10	.05	.01
☐ 190	Whitey Herzog MG	.06	.03	.00
☐ 191	Dave Smith	.08	.04	.01
☐ 192	Ed Ott	.03	.01	.00
☐ 193	Greg Luzinski	.12	.06	.01
☐ 194	Bill Lee	.06	.03	.00
☐ 195	Don Zimmer MG	.06	.03	.00
☐ 196	Hal McRae	.06	.03	.00
☐ 197	Mike Norris	.03	.01	.00
☐ 198	Duane Kuiper	.03	.01	.00
☐ 199	Rick Cerone	.03	.01	.00
☐ 200	Jim Rice	.30	.15	.03
☐ 201	Steve Yeager	.03	.01	.00
☐ 202	Tom Brookens	.03	.01	.00
☐ 203	Jose Morales	.03	.01	.00
☐ 204	Roy Howell	.03	.01	.00
☐ 205	Tippy Martinez	.03	.01	.00
☐ 206	Moose Haas	.03	.01	.00
☐ 207	Al Cowens	.03	.01	.00
☐ 208	Dave Stapleton	.03	.01	.00
☐ 209	Bucky Dent	.12	.06	.01
☐ 210	Ron Cey	.10	.05	.01
☐ 211	Jorge Orta	.03	.01	.00
☐ 212	Jamie Quirk	.03	.01	.00
☐ 213	Jeff Jones	.03	.01	.00
☐ 214	Tim Raines	1.00	.50	.10
☐ 215	Jon Matlack	.03	.01	.00
☐ 216	Rod Carew	.50	.25	.05
☐ 217	Jim Kaat	.15	.07	.01
☐ 218	Joe Pittman	.03	.01	.00
☐ 219	Larry Christenson	.03	.01	.00
☐ 220	Juan Bonilla	.03	.01	.00
☐ 221	Mike Easler	.03	.01	.00
☐ 222	Vida Blue	.08	.04	.01
☐ 223	Rick Camp	.03	.01	.00
☐ 224	Mike Jorgensen	.03	.01	.00
☐ 225	Jody Davis	.35	.17	.03
☐ 226	Mike Parrott	.03	.01	.00
☐ 227	Jim Clancy	.03	.01	.00
☐ 228	Hosken Powell	.03	.01	.00
☐ 229	Tom Hume	.03	.01	.00
☐ 230	Britt Burns	.03	.01	.00
☐ 231	Jim Palmer	.60	.30	.06
☐ 232	Bob Rodgers MG	.03	.01	.00
☐ 233	Milt Wilcox	.03	.01	.00

		MINT	EXC	G-VG
☐ 234	Dave Revering	.03	.01	.00
☐ 235	Mike Torrez	.03	.01	.00
☐ 236	Robert Castillo	.03	.01	.00
☐ 237	Von Hayes	1.00	.50	.10
☐ 238	Renie Martin	.03	.01	.00
☐ 239	Dwayne Murphy	.03	.01	.00
☐ 240	Rodney Scott	.03	.01	.00
☐ 241	Fred Patek	.03	.01	.00
☐ 242	Mickey Rivers	.06	.03	.00
☐ 243	Steve Trout	.03	.01	.00
☐ 244	Jose Cruz	.10	.05	.01
☐ 245	Manny Trillo	.03	.01	.00
☐ 246	Lary Sorensen	.03	.01	.00
☐ 247	Dave Edwards	.03	.01	.00
☐ 248	Dan Driessen	.03	.01	.00
☐ 249	Tommy Boggs	.03	.01	.00
☐ 250	Dale Berra	.03	.01	.00
☐ 251	Ed Whitson	.06	.03	.00
☐ 252	Lee Smith	.60	.30	.06
☐ 253	Tom Paciorek	.03	.01	.00
☐ 254	Pat Zachry	.03	.01	.00
☐ 255	Luis Leal	.03	.01	.00
☐ 256	John Castino	.03	.01	.00
☐ 257	Rich Dauer	.03	.01	.00
☐ 258	Cecil Cooper	.15	.07	.01
☐ 259	Dave Rozema	.03	.01	.00
☐ 260	John Tudor	.20	.10	.02
☐ 261	Jerry Mumphrey	.03	.01	.00
☐ 262	Jay Johnstone	.06	.03	.00
☐ 263	Bo Diaz	.06	.03	.00
☐ 264	Dennis Leonard	.06	.03	.00
☐ 265	Jim Spencer	.03	.01	.00
☐ 266	John Milner	.03	.01	.00
☐ 267	Don Aase	.03	.01	.00
☐ 268	Jim Sundberg	.06	.03	.00
☐ 269	Lamar Johnson	.03	.01	.00
☐ 270	Frank LaCorte	.03	.01	.00
☐ 271	Barry Evans	.03	.01	.00
☐ 272	Enos Cabell	.03	.01	.00
☐ 273	Del Unser	.03	.01	.00
☐ 274	George Foster	.12	.06	.01
☐ 275	Brett Butler	.75	.35	.07
☐ 276	Lee Lacy	.03	.01	.00
☐ 277	Ken Reitz	.03	.01	.00
☐ 278	Keith Hernandez	.35	.17	.03
☐ 279	Doug DeCinces	.06	.03	.00
☐ 280	Charlie Moore	.03	.01	.00
☐ 281	Lance Parrish	.20	.10	.02
☐ 282	Ralph Houk MG	.03	.01	.00
☐ 283	Rich Gossage	.20	.10	.02

		MINT	EXC	G-VG
☐ 284	Jerry Reuss	.06	.03	.00
☐ 285	Mike Stanton	.03	.01	.00
☐ 286	Frank White	.06	.03	.00
☐ 287	Bob Owchinko	.03	.01	.00
☐ 288	Scott Sanderson	.03	.01	.00
☐ 289	Bump Wills	.03	.01	.00
☐ 290	Dave Frost	.03	.01	.00
☐ 291	Chet Lemon	.06	.03	.00
☐ 292	Tito Landrum	.03	.01	.00
☐ 293	Vern Ruhle	.03	.01	.00
☐ 294	Mike Schmidt	1.00	.50	.10
☐ 295	Sam Mejias	.03	.01	.00
☐ 296	Gary Lucas	.03	.01	.00
☐ 297	John Candelaria	.08	.04	.01
☐ 298	Jerry Martin	.03	.01	.00
☐ 299	Dale Murphy	.90	.45	.09
☐ 300	Mike Lum	.03	.01	.00
☐ 301	Tom Hausman	.03	.01	.00
☐ 302	Glenn Abbott	.03	.01	.00
☐ 303	Roger Erickson	.03	.01	.00
☐ 304	Otto Velez	.03	.01	.00
☐ 305	Danny Goodwin	.03	.01	.00
☐ 306	John Mayberry	.06	.03	.00
☐ 307	Lenny Randle	.03	.01	.00
☐ 308	Bob Bailor	.03	.01	.00
☐ 309	Jerry Morales	.03	.01	.00
☐ 310	Rufino Linares	.03	.01	.00
☐ 311	Kent Tekulve	.06	.03	.00
☐ 312	Joe Morgan	.35	.17	.03
☐ 313	John Urrea	.03	.01	.00
☐ 314	Paul Householder	.03	.01	.00
☐ 315	Garry Maddox	.06	.03	.00
☐ 316	Mike Ramsey	.03	.01	.00
☐ 317	Alan Ashby	.03	.01	.00
☐ 318	Bob Clark	.03	.01	.00
☐ 319	Tony LaRussa MG	.06	.03	.00
☐ 320	Charlie Lea	.03	.01	.00
☐ 321	Danny Darwin	.03	.01	.00
☐ 322	Cesar Geronimo	.03	.01	.00
☐ 323	Tom Underwood	.03	.01	.00
☐ 324	Andre Thornton	.06	.03	.00
☐ 325	Rudy May	.03	.01	.00
☐ 326	Frank Tanana	.08	.04	.01
☐ 327	Dave Lopes	.08	.04	.01
☐ 328	Richie Hebner	.03	.01	.00
☐ 329	Mike Flanagan	.08	.04	.01
☐ 330	Mike Caldwell	.03	.01	.00
☐ 331	Scott McGregor	.06	.03	.00
☐ 332	Jerry Augustine	.03	.01	.00
☐ 333	Stan Papi	.03	.01	.00
☐ 334	Rick Miller	.03	.01	.00
☐ 335	Graig Nettles	.12	.06	.01
☐ 336	Dusty Baker	.06	.03	.00
☐ 337	Dave Garcia MG	.03	.01	.00
☐ 338	Larry Gura	.06	.03	.00
☐ 339	Cliff Johnson	.03	.01	.00
☐ 340	Warren Cromartie	.03	.01	.00
☐ 341	Steve Comer	.03	.01	.00
☐ 342	Rick Burleson	.06	.03	.00
☐ 343	John Martin	.03	.01	.00
☐ 344	Craig Reynolds	.03	.01	.00
☐ 345	Mike Proly	.03	.01	.00
☐ 346	Ruppert Jones	.03	.01	.00
☐ 347	Omar Moreno	.03	.01	.00
☐ 348	Greg Minton	.03	.01	.00
☐ 349	Rick Mahler	.25	.12	.02
☐ 350	Alex Trevino	.03	.01	.00
☐ 351	Mike Krukow	.06	.03	.00
☐ 352A	Shane Rawley ERR (photo actually Jim Anderson)	.75	.35	.07
☐ 352B	Shane Rawley COR	.10	.05	.01
☐ 353	Garth Iorg	.03	.01	.00
☐ 354	Pete Mackanin	.03	.01	.00
☐ 355	Paul Moskau	.03	.01	.00
☐ 356	Richard Dotson	.06	.03	.00
☐ 357	Steve Stone	.06	.03	.00
☐ 358	Larry Hisle	.06	.03	.00
☐ 359	Aurelio Lopez	.03	.01	.00
☐ 360	Oscar Gamble	.03	.01	.00
☐ 361	Tom Burgmeier	.03	.01	.00
☐ 362	Terry Forster	.06	.03	.00
☐ 363	Joe Charboneau	.06	.03	.00
☐ 364	Ken Brett	.03	.01	.00
☐ 365	Tony Armas	.08	.04	.01
☐ 366	Chris Speier	.03	.01	.00
☐ 367	Fred Lynn	.20	.10	.02
☐ 368	Buddy Bell	.12	.06	.01
☐ 369	Jim Essian	.03	.01	.00
☐ 370	Terry Puhl	.03	.01	.00
☐ 371	Greg Gross	.03	.01	.00
☐ 372	Bruce Sutter	.15	.07	.01
☐ 373	Joe Lefebvre	.03	.01	.00
☐ 374	Ray Knight	.08	.04	.01
☐ 375	Bruce Benedict	.03	.01	.00
☐ 376	Tim Foli	.03	.01	.00
☐ 377	Al Holland	.03	.01	.00
☐ 378	Ken Kravec	.03	.01	.00
☐ 379	Jeff Burroughs	.03	.01	.00
☐ 380	Pete Falcone	.03	.01	.00

		MINT	EXC	G-VG
☐ 381	Ernie Whitt	.06	.03	.00
☐ 382	Brad Havens	.03	.01	.00
☐ 383	Terry Crowley	.03	.01	.00
☐ 384	Don Money	.03	.01	.00
☐ 385	Dan Schatzeder	.03	.01	.00
☐ 386	Gary Allenson	.03	.01	.00
☐ 387	Yogi Berra MG	.15	.07	.01
☐ 388	Ken Landreaux	.03	.01	.00
☐ 389	Mike Hargrove	.06	.03	.00
☐ 390	Darryl Motley	.06	.03	.00
☐ 391	Dave McKay	.03	.01	.00
☐ 392	Stan Bahnsen	.03	.01	.00
☐ 393	Ken Forsch	.03	.01	.00
☐ 394	Mario Mendoza	.03	.01	.00
☐ 395	Jim Morrison	.03	.01	.00
☐ 396	Mike Ivie	.03	.01	.00
☐ 397	Broderick Perkins	.03	.01	.00
☐ 398	Darrell Evans	.12	.06	.01
☐ 399	Ron Reed	.03	.01	.00
☐ 400	Johnny Bench	.65	.30	.06
☐ 401	Steve Bedrosian	1.00	.50	.10
☐ 402	Bill Robinson	.06	.03	.00
☐ 403	Bill Buckner	.12	.06	.01
☐ 404	Ken Oberkfell	.03	.01	.00
☐ 405	Cal Ripken Jr.	8.50	4.25	.85
☐ 406	Jim Gantner	.03	.01	.00
☐ 407	Kirk Gibson	1.75	.85	.17
☐ 408	Tony Perez	.18	.09	.01
☐ 409	Tommy John	.18	.09	.01
☐ 410	Dave Stewart	3.75	1.85	.37
☐ 411	Dan Spillner	.03	.01	.00
☐ 412	Willie Aikens	.03	.01	.00
☐ 413	Mike Heath	.03	.01	.00
☐ 414	Ray Burris	.03	.01	.00
☐ 415	Leon Roberts	.03	.01	.00
☐ 416	Mike Witt	.75	.35	.07
☐ 417	Bob Molinaro	.03	.01	.00
☐ 418	Steve Braun	.03	.01	.00
☐ 419	Nolan Ryan	1.75	.85	.17
☐ 420	Tug McGraw	.10	.05	.01
☐ 421	Dave Concepcion	.12	.06	.01
☐ 422A	Juan Eichelberger ERR (photo actually Gary Lucas)	.65	.30	.06
☐ 422B	Juan Eichelberger COR	.08	.04	.01
☐ 423	Rick Rhoden	.08	.04	.01
☐ 424	Frank Robinson MG	.15	.07	.01
☐ 425	Eddie Miller	.03	.01	.00
☐ 426	Bill Caudill	.03	.01	.00

		MINT	EXC	G-VG
☐ 427	Doug Flynn	.03	.01	.00
☐ 428	Larry Andersen UER (misspelled Anderson on card front)	.03	.01	.00
☐ 429	Al Williams	.03	.01	.00
☐ 430	Jerry Garvin	.03	.01	.00
☐ 431	Glenn Adams	.03	.01	.00
☐ 432	Barry Bonnell	.03	.01	.00
☐ 433	Jerry Narron	.03	.01	.00
☐ 434	John Stearns	.03	.01	.00
☐ 435	Mike Tyson	.03	.01	.00
☐ 436	Glenn Hubbard	.03	.01	.00
☐ 437	Eddie Solomon	.03	.01	.00
☐ 438	Jeff Leonard	.08	.04	.01
☐ 439	Randy Bass	.06	.03	.00
☐ 440	Mike LaCoss	.03	.01	.00
☐ 441	Gary Matthews	.06	.03	.00
☐ 442	Mark Littell	.03	.01	.00
☐ 443	Don Sutton	.30	.15	.03
☐ 444	John Harris	.03	.01	.00
☐ 445	Vada Pinson CO	.06	.03	.00
☐ 446	Elias Sosa	.03	.01	.00
☐ 447	Charlie Hough	.06	.03	.00
☐ 448	Willie Wilson	.12	.06	.01
☐ 449	Fred Stanley	.03	.01	.00
☐ 450	Tom Veryzer	.03	.01	.00
☐ 451	Ron Davis	.03	.01	.00
☐ 452	Mark Clear	.03	.01	.00
☐ 453	Bill Russell	.06	.03	.00
☐ 454	Lou Whitaker	.25	.12	.02
☐ 455	Dan Graham	.03	.01	.00
☐ 456	Reggie Cleveland	.03	.01	.00
☐ 457	Sammy Stewart	.03	.01	.00
☐ 458	Pete Vuckovich	.08	.04	.01
☐ 459	John Wockenfuss	.03	.01	.00
☐ 460	Glenn Hoffman	.03	.01	.00
☐ 461	Willie Randolph	.10	.05	.01
☐ 462	Fernando Valenzuela	.90	.45	.09
☐ 463	Ron Hassey	.03	.01	.00
☐ 464	Paul Splittorff	.03	.01	.00
☐ 465	Rob Picciolo	.03	.01	.00
☐ 466	Larry Parrish	.06	.03	.00
☐ 467	Johnny Grubb	.03	.01	.00
☐ 468	Dan Ford	.03	.01	.00
☐ 469	Silvio Martinez	.03	.01	.00
☐ 470	Kiko Garcia	.03	.01	.00
☐ 471	Bob Boone	.15	.07	.01
☐ 472	Luis Salazar	.10	.05	.01
☐ 473	Randy Niemann	.03	.01	.00
☐ 474	Tom Griffin	.03	.01	.00

		MINT	EXC	G-VG				MINT	EXC	G-VG
☐ 475	Phil Niekro	.30	.15	.03	☐ 525	Dick Ruthven		.03	.01	.00
☐ 476	Hubie Brooks	.40	.20	.04	☐ 526	John McNamara MG		.06	.03	.00
☐ 477	Dick Tidrow	.03	.01	.00	☐ 527	Larry McWilliams		.03	.01	.00
☐ 478	Jim Beattie	.03	.01	.00	☐ 528	Johnny Ray		.75	.35	.07
☐ 479	Damaso Garcia	.06	.03	.00	☐ 529	Pat Tabler		.60	.30	.06
☐ 480	Mickey Hatcher	.06	.03	.00	☐ 530	Tom Herr		.10	.05	.01
☐ 481	Joe Price	.03	.01	.00	☐ 531A	San Diego Chicken		.90	.45	.09
☐ 482	Ed Farmer	.03	.01	.00		(with TM)				
☐ 483	Eddie Murray	.50	.25	.05	☐ 531B	San Diego Chicken		.75	.35	.07
☐ 484	Ben Oglivie	.06	.03	.00		(without TM)				
☐ 485	Kevin Saucier	.03	.01	.00	☐ 532	Sal Butera		.03	.01	.00
☐ 486	Bobby Murcer	.10	.05	.01	☐ 533	Mike Griffin		.03	.01	.00
☐ 487	Bill Campbell	.03	.01	.00	☐ 534	Kelvin Moore		.03	.01	.00
☐ 488	Reggie Smith	.08	.04	.01	☐ 535	Reggie Jackson		.75	.35	.07
☐ 489	Wayne Garland	.03	.01	.00	☐ 536	Ed Romero		.03	.01	.00
☐ 490	Jim Wright	.03	.01	.00	☐ 537	Derrel Thomas		.03	.01	.00
☐ 491	Billy Martin MG	.20	.10	.02	☐ 538	Mike O'Berry		.03	.01	.00
☐ 492	Jim Fanning MG	.03	.01	.00	☐ 539	Jack O'Connor		.03	.01	.00
☐ 493	Don Baylor	.15	.07	.01	☐ 540	Bob Ojeda		.60	.30	.06
☐ 494	Rick Honeycutt	.03	.01	.00	☐ 541	Roy Lee Jackson		.03	.01	.00
☐ 495	Carlton Fisk	.35	.17	.03	☐ 542	Lynn Jones		.03	.01	.00
☐ 496	Denny Walling	.03	.01	.00	☐ 543	Gaylord Perry		.30	.15	.03
☐ 497	Bake McBride	.03	.01	.00	☐ 544A	Phil Garner ERR		.75	.35	.07
☐ 498	Darrell Porter	.03	.01	.00		(reverse negative)				
☐ 499	Gene Richards	.03	.01	.00	☐ 544B	Phil Garner COR		.10	.05	.01
☐ 500	Ron Oester	.03	.01	.00	☐ 545	Garry Templeton		.08	.04	.01
☐ 501	Ken Dayley	.20	.10	.02	☐ 546	Rafael Ramirez		.03	.01	.00
☐ 502	Jason Thompson	.03	.01	.00	☐ 547	Jeff Reardon		.20	.07	.01
☐ 503	Milt May	.03	.01	.00	☐ 548	Ron Guidry		.25	.12	.02
☐ 504	Doug Bird	.03	.01	.00	☐ 549	Tim Laudner		.25	.12	.02
☐ 505	Bruce Bochte	.03	.01	.00	☐ 550	John Henry Johnson		.03	.01	.00
☐ 506	Neil Allen	.06	.03	.00	☐ 551	Chris Bando		.03	.01	.00
☐ 507	Joey McLaughlin	.03	.01	.00	☐ 552	Bobby Brown		.03	.01	.00
☐ 508	Butch Wynegar	.03	.01	.00	☐ 553	Larry Bradford		.03	.01	.00
☐ 509	Gary Roenicke	.03	.01	.00	☐ 554	Scott Fletcher		.40	.20	.04
☐ 510	Robin Yount	1.00	.50	.10	☐ 555	Jerry Royster		.03	.01	.00
☐ 511	Dave Tobik	.03	.01	.00	☐ 556	Shooty Babitt		.03	.01	.00
☐ 512	Rich Gedman	.40	.20	.04		(spelled Babbitt				
☐ 513	Gene Nelson	.08	.04	.01		on front)				
☐ 514	Rick Monday	.06	.03	.00	☐ 557	Kent Hrbek		3.00	1.50	.30
☐ 515	Miguel Dilone	.03	.01	.00	☐ 558	Yankee Winners		.12	.06	.01
☐ 516	Clint Hurdle	.03	.01	.00		Ron Guidry				
☐ 517	Jeff Newman	.03	.01	.00		Tommy John				
☐ 518	Grant Jackson	.03	.01	.00	☐ 559	Mark Bomback		.03	.01	.00
☐ 519	Andy Hassler	.03	.01	.00	☐ 560	Julio Valdez		.03	.01	.00
☐ 520	Pat Putnam	.03	.01	.00	☐ 561	Buck Martinez		.03	.01	.00
☐ 521	Greg Pryor	.03	.01	.00	☐ 562	Mike Marshall		1.00	.50	.10
☐ 522	Tony Scott	.03	.01	.00		(Dodger hitter)				
☐ 523	Steve Mura	.03	.01	.00	☐ 563	Rennie Stennett		.03	.01	.00
☐ 524	Johnnie LeMaster	.03	.01	.00	☐ 564	Steve Crawford		.03	.01	.00

		MINT	EXC	G-VG			MINT	EXC	G-VG
☐ 565	Bob Babcock	.03	.01	.00	☐ 608	Garry Hancock	.03	.01	.00
☐ 566	Johnny Podres CO	.06	.03	.00	☐ 609	Jerry Turner	.03	.01	.00
☐ 567	Paul Serna	.03	.01	.00	☐ 610	Bob Bonner	.03	.01	.00
☐ 568	Harold Baines	.75	.35	.07	☐ 611	Jim Dwyer	.03	.01	.00
☐ 569	Dave LaRoche	.03	.01	.00	☐ 612	Terry Bulling	.03	.01	.00
☐ 570	Lee May	.03	.01	.00	☐ 613	Joel Youngblood	.03	.01	.00
☐ 571	Gary Ward	.06	.03	.00	☐ 614	Larry Milbourne	.03	.01	.00
☐ 572	John Denny	.06	.03	.00	☐ 615	Gene Roof	.06	.03	.00
☐ 573	Roy Smalley	.03	.01	.00		(name on front			
☐ 574	Bob Brenly	.20	.10	.02		is Phil Roof)			
☐ 575	Bronx Bombers	.45	.22	.04	☐ 616	Keith Drumwright	.03	.01	.00
	Reggie Jackson				☐ 617	Dave Rosello	.03	.01	.00
	Dave Winfield				☐ 618	Rickey Keeton	.03	.01	.00
☐ 576	Luis Pujols	.03	.01	.00	☐ 619	Dennis Lamp	.03	.01	.00
☐ 577	Butch Hobson	.03	.01	.00	☐ 620	Sid Monge	.03	.01	.00
☐ 578	Harvey Kuenn MG	.06	.03	.00	☐ 621	Jerry White	.03	.01	.00
☐ 579	Cal Ripken Sr. CO	.08	.04	.01	☐ 622	Luis Aguayo	.03	.01	.00
☐ 580	Juan Berenguer	.03	.01	.00	☐ 623	Jamie Easterly	.03	.01	.00
☐ 581	Benny Ayala	.03	.01	.00	☐ 624	Steve Sax	2.75	1.35	.27
☐ 582	Vance Law	.20	.10	.02	☐ 625	Dave Roberts	.03	.01	.00
☐ 583	Rick Leach	.03	.01	.00	☐ 626	Rick Bosetti	.03	.01	.00
☐ 584	George Frazier	.03	.01	.00	☐ 627	Terry Francona	.08	.04	.01
☐ 585	Phillies Finest	1.00	.50	.10	☐ 628	Pride of Reds	.50	.25	.05
	Pete Rose					Tom Seaver			
	Mike Schmidt					Johnny Bench			
☐ 586	Joe Rudi	.06	.03	.00	☐ 629	Paul Mirabella	.03	.01	.00
☐ 587	Juan Beniquez	.03	.01	.00	☐ 630	Rance Mulliniks	.03	.01	.00
☐ 588	Luis DeLeon	.06	.03	.00	☐ 631	Kevin Hickey	.03	.01	.00
☐ 589	Craig Swan	.03	.01	.00	☐ 632	Reid Nichols	.03	.01	.00
☐ 590	Dave Chalk	.03	.01	.00	☐ 633	Dave Geisel	.03	.01	.00
☐ 591	Billy Gardner MG	.03	.01	.00	☐ 634	Ken Griffey	.10	.05	.01
☐ 592	Sal Bando	.06	.03	.00	☐ 635	Bob Lemon MG	.10	.05	.01
☐ 593	Bert Campaneris	.06	.03	.00	☐ 636	Orlando Sanchez	.03	.01	.00
☐ 594	Steve Kemp	.06	.03	.00	☐ 637	Bill Almon	.03	.01	.00
☐ 595A	Randy Lerch ERR	.65	.30	.06	☐ 638	Danny Ainge	.15	.07	.01
	(Braves)				☐ 639	Willie Stargell	.40	.20	.04
☐ 595B	Randy Lerch COR	.06	.03	.00	☐ 640	Bob Sykes	.03	.01	.00
	(Brewers)				☐ 641	Ed Lynch	.06	.03	.00
☐ 596	Bryan Clark	.03	.01	.00	☐ 642	John Ellis	.03	.01	.00
☐ 597	Dave Ford	.03	.01	.00	☐ 643	Ferguson Jenkins	.15	.07	.01
☐ 598	Mike Scioscia	.25	.12	.02	☐ 644	Lenn Sakata	.03	.01	.00
☐ 599	John Lowenstein	.03	.01	.00	☐ 645	Julio Gonzalez	.03	.01	.00
☐ 600	Rene Lachemann MG	.06	.03	.00	☐ 646	Jesse Orosco	.06	.03	.00
☐ 601	Mick Kelleher	.03	.01	.00	☐ 647	Jerry Dybzinski	.03	.01	.00
☐ 602	Ron Jackson	.03	.01	.00	☐ 648	Tommy Davis	.06	.03	.00
☐ 603	Jerry Koosman	.08	.04	.01	☐ 649	Ron Gardenhire	.06	.03	.00
☐ 604	Dave Goltz	.03	.01	.00	☐ 650	Felipe Alou CO	.06	.03	.00
☐ 605	Ellis Valentine	.03	.01	.00	☐ 651	Harvey Haddix CO	.03	.01	.00
☐ 606	Lonnie Smith	.10	.05	.01	☐ 652	Willie Upshaw	.06	.03	.00
☐ 607	Joaquin Andujar	.10	.05	.01	☐ 653	Bill Madlock	.10	.05	.01

	MINT	EXC	G-VG
☐ **654A** DK Checklist .... (unnumbered) (with Trammel)	.25	.03	.01
☐ **654B** DK Checklist .... (unnumbered) (with Trammel)	.12	.02	.01
☐ **655** Checklist 1 .... (unnumbered)	.08	.01	.00
☐ **656** Checklist 2 .... (unnumbered)	.08	.01	.00
☐ **657** Checklist 3 .... (unnumbered)	.08	.01	.00
☐ **658** Checklist 4 .... (unnumbered)	.08	.01	.00
☐ **659** Checklist 5 .... (unnumbered)	.08	.01	.00
☐ **660** Checklist 6 .... (unnumbered)	.08	.01	.00

1983 Donruss

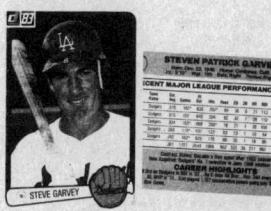

*The cards in this 660-card set measure 2 ½"
by 3 ½". The 1983 Donruss baseball set,
issued with a 63-piece Diamond King puzzle,
again leads off with a 26-card Diamond King
(DK) series. Of the remaining 634 cards, two
are combination cards, one portrays the San
Diego Chicken, one shows the completed Ty*

*Cobb puzzle, and seven are unnumbered
checklist cards. The seven unnumbered checklist cards are arbitrarily assigned numbers 654
through 660 and are listed at the end of the list
below. The Donruss logo and the year of issue
are shown in the upper left corner of the obverse. The card backs have black print on
yellow and white and are numbered on a small
ball design. The complete set price below includes only the more common of each variation
pair.*

	MINT	EXC	G-VG
COMPLETE SET (660)	65.00	32.50	6.50
COMMON PLAYER (1-660)	.03	.01	.00

		MINT	EXC	G-VG
☐	1 Fern. Valenzuela DK	.50	.10	.02
☐	2 Rollie Fingers DK ...	.20	.10	.02
☐	3 Reggie Jackson DK ..	.50	.25	.05
☐	4 Jim Palmer DK	.35	.17	.03
☐	5 Jack Morris DK	.15	.07	.01
☐	6 George Foster DK ..	.10	.05	.01
☐	7 Jim Sundberg DK ...	.06	.03	.00
☐	8 Willie Stargell DK ...	.35	.17	.03
☐	9 Dave Stieb DK	.15	.07	.01
☐	10 Joe Niekro DK	.08	.04	.01
☐	11 Rickey Henderson DK	.75	.35	.07
☐	12 Dale Murphy DK	.60	.30	.06
☐	13 Toby Harrah DK	.06	.03	.00
☐	14 Bill Buckner DK	.08	.04	.01
☐	15 Willie Wilson DK ...	.10	.05	.01
☐	16 Steve Carlton DK ...	.40	.20	.04
☐	17 Ron Guidry DK	.20	.10	.02
☐	18 Steve Rogers DK ...	.06	.03	.00
☐	19 Kent Hrbek DK	.40	.20	.04
☐	20 Keith Hernandez DK .	.30	.15	.03
☐	21 Floyd Bannister DK .	.06	.03	.00
☐	22 Johnny Bench DK ...	.50	.25	.05
☐	23 Britt Burns DK	.06	.03	.00
☐	24 Joe Morgan DK	.35	.17	.03
☐	25 Carl Yastrzemski DK	.80	.40	.08
☐	26 Terry Kennedy DK ..	.06	.03	.00
☐	27 Gary Roenicke	.03	.01	.00
☐	28 Dwight Bernard	.03	.01	.00
☐	29 Pat Underwood	.03	.01	.00
☐	30 Gary Allenson	.03	.01	.00
☐	31 Ron Guidry	.18	.09	.01
☐	32 Burt Hooton	.03	.01	.00
☐	33 Chris Bando	.03	.01	.00
☐	34 Vida Blue	.08	.04	.01

			MINT	EXC	G-VG				MINT	EXC	G-VG
☐	35	Rickey Henderson ..	.90	.45	.09	☐	84	Ron Cey	.10	.05	.01
☐	36	Ray Burris	.03	.01	.00	☐	85	Miguel Dilone	.03	.01	.00
☐	37	John Butcher	.03	.01	.00	☐	86	John Wathan	.06	.03	.00
☐	38	Don Aase	.03	.01	.00	☐	87	Kelvin Moore	.03	.01	.00
☐	39	Jerry Koosman	.08	.04	.01	☐	88A	Byrn Smith ERR	.50	.25	.05
☐	40	Bruce Sutter	.15	.07	.01			(sic, Bryn)			
☐	41	Jose Cruz	.08	.04	.01	☐	88B	Bryn Smith COR	1.00	.50	.10
☐	42	Pete Rose	1.00	.50	.10	☐	89	Dave Hostetler	.06	.03	.00
☐	43	Cesar Cedeno	.06	.03	.00	☐	90	Rod Carew	.50	.22	.04
☐	44	Floyd Chiffer	.03	.01	.00	☐	91	Lonnie Smith	.12	.06	.01
☐	45	Larry McWilliams ...	.03	.01	.00	☐	92	Bob Knepper	.06	.03	.00
☐	46	Alan Fowlkes	.03	.01	.00	☐	93	Marty Bystrom	.03	.01	.00
☐	47	Dale Murphy	.85	.40	.08	☐	94	Chris Welsh	.03	.01	.00
☐	48	Doug Bird	.03	.01	.00	☐	95	Jason Thompson	.03	.01	.00
☐	49	Hubie Brooks	.10	.05	.01	☐	96	Tom O'Malley	.03	.01	.00
☐	50	Floyd Bannister	.03	.01	.00	☐	97	Phil Niekro	.25	.12	.02
☐	51	Jack O'Connor	.03	.01	.00	☐	98	Neil Allen	.03	.01	.00
☐	52	Steve Senteney	.03	.01	.00	☐	99	Bill Buckner	.10	.05	.01
☐	53	Gary Gaetti	3.00	1.50	.30	☐	100	Ed VandeBerg	.03	.01	.00
☐	54	Damaso Garcia	.03	.01	.00	☐	101	Jim Clancy	.03	.01	.00
☐	55	Gene Nelson	.03	.01	.00	☐	102	Robert Castillo	.03	.01	.00
☐	56	Mookie Wilson	.10	.05	.01	☐	103	Bruce Berenyi	.03	.01	.00
☐	57	Allen Ripley	.03	.01	.00	☐	104	Carlton Fisk	.35	.17	.03
☐	58	Bob Horner	.15	.07	.01	☐	105	Mike Flanagan	.08	.04	.01
☐	59	Tony Pena	.15	.07	.01	☐	106	Cecil Cooper	.15	.07	.01
☐	60	Gary Lavelle	.03	.01	.00	☐	107	Jack Morris	.20	.10	.02
☐	61	Tim Lollar	.03	.01	.00	☐	108	Mike Morgan	.06	.03	.00
☐	62	Frank Pastore	.03	.01	.00	☐	109	Luis Aponte	.03	.01	.00
☐	63	Garry Maddox	.06	.03	.00	☐	110	Pedro Guerrero	.30	.15	.03
☐	64	Bob Forsch	.03	.01	.00	☐	111	Len Barker	.03	.01	.00
☐	65	Harry Spilman	.03	.01	.00	☐	112	Willie Wilson	.12	.06	.01
☐	66	Geoff Zahn	.03	.01	.00	☐	113	Dave Beard	.03	.01	.00
☐	67	Salome Barojas	.03	.01	.00	☐	114	Mike Gates	.03	.01	.00
☐	68	David Palmer	.03	.01	.00	☐	115	Reggie Jackson	.50	.25	.05
☐	69	Charlie Hough	.06	.03	.00	☐	116	George Wright	.03	.01	.00
☐	70	Dan Quisenberry ...	.12	.06	.01	☐	117	Vance Law	.06	.03	.00
☐	71	Tony Armas	.06	.03	.00	☐	118	Nolan Ryan	1.25	.60	.12
☐	72	Rick Sutcliffe	.15	.07	.01	☐	119	Mike Krukow	.06	.03	.00
☐	73	Steve Balboni	.06	.03	.00	☐	120	Ozzie Smith	.35	.17	.03
☐	74	Jerry Remy	.03	.01	.00	☐	121	Broderick Perkins ..	.03	.01	.00
☐	75	Mike Scioscia	.06	.03	.00	☐	122	Tom Seaver	.40	.20	.04
☐	76	John Wockenfuss ...	.03	.01	.00	☐	123	Chris Chambliss ...	.06	.03	.00
☐	77	Jim Palmer	.40	.20	.04	☐	124	Chuck Tanner MG ..	.03	.01	.00
☐	78	Rollie Fingers	.20	.10	.02	☐	125	Johnnie LeMaster ..	.03	.01	.00
☐	79	Joe Nolan	.03	.01	.00	☐	126	Mel Hall	.75	.35	.07
☐	80	Pete Vuckovich	.06	.03	.00	☐	127	Bruce Bochte	.03	.01	.00
☐	81	Rick Leach	.03	.01	.00	☐	128	Charlie Puleo	.03	.01	.00
☐	82	Rick Miller	.03	.01	.00	☐	129	Luis Leal	.03	.01	.00
☐	83	Graig Nettles	.12	.06	.01	☐	130	John Pacella	.03	.01	.00

		MINT	EXC	G-VG			MINT	EXC	G-VG
☐ 131	Glenn Gulliver	.03	.01	.00	☐ 178	Buck Martinez	.03	.01	.00
☐ 132	Don Money	.03	.01	.00	☐ 179	Kent Hrbek	.50	.25	.05
☐ 133	Dave Rozema	.03	.01	.00	☐ 180	Alfredo Griffin	.06	.03	.00
☐ 134	Bruce Hurst	.40	.20	.04	☐ 181	Larry Andersen	.03	.01	.00
☐ 135	Rudy May	.03	.01	.00	☐ 182	Pete Falcone	.03	.01	.00
☐ 136	Tom Lasorda MG	.06	.03	.00	☐ 183	Jody Davis	.08	.04	.01
☐ 137	Dan Spillner UER	.06	.03	.00	☐ 184	Glenn Hubbard	.03	.01	.00
	(photo actually				☐ 185	Dale Berra	.03	.01	.00
	Ed Whitson)				☐ 186	Greg Minton	.03	.01	.00
☐ 138	Jerry Martin	.03	.01	.00	☐ 187	Gary Lucas	.03	.01	.00
☐ 139	Mike Norris	.03	.01	.00	☐ 188	Dave Van Gorder	.03	.01	.00
☐ 140	Al Oliver	.08	.04	.01	☐ 189	Bob Dernier	.03	.01	.00
☐ 141	Daryl Sconiers	.03	.01	.00	☐ 190	Willie McGee	1.25	.60	.12
☐ 142	Lamar Johnson	.03	.01	.00	☐ 191	Dickie Thon	.03	.01	.00
☐ 143	Harold Baines	.25	.12	.02	☐ 192	Bob Boone	.15	.07	.01
☐ 144	Alan Ashby	.03	.01	.00	☐ 193	Britt Burns	.03	.01	.00
☐ 145	Garry Templeton	.06	.03	.00	☐ 194	Jeff Reardon	.15	.07	.01
☐ 146	Al Holland	.03	.01	.00	☐ 195	Jon Matlack	.03	.01	.00
☐ 147	Bo Diaz	.03	.01	.00	☐ 196	Don Slaught	.30	.15	.03
☐ 148	Dave Concepcion	.10	.05	.01	☐ 197	Fred Stanley	.03	.01	.00
☐ 149	Rick Camp	.03	.01	.00	☐ 198	Rick Manning	.03	.01	.00
☐ 150	Jim Morrison	.03	.01	.00	☐ 199	Dave Righetti	.25	.12	.02
☐ 151	Randy Martz	.03	.01	.00	☐ 200	Dave Stapleton	.03	.01	.00
☐ 152	Keith Hernandez	.30	.15	.03	☐ 201	Steve Yeager	.03	.01	.00
☐ 153	John Lowenstein	.03	.01	.00	☐ 202	Enos Cabell	.03	.01	.00
☐ 154	Mike Caldwell	.03	.01	.00	☐ 203	Sammy Stewart	.03	.01	.00
☐ 155	Milt Wilcox	.03	.01	.00	☐ 204	Moose Haas	.03	.01	.00
☐ 156	Rich Gedman	.08	.04	.01	☐ 205	Lenn Sakata	.03	.01	.00
☐ 157	Rich Gossage	.15	.07	.01	☐ 206	Charlie Moore	.03	.01	.00
☐ 158	Jerry Reuss	.06	.03	.00	☐ 207	Alan Trammell	.30	.15	.03
☐ 159	Ron Hassey	.03	.01	.00	☐ 208	Jim Rice	.30	.15	.03
☐ 160	Larry Gura	.06	.03	.00	☐ 209	Roy Smalley	.03	.01	.00
☐ 161	Dwayne Murphy	.03	.01	.00	☐ 210	Bill Russell	.06	.03	.00
☐ 162	Woodie Fryman	.03	.01	.00	☐ 211	Andre Thornton	.06	.03	.00
☐ 163	Steve Comer	.03	.01	.00	☐ 212	Willie Aikens	.03	.01	.00
☐ 164	Ken Forsch	.03	.01	.00	☐ 213	Dave McKay	.03	.01	.00
☐ 165	Dennis Lamp	.03	.01	.00	☐ 214	Tim Blackwell	.03	.01	.00
☐ 166	David Green	.03	.01	.00	☐ 215	Buddy Bell	.08	.04	.01
☐ 167	Terry Puhl	.03	.01	.00	☐ 216	Doug DeCinces	.06	.03	.00
☐ 168	Mike Schmidt	1.00	.50	.10	☐ 217	Tom Herr	.08	.04	.01
☐ 169	Eddie Milner	.08	.04	.01	☐ 218	Frank LaCorte	.03	.01	.00
☐ 170	John Curtis	.03	.01	.00	☐ 219	Steve Carlton	.35	.17	.03
☐ 171	Don Robinson	.03	.01	.00	☐ 220	Terry Kennedy	.03	.01	.00
☐ 172	Rich Gale	.03	.01	.00	☐ 221	Mike Easler	.03	.01	.00
☐ 173	Steve Bedrosian	.25	.12	.02	☐ 222	Jack Clark	.25	.12	.02
☐ 174	Willie Hernandez	.10	.05	.01	☐ 223	Gene Garber	.03	.01	.00
☐ 175	Ron Gardenhire	.03	.01	.00	☐ 224	Scott Holman	.03	.01	.00
☐ 176	Jim Beattie	.03	.01	.00	☐ 225	Mike Proly	.03	.01	.00
☐ 177	Tim Laudner	.03	.01	.00	☐ 226	Terry Bulling	.03	.01	.00

		MINT	EXC	G-VG			MINT	EXC	G-VG
☐ 227	Jerry Garvin	.03	.01	.00	☐ 274	Dan Driessen	.03	.01	.00
☐ 228	Ron Davis	.03	.01	.00	☐ 275	Rufino Linares	.03	.01	.00
☐ 229	Tom Hume	.03	.01	.00	☐ 276	Lee Lacy	.03	.01	.00
☐ 230	Marc Hill	.03	.01	.00	☐ 277	Ryne Sandberg	8.00	4.00	.80
☐ 231	Dennis Martinez	.06	.03	.00	☐ 278	Darrell Porter	.03	.01	.00
☐ 232	Jim Gantner	.03	.01	.00	☐ 279	Cal Ripken	1.25	.60	.12
☐ 233	Larry Pashnick	.03	.01	.00	☐ 280	Jamie Easterly	.03	.01	.00
☐ 234	Dave Collins	.03	.01	.00	☐ 281	Bill Fahey	.03	.01	.00
☐ 235	Tom Burgmeier	.03	.01	.00	☐ 282	Glenn Hoffman	.03	.01	.00
☐ 236	Ken Landreaux	.03	.01	.00	☐ 283	Willie Randolph	.08	.04	.01
☐ 237	John Denny	.08	.04	.01	☐ 284	Fernando Valenzuela	.30	.15	.03
☐ 238	Hal McRae	.06	.03	.00	☐ 285	Alan Bannister	.03	.01	.00
☐ 239	Matt Keough	.03	.01	.00	☐ 286	Paul Splittorff	.03	.01	.00
☐ 240	Doug Flynn	.03	.01	.00	☐ 287	Joe Rudi	.06	.03	.00
☐ 241	Fred Lynn	.18	.09	.01	☐ 288	Bill Gullickson	.03	.01	.00
☐ 242	Billy Sample	.03	.01	.00	☐ 289	Danny Darwin	.03	.01	.00
☐ 243	Tom Paciorek	.03	.01	.00	☐ 290	Andy Hassler	.03	.01	.00
☐ 244	Joe Sambito	.03	.01	.00	☐ 291	Ernesto Escarrega	.03	.01	.00
☐ 245	Sid Monge	.03	.01	.00	☐ 292	Steve Mura	.03	.01	.00
☐ 246	Ken Oberkfell	.03	.01	.00	☐ 293	Tony Scott	.03	.01	.00
☐ 247	Joe Pittman UER	.06	.03	.00	☐ 294	Manny Trillo	.03	.01	.00
	(photo actually Juan				☐ 295	Greg Harris	.03	.01	.00
	Eichelberger)				☐ 296	Luis DeLeon	.03	.01	.00
☐ 248	Mario Soto	.06	.03	.00	☐ 297	Kent Tekulve	.06	.03	.00
☐ 249	Claudell Washington	.08	.04	.01	☐ 298	Atlee Hammaker	.06	.03	.00
☐ 250	Rick Rhoden	.06	.03	.00	☐ 299	Bruce Benedict	.03	.01	.00
☐ 251	Darrell Evans	.10	.05	.01	☐ 300	Fergie Jenkins	.15	.07	.01
☐ 252	Steve Henderson	.03	.01	.00	☐ 301	Dave Kingman	.10	.05	.01
☐ 253	Manny Castillo	.03	.01	.00	☐ 302	Bill Caudill	.03	.01	.00
☐ 254	Craig Swan	.03	.01	.00	☐ 303	John Castino	.03	.01	.00
☐ 255	Joey McLaughlin	.03	.01	.00	☐ 304	Ernie Whitt	.06	.03	.00
☐ 256	Pete Redfern	.03	.01	.00	☐ 305	Randy Johnson	.03	.01	.00
☐ 257	Ken Singleton	.08	.04	.01	☐ 306	Garth Iorg	.03	.01	.00
☐ 258	Robin Yount	.65	.30	.06	☐ 307	Gaylord Perry	.25	.12	.02
☐ 259	Elias Sosa	.03	.01	.00	☐ 308	Ed Lynch	.03	.01	.00
☐ 260	Bob Ojeda	.10	.05	.01	☐ 309	Keith Moreland	.03	.01	.00
☐ 261	Bobby Murcer	.08	.04	.01	☐ 310	Rafael Ramirez	.03	.01	.00
☐ 262	Candy Maldonado	.40	.20	.04	☐ 311	Bill Madlock	.08	.04	.01
☐ 263	Rick Waits	.03	.01	.00	☐ 312	Milt May	.03	.01	.00
☐ 264	Greg Pryor	.03	.01	.00	☐ 313	John Montefusco	.06	.03	.00
☐ 265	Bob Owchinko	.03	.01	.00	☐ 314	Wayne Krenchicki	.03	.01	.00
☐ 266	Chris Speier	.03	.01	.00	☐ 315	George Vukovich	.03	.01	.00
☐ 267	Bruce Kison	.03	.01	.00	☐ 316	Joaquin Andujar	.08	.04	.01
☐ 268	Mark Wagner	.03	.01	.00	☐ 317	Craig Reynolds	.03	.01	.00
☐ 269	Steve Kemp	.03	.01	.00	☐ 318	Rick Burleson	.06	.03	.00
☐ 270	Phil Garner	.03	.01	.00	☐ 319	Richard Dotson	.06	.03	.00
☐ 271	Gene Richards	.03	.01	.00	☐ 320	Steve Rogers	.03	.01	.00
☐ 272	Renie Martin	.03	.01	.00	☐ 321	Dave Schmidt	.15	.07	.01
☐ 273	Dave Roberts	.03	.01	.00	☐ 322	Bud Black	.20	.10	.02

		MINT	EXC	G-VG			MINT	EXC	G-VG
☐ 323	Jeff Burroughs	.06	.03	.00	☐ 367	Brian Downing	.06	.03	.00
☐ 324	Von Hayes	.20	.10	.02	☐ 368	Mike Richardt	.03	.01	.00
☐ 325	Butch Wynegar	.03	.01	.00	☐ 369	Aurelio Rodriguez	.03	.01	.00
☐ 326	Carl Yastrzemski	.80	.40	.08	☐ 370	Dave Smith	.06	.03	.00
☐ 327	Ron Roenicke	.03	.01	.00	☐ 371	Tug McGraw	.10	.05	.01
☐ 328	Howard Johnson	9.00	4.50	.90	☐ 372	Doug Bair	.03	.01	.00
☐ 329	Rick Dempsey	.03	.01	.00	☐ 373	Ruppert Jones	.03	.01	.00
☐ 330A	Jim Slaton	.06	.03	.00	☐ 374	Alex Trevino	.03	.01	.00
	(bio printed				☐ 375	Ken Dayley	.06	.03	.00
	black on white)				☐ 376	Rod Scurry	.03	.01	.00
☐ 330B	Jim Slaton	.15	.07	.01	☐ 377	Bob Brenly	.03	.01	.00
	(bio printed				☐ 378	Scot Thompson	.03	.01	.00
	black on yellow)				☐ 379	Julio Cruz	.03	.01	.00
☐ 331	Benny Ayala	.03	.01	.00	☐ 380	John Stearns	.03	.01	.00
☐ 332	Ted Simmons	.12	.06	.01	☐ 381	Dale Murray	.03	.01	.00
☐ 333	Lou Whitaker	.25	.12	.02	☐ 382	Frank Viola	3.75	1.85	.37
☐ 334	Chuck Rainey	.03	.01	.00	☐ 383	Al Bumbry	.03	.01	.00
☐ 335	Lou Piniella	.12	.06	.01	☐ 384	Ben Oglivie	.06	.03	.00
☐ 336	Steve Sax	.50	.25	.05	☐ 385	Dave Tobik	.03	.01	.00
☐ 337	Toby Harrah	.06	.03	.00	☐ 386	Bob Stanley	.03	.01	.00
☐ 338	George Brett	.65	.30	.06	☐ 387	Andre Robertson	.03	.01	.00
☐ 339	Dave Lopes	.08	.04	.01	☐ 388	Jorge Orta	.03	.01	.00
☐ 340	Gary Carter	.35	.17	.03	☐ 389	Ed Whitson	.06	.03	.00
☐ 341	John Grubb	.03	.01	.00	☐ 390	Don Hood	.03	.01	.00
☐ 342	Tim Foli	.03	.01	.00	☐ 391	Tom Underwood	.03	.01	.00
☐ 343	Jim Kaat	.12	.06	.01	☐ 392	Tim Wallach	.18	.09	.01
☐ 344	Mike LaCoss	.03	.01	.00	☐ 393	Steve Renko	.03	.01	.00
☐ 345	Larry Christenson	.03	.01	.00	☐ 394	Mickey Rivers	.06	.03	.00
☐ 346	Juan Bonilla	.03	.01	.00	☐ 395	Greg Luzinski	.10	.05	.01
☐ 347	Omar Moreno	.03	.01	.00	☐ 396	Art Howe	.08	.04	.01
☐ 348	Chili Davis	.30	.15	.03	☐ 397	Alan Wiggins	.10	.05	.01
☐ 349	Tommy Boggs	.03	.01	.00	☐ 398	Jim Barr	.03	.01	.00
☐ 350	Rusty Staub	.10	.05	.01	☐ 399	Ivan DeJesus	.03	.01	.00
☐ 351	Bump Wills	.03	.01	.00	☐ 400	Tom Lawless	.06	.03	.00
☐ 352	Rick Sweet	.03	.01	.00	☐ 401	Bob Walk	.06	.03	.00
☐ 353	Jim Gott	.30	.15	.03	☐ 402	Jimmy Smith	.03	.01	.00
☐ 354	Terry Felton	.03	.01	.00	☐ 403	Lee Smith	.10	.05	.01
☐ 355	Jim Kern	.03	.01	.00	☐ 404	George Hendrick	.06	.03	.00
☐ 356	Bill Almon	.03	.01	.00	☐ 405	Eddie Murray	.45	.22	.04
☐ 357	Tippy Martinez	.03	.01	.00	☐ 406	Marshall Edwards	.03	.01	.00
☐ 358	Roy Howell	.03	.01	.00	☐ 407	Lance Parrish	.20	.10	.02
☐ 359	Dan Petry	.03	.01	.00	☐ 408	Carney Lansford	.20	.07	.01
☐ 360	Jerry Mumphrey	.03	.01	.00	☐ 409	Dave Winfield	.40	.20	.04
☐ 361	Mark Clear	.03	.01	.00	☐ 410	Bob Welch	.08	.04	.01
☐ 362	Mike Marshall	.25	.12	.02	☐ 411	Larry Milbourne	.03	.01	.00
☐ 363	Lary Sorensen	.03	.01	.00	☐ 412	Dennis Leonard	.06	.03	.00
☐ 364	Amos Otis	.08	.04	.01	☐ 413	Dan Meyer	.03	.01	.00
☐ 365	Rick Langford	.03	.01	.00	☐ 414	Charlie Lea	.03	.01	.00
☐ 366	Brad Mills	.03	.01	.00	☐ 415	Rick Honeycutt	.03	.01	.00

		MINT	EXC	G-VG			MINT	EXC	G-VG
☐ 416	Mike Witt	.15	.07	.01	☐ 460	Reid Nichols	.03	.01	.00
☐ 417	Steve Trout	.03	.01	.00	☐ 461	Oscar Gamble	.03	.01	.00
☐ 418	Glenn Brummer	.03	.01	.00	☐ 462	Dusty Baker	.06	.03	.00
☐ 419	Denny Walling	.03	.01	.00	☐ 463	Jack Perconte	.03	.01	.00
☐ 420	Gary Matthews	.06	.03	.00	☐ 464	Frank White	.08	.04	.01
☐ 421	Charlie Leibrandt UER	.06	.03	.00	☐ 465	Mickey Klutts	.03	.01	.00
	(Liebrandt on				☐ 466	Warren Cromartie	.03	.01	.00
	front of card)				☐ 467	Larry Parrish	.06	.03	.00
☐ 422	Juan Eichelberger				☐ 468	Bobby Grich	.06	.03	.00
	UER	.06	.03	.00	☐ 469	Dane Iorg	.03	.01	.00
	(photo actually				☐ 470	Joe Niekro	.10	.05	.01
	Joe Pittman)				☐ 471	Ed Farmer	.03	.01	.00
☐ 423	Matt Guante	.06	.03	.00	☐ 472	Tim Flannery	.03	.01	.00
☐ 424	Bill Laskey	.03	.01	.00	☐ 473	Dave Parker	.20	.10	.02
☐ 425	Jerry Royster	.03	.01	.00	☐ 474	Jeff Leonard	.08	.04	.01
☐ 426	Dickie Noles	.03	.01	.00	☐ 475	Al Hrabosky	.06	.03	.00
☐ 427	George Foster	.15	.07	.01	☐ 476	Ron Hodges	.03	.01	.00
☐ 428	Mike Moore	1.50	.75	.15	☐ 477	Leon Durham	.06	.03	.00
☐ 429	Gary Ward	.06	.03	.00	☐ 478	Jim Essian	.03	.01	.00
☐ 430	Barry Bonnell	.03	.01	.00	☐ 479	Roy Lee Jackson	.03	.01	.00
☐ 431	Ron Washington	.03	.01	.00	☐ 480	Brad Havens	.03	.01	.00
☐ 432	Rance Mulliniks	.03	.01	.00	☐ 481	Joe Price	.03	.01	.00
☐ 433	Mike Stanton	.03	.01	.00	☐ 482	Tony Bernazard	.03	.01	.00
☐ 434	Jesse Orosco	.06	.03	.00	☐ 483	Scott McGregor	.06	.03	.00
☐ 435	Larry Bowa	.10	.05	.01	☐ 484	Paul Molitor	.18	.09	.01
☐ 436	Biff Pocoroba	.03	.01	.00	☐ 485	Mike Ivie	.03	.01	.00
☐ 437	Johnny Ray	.12	.06	.01	☐ 486	Ken Griffey	.10	.05	.01
☐ 438	Joe Morgan	.30	.15	.03	☐ 487	Dennis Eckersley	.20	.10	.02
☐ 439	Eric Show	.35	.17	.03	☐ 488	Steve Garvey	.40	.20	.04
☐ 440	Larry Biittner	.03	.01	.00	☐ 489	Mike Fischlin	.03	.01	.00
☐ 441	Greg Gross	.03	.01	.00	☐ 490	U.L. Washington	.03	.01	.00
☐ 442	Gene Tenace	.03	.01	.00	☐ 491	Steve McCatty	.03	.01	.00
☐ 443	Danny Heep	.03	.01	.00	☐ 492	Roy Johnson	.03	.01	.00
☐ 444	Bobby Clark	.03	.01	.00	☐ 493	Don Baylor	.12	.06	.01
☐ 445	Kevin Hickey	.03	.01	.00	☐ 494	Bobby Johnson	.03	.01	.00
☐ 446	Scott Sanderson	.03	.01	.00	☐ 495	Mike Squires	.03	.01	.00
☐ 447	Frank Tanana	.08	.04	.01	☐ 496	Bert Roberge	.03	.01	.00
☐ 448	Cesar Geronimo	.03	.01	.00	☐ 497	Dick Ruthven	.03	.01	.00
☐ 449	Jimmy Sexton	.03	.01	.00	☐ 498	Tito Landrum	.03	.01	.00
☐ 450	Mike Hargrove	.03	.01	.00	☐ 499	Sixto Lezcano	.03	.01	.00
☐ 451	Doyle Alexander	.06	.03	.00	☐ 500	Johnny Bench	.50	.25	.05
☐ 452	Dwight Evans	.18	.09	.01	☐ 501	Larry Whisenton	.03	.01	.00
☐ 453	Terry Forster	.06	.03	.00	☐ 502	Manny Sarmiento	.03	.01	.00
☐ 454	Tom Brookens	.03	.01	.00	☐ 503	Fred Breining	.03	.01	.00
☐ 455	Rich Dauer	.03	.01	.00	☐ 504	Bill Campbell	.03	.01	.00
☐ 456	Rob Picciolo	.03	.01	.00	☐ 505	Todd Cruz	.03	.01	.00
☐ 457	Terry Crowley	.03	.01	.00	☐ 506	Bob Bailor	.03	.01	.00
☐ 458	Ned Yost	.03	.01	.00	☐ 507	Dave Stieb	.18	.09	.01
☐ 459	Kirk Gibson	.40	.20	.04	☐ 508	Al Williams	.03	.01	.00

		MINT	EXC	G-VG
☐ 509	Dan Ford	.03	.01	.00
☐ 510	Gorman Thomas	.08	.04	.01
☐ 511	Chet Lemon	.06	.03	.00
☐ 512	Mike Torrez	.03	.01	.00
☐ 513	Shane Rawley	.03	.01	.00
☐ 514	Mark Belanger	.06	.03	.00
☐ 515	Rodney Craig	.03	.01	.00
☐ 516	Onix Concepcion	.03	.01	.00
☐ 517	Mike Heath	.03	.01	.00
☐ 518	Andre Dawson	.35	.17	.03
☐ 519	Luis Sanchez	.03	.01	.00
☐ 520	Terry Bogener	.03	.01	.00
☐ 521	Rudy Law	.03	.01	.00
☐ 522	Ray Knight	.06	.03	.00
☐ 523	Joe Lefebvre	.03	.01	.00
☐ 524	Jim Wohlford	.03	.01	.00
☐ 525	Julio Franco	4.00	2.00	.40
☐ 526	Ron Oester	.03	.01	.00
☐ 527	Rick Mahler	.03	.01	.00
☐ 528	Steve Nicosia	.03	.01	.00
☐ 529	Junior Kennedy	.03	.01	.00
☐ 530A	Whitey Herzog MG (bio printed black on white)	.10	.05	.01
☐ 530B	Whitey Herzog MG (bio printed black on yellow)	.10	.05	.01
☐ 531A	Don Sutton (blue border on photo)	.40	.20	.04
☐ 531B	Don Sutton (green border on photo)	.40	.20	.04
☐ 532	Mark Brouhard	.03	.01	.00
☐ 533A	Sparky Anderson MG (bio printed black on white)	.10	.05	.01
☐ 533B	Sparky Anderson MG (bio printed black on yellow)	.10	.05	.01
☐ 534	Roger LaFrancois	.03	.01	.00
☐ 535	George Frazier	.03	.01	.00
☐ 536	Tom Niedenfuer	.06	.03	.00
☐ 537	Ed Glynn	.03	.01	.00
☐ 538	Lee May	.06	.03	.00
☐ 539	Bob Kearney	.03	.01	.00
☐ 540	Tim Raines	.50	.25	.05
☐ 541	Paul Mirabella	.03	.01	.00
☐ 542	Luis Tiant	.08	.04	.01

		MINT	EXC	G-VG
☐ 543	Ron LeFlore	.06	.03	.00
☐ 544	Dave LaPoint	.35	.17	.03
☐ 545	Randy Moffitt	.03	.01	.00
☐ 546	Luis Aguayo	.03	.01	.00
☐ 547	Brad Lesley	.03	.01	.00
☐ 548	Luis Salazar	.03	.01	.00
☐ 549	John Candelaria	.06	.03	.00
☐ 550	Dave Bergman	.03	.01	.00
☐ 551	Bob Watson	.06	.03	.00
☐ 552	Pat Tabler	.10	.05	.01
☐ 553	Brent Gaff	.03	.01	.00
☐ 554	Al Cowens	.03	.01	.00
☐ 555	Tom Brunansky	.60	.30	.06
☐ 556	Lloyd Moseby	.10	.05	.01
☐ 557A	Pascual Perez ERR (Twins in glove)	2.00	1.00	.20
☐ 557B	Pascual Perez COR (Braves in glove)	.20	.10	.02
☐ 558	Willie Upshaw	.03	.01	.00
☐ 559	Richie Zisk	.03	.01	.00
☐ 560	Pat Zachry	.03	.01	.00
☐ 561	Jay Johnstone	.06	.03	.00
☐ 562	Carlos Diaz	.03	.01	.00
☐ 563	John Tudor	.12	.06	.01
☐ 564	Frank Robinson MG	.15	.07	.01
☐ 565	Dave Edwards	.03	.01	.00
☐ 566	Paul Householder	.03	.01	.00
☐ 567	Ron Reed	.03	.01	.00
☐ 568	Mike Ramsey	.03	.01	.00
☐ 569	Kiko Garcia	.03	.01	.00
☐ 570	Tommy John	.15	.07	.01
☐ 571	Tony LaRussa MG	.06	.03	.00
☐ 572	Joel Youngblood	.03	.01	.00
☐ 573	Wayne Tolleson	.15	.07	.01
☐ 574	Keith Creel	.03	.01	.00
☐ 575	Billy Martin MG	.15	.07	.01
☐ 576	Jerry Dybzinski	.03	.01	.00
☐ 577	Rick Cerone	.03	.01	.00
☐ 578	Tony Perez	.15	.07	.01
☐ 579	Greg Brock	.30	.15	.03
☐ 580	Glenn Wilson	.35	.17	.03
☐ 581	Tim Stoddard	.03	.01	.00
☐ 582	Bob McClure	.03	.01	.00
☐ 583	Jim Dwyer	.03	.01	.00
☐ 584	Ed Romero	.03	.01	.00
☐ 585	Larry Herndon	.03	.01	.00
☐ 586	Wade Boggs	18.00	9.00	1.80
☐ 587	Jay Howell	.06	.03	.00
☐ 588	Dave Stewart	.50	.25	.05

		MINT	EXC	G-VG
☐ 589	Bert Blyleven	.20	.10	.02
☐ 590	Dick Howser MG	.06	.03	.00
☐ 591	Wayne Gross	.03	.01	.00
☐ 592	Terry Francona	.03	.01	.00
☐ 593	Don Werner	.03	.01	.00
☐ 594	Bill Stein	.03	.01	.00
☐ 595	Jesse Barfield	.75	.35	.07
☐ 596	Bob Molinaro	.03	.01	.00
☐ 597	Mike Vail	.03	.01	.00
☐ 598	Tony Gwynn	12.50	6.00	1.20
☐ 599	Gary Rajsich	.03	.01	.00
☐ 600	Jerry Ujdur	.03	.01	.00
☐ 601	Cliff Johnson	.03	.01	.00
☐ 602	Jerry White	.03	.01	.00
☐ 603	Bryan Clark	.03	.01	.00
☐ 604	Joe Ferguson	.03	.01	.00
☐ 605	Guy Sularz	.03	.01	.00
☐ 606A	Ozzie Virgil (green border on photo)	.10	.05	.01
☐ 606B	Ozzie Virgil (orange border on photo)	.10	.05	.01
☐ 607	Terry Harper	.03	.01	.00
☐ 608	Harvey Kuenn MG	.06	.03	.00
☐ 609	Jim Sundberg	.03	.01	.00
☐ 610	Willie Stargell	.35	.17	.03
☐ 611	Reggie Smith	.08	.04	.01
☐ 612	Rob Wilfong	.03	.01	.00
☐ 613	The Niekro Brothers Joe Niekro Phil Niekro	.12	.06	.01
☐ 614	Lee Elia MG	.03	.01	.00
☐ 615	Mickey Hatcher	.06	.03	.00
☐ 616	Jerry Hairston	.03	.01	.00
☐ 617	John Martin	.03	.01	.00
☐ 618	Wally Backman	.20	.10	.02
☐ 619	Storm Davis	.60	.30	.06
☐ 620	Alan Knicely	.03	.01	.00
☐ 621	John Stuper	.03	.01	.00
☐ 622	Matt Sinatro	.03	.01	.00
☐ 623	Geno Petralli	.15	.07	.01
☐ 624	Duane Walker	.03	.01	.00
☐ 625	Dick Williams MG	.03	.01	.00
☐ 626	Pat Corrales MG	.03	.01	.00
☐ 627	Vern Ruhle	.03	.01	.00
☐ 628	Joe Torre MG	.08	.04	.01
☐ 629	Anthony Johnson	.03	.01	.00
☐ 630	Steve Howe	.03	.01	.00

		MINT	EXC	G-VG
☐ 631	Gary Woods	.03	.01	.00
☐ 632	LaMarr Hoyt	.08	.04	.01
☐ 633	Steve Swisher	.03	.01	.00
☐ 634	Terry Leach	.25	.12	.02
☐ 635	Jeff Newman	.03	.01	.00
☐ 636	Brett Butler	.12	.06	.01
☐ 637	Gary Gray	.03	.01	.00
☐ 638	Lee Mazzilli	.03	.01	.00
☐ 639A	Ron Jackson ERR (A's in glove)	12.00	6.00	1.20
☐ 639B	Ron Jackson COR (Angels in glove, red border on photo)	.15	.07	.01
☐ 639C	Roh Jackson COR (Angels in glove, green border on photo)	.50	.25	.05
☐ 640	Juan Beniquez	.03	.01	.00
☐ 641	Dave Rucker	.03	.01	.00
☐ 642	Luis Pujols	.03	.01	.00
☐ 643	Rick Monday	.06	.03	.00
☐ 644	Hosken Powell	.03	.01	.00
☐ 645	The Chicken	.15	.07	.01
☐ 646	Dave Engle	.03	.01	.00
☐ 647	Dick Davis	.03	.01	.00
☐ 648	Frank Robinson Vida Blue Joe Morgan	.15	.07	.01
☐ 649	Al Chambers	.03	.01	.00
☐ 650	Jesus Vega	.03	.01	.00
☐ 651	Jeff Jones	.03	.01	.00
☐ 652	Marvis Foley	.03	.01	.00
☐ 653	Ty Cobb Puzzle Card	.03	.01	.00
☐ 654A	Dick Perez/Diamond King Checklist (unnumbered) (word "checklist" omitted from back)	.15	.02	.01
☐ 654B	Dick Perez/Diamond King Checklist (unnumbered) (word "checklist" is on back)	.15	.02	.01
☐ 655	Checklist 1 (unnumbered)	.07	.01	.00
☐ 656	Checklist 2 (unnumbered)	.07	.01	.00
☐ 657	Checklist 3	.07	.01	.00

			MINT	EXC	G-VG
☐	658	Checklist 4 .... (unnumbered)	.07	.01	.00
☐	659	Checklist 5 .... (unnumbered)	.07	.01	.00
☐	660	Checklist 6 .... (unnumbered)	.07	.01	.00

1984 Donruss

The 1984 Donruss set contains a total of 660 cards, each measuring 2 ½" by 3 ½"; however, only 658 are numbered. The first 26 cards in the set are again Diamond Kings (DK), although the drawings this year were styled differently and are easily differentiated from other DK issues. A new feature, Rated Rookies (RR), was introduced with this set with Bill Madden's 20 selections comprising numbers 27 through 46. Two "Living Legend" cards designated A (featuring Gaylord Perry and Rollie Fingers) and B (featuring Johnny Bench and Carl Yastrzemski) were issued as bonus cards in wax packs, but were not issued in the vending sets sold to hobby dealers. The seven unnumbered checklist cards are arbitrarily assigned numbers 652 through 658 and are listed at the end of the list below. The designs on the fronts of the Donruss cards changed considerably from the past two years. The backs contain statistics and are printed in green and black ink. The cards were distributed with a 63-piece puzzle of Duke Snider. There are no

extra variation cards included in the complete set price below.

		MINT	EXC	G-VG
	COMPLETE SET (658)	275.00	125.00	25.00
	COMMON PLAYER (1-658)	.10	.05	.01
☐	1A Robin Yount DK ERR (Perez Steel)	1.25	.60	.12
☐	1B Robin Yount DK COR	2.00	1.00	.20
☐	2A Dave Concepcion DK ERR (Perez Steel)	.15	.07	.01
☐	2B Dave Concepcion DK COR	.25	.12	.02
☐	3A Dwayne Murphy DK . ERR (Perez Steel)	.15	.07	.01
☐	3B Dwayne Murphy DK . COR	.25	.12	.02
☐	4A John Castino DK ERR .... (Perez Steel)	.15	.07	.01
☐	4B John Castino DK COR	.25	.12	.02
☐	5A Leon Durham DK ERR .... (Perez Steel)	.15	.07	.01
☐	5B Leon Durham DK COR	.25	.12	.02
☐	6A Rusty Staub DK ERR (Perez Steel)	.15	.07	.01
☐	6B Rusty Staub DK COR	.25	.12	.02
☐	7A Jack Clark DK ERR ... (Perez Steel)	.30	.15	.03
☐	7B Jack Clark DK COR ...	.50	.25	.05
☐	8A Dave Dravecky DK .. ERR (Perez Steel)	.15	.07	.01
☐	8B Dave Dravecky DK . COR	.25	.12	.02
☐	9A Al Oliver DK ERR ... (Perez Steel)	.15	.07	.01
☐	9B Al Oliver DK COR ...	.25	.12	.02
☐	10A Dave Righetti DK ... ERR (Perez Steel)	.20	.10	.02
☐	10B Dave Righetti DK .... COR	.30	.15	.03
☐	11A Hal McRae DK ERR . (Perez Steel)	.15	.07	.01
☐	11B Hal McRae DK COR	.25	.12	.02
☐	12A Ray Knight DK ERR . (Perez Steel)	.15	.07	.01

		MINT	EXC	G-VG
☐ 12B	Ray Knight DK COR	.25	.12	.02
☐ 13A	Bruce Sutter DK ERR (Perez Steel)	.15	.07	.01
☐ 13B	Bruce Sutter DK COR	.25	.12	.02
☐ 14A	Bob Horner DK ERR (Perez Steel)	.15	.07	.01
☐ 14B	Bob Horner DK COR	.25	.12	.02
☐ 15A	Lance Parrish DK ERR (Perez Steel)	.25	.12	.02
☐ 15B	Lance Parrish DK COR	.35	.17	.03
☐ 16A	Matt Young DK ERR (Perez Steel)	.15	.07	.01
☐ 16B	Matt Young DK COR	.25	.12	.02
☐ 17A	Fred Lynn DK ERR (A's logo on back)	.20	.10	.02
☐ 17B	Fred Lynn DK COR	.30	.15	.03
☐ 18A	Ron Kittle DK ERR (Perez Steel)	.20	.10	.02
☐ 18B	Ron Kittle DK COR	.30	.15	.03
☐ 19A	Jim Clancy DK ERR (Perez Steel)	.15	.07	.01
☐ 19B	Jim Clancy DK COR	.25	.12	.02
☐ 20A	Bill Madlock DK ERR (Perez Steel)	.15	.07	.01
☐ 20B	Bill Madlock DK COR	.25	.12	.02
☐ 21A	Larry Parrish DK ERR (Perez Steel)	.15	.07	.01
☐ 21B	Larry Parrish DK COR	.25	.12	.02
☐ 22A	Eddie Murray DK ERR (Perez Steel)	.90	.45	.09
☐ 22B	Eddie Murray DK COR	1.50	.75	.15
☐ 23A	Mike Schmidt DK ERR (Perez Steel)	1.25	.60	.12
☐ 23B	Mike Schmidt DK COR	2.00	1.00	.20
☐ 24A	Pedro Guerrero DK ERR (Perez Steel)	.35	.17	.03
☐ 24B	Pedro Guerrero DK COR	.50	.25	.05
☐ 25A	Andre Thornton DK ERR (Perez Steel)	.15	.07	.01
☐ 25B	Andre Thornton DK COR	.25	.12	.02

		MINT	EXC	G-VG
☐ 26A	Wade Boggs DK ERR (Perez Steel)	3.50	1.75	.35
☐ 26B	Wade Boggs DK COR	5.50	2.75	.55
☐ 27	Joel Skinner RR	.25	.12	.02
☐ 28	Tommy Dunbar RR	.15	.07	.01
☐ 29A	Mike Stenhouse RR ERR (no back number)	.25	.12	.02
☐ 29B	Mike Stenhouse RR COR (number on back)	3.00	1.50	.30
☐ 30A	Ron Darling RR ERR (no number on back)	6.00	3.00	.60
☐ 30B	Ron Darling RR COR	16.00	8.00	1.60
☐ 31	Dion James RR	.60	.30	.06
☐ 32	Tony Fernandez RR	8.00	4.00	.80
☐ 33	Angel Salazar RR	.15	.07	.01
☐ 34	Kevin McReynolds RR	11.00	5.50	1.10
☐ 35	Dick Schofield RR	.60	.30	.06
☐ 36	Brad Komminsk RR	.35	.17	.03
☐ 37	Tim Teufel RR	.40	.20	.04
☐ 38	Doug Frobel RR	.15	.07	.01
☐ 39	Greg Gagne RR	.35	.17	.03
☐ 40	Mike Fuentes RR	.15	.07	.01
☐ 41	Joe Carter RR	15.00	7.50	1.50
☐ 42	Mike Brown RR (Angels OF)	.15	.07	.01
☐ 43	Mike Jeffcoat RR	.15	.07	.01
☐ 44	Sid Fernandez RR	7.00	3.50	.70
☐ 45	Brian Dayett RR	.20	.10	.02
☐ 46	Chris Smith RR	.15	.07	.01
☐ 47	Eddie Murray	1.00	.50	.10
☐ 48	Robin Yount	1.50	.75	.15
☐ 49	Lance Parrish	.35	.17	.03
☐ 50	Jim Rice	.45	.22	.04
☐ 51	Dave Winfield	.85	.40	.08
☐ 52	Fernando Valenzuela	.45	.22	.04
☐ 53	George Brett	1.25	.60	.12
☐ 54	Rickey Henderson	2.00	1.00	.20
☐ 55	Gary Carter	.65	.30	.06
☐ 56	Buddy Bell	.15	.07	.01
☐ 57	Reggie Jackson	1.50	.75	.15
☐ 58	Harold Baines	.35	.17	.03
☐ 59	Ozzie Smith	.75	.30	.06
☐ 60	Nolan Ryan	3.25	1.60	.32
☐ 61	Pete Rose	2.50	1.25	.25
☐ 62	Ron Oester	.10	.05	.01
☐ 63	Steve Garvey	.90	.45	.09
☐ 64	Jason Thompson	.10	.05	.01

		MINT	EXC	G-VG				MINT	EXC	G-VG
☐	65	Jack Clark	.35	.17	.03	☐	110	Joe Niekro	.15	.07	.01
☐	66	Dale Murphy	1.50	.75	.15	☐	111	Steve Carlton	.90	.45	.09
☐	67	Leon Durham	.15	.07	.01	☐	112	Terry Kennedy	.10	.05	.01
☐	68	Darryl Strawberry	36.00	18.00	3.60	☐	113	Bill Madlock	.20	.10	.02
☐	69	Richie Zisk	.10	.05	.01	☐	114	Chili Davis	.20	.10	.02
☐	70	Kent Hrbek	.60	.30	.06	☐	115	Jim Gantner	.10	.05	.01
☐	71	Dave Stieb	.25	.12	.02	☐	116	Tom Seaver	1.00	.50	.10
☐	72	Ken Schrom	.10	.05	.01	☐	117	Bill Buckner	.20	.10	.02
☐	73	George Bell	1.75	.85	.17	☐	118	Bill Caudill	.10	.05	.01
☐	74	John Moses	.15	.07	.01	☐	119	Jim Clancy	.10	.05	.01
☐	75	Ed Lynch	.10	.05	.01	☐	120	John Castino	.10	.05	.01
☐	76	Chuck Rainey	.10	.05	.01	☐	121	Dave Concepcion	.20	.10	.02
☐	77	Biff Pocoroba	.10	.05	.01	☐	122	Greg Luzinski	.20	.10	.02
☐	78	Cecilio Guante	.10	.05	.01	☐	123	Mike Boddicker	.20	.10	.02
☐	79	Jim Barr	.10	.05	.01	☐	124	Pete Ladd	.10	.05	.01
☐	80	Kurt Bevacqua	.10	.05	.01	☐	125	Juan Berenguer	.10	.05	.01
☐	81	Tom Foley	.10	.05	.01	☐	126	John Montefusco	.10	.05	.01
☐	82	Joe Lefebvre	.10	.05	.01	☐	127	Ed Jurak	.10	.05	.01
☐	83	Andy Van Slyke	4.00	2.00	.40	☐	128	Tom Niedenfuer	.15	.07	.01
☐	84	Bob Lillis MG	.10	.05	.01	☐	129	Bert Blyleven	.25	.10	.02
☐	85	Ricky Adams	.10	.05	.01	☐	130	Bud Black	.10	.05	.01
☐	86	Jerry Hairston	.10	.05	.01	☐	131	Gorman Heimueller	.10	.05	.01
☐	87	Bob James	.20	.10	.02	☐	132	Dan Schatzeder	.10	.05	.01
☐	88	Joe Altobelli MG	.10	.05	.01	☐	133	Ron Jackson	.10	.05	.01
☐	89	Ed Romero	.10	.05	.01	☐	134	Tom Henke	.90	.45	.09
☐	90	John Grubb	.10	.05	.01	☐	135	Kevin Hickey	.10	.05	.01
☐	91	John Henry Johnson	.10	.05	.01	☐	136	Mike Scott	.60	.30	.06
☐	92	Juan Espino	.10	.05	.01	☐	137	Bo Diaz	.10	.05	.01
☐	93	Candy Maldonado	.20	.10	.02	☐	138	Glenn Brummer	.10	.05	.01
☐	94	Andre Thornton	.15	.07	.01	☐	139	Sid Monge	.10	.05	.01
☐	95	Onix Concepcion	.10	.05	.01	☐	140	Rich Gale	.10	.05	.01
☐	96	Donnie Hill (listed as P, should be 2B)	.15	.07	.01	☐	141	Brett Butler	.20	.10	.02
						☐	142	Brian Harper	.30	.15	.03
						☐	143	John Rabb	.10	.05	.01
☐	97	Andre Dawson UER (wrong middle name, should be Nolan)	.75	.35	.07	☐	144	Gary Woods	.10	.05	.01
						☐	145	Pat Putnam	.10	.05	.01
						☐	146	Jim Acker	.15	.07	.01
☐	98	Frank Tanana	.15	.07	.01	☐	147	Mickey Hatcher	.10	.05	.01
☐	99	Curt Wilkerson	.15	.07	.01	☐	148	Todd Cruz	.10	.05	.01
☐	100	Larry Gura	.10	.05	.01	☐	149	Tom Tellmann	.10	.05	.01
☐	101	Dwayne Murphy	.10	.05	.01	☐	150	John Wockenfuss	.10	.05	.01
☐	102	Tom Brennan	.10	.05	.01	☐	151	Wade Boggs	11.00	5.50	1.10
☐	103	Dave Righetti	.30	.15	.03	☐	152	Don Baylor	.20	.10	.02
☐	104	Steve Sax	.50	.25	.05	☐	153	Bob Welch	.15	.07	.01
☐	105	Dan Petry	.10	.05	.01	☐	154	Alan Bannister	.10	.05	.01
☐	106	Cal Ripken	1.75	.85	.17	☐	155	Willie Aikens	.10	.05	.01
☐	107	Paul Molitor	.30	.15	.03	☐	156	Jeff Burroughs	.10	.05	.01
☐	108	Fred Lynn	.25	.12	.02	☐	157	Bryan Little	.10	.05	.01
☐	109	Neil Allen	.10	.05	.01	☐	158	Bob Boone	.25	.12	.02

		MINT	EXC	G-VG			MINT	EXC	G-VG
☐ 159	Dave Hostetler	.10	.05	.01	☐ 208	Juan Agosto	.20	.10	.02
☐ 160	Jerry Dybzinski	.10	.05	.01	☐ 209	Bobby Ramos	.10	.05	.01
☐ 161	Mike Madden	.10	.05	.01	☐ 210	Al Bumbry	.10	.05	.01
☐ 162	Luis DeLeon	.10	.05	.01	☐ 211	Mark Brouhard	.10	.05	.01
☐ 163	Willie Hernandez	.25	.12	.02	☐ 212	Howard Bailey	.10	.05	.01
☐ 164	Frank Pastore	.10	.05	.01	☐ 213	Bruce Hurst	.35	.17	.03
☐ 165	Rick Camp	.10	.05	.01	☐ 214	Bob Shirley	.10	.05	.01
☐ 166	Lee Mazzilli	.10	.05	.01	☐ 215	Pat Zachry	.10	.05	.01
☐ 167	Scot Thompson	.10	.05	.01	☐ 216	Julio Franco	1.25	.60	.12
☐ 168	Bob Forsch	.10	.05	.01	☐ 217	Mike Armstrong	.10	.05	.01
☐ 169	Mike Flanagan	.15	.07	.01	☐ 218	Dave Beard	.10	.05	.01
☐ 170	Rick Manning	.10	.05	.01	☐ 219	Steve Rogers	.10	.05	.01
☐ 171	Chet Lemon	.15	.07	.01	☐ 220	John Butcher	.10	.05	.01
☐ 172	Jerry Remy	.10	.05	.01	☐ 221	Mike Smithson	.15	.07	.01
☐ 173	Ron Guidry	.25	.12	.02	☐ 222	Frank White	.15	.07	.01
☐ 174	Pedro Guerrero	.50	.25	.05	☐ 223	Mike Heath	.10	.05	.01
☐ 175	Willie Wilson	.20	.10	.02	☐ 224	Chris Bando	.10	.05	.01
☐ 176	Carney Lansford	.25	.12	.02	☐ 225	Roy Smalley	.10	.05	.01
☐ 177	Al Oliver	.20	.10	.02	☐ 226	Dusty Baker	.15	.07	.01
☐ 178	Jim Sundberg	.10	.05	.01	☐ 227	Lou Whitaker	.35	.17	.03
☐ 179	Bobby Grich	.15	.07	.01	☐ 228	John Lowenstein	.10	.05	.01
☐ 180	Rich Dotson	.15	.07	.01	☐ 229	Ben Oglivie	.15	.07	.01
☐ 181	Joaquin Andujar	.15	.07	.01	☐ 230	Doug DeCinces	.15	.07	.01
☐ 182	Jose Cruz	.15	.07	.01	☐ 231	Lonnie Smith	.20	.10	.02
☐ 183	Mike Schmidt	3.25	1.50	.30	☐ 232	Ray Knight	.15	.07	.01
☐ 184	Gary Redus	.40	.20	.04	☐ 233	Gary Matthews	.15	.07	.01
☐ 185	Garry Templeton	.15	.07	.01	☐ 234	Juan Bonilla	.10	.05	.01
☐ 186	Tony Pena	.20	.10	.02	☐ 235	Rod Scurry	.10	.05	.01
☐ 187	Greg Minton	.10	.05	.01	☐ 236	Atlee Hammaker	.10	.05	.01
☐ 188	Phil Niekro	.40	.20	.04	☐ 237	Mike Caldwell	.10	.05	.01
☐ 189	Ferguson Jenkins	.25	.12	.02	☐ 238	Keith Hernandez	.45	.22	.04
☐ 190	Mookie Wilson	.20	.10	.02	☐ 239	Larry Bowa	.15	.07	.01
☐ 191	Jim Beattie	.10	.05	.01	☐ 240	Tony Bernazard	.10	.05	.01
☐ 192	Gary Ward	.15	.07	.01	☐ 241	Damaso Garcia	.10	.05	.01
☐ 193	Jesse Barfield	.40	.20	.04	☐ 242	Tom Brunansky	.35	.17	.03
☐ 194	Pete Filson	.10	.05	.01	☐ 243	Dan Driessen	.10	.05	.01
☐ 195	Roy Lee Jackson	.10	.05	.01	☐ 244	Ron Kittle	.30	.15	.03
☐ 196	Rick Sweet	.10	.05	.01	☐ 245	Tim Stoddard	.10	.05	.01
☐ 197	Jesse Orosco	.10	.05	.01	☐ 246	Bob L. Gibson	.15	.07	.01
☐ 198	Steve Lake	.10	.05	.01		(Brewers Pitcher)			
☐ 199	Ken Dayley	.10	.05	.01					
☐ 200	Manny Sarmiento	.10	.05	.01	☐ 247	Marty Castillo	.10	.05	.01
☐ 201	Mark Davis	1.50	.75	.15	☐ 248	Don Mattingly UER	65.00	32.50	6.50
☐ 202	Tim Flannery	.10	.05	.01		("traiing," on back)			
☐ 203	Bill Scherrer	.10	.05	.01	☐ 249	Jeff Newman	.10	.05	.01
☐ 204	Al Holland	.10	.05	.01	☐ 250	Alejandro Pena	.60	.30	.06
☐ 205	Dave Von Ohlen	.10	.05	.01	☐ 251	Toby Harrah	.15	.07	.01
☐ 206	Mike LaCoss	.10	.05	.01	☐ 252	Cesar Geronimo	.10	.05	.01
☐ 207	Juan Beniquez	.10	.05	.01	☐ 253	Tom Underwood	.10	.05	.01
					☐ 254	Doug Flynn	.10	.05	.01

		MINT	EXC	G-VG				MINT	EXC	G-VG
☐ 255	Andy Hassler	.10	.05	.01	☐ 303	Darrell Porter		.10	.05	.01
☐ 256	Odell Jones	.10	.05	.01	☐ 304	Dickie Thon		.15	.07	.01
☐ 257	Rudy Law	.10	.05	.01	☐ 305	Garry Maddox		.10	.05	.01
☐ 258	Harry Spilman	.10	.05	.01	☐ 306	Cesar Cedeno		.15	.07	.01
☐ 259	Marty Bystrom	.10	.05	.01	☐ 307	Gary Lucas		.10	.05	.01
☐ 260	Dave Rucker	.10	.05	.01	☐ 308	Johnny Ray		.20	.10	.02
☐ 261	Ruppert Jones	.10	.05	.01	☐ 309	Andy McGaffigan		.10	.05	.01
☐ 262	Jeff R. Jones	.10	.05	.01	☐ 310	Claudell Washington		.15	.07	.01
	(Reds OF)				☐ 311	Ryne Sandberg		3.00	1.50	.30
☐ 263	Gerald Perry	1.50	.75	.15	☐ 312	George Foster		.25	.12	.02
☐ 264	Gene Tenace	.10	.05	.01	☐ 313	Spike Owen		.30	.15	.03
☐ 265	Brad Wellman	.10	.05	.01	☐ 314	Gary Gaetti		1.00	.50	.10
☐ 266	Dickie Noles	.10	.05	.01	☐ 315	Willie Upshaw		.15	.07	.01
☐ 267	Jamie Allen	.10	.05	.01	☐ 316	Al Williams		.10	.05	.01
☐ 268	Jim Gott	.15	.07	.01	☐ 317	Jorge Orta		.10	.05	.01
☐ 269	Ron Davis	.10	.05	.01	☐ 318	Orlando Mercado		.10	.05	.01
☐ 270	Benny Ayala	.10	.05	.01	☐ 319	Junior Ortiz		.10	.05	.01
☐ 271	Ned Yost	.10	.05	.01	☐ 320	Mike Proly		.10	.05	.01
☐ 272	Dave Rozema	.10	.05	.01	☐ 321	Randy Johnson		.10	.05	.01
☐ 273	Dave Stapleton	.10	.05	.01	☐ 322	Jim Morrison		.10	.05	.01
☐ 274	Lou Piniella	.20	.10	.02	☐ 323	Max Venable		.10	.05	.01
☐ 275	Jose Morales	.10	.05	.01	☐ 324	Tony Gwynn		5.00	2.50	.50
☐ 276	Broderick Perkins	.10	.05	.01	☐ 325	Duane Walker		.10	.05	.01
☐ 277	Butch Davis	.15	.07	.01	☐ 326	Ozzie Virgil		.10	.05	.01
☐ 278	Tony Phillips	.35	.17	.03	☐ 327	Jeff Lahti		.10	.05	.01
☐ 279	Jeff Reardon	.20	.10	.02	☐ 328	Bill Dawley		.15	.07	.01
☐ 280	Ken Forsch	.10	.05	.01	☐ 329	Rob Wilfong		.10	.05	.01
☐ 281	Pete O'Brien	1.50	.75	.15	☐ 330	Marc Hill		.10	.05	.01
☐ 282	Tom Paciorek	.10	.05	.01	☐ 331	Ray Burris		.10	.05	.01
☐ 283	Frank LaCorte	.10	.05	.01	☐ 332	Allan Ramirez		.10	.05	.01
☐ 284	Tim Lollar	.10	.05	.01	☐ 333	Chuck Porter		.10	.05	.01
☐ 285	Greg Gross	.10	.05	.01	☐ 334	Wayne Krenchicki		.10	.05	.01
☐ 286	Alex Trevino	.10	.05	.01	☐ 335	Gary Allenson		.10	.05	.01
☐ 287	Gene Garber	.10	.05	.01	☐ 336	Bobby Meacham		.15	.07	.01
☐ 288	Dave Parker	.40	.20	.04	☐ 337	Joe Beckwith		.10	.05	.01
☐ 289	Lee Smith	.20	.10	.02	☐ 338	Rick Sutcliffe		.35	.17	.03
☐ 290	Dave LaPoint	.15	.07	.01	☐ 339	Mark Huismann		.15	.07	.01
☐ 291	John Shelby	.45	.22	.04	☐ 340	Tim Conroy		.15	.07	.01
☐ 292	Charlie Moore	.10	.05	.01	☐ 341	Scott Sanderson		.10	.05	.01
☐ 293	Alan Trammell	.60	.30	.06	☐ 342	Larry Biittner		.10	.05	.01
☐ 294	Tony Armas	.15	.07	.01	☐ 343	Dave Stewart		.60	.30	.06
☐ 295	Shane Rawley	.10	.05	.01	☐ 344	Darryl Motley		.10	.05	.01
☐ 296	Greg Brock	.15	.07	.01	☐ 345	Chris Codiroli		.15	.07	.01
☐ 297	Hal McRae	.15	.07	.01	☐ 346	Rich Behenna		.10	.05	.01
☐ 298	Mike Davis	.10	.05	.01	☐ 347	Andre Robertson		.10	.05	.01
☐ 299	Tim Raines	.75	.35	.07	☐ 348	Mike Marshall		.25	.12	.02
☐ 300	Bucky Dent	.20	.10	.02	☐ 349	Larry Herndon		.10	.05	.01
☐ 301	Tommy John	.30	.15	.03	☐ 350	Rich Dauer		.10	.05	.01
☐ 302	Carlton Fisk	.50	.25	.05	☐ 351	Cecil Cooper		.15	.07	.01

		MINT	EXC	G-VG			MINT	EXC	G-VG
☐ 352	Rod Carew	.90	.45	.09	☐ 401	Bill Gullickson	.10	.05	.01
☐ 353	Willie McGee	.40	.20	.04	☐ 402	Geoff Zahn	.10	.05	.01
☐ 354	Phil Garner	.10	.05	.01	☐ 403	Billy Sample	.10	.05	.01
☐ 355	Joe Morgan	.60	.30	.06	☐ 404	Mike Squires	.10	.05	.01
☐ 356	Luis Salazar	.15	.07	.01	☐ 405	Craig Reynolds	.10	.05	.01
☐ 357	John Candelaria	.15	.07	.01	☐ 406	Eric Show	.15	.07	.01
☐ 358	Bill Laskey	.10	.05	.01	☐ 407	John Denny	.15	.07	.01
☐ 359	Bob McClure	.10	.05	.01	☐ 408	Dann Bilardello	.10	.05	.01
☐ 360	Dave Kingman	.20	.10	.02	☐ 409	Bruce Benedict	.10	.05	.01
☐ 361	Ron Cey	.15	.07	.01	☐ 410	Kent Tekulve	.15	.07	.01
☐ 362	Matt Young	.15	.07	.01	☐ 411	Mel Hall	.25	.12	.02
☐ 363	Lloyd Moseby	.20	.10	.02	☐ 412	John Stuper	.10	.05	.01
☐ 364	Frank Viola	1.25	.60	.12	☐ 413	Rick Dempsey	.10	.05	.01
☐ 365	Eddie Milner	.10	.05	.01	☐ 414	Don Sutton	.40	.20	.04
☐ 366	Floyd Bannister	.10	.05	.01	☐ 415	Jack Morris	.35	.17	.03
☐ 367	Dan Ford	.10	.05	.01	☐ 416	John Tudor	.30	.15	.03
☐ 368	Moose Haas	.10	.05	.01	☐ 417	Willie Randolph	.20	.10	.02
☐ 369	Doug Bair	.10	.05	.01	☐ 418	Jerry Reuss	.15	.07	.01
☐ 370	Ray Fontenot	.10	.05	.01	☐ 419	Don Slaught	.15	.07	.01
☐ 371	Luis Aponte	.10	.05	.01	☐ 420	Steve McCatty	.10	.05	.01
☐ 372	Jack Fimple	.10	.05	.01	☐ 421	Tim Wallach	.25	.12	.02
☐ 373	Neal Heaton	.30	.15	.03	☐ 422	Larry Parrish	.15	.07	.01
☐ 374	Greg Pryor	.10	.05	.01	☐ 423	Brian Downing	.15	.07	.01
☐ 375	Wayne Gross	.10	.05	.01	☐ 424	Britt Burns	.10	.05	.01
☐ 376	Charlie Lea	.10	.05	.01	☐ 425	David Green	.10	.05	.01
☐ 377	Steve Lubratich	.10	.05	.01	☐ 426	Jerry Mumphrey	.10	.05	.01
☐ 378	Jon Matlack	.10	.05	.01	☐ 427	Ivan DeJesus	.10	.05	.01
☐ 379	Julio Cruz	.10	.05	.01	☐ 428	Mario Soto	.10	.05	.01
☐ 380	John Mizerock	.10	.05	.01	☐ 429	Gene Richards	.10	.05	.01
☐ 381	Kevin Gross	.50	.25	.05	☐ 430	Dale Berra	.10	.05	.01
☐ 382	Mike Ramsey	.10	.05	.01	☐ 431	Darrell Evans	.20	.10	.02
☐ 383	Doug Gwosdz	.10	.05	.01	☐ 432	Glenn Hubbard	.10	.05	.01
☐ 384	Kelly Paris	.15	.07	.01	☐ 433	Jody Davis	.15	.07	.01
☐ 385	Pete Falcone	.10	.05	.01	☐ 434	Danny Heep	.10	.05	.01
☐ 386	Milt May	.10	.05	.01	☐ 435	Ed Nunez	.20	.10	.02
☐ 387	Fred Breining	.10	.05	.01	☐ 436	Bobby Castillo	.10	.05	.01
☐ 388	Craig Lefferts	.30	.15	.03	☐ 437	Ernie Whitt	.15	.07	.01
☐ 389	Steve Henderson	.10	.05	.01	☐ 438	Scott Ullger	.10	.05	.01
☐ 390	Randy Moffitt	.10	.05	.01	☐ 439	Doyle Alexander	.15	.07	.01
☐ 391	Ron Washington	.10	.05	.01	☐ 440	Domingo Ramos	.10	.05	.01
☐ 392	Gary Roenicke	.10	.05	.01	☐ 441	Craig Swan	.10	.05	.01
☐ 393	Tom Candiotti	.35	.17	.03	☐ 442	Warren Brusstar	.10	.05	.01
☐ 394	Larry Pashnick	.10	.05	.01	☐ 443	Len Barker	.10	.05	.01
☐ 395	Dwight Evans	.35	.17	.03	☐ 444	Mike Easler	.10	.05	.01
☐ 396	Goose Gossage	.25	.12	.02	☐ 445	Renie Martin	.10	.05	.01
☐ 397	Derrel Thomas	.10	.05	.01	☐ 446	Dennis Rasmussen	.65	.30	.06
☐ 398	Juan Eichelberger	.10	.05	.01	☐ 447	Ted Power	.15	.07	.01
☐ 399	Leon Roberts	.10	.05	.01	☐ 448	Charles Hudson	.25	.12	.02
☐ 400	Dave Lopes	.15	.07	.01	☐ 449	Danny Cox	.65	.30	.06

		MINT	EXC	G-VG
☐ 450	Kevin Bass	.20	.10	.02
☐ 451	Daryl Sconiers	.10	.05	.01
☐ 452	Scott Fletcher	.20	.10	.02
☐ 453	Bryn Smith	.20	.10	.02
☐ 454	Jim Dwyer	.10	.05	.01
☐ 455	Rob Picciolo	.10	.05	.01
☐ 456	Enos Cabell	.10	.05	.01
☐ 457	Dennis Boyd	.65	.30	.06
☐ 458	Butch Wynegar	.10	.05	.01
☐ 459	Burt Hooton	.10	.05	.01
☐ 460	Ron Hassey	.10	.05	.01
☐ 461	Danny Jackson	2.00	1.00	.20
☐ 462	Bob Kearney	.10	.05	.01
☐ 463	Terry Francona	.10	.05	.01
☐ 464	Wayne Tolleson	.10	.05	.01
☐ 465	Mickey Rivers	.10	.05	.01
☐ 466	John Wathan	.10	.05	.01
☐ 467	Bill Almon	.10	.05	.01
☐ 468	George Vukovich	.10	.05	.01
☐ 469	Steve Kemp	.15	.07	.01
☐ 470	Ken Landreaux	.10	.05	.01
☐ 471	Milt Wilcox	.10	.05	.01
☐ 472	Tippy Martinez	.10	.05	.01
☐ 473	Ted Simmons	.20	.10	.02
☐ 474	Tim Foli	.10	.05	.01
☐ 475	George Hendrick	.15	.07	.01
☐ 476	Terry Puhl	.10	.05	.01
☐ 477	Von Hayes	.25	.12	.02
☐ 478	Bobby Brown	.10	.05	.01
☐ 479	Lee Lacy	.10	.05	.01
☐ 480	Joel Youngblood	.10	.05	.01
☐ 481	Jim Slaton	.10	.05	.01
☐ 482	Mike Fitzgerald	.10	.05	.01
☐ 483	Keith Moreland	.10	.05	.01
☐ 484	Ron Roenicke	.10	.05	.01
☐ 485	Luis Leal	.10	.05	.01
☐ 486	Bryan Oelkers	.10	.05	.01
☐ 487	Bruce Berenyi	.10	.05	.01
☐ 488	LaMarr Hoyt	.15	.07	.01
☐ 489	Joe Nolan	.10	.05	.01
☐ 490	Marshall Edwards	.10	.05	.01
☐ 491	Mike Laga	.10	.05	.01
☐ 492	Rick Cerone	.10	.05	.01
☐ 493	Rick Miller (listed as Mike on card front)	.10	.05	.01
☐ 494	Rick Honeycutt	.10	.05	.01
☐ 495	Mike Hargrove	.15	.07	.01
☐ 496	Joe Simpson	.10	.05	.01

		MINT	EXC	G-VG
☐ 497	Keith Atherton	.10	.05	.01
☐ 498	Chris Welsh	.10	.05	.01
☐ 499	Bruce Kison	.10	.05	.01
☐ 500	Bobby Johnson	.10	.05	.01
☐ 501	Jerry Koosman	.20	.10	.02
☐ 502	Frank DiPino	.10	.05	.01
☐ 503	Tony Perez	.30	.15	.03
☐ 504	Ken Oberkfell	.10	.05	.01
☐ 505	Mark Thurmond	.15	.07	.01
☐ 506	Joe Price	.10	.05	.01
☐ 507	Pascual Perez	.30	.15	.03
☐ 508	Marvell Wynne	.15	.07	.01
☐ 509	Mike Krukow	.15	.07	.01
☐ 510	Dick Ruthven	.10	.05	.01
☐ 511	Al Cowens	.10	.05	.01
☐ 512	Cliff Johnson	.10	.05	.01
☐ 513	Randy Bush	.25	.12	.02
☐ 514	Sammy Stewart	.10	.05	.01
☐ 515	Bill Schroeder	.15	.07	.01
☐ 516	Aurelio Lopez	.10	.05	.01
☐ 517	Mike Brown (Red Sox pitcher)	.15	.07	.01
☐ 518	Graig Nettles	.20	.10	.02
☐ 519	Dave Sax	.10	.05	.01
☐ 520	Jerry Willard	.10	.05	.01
☐ 521	Paul Splittorff	.10	.05	.01
☐ 522	Tom Burgmeier	.10	.05	.01
☐ 523	Chris Speier	.10	.05	.01
☐ 524	Bobby Clark	.10	.05	.01
☐ 525	George Wright	.10	.05	.01
☐ 526	Dennis Lamp	.10	.05	.01
☐ 527	Tony Scott	.10	.05	.01
☐ 528	Ed Whitson	.10	.05	.01
☐ 529	Ron Reed	.10	.05	.01
☐ 530	Charlie Puleo	.10	.05	.01
☐ 531	Jerry Royster	.10	.05	.01
☐ 532	Don Robinson	.10	.05	.01
☐ 533	Steve Trout	.10	.05	.01
☐ 534	Bruce Sutter	.20	.10	.02
☐ 535	Bob Horner	.20	.10	.02
☐ 536	Pat Tabler	.20	.10	.02
☐ 537	Chris Chambliss	.15	.07	.01
☐ 538	Bob Ojeda	.20	.10	.02
☐ 539	Alan Ashby	.10	.05	.01
☐ 540	Jay Johnstone	.15	.07	.01
☐ 541	Bob Dernier	.10	.05	.01
☐ 542	Brook Jacoby	1.25	.60	.12
☐ 543	U.L. Washington	.10	.05	.01
☐ 544	Danny Darwin	.10	.05	.01

		MINT	EXC	G-VG
☐ 545	Kiko Garcia	.10	.05	.01
☐ 546	Vance Law UER (listed as P on card front)	.15	.07	.01
☐ 547	Tug McGraw	.20	.10	.02
☐ 548	Dave Smith	.15	.07	.01
☐ 549	Len Matuszek	.10	.05	.01
☐ 550	Tom Hume	.10	.05	.01
☐ 551	Dave Dravecky	.60	.30	.06
☐ 552	Rick Rhoden	.15	.07	.01
☐ 553	Duane Kuiper	.10	.05	.01
☐ 554	Rusty Staub	.20	.10	.02
☐ 555	Bill Campbell	.10	.05	.01
☐ 556	Mike Torrez	.10	.05	.01
☐ 557	Dave Henderson	.30	.15	.03
☐ 558	Len Whitehouse	.10	.05	.01
☐ 559	Barry Bonnell	.10	.05	.01
☐ 560	Rick Lysander	.10	.05	.01
☐ 561	Garth Iorg	.10	.05	.01
☐ 562	Bryan Clark	.10	.05	.01
☐ 563	Brian Giles	.10	.05	.01
☐ 564	Vern Ruhle	.10	.05	.01
☐ 565	Steve Bedrosian	.30	.15	.03
☐ 566	Larry McWilliams	.10	.05	.01
☐ 567	Jeff Leonard UER (listed as P on card front)	.20	.10	.02
☐ 568	Alan Wiggins	.10	.05	.01
☐ 569	Jeff Russell	.75	.35	.07
☐ 570	Salome Barojas	.10	.05	.01
☐ 571	Dane Iorg	.10	.05	.01
☐ 572	Bob Knepper	.15	.07	.01
☐ 573	Gary Lavelle	.10	.05	.01
☐ 574	Gorman Thomas	.15	.07	.01
☐ 575	Manny Trillo	.10	.05	.01
☐ 576	Jim Palmer	1.00	.50	.10
☐ 577	Dale Murray	.10	.05	.01
☐ 578	Tom Brookens	.10	.05	.01
☐ 579	Rich Gedman	.15	.07	.01
☐ 580	Bill Doran	1.00	.50	.10
☐ 581	Steve Yeager	.10	.05	.01
☐ 582	Dan Spillner	.10	.05	.01
☐ 583	Dan Quisenberry	.20	.10	.02
☐ 584	Rance Mulliniks	.10	.05	.01
☐ 585	Storm Davis	.20	.10	.02
☐ 586	Dave Schmidt	.15	.07	.01
☐ 587	Bill Russell	.15	.07	.01
☐ 588	Pat Sheridan	.25	.12	.02
☐ 589	Rafael Ramirez	.15	.07	.01

		MINT	EXC	G-VG
	ERR (A's on front)			
☐ 590	Bud Anderson	.10	.05	.01
☐ 591	George Frazier	.10	.05	.01
☐ 592	Lee Tunnell	.15	.07	.01
☐ 593	Kirk Gibson	.65	.30	.06
☐ 594	Scott McGregor	.15	.07	.01
☐ 595	Bob Bailor	.10	.05	.01
☐ 596	Tommy Herr	.15	.07	.01
☐ 597	Luis Sanchez	.10	.05	.01
☐ 598	Dave Engle	.10	.05	.01
☐ 599	Craig McMurtry	.15	.07	.01
☐ 600	Carlos Diaz	.10	.05	.01
☐ 601	Tom O'Malley	.10	.05	.01
☐ 602	Nick Esasky	3.50	1.75	.35
☐ 603	Ron Hodges	.10	.05	.01
☐ 604	Ed VandeBerg	.10	.05	.01
☐ 605	Alfredo Griffin	.15	.07	.01
☐ 606	Glenn Hoffman	.10	.05	.01
☐ 607	Hubie Brooks	.25	.12	.02
☐ 608	Richard Barnes UER (photo actually Neal Heaton)	.10	.05	.01
☐ 609	Greg Walker	.50	.25	.05
☐ 610	Ken Singleton	.15	.07	.01
☐ 611	Mark Clear	.10	.05	.01
☐ 612	Buck Martinez	.10	.05	.01
☐ 613	Ken Griffey	.20	.10	.02
☐ 614	Reid Nichols	.10	.05	.01
☐ 615	Doug Sisk	.10	.05	.01
☐ 616	Bob Brenly	.10	.05	.01
☐ 617	Joey McLaughlin	.10	.05	.01
☐ 618	Glenn Wilson	.15	.07	.01
☐ 619	Bob Stoddard	.10	.05	.01
☐ 620	Lenn Sakata UER (listed as Len on card front)	.10	.05	.01
☐ 621	Mike Young	.25	.12	.02
☐ 622	John Stefero	.15	.07	.01
☐ 623	Carmelo Martinez	.30	.15	.03
☐ 624	Dave Bergman	.10	.05	.01
☐ 625	Runnin' Reds (sic, Redbirds) David Green Willie McGee Lonnie Smith Ozzie Smith	.20	.10	.02
☐ 626	Rudy May	.10	.05	.01
☐ 627	Matt Keough	.10	.05	.01
☐ 628	Jose DeLeon	.75	.35	.07

		MINT	EXC	G-VG
☐ 629	Jim Essian	.10	.05	.01
☐ 630	Darnell Coles	.40	.20	.04
☐ 631	Mike Warren	.15	.07	.01
☐ 632	Del Crandall MG	.10	.05	.01
☐ 633	Dennis Martinez	.15	.07	.01
☐ 634	Mike Moore	.25	.12	.02
☐ 635	Lary Sorensen	.10	.05	.01
☐ 636	Ricky Nelson	.10	.05	.01
☐ 637	Omar Moreno	.10	.05	.01
☐ 638	Charlie Hough	.15	.07	.01
☐ 639	Dennis Eckersley	.30	.12	.03
☐ 640	Walt Terrell	.60	.30	.06
☐ 641	Denny Walling	.10	.05	.01
☐ 642	Dave Anderson	.25	.12	.02
☐ 643	Jose Oquendo	.75	.35	.07
☐ 644	Bob Stanley	.10	.05	.01
☐ 645	Dave Geisel	.10	.05	.01
☐ 646	Scott Garrelts	1.00	.50	.10
☐ 647	Gary Pettis	.50	.25	.05
☐ 648	Duke Snider Puzzle Card	.10	.05	.01
☐ 649	Johnnie LeMaster	.10	.05	.01
☐ 650	Dave Collins	.10	.05	.01
☐ 651	The Chicken	.20	.10	.02
☐ 652	DK Checklist (unnumbered)	.10	.01	.00
☐ 653	Checklist 1-130 (unnumbered)	.08	.01	.00
☐ 654	Checklist 131-234 (unnumbered)	.08	.01	.00
☐ 655	Checklist 235-338 (unnumbered)	.08	.01	.00
☐ 656	Checklist 339-442 (unnumbered)	.08	.01	.00
☐ 657	Checklist 443-546 (unnumbered)	.08	.01	.00
☐ 658	Checklist 547-651 (unnumbered)	.08	.01	.00
☐ A	Living Legends A Gaylord Perry Rollie Fingers	3.00	1.50	.30
☐ B	Living Legends B Carl Yastrzemski Johnny Bench	7.00	3.50	.70

1985 Donruss

The cards in this 660-card set measure 2 ½" by 3 ½". The 1985 Donruss regular issue cards have fronts that feature jet black borders on which orange lines have been placed. The fronts contain the standard team logo, player's name, position, and Donruss logo. The cards were distributed with puzzle pieces from a Dick Perez rendition of Lou Gehrig. The first 26 cards of the set feature Diamond Kings (DK), for the fourth year in a row; the artwork on the Diamond Kings was again produced by the Perez-Steele Galleries. Cards 27-46 feature Rated Rookies (RR). The unnumbered checklist cards are arbitrarily numbered below as numbers 654 through 660. This set is noted for containing the Rookie Cards of Roger Clemens, Alvin Davis, Eric Davis, Dwight Gooden, Orel Hershiser, Mark Langston, Kirby Puckett, Bret Saberhagen, and Danny Tartabull.

		MINT	EXC	G-VG
COMPLETE SET (660)		150.00	70.00	14.00
COMMON PLAYER (1-660)		.06	.03	.00
☐ 1	Ryne Sandberg DK	.60	.12	.02
☐ 2	Doug DeCinces DK	.10	.05	.01
☐ 3	Richard Dotson DK	.10	.05	.01
☐ 4	Bert Blyleven DK	.15	.07	.01
☐ 5	Lou Whitaker DK	.20	.10	.02
☐ 6	Dan Quisenberry DK	.15	.07	.01
☐ 7	Don Mattingly DK	6.00	3.00	.60
☐ 8	Carney Lansford DK	.15	.07	.01

			MINT	EXC	G-VG
☐	9	Frank Tanana DK	.10	.05	.01
☐	10	Willie Upshaw DK	.10	.05	.01
☐	11	Claudell Washington DK	.10	.05	.01
☐	12	Mike Marshall DK	.15	.07	.01
☐	13	Joaquin Andujar DK	.10	.05	.01
☐	14	Cal Ripken DK	.40	.20	.04
☐	15	Jim Rice DK	.25	.12	.02
☐	16	Don Sutton DK	.25	.12	.02
☐	17	Frank Viola DK	.40	.20	.04
☐	18	Alvin Davis DK	.40	.20	.04
☐	19	Mario Soto DK	.10	.05	.01
☐	20	Jose Cruz DK	.10	.05	.01
☐	21	Charlie Lea DK	.10	.05	.01
☐	22	Jesse Orosco DK	.10	.05	.01
☐	23	Juan Samuel DK	.30	.15	.03
☐	24	Tony Pena DK	.15	.07	.01
☐	25	Tony Gwynn DK	.75	.35	.07
☐	26	Bob Brenly DK	.10	.05	.01
☐	27	Danny Tartabull RR	5.00	2.50	.50
☐	28	Mike Bielecki RR	.75	.35	.07
☐	29	Steve Lyons RR	.15	.07	.01
☐	30	Jeff Reed RR	.10	.05	.01
☐	31	Tony Brewer RR	.10	.05	.01
☐	32	John Morris RR	.15	.07	.01
☐	33	Daryl Boston RR	.20	.10	.02
☐	34	Al Pulido RR	.10	.05	.01
☐	35	Steve Kiefer RR	.15	.07	.01
☐	36	Larry Sheets RR	.35	.17	.03
☐	37	Scott Bradley RR	.30	.15	.03
☐	38	Calvin Schiraldi RR	.25	.12	.02
☐	39	Shawon Dunston RR	2.50	1.25	.25
☐	40	Charlie Mitchell RR	.10	.05	.01
☐	41	Billy Hatcher RR	.45	.22	.04
☐	42	Russ Stephans RR	.10	.05	.01
☐	43	Alejandro Sanchez RR	.10	.05	.01
☐	44	Steve Jeltz RR	.10	.05	.01
☐	45	Jim Traber RR	.25	.12	.02
☐	46	Doug Loman RR	.15	.07	.01
☐	47	Eddie Murray	.45	.22	.04
☐	48	Robin Yount	.70	.35	.07
☐	49	Lance Parrish	.25	.12	.02
☐	50	Jim Rice	.30	.15	.03
☐	51	Dave Winfield	.40	.20	.04
☐	52	Fernando Valenzuela	.25	.12	.02
☐	53	George Brett	.70	.35	.07
☐	54	Dave Kingman	.12	.06	.01
☐	55	Gary Carter	.35	.17	.03
☐	56	Buddy Bell	.12	.06	.01
☐	57	Reggie Jackson	.60	.30	.06
☐	58	Harold Baines	.25	.12	.02
☐	59	Ozzie Smith	.35	.17	.03
☐	60	Nolan Ryan	1.75	.85	.17
☐	61	Mike Schmidt	1.50	.75	.15
☐	62	Dave Parker	.20	.10	.02
☐	63	Tony Gwynn	1.50	.75	.15
☐	64	Tony Pena	.12	.06	.01
☐	65	Jack Clark	.25	.12	.02
☐	66	Dale Murphy	.75	.35	.07
☐	67	Ryne Sandberg	.60	.30	.06
☐	68	Keith Hernandez	.35	.17	.03
☐	69	Alvin Davis	4.00	2.00	.40
☐	70	Kent Hrbek	.35	.17	.03
☐	71	Willie Upshaw	.06	.03	.00
☐	72	Dave Engle	.06	.03	.00
☐	73	Alfredo Griffin	.10	.05	.01
☐	74A	Jack Perconte (Career Highlights takes four lines)	.15	.07	.01
☐	74B	Jack Perconte (Career Highlights takes three lines)	.15	.07	.01
☐	75	Jesse Orosco	.06	.03	.00
☐	76	Jody Davis	.10	.05	.01
☐	77	Bob Horner	.12	.06	.01
☐	78	Larry McWilliams	.06	.03	.00
☐	79	Joel Youngblood	.06	.03	.00
☐	80	Alan Wiggins	.06	.03	.00
☐	81	Ron Oester	.06	.03	.00
☐	82	Ozzie Virgil	.06	.03	.00
☐	83	Ricky Horton	.20	.10	.02
☐	84	Bill Doran	.15	.07	.01
☐	85	Rod Carew	.50	.25	.05
☐	86	LaMarr Hoyt	.10	.05	.01
☐	87	Tim Wallach	.12	.06	.01
☐	88	Mike Flanagan	.10	.05	.01
☐	89	Jim Sundberg	.06	.03	.00
☐	90	Chet Lemon	.10	.05	.01
☐	91	Bob Stanley	.06	.03	.00
☐	92	Willie Randolph	.12	.06	.01
☐	93	Bill Russell	.10	.05	.01
☐	94	Julio Franco	.40	.20	.04
☐	95	Dan Quisenberry	.15	.07	.01
☐	96	Bill Caudill	.06	.03	.00
☐	97	Bill Gullickson	.06	.03	.00
☐	98	Danny Darwin	.06	.03	.00
☐	99	Curtis Wilkerson	.06	.03	.00

		MINT	EXC	G-VG			MINT	EXC	G-VG
☐ 100	Bud Black	.06	.03	.00	☐ 147	Dave Meier	.06	.03	.00
☐ 101	Tony Phillips	.06	.03	.00	☐ 148	Sammy Stewart	.06	.03	.00
☐ 102	Tony Bernazard	.06	.03	.00	☐ 149	Mark Brouhard	.06	.03	.00
☐ 103	Jay Howell	.10	.05	.01	☐ 150	Larry Herndon	.06	.03	.00
☐ 104	Burt Hooton	.06	.03	.00	☐ 151	Oil Can Boyd	.10	.05	.01
☐ 105	Milt Wilcox	.06	.03	.00	☐ 152	Brian Dayett	.06	.03	.00
☐ 106	Rich Dauer	.06	.03	.00	☐ 153	Tom Niedenfuer	.06	.03	.00
☐ 107	Don Sutton	.25	.12	.02	☐ 154	Brook Jacoby	.12	.06	.01
☐ 108	Mike Witt	.10	.05	.01	☐ 155	Onix Concepcion	.06	.03	.00
☐ 109	Bruce Sutter	.12	.06	.01	☐ 156	Tim Conroy	.06	.03	.00
☐ 110	Enos Cabell	.06	.03	.00	☐ 157	Joe Hesketh	.15	.07	.01
☐ 111	John Denny	.10	.05	.01	☐ 158	Brian Downing	.10	.05	.01
☐ 112	Dave Dravecky	.15	.07	.01	☐ 159	Tommy Dunbar	.06	.03	.00
☐ 113	Marvell Wynne	.06	.03	.00	☐ 160	Marc Hill	.06	.03	.00
☐ 114	Johnnie LeMaster	.06	.03	.00	☐ 161	Phil Garner	.06	.03	.00
☐ 115	Chuck Porter	.06	.03	.00	☐ 162	Jerry Davis	.06	.03	.00
☐ 116	John Gibbons	.10	.05	.01	☐ 163	Bill Campbell	.06	.03	.00
☐ 117	Keith Moreland	.06	.03	.00	☐ 164	John Franco	2.00	1.00	.20
☐ 118	Darnell Coles	.10	.05	.01	☐ 165	Len Barker	.06	.03	.00
☐ 119	Dennis Lamp	.06	.03	.00	☐ 166	Benny Distefano	.10	.05	.01
☐ 120	Ron Davis	.06	.03	.00	☐ 167	George Frazier	.06	.03	.00
☐ 121	Nick Esasky	.25	.12	.02	☐ 168	Tito Landrum	.06	.03	.00
☐ 122	Vance Law	.10	.05	.01	☐ 169	Cal Ripken	.60	.30	.06
☐ 123	Gary Roenicke	.06	.03	.00	☐ 170	Cecil Cooper	.12	.06	.01
☐ 124	Bill Schroeder	.06	.03	.00	☐ 171	Alan Trammell	.30	.15	.03
☐ 125	Dave Rozema	.06	.03	.00	☐ 172	Wade Boggs	5.50	2.75	.55
☐ 126	Bobby Meacham	.06	.03	.00	☐ 173	Don Baylor	.15	.07	.01
☐ 127	Marty Barrett	.35	.17	.03	☐ 174	Pedro Guerrero	.30	.15	.03
☐ 128	R.J. Reynolds	.25	.12	.02	☐ 175	Frank White	.10	.05	.01
☐ 129	Ernie Camacho UER	.06	.03	.00	☐ 176	Rickey Henderson	.90	.45	.09
	(photo actually				☐ 177	Charlie Lea	.06	.03	.00
	Rich Thompson)				☐ 178	Pete O'Brien	.15	.07	.01
☐ 130	Jorge Orta	.06	.03	.00	☐ 179	Doug DeCinces	.10	.05	.01
☐ 131	Lary Sorensen	.06	.03	.00	☐ 180	Ron Kittle	.20	.10	.02
☐ 132	Terry Francona	.06	.03	.00	☐ 181	George Hendrick	.10	.05	.01
☐ 133	Fred Lynn	.15	.07	.01	☐ 182	Joe Niekro	.10	.05	.01
☐ 134	Bob Jones	.06	.03	.00	☐ 183	Juan Samuel	1.00	.50	.10
☐ 135	Jerry Hairston	.06	.03	.00	☐ 184	Mario Soto	.06	.03	.00
☐ 136	Kevin Bass	.12	.06	.01	☐ 185	Goose Gossage	.15	.07	.01
☐ 137	Garry Maddox	.10	.05	.01	☐ 186	Johnny Ray	.12	.06	.01
☐ 138	Dave LaPoint	.10	.05	.01	☐ 187	Bob Brenly	.06	.03	.00
☐ 139	Kevin McReynolds	1.00	.50	.10	☐ 188	Craig McMurtry	.06	.03	.00
☐ 140	Wayne Krenchicki	.06	.03	.00	☐ 189	Leon Durham	.06	.03	.00
☐ 141	Rafael Ramirez	.06	.03	.00	☐ 190	Dwight Gooden	13.50	6.00	1.25
☐ 142	Rod Scurry	.06	.03	.00	☐ 191	Barry Bonnell	.06	.03	.00
☐ 143	Greg Minton	.06	.03	.00	☐ 192	Tim Teufel	.10	.05	.01
☐ 144	Tim Stoddard	.06	.03	.00	☐ 193	Dave Stieb	.15	.07	.01
☐ 145	Steve Henderson	.06	.03	.00	☐ 194	Mickey Hatcher	.06	.03	.00
☐ 146	George Bell	.65	.30	.06	☐ 195	Jesse Barfield	.25	.12	.02

		MINT	EXC	G-VG			MINT	EXC	G-VG
☐ 196	Al Cowens	.06	.03	.00	☐ 243	Dann Bilardello	.06	.03	.00
☐ 197	Hubie Brooks	.10	.05	.01	☐ 244	Rudy Law	.06	.03	.00
☐ 198	Steve Trout	.06	.03	.00	☐ 245	John Lowenstein	.06	.03	.00
☐ 199	Glenn Hubbard	.06	.03	.00	☐ 246	Tom Tellmann	.06	.03	.00
☐ 200	Bill Madlock	.10	.05	.01	☐ 247	Howard Johnson	2.00	1.00	.20
☐ 201	Jeff Robinson	.35	.17	.03	☐ 248	Ray Fontenot	.06	.03	.00
	(Giants pitcher)				☐ 249	Tony Armas	.10	.05	.01
☐ 202	Eric Show	.06	.03	.00	☐ 250	Candy Maldonado	.10	.05	.01
☐ 203	Dave Concepcion	.10	.05	.01	☐ 251	Mike Jeffcoat	.06	.03	.00
☐ 204	Ivan DeJesus	.06	.03	.00	☐ 252	Dane Iorg	.06	.03	.00
☐ 205	Neil Allen	.06	.03	.00	☐ 253	Bruce Bochte	.06	.03	.00
☐ 206	Jerry Mumphrey	.06	.03	.00	☐ 254	Pete Rose	1.50	.75	.15
☐ 207	Mike Brown	.06	.03	.00	☐ 255	Don Aase	.06	.03	.00
	(Angels OF)				☐ 256	George Wright	.06	.03	.00
☐ 208	Carlton Fisk	.30	.15	.03	☐ 257	Britt Burns	.06	.03	.00
☐ 209	Bryn Smith	.12	.06	.01	☐ 258	Mike Scott	.40	.20	.04
☐ 210	Tippy Martinez	.06	.03	.00	☐ 259	Len Matuszek	.06	.03	.00
☐ 211	Dion James	.10	.05	.01	☐ 260	Dave Rucker	.06	.03	.00
☐ 212	Willie Hernandez	.10	.05	.01	☐ 261	Craig Lefferts	.10	.05	.01
☐ 213	Mike Easler	.06	.03	.00	☐ 262	Jay Tibbs	.12	.06	.01
☐ 214	Ron Guidry	.20	.10	.02	☐ 263	Bruce Benedict	.06	.03	.00
☐ 215	Rick Honeycutt	.06	.03	.00	☐ 264	Don Robinson	.06	.03	.00
☐ 216	Brett Butler	.10	.05	.01	☐ 265	Gary Lavelle	.06	.03	.00
☐ 217	Larry Gura	.06	.03	.00	☐ 266	Scott Sanderson	.06	.03	.00
☐ 218	Ray Burris	.06	.03	.00	☐ 267	Matt Young	.06	.03	.00
☐ 219	Steve Rogers	.06	.03	.00	☐ 268	Ernie Whitt	.06	.03	.00
☐ 220	Frank Tanana	.10	.05	.01	☐ 269	Houston Jimenez	.06	.03	.00
☐ 221	Ned Yost	.06	.03	.00	☐ 270	Ken Dixon	.10	.05	.01
☐ 222	Bret Saberhagen	10.00	5.00	1.00	☐ 271	Pete Ladd	.06	.03	.00
☐ 223	Mike Davis	.10	.05	.01	☐ 272	Juan Berenguer	.06	.03	.00
☐ 224	Bert Blyleven	.20	.10	.02	☐ 273	Roger Clemens	15.00	7.50	1.50
☐ 225	Steve Kemp	.10	.05	.01	☐ 274	Rick Cerone	.06	.03	.00
☐ 226	Jerry Reuss	.10	.05	.01	☐ 275	Dave Anderson	.06	.03	.00
☐ 227	Darrell Evans	.15	.07	.01	☐ 276	George Vukovich	.06	.03	.00
☐ 228	Wayne Gross	.06	.03	.00	☐ 277	Greg Pryor	.06	.03	.00
☐ 229	Jim Gantner	.06	.03	.00	☐ 278	Mike Warren	.06	.03	.00
☐ 230	Bob Boone	.15	.07	.01	☐ 279	Bob James	.06	.03	.00
☐ 231	Lonnie Smith	.12	.06	.01	☐ 280	Bobby Grich	.10	.05	.01
☐ 232	Frank DiPino	.06	.03	.00	☐ 281	Mike Mason	.06	.03	.00
☐ 233	Jerry Koosman	.10	.05	.01	☐ 282	Ron Reed	.06	.03	.00
☐ 234	Graig Nettles	.15	.07	.01	☐ 283	Alan Ashby	.06	.03	.00
☐ 235	John Tudor	.15	.07	.01	☐ 284	Mark Thurmond	.06	.03	.00
☐ 236	John Rabb	.06	.03	.00	☐ 285	Joe Lefebvre	.06	.03	.00
☐ 237	Rick Manning	.06	.03	.00	☐ 286	Ted Power	.06	.03	.00
☐ 238	Mike Fitzgerald	.06	.03	.00	☐ 287	Chris Chambliss	.10	.05	.01
☐ 239	Gary Matthews	.10	.05	.01	☐ 288	Lee Tunnell	.06	.03	.00
☐ 240	Jim Presley	.90	.45	.09	☐ 289	Rich Bordi	.06	.03	.00
☐ 241	Dave Collins	.06	.03	.00	☐ 290	Glenn Brummer	.06	.03	.00
☐ 242	Gary Gaetti	.40	.20	.04	☐ 291	Mike Boddicker	.10	.05	.01

		MINT	EXC	G-VG			MINT	EXC	G-VG
☐ 292	Rollie Fingers	.20	.10	.02	☐ 341	David Palmer	.06	.03	.00
☐ 293	Lou Whitaker	.25	.12	.02	☐ 342	Gary Ward	.10	.05	.01
☐ 294	Dwight Evans	.18	.09	.01	☐ 343	Dave Stewart	.35	.17	.03
☐ 295	Don Mattingly	15.00	7.50	1.50	☐ 344	Mark Gubicza	2.50	1.25	.25
☐ 296	Mike Marshall	.15	.07	.01	☐ 345	Carney Lansford	.15	.07	.01
☐ 297	Willie Wilson	.12	.06	.01	☐ 346	Jerry Willard	.06	.03	.00
☐ 298	Mike Heath	.06	.03	.00	☐ 347	Ken Griffey	.12	.06	.01
☐ 299	Tim Raines	.50	.25	.05	☐ 348	Franklin Stubbs	.35	.17	.03
☐ 300	Larry Parrish	.10	.05	.01	☐ 349	Aurelio Lopez	.06	.03	.00
☐ 301	Geoff Zahn	.06	.03	.00	☐ 350	Al Bumbry	.06	.03	.00
☐ 302	Rich Dotson	.10	.05	.01	☐ 351	Charlie Moore	.06	.03	.00
☐ 303	David Green	.06	.03	.00	☐ 352	Luis Sanchez	.06	.03	.00
☐ 304	Jose Cruz	.10	.05	.01	☐ 353	Darrell Porter	.06	.03	.00
☐ 305	Steve Carlton	.50	.25	.05	☐ 354	Bill Dawley	.06	.03	.00
☐ 306	Gary Redus	.06	.03	.00	☐ 355	Charles Hudson	.06	.03	.00
☐ 307	Steve Garvey	.50	.25	.05	☐ 356	Garry Templeton	.10	.05	.01
☐ 308	Jose DeLeon	.10	.05	.01	☐ 357	Cecilio Guante	.06	.03	.00
☐ 309	Randy Lerch	.06	.03	.00	☐ 358	Jeff Leonard	.12	.06	.01
☐ 310	Claudell Washington	.10	.05	.01	☐ 359	Paul Molitor	.20	.10	.02
☐ 311	Lee Smith	.10	.05	.01	☐ 360	Ron Gardenhire	.06	.03	.00
☐ 312	Darryl Strawberry	5.00	2.50	.50	☐ 361	Larry Bowa	.10	.05	.01
☐ 313	Jim Beattie	.06	.03	.00	☐ 362	Bob Kearney	.06	.03	.00
☐ 314	John Butcher	.06	.03	.00	☐ 363	Garth Iorg	.06	.03	.00
☐ 315	Damaso Garcia	.06	.03	.00	☐ 364	Tom Brunansky	.25	.12	.02
☐ 316	Mike Smithson	.06	.03	.00	☐ 365	Brad Gulden	.06	.03	.00
☐ 317	Luis Leal	.06	.03	.00	☐ 366	Greg Walker	.10	.05	.01
☐ 318	Ken Phelps	.45	.22	.04	☐ 367	Mike Young	.10	.05	.01
☐ 319	Wally Backman	.10	.05	.01	☐ 368	Rick Waits	.06	.03	.00
☐ 320	Ron Cey	.10	.05	.01	☐ 369	Doug Bair	.06	.03	.00
☐ 321	Brad Komminsk	.06	.03	.00	☐ 370	Bob Shirley	.06	.03	.00
☐ 322	Jason Thompson	.06	.03	.00	☐ 371	Bob Ojeda	.10	.05	.01
☐ 323	Frank Williams	.12	.06	.01	☐ 372	Bob Welch	.10	.05	.01
☐ 324	Tim Lollar	.06	.03	.00	☐ 373	Neal Heaton	.06	.03	.00
☐ 325	Eric Davis	18.00	9.00	1.80	☐ 374	Danny Jackson UER	.40	.20	.04
☐ 326	Von Hayes	.15	.07	.01		(photo actually			
☐ 327	Andy Van Slyke	.50	.25	.05		Frank Wills)			
☐ 328	Craig Reynolds	.06	.03	.00	☐ 375	Donnie Hill	.06	.03	.00
☐ 329	Dick Schofield	.10	.05	.01	☐ 376	Mike Stenhouse	.06	.03	.00
☐ 330	Scott Fletcher	.10	.05	.01	☐ 377	Bruce Kison	.06	.03	.00
☐ 331	Jeff Reardon	.12	.06	.01	☐ 378	Wayne Tolleson	.06	.03	.00
☐ 332	Rick Dempsey	.06	.03	.00	☐ 379	Floyd Bannister	.06	.03	.00
☐ 333	Ben Oglivie	.10	.05	.01	☐ 380	Vern Ruhle	.06	.03	.00
☐ 334	Dan Petry	.06	.03	.00	☐ 381	Tim Corcoran	.06	.03	.00
☐ 335	Jackie Gutierrez	.06	.03	.00	☐ 382	Kurt Kepshire	.06	.03	.00
☐ 336	Dave Righetti	.15	.07	.01	☐ 383	Bobby Brown	.06	.03	.00
☐ 337	Alejandro Pena	.10	.05	.01	☐ 384	Dave Van Gorder	.06	.03	.00
☐ 338	Mel Hall	.12	.06	.01	☐ 385	Rick Mahler	.06	.03	.00
☐ 339	Pat Sheridan	.06	.03	.00	☐ 386	Lee Mazzilli	.06	.03	.00
☐ 340	Keith Atherton	.06	.03	.00	☐ 387	Bill Laskey	.06	.03	.00

		MINT	EXC	G-VG			MINT	EXC	G-VG
☐ 388	Thad Bosley	.06	.03	.00	☐ 434	Ron Darling	.90	.45	.09
☐ 389	Al Chambers	.06	.03	.00	☐ 435	Spike Owen	.06	.03	.00
☐ 390	Tony Fernandez	.75	.35	.07	☐ 436	Frank Viola	.45	.22	.04
☐ 391	Ron Washington	.06	.03	.00	☐ 437	Lloyd Moseby	.12	.06	.01
☐ 392	Bill Swaggerty	.06	.03	.00	☐ 438	Kirby Puckett	20.00	10.00	2.00
☐ 393	Bob L. Gibson	.06	.03	.00	☐ 439	Jim Clancy	.06	.03	.00
☐ 394	Marty Castillo	.06	.03	.00	☐ 440	Mike Moore	.12	.06	.01
☐ 395	Steve Crawford	.06	.03	.00	☐ 441	Doug Sisk	.06	.03	.00
☐ 396	Clay Christiansen	.06	.03	.00	☐ 442	Dennis Eckersley	.20	.10	.02
☐ 397	Bob Bailor	.06	.03	.00	☐ 443	Gerald Perry	.18	.09	.01
☐ 398	Mike Hargrove	.10	.05	.01	☐ 444	Dale Berra	.06	.03	.00
☐ 399	Charlie Leibrandt	.06	.03	.00	☐ 445	Dusty Baker	.10	.05	.01
☐ 400	Tom Burgmeier	.06	.03	.00	☐ 446	Ed Whitson	.06	.03	.00
☐ 401	Razor Shines	.10	.05	.01	☐ 447	Cesar Cedeno	.10	.05	.01
☐ 402	Rob Wilfong	.06	.03	.00	☐ 448	Rick Schu	.18	.09	.01
☐ 403	Tom Henke	.15	.07	.01	☐ 449	Joaquin Andujar	.10	.05	.01
☐ 404	Al Jones	.06	.03	.00	☐ 450	Mark Bailey	.10	.05	.01
☐ 405	Mike LaCoss	.06	.03	.00	☐ 451	Ron Romanick	.10	.05	.01
☐ 406	Luis DeLeon	.06	.03	.00	☐ 452	Julio Cruz	.06	.03	.00
☐ 407	Greg Gross	.06	.03	.00	☐ 453	Miguel Dilone	.06	.03	.00
☐ 408	Tom Hume	.06	.03	.00	☐ 454	Storm Davis	.12	.06	.01
☐ 409	Rick Camp	.06	.03	.00	☐ 455	Jaime Cocanower	.10	.05	.01
☐ 410	Milt May	.06	.03	.00	☐ 456	Barbaro Garbey	.06	.03	.00
☐ 411	Henry Cotto	.10	.05	.01	☐ 457	Rich Gedman	.10	.05	.01
☐ 412	David Von Ohlen	.06	.03	.00	☐ 458	Phil Niekro	.25	.12	.02
☐ 413	Scott McGregor	.10	.05	.01	☐ 459	Mike Scioscia	.10	.05	.01
☐ 414	Ted Simmons	.12	.06	.01	☐ 460	Pat Tabler	.10	.05	.01
☐ 415	Jack Morris	.18	.09	.01	☐ 461	Darryl Motley	.06	.03	.00
☐ 416	Bill Buckner	.10	.05	.01	☐ 462	Chris Codiroli	.06	.03	.00
☐ 417	Butch Wynegar	.06	.03	.00	☐ 463	Doug Flynn	.06	.03	.00
☐ 418	Steve Sax	.30	.15	.03	☐ 464	Billy Sample	.06	.03	.00
☐ 419	Steve Balboni	.06	.03	.00	☐ 465	Mickey Rivers	.06	.03	.00
☐ 420	Dwayne Murphy	.06	.03	.00	☐ 466	John Wathan	.06	.03	.00
☐ 421	Andre Dawson	.35	.17	.03	☐ 467	Bill Krueger	.06	.03	.00
☐ 422	Charlie Hough	.10	.05	.01	☐ 468	Andre Thornton	.10	.05	.01
☐ 423	Tommy John	.15	.07	.01	☐ 469	Rex Hudler	.18	.09	.01
☐ 424A	Tom Seaver ERR	1.00	.50	.10	☐ 470	Sid Bream	.35	.17	.03
	(photo actually				☐ 471	Kirk Gibson	.35	.17	.03
	Floyd Bannister)				☐ 472	John Shelby	.06	.03	.00
☐ 424B	Tom Seaver COR	10.00	5.00	1.00	☐ 473	Moose Haas	.06	.03	.00
☐ 425	Tommy Herr	.10	.05	.01	☐ 474	Doug Corbett	.06	.03	.00
☐ 426	Terry Puhl	.06	.03	.00	☐ 475	Willie McGee	.35	.17	.03
☐ 427	Al Holland	.06	.03	.00	☐ 476	Bob Knepper	.10	.05	.01
☐ 428	Eddie Milner	.06	.03	.00	☐ 477	Kevin Gross	.06	.03	.00
☐ 429	Terry Kennedy	.06	.03	.00	☐ 478	Carmelo Martinez	.06	.03	.00
☐ 430	John Candelaria	.10	.05	.01	☐ 479	Kent Tekulve	.05	.05	.01
☐ 431	Manny Trillo	.06	.03	.00	☐ 480	Chili Davis	.10	.05	.01
☐ 432	Ken Oberkfell	.06	.03	.00	☐ 481	Bobby Clark	.06	.03	.00
☐ 433	Rick Sutcliffe	.20	.10	.02	☐ 482	Mookie Wilson	.12	.06	.01

		MINT	EXC	G-VG
☐ 483	Dave Owen	.06	.03	.00
☐ 484	Ed Nunez	.06	.03	.00
☐ 485	Rance Mulliniks	.06	.03	.00
☐ 486	Ken Schrom	.06	.03	.00
☐ 487	Jeff Russell	.06	.03	.00
☐ 488	Tom Paciorek	.06	.03	.00
☐ 489	Dan Ford	.06	.03	.00
☐ 490	Mike Caldwell	.06	.03	.00
☐ 491	Scottie Earl	.06	.03	.00
☐ 492	Jose Rijo	.45	.22	.04
☐ 493	Bruce Hurst	.15	.07	.01
☐ 494	Ken Landreaux	.06	.03	.00
☐ 495	Mike Fischlin	.06	.03	.00
☐ 496	Don Slaught	.06	.03	.00
☐ 497	Steve McCatty	.06	.03	.00
☐ 498	Gary Lucas	.06	.03	.00
☐ 499	Gary Pettis	.10	.05	.01
☐ 500	Marvis Foley	.06	.03	.00
☐ 501	Mike Squires	.06	.03	.00
☐ 502	Jim Pankovits	.06	.03	.00
☐ 503	Luis Aguayo	.06	.03	.00
☐ 504	Ralph Citarella	.06	.03	.00
☐ 505	Bruce Bochy	.06	.03	.00
☐ 506	Bob Owchinko	.06	.03	.00
☐ 507	Pascual Perez	.15	.07	.01
☐ 508	Lee Lacy	.06	.03	.00
☐ 509	Atlee Hammaker	.06	.03	.00
☐ 510	Bob Dernier	.06	.03	.00
☐ 511	Ed VandeBerg	.06	.03	.00
☐ 512	Cliff Johnson	.06	.03	.00
☐ 513	Len Whitehouse	.06	.03	.00
☐ 514	Dennis Martinez	.10	.05	.01
☐ 515	Ed Romero	.06	.03	.00
☐ 516	Rusty Kuntz	.06	.03	.00
☐ 517	Rick Miller	.06	.03	.00
☐ 518	Dennis Rasmussen	.15	.07	.01
☐ 519	Steve Yeager	.06	.03	.00
☐ 520	Chris Bando	.06	.03	.00
☐ 521	U.L. Washington	.06	.03	.00
☐ 522	Curt Young	.35	.17	.03
☐ 523	Angel Salazar	.06	.03	.00
☐ 524	Curt Kaufman	.06	.03	.00
☐ 525	Odell Jones	.06	.03	.00
☐ 526	Juan Agosto	.06	.03	.00
☐ 527	Denny Walling	.06	.03	.00
☐ 528	Andy Hawkins	.25	.12	.02
☐ 529	Sixto Lezcano	.06	.03	.00
☐ 530	Skeeter Barnes	.06	.03	.00
☐ 531	Randy Johnson	.06	.03	.00
☐ 532	Jim Morrison	.06	.03	.00
☐ 533	Warren Brusstar	.06	.03	.00
☐ 534A	Jeff Pendleton ERR (wrong first name)	.75	.35	.07
☐ 534B	Terry Pendleton COR	3.50	1.75	.35
☐ 535	Vic Rodriguez	.10	.05	.01
☐ 536	Bob McClure	.06	.03	.00
☐ 537	Dave Bergman	.06	.03	.00
☐ 538	Mark Clear	.06	.03	.00
☐ 539	Mike Pagliarulo	.90	.45	.09
☐ 540	Terry Whitfield	.06	.03	.00
☐ 541	Joe Beckwith	.06	.03	.00
☐ 542	Jeff Burroughs	.06	.03	.00
☐ 543	Dan Schatzeder	.06	.03	.00
☐ 544	Donnie Scott	.06	.03	.00
☐ 545	Jim Slaton	.06	.03	.00
☐ 546	Greg Luzinski	.12	.06	.01
☐ 547	Mark Salas	.12	.06	.01
☐ 548	Dave Smith	.06	.03	.00
☐ 549	John Wockenfuss	.06	.03	.00
☐ 550	Frank Pastore	.06	.03	.00
☐ 551	Tim Flannery	.06	.03	.00
☐ 552	Rick Rhoden	.10	.05	.01
☐ 553	Mark Davis	.30	.15	.03
☐ 554	Jeff Dedmon	.10	.05	.01
☐ 555	Gary Woods	.06	.03	.00
☐ 556	Danny Heep	.06	.03	.00
☐ 557	Mark Langston	7.50	3.75	.75
☐ 558	Darrell Brown	.06	.03	.00
☐ 559	Jimmy Key	1.75	.85	.17
☐ 560	Rick Lysander	.06	.03	.00
☐ 561	Doyle Alexander	.10	.05	.01
☐ 562	Mike Stanton	.06	.03	.00
☐ 563	Sid Fernandez	.75	.35	.07
☐ 564	Richie Hebner	.06	.03	.00
☐ 565	Alex Trevino	.06	.03	.00
☐ 566	Brian Harper	.06	.03	.00
☐ 567	Dan Gladden	.45	.22	.04
☐ 568	Luis Salazar	.10	.05	.01
☐ 569	Tom Foley	.06	.03	.00
☐ 570	Larry Andersen	.06	.03	.00
☐ 571	Danny Cox	.10	.05	.01
☐ 572	Joe Sambito	.06	.03	.00
☐ 573	Juan Beniquez	.06	.03	.00
☐ 574	Joel Skinner	.06	.03	.00
☐ 575	Randy St. Claire	.06	.03	.00
☐ 576	Floyd Rayford	.06	.03	.00
☐ 577	Roy Howell	.06	.03	.00
☐ 578	John Grubb	.06	.03	.00

		MINT	EXC	G-VG
☐ 579	Ed Jurak	.06	.03	.00
☐ 580	John Montefusco	.06	.03	.00
☐ 581	Orel Hershiser	11.00	5.50	1.10
☐ 582	Tom Waddell	.10	.05	.01
☐ 583	Mark Huismann	.06	.03	.00
☐ 584	Joe Morgan	.30	.15	.03
☐ 585	Jim Wohlford	.06	.03	.00
☐ 586	Dave Schmidt	.10	.05	.01
☐ 587	Jeff Kunkel	.10	.05	.01
☐ 588	Hal McRae	.10	.05	.01
☐ 589	Bill Almon	.06	.03	.00
☐ 590	Carmen Castillo	.06	.03	.00
☐ 591	Omar Moreno	.06	.03	.00
☐ 592	Ken Howell	.15	.07	.01
☐ 593	Tom Brookens	.06	.03	.00
☐ 594	Joe Nolan	.06	.03	.00
☐ 595	Willie Lozado	.10	.05	.01
☐ 596	Tom Nieto	.10	.05	.01
☐ 597	Walt Terrell	.06	.03	.00
☐ 598	Al Oliver	.10	.05	.01
☐ 599	Shane Rawley	.06	.03	.00
☐ 600	Denny Gonzalez	.10	.05	.01
☐ 601	Mark Grant	.10	.05	.01
☐ 602	Mike Armstrong	.06	.03	.00
☐ 603	George Foster	.12	.06	.01
☐ 604	Dave Lopes	.10	.05	.01
☐ 605	Salome Barojas	.06	.03	.00
☐ 606	Roy Lee Jackson	.06	.03	.00
☐ 607	Pete Filson	.06	.03	.00
☐ 608	Duane Walker	.06	.03	.00
☐ 609	Glenn Wilson	.10	.05	.01
☐ 610	Rafael Santana	.25	.12	.02
☐ 611	Roy Smith	.10	.05	.01
☐ 612	Ruppert Jones	.06	.03	.00
☐ 613	Joe Cowley	.06	.03	.00
☐ 614	Al Nipper UER (photo actually Mike Brown)	.20	.10	.02
☐ 615	Gene Nelson	.06	.03	.00
☐ 616	Joe Carter	2.25	1.10	.22
☐ 617	Ray Knight	.10	.05	.01
☐ 618	Chuck Rainey	.06	.03	.00
☐ 619	Dan Driessen	.06	.03	.00
☐ 620	Daryl Sconiers	.06	.03	.00
☐ 621	Bill Stein	.06	.03	.00
☐ 622	Roy Smalley	.06	.03	.00
☐ 623	Ed Lynch	.06	.03	.00
☐ 624	Jeff Stone	.12	.06	.01
☐ 625	Bruce Berenyi	.06	.03	.00
☐ 626	Kelvin Chapman	.10	.05	.01
☐ 627	Joe Price	.06	.03	.00
☐ 628	Steve Bedrosian	.15	.07	.01
☐ 629	Vic Mata	.10	.05	.01
☐ 630	Mike Krukow	.06	.03	.00
☐ 631	Phil Bradley	1.00	.50	.10
☐ 632	Jim Gott	.10	.05	.01
☐ 633	Randy Bush	.10	.05	.01
☐ 634	Tom Browning	1.50	.75	.15
☐ 635	Lou Gehrig Puzzle Card	.06	.03	.00
☐ 636	Reid Nichols	.06	.03	.00
☐ 637	Dan Pasqua	.65	.30	.06
☐ 638	German Rivera	.10	.05	.01
☐ 639	Don Schulze	.06	.03	.00
☐ 640A	Mike Jones (Career Highlights, takes five lines)	.10	.05	.01
☐ 640B	Mike Jones (Career Highlights, takes four lines)	.10	.05	.01
☐ 641	Pete Rose	1.00	.50	.10
☐ 642	Wade Rowdon	.10	.05	.01
☐ 643	Jerry Narron	.06	.03	.00
☐ 644	Darrell Miller	.10	.05	.01
☐ 645	Tim Hulett	.10	.05	.01
☐ 646	Andy McGaffigan	.06	.03	.00
☐ 647	Kurt Bevacqua	.06	.03	.00
☐ 648	John Russell	.10	.05	.01
☐ 649	Ron Robinson	.20	.10	.02
☐ 650	Donnie Moore	.06	.03	.00
☐ 651A	Two for the Title Dave Winfield Don Mattingly (yellow letters)	5.00	2.50	.50
☐ 651B	Two for the Title Dave Winfield Don Mattingly (white letters)	7.50	3.75	.75
☐ 652	Tim Laudner	.06	.03	.00
☐ 653	Steve Farr	.30	.15	.03
☐ 654	DK Checklist 1-26 (unnumbered)	.09	.01	.00
☐ 655	Checklist 27-130 (unnumbered)	.07	.01	.00
☐ 656	Checklist 131-234 (unnumbered)	.07	.01	.00
☐ 657	Checklist 235-338 (unnumbered)	.07	.01	.00

			MINT	EXC	G-VG
☐	658	Checklist 339-442 .. (unnumbered)	.07	.01	.00
☐	659	Checklist 443-546 .. (unnumbered)	.07	.01	.00
☐	660	Checklist 547-653 .. (unnumbered)	.07	.01	.00

1985 Donruss Highlights

This 56-card set features the players and pitchers of the month for each league as well as a number of highlight cards commemorating the 1985 season. The Donruss Company dedicated the last two cards to their own selections for Rookies of the Year (ROY). This set proved to be more popular than the Donruss Company had predicted, as their first and only print run was exhausted before card dealers' initial orders were filled.

			MINT	EXC	G-VG
		COMPLETE SET (56)	25.00	12.50	2.50
		COMMON PLAYER (1-56)	.10	.05	.01
☐	1	Tom Seaver: Sets Opening Day Record	.50	.25	.05
☐	2	Rollie Fingers: Sets AL Save Mark	.20	.10	.02
☐	3	Mike Davis:	.10	.05	.01

			MINT	EXC	G-VG
☐	4	AL Player April Charlie Leibrandt: ...	.10	.05	.01
☐	5	AL Pitcher April Dale Murphy:	.75	.35	.07
☐	6	NL Player April Fernando Valenzuela:	.25	.12	.02
☐	7	NL Pitcher April Larry Bowa:	.10	.05	.01
☐	8	NL Shortstop Record Dave Concepcion: Joins	.10	.05	.01
☐	9	Reds' 2000 Hit Club Tony Perez:	.15	.07	.01
☐	10	Eldest Grand Slammer Pete Rose:	1.25	.60	.12
☐	11	NL Career Run Leader George Brett:	.75	.35	.07
☐	12	AL Player May Dave Stieb:	.15	.07	.01
☐	13	AL Pitcher May Dave Parker:	.15	.07	.01
☐	14	NL Player May Andy Hawkins:	.10	.05	.01
☐	15	NL Pitcher May Andy Hawkins: Records	.10	.05	.01
☐	16	11th Straight Win Von Hayes: Two .... Homers in First Inning	.15	.07	.01
☐	17	Rickey Henderson: .. AL Player June	.75	.35	.07
☐	18	Jay Howell: .... AL Pitcher June	.10	.05	.01
☐	19	Pedro Guerrero: ..... NL Player June	.20	.10	.02
☐	20	John Tudor: .... NL Pitcher June	.15	.07	.01
☐	21	Hernandez/Carter: .. Marathon Game Iron Men	.25	.12	.02
☐	22	Nolan Ryan: .... Records 4000th K	1.25	.60	.12
☐	23	LaMarr Hoyt: .... All-Star Game MVP	.10	.05	.01
☐	24	Oddibe McDowell: 1st Ranger to Hit for Cycle	.25	.12	.02
☐	25	George Brett:	.75	.35	.07

		MINT	EXC	G-VG
☐ 26	Bret Saberhagen: AL Player July	.75	.35	.07
☐ 27	Keith Hernandez: ... AL Pitcher July	.25	.12	.02
☐ 28	Fernando Valenzuela: NL Player July	.25	.12	.02
☐ 29	W. McGee/V. Coleman: Record Setting Base Stealers	.75	.35	.07
☐ 30	Tom Seaver: Notches 300th Career Win	.35	.17	.03
☐ 31	Rod Carew: Strokes 3000th Hit	.35	.17	.03
☐ 32	Dwight Gooden: .... Establishes Met Record	1.25	.60	.12
☐ 33	Dwight Gooden: .... Achieves Strikeout Milestone	1.25	.60	.12
☐ 34	Eddie Murray: ...... Explodes for 9 RBI	.35	.17	.03
☐ 35	Don Baylor: .... AL Career HBP Leader	.15	.07	.01
☐ 36	Don Mattingly: .... AL Player August	2.50	1.25	.25
☐ 37	Dave Righetti: ...... AL Pitcher August	.15	.07	.01
☐ 38	Willie McGee: ...... NL Player August	.25	.12	.02
☐ 39	Shane Rawley: ...... NL Pitcher August	.10	.05	.01
☐ 40	Pete Rose: .... Tie-Breaking Hit	1.25	.60	.12
☐ 41	Andre Dawson: Hits 3 HR's Drives in 8 Runs	.25	.12	.02
☐ 42	Rickey Henderson: .. Sets Yankee Theft Mark	.75	.35	.07
☐ 43	Tom Browning: 20 Wins .... in Rookie Season	.20	.10	.02
☐ 44	Don Mattingly: Yankee Milestone for Hits	2.50	1.25	.25
☐ 45	Don Mattingly: AL ... Player September	2.50	1.25	.25
☐ 46	Charlie Leibrandt: AL Pitcher September	.10	.05	.01

		MINT	EXC	G-VG
☐ 47	Gary Carter: NL .... Player September	.25	.12	.02
☐ 48	Dwight Gooden: NL . Pitcher September	1.25	.60	.12
☐ 49	Wade Boggs: Major League Record Setter	2.00	1.00	.20
☐ 50	Phil Niekro: Hurls Shutout for 300th Win	.20	.10	.02
☐ 51	Darrell Evans: ...... Venerable HR King	.10	.05	.01
☐ 52	Willie McGee: NL ... Switch-Hitting Record	.20	.10	.02
☐ 53	Dave Winfield: ...... Equals DiMaggio Feat	.30	.15	.03
☐ 54	Vince Coleman: .... Donruss NL ROY	2.00	1.00	.20
☐ 55	Ozzie Guillen: ...... Donruss AL ROY	.50	.25	.05
☐ 56	Checklist Card (unnumbered)	.10	.05	.01

1986 Donruss

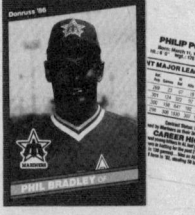
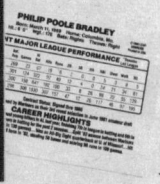

The cards in this 660-card set measure 2 ½"
by 3 ½". The 1986 Donruss regular issue
cards have fronts that feature blue borders.
The fronts contain the standard team logo,

player's name, position, and Donruss logo. The cards were distributed with puzzle pieces from a Dick Perez rendition of Hank Aaron. The first 26 cards of the set are Diamond Kings (DK), for the fifth year in a row; the artwork on the Diamond Kings was again produced by the Perez-Steele Galleries. Cards 27-46 again feature Rated Rookies (RR); Danny Tartabull is included in this subset for the second year in a row. The unnumbered checklist cards are arbitrarily numbered below as numbers 654 through 660.

		MINT	EXC	G-VG
COMPLETE SET (660)		130.00	65.00	13.00
COMMON PLAYER (1-660)		.05	.02	.00
☐ 1	Kirk Gibson DK	.35	.08	.01
☐ 2	Goose Gossage DK	.12	.06	.01
☐ 3	Willie McGee DK	.15	.07	.01
☐ 4	George Bell DK	.18	.09	.01
☐ 5	Tony Armas DK	.08	.04	.01
☐ 6	Chili Davis DK	.08	.04	.01
☐ 7	Cecil Cooper DK	.10	.05	.01
☐ 8	Mike Boddicker DK	.08	.04	.01
☐ 9	Dave Lopes DK	.08	.04	.01
☐ 10	Bill Doran DK	.08	.04	.01
☐ 11	Bret Saberhagen DK	.50	.25	.05
☐ 12	Brett Butler DK	.08	.04	.01
☐ 13	Harold Baines DK	.12	.06	.01
☐ 14	Mike Davis DK	.08	.04	.01
☐ 15	Tony Perez DK	.12	.06	.01
☐ 16	Willie Randolph DK	.08	.04	.01
☐ 17	Bob Boone DK	.10	.05	.01
☐ 18	Orel Hershiser DK	.90	.45	.09
☐ 19	Johnny Ray DK	.08	.04	.01
☐ 20	Gary Ward DK	.08	.04	.01
☐ 21	Rick Mahler DK	.08	.04	.01
☐ 22	Phil Bradley DK	.10	.05	.01
☐ 23	Jerry Koosman DK	.08	.04	.01
☐ 24	Tom Brunansky DK	.12	.06	.01
☐ 25	Andre Dawson DK	.25	.12	.02
☐ 26	Dwight Gooden DK	1.00	.50	.10
☐ 27	Kal Daniels RR	3.50	1.75	.35
☐ 28	Fred McGriff RR	15.00	7.50	1.50
☐ 29	Cory Snyder RR	2.25	1.10	.22
☐ 30	Jose Guzman RR	.25	.12	.02
☐ 31	Ty Gainey RR	.10	.05	.01
☐ 32	Johnny Abrego RR	.08	.04	.01
☐ 33A	Andres Galarraga RR	4.00	2.00	.40

		MINT	EXC	G-VG
	(no accent)			
☐ 33B	Andre's Galarraga RR	6.00	3.00	.60
	(accent over e)			
☐ 34	Dave Shipanoff RR	.08	.04	.01
☐ 35	Mark McLemore RR	.10	.05	.01
☐ 36	Marty Clary RR	.10	.05	.01
☐ 37	Paul O'Neill RR	1.75	.85	.17
☐ 38	Danny Tartabull RR	1.00	.50	.10
☐ 39	Jose Canseco RR	50.00	25.00	5.00
☐ 40	Juan Nieves RR	.30	.15	.03
☐ 41	Lance McCullers RR	.40	.20	.04
☐ 42	Rick Surhoff RR	.10	.05	.01
☐ 43	Todd Worrell RR	.90	.45	.09
☐ 44	Bob Kipper RR	.10	.05	.01
☐ 45	John Habyan RR	.10	.05	.01
☐ 46	Mike Woodard RR	.10	.05	.01
☐ 47	Mike Boddicker	.08	.04	.01
☐ 48	Robin Yount	.50	.25	.05
☐ 49	Lou Whitaker	.15	.07	.01
☐ 50	Oil Can Boyd	.08	.04	.01
☐ 51	Rickey Henderson	.60	.30	.06
☐ 52	Mike Marshall	.12	.06	.01
☐ 53	George Brett	.50	.25	.05
☐ 54	Dave Kingman	.10	.05	.01
☐ 55	Hubie Brooks	.10	.05	.01
☐ 56	Oddibe McDowell	.25	.12	.02
☐ 57	Doug DeCinces	.08	.04	.01
☐ 58	Britt Burns	.05	.02	.00
☐ 59	Ozzie Smith	.30	.15	.03
☐ 60	Jose Cruz	.08	.04	.01
☐ 61	Mike Schmidt	.90	.45	.09
☐ 62	Pete Rose	.75	.35	.07
☐ 63	Steve Garvey	.40	.20	.04
☐ 64	Tony Pena	.08	.04	.01
☐ 65	Chili Davis	.08	.04	.01
☐ 66	Dale Murphy	.50	.25	.05
☐ 67	Ryne Sandberg	.40	.20	.04
☐ 68	Gary Carter	.30	.15	.03
☐ 69	Alvin Davis	.30	.15	.03
☐ 70	Kent Hrbek	.25	.12	.02
☐ 71	George Bell	.30	.15	.03
☐ 72	Kirby Puckett	4.00	2.00	.40
☐ 73	Lloyd Moseby	.10	.05	.01
☐ 74	Bob Kearney	.05	.02	.00
☐ 75	Dwight Gooden	2.75	1.35	.27
☐ 76	Gary Matthews	.08	.04	.01
☐ 77	Rick Mahler	.05	.02	.00
☐ 78	Benny Distefano	.05	.02	.00
☐ 79	Jeff Leonard	.10	.05	.01

			MINT	EXC	G-VG				MINT	EXC	G-VG
☐	80	Kevin McReynolds	.50	.25	.05	☐	129	Pat Tabler	.08	.04	.01
☐	81	Ron Oester	.05	.02	.00	☐	130	Frank White	.08	.04	.01
☐	82	John Russell	.05	.02	.00	☐	131	Carney Lansford	.12	.06	.01
☐	83	Tommy Herr	.08	.04	.01	☐	132	Vance Law	.08	.04	.01
☐	84	Jerry Mumphrey	.05	.02	.00	☐	133	Dick Schofield	.08	.04	.01
☐	85	Ron Romanick	.05	.02	.00	☐	134	Wayne Tolleson	.05	.02	.00
☐	86	Daryl Boston	.05	.02	.00	☐	135	Greg Walker	.08	.04	.01
☐	87	Andre Dawson	.30	.15	.03	☐	136	Denny Walling	.05	.02	.00
☐	88	Eddie Murray	.35	.17	.03	☐	137	Ozzie Virgil	.05	.02	.00
☐	89	Dion James	.05	.02	.00	☐	138	Ricky Horton	.05	.02	.00
☐	90	Chet Lemon	.08	.04	.01	☐	139	LaMarr Hoyt	.08	.04	.01
☐	91	Bob Stanley	.05	.02	.00	☐	140	Wayne Krenchicki	.05	.02	.00
☐	92	Willie Randolph	.08	.04	.01	☐	141	Glenn Hubbard	.05	.02	.00
☐	93	Mike Scioscia	.08	.04	.01	☐	142	Cecilio Guante	.05	.02	.00
☐	94	Tom Waddell	.05	.02	.00	☐	143	Mike Krukow	.05	.02	.00
☐	95	Danny Jackson	.25	.12	.02	☐	144	Lee Smith	.08	.04	.01
☐	96	Mike Davis	.08	.04	.01	☐	145	Edwin Nunez	.05	.02	.00
☐	97	Mike Fitzgerald	.05	.02	.00	☐	146	Dave Stieb	.12	.06	.01
☐	98	Gary Ward	.08	.04	.01	☐	147	Mike Smithson	.05	.02	.00
☐	99	Pete O'Brien	.08	.04	.01	☐	148	Ken Dixon	.05	.02	.00
☐	100	Bret Saberhagen	1.75	.85	.17	☐	149	Danny Darwin	.05	.02	.00
☐	101	Alfredo Griffin	.08	.04	.01	☐	150	Chris Pittaro	.05	.02	.00
☐	102	Brett Butler	.08	.04	.01	☐	151	Bill Buckner	.08	.04	.01
☐	103	Ron Guidry	.15	.07	.01	☐	152	Mike Pagliarulo	.10	.05	.01
☐	104	Jerry Reuss	.08	.04	.01	☐	153	Bill Russell	.08	.04	.01
☐	105	Jack Morris	.15	.07	.01	☐	154	Brook Jacoby	.10	.05	.01
☐	106	Rick Dempsey	.05	.02	.00	☐	155	Pat Sheridan	.05	.02	.00
☐	107	Ray Burris	.05	.02	.00	☐	156	Mike Gallego	.05	.02	.00
☐	108	Brian Downing	.08	.04	.01	☐	157	Jim Wohlford	.05	.02	.00
☐	109	Willie McGee	.15	.07	.01	☐	158	Gary Pettis	.05	.02	.00
☐	110	Bill Doran	.10	.05	.01	☐	159	Toby Harrah	.08	.04	.01
☐	111	Kent Tekulve	.05	.02	.00	☐	160	Richard Dotson	.08	.04	.01
☐	112	Tony Gwynn	1.00	.50	.10	☐	161	Bob Knepper	.08	.04	.01
☐	113	Marvell Wynne	.05	.02	.00	☐	162	Dave Dravecky	.10	.05	.01
☐	114	David Green	.05	.02	.00	☐	163	Greg Gross	.05	.02	.00
☐	115	Jim Gantner	.05	.02	.00	☐	164	Eric Davis	3.50	1.75	.35
☐	116	George Foster	.12	.06	.01	☐	165	Gerald Perry	.12	.06	.01
☐	117	Steve Trout	.05	.02	.00	☐	166	Rick Rhoden	.08	.04	.01
☐	118	Mark Langston	.90	.45	.09	☐	167	Keith Moreland	.05	.02	.00
☐	119	Tony Fernandez	.25	.12	.02	☐	168	Jack Clark	.25	.12	.02
☐	120	John Butcher	.05	.02	.00	☐	169	Storm Davis	.10	.05	.01
☐	121	Ron Robinson	.05	.02	.00	☐	170	Cecil Cooper	.10	.05	.01
☐	122	Dan Spillner	.05	.02	.00	☐	171	Alan Trammell	.25	.12	.02
☐	123	Mike Young	.08	.04	.01	☐	172	Roger Clemens	3.50	1.75	.35
☐	124	Paul Molitor	.15	.07	.01	☐	173	Don Mattingly	5.00	2.50	.50
☐	125	Kirk Gibson	.25	.12	.02	☐	174	Pedro Guerrero	.25	.12	.02
☐	126	Ken Griffey	.10	.05	.01	☐	175	Willie Wilson	.10	.05	.01
☐	127	Tony Armas	.08	.04	.01	☐	176	Dwayne Murphy	.05	.02	.00
☐	128	Mariano Duncan	.15	.07	.01	☐	177	Tim Raines	.30	.15	.03

		MINT	EXC	G-VG			MINT	EXC	G-VG
☐ 178	Larry Parrish	.05	.02	.00	☐ 226	Orel Hershiser	2.00	1.00	.20
☐ 179	Mike Witt	.08	.04	.01	☐ 227	Willie Hernandez	.10	.05	.01
☐ 180	Harold Baines	.15	.07	.01	☐ 228	Lee Lacy	.05	.02	.00
☐ 181	Vince Coleman	2.25	1.10	.22	☐ 229	Rollie Fingers	.15	.07	.01
	(BA 2.67 on back)				☐ 230	Bob Boone	.12	.06	.01
☐ 182	Jeff Heathcock	.05	.02	.00	☐ 231	Joaquin Andujar	.10	.05	.01
☐ 183	Steve Carlton	.30	.15	.03	☐ 232	Craig Reynolds	.05	.02	.00
☐ 184	Mario Soto	.05	.02	.00	☐ 233	Shane Rawley	.05	.02	.00
☐ 185	Goose Gossage	.12	.06	.01	☐ 234	Eric Show	.08	.04	.01
☐ 186	Johnny Ray	.08	.04	.01	☐ 235	Jose DeLeon	.05	.02	.00
☐ 187	Dan Gladden	.08	.04	.01	☐ 236	Jose Uribe	.30	.15	.03
☐ 188	Bob Horner	.15	.07	.01	☐ 237	Moose Haas	.05	.02	.00
☐ 189	Rick Sutcliffe	.15	.07	.01	☐ 238	Wally Backman	.05	.02	.00
☐ 190	Keith Hernandez	.25	.12	.02	☐ 239	Dennis Eckersley	.15	.07	.01
☐ 191	Phil Bradley	.10	.05	.01	☐ 240	Mike Moore	.10	.05	.01
☐ 192	Tom Brunansky	.15	.07	.01	☐ 241	Damaso Garcia	.05	.02	.00
☐ 193	Jesse Barfield	.25	.12	.02	☐ 242	Tim Teufel	.05	.02	.00
☐ 194	Frank Viola	.35	.17	.03	☐ 243	Dave Concepcion	.10	.05	.01
☐ 195	Willie Upshaw	.05	.02	.00	☐ 244	Floyd Bannister	.05	.02	.00
☐ 196	Jim Beattie	.05	.02	.00	☐ 245	Fred Lynn	.15	.07	.01
☐ 197	Darryl Strawberry	2.50	1.25	.25	☐ 246	Charlie Moore	.05	.02	.00
☐ 198	Ron Cey	.10	.05	.01	☐ 247	Walt Terrell	.05	.02	.00
☐ 199	Steve Bedrosian	.12	.06	.01	☐ 248	Dave Winfield	.30	.15	.03
☐ 200	Steve Kemp	.08	.04	.01	☐ 249	Dwight Evans	.15	.07	.01
☐ 201	Manny Trillo	.05	.02	.00	☐ 250	Dennis Powell	.08	.04	.01
☐ 202	Garry Templeton	.08	.04	.01	☐ 251	Andre Thornton	.08	.04	.01
☐ 203	Dave Parker	.15	.07	.01	☐ 252	Onix Concepcion	.05	.02	.00
☐ 204	John Denny	.08	.04	.01	☐ 253	Mike Heath	.05	.02	.00
☐ 205	Terry Pendleton	.08	.04	.01	☐ 254A	David Palmer ERR	.10	.05	.01
☐ 206	Terry Puhl	.05	.02	.00		(position 2B)			
☐ 207	Bobby Grich	.08	.04	.01	☐ 254B	David Palmer COR	.60	.30	.06
☐ 208	Ozzie Guillen	.60	.30	.06		(position P)			
☐ 209	Jeff Reardon	.10	.05	.01	☐ 255	Donnie Moore	.05	.02	.00
☐ 210	Cal Ripken	.45	.22	.04	☐ 256	Curtis Wilkerson	.05	.02	.00
☐ 211	Bill Schroeder	.05	.02	.00	☐ 257	Julio Cruz	.05	.02	.00
☐ 212	Dan Petry	.05	.02	.00	☐ 258	Nolan Ryan	.90	.45	.09
☐ 213	Jim Rice	.20	.10	.02	☐ 259	Jeff Stone	.05	.02	.00
☐ 214	Dave Righetti	.12	.06	.01	☐ 260	John Tudor	.12	.06	.01
☐ 215	Fernando Valenzuela	.25	.12	.02	☐ 261	Mark Thurmond	.05	.02	.00
☐ 216	Julio Franco	.20	.10	.02	☐ 262	Jay Tibbs	.05	.02	.00
☐ 217	Darryl Motley	.05	.02	.00	☐ 263	Rafael Ramirez	.05	.02	.00
☐ 218	Dave Collins	.05	.02	.00	☐ 264	Larry McWilliams	.05	.02	.00
☐ 219	Tim Wallach	.10	.05	.01	☐ 265	Mark Davis	.15	.07	.01
☐ 220	George Wright	.05	.02	.00	☐ 266	Bob Dernier	.05	.02	.00
☐ 221	Tommy Dunbar	.05	.02	.00	☐ 267	Matt Young	.05	.02	.00
☐ 222	Steve Balboni	.05	.02	.00	☐ 268	Jim Clancy	.05	.02	.00
☐ 223	Jay Howell	.08	.04	.01	☐ 269	Mickey Hatcher	.05	.02	.00
☐ 224	Joe Carter	.60	.30	.06	☐ 270	Sammy Stewart	.05	.02	.00
☐ 225	Ed Whitson	.05	.02	.00	☐ 271	Bob L. Gibson	.05	.02	.00

		MINT	EXC	G-VG			MINT	EXC	G-VG
☐ 272	Nelson Simmons ...	.05	.02	.00	☐ 321	Bruce Sutter	.12	.06	.01
☐ 273	Rich Gedman	.05	.02	.00	☐ 322	Jason Thompson ...	.05	.02	.00
☐ 274	Butch Wynegar	.05	.02	.00	☐ 323	Bob Brenly	.05	.02	.00
☐ 275	Ken Howell	.05	.02	.00	☐ 324	Carmelo Martinez ...	.05	.02	.00
☐ 276	Mel Hall	.10	.05	.01	☐ 325	Eddie Milner	.05	.02	.00
☐ 277	Jim Sundberg	.05	.02	.00	☐ 326	Juan Samuel	.15	.07	.01
☐ 278	Chris Codiroli	.05	.02	.00	☐ 327	Tom Nieto	.05	.02	.00
☐ 279	Herm Winningham ..	.10	.05	.01	☐ 328	Dave Smith	.08	.04	.01
☐ 280	Rod Carew	.35	.17	.03	☐ 329	Urbano Lugo	.05	.02	.00
☐ 281	Don Slaught	.05	.02	.00	☐ 330	Joel Skinner	.05	.02	.00
☐ 282	Scott Fletcher	.05	.02	.00	☐ 331	Bill Gullickson	.05	.02	.00
☐ 283	Bill Dawley	.05	.02	.00	☐ 332	Floyd Rayford	.05	.02	.00
☐ 284	Andy Hawkins	.10	.05	.01	☐ 333	Ben Oglivie	.08	.04	.01
☐ 285	Glenn Wilson	.08	.04	.01	☐ 334	Lance Parrish	.15	.07	.01
☐ 286	Nick Esasky	.12	.06	.01	☐ 335	Jackie Gutierrez	.05	.02	.00
☐ 287	Claudell Washington .	.08	.04	.01	☐ 336	Dennis Rasmussen ..	.10	.05	.01
☐ 288	Lee Mazzilli	.05	.02	.00	☐ 337	Terry Whitfield	.05	.02	.00
☐ 289	Jody Davis	.05	.02	.00	☐ 338	Neal Heaton	.05	.02	.00
☐ 290	Darrell Porter	.05	.02	.00	☐ 339	Jorge Orta	.05	.02	.00
☐ 291	Scott McGregor	.08	.04	.01	☐ 340	Donnie Hill	.05	.02	.00
☐ 292	Ted Simmons	.10	.05	.01	☐ 341	Joe Hesketh	.05	.02	.00
☐ 293	Aurelio Lopez	.05	.02	.00	☐ 342	Charlie Hough	.08	.04	.01
☐ 294	Marty Barrett	.10	.05	.01	☐ 343	Dave Rozema	.05	.02	.00
☐ 295	Dale Berra	.05	.02	.00	☐ 344	Greg Pryor	.05	.02	.00
☐ 296	Greg Brock	.05	.02	.00	☐ 345	Mickey Tettleton ...	.60	.30	.06
☐ 297	Charlie Leibrandt ...	.05	.02	.00	☐ 346	George Vukovich ...	.05	.02	.00
☐ 298	Bill Krueger	.05	.02	.00	☐ 347	Don Baylor	.10	.05	.01
☐ 299	Bryn Smith	.10	.05	.01	☐ 348	Carlos Diaz	.05	.02	.00
☐ 300	Burt Hooton	.05	.02	.00	☐ 349	Barbaro Garbey	.05	.02	.00
☐ 301	Stu Cliburn	.08	.04	.01	☐ 350	Larry Sheets	.08	.04	.01
☐ 302	Luis Salazar	.05	.02	.00	☐ 351	Ted Higuera	1.50	.75	.15
☐ 303	Ken Dayley	.05	.02	.00	☐ 352	Juan Beniquez	.05	.02	.00
☐ 304	Frank DiPino	.05	.02	.00	☐ 353	Bob Forsch	.05	.02	.00
☐ 305	Von Hayes	.12	.06	.01	☐ 354	Mark Bailey	.05	.02	.00
☐ 306	Gary Redus	.05	.02	.00	☐ 355	Larry Andersen	.05	.02	.00
☐ 307	Craig Lefferts	.08	.04	.01	☐ 356	Terry Kennedy	.05	.02	.00
☐ 308	Sammy Khalifa	.08	.04	.01	☐ 357	Don Robinson	.05	.02	.00
☐ 309	Scott Garrelts	.12	.06	.01	☐ 358	Jim Gott	.05	.02	.00
☐ 310	Rick Cerone	.05	.02	.00	☐ 359	Earnie Riles	.25	.12	.02
☐ 311	Shawon Dunston ...	.35	.17	.03	☐ 360	John Christensen ...	.05	.02	.00
☐ 312	Howard Johnson ...	.60	.30	.06	☐ 361	Ray Fontenot	.05	.02	.00
☐ 313	Jim Presley	.10	.05	.01	☐ 362	Spike Owen	.05	.02	.00
☐ 314	Gary Gaetti	.25	.12	.02	☐ 363	Jim Acker	.05	.02	.00
☐ 315	Luis Leal	.05	.02	.00	☐ 364	Ron Davis	.08	.04	.01
☐ 316	Mark Salas	.05	.02	.00	☐ 365	Tom Hume	.05	.02	.00
☐ 317	Bill Caudill	.05	.02	.00	☐ 366	Carlton Fisk	.30	.15	.03
☐ 318	Dave Henderson ...	.10	.05	.01	☐ 367	Nate Snell	.05	.02	.00
☐ 319	Rafael Santana	.05	.02	.00	☐ 368	Rick Manning	.05	.02	.00
☐ 320	Leon Durham	.08	.04	.01	☐ 369	Darrell Evans	.10	.05	.01

		MINT	EXC	G-VG
☐ 370	Ron Hassey	.05	.02	.00
☐ 371	Wade Boggs	3.00	1.50	.30
☐ 372	Rick Honeycutt	.05	.02	.00
☐ 373	Chris Bando	.05	.02	.00
☐ 374	Bud Black	.05	.02	.00
☐ 375	Steve Henderson	.05	.02	.00
☐ 376	Charlie Lea	.05	.02	.00
☐ 377	Reggie Jackson	.50	.25	.05
☐ 378	Dave Schmidt	.08	.04	.01
☐ 379	Bob James	.05	.02	.00
☐ 380	Glenn Davis	3.75	1.85	.37
☐ 381	Tim Corcoran	.05	.02	.00
☐ 382	Danny Cox	.10	.05	.01
☐ 383	Tim Flannery	.05	.02	.00
☐ 384	Tom Browning	.20	.10	.02
☐ 385	Rick Camp	.05	.02	.00
☐ 386	Jim Morrison	.05	.02	.00
☐ 387	Dave LaPoint	.08	.04	.01
☐ 388	Dave Lopes	.08	.04	.01
☐ 389	Al Cowens	.05	.02	.00
☐ 390	Doyle Alexander	.08	.04	.01
☐ 391	Tim Laudner	.05	.02	.00
☐ 392	Don Aase	.05	.02	.00
☐ 393	Jaime Cocanower	.05	.02	.00
☐ 394	Randy O'Neal	.05	.02	.00
☐ 395	Mike Easler	.05	.02	.00
☐ 396	Scott Bradley	.05	.02	.00
☐ 397	Tom Niedenfuer	.05	.02	.00
☐ 398	Jerry Willard	.05	.02	.00
☐ 399	Lonnie Smith	.10	.05	.01
☐ 400	Bruce Bochte	.05	.02	.00
☐ 401	Terry Francona	.05	.02	.00
☐ 402	Jim Slaton	.05	.02	.00
☐ 403	Bill Stein	.05	.02	.00
☐ 404	Tim Hulett	.05	.02	.00
☐ 405	Alan Ashby	.05	.02	.00
☐ 406	Tim Stoddard	.05	.02	.00
☐ 407	Garry Maddox	.05	.02	.00
☐ 408	Ted Power	.05	.02	.00
☐ 409	Len Barker	.05	.02	.00
☐ 410	Denny Gonzalez	.05	.02	.00
☐ 411	George Frazier	.05	.02	.00
☐ 412	Andy Van Slyke	.25	.12	.02
☐ 413	Jim Dwyer	.05	.02	.00
☐ 414	Paul Householder	.05	.02	.00
☐ 415	Alejandro Sanchez	.05	.02	.00
☐ 416	Steve Crawford	.05	.02	.00
☐ 417	Dan Pasqua	.10	.05	.01
☐ 418	Enos Cabell	.05	.02	.00
☐ 419	Mike Jones	.05	.02	.00
☐ 420	Steve Kiefer	.05	.02	.00
☐ 421	Tim Burke	.35	.17	.03
☐ 422	Mike Mason	.05	.02	.00
☐ 423	Ruppert Jones	.05	.02	.00
☐ 424	Jerry Hairston	.05	.02	.00
☐ 425	Tito Landrum	.05	.02	.00
☐ 426	Jeff Calhoun	.05	.02	.00
☐ 427	Don Carman	.25	.12	.02
☐ 428	Tony Perez	.12	.06	.01
☐ 429	Jerry Davis	.05	.02	.00
☐ 430	Bob Walk	.05	.02	.00
☐ 431	Brad Wellman	.05	.02	.00
☐ 432	Terry Forster	.08	.04	.01
☐ 433	Billy Hatcher	.10	.05	.01
☐ 434	Clint Hurdle	.05	.02	.00
☐ 435	Ivan Calderon	.65	.30	.06
☐ 436	Pete Filson	.05	.02	.00
☐ 437	Tom Henke	.10	.05	.01
☐ 438	Dave Engle	.05	.02	.00
☐ 439	Tom Filer	.05	.02	.00
☐ 440	Gorman Thomas	.10	.05	.01
☐ 441	Rick Aguilera	.35	.17	.03
☐ 442	Scott Sanderson	.05	.02	.00
☐ 443	Jeff Dedmon	.05	.02	.00
☐ 444	Joe Orsulak	.10	.05	.01
☐ 445	Atlee Hammaker	.05	.02	.00
☐ 446	Jerry Royster	.05	.02	.00
☐ 447	Buddy Bell	.10	.05	.01
☐ 448	Dave Rucker	.05	.02	.00
☐ 449	Ivan DeJesus	.05	.02	.00
☐ 450	Jim Pankovits	.05	.02	.00
☐ 451	Jerry Narron	.05	.02	.00
☐ 452	Bryan Little	.05	.02	.00
☐ 453	Gary Lucas	.05	.02	.00
☐ 454	Dennis Martinez	.08	.04	.01
☐ 455	Ed Romero	.05	.02	.00
☐ 456	Bob Melvin	.10	.05	.01
☐ 457	Glenn Hoffman	.05	.02	.00
☐ 458	Bob Shirley	.05	.02	.00
☐ 459	Bob Welch	.08	.04	.01
☐ 460	Carmen Castillo	.05	.02	.00
☐ 461	Dave Leeper (outfielder)	.08	.04	.01
☐ 462	Tim Birtsas	.10	.05	.01
☐ 463	Randy St.Claire	.05	.02	.00
☐ 464	Chris Welsh	.05	.02	.00
☐ 465	Greg Harris	.05	.02	.00
☐ 466	Lynn Jones	.05	.02	.00

		MINT	EXC	G-VG			MINT	EXC	G-VG
☐ 467	Dusty Baker	.08	.04	.01	☐ 516	Bill Scherrer	.05	.02	.00
☐ 468	Roy Smith	.05	.02	.00	☐ 517	Bruce Hurst	.15	.07	.01
☐ 469	Andre Robertson	.05	.02	.00	☐ 518	Rich Bordi	.05	.02	.00
☐ 470	Ken Landreaux	.05	.02	.00	☐ 519	Steve Yeager	.05	.02	.00
☐ 471	Dave Bergman	.05	.02	.00	☐ 520	Tony Bernazard	.05	.02	.00
☐ 472	Gary Roenicke	.05	.02	.00	☐ 521	Hal McRae	.08	.04	.01
☐ 473	Pete Vuckovich	.05	.02	.00	☐ 522	Jose Rijo	.08	.04	.01
☐ 474	Kirk McCaskill	.60	.30	.06	☐ 523	Mitch Webster	.30	.15	.03
☐ 475	Jeff Lahti	.05	.02	.00	☐ 524	Jack Howell	.35	.17	.03
☐ 476	Mike Scott	.35	.17	.03	☐ 525	Alan Bannister	.05	.02	.00
☐ 477	Darren Daulton	.15	.07	.01	☐ 526	Ron Kittle	.10	.05	.01
☐ 478	Graig Nettles	.10	.05	.01	☐ 527	Phil Garner	.05	.02	.00
☐ 479	Bill Almon	.05	.02	.00	☐ 528	Kurt Bevacqua	.05	.02	.00
☐ 480	Greg Minton	.05	.02	.00	☐ 529	Kevin Gross	.05	.02	.00
☐ 481	Randy Ready	.05	.02	.00	☐ 530	Bo Diaz	.05	.02	.00
☐ 482	Len Dykstra	.75	.35	.07	☐ 531	Ken Oberkfell	.05	.02	.00
☐ 483	Thad Bosley	.05	.02	.00	☐ 532	Rick Reuschel	.12	.06	.01
☐ 484	Harold Reynolds	.60	.30	.06	☐ 533	Ron Meridith	.08	.04	.01
☐ 485	Al Oliver	.10	.05	.01	☐ 534	Steve Braun	.05	.02	.00
☐ 486	Roy Smalley	.05	.02	.00	☐ 535	Wayne Gross	.05	.02	.00
☐ 487	John Franco	.20	.10	.02	☐ 536	Ray Searage	.05	.02	.00
☐ 488	Juan Agosto	.05	.02	.00	☐ 537	Tom Brookens	.05	.02	.00
☐ 489	Al Pardo	.05	.02	.00	☐ 538	Al Nipper	.05	.02	.00
☐ 490	Bill Wegman	.10	.05	.01	☐ 539	Billy Sample	.05	.02	.00
☐ 491	Frank Tanana	.08	.04	.01	☐ 540	Steve Sax	.20	.10	.02
☐ 492	Brian Fisher	.20	.10	.02	☐ 541	Dan Quisenberry	.10	.05	.01
☐ 493	Mark Clear	.05	.02	.00	☐ 542	Tony Phillips	.05	.02	.00
☐ 494	Len Matuszek	.05	.02	.00	☐ 543	Floyd Youmans	.30	.15	.03
☐ 495	Ramon Romero	.05	.02	.00	☐ 544	Steve Buechele	.25	.12	.02
☐ 496	John Wathan	.05	.02	.00	☐ 545	Craig Gerber	.05	.02	.00
☐ 497	Rob Picciolo	.05	.02	.00	☐ 546	Joe DeSa	.05	.02	.00
☐ 498	U.L. Washington	.05	.02	.00	☐ 547	Brian Harper	.05	.02	.00
☐ 499	John Candelaria	.08	.04	.01	☐ 548	Kevin Bass	.08	.04	.01
☐ 500	Duane Walker	.05	.02	.00	☐ 549	Tom Foley	.05	.02	.00
☐ 501	Gene Nelson	.05	.02	.00	☐ 550	Dave Van Gorder	.05	.02	.00
☐ 502	John Mizerock	.05	.02	.00	☐ 551	Bruce Bochy	.05	.02	.00
☐ 503	Luis Aguayo	.05	.02	.00	☐ 552	R.J. Reynolds	.05	.02	.00
☐ 504	Kurt Kepshire	.05	.02	.00	☐ 553	Chris Brown	.20	.10	.02
☐ 505	Ed Wojna	.10	.05	.01	☐ 554	Bruce Benedict	.05	.02	.00
☐ 506	Joe Price	.05	.02	.00	☐ 555	Warren Brusstar	.05	.02	.00
☐ 507	Milt Thompson	.30	.15	.03	☐ 556	Danny Heep	.05	.02	.00
☐ 508	Junior Ortiz	.05	.02	.00	☐ 557	Darnell Coles	.05	.02	.00
☐ 509	Vida Blue	.08	.04	.01	☐ 558	Greg Gagne	.08	.04	.01
☐ 510	Steve Engel	.05	.02	.00	☐ 559	Ernie Whitt	.08	.04	.01
☐ 511	Karl Best	.05	.02	.00	☐ 560	Ron Washington	.05	.02	.00
☐ 512	Cecil Fielder	.20	.10	.02	☐ 561	Jimmy Key	.15	.07	.01
☐ 513	Frank Eufemia	.08	.04	.01	☐ 562	Billy Swift	.10	.05	.01
☐ 514	Tippy Martinez	.05	.02	.00	☐ 563	Ron Darling	.30	.15	.03
☐ 515	Billy Jo Robidoux	.10	.05	.01	☐ 564	Dick Ruthven	.05	.02	.00

		MINT	EXC	G-VG
☐ 565	Zane Smith	.25	.12	.02
☐ 566	Sid Bream	.05	.02	.00
☐ 567A	Joel Youngblood ERR (position P)	.10	.05	.01
☐ 567B	Joel Youngblood COR (position IF)	.60	.30	.06
☐ 568	Mario Ramirez	.05	.02	.00
☐ 569	Tom Runnels	.05	.02	.00
☐ 570	Rick Schu	.05	.02	.00
☐ 571	Bill Campbell	.05	.02	.00
☐ 572	Dickie Thon	.05	.02	.00
☐ 573	Al Holland	.05	.02	.00
☐ 574	Reid Nichols	.05	.02	.00
☐ 575	Bert Roberge	.05	.02	.00
☐ 576	Mike Flanagan	.08	.04	.01
☐ 577	Tim Leary	.35	.17	.03
☐ 578	Mike Laga	.05	.02	.00
☐ 579	Steve Lyons	.05	.02	.00
☐ 580	Phil Nickro	.20	.10	.02
☐ 581	Gilberto Reyes	.10	.05	.01
☐ 582	Jamie Easterly	.05	.02	.00
☐ 583	Mark Gubicza	.20	.10	.02
☐ 584	Stan Javier	.25	.12	.02
☐ 585	Bill Laskey	.05	.02	.00
☐ 586	Jeff Russell	.10	.05	.01
☐ 587	Dickie Noles	.05	.02	.00
☐ 588	Steve Farr	.08	.04	.01
☐ 589	Steve Ontiveros	.10	.05	.01
☐ 590	Mike Hargrove	.05	.02	.00
☐ 591	Marty Bystrom	.05	.02	.00
☐ 592	Franklin Stubbs	.08	.04	.01
☐ 593	Larry Herndon	.05	.02	.00
☐ 594	Bill Swaggerty	.05	.02	.00
☐ 595	Carlos Ponce	.05	.02	.00
☐ 596	Pat Perry	.10	.05	.01
☐ 597	Ray Knight	.08	.04	.01
☐ 598	Steve Lombardozzi	.12	.06	.01
☐ 599	Brad Havens	.05	.02	.00
☐ 600	Pat Clements	.10	.05	.01
☐ 601	Joe Niekro	.08	.04	.01
☐ 602	Hank Aaron Puzzle Card	.08	.04	.01
☐ 603	Dwayne Henry	.08	.04	.01
☐ 604	Mookie Wilson	.08	.04	.01
☐ 605	Buddy Biancalana	.05	.02	.00
☐ 606	Rance Mulliniks	.05	.02	.00
☐ 607	Alan Wiggins	.05	.02	.00
☐ 608	Joe Cowley	.05	.02	.00
☐ 609A	Tom Seaver	.50	.25	.05

		MINT	EXC	G-VG
	(green borders on name)			
☐ 609B	Tom Seaver (yellow borders on name)	1.50	.75	.15
☐ 610	Neil Allen	.05	.02	.00
☐ 611	Don Sutton	.25	.12	.02
☐ 612	Fred Toliver	.10	.05	.01
☐ 613	Jay Baller	.08	.04	.01
☐ 614	Marc Sullivan	.08	.04	.01
☐ 615	John Grubb	.05	.02	.00
☐ 616	Bruce Kison	.05	.02	.00
☐ 617	Bill Madlock	.10	.05	.01
☐ 618	Chris Chambliss	.08	.04	.01
☐ 619	Dave Stewart	.30	.15	.03
☐ 620	Tim Lollar	.05	.02	.00
☐ 621	Gary Lavelle	.05	.02	.00
☐ 622	Charles Hudson	.05	.02	.00
☐ 623	Joel Davis	.10	.05	.01
☐ 624	Joe Johnson	.10	.05	.01
☐ 625	Sid Fernandez	.25	.12	.02
☐ 626	Dennis Lamp	.05	.02	.00
☐ 627	Terry Harper	.05	.02	.00
☐ 628	Jack Lazorko	.05	.02	.00
☐ 629	Roger McDowell	.50	.25	.05
☐ 630	Mark Funderburk	.10	.05	.01
☐ 631	Ed Lynch	.05	.02	.00
☐ 632	Rudy Law	.05	.02	.00
☐ 633	Roger Mason	.10	.05	.01
☐ 634	Mike Felder	.12	.06	.01
☐ 635	Ken Schrom	.05	.02	.00
☐ 636	Bob Ojeda	.08	.04	.01
☐ 637	Ed VandeBerg	.05	.02	.00
☐ 638	Bobby Meacham	.05	.02	.00
☐ 639	Cliff Johnson	.05	.02	.00
☐ 640	Garth Iorg	.05	.02	.00
☐ 641	Dan Driessen	.05	.02	.00
☐ 642	Mike Brown OF	.05	.02	.00
☐ 643	John Shelby	.05	.02	.00
☐ 644	Pete Rose (Ty-Breaking)	.35	.17	.03
☐ 645	The Knuckle Brothers Phil Niekro Joe Niekro	.10	.05	.01
☐ 646	Jesse Orosco	.05	.02	.00
☐ 647	Billy Beane	.12	.06	.01
☐ 648	Cesar Cedeno	.08	.04	.01
☐ 649	Bert Blyleven	.12	.06	.01
☐ 650	Max Venable	.05	.02	.00

		MINT	EXC	G-VG
☐ 651	Fleet Feet Vince Coleman Willie McGee	.30	.15	.03
☐ 652	Calvin Schiraldi	.08	.04	.01
☐ 653	King of Kings (Pete Rose)	.75	.35	.07
☐ 654	CL: Diamond Kings (unnumbered)	.08	.01	.00
☐ 655A	CL 1: 27-130 (unnumbered) (45 Beane ERR)	.10	.01	.00
☐ 655B	CL 1: 27-130 (unnumbered) (45 Habyan COR)	.50	.05	.01
☐ 656	CL 2: 131-234 (unnumbered)	.06	.01	.00
☐ 657	CL 3: 235-338 (unnumbered)	.06	.01	.00
☐ 658	CL 4: 339-442 (unnumbered)	.06	.01	.00
☐ 659	CL 5: 443-546 (unnumbered)	.06	.01	.00
☐ 660	CL 6: 547-653 (unnumbered)	.06	.01	.00

1986 Donruss Rookies

The 1986 Donruss "The Rookies" set features 56 cards plus a 15-piece puzzle of Hank Aaron. Cards are in full color and are standard size,

2 ½" by 3 ½". The set was distributed in a small green box with gold lettering. Although the set was wrapped in cellophane, the top card was #1 Joyner, resulting in a percentage of Joyner cards arriving in less than perfect condition. Card fronts are similar in design to the 1986 Donruss regular issue except for the presence of "The Rookies" logo in the lower left corner and a bluish green border instead of a blue border.

		MINT	EXC	G-VG
	COMPLETE SET (56)	50.00	25.00	5.00
	COMMON PLAYER (1-56)	.08	.04	.01
☐ 1	Wally Joyner	4.00	2.00	.40
☐ 2	Tracy Jones	.35	.17	.03
☐ 3	Allan Anderson	.45	.22	.04
☐ 4	Ed Correa	.20	.10	.02
☐ 5	Reggie Williams	.15	.07	.01
☐ 6	Charlie Kerfeld	.15	.07	.01
☐ 7	Andres Galarraga	1.00	.50	.10
☐ 8	Bob Tewksbury	.15	.07	.01
☐ 9	Al Newman	.15	.07	.01
☐ 10	Andres Thomas	.25	.12	.02
☐ 11	Barry Bonds	1.50	.75	.15
☐ 12	Juan Nieves	.15	.07	.01
☐ 13	Mark Eichhorn	.15	.07	.01
☐ 14	Dan Plesac	.35	.17	.03
☐ 15	Cory Snyder	1.00	.50	.10
☐ 16	Kelly Gruber	.45	.22	.04
☐ 17	Kevin Mitchell	7.00	3.50	.70
☐ 18	Steve Lombardozzi	.08	.04	.01
☐ 19	Mitch Williams	.60	.30	.06
☐ 20	John Cerutti	.30	.15	.03
☐ 21	Todd Worrell	.45	.22	.04
☐ 22	Jose Canseco	9.00	4.50	.90
☐ 23	Pete Incaviglia	.85	.40	.08
☐ 24	Jose Guzman	.15	.07	.01
☐ 25	Scott Bailes	.15	.07	.01
☐ 26	Greg Mathews	.25	.12	.02
☐ 27	Eric King	.20	.10	.02
☐ 28	Paul Assenmacher	.15	.07	.01
☐ 29	Jeff Sellers	.20	.10	.02
☐ 30	Bobby Bonilla	1.50	.75	.15
☐ 31	Doug Drabek	.45	.22	.04
☐ 32	Will Clark	13.50	6.00	1.25
☐ 33	Bip Roberts	.25	.12	.02
☐ 34	Jim Deshaies	.45	.22	.04
☐ 35	Mike LaValliere	.25	.12	.02

			MINT	EXC	G-VG
☐	36	Scott Bankhead	.30	.15	.03
☐	37	Dale Sveum	.25	.12	.02
☐	38	Bo Jackson	11.00	5.50	1.10
☐	39	Rob Thompson	.45	.22	.04
☐	40	Eric Plunk	.25	.12	.02
☐	41	Bill Bathe	.15	.07	.01
☐	42	John Kruk	.50	.25	.05
☐	43	Andy Allanson	.15	.07	.01
☐	44	Mark Portugal	.25	.12	.02
☐	45	Danny Tartabull	.85	.40	.08
☐	46	Bob Kipper	.08	.04	.01
☐	47	Gene Walter	.15	.07	.01
☐	48	Rey Quinones	.20	.10	.02
☐	49	Bobby Witt	.45	.22	.04
☐	50	Bill Mooneyham	.15	.07	.01
☐	51	John Cangelosi	.15	.07	.01
☐	52	Ruben Sierra	7.50	3.75	.75
☐	53	Rob Woodward	.15	.07	.01
☐	54	Ed Hearn	.15	.07	.01
☐	55	Joel McKeon	.15	.07	.01
☐	56	Checklist card	.08	.01	.00

1986 Donruss Highlights

Donruss' second edition of Highlights was released late in 1986. These glossy-coated cards are standard size, measuring 2 1/2" by 3 1/2". Cards commemorate events during the 1986 season, as well as players and pitchers of the month from each league. The set was

distributed in its own red, white, blue, and gold box along with a small Hank Aaron puzzle. Card fronts are similar to the regular 1986 Donruss issue except that the Highlights logo is positioned in the lower left-hand corner and the borders are in gold instead of blue. The backs are printed in black and gold on white card stock.

			MINT	EXC	G-VG
		COMPLETE SET (56)	9.00	4.50	.90
		COMMON PLAYER (1-56)	.06	.03	.00
☐	1	Will Clark .... Homers in First At-Bat	1.00	.50	.10
☐	2	Jose Rijo .... Oakland Milestone for Strikeouts	.06	.03	.00
☐	3	George Brett .... Royals' All-Time Hit Man	.25	.12	.02
☐	4	Mike Schmidt ...... Phillies RBI Leader	.65	.30	.06
☐	5	Roger Clemens ..... KKKKKKKKKK KKKKKKKKKK	.40	.20	.04
☐	6	Roger Clemens ..... AL Pitcher April	.40	.20	.04
☐	7	Kirby Puckett ...... AL Player April	.50	.25	.05
☐	8	Dwight Gooden ..... NL Pitcher April	.40	.20	.04
☐	9	Johnny Ray .... NL Player April	.06	.03	.00
☐	10	Reggie Jackson .... Eclipses Mantle HR Record	.40	.20	.04
☐	11	Wade Boggs .... First Five Hit Game of Career	.65	.30	.06
☐	12	Don Aase .... AL Pitcher May	.06	.03	.00
☐	13	Wade Boggs .... AL Player May	.65	.30	.06
☐	14	Jeff Reardon ...... NL Pitcher May	.06	.03	.00
☐	15	Hubie Brooks ...... NL Player May	.06	.03	.00
☐	16	Don Sutton .... Notches 300th	.10	.05	.01

			MINT	EXC	G-VG
☐	17	Roger Clemens .... Starts 14-0	.40	.20	.04
☐	18	Roger Clemens .... AL Pitcher June	.40	.20	.04
☐	19	Kent Hrbek .... AL Player June	.15	.07	.01
☐	20	Rick Rhoden .... NL Pitcher June	.06	.03	.00
☐	21	Kevin Bass .... NL Player June	.06	.03	.00
☐	22	Bob Horner .... Blasts four HRs in one Game	.10	.05	.01
☐	23	Wally Joyner .... Starting All-Star Rookie	.50	.25	.05
☐	24	Darryl Strawberry ... Starts Third Straight All-Star Game	.50	.25	.05
☐	25	Fernando Valenzuela Ties All-Star Game Record	.15	.07	.01
☐	26	Roger Clemens .... All-Star Game MVP	.40	.20	.04
☐	27	Jack Morris .... AL Pitcher July	.10	.05	.01
☐	28	Scott Fletcher ...... AL Player July	.06	.03	.00
☐	29	Todd Worrell .... NL Pitcher July	.10	.05	.01
☐	30	Eric Davis .... NL Player July	.65	.30	.06
☐	31	Bert Blyleven ...... Records 3000th Strikeout	.15	.07	.01
☐	32	Bobby Doerr .... '86 HOF Inductee	.15	.07	.01
☐	33	Ernie Lombardi ..... '86 HOF Inductee	.15	.07	.01
☐	34	Willie McCovey ..... '86 HOF Inductee	.25	.12	.02
☐	35	Steve Carlton ...... Notches 4000th K	.25	.12	.02
☐	36	Mike Schmidt ...... Surpasses DiMaggio Record	.65	.30	.06
☐	37	Juan Samuel .... Records 3rd "Quadruple Double"	.10	.05	.01
☐	38	Mike Witt .... AL Pitcher August	.10	.05	.01
☐	39	Doug DeCinces .... AL Player August	.06	.03	.00
☐	40	Bill Gullickson ...... NL Pitcher August	.06	.03	.00
☐	41	Dale Murphy .... NL Player August	.30	.15	.03
☐	42	Joe Carter .... Sets Tribe Offensive Record	.15	.07	.01
☐	43	Bo Jackson .... Longest HR in Royals Stadium	1.50	.75	.15
☐	44	Joe Cowley .... Majors 1st No-Hitter in 2 Years	.06	.03	.00
☐	45	Jim Deshaies ...... Sets ML Strikeout Record	.06	.03	.00
☐	46	Mike Scott .... No Hitter Clinches Division	.15	.07	.01
☐	47	Bruce Hurst .... AL Pitcher September	.10	.05	.01
☐	48	Don Mattingly ...... AL Player September	1.00	.50	.10
☐	49	Mike Krukow .... NL Pitcher September	.06	.03	.00
☐	50	Steve Sax .... NL Player September	.15	.07	.01
☐	51	John Cangelosi ..... AL Rookie Steals Record	.10	.05	.01
☐	52	Dave Righetti ...... ML Save Mark	.10	.05	.01
☐	53	Don Mattingly ...... Yankee Record for Hits and Doubles	1.25	.60	.12
☐	54	Todd Worrell .... Donruss NL ROY	.15	.07	.01
☐	55	Jose Canseco ...... Donruss AL ROY	1.50	.75	.15
☐	56	Checklist Card	.06	.03	.00

1987 Donruss

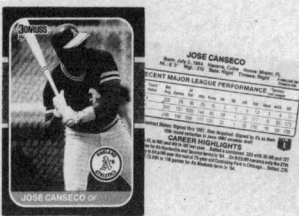

This 660-card set was distributed along with a puzzle of Roberto Clemente. The checklist cards are numbered throughout the set as multiples of 100. The wax pack boxes again contain four separate cards printed on the bottom of the box. Cards measure 2 ½" by 3 ½" and feature a black and gold border on the front; the backs are also done in black and gold on white card stock. The popular Diamond King subset returns for the sixth consecutive year. Some of the Diamond Kings (1-26) selections are repeats from prior years; Perez-Steele Galleries has indicated that a five-year rotation will be maintained in order to avoid depleting the pool of available worthy "kings" on some of the teams. Three of the Diamond Kings have a variation (on the reverse) where the yellow strip behind the words "Donruss Diamond Kings" is not printed and, hence, the background is white.

		MINT	EXC	G-VG
	COMPLETE SET (660)	75.00	35.00	7.00
	COMMON PLAYER (1-660)	.04	.02	.00
☐ 1	Wally Joyner DK	1.00	.15	.03
☐ 2	Roger Clemens DK	.60	.30	.06
☐ 3	Dale Murphy DK	.40	.20	.04
☐ 4	Darryl Strawberry DK	.50	.25	.05
☐ 5	Ozzie Smith DK	.15	.07	.01
☐ 6	Jose Canseco DK	1.50	.75	.15

		MINT	EXC	G-VG
☐ 7	Charlie Hough DK	.07	.03	.01
☐ 8	Brook Jacoby DK	.07	.03	.01
☐ 9	Fred Lynn DK	.12	.06	.01
☐ 10	Rick Rhoden DK	.07	.03	.01
☐ 11	Chris Brown DK	.07	.03	.01
☐ 12	Von Hayes DK	.10	.05	.01
☐ 13	Jack Morris DK	.12	.06	.01
☐ 14A	Kevin McReynolds DK (yellow strip missing on back)	1.00	.50	.10
☐ 14B	Kevin McReynolds DK	.30	.15	.03
☐ 15	George Brett DK	.40	.20	.04
☐ 16	Ted Higuera DK	.15	.07	.01
☐ 17	Hubie Brooks DK	.07	.03	.01
☐ 18	Mike Scott DK	.15	.07	.01
☐ 19	Kirby Puckett DK	.40	.20	.04
☐ 20	Dave Winfield DK	.25	.12	.02
☐ 21	Lloyd Moseby DK	.07	.03	.01
☐ 22A	Eric Davis DK (yellow strip missing on back)	3.00	1.50	.30
☐ 22B	Eric Davis DK	1.00	.50	.10
☐ 23	Jim Presley DK	.07	.03	.01
☐ 24	Keith Moreland DK	.07	.03	.01
☐ 25A	Greg Walker DK (yellow strip missing on back)	.75	.35	.07
☐ 25B	Greg Walker DK	.12	.06	.01
☐ 26	Steve Sax DK	.15	.07	.01
☐ 27	DK Checklist 1-26	.07	.01	.00
☐ 28	B.J. Surhoff RR	.45	.22	.04
☐ 29	Randy Myers RR	.60	.30	.06
☐ 30	Ken Gerhart RR	.15	.07	.01
☐ 31	Benito Santiago RR	1.50	.75	.15
☐ 32	Greg Swindell RR	1.50	.75	.15
☐ 33	Mike Birkbeck RR	.15	.07	.01
☐ 34	Terry Steinbach RR	.75	.35	.07
☐ 35	Bo Jackson RR	9.00	4.50	.90
☐ 36	Greg Maddux RR	1.50	.75	.15
☐ 37	Jim Lindeman RR	.15	.07	.01
☐ 38	Devon White RR	1.25	.60	.12
☐ 39	Eric Bell RR	.10	.05	.01
☐ 40	Willie Fraser RR	.10	.05	.01
☐ 41	Jerry Browne RR	.50	.25	.05
☐ 42	Chris James RR	.90	.45	.09
☐ 43	Rafael Palmeiro RR	2.00	1.00	.20
☐ 44	Pat Dodson RR	.15	.07	.01
☐ 45	Duane Ward RR	.20	.10	.02
☐ 46	Mark McGwire RR	8.00	4.00	.80

	#	Player	MINT	EXC	G-VG		#	Player	MINT	EXC	G-VG
☐	47	Bruce Fields RR (photo actually Darnell Coles)	.10	.05	.01	☐	94	Fernando Valenzuela	.18	.09	.01
☐	48	Eddie Murray	.25	.12	.02	☐	95	Andy Allanson	.07	.03	.01
						☐	96	Willie Wilson	.10	.05	.01
☐	49	Ted Higuera	.18	.09	.01	☐	97	Jose Canseco	6.50	3.25	.65
☐	50	Kirk Gibson	.25	.12	.02	☐	98	Jeff Reardon	.10	.05	.01
☐	51	Oil Can Boyd	.07	.03	.01	☐	99	Bobby Witt	.30	.15	.03
☐	52	Don Mattingly	2.25	1.10	.22	☐	100	Checklist	.07	.01	.00
☐	53	Pedro Guerrero	.15	.07	.01	☐	101	Jose Guzman	.04	.02	.00
☐	54	George Brett	.30	.15	.03	☐	102	Steve Balboni	.04	.02	.00
☐	55	Jose Rijo	.07	.03	.01	☐	103	Tony Phillips	.04	.02	.00
☐	56	Tim Raines	.25	.12	.02	☐	104	Brook Jacoby	.07	.03	.01
☐	57	Ed Correa	.12	.06	.01	☐	105	Dave Winfield	.30	.15	.03
☐	58	Mike Witt	.07	.03	.01	☐	106	Orel Hershiser	.40	.20	.04
☐	59	Greg Walker	.07	.03	.01	☐	107	Lou Whitaker	.12	.06	.01
☐	60	Ozzie Smith	.20	.10	.02	☐	108	Fred Lynn	.12	.06	.01
☐	61	Glenn Davis	.30	.15	.03	☐	109	Bill Wegman	.04	.02	.00
☐	62	Glenn Wilson	.04	.02	.00	☐	110	Donnie Moore	.04	.02	.00
☐	63	Tom Browning	.10	.05	.01	☐	111	Jack Clark	.18	.09	.01
☐	64	Tony Gwynn	.50	.25	.05	☐	112	Bob Knepper	.07	.03	.01
☐	65	R.J. Reynolds	.04	.02	.00	☐	113	Von Hayes	.07	.03	.01
☐	66	Will Clark	12.00	6.00	1.20	☐	114	Bip Roberts	.12	.06	.01
☐	67	Ozzie Virgil	.04	.02	.00	☐	115	Tony Pena	.07	.03	.01
☐	68	Rick Sutcliffe	.10	.05	.01	☐	116	Scott Garrelts	.07	.03	.01
☐	69	Gary Carter	.25	.12	.02	☐	117	Paul Molitor	.12	.06	.01
☐	70	Mike Moore	.07	.03	.01	☐	118	Darryl Strawberry	.75	.35	.07
☐	71	Bert Blyleven	.12	.06	.01	☐	119	Shawon Dunston	.12	.06	.01
☐	72	Tony Fernandez	.15	.07	.01	☐	120	Jim Presley	.07	.03	.01
☐	73	Kent Hrbek	.15	.07	.01	☐	121	Jesse Barfield	.15	.07	.01
☐	74	Lloyd Moseby	.07	.03	.01	☐	122	Gary Gaetti	.15	.07	.01
☐	75	Alvin Davis	.12	.06	.01	☐	123	Kurt Stillwell	.30	.15	.03
☐	76	Keith Hernandez	.20	.10	.02	☐	124	Joel Davis	.04	.02	.00
☐	77	Ryne Sandberg	.25	.12	.02	☐	125	Mike Boddicker	.07	.03	.01
☐	78	Dale Murphy	.40	.20	.04	☐	126	Robin Yount	.40	.20	.04
☐	79	Sid Bream	.04	.02	.00	☐	127	Alan Trammell	.20	.10	.02
☐	80	Chris Brown	.04	.02	.00	☐	128	Dave Righetti	.10	.05	.01
☐	81	Steve Garvey	.25	.12	.02	☐	129	Dwight Evans	.10	.05	.01
☐	82	Mario Soto	.04	.02	.00	☐	130	Mike Scioscia	.04	.02	.00
☐	83	Shane Rawley	.04	.02	.00	☐	131	Julio Franco	.12	.06	.01
☐	84	Willie McGee	.10	.05	.01	☐	132	Bret Saberhagen	.35	.17	.03
☐	85	Jose Cruz	.07	.03	.01	☐	133	Mike Davis	.04	.02	.00
☐	86	Brian Downing	.07	.03	.01	☐	134	Joe Hesketh	.04	.02	.00
☐	87	Ozzie Guillen	.07	.03	.01	☐	135	Wally Joyner	1.75	.85	.17
☐	88	Hubie Brooks	.07	.03	.01	☐	136	Don Slaught	.04	.02	.00
☐	89	Cal Ripken	.30	.15	.03	☐	137	Daryl Boston	.04	.02	.00
☐	90	Juan Nieves	.07	.03	.01	☐	138	Nolan Ryan	.50	.25	.05
☐	91	Lance Parrish	.10	.05	.01	☐	139	Mike Schmidt	.50	.25	.05
☐	92	Jim Rice	.18	.09	.01	☐	140	Tommy Herr	.07	.03	.01
☐	93	Ron Guidry	.12	.06	.01	☐	141	Garry Templeton	.07	.03	.01
						☐	142	Kal Daniels	.75	.35	.07

		MINT	EXC	G-VG
☐ 143	Billy Sample	.04	.02	.00
☐ 144	Johnny Ray	.07	.03	.01
☐ 145	Rob Thompson	.30	.15	.03
☐ 146	Bob Dernier	.04	.02	.00
☐ 147	Danny Tartabull	.30	.15	.03
☐ 148	Ernie Whitt	.04	.02	.00
☐ 149	Kirby Puckett	1.00	.50	.10
☐ 150	Mike Young	.04	.02	.00
☐ 151	Ernest Riles	.04	.02	.00
☐ 152	Frank Tanana	.07	.03	.01
☐ 153	Rich Gedman	.04	.02	.00
☐ 154	Willie Randolph	.07	.03	.01
☐ 155	Bill Madlock	.07	.03	.01
☐ 156	Joe Carter	.30	.15	.03
☐ 157	Danny Jackson	.10	.05	.01
☐ 158	Carney Lansford	.10	.05	.01
☐ 159	Bryn Smith	.07	.03	.01
☐ 160	Gary Pettis	.04	.02	.00
☐ 161	Oddibe McDowell	.10	.05	.01
☐ 162	John Cangelosi	.10	.05	.01
☐ 163	Mike Scott	.20	.10	.02
☐ 164	Eric Show	.07	.03	.01
☐ 165	Juan Samuel	.12	.06	.01
☐ 166	Nick Esasky	.10	.05	.01
☐ 167	Zane Smith	.07	.03	.01
☐ 168	Mike Brown (Pirates OF)	.04	.02	.00
☐ 169	Keith Moreland	.04	.02	.00
☐ 170	John Tudor	.10	.05	.01
☐ 171	Ken Dixon	.04	.02	.00
☐ 172	Jim Gantner	.04	.02	.00
☐ 173	Jack Morris	.12	.06	.01
☐ 174	Bruce Hurst	.12	.06	.01
☐ 175	Dennis Rasmussen	.07	.03	.01
☐ 176	Mike Marshall	.10	.05	.01
☐ 177	Dan Quisenberry	.10	.05	.01
☐ 178	Eric Plunk	.07	.03	.01
☐ 179	Tim Wallach	.07	.03	.01
☐ 180	Steve Buechele	.04	.02	.00
☐ 181	Don Sutton	.15	.07	.01
☐ 182	Dave Schmidt	.07	.03	.01
☐ 183	Terry Pendleton	.07	.03	.01
☐ 184	Jim Deshaies	.35	.17	.03
☐ 185	Steve Bedrosian	.12	.06	.01
☐ 186	Pete Rose	.55	.27	.05
☐ 187	Dave Dravecky	.10	.05	.01
☐ 188	Rick Reuschel	.10	.05	.01
☐ 189	Dan Gladden	.07	.03	.01
☐ 190	Rick Mahler	.04	.02	.00
☐ 191	Thad Bosley	.04	.02	.00
☐ 192	Ron Darling	.18	.09	.01
☐ 193	Matt Young	.04	.02	.00
☐ 194	Tom Brunansky	.12	.06	.01
☐ 195	Dave Stieb	.10	.05	.01
☐ 196	Frank Viola	.15	.07	.01
☐ 197	Tom Henke	.07	.03	.01
☐ 198	Karl Best	.04	.02	.00
☐ 199	Dwight Gooden	.75	.35	.07
☐ 200	Checklist	.07	.01	.00
☐ 201	Steve Trout	.04	.02	.00
☐ 202	Rafael Ramirez	.04	.02	.00
☐ 203	Bob Walk	.04	.02	.00
☐ 204	Roger Mason	.04	.02	.00
☐ 205	Terry Kennedy	.04	.02	.00
☐ 206	Ron Oester	.04	.02	.00
☐ 207	John Russell	.04	.02	.00
☐ 208	Greg Mathews	.20	.10	.02
☐ 209	Charlie Kerfeld	.04	.02	.00
☐ 210	Reggie Jackson	.40	.20	.04
☐ 211	Floyd Bannister	.04	.02	.00
☐ 212	Vance Law	.04	.02	.00
☐ 213	Rich Bordi	.04	.02	.00
☐ 214	Dan Plesac	.30	.15	.03
☐ 215	Dave Collins	.04	.02	.00
☐ 216	Bob Stanley	.04	.02	.00
☐ 217	Joe Niekro	.07	.03	.01
☐ 218	Tom Niedenfuer	.04	.02	.00
☐ 219	Brett Butler	.07	.03	.01
☐ 220	Charlie Leibrandt	.04	.02	.00
☐ 221	Steve Ontiveros	.04	.02	.00
☐ 222	Tim Burke	.07	.03	.01
☐ 223	Curtis Wilkerson	.04	.02	.00
☐ 224	Pete Incaviglia	.75	.35	.07
☐ 225	Lonnie Smith	.07	.03	.01
☐ 226	Chris Codiroli	.04	.02	.00
☐ 227	Scott Bailes	.10	.05	.01
☐ 228	Rickey Henderson	.40	.20	.04
☐ 229	Ken Howell	.04	.02	.00
☐ 230	Darnell Coles	.04	.02	.00
☐ 231	Don Aase	.04	.02	.00
☐ 232	Tim Leary	.10	.05	.01
☐ 233	Bob Boone	.10	.05	.01
☐ 234	Ricky Horton	.04	.02	.00
☐ 235	Mark Bailey	.04	.02	.00
☐ 236	Kevin Gross	.04	.02	.00
☐ 237	Lance McCullers	.07	.03	.01
☐ 238	Cecilio Guante	.04	.02	.00
☐ 239	Bob Melvin	.04	.02	.00

		MINT	EXC	G-VG
☐ 240	Billy Jo Robidoux	.04	.02	.00
☐ 241	Roger McDowell	.07	.03	.01
☐ 242	Leon Durham	.07	.03	.01
☐ 243	Ed Nunez	.04	.02	.00
☐ 244	Jimmy Key	.10	.05	.01
☐ 245	Mike Smithson	.04	.02	.00
☐ 246	Bo Diaz	.04	.02	.00
☐ 247	Carlton Fisk	.18	.09	.01
☐ 248	Larry Sheets	.07	.03	.01
☐ 249	Juan Castillo	.04	.02	.00
☐ 250	Eric King	.12	.06	.01
☐ 251	Doug Drabek	.30	.15	.03
☐ 252	Wade Boggs	1.50	.75	.15
☐ 253	Mariano Duncan	.04	.02	.00
☐ 254	Pat Tabler	.07	.03	.01
☐ 255	Frank White	.07	.03	.01
☐ 256	Alfredo Griffin	.07	.03	.01
☐ 257	Floyd Youmans	.07	.03	.01
☐ 258	Rob Wilfong	.04	.02	.00
☐ 259	Pete O'Brien	.07	.03	.01
☐ 260	Tim Hulett	.04	.02	.00
☐ 261	Dickie Thon	.04	.02	.00
☐ 262	Darren Daulton	.04	.02	.00
☐ 263	Vince Coleman	.40	.20	.04
☐ 264	Andy Hawkins	.07	.03	.01
☐ 265	Eric Davis	1.50	.75	.15
☐ 266	Andres Thomas	.18	.09	.01
☐ 267	Mike Diaz	.10	.05	.01
☐ 268	Chili Davis	.07	.03	.01
☐ 269	Jody Davis	.04	.02	.00
☐ 270	Phil Bradley	.07	.03	.01
☐ 271	George Bell	.25	.12	.02
☐ 272	Keith Atherton	.04	.02	.00
☐ 273	Storm Davis	.07	.03	.01
☐ 274	Rob Deer	.25	.12	.02
☐ 275	Walt Terrell	.04	.02	.00
☐ 276	Roger Clemens	1.50	.75	.15
☐ 277	Mike Easler	.04	.02	.00
☐ 278	Steve Sax	.15	.07	.01
☐ 279	Andre Thornton	.07	.03	.01
☐ 280	Jim Sundberg	.04	.02	.00
☐ 281	Bill Bathe	.07	.03	.01
☐ 282	Jay Tibbs	.04	.02	.00
☐ 283	Dick Schofield	.04	.02	.00
☐ 284	Mike Mason	.04	.02	.00
☐ 285	Jerry Hairston	.04	.02	.00
☐ 286	Bill Doran	.07	.03	.01
☐ 287	Tim Flannery	.04	.02	.00
☐ 288	Gary Redus	.04	.02	.00
☐ 289	John Franco	.10	.05	.01
☐ 290	Paul Assenmacher	.07	.03	.01
☐ 291	Joe Orsulak	.04	.02	.00
☐ 292	Lee Smith	.07	.03	.01
☐ 293	Mike Laga	.04	.02	.00
☐ 294	Rick Dempsey	.04	.02	.00
☐ 295	Mike Felder	.07	.03	.01
☐ 296	Tom Brookens	.04	.02	.00
☐ 297	Al Nipper	.04	.02	.00
☐ 298	Mike Pagliarulo	.07	.03	.01
☐ 299	Franklin Stubbs	.07	.03	.01
☐ 300	Checklist	.07	.01	.00
☐ 301	Steve Farr	.04	.02	.00
☐ 302	Bill Mooneyham	.07	.03	.01
☐ 303	Andres Galarraga	.40	.20	.04
☐ 304	Scott Fletcher	.07	.03	.01
☐ 305	Jack Howell	.07	.03	.01
☐ 306	Russ Morman	.10	.05	.01
☐ 307	Todd Worrell	.15	.07	.01
☐ 308	Dave Smith	.07	.03	.01
☐ 309	Jeff Stone	.04	.02	.00
☐ 310	Ron Robinson	.04	.02	.00
☐ 311	Bruce Bochy	.04	.02	.00
☐ 312	Jim Winn	.04	.02	.00
☐ 313	Mark Davis	.12	.06	.01
☐ 314	Jeff Dedmon	.04	.02	.00
☐ 315	Jamie Moyer	.15	.07	.01
☐ 316	Wally Backman	.04	.02	.00
☐ 317	Ken Phelps	.07	.03	.01
☐ 318	Steve Lombardozzi	.04	.02	.00
☐ 319	Rance Mulliniks	.04	.02	.00
☐ 320	Tim Laudner	.04	.02	.00
☐ 321	Mark Eichhorn	.10	.05	.01
☐ 322	Lee Guetterman	.12	.06	.01
☐ 323	Sid Fernandez	.12	.06	.01
☐ 324	Jerry Mumphrey	.04	.02	.00
☐ 325	David Palmer	.04	.02	.00
☐ 326	Bill Almon	.04	.02	.00
☐ 327	Candy Maldonado	.07	.03	.01
☐ 328	John Kruk	.35	.17	.03
☐ 329	John Denny	.04	.02	.00
☐ 330	Milt Thompson	.07	.03	.01
☐ 331	Mike LaValliere	.20	.10	.02
☐ 332	Alan Ashby	.04	.02	.00
☐ 333	Doug Corbett	.04	.02	.00
☐ 334	Ron Karkovice	.07	.03	.01
☐ 335	Mitch Webster	.04	.02	.00
☐ 336	Lee Lacy	.04	.02	.00
☐ 337	Glenn Braggs	.50	.25	.05

		MINT	EXC	G-VG			MINT	EXC	G-VG
☐ 338	Dwight Lowry	.10	.05	.01	☐ 387	Craig Lefferts	.07	.03	.01
☐ 339	Don Baylor	.07	.03	.01	☐ 388	Dave Parker	.12	.06	.01
☐ 340	Brian Fisher	.07	.03	.01	☐ 389	Bob Horner	.10	.05	.01
☐ 341	Reggie Williams	.10	.05	.01	☐ 390	Pat Clements	.04	.02	.00
☐ 342	Tom Candiotti	.04	.02	.00	☐ 391	Jeff Leonard	.07	.03	.01
☐ 343	Rudy Law	.04	.02	.00	☐ 392	Chris Speier	.04	.02	.00
☐ 344	Curt Young	.04	.02	.00	☐ 393	John Moses	.04	.02	.00
☐ 345	Mike Fitzgerald	.04	.02	.00	☐ 394	Garth Iorg	.04	.02	.00
☐ 346	Ruben Sierra	5.50	2.75	.55	☐ 395	Greg Gagne	.04	.02	.00
☐ 347	Mitch Williams	.45	.22	.04	☐ 396	Nate Snell	.04	.02	.00
☐ 348	Jorge Orta	.04	.02	.00	☐ 397	Bryan Clutterbuck	.07	.03	.01
☐ 349	Mickey Tettleton	.12	.06	.01	☐ 398	Darrell Evans	.07	.03	.01
☐ 350	Ernie Camacho	.04	.02	.00	☐ 399	Steve Crawford	.04	.02	.00
☐ 351	Ron Kittle	.10	.05	.01	☐ 400	Checklist	.07	.01	.00
☐ 352	Ken Landreaux	.04	.02	.00	☐ 401	Phil Lombardi	.12	.06	.01
☐ 353	Chet Lemon	.04	.02	.00	☐ 402	Rick Honeycutt	.04	.02	.00
☐ 354	John Shelby	.04	.02	.00	☐ 403	Ken Schrom	.04	.02	.00
☐ 355	Mark Clear	.04	.02	.00	☐ 404	Bud Black	.04	.02	.00
☐ 356	Doug DeCinces	.07	.03	.01	☐ 405	Donnie Hill	.04	.02	.00
☐ 357	Ken Dayley	.04	.02	.00	☐ 406	Wayne Krenchicki	.04	.02	.00
☐ 358	Phil Garner	.04	.02	.00	☐ 407	Chuck Finley	.50	.25	.05
☐ 359	Steve Jeltz	.04	.02	.00	☐ 408	Toby Harrah	.04	.02	.00
☐ 360	Ed Whitson	.04	.02	.00	☐ 409	Steve Lyons	.04	.02	.00
☐ 361	Barry Bonds	1.00	.50	.10	☐ 410	Kevin Bass	.07	.03	.01
☐ 362	Vida Blue	.07	.03	.01	☐ 411	Marvell Wynne	.04	.02	.00
☐ 363	Cecil Cooper	.07	.03	.01	☐ 412	Ron Roenicke	.04	.02	.00
☐ 364	Bob Ojeda	.07	.03	.01	☐ 413	Tracy Jones	.20	.10	.02
☐ 365	Dennis Eckersley	.12	.06	.01	☐ 414	Gene Garber	.04	.02	.00
☐ 366	Mike Morgan	.07	.03	.01	☐ 415	Mike Bielecki	.12	.06	.01
☐ 367	Willie Upshaw	.04	.02	.00	☐ 416	Frank DiPino	.04	.02	.00
☐ 368	Allan Anderson	.35	.17	.03	☐ 417	Andy Van Slyke	.20	.10	.02
☐ 369	Bill Gullickson	.04	.02	.00	☐ 418	Jim Dwyer	.04	.02	.00
☐ 370	Bobby Thigpen	.30	.15	.03	☐ 419	Ben Oglivie	.07	.03	.01
☐ 371	Juan Beniquez	.04	.02	.00	☐ 420	Dave Bergman	.04	.02	.00
☐ 372	Charlie Moore	.04	.02	.00	☐ 421	Joe Sambito	.04	.02	.00
☐ 373	Dan Petry	.04	.02	.00	☐ 422	Bob Tewksbury	.10	.05	.01
☐ 374	Rod Scurry	.04	.02	.00	☐ 423	Len Matuszek	.04	.02	.00
☐ 375	Tom Seaver	.30	.15	.03	☐ 424	Mike Kingery	.12	.06	.01
☐ 376	Ed VandeBerg	.04	.02	.00	☐ 425	Dave Kingman	.07	.03	.01
☐ 377	Tony Bernazard	.04	.02	.00	☐ 426	Al Newman	.07	.03	.01
☐ 378	Greg Pryor	.04	.02	.00	☐ 427	Gary Ward	.04	.02	.00
☐ 379	Dwayne Murphy	.04	.02	.00	☐ 428	Ruppert Jones	.04	.02	.00
☐ 380	Andy McGaffigan	.04	.02	.00	☐ 429	Harold Baines	.10	.05	.01
☐ 381	Kirk McCaskill	.04	.02	.00	☐ 430	Pat Perry	.04	.02	.00
☐ 382	Greg Harris	.04	.02	.00	☐ 431	Terry Puhl	.04	.02	.00
☐ 383	Rich Dotson	.07	.03	.01	☐ 432	Don Carman	.04	.02	.00
☐ 384	Craig Reynolds	.04	.02	.00	☐ 433	Eddie Milner	.04	.02	.00
☐ 385	Greg Gross	.04	.02	.00	☐ 434	LaMarr Hoyt	.07	.03	.01
☐ 386	Tito Landrum	.04	.02	.00	☐ 435	Rick Rhoden	.07	.03	.01

		MINT	EXC	G-VG
☐ 436	Jose Uribe	.04	.02	.00
☐ 437	Ken Oberkfell	.04	.02	.00
☐ 438	Ron Davis	.04	.02	.00
☐ 439	Jesse Orosco	.04	.02	.00
☐ 440	Scott Bradley	.04	.02	.00
☐ 441	Randy Bush	.04	.02	.00
☐ 442	John Cerutti	.20	.10	.02
☐ 443	Roy Smalley	.04	.02	.00
☐ 444	Kelly Gruber	.10	.05	.01
☐ 445	Bob Kearney	.04	.02	.00
☐ 446	Ed Hearn	.07	.03	.01
☐ 447	Scott Sanderson	.04	.02	.00
☐ 448	Bruce Benedict	.04	.02	.00
☐ 449	Junior Ortiz	.04	.02	.00
☐ 450	Mike Aldrete	.20	.10	.02
☐ 451	Kevin McReynolds	.30	.15	.03
☐ 452	Rob Murphy	.25	.12	.02
☐ 453	Kent Tekulve	.04	.02	.00
☐ 454	Curt Ford	.07	.03	.01
☐ 455	Dave Lopes	.07	.03	.01
☐ 456	Bob Grich	.07	.03	.01
☐ 457	Jose DeLeon	.07	.03	.01
☐ 458	Andre Dawson	.25	.12	.02
☐ 459	Mike Flanagan	.07	.03	.01
☐ 460	Joey Meyer	.45	.22	.04
☐ 461	Chuck Cary	.15	.07	.01
☐ 462	Bill Buckner	.07	.03	.01
☐ 463	Bob Shirley	.04	.02	.00
☐ 464	Jeff Hamilton	.25	.12	.02
☐ 465	Phil Niekro	.15	.07	.01
☐ 466	Mark Gubicza	.12	.06	.01
☐ 467	Jerry Willard	.04	.02	.00
☐ 468	Bob Sebra	.10	.05	.01
☐ 469	Larry Parrish	.04	.02	.00
☐ 470	Charlie Hough	.07	.03	.01
☐ 471	Hal McRae	.07	.03	.01
☐ 472	Dave Leiper	.07	.03	.01
☐ 473	Mel Hall	.10	.05	.01
☐ 474	Dan Pasqua	.07	.03	.01
☐ 475	Bob Welch	.07	.03	.01
☐ 476	Johnny Grubb	.04	.02	.00
☐ 477	Jim Traber	.07	.03	.01
☐ 478	Chris Bosio	.35	.17	.03
☐ 479	Mark McLemore	.04	.02	.00
☐ 480	John Morris	.04	.02	.00
☐ 481	Billy Hatcher	.07	.03	.01
☐ 482	Dan Schatzeder	.04	.02	.00
☐ 483	Rich Gossage	.10	.05	.01
☐ 484	Jim Morrison	.04	.02	.00

		MINT	EXC	G-VG
☐ 485	Bob Brenly	.04	.02	.00
☐ 486	Bill Schroeder	.04	.02	.00
☐ 487	Mookie Wilson	.07	.03	.01
☐ 488	Dave Martinez	.20	.10	.02
☐ 489	Harold Reynolds	.07	.03	.01
☐ 490	Jeff Hearron	.07	.03	.01
☐ 491	Mickey Hatcher	.04	.02	.00
☐ 492	Barry Larkin	2.25	1.10	.22
☐ 493	Bob James	.04	.02	.00
☐ 494	John Habyan	.04	.02	.00
☐ 495	Jim Adduci	.10	.05	.01
☐ 496	Mike Heath	.04	.02	.00
☐ 497	Tim Stoddard	.04	.02	.00
☐ 498	Tony Armas	.07	.03	.01
☐ 499	Dennis Powell	.04	.02	.00
☐ 500	Checklist	.07	.01	.00
☐ 501	Chris Bando	.04	.02	.00
☐ 502	David Cone	3.75	1.85	.37
☐ 503	Jay Howell	.07	.03	.01
☐ 504	Tom Foley	.04	.02	.00
☐ 505	Ray Chadwick	.07	.03	.01
☐ 506	Mike Loynd	.07	.03	.01
☐ 507	Neil Allen	.04	.02	.00
☐ 508	Danny Darwin	.04	.02	.00
☐ 509	Rick Schu	.04	.02	.00
☐ 510	Jose Oquendo	.04	.02	.00
☐ 511	Gene Walter	.04	.02	.00
☐ 512	Terry McGriff	.15	.07	.01
☐ 513	Ken Griffey	.10	.05	.01
☐ 514	Benny Distefano	.04	.02	.00
☐ 515	Terry Mulholland	.07	.03	.01
☐ 516	Ed Lynch	.04	.02	.00
☐ 517	Bill Swift	.07	.03	.01
☐ 518	Manny Lee	.07	.03	.01
☐ 519	Andre David	.04	.02	.00
☐ 520	Scott McGregor	.07	.03	.01
☐ 521	Rick Manning	.04	.02	.00
☐ 522	Willie Hernandez	.07	.03	.01
☐ 523	Marty Barrett	.07	.03	.01
☐ 524	Wayne Tolleson	.04	.02	.00
☐ 525	Jose Gonzalez	.20	.10	.02
☐ 526	Cory Snyder	.60	.30	.06
☐ 527	Buddy Biancalana	.04	.02	.00
☐ 528	Moose Haas	.04	.02	.00
☐ 529	Wilfredo Tejada	.07	.03	.01
☐ 530	Stu Cliburn	.04	.02	.00
☐ 531	Dale Mohorcic	.15	.07	.01
☐ 532	Ron Hassey	.04	.02	.00
☐ 533	Ty Gainey	.04	.02	.00

		MINT	EXC	G-VG			MINT	EXC	G-VG
☐ 534	Jerry Royster	.04	.02	.00	☐ 581	Tim Teufel	.04	.02	.00
☐ 535	Mike Maddux	.15	.07	.01	☐ 582	Odell Jones	.04	.02	.00
☐ 536	Ted Power	.04	.02	.00	☐ 583	Mark Ryal	.07	.03	.01
☐ 537	Ted Simmons	.10	.05	.01	☐ 584	Randy O'Neal	.04	.02	.00
☐ 538	Rafael Belliard	.07	.03	.01	☐ 585	Mike Greenwell	9.00	4.50	.90
☐ 539	Chico Walker	.07	.03	.01	☐ 586	Ray Knight	.07	.03	.01
☐ 540	Bob Forsch	.04	.02	.00	☐ 587	Ralph Bryant	.10	.05	.01
☐ 541	John Stefero	.04	.02	.00	☐ 588	Carmen Castillo	.04	.02	.00
☐ 542	Dale Sveum	.18	.09	.01	☐ 589	Ed Wojna	.04	.02	.00
☐ 543	Mark Thurmond	.04	.02	.00	☐ 590	Stan Javier	.07	.03	.01
☐ 544	Jeff Sellers	.15	.07	.01	☐ 591	Jeff Musselman	.15	.07	.01
☐ 545	Joel Skinner	.04	.02	.00	☐ 592	Mike Stanley	.15	.07	.01
☐ 546	Alex Trevino	.04	.02	.00	☐ 593	Darrell Porter	.04	.02	.00
☐ 547	Randy Kutcher	.07	.03	.01	☐ 594	Drew Hall	.10	.05	.01
☐ 548	Joaquin Andujar	.07	.03	.01	☐ 595	Rob Nelson	.15	.07	.01
☐ 549	Casey Candaele	.10	.05	.01	☐ 596	Bryan Oelkers	.04	.02	.00
☐ 550	Jeff Russell	.10	.05	.01	☐ 597	Scott Nielsen	.15	.07	.01
☐ 551	John Candelaria	.07	.03	.01	☐ 598	Brian Holton	.18	.09	.01
☐ 552	Joe Cowley	.04	.02	.00	☐ 599	Kevin Mitchell	5.00	2.50	.50
☐ 553	Danny Cox	.07	.03	.01	☐ 600	Checklist	.07	.01	.00
☐ 554	Denny Walling	.04	.02	.00	☐ 601	Jackie Gutierrez	.04	.02	.00
☐ 555	Bruce Ruffin	.15	.07	.01	☐ 602	Barry Jones	.12	.06	.01
☐ 556	Buddy Bell	.07	.03	.01	☐ 603	Jerry Narron	.04	.02	.00
☐ 557	Jimmy Jones	.25	.12	.02	☐ 604	Steve Lake	.04	.02	.00
☐ 558	Bobby Bonilla	1.00	.50	.10	☐ 605	Jim Pankovits	.04	.02	.00
☐ 559	Jeff Robinson	.10	.05	.01	☐ 606	Ed Romero	.04	.02	.00
	(Giants pitcher)				☐ 607	Dave LaPoint	.07	.03	.01
☐ 560	Ed Olwine	.06	.03	.00	☐ 608	Don Robinson	.04	.02	.00
☐ 561	Glenallen Hill	.90	.45	.09	☐ 609	Mike Krukow	.04	.02	.00
☐ 562	Lee Mazzilli	.04	.02	.00	☐ 610	Dave Valle	.04	.02	.00
☐ 563	Mike Brown	.04	.02	.00	☐ 611	Len Dykstra	.10	.05	.01
	(pitcher)				☐ 612	Roberto Clemente	.07	.03	.01
☐ 564	George Frazier	.04	.02	.00		Puzzle Card			
☐ 565	Mike Sharperson	.07	.03	.01	☐ 613	Mike Trujillo	.04	.02	.00
☐ 566	Mark Portugal	.20	.10	.02	☐ 614	Damaso Garcia	.04	.02	.00
☐ 567	Rick Leach	.04	.02	.00	☐ 615	Neal Heaton	.04	.02	.00
☐ 568	Mark Langston	.30	.15	.03	☐ 616	Juan Berenguer	.04	.02	.00
☐ 569	Rafael Santana	.04	.02	.00	☐ 617	Steve Carlton	.20	.10	.02
☐ 570	Manny Trillo	.04	.02	.00	☐ 618	Gary Lucas	.04	.02	.00
☐ 571	Cliff Speck	.07	.03	.01	☐ 619	Geno Petralli	.04	.02	.00
☐ 572	Bob Kipper	.04	.02	.00	☐ 620	Rick Aguilera	.04	.02	.00
☐ 573	Kelly Downs	.30	.15	.03	☐ 621	Fred McGriff	3.00	1.50	.30
☐ 574	Randy Asadoor	.07	.03	.01	☐ 622	Dave Henderson	.07	.03	.01
☐ 575	Dave Magadan	1.00	.50	.10	☐ 623	Dave Clark	.35	.17	.03
☐ 576	Marvin Freeman	.15	.07	.01	☐ 624	Angel Salazar	.04	.02	.00
☐ 577	Jeff Lahti	.04	.02	.00	☐ 625	Randy Hunt	.04	.02	.00
☐ 578	Jeff Calhoun	.04	.02	.00	☐ 626	John Gibbons	.04	.02	.00
☐ 579	Gus Polidor	.04	.02	.00	☐ 627	Kevin Brown	.65	.30	.06
☐ 580	Gene Nelson	.04	.02	.00	☐ 628	Bill Dawley	.04	.02	.00

		MINT	EXC	G-VG
☐	629 Aurelio Lopez	.04	.02	.00
☐	630 Charles Hudson	.04	.02	.00
☐	631 Ray Soff	.07	.03	.01
☐	632 Ray Hayward	.07	.03	.01
☐	633 Spike Owen	.04	.02	.00
☐	634 Glenn Hubbard	.04	.02	.00
☐	635 Kevin Elster	.60	.30	.06
☐	636 Mike LaCoss	.04	.02	.00
☐	637 Dwayne Henry	.04	.02	.00
☐	638 Rey Quinones	.20	.10	.02
☐	639 Jim Clancy	.04	.02	.00
☐	640 Larry Andersen	.04	.02	.00
☐	641 Calvin Schiraldi	.07	.03	.01
☐	642 Stan Jefferson	.25	.12	.02
☐	643 Marc Sullivan	.04	.02	.00
☐	644 Mark Grant	.04	.02	.00
☐	645 Cliff Johnson	.04	.02	.00
☐	646 Howard Johnson	.30	.15	.03
☐	647 Dave Sax	.04	.02	.00
☐	648 Dave Stewart	.15	.07	.01
☐	649 Danny Heep	.04	.02	.00
☐	650 Joe Johnson	.04	.02	.00
☐	651 Bob Brower	.15	.07	.01
☐	652 Rob Woodward	.04	.02	.00
☐	653 John Mizerock	.04	.02	.00
☐	654 Tim Pyznarski	.10	.05	.01
☐	655 Luis Aquino	.07	.03	.01
☐	656 Mickey Brantley	.15	.07	.01
☐	657 Doyle Alexander	.07	.03	.01
☐	658 Sammy Stewart	.04	.02	.00
☐	659 Jim Acker	.04	.02	.00
☐	660 Pete Ladd	.07	.03	.01

1987 Donruss Opening Day

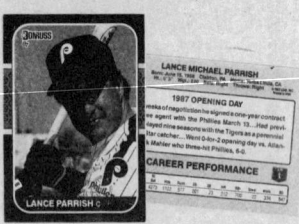

This innovative set of 272 cards features a card for each of the players in the starting line-ups of all the teams on Opening Day 1987. Cards are the standard size, 2 ½" by 3 ½", and are packaged as a complete set in a specially designed box. Cards are very similar in design to the 1987 regular Donruss issue except that these "OD" cards have a maroon border instead of a black border. The set features the first card in a Major League uniform of Joey Cora, Mark Davidson, Donnell Nixon, Bob Patterson, and Alonzo Powell. Teams in the same city share a checklist card. A 15-piece puzzle of Roberto Clemente is also included with every complete set. The error on Bobby Bonds was corrected very early in the press run; supposedly less than one percent of the sets have the error.

		MINT	EXC	G-VG
	COMPLETE SET (272)	18.00	9.00	1.80
	COMMON PLAYER (1-248)	.05	.02	.00
	COMMON LOGO (249-272)	.03	.01	.00
☐	1 Doug DeCinces	.05	.02	.00
☐	2 Mike Witt	.10	.05	.01
☐	3 George Hendrick	.05	.02	.00
☐	4 Dick Schofield	.05	.02	.00
☐	5 Devon White	.60	.30	.06
☐	6 Butch Wynegar	.05	.02	.00

		MINT	EXC	G-VG			MINT	EXC	G-VG
☐ 7	Wally Joyner	1.00	.50	.10	☐ 56	Ted Higuera	.15	.07	.01
☐ 8	Mark McLemore	.05	.02	.00	☐ 57	Rob Deer	.10	.05	.01
☐ 9	Brian Downing	.05	.02	.00	☐ 58	Robin Yount	.45	.22	.04
☐ 10	Gary Pettis	.05	.02	.00	☐ 59	Jim Lindeman	.10	.05	.01
☐ 11	Bill Doran	.10	.05	.01	☐ 60	Vince Coleman	.30	.15	.03
☐ 12	Phil Garner	.05	.02	.00	☐ 61	Tommy Herr	.05	.02	.00
☐ 13	Jose Cruz	.10	.05	.01	☐ 62	Terry Pendleton	.05	.02	.00
☐ 14	Kevin Bass	.10	.05	.01	☐ 63	John Tudor	.15	.07	.01
☐ 15	Mike Scott	.20	.10	.02	☐ 64	Tony Pena	.10	.05	.01
☐ 16	Glenn Davis	.25	.12	.02	☐ 65	Ozzie Smith	.25	.12	.02
☐ 17	Alan Ashby	.05	.02	.00	☐ 66	Tito Landrum	.05	.02	.00
☐ 18	Billy Hatcher	.10	.05	.01	☐ 67	Jack Clark	.20	.10	.02
☐ 19	Craig Reynolds	.05	.02	.00	☐ 68	Bob Dernier	.05	.02	.00
☐ 20	Carney Lansford	.20	.10	.02	☐ 69	Rick Sutcliffe	.10	.05	.01
☐ 21	Mike Davis	.05	.02	.00	☐ 70	Andre Dawson	.25	.12	.02
☐ 22	Reggie Jackson	.50	.25	.05	☐ 71	Keith Moreland	.05	.02	.00
☐ 23	Mickey Tettleton	.20	.10	.02	☐ 72	Jody Davis	.05	.02	.00
☐ 24	Jose Canseco	2.50	1.25	.25	☐ 73	Brian Dayett	.05	.02	.00
☐ 25	Rob Nelson	.05	.02	.00	☐ 74	Leon Durham	.05	.02	.00
☐ 26	Tony Phillips	.05	.02	.00	☐ 75	Ryne Sandberg	.25	.12	.02
☐ 27	Dwayne Murphy	.05	.02	.00	☐ 76	Shawon Dunston	.20	.10	.02
☐ 28	Alfredo Griffin	.05	.02	.00	☐ 77	Mike Marshall	.15	.07	.01
☐ 29	Curt Young	.05	.02	.00	☐ 78	Bill Madlock	.05	.02	.00
☐ 30	Willie Upshaw	.05	.02	.00	☐ 79	Orel Hershiser	.60	.30	.06
☐ 31	Mike Sharperson	.05	.02	.00	☐ 80	Mike Ramsey	.10	.05	.01
☐ 32	Rance Mulliniks	.05	.02	.00	☐ 81	Ken Landreaux	.05	.02	.00
☐ 33	Ernie Whitt	.05	.02	.00	☐ 82	Mike Scioscia	.05	.02	.00
☐ 34	Jesse Barfield	.15	.07	.01	☐ 83	Franklin Stubbs	.05	.02	.00
☐ 35	Tony Fernandez	.15	.07	.01	☐ 84	Mariano Duncan	.05	.02	.00
☐ 36	Lloyd Moseby	.10	.05	.01	☐ 85	Steve Sax	.15	.07	.01
☐ 37	Jimmy Key	.10	.05	.01	☐ 86	Mitch Webster	.05	.02	.00
☐ 38	Fred McGriff	.75	.35	.07	☐ 87	Reid Nichols	.05	.02	.00
☐ 39	George Bell	.25	.12	.02	☐ 88	Tim Wallach	.10	.05	.01
☐ 40	Dale Murphy	.35	.17	.03	☐ 89	Floyd Youmans	.10	.05	.01
☐ 41	Rick Mahler	.05	.02	.00	☐ 90	Andres Galarraga	.35	.17	.03
☐ 42	Ken Griffey	.10	.05	.01	☐ 91	Hubie Brooks	.10	.05	.01
☐ 43	Andres Thomas	.05	.02	.00	☐ 92	Jeff Reed	.05	.02	.00
☐ 44	Dion James	.05	.02	.00	☐ 93	Alonzo Powell	.10	.05	.01
☐ 45	Ozzie Virgil	.05	.02	.00	☐ 94	Vance Law	.05	.02	.00
☐ 46	Ken Oberkfell	.05	.02	.00	☐ 95	Bob Brenly	.05	.02	.00
☐ 47	Gary Roenicke	.05	.02	.00	☐ 96	Will Clark	2.50	1.25	.25
☐ 48	Glenn Hubbard	.05	.02	.00	☐ 97	Chili Davis	.10	.05	.01
☐ 49	Bill Schroeder	.05	.02	.00	☐ 98	Mike Krukow	.05	.02	.00
☐ 50	Greg Brock	.05	.02	.00	☐ 99	Jose Uribe	.05	.02	.00
☐ 51	Billy Jo Robidoux	.05	.02	.00	☐ 100	Chris Brown	.05	.02	.00
☐ 52	Glenn Braggs	.25	.12	.02	☐ 101	Rob Thompson	.10	.05	.01
☐ 53	Jim Gantner	.05	.02	.00	☐ 102	Candy Maldonado	.10	.05	.01
☐ 54	Paul Molitor	.15	.07	.01	☐ 103	Jeff Leonard	.10	.05	.01
☐ 55	Dale Sveum	.10	.05	.01	☐ 104	Tom Candiotti	.05	.02	.00

			MINT	EXC	G-VG				MINT	EXC	G-VG
☐	105	Chris Bando	.05	.02	.00	☐	154	Milt Thompson	.05	.02	.00
☐	106	Cory Snyder	.40	.20	.04	☐	155	Mike Easler	.05	.02	.00
☐	107	Pat Tabler	.05	.02	.00	☐	156	Juan Samuel	.15	.07	.01
☐	108	Andre Thornton	.05	.02	.00	☐	157	Steve Jeltz	.05	.02	.00
☐	109	Joe Carter	.20	.10	.02	☐	158	Glenn Wilson	.10	.05	.01
☐	110	Tony Bernazard	.05	.02	.00	☐	159	Shane Rawley	.05	.02	.00
☐	111	Julio Franco	.15	.07	.01	☐	160	Mike Schmidt	.75	.35	.07
☐	112	Brook Jacoby	.10	.05	.01	☐	161	Andy Van Slyke	.20	.10	.02
☐	113	Brett Butler	.10	.05	.01	☐	162	Johnny Ray	.10	.05	.01
☐	114	Donnell Nixon	.10	.05	.01	☐	163A	Barry Bonds ERR	150.00	75.00	15.00
☐	115	Alvin Davis	.20	.10	.02			(photo actually			
☐	116	Mark Langston	.35	.17	.03			Johnny Ray)			
☐	117	Harold Reynolds	.10	.05	.01	☐	163B	Barry Bonds COR	.30	.15	.03
☐	118	Ken Phelps	.05	.02	.00	☐	164	Junior Ortiz	.05	.02	.00
☐	119	Mike Kingery	.05	.02	.00	☐	165	Rafael Belliard	.05	.02	.00
☐	120	Dave Valle	.05	.02	.00	☐	166	Bob Patterson	.10	.05	.01
☐	121	Rey Quinones	.05	.02	.00	☐	167	Bobby Bonilla	.30	.15	.03
☐	122	Phil Bradley	.10	.05	.01	☐	168	Sid Bream	.05	.02	.00
☐	123	Jim Presley	.10	.05	.01	☐	169	Jim Morrison	.05	.02	.00
☐	124	Keith Hernandez	.20	.10	.02	☐	170	Jerry Browne	.10	.05	.01
☐	125	Kevin McReynolds	.25	.12	.02	☐	171	Scott Fletcher	.05	.02	.00
☐	126	Rafael Santana	.05	.02	.00	☐	172	Ruben Sierra	1.50	.75	.15
☐	127	Bob Ojeda	.10	.05	.01	☐	173	Larry Parrish	.05	.02	.00
☐	128	Darryl Strawberry	.90	.45	.09	☐	174	Pete O'Brien	.10	.05	.01
☐	129	Mookie Wilson	.05	.02	.00	☐	175	Pete Incaviglia	.35	.17	.03
☐	130	Gary Carter	.20	.10	.02	☐	176	Don Slaught	.05	.02	.00
☐	131	Tim Teufel	.05	.02	.00	☐	177	Oddibe McDowell	.10	.05	.01
☐	132	Howard Johnson	.25	.12	.02	☐	178	Charlie Hough	.05	.02	.00
☐	133	Cal Ripken	.35	.17	.03	☐	179	Steve Buechele	.05	.02	.00
☐	134	Rick Burleson	.05	.02	.00	☐	180	Bob Stanley	.05	.02	.00
☐	135	Fred Lynn	.10	.05	.01	☐	181	Wade Boggs	1.00	.50	.10
☐	136	Eddie Murray	.20	.10	.02	☐	182	Jim Rice	.20	.10	.02
☐	137	Ray Knight	.05	.02	.00	☐	183	Bill Buckner	.10	.05	.01
☐	138	Alan Wiggins	.05	.02	.00	☐	184	Dwight Evans	.15	.07	.01
☐	139	John Shelby	.05	.02	.00	☐	185	Spike Owen	.05	.02	.00
☐	140	Mike Boddicker	.05	.02	.00	☐	186	Don Baylor	.10	.05	.01
☐	141	Ken Gerhart	.10	.05	.01	☐	187	Marc Sullivan	.05	.02	.00
☐	142	Terry Kennedy	.05	.02	.00	☐	188	Marty Barrett	.10	.05	.01
☐	143	Steve Garvey	.30	.15	.03	☐	189	Dave Henderson	.10	.05	.01
☐	144	Marvell Wynne	.05	.02	.00	☐	190	Bo Diaz	.05	.02	.00
☐	145	Kevin Mitchell	1.00	.50	.10	☐	191	Barry Larkin	.75	.35	.07
☐	146	Tony Gwynn	.75	.35	.07	☐	192	Kal Daniels	.45	.22	.04
☐	147	Joey Cora	.10	.05	.01	☐	193	Terry Francona	.05	.02	.00
☐	148	Benito Santiago	1.00	.50	.10	☐	194	Tom Browning	.15	.07	.01
☐	149	Eric Show	.10	.05	.01	☐	195	Ron Oester	.05	.02	.00
☐	150	Garry Templeton	.10	.05	.01	☐	196	Buddy Bell	.10	.05	.01
☐	151	Carmelo Martinez	.05	.02	.00	☐	197	Eric Davis	1.00	.50	.10
☐	152	Von Hayes	.10	.05	.01	☐	198	Dave Parker	.15	.07	.01
☐	153	Lance Parrish	.10	.05	.01	☐	199	Steve Balboni	.05	.02	.00

		MINT	EXC	G-VG
☐ 200	Danny Tartabull	.25	.12	.02
☐ 201	Ed Hearn	.05	.02	.00
☐ 202	Buddy Biancalana	.05	.02	.00
☐ 203	Danny Jackson	.20	.10	.02
☐ 204	Frank White	.10	.05	.01
☐ 205	Bo Jackson	2.50	1.25	.25
☐ 206	George Brett	.35	.17	.03
☐ 207	Kevin Seitzer	1.00	.50	.10
☐ 208	Willie Wilson	.10	.05	.01
☐ 209	Orlando Mercado	.05	.02	.00
☐ 210	Darrell Evans	.10	.05	.01
☐ 211	Larry Herndon	.05	.02	.00
☐ 212	Jack Morris	.15	.07	.01
☐ 213	Chet Lemon	.05	.02	.00
☐ 214	Mike Heath	.05	.02	.00
☐ 215	Darnell Coles	.05	.02	.00
☐ 216	Alan Trammell	.25	.12	.02
☐ 217	Terry Harper	.05	.02	.00
☐ 218	Lou Whitaker	.15	.07	.01
☐ 219	Gary Gaetti	.20	.10	.02
☐ 220	Tom Nieto	.05	.02	.00
☐ 221	Kirby Puckett	.75	.35	.07
☐ 222	Tom Brunansky	.15	.07	.01
☐ 223	Greg Gagne	.05	.02	.00
☐ 224	Dan Gladden	.05	.02	.00
☐ 225	Mark Davidson	.10	.05	.01
☐ 226	Bert Blyleven	.15	.07	.01
☐ 227	Steve Lombardozzi	.05	.02	.00
☐ 228	Kent Hrbek	.25	.12	.02
☐ 229	Gary Redus	.05	.02	.00
☐ 230	Ivan Calderon	.10	.05	.01
☐ 231	Tim Hulett	.05	.02	.00
☐ 232	Carlton Fisk	.25	.12	.02
☐ 233	Greg Walker	.10	.05	.01
☐ 234	Ron Karkovice	.05	.02	.00
☐ 235	Ozzie Guillen	.15	.07	.01
☐ 236	Harold Baines	.15	.07	.01
☐ 237	Donnie Hill	.05	.02	.00
☐ 238	Rich Dotson	.10	.05	.01
☐ 239	Mike Pagliarulo	.10	.05	.01
☐ 240	Joel Skinner	.05	.02	.00
☐ 241	Don Mattingly	1.50	.75	.15
☐ 242	Gary Ward	.05	.02	.00
☐ 243	Dave Winfield	.25	.12	.02
☐ 244	Dan Pasqua	.10	.05	.01
☐ 245	Wayne Tolleson	.05	.02	.00
☐ 246	Willie Randolph	.10	.05	.01
☐ 247	Dennis Rasmussen	.10	.05	.01
☐ 248	Rickey Henderson	.45	.22	.04

		MINT	EXC	G-VG
☐ 249	Angels Logo	.03	.01	.00
☐ 250	Astros Logo	.03	.01	.00
☐ 251	A's Logo	.03	.01	.00
☐ 252	Blue Jays Logo	.03	.01	.00
☐ 253	Braves Logo	.03	.01	.00
☐ 254	Brewers Logo	.03	.01	.00
☐ 255	Cardinals Logo	.03	.01	.00
☐ 256	Dodgers Logo	.03	.01	.00
☐ 257	Expos Logo	.03	.01	.00
☐ 258	Giants Logo	.03	.01	.00
☐ 259	Indians Logo	.03	.01	.00
☐ 260	Mariners Logo	.03	.01	.00
☐ 261	Orioles Logo	.03	.01	.00
☐ 262	Padres Logo	.03	.01	.00
☐ 263	Phillies Logo	.03	.01	.00
☐ 264	Pirates Logo	.03	.01	.00
☐ 265	Rangers Logo	.03	.01	.00
☐ 266	Red Sox Logo	.03	.01	.00
☐ 267	Reds Logo	.03	.01	.00
☐ 268	Royals Logo	.03	.01	.00
☐ 269	Tigers Logo	.03	.01	.00
☐ 270	Twins Logo	.03	.01	.00
☐ 271	Chicago Logos	.03	.01	.00
☐ 272	New York Logos	.03	.01	.00

1987 Donruss Rookies

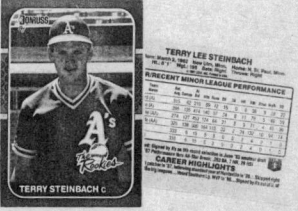

The 1987 Donruss "The Rookies" set features 56 cards plus a 15-piece puzzle of Roberto Clemente. Cards are in full color and are standard size, 2 ½" by 3 ½". The set was distributed in a small green and black box with gold lettering. Card fronts are similar in design to the 1987 Donruss regular issue except for the presence of "The Rookies" logo in the lower left corner and a green border instead of a black border.

		MINT	EXC	G-VG
COMPLETE SET (56)		20.00	9.00	1.80
COMMON PLAYER (1-56)		.06	.03	.00
☐ 1	Mark McGwire	3.00	1.00	.20
☐ 2	Eric Bell	.06	.03	.00
☐ 3	Mark Williamson	.12	.06	.01
☐ 4	Mike Greenwell	3.50	1.75	.35
☐ 5	Ellis Burks	2.50	1.25	.25
☐ 6	DeWayne Buice	.12	.06	.01
☐ 7	Mark McLemore	.06	.03	.00
☐ 8	Devon White	.45	.22	.04
☐ 9	Willie Fraser	.06	.03	.00
☐ 10	Les Lancaster	.20	.10	.02
☐ 11	Ken Williams	.25	.12	.02
☐ 12	Matt Nokes	.60	.30	.06
☐ 13	Jeff Robinson (Tigers pitcher)	.35	.17	.03
☐ 14	Bo Jackson	3.50	1.75	.35
☐ 15	Kevin Seitzer	1.25	.60	.12
☐ 16	Billy Ripken	.25	.12	.02
☐ 17	B.J. Surhoff	.15	.07	.01
☐ 18	Chuck Crim	.12	.06	.01
☐ 19	Mike Birkbeck	.06	.03	.00
☐ 20	Chris Bosio	.15	.07	.01
☐ 21	Les Straker	.12	.06	.01
☐ 22	Mark Davidson	.12	.06	.01
☐ 23	Gene Larkin	.35	.17	.03
☐ 24	Ken Gerhart	.10	.05	.01
☐ 25	Luis Polonia	.30	.15	.03
☐ 26	Terry Steinbach	.25	.12	.02
☐ 27	Mickey Brantley	.15	.07	.01
☐ 28	Mike Stanley	.10	.05	.01
☐ 29	Jerry Browne	.10	.05	.01
☐ 30	Todd Benzinger	.45	.22	.04
☐ 31	Fred McGriff	2.00	1.00	.20
☐ 32	Mike Henneman	.30	.15	.03
☐ 33	Casey Candaele	.10	.05	.01
☐ 34	Dave Magadan	.25	.12	.02
☐ 35	David Cone	1.00	.50	.10
☐ 36	Mike Jackson	.20	.10	.02
☐ 37	John Mitchell	.15	.07	.01
☐ 38	Mike Dunne	.25	.12	.02
☐ 39	John Smiley	.35	.17	.03
☐ 40	Joe Magrane	1.50	.75	.15
☐ 41	Jim Lindeman	.10	.05	.01
☐ 42	Shane Mack	.20	.10	.02
☐ 43	Stan Jefferson	.12	.06	.01
☐ 44	Benito Santiago	.60	.30	.06
☐ 45	Matt Williams	3.00	1.50	.30
☐ 46	Dave Meads	.10	.05	.01
☐ 47	Rafael Palmeiro	.75	.35	.07
☐ 48	Bill Long	.12	.06	.01
☐ 49	Bob Brower	.10	.05	.01
☐ 50	James Steels	.10	.05	.01
☐ 51	Paul Noce	.12	.06	.01
☐ 52	Greg Maddux	.45	.22	.04
☐ 53	Jeff Musselman	.10	.05	.01
☐ 54	Brian Holton	.10	.05	.01
☐ 55	Chuck Jackson	.12	.06	.01
☐ 56	Checklist Card	.06	.01	.00

1987 Donruss Highlights

Donruss' third (and last) edition of Highlights was released late in 1987. The cards are standard size, measuring 2 ½" by 3 ½", and are glossy in appearance. Cards commemorate events during the 1987 season, as well as players and pitchers of the month from each league. The set was distributed in its own red, black, blue, and gold box along with a small

Roberto Clemente puzzle. Card fronts are similar to the regular 1987 Donruss issue except that the Highlights logo is positioned in the lower right-hand corner and the borders are in blue instead of black. The backs are printed in black and gold on white card stock.

			MINT	EXC	G-VG
	COMPLETE SET (56)		8.00	4.00	.80
	COMMON PLAYER (1-56)		.06	.03	.00
☐	1	Juan Nieves	.06	.03	.00
		First No-Hitter			
☐	2	Mike Schmidt	.45	.22	.04
		Hits 500th Homer			
☐	3	Eric Davis	.35	.17	.03
		NL Player April			
☐	4	Sid Fernandez	.10	.05	.01
		NL Pitcher April			
☐	5	Brian Downing	.06	.03	.00
		AL Player April			
☐	6	Bret Saberhagen	.25	.12	.02
		AL Pitcher April			
☐	7	Tim Raines	.15	.07	.01
		Free Agent Returns			
☐	8	Eric Davis	.35	.17	.03
		NL Player May			
☐	9	Steve Bedrosian	.10	.05	.01
		NL Pitcher May			
☐	10	Larry Parrish	.06	.03	.00
		AL Player May			
☐	11	Jim Clancy	.06	.03	.00
		AL Pitcher May			
☐	12	Tony Gwynn	.25	.12	.02
		NL Player June			
		ERR (over "20" hits)			
☐	13	Orel Hershiser	.35	.17	.03
		NL Pitcher June			
☐	14	Wade Boggs	.50	.25	.05
		AL Player June			
☐	15	Steve Ontiveros	.06	.03	.00
		AL Pitcher June			
☐	16	Tim Raines	.15	.07	.01
		All Star Game Hero			
☐	17	Don Mattingly	.75	.35	.07
		Consecutive Game			
		Homerun Streak			
☐	18	Ray Dandridge	.15	.07	.01
		1987 HOF Inductee			
☐	19	Jim "Catfish" Hunter	.15	.07	.01

			MINT	EXC	G-VG
		1987 HOF Inductee			
☐	20	Billy Williams	.15	.07	.01
		1987 HOF Inductee			
☐	21	Bo Diaz	.06	.03	.00
		NL Player July			
☐	22	Floyd Youmans	.06	.03	.00
		NL Pitcher July			
☐	23	Don Mattingly	.75	.35	.07
		AL Player July			
☐	24	Frank Viola	.15	.07	.01
		AL Pitcher July			
☐	25	Bobby Witt	.15	.07	.01
		Strikes Out Four			
		Batters in One Inning			
☐	26	Kevin Seitzer	.45	.22	.04
		Ties AL 9-Inning			
		Game Hit Mark			
☐	27	Mark McGwire	.90	.45	.09
		Sets Rookie HR			
		Record			
☐	28	Andre Dawson	.20	.10	.02
		Sets Cubs' 1st Year			
		Homer Mark			
☐	29	Paul Molitor	.15	.07	.01
		Hits in 39			
		Straight Games			
☐	30	Kirby Puckett	.50	.25	.05
		Record Weekend			
☐	31	Andre Dawson	.20	.10	.02
		NL Player August			
☐	32	Doug Drabek	.06	.03	.00
		NL Pitcher August			
☐	33	Dwight Evans	.10	.05	.01
		AL Player August			
☐	34	Mark Langston	.20	.10	.02
		AL Pitcher August			
☐	35	Wally Joyner	.25	.12	.02
		100 RBI in 1st Two			
		Major League Seasons			
☐	36	Vince Coleman	.20	.10	.02
		100 SB in 1st Three			
		Major League Seasons			
☐	37	Eddie Murray	.20	.10	.02
		Orioles' All Time			
		Homer King			
☐	38	Cal Ripken	.20	.10	.02
		Ends Consecutive			
		Innings Streak			
☐	39	Blue Jays	.06	.03	.00

		MINT	EXC	G-VG
	Hit Record 10 Homers In One Game (McGriff/Ducey/Whitt)			
☐ 40	McGwire/Canseco ... Equal A's RBI Marks	1.00	.50	.10
☐ 41	Bob Boone .... Sets All-Time Catching Record	.10	.05	.01
☐ 42	Darryl Strawberry .... Sets Mets' One-Season Home Run Mark	.35	.17	.03
☐ 43	Howard Johnson .... NL's All-Time Switchhit HR King	.25	.12	.02
☐ 44	Wade Boggs .... Five Straight 200 Hit Seasons	.50	.25	.05
☐ 45	Benito Santiago .... Eclipses Rookie Game Hitting Streak	.35	.17	.03
☐ 46	Mark McGwire ..... Eclipses Jackson's A's HR Record	.90	.45	.09
☐ 47	Kevin Seitzer .... 13th Rookie to Collect 200 Hits	.45	.22	.04
☐ 48	Don Mattingly ...... Sets Slam Record	1.00	.50	.10
☐ 49	Darryl Strawberry ... NL Player September	.40	.20	.04
☐ 50	Pascual Perez ...... NL Pitcher September	.10	.05	.01
☐ 51	Alan Trammell ...... AL Player September	.15	.07	.01
☐ 52	Doyle Alexander .... AL Pitcher September	.06	.03	.00
☐ 53	Nolan Ryan .... Strikeout King Again	1.00	.50	.10
☐ 54	Mark McGwire ..... Donruss AL ROY	1.00	.50	.10
☐ 55	Benito Santiago .... Donruss NL ROY	.50	.25	.05
☐ 56	Checklist Card	.06	.03	.00

1988 Donruss

This 660-card set was distributed along with a puzzle of Stan Musial. The six regular checklist cards are numbered throughout the set as multiples of 100. Cards measure 2 ½" by 3 ½" and feature a distinctive black and blue border on the front. The popular Diamond King subset returns for the seventh consecutive year. Rated Rookies are featured again as cards 28-47. Cards marked as SP (short printed) from 648-660 are more difficult to find than the other 13 SP's in the lower 600s. These 26 cards listed as SP were apparently pulled from the printing sheet to make room for the 26 Bonus MVP cards. Six of the checklist cards were done two different ways to reflect the inclusion or exclusion of the Bonus MVP cards in the wax packs. In the checklist below, the A variations (for the checklist cards) are from the wax packs and the B variations are from the factory-collated sets.

		MINT	EXC	G-VG
COMPLETE SET (660)		28.00	14.00	2.80
COMMON PLAYER (1-647)		.03	.01	.00
COMMON PLAYER (648-660) ..		.08	.04	.01
☐ 1	Mark McGwire DK ...	.65	.15	.03
☐ 2	Tim Raines DK	.15	.07	.01
☐ 3	Benito Santiago DK ..	.15	.07	.01
☐ 4	Alan Trammell DK ...	.12	.06	.01
☐ 5	Danny Tartabull DK ..	.10	.05	.01
☐ 6	Ron Darling DK	.10	.05	.01

			MINT	EXC	G-VG				MINT	EXC	G-VG
☐	7	Paul Molitor DK	.12	.06	.01	☐	56	Floyd Youmans	.03	.01	.00
☐	8	Devon White DK	.12	.06	.01	☐	57	Ed Correa	.03	.01	.00
☐	9	Andre Dawson DK	.15	.07	.01	☐	58	DeWayne Buice	.08	.04	.01
☐	10	Julio Franco DK	.10	.05	.01	☐	59	Jose DeLeon	.03	.01	.00
☐	11	Scott Fletcher DK	.06	.03	.00	☐	60	Danny Cox	.03	.01	.00
☐	12	Tony Fernandez DK	.10	.05	.01	☐	61	Nolan Ryan	.40	.20	.04
☐	13	Shane Rawley DK	.06	.03	.00	☐	62	Steve Bedrosian	.08	.04	.01
☐	14	Kal Daniels DK	.10	.05	.01	☐	63	Tom Browning	.08	.04	.01
☐	15	Jack Clark DK	.12	.06	.01	☐	64	Mark Davis	.12	.06	.01
☐	16	Dwight Evans DK	.12	.06	.01	☐	65	R.J. Reynolds	.03	.01	.00
☐	17	Tommy John DK	.12	.06	.01	☐	66	Kevin Mitchell	.45	.22	.04
☐	18	Andy Van Slyke DK	.12	.06	.01	☐	67	Ken Oberkfell	.03	.01	.00
☐	19	Gary Gaetti DK	.10	.05	.01	☐	68	Rick Sutcliffe	.08	.04	.01
☐	20	Mark Langston DK	.15	.07	.01	☐	69	Dwight Gooden	.45	.22	.04
☐	21	Will Clark DK	.60	.30	.06	☐	70	Scott Bankhead	.12	.06	.01
☐	22	Glenn Hubbard DK	.06	.03	.00	☐	71	Bert Blyleven	.10	.05	.01
☐	23	Billy Hatcher DK	.06	.03	.00	☐	72	Jimmy Key	.06	.03	.00
☐	24	Bob Welch DK	.08	.04	.01	☐	73	Les Straker	.08	.04	.01
☐	25	Ivan Calderon DK	.08	.04	.01	☐	74	Jim Clancy	.03	.01	.00
☐	26	Cal Ripken Jr. DK	.20	.10	.02	☐	75	Mike Moore	.06	.03	.00
☐	27	DK Checklist 1-26	.06	.01	.00	☐	76	Ron Darling	.08	.04	.01
☐	28	Mackey Sasser RR	.20	.10	.02	☐	77	Ed Lynch	.03	.01	.00
☐	29	Jeff Treadway RR	.30	.15	.03	☐	78	Dale Murphy	.25	.12	.02
☐	30	Mike Campbell RR	.18	.09	.01	☐	79	Doug Drabek	.06	.03	.00
☐	31	Lance Johnson RR	.18	.09	.01	☐	80	Scott Garrelts	.06	.03	.00
☐	32	Nelson Liriano RR	.20	.10	.02	☐	81	Ed Whitson	.03	.01	.00
☐	33	Shawn Abner RR	.18	.09	.01	☐	82	Rob Murphy	.03	.01	.00
☐	34	Roberto Alomar RR	1.00	.40	.07	☐	83	Shane Rawley	.03	.01	.00
☐	35	Shawn Hillegas RR	.18	.09	.01	☐	84	Greg Mathews	.03	.01	.00
☐	36	Joey Meyer RR	.12	.06	.01	☐	85	Jim Deshaies	.06	.03	.00
☐	37	Kevin Elster RR	.15	.07	.01	☐	86	Mike Witt	.06	.03	.00
☐	38	Jose Lind RR	.20	.10	.02	☐	87	Donnie Hill	.03	.01	.00
☐	39	Kirt Manwaring RR	.20	.10	.02	☐	88	Jeff Reed	.03	.01	.00
☐	40	Mark Grace RR	4.00	2.00	.40	☐	89	Mike Boddicker	.03	.01	.00
☐	41	Jody Reed RR	.35	.17	.03	☐	90	Ted Higuera	.08	.04	.01
☐	42	John Farrell RR	.25	.12	.02	☐	91	Walt Terrell	.03	.01	.00
☐	43	Al Leiter RR	.50	.25	.05	☐	92	Bob Stanley	.03	.01	.00
☐	44	Gary Thurman RR	.20	.10	.02	☐	93	Dave Righetti	.08	.04	.01
☐	45	Vicente Palacios RR	.12	.06	.01	☐	94	Orel Hershiser	.20	.10	.02
☐	46	Eddie Williams RR	.15	.07	.01	☐	95	Chris Bando	.03	.01	.00
☐	47	Jack McDowell RR	.15	.07	.01	☐	96	Bret Saberhagen	.20	.10	.02
☐	48	Ken Dixon	.03	.01	.00	☐	97	Curt Young	.03	.01	.00
☐	49	Mike Birkbeck	.03	.01	.00	☐	98	Tim Burke	.06	.03	.00
☐	50	Eric King	.03	.01	.00	☐	99	Charlie Hough	.03	.01	.00
☐	51	Roger Clemens	.50	.25	.05	☐	100A	Checklist 28-137	.06	.01	.00
☐	52	Pat Clements	.03	.01	.00	☐	100B	Checklist 28-133	.06	.01	.00
☐	53	Fernando Valenzuela	.12	.06	.01	☐	101	Bobby Witt	.06	.03	.00
☐	54	Mark Gubicza	.10	.05	.01	☐	102	George Brett	.25	.12	.02
☐	55	Jay Howell	.03	.01	.00	☐	103	Mickey Tettleton	.06	.03	.00

		MINT	EXC	G-VG			MINT	EXC	G-VG
☐ 104	Scott Bailes	.03	.01	.00	☐ 153	Wade Boggs	.80	.40	.08
☐ 105	Mike Pagliarulo	.06	.03	.00	☐ 154	Wayne Tolleson	.03	.01	.00
☐ 106	Mike Scioscia	.03	.01	.00	☐ 155	Mariano Duncan	.03	.01	.00
☐ 107	Tom Brookens	.03	.01	.00	☐ 156	Julio Franco	.10	.05	.01
☐ 108	Ray Knight	.06	.03	.00	☐ 157	Charlie Leibrandt	.03	.01	.00
☐ 109	Dan Plesac	.06	.03	.00	☐ 158	Terry Steinbach	.12	.06	.01
☐ 110	Wally Joyner	.40	.20	.04	☐ 159	Mike Fitzgerald	.03	.01	.00
☐ 111	Bob Forsch	.03	.01	.00	☐ 160	Jack Lazorko	.03	.01	.00
☐ 112	Mike Scott	.15	.07	.01	☐ 161	Mitch Williams	.03	.01	.00
☐ 113	Kevin Gross	.03	.01	.00	☐ 162	Greg Walker	.06	.03	.00
☐ 114	Benito Santiago	.30	.15	.03	☐ 163	Alan Ashby	.03	.01	.00
☐ 115	Bob Kipper	.03	.01	.00	☐ 164	Tony Gwynn	.35	.17	.03
☐ 116	Mike Krukow	.03	.01	.00	☐ 165	Bruce Ruffin	.03	.01	.00
☐ 117	Chris Bosio	.06	.03	.00	☐ 166	Ron Robinson	.03	.01	.00
☐ 118	Sid Fernandez	.08	.04	.01	☐ 167	Zane Smith	.03	.01	.00
☐ 119	Jody Davis	.03	.01	.00	☐ 168	Junior Ortiz	.03	.01	.00
☐ 120	Mike Morgan	.06	.03	.00	☐ 169	Jamie Moyer	.03	.01	.00
☐ 121	Mark Eichhorn	.03	.01	.00	☐ 170	Tony Pena	.08	.04	.01
☐ 122	Jeff Reardon	.08	.04	.01	☐ 171	Cal Ripken	.20	.10	.02
☐ 123	John Franco	.08	.04	.01	☐ 172	B.J. Surhoff	.10	.05	.01
☐ 124	Richard Dotson	.03	.01	.00	☐ 173	Lou Whitaker	.10	.05	.01
☐ 125	Eric Bell	.03	.01	.00	☐ 174	Ellis Burks	1.50	.75	.15
☐ 126	Juan Nieves	.03	.01	.00	☐ 175	Ron Guidry	.10	.05	.01
☐ 127	Jack Morris	.10	.05	.01	☐ 176	Steve Sax	.12	.06	.01
☐ 128	Rick Rhoden	.03	.01	.00	☐ 177	Danny Tartabull	.20	.10	.02
☐ 129	Rich Gedman	.03	.01	.00	☐ 178	Carney Lansford	.08	.04	.01
☐ 130	Ken Howell	.03	.01	.00	☐ 179	Casey Candaele	.03	.01	.00
☐ 131	Brook Jacoby	.06	.03	.00	☐ 180	Scott Fletcher	.03	.01	.00
☐ 132	Danny Jackson	.08	.04	.01	☐ 181	Mark McLemore	.03	.01	.00
☐ 133	Gene Nelson	.03	.01	.00	☐ 182	Ivan Calderon	.06	.03	.00
☐ 134	Neal Heaton	.03	.01	.00	☐ 183	Jack Clark	.12	.06	.01
☐ 135	Willie Fraser	.03	.01	.00	☐ 184	Glenn Davis	.15	.07	.01
☐ 136	Jose Guzman	.03	.01	.00	☐ 185	Luis Aguayo	.03	.01	.00
☐ 137	Ozzie Guillen	.06	.03	.00	☐ 186	Bo Diaz	.03	.01	.00
☐ 138	Bob Knepper	.03	.01	.00	☐ 187	Stan Jefferson	.03	.01	.00
☐ 139	Mike Jackson	.12	.06	.01	☐ 188	Sid Bream	.03	.01	.00
☐ 140	Joe Magrane	.50	.25	.05	☐ 189	Bob Brenly	.03	.01	.00
☐ 141	Jimmy Jones	.06	.03	.00	☐ 190	Dion James	.03	.01	.00
☐ 142	Ted Power	.03	.01	.00	☐ 191	Leon Durham	.03	.01	.00
☐ 143	Ozzie Virgil	.03	.01	.00	☐ 192	Jesse Orosco	.03	.01	.00
☐ 144	Felix Fermin	.08	.04	.01	☐ 193	Alvin Davis	.10	.05	.01
☐ 145	Kelly Downs	.06	.03	.00	☐ 194	Gary Gaetti	.10	.05	.01
☐ 146	Shawon Dunston	.08	.04	.01	☐ 195	Fred McGriff	.45	.22	.04
☐ 147	Scott Bradley	.03	.01	.00	☐ 196	Steve Lombardozzi	.03	.01	.00
☐ 148	Dave Stieb	.08	.04	.01	☐ 197	Rance Mulliniks	.03	.01	.00
☐ 149	Frank Viola	.12	.06	.01	☐ 198	Rey Quinones	.03	.01	.00
☐ 150	Terry Kennedy	.03	.01	.00	☐ 199	Gary Carter	.15	.07	.01
☐ 151	Bill Wegman	.03	.01	.00	☐ 200A	Checklist 138-247	.06	.01	.00
☐ 152	Matt Nokes	.40	.20	.04	☐ 200B	Checklist 134-239	.06	.01	.00

		MINT	EXC	G-VG
☐ 201	Keith Moreland	.03	.01	.00
☐ 202	Ken Griffey	.08	.04	.01
☐ 203	Tommy Gregg	.18	.09	.01
☐ 204	Will Clark	1.50	.75	.15
☐ 205	John Kruk	.08	.04	.01
☐ 206	Buddy Bell	.06	.03	.00
☐ 207	Von Hayes	.08	.04	.01
☐ 208	Tommy Herr	.03	.01	.00
☐ 209	Craig Reynolds	.03	.01	.00
☐ 210	Gary Pettis	.03	.01	.00
☐ 211	Harold Baines	.08	.04	.01
☐ 212	Vance Law	.03	.01	.00
☐ 213	Ken Gerhart	.03	.01	.00
☐ 214	Jim Gantner	.03	.01	.00
☐ 215	Chet Lemon	.03	.01	.00
☐ 216	Dwight Evans	.10	.05	.01
☐ 217	Don Mattingly	1.25	.60	.12
☐ 218	Franklin Stubbs	.03	.01	.00
☐ 219	Pat Tabler	.06	.03	.00
☐ 220	Bo Jackson	1.00	.50	.10
☐ 221	Tony Phillips	.03	.01	.00
☐ 222	Tim Wallach	.06	.03	.00
☐ 223	Ruben Sierra	.50	.25	.05
☐ 224	Steve Buechele	.03	.01	.00
☐ 225	Frank White	.06	.03	.00
☐ 226	Alfredo Griffin	.06	.03	.00
☐ 227	Greg Swindell	.12	.06	.01
☐ 228	Willie Randolph	.06	.03	.00
☐ 229	Mike Marshall	.10	.05	.01
☐ 230	Alan Trammell	.15	.07	.01
☐ 231	Eddie Murray	.15	.07	.01
☐ 232	Dale Sveum	.03	.01	.00
☐ 233	Dick Schofield	.03	.01	.00
☐ 234	Jose Oquendo	.03	.01	.00
☐ 235	Bill Doran	.06	.03	.00
☐ 236	Milt Thompson	.03	.01	.00
☐ 237	Marvell Wynne	.03	.01	.00
☐ 238	Bobby Bonilla	.15	.07	.01
☐ 239	Chris Speier	.03	.01	.00
☐ 240	Glenn Braggs	.06	.03	.00
☐ 241	Wally Backman	.03	.01	.00
☐ 242	Ryne Sandberg	.20	.10	.02
☐ 243	Phil Bradley	.06	.03	.00
☐ 244	Kelly Gruber	.06	.03	.00
☐ 245	Tom Brunansky	.10	.05	.01
☐ 246	Ron Oester	.03	.01	.00
☐ 247	Bobby Thigpen	.08	.04	.01
☐ 248	Fred Lynn	.10	.05	.01
☐ 249	Paul Molitor	.12	.06	.01
☐ 250	Darrell Evans	.08	.04	.01
☐ 251	Gary Ward	.03	.01	.00
☐ 252	Bruce Hurst	.10	.05	.01
☐ 253	Bob Welch	.06	.03	.00
☐ 254	Joe Carter	.15	.07	.01
☐ 255	Willie Wilson	.06	.03	.00
☐ 256	Mark McGwire	1.25	.60	.12
☐ 257	Mitch Webster	.03	.01	.00
☐ 258	Brian Downing	.03	.01	.00
☐ 259	Mike Stanley	.06	.03	.00
☐ 260	Carlton Fisk	.12	.06	.01
☐ 261	Billy Hatcher	.06	.03	.00
☐ 262	Glenn Wilson	.03	.01	.00
☐ 263	Ozzie Smith	.15	.07	.01
☐ 264	Randy Ready	.03	.01	.00
☐ 265	Kurt Stillwell	.03	.01	.00
☐ 266	David Palmer	.03	.01	.00
☐ 267	Mike Diaz	.03	.01	.00
☐ 268	Rob Thompson	.03	.01	.00
☐ 269	Andre Dawson	.15	.07	.01
☐ 270	Lee Guetterman	.03	.01	.00
☐ 271	Willie Upshaw	.03	.01	.00
☐ 272	Randy Bush	.03	.01	.00
☐ 273	Larry Sheets	.06	.03	.00
☐ 274	Rob Deer	.08	.04	.01
☐ 275	Kirk Gibson	.18	.09	.01
☐ 276	Marty Barrett	.06	.03	.00
☐ 277	Rickey Henderson	.25	.12	.02
☐ 278	Pedro Guerrero	.15	.07	.01
☐ 279	Brett Butler	.06	.03	.00
☐ 280	Kevin Seitzer	.75	.35	.07
☐ 281	Mike Davis	.03	.01	.00
☐ 282	Andres Galarraga	.25	.12	.02
☐ 283	Devon White	.18	.09	.01
☐ 284	Pete O'Brien	.06	.03	.00
☐ 285	Jerry Hairston	.03	.01	.00
☐ 286	Kevin Bass	.06	.03	.00
☐ 287	Carmelo Martinez	.03	.01	.00
☐ 288	Juan Samuel	.08	.04	.01
☐ 289	Kal Daniels	.15	.07	.01
☐ 290	Albert Hall	.03	.01	.00
☐ 291	Andy Van Slyke	.12	.06	.01
☐ 292	Lee Smith	.06	.03	.00
☐ 293	Vince Coleman	.15	.07	.01
☐ 294	Tom Niedenfuer	.03	.01	.00
☐ 295	Robin Yount	.20	.10	.02
☐ 296	Jeff Robinson	.30	.15	.03
	(Tigers pitcher)			
☐ 297	Todd Benzinger	.30	.15	.03

		MINT	EXC	G-VG			MINT	EXC	G-VG
☐ 298	Dave Winfield	.20	.10	.02	☐ 346	Bob Brower	.03	.01	.00
☐ 299	Mickey Hatcher	.03	.01	.00	☐ 347	Larry Parrish	.03	.01	.00
☐ 300A	Checklist 248-357	.06	.01	.00	☐ 348	Thad Bosley	.03	.01	.00
☐ 300B	Checklist 240-345	.06	.01	.00	☐ 349	Dennis Eckersley	.10	.05	.01
☐ 301	Bud Black	.03	.01	.00	☐ 350	Cory Snyder	.12	.06	.01
☐ 302	Jose Canseco	1.25	.60	.12	☐ 351	Rick Cerone	.03	.01	.00
☐ 303	Tom Foley	.03	.01	.00	☐ 352	John Shelby	.03	.01	.00
☐ 304	Pete Incaviglia	.15	.07	.01	☐ 353	Larry Herndon	.03	.01	.00
☐ 305	Bob Boone	.08	.04	.01	☐ 354	John Habyan	.03	.01	.00
☐ 306	Bill Long	.08	.04	.01	☐ 355	Chuck Crim	.06	.03	.00
☐ 307	Willie McGee	.10	.05	.01	☐ 356	Gus Polidor	.03	.01	.00
☐ 308	Ken Caminiti	.18	.09	.01	☐ 357	Ken Dayley	.03	.01	.00
☐ 309	Darren Daulton	.03	.01	.00	☐ 358	Danny Darwin	.03	.01	.00
☐ 310	Tracy Jones	.08	.04	.01	☐ 359	Lance Parrish	.10	.05	.01
☐ 311	Greg Booker	.03	.01	.00	☐ 360	James Steels	.08	.04	.01
☐ 312	Mike LaValliere	.03	.01	.00	☐ 361	Al Pedrique	.08	.04	.01
☐ 313	Chili Davis	.06	.03	.00	☐ 362	Mike Aldrete	.03	.01	.00
☐ 314	Glenn Hubbard	.03	.01	.00	☐ 363	Juan Castillo	.03	.01	.00
☐ 315	Paul Noce	.08	.04	.01	☐ 364	Len Dykstra	.06	.03	.00
☐ 316	Keith Hernandez	.15	.07	.01	☐ 365	Luis Quinones	.06	.03	.00
☐ 317	Mark Langston	.12	.06	.01	☐ 366	Jim Presley	.06	.03	.00
☐ 318	Keith Atherton	.03	.01	.00	☐ 367	Lloyd Moseby	.06	.03	.00
☐ 319	Tony Fernandez	.10	.05	.01	☐ 368	Kirby Puckett	.50	.25	.05
☐ 320	Kent Hrbek	.12	.06	.01	☐ 369	Eric Davis	.50	.25	.05
☐ 321	John Cerutti	.03	.01	.00	☐ 370	Gary Redus	.03	.01	.00
☐ 322	Mike Kingery	.03	.01	.00	☐ 371	Dave Schmidt	.03	.01	.00
☐ 323	Dave Magadan	.10	.05	.01	☐ 372	Mark Clear	.03	.01	.00
☐ 324	Rafael Palmeiro	.25	.12	.02	☐ 373	Dave Bergman	.03	.01	.00
☐ 325	Jeff Dedmon	.03	.01	.00	☐ 374	Charles Hudson	.03	.01	.00
☐ 326	Barry Bonds	.20	.10	.02	☐ 375	Calvin Schiraldi	.03	.01	.00
☐ 327	Jeffrey Leonard	.06	.03	.00	☐ 376	Alex Trevino	.03	.01	.00
☐ 328	Tim Flannery	.03	.01	.00	☐ 377	Tom Candiotti	.03	.01	.00
☐ 329	Dave Concepcion	.06	.03	.00	☐ 378	Steve Farr	.03	.01	.00
☐ 330	Mike Schmidt	.35	.17	.03	☐ 379	Mike Gallego	.03	.01	.00
☐ 331	Bill Dawley	.03	.01	.00	☐ 380	Andy McGaffigan	.03	.01	.00
☐ 332	Larry Andersen	.03	.01	.00	☐ 381	Kirk McCaskill	.03	.01	.00
☐ 333	Jack Howell	.03	.01	.00	☐ 382	Oddibe McDowell	.06	.03	.00
☐ 334	Ken Williams	.15	.07	.01	☐ 383	Floyd Bannister	.03	.01	.00
☐ 335	Bryn Smith	.06	.03	.00	☐ 384	Denny Walling	.03	.01	.00
☐ 336	Billy Ripken	.15	.07	.01	☐ 385	Don Carman	.03	.01	.00
☐ 337	Greg Brock	.03	.01	.00	☐ 386	Todd Worrell	.08	.04	.01
☐ 338	Mike Heath	.03	.01	.00	☐ 387	Eric Show	.03	.01	.00
☐ 339	Mike Greenwell	1.25	.60	.12	☐ 388	Dave Parker	.10	.05	.01
☐ 340	Claudell Washington	.06	.03	.00	☐ 389	Rick Mahler	.03	.01	.00
☐ 341	Jose Gonzalez	.03	.01	.00	☐ 390	Mike Dunne	.08	.04	.01
☐ 342	Mel Hall	.06	.03	.00	☐ 391	Candy Maldonado	.06	.03	.00
☐ 343	Jim Eisenreich	.06	.03	.00	☐ 392	Bob Dernier	.03	.01	.00
☐ 344	Tony Bernazard	.03	.01	.00	☐ 393	Dave Valle	.03	.01	.00
☐ 345	Tim Raines	.18	.09	.01	☐ 394	Ernie Whitt	.03	.01	.00

			MINT	EXC	G-VG
☐ 395	Juan Berenguer	....	.03	.01	.00
☐ 396	Mike Young	....	.03	.01	.00
☐ 397	Mike Felder	....	.03	.01	.00
☐ 398	Willie Hernandez	....	.06	.03	.00
☐ 399	Jim Rice	....	.12	.06	.01
☐ 400A	Checklist 358-467	....	.06	.01	.00
☐ 400B	Checklist 346-451	....	.06	.01	.00
☐ 401	Tommy John	......	.10	.05	.01
☐ 402	Brian Holton	....	.03	.01	.00
☐ 403	Carmen Castillo	....	.03	.01	.00
☐ 404	Jamie Quirk	....	.03	.01	.00
☐ 405	Dwayne Murphy	....	.03	.01	.00
☐ 406	Jeff Parrett	....	.15	.07	.01
☐ 407	Don Sutton	....	.12	.06	.01
☐ 408	Jerry Browne	....	.06	.03	.00
☐ 409	Jim Winn	....	.03	.01	.00
☐ 410	Dave Smith	....	.03	.01	.00
☐ 411	Shane Mack	....	.10	.05	.01
☐ 412	Greg Gross	....	.03	.01	.00
☐ 413	Nick Esasky	....	.08	.04	.01
☐ 414	Damaso Garcia	....	.03	.01	.00
☐ 415	Brian Fisher	....	.03	.01	.00
☐ 416	Brian Dayett	....	.03	.01	.00
☐ 417	Curt Ford	....	.03	.01	.00
☐ 418	Mark Williamson	....	.08	.04	.01
☐ 419	Bill Schroeder	....	.03	.01	.00
☐ 420	Mike Henneman	....	.20	.10	.02
☐ 421	John Marzano	....	.08	.04	.01
☐ 422	Ron Kittle	....	.08	.04	.01
☐ 423	Matt Young	....	.03	.01	.00
☐ 424	Steve Balboni	....	.03	.01	.00
☐ 425	Luis Polonia	....	.15	.07	.01
☐ 426	Randy St.Claire	....	.03	.01	.00
☐ 427	Greg Harris	....	.03	.01	.00
☐ 428	Johnny Ray	....	.06	.03	.00
☐ 429	Ray Searage	....	.03	.01	.00
☐ 430	Ricky Horton	....	.03	.01	.00
☐ 431	Gerald Young	....	.30	.15	.03
☐ 432	Rick Schu	....	.03	.01	.00
☐ 433	Paul O'Neill	....	.08	.04	.01
☐ 434	Rich Gossage	....	.08	.04	.01
☐ 435	John Cangelosi	....	.03	.01	.00
☐ 436	Mike LaCoss	....	.03	.01	.00
☐ 437	Gerald Perry	....	.06	.03	.00
☐ 438	Dave Martinez	....	.06	.03	.00
☐ 439	Darryl Strawberry	....	.45	.22	.04
☐ 440	John Moses	....	.03	.01	.00
☐ 441	Greg Gagne	....	.03	.01	.00
☐ 442	Jesse Barfield	....	.10	.05	.01
☐ 443	George Frazier	......	.03	.01	.00
☐ 444	Garth Iorg	....	.03	.01	.00
☐ 445	Ed Nunez	....	.03	.01	.00
☐ 446	Rick Aguilera	....	.08	.04	.01
☐ 447	Jerry Mumphrey	....	.03	.01	.00
☐ 448	Rafael Ramirez	....	.03	.01	.00
☐ 449	John Smiley	....	.35	.17	.03
☐ 450	Atlee Hammaker	....	.03	.01	.00
☐ 451	Lance McCullers	....	.06	.03	.00
☐ 452	Guy Hoffman	....	.03	.01	.00
☐ 453	Chris James	....	.08	.04	.01
☐ 454	Terry Pendleton	....	.08	.04	.01
☐ 455	Dave Meads	....	.08	.04	.01
☐ 456	Bill Buckner	....	.08	.04	.01
☐ 457	John Pawlowski	....	.08	.04	.01
☐ 458	Bob Sebra	....	.03	.01	.00
☐ 459	Jim Dwyer	....	.03	.01	.00
☐ 460	Jay Aldrich	....	.08	.04	.01
☐ 461	Frank Tanana	....	.03	.01	.00
☐ 462	Oil Can Boyd	....	.03	.01	.00
☐ 463	Dan Pasqua	....	.03	.01	.00
☐ 464	Tim Crews	....	.08	.04	.01
☐ 465	Andy Allanson	....	.03	.01	.00
☐ 466	Bill Pecota	....	.08	.04	.01
☐ 467	Steve Ontiveros	....	.03	.01	.00
☐ 468	Hubie Brooks	....	.08	.04	.01
☐ 469	Paul Kilgus	....	.12	.06	.01
☐ 470	Dale Mohorcic	....	.03	.01	.00
☐ 471	Dan Quisenberry	....	.08	.04	.01
☐ 472	Dave Stewart	....	.12	.06	.01
☐ 473	Dave Clark	....	.06	.03	.00
☐ 474	Joel Skinner	....	.03	.01	.00
☐ 475	Dave Anderson	....	.03	.01	.00
☐ 476	Dan Petry	....	.03	.01	.00
☐ 477	Carl Nichols	....	.08	.04	.01
☐ 478	Ernest Riles	....	.03	.01	.00
☐ 479	George Hendrick	....	.03	.01	.00
☐ 480	John Morris	....	.03	.01	.00
☐ 481	Manny Hernandez	....	.08	.04	.01
☐ 482	Jeff Stone	....	.03	.01	.00
☐ 483	Chris Brown	....	.03	.01	.00
☐ 484	Mike Bielecki	....	.08	.04	.01
☐ 485	Dave Dravecky	....	.08	.04	.01
☐ 486	Rick Manning	....	.03	.01	.00
☐ 487	Bill Almon	....	.03	.01	.00
☐ 488	Jim Sundberg	....	.03	.01	.00
☐ 489	Ken Phelps	....	.06	.03	.00
☐ 490	Tom Henke	....	.06	.03	.00
☐ 491	Dan Gladden	....	.06	.03	.00

		MINT	EXC	G-VG			MINT	EXC	G-VG
☐ 492	Barry Larkin	.25	.12	.02	☐ 539	Greg Maddux	.18	.09	.01
☐ 493	Fred Manrique	.10	.05	.01	☐ 540	Jim Lindeman	.03	.01	.00
☐ 494	Mike Griffin	.03	.01	.00	☐ 541	Pete Stanicek	.15	.07	.01
☐ 495	Mark Knudson	.10	.05	.01	☐ 542	Steve Kiefer	.03	.01	.00
☐ 496	Bill Madlock	.06	.03	.00	☐ 543A	Jim Morrison ERR	.25	.12	.02
☐ 497	Tim Stoddard	.03	.01	.00		(no decimal before			
☐ 498	Sam Horn	.15	.07	.01		lifetime average)			
☐ 499	Tracy Woodson	.18	.09	.01	☐ 543B	Jim Morrison COR	.06	.03	.00
☐ 500A	Checklist 468-577	.06	.01	.00	☐ 544	Spike Owen	.03	.01	.00
☐ 500B	Checklist 452-557	.06	.01	.00	☐ 545	Jay Buhner	.45	.22	.04
☐ 501	Ken Schrom	.03	.01	.00	☐ 546	Mike Devereaux	.25	.12	.02
☐ 502	Angel Salazar	.03	.01	.00	☐ 547	Jerry Don Gleaton	.03	.01	.00
☐ 503	Eric Plunk	.03	.01	.00	☐ 548	Jose Rijo	.03	.01	.00
☐ 504	Joe Hesketh	.03	.01	.00	☐ 549	Dennis Martinez	.03	.01	.00
☐ 505	Greg Minton	.03	.01	.00	☐ 550	Mike Loynd	.03	.01	.00
☐ 506	Geno Petralli	.03	.01	.00	☐ 551	Darrell Miller	.03	.01	.00
☐ 507	Bob James	.03	.01	.00	☐ 552	Dave LaPoint	.03	.01	.00
☐ 508	Robbie Wine	.08	.04	.01	☐ 553	John Tudor	.08	.04	.01
☐ 509	Jeff Calhoun	.03	.01	.00	☐ 554	Rocky Childress	.08	.04	.01
☐ 510	Steve Lake	.03	.01	.00	☐ 555	Wally Ritchie	.08	.04	.01
☐ 511	Mark Grant	.03	.01	.00	☐ 556	Terry McGriff	.06	.03	.00
☐ 512	Frank Williams	.03	.01	.00	☐ 557	Dave Leiper	.03	.01	.00
☐ 513	Jeff Blauser	.25	.12	.02	☐ 558	Jeff Robinson	.08	.04	.01
☐ 514	Bob Walk	.03	.01	.00		(Pirates pitcher)			
☐ 515	Craig Lefferts	.06	.03	.00	☐ 559	Jose Uribe	.03	.01	.00
☐ 516	Manny Trillo	.03	.01	.00	☐ 560	Ted Simmons	.08	.04	.01
☐ 517	Jerry Reed	.03	.01	.00	☐ 561	Les Lancaster	.15	.07	.01
☐ 518	Rick Leach	.03	.01	.00	☐ 562	Keith Miller	.20	.10	.02
☐ 519	Mark Davidson	.12	.06	.01		(New York Mets)			
☐ 520	Jeff Ballard	.35	.17	.03	☐ 563	Harold Reynolds	.06	.03	.00
☐ 521	Dave Stapleton	.06	.03	.00	☐ 564	Gene Larkin	.25	.12	.02
☐ 522	Pat Sheridan	.03	.01	.00	☐ 565	Cecil Fielder	.03	.01	.00
☐ 523	Al Nipper	.03	.01	.00	☐ 566	Roy Smalley	.03	.01	.00
☐ 524	Steve Trout	.03	.01	.00	☐ 567	Duane Ward	.03	.01	.00
☐ 525	Jeff Hamilton	.06	.03	.00	☐ 568	Bill Wilkinson	.10	.05	.01
☐ 526	Tommy Hinzo	.08	.04	.01	☐ 569	Howard Johnson	.15	.07	.01
☐ 527	Lonnie Smith	.06	.03	.00	☐ 570	Frank DiPino	.03	.01	.00
☐ 528	Greg Cadaret	.20	.10	.02	☐ 571	Pete Smith	.15	.07	.01
☐ 529	Bob McClure	.03	.01	.00	☐ 572	Darnell Coles	.03	.01	.00
	("Rob" on front)				☐ 573	Don Robinson	.03	.01	.00
☐ 530	Chuck Finley	.06	.03	.00	☐ 574	Rob Nelson	.03	.01	.00
☐ 531	Jeff Russell	.06	.03	.00	☐ 575	Dennis Rasmussen	.06	.03	.00
☐ 532	Steve Lyons	.03	.01	.00	☐ 576	Steve Jeltz	.03	.01	.00
☐ 533	Terry Puhl	.03	.01	.00	☐ 577	Tom Pagnozzi	.10	.05	.01
☐ 534	Eric Nolte	.12	.06	.01	☐ 578	Ty Gainey	.03	.01	.00
☐ 535	Kent Tekulve	.03	.01	.00	☐ 579	Gary Lucas	.03	.01	.00
☐ 536	Pat Pacillo	.08	.04	.01	☐ 580	Ron Hassey	.03	.01	.00
☐ 537	Charlie Puleo	.03	.01	.00	☐ 581	Herm Winningham	.03	.01	.00
☐ 538	Tom Prince	.10	.05	.01	☐ 582	Rene Gonzales	.10	.05	.01

		MINT	EXC	G-VG
☐ 583	Brad Komminsk	.03	.01	.00
☐ 584	Doyle Alexander	.03	.01	.00
☐ 585	Jeff Sellers	.03	.01	.00
☐ 586	Bill Gullickson	.03	.01	.00
☐ 587	Tim Belcher	.40	.20	.04
☐ 588	Doug Jones	.30	.15	.03
☐ 589	Melido Perez	.25	.12	.02
☐ 590	Rick Honeycutt	.03	.01	.00
☐ 591	Pascual Perez	.08	.04	.01
☐ 592	Curt Wilkerson	.03	.01	.00
☐ 593	Steve Howe	.03	.01	.00
☐ 594	John Davis	.12	.06	.01
☐ 595	Storm Davis	.08	.04	.01
☐ 596	Sammy Stewart	.03	.01	.00
☐ 597	Neil Allen	.03	.01	.00
☐ 598	Alejandro Pena	.06	.03	.00
☐ 599	Mark Thurmond	.03	.01	.00
☐ 600A	Checklist 578-BC26	.06	.01	.00
☐ 600B	Checklist 558-660	.06	.01	.00
☐ 601	Jose Mesa	.12	.06	.01
☐ 602	Don August	.12	.06	.01
☐ 603	Terry Leach SP	.10	.05	.01
☐ 604	Tom Newell	.12	.06	.01
☐ 605	Randall Byers SP	.20	.10	.02
☐ 606	Jim Gott	.03	.01	.00
☐ 607	Harry Spilman	.03	.01	.00
☐ 608	John Candelaria	.06	.03	.00
☐ 609	Mike Brumley	.15	.07	.01
☐ 610	Mickey Brantley	.06	.03	.00
☐ 611	Jose Nunez SP	.20	.10	.02
☐ 612	Tom Nieto	.03	.01	.00
☐ 613	Rick Reuschel	.06	.03	.00
☐ 614	Lee Mazzilli SP	.08	.04	.01
☐ 615	Scott Lusader	.12	.06	.01
☐ 616	Bobby Meacham	.03	.01	.00
☐ 617	Kevin McReynolds SP	.15	.07	.01
☐ 618	Gene Garber	.03	.01	.00
☐ 619	Barry Lyons SP	.25	.12	.02
☐ 620	Randy Myers	.10	.05	.01
☐ 621	Donnie Moore	.03	.01	.00
☐ 622	Domingo Ramos	.03	.01	.00
☐ 623	Ed Romero	.03	.01	.00
☐ 624	Greg Myers	.12	.06	.01
☐ 625	Ripken Family	.08	.04	.01
☐ 626	Pat Perry	.03	.01	.00
☐ 627	Andres Thomas SP	.10	.05	.01
☐ 628	Matt Williams SP	1.25	.60	.12
☐ 629	Dave Hengel	.12	.06	.01

		MINT	EXC	G-VG
☐ 630	Jeff Musselman SP	.08	.04	.01
☐ 631	Tim Laudner	.03	.01	.00
☐ 632	Bob Ojeda SP	.10	.05	.01
☐ 633	Rafael Santana	.03	.01	.00
☐ 634	Wes Gardner	.20	.10	.02
☐ 635	Roberto Kelly SP	1.00	.50	.10
☐ 636	Mike Flanagan SP	.08	.04	.01
☐ 637	Jay Bell	.20	.10	.02
☐ 638	Bob Melvin	.03	.01	.00
☐ 639	Damon Berryhill	.45	.22	.04
☐ 640	David Wells SP	.25	.12	.02
☐ 641	Puzzle Card (Stan Musial)	.03	.01	.00
☐ 642	Doug Sisk	.03	.01	.00
☐ 643	Keith Hughes	.18	.09	.01
☐ 644	Tom Glavine	.35	.17	.03
☐ 645	Al Newman	.03	.01	.00
☐ 646	Scott Sanderson	.03	.01	.00
☐ 647	Scott Terry	.12	.06	.01
☐ 648	Tim Teufel SP	.08	.04	.01
☐ 649	Garry Templeton SP	.10	.05	.01
☐ 650	Manny Lee SP	.08	.04	.01
☐ 651	Roger McDowell SP	.10	.05	.01
☐ 652	Mookie Wilson SP	.10	.05	.01
☐ 653	David Cone SP	.60	.30	.06
☐ 654	Ron Gant SP	.60	.30	.06
☐ 655	Joe Price SP	.08	.04	.01
☐ 656	George Bell SP	.20	.10	.02
☐ 657	Gregg Jefferies SP	4.00	2.00	.40
☐ 658	Todd Stottlemyre SP	.35	.17	.03
☐ 659	Geronimo Berroa SP	.35	.17	.03
☐ 660	Jerry Royster SP	.08	.04	.01

1988 Donruss Bonus MVP's

Mike Schmidt 3B

		MINT	EXC	G-VG
☐ BC10	Andre Dawson	.15	.07	.01
☐ BC11	Alan Trammell	.10	.05	.01
☐ BC12	Mike Scott	.10	.05	.01
☐ BC13	Wally Joyner	.20	.10	.02
☐ BC14	Dale Murphy	.25	.12	.02
☐ BC15	Kirby Puckett	.45	.22	.04
☐ BC16	Pedro Guerrero	.10	.05	.01
☐ BC17	Kevin Seitzer	.30	.15	.03
☐ BC18	Tim Raines	.15	.07	.01
☐ BC19	George Bell	.15	.07	.01
☐ BC20	Darryl Strawberry	.45	.22	.04
☐ BC21	Don Mattingly	.75	.35	.07
☐ BC22	Ozzie Smith	.15	.07	.01
☐ BC23	Mark McGwire	.60	.30	.06
☐ BC24	Will Clark	.90	.45	.09
☐ BC25	Alvin Davis	.10	.05	.01
☐ BC26	Ruben Sierra	.35	.17	.03

This 26-card set was distributed along with the regular 1988 Donruss issue as random inserts with the rack and wax packs. These bonus cards are numbered with the prefix BC for bonus cards and were supposedly produced in the same quantities as the other 660 regular issue cards. The "most valuable" player was selected from each of the 26 teams. Cards measure 2 ½" by 3 ½" and feature the same distinctive black and blue border on the front as the regular issue. The cards are distinguished by the MVP logo in the upper left corner of the obverse. The last 13 cards numerically are considered to be somewhat tougher to find than the first 13 cards.

		MINT	EXC	G-VG
COMPLETE SET (26)		7.50	3.75	.75
COMMON CARD (BC1-BC13)		.05	.02	.00
COMMON CARD (BC14-BC26)		.10	.05	.01
☐ BC1	Cal Ripken	.25	.12	.02
☐ BC2	Eric Davis	.40	.20	.04
☐ BC3	Paul Molitor	.10	.05	.01
☐ BC4	Mike Schmidt	.40	.20	.04
☐ BC5	Ivan Calderon	.05	.02	.00
☐ BC6	Tony Gwynn	.30	.15	.03
☐ BC7	Wade Boggs	.50	.25	.05
☐ BC8	Andy Van Slyke	.10	.05	.01
☐ BC9	Joe Carter	.10	.05	.01

1988 Donruss Rookies

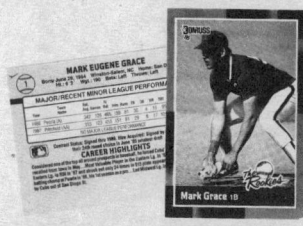

The 1988 Donruss "The Rookies" set features
56 cards plus a 15-piece puzzle of Stan Musial.
Cards are in full color and are standard size,
2 ½" by 3 ½". The set was distributed in a
small green and black box with gold lettering.
Card fronts are similar in design to the 1988
Donruss regular issue except for the presence
of "The Rookies" logo in the lower right corner
and a green and black border instead of a blue
and black border on the fronts.

	MINT	EXC	G-VG
COMPLETE SET (56)	13.00	6.50	1.30
COMMON PLAYER (1-56)	.06	.03	.00

			MINT	EXC	G-VG
☐	1	Mark Grace	4.00	1.00	.20
☐	2	Mike Campbell	.10	.05	.01
☐	3	Todd Frohwirth	.10	.05	.01
☐	4	Dave Stapleton	.06	.03	.00
☐	5	Shawn Abner	.10	.05	.01
☐	6	Jose Cecena	.10	.05	.01
☐	7	Dave Gallagher	.35	.17	.03
☐	8	Mark Parent	.15	.07	.01
☐	9	Cecil Espy	.15	.07	.01
☐	10	Pete Smith	.10	.05	.01
☐	11	Jay Buhner	.20	.10	.02
☐	12	Pat Borders	.25	.12	.02
☐	13	Doug Jennings	.25	.12	.02
☐	14	Brady Anderson	.35	.17	.03
☐	15	Pete Stanicek	.10	.05	.01

			MINT	EXC	G-VG
☐	16	Roberto Kelly	.40	.20	.04
☐	17	Jeff Treadway	.10	.05	.01
☐	18	Walt Weiss	1.25	.60	.12
☐	19	Paul Gibson	.10	.05	.01
☐	20	Tim Crews	.06	.03	.00
☐	21	Melido Perez	.15	.07	.01
☐	22	Steve Peters	.15	.07	.01
☐	23	Craig Worthington	.50	.25	.05
☐	24	John Trautwein	.15	.07	.01
☐	25	DeWayne Vaughn	.10	.05	.01
☐	26	David Wells	.10	.05	.01
☐	27	Al Leiter	.15	.07	.01
☐	28	Tim Belcher	.25	.12	.02
☐	29	Johnny Paredes	.15	.07	.01
☐	30	Chris Sabo	1.25	.60	.12
☐	31	Damon Berryhill	.25	.12	.02
☐	32	Randy Milligan	.20	.10	.02
☐	33	Gary Thurman	.15	.07	.01
☐	34	Kevin Elster	.20	.10	.02
☐	35	Roberto Alomar	.30	.15	.03
☐	36	Edgar Martinez UER (photo actually Edwin Nunez)	.25	.12	.02
☐	37	Todd Stottlemyre	.15	.07	.01
☐	38	Joey Meyer	.10	.05	.01
☐	39	Carl Nichols	.06	.03	.00
☐	40	Jack McDowell	.10	.05	.01
☐	41	Jose Bautista	.15	.07	.01
☐	42	Sil Campusano	.25	.12	.02
☐	43	John Dopson	.20	.10	.02
☐	44	Jody Reed	.15	.07	.01
☐	45	Darrin Jackson	.15	.07	.01
☐	46	Mike Capel	.12	.06	.01
☐	47	Ron Gant	.20	.10	.02
☐	48	John Davis	.06	.03	.00
☐	49	Kevin Coffman	.10	.05	.01
☐	50	Cris Carpenter	.25	.12	.02
☐	51	Mackey Sasser	.10	.05	.01
☐	52	Luis Alicea	.10	.05	.01
☐	53	Bryan Harvey	.25	.12	.02
☐	54	Steve Ellsworth	.15	.07	.01
☐	55	Mike Macfarlane	.20	.10	.02
☐	56	Checklist Card	.06	.01	.00

1988 Donruss Baseball's Best

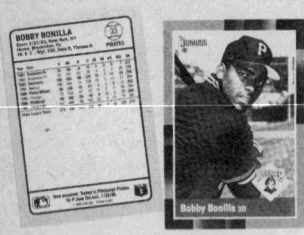

This innovative set of 336 cards was released by Donruss very late in the 1988 season to be sold in large national retail chains as a complete packaged set. Cards are the standard size, 2 ½" by 3 ½", and are packaged as a complete set in a specially designed box. Cards are very similar in design to the 1988 regular Donruss issue except that these cards have orange and black borders instead of blue and black borders. Six (2 ½" by 3 ½") 15-piece puzzles of Stan Musial are also included with every complete set.

	MINT	EXC	G-VG
COMPLETE SET (336)	20.00	10.00	2.00
COMMON PLAYER (1-336)	.04	.02	.00

			MINT	EXC	G-VG
☐	1	Don Mattingly	1.00	.50	.10
☐	2	Ron Gant	.35	.17	.03
☐	3	Bob Boone	.10	.05	.01
☐	4	Mark Grace	1.25	.60	.12
☐	5	Andy Allanson	.04	.02	.00
☐	6	Kal Daniels	.10	.05	.01
☐	7	Floyd Bannister	.04	.02	.00
☐	8	Alan Ashby	.04	.02	.00
☐	9	Marty Barrett	.07	.03	.01
☐	10	Tim Belcher	.15	.07	.01
☐	11	Harold Baines	.10	.05	.01
☐	12	Hubie Brooks	.07	.03	.01
☐	13	Doyle Alexander	.04	.02	.00
☐	14	Gary Carter	.20	.10	.02
☐	15	Glenn Braggs	.10	.05	.01
☐	16	Steve Bedrosian	.10	.05	.01
☐	17	Barry Bonds	.20	.10	.02
☐	18	Bert Blyleven	.10	.05	.01
☐	19	Tom Brunansky	.10	.05	.01
☐	20	John Candelaria	.04	.02	.00
☐	21	Shawn Abner	.10	.05	.01
☐	22	Jose Canseco	1.25	.60	.12
☐	23	Brett Butler	.07	.03	.01
☐	24	Scott Bradley	.04	.02	.00
☐	25	Ivan Calderon	.07	.03	.01
☐	26	Rich Gossage	.10	.05	.01
☐	27	Brian Downing	.04	.02	.00
☐	28	Jim Rice	.15	.07	.01
☐	29	Dion James	.04	.02	.00
☐	30	Terry Kennedy	.04	.02	.00
☐	31	George Bell	.15	.07	.01
☐	32	Scott Fletcher	.04	.02	.00
☐	33	Bobby Bonilla	.15	.07	.01
☐	34	Tim Burke	.04	.02	.00
☐	35	Darrell Evans	.07	.03	.01
☐	36	Mike Davis	.04	.02	.00
☐	37	Shawon Dunston	.10	.05	.01
☐	38	Kevin Bass	.07	.03	.01
☐	39	George Brett	.25	.12	.02
☐	40	David Cone	.30	.15	.03
☐	41	Ron Darling	.10	.05	.01
☐	42	Roberto Alomar	.35	.17	.03
☐	43	Dennis Eckersley	.15	.07	.01
☐	44	Vince Coleman	.20	.10	.02
☐	45	Sid Bream	.04	.02	.00
☐	46	Gary Gaetti	.15	.07	.01
☐	47	Phil Bradley	.07	.03	.01
☐	48	Jim Clancy	.04	.02	.00
☐	49	Jack Clark	.15	.07	.01
☐	50	Mike Krukow	.04	.02	.00
☐	51	Henry Cotto	.04	.02	.00
☐	52	Rich Dotson	.04	.02	.00
☐	53	Jim Gantner	.04	.02	.00
☐	54	John Franco	.07	.03	.01
☐	55	Pete Incaviglia	.15	.07	.01
☐	56	Joe Carter	.15	.07	.01
☐	57	Roger Clemens	.50	.25	.05
☐	58	Gerald Perry	.04	.02	.00
☐	59	Jack Howell	.04	.02	.00
☐	60	Vance Law	.04	.02	.00
☐	61	Jay Bell	.04	.02	.00
☐	62	Eric Davis	.50	.25	.05

		MINT	EXC	G-VG			MINT	EXC	G-VG
☐	63 Gene Garber	.04	.02	.00	☐	112 Tom Candiotti	.04	.02	.00
☐	64 Glenn Davis	.15	.07	.01	☐	113 Dale Murphy	.30	.15	.03
☐	65 Wade Boggs	.75	.35	.07	☐	114 Rick Mahler	.04	.02	.00
☐	66 Kirk Gibson	.20	.10	.02	☐	115 Wally Joyner	.40	.20	.04
☐	67 Carlton Fisk	.20	.10	.02	☐	116 Ryne Sandberg	.30	.15	.03
☐	68 Casey Candaele	.04	.02	.00	☐	117 John Farrell	.10	.05	.01
☐	69 Mike Heath	.04	.02	.00	☐	118 Nick Esasky	.10	.05	.01
☐	70 Kevin Elster	.10	.05	.01	☐	119 Bo Jackson	1.25	.60	.12
☐	71 Greg Brock	.04	.02	.00	☐	120 Bill Doran	.07	.03	.01
☐	72 Don Carman	.04	.02	.00	☐	121 Ellis Burks	.75	.35	.07
☐	73 Doug Drabek	.07	.03	.01	☐	122 Pedro Guerrero	.15	.07	.01
☐	74 Greg Gagne	.04	.02	.00	☐	123 Dave LaPoint	.07	.03	.01
☐	75 Danny Cox	.07	.03	.01	☐	124 Neal Heaton	.04	.02	.00
☐	76 Rickey Henderson	.35	.17	.03	☐	125 Willie Hernandez	.07	.03	.01
☐	77 Chris Brown	.04	.02	.00	☐	126 Roger McDowell	.07	.03	.01
☐	78 Terry Steinbach	.10	.05	.01	☐	127 Ted Higuera	.07	.03	.01
☐	79 Will Clark	1.25	.60	.12	☐	128 Von Hayes	.10	.05	.01
☐	80 Mickey Brantley	.07	.03	.01	☐	129 Mike LaValliere	.04	.02	.00
☐	81 Ozzie Guillen	.10	.05	.01	☐	130 Dan Gladden	.04	.02	.00
☐	82 Greg Maddux	.15	.07	.01	☐	131 Willie McGee	.10	.05	.01
☐	83 Kirk McCaskill	.04	.02	.00	☐	132 Al Leiter	.10	.05	.01
☐	84 Dwight Evans	.15	.07	.01	☐	133 Mark Grant	.04	.02	.00
☐	85 Ozzie Virgil	.04	.02	.00	☐	134 Bob Welch	.07	.03	.01
☐	86 Mike Morgan	.07	.03	.01	☐	135 Dave Dravecky	.10	.05	.01
☐	87 Tony Fernandez	.10	.05	.01	☐	136 Mark Langston	.20	.10	.02
☐	88 Jose Guzman	.04	.02	.00	☐	137 Dan Pasqua	.07	.03	.01
☐	89 Mike Dunne	.07	.03	.01	☐	138 Rick Sutcliffe	.10	.05	.01
☐	90 Andres Galarraga	.25	.12	.02	☐	139 Dan Petry	.04	.02	.00
☐	91 Mike Henneman	.07	.03	.01	☐	140 Rich Gedman	.07	.03	.01
☐	92 Alfredo Griffin	.04	.02	.00	☐	141 Ken Griffey Sr.	.10	.05	.01
☐	93 Rafael Palmeiro	.20	.10	.02	☐	142 Eddie Murray	.20	.10	.02
☐	94 Jim Deshaies	.04	.02	.00	☐	143 Jimmy Key	.07	.03	.01
☐	95 Mark Gubicza	.10	.05	.01	☐	144 Dale Mohorcic	.04	.02	.00
☐	96 Dwight Gooden	.50	.25	.05	☐	145 Jose Lind	.07	.03	.01
☐	97 Howard Johnson	.20	.10	.02	☐	146 Dennis Martinez	.07	.03	.01
☐	98 Mark Davis	.20	.10	.02	☐	147 Chet Lemon	.04	.02	.00
☐	99 Dave Stewart	.20	.10	.02	☐	148 Orel Hershiser	.35	.17	.03
☐	100 Joe Magrane	.15	.07	.01	☐	149 Dave Martinez	.04	.02	.00
☐	101 Brian Fisher	.04	.02	.00	☐	150 Billy Hatcher	.07	.03	.01
☐	102 Kent Hrbek	.15	.07	.01	☐	151 Charlie Leibrandt	.04	.02	.00
☐	103 Kevin Gross	.04	.02	.00	☐	152 Keith Hernandez	.15	.07	.01
☐	104 Tom Henke	.07	.03	.01	☐	153 Kevin McReynolds	.20	.10	.02
☐	105 Mike Pagliarulo	.07	.03	.01	☐	154 Tony Gwynn	.35	.17	.03
☐	106 Kelly Downs	.04	.02	.00	☐	155 Stan Javier	.04	.02	.00
☐	107 Alvin Davis	.10	.05	.01	☐	156 Tony Pena	.04	.02	.00
☐	108 Willie Randolph	.10	.05	.01	☐	157 Andy Van Slyke	.10	.05	.01
☐	109 Rob Deer	.10	.05	.01	☐	158 Gene Larkin	.07	.03	.01
☐	110 Bo Diaz	.04	.02	.00	☐	159 Chris James	.07	.03	.01
☐	111 Paul Kilgus	.04	.02	.00	☐	160 Fred McGriff	.35	.17	.03

			MINT	EXC	G-VG				MINT	EXC	G-VG
☐	161	Rick Rhoden	.07	.03	.01	☐	210	Lance McCullers	.07	.03	.01
☐	162	Scott Garrelts	.07	.03	.01	☐	211	Rick Honeycutt	.04	.02	.00
☐	163	Mike Campbell	.07	.03	.01	☐	212	John Tudor	.10	.05	.01
☐	164	Dave Righetti	.10	.05	.01	☐	213	Jim Gott	.04	.02	.00
☐	165	Paul Molitor	.15	.07	.01	☐	214	Frank Viola	.15	.07	.01
☐	166	Danny Jackson	.10	.05	.01	☐	215	Juan Samuel	.10	.05	.01
☐	167	Pete O'Brien	.10	.05	.01	☐	216	Jesse Barfield	.15	.07	.01
☐	168	Julio Franco	.15	.07	.01	☐	217	Claudell Washington	.07	.03	.01
☐	169	Mark McGwire	.75	.35	.07	☐	218	Rick Reuschel	.10	.05	.01
☐	170	Zane Smith	.07	.03	.01	☐	219	Jim Presley	.07	.03	.01
☐	171	Johnny Ray	.07	.03	.01	☐	220	Tommy John	.15	.07	.01
☐	172	Lester Lancaster	.07	.03	.01	☐	221	Dan Plesac	.07	.03	.01
☐	173	Mel Hall	.10	.05	.01	☐	222	Barry Larkin	.20	.10	.02
☐	174	Tracy Jones	.07	.03	.01	☐	223	Mike Stanley	.04	.02	.00
☐	175	Kevin Seitzer	.35	.17	.03	☐	224	Cory Snyder	.15	.07	.01
☐	176	Bob Knepper	.04	.02	.00	☐	225	Andre Dawson	.20	.10	.02
☐	177	Mike Greenwell	1.25	.60	.12	☐	226	Ken Oberkfell	.04	.02	.00
☐	178	Mike Marshall	.10	.05	.01	☐	227	Devon White	.15	.07	.01
☐	179	Melido Perez	.15	.07	.01	☐	228	Jamie Moyer	.07	.03	.01
☐	180	Tim Raines	.20	.10	.02	☐	229	Brook Jacoby	.07	.03	.01
☐	181	Jack Morris	.10	.05	.01	☐	230	Rob Murphy	.07	.03	.01
☐	182	Darryl Strawberry	.50	.25	.05	☐	231	Bret Saberhagen	.25	.12	.02
☐	183	Robin Yount	.35	.17	.03	☐	232	Nolan Ryan	.60	.30	.06
☐	184	Lance Parrish	.10	.05	.01	☐	233	Bruce Hurst	.10	.05	.01
☐	185	Darnell Coles	.04	.02	.00	☐	234	Jesse Orosco	.04	.02	.00
☐	186	Kirby Puckett	.50	.25	.05	☐	235	Bobby Thigpen	.07	.03	.01
☐	187	Terry Pendleton	.04	.02	.00	☐	236	Pascual Perez	.07	.03	.01
☐	188	Don Slaught	.04	.02	.00	☐	237	Matt Nokes	.10	.05	.01
☐	189	Jimmy Jones	.07	.03	.01	☐	238	Bob Ojeda	.07	.03	.01
☐	190	Dave Parker	.15	.07	.01	☐	239	Joey Meyer	.07	.03	.01
☐	191	Mike Aldrete	.04	.02	.00	☐	240	Shane Rawley	.04	.02	.00
☐	192	Mike Moore	.07	.03	.01	☐	241	Jeff Robinson	.07	.03	.01
☐	193	Greg Walker	.07	.03	.01	☐	242	Jeff Reardon	.10	.05	.01
☐	194	Calvin Schiraldi	.04	.02	.00	☐	243	Ozzie Smith	.15	.07	.01
☐	195	Dick Schofield	.04	.02	.00	☐	244	Dave Winfield	.20	.10	.02
☐	196	Jody Reed	.10	.05	.01	☐	245	John Kruk	.10	.05	.01
☐	197	Pete Smith	.07	.03	.01	☐	246	Carney Lansford	.15	.07	.01
☐	198	Cal Ripken	.25	.12	.02	☐	247	Candy Maldonado	.07	.03	.01
☐	199	Lloyd Moseby	.10	.05	.01	☐	248	Ken Phelps	.07	.03	.01
☐	200	Ruben Sierra	.35	.17	.03	☐	249	Ken Williams	.07	.03	.01
☐	201	R.J. Reynolds	.04	.02	.00	☐	250	Al Nipper	.04	.02	.00
☐	202	Bryn Smith	.07	.03	.01	☐	251	Mark McLemore	.04	.02	.00
☐	203	Gary Pettis	.04	.02	.00	☐	252	Lee Smith	.07	.03	.01
☐	204	Steve Sax	.15	.07	.01	☐	253	Albert Hall	.04	.02	.00
☐	205	Frank DiPino	.04	.02	.00	☐	254	Billy Ripken	.07	.03	.01
☐	206	Mike Scott	.15	.07	.01	☐	255	Kelly Gruber	.07	.03	.01
☐	207	Kurt Stillwell	.07	.03	.01	☐	256	Charlie Hough	.04	.02	.00
☐	208	Mookie Wilson	.07	.03	.01	☐	257	John Smiley	.07	.03	.01
☐	209	Lee Mazzilli	.04	.02	.00	☐	258	Tim Wallach	.10	.05	.01

		MINT	EXC	G-VG
☐ 259	Frank Tanana	.07	.03	.01
☐ 260	Mike Scioscia	.04	.02	.00
☐ 261	Damon Berryhill	.15	.07	.01
☐ 262	Dave Smith	.04	.02	.00
☐ 263	Willie Wilson	.07	.03	.01
☐ 264	Len Dykstra	.07	.03	.01
☐ 265	Randy Myers	.07	.03	.01
☐ 266	Keith Moreland	.04	.02	.00
☐ 267	Eric Plunk	.04	.02	.00
☐ 268	Todd Worrell	.10	.05	.01
☐ 269	Bob Walk	.04	.02	.00
☐ 270	Keith Atherton	.04	.02	.00
☐ 271	Mike Schmidt	.50	.25	.05
☐ 272	Mike Flanagan	.04	.02	.00
☐ 273	Rafael Santana	.04	.02	.00
☐ 274	Rob Thompson	.07	.03	.01
☐ 275	Rey Quinones	.04	.02	.00
☐ 276	Cecilio Guante	.04	.02	.00
☐ 277	B.J. Surhoff	.10	.05	.01
☐ 278	Chris Sabo	.45	.22	.04
☐ 279	Mitch Williams	.10	.05	.01
☐ 280	Greg Swindell	.10	.05	.01
☐ 281	Alan Trammell	.15	.07	.01
☐ 282	Storm Davis	.10	.05	.01
☐ 283	Chuck Finley	.07	.03	.01
☐ 284	Dave Stieb	.10	.05	.01
☐ 285	Scott Bailes	.04	.02	.00
☐ 286	Larry Sheets	.07	.03	.01
☐ 287	Danny Tartabull	.15	.07	.01
☐ 288	Checklist Card	.04	.02	.00
☐ 289	Todd Benzinger	.10	.05	.01
☐ 290	John Shelby	.04	.02	.00
☐ 291	Steve Lyons	.04	.02	.00
☐ 292	Mitch Webster	.04	.02	.00
☐ 293	Walt Terrell	.04	.02	.00
☐ 294	Pete Stanicek	.04	.02	.00
☐ 295	Chris Bosio	.07	.03	.01
☐ 296	Milt Thompson	.04	.02	.00
☐ 297	Fred Lynn	.10	.05	.01
☐ 298	Juan Berenguer	.04	.02	.00
☐ 299	Ken Dayley	.04	.02	.00
☐ 300	Joel Skinner	.04	.02	.00
☐ 301	Benito Santiago	.35	.17	.03
☐ 302	Ron Hassey	.04	.02	.00
☐ 303	Jose Uribe	.04	.02	.00
☐ 304	Harold Reynolds	.07	.03	.01
☐ 305	Dale Sveum	.04	.02	.00
☐ 306	Glenn Wilson	.04	.02	.00
☐ 307	Mike Witt	.07	.03	.01

		MINT	EXC	G-VG
☐ 308	Ron Robinson	.04	.02	.00
☐ 309	Denny Walling	.04	.02	.00
☐ 310	Joe Orsulak	.04	.02	.00
☐ 311	David Wells	.04	.02	.00
☐ 312	Steve Buechele	.04	.02	.00
☐ 313	Jose Oquendo	.04	.02	.00
☐ 314	Floyd Youmans	.04	.02	.00
☐ 315	Lou Whitaker	.10	.05	.01
☐ 316	Fernando Valenzuela	.15	.07	.01
☐ 317	Mike Boddicker	.07	.03	.01
☐ 318	Gerald Young	.07	.03	.01
☐ 319	Frank White	.07	.03	.01
☐ 320	Bill Wegman	.04	.02	.00
☐ 321	Tom Niedenfuer	.04	.02	.00
☐ 322	Ed Whitson	.04	.02	.00
☐ 323	Curt Young	.04	.02	.00
☐ 324	Greg Mathews	.04	.02	.00
☐ 325	Doug Jones	.10	.05	.01
☐ 326	Tommy Herr	.07	.03	.01
☐ 327	Kent Tekulve	.04	.02	.00
☐ 328	Rance Mulliniks	.04	.02	.00
☐ 329	Checklist Card	.04	.02	.00
☐ 330	Craig Lefferts	.04	.02	.00
☐ 331	Franklin Stubbs	.04	.02	.00
☐ 332	Rick Cerone	.04	.02	.00
☐ 333	Dave Schmidt	.04	.02	.00
☐ 334	Larry Parrish	.04	.02	.00
☐ 335	Tom Browning	.10	.05	.01
☐ 336	Checklist Card	.04	.02	.00

1989 Donruss

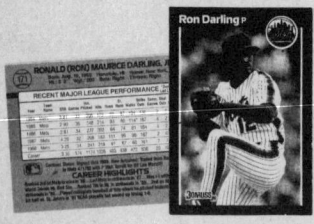

This 660-card set was distributed along with a puzzle of Warren Spahn. The six regular checklist cards are numbered throughout the set as multiples of 100. Cards measure 2 ½" by 3 ½" and feature a distinctive black side border with an alternating coating. The popular Diamond King subset returns for the eighth consecutive year. Rated Rookies are featured again as cards 28-47. The Donruss '89 logo appears in the lower left corner of every obverse. There are two variations that occur throughout most of the set. On the card backs "Denotes Led League" can be found with one asterisk to the left or with an asterisk on each side. On the card fronts the horizontal lines on the left and right borders can be glossy or nonglossy. Since both of these variation types are relatively minor and seem equally common, there is no premium value for either type. Rather than short printing 26 cards in order to make room for printing the Bonus MVP's this year, Donruss apparently chose to double print 106 cards. These double prints are listed below by DP.

		MINT	EXC	G-VG
COMPLETE SET (660)		25.00	12.50	2.50
COMMON PLAYER (1-660)		.03	.01	.00
☐ 1	Mike Greenwell DK	.50	.10	.02
☐ 2	Bobby Bonilla DK DP	.08	.04	.01
☐ 3	Pete Incaviglia DK	.08	.04	.01

		MINT	EXC	G-VG
☐ 4	Chris Sabo DK DP	.12	.06	.01
☐ 5	Robin Yount DK	.15	.06	.01
☐ 6	Tony Gwynn DK DP	.15	.06	.01
☐ 7	Carlton Fisk DK (OF on back)	.12	.06	.01
☐ 8	Cory Snyder DK	.10	.05	.01
☐ 9	David Cone DK UER (sic "hurdlers")	.15	.06	.01
☐ 10	Kevin Seitzer DK	.12	.06	.01
☐ 11	Rick Reuschel DK	.08	.04	.01
☐ 12	Johnny Ray DK	.08	.04	.01
☐ 13	Dave Schmidt DK	.06	.03	.00
☐ 14	Andres Galarraga DK	.10	.05	.01
☐ 15	Kirk Gibson DK	.12	.06	.01
☐ 16	Fred McGriff DK	.15	.07	.01
☐ 17	Mark Grace DK	.75	.35	.07
☐ 18	Jeff Robinson DT DK	.08	.04	.01
☐ 19	Vince Coleman DK DP	.08	.04	.01*
☐ 20	Dave Henderson DK	.06	.03	.00
☐ 21	Harold Reynolds DK	.06	.03	.00
☐ 22	Gerald Perry DK	.06	.03	.00
☐ 23	Frank Viola DK	.12	.06	.01
☐ 24	Steve Bedrosian DK	.08	.04	.01
☐ 25	Glenn Davis DK	.12	.06	.01
☐ 26	Don Mattingly DK UER (doesn't mention Don's previous DK in 1985)	.60	.30	.06
☐ 27	DK Checklist DP	.06	.01	.00
☐ 28	Sandy Alomar Jr. RR	1.25	.60	.12
☐ 29	Steve Searcy RR	.20	.10	.02
☐ 30	Cameron Drew RR	.20	.10	.02
☐ 31	Gary Sheffield RR	1.50	.75	.15
☐ 32	Erik Hanson RR	.20	.10	.02
☐ 33	Ken Griffey Jr. RR	3.75	1.85	.37
☐ 34	Greg Harris RR San Diego Padres	.20	.10	.02
☐ 35	Gregg Jefferies RR	1.50	.75	.15
☐ 36	Luis Medina RR	.25	.12	.02
☐ 37	Carlos Quintana RR	.30	.15	.03
☐ 38	Felix Jose RR	.25	.12	.02
☐ 39	Cris Carpenter RR	.20	.10	.02
☐ 40	Ron Jones RR	.30	.15	.03
☐ 41	Dave West RR	.35	.17	.03
☐ 42	Randy Johnson RR	.25	.12	.02
☐ 43	Mike Harkey RR	.30	.15	.03
☐ 44	Pete Harnisch RR DP	.15	.07	.01

			MINT	EXC	G-VG
☐	45	Tom Gordon RR DP	1.00	.50	.10
☐	46	Gregg Olson RR DP	1.00	.50	.10
☐	47	Alex Sanchez RR DP	.20	.10	.02
☐	48	Ruben Sierra	.25	.12	.02
☐	49	Rafael Palmeiro	.10	.05	.01
☐	50	Ron Gant	.10	.05	.01
☐	51	Cal Ripken	.15	.07	.01
☐	52	Wally Joyner	.15	.07	.01
☐	53	Gary Carter	.12	.06	.01
☐	54	Andy Van Slyke	.10	.05	.01
☐	55	Robin Yount	.18	.09	.01
☐	56	Pete Incaviglia	.10	.05	.01
☐	57	Greg Brock	.03	.01	.00
☐	58	Melido Perez	.06	.03	.00
☐	59	Craig Lefferts	.06	.03	.00
☐	60	Gary Pettis	.03	.01	.00
☐	61	Danny Tartabull	.10	.05	.01
☐	62	Guillermo Hernandez	.06	.03	.00
☐	63	Ozzie Smith	.12	.06	.01
☐	64	Gary Gaetti	.08	.04	.01
☐	65	Mark Davis	.12	.06	.01
☐	66	Lee Smith	.06	.03	.00
☐	67	Dennis Eckersley	.10	.05	.01
☐	68	Wade Boggs	.50	.25	.05
☐	69	Mike Scott	.10	.05	.01
☐	70	Fred McGriff	.18	.09	.01
☐	71	Tom Browning	.08	.04	.01
☐	72	Claudell Washington	.06	.03	.00
☐	73	Mel Hall	.06	.03	.00
☐	74	Don Mattingly	.85	.40	.08
☐	75	Steve Bedrosian	.08	.04	.01
☐	76	Juan Samuel	.08	.04	.01
☐	77	Mike Scioscia	.03	.01	.00
☐	78	Dave Righetti	.08	.04	.01
☐	79	Alfredo Griffin	.03	.01	.00
☐	80	Eric Davis UER	.30	.15	.03
		(165 games in 1988, should be 135)			
☐	81	Juan Berenguer	.03	.01	.00
☐	82	Todd Worrell	.08	.04	.01
☐	83	Joe Carter	.12	.06	.01
☐	84	Steve Sax	.10	.05	.01
☐	85	Frank White	.06	.03	.00
☐	86	John Kruk	.06	.03	.00
☐	87	Rance Mulliniks	.03	.01	.00
☐	88	Alan Ashby	.03	.01	.00
☐	89	Charlie Leibrandt	.03	.01	.00
☐	90	Frank Tanana	.03	.01	.00
☐	91	Jose Canseco	1.00	.50	.10

			MINT	EXC	G-VG
☐	92	Barry Bonds	.08	.04	.01
☐	93	Harold Reynolds	.06	.03	.00
☐	94	Mark McLemore	.03	.01	.00
☐	95	Mark McGwire	.50	.25	.05
☐	96	Eddie Murray	.12	.06	.01
☐	97	Tim Raines	.12	.06	.01
☐	98	Rob Thompson	.03	.01	.00
☐	99	Kevin McReynolds	.10	.05	.01
☐	100	Checklist	.06	.01	.00
☐	101	Carlton Fisk	.10	.05	.01
☐	102	Dave Martinez	.03	.01	.00
☐	103	Glenn Braggs	.06	.03	.00
☐	104	Dale Murphy	.18	.09	.01
☐	105	Ryne Sandberg	.15	.07	.01
☐	106	Dennis Martinez	.06	.03	.00
☐	107	Pete O'Brien	.06	.03	.00
☐	108	Dick Schofield	.03	.01	.00
☐	109	Henry Cotto	.03	.01	.00
☐	110	Mike Marshall	.08	.04	.01
☐	111	Keith Moreland	.03	.01	.00
☐	112	Tom Brunansky	.08	.04	.01
☐	113	Kelly Gruber UER	.06	.03	.00
		(wrong birthdate)			
☐	114	Brook Jacoby	.06	.03	.00
☐	115	Keith Brown	.10	.05	.01
☐	116	Matt Nokes	.08	.04	.01
☐	117	Keith Hernandez	.10	.05	.01
☐	118	Bob Forsch	.03	.01	.00
☐	119	Bert Blyleven UER	.08	.04	.01
		(. . . 3000 strikeouts in 1987, should be 1986)			
☐	120	Willie Wilson	.06	.03	.00
☐	121	Tommy Gregg	.03	.01	.00
☐	122	Jim Rice	.10	.05	.01
☐	123	Bob Knepper	.03	.01	.00
☐	124	Danny Jackson	.06	.03	.00
☐	125	Eric Plunk	.03	.01	.00
☐	126	Brian Fisher	.03	.01	.00
☐	127	Mike Pagliarulo	.06	.03	.00
☐	128	Tony Gwynn	.20	.10	.02
☐	129	Lance McCullers	.03	.01	.00
☐	130	Andres Galarraga	.10	.05	.01
☐	131	Jose Uribe	.03	.01	.00
☐	132	Kirk Gibson UER	.12	.06	.01
		(wrong birthdate)			
☐	133	David Palmer	.03	.01	.00
☐	134	R.J. Reynolds	.03	.01	.00
☐	135	Greg Walker	.06	.03	.00
☐	136	Kirk McCaskill UER	.03	.01	.00

		MINT	EXC	G-VG
	(wrong birthdate)			
☐ 137	Shawon Dunston	.08	.04	.01
☐ 138	Andy Allanson	.03	.01	.00
☐ 139	Rob Murphy	.03	.01	.00
☐ 140	Mike Aldrete	.03	.01	.00
☐ 141	Terry Kennedy	.03	.01	.00
☐ 142	Scott Fletcher	.03	.01	.00
☐ 143	Steve Balboni	.03	.01	.00
☐ 144	Bret Saberhagen	.15	.07	.01
☐ 145	Ozzie Virgil	.03	.01	.00
☐ 146	Dale Sveum	.03	.01	.00
☐ 147	Darryl Strawberry	.40	.20	.04
☐ 148	Harold Baines	.08	.04	.01
☐ 149	George Bell	.12	.06	.01
☐ 150	Dave Parker	.08	.04	.01
☐ 151	Bobby Bonilla	.10	.05	.01
☐ 152	Mookie Wilson	.06	.03	.00
☐ 153	Ted Power	.03	.01	.00
☐ 154	Nolan Ryan	.30	.15	.03
☐ 155	Jeff Reardon	.06	.03	.00
☐ 156	Tim Wallach	.06	.03	.00
☐ 157	Jamie Moyer	.03	.01	.00
☐ 158	Rich Gossage	.08	.04	.01
☐ 159	Dave Winfield	.12	.06	.01
☐ 160	Von Hayes	.08	.04	.01
☐ 161	Willie McGee	.08	.04	.01
☐ 162	Rich Gedman	.03	.01	.00
☐ 163	Tony Pena	.06	.03	.00
☐ 164	Mike Morgan	.06	.03	.00
☐ 165	Charlie Hough	.03	.01	.00
☐ 166	Mike Stanley	.03	.01	.00
☐ 167	Andre Dawson	.12	.06	.01
☐ 168	Joe Boever	.08	.04	.01
☐ 169	Pete Stanicek	.03	.01	.00
☐ 170	Bob Boone	.08	.04	.01
☐ 171	Ron Darling	.08	.04	.01
☐ 172	Bob Walk	.03	.01	.00
☐ 173	Rob Deer	.06	.03	.00
☐ 174	Steve Buechele	.03	.01	.00
☐ 175	Ted Higuera	.06	.03	.00
☐ 176	Ozzie Guillen	.06	.03	.00
☐ 177	Candy Maldonado	.03	.01	.00
☐ 178	Doyle Alexander	.03	.01	.00
☐ 179	Mark Gubicza	.08	.04	.01
☐ 180	Alan Trammell	.12	.06	.01
☐ 181	Vince Coleman	.10	.05	.01
☐ 182	Kirby Puckett	.30	.15	.03
☐ 183	Chris Brown	.03	.01	.00
☐ 184	Marty Barrett	.03	.01	.00

		MINT	EXC	G-VG
☐ 185	Stan Javier	.03	.01	.00
☐ 186	Mike Greenwell	.65	.30	.06
☐ 187	Billy Hatcher	.03	.01	.00
☐ 188	Jimmy Key	.06	.03	.00
☐ 189	Nick Esasky	.06	.03	.00
☐ 190	Don Slaught	.03	.01	.00
☐ 191	Cory Snyder	.10	.05	.01
☐ 192	John Candelaria	.06	.03	.00
☐ 193	Mike Schmidt	.25	.12	.02
☐ 194	Kevin Gross	.03	.01	.00
☐ 195	John Tudor	.08	.04	.01
☐ 196	Neil Allen	.03	.01	.00
☐ 197	Orel Hershiser	.20	.10	.02
☐ 198	Kal Daniels	.08	.04	.01
☐ 199	Kent Hrbek	.10	.05	.01
☐ 200	Checklist	.06	.01	.00
☐ 201	Joe Magrane	.08	.04	.01
☐ 202	Scott Bailes	.03	.01	.00
☐ 203	Tim Belcher	.08	.04	.01
☐ 204	George Brett	.20	.10	.02
☐ 205	Benito Santiago	.15	.07	.01
☐ 206	Tony Fernandez	.10	.05	.01
☐ 207	Gerald Young	.06	.03	.00
☐ 208	Bo Jackson	.75	.35	.07
☐ 209	Chet Lemon	.03	.01	.00
☐ 210	Storm Davis	.06	.03	.00
☐ 211	Doug Drabek	.06	.03	.00
☐ 212	Mickey Brantley UER	.06	.03	.00
	(photo actually			
	Nelson Simmons)			
☐ 213	Devon White	.10	.05	.01
☐ 214	Dave Stewart	.10	.05	.01
☐ 215	Dave Schmidt	.03	.01	.00
☐ 216	Bryn Smith	.03	.01	.00
☐ 217	Brett Butler	.06	.03	.00
☐ 218	Bob Ojeda	.06	.03	.00
☐ 219	Steve Rosenberg	.10	.05	.01
☐ 220	Hubie Brooks	.06	.03	.00
☐ 221	B.J. Surhoff	.06	.03	.00
☐ 222	Rick Mahler	.03	.01	.00
☐ 223	Rick Sutcliffe	.08	.04	.01
☐ 224	Neal Heaton	.03	.01	.00
☐ 225	Mitch Williams	.08	.04	.01
☐ 226	Chuck Finley	.06	.03	.00
☐ 227	Mark Langston	.12	.06	.01
☐ 228	Jesse Orosco	.03	.01	.00
☐ 229	Ed Whitson	.03	.01	.00
☐ 230	Terry Pendleton	.03	.01	.00
☐ 231	Lloyd Moseby	.06	.03	.00

	MINT	EXC	G-VG			MINT	EXC	G-VG
☐ 232 Greg Swindell	.08	.04	.01	☐ 280 Roger Clemens	.25	.12	.02
☐ 233 John Franco	.08	.04	.01	☐ 281 Greg Mathews	.03	.01	.00
☐ 234 Jack Morris	.10	.05	.01	☐ 282 Tom Niedenfuer	.03	.01	.00
☐ 235 Howard Johnson	.15	.07	.01	☐ 283 Paul Kilgus	.03	.01	.00
☐ 236 Glenn Davis	.12	.06	.01	☐ 284 Jose Guzman	.03	.01	.00
☐ 237 Frank Viola	.15	.07	.01	☐ 285 Calvin Schiraldi	.03	.01	.00
☐ 238 Kevin Seitzer	.15	.07	.01	☐ 286 Charlie Puleo UER	.03	.01	.00
☐ 239 Gerald Perry	.06	.03	.00	(career ERA 4.24,			
☐ 240 Dwight Evans	.08	.04	.01	should be 4.23)			
☐ 241 Jim Deshaies	.03	.01	.00	☐ 287 Joe Orsulak	.03	.01	.00
☐ 242 Bo Diaz	.03	.01	.00	☐ 288 Jack Howell	.03	.01	.00
☐ 243 Carney Lansford	.08	.04	.01	☐ 289 Kevin Elster	.06	.03	.00
☐ 244 Mike LaValliere	.03	.01	.00	☐ 290 Jose Lind	.03	.01	.00
☐ 245 Rickey Henderson	.25	.12	.02	☐ 291 Paul Molitor	.10	.05	.01
☐ 246 Roberto Alomar	.20	.10	.02	☐ 292 Cecil Espy	.10	.05	.01
☐ 247 Jimmy Jones	.03	.01	.00	☐ 293 Bill Wegman	.03	.01	.00
☐ 248 Pascual Perez	.08	.04	.01	☐ 294 Dan Pasqua	.03	.01	.00
☐ 249 Will Clark	.75	.35	.07	☐ 295 Scott Garrelts UER	.06	.03	.00
☐ 250 Fernando Valenzuela	.10	.05	.01	(wrong birthdate)			
☐ 251 Shane Rawley	.03	.01	.00	☐ 296 Walt Terrell	.03	.01	.00
☐ 252 Sid Bream	.03	.01	.00	☐ 297 Ed Hearn	.03	.01	.00
☐ 253 Steve Lyons	.03	.01	.00	☐ 298 Lou Whitaker	.08	.04	.01
☐ 254 Brian Downing	.03	.01	.00	☐ 299 Ken Dayley	.03	.01	.00
☐ 255 Mark Grace	1.50	.75	.15	☐ 300 Checklist	.06	.01	.00
☐ 256 Tom Candiotti	.03	.01	.00	☐ 301 Tommy Herr	.03	.01	.00
☐ 257 Barry Larkin	.12	.06	.01	☐ 302 Mike Brumley	.03	.01	.00
☐ 258 Mike Krukow	.03	.01	.00	☐ 303 Ellis Burks	.30	.15	.03
☐ 259 Billy Ripken	.03	.01	.00	☐ 304 Curt Young UER	.03	.01	.00
☐ 260 Cecilio Guante	.03	.01	.00	(wrong birthdate)			
☐ 261 Scott Bradley	.03	.01	.00	☐ 305 Jody Reed	.06	.03	.00
☐ 262 Floyd Bannister	.03	.01	.00	☐ 306 Bill Doran	.06	.03	.00
☐ 263 Pete Smith	.03	.01	.00	☐ 307 David Wells	.03	.01	.00
☐ 264 Jim Gantner UER	.03	.01	.00	☐ 308 Ron Robinson	.03	.01	.00
(wrong birthdate)				☐ 309 Rafael Santana	.03	.01	.00
☐ 265 Roger McDowell	.06	.03	.00	☐ 310 Julio Franco	.08	.04	.01
☐ 266 Bobby Thigpen	.06	.03	.00	☐ 311 Jack Clark	.10	.05	.01
☐ 267 Jim Clancy	.03	.01	.00	☐ 312 Chris James	.06	.03	.00
☐ 268 Terry Steinbach	.10	.05	.01	☐ 313 Milt Thompson	.03	.01	.00
☐ 269 Mike Dunne	.06	.03	.00	☐ 314 John Shelby	.03	.01	.00
☐ 270 Dwight Gooden	.25	.12	.02	☐ 315 Al Leiter	.08	.04	.01
☐ 271 Mike Heath	.03	.01	.00	☐ 316 Mike Davis	.03	.01	.00
☐ 272 Dave Smith	.03	.01	.00	☐ 317 Chris Sabo	.50	.25	.05
☐ 273 Keith Atherton	.03	.01	.00	☐ 318 Greg Gagne	.03	.01	.00
☐ 274 Tim Burke	.06	.03	.00	☐ 319 Jose Oquendo	.03	.01	.00
☐ 275 Damon Berryhill	.10	.05	.01	☐ 320 John Farrell	.03	.01	.00
☐ 276 Vance Law	.03	.01	.00	☐ 321 Franklin Stubbs	.03	.01	.00
☐ 277 Rich Dotson	.03	.01	.00	☐ 322 Kurt Stillwell	.03	.01	.00
☐ 278 Lance Parrish	.08	.04	.01	☐ 323 Shawn Abner	.06	.03	.00
☐ 279 Denny Walling	.03	.01	.00	☐ 324 Mike Flanagan	.06	.03	.00

		MINT	EXC	G-VG
☐ 325	Kevin Bass	.06	.03	.00
☐ 326	Pat Tabler	.06	.03	.00
☐ 327	Mike Henneman	.03	.01	.00
☐ 328	Rick Honeycutt	.03	.01	.00
☐ 329	John Smiley	.03	.01	.00
☐ 330	Rey Quinones	.03	.01	.00
☐ 331	Johnny Ray	.06	.03	.00
☐ 332	Bob Welch	.06	.03	.00
☐ 333	Larry Sheets	.03	.01	.00
☐ 334	Jeff Parrett	.03	.01	.00
☐ 335	Rick Reuschel UER	.08	.04	.01
	(for Don Robinson,			
	should be Jeff)			
☐ 336	Randy Myers	.08	.04	.01
☐ 337	Ken Williams	.03	.01	.00
☐ 338	Andy McGaffigan	.03	.01	.00
☐ 339	Joey Meyer	.06	.03	.00
☐ 340	Dion James	.03	.01	.00
☐ 341	Les Lancaster	.03	.01	.00
☐ 342	Tom Foley	.03	.01	.00
☐ 343	Geno Petralli	.03	.01	.00
☐ 344	Dan Petry	.03	.01	.00
☐ 345	Alvin Davis	.08	.04	.01
☐ 346	Mickey Hatcher	.03	.01	.00
☐ 347	Marvell Wynne	.03	.01	.00
☐ 348	Danny Cox	.03	.01	.00
☐ 349	Dave Stieb	.08	.04	.01
☐ 350	Jay Bell	.03	.01	.00
☐ 351	Jeff Treadway	.06	.03	.00
☐ 352	Luis Salazar	.03	.01	.00
☐ 353	Len Dykstra	.06	.03	.00
☐ 354	Juan Agosto	.03	.01	.00
☐ 355	Gene Larkin	.06	.03	.00
☐ 356	Steve Farr	.03	.01	.00
☐ 357	Paul Assenmacher	.03	.01	.00
☐ 358	Todd Benzinger	.03	.01	.00
☐ 359	Larry Andersen	.03	.01	.00
☐ 360	Paul O'Neill	.08	.04	.01
☐ 361	Ron Hassey	.03	.01	.00
☐ 362	Jim Gott	.03	.01	.00
☐ 363	Ken Phelps	.06	.03	.00
☐ 364	Tim Flannery	.03	.01	.00
☐ 365	Randy Ready	.03	.01	.00
☐ 366	Nelson Santovenia	.15	.07	.01
☐ 367	Kelly Downs	.06	.03	.00
☐ 368	Danny Heep	.03	.01	.00
☐ 369	Phil Bradley	.06	.03	.00
☐ 370	Jeff Robinson	.06	.03	.00
	Pittsburgh Pirates			

		MINT	EXC	G-VG
☐ 371	Ivan Calderon	.06	.03	.00
☐ 372	Mike Witt	.06	.03	.00
☐ 373	Greg Maddux	.10	.05	.01
☐ 374	Carmen Castillo	.03	.01	.00
☐ 375	Jose Rijo	.03	.01	.00
☐ 376	Joe Price	.03	.01	.00
☐ 377	Rene C. Gonzales	.03	.01	.00
☐ 378	Oddibe McDowell	.06	.03	.00
☐ 379	Jim Presley	.03	.01	.00
☐ 380	Brad Wellman	.03	.01	.00
☐ 381	Tom Glavine	.06	.03	.00
☐ 382	Dan Plesac	.06	.03	.00
☐ 383	Wally Backman	.03	.01	.00
☐ 384	Dave Gallagher	.20	.10	.02
☐ 385	Tom Henke	.06	.03	.00
☐ 386	Luis Polonia	.03	.01	.00
☐ 387	Junior Ortiz	.03	.01	.00
☐ 388	David Cone	.20	.10	.02
☐ 389	Dave Bergman	.03	.01	.00
☐ 390	Danny Darwin	.03	.01	.00
☐ 391	Dan Gladden	.03	.01	.00
☐ 392	John Dopson	.15	.07	.01
☐ 393	Frank DiPino	.03	.01	.00
☐ 394	Al Nipper	.03	.01	.00
☐ 395	Willie Randolph	.06	.03	.00
☐ 396	Don Carman	.03	.01	.00
☐ 397	Scott Terry	.03	.01	.00
☐ 398	Rick Cerone	.03	.01	.00
☐ 399	Tom Pagnozzi	.03	.01	.00
☐ 400	Checklist	.06	.01	.00
☐ 401	Mickey Tettleton	.06	.03	.00
☐ 402	Curtis Wilkerson	.03	.01	.00
☐ 403	Jeff Russell	.06	.03	.00
☐ 404	Pat Perry	.03	.01	.00
☐ 405	Jose Alvarez	.08	.04	.01
☐ 406	Rick Schu	.03	.01	.00
☐ 407	Sherman Corbett	.08	.04	.01
☐ 408	Dave Magadan	.08	.04	.01
☐ 409	Bob Kipper	.03	.01	.00
☐ 410	Don August	.06	.03	.00
☐ 411	Bob Brower	.03	.01	.00
☐ 412	Chris Bosio	.03	.01	.00
☐ 413	Jerry Reuss	.03	.01	.00
☐ 414	Atlee Hammaker	.03	.01	.00
☐ 415	Jim Walewander	.08	.04	.01
☐ 416	Mike Macfarlane	.12	.06	.01
☐ 417	Pat Sheridan	.03	.01	.00
☐ 418	Pedro Guerrero	.10	.05	.01
☐ 419	Allan Anderson	.06	.03	.00

		MINT	EXC	G-VG
☐ 420	Mark Parent	.12	.06	.01
☐ 421	Bob Stanley	.03	.01	.00
☐ 422	Mike Gallego	.03	.01	.00
☐ 423	Bruce Hurst	.08	.04	.01
☐ 424	Dave Meads	.03	.01	.00
☐ 425	Jesse Barfield	.08	.04	.01
☐ 426	Rob Dibble	.25	.12	.02
☐ 427	Joel Skinner	.03	.01	.00
☐ 428	Ron Kittle	.08	.04	.01
☐ 429	Rick Rhoden	.03	.01	.00
☐ 430	Bob Dernier	.03	.01	.00
☐ 431	Steve Jeltz	.03	.01	.00
☐ 432	Rick Dempsey	.03	.01	.00
☐ 433	Roberto Kelly	.15	.07	.01
☐ 434	Dave Anderson	.03	.01	.00
☐ 435	Herm Winningham	.03	.01	.00
☐ 436	Al Newman	.03	.01	.00
☐ 437	Jose DeLeon	.06	.03	.00
☐ 438	Doug Jones	.06	.03	.00
☐ 439	Brian Holton	.03	.01	.00
☐ 440	Jeff Montgomery	.15	.07	.01
☐ 441	Dickie Thon	.03	.01	.00
☐ 442	Cecil Fielder	.03	.01	.00
☐ 443	John Fishel	.10	.05	.01
☐ 444	Jerry Don Gleaton	.03	.01	.00
☐ 445	Paul Gibson	.10	.05	.01
☐ 446	Walt Weiss	.40	.20	.04
☐ 447	Glenn Wilson	.03	.01	.00
☐ 448	Mike Moore	.06	.03	.00
☐ 449	Chili Davis	.06	.03	.00
☐ 450	Dave Henderson	.06	.03	.00
☐ 451	Jose Bautista	.08	.04	.01
☐ 452	Rex Hudler	.03	.01	.00
☐ 453	Bob Brenly	.03	.01	.00
☐ 454	Mackey Sasser	.08	.04	.01
☐ 455	Daryl Boston	.03	.01	.00
☐ 456	Mike Fitzgerald	.03	.01	.00
	Montreal Expos			
☐ 457	Jeffrey Leonard	.06	.03	.00
☐ 458	Bruce Sutter	.08	.04	.01
☐ 459	Mitch Webster	.03	.01	.00
☐ 460	Joe Hesketh	.03	.01	.00
☐ 461	Bobby Witt	.06	.03	.00
☐ 462	Stew Cliburn	.03	.01	.00
☐ 463	Scott Bankhead	.06	.03	.00
☐ 464	Ramon Martinez	.35	.17	.03
☐ 465	Dave Leiper	.03	.01	.00
☐ 466	Luis Alicea	.10	.05	.01
☐ 467	John Cerutti	.03	.01	.00

		MINT	EXC	G-VG
☐ 468	Ron Washington	.03	.01	.00
☐ 469	Jeff Reed	.03	.01	.00
☐ 470	Jeff Robinson	.06	.03	.00
	Detroit Tigers			
☐ 471	Sid Fernandez	.08	.04	.01
☐ 472	Terry Puhl	.03	.01	.00
☐ 473	Charlie Lea	.03	.01	.00
☐ 474	Israel Sanchez	.08	.04	.01
☐ 475	Bruce Benedict	.03	.01	.00
☐ 476	Oil Can Boyd	.06	.03	.00
☐ 477	Craig Reynolds	.03	.01	.00
☐ 478	Frank Williams	.03	.01	.00
☐ 479	Greg Cadaret	.03	.01	.00
☐ 480	Randy Kramer	.10	.05	.01
☐ 481	Dave Eiland	.10	.05	.01
☐ 482	Eric Show	.03	.01	.00
☐ 483	Garry Templeton	.06	.03	.00
☐ 484	Wallace Johnson	.03	.01	.00
☐ 485	Kevin Mitchell	.35	.17	.03
☐ 486	Tim Crews	.03	.01	.00
☐ 487	Mike Maddux	.03	.01	.00
☐ 488	Dave LaPoint	.03	.01	.00
☐ 489	Fred Manrique	.03	.01	.00
☐ 490	Greg Minton	.03	.01	.00
☐ 491	Doug Dascenzo UER	.25	.12	.02
	(photo actually			
	Damon Berryhill)			
☐ 492	Willie Upshaw	.03	.01	.00
☐ 493	Jack Armstrong	.25	.12	.02
☐ 494	Kirt Manwaring	.03	.01	.00
☐ 495	Jeff Ballard	.08	.04	.01
☐ 496	Jeff Kunkel	.03	.01	.00
☐ 497	Mike Campbell	.03	.01	.00
☐ 498	Gary Thurman	.03	.01	.00
☐ 499	Zane Smith	.03	.01	.00
☐ 500	Checklist DP	.06	.01	.00
☐ 501	Mike Birkbeck	.03	.01	.00
☐ 502	Terry Leach	.06	.03	.00
☐ 503	Shawn Hillegas	.03	.01	.00
☐ 504	Manny Lee	.03	.01	.00
☐ 505	Doug Jennings	.20	.10	.02
☐ 506	Ken Oberkfell	.03	.01	.00
☐ 507	Tim Teufel	.03	.01	.00
☐ 508	Tom Brookens	.03	.01	.00
☐ 509	Rafael Ramirez	.03	.01	.00
☐ 510	Fred Toliver	.03	.01	.00
☐ 511	Brian Holman	.10	.05	.01
☐ 512	Mike Bielecki	.08	.04	.01
☐ 513	Jeff Pico	.10	.05	.01

		MINT	EXC	G-VG
☐ 514	Charles Hudson	.03	.01	.00
☐ 515	Bruce Ruffin	.03	.01	.00
☐ 516	Larry McWilliams UER	.03	.01	.00
	(New Richland, should be North Richland)			
☐ 517	Jeff Sellers	.03	.01	.00
☐ 518	John Costello	.10	.05	.01
☐ 519	Brady Anderson	.25	.12	.02
☐ 520	Craig McMurtry	.03	.01	.00
☐ 521	Ray Hayward DP	.03	.01	.00
☐ 522	Drew Hall DP	.03	.01	.00
☐ 523	Mark Lemke DP	.10	.05	.01
☐ 524	Oswald Peraza DP	.08	.04	.01
☐ 525	Bryan Harvey DP	.15	.07	.01
☐ 526	Rick Aguilera DP	.03	.01	.00
☐ 527	Tom Prince DP	.03	.01	.00
☐ 528	Mark Clear DP	.03	.01	.00
☐ 529	Jerry Browne DP	.03	.01	.00
☐ 530	Juan Castillo DP	.03	.01	.00
☐ 531	Jack McDowell DP	.06	.03	.00
☐ 532	Chris Speier DP	.03	.01	.00
☐ 533	Darrell Evans DP	.06	.03	.00
☐ 534	Luis Aquino DP	.03	.01	.00
☐ 535	Eric King DP	.03	.01	.00
☐ 536	Ken Hill DP	.12	.06	.01
☐ 537	Randy Bush DP	.03	.01	.00
☐ 538	Shane Mack DP	.03	.01	.00
☐ 539	Tom Bolton DP	.06	.03	.00
☐ 540	Gene Nelson DP	.03	.01	.00
☐ 541	Wes Gardner DP	.03	.01	.00
☐ 542	Ken Caminiti DP	.03	.01	.00
☐ 543	Duane Ward DP	.03	.01	.00
☐ 544	Norm Charlton DP	.10	.05	.01
☐ 545	Hal Morris DP	.15	.07	.01
☐ 546	Rich Yett DP	.03	.01	.00
☐ 547	Hensley Meulens DP	.50	.25	.05
☐ 548	Greg Harris DP Philadelphia Phillies	.03	.01	.00
☐ 549	Darren Daulton DP (posing as right-handed hitter)	.03	.01	.00
☐ 550	Jeff Hamilton DP	.03	.01	.00
☐ 551	Luis Aguayo DP	.03	.01	.00
☐ 552	Tim Leary DP (resembles M. Marshall)	.06	.03	.00
☐ 553	Ron Oester DP	.03	.01	.00

		MINT	EXC	G-VG
☐ 554	Steve Lombardozzi DP	.03	.01	.00
☐ 555	Tim Jones DP	.08	.04	.01
☐ 556	Bud Black DP	.03	.01	.00
☐ 557	Alejandro Pena DP	.03	.01	.00
☐ 558	Jose DeJesus DP	.08	.04	.01
☐ 559	Dennis Rasmussen DP	.03	.01	.00
☐ 560	Pat Borders DP	.10	.05	.01
☐ 561	Craig Biggio DP	.35	.17	.03
☐ 562	Luis De Los Santos DP	.15	.07	.01
☐ 563	Fred Lynn DP	.06	.03	.00
☐ 564	Todd Burns DP	.20	.10	.02
☐ 565	Felix Fermin DP	.03	.01	.00
☐ 566	Darnell Coles DP	.03	.01	.00
☐ 567	Willie Fraser DP	.03	.01	.00
☐ 568	Glenn Hubbard DP	.03	.01	.00
☐ 569	Craig Worthington DP	.35	.17	.03
☐ 570	Johnny Paredes DP	.08	.04	.01
☐ 571	Don Robinson DP	.03	.01	.00
☐ 572	Barry Lyons DP	.03	.01	.00
☐ 573	Bill Long DP	.03	.01	.00
☐ 574	Tracy Jones DP	.03	.01	.00
☐ 575	Juan Nieves DP	.03	.01	.00
☐ 576	Andres Thomas DP	.03	.01	.00
☐ 577	Rolando Roomes DP	.25	.12	.02
☐ 578	Luis Rivera UER DP (wrong birthdate)	.03	.01	.00
☐ 579	Chad Kreuter DP	.10	.05	.01
☐ 580	Tony Armas DP	.03	.01	.00
☐ 581	Jay Buhner	.10	.05	.01
☐ 582	Ricky Horton DP	.03	.01	.00
☐ 583	Andy Hawkins DP	.03	.01	.00
☐ 584	Sil Campusano	.20	.10	.02
☐ 585	Dave Clark	.06	.03	.00
☐ 586	Van Snider DP	.20	.10	.02
☐ 587	Todd Frohwirth DP	.03	.01	.00
☐ 588	Puzzle Card DP Warren Spahn	.03	.01	.00
☐ 589	William Brennan	.12	.06	.01
☐ 590	German Gonzalez	.10	.05	.01
☐ 591	Ernie Whitt DP	.03	.01	.00
☐ 592	Jeff Blauser	.03	.01	.00
☐ 593	Spike Owen DP	.03	.01	.00
☐ 594	Matt Williams	.25	.12	.02
☐ 595	Lloyd McClendon DP	.08	.04	.01
☐ 596	Steve Ontiveros	.03	.01	.00
☐ 597	Scott Medvin	.12	.06	.01

		MINT	EXC	G-VG
☐ 598	Hipolito Pena DP	.08	.04	.01
☐ 599	Jerald Clark DP	.20	.10	.02
☐ 600A	Checklist Card DP 635 Kurt Schilling	.25	.03	.01
☐ 600B	Checklist Card DP 635 Curt Schilling (MVP's not listed on checklist card)	.06	.01	.00
☐ 600C	Checklist Card DP 635 Curt Schilling (MVP's listed following #660)	.06	.01	.00
☐ 601	Carmelo Martinez DP	.03	.01	.00
☐ 602	Mike LaCoss	.03	.01	.00
☐ 603	Mike Devereaux	.06	.03	.00
☐ 604	Alex Madrid DP	.08	.04	.01
☐ 605	Gary Redus DP	.03	.01	.00
☐ 606	Lance Johnson	.03	.01	.00
☐ 607	Terry Clark DP	.08	.04	.01
☐ 608	Manny Trillo DP	.03	.01	.00
☐ 609	Scott Jordan	.10	.05	.01
☐ 610	Jay Howell DP	.03	.01	.00
☐ 611	Francisco Melendez	.20	.10	.02
☐ 612	Mike Boddicker	.03	.01	.00
☐ 613	Kevin Brown DP	.08	.04	.01
☐ 614	Dave Valle	.03	.01	.00
☐ 615	Tim Laudner DP	.03	.01	.00
☐ 616	Andy Nezelek UER (wrong birthdate)	.20	.10	.02
☐ 617	Chuck Crim	.03	.01	.00
☐ 618	Jack Savage DP	.08	.04	.01
☐ 619	Adam Peterson	.08	.04	.01
☐ 620	Todd Stottlemyre	.08	.04	.01
☐ 621	Lance Blankenship	.20	.10	.02
☐ 622	Miguel Garcia DP	.08	.04	.01
☐ 623	Keith Miller DP New York Mets	.03	.01	.00
☐ 624	Ricky Jordan DP	1.25	.60	.12
☐ 625	Ernest Riles DP	.03	.01	.00
☐ 626	John Moses DP	.03	.01	.00
☐ 627	Nelson Liriano DP	.03	.01	.00
☐ 628	Mike Smithson DP	.03	.01	.00
☐ 629	Scott Sanderson	.03	.01	.00
☐ 630	Dale Mohorcic	.03	.01	.00
☐ 631	Marvin Freeman DP	.03	.01	.00
☐ 632	Mike Young DP	.03	.01	.00
☐ 633	Dennis Lamp	.03	.01	.00
☐ 634	Dante Bichette DP	.18	.09	.01
☐ 635	Curt Schilling DP	.10	.05	.01

		MINT	EXC	G-VG
☐ 636	Scott May DP	.10	.05	.01
☐ 637	Mike Schooler	.35	.17	.03
☐ 638	Rick Leach	.03	.01	.00
☐ 639	Tom Lampkin UER (Throws Left, should be Throws Right)	.10	.05	.01
☐ 640	Brian Meyer	.10	.05	.01
☐ 641	Brian Harper	.03	.01	.00
☐ 642	John Smoltz	.50	.25	.05
☐ 643	Jose: 40/40 Club (Jose Canseco)	.50	.25	.05
☐ 644	Bill Schroeder	.03	.01	.00
☐ 645	Edgar Martinez	.10	.05	.01
☐ 646	Dennis Cook	.25	.12	.02
☐ 647	Barry Jones	.03	.01	.00
☐ 648	Orel: 59 and Counting (Orel Hershiser)	.15	.07	.01
☐ 649	Rod Nichols	.10	.05	.01
☐ 650	Jody Davis	.03	.01	.00
☐ 651	Bob Milacki	.25	.12	.02
☐ 652	Mike Jackson	.03	.01	.00
☐ 653	Derek Lilliquist	.30	.15	.03
☐ 654	Paul Mirabella	.03	.01	.00
☐ 655	Mike Diaz	.03	.01	.00
☐ 656	Jeff Musselman	.03	.01	.00
☐ 657	Jerry Reed	.03	.01	.00
☐ 658	Kevin Blankenship	.15	.07	.01
☐ 659	Wayne Tolleson	.03	.01	.00
☐ 660	Eric Hetzel	.12	.06	.01

1989 Donruss Bonus MVP's

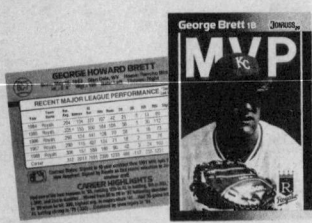

This 26-card set was distributed along with the regular 1989 Donruss issue as random inserts with the rack and wax packs. These bonus cards are numbered with the prefix BC for bonus cards and were supposedly produced in the same quantities as the other 660 regular issue cards. The "most valuable" player was selected from each of the 26 teams. Cards measure 2 ½" by 3 ½" and feature the same distinctive side border as the regular issue. The cards are distinguished by the bold MVP logo in the upper background of the obverse. Four of these cards were double printed with respect to the other cards in the set; these four are denoted by DP in the checklist below.

	MINT	EXC	G-VG
COMPLETE SET (26)	6.00	3.00	.60
COMMON CARD (BC1-BC26) ..	.07	.03	.01
☐ BC1 Kirby Puckett	.30	.15	.03
☐ BC2 Mike Scott	.12	.06	.01
☐ BC3 Joe Carter	.12	.06	.01
☐ BC4 Orel Hershiser	.20	.10	.02
☐ BC5 Jose Canseco	.60	.30	.06
☐ BC6 Darryl Strawberry ...	.35	.17	.03
☐ BC7 George Brett	.20	.10	.02
☐ BC8 Andre Dawson	.12	.06	.01
☐ BC9 Paul Molitor UER	.12	.06	.01
(Brewers logo missing			

	MINT	EXC	G-VG
the word Milwaukee)			
☐ BC10 Andy Van Slyke	.10	.05	.01
☐ BC11 Dave Winfield	.12	.06	.01
☐ BC12 Kevin Gross	.07	.03	.01
☐ BC13 Mike Greenwell	.40	.20	.04
☐ BC14 Ozzie Smith	.12	.06	.01
☐ BC15 Cal Ripken	.15	.07	.01
☐ BC16 Andres Galarraga ...	.10	.05	.01
☐ BC17 Alan Trammell	.12	.06	.01
☐ BC18 Kal Daniels	.10	.05	.01
☐ BC19 Fred McGriff	.15	.07	.01
☐ BC20 Tony Gwynn	.20	.10	.02
☐ BC21 Wally Joyner DP	.10	.05	.01
☐ BC22 Will Clark DP	.50	.25	.05
☐ BC23 Ozzie Guillen	.07	.03	.01
☐ BC24 Gerald Perry DP	.07	.03	.01
☐ BC25 Alvin Davis DP	.10	.05	.01
☐ BC26 Ruben Sierra	.25	.12	.02

1989 Donruss Traded

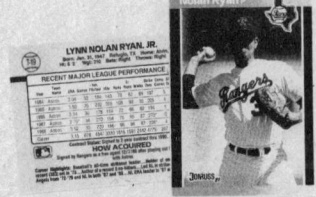

The 1989 Donruss Traded set contains 56 standard-size (2 ½" by 3 ½") cards. The fronts have yellowish-orange borders; the backs are yellow and feature recent statistics. The cards were distributed as a boxed set. The set was never very popular with collectors since it included (as the name implies) only traded players rather than rookies.

			MINT	EXC	G-VG
COMPLETE SET (56)			5.00	2.50	.50
COMMON PLAYER (1-55)			.05	.02	.00
☐	1	Jeffrey Leonard	.10	.05	.01
☐	2	Jack Clark	.15	.07	.01
☐	3	Kevin Gross	.05	.02	.00
☐	4	Tommy Herr	.10	.05	.01
☐	5	Bob Boone	.15	.07	.01
☐	6	Rafael Palmeiro	.25	.12	.02
☐	7	John Dopson	.05	.02	.00
☐	8	Willie Randolph	.10	.05	.01
☐	9	Chris Brown	.05	.02	.00
☐	10	Wally Backman	.05	.02	.00
☐	11	Steve Ontiveros	.05	.02	.00
☐	12	Eddie Murray	.15	.07	.01
☐	13	Lance McCullers	.05	.02	.00
☐	14	Spike Owen	.05	.02	.00
☐	15	Rob Murphy	.05	.02	.00
☐	16	Pete O'Brien	.10	.05	.01
☐	17	Ken Williams	.05	.02	.00
☐	18	Nick Esasky	.15	.07	.01
☐	19	Nolan Ryan	1.25	.60	.12
☐	20	Brian Holton	.05	.02	.00
☐	21	Mike Moore	.10	.05	.01
☐	22	Joel Skinner	.05	.02	.00
☐	23	Steve Sax	.15	.07	.01
☐	24	Rick Mahler	.05	.02	.00
☐	25	Mike Aldrete	.05	.02	.00
☐	26	Jesse Orosco	.05	.02	.00
☐	27	Dave LaPoint	.05	.02	.00
☐	28	Walt Terrell	.05	.02	.00
☐	29	Eddie Williams	.05	.02	.00
☐	30	Mike Devereaux	.05	.02	.00
☐	31	Julio Franco	.15	.07	.01
☐	32	Jim Clancy	.05	.02	.00
☐	33	Felix Fermin	.05	.02	.00
☐	34	Curt Wilkerson	.05	.02	.00
☐	35	Bert Blyleven	.15	.07	.01
☐	36	Mel Hall	.10	.05	.01
☐	37	Eric King	.05	.02	.00
☐	38	Mitch Williams	.10	.05	.01
☐	39	Jamie Moyer	.05	.02	.00
☐	40	Rick Rhoden	.05	.02	.00
☐	41	Phil Bradley	.10	.05	.01
☐	42	Paul Kilgus	.05	.02	.00
☐	43	Milt Thompson	.05	.02	.00
☐	44	Jerry Browne	.10	.05	.01
☐	45	Bruce Hurst	.10	.05	.01
☐	46	Claudell Washington	.10	.05	.01

			MINT	EXC	G-VG
☐	47	Todd Benzinger	.10	.05	.01
☐	48	Steve Balboni	.05	.02	.00
☐	49	Oddibe McDowell	.10	.05	.01
☐	50	Charles Hudson	.05	.02	.00
☐	51	Ron Kittle	.10	.05	.01
☐	52	Andy Hawkins	.05	.02	.00
☐	53	Tom Brookens	.05	.02	.00
☐	54	Tom Niedenfuer	.05	.02	.00
☐	55	Jeff Parrett	.05	.02	.00
☐	56	Checklist Card	.05	.02	.00

1989 Donruss Baseball's Best

The 1989 Donruss Baseball's Best set contains 336 standard-size (2 ½" by 3 ½") glossy cards. The fronts are green and yellow, and the backs feature career highlight information. The backs are green, and feature vertically oriented career stats. The cards were distributed as a set in a blister pack through various retail and department store chains.

			MINT	EXC	G-VG
COMPLETE SET (336)			20.00	10.00	2.00
COMMON PLAYER (1-336)			.04	.02	.00
☐	1	Don Mattingly	1.00	.50	.10
☐	2	Tom Glavine	.10	.05	.01
☐	3	Bert Blyleven	.10	.05	.01

			MINT	EXC	G-VG				MINT	EXC	G-VG
☐	4	Andre Dawson	.15	.07	.01	☐	53	Robin Yount	.35	.17	.03
☐	5	Pete O'Brien	.07	.03	.01	☐	54	Danny Jackson	.10	.05	.01
☐	6	Eric Davis	.45	.22	.04	☐	55	Nolan Ryan	.75	.35	.07
☐	7	George Brett	.35	.17	.03	☐	56	Joe Carter	.15	.07	.01
☐	8	Glenn Davis	.20	.10	.02	☐	57	Jose Canseco	1.00	.50	.10
☐	9	Ellis Burks	.30	.15	.03	☐	58	Jody Davis	.04	.02	.00
☐	10	Kirk Gibson	.20	.10	.02	☐	59	Lance Parrish	.07	.03	.01
☐	11	Carlton Fisk	.20	.10	.02	☐	60	Mitch Williams	.07	.03	.01
☐	12	Andres Galarraga	.20	.10	.02	☐	61	Brook Jacoby	.07	.03	.01
☐	13	Alan Trammell	.15	.07	.01	☐	62	Tom Browning	.07	.03	.01
☐	14	Dwight Gooden	.40	.20	.04	☐	63	Kurt Stillwell	.04	.02	.00
☐	15	Paul Molitor	.15	.07	.01	☐	64	Rafael Ramirez	.04	.02	.00
☐	16	Roger McDowell	.07	.03	.01	☐	65	Roger Clemens	.40	.20	.04
☐	17	Doug Drabek	.07	.03	.01	☐	66	Mike Scioscia	.04	.02	.00
☐	18	Kent Hrbek	.15	.07	.01	☐	67	Dave Gallagher	.07	.03	.01
☐	19	Vince Coleman	.20	.10	.02	☐	68	Mark Langston	.20	.10	.02
☐	20	Steve Sax	.15	.07	.01	☐	69	Chet Lemon	.04	.02	.00
☐	21	Roberto Alomar	.20	.10	.02	☐	70	Kevin McReynolds	.10	.05	.01
☐	22	Carney Lansford	.15	.07	.01	☐	71	Rob Deer	.07	.03	.01
☐	23	Will Clark	1.00	.50	.10	☐	72	Tommy Herr	.07	.03	.01
☐	24	Alvin Davis	.10	.05	.01	☐	73	Barry Bonds	.10	.05	.01
☐	25	Bobby Thigpen	.07	.03	.01	☐	74	Frank Viola	.15	.07	.01
☐	26	Ryne Sandberg	.25	.12	.02	☐	75	Pedro Guerrero	.15	.07	.01
☐	27	Devon White	.10	.05	.01	☐	76	Dave Righetti	.10	.05	.01
☐	28	Mike Greenwell	.60	.30	.06	☐	77	Bruce Hurst	.07	.03	.01
☐	29	Dale Murphy	.35	.17	.03	☐	78	Rickey Henderson	.35	.17	.03
☐	30	Jeff Ballard	.10	.05	.01	☐	79	Robby Thompson	.04	.02	.00
☐	31	Kelly Gruber	.07	.03	.01	☐	80	Randy Johnson	.07	.03	.01
☐	32	Julio Franco	.10	.05	.01	☐	81	Harold Baines	.10	.05	.01
☐	33	Bobby Bonilla	.10	.05	.01	☐	82	Calvin Schiraldi	.04	.02	.00
☐	34	Tim Wallach	.07	.03	.01	☐	83	Kirk McCaskill	.04	.02	.00
☐	35	Lou Whitaker	.10	.05	.01	☐	84	Lee Smith	.07	.03	.01
☐	36	Jay Howell	.07	.03	.01	☐	85	John Smoltz	.10	.05	.01
☐	37	Greg Maddux	.10	.05	.01	☐	86	Mickey Tettleton	.10	.05	.01
☐	38	Bill Doran	.07	.03	.01	☐	87	Jimmy Key	.07	.03	.01
☐	39	Danny Tartabull	.15	.07	.01	☐	88	Rafael Palmeiro	.15	.07	.01
☐	40	Darryl Strawberry	.40	.20	.04	☐	89	Sid Bream	.04	.02	.00
☐	41	Ron Darling	.10	.05	.01	☐	90	Dennis Martinez	.07	.03	.01
☐	42	Tony Gwynn	.30	.15	.03	☐	91	Frank Tanana	.04	.02	.00
☐	43	Mark McGwire	.60	.30	.06	☐	92	Eddie Murray	.20	.10	.02
☐	44	Ozzie Smith	.20	.10	.02	☐	93	Shawon Dunston	.10	.05	.01
☐	45	Andy Van Slyke	.10	.05	.01	☐	94	Mike Scott	.15	.07	.01
☐	46	Juan Berenguer	.04	.02	.00	☐	95	Bret Saberhagen	.20	.10	.02
☐	47	Von Hayes	.10	.05	.01	☐	96	David Cone	.20	.10	.02
☐	48	Tony Fernandez	.10	.05	.01	☐	97	Kevin Elster	.07	.03	.01
☐	49	Eric Plunk	.04	.02	.00	☐	98	Jack Clark	.15	.07	.01
☐	50	Ernest Riles	.04	.02	.00	☐	99	Dave Stewart	.20	.10	.02
☐	51	Harold Reynolds	.07	.03	.01	☐	100	Jose Oquendo	.04	.02	.00
☐	52	Andy Hawkins	.04	.02	.00	☐	101	Jose Lind	.04	.02	.00

		MINT	EXC	G-VG			MINT	EXC	G-VG
☐ 102	Gary Gaetti	.10	.05	.01	☐ 151	Steve Farr	.04	.02	.00
☐ 103	Ricky Jordan	.25	.12	.02	☐ 152	Gregg Jefferies	.75	.35	.07
☐ 104	Fred McGriff	.30	.15	.03	☐ 153	Randy Myers	.07	.03	.01
☐ 105	Don Slaught	.04	.02	.00	☐ 154	Garry Templeton	.07	.03	.01
☐ 106	Jose Uribe	.04	.02	.00	☐ 155	Walt Weiss	.15	.07	.01
☐ 107	Jeffrey Leonard	.07	.03	.01	☐ 156	Terry Pendleton	.04	.02	.00
☐ 108	Lee Guetterman	.04	.02	.00	☐ 157	John Smiley	.07	.03	.01
☐ 109	Chris Bosio	.07	.03	.01	☐ 158	Greg Gagne	.04	.02	.00
☐ 110	Barry Larkin	.20	.10	.02	☐ 159	Len Dykstra	.07	.03	.01
☐ 111	Ruben Sierra	.35	.17	.03	☐ 160	Nelson Liriano	.04	.02	.00
☐ 112	Greg Swindell	.10	.05	.01	☐ 161	Alvaro Espinoza	.04	.02	.00
☐ 113	Gary Sheffield	.50	.25	.05	☐ 162	Rick Reuschel	.10	.05	.01
☐ 114	Lonnie Smith	.07	.03	.01	☐ 163	Omar Vizquel UER	.15	.07	.01
☐ 115	Chili Davis	.04	.02	.00		(photo actually			
☐ 116	Damon Berryhill	.10	.05	.01		Darnell Coles)			
☐ 117	Tom Candiotti	.04	.02	.00	☐ 164	Clay Parker	.07	.03	.01
☐ 118	Kal Daniels	.10	.05	.01	☐ 165	Dan Plesac	.07	.03	.01
☐ 119	Mark Gubicza	.10	.05	.01	☐ 166	John Franco	.10	.05	.01
☐ 120	Jim Deshaies	.04	.02	.00	☐ 167	Scott Fletcher	.04	.02	.00
☐ 121	Dwight Evans	.10	.05	.01	☐ 168	Cory Snyder	.10	.05	.01
☐ 122	Mike Morgan	.07	.03	.01	☐ 169	Bo Jackson	1.00	.50	.10
☐ 123	Dan Pasqua	.04	.02	.00	☐ 170	Tommy Gregg	.07	.03	.01
☐ 124	Bryn Smith	.07	.03	.01	☐ 171	Jim Abbott	1.00	.50	.10
☐ 125	Doyle Alexander	.04	.02	.00	☐ 172	Jerome Walton	1.50	.75	.15
☐ 126	Howard Johnson	.15	.07	.01	☐ 173	Doug Jones	.07	.03	.01
☐ 127	Chuck Crim	.04	.02	.00	☐ 174	Todd Benzinger	.07	.03	.01
☐ 128	Darren Daulton	.04	.02	.00	☐ 175	Frank White	.07	.03	.01
☐ 129	Jeff Robinson	.07	.03	.01	☐ 176	Craig Biggio	.20	.10	.02
☐ 130	Kirby Puckett	.40	.20	.04	☐ 177	John Dopson	.04	.02	.00
☐ 131	Joe Magrane	.10	.05	.01	☐ 178	Alfredo Griffin	.04	.02	.00
☐ 132	Jesse Barfield	.10	.05	.01	☐ 179	Melido Perez	.07	.03	.01
☐ 133	Mark Davis	.20	.10	.02	☐ 180	Tim Burke	.07	.03	.01
☐ 134	Dennis Eckersley	.15	.07	.01	☐ 181	Matt Nokes	.10	.05	.01
☐ 135	Mike Krukow	.04	.02	.00	☐ 182	Gary Carter	.20	.10	.02
☐ 136	Jay Buhner	.10	.05	.01	☐ 183	Ted Higuera	.10	.05	.01
☐ 137	Ozzie Guillen	.07	.03	.01	☐ 184	Ken Howell	.04	.02	.00
☐ 138	Rick Sutcliffe	.07	.03	.01	☐ 185	Rey Quinones	.04	.02	.00
☐ 139	Wally Joyner	.20	.10	.02	☐ 186	Wally Backman	.04	.02	.00
☐ 140	Wade Boggs	.50	.25	.05	☐ 187	Tom Brunansky	.10	.05	.01
☐ 141	Jeff Treadway	.04	.02	.00	☐ 188	Steve Balboni	.04	.02	.00
☐ 142	Cal Ripken	.25	.12	.02	☐ 189	Marvell Wynne	.04	.02	.00
☐ 143	Dave Stieb	.10	.05	.01	☐ 190	Dave Henderson	.04	.02	.00
☐ 144	Pete Incaviglia	.10	.05	.01	☐ 191	Don Robinson	.04	.02	.00
☐ 145	Bob Walk	.04	.02	.00	☐ 192	Ken Griffey Jr.	1.50	.75	.15
☐ 146	Nelson Santovenia	.07	.03	.01	☐ 193	Ivan Calderon	.07	.03	.01
☐ 147	Mike Heath	.04	.02	.00	☐ 194	Mike Bielecki	.07	.03	.01
☐ 148	Willie Randolph	.07	.03	.01	☐ 195	Johnny Ray	.07	.03	.01
☐ 149	Paul Kilgus	.04	.02	.00	☐ 196	Rob Murphy	.04	.02	.00
☐ 150	Billy Hatcher	.04	.02	.00	☐ 197	Andres Thomas	.04	.02	.00

			MINT	EXC	G-VG				MINT	EXC	G-VG
☐	198	Phil Bradley	.07	.03	.01	☐	247	Kelly Downs	.04	.02	.00
☐	199	Junior Felix	.35	.17	.03	☐	248	Dave Valle	.04	.02	.00
☐	200	Jeff Russell	.07	.03	.01	☐	249	Ron Kittle	.10	.05	.01
☐	201	Mike LaValliere	.04	.02	.00	☐	250	Steve Wilson	.07	.03	.01
☐	202	Kevin Gross	.04	.02	.00	☐	251	Dick Schofield	.04	.02	.00
☐	203	Keith Moreland	.04	.02	.00	☐	252	Marty Barrett	.07	.03	.01
☐	204	Mike Marshall	.10	.05	.01	☐	253	Dion James	.04	.02	.00
☐	205	Dwight Smith	.75	.35	.07	☐	254	Bob Milacki	.10	.05	.01
☐	206	Jim Clancy	.04	.02	.00	☐	255	Ernie Whitt	.04	.02	.00
☐	207	Kevin Seitzer	.15	.07	.01	☐	256	Kevin Brown	.10	.05	.01
☐	208	Keith Hernandez	.15	.07	.01	☐	257	R.J. Reynolds	.04	.02	.00
☐	209	Bob Ojeda	.07	.03	.01	☐	258	Tim Raines	.20	.10	.02
☐	210	Ed Whitson	.04	.02	.00	☐	259	Frank Williams	.04	.02	.00
☐	211	Tony Phillips	.04	.02	.00	☐	260	Jose Gonzalez	.04	.02	.00
☐	212	Milt Thompson	.04	.02	.00	☐	261	Mitch Webster	.04	.02	.00
☐	213	Randy Kramer	.04	.02	.00	☐	262	Ken Caminiti	.04	.02	.00
☐	214	Randy Bush	.04	.02	.00	☐	263	Bob Boone	.10	.05	.01
☐	215	Randy Ready	.04	.02	.00	☐	264	Dave Magadan	.10	.05	.01
☐	216	Duane Ward	.04	.02	.00	☐	265	Rick Aguilera	.04	.02	.00
☐	217	Jimmy Jones	.07	.03	.01	☐	266	Chris James	.07	.03	.01
☐	218	Scott Garrelts	.07	.03	.01	☐	267	Bob Welch	.07	.03	.01
☐	219	Scott Bankhead	.07	.03	.01	☐	268	Ken Dayley	.04	.02	.00
☐	220	Lance McCullers	.07	.03	.01	☐	269	Junior Ortiz	.04	.02	.00
☐	221	B.J. Surhoff	.07	.03	.01	☐	270	Allan Anderson	.07	.03	.01
☐	222	Chris Sabo	.15	.07	.01	☐	271	Steve Jeltz	.04	.02	.00
☐	223	Steve Buechele	.04	.02	.00	☐	272	George Bell	.15	.07	.01
☐	224	Joel Skinner	.04	.02	.00	☐	273	Roberto Kelly	.20	.10	.02
☐	225	Orel Hershiser	.30	.15	.03	☐	274	Brett Butler	.07	.03	.01
☐	226	Derek Lilliquist	.10	.05	.01	☐	275	Mike Schooler	.10	.05	.01
☐	227	Claudell Washington	.07	.03	.01	☐	276	Ken Phelps	.07	.03	.01
☐	228	Lloyd McClendon	.04	.02	.00	☐	277	Glenn Braggs	.10	.05	.01
☐	229	Felix Fermin	.04	.02	.00	☐	278	Jose Rijo	.04	.02	.00
☐	230	Paul O'Neill	.10	.05	.01	☐	279	Bobby Witt	.07	.03	.01
☐	231	Charlie Leibrandt	.04	.02	.00	☐	280	Jerry Browne	.07	.03	.01
☐	232	Dave Sabo	.04	.02	.00	☐	281	Kevin Mitchell	.45	.22	.04
☐	233	Bob Stanley	.04	.02	.00	☐	282	Craig Worthington	.20	.10	.02
☐	234	Tim Belcher	.10	.05	.01	☐	283	Greg Minton	.04	.02	.00
☐	235	Eric King	.04	.02	.00	☐	284	Nick Esasky	.10	.05	.01
☐	236	Spike Owen	.04	.02	.00	☐	285	John Farrell	.07	.03	.01
☐	237	Mike Henneman	.04	.02	.00	☐	286	Rick Mahler	.04	.02	.00
☐	238	Juan Samuel	.10	.05	.01	☐	287	Tom Gordon	.50	.25	.05
☐	239	Greg Brock	.04	.02	.00	☐	288	Gerald Young	.10	.05	.01
☐	240	John Kruk	.10	.05	.01	☐	289	Jody Reed	.04	.02	.00
☐	241	Glenn Wilson	.07	.03	.01	☐	290	Jeff Hamilton	.04	.02	.00
☐	242	Jeff Reardon	.07	.03	.01	☐	291	Gerald Perry	.04	.02	.00
☐	243	Todd Worrell	.10	.05	.01	☐	292	Hubie Brooks	.07	.03	.01
☐	244	Dave LaPoint	.04	.02	.00	☐	293	Bo Diaz	.04	.02	.00
☐	245	Walt Terrell	.04	.02	.00	☐	294	Terry Puhl	.04	.02	.00
☐	246	Mike Moore	.07	.03	.01	☐	295	Jim Gantner	.04	.02	.00

1989 Donruss Rookies

		MINT	EXC	G-VG
☐ 296	Jeff Parrett	.04	.02	.00
☐ 297	Mike Boddicker	.04	.02	.00
☐ 298	Dan Gladden	.04	.02	.00
☐ 299	Tony Pena	.07	.03	.01
☐ 300	Checklist Card	.04	.02	.00
☐ 301	Tom Henke	.07	.03	.01
☐ 302	Pascual Perez	.07	.03	.01
☐ 303	Steve Bedrosian	.07	.03	.01
☐ 304	Ken Hill	.07	.03	.01
☐ 305	Jerry Reuss	.04	.02	.00
☐ 306	Jim Eisenreich	.07	.03	.01
☐ 307	Jack Howell	.04	.02	.00
☐ 308	Rick Cerone	.04	.02	.00
☐ 309	Tim Leary	.07	.03	.01
☐ 310	Joe Orsulak	.04	.02	.00
☐ 311	Jim Dwyer	.04	.02	.00
☐ 312	Geno Petralli	.04	.02	.00
☐ 313	Rick Honeycutt	.04	.02	.00
☐ 314	Tom Foley	.04	.02	.00
☐ 315	Kenny Rogers	.04	.02	.00
☐ 316	Mike Flanagan	.04	.02	.00
☐ 317	Bryan Harvey	.10	.05	.01
☐ 318	Billy Ripken	.04	.02	.00
☐ 319	Jeff Montgomery	.10	.05	.01
☐ 320	Erik Hanson	.07	.03	.01
☐ 321	Brian Downing	.04	.02	.00
☐ 322	Gregg Olson	.50	.25	.05
☐ 323	Terry Steinbach	.10	.05	.01
☐ 324	Sammy Sosa	.40	.20	.04
☐ 325	Gene Harris	.15	.07	.01
☐ 326	Mike Devereaux	.07	.03	.01
☐ 327	Dennis Cook	.07	.03	.01
☐ 328	David Wells	.04	.02	.00
☐ 329	Checklist Card	.04	.02	.00
☐ 330	Kirt Manwaring	.07	.03	.01
☐ 331	Jim Presley	.04	.02	.00
☐ 332	Checklist Card	.04	.02	.00
☐ 333	Chuck Finley	.07	.03	.01
☐ 334	Rob Dibble	.10	.05	.01
☐ 335	Cecil Espy	.07	.03	.01
☐ 336	Dave Parker	.10	.05	.01

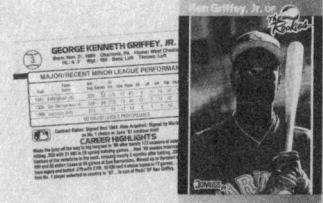

The 1989 Donruss Rookies set contains 56 standard-size (2 ½" by 3 ½") cards. The fronts have green and black borders; the backs are green and feature career highlights. The cards were distributed as a boxed set.

		MINT	EXC	G-VG
COMPLETE SET (56)		27.00	13.50	2.70
COMMON PLAYER (1-56)		.07	.03	.01
☐ 1	Gary Sheffield	1.00	.50	.10
☐ 2	Gregg Jefferies	1.00	.50	.10
☐ 3	Ken Griffey Jr.	3.00	1.50	.30
☐ 4	Tom Gordon	1.00	.50	.10
☐ 5	Billy Spiers	.35	.17	.03
☐ 6	Deion Sanders	1.25	.60	.12
☐ 7	Donn Pall	.10	.05	.01
☐ 8	Steve Carter	.20	.10	.02
☐ 9	Francisco Oliveras	.10	.05	.01
☐ 10	Steve Wilson	.15	.07	.01
☐ 11	Bob Geren	.45	.22	.04
☐ 12	Tony Castillo	.15	.07	.01
☐ 13	Kenny Rogers	.15	.07	.01
☐ 14	Carlos Martinez	.20	.10	.02
☐ 15	Edgar Martinez	.10	.05	.01
☐ 16	Jim Abbott	2.50	1.25	.25
☐ 17	Torey Lovullo	.15	.07	.01
☐ 18	Mark Carreon	.10	.05	.01
☐ 19	Geronimo Berroa	.07	.03	.01

		MINT	EXC	G-VG
☐ 20	Luis Medina	.15	.07	.01
☐ 21	Sandy Alomar Jr.	.50	.25	.05
☐ 22	Bob Milacki	.15	.07	.01
☐ 23	Joe Girardi	.35	.17	.03
☐ 24	German Gonzalez	.07	.03	.01
☐ 25	Craig Worthington	.35	.17	.03
☐ 26	Jerome Walton	4.50	2.25	.45
☐ 27	Gary Wayne	.20	.10	.02
☐ 28	Tim Jones	.10	.05	.01
☐ 29	Dante Bichette	.10	.05	.01
☐ 30	Alexis Infante	.15	.07	.01
☐ 31	Ken Hill	.10	.05	.01
☐ 32	Dwight Smith	1.50	.75	.15
☐ 33	Luis de los Santos	.15	.07	.01
☐ 34	Eric Yelding	.15	.07	.01
☐ 35	Gregg Olson	1.00	.50	.10
☐ 36	Phil Stephenson	.20	.10	.02
☐ 37	Ken Patterson	.10	.05	.01
☐ 38	Rick Wrona	.30	.15	.03
☐ 39	Mike Brumley	.10	.05	.01
☐ 40	Cris Carpenter	.10	.05	.01
☐ 41	Jeff Brantley	.20	.10	.02
☐ 42	Ron Jones	.20	.10	.02
☐ 43	Randy Johnson	.10	.05	.01
☐ 44	Kevin Brown	.15	.07	.01
☐ 45	Ramon Martinez	.20	.10	.02
☐ 46	Greg W. Harris	.15	.07	.01
☐ 47	Steve Finley	.30	.15	.03
☐ 48	Randy Kramer	.10	.05	.01
☐ 49	Erik Hanson	.15	.07	.01
☐ 50	Matt Merullo	.15	.07	.01
☐ 51	Mike Devereaux	.10	.05	.01
☐ 52	Clay Parker	.25	.12	.02
☐ 53	Omar Vizquel	.30	.15	.03
☐ 54	Derek Lilliquist	.15	.07	.01
☐ 55	Junior Felix	1.00	.50	.10
☐ 56	Checklist	.07	.01	.00

1990 Donruss

The 1990 Donruss set contains 716 standard-size (2 ½" by 3 ½") cards. The front borders are bright red. The horizontally oriented backs are amber. Cards numbered 1-26 are Diamond Kings; cards numbered 28-47 are Rated Rookies. Card #716 was added to the set shortly after the set's initial production, necessitating the checklist variation on card #700. The set is the largest ever produced by Donruss; unfortunately, it also has a large number of errors, which were corrected after the cards were released. Every All-Star selection in the set has two versions—the statistical heading on the back is either "Recent Major League Performance" or "All-Star Game Performance."

		MINT	EXC	G-VG
COMPLETE SET (716)		24.00	12.00	2.40
COMMON PLAYER (1-716)		.03	.01	.00
☐ 1	Bo Jackson DK	.50	.20	.04
☐ 2	Steve Sax DK	.08	.04	.01
☐ 3A	Ruben Sierra DK ERR (no small line on top border on card back)	1.50	.50	.07
☐ 3B	Ruben Sierra DK COR	.30	.10	.02
☐ 4	Ken Griffey Jr. DK	.50	.25	.05
☐ 5	Mickey Tettleton DK	.06	.03	.00
☐ 6	Dave Stewart DK	.08	.04	.01
☐ 7	Jim Deshaies DK	.06	.03	.00

		MINT	EXC	G-VG
☐	8 John Smoltz DK	.08	.04	.01
☐	9 Mike Bielecki DK	.06	.03	.00
☐	10A Brian Downing DK ERR (reverse negative on card front)	1.75	.75	.15
☐	10B Brian Downing DK COR	.10	.04	.01
☐	11 Kevin Mitchell DK	.15	.07	.01
☐	12 Kelly Gruber DK	.06	.03	.00
☐	13 Joe Magrane DK	.08	.04	.01
☐	14 John Franco DK	.08	.04	.01
☐	15 Ozzie Guillen DK	.06	.03	.00
☐	16 Lou Whitaker DK	.08	.04	.01
☐	17 John Smiley DK	.06	.03	.00
☐	18 Howard Johnson DK	.10	.05	.01
☐	19 Willie Randolph DK	.06	.03	.00
☐	20 Chris Bosio DK	.06	.03	.00
☐	21 Tommy Herr DK	.06	.03	.00
☐	22 Dan Gladden DK	.06	.03	.00
☐	23 Ellis Burks DK	.15	.07	.01
☐	24 Pete O'Brien DK	.06	.03	.00
☐	25 Bryn Smith DK	.06	.03	.00
☐	26 Ed Whitson DK	.06	.03	.00
☐	27 DK Checklist	.06	.01	.00
☐	28 Robin Ventura	.50	.25	.05
☐	29 Todd Zeile	1.25	.60	.12
☐	30 Sandy Alomar Jr.	.25	.12	.02
☐	31 Kent Mercker	.35	.17	.03
☐	32 Ben McDonald	1.75	.85	.17
☐	33A Juan Gonzalez ERR (reverse negative)	5.00	2.50	.50
☐	33B Juan Gonzalez COR	.75	.35	.07
☐	34 Eric Anthony	1.50	.75	.15
☐	35 Mike Fetters	.20	.10	.02
☐	36 Marquis Grissom	.50	.25	.05
☐	37 Greg Vaughn	1.25	.60	.12
☐	38 Brian Dubois	.15	.07	.01
☐	39 Steve Avery	.35	.17	.03
☐	40 Mark Gardner	.15	.07	.01
☐	41 Andy Benes	.40	.20	.04
☐	42 Delino DeShields	.35	.17	.03
☐	43 Scott Coolbaugh	.25	.12	.02
☐	44 Pat Combs	.35	.17	.03
☐	45 Alex Sanchez	.10	.05	.01
☐	46 Kelly Mann	.15	.07	.01
☐	47 Julio Machado	.20	.10	.02
☐	48 Pete Incaviglia	.08	.04	.01
☐	49 Shawon Dunston	.08	.04	.01
☐	50 Jeff Treadway	.03	.01	.00
☐	51 Jeff Ballard	.06	.03	.00
☐	52 Claudell Washington	.06	.03	.00
☐	53 Juan Samuel	.08	.04	.01
☐	54 John Smiley	.06	.03	.00
☐	55 Rob Deer	.06	.03	.00
☐	56 Geno Petralli	.03	.01	.00
☐	57 Chris Bosio	.06	.03	.00
☐	58 Carlton Fisk	.10	.05	.01
☐	59 Kirt Manwaring	.03	.01	.00
☐	60 Chet Lemon	.03	.01	.00
☐	61 Bo Jackson	.50	.25	.05
☐	62 Doyle Alexander	.03	.01	.00
☐	63 Pedro Guerrero	.08	.04	.01
☐	64 Allan Anderson	.06	.03	.00
☐	65 Greg Harris	.03	.01	.00
☐	66 Mike Greenwell	.25	.12	.02
☐	67 Walt Weiss	.08	.04	.01
☐	68 Wade Boggs	.25	.12	.02
☐	69 Jim Clancy	.03	.01	.00
☐	70 Junior Felix	.35	.17	.03
☐	71 Barry Larkin	.10	.05	.01
☐	72 Dave LaPoint	.03	.01	.00
☐	73 Joel Skinner	.03	.01	.00
☐	74 Jesse Barfield	.08	.04	.01
☐	75 Tommy Herr	.03	.01	.00
☐	76 Ricky Jordan	.20	.10	.02
☐	77 Eddie Murray	.10	.05	.01
☐	78 Steve Sax	.08	.04	.01
☐	79 Tim Belcher	.06	.03	.00
☐	80 Danny Jackson	.06	.03	.00
☐	81 Kent Hrbek	.08	.04	.01
☐	82 Milt Thompson	.03	.01	.00
☐	83 Brook Jacoby	.06	.03	.00
☐	84 Mike Marshall	.08	.04	.01
☐	85 Kevin Seitzer	.08	.04	.01
☐	86 Tony Gwynn	.20	.10	.02
☐	87 Dave Stieb	.08	.04	.01
☐	88 Dave Smith	.03	.01	.00
☐	89 Bret Saberhagen	.10	.05	.01
☐	90 Alan Trammell	.08	.04	.01
☐	91 Tony Phillips	.03	.01	.00
☐	92 Doug Drabek	.03	.01	.00
☐	93 Jeffrey Leonard	.06	.03	.00
☐	94 Wally Joyner	.08	.04	.01
☐	95 Carney Lansford	.08	.04	.01
☐	96 Cal Ripken	.12	.06	.01
☐	97 Andres Galarraga	.08	.04	.01
☐	98 Kevin Mitchell	.20	.10	.02
☐	99 Howard Johnson	.10	.05	.01

			MINT	EXC	G-VG				MINT	EXC	G-VG
☐	100	Checklist Card	.06	.01	.00	☐	149	Tony Fernandez	.08	.04	.01
☐	101	Melido Perez	.03	.01	.00	☐	150	Dave Stewart	.08	.04	.01
☐	102	Spike Owen	.03	.01	.00	☐	151	Gary Gaetti	.08	.04	.01
☐	103	Paul Molitor	.08	.04	.01	☐	152	Kevin Elster	.06	.03	.00
☐	104	Geronimo Berroa	.03	.01	.00	☐	153	Gerald Perry	.03	.01	.00
☐	105	Ryne Sandberg	.12	.06	.01	☐	154	Jesse Orosco	.03	.01	.00
☐	106	Bryn Smith	.06	.03	.00	☐	155	Wally Backman	.03	.01	.00
☐	107	Steve Buechele	.03	.01	.00	☐	156	Dennis Martinez	.03	.01	.00
☐	108	Jim Abbott	.75	.35	.07	☐	157	Rick Sutcliffe	.08	.04	.01
☐	109	Alvin Davis	.08	.04	.01	☐	158	Greg Maddux	.08	.04	.01
☐	110	Lee Smith	.06	.03	.00	☐	159	Andy Hawkins	.03	.01	.00
☐	111	Roberto Alomar	.08	.04	.01	☐	160	John Kruk	.06	.03	.00
☐	112	Rick Reuschel	.06	.03	.00	☐	161	Jose Oquendo	.03	.01	.00
☐	113	Kelly Gruber	.06	.03	.00	☐	162	John Dopson	.03	.01	.00
☐	114	Joe Carter	.10	.05	.01	☐	163	Joe Magrane	.08	.04	.01
☐	115	Jose Rijo	.03	.01	.00	☐	164	Bill Ripken	.03	.01	.00
☐	116	Greg Minton	.03	.01	.00	☐	165	Fred Manrique	.03	.01	.00
☐	117	Bob Ojeda	.06	.03	.00	☐	166	Nolan Ryan	.25	.12	.02
☐	118	Glenn Davis	.10	.05	.01	☐	167	Damon Berryhill	.08	.04	.01
☐	119	Jeff Reardon	.06	.03	.00	☐	168	Dale Murphy	.12	.06	.01
☐	120	Kurt Stillwell	.03	.01	.00	☐	169	Mickey Tettleton	.06	.03	.00
☐	121	John Smoltz	.10	.05	.01	☐	170	Kirk McCaskill	.03	.01	.00
☐	122	Dwight Evans	.08	.04	.01	☐	171	Dwight Gooden	.20	.10	.02
☐	123	Eric Yelding	.10	.05	.01	☐	172	Jose Lind	.03	.01	.00
☐	124	John Franco	.08	.04	.01	☐	173	B.J. Surhoff	.06	.03	.00
☐	125	Jose Canseco	.50	.25	.05	☐	174	Ruben Sierra	.25	.12	.02
☐	126	Barry Bonds	.08	.04	.01	☐	175	Dan Plesac	.06	.03	.00
☐	127	Lee Guetterman	.03	.01	.00	☐	176	Dan Pasqua	.03	.01	.00
☐	128	Jack Clark	.08	.04	.01	☐	177	Kelly Downs	.03	.01	.00
☐	129	Dave Valle	.03	.01	.00	☐	178	Matt Nokes	.06	.03	.00
☐	130	Hubie Brooks	.06	.03	.00	☐	179	Luis Aquino	.03	.01	.00
☐	131	Ernest Riles	.03	.01	.00	☐	180	Frank Tanana	.03	.01	.00
☐	132	Mike Morgan	.03	.01	.00	☐	181	Tony Pena	.06	.03	.00
☐	133	Steve Jeltz	.03	.01	.00	☐	182	Dan Gladden	.03	.01	.00
☐	134	Jeff Robinson	.06	.03	.00	☐	183	Bruce Hurst	.06	.03	.00
☐	135	Ozzie Guillen	.06	.03	.00	☐	184	Roger Clemens	.25	.12	.02
☐	136	Chili Davis	.06	.03	.00	☐	185	Mark McGwire	.25	.12	.02
☐	137	Mitch Webster	.03	.01	.00	☐	186	Rob Murphy	.03	.01	.00
☐	138	Jerry Browne	.03	.01	.00	☐	187	Jim Deshaies	.03	.01	.00
☐	139	Bo Diaz	.03	.01	.00	☐	188	Fred McGriff	.12	.06	.01
☐	140	Robby Thompson	.03	.01	.00	☐	189	Rob Dibble	.06	.03	.00
☐	141	Craig Worthington	.10	.05	.01	☐	190	Don Mattingly	.50	.25	.05
☐	142	Julio Franco	.08	.04	.01	☐	191	Felix Fermin	.03	.01	.00
☐	143	Brian Holman	.03	.01	.00	☐	192	Roberto Kelly	.10	.05	.01
☐	144	George Brett	.12	.06	.01	☐	193	Dennis Cook	.08	.04	.01
☐	145	Tom Glavine	.06	.03	.00	☐	194	Darren Daulton	.03	.01	.00
☐	146	Robin Yount	.25	.12	.02	☐	195	Alfredo Griffin	.03	.01	.00
☐	147	Gary Carter	.08	.04	.01	☐	196	Eric Plunk	.03	.01	.00
☐	148	Ron Kittle	.06	.03	.00	☐	197	Orel Hershiser	.10	.05	.01

			MINT	EXC	G-VG				MINT	EXC	G-VG
☐	198	Paul O'Neill	.08	.04	.01	☐	247	Gene Harris	.15	.07	.01
☐	199	Randy Bush	.03	.01	.00	☐	248	Kevin Gross	.03	.01	.00
☐	200	Checklist Card	.06	.01	.00	☐	249	Brett Butler	.06	.03	.00
☐	201	Ozzie Smith	.10	.05	.01	☐	250	Willie Randolph	.06	.03	.00
☐	202	Pete O'Brien	.06	.03	.00	☐	251	Roger McDowell	.06	.03	.00
☐	203	Jay Howell	.03	.01	.00	☐	252	Rafael Belliard	.03	.01	.00
☐	204	Mark Gubicza	.08	.04	.01	☐	253	Steve Rosenberg	.03	.01	.00
☐	205	Ed Whitson	.03	.01	.00	☐	254	Jack Howell	.03	.01	.00
☐	206	George Bell	.08	.04	.01	☐	255	Marvell Wynne	.03	.01	.00
☐	207	Mike Scott	.08	.04	.01	☐	256	Tom Candiotti	.03	.01	.00
☐	208	Charlie Leibrandt	.03	.01	.00	☐	257	Todd Benzinger	.03	.01	.00
☐	209	Mike Heath	.03	.01	.00	☐	258	Don Robinson	.03	.01	.00
☐	210	Dennis Eckersley	.08	.04	.01	☐	259	Phil Bradley	.06	.03	.00
☐	211	Mike LaValliere	.03	.01	.00	☐	260	Cecil Espy	.03	.01	.00
☐	212	Darnell Coles	.03	.01	.00	☐	261	Scott Bankhead	.06	.03	.00
☐	213	Lance Parrish	.08	.04	.01	☐	262	Frank White	.06	.03	.00
☐	214	Mike Moore	.06	.03	.00	☐	263	Andres Thomas	.03	.01	.00
☐	215	Steve Finley	.12	.06	.01	☐	264	Glenn Braggs	.06	.03	.00
☐	216	Tim Raines	.10	.05	.01	☐	265	David Cone	.08	.04	.01
☐	217	Scott Garrelts	.06	.03	.00	☐	266	Bobby Thigpen	.06	.03	.00
☐	218	Kevin McReynolds	.08	.04	.01	☐	267	Nelson Liriano	.03	.01	.00
☐	219	Dave Gallagher	.03	.01	.00	☐	268	Terry Steinbach	.08	.04	.01
☐	220	Tim Wallach	.06	.03	.00	☐	269	Kirby Puckett	.25	.12	.02
☐	221	Chuck Crim	.03	.01	.00	☐	270	Gregg Jefferies	.35	.17	.03
☐	222	Lonnie Smith	.06	.03	.00	☐	271	Jeff Blauser	.03	.01	.00
☐	223	Andre Dawson	.10	.05	.01	☐	272	Cory Snyder	.08	.04	.01
☐	224	Nelson Santovenia	.06	.03	.00	☐	273	Roy Smith	.03	.01	.00
☐	225	Rafael Palmeiro	.08	.04	.01	☐	274	Tom Foley	.03	.01	.00
☐	226	Devon White	.08	.04	.01	☐	275	Mitch Williams	.06	.03	.00
☐	227	Harold Reynolds	.06	.03	.00	☐	276	Paul Kilgus	.03	.01	.00
☐	228	Ellis Burks	.15	.07	.01	☐	277	Don Slaught	.03	.01	.00
☐	229	Mark Parent	.03	.01	.00	☐	278	Von Hayes	.08	.04	.01
☐	230	Will Clark	.50	.25	.05	☐	279	Vince Coleman	.08	.04	.01
☐	231	Jimmy Key	.06	.03	.00	☐	280	Mike Boddicker	.03	.01	.00
☐	232	John Farrell	.03	.01	.00	☐	281	Ken Dayley	.03	.01	.00
☐	233	Eric Davis	.20	.10	.02	☐	282	Mike Devereaux	.03	.01	.00
☐	234	Johnny Ray	.06	.03	.00	☐	283	Kenny Rogers	.10	.05	.01
☐	235	Darryl Strawberry	.25	.12	.02	☐	284	Jeff Russell	.06	.03	.00
☐	236	Bill Doran	.06	.03	.00	☐	285	Jerome Walton	1.00	.50	.10
☐	237	Greg Gagne	.03	.01	.00	☐	286	Derek Lilliquist	.03	.01	.00
☐	238	Jim Eisenreich	.03	.01	.00	☐	287	Joe Orsulak	.03	.01	.00
☐	239	Tommy Gregg	.03	.01	.00	☐	288	Dick Schofield	.03	.01	.00
☐	240	Marty Barrett	.03	.01	.00	☐	289	Ron Darling	.08	.04	.01
☐	241	Rafael Ramirez	.03	.01	.00	☐	290	Bobby Bonilla	.08	.04	.01
☐	242	Chris Sabo	.08	.04	.01	☐	291	Jim Gantner	.03	.01	.00
☐	243	Dave Henderson	.06	.03	.00	☐	292	Bobby Witt	.06	.03	.00
☐	244	Andy Van Slyke	.08	.04	.01	☐	293	Greg Brock	.03	.01	.00
☐	245	Alvaro Espinoza	.03	.01	.00	☐	294	Ivan Calderon	.06	.03	.00
☐	246	Garry Templeton	.06	.03	.00	☐	295	Steve Bedrosian	.08	.04	.01

		MINT	EXC	G-VG			MINT	EXC	G-VG
☐ 296	Mike Henneman	.03	.01	.00	☐ 345	Erik Hanson	.03	.01	.00
☐ 297	Tom Gordon	.40	.20	.04	☐ 346	Rich Gedman	.03	.01	.00
☐ 298	Lou Whitaker	.08	.04	.01	☐ 347	Bip Roberts	.03	.01	.00
☐ 299	Terry Pendleton	.03	.01	.00	☐ 348	Matt Williams	.12	.06	.01
☐ 300	Checklist Card	.06	.01	.00	☐ 349	Tom Henke	.06	.03	.00
☐ 301	Juan Berenguer	.03	.01	.00	☐ 350	Brad Komminsk	.03	.01	.00
☐ 302	Mark Davis	.08	.04	.01	☐ 351	Jeff Reed	.03	.01	.00
☐ 303	Nick Esasky	.06	.03	.00	☐ 352	Brian Downing	.03	.01	.00
☐ 304	Rickey Henderson	.20	.10	.02	☐ 353	Frank Viola	.08	.04	.01
☐ 305	Rick Cerone	.03	.01	.00	☐ 354	Terry Puhl	.03	.01	.00
☐ 306	Craig Biggio	.10	.05	.01	☐ 355	Brian Harper	.03	.01	.00
☐ 307	Duane Ward	.03	.01	.00	☐ 356	Steve Farr	.03	.01	.00
☐ 308	Tom Browning	.06	.03	.00	☐ 357	Joe Boever	.03	.01	.00
☐ 309	Walt Terrell	.03	.01	.00	☐ 358	Danny Heep	.03	.01	.00
☐ 310	Greg Swindell	.08	.04	.01	☐ 359	Larry Andersen	.03	.01	.00
☐ 311	Dave Righetti	.08	.04	.01	☐ 360	Rolando Roomes	.06	.03	.00
☐ 312	Mike Maddux	.03	.01	.00	☐ 361	Mike Gallego	.03	.01	.00
☐ 313	Len Dykstra	.06	.03	.00	☐ 362	Bob Kipper	.03	.01	.00
☐ 314	Jose Gonzalez	.03	.01	.00	☐ 363	Clay Parker	.10	.05	.01
☐ 315	Steve Balboni	.03	.01	.00	☐ 364	Mike Pagliarulo	.06	.03	.00
☐ 316	Mike Scioscia	.03	.01	.00	☐ 365	Ken Griffey Jr. UER (signed through 1990, should be 1991)	1.00	.50	.10
☐ 317	Ron Oester	.03	.01	.00					
☐ 318	Gary Wayne	.10	.05	.01					
☐ 319	Todd Worrell	.08	.04	.01	☐ 366	Rex Hudler	.03	.01	.00
☐ 320	Doug Jones	.06	.03	.00	☐ 367	Pat Sheridan	.03	.01	.00
☐ 321	Jeff Hamilton	.06	.03	.00	☐ 368	Kirk Gibson	.08	.04	.01
☐ 322	Danny Tartabull	.08	.04	.01	☐ 369	Jeff Parrett	.03	.01	.00
☐ 323	Chris James	.06	.03	.00	☐ 370	Bob Walk	.03	.01	.00
☐ 324	Mike Flanagan	.03	.01	.00	☐ 371	Ken Patterson	.08	.04	.01
☐ 325	Gerald Young	.03	.01	.00	☐ 372	Bryan Harvey	.03	.01	.00
☐ 326	Bob Boone	.08	.04	.01	☐ 373	Mike Bielecki	.06	.03	.00
☐ 327	Frank Williams	.03	.01	.00	☐ 374	Tom Magrann	.12	.06	.01
☐ 328	Dave Parker	.08	.04	.01	☐ 375	Rick Mahler	.03	.01	.00
☐ 329	Sid Bream	.03	.01	.00	☐ 376	Craig Lefferts	.03	.01	.00
☐ 330	Mike Schooler	.06	.03	.00	☐ 377	Gregg Olson	.25	.12	.02
☐ 331	Bert Blyleven	.08	.04	.01	☐ 378	Jamie Moyer	.03	.01	.00
☐ 332	Bob Welch	.06	.03	.00	☐ 379	Randy Johnson	.03	.01	.00
☐ 333	Bob Milacki	.06	.03	.00	☐ 380	Jeff Montgomery	.06	.03	.00
☐ 334	Tim Burke	.06	.03	.00	☐ 381	Marty Clary	.03	.01	.00
☐ 335	Jose Uribe	.03	.01	.00	☐ 382	Bill Spiers	.20	.08	.01
☐ 336	Randy Myers	.03	.01	.00	☐ 383	Dave Magadan	.08	.04	.01
☐ 337	Eric King	.03	.01	.00	☐ 384	Greg Hibbard	.10	.05	.01
☐ 338	Mark Langston	.10	.05	.01	☐ 385	Ernie Whitt	.03	.01	.00
☐ 339	Teddy Higuera	.06	.03	.00	☐ 386	Rick Honeycutt	.03	.01	.00
☐ 340	Oddibe McDowell	.03	.03	.00	☐ 387	Dave West	.06	.03	.00
☐ 341	Lloyd McClendon	.03	.01	.00	☐ 388	Keith Hernandez	.08	.04	.01
☐ 342	Pascual Perez	.06	.03	.00	☐ 389	Jose Alvarez	.03	.01	.00
☐ 343	Kevin Brown	.08	.04	.01	☐ 390	Joey Belle	.50	.25	.05
☐ 344	Chuck Finley	.06	.03	.00	☐ 391	Rick Aguilera	.03	.01	.00

		MINT	EXC	G-VG
☐ 392	Mike Fitzgerald	.03	.01	.00
☐ 393	Dwight Smith	.50	.25	.05
☐ 394	Steve Wilson	.10	.05	.01
☐ 395	Bob Geren	.12	.06	.01
☐ 396	Randy Ready	.03	.01	.00
☐ 397	Ken Hill	.03	.01	.00
☐ 398	Jody Reed	.03	.01	.00
☐ 399	Tom Brunansky	.08	.04	.01
☐ 400	Checklist Card	.06	.01	.00
☐ 401	Rene Gonzales	.03	.01	.00
☐ 402	Harold Baines	.08	.04	.01
☐ 403	Cecilio Guante	.03	.01	.00
☐ 404	Joe Girardi	.10	.05	.01
☐ 405	Sergio Valdez	.10	.05	.01
☐ 406	Mark Williamson	.03	.01	.00
☐ 407	Glenn Hoffman	.03	.01	.00
☐ 408	Jeff Innis	.08	.04	.01
☐ 409	Randy Kramer	.03	.01	.00
☐ 410	Charlie O'Brien	.03	.01	.00
☐ 411	Charlie Hough	.03	.01	.00
☐ 412	Gus Polidor	.03	.01	.00
☐ 413	Ron Karkovice	.03	.01	.00
☐ 414	Trevor Wilson	.10	.05	.01
☐ 415	Kevin Ritz	.15	.07	.01
☐ 416	Gary Thurman	.03	.01	.00
☐ 417	Jeff Robinson	.06	.03	.00
☐ 418	Scott Terry	.03	.01	.00
☐ 419	Tim Laudner	.03	.01	.00
☐ 420	Dennis Rasmussen	.03	.01	.00
☐ 421	Luis Rivera	.03	.01	.00
☐ 422	Jim Corsi	.06	.03	.00
☐ 423	Dennis Lamp	.03	.01	.00
☐ 424	Ken Caminiti	.03	.01	.00
☐ 425	David Wells	.03	.01	.00
☐ 426	Norm Charlton	.03	.01	.00
☐ 427	Deion Sanders	.50	.25	.05
☐ 428	Dion James	.03	.01	.00
☐ 429	Chuck Cary	.06	.03	.00
☐ 430	Ken Howell	.03	.01	.00
☐ 431	Steve Lake	.03	.01	.00
☐ 432	Kal Daniels	.08	.04	.01
☐ 433	Lance McCullers	.03	.01	.00
☐ 434	Lenny Harris	.10	.05	.01
☐ 435	Scott Scudder	.15	.07	.01
☐ 436	Gene Larkin	.03	.01	.00
☐ 437	Dan Quisenberry	.06	.03	.00
☐ 438	Steve Olin	.08	.04	.01
☐ 439	Mickey Hatcher	.03	.01	.00
☐ 440	Willie Wilson	.06	.03	.00
☐ 441	Mark Grant	.03	.01	.00
☐ 442	Mookie Wilson	.06	.03	.00
☐ 443	Alex Trevino	.03	.01	.00
☐ 444	Pat Tabler	.03	.01	.00
☐ 445	Dave Bergman	.03	.01	.00
☐ 446	Todd Burns	.06	.03	.00
☐ 447	R.J. Reynolds	.03	.01	.00
☐ 448	Jay Buhner	.08	.04	.01
☐ 449	Lee Stevens	.20	.10	.02
☐ 450	Ron Hassey	.03	.01	.00
☐ 451	Bob Melvin	.03	.01	.00
☐ 452	Dave Martinez	.03	.01	.00
☐ 453	Greg Litton	.20	.10	.02
☐ 454	Mark Carreon	.06	.03	.00
☐ 455	Scott Fletcher	.03	.01	.00
☐ 456	Otis Nixon	.03	.01	.00
☐ 457	Tony Fossas	.10	.05	.01
☐ 458	John Russell	.03	.01	.00
☐ 459	Paul Assenmacher	.03	.01	.00
☐ 460	Zane Smith	.03	.01	.00
☐ 461	Jack Daugherty	.12	.06	.01
☐ 462	Rich Monteleone	.10	.05	.01
☐ 463	Greg Briley	.20	.10	.02
☐ 464	Mike Smithson	.03	.01	.00
☐ 465	Benito Santiago	.08	.04	.01
☐ 466	Jeff Brantley	.10	.05	.01
☐ 467	Jose Nunez	.03	.01	.00
☐ 468	Scott Bailes	.03	.01	.00
☐ 469	Ken Griffey Sr.	.08	.04	.01
☐ 470	Bob McClure	.03	.01	.00
☐ 471	Mackey Sasser	.06	.03	.00
☐ 472	Glenn Wilson	.03	.01	.00
☐ 473	Kevin Tapani	.15	.07	.01
☐ 474	Bill Buckner	.06	.03	.00
☐ 475	Ron Gant	.06	.03	.00
☐ 476	Kevin Romine	.03	.01	.00
☐ 477	Juan Agosto	.03	.01	.00
☐ 478	Herm Winningham	.03	.01	.00
☐ 479	Storm Davis	.06	.03	.00
☐ 480	Jeff King	.08	.04	.01
☐ 481	Kevin Mmahat	.12	.06	.01
☐ 482	Carmelo Martinez	.03	.01	.00
☐ 483	Omar Vizquel	.12	.06	.01
☐ 484	Jim Dwyer	.03	.01	.00
☐ 485	Bob Knepper	.03	.01	.00
☐ 486	Dave Anderson	.03	.01	.00
☐ 487	Ron Jones	.06	.03	.00
☐ 488	Jay Bell	.03	.01	.00
☐ 489	Sammy Sosa	.35	.17	.03

		MINT	EXC	G-VG			MINT	EXC	G-VG
☐ 490	Kent Anderson	.10	.05	.01	☐ 538	Joey Cora	.06	.03	.00
☐ 491	Domingo Ramos	.03	.01	.00	☐ 539	Eric Hetzel	.03	.01	.00
☐ 492	Dave Clark	.06	.03	.00	☐ 540	Gene Nelson	.03	.01	.00
☐ 493	Tim Birtsas	.03	.01	.00	☐ 541	Wes Gardner	.03	.01	.00
☐ 494	Ken Oberkfell	.03	.01	.00	☐ 542	Mark Portugal	.03	.01	.00
☐ 495	Larry Sheets	.03	.01	.00	☐ 543	Al Leiter	.06	.03	.00
☐ 496	Jeff Kunkel	.03	.01	.00	☐ 544	Jack Armstrong	.06	.03	.00
☐ 497	Jim Presley	.03	.01	.00	☐ 545	Greg Cadaret	.03	.01	.00
☐ 498	Mike Macfarlane	.03	.01	.00	☐ 546	Rod Nichols	.03	.01	.00
☐ 499	Pete Smith	.03	.01	.00	☐ 547	Luis Polonia	.03	.01	.00
☐ 500	Checklist Card	.06	.01	.00	☐ 548	Charlie Hayes	.08	.04	.01
☐ 501	Gary Sheffield	.35	.17	.03	☐ 549	Dickie Thon	.03	.01	.00
☐ 502	Terry Bross	.12	.06	.01	☐ 550	Tim Crews	.03	.01	.00
☐ 503	Jerry Kutzler	.12	.06	.01	☐ 551	Dave Winfield	.10	.05	.01
☐ 504	Lloyd Moseby	.06	.03	.00	☐ 552	Mike Davis	.03	.01	.00
☐ 505	Curt Young	.03	.01	.00	☐ 553	Ron Robinson	.03	.01	.00
☐ 506	Al Newman	.03	.01	.00	☐ 554	Carmen Castillo	.03	.01	.00
☐ 507	Keith Miller	.03	.01	.00	☐ 555	John Costello	.03	.01	.00
☐ 508	Mike Stanton	.20	.10	.02	☐ 556	Bud Black	.03	.01	.00
☐ 509	Rich Yett	.03	.01	.00	☐ 557	Rick Dempsey	.03	.01	.00
☐ 510	Tim Drummond	.12	.06	.01	☐ 558	Jim Acker	.03	.01	.00
☐ 511	Joe Hesketh	.03	.01	.00	☐ 559	Eric Show	.03	.01	.00
☐ 512	Rick Wrona	.20	.10	.02	☐ 560	Pat Borders	.03	.01	.00
☐ 513	Luis Salazar	.03	.01	.00	☐ 561	Danny Darwin	.03	.01	.00
☐ 514	Hal Morris	.03	.01	.00	☐ 562	Rick Luecken	.10	.05	.01
☐ 515	Terry Mulholland	.03	.01	.00	☐ 563	Edwin Nunez	.03	.01	.00
☐ 516	John Morris	.03	.01	.00	☐ 564	Felix Jose	.03	.01	.00
☐ 517	Carlos Quintana	.03	.01	.00	☐ 565	John Cangelosi	.03	.01	.00
☐ 518	Frank DiPino	.03	.01	.00	☐ 566	Bill Swift	.03	.01	.00
☐ 519	Randy Milligan	.10	.05	.01	☐ 567	Bill Schroeder	.03	.01	.00
☐ 520	Chad Kreuter	.03	.01	.00	☐ 568	Stan Javier	.03	.01	.00
☐ 521	Mike Jeffcoat	.03	.01	.00	☐ 569	Jim Traber	.03	.01	.00
☐ 522	Mike Harkey	.06	.03	.00	☐ 570	Wallace Johnson	.03	.01	.00
☐ 523	Andy Nezelek UER (wrong birth year)	.03	.01	.00	☐ 571	Donell Nixon	.03	.01	.00
					☐ 572	Sid Fernandez	.08	.04	.01
☐ 524	Dave Schmidt	.03	.01	.00	☐ 573	Lance Johnson	.03	.01	.00
☐ 525	Tony Armas	.06	.03	.00	☐ 574	Andy McGaffigan	.03	.01	.00
☐ 526	Barry Lyons	.03	.01	.00	☐ 575	Mark Knudson	.03	.01	.00
☐ 527	Rick Reed	.10	.05	.01	☐ 576	Tommy Greene	.35	.17	.03
☐ 528	Jerry Reuss	.03	.01	.00	☐ 577	Mark Grace	.35	.17	.03
☐ 529	Dean Palmer	.30	.15	.03	☐ 578	Larry Walker	.20	.10	.02
☐ 530	Jeff Peterek	.12	.06	.01	☐ 579	Mike Stanley	.03	.01	.00
☐ 531	Carlos Martinez	.20	.10	.02	☐ 580	Mike Witt	.06	.03	.00
☐ 532	Atlee Hammaker	.03	.01	.00	☑ 581	Scott Bradley	.03	.01	.00
☐ 533	Mike Brumley	.03	.01	.00	☐ 582	Greg Harris	.03	.01	.00
☐ 534	Terry Leach	.03	.01	.00	☐ 583	Kevin Hickey	.03	.01	.00
☐ 535	Doug Strange	.12	.06	.01	☐ 584	Lee Mazzilli	.03	.01	.00
☐ 536	Jose DeLeon	.06	.03	.00	☐ 585	Jeff Pico	.03	.01	.00
☐ 537	Shane Rawley	.03	.01	.00	☐ 586	Joe Oliver	.12	.06	.01

		MINT	EXC	G-VG
☐ 587	Willie Fraser	.03	.01	.00
☐ 588	Carl Yastrzemski PUZ Puzzle Card	.06	.03	.00
☐ 589	Kevin Bass	.06	.03	.00
☐ 590	John Moses	.03	.01	.00
☐ 591	Tom Pagnozzi	.03	.01	.00
☐ 592	Tony Castillo	.08	.04	.01
☐ 593	Jerald Clark	.03	.01	.00
☐ 594	Dan Schatzeder	.03	.01	.00
☐ 595	Luis Quinones	.03	.01	.00
☐ 596	Pete Harnisch	.03	.01	.00
☐ 597	Gary Redus	.03	.01	.00
☐ 598	Mel Hall	.06	.03	.00
☐ 599	Rick Schu	.03	.01	.00
☐ 600	Checklist Card	.06	.01	.00
☐ 601	Mike Kingery	.03	.01	.00
☐ 602	Terry Kennedy	.03	.01	.00
☐ 603	Mike Sharperson	.03	.01	.00
☐ 604	Don Carman	.03	.01	.00
☐ 605	Jim Gott	.03	.01	.00
☐ 606	Donn Pall	.08	.04	.01
☐ 607	Rance Mulliniks	.03	.01	.00
☐ 608	Curt Wilkerson	.03	.01	.00
☐ 609	Mike Felder	.03	.01	.00
☐ 610	Guillermo Hernandez	.06	.03	.00
☐ 611	Candy Maldonado	.03	.01	.00
☐ 612	Mark Thurmond	.03	.01	.00
☐ 613	Rick Leach	.03	.01	.00
☐ 614	Jerry Reed	.03	.01	.00
☐ 615	Franklin Stubbs	.03	.01	.00
☐ 616	Billy Hatcher	.03	.01	.00
☐ 617	Don August	.03	.01	.00
☐ 618	Tim Teufel	.03	.01	.00
☐ 619	Shawn Hillegas	.03	.01	.00
☐ 620	Manny Lee	.03	.01	.00
☐ 621	Gary Ward	.03	.01	.00
☐ 622	Mark Guthrie	.12	.06	.01
☐ 623	Jeff Musselman	.03	.01	.00
☐ 624	Mark Lemke	.03	.01	.00
☐ 625	Fernando Valenzuela	.10	.05	.01
☐ 626	Paul Sorrento	.15	.07	.01
☐ 627	Glenallen Hill	.15	.07	.01
☐ 628	Les Lancaster	.03	.01	.00
☐ 629	Vance Law	.03	.01	.00
☐ 630	Randy Velarde	.06	.03	.00
☐ 631	Todd Frohwirth	.03	.01	.00
☐ 632	Willie McGee	.08	.04	.01
☐ 633	Dennis Boyd	.06	.03	.00
☐ 634	Cris Carpenter	.03	.01	.00

		MINT	EXC	G-VG
☐ 635	Brian Holton	.03	.01	.00
☐ 636	Tracy Jones	.03	.01	.00
☐ 637A	Terry Steinbach AS (Recent Major League Performance)	.50	.25	.05
☐ 637B	Terry Steinbach AS (All-Star Game Performance)	.10	.05	.01
☐ 638	Brady Anderson	.06	.03	.00
☐ 639	Jack Morris	.08	.04	.01
☐ 640	Jaime Navarro	.15	.07	.01
☐ 641	Darrin Jackson	.03	.01	.00
☐ 642	Mike Dyer	.15	.07	.01
☐ 643	Mike Schmidt	.25	.12	.02
☐ 644	Henry Cotto	.03	.01	.00
☐ 645	John Cerutti	.03	.01	.00
☐ 646	Francisco Cabrera	.20	.10	.02
☐ 647	Scott Sanderson	.03	.01	.00
☐ 648	Brian Meyer	.03	.01	.00
☐ 649	Ray Searage	.03	.01	.00
☐ 650A	Bo Jackson AS (Recent Major League Performance)	2.00	1.00	.20
☐ 650B	Bo Jackson AS (All-Star Game Performance)	.50	.20	.04
☐ 651	Steve Lyons	.03	.01	.00
☐ 652	Mike LaCoss	.03	.01	.00
☐ 653	Ted Power	.03	.01	.00
☐ 654A	Howard Johnson AS (Recent Major League Performance)	.75	.35	.07
☐ 654B	Howard Johnson AS (All-Star Game Performance)	.15	.07	.01
☐ 655	Mauro Gozzo	.15	.07	.01
☐ 656	Mike Blowers	.20	.10	.02
☐ 657	Paul Gibson	.03	.01	.00
☐ 658	Neal Heaton	.03	.01	.00
☐ 659A	Nolan Ryan 5000K (#665 King of Kings back) ERR	10.00	5.00	1.00
☐ 659B	Nolan Ryan 5000K COR	.75	.35	.07
☐ 660A	Harold Baines AS (black line through star on front; Recent Major League Performance)	10.00	4.00	.75

	MINT	EXC	G-VG
☐ 660B Harold Baines AS ... (black line through star on front; All-Star Game Performance)	10.00	4.00	.75
☐ 660C Harold Baines AS ... (black line behind star on front; Recent Major League Performance)	10.00	4.00	.75
☐ 660D Harold Baines AS ... (black line behind star on front; All-Star Game Performance)	.15	.07	.01
☐ 661 Gary Pettis	.03	.01	.00
☐ 662 Clint Zavaras	.12	.06	.01
☐ 663A Rick Reuschel AS ... (Recent Major League Performance)	.50	.25	.05
☐ 663B Rick Reuschel AS ... (All-Star Game Performance)	.10	.05	.01
☐ 664 Alejandro Pena	.03	.01	.00
☐ 665A Nolan Ryan KING (#659 5000 K back) ERR	10.00	5.00	1.00
☐ 665B Nolan Ryan KING COR	.75	.35	.07
☐ 666 Ricky Horton	.03	.01	.00
☐ 667 Curt Schilling	.03	.01	.00
☐ 668 Bill Landrum	.03	.01	.00
☐ 669 Todd Stottlemyre	.06	.03	.00
☐ 670 Tim Leary	.06	.03	.00
☐ 671 John Wetteland	.25	.12	.02
☐ 672 Calvin Schiraldi	.03	.01	.00
☐ 673A Ruben Sierra AS ... (Recent Major League Performance)	1.00	.50	.10
☐ 673B Ruben Sierra AS ... (All-Star Game Performance)	.20	.10	.02
☐ 674A Pedro Guerrero AS ... (Recent Major League Performance)	.50	.25	.05
☐ 674B Pedro Guerrero AS ... (All-Star Game Performance)	.10	.05	.01
☐ 675 Ken Phelps	.03	.01	.00
☐ 676A Cal Ripken AS ..... (Recent Major League Performance)	.75	.35	.07
☐ 676B Cal Ripken AS ..... (All-Star Game Performance)	.15	.07	.01
☐ 677 Denny Walling	.03	.01	.00
☐ 678 Goose Gossage	.06	.03	.00
☐ 679 Gary Mielke	.10	.05	.01
☐ 680 Bill Bathe	.03	.01	.00
☐ 681 Tom Lawless	.03	.01	.00
☐ 682 Xavier Hernandez	.12	.06	.01
☐ 683A Kirby Puckett AS .... (Recent Major League Performance)	1.00	.50	.10
☐ 683B Kirby Puckett AS .... (All-Star Game Performance)	.20	.10	.02
☐ 684 Mariano Duncan	.03	.01	.00
☐ 685 Ramon Martinez	.08	.04	.01
☐ 686 Tim Jones	.03	.01	.00
☐ 687 Tom Filer	.03	.01	.00
☐ 688 Steve Lombardozzi	.03	.01	.00
☐ 689 Bernie Williams	.40	.20	.04
☐ 690 Chip Hale	.15	.07	.01
☐ 691 Beau Allred	.15	.07	.01
☐ 692A Ryne Sandberg AS ... (Recent Major League Performance)	1.00	.50	.10
☐ 692B Ryne Sandberg AS ... (All-Star Game Performance)	.20	.10	.02
☐ 693 Jeff Huson	.12	.06	.01
☐ 694 Curt Ford	.03	.01	.00
☐ 695A Eric Davis AS .... (Recent Major League Performance)	1.00	.50	.10
☐ 695B Eric Davis AS ...... (All-Star Game Performance)	.20	.10	.02
☐ 696 Scott Lusader	.03	.01	.00
☐ 697A Mark McGwire AS ... (Recent Major League Performance)	1.00	.50	.10
☐ 697B Mark McGwire AS ... (All-Star Game Performance)	.20	.10	.02
☐ 698 Steve Cummings	.12	.06	.01
☐ 699 George Canale	.20	.10	.02

		MINT	EXC	G-VG
☐	700A Checklist Card ..... (#716 not listed)	1.00	.10	.02
☐	700B Checklist Card ..... (#716 listed)	.10	.01	.00
☐	701A Julio Franco AS .... (Recent Major League Performance)	.50	.25	.05
☐	701B Julio Franco AS .... (All-Star Game Performance)	.10	.05	.01
☐	702 Dave Johnson (P) ...	.15	.07	.01
☐	703A Dave Stewart AS ... (Recent Major League Performance)	.50	.25	.05
☐	703B Dave Stewart AS ... (All-Star Game Performance)	.10	.05	.01
☐	704 Dave Justice	.20	.10	.02
☐	705A Tony Gwynn AS .... (Recent Major League Performance)	.75	.35	.07
☐	705B Tony Gwynn AS .... (All-Star Game Performance)	.15	.07	.01
☐	706 Greg Myers	.03	.01	.00
☐	707A Will Clark AS ...... (Recent Major League Performance)	2.00	1.00	.20
☐	707B Will Clark AS ...... (All-Star Game Performance)	.40	.20	.04
☐	708A Benito Santiago AS . (Recent Major League Performance)	.50	.25	.05
☐	708B Benito Santiago AS . (All-Star Game Performance)	.10	.05	.01
☐	709 Larry McWilliams ...	.03	.01	.00
☐	710A Ozzie Smith AS .... (Recent Major League Performance)	.50	.25	.05
☐	710B Ozzie Smith AS .... (All-Star Game Performance)	.10	.05	.01
☐	711 John Olerud	2.50	1.00	.20
☐	712A Wade Boggs AS .... (Recent Major League Performance)	1.00	.50	.10
☐	712B Wade Boggs AS .... (All-Star Game Performance)	.20	.10	.02

		MINT	EXC	G-VG
☐	713 Gary Eave	.12	.06	.01
☐	714 Bob Tewksbury	.03	.01	.00
☐	715A Kevin Mitchell AS ... (Recent Major League Performance)	.75	.35	.07
☐	715B Kevin Mitchell AS ... (All-Star Game Performance)	.15	.07	.01
☐	716 Bart Giamatti	1.00	.50	.10

1990 Donruss Bonus MVP's

The 1990 Donruss Bonus MVP's set contains 26 standard-size (2 ½" by 3 ½") cards. The front borders are bright red. The horizontally oriented backs are amber. These cards were randomly distributed in all 1990 Donruss un-opened pack formats. The selection of players in the set is Donruss' opinion of each team's MVP. The complete set price below does not include any variation cards.

	MINT	EXC	G-VG
COMPLETE SET (26)	5.00	2.50	.50
COMMON CARD (BC1-BC26) ..	.05	.02	.00
☐ BC1 Bo Jackson	.40	.20	.04

		MINT	EXC	G-VG
☐	BC2 Howard Johnson	.10	.05	.01
☐	BC3 Dave Stewart	.08	.04	.01
☐	BC4 Tony Gwynn	.15	.07	.01
☐	BC5 Orel Hershiser	.12	.06	.01
☐	BC6 Pedro Guerrero	.08	.04	.01
☐	BC7 Tim Raines	.10	.05	.01
☐	BC8 Kirby Puckett	.20	.10	.02
☐	BC9 Alvin Davis	.08	.04	.01
☐	BC10 Ryne Sandberg	.12	.06	.01
☐	BC11 Kevin Mitchell	.12	.06	.01
☐	BC12 John Smoltz UER ... (photo actually Tom Glavine)	.75	.30	.06
☐	BC13 George Bell	.08	.04	.01
☐	BC14 Julio Franco	.08	.04	.01
☐	BC15 Paul Molitor	.08	.04	.01
☐	BC16 Bobby Bonilla	.08	.04	.01
☐	BC17 Mike Greenwell	.15	.07	.01
☐	BC18 Cal Ripken	.12	.06	.01
☐	BC19 Carlton Fisk	.10	.05	.01
☐	BC20 Chili Davis	.05	.02	.00
☐	BC21 Glenn Davis	.08	.04	.01
☐	BC22 Steve Sax	.08	.04	.01
☐	BC23 Eric Davis	.15	.07	.01
☐	BC24 Greg Swindell	.08	.04	.01
☐	BC25 Von Hayes	.08	.04	.01
☐	BC26 Alan Trammell	.10	.05	.01

1959 Fleer

Ted Williams & Jim Thorpe

The cards in this 80-card set measure 2 ½" by
3 ½". The 1959 Fleer set, designated as R418-
1 in the ACC, portrays the life of Ted Williams.
The wording of the wrapper, "Baseball's Great-
est Series," has led to speculation that Fleer
contemplated similar sets honoring other baseball immortals, but chose to develop instead
the format of the 1960 and 1961 issues. Card
number 68, which was withdrawn early in production, is considered scarce and has even
been counterfeited; the fake has a rosy color-
ation and a cross-hatch pattern visible over the
picture area.

		NRMT	VG-E	GOOD
	COMPLETE SET (80)	600.00	300.00	60.00
	COMMON CARDS (1-80)	3.00	1.50	.30
☐	1 The Early Years	15.00	2.00	.40
☐	2 Ted's Idol Babe Ruth	10.00	5.00	1.00
☐	3 Practice Makes ..... Perfect	3.00	1.50	.30
☐	4 Learns Fine Points ..	3.00	1.50	.30
☐	5 Ted's Fame Spreads	3.00	1.50	.30
☐	6 Ted Turns Pro	3.00	1.50	.30
☐	7 From Mound to Plate	3.00	1.50	.30
☐	8 1937 First Full ..... Season	3.00	1.50	.30
☐	9 First Step to Majors .	3.00	1.50	.30
☐	10 Gunning as Pastime .	3.00	1.50	.30
☐	11 First Spring Training . (with Jimmie Foxx)	6.00	3.00	.60

		NRMT	VG-E	GOOD
☐ 12	Burning Up Minors	3.00	1.50	.30
☐ 13	1939 Shows Will Stay	3.00	1.50	.30
☐ 14	Outstanding Rookie '39	3.00	1.50	.30
☐ 15	Licks Sophomore Jinx	3.00	1.50	.30
☐ 16	1941 Greatest Year	3.00	1.50	.30
☐ 17	How Ted Hit .400	3.00	1.50	.30
☐ 18	1941 All Star Hero	3.00	1.50	.30
☐ 19	Ted Wins Triple Crown	3.00	1.50	.30
☐ 20	On to Naval Training	3.00	1.50	.30
☐ 21	Honors for Williams	3.00	1.50	.30
☐ 22	1944 Ted Solos	3.00	1.50	.30
☐ 23	Williams Wins Wings	3.00	1.50	.30
☐ 24	1945 Sharpshooter	3.00	1.50	.30
☐ 25	1945 Ted Discharged	3.00	1.50	.30
☐ 26	Off to Flying Start	3.00	1.50	.30
☐ 27	7/9/46 One Man Show	3.00	1.50	.30
☐ 28	The Williams Shift	3.00	1.50	.30
☐ 29	Ted Hits for Cycle	3.00	1.50	.30
☐ 30	Beating Williams Shift	3.00	1.50	.30
☐ 31	Sox Lose Series	3.00	1.50	.30
☐ 32	Most Valuable Player	3.00	1.50	.30
☐ 33	Another Triple Crown	3.00	1.50	.30
☐ 34	Runs Scored Record	3.00	1.50	.30
☐ 35	Sox Miss Pennant	3.00	1.50	.30
☐ 36	Banner Year for Ted	3.00	1.50	.30
☐ 37	1949 Sox Miss Again	3.00	1.50	.30
☐ 38	1949 Power Rampage	3.00	1.50	.30
☐ 39	1950 Great Start	3.00	1.50	.30
☐ 40	Ted Crashes into Wall	3.00	1.50	.30
☐ 41	1950 Ted Recovers	3.00	1.50	.30
☐ 42	Slowed by Injury	3.00	1.50	.30
☐ 43	Double Play Lead	3.00	1.50	.30
☐ 44	Back to Marines	3.00	1.50	.30
☐ 45	Farewell to Baseball	3.00	1.50	.30
☐ 46	Ready for Combat	3.00	1.50	.30
☐ 47	Ted Crash Lands Jet	3.00	1.50	.30
☐ 48	1953 Ted Returns	3.00	1.50	.30
☐ 49	Smash Return	3.00	1.50	.30
☐ 50	1954 Spring Injury	3.00	1.50	.30
☐ 51	Ted is Patched Up	3.00	1.50	.30
☐ 52	1954 Ted's Comeback	3.00	1.50	.30
☐ 53	Comeback is Success	3.00	1.50	.30
☐ 54	Ted Hooks Big One	3.00	1.50	.30
☐ 55	Retirement "No Go"	3.00	1.50	.30
☐ 56	2000th Hit	3.00	1.50	.30
☐ 57	400th Homer	3.00	1.50	.30
☐ 58	Williams Hits .388	3.00	1.50	.30
☐ 59	Hot September for Ted	3.00	1.50	.30
☐ 60	More Records for Ted	3.00	1.50	.30
☐ 61	1957 Outfielder Ted	3.00	1.50	.30
☐ 62	1958 Sixth Batting Title	3.00	1.50	.30
☐ 63	Ted's All-Star Record	3.00	1.50	.30
☐ 64	Daughter and Daddy	3.00	1.50	.30
☐ 65	1958 August 30	3.00	1.50	.30
☐ 66	1958 Powerhouse	3.00	1.50	.30
☐ 67	Two Famous Fishermen	6.00	3.00	.60
☐ 68	Ted Signs for 1959	350.00	175.00	35.00
☐ 69	A Future Ted Williams	3.00	1.50	.30
☐ 70	Williams and Thorpe	6.00	3.00	.60
☐ 71	Hitting Fund. 1	3.00	1.50	.30
☐ 72	Hitting Fund. 2	3.00	1.50	.30
☐ 73	Hitting Fund. 3	3.00	1.50	.30
☐ 74	Here's How	3.00	1.50	.30
☐ 75	Williams' Value to Sox	3.00	1.50	.30
☐ 76	On Base Record	3.00	1.50	.30
☐ 77	Ted Relaxes	3.00	1.50	.30
☐ 78	Honors for Williams	3.00	1.50	.30
☐ 79	Where Ted Stands	3.00	1.50	.30
☐ 80	Ted's Goals for 1959	6.00	3.00	.60

1960 Fleer

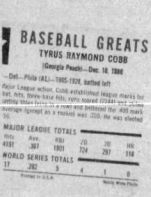

The cards in this 79-card set measure 2 ½" by 3 ½". The cards from the 1960 Fleer series of Baseball Greats are sometimes mistaken for 1930s cards by collectors not familiar with this set. The cards each contain a tinted photo of a baseball immortal, and were issued in one series. There are no known scarcities, although a number 80 card (Pepper Martin reverse with Eddie Collins obverse) exists (this is not considered part of the set). The catalog designation for 1960 Fleer is R418-2. The cards were printed on a 96-card sheet with 17 double prints. These are noted in the checklist below by DP. On the sheet the second Eddie Collins card is typically found in the #80 position.

		NRMT	VG-E	GOOD
	COMPLETE SET (79)	300.00	150.00	30.00
	COMMON PLAYER (1-79)	2.00	1.00	.20
	COMMON PLAYER DP	1.25	.60	.12
☐ 1	Napoleon Lajoie DP ...	10.00	1.00	.20
☐ 2	Christy Mathewson ..	7.50	3.75	.75
☐ 3	George H. Ruth	50.00	25.00	5.00
☐ 4	Carl Hubbell	3.00	1.50	.30
☐ 5	Grover Alexander ...	3.00	1.50	.30
☐ 6	Walter Johnson DP ..	5.00	2.50	.50
☐ 7	Charles A. Bender ..	2.00	1.00	.20
☐ 8	Roger P. Bresnahan .	2.00	1.00	.20
☐ 9	Mordecai P. Brown ..	2.00	1.00	.20
☐ 10	Tristram Speaker ...	3.00	1.50	.30
☐ 11	Arky Vaughan DP ...	1.25	.60	.12
☐ 12	Zachariah Wheat	2.00	1.00	.20
☐ 13	George Sisler	2.00	1.00	.20
☐ 14	Connie Mack	3.00	1.50	.30
☐ 15	Clark C. Griffith	2.00	1.00	.20
☐ 16	Louis Boudreau DP ..	2.00	1.00	.20
☐ 17	Ernest Lombardi	2.00	1.00	.20
☐ 18	Henry Manush	2.00	1.00	.20
☐ 19	Martin Marion	2.00	1.00	.20
☐ 20	Edward Collins DP ...	1.25	.60	.12
☐ 21	James Maranville DP .	1.25	.60	.12
☐ 22	Joseph Medwick	2.00	1.00	.20
☐ 23	Edward Barrow	2.00	1.00	.20
☐ 24	Gordon Cochrane ...	3.00	1.50	.30
☐ 25	James J. Collins	2.00	1.00	.20
☐ 26	Robert Feller DP	6.00	3.00	.60
☐ 27	Lucius Appling	3.00	1.50	.30
☐ 28	Lou Gehrig	25.00	12.50	2.50
☐ 29	Charles Hartnett	2.00	1.00	.20
☐ 30	Charles Klein	2.00	1.00	.20
☐ 31	Anthony Lazzeri DP ..	1.25	.60	.12
☐ 32	Aloysius Simmons ...	2.00	1.00	.20
☐ 33	Wilbert Robinson ...	2.00	1.00	.20
☐ 34	Edgar Rice	2.00	1.00	.20
☐ 35	Herbert Pennock	2.00	1.00	.20
☐ 36	Melvin Ott DP	2.00	1.00	.20
☐ 37	Frank O'Doul	2.00	1.00	.20
☐ 38	John Mize	3.00	1.50	.30
☐ 39	Edmund Miller	2.00	1.00	.20
☐ 40	Joseph Tinker	2.00	1.00	.20
☐ 41	John Baker DP	1.25	.60	.12
☐ 42	Tyrus Cobb	25.00	12.50	2.50
☐ 43	Paul Derringer	2.00	1.00	.20
☐ 44	Adrian Anson	2.00	1.00	.20
☐ 45	James Bottomley ...	2.00	1.00	.20
☐ 46	Edward S. Plank DP .	1.25	.60	.12
☐ 47	Denton (Cy) Young ..	5.00	2.50	.50
☐ 48	Hack Wilson	3.00	1.50	.30
☐ 49	Edward Walsh UER ... (photo actually Ed Walsh Jr.)	2.00	1.00	.20
☐ 50	Frank Chance	2.00	1.00	.20
☐ 51	Arthur Vance DP ...	1.25	.60	.12
☐ 52	William Terry	3.00	1.50	.30
☐ 53	James Foxx	5.00	2.50	.50
☐ 54	Vernon Gomez	3.00	1.50	.30
☐ 55	Branch Rickey	2.00	1.00	.20
☐ 56	Raymond Schalk DP .	1.25	.60	.12
☐ 57	John Evers	2.00	1.00	.20
☐ 58	Charles Gehringer ..	3.00	1.50	.30

			NRMT	VG-E	GOOD
☐	59	Burleigh Grimes	2.00	1.00	.20
☐	60	Robert (Lefty) Grove	4.00	2.00	.40
☐	61	George Waddell DP	1.25	.60	.12
☐	62	John (Honus) Wagner	7.50	3.75	.75
☐	63	Charles (Red) Ruffing	2.00	1.00	.20
☐	64	Kenesaw M. Landis	2.00	1.00	.20
☐	65	Harry Heilmann	2.00	1.00	.20
☐	66	John McGraw DP	2.00	1.00	.20
☐	67	Hugh Jennings	2.00	1.00	.20
☐	68	Harold Newhouser	2.00	1.00	.20
☐	69	Waite Hoyt	2.00	1.00	.20
☐	70	Louis (Bobo) Newsom	2.00	1.00	.20
☐	71	Earl Averill DP	1.25	.60	.12
☐	72	Theodore Williams	40.00	20.00	4.00
☐	73	Warren Giles	2.00	1.00	.20
☐	74	Ford Frick	2.00	1.00	.20
☐	75	Hazen (Kiki) Cuyler	2.00	1.00	.20
☐	76	Paul Waner DP	1.25	.60	.12
☐	77	Harold (Pie) Traynor	2.00	1.00	.20
☐	78	Lloyd Waner	2.00	1.00	.20
☐	79	Ralph Kiner	4.00	2.00	.40
☐	80	Pepper Martin SP (Eddie Collins pictured on obverse)	500.00	250.00	50.00

1961 Fleer

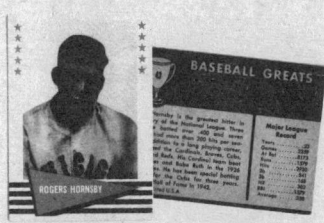

ROGERS HORNSBY

BASEBALL GREATS

*The cards in this 154-card set measure 2 ½"
by 3 ½". In 1961, Fleer continued its Baseball
Greats format by issuing this series of cards.
The set was released in two distinct series,*
*1-88 and 89-154 (of which the latter is more
difficult to obtain). The players within each series are conveniently numbered in alphabetical
order. It appears that this set continued to be
issued the following year by Fleer. The catalog
number for this set is F418-3. In each first series pack Fleer inserted a Major League team
decal and a pennant sticker honoring past
World Series winners.*

			NRMT	VG-E	GOOD
	COMPLETE SET (154)		600.00	300.00	60.00
	COMMON PLAYER (1-88)		1.50	.75	.15
	COMMON PLAYER (89-154)		3.00	1.50	.30
☐	1	Baker/Cobb/Wheat (checklist back)	15.00	2.50	.50
☐	2	Grover C. Alexander	3.00	1.50	.30
☐	3	Nick Altrock	1.50	.75	.15
☐	4	Cap Anson	1.50	.75	.15
☐	5	Earl Averill	1.50	.75	.15
☐	6	Frank Baker	1.50	.75	.15
☐	7	Dave Bancroft	1.50	.75	.15
☐	8	Chief Bender	1.50	.75	.15
☐	9	Jim Bottomley	1.50	.75	.15
☐	10	Roger Bresnahan	1.50	.75	.15
☐	11	Mordecai Brown	1.50	.75	.15
☐	12	Max Carey	1.50	.75	.15
☐	13	Jack Chesbro	1.50	.75	.15
☐	14	Ty Cobb	25.00	12.50	2.50
☐	15	Mickey Cochrane	2.50	1.25	.25
☐	16	Eddie Collins	1.50	.75	.15
☐	17	Earle Combs	1.50	.75	.15
☐	18	Charles Comiskey	1.50	.75	.15
☐	19	Kiki Cuyler	1.50	.75	.15
☐	20	Paul Derringer	1.50	.75	.15
☐	21	Howard Ehmke	1.50	.75	.15
☐	22	W. Evans	1.50	.75	.15
☐	23	Johnny Evers	1.50	.75	.15
☐	24	Urban Faber	1.50	.75	.15
☐	25	Bob Feller	7.50	3.75	.15
☐	26	Wes Ferrell	1.50	.75	.15
☐	27	Lew Fonseca	1.50	.75	.15
☐	28	Jimmy Foxx	5.00	2.50	.50
☐	29	Ford Frick	1.50	.75	.15
☐	30	Frank Frisch	2.50	1.25	.25
☐	31	Lou Gehrig	25.00	12.50	2.50
☐	32	Charlie Gehringer	2.50	1.25	.25
☐	33	Warren Giles	1.50	.75	.15
☐	34	Lefty Gomez	2.50	1.25	.25

		NRMT	VG-E	GOOD
☐ 35	Goose Goslin	1.50	.75	.15
☐ 36	Clark Griffith	1.50	.75	.15
☐ 37	Burleigh Grimes	1.50	.75	.15
☐ 38	Lefty Grove	3.00	1.50	.30
☐ 39	Chick Hafey	1.50	.75	.15
☐ 40	Jesse Haines	1.50	.75	.15
☐ 41	Gabby Hartnett	1.50	.75	.15
☐ 42	Harry Heilmann	1.50	.75	.15
☐ 43	Rogers Hornsby	4.00	2.00	.40
☐ 44	Waite Hoyt	1.50	.75	.15
☐ 45	Carl Hubbell	2.50	1.25	.25
☐ 46	Miller Huggins	1.50	.75	.15
☐ 47	Hugh Jennings	1.50	.75	.15
☐ 48	Ban Johnson	1.50	.75	.15
☐ 49	Walter Johnson	7.50	3.75	.75
☐ 50	Ralph Kiner	3.50	1.75	.35
☐ 51	Chuck Klein	1.50	.75	.15
☐ 52	Johnny Kling	1.50	.75	.15
☐ 53	K.M. Landis	1.50	.75	.15
☐ 54	Tony Lazzeri	1.50	.75	.15
☐ 55	Ernie Lombardi	1.50	.75	.15
☐ 56	Dolf Luque	1.50	.75	.15
☐ 57	Heine Manush	1.50	.75	.15
☐ 58	Marty Marion	1.50	.75	.15
☐ 59	Christy Mathewson	7.50	3.75	.75
☐ 60	John McGraw	2.50	1.25	.25
☐ 61	Joe Medwick	1.50	.75	.15
☐ 62	E. (Bing) Miller	1.50	.75	.15
☐ 63	Johnny Mize	3.50	1.75	.35
☐ 64	John Mostil	1.50	.75	.15
☐ 65	Art Nehf	1.50	.75	.15
☐ 66	Hal Newhouser	1.50	.75	.15
☐ 67	D. (Bobo) Newsom	1.50	.75	.15
☐ 68	Mel Ott	2.50	1.25	.25
☐ 69	Allie Reynolds	1.50	.75	.15
☐ 70	Sam Rice	1.50	.75	.15
☐ 71	Eppa Rixey	1.50	.75	.15
☐ 72	Edd Roush	1.50	.75	.15
☐ 73	Schoolboy Rowe	1.50	.75	.15
☐ 74	Red Ruffing	1.50	.75	.15
☐ 75	Babe Ruth	50.00	25.00	5.00
☐ 76	Joe Sewell	1.50	.75	.15
☐ 77	Al Simmons	1.50	.75	.15
☐ 78	George Sisler	1.50	.75	.15
☐ 79	Tris Speaker	3.00	1.50	.30
☐ 80	Fred Toney	1.50	.75	.15
☐ 81	Dazzy Vance	1.50	.75	.15
☐ 82	Jim Vaughn	1.50	.75	.15
☐ 83	Ed Walsh	1.50	.75	.15
☐ 84	Lloyd Waner	1.50	.75	.15
☐ 85	Paul Waner	1.50	.75	.15
☐ 86	Zack Wheat	1.50	.75	.15
☐ 87	Hack Wilson	2.50	1.25	.25
☐ 88	Jimmy Wilson	1.50	.75	.15
☐ 89	Sisler and Traynor (checklist back)	12.00	2.50	.50
☐ 90	Babe Adams	3.00	1.50	.30
☐ 91	Dale Alexander	3.00	1.50	.30
☐ 92	Jim Bagby	3.00	1.50	.30
☐ 93	Ossie Bluege	3.00	1.50	.30
☐ 94	Lou Boudreau	6.00	3.00	.60
☐ 95	Tom Bridges	3.00	1.50	.30
☐ 96	Donie Bush	3.00	1.50	.30
☐ 97	Dolph Camilli	3.00	1.50	.30
☐ 98	Frank Chance	4.50	2.25	.45
☐ 99	Jimmy Collins	4.50	2.25	.45
☐ 100	Stan Coveleskie	4.50	2.25	.45
☐ 101	Hugh Critz	3.00	1.50	.30
☐ 102	Alvin Crowder	3.00	1.50	.30
☐ 103	Joe Dugan	3.00	1.50	.30
☐ 104	Bibb Falk	3.00	1.50	.30
☐ 105	Rick Ferrell	4.50	2.25	.45
☐ 106	Art Fletcher	3.00	1.50	.30
☐ 107	Dennis Galehouse	3.00	1.50	.30
☐ 108	Chick Galloway	3.00	1.50	.30
☐ 109	Mule Haas	3.00	1.50	.30
☐ 110	Stan Hack	3.00	1.50	.30
☐ 111	Bump Hadley	3.00	1.50	.30
☐ 112	Billy B. Hamilton	4.50	2.25	.45
☐ 113	Joe Hauser	3.00	1.50	.30
☐ 114	Babe Herman	3.00	1.50	.30
☐ 115	Travis Jackson	6.00	3.00	.60
☐ 116	Eddie Joost	3.00	1.50	.30
☐ 117	Addie Joss	6.00	3.00	.60
☐ 118	Joe Judge	3.00	1.50	.30
☐ 119	Joe Kuhel	3.00	1.50	.30
☐ 120	Napoleon Lajoie	9.00	4.50	.90
☐ 121	Dutch Leonard	3.00	1.50	.30
☐ 122	Ted Lyons	4.50	2.25	.45
☐ 123	Connie Mack	9.00	4.50	.90
☐ 124	Rabbit Maranville	4.50	2.25	.45
☐ 125	Fred Marberry	3.00	1.50	.30
☐ 126	Joe McGinnity	6.00	3.00	.60
☐ 127	Oscar Melillo	3.00	1.50	.30
☐ 128	Ray Mueller	3.00	1.50	.30
☐ 129	Kid Nichols	4.50	2.25	.45
☐ 130	Lefty O'Doul	3.00	1.50	.30
☐ 131	Bob O'Farrell	3.00	1.50	.30

		NRMT	VG-E	GOOD
☐ 132	Roger Peckinpaugh	3.00	1.50	.30
☐ 133	Herb Pennock	4.50	2.25	.45
☐ 134	George Pipgras	3.00	1.50	.30
☐ 135	Eddie Plank	6.00	3.00	.60
☐ 136	Ray Schalk	4.50	2.25	.45
☐ 137	Hal Schumacher	3.00	1.50	.30
☐ 138	Luke Sewell	3.00	1.50	.30
☐ 139	Bob Shawkey	3.00	1.50	.30
☐ 140	Riggs Stephenson	3.00	1.50	.30
☐ 141	Billy Sullivan	3.00	1.50	.30
☐ 142	Bill Terry	7.50	3.75	.75
☐ 143	Joe Tinker	4.50	2.25	.45
☐ 144	Pie Traynor	6.00	3.00	.60
☐ 145	Hal Trosky	3.00	1.50	.30
☐ 146	George Uhle	3.00	1.50	.30
☐ 147	Johnny VanderMeer	4.50	2.25	.45
☐ 148	Arky Vaughan	4.50	2.25	.45
☐ 149	Rube Waddell	4.50	2.25	.45
☐ 150	Honus Wagner	25.00	12.50	2.50
☐ 151	Dixie Walker	3.00	1.50	.30
☐ 152	Ted Williams	50.00	25.00	5.00
☐ 153	Cy Young	15.00	7.50	-1.50
☐ 154	Ross Young	9.00	4.50	.90

1963 Fleer

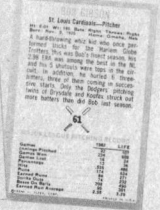

The cards in this 66-card set measure 2 ½" by 3 ½". The Fleer set of current baseball players was marketed in 1963 in a gum card-style waxed wrapper package, which contained a cherry cookie instead of gum. The cards were printed in sheets of 66 with the scarce card of

Adcock apparently being replaced by the un-numbered checklist card for the final press run. The complete set price includes the checklist card. The catalog designation for this set is R418-4.

		NRMT	VG-E	GOOD
☐ 1	Steve Barber	5.00	1.25	.25
☐ 2	Ron Hansen	2.50	1.25	.25
☐ 3	Milt Pappas	3.00	1.50	.30
☐ 4	Brooks Robinson	27.00	13.50	2.70
☐ 5	Willie Mays	50.00	25.00	5.00
☐ 6	Lou Clinton	2.50	1.25	.25
☐ 7	Bill Monbouquette	2.50	1.25	.25
☐ 8	Carl Yastrzemski	50.00	25.00	5.00
☐ 9	Ray Herbert	2.50	1.25	.25
☐ 10	Jim Landis	2.50	1.25	.25
☐ 11	Dick Donovan	2.50	1.25	.25
☐ 12	Tito Francona	2.50	1.25	.25
☐ 13	Jerry Kindall	2.50	1.25	.25
☐ 14	Frank Lary	3.00	1.50	.30
☐ 15	Dick Howser	4.00	2.00	.40
☐ 16	Jerry Lumpe	2.50	1.25	.25
☐ 17	Norm Siebern	2.50	1.25	.25
☐ 18	Don Lee	2.50	1.25	.25
☐ 19	Albie Pearson	2.50	1.25	.25
☐ 20	Bob Rodgers	3.00	1.50	.30
☐ 21	Leon Wagner	2.50	1.25	.25
☐ 22	Jim Kaat	6.00	3.00	.60
☐ 23	Vic Power	2.50	1.25	.25
☐ 24	Rich Rollins	2.50	1.25	.25
☐ 25	Bobby Richardson	5.00	2.50	.50
☐ 26	Ralph Terry	3.00	1.50	.30
☐ 27	Tom Cheney	2.50	1.25	.25
☐ 28	Chuck Cottier	2.50	1.25	.25
☐ 29	Jim Piersall	3.50	1.75	.35
☐ 30	Dave Stenhouse	2.50	1.25	.25
☐ 31	Glen Hobbie	2.50	1.25	.25
☐ 32	Ron Santo	5.00	2.50	.50
☐ 33	Gene Freese	2.50	1.25	.25
☐ 34	Vada Pinson	4.00	2.00	.40
☐ 35	Bob Purkey	2.50	1.25	.25
☐ 36	Joe Amalfitano	2.50	1.25	.25
☐ 37	Bob Aspromonte	2.50	1.25	.25
☐ 38	Dick Farrell	2.50	1.25	.25
☐ 39	Al Spangler	2.50	1.25	.25
☐ 40	Tommy Davis	3.50	1.75	.35
☐ 41	Don Drysdale	18.00	9.00	1.80
☐ 42	Sandy Koufax	50.00	25.00	5.00
☐ 43	Maury Wills	30.00	14.00	2.70
☐ 44	Frank Bolling	2.50	1.25	.25

COMPLETE SET (67)	750.00	375.00	75.00
COMMON PLAYER (1-66)	2.50	1.25	.25

			NRMT	VG-E	GOOD
☐	45	Warren Spahn	18.00	9.00	1.80
☐	46	Joe Adcock SP	85.00	42.50	8.50
☐	47	Roger Craig	4.00	2.00	.40
☐	48	Al Jackson	2.50	1.25	.25
☐	49	Rod Kanehl	2.50	1.25	.25
☐	50	Ruben Amaro	2.50	1.25	.25
☐	51	Johnny Callison	3.00	1.50	.30
☐	52	Clay Dalrymple	2.50	1.25	.25
☐	53	Don Demeter	2.50	1.25	.25
☐	54	Art Mahaffey	2.50	1.25	.25
☐	55	Smokey Burgess	3.00	1.50	.30
☐	56	Roberto Clemente	50.00	25.00	5.00
☐	57	Roy Face	3.50	1.75	.35
☐	58	Vern Law	3.00	1.50	.30
☐	59	Bill Mazeroski	5.00	2.50	.50
☐	60	Ken Boyer	5.00	2.50	.50
☐	61	Bob Gibson	18.00	9.00	1.80
☐	62	Gene Oliver	2.50	1.25	.25
☐	63	Bill White	5.00	2.50	.50
☐	64	Orlando Cepeda	6.00	3.00	.60
☐	65	Jim Davenport	2.50	1.25	.25
☐	66	Billy O'Dell	3.00	1.50	.30
☐	67	Checklist card (unnumbered)	250.00	50.00	10.00

(1-27), Kansas City (28-50), Houston (51-78), New York Yankees (79-109), Los Angeles (110-141), Montreal (142-168), Baltimore (169-195), Cincinnati (196-220), Boston (221-241), Atlanta (242-267), California (268-290), Chicago Cubs (291-315), New York Mets (316-338), Chicago White Sox (339-350 and 352-359), Pittsburgh (360-386), Cleveland (387- 408), Toronto (409-431), San Francisco (432-458), Detroit (459-483), San Diego (484-506), Milwaukee (507-527), St. Louis (528-550), Minnesota (551-571), Oakland (351 and 572-594), Seattle (595-616), and Texas (617-637). Cards 638-660 feature specials and checklists. The cards of pitchers in this set erroneously show a heading (on the card backs) of "Batting Record" over their career pitching statistics. There were three distinct printings: the two following the primary run were designed to correct numerous errors. The variations caused by these multiple printings are noted in the checklist below (P1, P2, or P3). The C. Nettles variation was corrected before the end of the first printing and thus is not included in the complete set consideration for a P1 (first printing) set.

1981 Fleer

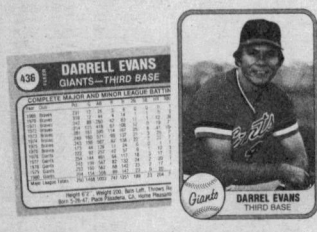

The cards in this 660-card set measure 2 ½ by 3 ½". This issue of cards marks Fleer's first entry into the current player baseball card market since 1963. Players from the same team are conveniently grouped together by number in the set. The teams are ordered (by 1980 standings) as follows: Philadelphia

			MINT	EXC	G-VG
	COMPLETE SET (P1)		33.00	16.00	3.00
	COMPLETE SET (P2)		27.00	13.50	2.70
	COMPLETE SET (P3)		30.00	15.00	3.00
	COMMON PLAYER (1-660)		.03	.01	.00
☐	1	Pete Rose	2.00	.50	.10
☐	2	Larry Bowa	.15	.07	.01
☐	3	Manny Trillo	.03	.01	.00
☐	4	Bob Boone	.20	.10	.02
☐	5	Mike Schmidt See also 640A	1.25	.60	.12
☐	6A	Steve Carlton P1 Pitcher of Year See also 660A Back "1066 Cardinals"	.75	.35	.07
☐	6B	Steve Carlton P2 Pitcher of Year Back "1966 Cardinals"	.65	.30	.06
☐	6C	Steve Carlton P3 "1966 Cardinals"	2.00	1.00	.20
☐	7	Tug McGraw See 657A	.10	.05	.01

			MINT	EXC	G-VG
☐	8	Larry Christenson ...	.03	.01	.00
☐	9	Bake McBride	.03	.01	.00
☐	10	Greg Luzinski	.12	.06	.01
☐	11	Ron Reed	.03	.01	.00
☐	12	Dickie Noles	.03	.01	.00
☐	13	Keith Moreland	.30	.15	.03
☐	14	Bob Walk	.30	.15	.03
☐	15	Lonnie Smith	.15	.07	.01
☐	16	Dick Ruthven	.03	.01	.00
☐	17	Sparky Lyle	.10	.05	.01
☐	18	Greg Gross	.03	.01	.00
☐	19	Garry Maddox	.06	.03	.00
☐	20	Nino Espinosa	.03	.01	.00
☐	21	George Vukovich ...	.03	.01	.00
☐	22	John Vukovich	.03	.01	.00
☐	23	Ramon Aviles	.03	.01	.00
☐	24A	Ken Saucier P1	.06	.03	.00
		Name on front "Ken"			
☐	24B	Ken Saucier P2	.06	.03	.00
		Name on front "Ken"			
☐	24C	Kevin Saucier P3 ...	.35	.17	.03
		Name on front "Kevin"			
☐	25	Randy Lerch	.03	.01	.00
☐	26	Del Unser	.03	.01	.00
☐	27	Tim McCarver	.15	.07	.01
☐	28	George Brett	1.00	.50	.10
		See also 655A			
☐	29	Willie Wilson	.15	.07	.01
		See also 653A			
☐	30	Paul Splittorff	.03	.01	.00
☐	31	Dan Quisenberry ...	.15	.07	.01
☐	32A	Amos Otis P1	.10	.05	.01
		Batting Pose			
		"Outfield"			
		(32 on back)			
☐	32B	Amos Otis P2	.10	.05	.01
		"Series Starter"			
		(483 on back)			
☐	33	Steve Busby	.03	.01	.00
☐	34	U.L. Washington	.03	.01	.00
☐	35	Dave Chalk	.03	.01	.00
☐	36	Darrell Porter	.03	.01	.00
☐	37	Marty Pattin	.03	.01	.00
☐	38	Larry Gura	.06	.03	.00
☐	39	Renie Martin	.03	.01	.00
☐	40	Rich Gale	.03	.01	.00
☐	41A	Hal McRae P1	.50	.25	.05
		"Royals" on front			
		in black letters			

			MINT	EXC	G-VG
☐	41B	Hal McRae P2	.10	.05	.01
		"Royals" on front			
		in blue letters			
☐	42	Dennis Leonard	.06	.03	.00
☐	43	Willie Aikens	.06	.03	.00
☐	44	Frank White	.10	.05	.01
☐	45	Clint Hurdle	.03	.01	.00
☐	46	John Wathan	.10	.05	.01
☐	47	Pete LaCock	.03	.01	.00
☐	48	Rance Mulliniks	.03	.01	.00
☐	49	Jeff Twitty	.03	.01	.00
☐	50	Jamie Quirk	.03	.01	.00
☐	51	Art Howe	.10	.05	.01
☐	52	Ken Forsch	.03	.01	.00
☐	53	Vern Ruhle	.03	.01	.00
☐	54	Joe Niekro	.10	.05	.01
☐	55	Frank LaCorte	.03	.01	.00
☐	56	J.R. Richard	.10	.05	.01
☐	57	Nolan Ryan	1.75	.85	.17
☐	58	Enos Cabell	.03	.01	.00
☐	59	Cesar Cedeno	.10	.05	.01
☐	60	Jose Cruz	.10	.05	.01
☐	61	Bill Virdon MG	.06	.03	.00
☐	62	Terry Puhl	.06	.03	.00
☐	63	Joaquin Andujar ...	.10	.05	.01
☐	64	Alan Ashby	.03	.01	.00
☐	65	Joe Sambito	.03	.01	.00
☐	66	Denny Walling	.03	.01	.00
☐	67	Jeff Leonard	.15	.07	.01
☐	68	Luis Pujols	.03	.01	.00
☐	69	Bruce Bochy	.03	.01	.00
☐	70	Rafael Landestoy ...	.03	.01	.00
☐	71	Dave Smith	.35	.17	.03
☐	72	Danny Heep	.20	.10	.02
☐	73	Julio Gonzalez	.03	.01	.00
☐	74	Craig Reynolds	.03	.01	.00
☐	75	Gary Woods	.03	.01	.00
☐	76	Dave Bergman	.03	.01	.00
☐	77	Randy Niemann	.03	.01	.00
☐	78	Joe Morgan	.40	.20	.04
☐	79	Reggie Jackson	1.00	.50	.10
		See 650A			
☐	80	Bucky Dent	.12	.06	.01
☐	81	Tommy John	.20	.10	.02
☐	82	Luis Tiant	.10	.05	.01
☐	83	Rick Cerone	.06	.03	.00
☐	84	Dick Howser MG ...	.10	.05	.01
☐	85	Lou Piniella	.12	.06	.01
☐	86	Ron Davis	.03	.01	.00

		MINT	EXC	G-VG
☐ 87A	Craig Nettles P1 ERR (Name on back misspelled "Craig")	11.00	5.50	1.10
☐ 87B	Graig Nettles P2 COR "Graig"	.30	.15	.03
☐ 88	Ron Guidry	.20	.10	.02
☐ 89	Rich Gossage	.20	.10	.02
☐ 90	Rudy May	.03	.01	.00
☐ 91	Gaylord Perry	.30	.15	.03
☐ 92	Eric Soderholm	.03	.01	.00
☐ 93	Bob Watson	.06	.03	.00
☐ 94	Bobby Murcer	.10	.05	.01
☐ 95	Bobby Brown	.03	.01	.00
☐ 96	Jim Spencer	.03	.01	.00
☐ 97	Tom Underwood	.03	.01	.00
☐ 98	Oscar Gamble	.03	.01	.00
☐ 99	Johnny Oates	.03	.01	.00
☐ 100	Fred Stanley	.03	.01	.00
☐ 101	Ruppert Jones	.03	.01	.00
☐ 102	Dennis Werth	.03	.01	.00
☐ 103	Joe Lefebvre	.06	.03	.00
☐ 104	Brian Doyle	.03	.01	.00
☐ 105	Aurelio Rodriguez	.03	.01	.00
☐ 106	Doug Bird	.03	.01	.00
☐ 107	Mike Griffin	.03	.01	.00
☐ 108	Tim Lollar	.03	.01	.00
☐ 109	Willie Randolph	.10	.05	.01
☐ 110	Steve Garvey	.65	.30	.06
☐ 111	Reggie Smith	.10	.05	.01
☐ 112	Don Sutton	.30	.15	.03
☐ 113	Burt Hooton	.03	.01	.00
☐ 114A	Dave Lopes P1 Small hand on back	.50	.25	.05
☐ 114B	Dave Lopes P2 No hand	.10	.05	.01
☐ 115	Dusty Baker	.06	.03	.00
☐ 116	Tom Lasorda MG	.10	.05	.01
☐ 117	Bill Russell	.06	.03	.00
☐ 118	Jerry Reuss	.06	.03	.00
☐ 119	Terry Forster	.06	.03	.00
☐ 120A	Bob Welch P1 Name on back is "Bob"	.20	.10	.02
☐ 120B	Bob Welch P2 Name on back is "Robert"	.20	.10	.02
☐ 121	Don Stanhouse	.03	.01	.00
☐ 122	Rick Monday	.03	.01	.00

		MINT	EXC	G-VG
☐ 123	Derrel Thomas	.03	.01	.00
☐ 124	Joe Ferguson	.03	.01	.00
☐ 125	Rick Sutcliffe	.30	.15	.03
☐ 126A	Ron Cey P1 Small hand on back	.50	.25	.05
☐ 126B	Ron Cey P2 No hand	.10	.05	.01
☐ 127	Dave Goltz	.03	.01	.00
☐ 128	Jay Johnstone	.06	.03	.00
☐ 129	Steve Yeager	.03	.01	.00
☐ 130	Gary Weiss	.03	.01	.00
☐ 131	Mike Scioscia	.60	.30	.06
☐ 132	Vic Davalillo	.03	.01	.00
☐ 133	Doug Rau	.03	.01	.00
☐ 134	Pepe Frias	.03	.01	.00
☐ 135	Mickey Hatcher	.10	.05	.01
☐ 136	Steve Howe	.10	.05	.01
☐ 137	Robert Castillo	.03	.01	.00
☐ 138	Gary Thomasson	.03	.01	.00
☐ 139	Rudy Law	.03	.01	.00
☐ 140	Fernand Valenzuela (sic, Fernando)	4.50	2.25	.45
☐ 141	Manny Mota	.06	.03	.00
☐ 142	Gary Carter	.50	.25	.05
☐ 143	Steve Rogers	.06	.03	.00
☐ 144	Warren Cromartie	.03	.01	.00
☐ 145	Andre Dawson	.40	.20	.04
☐ 146	Larry Parrish	.06	.03	.00
☐ 147	Rowland Office	.03	.01	.00
☐ 148	Ellis Valentine	.03	.01	.00
☐ 149	Dick Williams MG	.03	.01	.00
☐ 150	Bill Gullickson	.25	.12	.02
☐ 151	Elias Sosa	.03	.01	.00
☐ 152	John Tamargo	.03	.01	.00
☐ 153	Chris Speier	.03	.01	.00
☐ 154	Ron LeFlore	.06	.03	.00
☐ 155	Rodney Scott	.03	.01	.00
☐ 156	Stan Bahnsen	.03	.01	.00
☐ 157	Bill Lee	.06	.03	.00
☐ 158	Fred Norman	.03	.01	.00
☐ 159	Woodie Fryman	.03	.01	.00
☐ 160	David Palmer	.06	.03	.00
☐ 161	Jerry White	.03	.01	.00
☐ 162	Roberto Ramos	.03	.01	.00
☐ 163	John D'Acquisto	.03	.01	.00
☐ 164	Tommy Hutton	.03	.01	.00
☐ 165	Charlie Lea	.20	.10	.02
☐ 166	Scott Sanderson	.06	.03	.00
☐ 167	Ken Macha	.03	.01	.00

		MINT	EXC	G-VG
☐ 168	Tony Bernazard	.06	.03	.00
☐ 169	Jim Palmer	.60	.30	.06
☐ 170	Steve Stone	.06	.03	.00
☐ 171	Mike Flanagan	.10	.05	.01
☐ 172	Al Bumbry	.03	.01	.00
☐ 173	Doug DeCinces	.06	.03	.00
☐ 174	Scott McGregor	.06	.03	.00
☐ 175	Mark Belanger	.06	.03	.00
☐ 176	Tim Stoddard	.03	.01	.00
☐ 177A	Rick Dempsey P1	.50	.25	.05
	Small hand on front			
☐ 177B	Rick Dempsey P2	.10	.05	.01
	No hand			
☐ 178	Earl Weaver MG	.06	.03	.00
☐ 179	Tippy Martinez	.03	.01	.00
☐ 180	Dennis Martinez	.10	.05	.01
☐ 181	Sammy Stewart	.03	.01	.00
☐ 182	Rich Dauer	.03	.01	.00
☐ 183	Lee May	.06	.03	.00
☐ 184	Eddie Murray	.75	.35	.07
☐ 185	Benny Ayala	.03	.01	.00
☐ 186	John Lowenstein	.03	.01	.00
☐ 187	Gary Roenicke	.03	.01	.00
☐ 188	Ken Singleton	.10	.05	.01
☐ 189	Dan Graham	.03	.01	.00
☐ 190	Terry Crowley	.03	.01	.00
☐ 191	Kiko Garcia	.03	.01	.00
☐ 192	Dave Ford	.03	.01	.00
☐ 193	Mark Corey	.03	.01	.00
☐ 194	Lenn Sakata	.03	.01	.00
☐ 195	Doug DeCinces	.06	.03	.00
☐ 196	Johnny Bench	.75	.35	.07
☐ 197	Dave Concepcion	.15	.07	.01
☐ 198	Ray Knight	.10	.05	.01
☐ 199	Ken Griffey	.10	.05	.01
☐ 200	Tom Seaver	.60	.30	.06
☐ 201	Dave Collins	.03	.01	.00
☐ 202A	George Foster P1	.15	.07	.01
	Slugger			
	Number on back 216			
☐ 202B	George Foster P2	.15	.07	.01
	Slugger			
	Number on back 202			
☐ 203	Junior Kennedy	.03	.01	.00
☐ 204	Frank Pastore	.03	.01	.00
☐ 205	Dan Driessen	.03	.01	.00
☐ 206	Hector Cruz	.03	.01	.00
☐ 207	Paul Moskau	.03	.01	.00
☐ 208	Charlie Leibrandt	.30	.15	.03
☐ 209	Harry Spilman	.03	.01	.00
☐ 210	Joe Price	.06	.03	.00
☐ 211	Tom Hume	.03	.01	.00
☐ 212	Joe Nolan	.03	.01	.00
☐ 213	Doug Bair	.03	.01	.00
☐ 214	Mario Soto	.10	.05	.01
☐ 215A	Bill Bonham P1	.50	.25	.05
	Small hand on back			
☐ 215B	Bill Bonham P2	.06	.03	.00
	No hand			
☐ 216	George Foster	.15	.07	.01
	See #202			
☐ 217	Paul Householder	.03	.01	.00
☐ 218	Ron Oester	.06	.03	.00
☐ 219	Sam Mejias	.03	.01	.00
☐ 220	Sheldon Burnside	.03	.01	.00
☐ 221	Carl Yastrzemski	1.00	.50	.10
☐ 222	Jim Rice	.30	.15	.03
☐ 223	Fred Lynn	.20	.10	.02
☐ 224	Carlton Fisk	.40	.20	.04
☐ 225	Rick Burleson	.06	.03	.00
☐ 226	Dennis Eckersley	.25	.12	.02
☐ 227	Butch Hobson	.03	.01	.00
☐ 228	Tom Burgmeier	.03	.01	.00
☐ 229	Garry Hancock	.03	.01	.00
☐ 230	Don Zimmer MG	.06	.03	.00
☐ 231	Steve Renko	.03	.01	.00
☐ 232	Dwight Evans	.25	.12	.02
☐ 233	Mike Torrez	.06	.03	.00
☐ 234	Bob Stanley	.03	.01	.00
☐ 235	Jim Dwyer	.03	.01	.00
☐ 236	Dave Stapleton	.03	.01	.00
☐ 237	Glen Hoffman	.03	.01	.00
☐ 238	Jerry Remy	.03	.01	.00
☐ 239	Dick Drago	.03	.01	.00
☐ 240	Bill Campbell	.03	.01	.00
☐ 241	Tony Perez	.20	.10	.02
☐ 242	Phil Niekro	.30	.15	.03
☐ 243	Dale Murphy	1.25	.60	.12
☐ 244	Bob Horner	.15	.07	.01
☐ 245	Jeff Burroughs	.03	.01	.00
☐ 246	Rick Camp	.03	.01	.00
☐ 247	Bobby Cox MG	.03	.01	.00
☐ 248	Bruce Benedict	.03	.01	.00
☐ 249	Gene Garber	.03	.01	.00
☐ 250	Jerry Royster	.03	.01	.00
☐ 251A	Gary Matthews P1	.50	.25	.05
	Small hand on back			
☐ 251B	Gary Matthews P2	.10	.05	.01

		MINT	EXC	G-VG
	No hand			
☐ 252	Chris Chambliss	.10	.05	.01
☐ 253	Luis Gomez	.03	.01	.00
☐ 254	Bill Nahorodny	.03	.01	.00
☐ 255	Doyle Alexander	.06	.03	.00
☐ 256	Brian Asselstine	.03	.01	.00
☐ 257	Biff Pocoroba	.03	.01	.00
☐ 258	Mike Lum	.03	.01	.00
☐ 259	Charlie Spikes	.03	.01	.00
☐ 260	Glenn Hubbard	.03	.01	.00
☐ 261	Tommy Boggs	.03	.01	.00
☐ 262	Al Hrabosky	.06	.03	.00
☐ 263	Rick Matula	.03	.01	.00
☐ 264	Preston Hanna	.03	.01	.00
☐ 265	Larry Bradford	.03	.01	.00
☐ 266	Rafael Ramirez	.25	.12	.02
☐ 267	Larry McWilliams	.03	.01	.00
☐ 268	Rod Carew	.65	.30	.06
☐ 269	Bobby Grich	.10	.05	.01
☐ 270	Carney Lansford	.25	.10	.02
☐ 271	Don Baylor	.15	.07	.01
☐ 272	Joe Rudi	.06	.03	.00
☐ 273	Dan Ford	.03	.01	.00
☐ 274	Jim Fregosi	.06	.03	.00
☐ 275	Dave Frost	.03	.01	.00
☐ 276	Frank Tanana	.10	.05	.01
☐ 277	Dickie Thon	.10	.05	.01
☐ 278	Jason Thompson	.03	.01	.00
☐ 279	Rick Miller	.03	.01	.00
☐ 280	Bert Campaneris	.06	.03	.00
☐ 281	Tom Donohue	.03	.01	.00
☐ 282	Brian Downing	.06	.03	.00
☐ 283	Fred Patek	.03	.01	.00
☐ 284	Bruce Kison	.03	.01	.00
☐ 285	Dave LaRoche	.03	.01	.00
☐ 286	Don Aase	.03	.01	.00
☐ 287	Jim Barr	.03	.01	.00
☐ 288	Alfredo Martinez	.03	.01	.00
☐ 289	Larry Harlow	.03	.01	.00
☐ 290	Andy Hassler	.03	.01	.00
☐ 291	Dave Kingman	.15	.07	.01
☐ 292	Bill Buckner	.12	.06	.01
☐ 293	Rick Reuschel	.20	.10	.02
☐ 294	Bruce Sutter	.20	.10	.02
☐ 295	Jerry Martin	.03	.01	.00
☐ 296	Scot Thompson	.03	.01	.00
☐ 297	Ivan DeJesus	.03	.01	.00
☐ 298	Steve Dillard	.03	.01	.00
☐ 299	Dick Tidrow	.03	.01	.00

		MINT	EXC	G-VG
☐ 300	Randy Martz	.03	.01	.00
☐ 301	Lenny Randle	.03	.01	.00
☐ 302	Lynn McGlothen	.03	.01	.00
☐ 303	Cliff Johnson	.03	.01	.00
☐ 304	Tim Blackwell	.03	.01	.00
☐ 305	Dennis Lamp	.03	.01	.00
☐ 306	Bill Caudill	.03	.01	.00
☐ 307	Carlos Lezcano	.03	.01	.00
☐ 308	Jim Tracy	.03	.01	.00
☐ 309	Doug Capilla	.03	.01	.00
☐ 310	Willie Hernandez	.15	.07	.01
☐ 311	Mike Vail	.03	.01	.00
☐ 312	Mike Krukow	.06	.03	.00
☐ 313	Barry Foote	.03	.01	.00
☐ 314	Larry Biittner	.03	.01	.00
☐ 315	Mike Tyson	.03	.01	.00
☐ 316	Lee Mazzilli	.03	.01	.00
☐ 317	John Stearns	.03	.01	.00
☐ 318	Alex Trevino	.03	.01	.00
☐ 319	Craig Swan	.03	.01	.00
☐ 320	Frank Taveras	.03	.01	.00
☐ 321	Steve Henderson	.03	.01	.00
☐ 322	Neil Allen	.06	.03	.00
☐ 323	Mark Bomback	.03	.01	.00
☐ 324	Mike Jorgensen	.03	.01	.00
☐ 325	Joe Torre MG	.10	.05	.01
☐ 326	Elliott Maddox	.03	.01	.00
☐ 327	Pete Falcone	.03	.01	.00
☐ 328	Ray Burris	.03	.01	.00
☐ 329	Claudell Washington	.06	.03	.00
☐ 330	Doug Flynn	.03	.01	.00
☐ 331	Joel Youngblood	.03	.01	.00
☐ 332	Bill Almon	.03	.01	.00
☐ 333	Tom Hausman	.03	.01	.00
☐ 334	Pat Zachry	.03	.01	.00
☐ 335	Jeff Reardon	.75	.35	.07
☐ 336	Wally Backman	.35	.17	.03
☐ 337	Dan Norman	.03	.01	.00
☐ 338	Jerry Morales	.03	.01	.00
☐ 339	Ed Farmer	.03	.01	.00
☐ 340	Bob Molinaro	.03	.01	.00
☐ 341	Todd Cruz	.03	.01	.00
☐ 342A	Britt Burns P1	.40	.20	.04
	Small hand on front			
☐ 342B	Britt Burns P2	.20	.10	.02
	No hand			
☐ 343	Kevin Bell	.03	.01	.00
☐ 344	Tony LaRussa MG	.06	.03	.00
☐ 345	Steve Trout	.06	.03	.00

		MINT	EXC	G-VG
☐ 346	Harold Baines	2.25	1.10	.22
☐ 347	Richard Wortham	.03	.01	.00
☐ 348	Wayne Nordhagen	.03	.01	.00
☐ 349	Mike Squires	.03	.01	.00
☐ 350	Lamar Johnson	.03	.01	.00
☐ 351	Rickey Henderson	3.00	1.50	.30
☐ 352	Francisco Barrios	.03	.01	.00
☐ 353	Thad Bosley	.03	.01	.00
☐ 354	Chet Lemon	.06	.03	.00
☐ 355	Bruce Kimm	.03	.01	.00
☐ 356	Richard Dotson	.35	.17	.03
☐ 357	Jim Morrison	.03	.01	.00
☐ 358	Mike Proly	.03	.01	.00
☐ 359	Greg Pryor	.03	.01	.00
☐ 360	Dave Parker	.25	.12	.02
☐ 361	Omar Moreno	.03	.01	.00
☐ 362A	Kent Tekulve P1 Back "1071 Waterbury" and "1078 Pirates"	.15	.07	.01
☐ 362B	Kent Tekulve P2 "1971 Waterbury" and "1978 Pirates"	.10	.05	.01
☐ 363	Willie Stargell	.40	.20	.04
☐ 364	Phil Garner	.03	.01	.00
☐ 365	Ed Ott	.03	.01	.00
☐ 366	Don Robinson	.06	.03	.00
☐ 367	Chuck Tanner MG	.06	.03	.00
☐ 368	Jim Rooker	.03	.01	.00
☐ 369	Dale Berra	.03	.01	.00
☐ 370	Jim Bibby	.03	.01	.00
☐ 371	Steve Nicosia	.03	.01	.00
☐ 372	Mike Easler	.06	.03	.00
☐ 373	Bill Robinson	.06	.03	.00
☐ 374	Lee Lacy	.03	.01	.00
☐ 375	John Candelaria	.10	.05	.01
☐ 376	Manny Sanguillen	.06	.03	.00
☐ 377	Rick Rhoden	.06	.03	.00
☐ 378	Grant Jackson	.03	.01	.00
☐ 379	Tim Foli	.03	.01	.00
☐ 380	Rod Scurry	.03	.01	.00
☐ 381	Bill Madlock	.12	.06	.01
☐ 382A	Kurt Bevacqua P1 ERR (P on cap backwards)	.20	.10	.02
☐ 382B	Kurt Bevacqua P2 COR	.06	.03	.00
☐ 383	Bert Blyleven	.20	.10	.02
☐ 384	Eddie Solomon	.03	.01	.00
☐ 385	Enrique Romo	.03	.01	.00
☐ 386	John Milner	.03	.01	.00
☐ 387	Mike Hargrove	.06	.03	.00
☐ 388	Jorge Orta	.03	.01	.00
☐ 389	Toby Harrah	.06	.03	.00
☐ 390	Tom Veryzer	.03	.01	.00
☐ 391	Miguel Dilone	.03	.01	.00
☐ 392	Dan Spillner	.03	.01	.00
☐ 393	Jack Brohamer	.03	.01	.00
☐ 394	Wayne Garland	.03	.01	.00
☐ 395	Sid Monge	.03	.01	.00
☐ 396	Rick Waits	.03	.01	.00
☐ 397	Joe Charboneau	.10	.05	.01
☐ 398	Gary Alexander	.03	.01	.00
☐ 399	Jerry Dybzinski	.03	.01	.00
☐ 400	Mike Stanton	.03	.01	.00
☐ 401	Mike Paxton	.03	.01	.00
☐ 402	Gary Gray	.03	.01	.00
☐ 403	Rick Manning	.03	.01	.00
☐ 404	Bo Diaz	.06	.03	.00
☐ 405	Ron Hassey	.03	.01	.00
☐ 406	Ross Grimsley	.03	.01	.00
☐ 407	Victor Cruz	.03	.01	.00
☐ 408	Len Barker	.03	.01	.00
☐ 409	Bob Bailor	.03	.01	.00
☐ 410	Otto Velez	.03	.01	.00
☐ 411	Ernie Whitt	.10	.05	.01
☐ 412	Jim Clancy	.06	.03	.00
☐ 413	Barry Bonnell	.03	.01	.00
☐ 414	Dave Stieb	.35	.17	.03
☐ 415	Damaso Garcia	.10	.05	.01
☐ 416	John Mayberry	.06	.03	.00
☐ 417	Roy Howell	.03	.01	.00
☐ 418	Danny Ainge	.45	.22	.04
☐ 419A	Jesse Jefferson P1 Back says Pirates	.06	.03	.00
☐ 419B	Jesse Jefferson P2 Back says Pirates	.06	.03	.00
☐ 419C	Jesse Jefferson P3 Back says Blue Jays	.35	.17	.03
☐ 420	Joey McLaughlin	.03	.01	.00
☐ 421	Lloyd Moseby	.75	.35	.07
☐ 422	Alvis Woods	.03	.01	.00
☐ 423	Garth Iorg	.03	.01	.00
☐ 424	Doug Ault	.03	.01	.00
☐ 425	Ken Schrom	.06	.03	.00
☐ 426	Mike Willis	.03	.01	.00
☐ 427	Steve Braun	.03	.01	.00
☐ 428	Bob Davis	.03	.01	.00

		MINT	EXC	G-VG
☐ 429	Jerry Garvin	.03	.01	.00
☐ 430	Alfredo Griffin	.10	.05	.01
☐ 431	Bob Mattick MG	.03	.01	.00
☐ 432	Vida Blue	.10	.05	.01
☐ 433	Jack Clark	.30	.15	.03
☐ 434	Willie McCovey	.35	.17	.03
☐ 435	Mike Ivie	.03	.01	.00
☐ 436A	Darrel Evans P1 ERR Name on front "Darrel"	.40	.20	.04
☐ 436B	Darrell Evans P2 Name on front "Darrell"	.15	.07	.01
☐ 437	Terry Whitfield	.03	.01	.00
☐ 438	Rennie Stennett	.03	.01	.00
☐ 439	John Montefusco	.06	.03	.00
☐ 440	Jim Wohlford	.03	.01	.00
☐ 441	Bill North	.03	.01	.00
☐ 442	Milt May	.03	.01	.00
☐ 443	Max Venable	.03	.01	.00
☐ 444	Ed Whitson	.06	.03	.00
☐ 445	Al Holland	.06	.03	.00
☐ 446	Randy Moffitt	.03	.01	.00
☐ 447	Bob Knepper	.06	.03	.00
☐ 448	Gary Lavelle	.03	.01	.00
☐ 449	Greg Minton	.03	.01	.00
☐ 450	Johnnie LeMaster	.03	.01	.00
☐ 451	Larry Herndon	.03	.01	.00
☐ 452	Rich Murray	.03	.01	.00
☐ 453	Joe Pettini	.03	.01	.00
☐ 454	Allen Ripley	.03	.01	.00
☐ 455	Dennis Littlejohn	.03	.01	.00
☐ 456	Tom Griffin	.03	.01	.00
☐ 457	Alan Hargesheimer	.03	.01	.00
☐ 458	Joe Strain	.03	.01	.00
☐ 459	Steve Kemp	.06	.03	.00
☐ 460	Sparky Anderson MG	.10	.05	.01
☐ 461	Alan Trammell	.45	.22	.04
☐ 462	Mark Fidrych	.10	.05	.01
☐ 463	Lou Whitaker	.30	.15	.03
☐ 464	Dave Rozema	.03	.01	.00
☐ 465	Milt Wilcox	.03	.01	.00
☐ 466	Champ Summers	.03	.01	.00
☐ 467	Lance Parrish	.25	.12	.02
☐ 468	Dan Petry	.10	.05	.01
☐ 469	Pat Underwood	.03	.01	.00
☐ 470	Rick Peters	.03	.01	.00
☐ 471	Al Cowens	.03	.01	.00
☐ 472	John Wockenfuss	.03	.01	.00
☐ 473	Tom Brookens	.03	.01	.00
☐ 474	Richie Hebner	.03	.01	.00
☐ 475	Jack Morris	.25	.12	.02
☐ 476	Jim Lentine	.03	.01	.00
☐ 477	Bruce Robbins	.03	.01	.00
☐ 478	Mark Wagner	.03	.01	.00
☐ 479	Tim Corcoran	.03	.01	.00
☐ 480A	Stan Papi P1 Front as Pitcher	.15	.07	.01
☐ 480B	Stan Papi P2 Front as Shortstop	.10	.05	.01
☐ 481	Kirk Gibson	3.75	1.85	.37
☐ 482	Dan Schatzeder	.03	.01	.00
☐ 483A	Amos Otis P1 See card 32	.10	.05	.01
☐ 483B	Amos Otis P2 See card 32	.10	.05	.01
☐ 484	Dave Winfield	.50	.25	.05
☐ 485	Rollie Fingers	.35	.17	.03
☐ 486	Gene Richards	.03	.01	.00
☐ 487	Randy Jones	.03	.01	.00
☐ 488	Ozzie Smith	.50	.25	.05
☐ 489	Gene Tenace	.03	.01	.00
☐ 490	Bill Fahey	.03	.01	.00
☐ 491	John Curtis	.03	.01	.00
☐ 492	Dave Cash	.03	.01	.00
☐ 493A	Tim Flannery P1 Batting right	.15	.07	.01
☐ 493B	Tim Flannery P2 Batting left	.06	.03	.00
☐ 494	Jerry Mumphrey	.03	.01	.00
☐ 495	Bob Shirley	.03	.01	.00
☐ 496	Steve Mura	.03	.01	.00
☐ 497	Eric Rasmussen	.03	.01	.00
☐ 498	Broderick Perkins	.03	.01	.00
☐ 499	Barry Evans	.03	.01	.00
☐ 500	Chuck Baker	.03	.01	.00
☐ 501	Luis Salazar	.15	.07	.01
☐ 502	Gary Lucas	.06	.03	.00
☐ 503	Mike Armstrong	.06	.03	.00
☐ 504	Jerry Turner	.03	.01	.00
☐ 505	Dennis Kinney	.03	.01	.00
☐ 506	Willie Montanez	.03	.01	.00
☐ 507	Gorman Thomas	.10	.05	.01
☐ 508	Ben Oglivie	.06	.03	.00
☐ 509	Larry Hisle	.06	.03	.00
☐ 510	Sal Bando	.06	.03	.00
☐ 511	Robin Yount	1.00	.50	.10
☐ 512	Mike Caldwell	.03	.01	.00
☐ 513	Sixto Lezcano	.03	.01	.00

		MINT	EXC	G-VG
☐ 514A	Bill Travers P1 ERR "Jerry Augustine" with Augustine back	.20	.10	.02
☐ 514B	Bill Travers P2 COR	.10	.05	.01
☐ 515	Paul Molitor	.35	.17	.03
☐ 516	Moose Haas	.03	.01	.00
☐ 517	Bill Castro	.03	.01	.00
☐ 518	Jim Slaton	.03	.01	.00
☐ 519	Lary Sorensen	.03	.01	.00
☐ 520	Bob McClure	.03	.01	.00
☐ 521	Charlie Moore	.03	.01	.00
☐ 522	Jim Gantner	.06	.03	.00
☐ 523	Reggie Cleveland	.03	.01	.00
☐ 524	Don Money	.03	.01	.00
☐ 525	Bill Travers	.03	.01	.00
☐ 526	Buck Martinez	.03	.01	.00
☐ 527	Dick Davis	.03	.01	.00
☐ 528	Ted Simmons	.15	.07	.01
☐ 529	Garry Templeton	.10	.05	.01
☐ 530	Ken Reitz	.03	.01	.00
☐ 531	Tony Scott	.03	.01	.00
☐ 532	Ken Oberkfell	.03	.01	.00
☐ 533	Bob Sykes	.03	.01	.00
☐ 534	Keith Smith	.03	.01	.00
☐ 535	John Littlefield	.03	.01	.00
☐ 536	Jim Kaat	.20	.10	.02
☐ 537	Bob Forsch	.03	.01	.00
☐ 538	Mike Phillips	.03	.01	.00
☐ 539	Terry Landrum	.06	.03	.00
☐ 540	Leon Durham	.30	.15	.03
☐ 541	Terry Kennedy	.06	.03	.00
☐ 542	George Hendrick	.06	.03	.00
☐ 543	Dane Iorg	.03	.01	.00
☐ 544	Mark Littell	.03	.01	.00
☐ 545	Keith Hernandez	.35	.17	.03
☐ 546	Silvio Martinez	.03	.01	.00
☐ 547A	Don Hood P1 ERR "Pete Vuckovich" with Vuckovich back	.20	.10	.02
☐ 547B	Don Hood P2 COR	.10	.05	.01
☐ 548	Bobby Bonds	.12	.06	.01
☐ 549	Mike Ramsey	.03	.01	.00
☐ 550	Tom Herr	.15	.07	.01
☐ 551	Roy Smalley	.03	.01	.00
☐ 552	Jerry Koosman	.10	.05	.01
☐ 553	Ken Landreaux	.03	.01	.00
☐ 554	John Castino	.03	.01	.00
☐ 555	Doug Corbett	.06	.03	.00
☐ 556	Bombo Rivera	.03	.01	.00
☐ 557	Ron Jackson	.03	.01	.00
☐ 558	Butch Wynegar	.03	.01	.00
☐ 559	Hosken Powell	.03	.01	.00
☐ 560	Pete Redfern	.03	.01	.00
☐ 561	Roger Erickson	.03	.01	.00
☐ 562	Glenn Adams	.03	.01	.00
☐ 563	Rick Sofield	.03	.01	.00
☐ 564	Geoff Zahn	.03	.01	.00
☐ 565	Pete Mackanin	.03	.01	.00
☐ 566	Mike Cubbage	.03	.01	.00
☐ 567	Darrell Jackson	.03	.01	.00
☐ 568	Dave Edwards	.03	.01	.00
☐ 569	Rob Wilfong	.03	.01	.00
☐ 570	Sal Butera	.03	.01	.00
☐ 571	Jose Morales	.03	.01	.00
☐ 572	Rick Langford	.03	.01	.00
☐ 573	Mike Norris	.03	.01	.00
☐ 574	Rickey Henderson	3.00	1.50	.30
☐ 575	Tony Armas	.10	.05	.01
☐ 576	Dave Revering	.03	.01	.00
☐ 577	Jeff Newman	.03	.01	.00
☐ 578	Bob Lacey	.03	.01	.00
☐ 579	Brian Kingman	.03	.01	.00
☐ 580	Mitchell Page	.03	.01	.00
☐ 581	Billy Martin MG	.20	.10	.02
☐ 582	Rob Picciolo	.03	.01	.00
☐ 583	Mike Heath	.03	.01	.00
☐ 584	Mickey Klutts	.03	.01	.00
☐ 585	Orlando Gonzalez	.03	.01	.00
☐ 586	Mike Davis	.25	.12	.02
☐ 587	Wayne Gross	.03	.01	.00
☐ 588	Matt Keough	.03	.01	.00
☐ 589	Steve McCatty	.03	.01	.00
☐ 590	Dwayne Murphy	.03	.01	.00
☐ 591	Mario Guerrero	.03	.01	.00
☐ 592	Dave McKay	.03	.01	.00
☐ 593	Jim Essian	.03	.01	.00
☐ 594	Dave Heaverlo	.03	.01	.00
☐ 595	Maury Wills MG	.10	.05	.01
☐ 596	Juan Beniquez	.03	.01	.00
☐ 597	Rodney Craig	.03	.01	.00
☐ 598	Jim Anderson	.03	.01	.00
☐ 599	Floyd Bannister	.06	.03	.00
☐ 600	Bruce Bochte	.03	.01	.00
☐ 601	Julio Cruz	.03	.01	.00
☐ 602	Ted Cox	.03	.01	.00
☐ 603	Dan Meyer	.03	.01	.00
☐ 604	Larry Cox	.03	.01	.00
☐ 605	Bill Stein	.03	.01	.00

		MINT	EXC	G-VG
☐ 606	Steve Garvey	.65	.30	.06
☐ 607	Dave Roberts	.03	.01	.00
☐ 608	Leon Roberts	.03	.01	.00
☐ 609	Reggie Walton	.03	.01	.00
☐ 610	Dave Edler	.03	.01	.00
☐ 611	Larry Milbourne	.03	.01	.00
☐ 612	Kim Allen	.03	.01	.00
☐ 613	Mario Mendoza	.03	.01	.00
☐ 614	Tom Paciorek	.03	.01	.00
☐ 615	Glenn Abbott	.03	.01	.00
☐ 616	Joe Simpson	.03	.01	.00
☐ 617	Mickey Rivers	.06	.03	.00
☐ 618	Jim Kern	.03	.01	.00
☐ 619	Jim Sundberg	.06	.03	.00
☐ 620	Richie Zisk	.06	.03	.00
☐ 621	Jon Matlack	.03	.01	.00
☐ 622	Ferguson Jenkins	.15	.07	.01
☐ 623	Pat Corrales MG	.06	.03	.00
☐ 624	Ed Figueroa	.03	.01	.00
☐ 625	Buddy Bell	.15	.07	.01
☐ 626	Al Oliver	.12	.06	.01
☐ 627	Doc Medich	.03	.01	.00
☐ 628	Bump Wills	.03	.01	.00
☐ 629	Rusty Staub	.12	.06	.01
☐ 630	Pat Putnam	.03	.01	.00
☐ 631	John Grubb	.03	.01	.00
☐ 632	Danny Darwin	.03	.01	.00
☐ 633	Ken Clay	.03	.01	.00
☐ 634	Jim Norris	.03	.01	.00
☐ 635	John Butcher	.06	.03	.00
☐ 636	Dave Roberts	.03	.01	.00
☐ 637	Billy Sample	.03	.01	.00
☐ 638	Carl Yastrzemski	1.00	.50	.10
☐ 639	Cecil Cooper	.15	.07	.01
☐ 640A	Mike Schmidt P1 (Portrait) "Third Base" (number on back 5)	1.50	.75	.15
☐ 640B	Mike Schmidt P2 "1980 Home Run King" (640 on back)	1.25	.60	.12
☐ 641A	CL: Phils/Royals P1 41 is Hal McRae	.10	.05	.01
☐ 641B	CL: Phils/Royals P2 41 is Hal McRae, Double Threat	.10	.05	.01
☐ 642	CL: Astros/Yankees	.08	.04	.01
☐ 643	CL: Expos/Dodgers	.08	.04	.01

		MINT	EXC	G-VG
☐ 644A	CL: Reds/Orioles P1 202 is George Foster	.10	.05	.01
☐ 644B	CL: Reds/Orioles P2 202 is Foster Slugger	.10	.05	.01
☐ 645A	Rose/Bowa/Schmidt Triple Threat P1 (No number on back)	2.00	1.00	.20
☐ 645B	Rose/Bowa/Schmidt Triple Threat P2 (Back numbered 645)	1.00	.50	.10
☐ 646	CL: Braves/Red Sox	.08	.04	.01
☐ 647	CL: Cubs/Angels	.08	.04	.01
☐ 648	CL: Mets/White Sox	.08	.04	.01
☐ 649	CL: Indians/Pirates	.08	.04	.01
☐ 650A	Reggie Jackson Mr. Baseball P1 Number on back 79	1.25	.60	.12
☐ 650B	Reggie Jackson Mr. Baseball P2 Number on back 650	1.00	.50	.10
☐ 651	CL: Giants/Blue Jays	.08	.04	.01
☐ 652A	CL: Tigers/Padres P1 483 is listed	.10	.05	.01
☐ 652B	CL: Tigers/Padres P2 483 is deleted	.10	.05	.01
☐ 653A	Willie Wilson P1 Most Hits Most Runs Number on back 29	.10	.05	.01
☐ 653B	Willie Wilson P2 Most Hits Most Runs Number on back 653	.10	.05	.01
☐ 654A	CL:Brewers/Cards P1 514 Jerry Augustine 547 Pete Vuckovich	.10	.05	.01
☐ 654B	CL:Brewers/Cards P2 514 Billy Travers 547 Don Hood	.10	.05	.01
☐ 655A	George Brett P1 .390 Average Number on back 28	1.25	.60	.12
☐ 655B	George Brett P2 .390 Average Number on back 655	.90	.45	.09
☐ 656	CL: Twins/Oakland A's	.08	.04	.01
☐ 657A	Tug McGraw P1 Game Saver Number on back 7	.10	.05	.01
☐ 657B	Tug McGraw P2	.10	.05	.01

		MINT	EXC	G-VG
	Game Saver			
	Number on back 657			
☐ 658	CL: Rangers/Mariners	.08	.04	.01
☐ 659A	Checklist P1	.10	.05	.01
	of Special Cards			
	Last lines on front			
	Wilson Most Hits			
☐ 659B	Checklist P2	.10	.05	.01
	of Special Cards			
	Last lines on front			
	Otis Series Starter			
☐ 660A	Steve Carlton P1 ...	.80	.40	.08
	Golden Arm			
	Back "1066 Cardinals"			
	Number on back 6			
☐ 660B	Steve Carlton P2 ...	.65	.30	.06
	Golden Arm			
	Number on back 660			
	Back "1066 Cardinals"			
☐ 660C	Steve Carlton P3	2.00	1.00	.20
	Golden Arm			
	"1966 Cardinals"			

1981 Fleer Sticker Cards

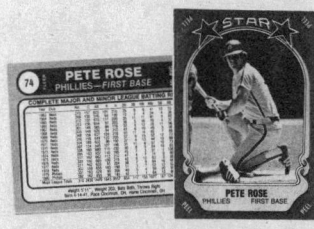

PETE ROSE
PHILLIES — FIRST BASE

74
PETE ROSE
PHILLIES   FIRST BASE

*The stickers in this 128-sticker set measure
2 ½" by 3 ½". The 1981 Fleer Baseball Star
Stickers consist of numbered cards with peel-
able, full-color sticker fronts and three unnumbered checklists. The backs of the*

*numbered player cards are the same as the
1981 Fleer regular issue cards except for the
numbers, while the checklist cards (cards 126-
128 below) have sticker fronts of Jackson (1-
42), Brett (43-83), and Schmidt (84-125).*

			MINT	EXC	G-VG
	COMPLETE SET (128)		45.00	22.50	4.50
	COMMON PLAYER (1-128)		.15	.07	.01
☐	1	Steve Garvey	2.00	.50	.10
☐	2	Ron LeFlore	.15	.07	.01
☐	3	Ron Cey	.20	.10	.02
☐	4	Dave Revering	.15	.07	.01
☐	5	Tony Armas	.15	.07	.01
☐	6	Mike Norris	.15	.07	.01
☐	7	Steve Kemp	.20	.10	.02
☐	8	Bruce Bochte	.15	.07	.01
☐	9	Mike Schmidt	3.50	1.75	.35
☐	10	Scott McGregor	.20	.10	.02
☐	11	Buddy Bell	.25	.12	.02
☐	12	Carney Lansford ...	.30	.15	.03
☐	13	Carl Yastrzemski ..	3.00	1.50	.30
☐	14	Ben Oglivie	.15	.07	.01
☐	15	Willie Stargell	1.25	.60	.12
☐	16	Cecil Cooper	.20	.10	.02
☐	17	Gene Richards	.15	.07	.01
☐	18	Jim Kern	.15	.07	.01
☐	19	Jerry Koosman	.20	.10	.02
☐	20	Larry Bowa	.25	.12	.02
☐	21	Kent Tekulve	.15	.07	.01
☐	22	Dan Driessen	.15	.07	.01
☐	23	Phil Niekro	.75	.35	.07
☐	24	Dan Quisenberry ...	.25	.12	.02
☐	25	Dave Winfield	1.50	.75	.15
☐	26	Dave Parker	.60	.30	.06
☐	27	Rick Langford	.15	.07	.01
☐	28	Amos Otis	.20	.10	.02
☐	29	Bill Buckner	.20	.10	.02
☐	30	Al Bumbry	.15	.07	.01
☐	31	Bake McBride	.15	.07	.01
☐	32	Mickey Rivers	.15	.07	.01
☐	33	Rick Burleson	.20	.10	.02
☐	34	Dennis Eckersley ..	.40	.20	.04
☐	35	Cesar Cedeno	.20	.10	.02
☐	36	Enos Cabell	.15	.07	.01
☐	37	Johnny Bench	3.00	1.50	.30
☐	38	Robin Yount	3.00	1.50	.30
☐	39	Mark Belanger	.15	.07	.01
☐	40	Rod Carew	2.00	1.00	.20

			MINT	EXC	G-VG
☐	41	George Foster	.60	.30	.06
☐	42	Lee Mazzilli	.15	.07	.01
☐	43	Triple Threat:	2.50	1.25	.25
		Pete Rose			
		Larry Bowa			
		Mike Schmidt			
☐	44	J.R. Richard	.20	.10	.02
☐	45	Lou Piniella	.20	.10	.02
☐	46	Ken Landreaux	.15	.07	.01
☐	47	Rollie Fingers	.60	.30	.06
☐	48	Joaquin Andujar	.20	.10	.02
☐	49	Tom Seaver	2.00	1.00	.20
☐	50	Bobby Grich	.20	.10	.02
☐	51	Jon Matlack	.15	.07	.01
☐	52	Jack Clark	.50	.25	.05
☐	53	Jim Rice	.90	.45	.09
☐	54	Rickey Henderson	3.00	1.50	.30
☐	55	Roy Smalley	.15	.07	.01
☐	56	Mike Flanagan	.20	.10	.02
☐	57	Steve Rogers	.15	.07	.01
☐	58	Carlton Fisk	.60	.30	.06
☐	59	Don Sutton	.60	.30	.06
☐	60	Ken Griffey	.25	.12	.02
☐	61	Burt Hooton	.15	.07	.01
☐	62	Dusty Baker	.20	.10	.02
☐	63	Vida Blue	.20	.10	.02
☐	64	Al Oliver	.20	.10	.02
☐	65	Jim Bibby	.15	.07	.01
☐	66	Tony Perez	.40	.20	.04
☐	67	Davy Lopes	.20	.10	.02
☐	68	Bill Russell	.15	.07	.01
☐	69	Larry Parrish	.15	.07	.01
☐	70	Garry Maddox	.15	.07	.01
☐	71	Phil Garner	.15	.07	.01
☐	72	Graig Nettles	.35	.17	.03
☐	73	Gary Carter	1.50	.75	.15
☐	74	Pete Rose	4.50	2.25	.45
☐	75	Greg Luzinski	.25	.12	.02
☐	76	Ron Guidry	.50	.25	.05
☐	77	Gorman Thomas	.20	.10	.02
☐	78	Jose Cruz	.20	.10	.02
☐	79	Bob Boone	.35	.17	.03
☐	80	Bruce Sutter	.25	.12	.02
☐	81	Chris Chambliss	.20	.10	.02
☐	82	Paul Molitor	.60	.30	.06
☐	83	Tug McGraw	.25	.12	.02
☐	84	Ferguson Jenkins	.45	.22	.04
☐	85	Steve Carlton	1.75	.85	.17
☐	86	Miguel Dilone	.15	.07	.01

			MINT	EXC	G-VG
☐	87	Reggie Smith	.25	.12	.02
☐	88	Rick Cerone	.15	.07	.01
☐	89	Alan Trammell	1.00	.50	.10
☐	90	Doug DeCinces	.25	.12	.02
☐	91	Sparky Lyle	.25	.12	.02
☐	92	Warren Cromartie	.15	.07	.01
☐	93	Rick Reuschel	.40	.20	.04
☐	94	Larry Hisle	.15	.07	.01
☐	95	Paul Splittorff	.20	.10	.02
☐	96	Manny Trillo	.15	.07	.01
☐	97	Frank White	.25	.12	.02
☐	98	Fred Lynn	.50	.25	.05
☐	99	Bob Horner	.50	.25	.05
☐	100	Omar Moreno	.15	.07	.01
☐	101	Dave Concepcion	.20	.10	.02
☐	102	Larry Gura	.15	.07	.01
☐	103	Ken Singleton	.20	.10	.02
☐	104	Steve Stone	.15	.07	.01
☐	105	Richie Zisk	.15	.07	.01
☐	106	Willie Wilson	.25	.12	.02
☐	107	Willie Randolph	.25	.12	.02
☐	108	Nolan Ryan	4.00	2.00	.40
☐	109	Joe Morgan	1.50	.75	.15
☐	110	Bucky Dent	.50	.25	.05
☐	111	Dave Kingman	.35	.17	.03
☐	112	John Castino	.15	.07	.01
☐	113	Joe Rudi	.15	.07	.01
☐	114	Ed Farmer	.15	.07	.01
☐	115	Reggie Jackson	2.50	1.25	.25
☐	116	George Brett	2.50	1.25	.25
☐	117	Eddie Murray	1.50	.75	.15
☐	118	Rich Gossage	.40	.20	.04
☐	119	Dale Murphy	2.00	1.00	.20
☐	120	Ted Simmons	.25	.12	.02
☐	121	Tommy John	.50	.25	.05
☐	122	Don Baylor	.40	.20	.04
☐	123	Andre Dawson	1.50	.75	.15
☐	124	Jim Palmer	1.50	.75	.15
☐	125	Garry Templeton	.20	.10	.02
☐	126	CL 1: Reggie Jackson	1.25	.60	.12
☐	127	CL 2: George Brett	1.25	.60	.12
☐	128	CL 3: Mike Schmidt	2.50	1.25	.25

1982 Fleer

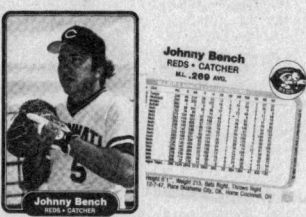

The cards in this 660-card set measure 2 ½"
by 3 ½". The 1982 Fleer set is again ordered
by teams; in fact, the players within each team
are listed in alphabetical order. The teams are
ordered (by 1981 standings) as follows: Los
Angeles (1-29), New York Yankees (30-56),
Cincinnati (57-84), Oakland (85-109), St. Louis
(110-132), Milwaukee (133-156), Baltimore
(157-182), Montreal (183-211), Houston (212-
237), Philadelphia (238-262), Detroit (263-
286), Boston (287-312), Texas (313-334),
Chicago White Sox (335-358), Cleveland (359-
382), San Francisco (383-403), Kansas City
(404-427), Atlanta (428-449), California (450-
474), Pittsburgh (475-501), Seattle (502-519),
New York Mets (520-544), Minnesota (545-
565), San Diego (566-585), Chicago Cubs
(586-607), and Toronto (608-627). Cards
numbered 628 through 646 are special cards
highlighting some of the stars and leaders of
the 1981 season. The last 14 cards in the set
(647-660) are checklist cards. The backs feature player statistics and a full-color team logo
in the upper right-hand corner of each card.
The complete set price below does not include
any of the more valuable variation cards listed.

		MINT	EXC	G-VG
COMPLETE SET (660)		35.00	17.50	3.50
COMMON PLAYER (1-660)		.03	.01	.00
☐ 1	Dusty Baker	.12	.03	.01

		MINT	EXC	G-VG
☐ 2	Robert Castillo	.03	.01	.00
☐ 3	Ron Cey	.10	.05	.01
☐ 4	Terry Forster	.06	.03	.00
☐ 5	Steve Garvey	.50	.25	.05
☐ 6	Dave Goltz	.03	.01	.00
☐ 7	Pedro Guerrero	.45	.22	.04
☐ 8	Burt Hooton	.03	.01	.00
☐ 9	Steve Howe	.03	.01	.00
☐ 10	Jay Johnstone	.06	.03	.00
☐ 11	Ken Landreaux	.03	.01	.00
☐ 12	Dave Lopes	.08	.04	.01
☐ 13	Mike Marshall	1.25	.60	.12
☐ 14	Bobby Mitchell	.03	.01	.00
☐ 15	Rick Monday	.03	.01	.00
☐ 16	Tom Niedenfuer	.20	.10	.02
☐ 17	Ted Power	.20	.10	.02
☐ 18	Jerry Reuss	.06	.03	.00
☐ 19	Ron Roenicke	.03	.01	.00
☐ 20	Bill Russell	.06	.03	.00
☐ 21	Steve Sax	2.75	1.35	.27
☐ 22	Mike Scioscia	.10	.05	.01
☐ 23	Reggie Smith	.08	.04	.01
☐ 24	Dave Stewart	3.75	1.85	.37
☐ 25	Rick Sutcliffe	.20	.10	.02
☐ 26	Derrel Thomas	.03	.01	.00
☐ 27	Fernando Valenzuela	.60	.30	.06
☐ 28	Bob Welch	.08	.04	.01
☐ 29	Steve Yeager	.03	.01	.00
☐ 30	Bobby Brown	.03	.01	.00
☐ 31	Rick Cerone	.03	.01	.00
☐ 32	Ron Davis	.03	.01	.00
☐ 33	Bucky Dent	.10	.05	.01
☐ 34	Barry Foote	.03	.01	.00
☐ 35	George Frazier	.03	.01	.00
☐ 36	Oscar Gamble	.03	.01	.00
☐ 37	Rich Gossage	.20	.10	.02
☐ 38	Ron Guidry	.20	.10	.02
☐ 39	Reggie Jackson	.75	.35	.07
☐ 40	Tommy John	.18	.09	.01
☐ 41	Rudy May	.03	.01	.00
☐ 42	Larry Milbourne	.03	.01	.00
☐ 43	Jerry Mumphrey	.03	.01	.00
☐ 44	Bobby Murcer	.08	.04	.01
☐ 45	Gene Nelson	.20	.10	.02
☐ 46	Graig Nettles	.12	.06	.01
☐ 47	Johnny Oates	.03	.01	.00
☐ 48	Lou Piniella	.10	.05	.01
☐ 49	Willie Randolph	.08	.04	.01
☐ 50	Rick Reuschel	.15	.07	.01

		MINT	EXC	G-VG			MINT	EXC	G-VG
☐ 51	Dave Revering	.03	.01	.00	☐ 100	Dave McKay	.03	.01	.00
☐ 52	Dave Righetti	1.50	.75	.15	☐ 101	Dwayne Murphy	.03	.01	.00
☐ 53	Aurelio Rodriguez	.03	.01	.00	☐ 102	Jeff Newman	.03	.01	.00
☐ 54	Bob Watson	.06	.03	.00	☐ 103	Mike Norris	.03	.01	.00
☐ 55	Dennis Werth	.03	.01	.00	☐ 104	Bob Owchinko	.03	.01	.00
☐ 56	Dave Winfield	.50	.25	.05	☐ 105	Mitchell Page	.03	.01	.00
☐ 57	Johnny Bench	.65	.30	.06	☐ 106	Rob Picciolo	.03	.01	.00
☐ 58	Bruce Berenyi	.03	.01	.00	☐ 107	Jim Spencer	.03	.01	.00
☐ 59	Larry Biittner	.03	.01	.00	☐ 108	Fred Stanley	.03	.01	.00
☐ 60	Scott Brown	.03	.01	.00	☐ 109	Tom Underwood	.03	.01	.00
☐ 61	Dave Collins	.03	.01	.00	☐ 110	Joaquin Andujar	.08	.04	.01
☐ 62	Geoff Combe	.03	.01	.00	☐ 111	Steve Braun	.03	.01	.00
☐ 63	Dave Concepcion	.10	.05	.01	☐ 112	Bob Forsch	.03	.01	.00
☐ 64	Dan Driessen	.03	.01	.00	☐ 113	George Hendrick	.06	.03	.00
☐ 65	Joe Edelen	.03	.01	.00	☐ 114	Keith Hernandez	.35	.17	.03
☐ 66	George Foster	.15	.07	.01	☐ 115	Tom Herr	.08	.04	.01
☐ 67	Ken Griffey	.10	.05	.01	☐ 116	Dane Iorg	.03	.01	.00
☐ 68	Paul Householder	.03	.01	.00	☐ 117	Jim Kaat	.15	.07	.01
☐ 69	Tom Hume	.03	.01	.00	☐ 118	Tito Landrum	.03	.01	.00
☐ 70	Junior Kennedy	.03	.01	.00	☐ 119	Sixto Lezcano	.03	.01	.00
☐ 71	Ray Knight	.08	.04	.01	☐ 120	Mark Littell	.03	.01	.00
☐ 72	Mike LaCoss	.03	.01	.00	☐ 121	John Martin	.03	.01	.00
☐ 73	Rafael Landestoy	.03	.01	.00	☐ 122	Silvio Martinez	.03	.01	.00
☐ 74	Charlie Leibrandt	.06	.03	.00	☐ 123	Ken Oberkfell	.03	.01	.00
☐ 75	Sam Mejias	.03	.01	.00	☐ 124	Darrell Porter	.03	.01	.00
☐ 76	Paul Moskau	.03	.01	.00	☐ 125	Mike Ramsey	.03	.01	.00
☐ 77	Joe Nolan	.03	.01	.00	☐ 126	Orlando Sanchez	.03	.01	.00
☐ 78	Mike O'Berry	.03	.01	.00	☐ 127	Bob Shirley	.03	.01	.00
☐ 79	Ron Oester	.03	.01	.00	☐ 128	Lary Sorensen	.03	.01	.00
☐ 80	Frank Pastore	.03	.01	.00	☐ 129	Bruce Sutter	.15	.07	.01
☐ 81	Joe Price	.03	.01	.00	☐ 130	Bob Sykes	.03	.01	.00
☐ 82	Tom Seaver	.50	.25	.05	☐ 131	Garry Templeton	.08	.04	.01
☐ 83	Mario Soto	.06	.03	.00	☐ 132	Gene Tenace	.03	.01	.00
☐ 84	Mike Vail	.03	.01	.00	☐ 133	Jerry Augustine	.03	.01	.00
☐ 85	Tony Armas	.06	.03	.00	☐ 134	Sal Bando	.06	.03	.00
☐ 86	Shooty Babitt	.03	.01	.00	☐ 135	Mark Brouhard	.03	.01	.00
☐ 87	Dave Beard	.03	.01	.00	☐ 136	Mike Caldwell	.03	.01	.00
☐ 88	Rick Bosetti	.03	.01	.00	☐ 137	Reggie Cleveland	.03	.01	.00
☐ 89	Keith Drumwright	.03	.01	.00	☐ 138	Cecil Cooper	.15	.07	.01
☐ 90	Wayne Gross	.03	.01	.00	☐ 139	Jamie Easterly	.03	.01	.00
☐ 91	Mike Heath	.03	.01	.00	☐ 140	Marshall Edwards	.03	.01	.00
☐ 92	Rickey Henderson	1.50	.75	.15	☐ 141	Rollie Fingers	.20	.10	.02
☐ 93	Cliff Johnson	.03	.01	.00	☐ 142	Jim Gantner	.03	.01	.00
☐ 94	Jeff Jones	.03	.01	.00	☐ 143	Moose Haas	.03	.01	.00
☐ 95	Matt Keough	.03	.01	.00	☐ 144	Larry Hisle	.06	.03	.00
☐ 96	Brian Kingman	.03	.01	.00	☐ 145	Roy Howell	.03	.01	.00
☐ 97	Mickey Klutts	.03	.01	.00	☐ 146	Rickey Keeton	.03	.01	.00
☐ 98	Rick Langford	.03	.01	.00	☐ 147	Randy Lerch	.03	.01	.00
☐ 99	Steve McCatty	.03	.01	.00	☐ 148	Paul Molitor	.25	.12	.02

		MINT	EXC	G-VG			MINT	EXC	G-VG
☐ 149	Don Money	.03	.01	.00	☐ 198	Rowland Office	.03	.01	.00
☐ 150	Charlie Moore	.03	.01	.00	☐ 199	David Palmer	.03	.01	.00
☐ 151	Ben Oglivie	.06	.03	.00	☐ 200	Larry Parrish	.06	.03	.00
☐ 152	Ted Simmons	.12	.06	.01	☐ 201	Mike Phillips	.03	.01	.00
☐ 153	Jim Slaton	.03	.01	.00	☐ 202	Tim Raines	2.00	1.00	.20
☐ 154	Gorman Thomas	.08	.04	.01	☐ 203	Bobby Ramos	.03	.01	.00
☐ 155	Robin Yount	1.00	.50	.10	☐ 204	Jeff Reardon	.20	.07	.01
☐ 156	Pete Vuckovich	.08	.04	.01	☐ 205	Steve Rogers	.06	.03	.00
☐ 157	Benny Ayala	.03	.01	.00	☐ 206	Scott Sanderson	.03	.01	.00
☐ 158	Mark Belanger	.06	.03	.00	☐ 207	Rodney Scott UER	.20	.10	.02
☐ 159	Al Bumbry	.03	.01	.00		(photo actually			
☐ 160	Terry Crowley	.03	.01	.00		Tim Raines)			
☐ 161	Rich Dauer	.03	.01	.00	☐ 208	Elias Sosa	.03	.01	.00
☐ 162	Doug DeCinces	.06	.03	.00	☐ 209	Chris Speier	.03	.01	.00
☐ 163	Rick Dempsey	.03	.01	.00	☐ 210	Tim Wallach	1.00	.50	.10
☐ 164	Jim Dwyer	.03	.01	.00	☐ 211	Jerry White	.03	.01	.00
☐ 165	Mike Flanagan	.08	.04	.01	☐ 212	Alan Ashby	.03	.01	.00
☐ 166	Dave Ford	.03	.01	.00	☐ 213	Cesar Cedeno	.08	.04	.01
☐ 167	Dan Graham	.03	.01	.00	☐ 214	Jose Cruz	.08	.04	.01
☐ 168	Wayne Krenchicki	.03	.01	.00	☐ 215	Kiko Garcia	.03	.01	.00
☐ 169	John Lowenstein	.03	.01	.00	☐ 216	Phil Garner	.03	.01	.00
☐ 170	Dennis Martinez	.08	.04	.01	☐ 217	Danny Heep	.03	.01	.00
☐ 171	Tippy Martinez	.03	.01	.00	☐ 218	Art Howe	.08	.04	.01
☐ 172	Scott McGregor	.06	.03	.00	☐ 219	Bob Knepper	.08	.04	.01
☐ 173	Jose Morales	.03	.01	.00	☐ 220	Frank LaCorte	.03	.01	.00
☐ 174	Eddie Murray	.50	.25	.05	☐ 221	Joe Niekro	.10	.05	.01
☐ 175	Jim Palmer	.45	.22	.04	☐ 222	Joe Pittman	.03	.01	.00
☐ 176	Cal Ripken	8.50	4.25	.85	☐ 223	Terry Puhl	.03	.01	.00
☐ 177	Gary Roenicke	.03	.01	.00	☐ 224	Luis Pujols	.03	.01	.00
☐ 178	Lenn Sakata	.03	.01	.00	☐ 225	Craig Reynolds	.03	.01	.00
☐ 179	Ken Singleton	.08	.04	.01	☐ 226	J.R. Richard	.08	.04	.01
☐ 180	Sammy Stewart	.03	.01	.00	☐ 227	Dave Roberts	.03	.01	.00
☐ 181	Tim Stoddard	.03	.01	.00	☐ 228	Vern Ruhle	.03	.01	.00
☐ 182	Steve Stone	.06	.03	.00	☐ 229	Nolan Ryan	1.75	.85	.17
☐ 183	Stan Bahnsen	.03	.01	.00	☐ 230	Joe Sambito	.03	.01	.00
☐ 184	Ray Burris	.03	.01	.00	☐ 231	Tony Scott	.03	.01	.00
☐ 185	Gary Carter	.45	.22	.04	☐ 232	Dave Smith	.08	.04	.01
☐ 186	Warren Cromartie	.03	.01	.00	☐ 233	Harry Spilman	.03	.01	.00
☐ 187	Andre Dawson	.40	.20	.04	☐ 234	Don Sutton	.30	.15	.03
☐ 188	Terry Francona	.08	.04	.01	☐ 235	Dickie Thon	.06	.03	.00
☐ 189	Woodie Fryman	.03	.01	.00	☐ 236	Denny Walling	.03	.01	.00
☐ 190	Bill Gullickson	.06	.03	.00	☐ 237	Gary Woods	.03	.01	.00
☐ 191	Grant Jackson	.03	.01	.00	☐ 238	Luis Aguayo	.03	.01	.00
☐ 192	Wallace Johnson	.06	.03	.00	☐ 239	Ramon Aviles	.03	.01	.00
☐ 193	Charlie Lea	.06	.03	.00	☐ 240	Bob Boone	.15	.07	.01
☐ 194	Bill Lee	.06	.03	.00	☐ 241	Larry Bowa	.12	.06	.01
☐ 195	Jerry Manuel	.03	.01	.00	☐ 242	Warren Brusstar	.03	.01	.00
☐ 196	Brad Mills	.03	.01	.00	☐ 243	Steve Carlton	.60	.30	.06
☐ 197	John Milner	.03	.01	.00	☐ 244	Larry Christenson	.03	.01	.00

		MINT	EXC	G-VG				MINT	EXC	G-VG
☐ 245	Dick Davis	.03	.01	.00	☐ 294	Rich Gedman	.35	.17	.03
☐ 246	Greg Gross	.03	.01	.00	☐ 295	Garry Hancock	.03	.01	.00
☐ 247	Sparky Lyle	.10	.05	.01	☐ 296	Glenn Hoffman	.03	.01	.00
☐ 248	Garry Maddox	.06	.03	.00	☐ 297	Bruce Hurst	.65	.30	.06
☐ 249	Gary Matthews	.06	.03	.00	☐ 298	Carney Lansford	.25	.12	.02
☐ 250	Bake McBride	.03	.01	.00	☐ 299	Rick Miller	.03	.01	.00
☐ 251	Tug McGraw	.10	.05	.01	☐ 300	Reid Nichols	.03	.01	.00
☐ 252	Keith Moreland	.03	.01	.00	☐ 301	Bob Ojeda	.60	.30	.06
☐ 253	Dickie Noles	.03	.01	.00	☐ 302	Tony Perez	.18	.09	.01
☐ 254	Mike Proly	.03	.01	.00	☐ 303	Chuck Rainey	.03	.01	.00
☐ 255	Ron Reed	.03	.01	.00	☐ 304	Jerry Remy	.03	.01	.00
☐ 256	Pete Rose	1.25	.60	.12	☐ 305	Jim Rice	.30	.15	.03
☐ 257	Dick Ruthven	.03	.01	.00	☐ 306	Joe Rudi	.06	.03	.00
☐ 258	Mike Schmidt	1.00	.50	.10	☐ 307	Bob Stanley	.03	.01	.00
☐ 259	Lonnie Smith	.12	.06	.01	☐ 308	Dave Stapleton	.03	.01	.00
☐ 260	Manny Trillo	.03	.01	.00	☐ 309	Frank Tanana	.06	.03	.00
☐ 261	Del Unser	.03	.01	.00	☐ 310	Mike Torrez	.03	.01	.00
☐ 262	George Vukovich	.03	.01	.00	☐ 311	John Tudor	.20	.10	.02
☐ 263	Tom Brookens	.03	.01	.00	☐ 312	Carl Yastrzemski	1.00	.50	.10
☐ 264	George Cappuzzello	.03	.01	.00	☐ 313	Buddy Bell	.10	.05	.01
☐ 265	Marty Castillo	.03	.01	.00	☐ 314	Steve Comer	.03	.01	.00
☐ 266	Al Cowens	.03	.01	.00	☐ 315	Danny Darwin	.03	.01	.00
☐ 267	Kirk Gibson	.75	.35	.07	☐ 316	John Ellis	.03	.01	.00
☐ 268	Richie Hebner	.03	.01	.00	☐ 317	John Grubb	.03	.01	.00
☐ 269	Ron Jackson	.03	.01	.00	☐ 318	Rick Honeycutt	.03	.01	.00
☐ 270	Lynn Jones	.03	.01	.00	☐ 319	Charlie Hough	.06	.03	.00
☐ 271	Steve Kemp	.06	.03	.00	☐ 320	Ferguson Jenkins	.15	.07	.01
☐ 272	Rick Leach	.03	.01	.00	☐ 321	John Henry Johnson	.03	.01	.00
☐ 273	Aurelio Lopez	.03	.01	.00	☐ 322	Jim Kern	.03	.01	.00
☐ 274	Jack Morris	.20	.10	.02	☐ 323	Jon Matlack	.03	.01	.00
☐ 275	Kevin Saucier	.03	.01	.00	☐ 324	Doc Medich	.03	.01	.00
☐ 276	Lance Parrish	.20	.10	.02	☐ 325	Mario Mendoza	.03	.01	.00
☐ 277	Rick Peters	.03	.01	.00	☐ 326	Al Oliver	.10	.05	.01
☐ 278	Dan Petry	.03	.01	.00	☐ 327	Pat Putnam	.03	.01	.00
☐ 279	Dave Rozema	.03	.01	.00	☐ 328	Mickey Rivers	.06	.03	.00
☐ 280	Stan Papi	.03	.01	.00	☐ 329	Leon Roberts	.03	.01	.00
☐ 281	Dan Schatzeder	.03	.01	.00	☐ 330	Billy Sample	.03	.01	.00
☐ 282	Champ Summers	.03	.01	.00	☐ 331	Bill Stein	.03	.01	.00
☐ 283	Alan Trammell	.35	.17	.03	☐ 332	Jim Sundberg	.06	.03	.00
☐ 284	Lou Whitaker	.25	.12	.01	☐ 333	Mark Wagner	.03	.01	.00
☐ 285	Milt Wilcox	.03	.01	.00	☐ 334	Bump Wills	.03	.01	.00
☐ 286	John Wockenfuss	.03	.01	.00	☐ 335	Bill Almon	.03	.01	.00
☐ 287	Gary Allenson	.03	.01	.00	☐ 336	Harold Baines	.35	.17	.03
☐ 288	Tom Burgmeier	.03	.01	.00	☐ 337	Ross Baumgarten	.03	.01	.00
☐ 289	Bill Campbell	.03	.01	.00	☐ 338	Tony Bernazard	.03	.01	.00
☐ 290	Mark Clear	.03	.01	.00	☐ 339	Britt Burns	.06	.03	.00
☐ 291	Steve Crawford	.03	.01	.00	☐ 340	Richard Dotson	.06	.03	.00
☐ 292	Dennis Eckersley	.20	.10	.02	☐ 341	Jim Essian	.03	.01	.00
☐ 293	Dwight Evans	.20	.10	.02	☐ 342	Ed Farmer	.03	.01	.00

		MINT	EXC	G-VG				MINT	EXC	G-VG
☐ 343	Carlton Fisk	.35	.17	.03	☐ 392	Gary Lavelle		.03	.01	.00
☐ 344	Kevin Hickey	.03	.01	.00	☐ 393	Johnnie LeMaster		.03	.01	.00
☐ 345	LaMarr Hoyt	.06	.03	.00	☐ 394	Jerry Martin		.03	.01	.00
☐ 346	Lamar Johnson	.03	.01	.00	☐ 395	Milt May		.03	.01	.00
☐ 347	Jerry Koosman	.08	.04	.01	☐ 396	Greg Minton		.03	.01	.00
☐ 348	Rusty Kuntz	.03	.01	.00	☐ 397	Joe Morgan		.35	.17	.03
☐ 349	Dennis Lamp	.03	.01	.00	☐ 398	Joe Pettini		.03	.01	.00
☐ 350	Ron LeFlore	.06	.03	.00	☐ 399	Allen Ripley		.03	.01	.00
☐ 351	Chet Lemon	.06	.03	.00	☐ 400	Billy Smith		.03	.01	.00
☐ 352	Greg Luzinski	.10	.05	.01	☐ 401	Rennie Stennett		.03	.01	.00
☐ 353	Bob Molinaro	.03	.01	.00	☐ 402	Ed Whitson		.06	.03	.00
☐ 354	Jim Morrison	.03	.01	.00	☐ 403	Jim Wohlford		.03	.01	.00
☐ 355	Wayne Nordhagen	.03	.01	.00	☐ 404	Willie Aikens		.03	.01	.00
☐ 356	Greg Pryor	.03	.01	.00	☐ 405	George Brett		.80	.40	.08
☐ 357	Mike Squires	.03	.01	.00	☐ 406	Ken Brett		.03	.01	.00
☐ 358	Steve Trout	.03	.01	.00	☐ 407	Dave Chalk		.03	.01	.00
☐ 359	Alan Bannister	.03	.01	.00	☐ 408	Rich Gale		.03	.01	.00
☐ 360	Len Barker	.03	.01	.00	☐ 409	Cesar Geronimo		.03	.01	.00
☐ 361	Bert Blyleven	.20	.07	.01	☐ 410	Larry Gura		.06	.03	.00
☐ 362	Joe Charboneau	.06	.03	.00	☐ 411	Clint Hurdle		.03	.01	.00
☐ 363	John Denny	.06	.03	.00	☐ 412	Mike Jones		.03	.01	.00
☐ 364	Bo Diaz	.03	.01	.00	☐ 413	Dennis Leonard		.06	.03	.00
☐ 365	Miguel Dilone	.03	.01	.00	☐ 414	Renie Martin		.03	.01	.00
☐ 366	Jerry Dybzinski	.03	.01	.00	☐ 415	Lee May		.06	.03	.00
☐ 367	Wayne Garland	.03	.01	.00	☐ 416	Hal McRae		.06	.03	.00
☐ 368	Mike Hargrove	.06	.03	.00	☐ 417	Darryl Motley		.06	.03	.00
☐ 369	Toby Harrah	.06	.03	.00	☐ 418	Rance Mulliniks		.03	.01	.00
☐ 370	Ron Hassey	.03	.01	.00	☐ 419	Amos Otis		.08	.04	.01
☐ 371	Von Hayes	1.00	.50	.10	☐ 420	Ken Phelps		.50	.25	.05
☐ 372	Pat Kelly	.03	.01	.00	☐ 421	Jamie Quirk		.03	.01	.00
☐ 373	Duane Kuiper	.03	.01	.00	☐ 422	Dan Quisenberry		.15	.07	.01
☐ 374	Rick Manning	.03	.01	.00	☐ 423	Paul Splittorff		.03	.01	.00
☐ 375	Sid Monge	.03	.01	.00	☐ 424	U.L. Washington		.03	.01	.00
☐ 376	Jorge Orta	.03	.01	.00	☐ 425	John Wathan		.06	.03	.00
☐ 377	Dave Rosello	.03	.01	.00	☐ 426	Frank White		.08	.04	.01
☐ 378	Dan Spillner	.03	.01	.00	☐ 427	Willie Wilson		.12	.06	.01
☐ 379	Mike Stanton	.03	.01	.00	☐ 428	Brian Asselstine		.03	.01	.00
☐ 380	Andre Thornton	.06	.03	.00	☐ 429	Bruce Benedict		.03	.01	.00
☐ 381	Tom Veryzer	.03	.01	.00	☐ 430	Tommy Boggs		.03	.01	.00
☐ 382	Rick Waits	.03	.01	.00	☐ 431	Larry Bradford		.03	.01	.00
☐ 383	Doyle Alexander	.06	.03	.00	☐ 432	Rick Camp		.03	.01	.00
☐ 384	Vida Blue	.08	.04	.01	☐ 433	Chris Chambliss		.08	.04	.01
☐ 385	Fred Breining	.03	.01	.00	☐ 434	Gene Garber		.03	.01	.00
☐ 386	Enos Cabell	.03	.01	.00	☐ 435	Preston Hanna		.03	.01	.00
☐ 387	Jack Clark	.25	.12	.02	☐ 436	Bob Horner		.15	.07	.01
☐ 388	Darrell Evans	.12	.06	.01	☐ 437	Glenn Hubbard		.03	.01	.00
☐ 389	Tom Griffin	.03	.01	.00	☐ 438A	All Hrabosky ERR		20.00	10.00	2.00
☐ 390	Larry Herndon	.03	.01	.00		(height 5'1",				
☐ 391	Al Holland	.03	.01	.00		All on reverse)				

		MINT	EXC	G-VG
☐ 438B	Al Hrabosky ERR (height 5'1")	1.25	.60	.12
☐ 438C	Al Hrabosky (height 5'10")	.10	.05	.01
☐ 439	Rufino Linares	.06	.03	.00
☐ 440	Rick Mahler	.25	.12	.02
☐ 441	Ed Miller	.03	.01	.00
☐ 442	John Montefusco	.06	.03	.00
☐ 443	Dale Murphy	.90	.45	.09
☐ 444	Phil Niekro	.30	.15	.03
☐ 445	Gaylord Perry	.30	.15	.03
☐ 446	Biff Pocoroba	.03	.01	.00
☐ 447	Rafael Ramirez	.03	.01	.00
☐ 448	Jerry Royster	.03	.01	.00
☐ 449	Claudell Washington	.08	.04	.01
☐ 450	Don Aase	.03	.01	.00
☐ 451	Don Baylor	.15	.07	.01
☐ 452	Juan Beniquez	.03	.01	.00
☐ 453	Rick Burleson	.06	.03	.00
☐ 454	Bert Campaneris	.06	.03	.00
☐ 455	Rod Carew	.50	.25	.05
☐ 456	Bob Clark	.03	.01	.00
☐ 457	Brian Downing	.06	.03	.00
☐ 458	Dan Ford	.03	.01	.00
☐ 459	Ken Forsch	.03	.01	.00
☐ 460A	Dave Frost (5 mm space before ERA)	.40	.20	.04
☐ 460B	Dave Frost (1 mm space)	.06	.03	.00
☐ 461	Bobby Grich	.08	.04	.01
☐ 462	Larry Harlow	.03	.01	.00
☐ 463	John Harris	.03	.01	.00
☐ 464	Andy Hassler	.03	.01	.00
☐ 465	Butch Hobson	.03	.01	.00
☐ 466	Jesse Jefferson	.03	.01	.00
☐ 467	Bruce Kison	.03	.01	.00
☐ 468	Fred Lynn	.20	.10	.02
☐ 469	Angel Moreno	.03	.01	.00
☐ 470	Ed Ott	.03	.01	.00
☐ 471	Fred Patek	.03	.01	.00
☐ 472	Steve Renko	.03	.01	.00
☐ 473	Mike Witt	.75	.35	.07
☐ 474	Geoff Zahn	.03	.01	.00
☐ 475	Gary Alexander	.03	.01	.00
☐ 476	Dale Berra	.03	.01	.00
☐ 477	Kurt Bevacqua	.03	.01	.00
☐ 478	Jim Bibby	.03	.01	.00
☐ 479	John Candelaria	.08	.04	.01
☐ 480	Victor Cruz	.03	.01	.00
☐ 481	Mike Easler	.06	.03	.00
☐ 482	Tim Foli	.03	.01	.00
☐ 483	Lee Lacy	.03	.01	.00
☐ 484	Vance Law	.20	.10	.02
☐ 485	Bill Madlock	.12	.06	.01
☐ 486	Willie Montanez	.03	.01	.00
☐ 487	Omar Moreno	.03	.01	.00
☐ 488	Steve Nicosia	.03	.01	.00
☐ 489	Dave Parker	.25	.12	.02
☐ 490	Tony Pena	.35	.17	.03
☐ 491	Pascual Perez	.30	.15	.03
☐ 492	Johnny Ray	.75	.35	.07
☐ 493	Rick Rhoden	.06	.03	.00
☐ 494	Bill Robinson	.06	.03	.00
☐ 495	Don Robinson	.06	.03	.00
☐ 496	Enrique Romo	.03	.01	.00
☐ 497	Rod Scurry	.03	.01	.00
☐ 498	Eddie Solomon	.03	.01	.00
☐ 499	Willie Stargell	.40	.20	.04
☐ 500	Kent Tekulve	.06	.03	.00
☐ 501	Jason Thompson	.03	.01	.00
☐ 502	Glenn Abbott	.03	.01	.00
☐ 503	Jim Anderson	.03	.01	.00
☐ 504	Floyd Bannister	.03	.01	.00
☐ 505	Bruce Bochte	.03	.01	.00
☐ 506	Jeff Burroughs	.06	.03	.00
☐ 507	Bryan Clark	.03	.01	.00
☐ 508	Ken Clay	.03	.01	.00
☐ 509	Julio Cruz	.03	.01	.00
☐ 510	Dick Drago	.03	.01	.00
☐ 511	Gary Gray	.03	.01	.00
☐ 512	Dan Meyer	.03	.01	.00
☐ 513	Jerry Narron	.03	.01	.00
☐ 514	Tom Paciorek	.03	.01	.00
☐ 515	Casey Parsons	.03	.01	.00
☐ 516	Lenny Randle	.03	.01	.00
☐ 517	Shane Rawley	.06	.03	.00
☐ 518	Joe Simpson	.03	.01	.00
☐ 519	Richie Zisk	.03	.01	.00
☐ 520	Neil Allen	.06	.03	.00
☐ 521	Bob Bailor	.03	.01	.00
☐ 522	Hubie Brooks	.40	.20	.04
☐ 523	Mike Cubbage	.03	.01	.00
☐ 524	Pete Falcone	.03	.01	.00
☐ 525	Doug Flynn	.03	.01	.00
☐ 526	Tom Hausman	.03	.01	.00
☐ 527	Ron Hodges	.03	.01	.00
☐ 528	Randy Jones	.03	.01	.00

		MINT	EXC	G-VG
☐ 529	Mike Jorgensen	.03	.01	.00
☐ 530	Dave Kingman	.12	.06	.01
☐ 531	Ed Lynch	.06	.03	.00
☐ 532	Mike Marshall (screwball pitcher)	.06	.03	.00
☐ 533	Lee Mazzilli	.03	.01	.00
☐ 534	Dyar Miller	.03	.01	.00
☐ 535	Mike Scott	.50	.25	.05
☐ 536	Rusty Staub	.10	.05	.01
☐ 537	John Stearns	.03	.01	.00
☐ 538	Craig Swan	.03	.01	.00
☐ 539	Frank Taveras	.03	.01	.00
☐ 540	Alex Trevino	.03	.01	.00
☐ 541	Ellis Valentine	.03	.01	.00
☐ 542	Mookie Wilson	.10	.05	.01
☐ 543	Joel Youngblood	.03	.01	.00
☐ 544	Pat Zachry	.03	.01	.00
☐ 545	Glenn Adams	.03	.01	.00
☐ 546	Fernando Arroyo	.03	.01	.00
☐ 547	John Verhoeven	.03	.01	.00
☐ 548	Sal Butera	.03	.01	.00
☐ 549	John Castino	.03	.01	.00
☐ 550	Don Cooper	.03	.01	.00
☐ 551	Doug Corbett	.03	.01	.00
☐ 552	Dave Engle	.03	.01	.00
☐ 553	Roger Erickson	.03	.01	.00
☐ 554	Danny Goodwin	.03	.01	.00
☐ 555A	Darrell Jackson (black cap)	1.00	.50	.10
☐ 555B	Darrell Jackson (red cap with T)	.10	.05	.01
☐ 555C	Darrell Jackson (red cap, no emblem)	5.00	2.50	.50
☐ 556	Pete Mackanin	.03	.01	.00
☐ 557	Jack O'Connor	.03	.01	.00
☐ 558	Hosken Powell	.03	.01	.00
☐ 559	Pete Redfern	.03	.01	.00
☐ 560	Roy Smalley	.03	.01	.00
☐ 561	Chuck Baker UER (shortstop on front)	.03	.01	.00
☐ 562	Gary Ward	.06	.03	.00
☐ 563	Rob Wilfong	.03	.01	.00
☐ 564	Al Williams	.03	.01	.00
☐ 565	Butch Wynegar	.03	.01	.00
☐ 566	Randy Bass	.06	.03	.00
☐ 567	Juan Bonilla	.03	.01	.00
☐ 568	Danny Boone	.03	.01	.00
☐ 569	John Curtis	.03	.01	.00
☐ 570	Juan Eichelberger	.03	.01	.00

		MINT	EXC	G-VG
☐ 571	Barry Evans	.03	.01	.00
☐ 572	Tim Flannery	.03	.01	.00
☐ 573	Ruppert Jones	.03	.01	.00
☐ 574	Terry Kennedy	.03	.01	.00
☐ 575	Joe Lefebvre	.03	.01	.00
☐ 576A	John Littlefield ERR (left handed)	150.00	75.00	15.00
☐ 576B	John Littlefield COR (right handed)	.06	.03	.00
☐ 577	Gary Lucas	.03	.01	.00
☐ 578	Steve Mura	.03	.01	.00
☐ 579	Broderick Perkins	.03	.01	.00
☐ 580	Gene Richards	.03	.01	.00
☐ 581	Luis Salazar	.06	.03	.00
☐ 582	Ozzie Smith	.35	.17	.03
☐ 583	John Urrea	.03	.01	.00
☐ 584	Chris Welsh	.03	.01	.00
☐ 585	Rick Wise	.03	.01	.00
☐ 586	Doug Bird	.03	.01	.00
☐ 587	Tim Blackwell	.03	.01	.00
☐ 588	Bobby Bonds	.10	.05	.01
☐ 589	Bill Buckner	.10	.05	.01
☐ 590	Bill Caudill	.03	.01	.00
☐ 591	Hector Cruz	.03	.01	.00
☐ 592	Jody Davis	.35	.17	.03
☐ 593	Ivan DeJesus	.03	.01	.00
☐ 594	Steve Dillard	.03	.01	.00
☐ 595	Leon Durham	.06	.03	.00
☐ 596	Rawly Eastwick	.03	.01	.00
☐ 597	Steve Henderson	.03	.01	.00
☐ 598	Mike Krukow	.06	.03	.00
☐ 599	Mike Lum	.03	.01	.00
☐ 600	Randy Martz	.03	.01	.00
☐ 601	Jerry Morales	.03	.01	.00
☐ 602	Ken Reitz	.03	.01	.00
☐ 603A	Lee Smith ERR (Cubs logo reversed)	1.25	.60	.12
☐ 603B	Lee Smith COR	.65	.30	.06
☐ 604	Dick Tidrow	.03	.01	.00
☐ 605	Jim Tracy	.03	.01	.00
☐ 606	Mike Tyson	.03	.01	.00
☐ 607	Ty Waller	.03	.01	.00
☐ 608	Danny Ainge	.15	.07	.01
☐ 609	Jorge Bell	6.50	3.25	.65
☐ 610	Mark Bomback	.03	.01	.00
☐ 611	Barry Bonnell	.03	.01	.00
☐ 612	Jim Clancy	.03	.01	.00
☐ 613	Damaso Garcia	.03	.01	.00
☐ 614	Jerry Garvin	.03	.01	.00

		MINT	EXC	G-VG
☐ 615	Alfredo Griffin	.06	.03	.00
☐ 616	Garth Iorg	.03	.01	.00
☐ 617	Luis Leal	.03	.01	.00
☐ 618	Ken Macha	.03	.01	.00
☐ 619	John Mayberry	.06	.03	.00
☐ 620	Joey McLaughlin	.03	.01	.00
☐ 621	Lloyd Moseby	.15	.07	.01
☐ 622	Dave Stieb	.20	.10	.02
☐ 623	Jackson Todd	.03	.01	.00
☐ 624	Willie Upshaw	.03	.01	.00
☐ 625	Otto Velez	.03	.01	.00
☐ 626	Ernie Whitt	.06	.03	.00
☐ 627	Alvis Woods	.03	.01	.00
☐ 628	All Star Game Cleveland, Ohio	.06	.03	.00
☐ 629	All Star Infielders Frank White and Bucky Dent	.06	.03	.00
☐ 630	Big Red Machine Dan Driessen Dave Concepcion George Foster	.08	.04	.01
☐ 631	Bruce Sutter Top NL Relief Pitcher	.08	.04	.01
☐ 632	"Steve and Carlton" Steve Carlton and Carlton Fisk	.20	.10	.02
☐ 633	Carl Yastrzemski 3000th Game	.35	.17	.03
☐ 634	Dynamic Duo Johnny Bench and Tom Seaver	.35	.17	.03
☐ 635	West Meets East Fernando Valenzuela and Gary Carter	.20	.10	.02
☐ 636A	Fernando Valenzuela: NL SO King ("he" NL)	.60	.30	.06
☐ 636B	Fernando Valenzuela: NL SO King ("the" NL)	.25	.12	.02
☐ 637	Mike Schmidt Home Run King	.35	.17	.03
☐ 638	NL All Stars Gary Carter and Dave Parker	.15	.07	.01
☐ 639	Perfect Game Len Barker and Bo Diaz (catcher actually Ron Hassey)	.06	.03	.00

		MINT	EXC	G-VG
☐ 640	Pete and Re-Pete Pete Rose and Son	1.50	.75	.15
☐ 641	Phillies Finest Lonnie Smith Mike Schmidt Steve Carlton	.35	.17	.03
☐ 642	Red Sox Reunion Fred Lynn and Dwight Evans	.08	.04	.01
☐ 643	Rickey Henderson Most Hits and Runs	.30	.15	.03
☐ 644	Rollie Fingers Most Saves AL	.10	.05	.01
☐ 645	Tom Seaver Most 1981 Wins	.20	.10	.02
☐ 646A	Yankee Powerhouse Reggie Jackson and Dave Winfield (comma on back after outfielder)	.75	.35	.07
☐ 646B	Yankee Powerhouse Reggie Jackson and Dave Winfield (no comma)	.40	.20	.04
☐ 647	CL: Yankees/Dodgers	.08	.01	.00
☐ 648	CL: A's/Reds	.07	.01	.00
☐ 649	CL: Cards/Brewers	.07	.01	.00
☐ 650	CL: Expos/Orioles	.07	.01	.00
☐ 651	CL: Astros/Phillies	.07	.01	.00
☐ 652	CL: Tigers/Red Sox	.07	.01	.00
☐ 653	CL: Rangers/White Sox	.07	.01	.00
☐ 654	CL: Giants/Indians	.07	.01	.00
☐ 655	CL: Royals/Braves	.07	.01	.00
☐ 656	CL: Angels/Pirates	.07	.01	.00
☐ 657	CL: Mariners/Mets	.07	.01	.00
☐ 658	CL: Padres/Twins	.07	.01	.00
☐ 659	CL: Blue Jays/Cubs	.07	.01	.00
☐ 660	Specials Checklist	.10	.01	.00

1983 Fleer

Mike Marshall
FIRST BASE

The cards in this 660-card set measure 2 ½"
by 3 ½". In 1983, for the third straight year,
Fleer has produced a baseball series numbering 660 cards. Of these, 1-628 are player
cards, 629-646 are special cards, and 647-660
are checklist cards. The player cards are again
ordered alphabetically within team. The team
order relates back to each team's on-field performance during the previous year, i.e., World
Champion Cardinals (1-25), AL Champion
Brewers (26-51), Baltimore (52-75), California
(76-103), Kansas City (104-128), Atlanta (129-
152), Philadelphia (153-176), Boston (177-
200), Los Angeles (201-227), Chicago White
Sox (228-251), San Francisco (252-276),
Montreal (277-301), Pittsburgh (302-326), Detroit (327-351), San Diego (352-375), New York
Yankees (376-399), Cleveland (400-423), Toronto (424-444), Houston (445-469), Seattle
(470-489), Chicago Cubs (490-512), Oakland
(513-535), New York Mets (536-561), Texas
(562-583), Cincinnati (584-606), and
Minnesota (607-628). The front of each card
has a colorful team logo at bottom left and the
player's name and position at lower right. The
reverses are done in shades of brown on white.
The cards are numbered on the back next to
a small black and white photo of the player.

	MINT	EXC	G-VG
COMPLETE SET (660)	65.00	32.50	6.50
COMMON PLAYER (1-660)	.03	.01	.00

		MINT	EXC	G-VG
☐	1 Joaquin Andujar	.12	.03	.01
☐	2 Doug Bair	.03	.01	.00
☐	3 Steve Braun	.03	.01	.00
☐	4 Glenn Brummer	.03	.01	.00
☐	5 Bob Forsch	.03	.01	.00
☐	6 David Green	.03	.01	.00
☐	7 George Hendrick ...	.06	.03	.00
☐	8 Keith Hernandez ...	.30	.15	.03
☐	9 Tom Herr	.08	.04	.01
☐	10 Dane Iorg	.03	.01	.00
☐	11 Jim Kaat	.12	.06	.01
☐	12 Jeff Lahti	.03	.01	.00
☐	13 Tito Landrum	.03	.01	.00
☐	14 Dave LaPoint	.35	.17	.03
☐	15 Willie McGee	1.25	.60	.12
☐	16 Steve Mura	.03	.01	.00
☐	17 Ken Oberkfell	.03	.01	.00
☐	18 Darrell Porter	.03	.01	.00
☐	19 Mike Ramsey	.03	.01	.00
☐	20 Gene Roof	.03	.01	.00
☐	21 Lonnie Smith	.10	.05	.01
☐	22 Ozzie Smith	.35	.17	.03
☐	23 John Stuper	.03	.01	.00
☐	24 Bruce Sutter	.12	.06	.01
☐	25 Gene Tenace	.03	.01	.00
☐	26 Jerry Augustine ...	.03	.01	.00
☐	27 Dwight Bernard ...	.03	.01	.00
☐	28 Mark Brouhard	.03	.01	.00
☐	29 Mike Caldwell	.03	.01	.00
☐	30 Cecil Cooper	.10	.05	.01
☐	31 Jamie Easterly	.03	.01	.00
☐	32 Marshall Edwards .	.03	.01	.00
☐	33 Rollie Fingers	.18	.09	.01
☐	34 Jim Gantner	.03	.01	.00
☐	35 Moose Haas	.03	.01	.00
☐	36 Roy Howell	.03	.01	.00
☐	37 Pete Ladd	.03	.01	.00
☐	38 Bob McClure	.03	.01	.00
☐	39 Doc Medich	.03	.01	.00
☐	40 Paul Molitor	.18	.09	.01
☐	41 Don Money	.03	.01	.00
☐	42 Charlie Moore	.03	.01	.00
☐	43 Ben Oglivie	.06	.03	.00
☐	44 Ed Romero	.03	.01	.00
☐	45 Ted Simmons	.12	.06	.01
☐	46 Jim Slaton	.03	.01	.00
☐	47 Don Sutton	.30	.15	.03
☐	48 Gorman Thomas ...	.08	.04	.01

		MINT	EXC	G-VG
☐ 49	Pete Vuckovich	.06	.03	.00
☐ 50	Ned Yost	.03	.01	.00
☐ 51	Robin Yount	.65	.30	.06
☐ 52	Benny Ayala	.03	.01	.00
☐ 53	Bob Bonner	.03	.01	.00
☐ 54	Al Bumbry	.03	.01	.00
☐ 55	Terry Crowley	.03	.01	.00
☐ 56	Storm Davis	.65	.30	.06
☐ 57	Rich Dauer	.03	.01	.00
☐ 58	Rick Dempsey (posing batting lefty)	.06	.03	.00
☐ 59	Jim Dwyer	.03	.01	.00
☐ 60	Mike Flanagan	.06	.03	.00
☐ 61	Dan Ford	.03	.01	.00
☐ 62	Glenn Gulliver	.03	.01	.00
☐ 63	John Lowenstein	.03	.01	.00
☐ 64	Dennis Martinez	.06	.03	.00
☐ 65	Tippy Martinez	.03	.01	.00
☐ 66	Scott McGregor	.06	.03	.00
☐ 67	Eddie Murray	.45	.22	.04
☐ 68	Joe Nolan	.03	.01	.00
☐ 69	Jim Palmer	.45	.22	.04
☐ 70	Cal Ripken Jr.	1.25	.60	.12
☐ 71	Gary Roenicke	.03	.01	.00
☐ 72	Lenn Sakata	.03	.01	.00
☐ 73	Ken Singleton	.08	.04	.01
☐ 74	Sammy Stewart	.03	.01	.00
☐ 75	Tim Stoddard	.03	.01	.00
☐ 76	Don Aase	.03	.01	.00
☐ 77	Don Baylor	.12	.06	.01
☐ 78	Juan Beniquez	.03	.01	.00
☐ 79	Bob Boone	.15	.07	.01
☐ 80	Rick Burleson	.06	.03	.00
☐ 81	Rod Carew	.50	.22	.04
☐ 82	Bobby Clark	.03	.01	.00
☐ 83	Doug Corbett	.03	.01	.00
☐ 84	John Curtis	.03	.01	.00
☐ 85	Doug DeCinces	.06	.03	.00
☐ 86	Brian Downing	.06	.03	.00
☐ 87	Joe Ferguson	.03	.01	.00
☐ 88	Tim Foli	.03	.01	.00
☐ 89	Ken Forsch	.03	.01	.00
☐ 90	Dave Goltz	.03	.01	.00
☐ 91	Bobby Grich	.06	.03	.00
☐ 92	Andy Hassler	.03	.01	.00
☐ 93	Reggie Jackson	.50	.25	.05
☐ 94	Ron Jackson	.03	.01	.00
☐ 95	Tommy John	.15	.07	.01
☐ 96	Bruce Kison	.03	.01	.00

		MINT	EXC	G-VG
☐ 97	Fred Lynn	.18	.09	.01
☐ 98	Ed Ott	.03	.01	.00
☐ 99	Steve Renko	.03	.01	.00
☐ 100	Luis Sanchez	.03	.01	.00
☐ 101	Rob Wilfong	.03	.01	.00
☐ 102	Mike Witt	.15	.07	.01
☐ 103	Geoff Zahn	.03	.01	.00
☐ 104	Willie Aikens	.03	.01	.00
☐ 105	Mike Armstrong	.03	.01	.00
☐ 106	Vida Blue	.06	.03	.00
☐ 107	Bud Black	.20	.10	.02
☐ 108	George Brett	.65	.30	.06
☐ 109	Bill Castro	.03	.01	.00
☐ 110	Onix Concepcion	.03	.01	.00
☐ 111ª	Dave Frost	.03	.01	.00
☐ 112	Cesar Geronimo	.03	.01	.00
☐ 113	Larry Gura	.03	.01	.00
☐ 114	Steve Hammond	.03	.01	.00
☐ 115	Don Hood	.03	.01	.00
☐ 116	Dennis Leonard	.06	.03	.00
☐ 117	Jerry Martin	.03	.01	.00
☐ 118	Lee May	.06	.03	.00
☐ 119	Hal McRae	.06	.03	.00
☐ 120	Amos Otis	.08	.04	.01
☐ 121	Greg Pryor	.03	.01	.00
☐ 122	Dan Quisenberry	.12	.06	.01
☐ 123	Don Slaught	.30	.15	.03
☐ 124	Paul Splittorff	.03	.01	.00
☐ 125	U.L. Washington	.03	.01	.00
☐ 126	John Wathan	.06	.03	.00
☐ 127	Frank White	.08	.04	.01
☐ 128	Willie Wilson	.12	.06	.01
☐ 129	Steve Bedrosian	.40	.20	.04
☐ 130	Bruce Benedict	.03	.01	.00
☐ 131	Tommy Boggs	.03	.01	.00
☐ 132	Brett Butler	.10	.05	.01
☐ 133	Rick Camp	.03	.01	.00
☐ 134	Chris Chambliss	.06	.03	.00
☐ 135	Ken Dayley	.06	.03	.00
☐ 136	Gene Garber	.03	.01	.00
☐ 137	Terry Harper	.03	.01	.00
☐ 138	Bob Horner	.15	.07	.01
☐ 139	Glenn Hubbard	.03	.01	.00
☐ 140	Rufino Linares	.03	.01	.00
☐ 141	Rick Mahler	.03	.01	.00
☐ 142	Dale Murphy	.85	.40	.08
☐ 143	Phil Niekro	.25	.12	.02
☐ 144	Pascual Perez	.10	.05	.01
☐ 145	Biff Pocoroba	.03	.01	.00

		MINT	EXC	G-VG			MINT	EXC	G-VG
☐ 146	Rafael Ramirez	.03	.01	.00	☐ 195	Bob Stanley	.03	.01	.00
☐ 147	Jerry Royster	.03	.01	.00	☐ 196	Dave Stapleton	.03	.01	.00
☐ 148	Ken Smith	.03	.01	.00	☐ 197	Mike Torrez	.03	.01	.00
☐ 149	Bob Walk	.06	.03	.00	☐ 198	John Tudor	.12	.06	.01
☐ 150	Claudell Washington	.08	.04	.01	☐ 199	Julio Valdez	.03	.01	.00
☐ 151	Bob Watson	.06	.03	.00	☐ 200	Carl Yastrzemski	.80	.40	.08
☐ 152	Larry Whisenton	.03	.01	.00	☐ 201	Dusty Baker	.06	.03	.00
☐ 153	Porfirio Altamirano	.03	.01	.00	☐ 202	Joe Beckwith	.03	.01	.00
☐ 154	Marty Bystrom	.03	.01	.00	☐ 203	Greg Brock	.30	.15	.03
☐ 155	Steve Carlton	.35	.17	.03	☐ 204	Ron Cey	.10	.05	.01
☐ 156	Larry Christenson	.03	.01	.00	☐ 205	Terry Forster	.06	.03	.00
☐ 157	Ivan DeJesus	.03	.01	.00	☐ 206	Steve Garvey	.45	.22	.04
☐ 158	John Denny	.08	.04	.01	☐ 207	Pedro Guerrero	.30	.15	.03
☐ 159	Bob Dernier	.03	.01	.00	☐ 208	Burt Hooton	.03	.01	.00
☐ 160	Bo Diaz	.03	.01	.00	☐ 209	Steve Howe	.03	.01	.00
☐ 161	Ed Farmer	.03	.01	.00	☐ 210	Ken Landreaux	.03	.01	.00
☐ 162	Greg Gross	.03	.01	.00	☐ 211	Mike Marshall	.25	.12	.02
☐ 163	Mike Krukow	.06	.03	.00	☐ 212	Candy Maldonado	.45	.22	.04
☐ 164	Garry Maddox	.03	.01	.00	☐ 213	Rick Monday	.06	.03	.00
☐ 165	Gary Matthews	.06	.03	.00	☐ 214	Tom Niedenfuer	.03	.01	.00
☐ 166	Tug McGraw	.10	.05	.01	☐ 215	Jorge Orta	.03	.01	.00
☐ 167	Bob Molinaro	.03	.01	.00	☐ 216	Jerry Reuss	.06	.03	.00
☐ 168	Sid Monge	.03	.01	.00	☐ 217	Ron Roenicke	.03	.01	.00
☐ 169	Ron Reed	.03	.01	.00	☐ 218	Vicente Romo	.03	.01	.00
☐ 170	Bill Robinson	.03	.01	.00	☐ 219	Bill Russell	.06	.03	.00
☐ 171	Pete Rose	1.00	.50	.10	☐ 220	Steve Sax	.50	.25	.05
☐ 172	Dick Ruthven	.03	.01	.00	☐ 221	Mike Scioscia	.06	.03	.00
☐ 173	Mike Schmidt	1.00	.50	.10	☐ 222	Dave Stewart	.50	.25	.05
☐ 174	Manny Trillo	.03	.01	.00	☐ 223	Derrel Thomas	.03	.01	.00
☐ 175	Ozzie Virgil	.03	.01	.00	☐ 224	Fernando Valenzuela	.30	.15	.03
☐ 176	George Vukovich	.03	.01	.00	☐ 225	Bob Welch	.08	.04	.01
☐ 177	Gary Allenson	.03	.01	.00	☐ 226	Ricky Wright	.03	.01	.00
☐ 178	Luis Aponte	.03	.01	.00	☐ 227	Steve Yeager	.03	.01	.00
☐ 179	Wade Boggs	18.00	9.00	1.80	☐ 228	Bill Almon	.03	.01	.00
☐ 180	Tom Burgmeier	.03	.01	.00	☐ 229	Harold Baines	.25	.12	.02
☐ 181	Mark Clear	.03	.01	.00	☐ 230	Salome Barojas	.03	.01	.00
☐ 182	Dennis Eckersley	.20	.10	.02	☐ 231	Tony Bernazard	.03	.01	.00
☐ 183	Dwight Evans	.18	.09	.01	☐ 232	Britt Burns	.03	.01	.00
☐ 184	Rich Gedman	.08	.04	.01	☐ 233	Richard Dotson	.06	.03	.00
☐ 185	Glenn Hoffman	.03	.01	.00	☐ 234	Ernesto Escarrega	.03	.01	.00
☐ 186	Bruce Hurst	.20	.10	.02	☐ 235	Carlton Fisk	.30	.15	.03
☐ 187	Carney Lansford	.20	.07	.01	☐ 236	Jerry Hairston	.03	.01	.00
☐ 188	Rick Miller	.03	.01	.00	☐ 237	Kevin Hickey	.03	.01	.00
☐ 189	Reid Nichols	.03	.01	.00	☐ 238	LaMarr Hoyt	.06	.03	.00
☐ 190	Bob Ojeda	.10	.05	.01	☐ 239	Steve Kemp	.06	.03	.00
☐ 191	Tony Perez	.15	.07	.01	☐ 240	Jim Kern	.03	.01	.00
☐ 192	Chuck Rainey	.03	.01	.00	☐ 241	Ron Kittle	1.00	.50	.10
☐ 193	Jerry Remy	.03	.01	.00	☐ 242	Jerry Koosman	.08	.04	.01
☐ 194	Jim Rice	.25	.12	.02	☐ 243	Dennis Lamp	.03	.01	.00

		MINT	EXC	G-VG
☐ 244	Rudy Law	.03	.01	.00
☐ 245	Vance Law	.06	.03	.00
☐ 246	Ron LeFlore	.06	.03	.00
☐ 247	Greg Luzinski	.10	.05	.01
☐ 248	Tom Paciorek	.03	.01	.00
☐ 249	Aurelio Rodriguez	.03	.01	.00
☐ 250	Mike Squires	.03	.01	.00
☐ 251	Steve Trout	.03	.01	.00
☐ 252	Jim Barr	.03	.01	.00
☐ 253	Dave Bergman	.03	.01	.00
☐ 254	Fred Breining	.03	.01	.00
☐ 255	Bob Brenly	.03	.01	.00
☐ 256	Jack Clark	.25	.12	.02
☐ 257	Chili Davis	.25	.12	.02
☐ 258	Darrell Evans	.10	.05	.01
☐ 259	Alan Fowlkes	.03	.01	.00
☐ 260	Rich Gale	.03	.01	.00
☐ 261	Atlee Hammaker	.03	.01	.00
☐ 262	Al Holland	.03	.01	.00
☐ 263	Duane Kuiper	.03	.01	.00
☐ 264	Bill Laskey	.03	.01	.00
☐ 265	Gary Lavelle	.03	.01	.00
☐ 266	Johnnie LeMaster	.03	.01	.00
☐ 267	Renie Martin	.03	.01	.00
☐ 268	Milt May	.03	.01	.00
☐ 269	Greg Minton	.03	.01	.00
☐ 270	Joe Morgan	.30	.15	.03
☐ 271	Tom O'Malley	.06	.03	.00
☐ 272	Reggie Smith	.06	.03	.00
☐ 273	Guy Sularz	.03	.01	.00
☐ 274	Champ Summers	.03	.01	.00
☐ 275	Max Venable	.03	.01	.00
☐ 276	Jim Wohlford	.03	.01	.00
☐ 277	Ray Burris	.03	.01	.00
☐ 278	Gary Carter	.30	.15	.03
☐ 279	Warren Cromartie	.03	.01	.00
☐ 280	Andre Dawson	.35	.17	.03
☐ 281	Terry Francona	.03	.01	.00
☐ 282	Doug Flynn	.03	.01	.00
☐ 283	Woodie Fryman	.03	.01	.00
☐ 284	Bill Gullickson	.03	.01	.00
☐ 285	Wallace Johnson	.06	.03	.00
☐ 286	Charlie Lea	.03	.01	.00
☐ 287	Randy Lerch	.03	.01	.00
☐ 288	Brad Mills	.03	.01	.00
☐ 289	Dan Norman	.03	.01	.00
☐ 290	Al Oliver	.08	.04	.01
☐ 291	David Palmer	.03	.01	.00
☐ 292	Tim Raines	.50	.25	.05

		MINT	EXC	G-VG
☐ 293	Jeff Reardon	.12	.06	.01
☐ 294	Steve Rogers	.03	.01	.00
☐ 295	Scott Sanderson	.03	.01	.00
☐ 296	Dan Schatzeder	.03	.01	.00
☐ 297	Bryn Smith	.50	.25	.05
☐ 298	Chris Speier	.03	.01	.00
☐ 299	Tim Wallach	.18	.09	.01
☐ 300	Jerry White	.03	.01	.00
☐ 301	Joel Youngblood	.03	.01	.00
☐ 302	Ross Baumgarten	.03	.01	.00
☐ 303	Dale Berra	.03	.01	.00
☐ 304	John Candelaria	.06	.03	.00
☐ 305	Dick Davis	.03	.01	.00
☐ 306	Mike Easler	.03	.01	.00
☐ 307	Richie Hebner	.03	.01	.00
☐ 308	Lee Lacy	.03	.01	.00
☐ 309	Bill Madlock	.08	.04	.01
☐ 310	Larry McWilliams	.03	.01	.00
☐ 311	John Milner	.03	.01	.00
☐ 312	Omar Moreno	.03	.01	.00
☐ 313	Jim Morrison	.03	.01	.00
☐ 314	Steve Nicosia	.03	.01	.00
☐ 315	Dave Parker	.18	.09	.01
☐ 316	Tony Pena	.15	.07	.01
☐ 317	Johnny Ray	.15	.07	.01
☐ 318	Rick Rhoden	.06	.03	.00
☐ 319	Don Robinson	.03	.01	.00
☐ 320	Enrique Romo	.03	.01	.00
☐ 321	Manny Sarmiento	.03	.01	.00
☐ 322	Rod Scurry	.03	.01	.00
☐ 323	Jimmy Smith	.03	.01	.00
☐ 324	Willie Stargell	.35	.17	.03
☐ 325	Jason Thompson	.03	.01	.00
☐ 326	Kent Tekulve	.06	.03	.00
☐ 327	Tom Brookens	.03	.01	.00
☐ 328	Enos Cabell	.03	.01	.00
☐ 329	Kirk Gibson	.40	.20	.04
☐ 330	Larry Herndon	.03	.01	.00
☐ 331	Mike Ivie	.03	.01	.00
☐ 332	Howard Johnson	9.00	4.50	.90
☐ 333	Lynn Jones	.03	.01	.00
☐ 334	Rick Leach	.03	.01	.00
☐ 335	Chet Lemon	.06	.03	.00
☐ 336	Jack Morris	.20	.10	.02
☐ 337	Lance Parrish	.20	.10	.02
☐ 338	Larry Pashnick	.03	.01	.00
☐ 339	Dan Petry	.03	.01	.00
☐ 340	Dave Rozema	.03	.01	.00
☐ 341	Dave Rucker	.03	.01	.00

		MINT	EXC	G-VG			MINT	EXC	G-VG
☐ 342	Elias Sosa	.03	.01	.00	☐ 391	Graig Nettles	.12	.06	.01
☐ 343	Dave Tobik	.03	.01	.00	☐ 392	Lou Piniella	.10	.05	.01
☐ 344	Alan Trammell	.30	.15	.03	☐ 393	Willie Randolph	.08	.04	.01
☐ 345	Jerry Turner	.03	.01	.00	☐ 394	Shane Rawley	.06	.03	.00
☐ 346	Jerry Ujdur	.03	.01	.00	☐ 395	Dave Righetti	.25	.12	.02
☐ 347	Pat Underwood	.03	.01	.00	☐ 396	Andre Robertson	.03	.01	.00
☐ 348	Lou Whitaker	.25	.12	.02	☐ 397	Roy Smalley	.03	.01	.00
☐ 349	Milt Wilcox	.03	.01	.00	☐ 398	Dave Winfield	.40	.20	.04
☐ 350	Glenn Wilson	.35	.17	.03	☐ 399	Butch Wynegar	.03	.01	.00
☐ 351	John Wockenfuss	.03	.01	.00	☐ 400	Chris Bando	.03	.01	.00
☐ 352	Kurt Bevacqua	.03	.01	.00	☐ 401	Alan Bannister	.03	.01	.00
☐ 353	Juan Bonilla	.03	.01	.00	☐ 402	Len Barker	.03	.01	.00
☐ 354	Floyd Chiffer	.03	.01	.00	☐ 403	Tom Brennan	.03	.01	.00
☐ 355	Luis DeLeon	.03	.01	.00	☐ 404	Carmelo Castillo	.06	.03	.00
☐ 356	Dave Dravecky	.75	.35	.07	☐ 405	Miguel Dilone	.03	.01	.00
☐ 357	Dave Edwards	.03	.01	.00	☐ 406	Jerry Dybzinski	.03	.01	.00
☐ 358	Juan Eichelberger	.03	.01	.00	☐ 407	Mike Fischlin	.03	.01	.00
☐ 359	Tim Flannery	.03	.01	.00	☐ 408	Ed Glynn UER	.03	.01	.00
☐ 360	Tony Gwynn	12.50	6.00	1.20		(photo actually			
☐ 361	Ruppert Jones	.03	.01	.00		Bud Anderson)			
☐ 362	Terry Kennedy	.03	.01	.00	☐ 409	Mike Hargrove	.06	.03	.00
☐ 363	Joe Lefebvre	.03	.01	.00	☐ 410	Toby Harrah	.06	.03	.00
☐ 364	Sixto Lezcano	.03	.01	.00	☐ 411	Ron Hassey	.03	.01	.00
☐ 365	Tim Lollar	.03	.01	.00	☐ 412	Von Hayes	.18	.09	.01
☐ 366	Gary Lucas	.03	.01	.00	☐ 413	Rick Manning	.03	.01	.00
☐ 367	John Montefusco	.03	.01	.00	☐ 414	Bake McBride	.03	.01	.00
☐ 368	Broderick Perkins	.03	.01	.00	☐ 415	Larry Milbourne	.03	.01	.00
☐ 369	Joe Pittman	.03	.01	.00	☐ 416	Bill Nahorodny	.03	.01	.00
☐ 370	Gene Richards	.03	.01	.00	☐ 417	Jack Perconte	.03	.01	.00
☐ 371	Luis Salazar	.03	.01	.00	☐ 418	Lary Sorensen	.03	.01	.00
☐ 372	Eric Show	.35	.17	.03	☐ 419	Dan Spillner	.03	.01	.00
☐ 373	Garry Templeton	.08	.04	.01	☐ 420	Rick Sutcliffe	.15	.07	.01
☐ 374	Chris Welsh	.03	.01	.00	☐ 421	Andre Thornton	.06	.03	.00
☐ 375	Alan Wiggins	.10	.05	.01	☐ 422	Rick Waits	.03	.01	.00
☐ 376	Rick Cerone	.03	.01	.00	☐ 423	Eddie Whitson	.06	.03	.00
☐ 377	Dave Collins	.03	.01	.00	☐ 424	Jesse Barfield	.75	.35	.07
☐ 378	Roger Erickson	.03	.01	.00	☐ 425	Barry Bonnell	.03	.01	.00
☐ 379	George Frazier	.03	.01	.00	☐ 426	Jim Clancy	.03	.01	.00
☐ 380	Oscar Gamble	.03	.01	.00	☐ 427	Damaso Garcia	.03	.01	.00
☐ 381	Goose Gossage	.15	.07	.01	☐ 428	Jerry Garvin	.03	.01	.00
☐ 382	Ken Griffey	.10	.05	.01	☐ 429	Alfredo Griffin	.06	.03	.00
☐ 383	Ron Guidry	.18	.09	.01	☐ 430	Garth Iorg	.03	.01	.00
☐ 384	Dave LaRoche	.03	.01	.00	☐ 431	Roy Lee Jackson	.03	.01	.00
☐ 385	Rudy May	.03	.01	.00	☐ 432	Luis Leal	.03	.01	.00
☐ 386	John Mayberry	.06	.03	.00	☐ 433	Buck Martinez	.03	.01	.00
☐ 387	Lee Mazzilli	.03	.01	.00	☐ 434	Joey McLaughlin	.03	.01	.00
☐ 388	Mike Morgan	.06	.03	.00	☐ 435	Lloyd Moseby	.10	.05	.01
☐ 389	Jerry Mumphrey	.03	.01	.00	☐ 436	Rance Mulliniks	.03	.01	.00
☐ 390	Bobby Murcer	.10	.05	.01	☐ 437	Dale Murray	.03	.01	.00

		MINT	EXC	G-VG			MINT	EXC	G-VG
☐ 438	Wayne Nordhagen	.03	.01	.00	☐ 487	Rick Sweet	.03	.01	.00
☐ 439	Geno Petralli	.15	.07	.01	☐ 488	Ed VandeBerg	.03	.01	.00
☐ 440	Hosken Powell	.03	.01	.00	☐ 489	Richie Zisk	.03	.01	.00
☐ 441	Dave Stieb	.15	.07	.01	☐ 490	Doug Bird	.03	.01	.00
☐ 442	Willie Upshaw	.03	.01	.00	☐ 491	Larry Bowa	.10	.05	.01
☐ 443	Ernie Whitt	.06	.03	.00	☐ 492	Bill Buckner	.10	.05	.01
☐ 444	Alvis Woods	.03	.01	.00	☐ 493	Bill Campbell	.03	.01	.00
☐ 445	Alan Ashby	.03	.01	.00	☐ 494	Jody Davis	.08	.04	.01
☐ 446	Jose Cruz	.08	.04	.01	☐ 495	Leon Durham	.06	.03	.00
☐ 447	Kiko Garcia	.03	.01	.00	☐ 496	Steve Henderson	.03	.01	.00
☐ 448	Phil Garner	.03	.01	.00	☐ 497	Willie Hernandez	.10	.05	.01
☐ 449	Danny Heep	.03	.01	.00	☐ 498	Ferguson Jenkins	.15	.07	.01
☐ 450	Art Howe	.08	.04	.01	☐ 499	Jay Johnstone	.06	.03	.00
☐ 451	Bob Knepper	.06	.03	.00	☐ 500	Junior Kennedy	.03	.01	.00
☐ 452	Alan Knicely	.03	.01	.00	☐ 501	Randy Martz	.03	.01	.00
☐ 453	Ray Knight	.08	.04	.01	☐ 502	Jerry Morales	.03	.01	.00
☐ 454	Frank LaCorte	.03	.01	.00	☐ 503	Keith Moreland	.03	.01	.00
☐ 455	Mike LaCoss	.03	.01	.00	☐ 504	Dickie Noles	.03	.01	.00
☐ 456	Randy Moffitt	.03	.01	.00	☐ 505	Mike Proly	.03	.01	.00
☐ 457	Joe Niekro	.10	.05	.01	☐ 506	Allen Ripley	.03	.01	.00
☐ 458	Terry Puhl	.03	.01	.00	☐ 507	Ryne Sandberg	8.00	4.00	.80
☐ 459	Luis Pujols	.03	.01	.00	☐ 508	Lee Smith	.10	.05	.01
☐ 460	Craig Reynolds	.03	.01	.00	☐ 509	Pat Tabler	.30	.15	.03
☐ 461	Bert Roberge	.03	.01	.00	☐ 510	Dick Tidrow	.03	.01	.00
☐ 462	Vern Ruhle	.03	.01	.00	☐ 511	Bump Wills	.03	.01	.00
☐ 463	Nolan Ryan	1.25	.60	.12	☐ 512	Gary Woods	.03	.01	.00
☐ 464	Joe Sambito	.03	.01	.00	☐ 513	Tony Armas	.06	.03	.00
☐ 465	Tony Scott	.03	.01	.00	☐ 514	Dave Beard	.03	.01	.00
☐ 466	Dave Smith	.06	.03	.00	☐ 515	Jeff Burroughs	.06	.03	.00
☐ 467	Harry Spilman	.03	.01	.00	☐ 516	John D'Acquisto	.03	.01	.00
☐ 468	Dickie Thon	.03	.01	.00	☐ 517	Wayne Gross	.03	.01	.00
☐ 469	Denny Walling	.03	.01	.00	☐ 518	Mike Heath	.03	.01	.00
☐ 470	Larry Andersen	.03	.01	.00	☐ 519	Rickey Henderson	.90	.45	.09
☐ 471	Floyd Bannister	.03	.01	.00	☐ 520	Cliff Johnson	.03	.01	.00
☐ 472	Jim Beattie	.03	.01	.00	☐ 521	Matt Keough	.03	.01	.00
☐ 473	Bruce Bochte	.03	.01	.00	☐ 522	Brian Kingman	.03	.01	.00
☐ 474	Manny Castillo	.03	.01	.00	☐ 523	Rick Langford	.03	.01	.00
☐ 475	Bill Caudill	.03	.01	.00	☐ 524	Dave Lopes	.08	.04	.01
☐ 476	Bryan Clark	.03	.01	.00	☐ 525	Steve McCatty	.03	.01	.00
☐ 477	Al Cowens	.03	.01	.00	☐ 526	Dave McKay	.03	.01	.00
☐ 478	Julio Cruz	.03	.01	.00	☐ 527	Dan Meyer	.03	.01	.00
☐ 479	Todd Cruz	.03	.01	.00	☐ 528	Dwayne Murphy	.03	.01	.00
☐ 480	Gary Gray	.03	.01	.00	☐ 529	Jeff Newman	.03	.01	.00
☐ 481	Dave Henderson	.35	.17	.03	☐ 530	Mike Norris	.03	.01	.00
☐ 482	Mike Moore	1.50	.75	.15	☐ 531	Bob Owchinko	.03	.01	.00
☐ 483	Gaylord Perry	.25	.12	.02	☐ 532	Joe Rudi	.06	.03	.00
☐ 484	Dave Revering	.03	.01	.00	☐ 533	Jimmy Sexton	.03	.01	.00
☐ 485	Joe Simpson	.03	.01	.00	☐ 534	Fred Stanley	.03	.01	.00
☐ 486	Mike Stanton	.03	.01	.00	☐ 535	Tom Underwood	.03	.01	.00

		MINT	EXC	G-VG
☐ 536	Neil Allen	.03	.01	.00
☐ 537	Wally Backman	.08	.04	.01
☐ 538	Bob Bailor	.03	.01	.00
☐ 539	Hubie Brooks	.10	.05	.01
☐ 540	Carlos Diaz	.03	.01	.00
☐ 541	Pete Falcone	.03	.01	.00
☐ 542	George Foster	.12	.06	.01
☐ 543	Ron Gardenhire	.03	.01	.00
☐ 544	Brian Giles	.03	.01	.00
☐ 545	Ron Hodges	.03	.01	.00
☐ 546	Randy Jones	.03	.01	.00
☐ 547	Mike Jorgensen	.03	.01	.00
☐ 548	Dave Kingman	.12	.06	.01
☐ 549	Ed Lynch	.03	.01	.00
☐ 550	Jesse Orosco	.03	.01	.00
☐ 551	Rick Ownbey	.03	.01	.00
☐ 552	Charlie Puleo	.03	.01	.00
☐ 553	Gary Rajsich	.03	.01	.00
☐ 554	Mike Scott	.30	.15	.03
☐ 555	Rusty Staub	.10	.05	.01
☐ 556	John Stearns	.03	.01	.00
☐ 557	Craig Swan	.03	.01	.00
☐ 558	Ellis Valentine	.03	.01	.00
☐ 559	Tom Veryzer	.03	.01	.00
☐ 560	Mookie Wilson	.10	.05	.01
☐ 561	Pat Zachry	.03	.01	.00
☐ 562	Buddy Bell	.10	.05	.01
☐ 563	John Butcher	.03	.01	.00
☐ 564	Steve Comer	.03	.01	.00
☐ 565	Danny Darwin	.03	.01	.00
☐ 566	Bucky Dent	.10	.05	.01
☐ 567	John Grubb	.03	.01	.00
☐ 568	Rick Honeycutt	.03	.01	.00
☐ 569	Dave Hostetler	.06	.03	.00
☐ 570	Charlie Hough	.06	.03	.00
☐ 571	Lamar Johnson	.03	.01	.00
☐ 572	Jon Matlack	.03	.01	.00
☐ 573	Paul Mirabella	.03	.01	.00
☐ 574	Larry Parrish	.06	.03	.00
☐ 575	Mike Richardt	.03	.01	.00
☐ 576	Mickey Rivers	.06	.03	.00
☐ 577	Billy Sample	.03	.01	.00
☐ 578	Dave Schmidt	.15	.07	.01
☐ 579	Bill Stein	.03	.01	.00
☐ 580	Jim Sundberg	.03	.01	.00
☐ 581	Frank Tanana	.08	.04	.01
☐ 582	Mark Wagner	.03	.01	.00
☐ 583	George Wright	.03	.01	.00
☐ 584	Johnny Bench	.60	.30	.06

		MINT	EXC	G-VG
☐ 585	Bruce Berenyi	.03	.01	.00
☐ 586	Larry Biittner	.03	.01	.00
☐ 587	Cesar Cedeno	.08	.04	.01
☐ 588	Dave Concepcion	.10	.05	.01
☐ 589	Dan Driessen	.03	.01	.00
☐ 590	Greg Harris	.03	.01	.00
☐ 591	Ben Hayes	.03	.01	.00
☐ 592	Paul Householder	.03	.01	.00
☐ 593	Tom Hume	.03	.01	.00
☐ 594	Wayne Krenchicki	.03	.01	.00
☐ 595	Rafael Landestoy	.03	.01	.00
☐ 596	Charlie Leibrandt	.03	.01	.00
☐ 597	Eddie Milner	.08	.04	.01
☐ 598	Ron Oester	.03	.01	.00
☐ 599	Frank Pastore	.03	.01	.00
☐ 600	Joe Price	.03	.01	.00
☐ 601	Tom Seaver	.40	.20	.04
☐ 602	Bob Shirley	.03	.01	.00
☐ 603	Mario Soto	.06	.03	.00
☐ 604	Alex Trevino	.03	.01	.00
☐ 605	Mike Vail	.03	.01	.00
☐ 606	Duane Walker	.03	.01	.00
☐ 607	Tom Brunansky	.60	.30	.06
☐ 608	Bobby Castillo	.03	.01	.00
☐ 609	John Castino	.03	.01	.00
☐ 610	Ron Davis	.03	.01	.00
☐ 611	Lenny Faedo	.03	.01	.00
☐ 612	Terry Felton	.03	.01	.00
☐ 613	Gary Gaetti	3.00	1.50	.30
☐ 614	Mickey Hatcher	.06	.03	.00
☐ 615	Brad Havens	.03	.01	.00
☐ 616	Kent Hrbek	1.25	.60	.12
☐ 617	Randy Johnson	.03	.01	.00
☐ 618	Tim Laudner	.06	.03	.00
☐ 619	Jeff Little	.03	.01	.00
☐ 620	Bobby Mitchell	.03	.01	.00
☐ 621	Jack O'Connor	.03	.01	.00
☐ 622	John Pacella	.03	.01	.00
☐ 623	Pete Redfern	.03	.01	.00
☐ 624	Jesus Vega	.03	.01	.00
☐ 625	Frank Viola	3.75	1.85	.37
☐ 626	Ron Washington	.06	.03	.00
☐ 627	Gary Ward	.06	.03	.00
☐ 628	Al Williams	.03	.01	.00
☐ 629	Red Sox All-Stars	.25	.12	.02
	Carl Yastrzemski			
	Dennis Eckersley			
	Mark Clear			
☐ 630	"300 Career Wins"	.10	.05	.01

		MINT	EXC	G-VG
	Gaylord Perry and Terry Bulling 5/6/82			
☐ 631	Pride of Venezuela ..	.06	.03	.00
	Dave Concepcion and Manny Trillo			
☐ 632	All-Star Infielders ...	.15	.07	.01
	Robin Yount and Buddy Bell			
☐ 633	Mr. Vet and Mr. Rookie	.20	.10	.02
	Dave Winfield and Kent Hrbek			
☐ 634	Fountain of Youth ..	.60	.30	.06
	Willie Stargell and Pete Rose			
☐ 635	Big Chiefs	.06	.03	.00
	Toby Harrah and Andre Thornton			
☐ 636	Smith Brothers	.08	.04	.01
	Ozzie and Lonnie			
☐ 637	Base Stealers' Threat	.10	.05	.01
	Bo Diaz and Gary Carter			
☐ 638	All-Star Catchers ...	.12	.06	.01
	Carlton Fisk and Gary Carter			
☐ 639	The Silver Shoe	.30	.15	.03
	Rickey Henderson			
☐ 640	Home Run Threats ..	.18	.09	.01
	Ben Oglivie and Reggie Jackson			
☐ 641	Two Teams Same Day	.06	.03	.00
	Joel Youngblood August 4, 1982			
☐ 642	Last Perfect Game ..	.06	.03	.00
	Ron Hassey and Len Barker			
☐ 643	Black and Blue	.06	.03	.00
	Bud Black			
☐ 644	Black and Blue	.06	.03	.00
	Vida Blue			
☐ 645	Speed and Power ...	.25	.12	.02
	Reggie Jackson			
☐ 646	Speed and Power ...	.30	.15	.03
	Rickey Henderson			
☐ 647	CL: Cards/Brewers ..	.07	.01	.00
☐ 648	CL: Orioles/Angels ..	.07	.01	.00
☐ 649	CL: Royals/Braves ..	.07	.01	.00

		MINT	EXC	G-VG
☐ 650	CL: Phillies/Red Sox	.07	.01	.00
☐ 651	CL: Dodgers/White Sox	.07	.01	.00
☐ 652	CL: Giants/Expos ...	.07	.01	.00
☐ 653	CL: Pirates/Tigers ...	.07	.01	.00
☐ 654	CL: Padres/Yankees .	.07	.01	.00
☐ 655	CL: Indians/Blue Jays	.07	.01	.00
☐ 656	CL: Astros/Mariners .	.07	.01	.00
☐ 657	CL: Cubs/A's	.07	.01	.00
☐ 658	CL: Mets/Rangers ...	.07	.01	.00
☐ 659	CL: Reds/Twins	.07	.01	.00
☐ 660	CL: Specials/Teams .	.09	.01	.00

1984 Fleer

George Brett
THIRD BASE

The cards in this 660-card set measure 2 ½" by 3 ½". The 1984 Fleer card set featured fronts with full-color team logos along with the player's name and position and the Fleer identification. The set features many imaginative photos, several multi-player cards, and many more action shots than the 1983 card set. The backs are quite similar to the 1983 backs except that blue rather than brown ink is used. The player cards are alphabetized within team and the teams are ordered by their 1983 season finish and won-lost record, e.g., Baltimore (1-23), Philadelphia (24-49), Chicago White Sox (50-73), Detroit (74-95), Los Angeles (96-118), New York Yankees (119-144), Toronto (145-169), Atlanta (170-193), Milwaukee (194-219), Houston (220-244), Pittsburgh (245-269),

Montreal (270-293), San Diego (294-317), St. Louis (318-340), Kansas City (341-364), San Francisco (365-387), Boston (388-412), Texas (413-435), Oakland (436-461), Cincinnati (462-485), Chicago (486-507), California (508-532), Cleveland (533-555), Minnesota (556-579), New York Mets (580-603), and Seattle (604-625). Specials (626-646) and checklist cards (647-660) make up the end of the set.

			MINT	EXC	G-VG
	COMPLETE SET (660)		135.00	60.00	12.00
	COMMON PLAYER (1-660)		.06	.03	.00
☐	1	Mike Boddicker	.20	.04	.01
☐	2	Al Bumbry	.06	.03	.00
☐	3	Todd Cruz	.06	.03	.00
☐	4	Rich Dauer	.06	.03	.00
☐	5	Storm Davis	.15	.07	.01
☐	6	Rick Dempsey	.06	.03	.00
☐	7	Jim Dwyer	.06	.03	.00
☐	8	Mike Flanagan	.10	.05	.01
☐	9	Dan Ford	.06	.03	.00
☐	10	John Lowenstein	.06	.03	.00
☐	11	Dennis Martinez	.10	.05	.01
☐	12	Tippy Martinez	.06	.03	.00
☐	13	Scott McGregor	.10	.05	.01
☐	14	Eddie Murray	.55	.27	.05
☐	15	Joe Nolan	.06	.03	.00
☐	16	Jim Palmer	.50	.25	.05
☐	17	Cal Ripken	1.00	.50	.10
☐	18	Gary Roenicke	.06	.03	.00
☐	19	Lenn Sakata	.06	.03	.00
☐	20	John Shelby	.35	.17	.03
☐	21	Ken Singleton	.10	.05	.01
☐	22	Sammy Stewart	.06	.03	.00
☐	23	Tim Stoddard	.06	.03	.00
☐	24	Marty Bystrom	.06	.03	.00
☐	25	Steve Carlton	.50	.25	.05
☐	26	Ivan DeJesus	.06	.03	.00
☐	27	John Denny	.10	.05	.01
☐	28	Bob Dernier	.06	.03	.00
☐	29	Bo Diaz	.06	.03	.00
☐	30	Kiko Garcia	.06	.03	.00
☐	31	Greg Gross	.06	.03	.00
☐	32	Kevin Gross	.35	.17	.03
☐	33	Von Hayes	.20	.10	.02
☐	34	Willie Hernandez	.20	.10	.02
☐	35	Al Holland	.06	.03	.00
☐	36	Charles Hudson	.25	.12	.02
☐	37	Joe Lefebvre	.06	.03	.00
☐	38	Sixto Lezcano	.06	.03	.00
☐	39	Garry Maddox	.06	.03	.00
☐	40	Gary Matthews	.10	.05	.01
☐	41	Len Matuszek	.06	.03	.00
☐	42	Tug McGraw	.10	.05	.01
☐	43	Joe Morgan	.35	.17	.03
☐	44	Tony Perez	.25	.12	.02
☐	45	Ron Reed	.06	.03	.00
☐	46	Pete Rose	1.25	.60	.12
☐	47	Juan Samuel	3.50	1.75	.35
☐	48	Mike Schmidt	2.25	1.10	.22
☐	49	Ozzie Virgil	.06	.03	.00
☐	50	Juan Agosto	.20	.10	.02
☐	51	Harold Baines	.25	.12	.02
☐	52	Floyd Bannister	.06	.03	.00
☐	53	Salome Barojas	.06	.03	.00
☐	54	Britt Burns	.06	.03	.00
☐	55	Julio Cruz	.06	.03	.00
☐	56	Richard Dotson	.10	.05	.01
☐	57	Jerry Dybzinski	.06	.03	.00
☐	58	Carlton Fisk	.40	.20	.04
☐	59	Scott Fletcher	.25	.12	.02
☐	60	Jerry Hairston	.06	.03	.00
☐	61	Kevin Hickey	.06	.03	.00
☐	62	Marc Hill	.06	.03	.00
☐	63	LaMarr Hoyt	.10	.05	.01
☐	64	Ron Kittle	.20	.10	.02
☐	65	Jerry Koosman	.10	.05	.01
☐	66	Dennis Lamp	.06	.03	.00
☐	67	Rudy Law	.06	.03	.00
☐	68	Vance Law	.10	.05	.01
☐	69	Greg Luzinski	.10	.05	.01
☐	70	Tom Paciorek	.06	.03	.00
☐	71	Mike Squires	.06	.03	.00
☐	72	Dick Tidrow	.06	.03	.00
☐	73	Greg Walker	.45	.22	.04
☐	74	Glenn Abbott	.06	.03	.00
☐	75	Howard Bailey	.06	.03	.00
☐	76	Doug Bair	.06	.03	.00
☐	77	Juan Berenguer	.06	.03	.00
☐	78	Tom Brookens	.06	.03	.00
☐	79	Enos Cabell	.06	.03	.00
☐	80	Kirk Gibson	.45	.22	.04
☐	81	John Grubb	.06	.03	.00
☐	82	Larry Herndon	.06	.03	.00
☐	83	Wayne Krenchicki	.06	.03	.00
☐	84	Rick Leach	.06	.03	.00
☐	85	Chet Lemon	.10	.05	.01

			MINT	EXC	G-VG				MINT	EXC	G-VG
☐	86	Aurelio Lopez	.06	.03	.00	☐	135	Graig Nettles	.15	.07	.01
☐	87	Jack Morris	.20	.10	.02	☐	136	Lou Piniella	.10	.05	.01
☐	88	Lance Parrish	.25	.12	.02	☐	137	Willie Randolph	.15	.07	.01
☐	89	Dan Petry	.06	.03	.00	☐	138	Shane Rawley	.06	.03	.00
☐	90	Dave Rozema	.06	.03	.00	☐	139	Dave Righetti	.20	.10	.02
☐	91	Alan Trammell	.40	.20	.04	☐	140	Andre Robertson	.06	.03	.00
☐	92	Lou Whitaker	.30	.15	.03	☐	141	Bob Shirley	.06	.03	.00
☐	93	Milt Wilcox	.06	.03	.00	☐	142	Roy Smalley	.06	.03	.00
☐	94	Glenn Wilson	.10	.05	.01	☐	143	Dave Winfield	.40	.20	.04
☐	95	John Wockenfuss	.06	.03	.00	☐	144	Butch Wynegar	.06	.03	.00
☐	96	Dusty Baker	.10	.05	.01	☐	145	Jim Acker	.10	.05	.01
☐	97	Joe Beckwith	.06	.03	.00	☐	146	Doyle Alexander	.10	.05	.01
☐	98	Greg Brock	.10	.05	.01	☐	147	Jesse Barfield	.30	.15	.03
☐	99	Jack Fimple	.06	.03	.00	☐	148	Jorge Bell	1.25	.60	.12
☐	100	Pedro Guerrero	.40	.20	.04	☐	149	Barry Bonnell	.06	.03	.00
☐	101	Rick Honeycutt	.06	.03	.00	☐	150	Jim Clancy	.06	.03	.00
☐	102	Burt Hooton	.06	.03	.00	☐	151	Dave Collins	.06	.03	.00
☐	103	Steve Howe	.06	.03	.00	☐	152	Tony Fernandez	4.50	2.25	.45
☐	104	Ken Landreaux	.06	.03	.00	☐	153	Damaso Garcia	.06	.03	.00
☐	105	Mike Marshall	.20	.10	.02	☐	154	Dave Geisel	.06	.03	.00
☐	106	Rick Monday	.10	.05	.01	☐	155	Jim Gott	.20	.10	.02
☐	107	Jose Morales	.06	.03	.00	☐	156	Alfredo Griffin	.10	.05	.01
☐	108	Tom Niedenfuer	.10	.05	.01	☐	157	Garth Iorg	.06	.03	.00
☐	109	Alejandro Pena	.40	.20	.04	☐	158	Roy Lee Jackson	.06	.03	.00
☐	110	Jerry Reuss	.10	.05	.01	☐	159	Cliff Johnson	.06	.03	.00
☐	111	Bill Russell	.10	.05	.01	☐	160	Luis Leal	.06	.03	.00
☐	112	Steve Sax	.35	.17	.03	☐	161	Buck Martinez	.06	.03	.00
☐	113	Mike Scioscia	.10	.05	.01	☐	162	Joey McLaughlin	.06	.03	.00
☐	114	Derrel Thomas	.06	.03	.00	☐	163	Randy Moffitt	.06	.03	.00
☐	115	Fernando Valenzuela	.30	.15	.03	☐	164	Lloyd Moseby	.15	.07	.01
☐	116	Bob Welch	.10	.05	.01	☐	165	Rance Mulliniks	.06	.03	.00
☐	117	Steve Yeager	.06	.03	.00	☐	166	Jorge Orta	.06	.03	.00
☐	118	Pat Zachry	.06	.03	.00	☐	167	Dave Stieb	.20	.10	.02
☐	119	Don Baylor	.15	.07	.01	☐	168	Willie Upshaw	.10	.05	.01
☐	120	Bert Campaneris	.10	.05	.01	☐	169	Ernie Whitt	.10	.05	.01
☐	121	Rick Cerone	.06	.03	.00	☐	170	Len Barker	.06	.03	.00
☐	122	Ray Fontenot	.06	.03	.00	☐	171	Steve Bedrosian	.20	.10	.02
☐	123	George Frazier	.06	.03	.00	☐	172	Bruce Benedict	.06	.03	.00
☐	124	Oscar Gamble	.06	.03	.00	☐	173	Brett Butler	.15	.07	.01
☐	125	Goose Gossage	.20	.10	.02	☐	174	Rick Camp	.06	.03	.00
☐	126	Ken Griffey	.15	.07	.01	☐	175	Chris Chambliss	.06	.03	.01
☐	127	Ron Guidry	.25	.12	.02	☐	176	Ken Dayley	.06	.03	.00
☐	128	Jay Howell	.30	.15	.03	☐	177	Pete Falcone	.06	.03	.00
☐	129	Steve Kemp	.10	.05	.01	☐	178	Terry Forster	.10	.05	.01
☐	130	Matt Keough	.06	.03	.00	☐	179	Gene Garber	.06	.03	.00
☐	131	Don Mattingly	36.00	18.00	3.60	☐	180	Terry Harper	.06	.03	.00
☐	132	John Montefusco	.06	.03	.00	☐	181	Bob Horner	.15	.07	.01
☐	133	Omar Moreno	.06	.03	.00	☐	182	Glenn Hubbard	.06	.03	.00
☐	134	Dale Murray	.06	.03	.00	☐	183	Randy Johnson	.06	.03	.00

		MINT	EXC	G-VG			MINT	EXC	G-VG
☐ 184	Craig McMurtry	.10	.05	.01	☐ 233	Jerry Mumphrey	.06	.03	.00
☐ 185	Donnie Moore	.06	.03	.00	☐ 234	Joe Niekro	.10	.05	.01
☐ 186	Dale Murphy	1.00	.50	.10	☐ 235	Terry Puhl	.06	.03	.00
☐ 187	Phil Niekro	.25	.12	.02	☐ 236	Luis Pujols	.06	.03	.00
☐ 188	Pascual Perez	.20	.10	.02	☐ 237	Craig Reynolds	.06	.03	.00
☐ 189	Biff Pocoroba	.06	.03	.00	☐ 238	Vern Ruhle	.06	.03	.00
☐ 190	Rafael Ramirez	.06	.03	.00	☐ 239	Nolan Ryan	2.50	1.25	.25
☐ 191	Jerry Royster	.06	.03	.00	☐ 240	Mike Scott	.40	.20	.04
☐ 192	Claudell Washington	.10	.05	.01	☐ 241	Tony Scott	.06	.03	.00
☐ 193	Bob Watson	.10	.05	.01	☐ 242	Dave Smith	.10	.05	.01
☐ 194	Jerry Augustine	.06	.03	.00	☐ 243	Dickie Thon	.06	.03	.00
☐ 195	Mark Brouhard	.06	.03	.00	☐ 244	Denny Walling	.06	.03	.00
☐ 196	Mike Caldwell	.06	.03	.00	☐ 245	Dale Berra	.06	.03	.00
☐ 197	Tom Candiotti	.30	.15	.03	☐ 246	Jim Bibby	.06	.03	.00
☐ 198	Cecil Cooper	.15	.07	.01	☐ 247	John Candelaria	.10	.05	.01
☐ 199	Rollie Fingers	.20	.10	.02	☐ 248	Jose DeLeon	.45	.22	.04
☐ 200	Jim Gantner	.06	.03	.00	☐ 249	Mike Easler	.10	.05	.01
☐ 201	Bob L. Gibson	.10	.05	.01	☐ 250	Cecilio Guante	.06	.03	.00
☐ 202	Moose Haas	.06	.03	.00	☐ 251	Richie Hebner	.06	.03	.00
☐ 203	Roy Howell	.06	.03	.00	☐ 252	Lee Lacy	.06	.03	.00
☐ 204	Pete Ladd	.06	.03	.00	☐ 253	Bill Madlock	.15	.07	.01
☐ 205	Rick Manning	.06	.03	.00	☐ 254	Milt May	.06	.03	.00
☐ 206	Bob McClure	.06	.03	.00	☐ 255	Lee Mazzilli	.06	.03	.00
☐ 207	Paul Molitor	.20	.10	.02	☐ 256	Larry McWilliams	.06	.03	.00
☐ 208	Don Money	.06	.03	.00	☐ 257	Jim Morrison	.06	.03	.00
☐ 209	Charlie Moore	.06	.03	.00	☐ 258	Dave Parker	.20	.10	.02
☐ 210	Ben Oglivie	.10	.05	.01	☐ 259	Tony Pena	.15	.07	.01
☐ 211	Chuck Porter	.06	.03	.00	☐ 260	Johnny Ray	.15	.07	.01
☐ 212	Ed Romero	.06	.03	.00	☐ 261	Rick Rhoden	.10	.05	.01
☐ 213	Ted Simmons	.15	.07	.01	☐ 262	Don Robinson	.06	.03	.00
☐ 214	Jim Slaton	.06	.03	.00	☐ 263	Manny Sarmiento	.06	.03	.00
☐ 215	Don Sutton	.30	.15	.03	☐ 264	Rod Scurry	.06	.03	.00
☐ 216	Tom Tellmann	.06	.03	.00	☐ 265	Kent Tekulve	.10	.05	.01
☐ 217	Pete Vuckovich	.10	.05	.01	☐ 266	Gene Tenace	.06	.03	.00
☐ 218	Ned Yost	.06	.03	.00	☐ 267	Jason Thompson	.06	.03	.00
☐ 219	Robin Yount	1.00	.50	.10	☐ 268	Lee Tunnell	.10	.05	.01
☐ 220	Alan Ashby	.06	.03	.00	☐ 269	Marvell Wynne	.10	.05	.01
☐ 221	Kevin Bass	.15	.07	.01	☐ 270	Ray Burris	.06	.03	.00
☐ 222	Jose Cruz	.10	.05	.01	☐ 271	Gary Carter	.40	.20	.04
☐ 223	Bill Dawley	.10	.05	.01	☐ 272	Warren Cromartie	.06	.03	.00
☐ 224	Frank DiPino	.06	.03	.00	☐ 273	Andre Dawson	.35	.17	.03
☐ 225	Bill Doran	.75	.35	.07	☐ 274	Doug Flynn	.06	.03	.00
☐ 226	Phil Garner	.06	.03	.00	☐ 275	Terry Francona	.06	.03	.00
☐ 227	Art Howe	.10	.05	.01	☐ 276	Bill Gullickson	.06	.03	.00
☐ 228	Bob Knepper	.10	.05	.01	☐ 277	Bob James	.15	.07	.01
☐ 229	Ray Knight	.10	.05	.01	☐ 278	Charlie Lea	.06	.03	.00
☐ 230	Frank LaCorte	.06	.03	.00	☐ 279	Bryan Little	.06	.03	.00
☐ 231	Mike LaCoss	.06	.03	.00	☐ 280	Al Oliver	.10	.05	.01
☐ 232	Mike Madden	.06	.03	.00	☐ 281	Tim Raines	.50	.25	.05

		MINT	EXC	G-VG			MINT	EXC	G-VG
☐ 282	Bobby Ramos	.06	.03	.00	☐ 331	Darrell Porter	.06	.03	.00
☐ 283	Jeff Reardon	.15	.07	.01	☐ 332	Jamie Quirk	.06	.03	.00
☐ 284	Steve Rogers	.06	.03	.00	☐ 333	Mike Ramsey	.06	.03	.00
☐ 285	Scott Sanderson	.06	.03	.00	☐ 334	Floyd Rayford	.06	.03	.00
☐ 286	Dan Schatzeder	.06	.03	.00	☐ 335	Lonnie Smith	.15	.07	.01
☐ 287	Bryn Smith	.15	.07	.01	☐ 336	Ozzie Smith	.50	.20	.04
☐ 288	Chris Speier	.06	.03	.00	☐ 337	John Stuper	.06	.03	.00
☐ 289	Manny Trillo	.06	.03	.00	☐ 338	Bruce Sutter	.15	.07	.01
☐ 290	Mike Vail	.06	.03	.00	☐ 339	Andy Van Slyke	2.50	1.25	.25
☐ 291	Tim Wallach	.15	.07	.01	☐ 340	Dave Von Ohlen	.06	.03	.00
☐ 292	Chris Welsh	.06	.03	.00	☐ 341	Willie Aikens	.06	.03	.00
☐ 293	Jim Wohlford	.06	.03	.00	☐ 342	Mike Armstrong	.06	.03	.00
☐ 294	Kurt Bevacqua	.06	.03	.00	☐ 343	Bud Black	.06	.03	.00
☐ 295	Juan Bonilla	.06	.03	.00	☐ 344	George Brett	1.00	.50	.10
☐ 296	Bobby Brown	.06	.03	.00	☐ 345	Onix Concepcion	.06	.03	.00
☐ 297	Luis DeLeon	.06	.03	.00	☐ 346	Keith Creel	.06	.03	.00
☐ 298	Dave Dravecky	.15	.07	.01	☐ 347	Larry Gura	.06	.03	.00
☐ 299	Tim Flannery	.06	.03	.00	☐ 348	Don Hood	.06	.03	.00
☐ 300	Steve Garvey	.50	.25	.05	☐ 349	Dennis Leonard	.10	.05	.01
☐ 301	Tony Gwynn	3.50	1.75	.35	☐ 350	Hal McRae	.10	.05	.01
☐ 302	Andy Hawkins	.60	.30	.06	☐ 351	Amos Otis	.10	.05	.01
☐ 303	Ruppert Jones	.06	.03	.00	☐ 352	Gaylord Perry	.25	.12	.02
☐ 304	Terry Kennedy	.10	.05	.01	☐ 353	Greg Pryor	.06	.03	.00
☐ 305	Tim Lollar	.06	.03	.00	☐ 354	Dan Quisenberry	.15	.07	.01
☐ 306	Gary Lucas	.06	.03	.00	☐ 355	Steve Renko	.06	.03	.00
☐ 307	Kevin McReynolds	6.50	3.25	.65	☐ 356	Leon Roberts	.06	.03	.00
☐ 308	Sid Monge	.06	.03	.00	☐ 357	Pat Sheridan	.20	.10	.02
☐ 309	Mario Ramirez	.06	.03	.00	☐ 358	Joe Simpson	.06	.03	.00
☐ 310	Gene Richards	.06	.03	.00	☐ 359	Don Slaught	.06	.03	.00
☐ 311	Luis Salazar	.06	.03	.00	☐ 360	Paul Splittorff	.06	.03	.00
☐ 312	Eric Show	.10	.05	.01	☐ 361	U.L. Washington	.06	.03	.00
☐ 313	Elias Sosa	.06	.03	.00	☐ 362	John Wathan	.06	.03	.00
☐ 314	Garry Templeton	.10	.05	.01	☐ 363	Frank White	.10	.05	.01
☐ 315	Mark Thurmond	.10	.05	.01	☐ 364	Willie Wilson	.15	.07	.01
☐ 316	Ed Whitson	.06	.03	.00	☐ 365	Jim Barr	.06	.03	.00
☐ 317	Alan Wiggins	.06	.03	.00	☐ 366	Dave Bergman	.06	.03	.00
☐ 318	Neil Allen	.06	.03	.00	☐ 367	Fred Breining	.06	.03	.00
☐ 319	Joaquin Andujar	.10	.05	.01	☐ 368	Bob Brenly	.06	.03	.00
☐ 320	Steve Braun	.06	.03	.00	☐ 369	Jack Clark	.30	.15	.03
☐ 321	Glenn Brummer	.06	.03	.00	☐ 370	Chili Davis	.15	.07	.01
☐ 322	Bob Forsch	.06	.03	.00	☐ 371	Mark Davis	.75	.35	.07
☐ 323	David Green	.06	.03	.00	☐ 372	Darrell Evans	.15	.07	.01
☐ 324	George Hendrick	.10	.05	.01	☐ 373	Atlee Hammaker	.06	.03	.00
☐ 325	Tom Herr	.10	.05	.01	☐ 374	Mike Krukow	.10	.05	.01
☐ 326	Dane Iorg	.06	.03	.00	☐ 375	Duane Kuiper	.06	.03	.00
☐ 327	Jeff Lahti	.06	.03	.00	☐ 376	Bill Laskey	.06	.03	.00
☐ 328	Dave LaPoint	.10	.05	.01	☐ 377	Gary Lavelle	.06	.03	.00
☐ 329	Willie McGee	.30	.15	.03	☐ 378	Johnnie LeMaster	.06	.03	.00
☐ 330	Ken Oberkfell	.06	.03	.00	☐ 379	Jeff Leonard	.10	.05	.01

		MINT	EXC	G-VG			MINT	EXC	G-VG
☐ 380	Randy Lerch	.06	.03	.00	☐ 428	Mike Smithson	.10	.05	.01
☐ 381	Renie Martin	.06	.03	.00	☐ 429	Bill Stein	.06	.03	.00
☐ 382	Andy McGaffigan	.06	.03	.00	☐ 430	Dave Stewart	.50	.25	.05
☐ 383	Greg Minton	.06	.03	.00	☐ 431	Jim Sundberg	.06	.03	.00
☐ 384	Tom O'Malley	.06	.03	.00	☐ 432	Frank Tanana	.10	.05	.01
☐ 385	Max Venable	.06	.03	.00	☐ 433	Dave Tobik	.06	.03	.00
☐ 386	Brad Wellman	.06	.03	.00	☐ 434	Wayne Tolleson	.10	.05	.01
☐ 387	Joel Youngblood	.06	.03	.00	☐ 435	George Wright	.06	.03	.00
☐ 388	Gary Allenson	.06	.03	.00	☐ 436	Bill Almon	.06	.03	.00
☐ 389	Luis Aponte	.06	.03	.00	☐ 437	Keith Atherton	.06	.03	.00
☐ 390	Tony Armas	.10	.05	.01	☐ 438	Dave Beard	.06	.03	.00
☐ 391	Doug Bird	.06	.03	.00	☐ 439	Tom Burgmeier	.06	.03	.00
☐ 392	Wade Boggs	8.00	4.00	.80	☐ 440	Jeff Burroughs	.10	.05	.01
☐ 393	Dennis Boyd	.45	.22	.04	☐ 441	Chris Codiroli	.10	.05	.01
☐ 394	Mike Brown	.10	.05	.01	☐ 442	Tim Conroy	.10	.05	.01
	(Red Sox pitcher)				☐ 443	Mike Davis	.10	.05	.01
☐ 395	Mark Clear	.06	.03	.00	☐ 444	Wayne Gross	.06	.03	.00
☐ 396	Dennis Eckersley	.25	.12	.02	☐ 445	Garry Hancock	.06	.03	.00
☐ 397	Dwight Evans	.25	.12	.02	☐ 446	Mike Heath	.06	.03	.00
☐ 398	Rich Gedman	.10	.05	.01	☐ 447	Rickey Henderson	1.50	.75	.15
☐ 399	Glenn Hoffman	.06	.03	.00	☐ 448	Donnie Hill	.10	.05	.01
☐ 400	Bruce Hurst	.25	.12	.02	☐ 449	Bob Kearney	.06	.03	.00
☐ 401	John Henry Johnson	.06	.03	.00	☐ 450	Bill Krueger	.10	.05	.01
☐ 402	Ed Jurak	.06	.03	.00	☐ 451	Rick Langford	.06	.03	.00
☐ 403	Rick Miller	.06	.03	.00	☐ 452	Carney Lansford	.15	.07	.01
☐ 404	Jeff Newman	.06	.03	.00	☐ 453	Dave Lopes	.10	.05	.01
☐ 405	Reid Nichols	.06	.03	.00	☐ 454	Steve McCatty	.06	.03	.00
☐ 406	Bob Ojeda	.10	.05	.01	☐ 455	Dan Meyer	.06	.03	.00
☐ 407	Jerry Remy	.06	.03	.00	☐ 456	Dwayne Murphy	.06	.03	.00
☐ 408	Jim Rice	.25	.12	.02	☐ 457	Mike Norris	.06	.03	.00
☐ 409	Bob Stanley	.06	.03	.00	☐ 458	Ricky Peters	.06	.03	.00
☐ 410	Dave Stapleton	.06	.03	.00	☐ 459	Tony Phillips	.25	.12	.02
☐ 411	John Tudor	.15	.07	.01	☐ 460	Tom Underwood	.06	.03	.00
☐ 412	Carl Yastrzemski	1.00	.50	.10	☐ 461	Mike Warren	.10	.05	.01
☐ 413	Buddy Bell	.15	.07	.01	☐ 462	Johnny Bench	.90	.45	.09
☐ 414	Larry Biittner	.06	.03	.00	☐ 463	Bruce Berenyi	.06	.03	.00
☐ 415	John Butcher	.06	.03	.00	☐ 464	Dann Bilardello	.06	.03	.00
☐ 416	Danny Darwin	.06	.03	.00	☐ 465	Cesar Cedeno	.10	.05	.01
☐ 417	Bucky Dent	.15	.07	.01	☐ 466	Dave Concepcion	.15	.07	.01
☐ 418	Dave Hostetler	.06	.03	.00	☐ 467	Dan Driessen	.06	.03	.00
☐ 419	Charlie Hough	.10	.05	.01	☐ 468	Nick Esasky	2.50	1.25	.25
☐ 420	Bobby Johnson	.06	.03	.00	☐ 469	Rich Gale	.06	.03	.00
☐ 421	Odell Jones	.06	.03	.00	☐ 470	Ben Hayes	.06	.03	.00
☐ 422	Jon Matlack	.06	.03	.00	☐ 471	Paul Householder	.06	.03	.00
☐ 423	Pete O'Brien	1.00	.50	.10	☐ 472	Tom Hume	.06	.03	.00
☐ 424	Larry Parrish	.10	.05	.01	☐ 473	Alan Knicely	.06	.03	.00
☐ 425	Mickey Rivers	.10	.05	.01	☐ 474	Eddie Milner	.06	.03	.00
☐ 426	Billy Sample	.06	.03	.00	☐ 475	Ron Oester	.06	.03	.00
☐ 427	Dave Schmidt	.10	.05	.01	☐ 476	Kelly Paris	.10	.05	.01

		MINT	EXC	G-VG			MINT	EXC	G-VG
☐ 477	Frank Pastore	.06	.03	.00	☐ 526	Gary Pettis	.35	.17	.03
☐ 478	Ted Power	.06	.03	.00	☐ 527	Luis Sanchez	.06	.03	.00
☐ 479	Joe Price	.06	.03	.00	☐ 528	Daryl Sconiers	.06	.03	.00
☐ 480	Charlie Puleo	.06	.03	.00	☐ 529	Ellis Valentine	.06	.03	.00
☐ 481	Gary Redus	.25	.12	.02	☐ 530	Rob Wilfong	.06	.03	.00
☐ 482	Bill Scherrer	.06	.03	.00	☐ 531	Mike Witt	.10	.05	.01
☐ 483	Mario Soto	.06	.03	.00	☐ 532	Geoff Zahn	.06	.03	.00
☐ 484	Alex Trevino	.06	.03	.00	☐ 533	Bud Anderson	.06	.03	.00
☐ 485	Duane Walker	.06	.03	.00	☐ 534	Chris Bando	.06	.03	.00
☐ 486	Larry Bowa	.10	.05	.01	☐ 535	Alan Bannister	.06	.03	.00
☐ 487	Warren Brusstar	.06	.03	.00	☐ 536	Bert Blyleven	.20	.10	.02
☐ 488	Bill Buckner	.10	.05	.01	☐ 537	Tom Brennan	.06	.03	.00
☐ 489	Bill Campbell	.06	.03	.00	☐ 538	Jamie Easterly	.06	.03	.00
☐ 490	Ron Cey	.10	.05	.01	☐ 539	Juan Eichelberger	.06	.03	.00
☐ 491	Jody Davis	.10	.05	.01	☐ 540	Jim Essian	.06	.03	.00
☐ 492	Leon Durham	.10	.05	.01	☐ 541	Mike Fischlin	.06	.03	.00
☐ 493	Mel Hall	.30	.15	.03	☐ 542	Julio Franco	1.50	.75	.15
☐ 494	Ferguson Jenkins	.20	.10	.02	☐ 543	Mike Hargrove	.10	.05	.01
☐ 495	Jay Johnstone	.10	.05	.01	☐ 544	Toby Harrah	.10	.05	.01
☐ 496	Craig Lefferts	.30	.15	.03	☐ 545	Ron Hassey	.06	.03	.00
☐ 497	Carmelo Martinez	.25	.12	.02	☐ 546	Neal Heaton	.25	.12	.02
☐ 498	Jerry Morales	.06	.03	.00	☐ 547	Bake McBride	.06	.03	.00
☐ 499	Keith Moreland	.06	.03	.00	☐ 548	Broderick Perkins	.06	.03	.00
☐ 500	Dickie Noles	.06	.03	.00	☐ 549	Lary Sorensen	.06	.03	.00
☐ 501	Mike Proly	.06	.03	.00	☐ 550	Dan Spillner	.06	.03	.00
☐ 502	Chuck Rainey	.06	.03	.00	☐ 551	Rick Sutcliffe	.25	.12	.02
☐ 503	Dick Ruthven	.06	.03	.00	☐ 552	Pat Tabler	.15	.07	.01
☐ 504	Ryne Sandberg	2.25	1.10	.22	☐ 553	Gorman Thomas	.10	.05	.01
☐ 505	Lee Smith	.15	.07	.01	☐ 554	Andre Thornton	.10	.05	.01
☐ 506	Steve Trout	.06	.03	.00	☐ 555	George Vukovich	.06	.03	.00
☐ 507	Gary Woods	.06	.03	.00	☐ 556	Darrell Brown	.06	.03	.00
☐ 508	Juan Beniquez	.06	.03	.00	☐ 557	Tom Brunansky	.30	.15	.03
☐ 509	Bob Boone	.20	.10	.02	☐ 558	Randy Bush	.25	.12	.02
☐ 510	Rick Burleson	.10	.05	.01	☐ 559	Bobby Castillo	.06	.03	.00
☐ 511	Rod Carew	.50	.25	.05	☐ 560	John Castino	.06	.03	.00
☐ 512	Bobby Clark	.06	.03	.00	☐ 561	Ron Davis	.06	.03	.00
☐ 513	John Curtis	.06	.03	.00	☐ 562	Dave Engle	.06	.03	.00
☐ 514	Doug DeCinces	.10	.05	.01	☐ 563	Lenny Faedo	.06	.03	.00
☐ 515	Brian Downing	.10	.05	.01	☐ 564	Pete Filson	.06	.03	.00
☐ 516	Tim Foli	.06	.03	.00	☐ 565	Gary Gaetti	.90	.45	.09
☐ 517	Ken Forsch	.06	.03	.00	☐ 566	Mickey Hatcher	.10	.05	.01
☐ 518	Bobby Grich	.10	.05	.01	☐ 567	Kent Hrbek	.50	.25	.05
☐ 519	Andy Hassler	.06	.03	.00	☐ 568	Rusty Kuntz	.06	.03	.00
☐ 520	Reggie Jackson	.75	.35	.07	☐ 569	Tim Laudner	.06	.03	.00
☐ 521	Ron Jackson	.06	.03	.00	☐ 570	Rick Lysander	.06	.03	.00
☐ 522	Tommy John	.18	.09	.01	☐ 571	Bobby Mitchell	.06	.03	.00
☐ 523	Bruce Kison	.06	.03	.00	☐ 572	Ken Schrom	.06	.03	.00
☐ 524	Steve Lubratich	.06	.03	.00	☐ 573	Ray Smith	.06	.03	.00
☐ 525	Fred Lynn	.20	.10	.02	☐ 574	Tim Teufel	.30	.15	.03

		MINT	EXC	G-VG
☐ 575	Frank Viola	1.00	.50	.10
☐ 576	Gary Ward	.10	.05	.01
☐ 577	Ron Washington	.06	.03	.00
☐ 578	Len Whitehouse	.06	.03	.00
☐ 579	Al Williams	.06	.03	.00
☐ 580	Bob Bailor	.06	.03	.00
☐ 581	Mark Bradley	.10	.05	.01
☐ 582	Hubie Brooks	.15	.07	.01
☐ 583	Carlos Diaz	.06	.03	.00
☐ 584	George Foster	.15	.07	.01
☐ 585	Brian Giles	.06	.03	.00
☐ 586	Danny Heep	.06	.03	.00
☐ 587	Keith Hernandez	.35	.17	.03
☐ 588	Ron Hodges	.06	.03	.00
☐ 589	Scott Holman	.06	.03	.00
☐ 590	Dave Kingman	.15	.07	.01
☐ 591	Ed Lynch	.06	.03	.00
☐ 592	Jose Oquendo	.60	.30	.06
☐ 593	Jesse Orosco	.06	.03	.00
☐ 594	Junior Ortiz	.06	.03	.00
☐ 595	Tom Seaver	.60	.30	.06
☐ 596	Doug Sisk	.06	.03	.00
☐ 597	Rusty Staub	.15	.07	.01
☐ 598	John Stearns	.06	.03	.00
☐ 599	Darryl Strawberry	24.00	12.00	2.40
☐ 600	Craig Swan	.06	.03	.00
☐ 601	Walt Terrell	.50	.25	.05
☐ 602	Mike Torrez	.06	.03	.00
☐ 603	Mookie Wilson	.15	.07	.01
☐ 604	Jamie Allen	.06	.03	.00
☐ 605	Jim Beattie	.06	.03	.00
☐ 606	Tony Bernazard	.06	.03	.00
☐ 607	Manny Castillo	.06	.03	.00
☐ 608	Bill Caudill	.06	.03	.00
☐ 609	Bryan Clark	.06	.03	.00
☐ 610	Al Cowens	.06	.03	.00
☐ 611	Dave Henderson	.20	.10	.02
☐ 612	Steve Henderson	.06	.03	.00
☐ 613	Orlando Mercado	.06	.03	.00
☐ 614	Mike Moore	.25	.12	.02
☐ 615	Ricky Nelson UER (Jamie Nelson's stats on back)	.15	.07	.01
☐ 616	Spike Owen	.25	.12	.02
☐ 617	Pat Putnam	.06	.03	.00
☐ 618	Ron Roenicke	.06	.03	.00
☐ 619	Mike Stanton	.06	.03	.00
☐ 620	Bob Stoddard	.06	.03	.00
☐ 621	Rick Sweet	.06	.03	.00

		MINT	EXC	G-VG
☐ 622	Roy Thomas	.06	.03	.00
☐ 623	Ed VandeBerg	.06	.03	.00
☐ 624	Matt Young	.10	.05	.01
☐ 625	Richie Zisk	.06	.03	.00
☐ 626	Fred Lynn 1982 AS Game RB	.10	.05	.01
☐ 627	Manny Trillo 1983 AS Game RB	.10	.05	.01
☐ 628	Steve Garvey NL Iron Man	.20	.10	.02
☐ 629	Rod Carew AL Batting Runner-Up	.20	.10	.02
☐ 630	Wade Boggs AL Batting Champion	.60	.30	.06
☐ 631	Tim,Raines: Letting Go of the Raines	.20	.10	.02
☐ 632	Al Oliver Double Trouble	.10	.05	.01
☐ 633	Steve Sax AS Second Base	.15	.07	.01
☐ 634	Dickie Thon AS Shortstop	.10	.05	.01
☐ 635	Ace Firemen Dan Quisenberry and Tippy Martinez	.10	.05	.01
☐ 636	Reds Reunited Joe Morgan Pete Rose Tony Perez	.40	.20	.04
☐ 637	Backstop Stars Lance Parrish Bob Boone	.10	.05	.01
☐ 638	Geo. Brett and G. Perry Pine Tar 7/24/83	.15	.07	.01
☐ 639	1983 No Hitters Dave Righetti Mike Warren Bob Forsch	.10	.05	.01
☐ 640	Bench and Yaz Retiring Superstars	.75	.35	.07
☐ 641	Gaylord Perry Going Out In Style	.15	.07	.01
☐ 642	Steve Carlton 300 Club and Strikeout Record	.20	.10	.02
☐ 643	Altobelli and Owens WS Managers	.10	.05	.01
☐ 644	Rick Dempsey	.10	.05	.01

		MINT	EXC	G-VG
	World Series MVP			
☐ 645	Mike Boddicker	.10	.05	.01
	WS Rookie Winner			
☐ 646	Scott McGregor	.10	.05	.01
	WS Clincher			
☐ 647	CL: Orioles/Royals ..	.08	.01	.00
☐ 648	CL: Phillies/Giants ..	.07	.01	.00
☐ 649	CL: White Sox/Red			
	Sox	.07	.01	.00
☐ 650	CL: Tigers/Rangers ..	.07	.01	.00
☐ 651	CL: Dodgers/A's	.07	.01	.00
☐ 652	CL: Yankees/Reds ...	.07	.01	.00
☐ 653	CL: Blue Jays/Cubs ..	.07	.01	.00
☐ 654	CL: Braves/Angels ...	.07	.01	.00
☐ 655	CL: Brewers/Indians ..	.07	.01	.00
☐ 656	CL: Astros/Twins ...	.07	.01	.00
☐ 657	CL: Pirates/Mets	.07	.01	.00
☐ 658	CL: Expos/Mariners ..	.07	.01	.00
☐ 659	CL: Padres/Specials ..	.07	.01	.00
☐ 660	CL: Cardinals/Teams ..	.08	.01	.00

1984 Fleer Update

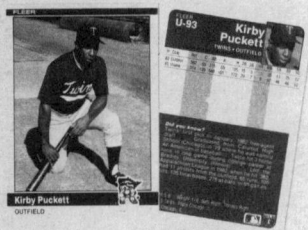

The cards in this 132-card set measure 2 ½"
by 3 ½". For the first time, the Fleer Gum Company issued a traded, extended, or update set.
The purpose of the set was the same as the
traded sets issued by Topps over the past four
years, i.e., to portray players with their proper
team for the current year and to portray rookies
who were not in their regular issue. Like the
Topps Traded sets of the past four years, the

Fleer Update sets were distributed through
hobby dealers only. The set was quite popular
with collectors, and, apparently, the print run
was relatively short, as the set was quickly in
short supply and exhibited a rapid and dra-
matic price increase. The cards are numbered
on the back with a U prefix; the order corre-
sponds to the alphabetical order of the
subjects' names. Collectors are urged to be
careful if purchasing single cards of Clemens,
Darling, Gooden, Puckett, Rose, or
Saberhagen, as these specific cards have
been illegally reprinted. These fakes are blurry
when compared to the real thing.

		MINT	EXC	G-VG
COMPLETE SET (132)		375.00	175.00	37.00
COMMON PLAYER (1-132) ..		.20	.10	.02
☐	U1 Willie Aikens	.30	.15	.03
☐	U2 Luis Aponte	.20	.10	.02
☐	U3 Mark Bailey	.30	.15	.03
☐	U4 Bob Bailor	.20	.10	.02
☐	U5 Dusty Baker	.30	.15	.03
☐	U6 Steve Balboni	.30	.15	.03
☐	U7 Alan Bannister	.20	.10	.02
☐	U8 Marty Barrett	3.50	1.75	.35
☐	U9 Dave Beard	.20	.10	.02
☐	U10 Joe Beckwith	.20	.10	.02
☐	U11 Dave Bergman	.20	.10	.02
☐	U12 Tony Bernazard	.20	.10	.02
☐	U13 Bruce Bochte	.20	.10	.02
☐	U14 Barry Bonnell	.20	.10	.02
☐	U15 Phil Bradley	4.00	2.00	.40
☐	U16 Fred Breining	.20	.10	.02
☐	U17 Mike Brown	.20	.10	.02
	(Angels OF)			
☐	U18 Bill Buckner	.40	.20	.04
☐	U19 Ray Burris	.20	.10	.02
☐	U20 John Butcher	.20	.10	.02
☐	U21 Brett Butler	.40	.20	.04
☐	U22 Enos Cabell	.20	.10	.02
☐	U23 Bill Campbell	.20	.10	.02
☐	U24 Bill Caudill	.20	.10	.02
☐	U25 Bobby Clark	.20	.10	.02
☐	U26 Bryan Clark	.20	.10	.02
☐	U27 Roger Clemens	85.00	42.50	8.50
☐	U28 Jaime Cocanower	.30	.15	.03
☐	U29 Ron Darling	9.00	4.50	.90
☐	U30 Alvin Davis	11.00	5.50	1.10

	MINT	EXC	G-VG		MINT	EXC	G-VG
☐ U31 Bob Dernier	.20	.10	.02	☐ U80 Joe Morgan	4.00	2.00	.40
☐ U32 Carlos Diaz	.20	.10	.02	☐ U81 Darryl Motley	.30	.15	.03
☐ U33 Mike Easler	.20	.10	.02	☐ U82 Graig Nettles	.90	.45	.09
☐ U34 Dennis Eckersley	1.00	.50	.10	☐ U83 Phil Niekro	2.50	1.25	.25
☐ U35 Jim Essian	.20	.10	.02	☐ U84 Ken Oberkfell	.20	.10	.02
☐ U36 Darrell Evans	.40	.20	.04	☐ U85 Al Oliver	.40	.20	.04
☐ U37 Mike Fitzgerald	.30	.15	.03	☐ U86 Jorge Orta	.20	.10	.02
☐ U38 Tim Foli	.20	.10	.02	☐ U87 Amos Otis	.30	.15	.03
☐ U39 John Franco	8.00	4.00	.80	☐ U88 Bob Owchinko	.20	.10	.02
☐ U40 George Frazier	.20	.10	.02	☐ U89 Dave Parker	2.00	1.00	.20
☐ U41 Rich Gale	.20	.10	.02	☐ U90 Jack Perconte	.20	.10	.02
☐ U42 Barbaro Garbey	.30	.15	.03	☐ U91 Tony Perez	1.50	.75	.15
☐ U43 Dwight Gooden	75.00	37.50	7.50	☐ U92 Gerald Perry	1.75	.85	.17
☐ U44 Goose Gossage	.75	.35	.07	☐ U93 Kirby Puckett	110.00	55.00	11.00
☐ U45 Wayne Gross	.20	.10	.02	☐ U94 Shane Rawley	.30	.15	.03
☐ U46 Mark Gubicza	7.00	3.50	.70	☐ U95 Floyd Rayford	.20	.10	.02
☐ U47 Jackie Gutierrez	.30	.15	.03	☐ U96 Ron Reed	.20	.10	.02
☐ U48 Toby Harrah	.30	.15	.03	☐ U97 R.J. Reynolds	1.25	.60	.12
☐ U49 Ron Hassey	.30	.15	.03	☐ U98 Gene Richards	.20	.10	.02
☐ U50 Richie Hebner	.20	.10	.02	☐ U99 Jose Rijo	3.00	1.50	.30
☐ U51 Willie Hernandez	.60	.30	.06	☐ U100 Jeff Robinson	1.25	.60	.12
☐ U52 Ed Hodge	.20	.10	.02	(Giants pitcher)			
☐ U53 Ricky Horton	.50	.25	.05	☐ U101 Ron Romanick	.30	.15	.03
☐ U54 Art Howe	.30	.15	.03	☐ U102 Pete Rose	15.00	7.50	1.50
☐ U55 Dane Iorg	.20	.10	.02	☐ U103 Bret Saberhagen	30.00	15.00	3.00
☐ U56 Brook Jacoby	2.00	1.00	.20	☐ U104 Scott Sanderson	.40	.20	.04
☐ U57 Dion James	.60	.30	.06	☐ U105 Dick Schofield	.65	.30	.06
☐ U58 Mike Jeffcoat	.30	.15	.03	☐ U106 Tom Seaver	8.00	4.00	.80
☐ U59 Ruppert Jones	.20	.10	.02	☐ U107 Jim Slaton	.20	.10	.02
☐ U60 Bob Kearney	.20	.10	.02	☐ U108 Mike Smithson	.20	.10	.02
☐ U61 Jimmy Key	5.00	2.50	.50	☐ U109 Lary Sorensen	.20	.10	.02
☐ U62 Dave Kingman	.40	.20	.04	☐ U110 Tim Stoddard	.20	.10	.02
☐ U63 Brad Komminsk	.40	.20	.04	☐ U111 Jeff Stone	.40	.20	.04
☐ U64 Jerry Koosman	.30	.15	.03	☐ U112 Champ Summers	.20	.10	.02
☐ U65 Wayne Krenchicki	.20	.10	.02	☐ U113 Jim Sundberg	.30	.15	.03
☐ U66 Rusty Kuntz	.20	.10	.02	☐ U114 Rick Sutcliffe	.75	.35	.07
☐ U67 Frank LaCorte	.20	.10	.02	☐ U115 Craig Swan	.30	.15	.03
☐ U68 Dennis Lamp	.20	.10	.02	☐ U116 Derrel Thomas	.20	.10	.02
☐ U69 Tito Landrum	.30	.15	.03	☐ U117 Gorman Thomas	.40	.20	.04
☐ U70 Mark Langston	24.00	12.00	2.40	☐ U118 Alex Trevino	.20	.10	.02
☐ U71 Rick Leach	.20	.10	.02	☐ U119 Manny Trillo	.20	.10	.02
☐ U72 Craig Lefferts	.40	.20	.04	☐ U120 John Tudor	.50	.25	.05
☐ U73 Gary Lucas	.20	.10	.02	☐ U121 Tom Underwood	.20	.10	.02
☐ U74 Jerry Martin	.20	.10	.02	☐ U122 Mike Vail	.20	.10	.02
☐ U75 Carmelo Martinez	.30	.15	.03	☐ U123 Tom Waddell	.30	.15	.03
☐ U76 Mike Mason	.30	.15	.03	☐ U124 Gary Ward	.30	.15	.03
☐ U77 Gary Matthews	.30	.15	.03	☐ U125 Terry Whitfield	.20	.10	.02
☐ U78 Andy McGaffigan	.20	.10	.02	☐ U126 Curtis Wilkerson	.30	.15	.03
☐ U79 Joey McLaughlin	.20	.10	.02	☐ U127 Frank Williams	.50	.25	.05

		MINT	EXC	G-VG
☐ U128	Glenn Wilson	.30	.15	.03
☐ U129	John Wockenfuss ...	.20	.10	.02
☐ U130	Ned Yost	.20	.10	.02
☐ U131	Mike Young	.50	.25	.05
☐ U132	Checklist: 1-132	.20	.03	.01

1985 Fleer

The cards in this 660-card set measure 2 ½"
by 3 ½". The 1985 Fleer set features fronts
that contain the team logo along with the
player's name and position. The borders enclosing the photo are color-coded to corre-
spond to the player's team. In each case, the
color is one of the standard colors of that team,
e.g., orange for Baltimore, red for St. Louis, etc.
The backs feature the same name, number,
and statistics format that Fleer has been using
over the past few years. The cards are ordered
alphabetically within team. The teams are ordered based on their respective performance
during the prior year, e.g., World Champion Detroit Tigers (1-25), Chicago Cubs (49-71), New York Mets
(72-95), Toronto (96-119), New York Yankees
(120-147), Boston (148-169), Baltimore (170-
195), Kansas City (196-218), St. Louis (219-
243), Philadelphia (244-269), Minnesota
(270-292), California (293-317), Atlanta (318-
342), Houston (343-365), Los Angeles (366-
391), Montreal (392-413), Oakland (414-436),
Cleveland (437-460), Pittsburgh (461-481),
Seattle (482-505), Chicago White Sox (506-

530), Cincinnati (531-554), Texas (555-575),
Milwaukee (576-601), and San Francisco (602-
625). Specials (626-643), Rookie Pairs (644-
653), and checklist cards (654-660) complete
the set. The black and white photo on the
reverse is included for the third straight year.
This set is noted for containing the Rookie
Cards of Roger Clemens, Alvin Davis, Eric
Davis, Glenn Davis, Dwight Gooden, Orel
Hershiser, Mark Langston, Kirby Puckett, Bret
Saberhagen, and Danny Tartabull.

			MINT	EXC	G-VG
		COMPLETE SET (660)	125.00	60.00	12.00
		COMMON PLAYER (1-660)	.05	.02	.00
☐	1	Doug Bair	.10	.02	.01
☐	2	Juan Berenguer	.05	.02	.00
☐	3	Dave Bergman	.05	.02	.00
☐	4	Tom Brookens	.05	.02	.00
☐	5	Marty Castillo	.05	.02	.00
☐	6	Darrell Evans	.12	.06	.01
☐	7	Barbaro Garbey	.05	.02	.00
☐	8	Kirk Gibson	.30	.15	.03
☐	9	John Grubb	.05	.02	.00
☐	10	Willie Hernandez ...	.12	.06	.01
☐	11	Larry Herndon	.05	.02	.00
☐	12	Howard Johnson ...	2.00	1.00	.20
☐	13	Ruppert Jones	.05	.02	.00
☐	14	Rusty Kuntz	.05	.02	.00
☐	15	Chet Lemon	.08	.04	.01
☐	16	Aurelio Lopez	.05	.02	.00
☐	17	Sid Monge	.05	.02	.00
☐	18	Jack Morris	.18	.09	.01
☐	19	Lance Parrish	.20	.10	.02
☐	20	Dan Petry	.05	.02	.00
☐	21	Dave Rozema	.05	.02	.00
☐	22	Bill Scherrer	.05	.02	.00
☐	23	Alan Trammell	.30	.15	.03
☐	24	Lou Whitaker	.25	.12	.02
☐	25	Milt Wilcox	.05	.02	.00
☐	26	Kurt Bevacqua	.05	.02	.00
☐	27	Greg Booker	.05	.02	.00
☐	28	Bobby Brown	.05	.02	.00
☐	29	Luis DeLeon	.05	.02	.00
☐	30	Dave Dravecky	.15	.07	.01
☐	31	Tim Flannery	.05	.02	.00
☐	32	Steve Garvey	.40	.20	.04
☐	33	Goose Gossage	.15	.07	.01
☐	34	Tony Gwynn	1.50	.75	.15

		MINT	EXC	G-VG			MINT	EXC	G-VG
☐	35 Greg Harris	.05	.02	.00	☐ 84	Danny Heep	.05	.02	.00
☐	36 Andy Hawkins	.10	.05	.01	☐ 85	Keith Hernandez	.30	.15	.03
☐	37 Terry Kennedy	.05	.02	.00	☐ 86	Ray Knight	.10	.05	.01
☐	38 Craig Lefferts	.08	.04	.01	☐ 87	Ed Lynch	.05	.02	.00
☐	39 Tim Lollar	.05	.02	.00	☐ 88	Jose Oquendo	.08	.04	.01
☐	40 Carmelo Martinez	.05	.02	.00	☐ 89	Jesse Orosco	.05	.02	.00
☐	41 Kevin McReynolds	1.00	.50	.10	☐ 90	Rafael Santana	.25	.12	.02
☐	42 Graig Nettles	.12	.06	.01	☐ 91	Doug Sisk	.05	.02	.00
☐	43 Luis Salazar	.08	.04	.01	☐ 92	Rusty Staub	.12	.06	.01
☐	44 Eric Show	.08	.04	.01	☐ 93	Darryl Strawberry	4.50	2.25	.45
☐	45 Garry Templeton	.08	.04	.01	☐ 94	Walt Terrell	.08	.04	.01
☐	46 Mark Thurmond	.05	.02	.00	☐ 95	Mookie Wilson	.10	.05	.01
☐	47 Ed Whitson	.05	.02	.00	☐ 96	Jim Acker	.05	.02	.00
☐	48 Alan Wiggins	.05	.02	.00	☐ 97	Willie Aikens	.05	.02	.00
☐	49 Rich Bordi	.05	.02	.00	☐ 98	Doyle Alexander	.08	.04	.01
☐	50 Larry Bowa	.10	.05	.01	☐ 99	Jesse Barfield	.30	.15	.03
☐	51 Warren Brusstar	.05	.02	.00	☐ 100	George Bell	.50	.25	.05
☐	52 Ron Cey	.10	.05	.01	☐ 101	Jim Clancy	.05	.02	.00
☐	53 Henry Cotto	.15	.07	.01	☐ 102	Dave Collins	.05	.02	.00
☐	54 Jody Davis	.08	.04	.01	☐ 103	Tony Fernandez	.45	.22	.04
☐	55 Bob Dernier	.05	.02	.00	☐ 104	Damaso Garcia	.05	.02	.00
☐	56 Leon Durham	.08	.04	.01	☐ 105	Jim Gott	.05	.02	.00
☐	57 Dennis Eckersley	.18	.09	.01	☐ 106	Alfredo Griffin	.08	.04	.01
☐	58 George Frazier	.05	.02	.00	☐ 107	Garth Iorg	.05	.02	.00
☐	59 Richie Hebner	.05	.02	.00	☐ 108	Roy Lee Jackson	.05	.02	.00
☐	60 Dave Lopes	.08	.04	.01	☐ 109	Cliff Johnson	.05	.02	.00
☐	61 Gary Matthews	.08	.04	.01	☐ 110	Jimmy Key	1.25	.60	.12
☐	62 Keith Moreland	.05	.02	.00	☐ 111	Dennis Lamp	.05	.02	.00
☐	63 Rick Reuschel	.12	.06	.01	☐ 112	Rick Leach	.05	.02	.00
☐	64 Dick Ruthven	.05	.02	.00	☐ 113	Luis Leal	.05	.02	.00
☐	65 Ryne Sandberg	.60	.30	.06	☐ 114	Buck Martinez	.05	.02	.00
☐	66 Scott Sanderson	.05	.02	.00	☐ 115	Lloyd Moseby	.10	.05	.01
☐	67 Lee Smith	.10	.05	.01	☐ 116	Rance Mulliniks	.05	.02	.00
☐	68 Tim Stoddard	.05	.02	.00	☐ 117	Dave Stieb	.15	.07	.01
☐	69 Rick Sutcliffe	.15	.07	.01	☐ 118	Willie Upshaw	.05	.02	.00
☐	70 Steve Trout	.05	.02	.00	☐ 119	Ernie Whitt	.05	.02	.00
☐	71 Gary Woods	.05	.02	.00	☐ 120	Mike Armstrong	.05	.02	.00
☐	72 Wally Backman	.08	.04	.01	☐ 121	Don Baylor	.12	.06	.01
☐	73 Bruce Berenyi	.05	.02	.00	☐ 122	Marty Bystrom	.05	.02	.00
☐	74 Hubie Brooks	.10	.05	.01	☐ 123	Rick Cerone	.05	.02	.00
☐	75 Kelvin Chapman	.08	.04	.01	☐ 124	Joe Cowley	.05	.02	.00
☐	76 Ron Darling	1.25	.60	.12	☐ 125	Brian Dayett	.05	.02	.00
☐	77 Sid Fernandez	1.25	.60	.12	☐ 126	Tim Foli	.05	.02	.00
☐	78 Mike Fitzgerald	.05	.02	.00	☐ 127	Ray Fontenot	.05	.02	.00
☐	79 George Foster	.12	.06	.01	☐ 128	Ken Griffey	.12	.06	.01
☐	80 Brent Gaff	.05	.02	.00	☐ 129	Ron Guidry	.15	.07	.01
☐	81 Ron Gardenhire	.05	.02	.00	☐ 130	Toby Harrah	.05	.02	.00
☐	82 Dwight Gooden	12.00	6.00	1.20	☐ 131	Jay Howell	.08	.04	.01
☐	83 Tom Gorman	.05	.02	.00	☐ 132	Steve Kemp	.08	.04	.01

		MINT	EXC	G-VG			MINT	EXC	G-VG
☐ 133	Don Mattingly	12.00	6.00	1.20	☐ 181	Dennis Martinez	.08	.04	.01
☐ 134	Bobby Meacham	.05	.02	.00	☐ 182	Tippy Martinez	.05	.02	.00
☐ 135	John Montefusco	.05	.02	.00	☐ 183	Scott McGregor	.08	.04	.01
☐ 136	Omar Moreno	.05	.02	.00	☐ 184	Eddie Murray	.40	.20	.04
☐ 137	Dale Murray	.05	.02	.00	☐ 185	Joe Nolan	.05	.02	.00
☐ 138	Phil Niekro	.25	.12	.02	☐ 186	Floyd Rayford	.05	.02	.00
☐ 139	Mike Pagliarulo	.75	.35	.07	☐ 187	Cal Ripken	.60	.30	.06
☐ 140	Willie Randolph	.10	.05	.01	☐ 188	Gary Roenicke	.05	.02	.00
☐ 141	Dennis Rasmussen	.25	.12	.02	☐ 189	Lenn Sakata	.05	.02	.00
☐ 142	Dave Righetti	.18	.09	.01	☐ 190	John Shelby	.05	.02	.00
☐ 143	Jose Rijo	.45	.22	.04	☐ 191	Ken Singleton	.08	.04	.01
☐ 144	Andre Robertson	.05	.02	.00	☐ 192	Sammy Stewart	.05	.02	.00
☐ 145	Bob Shirley	.05	.02	.00	☐ 193	Bill Swaggerty	.08	.04	.01
☐ 146	Dave Winfield	.35	.17	.03	☐ 194	Tom Underwood	.05	.02	.00
☐ 147	Butch Wynegar	.05	.02	.00	☐ 195	Mike Young	.15	.07	.01
☐ 148	Gary Allenson	.05	.02	.00	☐ 196	Steve Balboni	.05	.02	.00
☐ 149	Tony Armas	.08	.04	.01	☐ 197	Joe Beckwith	.05	.02	.00
☐ 150	Marty Barrett	.35	.17	.03	☐ 198	Bud Black	.05	.02	.00
☐ 151	Wade Boggs	4.00	2.00	.40	☐ 199	George Brett	.60	.30	.06
☐ 152	Dennis Boyd	.10	.05	.01	☐ 200	Onix Concepcion	.05	.02	.00
☐ 153	Bill Buckner	.10	.05	.01	☐ 201	Mark Gubicza	2.00	1.00	.20
☐ 154	Mark Clear	.05	.02	.00	☐ 202	Larry Gura	.05	.02	.00
☐ 155	Roger Clemens	12.00	6.00	1.20	☐ 203	Mark Huismann	.05	.02	.00
☐ 156	Steve Crawford	.05	.02	.00	☐ 204	Dane Iorg	.05	.02	.00
☐ 157	Mike Easler	.05	.02	.00	☐ 205	Danny Jackson	.85	.40	.08
☐ 158	Dwight Evans	.18	.09	.01	☐ 206	Charlie Leibrandt	.05	.02	.00
☐ 159	Rich Gedman	.10	.05	.01	☐ 207	Hal McRae	.08	.04	.01
☐ 160	Jackie Gutierrez	.15	.07	.01	☐ 208	Darryl Motley	.05	.02	.00
	(W. Boggs on deck)				☐ 209	Jorge Orta	.05	.02	.00
☐ 161	Bruce Hurst	.15	.07	.01	☐ 210	Greg Pryor	.05	.02	.00
☐ 162	John Henry Johnson	.05	.02	.00	☐ 211	Dan Quisenberry	.12	.06	.01
☐ 163	Rick Miller	.05	.02	.00	☐ 212	Bret Saberhagen	8.00	4.00	.80
☐ 164	Reid Nichols	.05	.02	.00	☐ 213	Pat Sheridan	.05	.02	.00
☐ 165	Al Nipper	.12	.06	.01	☐ 214	Don Slaught	.05	.02	.00
☐ 166	Bob Ojeda	.10	.05	.01	☐ 215	U.L. Washington	.05	.02	.00
☐ 167	Jerry Remy	.05	.02	.00	☐ 216	John Wathan	.05	.02	.00
☐ 168	Jim Rice	.25	.12	.02	☐ 217	Frank White	.08	.04	.01
☐ 169	Bob Stanley	.05	.02	.00	☐ 218	Willie Wilson	.12	.06	.01
☐ 170	Mike Boddicker	.10	.05	.01	☐ 219	Neil Allen	.05	.02	.00
☐ 171	Al Bumbry	.05	.02	.00	☐ 220	Joaquin Andujar	.08	.04	.01
☐ 172	Todd Cruz	.05	.02	.00	☐ 221	Steve Braun	.05	.02	.00
☐ 173	Rich Dauer	.05	.02	.00	☐ 222	Danny Cox	.10	.05	.01
☐ 174	Storm Davis	.12	.06	.01	☐ 223	Bob Forsch	.05	.02	.00
☐ 175	Rick Dempsey	.05	.02	.00	☐ 224	David Green	.05	.02	.00
☐ 176	Jim Dwyer	.05	.02	.00	☐ 225	George Hendrick	.08	.04	.01
☐ 177	Mike Flanagan	.08	.04	.01	☐ 226	Tom Herr	.08	.04	.01
☐ 178	Dan Ford	.05	.02	.00	☐ 227	Ricky Horton	.20	.10	.02
☐ 179	Wayne Gross	.05	.02	.00	☐ 228	Art Howe	.08	.04	.01
☐ 180	John Lowenstein	.05	.02	.00	☐ 229	Mike Jorgensen	.05	.02	.00

		MINT	EXC	G-VG
☐ 230	Kurt Kepshire	.08	.04	.01
☐ 231	Jeff Lahti	.05	.02	.00
☐ 232	Tito Landrum	.05	.02	.00
☐ 233	Dave LaPoint	.08	.04	.01
☐ 234	Willie McGee	.30	.15	.03
☐ 235	Tom Nieto	.05	.02	.00
☐ 236	Terry Pendleton	.45	.22	.04
☐ 237	Darrell Porter	.05	.02	.00
☐ 238	Dave Rucker	.05	.02	.00
☐ 239	Lonnie Smith	.12	.06	.01
☐ 240	Ozzie Smith	.35	.15	.03
☐ 241	Bruce Sutter	.12	.06	.01
☐ 242	Andy Van Slyke UER (Bats Right, Throws Left)	.50	.25	.05
☐ 243	Dave Von Ohlen	.05	.02	.00
☐ 244	Larry Andersen	.05	.02	.00
☐ 245	Bill Campbell	.05	.02	.00
☐ 246	Steve Carlton	.40	.20	.04
☐ 247	Tim Corcoran	.05	.02	.00
☐ 248	Ivan DeJesus	.05	.02	.00
☐ 249	John Denny	.08	.04	.01
☐ 250	Bo Diaz	.05	.02	.00
☐ 251	Greg Gross	.05	.02	.00
☐ 252	Kevin Gross	.08	.04	.01
☐ 253	Von Hayes	.18	.09	.01
☐ 254	Al Holland	.05	.02	.00
☐ 255	Charles Hudson	.05	.02	.00
☐ 256	Jerry Koosman	.08	.04	.01
☐ 257	Joe Lefebvre	.05	.02	.00
☐ 258	Sixto Lezcano	.05	.02	.00
☐ 259	Garry Maddox	.08	.04	.01
☐ 260	Len Matuszek	.05	.02	.00
☐ 261	Tug McGraw	.10	.05	.01
☐ 262	Al Oliver	.10	.05	.01
☐ 263	Shane Rawley	.05	.02	.00
☐ 264	Juan Samuel	.35	.17	.03
☐ 265	Mike Schmidt	.80	.40	.08
☐ 266	Jeff Stone	.12	.06	.01
☐ 267	Ozzie Virgil	.05	.02	.00
☐ 268	Glenn Wilson	.08	.04	.01
☐ 269	John Wockenfuss	.05	.02	.00
☐ 270	Darrell Brown	.05	.02	.00
☐ 271	Tom Brunansky	.20	.10	.02
☐ 272	Randy Bush	.08	.04	.01
☐ 273	John Butcher	.05	.02	.00
☐ 274	Bobby Castillo	.05	.02	.00
☐ 275	Ron Davis	.05	.02	.00
☐ 276	Dave Engle	.05	.02	.00
☐ 277	Pete Filson	.05	.02	.00
☐ 278	Gary Gaetti	.35	.17	.03
☐ 279	Mickey Hatcher	.05	.02	.00
☐ 280	Ed Hodge	.05	.02	.00
☐ 281	Kent Hrbek	.35	.17	.03
☐ 282	Houston Jimenez	.05	.02	.00
☐ 283	Tim Laudner	.05	.02	.00
☐ 284	Rick Lysander	.05	.02	.00
☐ 285	Dave Meier	.05	.02	.00
☐ 286	Kirby Puckett	18.00	9.00	1.80
☐ 287	Pat Putnam	.05	.02	.00
☐ 288	Ken Schrom	.05	.02	.00
☐ 289	Mike Smithson	.05	.02	.00
☐ 290	Tim Teufel	.05	.02	.00
☐ 291	Frank Viola	.40	.20	.04
☐ 292	Ron Washington	.05	.02	.00
☐ 293	Don Aase	.05	.02	.00
☐ 294	Juan Beniquez	.05	.02	.00
☐ 295	Bob Boone	.12	.06	.01
☐ 296	Mike Brown (Angels OF)	.05	.02	.00
☐ 297	Rod Carew	.40	.20	.04
☐ 298	Doug Corbett	.05	.02	.00
☐ 299	Doug DeCinces	.08	.04	.01
☐ 300	Brian Downing	.08	.04	.01
☐ 301	Ken Forsch	.05	.02	.00
☐ 302	Bobby Grich	.08	.04	.01
☐ 303	Reggie Jackson	.50	.25	.05
☐ 304	Tommy John	.15	.07	.01
☐ 305	Curt Kaufman	.08	.04	.01
☐ 306	Bruce Kison	.05	.02	.00
☐ 307	Fred Lynn	.15	.07	.01
☐ 308	Gary Pettis	.08	.04	.01
☐ 309	Ron Romanick	.05	.02	.00
☐ 310	Luis Sanchez	.05	.02	.00
☐ 311	Dick Schofield	.10	.05	.01
☐ 312	Daryl Sconiers	.05	.02	.00
☐ 313	Jim Slaton	.05	.02	.00
☐ 314	Derrel Thomas	.05	.02	.00
☐ 315	Rob Wilfong	.05	.02	.00
☐ 316	Mike Witt	.10	.05	.01
☐ 317	Geoff Zahn	.05	.02	.00
☐ 318	Len Barker	.05	.02	.00
☐ 319	Steve Bedrosian	.15	.07	.01
☐ 320	Bruce Benedict	.05	.02	.00
☐ 321	Rick Camp	.05	.02	.00
☐ 322	Chris Chambliss	.08	.04	.01
☐ 323	Jeff Dedmon	.08	.04	.01
☐ 324	Terry Forster	.08	.04	.01

			MINT	EXC	G-VG				MINT	EXC	G-VG
☐	325	Gene Garber	.05	.02	.00	☐	374	Ken Howell	.15	.07	.01
☐	326	Albert Hall	.10	.05	.01	☐	375	Ken Landreaux	.05	.02	.00
☐	327	Terry Harper	.05	.02	.00	☐	376	Candy Maldonado	.10	.05	.01
☐	328	Bob Horner	.12	.06	.01	☐	377	Mike Marshall	.15	.07	.01
☐	329	Glenn Hubbard	.05	.02	.00	☐	378	Tom Niedenfuer	.08	.04	.01
☐	330	Randy Johnson	.05	.02	.00	☐	379	Alejandro Pena	.08	.04	.01
☐	331	Brad Komminsk	.08	.04	.01	☐	380	Jerry Reuss	.08	.04	.01
☐	332	Rick Mahler	.05	.02	.00	☐	381	R.J. Reynolds	.25	.12	.02
☐	333	Craig McMurtry	.05	.02	.00	☐	382	German Rivera	.08	.04	.01
☐	334	Donnie Moore	.05	.02	.00	☐	383	Bill Russell	.08	.04	.01
☐	335	Dale Murphy	.60	.30	.06	☐	384	Steve Sax	.25	.12	.02
☐	336	Ken Oberkfell	.05	.02	.00	☐	385	Mike Scioscia	.08	.04	.01
☐	337	Pascual Perez	.12	.06	.01	☐	386	Franklin Stubbs	.30	.15	.03
☐	338	Gerald Perry	.30	.15	.03	☐	387	Fernando Valenzuela	.25	.12	.02
☐	339	Rafael Ramirez	.05	.02	.00	☐	388	Bob Welch	.10	.05	.01
☐	340	Jerry Royster	.05	.02	.00	☐	389	Terry Whitfield	.05	.02	.00
☐	341	Alex Trevino	.05	.02	.00	☐	390	Steve Yeager	.05	.02	.00
☐	342	Claudell Washington	.08	.04	.01	☐	391	Pat Zachry	.05	.02	.00
☐	343	Alan Ashby	.05	.02	.00	☐	392	Fred Breining	.05	.02	.00
☐	344	Mark Bailey	.08	.04	.01	☐	393	Gary Carter	.30	.15	.03
☐	345	Kevin Bass	.10	.05	.01	☐	394	Andre Dawson	.30	.15	.03
☐	346	Enos Cabell	.05	.02	.00	☐	395	Miguel Dilone	.05	.02	.00
☐	347	Jose Cruz	.10	.05	.01	☐	396	Dan Driessen	.05	.02	.00
☐	348	Bill Dawley	.05	.02	.00	☐	397	Doug Flynn	.05	.02	.00
☐	349	Frank DiPino	.05	.02	.00	☐	398	Terry Francona	.05	.02	.00
☐	350	Bill Doran	.15	.07	.01	☐	399	Bill Gullickson	.05	.02	.00
☐	351	Phil Garner	.05	.02	.00	☐	400	Bob James	.05	.02	.00
☐	352	Bob Knepper	.08	.04	.01	☐	401	Charlie Lea	.05	.02	.00
☐	353	Mike LaCoss	.05	.02	.00	☐	402	Bryan Little	.05	.02	.00
☐	354	Jerry Mumphrey	.05	.02	.00	☐	403	Gary Lucas	.05	.02	.00
☐	355	Joe Niekro	.10	.05	.01	☐	404	David Palmer	.05	.02	.00
☐	356	Terry Puhl	.05	.02	.00	☐	405	Tim Raines	.35	.17	.03
☐	357	Craig Reynolds	.05	.02	.00	☐	406	Mike Ramsey	.05	.02	.00
☐	358	Vern Ruhle	.05	.02	.00	☐	407	Jeff Reardon	.12	.06	.01
☐	359	Nolan Ryan	1.50	.75	.15	☐	408	Steve Rogers	.05	.02	.00
☐	360	Joe Sambito	.05	.02	.00	☐	409	Dan Schatzeder	.05	.02	.00
☐	361	Mike Scott	.35	.17	.03	☐	410	Bryn Smith	.10	.05	.01
☐	362	Dave Smith	.08	.04	.01	☐	411	Mike Stenhouse	.05	.02	.00
☐	363	Julio Solano	.08	.04	.01	☐	412	Tim Wallach	.12	.06	.01
☐	364	Dickie Thon	.05	.02	.00	☐	413	Jim Wohlford	.05	.02	.00
☐	365	Denny Walling	.05	.02	.00	☐	414	Bill Almon	.05	.02	.00
☐	366	Dave Anderson	.05	.02	.00	☐	415	Keith Atherton	.05	.02	.00
☐	367	Bob Bailor	.05	.02	.00	☐	416	Bruce Bochte	.05	.02	.00
☐	368	Greg Brock	.08	.04	.01	☐	417	Tom Burgmeier	.05	.02	.00
☐	369	Carlos Diaz	.05	.02	.00	☐	418	Ray Burris	.05	.02	.00
☐	370	Pedro Guerrero	.30	.15	.03	☐	419	Bill Caudill	.05	.02	.00
☐	371	Orel Hershiser	10.00	5.00	1.00	☐	420	Chris Codiroli	.05	.02	.00
☐	372	Rick Honeycutt	.05	.02	.00	☐	421	Tim Conroy	.05	.02	.00
☐	373	Burt Hooton	.05	.02	.00	☐	422	Mike Davis	.08	.04	.01

		MINT	EXC	G-VG			MINT	EXC	G-VG
☐ 423	Jim Essian	.05	.02	.00	☐ 472	Tony Pena	.12	.06	.01
☐ 424	Mike Heath	.05	.02	.00	☐ 473	Johnny Ray	.08	.04	.01
☐ 425	Rickey Henderson	.75	.35	.07	☐ 474	Rick Rhoden	.08	.04	.01
☐ 426	Donnie Hill	.05	.02	.00	☐ 475	Don Robinson	.05	.02	.00
☐ 427	Dave Kingman	.10	.05	.01	☐ 476	Rod Scurry	.05	.02	.00
☐ 428	Bill Krueger	.05	.02	.00	☐ 477	Kent Tekulve	.08	.04	.01
☐ 429	Carney Lansford	.12	.06	.01	☐ 478	Jason Thompson	.05	.02	.00
☐ 430	Steve McCatty	.05	.02	.00	☐ 479	John Tudor	.15	.07	.01
☐ 431	Joe Morgan	.25	.12	.02	☐ 480	Lee Tunnell	.05	.02	.00
☐ 432	Dwayne Murphy	.05	.02	.00	☐ 481	Marvell Wynne	.05	.02	.00
☐ 433	Tony Phillips	.05	.02	.00	☐ 482	Salome Barojas	.05	.02	.00
☐ 434	Lary Sorensen	.05	.02	.00	☐ 483	Dave Beard	.05	.02	.00
☐ 435	Mike Warren	.05	.02	.00	☐ 484	Jim Beattie	.05	.02	.00
☐ 436	Curt Young	.30	.15	.03	☐ 485	Barry Bonnell	.05	.02	.00
☐ 437	Luis Aponte	.05	.02	.00	☐ 486	Phil Bradley	1.00	.50	.10
☐ 438	Chris Bando	.05	.02	.00	☐ 487	Al Cowens	.05	.02	.00
☐ 439	Tony Bernazard	.05	.02	.00	☐ 488	Alvin Davis	3.00	1.50	.30
☐ 440	Bert Blyleven	.15	.07	.01	☐ 489	Dave Henderson	.12	.06	.01
☐ 441	Brett Butler	.10	.05	.01	☐ 490	Steve Henderson	.05	.02	.00
☐ 442	Ernie Camacho	.05	.02	.00	☐ 491	Bob Kearney	.05	.02	.00
☐ 443	Joe Carter	3.00	1.50	.30	☐ 492	Mark Langston	5.00	2.50	.50
☐ 444	Carmelo Castillo	.05	.02	.00	☐ 493	Larry Milbourne	.05	.02	.00
☐ 445	Jamie Easterly	.05	.02	.00	☐ 494	Paul Mirabella	.05	.02	.00
☐ 446	Steve Farr	.30	.15	.03	☐ 495	Mike Moore	.15	.07	.01
☐ 447	Mike Fischlin	.05	.02	.00	☐ 496	Edwin Nunez	.05	.02	.00
☐ 448	Julio Franco	.40	.20	.04	☐ 497	Spike Owen	.05	.02	.00
☐ 449	Mel Hall	.12	.06	.01	☐ 498	Jack Perconte	.05	.02	.00
☐ 450	Mike Hargrove	.08	.04	.01	☐ 499	Ken Phelps	.10	.05	.01
☐ 451	Neal Heaton	.05	.02	.00	☐ 500	Jim Presley	.75	.35	.07
☐ 452	Brook Jacoby	.25	.12	.02	☐ 501	Mike Stanton	.05	.02	.00
☐ 453	Mike Jeffcoat	.05	.02	.00	☐ 502	Bob Stoddard	.05	.02	.00
☐ 454	Don Schulze	.08	.04	.01	☐ 503	Gorman Thomas	.10	.05	.01
☐ 455	Roy Smith	.08	.04	.01	☐ 504	Ed VandeBerg	.05	.02	.00
☐ 456	Pat Tabler	.10	.05	.01	☐ 505	Matt Young	.05	.02	.00
☐ 457	Andre Thornton	.08	.04	.01	☐ 506	Juan Agosto	.05	.02	.00
☐ 458	George Vukovich	.05	.02	.00	☐ 507	Harold Baines	.20	.10	.02
☐ 459	Tom Waddell	.08	.04	.01	☐ 508	Floyd Bannister	.05	.02	.00
☐ 460	Jerry Willard	.05	.02	.00	☐ 509	Britt Burns	.05	.02	.00
☐ 461	Dale Berra	.05	.02	.00	☐ 510	Julio Cruz	.05	.02	.00
☐ 462	John Candelaria	.08	.04	.01	☐ 511	Richard Dotson	.08	.04	.01
☐ 463	Jose DeLeon	.08	.04	.01	☐ 512	Jerry Dybzinski	.05	.02	.00
☐ 464	Doug Frobel	.05	.02	.00	☐ 513	Carlton Fisk	.25	.12	.02
☐ 465	Cecilio Guante	.05	.02	.00	☐ 514	Scott Fletcher	.08	.04	.01
☐ 466	Brian Harper	.15	.07	.01	☐ 515	Jerry Hairston	.05	.02	.00
☐ 467	Lee Lacy	.05	.02	.00	☐ 516	Marc Hill	.05	.02	.00
☐ 468	Bill Madlock	.10	.05	.01	☐ 517	LaMarr Hoyt	.08	.04	.01
☐ 469	Lee Mazzilli	.05	.02	.00	☐ 518	Ron Kittle	.15	.07	.01
☐ 470	Larry McWilliams	.05	.02	.00	☐ 519	Rudy Law	.05	.02	.00
☐ 471	Jim Morrison	.05	.02	.00	☐ 520	Vance Law	.08	.04	.01

		MINT	EXC	G-VG			MINT	EXC	G-VG
☐ 521	Greg Luzinski	.10	.05	.01	☐ 570	Frank Tanana	.08	.04	.01
☐ 522	Gene Nelson	.05	.02	.00	☐ 571	Wayne Tolleson	.05	.02	.00
☐ 523	Tom Paciorek	.05	.02	.00	☐ 572	Gary Ward	.08	.04	.01
☐ 524	Ron Reed	.05	.02	.00	☐ 573	Curtis Wilkerson	.05	.02	.00
☐ 525	Bert Roberge	.05	.02	.00	☐ 574	George Wright	.05	.02	.00
☐ 526	Tom Seaver	.30	.15	.03	☐ 575	Ned Yost	.05	.02	.00
☐ 527	Roy Smalley	.05	.02	.00	☐ 576	Mark Brouhard	.05	.02	.00
☐ 528	Dan Spillner	.05	.02	.00	☐ 577	Mike Caldwell	.05	.02	.00
☐ 529	Mike Squires	.05	.02	.00	☐ 578	Bobby Clark	.05	.02	.00
☐ 530	Greg Walker	.10	.05	.01	☐ 579	Jaime Cocanower	.05	.02	.00
☐ 531	Cesar Cedeno	.08	.04	.01	☐ 580	Cecil Cooper	.12	.06	.01
☐ 532	Dave Concepcion	.10	.05	.01	☐ 581	Rollie Fingers	.15	.07	.01
☐ 533	Eric Davis	16.00	8.00	1.60	☐ 582	Jim Gantner	.05	.02	.00
☐ 534	Nick Esasky	.25	.12	.02	☐ 583	Moose Haas	.05	.02	.00
☐ 535	Tom Foley	.05	.02	.00	☐ 584	Dion James	.10	.05	.01
☐ 536	John Franco	1.50	.75	.15	☐ 585	Pete Ladd	.05	.02	.00
☐ 537	Brad Gulden	.05	.02	.00	☐ 586	Rick Manning	.05	.02	.00
☐ 538	Tom Hume	.05	.02	.00	☐ 587	Bob McClure	.05	.02	.00
☐ 539	Wayne Krenchicki	.05	.02	.00	☐ 588	Paul Molitor	.20	.10	.02
☐ 540	Andy McGaffigan	.05	.02	.00	☐ 589	Charlie Moore	.05	.02	.00
☐ 541	Eddie Milner	.05	.02	.00	☐ 590	Ben Oglivie	.08	.04	.01
☐ 542	Ron Oester	.05	.02	.00	☐ 591	Chuck Porter	.05	.02	.00
☐ 543	Bob Owchinko	.05	.02	.00	☐ 592	Randy Ready	.20	.10	.02
☐ 544	Dave Parker	.18	.09	.01	☐ 593	Ed Romero	.05	.02	.00
☐ 545	Frank Pastore	.05	.02	.00	☐ 594	Bill Schroeder	.05	.02	.00
☐ 546	Tony Perez	.18	.09	.01	☐ 595	Ray Searage	.05	.02	.00
☐ 547	Ted Power	.05	.02	.00	☐ 596	Ted Simmons	.12	.06	.01
☐ 548	Joe Price	.05	.02	.00	☐ 597	Jim Sundberg	.05	.02	.00
☐ 549	Gary Redus	.05	.02	.00	☐ 598	Don Sutton	.25	.12	.02
☐ 550	Pete Rose	1.00	.50	.10	☐ 599	Tom Tellmann	.05	.02	.00
☐ 551	Jeff Russell	.30	.15	.03	☐ 600	Rick Waits	.05	.02	.00
☐ 552	Mario Soto	.05	.02	.00	☐ 601	Robin Yount	.60	.30	.06
☐ 553	Jay Tibbs	.10	.05	.01	☐ 602	Dusty Baker	.08	.04	.01
☐ 554	Duane Walker	.05	.02	.00	☐ 603	Bob Brenly	.05	.02	.00
☐ 555	Alan Bannister	.05	.02	.00	☐ 604	Jack Clark	.20	.10	.02
☐ 556	Buddy Bell	.10	.05	.01	☐ 605	Chili Davis	.10	.05	.01
☐ 557	Danny Darwin	.05	.02	.00	☐ 606	Mark Davis	.25	.12	.02
☐ 558	Charlie Hough	.08	.04	.01	☐ 607	Dan Gladden	.40	.20	.04
☐ 559	Bobby Jones	.05	.02	.00	☐ 608	Atlee Hammaker	.05	.02	.00
☐ 560	Odell Jones	.05	.02	.00	☐ 609	Mike Krukow	.05	.02	.00
☐ 561	Jeff Kunkel	.08	.04	.01	☐ 610	Duane Kuiper	.05	.02	.00
☐ 562	Mike Mason	.08	.04	.01	☐ 611	Bob Lacey	.05	.02	.00
☐ 563	Pete O'Brien	.10	.05	.01	☐ 612	Bill Laskey	.05	.02	.00
☐ 564	Larry Parrish	.08	.04	.01	☐ 613	Gary Lavelle	.05	.02	.00
☐ 565	Mickey Rivers	.08	.04	.01	☐ 614	Johnnie LeMaster	.05	.02	.00
☐ 566	Billy Sample	.05	.02	.00	☐ 615	Jeff Leonard	.10	.05	.01
☐ 567	Dave Schmidt	.08	.04	.01	☐ 616	Randy Lerch	.05	.02	.00
☐ 568	Donnie Scott	.05	.02	.00	☐ 617	Greg Minton	.05	.02	.00
☐ 569	Dave Stewart	.35	.17	.03	☐ 618	Steve Nicosia	.05	.02	.00

		MINT	EXC	G-VG
☐ 619	Gene Richards	.05	.02	.00
☐ 620	Jeff Robinson ...... (Giants pitcher)	.35	.17	.03
☐ 621	Scot Thompson	.05	.02	.00
☐ 622	Manny Trillo	.05	.02	.00
☐ 623	Brad Wellman	.05	.02	.00
☐ 624	Frank Williams	.15	.07	.01
☐ 625	Joel Youngblood ...	.05	.02	.00
☐ 626	Cal Ripken IA	.20	.10	.02
☐ 627	Mike Schmidt IA ...	.35	.17	.03
☐ 628	Giving The Signs ... Sparky Anderson	.05	.02	.00
☐ 629	AL Pitcher's Nightmare .... Dave Winfield Rickey Henderson	.25	.12	.02
☐ 630	NL Pitcher's Nightmare .... Mike Schmidt Ryne Sandberg	.30	.15	.03
☐ 631	NL All-Stars .... Darryl Strawberry Gary Carter Steve Garvey Ozzie Smith	.25	.12	.02
☐ 632	A-S Winning Battery . Gary Carter Charlie Lea	.10	.05	.01
☐ 633	NL Pennant Clinchers Steve Garvey Goose Gossage	.12	.06	.01
☐ 634	NL Rookie Phenoms Dwight Gooden Juan Samuel	.90	.45	.09
☐ 635	Toronto's Big Guns .. Willie Upshaw	.05	.02	.00
☐ 636	Toronto's Big Guns .. Lloyd Moseby	.08	.04	.01
☐ 637	HOLLAND: Al Holland	.05	.02	.00
☐ 638	TUNNELL: Lee Tunnell	.05	.02	.00
☐ 639	500th Homer .... Reggie Jackson	.30	.15	.03
☐ 640	4000th Hit .... Pete Rose	.45	.22	.04
☐ 641	Father and Son ..... Cal Ripken Jr. and Sr.	.12	.06	.01

		MINT	EXC	G-VG
☐ 642	Cubs: Division Champs	.05	.02	.00
☐ 643	Two Perfect Games and One No-Hitter: Mike Witt David Palmer Jack Morris	.08	.04	.01
☐ 644	Willie Lozado and ... Vic Mata	.10	.05	.01
☐ 645	Kelly Gruber and ... Randy O'Neal	.90	.45	.09
☐ 646	Jose Roman and ... Joel Skinner	.10	.05	.01
☐ 647	Steve Kiefer and .... Danny Tartabull	4.00	2.00	.40
☐ 648	Rob Deer and ...... Alejandro Sanchez	1.25	.60	.12
☐ 649	Billy Hatcher and ... Shawon Dunston	2.25	1.10	.22
☐ 650	Ron Robinson and ... Mike Bielecki	.75	.35	.07
☐ 651	Zane Smith and .... Paul Zuvella	.35	.17	.03
☐ 652	Joe Hesketh and ... Glenn Davis	9.00	4.50	.90
☐ 653	John Russell and ... Steve Jeltz	.12	.06	.01
☐ 654	CL: Tigers/Padres ... and Cubs/Mets	.07	.01	.00
☐ 655	CL: Blue Jays/Yankees ..... and Red Sox/Orioles	.07	.01	.00
☐ 656	CL: Royals/Cardinals and Phillies/Twins	.07	.01	.00
☐ 657	CL: Angels/Braves ... and Astros/Dodgers	.07	.01	.00
☐ 658	CL: Expos/A's ..... and Indians/Pirates	.07	.01	.00
☐ 659	CL: Mariners/Wh.Sox and Reds/Rangers	.07	.01	.00
☐ 660	CL: Brewers/Giants .. and Special Cards	.10	.01	.00

1985 Fleer Update

This 132-card set was issued late in the collecting year and features new players and players on new teams compared to the 1985 Fleer regular issue cards. Cards measure 2 ½" by 3 ½" and were distributed together as a complete set in a special box. The cards are numbered with a U prefix and are ordered alphabetically by the player's name. This set features the Extended Rookie Cards of Vince Coleman, Ozzie Guillen, Teddy Higuera, and Mickey Tettleton.

	MINT	EXC	G-VG
COMPLETE SET (132)	16.00	8.00	1.60
COMMON PLAYER (1-132)	.06	.03	.00
□ U1 Don Aase	.10	.02	.01
□ U2 Bill Almon	.06	.03	.00
□ U3 Dusty Baker	.10	.05	.01
□ U4 Dale Berra	.06	.03	.00
□ U5 Karl Best	.10	.05	.01
□ U6 Tim Birtsas	.12	.06	.01
□ U7 Vida Blue	.10	.05	.01
□ U8 Rich Bordi	.06	.03	.00
□ U9 Daryl Boston	.10	.05	.01
□ U10 Hubie Brooks	.25	.12	.02
□ U11 Chris Brown	.20	.10	.02
□ U12 Tom Browning	1.25	.60	.12
□ U13 Al Bumbry	.06	.03	.00
□ U14 Tim Burke	.50	.25	.05
□ U15 Ray Burris	.06	.03	.00
□ U16 Jeff Burroughs	.06	.03	.00

	MINT	EXC	G-VG
□ U17 Ivan Calderon	.75	.35	.07
□ U18 Jeff Calhoun	.10	.05	.01
□ U19 Bill Campbell	.06	.03	.00
□ U20 Don Carman	.25	.12	.02
□ U21 Gary Carter	.75	.35	.07
□ U22 Bobby Castillo	.06	.03	.00
□ U23 Bill Caudill	.06	.03	.00
□ U24 Rick Cerone	.10	.05	.01
□ U25 Jack Clark	.35	.17	.03
□ U26 Pat Clements	.10	.05	.01
□ U27 Stewart Cliburn	.10	.05	.01
□ U28 Vince Coleman	4.50	2.25	.45
□ U29 Dave Collins	.06	.03	.00
□ U30 Fritz Connally	.10	.05	.01
□ U31 Henry Cotto	.06	.03	.00
□ U32 Danny Darwin	.06	.03	.00
□ U33 Darren Daulton	.15	.07	.01
□ U34 Jerry Davis	.10	.05	.01
□ U35 Brian Dayett	.10	.05	.01
□ U36 Ken Dixon	.12	.06	.01
□ U37 Tommy Dunbar	.06	.03	.00
□ U38 Mariano Duncan	.25	.12	.02
□ U39 Bob Fallon	.10	.05	.01
□ U40 Brian Fisher	.25	.12	.02
□ U41 Mike Fitzgerald	.06	.03	.00
□ U42 Ray Fontenot	.06	.03	.00
□ U43 Greg Gagne	.30	.15	.03
□ U44 Oscar Gamble	.06	.03	.00
□ U45 Jim Gott	.10	.05	.01
□ U46 David Green	.06	.03	.00
□ U47 Alfredo Griffin	.10	.05	.01
□ U48 Ozzie Guillen	1.25	.60	.12
□ U49 Toby Harrah	.10	.05	.01
□ U50 Ron Hassey	.06	.03	.00
□ U51 Rickey Henderson	2.00	1.00	.20
□ U52 Steve Henderson	.06	.03	.00
□ U53 George Hendrick	.10	.05	.01
□ U54 Teddy Higuera	2.00	1.00	.20
□ U55 Al Holland	.06	.03	.00
□ U56 Burt Hooton	.06	.03	.00
□ U57 Jay Howell	.15	.07	.01
□ U58 LaMarr Hoyt	.10	.05	.01
□ U59 Tim Hulett	.10	.05	.01
□ U60 Bob James	.10	.05	.01
□ U61 Cliff Johnson	.06	.03	.00
□ U62 Howard Johnson	2.25	1.10	.22
□ U63 Ruppert Jones	.06	.03	.00
□ U64 Steve Kemp	.10	.05	.01
□ U65 Bruce Kison	.06	.03	.00

		MINT	EXC	G-VG
☐ U66	Mike LaCoss	.06	.03	.00
☐ U67	Lee Lacy	.06	.03	.00
☐ U68	Dave LaPoint	.10	.05	.01
☐ U69	Gary Lavelle	.06	.03	.00
☐ U70	Vance Law	.10	.05	.01
☐ U71	Manny Lee	.12	.06	.01
☐ U72	Sixto Lezcano	.06	.03	.00
☐ U73	Tim Lollar	.06	.03	.00
☐ U74	Urbano Lugo	.10	.05	.01
☐ U75	Fred Lynn	.25	.12	.02
☐ U76	Steve Lyons	.10	.05	.01
☐ U77	Mickey Mahler	.06	.03	.00
☐ U78	Ron Mathis	.10	.05	.01
☐ U79	Len Matuszek	.06	.03	.00
☐ U80	Oddibe McDowell UER (part of bio actually Roger's)	.65	.30	.06
☐ U81	Roger McDowell UER (part of bio actually Oddibe's)	.85	.40	.08
☐ U82	Donnie Moore	.06	.03	.00
☐ U83	Ron Musselman	.10	.05	.01
☐ U84	Al Oliver	.15	.07	.01
☐ U85	Joe Orsulak	.20	.10	.02
☐ U86	Dan Pasqua	.40	.20	.04
☐ U87	Chris Pittaro	.10	.05	.01
☐ U88	Rick Rouschel	.25	.12	.02
☐ U89	Earnie Riles	.25	.12	.02
☐ U90	Jerry Royster	.06	.03	.00
☐ U91	Dave Rozema	.06	.03	.00
☐ U92	Dave Rucker	.06	.03	.00
☐ U93	Vern Ruhle	.06	.03	.00
☐ U94	Mark Salas	.12	.06	.01
☐ U95	Luis Salazar	.10	.05	.01
☐ U96	Joe Sambito	.06	.03	.00
☐ U97	Billy Sample	.06	.03	.00
☐ U98	Alejandro Sanchez	.10	.05	.01
☐ U99	Calvin Schiraldi	.20	.10	.02
☐ U100	Rick Schu	.15	.07	.01
☐ U101	Larry Sheets	.30	.15	.03
☐ U102	Ron Shephard	.10	.05	.01
☐ U103	Nelson Simmons	.10	.05	.01
☐ U104	Don Slaught	.06	.03	.00
☐ U105	Roy Smalley	.06	.03	.00
☐ U106	Lonnie Smith	.20	.10	.02
☐ U107	Nate Snell	.10	.05	.01
☐ U108	Lary Sorensen	.06	.03	.00
☐ U109	Chris Speier	.06	.03	.00

		MINT	EXC	G-VG
☐ U110	Mike Stenhouse	.10	.05	.01
☐ U111	Tim Stoddard	.06	.03	.00
☐ U112	John Stuper	.06	.03	.00
☐ U113	Jim Sundberg	.10	.05	.01
☐ U114	Bruce Sutter	.20	.10	.02
☐ U115	Don Sutton	.50	.25	.05
☐ U116	Bruce Tanner	.10	.05	.01
☐ U117	Kent Tekulve	.10	.05	.01
☐ U118	Walt Terrell	.15	.07	.01
☐ U119	Mickey Tettleton	1.00	.50	.10
☐ U120	Rich Thompson	.10	.05	.01
☐ U121	Louis Thornton	.10	.05	.01
☐ U122	Alex Trevino	.06	.03	.00
☐ U123	John Tudor	.20	.10	.02
☐ U124	Jose Uribe	.35	.17	.03
☐ U125	Dave Valle	.10	.05	.01
☐ U126	Dave Von Ohlen	.06	.03	.00
☐ U127	Curt Wardle	.10	.05	.01
☐ U128	U.L. Washington	.06	.03	.00
☐ U129	Ed Whitson	.10	.05	.01
☐ U130	Herm Winningham	.15	.07	.01
☐ U131	Rich Yett	.10	.05	.01
☐ U132	Checklist U1-U132	.06	.01	.00

1986 Fleer

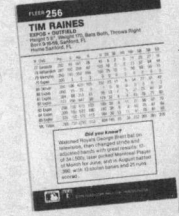

*The cards in this 660-card set measure 2 ½"
by 3 ½". The 1986 Fleer set features fronts
that contain the team logo along with the
player's name and position. The player cards
are alphabetized within team and the teams*

are ordered by their 1985 season finish and won-lost record, e.g., Kansas City (1-25), St. Louis (26-49), Toronto (50-73), New York Mets (74-97), New York Yankees (98-122), Los Angeles (123-147), California (148-171), Cincinnati (172-196), Chicago White Sox (197-220), Detroit (221-243), Montreal (244-267), Baltimore (268-291), Houston (292-314), San Diego (315-338), Boston (339-360), Chicago Cubs (361-385), Minnesota (386-409), Oakland (410-432), Philadelphia (433-457), Seattle (458-481), Milwaukee (482-506), Atlanta (507-532), San Francisco (533-555), Texas (556-578), Cleveland (579-601), and Pittsburgh (602-625). Specials (626-643), Rookie Pairs (644-653), and checklist cards (654-660) complete the set. The border enclosing the photo is dark blue. The backs feature the same name, number, and statistics format that Fleer has been using over the past few years. The Dennis and Tippy Martinez cards were apparently switched in the set numbering, as their adjacent numbers (279 and 280) were reversed on the Orioles checklist card.

		MINT	EXC	G-VG
COMPLETE SET (660)		100.00	50.00	10.00
COMMON PLAYER (1-660)		.05	.02	.00
☐ 1	Steve Balboni	.10	.02	.01
☐ 2	Joe Beckwith	.05	.02	.00
☐ 3	Buddy Biancalana	.05	.02	.00
☐ 4	Bud Black	.05	.02	.00
☐ 5	George Brett	.45	.22	.04
☐ 6	Onix Concepcion	.05	.02	.00
☐ 7	Steve Farr	.08	.04	.01
☐ 8	Mark Gubicza	.20	.10	.02
☐ 9	Dane Iorg	.05	.02	.00
☐ 10	Danny Jackson	.20	.10	.02
☐ 11	Lynn Jones	.05	.02	.00
☐ 12	Mike Jones	.05	.02	.00
☐ 13	Charlie Leibrandt	.05	.02	.00
☐ 14	Hal McRae	.08	.04	.01
☐ 15	Omar Moreno	.05	.02	.00
☐ 16	Darryl Motley	.05	.02	.00
☐ 17	Jorge Orta	.05	.02	.00
☐ 18	Dan Quisenberry	.12	.06	.01
☐ 19	Bret Saberhagen	1.25	.60	.12
☐ 20	Pat Sheridan	.05	.02	.00
☐ 21	Lonnie Smith	.10	.05	.01
☐ 22	Jim Sundberg	.05	.02	.00
☐ 23	John Wathan	.05	.02	.00
☐ 24	Frank White	.08	.04	.01
☐ 25	Willie Wilson	.10	.05	.01
☐ 26	Joaquin Andujar	.08	.04	.01
☐ 27	Steve Braun	.05	.02	.00
☐ 28	Bill Campbell	.05	.02	.00
☐ 29	Cesar Cedeno	.08	.04	.01
☐ 30	Jack Clark	.25	.12	.02
☐ 31	Vince Coleman	2.25	1.10	.22
☐ 32	Danny Cox	.10	.05	.01
☐ 33	Ken Dayley	.05	.02	.00
☐ 34	Ivan DeJesus	.05	.02	.00
☐ 35	Bob Forsch	.05	.02	.00
☐ 36	Brian Harper	.05	.02	.00
☐ 37	Tom Herr	.08	.04	.01
☐ 38	Ricky Horton	.05	.02	.00
☐ 39	Kurt Kepshire	.05	.02	.00
☐ 40	Jeff Lahti	.05	.02	.00
☐ 41	Tito Landrum	.05	.02	.00
☐ 42	Willie McGee	.15	.07	.01
☐ 43	Tom Nieto	.05	.02	.00
☐ 44	Terry Pendleton	.08	.04	.01
☐ 45	Darrell Porter	.05	.02	.00
☐ 46	Ozzie Smith	.25	.12	.02
☐ 47	John Tudor	.15	.07	.01
☐ 48	Andy Van Slyke	.25	.12	.02
☐ 49	Todd Worrell	.90	.45	.09
☐ 50	Jim Acker	.05	.02	.00
☐ 51	Doyle Alexander	.08	.04	.01
☐ 52	Jesse Barfield	.20	.10	.02
☐ 53	George Bell	.30	.15	.03
☐ 54	Jeff Burroughs	.05	.02	.00
☐ 55	Bill Caudill	.05	.02	.00
☐ 56	Jim Clancy	.05	.02	.00
☐ 57	Tony Fernandez	.25	.12	.02
☐ 58	Tom Filer	.05	.02	.00
☐ 59	Damaso Garcia	.05	.02	.00
☐ 60	Tom Henke	.25	.12	.02
☐ 61	Garth Iorg	.05	.02	.00
☐ 62	Cliff Johnson	.05	.02	.00
☐ 63	Jimmy Key	.12	.06	.01
☐ 64	Dennis Lamp	.05	.02	.00
☐ 65	Gary Lavelle	.05	.02	.00
☐ 66	Buck Martinez	.05	.02	.00
☐ 67	Lloyd Moseby	.10	.05	.01
☐ 68	Rance Mulliniks	.05	.02	.00
☐ 69	Al Oliver	.10	.05	.01
☐ 70	Dave Stieb	.12	.06	.01

		MINT	EXC	G-VG			MINT	EXC	G-VG
☐ 71	Louis Thornton	.10	.05	.01	☐ 120	Ed Whitson	.05	.02	.00
☐ 72	Willie Upshaw	.05	.02	.00	☐ 121	Dave Winfield	.30	.15	.03
☐ 73	Ernie Whitt	.05	.02	.00	☐ 122	Butch Wynegar	.05	.02	.00
☐ 74	Rick Aguilera	.35	.17	.03	☐ 123	Dave Anderson	.05	.02	.00
☐ 75	Wally Backman	.05	.02	.00	☐ 124	Bob Bailor	.05	.02	.00
☐ 76	Gary Carter	.30	.15	.03	☐ 125	Greg Brock	.05	.02	.00
☐ 77	Ron Darling	.25	.12	.02	☐ 126	Enos Cabell	.05	.02	.00
☐ 78	Len Dykstra	.75	.35	.07	☐ 127	Bobby Castillo	.05	.02	.00
☐ 79	Sid Fernandez	.15	.07	.01	☐ 128	Carlos Diaz	.05	.02	.00
☐ 80	George Foster	.12	.06	.01	☐ 129	Mariano Duncan	.20	.10	.02
☐ 81	Dwight Gooden	2.25	1.10	.22	☐ 130	Pedro Guerrero	.20	.10	.02
☐ 82	Tom Gorman	.05	.02	.00	☐ 131	Orel Hershiser	1.75	.85	.17
☐ 83	Danny Heep	.05	.02	.00	☐ 132	Rick Honeycutt	.05	.02	.00
☐ 84	Keith Hernandez	.25	.12	.02	☐ 133	Ken Howell	.05	.02	.00
☐ 85	Howard Johnson	.40	.20	.04	☐ 134	Ken Landreaux	.05	.02	.00
☐ 86	Ray Knight	.08	.04	.01	☐ 135	Bill Madlock	.10	.05	.01
☐ 87	Terry Leach	.15	.07	.01	☐ 136	Candy Maldonado	.10	.05	.01
☐ 88	Ed Lynch	.05	.02	.00	☐ 137	Mike Marshall	.12	.06	.01
☐ 89	Roger McDowell	.45	.22	.04	☐ 138	Len Matuszek	.05	.02	.00
☐ 90	Jesse Orosco	.05	.02	.00	☐ 139	Tom Niedenfuer	.05	.02	.00
☐ 91	Tom Paciorek	.05	.02	.00	☐ 140	Alejandro Pena	.08	.04	.01
☐ 92	Ronn Reynolds	.05	.02	.00	☐ 141	Jerry Reuss	.08	.04	.01
☐ 93	Rafael Santana	.05	.02	.00	☐ 142	Bill Russell	.08	.04	.01
☐ 94	Doug Sisk	.05	.02	.00	☐ 143	Steve Sax	.18	.09	.01
☐ 95	Rusty Staub	.10	.05	.01	☐ 144	Mike Scioscia	.08	.04	.01
☐ 96	Darryl Strawberry	2.00	1.00	.20	☐ 145	Fernando Valenzuela	.25	.12	.02
☐ 97	Mookie Wilson	.10	.05	.01	☐ 146	Bob Welch	.08	.04	.01
☐ 98	Neil Allen	.05	.02	.00	☐ 147	Terry Whitfield	.05	.02	.00
☐ 99	Don Baylor	.10	.05	.01	☐ 148	Juan Beniquez	.05	.02	.00
☐ 100	Dale Berra	.05	.02	.00	☐ 149	Bob Boone	.12	.06	.01
☐ 101	Rich Bordi	.05	.02	.00	☐ 150	John Candelaria	.08	.04	.01
☐ 102	Marty Bystrom	.05	.02	.00	☐ 151	Rod Carew	.30	.15	.03
☐ 103	Joe Cowley	.05	.02	.00	☐ 152	Stewart Cliburn	.08	.04	.01
☐ 104	Brian Fisher	.20	.10	.02	☐ 153	Doug DeCinces	.08	.04	.01
☐ 105	Ken Griffey	.10	.05	.01	☐ 154	Brian Downing	.08	.04	.01
☐ 106	Ron Guidry	.15	.07	.01	☐ 155	Ken Forsch	.05	.02	.00
☐ 107	Ron Hassey	.05	.02	.00	☐ 156	Craig Gerber	.05	.02	.00
☐ 108	Rickey Henderson	.60	.30	.06	☐ 157	Bobby Grich	.08	.04	.01
☐ 109	Don Mattingly	4.00	2.00	.40	☐ 158	George Hendrick	.08	.04	.01
☐ 110	Bobby Meacham	.05	.02	.00	☐ 159	Al Holland	.05	.02	.00
☐ 111	John Montefusco	.05	.02	.00	☐ 160	Reggie Jackson	.40	.20	.04
☐ 112	Phil Niekro	.18	.09	.01	☐ 161	Ruppert Jones	.05	.02	.00
☐ 113	Mike Pagliarulo	.10	.05	.01	☐ 162	Urbano Lugo	.05	.02	.00
☐ 114	Dan Pasqua	.12	.06	.01	☐ 163	Kirk McCaskill	.60	.30	.06
☐ 115	Willie Randolph	.10	.05	.01	☐ 164	Donnie Moore	.05	.02	.00
☐ 116	Dave Righetti	.12	.06	.01	☐ 165	Gary Pettis	.05	.02	.00
☐ 117	Andre Robertson	.05	.02	.00	☐ 166	Ron Romanick	.05	.02	.00
☐ 118	Billy Sample	.05	.02	.00	☐ 167	Dick Schofield	.05	.02	.00
☐ 119	Bob Shirley	.05	.02	.00	☐ 168	Daryl Sconiers	.05	.02	.00

		MINT	EXC	G-VG				MINT	EXC	G-VG
☐ 169	Jim Slaton	.05	.02	.00		☐ 218	Bruce Tanner	.08	.04	.01
☐ 170	Don Sutton	.18	.09	.01		☐ 219	Greg Walker	.08	.04	.01
☐ 171	Mike Witt	.10	.05	.01		☐ 220	Dave Wehrmeister	.05	.02	.00
☐ 172	Buddy Bell	.10	.05	.01		☐ 221	Juan Berenguer	.05	.02	.00
☐ 173	Tom Browning	.25	.12	.02		☐ 222	Dave Bergman	.05	.02	.00
☐ 174	Dave Concepcion	.10	.05	.01		☐ 223	Tom Brookens	.05	.02	.00
☐ 175	Eric Davis	3.00	1.50	.30		☐ 224	Darrell Evans	.10	.05	.01
☐ 176	Bo Diaz	.05	.02	.00		☐ 225	Barbaro Garbey	.05	.02	.00
☐ 177	Nick Esasky	.12	.06	.01		☐ 226	Kirk Gibson	.25	.12	.02
☐ 178	John Franco	.15	.07	.01		☐ 227	John Grubb	.05	.02	.00
☐ 179	Tom Hume	.05	.02	.00		☐ 228	Willie Hernandez	.10	.05	.01
☐ 180	Wayne Krenchicki	.05	.02	.00		☐ 229	Larry Herndon	.05	.02	.00
☐ 181	Andy McGaffigan	.05	.02	.00		☐ 230	Chet Lemon	.08	.04	.01
☐ 182	Eddie Milner	.05	.02	.00		☐ 231	Aurelio Lopez	.05	.02	.00
☐ 183	Ron Oester	.05	.02	.00		☐ 232	Jack Morris	.15	.07	.01
☐ 184	Dave Parker	.15	.07	.01		☐ 233	Randy O'Neal	.05	.02	.00
☐ 185	Frank Pastore	.05	.02	.00		☐ 234	Lance Parrish	.15	.07	.01
☐ 186	Tony Perez	.15	.07	.01		☐ 235	Dan Petry	.05	.02	.00
☐ 187	Ted Power	.05	.02	.00		☐ 236	Alejandro Sanchez	.05	.02	.00
☐ 188	Joe Price	.05	.02	.00		☐ 237	Bill Scherrer	.05	.02	.00
☐ 189	Gary Redus	.05	.02	.00		☐ 238	Nelson Simmons	.08	.04	.01
☐ 190	Ron Robinson	.05	.02	.00		☐ 239	Frank Tanana	.08	.04	.01
☐ 191	Pete Rose	.75	.35	.07		☐ 240	Walt Terrell	.05	.02	.00
☐ 192	Mario Soto	.05	.02	.00		☐ 241	Alan Trammell	.25	.12	.02
☐ 193	John Stuper	.05	.02	.00		☐ 242	Lou Whitaker	.15	.07	.01
☐ 194	Jay Tibbs	.05	.02	.00		☐ 243	Milt Wilcox	.05	.02	.00
☐ 195	Dave Van Gorder	.05	.02	.00		☐ 244	Hubie Brooks	.10	.05	.01
☐ 196	Max Venable	.05	.02	.00		☐ 245	Tim Burke	.35	.17	.03
☐ 197	Juan Agosto	.05	.02	.00		☐ 246	Andre Dawson	.30	.15	.03
☐ 198	Harold Baines	.12	.06	.01		☐ 247	Mike Fitzgerald	.05	.02	.00
☐ 199	Floyd Bannister	.05	.02	.00		☐ 248	Terry Francona	.05	.02	.00
☐ 200	Britt Burns	.05	.02	.00		☐ 249	Bill Gullickson	.05	.02	.00
☐ 201	Julio Cruz	.05	.02	.00		☐ 250	Joe Hesketh	.05	.02	.00
☐ 202	Joel Davis	.10	.05	.01		☐ 251	Bill Laskey	.05	.02	.00
☐ 203	Richard Dotson	.08	.04	.01		☐ 252	Vance Law	.05	.02	.00
☐ 204	Carlton Fisk	.25	.12	.02		☐ 253	Charlie Lea	.05	.02	.00
☐ 205	Scott Fletcher	.08	.04	.01		☐ 254	Gary Lucas	.05	.02	.00
☐ 206	Ozzie Guillen	.45	.22	.04		☐ 255	David Palmer	.05	.02	.00
☐ 207	Jerry Hairston	.05	.02	.00		☐ 256	Tim Raines	.30	.15	.03
☐ 208	Tim Hulett	.05	.02	.00		☐ 257	Jeff Reardon	.10	.05	.01
☐ 209	Bob James	.05	.02	.00		☐ 258	Bert Roberge	.05	.02	.00
☐ 210	Ron Kittle	.10	.05	.01		☐ 259	Dan Schatzeder	.05	.02	.00
☐ 211	Rudy Law	.05	.02	.00		☐ 260	Bryn Smith	.10	.05	.01
☐ 212	Bryan Little	.05	.02	.00		☐ 261	Randy St.Claire	.05	.02	.00
☐ 213	Gene Nelson	.05	.02	.00		☐ 262	Scot Thompson	.05	.02	.00
☐ 214	Reid Nichols	.05	.02	.00		☐ 263	Tim Wallach	.10	.05	.01
☐ 215	Luis Salazar	.05	.02	.00		☐ 264	U.L. Washington	.05	.02	.00
☐ 216	Tom Seaver	.35	.17	.03		☐ 265	Mitch Webster	.30	.15	.03
☐ 217	Dan Spillner	.05	.02	.00		☐ 266	Herm Winningham	.10	.05	.01

		MINT	EXC	G-VG				MINT	EXC	G-VG
☐ 267	Floyd Youmans	.30	.15	.03	☐ 316	Al Bumbry		.05	.02	.00
☐ 268	Don Aase	.05	.02	.00	☐ 317	Jerry Davis		.05	.02	.00
☐ 269	Mike Boddicker	.08	.04	.01	☐ 318	Luis DeLeon		.05	.02	.00
☐ 270	Rich Dauer	.05	.02	.00	☐ 319	Dave Dravecky		.12	.06	.01
☐ 271	Storm Davis	.10	.05	.01	☐ 320	Tim Flannery		.05	.02	.00
☐ 272	Rick Dempsey	.05	.02	.00	☐ 321	Steve Garvey		.35	.17	.03
☐ 273	Ken Dixon	.05	.02	.00	☐ 322	Goose Gossage		.12	.06	.01
☐ 274	Jim Dwyer	.05	.02	.00	☐ 323	Tony Gwynn		.75	.35	.07
☐ 275	Mike Flanagan	.08	.04	.01	☐ 324	Andy Hawkins		.10	.05	.01
☐ 276	Wayne Gross	.05	.02	.00	☐ 325	LaMarr Hoyt		.08	.04	.01
☐ 277	Lee Lacy	.05	.02	.00	☐ 326	Roy Lee Jackson		.05	.02	.00
☐ 278	Fred Lynn	.15	.07	.01	☐ 327	Terry Kennedy		.05	.02	.00
☐ 279	Tippy Martinez	.05	.02	.00	☐ 328	Craig Lefferts		.08	.04	.01
☐ 280	Dennis Martinez	.08	.04	.01	☐ 329	Carmelo Martinez		.05	.02	.00
☐ 281	Scott McGregor	.08	.04	.01	☐ 330	Lance McCullers		.35	.17	.03
☐ 282	Eddie Murray	.30	.15	.03	☐ 331	Kevin McReynolds		.35	.17	.03
☐ 283	Floyd Rayford	.05	.02	.00	☐ 332	Graig Nettles		.10	.05	.01
☐ 284	Cal Ripken	.40	.20	.04	☐ 333	Jerry Royster		.05	.02	.00
☐ 285	Gary Roenicke	.05	.02	.00	☐ 334	Eric Show		.08	.04	.01
☐ 286	Larry Sheets	.15	.07	.01	☐ 335	Tim Stoddard		.05	.02	.00
☐ 287	John Shelby	.05	.02	.00	☐ 336	Garry Templeton		.08	.04	.01
☐ 288	Nate Snell	.08	.04	.01	☐ 337	Mark Thurmond		.05	.02	.00
☐ 289	Sammy Stewart	.05	.02	.00	☐ 338	Ed Wojna		.08	.04	.01
☐ 290	Alan Wiggins	.05	.02	.00	☐ 339	Tony Armas		.08	.04	.01
☐ 291	Mike Young	.08	.04	.01	☐ 340	Marty Barrett		.10	.05	.01
☐ 292	Alan Ashby	.05	.02	.00	☐ 341	Wade Boggs		2.50	1.25	.25
☐ 293	Mark Bailey	.05	.02	.00	☐ 342	Dennis Boyd		.08	.04	.01
☐ 294	Kevin Bass	.08	.04	.01	☐ 343	Bill Buckner		.10	.05	.01
☐ 295	Jeff Calhoun	.08	.04	.01	☐ 344	Mark Clear		.05	.02	.00
☐ 296	Jose Cruz	.08	.04	.01	☐ 345	Roger Clemens		3.00	1.50	.30
☐ 297	Glenn Davis	1.25	.60	.12	☐ 346	Steve Crawford		.05	.02	.00
☐ 298	Bill Dawley	.05	.02	.00	☐ 347	Mike Easler		.05	.02	.00
☐ 299	Frank DiPino	.05	.02	.00	☐ 348	Dwight Evans		.15	.07	.01
☐ 300	Bill Doran	.10	.05	.01	☐ 349	Rich Gedman		.08	.04	.01
☐ 301	Phil Garner	.05	.02	.00	☐ 350	Jackie Gutierrez		.05	.02	.00
☐ 302	Jeff Heathcock	.05	.02	.00	☐ 351	Glenn Hoffman		.05	.02	.00
☐ 303	Charlie Kerfeld	.08	.04	.01	☐ 352	Bruce Hurst		.15	.07	.01
☐ 304	Bob Knepper	.08	.04	.01	☐ 353	Bruce Kison		.05	.02	.00
☐ 305	Ron Mathis	.08	.04	.01	☐ 354	Tim Lollar		.05	.02	.00
☐ 306	Jerry Mumphrey	.05	.02	.00	☐ 355	Steve Lyons		.05	.02	.00
☐ 307	Jim Pankovits	.05	.02	.00	☐ 356	Al Nipper		.05	.02	.00
☐ 308	Terry Puhl	.05	.02	.00	☐ 357	Bob Ojeda		.08	.04	.01
☐ 309	Craig Reynolds	.05	.02	.00	☐ 358	Jim Rice		.20	.10	.02
☐ 310	Nolan Ryan	.80	.40	.08	☐ 359	Bob Stanley		.05	.02	.00
☐ 311	Mike Scott	.35	.17	.03	☐ 360	Mike Trujillo		.05	.02	.00
☐ 312	Dave Smith	.08	.04	.01	☐ 361	Thad Bosley		.05	.02	.00
☐ 313	Dickie Thon	.05	.02	.00	☐ 362	Warren Brusstar		.05	.02	.00
☐ 314	Denny Walling	.05	.02	.00	☐ 363	Ron Cey		.08	.04	.01
☐ 315	Kurt Bevacqua	.05	.02	.00	☐ 364	Jody Davis		.05	.02	.00

		MINT	EXC	G-VG				MINT	EXC	G-VG
☐ 365	Bob Dernier	.05	.02	.00	☐ 414	Chris Codiroli	.05	.02	.00
☐ 366	Shawon Dunston	.25	.12	.02	☐ 415	Dave Collins	.05	.02	.00
☐ 367	Leon Durham	.08	.04	.01	☐ 416	Mike Davis	.05	.02	.00
☐ 368	Dennis Eckersley	.15	.07	.01	☐ 417	Alfredo Griffin	.08	.04	.01
☐ 369	Ray Fontenot	.05	.02	.00	☐ 418	Mike Heath	.05	.02	.00
☐ 370	George Frazier	.05	.02	.00	☐ 419	Steve Henderson	.05	.02	.00
☐ 371	Billy Hatcher	.10	.05	.01	☐ 420	Donnie Hill	.05	.02	.00
☐ 372	Dave Lopes	.08	.04	.01	☐ 421	Jay Howell	.08	.04	.01
☐ 373	Gary Matthews	.08	.04	.01	☐ 422	Tommy John	.15	.07	.01
☐ 374	Ron Meredith	.05	.02	.00	☐ 423	Dave Kingman	.12	.06	.01
☐ 375	Keith Moreland	.05	.02	.00	☐ 424	Bill Krueger	.05	.02	.00
☐ 376	Reggie Patterson	.05	.02	.00	☐ 425	Rick Langford	.05	.02	.00
☐ 377	Dick Ruthven	.05	.02	.00	☐ 426	Carney Lansford	.12	.06	.01
☐ 378	Ryne Sandberg	.30	.15	.03	☐ 427	Steve McCatty	.05	.02	.00
☐ 379	Scott Sanderson	.05	.02	.00	☐ 428	Dwayne Murphy	.05	.02	.00
☐ 380	Lee Smith	.08	.04	.01	☐ 429	Steve Ontiveros	.10	.05	.01
☐ 381	Lary Sorensen	.05	.02	.00	☐ 430	Tony Phillips	.05	.02	.00
☐ 382	Chris Speier	.05	.02	.00	☐ 431	Jose Rijo	.10	.05	.01
☐ 383	Rick Sutcliffe	.12	.06	.01	☐ 432	Mickey Tettleton	.60	.30	.06
☐ 384	Steve Trout	.05	.02	.00	☐ 433	Luis Aguayo	.05	.02	.00
☐ 385	Gary Woods	.05	.02	.00	☐ 434	Larry Andersen	.05	.02	.00
☐ 386	Bert Blyleven	.15	.07	.01	☐ 435	Steve Carlton	.25	.12	.02
☐ 387	Tom Brunansky	.15	.07	.01	☐ 436	Don Carman	.20	.10	.02
☐ 388	Randy Bush	.05	.02	.00	☐ 437	Tim Corcoran	.05	.02	.00
☐ 389	John Butcher	.05	.02	.00	☐ 438	Darren Daulton	.12	.06	.01
☐ 390	Ron Davis	.05	.02	.00	☐ 439	John Denny	.08	.04	.01
☐ 391	Dave Engle	.05	.02	.00	☐ 440	Tom Foley	.05	.02	.00
☐ 392	Frank Eufemia	.05	.02	.00	☐ 441	Greg Gross	.05	.02	.00
☐ 393	Pete Filson	.05	.02	.00	☐ 442	Kevin Gross	.05	.02	.00
☐ 394	Gary Gaetti	.20	.10	.02	☐ 443	Von Hayes	.10	.05	.01
☐ 395	Greg Gagne	.10	.05	.01	☐ 444	Charles Hudson	.05	.02	.00
☐ 396	Mickey Hatcher	.05	.02	.00	☐ 445	Garry Maddox	.05	.02	.00
☐ 397	Kent Hrbek	.25	.12	.02	☐ 446	Shane Rawley	.05	.02	.00
☐ 398	Tim Laudner	.05	.02	.00	☐ 447	Dave Rucker	.05	.02	.00
☐ 399	Rick Lysander	.05	.02	.00	☐ 448	John Russell	.05	.02	.00
☐ 400	Dave Meier	.05	.02	.00	☐ 449	Juan Samuel	.15	.07	.01
☐ 401	Kirby Puckett	3.50	1.75	.35	☐ 450	Mike Schmidt	.75	.35	.07
☐ 402	Mark Salas	.05	.02	.00	☐ 451	Rick Schu	.05	.02	.00
☐ 403	Ken Schrom	.05	.02	.00	☐ 452	Dave Shipanoff	.08	.04	.01
☐ 404	Roy Smalley	.05	.02	.00	☐ 453	Dave Stewart	.25	.12	.02
☐ 405	Mike Smithson	.05	.02	.00	☐ 454	Jeff Stone	.05	.02	.00
☐ 406	Mike Stenhouse	.05	.02	.00	☐ 455	Kent Tekulve	.05	.02	.00
☐ 407	Tim Teufel	.05	.02	.00	☐ 456	Ozzie Virgil	.05	.02	.00
☐ 408	Frank Viola	.30	.15	.03	☐ 457	Glenn Wilson	.08	.04	.01
☐ 409	Ron Washington	.05	.02	.00	☐ 458	Jim Beattie	.05	.02	.00
☐ 410	Keith Atherton	.05	.02	.00	☐ 459	Karl Best	.08	.04	.01
☐ 411	Dusty Baker	.08	.04	.01	☐ 460	Barry Bonnell	.05	.02	.00
☐ 412	Tim Birtsas	.10	.05	.01	☐ 461	Phil Bradley	.12	.06	.01
☐ 413	Bruce Bochte	.05	.02	.00	☐ 462	Ivan Calderon	.65	.30	.06

		MINT	EXC	G-VG			MINT	EXC	G-VG
☐ 463	Al Cowens	.05	.02	.00	☐ 512	Chris Chambliss	.08	.04	.01
☐ 464	Alvin Davis	.25	.12	.02	☐ 513	Jeff Dedmon	.05	.02	.00
☐ 465	Dave Henderson	.08	.04	.01	☐ 514	Terry Forster	.08	.04	.01
☐ 466	Bob Kearney	.05	.02	.00	☐ 515	Gene Garber	.05	.02	.00
☐ 467	Mark Langston	.60	.30	.06	☐ 516	Terry Harper	.05	.02	.00
☐ 468	Bob Long	.05	.02	.00	☐ 517	Bob Horner	.12	.06	.01
☐ 469	Mike Moore	.10	.05	.01	☐ 518	Glenn Hubbard	.05	.02	.00
☐ 470	Edwin Nunez	.05	.02	.00	☐ 519	Joe Johnson	.10	.05	.01
☐ 471	Spike Owen	.05	.02	.00	☐ 520	Brad Komminsk	.05	.02	.00
☐ 472	Jack Perconte	.05	.02	.00	☐ 521	Rick Mahler	.05	.02	.00
☐ 473	Jim Presley	.10	.05	.01	☐ 522	Dale Murphy	.50	.25	.05
☐ 474	Donnie Scott	.05	.02	.00	☐ 523	Ken Oberkfell	.05	.02	.00
☐ 475	Bill Swift	.10	.05	.01	☐ 524	Pascual Perez	.12	.06	.01
☐ 476	Danny Tartabull	.65	.30	.06	☐ 525	Gerald Perry	.10	.05	.01
☐ 477	Gorman Thomas	.10	.05	.01	☐ 526	Rafael Ramirez	.05	.02	.00
☐ 478	Roy Thomas	.05	.02	.00	☐ 527	Steve Shields	.08	.04	.01
☐ 479	Ed VandeBerg	.05	.02	.00	☐ 528	Zane Smith	.10	.05	.01
☐ 480	Frank Wills	.08	.04	.01	☐ 529	Bruce Sutter	.12	.06	.01
☐ 481	Matt Young	.05	.02	.00	☐ 530	Milt Thompson	.30	.15	.03
☐ 482	Ray Burris	.05	.02	.00	☐ 531	Claudell Washington	.08	.04	.01
☐ 483	Jaime Cocanower	.05	.02	.00	☐ 532	Paul Zuvella	.05	.02	.00
☐ 484	Cecil Cooper	.10	.05	.01	☐ 533	Vida Blue	.08	.04	.01
☐ 485	Danny Darwin	.05	.02	.00	☐ 534	Bob Brenly	.05	.02	.00
☐ 486	Rollie Fingers	.15	.07	.01	☐ 535	Chris Brown	.18	.09	.01
☐ 487	Jim Gantner	.05	.02	.00	☐ 536	Chili Davis	.10	.05	.01
☐ 488	Bob L. Gibson	.05	.02	.00	☐ 537	Mark Davis	.15	.07	.01
☐ 489	Moose Haas	.05	.02	.00	☐ 538	Rob Deer	.35	.17	.03
☐ 490	Teddy Higuera	1.25	.60	.12	☐ 539	Dan Driessen	.05	.02	.00
☐ 491	Paul Householder	.05	.02	.00	☐ 540	Scott Garrelts	.30	.15	.03
☐ 492	Pete Ladd	.05	.02	.00	☐ 541	Dan Gladden	.08	.04	.01
☐ 493	Rick Manning	.05	.02	.00	☐ 542	Jim Gott	.08	.04	.01
☐ 494	Bob McClure	.05	.02	.00	☐ 543	David Green	.05	.02	.00
☐ 495	Paul Molitor	.18	.09	.01	☐ 544	Atlee Hammaker	.05	.02	.00
☐ 496	Charlie Moore	.05	.02	.00	☐ 545	Mike Jeffcoat	.05	.02	.00
☐ 497	Ben Oglivie	.08	.04	.01	☐ 546	Mike Krukow	.05	.02	.00
☐ 498	Randy Ready	.05	.02	.00	☐ 547	Dave LaPoint	.08	.04	.01
☐ 499	Earnie Riles	.20	.10	.02	☐ 548	Jeff Leonard	.08	.04	.01
☐ 500	Ed Romero	.05	.02	.00	☐ 549	Greg Minton	.05	.02	.00
☐ 501	Bill Schroeder	.05	.02	.00	☐ 550	Alex Trevino	.05	.02	.00
☐ 502	Ray Searage	.05	.02	.00	☐ 551	Manny Trillo	.05	.02	.00
☐ 503	Ted Simmons	.10	.05	.01	☐ 552	Jose Uribe	.30	.15	.03
☐ 504	Pete Vuckovich	.08	.04	.01	☐ 553	Brad Wellman	.05	.02	.00
☐ 505	Rick Waits	.05	.02	.00	☐ 554	Frank Williams	.05	.02	.00
☐ 506	Robin Yount	.40	.20	.04	☐ 555	Joel Youngblood	.05	.02	.00
☐ 507	Len Barker	.05	.02	.00	☐ 556	Alan Bannister	.05	.02	.00
☐ 508	Steve Bedrosian	.12	.06	.01	☐ 557	Glenn Brummer	.05	.02	.00
☐ 509	Bruce Benedict	.05	.02	.00	☐ 558	Steve Buechele	.25	.12	.02
☐ 510	Rick Camp	.05	.02	.00	☐ 559	Jose Guzman	.25	.12	.02
☐ 511	Rick Cerone	.05	.02	.00	☐ 560	Toby Harrah	.05	.02	.00

		MINT	EXC	G-VG
□ 561	Greg Harris	.05	.02	.00
□ 562	Dwayne Henry	.08	.04	.01
□ 563	Burt Hooton	.05	.02	.00
□ 564	Charlie Hough	.08	.04	.01
□ 565	Mike Mason	.05	.02	.00
□ 566	Oddibe McDowell	.20	.10	.02
□ 567	Dickie Noles	.05	.02	.00
□ 568	Pete O'Brien	.10	.05	.01
□ 569	Larry Parrish	.05	.02	.00
□ 570	Dave Rozema	.05	.02	.00
□ 571	Dave Schmidt	.08	.04	.01
□ 572	Don Slaught	.05	.02	.00
□ 573	Wayne Tolleson	.05	.02	.00
□ 574	Duane Walker	.05	.02	.00
□ 575	Gary Ward	.08	.04	.01
□ 576	Chris Welsh	.05	.02	.00
□ 577	Curtis Wilkerson	.05	.02	.00
□ 578	George Wright	.05	.02	.00
□ 579	Chris Bando	.05	.02	.00
□ 580	Tony Bernazard	.05	.02	.00
□ 581	Brett Butler	.08	.04	.01
□ 582	Ernie Camacho	.05	.02	.00
□ 583	Joe Carter	.60	.30	.06
□ 584	Carmen Castillo	.05	.02	.00
□ 585	Jamie Easterly	.05	.02	.00
□ 586	Julio Franco	.20	.10	.02
□ 587	Mel Hall	.10	.05	.01
□ 588	Mike Hargrove	.08	.04	.01
□ 589	Neal Heaton	.05	.02	.00
□ 590	Brook Jacoby	.10	.05	.01
□ 591	Otis Nixon	.15	.07	.01
□ 592	Jerry Reed	.05	.02	.00
□ 593	Vern Ruhle	.05	.02	.00
□ 594	Pat Tabler	.08	.04	.01
□ 595	Rich Thompson	.05	.02	.00
□ 596	Andre Thornton	.08	.04	.01
□ 597	Dave Von Ohlen	.05	.02	.00
□ 598	George Vukovich	.05	.02	.00
□ 599	Tom Waddell	.05	.02	.00
□ 600	Curt Wardle	.05	.02	.00
□ 601	Jerry Willard	.05	.02	.00
□ 602	Bill Almon	.05	.02	.00
□ 603	Mike Bielecki	.10	.05	.01
□ 604	Sid Bream	.08	.04	.01
□ 605	Mike Brown OF	.05	.02	.00
□ 606	Pat Clements	.10	.05	.01
□ 607	Jose DeLeon	.08	.04	.01
□ 608	Denny Gonzalez	.05	.02	.00
□ 609	Cecilio Guante	.05	.02	.00

		MINT	EXC	G-VG
□ 610	Steve Kemp	.08	.04	.01
□ 611	Sammy Khalifa	.08	.04	.01
□ 612	Lee Mazzilli	.05	.02	.00
□ 613	Larry McWilliams	.05	.02	.00
□ 614	Jim Morrison	.05	.02	.00
□ 615	Joe Orsulak	.12	.06	.01
□ 616	Tony Pena	.10	.05	.01
□ 617	Johnny Ray	.10	.05	.01
□ 618	Rick Reuschel	.10	.05	.01
□ 619	R.J. Reynolds	.05	.02	.00
□ 620	Rick Rhoden	.08	.04	.01
□ 621	Don Robinson	.05	.02	.00
□ 622	Jason Thompson	.05	.02	.00
□ 623	Lee Tunnell	.05	.02	.00
□ 624	Jim Winn	.05	.02	.00
□ 625	Marvell Wynne	.05	.02	.00
□ 626	Dwight Gooden IA	.40	.20	.04
□ 627	Don Mattingly IA	1.50	.75	.15
□ 628	4192 (Pete Rose)	.40	.20	.04
□ 629	3000 Career Hits	.20	.10	.02
	Rod Carew			
□ 630	300 Career Wins	.15	.07	.01
	Tom Seaver			
	Phil Niekro			
□ 631	Ouch (Don Baylor)	.08	.04	.01
□ 632	Instant Offense	.25	.12	.02
	Darryl Strawberry			
	Tim Raines			
□ 633	Shortstops Supreme	.12	.06	.01
	Cal Ripken			
	Alan Trammell			
□ 634	Boggs and "Hero"	.50	.25	.05
	Wade Boggs			
	George Brett			
□ 635	Braves Dynamic Duo	.15	.07	.01
	Bob Horner			
	Dale Murphy			
□ 636	Cardinal Ignitors	.15	.07	.01
	Willie McGee			
	Vince Coleman			
□ 637	Terror on Basepaths	.20	.10	.02
	Vince Coleman			
□ 638	Charlie Hustle/Dr. K	.75	.35	.07
	Pete Rose			
	Dwight Gooden			
□ 639	1984 and 1985 AL	1.75	.85	.17
	Batting Champs			
	Wade Boggs			
	Don Mattingly			

		MINT	EXC	G-VG
☐ 640	NL West Sluggers .. Dale Murphy Steve Garvey Dave Parker	.15	.07	.01
☐ 641	Staff Aces .... Fernando Valenzuela Dwight Gooden	.30	.15	.03
☐ 642	Blue Jay Stoppers .. Jimmy Key Dave Stieb	.08	.04	.01
☐ 643	AL All-Star Backstops Carlton Fisk Rich Gedman	.08	.04	.01
☐ 644	Gene Walter and Benito Santiago	4.50	2.25	.45
☐ 645	Mike Woodard and Collin Ward	.10	.05	.01
☐ 646	Kal Daniels and Paul O'Neill	4.00	2.00	.40
☐ 647	Andres Galarraga and Fred Toliver	3.00	1.50	.30
☐ 648	Bob Kipper and Curt Ford	.10	.05	.10
☐ 649	Jose Canseco and Eric Plunk	35.00	17.50	3.50
☐ 650	Mark McLemore and Gus Polidor	.10	.05	.01
☐ 651	Rob Woodward and Mickey Brantley	.35	.17	.03
☐ 652	Billy Jo Robidoux and Mark Funderburk	.10	.05	.01
☐ 653	Cecil Fielder and Cory Snyder	2.25	1.10	.22
☐ 654	CL: Royals/Cardinals Blue Jays/Mets	.08	.01	.00
☐ 655	CL: Yankees/Dodgers Angels/Reds	.08	.01	.00
☐ 656	CL: White Sox/Tigers Expos/Orioles (279 Dennis, 280 Tippy)	.08	.01	.00
☐ 657	CL: Astros/Padres .. Red Sox/Cubs	.08	.01	.00
☐ 658	CL: Twins/A's ...... Phillies/Mariners	.08	.01	.00
☐ 659	CL: Brewers/Braves . Giants/Rangers	.08	.01	.00
☐ 660	CL: Indians/Pirates .. Special Cards	.08	.01	.00

1986 Fleer Sticker Cards

The stickers in this 132-sticker card set are standard card size, 2 ½" by 3 ½". The card photo on the front is surrounded by a yellow border and a cranberry frame. The backs are printed in blue and black on white card stock. The backs contain year-by-year statistical information. They are numbered on the back in the upper left-hand corner.

		MINT	EXC	G-VG
COMPLETE SET (132)		28.00	14.00	2.80
COMMON PLAYER (1-132)		.05	.02	.00
☐ 1	Harold Baines	.15	.07	.01
☐ 2	Jesse Barfield	.15	.07	.01
☐ 3	Don Baylor	.10	.05	.01
☐ 4	Juan Beniquez	.05	.02	.00
☐ 5	Tim Birtsas	.05	.02	.00
☐ 6	Bert Blyleven	.15	.07	.01
☐ 7	Bruce Bochte	.05	.02	.00
☐ 8	Wade Boggs	1.25	.60	.12
☐ 9	Dennis Boyd	.10	.05	.01
☐ 10	Phil Bradley	.10	.05	.01
☐ 11	George Brett	.75	.35	.07
☐ 12	Hubie Brooks	.10	.05	.01
☐ 13	Chris Brown	.05	.02	.00
☐ 14	Tom Browning	.15	.07	.01
☐ 15	Tom Brunansky	.15	.07	.01
☐ 16	Bill Buckner	.10	.05	.01
☐ 17	Britt Burns	.05	.02	.00

		MINT	EXC	G-VG				MINT	EXC	G-VG
☐	18 Brett Butler	.10	.05	.01	☐	67	Dave Kingman	.10	.05	.01
☐	19 Jose Canseco	3.00	1.50	.30	☐	68	Ron Kittle	.10	.05	.01
☐	20 Rod Carew	.40	.20	.04	☐	69	Charlie Leibrandt	.05	.02	.00
☐	21 Steve Carlton	.40	.20	.04	☐	70	Fred Lynn	.15	.07	.01
☐	22 Don Carman	.10	.05	.01	☐	71	Mike Marshall	.15	.07	.01
☐	23 Gary Carter	.30	.15	.03	☐	72	Don Mattingly	2.50	1.25	.25
☐	24 Jack Clark	.20	.10	.02	☐	73	Oddibe McDowell	.15	.07	.01
☐	25 Vince Coleman	1.00	.50	.10	☐	74	Willie McGee	.20	.10	.02
☐	26 Cecil Cooper	.10	.05	.01	☐	75	Scott McGregor	.05	.02	.00
☐	27 Jose Cruz	.05	.02	.00	☐	76	Paul Molitor	.20	.10	.02
☐	28 Ron Darling	.15	.07	.01	☐	77	Charlie Moore	.05	.02	.00
☐	29 Alvin Davis	.20	.10	.02	☐	78	Keith Moreland	.05	.02	.00
☐	30 Jody Davis	.05	.02	.00	☐	79	Jack Morris	.15	.07	.01
☐	31 Mike Davis	.05	.02	.00	☐	80	Dale Murphy	.50	.25	.05
☐	32 Andre Dawson	.25	.12	.02	☐	81	Eddie Murray	.40	.20	.04
☐	33 Mariano Duncan	.10	.05	.01	☐	82	Phil Niekro	.25	.12	.02
☐	34 Shawon Dunston	.10	.05	.01	☐	83	Joe Orsulak	.05	.02	.00
☐	35 Leon Durham	.05	.02	.00	☐	84	Dave Parker	.15	.07	.01
☐	36 Darrell Evans	.10	.05	.01	☐	85	Lance Parrish	.15	.07	.01
☐	37 Tony Fernandez	.15	.07	.01	☐	86	Larry Parrish	.05	.02	.00
☐	38 Carlton Fisk	.25	.12	.02	☐	87	Tony Pena	.10	.05	.01
☐	39 John Franco	.10	.05	.01	☐	88	Gary Pettis	.10	.05	.01
☐	40 Julio Franco	.10	.05	.01	☐	89	Jim Presley	.10	.05	.01
☐	41 Damaso Garcia	.05	.02	.00	☐	90	Kirby Puckett	1.00	.50	.10
☐	42 Scott Garrelts	.10	.05	.01	☐	91	Dan Quisenberry	.10	.05	.01
☐	43 Steve Garvey	.40	.20	.04	☐	92	Tim Raines	.20	.10	.02
☐	44 Rich Gedman	.05	.02	.00	☐	93	Johnny Ray	.10	.05	.01
☐	45 Kirk Gibson	.35	.17	.03	☐	94	Jeff Reardon	.10	.05	.01
☐	46 Dwight Gooden	1.00	.50	.10	☐	95	Rick Reuschel	.15	.07	.01
☐	47 Pedro Guerrero	.20	.10	.02	☐	96	Jim Rice	.20	.10	.02
☐	48 Ron Guidry	.15	.07	.01	☐	97	Dave Righetti	.15	.07	.01
☐	49 Ozzie Guillen	.15	.07	.01	☐	98	Earnie Riles	.05	.02	.00
☐	50 Tony Gwynn	.45	.22	.04	☐	99	Cal Ripken	.45	.22	.04
☐	51 Andy Hawkins	.05	.02	.00	☐	100	Ron Romanick	.05	.02	.00
☐	52 Von Hayes	.10	.05	.01	☐	101	Pete Rose	1.00	.50	.10
☐	53 Rickey Henderson	.75	.35	.07	☐	102	Nolan Ryan	1.50	.75	.15
☐	54 Tom Henke	.10	.05	.01	☐	103	Bret Saberhagen	.50	.25	.05
☐	55 Keith Hernandez	.25	.12	.02	☐	104	Mark Salas	.05	.02	.00
☐	56 Willie Hernandez	.10	.05	.01	☐	105	Juan Samuel	.15	.07	.01
☐	57 Tommy Herr	.05	.02	.00	☐	106	Ryne Sandberg	.45	.22	.04
☐	58 Orel Hershiser	.60	.30	.06	☐	107	Mike Schmidt	1.25	.60	.12
☐	59 Teddy Higuera	.40	.20	.04	☐	108	Mike Scott	.20	.10	.02
☐	60 Bob Horner	.15	.07	.01	☐	109	Tom Seaver	.35	.17	.03
☐	61 Charlie Hough	.05	.02	.00	☐	110	Bryn Smith	.10	.05	.01
☐	62 Jay Howell	.05	.02	.00	☐	111	Dave Smith	.05	.02	.00
☐	63 LaMarr Hoyt	.05	.02	.00	☐	112	Lonnie Smith	.10	.05	.01
☐	64 Kent Hrbek	.20	.10	.02	☐	113	Ozzie Smith	.25	.12	.02
☐	65 Reggie Jackson	.50	.25	.05	☐	114	Mario Soto	.05	.02	.00
☐	66 Bob James	.05	.02	.00	☐	115	Dave Stieb	.10	.05	.01

		MINT	EXC	G-VG
☐ 116	Darryl Strawberry	.75	.35	.07
☐ 117	Bruce Sutter	.10	.05	.01
☐ 118	Garry Templeton	.05	.02	.00
☐ 119	Gorman Thomas	.10	.05	.01
☐ 120	Andre Thornton	.05	.02	.00
☐ 121	Alan Trammell	.25	.12	.02
☐ 122	John Tudor	.15	.07	.01
☐ 123	Fernando Valenzuela	.20	.10	.02
☐ 124	Frank Viola	.20	.10	.02
☐ 125	Gary Ward	.05	.02	.00
☐ 126	Lou Whitaker	.15	.07	.01
☐ 127	Frank White	.10	.05	.01
☐ 128	Glenn Wilson	.05	.02	.00
☐ 129	Willie Wilson	.15	.07	.01
☐ 130	Dave Winfield	.30	.15	.03
☐ 131	Robin Yount	.50	.25	.05
☐ 132	Checklist Card	1.00	.50	.10
	Dwight Gooden			
	Dale Murphy			

1986 Fleer Update

This 132-card set was distributed by Fleer to dealers as a complete set in a custom box. In addition to the complete set of 132 cards, the box also contains 25 Team Logo Stickers. The card fronts look very similar to the 1986 Fleer regular issue. The cards are numbered (with a U prefix) alphabetically according to player's last name. Cards measure the standard size, 2 ½" by 3 ½".

		MINT	EXC	G-VG
	COMPLETE SET (132)	33.00	15.00	3.00
	COMMON PLAYER (1-132)	.06	.03	.00
☐ U1	Mike Aldrete	.25	.06	.01
☐ U2	Andy Allanson	.15	.07	.01
☐ U3	Neil Allen	.06	.03	.00
☐ U4	Joaquin Andujar	.10	.05	.01
☐ U5	Paul Assenmacher	.15	.07	.01
☐ U6	Scott Bailes	.15	.07	.01
☐ U7	Jay Baller	.10	.05	.01
☐ U8	Scott Bankhead	.35	.17	.03
☐ U9	Bill Bathe	.10	.05	.01
☐ U10	Don Baylor	.10	.05	.01
☐ U11	Billy Beane	.15	.07	.01
☐ U12	Steve Bedrosian	.15	.07	.01
☐ U13	Juan Beniquez	.06	.03	.00
☐ U14	Barry Bonds	1.25	.60	.12
☐ U15	Bobby Bonilla	1.25	.60	.12
	(wrong birthday)			
☐ U16	Rich Bordi	.06	.03	.00
☐ U17	Bill Campbell	.06	.03	.00
☐ U18	Tom Candiotti	.10	.05	.01
☐ U19	John Cangelosi	.15	.07	.01
☐ U20	Jose Canseco UER	8.00	4.00	.80
	(headings on back			
	for a pitcher)			
☐ U21	Chuck Cary	.20	.10	.02
☐ U22	Juan Castillo	.10	.05	.01
☐ U23	Rick Cerone	.10	.05	.01
☐ U24	John Cerutti	.25	.12	.02
☐ U25	Will Clark	12.00	6.00	1.20
☐ U26	Mark Clear	.06	.03	.00
☐ U27	Darnell Coles	.10	.05	.01
☐ U28	Dave Collins	.06	.03	.00
☐ U29	Tim Conroy	.06	.03	.00
☐ U30	Ed Correa	.15	.07	.01
☐ U31	Joe Cowley	.06	.03	.00
☐ U32	Bill Dawley	.06	.03	.00
☐ U33	Rob Deer	.20	.10	.02
☐ U34	John Denny	.10	.05	.01
☐ U35	Jim Deshaies	.35	.17	.03
☐ U36	Doug Drabek	.35	.17	.03
☐ U37	Mike Easler	.06	.03	.00
☐ U38	Mark Eichhorn	.10	.05	.01
☐ U39	Dave Engle	.06	.03	.00
☐ U40	Mike Fischlin	.06	.03	.00
☐ U41	Scott Fletcher	.10	.05	.01
☐ U42	Terry Forster	.10	.05	.01
☐ U43	Terry Francona	.06	.03	.00

		MINT	EXC	G-VG			MINT	EXC	G-VG
☐	U44 Andres Galarraga	.90	.45	.09	☐ U93 Rey Quinones	.20	.10	.02
☐	U45 Lee Guetterman	.20	.10	.02	☐ U94 Gary Redus	.06	.03	.00
☐	U46 Bill Gullickson	.06	.03	.00	☐ U95 Jeff Reed	.10	.05	.01
☐	U47 Jackie Gutierrez	.06	.03	.00	☐ U96 Bip Roberts	.25	.12	.02
☐	U48 Moose Haas	.06	.03	.00	☐ U97 Billy Jo Robidoux	.10	.05	.01
☐	U49 Billy Hatcher	.10	.05	.01	☐ U98 Gary Roenicke	.06	.03	.00
☐	U50 Mike Heath	.06	.03	.00	☐ U99 Ron Roenicke	.06	.03	.00
☐	U51 Guy Hoffman	.06	.03	.00	☐ U100 Angel Salazar	.06	.03	.00
☐	U52 Tom Hume	.06	.03	.00	☐ U101 Joe Sambito	.06	.03	.00
☐	U53 Pete Incaviglia	.75	.35	.07	☐ U102 Billy Sample	.06	.03	.00
☐	U54 Dane Iorg	.06	.03	.00	☐ U103 Dave Schmidt	.10	.05	.01
☐	U55 Chris James	.80	.40	.08	☐ U104 Ken Schrom	.06	.03	.00
☐	U56 Stan Javier	.25	.12	.02	☐ U105 Ruben Sierra	6.50	3.25	.65
☐	U57 Tommy John	.15	.07	.01	☐ U106 Ted Simmons	.20	.10	.02
☐	U58 Tracy Jones	.35	.17	.03	☐ U107 Sammy Stewart	.06	.03	.00
☐	U59 Wally Joyner	2.50	1.25	.25	☐ U108 Kurt Stillwell	.30	.15	.03
☐	U60 Wayne Krenchicki	.06	.03	.00	☐ U109 Dale Sveum	.25	.12	.02
☐	U61 John Kruk	.45	.22	.04	☐ U110 Tim Teufel	.10	.05	.01
☐	U62 Mike LaCoss	.06	.03	.00	☐ U111 Bob Tewksbury	.15	.07	.01
☐	U63 Pete Ladd	.06	.03	.00	☐ U112 Andres Thomas	.25	.12	.02
☐	U64 Dave LaPoint	.10	.05	.01	☐ U113 Jason Thompson	.06	.03	.00
☐	U65 Mike LaValliere	.25	.12	.02	☐ U114 Milt Thompson	.10	.05	.01
☐	U66 Rudy Law	.06	.03	.00	☐ U115 Robby Thompson	.40	.20	.04
☐	U67 Dennis Leonard	.10	.05	.01	☐ U116 Jay Tibbs	.06	.03	.00
☐	U68 Steve Lombardozzi	.10	.05	.01	☐ U117 Fred Toliver	.10	.05	.01
☐	U69 Aurelio Lopez	.06	.03	.00	☐ U118 Wayne Tolleson	.06	.03	.00
☐	U70 Mickey Mahler	.06	.03	.00	☐ U119 Alex Trevino	.06	.03	.00
☐	U71 Candy Maldonado	.10	.05	.01	☐ U120 Manny Trillo	.06	.03	.00
☐	U72 Roger Mason	.10	.05	.01	☐ U121 Ed VandeBerg	.06	.03	.00
☐	U73 Greg Mathews	.25	.12	.02	☐ U122 Ozzie Virgil	.06	.03	.00
☐	U74 Andy McGaffigan	.06	.03	.00	☐ U123 Tony Walker	.10	.05	.01
☐	U75 Joel McKeon	.10	.05	.01	☐ U124 Gene Walter	.10	.05	.01
☐	U76 Kevin Mitchell	6.50	3.25	.65	☐ U125 Duane Ward	.20	.10	.02
☐	U77 Bill Mooneyham	.10	.05	.01	☐ U126 Jerry Willard	.06	.03	.00
☐	U78 Omar Moreno	.06	.03	.00	☐ U127 Mitch Williams	.50	.25	.05
☐	U79 Jerry Mumphrey	.06	.03	.00	☐ U128 Reggie Williams	.10	.05	.01
☐	U80 Al Newman	.10	.05	.01	☐ U129 Bobby Witt	.40	.20	.04
☐	U81 Phil Niekro	.35	.17	.03	☐ U130 Marvell Wynne	.06	.03	.00
☐	U82 Randy Niemann	.06	.03	.00	☐ U131 Steve Yeager	.06	.03	.00
☐	U83 Juan Nieves	.15	.07	.01	☐ U132 Checklist 1-132	.06	.01	.00
☐	U84 Bob Ojeda	.15	.07	.01				
☐	U85 Rick Ownbey	.06	.03	.00				
☐	U86 Tom Paciorek	.06	.03	.00				
☐	U87 David Palmer	.06	.03	.00				
☐	U88 Jeff Parrett	.35	.17	.03				
☐	U89 Pat Perry	.15	.07	.01				
☐	U90 Dan Plesac	.35	.17	.03				
☐	U91 Darrell Porter	.06	.03	.00				
☐	U92 Luis Quinones	.15	.07	.01				

1987 Fleer

This 660-card set features a distinctive blue border, which fades to white on the card fronts. The backs are printed in blue, red, and pink on white card stock. The bottom of the card back shows an innovative graph of the player's ability, e.g., "He's got the stuff" for pitchers and "How he's hitting 'em," for hitters. Cards are numbered on the back and are again the standard 2 ½" by 3 ½". Cards are again organized numerically by teams, i.e., World Champion Mets (1-25), Boston Red Sox (26-48), Houston Astros (49-72), California Angels (73-95), New York Yankees (96-120), Texas Rangers (121-143), Detroit Tigers (144-168), Philadelphia Phillies (169-192), Cincinnati Reds (193-218), Toronto Blue Jays (219-240), Cleveland Indians (241-263), San Francisco Giants (264-288), St. Louis Cardinals (289-312), Montreal Expos (313-337), Milwaukee Brewers (338-361), Kansas City Royals (362-384), Oakland A's (385-410), San Diego Padres (411-435), Los Angeles Dodgers (436-460), Baltimore Orioles (461-483), Chicago White Sox (484-508), Atlanta Braves (509-532), Minnesota Twins (533-554), Chicago Cubs (555-578), Seattle Mariners (579-600), and Pittsburgh Pirates (601-624). The last 36 cards in this set consist of Specials (625-643), Rookie Pairs (644-653), and checklists (654-660). Fleer also produced a "limited" edition version of this set with glossy coating and packaged in a "tin." However, this tin set was apparently not limited enough (estimated be-

tween 75,000 and 100,000 1987 tin sets produced by Fleer), since the price of the "tin" glossy cards is now the same as the regular set.

		MINT	EXC	G-VG
	COMPLETE SET (660)	95.00	40.00	9.00
	COMMON PLAYER (1-660)	.05	.02	.00
☐ 1	Rick Aguilera	.10	.03	.01
☐ 2	Richard Anderson ...	.08	.04	.01
☐ 3	Wally Backman	.05	.02	.00
☐ 4	Gary Carter	.25	.12	.02
☐ 5	Ron Darling	.18	.09	.01
☐ 6	Len Dykstra	.12	.06	.01
☐ 7	Kevin Elster	.65	.30	.06
☐ 8	Sid Fernandez	.12	.06	.01
☐ 9	Dwight Gooden	1.00	.50	.10
☐ 10	Ed Hearn	.08	.04	.01
☐ 11	Danny Heep	.05	.02	.00
☐ 12	Keith Hernandez	.25	.12	.02
☐ 13	Howard Johnson	.30	.15	.03
☐ 14	Ray Knight	.08	.04	.01
☐ 15	Lee Mazzilli	.05	.02	.00
☐ 16	Roger McDowell	.08	.04	.01
☐ 17	Kevin Mitchell	9.00	4.50	.90
☐ 18	Randy Niemann	.05	.02	.00
☐ 19	Bob Ojeda	.08	.04	.01
☐ 20	Jesse Orosco	.05	.02	.00
☐ 21	Rafael Santana	.05	.02	.00
☐ 22	Doug Sisk	.05	.02	.00
☐ 23	Darryl Strawberry ...	1.00	.50	.10
☐ 24	Tim Teufel	.05	.02	.00
☐ 25	Mookie Wilson	.08	.04	.01
☐ 26	Tony Armas	.08	.04	.01
☐ 27	Marty Barrett	.08	.04	.01
☐ 28	Don Baylor	.10	.05	.01
☐ 29	Wade Boggs	1.50	.75	.15
☐ 30	Oil Can Boyd	.08	.04	.01
☐ 31	Bill Buckner	.08	.04	.01
☐ 32	Roger Clemens	1.50	.75	.15
☐ 33	Steve Crawford	.05	.02	.00
☐ 34	Dwight Evans	.12	.06	.01
☐ 35	Rich Gedman	.05	.02	.00
☐ 36	Dave Henderson	.08	.04	.01
☐ 37	Bruce Hurst	.12	.06	.01
☐ 38	Tim Lollar	.05	.02	.00
☐ 39	Al Nipper	.05	.02	.00
☐ 40	Spike Owen	.05	.02	.00
☐ 41	Jim Rice	.18	.09	.01

		MINT	\EXC	G-VG			MINT	EXC	G-VG
☐ 42	Ed Romero	.05	.02	.00	☐ 91	Vern Ruhle	.05	.02	.00
☐ 43	Joe Sambito	.05	.02	.00	☐ 92	Dick Schofield	.05	.02	.00
☐ 44	Calvin Schiraldi	.05	.02	.00	☐ 93	Don Sutton	.15	.07	.01
☐ 45	Tom Seaver	.35	.17	.03	☐ 94	Rob Wilfong	.05	.02	.00
☐ 46	Jeff Sellers	.15	.07	.01	☐ 95	Mike Witt	.08	.04	.01
☐ 47	Bob Stanley	.05	.02	.00	☐ 96	Doug Drabek	.45	.22	.04
☐ 48	Sammy Stewart	.05	.02	.00	☐ 97	Mike Easler	.05	.02	.00
☐ 49	Larry Andersen	.05	.02	.00	☐ 98	Mike Fischlin	.05	.02	.00
☐ 50	Alan Ashby	.05	.02	.00	☐ 99	Brian Fisher	.05	.02	.00
☐ 51	Kevin Bass	.10	.05	.01	☐ 100	Ron Guidry	.12	.06	.01
☐ 52	Jeff Calhoun	.05	.02	.00	☐ 101	Rickey Henderson	.50	.25	.05
☐ 53	Jose Cruz	.10	.05	.01	☐ 102	Tommy John	.15	.07	.01
☐ 54	Danny Darwin	.05	.02	.00	☐ 103	Ron Kittle	.10	.05	.01
☐ 55	Glenn Davis	.35	.17	.03	☐ 104	Don Mattingly	2.50	1.25	.25
☐ 56	Jim Deshaies	.35	.17	.03	☐ 105	Bobby Meacham	.05	.02	.00
☐ 57	Bill Doran	.10	.05	.01	☐ 106	Joe Niekro	.10	.05	.01
☐ 58	Phil Garner	.05	.02	.00	☐ 107	Mike Pagliarulo	.08	.04	.01
☐ 59	Billy Hatcher	.08	.04	.01	☐ 108	Dan Pasqua	.08	.04	.01
☐ 60	Charlie Kerfeld	.05	.02	.00	☐ 109	Willie Randolph	.08	.04	.01
☐ 61	Bob Knepper	.08	.04	.01	☐ 110	Dennis Rasmussen	.08	.04	.01
☐ 62	Dave Lopes	.08	.04	.01	☐ 111	Dave Righetti	.10	.05	.01
☐ 63	Aurelio Lopez	.05	.02	.00	☐ 112	Gary Roenicke	.05	.02	.00
☐ 64	Jim Pankovits	.05	.02	.00	☐ 113	Rod Scurry	.05	.02	.00
☐ 65	Terry Puhl	.05	.02	.00	☐ 114	Bob Shirley	.05	.02	.00
☐ 66	Craig Reynolds	.05	.02	.00	☐ 115	Joel Skinner	.05	.02	.00
☐ 67	Nolan Ryan	.90	.45	.09	☐ 116	Tim Stoddard	.05	.02	.00
☐ 68	Mike Scott	.25	.12	.02	☐ 117	Bob Tewksbury	.10	.05	.01
☐ 69	Dave Smith	.08	.04	.01	☐ 118	Wayne Tolleson	.05	.02	.00
☐ 70	Dickie Thon	.05	.02	.00	☐ 119	Claudell Washington	.08	.04	.01
☐ 71	Tony Walker	.08	.04	.01	☐ 120	Dave Winfield	.25	.12	.02
☐ 72	Denny Walling	.05	.02	.00	☐ 121	Steve Buechele	.05	.02	.00
☐ 73	Bob Boone	.12	.06	.01	☐ 122	Ed Correa	.15	.07	.01
☐ 74	Rick Burleson	.08	.04	.01	☐ 123	Scott Fletcher	.08	.04	.01
☐ 75	John Candelaria	.08	.04	.01	☐ 124	Jose Guzman	.08	.04	.01
☐ 76	Doug Corbett	.05	.02	.00	☐ 125	Toby Harrah	.05	.02	.00
☐ 77	Doug DeCinces	.08	.04	.01	☐ 126	Greg Harris	.05	.02	.00
☐ 78	Brian Downing	.08	.04	.01	☐ 127	Charlie Hough	.08	.04	.01
☐ 79	Chuck Finley	.75	.35	.07	☐ 128	Pete Incaviglia	1.00	.50	.10
☐ 80	Terry Forster	.08	.04	.01	☐ 129	Mike Mason	.05	.02	.00
☐ 81	Bob Grich	.08	.04	.01	☐ 130	Oddibe McDowell	.10	.05	.01
☐ 82	George Hendrick	.08	.04	.01	☐ 131	Dale Mohorcic	.15	.07	.01
☐ 83	Jack Howell	.15	.07	.01	☐ 132	Pete O'Brien	.10	.05	.01
☐ 84	Reggie Jackson	.45	.22	.04	☐ 133	Tom Paciorek	.05	.02	.00
☐ 85	Ruppert Jones	.05	.02	.00	☐ 134	Larry Parrish	.05	.02	.00
☐ 86	Wally Joyner	2.50	1.25	.25	☐ 135	Geno Petralli	.05	.02	.00
☐ 87	Gary Lucas	.05	.02	.00	☐ 136	Darrell Porter	.05	.02	.00
☐ 88	Kirk McCaskill	.10	.05	.01	☐ 137	Jeff Russell	.10	.05	.01
☐ 89	Donnie Moore	.05	.02	.00	☐ 138	Ruben Sierra	9.00	4.50	.90
☐ 90	Gary Pettis	.05	.02	.00	☐ 139	Don Slaught	.05	.02	.00

		MINT	EXC	G-VG			MINT	EXC	G-VG
☐ 140	Gary Ward	.05	.02	.00	☐ 189	Jeff Stone	.05	.02	.00
☐ 141	Curtis Wilkerson	.05	.02	.00	☐ 190	Kent Tekulve	.05	.02	.00
☐ 142	Mitch Williams	.65	.30	.06	☐ 191	Milt Thompson	.08	.04	.01
☐ 143	Bobby Witt	.35	.17	.03	☐ 192	Glenn Wilson	.05	.02	.00
☐ 144	Dave Bergman	.05	.02	.00	☐ 193	Buddy Bell	.10	.05	.01
☐ 145	Tom Brookens	.05	.02	.00	☐ 194	Tom Browning	.12	.06	.01
☐ 146	Bill Campbell	.05	.02	.00	☐ 195	Sal Butera	.05	.02	.00
☐ 147	Chuck Cary	.25	.12	.02	☐ 196	Dave Concepcion	.10	.05	.01
☐ 148	Darnell Coles	.08	.04	.01	☐ 197	Kal Daniels	.80	.40	.08
☐ 149	Dave Collins	.05	.02	.00	☐ 198	Eric Davis	1.50	.75	.15
☐ 150	Darrell Evans	.10	.05	.01	☐ 199	John Denny	.08	.04	.01
☐ 151	Kirk Gibson	.25	.12	.02	☐ 200	Bo Diaz	.05	.02	.00
☐ 152	John Grubb	.05	.02	.00	☐ 201	Nick Esasky	.10	.05	.01
☐ 153	Willie Hernandez	.10	.05	.01	☐ 202	John Franco	.10	.05	.01
☐ 154	Larry Herndon	.05	.02	.00	☐ 203	Bill Gullickson	.05	.02	.00
☐ 155	Eric King	.15	.07	.01	☐ 204	Barry Larkin	3.50	1.75	.35
☐ 156	Chet Lemon	.05	.02	.00	☐ 205	Eddie Milner	.05	.02	.00
☐ 157	Dwight Lowry	.10	.05	.01	☐ 206	Rob Murphy	.30	.15	.03
☐ 158	Jack Morris	.12	.06	.01	☐ 207	Ron Oester	.05	.02	.00
☐ 159	Randy O'Neal	.05	.02	.00	☐ 208	Dave Parker	.15	.07	.01
☐ 160	Lance Parrish	.12	.06	.01	☐ 209	Tony Perez	.15	.07	.01
☐ 161	Dan Petry	.05	.02	.00	☐ 210	Ted Power	.05	.02	.00
☐ 162	Pat Sheridan	.05	.02	.00	☐ 211	Joe Price	.05	.02	.00
☐ 163	Jim Slaton	.05	.02	.00	☐ 212	Ron Robinson	.05	.02	.00
☐ 164	Frank Tanana	.08	.04	.01	☐ 213	Pete Rose	.60	.30	.06
☐ 165	Walt Terrell	.05	.02	.00	☐ 214	Mario Soto	.05	.02	.00
☐ 166	Mark Thurmond	.05	.02	.00	☐ 215	Kurt Stillwell	.45	.22	.04
☐ 167	Alan Trammell	.18	.09	.01	☐ 216	Max Venable	.05	.02	.00
☐ 168	Lou Whitaker	.12	.06	.01	☐ 217	Chris Welsh	.05	.02	.00
☐ 169	Luis Aguayo	.05	.02	.00	☐ 218	Carl Willis	.08	.04	.01
☐ 170	Steve Bedrosian	.12	.06	.01	☐ 219	Jesse Barfield	.18	.09	.01
☐ 171	Don Carman	.05	.02	.00	☐ 220	George Bell	.35	.17	.03
☐ 172	Darren Daulton	.05	.02	.00	☐ 221	Bill Caudill	.05	.02	.00
☐ 173	Greg Gross	.05	.02	.00	☐ 222	John Cerutti	.30	.15	.03
☐ 174	Kevin Gross	.05	.02	.00	☐ 223	Jim Clancy	.05	.02	.00
☐ 175	Von Hayes	.10	.05	.01	☐ 224	Mark Eichhorn	.10	.05	.01
☐ 176	Charles Hudson	.05	.02	.00	☐ 225	Tony Fernandez	.25	.12	.02
☐ 177	Tom Hume	.05	.02	.00	☐ 226	Damaso Garcia	.05	.02	.00
☐ 178	Steve Jeltz	.05	.02	.00	☐ 227	Kelly Gruber ERR	.10	.05	.01
☐ 179	Mike Maddux	.15	.07	.01		(wrong birth year)			
☐ 180	Shane Rawley	.05	.02	.00	☐ 228	Tom Henke	.08	.04	.01
☐ 181	Gary Redus	.05	.02	.00	☐ 229	Garth Iorg	.05	.02	.00
☐ 182	Ron Roenicke	.05	.02	.00	☐ 230	Joe Johnson	.05	.02	.00
☐ 183	Bruce Ruffin	.18	.09	.01	☐ 231	Cliff Johnson	.05	.02	.00
☐ 184	John Russell	.05	.02	.00	☐ 232	Jimmy Key	.10	.05	.01
☐ 185	Juan Samuel	.12	.06	.01	☐ 233	Dennis Lamp	.05	.02	.00
☐ 186	Dan Schatzeder	.05	.02	.00	☐ 234	Rick Leach	.05	.02	.00
☐ 187	Mike Schmidt	.80	.40	.08	☐ 235	Buck Martinez	.05	.02	.00
☐ 188	Rick Schu	.05	.02	.00	☐ 236	Lloyd Moseby	.08	.04	.01

		MINT	EXC	G-VG
☐ 237	Rance Mulliniks	.05	.02	.00
☐ 238	Dave Stieb	.10	.05	.01
☐ 239	Willie Upshaw	.05	.02	.00
☐ 240	Ernie Whitt	.05	.02	.00
☐ 241	Andy Allanson	.08	.04	.01
☐ 242	Scott Bailes	.10	.05	.01
☐ 243	Chris Bando	.05	.02	.00
☐ 244	Tony Bernazard	.05	.02	.00
☐ 245	John Butcher	.05	.02	.00
☐ 246	Brett Butler	.08	.04	.01
☐ 247	Ernie Camacho	.05	.02	.00
☐ 248	Tom Candiotti	.05	.02	.00
☐ 249	Joe Carter	.35	.17	.03
☐ 250	Carmen Castillo	.05	.02	.00
☐ 251	Julio Franco	.15	.07	.01
☐ 252	Mel Hall	.10	.05	.01
☐ 253	Brook Jacoby	.08	.04	.01
☐ 254	Phil Niekro	.18	.09	.01
☐ 255	Otis Nixon	.10	.05	.01
☐ 256	Dickie Noles	.05	.02	.00
☐ 257	Bryan Oelkers	.05	.02	.00
☐ 258	Ken Schrom	.05	.02	.00
☐ 259	Don Schulze	.05	.02	.00
☐ 260	Cory Snyder	.75	.35	.07
☐ 261	Pat Tabler	.10	.05	.01
☐ 262	Andre Thornton	.08	.04	.01
☐ 263	Rich Yett	.05	.02	.00
☐ 264	Mike Aldrete	.20	.10	.02
☐ 265	Juan Berenguer	.05	.02	.00
☐ 266	Vida Blue	.08	.04	.01
☐ 267	Bob Brenly	.05	.02	.00
☐ 268	Chris Brown	.05	.02	.00
☐ 269	Will Clark	35.00	17.50	3.50
☐ 270	Chili Davis	.10	.05	.01
☐ 271	Mark Davis	.15	.07	.01
☐ 272	Kelly Downs	.35	.17	.03
☐ 273	Scott Garrelts	.08	.04	.01
☐ 274	Dan Gladden	.08	.04	.01
☐ 275	Mike Krukow	.05	.02	.00
☐ 276	Randy Kutcher	.10	.05	.01
☐ 277	Mike LaCoss	.05	.02	.00
☐ 278	Jeff Leonard	.08	.04	.01
☐ 279	Candy Maldonado	.08	.04	.01
☐ 280	Roger Mason	.05	.02	.00
☐ 281	Bob Melvin	.05	.02	.00
☐ 282	Greg Minton	.05	.02	.00
☐ 283	Jeff Robinson	.10	.05	.01
	(Giants pitcher)			
☐ 284	Harry Spilman	.05	.02	.00

		MINT	EXC	G-VG
☐ 285	Robby Thompson	.35	.17	.03
☐ 286	Jose Uribe	.05	.02	.00
☐ 287	Frank Williams	.05	.02	.00
☐ 288	Joel Youngblood	.05	.02	.00
☐ 289	Jack Clark	.20	.10	.02
☐ 290	Vince Coleman	.40	.20	.04
☐ 291	Tim Conroy	.05	.02	.00
☐ 292	Danny Cox	.08	.04	.01
☐ 293	Ken Dayley	.05	.02	.00
☐ 294	Curt Ford	.08	.04	.01
☐ 295	Bob Forsch	.05	.02	.00
☐ 296	Tom Herr	.08	.04	.01
☐ 297	Ricky Horton	.05	.02	.00
☐ 298	Clint Hurdle	.05	.02	.00
☐ 299	Jeff Lahti	.05	.02	.00
☐ 300	Steve Lake	.05	.02	.00
☐ 301	Tito Landrum	.05	.02	.00
☐ 302	Mike LaValliere	.20	.10	.02
☐ 303	Greg Mathews	.20	.10	.02
☐ 304	Willie McGee	.12	.06	.01
☐ 305	Jose Oquendo	.05	.02	.00
☐ 306	Terry Pendleton	.08	.04	.01
☐ 307	Pat Perry	.05	.02	.00
☐ 308	Ozzie Smith	.20	.10	.02
☐ 309	Ray Soff	.08	.04	.01
☐ 310	John Tudor	.10	.05	.01
☐ 311	Andy Van Slyke	.25	.12	.02
	ERR (Bats R, Throws L)			
☐ 312	Todd Worrell	.20	.10	.02
☐ 313	Dann Bilardello	.05	.02	.00
☐ 314	Hubie Brooks	.08	.04	.01
☐ 315	Tim Burke	.08	.04	.01
☐ 316	Andre Dawson	.30	.15	.03
☐ 317	Mike Fitzgerald	.05	.02	.00
☐ 318	Tom Foley	.05	.02	.00
☐ 319	Andres Galarraga	.35	.17	.03
☐ 320	Joe Hesketh	.05	.02	.00
☐ 321	Wallace Johnson	.05	.02	.00
☐ 322	Wayne Krenchicki	.05	.02	.00
☐ 323	Vance Law	.05	.02	.00
☐ 324	Dennis Martinez	.08	.04	.01
☐ 325	Bob McClure	.05	.02	.00
☐ 326	Andy McGaffigan	.05	.02	.00
☐ 327	Al Newman	.08	.04	.01
☐ 328	Tim Raines	.25	.12	.02
☐ 329	Jeff Reardon	.10	.05	.01
☐ 330	Luis Rivera	.08	.04	.01
☐ 331	Bob Sebra	.10	.05	.01

	MINT	EXC	G-VG		MINT	EXC	G-VG
☐ 332 Bryn Smith	.10	.05	.01	☐ 381 Lonnie Smith	.10	.05	.01
☐ 333 Jay Tibbs	.05	.02	.00	☐ 382 Jim Sundberg	.05	.02	.00
☐ 334 Tim Wallach	.10	.05	.01	☐ 383 Frank White	.08	.04	.01
☐ 335 Mitch Webster	.05	.02	.00	☐ 384 Willie Wilson	.10	.05	.01
☐ 336 Jim Wohlford	.05	.02	.00	☐ 385 Joaquin Andujar	.08	.04	.01
☐ 337 Floyd Youmans	.08	.04	.01	☐ 386 Doug Bair	.05	.02	.00
☐ 338 Chris Bosio	.45	.22	.04	☐ 387 Dusty Baker	.08	.04	.01
☐ 339 Glenn Braggs	.75	.35	.07	☐ 388 Bruce Bochte	.05	.02	.00
☐ 340 Rick Cerone	.05	.02	.00	☐ 389 Jose Canseco	8.00	4.00	.80
☐ 341 Mark Clear	.05	.02	.00	☐ 390 Chris Codiroli	.05	.02	.00
☐ 342 Bryan Clutterbuck	.08	.04	.01	☐ 391 Mike Davis	.05	.02	.00
☐ 343 Cecil Cooper	.10	.05	.01	☐ 392 Alfredo Griffin	.08	.04	.01
☐ 344 Rob Deer	.30	.15	.03	☐ 393 Moose Haas	.05	.02	.00
☐ 345 Jim Gantner	.05	.02	.00	☐ 394 Donnie Hill	.05	.02	.00
☐ 346 Ted Higuera	.15	.07	.01	☐ 395 Jay Howell	.08	.04	.01
☐ 347 John Henry Johnson	.05	.02	.00	☐ 396 Dave Kingman	.10	.05	.01
☐ 348 Tim Leary	.30	.15	.03	☐ 397 Carney Lansford	.12	.06	.01
☐ 349 Rick Manning	.05	.02	.00	☐ 398 Dave Leiper	.08	.04	.01
☐ 350 Paul Molitor	.12	.06	.01	☐ 399 Bill Mooneyham	.08	.04	.01
☐ 351 Charlie Moore	.05	.02	.00	☐ 400 Dwayne Murphy	.05	.02	.00
☐ 352 Juan Nieves	.15	.07	.01	☐ 401 Steve Ontiveros	.05	.02	.00
☐ 353 Ben Oglivie	.08	.04	.01	☐ 402 Tony Phillips	.05	.02	.00
☐ 354 Dan Plesac	.35	.17	.03	☐ 403 Eric Plunk	.05	.02	.00
☐ 355 Ernest Riles	.05	.02	.00	☐ 404 Jose Rijo	.08	.04	.01
☐ 356 Billy Jo Robidoux	.05	.02	.00	☐ 405 Terry Steinbach	1.25	.60	.12
☐ 357 Bill Schroeder	.05	.02	.00	☐ 406 Dave Stewart	.18	.09	.01
☐ 358 Dale Sveum	.18	.09	.01	☐ 407 Mickey Tettleton	.20	.10	.02
☐ 359 Gorman Thomas	.10	.05	.01	☐ 408 Dave Von Ohlen	.05	.02	.00
☐ 360 Bill Wegman	.08	.04	.01	☐ 409 Jerry Willard	.05	.02	.00
☐ 361 Robin Yount	.45	.22	.04	☐ 410 Curt Young	.05	.02	.00
☐ 362 Steve Balboni	.05	.02	.00	☐ 411 Bruce Bochy	.05	.02	.00
☐ 363 Scott Bankhead	.20	.10	.02	☐ 412 Dave Dravecky	.10	.05	.01
☐ 364 Buddy Biancalana	.05	.02	.00	☐ 413 Tim Flannery	.05	.02	.00
☐ 365 Bud Black	.05	.02	.00	☐ 414 Steve Garvey	.30	.15	.03
☐ 366 George Brett	.45	.22	.04	☐ 415 Goose Gossage	.10	.05	.01
☐ 367 Steve Farr	.08	.04	.01	☐ 416 Tony Gwynn	.60	.30	.06
☐ 368 Mark Gubicza	.15	.07	.01	☐ 417 Andy Hawkins	.08	.04	.01
☐ 369 Bo Jackson	18.00	9.00	1.80	☐ 418 LaMarr Hoyt	.08	.04	.01
☐ 370 Dartny Jackson	.12	.06	.01	☐ 419 Terry Kennedy	.05	.02	.00
☐ 371 Mike Kingery	.12	.06	.01	☐ 420 John Kruk	.45	.22	.04
☐ 372 Rudy Law	.05	.02	.00	☐ 421 Dave LaPoint	.08	.04	.01
☐ 373 Charlie Leibrandt	.05	.02	.00	☐ 422 Craig Lefferts	.08	.04	.01
☐ 374 Dennis Leonard	.05	.02	.00	☐ 423 Carmelo Martinez	.05	.02	.00
☐ 375 Hal McRae	.08	.04	.01	☐ 424 Lance McCullers	.08	.04	.01
☐ 376 Jorge Orta	.05	.02	.00	☐ 425 Kevin McReynolds	.30	.15	.03
☐ 377 Jamie Quirk	.05	.02	.00	☐ 426 Graig Nettles	.10	.05	.01
☐ 378 Dan Quisenberry	.10	.05	.01	☐ 427 Bip Roberts	.20	.10	.02
☐ 379 Bret Saberhagen	.45	.22	.04	☐ 428 Jerry Royster	.05	.02	.00
☐ 380 Angel Salazar	.05	.02	.00	☐ 429 Benito Santiago	1.00	.50	.10

	MINT	EXC	G-VG			MINT	EXC	G-VG
☐ 430 Eric Show	.08	.04	.01	☐ 479 Larry Sheets	.08	.04	.01
☐ 431 Bob Stoddard	.05	.02	.00	☐ 480 John Shelby	.05	.02	.00
☐ 432 Garry Templeton	.08	.04	.01	☐ 481 Nate Snell	.05	.02	.00
☐ 433 Gene Walter	.05	.02	.00	☐ 482 Jim Traber	.05	.02	.00
☐ 434 Ed Whitson	.05	.02	.00	☐ 483 Mike Young	.05	.02	.00
☐ 435 Marvell Wynne	.05	.02	.00	☐ 484 Neil Allen	.05	.02	.00
☐ 436 Dave Anderson	.05	.02	.00	☐ 485 Harold Baines	.12	.06	.01
☐ 437 Greg Brock	.05	.02	.00	☐ 486 Floyd Bannister	.05	.02	.00
☐ 438 Enos Cabell	.05	.02	.00	☐ 487 Daryl Boston	.05	.02	.00
☐ 439 Mariano Duncan	.05	.02	.00	☐ 488 Ivan Calderon	.12	.06	.01
☐ 440 Pedro Guerrero	.15	.07	.01	☐ 489 John Cangelosi	.10	.05	.01
☐ 441 Orel Hershiser	.40	.20	.04	☐ 490 Steve Carlton	.20	.10	.02
☐ 442 Rick Honeycutt	.05	.02	.00	☐ 491 Joe Cowley	.05	.02	.00
☐ 443 Ken Howell	.05	.02	.00	☐ 492 Julio Cruz	.05	.02	.00
☐ 444 Ken Landreaux	.05	.02	.00	☐ 493 Bill Dawley	.05	.02	.00
☐ 445 Bill Madlock	.07	.03	.01	☐ 494 Jose DeLeon	.05	.02	.00
☐ 446 Mike Marshall	.10	.05	.01	☐ 495 Richard Dotson	.08	.04	.01
☐ 447 Len Matuszek	.05	.02	.00	☐ 496 Carlton Fisk	.20	.10	.02
☐ 448 Tom Niedenfuer	.05	.02	.00	☐ 497 Ozzie Guillen	.10	.05	.01
☐ 449 Alejandro Pena	.08	.04	.01	☐ 498 Jerry Hairston	.05	.02	.00
☐ 450 Dennis Powell	.05	.02	.00	☐ 499 Ron Hassey	.05	.02	.00
☐ 451 Jerry Reuss	.05	.02	.00	☐ 500 Tim Hulett	.05	.02	.00
☐ 452 Bill Russell	.05	.02	.00	☐ 501 Bob James	.05	.02	.00
☐ 453 Steve Sax	.15	.07	.01	☐ 502 Steve Lyons	.05	.02	.00
☐ 454 Mike Scioscia	.08	.04	.01	☐ 503 Joel McKeon	.05	.02	.00
☐ 455 Franklin Stubbs	.05	.02	.00	☐ 504 Gene Nelson	.05	.02	.00
☐ 456 Alex Trevino	.05	.02	.00	☐ 505 Dave Schmidt	.05	.02	.00
☐ 457 Fernando Valenzuela	.18	.09	.01	☐ 506 Ray Searage	.05	.02	.00
☐ 458 Ed VandeBerg	.05	.02	.00	☐ 507 Bobby Thigpen	.35	.17	.03
☐ 459 Bob Welch	.08	.04	.01	☐ 508 Greg Walker	.08	.04	.01
☐ 460 Reggie Williams	.08	.04	.01	☐ 509 Jim Acker	.05	.02	.00
☐ 461 Don Aase	.05	.02	.00	☐ 510 Doyle Alexander	.08	.04	.01
☐ 462 Juan Beniquez	.05	.02	.00	☐ 511 Paul Assenmacher	.08	.04	.01
☐ 463 Mike Boddicker	.08	.04	.01	☐ 512 Bruce Benedict	.05	.02	.00
☐ 464 Juan Bonilla	.05	.02	.00	☐ 513 Chris Chambliss	.08	.04	.01
☐ 465 Rich Bordi	.05	.02	.00	☐ 514 Jeff Dedmon	.05	.02	.00
☐ 466 Storm Davis	.08	.04	.01	☐ 515 Gene Garber	.05	.02	.00
☐ 467 Rick Dempsey	.05	.02	.00	☐ 516 Ken Griffey	.10	.05	.01
☐ 468 Ken Dixon	.05	.02	.00	☐ 517 Terry Harper	.05	.02	.00
☐ 469 Jim Dwyer	.05	.02	.00	☐ 518 Bob Horner	.12	.06	.01
☐ 470 Mike Flanagan	.08	.04	.01	☐ 519 Glenn Hubbard	.05	.02	.00
☐ 471 Jackie Gutierrez	.05	.02	.00	☐ 520 Rick Mahler	.05	.02	.00
☐ 472 Brad Havens	.05	.02	.00	☐ 521 Omar Moreno	.05	.02	.00
☐ 473 Lee Lacy	.05	.02	.00	☐ 522 Dale Murphy	.40	.20	.04
☐ 474 Fred Lynn	.12	.06	.01	☐ 523 Ken Oberkfell	.05	.02	.00
☐ 475 Scott McGregor	.08	.04	.01	☐ 524 Ed Olwine	.08	.04	.01
☐ 476 Eddie Murray	.25	.12	.02	☐ 525 David Palmer	.05	.02	.00
☐ 477 Tom O'Malley	.05	.02	.00	☐ 526 Rafael Ramirez	.05	.02	.00
☐ 478 Cal Ripken Jr.	.30	.15	.03	☐ 527 Billy Sample	.05	.02	.00

		MINT	EXC	G-VG			MINT	EXC	G-VG
☐ 528	Ted Simmons	.10	.05	.01	☐ 574	Lee Smith	.08	.04	.01
☐ 529	Zane Smith	.08	.04	.01	☐ 575	Chris Speier	.05	.02	.00
☐ 530	Bruce Sutter	.10	.05	.01	☐ 576	Rick Sutcliffe	.10	.05	.01
☐ 531	Andres Thomas	.25	.12	.02	☐ 577	Manny Trillo	.05	.02	.00
☐ 532	Ozzie Virgil	.05	.02	.00	☐ 578	Steve Trout	.05	.02	.00
☐ 533	Allan Anderson	.45	.22	.04	☐ 579	Karl Best	.05	.02	.00
☐ 534	Keith Atherton	.05	.02	.00	☐ 580	Scott Bradley	.05	.02	.00
☐ 535	Billy Beane	.08	.04	.01	☐ 581	Phil Bradley	.08	.04	.01
☐ 536	Bert Blyleven	.12	.06	.01	☐ 582	Mickey Brantley	.08	.04	.01
☐ 537	Tom Brunansky	.12	.06	.01	☐ 583	Mike Brown	.05	.02	.00
☐ 538	Randy Bush	.05	.02	.00		(Mariners pitcher)			
☐ 539	George Frazier	.05	.02	.00	☐ 584	Alvin Davis	.18	.09	.01
☐ 540	Gary Gaetti	.15	.07	.01	☐ 585	Lee Guetterman	.20	.10	.02
☐ 541	Greg Gagne	.05	.02	.00	☐ 586	Mark Huismann	.05	.02	.00
☐ 542	Mickey Hatcher	.05	.02	.00	☐ 587	Bob Kearney	.05	.02	.00
☐ 543	Neal Heaton	.05	.02	.00	☐ 588	Pete Ladd	.05	.02	.00
☐ 544	Kent Hrbek	.15	.07	.01	☐ 589	Mark Langston	.35	.17	.03
☐ 545	Roy Lee Jackson	.05	.02	.00	☐ 590	Mike Moore	.10	.05	.01
☐ 546	Tim Laudner	.05	.02	.00	☐ 591	Mike Morgan	.08	.04	.01
☐ 547	Steve Lombardozzi	.05	.02	.00	☐ 592	John Moses	.05	.02	.00
☐ 548	Mark Portugal	.25	.12	.02	☐ 593	Ken Phelps	.08	.04	.01
☐ 549	Kirby Puckett	1.75	.85	.17	☐ 594	Jim Presley	.10	.05	.01
☐ 550	Jeff Reed	.05	.02	.00	☐ 595	Rey Quinones UER	.20	.10	.02
☐ 551	Mark Salas	.05	.02	.00		(Quinonez on front)			
☐ 552	Roy Smalley	.05	.02	.00	☐ 596	Harold Reynolds	.08	.04	.01
☐ 553	Mike Smithson	.05	.02	.00	☐ 597	Billy Swift	.05	.02	.00
☐ 554	Frank Viola	.18	.09	.01	☐ 598	Danny Tartabull	.35	.17	.03
☐ 555	Thad Bosley	.05	.02	.00	☐ 599	Steve Yeager	.05	.02	.00
☐ 556	Ron Cey	.08	.04	.01	☐ 600	Matt Young	.05	.02	.00
☐ 557	Jody Davis	.05	.02	.00	☐ 601	Bill Almon	.05	.02	.00
☐ 558	Ron Davis	.05	.02	.00	☐ 602	Rafael Belliard	.08	.04	.01
☐ 559	Bob Dernier	.05	.02	.00	☐ 603	Mike Bielecki	.12	.06	.01
☐ 560	Frank DiPino	.05	.02	.00	☐ 604	Barry Bonds	1.50	.75	.15
☐ 561	Shawon Dunston				☐ 605	Bobby Bonilla	1.50	.75	.15
	UER	.15	.07	.01	☐ 606	Sid Bream	.05	.02	.00
	(wrong birth year				☐ 607	Mike Brown	.05	.02	.00
	listed on card back)					(Pirates OF)			
☐ 562	Leon Durham	.08	.04	.01	☐ 608	Pat Clements	.05	.02	.00
☐ 563	Dennis Eckersley	.12	.06	.01	☐ 609	Mike Diaz	.10	.05	.01
☐ 564	Terry Francona	.05	.02	.00	☐ 610	Cecilio Guante	.05	.02	.00
☐ 565	Dave Gumpert	.05	.02	.00	☐ 611	Barry Jones	.10	.05	.01
☐ 566	Guy Hoffman	.05	.02	.00	☐ 612	Bob Kipper	.05	.02	.00
☐ 567	Ed Lynch	.05	.02	.00	☐ 613	Larry McWilliams	.05	.02	.00
☐ 568	Gary Matthews	.05	.02	.00	☐ 614	Jim Morrison	.05	.02	.00
☐ 569	Keith Moreland	.05	.02	.00	☐ 615	Joe Orsulak	.05	.02	.00
☐ 570	Jamie Moyer	.15	.07	.01	☐ 616	Junior Ortiz	.05	.02	.00
☐ 571	Jerry Mumphrey	.05	.02	.00	☐ 617	Tony Pena	.08	.04	.01
☐ 572	Ryne Sandberg	.35	.17	.03	☐ 618	Johnny Ray	.08	.04	.01
☐ 573	Scott Sanderson	.05	.02	.00	☐ 619	Rick Reuschel	.10	.05	.01

		MINT	EXC	G-VG
☐ 620	R.J. Reynolds	.05	.02	.00
☐ 621	Rick Rhoden	.08	.04	.01
☐ 622	Don Robinson	.05	.02	.00
☐ 623	Bob Walk	.05	.02	.00
☐ 624	Jim Winn	.05	.02	.00
☐ 625	Youthful Power	.60	.30	.06
	Pete Incaviglia			
	Jose Canseco			
☐ 626	300 Game Winners	.10	.05	.01
	Don Sutton			
	Phil Niekro			
☐ 627	AL Firemen	.07	.03	.01
	Dave Righetti			
	Don Aase			
☐ 628	Rookie All-Stars	1.25	.60	.12
	Wally Joyner			
	Jose Canseco			
☐ 629	Magic Mets	.50	.25	.05
	Gary Carter			
	Sid Fernandez			
	Dwight Gooden			
	Keith Hernandez			
	Darryl Strawberry			
☐ 630	NL Best Righties	.08	.04	.01
	Mike Scott			
	Mike Krukow			
☐ 631	Sensational Southpaws	.10	.05	.01
	Fernando Valenzuela			
	John Franco			
☐ 632	Count 'Em	.08	.04	.01
	Bob Horner			
☐ 633	AL Pitcher's Nightmare	.75	.35	.07
	Jose Canseco			
	Jim Rice			
	Kirby Puckett			
☐ 634	All-Star Battery	.25	.12	.02
	Gary Carter			
	Roger Clemens			
☐ 635	4000 Strikeouts	.15	.07	.01
	Steve Carlton			
☐ 636	Big Bats at First	.15	.07	.01
	Glenn Davis			
	Eddie Murray			
☐ 637	On Base	.35	.17	.03
	Wade Boggs			
	Keith Hernandez			
☐ 638	Sluggers Left Side	1.00	.50	.10

		MINT	EXC	G-VG
	Don Mattingly			
	Darryl Strawberry			
☐ 639	Former MVP's	.12	.06	.01
	Dave Parker			
	Ryne Sandberg			
☐ 640	Dr. K , Super K	.65	.30	.06
	Dwight Gooden			
	Roger Clemens			
☐ 641	AL West Stoppers	.08	.04	.01
	Mike Witt			
	Charlie Hough			
☐ 642	Doubles and Triples	.10	.05	.01
	Juan Samuel			
	Tim Raines			
☐ 643	Outfielders with Punch	.10	.05	.01
	Harold Baines			
	Jesse Barfield			
☐ 644	Dave Clark and Greg Swindell	2.50	1.25	.25
☐ 645	Ron Karkovice and Russ Morman	.10	.05	.01
☐ 646	Devon White and Willie Fraser	1.50	.75	.15
☐ 647	Mike Stanley and Jerry Browne	.45	.22	.04
☐ 648	Dave Magadan and Phil Lombardi	1.00	.50	.10
☐ 649	Jose Gonzalez and Ralph Bryant	.25	.12	.02
☐ 650	Jimmy Jones and Randy Asadoor	.20	.10	.02
☐ 651	Tracy Jones and Marvin Freeman	.30	.15	.03
☐ 652	John Stefero and Kevin Seitzer	5.00	2.50	.50
☐ 653	Rob Nelson and Steve Fireovid	.15	.07	.01
☐ 654	CL: Mets/Red Sox Astros/Angels	.08	.01	.00
☐ 655	CL: Yankees/Rangers Tigers/Phillies	.08	.01	.00
☐ 656	CL: Reds/Blue Jays Indians/Giants ERR (230/231 wrong)	.08	.01	.00
☐ 657	CL: Cardinals/Expos Brewers/Royals	.08	.01	.00
☐ 658	CL: A's/Padres Dodgers/Orioles	.08	.01	.00

		MINT	EXC	G-VG
□ 659	CL: White Sox/Braves Twins/Cubs	.08	.01	.00
□ 660	CL: Mariners/Pirates Special Cards ERR (580/581 wrong)	.08	.01	.00

1987 Fleer Sticker Cards

These Star Stickers were distributed as a separate issue by Fleer with five star stickers and a logo sticker in each wax pack. The 132-card (sticker) set features 2 ½" by 3 ½" full-color fronts and even statistics on the sticker back, which is an indication that the Fleer Company understands that these stickers are rarely used as stickers but more like traditional cards. The card fronts are surrounded by a green border and the backs are printed in green and yellow on white card stock.

		MINT	EXC	G-VG
COMPLETE SET (132)		25.00	12.50	2.50
COMMON PLAYER (1-132)		.05	.02	.00
□ 1	Don Aase	.05	.02	.00
□ 2	Harold Baines	.10	.05	.01
□ 3	Floyd Bannister	.05	.02	.00
□ 4	Jesse Barfield	.15	.07	.01

		MINT	EXC	G-VG
□ 5	Marty Barrett	.05	.02	.00
□ 6	Kevin Bass	.05	.02	.00
□ 7	Don Baylor	.10	.05	.01
□ 8	Steve Bedrosian	.10	.05	.01
□ 9	George Bell	.20	.10	.02
□ 10	Bert Blyleven	.15	.07	.01
□ 11	Mike Boddicker	.10	.05	.01
□ 12	Wade Boggs	1.50	.75	.15
□ 13	Phil Bradley	.10	.05	.01
□ 14	Sid Bream	.05	.02	.00
□ 15	George Brett	.45	.22	.04
□ 16	Hubie Brooks	.10	.05	.01
□ 17	Tom Brunansky	.15	.07	.01
□ 18	Tom Candiotti	.05	.02	.00
□ 19	Jose Canseco	2.50	1.25	.25
□ 20	Gary Carter	.30	.15	.03
□ 21	Joe Carter	.20	.10	.02
□ 22	Will Clark	2.50	1.25	.25
□ 23	Mark Clear	.05	.02	.00
□ 24	Roger Clemens	.75	.35	.07
□ 25	Vince Coleman	.35	.17	.03
□ 26	Jose Cruz	.10	.05	.01
□ 27	Ron Darling	.15	.07	.01
□ 28	Alvin Davis	.10	.05	.01
□ 29	Chili Davis	.10	.05	.01
□ 30	Eric Davis	1.00	.50	.10
□ 31	Glenn Davis	.30	.15	.03
□ 32	Mike Davis	.05	.02	.00
□ 33	Andre Dawson	.30	.15	.03
□ 34	Doug DeCinces	.05	.02	.00
□ 35	Brian Downing	.05	.02	.00
□ 36	Shawon Dunston	.15	.07	.01
□ 37	Mark Eichhorn	.05	.02	.00
□ 38	Dwight Evans	.20	.10	.02
□ 39	Tony Fernandez	.15	.07	.01
□ 40	Bob Forsch	.05	.02	.00
□ 41	John Franco	.10	.05	.01
□ 42	Julio Franco	.10	.05	.01
□ 43	Gary Gaetti	.20	.10	.02
□ 44	Gene Garber	.05	.02	.00
□ 45	Scott Garrelts	.10	.05	.01
□ 46	Steve Garvey	.45	.22	.04
□ 47	Kirk Gibson	.35	.17	.03
□ 48	Dwight Gooden	.75	.35	.07
□ 49	Ken Griffey Sr.	.10	.05	.01
□ 50	Ozzie Guillen	.10	.05	.01
□ 51	Bill Gullickson	.05	.02	.00
□ 52	Tony Gwynn	.50	.25	.05
□ 53	Mel Hall	.10	.05	.01

		MINT	EXC	G-VG
☐ 54	Greg Harris	.05	.02	.00
☐ 55	Von Hayes	.10	.05	.01
☐ 56	Rickey Henderson	.75	.35	.07
☐ 57	Tom Henke	.10	.05	.01
☐ 58	Keith Hernandez	.20	.10	.02
☐ 59	Willie Hernandez	.10	.05	.01
☐ 60	Ted Higuera	.15	.07	.01
☐ 61	Bob Horner	.15	.07	.01
☐ 62	Charlie Hough	.05	.02	.00
☐ 63	Jay Howell	.05	.02	.00
☐ 64	Kent Hrbek	.20	.10	.02
☐ 65	Bruce Hurst	.15	.07	.01
☐ 66	Pete Incaviglia	.25	.12	.02
☐ 67	Bob James	.05	.02	.00
☐ 68	Wally Joyner	1.00	.50	.10
☐ 69	Mike Krukow	.05	.02	.00
☐ 70	Mark Langston	.25	.12	.02
☐ 71	Carney Lansford	.15	.07	.01
☐ 72	Fred Lynn	.15	.07	.01
☐ 73	Bill Madlock	.05	.02	.00
☐ 74	Don Mattingly	2.50	1.25	.25
☐ 75	Kirk McCaskill	.05	.02	.00
☐ 76	Lance McCullers	.05	.02	.00
☐ 77	Oddibe McDowell	.10	.05	.01
☐ 78	Paul Molitor	.20	.10	.02
☐ 79	Keith Moreland	.05	.02	.00
☐ 80	Jack Morris	.15	.07	.01
☐ 81	Jim Morrison	.05	.02	.00
☐ 82	Jerry Mumphrey	.05	.02	.00
☐ 83	Dale Murphy	.40	.20	.04
☐ 84	Eddie Murray	.35	.17	.03
☐ 85	Ben Oglivie	.05	.02	.00
☐ 86	Bob Ojeda	.10	.05	.01
☐ 87	Jesse Orosco	.05	.02	.00
☐ 88	Dave Parker	.15	.07	.01
☐ 89	Larry Parrish	.05	.02	.00
☐ 90	Tony Pena	.05	.02	.00
☐ 91	Jim Presley	.10	.05	.01
☐ 92	Kirby Puckett	1.00	.50	.10
☐ 93	Dan Quisenberry	.10	.05	.01
☐ 94	Tim Raines	.25	.12	.02
☐ 95	Dennis Rasmussen	.05	.02	.00
☐ 96	Shane Rawley	.05	.02	.00
☐ 97	Johnny Ray	.10	.05	.01
☐ 98	Jeff Reardon	.10	.05	.01
☐ 99	Jim Rice	.20	.10	.02
☐ 100	Dave Righetti	.15	.07	.01
☐ 101	Cal Ripken Jr.	.40	.20	.04
☐ 102	Pete Rose	.75	.35	.07
☐ 103	Nolan Ryan	1.50	.75	.15
☐ 104	Juan Samuel	.15	.07	.01
☐ 105	Ryne Sandberg	.30	.15	.03
☐ 106	Steve Sax	.15	.07	.01
☐ 107	Mike Schmidt	1.25	.60	.12
☐ 108	Mike Scott	.20	.10	.02
☐ 109	Dave Smith	.05	.02	.00
☐ 110	Lee Smith	.10	.05	.01
☐ 111	Lonnie Smith	.10	.05	.01
☐ 112	Ozzie Smith	.20	.10	.02
☐ 113	Cory Snyder	.25	.12	.02
☐ 114	Darryl Strawberry	.60	.30	.06
☐ 115	Don Sutton	.20	.10	.02
☐ 116	Kent Tekulve	.05	.02	.00
☐ 117	Andres Thomas	.05	.02	.00
☐ 118	Alan Trammell	.25	.12	.02
☐ 119	John Tudor	.15	.07	.01
☐ 120	Fernando Valenzuela	.20	.10	.02
☐ 121	Bob Welch	.10	.05	.01
☐ 122	Lou Whitaker	.15	.07	.01
☐ 123	Frank White	.10	.05	.01
☐ 124	Reggie Williams	.05	.02	.00
☐ 125	Willie Wilson	.10	.05	.01
☐ 126	Dave Winfield	.25	.12	.02
☐ 127	Mike Witt	.10	.05	.01
☐ 128	Todd Worrell	.20	.10	.02
☐ 129	Curt Young	.05	.02	.00
☐ 130	Robin Yount	.75	.35	.07
☐ 131	Checklist	2.00	1.00	.20
	Jose Canseco			
	Don Mattingly			
☐ 132	Checklist	2.00	1.00	.20
	Bo Jackson			
	Eric Davis			

1987 Fleer Update

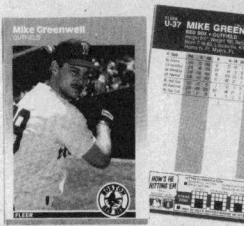

This 132-card set was distributed by Fleer to dealers as a complete set in a custom box. In addition to the complete set of 132 cards, the box also contains 25 Team Logo stickers.The card fronts look very similar to the 1987 Fleer regular issue. The cards are numbered (with a U prefix) alphabetically according to player's last name. Cards measure the standard size, 2 ½" by 3 ½". Fleer misalphabetized Jim Winn in their set numbering by putting him ahead of the next four players listed. Fleer also produced a "limited" edition version of this set with glossy coating and packaged in a "tin." However, this tin set was apparently not limited enough (estimated between 75,000 and 100,000 1987 Update tin sets produced by Fleer), since the price of the "tin" glossy cards is now the same as the regular set.

	MINT	EXC	G-VG
COMPLETE SET (132)	18.00	8.50	1.70
COMMON PLAYER (1-132)	.06	.03	.00
☐ U1 Scott Bankhead	.15	.04	.01
☐ U2 Eric Bell	.10	.05	.01
☐ U3 Juan Beniquez	.06	.03	.00
☐ U4 Juan Berenguer	.06	.03	.00
☐ U5 Mike Birkbeck	.15	.07	.01
☐ U6 Randy Bockus	.10	.05	.01
☐ U7 Greg Booker	.06	.03	.00
☐ U8 Thad Bosley	.06	.03	.00
☐ U9 Greg Brock	.06	.03	.00

		MINT	EXC	G-VG
☐	U10 Bob Brower	.12	.06	.01
☐	U11 Chris Brown	.10	.05	.01
☐	U12 Jerry Browne	.06	.03	.00
☐	U13 Ralph Bryant	.10	.05	.01
☐	U14 DeWayne Buice	.10	.05	.01
☐	U15 Ellis Burks	2.50	1.25	.25
☐	U16 Casey Candaele	.10	.05	.01
☐	U17 Steve Carlton	.35	.17	.03
☐	U18 Juan Castillo	.06	.03	.00
☐	U19 Chuck Crim	.10	.05	.01
☐	U20 Mark Davidson	.12	.06	.01
☐	U21 Mark Davis	.20	.10	.02
☐	U22 Storm Davis	.15	.07	.01
☐	U23 Bill Dawley	.06	.03	.00
☐	U24 Andre Dawson	.35	.17	.03
☐	U25 Brian Dayett	.06	.03	.00
☐	U26 Rick Dempsey	.06	.03	.00
☐	U27 Ken Dowell	.10	.05	.01
☐	U28 Dave Dravecky	.15	.07	.01
☐	U29 Mike Dunne	.20	.10	.02
☐	U30 Dennis Eckersley ...	.30	.15	.03
☐	U31 Cecil Fielder	.10	.05	.01
☐	U32 Brian Fisher	.10	.05	.01
☐	U33 Willie Fraser	.10	.05	.01
☐	U34 Ken Gerhart	.12	.06	.01
☐	U35 Jim Gott	.10	.05	.01
☐	U36 Dan Gladden	.10	.05	.01
☐	U37 Mike Greenwell	4.00	2.00	.40
☐	U38 Cecilio Guante	.06	.03	.00
☐	U39 Albert Hall	.06	.03	.00
☐	U40 Atlee Hammaker	.06	.03	.00
☐	U41 Mickey Hatcher	.06	.03	.00
☐	U42 Mike Heath	.06	.03	.00
☐	U43 Neal Heaton	.06	.03	.00
☐	U44 Mike Henneman ...	.30	.15	.03
☐	U45 Guy Hoffman	.10	.05	.01
☐	U46 Charles Hudson	.06	.03	.00
☐	U47 Chuck Jackson	.12	.06	.01
☐	U48 Mike Jackson	.15	.07	.01
☐	U49 Reggie Jackson	.50	.25	.05
☐	U50 Chris James	.30	.15	.03
☐	U51 Dion James	.10	.05	.01
☐	U52 Stan Javier	.10	.05	.01
☐	U53 Stan Jefferson	.20	.10	.02
☐	U54 Jimmy Jones	.12	.06	.01
☐	U55 Tracy Jones	.15	.07	.01
☐	U56 Terry Kennedy	.06	.03	.00
☐	U57 Mike Kingery	.10	.05	.01
☐	U58 Ray Knight	.10	.05	.01

		MINT	EXC	G-VG			MINT	EXC	G-VG
☐	U59 Gene Larkin	.35	.17	.03	☐	U106 Mark Salas	.06	.03	.00
☐	U60 Mike LaValliere	.10	.05	.01	☐	U107 Dave Schmidt	.10	.05	.01
☐	U61 Jack Lazorko	.10	.05	.01	☐	U108 Kevin Seitzer ERR	1.00	.50	.10
☐	U62 Terry Leach	.12	.06	.01		(wrong birth year)			
☐	U63 Rick Leach	.06	.03	.00	☐	U109 John Shelby	.06	.03	.00
☐	U64 Craig Lefferts	.10	.05	.01	☐	U110 John Smiley	.40	.20	.04
☐	U65 Jim Lindeman	.12	.06	.01	☐	U111 Lary Sorensen	.06	.03	.00
☐	U66 Bill Long	.12	.06	.01	☐	U112 Chris Speier	.06	.03	.00
☐	U67 Mike Loynd	.10	.05	.01	☐	U113 Randy St. Claire	.06	.03	.00
☐	U68 Greg Maddux	1.00	.50	.10	☐	U114 Jim Sundberg	.06	.03	.00
☐	U69 Bill Madlock	.12	.06	.01	☐	U115 B.J. Surhoff	.35	.17	.03
☐	U70 Dave Magadan	.35	.17	.03	☐	U116 Greg Swindell	.60	.30	.06
☐	U71 Joe Magrane	1.25	.60	.12	☐	U117 Danny Tartabull	.35	.17	.03
☐	U72 Fred Manrique	.12	.06	.01	☐	U118 Dorn Taylor	.10	.05	.01
☐	U73 Mike Mason	.06	.03	.00	☐	U119 Lee Tunnell	.06	.03	.00
☐	U74 Lloyd McClendon	.30	.15	.03	☐	U120 Ed VandeBerg	.06	.03	.00
☐	U75 Fred McGriff	2.25	1.10	.22	☐	U121 Andy Van Slyke	.20	.10	.02
☐	U76 Mark McGwire	3.00	1.50	.30	☐	U122 Gary Ward	.10	.05	.01
☐	U77 Mark McLemore	.06	.03	.00	☐	U123 Devon White	.35	.17	.03
☐	U78 Kevin McReynolds	.30	.15	.03	☐	U124 Alan Wiggins	.06	.03	.00
☐	U79 Dave Meads	.10	.05	.01	☐	U125 Bill Wilkinson	.10	.05	.01
☐	U80 Greg Minton	.06	.03	.00	☐	U126 Jim Winn	.06	.03	.00
☐	U81 John Mitchell	.15	.07	.01	☐	U127 Frank Williams	.06	.03	.00
☐	U82 Kevin Mitchell	2.00	1.00	.20	☐	U128 Ken Williams	.15	.07	.01
☐	U83 John Morris	.06	.03	.00	☐	U129 Matt Williams	2.50	1.25	.25
☐	U84 Jeff Musselman	.15	.07	.01	☐	U130 Herm Winningham	.10	.05	.01
☐	U85 Randy Myers	.50	.25	.05	☐	U131 Matt Young	.06	.03	.00
☐	U86 Gene Nelson	.06	.03	.00	☐	U132 Checklist	.06	.01	.00
☐	U87 Joe Niekro	.15	.07	.01					
☐	U88 Tom Nieto	.06	.03	.00					
☐	U89 Reid Nichols	.06	.03	.00					
☐	U90 Matt Nokes	.50	.25	.05					
☐	U91 Dickie Noles	.06	.03	.00					
☐	U92 Edwin Nunez	.06	.03	.00					
☐	U93 Jose Nunez	.15	.07	.01					
☐	U94 Paul O'Neill	.30	.15	.03					
☐	U95 Jim Paciorek	.10	.05	.01					
☐	U96 Lance Parrish	.12	.06	.01					
☐	U97 Bill Pecota	.12	.06	.01					
☐	U98 Tony Pena	.12	.06	.01					
☐	U99 Luis Polonia	.30	.15	.03					
☐	U100 Randy Ready	.10	.05	.01					
☐	U101 Jeff Reardon	.15	.07	.01					
☐	U102 Gary Redus	.06	.03	.00					
☐	U103 Rick Rhoden	.10	.05	.01					
☐	U104 Wally Ritchie	.10	.05	.01					
☐	U105 Jeff Robinson	.35	.17	.03					
	(wrong Jeff's								
	stats on back)								

1988 Fleer

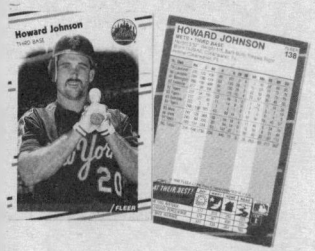

This 660-card set features a distinctive white background with red and blue diagonal stripes across the card. The backs are printed in gray and red on white card stock. The bottom of the card back shows an innovative breakdown of the player's demonstrated ability with respect to day, night, home, and road games. Cards are numbered on the back and are again the standard 2 ½" by 3 ½". Cards are again organized numerically by teams, i.e., World Champion Twins (1-25), St. Louis Cardinals (26-50), Detroit Tigers (51-75), San Francisco Giants (76-101), Toronto Blue Jays (102-126), New York Mets (127-154), Milwaukee Brewers (155-178), Montreal Expos (179-201), New York Yankees (202-226), Cincinnati Reds (227-250), Kansas City Royals (251-274), Oakland A's (275-296), Philadelphia Phillies (297-320), Pittsburgh Pirates (321-342), Boston Red Sox (343-367), Seattle Mariners (368-390), Chicago White Sox (391-413), Chicago Cubs (414-436), Houston Astros (437-460), Texas Rangers (461-483), California Angels (484-507), Los Angeles Dodgers (508-530), Atlanta Braves (531-552), Baltimore Orioles (553-575), San Diego Padres (576-599), and Cleveland Indians (600-621). The last 39 cards in the set consist of Specials (622-640), Rookie Pairs (641-653), and checklists (654-660). Cards 90 and 91 are incorrectly numbered on the checklist card #654. Fleer also produced a "limited" edition version of this set with glossy coating and packaged in a "tin." However, this tin set

was apparently not limited enough (estimated between 40,000 and 60,000 1988 tin sets produced by Fleer), since the price of the "tin" glossy cards is now only double the price of the regular set.

			MINT	EXC	G-VG
	COMPLETE SET (660)		32.00	16.00	3.20
	COMMON PLAYER (1-660)		.03	.01	.00
☐	1	Keith Atherton	.10	.02	.01
☐	2	Don Baylor	.08	.04	.01
☐	3	Juan Berenguer	.03	.01	.00
☐	4	Bert Blyleven	.08	.04	.01
☐	5	Tom Brunansky	.10	.05	.01
☐	6	Randy Bush	.03	.01	.00
☐	7	Steve Carlton	.18	.09	.01
☐	8	Mark Davidson	.10	.05	.01
☐	9	George Frazier	.03	.01	.00
☐	10	Gary Gaetti	.12	.06	.01
☐	11	Greg Gagne	.03	.01	.00
☐	12	Dan Gladden	.06	.03	.00
☐	13	Kent Hrbek	.12	.06	.01
☐	14	Gene Larkin	.25	.12	.02
☐	15	Tim Laudner	.03	.01	.00
☐	16	Steve Lombardozzi	.03	.01	.00
☐	17	Al Newman	.03	.01	.00
☐	18	Joe Niekro	.06	.03	.00
☐	19	Kirby Puckett	.60	.30	.06
☐	20	Jeff Reardon	.08	.04	.01
☐	21A	Dan Schatzeder ERR	.15	.07	.01
		(misspelled Schatza-			
		der on card front)			
☐	21B	Dan Schatzeder COR	.06	.03	.00
☐	22	Roy Smalley	.03	.01	.00
☐	23	Mike Smithson	.03	.01	.00
☐	24	Les Straker	.10	.05	.01
☐	25	Frank Viola	.15	.07	.01
☐	26	Jack Clark	.15	.07	.01
☐	27	Vince Coleman	.18	.09	.01
☐	28	Danny Cox	.03	.01	.00
☐	29	Bill Dawley	.03	.01	.00
☐	30	Ken Dayley	.03	.01	.00
☐	31	Doug DeCinces	.06	.03	.00
☐	32	Curt Ford	.03	.01	.00
☐	33	Bob Forsch	.03	.01	.00
☐	34	David Green	.03	.01	.00
☐	35	Tom Herr	.03	.01	.00
☐	36	Ricky Horton	.03	.01	.00
☐	37	Lance Johnson	.18	.09	.01

			MINT	EXC	G-VG				MINT	EXC	G-VG
☐	38	Steve Lake	.03	.01	.00	☐	81	Dave Dravecky	.08	.04	.01
☐	39	Jim Lindeman	.06	.03	.00	☐	82	Scott Garrelts	.06	.03	.00
☐	40	Joe Magrane	.75	.35	.07	☐	83	Atlee Hammaker	.03	.01	.00
☐	41	Greg Mathews	.03	.01	.00	☐	84	Dave Henderson	.06	.03	.00
☐	42	Willie McGee	.10	.05	.01	☐	85	Mike Krukow	.03	.01	.00
☐	43	John Morris	.03	.01	.00	☐	86	Mike LaCoss	.03	.01	.00
☐	44	Jose Oquendo	.03	.01	.00	☐	87	Craig Lefferts	.06	.03	.00
☐	45	Tony Pena	.06	.03	.00	☐	88	Jeff Leonard	.06	.03	.00
☐	46	Terry Pendleton	.03	.01	.00	☐	89	Candy Maldonado	.06	.03	.00
☐	47	Ozzie Smith	.15	.07	.01	☐	90	Eddie Milner	.03	.01	.00
☐	48	John Tudor	.08	.04	.01	☐	91	Bob Melvin	.03	.01	.00
☐	49	Lee Tunnell	.03	.01	.00	☐	92	Kevin Mitchell	1.00	.50	.10
☐	50	Todd Worrell	.10	.05	.01	☐	93	Jon Perlman	.08	.04	.01
☐	51	Doyle Alexander	.03	.01	.00	☐	94	Rick Reuschel	.08	.04	.01
☐	52	Dave Bergman	.03	.01	.00	☐	95	Don Robinson	.03	.01	.00
☐	53	Tom Brookens	.03	.01	.00	☐	96	Chris Speier	.03	.01	.00
☐	54	Darrell Evans	.08	.04	.01	☐	97	Harry Spilman	.03	.01	.00
☐	55	Kirk Gibson	.20	.10	.02	☐	98	Robbie Thompson	.06	.03	.00
☐	56	Mike Heath	.03	.01	.00	☐	99	Jose Uribe	.03	.01	.00
☐	57	Mike Henneman	.25	.12	.02	☐	100	Mark Wasinger	.15	.07	.01
☐	58	Willie Hernandez	.06	.03	.00	☐	101	Matt Williams	2.00	1.00	.20
☐	59	Larry Herndon	.03	.01	.00	☐	102	Jesse Barfield	.12	.06	.01
☐	60	Eric King	.03	.01	.00	☐	103	George Bell	.18	.09	.01
☐	61	Chet Lemon	.03	.01	.00	☐	104	Juan Beniquez	.03	.01	.00
☐	62	Scott Lusader	.15	.07	.01	☐	105	John Cerutti	.03	.01	.00
☐	63	Bill Madlock	.06	.03	.00	☐	106	Jim Clancy	.03	.01	.00
☐	64	Jack Morris	.10	.05	.01	☐	107	Rob Ducey	.20	.10	.02
☐	65	Jim Morrison	.03	.01	.00	☐	108	Mark Eichhorn	.03	.01	.00
☐	66	Matt Nokes	.40	.20	.04	☐	109	Tony Fernandez	.10	.05	.01
☐	67	Dan Petry	.03	.01	.00	☐	110	Cecil Fielder	.03	.01	.00
☐	68A	Jeff Robinson ERR	1.00	.50	.10	☐	111	Kelly Gruber	.06	.03	.00
		Detroit Tigers				☐	112	Tom Henke	.06	.03	.00
		(stats for other Jeff				☐	113A	Garth Iorg ERR	.15	.07	.01
		Robinson on card						(misspelled Iorq			
		back)						on card front)			
☐	68B	Jeff Robinson COR	.40	.20	.04	☐	113B	Garth Iorg COR	.06	.03	.00
		Detroit Tigers				☐	114	Jimmy Key	.06	.03	.00
☐	69	Pat Sheridan	.03	.01	.00	☐	115	Rick Leach	.03	.01	.00
☐	70	Nate Snell	.03	.01	.00	☐	116	Manny Lee	.06	.03	.00
☐	71	Frank Tanana	.03	.01	.00	☐	117	Nelson Liriano	.25	.12	.02
☐	72	Walt Terrell	.03	.01	.00	☐	118	Fred McGriff	1.75	.85	.17
☐	73	Mark Thurmond	.03	.01	.00	☐	119	Lloyd Moseby	.06	.03	.00
☐	74	Alan Trammell	.15	.07	.01	☐	120	Rance Mulliniks	.03	.01	.00
☐	75	Lou Whitaker	.12	.06	.01	☐	121	Jeff Musselman	.08	.04	.01
☐	76	Mike Aldrete	.03	.01	.00	☐	122	Jose Nunez	.15	.07	.01
☐	77	Bob Brenly	.03	.01	.00	☐	123	Dave Stieb	.08	.04	.01
☐	78	Will Clark	3.50	1.75	.35	☐	124	Willie Upshaw	.03	.01	.00
☐	79	Chili Davis	.06	.03	.00	☐	125	Duane Ward	.08	.04	.01
☐	80	Kelly Downs	.06	.03	.00	☐	126	Ernie Whitt	.03	.01	.00

		MINT	EXC	G-VG				MINT	EXC	G-VG
☐	127 Rick Aguilera	.03	.01	.00	☐	175 B.J. Surhoff	.15	.07	.01
☐	128 Wally Backman	.03	.01	.00	☐	176 Dale Sveum	.03	.01	.00
☐	129 Mark Carreon	.12	.06	.01	☐	177 Bill Wegman	.03	.01	.00
☐	130 Gary Carter	.15	.07	.01	☐	178 Robin Yount	.30	.15	.03
☐	131 David Cone	1.25	.60	.12	☐	179 Hubie Brooks	.08	.04	.01
☐	132 Ron Darling	.10	.05	.01	☐	180 Tim Burke	.06	.03	.00
☐	133 Len Dykstra	.08	.04	.01	☐	181 Casey Candaele	.03	.01	.00
☐	134 Sid Fernandez	.08	.04	.01	☐	182 Mike Fitzgerald	.03	.01	.00
☐	135 Dwight Gooden	.60	.30	.06	☐	183 Tom Foley	.03	.01	.00
☐	136 Keith Hernandez	.18	.09	.01	☐	184 Andres Galarraga	.25	.12	.02
☐	137 Gregg Jefferies	4.00	2.00	.40	☐	185 Neal Heaton	.03	.01	.00
☐	138 Howard Johnson	.20	.10	.02	☐	186 Wallace Johnson	.03	.01	.00
☐	139 Terry Leach	.06	.03	.00	☐	187 Vance Law	.03	.01	.00
☐	140 Barry Lyons	.25	.12	.02	☐	188 Dennis Martinez	.03	.01	.00
☐	141 Dave Magadan	.12	.06	.01	☐	189 Bob McClure	.03	.01	.00
☐	142 Roger McDowell	.06	.03	.00	☐	190 Andy McGaffigan	.03	.01	.00
☐	143 Kevin McReynolds	.15	.07	.01	☐	191 Reid Nichols	.03	.01	.00
☐	144 Keith Miller	.20	.10	.02	☐	192 Pascual Perez	.08	.04	.01
	(New York Mets)				☐	193 Tim Raines	.20	.10	.02
☐	145 John Mitchell	.15	.07	.01	☐	194 Jeff Reed	.03	.01	.00
☐	146 Randy Myers	.35	.17	.03	☐	195 Bob Sebra	.03	.01	.00
☐	147 Bob Ojeda	.06	.03	.00	☐	196 Bryn Smith	.06	.03	.00
☐	148 Jesse Orosco	.03	.01	.00	☐	197 Randy St. Claire	.03	.01	.00
☐	149 Rafael Santana	.03	.01	.00	☐	198 Tim Wallach	.08	.04	.01
☐	150 Doug Sisk	.03	.01	.00	☐	199 Mitch Webster	.03	.01	.00
☐	151 Darryl Strawberry	.50	.25	.05	☐	200 Herm Winningham	.03	.01	.00
☐	152 Tim Teufel	.03	.01	.00	☐	201 Floyd Youmans	.03	.01	.00
☐	153 Gene Walter	.03	.01	.00	☐	202 Brad Arnsberg	.10	.05	.01
☐	154 Mookie Wilson	.06	.03	.00	☐	203 Rick Cerone	.03	.01	.00
☐	155 Jay Aldrich	.08	.04	.01	☐	204 Pat Clements	.03	.01	.00
☐	156 Chris Bosio	.06	.03	.00	☐	205 Henry Cotto	.03	.01	.00
☐	157 Glenn Braggs	.08	.04	.01	☐	206 Mike Easler	.03	.01	.00
☐	158 Greg Brock	.03	.01	.00	☐	207 Ron Guidry	.08	.04	.01
☐	159 Juan Castillo	.06	.03	.00	☐	208 Bill Gullickson	.03	.01	.00
☐	160 Mark Clear	.03	.01	.00	☐	209 Rickey Henderson	.30	.15	.03
☐	161 Cecil Cooper	.08	.04	.01	☐	210 Charles Hudson	.03	.01	.00
☐	162 Chuck Crim	.10	.05	.01	☐	211 Tommy John	.10	.05	.01
☐	163 Rob Deer	.08	.04	.01	☐	212 Roberto Kelly	1.00	.50	.10
☐	164 Mike Felder	.03	.01	.00	☐	213 Ron Kittle	.08	.04	.01
☐	165 Jim Gantner	.03	.01	.00	☐	214 Don Mattingly	1.50	.75	.15
☐	166 Ted Higuera	.10	.05	.01	☐	215 Bobby Meacham	.03	.01	.00
☐	167 Steve Kiefer	.03	.01	.00	☐	216 Mike Pagliarulo	.06	.03	.00
☐	168 Rick Manning	.03	.01	.00	☐	217 Dan Pasqua	.03	.01	.00
☐	169 Paul Molitor	.12	.06	.01	☐	218 Willie Randolph	.06	.03	.00
☐	170 Juan Nieves	.03	.01	.00	☐	219 Rick Rhoden	.03	.01	.00
☐	171 Dan Plesac	.06	.03	.00	☐	220 Dave Righetti	.08	.04	.01
☐	172 Earnest Riles	.03	.01	.00	☐	221 Jerry Royster	.03	.01	.00
☐	173 Bill Schroeder	.03	.01	.00	☐	222 Tim Stoddard	.03	.01	.00
☐	174 Steve Stanicek	.12	.06	.01	☐	223 Wayne Tolleson	.03	.01	.00

		MINT	EXC	G-VG			MINT	EXC	G-VG
☐ 224	Gary Ward	.03	.01	.00	☐ 272	Gary Thurman	.25	.12	.02
☐ 225	Claudell Washington	.06	.03	.00	☐ 273	Frank White	.06	.03	.00
☐ 226	Dave Winfield	.25	.12	.02	☐ 274	Willie Wilson	.06	.03	.00
☐ 227	Buddy Bell	.08	.04	.01	☐ 275	Tony Bernazard	.03	.01	.00
☐ 228	Tom Browning	.08	.04	.01	☐ 276	Jose Canseco	1.75	.85	.17
☐ 229	Dave Concepcion	.08	.04	.01	☐ 277	Mike Davis	.03	.01	.00
☐ 230	Kal Daniels	.18	.09	.01	☐ 278	Storm Davis	.08	.04	.01
☐ 231	Eric Davis	.75	.35	.07	☐ 279	Dennis Eckersley	.12	.06	.01
☐ 232	Bo Diaz	.03	.01	.00	☐ 280	Alfredo Griffin	.06	.03	.00
☐ 233	Nick Esasky	.08	.04	.01	☐ 281	Rick Honeycutt	.03	.01	.00
☐ 234	John Franco	.08	.04	.01	☐ 282	Jay Howell	.06	.03	.00
☐ 235	Guy Hoffman	.03	.01	.00	☐ 283	Reggie Jackson	.30	.15	.03
☐ 236	Tom Hume	.03	.01	.00	☐ 284	Dennis Lamp	.03	.01	.00
☐ 237	Tracy Jones	.03	.01	.00	☐ 285	Carney Lansford	.10	.05	.01
☐ 238	Bill Landrum	.25	.12	.02	☐ 286	Mark McGwire	2.50	1.25	.25
☐ 239	Barry Larkin	.30	.15	.03	☐ 287	Dwayne Murphy	.03	.01	.00
☐ 240	Terry McGriff	.10	.05	.01	☐ 288	Gene Nelson	.03	.01	.00
☐ 241	Rob Murphy	.03	.01	.00	☐ 289	Steve Ontiveros	.03	.01	.00
☐ 242	Ron Oester	.03	.01	.00	☐ 290	Tony Phillips	.03	.01	.00
☐ 243	Dave Parker	.10	.05	.01	☐ 291	Eric Plunk	.03	.01	.00
☐ 244	Pat Perry	.03	.01	.00	☐ 292	Luis Polonia	.25	.12	.02
☐ 245	Ted Power	.03	.01	.00	☐ 293	Rick Rodriguez	.08	.04	.01
☐ 246	Dennis Rasmussen	.06	.03	.00	☐ 294	Terry Steinbach	.10	.05	.01
☐ 247	Ron Robinson	.03	.01	.00	☐ 295	Dave Stewart	.12	.06	.01
☐ 248	Kurt Stillwell	.06	.03	.00	☐ 296	Curt Young	.03	.01	.00
☐ 249	Jeff Treadway	.30	.15	.03	☐ 297	Luis Aguayo	.03	.01	.00
☐ 250	Frank Williams	.03	.01	.00	☐ 298	Steve Bedrosian	.08	.04	.01
☐ 251	Steve Balboni	.03	.01	.00	☐ 299	Jeff Calhoun	.03	.01	.00
☐ 252	Bud Black	.03	.01	.00	☐ 300	Don Carman	.03	.01	.00
☐ 253	Thad Bosley	.03	.01	.00	☐ 301	Todd Frohwirth	.15	.07	.01
☐ 254	George Brett	.30	.15	.03	☐ 302	Greg Gross	.03	.01	.00
☐ 255	John Davis	.15	.07	.01	☐ 303	Kevin Gross	.03	.01	.00
☐ 256	Steve Farr	.03	.01	.00	☐ 304	Von Hayes	.08	.04	.01
☐ 257	Gene Garber	.03	.01	.00	☐ 305	Keith Hughes	.18	.09	.01
☐ 258	Jerry Don Gleaton	.03	.01	.00	☐ 306	Mike Jackson	.15	.07	.01
☐ 259	Mark Gubicza	.10	.05	.01	☐ 307	Chris James	.15	.07	.01
☐ 260	Bo Jackson	2.50	1.25	.25	☐ 308	Steve Jeltz	.03	.01	.00
☐ 261	Danny Jackson	.08	.04	.01	☐ 309	Mike Maddux	.03	.01	.00
☐ 262	Ross Jones	.08	.04	.01	☐ 310	Lance Parrish	.10	.05	.01
☐ 263	Charlie Leibrandt	.03	.01	.00	☐ 311	Shane Rawley	.03	.01	.00
☐ 264	Bill Pecota	.08	.04	.01	☐ 312	Wally Ritchie	.08	.04	.01
☐ 265	Melido Perez	.25	.12	.02	☐ 313	Bruce Ruffin	.03	.01	.00
☐ 266	Jamie Quirk	.03	.01	.00	☐ 314	Juan Samuel	.08	.04	.01
☐ 267	Dan Quisenberry	.08	.04	.01	☐ 315	Mike Schmidt	.40	.20	.04
☐ 268	Bret Saberhagen	.25	.12	.02	☐ 316	Rick Schu	.03	.01	.00
☐ 269	Angel Salazar	.03	.01	.00	☐ 317	Jeff Stone	.03	.01	.00
☐ 270	Kevin Seitzer UER	.45	.22	.04	☐ 318	Kent Tekulve	.03	.01	.00
	(wrong birth year)				☐ 319	Milt Thompson	.03	.01	.00
☐ 271	Danny Tartabull	.20	.10	.02	☐ 320	Glenn Wilson	.03	.01	.00

		MINT	EXC	G-VG			MINT	EXC	G-VG
☐ 321	Rafael Belliard	.03	.01	.00	☐ 367	Bob Stanley	.03	.01	.00
☐ 322	Barry Bonds	.20	.10	.02	☐ 368	Scott Bankhead	.08	.04	.01
☐ 323	Bobby Bonilla UER	.20	.10	.02	☐ 369	Phil Bradley	.06	.03	.00
	(wrong birth year)				☐ 370	Scott Bradley	.03	.01	.00
☐ 324	Sid Bream	.03	.01	.00	☐ 371	Mickey Brantley	.06	.03	.00
☐ 325	John Cangelosi	.03	.01	.00	☐ 372	Mike Campbell	.15	.07	.01
☐ 326	Mike Diaz	.03	.01	.00	☐ 373	Alvin Davis	.10	.05	.01
☐ 327	Doug Drabek	.06	.03	.00	☐ 374	Lee Guetterman	.03	.01	.00
☐ 328	Mike Dunne	.10	.05	.01	☐ 375	Dave Hengel	.12	.06	.01
☐ 329	Brian Fisher	.03	.01	.00	☐ 376	Mike Kingery	.03	.01	.00
☐ 330	Brett Gideon	.10	.05	.01	☐ 377	Mark Langston	.12	.06	.01
☐ 331	Terry Harper	.03	.01	.00	☐ 378	Edgar Martinez	.25	.12	.02
☐ 332	Bob Kipper	.03	.01	.00	☐ 379	Mike Moore	.08	.04	.01
☐ 333	Mike LaValliere	.03	.01	.00	☐ 380	Mike Morgan	.06	.03	.00
☐ 334	Jose Lind	.20	.10	.02	☐ 381	John Moses	.03	.01	.00
☐ 335	Junior Ortiz	.03	.01	.00	☐ 382	Donnell Nixon	.15	.07	.01
☐ 336	Vincent Palacios	.08	.04	.01	☐ 383	Edwin Nunez	.03	.01	.00
☐ 337	Bob Patterson	.08	.04	.01	☐ 384	Ken Phelps	.06	.03	.00
☐ 338	Al Pedrique	.08	.04	.01	☐ 385	Jim Presley	.06	.03	.00
☐ 339	R.J. Reynolds	.03	.01	.00	☐ 386	Rey Quinones	.03	.01	.00
☐ 340	John Smiley	.25	.12	.02	☐ 387	Jerry Reed	.03	.01	.00
☐ 341	Andy Van Slyke UER	.15	.07	.01	☐ 388	Harold Reynolds	.06	.03	.00
	(wrong batting and				☐ 389	Dave Valle	.06	.03	.00
	throwing listed)				☐ 390	Bill Wilkinson	.10	.05	.01
☐ 342	Bob Walk	.03	.01	.00	☐ 391	Harold Baines	.10	.05	.01
☐ 343	Marty Barrett	.06	.03	.00	☐ 392	Floyd Bannister	.03	.01	.00
☐ 344	Todd Benzinger	.40	.20	.04	☐ 393	Daryl Boston	.03	.01	.00
☐ 345	Wade Boggs	1.00	.50	.10	☐ 394	Ivan Calderon	.06	.03	.00
☐ 346	Tom Bolton	.15	.07	.01	☐ 395	Jose DeLeon	.06	.03	.00
☐ 347	Oil Can Boyd	.06	.03	.00	☐ 396	Richard Dotson	.03	.01	.00
☐ 348	Ellis Burks	1.75	.85	.17	☐ 397	Carlton Fisk	.12	.06	.01
☐ 349	Roger Clemens	.75	.35	.07	☐ 398	Ozzie Guillen	.06	.03	.00
☐ 350	Steve Crawford	.08	.04	.01	☐ 399	Ron Hassey	.03	.01	.00
☐ 351	Dwight Evans	.10	.05	.01	☐ 400	Donnie Hill	.03	.01	.00
☐ 352	Wes Gardner	.20	.10	.02	☐ 401	Bob James	.03	.01	.00
☐ 353	Rich Gedman	.03	.01	.00	☐ 402	Dave LaPoint	.03	.01	.00
☐ 354	Mike Greenwell	2.50	1.25	.25	☐ 403	Bill Lindsey	.08	.04	.01
☐ 355	Sam Horn	.20	.10	.02	☐ 404	Bill Long	.08	.04	.01
☐ 356	Bruce Hurst	.10	.05	.01	☐ 405	Steve Lyons	.03	.01	.00
☐ 357	John Marzano	.10	.05	.01	☐ 406	Fred Manrique	.10	.05	.01
☐ 358	Al Nipper	.03	.01	.00	☐ 407	Jack McDowell	.20	.10	.02
☐ 359	Spike Owen	.03	.01	.00	☐ 408	Gary Redus	.03	.01	.00
☐ 360	Jody Reed	.40	.20	.04	☐ 409	Ray Searage	.03	.01	.00
☐ 361	Jim Rice	.15	.07	.01	☐ 410	Bobby Thigpen	.08	.04	.01
☐ 362	Ed Romero	.03	.01	.00	☐ 411	Greg Walker	.06	.03	.00
☐ 363	Kevin Romine	.10	.05	.01	☐ 412	Ken Williams	.15	.07	.01
☐ 364	Joe Sambito	.03	.01	.00	☐ 413	Jim Winn	.03	.01	.00
☐ 365	Calvin Schiraldi	.03	.01	.00	☐ 414	Jody Davis	.03	.01	.00
☐ 366	Jeff Sellers	.03	.01	.00	☐ 415	Andre Dawson	.20	.10	.02

		MINT	EXC	G-VG
☐ 416	Brian Dayett	.03	.01	.00
☐ 417	Bob Dernier	.03	.01	.00
☐ 418	Frank DiPino	.03	.01	.00
☐ 419	Shawon Dunston	.08	.04	.01
☐ 420	Leon Durham	.03	.01	.00
☐ 421	Les Lancaster	.20	.10	.02
☐ 422	Ed Lynch	.03	.01	.00
☐ 423	Greg Maddux	.75	.35	.07
☐ 424	Dave Martinez	.10	.05	.01
☐ 425A	Keith Moreland ERR (photo actually Jody Davis)	4.00	2.00	.40
☐ 425B	Keith Moreland COR (bat on shoulder)	.15	.07	.01
☐ 426	Jamie Moyer	.03	.01	.00
☐ 427	Jerry Mumphrey	.03	.01	.00
☐ 428	Paul Noce	.10	.05	.01
☐ 429	Rafael Palmeiro	.65	.30	.06
☐ 430	Wade Rowdon	.08	.04	.01
☐ 431	Ryne Sandberg	.25	.12	.02
☐ 432	Scott Sanderson	.03	.01	.00
☐ 433	Lee Smith	.06	.03	.00
☐ 434	Jim Sundberg	.03	.01	.00
☐ 435	Rick Sutcliffe	.08	.04	.01
☐ 436	Manny Trillo	.03	.01	.00
☐ 437	Juan Agosto	.03	.01	.00
☐ 438	Larry Andersen	.03	.01	.00
☐ 439	Alan Ashby	.03	.01	.00
☐ 440	Kevin Bass	.06	.03	.00
☐ 441	Ken Caminiti	.30	.15	.03
☐ 442	Rocky Childress	.08	.04	.01
☐ 443	Jose Cruz	.06	.03	.00
☐ 444	Danny Darwin	.03	.01	.00
☐ 445	Glenn Davis	.15	.07	.01
☐ 446	Jim Deshaies	.03	.01	.00
☐ 447	Bill Doran	.06	.03	.00
☐ 448	Ty Gainey	.03	.01	.00
☐ 449	Billy Hatcher	.06	.03	.00
☐ 450	Jeff Heathcock	.03	.01	.00
☐ 451	Bob Knepper	.06	.03	.00
☐ 452	Rob Mallicoat	.08	.04	.01
☐ 453	Dave Meads	.08	.04	.01
☐ 454	Craig Reynolds	.03	.01	.00
☐ 455	Nolan Ryan	.50	.25	.05
☐ 456	Mike Scott	.15	.07	.01
☐ 457	Dave Smith	.03	.01	.00
☐ 458	Denny Walling	.03	.01	.00
☐ 459	Robbie Wine	.08	.04	.01
☐ 460	Gerald Young	.30	.15	.03

		MINT	EXC	G-VG
☐ 461	Bob Brower	.08	.04	.01
☐ 462A	Jerry Browne ERR (photo actually Bob Brower, white player)	4.00	2.00	.40
☐ 462B	Jerry Browne COR (black player)	.15	.07	.01
☐ 463	Steve Buechele	.03	.01	.00
☐ 464	Edwin Correa	.03	.01	.00
☐ 465	Cecil Espy	.15	.07	.01
☐ 466	Scott Fletcher	.03	.01	.00
☐ 467	Jose Guzman	.03	.01	.00
☐ 468	Greg Harris	.03	.01	.00
☐ 469	Charlie Hough	.03	.01	.00
☐ 470	Pete Incaviglia	.15	.07	.01
☐ 471	Paul Kilgus	.12	.06	.01
☐ 472	Mike Loynd	.03	.01	.00
☐ 473	Oddibe McDowell	.06	.03	.00
☐ 474	Dale Mohorcic	.03	.01	.00
☐ 475	Pete O'Brien	.06	.03	.00
☐ 476	Larry Parrish	.03	.01	.00
☐ 477	Geno Petralli	.03	.01	.00
☐ 478	Jeff Russell	.06	.03	.00
☐ 479	Ruben Sierra	.75	.35	.07
☐ 480	Mike Stanley	.03	.01	.00
☐ 481	Curtis Wilkerson	.03	.01	.00
☐ 482	Mitch Williams	.08	.04	.01
☐ 483	Bobby Witt	.06	.03	.00
☐ 484	Tony Armas	.06	.03	.00
☐ 485	Bob Boone	.08	.04	.01
☐ 486	Bill Buckner	.06	.03	.00
☐ 487	DeWayne Buice	.10	.05	.01
☐ 488	Brian Downing	.03	.01	.00
☐ 489	Chuck Finley	.08	.04	.01
☐ 490	Willie Fraser UER (wrong bio stats, for George Hendrick)	.03	.01	.00
☐ 491	Jack Howell	.03	.01	.00
☐ 492	Ruppert Jones	.03	.01	.00
☐ 493	Wally Joyner	.50	.25	.05
☐ 494	Jack Lazorko	.03	.01	.00
☐ 495	Gary Lucas	.03	.01	.00
☐ 496	Kirk McCaskill	.03	.01	.00
☐ 497	Mark McLemore	.03	.01	.00
☐ 498	Darrell Miller	.03	.01	.00
☐ 499	Greg Minton	.03	.01	.00
☐ 500	Donnie Moore	.03	.01	.00
☐ 501	Gus Polidor	.03	.01	.00
☐ 502	Johnny Ray	.06	.03	.00

		MINT	EXC	G-VG			MINT	EXC	G-VG
☐ 503	Mark Ryal	.06	.03	.00	☐ 552	Ozzie Virgil	.03	.01	.00
☐ 504	Dick Schofield	.03	.01	.00	☐ 553	Don Aase	.03	.01	.00
☐ 505	Don Sutton	.12	.06	.01	☐ 554	Jeff Ballard	.45	.22	.04
☐ 506	Devon White	.15	.07	.01	☐ 555	Eric Bell	.06	.03	.00
☐ 507	Mike Witt	.06	.03	.00	☐ 556	Mike Boddicker	.03	.01	.00
☐ 508	Dave Anderson	.03	.01	.00	☐ 557	Ken Dixon	.03	.01	.00
☐ 509	Tim Belcher	.50	.25	.05	☐ 558	Jim Dwyer	.03	.01	.00
☐ 510	Ralph Bryant	.03	.01	.00	☐ 559	Ken Gerhart	.06	.03	.00
☐ 511	Tim Crews	.08	.04	.01	☐ 560	Rene Gonzales	.10	.05	.01
☐ 512	Mike Devereaux	.30	.15	.03	☐ 561	Mike Griffin	.03	.01	.00
☐ 513	Mariano Duncan	.03	.01	.00	☐ 562	John Habyan UER	.08	.04	.01
☐ 514	Pedro Guerrero	.15	.07	.01		(misspelled Hayban			
☐ 515	Jeff Hamilton	.12	.06	.01		on both sides of card)			
☐ 516	Mickey Hatcher	.03	.01	.00	☐ 563	Terry Kennedy	.03	.01	.00
☐ 517	Brad Havens	.03	.01	.00	☐ 564	Ray Knight	.06	.03	.00
☐ 518	Orel Hershiser	.25	.12	.02	☐ 565	Lee Lacy	.03	.01	.00
☐ 519	Shawn Hillegas	.15	.07	.01	☐ 566	Fred Lynn	.10	.05	.01
☐ 520	Ken Howell	.03	.01	.00	☐ 567	Eddie Murray	.15	.07	.01
☐ 521	Tim Leary	.08	.04	.01	☐ 568	Tom Niedenfuer	.03	.01	.00
☐ 522	Mike Marshall	.10	.05	.01	☐ 569	Bill Ripken	.15	.07	.01
☐ 523	Steve Sax	.15	.07	.01	☐ 570	Cal Ripken Jr.	.25	.12	.02
☐ 524	Mike Scioscia	.03	.01	.00	☐ 571	Dave Schmidt	.03	.01	.00
☐ 525	Mike Sharperson	.06	.03	.00	☐ 572	Larry Sheets	.06	.03	.00
☐ 526	John Shelby	.03	.01	.00	☐ 573	Pete Stanicek	.20	.10	.02
☐ 527	Franklin Stubbs	.03	.01	.00	☐ 574	Mark Williamson	.08	.04	.01
☐ 528	Fernando Valenzuela	.12	.06	.01	☐ 575	Mike Young	.03	.01	.00
☐ 529	Bob Welch	.06	.03	.00	☐ 576	Shawn Abner	.15	.07	.01
☐ 530	Matt Young	.03	.01	.00	☐ 577	Greg Booker	.03	.01	.00
☐ 531	Jim Acker	.03	.01	.00	☐ 578	Chris Brown	.03	.01	.00
☐ 532	Paul Assenmacher	.03	.01	.00	☐ 579	Keith Comstock	.08	.04	.01
☐ 533	Jeff Blauser	.30	.15	.03	☐ 580	Joey Cora	.10	.05	.01
☐ 534	Joe Boever	.20	.10	.02	☐ 581	Mark Davis	.06	.03	.00
☐ 535	Martin Clary	.06	.03	.00	☐ 582	Tim Flannery	.03	.01	.00
☐ 536	Kevin Coffman	.10	.05	.01		(with surfboard)			
☐ 537	Jeff Dedmon	.03	.01	.00	☐ 583	Goose Gossage	.08	.04	.01
☐ 538	Ron Gant	.60	.30	.06	☐ 584	Mark Grant	.03	.01	.00
☐ 539	Tom Glavine	.40	.20	.04	☐ 585	Tony Gwynn	.35	.17	.03
☐ 540	Ken Griffey	.08	.04	.01	☐ 586	Andy Hawkins	.03	.01	.00
☐ 541	Albert Hall	.03	.01	.00	☐ 587	Stan Jefferson	.15	.07	.01
☐ 542	Glenn Hubbard	.03	.01	.00	☐ 588	Jimmy Jones	.06	.03	.00
☐ 543	Dion James	.03	.01	.00	☐ 589	John Kruk	.08	.04	.01
☐ 544	Dale Murphy	.30	.15	.03	☐ 590	Shane Mack	.12	.06	.01
☐ 545	Ken Oberkfell	.03	.01	.00	☐ 591	Carmelo Martinez	.03	.01	.00
☐ 546	David Palmer	.03	.01	.00	☐ 592	Lance McCullers			
☐ 547	Gerald Perry	.06	.03	.00		UER	.06	.03	.00
☐ 548	Charlie Puleo	.03	.01	.00		(6'11" tall)			
☐ 549	Ted Simmons	.08	.04	.01	☐ 593	Eric Nolte	.12	.06	.01
☐ 550	Zane Smith	.03	.01	.00	☐ 594	Randy Ready	.03	.01	.00
☐ 551	Andres Thomas	.03	.01	.00	☐ 595	Luis Salazar	.03	.01	.00

		MINT	EXC	G-VG
☐ 596	Benito Santiago	.40	.20	.04
☐ 597	Eric Show	.03	.01	.00
☐ 598	Garry Templeton	.06	.03	.00
☐ 599	Ed Whitson	.03	.01	.00
☐ 600	Scott Bailes	.03	.01	.00
☐ 601	Chris Bando	.03	.01	.00
☐ 602	Jay Bell	.20	.10	.02
☐ 603	Brett Butler	.06	.03	.00
☐ 604	Tom Candiotti	.03	.01	.00
☐ 605	Joe Carter	.20	.10	.02
☐ 606	Carmen Castillo	.03	.01	.00
☐ 607	Brian Dorsett	.10	.05	.01
☐ 608	John Farrell	.25	.12	.02
☐ 609	Julio Franco	.10	.05	.01
☐ 610	Mel Hall	.03	.01	.00
☐ 611	Tommy Hinzo	.10	.05	.01
☐ 612	Brook Jacoby	.06	.03	.00
☐ 613	Doug Jones	.35	.17	.03
☐ 614	Ken Schrom	.03	.01	.00
☐ 615	Cory Snyder	.15	.07	.01
☐ 616	Sammy Stewart	.03	.01	.00
☐ 617	Greg Swindell	.20	.10	.02
☐ 618	Pat Tabler	.06	.03	.00
☐ 619	Ed VandeBerg	.03	.01	.00
☐ 620	Eddie Williams	.18	.09	.01
☐ 621	Rich Yett	.03	.01	.00
☐ 622	Slugging Sophomores	.12	.06	.01
	Wally Joyner			
	Cory Snyder			
☐ 623	Dominican Dynamite	.10	.05	.01
	George Bell			
	Pedro Guerrero			
☐ 624	Oakland's Power			
	Team	.75	.35	.07
	Mark McGwire			
	Jose Canseco			
☐ 625	Classic Relief	.10	.05	.01
	Dave Righetti			
	Dan Plesac			
☐ 626	All Star Righties	.10	.05	.01
	Bret Saberhagen			
	Mike Witt			
	Jack Morris			
☐ 627	Game Closers	.08	.04	.01
	John Franco			
	Steve Bedrosian			
☐ 628	Masters/Double Play .	.12	.06	.01
	Ozzie Smith			
	Ryne Sandberg			

		MINT	EXC	G-VG
☐ 629	Rookie Record Setter	.40	.20	.04
	Mark McGwire			
☐ 630	Changing the Guard .	.75	.35	.07
	Mike Greenwell			
	Ellis Burks			
	Todd Benzinger			
☐ 631	NL Batting Champs .	.18	.09	.01
	Tony Gwynn			
	Tim Raines			
☐ 632	Pitching Magic	.12	.06	.01
	Mike Scott			
	Orel Hershiser			
☐ 633	Big Bats at First	.25	.12	.02
	Pat Tabler			
	Mark McGwire			
☐ 634	Hitting King/Thief	.12	.06	.01
	Tony Gwynn			
	Vince Coleman			
☐ 635	Slugging Shortstops .	.10	.05	.01
	Tony Fernandez			
	Cal Ripken			
	Alan Trammell			
☐ 636	Tried/True Sluggers .	.12	.06	.01
	Mike Schmidt			
	Gary Carter			
☐ 637	Crunch Time	.35	.17	.03
	Darryl Strawberry			
	Eric Davis			
☐ 638	AL All-Stars	.15	.07	.01
	Matt Nokes			
	Kirby Puckett			
☐ 639	NL All-Stars	.10	.05	.01
	Keith Hernandez			
	Dale Murphy			
☐ 640	The O's Brothers ...	.08	.04	.01
	Billy Ripken			
	Cal Ripken			
☐ 641	Mark Grace and			
	Darrin Jackson	7.50	3.75	.75
☐ 642	Damon Berryhill and			
	Jeff Montgomery	1.25	.60	.12
☐ 643	Felix Fermin and			
	Jesse Reid	.12	.06	.01
☐ 644	Greg Myers and			
	Greg Tabor	.15	.07	.01
☐ 645	Joey Meyer and			
	Jim Eppard	.15	.07	.01
☐ 646	Adam Peterson and			
	Randy Velarde	.12	.06	.01

1988 Fleer Update

		MINT	EXC	G-VG
☐ 647	Peter Smith and Chris Gwynn	.35	.17	.03
☐ 648	Tom Newell and Greg Jelks	.12	.06	.01
☐ 649	Mario Diaz and Clay Parker	.35	.17	.03
☐ 650	Jack Savage and Todd Simmons	.15	.07	.01
☐ 651	John Burkett and Kirt Manwaring	.20	.10	.02
☐ 652	Dave Otto and Walt Weiss	1.25	.60	.12
☐ 653	Jeff King and Randell Byers	.35	.17	.03
☐ 654	CL: Twins/Cards .... Tigers/Giants UER (90 Bob Melvin, 91 Eddie Milner)	.06	.01	.00
☐ 655	CL: Blue Jays/Mets Brewers/Expos UER (Mets listed before Blue Jays on card)	.06	.01	.00
☐ 656	CL: Yankees/Reds .. Royals/A's	.06	.01	.00
☐ 657	CL: Phillies/Pirates .. Red Sox/Mariners	.06	.01	.00
☐ 658	CL: White Sox/Cubs .. Astros/Rangers	.06	.01	.00
☐ 659	CL: Angels/Dodgers Braves/Orioles	.06	.01	.00
☐ 660	CL: Padres/Indians .. Rookies/Specials	.06	.01	.00

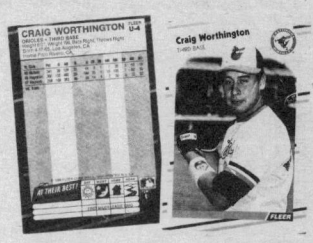

This 132-card set was distributed by Fleer to dealers as a complete set in a custom box. In addition to the complete set of 132 cards, the box also contains 25 Team Logo stickers. The card fronts look very similar to the 1987 Fleer regular issue. The cards are numbered (with a U prefix) alphabetically according to player's last name. Cards measure the standard size, 2 ½" by 3 ½". This was the first Fleer Update set to adopt the Fleer "alphabetical within team" numbering system. Fleer also produced a "limited" edition version of this set with glossy coating and packaged in a "tin." However, this tin set was apparently not limited enough (estimated between 40,000 and 60,000 1988 Update tin sets produced by Fleer), since the price of the "tin" glossy cards is now only double the price of the regular set.

		MINT	EXC	G-VG
	COMPLETE SET (132)	13.50	6.00	1.25
	COMMON PLAYER (1-132)	.05	.02	.00
☐ U1	Jose Bautista	.15	.07	.01
☐ U2	Joe Orsulak	.05	.02	.00
☐ U3	Doug Sisk	.05	.02	.00
☐ U4	Craig Worthington ...	.50	.25	.05
☐ U5	Mike Boddicker	.08	.04	.01
☐ U6	Rick Cerone	.05	.02	.00
☐ U7	Larry Parrish	.05	.02	.00
☐ U8	Lee Smith	.08	.04	.01
☐ U9	Mike Smithson	.05	.02	.00

		MINT	EXC	G-VG
☐ U10	John Trautwein	.10	.05	.01
☐ U11	Sherman Corbett	.12	.06	.01
☐ U12	Chili Davis	.08	.04	.01
☐ U13	Jim Eppard	.05	.02	.00
☐ U14	Bryan Harvey	.25	.12	.02
☐ U15	John Davis	.05	.02	.00
☐ U16	Dave Gallagher	.35	.17	.03
☐ U17	Ricky Horton	.05	.02	.00
☐ U18	Dan Pasqua	.05	.02	.00
☐ U19	Melido Perez	.12	.06	.01
☐ U20	Jose Segura	.12	.06	.01
☐ U21	Andy Allanson	.05	.02	.00
☐ U22	Jon Perlman	.05	.02	.00
☐ U23	Domingo Ramos	.08	.04	.01
☐ U24	Rick Rodriguez	.05	.02	.00
☐ U25	Willie Upshaw	.05	.02	.00
☐ U26	Paul Gibson	.12	.06	.01
☐ U27	Don Heinkel	.12	.06	.01
☐ U28	Ray Knight	.08	.04	.01
☐ U29	Gary Pettis	.08	.04	.01
☐ U30	Luis Salazar	.05	.02	.00
☐ U31	Mike MacFarlane	.18	.09	.01
☐ U32	Jeff Montgomery	.15	.07	.01
☐ U33	Ted Power	.05	.02	.00
☐ U34	Israel Sanchez	.12	.06	.01
☐ U35	Kurt Stillwell	.08	.04	.01
☐ U36	Pat Tabler	.08	.04	.01
☐ U37	Don August	.15	.07	.01
☐ U38	Darryl Hamilton	.25	.12	.02
☐ U39	Jeff Leonard	.08	.04	.01
☐ U40	Joey Meyer	.10	.05	.01
☐ U41	Allan Anderson	.12	.06	.01
☐ U42	Brian Harper	.05	.02	.00
☐ U43	Tom Herr	.05	.02	.00
☐ U44	Charlie Lea	.05	.02	.00
☐ U45	John Moses	.05	.02	.00
	(listed as Hohn on			
	checklist card)			
☐ U46	John Candelaria	.08	.04	.01
☐ U47	Jack Clark	.15	.07	.01
☐ U48	Richard Dotson	.05	.02	.00
☐ U49	Al Leiter	.25	.12	.02
☐ U50	Rafael Santana	.05	.02	.00
☐ U51	Don Slaught	.05	.02	.00
☐ U52	Todd Burns	.35	.17	.03
☐ U53	Dave Henderson	.08	.04	.01
☐ U54	Doug Jennings	.25	.12	.02
☐ U55	Dave Parker	.15	.07	.01
☐ U56	Walt Weiss	.60	.30	.06

		MINT	EXC	G-VG
☐ U57	Bob Welch	.08	.04	.01
☐ U58	Henry Cotto	.05	.02	.00
☐ U59	Mario Diaz UER	.08	.04	.01
	(listed as Marion			
	on card front)			
☐ U60	Mike Jackson	.08	.04	.01
☐ U61	Bill Swift	.08	.04	.01
☐ U62	Jose Cecena	.10	.05	.01
☐ U63	Ray Hayward	.10	.05	.01
☐ U64	Jim Steels UER	.10	.05	.01
	(listed as Jim Steele			
	on card back)			
☐ U65	Pat Borders	.20	.10	.02
☐ U66	Sil Campusano	.25	.12	.02
☐ U67	Mike Flanagan	.08	.04	.01
☐ U68	Todd Stottlemyre	.25	.12	.02
☐ U69	David Wells	.15	.07	.01
☐ U70	Jose Alvarez	.12	.06	.01
☐ U71	Paul Runge	.05	.02	.00
☐ U72	Cesar Jimenez UER	.15	.07	.01
	(card was intended			
	for German Jiminez,			
	it's his photo)			
☐ U73	Pete Smith	.12	.06	.01
☐ U74	John Smoltz	1.75	.85	.17
☐ U75	Damon Berryhill	.30	.15	.03
☐ U76	Goose Gossage	.12	.06	.01
☐ U77	Mark Grace	3.50	1.75	.35
☐ U78	Darrin Jackson	.12	.06	.01
☐ U79	Vance Law	.05	.02	.00
☐ U80	Jeff Pico	.15	.07	.01
☐ U81	Gary Varsho	.20	.10	.02
☐ U82	Tim Birtsas	.05	.02	.00
☐ U83	Rob Dibble	.50	.25	.05
☐ U84	Danny Jackson	.12	.06	.01
☐ U85	Paul O'Neill	.15	.07	.01
☐ U86	Jose Rijo	.10	.05	.01
☐ U87	Chris Sabo	1.00	.50	.10
☐ U88	John Fishel	.15	.07	.01
☐ U89	Craig Biggio	1.00	.50	.10
☐ U90	Terry Puhl	.05	.02	.00
☐ U91	Rafael Ramirez	.05	.02	.00
☐ U92	Louie Meadows	.10	.05	.01
☐ U93	Kirk Gibson	.25	.12	.02
☐ U94	Alfredo Griffin	.08	.04	.01
☐ U95	Jay Howell	.08	.04	.01
☐ U96	Jesse Orosco	.05	.02	.00
☐ U97	Alejandro Pena	.05	.02	.00
☐ U98	Tracy Woodson	.20	.10	.02

1988 Fleer Sticker Cards

		MINT	EXC	G-VG
☐ U99	John Dopson	.20	.10	.02
☐ U100	Brian Holman	.20	.10	.02
☐ U101	Rex Hudler	.05	.02	.00
☐ U102	Jeff Parrett	.08	.04	.01
☐ U103	Nelson Santovenia	.25	.12	.02
☐ U104	Kevin Elster	.15	.07	.01
☐ U105	Jeff Innis	.20	.10	.02
☐ U106	Mackey Sasser	.15	.07	.01
☐ U107	Phil Bradley	.08	.04	.01
☐ U108	Danny Clay	.12	.06	.01
☐ U109	Greg Harris	.05	.02	.00
☐ U110	Ricky Jordan	3.00	1.50	.30
☐ U111	David Palmer	.05	.02	.00
☐ U112	Jim Gott	.08	.04	.01
☐ U113	Tommy Gregg UER (photo actually Randy Milligan)	.25	.12	.02
☐ U114	Barry Jones	.05	.02	.00
☐ U115	Randy Milligan	.25	.12	.02
☐ U116	Luis Alicea	.12	.06	.01
☐ U117	Tom Brunansky	.10	.05	.01
☐ U118	John Costello	.15	.07	.01
☐ U119	Jose DeLeon	.08	.04	.01
☐ U120	Bob Horner	.10	.05	.01
☐ U121	Scott Terry	.12	.06	.01
☐ U122	Roberto Alomar	.50	.25	.05
☐ U123	Dave Leiper	.05	.02	.00
☐ U124	Keith Moreland	.05	.02	.00
☐ U125	Mark Parent	.15	.07	.01
☐ U126	Dennis Rasmussen	.08	.04	.01
☐ U127	Randy Bockus	.05	.02	.00
☐ U128	Brett Butler	.10	.05	.01
☐ U129	Donell Nixon	.08	.04	.01
☐ U130	Earnest Riles	.05	.02	.00
☐ U131	Roger Samuels	.12	.06	.01
☐ U132	Checklist U1-U132	.05	.01	.00

1988 Fleer Sticker Cards

These Star Stickers were distributed as a separate issue by Fleer, with five star stickers and a logo sticker in each wax pack. The 132-card (sticker) set features 2 ½" by 3 ½" full-color fronts and even statistics on the sticker back, which is an indication that the Fleer Company understands that these stickers are rarely used as stickers but more like traditional cards. The card fronts are surrounded by a silver-gray border and the backs are printed in red and black on white card stock.

		MINT	EXC	G-VG
COMPLETE SET (132)		20.00	10.00	2.00
COMMON PLAYER (1-132)		.05	.02	.00
☐ 1	Mike Boddicker	.10	.05	.01
☐ 2	Eddie Murray	.20	.10	.02
☐ 3	Cal Ripken	.25	.12	.02
☐ 4	Larry Sheets	.05	.02	.00
☐ 5	Wade Boggs	1.50	.75	.15
☐ 6	Ellis Burks	1.00	.50	.10
☐ 7	Roger Clemens	.90	.45	.09
☐ 8	Dwight Evans	.10	.05	.01
☐ 9	Mike Greenwell	1.00	.50	.10
☐ 10	Bruce Hurst	.10	.05	.01
☐ 11	Brian Downing	.05	.02	.00
☐ 12	Wally Joyner	.50	.25	.05
☐ 13	Mike Witt	.10	.05	.01
☐ 14	Ivan Calderon	.10	.05	.01

			MINT	EXC	G-VG
☐	15	Jose DeLeon	.10	.05	.01
☐	16	Ozzie Guillen	.10	.05	.01
☐	17	Bobby Thigpen	.15	.07	.01
☐	18	Joe Carter	.15	.07	.01
☐	19	Julio Franco	.15	.07	.01
☐	20	Brook Jacoby	.10	.05	.01
☐	21	Cory Snyder	.20	.10	.02
☐	22	Pat Tabler	.05	.02	.00
☐	23	Doyle Alexander	.05	.02	.00
☐	24	Kirk Gibson	.25	.12	.02
☐	25	Mike Henneman	.10	.05	.01
☐	26	Jack Morris	.15	.07	.01
☐	27	Matt Nokes	.20	.10	.02
☐	28	Walt Terrell	.05	.02	.00
☐	29	Alan Trammell	.25	.12	.02
☐	30	George Brett	.45	.22	.04
☐	31	Charlie Leibrandt	.05	.02	.00
☐	32	Bret Saberhagen	.30	.15	.03
☐	33	Kevin Seitzer	.35	.17	.03
☐	34	Danny Tartabull	.25	.12	.02
☐	35	Frank White	.10	.05	.01
☐	36	Rob Deer	.10	.05	.01
☐	37	Ted Higuera	.10	.05	.01
☐	38	Paul Molitor	.15	.07	.01
☐	39	Dan Plesac	.10	.05	.01
☐	40	Robin Yount	.45	.22	.04
☐	41	Bert Blyleven	.15	.07	.01
☐	42	Tom Brunansky	.15	.07	.01
☐	43	Gary Gaetti	.15	.07	.01
☐	44	Kent Hrbek	.20	.10	.02
☐	45	Kirby Puckett	.60	.30	.06
☐	46	Jeff Reardon	.10	.05	.01
☐	47	Frank Viola	.15	.07	.01
☐	48	Don Mattingly	2.00	1.00	.20
☐	49	Mike Pagliarulo	.10	.05	.01
☐	50	Willie Randolph	.10	.05	.01
☐	51	Rick Rhoden	.05	.02	.00
☐	52	Dave Righetti	.15	.07	.01
☐	53	Dave Winfield	.25	.12	.02
☐	54	Jose Canseco	2.00	1.00	.20
☐	55	Carney Lansford	.15	.07	.01
☐	56	Mark McGwire	1.00	.50	.10
☐	57	Dave Stewart	.15	.07	.01
☐	58	Curt Young	.05	.02	.00
☐	59	Alvin Davis	.10	.05	.01
☐	60	Mark Langston	.20	.10	.02
☐	61	Ken Phelps	.05	.02	.00
☐	62	Harold Reynolds	.05	.02	.00
☐	63	Scott Fletcher	.05	.02	.00
☐	64	Charlie Hough	.05	.02	.00
☐	65	Pete Incaviglia	.20	.10	.02
☐	66	Oddibe McDowell	.10	.05	.01
☐	67	Pete O'Brien	.10	.05	.01
☐	68	Larry Parrish	.05	.02	.00
☐	69	Ruben Sierra	.75	.35	.07
☐	70	Jesse Barfield	.15	.07	.01
☐	71	George Bell	.20	.10	.02
☐	72	Tony Fernandez	.15	.07	.01
☐	73	Tom Henke	.05	.02	.00
☐	74	Jimmy Key	.10	.05	.01
☐	75	Lloyd Moseby	.10	.05	.01
☐	76	Dion James	.05	.02	.00
☐	77	Dale Murphy	.40	.20	.04
☐	78	Zane Smith	.05	.02	.00
☐	79	Andre Dawson	.25	.12	.02
☐	80	Ryne Sandberg	.30	.15	.03
☐	81	Rick Sutcliffe	.10	.05	.01
☐	82	Kal Daniels	.15	.07	.01
☐	83	Eric Davis	.90	.45	.09
☐	84	John Franco	.10	.05	.01
☐	85	Kevin Bass	.05	.02	.00
☐	86	Glenn Davis	.15	.07	.01
☐	87	Bill Doran	.10	.05	.01
☐	88	Nolan Ryan	1.25	.60	.12
☐	89	Mike Scott	.15	.07	.01
☐	90	Dave Smith	.05	.02	.00
☐	91	Pedro Guerrero	.20	.10	.02
☐	92	Orel Hershiser	.45	.22	.04
☐	93	Steve Sax	.15	.07	.01
☐	94	Fernando Valenzuela	.15	.07	.01
☐	95	Tim Burke	.10	.05	.01
☐	96	Andres Galarraga	.25	.12	.02
☐	97	Tim Raines	.25	.12	.02
☐	98	Tim Wallach	.10	.05	.01
☐	99	Mitch Webster	.05	.02	.00
☐	100	Ron Darling	.10	.05	.01
☐	101	Sid Fernandez	.10	.05	.01
☐	102	Dwight Gooden	.50	.25	.05
☐	103	Keith Hernandez	.20	.10	.02
☐	104	Howard Johnson	.20	.10	.02
☐	105	Roger McDowell	.05	.02	.00
☐	106	Darryl Strawberry	.75	.35	.07
☐	107	Steve Bedrosian	.10	.05	.01
☐	108	Von Hayes	.10	.05	.01
☐	109	Shane Rawley	.05	.02	.00
☐	110	Juan Samuel	.15	.07	.01
☐	111	Mike Schmidt	.75	.35	.07
☐	112	Milt Thompson	.05	.02	.00

1989 Fleer

			MINT	EXC	G-VG
☐	113	Sid Bream	.05	.02	.00
☐	114	Bobby Bonilla	.15	.07	.01
☐	115	Mike Dunne	.05	.02	.00
☐	116	Any Van Slyke	.10	.05	.01
☐	117	Vince Coleman	.20	.10	.02
☐	118	Willie McGee	.15	.07	.01
☐	119	Terry Pendleton	.05	.02	.00
☐	120	Ozzie Smith	.15	.07	.01
☐	121	John Tudor	.10	.05	.01
☐	122	Todd Worrell	.15	.07	.01
☐	123	Tony Gwynn	.45	.22	.04
☐	124	John Kruk	.15	.07	.01
☐	125	Benito Santiago	.45	.22	.04
☐	126	Will Clark	2.00	1.00	.20
☐	127	Dave Dravecky	.15	.07	.01
☐	128	Jeff Leonard	.05	.02	.00
☐	129	Candy Maldonado	.05	.02	.00
☐	130	Rick Reuschel	.10	.05	.01
☐	131	Don Robinson	.05	.02	.00
☐	132	Checklist Card	.05	.02	.00

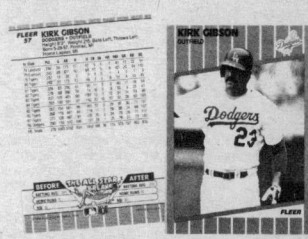

This 660-card set features a distinctive gray
border background with white and yellow trim.
The backs are printed in gray, black, and
yellow on white card stock. The bottom of the
card back shows an innovative breakdown of
the player's demonstrated ability with respect
to his performance before and after the All-Star
break. Cards are numbered on the back and
are again the standard 2 ½" by 3 ½". Cards
are again organized numerically by teams and
alphabetically within teams: Oakland A's (1-
26), New York Mets (27-52), Los Angeles
Dodgers (53-77), Boston Red Sox (78-101),
Minnesota Twins (102-127), Detroit Tigers
(128-151), Cincinnati Reds (152-175),
Milwaukee Brewers (176-200), Pittsburgh
Pirates (201-224), Toronto Blue Jays (225-
248), New York Yankees (249-274), Kansas
City Royals (275-298), San Diego Padres (299-
322), San Francisco Giants (323-347),
Houston Astros (348-370), Montreal Expos
(371-395), Cleveland Indians (396-417), Chicago Cubs (418-442), St. Louis Cardinals (443-
466), California Angels (467-490), Chicago
White Sox (491-513), Texas Rangers (514-
537), Seattle Mariners (538-561), Philadelphia
Phillies (562-584), Atlanta Braves (585-605),
and Baltimore Orioles (606-627). However,
pairs 148/149, 153/154, 272/273, 283/284, and
367/368 were apparently misalphabetized by
Fleer. The last 33 cards in the set consist of
Specials (628-639), Rookie Pairs (640-653),
and checklists (654-660). Due to the early be-

ginning of production of this set, it seems Fleer "presumed" that the A's would win the World Series, since they are listed as the first team in the numerical order; in fact, Fleer had the Mets over the underdog (but eventual World Champion) Dodgers as well. Approximately half of the California Angels players have white rather than yellow halos. Certain Oakland A's player cards have red instead of green lines for front photo borders. Checklist cards are available either with or without positions listed for each player. Fleer also produced a "limited" edition version of this set with glossy coating and packaged in a "tin." However, this tin set was apparently not limited enough (estimated between 30,000 and 45,000 1989 tin sets produced by Fleer), since the price of the "tin" glossy cards is now only double the price of the regular set.

		MINT	EXC	G-VG
	COMPLETE SET (660)	30.00	15.00	3.00
	COMMON PLAYER (1-660)	.03	.01	.00
☐ 1	Don Baylor	.10	.02	.01
☐ 2	Lance Blankenship ..	.25	.12	.02
☐ 3	Todd Burns UER ...	.35	.17	.03
	(wrong birthdate; before/after All-Star stats missing)			
☐ 4	Greg Cadaret	.10	.05	.01
	(All-Star Break stats show 3 losses, should be 2)			
☐ 5	Jose Canseco	1.25	.60	.12
☐ 6	Storm Davis	.06	.03	.00
☐ 7	Dennis Eckersley ...	.10	.05	.01
☐ 8	Mike Gallego	.03	.01	.00
☐ 9	Ron Hassey	.03	.01	.00
☐ 10	Dave Henderson ...	.06	.03	.00
☐ 11	Rick Honeycutt	.03	.01	.00
☐ 12	Glenn Hubbard	.03	.01	.00
☐ 13	Stan Javier	.03	.01	.00
☐ 14	Doug Jennings	.25	.12	.02
☐ 15	Felix Jose	.30	.15	.03
☐ 16	Carney Lansford ...	.08	.04	.01
☐ 17	Mark McGwire	.60	.30	.06
☐ 18	Gene Nelson	.03	.01	.00
☐ 19	Dave Parker	.08	.04	.01
☐ 20	Eric Plunk	.03	.01	.00

		MINT	EXC	G-VG
☐ 21	Luis Polonia	.03	.01	.00
☐ 22	Terry Steinbach	.08	.04	.01
☐ 23	Dave Stewart	.10	.05	.01
☐ 24	Walt Weiss	.25	.12	.02
☐ 25	Bob Welch	.06	.03	.00
☐ 26	Curt Young	.03	.01	.00
☐ 27	Rick Aguilera	.03	.01	.00
☐ 28	Wally Backman	.03	.01	.00
☐ 29	Mark Carreon UER ..	.03	.01	.00
	(after All-Star Break batting 7.14)			
☐ 30	Gary Carter	.12	.06	.01
☐ 31	David Cone	.20	.10	.02
☐ 32	Ron Darling	.08	.04	.01
☐ 33	Len Dykstra	.06	.03	.00
☐ 34	Kevin Elster	.06	.03	.00
☐ 35	Sid Fernandez	.08	.04	.01
☐ 36	Dwight Gooden	.30	.15	.03
☐ 37	Keith Hernandez ...	.12	.06	.01
☐ 38	Gregg Jefferies	1.50	.75	.15
☐ 39	Howard Johnson ...	.15	.07	.01
☐ 40	Terry Leach	.06	.03	.00
☐ 41	Dave Magadan UER .	.08	.04	.01
	(bio says 15 doubles, should be 13)			
☐ 42	Bob McClure	.03	.01	.00
☐ 43	Roger McDowell UER	.06	.03	.00
	(led Mets with 58, should be 62)			
☐ 44	Kevin McReynolds ..	.12	.06	.01
☐ 45	Keith Miller	.03	.01	.00
	New York Mets			
☐ 46	Randy Myers	.08	.04	.01
☐ 47	Bob Ojeda	.06	.03	.00
☐ 48	Mackey Sasser	.12	.06	.01
☐ 49	Darryl Strawberry ..	.40	.20	.04
☐ 50	Tim Teufel	.03	.01	.00
☐ 51	Dave West	.40	.20	.04
☐ 52	Mookie Wilson	.06	.03	.00
☐ 53	Dave Anderson	.03	.01	.00
☐ 54	Tim Belcher	.12	.06	.01
☐ 55	Mike Davis	.03	.01	.00
☐ 56	Mike Devereaux ...	.06	.03	.00
☐ 57	Kirk Gibson	.15	.07	.01
☐ 58	Alfredo Griffin	.03	.01	.00
☐ 59	Chris Gwynn	.06	.03	.00
☐ 60	Jeff Hamilton	.03	.01	.00
☐ 61A	Danny Heep	.90	.45	.09
	(Home: Lake Hills)			

		MINT	EXC	G-VG
☐	61B Danny Heep (Home: San Antonio)	.15	.07	.01
☐	62 Orel Hershiser	.25	.12	.02
☐	63 Brian Holton	.03	.01	.00
☐	64 Jay Howell	.03	.01	.00
☐	65 Tim Leary	.06	.03	.00
☐	66 Mike Marshall	.08	.04	.01
☐	67 Ramon Martinez	.45	.22	.04
☐	68 Jesse Orosco	.03	.01	.00
☐	69 Alejandro Pena	.03	.01	.00
☐	70 Steve Sax	.10	.05	.01
☐	71 Mike Scioscia	.03	.01	.00
☐	72 Mike Sharperson	.03	.01	.00
☐	73 John Shelby	.03	.01	.00
☐	74 Franklin Stubbs	.03	.01	.00
☐	75 John Tudor	.08	.04	.01
☐	76 Fernando Valenzuela	.12	.06	.01
☐	77 Tracy Woodson	.10	.05	.01
☐	78 Marty Barrett	.03	.01	.00
☐	79 Todd Benzinger	.03	.01	.00
☐	80 Mike Boddicker UER (Rochester in '76, should be '78)	.03	.01	.00
☐	81 Wade Boggs	.60	.30	.06
☐	82 "Oil Can" Boyd	.03	.01	.00
☐	83 Ellis Burks	.35	.17	.03
☐	84 Rick Cerone	.03	.01	.00
☐	85 Roger Clemens	.30	.15	.03
☐	86 Steve Curry	.10	.05	.01
☐	87 Dwight Evans	.08	.04	.01
☐	88 Wes Gardner	.03	.01	.00
☐	89 Rich Gedman	.03	.01	.00
☐	90 Mike Greenwell	.90	.45	.09
☐	91 Bruce Hurst	.10	.05	.01
☐	92 Dennis Lamp	.03	.01	.00
☐	93 Spike Owen	.03	.01	.00
☐	94 Larry Parrish UER (before All-Star Break batting 1.90)	.03	.01	.00
☐	95 Carlos Quintana	.35	.17	.03
☐	96 Jody Reed	.06	.03	.00
☐	97 Jim Rice	.10	.05	.01
☐	98A Kevin Romine ERR (photo actually Randy Kutcher batting)	.80	.40	.08
☐	98B Kevin Romine COR (arms folded)	.40	.20	.04
☐	99 Lee Smith	.06	.03	.00
☐	100 Mike Smithson	.03	.01	.00
☐	101 Bob Stanley	.03	.01	.00
☐	102 Allan Anderson	.06	.03	.00
☐	103 Keith Atherton	.03	.01	.00
☐	104 Juan Berenguer	.03	.01	.00
☐	105 Bert Blyleven	.08	.04	.01
☐	106 Eric Bullock UER (Bats/Throws Right, should be Left)	.12	.06	.01
☐	107 Randy Bush	.03	.01	.00
☐	108 John Christensen	.03	.01	.00
☐	109 Mark Davidson	.03	.01	.00
☐	110 Gary Gaetti	.08	.04	.01
☐	111 Greg Gagne	.03	.01	.00
☐	112 Dan Gladden	.03	.01	.00
☐	113 German Gonzalez	.08	.04	.01
☐	114 Brian Harper	.03	.01	.00
☐	115 Tom Herr	.03	.01	.00
☐	116 Kent Hrbek	.10	.05	.01
☐	117 Gene Larkin	.06	.03	.00
☐	118 Tim Laudner	.03	.01	.00
☐	119 Charlie Lea	.03	.01	.00
☐	120 Steve Lombardozzi	.03	.01	.00
☐	121A John Moses (Home: Tempe)	.90	.45	.09
☐	121B John Moses (Home: Phoenix)	.15	.07	.01
☐	122 Al Newman	.03	.01	.00
☐	123 Mark Portugal	.03	.01	.00
☐	124 Kirby Puckett	.35	.17	.03
☐	125 Jeff Reardon	.08	.04	.01
☐	126 Fred Toliver	.03	.01	.00
☐	127 Frank Viola	.15	.07	.01
☐	128 Doyle Alexander	.03	.01	.00
☐	129 Dave Bergman	.03	.01	.00
☐	130A Tom Brookens ERR (Mike Heath back)	2.00	1.00	.20
☐	130B Tom Brookens COR	.15	.07	.01
☐	131 Paul Gibson	.10	.05	.01
☐	132A Mike Heath ERR (Tom Brookens back)	2.00	1.00	.20
☐	132B Mike Heath COR	.15	.07	.01
☐	133 Don Heinkel	.08	.04	.01
☐	134 Mike Henneman	.03	.01	.00
☐	135 Guillermo Hernandez	.06	.03	.00
☐	136 Eric King	.03	.01	.00
☐	137 Chet Lemon	.03	.01	.00
☐	138 Fred Lynn UER ('74, '75 stats missing)	.10	.05	.01
☐	139 Jack Morris	.10	.05	.01

			MINT	EXC	G-VG
☐ 140	Matt Nokes		.10	.05	.01
☐ 141	Gary Pettis		.03	.01	.00
☐ 142	Ted Power		.03	.01	.00
☐ 143	Jeff M. Robinson		.08	.04	.01
	Detroit Tigers				
☐ 144	Luis Salazar		.03	.01	.00
☐ 145	Steve Searcy		.25	.12	.02
☐ 146	Pat Sheridan		.03	.01	.00
☐ 147	Frank Tanana		.03	.01	.00
☐ 148	Alan Trammell		.15	.07	.01
☐ 149	Walt Terrell		.03	.01	.00
☐ 150	Jim Walewander		.10	.05	.01
☐ 151	Lou Whitaker		.08	.04	.01
☐ 152	Tim Birtsas		.03	.01	.00
☐ 153	Tom Browning		.08	.04	.01
☐ 154	Keith Brown		.10	.05	.01
☐ 155	Norm Charlton		.15	.07	.01
☐ 156	Dave Concepcion		.08	.04	.01
☐ 157	Kal Daniels		.08	.04	.01
☐ 158	Eric Davis		.35	.17	.03
☐ 159	Bo Diaz		.03	.01	.00
☐ 160	Rob Dibble		.30	.15	.03
☐ 161	Nick Esasky		.08	.04	.01
☐ 162	John Franco		.08	.04	.01
☐ 163	Danny Jackson		.08	.04	.01
☐ 164	Barry Larkin		.15	.07	.01
☐ 165	Rob Murphy		.03	.01	.00
☐ 166	Paul O'Neill		.08	.04	.01
☐ 167	Jeff Reed		.03	.01	.00
☐ 168	Jose Rijo		.03	.01	.00
☐ 169	Ron Robinson		.03	.01	.00
☐ 170	Chris Sabo		.60	.30	.06
☐ 171	Candy Sierra		.10	.05	.01
☐ 172	Van Snider		.25	.12	.02
☐ 173A	Jeff Treadway		10.00	4.50	.75
	(target registration mark above head on front in light blue)				
☐ 173B	Jeff Treadway		.10	.05	.01
	(no target on front)				
☐ 174	Frank Williams		.03	.01	.00
	(after All-Star Break stats are jumbled)				
☐ 175	Herm Winningham		.03	.01	.00
☐ 176	Jim Adduci		.03	.01	.00
☐ 177	Don August		.06	.03	.00
☐ 178	Mike Birkbeck		.03	.01	.00
☐ 179	Chris Bosio		.06	.03	.00
☐ 180	Glenn Braggs		.06	.03	.00

			MINT	EXC	G-VG
☐ 181	Greg Brock		.03	.01	.00
☐ 182	Mark Clear		.03	.01	.00
☐ 183	Chuck Crim		.03	.01	.00
☐ 184	Rob Deer		.06	.03	.00
☐ 185	Tom Filer		.03	.01	.00
☐ 186	Jim Gantner		.03	.01	.00
☐ 187	Darryl Hamilton		.25	.12	.02
☐ 188	Ted Higuera		.06	.03	.00
☐ 189	Odell Jones		.03	.01	.00
☐ 190	Jeffrey Leonard		.06	.03	.00
☐ 191	Joey Meyer		.06	.03	.00
☐ 192	Paul Mirabella		.03	.01	.00
☐ 193	Paul Molitor		.10	.05	.01
☐ 194	Charlie O'Brien		.10	.05	.01
☐ 195	Dan Plesac		.06	.03	.00
☐ 196	Gary Sheffield		1.50	.75	.15
☐ 197	B.J. Surhoff		.08	.04	.01
☐ 198	Dale Sveum		.03	.01	.00
☐ 199	Bill Wegman		.03	.01	.00
☐ 200	Robin Yount		.18	.09	.01
☐ 201	Rafael Belliard		.03	.01	.00
☐ 202	Barry Bonds		.10	.05	.01
☐ 203	Bobby Bonilla		.10	.05	.01
☐ 204	Sid Bream		.03	.01	.00
☐ 205	Benny Distefano		.03	.01	.00
☐ 206	Doug Drabek		.06	.03	.00
☐ 207	Mike Dunne		.06	.03	.00
☐ 208	Felix Fermin		.03	.01	.00
☐ 209	Brian Fisher		.03	.01	.00
☐ 210	Jim Gott		.03	.01	.00
☐ 211	Bob Kipper		.03	.01	.00
☐ 212	Dave LaPoint		.03	.01	.00
☐ 213	Mike LaValliere		.03	.01	.00
☐ 214	Jose Lind		.03	.01	.00
☐ 215	Junior Ortiz		.03	.01	.00
☐ 216	Vicente Palacios		.03	.01	.00
☐ 217	Tom Prince		.08	.04	.01
☐ 218	Gary Redus		.03	.01	.00
☐ 219	R.J. Reynolds		.03	.01	.00
☐ 220	Jeff Robinson		.06	.03	.00
	Pittsburgh Pirates				
☐ 221	John Smiley		.06	.03	.00
☐ 222	Andy Van Slyke		.10	.05	.01
☐ 223	Bob Walk		.03	.01	.00
☐ 224	Glenn Wilson		.03	.01	.00
☐ 225	Jesse Barfield		.08	.04	.01
☐ 226	George Bell		.12	.06	.01
☐ 227	Pat Borders		.12	.06	.01
☐ 228	John Cerutti		.03	.01	.00

		MINT	EXC	G-VG
☐ 229	Jim Clancy	.03	.01	.00
☐ 230	Mark Eichhorn	.03	.01	.00
☐ 231	Tony Fernandez	.10	.05	.01
☐ 232	Cecil Fielder	.03	.01	.00
☐ 233	Mike Flanagan	.03	.01	.00
☐ 234	Kelly Gruber	.06	.03	.00
☐ 235	Tom Henke	.06	.03	.00
☐ 236	Jimmy Key	.06	.03	.00
☐ 237	Rick Leach	.03	.01	.00
☐ 238	Manny Lee UER	.03	.01	.00
	(bio says regular			
	shortstop, sic, Tony			
	Fernandez)			
☐ 239	Nelson Liriano	.03	.01	.00
☐ 240	Fred McGriff	.20	.10	.02
☐ 241	Lloyd Moseby	.06	.03	.00
☐ 242	Rance Mulliniks	.03	.01	.00
☐ 243	Jeff Musselman	.03	.01	.00
☐ 244	Dave Stieb	.08	.04	.01
☐ 245	Todd Stottlemyre	.15	.07	.01
☐ 246	Duane Ward	.03	.01	.00
☐ 247	David Wells	.08	.04	.01
☐ 248	Ernie Whitt UER	.03	.01	.00
	(HR total 21, should			
	be 121)			
☐ 249	Luis Aguayo	.03	.01	.00
☐ 250A	Neil Allen	2.00	1.00	.20
	(Home: Sarasota, FL)			
☐ 250B	Neil Allen	.25	.12	.02
	(Home: Syosset, NY)			
☐ 251	John Candelaria	.06	.03	.00
☐ 252	Jack Clark	.12	.06	.01
☐ 253	Richard Dotson	.03	.01	.00
☐ 254	Rickey Henderson	.25	.12	.02
☐ 255	Tommy John	.10	.05	.01
☐ 256	Roberto Kelly	.20	.10	.02
☐ 257	Al Leiter	.15	.07	.01
☐ 258	Don Mattingly	1.00	.50	.10
☐ 259	Dale Mohorcic	.03	.01	.00
☐ 260	Hal Morris	.20	.10	.02
☐ 261	Scott Nielsen	.03	.01	.00
☐ 262	Mike Pagliarulo UER	.06	.03	.00
	(wrong birthdate)			
☐ 263	Hipolito Pena	.12	.06	.01
☐ 264	Ken Phelps	.06	.03	.00
☐ 265	Willie Randolph	.06	.03	.00
☐ 266	Rick Rhoden	.03	.01	.00
☐ 267	Dave Righetti	.08	.04	.01
☐ 268	Rafael Santana	.03	.01	.00
☐ 269	Steve Shields	.03	.01	.00
☐ 270	Joel Skinner	.03	.01	.00
☐ 271	Don Slaught	.03	.01	.00
☐ 272	Claudell Washington	.06	.03	.00
☐ 273	Gary Ward	.03	.01	.00
☐ 274	Dave Winfield	.15	.07	.01
☐ 275	Luis Aquino	.03	.01	.00
☐ 276	Floyd Bannister	.03	.01	.00
☐ 277	George Brett	.20	.10	.02
☐ 278	Bill Buckner	.06	.03	.00
☐ 279	Nick Capra	.08	.04	.01
☐ 280	Jose DeJesus	.08	.04	.01
☐ 281	Steve Farr	.03	.01	.00
☐ 282	Jerry Don Gleaton	.03	.01	.00
☐ 283	Mark Gubicza	.08	.04	.01
☐ 284	Tom Gordon UER	1.25	.60	.12
	(16.2 innings in '88,			
	should be 15.2)			
☐ 285	Bo Jackson	.90	.45	.09
☐ 286	Charlie Leibrandt	.03	.01	.00
☐ 287	Mike Macfarlane	.15	.07	.01
☐ 288	Jeff Montgomery	.08	.04	.01
☐ 289	Bill Pecota UER	.03	.01	.00
	(photo actually Brad			
	Wellman)			
☐ 290	Jamie Quirk	.03	.01	.00
☐ 291	Bret Saberhagen	.15	.07	.01
☐ 292	Kevin Seitzer	.15	.07	.01
☐ 293	Kurt Stillwell	.03	.01	.00
☐ 294	Pat Tabler	.06	.03	.00
☐ 295	Danny Tartabull	.10	.05	.01
☐ 296	Gary Thurman	.03	.01	.00
☐ 297	Frank White	.06	.03	.00
☐ 298	Willie Wilson	.06	.03	.00
☐ 299	Roberto Alomar	.40	.20	.04
☐ 300	Sandy Alomar Jr. UER	1.50	.75	.15
	(wrong birthdate)			
☐ 301	Chris Brown	.03	.01	.00
☐ 302	Mike Brumley UER	.08	.04	.01
	(133 hits in '88,			
	should be 134)			
☐ 303	Mark Davis	.12	.06	.01
☐ 304	Mark Grant	.03	.01	.00
☐ 305	Tony Gwynn	.25	.12	.02
☐ 306	Greg W. Harris	.20	.10	.02
	San Diego Padres			
☐ 307	Andy Hawkins	.03	.01	.00
☐ 308	Jimmy Jones	.06	.03	.00

		MINT	EXC	G-VG
☐ 309	John Kruk	.06	.03	.00
☐ 310	Dave Leiper	.03	.01	.00
☐ 311	Carmelo Martinez	.03	.01	.00
☐ 312	Lance McCullers	.06	.03	.00
☐ 313	Keith Moreland	.03	.01	.00
☐ 314	Dennis Rasmussen	.06	.03	.00
☐ 315	Randy Ready UER (1214 games in '88, should be 114)	.03	.01	.00
☐ 316	Benito Santiago	.18	.09	.01
☐ 317	Eric Show	.03	.01	.00
☐ 318	Todd Simmons	.06	.03	.00
☐ 319	Garry Templeton	.06	.03	.00
☐ 320	Dickie Thon	.03	.01	.00
☐ 321	Ed Whitson	.03	.01	.00
☐ 322	Marvell Wynne	.03	.01	.00
☐ 323	Mike Aldrete	.03	.01	.00
☐ 324	Brett Butler	.06	.03	.00
☐ 325	Will Clark UER (three consecutive 100 RBI seasons)	1.00	.50	.10
☐ 326	Kelly Downs UER ('88 stats missing)	.06	.03	.00
☐ 327	Dave Dravecky	.08	.04	.01
☐ 328	Scott Garrelts	.06	.03	.00
☐ 329	Atlee Hammaker	.03	.01	.00
☐ 330	Charlie Hayes	.30	.15	.03
☐ 331	Mike Krukow	.03	.01	.00
☐ 332	Craig Lefferts	.06	.03	.00
☐ 333	Candy Maldonado	.06	.03	.00
☐ 334	Kirt Manwaring UER (Bats Rights)	.03	.01	.00
☐ 335	Bob Melvin	.03	.01	.00
☐ 336	Kevin Mitchell	.40	.20	.04
☐ 337	Donell Nixon	.03	.01	.00
☐ 338	Tony Perezchica	.12	.06	.01
☐ 339	Joe Price	.03	.01	.00
☐ 340	Rick Reuschel	.06	.03	.00
☐ 341	Earnest Riles	.03	.01	.00
☐ 342	Don Robinson	.03	.01	.00
☐ 343	Chris Speier	.03	.01	.00
☐ 344	Robby Thompson UER (West Plam Beach)	.03	.01	.00
☐ 345	Jose Uribe	.03	.01	.00
☐ 346	Matt Williams	.30	.15	.03
☐ 347	Trevor Wilson	.15	.07	.01
☐ 348	Juan Agosto	.03	.01	.00
☐ 349	Larry Andersen	.03	.01	.00
☐ 350A	Alan Ashby ERR (Throws Rig)	3.00	1.50	.30
☐ 350B	Alan Ashby COR	.06	.03	.00
☐ 351	Kevin Bass	.06	.03	.00
☐ 352	Buddy Bell	.06	.03	.00
☐ 353	Craig Biggio	.75	.35	.07
☐ 354	Danny Darwin	.03	.01	.00
☐ 355	Glenn Davis	.10	.05	.01
☐ 356	Jim Deshaies	.03	.01	.00
☐ 357	Bill Doran	.06	.03	.00
☐ 358	John Fishel	.10	.05	.01
☐ 359	Billy Hatcher	.03	.01	.00
☐ 360	Bob Knepper	.03	.01	.00
☐ 361	Louie Meadows UER (bio says 10 EBH's and 6 SB's in '88, should be 3 and 4)	.08	.04	.01
☐ 362	Dave Meads	.03	.01	.00
☐ 363	Jim Pankovits	.03	.01	.00
☐ 364	Terry Puhl	.03	.01	.00
☐ 365	Rafael Ramirez	.03	.01	.00
☐ 366	Craig Reynolds	.03	.01	.00
☐ 367	Mike Scott (card listed as 368 on Astros CL)	.12	.06	.01
☐ 368	Nolan Ryan (card listed as 367 on Astros CL)	.35	.17	.03
☐ 369	Dave Smith	.03	.01	.00
☐ 370	Gerald Young	.06	.03	.00
☐ 371	Hubie Brooks	.06	.03	.00
☐ 372	Tim Burke	.06	.03	.00
☐ 373	John Dopson	.25	.12	.02
☐ 374	Mike Fitzgerald	.03	.01	.00
	Montreal Expos			
☐ 375	Tom Foley	.03	.01	.00
☐ 376	Andres Galarraga UER (Home: Caracas)	.12	.06	.01
☐ 377	Neal Heaton	.03	.01	.00
☐ 378	Joe Hesketh	.03	.01	.00
☐ 379	Brian Holman	.15	.07	.01
☐ 380	Rex Hudler	.03	.01	.00
☐ 381	Randy Johnson UER (innings for '85 and '86 shown as 27 and 120, should be 27.1 and 119.2)	.25	.12	.02
☐ 382	Wallace Johnson	.03	.01	.00

		MINT	EXC	G-VG
☐ 383	Tracy Jones	.03	.01	.00
☐ 384	Dave Martinez	.03	.01	.00
☐ 385	Dennis Martinez	.06	.03	.00
☐ 386	Andy McGaffigan	.03	.01	.00
☐ 387	Otis Nixon	.03	.01	.00
☐ 388	Johnny Paredes	.10	.05	.01
☐ 389	Jeff Parrett	.10	.05	.01
☐ 390	Pascual Perez	.08	.04	.01
☐ 391	Tim Raines	.15	.07	.01
☐ 392	Luis Rivera	.03	.01	.00
☐ 393	Nelson Santovenia	.25	.12	.02
☐ 394	Bryn Smith	.06	.03	.00
☐ 395	Tim Wallach	.08	.04	.01
☐ 396	Andy Allanson UER (1214 hits in '88, should be 114)	.03	.01	.00
☐ 397	Rod Allen	.15	.07	.01
☐ 398	Scott Bailes	.03	.01	.00
☐ 399	Tom Candiotti	.03	.01	.00
☐ 400	Joe Carter	.12	.06	.01
☐ 401	Carmen Castillo UER (after All-Star Break batting 2.50)	.03	.01	.00
☐ 402	Dave Clark UER (card front shows position as Rookie; after All-Star Break batting 3.14)	.08	.04	.01
☐ 403	John Farrell UER (typo in runs allowed in '88)	.03	.01	.00
☐ 404	Julio Franco	.08	.04	.01
☐ 405	Don Gordon	.08	.04	.01
☐ 406	Mel Hall	.06	.03	.00
☐ 407	Brad Havens	.03	.01	.00
☐ 408	Brook Jacoby	.06	.03	.00
☐ 409	Doug Jones	.06	.03	.00
☐ 410	Jeff Kaiser	.10	.05	.01
☐ 411	Luis Medina	.30	.15	.03
☐ 412	Cory Snyder	.10	.05	.01
☐ 413	Greg Swindell	.10	.05	.01
☐ 414	Ron Tingley UER (hit HR in first ML at bat, should be first AL at bat)	.10	.05	.01
☐ 415	Willie Upshaw	.03	.01	.00
☐ 416	Ron Washington	.03	.01	.00
☐ 417	Rich Yett	.03	.01	.00
☐ 418	Damon Berryhill	.10	.05	.01
☐ 419	Mike Bielecki	.06	.03	.00
☐ 420	Doug Dascenzo	.15	.07	.01
☐ 421	Jody Davis UER (Braves stats for '88 missing)	.03	.01	.00
☐ 422	Andre Dawson	.12	.06	.01
☐ 423	Frank DiPino	.03	.01	.00
☐ 424	Shawon Dunston	.08	.04	.01
☐ 425	Goose Gossage	.08	.04	.01
☐ 426	Mark Grace UER (Minor League stats for '88 missing)	2.00	1.00	.20
☐ 427	Mike Harkey	.30	.15	.03
☐ 428	Darrin Jackson	.08	.04	.01
☐ 429	Les Lancaster	.03	.01	.00
☐ 430	Vance Law	.03	.01	.00
☐ 431	Greg Maddux	.12	.06	.01
☐ 432	Jamie Moyer	.03	.01	.00
☐ 433	Al Nipper	.03	.01	.00
☐ 434	Rafael Palmeiro UER (170 hits in '88, should be 178)	.12	.06	.01
☐ 435	Pat Perry	.03	.01	.00
☐ 436	Jeff Pico	.10	.05	.01
☐ 437	Ryne Sandberg	.15	.07	.01
☐ 438	Calvin Schiraldi	.03	.01	.00
☐ 439	Rick Sutcliffe	.08	.04	.01
☐ 440A	Manny Trillo ERR (Throws Rig)	3.00	1.50	.30
☐ 440B	Manny Trillo COR	.06	.03	.00
☐ 441	Gary Varsho UER (wrong birthdate; .303 should be .302; 11/28 should be 9/19)	.15	.07	.01
☐ 442	Mitch Webster	.03	.01	.00
☐ 443	Luis Alicea	.10	.05	.01
☐ 444	Tom Brunansky	.08	.04	.01
☐ 445	Vince Coleman UER (third straight with 83, should be fourth straight with 81)	.12	.06	.01
☐ 446	John Costello	.12	.06	.01
☐ 447	Danny Cox	.03	.01	.00
☐ 448	Ken Dayley	.03	.01	.00
☐ 449	Jose DeLeon	.06	.03	.00
☐ 450	Curt Ford	.03	.01	.00
☐ 451	Pedro Guerrero	.10	.05	.01
☐ 452	Bob Horner	.08	.04	.01
☐ 453	Tim Jones	.10	.05	.01

		MINT	EXC	G-VG
☐ 454	Steve Lake	.03	.01	.00
☐ 455	Joe Magrane UER (Des Moines, IO)	.08	.04	.01
☐ 456	Greg Mathews	.03	.01	.00
☐ 457	Willie McGee	.08	.04	.01
☐ 458	Larry McWilliams	.03	.01	.00
☐ 459	Jose Oquendo	.03	.01	.00
☐ 460	Tony Pena	.06	.03	.00
☐ 461	Terry Pendleton	.03	.01	.00
☐ 462	Steve Peters	.10	.05	.01
☐ 463	Ozzie Smith	.12	.06	.01
☐ 464	Scott Terry	.03	.01	.00
☐ 465	Denny Walling	.03	.01	.00
☐ 466	Todd Worrell	.08	.04	.01
☐ 467	Tony Armas UER (before All-Star Break batting 2.39)	.06	.03	.00
☐ 468	Dante Bichette	.20	.10	.02
☐ 469	Bob Boone	.08	.04	.01
☐ 470	Terry Clark	.12	.06	.01
☐ 471	Stew Cliburn	.03	.01	.00
☐ 472	Mike Cook UER (TM near Angels logo missing from front)	.10	.05	.01
☐ 473	Sherman Corbett	.10	.05	.01
☐ 474	Chili Davis	.06	.03	.00
☐ 475	Brian Downing	.03	.01	.00
☐ 476	Jim Eppard	.03	.01	.00
☐ 477	Chuck Finley	.06	.03	.00
☐ 478	Willie Fraser	.03	.01	.00
☐ 479	Bryan Harvey (ML record shows 0-0, should be 7-5)	.20	.10	.02
☐ 480	Jack Howell	.03	.01	.00
☐ 481	Wally Joyner UER (Yorba Linda, GA)	.20	.10	.02
☐ 482	Jack Lazorko	.03	.01	.00
☐ 483	Kirk McCaskill	.03	.01	.00
☐ 484	Mark McLemore	.03	.01	.00
☐ 485	Greg Minton	.03	.01	.00
☐ 486	Dan Petry	.03	.01	.00
☐ 487	Johnny Ray	.06	.03	.00
☐ 488	Dick Schofield	.03	.01	.00
☐ 489	Devon White	.10	.05	.01
☐ 490	Mike Witt	.06	.03	.00
☐ 491	Harold Baines	.08	.04	.01
☐ 492	Daryl Boston	.03	.01	.00
☐ 493	Ivan Calderon UER ('80 stats shifted)	.08	.04	.01
☐ 494	Mike Diaz	.03	.01	.00
☐ 495	Carlton Fisk	.10	.05	.01
☐ 496	Dave Gallagher	.25	.12	.02
☐ 497	Ozzie Guillen	.06	.03	.00
☐ 498	Shawn Hillegas	.03	.01	.00
☐ 499	Lance Johnson	.03	.01	.00
☐ 500	Barry Jones	.03	.01	.00
☐ 501	Bill Long	.03	.01	.00
☐ 502	Steve Lyons	.03	.01	.00
☐ 503	Fred Manrique	.03	.01	.00
☐ 504	Jack McDowell	.08	.04	.01
☐ 505	Donn Pall	.08	.04	.01
☐ 506	Kelly Paris	.03	.01	.00
▶ 507	Dan Pasqua	.03	.01	.00
☐ 508	Ken Patterson	.10	.05	.01
☐ 509	Melido Perez	.08	.04	.01
☐ 510	Jerry Reuss	.03	.01	.00
☐ 511	Mark Salas	.03	.01	.00
☐ 512	Bobby Thigpen UER ('86 ERA 4.69, should be 4.68)	.06	.03	.00
☐ 513	Mike Woodard	.03	.01	.00
☐ 514	Bob Brower	.03	.01	.00
☐ 515	Steve Buechele	.03	.01	.00
☐ 516	Jose Cecena	.08	.04	.01
☐ 517	Cecil Espy	.08	.04	.01
☐ 518	Scott Fletcher	.03	.01	.00
☐ 519	Cecilio Guante ('87 Yankee stats are off-centered)	.03	.01	.00
☐ 520	Jose Guzman	.03	.01	.00
☐ 521	Ray Hayward	.06	.03	.00
☐ 522	Charlie Hough	.03	.01	.00
☐ 523	Pete Incaviglia	.10	.05	.01
☐ 524	Mike Jeffcoat	.03	.01	.00
☐ 525	Paul Kilgus	.03	.01	.00
☐ 526	Chad Kreuter	.15	.07	.01
☐ 527	Jeff Kunkel	.03	.01	.00
☐ 528	Oddibe McDowell	.06	.03	.00
☐ 529	Pete O'Brien	.06	.03	.00
☐ 530	Geno Petralli	.03	.01	.00
☐ 531	Jeff Russell	.06	.03	.00
☐ 532	Ruben Sierra	.30	.15	.03
☐ 533	Mike Stanley	.03	.01	.00
☐ 534A	Ed VandeBerg ERR (Throws Left)	3.00	1.50	.30
☐ 534B	Ed VandeBerg COR	.06	.03	.00
☐ 535	Curtis Wilkerson ERR	.03	.01	.00

		MINT	EXC	G-VG
	(pitcher headings at bottom)			
☐ 536	Mitch Williams	.08	.04	.01
☐ 537	Bobby Witt UER ('85 ERA .643, should be 6.43)	.06	.03	.00
☐ 538	Steve Balboni	.03	.01	.00
☐ 539	Scott Bankhead	.06	.03	.00
☐ 540	Scott Bradley	.03	.01	.00
☐ 541	Mickey Brantley	.06	.03	.00
☐ 542	Jay Buhner	.20	.10	.02
☐ 543	Mike Campbell	.03	.01	.00
☐ 544	Darnell Coles	.03	.01	.00
☐ 545	Henry Cotto	.03	.01	.00
☐ 546	Alvin Davis	.08	.04	.01
☐ 547	Mario Diaz	.03	.01	.00
☐ 548	Ken Griffey Jr.	5.00	2.50	.50
☐ 549	Erik Hanson	.25	.12	.02
☐ 550	Mike Jackson UER (Lifetime ERA 3.345, should be 3.45)	.03	.01	.00
☐ 551	Mark Langston	.12	.06	.01
☐ 552	Edgar Martinez	.08	.04	.01
☐ 553	Bill McGuire	.10	.05	.01
☐ 554	Mike Moore	.06	.03	.00
☐ 555	Jim Presley	.03	.01	.00
☐ 556	Rey Quinones	.03	.01	.00
☐ 557	Jerry Reed	.03	.01	.00
☐ 558	Harold Reynolds	.06	.03	.00
☐ 559	Mike Schooler	.35	.17	.03
☐ 560	Bill Swift	.03	.01	.00
☐ 561	Dave Valle	.03	.01	.00
☐ 562	Steve Bedrosian	.08	.04	.01
☐ 563	Phil Bradley	.06	.03	.00
☐ 564	Don Carman	.03	.01	.00
☐ 565	Bob Dernier	.03	.01	.00
☐ 566	Marvin Freeman	.03	.01	.00
☐ 567	Todd Frohwirth	.03	.01	.00
☐ 568	Greg Gross	.03	.01	.00
☐ 569	Kevin Gross	.03	.01	.00
☐ 570	Greg Harris Philadelphia Phillies	.03	.01	.00
☐ 571	Von Hayes	.08	.04	.01
☐ 572	Chris James	.08	.04	.01
☐ 573	Steve Jeltz	.03	.01	.00
☐ 574	Ron Jones UER (Led IL in '88 with 85, should be 75)	.35	.17	.03
☐ 575	Ricky Jordan	1.75	.85	.17
☐ 576	Mike Maddux	.03	.01	.00
☐ 577	David Palmer	.03	.01	.00
☐ 578	Lance Parrish	.08	.04	.01
☐ 579	Shane Rawley	.03	.01	.00
☐ 580	Bruce Ruffin	.03	.01	.00
☐ 581	Juan Samuel	.08	.04	.01
☐ 582	Mike Schmidt	.35	.17	.03
☐ 583	Kent Tekulve	.03	.01	.00
☐ 584	Milt Thompson UER (19 hits in '88, should be 109)	.03	.01	.00
☐ 585	Jose Alvarez	.10	.05	.01
☐ 586	Paul Assenmacher	.03	.01	.00
☐ 587	Bruce Benedict	.03	.01	.00
☐ 588	Jeff Blauser	.03	.01	.00
☐ 589	Terry Blocker	.12	.06	.01
☐ 590	Ron Gant	.10	.05	.01
☐ 591	Tom Glavine	.03	.01	.00
☐ 592	Tommy Gregg	.12	.06	.01
☐ 593	Albert Hall	.03	.01	.00
☐ 594	Dion James	.03	.01	.00
☐ 595	Rick Mahler	.03	.01	.00
☐ 596	Dale Murphy	.25	.12	.02
☐ 597	Gerald Perry	.06	.03	.00
☐ 598	Charlie Puleo	.03	.01	.00
☐ 599	Ted Simmons	.08	.04	.01
☐ 600	Pete Smith	.03	.01	.00
☐ 601	Zane Smith	.03	.01	.00
☐ 602	John Smoltz	.60	.30	.06
☐ 603	Bruce Sutter	.08	.04	.01
☐ 604	Andres Thomas	.03	.01	.00
☐ 605	Ozzie Virgil	.03	.01	.00
☐ 606	Brady Anderson	.30	.15	.03
☐ 607	Jeff Ballard	.08	.04	.01
☐ 608	Jose Bautista	.08	.04	.01
☐ 609	Ken Gerhart	.03	.01	.00
☐ 610	Terry Kennedy	.03	.01	.00
☐ 611	Eddie Murray	.12	.06	.01
☐ 612	Carl Nichols (before All-Star Break batting 1.88)	.08	.04	.01
☐ 613	Tom Niedenfuer	.03	.01	.00
☐ 614	Joe Orsulak	.03	.01	.00
☐ 615	Oswald Peraza UER (shown as Oswaldo)	.10	.05	.01
☐ 616A	Bill Ripken ERR (Rick Face written on knob of bat)	18.00	9.00	1.80
☐ 616B	Bill Ripken	40.00	20.00	4.00

		MINT	EXC	G-VG
	(bat knob whited out)			
☐ 616C	Bill Ripken	18.00	9.00	1.80
	(words on bat knob scribbled out)			
☐ 616D	Bill Ripken	.75	.35	.07
	(black box covering bat knob			
☐ 617	Cal Ripken Jr.	.15	.07	.01
☐ 618	Dave Schmidt	.03	.01	.00
☐ 619	Rick Schu	.03	.01	.00
☐ 620	Larry Sheets	.03	.01	.00
☐ 621	Doug Sisk	.03	.01	.00
☐ 622	Pete Stanicek	.03	.01	.00
☐ 623	Mickey Tettleton	.08	.04	.01
☐ 624	Jay Tibbs	.03	.01	.00
☐ 625	Jim Traber	.03	.01	.00
☐ 626	Mark Williamson	.03	.01	.00
☐ 627	Craig Worthington ..	.50	.25	.05
☐ 628	Speed/Power	.60	.30	.06
	Jose Canseco			
☐ 629	Pitcher Perfect	.06	.03	.00
	Tom Browning			
☐ 630	Like Father/Like Sons	.25	.12	.02
	Roberto Alomar			
	Sandy Alomar Jr.			
	(names on card listed in wrong order) UER			
☐ 631	NL All Stars UER ...	.20	.10	.02
	Will Clark			
	Rafael Palmeiro			
	(Gallaraga, sic; Clark 3 consecutive 100 RBI seasons; third with 102 RBI's)			
☐ 632	Homeruns - Coast ..	.30	.15	.03
	to Coast UER			
	Darryl Strawberry			
	Will Clark (Homeruns should be two words)			
☐ 633	Hot Corners - Hot ..	.20	.10	.02
	Hitters UER			
	Wade Boggs			
	Carney Lansford			
	(Boggs hit .366 in '86, should be '88)			
☐ 634	Triple A's	.35	.17	.03
	Jose Canseco			
	Terry Steinbach			
	Mark McGwire			

		MINT	EXC	G-VG
☐ 635	Dual Heat	.20	.10	.02
	Mark Davis			
	Dwight Gooden			
☐ 636	NL Pitching Power			
	UER	.08	.04	.01
	Danny Jackson			
	David Cone			
	(Hersheiser, sic)			
☐ 637	Cannon Arms UER ..	.08	.04	.01
	Chris Sabo			
	Bobby Bonilla			
	(Bobby Bonds, sic)			
☐ 638	Double Trouble UER	.06	.03	.00
	Andres Galarraga			
	(misspelled Gallaraga on card back)			
	Gerald Perry			
☐ 639	Power Center	.20	.10	.02
	Kirby Puckett			
	Eric Davis			
☐ 640	Steve Wilson and			
	Cameron Drew	.20	.10	.02
☐ 641	Kevin Brown and			
	Kevin Reimer	.20	.10	.02
☐ 642	Brad Pounders and			
	Jerald Clark	.20	.10	.02
☐ 643	Mike Capel and			
	Drew Hall	.20	.10	.02
☐ 644	Joe Girardi and			
	Rolando Roomes ...	.40	.20	.04
☐ 645	Lenny Harris and			
	Marty Brown	.20	.10	.02
☐ 646	Luis De Los Santos			
	and Jim Campbell ...	.20	.10	.02
☐ 647	Randy Kramer and			
	Miguel Garcia	.15	.07	.01
☐ 648	Torey Lovullo and			
	Robert Palacios	.15	.07	.01
☐ 649	Jim Corsi and			
	Bob Milacki	.25	.12	.02
☐ 650	Grady Hall and			
	Mike Rochford	.15	.07	.01
☐ 651	Terry Taylor and			
	Vance Lovelace	.20	.10	.02
☐ 652	Ken Hill and			
	Dennis Cook	.50	.25	.05
☐ 653	Scott Service and			
	Shane Turner	.20	.10	.02
☐ 654	CL: Oakland/Mets ...	.06	.01	.00

	MINT	EXC	G-VG
Dodgers/Red Sox (10 Hendersor; 68 Jess Orosco)			
☐ 655 CL: Twins/Tigers .... Reds/Brewers (179 Boslo)	.06	.01	.00
☐ 656 CL: Pirates/Blue Jays Yankees/Royals (225 Jess Barfield)	.06	.01	.00
☐ 657 CL: Padres/Giants Astros/Expos (367/368 wrong)	.06	.01	.00
☐ 658 CL: Indians/Cubs Cardinals/Angels (449 Deleon)	.06	.01	.00
☐ 659 CL: White Sox/Rangers Mariners/Phillies	.06	.01	.00
☐ 660 CL: Braves/Orioles Specials/Checklists (632 hyphenated differently and 650 Hali; 595 Rich Mahler; 619 Rich Schu)	.06	.01	.00

1989 Fleer Update

The 1989 Fleer Update set contains 132 standard-size (2 ½" by 3 ½") cards. The fronts are gray with white pinstripes. The vertically oriented backs show lifetime stats and performance "Before and After the All-Star Break." The set does not include a card of 1989 AL Rookie of the Year Gregg Olson, but contains the first major card of Greg Vaughn and special cards for Nolan Ryan's 5,000th strikeout and Mike Schmidt's retirement.

		MINT	EXC	G-VG
COMPLETE SET (132)		20.00	10.00	2.00
COMMON PLAYER (1-132)		.06	.03	.00
☐ U1	Phil Bradley	.15	.03	.01
☐ U2	Mike Devereaux	.10	.05	.01
☐ U3	Steve Finley	.30	.15	.03
☐ U4	Kevin Hickey	.06	.03	.00
☐ U5	Brian Holton	.10	.05	.01
☐ U6	Bob Milacki	.15	.07	.01
☐ U7	Randy Milligan	.10	.05	.01
☐ U8	John Dopson	.10	.05	.01
☐ U9	Nick Esasky	.15	.07	.01
☐ U10	Rob Murphy	.10	.05	.01
☐ U11	Jim Abbott	2.50	1.25	.25
☐ U12	Bert Blyleven	.15	.07	.01
☐ U13	Jeff Manto	.30	.15	.03
☐ U14	Bob McClure	.06	.03	.00
☐ U15	Lance Parrish	.10	.05	.01
☐ U16	Lee Stevens	.50	.25	.05
☐ U17	Claudell Washington	.10	.05	.01
☐ U18	Mark Davis	.25	.12	.02
☐ U19	Eric King	.10	.05	.01
☐ U20	Ron Kittle	.15	.07	.01
☐ U21	Matt Merullo	.20	.10	.02
☐ U22	Steve Rosenberg	.15	.07	.01
☐ U23	Robin Ventura	1.50	.75	.15
☐ U24	Keith Atherton	.06	.03	.00
☐ U25	Joey Belle	1.00	.50	.10
☐ U26	Jerry Browne	.10	.05	.01
☐ U27	Felix Fermin	.06	.03	.00
☐ U28	Brad Komminsk	.10	.05	.01
☐ U29	Pete O'Brien	.10	.05	.01
☐ U30	Mike Brumley	.10	.05	.01
☐ U31	Tracy Jones	.10	.05	.01
☐ U32	Mike Schwabe	.15	.07	.01
☐ U33	Gary Ward	.06	.03	.00

		MINT	EXC	G-VG			MINT	EXC	G-VG
☐ U34	Frank Williams	.06	.03	.00	☐ U83	Todd Benzinger	.10	.05	.01
☐ U35	Kevin Appier	.20	.10	.02	☐ U84	Ken Griffey Sr.	.15	.07	.01
☐ U36	Bob Boone	.15	.07	.01	☐ U85	Rick Mahler	.06	.03	.00
☐ U37	Luis de los Santos	.20	.10	.02	☐ U86	Rolando Roomes	.15	.07	.01
☐ U38	Jim Eisenreich	.10	.05	.01	☐ U87	Scott Scudder	.30	.15	.03
☐ U39	Jaime Navarro	.40	.20	.04	☐ U88	Jim Clancy	.06	.03	.00
☐ U40	Bill Spiers	.35	.17	.03	☐ U89	Rick Rhoden	.06	.03	.00
☐ U41	Greg Vaughn	3.00	1.50	.30	☐ U90	Dan Schatzeder	.06	.03	.00
☐ U42	Randy Veres	.15	.07	.01	☐ U91	Mike Morgan	.10	.05	.01
☐ U43	Wally Backman	.06	.03	.00	☐ U92	Eddie Murray	.15	.07	.01
☐ U44	Shane Rawley	.06	.03	.00	☐ U93	Willie Randolph	.10	.05	.01
☐ U45	Steve Balboni	.06	.03	.00	☐ U94	Ray Searage	.06	.03	.00
☐ U46	Jesse Barfield	.15	.07	.01	☐ U95	Mike Aldrete	.06	.03	.00
☐ U47	Alvaro Espinoza	.10	.05	.01	☐ U96	Kevin Gross	.10	.05	.01
☐ U48	Bob Geren	.45	.22	.04	☐ U97	Mark Langston	.25	.12	.02
☐ U49	Mel Hall	.10	.05	.01	☐ U98	Spike Owen	.06	.03	.00
☐ U50	Andy Hawkins	.10	.05	.01	☐ U99	Zane Smith	.06	.03	.00
☐ U51	Hensley Meulens	.50	.25	.05	☐ U100	Don Aase	.06	.03	.00
☐ U52	Steve Sax	.15	.07	.01	☐ U101	Barry Lyons	.06	.03	.00
☐ U53	Deion Sanders	1.25	.60	.12	☐ U102	Juan Samuel	.15	.07	.01
☐ U54	Rickey Henderson	.40	.20	.04	☐ U103	Wally Whitehurst	.20	.10	.02
☐ U55	Mike Moore	.15	.07	.01	☐ U104	Dennis Cook	.15	.07	.01
☐ U56	Tony Phillips	.10	.05	.01	☐ U105	Len Dykstra	.15	.07	.01
☐ U57	Greg Briley	.75	.35	.07	☐ U106	Charlie Hayes	.15	.07	.01
☐ U58	Gene Harris	.30	.15	.03	☐ U107	Tommy Herr	.06	.03	.00
☐ U59	Randy Johnson	.15	.07	.01	☐ U108	Ken Howell	.06	.03	.00
☐ U60	Jeffrey Leonard	.10	.05	.01	☐ U109	John Kruk	.10	.05	.01
☐ U61	Dennis Powell	.06	.03	.00	☐ U110	Roger McDowell	.10	.05	.01
☐ U62	Omar Vizquel	.25	.12	.02	☐ U111	Terry Mulholland	.06	.03	.00
☐ U63	Kevin Brown	.15	.07	.01	☐ U112	Jeff Parrett	.10	.05	.01
☐ U64	Julio Franco	.15	.07	.01	☐ U113	Neal Heaton	.06	.03	.00
☐ U65	Jamie Moyer	.06	.03	.00	☐ U114	Jeff King	.15	.07	.01
☐ U66	Rafael Palmeiro	.15	.07	.01	☐ U115	Randy Kramer	.10	.05	.01
☐ U67	Nolan Ryan	1.50	.60	.12	☐ U116	Bill Landrum	.10	.05	.01
☐ U68	Francisco Cabrera	.30	.15	.03	☐ U117	Cris Carpenter	.10	.05	.01
☐ U69	Junior Felix	.90	.50	.10	☐ U118	Frank DiPino	.06	.03	.00
☐ U70	Al Leiter	.10	.05	.01	☐ U119	Ken Hill	.10	.05	.01
☐ U71	Alex Sanchez	.20	.10	.02	☐ U120	Dan Quisenberry	.10	.05	.01
☐ U72	Geronimo Berroa	.06	.03	.00	☐ U121	Milt Thompson	.06	.03	.00
☐ U73	Derek Lilliquist	.20	.10	.02	☐ U122	Todd Zeile	3.00	1.50	.30
☐ U74	Lonnie Smith	.15	.07	.01	☐ U123	Jack Clark	.12	.06	.01
☐ U75	Jeff Treadway	.10	.05	.01	☐ U124	Bruce Hurst	.12	.06	.01
☐ U76	Paul Kilgus	.06	.03	.00	☐ U125	Mark Parent	.06	.03	.00
☐ U77	Lloyd McClendon	.10	.05	.01	☐ U126	Bip Roberts	.06	.03	.00
☐ U78	Scott Sanderson	.06	.03	.00	☐ U127	Jeff Brantley UER	.25	.12	.02
☐ U79	Dwight Smith	1.50	.75	.15		(photo actually Joe			
☐ U80	Jerome Walton	4.50	2.25	.45		Kmak)			
☐ U81	Mitch Williams	.20	.10	.02	☐ U128	Terry Kennedy	.06	.03	.00
☐ U82	Steve Wilson	.10	.05	.01	☐ U129	Mike LaCoss	.06	.03	.00

		MINT	EXC	G-VG
☐ U130	Greg Litton	.30	.15	.03
☐ U131	Mike Schmidt	1.50	.60	.12
☐ U132	Checklist 1-132	.06	.01	.00

1990 Fleer

The 1990 Fleer set contains 660 standard-size (2 ½" by 3 ½") cards. The outer front borders are white; the inner, ribbon-like borders are different depending on the team. The vertically oriented backs are white, red, pink, and navy. The set is again ordered numerically by teams, followed by combination cards, rookie prospect pairs, and checklists. Just as with the 1989 set, Fleer incorrectly anticipated the outcome of the 1989 Playoffs according to the team ordering. The A's, listed first, did win the World Series, but their opponents were the Giants, not the Cubs.

		MINT	EXC	G-VG
COMPLETE SET (660)		24.00	12.00	2.40
COMMON PLAYER (1-160)		.03	.01	.00
☐ 1	Lance Blankenship	.10	.02	.01
☐ 2	Todd Burns	.06	.03	.00
☐ 3	Jose Canseco	.50	.25	.05
☐ 4	Jim Corsi	.03	.01	.00
☐ 5	Storm Davis	.06	.03	.00
☐ 6	Dennis Eckersley	.08	.04	.01
☐ 7	Mike Gallego	.03	.01	.00

		MINT	EXC	G-VG
☐ 8	Ron Hassey	.03	.01	.00
☐ 9	Dave Henderson	.03	.01	.00
☐ 10	Rickey Henderson	.25	.12	.02
☐ 11	Rick Honeycutt	.03	.01	.00
☐ 12	Stan Javier	.03	.01	.00
☐ 13	Felix Jose	.03	.01	.00
☐ 14	Carney Lansford	.08	.04	.01
☐ 15	Mark McGwire	.25	.12	.02
☐ 16	Mike Moore	.06	.03	.00
☐ 17	Gene Nelson	.03	.01	.00
☐ 18	Dave Parker	.08	.04	.01
☐ 19	Tony Phillips	.03	.01	.00
☐ 20	Terry Steinbach	.06	.03	.00
☐ 21	Dave Stewart	.08	.04	.01
☐ 22	Walt Weiss	.08	.04	.01
☐ 23	Bob Welch	.06	.03	.00
☐ 24	Curt Young	.03	.01	.00
☐ 25	Paul Assenmacher	.03	.01	.00
☐ 26	Damon Berryhill	.08	.04	.01
☐ 27	Mike Bielecki	.06	.03	.00
☐ 28	Kevin Blankenship	.08	.04	.01
☐ 29	Andre Dawson	.10	.05	.01
☐ 30	Shawon Dunston	.06	.03	.00
☐ 31	Joe Girardi	.08	.04	.01
☐ 32	Mark Grace	.35	.17	.03
☐ 33	Mike Harkey	.06	.03	.00
☐ 34	Paul Kilgus	.03	.01	.00
☐ 35	Les Lancaster	.03	.01	.00
☐ 36	Vance Law	.03	.01	.00
☐ 37	Greg Maddux	.06	.03	.00
☐ 38	Lloyd McClendon	.03	.01	.00
☐ 39	Jeff Pico	.03	.01	.00
☐ 40	Ryne Sandberg	.15	.07	.01
☐ 41	Scott Sanderson	.03	.01	.00
☐ 42	Dwight Smith	.50	.25	.05
☐ 43	Rick Sutcliffe	.06	.03	.00
☐ 44	Jerome Walton	1.25	.60	.12
☐ 45	Mitch Webster	.03	.01	.00
☐ 46	Curt Wilkerson	.03	.01	.00
☐ 47	Dean Wilkins	.15	.07	.01
☐ 48	Mitch Williams	.06	.03	.00
☐ 49	Steve Wilson	.03	.01	.00
☐ 50	Steve Bedrosian	.06	.03	.00
☐ 51	Mike Benjamin	.12	.06	.01
☐ 52	Jeff Brantley	.12	.06	.01
☐ 53	Brett Butler	.06	.03	.00
☐ 54	Will Clark	.50	.25	.05
☐ 55	Kelly Downs	.03	.01	.00
☐ 56	Scott Garreits	.06	.03	.00

		MINT	EXC	G-VG			MINT	EXC	G-VG
☐ 57	Atlee Hammaker	.03	.01	.00	☐ 106	Jim Eisenreich	.03	.01	.00
☐ 58	Terry Kennedy	.03	.01	.00	☐ 107	Steve Farr	.03	.01	.00
☐ 59	Mike LaCoss	.03	.01	.00	☐ 108	Tom Gordon	.40	.20	.04
☐ 60	Craig Lefferts	.03	.01	.00	☐ 109	Mark Gubicza	.08	.04	.01
☐ 61	Greg Litton	.20	.10	.02	☐ 110	Bo Jackson	.50	.25	.05
☐ 62	Candy Maldonado	.03	.01	.00	☐ 111	Terry Leach	.03	.01	.00
☐ 63	Kirt Manwaring	.06	.03	.00	☐ 112	Charlie Leibrandt	.03	.01	.00
☐ 64	Randy McCament	.12	.06	.01	☐ 113	Rick Luecken	.12	.06	.01
☐ 65	Kevin Mitchell	.20	.10	.02	☐ 114	Mike Macfarlane	.03	.01	.00
☐ 66	Donell Nixon	.03	.01	.00	☐ 115	Jeff Montgomery	.06	.03	.00
☐ 67	Ken Oberkfell	.03	.01	.00	☐ 116	Bret Saberhagen	.10	.05	.01
☐ 68	Rick Reuschel	.06	.03	.00	☐ 117	Kevin Seitzer	.08	.04	.01
☐ 69	Ernest Riles	.03	.01	.00	☐ 118	Kurt Stillwell	.03	.01	.00
☐ 70	Don Robinson	.03	.01	.00	☐ 119	Pat Tabler	.03	.01	.00
☐ 71	Pat Sheridan	.03	.01	.00	☐ 120	Danny Tartabull	.08	.04	.01
☐ 72	Chris Speier	.03	.01	.00	☐ 121	Gary Thurman	.03	.01	.00
☐ 73	Robby Thompson	.03	.01	.00	☐ 122	Frank White	.06	.03	.00
☐ 74	Jose Uribe	.03	.01	.00	☐ 123	Willie Wilson	.06	.03	.00
☐ 75	Matt Williams	.12	.06	.01	☐ 124	Matt Winters	.12	.06	.01
☐ 76	George Bell	.10	.05	.01	☐ 125	Jim Abbott	1.00	.50	.10
☐ 77	Pat Borders	.03	.01	.00	☐ 126	Tony Armas	.06	.03	.00
☐ 78	John Cerutti	.03	.01	.00	☐ 127	Dante Bichette	.03	.01	.00
☐ 79	Junior Felix	.35	.17	.03	☐ 128	Bert Blyleven	.08	.04	.01
☐ 80	Tony Fernandez	.08	.04	.01	☐ 129	Chili Davis	.06	.03	.00
☐ 81	Mike Flanagan	.03	.01	.00	☐ 130	Brian Downing	.03	.01	.00
☐ 82	Mauro Gozzo	.20	.10	.02	☐ 131	Mike Fetters	.12	.06	.01
☐ 83	Kelly Gruber	.06	.03	.00	☐ 132	Chuck Finley	.06	.03	.00
☐ 84	Tom Henke	.06	.03	.00	☐ 133	Willie Fraser	.03	.01	.00
☐ 85	Jimmy Key	.06	.03	.00	☐ 134	Bryan Harvey	.03	.01	.00
☐ 86	Manne Lee	.03	.01	.00	☐ 135	Jack Howell	.03	.01	.00
☐ 87	Nelson Liriano	.03	.01	.00	☐ 136	Wally Joyner	.10	.05	.01
☐ 88	Lee Mazzilli	.03	.01	.00	☐ 137	Jeff Manto	.15	.07	.01
☐ 89	Fred McGriff	.12	.06	.01	☐ 138	Kirk McCaskill	.03	.01	.00
☐ 90	Lloyd Moseby	.06	.03	.00	☐ 139	Bob McClure	.03	.01	.00
☐ 91	Rance Mulliniks	.03	.01	.00	☐ 140	Greg Minton	.03	.01	.00
☐ 92	Alex Sanchez	.12	.06	.01	☐ 141	Lance Parrish	.08	.04	.01
☐ 94	Todd Stottlemyre	.06	.03	.00	☐ 142	Dan Petry	.03	.01	.00
☐ 93	Dave Stieb	.08	.04	.01	☐ 143	Johnny Ray	.06	.03	.00
☐ 95	Duane Ward	.03	.01	.00	☐ 144	Dick Schofield	.03	.01	.00
☐ 96	David Wells	.03	.01	.00	☐ 145	Lee Stevens	.25	.12	.02
☐ 97	Ernie Whitt	.03	.01	.00	☐ 146	Claudell Washington	.06	.03	.00
☐ 98	Frank Wills	.03	.01	.00	☐ 147	Devon White	.08	.04	.01
☐ 99	Mookie Wilson	.06	.03	.00	☐ 148	Mike Witt	.06	.03	.00
☐ 100	Kevin Appier	.12	.06	.01	☐ 149	Roberto Alomar	.08	.04	.01
☐ 101	Luis Aquino	.03	.01	.00	☐ 150	Sandy Alomar Jr.	.30	.15	.03
☐ 102	Bob Boone	.08	.04	.01	☐ 151	Andy Benes	.50	.25	.05
☐ 103	George Brett	.12	.06	.01	☐ 152	Jack Clark	.08	.04	.01
☐ 104	Jose DeJesus	.03	.01	.00	☐ 153	Pat Clements	.03	.01	.00
☐ 105	Luis De Los Santos	.03	.01	.00	☐ 154	Joey Cora	.03	.01	.00

		MINT	EXC	G-VG
☐ 155	Mark Davis	.08	.04	.01
☐ 156	Mark Grant	.03	.01	.00
☐ 157	Tony Gwynn	.15	.07	.01
☐ 158	Greg W. Harris	.03	.01	.00
☐ 159	Bruce Hurst	.08	.04	.01
☐ 160	Darrin Jackson	.03	.01	.00
☐ 161	Chris James	.06	.03	.00
☐ 162	Carmelo Martinez	.03	.01	.00
☐ 163	Mike Pagliarulo	.06	.03	.00
☐ 164	Mark Parent	.08	.04	.01
☐ 165	Dennis Rasmussen	.03	.01	.00
☐ 166	Bip Roberts	.03	.01	.00
☐ 167	Benito Santiago	.08	.04	.01
☐ 168	Calvin Schiraldi	.03	.01	.00
☐ 169	Eric Show	.03	.01	.00
☐ 170	Garry Templeton	.06	.03	.00
☐ 171	Ed Whitson	.03	.01	.00
☐ 172	Brady Anderson	.03	.01	.00
☐ 173	Jeff Ballard	.06	.03	.00
☐ 174	Phil Bradley	.06	.03	.00
☐ 175	Mike Devereaux	.03	.01	.00
☐ 176	Steve Finley	.12	.06	.01
☐ 177	Pete Harnisch	.08	.04	.01
☐ 178	Kevin Hickey	.03	.01	.00
☐ 179	Brian Holton	.03	.01	.00
☐ 180	Ben McDonald	2.00	1.00	.20
☐ 181	Bob Melvin	.03	.01	.00
☐ 182	Bob Milacki	.10	.05	.01
☐ 183	Randy Milligan	.08	.04	.01
☐ 184	Gregg Olson	.30	.15	.03
☐ 185	Joe Orsulak	.03	.01	.00
☐ 186	Bill Ripken	.03	.01	.00
☐ 187	Cal Ripken	.15	.07	.01
☐ 188	Dave Schmidt	.03	.01	.00
☐ 189	Larry Sheets	.03	.01	.00
☐ 190	Mickey Tettleton	.06	.03	.00
☐ 191	Mark Thurmond	.03	.01	.00
☐ 192	Jay Tibbs	.03	.01	.00
☐ 193	Jim Traber	.03	.01	.00
☐ 194	Mark Williamson	.03	.01	.00
☐ 195	Craig Worthington	.10	.05	.01
☐ 196	Don Aase	.03	.01	.00
☐ 197	Blaine Beatty	.15	.07	.01
☐ 198	Mark Carreon	.03	.01	.00
☐ 199	Gary Carter	.08	.04	.01
☐ 200	David Cone	.08	.04	.01
☐ 201	Ron Darling	.08	.04	.01
☐ 202	Kevin Elster	.06	.03	.00
☐ 203	Sid Fernandez	.08	.04	.01

		MINT	EXC	G-VG
☐ 204	Dwight Gooden	.20	.10	.02
☐ 205	Keith Hernandez	.08	.04	.01
☐ 206	Jeff Innis	.10	.05	.01
☐ 207	Gregg Jefferies	.35	.17	.03
☐ 208	Howard Johnson	.10	.05	.01
☐ 209	Barry Lyons	.03	.01	.00
☐ 210	Dave Magadan	.06	.03	.00
☐ 211	Kevin McReynolds	.08	.04	.01
☐ 212	Jeff Musselman	.03	.01	.00
☐ 213	Randy Myers	.06	.03	.00
☐ 214	Bob Ojeda	.06	.03	.00
☐ 215	Juan Samuel	.06	.03	.00
☐ 216	Mackey Sasser	.06	.03	.00
☐ 217	Darryl Strawberry	.25	.12	.02
☐ 218	Tim Teufel	.03	.01	.00
☐ 219	Frank Viola	.08	.04	.01
☐ 220	Juan Agosto	.03	.01	.00
☐ 221	Larry Andersen	.03	.01	.00
☐ 222	Eric Anthony	1.75	.85	.17
☐ 223	Kevin Bass	.06	.03	.00
☐ 224	Craig Biggio	.10	.05	.01
☐ 225	Ken Caminiti	.03	.01	.00
☐ 226	Jim Clancy	.03	.01	.00
☐ 227	Danny Darwin	.03	.01	.00
☐ 228	Glenn Davis	.10	.05	.01
☐ 229	Jim Deshaies	.03	.01	.00
☐ 230	Bill Doran	.06	.03	.00
☐ 231	Bob Forsch	.03	.01	.00
☐ 232	Brian Meyer	.08	.04	.01
☐ 233	Terry Puhl	.03	.01	.00
☐ 234	Rafael Ramirez	.03	.01	.00
☐ 235	Rick Rhoden	.03	.01	.00
☐ 236	Dan Schatzeder	.03	.01	.00
☐ 237	Mike Scott	.08	.04	.01
☐ 238	Dave Smith	.03	.01	.00
☐ 239	Alex Trevino	.03	.01	.00
☐ 240	Glenn Wilson	.03	.01	.00
☐ 241	Gerald Young	.03	.01	.00
☐ 242	Tom Brunansky	.08	.04	.01
☐ 243	Cris Carpenter	.03	.01	.00
☐ 244	Alex Cole	.15	.07	.01
☐ 245	Vince Coleman	.08	.04	.01
☐ 246	John Costello	.03	.01	.00
☐ 247	Ken Dayley	.03	.01	.00
☐ 248	Jose DeLeon	.06	.03	.00
☐ 249	Frank DiPino	.03	.01	.00
☐ 250	Pedro Guerrero	.08	.04	.01
☐ 251	Ken Hill	.03	.01	.00
☐ 252	Joe Magrane	.08	.04	.01

		MINT	EXC	G-VG			MINT	EXC	G-VG
☐ 253	Willie McGee	.08	.04	.01	☐ 302	Mike Jeffcoat	.03	.01	.00
☐ 254	John Morris	.03	.01	.00	☐ 303	Chad Kreuter	.03	.01	.00
☐ 255	Jose Oquendo	.03	.01	.00	☐ 304	Jeff Kunkel	.03	.01	.00
☐ 256	Tony Pena	.06	.03	.00	☐ 305	Rick Leach	.03	.01	.00
☐ 257	Terry Pendleton	.03	.01	.00	☐ 306	Fred Manrique	.03	.01	.00
☐ 258	Ted Power	.03	.01	.00	☐ 307	Jamie Moyer	.03	.01	.00
☐ 259	Dan Quisenberry	.06	.03	.00	☐ 308	Rafael Palmeiro	.08	.04	.01
☐ 260	Ozzie Smith	.08	.04	.01	☐ 309	Geno Petralli	.03	.01	.00
☐ 261	Scott Terry	.03	.01	.00	☐ 310	Kevin Reimer	.03	.01	.00
☐ 262	Milt Thompson	.03	.01	.00	☐ 311	Kenny Rogers	.10	.05	.01
☐ 263	Denny Walling	.03	.01	.00	☐ 312	Jeff Russell	.06	.03	.00
☐ 264	Todd Worrell	.08	.04	.01	☐ 313	Nolan Ryan	.30	.15	.03
☐ 265	Todd Zeile	1.50	.75	.15	☐ 314	Ruben Sierra	.20	.10	.02
☐ 266	Marty Barrett	.03	.01	.00	☐ 315	Bobby Witt	.06	.03	.00
☐ 267	Mike Boddicker	.03	.01	.00	☐ 316	Chris Bosio	.06	.03	.00
☐ 268	Wade Boggs	.25	.12	.02	☐ 317	Glenn Braggs	.06	.03	.00
☐ 269	Ellis Burks	.15	.07	.011	☐ 318	Greg Brock	.03	.01	.00
☐ 270	Rick Cerone	.03	.01	.00	☐ 319	Chuck Crim	.03	.01	.00
☐ 271	Roger Clemens	.25	.12	.02	☐ 320	Rob Deer	.06	.03	.00
☐ 272	John Dopson	.03	.01	.00	☐ 321	Mike Felder	.03	.01	.00
☐ 273	Nick Esasky	.06	.03	.00	☐ 322	Tom Filer	.03	.01	.00
☐ 274	Dwight Evans	.08	.04	.01	☐ 323	Tony Fossas	.10	.05	.01
☐ 275	Wes Gardner	.03	.01	.00	☐ 324	Jim Gantner	.03	.01	.00
☐ 276	Rich Gedman	.03	.01	.00	☐ 325	Darryl Hamilton	.03	.01	.00
☐ 277	Mike Greenwell	.20	.10	.02	☐ 326	Teddy Higuera	.06	.03	.00
☐ 278	Danny Heep	.03	.01	.00	☐ 327	Mark Knudson	.08	.04	.01
☐ 279	Eric Hetzel	.08	.04	.01	☐ 328	Bill Krueger	.03	.01	.00
☐ 280	Dennis Lamp	.03	.01	.00	☐ 329	Tim McIntosh	.12	.06	.01
☐ 281	Rob Murphy	.03	.01	.00	☐ 330	Paul Molitor	.08	.04	.01
☐ 282	Joe Price	.03	.01	.00	☐ 331	Jaime Navarro	.15	.07	.01
☐ 283	Carlos Quintana	.06	.03	.00	☐ 332	Charlie O'Brien	.03	.01	.00
☐ 284	Jody Reed	.03	.01	.00	☐ 333	Jeff Peterek	.12	.06	.01
☐ 285	Luis Rivera	.03	.01	.00	☐ 334	Dan Plesac	.06	.03	.00
☐ 286	Kevin Romine	.03	.01	.00	☐ 335	Jerry Reuss	.03	.01	.00
☐ 287	Lee Smith	.06	.03	.00	☐ 336	Gary Sheffield	.30	.15	.03
☐ 288	Mike Smithson	.03	.01	.00	☐ 337	Bill Spiers	.30	.15	.03
☐ 289	Bob Stanley	.03	.01	.00	☐ 338	B.J. Surhoff	.06	.03	.00
☐ 290	Harold Baines	.08	.04	.01	☐ 339	Greg Vaughn	1.50	.75	.15
☐ 291	Kevin Brown	.08	.04	.01	☐ 340	Robin Yount	.25	.12	.02
☐ 292	Steve Buechele	.03	.01	.00	☐ 341	Hubie Brooks	.06	.03	.00
☐ 293	Scott Coolbaugh	.30	.15	.03	☐ 342	Tim Burke	.06	.03	.00
☐ 294	Jack Daugherty	.12	.06	.01	☐ 343	Mike Fitzgerald	.03	.01	.00
☐ 295	Cecil Espy	.03	.01	.00	☐ 344	Tom Foley	.03	.01	.00
☐ 296	Julio Franco	.08	.04	.01	☐ 345	Andres Galarraga	.08	.04	.01
☐ 297	Juan Gonzalez	.75	.35	.07	☐ 346	Damaso Garcia	.03	.01	.00
☐ 298	Cecilio Guante	.03	.01	.00	☐ 347	Marquis Grissom	.60	.30	.06
☐ 299	Drew Hall	.03	.01	.00	☐ 348	Kevin Gross	.03	.01	.00
☐ 300	Charlie Hough	.03	.01	.00	☐ 349	Joe Hesketh	.03	.01	.00
☐ 301	Pete Incaviglia	.08	.04	.01	☐ 350	Jeff Huson	.12	.06	.01

		MINT	EXC	G-VG
☐ 351	Wallace Johnson	.03	.01	.00
☐ 352	Mark Langston	.10	.05	.01
☐ 353	Dave Martinez	.03	.01	.00
☐ 354	Dennis Martinez	.03	.01	.00
☐ 355	Andy McGaffigan	.03	.01	.00
☐ 356	Otis Nixon	.03	.01	.00
☐ 357	Spike Owen	.03	.01	.00
☐ 358	Pascual Perez	.06	.03	.00
☐ 359	Tim Raines	.10	.05	.01
☐ 360	Nelson Santovenia	.03	.01	.00
☐ 361	Bryn Smith	.06	.03	.00
☐ 362	Zane Smith	.03	.01	.00
☐ 363	Larry Walker	.25	.12	.02
☐ 364	Tim Wallach	.06	.03	.00
☐ 365	Rick Aguilera	.03	.01	.00
☐ 366	Allan Anderson	.06	.03	.00
☐ 367	Wally Backman	.03	.01	.00
☐ 368	Doug Baker	.03	.01	.00
☐ 369	Juan Berenguer	.03	.01	.00
☐ 370	Randy Bush	.03	.01	.00
☐ 371	Carmen Castillo	.03	.01	.00
☐ 372	Mike Dyer	.15	.07	.01
☐ 373	Gary Gaetti	.08	.04	.01
☐ 374	Greg Gagne	.03	.01	.00
☐ 375	Dan Gladden	.03	.01	.00
☐ 376	German Gonzalez	.06	.03	.00
☐ 377	Brian Harper	.03	.01	.00
☐ 378	Kent Hrbek	.08	.04	.01
☐ 379	Gene Larkin	.03	.01	.00
☐ 380	Tim Laudner	.03	.01	.00
☐ 381	John Moses	.03	.01	.00
☐ 382	Al Newman	.03	.01	.00
☐ 383	Kirby Puckett	.20	.10	.02
☐ 384	Shane Rawley	.03	.01	.00
☐ 385	Jeff Reardon	.06	.03	.00
☐ 386	Roy Smith	.03	.01	.00
☐ 387	Gary Wayne	.12	.06	.01
☐ 388	Dave West	.06	.03	.00
☐ 389	Tim Belcher	.06	.03	.00
☐ 390	Tim Crews	.03	.01	.00
☐ 391	Mike Davis	.03	.01	.00
☐ 392	Rick Dempsey	.03	.01	.00
☐ 393	Kirk Gibson	.08	.04	.01
☐ 394	Jose Gonzalez	.03	.01	.00
☐ 395	Alfredo Griffin	.03	.01	.00
☐ 396	Jeff Hamilton	.03	.01	.00
☐ 397	Lenny Harris	.03	.01	.00
☐ 398	Mickey Hatcher	.03	.01	.00
☐ 399	Orel Hershiser	.10	.05	.01

		MINT	EXC	G-VG
☐ 400	Jay Howell	.03	.01	.00
☐ 401	Mike Marshall	.08	.04	.01
☐ 402	Ramon Martinez	.08	.04	.01
☐ 403	Mike Morgan	.03	.01	.00
☐ 404	Eddie Murray	.10	.05	.01
☐ 405	Alejandro Pena	.03	.01	.00
☐ 406	Willie Randolph	.06	.03	.01
☐ 407	Mike Scioscia	.03	.01	.00
☐ 408	Ray Searage	.03	.01	.00
☐ 409	Fernando Valenzuela	.10	.05	.01
☐ 410	Jose Vizcaino	.25	.12	.02
☐ 411	John Wetteland	.25	.12	.02
☐ 412	Jack Armstrong	.10	.05	.01
☐ 413	Todd Benzinger	.03	.01	.00
☐ 414	Tim Birtsas	.03	.01	.00
☐ 415	Tom Browning	.06	.03	.00
☐ 416	Norm Charlton	.03	.01	.00
☐ 417	Eric Davis	.20	.10	.02
☐ 418	Rob Dibble	.06	.03	.00
☐ 419	John Franco	.06	.03	.00
☐ 420	Ken Griffey Sr.	.06	.03	.00
☐ 421	Chris Hammond	.12	.06	.01
☐ 422	Danny Jackson	.06	.03	.00
☐ 423	Barry Larkin	.10	.05	.01
☐ 424	Tim Leary	.06	.03	.00
☐ 425	Rick Mahler	.03	.01	.00
☐ 426	Joe Oliver	.12	.06	.01
☐ 427	Paul O'Neill	.08	.04	.01
☐ 428	Luis Quinones	.03	.01	.00
☐ 429	Jeff Reed	.03	.01	.00
☐ 430	Jose Rijo	.03	.01	.00
☐ 431	Ron Robinson	.03	.01	.00
☐ 432	Rolando Roomes	.08	.04	.01
☐ 433	Chris Sabo	.08	.04	.01
☐ 434	Scott Scudder	.15	.07	.01
☐ 435	Herm Winningham	.03	.01	.00
☐ 436	Steve Balboni	.03	.01	.00
☐ 437	Jesse Barfield	.08	.04	.01
☐ 438	Mike Blowers	.20	.10	.02
☐ 439	Tom Brookens	.03	.01	.00
☐ 440	Greg Cadaret	.03	.01	.00
☐ 441	Alvaro Espinoza	.03	.01	.00
☐ 442	Bob Geren	.15	.07	.01
☐ 443	Lee Guetterman	.03	.01	.00
☐ 444	Mel Hall	.06	.03	.00
☐ 445	Andy Hawkins	.03	.01	.00
☐ 446	Roberto Kelly	.10	.05	.00
☐ 447	Don Mattingly	.50	.25	.05
☐ 448	Lance McCullers	.03	.01	.00

		MINT	EXC	G-VG			MINT	EXC	G-VG
☐ 449	Hensley Meulens	.20	.10	.02	☐ 498	Pete O'Brien	.06	.03	.00
☐ 450	Dale Mohorcic	.03	.01	.00	☐ 499	Steve Olin	.10	.05	.01
☐ 451	Clay Parker	.03	.01	.00	☐ 500	Jesse Orosco	.03	.01	.00
☐ 452	Eric Plunk	.03	.01	.00	☐ 501	Joel Skinner	.03	.01	.00
☐ 453	Dave Righetti	.08	.04	.01	☐ 502	Cory Snyder	.08	.04	.01
☐ 454	Deion Sanders	.50	.25	.05	☐ 503	Greg Swindell	.08	.04	.01
☐ 455	Steve Sax	.08	.04	.01	☐ 504	Rich Yett	.03	.01	.00
☐ 456	Don Slaught	.03	.01	.00	☐ 505	Scott Bankhead	.06	.03	.00
☐ 457	Walt Terrell	.03	.01	.00	☐ 506	Scott Bradley	.03	.01	.00
☐ 458	Dave Winfield	.10	.05	.01	☐ 508	Jay Buhner	.06	.03	.00
☐ 459	Jay Bell	.03	.01	.00	☐ 507	Greg Briley	.25	.12	.02
☐ 460	Rafael Belliard	.03	.01	.00	☐ 509	Darnell Coles	.03	.01	.00
☐ 461	Barry Bonds	.08	.04	.01	☐ 510	Keith Comstock	.03	.01	.00
☐ 462	Bobby Bonilla	.08	.04	.01	☐ 511	Henry Cotto	.03	.01	.00
☐ 463	Sid Bream	.03	.01	.00	☐ 512	Alvin Davis	.08	.04	.01
☐ 464	Benny Distefano	.03	.01	.00	☐ 513	Ken Griffey Jr.	1.00	.50	.10
☐ 465	Doug Drabek	.03	.01	.00	☐ 514	Erik Hanson	.03	.01	.00
☐ 466	Jim Gott	.03	.01	.00	☐ 515	Gene Harris	.15	.07	.01
☐ 467	Billy Hatcher	.03	.01	.00	☐ 516	Brian Holman	.03	.01	.00
☐ 468	Neal Heaton	.03	.01	.00	☐ 517	Mike Jackson	.03	.01	.00
☐ 469	Jeff King	.06	.03	.00	☐ 518	Randy Johnson	.03	.01	.00
☐ 470	Bob Kipper	.03	.01	.00	☐ 519	Jeffrey Leonard	.03	.01	.00
☐ 471	Randy Kramer	.03	.01	.00	☐ 520	Edgar Martinez	.03	.01	.00
☐ 472	Bill Landrum	.03	.01	.00	☐ 521	Dennis Powell	.03	.01	.00
☐ 473	Mike LaValliere	.03	.01	.00	☐ 522	Jim Presley	.03	.01	.00
☐ 474	Jose Lind	.03	.01	.00	☐ 523	Jerry Reed	.03	.01	.00
☐ 475	Junior Ortiz	.03	.01	.00	☐ 524	Harold Reynolds	.06	.03	.00
☐ 476	Gary Redus	.03	.01	.00	☐ 525	Mike Schooler	.06	.03	.00
☐ 477	Rick Reed	.12	.06	.01	☐ 526	Bill Swift	.03	.01	.00
☐ 478	R. J. Reynolds	.03	.01	.00	☐ 527	Dave Valle	.03	.01	.00
☐ 479	Jeff Robinson	.06	.03	.00	☐ 528	Omar Vizquel	.15	.07	.01
☐ 480	John Smiley	.06	.03	.00	☐ 529	Ivan Calderon	.06	.03	.00
☐ 481	Andy Van Slyke	.08	.04	.01	☐ 530	Carlton Fisk	.10	.05	.01
☐ 482	Bob Walk	.03	.01	.00	☐ 531	Scott Fletcher	.03	.01	.00
☐ 483	Andy Allanson	.03	.01	.00	☐ 532	Dave Gallagher	.03	.01	.00
☐ 484	Scott Bailes	.03	.01	.00	☐ 533	Ozzie Guillen	.06	.03	.00
☐ 485	Joey Belle	.50	.25	.05	☐ 534	Greg Hibbard	.12	.06	.01
☐ 486	Bud Black	.03	.01	.00	☐ 535	Shawn Hillegas	.03	.01	.00
☐ 487	Jerry Browne	.03	.01	.00	☐ 536	Lance Johnson	.03	.01	.00
☐ 488	Tom Candiotti	.03	.01	.00	☐ 537	Eric King	.03	.01	.00
☐ 489	Joe Carter	.10	.05	.01	☐ 538	Ron Kittle	.06	.03	.00
☐ 490	Dave Clark	.03	.01	.00	☐ 539	Steve Lyons	.03	.01	.00
☐ 491	John Farrell	.03	.01	.00	☐ 540	Carlos Martinez	.20	.10	.02
☐ 492	Felix Fermin	.03	.01	.00	☐ 541	Tom McCarthy	.10	.05	.01
☐ 493	Brook Jacoby	.06	.03	.00	☐ 542	Matt Merullo	.10	.05	.01
☐ 494	Dion James	.03	.01	.00	☐ 543	Donn Pall	.03	.01	.00
☐ 495	Doug Jones	.06	.03	.00	☐ 544	Dan Pasqua	.03	.01	.00
☐ 496	Brad Komminsk	.03	.01	.00	☐ 545	Ken Patterson	.03	.01	.00
☐ 497	Rod Nichols	.06	.03	.00	☐ 546	Melido Perez	.06	.03	.00

		MINT	EXC	G-VG
☐ 547	Steve Rosenberg ...	.08	.04	.01
☐ 548	Sammy Sosa	.40	.20	.04
☐ 549	Bobby Thigpen	.06	.03	.00
☐ 550	Robin Ventura	.50	.25	.05
☐ 551	Greg Walker	.03	.01	.00
☐ 552	Don Carman	.03	.01	.00
☐ 553	Pat Combs	.40	.20	.04
☐ 554	Dennis Cook	.06	.03	.00
☐ 555	Darren Daulton	.03	.01	.00
☐ 556	Len Dykstra	.06	.03	.00
☐ 557	Curt Ford	.03	.01	.00
☐ 558	Charlie Hayes	.06	.03	.00
☐ 559	Von Hayes	.08	.04	.01
☐ 560	Tommy Herr	.03	.01	.00
☐ 561	Ken Howell	.03	.01	.00
☐ 562	Steve Jeltz	.03	.01	.00
☐ 563	Ron Jones	.06	.03	.00
☐ 564	Ricky Jordan UER ...	.50	.25	.05
	(duplicate line of			
	statistics on back)			
☐ 565	John Kruk	.06	.03	.00
☐ 566	Steve Lake	.03	.01	.00
☐ 567	Roger McDowell	.06	.03	.00
☐ 568	Terry Mulholland	.03	.01	.00
☐ 569	Dwayne Murphy	.03	.01	.00
☐ 570	Jeff Parrett	.03	.01	.00
☐ 571	Randy Ready	.03	.01	.00
☐ 572	Bruce Ruffin	.03	.01	.00
☐ 573	Dickie Thon	.03	.01	.00
☐ 574	Jose Alvarez	.03	.01	.00
☐ 575	Geronimo Berroa ...	.08	.04	.01
☐ 576	Jeff Blauser	.03	.01	.00
☐ 577	Joe Boever	.03	.01	.00
☐ 578	Marty Clary	.03	.01	.00
☐ 579	Jody Davis	.03	.01	.00
☐ 580	Mark Eichhorn	.03	.01	.00
☐ 581	Darrell Evans	.06	.03	.00
☐ 582	Ron Gant	.06	.03	.00
☐ 583	Tom Glavine	.06	.03	.00
☐ 584	Tommy Greene	.40	.20	.04
☐ 585	Tommy Gregg	.03	.01	.00
☐ 586	Dave Justice	.20	.10	.02
☐ 587	Mark Lemke	.08	.04	.01
☐ 588	Derek Lilliquist	.08	.04	.01
☐ 589	Oddibe McDowell ...	.06	.03	.00
☐ 590	Kent Mercker	.40	.20	.04
☐ 591	Kent Mercker	.40	.20	.04
☐ 592	Gerald Perry	.06	.03	.00
☐ 593	Lonnie Smith	.06	.03	.00

		MINT	EXC	G-VG
☐ 594	Pete Smith	.03	.01	.00
☐ 595	John Smoltz	.08	.04	.01
☐ 596	Mike Stanton	.20	.10	.02
☐ 597	Andres Thomas	.03	.01	.00
☐ 598	Jeff Treadway	.03	.01	.00
☐ 599	Doyle Alexander ...	.03	.01	.00
☐ 600	Dave Bergman	.03	.01	.00
☐ 601	Brian Dubois	.12	.06	.01
☐ 602	Paul Gibson	.03	.01	.00
☐ 603	Mike Heath	.03	.01	.00
☐ 604	Mike Henneman ...	.03	.01	.00
☐ 605	Guillermo Hernandez .	.06	.03	.00
☐ 606	Shawn Holman	.12	.06	.01
☐ 607	Tracy Jones	.03	.01	.00
☐ 608	Chet Lemon	.03	.01	.00
☐ 609	Fred Lynn	.08	.04	.01
☐ 610	Jack Morris	.08	.04	.01
☐ 611	Matt Nokes	.06	.03	.00
☐ 612	Gary Pettis	.03	.01	.00
☐ 613	Kevin Ritz	.15	.07	.01
☐ 614	Jeff Robinson	.06	.03	.00
☐ 615	Steve Searcy	.03	.01	.00
☐ 616	Frank Tanana	.03	.01	.00
☐ 617	Alan Trammell	.08	.04	.01
☐ 618	Gary Ward	.03	.01	.00
☐ 619	Lou Whitaker	.08	.04	.01
☐ 620	Frank Williams	.03	.01	.00
☐ 621A	George Brett '80	5.00	2.00	.20
	ERR (had 10 .390 hitting seasons)			
☐ 621B	George Grett '80	.20	.08	.01
	COR			
☐ 622	Fern. Valenzuela '81 .	.08	.03	.01
☐ 623	Dale Murphy '82 ...	.12	.06	.01
☐ 624	Cal Ripken '83	.12	.06	.01
☐ 625	Ryne Sandberg '84 ..	.12	.06	.01
☐ 626	Don Mattingly '85 ..	.35	.17	.03
☐ 627	Roger Clemens '86 ..	.12	.06	.01
☐ 628	George Bell '87	.08	.04	.01
☐ 629	Jose Canseco '88 UER	.50	.25	.05
	(Reggie won MVP in '83, should say '73)			
☐ 630	Will Clark '89	.35	.17	.03
☐ 631	Game Savers	.08	.04	.01
	Mark Davis			
	Mitch Williams			
☐ 632	Boston Igniters	.20	.10	.02
	Wade Boggs			

		MINT	EXC	G-VG
☐ 633	Mike Greenwell Starter and Stopper ..	.06	.03	.00
	Mark Gubicza Jeff Russell			
☐ 634	League's Best Shortstops	.08	.04	.01
	Tony Fernandez Cal Ripken			
☐ 635	Human Dynamos ...	.25	.12	.02
	Kirby Puckett Bo Jackson			
☐ 636	300 Strikeout Club ...	.15	.07	.01
	Nolan Ryan Mike Scott			
☐ 637	The Dynamic Duo ..	.20	.10	.02
	Will Clark Kevin Mitchell			
☐ 638	AL All-Stars	.25	.12	.02
	Don Mattingly Mark McGwire			
☐ 639	NL East Rivals	.10	.05	.01
	Howard Johnson Ryne Sandberg			
☐ 640	Rudy Seanez	.20	.10	.02
	Colin Charland			
☐ 641	George Canale	.30	.15	.03
	Kevin Maas			
☐ 642	Kelly Mann	.20	.10	.02
	Dave Hansen			
☐ 643	Greg Smith	.20	.10	.02
	Stu Tate			
☐ 644	Tom Drees	.30	.15	.03
	Dan Howitt			
☐ 645	Mike Roesler	.25	.12	.02
	Derrick May			
☐ 646	Scott Hemond	.20	.10	.02
	Mark Gardner			
☐ 647	John Orton	.20	.10	.02
	Scott Leius			
☐ 648	Rich Monteleone	.20	.10	.02
	Dana Williams			
☐ 649	Mike Huff	.20	.10	.02
	Steve Frey			
☐ 650	Chuck McElroy	.20	.10	.02
	Moises Alou			
☐ 651	Bobby Rose	.20	.10	.02
	Mike Hartley			
☐ 652	Matt Kinzer	.20	.10	.02
	Wayne Edwards			

		MINT	EXC	G-VG
☐ 653	Delino DeShields ...	.40	.20	.04
	Jason Grimsley			
☐ 654	CL: A's/Cubs	.06	.01	.00
	Giants/Blue Jays			
☐ 655	CL: Royals/Angels ..	.06	.01	.00
	Padres/Orioles			
☐ 656	CL: Mets/Astros	.06	.01	.00
	Cards/Red Sox			
☐ 657	CL: Rangers/Brewers	.06	.01	.00
	Expos/Twins			
☐ 658	CL: Dodgers/Reds ..	.06	.01	.00
	Yankees/Pirates			
☐ 659	CL: Indians/Mariners	.06	.01	.00
	White Sox/Phillies			
☐ 660	CL: Braves/Tigers ..	.06	.01	.00
	Specials/Checklists			

1980-83 Pacific Legends

This 124-card set is actually four 30-card sub-sets plus a four-card wax box bottom panel. The set was distributed by series over several years beginning in 1980 with the first 30 cards. The set was produced by Pacific Trading Cards and is frequently referred to as "Cramer Legends," for the founder of Pacific Trading cards, Mike Cramer. Cards are standard size, 2 ½" by 3 ½" and are golden-toned. Even though the wax box cards are numbered from 121-124 and called "series 5", the set is considered complete without them.

			MINT	EXC	G-VG
		COMPLETE SET (120)	12.50	6.25	1.25
		COMMON PLAYER (1-120)	.10	.05	.01
		COMMON PLAYER (121-124)	.20	.10	.02
☐	1	Babe Ruth	1.00	.30	.06
☐	2	Heinie Manush	.10	.05	.01
☐	3	Rabbit Maranville	.10	.05	.01
☐	4	Earl Averill	.10	.05	.01
☐	5	Joe DiMaggio	.60	.30	.06
☐	6	Mickey Mantle	.80	.40	.08
☐	7	Hank Aaron	.30	.15	.03
☐	8	Stan Musial	.25	.12	.02
☐	9	Bill Terry	.10	.05	.01
☐	10	Sandy Koufax	.25	.12	.02
☐	11	Ernie Lombardi	.10	.05	.01
☐	12	Dizzy Dean	.20	.10	.02
☐	13	Lou Gehrig	.50	.25	.05
☐	14	Walter Alston	.10	.05	.01
☐	15	Jackie Robinson	.25	.12	.02
☐	16	Jimmie Foxx	.10	.05	.01
☐	17	Billy Southworth	.10	.05	.01
☐	18	Honus Wagner	.20	.10	.02
☐	19	Duke Snider	.20	.10	.02
☐	20	Rogers Hornsby	.20	.10	.02
☐	21	Paul Waner	.10	.05	.01
☐	22	Luke Appling	.10	.05	.01
☐	23	Billy Herman	.10	.05	.01
☐	24	Lloyd Waner	.10	.05	.01
☐	25	Fred Hutchinson	.10	.05	.01
☐	26	Eddie Collins	.10	.05	.01
☐	27	Lefty Grove	.20	.10	.02
☐	28	Chuck Connors	.20	.10	.02
☐	29	Lefty O'Doul	.10	.05	.01
☐	30	Hank Greenberg	.15	.07	.01
☐	31	Ty Cobb	.50	.25	.05
☐	32	Enos Slaughter	.10	.05	.01
☐	33	Ernie Banks	.20	.10	.02
☐	34	Christy Mathewson	.20	.10	.02
☐	35	Mel Ott	.10	.05	.01
☐	36	Pie Traynor	.10	.05	.01
☐	37	Clark Griffith	.10	.05	.01
☐	38	Mickey Cochrane	.10	.05	.01
☐	39	Joe Cronin	.10	.05	.01
☐	40	Leo Durocher	.10	.05	.01
☐	41	Home Run Baker	.10	.05	.01
☐	42	Joe Tinker	.10	.05	.01
☐	43	John McGraw	.10	.05	.01
☐	44	Bill Dickey	.10	.05	.01
☐	45	Walter Johnson	.20	.10	.02
☐	46	Frankie Frisch	.10	.05	.01
☐	47	Casey Stengel	.20	.10	.02
☐	48	Willie Mays	.35	.17	.03
☐	49	Johnny Mize	.10	.05	.01
☐	50	Roberto Clemente	.20	.10	.02
☐	51	Burleigh Grimes	.10	.05	.01
☐	52	Pee Wee Reese	.15	.07	.01
☐	53	Bob Feller	.20	.10	.02
☐	54	Brooks Robinson	.20	.10	.02
☐	55	Sam Crawford	.10	.05	.01
☐	56	Robin Roberts	.15	.07	.01
☐	57	Warren Spahn	.20	.10	.02
☐	58	Joe McCarthy	.10	.05	.01
☐	59	Jocko Conlan	.10	.05	.01
☐	60	Satchel Paige	.20	.10	.02
☐	61	Ted Williams	.25	.12	.02
☐	62	George Kelly	.10	.05	.01
☐	63	Gil Hodges	.10	.05	.01
☐	64	Jim Bottomley	.10	.05	.01
☐	65	Al Kaline	.20	.10	.02
☐	66	Harvey Kuenn	.10	.05	.01
☐	67	Yogi Berra	.20	.10	.02
☐	68	Nellie Fox	.10	.05	.01
☐	69	Harmon Killebrew	.15	.07	.01
☐	70	Ed Roush	.10	.05	.01
☐	71	Mordecai Brown	.10	.05	.01
☐	72	Gabby Hartnett	.10	.05	.01
☐	73	Early Wynn	.10	.05	.01
☐	74	Nap Lajoie	.10	.05	.01
☐	75	Charlie Grimm	.10	.05	.01
☐	76	Joe Garagiola	.20	.10	.02
☐	77	Ted Lyons	.10	.05	.01
☐	78	Mickey Vernon	.10	.05	.01
☐	79	Lou Boudreau	.10	.05	.01
☐	80	Al Dark	.10	.05	.01
☐	81	Ralph Kiner	.15	.07	.01
☐	82	Phil Rizzuto	.15	.07	.01
☐	83	Stan Hack	.10	.05	.01
☐	84	Frank Chance	.10	.05	.01
☐	85	Ray Schalk	.10	.05	.01
☐	86	Bill McKechnie	.10	.05	.01
☐	87	Travis Jackson	.10	.05	.01
☐	88	Pete Reiser	.10	.05	.01
☐	89	Carl Hubbell	.10	.05	.01
☐	90	Roy Campanella	.20	.10	.02

		MINT	EXC	G-VG
☐ 91	Cy Young	.10	.05	.01
☐ 92	Kiki Cuyler	.10	.05	.01
☐ 93	Chief Bender	.10	.05	.01
☐ 94	Richie Ashburn	.20	.10	.02
☐ 95	Riggs Stephenson	.10	.05	.01
☐ 96	Minnie Minoso	.10	.05	.01
☐ 97	Hack Wilson	.10	.05	.01
☐ 98	Al Lopez	.10	.05	.01
☐ 99	Willie Keeler	.10	.05	.01
☐ 100	Fred Lindstrom	.10	.05	.01
☐ 101	Roger Maris	.25	.12	.02
☐ 102	Roger Bresnahan	.10	.05	.01
☐ 103	Monty Stratton	.10	.05	.01
☐ 104	Goose Goslin	.10	.05	.01
☐ 105	Earl Combs	.10	.05	.01
☐ 106	Pepper Martin	.10	.05	.01
☐ 107	Joe Jackson	.40	.20	.04
☐ 108	George Sisler	.10	.05	.01
☐ 109	Red Ruffing	.10	.05	.01
☐ 110	Johnny Vander Meer	.10	.05	.01
☐ 111	Herb Pennock	.10	.05	.01
☐ 112	Chuck Klein	.10	.05	.01
☐ 113	Paul Derringer	.10	.05	.01
☐ 114	Addie Joss	.10	.05	.01
☐ 115	Bobby Thomson	.10	.05	.01
☐ 116	Chick Hafey	.10	.05	.01
☐ 117	Lefty Gomez	.15	.07	.01
☐ 118	George Kell	.10	.05	.01
☐ 119	Al Simmons	.10	.05	.01
☐ 120	Bob Lemon	.10	.05	.01
☐ 121	Hoyt Wilhelm (wax box card)	.25	.12	.02
☐ 122	Arky Vaughan (wax box card)	.20	.10	.02
☐ 123	Frank Robinson (wax box card)	.30	.15	.03
☐ 124	Grover Alexander (wax box card)	.20	.10	.02

1988 Pacific Legends

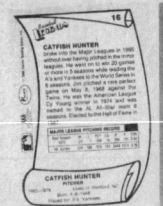

This attractive set of 110 full-color cards was produced by Mike Cramer's Pacific Trading Cards of Edmonds, Washington. The cards are silver bordered and are standard size, 2 ½" by 3 ½". Card backs are printed in yellow, black, and gray on white card stock. The cards were available either as wax packs or as collated sets. The players pictured in the set had retired many years before, but most are still well remembered. The statistics on the card backs give the player's career and "best season" statistics. The set was licensed by Major League Baseball Players Alumni.

		MINT	EXC	G-VG
COMPLETE SET (110)		10.00	5.00	1.00
COMMON PLAYER (1-110)		.05	.02	.00
☐ 1	Hank Aaron	.75	.35	.07
☐ 2	Red Schoendienst	.25	.12	.02
☐ 3	Brooks Robinson	.30	.15	.03
☐ 4	Luke Appling	.15	.07	.01
☐ 5	Gene Woodling	.05	.02	.00
☐ 6	Stan Musial	.60	.30	.06
☐ 7	Mickey Mantle	1.00	.50	.10
☐ 8	Richie Ashburn	.20	.10	.02
☐ 9	Ralph Kiner	.25	.12	.02
☐ 10	Phil Rizzuto	.15	.07	.01
☐ 11	Harvey Haddix	.05	.02	.00
☐ 12	Ken Boyer	.10	.05	.01
☐ 13	Clete Boyer	.05	.02	.00
☐ 14	Ken Harrelson	.10	.05	.01

			MINT	EXC	G-VG
☐	15	Robin Roberts	.20	.10	.02
☐	16	Catfish Hunter	.20	.10	.02
☐	17	Frank Howard	.10	.05	.01
☐	18	Jim Perry	.05	.02	.00
☐	19A	Elston Howard ERR	.10	.05	.01
		(reversed negative)			
☐	19B	Elston Howard COR	.10	.05	.01
☐	20	Jim Bouton	.10	.05	.01
☐	21	Pee Wee Reese	.25	.12	.02
☐	22A	Mel Stottlemyre ERR	.10	.05	.01
		(spelled Stottlemyer			
		on card front)			
☐	22B	Mel Stottlemyre COR	.10	.05	.01
☐	23	Hank Sauer	.05	.02	.00
☐	24	Willie Mays	.75	.35	.07
☐	25	Tom Tresh	.10	.05	.01
☐	26	Roy Sievers	.05	.02	.00
☐	27	Leo Durocher	.15	.07	.01
☐	28	Al Dark	.05	.02	.00
☐	29	Tony Kubek	.15	.07	.01
☐	30	Johnny VanderMeer	.10	.05	.01
☐	31	Joe Adcock	.05	.02	.00
☐	32	Bob Lemon	.15	.07	.01
☐	33	Don Newcombe	.10	.05	.01
☐	34	Thurman Munson	.30	.15	.03
☐	35	Earl Battey	.05	.02	.00
☐	36	Ernie Banks	.30	.15	.03
☐	37	Matty Alou	.05	.02	.00
☐	38	Dave McNally	.05	.02	.00
☐	39	Mickey Lolich	.10	.05	.01
☐	40	Jackie Robinson	.35	.17	.03
☐	41	Allie Reynolds	.10	.05	.01
☐	42A	Don Larsen ERR	.10	.05	.01
		(misspelled Larson			
		on card front)			
☐	42B	Don Larsen COR	.10	.05	.01
☐	43	Fergie Jenkins	.10	.05	.01
☐	44	Jim Gilliam	.10	.05	.01
☐	45	Bobby Thomson	.10	.05	.01
☐	46	Sparky Anderson	.10	.05	.01
☐	47	Roy Campanella	.35	.17	.03
☐	48	Marv Throneberry	.10	.05	.01
☐	49	Bill Virdon	.05	.02	.00
☐	50	Ted Williams	.50	.25	.05
☐	51	Minnie Minoso	.10	.05	.01
☐	52	Bob Turley	.05	.02	.00
☐	53	Yogi Berra	.35	.17	.03
☐	54	Juan Marichal	.20	.10	.02
☐	55	Duke Snider	.35	.17	.03
☐	56	Harvey Kuenn	.10	.05	.01
☐	57	Nellie Fox	.15	.07	.01
☐	58	Felipe Alou	.05	.02	.00
☐	59	Tony Oliva	.10	.05	.01
☐	60	Bill Mazeroski	.10	.05	.01
☐	61	Bobby Shantz	.05	.02	.00
☐	62	Mark Fidrych	.05	.02	.00
☐	63	Johnny Mize	.20	.10	.02
☐	64	Ralph Terry	.10	.05	.01
☐	65	Gus Bell	.05	.02	.00
☐	66	Jerry Koosman	.10	.05	.01
☐	67	Mike McCormick	.05	.02	.00
☐	68	Lou Burdette	.10	.05	.01
☐	69	George Kell	.20	.10	.02
☐	70	Vic Raschi	.10	.05	.01
☐	71	Chuck Connors	.20	.10	.02
☐	72	Ted Kluszewski	.15	.07	.01
☐	73	Bobby Doerr	.20	.10	.02
☐	74	Bobby Richardson	.15	.07	.01
☐	75	Carl Erskine	.10	.05	.01
☐	76	Hoyt Wilhelm	.20	.10	.02
☐	77	Bob Purkey	.05	.02	.00
☐	78	Bob Friend	.05	.02	.00
☐	79	Monte Irvin	.20	.10	.02
☐	80A	Jim Lonborg ERR	.10	.05	.01
		(misspelled Longborg			
		on card front)			
☐	80B	Jim Lonborg COR	.10	.05	.01
☐	81	Wally Moon	.05	.02	.00
☐	82	Moose Skowron	.10	.05	.01
☐	83	Tommy Davis	.10	.05	.01
☐	84	Enos Slaughter	.20	.10	.02
☐	85	Sal Maglie UER	.10	.05	.01
		(1945-1917 on back)			
☐	86	Harmon Killebrew	.20	.10	.02
☐	87	Gil Hodges	.20	.10	.02
☐	88	Jim Kaat	.10	.05	.01
☐	89	Roger Maris	.40	.20	.04
☐	90	Billy Williams	.20	.10	.02
☐	91	Luis Aparicio	.20	.10	.02
☐	92	Jim Bunning	.15	.07	.01
☐	93	Bill Freehan	.10	.05	.01
☐	94	Orlando Cepeda	.15	.07	.01
☐	95	Early Wynn	.20	.10	.02
☐	96	Tug McGraw	.10	.05	.01
☐	97	Ron Santo	.10	.05	.01
☐	98	Del Crandall	.05	.02	.00
☐	99	Sal Bando	.05	.02	.00
☐	100	Joe DiMaggio	.75	.35	.07

		MINT	EXC	G-VG
☐ 101	Bob Feller	.35	.17	.03
☐ 102	Larry Doby	.10	.05	.01
☐ 103	Rollie Fingers	.15	.07	.01
☐ 104	Al Kaline	.25	.12	.02
☐ 105	Johnny Podres	.10	.05	.01
☐ 106	Lou Boudreau	.20	.10	.02
☐ 107	Zoilo Versalles	.05	.02	.00
☐ 108	Dick Groat	.10	.05	.01
☐ 109	Warren Spahn	.25	.12	.02
☐ 110	Johnny Bench	.35	.17	.03

1989 Pacific Legends II

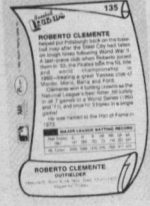

The 1989 Pacific Legends Series II set contains 110 standard-size (2 ½" by 3 ½") cards. The fronts have vintage color photos with silver borders. The backs are gray and feature career highlights and lifetime statistics. The cards were distributed as sets and in 10-card wax packs.

		MINT	EXC	G-VG
COMPLETE SET (110)		10.00	5.00	1.00
COMMON PLAYER (111-220)		.05	.02	.00
☐ 111	Reggie Jackson	.50	.25	.05
☐ 112	Rich Reese	.05	.02	.00
☐ 113	Frankie Frisch	.10	.05	.01
☐ 114	Ed Kranepool	.05	.02	.00

		MINT	EXC	G-VG
☐ 115	Al Hrabosky	.05	.02	.00
☐ 116	Eddie Mathews	.20	.10	.02
☐ 117	Ty Cobb	.40	.20	.04
☐ 118	Jim Davenport	.05	.02	.00
☐ 119	Buddy Lewis	.05	.02	.00
☐ 120	Virgil Trucks	.05	.02	.00
☐ 121	Del Ennis	.05	.02	.00
☐ 122	Dick Radatz	.05	.02	.00
☐ 123	Andy Pafko	.05	.02	.00
☐ 124	Wilbur Wood	.05	.02	.00
☐ 125	Joe Sewell	.10	.05	.01
☐ 126	Herb Score	.05	.02	.00
☐ 127	Paul Waner	.10	.05	.01
☐ 128	Lloyd Waner	.10	.05	.01
☐ 129	Brooks Robinson	.25	.12	.02
☐ 130	Bo Belinsky	.05	.02	.00
☐ 131	Phil Cavaretta	.05	.02	.00
☐ 132	Claude Osteen	.05	.02	.00
☐ 133	Tito Francona	.05	.02	.00
☐ 134	Billy Pierce	.05	.02	.00
☐ 135	Roberto Clemente	.30	.15	.03
☐ 136	Spud Chandler	.05	.02	.00
☐ 137	Enos Slaughter	.15	.07	.01
☐ 138	Ken Holtzman	.05	.02	.00
☐ 139	John Hopp	.05	.02	.00
☐ 140	Tony LaRussa	.05	.02	.00
☐ 141	Ryne Duren	.05	.02	.00
☐ 142	Glenn Beckert	.05	.02	.00
☐ 143	Ken Keltner	.05	.02	.00
☐ 144	Hank Bauer	.05	.02	.00
☐ 145	Roger Craig	.10	.05	.01
☐ 146	Frank Baker	.10	.05	.01
☐ 147	Jim O'Toole	.05	.02	.00
☐ 148	Rogers Hornsby	.20	.10	.02
☐ 149	Jose Cardenal	.05	.02	.00
☐ 150	Bobby Doerr	.15	.07	.01
☐ 151	Mickey Cochrane	.15	.07	.01
☐ 152	Gaylord Perry	.20	.10	.02
☐ 153	Frank Thomas	.05	.02	.00
☐ 154	Ted Williams	.50	.25	.05
☐ 155	Sam McDowell	.05	.02	.00
☐ 156	Bob Feller	.30	.15	.03
☐ 157	Bert Campaneris	.05	.02	.00
☐ 158	Thornton Lee	.05	.02	.00
☐ 159	Gary Peters	.05	.02	.00
☐ 160	Joe Medwick	.15	.07	.01
☐ 161	Joe Nuxhall	.05	.02	.00
☐ 162	Joe Schultz	.05	.02	.00
☐ 163	Harmon Killebrew	.20	.10	.02

		MINT	EXC	G-VG
☐ 164	Bucky Walters	.05	.02	.00
☐ 165	Bob Allison	.05	.02	.00
☐ 166	Lou Boudreau	.15	.07	.01
☐ 167	Joe Cronin	.15	.07	.01
☐ 168	Mike Torrez	.05	.02	.00
☐ 169	Rich Rollins	.05	.02	.00
☐ 170	Tony Cuccinello	.05	.02	.00
☐ 171	Hoyt Wilhelm	.20	.10	.02
☐ 172	Ernie Harwell	.05	.02	.00
	(announcer)			
☐ 173	George Foster	.10	.05	.01
☐ 174	Lou Gehrig	.50	.25	.05
☐ 175	Dave Kingman	.10	.05	.01
☐ 176	Babe Ruth	.75	.35	.07
☐ 177	Joe Black	.05	.02	.00
☐ 178	Roy Face	.05	.02	.00
☐ 179	Earl Weaver	.10	.05	.01
☐ 180	Johnny Mize	.15	.07	.01
☐ 181	Roger Cramer	.05	.02	.00
☐ 182	Jim Piersall	.05	.02	.00
☐ 183	Ned Garver	.05	.02	.00
☐ 184	Billy Williams	.15	.07	.01
☐ 185	Lefty Grove	.15	.07	.01
☐ 186	Jim Grant	.05	.02	.00
☐ 187	Elmer Valo	.05	.02	.00
☐ 188	Ewell Blackwell	.05	.02	.00
☐ 189	Mel Ott	.15	.07	.01
☐ 190	Harry Walker	.05	.02	.00
☐ 191	Bill Campbell	.05	.02	.00
☐ 192	Walter Johnson	.20	.10	.02
☐ 193	Catfish Hunter	.20	.10	.02
☐ 194	Charlie Keller	.05	.02	.00
☐ 195	Hank Greenberg	.15	.07	.01
☐ 196	Bobby Murcer	.10	.05	.01
☐ 197	Al Lopez	.15	.07	.01
☐ 198	Vida Blue	.05	.02	.00
☐ 199	Shag Crawford UMP	.05	.02	.00
☐ 200	Arky Vaughan	.15	.07	.01
☐ 201	Smoky Burgess	.05	.02	.00
☐ 202	Rip Sewell	.05	.02	.00
☐ 203	Earl Averill	.10	.05	.01
☐ 204	Milt Pappas	.05	.02	.00
☐ 205	Mel Harder	.05	.02	.00
☐ 206	Sam Jethroe	.05	.02	.00
☐ 207	Randy Hundley	.05	.02	.00
☐ 208	Jesse Haines	.05	.02	.00
☐ 209	Jack Brickhouse	.05	.02	.00
	(announcer)			
☐ 210	Whitey Ford	.25	.12	.02

		MINT	EXC	G-VG
☐ 211	Honus Wagner	.25	.12	.02
☐ 212	Phil Niekro	.15	.07	.01
☐ 213	Gary Bell	.05	.02	.00
☐ 214	Jon Matlack	.05	.02	.00
☐ 215	Moe Drabowsky	.05	.02	.00
☐ 216	Edd Roush	.15	.07	.01
☐ 217	Joel Horlen	.05	.02	.00
☐ 218	Casey Stengel	.20	.10	.02
☐ 219	Burt Hooton	.05	.02	.00
☐ 220	Joe Jackson	.50	.25	.05

1989-90 Pacific Senior League

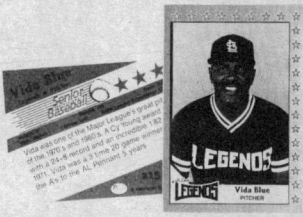

The 1989-90 Pacific Trading Cards Senior League set contains 220 standard-size (2 ½" by 3 ½") cards. The fronts feature color photos with silver borders and player names and positions at the bottom. The horizontally oriented backs are red, white, and blue, and show vital statistics and career highlights. The cards were distributed as a boxed set with 15 card-sized logo stickers/puzzle pieces as well as in wax packs. There are several In Action cards in the set, designated by IA in the checklist below.

	MINT	EXC	G-VG
COMPLETE SET (220)	15.00	7.00	1.00

			MINT	EXC	G-VG
	COMMON PLAYER (1-220)		.05	.02	.01
☐	1	Bobby Tolan	.10	.04	.01
☐	2	Sergio Ferrer	.05	.02	.01
☐	3	David Rajsich	.05	.02	.01
☐	4	Ron LeFlore	.10	.04	.01
☐	5	Steve Henderson	.05	.02	.01
☐	6	Jerry Martin	.05	.02	.01
☐	7	Gary Rajsich	.05	.02	.01
☐	8	Elias Sosa	.05	.02	.01
☐	9	Jon Matlock	.10	.04	.01
☐	10	Steve Kemp	.10	.04	.01
☐	11	Lenny Randle	.05	.02	.01
☐	12	Roy Howell	.05	.02	.01
☐	13	Milt Wilcox	.05	.02	.01
☐	14	Alan Bannister	.05	.02	.01
☐	15	Dock Ellis	.05	.02	.01
☐	16	Mike Williams	.05	.02	.01
☐	17	Luis Gomez	.05	.02	.01
☐	18	Joe Sambito	.05	.02	.01
☐	19	Bake McBride	.05	.02	.01
☐	20	Pat Zachry	.05	.02	.01
☐	21	Dwight Lowry	.05	.02	.01
☐	22	Ozzie Virgil Sr.	.05	.02	.01
☐	23	Randy Lerch	.05	.02	.01
☐	24	Butch Benton	.05	.02	.01
☐	25	Tom Zimmer	.05	.02	.01
☐	26	Al Holland	.05	.02	.01
☐	27	Sammy Stewart	.05	.02	.01
☐	28	Bill Lee	.10	.04	.01
☐	29	Ferguson Jenkins	.50	.20	.04
☐	30	Leon Roberts	.05	.02	.01
☐	31	Rick Wise	.05	.02	.01
☐	32	Butch Hobson	.05	.02	.01
☐	33	Pete LaCock	.05	.02	.01
☐	34	Bill Campbell	.05	.02	.01
☐	35	Doug Simunic	.05	.02	.01
☐	36	Mario Guerrero	.05	.02	.01
☐	37	Jim Willoughby	.05	.02	.01
☐	38	Joe Pittman	.05	.02	.01
☐	39	Mark Bomback	.05	.02	.01
☐	40	Tommy McMillian	.05	.02	.01
☐	41	Gary Allanson	.05	.02	.01
☐	42	Cecil Cooper	.10	.04	.01
☐	43	John LaRosa	.05	.02	.01
☐	44	Darrell Brandon	.05	.02	.01
☐	45	Bernie Carbo	.05	.02	.01
☐	46	Mike Cuellar	.10	.04	.01
☐	47	Al Bumbry	.05	.02	.01
☐	48	Gene Richards	.05	.02	.01
☐	49	Pedro Borbon	.05	.02	.01
☐	50	Julio Solo	.05	.02	.01
☐	51	Ed Nottle	.05	.02	.01
☐	52	Jim Bibby	.05	.02	.01
☐	53	Doug Griffin	.05	.02	.01
☐	54	Ed Clements	.05	.02	.01
☐	55	Dalton Jones	.05	.02	.01
☐	56	Earl Weaver MG	.50	.20	.04
☐	57	Jesus De La Rosa	.05	.02	.01
☐	58	Paul Casanova	.05	.02	.01
☐	59	Frank Riccelli	.05	.02	.01
☐	60	Rafael Landestoy	.05	.02	.01
☐	61	George Hendrick	.10	.04	.01
☐	62	Cesar Cedeno	.10	.04	.01
☐	63	Bert Campaneris	.10	.04	.01
☐	64	Derrell Thomas	.05	.02	.01
☐	65	Bobby Ramos	.05	.02	.01
☐	66	Grant Jackson	.05	.02	.01
☐	67	Steve Whitaker	.05	.02	.01
☐	68	Pedro Ramos	.05	.02	.01
☐	69	Joe Hicks	.05	.02	.01
☐	70	Taylor Duncan	.05	.02	.01
☐	71	Tom Shopay	.05	.02	.01
☐	72	Ken Clay	.05	.02	.01
☐	73	Mike Kekich	.05	.02	.01
☐	74	Ed Halicki	.05	.02	.01
☐	75	Ed Figueroa	.05	.02	.01
☐	76	Paul Blair	.10	.04	.01
☐	77	Luis Tiant	.25	.09	.01
☐	78	Stan Bahnsen	.05	.02	.01
☐	79	Rennie Stennett	.05	.02	.01
☐	80	Bobby Molinaro	.05	.02	.01
☐	81	Jim Gideon	.05	.02	.01
☐	82	Orlando Gonzalez	.05	.02	.01
☐	83	Amos Otis	.20	.08	.01
☐	84	Dennis Leonard	.10	.04	.01
☐	85	Pat Putman	.05	.02	.01
☐	86	Rick Manning	.05	.02	.01
☐	87	Pat Dobson	.10	.04	.01
☐	88	Marty Castillo	.05	.02	.01
☐	89	Steve McCatty	.05	.02	.01
☐	90	Doug Bird	.05	.02	.01
☐	91	Rick Waits	.05	.02	.01
☐	92	Ron Jackson	.05	.02	.01
☐	93	Tim Hosley	.05	.02	.01
☐	94	Steve Luebber	.05	.02	.01
☐	95	Rich Gale	.05	.02	.01
☐	96	Champ Summers	.05	.02	.01

		MINT	EXC	G-VG			MINT	EXC	G-VG
☐ 97	Dave LaRoche	.05	.02	.01	☐ 146	Gene Clines	.05	.02	.01
☐ 98	Bobby Jones	.05	.02	.01	☐ 147	Willie Aikens	.10	.04	.01
☐ 99	Kim Allen	.05	.02	.01	☐ 148	Tommy Moore	.05	.02	.01
☐ 100	Wayne Garland	.05	.02	.01	☐ 149	Clete Boyer	.10	.04	.01
☐ 101	Tom Spencer	.05	.02	.01	☐ 150	Stan Cliburn	.05	.02	.01
☐ 102	Dan Driessen	.10	.04	.01	☐ 151	Ken Kravec	.05	.02	.01
☐ 103	Ron Pruitt	.05	.02	.01	☐ 152	Garth Iorg	.05	.02	.01
☐ 104	Tim Ireland	.05	.02	.01	☐ 153	Rick Peterson	.05	.02	.01
☐ 105	Dan Driessen IA	.10	.04	.01	☐ 154	Wayne Nordhagen	.05	.02	.01
☐ 106	Pepe Frias	.05	.02	.01	☐ 155	Danny Meyer	.05	.02	.01
☐ 107	Eric Rasmussen	.05	.02	.01	☐ 156	Wayne Garrett	.05	.02	.01
☐ 108	Don Hood	.05	.02	.01	☐ 157	Wayne Krenchicki	.05	.02	.01
☐ 109	Joe Coleman	.05	.02	.01	☐ 158	Graig Nettles	.20	.08	.01
☐ 110	Jim Slaton	.05	.02	.01	☐ 159	Earl Stephenson	.05	.02	.01
☐ 111	Clint Hurdie	.05	.02	.01	☐ 160	Carl Taylor	.05	.02	.01
☐ 112	Larry Milbourne	.05	.02	.01	☐ 161	Rollie Fingers	.50	.20	.04
☐ 113	Al Holland	.05	.02	.01	☐ 162	Toby Harrah	.10	.04	.01
☐ 114	George Foster	.15	.06	.01	☐ 163	Mickey Rivers	.10	.04	.01
☐ 115	Graig Nettles	.15	.06	.01	☐ 164	Dave Kingman	.15	.06	.01
☐ 116	Oscar Gamble	.05	.02	.01	☐ 165	Paul Mirabella	.05	.02	.01
☐ 117	Ross Grimsley	.05	.02	.01	☐ 166	Dick Williams	.10	.04	.01
☐ 118	Bill Travers	.05	.02	.01	☐ 167	Luis Pujols	.05	.02	.01
☐ 119	Jose Beniquez	.10	.04	.01	☐ 168	Tito Landrum	.10	.04	.01
☐ 120	Jerry Grote IA	.05	.02	.01	☐ 169	Tom Underwood	.05	.02	.01
☐ 121	John D'Acquisto	.05	.02	.01	☐ 170	Mark Wagner	.05	.02	.01
☐ 122	Tom Murphy	.05	.02	.01	☐ 171	Odell Jones	.05	.02	.01
☐ 123	Walt Williams	.05	.02	.01	☐ 172	Doug Capilla	.05	.02	.01
☐ 124	Roy Thomas	.05	.02	.01	☐ 173	Allie Rondon	.05	.02	.01
☐ 125	Jerry Grote	.05	.02	.01	☐ 174	Lowell Palmer	.05	.02	.01
☐ 126	Jim Nettles	.05	.02	.01	☐ 175	Juan Eichelberger	.05	.02	.01
☐ 127	Randy Niemann	.05	.02	.01	☐ 176	Wes Clements	.05	.02	.01
☐ 128	Bobby Bonds	.25	.10	.01	☐ 177	Rodney Scott	.05	.02	.01
☐ 129	Ed Glynn	.05	.02	.01	☐ 178	Ron Washington	.10	.04	.01
☐ 130	Ed Hicks	.05	.02	.01	☐ 179	Al Hrabosky	.10	.04	.01
☐ 131	Ivan Murrell	.05	.02	.01	☐ 180	Sid Monge	.05	.02	.01
☐ 132	Graig Nettles	.20	.08	.01	☐ 181	Randy Johnson	.05	.02	.01
☐ 133	Hal McRae	.15	.06	.01	☐ 182	Tim Stoddard	.05	.02	.01
☐ 134	Pat Kelly	.05	.02	.01	☐ 183	Dick Williams MG	.10	.04	.01
☐ 135	Sammy Stewart	.05	.02	.01	☐ 184	Lee Lacy	.10	.04	.01
☐ 136	Bruce Kison	.05	.02	.01	☐ 185	Jerry White	.05	.02	.01
☐ 137	Jim Morrison	.05	.02	.01	☐ 186	Dave Kingman	.15	.06	.01
☐ 138	Omar Moreno	.05	.02	.01	☐ 187	Checklist 1-110	.15	.06	.01
☐ 139	Tom Brown	.05	.02	.01	☐ 188	Jose Cruz	.15	.06	.01
☐ 140	Steve Dillard	.05	.02	.01	☐ 189	Jamie Easterly	.05	.02	.01
☐ 141	Gary Alexander	.05	.02	.01	☐ 190	Ike Blessit	.05	.02	.01
☐ 142	Al Oliver	.20	.08	.01	☐ 191	Johnny Grubb	.05	.02	.01
☐ 143	Rick Lysander	.05	.02	.01	☐ 192	Dave Cash	.05	.02	.01
☐ 144	Tippy Martinez	.10	.05	.01	☐ 193	Doug Corbett	.05	.02	.01
☐ 145	Al Cowens	.10	.05	.01	☐ 194	Bruce Bochy	.05	.02	.01

1988 Score

			MINT	EXC	G-VG
☐	195	Mark Corey	.05	.02	.01
☐	196	Gil Rondon	.05	.02	.01
☐	197	Jerry Martin	.05	.02	.01
☐	198	Gerry Pirtle	.05	.02	.01
☐	199	Gates Brown	.10	.04	.01
☐	200	Bob Galasso	.05	.02	.01
☐	201	Bake McBride	.05	.02	.01
☐	202	Wayne Granger	.05	.02	.01
☐	203	Larry Milbourne	.05	.02	.01
☐	204	Tom Paciorek	.10	.04	.01
☐	205	U.L. Washington	.05	.02	.01
☐	206	Larvell Blanks	.05	.02	.01
☐	207	Bob Shirley	.05	.02	.01
☐	208	Pete Falcone	.05	.02	.01
☐	209	Sal Butera	.05	.02	.01
☐	210	Roy Branch	.05	.02	.01
☐	211	Dyar Miller	.05	.02	.01
☐	212	Paul Siebert	.05	.02	.01
☐	213	Ken Reitz	.05	.02	.01
☐	214	Bill Madlock	.15	.06	.01
☐	215	Vida Blue	.10	.04	.01
☐	216	Dave Hilton	.05	.02	.01
☐	217	Ramos and Bren	.05	.02	.01
☐	218	Checklist 111-220	.05	.02	.01
☐	219	Dobson and Weaver	.15	.06	.01
☐	220	Curt Flood	.20	.08	.01

This 660-card set was distributed by Major League Marketing. Cards measure 2 ½" by 3 ½" and feature six distinctive border colors on the front. Highlights (652-660) and Rookie Prospects (623-647) are included in the set. Reggie Jackson's career is honored with a 5-card subset on cards 500-504. The set is distinguished by the fact that each card back shows a full-color picture of the player. The company also produced a very limited "glossy" set, which is valued at eight times the value of the regular (non-glossy) set. Although exact production quantities of this glossy set are not known, it is generally accepted that the number of Score glossy sets produced in 1988 was much smaller (estimated only 10% to 15% as many) than the number of Topps Tiffany or Fleer Tin sets.

			MINT	EXC	G-VG
	COMPLETE SET (660)		25.00	12.50	2.50
	COMMON PLAYER (1-660)		.03	.01	.00
☐	1	Don Mattingly	1.50	.40	.08
☐	2	Wade Boggs	.75	.35	.07
☐	3	Tim Raines	.15	.07	.01
☐	4	Andre Dawson	.15	.07	.01
☐	5	Mark McGwire	1.25	.60	.12
☐	6	Kevin Seitzer	.65	.30	.06
☐	7	Wally-Joyner	.35	.17	.01
☐	8	Jesse Barfield	.10	.05	.01
☐	9	Pedro Guerrero	.12	.06	.01

			MINT	EXC	G-VG
☐	10	Eric Davis	.60	.30	.06
☐	11	George Brett	.25	.12	.02
☐	12	Ozzie Smith	.15	.07	.01
☐	13	Rickey Henderson	.25	.12	.02
☐	14	Jim Rice	.12	.06	.01
☐	15	Matt Nokes	.35	.17	.03
☐	16	Mike Schmidt	.25	.12	.02
☐	17	Dave Parker	.10	.05	.01
☐	18	Eddie Murray	.15	.07	.01
☐	19	Andres Galarraga	.15	.07	.01
☐	20	Tony Fernandez	.10	.05	.01
☐	21	Kevin McReynolds	.12	.06	.01
☐	22	B.J. Surhoff	.10	.05	.01
☐	23	Pat Tabler	.06	.03	.00
☐	24	Kirby Puckett	.40	.20	.04
☐	25	Benny Santiago	.40	.20	.04
☐	26	Ryne Sandberg	.20	.10	.02
☐	27	Kelly Downs	.08	.04	.01
		(Will Clark in back- ground, out of focus)			
☐	28	Jose Cruz	.06	.03	.00
☐	29	Pete O'Brien	.06	.03	.00
☐	30	Mark Langston	.12	.06	.01
☐	31	Lee Smith	.06	.03	.00
☐	32	Juan Samuel	.08	.04	.01
☐	33	Kevin Bass	.06	.03	.00
☐	34	R.J. Reynolds	.03	.01	.00
☐	35	Steve Sax	.12	.06	.01
☐	36	John Kruk	.08	.04	.01
☐	37	Alan Trammell	.12	.06	.01
☐	38	Chris Bosio	.06	.03	.00
☐	39	Brook Jacoby	.06	.03	.00
☐	40	Willie McGee	.08	.04	.01
☐	41	Dave Magadan	.12	.06	.01
☐	42	Fred Lynn	.10	.05	.01
☐	43	Kent Hrbek	.12	.06	.01
☐	44	Brian Downing	.03	.01	.00
☐	45	Jose Canseco	1.25	.60	.12
☐	46	Jim Presley	.06	.03	.00
☐	47	Mike Stanley	.06	.03	.00
☐	48	Tony Pena	.06	.03	.00
☐	49	David Cone	.75	.35	.07
☐	50	Rick Sutcliffe	.08	.04	.01
☐	51	Doug Drabek	.06	.03	.00
☐	52	Bill Doran	.06	.03	.00
☐	53	Mike Scioscia	.03	.01	.00
☐	54	Candy Maldonado	.06	.03	.00
☐	55	Dave Winfield	.18	.09	.01
☐	56	Lou Whitaker	.10	.05	.01

			MINT	EXC	G-VG
☐	57	Tom Henke	.06	.03	.00
☐	58	Ken Gerhart	.06	.03	.00
☐	59	Glenn Braggs	.08	.04	.01
☐	60	Julio Franco	.10	.05	.01
☐	61	Charlie Leibrandt	.03	.01	.00
☐	62	Gary Gaetti	.10	.05	.01
☐	63	Bob Boone	.08	.04	.01
☐	64	Luis Polonia	.20	.10	.02
☐	65	Dwight Evans	.10	.05	.01
☐	66	Phil Bradley	.08	.04	.01
☐	67	Mike Boddicker	.03	.01	.00
☐	68	Vince Coleman	.15	.07	.01
☐	69	Howard Johnson	.15	.07	.01
☐	70	Tim Wallach	.08	.04	.01
☐	71	Keith Moreland	.03	.01	.00
☐	72	Barry Larkin	.25	.12	.02
☐	73	Alan Ashby	.03	.01	.00
☐	74	Rick Rhoden	.03	.01	.00
☐	75	Darrell Evans	.06	.03	.00
☐	76	Dave Stieb	.08	.04	.01
☐	77	Dan Plesac	.06	.03	.00
☐	78	Will Clark	1.50	.75	.15
☐	79	Frank White	.06	.03	.00
☐	80	Joe Carter	.15	.07	.01
☐	81	Mike Witt	.06	.03	.00
☐	82	Terry Steinbach	.20	.10	.02
☐	83	Alvin Davis	.10	.05	.01
☐	84	Tommy Herr	.08	.04	.01
		(Will Clark shown slid- ing into second)			
☐	85	Vance Law	.03	.01	.00
☐	86	Kal Daniels	.12	.06	.01
☐	87	Rick Honeycutt UER	.03	.01	.00
		(wrong years for stats on back)			
☐	88	Alfredo Griffin	.06	.03	.00
☐	89	Bret Saberhagen	.20	.10	.02
☐	90	Bert Blyleven	.10	.05	.01
☐	91	Jeff Reardon	.08	.04	.01
☐	92	Cory Snyder	.12	.06	.01
☐	93A	Greg Walker ERR	3.00	1.00	.30
		(93 of 66)			
☐	93B	Greg Walker COR	.10	.04	.01
		(93 of 660)			
☐	94	Joe Magrane	.50	.25	.05
☐	95	Rob Deer	.08	.04	.01
☐	96	Ray Knight	.06	.03	.00
☐	97	Casey Candaele	.03	.01	.00
☐	98	John Cerutti	.03	.01	.00

			MINT	EXC	G-VG
☐	99	Buddy Bell	.06	.03	.00
☐	100	Jack Clark	.12	.06	.01
☐	101	Eric Bell	.03	.01	.00
☐	102	Willie Wilson	.06	.03	.00
☐	103	Dave Schmidt	.03	.01	.00
☐	104	Dennis Eckersley	.10	.05	.01
☐	105	Don Sutton	.12	.06	.01
☐	106	Danny Tartabull	.18	.09	.01
☐	107	Fred McGriff	1.00	.50	.10
☐	108	Les Straker	.08	.04	.01
☐	109	Lloyd Moseby	.06	.03	.00
☐	110	Roger Clemens	.50	.25	.05
☐	111	Glenn Hubbard	.03	.01	.00
☐	112	Ken Williams	.18	.09	.01
☐	113	Ruben Sierra	.35	.17	.03
☐	114	Stan Jefferson	.12	.06	.01
☐	115	Milt Thompson	.03	.01	.00
☐	116	Bobby Bonilla	.15	.07	.01
☐	117	Wayne Tolleson	.03	.01	.00
☐	118	Matt Williams	.75	.35	.07
☐	119	Chet Lemon	.03	.01	.00
☐	120	Dale Sveum	.03	.01	.00
☐	121	Dennis Boyd	.06	.03	.00
☐	122	Brett Butler	.06	.03	.00
☐	123	Terry Kennedy	.03	.01	.00
☐	124	Jack Howell	.03	.01	.00
☐	125	Curt Young	.03	.01	.00
☐	126A	Dave Valle ERR (misspelled Dale on card front)	.25	.12	.02
☐	126B	Dave Valle COR	.10	.05	.01
☐	127	Curt Wilkerson	.03	.01	.00
☐	128	Tim Teufel	.03	.01	.00
☐	129	Ozzie Virgil	.03	.01	.00
☐	130	Brian Fisher	.03	.01	.00
☐	131	Lance Parrish	.08	.04	.01
☐	132	Tom Browning	.08	.04	.01
☐	133A	Larry Andersen ERR (misspelled Anderson on card front)	.20	.10	.02
☐	133B	Larry Andersen COR	.06	.03	.00
☐	134A	Bob Brenly ERR (misspelled Brenley on card front)	.20	.10	.02
☐	134B	Bob Brenly COR	.06	.03	.00
☐	135	Mike Marshall	.08	.04	.01
☐	136	Gerald Perry	.06	.03	.00
☐	137	Bobby Meacham	.03	.01	.00
☐	138	Larry Herndon	.03	.01	.00
☐	139	Fred Manrique	.10	.05	.01
☐	140	Charlie Hough	.03	.01	.00
☐	141	Ron Darling	.08	.04	.01
☐	142	Herm Winningham	.03	.01	.00
☐	143	Mike Diaz	.03	.01	.00
☐	144	Mike Jackson	.12	.06	.01
☐	145	Denny Walling	.03	.01	.00
☐	146	Robby Thompson	.03	.01	.00
☐	147	Franklin Stubbs	.03	.01	.00
☐	148	Albert Hall	.03	.01	.00
☐	149	Bobby Witt	.06	.03	.00
☐	150	Lance McCullers	.06	.03	.00
☐	151	Scott Bradley	.03	.01	.00
☐	152	Mark McLemore	.03	.01	.00
☐	153	Tim Laudner	.03	.01	.00
☐	154	Greg Swindell	.12	.06	.01
☐	155	Marty Barrett	.06	.03	.00
☐	156	Mike Heath	.03	.01	.00
☐	157	Gary Ward	.03	.01	.00
☐	158A	Lee Mazzilli ERR (misspelled Mazilli on card front)	.20	.10	.02
☐	158B	Lee Mazzilli COR	.06	.03	.00
☐	159	Tom Foley	.03	.01	.00
☐	160	Robin Yount	.25	.12	.02
☐	161	Steve Bedrosian	.08	.04	.01
☐	162	Bob Walk	.03	.01	.00
☐	163	Nick Esasky	.08	.04	.01
☐	164	Ken Caminiti	.20	.10	.02
☐	165	Jose Uribe	.03	.01	.00
☐	166	Dave Anderson	.03	.01	.00
☐	167	Ed Whitson	.03	.01	.00
☐	168	Ernie Whitt	.03	.01	.00
☐	169	Cecil Cooper	.08	.04	.01
☐	170	Mike Pagliarulo	.06	.03	.00
☐	171	Pat Sheridan	.03	.01	.00
☐	172	Chris Bando	.03	.01	.00
☐	173	Lee Lacy	.03	.01	.00
☐	174	Steve Lombardozzi	.03	.01	.00
☐	175	Mike Greenwell	1.25	.60	.12
☐	176	Greg Minton	.03	.01	.00
☐	177	Moose Haas	.03	.01	.00
☐	178	Mike Kingery	.03	.01	.00
☐	179	Greg Harris	.03	.01	.00
☐	180	Bo Jackson	1.25	.60	.12
☐	181	Carmelo Martinez	.03	.01	.00
☐	182	Alex Trevino	.03	.01	.00
☐	183	Ron Oester	.03	.01	.00
☐	184	Danny Darwin	.03	.01	.00

		MINT	EXC	G-VG
☐ 185	Mike Krukow	.03	.01	.00
☐ 186	Rafael Palmeiro	.50	.25	.05
☐ 187	Tim Burke	.03	.01	.00
☐ 188	Roger McDowell	.06	.03	.00
☐ 189	Garry Templeton	.06	.03	.00
☐ 190	Terry Pendleton	.03	.01	.00
☐ 191	Larry Parrish	.03	.01	.00
☐ 192	Rey Quinones	.03	.01	.00
☐ 193	Joaquin Andujar	.06	.03	.00
☐ 194	Tom Brunansky	.10	.05	.01
☐ 195	Donnie Moore	.03	.01	.00
☐ 196	Dan Pasqua	.03	.01	.00
☐ 197	Jim Gantner	.03	.01	.00
☐ 198	Mark Eichhorn	.03	.01	.00
☐ 199	John Grubb	.03	.01	.00
☐ 200	Bill Ripken	.15	.07	.01
☐ 201	Sam Horn	.15	.07	.01
☐ 202	Todd Worrell	.10	.05	.01
☐ 203	Terry Leach	.06	.03	.00
☐ 204	Garth Iorg	.03	.01	.00
☐ 205	Brian Dayett	.03	.01	.00
☐ 206	Bo Diaz	.03	.01	.00
☐ 207	Craig Reynolds	.03	.01	.00
☐ 208	Brian Holton	.08	.04	.01
☐ 209	Marvell Wynne UER (misspelled Marvelle on card front)	.06	.03	.00
☐ 210	Dave Concepcion	.06	.03	.00
☐ 211	Mike Davis	.03	.01	.00
☐ 212	Devon White	.12	.06	.01
☐ 213	Mickey Brantley	.06	.03	.00
☐ 214	Greg Gagne	.03	.01	.00
☐ 215	Oddibe McDowell	.06	.03	.00
☐ 216	Jimmy Key	.06	.03	.00
☐ 217	Dave Bergman	.03	.01	.00
☐ 218	Calvin Schiraldi	.03	.01	.00
☐ 219	Larry Sheets	.06	.03	.00
☐ 220	Mike Easler	.03	.01	.00
☐ 221	Kurt Stillwell	.03	.01	.00
☐ 222	Chuck Jackson	.08	.04	.01
☐ 223	Dave Martinez	.06	.03	.00
☐ 224	Tim Leary	.08	.04	.01
☐ 225	Steve Garvey	.20	.10	.02
☐ 226	Greg Mathews	.03	.01	.00
☐ 227	Doug Sisk	.03	.01	.00
☐ 228	Dave Henderson	.06	.03	.00
☐ 229	Jimmy Dwyer	.03	.01	.00
☐ 230	Larry Owen	.03	.01	.00
☐ 231	Andre Thornton	.03	.01	.00

		MINT	EXC	G-VG
☐ 232	Mark Salas	.03	.01	.00
☐ 233	Tom Brookens	.03	.01	.00
☐ 234	Greg Brock	.03	.01	.00
☐ 235	Rance Mulliniks	.03	.01	.00
☐ 236	Bob Brower	.06	.03	.00
☐ 237	Joe Niekro	.06	.03	.00
☐ 238	Scott Bankhead	.06	.03	.00
☐ 239	Doug DeCinces	.03	.01	.00
☐ 240	Tommy John	.10	.05	.01
☐ 241	Rich Gedman	.03	.01	.00
☐ 242	Ted Power	.03	.01	.00
☐ 243	Dave Meads	.08	.04	.01
☐ 244	Jim Sundberg	.03	.01	.00
☐ 245	Ken Oberkfell	.03	.01	.00
☐ 246	Jimmy Jones	.10	.05	.01
☐ 247	Ken Landreaux	.03	.01	.00
☐ 248	Jose Oquendo	.03	.01	.00
☐ 249	John Mitchell	.10	.05	.01
☐ 250	Don Baylor	.08	.04	.01
☐ 251	Scott Fletcher	.03	.01	.00
☐ 252	Al Newman	.03	.01	.00
☐ 253	Carney Lansford	.08	.04	.01
☐ 254	Johnny Ray	.06	.03	.00
☐ 255	Gary Pettis	.03	.01	.00
☐ 256	Ken Phelps	.06	.03	.00
☐ 257	Rick Leach	.03	.01	.00
☐ 258	Tim Stoddard	.03	.01	.00
☐ 259	Ed Romero	.03	.01	.00
☐ 260	Sid Bream	.03	.01	.00
☐ 261A	Tom Niedenfuer ERR (misspelled Neidenfuer on card front)	.20	.10	.02
☐ 261B	Tom Niedenfuer COR	.06	.03	.00
☐ 262	Rick Dempsey	.03	.01	.00
☐ 263	Lonnie Smith	.08	.04	.01
☐ 264	Bob Forsch	.03	.01	.00
☐ 265	Barry Bonds	.15	.07	.01
☐ 266	Willie Randolph	.06	.03	.00
☐ 267	Mike Ramsey	.10	.05	.01
☐ 268	Don Slaught	.03	.01	.00
☐ 269	Mickey Tettleton	.08	.04	.01
☐ 270	Jerry Reuss	.03	.01	.00
☐ 271	Marc Sullivan	.03	.01	.00
☐ 272	Jim Morrison	.03	.01	.00
☐ 273	Steve Balboni	.03	.01	.00
☐ 274	Dick Schofield	.03	.01	.00
☐ 275	John Tudor	.08	.04	.01
☐ 276	Gene Larkin	.20	.10	.02

		MINT	EXC	G-VG			MINT	EXC	G-VG
☐ 277	Harold Reynolds	.06	.03	.00	☐ 323	Lee Guetterman	.03	.01	.00
☐ 278	Jerry Browne	.06	.03	.00	☐ 324	Dan Gladden	.06	.03	.00
☐ 279	Willie Upshaw	.03	.01	.00	☐ 325	Gary Carter	.15	.07	.01
☐ 280	Ted Higuera	.08	.04	.01	☐ 326	Tracy Jones	.06	.03	.00
☐ 281	Terry McGriff	.08	.04	.01	☐ 327	Floyd Youmans	.03	.01	.00
☐ 282	Terry Puhl	.03	.01	.00	☐ 328	Bill Dawley	.03	.01	.00
☐ 283	Mark Wasinger	.15	.07	.01	☐ 329	Paul Noce	.08	.04	.01
☐ 284	Luis Salazar	.03	.01	.00	☐ 330	Angel Salazar	.03	.01	.00
☐ 285	Ted Simmons	.08	.04	.01	☐ 331	Goose Gossage	.08	.04	.00
☐ 286	John Shelby	.03	.01	.00	☐ 332	George Frazier	.03	.01	.00
☐ 287	John Smiley	.25	.12	.02	☐ 333	Ruppert Jones	.03	.01	.00
☐ 288	Curt Ford	.03	.01	.00	☐ 334	Billy Jo Robidoux	.03	.01	.00
☐ 289	Steve Crawford	.03	.01	.00	☐ 335	Mike Scott	.12	.06	.01
☐ 290	Dan Quisenberry	.08	.04	.01	☐ 336	Randy Myers	.15	.07	.01
☐ 291	Alan Wiggins	.03	.01	.00	☐ 337	Bob Sebra	.03	.01	.00
☐ 292	Randy Bush	.03	.01	.00	☐ 338	Eric Show	.03	.01	.00
☐ 293	John Candelaria	.06	.03	.00	☐ 339	Mitch Williams	.08	.04	.01
☐ 294	Tony Phillips	.03	.01	.00	☐ 340	Paul Molitor	.10	.05	.01
☐ 295	Mike Morgan	.06	.03	.00	☐ 341	Gus Polidor	.03	.01	.00
☐ 296	Bill Wegman	.03	.01	.00	☐ 342	Steve Trout	.03	.01	.00
☐ 297A	Terry Francona ERR	.20	.10	.02	☐ 343	Jerry Don Gleaton	.03	.01	.00
	(misspelled Franconia				☐ 344	Bob Knepper	.03	.01	.00
	on card front)				☐ 345	Mitch Webster	.03	.01	.00
☐ 297B	Terry Francona COR	.06	.03	.00	☐ 346	John Morris	.03	.01	.00
☐ 298	Mickey Hatcher	.03	.01	.00	☐ 347	Andy Hawkins	.03	.01	.00
☐ 299	Andres Thomas	.03	.01	.00	☐ 348	Dave Leiper	.03	.01	.00
☐ 300	Bob Stanley	.03	.01	.00	☐ 349	Ernest Riles	.03	.01	.00
☐ 301	Al Pedrique	.08	.04	.01	☐ 350	Dwight Gooden	.40	.20	.04
☐ 302	Jim Lindeman	.06	.03	.00	☐ 351	Dave Righetti	.08	.04	.01
☐ 303	Wally Backman	.03	.01	.00	☐ 352	Pat Dodson	.08	.04	.01
☐ 304	Paul O'Neill	.10	.05	.01	☐ 353	John Habyan	.06	.03	.00
☐ 305	Hubie Brooks	.08	.04	.01	☐ 354	Jim Deshaies	.03	.01	.00
☐ 306	Steve Buechele	.03	.01	.00	☐ 355	Butch Wynegar	.03	.01	.00
☐ 307	Bobby Thigpen	.06	.03	.00	☐ 356	Bryn Smith	.06	.03	.00
☐ 308	George Hendrick	.03	.01	.00	☐ 357	Matt Young	.03	.01	.00
☐ 309	John Moses	.03	.01	.00	☐ 358	Tom Pagnozzi	.10	.05	.01
☐ 310	Ron Guidry	.08	.04	.01	☐ 359	Floyd Rayford	.03	.01	.00
☐ 311	Bill Schroeder	.03	.01	.00	☐ 360	Darryl Strawberry	.40	.20	.04
☐ 312	Jose Nunez	.12	.06	.01	☐ 361	Sal Butera	.03	.01	.00
☐ 313	Bud Black	.03	.01	.00	☐ 362	Domingo Ramos	.03	.01	.00
☐ 314	Joe Sambito	.03	.01	.00	☐ 363	Chris Brown	.03	.01	.00
☐ 315	Scott McGregor	.03	.01	.00	☐ 364	Jose Gonzalez	.08	.04	.01
☐ 316	Rafael Santana	.03	.01	.00	☐ 365	Dave Smith	.03	.01	.00
☐ 317	Frank Williams	.03	.01	.00	☐ 366	Andy McGaffigan	.03	.01	.00
☐ 318	Mike Fitzgerald	.03	.01	.00	☐ 367	Stan Javier	.03	.01	.00
☐ 319	Rick Mahler	.03	.01	.00	☐ 368	Henry Cotto	.03	.01	.00
☐ 320	Jim Gott	.03	.01	.00	☐ 369	Mike Birkbeck	.08	.04	.01
☐ 321	Mariano Duncan	.03	.01	.00	☐ 370	Len Dykstra	.06	.03	.00
☐ 322	Jose Guzman	.03	.01	.00	☐ 371	Dave Collins	.03	.01	.00

		MINT	EXC	G-VG
☐ 372	Spike Owen	.03	.01	.00
☐ 373	Geno Petralli	.03	.01	.00
☐ 374	Ron Karkovice	.03	.01	.00
☐ 375	Shane Rawley	.03	.01	.00
☐ 376	DeWayne Buice	.08	.04	.01
☐ 377	Bill Pecota	.08	.04	.01
☐ 378	Leon Durham	.03	.01	.00
☐ 379	Ed Olwine	.03	.01	.00
☐ 380	Bruce Hurst	.10	.05	.01
☐ 381	Bob McClure	.03	.01	.00
☐ 382	Mark Thurmond	.03	.01	.00
☐ 383	Buddy Biancalana	.03	.01	.00
☐ 384	Tim Conroy	.03	.01	.00
☐ 385	Tony Gwynn	.30	.15	.03
☐ 386	Greg Gross	.03	.01	.00
☐ 387	Barry Lyons	.20	.10	.02
☐ 388	Mike Felder	.03	.01	.00
☐ 389	Pat Clements	.03	.01	.00
☐ 390	Ken Griffey	.08	.04	.01
☐ 391	Mark Davis	.12	.06	.01
☐ 392	Jose Rijo	.06	.03	.00
☐ 393	Mike Young	.03	.01	.00
☐ 394	Willie Fraser	.03	.01	.00
☐ 395	Dion James	.03	.01	.00
☐ 396	Steve Shields	.03	.01	.00
☐ 397	Randy St.Claire	.03	.01	.00
☐ 398	Danny Jackson	.08	.04	.01
☐ 399	Cecil Fielder	.03	.01	.00
☐ 400	Keith Hernandez	.12	.06	.01
☐ 401	Don Carman	.03	.01	.00
☐ 402	Chuck Crim	.08	.04	.01
☐ 403	Rob Woodward	.03	.01	.00
☐ 404	Junior Ortiz	.03	.01	.00
☐ 405	Glenn Wilson	.03	.01	.00
☐ 406	Ken Howell	.03	.01	.00
☐ 407	Jeff Kunkel	.03	.01	.00
☐ 408	Jeff Reed	.03	.01	.00
☐ 409	Chris James	.10	.05	.01
☐ 410	Zane Smith	.03	.01	.00
☐ 411	Ken Dixon	.03	.01	.00
☐ 412	Ricky Horton	.03	.01	.00
☐ 413	Frank DiPino	.03	.01	.00
☐ 414	Shane Mack	.08	.04	.01
☐ 415	Danny Cox	.03	.01	.00
☐ 416	Andy Van Slyke	.12	.06	.01
☐ 417	Danny Heep	.03	.01	.00
☐ 418	John Cangelosi	.03	.01	.00
☐ 419A	John Christensen ERR	.20	.10	.02
	(Christiansen on card front)			
☐ 419B	John Christensen COR	.06	.03	.00
☐ 420	Joey Cora	.10	.05	.01
☐ 421	Mike LaValliere	.03	.01	.00
☐ 422	Kelly Gruber	.06	.03	.00
☐ 423	Bruce Benedict	.03	.01	.00
☐ 424	Len Matuszek	.03	.01	.00
☐ 425	Kent Tekulve	.03	.01	.00
☐ 426	Rafael Ramirez	.03	.01	.00
☐ 427	Mike Flanagan	.06	.03	.00
☐ 428	Mike Gallego	.03	.01	.00
☐ 429	Juan Castillo	.06	.03	.00
☐ 430	Neal Heaton	.03	.01	.00
☐ 431	Phil Garner	.03	.01	.00
☐ 432	Mike Dunne	.08	.04	.01
☐ 433	Wallace Johnson	.03	.01	.00
☐ 434	Jack O'Connor	.03	.01	.00
☐ 435	Steve Jeltz	.03	.01	.00
☐ 436	Donnell Nixon	.10	.05	.01
☐ 437	Jack Lazorko	.03	.01	.00
☐ 438	Keith Comstock	.08	.04	.01
☐ 439	Jeff Robinson (Pirates pitcher)	.06	.03	.00
☐ 440	Graig Nettles	.08	.04	.01
☐ 441	Mel Hall	.06	.03	.00
☐ 442	Gerald Young	.25	.12	.02
☐ 443	Gary Redus	.03	.01	.00
☐ 444	Charlie Moore	.03	.01	.00
☐ 445	Bill Madlock	.06	.03	.00
☐ 446	Mark Clear	.03	.01	.00
☐ 447	Greg Booker	.03	.01	.00
☐ 448	Rick Schu	.03	.01	.00
☐ 449	Ron Kittle	.08	.04	.01
☐ 450	Dale Murphy	.20	.10	.02
☐ 451	Bob Dernier	.03	.01	.00
☐ 452	Dale Mohorcic	.03	.01	.00
☐ 453	Rafael Belliard	.03	.01	.00
☐ 454	Charlie Puleo	.03	.01	.00
☐ 455	Dwayne Murphy	.03	.01	.00
☐ 456	Jim Eisenreich	.03	.01	.00
☐ 457	David Palmer	.03	.01	.00
☐ 458	Dave Stewart	.10	.05	.01
☐ 459	Pascual Perez	.08	.04	.01
☐ 460	Glenn Davis	.15	.07	.01
☐ 461	Dan Petry	.03	.01	.00
☐ 462	Jim Winn	.03	.01	.00
☐ 463	Darrell Miller	.03	.01	.00

		MINT	EXC	G-VG
☐ 464	Mike Moore	.06	.03	.00
☐ 465	Mike LaCoss	.03	.01	.00
☐ 466	Steve Farr	.03	.01	.00
☐ 467	Jerry Mumphrey	.03	.01	.00
☐ 468	Kevin Gross	.03	.01	.00
☐ 469	Bruce Bochy	.03	.01	.00
☐ 470	Orel Hershiser	.20	.10	.02
☐ 471	Eric King	.03	.01	.00
☐ 472	Ellis Burks	1.00	.50	.10
☐ 473	Darren Daulton	.03	.01	.00
☐ 474	Mookie Wilson	.06	.03	.00
☐ 475	Frank Viola	.12	.06	.01
☐ 476	Ron Robinson	.03	.01	.00
☐ 477	Bob Melvin	.03	.01	.00
☐ 478	Jeff Musselman	.08	.04	.01
☐ 479	Charlie Kerfeld	.03	.01	.00
☐ 480	Richard Dotson	.03	.01	.00
☐ 481	Kevin Mitchell	.45	.22	.04
☐ 482	Gary Roenicke	.03	.01	.00
☐ 483	Tim Flannery	.03	.01	.00
☐ 484	Rich Yett	.03	.01	.00
☐ 485	Pete Incaviglia	.12	.06	.01
☐ 486	Rick Cerone	.03	.01	.00
☐ 487	Tony Armas	.06	.03	.00
☐ 488	Jerry Reed	.03	.01	.00
☐ 489	Dave Lopes	.06	.03	.00
☐ 490	Frank Tanana	.03	.01	.00
☐ 491	Mike Loynd	.06	.03	.00
☐ 492	Bruce Ruffin	.03	.01	.00
☐ 493	Chris Speier	.03	.01	.00
☐ 494	Tom Hume	.03	.01	.00
☐ 495	Jesse Orosco	.03	.01	.00
☐ 496	Robbie Wine UER (misspelled Robby on card front)	.12	.06	.01
☐ 497	Jeff Montgomery	.35	.17	.03
☐ 498	Jeff Dedmon	.03	.01	.00
☐ 499	Luis Aguayo	.03	.01	.00
☐ 500	Reggie Jackson (Oakland A's)	.20	.10	.02
☐ 501	Reggie Jackson (Baltimore Orioles)	.20	.10	.02
☐ 502	Reggie Jackson (New York Yankees)	.20	.10	.02
☐ 503	Reggie Jackson (California Angels)	.20	.10	.02
☐ 504	Reggie Jackson (Oakland A's)	.20	.10	.02
☐ 505	Billy Hatcher	.03	.01	.00

		MINT	EXC	G-VG
☐ 506	Ed Lynch	.03	.01	.00
☐ 507	Willie Hernandez	.06	.03	.00
☐ 508	Jose DeLeon	.06	.03	.00
☐ 509	Joel Youngblood	.03	.01	.00
☐ 510	Bob Welch	.06	.03	.00
☐ 511	Steve Ontiveros	.03	.01	.00
☐ 512	Randy Ready	.03	.01	.00
☐ 513	Juan Nieves	.03	.01	.00
☐ 514	Jeff Russell	.06	.03	.00
☐ 515	Von Hayes	.08	.04	.01
☐ 516	Mark Gubicza	.10	.05	.01
☐ 517	Ken Dayley	.03	.01	.00
☐ 518	Don Aase	.03	.01	.00
☐ 519	Rick Reuschel	.08	.04	.01
☐ 520	Mike Henneman	.20	.10	.02
☐ 521	Rick Aguilera	.03	.01	.00
☐ 522	Jay Howell	.06	.03	.00
☐ 523	Ed Correa	.03	.01	.00
☐ 524	Manny Trillo	.03	.01	.00
☐ 525	Kirk Gibson	.18	.09	.01
☐ 526	Wally Ritchie	.08	.04	.01
☐ 527	Al Nipper	.03	.01	.00
☐ 528	Atlee Hammaker	.03	.01	.00
☐ 529	Shawon Dunston	.08	.04	.01
☐ 530	Jim Clancy	.03	.01	.00
☐ 531	Tom Paciorek	.03	.01	.00
☐ 532	Joel Skinner	.03	.01	.00
☐ 533	Scott Garrelts	.06	.03	.00
☐ 534	Tom O'Malley	.03	.01	.00
☐ 535	John Franco	.08	.04	.01
☐ 536	Paul Kilgus	.12	.06	.01
☐ 537	Darrell Porter	.03	.01	.00
☐ 538	Walt Terrell	.03	.01	.00
☐ 539	Bill Long	.08	.04	.01
☐ 540	George Bell	.15	.07	.01
☐ 541	Jeff Sellers	.03	.01	.00
☐ 542	Joe Boever	.15	.07	.01
☐ 543	Steve Howe	.03	.01	.00
☐ 544	Scott Sanderson	.03	.01	.00
☐ 545	Jack Morris	.10	.05	.01
☐ 546	Todd Benzinger	.25	.12	.02
☐ 547	Steve Henderson	.03	.01	.00
☐ 548	Eddie Milner	.03	.01	.00
☐ 549	Jeff Robinson (Tigers pitcher)	.25	.12	.02
☐ 550	Cal Ripken	.20	.10	.02
☐ 551	Jody Davis	.03	.01	.00
☐ 552	Kirk McCaskill	.03	.01	.00
☐ 553	Craig Lefferts	.06	.03	.00

		MINT	EXC	G-VG
☐ 554	Darnell Coles	.03	.01	.00
☐ 555	Phil Niekro	.12	.06	.01
☐ 556	Mike Aldrete	.03	.01	.00
☐ 557	Pat Perry	.03	.01	.00
☐ 558	Juan Agosto	.03	.01	.00
☐ 559	Rob Murphy	.03	.01	.00
☐ 560	Dennis Rasmussen	.06	.03	.00
☐ 561	Manny Lee	.03	.01	.00
☐ 562	Jeff Blauser	.20	.10	.02
☐ 563	Bob Ojeda	.06	.03	.00
☐ 564	Dave Dravecky	.08	.04	.01
☐ 565	Gene Garber	.03	.01	.00
☐ 566	Ron Roenicke	.03	.01	.00
☐ 567	Tommy Hinzo	.08	.04	.01
☐ 568	Eric Nolte	.08	.04	.01
☐ 569	Ed Hearn	.03	.01	.00
☐ 570	Mark Davidson	.08	.04	.01
☐ 571	Jim Walewander	.12	.06	.01
☐ 572	Donnie Hill	.03	.01	.00
☐ 573	Jamie Moyer	.03	.01	.00
☐ 574	Ken Schrom	.03	.01	.00
☐ 575	Nolan Ryan	.35	.17	.03
☐ 576	Jim Acker	.03	.01	.00
☐ 577	Jamie Quirk	.03	.01	.00
☐ 578	Jay Aldrich	.08	.04	.01
☐ 579	Claudell Washington	.06	.03	.00
☐ 580	Jeff Leonard	.06	.03	.00
☐ 581	Carmen Castillo	.03	.01	.00
☐ 582	Daryl Boston	.03	.01	.00
☐ 583	Jeff DeWillis	.08	.04	.01
☐ 584	John Marzano	.08	.04	.01
☐ 585	Bill Gullickson	.03	.01	.00
☐ 586	Andy Allanson	.03	.01	.00
☐ 587	Lee Tunnell	.03	.01	.00
☐ 588	Gene Nelson	.03	.01	.00
☐ 589	Dave LaPoint	.03	.01	.00
☐ 590	Harold Baines	.08	.04	.01
☐ 591	Bill Buckner	.08	.04	.01
☐ 592	Carlton Fisk	.10	.05	.01
☐ 593	Rick Manning	.03	.01	.00
☐ 594	Doug Jones	.25	.12	.02
☐ 595	Tom Candiotti	.03	.01	.00
☐ 596	Steve Lake	.03	.01	.00
☐ 597	Jose Lind	.20	.10	.02
☐ 598	Ross Jones	.08	.04	.01
☐ 599	Gary Matthews	.03	.01	.00
☐ 600	Fernando Valenzuela	.12	.06	.01
☐ 601	Dennis Martinez	.03	.01	.00
☐ 602	Les Lancaster	.12	.06	.01

		MINT	EXC	G-VG
☐ 603	Ozzie Guillen	.06	.03	.00
☐ 604	Tony Bernazard	.03	.01	.00
☐ 605	Chili Davis	.06	.03	.00
☐ 606	Roy Smalley	.03	.01	.00
☐ 607	Ivan Calderon	.06	.03	.00
☐ 608	Jay Tibbs	.03	.01	.00
☐ 609	Guy Hoffman	.03	.01	.00
☐ 610	Doyle Alexander	.03	.01	.00
☐ 611	Mike Bielecki	.06	.03	.00
☐ 612	Shawn Hillegas	.15	.07	.01
☐ 613	Keith Atherton	.03	.01	.00
☐ 614	Eric Plunk	.03	.01	.00
☐ 615	Sid Fernandez	.08	.04	.01
☐ 616	Dennis Lamp	.03	.01	.00
☐ 617	Dave Engle	.03	.01	.00
☐ 618	Harry Spilman	.03	.01	.00
☐ 619	Don Robinson	.03	.01	.00
☐ 620	John Farrell	.20	.10	.02
☐ 621	Nelson Liriano	.15	.07	.01
☐ 622	Floyd Bannister	.03	.01	.00
☐ 623	Randy Milligan	.30	.15	.03
☐ 624	Kevin Elster	.20	.10	.02
☐ 625	Jody Reed	.35	.17	.03
☐ 626	Shawn Abner	.15	.07	.01
☐ 627	Kurt Manwaring	.20	.10	.02
☐ 628	Pete Stanicek	.18	.09	.01
☐ 629	Rob Ducey	.20	.10	.02
☐ 630	Steve Kiefer	.03	.01	.00
☐ 631	Gary Thurman	.18	.09	.01
☐ 632	Darrel Akerfelds	.12	.06	.01
☐ 633	Dave Clark	.12	.06	.01
☐ 634	Roberto Kelly	.60	.30	.06
☐ 635	Keith Hughes	.15	.07	.01
☐ 636	John Davis	.12	.06	.01
☐ 637	Mike Devereaux	.25	.12	.02
☐ 638	Tom Glavine	.30	.15	.03
☐ 639	Keith Miller (New York Mets)	.20	.10	.02
☐ 640	Chris Gwynn UER (wrong batting and throwing on back)	.25	.12	.02
☐ 641	Tim Crews	.08	.04	.01
☐ 642	Mackey Sasser	.25	.12	.02
☐ 643	Vicente Palacios	.10	.05	.01
☐ 644	Kevin Romine	.08	.04	.01
☐ 645	Gregg Jefferies	2.50	1.25	.25
☐ 646	Jeff Treadway	.25	.12	.02
☐ 647	Ron Gant	.35	.17	.03

		MINT	EXC	G-VG
☐ 648	Mark McGwire and Matt Nokes .... (Rookie Sluggers)	.25	.12	.02
☐ 649	Eric Davis and Tim Raines .... (Speed and Power)	.18	.09	.01
☐ 650	Don Mattingly and Jack Clark	.40	.20	.04
☐ 651	Tony Fernandez, Alan Trammell, and Cal Ripken	.10	.05	.01
☐ 652	Vince Coleman HL 100 Stolen Bases	.10	.05	.01
☐ 653	Kirby Puckett HL ... 10 Hits in a Row	.15	.07	.01
☐ 654	Benito Santiago HL . Hitting Streak	.12	.06	.01
☐ 655	Juan Nieves HL .... No Hitter	.06	.03	.00
☐ 656	Steve Bedrosian HL . Saves Record	.06	.03	.00
☐ 657	Mike Schmidt HL ... 500 Homers	.15	.07	.01
☐ 658	Don Mattingly HL ... Home Run Streak	.40	.20	.04
☐ 659	Mark McGwire HL .. Rookie HR Record	.30	.15	.03
☐ 660	Paul Molitor HL .... Hitting Streak	.10	.05	.01

1988 Score Traded

This 110-card set featured traded players (1-65) and rookies (66-110) for the 1988 season. The cards are distinguishable from the regular Score set by the orange borders and by the fact that the numbering on the back has a T suffix. The cards are standard size, 2 ½" by 3 ½", and were distributed by Score as a collated set in a special collector box along with some trivia cards.

		MINT	EXC	G-VG
COMPLETE SET (110)		36.00	16.00	3.50
COMMON PLAYER (1-65)		.07	.03	.01
COMMON PLAYER (66-110) ...		.07	.03	.01
☐	1T Jack Clark	.25	.12	.02
☐	2T Danny Jackson	.15	.07	.01
☐	3T Brett Butler	.10	.05	.01
☐	4T Kurt Stillwell	.07	.03	.01
☐	5T Tom Brunansky	.15	.07	.01
☐	6T Dennis Lamp	.07	.03	.01
☐	7T Jose DeLeon	.10	.05	.01
☐	8T Tom Herr	.10	.05	.01
☐	9T Keith Moreland	.07	.03	.01
☐	10T Kirk Gibson	.25	.12	.02
☐	11T Bud Black	.07	.03	.01
☐	12T Rafael Ramirez	.07	.03	.01
☐	13T Luis Salazar	.07	.03	.01
☐	14T Goose Gossage	.15	.07	.01
☐	15T Bob Welch	.10	.05	.01
☐	16T Vance Law	.07	.03	.01
☐	17T Ray Knight	.07	.03	.01

	MINT	EXC	G-VG		MINT	EXC	G-VG
☐ 18T Dan Quisenberry	.10	.05	.01	☐ 67T Ray Hayward	.12	.06	.01
☐ 19T Don Slaught	.07	.03	.01	☐ 68T Ricky Jordan	4.50	2.25	.45
☐ 20T Lee Smith	.10	.05	.01	☐ 69T Tommy Gregg	.25	.12	.02
☐ 21T Rick Cerone	.07	.03	.01	☐ 70T Brady Anderson	.35	.17	.03
☐ 22T Pat Tabler	.07	.03	.01	☐ 71T Jeff Montgomery	.20	.10	.02
☐ 23T Larry McWilliams	.07	.03	.01	☐ 72T Darryl Hamilton	.25	.12	.02
☐ 24T Ricky Horton	.07	.03	.01	☐ 73T Cecil Espy	.20	.10	.02
☐ 25T Graig Nettles	.15	.07	.01	☐ 74T Gregg Briley	2.50	1.25	.25
☐ 26T Dan Petry	.07	.03	.01	☐ 75T Joey Meyer	.18	.09	.01
☐ 27T Jose Rijo	.10	.05	.01	☐ 76T Mike MacFarlane	.20	.10	.02
☐ 28T Chili Davis	.10	.05	.01	☐ 77T Oswald Peraza	.15	.07	.01
☐ 29T Dickie Thon	.07	.03	.01	☐ 78T Jack Armstrong	.35	.17	.03
☐ 30T Mackey Sasser	.15	.07	.01	☐ 79T Don Heinkel	.15	.07	.01
☐ 31T Mickey Tettleton	.15	.07	.01	☐ 80T Mark Grace	9.00	4.50	.90
☐ 32T Rick Dempsey	.07	.03	.01	☐ 81T Steve Curry	.15	.07	.01
☐ 33T Ron Hassey	.07	.03	.01	☐ 82T Damon Berryhill	.75	.35	.07
☐ 34T Phil Bradley	.10	.05	.01	☐ 83T Steve Ellsworth	.15	.07	.01
☐ 35T Jay Howell	.10	.05	.01	☐ 84T Pete Smith	.15	.07	.01
☐ 36T Bill Buckner	.10	.05	.01	☐ 85T Jack McDowell	.15	.07	.01
☐ 37T Alfredo Griffin	.10	.05	.01	☐ 86T Rob Dibble	.65	.30	.06
☐ 38T Gary Pettis	.07	.03	.01	☐ 87T Bryan Harvey	.35	.17	.03
☐ 39T Calvin Schiraldi	.07	.03	.01	☐ 88T John Dopson	.30	.15	.03
☐ 40T John Candelaria	.10	.05	.01	☐ 89T Dave Gallagher	.60	.30	.06
☐ 41T Joe Orsulak	.07	.03	.01	☐ 90T Todd Stottlemyre	.25	.12	.02
☐ 42T Willie Upshaw	.07	.03	.01	☐ 91T Mike Schooler	.50	.25	.05
☐ 43T Herm Winningham	.07	.03	.01	☐ 92T Don Gordon	.15	.07	.01
☐ 44T Ron Kittle	.15	.07	.01	☐ 93T Sil Campusano	.25	.12	.02
☐ 45T Bob Dernier	.07	.03	.01	☐ 94T Jeff Pico	.20	.10	.02
☐ 46T Steve Balboni	.07	.03	.01	☐ 95T Jay Buhner	.35	.17	.03
☐ 47T Steve Shields	.07	.03	.01	☐ 96T Nelson Santovenia	.35	.17	.03
☐ 48T Henry Cotto	.07	.03	.01	☐ 97T Al Leiter	.25	.12	.02
☐ 49T Dave Henderson	.10	.05	.01	☐ 98T Luis Alicea	.15	.07	.01
☐ 50T Dave Parker	.15	.07	.01	☐ 99T Pat Borders	.15	.07	.01
☐ 51T Mike Young	.07	.03	.01	☐ 100T Chris Sabo	1.75	.85	.17
☐ 52T Mark Salas	.07	.03	.01	☐ 101T Tim Belcher	.50	.25	.05
☐ 53T Mike Davis	.07	.03	.01	☐ 102T Walt Weiss	1.75	.85	.17
☐ 54T Rafael Santana	.07	.03	.01	☐ 103T Craig Biggio	2.25	1.10	.22
☐ 55T Don Baylor	.15	.07	.01	☐ 104T Don August	.20	.10	.02
☐ 56T Dan Pasqua	.10	.05	.01	☐ 105T Roberto Alomar	.75	.35	.07
☐ 57T Ernest Riles	.07	.03	.01	☐ 106T Todd Burns	.45	.22	.04
☐ 58T Glenn Hubbard	.07	.03	.01	☐ 107T John Costello	.20	.10	.02
☐ 59T Mike Smithson	.07	.03	.01	☐ 108T Melido Perez	.25	.12	.02
☐ 60T Richard Dotson	.07	.03	.01	☐ 109T Darrin Jackson	.20	.10	.02
☐ 61T Jerry Reuss	.07	.03	.01	☐ 110T Orestes Destrade	.20	.10	.02
☐ 62T Mike Jackson	.10	.05	.01				
☐ 63T Floyd Bannister	.07	.03	.01				
☐ 64T Jesse Orosco	.07	.03	.01				
☐ 65T Larry Parrish	.07	.03	.01				
☐ 66T Jeff Bittiger	.15	.07	.01				

1989 Score

This 660-card set was distributed by Major League Marketing. Cards measure 2 ½" by 3 ½" and feature six distinctive inner border (inside a white outer border) colors on the front. Highlights (652-660) and Rookie Prospects (621-651) are included in the set. The set is distinguished by the fact that each card back shows a full-color picture (portrait) of the player. Score "missed" many of the mid-season and later trades; there are numerous examples of inconsistency with regard to the treatment of these players. Study as examples of this inconsistency on handling of late trades, cards #49, 71, 77, 83, 106, 126, 139, 145, 173, 177, 242, 348, 384, 420, 439, 488, 494, and 525.

	MINT	EXC	G-VG
COMPLETE SET (660)	25.00	12.50	2.50
COMMON PLAYER (1-660)	.03	.01	.00

			MINT	EXC	G-VG
☐	1	Jose Canseco	1.00	.25	.05
☐	2	Andre Dawson	.12	.06	.01
☐	3	Mark McGwire UER (bio says 116 RBI's, should be 118)	.50	.25	.05
☐	4	Benny Santiago	.12	.06	.01
☐	5	Rick Reuschel	.06	.03	.00
☐	6	Fred McGriff	.15	.07	.01
☐	7	Kal Daniels	.08	.04	.01
☐	8	Gary Gaetti	.08	.04	.01
☐	9	Ellis Burks	.25	.12	.02
☐	10	Darryl Strawberry	.30	.15	.03
☐	11	Julio Franco	.08	.04	.01
☐	12	Lloyd Moseby	.06	.03	.00
☐	13	Jeff Pico	.10	.05	.01
☐	14	Johnny Ray	.06	.03	.00
☐	15	Cal Ripken Jr.	.15	.07	.01
☐	16	Dick Schofield	.03	.01	.00
☐	17	Mel Hall	.06	.03	.00
☐	18	Bill Ripken	.03	.01	.00
☐	19	Brook Jacoby	.06	.03	.00
☐	20	Kirby Puckett	.25	.12	.02
☐	21	Bill Doran	.06	.03	.00
☐	22	Pete O'Brien	.06	.03	.00
☐	23	Matt Nokes	.08	.04	.01
☐	24	Brian Fisher	.03	.01	.00
☐	25	Jack Clark	.10	.05	.01
☐	26	Gary Pettis	.03	.01	.00
☐	27	Dave Valle	.03	.01	.00
☐	28	Willie Wilson	.06	.03	.00
☐	29	Curt Young	.03	.01	.00
☐	30	Dale Murphy	.15	.07	.01
☐	31	Barry Larkin	.12	.06	.01
☐	32	Dave Stewart	.10	.05	.01
☐	33	Mike LaValliere	.03	.01	.00
☐	34	Glenn Hubbard	.03	.01	.00
☐	35	Ryne Sandberg	.15	.07	.01
☐	36	Tony Pena	.06	.03	.00
☐	37	Greg Walker	.03	.01	.00
☐	38	Von Hayes	.08	.04	.01
☐	39	Kevin Mitchell	.25	.12	.02
☐	40	Tim Raines	.12	.06	.01
☐	41	Keith Hernandez	.10	.05	.01
☐	42	Keith Moreland	.03	.01	.00
☐	43	Ruben Sierra	.20	.10	.02
☐	44	Chet Lemon	.03	.01	.00
☐	45	Willie Randolph	.06	.03	.00
☐	46	Andy Allanson	.03	.01	.00
☐	47	Candy Maldonado	.03	.01	.00
☐	48	Sid Bream	.03	.01	.00
☐	49	Denny Walling	.03	.01	.00
☐	50	Dave Winfield	.15	.07	.01
☐	51	Alvin Davis	.08	.04	.01
☐	52	Cory Snyder	.08	.04	.01
☐	53	Hubie Brooks	.06	.03	.00
☐	54	Chili Davis	.06	.03	.00
☐	55	Kevin Seitzer	.12	.06	.01
☐	56	Jose Uribe	.03	.01	.00
☐	57	Tony Fernandez	.08	.04	.01
☐	58	Tim Teufel	.03	.01	.00
☐	59	Oddibe McDowell	.06	.03	.00

		MINT	EXC	G-VG			MINT	EXC	G-VG
☐ 60	Les Lancaster	.03	.01	.00	☐ 104	Chris Sabo	.35	.17	.03
☐ 61	Billy Hatcher	.03	.01	.00	☐ 105	Danny Tartabull	.10	.05	.01
☐ 62	Dan Gladden	.03	.01	.00	☐ 106	Glenn Wilson	.03	.01	.00
☐ 63	Marty Barrett	.03	.01	.00	☐ 107	Mark Davidson	.03	.01	.00
☐ 64	Nick Esasky	.06	.03	.00	☐ 108	Dave Parker	.08	.04	.01
☐ 65	Wally Joyner	.15	.07	.01	☐ 109	Eric Davis	.25	.12	.02
☐ 66	Mike Greenwell	.50	.25	.05	☐ 110	Alan Trammell	.12	.06	.01
☐ 67	Ken Williams	.03	.01	.00	☐ 111	Ozzie Virgil	.03	.01	.00
☐ 68	Bob Horner	.08	.04	.01	☐ 112	Frank Tanana	.03	.01	.00
☐ 69	Steve Sax	.10	.05	.01	☐ 113	Rafael Ramirez	.03	.01	.00
☐ 70	Rickey Henderson	.20	.10	.02	☐ 114	Dennis Martinez	.03	.01	.00
☐ 71	Mitch Webster	.03	.01	.00	☐ 115	Jose DeLeon	.06	.03	.00
☐ 72	Rob Deer	.06	.03	.00	☐ 116	Bob Ojeda	.06	.03	.00
☐ 73	Jim Presley	.03	.01	.00	☐ 117	Doug Drabek	.06	.03	.00
☐ 74	Albert Hall	.03	.01	.00	☐ 118	Andy Hawkins	.03	.01	.00
☐ 75A	George Brett ERR	1.00	.50	.10	☐ 119	Greg Maddux	.15	.07	.01
	(at age 33)				☐ 120	Cecil Fielder UER	.06	.03	.00
☐ 75B	George Brett COR	.30	.15	.03		(photo on back			
	(at age 35)					reversed)			
☐ 76	Brian Downing	.03	.01	.00	☐ 121	Mike Scioscia	.03	.01	.00
☐ 77	Dave Martinez	.03	.01	.00	☐ 122	Dan Petry	.03	.01	.00
☐ 78	Scott Fletcher	.03	.01	.00	☐ 123	Terry Kennedy	.03	.01	.00
☐ 79	Phil Bradley	.06	.03	.00	☐ 124	Kelly Downs	.03	.01	.00
☐ 80	Ozzie Smith	.10	.05	.01	☐ 125	Greg Gross UER	.03	.01	.00
☐ 81	Larry Sheets	.03	.01	.00		(Gregg on back)			
☐ 82	Mike Aldrete	.03	.01	.00	☐ 126	Fred Lynn	.08	.04	.01
☐ 83	Darnell Coles	.03	.01	.00	☐ 127	Barry Bonds	.08	.04	.01
☐ 84	Len Dykstra	.06	.03	.00	☐ 128	Harold Baines	.08	.04	.01
☐ 85	Jim Rice	.10	.05	.01	☐ 129	Doyle Alexander	.03	.01	.00
☐ 86	Jeff Treadway	.03	.01	.00	☐ 130	Kevin Elster	.06	.03	.00
☐ 87	Jose Lind	.03	.01	.00	☐ 131	Mike Heath	.03	.01	.00
☐ 88	Willie McGee	.08	.04	.01	☐ 132	Teddy Higuera	.06	.03	.00
☐ 89	Mickey Brantley	.06	.03	.00	☐ 133	Charlie Leibrandt	.03	.01	.00
☐ 90	Tony Gwynn	.15	.07	.01	☐ 134	Tim Laudner	.03	.01	.00
☐ 91	R.J. Reynolds	.03	.01	.00	☐ 135A	Ray Knight ERR	1.00	.50	.10
☐ 92	Milt Thompson	.03	.01	.00		(reverse negative)			
☐ 93	Kevin McReynolds	.10	.05	.01	☐ 135B	Ray Knight COR	.10	.05	.01
☐ 94	Eddie Murray UER	.12	.06	.01	☐ 136	Howard Johnson	.12	.06	.01
	('86 batting .025,				☐ 137	Terry Pendleton	.03	.01	.00
	should be .305)				☐ 138	Andy McGaffigan	.03	.01	.00
☐ 95	Lance Parrish	.08	.04	.01	☐ 139	Ken Oberkfell	.03	.01	.00
☐ 96	Ron Kittle	.08	.04	.01	☐ 140	Butch Wynegar	.03	.01	.00
☐ 97	Gerald Young	.03	.01	.00	☐ 141	Rob Murphy	.03	.01	.00
☐ 98	Ernie Whitt	.03	.01	.00	☐ 142	Rich Renteria	.10	.05	.01
☐ 99	Jeff Reed	.03	.01	.00	☐ 143	Jose Guzman	.03	.01	.00
☐ 100	Don Mattingly	.75	.35	.07	☐ 144	Andres Galarraga	.10	.05	.01
☐ 101	Gerald Perry	.06	.03	.00	☐ 145	Ricky Horton	.03	.01	.00
☐ 102	Vance Law	.03	.01	.00	☐ 146	Frank DiPino	.03	.01	.00
☐ 103	John Shelby	.03	.01	.00	☐ 147	Glenn Braggs	.06	.03	.00

		MINT	EXC	G-VG			MINT	EXC	G-VG
☐ 148	John Kruk	.06	.03	.00	☐ 192	Jim Pankovits	.03	.01	.00
☐ 149	Mike Schmidt	.25	.12	.02	☐ 193	Dwight Evans	.08	.04	.01
☐ 150	Lee Smith	.06	.03	.00	☐ 194	Kelly Gruber	.06	.03	.00
☐ 151	Robin Yount	.15	.07	.01	☐ 195	Bobby Bonilla	.10	.05	.01
☐ 152	Mark Eichhorn	.03	.01	.00	☐ 196	Wallace Johnson	.03	.01	.00
☐ 153	DeWayne Buice	.03	.01	.00	☐ 197	Dave Stieb	.08	.04	.01
☐ 154	B.J. Surhoff	.06	.03	.00	☐ 198	Pat Borders	.12	.06	.01
☐ 155	Vince Coleman	.10	.05	.01	☐ 199	Rafael Palmeiro	.10	.05	.01
☐ 156	Tony Phillips	.03	.01	.00	☐ 200	Dwight Gooden	.25	.12	.02
☐ 157	Willie Fraser	.03	.01	.00	☐ 201	Pete Incaviglia	.08	.04	.01
☐ 158	Lance McCullers	.03	.01	.00	☐ 202	Chris James	.06	.03	.00
☐ 159	Greg Gagne	.03	.01	.00	☐ 203	Marvell Wynne	.03	.01	.00
☐ 160	Jesse Barfield	.08	.04	.01	☐ 204	Pat Sheridan	.03	.01	.00
☐ 161	Mark Langston	.12	.06	.01	☐ 205	Don Baylor	.08	.04	.01
☐ 162	Kurt Stillwell	.03	.01	.00	☐ 206	Paul O'Neill	.08	.04	.01
☐ 163	Dion James	.03	.01	.00	☐ 207	Pete Smith	.10	.05	.01
☐ 164	Glenn Davis	.10	.05	.01	☐ 208	Mark McLemore	.03	.01	.00
☐ 165	Walt Weiss	.30	.15	.03	☐ 209	Henry Cotto	.03	.01	.00
☐ 166	Dave Concepcion	.06	.03	.00	☐ 210	Kirk Gibson	.12	.06	.01
☐ 167	Alfredo Griffin	.03	.01	.00	☐ 211	Claudell Washington	.06	.03	.00
☐ 168	Don Heinkel	.08	.04	.01	☐ 212	Randy Bush	.03	.01	.00
☐ 169	Luis Rivera	.03	.01	.00	☐ 213	Joe Carter	.12	.06	.01
☐ 170	Shane Rawley	.03	.01	.00	☐ 214	Bill Buckner	.06	.03	.00
☐ 171	Darrell Evans	.06	.03	.00	☐ 215	Bert Blyleven UER	.08	.04	.01
☐ 172	Robby-Thompson	.03	.01	.00		(wrong birth year)			
☐ 173	Jody Davis	.06	.03	.00	☐ 216	Brett Butler	.06	.03	.00
☐ 174	Andy Van Slyke	.08	.04	.01	☐ 217	Lee Mazzilli	.03	.01	.00
☐ 175	Wade Boggs UER	.50	.25	.05	☐ 218	Spike Owen	.03	.01	.00
	(bio says .364,				☐ 219	Bill Swift	.03	.01	.00
	should be .356)				☐ 220	Tim Wallach	.06	.03	.00
☐ 176	Garry Templeton	.06	.03	.00	☐ 221	David Cone	.15	.07	.01
	('85 stats off-centered)				☐ 222	Don Carman	.03	.01	.00
☐ 177	Gary Redus	.03	.01	.00	☐ 223	Rich Gossage	.08	.04	.01
☐ 178	Craig Lefferts	.06	.03	.00	☐ 224	Bob Walk	.03	.01	.00
☐ 179	Carney Lansford	.08	.04	.01	☐ 225	Dave Righetti	.08	.04	.01
☐ 180	Ron Darling	.08	.04	.01	☐ 226	Kevin Bass	.06	.03	.00
☐ 181	Kirk McCaskill	.03	.01	.00	☐ 227	Kevin Gross	.03	.01	.00
☐ 182	Tony Armas	.06	.03	.00	☐ 228	Tim Burke	.06	.03	.00
☐ 183	Steve Farr	.03	.01	.00	☐ 229	Rick Mahler	.03	.01	.00
☐ 184	Tom Brunansky	.08	.04	.01	☐ 230	Lou Whitaker UER	.08	.04	.01
☐ 185	Bryan Harvey UER	.20	.10	.02		(252 games in '85,			
	('87 games 47,					should be 152)			
	should be 3)				☐ 231	Luis Alicea	.08	.04	.01
☐ 186	Mike Marshall	.08	.04	.01	☐ 232	Roberto Alomar	.30	.15	.03
☐ 187	Bo Diaz	.03	.01	.00	☐ 233	Bob Boone	.08	.04	.01
☐ 188	Willie Upshaw	.03	.01	.00	☐ 234	Dickie Thon	.03	.01	.00
☐ 189	Mike Pagliarulo	.06	.03	.00	☐ 235	Shawon Dunston	.08	.04	.01
☐ 190	Mike Krukow	.03	.01	.00	☐ 236	Pete Stanicek	.03	.01	.00
☐ 191	Tommy Herr	.03	.01	.00	☐ 237	Craig Biggio	.40	.20	.04

		MINT	EXC	G-VG			MINT	EXC	G-VG
	(inconsistent design, portrait on front)				☐ 284	Jeff Robinson Detroit Tigers	.06	.03	.00
☐ 238	Dennis Boyd	.06	.03	.00	☐ 285	Mike Dunne	.06	.03	.00
☐ 239	Tom Candiotti	.03	.01	.00	☐ 286	Greg Mathews	.03	.01	.00
☐ 240	Gary Carter	.12	.06	.01	☐ 287	Kent Tekulve	.03	.01	.00
☐ 241	Mike Stanley	.03	.01	.00	☐ 288	Jerry Mumphrey	.03	.01	.00
☐ 242	Ken Phelps	.06	.03	.00	☐ 289	Jack McDowell	.10	.05	.01
☐ 243	Chris Bosio	.06	.03	.00	☐ 290	Frank Viola	.12	.06	.01
☐ 244	Les Straker	.03	.01	.00	☐ 291	Mark Gubicza	.08	.04	.01
☐ 245	Dave Smith	.03	.01	.00	☐ 292	Dave Schmidt	.03	.01	.00
☐ 246	John Candelaria	.06	.03	.00	☐ 293	Mike Henneman	.03	.01	.00
☐ 247	Joe Orsulak	.03	.01	.00	☐ 294	Jimmy Jones	.03	.01	.00
☐ 248	Storm Davis	.06	.03	.00	☐ 295	Charlie Hough	.03	.01	.00
☐ 249	Floyd Bannister UER (NL Batting Record)	.03	.01	.00	☐ 296	Rafael Santana	.03	.01	.00
					☐ 297	Chris Speier	.03	.01	.00
☐ 250	Jack Morris	.08	.04	.01	☐ 298	Mike Witt	.06	.03	.00
☐ 251	Bret Saberhagen	.15	.07	.01	☐ 299	Pascual Perez	.08	.04	.01
☐ 252	Tom Niedenfuer	.03	.01	.00	☐ 300	Nolan Ryan	.30	.15	.03
☐ 253	Neal Heaton	.03	.01	.00	☐ 301	Mitch Williams	.08	.04	.01
☐ 254	Eric Show	.03	.01	.00	☐ 302	Mookie Wilson	.06	.03	.00
☐ 255	Juan Samuel	.08	.04	.01	☐ 303	Mackey Sasser	.08	.04	.01
☐ 256	Dale Sveum	.03	.01	.00	☐ 304	John Cerutti	.03	.01	.00
☐ 257	Jim Gott	.03	.01	.00	☐ 305	Jeff Reardon	.08	.04	.01
☐ 258	Scott Garrelts	.06	.03	.00	☐ 306	Randy Myers	.06	.03	.00
☐ 259	Larry McWilliams	.03	.01	.00		(6 hits in '87, should			
☐ 260	Steve Bedrosian	.08	.04	.01		be 61)			
☐ 261	Jack Howell	.03	.01	.00	☐ 307	Greg Brock	.03	.01	.00
☐ 262	Jay Tibbs	.03	.01	.00	☐ 308	Bob Welch	.06	.03	.00
☐ 263	Jamie Moyer	.03	.01	.00	☐ 309	Jeff Robinson	.06	.03	.00
☐ 264	Doug Sisk	.03	.01	.00		Pittsburgh Pirates			
☐ 265	Todd Worrell	.08	.04	.01	☐ 310	Harold Reynolds	.06	.03	.00
☐ 266	John Farrell	.03	.01	.00	☐ 311	Jim Walewander	.03	.01	.00
☐ 267	Dave Collins	.03	.01	.00	☐ 312	Dave Magadan	.08	.04	.01
☐ 268	Sid Fernandez	.08	.04	.01	☐ 313	Jim Gantner	.03	.01	.00
☐ 269	Tom Brookens	.03	.01	.00	☐ 314	Walt Terrell	.03	.01	.00
☐ 270	Shane Mack	.06	.03	.00	☐ 315	Wally Backman	.03	.01	.00
☐ 271	Paul Kilgus	.03	.01	.00	☐ 316	Luis Salazar	.03	.01	.00
☐ 272	Chuck Crim	.03	.01	.00	☐ 317	Rick Rhoden	.03	.01	.00
☐ 273	Bob Knepper	.03	.01	.00	☐ 318	Tom Henke	.06	.03	.00
☐ 274	Mike Moore	.06	.03	.00	☐ 319	Mike Macfarlane	.12	.06	.01
☐ 275	Guillermo Hernandez	.06	.03	.00	☐ 320	Dan Plesac	.06	.03	.00
☐ 276	Dennis Eckersley	.10	.05	.01	☐ 321	Calvin Schiraldi	.03	.01	.00
☐ 277	Graig Nettles	.08	.04	.01	☐ 322	Stan Javier	.03	.01	.00
☐ 278	Rich Dotson	.03	.01	.00	☐ 323	Devon White	.10	.05	.01
☐ 279	Larry Herndon	.03	.01	.00	☐ 324	Scott Bradley	.03	.01	.00
☐ 280	Gene Larkin	.03	.01	.00	☐ 325	Bruce Hurst	.08	.04	.01
☐ 281	Roger McDowell	.06	.03	.00	☐ 326	Manny Lee	.03	.01	.00
☐ 282	Greg Swindell	.08	.04	.01	☐ 327	Rick Aguilera	.03	.01	.00
☐ 283	Juan Agosto	.03	.01	.00	☐ 328	Bruce Ruffin	.03	.01	.00

		MINT	EXC	G-VG
☐ 329	Ed Whitson	.03	.01	.00
☐ 330	Bo Jackson	.50	.25	.05
☐ 331	Ivan Calderon	.06	.03	.00
☐ 332	Mickey Hatcher	.03	.01	.00
☐ 333	Barry Jones	.03	.01	.00
☐ 334	Ron Hassey	.03	.01	.00
☐ 335	Bill Wegman	.03	.01	.00
☐ 336	Damon Berryhill	.20	.10	.02
☐ 337	Steve Ontiveros	.03	.01	.00
☐ 338	Dan Pasqua	.03	.01	.00
☐ 339	Bill Pecota	.03	.01	.00
☐ 340	Greg Cadaret	.10	.05	.01
☐ 341	Scott Bankhead	.06	.03	.00
☐ 342	Ron Guidry	.08	.04	.01
☐ 343	Danny Heep	.03	.01	.00
☐ 344	Bob Brower	.03	.01	.00
☐ 345	Rich Gedman	.03	.01	.00
☐ 346	Nelson Santovenia	.15	.07	.01
☐ 347	George Bell	.12	.06	.01
☐ 348	Ted Power	.03	.01	.00
☐ 349	Mark Grant	.03	.01	.00
☐ 350A	Roger Clemens ERR (778 career wins)	4.00	2.00	.40
☐ 350B	Roger Clemens COR (78 career wins)	.60	.30	.06
☐ 351	Bill Long	.03	.01	.00
☐ 352	Jay Bell	.08	.04	.01
☐ 353	Steve Balboni	.03	.01	.00
☐ 354	Bob Kipper	.03	.01	.00
☐ 355	Steve Jeltz	.03	.01	.00
☐ 356	Jesse Orosco	.03	.01	.00
☐ 357	Bob Dernier	.03	.01	.00
☐ 358	Mickey Tettleton	.08	.04	.01
☐ 359	Duane Ward	.03	.01	.00
☐ 360	Darrin Jackson	.10	.05	.01
☐ 361	Rey Quinones	.03	.01	.00
☐ 362	Mark Grace	2.00	1.00	.20
☐ 363	Steve Lake	.03	.01	.00
☐ 364	Pat Perry	.03	.01	.00
☐ 365	Terry Steinbach	.08	.04	.01
☐ 366	Alan Ashby	.03	.01	.00
☐ 367	Jeff Montgomery	.08	.04	.01
☐ 368	Steve Buechele	.03	.01	.00
☐ 369	Chris Brown	.03	.01	.00
☐ 370	Orel Hershiser	.20	.10	.02
☐ 371	Todd Benzinger	.03	.01	.00
☐ 372	Ron Gant	.10	.05	.01
☐ 373	Paul Assenmacher	.03	.01	.00
☐ 374	Joey Meyer	.08	.04	.01
☐ 375	Neil Allen	.03	.01	.00
☐ 376	Mike Davis	.03	.01	.00
☐ 377	Jeff Parrett	.08	.04	.01
☐ 378	Jay Howell	.06	.03	.00
☐ 379	Rafael Belliard	.03	.01	.00
☐ 380	Luis Polonia UER (2 triples in '87, should be 10)	.03	.01	.00
☐ 381	Keith Atherton	.03	.01	.00
☐ 382	Kent Hrbek	.10	.05	.01
☐ 383	Bob Stanley	.03	.01	.00
☐ 384	Dave LaPoint	.03	.01	.00
☐ 385	Rance Mulliniks	.03	.01	.00
☐ 386	Melido Perez	.10	.05	.01
☐ 387	Doug Jones	.06	.03	.00
☐ 388	Steve Lyons	.03	.01	.00
☐ 389	Alejandro Pena	.03	.01	.00
☐ 390	Frank White	.06	.03	.00
☐ 391	Pat Tabler	.06	.03	.00
☐ 392	Eric Plunk	.03	.01	.00
☐ 393	Mike Maddux	.03	.01	.00
☐ 394	Allan Anderson	.06	.03	.00
☐ 395	Bob Brenly	.03	.01	.00
☐ 396	Rick Cerone	.03	.01	.00
☐ 397	Scott Terry	.03	.01	.00
☐ 398	Mike Jackson	.03	.01	.00
☐ 399	Bobby Thigpen UER (bio says 37 saves in '88, should be 34)	.06	.03	.00
☐ 400	Don Sutton	.10	.05	.01
☐ 401	Cecil Espy	.08	.04	.01
☐ 402	Junior Ortiz	.03	.01	.00
☐ 403	Mike Smithson	.03	.01	.00
☐ 404	Bud Black	.03	.01	.00
☐ 405	Tom Foley	.03	.01	.00
☐ 406	Andres Thomas	.03	.01	.00
☐ 407	Rick Sutcliffe	.08	.04	.01
☐ 408	Brian Harper	.03	.01	.00
☐ 409	John Smiley	.06	.03	.00
☐ 410	Juan Nieves	.03	.01	.00
☐ 411	Shawn Abner	.03	.01	.00
☐ 412	Wes Gardner	.08	.04	.01
☐ 413	Darren Daulton	.03	.01	.00
☐ 414	Juan Berenguer	.03	.01	.00
☐ 415	Charles Hudson	.03	.01	.00
☐ 416	Rick Honeycutt	.03	.01	.00
☐ 417	Greg Booker	.03	.01	.00
☐ 418	Tim Belcher	.20	.10	.02
☐ 419	Don August	.06	.03	.00

		MINT	EXC	G-VG			MINT	EXC	G-VG
☐ 420	Dale Mohorcic	.03	.01	.00	☐ 466	John Dopson	.15	.07	.01
☐ 421	Steve Lombardozzi	.03	.01	.00	☐ 467	Rich Yett	.03	.01	.00
☐ 422	Atlee Hammaker	.03	.01	.00	☐ 468	Craig Reynolds	.03	.01	.00
☐ 423	Jerry Don Gleaton	.03	.01	.00	☐ 469	Dave Bergman	.03	.01	.00
☐ 424	Scott Bailes	.03	.01	.00	☐ 470	Rex Hudler	.03	.01	.00
☐ 425	Bruce Sutter	.08	.04	.01	☐ 471	Eric King	.03	.01	.00
☐ 426	Randy Ready	.03	.01	.00	☐ 472	Joaquin Andujar	.06	.03	.00
☐ 427	Jerry Reed	.03	.01	.00	☐ 473	Sil Campusano	.20	.10	.02
☐ 428	Bryn Smith	.06	.03	.00	☐ 474	Terry Mulholland	.03	.01	.00
☐ 429	Tim Leary	.06	.03	.00	☐ 475	Mike Flanagan	.06	.03	.00
☐ 430	Mark Clear	.03	.01	.00	☐ 476	Greg Harris	.03	.01	.00
☐ 431	Terry Leach	.06	.03	.00		Philadelphia Phillies			
☐ 432	John Moses	.03	.01	.00	☐ 477	Tommy John	.08	.04	.01
☐ 433	Ozzie Guillen	.06	.03	.00	☐ 478	Dave Anderson	.03	.01	.00
☐ 434	Gene Nelson	.03	.01	.00	☐ 479	Fred Toliver	.03	.01	.00
☐ 435	Gary Ward	.03	.01	.00	☐ 480	Jimmy Key	.06	.03	.00
☐ 436	Luis Aguayo	.03	.01	.00	☐ 481	Donell Nixon	.03	.01	.00
☐ 437	Fernando Valenzuela	.10	.05	.01	☐ 482	Mark Portugal	.03	.01	.00
☐ 438	Jeff Russell	.06	.03	.00	☐ 483	Tom Pagnozzi	.03	.01	.00
☐ 439	Cecilio Guante	.03	.01	.00	☐ 484	Jeff Kunkel	.03	.01	.00
☐ 440	Don Robinson	.03	.01	.00	☐ 485	Frank Williams	.03	.01	.00
☐ 441	Rick Anderson	.03	.01	.00	☐ 486	Jody Reed	.06	.03	.00
☐ 442	Tom Glavine	.06	.03	.00	☐ 487	Roberto Kelly	.15	.07	.01
☐ 443	Daryl Boston	.03	.01	.00	☐ 488	Shawn Hillegas UER	.03	.01	.00
☐ 444	Joe Price	.03	.01	.00		(165 innings in '87,			
☐ 445	Stewart Cliburn	.03	.01	.00		should be 165.2)			
☐ 446	Manny Trillo	.03	.01	.00	☐ 489	Jerry Reuss	.03	.01	.00
☐ 447	Joel Skinner	.03	.01	.00	☐ 490	Mark Davis	.12	.06	.01
☐ 448	Charlie Puleo	.03	.01	.00	☐ 491	Jeff Sellers	.03	.01	.00
☐ 449	Carlton Fisk	.10	.05	.01	☐ 492	Zane Smith	.03	.01	.00
☐ 450	Will Clark	.60	.30	.06	☐ 493	Al Newman	.03	.01	.00
☐ 451	Otis Nixon	.03	.01	.00	☐ 494	Mike Young	.03	.01	.00
☐ 452	Rick Schu	.03	.01	.00	☐ 495	Larry Parrish	.03	.01	.00
☐ 453	Todd Stottlemyre				☐ 496	Herm Winningham	.03	.01	.00
	UER	.15	.07	.01	☐ 497	Carmen Castillo	.03	.01	.00
	(NL Batting Record)				☐ 498	Joe Hesketh	.03	.01	.00
☐ 454	Tim Birtsas	.03	.01	.00	☐ 499	Darrell Miller	.03	.01	.00
☐ 455	Dave Gallagher	.15	.07	.01	☐ 500	Mike LaCoss	.03	.01	.00
☐ 456	Barry Lyons	.03	.01	.00	☐ 501	Charlie Lea	.03	.01	.00
☐ 457	Fred Manrique	.03	.01	.00	☐ 502	Bruce Benedict	.03	.01	.00
☐ 458	Ernest Riles	.03	.01	.00	☐ 503	Chuck Finley	.06	.03	.00
☐ 459	Doug Jennings	.18	.09	.01	☐ 504	Brad Wellman	.03	.01	.00
☐ 460	Joe Magrane	.08	.04	.01	☐ 505	Tim Crews	.03	.01	.00
☐ 461	Jamie Quirk	.03	.01	.00	☐ 506	Ken Gerhart	.03	.01	.00
☐ 462	Jack Armstrong	.25	.12	.02	☐ 507	Brian Holton UER	.10	.05	.01
☐ 463	Bobby Witt	.06	.03	.00		(born 1/25/65 Denver,			
☐ 464	Keith Miller	.03	.01	.00		should be 11/29/59 in			
	New York Mets					McKeesport)			
☐ 465	Todd Burns	.30	.15	.03	☐ 508	Dennis Lamp	.03	.01	.00

		MINT	EXC	G-VG
☐ 509	Bobby Meacham UER	.10	.05	.01
	('84 games 099)			
☐ 510	Tracy Jones	.03	.01	.00
☐ 511	Mike Fitzgerald	.03	.01	.00
	Montreal Expos			
☐ 512	Jeff Bittiger	.12	.06	.01
☐ 513	Tim Flannery	.03	.01	.00
☐ 514	Ray Hayward	.06	.03	.00
☐ 515	Dave Leiper	.03	.01	.00
☐ 516	Rod Scurry	.03	.01	.00
☐ 517	Carmelo Martinez	.03	.01	.00
☐ 518	Curtis Wilkerson	.03	.01	.00
☐ 519	Stan Jefferson	.06	.03	.00
☐ 520	Dan Quisenberry	.08	.04	.01
☐ 521	Lloyd McClendon	.08	.04	.01
☐ 522	Steve Trout	.03	.01	.00
☐ 523	Larry Andersen	.03	.01	.00
☐ 524	Don Aase	.03	.01	.00
☐ 525	Bob Forsch	.03	.01	.00
☐ 526	Geno Petralli	.03	.01	.00
☐ 527	Angel Salazar	.03	.01	.00
☐ 528	Mike Schooler	.25	.12	.02
☐ 529	Jose Oquendo	.03	.01	.00
☐ 530	Jay Buhner	.15	.07	.01
☐ 531	Tom Bolton	.08	.04	.01
☐ 532	Al Nipper	.03	.01	.00
☐ 533	Dave Henderson	.06	.03	.00
☐ 534	John Costello	.10	.05	.01
☐ 535	Donnie Moore	.03	.01	.00
☐ 536	Mike Laga	.03	.01	.00
☐ 537	Mike Gallego	.03	.01	.00
☐ 538	Jim Clancy	.03	.01	.00
☐ 539	Joel Youngblood	.03	.01	.00
☐ 540	Rick Leach	.03	.01	.00
☐ 541	Kevin Romine	.03	.01	.00
☐ 542	Mark Salas	.03	.01	.00
☐ 543	Greg Minton	.03	.01	.00
☐ 544	Dave Palmer	.03	.01	.00
☐ 545	Dwayne Murphy UER (game-sinning)	.03	.01	.00
☐ 546	Jim Deshaies	.03	.01	.00
☐ 547	Don Gordon	.08	.04	.01
☐ 548	Ricky Jordan	1.50	.75	.15
☐ 549	Mike Boddicker	.03	.01	.00
☐ 550	Mike Scott	.10	.05	.01
☐ 551	Jeff Ballard	.18	.09	.01
☐ 552A	Jose Rijo ERR	1.00	.50	.10

		MINT	EXC	G-VG
	(uniform listed as 27 on back)			
☐ 552B	Jose Rijo COR	.15	.07	.01
	(uniform listed as 24 on back)			
☐ 553	Danny Darwin	.03	.01	.00
☐ 554	Tom Browning	.08	.04	.01
☐ 555	Danny Jackson	.08	.04	.01
☐ 556	Rick Dempsey	.03	.01	.00
☐ 557	Jeffrey Leonard	.06	.03	.00
☐ 558	Jeff Musselman	.03	.01	.00
☐ 559	Ron Robinson	.03	.01	.00
☐ 560	John Tudor	.08	.04	.01
☐ 561	Don Slaught	.03	.01	.00
☐ 562	Dennis Rasmussen	.06	.03	.00
☐ 563	Brady Anderson	.20	.10	.02
☐ 564	Pedro Guerrero	.10	.05	.01
☐ 565	Paul Molitor	.10	.05	.01
☐ 566	Terry Clark	.10	.05	.01
☐ 567	Terry Puhl	.03	.01	.00
☐ 568	Mike Campbell	.10	.05	.01
☐ 569	Paul Mirabella	.03	.01	.00
☐ 570	Jeff Hamilton	.03	.01	.00
☐ 571	Oswald Peraza	.08	.04	.01
☐ 572	Bob McClure	.03	.01	.00
☐ 573	Jose Bautista	.08	.04	.01
☐ 574	Alex Trevino	.03	.01	.00
☐ 575	John Franco	.06	.03	.00
☐ 576	Mark Parent	.10	.05	.01
☐ 577	Nelson Liriano	.03	.01	.00
☐ 578	Steve Shields	.03	.01	.00
☐ 579	Odell Jones	.03	.01	.00
☐ 580	Al Leiter	.10	.05	.01
☐ 581	Dave Stapleton	.08	.04	.01
☐ 582	World Series '88	.15	.07	.01
	Orel Hershiser			
	Jose Canseco			
	Kirk Gibson			
	Dave Stewart			
☐ 583	Donnie Hill	.03	.01	.00
☐ 584	Chuck Jackson	.03	.01	.00
☐ 585	Rene Gonzales	.08	.04	.01
☐ 586	Tracy Woodson	.08	.04	.01
☐ 587	Jim Adduci	.03	.01	.00
☐ 588	Mario Soto	.03	.01	.00
☐ 589	Jeff Blauser	.03	.01	.00
☐ 590	Jim Traber	.03	.01	.00
☐ 591	Jon Perlman	.08	.04	.01
☐ 592	Mark Williamson	.08	.04	.01

		MINT	EXC	G-VG
☐ 593	Dave Meads	.03	.01	.00
☐ 594	Jim Eisenreich	.03	.01	.00
☐ 595A	Paul Gibson P1	2.00	1.00	.20
☐ 595B	Paul Gibson P2	.15	.07	.01
	(airbrushed leg on			
	player in background)			
☐ 596	Mike Birkbeck	.03	.01	.00
☐ 597	Terry Francona	.03	.01	.00
☐ 598	Paul Zuvella	.03	.01	.00
☐ 599	Franklin Stubbs	.03	.01	.00
☐ 600	Gregg Jefferies	1.00	.50	.10
☐ 601	John Cangelosi	.03	.01	.00
☐ 602	Mike Sharperson	.03	.01	.00
☐ 603	Mike Diaz	.03	.01	.00
☐ 604	Gary Varsho	.12	.06	.01
☐ 605	Terry Blocker	.12	.06	.01
☐ 606	Charlie O'Brien	.08	.04	.01
☐ 607	Jim Eppard	.08	.04	.01
☐ 608	John Davis	.03	.01	.00
☐ 609	Ken Griffey Sr.	.08	.04	.01
☐ 610	Buddy Bell	.06	.03	.00
☐ 611	Ted Simmons UER	.08	.04	.01
	('78 stats Cardinal)			
☐ 612	Matt Williams	.15	.07	.01
☐ 613	Danny Cox	.03	.01	.00
☐ 614	Al Pedrique	.03	.01	.00
☐ 615	Ron Oester	.03	.01	.00
☐ 616	John Smoltz	.35	.17	.03
☐ 617	Bob Melvin	.03	.01	.00
☐ 618	Rob Dibble	.20	.10	.02
☐ 619	Kirt Manwaring	.03	.01	.00
☐ 620	Felix Fermin	.08	.04	.01
☐ 621	Doug Dascenzo	.15	.07	.01
☐ 622	Bill Brennan	.15	.07	.01
☐ 623	Carlos Quintana	.25	.12	.02
☐ 624	Mike Harkey UER	.30	.15	.03
	(13 and 31 walks in			
	'88, should be 35 and			
	33)			
☐ 625	Gary Sheffield	1.00	.50	.10
☐ 626	Tom Prince	.08	.04	.01
☐ 627	Steve Searcy	.18	.09	.01
☐ 628	Charlie Hayes	.15	.07	.01
	(listed as outfielder)			
☐ 629	Felix Jose	.25	.12	.02
☐ 630	Sandy Alomar	.75	.35	.07
☐ 631	Derek Lilliquist	.20	.10	.02
☐ 632	Geronimo Berroa	.10	.05	.01
☐ 633	Luis Medina	.25	.12	.02

		MINT	EXC	G-VG
☐ 634	Tom Gordon UER	1.00	.50	.10
	(height 6'0")			
☐ 635	Ramon Martinez	.35	.17	.03
☐ 636	Craig Worthington	.35	.17	.03
☐ 637	Edgar Martinez	.10	.05	.01
☐ 638	Chad Kreuter	.15	.07	.01
☐ 639	Ron Jones	.25	.12	.02
☐ 640	Van Snider	.20	.10	.02
☐ 641	Lance Blankenship	.20	.10	.02
☐ 642	Dwight Smith UER	2.00	1.00	.20
	(10 HR's in '87,			
	should be 18)			
☐ 643	Cameron Drew	.18	.09	.01
☐ 644	Jerald Clark	.18	.09	.01
☐ 645	Randy Johnson	.20	.10	.02
☐ 646	Norm Charlton	.15	.07	.01
☐ 647	Todd Frohwirth UER	.10	.05	.01
	(southpaw on back)			
☐ 648	Luis De Los Santos	.20	.10	.02
☐ 649	Tim Jones	.10	.05	.01
☐ 650	Dave West UER	.25	.12	.02
	(ML hits 3, should be			
	6)			
☐ 651	Bob Milacki	.25	.12	.02
☐ 652	Wrigley Field HL	.03	.01	.00
	(Let There Be Lights)			
☐ 653	Orel Hershiser HL	.15	.07	.01
	(The Streak)			
☐ 654A	Wade Boggs HL ERR	3.50	1.75	.35
	(Wade Whacks 'Em)			
	("seaason" on back)			
☐ 654B	Wade Boggs HL	.50	.25	.05
	COR			
	(Wade Whacks 'Em)			
☐ 655	Jose Canseco HL	.40	.20	.04
	(One of a Kind)			
☐ 656	Doug Jones HL	.06	.03	.00
	(Doug Sets Saves)			
☐ 657	Rickey Henderson HL	.20	.10	.02
	(Rickey Rocks 'Em)			
☐ 658	Tom Browning HL	.06	.03	.00
	(Tom Perfect Pitches)			
☐ 659	Mike Greenwell HL	.20	.10	.02
	(Greenwell Gamers)			
☐ 660	Boston Red Sox HL	.06	.03	.00
	(Joe Morgan MG,			
	Sox Sock 'Em)			

1989 Score Scoremasters

The 1989 Score Scoremasters set contains 42 standard-size (2½" by 3½") cards. The fronts are "pure" with attractively-drawn action portraits. The backs feature write-ups of the players' careers. The cards were distributed as a boxed set.

			MINT	EXC	G-VG
		COMPLETE SET (42)	10.00	5.00	1.00
		COMMON PLAYER (1-42)	.10	.05	.01
☐	1	Bo Jackson	1.00	.50	.10
☐	2	Jerome Walton	1.00	.50	.10
☐	3	Cal Ripken Jr.	.30	.15	.03
☐	4	Mike Scott	.20	.10	.02
☐	5	Nolan Ryan	1.00	.50	.10
☐	6	Don Mattingly	1.00	.50	.10
☐	7	Tom Gordon	.50	.25	.05
☐	8	Jack Morris	.10	.05	.01
☐	9	Carlton Fisk	.30	.15	.03
☐	10	Will Clark	1.00	.50	.10
☐	11	George Brett	.50	.25	.05
☐	12	Kevin Mitchell	.50	.25	.05
☐	13	Mark Langston	.30	.15	.03
☐	14	Dave Stewart	.20	.10	.02
☐	15	Dale Murphy	.40	.20	.04
☐	16	Gary Gaetti	.20	.10	.02
☐	17	Wade Boggs	1.00	.50	.10
☐	18	Eric Davis	.75	.35	.07
☐	19	Kirby Puckett	.90	.45	.09

			MINT	EXC	G-VG
☐	20	Roger Clemens	.75	.35	.07
☐	21	Orel Hershiser	.50	.25	.05
☐	22	Mark Grace	1.00	.50	.10
☐	23	Ryne Sandberg	.25	.12	.02
☐	24	Barry Larkin	.25	.12	.02
☐	25	Ellis Burks	.35	.17	.03
☐	26	Dwight Gooden	.40	.20	.04
☐	27	Ozzie Smith	.20	.10	.02
☐	28	Andre Dawson	.20	.10	.02
☐	29	Julio Franco	.10	.05	.01
☐	30	Ken Griffey Jr.	1.00	.50	.10
☐	31	Ruben Sierra	.50	.25	.05
☐	32	Mark McGwire	.75	.35	.07
☐	33	Andres Galarraga	.20	.10	.02
☐	34	Joe Carter	.20	.10	.02
☐	35	Vince Coleman	.25	.12	.02
☐	36	Mike Greenwell	.75	.35	.07
☐	37	Tony Gwynn	.60	.30	.06
☐	38	Andy Van Slyke	.15	.07	.01
☐	39	Gregg Jefferies	.75	.35	.07
☐	40	Jose Canseco	1.00	.50	.10
☐	41	Dave Winfield	.25	.12	.02
☐	42	Darryl Strawberry	.60	.30	.06

1989 Score Traded

The 1989 Score Traded set contains 110 standard-size (2½" by 3½") cards. The fronts have coral green borders with pink diamonds at the bottom. The vertically oriented backs have color facial shots, career stats, and biographical information. Cards 1-80 feature

traded players; cards 81-110 feature 1989
rookies. The set was distributed in a blue box
with 10 Magic Motion trivia cards.

		MINT	EXC	G-VG
	COMPLETE SET (110)	13.50	6.00	1.00
	COMMON PLAYER (1-80)	.05	.02	.00
	COMMON PLAYER (81-110)	.06	.03	.00
1	Rafael Palmeiro	.12	.02	.01
2	Nolan Ryan	1.25	.60	.12
3	Jack Clark	.10	.05	.01
4	Dave LaPoint	.05	.02	.00
5	Mike Moore	.10	.05	.01
6	Pete O'Brien	.10	.05	.01
7	Jeffrey Leonard	.10	.05	.01
8	Rob Murphy	.05	.02	.00
9	Tom Herr	.05	.02	.00
10	Claudell Washington	.10	.05	.01
11	Mike Pagliarulo	.05	.02	.00
12	Steve Lake	.05	.02	.00
13	Spike Owen	.05	.02	.00
14	Andy Hawkins	.10	.05	.01
15	Todd Benzinger	.05	.02	.00
16	Mookie Wilson	.10	.05	.01
17	Bert Blyleven	.15	.07	.01
18	Jeff Treadway	.05	.02	.00
19	Bruce Hurst	.10	.05	.01
20	Steve Sax	.15	.07	.01
21	Juan Samuel	.15	.07	.01
22	Jesse Barfield	.15	.07	.01
23	Carmen Castillo	.05	.02	.00
24	Terry Leach	.05	.02	.00
25	Mark Langston	.20	.10	.02
26	Eric King	.05	.02	.00
27	Steve Balboni	.05	.02	.00
28	Len Dykstra	.10	.05	.01
29	Keith Moreland	.05	.02	.00
30	Terry Kennedy	.05	.02	.00
31	Eddie Murray	.12	.06	.01
32	Mitch Williams	.20	.10	.02
33	Jeff Parrett	.10	.05	.01
34	Wally Backman	.05	.02	.00
35	Julio Franco	.15	.07	.01
36	Lance Parrish	.15	.07	.01
37	Nick Esasky	.15	.07	.01
38	Luis Polonia	.05	.02	.00
39	Kevin Gross	.05	.02	.00
40	John Dopson	.10	.05	.01
41	Willie Randolph	.10	.05	.01
42	Jim Clancy	.05	.02	.00
43	Tracy Jones	.10	.05	.01
44	Phil Bradley	.10	.05	.01
45	Milt Thompson	.05	.02	.00
46	Chris James	.10	.05	.01
47	Scott Fletcher	.05	.02	.00
48	Kal Daniels	.10	.05	.01
49	Steve Bedrosian	.10	.05	.01
50	Rickey Henderson	.50	.25	.05
51	Dion James	.05	.02	.00
52	Tim Leary	.10	.05	.01
53	Roger McDowell	.10	.05	.01
54	Mel Hall	.10	.05	.01
55	Dickie Thon	.05	.02	.00
56	Zane Smith	.05	.02	.00
57	Danny Heep	.05	.02	.00
58	Bob McClure	.05	.02	.00
59	Brian Holton	.05	.02	.00
60	Randy Ready	.05	.02	.00
61	Bob Melvin	.05	.02	.00
62	Harold Baines	.15	.07	.01
63	Lance McCullers	.05	.02	.00
64	Jody Davis	.05	.02	.00
65	Darrell Evans	.10	.05	.01
66	Joel Youngblood	.05	.02	.00
67	Frank Viola	.15	.07	.01
68	Mike Aldrete	.05	.02	.00
69	Greg Cadaret	.10	.05	.01
70	John Kruk	.10	.05	.01
71	Pat Sheridan	.05	.02	.00
72	Oddibe McDowell	.10	.05	.01
73	Tom Brookens	.05	.02	.00
74	Bob Boone	.15	.07	.01
75	Walt Terrell	.05	.02	.00
76	Joel Skinner	.05	.02	.00
77	Randy Johnson	.15	.07	.01
78	Felix Fermin	.05	.02	.00
79	Rick Mahler	.05	.02	.00
80	Richard Dotson	.05	.02	.00
81	Cris Carpenter	.15	.07	.01
82	Bill Spiers	.35	.17	.03
83	Junior Felix	.90	.45	.09
84	Joe Girardi	.30	.15	.03
85	Jerome Walton	3.50	1.75	.35
86	Greg Litton	.30	.15	.03
87	Greg W.Harris	.20	.10	.02
88	Jim Abbott	2.50	1.25	.25
89	Kevin Brown	.20	.10	.02
90	John Wetteland	.40	.20	.04

		MINT	EXC	G-VG
☐ 91	Gary Wayne	.20	.10	.02
☐ 92	Rich Monteleone	.20	.10	.02
☐ 93	Bob Geren	.30	.15	.03
☐ 94	Clay Parker	.20	.10	.02
☐ 95	Steve Finley	.20	.10	.02
☐ 96	Gregg Olson	1.25	.60	.12
☐ 97	Ken Patterson	.15	.07	.01
☐ 98	Ken Hill	.20	.10	.02
☐ 99	Scott Scudder	.30	.15	.03
☐ 100	Ken Griffey Jr.	2.50	1.25	.25
☐ 101	Jeff Brantley	.20	.10	.02
☐ 102	Donn Pall	.15	.07	.01
☐ 103	Carlos Martinez	.20	.10	.02
☐ 104	Joe Oliver	.30	.15	.03
☐ 105	Omar Vizquel	.30	.15	.03
☐ 106	Joey Belle	1.00	.50	.10
☐ 107	Kenny Rogers	.20	.10	.02
☐ 108	Mark Carreon	.15	.07	.01
☐ 109	Rolando Roomes	.20	.10	.02
☐ 110	Pete Harnisch	.20	.10	.02

1990 Score

The 1990 Score set contains 704 standard-size (2 ½" by 3 ½") cards. The front borders are red, blue, green or white. The vertically oriented backs are white with borders that match the fronts, and feature color mugshots. Cards numbered 661-682 contain the first round draft picks subset noted as DC for "draft choice" in the checklist below. Cards numbered 683-695

contain the "Dream Team" subset noted by DT in the checklist below.

		MINT	EXC	G-VG
COMPLETE SET (704)		24.00	12.00	2.40
COMMON PLAYER (1-704)		.03	.01	.00
☐ 1	Don Mattingly	.60	.20	.04
☐ 2	Cal Ripken	.12	.06	.01
☐ 3	Dwight Evans	.08	.04	.01
☐ 4	Barry Bonds	.08	.04	.01
☐ 5	Kevin McReynolds	.08	.04	.01
☐ 6	Ozzie Guillen	.06	.03	.00
☐ 7	Terry Kennedy	.03	.01	.00
☐ 8	Bryan Harvey	.03	.01	.00
☐ 9	Alan Trammell	.08	.04	.01
☐ 10	Cory Snyder	.08	.04	.01
☐ 11	Jody Reed	.03	.01	.00
☐ 12	Roberto Alomar	.08	.04	.01
☐ 13	Pedro Guerrero	.08	.04	.01
☐ 14	Gary Redus	.03	.01	.00
☐ 15	Marty Barrett	.03	.01	.00
☐ 16	Ricky Jordan	.20	.10	.02
☐ 17	Joe Magrane	.08	.04	.01
☐ 18	Sid Fernandez	.08	.04	.01
☐ 19	Richard Dotson	.03	.01	.00
☐ 20	Jack Clark	.08	.04	.01
☐ 21	Bob Walk	.03	.01	.00
☐ 22	Ron Karkovice	.03	.01	.00
☐ 23	Lenny Harris	.08	.04	.01
☐ 24	Phil Bradley	.06	.03	.00
☐ 25	Andres Galarraga	.08	.04	.01
☐ 26	Brian Downing	.03	.01	.00
☐ 27	Dave Martinez	.03	.01	.00
☐ 28	Eric King	.03	.01	.00
☐ 29	Barry Lyons	.03	.01	.00
☐ 30	Dave Schmidt	.03	.01	.00
☐ 31	Mike Boddicker	.03	.01	.00
☐ 32	Tom Foley	.03	.01	.00
☐ 33	Brady Anderson	.03	.01	.00
☐ 34	Jim Presley	.03	.01	.00
☐ 35	Lance Parrish	.08	.04	.01
☐ 36	Von Hayes	.08	.04	.01
☐ 37	Lee Smith	.06	.03	.00
☐ 38	Herm Winningham	.03	.01	.00
☐ 39	Alejandro Pena	.03	.01	.00
☐ 40	Mike Scott	.08	.04	.01
☐ 41	Joe Orsulak	.03	.01	.00
☐ 42	Rafael Ramirez	.03	.01	.00
☐ 43	Gerald Young	.03	.01	.00

		MINT	EXC	G-VG			MINT	EXC	G-VG
☐	44 Dick Schofield	.03	.01	.00	☐	93 Pete Incaviglia	.06	.03	.00
☐	45 Dave Smith	.03	.01	.00	☐	94 Ivan Calderon	.06	.03	.00
☐	46 Dave Magadan	.06	.03	.00	☐	95 Jeff Treadway	.03	.01	.00
☐	47 Dennis Martinez	.03	.01	.00	☐	96 Kurt Stillwell	.03	.01	.00
☐	48 Greg Minton	.03	.01	.00	☐	97 Gary Sheffield	.30	.15	.03
☐	49 Milt Thompson	.03	.01	.00	☐	98 Jeffrey Leonard	.06	.03	.00
☐	50 Orel Hershiser	.10	.05	.01	☐	99 Andres Thomas	.03	.01	.00
☐	51 Bip Roberts	.03	.01	.00	☐	100 Roberto Kelly	.08	.04	.01
☐	52 Jerry Browne	.03	.01	.00	☐	101 Alvaro Espinoza	.03	.01	.00
☐	53 Bob Ojeda	.06	.03	.00	☐	102 Greg Gagne	.03	.01	.00
☐	54 Fernando Valenzuela	.08	.04	.01	☐	103 John Farrell	.03	.01	.00
☐	55 Matt Nokes	.06	.03	.00	☐	104 Willie Wilson	.06	.03	.00
☐	56 Brook Jacoby	.06	.03	.00	☐	105 Glenn Braggs	.06	.03	.00
☐	57 Frank Tanana	.03	.01	.00	☐	106 Chet Lemon	.03	.01	.00
☐	58 Scott Fletcher	.03	.01	.00	☐	107 Jamie Moyer	.03	.01	.00
☐	59 Ron Oester	.03	.01	.00	☐	108 Chuck Crim	.03	.01	.00
☐	60 Bob Boone	.06	.03	.00	☐	109 Dave Valle	.03	.01	.00
☐	61 Dan Gladden	.03	.01	.00	☐	110 Walt Weiss	.08	.04	.01
☐	62 Darnell Coles	.03	.01	.00	☐	111 Larry Sheets	.03	.01	.00
☐	63 Gregg Olson	.30	.15	.03	☐	112 Don Robinson	.03	.01	.00
☐	64 Todd Burns	.06	.03	.00	☐	113 Danny Heep	.03	.01	.00
☐	65 Todd Benzinger	.03	.01	.00	☐	114 Carmelo Martinez	.03	.01	.00
☐	66 Dale Murphy	.12	.06	.01	☐	115 Dave Gallagher	.03	.01	.00
☐	67 Mike Flanagan	.03	.01	.00	☐	116 Mike LaValliere	.03	.01	.00
☐	68 Jose Oquendo	.03	.01	.00	☐	117 Bob McClure	.03	.01	.00
☐	69 Cecil Espy	.03	.01	.00	☐	118 Rene Gonzales	.03	.01	.00
☐	70 Chris Sabo	.06	.03	.00	☐	119 Mark Parent	.03	.01	.00
☐	71 Shane Rawley	.03	.01	.00	☐	120 Wally Joyner	.08	.04	.01
☐	72 Tom Brunansky	.08	.04	.01	☐	121 Mark Gubicza	.08	.04	.01
☐	73 Vance Law	.03	.01	.00	☐	122 Tony Pena	.06	.03	.00
☐	74 B.J. Surhoff	.06	.03	.00	☐	123 Carmen Castillo	.03	.01	.00
☐	75 Lou Whitaker	.08	.04	.01	☐	124 Howard Johnson	.10	.05	.01
☐	76 Ken Caminiti	.03	.01	.00	☐	125 Steve Sax	.08	.04	.01
☐	77 Nelson Liriano	.03	.01	.00	☐	126 Tim Belcher	.06	.03	.00
☐	78 Tommy Gregg	.06	.03	.00	☐	127 Tim Burke	.06	.03	.00
☐	79 Don Slaught	.03	.01	.00	☐	128 Al Newman	.03	.01	.00
☐	80 Eddie Murray	.10	.05	.01	☐	129 Dennis Rasmussen	.03	.01	.00
☐	81 Joe Boever	.03	.01	.00	☐	130 Doug Jones	.06	.03	.00
☐	82 Charlie Leibrandt	.03	.01	.00	☐	131 Fred Lynn	.06	.03	.00
☐	83 Jose Lind	.03	.01	.00	☐	132 Jeff Hamilton	.03	.01	.00
☐	84 Tony Phillips	.03	.01	.00	☐	133 German Gonzalez	.03	.01	.00
☐	85 Mitch Webster	.03	.01	.00	☐	134 John Morris	.03	.01	.00
☐	86 Dan Plesac	.06	.03	.00	☐	135 Dave Parker	.08	.04	.01
☐	87 Rick Mahler	.03	.01	.00	☐	136 Gary Pettis	.03	.01	.00
☐	88 Steve Lyons	.03	.01	.00	☐	137 Dennis Boyd	.03	.01	.00
☐	89 Tony Fernandez	.08	.04	.01	☐	138 Candy Maldonado	.03	.01	.00
☐	90 Ryne Sandberg	.12	.06	.01	☐	139 Rick Cerone	.03	.01	.00
☐	91 Nick Esasky	.06	.03	.00	☐	140 George Brett	.12	.06	.01
☐	92 Luis Salazar	.03	.01	.00	☐	141 Dave Clark	.03	.01	.00

		MINT	EXC	G-VG			MINT	EXC	G-VG
☐ 142	Dickie Thon	.03	.01	.00	☐ 184	Mike Henneman	.03	.01	.00
☐ 143	Junior Ortiz	.03	.01	.00	☐ 185	Eric Davis	.20	.10	.02
☐ 144	Don August	.03	.01	.00	☐ 186	Lance McCullers	.03	.01	.00
☐ 145	Gary Gaetti	.08	.04	.01	☐ 187	Steve Davis	.12	.06	.01
☐ 146	Kirt Manwaring	.03	.01	.00	☐ 188	Bill Wegman	.03	.01	.00
☐ 147	Jeff Reed	.03	.01	.00	☐ 189	Brian Harper	.03	.01	.00
☐ 148	Jose Alvarez	.03	.01	.00	☐ 190	Mike Moore	.06	.03	.00
☐ 149	Mike Schooler	.06	.03	.00	☐ 191	Dale Mohorcic	.03	.01	.00
☐ 150	Mark Grace	.35	.17	.03	☐ 192	Tim Wallach	.06	.03	.00
☐ 151	Geronimo Berroa	.03	.01	.00	☐ 193	Keith Hernandez	.08	.04	.01
☐ 152	Barry Jones	.03	.01	.00	☐ 194	Dave Righetti	.08	.04	.01
☐ 153	Geno Petralli	.03	.01	.00	☐ 195	Bret Saberhagen	.10	.05	.01
☐ 154	Jim Deshaies	.03	.01	.00	☐ 196	Paul Kilgus	.03	.01	.00
☐ 155	Barry Larkin	.08	.04	.01	☐ 197	Bud Black	.03	.01	.00
☐ 156	Alfredo Griffin	.03	.01	.00	☐ 198	Juan Samuel	.06	.03	.00
☐ 157	Tom Henke	.06	.03	.00	☐ 199	Kevin Seitzer	.08	.04	.01
☐ 158	Mike Jeffcoat	.03	.01	.00	☐ 200	Darryl Strawberry	.25	.12	.02
☐ 159	Bob Welch	.06	.03	.00	☐ 201	Dave Stieb	.08	.04	.01
☐ 160	Julio Franco	.06	.03	.00	☐ 202	Charlie Hough	.03	.01	.00
☐ 161	Henry Cotto	.03	.01	.00	☐ 203	Jack Morris	.08	.04	.01
☐ 162	Terry Steinbach	.06	.03	.00	☐ 204	Rance Mulliniks	.03	.01	.00
☐ 163	Damon Berryhill	.08	.04	.01	☐ 205	Alvin Davis	.08	.04	.01
☐ 164	Tim Crews	.03	.01	.00	☐ 206	Jack Howell	.03	.01	.00
☐ 165	Tom Browning	.06	.03	.00	☐ 207	Ken Patterson	.08	.04	.01
☐ 166	Fred Manrique	.03	.01	.00	☐ 208	Terry Pendleton	.03	.01	.00
☐ 167	Harold Reynolds	.06	.03	.00	☐ 209	Craig Lefferts	.03	.01	.00
☐ 168	Ron Hassey	.03	.01	.00	☐ 210	Kevin Brown	.10	.05	.01
☐ 169	Shawon Dunston	.06	.03	.00	☐ 211	Dan Petry	.03	.01	.00
☐ 170	Bobby Bonilla	.08	.04	.01	☐ 212	Dave Leiper	.03	.01	.00
☐ 171	Tommy Herr	.03	.01	.00	☐ 213	Daryl Boston	.03	.01	.00
☐ 172	Mike Heath	.03	.01	.00	☐ 214	Kevin Hickey	.03	.01	.00
☐ 173	Rich Gedman	.03	.01	.00	☐ 215	Mike Krukow	.03	.01	.00
☐ 174	Bill Ripken	.03	.01	.00	☐ 216	Terry Francona	.03	.01	.00
☐ 175	Pete O'Brien	.06	.03	.00	☐ 217	Kirk McCaskill	.03	.01	.00
☐ 176A	Lloyd McClendon ERR	1.00	.50	.10	☐ 218	Scott Bailes	.03	.01	.00
	(uniform number on back listed as 1)				☐ 219	Bob Forsch	.03	.01	.00
					☐ 220	Mike Aldrete	.03	.01	.00
					☐ 221	Steve Buechele	.03	.01	.00
☐ 176B	Lloyd McClendon COR	.08	.04	.01	☐ 222	Jesse Barfield	.08	.04	.01
	(uniform number on back listed as 10)				☐ 223	Juan Berenguer	.03	.01	.00
					☐ 224	Andy McGaffigan	.03	.01	.00
					☐ 225	Pete Smith	.03	.01	.00
☐ 177	Brian Holton	.03	.01	.00	☐ 226	Mike Witt	.06	.03	.00
☐ 178	Jeff Blauser	.03	.01	.00	☐ 227	Jay Howell	.03	.01	.00
☐ 179	Jim Eisenreich	.03	.01	.00	☐ 228	Scott Bradley	.03	.01	.00
☐ 180	Bert Blyleven	.08	.04	.01	☐ 229	Jerome Walton	1.00	.50	.10
☐ 181	Rob Murphy	.03	.01	.00	☐ 230	Greg Swindell	.08	.04	.01
☐ 182	Bill Doran	.06	.03	.00	☐ 231	Atlee Hammaker	.03	.01	.00
☐ 183	Curt Ford	.03	.01	.00	☐ 232	Mike Devereaux	.03	.01	.00

		MINT	EXC	G-VG			MINT	EXC	G-VG
☐ 233	Ken Hill	.08	.04	.01	☐ 282	Larry Andersen	.03	.01	.00
☐ 234	Craig Worthington	.08	.04	.01	☐ 283	Chris Bosio	.06	.03	.00
☐ 235	Scott Terry	.03	.01	.00	☐ 284	Juan Agosto	.03	.01	.00
☐ 236	Brett Butler	.06	.03	.00	☐ 285	Ozzie Smith	.08	.04	.01
☐ 237	Doyle Alexander	.03	.01	.00	☐ 286	George Bell	.08	.04	.01
☐ 238	Dave Anderson	.03	.01	.00	☐ 287	Rex Hudler	.03	.01	.00
☐ 239	Bob Milacki	.03	.01	.00	☐ 288	Pat Borders	.03	.01	.00
☐ 240	Dwight Smith	.35	.17	.03	☐ 289	Danny Jackson	.06	.03	.00
☐ 241	Otis Nixon	.03	.01	.00	☐ 290	Carlton Fisk	.10	.05	.01
☐ 242	Pat Tabler	.03	.01	.00	☐ 291	Tracy Jones	.03	.01	.00
☐ 243	Derek Lilliquist	.06	.03	.00	☐ 292	Allan Anderson	.06	.03	.00
☐ 244	Danny Tartabull	.08	.04	.01	☐ 293	Johnny Ray	.06	.03	.00
☐ 245	Wade Boggs	.25	.12	.02	☐ 294	Lee Guetterman	.03	.01	.00
☐ 246	Scott Garrelts	.06	.03	.00	☐ 295	Paul O'Neill	.08	.04	.01
☐ 247	Spike Owen	.03	.01	.00	☐ 296	Carney Lansford	.08	.04	.01
☐ 248	Norm Charlton	.03	.01	.00	☐ 297	Tom Brookens	.03	.01	.00
☐ 249	Gerald Perry	.06	.03	.00	☐ 298	Claudell Washington	.06	.03	.00
☐ 250	Nolan Ryan	.25	.12	.02	☐ 299	Hubie Brooks	.06	.03	.00
☐ 251	Kevin Gross	.03	.01	.00	☐ 300	Will Clark	.50	.25	.05
☐ 252	Randy Milligan	.03	.01	.00	☐ 301	Kenny Rogers	.12	.06	.01
☐ 253	Mike LaCoss	.03	.01	.00	☐ 302	Darrell Evans	.06	.03	.00
☐ 254	Dave Bergman	.03	.01	.00	☐ 303	Greg Briley	.20	.10	.02
☐ 255	Tony Gwynn	.15	.07	.01	☐ 304	Donn Pall	.08	.04	.01
☐ 256	Felix Fermin	.03	.01	.00	☐ 305	Teddy Higuera	.06	.03	.00
☐ 257	Greg Harris	.10	.05	.01	☐ 306	Dan Pasqua	.03	.01	.00
☐ 258	Junior Felix	.30	.15	.03	☐ 307	Dave Winfield	.10	.05	.01
☐ 259	Mark Davis	.08	.04	.01	☐ 308	Dennis Powell	.03	.01	.00
☐ 260	Vince Coleman	.08	.04	.01	☐ 309	Jose DeLeon	.06	.03	.00
☐ 261	Paul Gibson	.03	.01	.00	☐ 310	Roger Clemens	.20	.10	.02
☐ 262	Mitch Williams	.06	.03	.00	☐ 311	Melido Perez	.06	.03	.00
☐ 263	Jeff Russell	.06	.03	.00	☐ 312	Devon White	.08	.04	.01
☐ 264	Omar Vizquel	.12	.06	.01	☐ 313	Dwight Gooden	.20	.10	.02
☐ 265	Andre Dawson	.10	.05	.01	☐ 314	Carlos Martinez	.20	.10	.02
☐ 266	Storm Davis	.06	.03	.00	☐ 315	Dennis Eckersley	.08	.04	.01
☐ 267	Guillermo Hernandez	.06	.03	.00	☐ 316	Clay Parker	.10	.05	.01
☐ 268	Mike Felder	.03	.01	.00	☐ 317	Rick Honeycutt	.03	.01	.00
☐ 269	Tom Candiotti	.03	.01	.00	☐ 318	Tim Laudner	.03	.01	.00
☐ 270	Bruce Hurst	.06	.03	.00	☐ 319	Joe Carter	.10	.05	.01
☐ 271	Fred McGriff	.12	.06	.01	☐ 320	Robin Yount	.25	.12	.02
☐ 272	Glenn Davis	.10	.05	.01	☐ 321	Felix Jose	.03	.01	.00
☐ 273	John Franco	.06	.03	.00	☐ 322	Mickey Tettleton	.06	.03	.00
☐ 274	Rich Yett	.03	.01	.00	☐ 323	Mike Gallego	.03	.01	.00
☐ 275	Craig Biggio	.08	.04	.01	☐ 324	Edgar Martinez	.03	.01	.00
☐ 276	Gene Larkin	.03	.01	.00	☐ 325	Dave Henderson	.03	.01	.00
☐ 277	Rob Dibble	.06	.03	.00	☐ 326	Chili Davis	.06	.03	.00
☐ 278	Randy Bush	.03	.01	.00	☐ 327	Steve Balboni	.03	.01	.00
☐ 279	Kevin Bass	.06	.03	.00	☐ 328	Jody Davis	.03	.01	.00
☐ 280	Bo Jackson	.50	.25	.05	☐ 329	Shawn Hillegas	.03	.01	.00
☐ 281	Wally Backman	.03	.01	.00	☐ 330	Jim Abbott	.75	.35	.07

		MINT	EXC	G-VG
☐ 331	John Dopson	.03	.01	.00
☐ 332	Mark Williamson	.03	.01	.00
☐ 333	Jeff Robinson	.06	.03	.00
☐ 334	John Smiley	.06	.03	.00
☐ 335	Bobby Thigpen	.06	.03	.00
☐ 336	Garry Templeton	.06	.03	.00
☐ 337	Marvell Wynne	.03	.01	.00
☐ 338A	Ken Griffey Sr. ERR (uniform number on back listed as 25)	1.00	.50	.10
☐ 338B	Ken Griffey Sr. COR (uniform number on back listed as 30)	.08	.04	.01
☐ 339	Steve Finley	.12	.06	.01
☐ 340	Ellis Burks	.15	.07	.01
☐ 341	Frank Williams	.03	.01	.00
☐ 342	Mike Morgan	.03	.01	.00
☐ 343	Kevin Mitchell	.15	.07	.01
☐ 344	Joel Youngblood	.03	.01	.00
☐ 345	Mike Greenwell	.20	.10	.02
☐ 346	Glenn Wilson	.03	.01	.00
☐ 347	John Costello	.03	.01	.00
☐ 348	Wes Gardner	.03	.01	.00
☐ 349	Jeff Ballard	.06	.03	.00
☐ 350	Mark Thurmond	.03	.01	.00
☐ 351	Randy Myers	.06	.03	.00
☐ 352	Shawn Abner	.03	.01	.00
☐ 353	Jesse Orosco	.03	.01	.00
☐ 354	Greg Walker	.03	.01	.00
☐ 355	Pete Harnisch	.06	.03	.00
☐ 356	Steve Farr	.03	.01	.00
☐ 357	Dave LaPoint	.03	.01	.00
☐ 358	Willie Fraser	.03	.01	.00
☐ 359	Mickey Hatcher	.03	.01	.00
☐ 360	Rickey Henderson	.25	.12	.02
☐ 361	Mike Fitzgerald	.03	.01	.00
☐ 362	Bill Schroeder	.03	.01	.00
☐ 363	Mark Carreon	.06	.03	.00
☐ 364	Ron Jones	.06	.03	.00
☐ 365	Jeff Montgomery	.06	.03	.00
☐ 366	Bill Krueger	.03	.01	.00
☐ 367	John Cangelosi	.03	.01	.00
☐ 368	Jose Gonzalez	.03	.01	.00
☐ 369	Greg Hibbard	.12	.06	.01
☐ 370	John Smoltz	.08	.04	.01
☐ 371	Jeff Brantley	.15	.07	.01
☐ 372	Frank White	.06	.03	.00
☐ 373	Ed Whitson	.03	.01	.00
☐ 374	Willie McGee	.08	.04	.01
☐ 375	Jose Canseco	.50	.25	.05
☐ 376	Randy Ready	.03	.01	.00
☐ 377	Don Aase	.03	.01	.00
☐ 378	Tony Armas	.06	.03	.00
☐ 379	Steve Bedrosian	.06	.03	.00
☐ 380	Chuck Finley	.06	.03	.00
☐ 381	Kent Hrbek	.08	.04	.01
☐ 382	Jim Gantner	.03	.01	.00
☐ 383	Mel Hall	.06	.03	.00
☐ 384	Mike Marshall	.08	.04	.01
☐ 385	Mark McGwire	.25	.12	.02
☐ 386	Wayne Tolleson	.03	.01	.00
☐ 387	Brian Holman	.08	.04	.01
☐ 388	John Wetteland	.20	.10	.02
☐ 389	Darren Daulton	.03	.01	.00
☐ 390	Rob Deer	.06	.03	.00
☐ 391	John Moses	.03	.01	.00
☐ 392	Todd Worrell	.08	.04	.01
☐ 393	Chuck Cary	.06	.03	.00
☐ 394	Stan Javier	.03	.01	.00
☐ 395	Willie Randolph	.06	.03	.00
☐ 396	Bill Buckner	.06	.03	.00
☐ 397	Robby Thompson	.03	.01	.00
☐ 398	Mike Scioscia	.03	.01	.00
☐ 399	Lonnie Smith	.06	.03	.00
☐ 400	Kirby Puckett	.25	.12	.02
☐ 401	Mark Langston	.08	.04	.01
☐ 402	Danny Darwin	.03	.01	.00
☐ 403	Greg Maddux	.06	.03	.00
☐ 404	Lloyd Moseby	.06	.03	.00
☐ 405	Rafael Palmeiro	.06	.03	.00
☐ 406	Chad Kreuter	.03	.01	.00
☐ 407	Jimmy Key	.06	.03	.00
☐ 408	Tim Birtsas	.03	.01	.00
☐ 409	Tim Raines	.10	.05	.01
☐ 410	Dave Stewart	.08	.04	.01
☐ 411	Eric Yelding	.10	.05	.01
☐ 412	Kent Anderson	.10	.05	.01
☐ 413	Les Lancaster	.03	.01	.00
☐ 414	Rick Dempsey	.03	.01	.00
☐ 415	Randy Johnson	.06	.03	.00
☐ 416	Gary Carter	.08	.04	.01
☐ 417	Rolando Roomes	.08	.04	.01
☐ 418	Dan Schatzeder	.03	.01	.00
☐ 419	Bryn Smith	.06	.03	.00
☐ 420	Ruben Sierra	.20	.10	.02
☐ 421	Steve Jeltz	.03	.01	.00
☐ 422	Ken Oberkfell	.03	.01	.00
☐ 423	Sid Bream	.03	.01	.00

		MINT	EXC	G-VG			MINT	EXC	G-VG
☐ 424	Jim Clancy	.03	.01	.00	☐ 470	Harold Baines	.08	.04	.01
☐ 425	Kelly Gruber	.06	.03	.00	☐ 471	Dennis Lamp	.03	.01	.00
☐ 426	Rick Leach	.03	.01	.00	☐ 472	Tom Gordon	.35	.17	.03
☐ 427	Len Dykstra	.06	.03	.00	☐ 473	Terry Puhl	.03	.01	.00
☐ 428	Jeff Pico	.03	.01	.00	☐ 474	Curt Wilkerson	.03	.01	.00
☐ 429	John Cerutti	.03	.01	.00	☐ 475	Dan Quisenberry	.06	.03	.00
☐ 430	David Cone	.10	.05	.01	☐ 476	Oddibe McDowell	.06	.03	.00
☐ 431	Jeff Kunkel	.03	.01	.00	☐ 477	Zane Smith	.03	.01	.00
☐ 432	Luis Aquino	.03	.01	.00	☐ 478	Franklin Stubbs	.03	.01	.00
☐ 433	Ernie Whitt	.03	.01	.00	☐ 479	Wallace Johnson	.03	.01	.00
☐ 434	Bo Diaz	.03	.01	.00	☐ 480	Jay Tibbs	.03	.01	.00
☐ 435	Steve Lake	.03	.01	.00	☐ 481	Tom Glavine	.06	.03	.00
☐ 436	Pat Perry	.03	.01	.00	☐ 482	Manny Lee	.03	.01	.00
☐ 437	Mike Davis	.03	.01	.00	☐ 483	Joe Hesketh	.03	.01	.00
☐ 438	Cecilio Guante	.03	.01	.00	☐ 484	Mike Bielecki	.06	.03	.00
☐ 439	Duane Ward	.03	.01	.00	☐ 485	Greg Brock	.03	.01	.00
☐ 440	Andy Van Slyke	.08	.04	.01	☐ 486	Pascual Perez	.06	.03	.00
☐ 441	Gene Nelson	.03	.01	.00	☐ 487	Kirk Gibson	.08	.04	.01
☐ 442	Luis Polonia	.03	.01	.00	☐ 488	Scott Sanderson	.03	.01	.00
☐ 443	Kevin Elster	.06	.03	.00	☐ 489	Domingo Ramos	.03	.01	.00
☐ 444	Keith Moreland	.03	.01	.00	☐ 490	Kal Daniels	.08	.04	.01
☐ 445	Roger McDowell	.06	.03	.00	☐ 491A	David Wells ERR	2.50	1.00	.20
☐ 446	Ron Darling	.08	.04	.01		(reverse negative			
☐ 447	Ernest Riles	.03	.01	.00		photo on card back)			
☐ 448	Mookie Wilson	.06	.03	.00	☐ 491B	David Wells COR	.10	.04	.01
☐ 449A	Billy Spiers ERR	2.00	1.00	.20	☐ 492	Jerry Reed	.03	.01	.00
	(no birth year)				☐ 493	Eric Show	.03	.01	.00
					☐ 494	Mike Pagliarulo	.06	.03	.00
☐ 449B	Billy Spiers COR	.40	.20	.04	☐ 495	Ron Robinson	.03	.01	.00
	(born in 1966)				☐ 496	Brad Komminsk	.03	.01	.00
☐ 450	Rick Sutcliffe	.06	.03	.00	☐ 497	Greg Litton	.20	.10	.02
☐ 451	Nelson Santovenia	.03	.01	.00	☐ 498	Chris James	.06	.03	.00
☐ 452	Andy Allanson	.03	.01	.00	☐ 499	Luis Quinones	.03	.01	.00
☐ 453	Bob Melvin	.03	.01	.00	☐ 500	Frank Viola	.08	.04	.01
☐ 454	Benito Santiago	.08	.04	.01	☐ 501	Tim Teufel	.03	.01	.00
☐ 455	Jose Uribe	.03	.01	.00	☐ 502	Terry Leach	.03	.01	.00
☐ 456	Bill Landrum	.03	.01	.00	☐ 503	Matt Williams	.12	.06	.01
☐ 457	Bobby Witt	.06	.03	.00	☐ 504	Tim Leary	.06	.03	.00
☐ 458	Kevin Romine	.03	.01	.00	☐ 505	Doug Drabek	.06	.03	.00
☐ 459	Lee Mazzilli	.03	.01	.00	☐ 506	Mariano Duncan	.03	.01	.00
☐ 460	Paul Molitor	.08	.04	.01	☐ 507	Charlie Hayes	.06	.03	.00
☐ 461	Ramon Martinez	.08	.04	.01	☐ 508	Joey Belle	.50	.25	.05
☐ 462	Frank DiPino	.03	.01	.00	☐ 509	Pat Sheridan	.03	.01	.00
☐ 463	Walt Terrell	.03	.01	.00	☐ 510	Mackey Sasser	.06	.03	.00
☐ 464	Bob Geren	.15	.07	.01	☐ 511	Jose Rijo	.03	.01	.00
☐ 465	Rick Reuschel	.06	.03	.00	☐ 512	Mike Smithson	.03	.01	.00
☐ 466	Mark Grant	.03	.01	.00	☐ 513	Gary Ward	.03	.01	.00
☐ 467	John Kruk	.06	.03	.00	☐ 514	Dion James	.03	.01	.00
☐ 468	Gregg Jefferies	.35	.17	.03	☐ 515	Jim Gott	.03	.01	.00
☐ 469	R.J. Reynolds	.03	.01	.00					

	MINT	EXC	G-VG		MINT	EXC	G-VG
☐ 516 Drew Hall	.03	.01	.00	☐ 561B Ryne Sandberg HL COR	.50	.25	.05
☐ 517 Doug Bair	.03	.01	.00	☐ 562 Billy Hatcher	.03	.01	.00
☐ 518 Scott Scudder	.15	.07	.01	☐ 563 Jay Bell	.03	.01	.00
☐ 519 Rick Aguilera	.03	.01	.00	☐ 564 Jack Daugherty	.10	.05	.01
☐ 520 Rafael Belliard	.03	.01	.00	☐ 565 Rich Monteleone	.10	.05	.01
☐ 521 Jay Buhner	.06	.03	.00	☐ 566 Bo Jackson AS-MVP	.35	.17	.03
☐ 522 Jeff Reardon	.06	.03	.00	☐ 567 Tony Fossas	.10	.05	.01
☐ 523 Steve Rosenberg	.08	.04	.01	☐ 568 Roy Smith	.03	.01	.00
☐ 524 Randy Velarde	.06	.03	.00	☐ 569 Jaime Navarro	.20	.10	.02
☐ 525 Jeff Musselman	.03	.01	.00	☐ 570 Lance Johnson	.10	.05	.01
☐ 526 Bill Long	.03	.01	.00	☐ 571 Mike Dyer	.15	.07	.01
☐ 527 Gary Wayne	.10	.05	.01	☐ 572 Kevin Ritz	.15	.07	.01
☐ 528 Dave Johnson (P)	.12	.06	.01	☐ 573 Dave West	.06	.03	.00
☐ 529 Ron Kittle	.06	.03	.00	☐ 574 Gary Mielke	.10	.05	.01
☐ 530 Erik Hanson	.10	.05	.01	☐ 575 Scott Lusader	.03	.01	.00
☐ 531 Steve Wilson	.08	.04	.01	☐ 576 Joe Oliver	.15	.07	.01
☐ 532 Joey Meyer	.06	.03	.00	☐ 577 Sandy Alomar Jr.	.25	.12	.02
☐ 533 Curt Young	.03	.01	.00	☐ 578 Andy Benes	.35	.17	.03
☐ 534 Kelly Downs	.03	.01	.00	☐ 579 Tim Jones	.03	.01	.00
☐ 535 Joe Girardi	.12	.06	.01	☐ 580 Randy McCament	.12	.06	.01
☐ 536 Lance Blankenship	.03	.01	.00	☐ 581 Curt Schilling	.08	.04	.01
☐ 537 Greg Mathews	.03	.01	.00	☐ 582 John Orton	.15	.07	.01
☐ 538 Donell Nixon	.03	.01	.00	☐ 583A Milt Cuyler ERR	2.00	1.00	.20
☐ 539 Mark Knudson	.08	.04	.01	(989 games)			
☐ 540 Jeff Wetherby	.12	.06	.01	☐ 583B Milt Cuyler COR	.40	.20	.04
☐ 541 Darrin Jackson	.03	.01	.00	(98 games)			
☐ 542 Terry Mulholland	.03	.01	.00				
☐ 543 Eric Hetzel	.08	.04	.01	☐ 584 Eric Anthony	1.50	.75	.15
☐ 544 Rick Reed	.12	.06	.01	☐ 585 Greg Vaughn	1.25	.60	.12
☐ 545 Dennis Cook	.10	.05	.01	☐ 586 Deion Sanders	.50	.25	.05
☐ 546 Mike Jackson	.03	.01	.00	☐ 587 Jose DeJesus	.03	.01	.00
☐ 547 Brian Fisher	.03	.01	.00	☐ 588 Chip Hale	.15	.07	.01
☐ 548 Gene Harris	.15	.07	.01	☐ 589 John Olerud	2.50	1.00	.20
☐ 549 Jeff King	.10	.05	.01	☐ 590 Steve Olin	.12	.06	.01
☐ 550 Dave Dravecky	.08	.04	.01	☐ 591 Marquis Grissom	.50	.25	.05
☐ 551 Randy Kutcher	.03	.01	.00	☐ 592 Moises Alou	.25	.12	.02
☐ 552 Mark Portugal	.03	.01	.00	☐ 593 Mark Lemke	.08	.04	.01
☐ 553 Jim Corsi	.08	.04	.01	☐ 594 Dean Palmer	.25	.12	.02
☐ 554 Todd Stottlemyre	.06	.03	.00	☐ 595 Robin Ventura	.50	.25	.05
☐ 555 Scott Bankhead	.06	.03	.00	☐ 596 Tino Martinez	.35	.17	.03
☐ 556 Ken Dayley	.03	.01	.00	☐ 597 Mike Huff	.20	.10	.02
☐ 557 Rick Wrona	.15	.07	.01	☐ 598 Scott Hemond	.20	.10	.02
☐ 558 Sammy Sosa	.40	.20	.04	☐ 599 Wally Whitehurst	.05	.01	.01
☐ 559 Keith Miller	.03	.01	.00	☐ 600 Todd Zeile	1.25	.60	.12
☐ 560 Ken Griffey Jr.	1.00	.50	.10	☐ 601 Glenallen Hill	.20	.10	.02
☐ 561A Ryne Sandberg HL ERR	16.00	8.00	1.60	☐ 602 Hal Morris	.15	.07	.01
(position on front listed as 3B)				☐ 603 Juan Bell	.20	.10	.02
				☐ 604 Bobby Rose	.20	.10	.02
				☐ 605 Matt Merullo	.12	.06	.01

		MINT	EXC	G-VG			MINT	EXC	G-VG
☐ 606	Kevin Maas	.25	.12	.02	☐ 655	Terry Jorgenson	.12	.06	.01
☐ 607	Randy Nosek	.15	.07	.01	☐ 656	George Canale	.15	.07	.01
☐ 608	Billy Bates	.12	.06	.01	☐ 657	Brian Dubois	.12	.06	.01
☐ 609	Mike Stanton	.20	.10	.02	☐ 658	Carlos Quintana	.06	.03	.00
☐ 610	Mauro Gozzo	.20	.10	.02	☐ 659	Luis De Los Santos	.03	.01	.00
☐ 611	Charles Nagy	.20	.10	.02	☐ 660	Jerald Clark	.03	.01	.00
☐ 612	Scott Coolbaugh	.25	.12	.02	☐ 661	Donald Harris DC	.30	.15	.03
☐ 613	Jose Vizcaino	.20	.10	.02	☐ 662	Paul Coleman DC	.30	.15	.03
☐ 614	Greg Smith	.15	.07	.01	☐ 663	Frank Thomas DC	.30	.15	.03
☐ 615	Jeff Huson	.12	.06	.01	☐ 664	Brent Mayne DC	.20	.10	.02
☐ 616	Mickey Weston	.10	.05	.01	☐ 665	Eddie Zosky DC	.20	.10	.02
☐ 617	John Pawlowski	.08	.04	.01	☐ 666	Steve Hosey DC	.20	.10	.02
☐ 618	Joe Skalski	.12	.06	.01	☐ 667	Scott Bryant DC	.20	.10	.02
☐ 619	Bernie Williams	.45	.22	.04	☐ 668	Tom Goodwin DC	.40	.20	.04
☐ 620	Shawn Holman	.12	.06	.01	☐ 669	Cal Eldred DC	.20	.10	.02
☐ 621	Gary Eave	.12	.06	.01	☐ 670	Earl Cunningham DC	.40	.20	.04
☐ 622	Darrin Fletcher	.12	.06	.01	☐ 671	Alan Zinter DC	.20	.10	.02
☐ 623	Pat Combs	.30	.15	.03	☐ 672	Chuck Knoblauch DC	.20	.10	.02
☐ 624	Mike Blowers	.20	.10	.02	☐ 673	Kyle Abbott DC	.20	.10	.02
☐ 625	Kevin Appier	.12	.06	.01	☐ 674	Roger Salkeld DC	.20	.10	.02
☐ 626	Pat Austin	.12	.06	.01	☐ 675	Maurice Vaughn DC	.30	.15	.03
☐ 627	Kelly Mann	.12	.06	.01	☐ 676	Keith (Kiki) Jones DC	.40	.20	.04
☐ 628	Matt Kinzer	.10	.05	.01	☐ 677	Tyler Houston DC	.40	.20	.04
☐ 629	Chris Hammond	.15	.07	.01	☐ 678	Jeff Jackson DC	.25	.12	.02
☐ 630	Dean Wilkins	.12	.06	.01	☐ 679	Greg Gohr DC	.20	.10	.02
☐ 631	Larry Walker	.20	.10	.02	☐ 680	Ben McDonald DC	1.75	.85	.17
☐ 632	Blaine Beatty	.15	.07	.01	☐ 681	Greg Blosser DC	.20	.10	.02
☐ 633	Tommy Barrett	.08	.04	.01	☐ 682	Willie Green DC	.20	.10	.02
☐ 634	Stan Belinda	.10	.05	.01	☐ 683	Wade Boggs DT	.20	.10	.02
☐ 635	Mike (Tex) Smith	.10	.05	.01	☐ 684	Will Clark DT	.35	.17	.03
☐ 636	Hensley Meulens	.20	.10	.02	☐ 685	Tony Gwynn DT	.15	.07	.01
☐ 637	Juan Gonzalez	.60	.30	.06	☐ 686	Rickey Henderson DT	.20	.10	.02
☐ 638	Lenny Webster	.12	.06	.01					
☐ 639	Mark Gardner	.12	.06	.01	☐ 687	Bo Jackson DT	.35	.17	.03
☐ 640	Tommy Greene	.40	.20	.04	☐ 688	Mark Langston DT	.10	.05	.01
☐ 641	Mike Hartley	.10	.05	.01	☐ 689	Barry Larkin DT	.10	.05	.01
☐ 642	Phil Stephenson	.10	.05	.01	☐ 690	Kirby Puckett DT	.20	.10	.02
☐ 643	Kevin Mmahat	.20	.10	.02	☐ 691	Ryne Sandberg DT	.12	.06	.01
☐ 644	Ed Whited	.20	.10	.02	☐ 692	Mike Scott DT	.08	.04	.01
☐ 645	Delino DeShields	.30	.15	.03	☐ 693	Terry Steinbach DT	.06	.03	.00
☐ 646	Kevin Blankenship	.08	.04	.01	☐ 694	Bobby Thigpen DT	.06	.03	.00
☐ 647	Paul Sorrento	.15	.07	.01	☐ 695	Mitch Williams DT	.06	.03	.00
☐ 648	Mike Roesler	.12	.06	.01	☐ 696	Nolan Ryan HL	.25	.12	.02
☐ 649	Jason Grimsley	.15	.07	.01	☐ 697	Bo Jackson FB/BB	1.50	.50	.10
☐ 650	Dave Justice	.20	.10	.02	☐ 698	Rickey Henderson ALCS-MVP	.20	.10	.02
☐ 651	Scott Cooper	.20	.10	.02					
☐ 652	Dave Eiland	.08	.04	.01	☐ 699	Will Clark NLCS-MVP	.30	.15	.03
☐ 653	Mike Munoz	.12	.06	.01					
☐ 654	Jeff Fischer	.10	.05	.01	☐ 700	WS Games 1/2	.06	.03	.00

		MINT	EXC	G-VG
☐ 701	Candlestick	.06	.03	.00
☐ 702	WS Game 3	.06	.03	.00
☐ 703	WS Wrap-up	.06	.03	.00
☐ 704	Wade Boggs	.15	.07	.01

1986 Sportflics

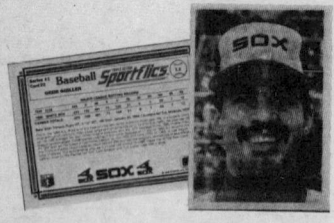

This 200-card set was marketed with 133 small trivia cards. This inaugural set for Sportflics was initially fairly well received by the public. Sportflics was distributed by Major League Marketing; the company is also affiliated with Wrigley and Amurol. The set features 139 single player "magic motion" cards (which can be tilted to show three different pictures of the same player), 50 "Tri-Stars" (which show three different players), 10 "Big Six" cards (which show six players who share similar achievements), and one World Champs card featuring 12 members of the victorious Kansas City Royals. All cards measure 2 ½" by 3 ½". Some of the cards also have (limited production and rarely seen) proof versions with some player selection differences; a proof version of #178 includes Jim Wilson instead of Mark Funderburk. Also a proof of #179 with Karl Best, Mark Funderburk, Andres Galarraga, Dwayne Henry, Pete Incaviglia, and Todd Worrell was produced.

			MINT	EXC	G-VG
	COMPLETE SET (200)		40.00	20.00	4.00
	COMMON PLAYER (1-200)		.12	.06	.01
☐	1	George Brett	1.25	.60	.12
☐	2	Don Mattingly	4.00	2.00	.40
☐	3	Wade Boggs	2.50	1.25	.25
☐	4	Eddie Murray	.75	.35	.07
☐	5	Dale Murphy	.90	.45	.09
☐	6	Rickey Henderson	1.00	.50	.10
☐	7	Harold Baines	.30	.15	.03
☐	8	Cal Ripken	1.00	.50	.10
☐	9	Orel Hershiser	1.00	.50	.10
☐	10	Bret Saberhagen	.75	.35	.07
☐	11	Tim Raines	.50	.25	.05
☐	12	Fernando Valenzuela	.40	.20	.04
☐	13	Tony Gwynn	.90	.45	.09
☐	14	Pedro Guerrero	.35	.17	.03
☐	15	Keith Hernandez	.35	.17	.03
☐	16	Ernie Riles	.20	.10	.02
☐	17	Jim Rice	.40	.20	.04
☐	18	Ron Guidry	.30	.15	.03
☐	19	Willie McGee	.35	.17	.03
☐	20	Ryne Sandberg	1.00	.50	.10
☐	21	Kirk Gibson	.60	.30	.06
☐	22	Ozzie Guillen	.40	.20	.04
☐	23	Dave Parker	.30	.15	.03
☐	24	Vince Coleman	1.25	.60	.12
☐	25	Tom Seaver	.75	.35	.07
☐	26	Brett Butler	.20	.10	.02
☐	27	Steve Carlton	.60	.30	.06
☐	28	Gary Carter	.50	.25	.05
☐	29	Cecil Cooper	.20	.10	.02
☐	30	Jose Cruz	.12	.06	.01
☐	31	Alvin Davis	.20	.10	.02
☐	32	Dwight Evans	.25	.12	.02
☐	33	Julio Franco	.25	.12	.02
☐	34	Damaso Garcia	.12	.06	.01
☐	35	Steve Garvey	.75	.35	.07
☐	36	Kent Hrbek	.40	.20	.04
☐	37	Reggie Jackson	1.00	.50	.10
☐	38	Fred Lynn	.30	.15	.03
☐	39	Paul Molitor	.40	.20	.04
☐	40	Jim Presley	.20	.10	.02
☐	41	Dave Righetti	.30	.15	.03
☐	42	Robin Yount	.75	.35	.07
☐	43	Nolan Ryan	1.50	.75	.15
☐	44	Mike Schmidt	1.50	.75	.15
☐	45	Lee Smith	.12	.06	.01
☐	46	Rick Sutcliffe	.20	.10	.02

			MINT	EXC	G-VG
☐	47	Bruce Sutter	.20	.10	.02
☐	48	Lou Whitaker	.25	.12	.02
☐	49	Dave Winfield	.65	.30	.06
☐	50	Pete Rose	1.50	.75	.15
☐	51	NL MVP's	.75	.35	.07
		Ryne Sandberg			
		Steve Garvey			
		Pete Rose			
☐	52	Slugging Stars	.40	.20	.04
		George Brett			
		Harold Baines			
		Jim Rice			
☐	53	No-Hitters	.20	.10	.02
		Phil Niekro			
		Jerry Reuss			
		Mike Witt			
☐	54	Big Hitters	1.00	.50	.10
		Don Mattingly			
		Cal Ripken			
		Robin Yount			
☐	55	Bullpen Aces	.20	.10	.02
		Dan Quisenberry			
		Goose Gossage			
		Lee Smith			
☐	56	Rookies of The Year .	1.00	.50	.10
		Darryl Strawberry			
		Steve Sax			
		Pete Rose			
☐	57	AL MVP's	.50	.25	.05
		Cal Ripken			
		Don Baylor			
		Reggie Jackson			
☐	58	Repeat Batting			
		Champs	.75	.35	.07
		Dave Parker			
		Bill Madlock			
		Pete Rose			
☐	59	Cy Young Winners ..	.12	.06	.01
		LaMarr Hoyt			
		Mike Flanagan			
		Ron Guidry			
☐	60	Double Award			
		Winners	.30	.15	.03
		Fernando Valenzuela			
		Rick Sutcliffe			
		Tom Seaver			
☐	61	Home Run Champs .	.65	.30	.06
		Reggie Jackson			
		Jim Rice			

			MINT	EXC	G-VG
		Tony Armas			
☐	62	NL MVP's	.75	.35	.07
		Keith Hernandez			
		Dale Murphy			
		Mike Schmidt			
☐	63	AL MVP's	.60	.30	.06
		Robin Yount			
		George Brett			
		Fred Lynn			
☐	64	Comeback Players ..	.12	.06	.01
		Bert Blyleven			
		Jerry Koosman			
		John Denny			
☐	65	Cy Young Relievers .	.20	.10	.02
		Willie Hernandez			
		Rollie Fingers			
		Bruce Sutter			
☐	66	Rookies of The Year .	.20	.10	.02
		Bob Horner			
		Andre Dawson			
		Gary Matthews			
☐	67	Rookies of The Year .	.35	.17	.03
		Ron Kittle			
		Carlton Fisk			
		Tom Seaver			
☐	68	Home Run Champs .	.35	.17	.03
		Mike Schmidt			
		George Foster			
		Dave Kingman			
☐	69	Double Award			
		Winners	1.00	.50	.10
		Cal Ripken			
		Rod Carew			
		Pete Rose			
☐	70	Cy Young Winners ..	.40	.20	.04
		Rick Sutcliffe			
		Steve Carlton			
		Tom Seaver			
☐	71	Top Sluggers	.50	.25	.05
		Reggie Jackson			
		Fred Lynn			
		Robin Yount			
☐	72	Rookies of The Year .	.25	.12	.02
		Dave Righetti			
		Fernando Valenzuela			
		Rick Sutcliffe			
☐	73	Rookies of The Year .	.50	.25	.05
		Fred Lynn			
		Eddie Murray			

			MINT	EXC	G-VG
		Cal Ripken			
☐	74	Rookies of The Year	.25	.12	.02
		Alvin Davis			
		Lou Whitaker			
		Rod Carew			
☐	75	Batting Champs	1.25	.60	.12
		Don Mattingly			
		Wade Boggs			
		Carney Lansford			
☐	76	Jesse Barfield	.30	.15	.03
☐	77	Phil Bradley	.25	.12	.02
☐	78	Chris Brown	.20	.10	.02
☐	79	Tom Browning	.30	.15	.03
☐	80	Tom Brunansky	.25	.12	.02
☐	81	Bill Buckner	.20	.10	.02
☐	82	Chili Davis	.20	.10	.02
☐	83	Mike Davis	.12	.06	.01
☐	84	Rich Gedman	.12	.06	.01
☐	85	Willie Hernandez	.20	.10	.02
☐	86	Ron Kittle	.20	.10	.02
☐	87	Lee Lacy	.12	.06	.01
☐	88	Bill Madlock	.20	.10	.02
☐	89	Mike Marshall	.20	.10	.02
☐	90	Keith Moreland	.12	.06	.01
☐	91	Graig Nettles	.20	.10	.02
☐	92	Lance Parrish	.30	.15	.03
☐	93	Kirby Puckett	1.25	.60	.12
☐	94	Juan Samuel	.30	.15	.03
☐	95	Steve Sax	.35	.17	.03
☐	96	Dave Stieb	.20	.10	.02
☐	97	Darryl Strawberry	1.25	.60	.12
☐	98	Willie Upshaw	.12	.06	.01
☐	99	Frank Viola	.30	.15	.03
☐	100	Dwight Gooden	1.25	.60	.12
☐	101	Joaquin Andujar	.12	.06	.01
☐	102	George Bell	.40	.20	.04
☐	103	Bert Blyleven	.25	.12	.02
☐	104	Mike Boddicker	.12	.06	.01
☐	105	Britt Burns	.12	.06	.01
☐	106	Rod Carew	.75	.35	.07
☐	107	Jack Clark	.35	.17	.03
☐	108	Danny Cox	.20	.10	.02
☐	109	Ron Darling	.35	.17	.03
☐	110	Andre Dawson	.50	.25	.05
☐	111	Leon Durham	.12	.06	.01
☐	112	Tony Fernandez	.25	.12	.02
☐	113	Tommy Herr	.12	.06	.01
☐	114	Teddy Higuera	.35	.17	.03
☐	115	Bob Horner	.20	.10	.02

			MINT	EXC	G-VG
☐	116	Dave Kingman	.20	.10	.02
☐	117	Jack Morris	.25	.12	.02
☐	118	Dan Quisenberry	.20	.10	.02
☐	119	Jeff Reardon	.20	.10	.02
☐	120	Bryn Smith	.20	.10	.02
☐	121	Ozzie Smith	.50	.25	.05
☐	122	John Tudor	.20	.10	.02
☐	123	Tim Wallach	.12	.06	.01
☐	124	Willie Wilson	.20	.10	.02
☐	125	Carlton Fisk	.30	.15	.03
☐	126	RBI Sluggers	.20	.10	.02
		Gary Carter			
		Al Oliver			
		George Foster			
☐	127	Run Scorers	.40	.20	.04
		Tim Raines			
		Ryne Sandberg			
		Keith Hernandez			
☐	128	Run Scorers	.35	.17	.03
		Paul Molitor			
		Cal Ripken			
		Willie Wilson			
☐	129	No-Hitters	.12	.06	.01
		John Candelaria			
		Dennis Eckersley			
		Bob Forsch			
☐	130	World Series MVP's	.60	.30	.06
		Pete Rose			
		Ron Coy			
		Rollie Fingers			
☐	131	All-Star Game MVP's	.12	.06	.01
		Dave Concepcion			
		George Foster			
		Bill Madlock			
☐	132	Cy Young Winners	.12	.06	.01
		John Denny			
		Fernando Valenzuela			
		Vida Blue			
☐	133	Comeback Players	.12	.06	.01
		Rich Dotson			
		Joaquin Andujar			
		Doyle Alexander			
☐	134	Big Winners	.35	.17	.03
		Rick Sutcliffe			
		Tom Seaver			
		John Denny			
☐	135	Veteran Pitchers	.50	.25	.05
		Tom Seaver			
		Phil Niekro			

		MINT	EXC	G-VG
	Don Sutton			
☐ 136	Rookies of The Year	.75	.35	.07
	Dwight Gooden			
	Vince Coleman			
	Alfredo Griffin			
☐ 137	All-Star Game MVP's	.40	.20	.04
	Gary Carter			
	Fred Lynn			
	Steve Garvey			
☐ 138	Veteran Hitters	.60	.30	.06
	Tony Perez			
	Rusty Staub			
	Pete Rose			
☐ 139	Power Hitters	.50	.25	.05
	Mike Schmidt			
	Jim Rice			
	George Foster			
☐ 140	Batting Champs	.25	.12	.02
	Tony Gwynn			
	Al Oliver			
	Bill Buckner			
☐ 141	No-Hitters	.50	.25	.05
	Nolan Ryan			
	Jack Morris			
	Dave Righetti			
☐ 142	No-Hitters	.30	.15	.03
	Tom Seaver			
	Bert Blyleven			
	Vida Blue			
☐ 143	Strikeout Kings	1.00	.50	.10
	Nolan Ryan			
	Fernando Valenzuela			
	Dwight Gooden			
☐ 144	Base Stealers	.20	.10	.02
	Tim Raines			
	Willie Wilson			
	Davey Lopes			
☐ 145	RBI Sluggers	.20	.10	.02
	Tony Armas			
	Cecil Cooper			
	Eddie Murray			
☐ 146	AL MVP's	.40	.20	.04
	Rod Carew			
	Jim Rice			
	Rollie Fingers			
☐ 147	World Series MVP's .	.35	.17	.03
	Alan Trammell			
	Rick Dempsey			
	Reggie Jackson			

		MINT	EXC	G-VG
☐ 148	World Series MVP's	.40	.20	.04
	Darrell Porter			
	Pedro Guerrero			
	Mike Schmidt			
☐ 149	ERA Leaders	.12	.06	.01
	Mike Boddicker			
	Rick Sutcliffe			
	Ron Guidry			
☐ 150	Comeback Players ..	.35	.17	.03
	Reggie Jackson			
	Dave Kingman			
	Fred Lynn			
☐ 151	Buddy Bell	.20	.10	.02
☐ 152	Dennis Boyd	.12	.06	.01
☐ 153	Dave Concepcion	.20	.10	.02
☐ 154	Brian Downing	.12	.06	.01
☐ 155	Shawon Dunston	.30	.15	.03
☐ 156	John Franco	.35	.17	.03
☐ 157	Scott Garrelts	.20	.10	.02
☐ 158	Bob James	.12	.06	.01
☐ 159	Charlie Leibrandt	.12	.06	.01
☐ 160	Oddibe McDowell	.25	.12	.02
☐ 161	Roger McDowell	.30	.15	.03
☐ 162	Mike Moore	.30	.15	.03
☐ 163	Phil Niekro	.50	.25	.05
☐ 164	Al Oliver	.20	.10	.02
☐ 165	Tony Pena	.20	.10	.02
☐ 166	Ted Power	.12	.06	.01
☐ 167	Mike Scioscia	.12	.06	.01
☐ 168	Mario Soto	.12	.06	.01
☐ 169	Bob Stanley	.12	.06	.01
☐ 170	Gary Templeton	.12	.06	.01
☐ 171	Andre Thornton	.12	.06	.01
☐ 172	Alan Trammell	.45	.22	.04
☐ 173	Doug DeCinces	.20	.10	.02
☐ 174	Greg Walker	.12	.06	.01
☐ 175	Don Sutton	.40	.20	.04
☐ 176	1985 Award Winners	.90	.45	.09
	Ozzie Guillen			
	Bret Saberhagen			
	Don Mattingly			
	Vince Coleman			
	Dwight Gooden			
	Willie McGee			
☐ 177	1985 Hot Rookies ...	.30	.15	.03
	Stew Cliburn			
	Brian Fisher			
	Joe Hesketh			
	Joe Orsulak			

		MINT	EXC	G-VG
	Mark Salas			
	Larry Sheets			
☐ 178	1986 Rookies To Watch	18.00	9.00	1.80
	Jose Canseco			
	Mark Funderburk			
	Mike Greenwell			
	Steve Lombardozzi			
	Billy Joe Robidoux			
	Danny Tartabull			
☐ 179	1985 Gold Glovers	.75	.35	.07
	George Brett			
	Ron Guidry			
	Keith Hernandez			
	Don Mattingly			
	Willie McGee			
	Dale Murphy			
☐ 180	Active Lifetime .300	.75	.35	.07
	Wade Boggs			
	George Brett			
	Rod Carew			
	Cecil Cooper			
	Don Mattingly			
	Willie Wilson			
☐ 181	Active Lifetime .300	.60	.30	.06
	Tony Gwynn			
	Bill Madlock			
	Pedro Guerrero			
	Dave Parker			
	Pete Rose			
	Keith Hernandez			
☐ 182	1985 Milestones	.75	.35	.07
	Rod Carew			
	Phil Niekro			
	Pete Rose			
	Nolan Ryan			
	Tom Seaver			
	Matt Tallman (fan)			
☐ 183	1985 Triple Crown	.75	.35	.07
	Wade Boggs			
	Darrell Evans			
	Don Mattingly			
	Willie McGee			
	Dale Murphy			
	Dave Parker			
☐ 184	1985 Highlights	.75	.35	.07
	Wade Boggs			
	Dwight Gooden			
	Rickey Henderson			

		MINT	EXC	G-VG
	Don Mattingly			
	Willie McGee			
	John Tudor			
☐ 185	1985 20 Game Winners	.75	.35	.07
	Dwight Gooden			
	Ron Guidry			
	John Tudor			
	Joaquin Andujar			
	Bret Saberhagen			
	Tom Browning			
☐ 186	World Series Champs	.35	.17	.03
	L. Smith, Dane Iorg			
	W. Wilson, Leibrandt			
	G. Brett, Saberhagen			
	Motley, Quisenberry			
	D. Jackson, Sundberg			
	S. Balboni, F. White			
☐ 187	Hubie Brooks	.20	.10	.02
☐ 188	Glenn Davis	.75	.35	.07
☐ 189	Darrell Evans	.20	.10	.02
☐ 190	Rich Gossage	.25	.12	.02
☐ 191	Andy Hawkins	.20	.10	.02
☐ 192	Jay Howell	.12	.06	.01
☐ 193	LaMarr Hoyt	.12	.06	.01
☐ 194	Davey Lopes	.12	.06	.01
☐ 195	Mike Scott	.50	.25	.05
☐ 196	Ted Simmons	.20	.10	.02
☐ 197	Gary Ward	.12	.06	.01
☐ 198	Bob Welch	.20	.10	.02
☐ 199	Mike Young	.12	.06	.01
☐ 200	Buddy Biancalana	.12	.06	.01

1986 Sportflics Rookies

This set of 50 three-phase "animated" cards features top rookies of 1986 as well as a few outstanding rookies from the past. These "Magic Motion" cards are standard size, 2 ½" by 3 ½", and feature a distinctive light blue border on the front of the card. Cards were distributed in a light blue box, which also contained 34 trivia cards, each measuring 1¾" by 2". There are 47 single player cards along with two Tri-Stars and one Big Six.

		MINT	EXC	G-VG
	COMPLETE SET (50)	18.00	9.00	1.80
	COMMON PLAYER (1-50)	.10	.05	.01
☐ 1	John Kruk	.30	.15	.03
☐ 2	Edwin Correa	.15	.07	.01
☐ 3	Pete Incaviglia	.75	.35	.07
☐ 4	Dale Sveum	.15	.07	.01
☐ 5	Juan Nieves	.15	.07	.01
☐ 6	Will Clark	4.50	2.25	.45
☐ 7	Wally Joyner	2.00	1.00	.20
☐ 8	Lance McCullers	.15	.07	.01
☐ 9	Scott Bailes	.15	.07	.01
☐ 10	Dan Plesac	.20	.10	.02
☐ 11	Jose Canseco	4.50	2.25	.45
☐ 12	Bobby Witt	.20	.10	.02
☐ 13	Barry Bonds	.75	.35	.07
☐ 14	Andres Thomas	.20	.10	.02
☐ 15	Jim Deshaies	.20	.10	.02

		MINT	EXC	G-VG
☐ 16	Ruben Sierra	2.50	1.25	.25
☐ 17	Steve Lombardozzi	.10	.05	.01
☐ 18	Cory Snyder	1.00	.50	.10
☐ 19	Reggie Williams	.10	.05	.01
☐ 20	Mitch Williams	.25	.12	.02
☐ 21	Glenn Braggs	.25	.12	.02
☐ 22	Danny Tartabull	.75	.35	.07
☐ 23	Charlie Kerfeld	.10	.05	.01
☐ 24	Paul Assenmacher	.10	.05	.01
☐ 25	Robby Thompson	.25	.12	.02
☐ 26	Bobby Bonilla	.75	.35	.07
☐ 27	Andres Galarraga	.75	.35	.07
☐ 28	Billy Jo Robidoux	.15	.07	.01
☐ 29	Bruce Ruffin	.15	.07	.01
☐ 30	Greg Swindell	.50	.25	.05
☐ 31	John Cangelosi	.10	.05	.01
☐ 32	Jim Traber	.10	.05	.01
☐ 33	Russ Morman	.15	.07	.01
☐ 34	Barry Larkin	1.50	.75	.15
☐ 35	Todd Worrell	.50	.25	.05
☐ 36	John Cerutti	.15	.07	.01
☐ 37	Mike Kingery	.10	.05	.01
☐ 38	Mark Eichhorn	.10	.05	.01
☐ 39	Scott Bankhead	.20	.10	.02
☐ 40	Bo Jackson	3.50	1.75	.35
☐ 41	Greg Mathews	.15	.07	.01
☐ 42	Eric King	.15	.07	.01
☐ 43	Kal Daniels	.75	.35	.07
☐ 44	Calvin Schiraldi	.15	.07	.01
☐ 45	Mickey Brantley	.20	.10	.02
☐ 46	Tri-Stars	.50	.25	.05
	Willie Mays			
	Pete Rose			
	Fred Lynn			
☐ 47	Tri-Stars	.50	.25	.05
	Tom Seaver			
	Fern. Valenzuela			
	Dwight Gooden			
☐ 48	Big Six	.50	.25	.05
	Eddie Murray			
	Lou Whitaker			
	Dave Righetti			
	Steve Sax			
	Cal Ripken Jr.			
	Darryl Strawberry			
☐ 49	Kevin Mitchell	2.00	1.00	.20
☐ 50	Mike Diaz	.15	.07	.01

1987 Sportflics

This 200-card set was produced by Sportflics and again features three sequence action pictures on each card. Cards measure 2 ½" by 3 ½" and are in full color. Also included with the cards were 136 small team logo and trivia cards. There are 165 individual players, 20 Tri-Stars (the top three players in each league at each position), and 15 other miscellaneous multi-player cards. The cards feature a red border on the front. A full-color face shot of the player is printed on the back of the card. Cards are numbered on the back in the upper right corner. The cards in the factory-collated sets are copyrighted 1986, while the cards in the wax packs are copyrighted 1987 or show no copyright year on the back. Cards from wax packs with 1987 copyright are 1-35, 41-75, 81-115, 121-155, and 161-200; the rest of the numbers (when taken from wax packs) are found without a copyright year.

	MINT	EXC	G-VG
COMPLETE SET (200)	35.00	17.50	3.50
COMMON PLAYER (1-200)	.12	.06	.01
☐ 1 Don Mattingly	3.00	1.50	.30
☐ 2 Wade Boggs	1.50	.75	.15
☐ 3 Dale Murphy	.90	.45	.09
☐ 4 Rickey Henderson	.90	.45	.09
☐ 5 George Brett	.75	.35	.07
☐ 6 Eddie Murray	.60	.30	.06
☐ 7 Kirby Puckett	.90	.45	.09

	MINT	EXC	G-VG
☐ 8 Ryne Sandberg	.50	.25	.05
☐ 9 Cal Ripken	.50	.25	.05
☐ 10 Roger Clemens	1.25	.60	.12
☐ 11 Ted Higuera	.25	.12	.02
☐ 12 Steve Sax	.25	.12	.02
☐ 13 Chris Brown	.12	.06	.01
☐ 14 Jesse Barfield	.25	.12	.02
☐ 15 Kent Hrbek	.30	.15	.03
☐ 16 Robin Yount	.75	.35	.07
☐ 17 Glenn Davis	.50	.25	.05
☐ 18 Hubie Brooks	.12	.06	.01
☐ 19 Mike Scott	.30	.15	.03
☐ 20 Darryl Strawberry ..	.90	.45	.09
☐ 21 Alvin Davis	.20	.10	.02
☐ 22 Eric Davis	1.25	.60	.12
☐ 23 Danny Tartabull	.45	.22	.04
☐ 24A Cory Snyder ERR '86 (photo on front is Pat Tabler)	3.00	1.50	.30
☐ 24B Cory Snyder ERR '87 (photos on front and back are Pat Tabler)	2.00	1.00	.20
☐ 24C Cory Snyder COR '86	2.00	1.00	.20
☐ 25 Pete Rose	1.00	.50	.10
☐ 26 Wally Joyner	1.00	.50	.10
☐ 27 Pedro Guerrero	.25	.12	.02
☐ 28 Tom Seaver	.60	.30	.06
☐ 29 Bob Knepper	.15	.07	.01
☐ 30 Mike Schmidt	1.00	.50	.10
☐ 31 Tony Gwynn	.75	.35	.07
☐ 32 Don Slaught	.12	.06	.01
☐ 33 Todd Worrell	.30	.15	.03
☐ 34 Tim Raines	.30	.15	.03
☐ 35 Dave Parker	.25	.12	.02
☐ 36 Bob Ojeda	.12	.06	.01
☐ 37 Pete Incaviglia	.50	.25	.05
☐ 38 Bruce Hurst	.20	.10	.02
☐ 39 Bobby Witt	.20	.10	.02
☐ 40 Steve Garvey	.60	.30	.06
☐ 41 Dave Winfield	.40	.20	.04
☐ 42 Jose Cruz	.12	.06	.01
☐ 43 Orel Hershiser	.75	.35	.07
☐ 44 Reggie Jackson	.90	.45	.09
☐ 45 Chili Davis	.12	.06	.01
☐ 46 Robby Thompson	.12	.06	.01
☐ 47 Dennis Boyd	.12	.06	.01
☐ 48 Kirk Gibson	.40	.20	.04
☐ 49 Fred Lynn	.20	.10	.02
☐ 50 Gary Carter	.40	.20	.04

			MINT	EXC	G-VG
☐	51	George Bell	.30	.15	.03
☐	52	Pete O'Brien	.12	.06	.01
☐	53	Ron Darling	.20	.10	.02
☐	54	Paul Molitor	.30	.15	.03
☐	55	Mike Pagliarulo	.12	.06	.01
☐	56	Mike Boddicker	.12	.06	.01
☐	57	Dave Righetti	.20	.10	.02
☐	58	Len Dykstra	.20	.10	.02
☐	59	Mike Witt	.20	.10	.02
☐	60	Tony Bernazard	.12	.06	.01
☐	61	John Kruk	.25	.12	.02
☐	62	Mike Krukow	.12	.06	.01
☐	63	Sid Fernandez	.25	.12	.02
☐	64	Gary Gaetti	.25	.12	.02
☐	65	Vince Coleman	.50	.25	.05
☐	66	Pat Tabler	.12	.06	.01
☐	67	Mike Scioscia	.12	.06	.01
☐	68	Scott Garrelts	.12	.06	.01
☐	69	Brett Butler	.12	.06	.01
☐	70	Bill Buckner	.20	.10	.02
☐	71A	Dennis Rasmussen ERR '86 copyright (photo on back is John Montefusco)	1.00	.50	.10
☐	71B	Dennis Rasmussen COR '87 copyright (photo with mustache)	.50	.25	.05
☐	72	Tim Wallach	.12	.06	.01
☐	73	Bob Horner	.20	.10	.02
☐	74	Willie McGee	.25	.12	.02
☐	75	Tri-Stars Don Mattingly Wally Joyner Eddie Murray	1.00	.50	.10
☐	76A	Jesse Orosco COR '86 copyright	.12	.06	.01
☐	76B	Jesse Orosco ERR '87 copyright (number on back is 96)	.12	.06	.01
☐	77	Tri-Stars Todd Worrell Jeff Reardon Lee Smith	.12	.06	.01
☐	78	Candy Maldonado	.12	.06	.01
☐	79	Tri-Stars Ozzie Smith Hubie Brooks Shawon Dunston	.20	.10	.02
☐	80	Tri-Stars George Bell Jose Canseco Jim Rice	1.00	.50	.10
☐	81	Bert Blyleven	.25	.12	.02
☐	82	Mike Marshall	.20	.10	.02
☐	83	Ron Guidry	.20	.10	.02
☐	84	Julio Franco	.20	.10	.02
☐	85	Willie Wilson	.20	.10	.02
☐	86	Lee Lacy	.12	.06	.01
☐	87	Jack Morris	.25	.12	.02
☐	88	Ray Knight	.12	.06	.01
☐	89	Phil Bradley	.12	.06	.01
☐	90	Jose Canseco	2.50	1.25	.25
☐	91	Gary Ward	.12	.06	.01
☐	92	Mike Easler	.12	.06	.01
☐	93	Tony Pena	.12	.06	.01
☐	94	Dave Smith	.12	.06	.01
☐	95	Will Clark	2.50	1.25	.25
☐	96	Lloyd Moseby (see also 76B)	.12	.06	.01
☐	97	Jim Rice	.30	.15	.03
☐	98	Shawon Dunston	.25	.12	.02
☐	99	Don Sutton	.35	.17	.03
☐	100	Dwight Gooden	.90	.45	.09
☐	101	Lance Parrish	.25	.12	.02
☐	102	Mark Langston	.35	.17	.03
☐	103	Floyd Youmans	.12	.06	.01
☐	104	Lee Smith	.12	.06	.01
☐	105	Willie Hernandez	.20	.10	.02
☐	106	Doug DeCinces	.12	.06	.01
☐	107	Ken Schrom	.12	.06	.01
☐	108	Don Carman	.12	.06	.01
☐	109	Brook Jacoby	.20	.10	.02
☐	110	Steve Bedrosian	.25	.12	.02
☐	111	Tri-Stars Roger Clemens Jack Morris Ted Higuera	.50	.25	.05
☐	112	Tri-Stars Marty Barrett Tony Bernazard Lou Whitaker	.12	.06	.01
☐	113	Tri-Stars Cal Ripken Scott Fletcher Tony Fernandez	.25	.12	.02
☐	114	Tri-Stars Wade Boggs	.75	.35	.07

		MINT	EXC	G-VG
	George Brett			
	Gary Gaetti			
☐ 115	Tri-Stars	.50	.25	.05
	Mike Schmidt			
	Chris Brown			
	Tim Wallach			
☐ 116	Tri-Stars	.25	.12	.02
	Ryne Sandberg			
	Johnny Ray			
	Bill Doran			
☐ 117	Tri-Stars	.25	.12	.02
	Dave Parker			
	Tony Gwynn			
	Kevin Bass			
☐ 118	Big Six Rookies	1.50	.75	.15
	Ty Gainey			
	Terry Steinbach			
	Dave Clark			
	Pat Dodson			
	Phil Lombardi			
	Benito Santiago			
☐ 119	Hi-Lite Tri-Stars	.25	.12	.02
	Dave Righetti			
	Fernando Valenzuela			
	Mike Scott			
☐ 120	Tri-Stars	.50	.25	.05
	Fernando Valenzuela			
	Mike Scott			
	Dwight Gooden			
☐ 121	Johnny Ray	.12	.06	.01
☐ 122	Keith Moreland	.12	.06	.01
☐ 123	Juan Samuel	.20	.10	.02
☐ 124	Wally Backman	.12	.06	.01
☐ 125	Nolan Ryan	1.25	.60	.12
☐ 126	Greg Harris	.12	.06	.01
☐ 127	Kirk McCaskill	.12	.06	.01
☐ 128	Dwight Evans	.25	.12	.02
☐ 129	Rick Rhoden	.12	.06	.01
☐ 130	Bill Madlock	.12	.06	.01
☐ 131	Oddibe McDowell	.20	.10	.02
☐ 132	Darrell Evans	.20	.10	.02
☐ 133	Keith Hernandez	.30	.15	.03
☐ 134	Tom Brunansky	.20	.10	.02
☐ 135	Kevin McReynolds	.50	.25	.05
☐ 136	Scott Fletcher	.12	.06	.01
☐ 137	Lou Whitaker	.20	.10	.02
☐ 138	Carney Lansford	.25	.12	.02
☐ 139	Andre Dawson	.35	.17	.03
☐ 140	Carlton Fisk	.30	.15	.03

		MINT	EXC	G-VG
☐ 141	Buddy Bell	.20	.10	.02
☐ 142	Ozzie Smith	.50	.25	.05
☐ 143	Dan Pasqua	.12	.06	.01
☐ 144	Kevin Mitchell	.75	.35	.07
☐ 145	Bret Saberhagen	.50	.25	.05
☐ 146	Charlie Kerfeld	.12	.06	.01
☐ 147	Phil Niekro	.35	.17	.03
☐ 148	John Candelaria	.12	.06	.01
☐ 149	Rich Gedman	.12	.06	.01
☐ 150	Fernando Valenzuela	.35	.17	.03
☐ 151	Tri-Stars	.20	.10	.02
	Gary Carter			
	Mike Scioscia			
	Tony Pena			
☐ 152	Tri-Stars	.30	.15	.03
	Tim Raines			
	Jose Cruz			
	Vince Coleman			
☐ 153	Tri-Stars	.25	.12	.02
	Jesse Barfield			
	Harold Baines			
	Dave Winfield			
☐ 154	Tri-Stars	.12	.06	.01
	Lance Parrish			
	Don Slaught			
	Rich Gedman			
☐ 155	Tri-Stars	.75	.35	.07
	Dale Murphy			
	Kevin McReynolds			
	Eric Davis			
☐ 156	Hi-Lite Tri-Stars	.45	.22	.04
	Don Sutton			
	Mike Schmidt			
	Jim Deshaies			
☐ 157	Speedburners	.30	.15	.03
	Rickey Henderson			
	John Cangelosi			
	Gary Pettis			
☐ 158	Big Six Rookies	2.00	1.00	.20
	Randy Asadoor			
	Casey Candaele			
	Kevin Seitzer			
	Rafael Palmeiro			
	Tim Pyznarski			
	Dave Cochrane			
☐ 159	Big Six	1.50	.75	.15
	Don Mattingly			
	Rickey Henderson			
	Roger Clemens			

		MINT	EXC	G-VG
	Dale Murphy			
	Eddie Murray			
	Dwight Gooden			
☐ 160	Roger McDowell	.20	.10	.02
☐ 161	Brian Downing	.12	.06	.01
☐ 162	Bill Doran	.20	.10	.02
☐ 163	Don Baylor	.20	.10	.02
☐ 164A	Alfredo Griffin ERR ..	.25	.12	.02
	(no uniform number			
	on card back) '87			
☐ 164B	Alfredo Griffin	.25	.12	.02
	COR '86			
☐ 165	Don Aase	.12	.06	.01
☐ 166	Glenn Wilson	.12	.06	.01
☐ 167	Dan Quisenberry ...	.20	.10	.02
☐ 168	Frank White	.12	.06	.01
☐ 169	Cecil Cooper	.12	.06	.01
☐ 170	Jody Davis	.12	.06	.01
☐ 171	Harold Baines	.25	.12	.02
☐ 172	Rob Deer	.20	.10	.02
☐ 173	John Tudor	.20	.10	.02
☐ 174	Larry Parrish	.12	.06	.01
☐ 175	Kevin Bass	.20	.10	.02
☐ 176	Joe Carter	.40	.20	.04
☐ 177	Mitch Webster	.12	.06	.01
☐ 178	Dave Kingman	.20	.10	.02
☐ 179	Jim Presley	.12	.06	.01
☐ 180	Mel Hall	.20	.10	.02
☐ 181	Shane Rawley	.12	.06	.01
☐ 182	Marty Barrett	.20	.10	.02
☐ 183	Damaso Garcia ...	.12	.06	.01
☐ 184	Bobby Grich	.20	.10	.02
☐ 185	Leon Durham	.12	.06	.01
☐ 186	Ozzie Guillen	.20	.10	.02
☐ 187	Tony Fernandez ...	.25	.12	.02
☐ 188	Alan Trammell	.35	.17	.03
☐ 189	Jim Clancy	.12	.06	.01
☐ 190	Bo Jackson	2.00	1.00	.20
☐ 191	Bob Forsch	.12	.06	.01
☐ 192	John Franco	.20	.10	.02
☐ 193	Von Hayes	.20	.10	.02
☐ 194	Tri-Stars	.12	.06	.01
	Don Aase			
	Dave Righetti			
	Mark Eichhorn			
☐ 195	Tri-Stars	.60	.30	.06
	Keith Hernandez			
	Will Clark			
	Glenn Davis			

		MINT	EXC	G-VG
☐ 196	Hi-Lite Tri-Stars	.45	.22	.04
	Roger Clemens			
	Joe Cowley			
	Bob Horner			
☐ 197	Big Six	.75	.35	.07
	George Brett			
	Hubie Brooks			
	Tony Gwynn			
	Ryne Sandberg			
	Tim Raines			
	Wade Boggs			
☐ 198	Tri-Stars	.50	.25	.05
	Kirby Puckett			
	Rickey Henderson			
	Fred Lynn			
☐ 199	Speedburners	.60	.30	.06
	Tim Raines			
	Vince Coleman			
	Eric Davis			
☐ 200	Steve Carlton	.40	.20	.04

1988 Sportflics

This 225-card set was produced by Sportflics and again features three sequence action pictures on each card. Cards measure 2 ½" by 3 ½" and are in full color. There are 219 individual players, 3 Highlights trios, and 3 Rookie Prospect trio cards. The cards feature a red border on the front. A full-color action picture of the player is printed on the back of the

card. Cards are numbered on the back in the lower right corner.

			MINT	EXC	G-VG
		COMPLETE SET (225)	40.00	20.00	4.00
		COMMON PLAYER (1-225)	.12	.06	.01
☐	1	Don Mattingly	2.50	1.25	.25
☐	2	Tim Raines	.40	.20	.04
☐	3	Andre Dawson	.40	.20	.04
☐	4	George Bell	.35	.17	.03
☐	5	Joe Carter	.30	.15	.03
☐	6	Matt Nokes	.40	.20	.04
☐	7	Dave Winfield	.40	.20	.04
☐	8	Kirby Puckett	.90	.45	.09
☐	9	Will Clark	1.50	.75	.15
☐	10	Eric Davis	.90	.45	.09
☐	11	Rickey Henderson	.75	.35	.07
☐	12	Ryne Sandberg	.45	.22	.04
☐	13	Jesse Barfield UER (misspelled Jessie on card back)	.30	.15	.03
☐	14	Ozzie Guillen	.20	.10	.02
☐	15	Bret Saberhagen	.35	.17	.03
☐	16	Tony Gwynn	.50	.25	.05
☐	17	Kevin Seitzer	.75	.35	.07
☐	18	Jack Clark	.30	.15	.03
☐	19	Danny Tartabull	.40	.20	.04
☐	20	Ted Higuera	.25	.12	.02
☐	21	Charlie Leibrandt UER (misspelled Liebrandt on card front)	.15	.07	.01
☐	22	Benny Santiago	.75	.35	.07
☐	23	Fred Lynn	.25	.12	.02
☐	24	Rob Thompson	.15	.07	.01
☐	25	Alan Trammell	.35	.17	.03
☐	26	Tony Fernandez	.25	.12	.02
☐	27	Rick Sutcliffe	.20	.10	.02
☐	28	Gary Carter	.35	.17	.03
☐	29	Cory Snyder	.35	.17	.03
☐	30	Lou Whitaker	.20	.10	.02
☐	31	Keith Hernandez	.30	.15	.03
☐	32	Mike Witt	.20	.10	.02
☐	33	Harold Baines	.20	.10	.02
☐	34	Robin Yount	.75	.35	.07
☐	35	Mike Schmidt	1.00	.50	.10
☐	36	Dion James	.12	.06	.01
☐	37	Tom Candiotti	.12	.06	.01
☐	38	Tracy Jones	.20	.10	.02

			MINT	EXC	G-VG
☐	39	Nolan Ryan	1.25	.60	.12
☐	40	Fernando Valenzuela	.35	.17	.03
☐	41	Vance Law	.12	.06	.01
☐	42	Roger McDowell	.20	.10	.02
☐	43	Carlton Fisk	.30	.15	.03
☐	44	Scott Garrelts	.20	.10	.02
☐	45	Lee Guetterman	.12	.06	.01
☐	46	Mark Langston	.30	.15	.03
☐	47	Willie Randolph	.20	.10	.02
☐	48	Bill Doran	.20	.10	.02
☐	49	Larry Parrish	.12	.06	.01
☐	50	Wade Boggs	1.25	.60	.12
☐	51	Shane Rawley	.12	.06	.01
☐	52	Alvin Davis	.20	.10	.02
☐	53	Jeff Reardon	.20	.10	.02
☐	54	Jim Presley	.12	.06	.01
☐	55	Kevin Bass	.12	.06	.01
☐	56	Kevin McReynolds	.40	.20	.04
☐	57	B.J. Surhoff	.20	.10	.02
☐	58	Julio Franco	.20	.10	.02
☐	59	Eddie Murray	.45	.22	.04
☐	60	Jody Davis	.12	.06	.01
☐	61	Todd Worrell	.20	.10	.02
☐	62	Von Hayes	.20	.10	.02
☐	63	Billy Hatcher	.12	.06	.01
☐	64	John Kruk	.20	.10	.02
☐	65	Tom Henke	.12	.06	.01
☐	66	Mike Scott	.30	.15	.03
☐	67	Vince Coleman	.35	.17	.03
☐	68	Ozzie Smith	.35	.17	.03
☐	69	Ken Williams	.20	.10	.02
☐	70	Steve Bedrosian	.20	.10	.02
☐	71	Luis Polonia	.20	.10	.02
☐	72	Brook Jacoby	.12	.06	.01
☐	73	Ron Darling	.20	.10	.02
☐	74	Lloyd Moseby	.12	.06	.01
☐	75	Wally Joyner	.45	.22	.04
☐	76	Dan Quisenberry	.20	.10	.02
☐	77	Scott Fletcher	.12	.06	.01
☐	78	Kirk McCaskill	.12	.06	.01
☐	79	Paul Molitor	.30	.15	.03
☐	80	Mike Aldrete	.12	.06	.01
☐	81	Neal Heaton	.12	.06	.01
☐	82	Jeffrey Leonard	.12	.06	.01
☐	83	Dave Magadan	.20	.10	.02
☐	84	Danny Cox	.12	.06	.01
☐	85	Lance McCullers	.12	.06	.01
☐	86	Jay Howell	.12	.06	.01
☐	87	Charlie Hough	.12	.06	.01

			MINT	EXC	G-VG
☐	88	Gene Garber	.12	.06	.01
☐	89	Jesse Orosco	.12	.06	.01
☐	90	Don Robinson	.12	.06	.01
☐	91	Willie McGee	.25	.12	.02
☐	92	Bert Blyleven	.25	.12	.02
☐	93	Phil Bradley	.20	.10	.02
☐	94	Terry Kennedy	.12	.06	.01
☐	95	Kent Hrbek	.30	.15	.03
☐	96	Juan Samuel	.25	.12	.02
☐	97	Pedro Guerrero	.30	.15	.03
☐	98	Sid Bream	.12	.06	.01
☐	99	Devon White	.30	.15	.03
☐	100	Mark McGwire	1.00	.50	.10
☐	101	Dave Parker	.25	.12	.02
☐	102	Glenn Davis	.35	.17	.03
☐	103	Greg Walker	.12	.06	.01
☐	104	Rick Rhoden	.12	.06	.01
☐	105	Mitch Webster	.12	.06	.01
☐	106	Lenny Dykstra	.20	.10	.02
☐	107	Gene Larkin	.12	.06	.01
☐	108	Floyd Youmans	.12	.06	.01
☐	109	Andy Van Slyke	.25	.12	.02
☐	110	Mike Scioscia	.12	.06	.01
☐	111	Kirk Gibson	.40	.20	.04
☐	112	Kal Daniels	.30	.15	.03
☐	113	Ruben Sierra	.75	.35	.07
☐	114	Sam Horn	.20	.10	.02
☐	115	Ray Knight	.12	.06	.01
☐	116	Jimmy Key	.12	.06	.01
☐	117	Bo Diaz	.12	.06	.01
☐	118	Mike Greenwell	1.25	.60	.12
☐	119	Barry Bonds	.30	.15	.03
☐	120	Reggie Jackson UER (463 lifetime homers)	.75	.35	.07
☐	121	Mike Pagliarulo	.12	.06	.01
☐	122	Tommy John	.25	.12	.02
☐	123	Bill Madlock	.12	.06	.01
☐	124	Ken Caminiti	.20	.10	.02
☐	125	Gary Ward	.12	.06	.01
☐	126	Candy Maldonado	.12	.06	.01
☐	127	Harold Reynolds	.12	.06	.01
☐	128	Joe Magrane	.40	.20	.04
☐	129	Mike Henneman	.20	.10	.02
☐	130	Jim Gantner	.12	.06	.01
☐	131	Bobby Bonilla	.35	.17	.03
☐	132	John Farrell	.25	.12	.02
☐	133	Frank Tanana	.12	.06	.01
☐	134	Zane Smith	.12	.06	.01
☐	135	Dave Righetti	.20	.10	.02
☐	136	Rick Reuschel	.20	.10	.02
☐	137	Dwight Evans	.25	.12	.02
☐	138	Howard Johnson	.35	.17	.03
☐	139	Terry Leach	.12	.06	.01
☐	140	Casey Candaele	.12	.06	.01
☐	141	Tom Herr	.12	.06	.01
☐	142	Tony Pena	.20	.10	.02
☐	143	Lance Parrish	.25	.12	.02
☐	144	Ellis Burks	1.25	.60	.12
☐	145	Pete O'Brien	.20	.10	.02
☐	146	Mike Boddicker	.12	.06	.01
☐	147	Buddy Bell	.12	.06	.01
☐	148	Bo Jackson	1.50	.75	.15
☐	149	Frank White	.20	.10	.02
☐	150	George Brett	.50	.25	.05
☐	151	Tim Wallach	.12	.06	.01
☐	152	Cal Ripken Jr.	.40	.20	.04
☐	153	Brett Butler	.12	.06	.01
☐	154	Gary Gaetti	.25	.12	.02
☐	155	Darryl Strawberry	.75	.35	.07
☐	156	Alredo Griffin	.12	.06	.01
☐	157	Marty Barrett	.12	.06	.01
☐	158	Jim Rice	.30	.15	.03
☐	159	Terry Pendleton	.12	.06	.01
☐	160	Orel Hershiser	.65	.30	.06
☐	161	Larry Sheets	.12	.06	.01
☐	162	Dave Stewart UER (Braves logo)	.50	.25	.05
☐	163	Shawon Dunston	.20	.10	.02
☐	164	Keith Moreland	.12	.06	.01
☐	165	Ken Oberkfell	.12	.06	.01
☐	166	Ivan Calderon	.20	.10	.02
☐	167	Bob Welch	.20	.10	.02
☐	168	Fred McGriff	.50	.25	.05
☐	169	Pete Incaviglia	.30	.15	.03
☐	170	Dale Murphy	.60	.30	.06
☐	171	Mike Dunne	.12	.06	.01
☐	172	Chili Davis	.20	.10	.02
☐	173	Milt Thompson	.12	.06	.01
☐	174	Terry Steinbach	.25	.12	.02
☐	175	Oddibe McDowell	.20	.10	.02
☐	176	Jack Morris	.25	.12	.02
☐	177	Sid Fernandez	.20	.10	.02
☐	178	Ken Griffey	.20	.10	.02
☐	179	Lee Smith	.12	.06	.01
☐	180	Highlights 1987 Kirby Puckett Juan Nieves Mike Schmidt	.45	.22	.04

		MINT	EXC	G-VG
☐ 181	Brian Downing	.12	.06	.01
☐ 182	Andres Galarraga	.35	.17	.03
☐ 183	Rob Deer	.20	.10	.02
☐ 184	Greg Brock	.12	.06	.01
☐ 185	Doug DeCinces	.12	.06	.01
☐ 186	Johnny Ray	.12	.06	.01
☐ 187	Hubie Brooks	.12	.06	.01
☐ 188	Darrell Evans	.12	.06	.01
☐ 189	Mel Hall	.12	.06	.01
☐ 190	Jim Deshaies	.12	.06	.01
☐ 191	Dan Plesac	.20	.10	.02
☐ 192	Willie Wilson	.20	.10	.02
☐ 193	Mike LaValliere	.12	.06	.01
☐ 194	Tom Brunansky	.25	.12	.02
☐ 195	John Franco	.20	.10	.02
☐ 196	Frank Viola	.30	.15	.03
☐ 197	Bruce Hurst	.20	.10	.02
☐ 198	John Tudor	.20	.10	.02
☐ 199	Bob Forsch	.12	.06	.01
☐ 200	Dwight Gooden	.75	.35	.07
☐ 201	Jose Canseco	1.50	.75	.15
☐ 202	Carney Lansford	.25	.12	.02
☐ 203	Kelly Downs	.12	.06	.01
☐ 204	Glenn Wilson	.12	.06	.01
☐ 205	Pat Tabler	.12	.06	.01
☐ 206	Mike Davis	.12	.06	.01
☐ 207	Roger Clemens	.90	.45	.09
☐ 208	Dave Smith	.12	.06	.01
☐ 209	Curt Young	.12	.06	.01
☐ 210	Mark Eichhorn	.12	.06	.01
☐ 211	Juan Nieves	.12	.06	.01
☐ 212	Bob Boone	.20	.10	.02
☐ 213	Don Sutton	.35	.17	.03
☐ 214	Willie Upshaw	.12	.06	.01
☐ 215	Jim Clancy	.12	.06	.01
☐ 216	Bill Ripken	.20	.10	.02
☐ 217	Ozzie Virgil	.12	.06	.01
☐ 218	Dave Concepcion	.12	.06	.01
☐ 219	Alan Ashby	.12	.06	.01
☐ 220	Mike Marshall	.20	.10	.02
☐ 221	Highlights 1987	.60	.30	.06
	Mark McGwire			
	Paul Molitor			
	Vince Coleman			
☐ 222	Highlights 1987	.75	.35	.07
	Benito Santiago			
	Steve Bedrosian			
	Don Mattingly			
☐ 223	Rookie Prospects	.45	.22	.04

		MINT	EXC	G-VG
	Shawn Abner			
	Jay Buhner			
	Gary Thurman			
☐ 224	Rookie Prospects	.30	.15	.03
	Tim Crews			
	Vincente Palacios			
	John Davis			
☐ 225	Rookie Prospects	.45	.22	.04
	Jody Reed			
	Jeff Treadway			
	Keith Miller			

1989 Sportflics

This 225-card set was produced by Sportflics (distributed by Major League Marketing) and again features three sequence action pictures on each card. Cards measure 2 ½" by 3 ½" and are in full color. There are 219 individual players, 2 Highlights trios, and 3 Rookie Prospect trio cards. The cards feature a white border on the front with red and blue inner trim colors. A full-color action picture of the player is printed on the back of the card. Cards are numbered on the back in the lower right corner.

		MINT	EXC	G-VG
COMPLETE SET (225)		40.00	20.00	4.00
COMMON PLAYER (1-225)		.10	.05	.01
☐ 1	Jose Canseco	1.50	.75	.15

			MINT	EXC	G-VG				MINT	EXC	G-VG
☐	2	Wally Joyner	.40	.20	.04	☐	51	David Cone	.50	.25	.05
☐	3	Roger Clemens	.75	.35	.07	☐	52	Kal Daniels	.25	.12	.02
☐	4	Greg Swindell	.30	.15	.03	☐	53	Carney Lansford	.20	.10	.02
☐	5	Jack Morris	.20	.10	.02	☐	54	Mike Marshall	.20	.10	.02
☐	6	Mickey Brantley	.15	.07	.01	☐	55	Kevin Seitzer	.30	.15	.03
☐	7	Jim Presley	.10	.05	.01	☐	56	Mike Henneman	.15	.07	.01
☐	8	Pete O'Brien	.15	.07	.01	☐	57	Bill Doran	.15	.07	.01
☐	9	Jesse Barfield	.25	.12	.02	☐	58	Steve Sax	.20	.10	.02
☐	10	Frank Viola	.20	.10	.02	☐	59	Lance Parrish	.15	.07	.01
☐	11	Kevin Bass	.10	.05	.01	☐	60	Keith Hernandez	.20	.10	.02
☐	12	Glenn Wilson	.10	.05	.01	☐	61	Jose Uribe	.10	.05	.01
☐	13	Chris Sabo	.35	.17	.03	☐	62	Jose Lind	.10	.05	.01
☐	14	Fred McGriff	.50	.25	.05	☐	63	Steve Bedrosian	.15	.07	.01
☐	15	Mark Grace	1.00	.50	.10	☐	64	George Brett	.30	.15	.03
☐	16	Devon White	.20	.10	.02	☐	65	Kirk Gibson	.30	.15	.03
☐	17	Juan Samuel	.15	.07	.01	☐	66	Cal Ripken Jr.	.25	.12	.02
☐	18	Lou Whitaker	.15	.07	.01	☐	67	Mitch Webster	.10	.05	.01
☐	19	Greg Walker	.10	.05	.01	☐	68	Fred Lynn	.20	.10	.02
☐	20	Roberto Alomar	.35	.17	.03	☐	69	Eric Davis	.75	.35	.07
☐	21	Mike Schmidt	1.00	.50	.10	☐	70	Bo Jackson	1.25	.60	.12
☐	22	Benny Santiago	.50	.25	.05	☐	71	Kevin Elster	.20	.10	.02
☐	23	Dave Stewart	.25	.12	.02	☐	72	Rick Reuschel	.15	.07	.01
☐	24	Dave Winfield	.40	.20	.04	☐	73	Tim Burke	.10	.05	.01
☐	25	George Bell	.20	.10	.02	☐	74	Mark Davis	.25	.12	.02
☐	26	Jack Clark	.20	.10	.02	☐	75	Claudell Washington	.15	.07	.01
☐	27	Doug Drabek	.10	.05	.01	☐	76	Lance McCullers	.10	.05	.01
☐	28	Ron Gant	.20	.10	.02	☐	77	Mike Moore	.15	.07	.01
☐	29	Glenn Braggs	.15	.07	.01	☐	78	Robby Thompson	.15	.07	.01
☐	30	Rafael Palmeiro	.30	.15	.03	☐	79	Roger McDowell	.15	.07	.01
☐	31	Brett Butler	.15	.07	.01	☐	80	Danny Jackson	.15	.07	.01
☐	32	Ron Darling	.20	.10	.02	☐	81	Tim Leary	.15	.07	.01
☐	33	Alvin Davis	.15	.07	.01	☐	82	Bobby Witt	.15	.07	.01
☐	34	Bob Walk	.10	.05	.01	☐	83	Jim Gott	.10	.05	.01
☐	35	Dave Stieb	.15	.07	.01	☐	84	Andy Hawkins	.15	.07	.01
☐	36	Orel Hershiser	.75	.35	.07	☐	85	Ozzie Guillen	.15	.07	.01
☐	37	John Farrell	.15	.07	.01	☐	86	John Tudor	.15	.07	.01
☐	38	Doug Jones	.15	.07	.01	☐	87	Todd Burns	.20	.10	.02
☐	39	Kelly Downs	.15	.07	.01	☐	88	Dave Gallagher	.15	.07	.01
☐	40	Bob Boone	.20	.10	.02	☐	89	Jay Buhner	.20	.10	.02
☐	41	Gary Sheffield	1.00	.50	.10	☐	90	Gregg Jefferies	1.00	.50	.10
☐	42	Doug Dascenzo	.20	.10	.02	☐	91	Bob Welch	.15	.07	.01
☐	43	Chad Kreuter	.20	.10	.02	☐	92	Charlie Hough	.10	.05	.01
☐	44	Ricky Jordan	1.00	.50	.10	☐	93	Tony Fernandez	.20	.10	.02
☐	45	Dave West	.30	.15	.03	☐	94	Ozzie Virgil	.10	.05	.01
☐	46	Danny Tartabull	.25	.12	.02	☐	95	Andre Dawson	.25	.12	.02
☐	47	Teddy Higuera	.15	.07	.01	☐	96	Hubie Brooks	.15	.07	.01
☐	48	Gary Gaetti	.15	.07	.01	☐	97	Kevin McReynolds	.30	.15	.03
☐	49	Dave Parker	.20	.10	.02	☐	98	Mike LaValliere	.10	.05	.01
☐	50	Don Mattingly	1.25	.60	.12	☐	99	Terry Pendleton	.15	.07	.01

		MINT	EXC	G-VG			MINT	EXC	G-VG
☐ 100	Wade Boggs	1.00	.50	.10	☐ 149	Julio Franco	.20	.10	.02
☐ 101	Dennis Eckersley	.20	.10	.02	☐ 150	Tim Raines	.20	.10	.02
☐ 102	Mark Gubicza	.20	.10	.02	☐ 151	Mitch Williams	.20	.10	.02
☐ 103	Frank Tanana	.15	.07	.01	☐ 152	Tim Laudner	.10	.05	.01
☐ 104	Joe Carter	.25	.12	.02	☐ 153	Mike Pagliarulo	.10	.05	.01
☐ 105	Ozzie Smith	.25	.12	.02	☐ 154	Floyd Bannister	.10	.05	.01
☐ 106	Dennis Martinez	.10	.05	.01	☐ 155	Gary Carter	.25	.12	.02
☐ 107	Jeff Treadway	.15	.07	.01	☐ 156	Kirby Puckett	.75	.35	.07
☐ 108	Greg Maddux	.25	.12	.02	☐ 157	Harold Baines	.15	.07	.01
☐ 109	Bret Saberhagen	.35	.17	.03	☐ 158	Dave Righetti	.15	.07	.01
☐ 110	Dale Murphy	.35	.17	.03	☐ 159	Mark Langston	.20	.10	.02
☐ 111	Rob Deer	.15	.07	.01	☐ 160	Tony Gwynn	.35	.17	.03
☐ 112	Pete Incaviglia	.25	.12	.02	☐ 161	Tom Brunansky	.15	.07	.01
☐ 113	Vince Coleman	.25	.12	.02	☐ 162	Vance Law	.10	.05	.01
☐ 114	Tim Wallach	.15	.07	.01	☐ 163	Kelly Gruber	.15	.07	.01
☐ 115	Nolan Ryan	1.00	.50	.10	☐ 164	Gerald Perry	.15	.07	.01
☐ 116	Walt Weiss	.35	.17	.03	☐ 165	Harold Reynolds	.15	.07	.01
☐ 117	Brian Downing	.10	.05	.01	☐ 166	Andy Van Slyke	.20	.10	.02
☐ 118	Melido Perez	.15	.07	.01	☐ 167	Jimmy Key	.10	.05	.01
☐ 119	Terry Steinbach	.20	.10	.02	☐ 168	Jeff Reardon	.15	.07	.01
☐ 120	Mike Scott	.25	.12	.02	☐ 169	Milt Thompson	.10	.05	.01
☐ 121	Tim Belcher	.20	.10	.02	☐ 170	Will Clark	1.25	.60	.12
☐ 122	Mike Boddicker	.10	.05	.01	☐ 171	Chet Lemon	.10	.05	.01
☐ 123	Len Dykstra	.15	.07	.01	☐ 172	Pat Tabler	.10	.05	.01
☐ 124	Fernando Valenzuela	.25	.12	.02	☐ 173	Jim Rice	.20	.10	.02
☐ 125	Gerald Young	.20	.10	.02	☐ 174	Billy Hatcher	.10	.05	.01
☐ 126	Tom Henke	.10	.05	.01	☐ 175	Bruce Hurst	.15	.07	.01
☐ 127	Dave Henderson	.10	.05	.01	☐ 176	John Franco	.15	.07	.01
☐ 128	Dan Plesac	.15	.07	.01	☐ 177	Van Snider	.20	.10	.02
☐ 129	Chili Davis	.15	.07	.01	☐ 178	Ron Jones	.20	.10	.02
☐ 130	Bryan Harvey	.15	.07	.01	☐ 179	Jerald Clark	.20	.10	.02
☐ 131	Don August	.10	.05	.01	☐ 180	Tom Browning	.20	.10	.02
☐ 132	Mike Harkey	.25	.12	.02	☐ 181	Von Hayes	.15	.07	.01
☐ 133	Luis Polonia	.15	.07	.01	☐ 182	Bobby Bonilla	.25	.12	.02
☐ 134	Craig Worthington	.25	.12	.02	☐ 183	Todd Worrell	.15	.07	.01
☐ 135	Joey Meyer	.15	.07	.01	☐ 184	John Kruk	.15	.07	.01
☐ 136	Barry Larkin	.30	.15	.03	☐ 185	Scott Fletcher	.10	.05	.01
☐ 137	Glenn Davis	.25	.12	.02	☐ 186	Willie Wilson	.15	.07	.01
☐ 138	Mike Scioscia	.10	.05	.01	☐ 187	Jody Davis	.10	.05	.01
☐ 139	Andres Galarraga	.20	.10	.02	☐ 188	Kent Hrbek	.20	.10	.02
☐ 140	Dwight Gooden	.50	.25	.05	☐ 189	Ruben Sierra	.60	.30	.06
☐ 141	Keith Moreland	.10	.05	.01	☐ 190	Shawon Dunston	.15	.07	.01
☐ 142	Kevin Mitchell	.50	.25	.05	☐ 191	Ellis Burks	.30	.15	.03
☐ 143	Mike Greenwell	1.00	.50	.10	☐ 192	Brook Jacoby	.15	.07	.01
☐ 144	Mel Hall	.15	.07	.01	☐ 193	Jeff Robinson	.15	.07	.01
☐ 145	Rickey Henderson	.60	.30	.06		Detroit Tigers			
☐ 146	Barry Bonds	.25	.12	.02	☐ 194	Rich Dotson	.10	.05	.01
☐ 147	Eddie Murray	.40	.20	.04	☐ 195	Johnny Ray	.10	.05	.01
☐ 148	Lee Smith	.15	.07	.01	☐ 196	Cory Snyder	.20	.10	.02

		MINT	EXC	G-VG
☐ 197	Mike Witt	.15	.07	.01
☐ 198	Marty Barrett	.10	.05	.01
☐ 199	Robin Yount	.50	.25	.05
☐ 200	Mark McGwire	.75	.35	.07
☐ 201	Ryne Sandberg	.30	.15	.03
☐ 202	John Candelaria	.15	.07	.01
☐ 203	Matt Nokes	.20	.10	.02
☐ 204	Dwight Evans	.20	.10	.02
☐ 205	Darryl Strawberry	.75	.35	.07
☐ 206	Willie McGee	.20	.10	.02
☐ 207	Bobby Thigpen	.15	.07	.01
☐ 208	B.J. Surhoff	.15	.07	.01
☐ 209	Paul Molitor	.20	.10	.02
☐ 210	Jody Reed	.15	.07	.01
☐ 211	Doyle Alexander	.10	.05	.01
☐ 212	Dennis Rasmussen	.10	.05	.01
☐ 213	Kevin Gross	.10	.05	.01
☐ 214	Kirk McCaskill	.10	.05	.01
☐ 215	Alan Trammell	.25	.12	.02
☐ 216	Damon Berryhill	.20	.10	.02
☐ 217	Rick Sutcliffe	.15	.07	.01
☐ 218	Don Slaught	.10	.05	.01
☐ 219	Carlton Fisk	.25	.12	.02
☐ 220	Allan Anderson	.20	.10	.02
☐ 221	Jose Canseco	1.25	.60	.12
	Wade Boggs			
	Mike Greenwell			
☐ 222	Orel Hershiser	.40	.20	.04
	Dennis Eckersley			
	Tom Browning			
☐ 223	Gary Sheffield	2.50	1.25	.25
	Gregg Jefferies			
	Sandy Alomar Jr.			
☐ 224	Bob Milacki	.30	.15	.03
	Randy Johnson			
	Ramon Martinez			
☐ 225	Cameron Drew	.30	.15	.03
	Geronimo Berroa			
	Ron Jones			

1990 Sportflics

The 1990 Sportflics set contains 225 standard-size (2 ½" by 3 ½") cards. On the fronts, the black, white, orange, and yellow borders surround two photos, which can each be seen depending on the angle. The set is considered an improvement over the previous years' versions by many collectors due to the increased clarity of the fronts, caused by having two images rather than three. The backs are dominated by large color photos.

		MINT	EXC	G-VG
COMPLETE SET (225)		40.00	20.00	4.00
COMMON PLAYER (1-225)		.10	.05	.01
☐ 1	Kevin Mitchell	.50	.25	.05
☐ 2	Wade Boggs	1.00	.50	.10
☐ 3	Cory Snyder	.20	.10	.02
☐ 4	Paul O'Neill	.20	.10	.02
☐ 5	Will Clark	1.25	.60	.12
☐ 6	Tony Fernandez	.20	.10	.02
☐ 7	Ken Griffey Jr.	1.25	.60	.12
☐ 8	Nolan Ryan	1.00	.50	.10
☐ 9	Rafael Palmeiro	.20	.10	.02
☐ 10	Jesse Barfield	.20	.10	.02
☐ 11	Kirby Puckett	.50	.25	.05
☐ 12	Steve Sax	.20	.10	.02
☐ 13	Fred McGriff	.30	.15	.03
☐ 14	Gregg Jefferies	.50	.25	.05
☐ 15	Mark Grace	.75	.35	.07
☐ 16	Ozzie Smith	.20	.10	.02
☐ 17	George Bell	.20	.10	.02

		MINT	EXC	G-VG			MINT	EXC	G-VG
☐ 18	Robin Yount	.40	.20	.04	☐ 67	Jerome Walton	1.00	.50	.10
☐ 19	Glenn Davis	.25	.12	.02	☐ 68	Ramon Martinez	.30	.15	.03
☐ 20	Jeffrey Leonard	.10	.05	.01	☐ 69	Tim Raines	.20	.10	.02
☐ 21	Chili Davis	.10	.05	.01	☐ 70	Matt Williams	.75	.35	.07
☐ 22	Craig Biggio	.30	.15	.03	☐ 71	Joe Oliver	.20	.10	.02
☐ 23	Jose Canseco	1.00	.50	.10	☐ 72	Nick Esasky	.20	.10	.02
☐ 24	Derek Lilliquist	.15	.07	.01	☐ 73	Kevin Brown	.20	.10	.02
☐ 25	Chris Bosio	.15	.07	.01	☐ 74	Walt Weiss	.30	.15	.03
☐ 26	Dave Stieb	.15	.07	.01	☐ 75	Roger McDowell	.15	.07	.01
☐ 27	Bobby Thigpen	.10	.05	.01	☐ 76	Jose DeLeon	.15	.07	.01
☐ 28	Jack Clark	.20	.10	.02	☐ 77	Brian Downing	.10	.05	.01
☐ 29	Kevin Ritz	.20	.10	.02	☐ 78	Jay Howell	.10	.05	.01
☐ 30	Tom Gordon	.40	.20	.04	☐ 79	Jose Uribe	.10	.05	.01
☐ 31	Bryan Harvey	.20	.10	.02	☐ 80	Ellis Burks	.50	.25	.05
☐ 32	Jim Deshaies	.10	.05	.01	☐ 81	Sammy Sosa	.40	.20	.04
☐ 33	Terry Steinbach	.20	.10	.02	☐ 82	Johnny Ray	.10	.05	.01
☐ 34	Tom Glavine	.10	.05	.01	☐ 83	Danny Darwin	.10	.05	.01
☐ 35	Bob Welch	.15	.07	.01	☐ 84	Carney Lansford	.15	.07	.01
☐ 36	Charlie Hayes	.15	.07	.01	☐ 85	Jose Oquendo	.10	.05	.01
☐ 37	Jeff Reardon	.15	.07	.01	☐ 86	John Cerutti	.10	.05	.01
☐ 38	Joe Orsulak	.10	.05	.01	☐ 87	Dave Winfield	.25	.12	.02
☐ 39	Scott Garrelts	.15	.07	.01	☐ 88	Dave Righetti	.15	.07	.01
☐ 40	Bob Boone	.20	.10	.02	☐ 89	Danny Jackson	.15	.07	.01
☐ 41	Scott Bankhead	.15	.07	.01	☐ 90	Andy Benes	.60	.30	.06
☐ 42	Tom Henke	.10	.05	.01	☐ 91	Tom Browning	.15	.07	.01
☐ 43	Greg Briley	.30	.15	.03	☐ 92	Pete O'Brien	.15	.07	.01
☐ 44	Teddy Higuera	.20	.10	.02	☐ 93	Roberto Alomar	.25	.12	.02
☐ 45	Pat Borders	.15	.07	.01	☐ 94	Bret Saberhagen	.30	.15	.03
☐ 46	Kevin Seitzer	.30	.15	.03	☐ 95	Phil Bradley	.15	.07	.01
☐ 47	Bruce Hurst	.15	.07	.01	☐ 96	Doug Jones	.15	.07	.01
☐ 48	Ozzie Guillen	.15	.07	.01	☐ 97	Eric Davis	.60	.30	.06
☐ 49	Wally Joyner	.30	.15	.03	☐ 98	Tony Gwynn	.45	.22	.04
☐ 50	Mike Greenwell	.75	.35	.07	☐ 99	Jim Abbott	1.00	.50	.10
☐ 51	Gary Gaetti	.20	.10	.02	☐ 100	Cal Ripken	.40	.20	.04
☐ 52	Gary Sheffield	.50	.25	.05	☐ 101	Andy Van Slyke	.20	.10	.02
☐ 53	Dennis Martinez	.10	.05	.01	☐ 102	Dan Plesac	.15	.07	.01
☐ 54	Ryne Sandberg	.30	.15	.03	☐ 103	Lou Whitaker	.20	.10	.02
☐ 55	Mike Scott	.20	.10	.02	☐ 104	Steve Bedrosian	.15	.07	.01
☐ 56	Todd Benzinger	.20	.10	.02	☐ 105	Dave Gallagher	.15	.07	.01
☐ 57	Kelly Gruber	.15	.07	.01	☐ 106	Keith Hernandez	.20	.10	.02
☐ 58	Jose Lind	.10	.05	.01	☐ 107	Duane Ward	.10	.05	.01
☐ 59	Allan Anderson	.10	.05	.01	☐ 108	Andre Dawson	.20	.10	.02
☐ 60	Robby Thompson	.10	.05	.01	☐ 109	Howard Johnson	.20	.15	.03
☐ 61	John Smoltz	.30	.15	.03	☐ 110	Mark Langston	.25	.12	.02
☐ 62	Mark Davis	.25	.12	.02	☐ 111	Jerry Browne	.15	.07	.01
☐ 63	Tom Herr	.10	.05	.01	☐ 112	Alvin Davis	.15	.07	.01
☐ 64	Randy Johnson	.15	.07	.01	☐ 113	Sid Fernandez	.15	.07	.01
☐ 65	Lonnie Smith	.15	.07	.01	☐ 114	Mike Devereaux	.15	.07	.01
☐ 66	Pedro Guerrero	.20	.10	.02	☐ 115	Benito Santiago	.25	.12	.02

		MINT	EXC	G-VG			MINT	EXC	G-VG
☐ 116	Bip Roberts	.10	.05	.01	☐ 165	Todd Worrell	.20	.10	.02
☐ 117	Craig Worthington	.20	.10	.02	☐ 166	Jim Eisenreich	.15	.07	.01
☐ 118	Kevin Elster	.15	.07	.01	☐ 167	Ivan Calderon	.15	.07	.01
☐ 119	Harold Reynolds	.15	.07	.01	☐ 168	Mauro Gozzo	.20	.10	.02
☐ 120	Joe Carter	.20	.10	.02	☐ 169	Kirk McCaskill	.10	.05	.01
☐ 121	Brian Harper	.10	.05	.01	☐ 170	Dennis Eckersley	.20	.10	.02
☐ 122	Frank Viola	.20	.10	.02	☐ 171	Mickey Tettleton	.20	.10	.02
☐ 123	Jeff Ballard	.20	.10	.02	☐ 172	Chuck Finley	.15	.07	.01
☐ 124	John Kruk	.20	.10	.02	☐ 173	Dave Magadan	.15	.07	.01
☐ 125	Harold Baines	.20	.10	.02	☐ 174	Terry Pendleton	.10	.05	.01
☐ 126	Tom Candiotti	.10	.05	.01	☐ 175	Willie Randolph	.15	.07	.01
☐ 127	Kevin McReynolds	.20	.10	.02	☐ 176	Jeff Huson	.15	.07	.01
☐ 128	Mookie Wilson	.15	.07	.01	☐ 177	Todd Zeile	1.00	.50	.10
☐ 129	Danny Tartabull	.20	.10	.02	☐ 178	Steve Olin	.15	.07	.01
☐ 130	Craig Lefferts	.10	.05	.01	☐ 179	Eric Anthony	1.00	.50	.10
☐ 131	Jose DeJesus	.10	.05	.01	☐ 180	Scott Coolbaugh	.30	.15	.03
☐ 132	John Orton	.15	.07	.01	☐ 181	Rick Sutcliffe	.20	.10	.02
☐ 133	Curt Schilling	.10	.05	.01	☐ 182	Tim Wallach	.15	.07	.01
☐ 134	Marquis Grissom	.45	.22	.04	☐ 183	Paul Molitor	.20	.10	.02
☐ 135	Greg Vaughn	1.00	.50	.10	☐ 184	Roberto Kelly	.30	.15	.03
☐ 136	Brett Butler	.15	.07	.01	☐ 185	Mike Moore	.15	.07	.01
☐ 137	Rob Deer	.15	.07	.01	☐ 186	Junior Felix	.30	.15	.03
☐ 138	John Franco	.15	.07	.01	☐ 187	Mike Schooler	.20	.10	.02
☐ 139	Keith Moreland	.10	.05	.01	☐ 188	Ruben Sierra	.60	.30	.06
☐ 140	Dave Smith	.10	.05	.01	☐ 189	Dale Murphy	.35	.17	.03
☐ 141	Mark McGwire	.75	.35	.07	☐ 190	Dan Gladden	.10	.05	.01
☐ 142	Vince Coleman	.35	.17	.03	☐ 191	John Smiley	.15	.07	.01
☐ 143	Barry Bonds	.20	.10	.02	☐ 192	Jeff Russell	.15	.07	.01
☐ 144	Mike Henneman	.10	.05	.01	☐ 193	Bert Blyleven	.20	.10	.02
☐ 145	Dwight Gooden	.45	.22	.04	☐ 194	Dave Stewart	.30	.15	.03
☐ 146	Darryl Strawberry	.60	.30	.06	☐ 195	Bobby Bonilla	.20	.10	.02
☐ 147	Von Hayes	.20	.10	.02	☐ 196	Mitch Williams	.20	.10	.02
☐ 148	Andres Galarraga	.20	.10	.02	☐ 197	Orel Hershiser	.40	.20	.04
☐ 149	Roger Clemens	.50	.25	.05	☐ 198	Kevin Bass	.10	.05	.01
☐ 150	Don Mattingly	1.00	.50	.10	☐ 199	Tim Burke	.10	.05	.01
☐ 151	Joe Magrane	.25	.12	.02	☐ 200	Bo Jackson	1.25	.60	.12
☐ 152	Dwight Smith	.60	.30	.06	☐ 201	David Cone	.25	.12	.02
☐ 153	Ricky Jordan	.75	.35	.07	☐ 202	Gary Pettis	.10	.05	.01
☐ 154	Alan Trammell	.20	.10	.02	☐ 203	Kent Hrbek	.20	.10	.02
☐ 155	Brook Jacoby	.15	.07	.01	☐ 204	Carlton Fisk	.20	.10	.02
☐ 156	Len Dykstra	.15	.07	.01	☐ 205	Bob Geren	.20	.10	.02
☐ 157	Mike LaValliere	.10	.05	.01	☐ 206	Bill Spiers	.25	.12	.02
☐ 158	Julio Franco	.15	.07	.01	☐ 207	Oddibe McDowell	.10	.05	.01
☐ 159	Joey Belle	.45	.22	.04	☐ 208	Rickey Henderson	.50	.25	.05
☐ 160	Barry Larkin	.25	.12	.02	☐ 209	Ken Caminiti	.15	.07	.01
☐ 161	Rick Reuschel	.15	.07	.01	☐ 210	Devon White	.15	.07	.01
☐ 162	Nelson Santovenia	.15	.07	.01	☐ 211	Greg Maddux	.15	.07	.01
☐ 163	Mike Scioscia	.10	.05	.01	☐ 212	Ed Whitson	.15	.07	.01
☐ 164	Damon Berryhill	.20	.10	.02	☐ 213	Carlos Martinez	.20	.10	.02

		MINT	EXC	G-VG
☐ 214	George Brett	.30	.15	.03
☐ 215	Gregg Olson	.50	.25	.05
☐ 216	Kenny Rogers	.15	.07	.01
☐ 217	Dwight Evans	.15	.07	.01
☐ 218	Pat Tabler	.15	.07	.01
☐ 219	Jeff Treadway	.10	.05	.01
☐ 220	Scott Fletcher	.10	.05	.01
☐ 221	Deion Sanders	.75	.35	.07
☐ 222	Robin Ventura	.50	.25	.05
☐ 223	Chip Hale	.20	.10	.02
☐ 224	Tommy Greene	.35	.17	.03
☐ 225	Dean Palmer	.35	.17	.03

1989 Upper Deck

Orel Hershiser

This attractive set was introduced in 1989 as an additional major card set. The cards feature full color on both the front and the back. The cards are distinguished by the fact that each card has a hologram on the reverse, thus making the cards essentially copy proof. Cards 668-693 feature a "Collector's Choice" (CC) colorful drawing of a player (by artist Vernon Wells) on the card front and a checklist of that team on the card back. On many cards "Rookie" and team logos can be found with either a "TM" or (R). Cards with missing or duplicate holograms appear to be relatively common and hence there is little, if any, premium value on these "variations." The more significant variations involving changed photos

or changed type are listed below. According to the company, the Murphy and Sheridan cards were corrected very early, after only 2% of the cards had been produced. This means, for example, that out of 1,000,000 Dale Murphy '89 Upper Deck cards produced, there are only 20,000 Murphy error cards. Similarly, the Sheffield was corrected after 15% had been printed; Varsho, Gallego, and Schroeder were corrected after 20%; and Holton, Manrique, and Winningham were corrected 30% of the way through. Collectors should also note that many dealers consider that Upper Deck's "planned" production of 1,000,000 of each player was increased (perhaps even doubled) later in the year due to the explosion in popularity of the Upper Deck cards.

		MINT	EXC	G-VG
	COMPLETE SET (700)	48.00	22.00	4.00
	COMMON PLAYER (1-700)	.06	.03	.00
☐ 1	Ken Griffey Jr.	9.00	3.00	.60
☐ 2	Luis Medina	.30	.15	.03
☐ 3	Tony Chance	.20	.10	.02
☐ 4	Dave Otto	.18	.09	.01
☐ 5	Sandy Alomar Jr. UER	1.50	.75	.15
	(wrong birthdate)			
☐ 6	Rolando Roomes	.30	.15	.03
☐ 7	Dave West	.45	.22	.04
☐ 8	Cris Carpenter	.25	.12	.02
☐ 9	Gregg Jefferies	2.50	1.25	.25
☐ 10	Doug Dascenzo	.20	.10	.02
☐ 11	Ron Jones	.35	.17	.03
☐ 12	Luis De Los Santos	.20	.10	.02
☐ 13A	Gary Sheffield ERR (SS upside down on card front)	4.00	2.00	.40
☐ 13B	Gary Sheffield COR	2.00	1.00	.20
☐ 14	Mike Harkey	.40	.20	.04
☐ 15	Lance Blankenship	.25	.12	.02
☐ 16	William Brennan	.18	.09	.01
☐ 17	John Smoltz	1.00	.50	.10
☐ 18	Ramon Martinez	.75	.30	.05
☐ 19	Mark Lemke	.18	.09	.01
☐ 20	Juan Bell	.30	.15	.03
☐ 21	Rey Palacios	.18	.09	.01
☐ 22	Felix Jose	.30	.15	.03
☐ 23	Van Snider	.25	.12	.02

			MINT	EXC	G-VG
☐	24	Dante Bichette	.20	.10	.02
☐	25	Randy Johnson	.25	.12	.02
☐	26	Carlos Quintana	.35	.17	.03
☐	27	Star Rookie Checklist	.06	.01	.00
☐	28	Mike Schooler	.35	.17	.03
☐	29	Randy St. Claire	.06	.03	.00
☐	30	Jerald Clark	.20	.10	.02
☐	31	Kevin Gross	.06	.03	.00
☐	32	Dan Firova	.12	.06	.01
☐	33	Jeff Calhoun	.06	.03	.00
☐	34	Tommy Hinzo	.06	.03	.00
☐	35	Ricky Jordan	2.00	1.00	.20
☐	36	Larry Parrish	.06	.03	.00
☐	37	Bret Saberhagen UER (hit total 931, should be 1031)	.20	.10	.02
☐	38	Mike Smithson	.06	.03	.00
☐	39	Dave Dravecky	.10	.05	.01
☐	40	Ed Romero	.06	.03	.00
☐	41	Jeff Musselman	.06	.03	.00
☐	42	Ed Hearn	.06	.03	.00
☐	43	Rance Mulliniks	.06	.03	.00
☐	44	Jim Eisenreich	.06	.03	.00
☐	45	Sil Campusano	.20	.10	.02
☐	46	Mike Krukow	.06	.03	.00
☐	47	Paul Gibson	.12	.06	.01
☐	48	Mike LaCoss	.06	.03	.00
☐	49	Larry Herndon	.06	.03	.00
☐	50	Scott Garrelts	.10	.05	.01
☐	51	Dwayne Henry	.06	.03	.00
☐	52	Jim Acker	.06	.03	.00
☐	53	Steve Sax	.12	.06	.01
☐	54	Pete O'Brien	.10	.05	.01
☐	55	Paul Runge	.06	.03	.00
☐	56	Rick Rhoden	.06	.03	.00
☐	57	John Dopson	.25	.12	.02
☐	58	Casey Candaele UER (no stats for Astros for '88 season)	.06	.03	.00
☐	59	Dave Righetti	.10	.05	.01
☐	60	Joe Hesketh	.06	.03	.00
☐	61	Frank DiPino	.06	.03	.00
☐	62	Tim Laudner	.06	.03	.00
☐	63	Jamie Moyer	.06	.03	.00
☐	64	Fred Toliver	.06	.03	.00
☐	65	Mitch Webster	.06	.03	.00
☐	66	John Tudor	.10	.05	.01
☐	67	John Cangelosi	.06	.03	.00
☐	68	Mike Devereaux	.12	.06	.01
☐	69	Brian Fisher	.06	.03	.00
☐	70	Mike Marshall	.10	.05	.01
☐	71	Zane Smith	.06	.03	.00
☐	72A	Brian Holton ERR (photo actually Shawn Hillegas)	2.50	1.25	.25
☐	72B	Brian Holton COR	.30	.15	.03
☐	73	Jose Guzman	.06	.03	.00
☐	74	Rick Mahler	.06	.03	.00
☐	75	John Shelby	.06	.03	.00
☐	76	Jim Deshaies	.06	.03	.00
☐	77	Bobby Meacham	.06	.03	.00
☐	78	Bryn Smith	.10	.05	.01
☐	79	Joaquin Andujar	.10	.05	.01
☐	80	Richard Dotson	.06	.03	.00
☐	81	Charlie Lea	.06	.03	.00
☐	82	Calvin Schiraldi	.06	.03	.00
☐	83	Les Straker	.06	.03	.00
☐	84	Les Lancaster	.06	.03	.00
☐	85	Allan Anderson	.10	.05	.01
☐	86	Junior Ortiz	.06	.03	.00
☐	87	Jesse Orosco	.06	.03	.00
☐	88	Felix Fermin	.10	.05	.01
☐	89	Dave Anderson	.06	.03	.00
☐	90	Rafael Belliard UER (wrong birth year)	.06	.03	.00
☐	91	Franklin Stubbs	.06	.03	.00
☐	92	Cecil Espy	.10	.05	.01
☐	93	Albert Hall	.06	.03	.00
☐	94	Tim Leary	.10	.05	.01
☐	95	Mitch Williams	.12	.06	.01
☐	96	Tracy Jones	.10	.05	.01
☐	97	Danny Darwin	.06	.03	.00
☐	98	Gary Ward	.06	.03	.00
☐	99	Neal Heaton	.06	.03	.00
☐	100	Jim Pankovits	.06	.03	.00
☐	101	Bill Doran	.10	.05	.01
☐	102	Tim Wallach	.10	.05	.01
☐	103	Joe Magrane	.12	.06	.01
☐	104	Ozzie Virgil	.06	.03	.00
☐	105	Alvin Davis	.12	.06	.01
☐	106	Tom Brookens	.06	.03	.00
☐	107	Shawon Dunston	.10	.05	.01
☐	108	Tracy Woodson	.10	.05	.01
☐	109	Nelson Liriano	.06	.03	.00
☐	110	Devon White UER (doubles total 46, should be 56)	.12	.06	.01
☐	111	Steve Balboni	.06	.03	.00

		MINT	EXC	G-VG
☐ 112	Buddy Bell	.10	.05	.01
☐ 113	German Jimenez	.10	.05	.01
☐ 114	Ken Dayley	.06	.03	.00
☐ 115	Andres Galarraga	.12	.06	.01
☐ 116	Mike Scioscia	.06	.03	.00
☐ 117	Gary Pettis	.06	.03	.00
☐ 118	Ernie Whitt	.06	.03	.00
☐ 119	Bob Boone	.12	.06	.01
☐ 120	Ryne Sandberg	.25	.12	.02
☐ 121	Bruce Benedict	.06	.03	.00
☐ 122	Hubie Brooks	.10	.05	.01
☐ 123	Mike Moore	.10	.05	.01
☐ 124	Wallace Johnson	.06	.03	.00
☐ 125	Bob Horner	.10	.05	.01
☐ 126	Chili Davis	.10	.05	.01
☐ 127	Manny Trillo	.06	.03	.00
☐ 128	Chet Lemon	.06	.03	.00
☐ 129	John Cerutti	.06	.03	.00
☐ 130	Orel Hershiser	.25	.12	.02
☐ 131	Terry Pendleton	.06	.03	.00
☐ 132	Jeff Blauser	.15	.07	.01
☐ 133	Mike Fitzgerald	.06	.03	.00
☐ 134	Henry Cotto	.06	.03	.00
☐ 135	Gerald Young	.10	.05	.01
☐ 136	Luis Salazar	.06	.03	.00
☐ 137	Alejandro Pena	.06	.03	.00
☐ 138	Jack Howell	.06	.03	.00
☐ 139	Tony Fernandez	.10	.05	.01
☐ 140	Mark Grace	2.50	1.25	.25
☐ 141	Ken Caminiti	.06	.03	.00
☐ 142	Mike Jackson	.06	.03	.00
☐ 143	Larry McWilliams	.06	.03	.00
☐ 144	Andres Thomas	.06	.03	.00
☐ 145	Nolan Ryan	2.00	1.00	.20
☐ 146	Mike Davis	.06	.03	.00
☐ 147	DeWayne Buice	.06	.03	.00
☐ 148	Jody Davis	.06	.03	.00
☐ 149	Jesse Barfield	.10	.05	.01
☐ 150	Matt Nokes	.10	.05	.01
☐ 151	Jerry Reuss	.06	.03	.00
☐ 152	Rick Cerone	.06	.03	.00
☐ 153	Storm Davis	.10	.05	.01
☐ 154	Marvell Wynne	.06	.03	.00
☐ 155	Will Clark	1.75	.85	.17
☐ 156	Luis Aguayo	.06	.03	.00
☐ 157	Willie Upshaw	.06	.03	.00
☐ 158	Randy Bush	.06	.03	.00
☐ 159	Ron Darling	.10	.05	.01
☐ 160	Kal Daniels	.10	.05	.01
☐ 161	Spike Owen	.06	.03	.00
☐ 162	Luis Polonia	.06	.03	.00
☐ 163	Kevin Mitchell UER ('88/total HR's 18/52, should be 19/53)	.60	.30	.06
☐ 164	Dave Gallagher	.30	.15	.03
☐ 165	Benito Santiago	.20	.10	.02
☐ 166	Greg Gagne	.06	.03	.00
☐ 167	Ken Phelps	.06	.03	.00
☐ 168	Sid Fernandez	.10	.05	.01
☐ 169	Bo Diaz	.06	.03	.00
☐ 170	Cory Snyder	.12	.06	.01
☐ 171	Eric Show	.06	.03	.00
☐ 172	Rob Thompson	.06	.03	.00
☐ 173	Marty Barrett	.06	.03	.00
☐ 174	Dave Henderson	.06	.03	.00
☐ 175	Ozzie Guillen	.10	.05	.01
☐ 176	Barry Lyons	.06	.03	.00
☐ 177	Kelvin Torve	.12	.06	.01
☐ 178	Don Slaught	.06	.03	.00
☐ 179	Steve Lombardozzi	.06	.03	.00
☐ 180	Chris Sabo	.60	.30	.06
☐ 181	Jose Uribe	.06	.03	.00
☐ 182	Shane Mack	.10	.05	.01
☐ 183	Ron Karkovice	.06	.03	.00
☐ 184	Todd Benzinger	.06	.03	.00
☐ 185	Dave Stewart	.15	.07	.01
☐ 186	Julio Franco	.12	.06	.01
☐ 187	Ron Robinson	.06	.03	.00
☐ 188	Wally Backman	.06	.03	.00
☐ 189	Randy Velarde	.10	.05	.01
☐ 190	Joe Carter	.15	.07	.01
☐ 191	Bob Welch	.10	.05	.01
☐ 192	Kelly Paris	.06	.03	.00
☐ 193	Chris Brown	.06	.03	.00
☐ 194	Rick Reuschel	.10	.05	.01
☐ 195	Roger Clemens	.50	.25	.05
☐ 196	Dave Concepcion	.10	.05	.01
☐ 197	Al Newman	.06	.03	.00
☐ 198	Brook Jacoby	.10	.05	.01
☐ 199	Mookie Wilson	.10	.05	.01
☐ 200	Don Mattingly	1.00	.50	.10
☐ 201	Dick Schofield	.06	.03	.00
☐ 202	Mark Gubicza	.10	.05	.01
☐ 203	Gary Gaetti	.10	.05	.01
☐ 204	Dan Pasqua	.06	.03	.00
☐ 205	Andre Dawson	.12	.06	.01
☐ 206	Chris Speier	.06	.03	.00
☐ 207	Kent Tekulve	.06	.03	.00

		MINT	EXC	G-VG			MINT	EXC	G-VG
☐ 208	Rod Scurry	.06	.03	.00	☐ 252	Mike Felder	.06	.03	.00
☐ 209	Scott Bailes	.06	.03	.00	☐ 253	Vince Coleman	.15	.07	.01
☐ 210	Rickey Henderson UER (Throws Right)	.35	.17	.03	☐ 254	Larry Sheets	.06	.03	.00
					☐ 255	George Bell	.12	.06	.01
					☐ 256	Terry Steinbach	.10	.05	.01
☐ 211	Harold Baines	.12	.06	.01	☐ 257	Jack Armstrong	.25	.12	.02
☐ 212	Tony Armas	.10	.05	.01	☐ 258	Dickie Thon	.06	.03	.00
☐ 213	Kent Hrbek	.12	.06	.01	☐ 259	Ray Knight	.10	.05	.01
☐ 214	Darrin Jackson	.12	.06	.01	☐ 260	Darryl Strawberry	.50	.25	.05
☐ 215	George Brett	.25	.12	.02	☐ 261	Doug Sisk	.06	.03	.00
☐ 216	Rafael Santana	.06	.03	.00	☐ 262	Alex Trevino	.06	.03	.00
☐ 217	Andy Allanson	.06	.03	.00	☐ 263	Jeffrey Leonard	.10	.05	.01
☐ 218	Brett Butler	.10	.05	.01	☐ 264	Tom Henke	.10	.05	.01
☐ 219	Steve Jeltz	.06	.03	.00	☐ 265	Ozzie Smith	.20	.10	.02
☐ 220	Jay Buhner	.25	.12	.02	☐ 266	Dave Bergman	.06	.03	.00
☐ 221	Bo Jackson	1.50	.75	.15	☐ 267	Tony Phillips	.06	.03	.00
☐ 222	Angel Salazar	.06	.03	.00	☐ 268	Mark Davis	.15	.07	.01
☐ 223	Kirk McCaskill	.06	.03	.00	☐ 269	Kevin Elster	.10	.05	.01
☐ 224	Steve Lyons	.06	.03	.00	☐ 270	Barry Larkin	.20	.10	.02
☐ 225	Bert Blyleven	.10	.05	.01	☐ 271	Manny Lee	.06	.03	.00
☐ 226	Scott Bradley	.06	.03	.00	☐ 272	Tom Brunansky	.12	.06	.01
☐ 227	Bob Melvin	.06	.03	.00	☐ 273	Craig Biggio	1.00	.50	.10
☐ 228	Ron Kittle	.10	.05	.01	☐ 274	Jim Gantner	.06	.03	.00
☐ 229	Phil Bradley	.10	.05	.01	☐ 275	Eddie Murray	.15	.07	.01
☐ 230	Tommy John	.12	.06	.01	☐ 276	Jeff Reed	.06	.03	.00
☐ 231	Greg Walker	.06	.03	.00	☐ 277	Tim Teufel	.06	.03	.00
☐ 232	Juan Berenguer	.06	.03	.00	☐ 278	Rick Honeycutt	.06	.03	.00
☐ 233	Pat Tabler	.06	.03	.00	☐ 279	Guillermo Hernandez	.10	.05	.01
☐ 234	Terry Clark	.15	.07	.01	☐ 280	John Kruk	.10	.05	.01
☐ 235	Rafael Palmeiro	.15	.07	.01	☐ 281	Luis Alicea	.10	.05	.01
☐ 236	Paul Zuvella	.06	.03	.00	☐ 282	Jim Clancy	.06	.03	.00
☐ 237	Willie Randolph	.10	.05	.01	☐ 283	Billy Ripken	.06	.03	.00
☐ 238	Bruce Fields	.06	.03	.00	☐ 284	Craig Reynolds	.06	.03	.00
☐ 239	Mike Aldrete	.06	.03	.00	☐ 285	Robin Yount	.30	.15	.03
☐ 240	Lance Parrish	.10	.05	.01	☐ 286	Jimmy Jones	.10	.05	.01
☐ 241	Greg Maddux	.20	.10	.02	☐ 287	Ron Oester	.06	.03	.00
☐ 242	John Moses	.06	.03	.00	☐ 288	Terry Leach	.10	.05	.01
☐ 243	Melido Perez	.15	.07	.01	☐ 289	Dennis Eckersley	.12	.06	.01
☐ 244	Willie Wilson	.10	.05	.01	☐ 290	Alan Trammell	.15	.07	.01
☐ 245	Mark McLemore	.06	.03	.00	☐ 291	Jimmy Key	.10	.05	.01
☐ 246	Von Hayes	.10	.05	.01	☐ 292	Chris Bosio	.10	.05	.01
☐ 247	Matt Williams	.30	.15	.03	☐ 293	Jose DeLeon	.10	.05	.01
☐ 248	John Candelaria UER (listed as Yankee for part of '87, should be Mets)	.10	.05	.01	☐ 294	Jim Traber	.06	.03	.00
					☐ 295	Mike Scott	.15	.07	.01
					☐ 296	Roger McDowell	.10	.05	.01
					☐ 297	Garry Templeton	.10	.05	.01
☐ 249	Harold Reynolds	.10	.05	.01	☐ 298	Doyle Alexander	.06	.03	.00
☐ 250	Greg Swindell	.12	.06	.01	☐ 299	Nick Esasky	.12	.06	.01
☐ 251	Juan Agosto	.06	.03	.00	☐ 300	Mark McGwire UER	.75	.35	.07

		MINT	EXC	G-VG			MINT	EXC	G-VG
	(doubles total 52, should be 51)				☐ 343	B.J. Surhoff	.10	.05	.01
☐ 301	Darryl Hamilton	.25	.12	.02	☐ 344	Billy Hatcher	.06	.03	.00
☐ 302	Dave Smith	.06	.03	.00	☐ 345	Pat Perry	.06	.03	.00
☐ 303	Rick Sutcliffe	.10	.05	.01	☐ 346	Jack Clark	.12	.06	.01
☐ 304	Dave Stapleton	.10	.05	.01	☐ 347	Gary Thurman	.06	.03	.00
☐ 305	Alan Ashby	.06	.03	.00	☐ 348	Tim Jones	.12	.06	.01
☐ 306	Pedro Guerrero	.12	.06	.01	☐ 349	Dave Winfield	.20	.10	.02
☐ 307	Ron Guidry	.10	.05	.01	☐ 350	Frank White	.10	.05	.01
☐ 308	Steve Farr	.06	.03	.00	☐ 351	Dave Collins	.06	.03	.00
☐ 309	Curt Ford	.06	.03	.00	☐ 352	Jack Morris	.10	.05	.01
☐ 310	Claudell Washington	.10	.05	.01	☐ 353	Eric Plunk	.06	.03	.00
☐ 311	Tom Prince	.10	.05	.01	☐ 354	Leon Durham	.06	.03	.00
☐ 312	Chad Kreuter	.15	.07	.01	☐ 355	Ivan DeJesus	.06	.03	.00
☐ 313	Ken Oberkfell	.06	.03	.00	☐ 356	Brian Holman	.15	.07	.01
☐ 314	Jerry Browne	.06	.03	.00	☐ 357A	Dale Murphy ERR	150.00	75.00	15.00
☐ 315	R.J. Reynolds	.06	.03	.00		(front reverse negative)			
☐ 316	Scott Bankhead	.10	.05	.01	☐ 357B	Dale Murphy COR	.75	.35	.07
☐ 317	Milt Thompson	.06	.03	.00	☐ 358	Mark Portugal	.06	.03	.00
☐ 318	Mario Diaz	.10	.05	.01	☐ 359	Andy McGaffigan	.06	.03	.00
☐ 319	Bruce Ruffin	.06	.03	.00	☐ 360	Tom Glavine	.10	.05	.01
☐ 320	Dave Valle	.06	.03	.00	☐ 361	Keith Moreland	.06	.03	.00
☐ 321A	Gary Varsho ERR	2.50	1.25	.25	☐ 362	Todd Stottlemyre	.12	.06	.01
	(back photo actually Mike Bielecki bunting)				☐ 363	Dave Leiper	.06	.03	.00
					☐ 364	Cecil Fielder	.06	.03	.00
☐ 321B	Gary Varsho COR	.30	.15	.03	☐ 365	Carmelo Martinez	.06	.03	.00
	(in road uniform)				☐ 366	Dwight Evans	.12	.06	.01
☐ 322	Paul Mirabella	.06	.03	.00	☐ 367	Kevin McReynolds	.12	.06	.01
☐ 323	Chuck Jackson	.10	.05	.01	☐ 368	Rich Gedman	.06	.03	.00
☐ 324	Drew Hall	.06	.03	.00	☐ 369	Len Dykstra	.10	.05	.01
☐ 325	Don August	.10	.05	.01	☐ 370	Jody Reed	.10	.05	.01
☐ 326	Israel Sanchez	.10	.05	.01	☐ 371	Jose Canseco UER	1.50	.75	.15
☐ 327	Denny Walling	.06	.03	.00		(strikeout total 391, should be 491)			
☐ 328	Joel Skinner	.06	.03	.00	☐ 372	Rob Murphy	.06	.03	.00
☐ 329	Danny Tartabull	.12	.06	.01	☐ 373	Mike Henneman	.06	.03	.00
☐ 330	Tony Pena	.10	.05	.01	☐ 374	Walt Weiss	.75	.35	.07
☐ 331	Jim Sundberg	.06	.03	.00	☐ 375	Rob Dibble	.35	.17	.03
☐ 332	Jeff Robinson Pittsburgh Pirates	.10	.05	.01	☐ 376	Kirby Puckett (Mark McGwire in background)	.60	.30	.06
☐ 333	Oddibe McDowell	.10	.05	.01					
☐ 334	Jose Lind	.06	.03	.00	☐ 377	Dennis Martinez	.06	.03	.00
☐ 335	Paul Kilgus	.06	.03	.00	☐ 378	Ron Gant	.35	.17	.03
☐ 336	Juan Samuel	.12	.06	.01	☐ 379	Brian Harper	.06	.03	.00
☐ 337	Mike Campbell	.12	.06	.01	☐ 380	Nelson Santovenia	.25	.12	.02
☐ 338	Mike Maddux	.06	.03	.00	☐ 381	Lloyd Moseby	.10	.05	.01
☐ 339	Darnell Coles	.06	.03	.00	☐ 382	Lance McCullers	.10	.05	.01
☐ 340	Bob Dernier	.06	.03	.00	☐ 383	Dave Stieb	.10	.05	.01
☐ 341	Rafael Ramirez	.06	.03	.00	☐ 384	Tony Gwynn	.35	.17	.03
☐ 342	Scott Sanderson	.06	.03	.00	☐ 385	Mike Flanagan	.06	.03	.00

		MINT	EXC	G-VG			MINT	EXC	G-VG
☐	386 Bob Ojeda	.10	.05	.01	☐	435 Ed Olwine	.06	.03	.00
☐	387 Bruce Hurst	.10	.05	.01	☐	436 Dave Rucker	.06	.03	.00
☐	388 Dave Magadan	.10	.05	.01	☐	437 Charlie Hough	.06	.03	.00
☐	389 Wade Boggs	.75	.35	.07	☐	438 Bob Walk	.06	.03	.00
☐	390 Gary Carter	.15	.07	.01	☐	439 Bob Brower	.06	.03	.00
☐	391 Frank Tanana	.06	.03	.00	☐	440 Barry Bonds	.10	.05	.01
☐	392 Curt Young	.06	.03	.00	☐	441 Tom Foley	.06	.03	.00
☐	393 Jeff Treadway	.15	.07	.01	☐	442 Rob Deer	.10	.05	.01
☐	394 Darrell Evans	.10	.05	.01	☐	443 Glenn Davis	.15	.07	.01
☐	395 Glenn Hubbard	.06	.03	.00	☐	444 Dave Martinez	.06	.03	.00
☐	396 Chuck Cary	.06	.03	.00	☐	445 Bill Wegman	.06	.03	.00
☐	397 Frank Viola	.15	.07	.01	☐	446 Lloyd McClendon	.15	.07	.01
☐	398 Jeff Parrett	.12	.06	.01	☐	447 Dave Schmidt	.06	.03	.00
☐	399 Terry Blocker	.12	.06	.01	☐	448 Darren Daulton	.06	.03	.00
☐	400 Dan Gladden	.06	.03	.00	☐	449 Frank Williams	.06	.03	.00
☐	401 Louie Meadows	.10	.05	.01	☐	450 Don Aase	.06	.03	.00
☐	402 Tim Raines	.15	.07	.01	☐	451 Lou Whitaker	.12	.06	.01
☐	403 Joey Meyer	.10	.05	.01	☐	452 Goose Gossage	.10	.05	.01
☐	404 Larry Andersen	.06	.03	.00	☐	453 Ed Whitson	.06	.03	.00
☐	405 Rex Hudler	.06	.03	.00	☐	454 Jim Walewander	.10	.05	.01
☐	406 Mike Schmidt	.75	.35	.07	☐	455 Damon Berryhill	.30	.15	.03
☐	407 John Franco	.10	.05	.01	☐	456 Tim Burke	.10	.05	.01
☐	408 Brady Anderson	.30	.15	.03	☐	457 Barry Jones	.06	.03	.00
☐	409 Don Carman	.06	.03	.00	☐	458 Joel Youngblood	.06	.03	.00
☐	410 Eric Davis	.35	.17	.03	☐	459 Floyd Youmans	.06	.03	.00
☐	411 Bob Stanley	.06	.03	.00	☐	460 Mark Salas	.06	.03	.00
☐	412 Pete Smith	.10	.05	.01	☐	461 Jeff Russell	.10	.05	.01
☐	413 Jim Rice	.12	.06	.01	☐	462 Darrell Miller	.06	.03	.00
☐	414 Bruce Sutter	.08	.04	.01	☐	463 Jeff Kunkel	.06	.03	.00
☐	415 Oil Can Boyd	.08	.04	.01	☐	464 Sherman Corbett	.10	.05	.01
☐	416 Ruben Sierra	.40	.20	.04	☐	465 Curtis Wilkerson	.06	.03	.00
☐	417 Mike LaValliere	.06	.03	.00	☐	466 Bud Black	.06	.03	.00
☐	418 Steve Buechele	.06	.03	.00	☐	467 Cal Ripken Jr.	.20	.10	.02
☐	419 Gary Redus	.06	.03	.00	☐	468 John Farrell	.06	.03	.00
☐	420 Scott Fletcher	.06	.03	.00	☐	469 Terry Kennedy	.06	.03	.00
☐	421 Dale Sveum	.06	.03	.00	☐	470 Tom Candiotti	.06	.03	.00
☐	422 Bob Knepper	.06	.03	.00	☐	471 Roberto Alomar	.35	.17	.03
☐	423 Luis Rivera	.06	.03	.00	☐	472 Jeff Robinson	.10	.05	.01
☐	424 Ted Higuera	.10	.05	.01		Detroit Tigers			
☐	425 Kevin Bass	.10	.05	.01	☐	473 Vance Law	.06	.03	.00
☐	426 Ken Gerhart	.06	.03	.00	☐	474 Randy Ready UER	.06	.03	.00
☐	427 Shane Rawley	.06	.03	.00		(strikeout total 136,			
☐	428 Paul O'Neill	.10	.05	.01		should be 115)			
☐	429 Joe Orsulak	.06	.03	.00	☐	475 Walt Terrell	.06	.03	.00
☐	430 Jackie Gutierrez	.06	.03	.00	☐	476 Kelly Downs	.06	.03	.00
☐	431 Gerald Perry	.10	.05	.01	☐	477 Johnny Paredes	.10	.05	.01
☐	432 Mike Greenwell	1.00	.50	.10	☐	478 Shawn Hillegas	.06	.03	.00
☐	433 Jerry Royster	.06	.03	.00	☐	479 Bob Brenly	.06	.03	.00
☐	434 Ellis Burks	.45	.22	.04	☐	480 Otis Nixon	.06	.03	.00

		MINT	EXC	G-VG			MINT	EXC	G-VG
☐ 481	Johnny Ray	.10	.05	.01	☐ 528	Larry Owen	.06	.03	.00
☐ 482	Geno Petralli	.06	.03	.00	☐ 529	Jerry Reed	.06	.03	.00
☐ 483	Stu Cliburn	.06	.03	.00	☐ 530	Jack McDowell	.10	.05	.01
☐ 484	Pete Incaviglia	.12	.06	.01	☐ 531	Greg Mathews	.06	.03	.00
☐ 485	Brian Downing	.06	.03	.00	☐ 532	John Russell	.06	.03	.00
☐ 486	Jeff Stone	.06	.03	.00	☐ 533	Dan Quisenberry	.10	.05	.01
☐ 487	Carmen Castillo	.06	.03	.00	☐ 534	Greg Gross	.06	.03	.00
☐ 488	Tom Niedenfuer	.06	.03	.00	☐ 535	Danny Cox	.06	.03	.00
☐ 489	Jay Bell	.12	.06	.01	☐ 536	Terry Francona	.06	.03	.00
☐ 490	Rick Schu	.06	.03	.00	☐ 537	Andy Van Slyke	.12	.06	.01
☐ 491	Jeff Pico	.10	.05	.01	☐ 538	Mel Hall	.10	.05	.01
☐ 492	Mark Parent	.12	.06	.01	☐ 539	Jim Gott	.06	.03	.00
☐ 493	Eric King	.06	.03	.00	☐ 540	Doug Jones	.10	.05	.01
☐ 494	Al Nipper	.06	.03	.00	☐ 541	Craig Lefferts	.06	.03	.00
☐ 495	Andy Hawkins	.06	.03	.00	☐ 542	Mike Boddicker	.06	.03	.00
☐ 496	Daryl Boston	.06	.03	.00	☐ 543	Greg Brock	.06	.03	.00
☐ 497	Ernie Riles	.06	.03	.00	☐ 544	Atlee Hammaker	.06	.03	.00
☐ 498	Pascual Perez	.10	.05	.01	☐ 545	Tom Bolton	.10	.05	.01
☐ 499	Bill Long UER	.06	.03	.00	☐ 546	Mike Macfarlane	.12	.06	.01
	(games started total				☐ 547	Rich Renteria	.12	.06	.01
	70, should be 44)				☐ 548	John Davis	.06	.03	.00
☐ 500	Kirt Manwaring	.12	.06	.01	☐ 549	Floyd Bannister	.06	.03	.00
☐ 501	Chuck Crim	.06	.03	.00	☐ 550	Mickey Brantley	.10	.05	.01
☐ 502	Candy Maldonado	.06	.03	.00	☐ 551	Duane Ward	.06	.03	.00
☐ 503	Dennis Lamp	.06	.03	.00	☐ 552	Dan Petry	.06	.03	.00
☐ 504	Glenn Braggs	.10	.05	.01	☐ 553	Mickey Tettleton UER	.12	.06	.01
☐ 505	Joe Price	.06	.03	.00		(walks total 175,			
☐ 506	Ken Williams	.10	.05	.01		should be 136)			
☐ 507	Bill Pecota	.06	.03	.00	☐ 554	Rick Leach	.06	.03	.00
☐ 508	Rey Quinones	.06	.03	.00	☐ 555	Mike Witt	.10	.05	.01
☐ 509	Jeff Bittiger	.12	.06	.01	☐ 556	Sid Bream	.06	.03	.00
☐ 510	Kevin Seitzer	.20	.10	.02	☐ 557	Bobby Witt	.10	.05	.01
☐ 511	Steve Bedrosian	.10	.05	.01	☐ 558	Tommy Herr	.06	.03	.00
☐ 512	Todd Worrell	.10	.05	.01	☐ 559	Randy Milligan	.12	.06	.01
☐ 513	Chris James	.10	.05	.01	☐ 560	Jose Cecena	.10	.05	.01
☐ 514	Jose Oquendo	.06	.03	.00	☐ 561	Mackey Sasser	.12	.06	.01
☐ 515	David Palmer	.06	.03	.00	☐ 562	Carney Lansford	.12	.06	.01
☐ 516	John Smiley	.06	.03	.00	☐ 563	Rick Aguilera	.06	.03	.00
☐ 517	Dave Clark	.06	.03	.00	☐ 564	Ron Hassey	.06	.03	.00
☐ 518	Mike Dunne	.06	.03	.00	☐ 565	Dwight Gooden	.40	.20	.04
☐ 519	Ron Washington	.06	.03	.00	☐ 566	Paul Assenmacher	.06	.03	.00
☐ 520	Bob Kipper	.06	.03	.00	☐ 567	Neil Allen	.06	.03	.00
☐ 521	Lee Smith	.10	.05	.01	☐ 568	Jim Morrison	.06	.03	.00
☐ 522	Juan Castillo	.06	.03	.00	☐ 569	Mike Pagliarulo	.10	.05	.01
☐ 523	Don Robinson	.06	.03	.00	☐ 570	Ted Simmons	.12	.06	.01
☐ 524	Kevin Romine	.06	.03	.00	☐ 571	Mark Thurmond	.06	.03	.00
☐ 525	Paul Molitor	.10	.05	.01	☐ 572	Fred McGriff	.30	.15	.03
☐ 526	Mark Langston	.15	.07	.01	☐ 573	Wally Joyner	.25	.12	.02
☐ 527	Donnie Hill	.06	.03	.00	☐ 574	Jose Bautista	.10	.05	.01

		MINT	EXC	G-VG
☐ 575	Kelly Gruber	.10	.05	.01
☐ 576	Cecilio Guante	.06	.03	.00
☐ 577	Mark Davidson	.06	.03	.00
☐ 578	Bobby Bonilla UER	.12	.06	.01
	(total steals 2 in '87, should be 3)			
☐ 579	Mike Stanley	.06	.03	.00
☐ 580	Gene Larkin	.06	.03	.00
☐ 581	Stan Javier	.06	.03	.00
☐ 582	Howard Johnson	.20	.10	.02
☐ 583A	Mike Gallego ERR	2.50	1.25	.25
	(front reversed negative)			
☐ 583B	Mike Gallego COR	.30	.15	.03
☐ 584	David Cone	.30	.15	.03
☐ 585	Doug Jennings	.25	.12	.02
☐ 586	Charles Hudson	.06	.03	.00
☐ 587	Dion James	.06	.03	.00
☐ 588	Al Leiter	.20	.10	.02
☐ 589	Charlie Puleo	.06	.03	.00
☐ 590	Roberto Kelly	.35	.17	.03
☐ 591	Thad Bosley	.06	.03	.00
☐ 592	Pete Stanicek	.10	.05	.01
☐ 593	Pat Borders	.12	.06	.01
☐ 594	Bryan Harvey	.20	.10	.02
☐ 595	Jeff Ballard	.25	.12	.02
☐ 596	Jeff Reardon	.10	.05	.01
☐ 597	Doug Drabek	.10	.05	.01
☐ 598	Edwin Correa	.06	.03	.00
☐ 599	Keith Atherton	.06	.03	.00
☐ 600	Dave LaPoint	.06	.03	.00
☐ 601	Don Baylor	.10	.05	.01
☐ 602	Tom Pagnozzi	.10	.05	.01
☐ 603	Tim Flannery	.06	.03	.00
☐ 604	Gene Walter	.06	.03	.00
☐ 605	Dave Parker	.10	.05	.01
☐ 606	Mike Diaz	.06	.03	.00
☐ 607	Chris Gwynn	.12	.06	.01
☐ 608	Odell Jones	.06	.03	.00
☐ 609	Carlton Fisk	.12	.06	.01
☐ 610	Jay Howell	.10	.05	.01
☐ 611	Tim Crews	.06	.03	.00
☐ 612	Keith Hernandez	.12	.06	.01
☐ 613	Willie Fraser	.06	.03	.00
☐ 614	Jim Eppard	.10	.05	.01
☐ 615	Jeff Hamilton	.06	.03	.00
☐ 616	Kurt Stillwell	.06	.03	.00
☐ 617	Tom Browning	.10	.05	.01
☐ 618	Jeff Montgomery	.25	.12	.02

		MINT	EXC	G-VG
☐ 619	Jose Rijo	.06	.03	.00
☐ 620	Jamie Quirk	.06	.03	.00
☐ 621	Willie McGee	.12	.06	.01
☐ 622	Mark Grant	.06	.03	.00
	(glove on wrong hand)			
☐ 623	Bill Swift	.06	.03	.00
☐ 624	Orlando Mercado	.06	.03	.00
☐ 625	John Costello	.12	.06	.01
☐ 626	Jose Gonzalez	.10	.05	.01
☐ 627A	Bill Schroeder ERR	2.50	1.25	.25
	(back photo actually Ronn Reynolds buckling shin guards)			
☐ 627B	Bill Schroeder COR	.30	.15	.03
☐ 628A	Fred Manrique ERR	2.50	1.25	.25
	(back photo actually Ozzie Guillen throwing)			
☐ 628B	Fred Manrique COR	.30	.15	.03
	(swinging bat on back)			
☐ 629	Ricky Horton	.06	.03	.00
☐ 630	Dan Plesac	.10	.05	.01
☐ 631	Alfredo Griffin	.06	.03	.00
☐ 632	Chuck Finley	.10	.05	.01
☐ 633	Kirk Gibson	.15	.07	.01
☐ 634	Randy Myers	.10	.05	.01
☐ 635	Greg Minton	.06	.03	.00
☐ 636A	Herm Winningham ERR	2.50	1.25	.25
	(Winningham on back)			
☐ 636B	Herm Winningham COR	.30	.15	.03
☐ 637	Charlie Leibrandt	.06	.03	.00
☐ 638	Tim Birtsas	.06	.03	.00
☐ 639	Bill Buckner	.10	.05	.01
☐ 640	Danny Jackson	.10	.05	.01
☐ 641	Greg Booker	.06	.03	.00
☐ 642	Jim Presley	.06	.03	.00
☐ 643	Gene Nelson	.06	.03	.00
☐ 644	Rod Booker	.10	.05	.01
☐ 645	Dennis Rasmussen	.06	.03	.00
☐ 646	Juan Nieves	.06	.03	.00
☐ 647	Bobby Thigpen	.10	.05	.01
☐ 648	Tim Belcher	.20	.10	.02
☐ 649	Mike Young	.06	.03	.00
☐ 650	Ivan Calderon	.10	.05	.01
☐ 651	Oswaldo Peraza	.10	.05	.01
☐ 652A	Pat Sheridan ERR	50.00	25.00	5.00
	(no position on front)			
☐ 652B	Pat Sheridan COR	.25	.12	.02

		MINT	EXC	G-VG
☐ 653	Mike Morgan	.10	.05	.01
☐ 654	Mike Heath	.06	.03	.00
☐ 655	Jay Tibbs	.06	.03	.00
☐ 656	Fernando Valenzuela	.12	.06	.01
☐ 657	Lee Mazzilli	.06	.03	.00
☐ 658	AL CY: Frank Viola	.12	.06	.01
☐ 659A	AL MVP: Jose Canseco (eagle logo in black)	.50	.25	.05
☐ 659B	AL MVP: Jose Canseco (eagle logo in blue)	.50	.25	.05
☐ 660	AL ROY: Walt Weiss	.12	.06	.01
☐ 661	NL CY: Orel Hershiser	.20	.10	.02
☐ 662	NL MVP: Kirk Gibson	.12	.06	.01
☐ 663	NL ROY: Chris Sabo	.12	.06	.01
☐ 664	ALCS MVP: D. Eckersley	.35	.17	.03
☐ 665	NLCS MVP: O. Hershiser	.20	.10	.02
☐ 666	Great WS Moment (Kirk Gibson's homer)	.12	.06	.01
☐ 667	WS MVP: O. Hershiser	.20	.10	.02
☐ 668	Angels Checklist Wally Joyner	.15	.07	.01
☐ 669	Astros Checklist Nolan Ryan	.35	.17	.03
☐ 670	Athletics Checklist Jose Canseco	.50	.25	.05
☐ 671	Blue Jays Checklist Fred McGriff	.15	.07	.01
☐ 672	Braves Checklist Dale Murphy	.18	.09	.01
☐ 673	Brewers Checklist Paul Molitor	.10	.05	.01
☐ 674	Cardinals Checklist Ozzie Smith	.12	.06	.01
☐ 675	Cubs Checklist Ryne Sandberg	.12	.06	.01
☐ 676	Dodgers Checklist Kirk Gibson	.12	.06	.01
☐ 677	Expos Checklist Andres Galarraga	.10	.05	.01
☐ 678	Giants Checklist Will Clark	.50	.25	.05
☐ 679	Indians Checklist Cory Snyder	.10	.05	.01
☐ 680	Mariners Checklist	.10	.05	.01

		MINT	EXC	G-VG
	Alvin Davis			
☐ 681	Mets Checklist Darryl Strawberry	.40	.20	.04
☐ 682	Orioles Checklist Cal Ripken	.15	.07	.01
☐ 683	Padres Checklist Tony Gwynn	.20	.10	.02
☐ 684	Phillies Checklist Mike Schmidt	.35	.17	.03
☐ 685	Pirates Checklist Andy Van Slyke UER (96 Junior Ortiz)	.10	.05	.01
☐ 686	Rangers Checklist Ruben Sierra	.20	.10	.02
☐ 687	Red Sox Checklist Wade Boggs	.35	.17	.03
☐ 688	Reds Checklist Eric Davis	.20	.10	.02
☐ 689	Royals Checklist George Brett	.15	.07	.01
☐ 690	Tigers Checklist Alan Trammell	.10	.05	.01
☐ 691	Twins Checklist Frank Viola	.12	.06	.01
☐ 692	White Sox Checklist Harold Baines	.10	.05	.01
☐ 693	Yankees Checklist Don Mattingly	.50	.25	.05
☐ 694	Checklist 1-100	.06	.01	.00
☐ 695	Checklist 101-200	.06	.01	.00
☐ 696	Checklist 201-300	.06	.01	.00
☐ 697	Checklist 301-400	.06	.01	.00
☐ 698	Checklist 401-500 UER 467 Cal Ripkin Jr.	.06	.01	.00
☐ 699	Checklist 501-600 UER 543 Greg Booker	.06	.01	.00
☐ 700	Checklist 601-700	.06	.01	.00

1989 Upper Deck Extended

Todd Zeile

The 1989 Upper Deck Extended set contains 100 standard-size (2 ½" by 3 ½") cards. The fronts have pure white borders; the backs have recent stats and anti-counterfeit holograms. Both sides feature attractive color photos. The cards were distributed in "high number" packs, along with factory sets, and as a separate set in their own box.

	MINT	EXC	G-VG
COMPLETE SET (100)	36.00	18.00	3.60
COMMON PLAYER (701-800) ..	.08	.04	.01
☐ 701 Checklist 701-800	.08	.01	.00
☐ 702 Jesse Barfield	.15	.07	.01
☐ 703 Walt Terrell	.08	.04	.01
☐ 704 Dickie Thon	.08	.04	.01
☐ 705 Al Leiter	.15	.07	.01
☐ 706 Dave LaPoint	.08	.04	.01
☐ 707 Charlie Hayes	.30	.15	.03
☐ 708 Andy Hawkins	.08	.04	.01
☐ 709 Mickey Hatcher	.08	.04	.01
☐ 710 Lance McCullers	.08	.04	.01
☐ 711 Ron Kittle	.15	.07	.01
☐ 712 Bert Blyleven	.20	.10	.02
☐ 713 Rick Dempsey	.08	.04	.01
☐ 714 Ken Williams	.08	.04	.01
☐ 715 Steve Rosenberg	.20	.10	.02
☐ 716 Joe Skalski	.20	.10	.02
☐ 717 Spike Owen	.08	.04	.01
☐ 718 Todd Burns	.35	.17	.03
☐ 719 Kevin Gross	.08	.04	.01
☐ 720 Tommy Herr	.08	.04	.01
☐ 721 Rob Ducey	.20	.10	.02
☐ 722 Gary Green	.20	.10	.02
☐ 723 Gregg Olson	3.00	1.50	.30
☐ 724 Greg W. Harris	.20	.10	.02
☐ 725 Craig Worthington ...	.50	.25	.05
☐ 726 Tom Howard	.35	.17	.03
☐ 727 Dale Mohorcic	.08	.04	.01
☐ 728 Rich Yett	.08	.04	.01
☐ 729 Mel Hall	.15	.07	.01
☐ 730 Floyd Youmans	.08	.04	.01
☐ 731 Lonnie Smith	.15	.07	.01
☐ 732 Wally Backman	.08	.04	.01
☐ 733 Trevor Wilson	.20	.10	.02
☐ 734 Jose Alvarez	.20	.10	.02
☐ 735 Bob Milacki	.15	.07	.01
☐ 736 Tom Gordon	3.00	1.50	.30
☐ 737 Wally Whitehurst	.30	.15	.03
☐ 738 Mike Aldrete	.08	.04	.01
☐ 739 Keith Miller	.20	.10	.02
☐ 740 Randy Milligan	.15	.07	.01
☐ 741 Jeff Parrett	.15	.07	.01
☐ 742 Steve Finley	.30	.15	.03
☐ 743 Junior Felix	1.50	.75	.15
☐ 744 Pete Harnisch	.20	.10	.02
☐ 745 Bill Spiers	.60	.30	.06
☐ 746 Hensley Meulens ...	.60	.30	.06
☐ 747 Juan Bell	.20	.10	.02
☐ 748 Steve Sax	.20	.10	.02
☐ 749 Phil Bradley	.15	.07	.01
☐ 750 Rey Quinones	.08	.04	.01
☐ 751 Tommy Gregg	.08	.04	.01
☐ 752 Kevin Brown	.35	.17	.03
☐ 753 Derek Lilliquist	.30	.15	.03
☐ 754 Todd Zeile	6.50	3.25	.65
☐ 755 Jim Abbott	7.50	3.75	.75
☐ 756 Ozzie Canseco	1.00	.50	.10
☐ 757 Nick Esasky	.20	.10	.02
☐ 758 Mike Moore	.15	.07	.01
☐ 759 Rob Murphy	.08	.04	.01
☐ 760 Rick Mahler	.08	.04	.01
☐ 761 Fred Lynn	.15	.07	.01
☐ 762 Kevin Blankenship ..	.20	.10	.02
☐ 763 Eddie Murray	.20	.10	.02
☐ 764 Steve Searcy	.20	.10	.02
☐ 765 Jerome Walton	8.50	4.25	.85
☐ 766 Erik Hanson	.30	.15	.03

1990 Upper Deck

			MINT	EXC	G-VG
☐	767	Bob Boone	.20	.10	.02
☐	768	Edgar Martinez	.20	.10	.02
☐	769	Jose DeJesus	.15	.07	.01
☐	770	Greg Briley	1.50	.75	.15
☐	771	Steve Peters	.20	.10	.02
☐	772	Rafael Palmeiro	.20	.10	.02
☐	773	Jack Clark	.20	.10	.02
☐	774	Nolan Ryan	4.00	2.00	.40
☐	775	Lance Parrish	.15	.07	.01
☐	776	Joe Girardi	.35	.17	.03
☐	777	Willie Randolph	.15	.07	.01
☐	778	Mitch Williams	.20	.10	.02
☐	779	Dennis Cook	.30	.15	.03
☐	780	Dwight Smith	3.00	1.50	.30
☐	781	Lenny Harris	.30	.15	.03
☐	782	Torey Lovullo	.20	.10	.02
☐	783	Norm Charlton	.20	.10	.02
☐	784	Chris Brown	.08	.04	.01
☐	785	Todd Benzinger	.15	.07	.01
☐	786	Shane Rawley	.08	.04	.01
☐	787	Omar Vizquel	.30	.15	.03
☐	788	LaVel Freeman	.50	.25	.05
☐	789	Jeffrey Leonard	.15	.07	.01
☐	790	Eddie Williams	.08	.04	.01
☐	791	Jamie Moyer	.08	.04	.01
☐	792	Bruce Hurst UER (World Series)	.15	.07	.01
☐	793	Julio Franco	.20	.10	.02
☐	794	Claudell Washington	.15	.07	.01
☐	795	Jody Davis	.08	.04	.01
☐	796	Oddibe McDowell	.15	.07	.01
☐	797	Paul Kilgus	.08	.04	.01
☐	798	Tracy Jones	.08	.04	.01
☐	799	Steve Wilson	.20	.10	.02
☐	800	Pete O'Brien	.15	.07	.01

Craig Biggio

The 1990 Upper Deck set contains 700 standard-size (2 ½" by 3 ½") cards. The front and back borders are white, and both sides feature full-color photos. The horizontally oriented backs have recent stats and anti-counterfeiting holograms. Unlike the 1989 Upper Deck set, the team checklist cards are not grouped numerically at the end of the set, but are mixed in with the first 100 cards.

			MINT	EXC	G-VG
	COMPLETE SET (700)		45.00	22.50	4.50
	COMMON PLAYER (1-700)		.05	.02	.00
☐	1	Star Rookie Checklist	.15	.02	.01
☐	2	Randy Nosek	.15	.07	.01
☐	3	Tom Drees	.25	.12	.02
☐	4	Curt Young	.05	.02	.00
☐	5	Devon White TC California Angels	.08	.04	.01
☐	6	Luis Salazar	.05	.02	.00
☐	7	Von Hayes TC Philadelphia Phillies	.08	.04	.01
☐	8	Jose Bautista	.05	.02	.00
☐	9	Marquis Grissom	.75	.35	.07
☐	10	Orel Hershiser TC Los Angeles Dodgers	.15	.07	.01
☐	11	Rick Aguilera	.05	.02	.00
☐	12	Benito Santiago TC San Diego Padres	.10	.05	.01
☐	13	Deion Sanders	.50	.25	.05
☐	14	Marvell Wynne	.05	.02	.00

		MINT	EXC	G-VG
☐ 15	Dave West	.05	.02	.00
☐ 16	Bobby Bonilla TC	.08	.04	.01
	Pittsburgh Pirates			
☐ 17	Sammy Sosa	.50	.25	.05
☐ 18	Steve Sax TC	.10	.05	.01
	New York Yankees			
☐ 19	Jack Howell	.05	.02	.00
☐ 20	Mike Schmidt Special	.35	.17	.03
☐ 21	Robin Ventura	.75	.35	.07
☐ 22	Brian Meyer	.10	.05	.01
☐ 23	Blaine Beatty	.20	.10	.02
☐ 24	Ken Griffey Jr. TC	.40	.20	.04
	Seattle Mariners			
☐ 25	Greg Vaughn	1.50	.75	.15
☐ 26	Xavier Hernandez	.15	.07	.01
☐ 27	Jason Grimsley	.15	.07	.01
☐ 28	Eric Anthony	2.00	1.00	.20
☐ 29	Tim Raines TC	.10	.05	.01
	Montreal Expos			
☐ 30	David Wells	.05	.02	.00
☐ 31	Hal Morris	.10	.05	.01
☐ 32	Bo Jackson TC	.35	.17	.03
	Kansas City Royals			
☐ 33	Kelly Mann	.15	.07	.01
☐ 34	Nolan Ryan Special	.40	.20	.04
☐ 35	Scott Service	.15	.07	.01
☐ 36	Mark McGwire TC	.25	.12	.02
	Oakland A's			
☐ 37	Tino Martinez	.50	.25	.05
☐ 38	Chili Davis	.08	.04	.01
☐ 39	Scott Sanderson	.05	.02	.00
☐ 40	Kevin Mitchell TC	.15	.07	.01
	San Francisco Giants			
☐ 41	Lou Whitaker TC	.08	.04	.01
	Detroit Tigers			
☐ 42	Scott Coolbaugh	.30	.15	.03
☐ 43	Jose Cano	.30	.15	.03
☐ 44	Jose Vizcaino	.30	.15	.03
☐ 45	Bob Hamelin	.80	.40	.08
☐ 46	Jose Offerman	1.50	.75	.15
☐ 47	Kevin Blankenship	.10	.05	.01
☐ 48	Kirby Puckett TC	.20	.10	.02
	Minnesota Twins			
☐ 49	Tommy Greene	.50	.25	.05
☐ 50	Will Clark Special	.40	.20	.04
☐ 51	Rob Nelson	.05	.02	.00
☐ 52	Chris Hammond	.15	.07	.01
☐ 53	Joe Carter TC	.10	.05	.01
	Cleveland Indians			

		MINT	EXC	G-VG
☐ 54A	Ben McDonald ERR	75.00	30.00	6.00
	(no Rookie designation on card front)			
☐ 54B	Ben McDonald COR	3.50	1.75	.35
☐ 55	Andy Benes	.75	.35	.07
☐ 56	John Olerud	4.00	1.50	.25
☐ 57	Roger Clemens TC	.15	.07	.01
	Boston Red Sox			
☐ 58	Tony Armas	.08	.04	.01
☐ 59	George Canale	.20	.10	.02
☐ 60A	Mickey Tettleton TC	3.00	1.00	.25
	Baltimore Orioles (683 Jamie Weston)			
☐ 60B	Mickey Tettleton TC	.20	.10	.02
	Baltimore Orioles (683 Mickey Weston)			
☐ 61	Mike Stanton	.20	.10	.02
☐ 62	Dwight Gooden TC	.15	.07	.01
	New York Mets			
☐ 63	Kent Mercker	.50	.25	.05
☐ 64	Francisco Cabrera	.20	.10	.02
☐ 65	Steve Avery UER	.50	.25	.05
	(born NJ, should be MI)			
☐ 66	Jose Canseco	.60	.30	.06
☐ 67	Matt Merullo	.15	.07	.01
☐ 68	Vince Coleman TC	.08	.04	.01
	St. Louis Cardinals			
☐ 69	Ron Karkovice	.05	.02	.00
☐ 70	Kevin Maas	.40	.20	.04
☐ 71	Dennis Cook	.15	.07	.01
☐ 72	Juan Gonzalez	.75	.35	.07
☐ 73	Andre Dawson TC	.10	.05	.01
	Chicago Cubs			
☐ 74	Dean Palmer	.35	.17	.03
☐ 75	Bo Jackson Special	.50	.25	.05
☐ 76	Rob Richie	.15	.07	.01
☐ 77	Bobby Rose	.30	.15	.03
☐ 78	Brian Dubois	.15	.07	.01
☐ 79	Ozzie Guillen TC	.08	.04	.01
	Chicago White Sox			
☐ 80	Gene Nelson	.05	.02	.00
☐ 81	Bob McClure	.05	.02	.00
☐ 82	Julio Franco TC	.08	.04	.01
	Texas Rangers			
☐ 83	Greg Minton	.05	.02	.00
☐ 84	John Smoltz TC	.10	.05	.01
	Atlanta Braves			
☐ 85	Willie Fraser	.05	.02	.00

		MINT	EXC	G-VG
☐ 86	Neal Heaton	.05	.02	.00
☐ 87	Kevin Tapani	.20	.10	.02
☐ 88	Mike Scott TC	.10	.05	.01
	Houston Astros			
☐ 89A	Jim Gott ERR	12.00	6.00	1.20
	(photo actually			
	Rick Reed)			
☐ 89B	Jim Gott COR	.15	.07	.01
☐ 90	Lance Johnson	.10	.05	.01
☐ 91	Robin Yount TC	.15	.07	.01
	Milwaukee Brewers			
☐ 92	Jeff Parrett	.05	.02	.00
☐ 93	Julio Machado	.20	.10	.02
☐ 94	Ron Jones	.08	.04	.01
☐ 95	George Bell TC	.08	.04	.01
	Toronto Blue Jays			
☐ 96	Jerry Reuss	.05	.02	.00
☐ 97	Brian Fisher	.05	.02	.00
☐ 98	Kevin Ritz	.20	.10	.02
☐ 99	Barry Larkin TC	.10	.05	.01
	Cincinnati Reds			
☐ 100	Checklist 1-100	.05	.01	.00
☐ 101	Gerald Perry	.05	.02	.00
☐ 102	Kevin Appier	.15	.07	.01
☐ 103	Julio Franco	.08	.04	.01
☐ 104	Craig Biggio	.10	.05	.01
☐ 105	Bo Jackson	.60	.30	.06
☐ 106	Junior Felix	.35	.17	.03
☐ 107	Mike Harkey	.08	.04	.01
☐ 108	Fred McGriff	.15	.07	.01
☐ 109	Rick Sutcliffe	.08	.04	.01
☐ 110	Pete O'Brien	.08	.04	.01
☐ 111	Kelly Gruber	.08	.04	.01
☐ 112	Pat Borders	.05	.02	.00
☐ 113	Dwight Evans	.08	.04	.01
☐ 114	Dwight Gooden	.25	.12	.02
☐ 115	Kevin Batiste	.20	.10	.02
☐ 116	Eric Davis	.25	.12	.02
☐ 117	Kevin Mitchell	.20	.10	.02
☐ 118	Ron Oester	.05	.02	.00
☐ 119	Brett Butler	.08	.04	.01
☐ 120	Danny Jackson	.08	.04	.01
☐ 121	Tommy Gregg	.08	.04	.01
☐ 122	Ken Caminiti	.05	.02	.00
☐ 123	Kevin Brown	.15	.07	.01
☐ 124	George Brett	.15	.07	.01
☐ 125	Mike Scott	.10	.05	.01
☐ 126	Cory Snyder	.10	.05	.01
☐ 127	George Bell	.10	.05	.01
☐ 128	Mark Grace	.40	.20	.04
☐ 129	Devon White	.10	.05	.01
☐ 130	Tony Fernandez	.10	.05	.01
☐ 131	Don Aase	.05	.02	.00
☐ 132	Rance Mulliniks	.05	.02	.00
☐ 133	Marty Barrett	.05	.02	.00
☐ 134	Nelson Liriano	.05	.02	.00
☐ 135	Mark Carreon	.10	.05	.01
☐ 136	Candy Maldonado	.05	.02	.00
☐ 137	Tim Birtsas	.05	.02	.00
☐ 138	Tom Brookens	.05	.02	.00
☐ 139	John Franco	.08	.04	.01
☐ 140	Mike LaCoss	.05	.02	.00
☐ 141	Jeff Treadway	.05	.02	.00
☐ 142	Pat Tabler	.05	.02	.00
☐ 143	Darrell Evans	.08	.04	.01
☐ 144	Rafael Ramirez	.05	.02	.00
☐ 145	Oddibe McDowell	.08	.04	.01
☐ 146	Brian Downing	.05	.02	.00
☐ 147	Curt Wilkerson	.05	.02	.00
☐ 148	Ernie Whitt	.05	.02	.00
☐ 149	Bill Schroeder	.05	.02	.00
☐ 150	Domingo Ramos	.05	.02	.00
☐ 151	Rick Honeycutt	.05	.02	.00
☐ 152	Don Slaught	.05	.02	.00
☐ 153	Mitch Webster	.05	.02	.00
☐ 154	Tony Phillips	.05	.02	.00
☐ 155	Paul Kilgus	.05	.02	.00
☐ 156	Ken Griffey Jr.	1.75	.85	.17
☐ 157	Gary Sheffield	.35	.17	.03
☐ 158	Wally Backman	.05	.02	.00
☐ 159	B.J. Surhoff	.08	.04	.01
☐ 160	Louie Meadows	.05	.02	.00
☐ 161	Paul O'Neill	.10	.05	.01
☐ 162	Jeff McKnight	.20	.10	.02
☐ 163	Alvaro Espinoza	.05	.02	.00
☐ 164	Scott Scudder	.20	.10	.02
☐ 165	Jeff Reed	.05	.02	.00
☐ 166	Gregg Jefferies	.50	.25	.05
☐ 167	Barry Larkin	.10	.05	.01
☐ 168	Gary Carter	.10	.05	.01
☐ 169	Robby Thompson	.05	.02	.00
☐ 170	Rolando Roomes	.08	.04	.01
☐ 171	Mark McGwire	.25	.12	.02
☐ 172	Steve Sax	.10	.05	.01
☐ 173	Mark Williamson	.05	.02	.00
☐ 174	Mitch Williams	.08	.04	.01
☐ 175	Brian Holton	.05	.02	.00
☐ 176	Rob Deer	.08	.04	.01

		MINT	EXC	G-VG
☐ 177	Tim Raines	.10	.05	.01
☐ 178	Mike Felder	.05	.02	.00
☐ 179	Harold Reynolds	.08	.04	.01
☐ 180	Terry Francona	.05	.02	.00
☐ 181	Chris Sabo	.10	.05	.01
☐ 182	Darryl Strawberry	.30	.15	.03
☐ 183	Willie Randolph	.08	.04	.01
☐ 184	Bill Ripken	.05	.02	.00
☐ 185	Mackey Sasser	.08	.04	.01
☐ 186	Todd Benzinger	.05	.02	.00
☐ 187	Kevin Elster	.08	.04	.01
☐ 188	Jose Uribe	.05	.02	.00
☐ 189	Tom Browning	.08	.04	.01
☐ 190	Keith Miller	.05	.02	.00
☐ 191	Don Mattingly	.60	.30	.06
☐ 192	Dave Parker	.10	.05	.01
☐ 193	Roberto Kelly	.10	.05	.01
☐ 194	Phil Bradley	.08	.04	.01
☐ 195	Ron Hassey	.05	.02	.00
☐ 196	Gerald Young	.05	.02	.00
☐ 197	Hubie Brooks	.08	.04	.01
☐ 198	Bill Doran	.08	.04	.01
☐ 199	Al Newman	.05	.02	.00
☐ 200	Checklist 101-200	.05	.01	.00
☐ 201	Terry Puhl	.05	.02	.00
☐ 202	Frank DiPino	.05	.02	.00
☐ 203	Jim Clancy	.05	.02	.00
☐ 204	Bob Ojeda	.08	.04	.01
☐ 205	Alex Trevino	.05	.02	.00
☐ 206	Dave Henderson	.05	.02	.00
☐ 207	Henry Cotto	.05	.02	.00
☐ 208	Rafael Belliard	.05	.02	.00
☐ 209	Stan Javier	.05	.02	.00
☐ 210	Jerry Reed	.05	.02	.00
☐ 211	Doug Dascenzo	.05	.02	.00
☐ 212	Andres Thomas	.05	.02	.00
☐ 213	Greg Maddux	.08	.04	.01
☐ 214	Mike Schooler	.08	.04	.01
☐ 215	Lonnie Smith	.08	.04	.01
☐ 216	Jose Rijo	.05	.02	.00
☐ 217	Greg Gagne	.05	.02	.00
☐ 218	Jim Gantner	.05	.02	.00
☐ 219	Allan Anderson	.08	.04	.01
☐ 220	Rick Mahler	.05	.02	.00
☐ 221	Jim Deshaies	.05	.02	.00
☐ 222	Keith Hernandez	.10	.05	.01
☐ 223	Vince Coleman	.10	.05	.01
☐ 224	David Cone	.10	.05	.01
☐ 225	Ozzie Smith	.10	.05	.01
☐ 226	Matt Nokes	.08	.04	.01
☐ 227	Barry Bonds	.08	.04	.01
☐ 228	Felix Jose	.05	.02	.00
☐ 229	Dennis Powell	.05	.02	.00
☐ 230	Mike Gallego	.05	.02	.00
☐ 231	Shawon Dunston UER ('89 stats are Andre Dawson's)	.10	.04	.01
☐ 232	Ron Gant	.08	.04	.01
☐ 233	Omar Vizquel	.15	.07	.01
☐ 234	Derek Lilliquist	.10	.05	.01
☐ 235	Erik Hanson	.10	.05	.01
☐ 236	Kirby Puckett	.30	.15	.03
☐ 237	Bill Spiers	.30	.15	.03
☐ 238	Dan Gladden	.05	.02	.00
☐ 239	Bryan Clutterbuck	.05	.02	.00
☐ 240	John Moses	.05	.02	.00
☐ 241	Ron Darling	.10	.05	.01
☐ 242	Joe Magrane	.08	.04	.01
☐ 243	Dave Magadan	.08	.04	.01
☐ 244	Pedro Guerrero	.10	.05	.01
☐ 245	Glenn Davis	.10	.05	.01
☐ 246	Terry Steinbach	.08	.04	.01
☐ 247	Fred Lynn	.08	.04	.01
☐ 248	Gary Redus	.05	.02	.00
☐ 249	Ken Williams	.05	.02	.00
☐ 250	Sid Bream	.05	.02	.00
☐ 251	Bob Welch	.08	.04	.01
☐ 252	Bill Buckner	.08	.04	.01
☐ 253	Carney Lansford	.10	.05	.01
☐ 254	Paul Molitor	.10	.05	.01
☐ 255	Jose DeJesus	.05	.02	.00
☐ 256	Orel Hershiser	.12	.06	.01
☐ 257	Tom Brunansky	.10	.05	.01
☐ 258	Mike Davis	.05	.02	.00
☐ 259	Jeff Ballard	.08	.04	.01
☐ 260	Scott Terry	.05	.02	.00
☐ 261	Sid Fernandez	.08	.04	.01
☐ 262	Mike Marshall	.08	.04	.01
☐ 263	Howard Johnson	.12	.06	.01
☐ 264	Kirk Gibson	.12	.06	.01
☐ 265	Kevin McReynolds	.10	.05	.01
☐ 266	Cal Ripken Jr.	.12	.06	.01
☐ 267	Ozzie Guillen	.05	.02	.00
☐ 268	Jim Traber	.05	.02	.00
☐ 269	Bobby Thigpen	.08	.04	.01
☐ 270	Joe Orsulak	.05	.02	.00
☐ 271	Bob Boone	.08	.04	.01

		MINT	EXC	G-VG			MINT	EXC	G-VG
☐ 272	Dave Stewart	.10	.05	.01	☐ 321	Jody Reed	.05	.02	.00
☐ 273	Tim Wallach	.08	.04	.01	☐ 322	Damon Berryhill	.10	.05	.01
☐ 274	Luis Aquino	.08	.04	.01	☐ 323	Roger Clemens	.25	.12	.02
☐ 275	Mike Moore	.08	.04	.01	☐ 324	Ryne Sandberg	.15	.07	.01
☐ 276	Tony Pena	.08	.04	.01	☐ 325	Benito Santiago	.12	.06	.01
☐ 277	Eddie Murray	.12	.06	.01	☐ 326	Bret Saberhagen	.12	.06	.01
☐ 278	Milt Thompson	.05	.02	.00	☐ 327	Lou Whitaker	.10	.05	.01
☐ 279	Alejandro Pena	.05	.02	.00	☐ 328	Dave Gallagher	.05	.02	.00
☐ 280	Ken Dayley	.05	.02	.00	☐ 329	Mike Pagliarulo	.08	.04	.01
☐ 281	Carmen Castillo	.05	.02	.00	☐ 330	Doyle Alexander	.05	.02	.00
☐ 282	Tom Henke	.08	.04	.01	☐ 331	Jeffrey Leonard	.08	.04	.01
☐ 283	Mickey Hatcher	.05	.02	.00	☐ 332	Torey Lovullo	.08	.04	.01
☐ 284	Roy Smith	.05	.02	.00	☐ 333	Pete Incaviglia	.08	.04	.01
☐ 285	Manny Lee	.05	.02	.00	☐ 334	Ritkey Henderson	.25	.12	.02
☐ 286	Dan Pasqua	.05	.02	.00	☐ 335	Rafael Palmeiro	.10	.05	.01
☐ 287	Larry Sheets	.05	.02	.00	☐ 336	Ken Hill	.08	.04	.01
☐ 288	Garry Templeton	.08	.04	.01	☐ 337	Dave Winfield	.12	.06	.01
☐ 289	Eddie Williams	.08	.04	.01	☐ 338	Alfredo Griffin	.05	.02	.00
☐ 290	Brady Anderson	.05	.02	.00	☐ 339	Andy Hawkins	.05	.02	.00
☐ 291	Spike Owen	.05	.02	.00	☐ 340	Ted Power	.05	.02	.00
☐ 292	Storm Davis	.08	.04	.01	☐ 341	Steve Wilson	.10	.05	.01
☐ 293	Chris Bosio	.08	.04	.01	☐ 342	Jack Clark	.10	.05	.01
☐ 294	Jim Eisenreich	.05	.02	.00	☐ 343	Ellis Burks	.20	.10	.02
☐ 295	Don August	.05	.02	.00	☐ 344	Tony Gwynn	.20	.10	.02
☐ 296	Jeff Hamilton	.05	.02	.00	☐ 345	Jerome Walton	1.50	.75	.15
☐ 297	Mickey Tettleton	.08	.04	.01	☐ 346	Roberto Alomar	.12	.06	.01
☐ 298	Mike Scioscia	.05	.02	.00	☐ 347	Carlos Martinez	.20	.10	.02
☐ 299	Kevin Hickey	.05	.02	.00	☐ 348	Chet Lemon	.05	.02	.00
☐ 300	Checklist 201-300	.05	.01	.00	☐ 349	Willie Wilson	.08	.04	.01
☐ 301	Shawn Abner	.10	.05	.01	☐ 350	Greg Walker	.05	.02	.00
☐ 302	Kevin Bass	.08	.04	.01	☐ 351	Tom Bolton	.05	.02	.00
☐ 303	Bip Roberts	.05	.02	.00	☐ 352	German Gonzalez	.08	.04	.01
☐ 304	Joe Girardi	.15	.07	.01	☐ 353	Harold Baines	.10	.05	.01
☐ 305	Danny Darwin	.05	.02	.00	☐ 354	Mike Greenwell	.25	.12	.02
☐ 306	Mike Heath	.05	.02	.00	☐ 355	Ruben Sierra	.20	.10	.02
☐ 307	Mike Macfarlane	.05	.02	.00	☐ 356	Andres Galarraga	.10	.05	.01
☐ 308	Ed Whitson	.05	.02	.00	☐ 357	Andre Dawson	.10	.05	.01
☐ 309	Tracy Jones	.05	.02	.00	☐ 358	Jeff Brantley	.15	.07	.01
☐ 310	Scott Fletcher	.05	.02	.00	☐ 359	Mike Bielecki	.08	.04	.01
☐ 311	Darnell Coles	.05	.02	.00	☐ 360	Ken Oberkfell	.05	.02	.00
☐ 312	Mike Brumley	.08	.04	.01	☐ 361	Kurt Stillwell	.05	.02	.00
☐ 313	Bill Swift	.05	.02	.00	☐ 362	Brian Holman	.05	.02	.00
☐ 314	Charlie Hough	.05	.02	.00	☐ 363	Kevin Seitzer	.12	.06	.01
☐ 315	Jim Presley	.05	.02	.00	☐ 364	Alvin Davis	.08	.04	.01
☐ 316	Luis Polonia	.05	.02	.00	☐ 365	Tom Gordon	.75	.35	.07
☐ 317	Mike Morgan	.05	.02	.00	☐ 366	Bobby Bonilla	.10	.05	.01
☐ 318	Lee Guetterman	.05	.02	.00	☐ 367	Carlton Fisk	.10	.05	.01
☐ 319	Jose Oquendo	.05	.02	.00	☐ 368	Steve Carter	.15	.07	.01
☐ 320	Wayne Tolleson	.05	.02	.00	☐ 369	Joel Skinner	.05	.02	.00

		MINT	EXC	G-VG
☐ 370	John Cangelosi	.05	.02	.00
☐ 371	Cecil Espy	.05	.02	.00
☐ 372	Gary Wayne	.12	.06	.01
☐ 373	Jim Rice	.12	.06	.01
☐ 374	Mike Dyer	.15	.07	.01
☐ 375	Joe Carter	.12	.06	.01
☐ 376	Dwight Smith	.75	.35	.07
☐ 377	John Wetteland	.35	.17	.03
☐ 378	Ernie Riles	.05	.02	.00
☐ 379	Otis Nixon	.05	.02	.00
☐ 380	Vance Law	.05	.02	.00
☐ 381	Dave Bergman	.05	.02	.00
☐ 382	Frank White	.08	.04	.01
☐ 383	Scott Bradley	.05	.02	.00
☐ 384	Israel Sanchez UER	.05	.02	.00
	(totals don't include			
	'89 stats)			
☐ 385	Gary Pettis	.05	.02	.00
☐ 386	Donn Pall	.08	.04	.01
☐ 387	John Smiley	.08	.04	.01
☐ 388	Tom Candiotti	.05	.02	.00
☐ 389	Junior Ortiz	.05	.02	.00
☐ 390	Steve Lyons	.05	.02	.00
☐ 391	Brian Harper	.05	.02	.00
☐ 392	Fred Manrique	.05	.02	.00
☐ 393	Lee Smith	.08	.04	.01
☐ 394	Jeff Kunkel	.05	.02	.00
☐ 395	Claudell Washington	.08	.04	.01
☐ 396	John Tudor	.08	.04	.01
☐ 397	Terry Kennedy	.05	.02	.00
☐ 398	Lloyd McClendon	.05	.02	.00
☐ 399	Craig Lefferts	.05	.02	.00
☐ 400	Checklist 301-400	.05	.01	.00
☐ 401	Keith Moreland	.05	.02	.00
☐ 402	Rich Gedman	.05	.02	.00
☐ 403	Jeff Robinson	.08	.04	.01
☐ 404	Randy Ready	.05	.02	.00
☐ 405	Rick Cerone	.05	.02	.00
☐ 406	Jeff Blauser	.05	.02	.00
☐ 407	Larry Andersen	.05	.02	.00
☐ 408	Joe Boever	.05	.02	.00
☐ 409	Felix Fermin	.05	.02	.00
☐ 410	Glenn Wilson	.05	.02	.00
☐ 411	Rex Hudler	.05	.02	.00
☐ 412	Mark Grant	.05	.02	.00
☐ 413	Dennis Martinez	.05	.02	.00
☐ 414	Darrin Jackson	.05	.02	.00
☐ 415	Mike Aldrete	.05	.02	.00
☐ 416	Roger McDowell	.08	.04	.01

		MINT	EXC	G-VG
☐ 417	Jeff Reardon	.08	.04	.01
☐ 418	Darren Daulton	.05	.02	.00
☐ 419	Tim Laudner	.05	.02	.00
☐ 420	Don Carman	.05	.02	.00
☐ 421	Lloyd Moseby	.08	.04	.01
☐ 422	Doug Drabek	.08	.04	.01
☐ 423	Lenny Harris	.10	.05	.01
☐ 424	Jose Lind	.05	.02	.00
☐ 425	Dave Johnson (P)	.15	.07	.01
☐ 426	Jerry Browne	.05	.02	.00
☐ 427	Eric Yelding	.10	.05	.01
☐ 428	Brad Komminsk	.05	.02	.00
☐ 429	Jody Davis	.05	.02	.00
☐ 430	Mariano Duncan	.05	.02	.00
☐ 431	Mark Davis	.10	.05	.01
☐ 432	Nelson Santovenia	.05	.02	.00
☐ 433	Bruce Hurst	.08	.04	.01
☐ 434	Jeff Huson	.12	.06	.01
☐ 435	Chris James	.08	.04	.01
☐ 436	Mark Guthrie	.12	.06	.01
☐ 437	Charlie Hayes	.10	.05	.01
☐ 438	Shane Rawley	.05	.02	.00
☐ 439	Dickie Thon	.05	.02	.00
☐ 440	Juan Berenguer	.05	.02	.00
☐ 441	Kevin Romine	.05	.02	.00
☐ 442	Bill Landrum	.05	.02	.00
☐ 443	Todd Frohwirth	.08	.04	.01
☐ 444	Craig Worthington	.10	.05	.01
☐ 445	Fernando Valenzuela	.12	.06	.01
☐ 446	Joey Belle	.75	.35	.07
☐ 447	Ed Whited	.20	.10	.02
☐ 448	Dave Smith	.05	.02	.00
☐ 449	Dave Clark	.05	.02	.00
☐ 450	Juan Agosto	.05	.02	.00
☐ 451	Dave Valle	.05	.02	.00
☐ 452	Kent Hrbek	.10	.05	.01
☐ 453	Von Hayes	.08	.04	.01
☐ 454	Gary Gaetti	.10	.05	.01
☐ 455	Greg Briley	.30	.15	.03
☐ 456	Glenn Braggs	.08	.04	.01
☐ 457	Kirt Manwaring	.05	.02	.00
☐ 458	Mel Hall	.08	.04	.01
☐ 459	Brook Jacoby	.08	.04	.01
☐ 460	Pat Sheridan	.05	.02	.00
☐ 461	Rob Murphy	.05	.02	.00
☐ 462	Jimmy Key	.08	.04	.01
☐ 463	Nick Esasky	.08	.04	.01
☐ 464	Rob Ducey	.05	.02	.00
☐ 465	Carlos Quintana	.08	.04	.01

		MINT	EXC	G-VG			MINT	EXC	G-VG
☐ 466	Larry Walker	.35	.17	.03	☐ 512	Joe Hesketh	.05	.02	.00
☐ 467	Todd Worrell	.10	.05	.01	☐ 513	Dennis Eckersley	.10	.05	.01
☐ 468	Kevin Gross	.05	.02	.00	☐ 514	Greg Brock	.05	.02	.00
☐ 469	Terry Pendleton	.05	.02	.00	☐ 515	Tim Burke	.08	.04	.01
☐ 470	Dave Martinez	.05	.02	.00	☐ 516	Frank Tanana	.05	.02	.00
☐ 471	Gene Larkin	.05	.02	.00	☐ 517	Jay Bell	.05	.02	.00
☐ 472	Len Dykstra	.08	.04	.01	☐ 518	Guillermo Hernandez	.08	.04	.01
☐ 473	Barry Lyons	.05	.02	.00	☐ 519	Randy Kramer	.10	.05	.01
☐ 474	Terry Mulholland	.05	.02	.00	☐ 520	Charles Hudson	.05	.02	.00
☐ 475	Chip Hale	.20	.10	.02	☐ 521	Jim Corsi	.10	.05	.01
☐ 476	Jesse Barfield	.10	.05	.01	☐ 522	Steve Rosenberg	.08	.04	.01
☐ 477	Dan Plesac	.08	.04	.01	☐ 523	Cris Carpenter	.05	.02	.00
☐ 478A	Scott Garrelts ERR	4.00	1.50	.20	☐ 524	Matt Winters	.20	.10	.02
	(photo actually Bill				☐ 525	Melido Perez	.08	.04	.01
	Bathe)				☐ 526	Chris Gwynn UER	.05	.02	.00
☐ 478B	Scott Garrelts COR	.10	.05	.01		(Albeguerque)			
☐ 479	Dave Righetti	.10	.05	.01	☐ 527	Bert Blyleven	.10	.05	.01
☐ 480	Gus Polidor	.05	.02	.00	☐ 528	Chuck Cary	.08	.04	.01
☐ 481	Mookie Wilson	.08	.04	.01	☐ 529	Daryl Boston	.05	.02	.00
☐ 482	Luis Rivera	.05	.02	.00	☐ 530	Dale Mohorcic	.05	.02	.00
☐ 483	Mike Flanagan	.05	.02	.00	☐ 531	Geronimo Berroa	.08	.04	.01
☐ 484	Dennis Boyd	.05	.02	.00	☐ 532	Edgar Martinez	.05	.02	.00
☐ 485	John Cerutti	.05	.02	.00	☐ 533	Dale Murphy	.15	.07	.01
☐ 486	John Costello	.05	.02	.00	☐ 534	Jay Buhner	.08	.04	.01
☐ 487	Pascual Perez	.08	.04	.01	☐ 535	John Smoltz UER	.10	.05	.01
☐ 488	Tommy Herr	.05	.02	.00		(HEA Stadium)			
☐ 489	Tom Foley	.05	.02	.00	☐ 536	Andy Van Slyke	.10	.05	.01
☐ 490	Curt Ford	.05	.02	.00	☐ 537	Mike Henneman	.05	.02	.00
☐ 491	Steve Lake	.05	.02	.00	☐ 538	Miguel Garcia	.08	.04	.01
☐ 492	Tim Teufel	.05	.02	.00	☐ 539	Frank Williams	.05	.02	.00
☐ 493	Randy Bush	.05	.02	.00	☐ 540	R.J. Reynolds	.05	.02	.00
☐ 494	Mike Jackson	.05	.02	.00	☐ 541	Shawn Hillegas	.05	.02	.00
☐ 495	Steve Jeltz	.05	.02	.00	☐ 542	Walt Weiss	.10	.05	.01
☐ 496	Paul Gibson	.05	.02	.00	☐ 543	Greg Hibbard	.15	.07	.01
☐ 497	Steve Balboni	.05	.02	.00	☐ 544	Nolan Ryan	.40	.20	.04
☐ 498	Bud Black	.05	.02	.00	☐ 545	Todd Zeile	1.75	.85	.17
☐ 499	Dale Sveum	.05	.02	.00	☐ 546	Hensley Meulens	.30	.15	.03
☐ 500	Checklist 401-500	.05	.01	.00	☐ 547	Tim Belcher	.10	.05	.01
☐ 501	Tim Jones	.05	.02	.00	☐ 548	Mike Witt	.08	.04	.01
☐ 502	Mark Portugal	.05	.02	.00	☐ 549	Greg Cadaret	.10	.05	.01
☐ 503	Ivan Calderon	.08	.04	.01	☐ 550	Franklin Stubbs	.05	.02	.00
☐ 504	Rick Rhoden	.05	.02	.00	☐ 551	Tony Castillo	.08	.04	.01
☐ 505	Willie McGee	.08	.04	.01	☐ 552	Jeff Robinson	.08	.04	.01
☐ 506	Kirk McCaskill	.05	.02	.00	☐ 553	Steve Olin	.10	.05	.01
☐ 507	Dave LaPoint	.05	.02	.00	☐ 554	Alan Trammell	.10	.05	.01
☐ 508	Jay Howell	.05	.02	.00	☐ 555	Wade Boggs	.30	.15	.03
☐ 509	Johnny Ray	.08	.04	.01	☐ 556	Will Clark	.60	.30	.06
☐ 510	Dave Anderson	.05	.02	.00	☐ 557	Jeff King	.15	.07	.01
☐ 511	Chuck Crim	.05	.02	.00	☐ 558	Mike Fitzgerald	.05	.02	.00

		MINT	EXC	G-VG
☐ 559	Ken Howell	.05	.02	.00
☐ 560	Bob Kipper	.05	.02	.00
☐ 561	Scott Bankhead	.08	.04	.01
☐ 562A	Jeff Innis ERR (photo actually David West)	4.00	1.50	.20
☐ 562B	Jeff Innis COR	.20	.10	.02
☐ 563	Randy Johnson	.05	.02	.00
☐ 564	Wally Whitehurst	.10	.05	.01
☐ 565	Gene Harris	.15	.07	.01
☐ 566	Norm Charlton	.10	.05	.01
☐ 567	Robin Yount UER (7606 career hits, should be 2606)	.35	.15	.03
☐ 568	Joe Oliver	.15	.07	.01
☐ 569	Mark Parent	.05	.02	.00
☐ 570	John Farrell	.05	.02	.00
☐ 571	Tom Glavine	.08	.04	.01
☐ 572	Rod Nichols	.10	.05	.01
☐ 573	Jack Morris	.10	.05	.01
☐ 574	Greg Swindell	.10	.05	.01
☐ 575	Steve Searcy	.12	.06	.01
☐ 576	Ricky Jordan	.20	.10	.02
☐ 577	Matt Williams	.15	.07	.01
☐ 578	Mike LaValliere	.05	.02	.00
☐ 579	Bryn Smith	.08	.04	.01
☐ 580	Bruce Ruffin	.05	.02	.00
☐ 581	Randy Myers	.08	.04	.01
☐ 582	Rick Wrona	.15	.07	.01
☐ 583	Juan Samuel	.10	.05	.01
☐ 584	Les Lancaster	.05	.02	.00
☐ 585	Jeff Musselman	.05	.02	.00
☐ 586	Rob Dibble	.08	.04	.01
☐ 587	Eric Show	.05	.02	.00
☐ 588	Jesse Orosco	.05	.02	.00
☐ 589	Herm Winningham	.05	.02	.00
☐ 590	Andy Allanson	.05	.02	.00
☐ 591	Dion James	.05	.02	.00
☐ 592	Carmelo Martinez	.05	.02	.00
☐ 593	Luis Quinones	.05	.02	.00
☐ 594	Dennis Rasmussen	.05	.02	.00
☐ 595	Rich Yett	.05	.02	.00
☐ 596	Bob Walk	.05	.02	.00
☐ 597	Andy McGaffigan	.05	.02	.00
☐ 598	Billy Hatcher	.05	.02	.00
☐ 599	Bob Knepper	.05	.02	.00
☐ 600	Checklist 501-600	.05	.01	.00
☐ 601	Joey Cora	.08	.04	.01
☐ 602	Steve Finley	.10	.05	.01
☐ 603	Kal Daniels	.10	.05	.01
☐ 604	Gregg Olson	.40	.20	.04
☐ 605	Dave Stieb	.10	.05	.01
☐ 606	Kenny Rogers	.15	.07	.01
☐ 607	Zane Smith	.05	.02	.00
☐ 608	Bob Geren	.20	.10	.02
☐ 609	Chad Kreuter	.05	.02	.00
☐ 610	Mike Smithson	.05	.02	.00
☐ 611	Jeff Wetherby	.20	.10	.02
☐ 612	Gary Mielke	.10	.05	.01
☐ 613	Pete Smith	.05	.02	.00
☐ 614	Jack Daugherty	.15	.07	.01
☐ 615	Lance McCullers	.05	.02	.00
☐ 616	Don Robinson	.05	.02	.00
☐ 617	Jose Guzman	.05	.02	.00
☐ 618	Steve Bedrosian	.08	.04	.01
☐ 619	Jamie Moyer	.05	.02	.00
☐ 620	Atlee Hammaker	.05	.02	.00
☐ 621	Rick Luecken	.15	.07	.01
☐ 622	Greg W. Harris	.12	.06	.01
☐ 623	Pete Harnisch	.08	.04	.01
☐ 624	Jerald Clark	.05	.02	.00
☐ 625	Jack McDowell	.05	.02	.00
☐ 626	Frank Viola	.10	.05	.01
☐ 627	Teddy Higuera	.08	.04	.01
☐ 628	Marty Pevey	.10	.05	.01
☐ 629	Bill Wegman	.05	.02	.00
☐ 630	Eric Plunk	.05	.02	.00
☐ 631	Drew Hall	.05	.02	.00
☐ 632	Doug Jones	.08	.04	.01
☐ 633	Geno Petralli	.05	.02	.00
☐ 634	Jose Alvarez	.05	.02	.00
☐ 635	Bob Milacki	.12	.06	.01
☐ 636	Bobby Witt	.08	.04	.01
☐ 637	Trevor Wilson	.08	.04	.01
☐ 638	Jeff Russell	.08	.04	.01
☐ 639	Mike Krukow	.05	.02	.00
☐ 640	Rick Leach	.05	.02	.00
☐ 641	Dave Schmidt	.05	.02	.00
☐ 642	Terry Leach	.05	.02	.00
☐ 643	Calvin Schiraldi	.05	.02	.00
☐ 644	Bob Melvin	.05	.02	.00
☐ 645	Jim Abbott	1.50	.75	.15
☐ 646	Jaime Navarro	.20	.10	.02
☐ 647	Mark Langston	.12	.06	.01
☐ 648	Juan Nieves	.05	.02	.00
☐ 649	Damaso Garcia	.05	.02	.00
☐ 650	Charlie O'Brien	.05	.02	.00
☐ 651	Eric King	.05	.02	.00

		MINT	EXC	G-VG
☐ 652	Mike Boddicker	.05	.02	.00
☐ 653	Duane Ward	.05	.02	.00
☐ 654	Bob Stanley	.05	.02	.00
☐ 655	Sandy Alomar Jr.	.35	.17	.03
☐ 656	Danny Tartabull	.10	.04	.01
☐ 657	Randy McCament	.12	.06	.01
☐ 658	Charlie Leibrandt	.05	.02	.00
☐ 659	Dan Quisenberry	.08	.04	.01
☐ 660	Paul Assenmacher	.05	.02	.00
☐ 661	Walt Terrell	.05	.02	.00
☐ 662	Tim Leary	.08	.04	.01
☐ 663	Randy Milligan	.08	.04	.01
☐ 664	Bo Diaz	.05	.02	.00
☐ 665	Mark Lemke	.05	.02	.00
☐ 666	Jose Gonzalez	.08	.04	.01
☐ 667	Chuck Finley	.08	.04	.01
☐ 668	John Kruk	.08	.04	.01
☐ 669	Dick Schofield	.05	.02	.00
☐ 670	Tim Crews	.05	.02	.00
☐ 671	John Dopson	.05	.02	.00
☐ 672	John Orton	.20	.10	.02
☐ 673	Eric Hetzel	.10	.05	.01
☐ 674	Lance Parrish	.10	.05	.01
☐ 675	Ramon Martinez	.10	.05	.01
☐ 676	Mark Gubicza	.10	.05	.01
☐ 677	Greg Litton	.20	.10	.02
☐ 678	Greg Mathews	.05	.02	.00
☐ 679	Dave Dravecky	.10	.05	.01
☐ 680	Steve Farr	.05	.02	.00
☐ 681	Mike Devereaux	.05	.02	.00
☐ 682	Ken Griffey Sr.	.08	.04	.01
☐ 683A	Mickey Weston ERR (listed as Jamie on card)	9.00	4.50	.90
☐ 683B	Mickey Weston COR	.35	.17	.03
☐ 684	Jack Armstrong	.08	.04	.01
☐ 685	Steve Buechele	.05	.02	.00
☐ 686	Bryan Harvey	.05	.02	.00
☐ 687	Lance Blankenship	.05	.02	.00
☐ 688	Dante Bichette	.05	.02	.00
☐ 689	Todd Burns	.20	.10	.02
☐ 690	Dan Petry	.05	.02	.00
☐ 691	Kent Anderson	.15	.07	.01
☐ 692	Todd Stottlemyre	.08	.04	.01
☐ 693	Wally Joyner	.12	.06	.01
☐ 694	Mike Rochford	.12	.06	.01
☐ 695	Floyd Bannister	.05	.02	.00
☐ 696	Rick Reuschel	.08	.04	.01
☐ 697	Jose DeLeon	.08	.04	.01

		MINT	EXC	G-VG
☐ 698	Jeff Montgomery	.08	.04	.01
☐ 699	Kelly Downs	.05	.02	.00
☐ 700A	Checklist 601-700 (#683 Jamie Weston)	2.00	.50	.10
☐ 700B	Checklist 601-700 (#683 Mickey Weston)	.10	.05	.01

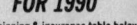

BILL HENDERSON'S CARDS
"King of the Commons"

2320 RUGER AVE. PG12
JANESVILLE, WISCONSIN 53545
1-608-755-0922

"ALWAYS BUYING" Call or Write for Quote

"ALWAYS BUYING" Call or Write for Quote

HI # OR SCARCE SERIES		COMMONS EACH		EX/MT TO MINT CONDITION GROUP LOTS FOR SALE				VG+ to EX Condition		
				50 Diff.	100 Diff.	300 Asst.	500 Asst.	50 Different	100	200
1948 BOWMAN	(37-48) 25.00	15.00								
1949 BOWMAN	(145-240) 80.00	15.00		675.				400.		
50-51 BOWMAN	50(1-72) 51(253-324) 50.00	15.00	51 (2-36) 20.00	675.				400.		
1952 TOPPS	(311-407) P.O.R.	30.00	(2-80) 60.00	1350.				800.		
1952 TOPPS	(217-252) 30.00	15.00	(2-36) 20.00	675.				400.		
1953 TOPPS	(220-280) 80.00	20.00	(2-165) 30.00	900.				600.		
1953 BOWMAN	(129-160) 40.00	30.00	(113-128) 50.00	1350.				800.		
1954 TOPPS		12.00	(51-75) 25.00	540.				360.		
1954 BOWMAN		7.00	(129-224) 8.00	315.	600.			210.		
1955 TOPPS	(161-210) 18.00		(151-160) 12.00	315.				210.		
1955 BOWMAN	(225-320) 15.-20. Umps	6.00	(2-96) 8.00	270.	500.			180.	350.	
1956 TOPPS		7.00	(181-260) 12.00	315.				210.	400.	
1957 TOPPS	(265-352) 17.50	5.00	(353-407) 5.00	220.	420.			155.	300.	
1958 TOPPS		3.50	(1-110) 5.00	155.	300.	850.		105.	200.	
1959 TOPPS	(507-572) 12.50	3.00	(1-110) 4.00	135.	260.	750.		90.	175.	385.
1960 TOPPS	(523-572) 12.50	1.75	(441-506) 3.50	85.	165.	450.	750.	52.	100.	190.
1961 TOPPS	(523-589) 25.00	1.50	(371-522) 2.00	65.	125.	360.	700.	45.	80.	155.
1962 TOPPS	(523-590) 12.50	1.50	(371-522) 2.00	65.	125.	360.		45.	80.	155.
1963 TOPPS	(447-576) 8.00	1.00	(197-446) 2.00	45.	90.			32.	60.	
1964 TOPPS	(523-587) 7.50	1.00	(371-522) 2.00	45.	90.			32.	60.	115.
1965 TOPPS	(447-522) 3.00 (523-598) 5.00	1.00	(371-446) 1.50	45.	90.			32.	60.	115.
1966 TOPPS	(523-598) 15.00	1.00	(447-522) 4.00	45.	90.			32.	60.	115.
1967 TOPPS	(534-609) 10.00	1.00	(458-533) 4.00	45.	90.			32.	60.	115.
1968 TOPPS		.75	(458-533) 1.00	35.	65.			23.	45.	85.
1969 TOPPS	(589-664) 1.00	.60	(219-327) 1.00	28.	55.	155.		18.	35.	65.
1970 TOPPS	(634-720) 2.50	.45	(547-633) 1.25	22.	42.	120.	190.	14.	26.	50.
1971 TOPPS	(644-752) 2.50	.45	(524-643) 1.50	22.	42.	120.	190.	14.	26.	50.
1972 TOPPS	(657-787) 3.00	.45	(526-656) 1.50	22.	42.	*120.	190.	14.	26.	50.
1973 TOPPS	(528-660) 2.00	.35	(397-528) .60	16.	32.	*90.		12.	22.	40.
1974 TOPPS		.35		16.	32.	*90.	*150.		22.	40.
1975 TOPPS	(8-132 .50)	.35		16.	32.	*90.			22.	40.
1976-77		.20		18.	*50.	*85.		10.	18.	
1978-1980		.15		13.	*38.	*65.		8.	15.	
1981 thru 1990 Topps, Fleer or Donrus Specify Year & Company except below		.10		8. Per Yr.	*22. Per Yr.	*35. Per Yr.		5.	10.	
1984-86 DONRUS		.15		7.	13.	*38.	*60.			

SPECIAL IN VG+ to EX CONDITION-POSTPAID

250	58-62	300.00
500	58-62	550.00
250	60-69	170.00
500	60-69	320.00
1000	60-69	600.00
250	70-79	50.00
500	70-79	90.00
1000	70-79	160.00
250	80-84	15.00
500	80-84	28.00
1000	80-84	55.00

*These lots are all different.

Special 1 Different from each year 1949-80 - $130.00 postpaid.
Special 100 Different from each year 1956-80 - $2600.00 postpaid.
Special 10 Different from each year 1956-80 - $280.00 postpaid.
All lot groups are my choice only.

All assorted lots will contain as many different as possible.
Please list alternates whenever possible.
Send your want list and I will fill them at the above price for commons. High numbers, specials, scarce series, and stars extra.
You can use your Master Card or Visa to charge your purchases.
Minimum order $7.50 - Postage and handling .50 per 100 cards (minimum $1.75)
Also interested in purchasing your collection.
Groups include various years of my choice.

SETS AVAILABLE
Topps 1988, 1989, 1990
19.95 ea + 2.50 UPS
6 for 19.75 ea + 9.00 UPS
18 for 19.25 ea + 20.00 UPS
54 for 18.75 ea + 60.00 UPS
MIX OR MATCH

ANY CARD NOT LISTED ON PRICE SHEET IS PRICED AT BECKETT-SPORTS AMERICANA PRICE GUIDE XII

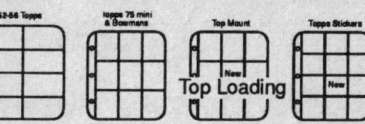

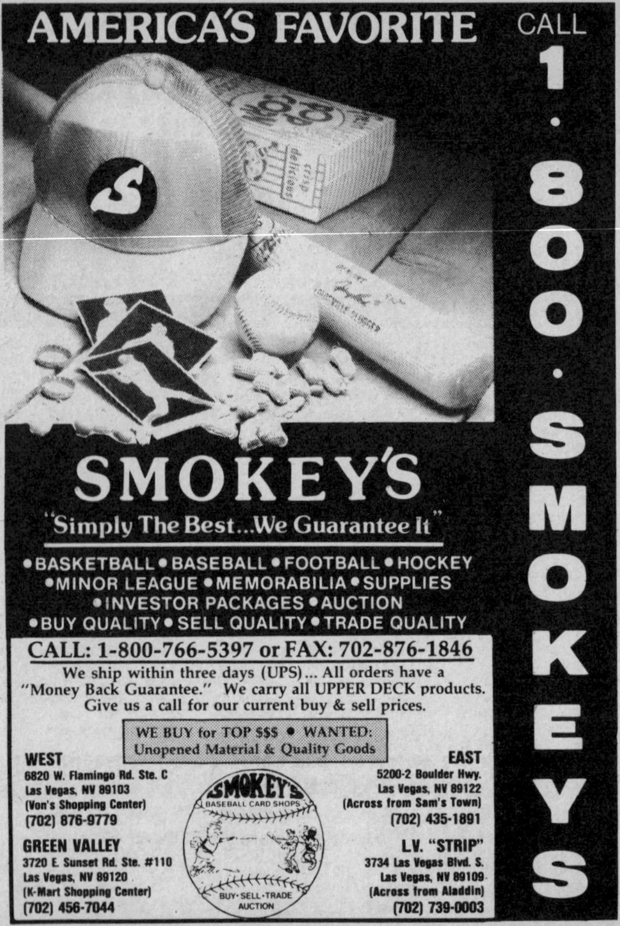
AMERICA'S FAVORITE
CALL 1·800·SMOKEYS
SMOKEY'S
"Simply The Best...We Guarantee It"
•BASKETBALL •BASEBALL •FOOTBALL •HOCKEY
•MINOR LEAGUE •MEMORABILIA •SUPPLIES
•INVESTOR PACKAGES •AUCTION
•BUY QUALITY •SELL QUALITY •TRADE QUALITY
CALL: 1-800-766-5397 or FAX: 702-876-1846
We ship within three days (UPS)... All orders have a "Money Back Guarantee." We carry all UPPER DECK products. Give us a call for our current buy & sell prices.
WE BUY for TOP $$$ • WANTED: Unopened Material & Quality Goods
WEST
6820 W. Flamingo Rd. Ste. C
Las Vegas, NV 89103
(Von's Shopping Center)
(702) 876-9779
EAST
5200-2 Boulder Hwy.
Las Vegas, NV 89122
(Across from Sam's Town)
(702) 435-1891
SMOKEY'S
BASEBALL CARD SHOPS
BUY·SELL·TRADE
AUCTION
GREEN VALLEY
3720 E. Sunset Rd. Ste. #110
Las Vegas, NV 89120
(K-Mart Shopping Center)
(702) 456-7044
LV. "STRIP"
3734 Las Vegas Blvd. S.
Las Vegas, NV 89109
(Across from Aladdin)
(702) 739-0003

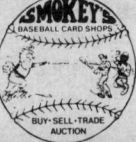

BUYING - SELLING

19th CENTURY TO DATE
BASEBALL - FOOTBALL
SPORT CARDS

ALSO BUYING EARLY SPORT MEMORABILIA

COMICS .   PULPS   . SF BOOKS

AND COLLECTOR PAPERBACKS

COLLECTOR'S CHOICE

LAUREL SHOPPING CENTRE
LAUREL, MARYLAND 20707
near Laurel Cinema

1-301-725-0887

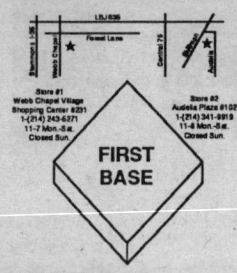

Store #1
Webb Chapel Village
Shopping Center #231
1-(214) 243-5271
11-7 Mon.-Sat.
Closed Sun.

Store #2
Audelia Plaza #102
1-(214) 341-9919
11-6 Mon.-Sat.
Closed Sun.

FIRST
BASE

BASEBALL CARD LOTS
Our Choice - No Superstars

1959 Topps 10 diff (f-vg)	$10.00
1960 Topps 10 diff (f-vg)	7.50
1961 Topps 10 diff (f-vg)	7.50
1962 Topps 10 diff (f-vg)	7.00
1963 Topps 10 diff (f-vg)	6.50
1964 Topps 10 diff (f-vg)	5.00
1965 Topps 10 diff (f-vg)	5.00
1966 Topps 10 diff (f-vg)	3.50
1967 Topps 10 diff (f-vg)	3.50
1968 Topps 10 diff (f-vg)	3.00
1969 Topps 25 diff (f-vg)	5.95
1970 Topps 25 diff (f-vg)	3.95
1971 Topps 25 diff (f-vg)	3.95
1972 Topps 25 diff (f-vg)	3.95
1973 Topps 25 diff (f-vg)	3.95
1974 Topps 25 diff (f-vg)	3.95
1975 Topps 25 diff (f-vg)	3.95
1976 Topps 25 diff (f-vg)	2.95
1977 Topps 25 diff (f-vg)	2.95
1978 Topps 50 diff (f-vg)	2.95
1979 Topps 25 diff (f-vg)	2.95
1980 Topps 25 diff (f-vg)	2.95
1981 Donruss 50 diff (ex-m)	2.50
1981 Fleer 50 diff (ex-m)	2.50
1982 Fleer 50 diff (ex-m)	2.50

FOOTBALL CARD LOTS
Our Choice - No Superstars

1969 Topps 25 diff (f-vg)	$6.95
1970 Topps 25 diff (f-vg)	5.95
1971 Topps 25 diff (f-vg)	4.95
1972 Topps 25 diff (f-vg)	4.95
1973 Topps 25 diff (f-vg)	4.95
1974 Topps 25 diff (f-vg)	2.50
1975 Topps 25 diff (f-vg)	2.50
1976 Topps 25 diff (f-vg)	2.50
1977 Topps 25 diff (f-vg)	2.00
1978 Topps 50 diff (f-vg)	3.00
1979 Topps 50 diff (f-vg)	3.00
1980 Topps 50 diff (f-vg)	2.50

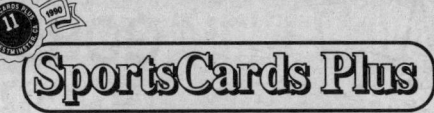

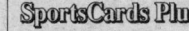

COMPLETE BASEBALL CARD SETS

REGULAR ISSUES

1990 Topps (792)	$25.00
1989 Topps (792)	26.00
1988 Topps (792)	25.00
1987 Topps (792)	35.00
1986 Topps (792)	35.00
All 5 above Topps Sets	135.00
1985 Topps (792)	100.00
1984 Topps (792)	100.00
1989 Bowman (484)	23.00
1990 Fleer (660)	28.00
1989 Fleer (660)	30.00
1988 Fleer (660)	35.00
1986 Fleer (660)	100.00
1990 Donruss (716)	28.00
1989 Donruss (660)	30.00
1988 Donruss (660)	35.00
1990 Score (714)	23.00
1989 Score (660)	22.00
1988 Score (660)	24.00
1990 Sportflics (225)	40.00
1989 Sportflics (225)	42.00
1988 Sportflics (225)	50.00
1987 Sportflics (200)	32.00

TRADED OR UPDATE ISSUES

1989 Topps (132)	$15.00
1988 Topps (132)	26.00
1987 Topps (132)	14.00
1985 Topps (132)	16.00
1982 Topps (132)	32.00
1989 Fleer (132)	22.00
1988 Fleer (132)	13.00
1987 Fleer (132)	18.00
1986 Fleer (132)	34.00
1985 Fleer (132)	16.00
1989 Score (110)	15.00
1988 Score (110)	38.00
1989 Donruss (56)	7.00
1989 Upper Deck (100)	50.00
1987 Topps Tiffany (132)	35.00
1988 Fleer Tin (132)	25.00
1987 Fleer Tin (132)	25.00

ROOKIE SETS

1989 Donruss (56)	$28.00
1988 Donruss (56)	14.00
1987 Donruss (56)	20.00
1987 Sportflics-Pt. 1 (25)	12.00
1987 Sportflics-Pt. 2 (25)	12.00
1986 Sportflics (50)	13.00
1989 Topps (22)	10.00

TOPPS GLOSSY ALL-STARS

All 22 cards per set

1990, 1989, 1988	$5.00 each
1985, 1984	6.00 each

CANADIAN ISSUES

1990 O.P.C. (792)	$32.00
1989 O.P.C. (396)	16.00
1988 O.P.C. (396)	16.00
1984 O.P.C. (396)	40.00
1988 Leaf (264)	16.00

MINI SETS

1988 Fleer (120)	$14.00
1987 Fleer (120)	10.00
1986 Fleer (120)	12.00

DONRUSS ALL-STAR SETS

60 or 64 cards per set

1989, 1988, 1987, 1986	$9.00 each

DONRUSS POP-UP SETS

18 or 20 cards per set

1989, 1988, 1987, 1986	$5.00 each

DONRUSS LARGE DIAMOND KINGS (5" x 7")

28 cards per set

1990, 1989, 1988, 1986, 1985	$12.00 each

OTHER ISSUES

1990 Topps Major League Debut (152)	$16.00
1989 Topps 'Big' Cards (330)	32.00
1989 Score Young Superstars	
Series 1 (40)	11.00
Series 2 (40)	11.00
Both Series 1 & 2	20.00
1989 Score Masters (42)	13.00
1988 Topps 'Big' Cards (264)	30.00
1988 Topps United Kingdom (88)	10.00
1988 Topps Glossy Send In (60)	12.00
1988 Score Young Superstars	
Series 1 (40)	12.00
Series 2 (40)	12.00
Both Series 1 & 2	22.00
1987 Topps Tiffany (792)	120.00
1987 Donruss Opening Day (272)	18.00
1987 Sportflics Team Preview (26)	7.00
1987 Sportflics Rookie Packs (10)	10.00
1987 Sportflics Superstar Sheets (4)	15.00
1987 Donruss Highlights (56)	5.00
1986 Topps Supers (60)	8.00
1985 Topps Pete Rose (120)	18.00
1985 Donruss Highlights (56)	28.00
1982 Topps Stickers (260 + album)	10.00
1982 Fleer Stamps (Box of 600)	10.00
1981 Topps Stickers (262 + album)	10.00

BILL DODGE
P.O. BOX 40154
BAY VILLAGE, OH 44140
Phone: (216) 835-4146

TEMDEE
Wholesale & Retail

We Carry A Full Line Of:

- **Complete Sets** In Football, Baseball, Hockey, Basketball & Non Sports Cards.
- **Manufacturers** Include Topps, Fleer, Donruss, Score, Bowman, Leaf, Star, O-P-C, Upper Deck, Kelloggs, Pro Set Football, Hoops, Sportflics & Others.
- **Supplies** Card Pages (all sizes), Binders (2"&3"), Boxes (100, 400, 500, 600 & 800), Single Card Sleeves, Lucite Holders, Ball & Bat Holders, Plastic Cases and much more!
- **Pennants** All sports and major colleges plus specials.
- **Autographed Baseballs**
- **Photographs**
- **Porcelain Figurines & Plates**-Sports Impressions & Gartlans.
- **Unopened Boxes & Packs**
- **Yearbooks & Price Guides**
- **Souvenirs** Hats, Scarfs, Bobble Dolls, Buttons & More.
- **Starting Line Ups** For 88 & 89 in Baseball, Football & Basketball.
- **Minor League Sets** Pro Cards, Star Co. & Grand Slam.
- **Want Lists** Filled for all sports. Send for specific wants or needs with an S.A.S.E.

WE BUY AND SELL

Temdee
15 Whitman Square & Black Horse Pike
Turnersville, N.J. 08012
(609) 228-8645

Store hours: Mon.- Fri. Noon - 8:00 p.m.
Sat.. 10 a.m. - 5 p.m. Sun. Noon - 5:00 p.m.

Let us know what your interests are. To get our FREE catalog send
55 cents or large 45-cent self-addressed stamped envelope.

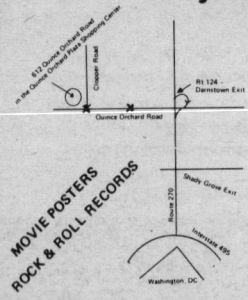

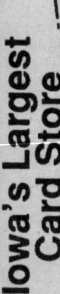

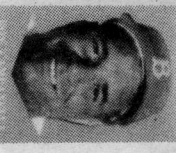

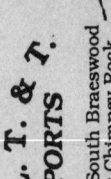

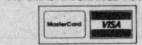

CLASSIFIED ADS

MORE FOR LESS!

More color superstar covers, answers to your hobby questions, monthly profiles on the big guns in the hobby, accurate prices to all the new sets, national rankings to keep you in the know, informative features to help you collect better, explanations of the hobby's hottest errors & variations, interviews with baseball's current superstars — more fun for the hobby!

It's simple. Now, Beckett Monthly subscribers get even more hobby enjoyment for less money. Subscribe today!

TWO GREAT NEW MAGAZINES

from the people that brought you Beckett Baseball Card Monthly

---

🏈 Beckett Football Card Magazine Subscriptions

Name _____ Age _____

(Please Print)

Address _____

City _____ State _____ Zip _____

Type of Subscription: ☐ New Subscription ☐ Renewal

Payment enclosed via: ☐ Check or Money Order ☐ VISA/MasterCard

Signature _____

Acct. # _____ Exp. _____

Check one please:	Your Price
8 issues (a savings of $8.65)	**$14.95**
16 issues (a savings of $21.25)	**$25.95**
24 issues (a savings of $33.85)	**$36.95**
32 issues (a savings of $46.45)	**$47.95**

All foreign addresses add $12 per 8 issues for postage. All payments payable in U.S. funds.
Beckett Football Card Magazine is published 8 times a year.

Mail to: Beckett Publications, Football Subscriptions, 4887 Alpha Rd., Suite 200,
Dallas, Texas 75244

🏀 Beckett Basketball Card Magazine Subscriptions

Name _____ Age _____

(Please Print)

Address _____

City _____ State _____ Zip _____

Type of Subscription: ☐ New Subscription ☐ Renewal

Payment enclosed via: ☐ Check or Money Order ☐ VISA/MasterCard

Signature _____

Acct. # _____ Exp. _____

Check one please:	Your Price
6 issues (a savings of $4.75)	**$12.95**
12 issues (a savings of $13.45)	**$21.95**
18 issues (a savings of $23.15)	**$29.95**
24 issues (a savings of $33.85)	**$36.95**

All foreign addresses add $9 per 6 issues for postage. All payments payable in U.S. funds.
Beckett Basketball Card Magazine is published 6 times a year.

Mail to: Beckett Publications, Basketball Subscriptions, 4887 Alpha Rd., Suite 200,
Dallas, Texas 75244